October 17–21, 2011
Chicago, Illinois, USA

Association for
Computing Machinery

Advancing Computing as a Science & Profession

CCS'11

Proceedings of the 18th ACM Conference on Computer & Communications Security

Sponsored by:

ACM SIGSAC

Supported by:

US Army Research Office, National Science Foundation, Google, IBM, Microsoft Research, Nokia, Northwestern University, Pearson, Springer, & Technicolor

Association for Computing Machinery

Advancing Computing as a Science & Profession

The Association for Computing Machinery
2 Penn Plaza, Suite 701
New York, New York 10121-0701

Notice to Past Authors of ACM-Published Articles

ACM intends to create a complete electronic archive of all articles and/or other material previously published by ACM. If you have written a work that has been previously published by ACM in any journal or conference proceedings prior to 1978, or any SIG Newsletter at any time, and you do NOT want this work to appear in the ACM Digital Library, please inform permissions@acm.org, stating the title of the work, the author(s), and where and when published.

ISBN: 978-1-4503-1075-8

Additional copies may be ordered prepaid from:

ACM Order Department
PO Box 30777
New York, NY 10087-0777, USA

Phone: 1-800-342-6626 (USA and Canada)
+1-212-626-0500 (Global)
Fax: +1-212-944-1318
E-mail: acmhelp@acm.org
Hours of Operation: 8:30 am – 4:30 pm ET

Printed in the USA

CCS 2011 General Chair's Welcome

ACM Conference on Computer and Communications Security (CCS) is the flagship annual conference of the Special Interest Group on Security, Audit and Control (SIGSAC) of the Association for Computing Machinery. CCS is ACM's oldest conference in security area. It brings together researchers and developers for academics, government agencies, research labs and corporate sectors from all over the world. It provides an environment to conduct intellectual discussions and exchange ideas that are instrumental in shaping the future of computer and communications security. From its inception, CCS has established itself as a high standard research conference in the area of computer and communications security. This reputation continues to grow and is reflected in high selective and prestige of the technical programs.

From 2002- 2010, the number of paper submissions increased from ~150 to ~300 submissions, and reached the record of 325 in 2010. For this year, I am proud to announce that we have a much higher new record: 429 submissions. CCS 2011 received funding support of over $50,000 from NSF, ARL, Google, IBM, Microsoft Research, Nokia, Northwestern University, Pearson, Springer, and Technicolor. The Organizing Committee of CCS 2010 has put together an outstanding program that includes 60 papers (another record!) in 16 technical sessions, two invited talks, 7 pre- and post-conferences specialized workshops, 4 tutorials, 41 posters, and two social events.

The CCS 2011 conference would not have been possible without the genuine and tireless efforts of the entire CCS 2011 Organizing Committee. We would like to congratulate them for their professionalism and commitment. We are most grateful to the authors who submitted their work to the main conference, workshops or posters. We would also like to thank the technical program committee members, the reviewers who diligently supported the peer review process, the workshop chairs who worked hard to organize the workshops, session chairs, and everyone else for their time and dedication to put together an outstanding program, as usual. We are also extremely grateful to those who are involved in making the local arrangements, designing the website, creating the publications and promotional materials, and handling registrations. Special acknowledgements go to the Steering Committee, especially the Chair Prof. Elisa Bertino, and the staff of the ACM who supported us throughout. Last, but far from least, we would like to express our gratitude to the patrons who so generously contributed to the conference and/or workshops.

I hope that that you will enjoy staying in Chicago. Two social local events (Happy Hour and Banquet) have been arranged to provide an opportunity for you to get together with friends and colleagues. I hope that you will have a rewarding and enjoyable experience in CCS 2011.

Yan Chen
CCS 2011 General Chair
Northwestern University, USA

CCS 2011 Program Chairs' Welcome

It is a pleasure to present to you the proceedings of this year's ACM Conference on Computer and Communications Security (CCS 2011), held October 17-21 in Chicago, Illnois, USA.

This year we received a record 429 submissions from 39 countries. Each submission was reviewed by the technical program committee of 53 experts, as well as over 280 external reviewers. The final program contains 60 full papers, representing the acceptance rate of 14%.

The single-blind review process was organised in two rounds spanning 10 weeks. It included an opportunity for the authors to respond to reviews after the first round. Author response was followed by an electronic discussion among the PC members. Many reviews were assigned to PC members dynamically to maximise scrutiny and discussion of the submissions whose inclusion in the program was most uncertain. Overall, 1366 reviews were filed, including 430 from external reviewers. Despite the unexpected increase in submissions relative to CCS 2010, 327 papers received at least 3 reviews and 158 papers received at least 4 reviews, with some receiving as many as 5 or 6 reviews. The decision to allocate fewer than 3 reviews to some papers was taken on the basis of both the qualitative feedback from the first-round reviewers and a systematic quantitative analysis of the likelihood of their acceptance given the first-round reviews.

Many papers that could not be selected for presentation contained interesting results and ideas. We hope that the reviews will help improve these papers for future re-submissions. We also worked closely with the program chairs of CCS-affiliated workshops to ensure that the authors of rejected papers had an opportunity to submit their work to those venues.

We are deeply indebted to all members of the program committee for their hard work and the graciousness with which they engaged with a much higher workload than anticipated. On average, each PC member filed 23 reviews, with some volunteering for more than 30 reviews. We would also like to thank them for their enthusiastic participation in the discussions, and the valuable feedback to authors they included into their reviews. We would also like to recognise the hard work of external reviewers on whom we relied heavily this year. Some were kind enough to review bundles of papers on a particular subject – sometimes over 3 or 4 – a level of work that merits more than a casual acknowledgement.

We are grateful to all CCS 2011 organizers and members of the CCS steering committee for smoothly dealing with all other aspects of the conference and allowing us to concentrate on selecting quality papers for the technical program. Last, but certainly not least, our thanks go to all the authors who submitted papers and all attendees. We hope that you enjoy the program, and your participation at CCS helps you advance computer security research.

Vitaly Shmatikov
ACM CCS 2011 Program Chair
The University of Texas at Austin, USA

George Danezis
ACM CCS 2011 Program Chair
Microsoft Research, Cambridge, UK

Table of Contents

Keynote Address

Session 9: Virtual Machines and Hypervisors

Session 10: Applied Cryptography

Session 11: Wild Woolly Web

Session 12: Cloud Computing

Session 13: Side-channel Attacks and Defenses

Session 14: Securing Web Applications

Session 15: Privacy and Mobile Security

Session 16: Making Secure Computation Practical

ACM CCS 2011 Conference Organization

General Chair: Yan Chen *(Northwestern University, USA)*

Program Co-Chairs: George Danezis *(Microsoft Research Cambridge, UK)*
Vitaly Shmatikov *(University of Texas at Austin, USA)*

Workshop Co-Chairs: Ninghui Li *(Purdue University, USA)*
V. N. Venkatakrishnan *(University of Illinois Chicago, USA)*

Tutorial Co-Chairs: Gail-Joon Ahn *(Arizona State University)*
Brent Byunghoon Kang *(George Mason University, USA)*

Treasurer: Bin Xiao *(Hongkong Polytechnic University, China)*

Publication Chair: Dongyan Xu *(Purdue University, USA)*

Web Chair: Zhichun Li *(NEC Laboratories America, USA)*

Student Travel Grant Co-Chairs: Kang Li *(University of Georgia, USA)*
Phillip Porras *(SRI International, USA)*

Poster and Demo Co-Chairs: Adam Lee *(University of Pittsburgh, USA)*
Haining Wang *(College of William and Mary, USA)*

Publicity Co-Chairs: Guofei Gu *(Texas A&M University, USA)*
Carlos Becker Westphall *(Federal University of Santa Catarina, Brazil)*

Patron Co-Chairs: Bei-Tseng Chu *(University of North Carolina Charlotte, USA)*
Yong Guan *(Iowa State University, USA)*

Local Arrangements Chair: Xiaofeng Wang *(Indiana University at Bloomington, USA)*

Local Arrangements Committee: Kui Ren *(Illinois Institute of Technology, USA)*
Dingbang Xu *(Governors State University, USA)*

Steering Committee Chair: Elisa Bertino *(Purdue University, USA)*

Steering Committee: Carl Landwehr *(University of Maryland, USA)*
John Mitchell *(Stanford University, USA)*
Peng Ning *(North Carolina State University, USA)*
Rei Safavi-Naini *(University of Calgary, Canada)*
Paul Syverson *(Naval Research Laboratory, USA)*
Gene Tsudik *(University of California, Irvine, USA)*
Marianne Winslett *(University of Illinois at Urbana-Champaign, USA)*
Moti Yung *(Google, USA)*

Program Committee: Michael Backes *(Saarland Univ. and MPI-SWS, Germany)*
Bruno Blanchet *(CNRS, ENS, INRIA, France)*
Dan Boneh *(Stanford, USA)*
Nikita Borisov *(UIUC, USA)*
Herbert Bos *(VU, Netherlands)*

Program Committee (continued):

Srdjan Capkun *(ETHZ, Switzerland)*
Avik Chaudhuri *(Adobe Advanced Technology Labs, USA)*
Shuo Chen *(Microsoft Research, USA)*
Manuel Costa *(Microsoft Research, UK)*
Anupam Datta *(CMU, USA)*
Stephanie Delaune *(CNRS and ENS-Cachan, France)*
Roger Dingledine *(The Tor Project, USA)*
Orr Dunkelman *(University of Haifa and Weizmann Institute, Israel)*
Ulfar Erlingsson *(Google, USA)*
Nick Feamster *(Georgia Tech, USA)*
Bryan Ford *(Yale University, USA)*
Cedric Fournet *(Microsoft Research, UK)*
Paul Francis *(MPI-SWS, Germany)*
Michael Freedman *(Princeton University, USA)*
Guofei Gu *(Texas A&M University, USA)*
Nicholas Hopper *(University of Minnesota, USA)*
Jean-Pierre Hubaux *(EPFL, Switzerland)*
Collin Jackson *(CMU Silicon Valley, USA)*
Markus Jakobsson *(Paypal, USA)*
Jaeyeon Jung *(Intel Labs Seattle, USA)*
Apu Kapadia *(Indiana University, USA)*
Jonathan Katz *(University of Maryland, USA)*
Stefan Katzenbeisser *(TU Darmstadt, Germany)*
Arvind Krishnamurthy *(University of Washington, USA)*
Christopher Kruegel *(UCSB, USA)*
Ralf Kuesters *(University of Trier, Germany)*
Ninghui Li *(Purdue University, USA)*
Benjamin Livshits *(Microsoft Research, USA)*
Heiko Mantel *(TU Darmstadt, Germany)*
John Mitchell *(Stanford, USA)*
Fabian Monrose *(UNC at Chapel Hill, USA)*
Steven Murdoch *(University of Cambridge, UK)*
David Naccache *(Ecole Normale Superieure, France)*
Arvind Narayanan *(Stanford, USA)*
Kenny Paterson *(Royal Holloway, University of London, UK)*
Niels Provos *(Google, USA)*
Mike Reiter *(UNC at Chapel Hill, USA)*
Thomas Ristenpart *(University of Wisconsin, USA)*
Hovav Shacham *(UCSD, USA)*
Anil Somayaji *(Carleton University, Canada)*
Francois-Xavier Standaert *(UCL, Belgium, UK)*
Eran Tromer *(Tel Aviv University, Israel)*
Leendert Van Doorn *(AMD, USA)*
Paul Van Oorschot *(Carleton University, Canada)*
Bogdan Warinschi *(University of Bristol, UK)*
Brent Waters *(University of Texas Austin, USA)*
Robert Watson *(University of Cambridge, UK)*
Xiaowei Yang *(Duke University, USA)*
Haifeng Yu *(NUS, Singapore)*

ACM CCS 2011 Additional Reviewers

Michel Abdalla
Moheeb Abu Rajab
Markus Aderhold
Ben Adida
Ruj Akavipat
Nadhem Alfardan
Mansour Alsaleh
Elena Andreeva
Baskar Anguraj
Jacob Appelbaum
Aslan Askarov
Arthur Asuncion
Brandon Baker
Lucas Ballard
David Barrera
Jason Bau
Kevin Bauer
Josh Benaloh
Emery Berger
Daniel J. Bernstein
Igor Bilogrevic
Arnar Birgisson
Jeremiah Blocki
Dan Bogdanov
Rainer Bohme
Alexandra Boldyreva
Joseph Bonneau
Andrew Bortz
Michael Brennan
Christina Brzuska
Mihai Budiu
Philippe Bulens
Elie Bursztein
David Cad
David Cash
Sagar Chaki
Melissa Chase
Binbin Chen
Brad Chen
Eric Chen
Vincent Cheval
Csine Chevalier
Yannick Chevalier
Alessandro Chiesa
Seung Geol Choi
Sherman S. M. Chow
Shane Clark
Richard Clayton
Allen Clement
Iwen Coisel
Scott Coull
Jason Crampton
Jed Crandall
Cas Cremers
Jon Crowcroft
Weidong Cui
Boris Danev
Anupam Das
Lucas Davi
Emiliano De Cristofaro
Alex Dent
Alan Dunn
William Enck
Sarah Ereth
Pooya Farshim
Kathi Fisler
Riccardo Focardi
Jason Franklin
Pierre Francis
Matt Fredrikson
David Freeman
Keith Frikken
Shailendra Fuloria
Sebastian Gajek
Tal Garfinkel
Deepak Garg
Sanjam Garg
Chris Gates
Richard Gay
Daniel Genkin
Benedikt Gierlichs
Peter Gilbert
Damien Giry
Mikhail Gofman
Philippe Golle
Xun Gong
Vipul Goyal
Rachel Greenstadt
Adam Groce
Thomas Gross
Krishna Gummadi
Beno Gard
J. Alex Halderman
Shai Halevi
Mike Hamburg
William Harris
Carmit Hazay
Ryan Henry
Cormac Herley
Clemens Hlauschek
Jeff Hodges
Owen Hofmann
Susan Hohenberger
Thorsten Holz
Amir Houmansadr

David Huang
Yan Huang
Mathias Humbert
Tomas Isdal
Yuval Ishai
Murtuza Jadliwala
Sonia Jahid
Limin Jia
Xuxian Jiang
Maritza Johnson
Ari Juels
Joshua Juen
Mike Just
Seny Kamara
Emilia Kasper
Aniket Kate
Dilsun Kaynar
Michelle Kendal
Samuel King
Felix Klaedtke
Francis Koeune
Markulf Kohlweiss
Clemens Kolbitsch
Vladimir Kolesnikov
Steve Kremer
Shriram Krishnamurthi
Srinivas Krishnan
Markus Kuhn
Klaus Kursawe
William Leddy
Adam J. Lee
Chris Lesniewski-Laas
Allison Lewko
Ang Li
Peng Li
Shujun Li
Benoit Libert
Jay Ligatti
Zhiqiang Lin
Zi Lin
Debin Liu
Xin Liu
Michael Locasto
Alexander Lux
Phil Mackenzie
Phillip Mackenzie
Mohammad Hossein Manshaei
Petr Marchenko
Ramya Masti
Nick Mathewson
Michael May
Jonathan Mayer
Jonathan Mccune
John Mchugh
Frank Mcsherry
Sebastian Meiser
Filippo Menczer
Kazuhiro Minami
Chris Mitchell
Prateek Mittal
Abadelaziz Mohaisen
Esfandiar Mohammadi
Payman Mohassel
Andres Molina
David Molnar
Hart Montgomery
Tyler Moore
Alexander Moshchuk
Sascha Mler
Shishir Nagaraja
Sanjai Narain
Gregory Neven
Giang Nguyen
Kobbi Nissim
Adam O'Neill
Yossi Oren
Claudio Orlandi
Xinming Ou
Miriam Paiola
Sameer Patil
Karthik Pattabiraman
Kim Pecina
Roberto Perdisci
Olivier Pereira
Matthias Perner
Andreas Peter
Duong-Hieu Phan
Frank Piessens
Benny Pinkas
Jeremy Planul
David Pointcheval
Alex Popa
Christina Popper
Phil Porras
Marcin Poturalski
Shi Pu
Elizabeth Quaglia
Moheeb Rajab
Kasper Rasmussen
Rob Reeder
Francesco Regazzoni
Tzachy Reinman
Tamara Rezk
Christian Rossow
Aaron Roth
Guy Rothblum
Yannis Rouselakis
Indrajit Roy

Mark Ryan
Andrei Sabelfeld
Amit Sahai
Len Sassaman
Damien Saucez
Prateek Saxena
Stuart Schechter
Roman Schlegel
Thomas Schneider
Dominique Schroeder
Jacob Schuldt
Eric Seidel
Andrei Serjantov
Monirul Sharif
Weidong Shi
Seungwon Shin
Reza Shokri
Arunesh Sinha
Michael Sirivianos
Asia Slowinska
Adam Smith
Barbara Sprick
Sid Stamm
Artem Starostin
Angelos Stavrou
Gianluca Stringhini
Henning Sudbrock
Ankur Taly
Eno Thereska
Mohammad Torabi Dashti
Patrick Traynor
Nikos Triandopoulos
Carmela Troncoso
Tomasz Truderung
Max Tuengerthal
Dominique Unruh
Berkant Ustaoglu
Eugene Vasserman
Ingrid Verbauwhede
Damien Vergnaud
Andreas Vogt
Marko Vukolic
Qiyan Wang
Rui Wang
Tielei Wang
Xiaofeng Wang
Lei Wei
Joel Weinberger
Emmett Witchel
Marcin Wojcik
Edmund Wong
Matthew Wright
Rebecca Wright
Zhaoyan Xu
Jeff Yan
Chao Yang
Liu Yang
Bennet Yee
Yves Younan
Murtaza Zafer
Davide Zanetti
Jialong Zhang
Xiaolan Zhang
Alice Zheng
Joe Zimmerman

CCS 2011 Sponsor & Supporters

Sponsor:

acm SIGSAC

Supporters:

Army Research Office

NSF

Google

IBM

Microsoft Research

NOKIA
CONNECTING PEOPLE

NORTHWESTERN UNIVERSITY

PEARSON

Springer
science+business media

technicolor

Reflections on the Evolution of Internet Threats: The Growing Imperative for a Cyber Secure Society

Farnam Jahanian
Directorate for Computer and Information Science and Engineering
National Science Foundation
Arlington, VA, USA
fjahania@nsf.gov

Abstract

Critical infrastructure, including the Internet, plays a vital role in the economic, political, and social fabric of society. This interdependency leaves society vulnerable to a wide range of threats that impact the security, reliability, availability, and overall trustworthiness of information technology resources. Assuring these properties in the face of adversarial behavior and an Internet that has changed dramatically in size, complexity, and diversity over the last decade has proven to be a critical challenge.

In this talk, I will reflect on the evolution of Internet threats – from early threats, such as viruses and worms, to modern botnets. I will explore how changing attacker's technological means (e.g., resilient infrastructure, covert communication) have intertwined with attacker's changing social, behavioral, and economic motives (e.g., vandalism, crime, activism) to create today's large, complex, and diverse ecosystem of threats. I will also touch on how future innovation in the threat landscape will likely be driven by Internet adoption patterns such as the explosive growth of on-line data, the proliferation of mobile devices, and the emergence of the "cloud" computing paradigm.

In response to these challenges, I will discuss the need for sustained, long-term research investments in a spectrum of scientific and technical areas with particular emphasis on calls to develop the scientific foundations of cyber-security and to accelerate the transition of knowledge into practice. I will articulate a vision in which a cyber secure society is necessary if we are to achieve the promise of computing to address a wide range of national priorities including health, energy, transportation, education and life-long learning, and public safety/emergency preparedness.

Categories & Subject Descriptors: K.6.5

[Management of Computing and Information Systems]: Security and Protection; K.4.0 [Computers and Society]: General

General Terms: Security, Reliability, Algorithms, Experimentation, Human Factors

Bio

Farnam Jahanian serves as the National Science Foundation Assistant Director for the Computer and Information Science and Engineering (CISE) Directorate. He is on leave from the University of Michigan, where he holds the Edward S. Davidson Collegiate Professorship and served as Chair for Computer Science and Engineering from 2007 – 2011 and as Director of the Software Systems Laboratory from 1997 – 2000. His research on Internet infrastructure security formed the basis for the Internet security company Arbor Networks, which he co-founded in 2001. He served as Chairman until its acquisition by Tektronix Communication in 2010.

Dr. Jahanian guides CISE, with a budget of over $600 million, in its mission to uphold the nation's leadership in computer and information science and engineering through its support for fundamental and transformative advances. Dr. Jahanian is also co-chair of the Networking and Information Technology Research and Development (NITRD) Subcommittee of the National Science and Technology Council Committee on Technology, providing overall coordination for the activities of 14 government agencies.

Dr. Jahanian holds a master's degree and a Ph.D. in Computer Science from the University of Texas at Austin. He is a Fellow of the Association for Computing Machinery (ACM), the Institute of Electrical and Electronic Engineers (IEEE), and the American Association for the Advancement of Science (AAAS).

CCS'11, October 17-21, 2011, Chicago, Illinois, USA.
ACM 978-1-4503-0948-6/11/10.

VIPER: Verifying the Integrity of PERipherals' Firmware

Yanlin Li, Jonathan M. McCune, and Adrian Perrig
CyLab, Carnegie Mellon University
Pittsburgh, PA, USA
{yanlli,jonmccune,perrig}@cmu.edu

ABSTRACT

Recent research demonstrates that malware can infect peripherals' firmware in a typical x86 computer system, e.g., by exploiting vulnerabilities in the firmware itself or in the firmware update tools. Verifying the integrity of peripherals' firmware is thus an important challenge. We propose software-only attestation protocols to verify the integrity of peripherals' firmware, and show that they can detect all known software-based attacks. We implement our scheme using a Netgear GA620 network adapter in an x86 PC, and evaluate our system with known attacks.

Categories and Subject Descriptors

D.4.6 [**Software**]: Operating Systems—*Security and Protection*

General Terms

Security, Verification

Keywords

Integrity of Peripherals' Firmware, Proxy Attack, Software-based Attestation

1. INTRODUCTION

An often-overlooked software attack target is the firmware that executes in peripheral devices. Attackers can exploit vulnerabilities in peripherals' firmware or their firmware update tools [5, 7]. The malware, once inside a peripheral, may also compromise other peripherals' firmware. In 2008, Triulzi demonstrated how to exploit a vulnerability in a Broadcom Tigon network interface card (NIC), and inject malware into the NIC to eavesdrop on all traffic [35]. Triulzi also showed that the malware on the NIC can deploy malicious code into the GPU, causing the GPU to store and analyze the data sent through the NIC [36]. In 2009, Chen exploited a vulnerability in the Apple keyboard firmware update tool, which enables attackers to inject malicious code into the firmware of an Apple Aluminum Keyboard during firmware update [5]. Such malicious code can be a key-logger or script that can compromise the host operating system. In 2010, a buffer overflow vulnerability in a Broadcom NIC firmware was published [7], through which a remote attacker can compromise the NIC firmware by sending malicious packets to this NIC, then execute arbitrary code on the NIC.

We expect that malware on peripherals' firmware will be a popular trend for next-generation malware. Unfortunately, it is still an open challenge to detect malware on peripherals or verify the integrity of peripherals' firmware because (1) the limited memory and computational resources on peripherals make it difficult to deploy complex security primitives on peripherals themselves; and (2) hardware-based protection is impractical because it would add cost and complexity to devices already under severe economic constraints.

Problem Definition. In today's computer systems, all peripheral devices with firmware, such as network adapters, USB and disk controllers, and even the BIOS, are at risk from computer malware. Verifying the integrity of these components' firmware, and guaranteeing the absence of malware, is the main problem we address in this paper.

At first glance, software-based attestation [30, 31] may provide an approach for verifying the integrity of firmware. Device vendors could embed an attestation function in their firmware, which driver code executing on the main CPU could query to verify firmware integrity. The advantages of software-based attestation are that no costly hardware changes are needed, and that the OS can validate firmware integrity (e.g., as a standard part of device driver initialization). Unfortunately, previously proposed approaches for software-based attestation have several shortcomings that preclude applicability in this context. The most serious shortcoming is a *proxy attack* (Figure 1), in which a queried device contacts a faster device (the proxy) to compute the correct answer to the time-sensitive checksum computation, which enables malware on the device to go undetected. Peripherals, such as a NIC, can communicate with a remote proxy server to compute the expected answer. Also, faster peripherals can work as a proxy server to compute correct answers for slower peripherals in the face of previous software-based attestation mechanisms.

Thanks to several new approaches, we improve software-based attestation for devices and bring these approaches into the realm of practicality. In fact, we leverage intricacies of the system buses to create a software-based attestation function that prevents proxy attacks and dramatically increases

CCS'11, October 17–21, 2011, Chicago, Illinois, USA.

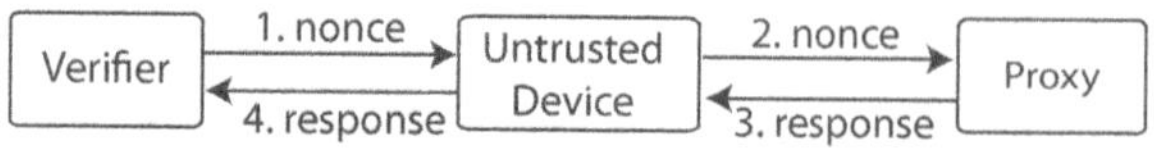

Figure 1: A Proxy Attack.

the time overhead that malicious code exhibits. More specifically, we propose to verify the peripheral firmware integrity on a modern computer system, and propose a software-only primitive, Verifying Integrity of PERipherals (VIPER). In the spirit of software-based attestation, VIPER is based on a timed challenge-response protocol between the host CPU and each peripheral. Our attestation protocols can detect all known software-based attacks on peripherals.

This paper makes the following contributions:

1. We systematically analyze the features of malware on computer peripherals.
2. We propose a software-only primitive, VIPER, to verify the integrity of peripheral devices' firmware.
3. We propose novel attestation protocols that prevent all known software-only attacks. Specifically, our attestation protocols can prevent a proxy attack that would have been successful against previous software-based attestation mechanisms.
4. We fully implement VIPER on a Netgear GA620 network adapter in an off-the-shelf computer, and also implement an Ethernet-based proxy attack. Our evaluation shows that VIPER can efficiently verify the integrity of peripherals' firmware.

The remainder of this paper is organized as follows: Section 2 provides background knowledge on the system bus and architecture of a modern computer system, and malware on peripherals. Section 3 describes our assumptions and attacker model. The VIPER architecture and attestation protocols are detailed in Section 4. Section 5 describes our implementation, and Section 6 gives evaluation results with the best known attacks. Open problems and limitations are treated in Section 7, related work in Section 8, and conclusions in Section 9.

2. BACKGROUND

We provide the necessary background on the system buses and architecture of a modern motherboard, and the features of malware on peripherals.

Modern System Buses and Architecture. Figure 2 shows a diagram of a modern motherboard. Two logical chipsets (north- and southbridge) connect the host CPU(s) with memory, PCI-family buses, and numerous other buses and peripherals. The northbridge (memory controller hub) typically deals with communication among the CPU, main memory, any PCI Express (PCIe) peripherals, and the southbridge (I/O controller hub). The southbridge primarily handles communication among the northbridge, IDE, SATA, USB, LPC, PCI or PCI-X buses / peripherals, and so on. On a modern motherboard, the clock speed of the northbridge and southbridge can exceed 1 GHz. The capacity of various versions of PCI buses are from 1066 Mbps (32-bit at 33.3 MHz) to 4266 Mbps (64-bit at 66.6 MHz). The capacity of a PCI-X bus is 4266 Mbps (64-bit at 66.6 MHz) or 8512 Mbps (64-bit at 133 MHz) [21]. PCIe supports 2 Gbps (v1), 4 Gbps (v2), and 8 Gbps (v3) on each lane, with up to 32 lanes in each PCIe slot [20].

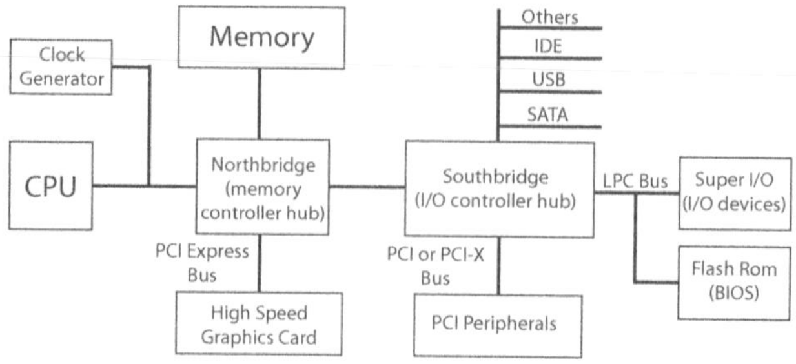

Figure 2: Hardware Architecture of a Modern Motherboard.

Memory-mapped I/O (MMIO) [13] maps part of the memory inside peripherals (MMIO memory) to the main memory address space of the host CPU, and enables the host CPU to access the MMIO memory on peripherals through ordinary memory read or write instructions. A separate I/O address space also exists and can be used to interface with some peripherals, in which case the host CPU accesses the peripherals through special I/O instructions (e.g., `outb`).

Direct Memory Access (DMA) enables peripherals to transfer data between main memory and the device's local memory without involving the host CPU. The memory addresses in the main memory that a peripheral can access through DMA can be controlled in newer systems with hardware support for virtualization by using an input/output memory management unit (IOMMU) [1, 2, 14].

Peer-to-Peer Peripheral Communication. Based on the PCI and PCIe specifications [20, 21], two PCI / PCIe peripherals can engage in peer-to-peer communication. However, under typical workloads on a commodity PC, one endpoint is almost always the host CPU or main memory. Nevertheless, on a modern motherboard, DMA potentially enables a peripheral device to read or write other peripherals' MMIO memory. For instance, the GPU often has a large amount of memory (1 GB or more) mapped into the main memory address space using MMIO. A NIC can write or read the GPU's MMIO memory using DMA [27, 36]. In today's systems, the IOMMU is in the northbridge, and it is responsible for configuring the main memory addresses that peripherals can access through DMA. Any DMA access to main memory must go through the IOMMU. However, two PCI peripherals can often avoid the IOMMU, especially if both peripherals connect via the southbridge [27].

Malware on Peripherals. Once malware infects computer peripherals, it has the following features:

1. Malware on a peripheral can eavesdrop on sensitive data handled by the peripheral (e.g., passwords).
2. Malware on a peripheral may modify executable programs or scan sensitive data in main memory via DMA if the IOMMU is not perfectly configured or not present on a computer system.
3. Malware on one peripheral may spread malicious code to other peripherals through DMA.
4. Malicious peripherals can collude using peer-to-peer bus communication without involving the host CPU.
5. Malware on peripherals cannot be removed by firmware

update tools if the firmware update procedure assumes that the existing firmware is benign.

3. ASSUMPTIONS & ATTACKER MODEL

Assumptions. Our focus is in protecting peripherals from network-based threats. Attacks where an attacker physically accesses the target device to change its hardware configuration (e.g., over-clocking peripherals' CPUs or increasing their memory) are out of scope. We assume that the verification program on the host CPU is correct, and that the operating system on the host CPU is secure and trustworthy during verification. While this is a strong assumption [26], recent work in OS-level security and trustworthy computing may in fact provide a reasonable platform from which to attempt peripheral device verification [3, 19, 37]. We also require that the verifier program on the host CPU has been configured with sufficient information about peripheral devices installed in a computer system, i.e., the verifier knows what is *supposed* to be there.

Attacker Model. The attacker may compromise firmware executing inside peripheral devices. The attacker may also control remote machines that may assist a compromised device in responding to challenges. This machine may have considerable computation and memory resources, though the attacker is still unable to break standard cryptographic primitives [23]. However, we assume practical communication constraints, such as the bandwidth and latency characteristics of PCI [20, 21] and Gigabit Ethernet.

4. VIPER: VERIFYING THE INTEGRITY OF PERIPHERALS' FIRMWARE

We describe the VIPER system architecture, attestation protocols, and checksum function.

4.1 VIPER Overview

VIPER is a software-only solution to verify the integrity of peripherals' firmware using a timed challenge-response protocol between the host CPU and peripherals.

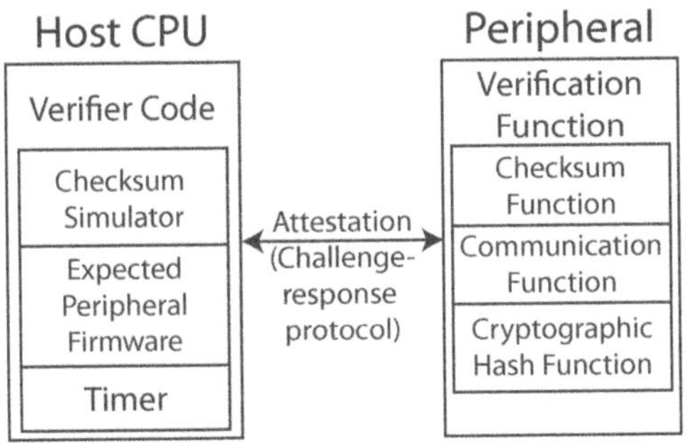

Figure 3: VIPER system architecture.

System Architecture. In VIPER (Figure 3), a verifier program executes on the host CPU and performs the verification procedure over all peripherals one-by-one on a computer system. The verifier program has correct copies of all peripheral firmware (e.g., bundled with device drivers) in the computer. A checksum simulator in the verifier program generates challenges (cryptographic nonces) and the corresponding expected responses by simulating the verification procedure over the correct copies of peripherals' firmware. A timer is used to measure the time of the verification procedure from inside the verifier program ("Verifier Code" in Figure 3). On each peripheral device, a verification function comprised of three main parts engages in the VIPER verification protocol to set up an untampered execution environment and compute a special checksum function over the contents of the verification function's components (the checksum function itself, a communication function, and a cryptographic hash function). The checksum function is carefully designed to offer optimal performance. Any malicious code or operations during verification either invalidate the checksum result, or cause a detectable delay in the verification function's response. When the checksum computation finishes, the checksum function invokes the hash function over the entire memory contents of the peripheral. By verifying the checksum result and the computation time, the verifier program obtains the guarantee that an untampered execution environment has been set up inside the peripheral device, and that the subsequent computation of the complete hash of the peripheral's firmware is trustworthy.

Full System Verification. In VIPER, the host CPU verifies the firmware integrity of all peripherals one-by-one. However, a faster peripheral on the motherboard can work as a proxy helper for a slower peripheral. Consider a resource-impoverished device such as a keyboard. Such devices are likely equipped with 8-bit microcontrollers running at a few tens of MHz. The computational latency imposed by running a checksum algorithm on such devices may actually be large enough to cover up the communication latency induced by forwarding nonces and responses to a faster malicious device elsewhere in the system or even on an external system.

The solution for verifying a device with a particular level of computational capability is that all devices with greater capabilities must be verified first. For example, to verify a slow 8-bit microcontroller, all high-speed peripheral devices (e.g., NIC, SATA controller, GPU, USB 3.0) must first be verified. After the attestation of a faster peripheral, the verification function on the faster peripheral continues running until all peripherals have been verified. In this way, VIPER can prevent the faster peripheral from being compromised during the time interval between initial verification of the faster peripheral and completion of the verification of all peripherals. Thus, the verifier program on the host CPU can conclude that the devices capable of masquerading as the weak device are all benign, and will not interfere with the verification process.

Verification Procedure. We now detail the verification procedure for a single peripheral.

1. The verifier program calls the checksum simulator to generate nonces, and expected checksum and hash results by simulating the verification procedure.
2. The verifier program sends an attestation request to the peripheral. The checksum function on the peripheral resets the peripheral into a known-good state.
3. The verifier program starts a timer, and begins to perform the attestation by sending the nonces generated by the checksum simulator to the target peripheral over the system's bus (Section 4.2).
4. The verification function executing inside the peripheral sets up an untampered execution environment, performs the checksum computation, and sends the result back to

the verifier program on the host CPU. The verification function then calls the hash function to compute a hash over the full memory contents of the target peripheral.

5. The verifier program confirms that the checksum results are correct and timely.
6. The verification function on the peripheral sends the hash result to the verifier program.
7. The verifier program validates the hash result.

4.2 Attestation Protocol

Though an on-board proxy attack can be prevented or detected as described in Section 4.1, it is a challenge to detect a remote proxy attack. A network-enabled peripheral device can communicate with a remote proxy helper through its network interface. Also, the network-enabled peripheral can work as a communication medium in a hybrid proxy attack, e.g., when a USB peripheral is being verified, a NIC may help the USB peripheral to contact a remote proxy helper, even if the NIC's CPU is slower than the USB peripheral's. In this section, we propose novel attestation protocols that detect such remote proxy attacks.

4.2.1 *Latency-based Attestation Protocol*

In a proxy attack, the peripheral to be verified always incurs some latency to communicate with a proxy helper. If the checksum computation time is well-controlled and smaller than the minimal communication latency between the peripheral and a proxy helper, the additional latency caused by the proxy attack is detectable, even if the proxy helper has infinitely fast computation resources. In this section, we detail a latency-based attestation protocol based on these observations. Also, we describe a technique to increase the communication overhead between a peripheral and a proxy helper, and a technique to accelerate the attestation procedure by synchronizing the host CPU and peripheral. Figure 4 shows the time line of one challenge-response pair in a latency-based attestation protocol, including both the normal computation, and the proxy attack.

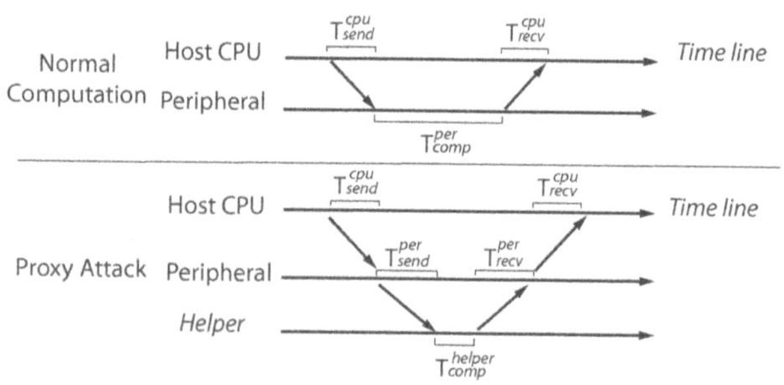

Figure 4: One challenge-response pair for latency-based attestation under both normal computation and a proxy attack.

Under normal conditions, the host CPU sends a challenge to the peripheral requiring time T_{send}^{cpu}, and the checksum computation consumes time T_{comp}^{per}. After checksum computation, communication consumes time T_{recv}^{cpu} to send the checksum back to the host CPU. Thus, the time of one challenge-response pair is:

$$T_{comp}^{normal} = T_{send}^{cpu} + T_{comp}^{per} + T_{recv}^{cpu} \quad (1)$$

In a proxy attack, the peripheral forwards the challenge sent by the host CPU to a proxy helper, which consumes time T_{send}^{per}. The remote helper consumes T_{comp}^{helper} to compute the correct checksum, and then takes T_{recv}^{per} to send the result back to the peripheral. Thus, in the proxy attack, the time of each challenge-response pair is:

$$T_{comp}^{proxy} = T_{send}^{cpu} + T_{send}^{per} + T_{comp}^{helper} + T_{recv}^{per} + T_{recv}^{cpu} \quad (2)$$

We assume that T_{comp}^{helper} is zero because we conservatively assume that the remote helper has massive computational and memory resources available. Then, the overhead caused by a proxy attack is:

$$T_{overhead}^{proxy} = T_{send}^{per} + T_{recv}^{per} - T_{comp}^{per} \quad (3)$$

To detect a proxy attack, $T_{overhead}^{proxy}$ must be positive and detectable. Therefore, T_{comp}^{per} must be well-controlled to guarantee that T_{comp}^{per} is smaller than the minimal detectable proxy overhead. Note that modern network interfaces can have extremely low latency for short connections (e.g., consider a gigabit Ethernet crossover cable). Thus, the practical bound for minimal proxy overhead is a function of the application scenario. Internet-based attacks are unlikely to be less than one millisecond away, but an "evil maid" attack can easily manage sub-millisecond latencies.

If T_{comp}^{per} must be small, it is unlikely that the entire memory region containing the verification function can be checked during a single challenge-response pair. Thus, VIPER employs multiple challenge-response iterations to guarantee that the entire verification function memory region is verified. Between two consecutive challenge-response pairs, the communication function waits for the next challenge. Note that the communication function is also part of the verification function (Figure 3) and is verified by the checksum function. However, during the time interval between two consecutive challenge-response pairs, an adversary can accurately guess the expected behavior of the checksum function. To remove this potential attack surface, we work to minimize any idle waiting time by overlapping checksum computation and challenge-response exchange.

Increasing Proxy Communication Overhead. The checksum function maintains state as an array of bit vectors. During one iteration of the checksum computation, several checksum vectors may be updated. However, to make the communication between the verifier program and the peripheral efficient, only one randomly-selected checksum vector is returned to the host CPU during each challenge-response pair. To increase the communication overhead between peripherals and the proxy helper, we design the protocol such that the host CPU sends a new challenge to the peripheral before the checksum vector is returned, and the checksum vector to be returned is chosen based on this newly-received challenge sent by the verifier program. This is illustrated in Figure 5, where *cksum*[*i*] denotes a single checksum vector randomly selected from the full checksum state as it exists after an iteration computed with *nonce*[*i*] as an input. The random selection is chosen based on the value of *nonce*[*i + 1*]. T_{diff}^{n}, the time interval between receiving the new challenge and sending the correct checksum result, is so small that a proxy helper is forced to return the entire set of correct checksum vectors or at least all the checksum vectors that have been updated during the checksum computation back to the peripheral before missing the time deadline. (A proxy that randomly guesses which vector to return will quickly be detected as additional checksum iterations drive the probability of repeated successful guessing to a negligible level.) This technique then increases the value of T^{per}_{recv}. The additional communication overhead of sending the entire set of vectors makes it overwhelmingly likely that the attacker will miss the deadline.

Continuous Checksum Computation. It is desirable to eliminate any idle waiting on the peripheral between checksum iterations, both for efficiency and to reduce the time during which an attacker knows that the checksum's internal state remains constant. The previous paragraph describes how a portion of the checksum state as influenced by $nonce[i]$ is not returned to the host CPU until $nonce[i+1]$ is received. If the peripheral device supports concurrent computation and data exchange (as is commonly the case with memory-mapped IO), then the reception of new nonces can be closely synchronized with the runtime of checksum iterations, thereby enabling continuous checksum computation. This is evident in Figure 5, when viewing a checksum iteration as the elapsed time at the host CPU between transmission of $nonce[i]$ and reception of $chsum[i]$. Excluding the very first and last checksum iterations, T^{cpu}_{send} for iteration $i+1$ and T^{cpu}_{recv} for iteration i do not impose any additional latency on the total checksum computation time.

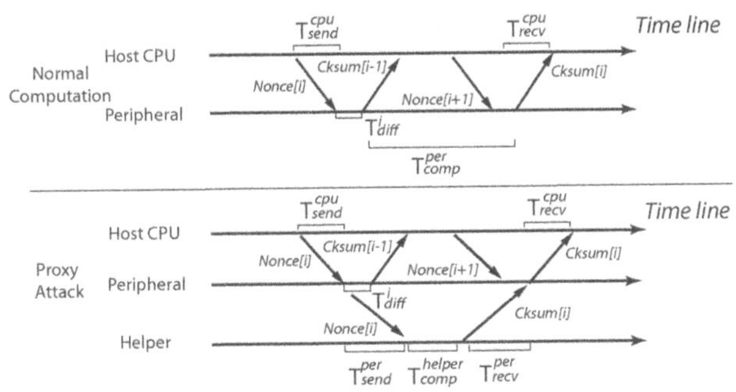

Figure 5: The latency-based attestation procedure after speed-up under benign and (hypothetically successful) attack conditions.

The time for a single challenge-response pair is:

$$T^{normal}_{comp} = T^{cpu}_{send} + T^{n}_{diff} + T^{per}_{comp} + T^{cpu}_{recv} \quad (4)$$

In this equation, T^{n}_{diff} is the time interval between receiving the nth nonce and sending the $(n-1)^{th}$ checksum result on the peripheral.

In a proxy attack, the malicious code on the peripheral sends the challenge to a proxy helper as soon as it receives the challenge. The time of a challenge-response pair in the proxy attack is:

$$T^{proxy}_{comp} = T^{cpu}_{send} + T^{per}_{send} + T^{helper}_{comp} + T^{per}_{recv} + T^{cpu}_{recv} \quad (5)$$

We still assume that T^{helper}_{comp} is zero. Thus, the time overhead caused by a proxy attack is:

$$T^{proxy}_{overhead} = T^{per}_{send} + T^{per}_{recv} - T^{n}_{diff} - T^{per}_{comp} \quad (6)$$

Through this equation, we can see that T^{n}_{diff} decreases the value of $T^{proxy}_{overhead}$. Thus, it is desirable that the CPU and peripheral are well-synchronized so that $T^{proxy}_{overhead}$ remains positive and detectable.

4.2.2 *Other Potential Attestation Solutions*

Other features of communication channels, such as communication latency variance, packet loss, and throughput, may also be viable tools to detect a proxy attack when verifying the integrity of peripherals' firmware. Compared with Ethernet communication, the communication channel between the host CPU and the peripheral is very efficient and stable, with low communication latency variance and near-zero packet loss rate. In a communication latency variance-based attestation protocol, if the communication variance on the proxy communication channel is larger than the well controlled checksum computation time, the proxy helper cannot always send the expected checksum result back to the peripheral in time. A packet loss-based attestation protocol is similar. Network devices suffer from different levels of packet loss with Ethernet. However, on the motherboard, the communication between the host CPU and peripherals over system buses has near-zero loss rate. Therefore, a packet loss-based attestation protocol may also represent a practical solution to verify the integrity of peripherals' firmware in a computer system. A throughput-based attestation protocol requires that the throughput between the host CPU and the peripheral is larger than the throughput between the peripheral and the proxy helper. The host CPU can send a large amount of random data to the peripheral and require that the random data is incorporated into the checksum computation. To attempt an attack, all of the random data must be sent from the peripheral to the proxy helper. The protocol can be constructed such that the checksum computation on the NIC will complete before the necessary challenge and response can be exchanged with the proxy. We leave the detailed investigation of these mechanisms as future work.

4.3 Design of the Checksum Function

In this section, we describe the design of our checksum function in detail. Similar to other software-based attestation schemes [18, 30, 31], our checksum function sets up an untampered execution environment, computes a fingerprint over the contents of the verification function (i.e., the checksum function itself, and communication and hash functions). Through the checksum result and elapsed computation time, the checksum function provides a guarantee to the verifier program that the verification function has not been modified and the following hash computation was carried out in the untampered execution environment, and is therefore trustworthy. As discussed in the above sections, the checksum function needs to be carefully designed to achieve the necessary timing properties.

There are many different system architectures and instruction sets on peripheral devices. It is difficult to design a single generic checksum function for all cases. However, we first discuss the general principles that apply to the design of the checksum function for any peripheral:

1. All available registers are used during checksum computation. For any additional operations (malicious operations), an attacker has to utilize memory operations (read and write) to save the register values first. This causes large computational overhead since memory operations are much slower than register operations.
2. Each iteration of the checksum function should fit into the Instruction Cache if there is an Instruction Cache, and cause as few cache misses as possible. Any ad-

ditional operations inserted by malicious code should cause more cache misses.

3. To prevent an attacker from predicting the memory addresses to read, the checksum function reads from memory addresses in a pseudo-random pattern.
4. To prevent an attacker from computing the expected checksum result over a correct copy of the verification function located in some other memory address, the data pointer (DP) value used to address memory should be included in the checksum computation, i.e., the checksum computation is position-*dependent*.
5. To further prevent malicious code from performing the computation at other memory addresses, the program counter (PC) value is also included in the checksum computation if the PC value can be efficiently read by the checksum function.
6. The checksum function is simple enough that it is feasible to determine that the implementation is optimal but non-parallelizable.

We design our checksum function using a sequence of strongly-ordered ADD and XOR operations, since they are naturally non-parallelizable. Strongly-ordered means that the sequence of checksum operations cannot be changed without causing the checksum result to be different with high probability. Each checksum state update incorporates the value of the program counter (PC), data pointer (DP), contents of the memory referenced by the DP, the most recent nonce sent by the verifier, and the existing checksum states. The carry bit should be included during addition operations if a carry bit is supported on the target peripheral, to avoid losing entropy due to repeated invocation of the checksum. We use intermediate checksum results to select the memory addresses to read in a pseudo-random fashion. This helps to optimize the implementation of the checksum function, since we do not need additional instructions to generate pseudo-random numbers. Malware, in an attempt to remain undetected, must forge the correct PC or DP values during checksum computation. However, forging the PC or DP value will require additional register and memory operations, and cause cache misses and extra memory operations, which will result in detectable computational overhead. We describe our specific implementation of the checksum function on a Netgear GA620 NIC [12] in Section 5.3.

5. IMPLEMENTATION

We implement and evaluate VIPER on an x86-class computer system. Because of the limited availability of source code for peripherals' firmware, we focus on a PCI-X Netgear GA620 Gigabit Ethernet Adapter (NIC) that uses open source firmware [11]. We installed this card in a Sun Fire V20z 1U rack-mount server that includes a single-core AMD Opteron processor running at 1.795 GHz, 2 GB of RAM, and two PCI-X expansion slots. In this section, we describe the hardware architecture of the Netgear GA620 NIC, and present the detailed implementation of our latency-based attestation scheme.

5.1 Netgear GA620 Network Adapter

The Netgear GA620 is a Gigabit Ethernet adapter with a 64-bit PCI-X interface. The theoretical maximum throughput between the host CPU and the GA620 NIC is 8.5 Gbps on a 133.3 MHz, 64-bit PCI-X bus. The maximal bandwidth of the Ethernet link of the Netgear GA620 is 1 Gbps. Figure 6 illustrates the architecture of a Netgear GA620. The GA620 features two MIPS microcontrollers "A" and "B" running at 200 MHz. The two microcontrollers work simultaneously, and the firmware assigns work to both microcontrollers. In firmware version 12.4.3 [11], Microcontroller A works as the main controller in charge of packet transmission, and microcontroller B assists by preparing DMA descriptors. On each microcontroller, there is a 64-byte Instruction Cache (which fits 16 instructions), and an 8-byte Data Cache. On microcontroller A there are 16 KB of scratch pad memory, though microcontroller B has only 8 KB of scratch pad memory. The scratch pad memory of each microcontroller is located in the same memory address range, and one microcontroller physically cannot address the other's scratch pad memory. The host CPU and DMA transactions are also unable to address either scratch pad memory region. During NIC initialization, the firmware moves some time-critical functions into the scratch pad memory. A 4 MB SRAM is shared by both microcontrollers.

Instruction Set Architecture. The microcontrollers implement a 32-bit MIPS instruction set architecture. There are 32 registers, where r0 is always zero, and r1 – r31 are used for common operations. All arithmetic operations, logical operations, memory operations, and jump operations are supported while the rotation-shift, multiply, and divide operations, which are available in general MIPS microcontrollers, are removed. In arithmetic operations the carry bit value is not included, which makes the design of an attestation function significantly more challenging because the lack of the carry bit results in entropy loss. The lack of a multiplier or rotation shift also complicates implementation of a size-optimized cryptographic hash function. However, firmware can read the program counter value indirectly using jump instructions (e.g., *JAL* or *JALR*).

Memory Layout. Figure 7 illustrates the memory layout of the external SRAM on a Netgear GA620 NIC. The first 16 KB of the external SRAM is mapped into the memory addresses of the host CPU via a memory-mapped IO (MMIO) interface. Both the host CPU and NIC firmware can read or write this MMIO memory. Following the shared MMIO memory, the NIC firmware is in the space from 0x04000 to 0x16000. After the firmware space follows the space for each microcontroller's stack, RX/TX DMA descriptors and RX/TX buffers. On microcontroller A, the 16 KB internal scratch pad memory is addressable from 0x00c00000 to 0x00c04000. On microcontroller B, the 8 KB internal scratch pad memory occupies 0x00c00000 to 0x00c02000.

NIC – Host CPU Communication. The Netgear GA620 NIC and host CPU communicate via a *Mailbox* abstraction, which is a bank of 32 8-byte communication registers that are mapped into the host CPU's MMIO address space. Microcontroller A uses the lower 16 mailbox registers and microcontroller B uses the higher 16 mailbox registers. The host CPU can read or write to the mailbox registers directly using ordinary memory operations (e.g., `mov`). When the host CPU writes a mailbox register, an event is generated on the GA620 NIC and the NIC firmware can detect the event by checking the event register. However, the GA620 NIC cannot cause interrupts to the host CPU by writing values into the mailbox registers, because the interrupt mechanism on the host CPU is too slow to support Gigabit-speed

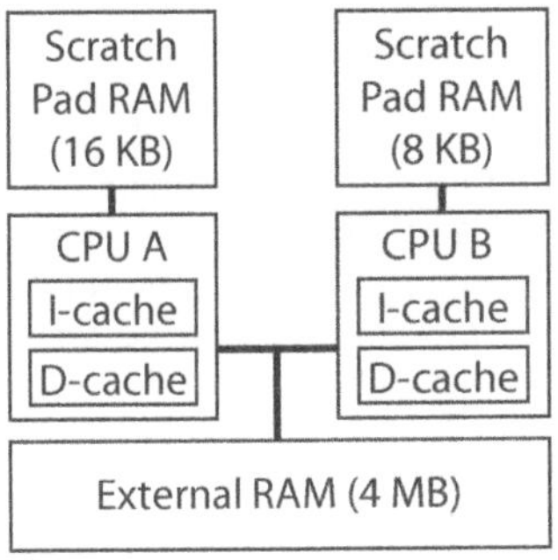

Figure 6: Netgear GA620 System Architecture.

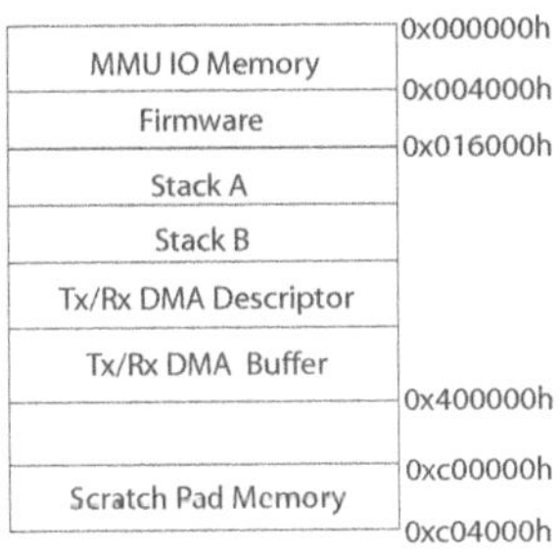

Figure 7: Netgear GA620 Memory Layout.

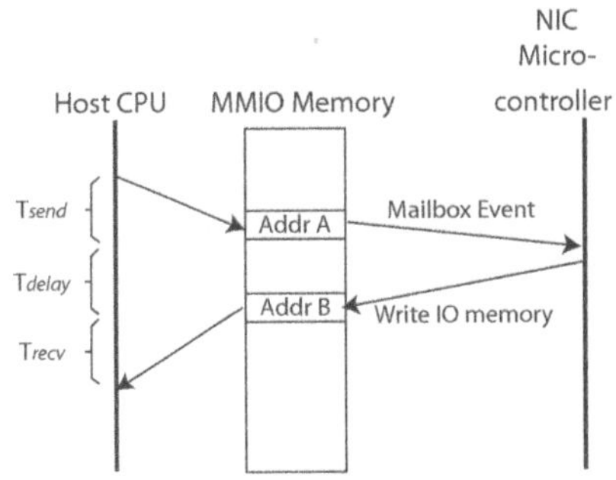

Figure 8: Host CPU to NIC communication via GA620's *mailbox*.

communication. For large amounts of data, such as network packets, the NIC transmits the data between local memory (TX/RX buffer) and main memory through DMA.

5.2 Verification for Microcontrollers A and B

We conduct the attestation protocol on both microcontrollers A and B to verify the entire memory contents of the Netgear GA620 NIC. To prevent the verification functions running on one microcontroller from being modified by malicious code running on the other microcontroller, we execute the verification functions within the scratch-pad memory of each microcontroller. On each microcontroller, we implement: a checksum function *VCF* (*Viper Checksum Function*) (Section 4.3) that computes a checksum over the entire verification function memory contents; a communication function that initializes the checksum states, reads nonces from the host CPU, and randomly returns a 32-bit checksum state vector to the host CPU for each nonce-checksum pair. *VCF* and the communication function are implemented using 656 MIPS instructions, and are deployed into the scratch pad memory of each microcontroller. A SHA-1 hash function is deployed into the scratch pad memory of Microcontroller A and its binary code consumes 2 KB. In detail, the attestation procedure performs the following operations:

1. The verifier program on the host CPU sends an attestation request to both microcontrollers A and B on the NIC. The checksum functions on both microcontrollers A and B set the NIC to a known state.
2. The verifier program conducts the latency-based attestation protocol for microcontroller B first.
3. During the attestation, *VCF*, which is in microcontroller B's scratch-pad memory, sets up an untampered execution environment and computes a checksum over the entire 8 KB scratch pad memory on Microcontroller B. Because microcontroller A cannot access microcontroller B's scratch pad memory, any malicious code on microcontroller A cannot tamper with the execution environment on microcontroller B.
4. Because *VCF* verifies the entire scratch pad memory on Microcontroller B, it is not necessary to call the SHA-1 hash function to compute a hash over the scratch pad memory on Microcontroller B. After the attestation procedure for microcontroller B, the communication function on microcontroller B continues to run but waits for an *EXIT* command from the host CPU. The host CPU will not send an *EXIT* until the attestation for both microcontrollers B and A are complete. Note that while it waits, the program counter of microcontroller B remains within the scratch-pad memory that has just been verified, so its behavior is known.
5. The verifier program on the host CPU verifies the checksum results and computation time during the attestation for microcontroller B. If the attestation for microcontroller B is successful, the verifier program conducts the attestation for microcontroller A, also using the latency-based attestation protocol.
6. During the attestation for microcontroller A, *VCF* on microcontroller A first sets up an untampered execution environment, and computes checksums over *VCF* itself, the communication function, and the SHA-1 hash function.
7. The *VCF* calls the SHA-1 hash function to compute a cryptographic hash over the memory contents of the entire scratch-pad memory on microcontroller A, and of the external SRAM. It then sends the hash result to the host CPU. Because the verification function on microcontroller B is running during the attestation of microcontroller A, the attestation procedure of microcontroller A cannot be tampered with by B.
8. The verifier program on the host CPU confirms the attestation results (checksum results, timing results, and hash result) of the attestation for microcontroller A.
9. The verifier program informs both microcontrollers A and B to exit their attestation functions.

5.3 Checksum Function Implementation

We implement the checksum function *VCF* as 32 checksum computation blocks. Each block has 16 MIPS CPU instructions and fits precisely into the 64-byte instruction cache, since all instructions are 32 bits long. As each block executes, one 32-bit checksum vector, out of a total of 26 checksum state vectors, are updated using alternating ADD and XOR operations. Each block takes as input: a subset of the contents of scratch pad memory in the NIC, other checksum states, nonces from the verifier program on the host CPU, the memory addresses being read (data pointer), and the program counter. Figure 9 shows the pseudo-code to update one checksum state in each block. All 31 available general purpose registers ($r1$ to $r31$) are used by the checksum computation: 26 registers ($r5$ to $r30$) are used to save checksum states; $r1$ and $r31$ are used as temporary variables to save memory addresses and the values of recently read memory; $r2$ stores the nonce provided by the host CPU; $r3$ stores the end address of each checksum block; $r4$ stores the starting address of each checksum block (both $r3$ and $r4$ essentially reflect program counter values).

```
/* Pseudo Code to update one checksum state:
   C is the checksum vector,
   i is the index of a checksum vector register,
   tmp is a temporary variable,
   addr is the memory address to read,
   memory_base can be the beginning address of
   a checksum block or the end address of
   a checksum block. */
/* in odd blocks */
tmp = mem[addr] xor C[(i-2) mod 26] + addr
/* construct another memory address */
addr = memory_base xor ( tmp & mask )
/* update one checksum state */
C[i] = mem[addr] xor C[i] + PC xor nonce + tmp
/* create dependency on C[i] for next iteration */
nonce = nonce + C[i]

/* in even blocks */
tmp = mem[addr] + C[(i-2) mod 26] + addr
/* construct another memory address */
addr = memory_base xor ( tmp & mask )
/* update one checksum state */
C[i] = mem[addr] + C[i] xor PC + nonce xor tmp
/* create dependency on C[i] for next iteration */
nonce = nonce xor C[i]
```

Figure 9: Pseudo-code to update one checksum state vector.

Assembly Instruction	Explanation
xor r31, r4, r1	$addr = memory\_base \oplus offset$
lw r1, 0(r31)	*memory read*
xor r1, r5, r1	$tmp1 = r5 \oplus mem[addr]$
add r31, r31, r1	$tmp2 = addr + tmp1$
andi r1, r31, 0x1ffc	$offset = tmp2 \ \&\ mask$
xor r1, r3, r1	$addr = memory\_base \oplus offset$
lw r1, 0(r1)	*memory read*
xor r1, r7, r1	$tmp3 = r7 \oplus mem[addr]$
add r1, r3, r1	$tmp3 = PC + tmp3$
xor r1, r2, r1	$tmp3 = nonce \oplus tmp3$
add r7, r31, r1	$r7 = tmp2 + tmp3$
add r2, r7, r2	$nonce = r7 + nonce$
andi r1, r7, 0x7c0	$tmp4 = r7 \ \&\ mask1$
xor r4, r4, r1	$r4 = r4 \oplus tmp4$
jalr r3, r4	$r3 = PC + 8; jump\ to\ r4$
andi r1, r2, 0x1ffc	$offset = nonce \ \&\ mask$

Figure 10: Assembly instructions for one checksum block.

Figure 10 shows the assembly code of one checksum computation block. In this checksum block, one checksum state ($r7$) is updated based on the contents of two memory addresses, the values in $r3$, and another checksum state ($r5$). At the end of this checksum block, the value of $r3$ is updated by the instruction $JALR$, which reads the program counter (PC) value into $r3$ as part of a jump to the memory address saved in $r4$. Note that MIPS executes the instruction following a jump instruction even if the jump is taken; it executes prior to the instruction residing at the jump target. The value of $r4$ is updated using five bits (bits 6 to bits 10) of $r7$. Because the target address ($r4$) of the $JALR$ instruction is updated randomly, the PC jumps to the beginning address of one of the 32 checksum blocks at the end of each checksum block in a pseudo-random fashion. *In this way, we can prevent an attacker from predicting the target address of the jump instruction.* Out of the 32 checksum blocks, 4 checksum blocks are chosen as 'exit' blocks, which deterministically jump to the communication code following checksum computation. The communication code returns one 32-bit checksum state vector to the host CPU and reads the nonce most recently sent from the host CPU (i.e., the verifier program).

One checksum state is read in each block, and one state is updated (written) in each block. Cumulatively across all 32 checksum blocks, all 26 checksum states are updated. Since an attacker cannot predict which block will be used for computation until the current block has completed, the attacker cannot use any of the registers that store checksum states for malicious operations, unless the attacker first uses memory operations to save the values stored in those registers.

5.4 Latency-Based Attestation

As described in Section 4.2.1, to prevent a proxy attack, the checksum computation time must be well controlled, and small enough that the overhead of a proxy attack ($T^{proxy}_{overhead}$ from Eqn. 3) is detectable. In this section, we calculate the theoretical minimal time of a proxy attack over a 1 Gbps Ethernet link. Then, we describe the mailbox communication overhead between the host CPU and the GA620 NIC, the checksum computation time for one challenge-response pair, and an optimization to speed up the attestation procedure via synchronization.

5.4.1 Theoretical Fastest Time for a Proxy Attack

In an Ethernet-based proxy attack, to explore the best case for the attacker, we assume that both the peripheral and the proxy helper need no time to prepare the network packets. However, the packets used in a proxy attack must go through the hardware Ethernet MAC (physical serial communications port) of the NIC. Therefore, theoretically the fastest time of an Ethernet-based proxy attack is the time that it takes the packets to go through the Ethernet MAC of both the sender's and receiver's NICs, and the time that the data actually spends on the wire. We assume that the peripheral and the proxy helper utilize 72 byte raw Ethernet frames to exchange data during a proxy attack, as 72 bytes is the minimal allowable Ethernet frame size [10]. Assuming that both the peripheral and the proxy helper use 1 Gbps Ethernet MAC, the time consumed by packet transmission is 1152 nanoseconds for a round trip.[1] This is useful to set a lower bound for the shortest possible proxy attack (i.e., the fastest attack that could ever be performed with this hardware configuration), and sets $T^{per}_{send} + T^{per}_{recv} = 1152\ ns$ from Eqns. 3 and 6. Under these conditions, to detect a proxy attack, T^{per}_{comp} (Eqn. 3) and (if using the synchronized version) T^{n}_{diff} (Eqn. 6) must be sufficiently small that $T^{proxy}_{overhead}$ remains positive and detectable.

[1] $2 \cdot \frac{72\ bytes \cdot 8\ bits/byte}{1{,}000{,}000{,}000\ bits/second} = 1152\ ns$. 72 bytes is the minimal usable Ethernet frame size with payload [10].

5.4.2 *Communication Overhead*

During attestation, the host CPU measures the time for each challenge-response pair between the host CPU and the peripheral device. To detect the time overhead caused by malicious operations, the communication between the host CPU and peripheral should be efficient and stable. Figure 8 shows the mailbox communication architecture between the host CPU and the microcontrollers on the GA620 NIC.

Determining Communication Delay. We now describe our approach to empirically determine the CPU-NIC communication overheads (T^{cpu}_{send} and T^{cpu}_{recv} from Section 4.2.1). Essentially, we exchange the smallest possible amount of data between the CPU and the NIC, with the NIC performing the absolute minimum amount of computation to return a result. This is as close as we can practically come to setting $T^{per}_{comp} = 0$. First, the host CPU writes a 32-bit value into address A (a mailbox register address), which generates an event on the GA620 NIC. As soon as it detects the mailbox event, the firmware on the GA620 NIC updates the 32-bit value in address B. After a time delay, the host CPU repeatedly reads address B until it obtains the updated value from address B.

Since memory operations can take hundreds of CPU cycles, the communication between the host CPU and NIC is the most efficient when the host CPU can predict the precise time to read the updated value, and obtain the updated value from address B in a single read operation. Therefore, we design an experiment to predict the time delay between a mailbox write and mailbox read on the host CPU, so that the host CPU can communicate efficiently and reliably. In our experiment, the host CPU stalls for a fixed delay interval between the MMIO write and MMIO read. For each delay period, we repeat the MMIO write and MMIO read 200 times, and record the frequency that the host CPU obtains the updated value from address B in a single MMIO read. We then increase the delay, and repeat the same experiment until the delay is large enough that the host CPU can always read the updated value in a single MMIO read.

We implement the measurement code on both the host CPU and the GA620 NIC in assembly for efficiency. On the host CPU, we disable all interrupts on the CPU core where the measurement code is executing. We choose the instruction *RDTSC* to read the current CPU counter as a timer, taking care to incorporate a serializing instruction (i.e., *CPUID*) to prevent instruction reordering from impacting the accuracy of our measurements. We implement the delay by spinning in a tight loop that consumes exactly two clock cycles per loop iteration.

Figure 11 shows our experimental results. In this figure, the X-axis is the delay in nanoseconds, N. The Y-axis is the probability that the host CPU reads the updated value from address B in a single MMIO read when the host CPU stalls for N nanoseconds between writing the mailbox at address A and reading the value from address B. The experimental results show that when the delay is larger than 790 ns, the probability is 1.

Demonstrating Communication Reliability. We then fix the delay at 790 ns (determined from the previous results), and repeat the measurement another 200 times to confirm that communication is reliable. In this experiment, the host CPU measures the time between writing the mailbox event and obtaining the updated value from address B after a delay of 790 ns. Figure 12 shows our measurement results. The X-axis is individual trials and the Y-axis is the timing result in nanoseconds computed from CPU cycles. The average result of the 200 trials is $T^{cpu}_{send} + T^{cpu}_{recv} = 1375$ ns. The standard deviation is 4 nanoseconds.

5.4.3 *Checksum Computation Time*

We conduct two experiments to measure the time for checksum computation on the GA620 NIC. These experiments are similar to the experiments used to measure the communication overhead between the host CPU and NIC in Section 5.4.2. The only difference is that in the communication overhead measurement, the NIC writes a 4-byte value to MMIO memory immediately upon receiving a mailbox event, while in these experiments the NIC executes three checksum blocks before writing to MMIO memory. *Because we have implemented a checksum simulator, the checksum simulator always selects nonces where the NIC returns a checksum state after executing precisely three checksum blocks.*

As with the communication overhead measurement, we first perform experiments to predict the necessary delay on the host CPU to guarantee that the host CPU can obtain the expected checksum result in a single MMIO read operation. Figure 11 shows the probability that the host CPU gets the expected checksum result using a single MMIO read operation while varying the delay. For each delay period, the experiments are repeated 200 times. The experimental results show that after the delay reaches 1616 ns, the host CPU starts to read the expected checksum result for all 200 experiments, i.e., it becomes sufficiently reliable.

We conduct a second experiment to measure the entire time between the host CPU writing the mailbox event to MMIO memory, and reading the checksum result after a delay of 1616 ns (one challenge-response pair). In each trial, the checksum function on the NIC computes three checksum blocks. Figure 12 shows the time of 200 challenge-response pairs measured by the host CPU. The average value of a single challenge-response pair (T^{normal}_{comp}) is 2202 nanoseconds, with a standard deviation 4 nanoseconds. Based on these results, we can calculate that the time required for computing three checksums blocks (T^{per}_{comp}) on the NIC is about 827 nanoseconds, (i.e., $T^{per}_{comp} = T^{normal}_{comp} - (T^{cpu}_{send} + T^{cpu}_{recv}) =$ 2202 ns $-$ 1375 ns $=$ 827 ns). Thus, the overhead caused by the theoretical fastest proxy attack over 1 Gbps Ethernet is about 325 nanoseconds ($T^{proxy}_{overhead} = (T^{per}_{send} + T^{per}_{recv}) - T^{per}_{comp} =$ 1152 ns $-$ 827 ns $=$ 325 ns).

5.4.4 *Host CPU – NIC Synchronization*

A design goal of VIPER is to maximize the utilization of the system buses and the CPUs in the NIC, and to minimize the overall attestation runtime. Recall (Section 4.2.1) that we can parallelize bus communication and NIC computation; the host CPU sends the *next* nonce before the NIC writes the *current* checksum result into MMIO memory. These tight timing constraints require that the host CPU and NIC be synchronized, to guarantee (1) that the host CPU is able to send the nonce to the NIC before the NIC starts to return current checksum states, and (2) that the host CPU reads the checksum result from MMIO memory only after the NIC has updated the result. We describe the design and implementation of our synchronization mechanisms and the experiments that demonstrate their effectiveness.

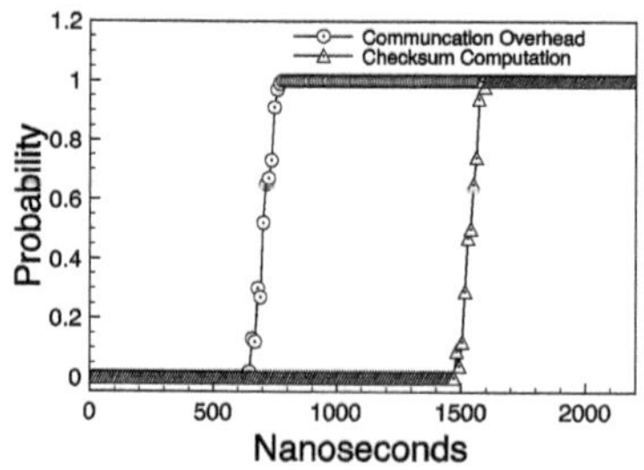

Figure 11: Impact of delay on probability that host CPU reads expected value from address B in a single MMIO read.

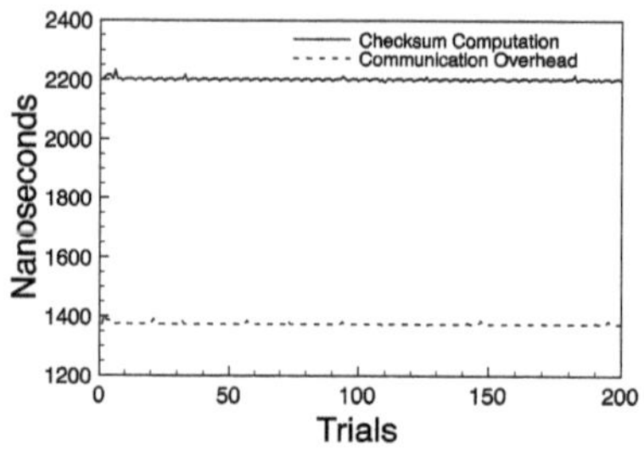

Figure 12: Communication overhead and checksum computation time (time of a challenge-response pair) measured by the host CPU.

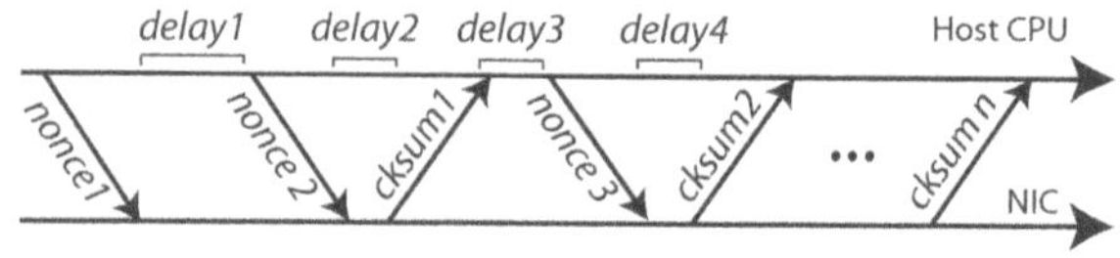

Figure 13: Verification procedure with synchronization between host CPU and NIC.

To remain synchronized, the time interval between two consecutive MMIO reads by the host CPU should match the time required to compute checksum blocks on the NIC CPU. Therefore, given the initiation time of a read of $cksum[i]$, the time when the host CPU should start to read the value of $cksum[i+1]$ can be predicted. In our implementation, the verifier code again uses *RDTSC* to read the CPU time stamp counter before starting to read $cksum[i]$, and then predicts the future time stamp counter value when the host CPU should start to read the following checksum state. The host CPU busy-waits in a tight loop that consumes exactly 2 CPU cycles per iteration until the necessary time arrives, although we convert iterations to nanoseconds to streamline presentation here. Figure 13 shows the verification procedure with synchronization between the host CPU and NIC. $nonce1$ is the first nonce that the host CPU sends to the NIC, while $cksum1$ is the first checksum result that the NIC returns to the host CPU.

To implement synchronization between the host CPU and NIC, the checksum computation time must be long enough that the host can perform one MMIO read operation (read a checksum result) and one MMIO write operation (write a nonce to the NIC) inside the time interval where two consecutive checksum results are returned by the NIC. When the NIC computes three checksum blocks for each nonce-checksum pair, the checksum computation time is not long enough to keep synchronization between the host CPU and NIC. Therefore, we increase the number of checksum blocks to compute on the NIC for each nonce-checksum pair. Our synchronization experiments show that the host CPU and NIC can remain synchronized for over 300 nonce-checksum response pairs when the NIC computes six checksum blocks for each nonce-response pair.[2] Figure 14 illustrates the first few iterations of this procedure, yielding $delay1 = 780$ ns, $delay2 = 670$ ns, and $delay3 = 390$ ns. Although 300 nonce-response iterations are not sufficient to verify the entire memory contents of the verification function (this is a simple application of the coupon collector's problem), the same procedure can be repeated multiple times to verify the entire memory with overwhelming probability.

The average time for a single challenge-response pair is 3106 ns (T_{comp}^{normal} from Eqn. 4), with a standard deviation of 19 ns. The entire time for performing 300 challenge-response pairs is 535 microseconds. The entire verification procedure (excluding the time for SHA-1 to process the firmware in SRAM on the NIC) consumes about 2 milliseconds.

[2]Note that the time for computing six checksum blocks on the NIC is longer than the time of the theoretical fastest proxy attack described in Section 5.4.1. However, it is much shorter than the time of the real proxy attack we have implemented. We discuss this discrepancy further in Section 7.

6. EVALUATION

We implement a real Ethernet-based proxy attack, the *forging DP attack*, and the *forging PC attack* on the Netgear GA620 NIC to evaluate VIPER's ability to detect the attacks.

Ethernet-based proxy attack. We implement a real Ethernet-based proxy attack (Figure 15). Computers A and B connect directly (without a switch) through a crossover cable. The NICs in both computers are 1 Gbps Netgear GA620s. On computer A, the host CPU verifies the firmware integrity of the GA620 NIC using the latency-based attestation protocol. Once the NIC on computer A receives a challenge from the host CPU, it sends the challenge to computer B (the proxy) over the crossover cable. It then waits for the reply from computer B. In the real implementation, we assume that the proxy is very fast, and needs no time to compute the excepted checksum result. Therefore, on computer B, as soon the NIC receives the packet that contains the challenge for attestation, it sends the response, which includes the expected checksum, to computer A. The NIC on computer B (the proxy) generates the response immediately within its firmware, without bus activity and without involving the host CPU. Then, on computer A, the NIC receives the checksum from computer B, and returns the checksum to the host CPU.

Note that there is no timer on the NIC. Thus, the host CPU measures the time of the proxy attack indirectly, since it measures the time of the proxy procedure plus the communication overhead between the host CPU and the NIC. The average latency of a single challenge-response pair measured by the host CPU over 200 trials during the proxy procedure is 43.72 ± 0.38 microseconds. The proxy attack we implement consumes much more time than the checksum computation time for each challenge-response pair in our implementation on the GA620 NIC. Our implementation shows that computer B cannot send the expected checksum back to the NIC on computer A on time because the latency to communicate with the proxy is longer than the expected checksum computation time. Note that our simple C code

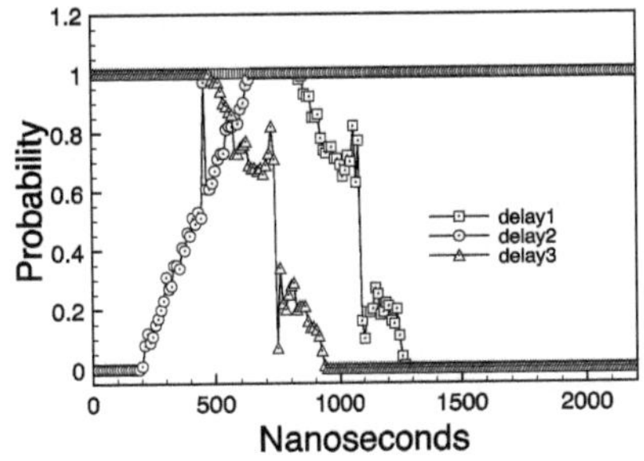

Figure 14: Impact of *delay*1, *delay*2, **and** *delay*3 **in Figure 13.**

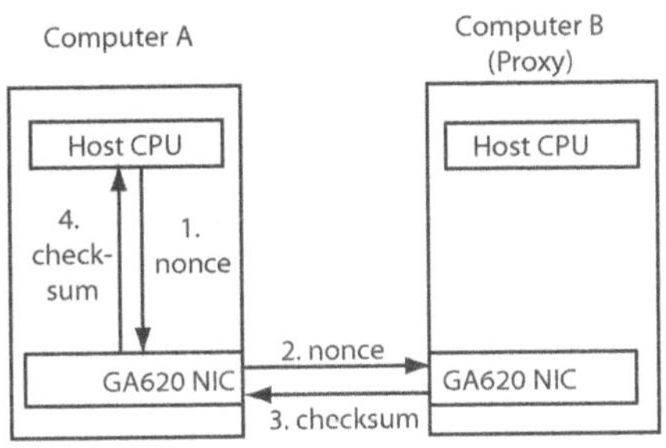

Figure 15: Proxy attack implementation.

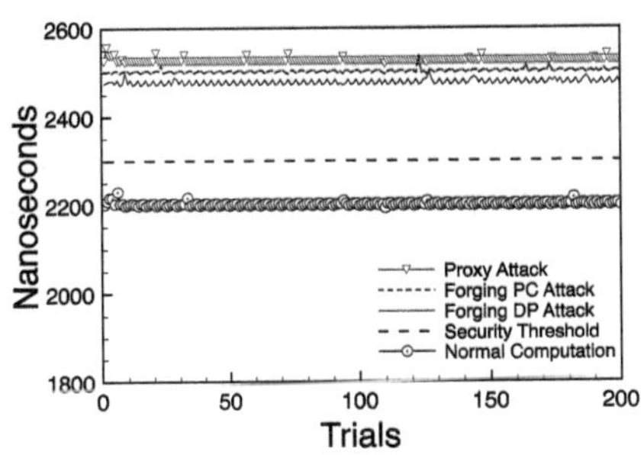

Figure 16: Attacker performance.

implementation in the NIC firmware is slower than the theoretical fastest gigabit Ethernet proxy attack, although this limitation is only a weakness for an attacker with a direct physical connection (no intermediate network hops) to the target system's Ethernet port. Further optimization of our attack is interesting future work.

Forging Data Pointer (DP) attack. In a *forging DP attack*, the attacker maintains a shadow copy of the correct verification function in unused memory, and then executes malicious code out of the original address range of the checksum function, computing the expected checksum over the shadow copy. In this attack, the malicious code needs to add or subtract a constant offset to the DP value to redirect the memory addresses to read (one instruction). Because the DP value is also included in the checksum computation, the malicious code also needs to forge its value before the computation (another instruction). To keep the PC value correct, the malicious code cannot inject additional instructions in the checksum computation block. Thus, the malicious code has to jump out of the main checksum computation block (one jump instruction) to change the DP value to compute the expected checksum. After the computation, malicious code has to jump back (another jump instruction) to the main checksum computation block to obtain the expected PC value. In our current checksum design, two memory addresses (DP) are checked in each checksum block and the DP value is included in the checksum computation once in each checksum block, so a *forging DP attack* needs five additional instructions (two jump instructions and three arithmetic or logical instructions) to compute the expected checksum result in each checksum block. The two jump instructions also cause two cache misses in each checksum block.

Forging PC attack. In a *forging PC attack*, malicious code is deployed in some other memory address and computes the expected checksum over the original copy of the verification function. In this attack, the malicious code does not need to forge the DP value since the checksum is computed over the original copy of the verification function. However, the malicious code does need to forge the correct PC. In *VCF*, $r4$ stores the beginning address of the current checksum computation block while $r3$ stores the end address of the previous checksum computation block. $r4$ and $r3$ are updated at the end of each checksum computation block. In the forging PC attack, the memory address of the malicious checksum computation block has a constant offset from the address of the original checksum computation block. To jump to the malicious code block, the malicious code adds a constant offset to $r4$ (one instruction) before the jump instruction in each checksum block. To forge the correct PC values (both $r3$ and $r4$) before the checksum computation, the malicious code also needs to subtract a constant value from $r3$ and $r4$ (two instructions). As with the forging DP attack, to guarantee that the value of $r3$ and $r4$ have a constant offset from the correct value, the malicious code has to jump out of the malicious checksum block (one jump instruction) to modify the PC value, and then jump back (another jump instruction) before the jump instruction at end of each checksum block. Therefore, the forging PC attack needs five additional instructions (two jump instructions, three arithmetic or logical instructions) and causes two additional cache misses for each checksum computation block to compute the expected checksum result.

Evaluation Results. Figure 16 shows the verification time (checksum computation time plus communication overhead) of normal computation (the host CPU and NIC are not synchronized; three checksum blocks are computed for each nonce-checksum pair), a *forging PC attack*, a *forging DP attack*, the theoretical best proxy attack, and a time threshold to detect attacks. The theoretical proxy attack line represents the communication overhead between the host CPU and the NIC plus the time of the theoretically fastest proxy attack (1152 nanoseconds for a round-trip) between the NIC and a proxy helper over 1 Gbps Ethernet. Our results show that a *forging PC attack* or a *forging DP attack* cause over 280 nanoseconds of computation overhead, while the theoretical fastest proxy attack causes over 325 nanoseconds of overhead compared with the normal computation. These overheads are readily detected by the host CPU executing in a tight loop with interrupts disabled. Thus, VIPER successfully detects all of the attacks.

7. DISCUSSION

We now discuss open problems, limitations, and known issues with VIPER.

It remains an open problem to prove that a program of any appreciable complexity is time-optimal. This has been a significant hurdle for all software-based attestation proposals to date. Two requirements have proven especially challenging: (1) The Checksum algorithm design does not have any flaws that allow an attacker to obtain the expected result with less than the expected data available. (2) The code design of the checksum algorithm must require precisely the smallest number of cycles to complete.

A primary goal of the present work has been to suggest

that additional sources of asymmetry may be viable primitives for software-based attestation, and that these other sources of asymmetry are easier to quantify. We used the asymmetry of the latencies from CPU-to-peripheral, as compared to the latencies from peripheral-to-proxy.

Interestingly, we also face the challenge of being unsure as to whether our attack implementations are optimal. For example, the theoretically fastest RTT for an Ethernet frame is significantly shorter than the RTT that we observed with our implementation of a proxy attack. We believe our VIPER prototype to be secure against proxy attacks facing the empirically measured proxy attack time, but an attacker who can communicate at gigabit Ethernet's theoretical speeds may have an advantage. In practice, this limitation is minor, since we primarily consider attacks arriving via multiple network hops on the Internet, which even today entails several orders of magnitude higher latency.

Full System Verification. An overview of full-system verification with VIPER is presented in Section 4.1. While theoretically straightforward, learning the expected configuration of all programmable elements of a computer system is a considerable practical challenge. Today's vendor ecosystem does not propagate such information, and we were unable to obtain enough information about a complete system to attempt such verification. We suggest such endeavors as fertile ground for future research.

Quiescing the System to Enable Verification. We ran our experiments (Section 6) on hardware that is several generations removed from the latest systems. Our motivation for doing so was in reducing the amount of system activity for which we could not account. Multicore processors, system management interrupts (SMIs), and platform management tools such as OPMA, IPMI, or Intel AMT are all capable of generating system activity that may be difficult or impossible to quantify from a vantage point on a single platform CPU. We view this as one instance of the challenges faced in attempting to identify expected or baseline system behavior with high-assurance.

It is also worth mentioning that modern platforms include significant support for power management. While the logic that governs these operations is itself in scope for verification, one way to achieve necessary levels of system quiescence may be to power down peripherals that cause (possibly benign) interference. Failure to respond to power-down requests is itself an indictment of a particular peripheral.

Hardware Variability. Nightingale et al. study 1,000,000 consumer PCs and find that a full 1% run outside 0.5% of their rated clock speed, even when intentional overclocking is taken into consideration [22]. This level of variability may complicate the process of establishing baseline, or expected, behavior for VIPER on a particular platform. Additional investigation is warranted.

The Keyboard Conundrum. Passwords and bank account information frequently enter systems via the keyboard. Unfortunately, it is among the most resource-impoverished, and thus the most susceptible to being impersonated by other devices. It may be more practical to empower keyboards with some level of cryptographic awareness, than to truly verify every last legacy peripheral that gets dragged along in today's SuperIO chips.

Why Not Hide? Attackers may be incentivized to infect peripherals with malware that deletes itself when interrogated for verification. In principle the system must have had a vulnerability somewhere, and the attacker may be able to reinfect the system post-verification. However, it is not easy to correlate infected firmware in one device with a vulnerability in that device's expected firmware, e.g., the vulnerability may have been in the OS and the driver that updates device firmware may have been compromised.

Network Infrastructure as the Verifier. In an enterprise network it may be reasonable to let network infrastructure such as gateway systems act as verifiers. While feasible for verifying NIC firmware, this approach does not trivially allow verification of all other peripherals in a full system.

Denial of Service. One malicious device can easily create excessive bus traffic such that verification of another device would fail. This can be interpreted as potentially being a form of inter-device "blackmail", but ultimately one has detected that something is amiss in the system. Localizing the source of the attack is a secondary problem.

8. RELATED WORK

To identify malware on devices within a computer system, Li et al. propose using software-based attestation to verify the firmware of an Apple aluminum keyboard that runs an 8-bit microcontroller [18]. The current work represents a significant extension in the same spirit as this work.

Duflot et al. [6] propose runtime firmware integrity verification of a network adapter by utilizing the debugging features available on a Broadcom network adapter. The debugging features enable the host CPU to single-step the microcontroller on the Broadcom NIC and inspect the memory contents on the NIC by accessing the NIC's MMIO registers. Unfortunately, similar debugging features are not available on all peripherals, and these features may themselves be susceptible to impersonation. A more general mechanism is needed to conduct the firmware integrity verification.

Lone Sang et al. discuss peer-to-peer attacks within computer systems by leveraging DMA-based communication [27]. They propose approaches to prevent unauthorized communication between devices within a computer system, but they do not propose any detection mechanisms for verifying the integrity of the firmware of devices.

We now chronologically review previous work on software-based attestation. Spinellis proposes "reflection" as an approach to verify the software running on a system [34]. Spinellis sketches an approach that fills the memory with random content, clears the system state and disables all interrupts, computes a hash function over the entire memory, and finally returns the system state and hash to a verifier. The verifier checks the execution time and returned information. Unfortunately, Spinellis only presents a high-level approach but no implementation details.

Kennell and Jamieson present Genuinity [17], an approach where a verifier executes a verification function on an untrusted system to validate the system configuration. Genuinity is based on the observation that simulating low-level hardware is slower than actual execution on that hardware, and intentionally creates randomized memory accesses that create many cache misses. By validating the number of cache misses the verifier can inspect whether the code was correctly executed. Shankar, Chew, and Tygar, however, point out several issues with their approach [33].

Seshadri et al. introduced software-based attestation and

developed SWATT, a system to verify the software of an embedded device [31]. SWATT relies on a checksum function that computes a checksum over the entire memory contents and is constructed to force an attacker to induce overhead to compute the correct checksum. Seshadri et al. proposed a variety of extensions: enable verification of a small amount of memory on sensor nodes through the ICE function [29], verification of code running on an Intel Pentium IV processor through the Pioneer function [30], and code running on an AMD Opteron K8 architecture through the Outpost function [28]. Castelluccia et al. point out weaknesses in the specific SWATT and ICE functions [4], triggering significant discussion [25, 8]. The basic approach of software-based attestation remains sound, but special care has to be paid to ensure security, as the current work demonstrates.

Concurrently, Gratzer and Naccache have presented a more theoretical treatment of software-based attestation, which relies on the assumption that the verifier can physically observe and reset the untrusted device and assuming that the reset and execution times can be accurately observed [9]. Park and Shin have proposed soft tamper-proofing, an approach that fills memory with random data and executes a hash function, however, without considering timing [24]. Shaneck et al. explore the use of encrypted and self-modifying code to verify software on sensor nodes [32]. Their approach also relies on randomized traversal and timing. Jakobsson and Johansson have studied new approaches to software-based attestation on mobile devices [15, 16].

9. CONCLUSIONS

Attackers have elevated malware to a new frontier: executing invisibly on devices within a computer system. Such malware can exploit DMA to compromise the OS or misuse PCI buses to compromise other devices. We address the research challenge of how to reliably detect such malware. This work shows how we extend previous software-based attestation mechanisms to defend against proxy attacks, where the untrusted system obtains help for computing the time-critical checksum from a remote party. By harnessing the inherent properties of PCI buses, we have developed a new approach for software-based attestation that can prevent the proxy attack and simultaneously achieve lower verification time overhead. We anticipate that our proposed techniques will make software-based attestation practical on current platforms and provide uncircumventable advantages to defenders without relying on specialized hardware.

Acknowledgements

We are particularly grateful to Loïc Duflot, Arrigo Triulzi, and Fernand Lone Sang for their help with peer-to-peer PCI transfers. We also wish to thank the (surprisingly many) anonymous reviewers for their time, attention, and valuable suggestions. We are grateful to Michael Stroucken for lending us the Sun Fire machine. Finally, we wish to thank Michael Strouchen for providing a Sun Fire V20z 1U rack-mount server to us, Michael Farb and Julie Bowman for improving the writing in the paper, and Virgil Gligor and Jim Newsome for stimulating conversations about new approaches for software-based attestation.

This research was supported in part by CyLab at Carnegie Mellon under grants DAAD19-02-1-0389, MURI W 911 NF 0710287, and W911NF-09-1-0273 from the Army Research Office, and by a gift from Lockheed Martin Corporation. The views and conclusions contained here are those of the authors and should not be interpreted as necessarily representing the official policies or endorsements, either express or implied, of ARO, CMU, LMC, or the U.S. Government or any of its agencies.

10. REFERENCES

[1] Advanced Micro Devices, Inc. AMD I/O virtualization technology (IOMMU) specification. Publication No. 34434, Revision: 1.26, Feb. 2009.

[2] Advanced Micro Devices, Inc. AMD64 architecture programmer's manual volume 2: System programming. Publication No. 24593, Revision: 3.17, June 2010.

[3] A. M. Azab, P. Ning, Z. Wang, X. Jiang, X. Zhang, and N. C. Skalsky. HyperSentry: enabling stealthy in-context measurement of hypervisor integrity. In *Proceedings of the ACM conference on Computer and Communication Security*, 2010.

[4] C. Castelluccia, A. Francillon, D. Perito, and C. Soriente. On the difficulty of software-based attestation of embedded devices. In *Proceedings of the ACM Conference on Computer and Communications Security*, Nov. 2009.

[5] K. Chen. Reversing and exploiting an Apple firmware update. In *Black Hat*, 2009.

[6] L. Duflot, Y.-A. Perez, and B. Morin. Run-time firmware integrity verification: what if you can not trust your network card? In *CanSecWest*, 2011.

[7] L. Duflot, Y.-A. Perez, G. Valadon, and O. Levillain. Can you still trust your network card? CanSecWest, 2010.

[8] A. Francillon, C. Castelluccia, D. Perito, and C. Soriente. Comments on "refutation of on the difficulty of software-based attestation of embedded devices". `http://planete.inrialpes.fr/~perito/papers/2010_CCS_attestation_comments_on_rebutal.pdf`, Oct. 2010.

[9] V. Gratzer and D. Naccache. Alien vs. quine, the vanishing circuit and other tales from the industry's crypt. In *Proceedings of Eurocrypt*, May 2006.

[10] IEEE Computer Society: 802.3 Working Group. IEEE standard 802.3x-1997, 1997.

[11] A. N. Inc. Tigon Open Firmware. `http://alteon.shareable.org`.

[12] A. N. Inc. Tigon/PCI Ethernet Controlller (revision 1.04). `http://alteon.shareable.org`, 1997.

[13] Intel Corporation. Intel 64 and IA-32 architectures software developer's manual volume 1: Basic architecture. Order Number: 253665-073US, Jan. 2011.

[14] Intel Corporation. Intel 64 and IA-32 architectures software developer's manual volume 3b: System programming guide, part 2. Order Number: 253669-037US, Jan. 2011.

[15] M. Jakobsson and K.-A. Johansson. Assured detection of malware with applications to mobile platforms. DIMACS Technical Report 2010-03, `http://dimacs.rutgers.edu/TechnicalReports/abstracts/2010/2010-03.html`, 2010.

[16] M. Jakobsson and K.-A. Johansson. Assured detection of malware with applications to mobile platforms. In *Proceedings of the Workshop on Hot Topics in Security (HotSec)*, Aug. 2010.

[17] R. Kennell and L. H. Jamieson. Establishing the genuinity of remote computer systems. In *Proceedings of the USENIX Security Symposium*, 2003.

[18] Y. Li, J. M. McCune, and A. Perrig. SBAP: Software-Based Attestation for Peripherals. In *Proceedings of the 3rd International Conference on Trust and Trustworthy Computing*, 2010.

[19] J. M. McCune, B. Parno, A. Perrig, M. K. Reiter, and H. Isozaki. Flicker: An execution infrastructure for TCB minimization. In *Proceedings of the European Conference on Computer Systems (EuroSys)*, Apr. 2008.

[20] Mindshare Inc., R. Budruk, D. Anderson, and T. Shanley. *PCI Express System Architecture.* Addison-Wesley Professional, Sept. 2003.

[21] MindShare Inc., T. Shanley, and D. Anderson. *PCI System Architecture (4th Edition).* Addison-Wesley Professional, June 1999.

[22] E. B. Nightingale, J. R. Douceur, and V. Orgovan. Cycles, cells and platters: an empirical analysisof hardware failures on a million consumer PCs. In *Proceedings of the European Conference on Computer systems (EuroSys)*, 2011.

[23] NIST. Recommendation for key management. Special Publication 800-57 Part 1, Mar. 2007.

[24] T. Park and K. G. Shin. Soft tamper-proofing via program integrity verification in wireless sensor networks. *IEEE Transactions on Mobile Computing (TMC)*, 2005.

[25] A. Perrig and L. van Doorn. Refutation of "on the difficulty of software-based attestation of embedded devices". `http://sparrow.ece.cmu.edu/group/pub/perrig-vandoorn-refutation.pdf`, 2010.

[26] F. L. Sang, Èric Lacombe, V. Nicomette, and Y. Deswarte. Exploiting an I/OMMU vulnerability. In *Proceedings of IEEE Conference on Malicious and Unwanted Software (Malware)*, 2010.

[27] F. L. Sang, V. Nicomette, Y. Deswarte, and L. Duflot. Attaques DMA peer-to-peer et contremesures. In *Proceedings of the Symposium sur la Sécurité des Technologies de L'Information et des Communications (SSTIC)*, June 2011.

[28] A. Seshadri. *A Software Primitive for Externally-verifiable Untampered Execution and its Applications to Securing Computing Systems.* PhD thesis, Electrical and Computer Engineering Department, Carnegie Mellon University, 2009.

[29] A. Seshadri, M. Luk, A. Perrig, L. van Doorn, and P. Khosla. SCUBA: Secure code update by attestation in sensor networks. In *Proceedings of ACM Workshop on Wireless Security (WiSe)*, Sept. 2006.

[30] A. Seshadri, M. Luk, E. Shi, A. Perrig, L. van Doorn, and P. Khosla. Pioneer: Verifying Integrity and Guaranteeing Execution of Code on Legacy Platforms. In *Proceedings of ACM Symposium on Operating Systems Principles*, Oct. 2005.

[31] A. Seshadri, A. Perrig, L. van Doorn, and P. Khosla. SWATT: SoftWare-based ATTestation for embedded devices. In *Proceedings of the IEEE Symposium on Security and Privacy*, 2004.

[32] M. Shaneck, K. Mahadevan, V. Kher, and Y. Kim. Remote software-based attestation for wireless sensors. In *Proceedings of the European Workshop on Security and Privacy in Ad Hoc and Sensor Networks (ESAS)*, 2005.

[33] U. Shankar, M. Chew, and J. Tygar. Side effects are not sufficient to authenticate software. In *Proceedings of the USENIX Security Symposium*, 2004.

[34] D. Spinellis. Reflection as a mechanism for software integrity verification. *ACM Transactions on Information and System Security*, Feb. 2000.

[35] A. Triulzi. Project Maux Mk.II, I Own the NIC, now I want a shell. In *The 8th annual PacSec conference*, 2008.

[36] A. Triulzi. The Jedi Packet takes over the Deathstar, taking NIC backdoor to the next level. In *The 12th annual CanSecWest conference*, 2010.

[37] J. Wang, A. Stavrou, and A. K. Ghosh. HyperCheck: A Hardware-Assisted Integrity Monitor. In *Proceedings of International Symposium on Recent Advances in Intrusion Detection (RAID)*, 2010.

Unicorn: Two-Factor Attestation for Data Security*

Mohammad Mannan
Concordia Institute for Information Systems Engineering
Concordia University
Montreal, Canada

Beom Heyn Kim
Computer Science
University of Toronto
Toronto, Canada

Afshar Ganjali and David Lie
Electrical and Computer Engineering
University of Toronto
Toronto, Canada

ABSTRACT

Malware and phishing are two major threats for users seeking to perform security-sensitive tasks using computers today. To mitigate these threats, we introduce Unicorn, which combines the phishing protection of standard security tokens and malware protection of trusted computing hardware. The Unicorn security token holds user authentication credentials, but only releases them if it can verify an attestation that the user's computer is free of malware. In this way, the user is released from having to remember passwords, as well as having to decide when it is safe to use them. The user's computer is further verified by either a TPM or a remote server to produce a *two-factor attestation scheme.*

We have implemented a Unicorn prototype using commodity software and hardware, and two Unicorn example applications (termed as uApps, short for Unicorn Applications), to secure access to both remote data services and encrypted local data. Each uApp consists of a small, hardened and immutable OS image, and a single application. Our Unicorn prototype co-exists with a regular user OS, and significantly reduces the time to switch between the secure environment and general purpose environment using a novel mechanism that removes the BIOS from the switch time.

Categories and Subject Descriptors

D.4.6 [**Security and Protection**]: Access controls, Authentication

General Terms

Human Factors, Security

Keywords

Trusted Computing, Authentication, Attestation, Security Token, Malware, Phishing

*Contact: `mmannan@ciise.concordia.ca`. Majority of this work was done when the first author was a post-doctoral fellow at the University of Toronto.

CCS'11, October 17–21, 2011, Chicago, Illinois, USA.

1. INTRODUCTION

Malware is one of the greatest security threats for Internet users today. Evidence suggests that 53% of computers (out of 21 millions scanned worldwide) are infected with malware [1]. Much of this malware is designed to steal sensitive information from and invade the privacy of the computer user. Aside from malware, computer users also have to contend with phishing attacks, where the adversary social engineers the user into leaking authentication credentials by producing a web page or interface that appears similar to a legitimate one. By acquiring these credentials the attacker can then proceed to steal the user's identity and access sensitive information that belongs to the user.

Passwords and other authentication credentials can be protected using security tokens that implement one-time passwords, or that are able to respond to cryptographic challenges (e.g., RSA SecurID, and the split trust paradigm [3]). By introducing the security token, users are protected from phishing since convincing the user to leak an authentication credential they know (such as a password) is not sufficient for the adversary to gain access to the user's data. However, even with token authentication, the user's data is still vulnerable to theft during an active session by malware on their computer.

In contrast, trusted-computing hardware can be used to measure and report integrity of the software stack running on a computer [7,8,20,21,25,35]. Trusted-computing hardware, developed by the Trusted Computing Group (TCG), Intel and AMD enables software to utilize a root of trust based in hardware, which is significantly more difficult for a remote attacker to subvert than a root of trust based in software. These systems use hardware to measure the integrity of software running on the computer, allowing the hardware to assert, via an attestation, that a system is free of malware. This attestation may be conveyed to the user over a trusted channel. Unfortunately, interpreting this attestation is difficult for humans and user studies have shown that users are not always diligent enough to interpret or notice signals that indicate that the attestation has failed [16] (cf. "the barn door property" [36]).

Our key insight is that security tokens and trusted computing can be combined to produce a system that is as resistant to phishing as standard security token authentication, but is additionally resistant to attacks by malware. We propose the use of a Personal Security Device (PSD), which, like a security token, holds personal authentication credentials, but differs in that a PSD can verify an attestation from the user's computer. Thus, rather than having the user decide when to release their authentication credential, the PSD verifies the attestation from the user's computer and releases the authentication credential on behalf of the user only if the attestation is correct. In addition to the attestation by the PSD, the computer's software stack is also verified either by a remote server that holds user data or the trusted computing hardware on the computer. Thus user data is in effect protected by a *two-factor attestation.*

To evaluate this idea, we have designed a system called Unicorn.[1] Rather than trying to preventing malware and phishing attacks altogether, Unicorn takes a mitigating approach by safe-guarding Unicorn-protected data from these attacks. We implement a Unicorn prototype that uses Intel TXT and TPM as the trusted computing implementation, and an Android smartphone as the user's PSD.[2] In our prototype, a user starts initially from an untrusted *user operating system (OS)*, which could be infected with malware. When the user wishes to access their secure data, which could be stored on a remote service requiring authentication (such as banking information), or encrypted on the local disk, the user uses Unicorn to invoke a *Unicorn application* (uApp) from her computer. A uApp is a small, hardened and immutable OS image with a single application that will be used to access the user's sensitive data. Unicorn uses the trusted computing hardware on the user's computer to boot and measure the uApp, generating an attestation that the user's PSD will verify. Only by combining this attestation with the authentication credential on the PSD will the uApp be able to access the user's data.

The result is that an adversary may only gain unauthorized access to data protected by Unicorn in one of two ways: the adversary must either (1) simultaneously gain physical access to the user's computer and compromise or clone the user's PSD, or (2) find and exploit a run time vulnerability in the uApp that has access to the sensitive data. In the first case, requiring the adversary to compromise two components simultaneously is a straightforward application of the principle of defense in depth. In the second case, uApps are intended to be smaller and simpler than the commodity user OS, giving the adversary fewer vulnerabilities that they can find and exploit. Consequently, Unicorn serves as a second line of defense so that a successful malware or phishing attack does not expose Unicorn-protected data.

Contributions.

1. We present and perform a security analysis of the design of Unicorn, which combines an authentication token with trusted computing to implement two-factor authentication protection for user data. Unicorn raises the bar for attackers, forcing them to either gain physical access to the user's computer and compromise the user's PSD simultaneously, or to find and exploit a run time compromise in a small hardened uApp.
2. We implement a Unicorn prototype using widely available commodity hardware and software tools. Unicorn enables users to use trusted and untrusted systems on the same computer, switching between them without a full reboot. Compared to existing solutions, Unicorn does not require hypervisor support, and does not suffer from performance degradation, while achieving significantly faster switching time. Our prototype uses a novel mechanism that reduces the time to invoke a uApp to approximately 25.5 seconds, which is almost twice as fast as existing systems [35].
3. We demonstrate the utility of Unicorn with two representative uApps. The first is a banking application, which represents a scenario where sensitive user data is stored on a remote service requiring authentication. The second uApp is a secure document reader, which represents a scenario where sensitive user data is encrypted and stored locally on the user's computer.

We first begin in Section 2 by defining the attacker model that Unicorn defends against, the guarantees that Unicorn provides and the limitations that Unicorn has. We then describe the design and operation of Unicorn in Section 3. The implementation of our prototype is given in Section 4 and we describe the two representative uApps we created in Section 5. We evaluate both the security of our Unicorn design and the performance of our Unicorn prototype in Section 6. Finally we discuss related work in Section 7 and give our conclusions in Section 8.

2. SECURITY MODEL AND GUARANTEES

2.1 Attacker Model

The goals of the attacker are to compromise the user's Unicorn-protected sensitive data in the local machine or a remote server, or to assume control of a Unicorn-session between the user and server (*session hijacking*). We explicitly distinguish Unicorn-protected data from arbitrary data that the user may know or have on their computer, which we consider out of scope for Unicorn. Unicorn-protected data must either be stored on a secure remote server, which requires authentication for access, or in encrypted format with keys available only to the user's computer and PSD.

We assign the attacker the following capabilities. First, the attacker is capable of infecting the user OS with arbitrary malware such that she has full control over the user's software platform. For example, she may tamper with the Master Boot Record (MBR), bootloader, user OS kernel, applications running on the user OS, and uApp binary images. Attackers can also tamper with device, BIOS and CPU configurations, and send arbitrary commands to devices before invoking a uApp. Second, the attacker can fake interaction with the user to try to convince them that they have correctly launched a uApp. We note that Unicorn does not prevent such an attacker from extracting secrets from the user through the equivalent of a phishing attack, but will ensure that Unicorn-protected data is not compromised. Third, the attacker may either gain physical access to the user's computer, or compromise the user's PSD, but not both. Compromising the user's PSD includes infecting the PSD with malware, cloning the PSD, gaining access to PSD secrets, or stealing the PSD. We note that there have been instances where attackers have compromised both the computer and PSD at the same time, e.g., the Zeus banking trojan [6]. However, compromising the user's computer and having physical access are not equivalent.

The following attacks are out of scope for Unicorn. While the attacker may have physical access to user's computer, we assume that he cannot subvert the hardware root of trust as provided by the TPM version 1.2 chip and CPU's late launch

[1] A unicorn is a mythical single-horned creature, commonly known as a protector of innocence, and a symbol of purity.
[2] For background on trusted computing, see Appendix A.

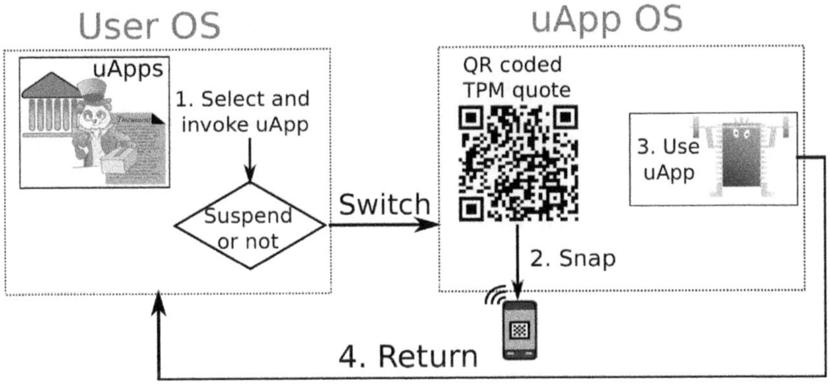

Figure 1: Overview of Unicorn user steps

feature; i.e., attacks against hardware trust (e.g., [11,37]) are considered out of scope. However, the attacker can reset the TPM and change ownership password. We also assume that compromises of the remote server storing Unicorn-protected data are out of scope. Unicorn does not mitigate flaws in the remote server storing the user data. Finally, we assume that the attacker cannot compromise the operation of a uApp after it has launched. This is a standard limitation of trusted computing hardware, which can only attest to the state of the computer at the time the measurements are made.

For the communication between the user's computer and remote server, a Dolev-Yao (DY) attacker is assumed, who also can arbitrarily modify and observe any plain text data in transit. However, the attacker is unable to circumvent any standard cryptographic mechanisms (e.g., SSL).

2.2 Properties, Guarantees and Limitations

Properties. Unicorn provides two properties from which we may derive the security guarantee it provides. (1) Unicorn-protected data is accessible only from the user's computer. Access is bound to a secret signing key stored in the TPM of the user's computer. Unicorn also deals with relaying attacks [32], as described in Section 6.1 (under item (d)). (2) Access to protected data is only granted if the PSD is present, which will release its secret only if it can verify the running uApp on the computer.

Guarantee. Unicorn protects user data unless (1) the adversary simultaneously gets physical access to the user computer, and compromises/clones the PSD; or (2) adversary finds and exploits a run time vulnerability in a uApp. Malware is defeated because Unicorn-protected data is only accessible from a verified environment. Unicorn provides equivalent protection to phishing attacks as security tokens – phishing attacks targeting Unicorn credentials cannot succeed since Unicorn authentication requires the presence of the PSD to succeed.

Limitations. Unicorn's major limitations are the following. (1) Unicorn requires a secure setup phase where the user must be diligent. Both TPM secrets and authentication credentials for the PSD must be transmitted securely and to the correct parties (e.g., by out-of-band methods). Resetting a Unicorn-protected account also requires a similar secure bootstrap. (2) Unicorn's phishing protection is limited to the user data explicitly protected by Unicorn. Phishing and social engineering attacks that trick user into revealing arbitrary information that users know (including information that Unicorn is protecting) cannot be prevented by Unicorn. (3) Unicorn is not an intrusion detection system and cannot detect if a uApp has been compromised after the measurements are taken. An attacker who compromises a uApp after the measurement phase will be able to usurp all privileges the uApp has, including access to the Unicorn-protected data.

3. SYSTEM DESCRIPTION

3.1 Unicorn Architecture

Unicorn requires a setup phase where the PSD is initialized with a long-term authentication credential and correct measurements of the user's uApps. This phase requires users to be diligent, as described below. After this, the regular use of Unicorn is broken into four steps as described in Figure 1. In the first step, the user uses Unicorn to invoke a uApp on their computer. Unicorn suspends or terminates the user OS and invokes the uApp in a Measured Launch Environment (MLE). The MLE uses trusted computing hardware to perform a *quote* by computing a hash of the uApp and signing it with a key in the TPM. This quote is then displayed as a QR-code image on the screen of the user's computer. In the second step, the user scans the quote using her PSD, which then verifies the correctness of the quote. If correct, the PSD uses the long-term secret to proceed to the third step, which grants the uApp access to the user's data and allows the user to access the remote service if applicable. If the quote is not correct, indicating tampering of the software stack, Unicorn halts and the user will be unable to use the uApp or access her data. In the final step, the user can terminate the uApp and return to the user OS.

Setup phase. In this phase, the PSD must be securely initialized with the two pieces of information: (1) user authentication credentials (e.g., a user ID and high-entropy secret); and (2) the hashes of the uApp, in the form of expected PCR values. In addition, if the uApp uses a remote service, the remote service must be given the public half of the AIK of the user's computer. If the uApp accesses encrypted data stored on the user's computer, then a sub-key of the encryption key must be sealed to the uApp on the TPM of the user's computer. If the user plans to access their data from more than one computer, then the AIK or sub-key must be initialized for each such computer. Note that sharing of AIKs with remote services will mandate a re-initialization of Unicorn in some cases, including: updating or resetting the TPM hardware. For distributing uApps, vendors may choose any channel, including web download. However, we assume that the vendor's copy of a uApp is malware-free.

It is important that the authentication credentials are not leaked to an adversary, since this would allow the adversary to clone the PSD. Similarly, if an adversary is able to modify the values of the hashes associated with a uApp before they are saved on the PSD, the adversary will be able to cause the authentication secret to be used with a tampered uApp. Finally, if an AIK of a computer other than the user's is transmitted to the remote server, or the sub-key of the encryption key for local data is leaked, this would allow the adversary to access the user data from a computer other than the user's.

Unicorn requires an out-of-band secure channel during the setup phase. For example, in our online banking example of a uApp with a remote service, the PCR hashes of the uApp and authentication credentials must be transmitted through a secure channel. Such a channel might be in-person registration at a branch or postal mail. In these cases, the information can be conveniently installed via a QR-coded image. Similarly, the secure channel can also be used to transmit a one-time authentication credential, with which the user may login to the remote service and initialize it with the AIK public-key(s) of their computer(s). The user must be diligent throughout this process and not inadvertently leak their credentials to the adversary, provide the wrong AIKs to the service, or install the wrong hashes.

Starting a uApp. When invoking a uApp, the user may choose one of two options as shown in Figure 1: (1) immediate execution of the uApp loader; or (2) save the user OS and application states into disk using e.g., suspend-to-disk before executing the uApp loader. The former option mandates that users will save any unsaved documents before initiating the switch. The later allows users to resume the saved environment, but adds the suspend time to switch.

After the user OS has suspended itself to disk (if users choose this option), it would normally power off the hardware. To invoke the uApp, we modify the user OS to load the *uApp loader* into memory and transfer control to it. The uApp loader sets up the MLE and then transfers control to the *uApp kernel*, which then resets the devices to a known state, completes its boot process and starts the application in the uApp. Since the uApp kernel now has control of all the devices, the entire system acts as a shared platform for both the user OS and the uApp.

Verifying the uApp. Once the user OS transfers control to the uApp loader, the loader will take measurements of itself, the hardware state, the uApp kernel and boot parameters, and store them in the TPM. The uApp kernel then measures the entire file system image it will use before mounting the image, and also extends the measurement into the TPM. uApps are immutable so the measurement of a correct uApp will produce the same value every time. These measurements are used to attest the state of the software platform. This attestation ensures that the uApp has not been tampered with in anyway.

The exact attestation procedure depends on the uApp being invoked. For uApps that interact with remote servers, attestation is performed with both the user's PSD and the remote server, while uApps that do not interact with remote servers only require attestation with the PSD. We discuss different attestation and authentication modes in more detail in Section 3.2.

Switch back to user OS. To return to the user OS, the uApp kernel loads the image of the user OS kernel into memory and transfers control to it. Since uApp images are immutable, any persistent state (e.g., user data) must be saved outside of the uApp, either on the remote server, or encrypted and saved on the local disk. After this, when control is transferred to the user OS kernel, it will load a new OS instance or restore the suspended image.

Hardening uApps. uApps must be resistant to run time attacks since a compromise of the uApp after it has loaded means that the adversary will gain access to the user data. Several standard mechanisms can be used to harden uApps. First, uApps should be built with a smaller trusted computing base (TCB). Unnecessary code and functionality should be removed as uApps are meant to be task-specific appliances. Second, uApps can be built on top of hardened operating systems, such as SELinux, which have stronger access control mechanisms designed to mitigate attacks. Finally, the attack surface of a uApp may also be restricted by limiting its functionality. For example, in the case of a banking uApp, one could restrict the uApp to only be able to connect to IP addresses or domain names belonging to the bank, or modify the browser to only accept SSL certificates that belong to the bank.

Updating uApps. To fix vulnerabilities or to offer new features, vendors may distribute updated uApps (a new image or only the differences) via any channel, secure or otherwise (e.g., downloaded from a website). However, measurements of the new image must be updated securely on user's PSD. For example, the PSD client may accept only signed measurements from a vendor (the signature verification key is also stored on the PSD) and only when the updating version is newer than the existing one; cf. [26, 34].

3.2 Attestation and Authentication

Unicorn supports two scenarios in which user data may be stored. The first is where the data is stored on a remote server, such as financial information stored on a bank website. The second is where data is stored locally encrypted on the user's computer. An example of this might be an encrypted document repository.

Remote server. Our combined attestation and authentication protocol is shown in Figure 2. When the uApp is launched, the client browser loads the remote site over SSL and initiates attestation (e.g., by sending an attestation request). The server responds with a random nonce N_S, a list of PCR indices P_i to be included in the TPM quote, and the server ID (ID_S). Let K_U be a key that represents the long-term authentication secret stored on the PSD. The uApp then retrieves PCR values P_v, generates a quote T_Q using the TPM, and forwards this quote, server ID and nonce to the PSD. If PSD can verify the quote (with the help of the pre-stored AIK and expected values of PCRs as indexed by ID_S), it generates an HMAC h of $(T_Q.ID_U.ID_S)$ using K_U. User ID and h are forwarded to the client browser, which then forwards these values along with the TPM quote to the server. If the server can verify the quote, and can calculate the same h, access is granted to the user. Note that, if the PSD has Internet connectivity, it can directly forward

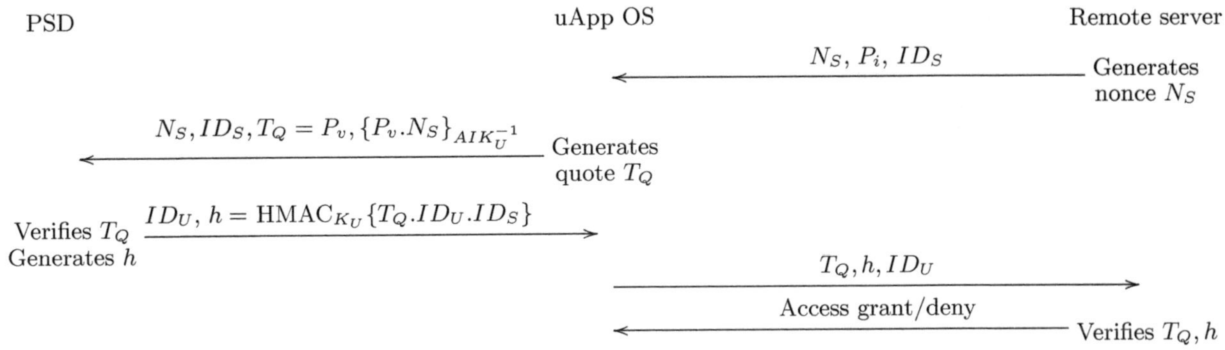

Figure 2: Attestation message flow for remote server. The setup phase initiates the PSD and the remote server with the shared authentication key K_U, AIK_U, and expected PCR values.

(T_Q, h, ID_U) to the server instead of requiring another PSD-to-computer communication channel. The remote server will only accept quotes signed with an AIK private key matching the AIK public that was registered with it during the setup phase, preventing access to the user data from any computer that wasn't registered during the setup phase. Security of the protocol remains unaffected even if attackers can collect and replay the response from the PSD as the server will check freshness of its nonce as used in the protocol. The protocol in Figure 2 does not establish a session key between the uApp and remote server. We assume that they negotiate a session key as part of the secure channel setup (e.g., SSL session key); see e.g., Goldman [9] for alternatives.

One might be concerned that the PSD does not generate a nonce and send it to the computer, allowing an attacker with a tampered uApp to replay quotes to the PSD. In this case, the PSD will generate HMAC of the quote with the replayed nonce in it. However, the tampered uApp will still be unable to authenticate to the remote server, since the server checks freshness of its nonces. On top of the key-based authentication, an optional password authentication mechanism may be deployed.

Locally encrypted data. For applications that do not access a remote server, there is no party to share the public AIK with. Instead, we break the key used to encrypt the user's data into two sub-keys. One sub-key is stored on the PSD as the user's authentication secret, and the other is sealed in the TPM to the uApp. Unlike the remote server scenario, the PSD must send a nonce (N_D) to prevent replay attacks against the quote operation. The PSD's sub-key (K_{psd}) is released to the uApp application only if the PSD can verify the quote. See Figure 3. In this example, we assume the PSD-to-computer channel is physically secure, otherwise an attacker may learn K_{psd}. When the uApp receives K_{psd}, it will retrieve the sealed part of the encryption key from the TPM (K_{tpm}), which will succeed only if the correct uApp is loaded. The decryption key is then generated as follows: $K_{dec} = K_{psd} \oplus K_{tpm}$.

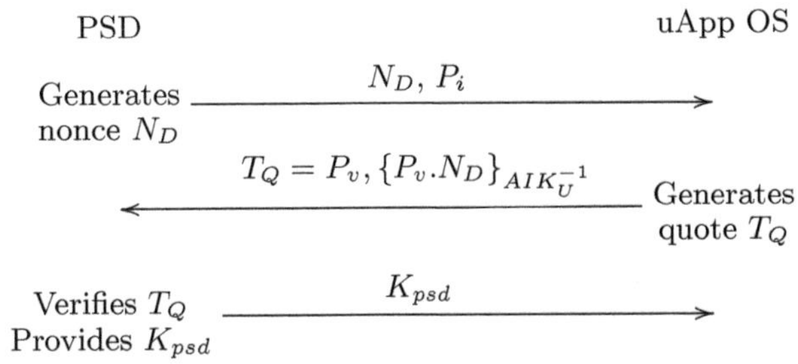

Figure 3: Attestation flow for locally encrypted data

4. IMPLEMENTATION

In this section, we give implementation details of our Unicorn prototype, including how we are able to quickly switch between the user OS and uApp OS, and the implementations of the uApp OS and our server- and PSD-based attestors. Because our prototype is intended more of a proof of concept than a polished implementation, we relax some of the security requirements on the components in our Unicorn implementation for convenience. First, instead of running a specialized security OS with a minimal TCB, our uApp OS is based on a stock Ubuntu 10.04 Linux distribution running the Linux 2.6.34 kernel. This allows us to make use of existing open source software packages in our prototype. Second, because we don't have the means to program and implement a real security token as our PSD, we implement our PSD as an application running on an Android smartphone. In reality, there should not be any other applications running on our PSD that could allow the adversary to gain access to the authentication secrets.

4.1 Switching between User OS and uApp

Tools used. To implement fast switching between user OS and uApp, we leverage two components already present in the Linux kernel – suspend-to-disk and kexec. Suspend-to-disk enables the kernel to save its running state to a disk so that the machine may be powered down and then later resumed back to the same running state. This functionality can be found on most commodity OSs. Kexec [22] is a feature in the Linux kernel that can load another kernel into memory and transfer control to the new kernel. Kexec is intended to be used during kernel development to invoke a crash kernel for debugging after a kernel crash. The kernel image can be loaded into memory and executed immediately, or at a later time (e.g., when a crash actually happens). Because kexec transfers control directly to the new kernel, it does not need to reset the machine and or invoke the BIOS.

User interaction. When the user wishes to invoke a uApp, she calls a user-space application. First, we use kexec to load the uApp loader, uApp kernel, initrd and Authenticated Code (AC) module into kernel memory, but we do not transfer control to the uApp loader yet. We then invoke the suspend-to-disk operation in the user OS kernel, if the user chooses to save her OS and application states. The user can also use kexec to invoke the uApp loader directly without suspend-to-disk; this enables faster switching at the expense of not being able to resume the user OS. When suspend-to-disk is complete, the Linux kernel normally powers down the machine. We modify the kernel implementation of suspend-to-disk to instead call a kexec function that transfers control to the uApp loader. If the uApp loader is not present in memory, the transfer of control fails. This would happen if the user directly called suspend-to-disk in the user OS with the intention of rebooting or powering down the machine. In this case, we proceed with the standard suspend-to-disk code to retain the existing kernel functionality. This change required only to add a single line of C code to the kernel.

4.2 uApp Loader and OS Implementation

uApp loader. Our uApp loader builds on tboot [13], an open-source project initiated by Intel. Tboot currently provides a pre-kernel module as an MLE that uses Intel TXT to perform a measured and verified launch of the Linux kernel or Xen hypervisor. Normally, tboot is invoked by the GRUB bootloader. However, to remove the bootloader and BIOS execution from the switch time, Unicorn invokes tboot using kexec as discussed above. Tboot creates the MLE and then extends PCR 17 with several chipset and AC module specific measurements using GETSEC[SENTER], PCR 18 with measurements of the tboot kernel binary, uApp kernel binary and boot parameters, and PCR 19 with hashes of the initrd binary used to boot the uApp Linux kernel. It is important to measure boot parameters as well as the binaries, since kernel behavior can be significantly altered by changing the boot parameters. The final component of the uApp that must be measured is the partition that will be used to boot the uApp OS. Unfortunately, tboot is unable to access the disk directly to perform the measurement, so we modify the uApp kernel to measure its root partition just before the kernel mounts the partition, and extend PCR 20 with this measurement. We set the TPM locality of the uApp kernel to 1 (default is 0), as PCR 20 cannot be extended from locality 0. This PCR is reset by tboot during initialization.

Cleanup at exit. When exiting from a uApp, we must ensure TXT tear down and clean up of residual states so that secrets used in the uApp session are not exposed to the user OS. Tboot contains this functionality, so one possibility was to simply reuse this functionality by exiting the uApp kernel and returning execution back to tboot. However, tboot does not have support for kexec, so it would not be able to return directly back to the user OS and instead would have to reboot the machine to return to the user OS. Thus, we reimplement the tboot cleanup code in the uApp kernel and then use kexec to load the user OS kernel and transfer control to it. We also reset the TPM locality to 0 from the uApp kernel.

Hardening uApp OS. We take two approaches to harden the OS in our uApp prototype. First, we reduce the network attack surface by constraining the uApp to only being able to access a minimal set of network services. We also cryptographically authenticate the remote services. Network restriction is achieved by using the `iptables` firewall to constrain network connections by IP address, and SSL with client-side verification to authenticate remote servers (without allowing any user-end override options if certificate errors are detected). Second, we reduce the code footprint of uApps to keep the TCB as small as possible. For our prototype, this meant removing unnecessary services and binaries from the uApp OS. Hardening of the uApp OS could be taken further by using a security-oriented high-assurance OS instead of a commodity OS like Linux. Candidate systems include: formally verified seL4 micro-kernel [15], enforcing security policies via SELinux [17], ensuring kernel integrity with SecVisor [27], continuous integrity monitoring using HyperSentry [2], and the Nexus OS [28] designed with trusted computing in mind.

Read-only uApp image and reducing image size. To make the uApp OS verification possible, we need a read-only uApp base image which is not changed after being invoked. However, a read-only root image is problematic to a regular Linux OS, as certain utilities in Linux require a modifiable root file system. For example, it is common for applications to write their PIDs (e.g., into `/var/run`), and log messages to disk. To address these issues, we use AUFS (Another Union File System [23]), which allows several file systems to be simultaneously mounted at a single mount point and act as a single file system. AUFS overlays the file systems, creating a unified hierarchy. Each file system can be configured as read-only or writable. During boot, the uApp creates a temporary rewritable in-memory file system using `tmpfs`. It then combines the root read-only uApp file system with temporary file system using AUFS. This combined file system is mounted as the root file system for our uApp OS. As a result, modifications will be stored in the in-memory file system and will be discarded when the user exits the uApp. The uApp starts from its pristine state the next time it is invoked.

Another challenge is the large size of the uApp base image. Since a hash must be performed over the entire uApp root partition, it is critical that the partition be as small as possible. To achieve this, one might start by removing unnecessary applications and kernel modules from the uApp OS. We made a smaller image by installing Ubuntu in command line mode and adding X server (Xorg), a simple window manager (openbox) and a login manager (SLiM).[3] Another way of reducing the image size is using a compressed file system. We use squashfs [30], an open source compressed read-only file system for Linux. In our setup, squashfs shrinks the size of our uApp base image to less than one-third of its original size. Altogether, with our optimizations we made a uApp base image of size less than 260 MB (about 900MB in ext4). We then copy this image to a 275MB partition.

4.3 Server and PSD Attestors

Attestation can be performed by the remote server, a PSD, or both. To demonstrate remote server attestation, we implement a web server that performs attestation of clients connecting to it using the Twisted [33] networking engine version 10.0.0 written in python. The web server's python

[3]We use auto-login, but without the login manager, Ubuntu boots into a command-line mode.

module uses a signature verification function we developed in C through `ctypes` (a Python wrapper of C library). Verification of the TPM quote received from the uApp client requires the RSA signature algorithm and SHA-1 hash function; we use the openssl library (version 0.9.8k) for these cryptographic operations.

To perform a quote operation of a uApp client connecting to it, our web server sends a quote request to another Twisted instance, called the TPM server, running in the uApp. When the user connects to the remote service, it contacts the TPM server on the uApp client with a nonce, PCR indices, and requests a quote. The TPM server retrieves the quote from TPM, and responds to the web server. We note that in reality, uApp clients are likely to be behind firewalls so it may not be possible for the remote service to initiate a connection to the uApp instance in the same way as our prototype. In this case, we would have to tunnel the quote request over the existing connection that was initiated by the uApp client. We leave this for future work.

Our PSD client prototype is implemented on an Android phone. This client is used for verification and authentication as follows. First we copy the expected platform measurement values, public part of the AIK, and the long-term shared secret to the PSD. Communications between the PSD and uApp are done via QR-codes. After receiving the server nonce, the TPM server on uApp generates the TPM quote, converts the quote data into a QR-code image and displays the image on a browser page. The user scans the image by the PSD. After the PSD client retrieves the quote data from the scanned image, it attempts to verify the quote using the stored AIK and PCR values. We use Java crypto packages for performing crypto operations on Android. If verification is successful, an HMAC response is generated (see Figure 2) and displayed as a base64 response. Normally, the HMAC response would be transmitted automatically to the uApp, but in our prototype we manually copy the response to the uApp TPM server. Note that ease of use is not the focus of our prototype implementation; see below. The HMAC value and quote are then sent to the web server, which can now verify the platform, and authenticate the user.

Communication channels. As shown in Figures 2 and 3, we assume communication channels exist between the remote server, uApp OS, and PSD. Between the remote server and uApp OS, we secure the connection using SSL. The server's domain name is included in the uApp OS. The OS does not allow any connection beyond this embedded domain. This prevents relay attacks. To defeat rogue or compromised CA attacks [29], hash of the server's SSL certificate may be included in the uApp OS, and checked during connection establishment. Similar to current browser-initiated SSL connections, this process remains transparent to users.

For transferring data from uApp to PSD, we use QR-code as outlined above. This provides an intuitive and secure channel for users without requiring any setup. For PSD-to-computer data transfer, the PSD may communicate directly with the computer over the network, or through a common 3rd party Internet site (such as a Twitter account or Google Docs page). This channel need not be secure. Instead, keys for encryption and signing are transferred from computer to PSD via the QR-code displayed in Step 2 of Figure 1. We are also exploring the feasibility of a *reverse QR-code* channel where the PSD's QR-coded response is scanned by a PC webcam.

5. UNICORN APPLICATION EXAMPLES

We built two applications as examples of how the Unicorn architecture may be realized in practice. We chose these example uApps to be representative of different types of applications people use often. Since these are proof-of-concept applications, we envision that commercial deployments may have updated authentication mechanisms, incorporate better security techniques (e.g., strict SELinux policies) and have spent more effort in reducing the uApp image size (e.g., dropping unnecessary functionality).

Secure online financial transactions. Our online-banking application represents services that would like to verify the integrity of the user platform and authenticate users before serving sensitive data and allowing financial transactions (recall Figure 2). The banking application uses both the local TPM server and the remote bank server. After booting into the uApp OS, the Chromium web browser is opened with the bank server's URL. The user requests for validation by clicking on a button on the page. The web server then contacts the TPM server with a nonce, PCR indices, and requests a quote. A pre-distributed shared secret is stored on the PSD. The TPM server retrieves the quote from TPM (via a Python C wrapper), and displays the QR-coded quote data on a web page to be scanned by the PSD. If the PSD client can verify the quote, it uses the stored shared secret to generate the HMAC response. After receiving the HMAC value from PSD, the TPM server responds to the bank server with this value and the quote. The user is logged into her bank account only if verification is successful at the server. She can then continue using her account from the browser without involving her PSD again.

Secure access to encrypted data. For this case, we built a uApp with a PDF reader application which represents environments that would want to verify the integrity of the user platform locally before allowing access to encrypted data stored on the user PC or a mobile storage (recall Figure 3). Assume a corporate IT department where administrators want that their users can access sensitive data from anywhere as long as a verified environment is used. This application does not involve a remote party. Half of the decryption key is stored on the PSD (K_{psd}), and the other half is sealed into the computer's TPM (K_{tpm}, with PCR values dependent on the uApp binary). After booting into this uApp, we use a custom program to get K_{psd} from the PSD if attestation is successful, and unseal K_{tpm} from the TPM if correct PCR values are initialized by the loaded uApp; these keys then form the decryption key (K_{dec}, see Section 3.2). Retrieving the decryption key implicitly indicates the uApp's correctness. We use openssl to encrypt a PDF file, and store the encryption key parts in the PSD, and TPM. Afterwards, when we boot into this uApp, the decryption key is formed upon a successful verification, openssl is used to decrypt the file, and then the PDF reader displays the content; cf. Kells [5] which enables a mobile storage system to perform attestation to verify a host's integrity state before allowing access to sensitive data.

6. EVALUATION

We evaluate Unicorn along two axes. First, we qualitatively evaluate the security of Unicorn against a variety of attacks. Then, we evaluate the time it takes to switch between the user OS and a uApp.

6.1 Security Evaluation

(a) Tampering with uApp before launch. As mentioned in Section 2, we assume the attacker can compromise and gain complete control over the user OS. Since the uApp image is stored on storage accessible to the user OS, the attacker may arbitrarily modify the uApp image. However, the integrity of the entire uApp image is measured and stored in the TPM so any tampering of any component of the uApp will necessarily alter those measurements. This will result in a failed uApp launch as the integrity verification test by the PSD will fail. We note that this allows an adversary to mount a denial of service attack. Moreover, by controlling the user OS, the adversary could encourage the user to re-enter the setup phase when the uApp launch fails. Thus, it is important that the setup phase be constructed to ensure user diligence, even at the cost of convenience, since the setup phase should be a rare event in benign scenarios.

(b) Run time attacks. The attacker can try to mount run time attacks against the uApp in three ways. First, she may try to tamper with the hardware platform the uApp will run on so that the effect of the tampering will only be felt after the uApp is running. Second, she may try to find a vulnerability in the uApp and exploit it while it is running. Finally, she may try to extract information left in the machine after the uApp has terminated.

To tamper with the platform, the attacker initiates residual commands on a device from the user OS that would be executed after the uApp is launched (e.g., after measurements have been taken and stored in the TPM). For example, before being suspended, a sophisticated attacker might schedule a DMA transfer to overwrite critical memory pages in the uApp. Such attacks are not possible because the MLE protects its content from being tampered by DMA. Also, our uApp kernel enables DMA remapping using VT-d, which restricts all DMA-capable devices to only be able to write to regions for which they are authorized.

Another potential vector for hardware tampering is to modify the contents of the TPM. If the attacker can learn the TPM ownership password, she can create new AIKs and delete existing AIKs from the TPM. However, new AIKs are not a threat unless the attacker can convince the user to add them to their PSD. Deleting an AIK will make the TPM unable to attest the state of the uApp to the remote server or the user's PSD. This means the user will not be able to use the uApp, but does not result in the compromise of any user information.

The attacker may attempt to find and exploit a vulnerability in the uApp while it is running (known as time of check to time of use attacks, see, e.g., [4]). We believe that the smaller attack surface of the uApp, achieved by constraining the network servers it communicates with, along with the smaller TCB of the uApp, achieved through reducing the functionality in the uApp OS, make such an attack difficult for an adversary to mount. Other hardening techniques can also be employed to limit these attacks; see Section 4.2.

Finally, after uApp terminates and the user OS is resumed, attackers can look for sensitive information on the memory and disk. On exiting uApp, we tear down the MLE and zero-out in-memory states. To prevent accidental storage of Unicorn secrets on the disk (e.g., due to swapping), uApps may be run without a swap partition or file; this may however affect some applications' functionality.

(c) Communication channel attacks. We assume the communication channel between a trusted application and the remote server is encrypted and integrity-checked. In addition, since the uApps have a specific use, we constrain their network access capabilities to the bare minimum necessary – thus they may only communicate with (trusted) servers which are needed for the uApp's operation. This severely limits an adversary's ability to find and exercise a vulnerability in a uApp.

Because the PSD has a direct communication channel with the user's computer, we assume that an attacker cannot tamper or snoop on this channel. If part of this channel uses a wireless technology, like 802.11 or bluetooth, this must be protected via cryptographic means, depending on how this channel is used (see Section 3.2).

(d) Attestor attacks. The attacker may attempt to fool the attestors in two ways. First, she may try to mount a spoofing attack by tricking the user into believing that the uApp has started, when in fact the computer is still running a malicious user OS. Second, she may try to use a relaying attack [32], where she relays attestation requests to a valid uApp running on another machine.

A spoofing attack is detected by the user's PSD since the spoofed uApp cannot generate a proper response to the quote request from the PSD. A correct quote response is signed by the AIK private key, which is only stored on the TPM. The user may not notice the spoofed uApp and continue to interact with it, but since she does not input any authentication credentials, no passwords or such may be leaked. In addition, no sensitive information the server can be compromised.

In a relaying attack, the adversary loads a tampered uApp. To generate a proper quote response, she can have a second machine running a valid uApp to which she relays the quote request, records the response and relays that back to the attestor. However, this attack is defeated by our Unicorn design. If the attestor is a remote server, the authentic uApp client will not respond to an attestation request from the attacker because its network interface is constrained to communicate only with authentic servers. In the case where the attestor is the user's PSD, then the AIK of the user's machines has been registered with the PSD and it will not accept a quote request by an AIK other than the one stored on the PSD. The quote response format for user and server attestation requests are different so that an attacker cannot convert one to the other without forging the AIK signature.

6.2 Performance Evaluation

Because uApps run natively on the hardware, there is no run time overhead for applications running inside a uApp. Therefore we focus our evaluation on the time to switch from the user OS to a uApp and back. All measurements are performed on a machine with an Intel Core 2 Quad processor Q9550 (2.83 GHz, 12M cache), Intel DQ45CB motherboard (Intel Q45 chipset and TPM 1.2), 4GB DDR2 memory, and a 500GB SATA2 disk (Western Digital WD5000AAKS, 7200RPM, 16MB cache). Ubuntu 10.04 (x86_64) with kernel 2.6.34 is used as user OS and uApp OS. The user OS has been used a kernel/application development platform.

Switching from user OS to uApp. As mentioned in Section 4, the uApp OS image is stored in a 275MB partition using the squashfs file system. The user OS is initially

	uApp loader	kernel, X	OS hash	**Total**	Suspend	**Total with suspend**	Resume	Switch with reboot	Resume with reboot
Run 1	3.40	7.19	3.95	14.54	11.34	25.88	24.8	48.57	45.6
Run 2	2.87	7.49	3.85	14.21	11.09	25.30	24.7	47.75	45.3
Run 3	3.02	6.98	3.85	13.85	11.06	24.91	23.6	45.72	44.1
Run 4	3.76	7.30	3.83	14.89	11.32	26.21	22.5	47.83	44.8
Run 5	3.40	7.04	3.76	14.20	11.00	25.20	23.1	48.61	46.4
Average	3.29	7.20	3.85	14.34	11.16	25.50	23.7	47.70	45.2

Table 1: Time distribution (in seconds) for switching user OS to uApp OS and back

configured to use 1GB of memory. To simulate an activity on the user OS when a uApp is invoked, we run the Firefox browser with five open tabs and play a movie using the VLC media player. In addition, default Ubuntu services, such as SSH and the Gnome desktop are also running. Under this load, the user OS had about 300MB of active memory usage.

We measure the time from when the user gives a user-level command to switch to the uApp to the time the X server in the uApp comes online (note that the uApp is configured to automatically log in). We break this process into several components and also record the intermediate times for each component. The components are: (1) the time for the user OS to suspend its state to disk; (2) the time from the end of suspend to when the uApp loader (tboot) transfers control to the uApp kernel; (3) the time from when the uApp kernel starts booting, to when X becomes available, excluding the uApp image's hash measurement time; and (4) the time to measure the hash of the uApp image. We measure the above times using `do_gettimeofday` inside the kernel, and the `date` and `time` shell commands. We do not include the time to load the uApp loader into memory as this usually took below one second to complete.

We switched between user OS and uApp OS for five rounds and give the results in Table 1.[4] We also performed a full reboot between each round to initiate switching from a similar state. Without suspending the user OS, the switch time is 14.34 seconds on average (std. deviation 0.39); in this case, after using a uApp, the user initiates a new user OS instance via kexec or regular reboot (as opposed to resume). The switching time including the time to save a suspended user OS takes an average of 25.5 seconds (std. deviation 0.53). While fairly fast, there are several parameters that could vary depending on the implementation and usage environment of the uApp. Because our uApp loader is based on tboot, there is a significant amount of functionality that is performed but not needed by the uApp. We believe that with more tuning, the uApp loader time could be reduced.

The suspend time is dependent on the amount of user OS state that must be saved to disk, which in turn depends on the amount of memory used by applications and the user OS kernel, and the total amount of memory that the user OS kernel has. To illustrate, we varied the amount of memory allocated to the user OS and found that average suspend durations for 2GB and 4GB memory are 11.86 and 16.64 seconds respectively (std. deviation 0.4 and 0.85 respectively). However, we note that if the uApp has lower memory requirements than the user OS, the suspend-to-disk code in the user OS could be modified to only write the amount of memory needed by the uApp to disk. Thus, with enough engineering, the suspend time of the user OS will be ultimately dependent on the lesser of the memory requirements of the uApp and the amount of active state in the user OS.

Another highly variable factor is the size of the uApp disk image. Our measurements on the test machine show that it takes about 1.4 seconds to hash every 100MB of the uApp OS partition, and that this time is dominated by the disk bandwidth, so it is unlikely to change even with a faster CPU. By using a smaller Linux distribution instead of Ubuntu (as used in our prototype), the uApp image size may be further reduced.

Switching from uApp to user OS. To measure the time to switch back to the user OS, we measure the time from when the user initiates shutdown of the uApp to the time the video running in the VLC player resumes in the user OS (assuming the user chooses suspend-to-disk before switching to uApp). Because there is no easy way to programmatically measure when the video resumes, and the switch time takes on the order of seconds, we measure the time to perform this switch operation using a stop watch. We also believe this better represents the user experience. This was measured to be an average of 23.7 seconds over 5 runs (std. deviation 1.0); see the "Resume" column in Table 1.

Switching with regular reboot. We also measure switch time with regular reboot, i.e., going through the BIOS and GRUB boot loader. We run applications in the user OS, and then suspend to disk with the reboot option. We do not load the uApp image via kexec into memory, which causes the suspend code in user OS kernel to initiate a regular reboot after suspend. We use GRUB to load the uApp loader (from a separate disk partition as GRUB cannot read from a squashfs partition), and continue to boot into the uApp OS. For switch back, we use the regular reboot command, and then initiate the resume of the user OS via GRUB. Results are in the last two columns of Table 1. Both switching to uApp and resume took much longer (nearly twice as long) than the uApp switch. Thus, bypassing the BIOS and bootloader indeed saved us significant amount of time.

7. RELATED WORK AND COMPARISON

There have been numerous publications on establishing trust in computers via hardware support; for a summary, see e.g., Parno et al. [24]. We discuss only few here which are most relevant to our work.

Secure kiosk computing. To enable users to use their own computing environment (e.g., a VM) on a public kiosk computer, Garriss et al. [8] designed a protocol for establishing trust on the kiosk. Unicorn is not intended for kiosk computing; technical differences with secure kiosk computing include the following. First, kiosk computing requires the user to notice whether the trusted PSD successfully ver-

[4]Ideally, we would have preferred more rounds for deriving our results. However, each round requires manual operations. Also, note that standard deviations were small for each measured item.

ifies the kiosk before the user proceeds to use the kiosk. In contrast, Unicorn relies on the PSD to make such decisions on the user's behalf. Second, kiosk computing uses IMA [25] to measure the VMM/OS software and verifies only what is loaded up to the point of the attestation request. In addition, variances in loading order and software execution can result in different PCR values and the attestor must be aware of all valid PCR values that could be returned in a quote response. Unicorn performs verification on the entire uApp image, which includes all software that could be executed while using the uApp. Finally, to switch from the untrusted to the trusted OS, the kiosk computer is then rebooted (i.e., shutdown, run BIOS and bootloader, late launch, run the OSLO secure loader [14], and boot into OS/VMM). Since uApps short circuit the process by avoiding the BIOS and bootloader, switching is nearly 10 times faster with uApps.

Lockdown. Lockdown [35] is a small hypervisor that provides one environment for regular tasks and another for all sensitive web transactions. Lockdown uses Advanced Configuration and Power Interface (ACPI) and AMD's Nested Page Table (NPT) features to partition system resources. A trusted BIOS is required for installation and booting of Lockdown. Lockdown runs at AMD SVM's hypervisor mode and OSs run in the guest mode. The trusted OS and applications are installed in separate disks after Lockdown is in control. Lockdown restricts the list of Internet servers the trusted environment can connect to, but since the trusted environment can be changed, the list must be updated by users as new applications are added. In contrast, uApps do not change and adding a new uApp does not affect the restrictions on any existing uApps. Also, remote servers in Lockdown receive no guarantee about user environments.

Another difference is the way the systems switch between trusted and untrusted environments. Lockdown maintains both environments in memory at the same time and interposes on hardware requests from both environments to enforce partitioning. Switching between environments requires ACPI operations and takes slightly longer than uApp switching (42–46 seconds vs. 25.5 seconds). However, system resources are inefficiently used by Lockdown, e.g., memory is exclusively partitioned between trusted and untrusted environments. The trusted environment also suffers significant performance degradation, with 15–55% CPU and memory overhead, 3-6 seconds additional network latency, and four times slower download speed. uApps have direct access to all hardware and thus do not suffer any performance penalty.

Flicker & Bumpy. Bumpy [21] is designed to secure sensitive user inputs (e.g., online passwords), by processing them in a separate Flicker [20] module, which can be loaded *on-demand* bypassing the untrusted user OS. Users must start sensitive input with @@, and also verify that a Flicker session has actually been initiated from the feedback received (e.g., beeps) on a trusted PSD, and that the receiving URL on the device is correct. For safe operation, users must also notice the transition between protected and unprotected input fields. These complexities could be attributed to using the untrusted OS and applications for everything except sensitive user input (for keeping the TCB small). A user study of Bumpy's input mechanisms [16] also highlights several user interface issues. Unicorn sidesteps many of these issues by taking the user out of the loop during all operations except setup. TrustVisor [19] improves the performance of Flicker by implementing a software-based micro-TPM module that executes on the primary CPU instead of the slow TPM hardware.

Root of trust installation. Immutability of uApps images is similar to the root of trust installation (ROTI [31]) system. Installers distributed by trusted parties are used for installing all system software and system-specific data and secrets. At the end of an installation, ROTI computes the hash of all (static) files in the root file system, and seals a file containing those hashes to the TPM. Sealing ensures that this hash file can be opened only if the system is loaded again in the same state (i.e., the same PCR values in the TPM). ROTI enables attestation to remote parties but does not address user authentication.

Terra: VM-based trusted computing. Terra [7] enables users to simultaneously use *open-box* VMs (with a commodity OS and user applications) and *closed-box* VMs (with a custom OS and application) on the same computer. Terra depends on a trusted virtual machine monitor (TVMM), and the hardware and TVMM enable closed-box VMs to identify their software stack to a remote party. However, user attestation and secure UI issues remain unaddressed by Terra.

Other authentication methods. A large amount of work has gone into protecting user credentials from theft or leakage through social engineering. For example, *split-trust* mechanisms (e.g., Balfanz and Felten [3], and MP-Auth [18]), and two-factor authentication mechanisms all protect user credentials (and optionally parts of a session). However, none protects the confidentiality of an entire user session. To achieve a malware-free execution environment, we rely on DRTM CPU instructions; current malware cannot evade hardware-based protections of these instructions. Additionally, Unicorn effectively enables *two-factor* attestation: malware cannot bypass the attestation checks either at the user-end, or at the server-end. As the PSD links attestation with authentication, Unicorn can guarantee both a malware-free user session, and resistance to social engineering attacks.

8. CONCLUSION

We have presented Unicorn, which both reduces the burden on the user by removing them from the attestation and authentication process and enables fast switching between a general-purpose user OS and a secure uApp OS using a novel mechanism that avoids a full machine reboot. The key idea behind Unicorn is a PSD that is able to verify the integrity of the user's computer and only use the user's authentication secrets if the integrity can be verified. Combining this with verification of the attestation by a remote server or the local TPM via sealed-storage produces a two-factor authentication, which forces the attacker to both gain physical access to the user's computer and compromise the PSD to successfully gain access to Unicorn-protected user data.

In building our Unicorn prototype we found that a great deal of standard functionality in commodity desktop systems could be repurposed to make implementing Unicorn easy: suspend-to-disk functionality on the desktop system was used to save the running state of the user OS to disk, and hardware Intel TXT support for confining buggy device drivers using DMA-remapping was used to protect against malicious commands left on devices by the user OS. We also found that the implementation of the Unicorn attestor on

Android was straightforward and many of the required components, such as crypto libraries and QR code libraries are relatively mature. While commodity code doesn't always meet the ideal security requirements of a small code footprint and strict access controls, we find it encouraging that much of the technology to implement the components of Unicorn already exists. This suggests that with more engineering effort, a deployable version of Unicorn could be implemented with relatively little effort.

Acknowledgments

We are grateful to our shepherd Mike Reiter and the anonymous reviewers for their insightful comments and advice. The first author was supported by an NSERC post-doctoral fellowship. This work was also supported by funding from the NSERC ISSNet Strategic Network, an NSERC Engage Grant, and an ORF Grant.

9. REFERENCES

[1] Anti-Phishing Working Group (APWG). Phishing activity trends report: 1st quarter 2010. `http://www.antiphishing.org/reports/apwg_report_Q1_2010.pdf`.

[2] A. M. Azab, P. Ning, Z. Wang, X. Jiang, X. Zhang, and N. C. Skalsky. HyperSentry: enabling stealthy in-context measurement of hypervisor integrity. In *ACM CCS'10*, Chicago, IL, USA, Oct. 2010.

[3] D. Balfanz and E. Felten. Hand-held computers can be better smart cards. In *USENIX Security Symposium*, Washington, DC, USA, Aug. 1999.

[4] S. Bratus, N. D'Cunha, E. Sparks, and S. W. Smith. TOCTOU, traps, and trusted computing. In *Trusted Computing—Challenges and Applications (TRUST'08)*, Villach, Austria, Mar. 2008.

[5] K. Butler, S. McLaughlin, and P. McDaniel. Kells: A protection framework for portable data. In *ACSAC'10*, Austin, TX, USA, Dec. 2010.

[6] eWeek.com. Zeus trojan mobile variant intercepts SMS passcodes from bank sites. News article (Feb. 22, 2011).

[7] T. Garfinkel, B. Pfaff, J. Chow, M. Rosenblum, and D. Boneh. Terra: A virtual machine-based platform for trusted computing. In *SOSP'03*, Bolton Landing, NY, USA, Oct. 2003.

[8] S. Garriss, R. Cáceres, S. Berger, R. Sailer, L. van Doorn, and X. Zhang. Trustworthy and personalized computing on public kiosks. In *Mobile Systems, Applications and Services (Mobisys'08)*, Breckenridge, CO, USA, June 2008.

[9] K. Goldman, R. Perez, and R. Sailer. Linking remote attestation to secure tunnel endpoints. In *Scalable Trusted Computing (STC'06)*, Fairfax, VA, USA, Nov. 2006.

[10] D. Grawrock. *The Intel Safer Computing Initiative: Building Blocks for Trusted Computing.* Intel Press, 2006.

[11] H-online.com. Hacker extracts crypto key from TPM chip. News article (Feb. 10, 2010).

[12] Intel. Intel trusted execution technology (TXT) software development guide. Technical article (Dec. 2009). `http://download.intel.com/technology/security/downloads/315168.pdf`.

[13] Intel. Trusted boot. Open-source project (version Oct. 5, 2010). `http://sourceforge.net/projects/tboot/`.

[14] B. Kauer. OSLO: Improving the security of trusted computing. In *USENIX Security Symposium*, Boston, MA, USA, Aug. 2007.

[15] G. Klein, K. Elphinstone, G. Heiser, J. Andronick, D. Cock, P. Derrin, D. Elkaduwe, K. Engelhardt, R. Kolanski, M. Norrish, T. Sewell, H. Tuch, and S. Winwood. seL4: Formal verification of an OS kernel. In *SOSP'09*, Big Sky, MT, USA, Oct. 2009.

[16] A. Libonati, J. M. McCune, and M. K. Reiter. Usability testing a malware-resistant input mechanism. In *NDSS'11*, San Diego, CA, USA, Feb. 2011.

[17] P. Loscocco and S. Smalley. Integrating flexible support for security policies into the Linux operating system. In *USENIX Annual Technical Conference*, Boston, MA, USA, June 2001.

[18] M. Mannan and P. van Oorschot. Leveraging personal devices for stronger password authentication from untrusted computers. *Journal of Computer Security*, 19(4):703–750, 2011.

[19] J. M. McCune, Y. Li, N. Qu, Z. Zhou, A. Datta, V. Gligor, and A. Perrig. TrustVisor: Efficient TCB reduction and attestation. In *IEEE Symposium on Security and Privacy*, Oakland, CA, USA, May 2010.

[20] J. M. McCune, B. Parno, A. Perrig, M. K. Reiter, and H. Isozaki. Flicker: An execution infrastructure for TCB minimization. In *The European Conference on Computer Systems (EuroSys'08)*, Glasgow, Scotland, UK, Apr. 2008.

[21] J. M. McCune, A. Perrig, and M. K. Reiter. Safe passage for passwords and other sensitive data. In *NDSS'09*, San Diego, CA, USA, Feb. 2009.

[22] H. Nellitheertha. Reboot Linux faster using kexec. IBM technical library (May 4, 2004). `http://www.ibm.com/developerworks/linux/library/l-kexec.html`.

[23] J. R. Okajima. Advanced multi layered unification filesystem. Open-source project (version 2.1). `http://aufs.sourceforge.net/`.

[24] B. Parno, J. M. McCune, and A. Perrig. Bootstrapping trust in commodity computers. In *IEEE Symposium on Security and Privacy*, Oakland, CA, USA, May 2010.

[25] R. Sailer, X. Zhang, T. Jaeger, and L. van Doorn. Design and implementation of a TCG-based integrity measurement architecture. In *USENIX Security Symposium*, San Diego, CA, USA, Aug. 2004.

[26] J. Samuel, N. Mathewson, J. Cappos, and R. Dingledine. Survivable key compromise in software update systems. In *ACM CCS'10*, Chicago, IL, USA, Oct. 2010.

[27] A. Seshadri, M. Luk, N. Qu, and A. Perrig. SecVisor: A tiny hypervisor to provide lifetime kernel code integrity for commodity OSes. In *SOSP'07*, Stevenson, WA, USA, Oct. 2007.

[28] A. Shieh, D. Williams, E. G. Sirer, and F. B. Schneider. Nexus: A new operating system for trustworthy computing. In *SOSP'05*, Brighton, UK, Oct. 2005.

[29] C. Soghoian and S. Stamm. Certified lies: Detecting and defeating government interception attacks against SSL. In *Financial Cryptography and Data Security (FC'11)*, St. Lucia, 2011.

[30] A squashed read-only file system for Linux. Open-source project (version 4.1, Sept. 19, 2010). `http://squashfs.sourceforge.net/`.

[31] L. St. Clair, J. Schiffman, T. Jaeger, and P. McDaniel. Establishing and sustaining system integrity via root of trust installation. In *ACSAC'07*, Miami, FL, USA, Dec. 2007.

[32] F. Stumpf, O. Tafreschi, P. Röder, and C. Eckert. A robust integrity reporting protocol for remote attestation. In *Workshop on Advances in Trusted Computing (WATC'06)*, Tokyo, Japan, Nov. 2006.

[33] Twisted Matrix Labs. Twisted: Event-driven networking engine. Open-source project. `http://twistedmatrix.com/trac/wiki`.

[34] P. van Oorschot and G. Wurster. Reducing unauthorized modification of digital objects. *IEEE Transactions on Software Engineering*, 2011. To appear.

[35] A. Vasudevan, B. Parno, N. Qu, V. D. Gligor, and A. Perrig. Lockdown: A safe and practical environment for security applications. Technical Report CMU-CyLab-09-011, CyLab, Carnegie Mellon University, July 2009. `http://repository.cmu.edu/cylab/5/`.

[36] A. Whitten and J. D. Tygar. Why Johnny can't encrypt: A usability evaluation of PGP 5.0. In *USENIX Security Symposium*, Washington, D.C., USA, Aug. 1999.
[37] R. Wojtczuk, J. Rutkowska, and A. Tereshkin. Another way to circumvent Intel Trusted Execution Technology: Tricking SENTER into misconfiguring VT-d via SINIT bug exploitation. Technical article (Dec., 2009). `http://theinvisiblethings.blogspot.com/2009/12/another-txt-attack.html`.

APPENDIX

A. BACKGROUND

In this section, we give some background on Intel Trusted Execution Technology (TXT) and its interaction with the Trusted Platform Module (TPM) chip. We only briefly discuss TXT here; see e.g., Grawrock [10], TXT software development guide [12], and the tboot project [13] for details.

Trusted Platform Module. A TPM is a hardware chip that provides the following functionality: (1) protected storage for persistent secrets (NV-RAM) and for Platform Configuration Registers (PCRs), which contain measurements of the running state of the machine; (2) a protected execution environment for certain cryptographic operations (e.g., SHA-1 hash, RSA encryption/signature); (3) and the ability to generate attestation quote responses with current PCR values. TPMs implement two types of PCRs: static PCRs, which can only be reset by a system reboot, and dynamic PCRs, which can be reset by Dynamic Root of Trust Measurement (DRTM). Each layer of software stack in the platform is measured (i.e., hashed) and the measurements are stored to a PCR using the *extend* operation. Extend appends the hash to a PCR by concatenating the current PCR value with the new measurement and then computing a hash over the combined value. This new hash value is then stored in the PCR. Thus, PCRs contain a hash chain describing all software that was loaded on the system since the PCR was reset. Remote parties can request attestations of the PCR values using the *quote* operation. To perform a quote operation, the TPM must be initialized with an Attestation Identity Key (AIK) pair. This AIK pair is generated by a TPM and the private part of the key pair never leaves the TPM chip. The public part of the key pair is certified by a trusted Privacy Certificate Authority (CA) and should be distributed to the attestor prior to the attestation request. A quote request contains a specification of which PCR values need to be retrieved as well as a nonce used for freshness. In response, the TPM computes a hash of the nonce and PCR values, signs the hash with the AIK private key, and returns the signature with the PCR values. The TPM 1.2 specification also defines *localities*, which restrict how the dynamic PCRs can be modified. By default, all untrusted code executes in locality zero, the lowest privilege level. By executing code in more privileged localities, software gains the ability to extend/reset certain PCRs. TPMs also support sealing and unsealing operations which bind data (e.g., a secret key) to the current platform configuration, as specified by the chosen PCRs. Sealing takes a set of PCRs and data as input, and encrypts the given data using the TPM's Storage Root Key (SRK), which never leaves the TPM. Unsealing of the sealed data can be done only when the pre-specified PCRs have the same values as during sealing.

Intel TXT. On their own, TPMs implement Static Root of Trust Measurements (SRTM), where static PCRs can only be reset by a full reboot of the machine. Intel TXT, formally known as LaGrande Technology (LT), is a set of hardware extensions available on recent Intel CPUs and chipsets that implements Dynamic Root of Trust Measurement (DRTM), also known as *late launch.* DRTM allows the dynamic PCRs (PCRs 17-23) to be reset at any time by entering a measured launch environment (MLE). The CPU enters into and exits from the MLE via GETSEC[SENTER] and GETSEC[SEXIT] instructions respectively. Before executing SENTER, an authenticated code (AC) module is loaded into the processor's internal memory (which is out of reach of DMA devices or the external processor bus). The CPU initially protects an MLE from DMA modifications by loading it into one of two memory regions: (i) the DMA protected range (DPR), a contiguous region (currently 3MB in size) in the physical memory which is protected from all DMA accesses; or (ii) the Intel VT-d protected memory regions (PMRs), two ranges of physical memory addresses (one in the lower 4GB and the other in the upper 4GB) which are also DMA protected. The AC module is chipset-specific, distributed in a binary form by Intel, and is authenticated through a digital signature check (signed by Intel) by the processor. SENTER proceeds only if the AC module can be authenticated, and the MLE is loaded into the DPR or in a PMR. The AC module checks several chipset and processor configurations, and if successful, it then executes the MLE. After an MLE has been established, it can facilitate trusted boot into an OS kernel or hypervisor.

Combining Control-Flow Integrity and Static Analysis for Efficient and Validated Data Sandboxing

Bin Zeng
Department of Computer Science and Engineering
Lehigh University
zeb209@lehigh.edu

Gang Tan
Department of Computer Science and Engineering
Lehigh University
gtan@cse.lehigh.edu

Greg Morrisett
School of Engineering and Applied Sciences
Harvard University
greg@eecs.harvard.edu

ABSTRACT

In many software attacks, inducing an illegal control-flow transfer in the target system is one common step. Control-Flow Integrity (CFI [1]) protects a software system by enforcing a pre-determined control-flow graph. In addition to providing strong security, CFI enables static analysis on low-level code. This paper evaluates whether CFI-enabled static analysis can help build efficient and validated data sandboxing. Previous systems generally sandbox memory writes for integrity, but avoid protecting confidentiality due to the high overhead of sandboxing memory reads. To reduce overhead, we have implemented a series of optimizations that remove sandboxing instructions if they are proven unnecessary by static analysis. On top of CFI, our system adds only 2.7% runtime overhead on SPECint2000 for sandboxing memory writes and adds modest 19% for sandboxing both reads and writes. We have also built a principled data-sandboxing verifier based on range analysis. The verifier checks the safety of the results of the optimizer, which removes the need to trust the rewriter and optimizer. Our results show that the combination of CFI and static analysis has the potential of bringing down the cost of general inlined reference monitors, while maintaining strong security.

Categories and Subject Descriptors

D.4.6 [**Operating Systems**]: Security and Protection; D.2.4 [**Software Engineering**]: Software/Program Verification; D.3.4 [**Programming Languages**]: Processors

General Terms

Security, Verification

Keywords

Control-Flow Integrity, Static Analysis, Binary Rewriting, Inlined Reference Monitors

CCS'11, October 17–21, 2011, Chicago, Illinois, USA.

1. INTRODUCTION

Software attacks often exploit vulnerabilities such as buffer overflows and format-string handling errors that are common in large software systems. In many attacks, one essential step is to induce an illegal control transfer through, for example, overwriting a return address or a function pointer. The illegal control transfer might jump to new code injected by attackers, as in code-injection attacks; it might jump to code already in the target program, as in return-into-libc attacks. The extreme case is Return-Oriented Programming (ROP [9, 26]), which can induce any malicious behavior by combining code snippets in the program with arbitrary control flow. In all these attacks, the expected control-flow graph of the target program is violated.

Control-Flow Integrity (CFI [1,2]) is a defensive technique that can foil attacks based on illegal control transfers. A program satisfies control-flow integrity if it follows a pre-determined control-flow graph. The expected control-flow graph serves as a specification of control transfers allowed in the program. A software-based CFI implementation inserts runtime checks to enforce the specification. The runtime checks will catch and prevent illegal control transfers attempted by attacks.

It is generally believed that CFI is a principled defense mechanism against Return-Oriented Programming (ROP). Previous research has shown that ad-hoc defenses fail to prevent simple variants of ROP [9]. The inventors of ROP have argued that research should instead focus on comprehensive defenses such as CFI.

An attractive property of CFI is that it can be enforced on almost all software, including legacy C and C++ code, and even assembly code without breaking applications and without requiring special hardware features (e.g., segment registers). Software-based Fault Isolation (SFI) [31] is another policy that can be applied in a language-agnostic way. However, SFI only provides weak integrity for control-flow and as such, does not prevent return-into-libc and ROP attacks completely. Furthermore, the lack of an enforced control-flow graph prevents the use of standard compiler techniques for optimizing SFI enforcement mechanisms. In contrast, the enforced control-flow graph of CFI supports standard dataflow analysis and optimizations. Thus, in addition to protecting applications from control-hijacking attacks, CFI provides a basis for efficient enforcement of any inlined reference monitor. In particular:

- *Optimization.* Optimizers can perform static analysis to eliminate unnecessary security checks if they are statically proven unnecessary. This reduces the runtime overhead of enforcing security.

- *Verification.* Static analysis can be used to verify the result of binary rewriting and optimizations. The verification checks whether the rewritten and optimized code obeys the desired security policy, removing the binary rewriter and the optimizer from the TCB.

The original work on CFI recognized the potential for static analysis, but did not take advantage of it. In this paper, we investigate how CFI-enabled static analysis can be used to cut the overheads of SFI-style data sandboxing. Previous implementations of SFI either rely upon segment registers to enforce data sandboxing, or else use software-based techniques but only instrument memory writes due to the high overhead of sandboxing reads. In contrast, we consider software-only techniques, which are applicable to a much wider class of architectures, and consider sandboxing both memory writes as well as reads.

We highlight key contributions of the paper as follows:

- We describe a series of optimizations for efficient data sandboxing in Sec. 4. These optimizations utilize static analysis including liveness analysis and range analysis to eliminate unneeded security checks. Our implementation on x86-32 adds modest runtime overheads on top of CFI (an average of 2.7% for write protection and 19% for read-and-write protection on SPECint2000).

- We propose to use range analysis as a principled way to verify data-sandboxing optimizations in Sec. 5. A single verifier can verify all our implemented optimizations and beyond.

- Since CFI is used as the basis for static analysis, reducing the overhead of the CFI enforcement itself is beneficial. In Sec. 6, we describe two simple optimizations for faster CFI. The optimizations cut the runtime cost of CFI by more than half.

- Our ideas have been implemented in LLVM and fully evaluated using benchmark programs. Sec. 7 describes our implementation and evaluation.

2. RELATED WORK

We divide closely related work into three categories.

SFI. Software-based fault isolation (SFI, [12, 14, 21, 25, 28, 31, 34]) rewrites unsafe code to insert sandboxing instructions before memory and control-transfer instructions. The inserted instructions prevent the code from accessing memory outside of a designated data region and executing instructions outside of a designated code region. For avoiding high overhead, most SFI systems sandbox memory writes but not memory reads. NaCl x86-32 [34] restrains memory access through hardware segmentation that applies to memory reads as well as writes. Hardware segmentation, however, is unavailable on x86-64 and ARM. As a result, NaCl's implementations on these processors rely on SFI to sandbox memory writes [25] (or both reads and writes with a significant performance penalty [6]). Our SFI support reduces overhead through static analysis and in principle applies to processors with or without segmentation.

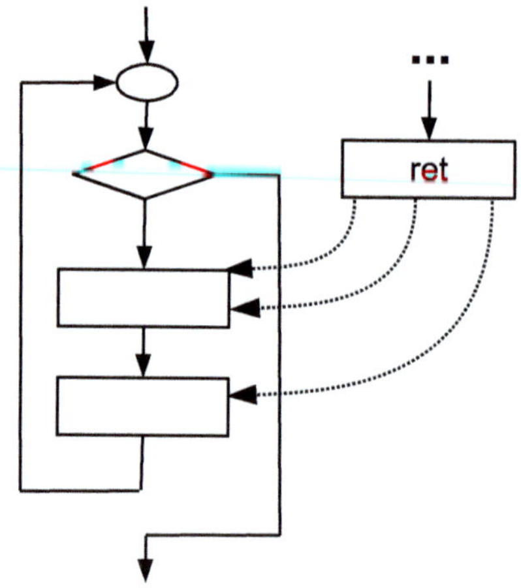

Figure 1: The insufficiency of chunk-based control-flow integrity for static analysis.

One subtle requirement of SFI is that some form of control-flow integrity should be enforced so that inserted checks cannot be bypassed. PittSFIeld [21] and NaCl [25, 34] adopt the *chunk-based control-flow integrity*. Code is divided into atomic chunks of fixed sizes such as 16 bytes. A computed jump is restricted by runtime checks to target only beginnings of chunks. Checks before memory operations cannot be bypassed as long as they are in the same chunk.

The chunk-based control-flow integrity guarantees only an imprecise control-flow graph and is insufficient for most static analyses. To illustrate this point, we use loop optimizations as an example. The control-flow graph in Fig. 1 would contain a loop if those dotted edges do not exist. In chunk-based control flow integrity, a `ret` instruction can jump to any chunk beginnings (because the instruction makes a control transfer according to a value from the untrusted stack). These control transfers are represented by dotted edges in the figure. Therefore, basic blocks in the loop body have to be broken into chunks. Worse, the control-flow graph in the figure is no longer a loop because by definition there should be no edges from nodes outside of the loop to the loop's internal nodes. Consequently, loop optimizations cannot be performed.

SFI traditionally provides coarse-grained data sandboxing with respect to one big, contiguous data region. Recent work [4, 5, 8] extends SFI to provide fine-grained data integrity, which accommodates multiple data regions of various granularity (e.g., at the byte level). However, confidentiality is not supported. Furthermore, the implementation seems to rely upon re-compiling the source, whereas our rewriter and verifier work directly on the assembly language. Consequently, the compiler is not in the TCB in our system. Finally, their techniques do not work for multi-threaded applications; our system is thread safe since it assumes a concurrent attack model. We believe the general idea of using static analysis for optimization and verification should also benefit fine-grained data sandboxing.

XFI. Extended Fault Isolation (XFI, [11]) is a closely related system in its approach. Similar to our system, XFI builds on CFI and exploits the control-flow graph for stronger security and for performance. On the one hand, XFI's goal is to provide a more comprehensive protection system for loading untrusted code. For instance, it also provides a high-integrity stack for protecting return addresses. On the other hand, our system explores more aggressive optimizations such as loop optimizations. The static analysis enables our system to have more efficient support for data sandboxing (more comparison with XFI will be in the following sections).

Program shepherding. Instead of static rewriting, program shepherding [18] (as well as systems in [22, 24]) relies on dynamic binary rewriting to enforce security. One downside of dynamic rewriting is the whole dynamic optimization and monitoring framework is in the TCB, whereas only a verifier needs to be trusted in static rewriting. Furthermore, program shepherding relies on page protection for memory protection; it cannot prevent untrusted application code from reading outside its data region (e.g., the dynamic rewriter's own code and data regions are readable).

Static analysis on low-level code. Analyzing low-level code such as assembly code is more difficult than analyzing source code due to the lack of structured information. Despite this difficulty, there has been plenty of research that applies static analysis to low-level code for various purposes (e.g., [7, 29, 33]). We use static analysis to reduce runtime overhead of SFI-style data sandboxing. Compared with previous low-level code analysis, our static analysis is simpler and more specialized. First, since our attack model (described in Sec. 3) assumes data memory can change between instructions, our static analysis only needs to track properties of registers. Second, some of our static analysis such as range analysis is geared toward the purpose of optimizing checks for guaranteeing safe access within data memory.

Code sandboxing. Also related is the general idea of sandboxing. SFI-style sandboxing, the topic of this paper, is a particular form of sandboxing untrusted code. Isolating untrusted code in a trusted environment has long been a goal of computer-security research. This line of work includes systems that monitor and restrict OS system calls [15–17, 23], systems that isolate device drivers from kernel code [30], systems that isolate web applications from browsers [10, 34], and systems that isolate native code from language virtual machines [19, 27].

3. ATTACK MODEL AND SECURITY POLICY

We adopt the CFI attack model. It is both conceptually simple and realistic. It assumes separate code and data regions for an untrusted program. The data region is not executable.[1] An attacker is then modeled as a thread that runs in parallel with the program. The concurrent attacker thread can overwrite any part of the data region, including the stack, the heap, and global data. This model effectively assumes that contents in the data region can arbitrarily change between any two instructions in the program. This rather pessimistic assumption captures real attack scenarios and is also amenable to formal analysis [2].

One implication of the attack model is that the code region and registers cannot be changed by the attacker directly. Note this assumption by itself does not prevent indirect changes induced by the attacker to the code region and registers. For instance, if the program loads into a register some contents from the data region, the register can afterwards hold any value supplied by the attacker as he/she controls the data region. As another example, an unconstrained memory write in the program could possibly change the code region—one goal of data sandboxing is to prevent this from happening by sandboxing memory writes.

Control-flow security policy. A CFI policy for a program is a graph whose nodes consist of addresses of basic blocks, and whose edges connect control instructions (i.e., jumps and branches) to allowed destination basic blocks. Within a procedure, this corresponds directly to a basic control-flow graph. For dynamic control flow (i.e., a jump through a register, a return, or other computed jumps), the outgoing edges correspond to the possible addresses where control is allowed to transfer.

DEFINITION 1. *Code C respects its CFI policy P if and only if when executed, all control transfers in C respect the graph P.*

CFI policies are in essence NDFA's or regular expressions denoting sets of possible control traces. In contrast, XFI provides a richer language of policies (corresponding to pushdown automata), which can ensure that functions only return to the code that called them. CFI can only ensure that functions return to *some* possible caller. On the other hand, XFI requires a high-integrity stack to store return addresses (which is broken by our strong attack model) and introduces issues with setjmp, exceptions, continuations, and other unconventional control-transfers. Thus, CFI has the attractive property that it breaks fewer applications than XFI, supports a strong, concurrent attack model, and provides tighter bounds on control-flow than SFI.

Data sandboxing policy. This policy dictates that any memory access in the untrusted program must be within the data region. Consequently, integrity and confidentiality of memory outside of the data region are ensured. Integrity is usually more important for security than confidentiality. But in highly sensitive applications such as military applications, protecting confidentiality can be as important.

We next formalize the data sandboxing policy. We assume there is a large, contiguous region of data memory that untrusted code can read and write. We assume the data region begins with the address `DB` (Data Begin) and ends with the address `DL` (Data Limit). That is, the address range of the data region is `[DB, DL]`, inclusive. Following previous SFI systems, we set up *guard zones* of size `GSize` before and after the data region. The size of a guard zone can vary depending on the host policy. It is further assumed that memory access to locations in guard zones can be efficiently trapped (through page protection). Fig. 2 depicts the data region, the guard zones, and relevant parameters.

DEFINITION 2. *A memory access is allowed if the address is within the range `[DB-GSize, DL+GSize]`.*[2]

[1]This assumption can be discharged either by the hardware No-eXecute (NX) protection or by a pure software approach; the software approach sandboxes indirect jumps so that control always stays in the code region.

[2]The size of the memory access is irrelevant because of the presence of the guard zones and the assumption that access to guard zones is trapped. Furthermore, the policy in our implementation also allows reading the code region because the inserted CFI checks read IDs from the code region. This is a special case and will be ignored in the rest of the paper.

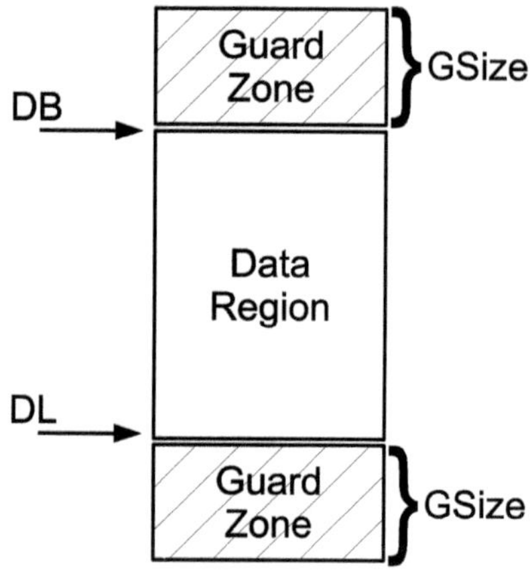

Figure 2: Data region and guard zones.

4. DATA SANDBOXING OPTIMIZATIONS

We next present a series of optimizations that significantly cut the data-sandboxing cost. The data-sandboxing optimizations utilize static analysis to identify optimization opportunities. The optimizations are similar to those performed in an optimizing compiler, except they need to not only improve performance but also maintain the security.

Note this section assumes CFI is already in place; Sec. 6 will discuss CFI and its own optimizations. One immediate benefit of CFI is it obviates the need for chunk-based control-flow integrity [21, 25]. CFI provides better security as its control-flow graph is more precise. Moreover, it also avoids the large number of no-ops that have to be inserted for instruction alignment. The extra no-ops add both spatial and temporal overheads. PittSFIeld [21] reports that inserted no-ops account for about half of the runtime overhead of enforcing data integrity. NaCl [25] reports that instruction alignment accounts for most of its performance overhead.

In addition, CFI enables many other optimizations. Before we discuss these optimizations, we present a running example that will be used to illustrates how the optimizations work.

A running example. Fig. 3 presents the example. For clarity, this and other programs in the paper use a pseudo-assembly syntax whose notation is described as follows. We use "`:=`" for an assignment. When an operand represents a memory address, it is put into square brackets. For instance, `[esp]` denotes a memory-address operand with the address in `esp`, while `esp` (without square brackets) represents a register operand. We will also use the syntax "`if ... goto ...`" to represent a comparison followed by a conditional jump instruction (i.e., `jcc`).

Fig. 3(a) shows an instruction that transfers the contents at memory location `ecx+4` to `ebx`. For protecting confidentiality, the address has to be sandboxed before the memory read. Fig. 3(b) presents an unoptimized sequence of instructions that performs the sandboxing. In the sequence, `eax` is used as a scratch register for holding the intermediate value. Since the old value of `eax` might be needed afterwards, the sequence pushes `eax` onto the stack and later restores its value. The flags register, which stores status flags such as the overflow flag, also needs to be saved and restored since the bitwise-and instruction changes the status flags and the old flags might be needed for the subsequent computation. The constant `$DMask` denotes the data-region mask. Following PittSFIeld [21], a single bitwise-and sandboxing instruction is used to ensure that the resulting address is in the data region. For instance, if the data region starts from 0x20000000 and is of 16MB size, then `$DMask` is `0x20ffffff`. The sandboxing instruction will also be called a check in the rest of the paper.

4.1 Liveness analysis

Our system performs liveness analysis on registers and the flags register to remove operations that save and restore old values when they are unnecessary.

Register liveness analysis. Oftentimes inlined reference monitors require the use of scratch registers for storing intermediate results. For instance, `eax` is used as a scratch register in Fig. 3(b). One simple approach to avoiding the overhead of saving and restoring scratch registers is to reserve a dedicated scratch register. As an example, PittSFIeld [21] reserves `ebx` as the scratch register. This approach has the downside of increasing the register pressure, especially on machines with few general-purpose registers.

Our alternative approach relies on register liveness analysis. Liveness analysis is a classic compiler analysis technique. At each program point, the liveness analysis calculates the set of live registers; that is, those registers whose values are used in the future. A register is dead if it is not live. At a program point, a dead register can be used as the scratch register without saving its old value (since the old value will no longer be needed). When no dead register is available, we can resort to the old way of saving the scratch register on the stack.

For the running example in Fig. 3, if register liveness analysis determines that `eax` is dead after the instruction `ebx := [ecx + 4]`, then there is no need to save and restore its old value; the sequence in Fig. 3(c) is then sufficient.

We implemented an intra-procedural register liveness analysis with extra assumptions about the calling convention. It is a backward dataflow analysis and uses a standard work-list algorithm. The analysis takes advantage of the `cdecl` calling convention to deal with function calls and returns. In particular, the live-out of a return instruction is those callee-saved registers (including `ebx`, `esi`, and `edi`) together with registers that contain the return value. The live-in of a call instruction is the live-out subtracted by the set of caller-saved registers (including `eax`, `ecx`, and `edx`).

We note the correctness of liveness analysis (including the assumption about the calling convention) does not affect security. When liveness analysis produced wrong results, some registers would not be properly saved and restored; this would affect the correctness of the program, but not the security of its memory operations.

Flags-register liveness analysis. We also perform the flags-register liveness analysis to remove unnecessary operations for saving and restoring the flags register. Saving and restoring the status flags are costly on modern processors. For the running example, if the analysis determines that the flags register is dead after the instruction `ebx := [ecx + 4]`, then the sequence in Fig. 3(d) can be used.

For simplicity, we perform the flags-register liveness analysis only within basic blocks. We assume flags are not used across basic blocks (meaning the register is assumed dead at

(a) Original instruction

```
ebx := [ecx + 4]
```

(b) Unoptimized instruction sequence

```
push eflags
push eax
eax := ecx + 4
eax := eax & $DMask
ebx := [eax]
pop eax
pop eflags
```

(c) When **eax** is a dead register

```
push eflags
eax := ecx + 4
eax := eax & $DMask
ebx := [eax]
pop eflags
```

(d) When the flags register is dead

```
eax := ecx + 4
eax := eax & $DMask
ebx := [eax]
```

(e) After in-place sandboxing

```
ecx := ecx & $DMask
ebx := [ecx + 4]
```

Figure 3: A running example for illustrating optimizations. `DMask` is the data-region mask.

the end of a basic block). This seems to be an assumption used by compilers and has been confirmed by our experiments on SPECint2000.[3]

PittSFIeld [21] avoids saving and restoring the flags register by disabling instruction scheduling in compilers. It prevents compilers from moving comparisons away from their corresponding branching instructions. In contrast, our approach allows instruction scheduling within basic blocks.

4.2 In-place sandboxing

Thanks to the guard zones before and after the data region, there are special cases where we can avoid using a scratch register. A commonly used address pattern in memory operations is a base register plus a small displacement (which is a static constant value). For instance, this pattern is used to access fields of a data structure; the base register holds the base address of the data structure and the displacement is the offset of a field. When a memory address of this pattern is used, we can perform the optimization that sandboxes just the base register. The running example in Fig. 3 uses address `ecx+4`. Therefore, the sequence in Fig. 3(e) sandboxes the base register `ecx` directly.

The safety of this transformation is straightforward to see. After "`ecx := ecx & $DMask`", register `ecx` is constrained within the data region. Consequently, `ecx+4` must be within the data region plus the guard zones (assuming `GSize` ≥ 4). The memory operation is then allowed according to the data security policy.

We call this optimization *in-place sandboxing* since it sandboxes the base register directly and avoids the use of an extra scratch register. Additionally, it has the benefit of making it convenient to remove redundant checks, as shown next.

4.3 Optimizations based on range analysis

According to the data-sandboxing policy, a memory access is allowed if the address range is within the valid range of the data region plus guard zones. This definition naturally leads to a strategy of removing unnecessary checks: if the address range of a memory access can be statically determined to

```
        ecx ∈ [−∞, +∞]
ecx := ecx & $DMask
        ecx ∈ [DB, DL]
eax := [ecx + 4]
        ecx ∈ [DB, DL]
... // assume ecx not changed in between
        ecx ∈ [DB, DL]
ecx := ecx & $DMask
        ecx ∈ [DB, DL]
ebx := [ecx + 8]
        ecx ∈ [DB, DL]
```

Figure 4: An example demonstrating redundant check elimination.

be within the valid range, then it is unnecessary to have a check before the memory access.

To realize this idea, we have implemented *range analysis* on low-level code. At each program point, the range analysis determines the ranges of values in registers. The range $[-\infty, +\infty]$ is the universe and gives no information. For instance, after an operation that loads contents from the data region into a register, the register's range becomes $[-\infty, +\infty]$; this reflects that the attack model allows arbitrary changes to the data region. In many other situations, a more accurate range can be obtained. For instance, after "`ecx := ecx & $DMask`", the range of `ecx` is `[DB, DL]` (i.e., the data region).

We have implemented two optimizations that take advantage of range analysis. We discuss them next.

Redundant check elimination. This optimization takes an input program with checks embedded in and aims to eliminate redundant checks. It is performed in two steps. In the first step, range analysis is performed on the input program. In the second step, it uses the results of range analysis and heuristics to decide whether a check can be eliminated. For instance, if the range of `r` is within the data region before "`r := r & $DMask`", then the check is equivalent to a no-op and thus unnecessary. As another example, suppose (1) the instruction sequence is "`r := r & $DMask`" immediately followed by a memory dereference through `r`; (2) the range of `r` before the sequence is within the data region plus the guard zones, then the check can also be removed because the memory dereference is safe without the check. The general

[3]This might be broken by hand-written assembly code. But similar to register liveness analysis, the correctness of this analysis does not affect security.

(a) Unoptimized sequence

```
  esi := eax
  ecx := eax + ebx * 4
  edx := 0
loop:
  if  esi≥uecx goto end
  esi := esi & $DMask
  edx := edx + [esi]
  esi := esi + 4
  jmp loop
end:
```

(b) Hoisting checks outside of the loop

```
  esi := eax
  ecx := eax + ebx * 4
  edx := 0
  esi := esi & $DMask
loop:
  if  esi≥uecx goto end
  edx := edx + [esi]
  esi := esi + 4
  jmp loop
end:
```

Figure 5: An example demonstrating loop check hoisting.

criterion for a removal is if it can be statically determined that the removal will not result in unsafe access in the following memory dereference.

We next examine a simple example in Fig. 4. Imagine `ecx` is the base address of a C struct. The program then loads two fields from the struct. Each memory read is preceded by a check. The figure also shows the ranges of `ecx` at each program point. With range analysis, the optimizer can tell that the second check can be removed because the range of `ecx` is already in the data region before the check.

Loop check hoisting. This optimization hoists checks so that one single check outside the loop is sufficient to guarantee safety of all memory access in the loop.

Fig. 5 presents an example program showing how static analysis enables hoisting checks outside of loops. The assembly program in the figure calculates the sum of an integer array (with base address `a` and length `len`) and roughly corresponds to the following C program:

```
sum = 0;
int *p = a;
while (p < a + len) {
  sum = sum + *p;
  p = p + 1;
}
```

In Fig. 5, `eax` holds the initial address of the array, `ebx` holds the length, and `esi` holds the pointer value `p`. Without optimization, `esi` needs to be sandboxed within the loop body. The sandboxing instruction is underlined in Fig. 5. That sandboxing instruction can actually be moved outside of the loop, avoiding the per-iteration sandboxing (how the optimization is achieved will be discussed shortly). The optimized code is shown in Fig. 5(b).

It is instructive to understand why the code in Fig. 5(b) is safe even though it sandboxes only the beginning address of the array and there is no restriction on the array length. To show its safety, it is sufficient to show that `esi ∈ [DB, DL+4]` is a loop invariant. The condition is clearly true at the beginning of the loop since the sandboxing instruction gives `esi ∈ [DB, DL]`. Next, assuming the condition holds at the beginning of the loop body, we try to re-establish it at the end of the loop body. The key step in the reasoning is that `esi ∈ [DB, DL]` holds after `edx := edx + [esi]`—a hardware trap would be generated if `esi` were in guard zones. With that result, the following add-by-four operation clearly re-establishes the loop invariant. What has been exploited is the following observation: since access to guard zones can be efficiently trapped, a successful (untrapped) memory access actually serves as a "check" and narrows the range down to the data region.

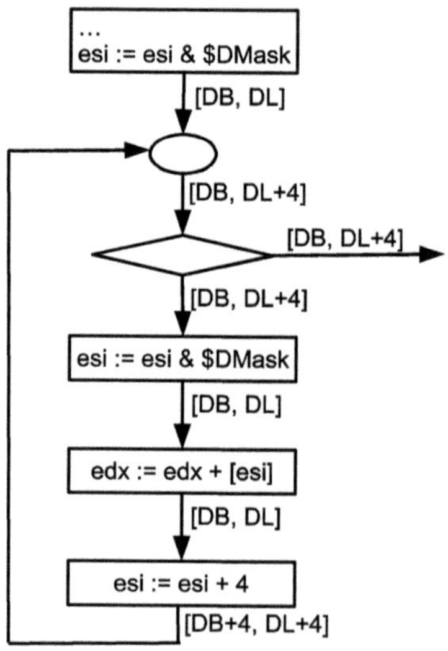

Figure 6: Range analysis result for the program in Figure 5(a), after the check is duplicated at the loop pre-head. Only the ranges of `esi` are included.

The loop optimization is implemented in multiple steps, outlined as follows:

(1) *Dominator trees* are used to identify loops in assembly code. Backward edges in a dominator tree is then used to locate loops. Calculation of the dominator tree and loop identification are standard techniques in an optimizing compiler [3].

(2) Given an input program, any check that appears in the loop body is duplicated at the beginning of a loop. For the program in Fig. 5(a), this step results in the program depicted in Fig. 6. Notice the instruction "`esi := esi & $DMask`" is duplicated before the loop. One worry of eagerly sandboxing before the loop is it might change the program behavior. However, if we assume good code will always have pointers that point into the data region, then eager sandboxing should be an idempotent operation for good code and it breaks only programs that would violate the policy.[4]

[4]Certain programming practices use pointers that are out-

(3) A range analysis is then performed to decide if any check is unnecessary. Fig. 6 also presents the ranges of **esi** at each program point. Notice the range of **esi** is within the data region plus guard zones (assuming $\texttt{GSize} \geq 4$). This enables the optimizer to remove the check in the loop body. After its removal, we get the optimized program in Fig. 5(b). There is also a possibility that the optimizer decides that the check in the loop cannot be removed; in this case, the corresponding one that was added before the loop is removed.

The above strategy of loop optimizations has the benefit of performing only one round of range analysis even if the program has multiple loops or nested loops. However, it does not capture every loop-hoisting opportunity. Another strategy is to hoist checks outside the loop one by one, and use the verifier (discussed in the next section) to check the safety of intermediate results; but it involves backtracking and performing a range analysis after each intermediate step.

5. VALIDATING DATA SANDBOXING

Of the three SFI optimizations we have discussed, liveness analysis is not security critical: security would not be affected even if it produced wrong results. On the other hand, the other two optimizations change checks, remove checks, or move checks to a different place. Security would be affected if they were wrong. Since low-level optimizations are extremely error prone, it is always a good idea to have a separate verifier to verify the results of optimizations, instead of trusting the optimizer.

Previous SFI verifiers assume checks appear immediately before memory operations. With that assumption, a simple linear scan of the code is sufficient to check the code's safety. Since our optimizer eliminates checks and moves checks away from memory operations, a more complex verifier is needed to check the result of optimizations. This does increase the size of the TCB, but seems unavoidable when verifying the optimization results.

We have implemented a verifier based on range analysis which can check the results of our optimizations. The basic idea is to perform range analysis over the optimized program and determine the range of addresses used in memory operations; the program is verified if every such address is statically determined to be within `[DB-GSize, DL+GSize]`.

The following example is the code in Fig. 4 after the optimizer has removed the second check. Range analysis determines that the address range in the first memory access is `[DB+4, DL+4]` and the address range in the second memory access is `[DB+8, DL+8]`. Assuming $\texttt{GSize} \geq 8$, both are safe according to the policy.

```
                ecx ∈ [−∞, +∞]
ecx := ecx & $DMask
                ecx ∈ [DB, DL]
eax := [ecx + 4]
                ecx ∈ [DB, DL]
... // assume ecx not changed in between
                ecx ∈ [DB, DL]
ebx := [ecx + 8]
                ecx ∈ [DB, DL]
```

side the object bounds, but those pointers should stay inside the data region. For instance, pointers that are one element past the end of an array in the heap stay in the data region if the stack is in the upper portion of the data region.

In a similar fashion, range analysis can determine the safety of the program in Fig. 5(b), which is the result after loop optimizations.

Our verifier is robust in the sense it can verify many more optimizations, including those we have not implemented. New optimizations, including more aggressive loop optimizations, can be verified by the same verifier. Another use of the verifier is for *speculative optimizations*. The optimizer can eliminate a check or move a check to a different place even when it is not clear whether that transformation would result in a safe program. After the transformation, the verifier can be used to check the safety of the resulting program; if the verifier fails, the optimizer can resort to the old program. We have not tried any speculative optimizations.

6. MORE EFFICIENT CONTROL-FLOW SANDBOXING

We describe two simple CFI optimizations that result in a more efficient implementation. This reduces the overhead of protection schemes that build on CFI, including our data-sandboxing scheme.

6.1 Original CFI instrumentation

As background information, we discuss CFI's original mechanism for ensuring that a program's execution follows a predetermined control-flow graph [1, 2]. CFI uses a combination of static verification and dynamic instrumentation for enforcement. For a direct jump instruction, a static verifier can easily check that the target is allowed by the control-flow graph, without incurring any runtime overhead. For a computed jump, CFI inserts runtime checks into the program being protected to ensure that the control transfer is consistent with the control-flow graph.

Fig. 7 presents an example illustrating how CFI checks are performed. It shows how a direct function call is instrumented in CFI. Instruction "`call fun`" invokes a known function with name `fun`. The direct call itself does not need instrumentation—whether this is legitimate is checked statically. The return instruction in the body of `fun`, however, needs instrumentation since it takes from the data region a return address, which may be corrupted by the attacker.

The instrumentation is performed in two steps. First, an ID is inserted after the call instruction (note the same ID is inserted after all possible call sites to `fun`). Second, the return instruction is changed to a sequence of instructions that checks the correct ID is at the target before the control transfer. The ID is embedded in a side-effect free `prefetch` instruction. The instruction takes a memory location as its operand, and moves data from memory closer to a location in the cache hierarchy. It is a hint to the processor and does not affect program semantics. Instrumentation of other computed jumps is similar: IDs are inserted at the allowed targets and runtime checks ensure correct IDs are there before control transfers. Note that IDs are inserted into the code region and cannot be changed by the attacker. Furthermore, since the data region is not executable, the attacker cannot manufacture new code in the data region with the correct ID in it and jump to it for execution.

6.2 CFI optimizations

We next describe two simple CFI optimizations.

Jumping over prefetch instructions. The original CFI

Original code	Code after instrumentation	Comment
`call fun`	`call fun`	
	`prefetchnta [$ID]`	a side-effect free instruction with an ID embedded
`ret`	`ecx := [esp]`	retrieve the return address
	`esp := esp + 4`	adjust the stack pointer
	`if [ecx+3]≠$ID goto error`	check ID; ecx+3 is the address of the ID since the opcode of the prefetch instruction takes three bytes
	`jmp ecx`	transfer the control

Figure 7: A CFI example.

Original code	Code after instrumentation
`call fun`	`call fun`
	`prefetchnta [$ID]`
`ret`	`ecx := [esp]`
	`esp := esp + 4`
	`if [ecx+3]≠$ID goto error`
	<u>`ecx := ecx + 7`</u>
	`jmp ecx`

Figure 8: New CFI instrumentation by skipping over prefetch instructions.

implementation inserts prefetch instructions at targets of computed jumps. However, prefetch instructions incur significant overhead by fetching data from memory and increasing cache pressure. Therefore, the first optimization jumps over prefetch instructions to avoid their execution. Fig. 8 presents the new code sequence after the optimization. The only difference is a new instruction (underlined) that adds seven to the register that holds the target address.[5] Since the size of a prefetch instruction is seven, it is skipped over. This optimization trades a `prefetch` instruction for a cheaper `add` instruction. Our evaluation shows this alternative significantly cuts the runtime overhead of CFI (from 24.90% to 7.74%). Designers of the original CFI mentioned this alternative, but it seems it has not been evaluated for performance comparison.

Jump table check optimization. Computed jumps are often used for efficient compilation of switch statements. Most compilers generate a jump table for a switch statement. The starting address of each branch of the switch statement is stored as an entry in the jump table. Fig. 9 presents an example. The first column presents the typical sequence of instructions used by compilers to transfer the control to a branch of a switch statement. It assumes `edx` stores an index into the jump table and `JT` is a constant denoting the start address of the jump table. `edx` is scaled by a factor of four when loading an entry from the jump table because each entry is assumed to be a four-byte address.

The middle column lists the code sequence after the CFI instrumentation. Because "`jmp ecx`" is a computed jump, the instruction checks that there is a correct ID at the target.

Jump tables are usually stored in read-only sections of object code. If we assume jump tables cannot be modified by attackers[6], then control-flow integrity is satisfied if (1) the index into the jump table is within bounds and (2) all jump targets in the jump table are legal according to the control-flow graph. The second condition can be checked statically and the first condition needs a bounds check. The last column in Fig. 9 presents the new sequence with the bounds check, assuming the size of the jump table is 16. We use $>_u$ for the unsigned comparison so that large numbers would not be treated as negative. The bounds check involves only register values and avoids retrieving IDs from memory. Furthermore, it turns out that the LLVM compiler, in which our prototype implementation is developed, already inserts bounds checks before using a jump table. This further simplifies the work of our CFI rewriter. Note our system does not depend on the assumption that LLVM emits bounds checks since the CFI verifier would complain if it did not.

This jump-table check optimization is essentially a special case of the idea of encoding target tables for computed jumps, as implemented in HyperSafe [32]. The effectiveness of this optimization depends on how often switch statements are used in programs.

7. IMPLEMENTATION AND EVALUATION

We next discuss our prototype implementation and evaluation of the implementation on benchmark programs.

7.1 Prototype implementation

Our implementation is built in LLVM 2.8 [20], a widely used compiler infrastructure. We inserted a pass for CFI rewriting, a pass for data sandboxing rewriting and optimization, and a pass for CFI and data-sandboxing verification. All these passes are inserted right before the code-emission pass. There are approximately 14,000 lines of C++ code in total added to LLVM (including comments and code for dumping debugging information). Our rewriters essentially perform assembly-level rewriting. We chose LLVM as our implementation platform because LLVM preserves helpful meta-information at assembly level (such as the control flow graph). It also provides a clean representation of compiled programs, which benefits instrumentation and optimization. In addition, it is easy to extend LLVM since inserting an extra pass into its compilation process requires nothing more than a registration of the pass.

Control flow graph. Control-flow graphs are constructed with the help of LLVM. In particular, the LLVM compiler preserves meta-information so that a precise intra-procedural

[5]The sequence takes care of only control-flow sandboxing. In our implementation for data confidentiality, `esp` is sandboxed to stay in the data region and `ecx` is sandboxed to stay in the code region.

[6]This assumption can be discharged by either putting jump tables into code region as in HyperSafe [32] or have read-only data write-protected through page protection.

Original code	CFI instrumentation	After optimization
`ecx := [$JT + edx*4]`	`ecx := [$JT + edx*4]`	`if edx>`$_u$`15 goto error`
`jmp ecx`	`if [ecx+3]`$\neq$`$ID goto error`	`ecx := [$JT + edx*4]`
	`ecx := ecx + 7`	`ecx := ecx + 7`
	`jmp ecx`	`jmp ecx`

Figure 9: Jump table check optimization. Assume `JT` is a constant denoting the start address of the jump table, `edx` holds the index into the jump table, and the jump table is of size 16.

control-flow graph can be reconstructed at the assembly level. The inter-procedural control-flow graph (or the call graph) is conservatively estimated by allowing a computed call instruction to target any function. The precision of the call graph could certainly be improved through further static analysis such as inter-procedural control flow analysis and it would benefit security. On the other hand, since all our optimizations are intra-procedural, the precision of the call graph is not critical to these optimizations. In fact, we suspect inter-procedural static analysis would not result in significant performance improvement; the attack model assumes the data region can arbitrarily change between instructions and thus inter-procedural analysis on the data region such as shape analysis would be inapplicable.

Linker scripts, loader, and libraries. LLVM generates object code with multiple sections (.bss, .data, .text, .rodata, and others). We developed linker scripts to link multiple sections into three sections (code, data and read-only data) at certain start addresses. We modified PittSFIeld's loader to set up code and data regions and load executable code. PittSFIeld's loader does not protect confidentiality and allows sandboxed code to read outside of the sandbox; we modified the loader so that it copies arguments into the sandbox. Furthermore, the three sections are locked down with the desired permissions with `mprotect`: the code section is readable and executable; the data section is readable and writable; the read-only data section is readable (it includes data such as jump tables and string literals). We also reused PittSFIeld's library wrappers and libraries, including its reimplementation of library functions for dynamic memory allocation (malloc, free, and so on).

Verifier. We have implemented a CFI and a data sandboxing verifier. The CFI verifier is similar to previous CFI verifiers and checks whether IDs and checks are inserted at appropriate places. We do not elaborate on its details. The implementation of the data-sandboxing verifier contains approximately 7,000 lines of C++ code. The majority of the code is a large switch statement that calculates the ranges of registers for machine instructions. There are over 3261 distinct machine opcodes inside LLVM including opcodes and pseudo opcodes for IA-32, IA-64, x87 FPU, SSE, SSE2, SSE3, and others. The verifier could be shortened by grouping instructions into cases and omitting instructions that IA-32 does not support. Given its large size, its own trustworthiness should be independently validated (e.g., by testing or by developing its correctness proof in a theorem prover); we leave this to future work.

At the beginning of a function and any basic block that a computed jump might target, the ranges of general-purpose registers (`eax`, `ebx`, `ecx`, `edx`, `esi` and `edi`) are assumed to be the universe ($[-\infty, +\infty]$) and the ranges of `esp` and `ebp` to be the data region.[7] For each instruction, the verifier updates the ranges of the registers that are defined by the instruction or used to compute a memory location. For example, after "`movl (%ebx), %eax`", the range of `ebx` is narrowed down to the data region if the old range of `ebx` is within the data region plus guard zones; furthermore, the range of `eax` is set to be the universe because it is loaded from the untrusted data region.

Since the lattice in range analysis is of infinite height, its termination is not guaranteed unless some widening strategy is adopted. Our implementation uses a simple one: if a node has been processed more than a constant number of times, the ranges of registers that have not been stabilized are set to be the universe. Other than this aspect, our implementation of range analysis follows a standard worklist algorithm.

During the development, the verifier helped us catch several implementation errors in early versions of the optimizer; these errors would be hard to find by hand.

7.2 Performance evaluation

To evaluate our implementation, we conducted experiments to test its runtime overhead on SPECint2000. Experiments were conducted on a Linux CentOS 5.3 box with Intel Xeon X5550 CPU at 2.66 GHz and 12GB of RAM. All experiments were averaged over six runs. Three benchmark programs in SPECint2000 could not be compiled by LLVM: `eon` is written in C++ and LLVM's front end (clang) does not support the version of the standard C++ library in CentOS 5.3; `perlbmk` and `parser` could not be compiled with the optimization level 3 and seem incompatible with LLVM. All other benchmark programs were compiled with the optimization level 3.

Table 1 presents the runtime percentage increases of CFI compared to uninstrumented programs for SPECint2000. The CFI row reports the results of our CFI implementation. On average, it adds 7.74% runtime overhead. The *CFI.jt.no-skip* row shows the results of disabling the optimization of jumping over prefetch instructions. Disabling this optimization results in significant performance degradation: the overhead shoots up to almost 25%. This is due to the execution of costly prefetch instructions. The *CFI.no-jt.skip* row reports the results when the optimization for jump-table checks is disabled. The performance improvement by this optimization is modest, suggesting opportunities for this optimization in SPECint2000 are limited. *CFI.no-jt.no-skip* is the same as the original CFI implementation by Abadi *et al* [2]. They reported an average overhead of 16% on SPECint2000 on an older system (Pentium 4 x86 processor at 1.8 GHz with 512 MB of memory and Windows XP SP2). The experiments show that our CFI implemen-

[7]Before a function call and a computed jump, the verifier checks that `esp` and `ebp` are indeed in the data region.

	gzip	vpr	gcc	mcf	crafty	gap	vortex	bzip2	twolf	average
CFI (%)	3.47	1.05	2.52	0.09	11.47	13.87	26.78	6.36	4.04	7.74
CFI.jt.no-skip (%)	14.72	3.23	4.14	0.14	25.28	82.03	67.66	22.18	4.74	24.90
CFI.no-jt.skip (%)	3.84	1.01	2.46	0.04	15.28	13.61	28.39	6.32	3.18	8.24
CFI.no-jt.no-skip (%)	14.45	3.77	5.73	0.09	34.11	81.73	72.96	22.29	5.68	26.76

Table 1: CFI runtime overheads for SPECint2000.

	gzip	vpr	gcc	mcf	crafty	gap	vortex	bzip2	twolf	average
DS-W.CFI (%)	6.21	5.82	2.29	1.80	12.80	13.16	29.77	14.18	7.55	10.40
DS-RW.CFI.no-opt (%)	384.34	429.38	129.36	452.51	523.66	1092.98	690.73	748.27	476.25	547.50
DS-RW.live (%)	24.38	28.06	6.30	8.15	39.67	58.02	43.04	23.58	52.91	31.57
DS-RW.live.in-place (%)	24.29	26.69	5.81	5.13	39.12	49.23	39.08	23.65	48.69	29.08
DS-RW.CFI (%)	23.66	25.12	4.96	4.53	37.70	44.49	34.55	23.41	45.94	27.15

Table 2: Runtime overheads of data sandboxing plus CFI for SPECint2000.

tation is efficient even though we have not yet implemented sophisticated CFI optimizations.

Table 2 presents the runtime percentage increases for data sandboxing. All numbers in the table include the CFI overhead because our data-sandboxing optimizations build on top of CFI. The row of *DS-w.CFI* contains the numbers when sandboxing only the writes. The average overhead is 10.40%, which means it adds roughly 2.7% on top of CFI. The overhead is low considering it sandboxes memory writes and enforces CFI.

Table 2 also presents the overheads when sandboxing both reads and writes. To understand the overhead reduction of the three data-sandboxing optimizations, it presents the overheads incrementally with respect to the optimizations. The row of *DS-RW.CFI.no-opt* contains the numbers when all optimizations are disabled. In this case, a check is inserted before every memory access; scratch registers and the flags register are saved on and restored from the stack. Overheads are high because the saving and restoring registers and the flags register are costly. The row of "DS-RW.CFI.live" contains the numbers after performing liveness analysis to remove unnecessary saving and restoring operations. After this optimization, the overheads are significantly lower. The row of "DS-RW.CFI.live.in-place" contains the numbers with both liveness analysis and the technique of in-place sandboxing; this drives down about 2% of the overhead. Finally, the last row contains numbers when optimizations based on range analysis are turned on; they cut down another 2% of the overhead. When all optimizations are turned on, data sandboxing adds about 19% on top of CFI. The overhead for protecting both reads and writes is modest and it is acceptable for applications where confidentiality is of great concern.

Performance comparison with related systems. We next compare our system with PittSFIeld and XFI, two systems that adopt software-only techniques for protection. PittSFIeld reports an average of 21% for SPECint2000 for sandboxing both memory writes and jumps. Our system has a lower overhead (10.4% for CFI and write protection) and provides stronger control-flow integrity; it can additionally sandbox memory reads with acceptable overheads.

To compare with XFI, we have evaluated our implementation on the Independent JPEG Group's image-decoding reference implementation. The XFI paper reports both fastpath and slowpath overheads for the JPEG program; the XFI fastpath overhead is directly comparable with our implementation. The following table shows the performance overheads of our implementation compared to XFI's fastpath implementation, for images of different sizes. The columns of *DS-W.CFI* and *DS-RW.CFI* report the numbers of our system for write protection and read-write protection, respectively. The columns of *XFI-W* and *XFI-RW* report XFI's numbers for write protection and read-write protection, respectively. In both cases, our implementation reports lesser overheads. It seems that our optimizations are effective at bringing down the overheads. Note the comparison is preliminary as we have tested only on one program and LLVM is a different compiler from the one used in XFI.

Size	DS-W.CFI	DS-RW.CFI	XFI-W	XFI-RW
4k (%)	2.90	15.53	18	78
14k (%)	2.32	13.09	18	80
63k (%)	9.99	25.27	17	75
229k (%)	9.09	14.17	15	68

8. FUTURE WORK

We plan to implement more static-analysis based optimizations. First, more aggressive loop optimizations based on induction variable analysis should further bring down the data sandboxing overhead. Second, CFI can also benefit from static analysis—an ID check for a computed jump is unnecessary if the jump targets can be statically determined to obey the control-flow policy.

Our prototype implementation is built for x86-32 and we have not addressed the portability issue. We plan to port our implementation to newer architectures including x86-64 and ARM. These architectures should benefit more since they do not have the hardware segmentation support.

SFI is a special kind of Inlined Reference Monitors (IRM [12, 13]). IRMs can enforce fine-grained safety properties. Clearly, the methodology of combining CFI with static analysis to reduce the runtime overhead applies to general IRMs. For instance, fine-grained memory protection, which allows access control of multiple data regions of small sizes [4, 5, 8], can also benefit from CFI-enabled optimizations. Dynamic taint tracking is another example.

9. CONCLUSIONS

In this research, we have explored how CFI-enabled static analysis can help build efficient and validated system for data sandboxing, for the case of protecting both integrity and confidentiality. We believe the combination of CFI and static analysis provides a sweet point in design space for enforcing security policies on untrusted or buggy software: it provides strong security, enables sound optimization strategies, is thread safe, and can be easily integrated into the software tool chain. The combination can possibly serve as a foundation for improving efficiency of general inlined reference monitors for enforcing advanced security polices.

Acknowledgments

This research is supported in part by NSF grant CCF-0915157, CCF-0915030, a research grant from Google, and by AFOSR MURI grant FA9550-09-1-0539.

10. REFERENCES

[1] M. Abadi, M. Budiu, Ú. Erlingsson, and J. Ligatti. Control-flow integrity. In *12th CCS*, pages 340–353, 2005.

[2] M. Abadi, M. Budiu, Ú. Erlingsson, and J. Ligatti. Control-flow integrity principles, implementations, and applications. *ACM Transactions on Information and System Security*, 13:4:1–4:40, Nov. 2009.

[3] A. V. Aho, R. Sethi, and J. D. Ullman. *Compilers: Principles, Techniques, and Tools*. Addison-Wesley, Reading, MA, 1986.

[4] P. Akritidis, C. Cadar, C. Raiciu, M. Costa, and M. Castro. Preventing memory error exploits with wit. In *IEEE S&P*, pages 263–277, 2008.

[5] P. Akritidis, M. Costa, M. Castro, and S. Hand. Baggy bounds checking: An efficient and backwards-compatible defense against out-of-bounds errors. In *18th Usenix Security Symposium*, pages 51–66, 2009.

[6] J. Ansel, P. Marchenko, Ú. Erlingsson, E. Taylor, B. Chen, D. Schuff, D. Sehr, C. Biffle, and B. Yee. Language-independent sandboxing of just-in-time compilation and self-modifying code. In *PLDI*, pages 355–366, 2011.

[7] G. Balakrishnan and T. Reps. Analyzing memory accesses in x86 executables. In *13th International Conference on Compiler Construction (CC)*, pages 5–23, 2004.

[8] M. Castro, M. Costa, J.-P. Martin, M. Peinado, P. Akritidis, A. Donnelly, P. Barham, and R. Black. Fast byte-granularity software fault isolation. In *SOSP*, pages 45–58, 2009.

[9] S. Checkoway, L. Davi, A. Dmitrienko, A.-R. Sadeghi, H. Shacham, and M. Winandy. Return-oriented programming without returns. In *17th CCS*, pages 559–572, 2010.

[10] J. R. Douceur, J. Elson, J. Howell, and J. R. Lorch. Leveraging legacy code to deploy desktop applications on the web. In *OSDI*, pages 339–354, 2008.

[11] Ú. Erlingsson, M. Abadi, M. Vrable, M. Budiu, and G. Necula. XFI: Software guards for system address spaces. In *OSDI*, pages 75–88, 2006.

[12] Ú. Erlingsson and F. Schneider. SASI enforcement of security policies: A retrospective. In *Proceedings of the New Security Paradigms Workshop (NSPW)*, pages 87–95. ACM Press, 1999.

[13] Ú. Erlingsson and F. Schneider. IRM enforcement of Java stack inspection. In *IEEE S&P*, pages 246–255, 2000.

[14] B. Ford and R. Cox. Vx32: Lightweight user-level sandboxing on the x86. In *USENIX Annual Technical Conference*, pages 293–306, 2008.

[15] T. Garfinkel, B. Pfaff, and M. Rosenblum. Ostia: A delegating architecture for secure system call interposition. In *NDSS*, 2004.

[16] I. Goldberg, D. Wagner, R. Thomas, and E. A. Brewer. A secure environment for untrusted helper applications: Confining the wily hacker. In *Proceedings of the 6th conference on USENIX Security Symposium*, 1996.

[17] S. Ioannidis, S. M. Bellovin, and J. M. Smith. Sub-operating systems: a new approach to application security. In *ACM SIGOPS European Workshop*, pages 108–115, 2002.

[18] V. Kiriansky, D. Bruening, and S. Amarasinghe. Secure execution via program shepherding. In *11th Usenix Security Symposium*, pages 191–206, 2002.

[19] P. Klinkoff, E. Kirda, C. Kruegel, and G. Vigna. Extending .NET security to unmanaged code. *Internation Journal of Information Security*, 6(6):417–428, 2007.

[20] LLVM 2.8. http://llvm.org.

[21] S. McCamant and G. Morrisett. Evaluating SFI for a CISC architecture. In *15th Usenix Security Symposium*, 2006.

[22] M. Payer and T. R. Gross. Fine-grained user-space security through virtualization. In *Proceedings of the 7th ACM SIGPLAN/SIGOPS international conference on Virtual execution environments (VEE)*, pages 157–168, 2011.

[23] N. Provos. Improving host security with system call policies. In *12th Usenix Security Symposium*, pages 257–272, 2003.

[24] K. Scott and J. Davidson. Safe virtual execution using software dynamic translation. In *Proceedings of the 18th Annual Computer Security Applications Conference*, ACSAC '02, pages 209–218, 2002.

[25] D. Sehr, R. Muth, C. Biffle, V. Khimenko, E. Pasko, K. Schimpf, B. Yee, and B. Chen. Adapting software fault isolation to contemporary CPU architectures. In *19th Usenix Security Symposium*, pages 1–12, 2010.

[26] H. Shacham. The geometry of innocent flesh on the bone: return-into-libc without function calls (on the x86). In *14th CCS*, pages 552–561, 2007.

[27] J. Siefers, G. Tan, and G. Morrisett. Robusta: Taming the native beast of the JVM. In *17th CCS*, pages 201–211, 2010.

[28] C. Small. A tool for constructing safe extensible C++ systems. In *COOTS'97: Proceedings of the 3rd conference on USENIX Conference on Object-Oriented Technologies (COOTS)*, pages 174–184, 1997.

[29] D. Song, D. Brumley, H. Yin, J. Caballero, I. Jager, M. G. Kang, Z. Liang, J. Newsome, P. Poosankam, and P. Saxena. BitBlaze: A new approach to computer security via binary analysis. In *Proceedings of the 4th International Conference on Information Systems Security. Keynote invited paper*, Hyderabad, India, Dec. 2008.

[30] M. M. Swift, M. Annamalai, B. N. Bershad, and H. M. Levy. Recovering device drivers. In *OSDI*, pages 1–16, 2004.

[31] R. Wahbe, S. Lucco, T. Anderson, and S. Graham. Efficient software-based fault isolation. In *SOSP*, pages 203–216, New York, 1993. ACM Press.

[32] Z. Wang and X. Jiang. Hypersafe: A lightweight approach to provide lifetime hypervisor control-flow integrity. In *IEEE S&P*, pages 380–395, 2010.

[33] Z. Xu, B. Miller, and T. Reps. Safety checking of machine code. In *PLDI*, pages 70–82, 2000.

[34] B. Yee, D. Sehr, G. Dardyk, B. Chen, R. Muth, T. Ormandy, S. Okasaka, N. Narula, and N. Fullagar. Native client: A sandbox for portable, untrusted x86 native code. In *IEEE S&P*, May 2009.

Composition Theorems Without Pre-Established Session Identifiers

Ralf Küsters
University of Trier
Trier, Germany
kuesters@uni-trier.de

Max Tuengerthal
University of Trier
Trier, Germany
tuengerthal@uni-trier.de

ABSTRACT

Canetti's universal composition theorem and the joint state composition theorems by Canetti and Rabin are useful and widely employed tools for the modular design and analysis of cryptographic protocols. However, these theorems assume that parties participating in a protocol session have pre-established a unique session ID (SID). While the use of such SIDs is a good design principle, existing protocols, in particular real-world security protocols, typically do not use pre-established SIDs, at least not explicitly and not in the particular way stipulated by the theorems. As a result, the composition theorems cannot be applied for analyzing such protocols in a modular and faithful way.

In this paper, we therefore present universal and joint state composition theorems which do not assume pre-established SIDs. In our joint state composition theorem, the joint state is an ideal functionality which supports several cryptographic operations, including public-key encryption, (authenticated and unauthenticated) symmetric encryption, MACs, digital signatures, and key derivation. This functionality has recently been proposed by Küsters and Tuengerthal and has been shown to be realizable under standard cryptographic assumptions and for a reasonable class of environments. We demonstrate the usefulness of our composition theorems by several case studies on real-world security protocols, including IEEE 802.11i, SSL/TLS, SSH, IPsec, and EAP-PSK. While our applications focus on real-world security protocols, our theorems, models, and techniques should be useful beyond this domain.

Categories and Subject Descriptors

C.2.2 [**Computer-Communication Networks**]: Network Protocols—*Protocol Verification*

General Terms

Security, Verification

1. INTRODUCTION

Universal composition theorems, such as Canetti's composition theorem in the UC model [7] and Küsters' composition theorem in the IITM model [19], allow to obtain security for multiple sessions of a protocol by analyzing just a single protocol session. These theorems assume that different protocol sessions have disjoint state; in particular, each session has to use fresh randomness. This can lead to inefficient and impractical protocols, since, for example, every session has to use fresh long-term symmetric and public/private keys. Canetti and Rabin [11] therefore proposed to combine universal composition theorems with what they called composition theorems with joint state. As the name suggests, such theorems yield systems in which different sessions may use some joint state, e.g., the same long-term and public/private keys.

However, these theorems, both for universal and joint state composition, assume that parties participating in a protocol session have pre-established a unique session ID (SID), and as a result (see Section 3), make heavy use of this SID in a specific way stipulated by the universal and joint state composition theorems. On the one hand, the use of such SIDs is a good design principle and as discussed by Canetti [8] and Barak et al. [2] establishing such SIDs is simple. On the other hand, many existing protocols, including most real-world security protocols, do not make use of such pre-established SIDs, at least not explicitly and not in the particular way stipulated by the theorems. As a result, these theorems cannot be used for the faithful modular analysis of such protocols; at most for analyzing idealized variants of the original protocols, which is unsatisfactory and risky, in the sense that attacks on the original protocols might be missed (see Section 4). The problems resulting from pre-established SIDs in the existing composition theorems do not seem to have been brought out in previous work.

The goal of this paper is therefore to obtain general universal composition and joint state composition theorems that do not assume pre-established SIDs and their use in cryptographic protocols, and hence, to enable modular, yet faithful analysis of protocols, without the need to modify/idealize these protocols. A main motivation for our work comes from the analysis of real-world security protocols. While many attacks on such protocols have been uncovered (see, e.g., [12, 15, 1, 27, 25] for recent examples), their comprehensive analysis still poses a big challenge, as often pointed out in the literature (see, e.g., [26, 18, 10]). A central problem is the complexity of these protocols. In order to tame the complexity, *modular* analysis of such protocols should be pushed as far as possible, but without giving up on accurate modeling. Our composition theorems are useful tools for this kind of modular and faithful analysis. They should be of interest also beyond the analysis of real-world security protocols. More precisely, the main contributions of our work are as follows:

Contribution of this Paper. Our universal composition theorem without pre-established SIDs states that if a protocol realizes an ideal functionality for a single session, then it also realizes the ideal

CCS'11, October 17–21, 2011, Chicago, Illinois, USA.

functionality for multiple sessions, subject to mild restrictions on the single-session simulator. The important point is that a user invokes a protocol instance simply with a *local* SID, locally chosen and managed by the user herself, rather than with an SID pre-established with other users for that session. This not only provides the user with a more common and convenient interface, where the user addresses her protocol instances with the corresponding local SIDs, but, more importantly, as explained in Section 3, frees the real protocol from the need to use pre-established SIDs and allows for realizations that faithfully model existing (real-world) protocols.

In our joint state composition theorem without pre-established SIDs we consider protocols that use an ideal crypto functionality $\mathcal{F}_{\text{crypto}}$ proposed in [23]. The functionality $\mathcal{F}_{\text{crypto}}$ allows its users to perform several cryptographic operations in an ideal way, including public-key encryption, authenticated and unauthenticated symmetric encryption, MACs, digital signatures, key derivation, and establishing pre-shared keys. As shown in [23], $\mathcal{F}_{\text{crypto}}$ can be realized under standard cryptographic assumptions, subject to reasonable restrictions on the environment. Now, our joint state composition theorem states that under a certain condition on the protocol, which we call *implicit (session) disjointness*, it suffices to show that the protocol (which may use $\mathcal{F}_{\text{crypto}}$) realizes an ideal functionality for a single session of the protocol to obtain security for multiple sessions of the protocol, where all sessions may use the *same* ideal crypto functionality $\mathcal{F}_{\text{crypto}}$; again we put mild restrictions on the single-session simulator. So, $\mathcal{F}_{\text{crypto}}$ (or its realization), with the keys stored in it, constitutes the joint state across sessions. As in the case of the universal composition theorem, users again invoke protocol instances with locally chosen and managed SIDs. Unlike joint state composition theorems with pre-established SIDs, our joint state composition theorem does not modify/idealize the original protocol.

Given our theorems, (real-world) security protocols can be analyzed with a high degree of modularity and without giving up on precision: Once implicit disjointness is established for a protocol—first proof step—, it suffices to carry out single-session analysis for the protocols—second proof step—in order to obtain multi-session security with joint state for the original protocol, not just an idealized version with pre-established SIDs added in various places, as explained in Sections 3 and 4. We emphasize that, due to the use of $\mathcal{F}_{\text{crypto}}$, in all proof steps often merely information-theoretic or purely syntactical reasoning, without reasoning about probabilities and without reduction proofs, suffices.

We demonstrate the usefulness of our theorems and approach by several case studies on real-world security protocols, namely (sub-protocols of) IEEE 802.11i, SSL/TLS, SSH, IPsec, and EAP-PSK. More precisely, we show that all these protocols satisfy implicit disjointness, confirming our believe that this property is satisfied by many (maybe most) real-world security protocols. While proving implicit disjointness requires to reason about multiple sessions of a protocol, this step is nevertheless relatively easy. In fact, as demonstrated by our case studies, to prove implicit disjointness, typically the security properties of only a fraction of the primitives used in a protocol need to be considered. For example, to prove that the SSH key exchange protocol satisfies implicit disjointness, only collision resistance of the hash function is needed, but not the security of the encryption scheme, the MAC, or the Diffie-Hellman key exchange used in SSH. Now since the above mentioned protocols satisfy implicit disjointness, to show that these protocols are secure key exchange or secure channel protocols, single-session analysis suffices. Performing this single-session analysis for all these protocols is out of the scope of this paper. (The main point of this paper is to provide the machinery for faithful and highly modular analysis, not to provide a full-fledged analysis of these protocols.) However, for some of the mentioned protocols single-session analysis has been carried out in other works (see Section 5). For example, this has been done for SSL/TLS by Gajek et al. in [16]. However, they used the original joint state theorem to lift their security result to the multi-session case, resulting in an idealized version of SSL/TLS (see Section 5.2). With our theorems and since SSL/TLS satisfies implicit disjointness, multi-session security follows for the original, unmodified protocol.

Structure of this Paper. In Section 2, we recall basics on simulation-based security and introduce some notation. Our universal composition and joint state composition theorems without pre-established SIDs are then presented in Sections 3 and 4, respectively, with applications discussed in Section 5. Full details and proofs are provided in our technical report [22].

2. SIMULATION-BASED SECURITY

We briefly recall the framework of simulation-based security, following [19] (see also [22]). We provide a quite model-independent account as the details of the model are not important to be able to follow the rest of this paper.

The General Computational Model. The general computational model is defined in terms of systems of interactive Turing machines. An interactive Turing machine (shortly, machine) is a probabilistic polynomial-time Turing machine with named input and output tapes. The names determine how different machines are connected in a system of machines. A *system* $\mathcal{S}$ of machines is of the form $\mathcal{S} = M_1 \mid \cdots \mid M_k \mid !M'_1 \mid \cdots \mid !M'_{k'}$ where the M_i and M'_j are machines such that the names of input tapes of different machines in the system are disjoint. We say that the machines M'_j are in the scope of a bang operator. This operator indicates that in a run of a system an unbounded number of (fresh) copies of a machine may be generated. Conversely, machines which are not in the scope of a bang operator may not be copied. Systems in which multiple copies of a machine may be generated are often needed, e.g., in case of multi-party protocols or in case a system describes the concurrent execution of multiple instances of a protocol. In a run of a system $\mathcal{S}$ at any time only one machine is active and all other machines wait for new input. A (copy of a) machine M can trigger another (copy of a) machine M' by sending a message on an output tape corresponding to an input tape of M'. Identifiers, e.g., session or party identifiers, contained in the message can be used to address a specific copy of M'. If a new identifier is used, a fresh copy of M' would be generated. The first machine to be triggered is the so-called master machine. This machine is also triggered if a machine does not produce output. A run stops if the master machine does not produce output or a machine outputs a message on a tape named decision. Such a message is considered to be the overall output of the system. Systems will always have polynomial runtime in the security parameter (and possibly the length of auxiliary input).

Two systems $\mathcal{P}$ and $\mathcal{Q}$ are called *indistinguishable* ($\mathcal{P} \equiv \mathcal{Q}$) iff the difference between the probability that $\mathcal{P}$ outputs 1 (on the decision tape) and the probability that $\mathcal{Q}$ outputs 1 is negligible in the security parameter.

Notions of Simulation-Based Security. We need the following terminology. For a system $\mathcal{S}$, the input/output tapes of machines in $\mathcal{S}$ that do not have a matching output/input tape are called *external*. These tapes are grouped into *I/O* and *network tapes*. We consider three different types of systems, modeling i) real and ideal protocols/functionalities, ii) adversaries and simulators, and iii) environments: *Protocol systems* and *environmental systems* are systems which have an I/O and network interface, i.e., they may have I/O and network tapes. *Adversarial systems* only have a network interface. Environmental systems may contain a master machine and may produce output on the decision tape. We can now define strong simulatability; other equivalent security notions, such as (dummy) UC, can be defined in a similar way [19].

DEFINITION 1 ([19]). *Let $\mathcal{P}$ and $\mathcal{F}$ be protocol systems with the same I/O interface, the real and the ideal protocol, respectively. Then, $\mathcal{P}$* realizes *$\mathcal{F}$ ($\mathcal{P} \leq \mathcal{F}$) iff there exists an adversarial system $\mathcal{S}$ (a simulator or an ideal adversary) such that the systems $\mathcal{P}$ and $\mathcal{S} \,|\, \mathcal{F}$ have the same external interface and for all environmental systems $\mathcal{E}$, connecting only to the external interface of $\mathcal{P}$ (and hence, $\mathcal{S} \,|\, \mathcal{F}$), it holds that $\mathcal{E} \,|\, \mathcal{P} \equiv \mathcal{E} \,|\, \mathcal{S} \,|\, \mathcal{F}$.*

Composition Theorems. We restate the composition theorems from [19], in a slightly simplified way. The first composition theorem handles concurrent composition of a fixed number of protocol systems. The second one guarantees secure composition of an unbounded number of copies of a protocol system.

THEOREM 1 ([19]). *Let $\mathcal{P}_1, \mathcal{P}_2, \mathcal{F}_1, \mathcal{F}_2$ be protocol systems such that $\mathcal{P}_1$ and $\mathcal{P}_2$ as well as $\mathcal{F}_1$ and $\mathcal{F}_2$ only connect via their I/O interfaces and $\mathcal{P}_i \leq \mathcal{F}_i$, for $i \in \{1, 2\}$. Then, $\mathcal{P}_1 \,|\, \mathcal{P}_2 \leq \mathcal{F}_1 \,|\, \mathcal{F}_2$.*

Let $\mathcal{F}$ and $\mathcal{P}$ be protocol systems, which, for example, describe one session of an ideal/real protocol. By $\underline{\mathcal{F}}$ and $\underline{\mathcal{P}}$ we denote the so-called session versions of $\mathcal{F}$ and $\mathcal{P}$, which allow an environment to address different sessions of $\mathcal{F}$ and $\mathcal{P}$, respectively, in the multi-session versions $!\underline{\mathcal{F}}$ and $!\underline{\mathcal{P}}$ of $\mathcal{F}$ and $\mathcal{P}$ by prefixing messages with session identifiers (SIDs); an instance of $\underline{\mathcal{P}}/\underline{\mathcal{F}}$ is accessed via a unique SID. Conversely, messages output by $\underline{\mathcal{F}}$ and $\underline{\mathcal{P}}$ will be prefixed by their respective SID.

THEOREM 2 ([19]). *Let $\mathcal{P}, \mathcal{F}$ be protocol systems such that $\mathcal{P} \leq \mathcal{F}$. Then, $!\underline{\mathcal{P}} \leq !\underline{\mathcal{F}}$.*

These theorems can be applied iteratively to construct more and more complex systems. For example, using that $\leq$ is reflexive, we obtain, as a corollary of the above theorems, that for any protocol system Q: $\mathcal{P} \leq \mathcal{F}$ implies $Q \,|\, !\underline{\mathcal{P}} \leq Q \,|\, !\underline{\mathcal{F}}$, i.e., Q using an unbounded number of copies of $\mathcal{P}$ realizes Q using an unbounded number of copies of $\mathcal{F}$. This corollary is in the spirit of Canetti's universal composition theorem [7].

3. UNIVERSAL COMPOSITION WITHOUT PRE-ESTABLISHED SIDS

Universal composition theorems, such as Theorem 2 and the composition theorem by Canetti, allow to obtain security for multiple sessions of a protocol by analyzing just a single session. Such theorems can therefore greatly simplify protocol analysis. However, these theorems rely on the setup assumption that the parties participating in a protocol session agree upon a unique SID and that they invoke their instance of the protocol with that SID. This is due to the way multi-session versions of ideal functionalities are defined in these composition theorems: A multi-session version of an ideal functionality F is such that parties which want to access an instance of F have to agree on a unique SID in order to be able to all invoke the same instance of F with that SID. As a consequence, the composition theorems implicitly require that a session of a real protocol with SID s realizes a session of the ideal functionality with SID s. (For example, if a session of the real protocol consists of two instances, e.g., an initiator instance and a responder instance, then the initiator with SID s and the responder with SID s together have to realize the ideal functionality with SID s.) This, in turn, implies that the real protocol has to use the SID s in some way, since otherwise there is nothing that prevents grouping instances with different SIDs (e.g., an initiator with SID s and a responder with SID s') into one session. One usage of the SID s is, for example, to access a resource for the specific session, e.g., a functionality (with SID s) that provides the parties with fresh keys or certain communication channels for that specific session. In realizations with joint state, s is typically used in *all* messages exchanged between parties in order to prevent interference with other sessions (see also Section 4).

Canetti [8] discusses three methods of how such unique SIDs could be established, including a method proposed by Barak et al. [2], where parties simply exchange nonces in clear and then form a unique SID by concatenating these nonces and the party names. We will refer to such uniquely established SIDs (using whatever method) by *pre-established* SIDs. The use of pre-established SIDs is certainly a good design principle. However, assuming pre-established SIDs and, as a result, forcing their use in the protocols greatly limits the scope of the composition theorems for the analysis of existing protocols. In particular, they cannot be used for the modular analysis of real-world security protocols since such protocols typically do not make use of SIDs in this explicit and specific way. In other words, the composition theorems could only be used to analyze idealized/modified versions of such protocols. However, this is dangerous: While the idealized/modified version of a protocol might be secure, its original version may not be secure (see Section 4). We note that, alternatively, protocols could of course directly be analyzed in the multi-session settings, instead of first analyzing the single-session setting and then lifting the analysis to the multi-session setting by a composition theorem. But this kind of analysis would be more involved and would not exploit the potential of modular analysis, which for the comprehensive analysis of complex protocols, such as real-world security protocols, is essential.

In this section, we therefore present a general universal composition theorem that does not assume pre-established SIDs (and their use in protocols). For this purpose, we first provide a new definition of the multi-session version of an ideal functionality. Our new multi-session version models the more realistic scenario that a party accesses an instance of an ideal functionality F simply by a *local* SID, which is locally chosen and managed by the party itself. It is then left to an adversary (simulator) to determine which group of local sessions may use one instance of F, where the grouping into what we call a (global) session is subject to certain restrictions (see below). This seemingly harmless modification not only provides a more realistic and common interface to the functionality (and its realization), but, as explained above, more importantly frees the realization from the need to use pre-established SIDs and allows for realizations that faithfully model existing (real-world) protocols. Before presenting the new multi-session versions of ideal functionalities and our composition theorem, we fix some notation and terminology for modeling arbitrary real protocols.

3.1 Multi-Session Real Protocols

A multi-session real protocol is an arbitrary real protocol with n roles, for some $n \geq 2$, which may use arbitrary subprotocols/functionalities to perform its tasks. More precisely, a *multi-session (real) protocol* $\mathcal{P}$ is a protocol system of the form $\mathcal{P} = !M_1 \,|\, \cdots \,|\, !M_n$ for some $n \geq 2$ and machines $M_1, \ldots, M_n$. Each machine M_r represents one role in the protocol and, since these machines are under the scope of a bang operator, there can be multiple instances of each machine in a run of the system (see below). Every machine M_r has

i) an I/O input and output tape for communication with the environment (users), ii) a network input and output tape for communication with the adversary (modeling the network), and iii) an I/O input and output tape for communication with a subprotocol/ideal functionality $\mathcal{F}$. We require that the I/O interface of $\mathcal{F}$ consists of n pairs of I/O input and output tapes, one for each role. Note that $\mathcal{F}$ may include several subprotocols/functionalities. We say that $\mathcal{P}$ *uses* $\mathcal{F}$.

A machine M_r expects inputs to be prefixed with a tuple of the form $(lsid, p)$ from the environment (user) and the adversary, and it prefixes all messages it outputs with $(lsid, p)$. Intuitively, p is a party identifier (PID) and $lsid$ a *local* SID (LSID), locally chosen and managed by party p. In a run of $\mathcal{P}$ there will be at most one instance of M_r with ID $(lsid, p)$, representing the local session $lsid$ of party p in role r.

To model corruption, we assume that every (instance of) M_r stores a flag **corrupted** $\in$ {false, true} in its state, which initially is false. At some point, M_r might set it to true in which case we call M_r *corrupted*. We require that once M_r sets the flag to true, it stays true. Furthermore, whenever the environment sends the message $(lsid, p, \text{Corrupted?})$ to M_r (on the I/O tape), M_r replies with $(lsid, p, \text{Corrupted}, \textbf{corrupted})$. This allows the environment to know which instances are corrupted. (As usual, this is necessary in simulation-based settings.) However, we do not fix how M_r behaves when corrupted; we leave this entirely up to the definition of M_r. One possible behavior could be, for example, that when corrupted, M_r gives complete control to the adversary by forwarding all messages between the environment and the adversary. We note that the possibility of corrupting single instances of M_r is quite fine-grained and allows several forms corruption, including complete corruption of a party: the adversary can simply corrupt all instances of that party.

3.2 A New Multi-Session Version of Ideal Functionalities

Let F be any machine, modeling an ideal functionality, with n pairs of input and output I/O tapes, one for each role, and one pair of input and output network tapes. We now define the new multi-session version of F, informally explained above. We call this new multi-session version *multi-session local-SID (ideal) functionality* and denote it by $\mathcal{F}[F]$ or simply $\mathcal{F}$:

A *user* of $\mathcal{F}$ is identified within $\mathcal{F}$ by the tuple $(p, lsid, r)$, where p is a party identifier (PID), $r \leq n$ a role, and $lsid$ a *local* SID (LSID), which can be chosen and managed by the party itself. In particular, on the tape for role r, $\mathcal{F}$ expects requests to be prefixed by tuples of the form $(lsid, p)$, and conversely, $\mathcal{F}$ prefixes answers sent on that tape with a tuple of the form $(lsid, p)$.

A user of $\mathcal{F}$, say $(p, lsid, r)$, can initiate a session by sending a *session-start* message of the form $(lsid, p, \text{Start}, m)$ where m is an optional bit string, which can be used to set parameters of the session, e.g., the desired partners or the name of a key distribution server. For example, in the case of two-party key exchange, a user with PID p who wants to exchange a key with party p' could set $m = (p, p')$. We emphasize that the interpretation of m is left to F. Upon such a *session-start* request, $\mathcal{F}$ records this request (if it is the first such request from $(p, lsid, r)$) as a *local session* for user $(p, lsid, r)$ and forwards this information to the adversary.

The adversary (simulator) determines to which *global* session local sessions belong, by sending a *session-create* message of the form (Create, sid) to $\mathcal{F}$ where $sid = (p_1, lsid_1, 1), \ldots, (p_n, lsid_n, n)$ contains one local session for every role. (We note that $\mathcal{F}$ could easily be extended to deal with multiple local sessions per role.) The machine $\mathcal{F}$ only accepts such a message if it is consistent with the local sessions: The mentioned local sessions all exist, are not corrupted (see below), and are not already part of another global session. If $\mathcal{F}$ accepts such a *session-create* message, $\mathcal{F}$ internally creates a new instance of F identifying it by sid. Then, $\mathcal{F}$ sends the message $(\text{Create}, m_1, \ldots, m_n)$ to this instance of F where, for all $r \leq n$, m_r is the optional bit string contained in the *session-start* message of user $(p_r, lsid_r, r)$. The adversary can address this instance of F (via the network interface) by prefixing messages with sid; conversely, messages output by F on its network interface are prefixed with sid.

For a message m of a user $(p, lsid, r)$, which is not a *session-start* message or a message of the form Corrupted? (see below), $\mathcal{F}$ checks whether $(p, lsid, r)$ is part of a global session. If not, $\mathcal{F}$ drops m, i.e., this message is ignored. Otherwise, $\mathcal{F}$ forwards m to the corresponding instance of F. Conversely, $\mathcal{F}$ forwards all messages from an instance of F on tape r to the corresponding user in role r.

We model corruption as follows in $\mathcal{F}$. The adversary can send a *corrupt* message of the form $(\text{Corrupt}, (p, lsid, r))$ for a local session $(p, lsid, r)$ to $\mathcal{F}$. The machine $\mathcal{F}$ only accepts this message if the local session $(p, lsid, r)$ is not already part of a global session, and in this case records $(p, lsid, r)$ as *corrupted*. For every corrupted local session, $\mathcal{F}$ forwards all messages from a user of that local session to the adversary (instead of forwarding them to F) and vice versa. This models that the adversary has full control over corrupted local sessions. Note that once a local session is part of a global session, the local session or its corresponding global session can still be corrupted at any time according to the way corruption is defined in F, which we do not restrict.

Finally, a user may ask $\mathcal{F}$ whether or not a local session was corrupted before being part of a global session by sending the message $(lsid, p, \text{Corrupted?})$. Then, $\mathcal{F}$ replies accordingly with true or false. This, as usual, guarantees that the environment is aware of who is corrupted, preventing the simulator from simply corrupting all local sessions. Whether or not a user can ask about the corruption status of F is completely up to the definition of F, which, again, we do not restrict.

We note that the above definition of a multi-session version of an ideal functionality applies to any ideal functionality F.

Technically, for a real protocol to realize a multi-session local-SID functionality the simulator must be able to group instances of the simulated real protocol into a global session before interaction with the functionality F is possible. This means that a real protocol needs to allow for the grouping of instances by whatever mechanism (where the mechanisms is typically intertwined with the rest of the protocol). In particular, the grouping is part of the protocol, and hence, can now be precisely modeled and analyzed. For example, for authentication, key exchange, secure channel protocols and the like, being able to tell which instances are grouped together is an essential part of what these protocols (have to) guarantee and different protocols use different mechanisms; these mechanisms should be part of the analysis. Conversely, before there was one fixed mechanism for grouping instances, namely pre-established SIDs. Real protocols needed to make sure that they in fact can be grouped according to the SID they obtained, and hence, they had to use the SID in some essential way. Moreover, the SIDs came from outside of the protocol, and hence, their establishment was not part of the protocol.

3.3 The Universal Composition Theorem Without Pre-Established SIDs

We now present our universal composition theorem. Let $\mathcal{P}$ be a multi-session protocol using a multi-session local-SID functionality $\mathcal{F}'$ and let $\mathcal{F}$ be a multi-session local-SID functionality. Informally, our theorem states that if $\mathcal{P}\,|\,\mathcal{F}'$ realizes $\mathcal{F}$ in the single-session setting, then $\mathcal{P}\,|\,\mathcal{F}'$ realizes $\mathcal{F}$ in the multi-session setting. The important point here is that, by the definition of multi-session local-SID functionalities, no pre-established SIDs (nor their use in the protocol) are required.

To formulate this theorem, we consider a machine F_{single} that is put on top of $\mathcal{P}\,|\,\mathcal{F}'$ and $\mathcal{F}$, respectively, and that allows an environment to create *at most one* session, i.e., only one user is allowed per role. We note that an alternative to using F_{single} would be to restrict the environment explicitly.

To be able to prove the composition theorem, we need to restrict the class of simulators used to prove that $\mathcal{P}\,|\,\mathcal{F}'$ realizes $\mathcal{F}$ in the single-session case. For this purpose, we define the following simulation relation: We say that $\mathcal{P}\,|\,\mathcal{F}'$ *single-session realizes* $\mathcal{F}$ (denoted by $F_{\text{single}}\,|\,\mathcal{P}\,|\,\mathcal{F}' \leq^* F_{\text{single}}\,|\,\mathcal{F}$) if i) $F_{\text{single}}\,|\,\mathcal{P}\,|\,\mathcal{F}' \leq F_{\text{single}}\,|\,\mathcal{F}$, i.e., according to Definition 1, there exists a simulator *Sim* such that for all $\mathcal{E}$ it holds that $\mathcal{E}\,|\,F_{\text{single}}\,|\,\mathcal{P}\,|\,\mathcal{F}' \equiv \mathcal{E}\,|\,Sim\,|\,F_{\text{single}}\,|\,\mathcal{F}$, and ii) *Sim* is a machine which operators in two stages as follows: In the first stage, *Sim* simply emulates the system $\mathcal{P}\,|\,\mathcal{F}'$, where *session-start* messages from $\mathcal{F}$ are forward to the emulated $\mathcal{P}$. If *Sim* receives a) a *session-create* message for the emulated $\mathcal{F}'$ from the adversary and this message is accepted by $\mathcal{F}'$ or b) the **corrupted** flag of an emulated instance M_r in $\mathcal{P}$ is set to true, then *Sim* enters its second stage. Once in the second stage, *Sim* is not restricted whatsoever. If, in the first stage, the emulated $\mathcal{P}\,|\,\mathcal{F}'$ produces I/O output, then *Sim* terminates. (In this case the simulation fails.) This is in fact not a restriction: Every protocol that produces I/O output if *Sim* is in its first stage would not realize $\mathcal{F}$, i.e., $F_{\text{single}}\,|\,\mathcal{P}\,|\,\mathcal{F}' \not\leq F_{\text{single}}\,|\,\mathcal{F}$. The reason is that in the first stage, the instances in $\mathcal{P}$ run independently. Now, if an environment emulated all but one instance, in $F_{\text{single}}\,|\,\mathcal{F}$ no session would be created, and hence, no output at the I/O interface would be produced.

So, altogether the only restriction we put on *Sim* is that it emulates the real protocol in its first stage. This is what simulators would typically do anyway. In fact, we think that for most applications $F_{\text{single}}\,|\,\mathcal{P}\,|\,\mathcal{F}' \leq F_{\text{single}}\,|\,\mathcal{F}$ implies $F_{\text{single}}\,|\,\mathcal{P}\,|\,\mathcal{F}' \leq^* F_{\text{single}}\,|\,\mathcal{F}$.

Moreover, our restriction seems unavoidable in order to prove our composition theorem. First recall that for the classical universal composition theorems (Theorem 2 and Canetti's composition theorem) the proof is by a hybrid argument. In the i-th hybrid system the environment emulates the first $< i$ sessions as real protocols (real sessions) and the last $> i$ sessions as ideal (single-session simulator plus ideal functionality). The i-th session is external. Since every session is identified by a pre-established SID, the environment knows exactly and from the start on which instances of machines form one session. In particular, it knows from the start on whether a session should be emulated as real or ideal and which messages must be relayed to the external session. In our setting, this does not work since we do not assume pre-established SIDs: Initially, the (hybrid) environment does not know to which session an instance $(p, lsid, r)$ will belong. In particular, it does not know whether it will belong to an ideal or real session. This is only determined if $(p, lsid, r)$ is included in a (valid) *session-create* message to $\mathcal{F}'$. So unless an instance $(p, lsid, r)$ does not behave the same in the ideal and real session up to this point, consistent simulation would not be possible. Now, by our assumption that the simulator in its first stage simulates the real protocol, the environment can first simulate the real protocol for the instance $(p, lsid, r)$. Once this instance is included in a (valid) *session-create* message to $\mathcal{F}'$, and hence, the environment knows whether the instance belongs to an ideal or real session, the simulation can be continued accordingly. More concretely, if it turns out that $(p, lsid, r)$ belongs to an ideal session, the environment starts the emulation of the simulator for that session with the current configurations of all emulated instances for that session. Again, this is possible because up to this point the simulator too would have only simulated these instance as real protocols. For the i-th session, the environment guesses the instances that shall belong to it. Following this idea, we proved our composition theorem stated next.

THEOREM 3. *Let $\mathcal{F}$ and $\mathcal{F}'$ be two multi-session local-SID functionalities and let $\mathcal{P}$ be a multi-session real protocol that uses $\mathcal{F}'$. If $F_{\text{single}}\,|\,\mathcal{P}\,|\,\mathcal{F}' \leq^* F_{\text{single}}\,|\,\mathcal{F}$, then $\mathcal{P}\,|\,\mathcal{F}' \leq \mathcal{F}$.*

We note that Theorem 3 can be applied iteratively: For example, if we have that $F_{\text{single}}\,|\,\mathcal{P}_1\,|\,\mathcal{F}_1 \leq^* F_{\text{single}}\,|\,\mathcal{F}_2$ and $F_{\text{single}}\,|\,\mathcal{P}_2\,|\,\mathcal{F}_2 \leq^* F_{\text{single}}\,|\,\mathcal{F}_3$, then, by Theorem 3 and Theorem 1, $\mathcal{P}_2\,|\,\mathcal{P}_1\,|\,\mathcal{F}_1 \leq \mathcal{F}_3$.

4. JOINT STATE COMPOSITION WITHOUT PRE-ESTABLISHED SIDS

Universal composition theorems, such as Theorem 2 and the composition theorem of Canetti, assume that different protocol sessions have disjoint state; in particular, each session has to use fresh randomness. (Theorem 3 makes this assumption too, but we exclude this theorem from the following discussion since it does not assume pre-established SIDs.) This can lead to inefficient and impractical protocols, since, for example, in every session fresh long-term symmetric and public/private keys have to be used. Canetti and Rabin [11] therefore proposed to combine the universal composition theorems with what they called composition theorems with joint state. By now, joint state composition theorems for several cryptographic primitives are available, including joint state composition theorems for digital signatures [11, 20] and public-key encryption [20] as well as encryption with long-term symmetric keys [21]. These theorems provide mechanisms that allow to turn a system with independent sessions (i.e., sessions with disjoint state) into a system where the same (long-term symmetric and public/private) keys may be used in different sessions. This joint state comes "for free" in the sense that it does not require additional proofs. However, there is a price to pay: Just as the universal composition theorems, the joint state composition theorems assume pre-established SIDs. Moreover, the mechanisms used by existing joint state theorems for specific cryptographic primitives, such as encryption and digital signatures, prefix *all* plaintexts to be encrypted (with long-term symmetric or public/private keys) and messages to be signed by the unique pre-established SIDs; by this, interference between different sessions is prevented. While this is a good design principle, these theorems are unsuitable for the modular analysis of an existing protocol that does not employ these mechanisms: If such a protocol is secure in the single-session setting, then its multi-session version obtained by combining universal composition with joint state composition, and hence, the version of the protocol in which messages are prefixed with pre-established SIDs, is secure as well. But from this it does in general not follow that the original protocol, which may be drastically different, is also secure in the multi-session setting. In fact, by the above joint-state constructions insecure protocols can be turned into secure ones (see Figure 1). In particular, since real-world security protocols typically do not use pre-established SIDs, at least not explicitly and not in the particular way stipulated by the theorems, the joint state composition theorems are unsuitable for the modular and faithful analysis of such protocols; at most idealized/modified protocols, but not the original real-world protocols, can be analyzed in this modular way. For example, in Step 3 of the TLS Handshake Protocol (see Figure 2), the client sends the pre-master key encrypted to the server. In the variant of TLS obtained by the joint state theorems, a unique SID

		original	modified
1.	$A \to B$:	$\{\!|N_A, A|\!\}_{k_B}$	$\{\!|sid, N_A, A|\!\}_{k_B}$
2.	$B \to A$:	$\{\!|N_A, N_B|\!\}_{k_A}$	$\{\!|sid, N_A, N_B|\!\}_{k_A}$
3.	$A \to B$:	$\{\!|N_B|\!\}_{k_B}$	$\{\!|sid, N_B|\!\}_{k_B}$

Figure 1: The original Needham-Schroeder Public-Key Protocol is insecure [24]. Its modified version, resulting from the joint-state construction, which prefixes every plaintext with a pre-established SID *sid* is secure (see [22] for details).

sid would be included in the plaintext as well. By this alone, unlike the original version of TLS, this message is bound to session *sid*.

In this section, we therefore propose a joint state composition theorem which does not require to modify the protocol under consideration. In particular, it does not rely on pre-established SIDs and the mechanism of prefixing messages with such SIDs.

In our joint state theorem we consider a multi-session real protocol $\mathcal{P}$ which uses an ideal crypto functionality $\mathcal{F}_{\text{crypto}}$ proposed in [23]. The functionality $\mathcal{F}_{\text{crypto}}$ allows its users to perform the following operations in an ideal way: i) generate symmetric keys, including pre-shared keys, ii) generate public/private keys, iii) derive symmetric keys from other symmetric keys, iv) encrypt and decrypt messages and ciphertexts, respectively (public-key encryption and both unauthenticated and authenticated symmetric encryption are supported), v) compute and verify MACs and digital signatures, and vi) generate fresh nonces. All symmetric and public keys can be part of plaintexts to be encrypted under other symmetric and public keys. Derived keys can be used just as freshly generated symmetric keys. As shown in [23], $\mathcal{F}_{\text{crypto}}$ can be realized under standard cryptographic assumptions, subject to natural restrictions on the environment. We briefly recall $\mathcal{F}_{\text{crypto}}$ and its realization in Section 4.1.

Every instance of a machine M_r in $\mathcal{P}$ has access to $\mathcal{F}_{\text{crypto}}$. In other words, $\mathcal{F}_{\text{crypto}}$ is the joint state of all sessions of $\mathcal{P}$: Different sessions may have access to the same public/private and symmetric keys in $\mathcal{F}_{\text{crypto}}$.

Now, informally speaking, our joint state composition theorem states that under a certain condition on $\mathcal{P}$, which we call *implicit (session) disjointness*, it is sufficient to analyze $\mathcal{P}$ (which may use $\mathcal{F}_{\text{crypto}}$) in the single-session setting to obtain security in the multi-session setting, where all sessions may use the *same* ideal crypto functionality $\mathcal{F}_{\text{crypto}}$. (We note that by the universal composition theorem, $\mathcal{F}_{\text{crypto}}$ can be replaced by its realization.) It seems that most real-world protocols satisfy implicit disjointness and that this property can be verified easily, as illustrated by our case studies in Section 5.

In what follows, we briefly recall the ideal crypto functionality $\mathcal{F}_{\text{crypto}}$ and its realization. We then introduce the notion of implicit disjointness and present our joint state composition theorem.

4.1 The Ideal Crypto Functionality

We now briefly recall the ideal functionality $\mathcal{F}_{\text{crypto}}$, proposed in [23], which, as mentioned, supports several cryptographic operations. The formulation here is slightly modified (see below).

Description of $\mathcal{F}_{\text{crypto}}$. Just as multi-session local-SID functionalities introduced in Section 3, $\mathcal{F}_{\text{crypto}}$ is parametrized by a number n of roles. For every role, $\mathcal{F}_{\text{crypto}}$ has one I/O input and output tape. Again, a user of $\mathcal{F}_{\text{crypto}}$ is identified within $\mathcal{F}_{\text{crypto}}$ by a tuple $(p, lsid, r)$, where p is a PID, $lsid$ a LSID, and r a role.

Users of $\mathcal{F}_{\text{crypto}}$, and its realization, do not get their hands on the actual symmetric keys stored in the functionality, but only on pointers to these keys, since otherwise no security guarantees could be provided; users obtain the actual public keys though. A user can perform the operations mentioned above (encryption, etc.). Upon a key generation request, an adversary can corrupt a key, which is then marked "known" in $\mathcal{F}_{\text{crypto}}$ (see below). A user can ask whether a key one of her pointers points to is corrupted.

The functionality $\mathcal{F}_{\text{crypto}}$ keeps track of which user has access to which symmetric keys (via pointers) and which keys are known to the environment/adversary, i.e., have been corrupted or have been encrypted under a known key, and as a result became known. For this purpose, $\mathcal{F}_{\text{crypto}}$ maintains a set $\mathcal{K}$ of all symmetric keys stored within $\mathcal{F}_{\text{crypto}}$, a set $\mathcal{K}_{\text{known}} \subseteq \mathcal{K}$ of *known* keys, and a set $\mathcal{K}_{\text{unknown}} := \mathcal{K} \setminus \mathcal{K}_{\text{known}}$ of *unknown* keys.

To illustrate the internal behavior of $\mathcal{F}_{\text{crypto}}$ and to point out the mentioned modification to the original version of $\mathcal{F}_{\text{crypto}}$, we sketch the behavior of $\mathcal{F}_{\text{crypto}}$ for authenticated encryption and decryption, with requests (Enc, ptr, x) and (Dec, ptr, y): We first consider the case that ptr points to an unknown key, i.e., a key in $\mathcal{K}_{\text{unknown}}$. The plaintext x may contain pointers to symmetric keys. Before x is actually encrypted, such pointers are replaced by the keys they refer to, resulting in a message x'. Now, not the actual message, but a random message of the same length is encrypted. If this results in a ciphertext y', then the pair (x', y') is stored in $\mathcal{F}_{\text{crypto}}$ and y' is returned to the user. Decryption of y succeeds only if exactly one pair of the form (x'', y) is stored. In this case, x'' with embedded keys replaced by pointers is returned. In case ptr points to a key marked known, i.e., a key in $\mathcal{K}_{\text{known}}$, the adversary is asked for a ciphertext (in case of encryption) or a plaintext (in case of decryption).[1] Furthermore, all keys contained in x' are marked known as they are encrypted under a known key.

Realization of $\mathcal{F}_{\text{crypto}}$. In [23], a realization $\mathcal{P}_{\text{crypto}}$ of $\mathcal{F}_{\text{crypto}}$ has been proposed based on standard cryptographic assumptions on schemes: IND-CCA2-secure schemes for public-key and unauthenticated symmetric encryption, an IND-CPA- and INT-CTXT-secure scheme for authenticated symmetric encryption, UF-CMA-secure MAC and digital signature schemes, and pseudo-random functions for key derivation. These schemes are used to realize $\mathcal{F}_{\text{crypto}}$ in the expected way. To show that $\mathcal{P}_{\text{crypto}}$ realizes $\mathcal{F}_{\text{crypto}}$ it is necessary to restrict the environment: Environments should not cause the so-called commitment problem (once an unknown symmetric key was used for encryption, it should not become known) and should not generate key cycles; without these restrictions, much stronger cryptographic assumptions would be necessary, which go beyond what is typically assumed for the security of real-world security protocols. Protocols (in particular, real-world security protocols) using $\mathcal{F}_{\text{crypto}}$ typically satisfy these restrictions and this is easy to verify for a given protocol, as discussed and illustrated in [23].

4.2 Our Criterion: Implicit Disjointness

We now introduce the notion of *implicit (session) disjointness*, already mentioned at the beginning of Section 4. Recall that we are interested in the security of the system $\mathcal{P} \,|\, \mathcal{F}_{\text{crypto}}$, where $\mathcal{P}$ is a multi-session protocol in which all sessions may use the same $\mathcal{F}_{\text{crypto}}$. As explained before, implicit disjointness is a condition on $\mathcal{P}$ which should allow to analyze the security of $\mathcal{P}$ in a single-session setting in order to obtain security of $\mathcal{P}$ in a multi-session setting, without assuming pre-established SIDs and without modifying $\mathcal{P}$. Intuitively, implicit disjointness is a condition that en-

[1] This constitutes a slight modification to the original ideal functionality in [23], where in this case encryption and decryption were performed with algorithms previously provided by the adversary. The new version helps in the proof of our joint state theorem. It is just as useful for analyzing protocols and can be realized in exactly the same way as the original version.

sures that different sessions of $\mathcal{P}$ cannot "interfere", even though they share state, in the form of information stored in $\mathcal{F}_{\text{crypto}}$, including public/private and pre-shared keys, and the information stored along with these keys, e.g., plaintext-ciphertext pairs. In order to define the notion of implicit disjointness, we first introduce some notation and terminology.

Partnering Functions. In the definition of implicit disjointness, we assume the existence of a partnering function[2] which groups users $(p, lsid, r)$, more precisely, the corresponding instances of machines M_r in a run of $\mathcal{P}$, into sessions. Formally, a *partnering function* τ for $\mathcal{P}\,|\,\mathcal{F}_{\text{crypto}}$ is a polynomial-time computable, partial function that maps every sequence α of configurations of an instance of a machine M_r in $\mathcal{P}$ to an SID (which is an arbitrary bit string) or $\perp$. For every environment $\mathcal{E}$, (partial) run ρ of $\mathcal{E}\,|\,\mathcal{P}\,|\,\mathcal{F}_{\text{crypto}}$, and every user $(p, lsid, r)$, we define $\tau_{(p,lsid,r)}(\rho) := \tau(\alpha)$ where α is the projection of ρ to the sequence of configurations of the machine M_r with PID p and LSID $lsid$. We say that $(p, lsid, r)$ and $(p', lsid', r')$ *are partners* (or *belong to the same session*) in a (partial) run ρ if $\tau_{(p,lsid,r)}(\rho) = \tau_{(p',lsid',r')}(\rho) \neq \perp$.

We say that τ is *valid* for $\mathcal{P}$ if, for every environment $\mathcal{E}$ for $\mathcal{P}\,|\,\mathcal{F}_{\text{crypto}}$, the following holds with overwhelming probability (the probability is taken over runs ρ of $\mathcal{E}\,|\,\mathcal{P}\,|\,\mathcal{F}_{\text{crypto}}$): For every user $(p, lsid, r)$ in ρ, the following conditions are satisfied. i) Once an SID is assigned, it is fixed, i.e., if $\tau_{(p,lsid,r)}(\rho'') \neq \perp$, then it holds $\tau_{(p,lsid,r)}(\rho') = \tau_{(p,lsid,r)}(\rho'')$ for every prefix ρ' of ρ and every prefix ρ'' of ρ'. ii) Corrupted users do not belong to sessions, i.e., if $(p, lsid, r)$ is corrupted in ρ (i.e., the flag **corrupted** is set to `true` in the corresponding instances of M_r), then $\tau_{(p,lsid,r)}(\rho) = \perp$. iii) Every session contains at most one user per role, i.e., for every partner $(p', lsid', r')$ of $(p, lsid, r)$ in ρ, it holds that $r \neq r'$ or $(p', lsid', r') = (p, lsid, r)$.

In practice, partnering functions are typically very simple. In our case studies (Section 5), we use conceptually the same partnering function for all protocols; basically partners are determined based on the exchanged nonces.

Construction and Destruction Requests. We call an encryption, MAC, and sign request (for $\mathcal{F}_{\text{crypto}}$ by an instance M_r of $\mathcal{P}$, i.e., a user) a *construction* request and a decryption, MAC verification, and signature verification request a *destruction* request.

Now, roughly speaking, implicit disjointness says that whenever some user sends a destruction request, then the user who sent the "corresponding" construction request belongs to the same session according to τ. This formulation is, however, too strong. For example, an adversary could send a ciphertext coming from one session to a different session where it is successfully decrypted. But further inspection of the plaintext might lead to the rejection of the message (e.g., because excepted nonces did not appear or MAC/signature verification failed). We therefore need to introduce the notion of a *successful* destruction request. For this purpose, we also introduce what we call *tests*.

Tests and Successful Destruction Requests. We imagine that a user $(p, lsid, r)$ (more precisely, the corresponding instance of M_r) after every destruction request runs some deterministic algorithm `test` which outputs *accept* or *reject*, where, besides the response received, the run of `test` may depend on and may even modify the state of $(p, lsid, r)$. We require that `test` satisfies the following conditions: If the destruction request is a MAC/signature verification request, then `test` simply outputs the result of the verification. If the destruction request is a decryption request, but decryption failed (i.e., $\mathcal{F}_{\text{crypto}}$ returned an error message), then `test` returns *reject*. Otherwise, if decryption did not fail, and hence, a plaintext was returned, `test` is free to output *accept* or *reject*. In the latter case—reject—, we require the state of $(p, lsid, r)$ to be the same as if decryption had failed (i.e., as if $\mathcal{F}_{\text{crypto}}$ had returned an error message) in the first place; this ensures that the state of $(p, lsid, r)$ does not depend on the plaintext that was returned. The algorithm `test` may itself make destruction requests (but no construction requests), e.g., decrypt nested ciphertexts or verify embedded MACs/signatures, which are subject to the same constraints. Also, key generation and key derivation are allowed within a test. The requirements on `test` reflect what protocols typically do (see Section 5.2 for an example).

Now, we say that a destruction request is *accepted* if the test performed after the request returns *accept*. We say that it is *ideal* if the key used in the destruction request is marked unknown in $\mathcal{F}_{\text{crypto}}$ or is an uncorrupted public/private key in $\mathcal{F}_{\text{crypto}}$ and, in case of a decryption request, the ciphertext in that request is stored in $\mathcal{F}_{\text{crypto}}$ (and hence, it was produced by $\mathcal{F}_{\text{crypto}}$ and the corresponding stored plaintext is returned).

Correspondence Between Construction and Destruction Requests. We now define when a construction request corresponds to a destruction request. Let ρ be a run of the system $\mathcal{E}\,|\,\mathcal{P}\,|\,\mathcal{F}_{\text{crypto}}$ and let m_c and m_d be construction and destruction request, respectively, such that m_c was sent by some instance to $\mathcal{F}_{\text{crypto}}$ before m_d was sent by some (possibly other) instance to $\mathcal{F}_{\text{crypto}}$ in ρ. Then, we say that m_c *corresponds* to m_d in ρ if i) m_c is an encryption and m_d a decryption request under the same key (for public-key encryption/decryption, under corresponding public/private keys) such that the ciphertext in the response to m_c from $\mathcal{F}_{\text{crypto}}$ coincides with the ciphertext in m_d, ii) m_c is a MAC/signature and m_d a MAC/signature verification request under the same key/corresponding keys such that the message in m_c coincides with the message in m_d (the MACs/signatures do not need to coincide).

Explicitly Shared (Symmetric) Keys. For implicit disjointness, we only impose restrictions on what we call explicitly shared (symmetric) keys. These are pre-shared symmetric keys or keys (directly or indirectly) derived from such keys in different sessions with the same seed. We note that in most protocols pre-shared keys are the only explicitly shared keys since derived keys are typically derived from seeds that are unique to the session.

DEFINITION 2 (IMPLICIT DISJOINTNESS). *Let $\mathcal{P}$ be a multi-session protocol that uses $\mathcal{F}_{\text{crypto}}$ and τ be a valid partnering function for $\mathcal{P}\,|\,\mathcal{F}_{\text{crypto}}$. Then, $\mathcal{P}$ satisfies* implicit (session) disjointness *w.r.t. τ if for every environment $\mathcal{E}$ for $\mathcal{P}\,|\,\mathcal{F}_{\text{crypto}}$ the following holds with overwhelming probability for runs ρ of $\mathcal{E}\,|\,\mathcal{P}\,|\,\mathcal{F}_{\text{crypto}}$:*

(a) Every explicitly shared key is either always marked unknown or always marked known in $\mathcal{F}_{\text{crypto}}$.

(b) Whenever some user $(p, lsid, r)$ (i.e., an instance of M_r) performed an accepted and ideal destruction request with an explicitly shared key or a public/private key at some point in ρ, say after the partial run ρ', then there exists some user $(p', lsid', r')$ that has sent a corresponding construction request such that both users are partners or both users are corrupted in ρ'.

Most protocols can easily be seen to satisfy (a) because explicitly shared keys are typically not sent around (i.e., encrypted by other keys), and hence, since they can be corrupted upon generation only, they are either corrupted (i.e., always known) or always unknown. As already mentioned, our case studies (Section 5) demonstrate that

[2]The concept of partnering functions has been used to define security in game-based definitions, which led to discussions whether the obtained security notions are reasonable [4, 5, 3, 9, 13, 17]. Here, we use partnering functions as part of our *criterion* (implicit disjointness) but not as part of the security definition itself; security means realizing an ideal functionality (see Theorem 4).

(b) too is typically satisfied by real-world protocols and can easily be checked. We note that (b) can be interpreted as a specific correspondence assertion, and it might be possible to check (b) using automated techniques, such as CryptoVerif [6].

4.3 The Joint State Composition Theorem Without Pre-Established SIDs

In this section, we present our joint state composition theorem. To be able to prove this theorem, we need to restrict the class of simulators used to prove that $\mathcal{P}\,|\,\mathcal{F}_{\text{crypto}}$ realizes $\mathcal{F}$ in the single-session case. For this purpose, similarly to Section 3.3, we define the following simulation relation, where τ is a valid partnering function for $\mathcal{P}\,|\,\mathcal{F}_{\text{crypto}}$ and $\mathcal{F}$ is a multi-session local-SID functionality: We say that $\mathcal{P}\,|\,\mathcal{F}_{\text{crypto}}$ *single-session realizes* $\mathcal{F}$ *w.r.t.* τ (denoted by $F_{\text{single}}\,|\,\mathcal{P}\,|\,\mathcal{F}_{\text{crypto}} \leq^{\tau} F_{\text{single}}\,|\,\mathcal{F}$) if i) $F_{\text{single}}\,|\,\mathcal{P}\,|\,\mathcal{F}_{\text{crypto}} \leq F_{\text{single}}\,|\,\mathcal{F}$, i.e., according to Definition 1, there exists a simulator Sim_{τ} such that for all $\mathcal{E}$ it holds that $\mathcal{E}\,|\,F_{\text{single}}\,|\,\mathcal{P}\,|\,\mathcal{F}_{\text{crypto}} \equiv \mathcal{E}\,|\,Sim_{\tau}\,|\,F_{\text{single}}\,|\,\mathcal{F}$, and ii) Sim_{τ} is a machine which operators in two stages: Analogously to the simulators defined in Section 3.3, in the first stage Sim_{τ} emulates the system $\mathcal{P}\,|\,\mathcal{F}_{\text{crypto}}$. Just as in Section 3.3, Sim_{τ} enters its second stage, in which Sim_{τ} is unrestricted, if an emulated instance of M_r in $\mathcal{P}$ set its **corrupted** flag to true. In Section 3.3, simulators also entered the second stage if a *session-create* message (addressed to $\mathcal{F}'$) was received. Such messages do not occur here. Instead, whenever activated, Sim_{τ} computes $\tau(\alpha_r)$ for all $r \leq n$, where α_r is the current sequence of configurations of the emulated instance of M_r. If τ signals a session, i.e., $\tau(\alpha_1) = \cdots = \tau(\alpha_n) \neq \bot$, then Sim_{τ} enters its second stage, in which it is unrestricted.

Analogously to Section 3.3, we can observe that the only restriction we put on Sim_{τ} is that it emulates the real protocol in its first stage. As already argued in Section 3.3, this appears to be unavoidable and does not seem to be a restriction in practice.

We are now ready to present our joint state composition theorem, with $\mathcal{F}_{\text{crypto}}$ serving as the joint state. Since our theorem does not assume pre-established SIDs, protocols analyzed using this theorem do not need to be modify/idealize by prefixing SIDs to messages. The usage of our theorem is discussed in more detail in Section 5.

THEOREM 4. *Let* $\mathcal{F}$ *be a multi-session local-SID functionality and let* $\mathcal{P}$ *be a multi-session protocol that uses* $\mathcal{F}_{\text{crypto}}$ *and satisfies implicit disjointness w.r.t.* τ.

If $F_{\text{single}}\,|\,\mathcal{P}\,|\,\mathcal{F}_{\text{crypto}} \leq^{\tau} F_{\text{single}}\,|\,\mathcal{F}$, *then* $\mathcal{P}\,|\,\mathcal{F}_{\text{crypto}} \leq \mathcal{F}$.

PROOF SKETCH. We first construct a machine Q_{τ} which simulates $\mathcal{P}\,|\,\mathcal{F}_{\text{crypto}}$ except that it uses a different copy of $\mathcal{F}_{\text{crypto}}$ for every session (according to τ). Using implicit disjointness, we can show that $\mathcal{E}\,|\,\mathcal{P}\,|\,\mathcal{F}_{\text{crypto}} \equiv \mathcal{E}\,|\,Q_{\tau}$ for every environment $\mathcal{E}$. We then show that Q_{τ} realizes $\mathcal{F}$, using $F_{\text{single}}\,|\,\mathcal{P}\,|\,\mathcal{F}_{\text{crypto}} \leq^{\tau} F_{\text{single}}\,|\,\mathcal{F}$. □

5. APPLICATIONS

In this section, we discuss, using key exchange and secure channels as an example, how Theorems 3 and 4 can be used to analyze protocols in a modular and faithful way. While our discussion focuses on the analysis of properties of real-world security protocols, our theorems should be useful beyond this domain.

5.1 Proving Security of Key Exchange and Secure Channel Protocols

We consider a standard secure channel ideal functionality F_{sc} and an ideal functionality $F_{\text{key-use}}$ for key usability. The latter functionality, which is inspired by the notion of key usability proposed in [14], is new and of independent interest. It is very similar to a standard key exchange functionality. However, parties do not obtain the actual exchanged key but only a pointer to this key. They can then use this key to perform *ideal* cryptographic operations, e.g., encryption, MACing, key derivation, etc., similarly to $\mathcal{F}_{\text{crypto}}$. Compared to the standard key exchange functionality, $F_{\text{key-use}}$ has two big advantages: i) One can reason about the session key (and keys derived from it) still in an *ideal* way, which greatly simplifies the analysis when used in higher level protocols. ii) $F_{\text{key-use}}$ can be realized by protocols which use the session key in the key exchange, e.g., for key confirmation. In what follows, let $\mathcal{F}_{\text{sc}} = \mathcal{F}[F_{\text{sc}}]$ and $\mathcal{F}_{\text{key-use}} = \mathcal{F}[F_{\text{key-use}}]$ denote the multi-session local-SID functionalities of F_{sc} and $F_{\text{key-use}}$, respectively.

To illustrate the use of Theorems 3 and 4, consider, for example, the task of proving that a multi-session protocol Q which is based on a multi-session key exchange protocol $\mathcal{P}$ realizes $\mathcal{F}_{\text{sc}}$, where both Q and $\mathcal{P}$ could be real-world security protocols.

While a proof from scratch would, similarly to proofs in a game-based setting, require involved reduction arguments and would be quite complex, using our framework the proof is very modular, with every proof step being relatively small and simple: First, instead of using the actual cryptographic schemes, $\mathcal{P}$ can use $\mathcal{F}_{\text{crypto}}$ (at least for the operations supported by $\mathcal{F}_{\text{crypto}}$). As a result, for the rest of the proof merely information-theoretic reasoning is needed, often not even probabilistic reasoning, in particular no reduction proofs (at least as far as the operations supported by $\mathcal{F}_{\text{crypto}}$ are concerned). The remaining proof steps are to show: i) $\mathcal{P}\,|\,\mathcal{F}_{\text{crypto}}$ satisfies implicit disjointness, ii) $\mathcal{P}\,|\,\mathcal{F}_{\text{crypto}}$ single-session realizes $\mathcal{F}_{\text{key-use}}$, and iii) $Q\,|\,\mathcal{F}_{\text{key-use}}$ single-session realizes $\mathcal{F}_{\text{sc}}$. (Since, the session key established by $\mathcal{F}_{\text{key-use}}$ can be used for ideal cryptographic operations, the argument for Step iii) is still information-theoretic.) We note that only Step i) needs some (information-theoretic) reasoning on multiple sessions, but only to show implicit disjointness. This is easy, as illustrated by our case studies (see below); the proof often merely needs to consider the security properties of a small fraction of the primitives used in the protocol. Now, by i), ii), and Theorem 4, we obtain $\mathcal{P}\,|\,\mathcal{F}_{\text{crypto}} \leq \mathcal{F}_{\text{key-use}}$. Theorem 3 and iii) imply $Q\,|\,\mathcal{F}_{\text{key-use}} \leq \mathcal{F}_{\text{sc}}$. By Theorem 1 and since $Q \leq Q$, we have $Q\,|\,\mathcal{P}\,|\,\mathcal{F}_{\text{crypto}} \leq Q\,|\,\mathcal{F}_{\text{key-use}}$, and hence, $Q\,|\,\mathcal{P}\,|\,\mathcal{F}_{\text{crypto}} \leq \mathcal{F}_{\text{sc}}$ by transitivity of $\leq$.

5.2 Case Studies

In our case studies (see [22] for details), we consider real-world key exchange protocols, namely IEEE 802.11i, SSH, SSL/TLS, IPsec, and EAP-PSK. We show that these protocols, for which we model the cryptographic core, satisfy implicit disjointness (see below); we also give an example of a (secure) protocol, namely the Needham-Schroeder-Lowe Public-Key Protocol, that does not satisfy implicit disjointness. Step iii) (see above), and hence, with Theorem 3, also $Q\,|\,\mathcal{F}_{\text{key-use}} \leq \mathcal{F}_{\text{sc}}$, is proved for a generic secure channel protocol Q of which many real-world protocols are instances (see [22]). Providing full proofs for Step ii) for the key exchange protocols of our case studies is beyond the scope of this paper. However, ii) partly follows from existing work, from [23] for IEEE 802.11i and from [16] for SSL/TLS. For example, in [16] Gajek et al. showed single-session security of TLS; they use the joint state composition theorem by Canetti and Rabin to obtain security in the multi-session setting, which, however, as discussed only proves security of a modified/idealized version of TLS (see the remarks on TLS at the beginning of Section 4 and Figure 2). Using our theorems and the fact that TLS satisfies implicit disjointness, the result by Gajek et al. now also implies security of the (original) version of TLS in the multi-session setting, without pre-established SIDs prefixed to all plaintexts and signed messages.

		original	*modified*
1.	$C \to S$:	c_1, N_C	c_1, N_C
2.	$S \to C$:	$S, k_S, c_2, N_S,$	$S, k_S, c_2, N_S,$
3.	$C \to S$:	$C, k_C, \{\!\vert PMS \vert\!\}_{k_S}, \text{sig}_{k_C}(\mathit{handshake}),$ $\{F(MS, c_3 \Vert \mathit{handshake})\}_{IKCS,EKCS}$	$C, k_C, \{\!\vert sid, PMS \vert\!\}_{k_S}, \text{sig}_{k_C}(sid, \mathit{handshake}),$ $\{F(MS, c_3 \Vert \mathit{handshake})\}_{IKCS,EKCS}$
4.	$S \to C$:	$\{F(MS, c_4 \Vert \mathit{handshake})\}_{IKSC,EKSC}$	$\{F(MS, c_4 \Vert \mathit{handshake})\}_{IKSC,EKSC}$

Figure 2: The TLS Handshake Protocol (Key Exchange Method: RSA) and its modified version.

For SSL/TLS and SSH, we now show that they satisfy implicit disjointness; for details and the proofs for other protocols see [22].

Implicit Disjointness of SSL/TLS. The cryptographic core of the TLS Handshake Protocol with RSA encryption is depicted in Figure 2 on the left (we consider the variant where the client authenticates itself using digital signatures): N_C and N_S are nonces generated by C and S, respectively; the premaster secret *PMS* is chosen randomly by C and is encrypted under the public key of S ($\{\!\vert PMS \vert\!\}_{k_S}$); $c_0, \ldots, c_4$ are distinct constants; F is a pseudo-random function; the master secret *MS* is derived from *PMS* as follows: $MS = F(PMS, c_0 \Vert N_C \Vert N_S)$; $\{m\}_{k_1,k_2}$ denotes MAC-then-encrypt, i.e., $\{m\}_{k_1,k_2} = \{m, \text{mac}_{k_1}(m)\}_{k_2}$; the symmetric encryption and MAC keys *EKCS*, *EKSC*, *IKCS*, *IKSC* are derived from *MS* using F and the nonces N_C and N_S as a seed; *handshake* stands for the concatenation of all previous messages, that is, $\mathit{handshake} = c_1 \Vert N_C \Vert S \Vert k_S \Vert c_2 \Vert N_S \Vert C \Vert k_C \Vert \{\!\vert PMS \vert\!\}_{k_S}$. In Step 3 of the protocol, the server performs the following test (as soon as a check fails, the whole message is dropped): It first decrypts the first ciphertext (using $\mathcal{F}_{\text{crypto}}$). If successful, it checks that the signature is over the expected message. If so, it verifies the signature $\text{sig}_{k_C}(\mathit{handshake})$ (using $\mathcal{F}_{\text{crypto}}$). If successful, S derives the keys *MS*, *EKCS*, etc. and decrypts the second ciphertext (using $\mathcal{F}_{\text{crypto}}$). If this succeeds, the MAC within the plaintext is verified (using $\mathcal{F}_{\text{crypto}}$). If successful, the test accepts and S continues the protocol.

Modeling this protocol as a multi-session real protocol $\mathcal{P}_{\text{TLS}} = !M_C \,|\, !M_S$ that uses $\mathcal{F}_{\text{crypto}}$ for all cryptographic operations (i.e., public-key and symmetric encryption, key derivation, digital signatures, and MAC) is straightforward. The protocol $\mathcal{P}_{\text{TLS}}$ is meant to realize $\mathcal{F}_{\text{key-use}}$, i.e., after the keys are established, the parties can send encryption and decryption requests to M_C and M_S which are MACed and encrypted under the corresponding keys. Corruption is defined such that the adversary can corrupt the public/private keys of parties (via $\mathcal{F}_{\text{crypto}}$) and can corrupt instances of M_C and M_S when they are created. In particular, the adversary can gain complete control over a party by corrupting her public/private keys and all her instances of M_C and M_S.

We provide a proof sketch that $\mathcal{P}_{\text{TLS}}$ satisfies implicit disjointness (see [22] for details). The proof does not need to exploit security of symmetric encryption. Moreover, the proof merely requires syntactic arguments (rather than probabilistic reasoning or reduction arguments) since we can use $\mathcal{F}_{\text{crypto}}$ for the cryptographic primitives.

The partnering function τ_{TLS} for $\mathcal{P}_{\text{TLS}}$ we use is the obvious one: Let ρ be a run of $\mathcal{E} \,|\, \mathcal{P}_{\text{TLS}} \,|\, \mathcal{F}_{\text{crypto}}$ for some environment $\mathcal{E}$ and α be the projection of ρ to an instance of M_r for some user $(p, lsid, r)$ (where $r \in \{C, S\}$). If $(p, lsid, r)$ is corrupted, then $\tau_{\text{TLS}}(\alpha) := \bot$. Otherwise, if $r = C$ and α contains at least the first two messages of the protocol, then $\tau_{\text{TLS}}(\alpha) := (N_C, N_S)$, where N_S is the server's nonce $(p, lsid, r)$ received and N_C is the nonce $(p, lsid, r)$ generated; analogously for the case $r = S$. It is easy to see that τ_{TLS} is valid for $\mathcal{P}_{\text{TLS}}$ because ideal nonces (i.e., nonces generated using $\mathcal{F}_{\text{crypto}}$) do not collide.

THEOREM 5. *$\mathcal{P}_{\text{TLS}}$ satisfies implicit disjointness w.r.t. τ_{TLS}.*

PROOF SKETCH. All symmetric keys (*PMS*, *MS*, *EKSC*, etc.) are, by definition, not explicitly shared: *PMS* is not a pre-shared key but a freshly generated symmetric key; *MS* is derived from *PMS* and all other keys are derived from *MS*. Hence, we only have to show (b) of Definition 2 for public-key encryption and digital signatures. More precisely, the only relevant cases are when the server performs a decryption request with k_S (to obtain *PMS*) or when it performs a verification request to verify the signature of the client.

We now consider the former case (decryption request with k_S); the latter follows a similar (even simpler) argumentation. In this proof sketch, we only consider the case where the server which makes the decryption request is uncorrupted and where the key k_C he received is uncorrupted (in $\mathcal{F}_{\text{crypto}}$) as well. (We refer to our technical report [22] for the case of corruption. The argument there requires a more precise description of our protocol and corruption model than what we can present in this extended abstract.)

So, let us assume that an uncorrupted instance of the server, say $\hat{M}_S$, performed an accepted and ideal decryption request. Let N_C be the nonce $\hat{M}_S$ received, let N_S be the nonce generated by $\hat{M}_S$, let k_S be its public key, let k_C be the public key received, and *ct* be the ciphertext received (containing *PMS*) and on which $\hat{M}_S$ performed the decryption request under consideration. Since the decryption request is accepted, by the definition of the test the server performs, we know that the *handshake* message has the required format and the signature verified. From this we can conclude that an uncorrupted instance made a signing request to $\mathcal{F}_{\text{crypto}}$ with (a pointer to) the private key of k_C and the message *handshake*; a corrupted instance would not have had access to an uncorrupted signing key. This instance must be in role C (so say the instance is $\hat{M}_C$), since uncorrupted server instances do not produce signatures. Since *handshake* contains N_C and N_S, we know that these are the nonces generated and received, respectively, by $\hat{M}_C$. Consequently, $\hat{M}_C$ and $\hat{M}_S$ are partners according to τ_{TLS}. Since the ciphertext *ct* and the public key k_S are contained in *handshake*, it follows that $\hat{M}_C$ must have encrypted *PMS* under k_S and obtained the ciphertext *ct* from $\mathcal{F}_{\text{crypto}}$. Hence, we have shown, as desired, that the partner $\hat{M}_C$ of $\hat{M}_S$ has issued the corresponding encryption request. □

Implicit Disjointness of SSH. The cryptographic core of the key exchange protocol of SSH—for which we show implicit disjointness—is depicted in Figure 3, with $K = g^{xy}$ and $sid = H(N_C, N_S, k_S, g^x, g^y, K)$, where H is a hash function. The symmetric encryption and MAC keys *EKCS*, *EKSC*, *IKCS*, *IKSC* are derived from K using H and *sid* as a seed. (The details are not relevant for proving implicit disjointness.) By $\{m\}_{k_1,k_2}$ we denote encrypt-and-MAC, i.e., $\{m\}_{k_1,k_2} = \{m\}_{k_2}, \text{mac}_{k_1}(m)$. The formal model of SSH as a multi-session real protocol $\mathcal{P}_{\text{SSH}} = !M_C \,|\, !M_S$ is similar to the one for TLS. However, $\mathcal{P}_{\text{SSH}}$ only uses $\mathcal{F}_{\text{crypto}}$ for digital signatures; all other cryptographic operations (i.e., encryption, MAC, hashing) are carried out by M_C and M_S itself because $\mathcal{F}_{\text{crypto}}$ does not support Diffie-Hellman key exchange yet, and hence, K (and all derived keys) cannot be a key in $\mathcal{F}_{\text{crypto}}$. Still, in the proof that $\mathcal{P}_{\text{SSH}}$ satisfies implicit disjointness, we only need to do a reduction argument to the collision resistance of the hash function, since $\mathcal{P}_{\text{SSH}}$ uses $\mathcal{F}_{\text{crypto}}$

1.	$C \to S$:	c_1, N_C
2.	$S \to C$:	c_2, N_S
3.	$C \to S$:	g^x
4.	$S \to C$:	$k_S, g^y, \mathrm{sig}_{k_S}(sid)$
5.	$C \to S$:	$\{C, k_C, \mathrm{sig}_{k_C}(sid, C, k_C)\}_{IKCS,EKCS}$
6.	$S \to C$:	$\{\text{"success"}\}_{IKSC,EKSC}$

Figure 3: The SSH Key Exchange Protocol.

for digital signatures and security of the encryption scheme, the MAC scheme, or the Diffie-Hellman key exchange is not needed.

The partnering function τ_{SSH} for $\mathcal{P}_{\text{SSH}}$ is the obvious one: It is defined similarly to TLS except that the SID is $sid = H(N_C, N_S, k_S, g^x, g^y, K)$ instead of (N_C, N_S). To show that it is valid, we need that the hash function is collision resistant; alternatively, one could define $sid = (N_C, N_S)$, in which case collision resistance is not needed to show that τ_{SSH} is valid, but then collision resistance would be necessary to show implicit disjointness. With τ_{SSH}, implicit disjointness of $\mathcal{P}_{\text{SSH}}$ follows very easily since *sid* is part of every signature.

THEOREM 6. *$\mathcal{P}_{\text{SSH}}$ satisfies implicit disjointness w.r.t. τ_{SSH}.*

6. REFERENCES

[1] M. R. Albrecht, K. G. Paterson, and G. J. Watson. Plaintext Recovery Attacks against SSH. In *S&P 2009*, pages 16–26. IEEE Computer Society, 2009.

[2] B. Barak, Y. Lindell, and T. Rabin. Protocol Initialization for the Framework of Universal Composability. Technical Report 2004/006, Cryptology ePrint Archive, 2004. `http://eprint.iacr.org`.

[3] M. Bellare, D. Pointcheval, and P. Rogaway. Authenticated Key Exchange Secure against Dictionary Attacks. In B. Preneel, editor, *EUROCRYPT 2000*, volume 1807 of *LNCS*, pages 139–155. Springer, 2000.

[4] M. Bellare and P. Rogaway. Entity Authentication and Key Distribution. In D. Stinson, editor, *CRYPTO'93*, volume 773 of *LNCS*, pages 232–249. Springer, 1993.

[5] M. Bellare and P. Rogaway. Provably Secure Session Key Distribution: The Three Party Case. In *STOC'95*, pages 57–66. ACM, 1995.

[6] B. Blanchet. Computationally Sound Mechanized Proofs of Correspondence Assertions. In *CSF 2007*, pages 97–111. IEEE Computer Society, 2007.

[7] R. Canetti. Universally Composable Security: A New Paradigm for Cryptographic Protocols. In *FOCS 2001*, pages 136–145. IEEE Computer Society, 2001.

[8] R. Canetti. Universally Composable Security: A New Paradigm for Cryptographic Protocols. Technical Report 2000/067, Cryptology ePrint Archive, December 2005. `http://eprint.iacr.org`.

[9] R. Canetti and H. Krawczyk. Analysis of Key-Exchange Protocols and Their Use for Building Secure Channels. In B. Pfitzmann, editor, *EUROCRYPT 2001*, volume 2045 of *LNCS*, pages 453–474. Springer, 2001.

[10] R. Canetti and H. Krawczyk. Security Analysis of IKE's Signature-Based Key-Exchange Protocol. In M. Yung, editor, *CRYPTO 2002*, volume 2442 of *LNCS*, pages 143–161. Springer, 2002.

[11] R. Canetti and T. Rabin. Universal Composition with Joint State. In *CRYPTO 2003*, volume 2729 of *LNCS*, pages 265–281. Springer, 2003.

[12] I. Cervesato, A. D. Jaggard, A. Scedrov, J.-K. Tsay, and C. Walstad. Breaking and Fixing Public-key Kerberos. *Inf. Comput.*, 206(2-4):402–424, 2008.

[13] K.-K. R. Choo and Y. Hitchcock. Security Requirements for Key Establishment Proof Models: Revisiting Bellare-Rogaway and Jeong-Katz-Lee Protocols. In C. Boyd and J. M. G. Nieto, editors, *ACISP 2005*, volume 3574 of *LNCS*, pages 429–442. Springer, 2005.

[14] A. Datta, A. Derek, J. C. Mitchell, and B. Warinschi. Computationally Sound Compositional Logic for Key Exchange Protocols. In *CSFW 2006*, pages 321–334. IEEE Computer Society, 2006.

[15] J. P. Degabriele and K. G. Paterson. On the (In)Security of IPsec in MAC-then-Encrypt Configurations. In *CCS 2010*. ACM, 2010.

[16] S. Gajek, M. Manulis, O. Pereira, A. Sadeghi, and J. Schwenk. Universally Composable Security Analysis of TLS. In J. Baek, F. Bao, K. Chen, and X. Lai, editors, *ProvSec 2008*, volume 5324 of *LNCS*, pages 313–327. Springer, 2008.

[17] K. Kobara, S. Shin, and M. Strefler. Partnership in key exchange protocols. In W. Li, W. Susilo, U. K. Tupakula, R. Safavi-Naini, and V. Varadharajan, editors, *ASIACCS 2009*, pages 161–170. ACM, 2009.

[18] H. Krawczyk. SIGMA: The 'SIGn-and-MAc' Approach to Authenticated Diffie-Hellman and Its Use in the IKE-Protocols. In D. Boneh, editor, *CRYPTO 2003*, volume 2729 of *LNCS*, pages 400–425. Springer, 2003.

[19] R. Küsters. Simulation-Based Security with Inexhaustible Interactive Turing Machines. In *CSFW 2006*, pages 309–320. IEEE Computer Society, 2006.

[20] R. Küsters and M. Tuengerthal. Joint State Theorems for Public-Key Encryption and Digitial Signature Functionalities with Local Computation. In *CSF 2008*, pages 270–284. IEEE Computer Society, 2008.

[21] R. Küsters and M. Tuengerthal. Universally Composable Symmetric Encryption. In *CSF 2009*, pages 293–307. IEEE Computer Society, 2009.

[22] R. Küsters and M. Tuengerthal. Composition Theorems Without Pre-Established Session Identifiers. Technical Report 2011/406, Cryptology ePrint Archive, 2011. `http://eprint.iacr.org`.

[23] R. Küsters and M. Tuengerthal. Ideal Key Derivation and Encryption in Simulation-based Security. In A. Kiayias, editor, *CT-RSA 2011*, volume 6558 of *LNCS*, pages 161–179. Springer, 2011.

[24] G. Lowe. An attack on the Needham-Schroeder public-key authentication protocol. *Information Processing Letters*, 56:131–133, 1995.

[25] M. Ray and S. Dispensa. Renegotiating TLS. November 2009. Available at `http://extendedsubset.com/Renegotiating_TLS.pdf`.

[26] P. Rogaway and T. Stegers. Authentication without Elision: Partially Specified Protocols, Associated Data, and Cryptographic Models Described by Code. In *CSF 2009*, pages 26–39. IEEE Computer Society, 2009.

[27] E. Tews and M. Beck. Practical Attacks against WEP and WPA. In D. A. Basin, S. Capkun, and W. Lee, editors, *WISEC 2009*, pages 79–86. ACM, 2009.

Composability of Bellare-Rogaway Key Exchange Protocols*

Christina Brzuska Marc Fischlin
Darmstadt University & CASED

Bogdan Warinschi Stephen C. Williams
University of Bristol

ABSTRACT

In this paper we examine composability properties for the fundamental task of key exchange. Roughly speaking, we show that key exchange protocols secure in the prevalent model of Bellare and Rogaway can be composed with arbitrary protocols that require symmetrically distributed keys. This composition theorem holds if the key exchange protocol satisfies an additional technical requirement that our analysis brings to light: it should be possible to determine which sessions derive equal keys given only the publicly available information.

What distinguishes our results from virtually all existing work is that we do not rely, neither directly nor indirectly, on the simulation paradigm. Instead, our security notions and composition theorems exclusively use a game-based formalism. We thus avoid several undesirable consequences of simulation-based security notions and support applicability to a broader class of protocols. In particular, we offer an abstract formalization of game-based security that should be of independent interest in other investigations using game-based formalisms.

Categories and Subject Descriptors

F.0 [**Theory of Computation**]: General

General Terms

Security, Theory

Keywords

key exchange, Bellare-Rogaway, composition

*A full version of this paper, including all proofs, is available at http://www.eprint.iacr.org/2011/. This work has been supported in part by the European Commission through the ICT Programme under Contract ICT-2007-216676 ECRYPT II. The first two authors were supported by grant 50021949 of the German Academic Exchange Service (DAAD). The second author was also supported by grants Fi 940/2-1 and Fi 940/3-1 of the German Research Foundation (DFG). This work was supported by CASED.

1. INTRODUCTION

1.1 Background

Typical security proofs of modern-day cryptography involve sophisticated reductions based on probabilistic arguments that are error prone and often difficult to verify. One of the few available approaches to make the analysis of complex systems even remotely possible is compositional design and analysis. Here, one concludes the security of a larger system from the security of individual components via general composition principles. This paper is a contribution to this line of research. Our work is focused on the composability of one of the most fundamental cryptographic tasks, secure key exchange.

There are two main approaches to capture security of protocols. One is based on the simulation paradigm such as the universal composition (UC) framework and related models [7, 2, 15]. The other approach uses games to model security. Simulation-based security offers structured, intuitively appealing means for defining security, and often allow to conclude security of composed protocols automatically. At the same time, the resulting frameworks can be complex and involve hard to grasp subtleties. Additionally, the strong security requirements imposed by simulation prevent efficient secure realisations for many important tasks. Furthermore, and in some sense this is the main motivation for the present work, simulation frameworks (e.g. [9]) are often simply not suitable for the analysis of existing protocols of practical importance, mainly because such protocols do not meet the highly stringent requirements that simulation-based security demands. The only remaining alternative is to then use game-based formalisms (e.g. [5, 6, 3, 8, 17]). Their requirements are less onerous, yet the level of security for the keys that are derived is usually quite high: they are indistinguishable from random keys. Unfortunately, while we have a good understanding of the level of security that standard game-based models entail for key-exchange protocols when these are executed stand-alone, there are no rigorously demonstrated —or even defined!— guarantees for their composition with other tasks. Our work fills this gap.

In this paper we study composability of key exchange protocols with arbitrary tasks that use symmetric keys. A typical application example is the use of a key exchange protocol to establish symmetric keys used later in a secure channel protocol. The security definitions that we consider, for both stand alone and composed protocol are within the traditional game-based setting. Our main result is a theorem that allows composition of key exchange with arbitrary protocols that use symmetrically shared keys. Perhaps surprisingly, the main requirement on the key exchange is a mild refinement of the original security definition by Bellare and Rogaway [4] (BR model). We note that one can, for instance, easily incorporate the eCK derivative [17] of the BR model into our framework by adapting the corresponding stronger corruption type accordingly. An additional requirement for our composition result is a technical condition on matching sessions which we show to be (in a formal sense) necessary.

1.2 Summary of results

ABSTRACT FRAMEWORK FOR GAMES. We first develop a framework for specifying cryptographic games (for two-party protocols). Our formalization reflects standard definitional ideas in cryptography that originate in the work of Bellare and Rogaway [4]. Here, an adversary controls all communication between the participating parties and interacts with the algorithms that define the protocol, through an interface offered by the cryptographic game. The goal of the adversary is to trigger a specific event that the game considers "bad". We model this goal as a predicate on the complete state of the execution. This abstract way of defining security is sufficiently flexible to generalize most, if not all, existing game-based security definitions. Our abstract model for games should be of independent interest.

SECURITY OF KEY EXCHANGE PROTOCOLS. Interestingly, the crucial security notion we demand from the key exchange protocol is based on the original proposal of Bellare and Rogaway [4], as refined by Blake-Wilson et al. [6] for the public-key setting. Recall, their model ensures that an adversary cannot distinguish keys derived via the protocol from random strings (selected from the key space). Additionally, they identify the two local "partner" sessions involved in an execution of the protocol via the concept of matching conversations. They demand that at most two sessions can have the same matching conversation. As a stepping stone towards our result we show how to cast the BR security definition in our abstract framework. Our formulation maintains the key-indistinguishability requirement. However, we pair local sessions via the more general concept of session identifiers as introduced by Bellare, Pointcheval and Rogaway [3]. These identifiers are generated on the fly during protocol execution and match more closely how real world protocols define their partners. For example the TLS [13] and SSH protocols [19] both have session identifiers set during the course of execution. We demand that at most two local sessions agree on the same (global) session identifier.

PUBLIC SESSION MATCHING. In the above definition we match sessions via session identifiers that are locally computed on the fly. Thus, they may be unknown to third parties, in particular to the adversary. However, we were only able to prove general composability for key exchange protocols which satisfy an additional technical requirement, namely the existence of a *public session matching algorithm.* Roughly, such an algorithm is able to determine which sessions have derived equal session identifiers, only using public information. Note this is not as restrictive as it may seem: protocols where sessions are defined via matching conversations [4] fall into this class. Therefore, session matching is more of a functional requirement than a security requirement.

DEFINING COMPOSITION. We compose key exchange protocols with arbitrary two-party *symmetric key protocols*, i.e., protocols, whose execution relies on a shared secret key.

Given a game G_{ke} defining the security of the key exchange protocol, ke, and given the game G_π defining the security of the symmetric key protocol, π, we generically define the execution of the composed protocol, and a game $G_{\mathsf{ke};\pi}$, capturing its security. In the composed protocol, each session first runs an instance of the key exchange protocol and then uses the derived key to execute the symmetric key protocol while not using any other information from the key exchange stage. The game $G_{\mathsf{ke};\pi}$ allows the adversary to interact with ke and π simultaneously: at any given point some sessions may be in the key exchange stage, while others are in the symmetric key protocol stage. The security requirement on the composition is inherited from G_π: the adversary wins against the composition if it breaks the symmetric key protocol. The game $G_{\mathsf{ke};\pi}$ does not place any explicit security requirement on the key exchange protocol.

COMPOSITION THEOREM. Our main result is that BR-secure key exchange protocols, for which a session matching algorithm exists, can be securely composed with arbitrary symmetric key protocols. In practice, assume you want to run a key exchange protocol to use the keys for a secure channel. To conclude security of the entire protocol, one would usually analyse the protocol as a whole. Instead, with our theorem, one can now analyse the two components seperately, and more importantly, if one uses an existing provable secure key exchange protocol (i.e. BR-secure), one can simply re-use the existing security analysis without further investigation; and the same applies to secure channels.

We notice that secure channel protocols usually fall into the class of so-called *single session reducible* protocols, a notion we introduce in this paper. For protocols in this class, it suffices to analyse a single session of the protocol and security for concurrent execution follows automatically.

Overall, in the case of a composed protocol consisting of a key exchange part and a secure channel part, the analysis boils down to a single session analysis of the secure channel protocol and a (possibly existing) BR-analysis of the key exchange part. For clarity, we emphasise that single session reducibility is not a requirement of our framework, but a useful tool to shorten a complex analysis if applicable.

We now take a closer look at the public session matching we assume to exist: one might think that this requirement is a necessary artifact for our proof to work. However, this is (provably) not the case. In the full version, we show that if a key exchange protocol is composable with arbitrary symmetric key protocols and security is shown via a specific kind of black-box reduction, then (a weak form of) a session matching algorithm exists. We emphasize that the public session matching is only on the key exchange protocol, and *not* on the subsequent uses of the key; hence, it does not impact the protocol with which the key exchange is composed.

We finally note that it may look impossible to provide secure composition of key exchange protocols with *arbitrary* symmetric key protocols. The seemingly intuitive counter argument is that, if the symmetric key protocol "misbehaves" in the sense that it duplicates some steps of the key exchange protocol in a bad way, then the composition would easily become insecure. As an example assume that the key exchange somehow involves (in a secure way) a step in which a nonce is encrypted under the new session key, and that the first step of the subsequent protocol is that a party, exceptionally receiving such an encrypted message, would immediately disclose the session key. Then replaying the previous message from the key exchange phase should violate the security of the overall protocol. This line of reasoning, however, is incorrect. Key indistinguishability of a key exchange protocol essentially says that one can replace the actual key by an independent random key, more or less decoupling the two phases. This is even true in presence of key leakage in the symmetric key protocol, as such leakage can be already captured in the Bellare-Rogaway model through special key reveals the adversary can enforce. This implies that the "misbehaving" symmetric key protocol either contradicts the indistinguishability of the key exchange protocol, or that the duplication of steps is harmless because the derived key is independent of the information flow in the key exchange phase. Carrying out this argument formally requires some care, especially with the session matching, but our theorem shows that general composition indeed holds.

1.3 Related work

The work of Canetti and Krawczyk on session-key (SK) security [8, 9] is probably closest in spirit and motivation with ours. They spell out why game based techniques may sometime be preferable to simulation based ones. Their formalization of SK security uses game-based techniques (explicitly avoiding the simulation paradigm) and provides a limited form of composition: SK-secure protocols can be composed with secure channels. Notice that this result is specific to secure channels and does not apply to other tasks.

In follow-up work Canetti and Krawczyk obtain more general composability properties for the SK-security notion [9]. The approach is however not direct: they show that protocols that satisfy a variant of SK-security implement, in a UC sense an ideal functionality for key exchange. They therefore conclude that SK-security is composable. The crucial difference between this composition result and ours is the composability properties that SK-security enjoys are still obtained (indirectly) via a simulation-based framework (and thus inherit the associated problems). Furthermore, the equivalence with UC key exchange functionality is imperfect. One either requires that protocols conform to a particular form (requirement not met by practical protocols), or equivalence is proven with respect to a weaker version of UC.

Shoup presents a security framework for key exchange which resembles the BR model, even though it is cast as a simulation-based approach [18]. Shoup takes into account protocol interference of the subsequent symmetric key protocol with the key exchange protocol. That is, his notion of a secure key exchange protocol requires key indistinguishability in presence of arbitrary applications using the keys. Still, his model does not allow to reason about the security of the composed protocol, i.e., when the symmetric key protocol uses keys derived from the key exchange protocol.

The work of Datta et al. [11] is also aimed at compositional analysis of protocols. They use the logical framework called *Protocol Compositional Logic* [12]. One can regard this line of research as an effort to add some structure to a game-based formalism. In this case, the structure is in the form of an additional layer of logical formalism: formulas in the logic express security properties specified in a game-based framework. By working directly within the game-based framework we present a more general framework where the language for specifying protocols is left unspecified. We therefore impose no restrictions on the primitives used in the construction of our protocols. In contrast, adding new primitives to the formalism of [11] would require re-proving the validity of many of the axioms and inference rules from scratch.

Recent works get around some of the technical issues that make the UC framework non-applicable to practical protocols. For example Küsters and Tuengerthal [16] eliminated the need for pre-establish session identifiers. However, some of the other problems (e.g., the limitation to static corruption) still seems to present an insurmountable obstacle.

2. PROTOCOLS

Games are a standard modelling approach for security of schemes. In such a game, an arbitrary adversary interacts with the algorithms that define the protocol, via a set of queries that capture the use of the protocol in a real system. The adversary sends queries to the game, which computes responses using the algorithms under attack. The adversary tries to trigger an event which the game deems bad.

In this section we first give a general abstract definition for cryptographic games and then specialise it in two ways. First we explain how key exchange is an instance of our abstract framework. Then we identify a class of protocols, which we call "symmetric key protocols".

IDENTITIES. We fix an integer n_i of size polynomial in the security parameter. Identities, used to model the users of a system, are identified by some integer i, with $0 \leq i < n_i$.

PROTOCOLS. A protocol is a pair of algorithms (kg, ξ), where kg is a randomized key generation algorithm taking as input the security parameter and outputting keys from some key space. The algorithm ξ is the algorithm executed locally by a party that executes the protocol.

Local sessions of a protocol are identified by *local session identifiers* $\mathsf{lsid} \in \mathbb{Z} \times \mathbb{Z} \times \mathbb{Z}$, where the local identifier $\mathsf{lsid} = (i, j, k)$ refers to the k-th local session of the identity i, where the intended partner identity is j. These identifiers are only for bookkeeping. They allow the adversary to uniquely identify each session within the game and are not used by the protocol.

GAMES. Formally, a game is a probabilistic Turing machine with an input tape to receive queries from the adversary, an output tape to return responses to the adversary, a random tape and internal state. The internal state consists of the following:

- LSID: The set of all local session identifiers valid for use within the game. This set is assumed to be hardwired in the model.
- $\mathsf{SST} : \mathsf{LSID} \to \{0,1\}^*$: This function provides *session state* information for a given session $\mathsf{lsid} \in \mathsf{LSID}$. Session state information is specific to the type of protocol being executed and usually denotes user-specific data.
- $\mathsf{LST} : \mathsf{LSID} \to \{0,1\}^*$: The *local session state* is the state for a specific session containing the game-relevant variables for this session.
- $\mathsf{EST} \in \{0,1\}^*$: The game *execution state* stores information needed for the execution model which is not used on a session-by-session basis. For example this may contain long term keys of identities.
- $\mathsf{MST} \in \{0,1\}^*$: The *model state* for the security requirement being modeled provides information to the game which is not session specific. For example this may be some bit which the adversary is attempting to discover.

Many previous models for protocols do not separate the session state and local session state. We do this to provide a clear boundary between variables used and updated by the protocol's algorithm and those used by the game to model various security requirements. For example, the session state may contain the session key computed by running a key exchange algorithm, while the local session state would consist of flags to mark individual sessions as corrupted or revealed. Naturally, this local session information shall neither be used by, nor be available to the algorithm that defines the behaviour of a session. Note, although we require the internal state to consist of these components, one may still model any arbitrary game via these requirements: if any arbitrary variable is used directly by the protocol it is stored in either SST or EST, otherwise it is stored in LST or MST. For example, if the game's security requirement required a history of all queries made, this would be stored in MST.

Consequently we use two setup algorithms for initialising these two separate sets of state within the game. The first initialises the state specific to the execution model of the protocol, while the second initialises the state used for the security requirement being modelled.

- (SST, EST) $\leftarrow$ setupE(LSID, kg, 1^η): Initialises the session state and game execution state, where kg is the protocol's key generation algorithm and 1^η is the security parameter.
- (LST, MST) $\leftarrow$ setupG(LSID, SST, EST, 1^η): Initialises the local session state and model state.

An adversary is a probabilistic polynomial time algorithm that interacts with a game through a finite number of well defined queries in a set $\mathcal{Q}$. The game processes each query in a given way, i.e., according to its *behaviour*, the algorithm χ, which runs on the internal game state and the query provided; a response is then passed back to the adversary. The game behaviour χ makes calls to underlying protocol algorithms, i.e. for a query to a left-or-right oracle in a typical encryption game, χ computes the appropriate response with the help of the underlying encryption algorithm.

As usual, not all queries are valid at all points within a game's execution. We model this possibility via a predicate, **Valid**, which the game tests each time it receives a query. The **Valid** predicate takes as input the entire game state and the query received; either true or false is returned, indicating whether the game processes or ignores the query. It is required that all **Valid** predicates check that any local session identifiers are in the set LSID, and if a query has no specified **Valid** predicate we assume this is the only check made. Throughout the paper we give only informal descriptions for all **Valid** predicates. However the formal descriptions are available in the full version of this paper.

When the game receives a query $q \in \mathcal{Q}$ it executes in the following way:

If **Valid**(q, (LSID, SST, LST, EST, MST)) returns false then do nothing and return invalid to the adversary.
Else ((SST′, LST′, EST′, MST′), response) $\leftarrow \chi(q$, (LSID, SST, LST, EST, MST), (kg, ξ), 1^η), set SST $\leftarrow$ SST′, LST $\leftarrow$ LST′, EST $\leftarrow$ EST′, MST $\leftarrow$ MST′ and return response to the adversary.

Definition 1. *A game G is a Turing machine parameterised by* (kg, ξ) *maintaining state* (LSID, SST, LST, EST, MST) *with setup algorithms* setupE, setupG, *some behavior χ and predicates defined by* **Valid**.

The set of queries, $\mathcal{Q}$, always includes a Send query, taking as input lsid $\in$ LSID and message msg $\in \{0,1\}^*$. Typically for a Send query, the behaviour χ executes the algorithm ξ on the local session state of session lsid and message msg. This algorithm then returns an updated session state and a response to be passed back to the adversary. Formally this is defined as follows; note for brevity we omit the full notation of χ taking as input the game's state, and assume this implicitly.

Send(lsid, msg):
  SST′ $\leftarrow$ SST
  (sst′, response) $\leftarrow \xi$(SST(lsid), msg)
  SST′(lsid) $\leftarrow$ sst′
  Return ((SST′, LST, EST, MST), response).

The Send query is used to allow the adversary to simulate messages being sent over a network. It receives back a response which is computed by running the protocol algorithm. This gives the adversary complete control over the network so it can alter, delay, create or delete messages.

The goal of the adversary is to trigger some event which is deemed "bad", i.e. the adversary has in some sense broken the security of the protocol. In order to test for such an event there exists a predicate P associated to the game G which is an algorithm of the form $b \leftarrow$ P(LSID, SST, LST, EST, MST), where $b \in \{0,1\}$, and $b = 1$ if and only if the adversary has succeeded in its goal.

The entire process of the adversary interacting with the game, through to the predicate being applied, is called the *experiment*, which is executed in the following way.

- The game runs (SST, EST) $\leftarrow$ setupE(LSID, kg, 1^η) and (LST, MST) $\leftarrow$ setupG(LSID, SST, EST, 1^η).
- The adversary now proceeds to send queries from the set $\mathcal{Q}$ to the game.
- When the adversary terminates the predicate $b \leftarrow$ P(LSID, SST, LST, EST, MST) is run.
- Output b.

Note that the game may pass some information of the initialisation phase to the adversary, like the users' public keys, by introducing a special query to $\mathcal{Q}$ which can be made only once, at the beginning.

We write $\mathrm{Exp}^G_{\pi,\mathcal{A}}(1^\eta)$ for the experiment where $\mathcal{A}$ is the adversary, π is the protocol and G is the game. We write $\mathrm{Exp}^G_{\pi,\mathcal{A}}(1^\eta) = b$ for the event that the predicate P associated to G outputs bit b. Note that our notion of protocols and games is general enough to subsume distinct protocols and their games under a single one, with the parties using some identifier to address different sub protocols, and usually demanding that the adversary only needs to win some of the games to break the composed game. This is particularly interesting for our composition theorem, because it immediately allows one to conclude security even if pairs of parties subsequently run different protocols.

3. KEY EXCHANGE PROTOCOLS

A key exchange protocol allows two local sessions, which use long term keys of identities, to agree upon a short term session key. We consider identities who have asymmetric long term keys. (The case of symmetric long term keys can be done analogously.) In order to "partner" two sessions we use the notion of a session identifier value. This value is computed by the key exchange protocol. Using a session identifier still allows one to base partnering on notions such as matching conversation as done by Bellare et al. [4]; using the message transcript one can achieve a similar, while not equivalent notion. Partnered sessions are required to compute the same session key, and this session key must be indistinguishable from random. Further, as we consider two party protocols at most two sessions should ever share the same session identifier.

The session identifier is distinct to the local session identifier lsid. The former is computed by the key exchange algorithm to determine which sessions are partners, whilst the latter is simply a unique label for the adversary to address queries to a particular session.

We assume that when a key exchange protocol session agrees upon or rejects a key, the adversary knows this has taken place. We require this property explicitly, but one can see that in the models of [4, 6], by sending a 'Reveal' query after every 'Send' query it is possible for an adversary to learn when sessions accept or reject a key.

To model the above requirements of a key exchange protocol we introduce two security games. The first requirement, secrecy, is modelled using the methods of Bellare-Rogaway security: the adversary chooses a session of the game and receives either a random key or the real session key agreed. It wins the game if it determines correctly with which it was provided. We model only protocols that provide forward security, i.e. if a long term key is corrupted by an adversary, any session keys (including those computed using the corrupted long term key) already agreed will still be considered secure. [1] The second security game places restrictions on the partnered sessions: The adversary attempts to cause partnered sessions to agree upon different keys, or force at least three sessions to agree upon the same session identifier.

Both security games have the same execution model, and share many of the same characteristics in terms of game state. Therefore we first introduce the common elements and introduce game-specific properties later. In particular, both games share Send, $\mathsf{Corrupt}$ and Reveal queries. The two games have different winning conditions, and the BR-secrecy game allows the adversary the additional Test and Guess queries.

GAME EXECUTION STATE. The execution state for key exchange games consists of a list $\mathcal{L}_{\mathsf{keys}}$ with tuples $(i, pk_i, sk_i, \delta_i)$, where i is some identity, $pk_i \in \{0,1\}^*$ is the public key of the identity i, $sk_i \in \{0,1\}^*$ is the secret key of i and $\delta_i \in \{\mathsf{honest}, \mathsf{corrupted}\}$ denotes whether i has been corrupted by the adversary or not. This model assumes there is some secure PKI to distribute keys to identities.

SESSION STATE. For key exchange protocols the session state for the local session identified by $\mathsf{lsid} = (i, j, k)$ consists of the following:

- $(pk_i, sk_i) \in \{0,1\}^* \times \{0,1\}^*$: This is the long term key pair for the identity i to whom this session belongs.
- $pk_j \in \{0,1\}^*$: This is the public key, for the identity j, who is the intended partner of this session.
- $\mathsf{sid} \in \{0,1\}^* \cup \{\perp\}$: This is the *session identifier* for the session. We say that two sessions are *partners* if they share the same session identifier and $\mathsf{sid} \neq \perp$. Once sid is set to a value different from $\perp$, it may not be changed.

[1] Note that the corruption model is essentially a parameter of our model. One can equally define non-forward secure protocols where the adversary receives the state of parties, or forward-secure protocols where the adversary is allowed to communicate with sessions after corrupting them. If modelled correctly, consistency of the composed game is preserved, and our overall composition result should still holds.

```
setupE(LSID, kg, 1^η):
  L_keys ← [ ]
  For i = 1 to n_i do
    Run (pk_i, sk_i) ← kg(1^η)
    Add (i, pk_i, sk_i, honest) to the list L_keys
  For each (i, j, k) ∈ LSID do
    SST((i, j, k)) ← ((pk_i, sk_i), pk_j, ⊥, ⊥, running, ⊥)
  EST ← L_keys
  Return (SST, EST)
```

Figure 1: The setup algorithm for the execution model of key exchange algorithms.

- $\kappa \in \{0,1\}^* \cup \{\perp\}$: This is the *session key* for the protocol, where $\perp$ indicates no session key has yet been agreed.
- $\gamma \in \{\mathsf{running}, \mathsf{accepted}, \mathsf{rejected}\}$: This provides the current execution state of the protocol, indicating the session's acceptance (or rejection) of a session key. It is required if $\kappa \neq \perp$ then $\gamma = \mathsf{accepted}$ and if $\gamma = \mathsf{accepted}$ then $\mathsf{sid} \neq \perp$. Furthermore if $\gamma \neq \mathsf{running}$ then execution for this session has "finished", therefore no further updates to the session state are allowed.
- $\mathsf{sinfo} \in \{0,1\}^* \cup \{\perp\}$: This is any *additional session state* required for specific key exchange protocols.

Note, these requirements mean, in the final step of a key exchange protocol (in response to a Send query), the value κ is set to some value and γ is set to $\mathsf{accepted}$ before a response is returned to the adversary.

We write $\mathsf{SST}(\mathsf{lsid}) = ((pk_i, sk_i), pk_j, \mathsf{sid}, \kappa, \gamma, \mathsf{sinfo})$ for the session state of the session identified by lsid. For clarity we provide notation for accessing individual elements of the session state. For example we write $\mathsf{SST}(\mathsf{lsid}).\kappa$ for the session key κ of local session lsid. Individual elements of a game's state are also updated via similar notation.

LOCAL SESSION STATE. The local session state for key exchange protocols is composed of:

- $\delta \in \{\mathsf{honest}, \mathsf{corrupted}\}$: Details whether the identity associated to this session was corrupted before the session was completed (i.e. while $\gamma = \mathsf{running}$).
- $\delta_{\mathsf{pnr}} \in \{\mathsf{honest}, \mathsf{corrupted}\}$: Details whether the identity of the partner associated to this session was corrupted before the session was completed.
- $\omega \in \{\mathsf{fresh}, \mathsf{revealed}\}$: Shows if the session key for this session has been revealed to the adversary.

Although we keep track of the value δ_i for each identity within the execution state, keeping track of δ for each session allows sessions that have completed before an identity is corrupted, to continue being thought of as not corrupt. In turn, this is used to model forward secrecy[2]. We write $\mathsf{LST}(\mathsf{lsid}) = (\delta, \delta_{\mathsf{pnr}}, \omega)$ for the local session state of the session lsid.

SETUP. To initialise the games for key exchange protocols the setupE algorithm is used to generate all asymmetric keys for identities. Each session is then initialised with the correct asymmetric keys, while all other variables are initially set to be undefined. This is shown in Figure 1.

QUERIES. For the Send query in key exchange protocol games, we require that the algorithm ξ_{ke} outputs a $\mathsf{response} =$

[2] In forward secure protocols, sessions that accepted a key before the corresponding user gets corrupted are still considered honest after the corruption occurs. When modelling non-forward secure protocols all sessions of a user are considered corrupted when the adversary makes a corruption query for this user.

$\mathsf{Corrupt}(i)$:
  $\mathsf{LST}' \leftarrow \mathsf{LST}$
  For $(i, pk_i, sk_i, \delta_i) \in \mathcal{L}_{\mathsf{keys}}$ do
    $\delta_i \leftarrow$ corrupted
  For all $\mathsf{lsid} \in \mathsf{LSID}$ s.t. $\mathsf{lsid} = (i, *, *)$ do
    //set all running executions of party i to corrupted
    If $\mathsf{SST}(\mathsf{lsid}).\gamma =$ running then $\mathsf{LST}'(\mathsf{lsid}).\delta \leftarrow$ corrupted
  For all $\mathsf{lsid} \in \mathsf{LSID}$ s.t. $\mathsf{lsid} = (*, i, *)$ do
    //set pointer to i in all running partner executions to corrupted
    If $\mathsf{SST}(\mathsf{lsid}).\gamma =$ running then set $\mathsf{LST}'(\mathsf{lsid}).\delta_{\mathsf{pnr}} \leftarrow$ corrupted
  Return $((\mathsf{SST}, \mathsf{LST}', \mathsf{EST}, \mathsf{MST}), sk_i)$
$\mathsf{Reveal}(\mathsf{lsid})$:
  $\mathsf{LST}' \leftarrow \mathsf{LST}$ and $\mathsf{LST}'(\mathsf{lsid}).\omega \leftarrow$ revealed
  Return $((\mathsf{SST}, \mathsf{LST}', \mathsf{EST}, \mathsf{MST}), \mathsf{SST}(\mathsf{lsid}).\kappa)$

Figure 2: The queries for key exchange protocols.

(γ, msg'). This explicitly tells the adversary when a session accepts or rejects a key.

Additionally to the Send query, the adversary may make Corrupt and Reveal queries, formally given in Figure 2. The Corrupt query allows the adversary to take control of all sessions of an identity by receiving its long term secret key. This query marks the identity as corrupt and all sessions of this identity which have not completed are also marked as corrupt. As completed sessions are not set to be corrupt we only consider key exchange protocols which provide forward security. The Reveal query returns the derived session key to the adversary and marks the session as revealed. Using a **Valid** predicate, we restrict adversaries to only make Send queries to un-revealed sessions of non-corrupt users where the key has not been accepted or rejected.

BR-SECRECY GAME. To provide secrecy guarantees of the session key we ask an adversary to decide whether it received the real session key, or a random value, for a session of its choice. It is assumed any random value is drawn from some key distribution $\mathcal{D}$ (often the uniform distribution for bit strings of length $|\kappa|$). We write $\kappa \xleftarrow{\$} \mathcal{D}$ for the value of κ drawn randomly from the distribution $\mathcal{D}$. We call this game the BR-secrecy game and use the execution model of key exchange protocols as described so far. We now set out the additional details of the model for the secrecy property.

The model state for the BR-secrecy game contains two bits, $b_{\mathsf{test}} \in \{0,1\}$ and $b_{\mathsf{guess}} \in \{0,1,\perp\}$ along with a session identifier $\mathsf{lsid}_{\mathsf{tested}} \in \mathsf{LSID} \cup \{\perp\}$. We write $\mathsf{MST} = (b_{\mathsf{test}}, b_{\mathsf{guess}}, \mathsf{lsid}_{\mathsf{tested}})$ for the model state in the BR-secrecy game. The bit b_{test} determines whether the adversary is given the real session key, or random value in response to the Test query.[3] The bit b_{guess} stores the adversary's guess for the value of b_{test}. The session identifier $\mathsf{lsid}_{\mathsf{tested}}$ is the local session identifier for which the Test query was made.

The algorithm setupG initialises the model state by selecting the random value for b_{test}. Upon initialisation b_{guess} and $\mathsf{lsid}_{\mathsf{tested}}$ are undefined, so set to $\perp$. This is shown in Figure 3.

There are two additional queries required to model the BR-security of a key exchange protocol, namely Test and Guess. The Test query provides the adversary with either the real session key for a given session, or a random value. The Guess query provides the game with the adversary's guess to the value b_{test}. The queries are given in Figure 3.

In order to prevent trivial attacks, we place restrictions

[3] We assume that the adversary only makes a single Test query. Security with respect to many Test queries then follows by a hybrid argument [4].

$\mathsf{setupG}(\mathsf{LSID}, \mathsf{SST}, \mathsf{EST}, 1^\eta)$:
  Draw $b_{\mathsf{test}} \xleftarrow{\$} \{0,1\}$
  Set $b_{\mathsf{guess}} \leftarrow \perp$, $\mathsf{lsid}_{\mathsf{tested}} \leftarrow \perp$
  For all $\mathsf{lsid} \in \mathsf{LSID}$, $\mathsf{LST}(\mathsf{lsid})$ $\leftarrow$ (honest, honest, fresh)
  Return
  $(\mathsf{LST}, (b_{\mathsf{test}}, b_{\mathsf{guess}}, \mathsf{lsid}_{\mathsf{tested}}))$

$\mathsf{Test}(\mathsf{lsid})$:
  If $\mathsf{MST}.b_{\mathsf{test}} = 0$ then $\kappa \xleftarrow{\$} \mathcal{D}$
  Else set $\kappa \leftarrow \mathsf{SST}(\mathsf{lsid}).\kappa$,
  $\mathsf{MST}' \leftarrow \mathsf{MST}$, $\mathsf{MST}'.\mathsf{lsid}_{\mathsf{tested}} \leftarrow \mathsf{lsid}$
  Return $(\mathsf{SST}, \mathsf{LST}, \mathsf{EST}, \mathsf{MST}'), \kappa$
$\mathsf{Guess}(b)$:
  $\mathsf{MST}' \leftarrow \mathsf{MST}$, $\mathsf{MST}'.b_{\mathsf{guess}} \leftarrow b$
  Return $(\mathsf{SST}, \mathsf{LST}, \mathsf{EST}, \mathsf{MST}')$, okay

Figure 3: Model state setup for BR-secrecy game and the Test and Guess queries for the BR-secrecy game.

$\mathsf{P_{BR}}(\mathsf{LSID}, \mathsf{SST}, \mathsf{LST}, \mathsf{EST}, \mathsf{MST})$:
  If $\mathsf{MST}.\mathsf{lsid}_{\mathsf{tested}} = \perp$ then return 0. //No Test query made
  For each $\mathsf{lsid} \in \mathsf{LSID}$ s.t. $\mathsf{SST}(\mathsf{lsid}).\mathsf{sid} = \mathsf{SST}(\mathsf{MST}.\mathsf{lsid}_{\mathsf{tested}}).\mathsf{sid}$ do
    //Test for exposure of partner key or key itself
    If $\mathsf{LST}(\mathsf{lsid}).\omega =$ revealed then return 0.
  If $\mathsf{MST}.b_{\mathsf{test}} \neq \mathsf{MST}.b_{\mathsf{guess}}$ then return 0. //Wrong guess
  Else return 1.

Figure 4: Predicate for the BR-secrecy game.

on the admissibility of the Test query. An adversary is not allowed to Test a session which is corrupt, has not accepted, or whose partner is corrupt, or to test more than a session. In these cases, the **Valid** predicate for the Test query returns false. Note that these cases are publicly verifiable. The **Valid** predicate checks if a session (or partner session) is corrupt by checking the value of δ or δ_{pnr} stored in the local session state, LST. Moreover, the adversary should not Test a session which is revealed or where the partner session has been revealed. In these cases though, the **Valid** predicate does not return false but instead lets the adversary continue. This is in order to prevent leakage of partnering information through the Test query. The adversary may not be aware this has occurred; however at the end of execution the predicate checks for this, and causes the experiment to be lost if such an action has occurred. We also forbid Reveal queries on the tested session or its partner. Again, the adversary is later declared to lose if such a Reveal query happens (but again without being informed immediately). Furthermore we only allow the adversary one Guess query.

The predicate for the BR-secrecy game checks if the adversary's guess for the value of b_{test} is correct. Furthermore, the predicate causes the adversary to lose the game if the tested session (or its partner) have been revealed. No checks relating to corruption are required, as we only consider protocols which are forward secure; hence if an identity is corrupted after the Test query is made, key indistinguishability should still hold. The predicate $\mathsf{P_{BR}}$ is defined in Figure 4.

We write the BR-secrecy game as $G_{\mathsf{BR},\mathcal{D}}$, where $\mathcal{D}$ is the key distribution from which random keys are chosen during the Test query. Furthermore we denote the game $G_{\mathsf{BR},\mathcal{D}}$ with the secret bit b_{test} as $G^{b_{\mathsf{test}}}_{\mathsf{BR},\mathcal{D}}$.

DEFINITION 2. *We define the advantage of the adversary $\mathcal{A}$ against the BR-secrecy property as*

$$\mathrm{Adv}^{G_{\mathsf{BR},\mathcal{D}}}_{\mathsf{ke},\mathcal{A}}(1^\eta) = \left| \Pr\left[\mathrm{Exp}^{G^0_{\mathsf{BR},\mathcal{D}}}_{\mathsf{ke},\mathcal{A}}(1^\eta) = 0\right] - \Pr\left[\mathrm{Exp}^{G^1_{\mathsf{BR},\mathcal{D}}}_{\mathsf{ke},\mathcal{A}}(1^\eta) = 1\right] \right|$$

where ke *is the key exchange protocol analysed.*

PARTNERING SECURITY GAME. In the partnering security

$\mathsf{P_{sid}}(\mathsf{LSID}, \mathsf{SST}, \mathsf{LST}, \mathsf{EST}, \mathsf{MST})$:
  For each $\mathsf{lsid} = (i, j, k) \in \mathsf{LSID}$ do
    If $\mathsf{SST}(\mathsf{lsid}).\mathsf{sid} \neq \perp$ then for all triples
    $(j', i', k') \in \mathsf{LSID}$ with $\mathsf{SST}((j', i', k')).\mathsf{sid} = \mathsf{SST}(\mathsf{lsid}).\mathsf{sid}$ do
      If $(j', i') \notin \{(i, j), (j, i)\}$ then return 1.
      //distinct intended partners
      If $i = i'$, $j = j'$, $\mathsf{LST}(i, j, k).\delta = \mathsf{LST}(j', i', k').\delta = \mathsf{accepted}$ but
      $\mathsf{SST}(i', j', k').\kappa \neq \mathsf{SST}(\mathsf{lsid}).\kappa$ then return 1. //distinct keys
    If the number of triples $(j', i', k') \in \mathsf{LSID}$ with
    $\mathsf{SST}((j', i', k')).\mathsf{sid} = \mathsf{SST}(\mathsf{lsid}).\mathsf{sid}$ is strictly larger than 2,
    then return 1. //Too many partners
  Return 0.

Figure 5: Predicate for the partnering key exchange game.

$\mathsf{setupG}(\mathsf{LSID}, \mathsf{SST}, \mathsf{EST}, 1^\eta)$:
  For each $\mathsf{lsid} \in \mathsf{LSID}$ set $\mathsf{LST}(\mathsf{lsid}) \leftarrow (\mathsf{honest}, \mathsf{honest}, \mathsf{fresh})$
  Return $(\mathsf{LST}, \perp)$

Figure 6: Model state setup algorithm for BR partnering game.

game the adversary attempts to cause the session identifiers within the game to be considered invalid in some way. This is done by causing more than two sessions to share the same session identifier, making a session accept a key without setting the session identifier, or causing two sessions to hold the same session identifier, but where the intended partner identity of such sessions are incorrect. Moreover, the adversary wins if two sessions have the same session identifier and different keys. All these properties are modelled via the winning condition of the partnering which is defined through $\mathsf{P_{sid}}$, see Figure 5.

The partnering security game requires no model state or additional queries to those required for general execution of a key exchange protocol. The setupG algorithm sets the LST function and leaves the model state undefined. We give the formal description in Figure 6.

The partnering security game is written as G_{sid}, and the advantage of the adversary $\mathcal{A}$ against the partnering security property as

$$\mathrm{Adv}_{\mathsf{ke},\mathcal{A}}^{G_{\mathsf{sid}}}(1^\eta) = \Pr\left[\mathrm{Exp}_{\mathsf{ke},\mathcal{A}}^{G_{\mathsf{sid}}}(1^\eta) = 1\right].$$

Definition 3 (BR-secure protocol). *We call a key exchange protocol* ke *BR-secure w.r.t.* $\mathcal{D}$ *if for all adversaries* $\mathcal{A}$, $\mathrm{Adv}_{\mathsf{ke},\mathcal{A}}^{G_{\mathsf{BR},\mathcal{D}}}(1^\eta)$ *and* $\mathrm{Adv}_{\mathsf{ke},\mathcal{A}}^{G_{\mathsf{sid}}}(1^\eta)$ *are negligible functions in the security parameter.*

Session Matching. For composability, we need an additional property, called *session matching*. Roughly, this means that an eavesdropper on the communication between the BR-adversary and the BR-secrecy game should be able to deduce which sessions are partnered, i.e. at any time, the eavesdropper should be able to produce a list of pairs of all partnered (accepted) sessions. Note that this is trivially satisfied when defining session identifiers through matching conversations. However, when using abstract session identifiers, sid, this need not be the case. For instance, consider a BR-secure key exchange that uses matching conversations as the session identifier. We now transform the protocol as follows: The participants encrypt all messages they send. The session identifiers are now defined as matching conversations *on the plaintexts*. First note that the resulting key exchange protocol is as secure as the original, assuming secure encryption. But the protocol has an interesting property: Assume the encryption scheme is re-randomizable. Then, an eavesdropper on the communication is unable to deduce which sessions between two parties are partnered, as the BR-adversary may re-randomize all messages sent.

$\mathsf{P_{partner}}(\mathsf{LSID}, \mathsf{SST}, \mathsf{LST}, \mathsf{EST}, \mathsf{MST}, \mathsf{LSID_{partner}}, \mathsf{LSID_{single}})$:
  For each $\mathsf{lsid} \in \mathsf{LSID_{single}}$ do
    //Alleged single parties don't have partners
    If $\mathsf{SST}(\mathsf{lsid}).\gamma \neq \mathsf{accepted}$ then return 0.
    Else if there exists $\mathsf{lsid}' \in \mathsf{LSID} \setminus \{\mathsf{lsid}\}$ with $\mathsf{SST}(\mathsf{lsid}').\mathsf{sid} =$
    $\mathsf{SST}(\mathsf{lsid}).\mathsf{sid}$ then return 0.
  For each $(\mathsf{lsid}, \mathsf{lsid}') \in \mathsf{LSID_{partner}}$ do
    //Alleged partners have accepted and are really partnered
    If $(\mathsf{SST}(\mathsf{lsid}).\gamma, \mathsf{SST}(\mathsf{lsid}').\gamma) \neq (\mathsf{accepted}, \mathsf{accepted})$ then return 0.
    If $\mathsf{SST}(\mathsf{lsid}).\mathsf{sid} \neq \mathsf{SST}(\mathsf{lsid}').\mathsf{sid}'$ then return 0.
  For each $\mathsf{lsid} \in \mathsf{LSID}$ do
    //Each accepted session is assigned as single or partnered
    If $\mathsf{SST}(\mathsf{lsid}).\gamma = \mathsf{accepted}$, $\mathsf{lsid} \notin \mathsf{LSID_{single}}$ and for all
    $(\mathsf{lsid}_0, \mathsf{lsid}_1) \in \mathsf{LSID_{partner}}$, one has $\mathsf{lsid}_0 \neq \mathsf{lsid}$ and $\mathsf{lsid}_1 \neq \mathsf{lsid}$
    then return 0.
  Return 1.

Figure 7: Session matching predicate.

We therefore define an efficient session matching algorithm $\mathcal{M}$ which can deduce from the communication between the BR-secrecy adversary and BR-secrecy game which sessions are partnered. Algorithm $\mathcal{M}$ is allowed to see all queries and answers exchanged between a key exchange and an adversary $\mathcal{A}$; this includes all public parameters of the system. The requirement on $\mathcal{M}$ is independent of the winning condition of $\mathcal{A}$ in the game; algorithm $\mathcal{M}$ needs to provide correct matchings constantly.

More formally, a *session matching algorithm* $\mathcal{M}$ for the key exchange protocol is defined as an efficient algorithm that receives all information exchanged between a key exchange game G_{BR} and an adversary $\mathcal{A}$ against G_{BR}. We require that each time the key exchange game sends a response to the adversary $\mathcal{A}$, algorithm $\mathcal{M}$ is able to output two sets $\mathsf{LSID_{partner}}$ and $\mathsf{LSID_{single}}$, where $\mathsf{LSID_{partner}}$ contains pairs $(\mathsf{lsid}_0, \mathsf{lsid}_1)$, and $\mathsf{LSID_{single}}$ consists of session identifiers lsid. We define the predicate $\mathsf{P_{partner}}$ to specify correctness of these sets by checking all pairs $(\mathsf{lsid}_0, \mathsf{lsid}_1)$ are sessions which share the same session identifier, and all identifiers in the set $\mathsf{LSID_{single}}$ are sessions which are currently unpartnered. This is formally described in Figure 7.

Definition 4 (Session matching algorithm). *A session matching algorithm* $\mathcal{M} : \{0,1\}^* \to \{0,1\}^*$ *for a key exchange protocol* ke *is an efficient algorithm such that the following holds for any adversary* $\mathcal{A}$ *playing against* G_{BR}*: After each response of the key exchange game, the algorithm* $\mathcal{M}$ *is given an ordered list of all queries and responses made between* $\mathcal{A}$ *and* $G_{\mathsf{BR},\mathcal{D}}$*, along with the public parameters of the system. Algorithm* $\mathcal{M}$ *then outputs sets* $\mathsf{LSID_{partner}}$ *and* $\mathsf{LSID_{single}}$ *such that, for the current state* $(\mathsf{LSID}, \mathsf{SST}, \mathsf{LST}, \mathsf{EST}, \mathsf{MST})$ *of the game, the sets* $\mathsf{LSID_{partner}}$, $\mathsf{LSID_{single}}$ *always satisfy the predicate* $\mathsf{P_{partner}}(\mathsf{LSID}, \mathsf{SST}, \mathsf{LST}, \mathsf{EST}, \mathsf{MST}, \mathsf{LSID_{partner}}, \mathsf{LSID_{single}})$.

We remark that the idea of a session matching algorithm has already appeared in different forms in the literature. As mentioned above, in the original paper [4] the notion of matching conversations via the communication transcripts (and their order) supports a straightforward session matching algorithm. In [5] Bellare and Rogaway introduce a partner function which resembles our notion of a session matching algorithm, but their function does not need to be efficiently computable. Finally, in [3] the authors require the session identifiers, defining essentially the partners, to be given to the adversary upon acceptance of a session, again yielding a session matching algorithm straightforwardly. As we show in the full version, a weak form of session matching algorithm is in fact necessary to ensure secure composition.

4. SYMMETRIC-KEY PROTOCOLS

We now introduce the class of symmetric key protocols. They use a symmetric session key which is shared between pairs of sessions, i.e. these are the protocols that run after a key agreement protocol has completed. Games for symmetric key protocols allow the adversary to initialise sessions, causing the game to generate a new session key. The adversary can partner two sessions, so that they share the same key. Finally the adversary may choose session keys, and initialise sessions with its chosen key. The latter forces any model to cope with sessions where the key is known to the adversary. For example an adversary should not be considered to have broken the security requirement if it does so against a session for which it has chosen the key. Potentially, the adversary has access to additional queries which depend on the precise requirements of the protocol being modeled.

As for all protocols a symmetric key protocol $\pi = (\mathsf{kg}, \xi)$ consists of a randomized key generation algorithm and protocol algorithm. We write $\mathcal{D}_{\mathsf{kg}}$ as the distribution of keys output from the key generation algorithm. The key generation algorithm of π is used to generate the session keys.

We consider arbitrary protocols π and so the security requirements depend on the protocol being analysed. We now provide the minimum requirements of games for symmetric key protocols.

Game execution state. The game execution state EST is not required for the execution of a symmetric key protocol and so is assumed to be undefined for the duration of execution.

Session state. The session state for symmetric key protocols consists of two variables:

> $\kappa \in \{0,1\}^* \cup \{\bot\}$: This is the symmetric session key for the protocol.
>
> sinfo $\in \{0,1\}^* \cup \{\bot\}$: This is any additional session state required for specific symmetric key protocols.

Local session state. The local session state for symmetric key protocols consists of two variables:

> $\psi \in$ {secret, known}: This denotes whether a key is "known" by the adversary.
>
> lst $\in \{0,1\}^* \cup \{\bot\}$: This contains any other local session state required to model the security required of a symmetric key protocol.

Setup. The setupE algorithm to initialise the session states simply sets all initial values to be undefined, running as given in Figure 8. The setupG algorithm is required to initialise the model state and local session state. The value of ψ in the local session state must be set to secret initially. However as other details of model state and local session state are unknown due to the generic nature of our model, we do not specify the setupG algorithm here.

setupE(LSID, kg, 1^η):	InitP(lsid$_1$, lsid$_2$):
For each lsid $\in$ LSID	SST$'$ $\leftarrow$ SST and LST$'$ $\leftarrow$ LST
set SST(lsid) $\leftarrow (\bot, \bot)$	SST$'$(lsid$_2$) $\leftarrow$ (SST(lsid$_1$).κ, $\bot$)
Return (SST, $\bot$)	LST$'$(lsid$_2$).ψ $\leftarrow$ LST(lsid$_1$).ψ
InitS(lsid):	Return (SST$'$, LST$'$, EST, MST), okay
SST$'$ $\leftarrow$ SST	InitK(lsid, κ):
Run $\kappa \leftarrow$ kg(1^η)	SST$'$ $\leftarrow$ SST and LST$'$ $\leftarrow$ LST
SST$'$(lsid) $\leftarrow (\kappa, \bot)$	SST$'$(lsid) $\leftarrow (\kappa, \bot)$
Return	LST$'$(lsid).ψ $\leftarrow$ known
(SST$'$, LST, EST, MST), okay	Return (SST$'$, LST$'$, EST, MST), okay

Figure 8: Execution state setup algorithm for symmetric key protocols and initialisation queries for symmetric key protocol games.

Queries. There are a minimum of four queries available to the adversary in symmetric protocol games. The Send query is available and behaves as described previously. There are three queries to allow the adversary to initialise sessions. The first, InitS, causes the game to generate a new session key using the key generation algorithm. The second, InitP, partners two sessions by keying the second session with the key of the first one. The third, InitK, allows the adversary to choose a key, which is then used as the session key. This final method of initialisation sets the value of ψ for the current session to known.

These different initialisation methods correspond to what can happen in situations where protocols are composed with key exchange: Sometimes, keys known to the adversary are used in the protocol, so that this needs to be reflected in the syntax. Also, initialisation of two parties never happens simultaneously as parties accept keys one after the other. Now, formally the initialisation queries are given in Figure 8. Additionally to the output okay, the game is allowed to output further information.

Sanity checks are required for the Send, InitS, InitP and InitK queries. The **Valid** condition for Send checks the session key κ has been initialised to some value and can be used. This is the minimum check required and may be augmented for specific games. The checks for initialisation queries ensure that one cannot change the keys for sessions already initialised with a session key. Also when performing the InitP query a check is made that the first session already has a session key.

Predicate. The predicate for the symmetric key protocol game depends on the security model required for the protocol π. However we note it may be necessary for the predicate to take into account the value of ψ in the local session state.

We typically denote the game of the protocol π as G_π. The advantage of an adversary against a symmetric key protocol may depend on some constant Δ (typically 0 for computational games or 1/2 for decisional games) and we define the advantage by

$$\mathrm{Adv}_{\pi,\mathcal{A}}^{G_\pi}(1^\eta) = \left|\Pr\left[\mathrm{Exp}_{\pi,\mathcal{A}}^{G_\pi}(1^\eta) = 1\right] - \Delta\right|.$$

We say that the protocol π is secure with respect to G_π if the advantage $\mathrm{Adv}_{\pi,\mathcal{A}}^{G_\pi}(1^\eta)$ is a negligible function in the security parameter for all PPT adversaries $\mathcal{A}$.

We remark that, at a superficial glance, the session matching algorithm for the key exchange protocol seems to impose some restrictions on the communication privacy or anonymity for the symmetric key protocol. This, however, is not true, as session matching for key exchange does not refer to the actual usage of the derived keys in the subsequent protocol. In particular, the symmetric key protocol and its security game may well cover anonymity-related properties such as the key-hiding property [14, 1], i.e. which of two keys has been used to encrypt messages.

SINGLE SESSION GAME. Usually, game based notions of protocol security require one to consider multiple sessions executed concurrently in order to draw conclusions about the security of the scheme. Notice that when different sessions of the protocol depend only on independent, efficiently samplable states, then it may be possible to reduce the security of the many session scenario to that of a single session. This greatly simplifies the analysis of the protocol and thus allows one to conclude security of the composed protocol more easily.

In symmetric key protocol games, all unknown keys are independent. Thus, in many cases one is able to analyse only the security of a single pair of sessions and, provided this is secure, may conclude the standard multi-session scenario is secure. For example, consider an authenticated channel. An adversary is required to cause any one session to accept some invalid (non-authenticated) message. It is clear, any adversary who is able to do this when there are multiple, concurrently executing sessions, will be able to achieve the same goal when there is only a single run of the protocol being executed. We note that for key exchange protocols, individual runs are not independent due to the session keys depending upon the shared long term asymmetric keys in some way.

The *single session game* is a symmetric key game where the adversary is allowed to query at most one InitS query and one InitP query, i.e. the adversary is given access to at most one pair of "honest" sessions. The **Valid** predicate is modified to restrict the number of InitS and InitP queries. We denote this game by $G_{\pi-1}$. Note that any (multi-session) symmetric key game G_π has a single session version $G_{\pi-1}$. A symmetric key game is called *single session reducible* if its (multi-session) security can be reduced to the security of the corresponding single session game.

DEFINITION 5 (SINGLE-SESSION REDUCIBILITY). *A security game G_π is* single session reducible *if for any PPT adversary $\mathcal{A}$ against G_π where $\mathrm{Adv}_{\pi,\mathcal{A}}^{G_\pi}(1^\eta)$ is non-negligible, then there exists a PPT adversary $\mathcal{B}$ against $G_{\pi-1}$ such that $\mathrm{Adv}_{\pi,\mathcal{B}}^{G_{\pi-1}}(1^\eta)$ is non-negligible.*

We stress again that single-session reducibility is not a prerequisite for our general composition theorem to work. This class of protocols only supports a simpler analysis.

In the full version we treat necessary conditions for single session reducibility. We show that the game of authenticated channels satisfies this condition. Hence, a single session secure authenticated channel remains secure when putting the protocol into a multi-session setting where the symmetric key generation of the protocol is replaced by a BR-secure key exchange protocol.

5. DEFINING COMPOSITION

In this section we discuss the composition of key exchange protocols with symmetric key protocols. The composition of a key exchange protocol and symmetric key protocol is as expected: Intuitively, once a session of the key exchange is successfully finished, the derived key is used to initialise and run a session of the symmetric key protocol. Secondly, we define security for the resulting composition.

$\xi_{\mathsf{ke};\pi}(((pk_i, sk_i), pk_j, \mathsf{sid}, \kappa_{\mathsf{ke}}, \gamma, \mathsf{sinfo}_{\mathsf{ke}}, \kappa_\pi, \mathsf{sinfo}_\pi), \mathsf{msg})$:
  If $\gamma \neq \mathsf{accepted}$ then `//Hand message to key exchange`
    Run $(((pk_i, sk_i), pk_j, \mathsf{sid}', \kappa'_{\mathsf{ke}}, \gamma', \mathsf{sinfo}'_{\mathsf{ke}}), \mathsf{response})$
    $\leftarrow \xi_{\mathsf{ke}}(((pk_i, sk_i), pk_j, \mathsf{sid}, \kappa_{\mathsf{ke}}, \gamma, \mathsf{sinfo}_{\mathsf{ke}}), \mathsf{msg})$
    If $\gamma' = \mathsf{accepted}$ then set $\kappa_\pi := \kappa_{\mathsf{ke}}$
    $(\kappa'_\pi, \mathsf{sinfo}'_\pi) \leftarrow (\kappa_\pi, \mathsf{sinfo}_\pi)$
  If $\gamma = \mathsf{accepted}$ then `//Pass message to symmetric protocol`
    Run $((\kappa'_\pi, \mathsf{sinfo}'_\pi), \mathsf{response}) \leftarrow \xi_\pi((\kappa_\pi, \mathsf{sinfo}_\pi), \mathsf{msg})$
    $(\mathsf{sid}', \kappa'_{\mathsf{ke}}, \gamma', \mathsf{sinfo}'_{\mathsf{ke}}) \leftarrow (\mathsf{sid}, \kappa_{\mathsf{ke}}, \gamma, \mathsf{sinfo}_{\mathsf{ke}})$
  Return $(((pk_i, sk_i), pk_j, \mathsf{sid}', \kappa'_{\mathsf{ke}}, \gamma', \mathsf{sst}'_{\mathsf{ke}}, \kappa'_\pi, \mathsf{sst}'_\pi), \mathsf{response})$

Figure 9: Algorithm for composed protocol, using ξ_{ke} and ξ_π.

5.1 Syntax of composed protocols

Given the key exchange protocol $\mathsf{ke} = (\mathsf{kg}_{\mathsf{ke}}, \xi_{\mathsf{ke}})$ and the symmetric key protocol $\pi = (\mathsf{kg}_\pi, \xi_\pi)$ we write the composed protocol as $\mathsf{ke};\pi = (\mathsf{kg}_{\mathsf{ke};\pi}, \xi_{\mathsf{ke};\pi})$. The key generation algorithm of the composed protocol generates the (long-term) keys for the key exchange protocol, so we set $\mathsf{kg}_{\mathsf{ke};\pi} = \mathsf{kg}_{\mathsf{ke}}$. We now detail the construction of the composed protocol's algorithm, namely $\xi_{\mathsf{ke};\pi}$.

COMPOSED ALGORITHM. Recall, a session of the key exchange protocol (resp. symmetric key protocol) executes by running the algorithm ξ_{ke} (resp. ξ_π). We describe a *composed algorithm* $\xi_{\mathsf{ke};\pi}$, which, for each session, first runs using ξ_{ke}, and upon a session key being accepted, then runs using ξ_π. To decide which sub-algorithm to call, the composed algorithm $\xi_{\mathsf{ke};\pi}$ examines the value γ. If the key exchange session has not yet accepted ($\gamma \neq \mathsf{accepted}$) it calls ξ_{ke}, otherwise it calls ξ_π. In either case, $\xi_{\mathsf{ke};\pi}$ passes only the required variables, and updates the variables of the composed game in a consistent way. Formally, the composed algorithm $\xi_{\mathsf{ke};\pi}$ is defined in Figure 9.

5.2 Syntax of composed games

The composed game, denoted $G_{\mathsf{ke};\pi}$, allows the adversary to simultaneously interact with multiple sessions of the composed protocol; some of these sessions may be executing the key exchange, while others are executing the symmetric key protocol. Note that the adversary's goal within the composed game is to "break" the security of the symmetric key protocol and not the key exchange protocol. We write $\mathrm{Adv}_{\mathsf{ke};\pi,\mathcal{A}}^{G_{\mathsf{ke};\pi}}(1^\eta)$ for its advantage.

We construct the composed game $G_{\mathsf{ke};\pi}$ using the internal state and queries of the games for key exchange and symmetric key protocols. Given the partnering game G_{sid} for the key exchange game and G_π for the symmetric key protocol we use an index notation to distinguish between the states of the different games, e.g. $\mathsf{SST}_{\mathsf{ke}}$ (resp. SST_π) for the session state of the key exchange partnering game (resp. symmetric key protocol game).

GAME STATE. The composed game contains all the internal state of the key exchange and symmetric protocol games. The session state function for the composed game $\mathsf{SST}_{\mathsf{ke};\pi}$ is defined as the pair of key exchange session state, $\mathsf{SST}_{\mathsf{ke}}$, and symmetric key protocol state, SST_π. Thus, $\mathsf{SST}_{\mathsf{ke};\pi} := (\mathsf{SST}_{\mathsf{ke}}, \mathsf{SST}_\pi)$, i.e. for all $\mathsf{lsid} \in \mathsf{LSID}$, $\mathsf{SST}_{\mathsf{ke};\pi}(\mathsf{lsid}) := (\mathsf{SST}_{\mathsf{ke}}(\mathsf{lsid}), \mathsf{SST}_\pi(\mathsf{lsid}))$. Similarly, the composed local session state

$\mathsf{setupE}_{\mathsf{ke};\pi}(\mathsf{LSID}, \mathsf{kg}, 1^\eta)$:
$(\mathsf{SST}_{\mathsf{ke}}, \mathsf{EST}_{\mathsf{ke}}) \leftarrow \mathsf{setupE}_{\mathsf{ke}}(\mathsf{LSID}, \mathsf{kg}_{\mathsf{ke}}, 1^\eta)$
$(\mathsf{SST}_\pi, \perp) \leftarrow \mathsf{setupE}_\pi(\mathsf{LSID}, \mathsf{kg}_\pi, 1^\eta)$
Return $((\mathsf{SST}_{\mathsf{ke}}, \mathsf{SST}_\pi), \mathsf{EST}_{\mathsf{ke}})$
$\mathsf{setupG}_{\mathsf{ke};\pi}(\mathsf{LSID}, (\mathsf{SST}_{\mathsf{ke}}, \mathsf{SST}_\pi), \mathsf{EST}_{\mathsf{ke}}, 1^\eta)$:
$(\mathsf{LST}_{\mathsf{ke}}, \perp) \leftarrow \mathsf{setupG}_{\mathsf{ke}}(\mathsf{LSID}, \mathsf{SST}_{\mathsf{ke}}, \mathsf{EST}_{\mathsf{ke}}, 1^\eta)$
$(\mathsf{LST}_\pi, \mathsf{MST}_\pi) \leftarrow \mathsf{setupG}_\pi(\mathsf{LSID}, \mathsf{SST}_\pi, \mathsf{EST}_\pi, 1^\eta)$
Return $((\mathsf{LST}_{\mathsf{ke}}, \mathsf{LST}_\pi), \mathsf{MST}_\pi)$

Figure 10: Setup algorithms for composed games.

is defined by the pair $\mathsf{LST}_{\mathsf{ke};\pi} := (\mathsf{LST}_{\mathsf{ke}}, \mathsf{LST}_\pi)$. The execution state for the composed game, $\mathsf{EST}_{\mathsf{ke};\pi}$, equals the execution state of the key exchange game, $\mathsf{EST}_{\mathsf{ke}}$, since the execution state of the symmetric key protocol game is always undefined. The model state in the composed game is the model state of the symmetric key protocol game, i.e. $\mathsf{MST}_{\mathsf{ke};\pi} := \mathsf{MST}_\pi$, since the model state for the partnering key exchange game is undefined. When clear from context, we write SST instead of $\mathsf{SST}_{\mathsf{ke};\pi}$ and LST instead of $\mathsf{LST}_{\mathsf{ke};\pi}$.

The session state $\mathsf{SST}(\mathsf{lsid})$ of a session lsid then is a tuple $((pk_i, sk_i), pk_j, \mathsf{sid}, \kappa_{\mathsf{ke}}, \gamma, \mathsf{sinfo}_{\mathsf{ke}}, \kappa_\pi, \mathsf{sinfo}_\pi)$, and the local session state $\mathsf{LST}(\mathsf{lsid})$ of a session lsid is a tuple $(\delta, \delta_{\mathsf{pnr}}, \omega, \psi, \mathsf{lst}_\pi)$. We omit additional brackets one could use to separate $\mathsf{LST}_{\mathsf{ke}}(\mathsf{lsid})$ from $\mathsf{LST}_\pi(\mathsf{lsid})$.

SETUP. To set the composed game's initial state we use the key exchange setup algorithms to initialise the key exchange portions of the composed game's state (e.g. $\mathsf{SST}_{\mathsf{ke}}$), and similarly use the symmetric key protocol's setup algorithm for the remainder, see Figure 10.

QUERIES. The adversary has similar abilities as previously described. It can send messages to sessions, corrupt long-term keys as well as interact with the symmetric key protocol in any way described by the game G_π (excluding the InitS, InitP and InitK queries). Notice that we do not allow the adversary access to the Reveal query from the key exchange game in the composed game. The Reveal query was used in the BR-secrecy game to ensure if a session key was compromised, it did not compromise the BR-security of other keys, and to model potential key leakage through the deployment in a potential subsequent protocol (which is now actual in our case). However, we are now considering the security of the symmetric key protocol (in the composed setting), thus the Reveal query is no longer allowed, unless the symmetric key protocol itself provides an equivalent query.

We modify the Send query slightly to set the value of ψ to known if a key exchange session accepts when its partner is corrupted. The rest of the behaviour of the Send query remains unchanged. We denote the behaviour of the partnering key exchange game by χ_{ke} and the behaviour of the symmetric protocol game by χ_π. The behaviour of the composed game is given in Figure 11.

Remember that $\mathsf{SST}'_{\mathsf{ke};\pi} := (\mathsf{SST}'_{\mathsf{ke}}, \mathsf{SST}'_\pi)$ and $\mathsf{LST}'_{\mathsf{ke};\pi} := (\mathsf{LST}'_{\mathsf{ke}}, \mathsf{LST}'_\pi)$. Informally, the behaviour $\chi_{\mathsf{ke};\pi}$ processes key exchange queries by calling the behaviour χ_{ke}, and symmetric key protocol queries by calling χ_π. The Send query constitutes an exception, as it is used by both the ke and π stage of the composition. Here, the behaviour $\chi_{\mathsf{ke};\pi}$ uses the composed algorithm $\xi_{\mathsf{ke};\pi}$ to process the Send query, noting the above modification, where the value ψ is set appropriately when a session accepts a key at the key exchange stage.

The **Valid** predicate for the InitS, InitP, InitK and Reveal queries always return false to make these queries invalid.

$\chi_{\mathsf{ke};\pi}(q, (\mathsf{LSID}, (\mathsf{SST}_{\mathsf{ke}}, \mathsf{SST}_\pi), (\mathsf{LST}_{\mathsf{ke}}, \mathsf{LST}_\pi), \mathsf{EST}_{\mathsf{ke}}, \mathsf{MST}_\pi))$:
If q is a Send query then `//Call` $\xi_{\mathsf{ke};\pi}$`, if the session accepts`
`//a key then mark this key as 'known' if appropriate`
Parse q into $\mathsf{Send}(\mathsf{lsid}, \mathsf{msg})$.
Set $\mathsf{SST}'_{\mathsf{ke};\pi} \leftarrow \mathsf{SST}_{\mathsf{ke};\pi}$, $\mathsf{LST}'_{\mathsf{ke};\pi} \leftarrow \mathsf{LST}_{\mathsf{ke};\pi}$.
Run $(\mathsf{SST}'_{\mathsf{ke};\pi}(\mathsf{lsid}), \mathsf{response}) \leftarrow \xi_{\mathsf{ke};\pi}(\mathsf{SST}_{\mathsf{ke};\pi}(\mathsf{lsid}), \mathsf{msg})$
If $\mathsf{SST}_{\mathsf{ke};\pi}(\mathsf{lsid}).\gamma \neq \mathsf{SST}'_{\mathsf{ke};\pi}(\mathsf{lsid}).\gamma$, $\mathsf{SST}'_{\mathsf{ke};\pi}(\mathsf{lsid}).\gamma = \mathsf{accepted}$
and there exists $\mathsf{lsid}^* \in \mathsf{LSID} \setminus \{\mathsf{lsid}\}$ such that
$\mathsf{SST}_{\mathsf{ke};\pi}(\mathsf{lsid}^*).\mathsf{sid} = \mathsf{SST}'_{\mathsf{ke};\pi}(\mathsf{lsid}).\mathsf{sid}$ then
set $\mathsf{LST}'_{\mathsf{ke};\pi}(\mathsf{lsid}).\psi \leftarrow \mathsf{LST}_{\mathsf{ke};\pi}(\mathsf{lsid}^*).\psi$
Else if $\mathsf{SST}_{\mathsf{ke};\pi}(\mathsf{lsid}).\gamma \neq \mathsf{SST}'_{\mathsf{ke};\pi}(\mathsf{lsid}).\gamma$
and $\mathsf{SST}'_{\mathsf{ke};\pi}(\mathsf{lsid}).\gamma' = \mathsf{accepted}$ then:
If $\mathsf{LST}_{\mathsf{ke};\pi}(\mathsf{lsid}).\delta_{\mathsf{pnr}} = \mathsf{corrupt}$ then
set $\mathsf{LST}'_{\mathsf{ke};\pi}(\mathsf{lsid}).\psi \leftarrow \mathsf{known}$
Return $((\mathsf{SST}'_{\mathsf{ke};\pi}, \mathsf{LST}'_{\mathsf{ke};\pi}, \mathsf{EST}_{\mathsf{ke}}, \mathsf{MST}_\pi), \mathsf{response})$
If q is a Corrupt query then `//Corrupt as for key exchange`
Run $((\mathsf{SST}'_{\mathsf{ke}}, \mathsf{LST}'_{\mathsf{ke}}, \mathsf{EST}'_{\mathsf{ke}}, \perp), \mathsf{response})$
$\leftarrow \chi_{\mathsf{ke}}(q, (\mathsf{LSID}, \mathsf{SST}_{\mathsf{ke}}, \mathsf{LST}_{\mathsf{ke}}, \mathsf{EST}_{\mathsf{ke}}, \perp))$
Set $\mathsf{SST}'_\pi \leftarrow \mathsf{SST}_\pi$, $\mathsf{LST}'_\pi \leftarrow \mathsf{LST}_\pi$, $\mathsf{MST}'_\pi \leftarrow \mathsf{MST}_\pi$
Return $((\mathsf{SST}'_{\mathsf{ke};\pi}, \mathsf{LST}'_{\mathsf{ke};\pi}, \mathsf{EST}'_{\mathsf{ke}}, \mathsf{MST}'_\pi), \mathsf{response})$
If q is a query from $\mathcal{Q}$ that is neither a Send nor a Corrupt query then: `//Execute as for symmetric protocols`
Run $((\mathsf{SST}'_\pi, \mathsf{LST}'_\pi, \perp, \mathsf{MST}'_\pi), \mathsf{response})$
$\leftarrow \chi_\pi(q, (\mathsf{LSID}, \mathsf{SST}_\pi, \mathsf{LST}_\pi, \perp, \mathsf{MST}_\pi))$
$\mathsf{SST}'_{\mathsf{ke}} \leftarrow \mathsf{SST}_{\mathsf{ke}}$, $\mathsf{LST}'_{\mathsf{ke}} \leftarrow \mathsf{LST}_{\mathsf{ke}}$, $\mathsf{EST}'_{\mathsf{ke}} \leftarrow \mathsf{EST}_{\mathsf{ke}}$
Return $((\mathsf{SST}'_{\mathsf{ke};\pi}, \mathsf{LST}'_{\mathsf{ke};\pi}, \mathsf{EST}'_{\mathsf{ke}}, \mathsf{MST}'_\pi), \mathsf{response})$

Figure 11: Behaviour $\chi_{\mathsf{ke};\pi}$ of composed games.

The **Valid** predicate for the Send query either calls the **Valid** predicate from the key exchange state, namely **Valid**$_{\mathsf{ke}}$, or the **Valid** predicate from the symmetric key protocol state, **Valid**$_\pi$. This depends on the value γ. If the queried session has not accepted a key yet then **Valid**$_{\mathsf{ke}}$ is used. Otherwise, the game evaluates **Valid**$_\pi$.

PREDICATE. We consider that an adversary breaks the security of the composition if it breaks the security of the symmetric key protocol (as captured by the predicate P_π). Therefore $\mathsf{P}_{\mathsf{ke};\pi}$ is defined as $\mathsf{P}_\pi(\mathsf{LSID}, \mathsf{SST}_\pi, \mathsf{LST}_\pi, \perp, \mathsf{MST}_\pi)$, i.e. we evaluate the predicate P_π on the state of the symmetric key protocol, π, maintained by the composed game.

6. COMPOSITION RESULT

We now present our main results. In Theorem 1 we show that a BR-secure key exchange, with the additional property of having an efficient session matching algorithm, securely composes with a symmetric key protocol.

THEOREM 1. *Let* ke *be a BR-secure key exchange protocol w.r.t. $\mathcal{D}$, where an efficient session matching algorithm exists. Let π be a secure protocol w.r.t. G_π. If the key generation algorithm of π outputs keys with distribution $\mathcal{D}$ then the composition* ke;π *is secure w.r.t. $G_{\mathsf{ke};\pi}$ and for any efficient $\mathcal{A}$ we have*

$$\mathrm{Adv}_{\mathsf{ke};\pi,\mathcal{A}}^{G_{\mathsf{ke};\pi}}(1^\eta) \leq {n_i}^2 \cdot n_s \cdot \mathrm{Adv}_{\mathsf{ke},\mathcal{B}}^{G_{\mathsf{BR},\mathcal{D}}}(1^\eta) + \mathrm{Adv}_{\pi,\mathcal{C}}^{G_\pi}(1^\eta)$$

for some efficient algorithms $\mathcal{B}$ and $\mathcal{C}$, where n_i is the maximum number of participants and n_s is the maximum number of sessions, and thus ${n_i}^2 \cdot n_s$ is the size of the set LSID.

The proof proceeds in two stages. First, we show that we can replace all the session keys one-by-one with random keys, where partner sessions are keyed with the same random value. This results in a composed game, where keys used by the symmetric protocol are independent of the key exchange. Next, we show this is then equivalent to the symmetric key protocol game G_π. Intuitively this means a break against this composition is a break against the symmetric key protocol, where keys are generated randomly. A complete proof of Theorem 1 can be found in the full version of the paper.

The following corollary is an immediate application of Theorem 1, for single session reducible protocols. Essentially, if a symmetric key protocol is single session reducible, then it securely composes with a BR-secure key exchange protocol.

COROLLARY 1. *Let* ke *be a BR-secure key exchange protocol w.r.t.* $\mathcal{D}$*, where an efficient session matching algorithm exists. Let* G_π *be a single session reducible security game, and let* π *be a secure protocol w.r.t.* $G_{\pi-1}$*. If the key generation algorithm of* π *outputs keys with distribution* $\mathcal{D}$ *then the composition* $\mathsf{ke};\pi$ *is secure w.r.t.* $G_{\mathsf{ke};\pi}$*.*

PROOF. Since π is secure w.r.t $G_{\pi-1}$, and G_π is single session reducible we have that π is secure w.r.t. G_π by definition. Therefore we can now apply Theorem 1 and the result holds. □

7. CONCLUSION

We have developed a formal abstract framework for specifying cryptographic games, to enable the modelling of two-party protocols. We specialise our abstract framework to allow the analysis of key exchange protocols, following the original security notions of Bellare and Rogaway. Further, we identify a general class of protocols, called symmetric key protocols, which *use* the session key exchanged by a key exchange protocol. We show that a key exchange protocol, which is secure in the Bellare-Rogaway sense, *i.e.* keys are indistinguishable from random, composed with a symmetric key protocol that is secure when session keys are generated randomly, results in a secure composition. Interestingly, for such a composition, it is required that there exists a session matching algorithm, which is able to identify partner sessions of the key exchange protocol. Conversely, we also show, for any BR-secure key exchange protocol (a weak form of) such a session matching algorithm must exist. Yet, exploring the full relationship is an interesting open problem.

Our composition results apply to BR-secure protocols such as EAC [10]. It would be interesting to extend our work to allow for key confirmation in key exchange protocols. If the parties apply such a confirmation step *during the key exchange phase* to check if they have agreed upon the same key, without performing a key refresh afterward, then the key exchange protocol cannot be secure in the model of Bellare and Rogaway. This, however, is a common technique in protocols like TLS. It may sometimes be possible to decouple the confirmation step from the key-exchange part (and essentially consider it as part of the symmetric-key protocol). In this situation our composition result should still apply. An interesting open problem is to allow for such a modular analysis in a generic way.

8. REFERENCES

[1] M. Abadi and P. Rogaway. Reconciling two views of cryptography (the computational soundness of formal encryption). In *IFIP TCS*, volume 1872 of *LNCS*, pages 3–22. Springer, 2000.

[2] M. Backes, B. Pfitzmann, and M. Waidner. The reactive simulatability (rsim) framework for asynchronous systems. *Information and Computation*, 205(12):1685–1720, 2007.

[3] M. Bellare, D. Pointcheval, and P. Rogaway. Authenticated key exchange secure against dictionary attacks. In *EUROCRYPT 2000*, pages 139–155. Springer LNCS 1807, 2000.

[4] M. Bellare and P. Rogaway. Entity authentication and key distribution. In *CRYPTO 1993*, pages 232–249. Springer Berlin / Heidelberg LNCS 773, 1993.

[5] M. Bellare and P. Rogaway. Provably secure session key distribution: the three party case. In *STOC 1995*, pages 57–66. ACM, 1995.

[6] S. Blake-Wilson, D. Johnson, and A. Menezes. Key agreement protocols and their security analysis. In *IMA International Conference on Cryptography and Coding*, pages 30–45. Springer, 1997.

[7] R. Canetti. Security and composition of multiparty cryptographic protocols. *Journal of Cryptology*, 13(1):143–202, 2000.

[8] R. Canetti and H. Krawczyk. Analysis of Key Exchange Protocols and Their Use for Building Secure Channels. In *EUROCRYPT 2001*, pages 453–474. Springer LNCS 2045, 2001.

[9] R. Canetti and H. Krawczyk. Universally Composable Notions of Key Exchange and Secure Channels. In *EUROCRYPT 2002*, pages 337–351. Springer LNCS 2332, 2002.

[10] Ö. Dagdelen and M. Fischlin. Security analysis of the extended access control protocol for machine readable travel documents. In *ISC*, volume 6531 of *LNCS*, pages 54–68. Springer, 2010.

[11] A. Datta, A. Derek, J. Mitchell, and B. Warinschi. Computationally sound compositional logic for key exchange protocols. In *CSFW*, pages 321–334. IEEE Computer Society, 2006.

[12] A. Datta, A. Derek, J. C. Mitchell, V. Shmatikov, and M. Turuani. Probabilistic Polynomial-time Semantics for a Protocol Security Logic. In *ICALP 2005*, pages 16–29. Springer LNCS 3580, 2005.

[13] T. Dierks and C. Allen. The TLS Protocol Version 1.2, 2006. RFC 4346.

[14] M. Fischlin. Pseudorandom function tribe ensembles based on one-way permutations: Improvements and applications. In *EUROCRYPT*, pages 432–445. Springer, 1999.

[15] R. Küsters. Simulation-based security with inexhaustible interactive turing machines. In *CSFW*, pages 309–320. IEEE Computer Society, 2006.

[16] R. Küsters and M. Tuengerthal. Composition Theorems Without Pre-Established Session Identifiers. In *Proceedings of the 18th ACM Conference on Computer and Communications Security (CCS 2011)*. ACM Press, 2011. To appear.

[17] B. LaMacchia, K. Lauter, and A. Mityagin. Stronger security of authenticated key exchange. eprint: `http://eprint.iacr.org/2006/073`, 2006.

[18] V. Shoup. On formal models for secure key exchange. eprint: `http://eprint.iacr.org/1999/012`, 1999.

[19] T. Ylonen and C. Lonvick. The Secure Shell (SSH) Transport Layer Protocol, 2006. RFC 4253.

A Composable Computational Soundness Notion

Véronique Cortier
LORIA - CNRS
Nancy, France
cortier@loria.fr

Bogdan Warinschi
University of Bristol
Bristol, United Kingdom
bogdan@cs.bris.ac.uk

ABSTRACT

Computational soundness results show that under certain conditions it is possible to conclude computational security whenever symbolic security holds. Unfortunately, each soundness result is usually established for some set of cryptographic primitives and extending the result to encompass new primitives typically requires redoing most of the work. In this paper we suggest a way of getting around this problem.

We propose a notion of computational soundness that we term *deduction soundness*. As for other soundness notions, our definition captures the idea that a computational adversary does not have any more power than a symbolic adversary. However, a key aspect of deduction soundness is that it considers, intrinsically, the use of the primitives in the presence of functions specified by the adversary. As a consequence, the resulting notion is amenable to modular extensions. We prove that a deduction sound implementation of some arbitrary primitives can be extended to include asymmetric encryption and public data-structures (e.g. pairings or list), without repeating the original proof effort.

Furthermore, our notion of soundness concerns cryptographic primitives in a way that is independent of any protocol specification language. Nonetheless, we show that deduction soundness leads to computational soundness for languages (or protocols) that satisfy a so called *commutation property*.

Categories and Subject Descriptors

F.0 [**Theory of Computation**]: General

General Terms

Security, Theory

Keywords

Computational soundness, Composability

1. INTRODUCTION

Security protocols are programs that aim at securing communications over public (insecure) networks. Their design is notoriously error prone and multiple approaches have been devised for rigorous protocol analysis. These techniques fall under one of two categories. Symbolic models ignore most of the cryptographic details using abstract structures like terms (a variant of labeled finite trees). What an adversary can compute out of a set of messages is then typically captured by a symbolic deduction system (that states e.g. that the adversary can decrypt whenever he has the corresponding decryption key). This approach leads to simple models that allow the development of fully automatic decision procedures for security (e.g. [19, 2]). The second category employs computational models. These models are more accurate: they consider a lower level of abstraction and powerful (probabilistic) polynomial time adversaries. Here security does not rely on an axiomatization of the basic primitives, but rather on the difficulty of solving various computational tasks (e.g. factoring or taking discrete logarithms). Proofs in the computational model thus imply stronger guarantees than those in the symbolic models but devising and verifying such proofs is tedious. Even for moderately-sized protocols proofs become extremely long, difficult, and error prone.

An important research direction [7, 1, 5, 4, 20, 13] aims to bridge the gap between the symbolic and the cryptographic approaches via computational soundness results. These results typically show that under reasonable standard cryptographic assumptions, proofs of security with respect to symbolic models directly imply security with respect to the more detailed computational ones. This is a promising approach that allows to obtain strong guarantees while benefiting from the simplicity of symbolic models.

Soundness results have been established for various primitives such as concatenation, asymmetric encryption [5, 13], symmetric encryption [9, 18], signatures [7, 13], hash functions [17, 11], zero-knowledge proofs [6], and non-malleable commitments [14]. See the recent survey [12] for an extensive list. However, each result is dedicated to a small subset of these primitives, typically for a few primitives at a time.

Each of the above results typically considers the security of a few primitives at a time and it is likely the techniques can be extended to cope with new primitives (as long as sound axiomatizations for such primitives are possible). However, the approach of sequentially extending existing results with new primitives has an important drawback. Each new extension requires duplicating large amounts of work and this renders a "unifying" soundness result difficult to obtain. What is missing is a more modular approach where it is possible to study the soundness of various axiomatizations in isolation and still conclude that the abstraction remains sound when the primitives are used together.

For existent approaches to computational soundness such a result is probably too optimistic. An intuitive counterexample is as follows. Consider some simple programming language that involves only pairing, nonces, and asymmetric encryption. A soundness result for such a language would require that the encryption scheme be IND-CCA secure, but only when used to encrypt bitstrings that arise naturally in the execution of the protocols (i.e. pairs, nonces, ciphertexts). When applied to other bitstrings (say to digital signatures) encryption can be completely insecure (e.g. the identity function) without affecting the soundness result. The extensibility now becomes problematic: adding to the specification language digital signatures would lead to an unsound axiomatization. Protocols may still be symbolically secure but their implementation would be insecure due to the use of an insecure encryption scheme. The example can be easily adapted to show that it is equally problematic to add even a simple datastructures (like lists) in a modular way to existing computational soundness. In both cases the source of the problem is the same: the starting soundness result for encryption does not account for other primitives (or data structures) but those in the programming language under consideration. One can cope with this problem by changing the axiomatization for encryption to reflect its insecurity when encrypting signatures, but this direction is ad-hoc and not modular. More structured approaches to computational soundness that use general compositional frameworks (e.g. [5, 8, 18]) alleviate the scalability problems, but do not yield easily extendable frameworks.

Our results

In this paper we propose and study a computational soundness notion that is amenable to modular extensions. This notion, which we term *deduction soundness* reflects the idea that a symbolic deduction system soundly abstracts the security of the computational implementation for a set of primitives, even when these primitives are used in the presence of other functions for which the implementation is provided by the adversary. This should allow to establish soundness of an implementation, even when additional primitives are around: adding new primitives essentially boils down to fixing the implementation of some of the unspecified functions (as opposed to letting the adversary provide their implementation).

Importantly, in the deduction soundness game, the adversary is only allowed to provide implementations that are *transparent*, which simply means that the implementations must be efficiently invertible. Nonetheless, we confirm that the resulting notion enjoys modular extensibility. We first show that deduction soundness can be extended, essentially for free, with arbitrary data-structures. This is perhaps not surprising as public data structures are given by transparent functions. More interestingly however, we show that deduction soundness can also be extended to asymmetric encryption. The intuition is that encryption under keys for which the adversary knows the corresponding decryption key is essentially a transparent function whereas for other keys encryption can be modelled via transparent constants. We expect that similar extensions can be proved for hash functions (modelled as random oracles) and symmetric encryption.

An important question is whether transparent function can be used to model any other cryptographic primitive. The answer is unfortunately "no". The axioms that define transparent functions only talk about the secrecy (or rather non-secrecy) of their arguments and thus they provide no authentication guarantees. Extensions of our notion with authentication primitives (e.g. signatures and message authentication codes) needs to account for the possible more intricate interaction of the axioms with those for signatures and message authentication codes.

A second aspect of deduction soundness is that it is solely concerned with the implementation of the primitives, and is independent of any protocol structure or programming language where the primitives may be used. The idea to focus only on the axiomatization of individual primitives while disregarding the protocols where the primitives are used can be traced from the work of Herzog [15], through to that of Backes, Pfitzmann, and Waidner [5], and to the more recent CoSP framework of Backes, Hofheinz, and Unruh [3]. As in these latter works we show that soundness (in the form of a mapping lemma) for protocol specification languages can be recovered using our notion. In turn this allows for the translation of trace properties from symbolic models to computational ones.

2. MODELS

In this section we introduce some notations and set our abstract and concrete models. Throughout we assume familiarity of basic cryptographic security notion like indistinguishability under chosen cipher attacks(IND-CCA) for asymmetric encryption schemes, existential unforgeability under chosen message attacks for digital signature and message authentication codes (EU-CMA).

2.1 Abstract algebras

Our abstract models—called *abstract algebras*—consist of term algebras defined on a first-order signature with sorts.

Specifically a *signature* $(\mathcal{S}, \mathcal{F})$ consists of a set of *sorts* $S = \{s, s_1 \ldots\}$, a set of labels $\mathsf{labels} = \mathsf{labelsH} \cup \mathsf{labelsA}$, and a set of *symbols* $\mathcal{F} = \{f, f_1 \ldots\}$ together with arities of the form $\mathrm{ar}(f) = s_1 \times \ldots \times s_k \to s$, $k \geq 0$. Symbols that take $k = 0$ arguments are called *constants*; their arity is simply written s. We fix an infinite set of *variables* $\mathcal{X} = \{x, y \ldots\}$. We assume that variables are given with sorts. The set of *terms of sort* s is defined inductively by

t ::=		term of sort s
|	x	variable x of sort s
|	$f^l(t_1, \ldots, t_k)$	application of symbol $f \in \mathcal{F}$

where for the last case, we further require that $l \in \mathcal{L}$, t_i is a term of some sort s_i and $\mathrm{ar}(f) = s_1 \times \ldots \times s_k \to s$.

Intuitively, for names, we use (randomized) constants. For example, assume that $n \in \mathcal{F}$ is a constant. Then usual nonces can be represented by $n^{r_1}, n^{r_2}, \ldots$ where $r_1, r_2 \in \mathcal{L}$ are labels. Labels in labelsH will be used when the function has been applied by an honest agent (thus the randomness has been honestly generated) whereas labels in labelsA will be used when the randomness has been generated by the adversary. Often when the label for a functional symbol is clear from the context (e.g. when there is only one label that suits a particular functional symbol) we may omit this label.

We always assume a supersort term containing all other sorts. We also assume a constant $g_s \in \mathcal{F}$ for any $s \in \mathcal{S}$ that will be used for representing garbage of sort s. Garbage will typically be the terms associated to bit-strings produced by the adversary and which cannot be parsed as a meaningful term. Therefore we require in what follows that for any term g_s^l, the randomness l has to be adversarial: $l \in \mathsf{labelsA}$. As usual, we write $\mathrm{var}(t)$ for the set of variables occurring in t. A term is *ground* or *closed* iff it has no variables. The set of terms is denoted by Term.

Substitutions are written $\sigma = \{x_1 = t_1, \ldots, x_n = t_n\}$ with $\mathrm{dom}(\sigma) = \{x_1, \ldots, x_n\}$. We only consider *well-sorted* substitutions, that is substitutions $\sigma = \{x_1 = t_1, \ldots, x_n = t_n\}$ for which x_i and t_i have the same sort. σ is *closed* iff all of the t_i are closed. We extend the notation var(.) from terms to substitutions in the obvious way. The application of a substitution σ to a term t is written $\sigma(t) = t\sigma$.

Symbols in $\mathcal{F}$ are intended to model cryptographic primitives, including generation of random data like e.g. nonces or keys. Identities will be typically represented by constants. The term algebra is equipped with a *deduction* relation $\vdash \subseteq 2^{\mathsf{Term}} \times \mathsf{Term}$ that models the information available to a formal adversary. $S \vdash m$ means that a formal adversary can build m out of S, where m is a term and S a set of terms. We say that m is *deducible* from S. Deduction relations are typically defined through deductions rules systems.

DEFINITION 1. *A deduction system $\mathcal{D}$ is a set of rules $\frac{u_1 \quad \cdots \quad u_k}{u}$ such that $u_1, \ldots, u_k, u \in \mathsf{Term}$. The deduction relation $\vdash_{\mathcal{D}} \subseteq 2^{\mathsf{Term}} \times \mathsf{Term}$ associated to $\mathcal{D}$ is the smallest relation S satisfying:*

- *for any $t \in S$, $S \vdash_{\mathcal{D}} t$;*
- *If $S \vdash_{\mathcal{D}} u_1\theta, \ldots S \vdash_{\mathcal{D}} u_k\theta$ for some substitution θ and $\frac{u_1 \quad \cdots \quad u_k}{u} \in \mathcal{D}$ then $S \vdash_{\mathcal{D}} u\theta$.*

We may omit the subscript $\mathcal{D}$ in $\vdash_{\mathcal{D}}$ when it is clear from the context.

2.1.1 *Specification for signatures and MACs*

For example, digital signatures and message authentication codes could be formalized using algebras with the signature Σ_{sm} defined as follows. The set of sorts are given by $\mathcal{S}_{sm} = \{\mathsf{id}, \mathsf{spair}, \mathsf{vkey}, \mathsf{skey}, \mathsf{sigs}, \mathsf{macs}, \mathsf{mkey}\}$ and the set of operations $\mathcal{F}_{sm}$ are given by:

$\mathsf{id}_i : \rightarrow \mathsf{id}$ for $i \in \mathbb{N}$

$\mathsf{skeypair} : \mathsf{id} \rightarrow \mathsf{spair}$	$\mathsf{mackey} : \mathsf{id} \times \mathsf{id} \rightarrow \mathsf{mkey}$
$\mathsf{vk} : \mathsf{spair} \rightarrow \mathsf{vkey}$	$\mathsf{sk} : \mathsf{spair} \rightarrow \mathsf{skey}$
$\mathsf{sign} : \mathsf{skey} \times \mathsf{term} \rightarrow \mathsf{sigs}$	$\mathsf{mac} : \mathsf{mkey} \times \mathsf{term} \rightarrow \mathsf{macs}$

Abusing notation, we often write $\mathsf{sk}(id)$ for $\mathsf{sk}(\mathsf{skeypair}(id))$, write $\mathsf{vk}(id)$ for $\mathsf{vk}(\mathsf{skeypair}(id))$ and write mackey_{ij} for $\mathsf{mackey}(id_i, id_j)$. Also, recall that by an earlier assumption the signature also contains constant garbage symbols of each sort.

The deduction system $\mathcal{D}_{\mathsf{sm}}$ that models the security of signatures and macs is given by rules in Figure 1. The first line specifies that the adversary can recover the verification key of any party, and that it can produce garbage of any type. The next two lines specify, for signature and macs, respectively, that signatures and macs always reveal the message that is being authenticated (even when produced honestly), and that given the secret key the adversary can produce signatures and macs.

$$\frac{}{\mathsf{vk}(x)} \qquad \frac{}{g_s^l}$$

$$\frac{\mathsf{sign}^l(\mathsf{sk}(x), t)}{t} \qquad \frac{\mathsf{sk}(x) \quad t}{\mathsf{sign}^{l_A}(\mathsf{sk}(x), t)}$$

$$\frac{\mathsf{mac}^l(\mathsf{mkey}(x,y), t)}{t} \qquad \frac{\mathsf{mackey}(x,y) \quad t}{\mathsf{mac}^{l_A}(\mathsf{mackey}(x,y), t)}$$

where $x, y \in \mathsf{id}, s \in \mathcal{S}, t \in \mathsf{term}, l \in \mathsf{labels}, l_A \in \mathsf{labelsA}$.

Figure 1: Deduction rules for signatures and macs.

2.2 Concrete implementations for algebras

If A is a randomized algorithm we write $y \leftarrow A(x; r)$ for the process of obtaining y by running A on x with random coins r. We assume a non-empty set of bit-strings $[\![s]\!] \subseteq \{0,1\}^*$ for each sort $s \in \mathcal{S}$. For the supersort term , we assume $[\![\mathsf{term}]\!] = \{0,1\}^*$. We now give terms a concrete semantics, parametrized by:

- a security parameter η,
- an $(\mathcal{S}, \mathcal{F})$-*concrete implementation* of the primitives, given by some Turing Machine M such that for any $f \in \mathcal{F}$, with $\mathrm{ar}(f) = s_1 \times \ldots \times s_k \rightarrow s$,

$$(M\ f) : [\![s_1]\!] \times \cdots \times [\![s_k]\!] \times \{0,1\}^\eta \rightarrow [\![s]\!]$$

The concrete implementation is used in the game that defines computational soundness. In particular, the implementation determines how to parse bitstrings as terms and how to generate the bitstrings that correspond to terms. Next we give some specifics related to these two points.

2.2.1 *Assignation sets*

The concrete interpretation of a symbolic term is usually obtained by replacing each symbolic function in the term with its concrete implementation. In cryptographic applications functions are often randomized and the same random coins may occur in different places within the same term. This is the case for instance when the same nonce occurs twice in the same term. We record this information via *assignation sets*. Such a set L is simply a set of couples (c, U) where c is a bitstring and U is a list of terms. The idea is that the terms in U are the possible interpretations of the bitstring c. In particular, each such U is either of the form $[g^{l(c)}]$ or of the form $[f^l(g_1, \ldots, g_k); g^{l(c)}]$ where $g^{l(c)}, g_1, \ldots, g_k$ are garbage symbols. The two different forms for U corresponds to the following two situations, respectively. In the first case, c is interpreted as a garbage (i.e. we do not have any special information on it, except possibly its sort). In the second case c is interpreted as $f^l(g_1, \ldots, g_k)$ meaning that c is interpreted as the application of f^l to the interpretation of $g_1, \ldots, g_k$. In the second case, for convenience, we store the two possible interpretations of c which usually are obtained through successive refinements. We may write $(b, u) \in L$ instead of $(b, [u]) \in L$ when $[u]$ is a list with a single element. We say that an assignation set L is *one-to-one and onto* if for any $(c, U_1), (c, U_2) \in L$, we have $U_1 = U_2$ and for any $(c_1, U), (c_2, U) \in L$, we have $c_1 = c_2$.

An assignation set L defines the substitution θ_L *associated to an assignation set* L. This is simply the union of the substitutions $g \mapsto f^l(g_1, \ldots, g_k)$ for any $(c, [f^l(g_1, \ldots, g_k); g]) \in L$. For this notion to be well-defined, the substitution needs to be loop free, and in what follows we will ensure that this property is satisfied. A *partial substitution associated to* L is a substitution associated to some assignation set $L' \subseteq L$.

2.2.2 Generating function.

Given an assignation set L we define a generating function that associates a concrete semantics for terms (given the terms already interpreted in L). For reasons that will be clear later, we are only interested in giving semantics to terms labeled by an honest label.

The generation function uses a random tape $\mathcal{R}$ that essentially implements a mapping $\mathcal{R} : \mathsf{Term} \to \{0,1\}^\eta$, mapping a term to random coins used by the randomized operations in that term. Given a closed term t and an assignation set L, $\mathsf{generate}(t, L)$ is defined as follows. We have that t is of the form $f^l(t_1, \ldots, t_n)$ (with possibly $n = 0$).

- If there is $(c, u :: U) \in L$ with $t = u\theta$ for some θ partial substitution associated to L, then return (c, L).
- Otherwise, if $l \in \mathsf{labelsA}$ then the request is rejected ($\mathsf{generate}$ is undefined).
  Otherwise, let $r = \mathcal{R}(f^l(t_1, \ldots, t_n))$, let $(c_i, L) = \mathsf{generate}(t_i, L)$, $1 \leq i \leq n$ and let $c = (M\ f)(c_1, \ldots, c_n, r)$. Then the function returns $(c, L \cup \{(c, [f^l(g^{l(c_1)}, \ldots, g^{l(c_n)}); g^l])\})$.

Note that $\mathsf{generate}(t, L)$ not only returns a bitstring c associated to t but also updates L (to remember, for example, the value associated to t). Note also that $\mathsf{generate}$ depends on the concrete implementation M and the random tape $\mathcal{R}$. When needed, we show explicitly this dependency, but in general we avoid it for readability.

2.2.3 Parsing function

Conversely, we define a function to convert bitstring into terms. A *parsing function* for a $(\mathcal{S}, \mathcal{F})$-concrete implementation M is a function that takes as input a bitstring c and a (one-to-one and onto) assignation set L and returns a term t and a (one-to-one and onto) assignation set that extends L. We impose a particular structure for the function parse. This assumption allows to later extend the parse function associated to an implementation when other primitives are added to the implementation. More precisely, the parse function uses an auxiliary function $\mathsf{saturate}$ (which does the actual parsing). Formally, we assume that the parse function is defined as follows:

$\mathsf{parse}(c, L)$:
If there exists $(c, t :: U) \in L$
  then output $t\theta_L$;
  else let $L = \mathsf{saturate}(L \cup \{(c, [g^{l(c)}])\})$;
    (we assign a new garbage symbol to c with label $l(c) \in \mathsf{labelsA}$)
  let $(c, t :: U) \in L$, output $t\theta_L$;

The $\mathsf{saturate}$ function takes as input an assignation set and outputs an assignation set. Intuitively, the saturate function tries to interpret as a term any bitstring left uninterpreted (to which the current interpretation is set to garbage), given the information present in the assignation set. Notice that when $\mathsf{saturate}$ is called, a new bitstring that is interpreted as garbage had just been added to the assignation set. While interpreting such a bitstring, new bitstrings without an interpretation can be discovered and these are added to the assignation set. The process is repeated until the assignation set does not change.

The exact definition of $\mathsf{saturate}$ function is left unspecified, as it depends on the particular implementation. However, we demand two properties from any $\mathsf{saturate}$ functions used to define parsing. First, if $\mathsf{saturate}$ adds a new bitstring to the assignation set then, the term associated to this bitstring is by default a garbage symbol with adversarial label. Formally, we assume that for any L_1, L_2 such that $L_2 = \mathsf{saturate}(L_1)$ then for any $(b, f^l(g_1, \ldots, g_k) :: U) \in L_2$ if $l \in \mathsf{labelsH}$ then $(b, f^l(g_1, \ldots, g_k) :: U) \in L_1$: no new term with honest labels are introduced. The second assumption is that the order in which the function processes an assignation set does not matter.

$$\mathsf{saturate}(\mathsf{saturate}(L_1) \cup L_2) = \mathsf{saturate}(L_1 \cup L_2)$$

The examples that we give later in the paper satisfy these properties.

2.2.4 Implementation for signatures and MACs

For the implementation that we use for our running example, we assume an efficiently computable, efficiently invertible, one-to-one encoding function $\langle \_ \rangle$ that takes a tuple of bitstrings as input (separated by commas) and returns an encoding of that tuple. If A is a set of bitstrings, and x is a bitstring, then by a slight abuse, we write $\langle A, x\rangle$ for the set $\{\langle a, x\rangle \mid a \in A\}$, and we extend this notation in the obvious way to the case when encode receives several arguments as input. The concrete support sets for every sort s of the signature Σ_{sm} is given by $[\![s]\!] = \langle \{0,1\}^*, s\rangle$, that is any element of the support set is an encoding of a bit-string followed by the name of the support set. The concrete implementation M_{sm} (which we define below) depends on a digital signature scheme $\mathsf{DigSig} = (\mathcal{K}, \mathcal{S}, \mathcal{V})$ and a message authentication code $\mathsf{Mac} = (\mathcal{MK}, \mathcal{T}, \mathcal{MV})$. We assume that from any secret key sk produced by the key generation algorithm of the signature, one can immediately recover its associated verification key vk. Below, (and elsewhere) we write $[\![f]\!]$ for the algorithm that gives the concrete semantics for operation f. We assume some public (efficiently computable) mapping that maps each constant id_i of the signature to some bitstring id_i.

- $(M_{\mathsf{sm}}\ \mathsf{id}_i)$: output $\langle id_i, \mathsf{id}\rangle$
- $(M_{\mathsf{sm}}\ \mathsf{skeypair})$: is $\mathcal{K}(\eta)$ (to the output of which we tag spair)
- $(M_{\mathsf{sm}}\ \mathsf{sk})(s)$: parse s as $\langle (sk, vk), \mathsf{spair}\rangle$ and outputs $\langle sk, \mathsf{skey}\rangle$.
- $(M_{\mathsf{sm}}\ \mathsf{vk})(s)$: parse s as $\langle (sk, vk), \mathsf{spair}\rangle$ and outputs $\langle vk, \mathsf{vkey}\rangle$
- $(M_{\mathsf{sm}}\ \mathsf{sign})(s_1, s_2, r)$: parse s_1 as $\langle sk, \mathsf{skey}\rangle$, calculate $\sigma \leftarrow \mathcal{S}(sk, s_2; r)$, output $\langle \sigma, s_2, vk, \mathsf{sigs}\rangle$, where vk is the verification key associated to sk.

- (M_{sm} mackey): is just $\mathcal{MK}(\eta)$ (to the output of which we tag mackey)
- (M_{sm} mac)(s_1, s_2): parse s_1 as $\langle k, \mathsf{mkey}\rangle$ and output $\langle s_2, \mathcal{T}(k, s_2), \mathsf{macs}\rangle$.

Next, we give the parsing algorithm (that is we specify the function $\mathsf{saturate}_{\mathsf{sm}}$) for the implementation $\mathcal{M}_{\mathsf{sm}}$.

$\mathsf{saturate}_{\mathsf{sm}}(L)$
let $L' = L$
repeat
  let $L = L'$
  for all $(c, [g^{l(c)}]) \in L$ s.t. c is of the form $\langle m, t\rangle$ with $t \in \mathcal{S}_{sm}$
    if $t = \mathsf{id}$ then if $m = id_i$ for some i
      then $L \leftarrow L \setminus \{(c, [g^{l(c)}])\} \cup \{(c, [\mathsf{id}_i, g^{l(c)}])\}$
    if $t = \mathsf{vkey}$ then $L \leftarrow L \setminus \{(c, [g^{l(c)}])\} \cup \{(c, [g^{l(c)}_{\mathsf{vkey}}, g^{l(c)}])\}$
    if $t = \mathsf{skey}$ then $L \leftarrow L \setminus \{(c, [g^{l(c)}])\} \cup \{(c, [g^{l(c)}_{\mathsf{skey}}, g^{l(c)}])\}$
    if $t = \mathsf{sigs}$ and $m = s_1, s_2, s_3$ and there is a such that
      $(s_3, \mathsf{vk}(a) :: U) \in L)$ and $\mathcal{V}(s_3, (s_2, s_1)) = \mathsf{true}$
        then $L \leftarrow L \setminus \{(c, [g^{l(c)}])\} \cup$
          $\{(c, [\mathsf{sign}^{l(c)}(\mathsf{sk}(a), g^{l(s_2)}); g^{l(c)}]), (s_2, g^{l(s_2)})\}$
    if $t = \mathsf{macs}$ and $m = s_2, s_3$ and there exist some a, b
      such that $(s_1, \mathsf{mackey}(a, b) :: U) \in L$ and
      $\mathcal{MV}(s_1, s_2, s_3) = \mathsf{true}$
        then $L \leftarrow L \setminus \{(c, [g^{l(c)}])\} \cup$
      $\{(c, [\mathsf{mac}^{l(c)}(\mathsf{mackey}(a, b), g^{l(s_2)}); g^{l(c)}]), (s_2, g^{l(s_2)})\})$
until $L = L'$
return L

As explained earlier the function saturate attempts to parse all bitstrings in L that are currently interpreted as garbage symbols. For each such occurrence, if the bitstring does not have associated a type, then nothing happens (i.e. the associated term remains a garbage constant). Otherwise the procedure attempts to parse the bitstring depending on the type of the bitstring. For example, when the type is sigs (that is the bitstring is supposedly a signature) the procedure determines that this is a valid signature on some message s_2 for the public key of some party. If this is so, a new interpretation for c is added to the assignation list, as a signature on some new garbage symbol associated to s_2, and $(s_2, g^{l(s_2)})$ is added to the assignation list (to be parsed in the next pass over the repeat loop).

2.3 Transparent implementation

Typical primitives that are usually considered in soundness results include encryption, signature scheme, hash function, etc. We define and study soundness of such primitives when they are used together with a class of functions which we call *transparent* functions.

Intuitively, such functions are efficiently invertible, and the type of their output can be efficiently determined. An example of such functions are data structures (i.e. pairs, lists, XML documents etc.). Formally, a transparent implementation of a signature $(\mathcal{S}, \mathcal{F})$ is a polynomial-time Turing machine M such that for all $f \in \mathcal{F}$, with $\mathrm{ar}(f) = s_1 \times \ldots \times s_k \to s$,

$$(M\ \mathsf{evaluate}\ f) : [\![s_1]\!] \times \cdots \times [\![s_k]\!] \times \{0,1\}^\eta \to [\![s]\!]$$
$$(M\ \mathsf{type}) : \{0,1\}^* \to \mathcal{F} \cup \{\bot\}$$
$$(M\ \mathsf{proj}\ f\ i) : \{0,1\}^* \to \{0,1\}^* \cup \{\bot\}$$

such that for any $m_i \in [\![s_i]\!]$, $1 \le i \le k$, for any r,

$$(M\ \mathsf{proj}\ f\ i)((M\ \mathsf{evaluate}\ f)(m_1, \ldots, m_k, r)) = m_i$$
$$(M\ \mathsf{type})((M\ \mathsf{evaluate}\ f)(m_1, \ldots, m_k, r)) = f$$

As hinted above, our notion of soundness does not consider primitives when used stand-alone, but considers their use together with a (infinite, but countable) set of transparent functions.

We next explain how to extend, generically, an algebraic signature and its associated deduction system with transparent functions. Furthermore, we explain how to extend the parsing algorithm associated to an implementation when one adds an implementation for transparent functions.

Let $\Sigma_1 = (\mathcal{S}_1, \mathcal{F}_1)$ be a signature and $\mathcal{D}_{\Sigma_1}$ be a set of deduction rules inducing a deduction system such as the deduction system defined in Example 2.1.1. Let $\Sigma_{\mathsf{tran}} = (\mathcal{S}_{\mathsf{tran}}, \mathcal{F}_{\mathsf{tran}})$ be a signature representing a set of transparent functions. Then we define its associated deduction system $\mathcal{D}_{\mathsf{tran}(\Sigma_{\mathsf{tran}})}$ as follows.

$$\mathcal{D}_{\mathsf{tran}(\Sigma_{\mathsf{tran}})} = \left\{ \begin{array}{ll} \frac{t_1 \ \cdots\ t_k}{f^l(t_1,\ldots,t_k)} & l \in \mathsf{labelsA}, f \in \mathcal{F}_{\mathsf{tran}} \\ \\ \frac{f^l(t_1,\ldots,t_k)}{t_i} & 1 \le i \le k, l \in \mathsf{labels}, f \in \mathcal{F}_{\mathsf{tran}} \end{array} \right\}$$

The deduction relation $\vdash_{\Sigma_1 \cup \Sigma_{\mathsf{tran}}}$ is the deduction relation induced by $\mathcal{D}_{\Sigma_1} \cup \mathcal{D}_{\mathsf{tran}(\Sigma_{\mathsf{tran}})}$.

Given a parsing algorithm parse (that is, the saturate algorithm) for signature Σ_1 and given an implementation M for the transparent functions in $\mathcal{F}_{\mathsf{tran}}$, we define the algorithm $\mathsf{parse}^{\mathsf{tran}}(M)$. This algorithm parses bitstrings as terms over $\mathcal{F}_1 \cup \mathcal{F}_{\mathsf{tran}}$. In Figure 2 we specify the function $\mathsf{saturate}^{\mathsf{tran}}$ (that defines $\mathsf{parse}^{\mathsf{tran}}$). Notice that we will from now on omit the dependency of this extension on M, since M will always be clear from the context. The extension is (necessarily) a bit technical: Here we are attempting to parse a bitstring as a term over the functions in $\mathcal{F}_1 \cup \mathcal{F}_{\mathsf{tran}}$, but have only black-box access to the parsing (saturate) algorithm corresponding to $\mathcal{F}_1$. This algorithm may classify as garbage strings that can potentially be successfully interpreted as terms over $\mathcal{F}_2$. We need therefore to maintain the link between the interpretation of the same bitstring as garbage with respect to $\mathcal{F}_1$, but as some term with respect to $\mathcal{F}_{\mathsf{tran}}$. For this we introduce a mechanism which uses an auxiliary function collapse. Given two signatures Σ_1, Σ_2, the collapse function takes as input an assignation set L and replaces any subterm with its head symbol in Σ_2 with a fresh garbage of the same sort. Since the labels of the term and of the garbage symbol are the same (i.e. the bitstring to which they correspond) the result is simply a substitution that replaces garbage symbols in Σ_1 with terms in Σ_2.

Function $\mathsf{collapse}_{\Sigma_1,\Sigma_2}(L)$
  Let $\mathsf{Mem} = \emptyset$; (memorizes garbage symbols and their associated terms)
  for any $f^l(t_1, \ldots, t_k)$ occurring as subterm in u,
    where $(c, u) \in L$ and $f \in \Sigma_2$ is of sort $s_1 \times \cdots \times s_k \to s$
    let $\mathsf{Mem} = \mathsf{Mem} \cup \{(g_s^{f^l(t_1,\ldots,t_k)}, f^l(t_1, \ldots, t_k))\}$
  return Mem

As explained above, the collapse function returns the set Mem which we view as a substitution. Its application to a term or (more generally) to an assignation set L is written by $L\mathsf{Mem}$. We define Mem^{-1} to be $\{(u, g) \mid (g, u) \in \mathsf{Mem}\}$. It can be viewed as a replacement function. $L\mathsf{Mem}^{-1}$ denotes

L where each term u occurring as subterm in L such that $(u, g) \in \mathsf{Mem}^{-1}$ is replaced by g, where the replacement is applied top-most.

Function $\mathsf{saturate}^{\mathsf{tran}}(L)$
Let $\mathsf{Mem} = \mathsf{collapse}_{\Sigma_1, \Sigma_{\mathsf{tran}}}(L)$;
  (Mem links terms headed by transp. functions to garbage)
let $L' = L$
repeat
  let $L = L'$;
  let $L' = \mathsf{saturate}(L'\mathsf{Mem}^{-1})\mathsf{Mem}$;
    (L' is parsed according to the signature Σ_1)
    if there is $(b, g^l) \in L$ s.t. g^l is of sort term
    and $(M\mathsf{type})(b) \neq \bot$
      let $f = (M\mathsf{type})(b)$, f is of arity $s_1 \times \cdots \times s_k \to s$
    if there is $1 \leq i \leq k$ s.t. $(M \; \mathsf{proj} \; f \; i)(b) = \bot$
      then $L' = \overline{L'}^{g^l \mapsto g^l_s}$
      else let $b_i = (M \; \mathsf{proj} \; f \; i)(b)$, $1 \leq i \leq k$
      let $V_i = U_i$ if there exists $(b_i, U_i) \in L$,
        otherwise $V_i = [g^{l(b_i)}]$ with $l(b_i) \in \mathsf{labelsA}$;
      let $L' = L' \setminus \{(b, g^l)\} \cup$
      $\{(b, [f^l(g^{l(b_1)}, \ldots, g^{l(b_k)}); g^l]), (b_1, V_1), \ldots, (b_k, V_k)\}$
      (We update L' with the bitstring obtained
       by projection.)
      let $\mathsf{Mem} = \mathsf{Mem} \cup \{(g^l, f^l(g^{l(b_1)}, \ldots, g^{l(b_k)}))\}$
until $L = L'$
return L.

Above, $L^{u \mapsto v}$ is obtained from L by replacing each element $(c, [u])$ of L with $(c, [u, v])$

Figure 2: Extending parsing to transparent functions.

Game $\mathsf{Game}_{\mathcal{S}, \mathcal{F}, A, M_1, \mathsf{parse}, \mathcal{D}}(\eta)$:
Set $S = \emptyset$;   (set of requested terms)
Set $L = \emptyset$;   (assignation set)
$\mathsf{DY} = \top$;   (only deducible terms have been received)
$\mathsf{Valid} = \top$;   (only valid requests have been received)
$\mathcal{R} \leftarrow \{0,1\}^*$
$M_2 \leftarrow \mathcal{A}(\eta)$; where M_2 has to be a transparent
    implementation for $(\mathcal{S}, \mathcal{F} \setminus \mathcal{F}_1)$
On request parse c do:
  Compute $(t, L') := \mathsf{parse}^{\mathsf{tran}}(c, L)$;
  Let $L := L'$;
  If $S \not\vdash_{\mathcal{D} \cup \mathcal{D}_{\mathsf{tran}(\mathcal{S}, \mathcal{F} \setminus \mathcal{F}_1)}} t$
    then $\mathsf{DY} = \bot$, output $(\mathsf{DY}, \mathsf{Valid})$, stop
    else return t
On request evaluate t do
  $S := S \cup \{t\}$;
  If $\neg P_{\mathsf{valid}}(S)$
    then $\mathsf{Valid} = \bot$, output $(\mathsf{DY}, \mathsf{Valid})$, stop
    else compute $(c, L') := \mathsf{generate}_{M_1 \cup M_2, \mathcal{R}}(t, L)$
    Let $L := L'$;
    return c
On request stop do
  output $(\mathsf{DY}, \mathsf{Valid})$, stop

Figure 3: Game defining deduction soundness.

3. DEDUCTION SOUNDNESS

In this section we give a notion of soundness of an implementation with respect to a symbolic deduction relation. The definition is through a game which, informally, is as follows. The game, maintains internally an assignation set (that is, the interpretation of bitstrings as terms). The adversary is allowed two types of actions. First, he can see interpretation of whatever terms it wants: here the game runs internally the generate function defined earlier using the current assignation set and returns the bitstring that is obtained this way. Secondly, the adversary is allowed to see parsings of whatever bitstrings it wants: here the game runs internally the parse algorithm and returns the term that it obtains. Soundness holds if with overwhelming probability the bitstrings that the adversary asks to be parsed correspond to terms that can be deduced by the adversary from the terms for which it had seen interpretations. This definitional idea can be traced back to the work of Herzog [15] and captures the idea that a computational adversary (that operates with bitstrings) is essentially limited to performing Dolev-Yao operations on the bit-strings that it receives.

The novel aspect of our definition is that the implementation of primitives is not analyzed standalone. Instead, we consider an extended signature that includes a countable number of transparent functions. The implementation for these functions is selected by the adversary. In effect, our game demands that the axiomatization of the primitives remains sound, even if the primitive is used in conjunction with arbitrary (adversarially chosen) other functions. This aspect of the definition is what enables compositionality of our notion.

Let $\Sigma = (\mathcal{S}, \mathcal{F})$ be a signature, a (symbolic) deduction system $\mathcal{D}$ associated to Σ and a concrete implementation M_1 for the functions $\mathcal{F}_1 \subset \mathcal{F}$. We define a game that captures the soundness of M_1 with respect to the deduction relation $\mathcal{D}$ in Figure 3. The game is parametrized by an adversary $\mathcal{A}$, the set of sorts $\mathcal{S}$ and a set of symbols $\mathcal{F}$ as above, a $(\mathcal{S}, \mathcal{F}_1)$-*concrete implementation* M_1 and, importantly, a predicate P_{valid} on a set of terms. This predicate restricts the queries of the adversary in various ways. For example, P_{valid} can be used to specify that the adversary is not allowed to create key cycles, only ask for well-formed terms, etc.. The last parameter is a parsing function parse. The game also maintains two flags DY and Valid initially set to true. The game allows three kinds of requests:

- The adversary sends a bit-string and gets a term that should represent the bit-string;
- The adversary sends a term t and gets its computational interpretation. In producing these interpretations the game needs random coins. These coins are generated as needed, so strictly speaking they are uniformly distributed in a finite set that depends on the running time of the adversary $\mathcal{A}$. To avoid introducing explicit bounds for this set we abuse notation and write $\mathcal{R} \leftarrow \{0,1\}^*$ for the (online) process of generating these coins.
- Finally, the adversary may decide to stop the game.

Two events may occur during the game:

- The flag DY is set to false if the adversary sends a request parse c such that the returned term t is non deducible symbolically, that is $S \not\vdash t$. This corresponds intuitively to cases where the adversary deviates from symbolic Dolev-Yao behaviors.
- The flag Valid is set to false if the list of requests S does not satisfy the predicate P_{valid} (which, as explained above, ensures that the adversary's requests are benign.)

We say that a computational implementation is *deduction sound* if the deduction relation $\vdash$ reflects the power of a computational adversary, that is if any bit-string sent by the adversary can be associated to a term deducible from previously seen terms.

DEFINITION 2. *Let $\mathcal{S}$ be a set of sorts and let $\mathcal{F}$ be a set of symbols. A $(\mathcal{S}, \mathcal{F}_1)$-*concrete implementation M_1 *is* deduction sound *w.r.t. a deduction system $\mathcal{D}$, a parsing function* parse *and a predicate P_{valid} if for any probabilistic polynomial time Turing machine (p.p.t) $\mathcal{A}$ (for which the game always stops)*

$$\mathbb{P}\left[\mathsf{Game}_{\mathcal{S},\mathcal{F},\mathcal{A},M_1,\mathsf{parse},\mathcal{D}}(\eta) = (\bot, \top)\right]$$

is a negligible *function of η, that is, remains eventually smaller than any η^{-n} $(n > 0)$ as η tends to infinity.*

Proving soundness in the sense of the definition above is not really more complex than when using other definitions in the literature. As an example, we prove the soundness of the implementation that we gave in our running example.

3.1 Soundness for signatures and MACs

In this section we show that the implementation of signatures and MACs specified in Section 2.2.4 is deduction sound. The predicate P_{sm} that restricts the queries of the adversary in the deduction soundness game only checks that signing keys have been generated before any signature generation request is issued (i.e. before the adversary sees the interpretation of a term that contains a signature).

PROPOSITION 1. *Let $\mathcal{F}_{\mathsf{tran}}$ be an arbitrary set of functional symbols with arity of the form* term $\times \ldots \times$ term $\to$ term. *Assume that the digital signature scheme and MAC scheme used to define M_{sm} are* EU-CMA *secure. Then M_{sm} is a $(\mathcal{S}, \mathcal{F}_{\mathsf{sm}} \cup \mathcal{F}_{\mathsf{tran}})$-concrete implementation that is deduction sound with respect to $\mathcal{D}_{\mathsf{sm}}$, parsing function* $\mathsf{parse}_{\mathsf{sm}}$ *and predicate P_{sm}.*

Assume that there exists an adversary $\mathcal{A}$ which wins the game for deduction soundness with non-negligible probability. A simple structural induction shows that the term $f(t_1, t_2, \ldots, t_k)$ that is non Dolev-Yao (nonDY) according to the deduction relation induced by $\mathcal{D}_{\mathsf{sm}} \cup \mathcal{D}_{\mathsf{tran}}$ must contain a subterm which has its head symbol in $\mathcal{F}_{\mathsf{sm}}$. The only non-deducible terms in $\mathcal{F}_{\mathsf{sm}}$ are secret keys (signing or mac keys), and signatures or macs on messages that have not been signed (or mac'ed) before. Intuitively, this corresponds to the adversary breaking the primitives underlying the implementation M_{sm}. We formalize this intuition by constructing adversaries against the primitives, one against the signature scheme, and one against the mac scheme.

Here, we only explain how the adversary against the signature scheme works – the other adversary works analogously. Assume that we know which of the messages of the adversary $\mathcal{A}$ contains the nonDY subterm, and that this subterm is a signature valid under the public key of some party a on a message that this party did not produce. Also assume that we know the identity a of this party. Both of these quantities can be guessed with non-negligible probability. Adversary $\mathcal{B}$ that we construct against the digital signature receives as input some verification key vk and access to a signing oracle under the corresponding secret key sk. Adversary $\mathcal{B}$ then simulates the deduction soundness game for $\mathcal{A}$ in such a way that the signing key of party a, that is, the interpretation of $\mathsf{vk}(a)$ is set to vk. All of the other secrets in the game (mac keys, signing keys) are generated by $\mathcal{B}$. Adversary $\mathcal{B}$ simulates the behaviour of the game (that is algorithms $\mathsf{parse}^{\mathsf{tran}}$ and generate) as if on the internal assignation list where the verification key of a is set to vk. Whenever $\mathcal{B}$ needs to produce signatures under vk it uses its signing oracle. Notice that the adversary $\mathcal{A}$ never asks for the interpretation of $\mathsf{sk}(a)$ (which $\mathcal{B}$ cannot provide), as otherwise the signature would actually be a Dolev-Yao message. The nonDY message that $\mathcal{A}$ produces contains a signature that verifies under vk on some message m that a did not previously sign (and which thus was not queried to the signing oracle of $\mathcal{B}$). The same simulation can be provided by $\mathcal{B}$ when the nonDY message is the signing key associated to a. In this case, $\mathcal{B}$ simply signs some fresh message to produce its forgery.

4. COMPOSITION THEOREMS

Our notion of deduction soundness enjoys the nice property of being easily extendable: if a computational algebra is deduction sound for a given set of primitives, it is possible to add other primitives, one by one, without having to prove deduction soundness, from scratch for the resulting set of primitives. In this paper we provide two results: we show how to extend in a modular way deduction soundness to encompass public data structures and asymmetric encryption.

4.1 Adding public datastructures

An immediate observation with interesting implications is the following. Consider some implementation M_1 for the functions in $\mathcal{F}_1 \subseteq \mathcal{F}$ for some signature $(\mathcal{S}, \mathcal{F})$. Now, extend M_1 to implement, in a transparent way additional functions in $\mathcal{F} \backslash \mathcal{F}_1$. Then, the resulting implementation is also deduction sound. The intuition behind this result is simple: if M_1 is sound when the functions in $\mathcal{F} \setminus \mathcal{F}_1$ are implemented via a transparent implementation selected by the adversary, implementing some (or even all) of the functions in $\mathcal{F} \backslash \mathcal{F}_1$ with some fixed transparent implementation preserves soundness. This idea is formalized by the following theorem.

THEOREM 1. *Assume that M_1 is an $(\mathcal{S}, \mathcal{F}_1)$-concrete implementation for some signature $(\mathcal{S}, \mathcal{F}_1 \cup \mathcal{F}_2 \cup \mathcal{F}_3)$ that is computationally sound with respect to deduction $\mathcal{D}$, parse function* parse *and predicate P_{valid}. Then, if M_2 is an arbitrary transparent implementation for the functions in $\mathcal{F}_2$, then $M_1 || M_2$ (the implementation that implements functions in $\mathcal{F}_1$ with M_1 and functions in $\mathcal{F}_2$ with M_2) is a $(\mathcal{S}, \mathcal{F}_1 \cup \mathcal{F}_2)$-concrete implementation for $(\mathcal{S}, \mathcal{F}_1 \cup \mathcal{F}_2 \cup \mathcal{F}_3)$ that is deduction sound with respect to $\mathcal{D} \cup \mathcal{D}_{\mathsf{tran}}(\mathcal{F}_2)$, parse function* $\mathsf{parse}^{\mathsf{tran}}$ *and predicate P_{valid}. The function* $\mathsf{parse}^{\mathsf{tran}}$ *is defined via* $\mathsf{saturate}^{\mathsf{tran}}$ *(Figure 2) with the transparent implementation set to M_2.*

The proof of the theorem is by reduction. Consider an adversary $\mathcal{A}$ that breaks deduction soundness for the $(\mathcal{S}, \mathcal{F}_1 \cup \mathcal{F}_2)$-concrete implementation. We construct the following adversary $\mathcal{B}$ against the soundness of the implementation M_1. Adversary $\mathcal{B}$ runs internally $\mathcal{A}$: when $\mathcal{A}$ outputs its transparent interpretation M_3 for the functions in $\mathcal{F}_3$, adversary $\mathcal{B}$ outputs $M_2 || M_3$ as its transparent interpretation for the functions in $\mathcal{F}_2 \cup \mathcal{F}_3$. After this, $\mathcal{B}$ simply forwards the queries of $\mathcal{A}$ to the game and forwards the returns. When $\mathcal{A}$ requests the parse of a string that corresponds to a nonDY term with respect to $\mathcal{D} \cup \mathcal{D}_{\mathsf{tran}(\mathcal{F}_2)}$ this term is in fact nonDY with respect to $\mathcal{D}$, so $\mathcal{B}$ wins its own game.

The above theorem is important as it allows to add, essentially for free, public data structures to any implementation that is deduction sound (in the sense of our definition) as typically data structures are implemented by transparent implementations.

For example lists can be added to a deduction soundness results as follows. Assume that the set of transparent functions $\mathcal{F}_{\mathsf{list}}$ contains two functions empty and $@$ with arities $\mathsf{empty} :\rightarrow \mathsf{term}$ and $@ : \mathsf{term} \rightarrow \mathsf{term}$, respectively. Consider the following implementation M_{list} for lists.

- (M_{list} $\mathsf{evaluate\ empty}$) outputs $\langle \epsilon, \mathsf{list} \rangle$ where ϵ is some fixed bitstring.
- (M_{list} $\mathsf{evaluate}$ $@$) on input x_0 and U, parses U as $\langle x_1, x_2, \ldots, x_k, \mathsf{list} \rangle$ for some k. If $k = 1$ and x_1 is ϵ then return $\langle x_0, \mathsf{list} \rangle$, otherwise return $\langle x_0, x_1, \ldots, x_k, \mathsf{list} \rangle$.
- (M_{list} type) on input x parses U as $\langle x_1, \ldots, x_k, \mathsf{list} \rangle$ for some $k \geq 0$ and $x_1, x_2, \ldots, x_k$ arbitrary bitstrings. If parsing fails, then the algorithm returns $\perp$. If $k = 1$ and $x_1 = \epsilon$ then return empty, otherwise return $@$.
- (M_{list} proj $@$ 1) on input x attempts to parse x as $\langle x_1, x_2, \ldots, x_k, \mathsf{list} \rangle$. If this does not succeed it outputs $\perp$. Otherwise it outputs x_1.
- (M_{list} proj $@$ 2) on input x attempts to parse x as $\langle x_1, x_2, \ldots, x_k, \mathsf{list} \rangle$. If this does not succeed it outputs $\perp$. If $k = 1$ then return $\langle \epsilon, \mathsf{list} \rangle$, otherwise output $\langle x_2, x_3, \ldots, x_k, \mathsf{list} \rangle$.

The above implementation clearly satisfies the properties of a transparent implementation. Theorem 1 works for arbitrary sets of transparent symbols. By replacing in the statement of the theorem $\mathcal{F}_2$ with $\mathcal{F}_{\mathsf{list}}$, and M_2 with $\mathcal{M}_{\mathsf{list}}$ one obtains a soundness result for the extension of the implementation of M_1 with M_{list} with respect to the deducibility relation induced by $\mathcal{D}_{\mathsf{sm}} \cup \mathcal{D}_{\mathsf{list}}$. Here, D_{list} is simply $\mathcal{D}_{\mathsf{tran}}(\mathcal{F}_{\mathsf{list}})$. We use this notation later in the paper.

Of course, other possible implementations for lists are possible and the theorem can be reused for each of these different implementations (as long as they are transparent). It is also possible to provide similar specifications for the usual pairing operation or more complex data structures (e.g. XML documents), and the corresponding extension result holds.

4.2 Adding asymmetric encryption

In this section we give a theorem that allows to extend a deduction sound implementation with asymmetric encryption. Our modeling assumes that corrupted keys are "honestly" generated by the key generation for the primitive. This assumption is quite common in existing soundness results (e.g.[5, 13, 16]) and is rarely circumvented (e.g.[8, 18]). For asymmetric primitives, as in the case of asymmetric encryption, the assumption can be ensured through a PKI. The reason for this assumption is that the problems outlined in [10] for the case of symmetric encryption also apply for asymmetric encryption.

For an algebraic signature $\mathcal{S}, \mathcal{F}$ we define its extension $\mathcal{S}_{\mathsf{enc}}, \mathcal{F}_{\mathsf{enc}}$ to asymmetric encryption. We define

$$\mathcal{S}_{\mathsf{enc}} = \mathcal{S} \cup \{\mathsf{id}, \mathsf{keypair}, \mathsf{ekey}, \mathsf{dkey}\}$$

where id represents agent identities and sorts $\mathsf{keypair}$, ekey, dkey contain key pairs, keys for encryption, and decryption respectively. We assume $\mathsf{keypair}, \mathsf{ekey}, \mathsf{dkey} \notin \mathcal{S}$ while id may already be in $\mathcal{S}$. Moreover, id is a sub-sort of term. We consider $\mathcal{F}_{\mathsf{enc}} = \mathcal{F} \uplus \{\mathsf{keypair}, \mathsf{ek}, \mathsf{dk}, \mathsf{enc}\}$. The function $\mathsf{keypair}$ of arity $\mathsf{id} \rightarrow \mathsf{keypair}$ takes on input an identity and returns the key pair associated to the identity. The function ek of arity $\mathsf{keypair} \rightarrow \mathsf{ekey}$ (resp dk of arity $\mathsf{keypair} \rightarrow \mathsf{dkey}$) is defined on the sort $\mathsf{keypair}$ and returns the encryption key (resp. the decryption key) associated to the key pair. The encryption function enc has arity $\mathsf{ekey} \times \mathsf{term} \rightarrow \mathsf{ciphertext}$. Note that, by construction, well-sorted terms do not contain strict subterms of sort dkey. By abuse of notation, we will often write $\mathsf{ek}(a)$ instead of $\mathsf{ek}(\mathsf{keypair}(a))$.

Let $\vdash$ be a deduction relation defined by a deduction system $\mathcal{D}$. We extend this deduction system with rules that capture the security of encryption:

$$\mathcal{D}_{\mathsf{enc}} = \left\{ \begin{array}{c} \frac{\mathsf{enc}^l(\mathsf{ek}(v),u) \quad \mathsf{dk}(v)}{u}, \qquad \frac{\mathsf{ek}(v) \quad u}{\mathsf{enc}^l(\mathsf{ek}(v),u)} l \in \mathsf{labelsA}, \\ \\ \frac{\mathsf{enc}^l(\mathsf{ek}(v),u)}{u} l \in \mathsf{labelsA} \end{array} \right\}$$

where v is a variable of sort id and u is a variable of sort term. We write $\vdash_{\mathsf{enc}}$ for the deduction relation induced by $\mathcal{D} \cup \mathcal{D}_{\mathsf{enc}}$

We now give a concrete implementation M_{enc} for encryption. The implementation uses some asymmetric encryption scheme $\Pi = (\mathcal{G}, \mathcal{E}, \mathcal{D})$. As usual, here $\mathcal{G}$ is a generation algorithm for key pairs, $\mathcal{E}$ is an encryption algorithm and $\mathcal{D}$ is a decryption algorithm. Note that $\mathcal{E}$ is an algorithm that takes three inputs: the encryption key, the message to be encrypted and the randomness that is used for encryption. We consider an implementation that affixes to bitstring a tag that indicates how it has been generated. The four possible tags are $\mathsf{tenc}, \mathsf{tkeypair}, \mathsf{tek}$ and tdk for cyphertexts, keypairs, encryption keys and decryption keys resp. The computable interpretations of $\mathsf{keypair}, \mathsf{ek}, \mathsf{dk}, \mathsf{enc}$ are as follows:

- (M_{enc} $\mathsf{keypair}$ a) is $\mathcal{G}(\eta)$ to the output of which we append the tag $\mathsf{tkeypair}$;
- (M_{enc} enc) : (k, m, r): parse k as $\langle pk, \mathsf{tek} \rangle$, compute $c \leftarrow \mathcal{E}(pk, m, r)$ and output $\langle c, pk, \mathsf{enc} \rangle$.
- (M_{enc} ek) is the function that extracts the encryption key from a key pair and adds the tag tek;
- (M_{enc} dk) is the function that extracts the decryption key from a key pair and adds the tag tdk.

Next, we show how to extend the parsing parse algorithm for the original implementation M to take into account the newly added primitive. In Figure 4 we define the function $\mathsf{saturate}^{\mathsf{enc}}$ (that in turn defines the parsing algorithm

$\mathsf{parse}^{\mathsf{enc}}$), starting from the abstract algorithm saturate underlying the parsing algorithm for the implementation M. The algorithm works as expected: it tries to interpret the strings that are parsed as garbage symbols by the original algorithm (i.e. saturate) as encryptions. If this does not succeed, the interpretation of these bitstrings does not change. Otherwise, the bitstrings are decrypted and the plaintext is then parsed according to saturate. The process is repeated until the assignation set remains unchanged (i.e. it is not possible to parse some bitstring that is interpreted as garbage in the current assignation set).

We assume that whenever there is $(ek, \mathsf{ek}(a)) \in L$ then there is (a unique) $(dk, \mathsf{dk}(a)) \in L$. It is easy to check that this property is preserved by the $\mathsf{saturate}^{\mathsf{enc}}$ function.

Function $\mathsf{saturate}^{\mathsf{enc}}(L)$
Let $\mathsf{Mem} = \mathsf{collapse}_{\Sigma,\Sigma_{\mathsf{enc}}}(L)$;
  (Mem links terms headed by functions outside Σ to garbage)
let $L' = L$
repeat
  let $L = L'$;
  let $L' = \mathsf{saturate}(L'\mathsf{Mem}^{-1})\mathsf{Mem}$;
    (L' is parsed according to the signature Σ)
  if there is $(b, g^l) \in L$ where g is of sort term
    and b is of the form $\langle b', ek, \mathsf{enc}\rangle$,
    and there is $(ek, \mathsf{ek}(a)) \in L$ thus a unique $(dk, \mathsf{dk}(a)) \in L$,
    and $\mathcal{D}(b', dk) \neq \perp$, do
    let $m = \mathcal{D}(b', dk)$,
    if there is $(m, U) \in L'$ then let $V = U$
      otherwise let $V = [g^{l(m)}]$ where $l(m) \in \mathsf{labelsA}$;
    let $L' = L' \setminus \{(b, g^l)\} \cup \{(b, [\mathsf{enc}^l(\mathsf{ek}(a), g^{l(m)}); g^l]), (m, V)\}$
    let $\mathsf{Mem} = \mathsf{Mem} \cup \{(g^l, \mathsf{enc}^l(\mathsf{ek}(a), g^{l(m)}))\}$
until $L = L'$
return L

Figure 4: Extending parsing to asymmetric encryption.

We now show that the extension of a deduction-sound implementation with asymmetric encryption, as specified above remains deduction-sound, provided that the encryption scheme used in the implementation is IND-CCA secure. More precisely, we show that soundness of the extension holds with respect to deduction system $\mathcal{D} \cup \mathcal{D}_{\mathsf{enc}}$ and parsing function $\mathsf{parse}^{\mathsf{enc}}$. The predicate that validates the requests of the adversary needs to be changed (as the signature has changed). In particular, the generate requests in the new game should satisfy that requests remain valid w.r.t. to the initial signature and some additional constraints due to the use of encryption. Formally, given a predicate P_{valid} for a signature $(\mathcal{S}, \mathcal{F}_1 \cup \mathcal{F}_{\mathsf{tran}})$, $\overline{P_{\mathsf{valid}}}^{\mathsf{enc}}$ is any predicate that conforms to the following restrictions (one would consider the least restrictive version).

- The adversary may generate keys (i.e. perform requests generate $\mathsf{ek}(\mathsf{keypair}(a))$ or generate $\mathsf{keypair}(a)$, with $a \in \mathsf{id}$) but only at the beginning of the game (before any encryption request is made); this requirement corresponds to allowing only static corruption of encryption keys.
- After this first phase, $\mathsf{keypair}(a)$ do not do not appear in terms except inside a sub-term of the form $\mathsf{ek}(\mathsf{keypair}(a))$;
- Importantly, the requests for the implementation that includes encryption, should remain valid w.r.t. the initial signature. To specify an appropriate extension of P_{valid} we remark the following about the workings of the game. As far as the adversary is concerned, ciphertexts are either entirely opaque (encrypted under honest keys) or entirely transparent (encrypted under corrupted keys). We can interpret then bitstrings with respect to the original signature as either garbage constants or as transparent functions. The validity requirement is then that terms with respect to the joint signature are, under this substitution valid with respect to the game for the original signature. Formally, we capture this idea as follows.

We define the auxiliary function $\mathsf{replace}_{(H,C)}$ which is parameterized by two sets of agents H and C such that $\mathsf{id} = H \cup C$, from terms in $\mathcal{F}_1 \cup \mathcal{F}_{\mathsf{tran}} \cup \mathcal{F}_{\mathsf{enc}}$ to terms in $\mathcal{F}_1 \cup \mathcal{F}_{\mathsf{tran}}$ as follows:

- $\mathsf{replace}_{(H,C)}(f^l(t_1, \ldots, t_n)) =$ $f^l(\mathsf{replace}_{(H,C)}(t_1), \ldots, \mathsf{replace}_{(H,C)}(t_n))$ if $f \neq \mathsf{enc}$;
- $\mathsf{replace}_{(H,C)}(\mathsf{enc}^l(\mathsf{ek}(b), t)) = f^l_{\mathsf{ek}(b)}(\mathsf{replace}_{(H,C)}(t))$ if $b \in C$;
- $\mathsf{replace}_{(H,C)}(\mathsf{enc}^l(\mathsf{ek}(a), t)) = f^{l(\mathsf{enc}^l(\mathsf{ek}(a),t))}_{\mathsf{ek}(a)}$ if $a \in H$ and $l \in \mathsf{labelsH}$;
- $\mathsf{replace}_{(H,C)}(\mathsf{enc}^l(\mathsf{ek}(a), t)) = g^{\mathsf{enc}^l(\mathsf{ek}(a),t)}$ if $a \in H$ and $l \in \mathsf{labelsA}$;

Then, $\overline{P_{\mathsf{valid}}}$ is any predicate such that for any choice of H and C such that $\mathsf{id} = H \cup C$ the following holds:

$$\mathsf{replace}_{(H,C)}(\overline{P_{\mathsf{valid}}}^{\mathsf{enc}}) \subseteq P_{\mathsf{valid}} \qquad (1)$$

where $f^l_{\mathsf{ek}(b)}$ is a unary symbol and $f^{l(\mathsf{enc}^l(\mathsf{ek}(a),t))}_{\mathsf{ek}(a)}$ is a constant symbol.

Our next theorem shows that any deduction sound set of primitives can be automatically extended to asymmetric encryption.

THEOREM 2. *Let $\mathcal{S}_1$ be a set of sorts, $\mathcal{F}_1$ be a set of symbols. Let $\mathcal{F}_{\mathsf{tran}}$ and $\mathcal{F}_{\mathsf{tran}'}$ be two disjoint sets of functions symbols of arity of the form* $\mathsf{term} \times \cdots \times \mathsf{term} \to \mathsf{term}$ *such that they contain an infinite countable number of functions of each arity. Let M_1 be a $(\mathcal{S}_1, \mathcal{F}_1 \cup \mathcal{F}_{\mathsf{tran}} \cup \mathcal{F}_{\mathsf{tran}'})$-concrete implementation which is deduction sound w.r.t. a deduction system $\mathcal{D}$, a parsing function* parse *and a predicate P_{valid}. Let $\mathcal{S}_{\mathsf{enc}}$, $\mathcal{F}_{\mathsf{enc}}$, $\mathcal{D}_{\mathsf{enc}}$, M_{enc} as defined in Section 4.2.*

Then $(M_1 \| M_{\mathsf{enc}})$ is a deduction sound $((\mathcal{S}_1 \cup \mathcal{S}_{\mathsf{enc}}, \mathcal{F}_1 \cup \mathcal{F}_{\mathsf{enc}} \cup \mathcal{F}_{\mathsf{tran}}))$-concrete implementation w.r.t. the deduction system $\mathcal{D} \cup \mathcal{D}_{\mathsf{enc}}$, the parsing function $\mathsf{parse}^{\mathsf{enc}}$ and any predicate $\overline{P_{\mathsf{valid}}}^{\mathsf{enc}}$ that satisfies Equation 1, provided that the encryption scheme used by M_{enc} is IND-CCA.

The proof of Theorem 2 works in two stages. First, we transform the deduction-soundness game for the $(\mathcal{S}_1 \cup \mathcal{S}_{\mathsf{enc}}, \mathcal{F}_1 \cup \mathcal{F}_{\mathsf{enc}} \cup \mathcal{F}_{\mathsf{tran}})$-concrete implementation $(M_1 \| M_{\mathsf{enc}})$ into a game $\mathsf{Game}^{\mathsf{fake}}$ where the encryption function is replaced by a function that encrypts with zeros when called on "honest" identities. The sets H and D of honest and dishonest identities are determined during the first phase of the game, when the adversary does not request any encryption: dishonest identities are those for which the adversary knows both the public and private corresponding keys while honest identities are the remaining ones. The IND-CCA assumption on the encryption function ensures that the two games are indistinguishable.

The second (and main) step of the proof is a reduction. Assume the existence of an adversary $\mathcal{A}$ that breaks the game $\mathsf{Game}^{\mathsf{fake}}$. Building upon $\mathcal{A}$, we construct an adversary $\mathcal{B}$ that wins the game $\mathsf{Game}_{\mathcal{S}_1,\mathcal{F}_1\cup\mathcal{F}_{\mathsf{tran}}\cup\mathcal{F}_{\mathsf{tran}'},\mathcal{B},M_1,\mathsf{parse},\mathcal{D}}$, that is, an adversary that contradicts the soundness of implementation M_1. In the first phase, $\mathcal{B}$ generates the key pairs (honest and dishonest) itself. The key idea is to show how the transparent functions in $\mathcal{F}_{\mathsf{tran}'}$ can be used by $\mathcal{B}$ to apply encryption inside terms it does not have access to. The simulation of encryption by transparent function works as follows. For each dishonest key $\mathsf{ek}(b) \in D$, we assume given a transparent function $f_{\mathsf{ek}(b)} \in \mathcal{F}_{\mathsf{tran}'}$ of arity 1, whose interpretation (provided by $\mathcal{B}$) is to encrypt with $\mathsf{ek}(b)$. The associated projector is simply the decryption with the corresponding decryption key. For each honest key $\mathsf{ek}(a)$ and length $l \in \mathbb{N}$, we assume given a transparent function $f_{\mathsf{ek}(a),l} \in \mathcal{F}_{\mathsf{tran}'}$ of arity 0 (a constant) that simply encrypts 0^l by $\mathsf{ek}(a)$. This function symbol being a constant, it does not have a projector. We can then conclude the proof by showing that $\mathcal{B}$ interacting with $\mathsf{Game}_{\mathcal{S}_1,\mathcal{F}_1\cup\mathcal{F}_{\mathsf{tran}}\cup\mathcal{F}_{\mathsf{tran}'},\mathcal{B},M_1,\mathsf{parse},\mathcal{D}}$ exactly simulates $\mathsf{Game}^{\mathsf{fake}}$.

5. APPLICATIONS

In this section we present two applications of our notion. First, we show that the composability property of our soundness notion allows to combine, several different primitives: we obtain deduction soundness for mac, signatures, lists and asymmetric encryption. In the following proposition $\mathsf{parse}_{\mathsf{sm,list,sm}}$ is the parsing algorithm $\mathsf{parse}_{\mathsf{sm}}$ extended to lists and encryption as specified earlier in the paper and predicate $\overline{P_{\mathsf{sm}}}$ is any predicate that satisfies Equation 1 (where P_{valid} is replaced by P_{sm}) and $\mathsf{parse}_{\mathsf{sm,list,sm}}$.

PROPOSITION 2. *$M_{\mathsf{sm}}||M_{\mathsf{list}}||M_{\mathsf{enc}}$ is a concrete implementation for $(\mathcal{S}_{\mathsf{enc}}, (\mathcal{F}_{\mathsf{sm}} \cup \mathcal{F}_{\mathsf{list}})_{\mathsf{enc}})$ that is deduction sound with respect to $\mathcal{D}_{\mathsf{sm}} \cup \mathcal{D}_{\mathsf{list}} \cup \mathcal{D}_{\mathsf{enc}}$, parsing function $\mathsf{parse}_{\mathsf{sm,list,enc}}$ and predicate $\overline{P_{\mathsf{sm}}}$, if the digital signature scheme and the MAC scheme used in M_{sm} are EU-CMA secure and the encryption scheme used in M_{enc} is IND-CCA secure.*

The proof of the proposition is an immediate consequence of Proposition 1 and Theorems 1 and 2.

Next, we show that deduction soundness allows computationally sound symbolic analysis for a wide class of protocols. We specify this class through an abstract property that links symbolic and computational versions of the same protocol. To this end, we regard protocols as state transition systems. So, a *symbolic protocol* is simply a state-based transition system that takes terms as inputs and outputs terms. A *computational protocol* is state-based transition system that takes bitstrings as inputs and outputs bitstrings. Symbolic protocols could be specified for instance using some process calculus, whereas computational protocols are specified through communicating Turing machines.

The property that we define next, and which we call *commutation property* links symbolic and computational protocols. Intuitively the property says that the computational interpretation of the symbolic behavior of the protocol correspond to its implementation.

DEFINITION 3 (COMMUTATION PROPERTY). *Let P^s be a symbolic protocol and P^c be a computational protocol. Intuitively, P^s and P^c should be respectively the symbolic and computational interpretation of the same protocol P. Let $\mathcal{S}$ be a set of sorts, $\mathcal{F}$ be a set of symbols. Let M_1 be a $(\mathcal{S},\mathcal{F}_1)$-concrete implementation and parse be a parsing function. We say that (P^s, P^c)* has the commutation property *if the two following games are computationally indistinguishable by any polynomial adversary.*

1. *Game 1: $\mathcal{A}$ interacts with P^c directly.*
2. *Game 2:*

   Set $L = \emptyset$; (assignation set)
   On input c from $\mathcal{A}$ do:
   $(t, L) := \mathsf{parse}(c, L)$
   send t to P^s, getting u
   $(c', L) := \mathsf{generate}_{M_1}(u, L)$
   return c' to $\mathcal{A}$

For example, for any protocol described by the language of [13] (with input and output of messages, conditional with no else branch and replication of processes) the formal and computational interpretations of the protocol enjoy the commutation property. A similar property has been identified by Backes, Hofheinz, and Unruh as a sufficient condition to obtain soundness results in their CoSP framework [3]. They elaborate in the full version of their paper and show how to prove this commutation property for all protocols written in a specific language. Similar results are possible within the framework that we propose.

Next, we show that for protocols that satisfy this commutation property one can prove a soundness result: whenever a formal protocol enjoys a security property (for a symbolic adversary), the corresponding computational protocol also enjoys the same security property. The focus of this paper is on trace-based properties which are naturally specified in terms of deducibility relations.

We write $P \xrightarrow{?u!v} P'$ if a protocol at state P outputs v on input u, moving to state P'. A trace is then a sequence of input/output messages. Formally, a *formal* (resp. *computational*) *execution trace* of a formal (resp. computational) protocol P is a sequence of the form $?u_1!v_1?u_2!v_2\cdots?u_n!v_n$ such that the u_i, v_i are terms (resp. bitstrings) and $P \xrightarrow{?u_1!v_1} P_1 \xrightarrow{?u_2!v_2} P_2 \cdots \xrightarrow{?u_n!v_n} P_n$. For formal protocols, we say that a formal execution trace $?u_1!v_1?u_2!v_2\cdots?u_n!v_n$ is *valid* w.r.t. to a deduction system $\mathcal{D}$ if $\{v_1,\ldots,v_{i-1} \vdash_{\mathcal{D}} u_i\}$ for any $1 \leq i \leq n$. Valid execution traces ensures that the symbolic adversary only makes valid (deducible) queries. A security property can be any predicate on the execution traces.

DEFINITION 4. *Let ϕ^s (resp. ϕ^c) be a predicate on formal (resp. computational) traces. Let P^s be a symbolic protocol and P^c be a computational protocol. Let $\mathcal{D}$ be a deduction system. We say that P^s satisfies ϕ^s, denoted $P^s \models^s \phi^s$ if ϕ^s holds for any valid execution trace of P^s, w.r.t. $\mathcal{D}$. Similarly, we say P^c satisfies ϕ^c, denoted $P^c \models^c \phi^c$ if for any p.p.t. adversary $\mathcal{A}$, the predicate ϕ^c holds with overwhelming probability on execution traces of P^c interacting with $\mathcal{A}$.*

Deduction soundness allows the transfer of security properties for any formal / computation interpretation that enjoys the commutation property from the symbolic to the computational setting.

PROPOSITION 3. *Let P^s be a symbolic protocol and P^c be a computational protocol. Let ϕ^s be a predicate on formal traces. Let $\mathcal{S}$ be a set of sorts, $\mathcal{F}$ a set of symbols, $\mathcal{D}$ a deduction system, P_{valid} a predicate and* parse *a parsing function. Assume M_1 is a deduction sound $(\mathcal{S}, \mathcal{F}_1)$-concrete implementation, w.r.t. $\mathcal{D}$, P_{valid} and* parse*. Assume that (P^s, P^c) has the commutation property and that all valid executions of P_s satisfy P_{valid}. Then*

$$P^s \models^s \phi^s \Rightarrow P^c \models^c \phi^c$$

where ϕ^c is the image of ϕ^s. Formally, $\phi^c = \{t^c \mid t^c = L(t^s)$ for some $t^s \in \phi^s, L \in \mathcal{L}\}$ where $\mathcal{L}$ is the set of all L that can be constructed in Game 2.

6. CONCLUSION

In this paper we propose *deduction soundness*, a novel computational soundness framework. The key feature of our notion is that it allows for modular extensions and we provide two concrete examples. We show that implementations for arbitrary cryptographic primitives that are deduction sound can be extended with public data structures and asymmetric encryption without repeating the original proof effort.

There are several obviously interesting directions for further work. The first is to show that deduction soundness can be extended, modularly, to other cryptographic primitives. We expect that the techniques developed in this paper for the case of asymmetric encryption would apply virtually unchanged to the case of hash functions (modeled as random oracles) and symmetric encryption schemes. However, in its present form, deduction soundness does not extend to authentication primitives (e.g. digital signature and message authentication codes). The main reason is that the current definition does not account for the interaction between the axioms that are proved deduction sound and those that characterize the implementation provided by the adversary, as far as authentication aspects are concerned. A modular extension with signatures and macs needs to limit, in a fairly non-restrictive manner, the interaction between the axioms for these authentication primitives and those of for which soundness had already been proved. We leave such an extension for further work.

The notion of deduction soundness is concerned directly with the implementation of cryptographic primitives and is independent of any particular protocol specification language. Computational soundness for such languages can however still be established if a certain property which we call a commutation property holds. The commutation property ensures that a real execution of a protocol (with primitives implemented as expected) is the same as the execution of the protocol with primitives implemented as in the game that defines soundness. If this property holds, then a real execution of the protocol can be mapped to a symbolic one and this, in turn, leads to a soundness result in the form of a mapping lemma.

Mapping lemmas allow for the translation of authentication properties from symbolic models to computational ones but they do not directly yield similar results for secrecy properties. An intriguing open question is therefore to develop modularly extensible frameworks for computational soundness that allow for the transfer of secrecy properties. Specification through equivalence notions (rather than deducibility) lend themselves naturally to capturing secrecy properties (both symbolically and computationally). A possible direction would therefore be to define *equivalence soundness*, the analogous of our notion for equivalences (rather than deducibility).

Finally, we note that proving that the commutation property holds for a general specification language is not particularly difficult, but it is rather tedious, as evidenced by the work of Backes, Hofheinz, and Unruh (in the long version of [3]), where such a property had been proved. An interesting research question is to find ways to prove, also in a modular way that the commutation property holds.

Acknowledgement.

We would like to thank Steve Kremer, Hubert Common Lundh, Ralf Küsters, and Dominique Unruh for useful discussions and suggestions. In particular, Dominique suggested the search for a modular way of proving the commutation property. This work has been supported in part by the European Commission through the ICT Programme under Contract ICT-2007-216676 ECRYPT II and by the European Research Council under the European Union's Seventh Framework Programme (FP72007–2013)/ERC grant agreement 258865 - project ProSecure.

7. REFERENCES

[1] M. Abadi and P. Rogaway. Reconciling two views of cryptography (the computational soundness of formal encryption). *Journal of Cryptology*, 15(2):103–127, 2002.

[2] A. Armando, R. Carbone, L. Compagna, J. Cuellar, and L. T. Abad. Formal analysis of saml 2.0 web browser single sign-on: Breaking the saml-based single sign-on for google apps. In *Proceedings of the 6th ACM Workshop on Formal Methods in Security Engineering (FMSE 2008)*, pages 1–10, 2008.

[3] M. Backes, D. Hofheinz, and D. Unruh. Cosp: A general framework for computational soundness proofs. In *ACM CCS 2009*, pages 66–78, November 2009. Preprint on IACR ePrint 2009/080.

[4] M. Backes and B. Pfitzmann. Symmetric encryption in a simulatable Dolev-Yao style cryptographic library. In *Proc. 17th IEEE Computer Science Foundations Workshop (CSFW'04)*, pages 204–218, 2004.

[5] M. Backes, B. Pfitzmann, and M. Waidner. A composable cryptographic library with nested operations. In *Proc. 10th ACM Conference on Computer and Communications Security (CCS'03)*, 2003.

[6] M. Backes and D. Unruh. Computational soundness of symbolic zero-knowledge proofs against active attackers. In *Proceedings of the 21st IEEE Computer Security Foundations Symposium (CSF'08)*, pages 255–269, Pittsburgh, PA, USA, June 2008. IEEE Computer Society Press.

[7] R. Canetti. Universally composable signature, certification, and authentication. In *Proc. 17th IEEE*

Computer Security Foundations Workshop (CSFW'04), pages 219–235, 2004.

[8] R. Canetti and J. Herzog. Universally composable symbolic analysis of mutual authentication and key-exchange protocols (extended abstract). In *Proc. 3rd Theory of Cryptography Conference (TCC'06)*, volume 3876 of *LNCS*, pages 380–403. Springer, 2006.

[9] H. Comon-Lundh and V. Cortier. Computational soundness of observational equivalence. In *Proceedings of the 15th ACM Conference on Computer and Communications Security (CCS'08)*, Alexandria, Virginia, USA, Oct. 2008. ACM Press.

[10] H. Comon-Lundh and V. Cortier. How to prove security of communication protocolsň A discussion on the soundness of formal models w.r.t. computational ones. In *28th International Symposium on Theoretical Aspects of Computer Science (STACS 2011)*, volume 9 of *Leibniz International Proceedings in Informatics (LIPIcs)*, pages 29–44, 2011.

[11] V. Cortier, S. Kremer, R. Küsters, and B. Warinschi. Computationally sound symbolic secrecy in the presence of hash functions. In *Proceedings of the 26th Conference on Fundations of Software Technology and Theoretical Computer Science (FSTTCS'06)*, volume 4337 of *LNCS*, pages 176–187, Kolkata, India, 2006. Springer.

[12] V. Cortier, S. Kremer, and B. Warinschi. A survey of symbolic methods in computational analysis of cryptographic systems. *J. Autom. Reasoning*, 46(3-4):225–259, 2011.

[13] V. Cortier and B. Warinschi. Computationally sound, automated proofs for security protocols. In *European Symposium on Programming (ESOP'05)*, volume 3444 of *LNCS*, pages 157–171, Edinburgh, UK, 2005. Springer.

[14] D. Galindo, F. D. Garcia, and P. van Rossum. Computational soundness of non-malleable commitments. In *Proc. 4th Information Security Practice and Experience Conference (ISPEC'08)*, LNCS, 2008. To appear.

[15] J. Herzog. A computational interpretation of Dolev-Yao adversaries. *Theoretical Computer Science*, 340:57–81, June 2005.

[16] R. Janvier, Y. Lakhnech, and L. Mazaré. Completing the picture: Soundness of formal encryption in the presence of active adversaries. In *European Symposium on Programming (ESOP'05)*, volume 3444 of *LNCS*, pages 172–185. Springer, 2005.

[17] R. Janvier, Y. Lakhnech, and L. Mazaré. Computational soundness of symbolic analysis for protocols using hash functions. In *Proceedings of the Workshop on Information and Computer Security (ICS'06)*, Electronic Notes in Theoretical Computer Science, Timisoara, Romania, Sept. 2006. Elsevier Science Publishers.

[18] R. Küsters and M. Tuengerthal. Computational Soundness for Key Exchange Protocols with Symmetric Encryption. In E. Al-Shaer, S. Jha, and A. D. Keromytis, editors, *Proceedings of the 16th ACM Conference on Computer and Communications Security (CCS 2009)*, pages 91–100. ACM Press, 2009.

[19] G. Lowe. Breaking and fixing the Needham-Schroeder public-key protocol using FDR. In *Tools and Algorithms for the Construction and Analysis of Systems (TACAS'96)*, volume 1055 of *LNCS*, pages 147–166. Springer-Verlag, March 1996.

[20] D. Micciancio and B. Warinschi. Soundness of formal encryption in the presence of active adversaries. In *Proc. 1st Theory of Cryptography Conference (TCC'04)*, volume 2951 of *LNCS*, pages 133–151. Springer, 2004.

On the Requirements for Successful GPS Spoofing Attacks

Nils Ole Tippenhauer
Dept. of Computer Science
ETH Zurich, Switzerland
tinils@inf.ethz.ch

Christina Pöpper
Dept. of Computer Science
ETH Zurich, Switzerland
poepperc@inf.ethz.ch

Kasper B. Rasmussen
Computer Science Dept.
UCI, Irvine, CA
kbrasmus@ics.uci.edu

Srdjan Čapkun
Dept. of Computer Science
ETH Zurich, Switzerland
capkuns@inf.ethz.ch

ABSTRACT

An increasing number of wireless applications rely on GPS signals for localization, navigation, and time synchronization. However, civilian GPS signals are known to be susceptible to spoofing attacks which make GPS receivers in range believe that they reside at locations different than their real physical locations. In this paper, we investigate the requirements for successful GPS spoofing attacks on individuals and groups of victims with civilian or military GPS receivers. In particular, we are interested in identifying from which locations and with which precision the attacker needs to generate its signals in order to successfully spoof the receivers.

We will show, for example, that any number of receivers can easily be spoofed to one arbitrary location; however, the attacker is restricted to only few transmission locations when spoofing a group of receivers while preserving their constellation.

In addition, we investigate the practical aspects of a satellite-lock takeover, in which a victim receives spoofed signals after first being locked on to legitimate GPS signals. Using a civilian GPS signal generator, we perform a set of experiments and find the minimal precision of the attacker's spoofing signals required for covert satellite-lock takeover.

Categories and Subject Descriptors

C.2.1 [**Computer Systems Organization**]: Computer-Communication Networks—*Network Architecture and Design*

General Terms

Security, Experimentation

1. INTRODUCTION

The Global Positioning System (GPS), originally introduced by the US military, has become an essential component for numerous civilian applications. Unlike military GPS signals, civilian GPS signals are not encrypted or authenticated and were never intended for safety- and security-critical applications. Nevertheless, GPS-provided locations are being used in applications such as vehicular navigation and aviation, asset monitoring (e. g., cargo tracking), and location-based services (e. g., routing) [23]. The use of the GPS system also includes time synchronization; examples are time stamping in security videos and critical time synchronization in financial, telecommunications and computer networks. Users highly rely on the precision and correctness of GPS location and time: transport companies track trucks, cargoes, and goods under GPS surveillance, and courts rely on criminals being correctly tracked by GPS-based ankle monitors.

This heavy reliance on civilian GPS—following the discontinuation of the selective availability feature of GPS in the year 2000—motivated a number of investigations on the security of GPS. These investigations found that civilian GPS is susceptible to jamming and spoofing attacks [9, 11, 16, 19]. Successful spoofing experiments on standard receivers have been reported [7, 24], showing that commercial-off-the-shelf receivers do not detect such attacks. The increased availability of programmable radio platforms such as USRPs [5] leads to a reduced cost of attacks on GPS. However, the requirements for GPS spoofing were so far not analyzed systematically and many of the previously proposed countermeasures [8, 16] assume a weak attacker that is, e. g., not able to generate signals with sufficient precision.

In this work, we investigate spoofing attacks on civilian and military GPS and analyze the requirements for their success as well as their limitations in practice. We divide the problem of GPS spoofing into the following two problems: (i) sending the correct spoofing signals such that they reach the receiver with the right timing, and (ii) getting a victim that is already synchronized to the legitimate GPS service to lock onto the attacker's spoofing signal. Regarding the first problem, we analyze the effects of GPS spoofing signals on multiple receivers and analyze under which conditions a *group* of victims can be spoofed such that, e. g., their mutual distances are preserved. Our analysis shows that, in order to spoof a group of victims while preserving the mutual distances, the attacker can only transmit from a restricted set of locations. To the best of our knowledge, such an analysis has not been done before. The second problem of taking over the satellite lock is relevant for performing attacks in real-world situations. In most cases, the victim will have been receiving legitimate GPS signals when the spoofing attack starts. It is thus important to know the required *precision* of the spoofing signal such that the victim seamlessly (i. e., without detection) switches lock from the legitimate GPS signal to the attacker's spoofing signal. We explore the influence of imperfections (in different aspects of signal power and timing) in a series of experiments and discuss the findings.

The structure of the paper is as follows. We give background information on GPS positioning and discuss related work on GPS spoofing in Section 2. We introduce the GPS spoofing problem and our system and attacker models in Section 3. In Section 4,

CCS'11, October 17–21, 2011, Chicago, Illinois, USA.
Copyright 2011 ACM 978-1-4503-0948-6/11/10 ...$10.00.

we analyze under which conditions GPS spoofing attacks are successful on single victims and groups of victims. The results of our experimental evaluation are presented in Section 5. In Section 6, we introduce a novel countermeasure which is based on multiple receivers. We conclude the paper in Section 7.

2. BACKGROUND

In this section, we introduce the fundamental concepts of GPS (based on [11]) which are necessary for this work. We also summarize related work on the security of GPS.

2.1 The Global Positioning System

The Global Positioning System (GPS) uses a number of satellite transmitters S_i located at known locations $L_i^S \in \mathbb{R}^3$. Each transmitter is equipped with a synchronized clock with no clock offset to the exact system time t^S and broadcasts a carefully chosen navigation signal $s_i(t)$ (low auto-/cross-correlation[1], including timestamps and information on the satellites' deviation from the predicted trajectories). The signal propagates with speed c (see Figure 1).

A receiver V located at the coordinates $L \in \mathbb{R}^3$ (to be determined) and using an omnidirectional antenna will receive the combined signal of all satellites in range:

$$g(L,t) = \sum_i A_i s_i\left(t - \frac{|L_i^S - L|}{c}\right) + n(L,t) \quad (1)$$

where A_i is the attenuation that the signal suffers on its way from L_i^S to L, $|L_i^S - L|$ denotes the Euclidean distance between L_i^S and L, and $n(L,t)$ is background noise.

Due to the properties of the signals $s_i(t)$, the receiver can separate the individual terms of this sum and extract the relative spreading code phase, satellite ID, and data content using a replica of the used spreading code. Given the data and relative phase offsets, the receiver can identify the time delay $|L_i^S - L|/c$ for each satellite and from that infer the "ranges"

$$d_i = |L_i^S - L|. \quad (2)$$

With three known ranges d_i to known transmitter positions L_i^S, three equations (2) can be solved unambiguously for L (unless all three S_i are located on a line). Since highly stable clocks (e. g., cesium oscillators) are costly and GPS receivers cannot participate in two-way clock synchronization, in practice, V will have a clock offset δ to the exact system time: $t = t^S + \delta$. With this, Eq. 1 can be rewritten:

$$g(L,t^S) = \sum_i A_i s_i\left(t - \frac{d_i}{c} - \delta\right) + n(L,t^S) \quad (3)$$

where the receiver can only infer the "pseudoranges" R_i from the delays $d_i/c + \delta$:

$$R_i = d_i + c \cdot \delta. \quad (4)$$

The clock offset δ adds a fourth unknown scalar. With pseudorange measurements to at least four transmitters S_i, the resulting system of equations (4) can be solved for both L and δ, providing both the exact position and time, without requiring a precise local clock. Given $L_i^S = (x_i^S, y_i^S, z_i^S)$, $L = (x,y,z)$, and $\Delta = c \cdot \delta$, we can transform (4) into the following set of equations [1]:

$$(x - x_i^S)^2 + (y - y_i^S)^2 + (z - z_i^S)^2 = (R_i - \Delta)^2 \quad \forall S_i \quad (5)$$

[1]In civilian GPS, the signals are spread using publicly known spreading codes. The codes used for military GPS are kept secret; they serve for signal hiding and authentication.

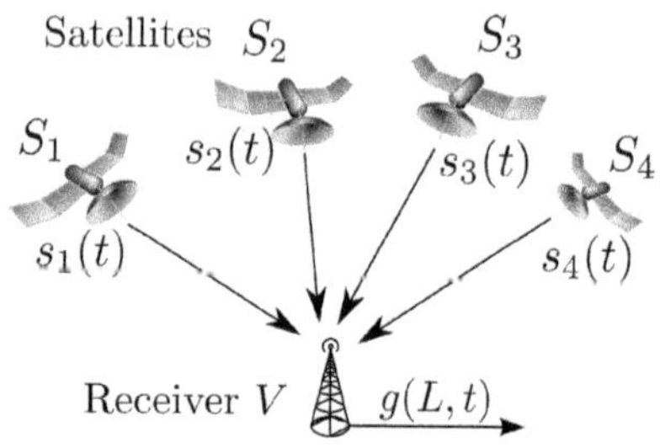

Figure 1: A GPS receiver V works by observing the signals from a set of satellites. The relative delays of the signals $s_i(t)$ can be used to solve four equations which determine the 3-dimensional position L and the time offset δ of the receiver V.

Geometrically, given a Δ, each S_i's equation translates into a sphere with L_i^S being the center. The set of equations (5) is overdetermined for more than four satellites and generally does not have a unique solution for L because of data noise. It can be solved by numerical methods such as a least-mean-square approach or Newton's method [1].

2.2 Related Work

In 2001, the Volpe report [8] identified that (malicious) interference with the civilian GPS signal is a serious problem. Starting with this report, practical spoofing attacks were discussed in several publications. In [24], the authors use a WelNavigate GS720 satellite simulator mounted in a truck to attack a target receiver in a second truck. The authors succeeded in taking over the victim's satellite lock by manually placing an antenna close to the victim's receiver. After the victim was locked onto the attacker's signal the spoofing signal could be sent from a larger distance. Instead of using a GPS simulator, the authors of [7] create GPS spoofing signals by decoding legitimate GPS signals and generating time-shifted copies which are then transmitted with higher energy to overshadow the original signals; a similar approach is also used in [14]. This approach requires less expensive equipment but introduces considerable delays between the legitimate and the spoofed signals. GPS spoofing attacks are discussed analytically in [11], showing that an attacker can manipulate the arrival times of military and civilian GPS signals by pulse-delaying or replaying (individual) navigation signals with a delay. We note that there is no unique attacker model used for spoofing attacks, and thus the assumptions on the attacker's capabilities vary between these works.

Given the lack of attacker models, the proposed countermeasures range from simple measures to constant monitoring of the channel. In [8], consistency checks based on inertial sensors, cryptographic authentication, and discrimination based on signal strength, time-of-arrival, polarization, and angle-of-arrival are proposed. The authors of [16, 17, 25] propose countermeasures based on detecting the side effects of a (not seamless) hostile satellite-lock takeover, e. g., by monitoring the local clock and Doppler shift of the signals. Kuhn proposes an asymmetric scheme in [11], based on the delayed disclosure of the spreading code and timing information. In general, countermeasures that rely on modifications of the GPS satellite signals or the infrastructure (such as [11] and certain proposals in [8]) are unlikely to be implemented in the near future due to long procurement and deployment cycles. At the same time, countermeasures based on lock interrupts or signal jumps do not detect seamless satellite-lock takeovers.

Few publications [3, 12–14] present experimental data on the effects seen by the victim during a spoofing attack. The authors

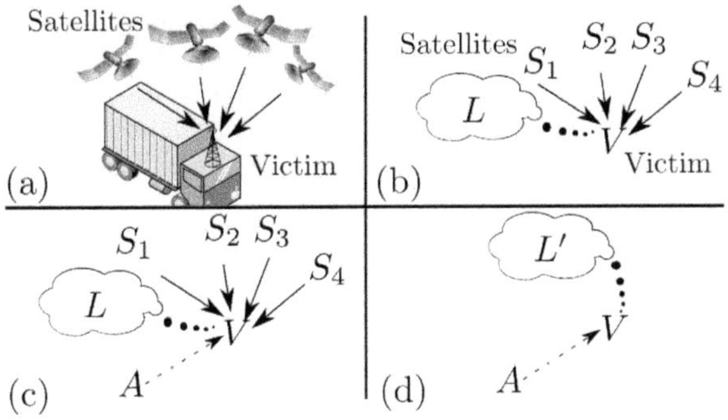

Figure 2: Basic attack scenario. (a) Visualization of the setup. The victim uses a GPS-based localization system and is synchronized to the legitimate satellites. (b) Abstract representation of the scene. (c) The attacker starts sending own spoofing and jamming signals. (d) The victim synchronizes to the attacker's signals.

of [13] use a setup based on two antennas to measure the phase difference for each satellite to detect the lock takeover. [3] and [14] analyze the spoofing effect on the carrier and code level. The authors of [12] present a device that prevents spoofing by monitoring and potentially suppressing the received signals before they are processed by the GPS receiver.

All works above only consider attacks on single GPS receivers but not on groups of receivers. In addition, none of them investigated the requirements for successful attacks on public GPS receivers, such as required precision of the attacker's spoofing signals. Although we expect that more works on GPS spoofing and anti-spoofing countermeasures were performed in classified (military) settings, they are not accessible to the public.

3. PROBLEM FORMULATION

In order to give an intuition of the problem, we present our motivation and an exemplary use case. Then, we define our system and attacker models and formulate the GPS spoofing problem.

3.1 Motivation

The fundamental reasons why GPS spoofing works have been discussed in the literature before, and spoofing attacks have been demonstrated on single receivers experimentally. In this work, we show under which conditions the attacker can establish the correct parameters to launch a successful spoofing attack on one or more victims, and later in the experiments, how inaccuracies in these parameters influence the lock takeover during the attack. This analysis enables us to identify which attacks are theoretically possible and which attacks would be noticeable as (potentially non-malicious) signal loss at the GPS receivers. This is important for proposing effective receiver-based countermeasures, which are not implemented yet in current standard GPS receivers.

Our work is further motivated by the real-life spoofing attacks, e. g. the one reported in [24]. In this scenario, a cargo truck (the victim), had a GPS unit that was housed in a tamper-proof casing and was sending cryptographically authenticated status updates with a fixed rate to a monitoring center. The attacker planned to steal the truck to get access to its loaded goods at a remote place. He got close to the victim and started transmitting forged (spoofed) signals in order to modify the location computed by the receiver (see Figure 2). In this setting, if the attacker can influence the localization process, he can make the victim report any position to the monitoring center and thus steal the truck without raising suspicion or revealing the truck's real location.

S_i	i-th satellite	A_i	i-th attacker unit
L_i^S	coordinates of S_i	P_i^A	physical coordinates of A_i
s_i	signal sent by S_i	L_i^A	claimed coordinates of A_i
V_j	j-th victim (receiver)	s_i^A	signal sent by A_i
L_j	GPS coordinates of V_j	δ_i^A	time offset of s_i^A
L'_j	spoofed coordinates of V_j	δ_j	GPS clock offset of V_j
P_j	physical coordinates of V_j	δ'_j	spoofed clock offset of V_j
R'_{ij}	V_j's calculated PR to S_i	c	signal propagation speed
R_{ij}^A	V_j's spoofed PR (by A_i)	Δ'_j	$= \delta'_j \cdot c$

Table 1: Summary of notations (PR = pseudorange).

3.2 System Model

Our system consists of a set of legitimate GPS satellites and a set $\mathcal{V}$ of victims (see Table 1 for notations used). Each victim is equipped with a GPS receiver that can compute the current position and time as described in Section 2. We assume that each receiver $V_j \in \mathcal{V}$ is able to receive wireless GPS signals, compute its position, and store its position/time-tuples. If several GPS receivers belong to a common group (e. g., they are mounted on the same vehicle), we assume that they can communicate to exchange their computed locations or are aware of the group's (fixed) formation.

The GPS location of each individual victim $V_j \in \mathcal{V}$ is given by its coordinates $L_j \in \mathbb{R}^3$ in space and the victim's clock offset δ_j with respect to the GPS system time t^S. We note that the computed GPS coordinates L_j and clock offset δ_j do not necessarily correspond to the true (physical) coordinates $P_j \in \mathbb{R}^3$ and time.[2] We define the local time of V_j as $t_j = t^S + \delta_j$, i. e., $\delta_j < 0$ refers to an internal clock that lags behind. We use $\mathcal{L}$ to denote the set of GPS locations of the victims in $\mathcal{V}$. A GPS spoofing attack may manipulate a receiver's coordinates in space and/or its local time. We denote a victim's spoofed coordinates by $L'_j \in \mathbb{R}^3$ and the spoofed time offset by δ'_j. We use $\mathcal{L}'$ for the set of spoofed victim locations.

In our analysis in Section 4, we distinguish between *civilian GPS*, which uses the public C/A codes so that each satellite signal s_i contains only public information, and *military GPS*, which provides authentic, confidential signals using the secret P(Y) codes. In the experimental evaluation in Section 5, we use a satellite signal generator for civilian GPS.

3.3 Attacker Model

GPS signals can be trivially spoofed under a Dolev-Yao [4]-like attacker that is able to fully control the wireless traffic by intercepting, injecting, modifying, replaying, delaying, and blocking messages without temporal constraints *for individual receivers*, see Figure 3(b). If the attacker has full control over the input to each individual receiver antenna, he can send the signals as they would be received at any location L'_j. This would, however, require the attacker to either be very close to each receiver or to use directional antennas with narrow beam widths and shielding to prevent that the signals intended for one victim are also received by another victim; in both cases, the number of required attacker antennas would be linear in the number of victims. In this work we assume that the signals sent by the attacker are transmitted wirelessly and that they will be received by all victims in $\mathcal{V}$, see Figure 3(a).

The attacker controls a set of wireless transmitters that he can move and position independently. We denote by $P_i^A \in \mathbb{R}^3$ the

[2]Typically, the difference $|L - P|$ is less than a few meters [22].

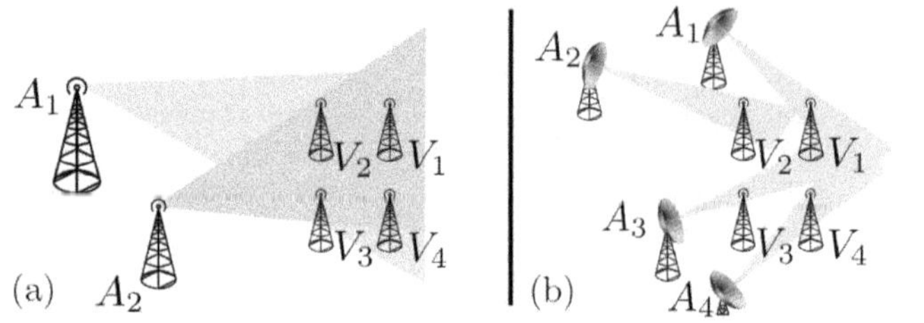

Figure 3: Models of the attacker's antenna coverage. (a) The attacker's signals reach all victims (used in the analysis of this paper). (b) The attacker's antennas each only reach one victim. This requires the attacker to be in close proximity to the victims if the distances between the receivers are small.

physical location of the i-th transmission unit of the attacker (manipulating the signals of satellite S_i), and the set of all physical attacker locations from where the attacker is transmitting by $\mathcal{P}^A$. We assume that the attacker's inherent, unwanted clock offset to the GPS system time is negligible[3] and use δ_i^A to capture the time shift introduced by the attacker in the transmission of signal s_i^A with respect to the signal s_i and the system time t^S. For example, for $\delta_1^A = 10\,\text{ms}$, the attacker transmits the spoofed signal 10 ms after the signal s_1 was transmitted by satellite S_1.

For our analysis, we assume that the attacker is aware of the victims' physical locations (the influence of errors in the attackers location estimates is evaluated in Section 5). We further denote by $|L_i^S - P_j|$ the physical distance between satellite S_i and victim V_j. Similarly, $|P_i^A - P_j|$ denotes the physical distance between the attacker's antenna at P_i^A and victim V_j. Given this setting, we distinguish the following two types of attacks:

Attacks on civilian (unauthenticated) GPS: The attacker can delay signals or send them prematurely, i. e., $\delta_i^A \in \mathbb{R}$. He can modify the content of received GPS signals or arbitrarily generate the spoofing signals s_i^A using the public GPS parameters (e. g., by using a GPS signal generator). This is possible because civilian GPS signals are not authenticated—given the right hardware, anyone can transmit his own GPS signals. Thus the attacker can also modify the claimed locations of the satellites: $L_i^A \neq L_i^S$. We note that on standard GPS receivers, the data content in the received GPS signals is not checked for plausibility or consistency [15].

Attacks on military (authenticated) GPS: The attacker is not able to generate valid military GPS signals. All he can do is to capture and relay existing signals, e. g. by separating signals from different satellites using high-gain directional antennas and broadband transceivers (called *Selective-Delay* in [11]). This means that the attacker can delay existing GPS signals and amplify or attenuate them. He is restricted by $\delta_i^A \geq |L_i^S - P_i^A|/c$, i. e., signals can be delayed but not sent prior to their reception. We note that neither the spreading codes nor the data content of the signal need to be known to the attacker for a successful selective-delay attack.

We note that these attacker models are very strong. Nevertheless, we consider them appropriate for our analysis because we want to make general statements that hold even under very strong (worst-case) attackers with sophisticated equipment.

3.4 Formulation of GPS Spoofing Problems

We first define GPS spoofing attacks and then present two GPS spoofing problems for the attacker.

[3]The attacker can synchronize his time to legitimate GPS signals.

Definition 1 (GPS Spoofing Attack). *Let a victim V compute its GPS location as L and its GPS time as t in the absence of an attacker. In a* GPS spoofing attack, *the attacker sends spoofing signals to manipulate the victim's GPS-based location calculations. As a result, V computes its location as $L' \neq L$ and/or time as $t' \neq t$.*

Definition 1 can also be extended to groups of victims:

Definition 2 (GPS Group Spoofing Problem). *Let $\mathcal{L}'$ be a set of target locations for each $V_j \in \mathcal{V}$ and let $t'_j \in \mathcal{T}'$ denote the target time for V_j. The* GPS Group Spoofing Problem *is the problem of finding combinations of GPS signals s_i^A (sent by the attacker), transmission times $t_i^A = t^S + \delta_i^A$ (when the spoofing signals are sent), and physical transmission locations P_i^A (from where the attacker transmits) such that the location or time of each $V_j \in \mathcal{V}$ is spoofed according to Definition 1.*

We note that the physical attacker locations P_i^A do not have to correspond to the claimed satellite positions L_i^A in the GPS messages (for civilian GPS, L_i^A can even be chosen by the attacker). As we will show in Section 4.2, the GPS spoofing problem for a single victim has a trivial solution for any target location.

In Section 4.3, we will analyze the necessary restrictions on the spoofed locations such that the GPS Group Spoofing Problem can be solved. We therefore define a decisional version of the GPS Group Spoofing Problem.

Definition 3 (Decisional GPS Group Spoofing Problem). *Let $\mathcal{P}$ be the set of physical locations of the victims in $\mathcal{V}$. Let $\mathcal{L}'$ and $\mathcal{T}'$ be defined according to Definition 2. The* Decisional GPS Group Spoofing Problem *for $\mathcal{P}, \mathcal{L}', \mathcal{T}'$ is the decision problem whether there exists at least one set of attacker locations $\mathcal{P}^A$ from where the attacker can send the spoofing signals s_i^A such that the location or time of each $V_j \in \mathcal{V}$ is spoofed according to Definition 1.*

In practice, the GPS Group Spoofing Problems (Definitions 2 and 3) may be restricted in terms of attacker capabilities. For example, the attacker may only be able to position his transmission antennas at a restricted set of physical locations $\mathcal{P}_*^A$, at a restricted set of claimed satellite positions $\mathcal{L}_*^A$, or he may only be able to send the spoofing signals at a restricted set of transmission times $\mathcal{T}_*^A$ (e. g., if he must receive legitimate signals before he can send the spoofing signals). In these cases, the GPS Group Spoofing Problems can be modified to take the restricted attacker capabilities $\mathcal{L}_*^A$, $\mathcal{P}_*^A$, $\mathcal{T}_*^A$ as additional input and find solutions that fulfill $\mathcal{P}^A \subset \mathcal{P}_*^A$, $\mathcal{L}^A \subset \mathcal{L}_*^A$, or $\mathcal{T}^A \subset \mathcal{T}_*^A$.

4. SOLVING GPS SPOOFING PROBLEMS

We now analyze how our attacker (as defined in Section 3.3) can spoof the locations of one or more receivers. In this section, we abstract away from implementation issues (such as taking over an established lock to legitimate satellites, see Section 5) and assume that there are no legitimate signals present on the channel. The intuition underlying the results that we will present is the following: spoofing requires the attacker to send out signals precisely aligned in time. This will be harder—if not impossible—for increasing numbers of victims (as summarized in Table 2 and visualized in Figure 5).

4.1 Construction of Pseudoranges

The attacker's physical location P_i^A, his transmission time offset δ_i^A, and the claimed satellite position L_i^A all influence the location L'_j as computed by a victim V_j (see Sections 2 and 3.2). By setting his physical location P_i^A and transmission offset δ_i^A, the

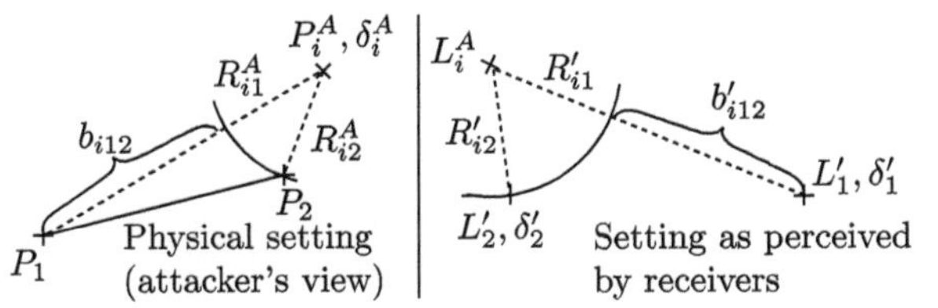

Figure 4: The GPS spoofing scenario for two victims in 2 dimensions. The attacker is impersonating a satellite with the claimed (forged) location L_i^A, using an antenna positioned at P_i^A. The victims are two receivers with physical positions at P_1 and P_2. For each signal s_i^A, the attacker ensures that R_{i1}^A and R_{i2}^A match R'_{i1} and R'_{i2}, and therefore V_1 and V_2 compute their locations as L'_1 and L'_2 with clock offsets δ'_1 and δ'_2. Here, b_{i12} and b'_{i12} are the differences of pseudoranges between V_1 and V_2.

attacker can influence the pseudorange computation at the victim. The expected pseudorange that a victim at physical position P_j will compute based on the attacker's signal s_i^A is

$$R_{ij}^A = |P_j - P_i^A| + \delta_i^A \cdot c \tag{6}$$

To determine its location, each victim solves a system of equations with the calculated pseudoranges (see Figure 4):

$$|L'_j - L_i^A| = R'_{ij} - \Delta'_j \tag{7}$$

Here, L_i^A are the (claimed) satellite coordinates of S_i extracted by V_j from the GPS message, R'_{ij} is the pseudorange to satellite S_i as calculated by V_j based on the received signal, and $\Delta'_j = \delta'_j \cdot c$ is the time offset times propagation speed as calculated by the victim.

For each impersonated satellite, the attacker must send a signal s_i^A such that solving Equation 7 by the victim yields the target location L'_j and the target time offset δ'_j. This requires $R_{ij}^A = R'_{ij}$, or:

$$|P_j - P_i^A| + \Delta_i^A = |L'_j - L_i^A| + \Delta'_j. \tag{8}$$

In attacks on civilian GPS, the attacker is free to choose P_i^A, δ_i^A, and L_i^A. This means that the system of equations (8) is underdetermined for a single victim. The attacker can fix two of the variables to his liking and solve for the third.

When the attack targets a military GPS receiver, the attacker cannot change the data content of the messages and is restricted to δ_i^A, which is greater than or equal to the transmission delay from the satellite to the attacker. Hence, the claimed satellite location in the message is the correct location of the legitimate satellite: $L_i^A = L_i^S$. In addition, the attacker is restricted by $\Delta_i^A \geq |P_i^A - L_i^S|$. We can therefore rewrite Equation 8 as

$$|P_j - P_i^A| + |P_i^A - L_i^S| \leq |L'_j - L_i^A| + \Delta'_j. \tag{9}$$

Or, using the triangle inequality

$$|P_j - L_i^S| \leq |L'_j - L_i^A| + \Delta'_j. \tag{10}$$

In the following, let b_{ijk} be the difference in pseudoranges to P_i^A between V_j and V_k (see Equation 6):

$$b_{ijk} = R_{ij}^A - R_{ik}^A = |P_j - P_i^A| - |P_k - P_i^A|. \tag{11}$$

Equally, we define b'_{ijk} as the difference of pseudoranges of the claimed satellite location L_i^A and the spoofed victim locations L'_j and L'_k (see Figure 4):

$$\begin{aligned} b'_{ijk} &= R'_{ij} - R'_{ik} \\ &= |L'_j - L_i^A| - |L'_k - L_i^A| + \Delta'_j - \Delta'_k. \end{aligned} \tag{12}$$

4.2 Spoofing to One Location

Result 1. *One or more receivers $V_j \in \mathcal{V}$ can be spoofed to any one location L' using a single attacker antenna. Spoofing multiple receivers to the same location L' will generally lead to different time offsets δ'_j at each victim.*

The reason for this is that the time-differences of arrival of the individual satellite signals determine the location that each receiver will compute. If the spoofed signals are all sent from the same attacker antenna, all victims will obtain the same time-differences. A detailed proof is given in Appendix A, along with a discussion of the resulting time differences at the victims.

4.3 Spoofing to Multiple Locations

We next consider multiple receivers at distinct physical locations $P_1, \ldots, P_n$ that the attacker tries to spoof to the locations $L'_1, \ldots, L'_n$. Following Result 1, an attacker can spoof any number of receivers in the transmission range to the same coordinates L' with differing δ'_j. If the victims have a way of establishing (coarse) relative distances, e. g., by estimating their respective distances visually, or can detect their mutual time offsets, they are able to detect such attacks. Therefore, we will now focus on attacks in which multiple victims are shifted to a set of new locations that preserve their mutual distances and mutual time offsets.

As stated in Result 1, if the attacker is using only one transmission antenna, any possible placement of this antenna will lead to two victims computing their location to the same coordinates L', with a small time synchronization error. Hence, the attacker cannot use only one antenna to shift the victims to different locations. We will now show that, using multiple antennas, the attacker can spoof two victims to any locations while preserving their mutual time offsets, with certain restrictions on the time offset in the case of military GPS receivers.

Result 2. *Two receivers at the physical locations $P_1 \neq P_2$ can be spoofed to the locations $L'_1 \neq L'_2$ and time offsets δ'_1, δ'_2 if the attacker is free to choose any P_i^A and L_i^A. For each s_i^A, the possible transmission locations P_i^A lie on one half of a two-sheeted hyperboloid defined by $L'_1, L'_2, \delta'_1, \delta'_2, L_i^A$, and P_1, P_2.*

In order to spoof V_1, V_2 to L'_1, L'_2 and Δ'_1, Δ'_2, the attacker must send each s_i such that it arrives with the correct delay at the physical locations of the victims, i. e., $b_{i12} = b'_{i12}\ \forall s_i$. As b_{ijk} is defined by P_i^A and, likewise, b'_{ijk} is defined by L_i^A, the attacker can always find combinations of P_i^A and L_i^A that yield the correct pseudorange (for attacks on civilian GPS). He can then use Equation 8 to find the appropriate δ_i^A. □

In the case of military GPS, the attacker cannot change the claimed placements of the satellites: $L_i^A = L_i^S$. Hence, b'_{i12} is determined by the selection of L'_1, L'_2 and δ'_1, δ'_2. In this case, Equation 8 yields one hyperboloid for each s_i^A with possible values of P_i^A and δ_i^A.

We demonstrate this by giving a simple example: the victims are located at $P_1 = (1, 0, 0)$ and $P_2 = (-1, 0, 0)$, the physical distance between the victims is $|P_1 - P_2| = 2$. The attacker wants to spoof the two victims to the locations $L'_1 = (0, 0, 0)$ and $L'_2 = (0, 2, 0)$, both with time offset zero: $\Delta'_1 = \Delta'_2 = 0$. The attacker now (arbitrarily) chooses $L_1^A = (-3, -2, 0)$, $L_2^A = (-2, 0, 0)$,

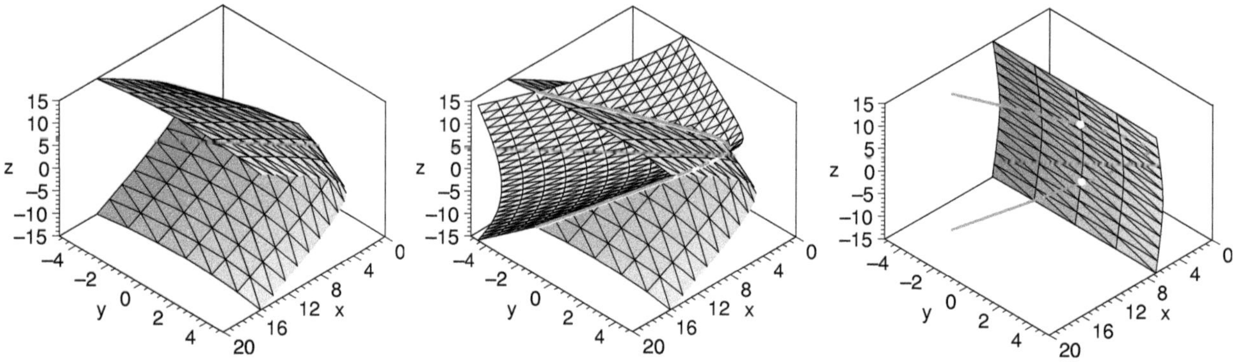

(a) 2 receivers (b) 3 receivers (c) 4 receivers

Figure 5: Visualization of possible attacker placements. For (a) two victims, all points on the hyperboloid are viable solutions; for (b) three victims the solutions lie on a curve (red/white intersection); and (c) for four victims only two points are viable solutions (white dots).

and $L_3^A = (-2, 2, 0)$ for the claimed satellite positions in the GPS messages. This determines three hyperboloids relative to P_1 and P_2 based on b'_{112}, b'_{212}, and b'_{312}.

Result 3. *A necessary condition for a successful GPS group spoofing attack is that* $\forall V_j, V_k, \forall s_i, b'_{ijk} \leq |P_j - P_k|$.

In other words, the difference b'_{ijk} of the perceived pseudoranges of each signal s_i^A at any two spoofed victim locations L'_j and L'_k must be smaller than or equal to the distance between the victims' physical locations P_j and P_k. From Equation 11 and the triangle inequality it follows that $b_{ijk} \leq |P_j - P_k|$. Since it must hold that $b'_{ijk} = b_{ijk}$, if $b'_{ijk} > |P_j - P_k|$ for *any* s_i, then there is no possible solution for the attacker's placement P_i^A. Thus we get

$$|P_j - P_k| \geq |L'_j - L_i^A| - |L'_k - L_i^A| + \Delta'_j - \Delta'_k \tag{13}$$

as a necessary condition for a successful attack. □

As we know from Result 2, for two victims, all possible antenna placements for the attacker lie on a hyperboloid defined by P_j, L'_j, δ'_j and L_i^A. We will now extend this result to the case of three and more victims. In the following, we assume that $b'_{ijk} \leq |P_j - P_k|$ is fulfilled $\forall V_j, V_k$ and $\forall s_i$, i.e., it is physically possible to spoof the locations of the receivers.

Result 4. *In a GPS group spoofing attack on three victims V_1, V_2, V_3 to specific locations L'_j and time offsets δ'_j, all possible attacker placements P_i^A lie on the intersection of two hyperboloids defined by b'_{i12}, b'_{i13}.*

This can be shown by constructing two hyperboloids using b'_{i12} and b'_{i13} as in Result 2. Both hyperboloids yield the possible placements of attacker's antennas to achieve the correct pseudorange for V_1, V_2 or V_1, V_3, respectively. Each point on the intersection of the two hyperboloids has a specific δ_i^A and is at the correct distance to all three victims. Therefore, all points of this space curve are valid P_i^A to solve the group spoofing problem. □

We can extend our example from Result 2 by a third victim placed at $P_3 = (1, 5, 0)$, which is spoofed to $L'_3 = (1, 1, 0)$ with $\delta'_3 = 0$. This reduces the possible locations from the hyperboloid as shown in Figure 5(a) to the intersection curve of the hyperboloids constructed using b'_{i12} and b'_{i13}, as shown in Figure 5(b).

Result 5. *In a GPS group spoofing attack on four victims $V_1, \ldots, V_4$ to specific locations L'_j and time offsets δ'_j, there are at most two possible placements for P_i^A to impersonate a satellite at L_i^A. These are the intersection points of three hyperboloids defined by b'_{i12}, b'_{i13}, b'_{i14}.*

As previously, to show this, we consider each signal s_i^A separately. By computing $b'_{i12}, b'_{i13}, b'_{i14}$ (and $b'_{i11} = 0$) according to Equation 11 and setting $b_{ijk} = b'_{ijk}$, we can construct three hyperboloids. Their intersection points are possible placements for the antennas of the attacker. As the intersection of two hyperboloids yields a spaced curve, the intersection of three hyperboloids is an intersection of this curve with a third hyperboloid, which results in at most two points. We can also arrive at this number of solutions by considering the system of four quadratic equations based on Equation 7. These can be transformed into three linear and one quadratic equation [1], defining the solutions for the location L_i^A and time offset δ_i^A. As the quadratic equation has at most two solutions [1], and each of the linear equations has one unique solution, there are at most two solutions for the attacker's position and transmission time. □

This result can also be observed in our example by adding a fourth victim placed at $P_4 = (10, 0, 0)$, which is spoofed to $L'_4 = (-1, 0, 0)$ with $\delta'_4 = 0$. The possible placements for the attacker's antenna is now the intersection of the previously obtained curve with another hyperboloid, yielding two points only (Figure 5(c)).

Result 6. *In a GPS group spoofing attack on five or more victims $V_1, \ldots, V_n$ to specific locations L'_j and time offsets δ'_j, there is at most one possible placement for P_i^A to impersonate a satellite at L_i^A. This is the intersection point of $n - 1$ hyperboloids defined by $b'_{i12}, \ldots, b'_{i1n}$.*

This result directly continues our previous reasoning: Each added victim adds another hyperboloid to the set of hyperboloids which must intersect to yield a possible P_i^A. For five or more receivers, the set of $(n - 1)$ linear equations and one quadratic equation is overdetermined, and therefore has at most one solution. □

From Result 5, we know that for military GPS receivers, there are at most two solutions for a given combination of P_j, L'_j, δ'_j, and $L_i^A = L_i^S$. For attacks on civilian GPS receivers, the attacker can influence the position of the two solutions of the system of equations by changing the claimed satellite location L_i^A. We will now

	Spoofing to one location	Spoofing to multiple locations (preserved formation)	
n	Civ. & Mil. GPS	Civilian GPS	Military GPS
1	$P_i^A \in \mathbb{R}^3$	-	-
2	$P_i^A \in \mathbb{R}^3$	set of hyperboloids	one hyperboloid
3	$P_i^A \in \mathbb{R}^3$	set of intersections of two hyperboloids	intersection of two hyperboloids
4	$P_i^A \in \mathbb{R}^3$	set of 2 points	2 points
≥5	$P_i^A \in \mathbb{R}^3$	set of points	1 point

Table 2: Summary of results for the number of possible attacker locations P_i^A for n victims.

give an intuition where these solutions are located for a formation-preserving GPS spoofing attack.

Result 7. *When spoofing a group of GPS receivers $V_1, \ldots, V_n$ such that the* formation *(i. e., the mutual distances and relative time offsets) is preserved, there is always at least one solution to the decisional group GPS spoofing problem.*

One way to show this result is to use an affine transformation to describe the relation between physical and spoofed locations of the receivers and senders. If the formation of the victims is preserved, there exists a bijective affine augmented transformation matrix T which describes this translation and rotation. Assuming that L and P are represented as augmented row vectors, we can therefore write $T \cdot L_j = L'_j$. Then, the inverse transformation T^{-1} applied to L_i^A will yield a possible antenna placement $P_i^A = T^{-1} \cdot L_i^A$, because all pseudoranges R'_{ij} between L'_j and L_i^A and the measured range R_{ij} between P_i^A and P_j will be the same (the transformation preserves the Euclidean distance). □

As a consequence of Results 6 and 7, spoofing five or more receivers while retaining their formation has exactly one solution, an affine transformation of the claimed satellite position L_i^A.

Summary of results: Table 2 gives an overview of sets of possible positions P_i^A for the attacker's antenna depending on the number of victims and on the target locations: spoofing all receivers to one location or each victim to a different location with a preserved formation. The results are shown for civilian and military GPS; 'hyperboloid' refers to half of a two-sheeted hyperboloid. In the table we assume that the condition of Result 3 holds.

The results in Table 2 show that there are no restrictions on the attacker's position for spoofing any number of victims to one location ($P_i^A \in \mathbb{R}^3$). With an increasing number of victims and a constant formation, the attacker is getting more and more restricted in terms of his antenna placement. For civilian GPS, the attacker has more degrees of freedom because he can select claimed (false) satellite locations L_i^A and thus influence the hyperboloid, intersection of hyperboloids, etc., whereas these are fixed for military GPS (i. e., there is only one specific hyperboloid of attacker positions for each transmitted signal per pair of victims).

5. EXPERIMENTS ON SATELLITE-LOCK TAKEOVER

A GPS spoofing attack in the presence of legitimate GPS satellite signals requires the attacker to make the victim stop receiving signals from the legitimate satellites and start receiving the attacker's signals. If this takeover is noticed by the victim, e. g. because the victim suddenly loses contact to previously seen satellites, it can detect the spoofing attack. While the victim might lose contact due to random noise or environmental changes, the attacker ideally should take over without being noticed. We say that the receiver has a *lock* on a specific transmitter when it is already receiving data from that satellite. The satellite lock makes spoofing attacks harder since a spoofing signal is likely to be misaligned (in phase, Doppler shift, or data content) to the legitimate signal. When the attacker's signal is turned on, this momentary interruption in the data-flow from that satellite could cause the victim to be temporarily unable to compute his position. Therefore, we now investigate how the attacker can take over the victim's lock with the victim losing the ability to calculate its position, even for a moment.

In Section 3 we assumed a strong attacker, who is always able to generate signals with perfect timing and power level, and who has perfect knowledge of his own and the victim's position. In a practical attack, many of these assumptions might be invalid. We conduct experiments to evaluate the influence of such imperfections. Because we do not change the claimed location of the satellite in the data sent by the attacker, all discussed imperfections should apply equally for military and public GPS receivers.

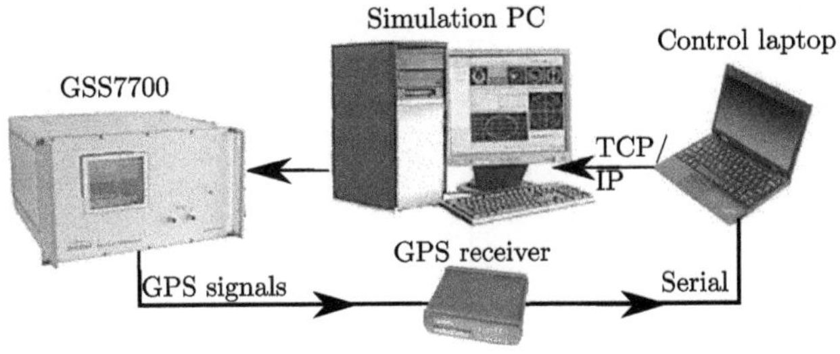

Figure 6: The experimental setup.

5.1 Experimental Setup and Procedure

In our experiments, the spoofing signals and the legitimate GPS signals are sent over a cable to eliminate the influence of the transmission channel. This enables us to measure the unique influence of the parameters of interest while disregarding channel and antenna noise.

We conduct the lock takeover attacks using a Spirent GSS7700 GPS simulator (see Figure 6). The GPS signal simulator is a hardware device that generates GPS signals and is controlled by a dedicated simulation PC running the SimGen simulation software package [20]. The GSS7700 GPS simulator generates two independent GPS constellations with up to 16 satellites in each. One constellation is simulating the signals from the legitimate GPS satellites, and the other is simulating the attacker's signals. Both are mixed together and sent to the GPS receiver via a wired connection. The GPS receiver in our experiments is an Antaris evaluation kit by u-blox, containing the ATR0600 GPS chip from Atmel.

At the start of each experiment, we send only the legitimate GPS signals for a static location. We reset the GPS receiver to make sure all experiments are independent and no internal state is kept from a previous experiment. After about 30 seconds the GPS receiver will lock on to enough satellites to be able to calculate a stable position. This position is the legitimate position L and the goal of the attacker is now to move the victim to a new location L' such that (i) the victim is continuously able to compute its position (ii) no noticeable discontinuities in the location occur.

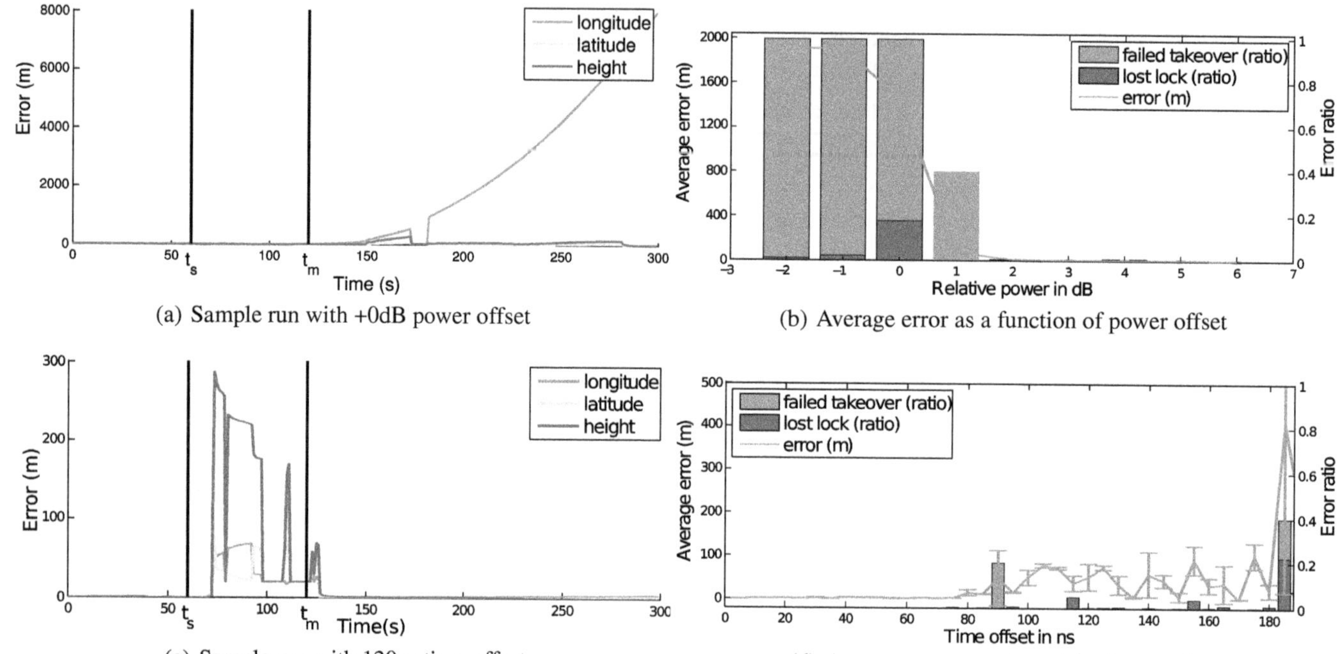

(a) Sample run with +0dB power offset

(b) Average error as a function of power offset

(c) Sample run with 120ns time offset

(d) Average error as a function of time offset

Figure 7: (a-b) Effects of relative signal power. (a) Example of unsuccessful takeover with too little power used. The spoofing signal is switched on at $t_s = 60$s and starts moving at t_m. (b) Average error over the measurement as a function of relative power. (c-d) Example of effects of spoofing signals with time offset. (c) During the takeover, the location jumps, in particular the height. The spoofing signal is switched on at $t = 60$s. (d) Average error over the measurement as a function of the time offset.

The attack then consists of two phases: first, the attacker sends signals which are supposed to match the legitimate satellites' signals at the location of the victim. These are generated by the attacker by approximating the current location of the victim as L_{init}, and constructing signals with time delays and data content appropriate for that location (see Section 4.1). This first phase lasts for one minute to allow the victim to lock on to the new signals. In the second phase, the attacker start to move the spoofed location towards the final location L', imitating an acceleration of 0.5m/s^2. After 3 minutes, the final location is reached. If this final location is not remotely close to L' (height difference $\leq$150m, horizontal distance $\leq$1km), we consider the takeover failed.

We vary the distance between the victim's true location L and its initial location as assumed by the attacker L_{init} as one of the parameters in the experiments. We refer to this distance as the *location offset* $d_{init} = |L - L_{init}|$. The other parameters we investigate are *relative signal power*, *relative time offset* and *constant time offset*. For each parameter value, five experiments were run.

We say that the lock takeover was successful if at the end of the experiment the victim's final location is close to L'. If the victim is close to L' but was unable to compute a valid position for more than one second during the lock takeover, we consider the attack a partial success and use the number of seconds the victim was not able to calculate a valid position as an error metric.

5.2 Results of the Experiments

Relative signal power of the spoofing signal: In this experiment, ideal spoofing signals are sent, but the power of the spoofing signals is varied between -2dB and $+8$dB relative to the legitimate signals. Figure 7(a) shows the effect of using spoofing signals that have the same power as the legitimate signals. In this figure, t_s marks the time at which the spoofing signals are turned on and t_m the time when the spoofed location starts to move away from L_{init}. The errors in longitude, latitude, and height are shown separately and are measured between the location as reported by the receiver and the one sent by the simulator. Although the victim reports the spoofed location for some time, it switches back to L after 170s of the experiment, which causes the growing error in longitude.

Figure 7(b) shows the error in meters between the position reported by the GPS receiver and the location sent by the attacker, as a function of the relative power of the attacker's signals. The error bars show the standard deviation for the error value over the five experimental runs. The gray bars indicate the ratio of experiments in which the receiver was unable to determine its position during the experiment. We use this as a metric to evaluate the smoothness of the lock takeover. If the receiver reported a location too far away from L', we count this run as failed takeover. Blue bars in the figure denote the ratio of attempts in which the GPS receiver was unable to compute a valid location.

It can be seen that for at least 2dB more power, the receiver consistently locks onto the spoofing signals without any offset occurring. 2dB of power is sufficiently low to not be detected by power based spoofing-countermeasures in practice.

Constant time offset influence: The second question we investigate is the effect of a general delay on all signals sent by the attacker relative to the legitimate signals. Such time delays can occur if the attacker's system setup is not perfectly compensating for internal delays, the distance to the victim is unknown or the system clock of the attacker is not synchronized perfectly to the clock of the legitimate GPS satellites. The interesting question is if such a general time offset will result in detectable errors in the victim's reported position, and if such a time offset will increase the chance of the victim losing lock completely during the takeover. To evaluate the influence of a constant time offset, we run the tests with time off-

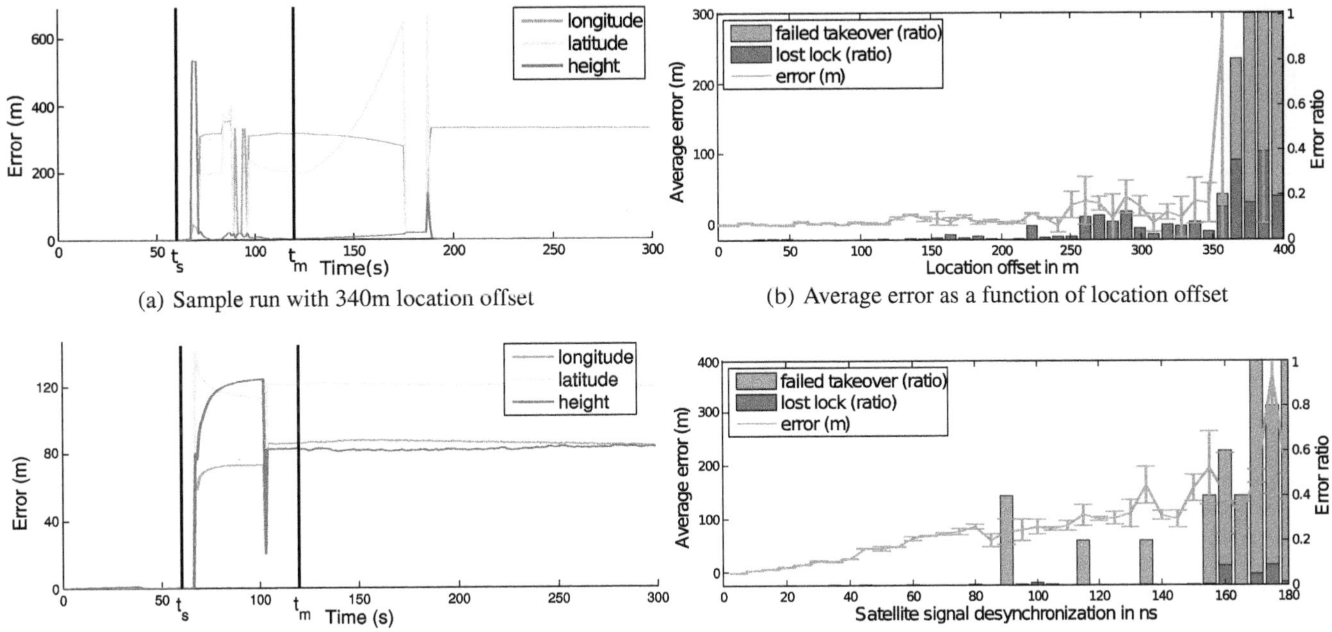

(a) Sample run with 340m location offset

(b) Average error as a function of location offset

(c) Sample run with 140ns time delay mismatch offset

(d) Average error as a function of time delay mismatch

Figure 8: (a-b) Example of effects of spoofing signals with location offset. (a) Example with 340m offset. During the takeover, the location is unstable. The spoofing signal is switched on at t = 60s. (b) Average error over the measurement as a function of the location offset. (c-d) Example of effects of spoofing signals with inconsistent time offset for half of the satellites. (c) With a 140ns time offset between the attacker's satellites, the takeover leads to an unstable lock. The spoofing signal is switched on at t = 60s. (d) Average error over the measurement as a function of the time delay mismatch.

sets between 0ns and 240ns. We plot the location error between the attacker's intended location and the actual location reported by the victim an example run in Figure 7(c). The effects are consistent over several runs with the same parameters, but can vary quite a lot with these parameters.

In Figure 7(d), we show the general relation between the average errors during the measurement as a function of the time offset for the first 120ns. After this time, lock takeover was not working consistently any more.

Location offset influence: In this series of experiments we determine the influence of an offset d_{init} between the position of the victim as determined from the legitimate satellites L and the spoofing signals sent by the attacker L_{init}. We evaluate the influence of such a location offset for values between 0 and 450m. Similarly to the time offset, this location offset can lead to a relatively large error during the lock takeover. An example with offset of 340m is given in Figure 8(a).

In Figure 8(b), we show the average error as a function of the location offset. Regardless of the intermediate errors, eventually the victim always synchronizes to the attacker's signals in all our experiments. This shows that the initial position is not very sensitive to small errors. If an attacker knows the location of his victim to within about 100 meters, he can perform a smooth takeover without the victim losing lock. There will of course be a detectable jump in position from L to L_{init} when the attackers signal is turned on but the victim will not lose lock with any satellite.

Relative time offset influence: In the case where the attacker has access to more than one transmission antenna, he can send the spoofing signals using two or more omnidirectional antennas (see Section 4). Depending on the relative position of the individual antennas, the victim will receive the spoofing signals with different time delays. Relative time offsets of the signals can also be caused

	Parameter value required for successful spoofing
Relative signal power	$\geq$ +2dB
Constant time offset	$\leq$ 75ns
Location offset	$\leq$ 500m
Relative time offset	$\leq$ 80ns

Table 3: Required parameter ranges for seamless lock-takeover in a GPS spoofing attack in our experiments.

by inaccuracies in the delay setup in the case of military GPS signals. In this experiment, we evaluate the consequences of having half of the spoofed satellite signals shifted by a fixed amount of time relative to the other half of the signals. In Figure 8(c), we show an example run with a time delay mismatch of 140ns. Our results for all tested values are presented in Figure 8(d).

Summary of experiments: We conducted the above experiments in order to evaluate the effects of imperfections in the attacker's signals for lock-takeovers. As these effects are influenced by the actual hardware at the receivers, the exact values might differ for other types of receivers, but the fundamental relations will remain the same. The results are summarized in Table 3.

According to our experiments, the attacker must ensure that his *time offset* to the system time is less than 75ns. Any greater offset will cause the GPS receiver to lose lock when the spoofing signal is turned on. A value of 75ns roughly corresponds to a distance of 22.5m, meaning that the attacker must know his distance from the victim with an accuracy of 22.5m (or better)— a higher offset will cause the victim to lose lock due to the signal (chip phase) misalignment. We confirmed that the *initial location offset* will cause

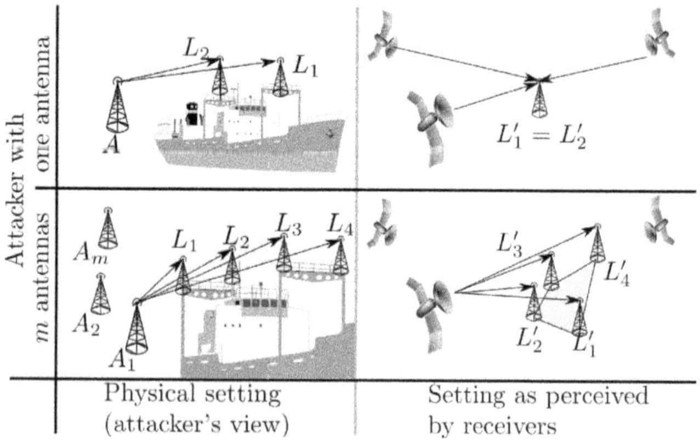

Figure 9: Proposed countermeasures: For an attacker with a single antenna, the two-receiver countermeasure is enough. If the attacker uses multiple antennas, four (or more) receivers severely restrict the attacker's antenna placements. Wrong antenna placements will change the distances of the receivers and can thus be detected.

a noticeable jump of the victim's reported position during the attack. Large offsets could therefore be detected by the victim by monitoring its position. Any imperfections in the *arrival time* of the signal from different antennas will directly impact the position calculated by the victim. If the relative time offset gets above 80ns, the signals will even cause the receiver to lose lock. This means that, if an attacker has multiple antennas, he must precisely know the distance from each antenna to the attacker in order to be able to spoof a desired location. We could also observe a general localization error as predicted in our theoretical analysis, even for smaller mismatches in the arrival times.

6. GPS SPOOFING COUNTERMEASURE

Spoofing detection based on lock loss has two disadvantages: (i) strong attackers can achieve a seamless satellite-lock takeover, and (ii) lock loss can occur due to natural causes (e. g. signal loss in a tunnel). We propose a countermeasure against GPS spoofing attacks that does *not* rely on the signal analysis or on the lock loss of signal. Instead, our mechanism is based on our insights of Section 4 and relies on the use of several GPS receivers. These GPS receivers can be deployed in a static, known formation, e. g., they are fixed on the deck of a cargo ship (see Figure 9). The basic idea of the countermeasure is the following: If the GPS receivers can exchange their individual GPS locations, they can check if their calculated locations preserve their physical formation (within certain error bounds). In the case that the calculated GPS locations do not match the known formation, an attack must be suspected and there should be a warning message.

Even if only two GPS receivers are used, this countermeasure can detect any attacker that is only using a single antenna. As shown in Result 1, in case of a single-antenna attack both GPS receivers would report the same location (with small time offsets).

As shown in Results 4–6, a strong attacker using multiple antennas could attempt to send signals such that the mutual distances between multiple receivers are preserved. Nevertheless, each additional receiver of the victim makes these spoofing attacks exceedingly more difficult because the space of possible antenna placements for the attacker gets reduced significantly (see Table 2). From Results 6 and 7 we know that there exists only one location per satellite where the attacker can place his antenna; this location is the rotated and translated satellite position of the GPS signal. Conducting such an attack is very difficult. It becomes even impossible if the victim can hide the exact positioning of at least one GPS receiver from the attacker (e. g., by keeping it mobile on the vehicle) such that the attacker cannot adapt to its position.

In summary, our countermeasure requires no modifications of the GPS signal, the satellite infrastructure, or the GPS receiver, it is resistant against a wide range of attackers, and it can be deployed using multiple standard GPS receivers.

Outlook: Further possible applications are not restricted to mobile scenarios with a fixed formation (such as in the cargo ship example above). The countermeasure can also be applied (i) to fixed and static (i. e., immobile) settings where GPS is used for time synchronization and (ii) to mobile settings with varying formations (e. g., mobile formation of cars, robots, etc.). In the latter case, the devices can apply additional ranging techniques to identify their formation and use it in the sanity check with the calculated GPS locations (as long as the ranging techniques are secure [2,6,10,18,21]). We leave the elaboration of these ideas for future work.

7. CONCLUSION

In this paper, we analyzed the requirements for successful GPS spoofing attacks on individuals and groups of victims with civilian or military GPS receivers. In particular, we identified from which locations and with which precision the attacker needs to generate its signals in order to successfully spoof the receivers.

For example, we show how spoofing a group of victims can only be achieved from a restricted set of locations, if the attacker aims to preserve the mutual distances and time offsets of the victims. With growing size of the group of victims, less spoofing location become available, until only single points remain for 5 victims or more. In addition, we discussed the practical aspects of seamless satellite-lock takeover. We used a GPS signal generator to perform a set of experiments in which we investigated the required precision of the attacker's spoofing signals. Besides demonstrating the effects of such lock takeovers on the victim, our results include minimal bounds for critical parameters to allow a seamless takeover of our target platform. Finally, we proposed a technique for the detection of spoofing based on a group of standard GPS receivers (without specific spoofing detection measures) in a static formation.

Acknowledgments

This work was partially supported by the Zurich Information Security Center. It represents the views of the authors.

8. REFERENCES

[1] Bensky, A. *Wireless Positioning Technologies and Applications.* GNSS Technology and Applications Series. Artech House, 2008.

[2] Brands, S., and Chaum, D. Distance-bounding protocols. In *Workshop on the theory and application of cryptographic techniques on Advances in cryptology (EUROCRYPT)* (1994), Springer.

[3] Cavaleri, A., Motella, B., Pini, M., and Fantino, M. Detection of spoofed GPS signals at code and carrier tracking level. In *Proceedings of ESA Workshop on Satellite Navigation Technologies and European Workshop on GNSS Signals and Signal Processing (Navitec)* (2010).

[4] Dolev, D., and Yao, A. C. On the security of public key protocols. *IEEE Trans. on Information Theory 29* (1983).

[5] Ettus. Universal software radio peripheral (USRP). http://www.ettus.com.

[6] HANCKE, G. P., AND KUHN, M. G. An RFID Distance Bounding Protocol. IEEE Computer Society.

[7] HUMPHREYS, T. E., LEDVINA, B. M., PSIAKI, M. L., O'HANLON, B. W., AND KINTNER, P. M. Assessing the spoofing threat: Development of a portable GPS civilian spoofer. In *Proceedings of the ION GNSS International Technical Meeting of the Satellite Division* (2008).

[8] JOHN A. VOLPE NATIONAL TRANSPORTATION SYSTEMS CENTER. Vulnerability assessment of the transportation infrastructure relying on the global positioning system. Final Report, 2001.

[9] JOHNSTON, R. G., AND WARNER, J. S. Think GPS cargo tracking = high security? Think again. In *Proceedings of Transport Security World* (2003).

[10] KUHN, M., LUECKEN, H., AND TIPPENHAUER, N. O. UWB impulse radio based distance bounding. In *Proceedings of the Workshop on Positioning, Navigation and Communication (WPNC)* (2010).

[11] KUHN, M. G. An asymmetric security mechanism for navigation signals. In *Proceedings of the Information Hiding Workshop* (2004).

[12] LEDVINA, B. M., BENCZE, W. J., GALUSHA, B., AND MILLER, I. An in-line anti-spoofing device for legacy civil GPS receivers. In *Proceedings of the ION International Technical Meeting* (2010).

[13] MONTGOMERY, P. Y., HUMPHREYS, T. E., AND LEDVINA, B. M. Receiver-autonomous spoofing detection: Experimental results of a multi-antenna receiver defense against a portable civil GPS spoofer. In *Proceedings of the ION International Technical Meeting* (2009).

[14] MOTELLA, B., PINI, M., FANTINO, M., MULASSANO, P., NICOLA, M., FORTUNY-GUASCH, J., WILDEMEERSCH, M., AND SYMEONIDIS, D. Performance assessment of low cost GPS receivers under civilian spoofing attacks. In *Proceedings of ESA Workshop on Satellite Navigation Technologies and European Workshop on GNSS Signals and Signal Processing (Navitec)* (2010).

[15] NAVIGATION CENTER, U.S. DEPARTMENT OF HOME SECURITY. Global Positioning System, Standard Positioning Service: Signal Specification. http://www.navcen.uscg.gov, June 1995. 2nd edition.

[16] PAPADIMITRATOS, P., AND JOVANOVIC, A. GNSS-based Positioning: Attacks and countermeasures. In *Proceedings of the IEEE Military Communications Conference (MILCOM)* (2008).

[17] PAPADIMITRATOS, P., AND JOVANOVIC, A. Protection and fundamental vulnerability of GNSS. In *Proceedings of the International Workshop on Satellite and Space Communications* (2008).

[18] RASMUSSEN, K. B., AND ČAPKUN, S. Realization of RF distance bounding. In *Proceedings of the USENIX Security Symposium* (2010).

[19] SCOTT, L. Anti-spoofing & authenticated signal architectures for civil navigation systems. In *Proceedings of the ION GNSS International Technical Meeting of the Satellite Division* (2003).

[20] SPIRENT COMMUNICATIONS PLC. SimGEN simulation software. http://www.spirent.com.

[21] TIPPENHAUER, N. O., RASMUSSEN, K. B., AND ČAPKUN, S. Secure ranging with message temporal integrity. In *Cryptology ePrint Archive: Report 2009/602* (2009).

[22] U. S. DEPARTEMENT OF DEFENSE. Global positioning system. standard positioning service. performance standard, Sep 2008.

[23] U. S. GOVERNMENT. Global positioning system. http://www.gps.gov, 2010.

[24] WARNER, J. S., AND JOHNSTON, R. G. A simple demonstration that the global positioning system (GPS) is vulnerable to spoofing. *Journal of Security Administration* (2002).

[25] WARNER, J. S., AND JOHNSTON, R. G. GPS spoofing countermeasures. *Homeland Security Journal* (2003).

APPENDIX

A. PROOF OF RESULT 1

To show Result 1, we first focus on a single receiver V_1 and **civilian GPS** . The attacker selects a target location L', a target time offset δ'_1, and any arbitrary attacker location P_i^A. Given this, Equation 8 yields Δ_i^A. Using one transmission antenna (i. e. $P_1^A = P_j^A \forall j$)[4], the attacker transmits all signals s_i^A with the delay $\delta_i^A = \Delta_i^A/c$.

While this will successfully spoof the location and time of one victim, other victims in the vicinity will receive the same signals with slight time delay or advancement. We now consider a set of receivers $\mathcal{V} = \{V_1, \ldots, V_n\}$ that are positioned at different physical locations $\mathcal{P} = \{P_1, \ldots, P_n\}$.

Since the attacker sends all signals s_i^A from the same position $P_1^A = P_2^A = \ldots$, we can follow that $b_{1jk} = b_{2jk} = \ldots$ for all signals s_i^A. To compute the effect of the offset on the pseudoranges on each victim, we can express each victims' pseudorange relative to the pseudorange of the first victim: $R_{ij} = R_{i1} + b_{1j1}$. Each victim will measure pseudoranges based on their physical distances to the attacker: $R'_{ij} = R_{ij}^A$. We can now substitute (11) into (7) and get the following equation for each signal s_i^A and V_j:

$$|L'_j - L_i^A| = R'_{i1} - (\Delta'_j - b_{1j1}). \tag{14}$$

Thus, for every V_j, these equations only differ by the different value $(\Delta'_j - b_{1j1}) = \Delta'_1$. This means that all V_j compute an identical location L', but different clock offsets δ'_j:

$$\delta'_j = \delta'_1 + \frac{1}{c}\Big(|P_j - P_i^A| - |P_1 - P_i^A|\Big).$$

□

Result 1 shows that an attacker can make a group of victims believe to be at a specific location by sending one set of satellite signals from the same antenna. All victims will believe to be at the same location L', but with different time offsets. The additional time offset $\delta'_j - \delta'_k$ between victim V_j and V_k introduced by the attacker is bounded by their mutual distance $|\delta'_j - \delta'_k| \leq \frac{|L_j - L_k|}{c}$ and is typically on the order of nanoseconds for victims a few meters apart.

In attacks on military GPS, Equation 10 can be used to derive the additional constraints on the relation between the resulting time offset of the main victim δ'_1 and the distance between the spoofed location and each satellite.

[4]For the victim to be able to compute its location, it must hold that the claimed locations are mutually different $L_1^A \neq L_2^A \neq \ldots$.

Protecting Consumer Privacy from Electric Load Monitoring

Stephen McLaughlin Patrick McDaniel
Systems and Internet Infrastructure Security Lab
Pennsylvania State Univesity
University Park, PA, USA
{smclaugh,mcdaniel}@cse.psu.edu

William Aiello
Networks, Systems, and Security Lab
University of British Columbia
Vancouver, B.C., Canada
aiello@cs.ubc.ca

ABSTRACT

The smart grid introduces concerns for the loss of consumer privacy; recently deployed smart meters retain and distribute highly accurate profiles of home energy use. These profiles can be mined by Non Intrusive Load Monitors (NILMs) to expose much of the human activity within the served site. This paper introduces a new class of algorithms and systems, called Non-Intrusive Load Leveling (NILL) to combat potential invasions of privacy. NILL uses an in-residence battery to mask variance in load on the grid, thus eliminating exposure of the appliance-driven information used to compromise consumer privacy. We use real residential energy use profiles to drive four simulated deployments of NILL. The simulations show that NILL exposes only 1.1 to 5.9 useful energy events per day hidden amongst hundreds or thousands of similar battery-suppressed events. Thus, the energy profiles exhibited by NILL are largely useless for current NILM algorithms. Surprisingly, such privacy gains can be achieved using battery systems whose storage capacity is far lower than the residence's aggregate load average. We conclude by discussing how the costs of NILL can be offset by energy savings under tiered energy schedules.

Categories and Subject Descriptors

J.m [**Computer Applications**]: Miscellaneous

General Terms

Security

Keywords

smart meter, privacy, load monitor

1. INTRODUCTION

Smart meters are being aggressively deployed in homes and businesses as part of a move to global smart grids [23]. This digitization of grid systems offers substantial benefits for society; increased efficiencies and information availability can enable cheaper and greener energy generation, less loss in energy storage and transmission, better fault isolation and recovery, and support for alternative energy sources, e.g., consumer generated wind and solar energy.

The move to digital grid control systems also introduces concerns about security [19, 24, 27]. The smart grid is a complex system of sensors, networks, and computing resources. Attacks against the smart-grid networks and computing elements can range from fraud, to denial of service, to privacy loss [27]. While some regulatory agencies have begun to explore security concerns, no comprehensive system has emerged to address these threats.

One area of particular concern is the loss of consumer privacy. Replacements for the antiquated in-home electromechanical meters, smart meters are embedded systems that use power and voltage sensors to collect and report *load profiles*. Load profiles are histories of energy usage collected at a configured granularity, e.g., seconds or minutes. While instrumental to managing energy use at the local and regional levels, such profiles are also sufficient to determine occupant behavior in residential settings [22, 21, 11]. Depicted here, this behavioral inference is made possible by a class of algorithms known as Non-Intrusive Load Monitoring (NILM):

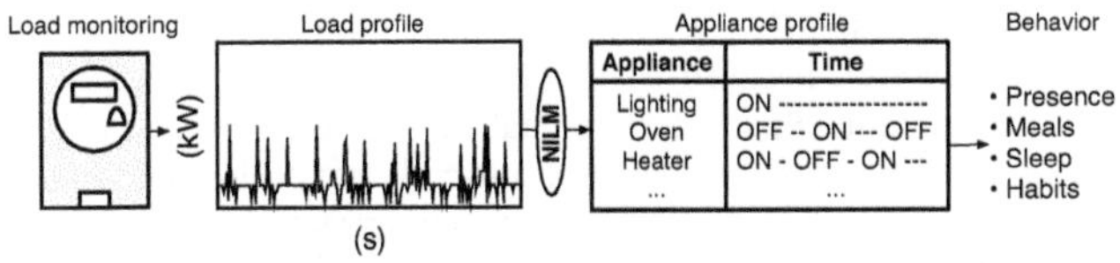

To simplify, NILM algorithms decompose load profiles into composite *appliance profiles* based on known or learned signatures. For example, traces of discrete changes in energy use can be mapped directly to ON/OFF events associated with identifiable appliances. The profile is a detailed description of appliance use and indirectly a surprisingly accurate model of human activity [22].

The concerns surrounding potential invasions of privacy via energy profiles appear to be more than hypothetical [15, 6]. Reuse of data by direct marketers, criminals, or law enforcement without prior approval or notification is often in conflict with privacy regulations, but may be occurring anyway [22]. Undercutting existing regulatory structures is a maze of often conflicting laws and court decisions relating to consumer privacy. For example, the 1939 Supreme Court *United State v. Miller* decision indicates that there is no reasonable expectation of privacy for information shared with third parties. State and regional agencies have built legal and regulatory structures to buttress privacy in the face of such decisions, but consumer rights remain, at best, murky.

The potential exposure of living conditions, occupancy, and family routines, through energy profiles warrants vigilance [15]. This prompts the goal of this work: we aim to protect consumer privacy

CCS'11, October 17–21, 2011, Chicago, Illinois, USA.

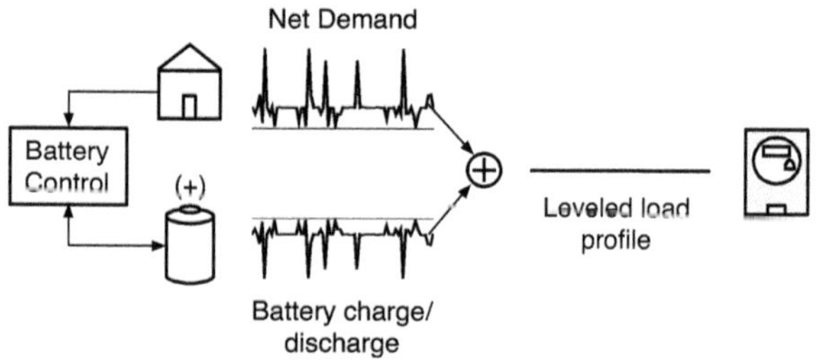

Figure 1: Idealized non-invasive load leveling (NILL).

in the face of profile-exposing smart meters while acknowledging two practical constraints of the current grid environment:

- *Energy usage must always be accurately reported.* Any modification of usage data would undermine grid management, and introduce inaccuracies in billing and grid controls.
- *The privacy solution must not require any modification to the meters, appliances, grid control systems, or provider operation.* The metering infrastructure, which is not under the control of the consumer, is assumed to be untrusted. Moreover, with millions of smart meters already installed and many more in deployment,[1] any solution requiring new grid systems will not be logistically and economically viable [27].

We address threats to electricity consumer privacy through *Non-Intrusive Load Leveling* (NILL), a novel technique to mask appliance features in a home's net load. Illustrated in Figure 1, NILL is conceptually simple; a consumer places a battery and control system between the smart meter and the circuit breaker of their residence. The load observed by the meter is smoothed by offsetting spikes and dips in usage by charging or discharging the battery. Hence, NILL removes the information content that reveals appliance usage. Because we make no assumptions about adversary motivations, NILL aims to smooth all appliance features in a house. However, because of the physical limits and structure of electrical systems, this is a more challenging task than one might initially surmise. Note that NILL is currently not designed to mask longer term energy usage such as day/night diurnal energy patterns, but only the instantaneous energy transitions that expose minute-to-minute human behavior exploited by NILM algorithms. However, we do explore the challenges and countermeasures posed by currently undeveloped NILM techniques that use more sophisticated learning and inference techniques in Appendix A.

NILL is an algorithm and control system that attempts to remove the fine-grained appliance signal represented by changes in the reported load. The control system directs the battery charges and discharges to obscure energy usage. This is conceptually similar to queue delay perturbation countermeasures that prevent networking timing analysis [5]. By de-correlating both the timing and amplitude of ON/OFF events in the load profile, we remove the signal that NILM algorithms use to identify behavior.

The idea of using a battery to provide "best effort" privacy protection is not new. For example, one short paper [16] has suggested the use of a power router to allow a battery to offset appliance loads, though the existing technology in this area limits the battery to handling one appliance at a time. Furthermore, none of the physical challenges of introducing a battery into a residential setting were evaluated. Ours is the first work to perform a rigorous physical simulation of such a system under substantial real-word data. The NILL approach presented here attempts to provide privacy for all appliances under all battery states. Our analysis also extends beyond previous results by examining NILL's effect on the basic unit of load monitoring, the feature pair, and by measuring the amount of privacy afforded over time due to changes in battery states.

The remainder of this paper identifies and evaluates a candidate NILL algorithm. A simulation of NILL is built on the widely-used SimPowerSystems [26] platform. We simulate four homes using energy profile data collected from real residential use. These experiments show that NILL exposed 1.1 and 5.9 identifiable appliance events per day. Such features reside amongst hundreds or thousands of battery-suppressed events, making reliable recovery of appliance profiles virtually impossible under current NILM. Further, we showed that such privacy can be achieved in the tested environments using only a moderately priced 50 amp-hour battery system–far smaller than the aggregate loads of protected residences.

[1]$4.3 billion dollars has been allocated by the U.S government for the smart grids [28], with similar programs in progress in Asia and the EU.

Table 1: Commodity smart meters [29].

Epoch	Product(s)	Deployed
monthly	electromechanical meters	N/A
(no data)	Sensus iCon [34]	7.6 million
15 min	Elster REX 2 [8]	4.0 million
5 min	Echelon NES echelon	4.4 million
1 min	Itron Centron [14]	14.4 million
1 s	TED 5000 [37]	(no data)

2. BACKGROUND

2.1 Load Profiles

Conventional electromechanical watt-hour meters do not record instantaneous demand, only net energy consumed over time. Thus, they act as memoryless accumulators whose readouts are physically spinning dials. Energy use is measured by computing dial position changes since the last reading (typically by a human meter reader once a month). In contrast, smart meters generate *load profiles*, time series of electric demand, that are delivered to the provider at or near real time. The level of detail in load profiles is useful for load forecasting and fraud detection [23]. Common low cost meters measure epochs at 15 minutes, but more sophisticated models can generate profiles at a second or lower granularity. Table 1 summarizes the capabilities of several market-leading meters with different capabilities.[2]

The three-day load profile for a large 5-bedroom home is shown in Figure 2. A diurnal pattern is observable: peaks are felt in the morning, mid-day, and evening. The drop-out box shows an event occurring about 7pm on the 18th. A plasma television connected to a home theater system was turned on and then off about 5 seconds later using a master switch. The initial large spike represents the power-hungry television, followed by the theater receiver and speaker system powering on. The OFF event shows a symmetric decrease in power draw. NILM algorithms match these *sister* features (ON/OFF features of equal amplitude) against known appliance profiles to uncover in-residence behavior.

2.2 Non-Intrusive Load Monitoring

NILM algorithms extract *appliance profiles* from load profiles. It is considered "non-intrusive" because it does this at the electric meter without instrumenting individual appliances. An appli-

[2]Note that TED identified in the table is not a smart meter, but a in-home device used to monitor energy usage (see Section 4.1).

Basic Definitions

t	A time variable (t_0 is used for an initial time when needed.)
$d(t)$	The net demand from all appliances in the house over time
$u(t)$	The load measured by the smart meter (This includes battery charging)
$c(t)$	The battery's state of charge over time
$b(t)$	The battery's rate of charging over time
	$b(t) > 0$ The battery is charging
	$b(t) < 0$ The battery is discharging
H	The upper safe limit on the battery's state of charge
L	The lower safe limit on the battery's state of charge
K_{SS}	The target constant load value for u(t)

Relations

$u(t) = d(t) + b(t)$ (utility observable profile)

$c(t) = \int_{t_0}^{t} b(t)\,dt + c(t_0) = K_{SS}[t - t_0] - \int_{t_0}^{t} d(t)\,dt + c(t_0)$ (state of charge)

NILL Constraints

$u(t) = K_{SS}$ for some constant K_{SS} (leveled load)

$L < c(t) < H$ (safe state of charge)

Figure 3: Summary of the house and battery model used for NILL.

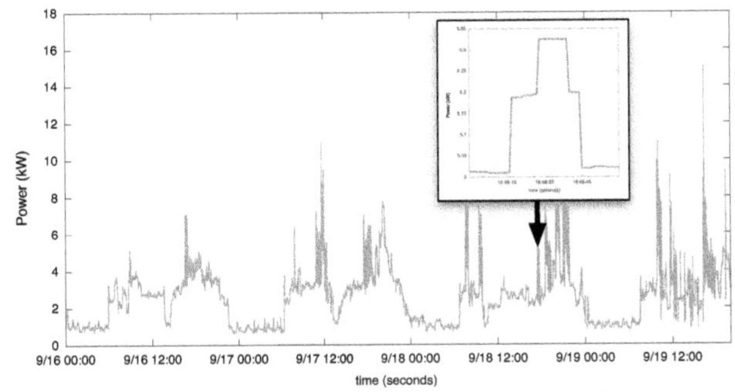

Figure 2: Three-day load profile for large home taken in September 2010. The drop-out box shows a higher resolution view of a television power ON and OFF.

ance profile consists of the types of appliances and the times during which each is operational during the day. Load profiling techniques classify devices by the changes in steady state load caused by their being turned ON and OFF [18]. The approach is to decompose the load profile into a composite of individual appliances features, i.e., representative pairs of ON/OFF events. For example, periodic spikes in energy use are visible in homes with electric furnaces during cold weather. NILM algorithms can extract the expected furnace load from the load profile to expose other, possibly smaller, appliance loads. These techniques use appliance models and information learned about a residence over time to reconstruct behavior from a single aggregate signature. Such techniques have been shown to be highly accurate in practice [25, 21, 33, 22]. We discuss other classes of NILM that are not relevant to residential smart meters in Section 5.3.

2.3 Energy Storage

NILL requires one of a particular class of *deep-cycle* batteries. Deep cycle batteries are designed to be able to operate adequately during long cycles of charging and discharging without significantly reducing their lifetime. Such batteries are frequently used in recreational vehicles such as RVs and boats. There are several types of deep cycle batteries that support highly variable load profiles (at short timescales) present in home energy consumption. The Absorbed Glass Mat (AGM) battery (which has a lead-acid chemistry) has several properties that make it ideal for home use; they work well at extreme temperatures, have low internal resistance, can be charged at high voltages, and are designed to prevent leakage. To avoid sulfation (inability to hold charge due to crystallization of the lead sulfate), deep cycle batteries should not be allowed to discharge below 20% of their total capacity, and staying above 50% is optimal. When a battery is to be charged beyond 90%, its charger should switch to a lower constant voltage than what was used for previous charging [13].

For our evaluation of NILL, we model a 50 Ah[3] lead-acid battery operating at a nominal voltage of 120V. This is achievable by connecting typical 50 Ah sealed DC batteries, which typically retail for approximately \$100 [2], in series. One of the most common voltages for these types of batteries is 12V, requiring 10 such batteries (approx. \$1,000) to achieve the necessary characteristics. We use a 60 ampere (A) maximum discharge current system as available in modern home solar setups [1].

3. Non-Intrusive Load Leveling

The goal of a NILL system is to level the load profile to a constant *target load*, thus removing appliance features. To achieve this, NILL relies on a battery to offset the power consumed by appliances. When an appliance turns ON, it will exert a load beyond the target load. Thus, NILL will discharge the battery to partially supply the load created by the appliance, maintaining the target load.[4] Similarly, if an appliance enters the OFF state, the load profile will decrease below the target load. These opportunities are used to charge the battery while restoring the target load. The NILL system presented here consists of two parts: a battery and a control system that regulates the battery's charge and discharge based on the present load and battery state. The controller attempts to maintain a steady state target load K_{SS}, but will go into one of two special states K_L or K_H if the battery needs to recover from a low or high state of charge. This section describes the NILL runtime control system and the calculation of the initial system parameters.

3.1 Run Time Control

In a perfect NILL implementation, there would be no runtime control as the battery would have sufficient capacity for maintaining the target load. For any reasonably sized battery, there will be times when the state of charge is insufficient to maintain the target load under a heavy load. We call this a *low recovery state* because the battery's SOC has become too low to maintain the target load.

[3] Ah stands for amp-hours, which is a measure of the battery charge capacity.

[4] The battery is only used to supply appliances in the house. It is never discharged back into the grid as is done in *net metering*.

Similarly, in times of light load, the battery will draw from the utility to maintain the constant load. If however, the load remains light, eventually the battery will reach its maximum SOC. We call this a *high recovery state*.

We use the model shown in Figure 3 in describing the control system and bootstrapping phase in the next section. The model captures both the actual load profile of the house $d(t)$, as well as the load under the influence of NILL as perceived by the electric meter $u(t)$. The essence of NILL is described by the equation, $u(t) = d(t) + b(t)$, where b is the battery's rate of charge over time. If $b(t) > 0$, the battery is charging, otherwise $b(t) < 0$ and the battery is discharging. Finally, $c(t)$ is used to represent the battery's state of charge (SOC).[5] The NILL controller must maintain the target load and respond to low and high recovery states. The controller sits next to the battery at the service-panel or electric meter. A sensor placed on the same line as the meter is used to monitor d, and one on the battery to monitor c. Using these two parameters, the controller selects b to maintain a constant u within the battery's operational constraints.

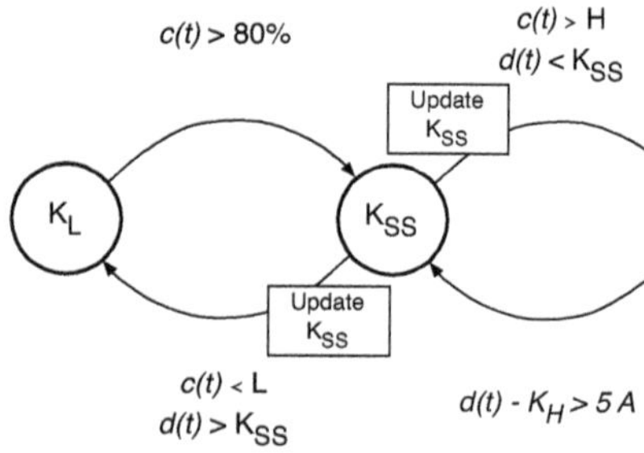

Figure 4: The transitions between the steady state target load and the high and low recovery loads. In state K_i, the battery output is calculated using $K_i - d$.

If the controller enters one of two recovery states, the target load will be altered to allow the battery to reach a safe state while still attempting to mask features present in the load profile. We denote the target load during steady state operation as K_{SS}, and the targets for the low and high recovery states as K_L and K_H respectively. Because entering a recovery state is a sign that the target load was either too high or too low to maintain, it is adjusted each time the controller transitions to a recovery state. Figure 4 illustrates the conditions under which the controller changes states and adjusts K_{SS}. While in state K_i, the battery is controlled using $b = K_i - d$.

In a low recovery state, a new target load K_L is chosen to allow the battery to recharge while still hiding the majority of load events. Thus, K_L is set equal to the battery's maximum sustained charge amperage, masking all load events with amperages less than or equal to this maximum. To reduce the frequency of recovery states over time, the controller will adapt K_{SS} each time a low or high recovery state occurs. This is done using the exponential weighted moving average of the instantaneous demand since the last recovery state at t_r: $K_{SS} \leftarrow \alpha \frac{D}{t-t_r} + (1-\alpha)K_{SS}$.[6] Once the battery reaches 80% SOC, the system returns to steady state. The effects of low recovery states in our experimental results are shown in Section 4.4.

In a high recovery state, the battery is at its maximum SOC, and the load is below K_{SS}. Once in this state, the only choices are idling the battery, which allows all events to appear in the load profile, or discharging the battery. Because NILL's goal is to cancel appliance level features, we choose the latter. The only question left is the choice of K_H. For this, the controller uses the most recent load samples to guess at a K_H that will be just below the current load (by approximately 1 to 5 amperes). If this guess is not successful after the first few seconds, a more conservative guess is made. With $K_H < d$, the battery can discharge minimally while producing a flat area in the load profile. If the load increases by 5 or more amps, the system returns to steady state. An example of a low recovery state in our experimental results is shown in section 4.3.

[5]Some literature uses Depth of Discharge (DOD), the complementary quantity to SOC.

[6]Note that this is not an EWMA over continuous time samples, but over discrete steady state periods.

3.2 Determining Initial Target Loads

A NILL system requires an initial value for K_{SS} to bootstrap normal operation. A good target load is one that can be sustained with little variation over time. Target load selection is also useful for battery sizing, i.e., if there is no feasible target load for a given battery capacity, a larger battery should be used. For the remainder of this section, we refer to the initial K_{SS} as simply K to distinguish from the steady state target load during run time operation. Two constraints must be satisfied for the target load K to be considered feasible. First, the utility observable profile should be leveled to K at all times. Second, the battery charge and discharge required to achieve $u(t) = K$ must not cause the battery to exceed its safe capacity limits L and H. Under these constraints, the equation for battery SOC can be rewritten in terms of d and K as shown in the RHS of the state of charge relation. This rewriting is used in the algorithm for finding a minimal target load.

Algorithm 1 $FindMinTargetLoad$

1: Given demand $d(t)$, start time t_0, end time t and initial charge $c(t_0)$
2: $D \leftarrow \int_{t_0}^{t} d(t)\, dt$
3: $d_{max} \leftarrow \max_{[t_0,t]} d(t)$
4: Binary search $K \in [0, d_{max}]$
5: Check that $L \leq K[t - t_0] - D + Hc(t_0) \leq H$ over $[t_0, t]$
6: Output minimal satisfactory K

We use Algorithm 1 to find the minimal target load for a given battery capacity. The minimal feasible K is chosen to put the least stress on the battery when coming on line. The input $d(t)$ is a sample of a load profile from the residence hosting the NILL installation. The output is the initial target K. In practice, we select $c(t_0) = 50\%$ SOC, $L = 20\%$ SOC, and $H = 90\%$ SOC to model the safe bounds on battery charge.

4. EVALUATION

4.1 Source Data Collection

The data used in the experiments was collected from devices installed in four homes in the Northeast United States. A TED 5000 [37] measuring transmitting unit (MTU) device was installed in each monitored location and collected real power (kW) and voltage data. TEDs passively measure power and voltage crossing the main circuit between the meter and the circuit panel. Energy readings are transmitted to a TED gateway over the house electrical circuits via power line communications. The gateway is connected via a wired network to a personal computer, which can access readings via HTTP. The TEDs were polled at half-hour intervals to collect per-second load profiles.

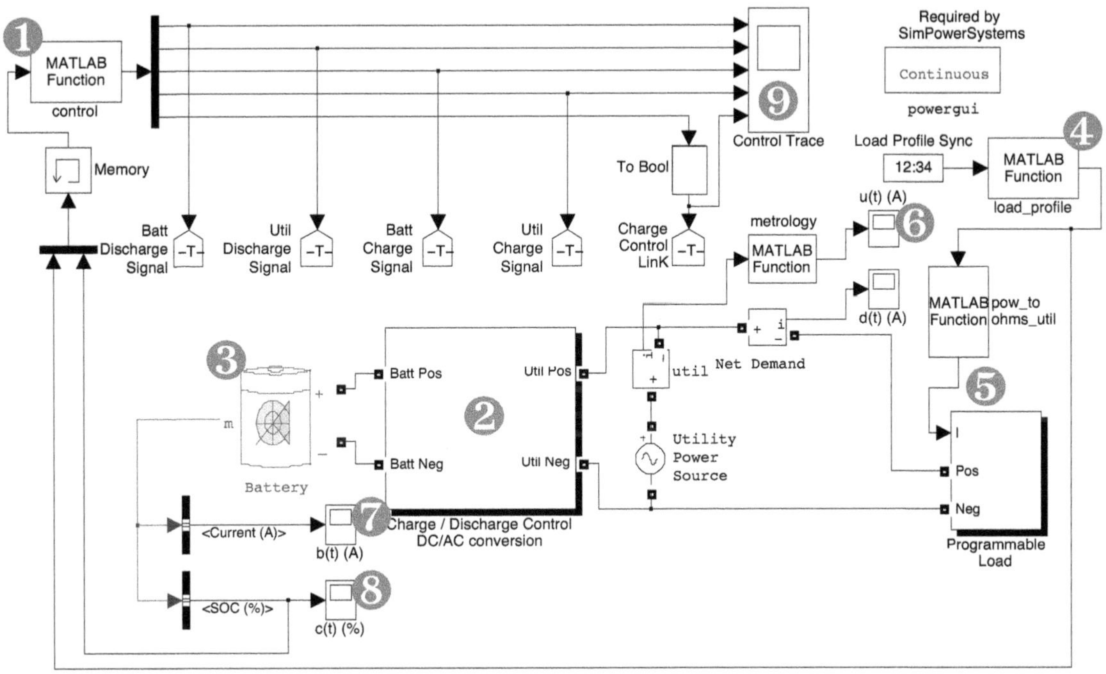

Figure 6: The NILL Simulator. Signals from the control algorithm (1) regulate the switching circuitry (2) that connects the battery (3) and load. The load profile data is inserted at (4) and exerted by a variable resistor (5). The sum of load and battery ($u(t)$) is measured by the meter (6), and rate and state of charge are measured at (7) and (8) respectively. A trace of the control signals (9) was used for debugging purposes.

Table 2: Experimental data sources - energy usage traces collected from residences in spring of 2010

Residence	H1	H2	A1	T1
Start	3/1 9am	4/17 12am	3/15 12am	4/18 11:15am
End	5/1 9am	5/16 12am	4/14 12am	5/17 11am
Length	61 days	30 days	30 days	29 days
Bedrooms	5	2	3	2
Residents	4	3	3	2
Init. K_{SS}	4.64 kW	4.08 kW	3.85 kW	8.20 kW

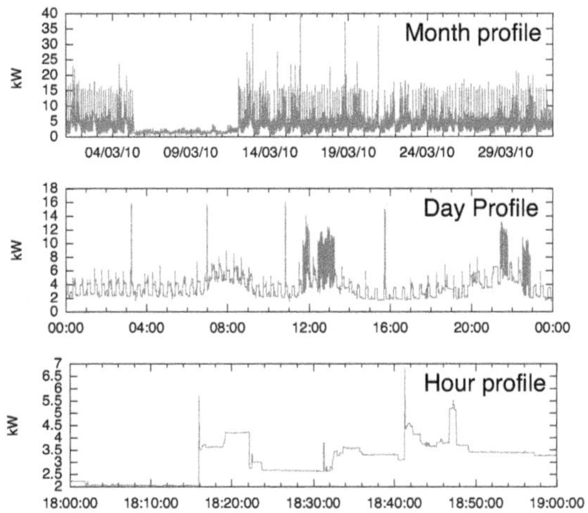

Figure 5: Residence monthly, daily, and hourly profiles.

The experiments in the following section use load profiles collected in the spring of 2010 in the four residences, as described in Table 2. We refer to the data sets as H1, H2, A2, and T1 throughout (homes 1 and 2, apartment 1 and townhouse 1, respectively). The data collection process introduced a small number of sample outages in which no data was collected. This was due to brief power cycles of the TED or lost communication between the TED collector and usage sensor. We repair these gaps by placing repeated samples of the constant average of the surrounding 100 seconds. The H1 data contained two such gaps (1 hour, 3 minutes), H2 contained one gap (19 minutes), A1 contained no outages, and T1 had 2 gaps (11 minutes, 13 minutes). Given their relatively small size, these gaps have little influence on our experimental results.

Figure 5 illustrates energy use over different time scales for one residence, H1. The month profile highlights the relatively constant rate of use over time. Note that during the week of March 3rd, the usage drops off substantially. The occupants left for a spring break during this period, turned down the thermostat, and unplugged appliances throughout the house. The daily energy use exhibits similar diurnal patters as described in Section 2.1. The periodic usage spikes observed in the day-scale data was the result of the home's furnace turning ON and OFF blower motors to force heat in the gas-heated house. Finally, the hourly readings show the enormous sensitivity of these devices to internal use; while spikes caused by starting dryers and heat pump blowers are very clear, small changes caused by appliances such as lamps are also visible.

4.2 Full System Simulation

The NILL system simulation answers the question of how effectively the battery and controller can remove appliance features from a metered load profile. To achieve a realistic battery model, we implemented the simulation in Simulink with the SimPowerSystems extension [26]. This was necessary, as using an oversimplified battery model, e.g. one with linear discharge characteristics, would lead to an inaccurate assessment of NILL's capabilities.

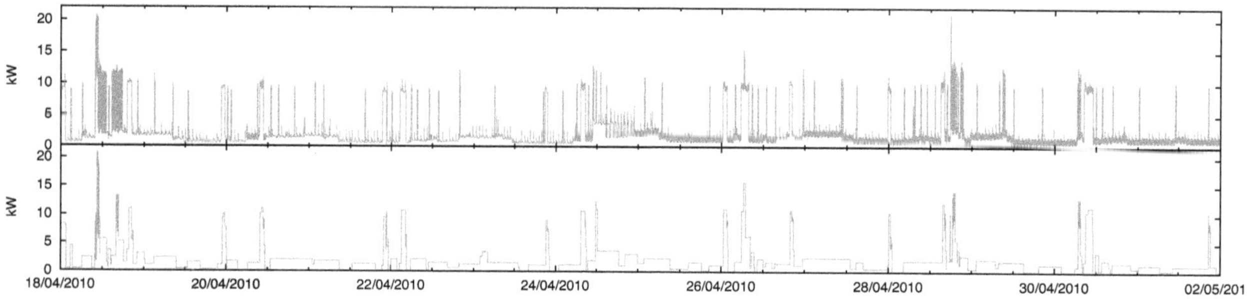

Figure 7: Top: The net load (d) consumed by T1 between Apr. 18 and Apr 30. Bottom: The same load under the simulated NILL system with a 50 Ah battery (u).

Our simulation is shown in Figure 6. At the heart of the system is a circuit with three elements: a net load exerted by appliances, a voltage source for the utility, and a battery. The appliance load is supplied by demand data collected from the TEDs. It is injected into the system as a real valued signal, and converted to an electrical load by a variable resistor in the programmable load. (Like several other residential NILM studies [10, 4, 22], we focus on real power consumption.) The programmable load is supplied by the utility and potentially the battery, which sit in parallel on the circuit. The part of the net load not supplied by the battery will be supplied by the utility voltage source according to Kirchhoff's circuit laws. Battery charging is controlled by the switching connecting the battery to the rest of the circuit. To avoid severe performance slowdowns in our simulation, we implement the battery switching using variable resistance and voltage sources in place of simulating non-linear power electronics. When the battery is discharging, a variable resistance is used to draw current from the battery, and a current source supplies the load proportionally. This process is reversed during charging.

With regards to timing in the circuit, the load profile data is inserted at the rate of one sample per second, the same rate at which it was recorded. The metrology unit on the utility meter decimates the signal to have 1/4 the resolution of the control unit. In reality, control units with MHz clocks can have orders of magnitude higher resolution than solid state metering, giving a full implementation a greater advantage. Forcing sampling at these rates however would have made the simulation run prohibitively slow. Finally, the memory block placed before the control serves to add a one-step delay between the propagation of the sensor signals to the simulator, and the propagation of the resulting control signals to the circuit.

The battery model used in the simulator was originally designed for SimPowerSystems in [38]. It maintains only a single state variable, the state of charge, as well as several other parameters to model voltage during the two phases of battery discharge: the exponential and nominal zones. The additional parameters, including internal resistance, are derived from the battery type, nominal voltage, and capacity. The model has been shown to accurately produce the original manufacturer voltage curves for lead acid batteries, as well as several other basic battery types.

The control unit receives two variables, the net demand and the battery's state of charge. Based on the control model presented in section 3.1, these are used to calculate the charge state and rate of charge for the target K_{SS}. The control also checks the conditions for entering a recovery state and adjusts K_{SS} using EWMA. The control system is implemented in just under 900 lines of Matlab code.

4.2.1 Simulation Procedure

We ran the simulator on each of the four load profile data sets. The runs for H2, A1, and T1 lasted for approximately 3 hours each, and H1 ran for 6 hours. The initial target load K_{SS} for each simulation was calculated by running Algorithm 1 over one week of sample data occurring prior to the load profiles used in the simulation. The initial K_{SS} for each residence is shown in Table 2. Though the initial values are not closely aligned with the longer term run-time steady states, they err on the side of caution due to the strict SOC constraint on line 5 of Algorithm 1. In each case, K_{SS} was either close to the immediate load at the beginning of the trace, or led to a high recovery state with no leaked features. Along with the metered power under NILL $u(t)$, the SOC over time $c(t)$ was included in the output of each simulation.

The results report below were collected using a simulated 50 Ah battery with a 60 A maximum discharge. The α value for the EWMA used to adjust K_{SS} was calibrated experimental to 0.5. Methods for choosing an optimal α and other parameters are covered in Section 5.2. The lower bound on charge was chosen to be 20% SOC. The initial state of the battery was set to 80% SOC.

4.3 Simulation Results

A two-week example of the load profile witnessed by the electric meter (u) compared with the total load (d) is shown in Figure 7. From this example, several things are apparent. First, there are extended periods of hours to days during which no appliance features are visible in u. Second, the majority of features that do occur in u have high amplitudes, and are among the largest present in d. Third, periods of light load in d are accompanied by periods of very light or nearly zero load in u. And finally, the emergent shape of the load profile remains the same for both d and u, and the area under the two curves is approximately the same. We now inspect each of these facets in detail.

Steady state loads comprise the majority of the NILL load profile. During these periods, the controller is able to maintain the target steady state load K_{SS} without depleting or fully charging the battery. Thus, the better the choice of K_{SS}, the longer the steady state can be maintained. Following several high amplitude loads at the beginning of the trace, the steady state converges to durations of half a day or more by Apr. 22nd.

A number of large features appear in u outside of the steady state. These features tend to appear at the peaks of comparatively steady high-amplitude loads. Examples of such events occur on Apr. 18th and 28th. These features, which are also some of the largest in d, either cause or occur during low recovery state. When the battery is recharging, the target load K_L is set to allow the maximum rate of charge, causing the large yet steady load below the visible features.

Table 3: NILL feature reduction

Residence	Non-NILL	NILL	Change
Total Features			
H1	1047099	61793	-94.10%
H2	286960	20713	-92.78%
A1	430214	24893	-94.21%
T1	384847	33413	-91.32%
Features per hour			
H1	358	21	-94.10%
H2	199	14	-92.79%
A1	289	16	-94.21%
T1	277	24	-91.32%
Sister feature pairs			
H1	340986	10552	-96.91%
H2	110994	4735	-95.73%
A1	176540	6030	-96.58%
T1	147982	8120	-94.51%

After sustained periods of steady state operation or light loads in d, a sharp decrease will occur in u as NILL enters a high recovery state. This happens when the battery has reached full charge while maintaining K_{SS}. In this state, the target load K_H is chosen to be just below some of the recently sampled demand values, so as to allow the battery to discharge at a low rate. As can be seen, in the majority of cases, the choice of K_H is correct on the first try. On a few occasions, most notably after mid day on Apr. 18th, the initial guess is too high, and K_H is lowered by 0.6 kW to allow the battery to discharge. In several instances (such as just prior to Apr. 26th) the NILL controller chose K_H to be slightly below zero, meaning that the battery is effectively discharging to the grid. This is only a concern if the meter can detect reverse power flows, in which case the NILL system can be configured to never set K_L below zero.

Having now covered how NILL reacts to loads, it should not be surprising that on the larger scale of days to weeks, the NILL graph looks similar to the original load. This is result of both the limited capacity batteries afforded by current technology, and typical weather and occupant behavioral patterns. While these larger trends reveal information about customers, most notably the likelihood of human presence in the house, they do not reveal the more fine-grained details such as how many occupants are at home or what their activities are. Thus, we now turn our analysis to quantifying NILL's effectiveness in removing individual appliance features from load profiles.

4.4 Countering NILM

NILM algorithms exploit the amplitude changes in load profiles. These "features" are indicative appliance ON/OFF events (and appliance-internal state changes that effect energy consumption, e.g., washing machine cycles [3]). Features exploited by NILM are represented by $(time, amplitude)$. Here, amplitude is not the absolute metric of energy, but the relative change in energy use from the last sample. For example, a system exhibiting a 5-second load profile: $\{t_0 : 0\text{W},\ t_1 : 100\text{W},\ t_2 : 200\text{W},\ t_3 : 200\text{W},\ t_4 : 200\text{W},\ t_5 : 100\text{W}\}$ would yield features: $\{(t_1, +100\text{W}), (t_2, +100\text{W}), (t_3, 0\text{W}), (t_4, 0\text{W}), (t_5, -100\text{W})\}$. Samples with amplitude with no change are not features, and are ignored for analysis.

Table 3 shows the feature reduction for the simulated environments. The original TED profile data (Non-NILL) contains just over 1 million features on the 60 day profile of the large house H1, down to the 380 thousand features in the 29 day profile for the small townhouse T1. When the load profile is simulated in NILL-enabled residences (NILL), the number of features drops significantly (around 95% or more). This reduces the number of features from several hundred an hour to as few as 16 in the case of T1.

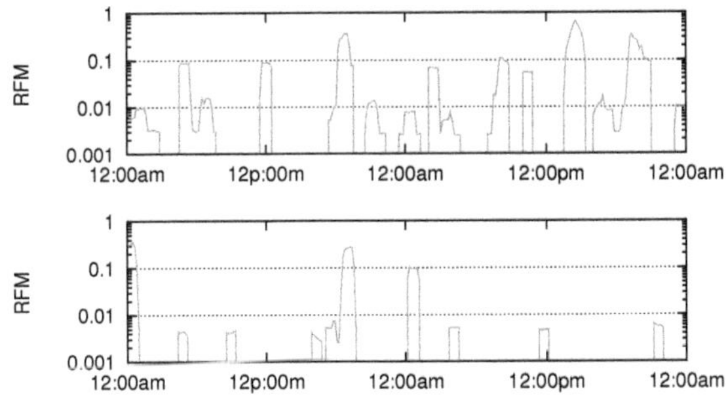

Figure 8: Relative feature mass over two day simulation for H1 (top) and A1 (bottom).

A key question asks if the residual features left after NILL are useful for the NILM analysis. Recall from Section 2 that NILM rely on pairs of symmetric ON/OFF "sister" features to infer appliance usage. We performed a sister matching algorithm that would match all events of greater than 10 W –about 1/6th the draw of a light bulb–as a pairing of positive charge increase and decrease (with a tolerance of 5 W). The matching algorithm linearly scans forward in the trace for the equal and opposite OFF event for each ON event. Table 3 shows that each simulated environment experienced 94% or greater reduction in identifiable sister features.

Raw feature reduction sketches the aggregate behavior of NILL, but only provides a crude estimate of privacy-preservation over time. A *feature mass* ($FM(w, D)$) is the number of non-zero features from over a discrete sample set $D = (d_0, d_1, \ldots, d_w)$, e.g., the number of features over a given time window of size w. In this work, the feature mass is the number of non-zero energy transitions occurring within a time-series interval sample D of length w:

$$FM(w, D) = \sum_{i=0}^{w} (d_i \neq 0)$$

The *relative feature mass* (RFM) for an interval w is the ratio of the feature mass for two sample sets (in this case NILL over non-NILL) over w, e.g.:

$$RFM(w, D) = \frac{FM(w, D_{NILL})}{FM(w, D_{NON\_NILL})}$$

RFM measures the relative number of features of the original and NILL data. Intuitively, as RFM approaches zero, there is very little signal relative to the original profile for a NILM algorithm to operate on. Figure 8 shows the RFM computed at ten minute intervals with a one hour sliding window, i.e., $w = 1\ hour$, over two days at A1 (11 days into the trace) and H1 (29 days into the trace).

The most visible characteristic in Figure 8 is the oscillation of RFM. Most of the trace shows the RFM at 1% or less, and at zero for some of the time (note that the Y axis is on a log scale). The reason for this is the nature of the battery system. When the battery is in the low recovery state, it is unable to suppress most appliance features, and they become visible in the load profile. (We investigate the impact of features occurring during low recovery state in the next section). RFM increases in this off state, peaking in the case of H1 at almost 0.5 RFM for a few minutes. T1 has fewer and less pronounced increases in RFM. Note that the prolonged RFM of zero represents perfect privacy.

To get a sense for the behavior of steady state NILL, consider the normal steady state. We arbitrarily define the system to be in a *NILL-effective* state when the RFM is less than 0.1–which repre-

Table 6: Residual Features

Residence	Features	Sisters	Residual Features (%)	Residual Sisters (%)
H1	1047099	340986	35969 (3.4%)	5526 (1.6%)
H2	286960	110994	13230 (4.6%)	3112 (2.8%)
A1	430214	176540	15556 (3.6%)	3648 (2.0%)
T1	384847	147982	30861 (8.0%)	7640 (5.1%)

Table 4: Feature reduction during NILL-effective ($RFM < 0.1$) state in simulated environments.

Residence	Non-NILL	NILL	Change
Total Features			
H1	879054	6808	-99.23%
H2	225088	1176	-99.48%
A1	354102	1508	-99.57%
T1	265400	1262	-99.52%
Features per hour			
H1	354	3	-99.09%
H2	186	1	-99.12%
A1	279	1	-99.32%
T1	260	2	-99.25%
Sister feature pairs			
H1	291718	561	-99.81%
H2	89558	118	-99.87%
A1	148446	128	-99.91%
T1	104012	161	-99.99%

Table 5: Simulated time in NILL-effective state

Residence	Non-NILL (sec)	NILL (sec)	% of sim.
H1	10527597	8928597	84.81%
H2	5183997	4345199	83.82%
A1	5356797	4570797	85.33%
T1	5009397	3255535	64.99%

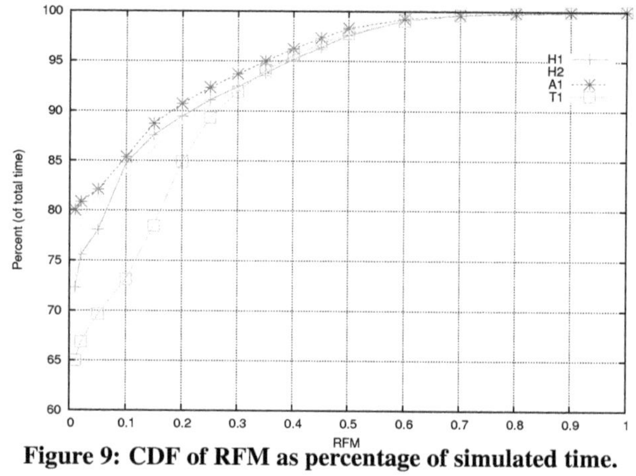

Figure 9: CDF of RFM as percentage of simulated time.

Table 7: Feature Exposure in the Low Recovery State

Res.	Time in Low State (%)	Residual Features (%)	Residual Sisters (%)
H1	891913 (8.5%)	18292 (50.8%)	3363 (60.8%)
H2	340685 (6.6%)	5248 (39.6%)	1414 (45.3%)
A1	435090 (8.1%)	8814 (56.6%)	2524 (69.1%)
T1	390279 (7.8%)	7456 (24.1%)	2172 (28.4%)

sents 10% residual features resulting from NILL. Table 4 shows the features present during intervals when the system is NILL-effective. In all experiments the features, features per hour, and sister features are reduced by over 99%. Table 5 shows that this state is the norm–where between 65% to over 85% of the simulated time was in this state in the simulated environment. One might (incorrectly) attribute the success of in these instances to periods when the load is quiescent. Quite the contrary, the majority of total features in the original data are present during these periods. 83% of the original features for H1 are observed during a NILL effective state, 78.5% of H2, 82% of A1, and 90% of T1.

Figure 9 shows RFM as a CDF–the Y-axis indicates the simulated time in which the system encounters a RFM (X-axis) or less. For all traces the feature mass is zero for 65% to over 80% of the time. Trace time rises steadily until around an RFM of 50%, which is around 2% of the trace for all simulated environments.

4.5 Residual Features

A residual feature is any feature that appears in the original profile that also appears in the NILL trace, e.g., an energy transition that appears at (or about) the same time with similar amplitude (within few watts). Because they precisely reflect appliance activities, these are the only features that are of value to current NILM algorithms. Such features slip through the NILL control system and are observable by the adversary. Table 6 shows the residual features occurring in the simulated environments.

One reason for the presence of residual features is the low recovery state, hereafter called simply low state for brevity, during which the battery is recharging. Table 7 describes NILL behavior in low battery states. Here, we see only 24-56% of the residual features are present in the low state (which occurs less than 10% of the time). Thus, while low state charging explains some of the residual features, many are present in the also steady (non-charging) state.

One can partition residual features into three classes. The first class of features contains very small changes, e.g., less than 60 W, about the load of a typical light bulb. Such loads, the most common in load profiles, are driven by numerous causes including small lighting fixtures, appliance state changes, and small electronics requiring standby power. Because they reside in the band on the smaller end of the power spectrum, it would not be difficult for a NILL system to mimic their arrivals and departures using small variations in the battery charge and discharge rate. We thus do not consider them for the remainder of this analysis.

A second class of features contains large transitions caused by often short-lived heavy loads, e.g., kitchen microwave. The aggregate draw of the large loads combined with ongoing draws exceeds the target load (K_L) plus the maximum output of the battery (60 A for the simulated battery we tested). There is little NILL can do about these loads because it simply cannot safely supply the necessary current. The last class are legitimate loads that are not managed by NILL because of low state. Table 8 provides a breakdown of the residual features present in the simulated environment. Interestingly, 70-85% of the features and 92-98% of the sister features are of the small variety.

Regardless of the reason for their presence, the features usable by NILM to correctly uncover are the large and medium residual sister features. To summarize:

Table 8: Classification of residual features

Residence	Features			Sister Features		
	Small (%)	Medium (%)	Large (%)	Small (%)	Medium (%)	Large (%)
H1	25334 (70.4%)	6257 (17.4%)	4378 (12.1%)	5167 (93.50%)	214 (3.87%)	145 (2.62%)
H2	11319 (85.5%)	1193 (9.0%)	718 (5.4%)	3079 (98.94%)	21 (0.67%)	12 (0.39%)
A1	13139 (84.4%)	1249 (8.0%)	1168 (7.5%)	3555 (97.45%)	45 (1.23%)	48 (1.32%)
T1	25823 (83.7%)	4717 (15.3%)	321 (1.0%)	7512 (98.32%)	118 (1.54%)	10 (0.13%)

Residence	Sister features	Per Day
H1	359 (0.11%)	5.9
H2	33 (0.03%)	1.1
A1	93 (0.05%)	3.1
T1	128 (0.09%)	4.4

Fewer than ten and as little as one true feature per day that are available to NILM algorithms in our simulated environment. This represents about 3 to 11 out of a thousand features exposed, a minuscule exposure of privacy.

One of the challenges a NILM algorithm might have in the presence of NILL is that it must identify which of the features out of the total trace are legitimate. For example, there are 473 true sister features hidden in 10,552 for H1. Unless there is a clear marker identifying a true feature in the timing/amplitude, then it would be virtually impossible to separate the real and synthetic transitions.

4.6 Entropy Analysis

In addition to comparing the number of features between the load seen by the battery and that seen by the utility, comparing the empirical entropy of two loads is also useful. As in the above discussion, distinguishing information about which appliance or type of appliance was just turned ON (or OFF) lies not in the d and u time series of aggregate load versus time but rather lies in the features (i.e., non-zero impulses) that. Define $\delta d(t) = d(t) - d(t-1)$ and $\delta u(t) = u(t) - u(t-1)$ as the time series of impulses generated by the appliances and seen by the utility, respectively. For each time series we define a probability mass function, $P_{\delta d}$ and $P_{\delta u}$, respectively, which takes a bin size b as a parameter. For concreteness define the ith bin as being the range $[ib, (i+1)b)$ in units of watts. $P_{\delta d}(i|b)$ is just the fraction of the values of δd that are in bin i. $P_{\delta u}$ is defined similarly. Given an empirical probability mass function $P(i)$ we calculate the empirical entropy using base 2 in the standard way:

$$H(P) = -\frac{1}{|I|}\sum_{i\in I} P(i)\log_2 P(i),$$

where I is the support of P, i.e., $I = \{i|P(i) > 0\}$.

Here, $H(P_{\delta d})$ can be interpreted as an upper bound on the number of bits of information a NILM algorithm could extract on average for each impulse sample in δd (if it had access to δd, as it would in the case that our NILL hardware and software were not deployed). Likewise, $H(P_{\delta u})$ can be interpreted as upper bound on the number of bits of information a NILM algorithm could extract on average for each impulse sample in δu, i.e., after the signal has been smoothed by our NILL algorithm. Table 9 reports the empirical entropies for our four data sets, computed using a bin size of 1 W. The bin size was chosen this small to allow for the potential of higher entropy due to higher precision but not any smaller in order to mitigate the introduction of undue noise.

As noted above, the empirical entropy is an upper bound on the information extractable by a NILM algorithm from a time series. Strictly speaking, showing a gap between an upper bound on the information extractable from d and an upper bound on the information extractable from u does not prove that the NILL algorithm decreases the information content of d. That is, the actual information content extractable from d may be below the upper bound on the information extractable from u. However, this would require that the information content of the two signals have significantly different characteristics. In the event that the sequences have similar characteristics, the ratio between the upper bound and the actual information extractable should be similar for each time series.

Note that if a time series is highly correlated, the empirical entropy will overestimate the information in the series. (For example, a series of 100 1's followed by 100 2's will have empirical entropy of 1 bit per time step although the series clearly does not contain 200 bits of information.) There are clearly examples of correlations in our time series. As mentioned above, when a home theatre system was turned on in H1 and H2, several features occurred in succession over a short period of time. In addition to such intra-appliance correlations, some home loads have quasi-periodic behavior. Examples of such loads include refrigerator compressors and home furnace systems.

To understand the extent of these time correlations we computed the autocorrelation function (Pearson variant) of δd and δu. The autocorrelation on input k of an n element times series s compares $s(i)$ with $s(i+k)$ for all $1 \le i \le n-k$. The autocorrelation is always at most 1 and at least -1, with values near 1 implying a high degree of correlation, values near -1 implying a high degree of anti-correlation, and values near 0 implying a high degree of independence. The autocorrelation of δd had absolute value less than 0.02 for all values of the lag k. Thus, in spite of the fact that there are some correlated impulses in the data set, the vast majority of impulses appear to be uncorrelated. The non-zero impulses of δu essentially constitute a subsequence of δd. (That is, if at time t, $\delta u(t)$ is non-zero then at the same time $\delta d(t)$ is non-zero as well. If fact, the size of the impulse is often the same in this case.) Since a subsequence of a sequence of independent events is itself independent, it follows that the impulses of δu are largely uncorrelated as well. Indeed, the autocorrelation of the δu time series was similarly small. This argues against the introduction of a systematic bias in empirical entropy of one series versus the other due to differences in time correlations between the two series.

In Table 9, the entropy is computed in two ways: one in which zero values of the respective time series are included when calculating a probability mass function for the time series, and one in which the zero values are excluded. Including the zero values has intuitive appeal as the fact that there are many more zeroes in the NILL time series does reflect that fact that the NILL time series conveys less information to a NILM algorithm. However, to ensure that the number of zeroes in the NILL time series were not biasing the results unduly, we also calculated the entropy of the various time series without the zeroes included. As the entropy represents the average amount of information per sample, and as there are more samples in the Non-NILL time series, we have in-

Table 9: Empirical Entropy

Residence	Non-NILL	NILL	Ratio	Non-NILL w/o zeroes	NILL w/o zeroes	Normalized Ratio
H1	0.633267	0.054265	0.085690	5.663782	7.519812	0.078346
H2	0.235150	0.029554	0.125681	4.516394	6.340144	0.101323
A1	0.363826	0.038459	0.1057071	4.468669	6.526919	0.039289
T1	0.360635	0.019137	0.0530647	5.114588	6.460732	0.084519

Table 10: NILL Cost Reduction per Month in Simulated Environments

Residence	O&R	Ont.	PG&E
H1	$8.94 (2.09%)	$11.11 (2.00%)	$18.67 (1.81%)
H2	$2.49 (5.16%)	$3.78 (4.27%)	$6.17 (4.28%)
A1	$3.41 (3.37%)	$4.96 (3.81%)	$10.22 (4.67%)
T1	$2.67 (2.53%)	$3.72 (2.97%)	$6.92 (2.62%)

cluded a ratio which normalizes for this fact. The numerator of the ratio represents the total information available in the NILL time series (i.e., the entropy times the number of terms in the NILL series without zeroes) and the denominator represents the total information available in the Non-NILL time series (i.e., the entropy times the number of terms in the Non-NILL series without zeroes).

Table 9 reports the empirical entropies for our four data sets. When including the zeroes of the time series, the ratio of the NILL to Non-NILL entropies varies from 0.53 on the low side for data set T1 to 0.126 on the high side for data set H2. When the zeroes are included, the normalized ratio varies from 0.039 on the low side for data set A1 to 0.101 on the high side for data set H2.

5. DISCUSSION

5.1 Energy Efficiency and Consumer Cost

Because the cost of energy generation increases substantially with mid-day demand, the Time of Use (TOU) pricing scheme is being introduced to shave demand during peak hours [17]. TOU creates a cost schedule that is tied to the demand curve observed by the provider. Energy costs rise with expected demand. For example, Orange and Rockland power in New York charges 1.280¢/kWh for off-peak use (9:00pm-10:00am year round), and 7.17¢/kWh for peak use (10:00am-9:00pm) October through May. During June through September, peak charges increase to 7.17¢/kWh for shoulder peak use (10:00am-noon and 7:00pm-9:00pm) and 19.899¢/kWh for high peak use (noon-7:00pm) [30]. TOU is touted as a way to control costs by creating incentives for customers to use energy during non-peak hours.

NILL may positively or negatively impact consumer cost under a TOU schedule. Consider a simplified model of consumer cost in a NILL and non-NILL household. Assume that the total kWh usage for the home is U, the percentage of use at peak is U_p, and the provider costs for peak and off-peak are C_p and C_o per kWh, respectively. The total monthly bill for the home is:

$$T = (U * U_p) * C_p + (U * (1 - U_p)) * C_o$$

According to the U.S. Energy Information Administration, the average home uses 920 kWh per month [39]. Using this figure, we can bound on the cost or savings observable by an average residence under Orange and Rockland TOU cost schedule. In the extreme cases, the costs of using NILL can increase by $24.84 (where the home uses no energy during peak hours) or decrease by as much as $29.35 (where the home no energy during off-peak hours). Based on usage statistics, the load of the average home will use slightly more energy during peak hours ($U_p > \%50$), with more pronounced peak loads in the summer months (due to air conditioning).

Table 10 shows the energy costs in the simulated environments under three time-of-use pricing schemes including Orange and Rockland, Ontario Power Generation [9] (Ontario, Canada), and Pacific Gas and Electric [31] (California). The simulated environments observed cost savings ranging from 1.8% to 5.2%. This reflects the smoothing of load by the battery, where some amount of the peak load is shifted into the off-peak hours. Note that the price of energy is significantly higher in California than the other simulated environments, and thus the costs are about double that of the upper-mid Atlantic and Ontario regions. The costs savings of $2 to $10 may partially offset the costs of the NILL system.

Also contributing to the long-term cost of a NILL scheme is the cost of battery maintenance and replacement as a function of battery lifetime. Under a NILL scheme that exercises a lead-acid battery to between 50 to 80% DOD, the battery can be expected to last between 500 to 1,000 cycles [7], which equates to one or two years. One way to extend battery lifetime is to only use NILL when occupants are at home. Additional measures to reduce cycle frequency are the primary goal of future work for this project.

5.2 Optimizing NILL Parameters

The NILL system simulated in this paper relies on a number of important parameters for its operation. While some guidance has been given for parameter choice, such as the calculation of K_{SS}, others were chosen using expert knowledge. In practice, set rules should be used to choose K_H, K_L, and the EWMA parameter α.

The K_L value chosen in a low recovery state allows the battery to recharge quickly to just below a maximum SOC (80% in our experiments). For many lead acid batteries, optimal lifetime and performance can be achieved by recharging to between 50% and 80% SOC at a high rate, and then throttling back to charge to between 90% to 100% [13]. K_H was chosen using the previous few data points from the net load. While this results in a low discharge from the battery, it is not guaranteed to be minimal. As lead-acid batteries tend to perform best at a high SOC, K_H should be chosen to maximize efficient performance. The EWMA was used to adapt K_{SS} over time as the net load caused recovery states. The better the choice of K_{SS}, the longer a steady state may be maintained. While we achieved good results with $\alpha = 0.5$, this heuristic is not guaranteed to work under arbitrary conditions. Instead, a full implementation should consider techniques such as minimizing Mean Squared Error (MSE).

5.3 Power Signatures and Disaggregation

Two NILM techniques under research that may pose a challenge to NILL are power signature analysis and load disaggregation. Power signature based NILMs collect high-resolution data to detect unique appliance signatures. One example of a device power signature is the turn on transient in demand when starting a motor [35, 41]. Similarly, power signatures can be found in loads with a small capacitance such as fluorescent lighting and electronic devices [40]. This technique can be highly accurate, but requires equally accurate measurements with a sampling rate of at least 600 samples per second and a resolution of tenths of amps. In the most extreme case a signature-based NILM can characterize the line noise caused by different appliances during transitional phases using MHz sampling rates [32]. As modern residential smart meters simply do not support the sampling rate or computation needed for detecting load signatures, we do not consider them further here.

Load disaggregation techniques attempt to find the set of appliance loads contributing to a net load by solving a discrete knapsack problem. Though this technique was originally considered to be computationally impractical [12], it has recently been demonstrated as feasible for residential loads [20]. In this scenario, the NILL battery represents an unknown quantity in the knapsack problem. At one-watt resolution, there are thousands of possible values for the battery quantity, many of which will have valid solutions to the knapsack fitting. Thus, we believe that load disaggregation based NILMs are not a significant threat to the privacy afforded by NILL.

6. CONCLUSIONS

We have introduced a new class of privacy-preserving algorithms called non-intrusive load leveling (NILL). NILL blinds privacy-exposing NILM algorithms by removing the majority of useful energy use transitions sensed by recently introduced smart meters. Simulations of NILL over real usage profiles in four homes showed that between 1.1 and 5.9 meaningful events were exposed to NILM algorithms per day. Such features reside amongst hundreds or thousands of false events, making recovery of appliance profiles virtually impossible under current algorithms. Future efforts will expand on the analysis to explore tradeoffs between different battery systems and the integration with existing in-home alternative energy generation technology.

7. REFERENCES

[1] Blue Sky Solar Boost 6024HDL. http://www.ecodirect.com/Blue-Sky-Solar-Boost-6024HL-60Amp-12-24-Volt-p/blue-sky-solar-boost-6024hdl.htm.

[2] Rechargeable Sealed Lead Acid Battery. http://www.lowcostbatteries.com/product_p/12v-50ah.htm.

[3] BARANSKI, M., AND VOSS, J. Detecting Patterns of Appliances from Total Load Data Using a Dynamic Programming Approach. *IEEE International Conference on Data Mining* (2004).

[4] BARANSKI, M., AND VOSS, J. Genetic Algorithm for Pattern Detection in NIALM Systems. In *Proceedings of the IEEE International Conference on Systems, Man and Cybernetics* (2004).

[5] BRUMLEY, D., AND BONEH, D. Remote Timing Attacks are Practical. In *Proceedings of the 12th USENIX Security Symposium* (2003).

[6] CARSON, A. Smart Grids and the Future of Privacy. http://www.greentechmedia.com/articles/read/smart-grids-and-the-future-of-privacy/, 2010.

[7] ELECTROPEDIA. Battery Life (and Death). http://www.mpoweruk.com/life.htm.

[8] ELSTER. REX2-EA meter. http://www.elstermetering.com, 2010.

[9] GREENTERRAFIRMA.COM. Time Of Use Electrical Pricing. http://greenterrafirma.com/time-of-use-electrical-pricing.html, 2010.

[10] GUEDRI, M. E., D'URSO, G., LAJAUNIE, C., AND FLEURY, G. Time-Frequency Characterisation for Electric Load Monitoring. In *Proceedings of the 17th European Signal Processing Conference (EUSIPCO)* (2009).

[11] HART, G. W. Residential Energy Monitoring and Computerized Surveillance via Utility Power Flows. *IEEE Technology and Society Magazine* (1989).

[12] HART, G. W. Nonintrusive Appliance Load Monitoring. *Proceedings of the IEEE* (2004).

[13] HUANG, B., HSU, P., WU, M., AND HO, P. System Dynamic Model and Charging Control of Lead-Acid Battery for Stand-Alone Solar PV System. *Solar Energy 84* (2010).

[14] ITRON. CENTRON Meter. http://www.itron.com, 2010.

[15] JOHN, J. S. Smart Grid Data: Too Much For Privacy, Not Enough For Innovation? http://gigaom.com, 2010.

[16] KALOGRIDIS, G., EFTHYMIOU, C., DENIC, S., LEWIS, T., AND CEPEDA, R. Privacy for Smart Meters: Towards Undetectable Appliance Load Signatures. In *First IEEE International Conference on Smart Grid Communications (SmartGridComm)* (2010).

[17] KING, C. S. The Economics of Real-Time and Time-of-Use Pricing For Residential Consumers. Tech. rep., American Energy Institute, 2001.

[18] LAUGHMAN, C., LEE, K., COX, R., SHAW, S., LEEB, S., NORFORD, L., AND ARMSTRONG, P. Power signature analysis. *IEEE Power and Energy Magazine 1* (2003).

[19] LEMAY, M., GROSS, G., GUNTER, C. A., AND GARG, S. Unified Architecture for Large-Scale Attested Metering. In *Hawaii International Conference on System Sciences* (2007).

[20] LEMAY, M., HAAS, J. J., AND GUNTER, C. A. Collaborative Recommender Systems for Building Automation. In *Hawaii International Conference on System Sciences* (2009).

[21] LEO, A. The measure of power. *MIT Technology Review* (2001).

[22] LISOVICH, M. A., MULLIGAN, D. K., AND WICKER, S. B. Inferring Personal Information from Demand-Response Systems. *IEEE Security and Privacy 8* (2010).

[23] LITOS STRATEGIC COMMUNICATION. The Smart Grid: An Introduction. http://www.oe.energy.gov/SmartGridIntroduction.htm, 2008.

[24] LIU, Y., NING, P., AND REITER, M. K. False Data Injection Attacks against State Estimation in Electric Power Grids. In *Proceedings of the 16th ACM Conference on Computer and Communications Security* (2009).

[25] MARCEAU, M. L., AND ZMEUREANU, R. Nonintrusive Load Disaggregation Computer Program to Estimate the Energy Consumption of Major End Uses in Residential Buildings. *Energy Conversion and Management 41*, 13 (2000).

[26] MATHWORKS. Simpowersystems 5.3. http://www.mathworks.com/products/simpower/, 2010.

[27] MCDANIEL, P., AND MCLAUGHLIN, S. Security and Privacy Challenges in the Smart Grid. *IEEE Security & Privacy Magazine* (2009).

[28] MERITT, R. Stimulus: DoE Readies $4.3 Billion for Smart Grid. *EE Times* (2009).

[29] METERPEDIA.COM. Meter Manufactuer Data, 2010.

[30] ORANGE, AND ROCKLAND. Time of Use Rate. http://www.oru.com/programsandservices/incentivesandrebates/timeofuse.html, 2010.

[31] PACFIC GAS AND ELECTRIC COMPANY. Electric Schedule E-6, Residential Time-Of-Use Service. http://greenterrafirma.com/time-of-use-electrical-pricing.html, 2010.

[32] PATEL, S. N., ROBERTSON, T., KIENTZ, J. A., REYNOLDS, M. S., AND ABOWD, G. D. At the Flick of a Switch: Detecting and Classifying Unique Electrical Events

on the Residential Power Line. In *Proceedings of Ubicomp* (2007).

[33] PRUDENZI, A. A Neuron Nets Based Procedure for Identifying Domestic Appliances Pattern-of-Use From Energy Recordings at Meter Panel. In *Power Engineering Society Winter Meeting* (2002).

[34] SENSUS. iCon APX C&I Meter. http://na.sensus.com/, 2010.

[35] SULTANEM, F. Using Appliance Signatures for Monitoring Residential Loads at Meter Panel Level. *IEEE Transactions on Power Delivery 6*, 4 (1991).

[36] TANG, H., AND MCMILLIN, B. M. Security Property Violation in CPS through Timing. *International Conference on Distributed Computing Systems Workshops 0* (2008).

[37] THE ENERGY DETECTIVE. The TED 5000 Overview. http://www.theenergydetective.com/, 2010.

[38] TREMBLAY, O., DESSAINT, L. A., AND DEKKICHE, A. A Generic Battery Model for the Dynamic Simulation of Hybrid Electric Vehicles. In *2007 IEEE Vehicle Power and Propulsion Conference* (September 2007), IEEE, pp. 284–289.

[39] US ENERGY INFORMATION ADMINISTRATION. Frequently Asked Questions – Electricity. http://tonto.eia.doe.gov/ask/electricity_faqs.asp#electricity_use_home, 2010.

[40] W. K. LEE AND G. S. K FUNG AND H. Y. LAM AND F. H. Y. CHAN AND MARK LUCENTE. Exploration on Load Signatures. In *International Conference on Electrical Engineering* (2004).

[41] YANG, H.-T., CHANG, H.-H., AND LIN, C.-L. Design a Neural Network for Features Selection in Non-intrusive Monitoring of Industrial Electrical Loads. In *11th International Conference on Computer Supported Cooperative Work in Design* (2007).

APPENDIX

A. FUTURE NILM ALGORITHMS

The analysis discussed in the previous section only considered currently available NILM algorithms. Future approaches will apply more powerful machine learning and data mining techniques. Consider the threat models of as-yet-unknown NILM algorithms that may use features more profitably or exploit knowledge of NILL to expose energy usage. In particular, the NILM algorithms considered thus far have been oblivious to the potential presence of NILL. This raises the question, could a NILM aware of the operations of a NILL algorithm recover more information about the actual demand d from the observed demand u than a basic feature-based NILM? While the answer to this question is almost certainly yes, it is currently unclear how this inference could be done, or how it could be countered.

A.1 Feature Correlation

In the evaluation, we saw that there are features in u that do not overlap with those visible in d, i.e., the non residual features. To a basic steady state NILM, these features reveal little to nothing about the appliance that caused the feature. An adversarial NILM, however, may be able to learn a mapping from some of the features present only in u to those in d. This may be done under three separate circumstances. First, the NILL system may have been installed before the NILM. When this is the case, there is no non-NILL data available for training, forcing the NILM to first cluster features from the NILL load profile. If a correlation is found between the NILL clustering and clusters for known appliance features, a mapping may potentially be found between the two sets.

In the second scenario, NILL is installed some time after NILM, revealing both NILL and non-NILL load profiles over mutually exclusive time span–thus allowing a differential analysis of the pre- and post-NILL data. Similar to the previous case, the NILM must find the clustering of the NILL data that most closely matches that of the non-NILL data. Any assumption about the significance of such a correlation, however, can be further leveraged NILL algorithms to cause false inference by the adversary. In the final scenario, which is both the least likely yet most advantageous for the adversary, there may be temporally overlapping NILL and non-NILL samples. If the non-identical features in these two sample sets are highly correlated, a linear mapping from NILL to non-NILL would give a fair approximation of the mapping between features. Once again, a NILM's reliance on any such mapping could be leveraged by NILL to cause false positive appliance classifications by adding random noise or phantom features.

A.2 Inference from NILL Internal State

It has been previously shown that the high level behavior of cyber-physical systems can be determined based on their low level signaling [36]. Similarly, adversarial NILMs may attempt to infer properties of the NILL system's internal state based on features in the NILL load profile. For example, a sudden spike in feature mass is likely indicative of a low recovery state. A low recovery state in turn reveals the state of the battery, i.e. that the state of charge $c \leq L$ and rate of charge $b(t) > 0$. Once the state is known at a point in time, it is possible to determine the state at any future time by observing transitions in the target load. The question that remains is whether or not an adversarial NILM can infer more about d from knowing the internal system state and u, than from knowing u alone.

To infer anything about d beyond the features already overlapping with u, the NILM must know something about b, because $u - b = d$. But can anything be implied about b from knowing NILL's internal state? The previous example demonstrated that in the low recovery scenario it is known that $b > 0$ and likely close to the battery's maximum safe charge rate. However, as was shown experimentally in Section 4.4, there is already a high RFM during a low recovery state, making the overlap between d and u fairly substantial. Whether the remainder of features in u reveal information about d during a recovery scenario is left to future analysis.

If the NILL is in steady state, then b may be either positive or negative depending completely on $K_{SS} - d$. Thus it seems highly unlikely that a NILM can make inferences based on knowing that the NILL is in steady state. Finally, in a high recovery scenario, K_H is chosen to be slightly below the most recent several d values, allowing the battery to discharge at a low rate. In this case, it is known that $b < 0$, and that $K_H - d$ is fairly small. While this is an indication that d is a light load for the duration of the high recovery state, it reveals only the general size of appliances, but not specific information as to which appliances or whether they are automatic or manually operated.

PaperSpeckle: Microscopic Fingerprinting of Paper

Ashlesh Sharma†
ashlesh@cs.nyu.edu

Lakshminarayanan Subramanian†
lakshmi@cs.nyu.edu

Eric Brewer*
brewer@cs.berkeley.edu

†Courant Institute of Mathematical Sciences
New York University
*Department of Computer Science
University of California, Berkeley

ABSTRACT

Paper forgery is among the leading causes of corruption in many developing regions [2]. In this paper, we introduce PaperSpeckle, a robust system that leverages the natural randomness property present in paper to generate a fingerprint for any piece of paper. Our goal in developing PaperSpeckle is to build a low-cost paper based authentication mechanism for applications in rural regions such as microfinance, healthcare, land ownership records, supply chain services and education which heavily rely on paper based records. Unlike prior paper fingerprinting techniques that have extracted fingerprints based on the fiber structure of paper, PaperSpeckle uses the *texture speckle pattern*, a random bright/dark region formation at the microscopic level when light falls on to the paper, to extract a unique fingerprint to identify paper. In PaperSpeckle, we show how to extract a "repeatable" texture speckle pattern of a microscopic region of a paper using low-cost machinery involving paper, pen and a cheap microscope. Using extensive testing on different types of paper, we show that PaperSpeckle can produce a robust repeatable fingerprint even if paper is damaged due to crumpling, printing or scribbling, soaking in water or aging with time.

Categories and Subject Descriptors

K.6.5 [**Management of Computing and Information Systems**]: Security and Protection
; I.4.7 [**Computing Methodologies**]: Image Processing And Computer Vision–Feature Measurement

General Terms

Algorithms, Design, Experimentation, Security

Keywords

paper fingerprinting, paper speckle

1. INTRODUCTION

Forgery of paper documents has been a major cause of corruption in several countries around the world, especially in developing regions. In these regions, most of the important essential services such as financial systems, healthcare, governance, land records completely rely on paper as the basic medium for storing critical information. In addition, these services use paper as the primary means for establishing identity and verifying the authenticity of information. Hence, any form of mass paper forgery can negatively impact the functioning of essential services and affect large populations. For example, the recent stamp paper scam in India unearthed an underground racket that produced fake stamp papers to forge important land and governance records resulting in a massive loss of over $10 billion dollars to the exchequer [2].

In this paper, we introduce PaperSpeckle, a robust system that leverages the natural randomness property present in paper to generate a fingerprint for any piece of paper.

The basic idea used in PaperSpeckle is the concept of *texture speckles* - when light falls onto an object, the scattered light when projected to a screen produces bright and dark regions formed due to paper's texture and underlying physical non-uniformities. Texture speckles are randomly distributed making them a worthy candidate for generating fingerprints. The concept of *speckles* has been used in the area of laser speckles to profile objects [15]. Typically, extracting good speckle patterns requires expensive equipment. In PaperSpeckle, we show a simple repeatable texture speckle pattern extraction using paper, pen and a low cost microscope. We capture the phenomena of multiple scattering of partially coherent light (natural light) from the complex microscopic structure (surface irregularities and particles) of the paper to obtain the texture speckle pattern and use this information to produce a fingerprint of a specific region of the document.

Based on our experiences working in several rural developing regions, PaperSpeckle also addresses many of the practical constraints that occur in developing regions. PaperSpeckle is low-cost, portable and compact. PaperSpeckle can work with sub-$100 USB microscope connected to a simple mobile device. Paper based documents are very poorly maintained in developing regions and can easily get damaged due to a variety of factors: bad storage environments, damage due to rain, crumpling and aging of paper. Based on extensive stress testing, we show that PaperSpeckle is robust and can withstand severe environmental conditions. To illustrate the magnitude of robustness and damage resistance, PaperSpeckle can match fingerprints even when the conditions are non-ideal: (a) crumpling; (b) soaking the paper in water; (c) generating the fingerprint under different lighting conditions (different microscopes) and (d) aging of paper over time.

The rest of the sections are organized as follows: Section 2 provides a brief description of speckles in general and introduces the concept of paper speckle and how texture speckle patterns can be extracted from a paper. Section 3 presents fingerprint generation algorithm, that is used to compare and distinguish speckle patterns, Section 4 presents our implementation of the PaperSpeckle system on a desktop/laptop setting and also on a cellphone. Section 5 presents a detailed evaluation of PaperSpeckle system and Section 6 discusses the application scenarios. In Section 7, we discuss some of the issues regarding cloning or fabrication of paper and some its limitations and we conclude with a look into the future in Section 8.

1.1 Related Work

There have been a variety of paper fingerprinting solutions [8, 18, 16, 9, 30, 25, 7, 31, 3, 29] that have been proposed to deal with this problem of paper forgery. One canonical solution is to manufacture watermarked paper that uses a special form of paper or ink material that is hard to reproduce [29, 8, 18, 16, 9, 30]. Another approach is to use different types of lithography techniques [10] to embed a unique watermark in paper that would be hard to remove or duplicate. The problem with both these approaches is that they require expensive machinery or access to specialized paper (which can be limited) which can constrain their applicability to specialized applications such as currency notes, checks, official government paper records *etc.* In addition, the paper/inks used in some of these techniques [29, 16, 9] are specially prepared (using physical or chemical means). Another problem with these watermarking techniques is that they embed the same watermark across a bulk collection of documents (eg. currency notes, checks, official paper); hence watermarked documents of the same type are *indistinguishable*. In many common applications (healthcare, finance) which use paper-based records, it is essential to distinguish individual paper documents from each other and prove its authenticity. While standard bar-coding techniques [27] can embed a unique code into each paper, such codes can easily be reproduced and duplicated. PaperSpeckle differs from these standard techniques in that it uses the natural randomness in paper and provides a low-cost distinguishable fingerprint for any piece of paper.

Smith *et. al.* introduced fiber fingerprinting [7, 25] which uses the fiber structure of the paper to provide unique signature of the paper. There have been patents on authenticating paper documents based on their grain or fiber structure [19, 12]. The Print Signatures work by Zhu *et. al.* [31] uses the randomness in character printing by a laser printer to provide a unique signature of that region of paper. They use a microscope to zoom into the minor ink splatters near a character and extract the random pattern associated in the ink splatter. Recently, Clarkson *et. al.* [4] used mid-range scanners to model the 3D fiber structure of a paper and provide unique fingerprints based on it. Cowburn *et. al.* [3, 1] use laser microscopy to look into the complex fiber structure of paper to produce a unique fingerprint of the paper.

Our approach differs from these related works in three significant ways. First, in PaperSpeckle we do not form a 3D representation of the underlying paper structure nor do we use laser microscopy. We capture the phenomena of multiple scattering of partially coherent light (natural light) from the complex microscopic structure (surface irregularities and particles) of the paper region using a microscope to obtain the texture speckle pattern and use this information to produce a unique fingerprint of a region of the document. The physical property that we use to fingerprint the paper is very different from existing solutions. The scale at which the speckle pattern is extracted is at a microscopic level: a pixel in a speckle pattern is about 1-2 microns. To give a sense of the scale, the size of a red blood cell in the human body is about 8 microns.

Second, the technique used in fingerprint generation is different from existing solutions and the fingerprint is much more compact. In addition to this, we also provide a detailed evaluation with respect to adverse environmental conditions and show that our system is robust in real world settings. Not only our system works without any modification to the paper document, it can be used with any specialized ink (such as the Uniball 207 Gel ink) to provide robust security in various scenarios. Texture speckle patterns can be extracted even when specialized ink or paper is used. We do not generate secure sketch of the fingerprint, since in developing regions authentication of a piece of paper is performed in an offline manner with an untrusted device. Also, the adversary might have access to the original document, which makes the secure sketch non-useful.

Third, unlike bulky equipment like scanners and laser surface authentication devices, we use a portable, handheld microscope to obtain the speckle pattern, that can be used in a widespread fashion in developing regions. Our system works both on a desktop/laptop and a cellphone. Cellphone is widely prevalent in the developing regions across the world and since our system also works on a cellphone, it can be readily used in a variety of settings.

Optical marks [17] are used to authenticate paper documents using latent images in different layers of a paper document. In our application, we do not manufacture paper documents, nor do we modify the document in any way. Due to the effect of multiple scattering of light through the structure of the paper, *texture speckle pattern* arises; and the fingerprint generated from this *texture speckle pattern* is used to authenticate that piece of paper.

2. SPECKLES

In this section we provide a brief background on laser speckles and then introduce paper speckles which are based on partially coherent light source (light of finite bandwidth). We discuss its advantages over laser speckles, describe the device setup and finally show how repeatable paper speckle patterns can be extracted using a microscope (with inbuilt LED) and a piece of paper.

2.1 Laser Speckles

When light falls onto an object and the scattered light is projected onto a screen, the screen is speckled with bright and dark regions which represents a speckle pattern [11]. A Speckle pattern is a random intensity pattern produced by the mutual interference of coherent or partially coherent wavefronts that are subject to phase differences or intensity fluctuations. At the screen these rays have a different op-

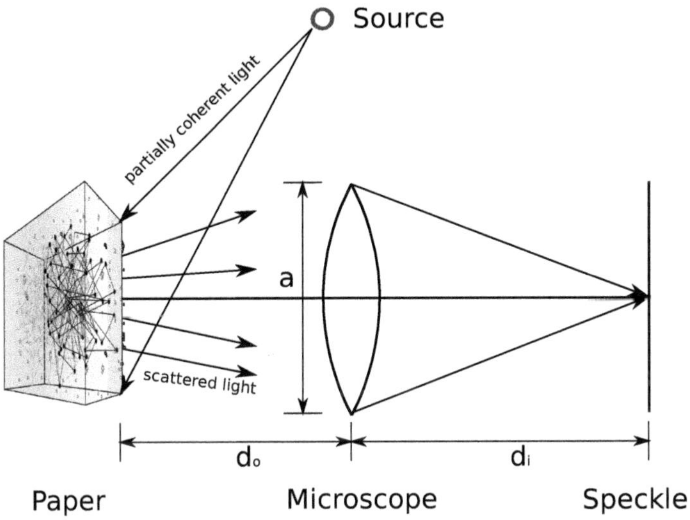

Figure 1: The light source is in the same plane as the observation point. The structure is the three dimensional cross section of the paper and the dark edges are light rays that undergo multiple scattering. The rays exiting the paper have a different optical path length that give rise to bright and dark regions representing a texture speckle pattern

tical path lengths; therefore the rays interfere and result in speckles.

The concept of speckles have been widely used in the field of laser speckles where a random speckle pattern is created when a coherent laser beam is reflected of a rough surface. Laser speckles have been used in research literature to fingerprint a wide range of objects including finger, paper documents, plastic cards, product packages [3]; the randomness in the laser speckle pattern can be used to uniquely identify the object. Using diffuse scattering of a focused laser, the fine structure of different surfaces can be extracted. However, the speckle pattern is very much dependent on the angle of measurement; hence laser speckle extraction requires expensive machinery to align laser as well as carefully extract the object surface pattern.

2.2 Paper Speckles

While laser speckles make a good candidate for extracting speckle patterns from paper, the underlying machinery is very expensive, delicate and fairly impractical in rural, developing country settings. Similarly, the extraction of speckles from partially coherent light source require expensive machinery, delicate experimental setup and careful modification of light source (to achieve either temporal or spatial coherence) [13, 23, 14]. Instead, we show that in practice we do not need to depend on lasers or specific partial coherent light sources and can capture light scattered from microscopic non-uniformities of an object illuminated by any partially coherent light source (such as LED) to identify and fingerprint the object. We call this type of patterns as *texture speckle patterns*. They are essentially, scattered light captured from the complex underlying microscopic structure of an object.

Consider the setup in Figure 1; using a simple microscope (with a 10-200X zoom) with an inbuilt LED source, we can extract a *texture* speckle pattern when we focus the microscope on a specific portion of the paper. Here, the texture

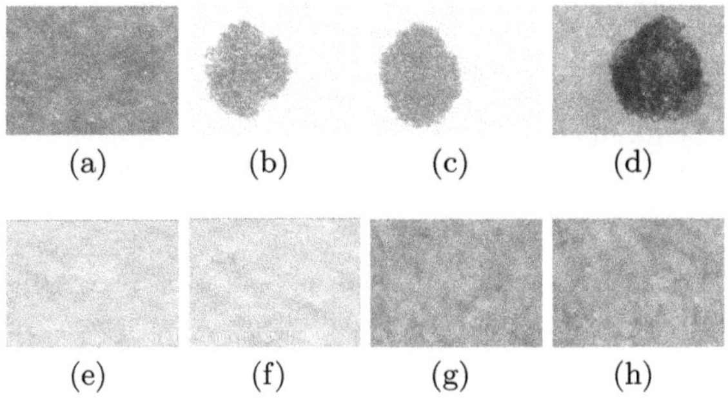

Figure 2: Speckles captured using USB microscope (a) a region of paper at 200X (b)-(d) speckles with ink stain (e)-(h) speckles without ink stain

speckle pattern represents how partially coherent light from the LED gets scattered through the rough surface and the underlying microscopic structures of the region of the paper focused on.

These texture speckle patterns generated from a simple microscope with an inbuilt LED light source makes an excellent choice for a paper fingerprint due to a variety of factors. First, as shown in prior work on laser speckles [3], speckle patterns generated from lasers are tamperproof even if paper is soaked in water, crumpled, affected by aging etc. - the chances that the microscopic structure gets affected are small. As we show in this paper, the fingerprint generated from texture speckle patterns from partially coherent light source is sufficient to achieve the same objectives. Second, generating these texture speckle patterns is cheap (when compared to laser speckles), and is easy to use which make them a great choice for developing regions. Third, extracting just the fiber structure of the paper at a relative macroscopic level with a small zoom might be susceptible to cloning by the adversary. While the field of view of our microscopes are about 0.5mm (or much smaller based on the magnification) in diameter, fiber fingerprinting uses a much larger region of about 2.5 cm x 2.5 cm.

The light from the LED is focused on the paper and the scattered light from the paper is captured by the imaging system, which consists of an optical microscope arrangement. The microscope has two controls, one is the magnification and another is the focus. The images are captured using a fixed magnification of 200x, but the focus is varied to provide a more crisp image, with minimal blur.

The texture speckle pattern is dependent on the properties of the imaging system: the type of incident light source, the distance between the light source and the object, the distance between the lens and the object d_o, the distance between the lens and the image capture plane d_i and the diameter of the lens a; the roughness characteristics and the configuration of microscopic structures in the object. Therefore, in order to obtain repeatable texture speckle patterns generated from partially coherent light, the properties of imaging system (d_i,d_o,a) have to be fixed, across trials. The two types of imaging systems of microscope assemblies that we use (Digital Blue QX5^{TM}and PC Gears AM2011^{TM}), can be configured such that its properties can be fixed across trials.

While we observe a texture speckle pattern, repeatedly extracting the pattern is not straightforward, as it is difficult to point to the exact region on the paper each time to obtain measurements. This is primarily due to the scale at which texture speckle is observed. To address this problem, we use a pen to stain a small region with an arbitrary contour; thereby producing an *arbitrary contour shaded region* which is about 0.5mm in diameter. Figure 2(a)-(d), illustrates different texture speckle pattern pictures extracted using this technique.

Using arbitrary contour shaded regions is important for several reasons. First, having a small shaded region aids in focusing within the same region for repetitive attempts since the goal would be to have the entire region appear within the microscope's field of view. Second, the arbitrary contour helps in orienting the images in a specific direction, as it helps in texture speckle image comparison.

Without the stain, texture speckles can be compared and matched, but the registration process (image registration) has to be standardized. The microscope and the paper need to be arranged in a specific way and this arrangement should provide the same texture speckle pattern from the same region of the paper on repeated measurements. Essentially, the extraction of the texture speckle pattern from the same region of the paper should be *repeatable*. If such a type of system is conceived, then the ink stain need not be used.

In this paper, we have used the ink stain, as we have performed experiments on a large scale to evaluate PaperSpeckle (on over 1500 pieces of paper), and not conformed to any sort of standardization. (In the rest of the paper, when we refer to speckles, we mean texture speckles).

3. FINGERPRINT GENERATION

To generate a fingerprint for a speckle pattern and to satisfy the properties that are required of the fingerprint we employ a technique that is used in texture analysis called Gabor transform and then use Singular Value Decomposition (SVD) to obtain eigenvalues (or singular values) of the Gabor transformed speckle. The details of the algorithm and the rationale are described below. First, we discuss Gabor transform and explain how Gabor bit sequences can be distinguished from each other. Second, we discuss the method of fingerprint generation from Gabor bit sequences.

3.1 Gabor transform

We convert the speckle image into a bit representation by applying Gabor transform to a speckle image. There are three reasons for using Gabor transforms:

1. It is used in laser speckle evaluation [22], iris recognition [6], as it is used to show statistical independence of speckles: empirically show that any two speckles are never the same.
2. Due to the statistical independence property obtained by using Gabor transform, it is a simple method to obtain a compact bit representation of a speckle image and distinguish any two bit patterns using the Hamming distance.
3. Gabor transform applied to speckles is robust to global changes in illumination and minor modifications of the speckle image [20].

Using the above technique, pairs of speckle patterns can be compared to find similarity (or dissimilarity). To compare two speckle patterns, we first convert each speckle image into bits using 2D Gabor transforms. Next, we compare the two speckle bits using the Fractional Hamming distance (FHD) metric to check if the speckles are similar or dissimilar. Comparing speckles using FHD shows the statistical independence property of Gabor transformed bit patterns.

i) Gabor transforms: We apply Gabor transforms [5] to speckle images and extract bits using the imaginary part of the complex phase of the Gabor wavelets,

$$g(x_0, y_0, f, \theta) = e^{-[\pi(a^2(x-x_0)^2+b^2(y-y_0)^2)]}e^{[i2\pi f(xcos\theta+ysin\theta)]}$$

The first term is a 2D Gaussian function located at (x_0, y_0) where a is width along the x-axis and b along the y-axis. The second term is a complex 2D sinusoid of frequency f and an orientation defined by θ. These parameters can be varied and Gabor transforms (or filters) can be applied to any location, scale or orientation of an image. The procedure to extract bits from the Gabor transforms can be stated as follows:

1. Compute the imaginary part of the complex phase of the Gabor transform for one orientation and one level.
2. Use the complex phase and apply zero as threshold to extract a binary sequence or a binary image.
3. Repeat this procedure for various orientations (θ) and levels (f).

The importance of using only the complex phase of the Gabor wavelet to extract bits is that, we eliminate any illumination effects, contrast or poor focus, present in the speckle image. Due to this, the extraction of speckle images need not be too precise. Also, mask bits are computed to remove the extraneous effects surrounding the speckle image. Mask bits are computed by thresholding the pixel values to 1 beyond the boundary of the speckle and 0 inside the speckle. If the speckle covers the entire image, then mask bits are not needed. Since, the region where the speckle pattern is extracted is known (marker, ink stain etc), any region outside of that is unnecessary. This unnecessary region is considered as the mask bits. These mask bits help in applying Gabor transforms to only the region within the image where speckles are present.

ii) Fractional Hamming Distance (FHD): Let A and B be the sequence of bits extracted from after applying Gabor transforms to two speckle images; $maskA$ and $maskB$ be the two mask bits of the respective speckle images. The similarity between two sequence of bits A and B can be computed using the Fractional Hamming Distance:

$$FHD = \frac{||(A \otimes B) \cap maskA \cap maskB||}{||maskA \cap maskB||}$$

$A \otimes B$ gives the difference between bits and the $\cap$ with mask bits prevents any extraneous (unnecessary) bits to be considered in computing FHD ($||\ ||$ is the norm of the vector). The FHD provides a ratio, that defines whether the sequence of bits are either similar or dissimilar. Ideally a FHD of 0 would represent equal bits and therefore, a perfect match of the speckles images and a FHD of 0.5 would represent dissimilar bits (and therefore different speckle images), where the likelihood of 0 or 1 occurring in a bit sequence is equally probable.

Figure 3 shows the Gabor kernel convolved with a speckle image under various orientations (6 orientations, $\theta = 0, 60^o$, 120°, 180°, 240°, 300°) and levels (5 levels, where f is the scaling factor between successive levels) and the complex phase is thresholded to zero to extract the bit sequence. Level 4 and level 5 provide the required FHD, to statisti-

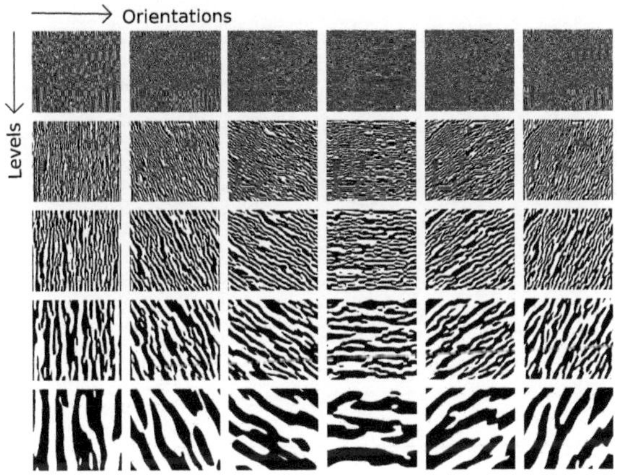

Figure 3: Gabor transform applied to a speckle image for various orientations and levels.

	Level 1	Level 2	Level 3	Level 4	Level 5
Instance 1	0.4898	0.4773	0.4636	0.3298	0.1654
Instance 2	0.4936	0.4798	0.3628	0.2146	0.1094
Instance 3	0.4507	0.4633	0.2863	0.1588	0.0662
Instance 4	0.4814	0.4897	0.4787	0.4245	0.2355

Table 1: Fractional Hamming Distance of a speckle with its own different instances across various levels. Each instance is a new measurement of the same speckle pattern.

cally distinguish two speckles. Table 1, shows the variation of FHD for various levels, for same speckle pattern extracted at different periods of time. (We have chosen orientation 5, which corresponds to $\theta = 240^0$ at each level, since the FHD values are similar for different orientations at a level). The FHD values at level 4 and level 5 are close to 0, which shows that these are the same speckle patterns. Table 2, shows the variation of FHD, when a candidate speckle is compared with different speckle patterns. The FHD values at level 4 and level 5 are close to 0.5, which show that these are different speckle patterns. We have found relatively similar FHD values (as described in Tables 1, 2) when trying to distinguish speckles in all of our experiments. In this paper, for statistical evaluation, we have chosen level 5 and orientation 5 as the Gabor bit sequence to compare speckle patterns using FHD. We have found similar statistical results for Gabor bit sequences extracted from different orientations of level 4 and level 5.

Figure 4 shows the FHD values of comparing 60,000 pairs of "different" Gabor bit sequences with mean 0.4875 and standard deviation 0.00577. When we say "different", we mean Gabor bit sequences in each pair correspond to speckle images taken from different regions of either the same paper or different paper. The least FHD value is 0.47. Each

	Level 1	Level 2	Level 3	Level 4	Level 5
Speckle 1	0.4789	0.4737	0.4625	0.4591	0.4573
Speckle 2	0.4844	0.4803	0.4686	0.4410	0.4649
Speckle 3	0.4941	0.4662	0.4520	0.4706	0.4691
Speckle 4	0.4888	0.4876	0.4690	0.4608	0.4657

Table 2: Fractional Hamming Distance of candidate speckle with different speckles across various levels.

speckle image is of size 512 $\times$ 384 pixels. The Gabor transform of each speckle image provides a Gabor bit sequence of 196608 bits. Figure 5 shows the FHD values of comparing 200 pairs of "same" Gabor bit sequences with mean 0.1675 and standard deviation 0.0594. Here, "same" means Gabor bit sequences in each pair correspond to speckle images taken from the same region of the paper. The maximum FHD value is 0.28.

The two distributions are well separated and as seen from the figures any FHD value between 0.28 and 0.47 would distinguish two speckles and provide no false positive/negatives. How well are the two distributions separated? It would take the modification of at least 39321 bits for the two distributions to intersect each other, which around 20% of the total number of bits in the Gabor sequence. For the mean (peak) of two distributions to meet, around 32% (62914 bits) of the total number of bits in the Gabor sequence has to be modified.

We process 200 speckle images from four different kinds of paper and we examine each pixel value (intensity) of these speckle images. The mean of each pixel (across 200 speckle images) is computed and the mean value is plotted. The entropy of the Gabor bit sequence is maximized if each pixel value is 0.5 (the probability of each pixel being either 0 or 1). Figure 6 shows the probability of a bit being set in a Gabor bit sequence of a paper speckle is almost 0.5, which suggests that the entropy of Gabor bit sequence is high.

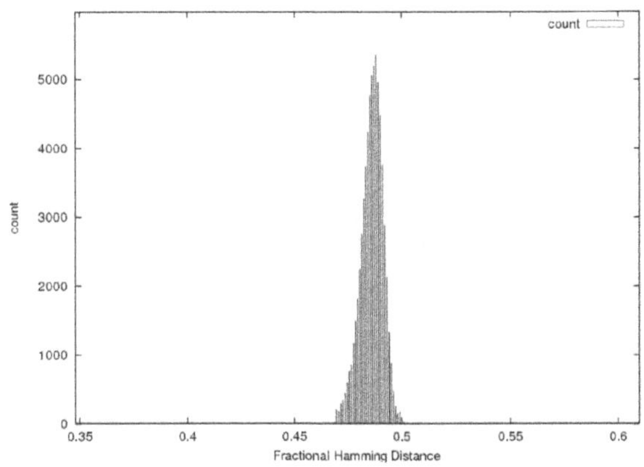

Figure 4: Fractional Hamming Distance of 60,000 pairs of different speckle image bits with mean = 0.48705 and standard deviation = 0.00577.

3.2 Fingerprint

Once we have the Gabor bit sequence for a speckle image, we convert the bit sequence into a binary matrix S_G such that its dimensions match the dimensions of the speckle image. Let S_G be the Gabor binary matrix. We apply SVD to S_G to obtain singular values, which we use as the fingerprint of the region of paper.

In SVD, we decompose S_G as, $S_G = U \Sigma V^T$ where orthogonal matrices U and V contain left and right singular vectors of S_G, respectively, and the diagonal of Σ contains the singular values of S_G. The singular values of any arbitrary matrix are uniquely determined [26]. These singular values are the square root of eigenvalues of $S_G S_G^T$.

Gabor binary matrix S_G is a binary (0,1) matrix and $S_G S_G^T$ is a real valued symmetric matrix. Therefore, the

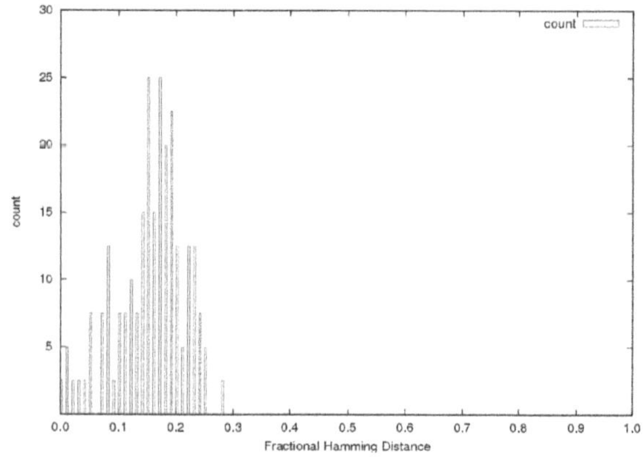

Figure 5: Fractional Hamming Distance of 200 "like" speckle bits with mean = 0.16751 and standard deviation = 0.05948.

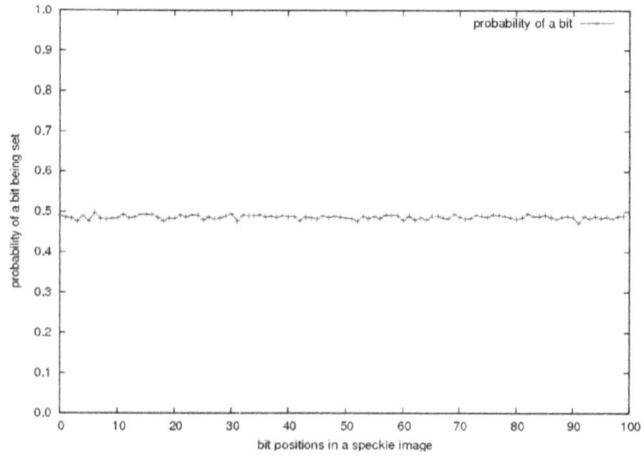

Figure 6: The probability of a bit being set in a Gabor bit sequence of the paper speckle image.

eigenvalues of $S_G S_G^T$ are real and well conditioned. Perturbations in $S_G S_G^T$ lead to perturbations of the same size in its eigenvalues (The proof is due to Stewart [26] and Papadimitriou *et. al.* [21] and states that if some large k singular values are sufficiently away from rest of the singular values, then the subspace spanned by the singular vectors are preserved if a small perturbation is added to S_G.)

Let $S1_G$ and $S2_G$ be Gabor bit sequences of the same region (where $S1_G$ is the Gabor bit sequence of the speckle image extracted in the first trial and $S2_G$ is the Gabor bit sequence of the same region extracted in the next trial) and $S3_G$ be a Gabor bit sequence of a different region. When we compare $S1_G$ and $S2_G$, we know that the Fractional Hamming Distance (FHD) between these are small (less than 4% of the total number of bits) as evidenced from the analysis of the FHDs Gabor bit sequences of "same" speckles. Hence, the difference in singular values of $S1_G$ and $S2_G$ would be a small number, indicating that $S1_G$ and $S2_G$ are the same speckle pattern. When we compare $S1_G$ and $S3_G$ (or $S2_G$ and $S3_G$), their FHDs would differ by a large amount (more than 20%) as evidenced from the analysis of FHDs of Gabor bit sequences of "different" speckles. Hence, the difference in singular values of $S1_G$ and $S3_G$ would be large, indicating that these are not the same speckles.

Next, we discuss the variation of singular values of S_G as the number of bits are varied.

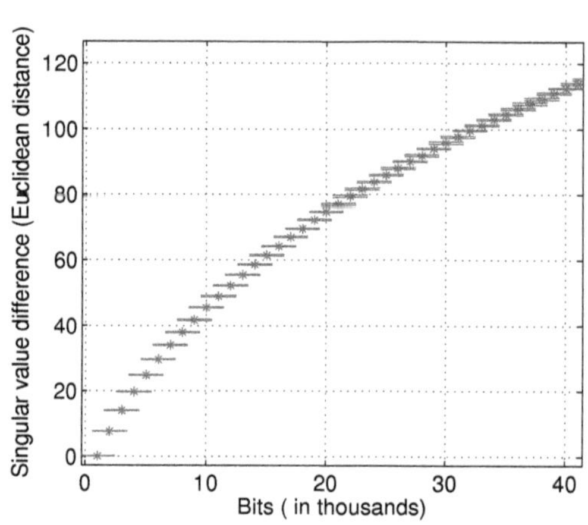

Figure 7: Singular value difference as the Gabor binary matrix is perturbed.

3.2.1 Singular value perturbation

We empirically examine the singular values of a Gabor binary matrix S_G as it is varied or perturbed. We consider one Gabor binary matrix S_G of size 512×384, and perturb the matrix randomly by modifying $10i$ bits in each step i of the experiment. In each step i, we perturb (flip) $10 \times i$ bits, where i is varied from 1000 to 196000. We conduct 20 trials in each step, compute mean and standard deviation and plot the results with error bars. Figure 7 shows the difference in the Euclidean distance between singular values of S_G and the singular values of the perturbed S_G, as the number of bits are modified. There is almost a linear increase in the difference of singular values as the perturbation of S_G increases. If the perturbation is small then the singular value difference is small, and if the perturbation is large, then the singular value difference is large. The difference in singular values of "same" Gabor bit sequences tend to be small as the change in bits is small (2000 bits). While the difference in singular values of "different" Gabor bit sequences tend to be large as the change in bits is large (20000 bits). Based on these results, we can distinguish fingerprints of "same" and "different" speckles and we show the detailed results in Section 5. Another important property that needs to be fulfilled is that the fingerprint has to be compact. To achieve this property, we analyze the scree plots of the singular values of large number of Gabor binary matrices. (Scree plot helps to analyze the relative importance of the singular values and a sharp drop in the plot signals that subsequent singular values can be ignored.) Figure 8, shows the singular values of one representative Gabor binary matrix, and it is clear from the scree plot that the "energy" or magnitude of singular values is clustered in the first few singular values. We choose the 64 and 128 largest singular values as the fingerprints of the speckle pattern. These 64 and 128 singular values hold 88% and 96% of the magnitude of the entire set of singular values respectively. The size of the fingerprint would be 768 digits if we use 128 singular values (using 6 digits of each singular value).

The evaluation of fingerprints across various types of paper are provided in Section 5.

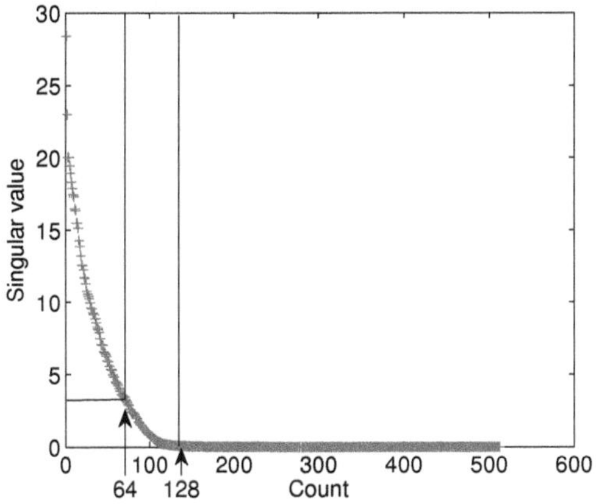

Figure 8: Scree plot of singular values. The first 64 and 128 singular values, which are inside the rectangles, contain 88% and 96% of the magnitude of the set of singular values respectively.

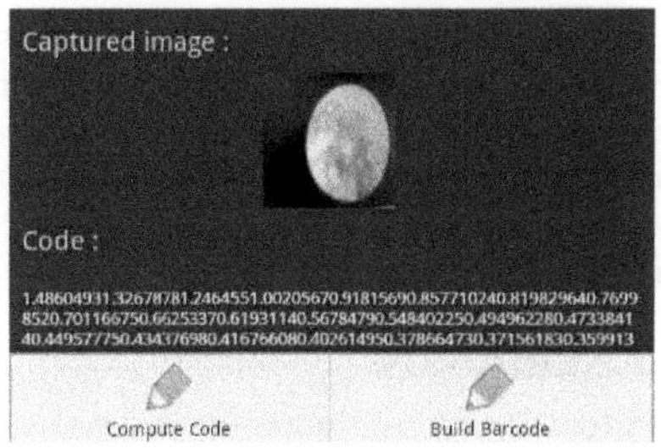

(a)

(b)

Figure 9: (a) A speckle image taken on the cellphone and the fingerprint of the speckle image; menu options: i) Compute Code, or ii) Build Barcode. (b) QR code of the fingerprint which is shown on the right side.

4. IMPLEMENTATION

We have implemented PaperSpeckle on two kinds of setup. One is a desktop/laptop attached with a USB microscope and another is a Google Nexus One mobile phone with a microscope attached to its camera.

In the laptop version we have tested the system with two types of microscopes: Digital Blue QX5 ™and PC Gears AM2011 ™. The detailed evaluation of speckles based on this system are presented in Section 5.

For the mobile phone version, we developed our application on the Android 2.1 platform on the Nexus One. We use standard image capture routines to capture the speckle patterns from the mobile device camera. The mobile phone camera is attached with a consumer grade microscope (Carson MM-200) that has a variable magnification from 10x to 100x, to extract speckles. (We fixed our resolution to 100x). These portable microscopes are low cost devices typically ranging from anywhere between $10 to $50. The fingerprint generation algorithm consists of two mathematically heavy operations: (a) computing Gabor transforms; (b) computing SVD of a large matrix. We implemented a lot of specific optimizations to reduce the compute time of these operations on the Android platform. Specifically, Android is relatively slow for floating point operations in comparison to integer operations; many of the previous Android phone hardware (1.5,1.6 phones) did not even support a hardware floating point unit. We implemented a lightweight floating point library using integer based calculations. While our initial unoptimized version took over 180 seconds of processing time to compute a fingerprint per image, our optimizations reduced the compute time to less than 5 seconds per image. In addition, our code can be easily ported to any Java enabled phone with an inbuilt camera. To support applications in emerging regions, making the system work on low-end mobile devices is essential.

Figure 9a shows the speckle pattern with a menu to generate the fingerprint (menu option: Compute Code) and the corresponding barcode (menu option: Build Barcode). Figure 9b shows the QR code with the corresponding fingerprint. This QR code can be scanned using any standard barcode scanner application on any cellphone to reveal the fingerprint. This fingerprint is compared for a match with the candidate speckle fingerprint that is computed after reading the speckle pattern. Our implementation can be used for: (a) generating fingerprints (2D barcodes) of new speckle images; (b) comparing a fingerprint of a new speckle pattern with a database fingerprints of speckle patterns; (c) reading a new speckle pattern and a barcode separately and comparing the fingerprint of the speckle pattern and the barcode to see if they both match.

The mobile phone is attached with a microscope with a different magnification (100x) and field of view than the microscope attached to the laptop. So, the fingerprints generated by this setup would be different than the laptop setup. The microscopes used with the laptop can be varied to extract speckles at 100x magnification, and we use a reduced field of view that is equal in dimensions to the field of view of the mobile microscope, to obtain the same fingerprint as the mobile version.

5. EVALUATION

We evaluate the fingerprints across different types of paper in both ideal and non-ideal conditions.

We considered four completely different categories of paper in our analysis: (a) Letter size print paper; (b) thin notebook style paper (ruled notebooks); (c) Thick print poster-style paper; (d) brown-colored binding/package paper. Also, we tested our results on three different microscopes; two by Digital Blue™and one by Dino-Lite™AM2011. The reason for considering different microscopes is to ensure better validity of our results across different microscopes. In this section, we provide important evaluations that stress test the fingerprint under varied conditions. Due to space limitations, we have only presented the results for the fingerprints that represent the 64 singular values. The results for fingerprints that represent 128 singular values are similar to the fingerprints that represent 64 singular values. The evaluations shown here are done on the laptop version of the system (with 200x magnification). We have also evaluated mobile phone version on the four different types of paper (which are stated above) and have found that the results are similar to the laptop version.

5.1 Ideal conditions

In ideal conditions, where the paper was not tampered, we extracted 300 speckles from each type of paper, totalling up to 1200 different speckles. To analyze the variation in fingerprints of speckles of different paper (or region), we made $\binom{300}{2} = 44850$ comparisons. To analyze the variation in fingerprints of "same" speckles , we made 300 pairs of comparisons of each type of speckle. The results are presented in Figures 10a, 10c, 10e. In each figure, the distribution to the left represents the difference in the Euclidean distance of fingerprints of "same" speckles. "Same" speckle means pairs of speckles are compared, where each pair represents two speckle patterns that is extracted from the same region of the paper (multiple measurement of the same speckle pattern). In each figure, the distribution to the left represents the difference in the Euclidean distance of fingerprints of "different" speckles. "Different" speckle means pairwise comparison of speckle patterns extracted from regions of different papers. The two distributions are well separated and any value that is in between the two distributions (greater than the maximum of the left distribution and lesser than the minimum of the right distribution) can be used as a threshold to provide no false positives in identifying or matching two fingerprints. The mean for "same" fingerprints across various types of paper is around 1.5 and the mean for "different" fingerprints across various types of paper is around 85. Based on our analysis in Section 3.2, we know that if the difference (of Euclidean distance of singular values) between a Gabor binary matrix and a randomly perturbed Gabor binary matrix is around 1.5, then the number of bits they disagree is less than 1000. If the difference is above 85, then the number of bits that they disagree is more than 20000. By applying the same analysis to this context, we could say that for the mean of two distributions to meet at least 19000 bits of a Gabor binary matrix have to be modified. Similarly, for a single false positive to occur, at least 9200 bits of a Gabor binary matrix have to be modified.

5.2 Non-ideal conditions

To simulate non-ideal conditions, we tampered the paper in four ways: crumpling, printing or scribbling, soaking in water and aging.

5.2.1 *Crumpling*

We extracted speckles from 50 pieces of paper and then crumpled each paper thoroughly. Since, the scale at which we operate is around 1 micron, most of the region of interest was not tampered. On an average, 5% of each of the speckle images were modified. This statistic was found out by extracting the 50 speckles again from the same regions and comparing it with the original 50 speckles. Figure 10b, shows the result of comparing "same" speckle on the left and "different" speckle on the right. As we can observe, the two distributions are well separated and the fingerprints can be distinguished with no false positives. For a single false positive to occur, at least 12000 bits of a Gabor binary matrix need to be modified. This shows that PaperSpeckle is able to distinguish fingerprints even when the paper is crumpled.

5.2.2 *Printing*

Once a speckle is extracted from a region, if the entire region is scribbled or printed, the speckle from the same region would be different when speckle is extracted in the next trial. Ink on the surface of the paper scatters the light in unexpected ways and changes the original speckle pattern. (On the other hand speckle pattern can be extracted after the text is printed or written). In spite of this limitation, our approach sustains printing or scribbling up to 6% to the speckle region. We extracted speckles from 50 papers and then printed or scribbled near the region of extraction. On an average, 6% of each of the speckles were modified. Figure 10d, shows the results of comparing "same" fingerprints (on the left) and "different" fingerprints (on the right). The two distributions are well separated and the fingerprints can be distinguished with no false positives. For a single false positive to occur, the at least 7000 bits of a Gabor binary matrix need to be modified. This shows the even if there is printing or scribbling on the paper, PaperSpeckle is able to distinguish fingerprints.

5.2.3 *Soaking in water*

We extracted 25 speckles from different pieces of paper and submerged the pieces of paper under water for a few minutes. To make sure we extract speckle from the same region, we used UniBall 207 Gel pen to pigment the papers and mark the region (special ink from the Uniball pen doesn't fade when a paper is soaked in water). After pigmenting the papers, it was submerged in water for a few minutes. Figure 10f, shows the results of comparing "same" fingerprints (on the left) and "different" fingerprints (on the right). The two distributions are well separated and the fingerprints can be distinguished with no false positives. For a single false positive to occur, at least 5000 bits of a Gabor binary matrix need to be modified. This shows that PaperSpeckle is robust and is able to withstand extreme conditions such as water soaking.

5.2.4 *Aging*

We extracted 50 speckles from different pieces of paper and stored it for around two years in a storage closet. Then, we extracted the speckles from the same set of papers, generated the fingerprints and compared them. The mean and standard deviation for "same" fingerprints is 1.52 and 1.61. The mean and standard deviation for "different" fingerprints is 87.56 and 12.98. For a single false positive to occur, at least 10000 bits of a Gabor binary matrix need to be modified. This shows that PaperSpeckle works on aged paper without any false positives.

6. APPLICATIONS

PaperSpeckle can be used in a variety of ways where verifying the authenticity of a paper document is of utmost importance.

The main benefit of fingerprints corresponding to a speckle pattern is that the fingerprint can be printed on the same piece of paper containing the paper speckle. Any piece of paper can be made *self-verifiable* by extracting the speckle pattern from a small region on the paper and imprinting the fingerprint of the speckle pattern of the region in the

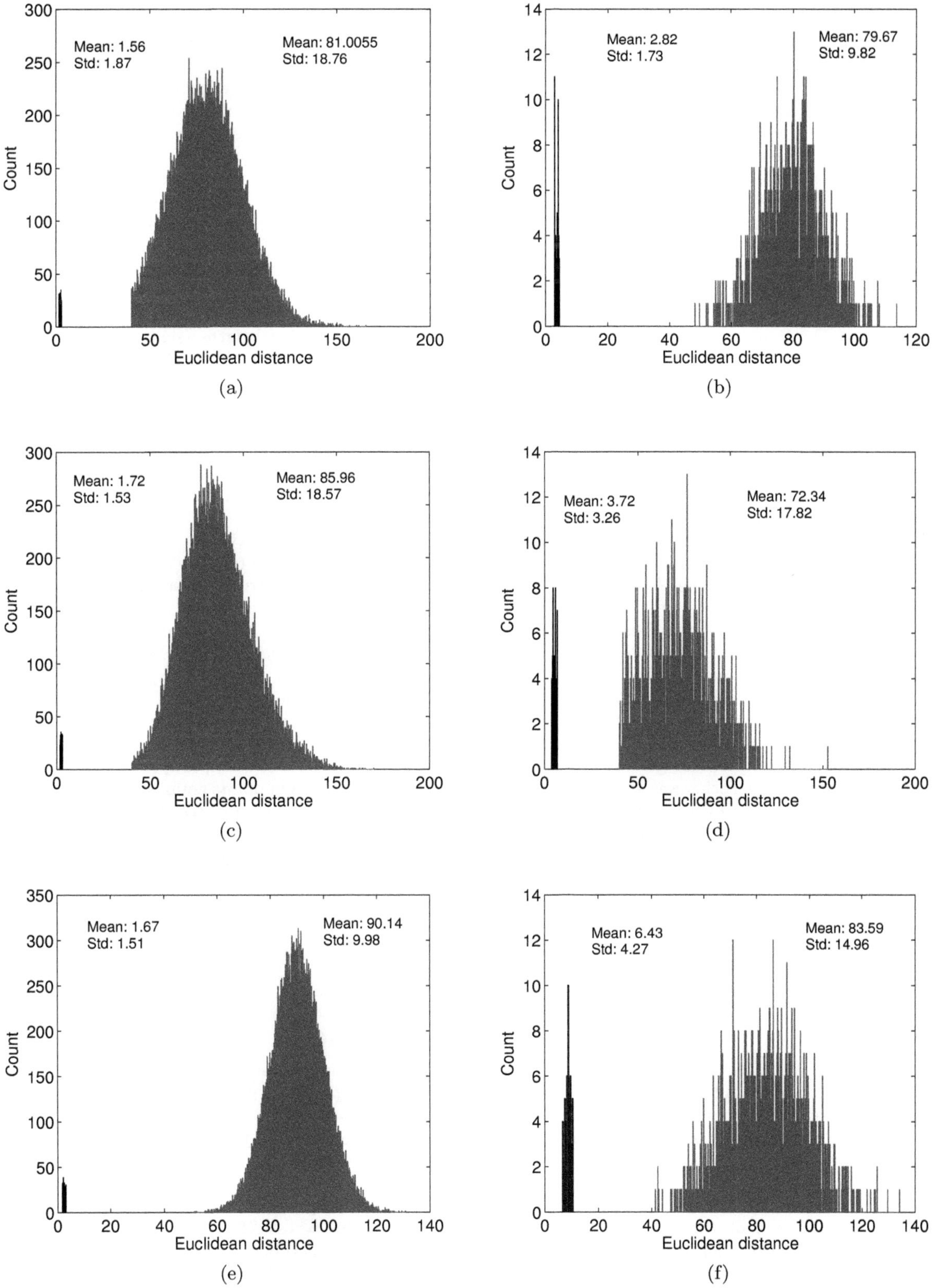

Figure 10: Histogram of pairwise Euclidean distances between fingerprints. (a) Letter size print paper; (c) thin notebook style paper (ruled notebooks); (e) Thick print poster-style paper; (b) Crumpling. (d) Printing and scribbling. (f) Soaking in water.

same paper. This self-verifiable paper can be used for offline verification of paper documents.

Paper check, receipt or voucher is issued by a trusted authority such as a Bank or Government Authority. The first step of the offline authentication mechanism is the paper check generation. The issuing authority is associated with a cryptographic key pair $K = (P, Q)$, where P is the public-key and Q is the corresponding private-key. While Q is only known to the trusted authority creating the official paper documents, P is known to any entity who wishes to authenticate the paper document in an offline manner. Given any piece of paper, the issuing authority can convert the paper into an authentic offline verifiable paper document using the following paper check generation steps. i) Make the paper self-verifiable by reading a region of the paper, extracting the speckle mark M and imprinting the corresponding fingerprint $D(M)$ computed using any computing device with an attached microscope. ii) The Bank signs $D(M)$ using its private key Q. We denote this as $S_Q(D)$ and the bank prints $S_Q(D)$ on the paper check. In practice, $S_Q(D)$ can be represented as a compact 2D barcode. iii) The paper check contains three artifacts: speckle pattern M, fingerprint $D(M)$, signed number $S_Q(D)$. In practice, this can be extended to authenticate any additional information T embedded such as serial number (for currency notes, checks), transaction details or personal information. To achieve this, we can simply replace $S_Q(D)$ with $S_Q(D, T)$. To authenticate this paper in an offline manner, a mobile device (cellphone) equipped with a microscope, extracts the speckle image M from the region, generates the fingerprint $D(M)'$ of the speckle M and checks if generated fingerprint $D(M)'$ matches $D(M)$ printed on the paper. (If $D(M)$ is represented as a 2-D barcode, then $D(M)$ is read using inbuilt camera in the mobile device coupled with a standard barcode library). If the fingerprints do not match, the paper is a counterfeit. Else, if the fingerprints match, then it is guaranteed that the paper is genuine. Once the paper is determined to be genuine, the next step is to verify whether the fingerprint was signed by the trusted authority (bank). $S_Q(D)$ which is represented as a 2D barcode is read using the barcode scanner in the mobile device. Using the authentic public-key P stored in the mobile device, it is checked if $S_Q(D)$ is a valid signature of $D(M)$.

In a similar fashion, PaperSpeckle can be used to authenticate currency notes, lottery tickets, land records, degree certificates, receipts in microfinance and in other areas where the possession of paper is used as a primary record of ownership.

7. DISCUSSION

In this section, we briefly discuss the robustness of PaperSpeckle in the face of photocopying or fabrication of paper.

Photocopying paper: Photocopying paper will clearly not preserve the speckle pattern in the original paper since the microscopic region of the copied paper is inherently very different. In addition, the speckle region in a paper is in the micrometer range. The field of view of a microscope with 200x magnification is 2mm and each pixel in the image is around 1-2 microns. Even the shape of the contour at a microscopic level may be very different in the photocopied paper. This was observed by Zhu *et. al.* [31] where they state that due to the halftoning effects of the photocopying process, the shape of the contour would differ from the original one. To test this hypothesis, we photocopied 100 speckles and compared their fingerprints. The results we obtained were similar to the results we obtained for "different" fingerprints in Section 5.

Fabrication of paper speckle: Pappu [24] discusses some of the current 3D fabrication techniques. Fabricating paper using photolithography techniques is an expensive process usually in the order of hundreds of millions of dollars [24]. Also, these processes manufacture large number of identical structures and they are not economically suited for producing just one cloned copy of a single microscopic paper structure.

Optical scattering based systems are hard to copy/clone for two reasons [28]. i) The light diffusion obscures the location of the scatterers (scatterers or scattering elements, are particles that scatter light in an object). The state-of-the-art techniques can probe strong diffusive materials only up to a depth of 10 scattering lengths (scattering of light between particles). ii) Even if we know the position of the all scatterers, the precise positioning of large number of scattering elements is very expensive.

Even the forward problem is hard. Given the details of all the scattering elements, computing or simulating the speckle pattern is computationally expensive where the complexity increases exponentially with the number of scattering events [28].

Destroying a speckle pattern: The simplest manner to destroy a speckle pattern is to scratch the speckled region with a sharp object that destroys the surface characteristics of the region of interest. Alternatively, the speckled region can be excessively scribbled upon (using a pen or pencil) thereby changing the boundary specification of a speckled region or one can tear the piece of paper at exactly the speckled spot. Any of these techniques have to be precise since the speckled region is typically very small in diameter (0.5 mm). To enhance the robustness of PaperSpeckle in the face of inadvertent incidents, a simple approach is to speckle a piece of paper at multiple points coupled with their corresponding self-verifiable compact codes of each of the speckle regions. A determined adversary who wishes to destroy a speckled piece of paper has to destroy each of the speckle points in the piece of paper which would essentially render the paper useless.

8. CONCLUSIONS

In this paper, we have presented PaperSpeckle, a low-cost, robust, portable paper fingerprinting system that can identify and authenticate paper. The key contributions of the paper can be summarized as follows. We show how to extract repeatable texture speckle patterns from a region of paper and present an algorithm to generate fingerprint from a region of paper. We provide detailed evaluation of our fingerprinting algorithm across different types of paper and also show how our system is robust against tampering by evaluating texture speckles in adverse environmental conditions. We implement the fingerprinting mechanism on a cellphone and discuss how our system can be used in an offline manner, which has a high potential in mitigating forgery and enhancing physical security of paper in developing regions.

Acknowledgements

We thank Varun Tamminedi, Alpesh Shah and Brinsley D. Cunha for their involvement in the early part of the project (NYU class project report: "Speckles: Low-cost Paper Watermarking").

9. REFERENCES

[1] Ingenia technology ltd. http://www.ingeniatechnology.com/.

[2] Telgi Scam. http://www.financialexpress.com/news/telgi-scam/83736/.

[3] J. D. R. Buchanan, R. P. Cowburn, A.-V. Jausovec, D. Petit, P. Seem, G. Xiong, D. Atkinson, K. Fenton, D. A. Allwood, and M. T. Bryan. Forgery: 'Fingerprinting' documents and packaging. *Nature*, 436:475, July 2005.

[4] William Clarkson, Tim Weyrich, Adam Finkelstein, Nadia Heninger, Alex Halderman, and Ed Felten. Fingerprinting blank paper using commodity scanners. In *IEEE Security and Privacy*, 2009.

[5] J.G. Daugman. Complete discrete 2-d gabor transforms by neural networks for image analysis and compression. *IEEE Transactions on Acoustics, Speech, and Signal Processing*, 36(7):1169–1179, Jul 1988.

[6] John Daugman. The importance of being random: statistical principles of iris recognition. *Pattern Recognition*, 36(2):279–291, February 2003.

[7] N. Salzman E. Metois, P. Yarin and J. R. Smith. Fiberfingerprint identification. In *Third Workshop on Automatic Identification*, 2002.

[8] Borowski Jr. et. al. Surface treated security paper and method and device for producing surface treated security paper, US Patent Number 5,193,854, 1993.

[9] E. B. Greene et al. Coatings and ink designs for negotiable instruments, us patent number 6,155,604, 2000.

[10] Kailath T et al. Multivariable control, simulation, optimization and signal processing for the microlithographic process, 1997.

[11] K. L. van der Molen F. van Beijnum, E.G. van Putten and A. P. Mosk. Recognition of paper samples by correlation of their speckle patterns. *Arxiv.org preprint physics/0610089*, 2006.

[12] Lin Feng. US Patent Application Number: 20100067691, Document certification and authentication system, 2010.

[13] H. Fujii and T. Asakura. A contrast variation of image speckle intensity under illumination of partially coherent light. *Optics Communications*, 12(1):32 – 38, 1974.

[14] Nicholas George and Atul Jain. Speckle reduction using multiple tones of illumination. *Appl. Opt.*, 12(6):1202–1212, Jun 1973.

[15] J. W. Goodman. Some fundamental properties of speckle. *Journal of the Optical Society of America (1917-1983)*, 66:1145–1150, 1976.

[16] E. B. Greene. Negotiable instrument, us patent number 4,634,148, 1987.

[17] Sheng Huang and Jian Kang Wu. Optical Watermark (WO/2002/023481), 2002.

[18] Kimura and Yoshihiro. Woven security label, us patent number 6,068,895, 2000.

[19] Roger D Melen. US Patent Number: 5325167, Record document authentication by microscopic grain structure and method, 1994.

[20] Margarita Osadchy, David W. Jacobs, and Michael Lindenbaum. Surface dependent representations for illumination insensitive image comparison. *IEEE Trans. Pattern Anal. Mach. Intell.*, 29:98–111, January 2007.

[21] Christos H. Papadimitriou, Hisao Tamaki, Prabhakar Raghavan, and Santosh Vempala. Latent semantic indexing: a probabilistic analysis. In *PODS '98: Proceedings of the seventeenth ACM SIGACT-SIGMOD-SIGART symposium on Principles of database systems*, pages 159–168, New York, NY, USA, 1998. ACM.

[22] R. Pappu, B. Recht, J. Taylor, and N. Gershenfeld. Physical One-Way Functions. *Science*, 297:2026–2030, September 2002.

[23] G. Parry. Speckle patterns in partially coherent light. In *Laser Speckle and Related Phenomena*, volume 9 of *Topics in Applied Physics*, pages 77–121. Springer Berlin / Heidelberg, 1975. 10.1007/BFb0111437.

[24] Pappu Srinivasa Ravikanth. *Physical one-way functions*. PhD thesis, 2001. Chair-Stephen A. Benton, Massachusetts Institute of Technology.

[25] Joshua R. Smith and Andrew V. Sutherland. Microstructure based indicia. In *Proceedings of the Second Workshop on Automatic Identification Advanced Technologies*, pages 79–83, New York, NY, USA, 1999. ACM.

[26] G. W. Stewart. *Matrix Algorithms: Volume 2 Eigensystems*. SIAM, 2001.

[27] J. Swartz T. Pavlidis and Y. P. Wang. Fundamentals of bar code information theory. *Computer*, 23(4):74âĂŞ85, 1990.

[28] P. Tuyls, B. Skoric, T. Akkermans, W. Ophey, and S. Stallinga. Security analysis of physical uncloneable functions, 2004.

[29] R. L. van Renesse. *Optical Document Security, Second Edition*. Artech House, Inc, Norwood, MA, 1998.

[30] Daniel; Zeira, Eitan; Ellett. Verification methods employing thermally–imageable substrates, us patent number 6107244, August 2000.

[31] Baoshi Zhu, Jiankang Wu, and Mohan S. Kankanhalli. Print signatures for document authentication. In *ACM CCS '03*, pages 145–154, New York, NY, USA, 2003.

On the Vulnerability of FPGA Bitstream Encryption against Power Analysis Attacks

Extracting Keys from Xilinx Virtex-II FPGAs

Amir Moradi
Horst Görtz Institute
for IT-Security
Ruhr University Bochum
Germany
amir.moradi@rub.de

Alessandro Barenghi
Dipartimento di
Elettronica e Informazione
Politecnico di Milano
Italy
barenghi@elet.polimi.it

Timo Kasper
Horst Görtz Institute
for IT-Security
Ruhr University Bochum
Germany
timo.kasper@rub.de

Christof Paar
Horst Görtz Institute
for IT-Security
Ruhr University Bochum
Germany
christof.paar@rub.de

ABSTRACT

Over the last two decades FPGAs have become central components for many advanced digital systems, e.g., video signal processing, network routers, data acquisition and military systems. In order to protect the intellectual property and to prevent fraud, e.g., by cloning a design embedded into an FPGA or manipulating its content, many current FPGAs employ a bitstream encryption feature. We develop a successful attack on the bitstream encryption engine integrated in the widespread Virtex-II Pro FPGAs from Xilinx, using side-channel analysis. After measuring the power consumption of a single power-up of the device and a modest amount of off-line computation, we are able to recover all three different keys used by its triple DES module. Our method allows extracting secret keys from any real-world device where the bitstream encryption feature of Virtex-II Pro is enabled. As a consequence, the target product can be cloned and manipulated at the will of the attacker since no side-channel protection was included into the design of the decryption module. Also, more advanced attacks such as reverse engineering or the introduction of hardware Trojans become potential threats. While performing the side-channel attack, we were able to deduce a hypothetical architecture of the hardware encryption engine. To our knowledge, this is the first attack against the bitstream encryption of a commercial FPGA reported in the open literature.

CCS'11, October 17–21, 2011, Chicago, Illinois, USA.

Categories and Subject Descriptors

K.6.5 [**Security and Protection**]: [Unauthorized access]; D.4.6 [**Security and Protection**]: [Cryptographic controls]

General Terms

Security, Experimentation

Keywords

Side-channel attacks, FPGA, bitstream encryption, triple DES

1. INTRODUCTION

Electronic devices have become essential parts of our private life (e.g., cell phones, e-readers or set-top boxes), at work (e.g., laptops or routers) and in industrial environments (e.g., control systems or sensors). Virtually all of today's IT, communication and consumer electronic systems employ digital technology. As a flip side of this well-known development, reverse-engineering and product piracy have become important issues for a wide variety of electronic products since the creation of exact copies of digital information is often straightforward. Examples include consumer products, network routers and set-top boxes, or military systems. The threat is not limited to merely counterfeiting products; once a product has been reverse-engineered it becomes vulnerable to various other attacks. For instance, ill-intended malfunctioning of the device or circumvention of business models based on the electronic content, as it is regularly happening in the pay-TV sector, become possible. Not only consumer products, but also industrial and military applications can be affected. For instance, the recent discovery of details of the STUXNET virus shows the potential implications that embedded malware can have [12]. Another flavor of malicious manipulation of digital systems was described in a 2005 report by the US Defense Science

Board, where the clandestine introduction of hardware Trojans was underlined as a serious threat [1]. In summary, protection of digital secrets and intellectual property is a key factor for developing and successfully marketing electronic products nowadays.

1.1 FPGA Basics

When developing embedded systems, the main target platform choices are software, i.e. running the application on a microprocessor, or hardware, i.e realize an application-specific integrated circuits (ASIC). A third form of device, Field Programmable Gate Arrays (FPGAs), combines some advantages of software (fast development, low non-recurring engineering costs) with those of hardware (performance, power efficiency). These advantages have made FPGAs an important fixture in embedded system design, especially for applications that require heavy processing, e.g., for routing, signal processing or encryption. Modern high-end FPGAs have the functional equivalent of several tens of millions of Boolean gates, making them formidable devices for a large spectrum of applications. Most of today's FPGAs are (re)configured via a blob of binary data, called *bitstream*, which completely determines the functionality of the device. As described in Sect. 2.1, programming them is quite similar to developing software for a microprocessor, allowing for fast development and a quick time-to-market.

Nowadays FPGAs have applications in banking, defence, aerospace, and many sophisticated commercial technical applications such as video signal processing, e.g., for HDTV, or network routing. Even hitherto totally mechanical devices such as guns nowadays incorporate FPGAs, e.g., the XM25 Individual Airburst Weapon System [8]. Noteworthy for this contribution, satellite communication and other mission-critical systems as well as high-security applications also employ FPGAs [20]. As a key advantage, a product relying on FPGAs can be regularly improved during its life-cycle by simply changing the bitstream, e.g., if a design bug is found or to provide new functionality. To name two examples, today's network routers are easily upgraded in the field via the Internet and set-top boxes obtain an updated firmware via cable or a satellite link. One of the disadvantages of FPGAs, especially with respect to custom hardware such as ASICs, is that an attacker who has access to the bitstream can clone the system and extract the intellectual property of the design. Note that the bitstream is in the vast majority of systems stored externally to the FPGA in a dedicated configuration memory and is from there loaded into the FPGA on every power-up or reset — an adversary wire-tapping the relevant data signals can hence easily monitor the bitstream. The main answer of the industry for protecting the design is a security feature called *bitstream encryption*.

1.2 Bitstream Encryption Basics

The idea of bitstream encryption is to establish end-to-end confidentiality by means of symmetric cryptography. It protects the entire path of an FPGA bitstream: the development environment of the manufacturer, the insecure channel into the product, the storage inside the product, and finally the loading of the design into the FPGA.

Figure 1 illustrates an example for a secure firmware upgrade of an FPGA-based network router. As a prerequisite, the manufacturer and the FPGA in the network router

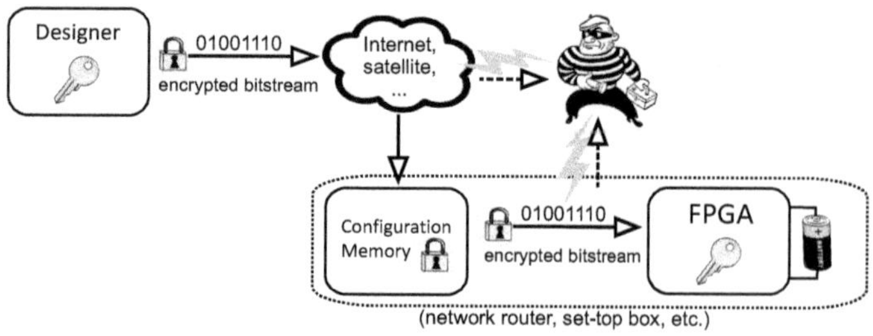

Figure 1: Bitstream encryption enables to securely transfer the content of an FPGA, e.g., a firmware update for a network router via the Internet.

possess the same secret key, that should be created individually for every device and securely stored both inside the FPGA (k_{FPGA}) and at the manufacturer site (k_{design}). After generating the bitstream, the designer encrypts it with a secure symmetric cipher such as triple DES or AES using a secret key k_{design}. This encrypted bitstream can now be safely sent, e.g., via the Internet, to the configuration memory of the target network router, from where it is loaded into the FPGA. The latter possesses an internal decryption engine and uses its secret key k_{FPGA} to decrypt each bitstream. Finally, the FPGA configures its internal circuitry according to the decrypted bitstream. The configuration is successful if and only if the secret keys used for the encryption and decryption of the bitstream are identical, i.e., $k_{design} = k_{FPGA}$.

A third party who gets hold of the encrypted bitstream — e.g., from the Internet or by wire-tapping the internal data bus that is used for the configuration inside the product — will not be able to extract any useful information. Without knowing the secret key for the decryption, she will not be able to deduce the design or configure another FPGA correctly. As a major consequence, counterfeiting or attacking the product becomes unfeasible, and no confidential or proprietary information contained in the bitstream can fall into the hands of the attacker.

1.3 Side-Channel Attacks

Side-channel attacks exploit physical information leakage of a cryptographic implementation in order to extract secret information, in particular the cryptographic key used. In the case of power analysis, the consumption of electric current or the electromagnetic emanations of the cryptographic device are used as a side channel for key extraction. Since both power consumption and EM emissions of a digital device depend on the values being computed, side channel attacks employ a divide-and-conquer approach, to model a part of the circuit employing guesses on small parts of the key, (e.g., 6 bits). The consumption (or EM emission) models are subsequently correlated with real world measurements: only the model dependent on the correct key guess will predict the behaviour of the actual device. Contrary to mathematical or brute-force attacks, where typically pairs of plaintexts and ciphertexts are required for a key-recovery, side-channel attacks require only one of them, i.e., either the plaintext or the ciphertext [15, 18]. While the open literature reports a number of successful attacks against cryptographic architectures implemented on the FPGA *fabric* [25, 27], no publicly known attack on the bitstream encryption has been reported in the open literature. We also refer to a number of surveys dealing with FPGA security which have not addressed bitstream reverse engineering as a real-world threat [14, 30].

1.4 Content of this Paper

In this paper we investigate the level of security provided by the bitstream encryption used in the widespread Virtex-II family of FPGAs produced by Xilinx. A detailed description of these FPGAs and their bitstream encryption feature, as well as an introduction to power analysis, are given in Sect. 2. The manufacturer claims that the bitstream encryption as implemented in Xilinx Virtex-II Pro FPGAs can thwart even most Class III attacks [28], i.e., attacks by well-funded intelligence agencies [5]. However, our research does not support this claim as shown in Sect. 3: starting without any previous knowledge about the implementation, i.e., a typical black box scenario, we demonstrate step-by-step how to conclude from the power consumption and timing behaviour of the FPGA to the detailed internal structure of the decryption hardware that we found not side-channel protected. Finally, we develop a side-channel attack that exploits the power consumption of the FPGA during the decryption of one bitstream to recover the secret keys used for the bitstream encryption. Some of the dramatic implications of our attack are illustrated in Sect. 4.

2. PRELIMINARIES

This section introduces Field Programmable Gate Arrays (FPGA) in general, and in particular the Virtex-II Pro device and its security features. We further describe the side-channel analysis and digital signal processing techniques used for our attack.

2.1 Flexible Hardware: FPGA Details

An FPGA is a reconfigurable integrated circuit that can host highly complex digital circuitry, e.g., a complete microcontroller, digital signal processing algorithms, or almost any other design that can be put in silicon.

Analyzing the worldwide **FPGA market**, *Xilinx* (51.2 %) and *Altera* (35.5 %) together account for more than 85 % market share, followed by *Actel* and *Lattice* with about 6 % market share each (Gartner Inc., 2008) [13]. Both market leaders offer security solutions for commercial and military environments that aim at protecting the bitstream by means of symmetric encryption. Altera programs the respective secret keys in non-volatile e-fuses on the silicon die of the FPGA that are covered by layers of metal to hinder extraction of the key by invasive physical attacks [7]. Xilinx on the other hand states that programmable fuses are easy to reverse-engineer [20] and instead promotes a battery-backed solution to store the keys in volatile memory, ensuring that the key is instantly zeroed if the FPGA is removed from the product, e.g., to conduct physical attacks. In this paper we focus on the advertised to be more secure solution of the — in terms of FPGAs sold — leading manufacturer Xilinx.

The essential **building blocks** of an FPGA are configurable logical blocks (CLB) which consist of *slices*. Each slice in turn contains small look-up tables (LUTs) that realize arbitrary combinational functions, i.e., small Boolean circuits, and usually also simple memory elements, e.g., latches storing one bit. Programmable switches allow altering of the signal path inside the slices, as well as routing the data to other CLBs on the FPGA. Depending on the particular type of FPGA various other auxiliary resources are available, for instance, multiply-and-add units, BlockRAMs that can be accessed by several CLBs, and even entire CPUs. By appropriately configuring the slices and combining the inputs and outputs of tens of thousands CLBs, an FPGA can realize the most elaborate tasks in parallel and hence achieves very high computational power. Obviously, the vast complexity of this configuration process cannot be managed manually, thus software tools are required for the design of an application. The tools ultimately generate the configuration information, i.e., the bitstream, for the FPGA.

The **design flow** for reconfigurable hardware starts with expressing the function to be realized by means of a high-level hardware description language (HDL) such as VHDL or Verilog. The FPGA manufacturers provide integrated development environments for their products, e.g., the Xilinx ISE Design Suite [3]. They allow HDL descriptions to be synthesized into a schematic representing the internal wiring of the corresponding FPGA, commonly called *netlist*. The synthesized netlist can be simulated on the development PC for debugging the implementation. Finally, the netlist is translated into a low-level circuit description, the *bitstream*, that specifies the exact content of each slice, each programmable switch, and every other configurable component inside the FPGA. Configuring the target device with this bitstream uniquely sets the initial state of the whole circuitry to realize the designed function.

2.2 Device Under Attack: Virtex-II Pro

As the target for our analysis we opted for a Virtex-II Pro XC2VP7 FPGA. According to the data sheet [33] its silicon die consists of nine metal layers manufactured in a 130 nm process with 90 nm high-speed transistors, allowing for designs with clock frequencies up to 600 MHz for internal components. Amongst others, the FPGA provides more than 11,000 internal registers and LUTs and an embedded PowerPC 401 processor core, wired to the fabric, in case a general purpose processor is needed alongside application specific hardware. For configuring all of its internal circuitry the FPGA requires a bitstream consisting of 560,700 bytes.

During our analysis, the power supply pins of the FPGA are of special interest, as they form the entry point for the side channel. The pins are divided in three main groups according to the parts of the device they are providing energy to: VCC_{INT} for a 1.5 V supply of the internal core logic, VCC_{AUX} for a 3.3 V supply of auxiliary circuits, and VCC_O for a 3.3 V supply of the input and output buffers. Note, that the 1.5 V of the core voltage VCC_{INT} can be distinguished from the other 3.3 V supply voltages and can hence be easily identified on the unknown printed circuit board of a real-world product.

Both Xilinx and Altera FPGAs rely on volatile static random access memory (SRAM) for holding the configuration information and, as a consequence, lose it when the power is switched off. In order to keep the crucial cryptographic key, in Xilinx products a lithium battery providing 1.0–3.6 V has to be connected to the VCC_{Batt} pin. The battery supplies the SRAM-based secret key storage used to decrypt the encrypted bitstream and provides the basis to use Virtex-II Pro devices in FIPS 140-2 Level 4 security devices, the highest security standard indicated by NIST. The standard mandates that all cryptographic keys must be instantly zeroed if physical tamper actions are detected on the secure device.

In case the battery is disconnected and the FPGA is not powered up the keys are instantly flushed away, forcing the customer to return the device to the producer for re-keying. While power is applied to the VCC_{AUX} pin of a Virtex-II Pro, the battery is not required to buffer the key storage and can be replaced [31].

2.2.1 Configuration Process and Protocols

As stated above, the configuration of the FPGA is completely erased every time the FPGA is powered off. It is thus necessary to reprogram the device after every boot, even when it is deployed in the field. Xilinx provides five different configuration protocols to configure the device, namely Master or Slave Serial mode, Master or Slave SelectMAP mode and IEEE-1149.1-2001 standard JTAG boundary scanning mode [4]. The first two modes input the bitstream into the device, one bit per clock cycle, through a specific pin which serves as a data-in line. The SelectMAP modes represent an evolution of the simple serial mode as they are able to send a byte of the bitstream at a time, thus decreasing significantly the time needed for configuration. The JTAG mode allows to input the whole bitstream into the device considering the internal configuration memory as one of the data registers of a standard JTAG chain. It is thus possible to insert the configuration information one bit at a time via JTAG, taking proper care of setting all the other devices on the JTAG chain into bypass mode.

Due to the widespread adoption and standardization of the JTAG protocol, we chose the JTAG interface of the FPGA for supplying the bitstream during our attack. The vast majority of commercial products retain the JTAG line contacts for post-production testing, hence this port is also the most suitable for real-world attacks. The JTAG interface is based on four lines: two for data input and output (TDI and TDO), one to supply the clock to the whole JTAG chain (TCK) and one to supply commands to the finite state machine implementing the JTAG port on every device (TMS). All the modules belonging to a JTAG chain, e.g., the configuration memory and the FPGA itself, have their TDI and TDO port daisy chained together and form a single loop. The number of devices connected to the JTAG testing chain and the order in which they are linked to the JTAG loop can be easily reverse-engineered [26].

2.2.2 Bitstream Encryption in the Virtex-II

The bitstream encryption feature [19] enables to configure the Virtex-II Pro FPGA with a bitstream that is encrypted by means of the symmetric-key cipher triple DES [32]. *Triple DES* is a block cipher constructed by chaining three subsequent executions of the Data Encryption Standard [23] (DES) by using either two or three different DES keys. In order to provide backwards compatibility, the three executions of DES are actually an encryption-decryption-encryption pattern: in this way, if a the same key is employed for all three cipher instances, the triple DES is effectively reduced to a single DES. The DES cipher encrypts blocks of 64 bits employing a 56-bit key, hence the possible key lengths of triple DES are 112 or 168 bits. Whilst single DES is vulnerable to brute-force attacks due to its short key length, e.g., using the COPACOBANA code breaking machine [17] or with commodity hardware such as GPUs [6], there are no theoretical or brute-force attacks against triple DES known with any realistic chance of success. Hence, neither mathematical cryptanalysis nor an exhaustive search can endanger the secrecy of a design protected by the bitstream encryption.

Since the bitstream is processed by the cipher in blocks of 64 bits, *Cipher Block Chaining* (CBC) [22] is implemented to combine subsequent blocks of the bitstream. During a decryption, this mode of operation defines that the ciphertext of one block should be added via a bitwise XOR to the output of the following triple DES decryption to obtain the plaintext. Since the first block to be decrypted does not have a predecessor, a 64-bit initialization vector (IV) is used to mask it. This IV may be publicly known and can hence be transmitted in plain without loss of security. The analyzed FPGA can store up to six single DES encryption keys, which can be independently marked for use in either the first, the second or the third DES run of the triple DES. This feature allows for either 3 key sets (for 2-key standard triple DES) or 2 key sets (for use with 3-key triple DES) and enables the manufacturer to update the bitstream even if a key set has been compromised. Xilinx states that there is no read port for the key storage, except for the one internally employed by the decryption engine [32]. The only way to program the keys into the device is through the JTAG programming mode, although no details of the key entering mode are provided by Xilinx in the technical specification. In order to avoid incorrect configuration of the FPGA due to a faulty decrypted bitstream and the subsequent possible damage to the device, Xilinx states that the FPGA performs a CRC check on the decrypted bitstream. For this purpose, a CRC16 standard checksum embedded in the configuration file is being used. In fact, there is no other authentication scheme implemented in the bitstream (encryption) mechanism of Virtex-II.

2.3 Power Analysis and Power Models

The power consumption of modern CMOS-based devices mostly depends on the ongoing switching activity. It is possible to exploit this relation in order to gain insights into the values being involved in a computation. For power analysis, the power dissipation is measured during the regular functioning of a secure device in order to infer the secret keys. The literature divides this class of attacks into two general families, "simple" (SPA) and "differential" (DPA) attacks [18]. *SPA attacks* involve visually interpreting power consumption measurements as a function of time in order to detect data-dependent properties between the computed value and the power consumption, in precise intervals of time. This methodology assumes that it is possible to discern a subset of keys thanks to their peculiar consumption behavior, e.g., to distinguish a square and multiply step in a modular exponentiation from a simple squaring. In public-key algorithms such as RSA this can lead to a complete leakage of the secret key. SPA is rarely applicable against symmetric ciphers, as the one used in our target device. *DPA attacks* rely on building a power model of a computing circuit, employing the input values to the circuit as inputs to the model, and a set of possible values of the unknown key as a parameter. To verify a correct key hypothesis, the attacker correlates the predicted values with the actual measurements from the device under attack through a statistical tool of her choice. Commonly, for a DPA it is assumed that the values of the measurement set and the hypothesis set are normally distributed random variables with mean μ and standard deviation σ, where μ is the mean consumption of the circuit for a precise key value at a specific time instant. Since the dynamic power consumption of a device is caused by the switching activity of the logic gates [16], a proper dynamic consumption model tries to express the power consumption depending on the intensity of the switching activity. This switching activity may be caused, e.g., by the combinational logic computing the result of a Boolean function, or by a latch storing a single bit value. A first order approximation of the switching activity of many circuits is provided by the *Hamming weight* (HW) of the input value. This results in a quite approximate model and has the advantage of requiring no precise knowledge about the implementation, since only the data processed at one instant in time has to be predicted. The switching activity induced by a latch storing a value is often better modeled by the *Hamming distance* (HD) between the former value stored by the latch and the new one. A latch toggles internally (and thereby consumes a noticeable amounts of energy) only if the previous value being held is different from the new one to be memorized, i.e., when their HD is 1 [11]. Consequentially, the model requires to predict two intermediate values, i.e., those stored in a register before and after the targeted operation. This requires some additional knowledge about the implementation, compared to a HW model.

Once a power model has been chosen, the attacker predicts an intermediate value depending on both a known input value and a part of the secret key. She then computes a set of hypothetical power consumption values, one for each of the possible values taken by the part of the secret key. The size of the part of the secret key hypothesized during one step of the attack is a trade-off between building an accurate model of the power consumption, which requires more key bits to be considered in a single time, and the computational complexity involved in computing a power hypothesis for every possible value which may be taken by the key portion. However, since attacking one key portion is performed independently from attacking the others, the attacker is free to divide the whole key in portions that are small enough to be processed. To recover the whole key, multiple attacks are performed (on the same set of measurements). After collecting a large number of measurements during the cryptographic operation to be attacked, the adversary employs a statistical tool to compare the hypothesized power values with those that have been measured, in order to infer the correct value of the key part. The typical methodology to correlate the predicted and actual power consumption of the circuit is to employ Pearson's linear correlation coefficient: if the model correctly predicts the consumption of the circuit, the linear correlation among the synthetic values and the recorded ones will be close to 1, while it is expected for a wrong model to have negligible correlation values. Conducting the correlation analysis time-wise, i.e., for each time instance of the consumption values recorded from the circuit, gives the attacker additional information about the exact moment when a side-channel leakage occurs in the power traces: the values of the correlation coefficient of the correct key hypothesis spike only in the time interval in which the operation is executed.

2.3.1 Processing the Measurements

For a successful power analysis attack the collected power traces need to fulfill a number of requirements. The first and foremost, due to the time-wise nature of the analysis, it is fundamental for obtaining correct results in the analysis, that the traces are perfectly synchronized. Due to either instrumental issues or the fact that the instant of the beginning of a sensitive operation is not always in full control of the attacker, it can be necessary to process the obtained traces in order to compensate for the possible phase shifts. The problem of realignment can be solved through choosing a single trace as a reference and detecting the most likely time delay that needs to be applied to each other measurement in order to achieve correct synchronization. Since the measurements are taken in very comparable situations (i.e., encryptions of different plaintexts with the same algorithm), the most natural figure of merit to detect the appropriate time delays is cross-correlation. Cross-correlation is a measure of the similarity of two signals as a function of a time-lag applied to one of them. The time delay maximizing the cross-correlation between the reference and the current trace is taken as the optimal time delay to achieve alignment.

A further key point for a successful power analysis is minimizing the amount of noise in the traces. Regardless of the quality of the measurement setup the measurements always contain noise, since the traces represent an aggregate measurement of the power consumption of the entire chip and its environment. **Digital signal processing** techniques can be employed to separate the side-channel leakage from the unwanted signals and thereby extract only the relevant information. Their usage turns out to be of crucial importance when dealing with large digital components as in [9]. Proper signal filtering can also be useful to evict any components of the measured trace which are not pertaining to the hardware under attack, provided they pertain to different harmonic components [10], removing even large amounts of unrelated signal.

3. ATTACKING A BLACK BOX

This section will provide a detailed description of the steps performed to successfully reverse engineer and break the protection scheme of Xilinx's Virtex-II Pro. The first subsection illustrates the implementation details of the encrypted bitstream that were gathered through the analysis of the output of the Xilinx ISE synthesis tool. After presenting the in-vitro analysis on the bitstream, the section will describe the custom communication device we built to program the FPGA and the measurement setup employed to record the power consumption profiles of the Virtex-II Pro. Subsequently we describe the preliminary chip analysis oriented at identifying the moment in time when the decryption is performed and provide an analysis of the power profile of the device. The section then infers the inner architecture of the DES decryption engine according to our findings about the time instances in which the intermediate values are processed. Finally, the precise attack techniques that allow to recover the whole triple DES key used for the decryption of the bitstream are illustrated and the minimal number of traces required for the full-key recovery is determined.

3.1 Reverse Engineering of the Bitstream

As a first step, the precise format of the bitstream needs to be analyzed. Understanding the bitstream is a prerequisite to find out how the configuration information is processed by the internal decryption engine of the device. We assume that the attacker is able to monitor the entire encrypted bitstream of the target FPGA, since the bitstream of an FPGA

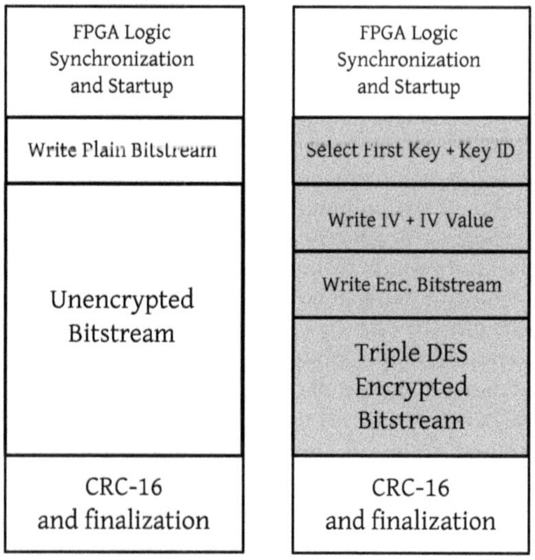

Figure 2: Comparison between the structure of an encrypted and an unencrypted bitstream

retains the same size regardless of the design implemented (the FPGA needs to be configured in full at least during its boot phase). Moreover, in case the bitstream encryption feature is enabled, the device cannot use the partial reconfiguration features — it is hence forced to perform a full reconfiguration for each update. To obtain the full (encrypted) bitstream an attacker has two options: *i*) she can wire-tap the data pin and command lines in order to eavesdrop on the communication while the FPGA is being configured, or *ii*) she can read out the content of the non-volatile memory attached to the FPGA which is responsible to configure the FPGA on power-ups. Note that this external memory is not necessarily connected via JTAG, and feeding the encrypted bitstream using different configuration schemes, e.g., Slave Serial, is also possible, but this does not have any impact on the attack that we present here. From now on, we assume that the attacker is in possession of the full encrypted bitstream through one of these methods.

Comparing Bitstreams.

While the Virtex-II Pro user guide [31] from Xilinx documents all the common configuration registers and gives a brief description of the inner addressing modes of the device, the internal registers driving the decryption are not explicitly mentioned. The the Virtex-II Pro user guide [31] describes the bitstream as split into packets which may target a specific configuration register to set configuration options, write to the SRAM configuration memory, or toggle internal signals, and are formed by a 32-bit header and a variable length body. Depending on the packet length they are split into two types: Type 1 packets may only handle a body shorter than $2^{11} - 1$ 32-bit words (i.e., 8 kB of data), while Type 2 packets, used to write the bitstream to the inner configuration mechanisms, handle up to $2^{27} - 1$ words (i.e., 512 MB of data). A peculiarity of the architecture mandates that only Type 1 packets may change the destination of a read or write operation which is not changed during a Type 2 packet operation. In order to understand which parts of the bitstream drive the decryption, we start the reverse engineering on the basis of a very simple test design comprising just a single boolean gate. We synthesized the test design once without activating the bitstream encryption feature, to obtain an unencrypted bitstream, and then again with varying keys for the encryption, producing several bit streams that are encrypted with the different keys. In the following we reveal the relevant details of the configuration by comparing the files containing the different bitstreams.

The differences deduced from the comparison are summarized in Fig. 2. The content of the bitstream is organized in packets, preceded by a single 32-bit synchronization word (namely, `0xAA995566`). This initialization header is the same for both encrypted and unencrypted bitstreams and has the purpose to synchronize the FPGA logic and reset the inner programming logic to a default state. After this phase, the unencrypted variant of the bitstream simply consists of a large packet with the whole configuration information. In contrast, the encrypted bitstream contains some extra information for initializing the cryptographic engine. The first value indexes the first key in the key storage to be employed for the triple DES decryption. The two remaining keys are determined by flags marking two cells of the 6-keys buffer as "middle" and "last". After the key indexes, the value of the IV required for the CBC mode is passed in plain. Following the IV value, the bitstream continues with a large packet containing the whole configuration information encrypted with triple DES. The writing command is the same as for the unencrypted bitstream, with the exception of an extra bit which is set to 1: we thus infer that setting the bit effectively enables the decryption engine. The next step was to reverse-engineer how the 64-bit secret keys input to the ISE synthesis tool are processed before being used for the encryption of a bitstream. In contrast to the DES standard, which suggests either to discard the eighth bit of every byte of the DES key or to employ it for a parity check, we have discovered that the ISE tool discards the full first byte of the 64-bit supplied key in order to obtain the 56-bit key for the DES encryption/decryption.This is done regardless of the fact that the manuals point out that the first byte is employed only for key indexing in the storage. As a final check to all our inferences and in order to understand the endianness of the bitstream, we generated a special bitstream that is encrypted with triple DES employing one of the known *weak keys* of DES — the same for all three executions of DES. These special weak keys have the property that a DES encryption involving one of them becomes an involutary operation, i.e., encrypting a second time with the same weak key is identical to a decryption and hence yields the plaintext. Through generating a bitstream that is encrypted with weak keys and with the IV of the CBC mode set to zero, due to the properties of the CBC mode the second 64-bit block contained in the bitstream is equal to the plaintext corresponding to the first block in the bitstream — thus we obtain a correctly deciphered plaintext in the generated bitstream file. Comparing this deciphered plaintext with the available unencrypted bitstream we confirmed that we correctly understood the triple DES engine input format and in particular the order in which the bits are processed internally.

Timing Issues.

The last information we were able to infer before tackling the device pertains the minimum throughput of the internal decryption engine. The Xilinx user guide reports that the maximum clock rate to be externally supplied during JTAG programming of an encrypted bitstream is $f_{clk} = 33$ MHz. In every clock cycle, one new bit of the bitstream is supplied to the FPGA. This in turn implies that the triple DES engine must be able to perform a full triple DES decryption of a 64-bit block in a time less than $64 \times T_{clk}$, where $T_{clk} = \frac{1}{f_{clk}}$ denotes the duration of a clock cycle. This gives us the expected time for a full triple DES of around $64 \times T_{clk} = 1.94\,\mu s$ which implies that, assuming all 48 rounds of the triple DES take roughly the same time, a single round of the DES must be executed in around 40 ns. Accordingly, the hypothesis of the DES being perfomed by means of a software implementation running on an internal microcontroller becomes highly unlikely, since it would be too slow — instead we now assume a hardware implementation. If the decryption was realized by implementing one DES round in hardware and execute it 48 times for the triple DES, the above details about the timing give a lower bound for the clock rate of the inner cryptographic engine of 24.75 MHz.

3.2 Customizing the Measurement Setup

After analyzing the format of the bitstream and the specifications of the target device, we moved on to develop a measurement workbench in order to record the power profile of our target FPGA during its operation in a real-world scenario. The first step in this direction was to develop a customized *communication module* that is able to correctly configure an FPGA via JTAG. Hence, we designed an in-system programmable board that is based on an Atmel ATMega256 8-bit microcontroller and provides a JTAG port, a universal serial bus (USB) as well as a dedicated pin for triggering the oscilloscope. We implemented a framework on the microcontroller comprising the JTAG protocol and a serial protocol for communicating via USB. The firmware allows to freeze the configuration process through stopping the clock signal fed to the Virtex-II Pro and enables to issue the trigger signal to the oscilloscope before the clocking in of any chosen bit, i.e., with a resolution of 125 ns. While the fixed header of the bitstream (see Fig. 2) fits into the memory of the microcontroller, the remaining bits to be sent are provided by the control PC and sent to the communication module. The latter then wraps the bitstream in the JTAG protocol and forwards it to the device under attack while issuing trigger signals at the appropriate time instants.

As the *target platform* for attacking the bitstream encryption we chose the customized FPGA development board SASEBO [2]. It contains an XC2VP7 Virtex-II Pro FPGA and provides stable and suitable voltages by means of on-board voltage regulators. A JTAG connector is provided to configure both the FPGA and a dedicated PROM which are connected in a daisy chain form. During the analyses we slightly modified the board by inserting resistors that allow measuring the power consumption of the VCC_{INT}, VCC_{AUX} and GND paths. Similar modifications are also required for attacking other real-world products comprising a bitstream encryption.

A LeCroy WP715Zi digital oscilloscope with a maximum sampling rate of 20 GSamples/s and an analog bandwidth of 1.5 GHz was employed to record the instantaneous power consumption of the target FPGA at a maximum vertical precision of 2 mV/division.All the traces where acquired at 10 GSamples/s to avoid any possible aliasing due to undersampling. The program feeding the encrypted bitstreams to our customized programmer and controlling the acquisition of the power consumption traces runs on the oscilloscope itself, i.e., the communication module is connected to it via USB. The employed probe connecting the oscilloscope to the measurement resistor on the board is a LeCroy AP033 active differential probe, which includes a low noise 10x analog amplifier that boosts the effective vertical resolution of our measurement subsystem to 200 μV/division.

For verifying that our setup allows to correctly configure the target FPGA with custom (encrypted) bitstreams, we again synthesized our test design comprising a single boolean gate and connected the appropriate pins of the FPGA to two external switches serving as inputs and an LED displaying the output of the logical operation. Experimenting with various self-generated bitstreams, e.g., by means of arbitrary IVs, we used the simple circuit as a practical means to debug the proper configuration of the FPGA and successfully verified the functionality of our setup.

3.3 Timing and Power Profile Analysis

With the framework for configuring the FPGA and acquiring its power consumption at hand we now proceed to analyze the power profile of the target FPGA, in order to identify the point in time when the targeted triple DES decryption takes place. We started our analyses from the VCC_{INT} line, which, according to the specifications provided by Xilinx, powers the whole FPGA fabric and inner circuits. This line turned out to be the actual line feeding the decryption engine. For the sake of completeness, the detection analyses have been repeated also on VCC_{AUX}, which did not show any change in the power consumption whether or not the decryption engine is enabled. We may thus conclude that only VCC_{INT} is effectively powering the FPGA decryption engine. To record the power consumption of the internal circuits connected to VCC_{INT}, there are two options: the power consumption can be sampled either by measuring the voltage drop across resistor between VCC_{INT} and the device, or one between the device and GND.

Trying the second option first, we detected a strong echo from the ground plane, implying a strong variation of the offset of the measured power consumption that rendered the power traces useless for further analysis. The disturbing effect turned out to be related to the activities at the input and output ports of the FPGA during the configuration, i.e., the communication via JTAG: the power consumption of all voltage supply inputs (VCC_{INT}, VCC_{AUX} and VCC_O) is summed up when measuring at the GND path, as a consequence the data and clock signal of the JTAG port caused the undesired variations in the offset. As a remedy for the problem we finally decided to acquire all our measurements between VCC_{INT} and the device and thereby solely record the power consumption of this pin, separated from all other activities on the other power pins.

To learn more about the internal configuration process we performed tests with bitstreams that were generated intentionally wrong, i.e., configuring an FPGA with them results in an unpredictable behavior. During the tests, the consumption of the FPGA spiked after a while, the device heated up and the configuration process effectively stopped: we proceeded no further in order to avoid damage to the device. These findings let us suggest that the configuration information is written to the SRAM memory of the configuration fabric instantly upon reception of each configuration block, even before the actual boot command is given and before the CRC checksum is properly verified.

The first step in the detection of the time period in which the decryption takes place was done through recording power traces during the loading of 64 bits of the bitstream. Two long traces have been collected: one from an encrypted bitstream and the other one from a plain bitstream.

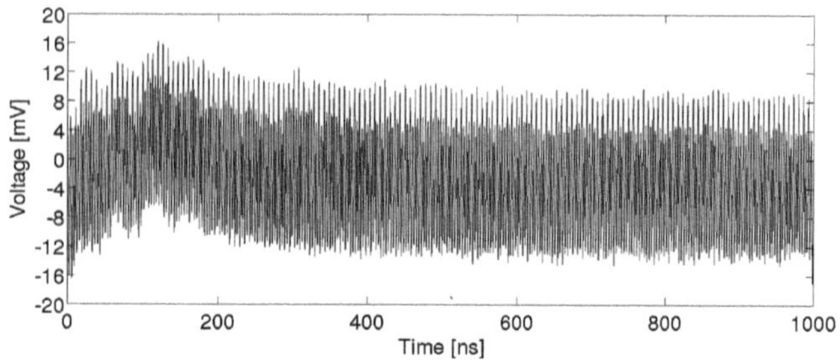

(a) Not encrypted

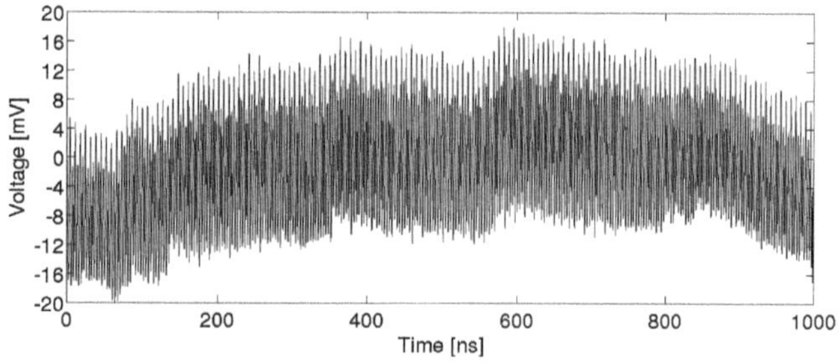

(b) Encrypted

Figure 3: Raw measurements of the power consumption at VCC_{INT} during the time period of the decryption

Through comparison we spotted the key difference in power consumption after the second bit of the 64-bit block is clocked in. Fig. 3 depicts the power consumption of the FPGA for the case of an encrypted bitstream (at the bottom) and its unencrypted counterpart (at the top), revealing a clear increment in the dynamic power consumption occurring at this time instant only if the bitstream encryption feature is used.

Filtering the Measurements.

A strong oscillating signal with a frequency of 295 MHz can be noticed in both traces. Being present also in the unencrypted bitstream trace we followed the intuition that it is not related to the decryption engine and tried to remove it by means of a band block filter. The latter is realized in the digital domain and suppresses the components of the signal at 295 MHz, employing a narrow Chebyshev type 2 window in order to minimize the effects of the aliasing on other harmonic components. The results of the filtering are depicted in Fig. 4: it is now possible to clearly distinguish the shape of the three DES executions, followed by the same peak in power consumption regarding what we suppose is the writeback operation of the 64-bit word into the configuration fabric.

In order to confirm that we did not discard any information relevant for further power analysis, we computed the variance of both the filtered measurements and also the part of the measurements that has been discarded by the filter,

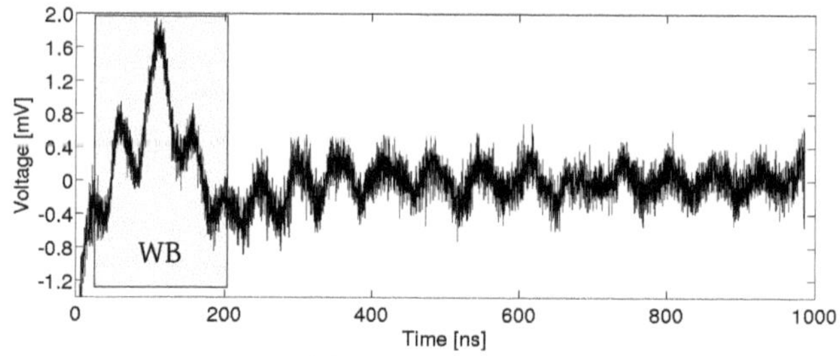

(a) Not encrypted

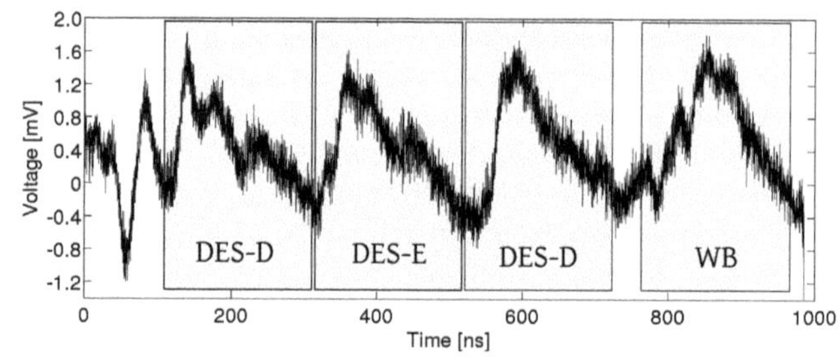

(b) Encrypted

Figure 4: Filtered power consumption measured at VCC_{INT} during the time period of the decryption.

i.e., containing the frequency components that have been blocked by the band block filter. We recall that, since differential power analysis relies on exploiting the differences in the power consumption caused by different inputs, the time-wise variance computed over a significant number of traces is a reasonable index of the information contained in the signal.

Figure 5 presents the computed variances for the time window pertaining the decryption-encryption-decryption operations, based on processing 50,000 different inputs. As we can see, the variance of the part of the signal kept by the filter features three distinct peaks at the beginning of each DES execution and is higher during the encryption process, with respect to the lower values assumed before and after. In contrast, the variance of the discarded signal is practically flat, suggesting that no information relevant to the decryption process has been omitted. Therefore it is conceivable that the oscillating power consumption is actually the power profile of the PowerPC 401 core embedded in the FPGA. The core has a reference working frequency of 300 MHz which seems compatible with our measurements.

The analysis suggests the presence of a large buffer employed to store the result of a whole DES decryption (or encryption) operation, due to the high variance at the beginning of every DES computation. It is also possible to infer the duration of a single DES round from the variance figure by simply computing the distance between the peaks: exactly one DES execution is encompassed between them. Through calculating this distance we obtain a computation time for the DES of 217 ns, corresponding to 651 ns for the execution of three full DES computations. This figure is well within the maximum bounds enforced by the JTAG input rate calculated in Sect. 3.1 which mandates the triple DES to be faster than 1.94 μs. The peak to peak amplitude of the decryption signal is roughly 2.8 mV, thus the measurement

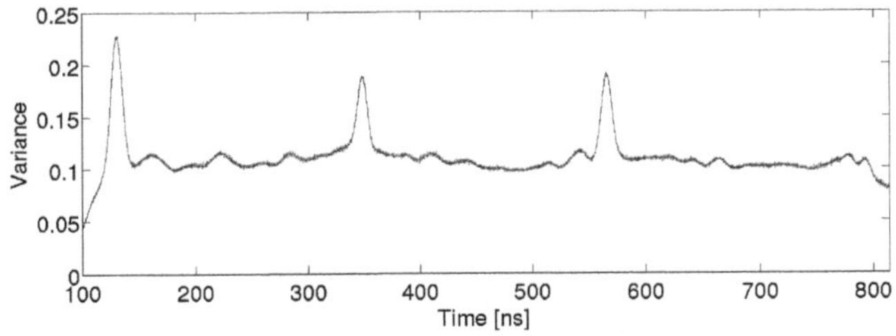

(a) Kept by the filter

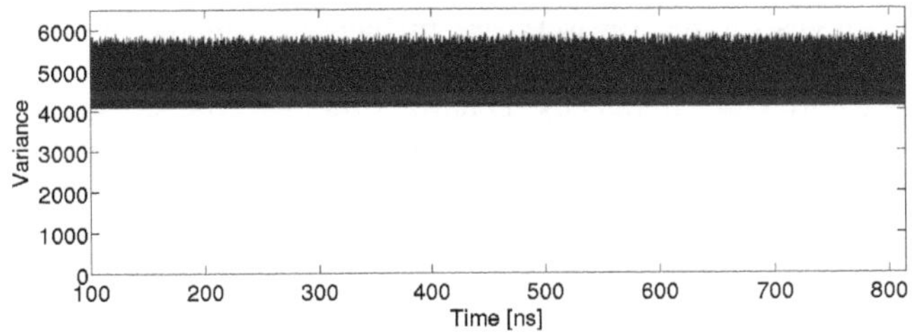

(b) Discarded by the filter

Figure 5: Variance of the power consumption for the part of the signal kept and discarded by the filter

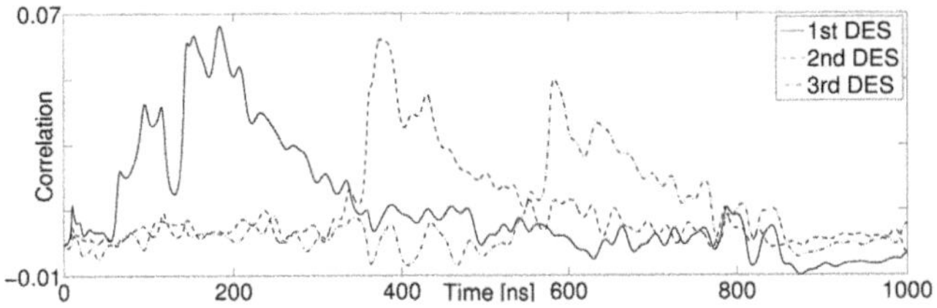

Figure 6: Correlation for hypothesizing the HD between the output of the first two rounds of each DES module

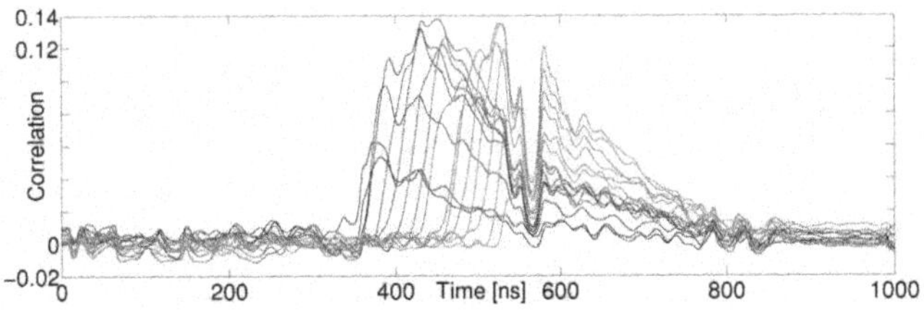

Figure 7: Correlation peaks for HD between the outputs of all the 16 rounds of the second DES

setup should have enough sensitivity to capture the differences in the consumptions of the decryptions of different plaintexts.

3.3.1 *Power-Profiling the Decryption Engine*

Performing a power analysis attack requires to know the architecture of the target device to select a power model which matches to its power consumption characteristics. This information is missing when attacking a black box. Having identified the point in time where the triple DES decryption is performed by the device we thus proceed with investigating the correct model for the power consumption. During this profiling phase, that aims at determining the underlying hardware structure of the decryption engine, the secret keys used for the 3DES are known. Accordingly, we are able to fully compute the intermediate results of the cipher in every encryption/decryption round.

We selected three different keys in the Xilinx ISE tools and generated the corresponding key file and an encrypted bitstream. After configuring the keys into the FPGA using a Xilinx programming device we collected $50,000$ power traces for the same number of ciphertexts (64-bit blocks)[1] while sending the encrypted bitstream to the target device by means of our customized configuration module. In the following, in order to perform a power analysis of the acquired measurements one needs to align them. For this purpose we applied the cross correlation alignment explained in Sect. 2.3.1 on the whole trace, band block filter.

Section 3.3 pinpoints the relevant part of the configuration process, i.e., when the second bit of a 64-bit ciphertext packet is sent to the FPGA. The acquired power traces must hence be related to one of the previous ciphertexts (depending on the size of the internal buffer of the device). In order to determine which ciphertext belongs to which power trace we calculated the intermediate values of every DES round, considering the first ciphertext block in the bitstream and the known key as inputs.

The power consumption model for the analysis was chosen based on an assumption about the internal DES hardware, i.e, the common design choice that the state of the cipher is saved in a buffer in every round. Consequently, we computed the correlation coefficient between the processed measurements and the HD of two consecutive round outputs of the first DES decryption, which is a typical hypothetical power model when attacking hardware. We supposed different relations between the ciphertexts and power traces. For the hypothesis that the previously sent ciphertext is processed when sending the current 64-bit packet a strong correlation appears right after the trigger point (see Fig. 6). As a result, we could deduce that a 64 bit ciphertext block is processed two clock cycles after it is fully input into the device. To gain further insights into the hardware architecture we repeated the same for the input of the second and the third DES executions. The results are shown in Fig. 6: clearly, the correlation corresponding to each of the three DES runs can be spotted.

In order to further confirm the presence of a buffer between every round of the DES cipher, we ran a series of power analyses, this time hypothesizing the HD between the input and the output of every DES round. Fig.7 depicts the correlation related to the 16 rounds at hand of the second DES execution. The correlation peak for the inner buffers is clearly present and the position of the peak shifts forward in time, increasing with the number of the hypothesized round.

An important point here is the role of the initial permutation (IP) of DES. By trial-and-error we found that reliable correlation results are obtained when excluding IP and IP^{-1} in the hypothesis. A self-evident hypothetical power model for attacking the first round of the first DES is $\mathrm{HD} = \mathrm{HW}(\mathrm{IP}(C) \oplus \mathrm{Round}(\mathrm{IP}(C), K))$, where C is a 64-bit ciphertext, "Round" represents the 64-bit DES round function, and K is the last 48-bit subkey of the first DES.

[1]Configuring this FPGA, a maximum of around $70,000$ ciphertexts are available.

Accordingly, all the correlation results shown above base on this hypothetical power model.

Observing that the features of the correlation figures do not sport any high frequency features, we tried a more restrictive filtering strategy: an additional low-pass filter with a cut-off frequency of 50 MHz was applied to all the collected traces and the HD-based correlation analysis was repeated. The results did not show any significant change in the shape and the amplitude of the correlations, thus we proceed in the actual attack with low-pass filtered traces.

3.4 The V2 DES Engine Internals

We conclude the profiling with some assumptions about the hardware implementation of the 3DES engine inside the Virtex-II Pro. It is conceivable that it employs a round function executing a round of the cipher per clock cycle, since DES employs 8 different S-boxes that cannot be shared during a round computation. The correlation peaks in Fig. 7 moving forward in time with the targeted round of DES supports this assumption. The corresponding hypothetical architecture is depicted in Fig. 8. Due to the Feistel structure of the cipher, the encryption and decryption can be realized by 48 successive rounds, supplying the subkeys in the correct order, and applying the IP before the start of the first round and IP^{-1} after the last round.

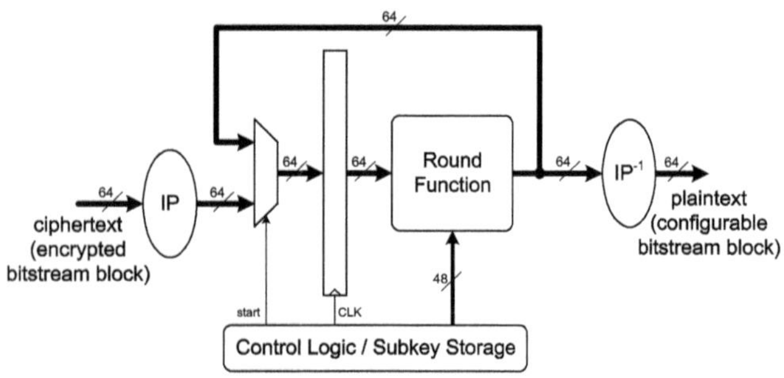

Figure 8: Our hypothetical architecture of the internal triple DES module of Virtex-II Pro FPGA

3.5 Extracting Keys from the Virtex-II

After choosing the proper information leakage model in the previous section, we now proceed to perform the attack in a real-world scenario: this time, an FPGA with an unknown set of keys is attacked. During a normal power-up of the target device, the adversary measures the power traces and collects the corresponding ciphertexts contained in the bitstream. Since the bitstream is encrypted with a secure cipher, even the simplest design results in the ciphertexts being uniformly distributed. This allows the attacker to measure the encryption operation of a whole codebook of plaintexts for each reasonably sized key hypothesis.

In the case of DES, each subkey of length 48-bit can be divided into 6-bit parts, since the value of a single bit of the output of a DES round is influenced by 6 key bits added to the input of the S-box computing it, because of the input width of the DES S-boxes. This allowed us to choose a 6-bit wide key hypothesis, thus, to reveal the first round key the attack therefore has to be repeated eight times, once for each key portion considered in the attack. After the first 48 bits of the round key have been recovered, the remaining 6 bits of the 56-bit DES key are exposed by attacking the second round of the DES operation. We performed a full key recovery involving 50,000 traces by hypothesizing the HD between a single bit of the output from a DES round and the previous value being stored in the round buffer (for simplicity consider a bit of the round buffer in Fig. 8). Once the 56-bit key for the first DES decryption is known the input for the subsequent DES encryption is computed and its 56-bit key (and finally that of the last DES decryption) is revealed similarly.

To quantify the minimum sampling frequency required for a successful key recovery, we further investigated the fact that the attacks still works if the traces are sampled at a sensibly lower frequency. Following the fact that we applied a lowpass filter at 50 MHz, we applied a 100 times decimation to the traces, i.e., use only every hundredth sampling point and discard the rest, and repeated all the attacks in order to see if the reduced traces are still containing enough information. As a result, all the attacks mentioned up to now are repeatable on the decimated traces, thus yielding a significant speedup in the required computation time and a reduction in the memory footprint.

It is possible to recover a 6-bit DES subkey in less than 4 seconds of computation time on a common desktop PC, with a memory footprint smaller than 20 MB. The whole 112-bit key of a 2-key triple DES is hence revealed by our attack in roughly two minutes and the 168-bit key of a 3-key triple DES in three minutes. The trace decimation also impacts on the minimum sampling frequency required for the digital oscilloscope: since the decimated traces are now sampled at a rate of 100 MS/s this can be regarded as a new lower bound for the required sampling frequency of the oscilloscope.

3.5.1 *Practical Results*

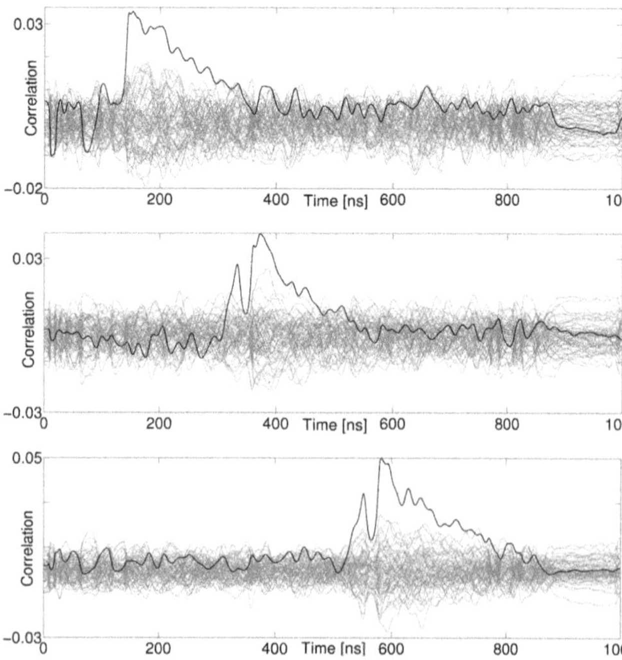

Figure 9: Results of the DPA attack on 50,000 traces employing non decimated lowpass traces targeting the (a) first (b) second (c) third DES execution (correct key guess in black, the others in gray)

So far, the same set of 50,000 power traces (acquired from loading a single bitstream into the FPGA) was used to profile the power consumption characteristics of the device and to perform the actual attacks. To determine the minimum number of traces required to reveal the complete triple DES key we have examined all subkeys of all three DES executions accordingly. As illustrated in Fig. 9 the power consumption right after the trigger signal is disturbed by the I/O activity, causing that a key-recovery attack on the first DES execution is harder than the others. The result of the attack over the number of traces for the worst case is shown by Fig. 10 indicating that with the current attack setup a minimum of 25,000 measurements is required for the correct hypothesis to emerge, albeit the statistical confidence margin is not high.

The minimum number of required traces is largely affected by the measurement setup and environmental noise. Depending on these parameters therefore the attacker may need more traces. Our target FPGA, i.e., XC2VP7, is one of the smallest variants on the market. Still, the size of its configuration bitstream (independent of the size of the design) suffices to acquire more than 70,000 measurements of different ciphertexts being encrypted by the 3DES engine. Hence, loading of a single bitstream into our target FPGA during a power-up suffices to acquire close to two times more measurements than required for a successful recovery of the full secret key — this indicates that our attack can be conducted on real-world products even in a very noisy measurement environment, and while large scale ASIC components are embedded in the FPGA chip. Note, that repeating the measurements for more power-ups does not increase the number of different ciphertexts — still averaging over the power-ups allows to reduce the noise level.

4. IMPLICATIONS

In the previous section we have shown that the bitstream encryption feature aiming to provide IP protection can be circumvented by extracting the secret keys used for the encryption via power analysis. The complete content of any Virtex-II Pro protected with bitstream encryption can fall into the hands of a competitor or criminal — this may imply system-wide damage, if IP such as encryption schemes and keys programmed into the FPGA, or similar secrets, are misused or become public. The attacks hence have a devastating impact on the security of products employing bitstream encryption in the real-world.

For performing our key-recovery, an attacker needs knowledge about side-channel cryptanalysis, a basic lab measurement setup and physical access to the target device in which

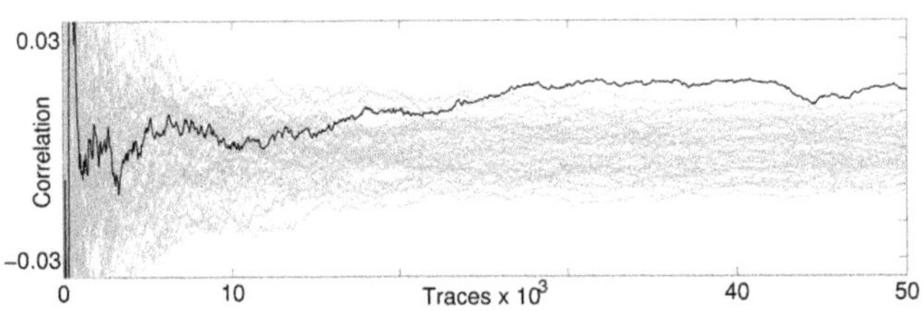

Figure 10: Result of the DPA attacks targeting the first DES as a function of number of traces (correct key guess in black, the others in gray)

the Virtex-II Pro FPGA is embedded. The only modification required to be performed on the product to be attacked is removing the capacitances which have negative effect on power measurements. Also, the lithium battery must remain connected to the FPGA to ensure that the secret keys are not zeroed. The adversary connects her measurement equipment and powers up the product-under-attack once, while monitoring the loading of the encrypted bitstream. Finally, she performs the statistical evaluation on a standard PC to recover the full secret key of the 3DES. Applying the methods described in this paper, the keys used for the bitstream encryption can be recovered with modest efforts in less than one hour, using the measurements of only one single configuration process.

After the key recovery the attacker can decrypt the protected bitstream from the Virtex-II Pro FPGA, and hence possesses its complete content. As a consequence, she can produce a clone of the original FPGA on the basis of an empty device by simply configuring it with the extracted bitstream, even without using the encryption feature, for example to replicate the product of a competitor.

Furthermore, by reverse-engineering the internal wiring of the FPGA from the bitstream a stolen design can be analyzed, the internal secrets extracted and used for malicious purposes. The stolen design could even be improved and disguised as an own product that outrivals the original. While Xilinx tries to establish security by obscurity by keeping the exact mapping of the bitstream to the internal circuitry of their product confidential, there already exist methods to recover the original design of an FPGA from a bitstream [24, 30].

In addition to lost IP, in a security-critical environment reprogramming the attacked FPGA with an ill-intended modified code, e.g., to accomplish malfunctioning or to unnoticedly implement a hardware trojan [21], is a particularly damaging option. In the following we illustrate possible implications that our attacks may have at hand of two examples from the commercial sector[2], without naming manufacturers.

4.1 Real-World Example 1: Set Top Box

Set-top boxes are widely used in the field for receiving digital TV and radio programmes, pay-per-view special events, allow to watch recent movies on a subscription basis and enable video on demand, i.e., remotely renting a video including the ability to pause, rewind, and fast forward. A set-top box is an ideal candidate for using FPGAs with bitstream encryption: In addition to the computationally highly demanding demodulating and decompressing algorithms for descrambling the transmitted TV and radio programmes, the manufacturers often employ their proprietary encryption schemes, e.g., for the above mentioned applications. The secure bitstream encryption feature enables to regularly update and improve the firmware running on the set-top boxes in the households, for example by cable or a satellite link, and establish corresponding business models without disclosing the descrambling schemes or secret keys to potential attackers.

Our key-recovery attack puts set-top boxes relying on the investigated or similar FPGAs using bitstream encryption at a high risk: an attacker extracting the firmware of a set-

[2]for obvious reasons we do not cover military applications here.

top box knows amongst others the scrambling scheme and secret keys, can gain access to all digital content without paying and is thus able to circumvent the above mentioned business models. A criminal can make high financial gain (and cause high financial losses for the service provider) by producing new set-top boxes or modifying the firmware of existing set-top boxes to enable the usage of the services free of cost by the customers.

4.2 Real-World Example 2: Router

Network routers redirect data traffic with a speed of hundreds of Gigabits per second in local networks and often constitute the interface to the outside world, e.g., the Internet, for companies, government agencies and private households. In addition to routing data, an FPGA in common products often realizes security-relevant functions such as a firewall to separate private local networks from other insecure ones. In case of a bug in the firmware or if a security fix is required, some routers can be updated remotely — again, the bitstream encryption is the basis for establishing this functionality. Assuming a router that is based on a Virtex-II Pro, an attacker having one-time physical access to it can perform our key-recovery attack. From there on, she can remotely initiate firmware updates, e.g., via the Internet, to modify the functionality of the router according to her demands.

A denial-of-service attack, aiming at malfunctioning or to destroy the device or other connected equipment is one option. More likely, a modified firmware can be used to open a covered channel allowing the adversary to spy out and access data from the internally connected computers and other devices, e.g., by implementing a trojan horse that secretly forwards all internal traffic to the adversary. The user typically has no means to verify whether his firmware has been manipulated or if it is original, hence — depending on the location where the manipulated router is used — a modified firmware can have a devastating impact on the privacy and security, and even the safety, of the attacked individual or company.

4.3 Scope of our Findings

As researchers of a university with this paper we intend to inform about possible vulnerabilities when using bitstream encryption and warn the end-users of products incorporating this feature from possible damage. We believe there can be fairly severe real-world implications (depending on the commercial devices in which Virtex-II Pro FPGAs are used) due to our findings. Furthermore, it seems highly likely that certain determined attackers, e.g., foreign intelligence services, are already capable of extracting and altering FPGA designs using power analysis techniques. Since the success of a power analysis attack in general does not depend on the cipher employed, it is conceivable that similar attacks can be applied to newer generations of FPGAs from different manufacturers, employing different ciphers, such as the Virtex 4 family or Altera products using AES-256 in their bit encryption schemes [7, 29].

5. CONCLUSION

We presented the first attacks targeting the bitstream encryption of FPGAs in the literature. By profiling the power consumption of the target FPGA we reverse-engineered all relevant details of the security feature and pinpointed the time instant when the decryption of the ciphertext blocks of the bitstream is performed by a dedicated hardware contained in the FPGA. We identified the appropriate power model for attacking the triple DES engine by means of power analysis and deduced the internal architecture of the hardware. Our proposed techniques for the digital signal processing of the power measurements enable a highly efficient power analysis attack that allows the full secret key of the triple DES to be extracted in only 3 minutes of computation time from only 25,000 measurements, obtainable with a single boot up of the device. Our findings indicate that the attacks are possible using a low-cost oscilloscope with a sample rate as little as 100 MS/s.

In particular, we have successfully exemplified our attack at hand of the bitstream decryption of a Virtex-II Pro XC2CP7 FPGA manufactured by the market leader Xilinx. We are able to recover all three different keys used by its triple DES module from a single power-up of the device in a real-world scenario. The lithium battery for the key storage, providing extra security according to Xilinx, does not have to be removed for the attack. It is highly conceivable that similar attacks can be applied to other series of FPGAs, e.g., from other manufacturers.

Besides the obscurity that emerges from Xilinx keeping the details of their bitstream files secret we encountered no countermeasures against side-channel analysis — an alarming fact considering the protection of many devices deployed in the field: an attacker knowing the secret key used for the encryption of the bitstream can obtain all secrets and intellectual property contained in commercial products, e.g., proprietary encryption schemes or processing algorithms.

As a consequence of our attacks, cloning of the products protected by the bitstream encryption scheme becomes straightforward. After reverse engineering the content of the FPGA from the bitstream, improved products could be marketed by a competitor that outrival the original. Much worse, the content of commercial products can be updated remotely, e.g., via Internet, with a maliciously modified new firmware. This poses a severe threat to the reliability of the products, puts the privacy of individuals and companies at a high risk and further enables to infect the devices with embedded malware.

6. REFERENCES

[1] Defense Science Board. `http://www.acq.osd.mil/dsb/`.

[2] Side-channel Attack Standard Evaluation Board (SASEBO). Further information are available via `http://www.rcis.aist.go.jp/special/SASEBO/`.

[3] Xilinx ISE Design Suite. `http://www.xilinx.com/tools/designtools.htm`.

[4] IEEE Standard Test Access Port and Boundary-Scan Architecture. *IEEE Std 1149.1-2001*, pages i –200, 2001.

[5] D. Abraham, G. Dolan, G. Double, and J. Stevens. Transaction Security System. In *IBM Systems Journal 30*, pages 206–229, 1991.

[6] G. Agosta, A. Barenghi, F. D. Santis, and G. Pelosi. Record Setting Software Implementation of DES Using CUDA. *Information Technology: New Generations, Third International Conference on*, pages 748–755, 2010.

[7] ALTERA. Using the Design Security Feature in Stratix II and Stratix II GX Devices (AN 341 version 2.3). Technical report, August 2009. http://www.altera.com/literature/an/an341.pdf.

[8] ATK. XM25 Counter Defilade Target Engagement System. http://www.atk.com/customer_solutions_missionsystems/documents/sw_iw_xm25.pdf, May 2009. Post "FPGAs in interesting places – the XM25 Airburst Weapon System" by Saar Drimer on www.fpgasecurity.com.

[9] A. Barenghi, G. Pelosi, and Y. Teglia. Improving first order differential power attacks through digital signal processing. In *ACM-SIGSAC International Conference on Security of Information and Networks*, pages 124–133. ACM, 2010.

[10] A. Barenghi, G. Pelosi, and Y. Teglia. Information leakage discovery techniques to enhance secure chip design. In C. A. Ardagna and J. Zhou, editors, *WISTP*, volume 6633 of *Lecture Notes in Computer Science*, pages 128–143. Springer, 2011.

[11] E. Brier, C. Clavier, and F. Olivier. Correlation Power Analysis with a Leakage Model. In *CHES 2004*, volume 3156 of *LNCS*, pages 16–29. Springer, 2004.

[12] W. J. Broad, J. Markoff, and D. E. Sanger. Israeli Test on Worm Called Crucial in Iran Nuclear Delay. Technical report, New York Times, January 2011. http://www.nytimes.com/2011/01/16/world/middleeast/16stuxnet.html.

[13] O. Coudert. Why FPGA startups keep failing, 2009. FPGA market shares according to Gartner Inc, 2008.

[14] S. Drimer. Security for volatile FPGAs. Technical Report UCAM-CL-TR-763, University of Cambridge, Computer Laboratory, Novembre 2009. ISSN 1476-2986 http://www.cl.cam.ac.uk/techreports/UCAM-CL-TR-763.pdf.

[15] T. Eisenbarth, T. Kasper, A. Moradi, C. Paar, M. Salmasizadeh, and M. T. M. Shalmani. On the Power of Power Analysis in the Real World: A Complete Break of the KeeLoq Code Hopping Scheme. In *CRYPTO 2008*, volume 5157 of *LNCS*, pages 203–220. Springer.

[16] Eric Peeters and François-Xavier Standaert and Jean-Jacques Quisquater. Power and Electromagnetic Analysis: Improved Model, Consequences and Comparisons. *Integr. VLSI J.*, 40(1):52–60, 2007.

[17] T. Güneysu, T. Kasper, M. Novotný, C. Paar, and A. Rupp. Cryptanalysis with COPACOBANA. *IEEE Transactions on Computers*, 57(11):1498–1513, 2008.

[18] P. Kocher, J. Jaffe, and B. Jun. Differential Power Analysis. In *CRYPTO 99*, volume 1666 of *LNCS*, pages 388–397. Springer, 1999.

[19] R. Krueger. Application Note XAPP766: Using High Security Features in Virtex-II Series FPGAs. Technical report, XILINX, 2004. http://www.xilinx.com/support/documentation/application_notes/xapp766.pdf.

[20] A. Lesea. IP Security in FPGAs, White Paper WP 261. Technical report, XILINX, February 2007.

[21] L. Lin, M. Kasper, T. Güneysu, C. Paar, and W. Burleson. Trojan Side-Channels: Lightweight Hardware Trojans through Side-Channel Engineering. In *CHES*, volume 5747 of *LNCS*, pages 382–395. Springer, 2009.

[22] A. Menezes, P. C. van Oorschot, and S. A. Vanstone. *Handbook of Applied Cryptography.* CRC Press, 1996.

[23] NIST. FIPS-46-3: Data Encryption Standard (DES), 1999.

[24] J.-B. Note and É. Rannaud. From the bitstream to the netlist. In M. Hutton and P. Chow, editors, *16th International Symposium on Field Programmable Gate Arrays, FPGA 2008*. ACM, 2008.

[25] S. B. Örs, E. Oswald, and B. Preneel. Power-Analysis Attacks on an FPGA - First Experimental Results. In *CHES 2003*, volume 2779 of *LNCS*, pages 35–50. Springer, 2003.

[26] Recurity Labs. Embedded Analysis. 27th Chaos Communication Congress, Dec. 2010. http://events.ccc.de/congress/2010/wiki/Embedded_Analysis.

[27] F.-X. Standaert, S. B. Örs, J.-J. Quisquater, and B. Preneel. Power Analysis Attacks Against FPGA Implementations of the DES. In *FPL 2004*, volume 3203 of *LNCS*, pages 84–94. Springer, 2004.

[28] A. Telikepalli. Is Your FPGA Design Secure? XCell Journal, XILINX, Fall 2003.

[29] C. W. Tseng. Lock Your Designs with the Virtex-4 Security Solution. XCell Journal, XILINX, Spring 2005.

[30] T. J. Wollinger, J. Guajardo, and C. Paar. Security on FPGAs: State-of-the-art implementations and attacks. *ACM Transactions in Embedded Computing Systems (TECS)*, 3(3):534–574, 2004.

[31] XILINX. Virtex-2 Platform FPGA User Guide (UG002 version 2.2). Technical report, November 2007. http://www.xilinx.com/support/documentation/user_guides/ug002.pdf.

[32] XILINX. Virtex-II Pro and Virtex-II Pro X FPGA User Guide. Technical report, 2007. http://www.xilinx.com/support/documentation/user_guides/ug012.pdf.

[33] XILINX. Virtex-II Pro Platform FPGAs: Complete Data Sheet (DS 083 version 4.7). Technical report, November 2007. http://www.xilinx.com/support/documentation/data_sheets/ds083.pdf.

Text-based CAPTCHA Strengths and Weaknesses

Elie Bursztein, Matthieu Martin, and John C. Mitchell
Stanford University
elie@cs.stanford.edu, mamartin@stanford.edu, mitchell@cs.stanford.edu

ABSTRACT

We carry out a systematic study of existing visual CAPTCHAs based on distorted characters that are augmented with anti-segmentation techniques. Applying a systematic evaluation methodology to 15 current CAPTCHA schemes from popular web sites , we find that 13 are vulnerable to automated attacks. Based on this evaluation, we identify a series of recommendations for CAPTCHA designers and attackers, and possible future directions for producing more reliable human/computer distinguishers.

Categories and Subject Descriptors

K.6.5 [**Computing Milieux**]: Management of Computing and Information Systems—*Security and Protection*

General Terms

Security, Theory

Keywords

CAPTCHA, reverse Turing test, machine learning, vision algorithm, SVM, KNN classifier.

1. INTRODUCTION

Many websites use CAPTCHAs [25], or *Completely Automated Public Turing tests to tell Computers and Humans Apart,* in an attempt to block automated interactions with their sites. These efforts may be crucial to the success of these sites in various ways. For example, Gmail improves its service by blocking access to automated spammers, eBay improves its marketplace by blocking bots from flooding the site with scams, and Facebook limits creation of fraudulent profiles used to spam honest users or cheat at games. The most widely used CAPTCHA [1] schemes use combinations of distorted characters and obfuscation techniques that humans can recognize but that may be difficult for automated scripts.

[1]For readability purpose, we will write the acronym in lowercase.

CCS'11, October 17–21, 2011, Chicago, Illinois, USA.

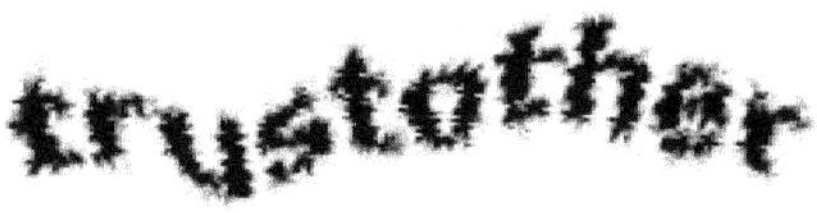

Figure 1: Wikipedia captcha example

Captchas are sometimes called "*reverse Turing tests*": because they are intended to allow a computer to determine if a remote client is human or not. In spite of their importance, their extremely widespread use, and a growing number of research studies [7, 8, 31] there is currently no systematic methodology for designing or evaluating captchas. In fact, as we substantiate by thorough study, many popular websites still rely on schemes that are vulnerable to automated attacks. For example, our automated **Decaptcha** tool breaks the Wikipedia scheme, illustrated in figure 1, approximately *25%* of the time. *13* out of *15* of the most widely used current schemes are similarly vulnerable to automated attack by our tool. Therefore, there is a clear need for a comprehensive set of design and testing principles that will lead to more robust captchas.

While fine previous work [7] suggests that captcha security depends on preventing segmentation, we find in our study that relying on segmentation alone does not provide reliable defense against automated attacks. For example, it is possible to exploit the fact that the captcha length is fixed to make an educated guess where to segment the captcha, even if its anti-segmentation technique can't be broken directly. We found that this type of attacks apply to numerous captcha schemes, including eBay and Baidu.

Reflecting on techniques described in the literature [10, 32], available machine-learning techniques [11, 20, 26] available vision algorithms [1, 13, 14], and our own experience with captcha analysis [2, 4, 5], we divide the automated captcha-solving process into five generic steps: *pre-processing, segmentation, post-segmentation, recognition, and post-processing.* While segmentation, the separation of a sequence of characters into individual characters, and recognition, identifying those characters, are intuitive and generally understood, there are good reasons for considering the additional pre-processing and post-processing steps as part of a standard process. For example, preprocessing can remove background patterns or eliminate other additions to the image that could interfere with segmentation, while post-segmentation steps can "clean up" the segmentation output by normalizing the size of each image or otherwise performing steps distinct from segmentation.

After recognition, post-processing can improve accuracy by, for example, applying spell checking to any captcha that is based on actual words (such as Slashdot). Based on this generic captcha-solving architecture, we experimented with various specific algorithms and tried them on various popular website captchas. From these corpus, we identified a set of techniques that make captchas more difficult to solve automatically. By varying these techniques, we created a larger synthetic corpus that allowed us to study the effect of each of these features in detail and refine our automated attack methods. Based on our previous study of how solvable captchas are for humans [3, 5], we focused our attention on a range of techniques that are within the grasp of human solvers, although we did consider possible captchas that could be uncomfortably difficult for some humans.

We tested the efficiency of our tool Decaptcha against real captchas from *Authorize, Baidu, Blizzard, Captcha.net, CNN, Digg, eBay, Google, Megaupload, NIH, Recaptcha, Reddit, Skyrock, Slashdot, and Wikipedia*. As far as we know none of these captcha schemes had been reported broken prior to this work. Of these 15 captchas, we had *1%-10%* success rate on two (*Baidu, Skyrock*), *10-24%* on two (*CNN, Digg*), *25-49%* on four (*eBay, Reddit, Slashdot, Wikipedia*), and *50%* or greater on five (*Authorize, Blizzard, Captcha.net, Megaupload, NIH*). To achieve such a high success rate we developed the first successful attacks against captcha schemes that use collapsed characters (*eBay, Megaupload, and Baidu*). Only Google and Recaptcha resisted to our attack attempts, and we reached some informative understanding of why we couldn't break them. Because of Decaptcha genericity we were able to break 7 of these 15 schemes (*Authorize, Baidu, CNN, Megaupload, NIH, Reddit, Wikipedia*) without writing a new algorithm.

Based on our evaluation of real-world and synthetic captchas, we extracted several guidelines and suggestions that we believe will be useful to captcha designers and attackers. For example, randomizing the captcha length and individual relative character size, while relatively painless for humans, are important steps for resisting automated attacks. Similarly, if all characters are the same size, partial segmentation then gives a good estimate of the number of characters, again aiding segmentation. Conversely, creating a wave shape and collapsing or overlayed lines can be effective, relatively speaking. We also find that complex character sets, which can be confusing for humans, are not particularly effective, and we comment on the relative importance of anti-recognition techniques, implementation errors, preparing alternative "backup" schemes in case vulnerabilities are discovered. The main contributions of this work include:

- A generic evaluation tool, **Decaptcha**, designed to evaluate quickly captcha security.
- A state-of-the-art evaluation of anti-recognition techniques and anti-segmentation techniques, and captchas used by the popular websites.
- Successful attacks by a single tool against 13 out of 15 real captcha schemes from popular websites and the first successful attacks on captchas that use collapsed characters (e.g eBay and Baidu).
- A publicly available synthetic corpus designed to replicate security features of real-world captchas, in ranges potentially acceptable to humans, so that designers may test new attack algorithms on them.
- A defense taxonomy and an evaluation of the impact of anti-recognition techniques on the learnability of captchas by automated tools.

2. BACKGROUND

Measuring attack effectiveness. A first step to evaluate attack effectiveness is to measure its **accuracy**, the fraction of captchas that were answered correctly by the captcha solver. However, a particular attacker may choose to respond to some captchas and not others, depending on the confidence in their guess, as web services usually limit the number of attempts per IP [2]. Therefore, a more precise way to evaluate attack effectiveness is through coverage and precision metrics.

Coverage is the fraction of captchas that the solver attempts to answer. **Precision** is the fraction of captchas answered correctly [2]. The captcha design goal is that "*automatic scripts should not be more successful than 1 in 10,000*" attempts (i.e. a precision of 0.01%) [18]. However, we believe that this security goal is too ambitious, random guesses can be sucessful, so we *deem a captcha scheme broken when the attacker is able to reach a precision of at least 1%.*

Another important consideration is how to choose the test set on which the solver is evaluated. We argue that cross-validation is useful for initial experimentation but is not sufficient to deem a captcha scheme insecure as it does not reflect real-world conditions where the solver attacking a website is presented with previously unknown captchas. Instead we adopt the machine learning community's best practices. We use a test set that is entirely different from the training set to evaluate the solver's effectiveness. We must avoid skewing the precision evaluation due to a single easy captcha in the test set. This is especially important when the solver's precision is close to 1% mark. Therefore, we advocate to *use a large test set, of at least 1,000 captchas.* Now, the solver must solve at least 10 unseen captchas before reaching the 1% precision mark required to deem a scheme insecure. Every evaluation performed in this work follows these best practices.

Attacking captchas. Prior to this work, state of the art automated solvers used a three-stage approach consisting of **preprocessing**, **segmentation** and **classification** stages [9]. Previous experiments have established that systems combining custom segmentation with machine learning greatly outperform off-the-shelf OCR system at breaking captchas. For example, [2] showed that on the eBay audio captcha, the accuracy of a state of the art speech recognizer does not exceed 1%, whereas a custom classifier can exceed 75%. This three-stage approach works as follow: first, the solver pre-processes the captcha to make it easier to analyze, for instance by removing colors or by applying noise reduction techniques. Next, the solver attempts to segment the captcha into chunks that contain exactly one character, for example by using a clustering algorithm on the image. Finally, a classifier, such as a support vector machine (SVM) or a neural network, is used to recognize which character is contained in each chunk. Accordingly, we will refer to **anti-recognition techniques** to describe the image/text manipulations that aim at preventing the recognition of individual characters and to **anti-segmentation techniques** to describe image/text manipulations that aim at preventing the solver from splitting the captcha into individual characters. We will refer to the **core-features** to describe the captcha's basic design features, including its charset, font, length, whether this length is random, and so forth.

Many experiments [7] and attacks [32] have demonstrated that most captcha schemes are broken if they can be reliably segmented. Accordingly robust text-based schemes must make it difficult for the solver to determine *where* each character is. However, even if anti-segmentation techniques are essential to captcha security, they are only effective when the captcha core features and anti-recognition techniques are properly designed and implemented. Instead of solely focusing on preventing segmentation, we will show in this evaluation section that secure design principles need to be applied at all layers to create a secure scheme to avoid "side-channel attacks". Finally we introduced in [4] a new metric called **Learnability** which evaluates captcha strength based on the number of labeled examples required to train a classifier to a given precision level. Our learnability metric provides insight into how to properly choose anti-recognition techniques and core-features.

3. CORPUS

In this section we present the captcha corpus we used to establish our design principles and breaking techniques. As a starting point we collected and annotated 15 real-world schemes used by popular websites to evaluate Decaptcha performances against top-of-the-line captchas schemes. Decaptcha was able to break 13 of these 15 schemes. We analyzed these captchas to come up with a set of relevant security features that we used to create our synthetic corpus designed to study the effect of each of these features in detail and refine attacking techniques.

3.1 Popular Real World Captchas

To collect a representative sample of captchas, we consulted the Alexa list of most used websites[2] and identified the top sites which presented captchas as part of their account registration process. Additionally, we collected captchas from sites which provide captchas to other sites, e.g. Recaptcha.net and captchas.net. For each website or captcha scheme presented in figure 2, we collected directly from the website, *11,000* captchas that we had labeled by humans via Amazon crowd-sourcing service Mechanical Turk [5]. Decaptcha is able to break all of them except Recaptcha and Google.

3.1.1 Real-world Captcha Security Features

As visible in figure 2, real-world captchas exhibit a lot of variation in their design. By analyzing how each scheme is constructed we grouped the security defenses used in these schemes into the following ten techniques. Following the taxonomy presented in section 2, these techniques were assigned into the anti-recognition or the anti-segmentation category. We assigned to the anti-recognition category every feature that didn't directly prevent segmentation.

The anti-recognition techniques considered are: 1. **Multi-fonts** Using multiple fonts or font-faces. 2. **Charset** Which charset the scheme uses. 3. **Font size** Using variable font size. 4. **Distortion** Distorting the captcha globally using attractor fields. 5. **Blurring** Blurring letters. 6. **Tilting** Rotating characters with various angles. 7. **Waving** Rotating the characters in a wave fashion.

The anti-segmentation techniques considered are: 1. **Complex background** Try to hide the text in a complex background to "confuse" the solver. 2. **Lines** Add extra lines to prevent the solver from knowing what are the real character segments. 3. **Collapsing** Remove the space between characters to prevent segmentation.

[2]http://www.alexa.com/topsites

Scheme	Range from [5]	Generated
Authorize	95 – 98	92
Baidu	90 – 93	90
Blizzard	89 – 95	91
Ebay	93 – 93	94
Recaptcha	72 – 75	93

Table 1: Optimistic solving accuracy across schemes, comparing real world captchas to generated versions

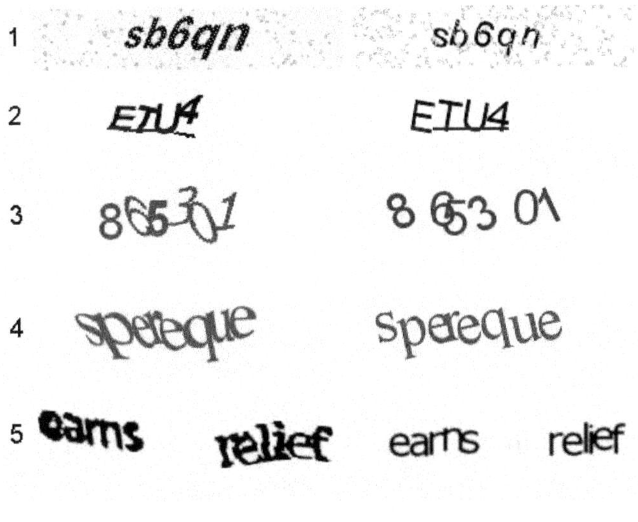

Figure 3: Real world captchas and our generated versions (generated on the left, real on the right) Captcha schemes depicted 1:Authorize, 2:Baidu, 3:eBay, 4:Google, 5:Recaptcha

3.2 Synthetic corpus

To generate our synthetic corpus we created a captcha generator. Using Mechnical turk we experimentally validated that our captcha generator is able to replicate real-world captchas. Synthetic captchas created by our generator have a similar accuracy to real world-captcha. Each generated captcha, (Figure 3), was annotated *1000* time by human using Mechanical Turk. We then measured the overall accuracy of each scheme, and compared these results to the scheme-level accuracies reported in [5]. While solving accuracy can be measured exactly for our fake captchas, the real ones used in our previous work were scraped from the web, and accordingly their true solutions were not known. So we can only compare our result to the *optimistic solving accuracy* metric we used previously. The table 1 shows for each scheme the optimistic solving accuracies reported in [5] (one for Mechanical Turk and one for an underground service) and the solving accuracy we measured on our generated captchas. As shown in table 1, the solving accuracy for our fake captchas are similar to the one observed on real world captchas except for Recaptcha. This experiment support the hypothesis that our taxonomy and its implementation are able to accurately replicate real world designs.

4. ATTACKING RECOGNITION

In this section we discuss how to represent a captcha so it is easy to process by machine learning algorithms. We motivate our algorithmic choices and evaluate their effectiveness on various anti-recognitions features. Based on the performance of the different machine learning algorithms, we can compare and recommend anti-recognition techniques.

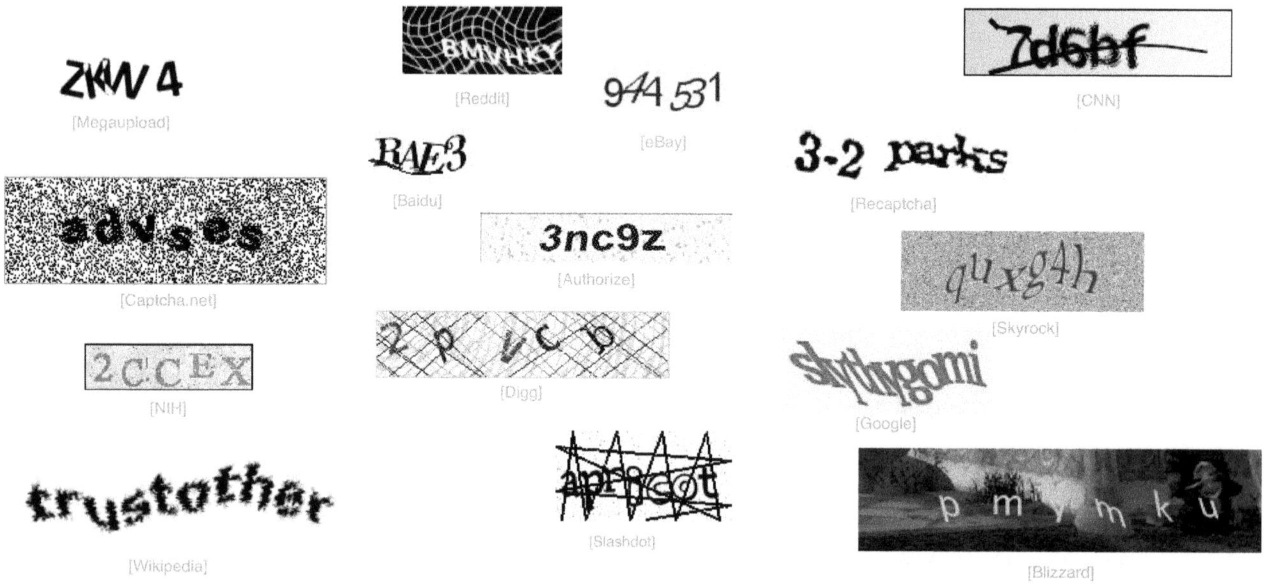

Figure 2: Samples of the 15 popular real world captcha schemes analyzed during our evaluation

4.1 Captcha representation recommendations

Character recognition is a core problem in machine learning. In the context of captchas prehaps the most relevant work produced by the machine learning community is on the MNIST database of handwritten digits challenge [21] which aims to recognize (distorted) handwritten digits. From this body of work, the most useful article for captcha security research is [20] which provide a deep analysis on how to efficiently recognize digits.

Based on this work and confirmed by our experimentations with Decaptcha on multiples schemes, we recommend:

- **Binarize letters**: While keeping letters in gray scale is useful for certain image algorithms, classifiers work better and faster on binary features so binarizing the letters in black and white is recommended. For example our custom distance algorithm is 35% faster on binary vectors than integer (gray scale/color) vectors.

- **Work at the pixel level**: The most efficient way to represent letter is to use a matrix that encodes their pixel representation. Using "receptors" as, sometime recommended while doing standard OCR, is not efficient in our case because of the distortion, rotations and other captcha deformations.

When the captchas can't be segmented and we have to recognize the letters without segmentation, an alternative promising approach. would be to use very high level and complex image descriptors, such as SURF [1] and SIFT [23], that are invariant to rotation and very stable against distortion. In theory describing letters with robust "interest points" will make the approach faster and more stable. A huge hurdle for using this kind of descriptors to break captchas is the fact that the number of points that describe each letter can't be normalized, which prevents the use of the classifiers that are so efficient at recognizing characters when combined with the standard approach.

4.2 Recommended Classifiers

In terms of accuracy, the choice of classifier does not matter greatly because many modern classifiers perform strikingly well (i.e. 97% - 99.5%) on the MNIST dataset. Recall that to deem a scheme insecure our system only needs to reach 1% precision. In practice, small differences in classifier accuracy never substantially changed system performance. Accordingly instead of using the classifier that have the best accuracy we choose to evaluate the classifiers that are the easiest to use. Specifically, we focused on classifiers that are fast to train and require minimal parameter tuning.

We argue that having a classifier that is easy to parameterize and which is fast is the best choice for captcha security evaluation because most of the work is done before the recognition phase, so this phase should be as stable and as fast as possible. Waiting a couple of hours or even 15 minutes to see if a modification in the pipeline had an impact on the breaker performance would make the evaluation a very tedious process. We choose to **use SVM** [11] (Support Vector Machines) because this class of classifiers has become the de-facto classifier over the last few years and is known to almost always yield very good performance regardless of the problem. We choose to use a linear kernel rather than a polynomial kernel which would have achieved better performance because a linear kernel is an order of magnitude faster to train and does not require any parameter tweaking. We also recommend **using KNN** [12] (K Nearest Neighbors) classifier because it is the fastest classifier and it has nice stability properties that make it very reliable. The relative simplicity of the KNN allowed us to write our own version which was optimized to work on our binary vectors and with our sliding windows algorithm.

KNN requires more configuration than SVM as the number of neighbors (K) needs to be selected. To remove the burden of setting it by hand, we rely on a heuristic that computes the optimal K value, which is often 1, by performing a cross validation on the training set to find the optimal maximal K value. Because this heuristic requires quadratic time in the number of vectors in the dataset, we use the random sampling method when the vector set is too big (> 300). On our desktop computers, our KNN algorithm takes 20 seconds to learn a data set of 500 captchas and 2 minutes to classify 1,000 captchas. Because of its speed, KNN is our algorithm of choice when evaluating real world captcha schemes.

4.3 Anti-recognition features evaluation

Before evaluating real-world captchas, we wanted to compare the effectiveness of the anti-segmentation features in isolation to understand their impact on the classifier performance. Effectiveness here is quantified by the scheme learnability and the classifier success rate. To compute these numbers we repeatedly trained our classifier varying the size of the training set from 10 to 500 examples. Each testing phase was done on 1,000 captchas coming from a different set. The SVM results are summarized in the chart 4(a) and the KNN results are summarized in the chart 4(b).

The first observation we can make about these results is the fact that they support our claims that any reasonable classifier is "good enough" to build a captcha breaker. Overall, the SVM and the KNN classifiers both achieve very good results and exhibit a very similar learning rate. The only two major differences is that SVM does better on distortion (61% vs 50%) and KNN performs better with the mix of five complex fonts (62% vs 59%). As predicted by the theory, the KNN results are also more stable than the SVM ones, but as visible in the charts, the SVM accuracy jittering is minimal (at most 5%) and is unlikely to affect the outcome of a security evaluation.

Recommendation. The results of our evaluation lead us to the following recommendations regarding anti-segmentation features.

- **Use a small non-confusable charset**: While using a larger charset slightly impacts the classifier accuracy and decreases the scheme's learnability, the security gain is too small to be useful: forcing the attacker to learn on 40 captchas instead of 10 reduces the accuracy from 100% to 92% which negligible compared to the loss in human accuracy (98% for 0-9 down to 82% for azAZ09 [3]). Accordingly, since increasing the charset does not offer a significant security gain, a captcha charset should be small, with no caps at the very least, and should not contain confusing letters (e.g. i-j) to make it easy for humans to solve.

- **Don't use distortion**: Applying a distortion is the most effective way for reducing classifier accuracy and decreasing scheme learnability. However, this is not sufficient to prevent a classifier from being effective - this should be avoided and replaced with a proper anti-segmentation technique as distortion also harms user accuracy significantly [3].

- **Use rotation only in conjunction with anti-segmentation**: Rotating characters by itself doesn't significantly impede classifier accuracy and learnability; accordingly, their sole use is in conjunction with anti-segmentation techniques to make the size of each character unpredictable (See section 5.3).

  It is interesting to note here that we ran an additional experiment, in which we tried to learn on straight characters and tried to classify examples from this dataset. As predicted by the theory, SVM and KNN can't recognize rotated characters if they don't learn on them. Having classifiers insensitive to rotation is one of the main rationales behind the creation and use of more complex classifiers such as CNN (Convolutional Neural Networks) [20].

- **Use multiple fonts**: Using multiple fonts is an effective principle as it decreases significantly the classifier accuracy and will render the segmentation more difficult by making the size of characters unpredictable.

5. SEGMENTATION

As seen in the previous section 4, while carefully chosen anti-recognition techniques help slow down the learning process and reduce classifier accuracy, they are not sufficient by themselves. In this section we analyze the effectiveness of the 7 anti-segmentation techniques we found in the wild on real captchas schemes and show their limitations. Note that we made the choice to focus on attacking techniques that are as generic as possible rather that technique optimized to break a specific captcha scheme. This choice make the techniques described below applicable to other schemes (we were able to break 13 schemes with the 7 techniques described below) at the expense of a couple of accuracy points. Based on the following analysis, we provide recommendations on which technique to use and how to implement them.

5.1 Background Confusion

Under the term **background confusion** we regroup all the techniques that try to prevent segmentation by "blending" the captcha text with the background. There are three main ways to achieve this: using a complex image background (figure 5), having a background that has "very" similar colors to the text (figure 6) and adding noise to the captcha (figure 7).

Some captchas schemes combine multiples background confusion techniques. However instead of increasing the security, combining background confusion techniques often lead to decrease it as it makes the scheme susceptible to more attacks. This is for example the case for Authorize (figure 8) which combines color similarity and noise: using gray noises make it susceptible to de-noising and anti-color attacks.

Complex background. The idea behind using a complex background is that the lines/shapes "inside it" will be confused with the real text and thus will prevent the breaker from isolating and segmenting the captcha. Eventhough previous works [31] have demonstrated that usually this type of defense is insecure, many captchas still rely on it. One of the most prominent examples of captcha using this type of defense is the one (figure 5) that Blizzard uses for all their websites (World of Warcraft, Starcraft II and Battle.net) . While they are using random backgrounds generated from game screenshots to prevent breakers from learning its shape they still have to make letters "stand out" from the background so that humans can decipher the captcha. We found out that that the easiest way to deal with captcha schemes that use random backgrounds but a finite number of colors is to use a technique that we call *anti-pattern*: for all the possible font colors remove everything from the captcha that is not close to this color and test if you get a reasonable number of clusters (letters) with the right amount of pixels. As visible in figure 5, this is very effective against Blizzard captchas and Decaptcha solves 70% on them.

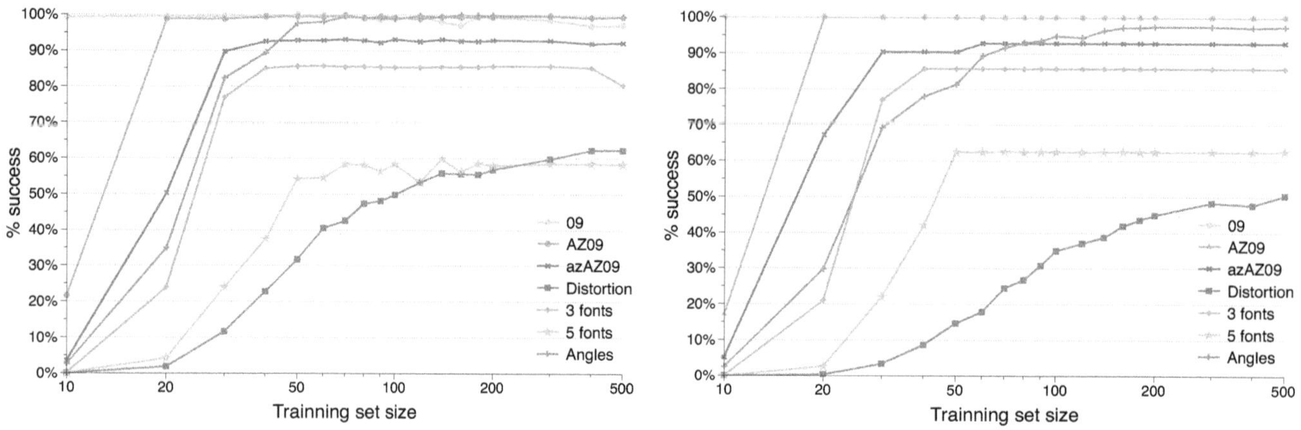

(a) SVM classifier

(b) KNN classifier

Figure 4: Effectiveness of classifiers on various anti-recognition features. These graphs depict how fast each classifier precision improves as more examples are added to the training set.

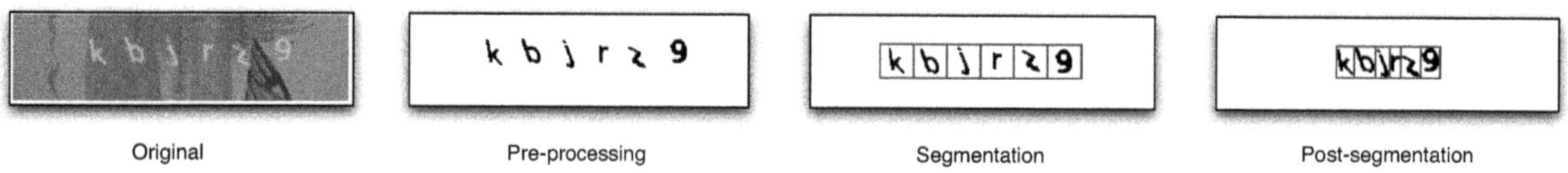

Figure 5: Example of the Blizzard pipeline

Color similarity. A related approach to the complex background techniques is to use colors that are perceived as very different by humans but are in reality very close in the RGB spectrum. The best and most sophisticated example of captcha scheme that uses this kind of technique is the Skyrock scheme visible in figure 6. While the letters appear very distinct to the human eye, when represented on the RGB spectrum they are so close that it is almost impossible to use the CFS [32] or the Anti-pattern techniques on it. However, as visible in figure 6, an effective way to counter this defense is to have the breaker work on a different color representation that is closer to the human perception, namely the HSV or HSL [29] ones, and *binarize* the captcha by using a threshold based on the hue or the saturation. For Skyrock we use a threshold based on the hue value. Changing the color space representation allows Decaptcha to get 2% precision on Skyrock.

Noise. The last and "most efficient" technique used to confuse the segmentation is to add random noise to the image. For example, this technique is used in Captcha.net as visible in figure 7. Note that the noise must have the same color as the text because otherwise the anti-pattern technique can be applied to remove it. To de-noise captchas many techniques have been proposed over the years, including using the standard image filter *erode* [30]. However it turns out that using a MRF (Markov Random Field) aka Gibbs algorithm [14] is far more effective. A Gibbs de-noising algorithm is an iterative algorithm that works by computing the energy of each pixel based on its surroundings and removing pixels that have an energy below a certain threshold. The algorithm completes when there are no more pixels to remove. The energy of a given pixel is computed by summing the values on a gray scale of its 8 surrounding pixels and dividing by 8. As visible in figure 7 this algorithm completely negates the Captcha.net anti-segmentation defense and, accordingly, decaptcha is able to achieve 73% precision on Captcha.net.

For Authorize, which also use noise, Decaptcha also achieves 66% precision. As we will see in the next section using the Gibbs algorithm is also the best approach when the lines are smaller that the characters.

Recommendation. Overall, we believe that using any background confusion technique as a security mechanism is **not secure** and we recommend not relying on these kinds of techniques. While it is true that certain complex backgrounds are harder than others to remove, with sufficient effort and custom pre-processing, it is likely than any of these backgrounds can be processed. Accordingly, we recommend using background **only for cosmetic purposes**.

5.2 Using lines

A second approach to prevent segmentation is to use line(s) that cross multiple characters. This approach is used by Digg (figure 9) and Slashdot (figure 10) for instance. While it is possible to use lines that do not cross multiples characters , like the old Microsoft captcha, it has been proven to be a totally insecure approach [32] and is, therefore, not discussed here. In the wild we saw two types of lines used to prevent segmentation: *small lines* that cross the captcha's letters (e.g. Digg) and *large lines* of the width as the characters' lines that cross entire captchas (e.g. Slashdot and CNN).

Small lines. The first approach is to use small lines that will prevent the captcha from being segmented. This is the strategy used by Digg (figure 9). The standard approach to deal with small lines is to use a histogram-based segmentation [17, 31] that projects the captcha pixels to the X or Y coordinates.

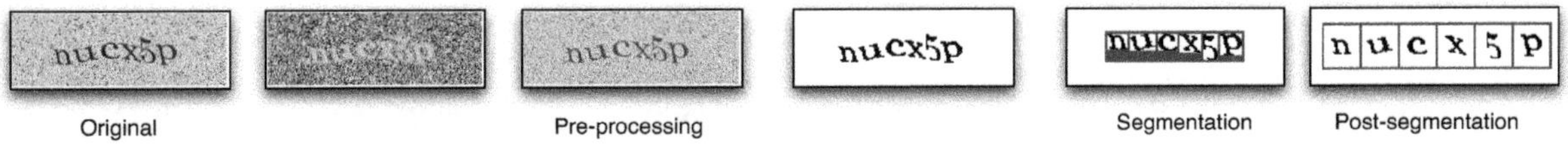

Figure 6: Example of the Skyrock pipeline

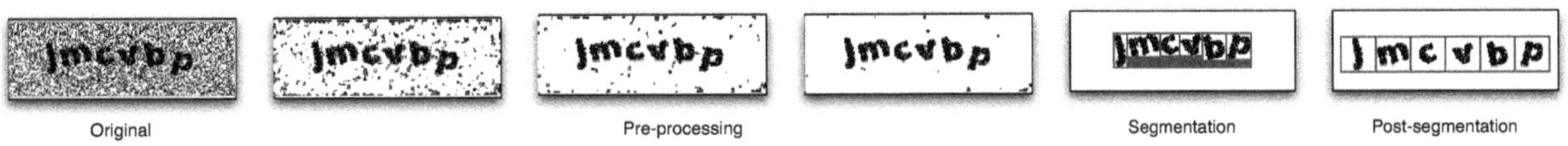

Figure 7: Example of the Captcha.net pipeline

This approach "works" because the region where the characters are is denser and therefore will create peaks in the histogram. The problem with this approach is how to determine the threshold and the size of the windows around it. It turns out that binarizing the captcha and then using a Gibbs de-noising algorithm with character reconstruction (see figure 9) is actually more efficient as it does not require such a brittle and complex tuning. Using Gibbs Decaptcha is able to achieve 86% recall and 20% precision on Digg captchas.

Big lines. The second approach is to use lines that have the same "width" as the character segments. The main advantage of this approach is that it is not susceptible to de-noising algorithms. However, it is susceptible to line-finding algorithms, such as the Canny edge detection [6] and the Hough Transform [13], because the lines cross the entire captcha. An illustration of our own implementation of the Hough Transform that preserves letters is visible in figure 10. As one can see, our implementation is able to find all the lines very accurately. The difficulty lies in the removal process that must preserve the letters. To do this, before removing a pixel we look at its surroundings to decide whether or not to remove it. The main reason behind Decaptcha's relatively low precision (35% precision) on Slashdot is the fact that Slashdot fonts have hollow characters that end up oftentimes damaged beyond repair when the lines are removed.

Recommendation. Based on our evaluation of captcha schemes we believe that using lines is a secure anti-segmentation defense when properly implemented. Overall, the goal of these principles is to prevent the attacker from finding a discriminator that will allow him to to tell apart character segments and lines. We recommend that in addition to the general security principles discussed in section 6, designers follow the following design principles when implementing this defense:

- **Use large lines:** Using lines that are not as wide as the character segments gives an attacker a robust discriminator and makes the line anti-segmentation technique vulnerable to many attack techniques including de-noising, projection-based segmentation and, in some rare cases, even the simple erode filter.

- **Keep the line within the captchas:** Line finding algorithms, such as the Hough transform, are very efficient at finding lines so for a defense mechanism to be effective, lines must cross only some of the captcha letters, so that it is impossible to tell whether it is a line or a character segment.

- **Don't use a strange slope:** Keep the angle of the line on par with the character segments otherwise the line slope will be used as a discriminator by the attacker. When using lines as anti-segmentation waving the captcha and tilting the characters will help ensure that it is hard for the attacker to distinguish between the lines and the character segments.

- **Match slopes:** The slope of the anti-segmentation lines must be roughly equivalent to the slope of a subset of the character segments. Otherwise when projecting in a Hough space the anti-segmentation lines will appear as outliners that are easily spotted.

- **Match color:** Anti-segmentation lines must be in the same color as the characters.

- **Randomize the length:** Make sure that the length of the line is variable to prevent the attacker from using its size as a discriminator.

5.3 Collapsing

Collapsing is considered by far to be the most secure anti-segmentation technique. While this is generally true, in practice the security of collapsing is often impeded by design flaws at the core feature level or at the anti-recognition level. That is why we distinguish two cases: one where the attacker can exploit a design flaw to predict the characters' segmentation despite the collapsing and the case where there is no flaw and the attacker is forced to "brute force" the captcha.

Predictable collapsing. Having the characters collapsed either by removing the space between characters ala Recaptcha or tilting them sufficiently ala eBay (figure 11) is insufficient to prevent the segmentation because the attacker can still guess where the cuts are likely to occur if the width of the letters is too regular and/or the number of letters is known in advance. As visible in figure 11 this is the case for eBay - we can't figure out where to cut but we know that there are 6 digits in their captchas and because the letter width is roughly always the same, we can make an educated guess and segment with reasonable success. We call this technique the **opportunistic segmentation** because it relies on"side channel information" to work. Overall, this segmentation works, as visible in figure 11, by first applying the standard CFS segmentation and then, based on the size of each segmented block, deciding how many characters each block contains using the fact that we either know the length of the captcha or the average size of the letters. Using this technique Decaptcha is able to achieve 43% precision on eBay captchas.

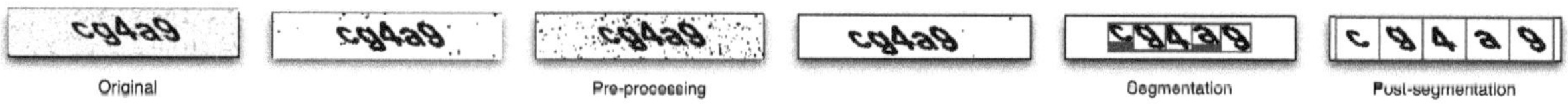

Figure 8: Example of the Authorize pipeline

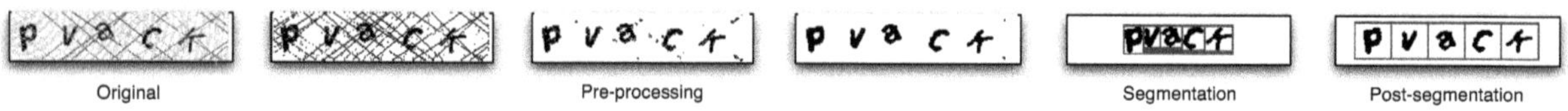

Figure 9: Example of the Digg pipeline using Gibbs

Figure 10: Example of the Slashdot pipeline

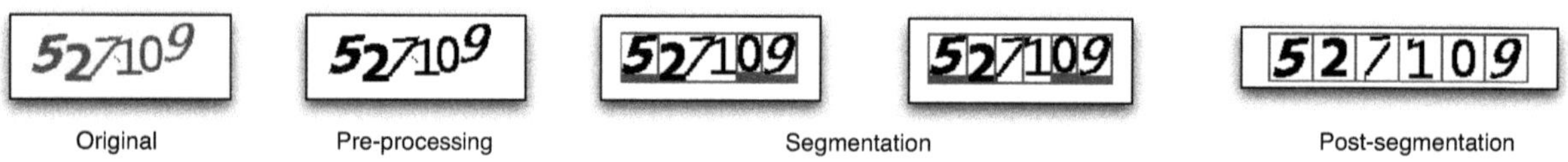

Figure 11: Example of the eBay pipeline

Figure 12: Example of the Baidu pipeline

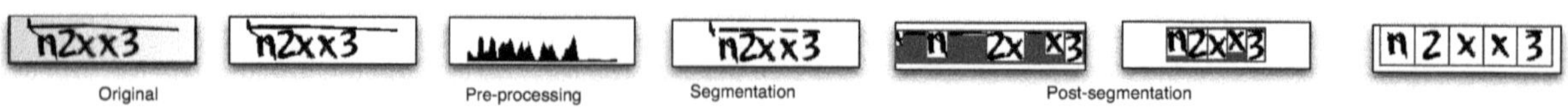

Figure 13: Example of the CNN pipeline

Even if it seems at first sight that randomizing either the size of the letters or the length would be sufficient to prevent this kind of attack, this is not the case. Take Baidu (figure 12) for example. Even if Baidu performs heavy tilting and uses lines to prevent the attacker from guessing where to cut, knowing that the captcha has a length of 4 and using a projection based segmentation to get rid of the trailing lines allows Decaptcha to have a *5%* precision on Baidu captchas. It works better on CNN (figure 13) where we get *50%* recall and *16%* accuracy.

Unpredictable collapsing. When the number of characters is unknown and the average size of each character is unpredictable as in the Google captcha case, then the only option is to try to recognize each letter of the captcha directly without segmenting it. This kind of approach is fairly common and one solution might be to train on character templates segmented by hand and then use a space displacement neural network [24] to recognize the characters without segmenting first.

Recommendation. We recommend to **use collapsing as the main anti-segmentation technique**. Provided that all the other aspects of the captcha are properly designed, this anti-segmentation technique provides an efficient defense against segmentation. It is also advised to not use too aggressive collapsing, as after a certain threshold (-5px) the human accuracy drops drastically [3].

6. DESIGN PRINCIPLES FOR CREATING A SECURE CAPTCHA

In this section we briefly summarize our results, on both our synthetic corpus and on real-world captchas, to provide a comprehensive assessment of the state of the art. We then provide general principles for how to design secure captchas based on the lessons learned while doing this massive evaluation. We finish by discussing future research directions that are likely to change the current state of the art sooner or later.

6.1 Real World Captchas Evaluation Summary

Table 2 summarizes Decaptcha recall and precision on the *15* real-world schemes that we use as the basis of evaluation during the course of this work. For all the results provided in this table, we followed our recommended best practices and tested Decaptcha on 1,000 testing examples that were never used during the exploration or training phase. We only report in this table the precision achieved by KNN on 500 examples as SVM achieved very similar results. Our results also support our proposal to use the 1% precision mark to deem a scheme broken as we either clearly break a scheme or we don't, but we are never in the range of the 0.5% success rate. This evaluation also supports our claim (Section 4) that the best classifiers to evaluate image captcha security are those which are the simplest to configure and fastest to run, as recognition was never the bottleneck. Another thing we learned from this evaluation is that the design flaws introduced at the core feature and anti-recognition levels make a huge difference in the captcha scheme's overall security, regardless of the anti-segmentation technique(s) used. For example, because Slashdot used words we were able to bump Decaptcha accuracy from *24%* to *35%* by loosening the segmentation process and relying heavily on the spellchecking process. Similarly, we wouldn't have been able to achieve *43%* precision on eBay captchas without exploiting the fact that they are using a fixed number of digits and a very regular font width.

Overall, while we were able to break every scheme except Google and Recaptcha to a certain extent, it is clear that some schemes were more broken than others. When compared to the anti-segmentation technique used it is clear that relying on lines or collapsing is more secure than relying on a confusion background.

The figure 14 depicts the learning rate of Decaptcha against the various real-world schemes. The first observation we can make is that with 100 captchas we are already able to know if the scheme is broken or not. The second thing that we can notice is that the anti-segmentation techniques affect the learning rate: when these curves are compared to the earlier ones that focused on anti-recognition techniques only (Figures 4(a), 4(b)) it is apparent that the learning rate is slower when anti-recognition techniques are solely used. The shape of the real world scheme learning curves are very similar to the shape of the distortion technique curve which also tampers with letters integrity.

Scheme	Recall	Precision	Anti-segmentation
Authorize	84%	66%	background confusion
Baidu	98%	5%	collapsing
Blizzard	75%	70%	background confusion
Captcha.net	96%	73%	background confusion
CNN	50%	16%	line
Digg	86%	20%	line
eBay	95%	43%	collapsing
Google	0%	0%	collapsing
Megaupload	n/a	93%	collapsing
NIH	87%	72%	background confusion
Recaptcha	0%	0%	collapsing
Reddit	71%	42%	background confusion
Skyrock	30%	2%	background confusion
Slashdot	52%	35%	lines
Wikipedia	57%	25%	n/a

Table 2: Real world captchas summary

6.2 Design principles

Based on our evaluation results and experimentation with Decaptcha , we derived the following core set of design principles that captcha designers need to follow to create schemes resilient to state of the art attackers. Overall, captcha scheme security comes from having a sound and coherent design at the core design, anti-recognition and anti-segmentation levels. Anti-segmentation techniques are only effective if the anti-recognition techniques and core design are sound. For example, using collapsing is only effective if the size and the number of characters are random. Failling to randomize either of these leaves the scheme vulnerable to an opportunistic segmentation such as in the eBay scheme. The Google scheme that implements all the design principles proposed in this section remains unbroken even-though it is in use for more than 4 years.

Core feature principles. The following principles apply to the design of the captcha core features:

1. **Randomize the captcha length**: Don't use a fixed length, it gives too much information to the attacker.

2. **Randomize the character size**: Make sure the attacker can't make educated guesses by using several font sizes / several fonts. As reported in section 4, using several fonts reduces the classifier accuracy and the scheme's learnability.

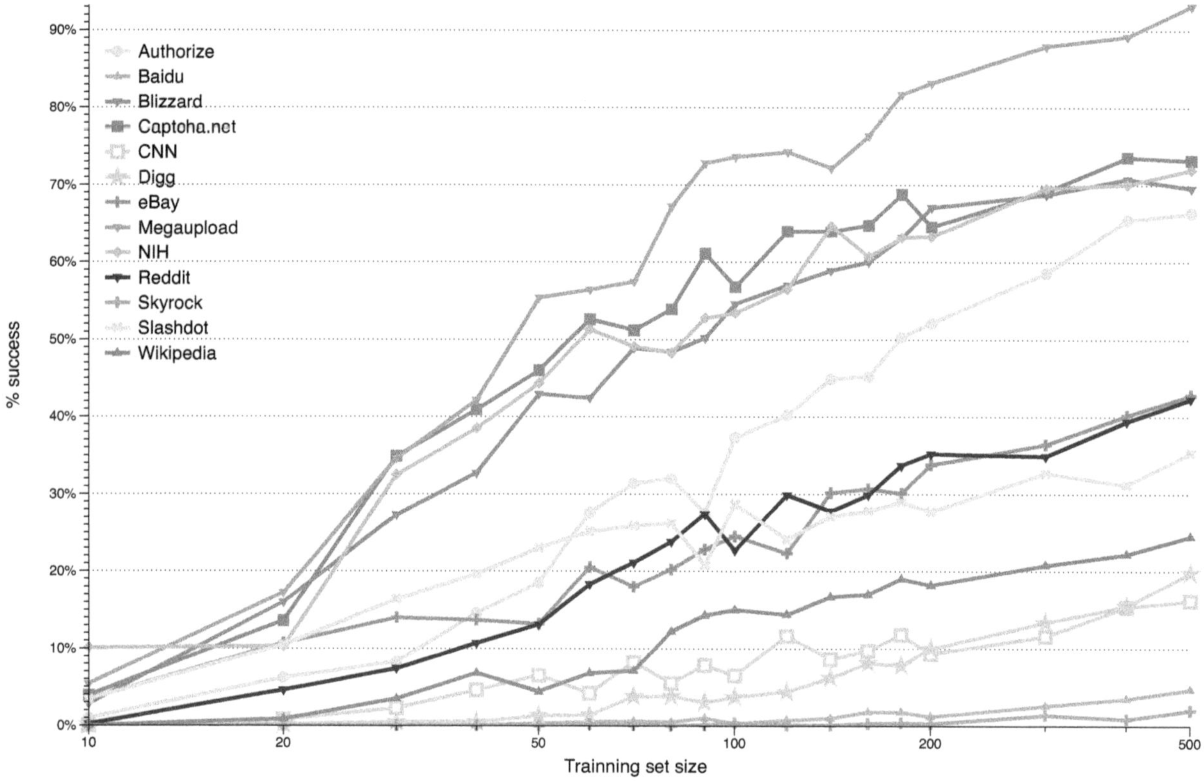

Figure 14: Real schemes learnability: Accuracy of Decaptcha using KNN vs the size of the training set. Logarithmic scale

3. **Wave the captcha**: Waving the captcha increases the difficulty of finding cut points in case of collapsing and helps mitigate the risk of the attacker finding the added line based on its slope when using lines.

Anti-recognition.

1. **Use anti-recognition techniques as a means of strengthening captcha security**: Don't rely on anti-recognition techniques to protect your scheme, use them to strengthen the overall captcha scheme security. Because most classifier efficiency is sensitive to rotation, scaling and rotating some characters and using various font sizes will reduce the recognition efficiency and increase the anti-segmentation security by making character width less predictable.

2. **Don't use a complex charset**: Using a large charset does not improve significantly the captcha scheme's security and really hurts human accuracy, thus using a non-confusable charset is the best option.

Anti-Segmentation.

1. **Use collapsing or lines**: Given the current state of the art, using any sort of complex background as an anti-segmentation technique is considered to be insecure. Using lines or collapsing correctly are the only two secure options currently. Complex background can be used as a second line of defense (e.g. the ellipses used in some Recaptcha's captchas).

2. **Be careful while implementing**: To be effective, anti-segmentation techniques must be implemented very carefully. When using lines, follow all the recommendations provided in section 5.2 and when implementing collapsing, make sure to follow the recommendations provided in section 5.3.

3. **Create alternative schemes**: As with cryptography algorithms, it is good practice to have alternative captcha schemes that can be rolled out in case of a break. Variations of the same battle-hardened schemes with additional security features is likely the easiest way to prepare alternative schemes. This seems to be the strategy of Recaptcha, which has alternative schemes that surface from time to time.

7. DECAPTCHA

In this section we present our captcha breaker, *Decaptcha*, which is able to break many popular captchas including eBay, Wikipedia and Digg. Then we discuss the rationale behind its five stage pipeline, its benefits, and its drawbacks, and conclude by deriving principles on how do build a successful solver.

Decaptcha implements a refined version of the three stage approach in 15,000 lines of code in C#. We chose C# because it offers a good tradeoff between speed, safety, robustness and the availability of AI/Vision libraries. We also chose C# because of the visual studio interface builder quality, as evaluating captcha security efficiently requires designing a fairly complex UI for debugging and tweaking purposes. Decaptcha uses the aForge framework [19] and the Accord framework that provide easy access to image manipulation filters, and standard machine learning algorithms such as SVM [11].

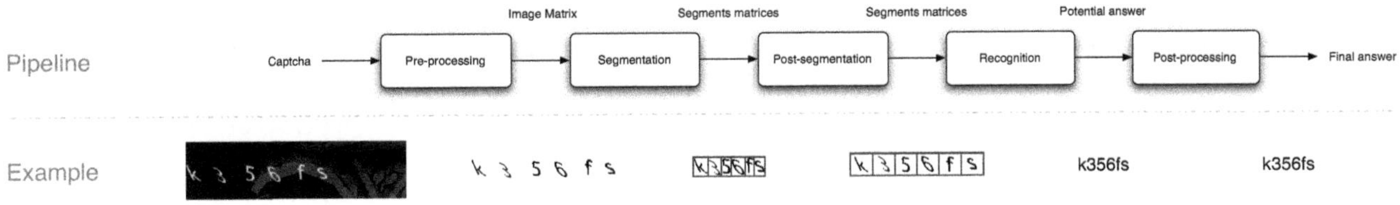

Figure 15: Decaptcha pipeline

Overall, although we tried to use existing libraries as much as possible we ended up writing roughly 80% of Decaptcha code, which took us at least a year of development. For example, we rewrote a KNN algorithm [12] because we needed a confidence metric and we rewrote various distance algorithms to maximize the speed on binary vectors. Note that Decaptcha in its current version is able to work on audio and image captchas.

7.1 Decaptcha pipeline

Decaptcha uses the five stage pipeline illustrated in figure 15. These stages are:

1. **Preprocessing**: In this first stage, the captcha's background is removed using several algorithms and the captcha is binarized (represented in black and white) and stored in a matrix of binary values. Transforming the captcha into a binary matrix makes the rest of the pipeline easier to implement, as the remaining algorithm works on a well-defined abstract object. The downside of using a binary representation is that we lose the pixel intensity. However in practice this was never an issue.

2. **Segmentation**: In this stage Decaptcha attempts to segment the captchas using various segmentation techniques, the most common being **CFS [32] (Color Filling Segmentation)** which uses a paint bucket flood filling algorithm [28]. This is the default segmentation technique because it allows us to segment the captcha letters even if they are tilted, as long as they are not contiguous.

3. **Post-Segmentation**: At this stage the segments are processed individually to make the recognition easier. During this phase the segments' sizes are always normalized.

4. **Recognition**: In training mode, this stage is used to teach the classifier what each letter looks like after the captcha has been segmented. In testing mode, the classifier is used in predictive mode to recognize each character.

5. **Post-processing**: During this stage the classifier's output is improved when possible. For example, spell checking is performed on the classifier's output for Slashdot because we know that this captcha scheme uses dictionary words. Using spellchecking allows us to increase our precision on Slashdot from 24% to 35%.

7.2 Design principles to write a captcha solver

Before writing the full blown version of Decaptcha in C#, we wrote a prototype in Ruby two years ago. Building this prototype allowed us to learn a couple of key principles that need to be applied to create a sucessful evaluation framework.

Here is the list of the four main design principles specific to captcha breaking that made the current Decaptcha implementation (Figure 16) an effective attack framework:

1. **Aiming for generality**: Decaptcha development was focused on algorithm generality and simplicity rather than accuracy optimization. We made this choice very early as we believed that on the long run it will yield better results. The fact that we were able to break the last three schemes evaluated in this paper, namely CNN, Megaupload and Reddit, in less than 3 hours without writing a new algorithm support this hypothesis. Overall we believe that this focus on generality and simplicity is what makes Decaptcha truly different from the previous add-hoc designed to break a single scheme.

2. **Immediate visual feedback**: When trying to break a captcha scheme most of the time is spend on trying and tweaking various algorithms, so it is essential to have quick feedback on how the change affected the attack's performance. We discovered that it is far more effective to provide this feedback in a pie chart form with a defined color code than use a table with raw numbers. As visible in figure 16 in Decaptcha the pie chart is in the center of the interface, which allows us to immediately see how efficient the current pipeline is. For example, in the screenshot it is very easy to see that in this tryout we have an overall *success of 66% (green)* on Blizzard captchas, that 5% of the failures occur at the *recognition stage (yellow)*, *18%* - at the *segmentation stage (orange)* and *11%* - at the *pre-processing stage (red)*.

3. **Visual debugging**: Similarly, we discovered that the only way to understand quickly how an algorithm is behaving is to look at how it affects and interacts with the captchas. That is why the ability to view the visual pipeline for a given captcha sample with a simple click is essential. In Decaptcha we implemented this principle by allowing the user to display a given captcha pipeline stage on the right side of the interface by clicking on a captcha from the list located in the middle of the interface. For example, in the example of figure 16, we selected a captcha that failed the segmentation stage and the fact that the failure occurs at the segmentation is clear by looking at the pipeline states. It also makes it very easy to understand that this segmentation failure is due to an error of our anti-pattern algorithm, which removed most of the background pattern except a few pixels at the bottom right, due to the similarity of their color to the text color.

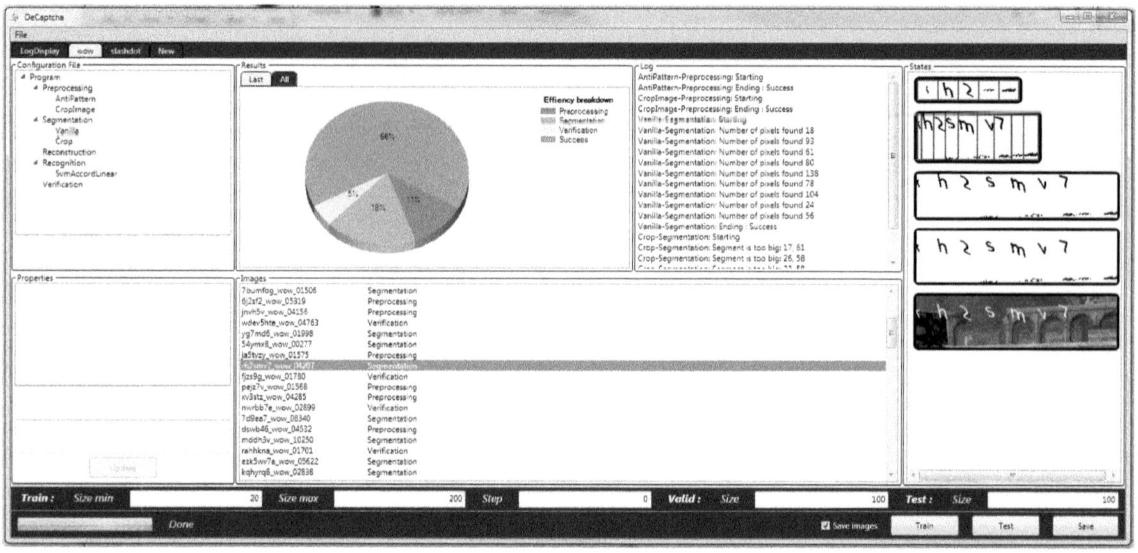

Figure 16: Decaptcha interface

4. **Algorithm independence**: Finding the optimal set of algorithms to break a given scheme is not trivial and often we ended up swapping one algorithm for another either because we found a better-performing algorithm or because we changed the approach. For example, for de-noising a captcha we moved from using an anti-pattern algorithm to a Markov Random Field algorithm [14]. Being able to combine algorithms as "lego bricks" without worrying about side effects is one of the keys to Decaptcha 's success. Having a flexible pipeline is achieved by abstracting the image representation as a matrix and ensuring that every algorithm has no side effects. This design also allows us to parallelize pipeline executions which is important because image processing and machine learning algorithms are usually slow. The algorithm independence principle is also what allows Decaptcha to work on image and audio captchas indistinctly.

5. **Exposing algorithm attributes**: Being able to change algorithm parameters such as a threshold without editing and recompiling the code makes a huge difference. Oftentimes, by tweaking parameters we were able to gain up to 40% in accuracy or segmentation efficiency. We tried to find a way to automatically optimize parameters but it turned out that modifying the parameters in one algorithm in isolation is not effective, as changing the behavior of one algorithm often requires re-adjusting parameters of algorithms used later in the pipeline. For example, being more aggressive when de-noising will force us to be more aggressive when reconstructing the captcha's characters afterward.

8. FURTHER RELEVANT WORK

In this section we summarize the related work cited in the paper and discuss further relevant work.

Captcha. In [10] the authors propose using machine learning classifiers to attacks captchas. In [7] the same authors study how efficient statistical classifier are at recognizing captcha letters. In [5] the authors study how good humans are at solving well-known captchas using Mechanical Turk.

In [15] the authors were able to break the Microsoft ASIRRA captcha using SVM. In [32] the authors were able to break the old Microsoft captcha using the two phase approach. In [30] the author proposes using the erode and dilate filter to segment captchas. [31] is one of the first papers to propose the use of histogram-based segmentation against captchas.

Recognition algorithm. The perceptron, the simplest neural network, has been used as a linear classifier since 1957 [27]. The convolutive neural networks which are considered to be the most efficient neural network to recognize letters were introduced in [20]. The space displacement neural network that attempts to recognize digits without segmentation was introduced in [24]. The support vector machines were introduced in [11]. The KNN algorithm is described in detail in [12]. The use of a bag of features to recognize objects in images is a very active field. The closest work to ours in this area is by [22], where the authors try to segment and categorize objects using this approach.

Machine vision algorithms. Detecting and removing lines is a well studied field in computer vision since the '70s. Two well-known and efficient algorithms that can be used against captchas with lines are the Canny detection [6] and the Hough Transform [13]. Removing noise using a Markov Random Field (Gibbs) was introduced in [14]. Many image descriptors have been proposed over the last decades: one of the first and most used descriptors is the the Harris Corner detector [16] introduced in 1988. However, recently it has been replaced by more complex descriptors that are insensitive to scale and rotation (to a certain extent). Of these, the two most notable and promising for dealing with captchas are SIFT [23] and SURF [1].

9. CONCLUSION

As a contribution toward improving the systematic evaluation and design of visual captchas, we evaluated various automated methods on real world captchas and synthetic one generated by varying significant features in ranges potentially acceptable to human users. We evaluated state-of-the-art anti-segmentation techniques, state-of-the-art anti-recognition techniques, and captchas used by the most popular websites.

We tested the efficiency of our tool Decaptcha against real captchas from *Authorize, Baidu, Blizzard, Captcha.net, CNN, Digg, eBay, Google, Megaupload, NIH, Recaptcha, Reddit, Skyrock, Slashdot, and Wikipedia.* On these 15 captchas, we had *1%-10%* success rate on two (*Baidu, Skyrock*), *10-24%* on two (*CNN, Digg*), *25-49%* on four (*eBay, Reddit, Slashdot, Wikipedia*), and *50%* or greater on five (*Authorize, Blizzard, Captcha.net, Megaupload, NIH*). To achieve such a high success rate we developed the first successful attacks on captchas that use collapsed characters (*eBay and Baidu*). Only Google and Recaptcha resisted to our attack attempts, and we reached some informative understanding of why we couldn't break them. Because of Decaptcha genericity we were able to break 7 of these 15 schemes without writing a new algorithm. Overall, our analysis led to a series of recommendations for captcha designers, including recommendations to use some anti-segmentation techniques, and recommendations not to use features that are ineffective against automated attacks but counterproductive for humans.

Acknowledgment

We thank Markus Jakobsson, Dave Jackson, Aleksandra Korolova and our anonymous reviewers for their comments and suggestions. This work was partially supported by the National Science Foundation, the Air Force Office of Scientific Research, and the Office of Naval Research.

10. REFERENCES

[1] H. Bay, T. Tuytelaars, and L. Van Gool. Surf: Speeded up robust features. *Computer Vision–ECCV 2006*, pages 404–417, 2006.

[2] E. Bursztein and S. Bethard. Decaptcha: breaking 75% of eBay audio CAPTCHAs. In *Proceedings of the 3rd USENIX conference on Offensive technologies*, page 8. USENIX Association, 2009.

[3] E. Bursztein, S. Bethard, Fabry C., Dan Jurafsky, and John C. Mitchell. Design parameters and human-solvability of text-based captchas. To appears.

[4] Elie Bursztein, Romain Bauxis, Hristo Paskov, Daniele Perito, Celine Fabry, and John C. Mitchell. The failure of noise-based non-continuous audio captchas. In *Security and Privacy*, 2011.

[5] Elie Bursztein, Steven Bethard, John C. Mitchell, Dan Jurafsky, and Celine Fabry. How good are humans at solving captchas? a large scale evaluation. In *Security and Privacy*, 2010.

[6] J. Canny. A computational approach to edge detection. *Readings in computer vision: issues, problems, principles, and paradigms*, 184:87–116, 1987.

[7] K. Chellapilla, K. Larson, P.Y. Simard, and M. Czerwinski. Computers beat humans at single character recognition in reading based human interaction proofs (hips). In *CEAS*, 2005.

[8] K Chellapilla and P Simard. Using machine learning to break visual human interaction proofs. In MIT Press, editor, *Neural Information Processing Systems (NIPS)*, 2004.

[9] K. Chellapilla and P. Simard. Using machine learning to break visual human interaction proofs (HIPs). *Advances in Neural Information Processing Systems*, 17, 2004.

[10] K. Chellapilla and P.Y. Simard. Using machine learning to break visual hips. In *Conf. on Neural Information Processing Systems, NIPS 2004*, 2004.

[11] C. Cortes and V. Vapnik. Support-vector networks. *Machine learning*, 20(3):273–297, 1995.

[12] B.V. Dasarathy. Nearest Neighbor ({NN}) Norms:{NN} Pattern Classification Techniques. 1991.

[13] R.O. Duda and P.E. Hart. Use of the Hough transformation to detect lines and curves in pictures. *Communications of the ACM*, 15(1):11–15, 1972.

[14] S. Geman and D. Geman. Stochastic relaxation, Gibbs distributions and the Bayesian restoration of images*. *Journal of Applied Statistics*, 20(5):25–62, 1993.

[15] P. Golle. Machine learning attacks against the asirra captcha. In *ACM CCS 2008*, 2008.

[16] C. Harris and M. Stephens. A combined corner and edge detector. In *Alvey vision conference*, volume 15, page 50. Manchester, UK, 1988.

[17] S.Y. Huang, Y.K. Lee, G. Bell, and Z. Ou. A projection-based segmentation algorithm for breaking MSN and YAHOO CAPTCHAs. In *Proceedings of the World Congress on Engineering*, volume 1. Citeseer, 2008.

[18] P Simard K Chellapilla, K Larson and M Czerwinski. Building segmentation based human- friendly human interaction proofs. In Springer-Verlag, editor, *2nd Int'l Workshop on Human Interaction Proofs*, 2005.

[19] Andrew Kirillov. aforge framework. `http://www.aforgenet.com/framework/`.

[20] Y. LeCun, L. Bottou, Y. Bengio, and P. Haffner. Gradient-based learning applied to document recognition. *Proceedings of the IEEE*, 86(11):2278–2324, 1998.

[21] Yann Lecun. The mnist database of handwritten digits algorithm results. `http://yann.lecun.com/exdb/mnist/`.

[22] B. Leibe, A. Leonardis, and B. Schiele. Robust object detection with interleaved categorization and segmentation. *International Journal of Computer Vision*, 77(1):259–289, 2008.

[23] D.G. Lowe. Object recognition from local scale-invariant features. In *iccv*, page 1150. Published by the IEEE Computer Society, 1999.

[24] O. Matan, C.J.C. Burges, and J.S. Denker. Multi-digit recognition using a space displacement neural network. *Advances in Neural Information Processing Systems*, pages 488–488, 1993.

[25] Moni Naor. Verification of a human in the loop or identification via the turing test. Available electronically: `http://www.wisdom.weizmann.ac.il/~naor/PAPERS/human.ps`, 1997.

[26] R. Quinlan. *Machine Learning*. Morgan Kaufmann Pub.

[27] F. Rosenblatt. The perceptron: a perceiving and recognizing automation (projet PARA), Cornell Aeronautical Laboratory Report. 1957.

[28] Wikipedia. Flood fill algorithm. `http://en.wikipedia.org/wiki/Flood_fill`.

[29] Wikipedia. Hsl and hsv color representaiton. `http://en.wikipedia.org/wiki/HSL_and_HSV`.

[30] J. Wilkins. Strong captcha guidelines v1. 2. *Retrieved Nov*, 10:2010, 2009.

[31] J. Yan and A.S.E. Ahmad. Breaking visual captchas with naive pattern recognition algorithms. In *ACSAC 2007*, 2007.

[32] J. Yan and A.S. El Ahmad. A Low-cost Attack on a Microsoft CAPTCHA. In *Proceedings of the 15th ACM conference on Computer and communications security*, pages 543–554. ACM, 2008.

An Efficient User Verification System via Mouse Movements

Nan Zheng, Aaron Paloski, and Haining Wang
Department of Computer Science
The College of William and Mary
Williamsburg, VA 23185, USA
{nzheng,appalo,hnw}@cs.wm.edu

Abstract

Biometric authentication verifies a user based on its inherent, unique characteristics—who you are. In addition to physiological biometrics, behavioral biometrics has proven very useful in authenticating a user. Mouse dynamics, with their unique patterns of mouse movements, is one such behavioral biometric. In this paper, we present a user verification system using mouse dynamics, which is both accurate and efficient enough for future usage. The key feature of our system lies in using much more fine-grained (point-by-point) angle-based metrics of mouse movements for user verification. These new metrics are relatively unique from person to person and independent of the computing platform. Moreover, we utilize support vector machines (SVMs) for accurate and fast classification. Our technique is robust across different operating platforms, and no specialized hardware is required. The efficacy of our approach is validated through a series of experiments. Our experimental results show that the proposed system can verify a user in an accurate and timely manner, and induced system overhead is minor.

Categories and Subject Descriptors

K.6.5 [**Management of Computing and Information Systems**]: Security and Protection—*authentication*

General Terms

Security, Human Factors

Keywords

User verification, mouse dynamics, angle-based metrics

1. INTRODUCTION

In today's Internet-centered world, the tasks of user authentication and verification have become more important than ever before [2, 7, 19, 24]. For highly sensitive systems such as online banking, it is crucial to secure users' accounts and protect their assets from malicious hands. Even in less critical systems such as desktop machines in a computing laboratory, online forums, or social networks, a hijacked session can still be misused to spread viruses or post spam, possibly damaging a user's reputation and other systems. The most common approach to securing access to systems is the use of a password [9, 11]. Unfortunately, passwords suffer from two serious problems: password cracking and password theft [25, 32]. Once a password is compromised, an adversary can easily abuse a victim's account. Thus, there is a great demand to quickly and accurately verify that the person controlling a given user's account is who the user claims to be, termed re-authentication [24].

Existing user verification and re-authentication methods require human involvement, such as providing secret answers to agreed-upon questions. Unfortunately, they only provide one-time verification, and the verified users are still vulnerable to both session hijacking and the divulging of the secret information. To achieve a timely response to an account breach, more frequent user verification is needed. However, frequent verification must be passive and transparent to users, as continually requiring a user's involvement for re-authentication is too obtrusive and inconvenient to be acceptable.

In this paper, we propose a biometric-based approach to verifying users based on passively observable mouse movement behaviors. In general, in order for a re-authentication system to be practical, it must have the following features:

- Accuracy. Not only must the system accurately identify an impostor, it must also have the probability of rejecting a true user close to zero, to avoid inconvenience to true users.
- Quick response. The system should make a quick verification decision. In other words, it should be able to distinguish a user in a timely manner.
- Difficult to forge. Even if a user's profile template is known by an impostor, it will be very hard to mimic the normal biometric behaviors in a consistent manner and then evade the verification system.

Our new approach meets all of these challenges, delivering an accurate and quick verification based on biometrics which are difficult to forge. The basic working mechanism of our approach is to passively monitor the mouse movements of a user, extract angle-based metrics, and then use Support Vector Machines (SVMs) for accurate user verification. The key feature of our approach is to exploit the point-by-point angle-based metrics of mouse movements, which are relatively unique from person to person and independent of the computing platform, for user verification.

Current biometric approaches are limited in applicability: physiological biometrics, such as fingerprints and retinal scans, provide accurate one-time authentication but require specialized hardware which may be expensive or unavailable on all users' machines. On the other hand, behavioral biometrics such as keystroke and mouse dynamics hold promise, because they can be obtained from common user interface (UI) devices that nearly every user can be assumed to own. Compared with keystroke dynamics [16, 20, 23], mouse dynamics has its own advantage for two reasons. First, keystroke monitoring can record sensitive user credentials like usernames and passwords, raising much more serious privacy concerns than mouse movement monitoring. Second, keyboard is much more complex than mouse in structure, and thus keystroke dynamics are more easily affected by different kinds of keyboards in terms of shape, size, and layout.

However, to date the existing mouse-based user verification approaches have either resulted in unacceptably low accuracy or have required an unacceptably long amount of time to reach a decision, making them unsuitable for online re-authentication. In contrast to previous research, our approach introduces a novel way—point-by-point angle-based metrics—to characterize users' mouse movements, which significantly reduces verification time while keeping high accuracy.

We perform a measurement-based study, derived from 30 *controllable* users and a corpus of more than 1,000 real users in the field. Based on these two sets of mouse movement data, we evaluate the effectiveness of the proposed system through a series of experiments, using the set of angle-based metrics specifically chosen for being both platform-independent and widely variant from user to user.

In summary, the major contributions of this paper include:

- We model behavioral biometrics using mouse dynamics, and develop an efficient user verification system. It achieves high accuracy and significantly outperforms existing systems in terms of verification time.

- We propose a novel measurement strategy involving a carefully chosen set of angle-based metrics, which is relatively independent of the operating environment and capable of uniquely identifying individual users.

- We conduct an experiment involving sessions from over 1,000 unique users, which is able to re-authenticate a user within just a few clicks with a high accuracy. This promising result could lead to a practical user verification system, suitable for online deployment in the future.

The remainder of the paper is structured as follows. Section 2 reviews the background and related work in the area of mouse dynamics. Section 3 describes our data collection and measurement, including our choice of angle-based metrics over more traditional metrics. Section 4 details the proposed classifier for user verification. Section 5 presents our experimental design and results. Section 6 discusses issues which arise from the details of our approach, and Section 7 concludes.

2. BACKGROUND AND RELATED WORK

The underlying principle of biometric-based user authentication is centered on "who you are". This is very different from conventional user authentication approaches, which are mainly based on either "what you have" or "what you know". Unfortunately, a physical object such as a key or an ID card can be lost or stolen. Similarly, a memorized password could be forgotten or divulged to malicious users. Conversely, a biometric-based approach relies on inherent and unique characteristics of a human user being authenticated. The biometrics can never be lost or forgotten, nor can another user easily steal or acquire them. This makes biometrics very attractive for user authentication.

Biometrics are categorized as either physiological or behavioral [31]. Physiological biometrics, like fingerprint and facial recognition, have attracted considerable attention in research [13, 18]. The downside of these biometrics is that they need specialized hardware, which can be problematic for wide deployment. For user authentication over the Internet, one cannot always rely on the existence of hardware at the client side. In contrast, behavioral biometrics using human-computer interaction (HCI) can record data from common input devices, such as keyboards and mice, providing user authentication in an accessible and convenient manner.

Behavioral biometrics first gained popularity with keystroke dynamics with Monrose et al.'s work on password hardening in 1999 [19]. Later on, Ahmed and Traore [1] proposed an approach combining keystroke dynamics with mouse dynamics. Mouse dynamics for re-authentication have been previously studied as a standalone biometric by Pusara and Brodley [24]. Unfortunately, their study is inconclusive with only eleven users involved, prompting the authors to conclude that mouse biometrics are insufficient for user re-authentication. Our study relies on an improved verification methodology and far more users, leading us to reverse their hypothesis.

In Ahmed et al.'s work [1, 2, 21], while achieving very high accuracy, the number of mouse actions needed to verify a user's identity[1] is too high to be practical. Specifically, their experiment requires as many as 2,000 aggregate mouse actions before a user can be recognized, and is not practical for real-time deployment. Conversely, we aim to provide a system suitable for online re-authentication. We first employ a finer-grained data collection methodology, allowing us to collect far more data in less time. We also employ support vector machines (SVMs), which are considerably faster than the neural networks employed in [2, 21]. Thus, our system can make a decision in just several mouse clicks.

More recently, a survey covering the existing works in mouse dynamics has been conducted with a comparative experiment [15]. It points out that mouse dynamics research should be more aware to reduce verification time and take the effect of environmental variables into account. It can be seen later that, compared to other works, our approach also achieves high accuracy but only requires a small amount of biometric data. Moreover, we explore the effects of environmental factors (different machines, mice, and time) and show that our approach is relatively robust across different operating environments and times.

Graphical passwords [7, 27] are a related form of user authentication, relying on HCI through a pointing device to

[1]referred to as *session length* in [2, 21].

authenticate a user. Mouse dynamics differ in that they differentiate between users by *how* the users move and click the mouse, rather than *where* the users click. Graphical passwords record where the user clicks on the screen, and subsequently use this sequence as a substitute password. Systems such as these are complementary to our work, and can be deployed together. For instance, one might employ a graphical password system while passively recording a user's mouse dynamics, utilizing the passively recorded measurements as a secondary fail-safe to verify the user's identity. This is similar in spirit to using keystroke dynamics with password hardening as in [19].

3. MOUSE MOVEMENT MEASUREMENT AND CHARACTERIZATION

3.1 Data Collection

We collect two sets of data. The first data set is from a controllable environment, referred to as the controllable set; while the second data set is from an online forum in the field, referred to as the field set. We have obtained approval from the Institutional Review Board (IRB) of our university, which ensures the appropriate and ethical use of human input data in our work.

For the controllable set, 30 users are invited personally to participate in the data collection. They are from different ages, educational backgrounds, and occupations. We intentionally set a normal environment for these users and inform them to behave as naturally as possible. Mouse movement data are recorded during their routine computing activities. These activities range among word processing, surfing the Internet, programming, online chatting, and playing games. We make use of a logging tool RUI [17] to record their mouse movement activities.

For the field set, more than 1,000 unique forum users' mouse movements are recorded by JavaScript code, and submitted passively via AJAX requests to the web server. On one hand, these users are anonymous but identifiable through unique login names. However, there is no guarantee on the amount of data collected for a certain user. A forum user could be logged in for a long time with frequent mouse activities, or could perform just one click and then leave. On the other hand, the breadth of this corpus of users is utilized to serve as the base profile for both training and testing purposes.

The raw mouse movements are represented as tuples of timestamp and Cartesian coordinate pairs. Each tuple is in the form of $\langle \text{ACTION-TYPE}, t, x, y \rangle$, where ACTION-TYPE is the mouse action type (a *mouse-move* or *mouse-click*), t is the timestamp of the mouse action, x is the x-coordinate, and y is the y-coordinate. Timestamps in our data collection are collected in milliseconds.

3.1.1 Data Processing

The purpose of preprocessing is to identify every point-and-click action, which is defined as continuous mouse movements followed by a click. *Continuous* mouse movements are series of mouse movements with little or no pause between each adjacent step. Within the ith point-and-click action for a user c, we denote the jth mouse move record as $\langle \text{MOUSE-MOVE}, t_i, x_i, y_i \rangle_{c,j}$, where t_i is the timestamp of the ith mouse movement. Based on the record that belongs to each point-and-click action, we calculate angle-based metrics.

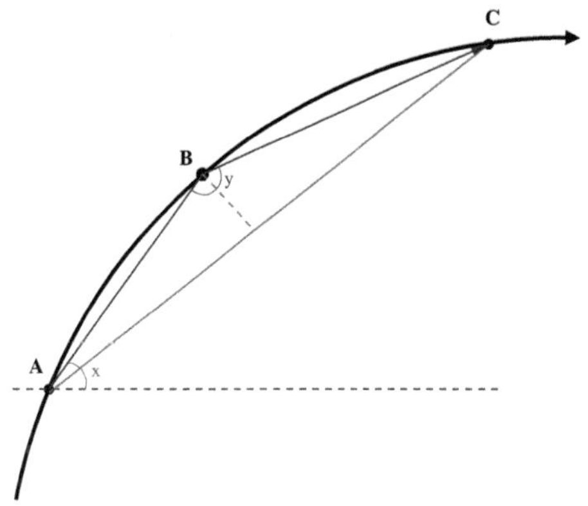

Figure 1: Illustration of angle-based metrics.

3.1.2 Metrics

To analyze the mouse movement data, we define three fine-grained angle-based metrics: direction, angle of curvature, and curvature distance. These newly-defined metrics are different from the conventional metrics, such as speed and acceleration, and can accurately characterize a user's unique mouse moving behaviors, independent of its running platform.

- Direction. For any two consecutive recorded points A and B, we record the direction traveled along the line $\overrightarrow{AB}$ from the first point to the second. The direction is defined as the angle between that line $\overrightarrow{AB}$ and the horizontal (see angle x in Figure 1).
- Angle of Curvature. For any three consecutive recorded points A, B, and C, the angle of curvature is angle $\angle ABC$; i.e., the angle between the line from A to B ($\overrightarrow{AB}$) and the line from B to C ($\overrightarrow{BC}$) (see angle y in Figure 1).
- Curvature Distance. For any three recorded points A, B, and C, consider the length of the line connecting A to C ($\overrightarrow{AC}$). The curvature distance is the ratio of the length of $\overrightarrow{AC}$ to the perpendicular distance from point B to the line $\overrightarrow{AC}$ (see the perpendicular lines in Figure 1). Note that this metric is unitless because it is the ratio of two distances.

As a comparison, we list the definition of two traditional mouse movement metrics, speed and pause-and-click, as follows.

- Speed. For each point-and-click action, we calculate the speed as the ratio of the total distance traveled for that action divided by the total time taken to complete the action.
- Pause-and-Click. For each point-and-click action, we measure the amount of time between the end of the movement and the click event. In other words, this metric measures the amount of time spent pausing between pointing to an object and actually clicking on it.

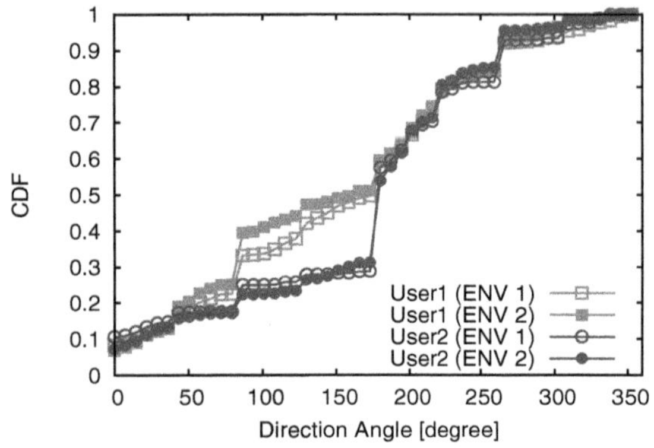

Figure 2: Direction Angle metric plotted for two different users on two different machines each.

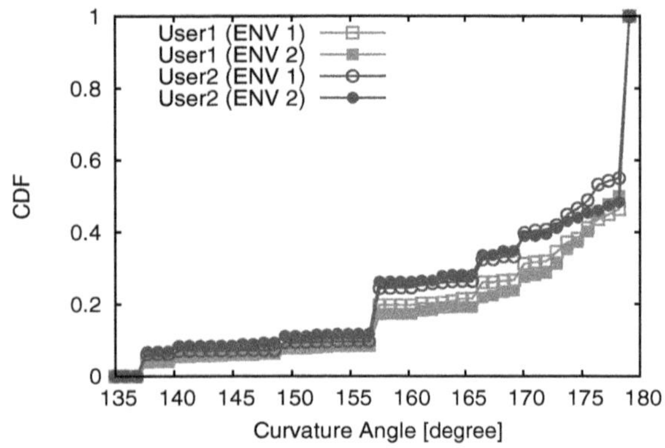

Figure 3: Angle of Curvature metric plotted for two different users on two different machines each.

3.2 Mouse Movement Characterization

3.2.1 Dependence on Different Platforms

One problem we came across in analyzing our data is that it may be difficult or meaningless to compare two users who are using very different machines. The entire user's environment can affect its data: the OS used, screen size and resolution, font size, mouse pointer sensitivity, brand of mouse, and even the amount of space available on the desk near the mousepad. Metrics such as speed and acceleration, then, are poor choices for comparison between users of arbitrary platforms. This is because these two metrics can be skewed by differences in screen resolution and pointer sensitivity. On the other hand, metrics such as pause-and-click are highly dependent on the content a user is reading. For example, a user tends to pause longer before clicking a link on a rich content page such as a wiki article, and hesitates for a much shorter time before clicking a "submit" button.

This makes a good case to use angle-based metrics for arbitrary user comparison instead. Direction and angle of curvature are not based on screen size or any other element of the user's environment, and thus are relatively platform-independent. Likewise, curvature distance is a ratio of distances on the screen, and thus self-adjusts for the user's specific environment. A ratio can be compared to another user's ratio across platforms.

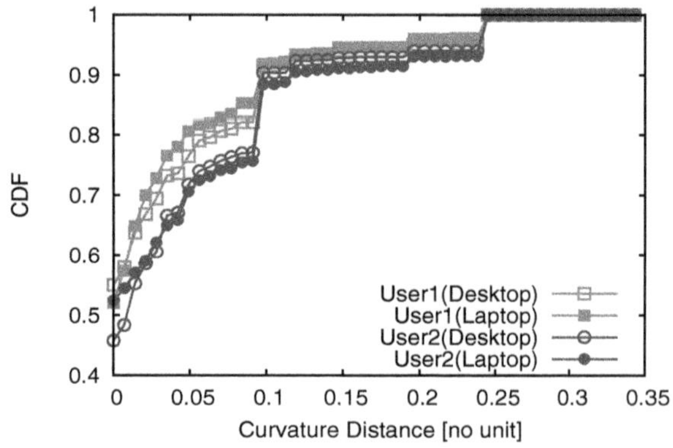

Figure 4: Curvature Distance metric plotted for two different users on two different machines each.

Figures 2, 3, and 4 show the comparison of two users with angle-based metrics. We can see that the cumulative distribution function (CDF) curves for the same user's individual data are very similar and well synchronized in shape, even across platforms. This indicates that angle-based metrics are relatively stable on different platforms.

3.2.2 Uniqueness of Angle-Based Metrics Across Users

The other distinctive feature of angle-based metrics is that they are unique across users. Not only does the same user have very similar angle-based results on different platforms, but different users have clearly different angle-based results, even on similar platforms.

Again, as Figures 2, 3, and 4 show, even though each user's CDF is consistent across different platforms, there is a distinct gap between different users' CDF curves, even on the same platform. As a comparison, Figure 5 shows the CDF curves with respect to the speed of the two users, a more commonly-used metric. Figure 6 shows the CDF curves with respect to the pause-and-click of the two users. While the different users' CDF curves in both speed and pause-and-click are closely coupled on the same environment, there is a distinct gap between the same user's two curves for different environments. Since the closest matching curve for either user is the curve of the *other* user under the same environment, it can be very hard to uniquely differentiate people using these metrics.

Together with the platform independence discussed above, this makes angle-based metrics superior to speed and pause-and-click for user verification. Note that for easy presentation, we only compare the difference of the mouse dynamics between a pair of users. However, the similar observation holds for the other users.

3.2.3 Distance Between Distributions

Using the *distance* between two probability distributions, we further verify if the angle-based features of a user remain relatively stable across different types of mice, platforms, and time, in comparison with those of the other controllable users.

We define the distance between two probability distributions as follows. Since angle-based features are continuous

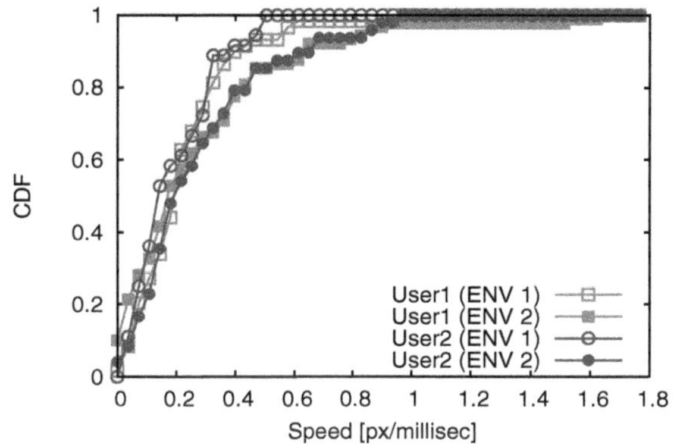

Figure 5: Speed metric plotted for two different users under two different environments each.

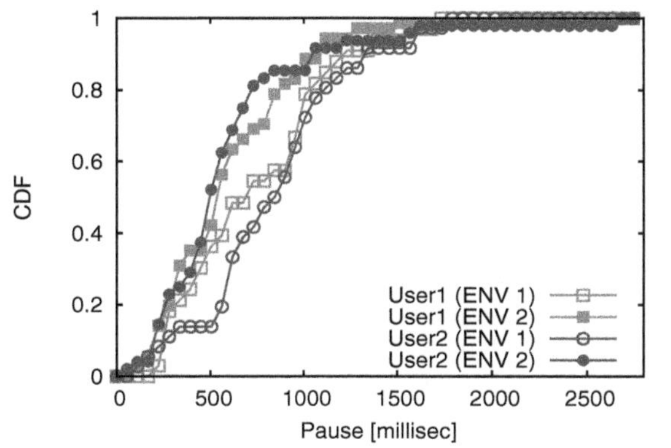

Figure 6: Pause-and-click metric plotted for two different users under two different environments each.

variables, we divide their whole range into discrete intervals, called *bins*, and calculate the probability density functions (PDFs) regarding to each bin. Consider two distributions: the first is expressed as PDF $\{p_1, p_2, ..., p_n\}$, where p_i represents the probability of falling into the ith bin; the second distribution is expressed similarly as PDF $\{q_1, q_2, ..., q_n\}$. The *distance* between the two distributions is the accumulated deviation from each other over all bins:

$$D(p, q) = \sum_i |p_i - q_i|.$$

Of course, the distance here is dependent on the size of each interval. The smaller we divide the interval, the more subtle differences the distance reflects. However, the bin should not be so small as to enlarge noise.

Figure 7 plots the distances of a user from the other users, as well as from itself using a different mouse on a different machine at very different time. Each user's PDF is computed over 1,000 curvature angles randomly selected from its data, and loops for 10 times. The height of each bar is the average distance from the target user (labeled as user 1) in setting A (indexed by 1-A in the figure), and each error bar is standard deviation over the 10 times. Data 1-A, 1-B, and 1-C are all from user 1. The details of these three settings are listed in Table 1. Moreover, data 1-B are recorded

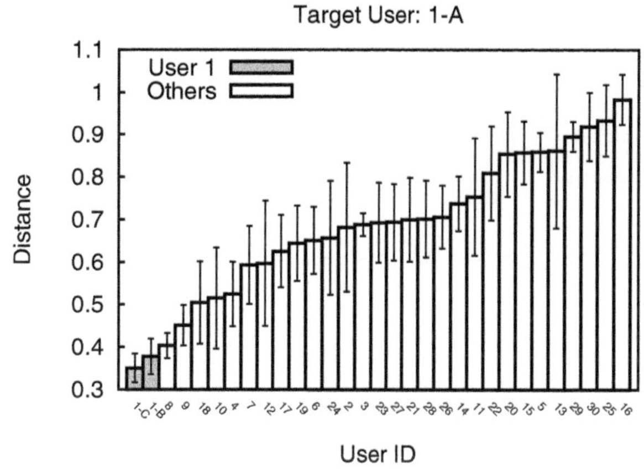

Figure 7: Distances from one user's curvature angle distribution to those of others, as well as to itself in different settings.

Setting	Machine Type	Mouse Type
1-A	Dell Precision T3500	Dell MOC5UO Two-Button Scroll-Wheel
1-B	Apple Macbook MB990LL/A	Apple A1152 One-Button Trackball
1-C	Apple Macbook MB990LL/A	Dell MOC5UO Two-Button Scroll-Wheel

Table 1: Setting Details

two and half months later than data 1-A, and data 1-C are recorded two days later than data 1-B.

It is clear that the distances from user 1 to itself using different mice, at different machines, and over different times are the two smallest in the figure, i.e., both are smaller than the distances from user 1 to any other users with the same setting. This implies that the angle-based behavior of a user has its own inherent pattern which is relatively stable across different settings and times; meanwhile, it is also distinguishable from the behaviors of other users. Note that in Figure 7, the distance values between user 1-A and some users are very close to each other (e.g. the distance value of user 23 and that of user 27). However, it does not indicate that the behaviors of those users are similar, because the definition of distance here is an accumulation of deviations at different bins. The dynamics of two users' PDFs could be totally different, but at the same time both deviate equally from a third user.

Note that to achieve accurate measurement results, there are two prerequisites in characterizing mouse movement under different environments. First, the polling rates of mouse recorders at different platforms should be configured to the same level. Second, prior to characterizing a user's mouse movement, sufficient mouse events must be collected to create a profile of the user's mouse movement. In particular, we observed that 1,000 mouse actions (which on average can be collected in 2 hours) are large enough to profile a user's mouse behavior well.

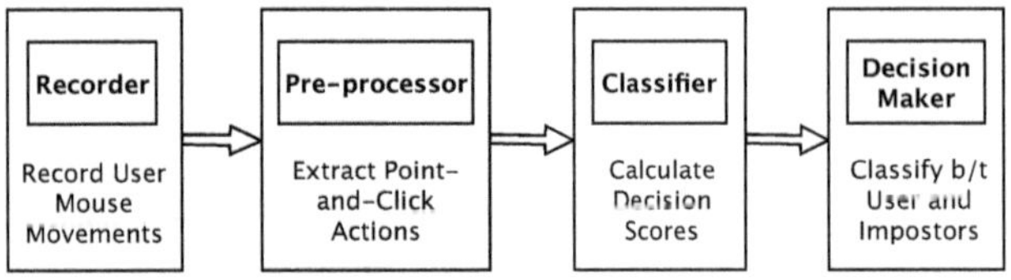

Figure 8: System Architecture

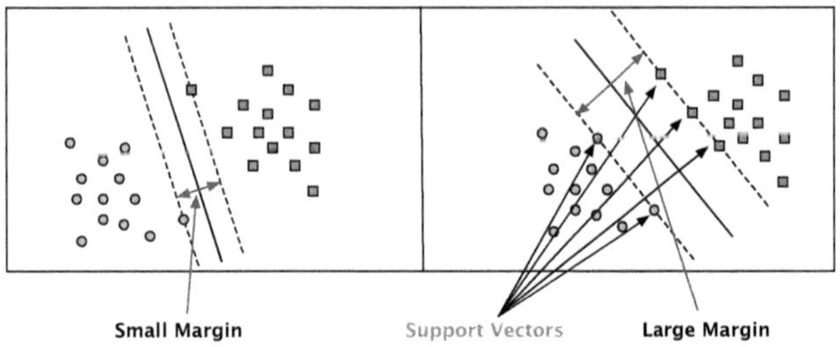

Figure 9: SVM hyperplane in two dimensional feature space [10].

3.2.4 *Number of Mouse Clicks in a Real Session*

For the field set, drawn from 1,074 real users on an online forum over the course of an hour, we recorded an average of 15.14 clicks per user session. Note that because this data was gathered over a one-hour window, this value is a lower bound on the actual number of clicks in an average user session. Any user who was logged in before the window began or stayed logged in after the window ended (including users who stayed logged in longer than an hour) would necessarily have more clicks than recorded. Thus, the actual average is almost certainly higher, and probably much higher.

The number of mouse clicks per user session is closely related to verification time. With the average number of mouse clicks per session being about 15, a verification system based on mouse dynamics must be able to identify a user in fewer than 15 clicks in order to ensure that, on average, a decision is made within one user session. As shown in Section 5, our approach can verify a user's identity with high accuracy in only 15 clicks, so our system can reliably make the right decision before the user logs off in a majority of cases.

4. SYSTEM ARCHITECTURE

As shown in Figure 8, our proposed user verification system consists of four components—recorder, preprocessor, classifier, and decision maker.

The design of the first two components is straightforward. The main task of the recorder is to record users' mouse movements, while the preprocessor computes the angle-based metrics based on the recorded raw data. The focus of this section is on the design of the classifier and that of the decision maker.

4.1 SVM Classifier

We choose Support Vector Machines (SVMs) as our classifier to differentiate users based on their mouse movement dynamics. SVMs have been successfully used in resolving real-life classification problems, including handwritten digit recognition [29], object recognition [22], text classification [14], and image retrieval [28]. In general, SVMs are able to achieve comparable or even higher accuracy with a simpler and thus faster scheme than neural networks.

In the two-class formulation, the basic idea of SVMs is to map feature vectors to a high dimensional space and compute a hyperplane, which separates the training vectors from different classes and further maximizes this separation by making the margin as large as possible. SVMs classify data by determining a set of support vectors, which are members of the set of training inputs outlining a hyper plane in feature space [30].

For a binary classification problem, given l training samples $\{\mathbf{x}_i, y_i\}, i = 1, \ldots, l$, each sample has d features, expressed as a d-dimensional vector $\mathbf{x}_i$ ($\mathbf{x}_i \in \mathbb{R}^d$), and a class label y_i with one of two values ($y_i \in \{-1, 1\}$). A hyperplane in d-dimensional space can be expressed as $\mathbf{w} \cdot \mathbf{x} + b = 0$, where $\mathbf{w}$ is a constant vector in d dimensions, and b is a scalar constant. We aim to find a hyperplane that not only separates the data points but also *maximizes* the separation. As Figure 9 shows, the distance between the dashed lines is called the *margin*. The vectors (points) that constrain the width of the margin are the *support vectors*. The formulation of our binary class SVM problem is to:

$$\text{minimize:} \quad W(\alpha) = -\alpha^T \mathbf{1} + \frac{1}{2}\alpha^T H \alpha,$$
$$\text{such that:} \quad \alpha^T y = 0, \qquad \mathbf{0} \le \alpha \le C\mathbf{1},$$

where matrix $(H)_{ij} = y_i y_j (\mathbf{x}_i \cdot \mathbf{x}_j)$, α is the vector of l non-negative Lagrangian multipliers to be determined, and C is a constant. This minimization problem is known as a *Quadratic Programming Problem (QP)*, which is well studied with many proposed efficient algorithms.

In reality, not all data points can be linearly separated as we assumed. To handle this issue, SVMs use a "kernel trick". The data are pre-processed in such a way that the problem is transformed into a higher dimension, where they are linearly separable in the new feature space. Given a mapping $\mathbf{z} = \phi(\mathbf{x})$, and defining the *kernel function* as $K(\mathbf{x}_a, \mathbf{x}_b) = \phi(\mathbf{x}_a) \cdot \phi(\mathbf{x}_b)$, our classifier would be

$$f(\mathbf{x}) = \text{sign}\left(\sum_i \alpha_i y_i (K(\mathbf{x}_i, \mathbf{x})) + b\right).$$

A popular choice of kernel function is the Gaussian Radial Basis Function (RBF) $K(\mathbf{x}_a, \mathbf{x}_b) = \exp\left(-\gamma \|\mathbf{x}_a - \mathbf{x}_b\|^2\right)$, where $\gamma > 0$, and is a tunable parameter. In practice, RBF is a reasonable first choice among other kernels, due to its generality and computational efficiency [6].

Thus, the procedure to resolve a classification problem using SVMs is: (1) choosing a kernel function, (2) setting the penalty parameter C and kernel parameters as well, if any, (3) resolving the quadratic programming problem, and (4) constructing the discriminant function from the support vectors. In particular, we view the user verification problem as a two-class classification problem, and the learning task is to build a classifier based on the user mouse movements.

In our proof-of-concept implementation, we used the open source SVM package LIBSVM 3.0 [6] for building the prototype. LIBSVM is an integrated tool for support vector classification. We used the default RBF kernel and the cross-validation to find the best parameter C and γ. In our study, all impostors are classified as +1, and normal data are classified as -1. The detailed experiment setups will be discussed in Section 5.

4.2 Decision Making

In the design of the decision maker, we use two mechanisms, threshold and majority vote, to further improve verification accuracy.

4.2.1 Threshold

The threshold determines how SVMs' output is interpreted: a value over the threshold indicates an impostor, while a value under the threshold indicates a true user. To make a user verification system deployable in practice, minimizing the probability of rejecting a true user is sometimes even more important than lowering the probability of accepting an impostor.

By default, in a binary classification problem with labels in $\{+1, -1\}$, LIBSVM outputs a score called a *decision value* for each testing sample. If the decision value is greater than 0, the sample is classified as $+1$, otherwise it is classified as -1.

4.2.2 Majority Votes

To build the profile for an authorized user, in training, we randomly pick $m/2$ samples that belong to the user, labeled as negative (non-impostor), and another random $m/2$ from the field set, labeled as positive (impostor). We employ a simple *majority vote* decision making scheme in order to improve and stabilize the verification accuracy. Specifically, before verifying if a sample belongs to the target user, we train the user's profile $2n+1$ times. Each time the training samples are different since they are randomly selected. In this way, there will be $2n+1$ votes about the predicted label for each testing sample.The label that is voted by the majority, i.e., with greater than n votes, will be the final predicted label. With majority votes, the decision maker can significantly reduce the randomness of the results and improve verification accuracy.

5. EXPERIMENTAL EVALUATION

In this section, we evaluate the effectiveness of our mouse movement based verification system through a series of experiments, in terms of verification accuracy, verification time, and system overhead. The verification accuracy of our system is measured using (1) the false reject rate (FRR), which is the probability that a user is wrongly identified as an impostor, and (2) the false accept rate (FAR), which is the probability that an impostor is incorrectly identified as a user. Here we define a block as follows:

Block (or detecting block) A *block* is composed of mouse movements in a group of point-and-click actions. Statistical features are calculated based on all mouse movements in one *block*.

Note that choosing different sizes (that is, choosing different number of point-and-click actions contained) of a *block* greatly affects verification accuracy, in terms of FAR and FRR.

The verification time is the mean time needed to detect an identity mismatch. This corresponds to the sum of the time for the user to generate mouse actions needed to make a decision, the time to extract the features for this session, and the time to classify the identity. In our approach, the number of mouse actions needed to make a decision equals to the number of clicks contained in one *block*. As described before, a *block* corresponds to one sample in either training or testing. Verification time is determined by the total number of actions needed to make decisions and the average time cost per action. In general, the larger the number of actions required for decisions and the higher the average time cost per action, the longer the verification time becomes.

5.1 Experimental Setup

As described in Section 3.1, our experiments are based on two sets of data. The first data set is collected in controllable environments. A total of 81,218 point-and-click actions are captured, with an average 5,801 point-and-click actions per user. Overall, 150 hours of raw mouse data are collected. The second data set is recorded from 1,074 anonymous users in an online forum for one hour.

These two data sets serve different purposes. A *target user* is selected from the first data set as the user to be verified, while forum users from the second data set are used as the background. Whereas we can identify a forum user based on its unique login name, the lack of guarantee on its collected data makes it unsuitable to be the verified target. The preprocessor extracts each user's point-and-click actions and computes the angle-based metrics corresponding to each point-and-click. Each of those generated files containing point-and-click actions is divided into two halves. The training data will be extracted from the first half, while the testing data will be from the second half. Therefore, there is no overlap between the training data and the testing data.

5.2 Verification Results

We construct our classification model based on self and non-self discrimination. That is, for a given user, its profile is learned from a certain number of its own mouse movement samples and an equal number of others' mouse movement samples. Therefore, the training data is composed of positive samples and an equal number of negative samples. We train a separate model for each user in the controllable set. In the training file for a given user, a negative case is a block of point-and-click actions that belongs to itself, while a positive case is a block of clicks that belongs to *others*. Here, *others*' mouse movement blocks are randomly chosen from the forum set, due to its large user population.

There are four configurable parameters in our system: the size of a detecting block, the size of the training data, the threshold, and the number of votes. The first two are associated with the SVM training process. Increasing the threshold value directly lowers false reject rate (FRR), but at the cost of raising false accept rate (FAR). Increasing the number of votes improves verification accuracy in terms of both FRR and FAR, but increases the verification time.

To fully evaluate verification accuracy, we conduct two sets of experiments. In the first set of experiments, we test our classification model trained in the same environment. In the second set of experiments, we test the classification model trained in a different environment.

5.2.1 Self and Non-Self Discrimination in Same Environment

We first configure the number of mouse clicks per block and the size of the training data. The FRR and FAR with different sizes of detecting blocks and training data are shown in Figures 10(a) and 10(b), respectively. These tests are

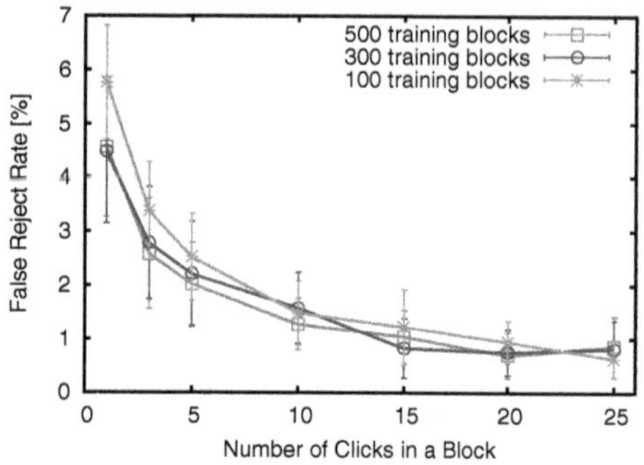

(a) False Reject Rate

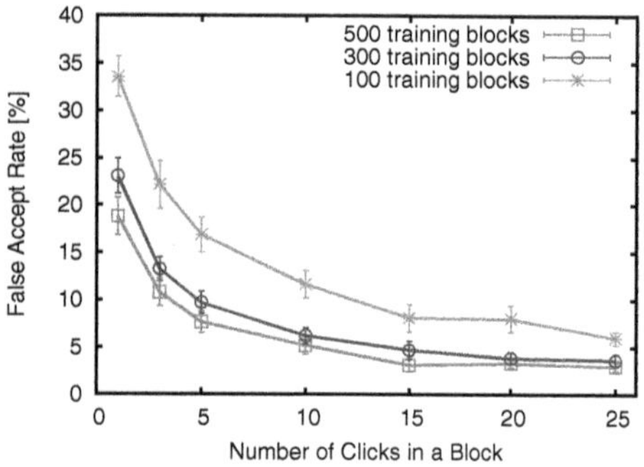

(b) False Accept Rate

Figure 10: Variation of FRR and FAR with the number of clicks. Error bars indicate standard deviation.

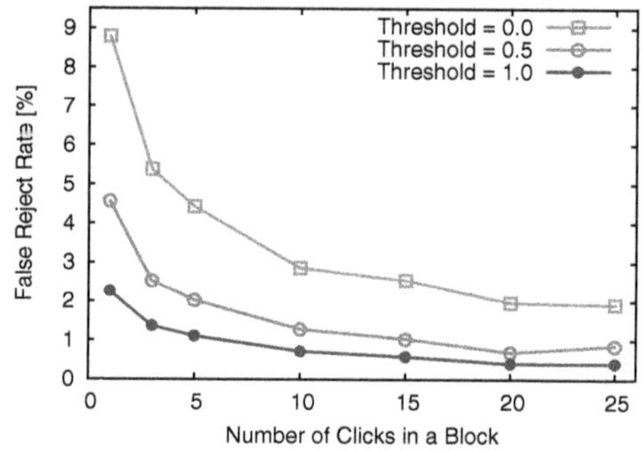

(a) False Reject Rate

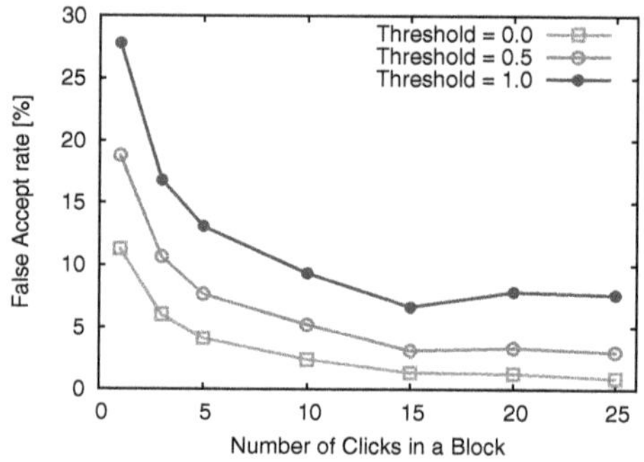

(b) False Accept Rate

Figure 11: Variation of FRR and FAR with threshold.

performed with the default threshold of 0.5 and 5 out of 9 (5/9) majority votes. As larger detecting block size and training data are provided, the SVM classifier becomes more accurate, but we see diminishing returns in accuracy as the number of actions increases, e.g., going from 10 clicks to 25 clicks requires 150% more input but only provides a relatively small increase in verification accuracy; also going from 100 training samples to 300 training samples requires 200% more data, but only returns a relatively small increase in verification accuracy.

With the SVM classifier configured, the last two parameters, the threshold and the number of votes, determine the overall performance of the system.

The threshold can be increased or decreased from the default value of 0.0 to bias the classifier towards authentic users or impostors, lowering the FRR or FAR, respectively. As mentioned in Section 4.2.1, this is a tradeoff between user inconvenience level and system security level. After multiple tests, we observe that setting the threshold value to 0.5 yields a false reject rate 1% on average. Therefore, throughout this paper, we only show results with a threshold value of 0.5. Setting the threshold value affects both FRR and FAR. Figure 11 shows that increasing the threshold value greatly lowers FRR at different sizes of a detecting block.

The use of majority votes increases the verification accuracy of the system, in terms of both FRR and FAR. Figure 12 shows the improvement of FRR by majority votes. However, increasing the number of votes means longer verification time, since for n votes the classifier needs to be run n times. Figure 12 indicates that the improvement by 2/3 majority votes is comparable to that of 3/5 majority votes.

With a fully configured system (500 training blocks, a threshold of 0.5, and 3/5 majority votes), Table 2 lists FRR and FAR averaged over 30 users in the controllable set. It can be seen that, if there are 25 clicks in one *block*, the average false reject rate is 0.86%, so there is only a little chance that an authenticated user is misclassified as an impostor. Meanwhile, we achieve an average false accept rate of 2.96%.

Number of Clicks	FRR	FAR
1	4.57%	18.79%
3	2.59%	10.81%
5	2.02%	7.67%
10	1.27%	5.23%
15	1.03%	3.13%
20	0.70%	3.32%
25	0.86%	2.96%

Table 2: Variation of FRR and FAR with different number of clicks in one block

5.2.2 *Self and Non-Self Discrimination in Different Environment*

To verify that our approach also works in different environments with different machines, we conduct another self vs. non-self discrimination experiment on two different machines. More specifically, the user's profile is trained from its mouse movements in a work environment on a desktop,

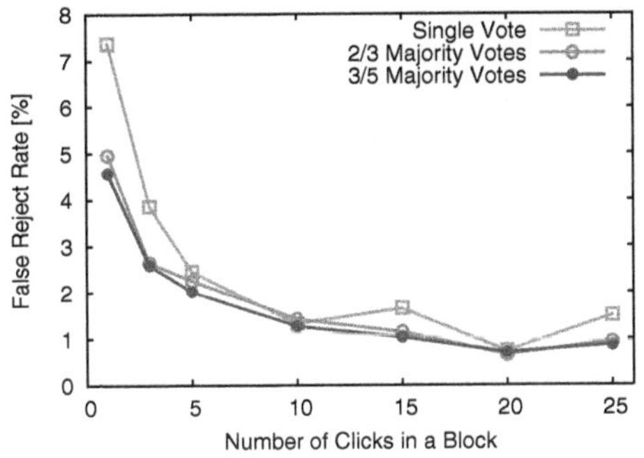

(a) False Reject Rate

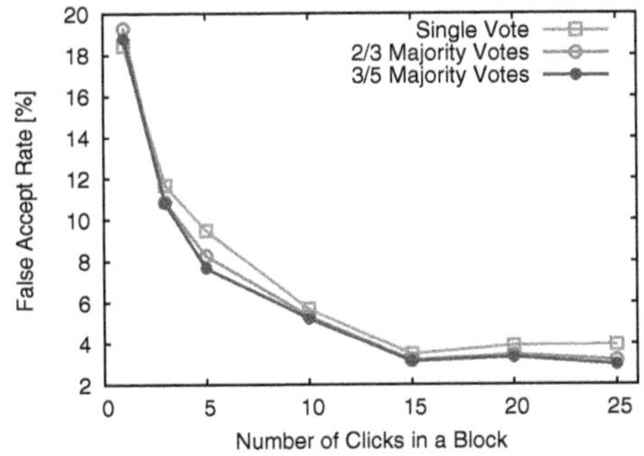

(b) False Accept Rate

Figure 12: Variation of FRR and FAR with majority votes.

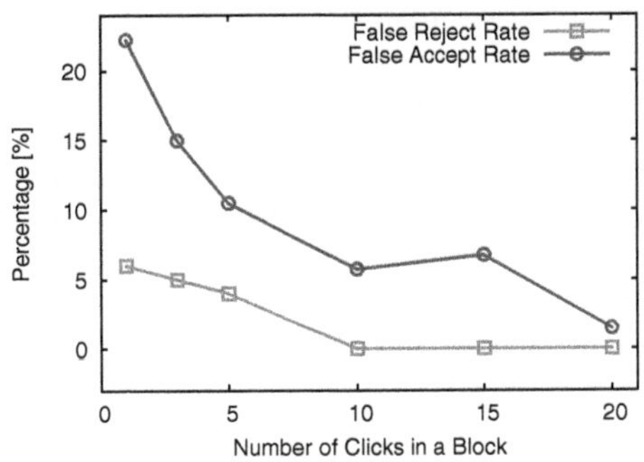

Figure 13: FRR and FAR for one user profiled on one platform and tested on another platform.

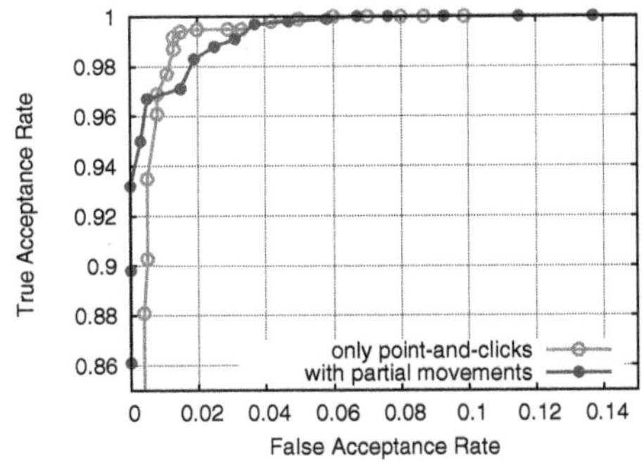

Figure 14: ROC curves with and without partial movements.

while its mouse movements in a home environment on a laptop are tested. The testing user base includes 5 users. The corresponding FRR and FAR are shown in Figure 13, each represented by a single curve, respectively. Note that a user is profiled on one platform but tested on a different one, and hence a single plot shows the result of the test.

It can be seen that our approach works well across different environments and platforms. It further confirms that our classification model indeed captures those features that are intrinsic to a user and not affected by environmental factors.

5.2.3 Partial Movements

Partial movements are a series of continuous mouse movements *without* ending in a click. On one hand, unlike point-and-click actions that have a certain object to reach as a target, some partial movements could be aimless. For example, a user may move its mouse just to stop the screen saver when watching a video. Thus, we observe that the movements of point-and-clicks demonstrate a more consistent pattern than those of partial movements. However, most partial movements are intentionally performed. For example, a user may often move its mouse to aid reading. In addition, some partial movements are just as well-motivated as point-and-clicks. A user could start moving the mouse to a link, but then decide not to click on it.

Moreover, in a real user session, partial movements occur much more frequently than point-and-clicks. From the forum data we collected, there are only 0.53 mouse clicks per minute on average, but 6.58 partial mouse movements per minute. Figure 14 shows the comparison of ROC (Receiver Operating Characteristic) curves with and without partial movements for a randomly selected user (other users' ROC curves are similar).

Suppose we choose 20 mouse clicks in a detecting block. On one hand, without partial movements – that is, when only point-and-clicks are included – the EER (equal error rate) is 1.3%; with partial movements, the EER increases to 1.9%. On the other hand, using partial movements can lower the average verification time by one order of magnitude (about 12 times) in our experiments. Therefore, using partial movements will significantly reduce verification time, but at the cost of accuracy degradation.

5.2.4 Subtleties on Verification Time

The verification time is the time required by a verification system to collect sufficient behavioral data and then make a classification decision. The value of the verification time heavily depends on two factors: (1) the number of required mouse clicks (or mouse movements if partial movements are included) in a detecting block, and (2) how frequently a user generates mouse actions. If the number of mouse actions in a detecting block is already configured, the verification time will be mainly determined by the latter.

There are two verification scenarios, static and continuous, when estimating the number of mouse actions a user generates per unit time. In the scenario of *static* verification, a user is required to perform a series of mouse movements and its mouse data is verified within a certain amount of time (e.g., login time). A good example of this scenario is a click-based graphical password for user login, where five clicks are estimated to be made in no more than 25 seconds [4, 8]. This implies that the verification time will be less than 100 seconds if 20 mouse clicks are needed in a testing block. By contrast, in the scenario of *continuous* verification, a user's mouse data is continuously collected and verified throughout the entire session. This is non-intrusive to users and meets the goal of passive monitoring. However, the frequency of user mouse actions varies significantly in different sessions. In general, the average frequency of user mouse actions will be much lower than that of the static scenario. The reason is that often there is a period of silence between a user's previous and next mouse actions while a user is reading or typing. An observation from the forum data we collected indicates, on average, it takes 1.89 minutes for one mouse click to happen. If we choose 20 mouse clicks in a detecting block, the verification time could be as long as 37.73 minutes; however, the verification time will be reduced to 3.03 minutes if partial movements are used.

5.2.5 System Overhead

The verification system can be deployed in two different scenarios. In the first scenario, for example, it can be used for access control in a computer lab or on a personal computer. In this case, it will be installed at the client side by the system administrator. In this standalone scenario, normally only a single user is present for verification at any one time, and the end host has a plenty of resources to fulfill the verification tasks. Thus, the performance impact caused by the verification on the host is minor.

In the second scenario, for an online application such as banking account verification, the system will be placed at the server side, with JavaScript embedded inside users' account home page. Deployed at the server side, our system needs to be able verify hundreds or even thousands of users simultaneously in real-time. Thus, system overhead becomes an issue, and the system must be efficient in terms of memory and CPU costs.

We first estimate the memory overhead of the verification process. We profile the verification process using the Linux tool `valgrind`, and find out that it only consumes 3.915 KBytes of memory per testing block during the operation. The prototype of our system is designed to use a single-thread multiple-client model with time-multiplexing, and thus only one process is used. The primary memory cost is to accommodate the accumulated user-input actions and SVM outputs for each online user. A single user-input action consumes 12 bytes, 4 bytes each for the 3 angle-based metrics. A detecting block of 10 user-input actions consumes 120 bytes, and this is the per-user memory requirement. If 120 bytes is scaled to 1,000 online users, it is only 117.19KBytes in total, which is negligible considering that online websites currently store the user name, password, IP address, security questions and literally dozens of other attributes for each user.

The computational overhead is the sum of CPU costs in pre-processing and detecting (including classifying and decision making). The pre-processing on 15 minutes' user inputs from more than 1,000 users in a typical website, including 5,270 point-and-click actions, takes only 20.937 seconds. The CPU cost is measured on a Pentium 4 Xeon 3.0Ghz, using the Linux command `time`. Note that the forum trace is collected during 15 minutes from about 1,000 online users, implying that it takes about 23.3 milliseconds to process data generated in one second. At the same time, the verification takes only 229 milliseconds over 5,801 point-and-click actions. In comparison to pre-processing, this is negligible. Therefore, the induced computational overhead is minor on the server.

In terms of disk space for storing user profiles, the signature of a single user profile generated by the training process consumes 203.32KBytes. If it is scaled to 100,000 users, that is 19.4GBytes, which is very affordable at a personal computer, let alone a high end server.

5.3 Comparison with Existing Works

We compare our evaluation results with those of existing works in terms of verification accuracy and time, which are listed in Table 3. As described in Section 5.2.4, the verification time is highly dependent on the number of mouse events needed to make a decision, the type of mouse events used (mouse click, mouse move, or drag-and-drop), as well as how fast a user generates mouse events. Even for the same user at different times, the number of mouse events per unit time varies a lot. However, to the best of our knowledge, our work is the first to achieve high accuracy with a reasonably small number of mouse events.

6. DISCUSSION

Since our verification system records users' mouse movements and clicks, privacy concerns may arise. However, compared to keystroke dynamics, the amount of personal information included in mouse dynamics is minimal. In the process of recording keystrokes, the system would record the user's passwords, user names, and other sensitive textual information. By contrast, recording mouse dynamics only reveals the physical movements of a mouse and its clicks within a certain period of time, giving away little to no information about user credentials. Even with the perfect knowledge of a user's mouse movements, the only things an adversary can figure out are when the user clicked and on which position of the screen. Thus, we believe that our verification system will not cause any privacy violations.

In general, mouse-dynamics-based re-authentication techniques are robust against online forgery. A person's unique mouse dynamics are similar to its signature, and like a signature, it is difficult to mimic even with the complete knowledge of the original. In fact, a user's mouse dynamics is a continuous process, making it much harder to forge than a signature. Unlike forging a signature, which only has to be accomplished once, the adversary of our verification system would need to mimic the true user's mouse patterns continuously for the entire length of the session. It is extremely difficult for one user to force itself to consistently move the mouse in such a mechanical way that it matches specific angles, even if those metrics are known ahead of time. Thus, mouse dynamics generally and our fine-grained angle-based approach in particular, are very robust against online forgery. However, how vulnerable mouse-dynamics-based approaches are to offline attacks, especially generative attacks which create concatenative synthetic forgeries [3], is still an open question and will be investigated in our future work.

The retraining of our classifier is necessary to deal with sudden, perhaps temporary, changes in a user's mouse profile. If the user's behavior suddenly changes, due to an unex-

Source	FRR	FAR	Data required	Settings	Notes
[2]	2.4649%	2.4614%	2000 mouse actions	Continuous	Free mouse movements
[21]	0%	0.36%	2000 mouse actions	Continuous	Free mouse movements
[12]	2%	2%	50 mouse strokes	Static	Mouse movements from a memory game
[24]	1.75%	0.43%	Not specified	Continuous	Applies to a certain application
[26]	11.2%	11.2%	3600 mouse curves	Continuous	Free mouse movements
Ours	1.3%	1.3%	20 mouse clicks	Continuous	Free mouse movements

Table 3: Comparison with Existing Works

pected complication such as a sprained wrist, the difference in mouse usage could be large enough for the user to be unrecognizable by the verification system. The system would classify the user as an impostor and prevent that user from accessing its own account. While these sorts of occurrences are relatively rare, to avoid the possible rejection, the user can easily appeal to a system administrator to retrain the classifier with the user's new movement patterns. Once the user's behavior returns to normal (for example, the user's wrist heals), we can either retrain the system again, or simply reuse the previous classifier if a backup is available.

Although our approach is relatively independent of the running environments, it is sensitive to the polling rate of mouse movement recording. In the mouse data collection, a continuous mouse movement is discretized to a set of mouse coordinates, which are sampled at a certain rate. Thus, the measured resolution of mouse movements is dependent on the polling rate of a recorder. The faster the polling rate is, the more fine-grained movements we capture. For example, given a mouse movement curve, a high polling rate can render a smooth accurate shape, but a low polling rate more likely profiles it as a zigzag path. For this reason, in our data collection on different environments, the polling rates of the recorders are configured to the same value. In fact, it is not difficult to maintain a given polling rate under different running environments. Through I/O methods provided in most common programming languages, we are able to set timers and capture mouse cursor position at a fixed interval.

It is true that with an increase in user population, there is a higher chance that two users share the similar mouse movements. In fact, known as "the scalability problem", this is a common problem for almost all biometrics approaches. In face recognition, if more people are tested, it is more likely that two users' faces are similar and could make the classifier fail. The same thing happens in keystroke dynamics, and it has been determined that the accuracy of keystroke dynamics decreases with the increase in sample size [5, 23].

Though promising, our accuracy is unable to reach the European Standard for Access Control Systems, which requires a false acceptance rate (FAR) of under 0.001% and a false rejection rate (FRR) of under 1%. Therefore, we believe that our scheme is more suitable to work together with other authentication methods for user verification, instead of working as a stand-alone authentication system.

7. CONCLUSION

In this paper, we present a new approach to user re-authentication using the behavioral biometrics provided by mouse dynamics. Our approach focuses on fine-grained angle-based metrics, which have two advantages over previously studied metrics. First, angle-based metrics can distinguish a user accurately with very few mouse clicks. Second, angle-based metrics are relatively independent of the operating environment of a user, making them suitable for online re-authentication.

Our system mainly consists of a recorder, which gathers a user's mouse dynamics, and a support vector machine (SVM) classifier, which seeks to verify a user as either an impostor or an authenticated party. We gathered two sets of data: one set of 30 users under controlled circumstances, and another set of over 1,000 users on a forum website. We evaluated the system performance in terms of verification accuracy and time, resulting in a equal error rate (EER) of 1.3% with just 20 mouse clicks. We also showed that, for a system deployed at server side, the overhead required for online verification is negligible.

Acknowledgments

We would like to thank Aaron Koehl, Steven Gianvecchio, and Xin Ruan for their invaluable assistance in data collection and technical support. We would also like to thank the anonymous reviewers for their insightful comments.

8. REFERENCES

[1] A. A. E. Ahmed and I. Traore. Anomaly intrusion detection based on biometrics. In *Proceedings of the 2005 IEEE Workshop on Information Assurance*, 2005.

[2] A. A. E. Ahmed and I. Traore. A new biometric technology based on mouse dynamics. *IEEE Transactions on Dependable and Secure Computing*, 4(3):165–179, 2007.

[3] L. Ballard, F. Monrose, and D. Lopresi. Biometric authentication revisited: Understanding the impact of wolves in sheep's clothing. In *USENIX Security Symposium*, 2006.

[4] R. Biddle, S. Chiasson, and P. van Oorschot. Graphical passwords: Learning from the first twelve years. *ACM Computing Surveys*, 2011. (to appear).

[5] T. Buch, A. Cotoranu, E. Jeskey, et al. An enhanced keystroke biometric system and associated studies. In *Proceedings of Student-Faculty Research Day, CSIS, Pace University*, pages C4.2–C4.7, 2008.

[6] C.-C. Chang and C.-J. Lin. *LIBSVM: a library for support vector machines*, 2001. Software available at `http://www.csie.ntu.edu.tw/~cjlin/libsvm`.

[7] S. Chiasson, A. Forget, E. Stobert, P. van Oorschot, and R. Biddle. Multiple password interference in text passwords and click-based graphical passwords. In *ACM Conference on Computer and Communications Security (CCS)*, 2009.

[8] S. Chiasson, P. C. V. Oorschot, and R. Biddle. Graphical password authentication using cued click-points. In *12th European Symposium On Research In Computer Security (ESORICS), 2007*. Springer-Verlag, 2007.

[9] S. Chiasson, P. van Oorschot, and R. Biddle. A usability study and critique of two password managers. In *USENIX Security Symposium*, 2006.

[10] DTREG. SVM - Support Vector Machines. `http://www.dtreg.com/svm.htm`, Feb 2011.

[11] D. Florencio and C. Herley. A large scale study of web password habits. In *Proceedings of WWW 2007*, 2007.

[12] H. Gamboa and A. Fred. A behavioral biometric system based on human-computer interaction. In *Society of Photo-Optical Instrumentation Engineers (SPIE) Conference Series*, volume 5404, pages 381–392, Aug. 2004.

[13] P. Gupta, S. Ravi, A. Raghunathan, and N. K. Jha. Efficient fingerprint-based user authentication for embedded systems. In *Proceedings of the 42nd annual Design Automation Conference (DAC)*, pages 244–247, 2005.

[14] T. Joachims. Text categorization with support vector machines: Learning with many relevant features. In *Proc. of European Conference on Machine Learning*, pages 137–142, 1998.

[15] Z. Jorgensen and T. Yu. On mouse dynamics as a behavioral biometric for authentication. In *Proceedings of the 6th ACM Symposium on Information, Computer and Communications Security*, ASIACCS '11, pages 476–482, 2011.

[16] K. Killourhy and R. Maxion. Why did my detector do that?!: predicting keystroke-dynamics error rates. In *Proceedings of RAID'10*, pages 256–276, 2010.

[17] U. Kukreja, W. E. Stevenson, and F. E. Ritter. RUI: Recording user input from interfaces under windows and mac os x. *Behavior Research Methods*, 38(4):656–659, 2006.

[18] C. Mallauran, J.-L. Dugelay, F. Perronnin, and C. Garcia. Online face detection and user authentication. In *Proceedings of the 13th annual ACM international conference on Multimedia (MM)*, pages 219–220, 2005.

[19] F. Monrose, M. K. Reiter, and S. Wetzel. Password hardening based on keystroke dynamics. In *ACM Conference on Computer and Communications Security (CCS)*, pages 73–82, 1999.

[20] F. Monrose and A. D. Rubin. Authentication via keystroke dynamics. In *ACM Conference on Computer and Communications Security (CCS)*, pages 48–56, 1997.

[21] Y. Nakkabi, I. Traore, and A. A. E. Ahmed. Improving mouse dynamics biometric performance using variance reduction via extractors with separate features. *IEEE Transactions on Systems, Man, and Cybernetics*, 40(6):1345–1353, 2010.

[22] C. Papageorgiou, M. Oren, and T. Poggio. A general framework for object detection. In *Proceedings of the International Conference on Computer Vision*, 1998.

[23] A. Peacok, X. Ke, and M. Wilkerson. Typing patterns: A key to user identification. *IEEE Security and Privacy*, 2(5):40–47, 2004.

[24] M. Pusara and C. E. Brodley. User re-authentication via mouse movements. In *Proceedings of the 2004 ACM workshop on Visualization and data mining for computer security*, pages 1–8, 2004.

[25] B. Ross, C. Jackson, N. Miyake, D. Boneh, and J. Mitchell. Stronger password authentication using browser extensions. In *USENIX Security Symposium*, 2005.

[26] D. Schulz. Mouse curve biometrics. In *Biometric Consortium Conference, 2006 Biometrics Symposium*, pages 1–6. IEEE, 2006.

[27] E. Stobert, A. Forget, S. Chiasson, et al. Exploring usability effects of increasing security in click-based graphical passwords. In *Annual Computer Security Applications Conference (ACSAC)*, 2010.

[28] S. Tong. Support vector machine active learning for image retrieval. In *Proceedings of the ninth ACM international conference on Multimedia*, 2001.

[29] V. Vapnik. *Statistical Learning Theory*. Wiley, 1998.

[30] V. N. Vladimir. *The Nature of Statistical Learning Theory*. Springer, Berline Heidelberg, New York, 1995.

[31] R. V. Yampolskiy and V. Govindaraju. Behavioural biometrics: a survey and classification. *Int. J. Biometrics*, 1(1):81–113, 2008.

[32] Y. Zhang, F. Monrose, and M. K. Reiter. The security of modern password expiration: An algorithmic framework and empirical analysis. In *ACM Conference on Computer and Communications Security (CCS)*, 2010.

Policy Auditing over Incomplete Logs: Theory, Implementation and Applications

Deepak Garg
Carnegie Mellon University
Pittsburgh, USA
dg@cs.cmu.edu

Limin Jia
Carnegie Mellon University
Pittsburgh, USA
liminjia@cmu.edu

Anupam Datta
Carnegie Mellon University
Pittsburgh, USA
danupam@cmu.edu

ABSTRACT

We present the design, implementation and evaluation of an algorithm that checks audit logs for compliance with privacy and security policies. The algorithm, which we name reduce, addresses two fundamental challenges in compliance checking that arise in practice. First, in order to be applicable to realistic policies, reduce operates on policies expressed in a first-order logic that allows *restricted quantification* over infinite domains. We build on ideas from logic programming to identify the restricted form of quantified formulas. The logic can, in particular, express all 84 disclosure-related clauses of the HIPAA Privacy Rule, which involve quantification over the infinite set of messages containing personal information. Second, since audit logs are inherently *incomplete* (they may not contain sufficient information to determine whether a policy is violated or not), reduce proceeds iteratively: in each iteration, it provably checks as much of the policy as possible over the current log and outputs a residual policy that can only be checked when the log is extended with additional information. We prove correctness, termination, time and space complexity results for reduce. We implement reduce and optimize the base implementation using two heuristics for database indexing that are guided by the syntactic structure of policies. The implementation is used to check simulated audit logs for compliance with the HIPAA Privacy Rule. Our experimental results demonstrate that the algorithm is fast enough to be used in practice.

Categories and Subject Descriptors

F.4.1 [**Mathematical Logic and Formal Languages**]: Mathematical Logic—*Temporal logic*; H.2.1 [**Database Management**]: Logical Design; I.2.4 [**Artificial Intelligence**]: Knowledge Representation Formalisms and Methods; K.4.3 [**Computers and Society**]: Organizational Impacts—*Automation*

General Terms

Experimentation, Legal Aspects, Security, Theory

Keywords

Audit, Formal logic, Incomplete logs, Privacy policy

1. INTRODUCTION

Organizations, such as hospitals, banks, and universities, that collect, use, and share personal information have to ensure that they do so in a manner that respects the privacy of the information's subjects. In fact, designing effective processes to ensure compliance with internal policies and privacy regulations, such as the Health Insurance Portability and Accountability Act (HIPAA) [34] and the Gramm-Leach-Bliley Act (GLBA) [33], has become one of the greatest challenges facing organizations today (see, for example, a survey from Deloitte and the Ponemon Institute [13]). This paper presents an approach to address this challenge.

We design and implement an algorithm that checks audit logs for compliance with a rich class of privacy and security policies. The algorithm, which we name reduce, addresses two fundamental challenges in compliance checking that arise in practice. First, in order to be applicable to realistic policies, reduce operates on policies expressed in a first-order logic that allows *restricted quantification* over infinite domains. We design this logic by starting from our prior work on a logic for specifying privacy regulations [15], and restricting the syntax of quantifiers in order to ensure that reduce terminates. In more detail, we note that many HIPAA clauses are of the form $\forall p_1, p_2, m.(\mathtt{send}(p_1, p_2, m) \supset \varphi)$ where p_1 and p_2 are principals and m is a message. This formula quantifies over the infinite set of messages, so if an enforcement algorithm were to blindly instantiate the quantifiers with all possible values in the domain, it would not terminate. However, since the number of messages transmitted from a hospital is finite, the predicate $\mathtt{send}(p_1, p_2, m)$ is true for only a finite number of substitutions for the variable m (and similarly for p_1 and p_2). At a technical level, we use the idea of *mode checking* from logic programming [2] to ensure that the number of relevant substitutions for every quantified variable is always finite, thus ensuring that reduce terminates. The resulting logic is more expressive than prior logics used for compliance-checking, including propositional temporal logics [6, 18] and first-order metric temporal logic [9], and, in contrast to these logics, can express all 84 disclosure-related clauses in the HIPAA Privacy Rule.

Second, a significant challenge in automated compliance checking is that logs maintained by organizations may be *incomplete*, i.e., they may not contain enough information to decide whether or not the policy has been violated. There are many different sources of incompleteness. Specifically, privacy regulations often permit disclosures based on subjective beliefs (e.g., allowing a hospital to share health information with law enforcement officers if the hospital believes that a death could have been the result of a criminal act) and future obligations (e.g., requiring organizations to notify customers within a prescribed time period if a data breach has occurred). These two classes of policies (which abound in privacy regulations) illustrate why we cannot hope to have an automated enforcement mechanism that decides whether a disclosure is permitted or not at the time the disclosure occurs—in other words, why a preventive enforcement regime is not sufficient for enforcement of such policies. In addition to these inherent forms of incompleteness, sometimes not all relevant information is recorded in a single log, i.e., logs may be spatially distributed. As an important contribution, we observe that such incomplete logs can be abstractly represented as three-valued, *partial structures* that map each atomic formula to either true, false, or unknown [11, 19]. We define the semantics of our logic over such structures. We design reduce to work with partial structures, thus providing a uniform method of compliance checking that accounts for different sources of incompleteness in audit logs. Since logs evolve over time by gathering more information, reduce proceeds iteratively: In each iteration, it checks as much of the policy as possible over the current log and outputs a residual policy that can only be checked when the log is extended with additional information.

We formally prove the following properties of reduce, using reduce$(\mathcal{L}, \varphi) = \varphi'$ to denote one iteration of reduce: (1) The residual policy φ' output by reduce is *minimal*: it only contains predicates whose truth value is unknown in the current partial structure $\mathcal{L}$; (2) reduce *terminates*: as noted earlier, the finite substitution property of variables quantified over infinite domains is crucial for termination; (3) reduce is *correct*: any extension of $\mathcal{L}$ satisfies the policy φ if and only if it satisfies the residual formula φ'; (4) Assuming that finding an entry in the audit log takes unit time, reduce runs in time polynomial in the size of the audit log where the degree of the polynomial is the size of the policy formula (i.e., TIME($|\mathcal{L}|^{O(|\varphi|)}$)), and uses space that is polynomial in the size of the policy formula (i.e., PSPACE($|\varphi|$)).

We implement reduce and optimize the base implementation with heuristics for database indexing that are guided by the syntactic structure of policies. The implementation is used to check simulated audit logs for compliance with the HIPAA Privacy Rule. Our experimental results demonstrate that the algorithm is practical—the average time for checking compliance for each disclosure of protected health information is 0.12 seconds for a log of size 15MB.

In practice, we expect that the reduce algorithm will be an integral component of an *after-the-fact audit* tool for policy violations. The other component of such a tool would be a front-end that allows an auditor to select a part of the policy (or the whole of it) and simplify it through the reduce algorithm. The auditor may also provide additional information about incomplete parts of the audit log and repeat the reduction. In ongoing work, we are building such a front-end.

Organization. Section 2 presents the syntax of the policy logic, and defines partial structures and the semantics of the logic over them. Section 3 presents the reduce algorithm and its properties. Section 4 describes the base implementation of the algorithm and its optimization. Section 5 describes our empirical evaluation of the implementation. Section 6 provides a detailed comparison with related work and Section 7 presents conclusions and directions for future work. The source code of our implementation and a technical report [17] with proofs of theorems and other details (TR in the sequel) are available online at the URL `http://www.cs.cmu.edu/~dg/`.

2. POLICY LOGIC

We represent policies in a first-order logic with restricted quantifiers (also called guarded quantifiers in the literature).

Atoms	P	$::=$	$p(t_1, \ldots, t_n)$
Formulas	φ	$::=$	$P \mid \top \mid \bot \mid \varphi_1 \wedge \varphi_2 \mid \varphi_1 \vee \varphi_2 \mid$ $\forall \vec{x}.(c \supset \varphi) \mid \exists \vec{x}.(c \wedge \varphi)$
Restrictions	c	$::=$	$P \mid \top \mid \bot \mid c_1 \wedge c_2 \mid c_1 \vee c_2 \mid \exists x.c$

Predicates p represent relations between terms t. Terms are variables $(x, y, \ldots)$, constants, or terms applied to uninterpreted function symbols. An atom is a predicate applied to a list of terms. Propositional connectives $\top$ (true), $\bot$ (false), $\wedge$ (conjunction), and $\vee$ (disjunction) have their usual meanings. First order quantifiers — forall ($\forall$) and exists ($\exists$) — may range over infinite domains. Anticipating the requirements of our audit algorithm (Section 3), we restrict these quantifiers to the forms $\forall \vec{x}.(c \supset \varphi)$ and $\exists \vec{x}.(c \wedge \varphi)$ by including a formula c called a *restriction*. By definition, $\forall \vec{x}.(c \supset \varphi)$ is true iff all instances of variables $\vec{x}$ that satisfy c, also satisfy φ. Similarly, $\exists \vec{x}.(c \wedge \varphi)$ holds iff there is an instance of $\vec{x}$ that satisfies both c and φ. To ensure that our enforcement algorithm terminates, we require that only a finite number of substitutions for quantified variables make a restriction true. The latter is forced by the limited syntax of restrictions (note that universal quantifiers and implications are not allowed in restrictions) and other checks that we describe in Section 3.

For technical reasons, we do not include negation in the logic. Instead we assume that each predicate p has a dual $\overline{p}$ such that $p(t_1, \ldots, t_n)$ is true iff $\overline{p}(t_1, \ldots, t_n)$ is false and define a dual $\overline{\varphi}$ that behaves exactly as $\neg\varphi$ would. For example,

$$\begin{array}{rcl}
\overline{p(t_1, \ldots, t_n)} & = & \overline{p}(t_1, \ldots, t_n) \\
\overline{\varphi \wedge \psi} & = & \overline{\varphi} \vee \overline{\psi} \\
\overline{\forall \vec{x}.(c \supset \varphi)} & = & \exists \vec{x}.(c \wedge \overline{\varphi}) \\
\overline{\exists \vec{x}.(c \wedge \varphi)} & = & \forall \vec{x}.(c \supset \overline{\varphi})
\end{array}$$

To represent time-dependent (temporal) properties, we assume a domain of integers (both negative and positive integers), denoted τ, that count time in seconds from a fixed point of reference and make the time of occurrence of an event explicit in the predicate that represents the event. For example, the atom $\mathsf{send}(p_1, p_2, m, \tau)$ means that principal p_1 sends to principal p_2 the message m *at time* τ. The relation $\tau_1 \leq \tau_2$ represents the total order on integers. All of linear-time temporal logic (LTL) [24] and its extension TPTL [1] can be encoded in our logic. For details of the encoding see our prior work [15].

Example 2.1. Consider the following policy about transmission of health information from one entity (e.g., a hospital or doctor) to another. This policy is motivated by similar requirements in HIPAA, but is simpler and serves as a good illustration.

> An entity may send an individual's protected health information (phi) to another entity only if the receiving entity is the individual's doctor and the purpose of the transmission is treatment, or the individual has previously consented to the transmission.

To formalize this policy in our logic, we start by assuming that all transmissions made by an entity are recorded in a log. The predicate $\texttt{send}(p_1, p_2, m, \tau)$ is true if the transmission of message m from principal p_1 to principal p_2 at time τ occurs in this log. Similarly, we assume that transmission consents given by individuals are also recorded in a database table. The predicate $\texttt{consents}(q, a, \tau)$, which means that individual q consents to the action a at time τ, holds if the corresponding consent exists in this table.

We further assume that each transmitted message m is *tagged* by the sender (in a machine-readable format) with the names of individuals whose information it carries as well as the attributes of information it carries (attributes include "address", "social security number", "medications", "medical history", etc.). The predicate $\texttt{tagged}(m, q, t)$ means that message m is tagged as carrying individual q's attribute t. Tags may or may not be accurate. Similarly, we assume that each message m is labeled in a machine readable format with a purpose u (e.g., "treatment", "healthcare", etc.). This is represented by the predicate $\texttt{purp}(m, u)$.

Attributes and purposes are assumed to have separate hierarchies, e.g., the attribute "medications" is contained in "medical history". This is formalized as the predicate $\texttt{attr\_in}(\text{medications}, \text{medical-history})$. Similarly, the predicate $\texttt{purp\_in}(u, u')$ means that purpose u is a special case of purpose u', e.g., $\texttt{purp\_in}(\text{surgery}, \text{treatment})$. Finally, $\texttt{doctorOf}(p_2, q, \tau)$ means that q is a doctor of p_2 at time τ.

The policy above can be formalized in our logic as follows (terms *phi* and *treatment* are constants).

$$\begin{aligned}
&\varphi_{pol} = \\
&\forall p_1, p_2, m, u, q, t, \tau.\ (\texttt{send}(p_1, p_2, m, \tau) \wedge \texttt{purp}(m, u) \wedge \\
&\qquad\qquad\qquad \texttt{tagged}(m, q, t)) \\
&\quad \supset \overline{\texttt{attr_in}}(t, \mathit{phi}) \\
&\qquad \vee (\texttt{doctorOf}(p_2, q, \tau) \wedge \texttt{purp_in}(u, \mathit{treatment})) \\
&\qquad \vee \exists \tau'.(\tau' < \tau \wedge \\
&\qquad\qquad \texttt{consents}(q, \texttt{sendaction}(p_1, p_2, (q, t)), \tau'))
\end{aligned}$$

In words, if entity p_1 sends to entity p_2 a message m at time τ, m is tagged as carrying attribute t of individual q, and m is labeled with purpose u, then either the attribute t is not a form of protected health information (so the policy does not apply) or the recipient p_2 is a doctor of q at time τ (atom $\texttt{doctorOf}(p_2, q, \tau)$) and u is a type of treatment, or q has consented to this transmission in the past (last two lines of φ_{pol}).

Predicates may be verified in different ways in an implementation. The predicates **send** and **consents** can be verified by looking up respective logs. Predicates $\texttt{tagged}(m, q, t)$ and $\texttt{purp}(m, u)$ can be verified by examining the tags in m, i.e., through a pre-defined computable function. Similarly, predicates **attr_in** and **purp_in** may be verified through a function that checks stipulated hierarchies over attributes and purposes, respectively. Finally, the predicate $\texttt{doctorOf}(p_2, q, \tau)$ may require human input to resolve because, in general, information about all of q's doctors may be unavailable to the audit mechanism. Our implementation (Section 4) requires the policy designer to categorize predicates based on how they are verified, but our audit algorithm uses a single, abstract representation of these verification methods, called partial structures, to which we turn next.

2.1 Partial Structures and Semantics

We formally abstract the information about truth and falsity of atoms available to our audit algorithm as functions called *partial structures* and define semantics of logical formulas over such structures. Given a possibly infinite domain D of terms, a partial structure (abbrev. structure) $\mathcal{L}$ is a map from atoms over D to the three-value set $\{\texttt{tt}, \texttt{ff}, \texttt{uu}\}$. We say that the atom P is true, false, or unknown in the structure $\mathcal{L}$ if $\mathcal{L}(P)$ is **tt**, **ff**, or **uu**, respectively. The possibility of mapping an atom to "unknown" captures the common phenomena that, during audit, not every atom may be classifiable as true or false. In particular, partial structures abstract the following different kinds of *incompleteness* in information available to the audit algorithm.

- Future incompleteness: Information about events in the future cannot be available to an audit algorithm. For instance, the policy may allow a disclosure if the subject of the information disclosed is notified within a month. However, if an audit occurs immediately after a disclosure, it will not be known whether or not a corresponding notification will be sent in future. This is easily modeled by a partial structure $\mathcal{L}$ satisfying $\mathcal{L}(\texttt{send}(p_1, p_2, m, \tau)) = \texttt{uu}$ for every τ greater than the time of audit.

- Spatial incompleteness: Not all relevant audit logs may be available to the audit system. For instance, with reference to Example 2.1, it is conceivable that the predicates **send** and **consents** are stored on separate physical sites. If we audit at the first site, information about **consents** may be unavailable. This incompleteness is easily modeled by requiring $\mathcal{L}(\texttt{consents}(p, a, \tau)) = \texttt{uu}$ for all p, a and τ.

- Subjective incompleteness: A mechanized audit system is unlikely to resolve predicates that rely on human input. In Example 2.1, assuming that the set of doctors of a patient is not known to the audit algorithm, resolving the predicate $\texttt{doctorOf}(p_2, q, \tau)$ may require human input. Formally, this is modeled by a partial structure $\mathcal{L}$ satisfying $\mathcal{L}(\texttt{doctorOf}(p_2, q, \tau)) = \texttt{uu}$ for all p_2 , q, and τ. Similarly, predicates that rely on human belief or professional judgment, which constitute a significant fraction of all predicates used in a prior formalization of HIPAA [15], can be modeled by mapping them to **uu** in a structure.

Because our audit algorithm (Section 3) works with partial structures, it takes into account all these forms of incompleteness. We note that real audit logs often only list atoms that are true (**tt**), and cannot distinguish atoms that are false (**ff**) from those that are unknown (**uu**). Consequently, for modeling real scenarios, we define partial structures $\mathcal{L}$ from system logs and additional information about their completeness, as explained in Section 4.1.

Semantics. We formalize the semantics of logical formulas as the relation $\mathcal{L} \models \varphi$, read "$\varphi$ is true in the partial structure $\mathcal{L}$". Restrictions c are a subsyntax of formulas φ, so we do not define the relation separately for them.

- $\mathcal{L} \models P$ iff $\mathcal{L}(P) = \mathtt{tt}$
- $\mathcal{L} \models \top$
- $\mathcal{L} \models \varphi \wedge \psi$ iff $\mathcal{L} \models \varphi$ and $\mathcal{L} \models \psi$
- $\mathcal{L} \models \varphi \vee \psi$ iff $\mathcal{L} \models \varphi$ or $\mathcal{L} \models \psi$
- $\mathcal{L} \models \forall \vec{x}.(c \supset \varphi)$ iff for all $\vec{t} \in \mathrm{D}$ either $\mathcal{L} \models \overline{c}[\vec{t}/\vec{x}]$ or $\mathcal{L} \models \varphi[\vec{t}/\vec{x}]$
- $\mathcal{L} \models \exists \vec{x}.(c \wedge \varphi)$ iff there exists $\vec{t} \in \mathrm{D}$ such that $\mathcal{L} \models c[\vec{t}/\vec{x}]$ and $\mathcal{L} \models \varphi[\vec{t}/\vec{x}]$

For dual atoms, we define $\mathcal{L}(\overline{P}) = \overline{\mathcal{L}(P)}$, where $\overline{\mathtt{tt}} = \mathtt{ff}$, $\overline{\mathtt{ff}} = \mathtt{tt}$, and $\overline{\mathtt{uu}} = \mathtt{uu}$. We say that a formula φ is *false* on the structure $\mathcal{L}$ if $\mathcal{L} \models \overline{\varphi}$. The following two properties hold:

1. Consistency: A formula φ cannot be simultaneously true and false in the structure $\mathcal{L}$, i.e., either $\mathcal{L} \not\models \varphi$ or $\mathcal{L} \not\models \overline{\varphi}$
2. Incompleteness: A formula φ may be neither true nor false in a structure $\mathcal{L}$, i.e., $\mathcal{L} \not\models \varphi$ and $\mathcal{L} \not\models \overline{\varphi}$ may both hold.

The first property follows by induction on φ. The second property follows from a simple example. Consider a structure $\mathcal{L}$ and an atom P such that $\mathcal{L}(P) = \mathtt{uu}$. Then, $\mathcal{L} \not\models P$ and $\mathcal{L} \not\models \overline{P}$.

Structure Extension. In practice, system logs evolve over time by gathering more information. This leads to a partial order, $\mathcal{L}_1 \leq \mathcal{L}_2$ on structures ($\mathcal{L}_2$ *extends* $\mathcal{L}_1$), meaning that $\mathcal{L}_2$ has more information than $\mathcal{L}_1$. Formally, $\mathcal{L}_1 \leq \mathcal{L}_2$ if for all ground atoms P (atoms P without free variables), $\mathcal{L}_1(P) \in \{\mathtt{tt}, \mathtt{ff}\}$ implies $\mathcal{L}_2(P) = \mathcal{L}_1(P)$. Thus, as structures extend, the valuation of an atom may change from $\mathtt{uu}$ to either $\mathtt{tt}$ or $\mathtt{ff}$, but cannot change once it is either $\mathtt{tt}$ or $\mathtt{ff}$. The following property follows by induction on φ:

- Monotonicity: $\mathcal{L}_1 \leq \mathcal{L}_2$ and $\mathcal{L}_1 \models \varphi$ imply $\mathcal{L}_2 \models \varphi$.

Replacing φ with $\overline{\varphi}$, we also obtain that $\mathcal{L}_1 \leq \mathcal{L}_2$ and $\mathcal{L}_1 \models \overline{\varphi}$ imply $\mathcal{L}_2 \models \overline{\varphi}$. Hence, if $\mathcal{L}_1 \leq \mathcal{L}_2$ then $\mathcal{L}_2$ preserves both the $\mathcal{L}_1$-truth and $\mathcal{L}_1$-falsity of every formula φ.

3. AUDIT ALGORITHM

Our main technical contribution is an iterative process that checks for violations of policies written in the logic. At each iteration, our algorithm takes as input a policy φ and information about atoms abstracted as a partial structure $\mathcal{L}$, and outputs a residual policy ψ that contains exactly the parts of φ that could not be verified due to lack of information in $\mathcal{L}$. Such an iteration is written $\mathsf{reduce}(\mathcal{L}, \varphi) = \psi$. When more information becomes available, extending $\mathcal{L}$ to $\mathcal{L}'$ ($\mathcal{L} \leq \mathcal{L}'$), another iteration of the algorithm can be used with inputs ψ and $\mathcal{L}'$ to obtain a new formula ψ'. This process can be continued until the output is either $\top$ (no violation), $\bot$ (violation) or a human auditor inspects the output. By design, our algorithm satisfies three important properties:

- Termination: Each iteration terminates.
- Correctness: If $\mathsf{reduce}(\mathcal{L}, \varphi) = \psi$, then for all extensions $\mathcal{L}'$ of $\mathcal{L}$, $\mathcal{L}' \models \varphi$ iff $\mathcal{L}' \models \psi$.
- Minimality: If $\mathsf{reduce}(\mathcal{L}, \varphi) = \psi$, then an atom occurs in ψ only if it occurs in φ and its valuation on $\mathcal{L}$ is $\mathtt{uu}$.

The technically difficult part of reduce is its treatment of quantifiers over infinite domains. Consider, for instance, the behavior of an algorithm satisfying the above three properties on input $\forall x.\varphi$. Because the output must be minimal, in order to reduce $\forall x.\varphi$, a naive algorithm will instantiate x with each possible element of the domain D and check the truth or falsity of φ for that instance on $\mathcal{L}$. This immediately leads to non-termination if the domain D is infinite, which does happen for real policies (e.g., HIPAA contains quantification over the infinite domain of messages).

Given the need for infinite domains, something intrinsic in quantification must limit the number of *relevant instances* of x that need to be checked to a finite number. To this end, we rely on the restrictions c in quantifiers, $\forall \vec{x}.(c \supset \varphi)$ and $\exists \vec{x}.(c \wedge \varphi)$, and use the technique of *mode analysis* from logic programming [2] to ensure that the restriction c has only a finite number of satisfying instances in any structure and that these instances are *computable.*

Briefly, mode analysis requires the policy designer to specify which argument positions of a predicate can be *computed finitely* from others. For instance, in Example 2.1 we assumed that the purpose of a message is written on it in machine-readable format and, hence, can be computed from the message. Denoting required inputs by $+$ and computable outputs by $-$, we may give the predicate $\mathtt{purp}(m, u)$ the *mode* $\mathtt{purp}(+, -)$, meaning that from the input m, the output u can be computed. The mode $\mathtt{purp}(-, +)$ is incorrect because given a fixed second argument (purpose), there may be an infinite number of first arguments (messages) annotated with that purpose, so the latter set cannot be finitely computed. Similarly, if the predicate $\mathtt{mult}(x, y, z)$ means that $x = yz$, where x, y, z are integers, then any of the modes $\mathtt{mult}(+, +, -)$, $\mathtt{mult}(-, +, +)$, and $\mathtt{mult}(+, -, +)$ are okay, but $\mathtt{mult}(-, -, +)$ is not.

Given the mode information of all predicates in a policy, a static, linear-time check of the policy, called a *mode check*, ensures that there are only a finite number of instances of free variables that can satisfy a restriction c in the policy. To keep the presentation accessible, we omit a technical description of mode checking, but its details are present in our TR. We note that mode checking is very permissive even though not every policy in the syntax of the logic passes the mode check. In particular, our entire prior formalization of HIPAA [15] passes the check.

To actually *compute* the satisfying instances of a restriction, we define a function $\widehat{\mathtt{sat}}(\mathcal{L}, c)$ that returns all substitutions σ for free variables of c such that $\mathcal{L} \models c\sigma$ (Section 3.1). This definition assumes a function $\mathtt{sat}(\mathcal{L}, P)$ that returns all substitutions σ for free variables of P such that $\mathcal{L} \models P\sigma$ if all input positions in P are ground. In practice, $\mathtt{sat}(\mathcal{L}, P)$ is implemented by looking up system logs or calling domain-specific solvers, depending on the predicate in

P (see Section 4 for the definition of $\mathtt{sat}$ that we use in our implementation).

Finally, the main audit function $\mathsf{reduce}(\mathcal{L}, \varphi)$ is defined by induction on φ, using $\widehat{\mathtt{sat}}(\mathcal{L}, c)$ as a black-box. Because $\mathtt{sat}(\mathcal{L}, P)$ may only be defined for P with ground input arguments, $\mathsf{reduce}(\mathcal{L}, \varphi)$ is a partial function. However, we show that if φ passes the mode check, then $\mathsf{reduce}(\mathcal{L}, \varphi)$ is defined (Theorem 3.3).

3.1 Iterative Reduction

At the core of our audit regime is a computable function $\mathsf{reduce}(\mathcal{L}, \varphi) = \psi$, that instantiates quantifiers in, and simplifies, the prevalent policy φ using information from the extant structure $\mathcal{L}$ to obtain a residual policy ψ. Given an initial policy φ_0 and a sequence of structures $\mathcal{L}_1 \leq \mathcal{L}_2 \leq \ldots \leq \mathcal{L}_n$, the reduction algorithm can be applied repeatedly to obtain $\varphi_1, \ldots, \varphi_n$ such that $\mathsf{reduce}(\mathcal{L}_i, \varphi_{i-1}) = \varphi_i$. We write this process in symbols as $\varphi_0 \xrightarrow{\mathcal{L}_1} \varphi_1 \ldots \xrightarrow{\mathcal{L}_n} \varphi_n$.

The definition of reduce is shown in Figure 1. It relies on the function $\widehat{\mathtt{sat}}(\mathcal{L}, c)$, which we define later. $\widehat{\mathtt{sat}}(\mathcal{L}, c)$ computes the finite set of substitutions σ such that $\mathcal{L} \models c\sigma$. For atoms P, $\mathsf{reduce}(\mathcal{L}, P)$ equals $\top$, $\bot$, or P, if $\mathcal{L}(P)$ equals $\mathtt{tt}$, $\mathtt{ff}$, or $\mathtt{uu}$, respectively. The clauses for the connectives $\top$, $\bot$, $\wedge$, and $\vee$ are straightforward. To evaluate $\mathsf{reduce}(\mathcal{L}, \forall\vec{x}.(c \supset \varphi))$, we first determine the set of instances of $\vec{x}$ that satisfy c by calling $\widehat{\mathtt{sat}}(\mathcal{L}, c)$. For each such instance $\vec{t_1}, \ldots, \vec{t_n}$, we reduce $\varphi[\vec{t_i}/\vec{x}]$ to ψ_i through a recursive call to reduce. Because all instances of φ must hold in order for $\forall\vec{x}.(c \supset \varphi)$ to be true, the output is $\psi_1 \wedge \ldots \wedge \psi_n \wedge \psi'$, where the last conjunct ψ' records the fact that instances of $\vec{x}$ *other than* $\vec{t_1}, \ldots, \vec{t_n}$ have not been considered. The latter is necessary because there may be instances of $\vec{x}$ satisfying c in extensions of $\mathcal{L}$, but not $\mathcal{L}$ itself. Precisely, we define $S = \{\vec{t_1}, \ldots, \vec{t_n}\}$ and $\psi' = \forall\vec{x}.((c \wedge \vec{x} \notin S) \supset \varphi)$. The new conjunct $\vec{x} \notin S$ prevents the instances $\vec{t_1}, \ldots, \vec{t_n}$ from being checked again in subsequent iterations. Formally, $\vec{x} \notin S$ encodes the negation of the usual finite-set membership. The treatment of $\exists\vec{x}.(c \wedge \varphi)$ is dual; in that case, the output contains disjunctions because the truth of any one instance of φ suffices for the formula to hold.

Our implementation also performs trivial rewriting to simplify the output of reduce. Specifically, it rewrites $\psi \wedge \top$ to ψ, $\psi \wedge \bot$ to $\bot$, $\psi \vee \top$ to $\top$, and $\psi \vee \bot$ to ψ.

Definition of $\widehat{\mathtt{sat}}$. The function $\widehat{\mathtt{sat}}(\mathcal{L}, c)$ which computes the set of substitutions σ such that $\mathcal{L} \models c\sigma$, is defined below. This function relies on a given function $\mathtt{sat}(\mathcal{L}, P)$ that computes the set of substitutions σ such that $\mathcal{L} \models P\sigma$. The latter function is application-dependent, as described in Section 4.

$$
\begin{array}{lcl}
\widehat{\mathtt{sat}}(\mathcal{L}, p(t_1, \ldots, t_n)) & = & \mathtt{sat}(\mathcal{L}, p(t_1, \ldots, t_n)) \\
\widehat{\mathtt{sat}}(\mathcal{L}, \top) & = & \{\bullet\} \\
\widehat{\mathtt{sat}}(\mathcal{L}, \bot) & = & \{\} \\
\widehat{\mathtt{sat}}(\mathcal{L}, c_1 \wedge c_2) & = & \bigcup_{\sigma \in \widehat{\mathtt{sat}}(\mathcal{L}, c_1)} \sigma + \widehat{\mathtt{sat}}(\mathcal{L}, c_2\sigma) \\
\widehat{\mathtt{sat}}(\mathcal{L}, c_1 \vee c_2) & = & \widehat{\mathtt{sat}}(\mathcal{L}, c_1) \cup \widehat{\mathtt{sat}}(\mathcal{L}, c_2) \\
\widehat{\mathtt{sat}}(\mathcal{L}, \exists x.c) & = & \widehat{\mathtt{sat}}(\mathcal{L}, c) \backslash \{x\} \quad (x \text{ fresh})
\end{array}
$$

For atoms, the definition of $\widehat{\mathtt{sat}}$ coincides with that of $\mathtt{sat}$. Since $\top$ must always be true, $\widehat{\mathtt{sat}}(\mathcal{L}, \top)$ contains only the empty substitution (denoted $\bullet$). Since $\bot$ can never be satisfied, $\widehat{\mathtt{sat}}(\mathcal{L}, \bot)$ is empty (denoted $\{\}$). For $c_1 \wedge c_2$, the set of satisfying instances is obtained by taking those of

$$
\mathsf{reduce}(\mathcal{L}, P) = \begin{cases} \top & \text{if } \mathcal{L}(P) = \mathtt{tt} \\ \bot & \text{if } \mathcal{L}(P) = \mathtt{ff} \\ P & \text{if } \mathcal{L}(P) = \mathtt{uu} \end{cases}
$$

$$
\begin{array}{lcl}
\mathsf{reduce}(\mathcal{L}, \top) & = & \top \\
\mathsf{reduce}(\mathcal{L}, \bot) & = & \bot \\
\mathsf{reduce}(\mathcal{L}, \varphi_1 \wedge \varphi_2) & = & \mathsf{reduce}(\mathcal{L}, \varphi_1) \wedge \mathsf{reduce}(\mathcal{L}, \varphi_2) \\
\mathsf{reduce}(\mathcal{L}, \varphi_1 \vee \varphi_2) & = & \mathsf{reduce}(\mathcal{L}, \varphi_1) \vee \mathsf{reduce}(\mathcal{L}, \varphi_2)
\end{array}
$$

$$
\begin{array}{lcl}
\mathsf{reduce}(\mathcal{L}, \forall\vec{x}.(c \supset \varphi)) & = & \text{let} \\
& & \quad \{\sigma_1, \ldots, \sigma_n\} \leftarrow \widehat{\mathtt{sat}}(\mathcal{L}, c) \\
& & \quad \{\vec{t_i} \leftarrow \sigma_i(\vec{x})\}_{i=1}^n \\
& & \quad S \leftarrow \{\vec{t_1}, \ldots, \vec{t_n}\} \\
& & \quad \{\psi_i \leftarrow \mathsf{reduce}(\mathcal{L}, \varphi[\vec{t_i}/\vec{x}])\}_{i=1}^n \\
& & \quad \psi' \leftarrow \forall\vec{x}.((c \wedge \vec{x} \notin S) \supset \varphi) \\
& & \text{return} \\
& & \quad \psi_1 \wedge \ldots \wedge \psi_n \wedge \psi'
\end{array}
$$

$$
\begin{array}{lcl}
\mathsf{reduce}(\mathcal{L}, \exists\vec{x}.(c \wedge \varphi)) & = & \text{let} \\
& & \quad \{\sigma_1, \ldots, \sigma_n\} \leftarrow \widehat{\mathtt{sat}}(\mathcal{L}, c) \\
& & \quad \{\vec{t_i} \leftarrow \sigma_i(\vec{x})\}_{i=1}^n \\
& & \quad S \leftarrow \{\vec{t_1}, \ldots, \vec{t_n}\} \\
& & \quad \{\psi_i \leftarrow \mathsf{reduce}(\mathcal{L}, \varphi[\vec{t_i}/\vec{x}])\}_{i=1}^n \\
& & \quad \psi' \leftarrow \exists\vec{x}.((c \wedge \vec{x} \notin S) \wedge \varphi) \\
& & \text{return} \\
& & \quad \psi_1 \vee \ldots \vee \psi_n \vee \psi'
\end{array}
$$

Figure 1: Definition of $\mathsf{reduce}(\mathcal{L}, \varphi)$

c_1 (denoted σ above), and conjoining those with satisfying instances of $c_2\sigma$ (the operation $\sigma + \Sigma$ appends σ to every substitution in Σ). The set of satisfying instances of $c_1 \vee c_2$ is the union of the satisfying instances of c_1 and c_2. Satisfying instances of $\exists x.c$ are obtained by taking those of c, and removing the substitutions for x ($\Sigma \backslash \{x\}$ removes x from the domain of every substitution in Σ).

Example 3.1. We illustrate iterative audit on the policy φ_{pol} from Example 2.1. For notational convenience, let $\vec{x}$ denote the sequence of variables $p_1, p_2, m, u, q, t, \tau$ and define $c(\vec{x})$ and $\varphi(\vec{x})$ by pattern matching as the restriction and formula satisfying $\varphi_{pol} = \forall\vec{x}.\ c(\vec{x}) \supset \varphi(\vec{x})$. Intuitively, $\varphi(p_1, p_2, m, u, q, t, \tau)$ is the formula that must be satisfied if p_1 sends to p_2 the message m at time τ and m is tagged as containing attribute t about principal q for purpose u. Further, define φ_2 and φ_3 by pattern matching as follows: $\varphi(\vec{x}) = \mathtt{attr\_in}(t, phi) \vee \varphi_2(p_2, q, \tau, u) \vee \varphi_3(\tau, q, p_1, p_2, t)$.

Consider a structure $\mathcal{L}$ with the following information: (1) Alice sends to Bob the message M at time 4, tagged as containing information about Charlie's address for the purpose of billing, (2) Charlie authorized this transmission at time 2. This information implies that $\widehat{\mathtt{sat}}(\mathcal{L}, c(\vec{x})) = \{\sigma\}$, where $\sigma = [\vec{x} \mapsto (\text{Alice}, \text{Bob}, M, \text{billing}, \text{Charlie}, \text{address}, 4)]$. Applying the definition of reduce, we obtain $\mathsf{reduce}(\mathcal{L}, \varphi_{pol}) = \psi_1 \wedge \varphi'_{pol}$ where $\psi_1 = \mathsf{reduce}(\mathcal{L}, \varphi(\vec{x})\sigma)$ and $\varphi'_{pol} = \forall\vec{x}.\ (c(\vec{x}) \wedge \vec{x} \notin \{\sigma\}) \supset \varphi(\vec{x})$.

Since $\varphi(\vec{x})$ is a disjunction of three formulas, the third of which is $\varphi_3(\tau, q, p_1, p_2, t)$, ψ_1 is also a disjunction of three formulas, the third of which is $\mathsf{reduce}(\mathcal{L}, \varphi_3(\tau, q, p_1, p_2, t)\sigma)$. It can easily be shown using (2) that this third disjunct is $\top$, so ψ_1 also simplifies to $\top$. This indicates that there is no violation of the policy so far, which should be intuitively clear from the description of the structure $\mathcal{L}$ and an inspection of the policy φ_{pol}. Succinctly, we have $\mathsf{reduce}(\mathcal{L}, \varphi_{pol}) = \varphi'_{pol}$.

Next, consider an extension $\mathcal{L}'$ which adds new information: (3) Alice sends to Bob a message M' at time 5, tagged as containing Dan's lab report for the purpose of surgery, (4) $\mathcal{L}'(\mathtt{consents}(\text{Dan}, a, \tau')) = \mathtt{ff}$ for every action a and every time τ' (in particular, Dan has not consented to Alice's transmission), and (5) $\mathcal{L}'(\mathtt{doctorOf}(\text{Bob}, \text{Dan}, 5)) = \mathtt{ff}$ (so Bob is not Dan's doctor at time 5). Then, the restriction in the top-level universal quantifier of φ'_{pol}, i.e., $c'(\vec{x}) = c(\vec{x}) \wedge \vec{x} \notin \{\sigma\}$ satisfies $\widehat{\mathtt{sat}}(\mathcal{L}', c'(\vec{x})) = \{\sigma'\}$, where $\sigma' = [\vec{x} \mapsto (\text{Alice}, \text{Bob}, M', \text{surgery}, \text{Dan}, \text{labreport}, 5)]$. Hence, $\mathsf{reduce}(\mathcal{L}', \varphi'_{pol}) = \psi_2 \wedge \varphi''_{pol}$, where $\psi_2 = \mathsf{reduce}(\mathcal{L}', \varphi(\vec{x})\sigma')$ and φ''_{pol} enforces the policy on transmissions other than the two already considered. Calculation using (4) and (5) yields $\psi_2 = \overline{\mathtt{attr\_in}}(\text{labreport}, \textit{phi})$, meaning that Alice's transmission of Bob's record satisfies the policy only if labreport is not a form of *phi* (protected health information). The same conclusion may also be expected from an informal inspection of the policy.

Reporting Causes of Policy Violations. From what we have presented so far, it may appear that the output of $\mathsf{reduce}(\mathcal{L}, \varphi)$ can only say that there has been a policy violation but cannot indicate *which instances* of quantifiers in φ have led to the violation. For instance, consider the policy $\varphi_{pol} = \forall \vec{x}.\ (c(\vec{x}) \supset \varphi(\vec{x}))$ defined in the beginning of Example 3.1. If $c(\vec{a})$ is true for some instance $\vec{a}$ of $\vec{x}$ on structure $\mathcal{L}$, but $\varphi(\vec{a})$ is false, then $\mathsf{reduce}(\mathcal{L}, \varphi_{pol})$ will evaluate to $\bot$, indicating a violation of the policy. However, this output does not indicate the instance $\vec{a}$ which actually causes the violation.

Violating instances of a policy can be reported in the output of reduce by slightly rewriting the policy formula (but without changing the the reduce algorithm). The idea is straightforward and easily illustrated with the example of φ_{pol}. Consider a new predicate $\mathtt{violated}(\vec{x})$ which means that the list of terms $\vec{x}$ causes a violation of the policy φ_{pol}. Further, and importantly, assume that $\mathtt{violated}$ is uninterpreted, i.e., for all $\vec{t}$, $\mathcal{L}(\mathtt{violated}(\vec{t})) = \mathtt{uu}$ (in our implementation, we call such uninterpreted predicates subjective or SUBJ; see Section 4). Consider the revised policy $\varphi'_{pol} = \forall \vec{x}.(c(\vec{x}) \supset (\mathtt{violated}(\vec{x}) \vee \varphi(\vec{x})))$. Intuitively, φ'_{pol} says that for all instances $\vec{a}$ of $\vec{x}$, if $c(\vec{a})$ is true, then either $\vec{a}$ violates the policy or $\varphi(\vec{a})$ is true. This is also the intended meaning of φ_{pol}, so replacing it with φ'_{pol} does not change the meaning of the policy itself. However, when reduce is executed on φ'_{pol} instead of φ_{pol}, the top-level of the output contains $\mathtt{violated}(\vec{a_1}) \wedge \ldots \wedge \mathtt{violated}(\vec{a_n})$, where $\vec{a_1}, \ldots, \vec{a_n}$ are exactly those instances of $\vec{x}$ for which c is true and φ is false. So, all instances of the quantifier $\vec{x}$ that cause policy violation can be read from the output of reduce on the revised policy φ'_{pol}. The technique illustrated by this example generalizes easily; any quantified formula (either universal or existential) can be modified by adding a new uninterpreted predicate to cause reduce to report all instances of quantified variables that violate the formula.

3.2 Properties of the Audit Algorithm

Partial Correctness. The function reduce is partially correct: If $\mathsf{reduce}(\mathcal{L}, \varphi) = \psi$, then in all extensions of $\mathcal{L}$, φ and ψ are logically equivalent.

Theorem 3.2 (Partial correctness of reduce). *If* $\mathsf{reduce}(\mathcal{L}, \varphi) = \psi$ *and* $\mathcal{L} \leq \mathcal{L}'$, *then (1)* $\mathcal{L}' \models \varphi$ *iff* $\mathcal{L}' \models \psi$ *and (2)* $\mathcal{L}' \models \overline{\varphi}$ *iff* $\mathcal{L}' \models \overline{\psi}$.

Partial correctness of iterative audit is an immediate corollary of Theorem 3.2. We can prove by induction on n that if $\varphi_0 \xrightarrow{\mathcal{L}_1} \varphi_1 \ldots \xrightarrow{\mathcal{L}_n} \varphi_n$, then for all structures $\mathcal{L}'$ satisfying $\mathcal{L}_n \leq \mathcal{L}'$, $\mathcal{L}' \models \varphi_n$ iff $\mathcal{L}' \models \varphi_0$ and $\mathcal{L}' \models \overline{\varphi_n}$ iff $\mathcal{L}' \models \overline{\varphi_0}$.

Totality. Let $\vdash \varphi$ mean that φ passes the mode check. The following theorem states that reduce is defined on every such φ and, further, that the output also passes the mode check.

Theorem 3.3 (Totality of reduce). *If* $\vdash \varphi$ *then there is a* ψ *such that* $\mathsf{reduce}(\mathcal{L}, \varphi) = \psi$ *and* $\vdash \psi$.

Complexity. The function $\mathsf{reduce}(\mathcal{L}, \varphi)$ can be implemented using auxiliary space polynomial in the size of the formula φ, and in time polynomial in the maximum number of substitutions returned by $\mathtt{sat}$ (denoted $|\mathcal{L}|$) where the degree of the polynomial is proportional to the size of the formula φ. This analysis assumes that computation of each output returned by $\mathtt{sat}$ takes unit time which, in turn means that finding a single row in a system log and reading it takes unit time. In practice, $|\mathcal{L}|$ is bounded by the size of the system logs, so the execution time of reduce for a fixed policy is polynomial in the size of the system logs.

Theorem 3.4 (Complexity of reduce). *Assuming that computing each output returned by* $\mathtt{sat}$ *takes unit time, the algorithm* $\mathsf{reduce}(\mathcal{L}, \varphi)$ *lies in the intersection of the complexity classes* $TIME(|\mathcal{L}|^{O(|\varphi|)})$ *and* $PSPACE(|\varphi|)$.

Minimality. If $\mathsf{reduce}(\mathcal{L}, \varphi) = \psi$ then ψ is minimal with respect to φ and $\mathcal{L}$, i.e., an atom occurs in ψ only if it occurs in φ and its valuation in $\mathcal{L}$ is unknown. Unfortunately, owing to quantification, there is no standard definition of the set of atoms of a formula of first-order logic. In the following, we provide one natural definition of the atoms of a formula and characterize minimality with respect to it. For a formula φ that passes the mode check, we define the set of atoms of φ with respect to a structure $\mathcal{L}$ as follows.

$$
\begin{array}{lcl}
\mathtt{atoms}(\mathcal{L}, P) & = & \{P\} \\
\mathtt{atoms}(\mathcal{L}, \top) & = & \{\} \\
\mathtt{atoms}(\mathcal{L}, \bot) & = & \{\} \\
\mathtt{atoms}(\mathcal{L}, \varphi_1 \wedge \varphi_2) & = & \mathtt{atoms}(\mathcal{L}, \varphi_1) \cup \mathtt{atoms}(\mathcal{L}, \varphi_2) \\
\mathtt{atoms}(\mathcal{L}, \varphi_1 \vee \varphi_2) & = & \mathtt{atoms}(\mathcal{L}, \varphi_1) \cup \mathtt{atoms}(\mathcal{L}, \varphi_2) \\
\mathtt{atoms}(\mathcal{L}, \forall \vec{x}.(c \supset \varphi)) & = & \bigcup_{\sigma \in \widehat{\mathtt{sat}}(\mathcal{L}, c)} \mathtt{atoms}(\mathcal{L}, \varphi\sigma) \\
\mathtt{atoms}(\mathcal{L}, \exists \vec{x}.(c \wedge \varphi)) & = & \bigcup_{\sigma \in \widehat{\mathtt{sat}}(\mathcal{L}, c)} \mathtt{atoms}(\mathcal{L}, \varphi\sigma)
\end{array}
$$

Theorem 3.5 (Minimality). *If* $\vdash \varphi$ *and* $\mathsf{reduce}(\mathcal{L}, \varphi) = \psi$, *then* $\mathtt{atoms}(\mathcal{L}, \psi) \subseteq \mathtt{atoms}(\mathcal{L}, \varphi) \cap \{P \mid \mathcal{L}(P) = \mathtt{uu}\}$.

4. IMPLEMENTATION

We have implemented the iterative algorithm $\mathsf{reduce}(\mathcal{L}, \varphi)$ described in Section 3 as well as the mode analysis on formulas. The implementation is written in Standard ML. This section describes the implementation of $\mathsf{reduce}(\mathcal{L}, \varphi)$ and syntax-directed optimizations on it. Section 5 reports on the implementation's experimental evaluation.

4.1 Application-Specific Structures

Our implementation of reduce closely follows its abstract definition from Section 3.1. The implementation must be *instantiated* for a specific application by providing enough information to define a structure $\mathcal{L}$, specifically, the two functions $\mathtt{sat}(\mathcal{L}, P)$ and $\mathcal{L}(P)$, on which reduce relies. This information includes audit logs (e.g., transmission or access logs) and relevant system databases (e.g., the roles database), and is structured into five different components that we describe next. Later, we describe how these four components are used to define $\mathtt{sat}(\mathcal{L}, P)$ and $\mathcal{L}(P)$.

First, the implementation of reduce must be told how each predicate is verified. This is called the *category* of the predicate, and is provided to the implementation through a file in a custom syntax. Our current implementation supports the following three common categories, but can be extended modularly to include other forms of verification if needed.

A. DB (Database): The predicate maps directly to a table in a relational database and is computed by looking up the table. The name of the table and the column name corresponding to each argument of the predicate must also be provided. We assume that audit logs are also represented as database tables, so predicates corresponding to these logs (e.g., `send` from Example 2.1) are also in the category DB.

B. EVAL (Evaluable): The predicate is verified through a given computable function (e.g., $\mathtt{mult}(x, y, z)$ meaning $x = yz$ would lie in this category).

C. SUBJ (Subjective): The predicate has no mechanized definition; it is checked by a human auditor.

To illustrate, the predicates `send` and `consents` in Example 2.1 are DB because they correspond to tables in the system logs; predicates `tagged` and `purp` are EVAL because they are implemented by analysis of messages (their first arguments); predicate `doctorOf` is SUBJ because its verification requires knowledge of all of a principal's doctors, which is unlikely to be available in mechanized form.

Second, a function, lookup, to query the database must be provided. Our current implementation requires that lookup support standard SQL SELECT queries. Using this function, we define a function $\mathsf{sat\_db}(P)$ that finds all satisfying substitutions for variables in a DB atom P by running a query on the database table corresponding to P.

Third, a function $\mathsf{eval}(P)$ to evaluate EVAL atoms P must be provided. This function has the same specification as `sat`, except that it need be defined only for EVAL atoms.

Fourth, we require a function $\mathsf{isFinal}(P)$ that takes as input a DB or EVAL atom P with ground input arguments and returns true iff in future extensions of the structure, no additional substitutions satisfying P will be found (i.e., substitutions other than those found by looking up its corresponding table or by running eval on it). The implementation of $\mathsf{isFinal}(P)$ will vary based on the predicate in P, but a simple heuristic works for DB atoms P if the database table corresponding to P is available in its entirety at the time of audit: $\mathsf{isFinal}(P) =$ true iff the time argument of P (which specifies the time at which the truth of P is being ascertained) is less than the time at which the database table was last updated.

Fifth, we require two tables of ground SUBJ atoms subjTrue and subjFalse that contain SUBJ atoms that have been marked true and false respectively by human auditors earlier. These tables are initially empty and an interactive front-end could allow a human auditor to add entries to both tables, making sure that no atom appears in both tables simultaneously.

Given these five components defining a structure $\mathcal{L}$, `sat` can be defined on $\mathcal{L}$ as follows.

$$\mathtt{sat}(\mathcal{L}, P) = \begin{cases} \mathsf{sat\_db}(P) & \text{if category}(P) = \text{DB} \\ \mathsf{eval}(P) & \text{if category}(P) = \text{EVAL} \\ \text{undefined} & \text{if category}(P) = \text{SUBJ} \end{cases}$$

(Our mode check ensures that a SUBJ atom never appears in a restriction so, following the definition of reduce, $\mathtt{sat}(\mathcal{L}, P)$ is never called if P is SUBJ. Hence, it is okay to have $\mathtt{sat}(\mathcal{L}, P) =$ undefined when P is SUBJ.)

Finally, we define $\mathcal{L}(P)$. Note that $\mathcal{L}(P)$ is meaningful only for P without free variables, and for such P, $\mathtt{sat}(\mathcal{L}, P)$ must be either $\{\}$ (no satisfying substitution) or $\{\bullet\}$ (only the trivial satisfying substitution) or undefined.

$$\mathcal{L}(P) = \begin{cases} \mathtt{tt} & \text{if } \mathtt{sat}(\mathcal{L}, P) = \{\bullet\} \text{ or } P \in \mathsf{subjTrue} \\ \mathtt{ff} & \text{if } (\mathtt{sat}(\mathcal{L}, P) = \{\} \text{ and } \mathsf{isFinal}(P) = \text{true}) \\ & \quad \text{or } P \in \mathsf{subjFalse} \\ \mathtt{uu} & \text{otherwise} \end{cases}$$

The valuation of a variable-free atom P is `tt` if either it has a satisfying substitution or it exists in the table subjTrue; the valuation is `ff` if either P does not have a satisfying substitution and it cannot become true in any extension of the structure or it exists in the table subjFalse; in all other cases, the valuation of P is `uu`.

4.2 Optimizations

We discuss some optimizations to simplify the output of reduce and improve the performance of its implementation.

Removing Residual Terms. The residual formula $\psi' = \forall\vec{x}.((c \wedge \vec{x} \notin S) \supset \varphi)$ or $\psi' = \exists\vec{x}.((c \wedge \vec{x} \notin S) \wedge \varphi)$ in the output of reduce in Figure 1 can be very large because it contains all substitutions S in the output of $\widehat{\mathtt{sat}}(\mathcal{L}, c)$. Accordingly, we remove this residual formula from the output of reduce using the following simple heuristic: If during the evaluation of $\widehat{\mathtt{sat}}(\mathcal{L}, c)$ in the reduction of a quantifier $\forall\vec{x}.(c \supset \varphi)$ or $\exists\vec{x}.(c \wedge \varphi)$, every recursive call of the form $\mathtt{sat}(\mathcal{L}, P)$ satisfies $\mathsf{isFinal}(P) =$ true, then the $c \wedge \vec{x} \notin S$ cannot be satisfied in any extension of $\mathcal{L}$, so the residual term ψ' can be omitted. Whether or not $\mathsf{isFinal}(P) =$ true in every recursive call is easily checked by maintaining a boolean variable during evaluation of $\widehat{\mathtt{sat}}$.

Database Indexing. As may be expected, indexing tables in system databases has a significant impact on performance. We list two reasonable syntax-directed heuristics for choosing tables and columns to index. These heuristics are justified through experiments in Section 5.

- Index deeper: More performance gains may be expected by indexing tables corresponding to DB predicates that are nested deeper inside quantifiers in the policy because our reduce procedure replicates formulas for each instance of a quantifier and this has a multiplicative effect for nested quantifiers.

- Index input modes: A table corresponding to the DB predicate p should be indexed on columns that correspond to input arguments in the mode of p because these columns are guaranteed to be known in any look-up query on the table.

Database Caching. We mention that in-memory caching of previously read entries of a database table is unlikely to improve performance when policies contain quantifiers. This is because the atoms checked against a database change every time quantifiers are instantiated differently. On the other hand, in-memory caching of database entries is very beneficial for policies without quantifiers.

5. EVALUATION

We evaluate our implementation of the algorithm reduce on policies that regulate the transmission of protected health information in the HIPAA Privacy Rule using synthetic logs generated by a simulator. Section 5.1 explains the setup of our experiments and Section 5.2 reports measurements of running time and memory consumed.

5.1 System Setup

HIPAA Policies. In prior work, we formalized all 84 transmission related clauses of HIPAA in a first-order logic PrivacyLFP [15]. To use our audit algorithm reduce on the formalized policy, we made semantics-preserving changes to our earlier encoding to make it fit our restricted quantifier syntax and to make it pass our mode check. These changes are minor and mostly involve refactoring parts of formulas under quantifiers into the restrictions required by our reduced syntax.

We show below the top-level formula of the HIPAA policy, φ_{HIPAA}. Predicates in φ_{HIPAA} have the same meaning as predicates of the same names in Example 2.1. The new predicate $\mathbf{contains}(m, q, t, u)$ means that the disclosed message m is both *correctly* tagged with the subject q and the attribute t of the information it is carrying and is correctly labeled with the purpose of the disclosure u. Verification of correctness of tags requires manual analysis of the content of m, which may be free text and, therefore, the predicate **contains** has category SUBJ. The body of the HIPAA policy is a conjunction of three components: 1) The **contains** predicate, 2) a disjunction of the so-called positive norms φ_i^+, of which at least one must be satisfied for every disclosure, and 3) a conjunction of the so-called negative norms φ_i^-, all of which must be satisfied for every disclosure [15].

$$\begin{aligned}
&\varphi_{\text{HIPAA}} = \\
&\quad \forall p_1, p_2, m, u, \tau.\ (\mathbf{send}(p_1, p_2, m, \tau) \wedge \mathbf{purp}(m, u)) \\
&\qquad \supset \forall q, t.\ \mathbf{tagged}(m, q, t) \\
&\qquad\qquad \supset (\mathbf{contains}(m, q, t, u) \wedge \textstyle\bigvee_i \varphi_i^+ \wedge \bigwedge_i \varphi_i^-)
\end{aligned}$$

Synthesizing Audit Logs. We test the algorithm reduce on synthetic logs generated by a discrete event-driven simulation that considers several disclosure scenarios governed by HIPAA. In particular, we simulate disclosures of protected health information by a HIPAA covered entity in the following scenarios: For its own treatment, payment and health operations; for another health provider's treatment, payment and health operations; for law-enforcement activities; for judicial administrative proceedings; for notification to friends and family to assist in treatment; and for marketing purposes.

Generated logs contain different types of events (disclosures, role changes, etc.). Each type of event is represented in the logic by a predicate (e.g., disclosures correspond to the predicate **send**) and is stored in a separate table in a SQLite database.

More precisely, the simulator implements a probabilistic event scheduler. Each scenario is repeated after a probabilistic gap, whose average value is an input to the simulator. For instance, we may assume that, on average, a hospital releases some patient's protected health information for judicial administrative proceedings every 30 days. During the execution of a scenario, the simulator adds relevant events to the database. In some cases, events may not be added with certain probabilities to model policy violations. For instance, one of our scenarios discloses protected health information to a coroner for the purpose of determining the cause of death of a patient. During this scenario, an entry corresponding to the disclosure is created in the database. In addition, two other facts are added to the database, but with probabilities less than 1: The first fact asserts that the receiver is actually in the role of a coroner and the second fact asserts that the purpose of the disclosure is determining the cause of death. Failure to add either of these two facts models a policy violation.

During simulation, we tag each disclosed message with a fresh symbolic attribute, and create entries in a table **attr_in_db** to record sub-attribute relations between such symbolic attributes. An entry (t_1, t_2) in table **attr_in_db** means that attribute t_1 is a sub-attribute of t_2. The table **attr_in_db** is used to compute the EVAL predicate **attr_in**.

5.2 Performance Evaluation

We perform two sets of experiments: one evaluates a single run of reduce, and the other evaluates iterative runs of reduce in the sense described at the beginning of Section 3.1. All experiments were performed on a 3GHz Intel Core 2 Duo CPU running Linux with 8GB RAM and a 7200 RPM hard disk drive. The database used for storing logs is SQLite version 3.7.2. Our implementation was compiled using the MLton compiler for Standard ML.

In the first set of experiments, we evaluate the impact of database indexing, the size of the database and the rate of policy violations on running time and memory consumption of reduce, by executing it on logs generated by the simulator. We vary the size of, and indexes on, three tables: **send**, **tagged**, and **attr_in_db**. These tables correspond to predicates that are nested progressively deeper inside quantifiers in φ_{HIPAA}. For each experiment, we record the size of the entire log (actually the size of the database containing all logs and indexes on them) and for each table we record the number of entries in the table, and whether or not it is indexed.

Figure 2 summarizes the evaluation results. For instance, in Experiment 1, the size of the entire database is 2.68MB, the table **send** contains 5401 entries, and it is not indexed (symbols N in the last four columns). Following the heuristic "index input modes" from Section 4.2, whenever we index a database table (entry Y in the last four columns), the index is created only on columns that correspond to input arguments of the corresponding predicate. The fifth column of Figure 2 is the probability that a disclosure in any scenario violates the policy.

Experiments 1–5 demonstrate the effect of indexing the database tables. Indexing a database table allows efficient random read access to data. As mentioned in Section 4.2,

Exp No.	Ave. Time per disclosure (s)	Total time (s)	Memory used (KB)	Prob. of violation	Log size (MB)	Number of entries/indexed (Y or N)			
						send	tagged	attr_in_db	the rest
1	0.27	1453.12	592440	0.10	2.68	5401/N	4947/N	5100/N	-/N
2	0.27	1456.43	592536	0.10	2.99	5401/Y	4947/N	5100/N	-/N
3	0.27	1448.53	592604	0.10	3.14	5401/Y	4947/Y	5100/N	-/N
4	0.26	1378.62	657436	0.10	3.29	5401/Y	4947/Y	5100/Y	-/N
5	0.04	209.21	662080	0.10	3.98	5401/Y	4947/Y	5100/Y	-/Y
6	0.07	725.19	1336808	0.10	7.68	10866/Y	9040/Y	9314/Y	-/Y
7	0.12	2674.77	2375564	0	15.11	21684/Y	16945/Y	17565/Y	-/Y
8	0.12	2680.25	2667132	0.10	15.10	21742/Y	17182/Y	17732/Y	-/Y
9	0.11	2306.93	3565964	1	14.41	21626/Y	16865/Y	17465/Y	-/Y

Figure 2: Experimental evaluation of single runs of the algorithm reduce

we may expect that indexing of predicates that are nested deeper in the policy would improve performance more. The results of Experiments 1–5 verify this expectation. For example, indexing the table of the predicate **send** (Experiment 2), which appears only in the restriction of the top-level quantifier of φ_{HIPAA} does not improve the running time at all over the baseline without any indexing (Experiment 1) because during the execution of reduce on φ_{HIPAA}, the **send** table is not accessed randomly. Instead, it is scanned linearly to instantiate the top-level quantifier in φ_{HIPAA}. Adding an index on the table **tagged** (Experiment 3), which is nested under two quantifiers, improves performance slightly over indexing **send** alone. Indexing **attr_in_db** (Experiment 4), which is nested very deep under quantifiers in the policy results in a noticeable improvement in performance. When we index all other tables in our database, of which six correspond to predicates that are nested very deep under quantifiers in the policy formula, we notice a large improvement in performance (Experiment 5).

Experiments 5, 6 and 8 measure the impact of log size on audit time for fully indexed tables. As expected, both the overall audit time and the per-disclosure audit time increase as the size of the logs increases.

Experiments 7–9 measure the effect of changing the ratio of policy violating disclosures to policy compliant disclosures. As can be seen, the average time per disclosure *decreases* slightly when more disclosures are violations. This is because the main body of φ_{HIPAA} contains conjunctions after the outermost quantifier. For an instance of the quantifier corresponding to a policy violation, reduce terminates as soon as any one formula in the conjunction reduces to false. On the other hand, for an instance of the quantifier corresponding to a policy compliant disclosure, the entire formula must be reduced.

Consequently, an experiment without policy violations (e.g., Experiment 7) measures the worst case performance of audit. Even this performance is very practical — for a database of size 15MB containing 21,684 disclosures without any violations, reduce can audit each disclosure in an average time of 0.12s.

In the second set of experiments, we simulate a run of our algorithm with three iterations on progressively larger logs, and measure the size of the residual formula after each iteration. The input to the first iteration is the formula φ_{HIPAA} and a log containing 5401 disclosures.

Figure 3 summarizes the evaluation results. The first column is the size of a textual rendering of the policy formula that is the input of reduce, and the second column is the size of the resulting output formula. The remaining columns document the running times, memory consumption, the size of the log in an iteration, and the number of disclosures in the log. The output formulas are quite large, e.g., after the first run, the output formula has a size 4,654.07 KB. The output formula is large because for each disclosure in the log, most of the policy formula is replicated in the output, but owing to a large number of SUBJ atoms in φ_{HIPAA}, these replicated formulas are not eliminated completely (67 out of the 84 clauses contain SUBJ atoms [15]). Although large output formulas slow subsequent iterations, such automatic iterations are not the intended application of reduce. Instead, we expect that our reduce algorithm will be used with an interactive front-end that allows an auditor to select specific subformulas of interest (e.g., those pertaining to disclosures by a specific agent) and run the reduce algorithm only on them. The front-end may also allow the auditor to provide information about subjective atoms and record such information for subsequent use.

6. RELATED WORK

Runtime Monitoring with Temporal Logic. A lot of prior work addresses the problem of *runtime monitoring* of policies expressed in Linear Temporal Logic (LTL) [32, 3, 29, 31, 9, 5] and its extensions [30, 5, 31]. Although similar in the spirit of enforcing policies, the intended deployment of our work is different: We assume that system logs are accumulated independently and given to our algorithm, whereas an integral component of runtime monitoring is accumulation of system logs on the fly. Our assumption about the availability of system logs fits practical situations like health organizations, which collect transmission, disclosure and other logs to comply with regulations such as HIPAA even if no computerized policy enforcement mechanism is in place.

Comparing only the expressiveness of the logic, our work is more advanced than all existing work on policy enforcement. First, LTL can be encoded in our logic easily [15]. Second, we allow expressive quantification in our logic, whereas prior work is either limited to propositional logic [32, 3, 29], or, when quantifiers are considered, they are severely restricted [30, 5, 31]. A recent exception to such syntactic restrictions is the work of Basin et al. [9], to which we compare in detail below. Third, no prior work considers the possibility of incompleteness in structures, which our reduce algorithm takes into account.

Recent work by Basin et al. [9] considers runtime monitoring over an expressive fragment of Metric First-order Temporal Logic. Similar to our work, Basin et al. allow quantification over infinite domains, and use a form of mode analysis (called a safe-range analysis) to ensure finiteness during en-

Policy size (KB)	Residual policy size (KB)	Ave. Time per disclosure(s)	Total time (s)	Memory used (KB)	Log size (MB)	Number of disclosures
39.52	4654.07	0.04	209.68	662080	3.98	5401
4654.07	9369.32	0.75	8193.76	4063472	7.68	10866
9369.32	19186.84	2.99	65009.30	4033484	15.1	21742

Figure 3: Experimental evaluation of iterative runs of the algorithm reduce

forcement. However, Basin et al.'s mode analysis is weaker than ours; in particular, it cannot relate the same variable in the input and output positions of two different conjuncts of a restriction and requires that each free variable appear in at least one predicate with a finite model. As a consequence, some policies such as the HIPAA policy φ_{HIPAA} from Section 5, whose top-level restriction ($\mathtt{send}(p_1, p_2, m, \tau) \wedge \mathtt{purp}(m, u)$) contains a variable u not occurring in any predicate with a finite model, cannot be enforced in their framework, but can be enforced in ours.

Formal Frameworks for Policy Audit. Cederquist et al. [12] present a proof-based system for a-posteriori audit, where policy obligations are discharged by constructing formal proofs. The leaves of proofs are established from logs, but the audit process only checks that an obligation has been satisfied somewhere in the past. Further, there is no systematic mechanism to instantiate quantifiers in proofs. However, using connectives of linear logic, the mechanism admits policies that rely on use-once permissions.

Iterative Enforcement. The idea of iteratively rewriting the policy over evolving logs has been considered previously [29, 32], but only for propositional logic where the absence of quantifiers simplifies the problem considerably. Bauer et al. [3] use a different approach for iterative enforcement: they convert an LTL formula with limited first-order quantification to a Büchi automaton and check whether the automaton accepts the input log. Further, they also use a three-valued semantic model similar to ours, but assume that logs record all information about past events (past-completeness). Three-valued structures have also been considered in work on generalized model checking [11, 19]. However, the problems addressed in that line of work are different; the objective there is to check whether there exist extensions of a given structure in which a formula is satisfied (or falsified).

Compliance Checking. Barth et al. [6] present two formal definitions of compliance of an action with a policy, called strong and weak compliance. An action is *strongly compliant* with a policy given a trace if there exists an extension of the trace that contains the action and satisfies the policy. We do not consider strong compliance in this paper. An action is *weakly compliant* with a policy in Propositional LTL (PLTL) given a trace if the trace augmented with the action satisfies the present requirements of the policy. However, a weakly compliant action might incur unsatisfiable future requirements. The technical definition is stated in terms of a standard tableau construction for PLTL [24] that syntactically separates present and future requirements. Our correctness property for reduce generalizes weak compliance to a richer class of policies and structures: PLTL can be encoded in our policy logic, the residual formula generalizes future requirements, and past-complete traces are a special case of our partial structures.

In a related paper, Barth et al. [7] present an algorithm that examines audit logs to detect policy violations and identify agents to blame for policy violations. While our audit algorithm can be used to detect violations of a much richer class of policies than the propositional logics considered by Barth et al., it does not identify agents to be blamed for violations.

Lam et al. [22] represent policy requirements of a part of the HIPAA Privacy Rule in an extension of Prolog with stratified negation, called pLogic, and use it to implement a compliance checker for a medical messaging system. The compliance checker makes decisions about legitimacy of messages entering the system based on eight attributes attached to each message (such as its sender, intended recipient, subject, type of information and purpose). The prototype tool has a usable front-end and provides a useful interface for understanding what types of disclosures and uses of personal health information are permitted and forbidden by the HIPAA Privacy Rule. However, as recognized by the authors, the approach has certain limitations in demonstrating compliance with the HIPAA Privacy Rule. First, it does not support temporal conditions. While pLogic uses specialized predicates to capture that certain events happened in the past, it cannot represent future obligations needed to formalize many clauses in HIPAA. In contrast, our policy logic and the reduce algorithm handle temporal conditions, including real-time conditions. Second, reasoning in pLogic proceeds assuming that all asserted beliefs, purposes and types of information associated with messages are correct. In contrast, since reduce mines logs to determine truth values of atoms, it does not assume facts unless there is evidence in logs to back them up. Typically, a purpose or belief will be taken as true only if a human auditor (or some other oracle) supplies evidence to that effect. Finally, our prototype implementation was evaluated with a formalization of the entire HIPAA Privacy Rule, whereas Lam et al. formalize only §§164.502, 164.506 and 164.510.

Policy Specification and Analysis. Several variants of LTL have been used to *specify* the properties of programs, business processes and security and privacy policies [6, 15, 8, 18, 23]. The logic we use as well as the formalization of HIPAA used in our experiments are adapted from our prior work on the logic PrivacyLFP [15]. PrivacyLFP, in turn, draws inspiration from earlier work on the logic LPU [6]. However, PrivacyLFP is more expressive than LPU because it allows first-order quantification over infinite domains.

Further, several access-control models have extensions for specifying usage control and future obligations [20, 10, 28, 21, 26, 16, 27]. Some of these models assume a pre-defined notion of obligations [21, 26]. For instance, Irwin et al. [21] model obligations as tuples containing the subject of the obligation, the actions to be performed, the objects that are targets of the actions and the time frames of the obligations. Other models leave specifications for obligations abstract [20, 10, 28]. Such specific models and the ensuing policies can be encoded in our logic using quantifiers.

There also has been much work on analyzing the properties of policies represented in formal models. For instance, Ni et al. study the interaction between obligation and authorization [26], Irwin et al. have analyzed accountability problems with obligations [21], and Dougherty et al. have modeled the interaction between obligations and programs [16]. These methods are orthogonal to our objective of policy enforcement.

Finally, privacy languages such as EPAL [4] and privacyAPI [25] do not include obligations or temporal modalities as primitives, and are less expressive than our framework.

7. CONCLUSION AND FUTURE WORK

We have presented the design, implementation, and evaluation of a provably correct iterative algorithm for policy audit, reduce, that works even with incomplete audit logs. Our policy logic is expressive enough to represent real privacy legislation like HIPAA, yet tractable due to a carefully designed static analysis. Our empirical evaluation shows that reduce is efficient enough to be used in practice.

In future work, we plan to investigate two applications besides after-the-fact auditing using the reduce algorithm as a core. The first application is *runtime monitoring* of policies. In this context, reduce can be applied to the part of the policy relevant to an action to be performed with a hypothetical log that includes the future action. If the resulting formula is unsatisfiable, then the action to be performed is a violation. If the resulting formula is satisfied, then the action is permitted. Finally, if reduce outputs a non-trivial residual formula (involving, for example, beliefs, purposes, or future obligations), the residual policy can be used to guide agents about legitimacy of actions they are about to perform. Such a tool will be useful to organizations in educating their employees about appropriate disclosures and uses of personal information as described in complex policies, such as the HIPAA Privacy Rule.

The second application is *accounting* of actions involving personal information of individual data subjects. Proposals for informing patients about disclosures and uses of their personal health information are currently being debated in the U.S. [14]. reduce can be run on the entire policy with a subset of the logs that pertain to a specific agent to discover all disclosures related to that agent and evidence supporting whether the disclosures were violations, permitted, or conditionally permitted.

We also plan to integrate our audit algorithm into a policy-aware health information exchange system that is being developed as part of the SHARPS project (`http://sharps.org`) that we participate in. Ensuring that disclosures of protected health information are made in accordance with privacy regulations is critical in this setting. This project also provides a vehicle to deploy and evaluate the effectiveness of this algorithm over real hospital logs. Another direction of ongoing and future work is to develop semantic foundations and enforcement techniques for concepts in privacy policies related to purposes and beliefs that at first glance appear difficult to formalize and enforce using computational methods.

Acknowledgments. This work was partially supported by the U.S. Army Research Office contract "Perpetually Available and Secure Information Systems" (DAAD19-02-1-0389) to Carnegie Mellon CyLab, the NSF Science and Technology Center TRUST, the NSF CyberTrust grant "Privacy, Compliance and Information Risk in Complex Organizational Processes", the AFOSR MURI "Collaborative Policies and Assured Information Sharing", and HHS Grant no. HHS 90TR0003/01.

8. REFERENCES

[1] R. Alur and T. A. Henzinger. A really temporal logic. *Journal of the ACM*, 41(1):181–203, 1994.

[2] K. R. Apt and E. Marchiori. Reasoning about Prolog programs: From modes through types to assertions. *Formal Aspects of Computing*, 6(6):743–765, 1994.

[3] F. Baader, A. Bauer, and M. Lippmann. Runtime verification using a temporal description logic. In *Proceedings of the 7th International Conference on Frontiers of Combining Systems (FroCos)*, pages 149–164, 2009.

[4] M. Backes, B. Pfitzmann, and M. Schunter. A toolkit for managing enterprise privacy policies. In *Proceedings of the 8th European Symposium on Research in Computer Security (ESORICS)*, LNCS 2808, pages 101–119, 2003.

[5] H. Barringer, A. Goldberg, K. Havelund, and K. Sen. Rule-based runtime verification. In *Proceedings of the 5th International Conference on Verification, Model Checking, and Abstract Interpretation (VMCAI)*, pages 44–57, 2004.

[6] A. Barth, A. Datta, J. C. Mitchell, and H. Nissenbaum. Privacy and contextual integrity: Framework and applications. In *Proceedings of the 27th IEEE Symposium on Security and Privacy (Oakland)*, pages 184–198, 2006.

[7] A. Barth, J. C. Mitchell, A. Datta, and S. Sundaram. Privacy and utility in business processes. In *Proceedings of the 20th IEEE Computer Security Foundations Symposium (CSF)*, pages 279–294, 2007.

[8] D. Basin, F. Klaedtke, and S. Müller. Monitoring security policies with metric first-order temporal logic. In *Proceeding of the 15th ACM Symposium on Access Control Models and Technologies (SACMAT)*, pages 23–34, 2010.

[9] D. A. Basin, F. Klaedtke, and S. Müller. Policy monitoring in first-order temporal logic. In *Proceedings of the 22nd International Conference on Computer Aided Verification (CAV)*, pages 1–18, 2010.

[10] C. Bettini, S. Jajodia, X. S. Wang, and D. Wijesekera. Provisions and obligations in policy rule management. *Journal of Network and Systems Management*, 11:351–372, 2003.

[11] G. Bruns and P. Godefroid. Generalized model checking: Reasoning about partial state spaces. In *Proceedings of the 11th International Conference on Concurrency Theory (CONCUR)*, pages 168–182, 2000.

[12] J. G. Cederquist, R. Corin, M. A. C. Dekker, S. Etalle, J. I. den Hartog, and G. Lenzini. Audit-based compliance control. *International Journal of Information Security*, 6(2):133–151, 2007.

[13] Deloitte & Touche and the Ponemon Institute.

Enterprise@Risk: 2007 Privacy and Data Protection Survey. White Paper, December 2007.

[14] Department of Health and Human Services, Office of the Secretary. HIPAA Privacy Rule accounting of disclosures under the health information technology for economic and clinical health act. 45 CFR 164, 2011. Available at `http://www.gpo.gov/fdsys/pkg/FR-2011-05-31/pdf/2011-13297.pdf`.

[15] H. DeYoung, D. Garg, L. Jia, D. Kaynar, and A. Datta. Experiences in the logical specification of the HIPAA and GLBA privacy laws. In *Proceedings of the 9th Annual ACM Workshop on Privacy in the Electronic Society (WPES)*, 2010. Full version: Carnegie Mellon University Technical Report CMU-CyLab-10-007.

[16] D. J. Dougherty, K. Fisler, and S. Krishnamurthi. Obligations and their interaction with programs. In *Proceedings of the 12th European Symposium on Research in Computer Security (ESORICS)*, pages 375–389, 2007.

[17] D. Garg, L. Jia, and A. Datta. A logical method for policy enforcement over evolving audit logs. Technical Report CMU-CyLab-11-002, Carnegie Mellon University, 2011.

[18] C. Giblin, A. Y. Liu, S. Müller, B. Pfitzmann, and X. Zhou. Regulations expressed as logical models (REALM). In *Proceeding of the 18th Annual Conference on Legal Knowledge and Information Systems (JURIX)*, pages 37–48, 2005.

[19] P. Godefroid and M. Huth. Model checking vs. generalized model checking: Semantic minimizations for temporal logics. In *Proceedings of the 20th Annual IEEE Symposium on Logic in Computer Science (LICS)*, pages 158–167, 2005.

[20] M. Hilty, D. A. Basin, and A. Pretschner. On obligations. In *Proceedings of the 10th European Symposium on Research in Computer Security (ESORICS)*, pages 98–117, 2005.

[21] K. Irwin, T. Yu, and W. H. Winsborough. On the modeling and analysis of obligations. In *Proceedings of the 13th ACM Conference on Computer and Communications Security (CCS)*, pages 134–143, 2006.

[22] P. E. Lam, J. C. Mitchell, and S. Sundaram. A formalization of HIPAA for a medical messaging system. In *Proceedings of the 6th International Conference on Trust, Privacy and Security in Digital Business (TrustBus)*, pages 73–85, 2009.

[23] Y. Liu, S. Müller, and K. Xu. A static compliance-checking framework for business process models. *IBM Systems Journal*, 46:335–361, 2007.

[24] Z. Manna and A. Pnueli. *Temporal Verification of Reactive Systems: Safety*. Springer-Verlag, 1995.

[25] M. J. May, C. A. Gunter, and I. Lee. Privacy APIs: Access control techniques to analyze and verify legal privacy policies. In *Proceedings of the 19th IEEE Workshop on Computer Security Foundations (CSFW)*, pages 85–97, 2006.

[26] Q. Ni, E. Bertino, and J. Lobo. An obligation model bridging access control policies and privacy policies. In *Proceedings of the 13th ACM Symposium on Access Control Models and Technologies (SACMAT)*, pages 133–142, 2008.

[27] OASIS XACML Committee. Extensible access control markup language (XACML) v2.0, 2004. Available at `http://www.oasis-open.org/specs/#xacmlv2.0`.

[28] J. Park and R. Sandhu. Towards usage control models: beyond traditional access control. In *Proceedings of the 7th ACM Symposium on Access Control Models and Technologies (SACMAT)*, pages 57–64, 2002.

[29] G. Roşu and K. Havelund. Rewriting-based techniques for runtime verification. *Automated Software Engineering*, 12:151–197, 2005.

[30] M. Roger and J. Goubault-Larrecq. Log auditing through model-checking. In *Proceedings of the 14th IEEE Workshop on Computer Security Foundations (CSF)*, pages 220–236, 2001.

[31] O. Sokolsky, U. Sammapun, I. Lee, and J. Kim. Run-time checking of dynamic properties. *Electronic Notes in Theoretical Computer Science*, 144:91–108, 2006.

[32] P. Thati and G. Roşu. Monitoring algorithms for metric temporal logic specifications. *Electronic Notes in Theoretical Computer Science*, 113:145–162, 2005.

[33] US Congress. Gramm-Leach-Bliley Act, Financial Privacy Rule. 15 USC §6801–§6809, November 1999. Available at `http://www.law.cornell.edu/uscode/usc_sup_01_15_10_94_20_I.html`.

[34] US Congress. Health Insurance Portability and Accountability Act of 1996, Privacy Rule. 45 CFR 164, 2002. Available at `http://www.access.gpo.gov/nara/cfr/waisidx_07/45cfr164_07.html`.

Automatic Error Finding in Access-Control Policies

Karthick Jayaraman*
Microsoft
karjay@microsoft.com

Vijay Ganesh
MIT
vganesh@csail.mit.edu

Mahesh Tripunitara
University of Waterloo
tripunit@uwaterloo.ca

Martin Rinard
MIT
rinard@csail.mit.edu

Steve Chapin
Syracuse University
chapin@syr.edu

ABSTRACT

Verifying that access-control systems maintain desired security properties is recognized as an important problem in security. Enterprise access-control systems have grown to protect tens of thousands of resources, and there is a need for verification to scale commensurately. We present a new abstraction-refinement technique for automatically finding errors in Administrative Role-Based Access Control (ARBAC) security policies. ARBAC is the first and most comprehensive administrative scheme for Role-Based Access Control (RBAC) systems. Underlying our approach is a change in mindset: we propose that error finding complements verification, can be more scalable, and allows for the use of a wider variety of techniques. In our approach, we use an abstraction-refinement technique to first identify and discard roles that are unlikely to be relevant to the verification question (the abstraction step), and then restore such abstracted roles incrementally (the refinement steps). Errors are one-sided: if there is an error in the abstracted policy, then there is an error in the original policy. If there is an error in a policy whose role-dependency graph diameter is smaller than a certain bound, then we find the error. Our abstraction-refinement technique complements conventional state-space exploration techniques such as model checking. We have implemented our technique in an access-control policy analysis tool. We show empirically that our tool scales well to realistic policies, and is orders of magnitude faster than prior tools.

Categories and Subject Descriptors: K.6.5 [Management and Information Systems]: Security and Protection; D.4.6 [Operating Systems]: Security and Protection; D2.4 [Software Engineering]: Software/Program Verification;

General Terms: Security, verification.

*This work was performed when the author was a graduate student at Syracuse University.

CCS'11, October 17–21, 2011, Chicago, Illinois, USA.

1. INTRODUCTION

This paper presents a technique and a tool for finding errors in access-control policies. Specifying and managing access-control policies is a problem of critical importance in system security. Researchers have proposed access-control frameworks (e.g., Administrative Role Based Access Control — ARBAC [36]) that have considerable expressive power, and can be used to specify complex policies. However, we do not have adequate tools for analyzing such complex policies. Without tools for analyzing these policies, administrators cannot determine the correctness of policies. As a consequence, several of these sophisticated frameworks are not deployed in practice.

An access-control policy contains an error if it allows an unauthorized user to access a resource. This is considered an error because a security property that an enterprise wants to (or even is legally required to) maintain, such as separation of privilege [35], is violated by the user's access to the resource. In RBAC, for example, if a user is already a member of a sensitive role, we may want to ensure that there exists no reachable state in which he is authorized to another sensitive role.

Administrators require efficient tools for identifying such errors in policies prior to deployment. Access-control policies for reasonably large systems feature several complexity sources that make it difficult to find errors in them. An access-control policy is essentially a finite-state machine that accepts valid requests. Depending on the framework, the policy may comprise states only or comprise both states and state changes. The nature of the states and state changes are sources of complexity (We explain the sources of complexity in Section 4). We need tools that are effective irrespective of the complexity of the access-control policies.

Automated analysis and verification of access-control policies is both an area of active research [11,13,17–21,26,28,30, 39,43,46–48] and practical interest [1,2]. Model checking [8] has emerged as a promising, automated approach to the verification problem [13, 21, 46]. In this approach, a model checker takes as input an access-control policy and a security property, and declares whether or not the policy adheres to the input security property. The idea is similar to verifying computer programs; the access-control policy is analogous to a computer program, and the security property is analogous to a program property. Ideally, the model checker checks whether the property always holds for all possible authorizations that the policy allows. However, the model-checking problem for the class of access-control policies that we consider is intractable in general (PSPACE-complete [21, 39]), and scalability for practical verification tools remains a significant issue despite considerable progress (see Section 5).

We present a new technique that combines abstraction refinement [6] and bounded model checking for analyzing complex security policies. Abstraction refinement is a paradigm for efficiently verifying a property on a system's abstraction that is iteratively constructed to contain only the relevant parts; the techniques vary depending on the specific system and property [4, 6, 12]. The use of a sophisticated abstraction-refinement algorithm makes our technique significantly more efficient than previous approaches. In realistic policies, our algorithm is often able to abstract most of the access-control policy while preserving the presence of any errors. This abstraction enables the underlying bounded model checker to find the error in much less time.

The insight behind the abstraction we use is that the dependency graph of the roles for many real-world access-control policies often contains many *tightly-knit sets of roles* that are *loosely-connected* to other tightly-knit sets of roles. This structure reflects the organization of large institutions (such as corporations, hospitals, and universities) as a conglomeration of loosely coupled tightly-knit departments or groups. Abstracting the policy produces a much smaller policy because it eliminates a large number of loosely-coupled roles that do not directly interact with the target set of tightly-coupled roles. If the loosely-coupled roles are indirectly involved in the error, the refinement step will incrementally add them back to the abstraction, enabling the analysis to find the error. Our results show that even when these roles are required to find the error, the analysis can usually find the error after applying a few refinement steps.

We have implemented this technique in the MOHAWK access-control policy analysis tool. MOHAWK accepts as input an access-control policy and a safety question. If MOHAWK finds an error in the input policy, it terminates and produces as output a sequence of actions that cause the error. We show that MOHAWK scales very well as the complexity of the input policies increase, and is orders of magnitude faster than competing tools. The MOHAWK tool is open source and is available from the Google Code website: `http://code.google.com/p/mohawk/`.

Contributions

We make the following contributions in this paper:

1. We describe an *abstraction-refinement* based approach for automatically finding errors in access-control policies (specifically, ARBAC policies). The resulting technique, implemented on top of a bounded model checker, scales very well as the size and complexity of the input policies increase. Our technique effectively tackles the sources of complexity (Section 4) in large, complex, real-world policies. Although we focus on error finding in this paper, our abstraction-refinement technique can be used in conjunction with model checking to perform verification.

   Our technique can also be used for error finding in frameworks other than ARBAC as the sources of complexity that we identify in Section 4 are not unique to ARBAC. They exist in other access-control schemes as well, such as administrative scope [9] and even the original access matrix scheme due to Harrison et al. [17].

2. An implementation of our technique in a tool called MOHAWK. MOHAWK accepts as input an access-control policy and a safety question, and outputs whether or not it found an error. Following similar techniques from software verification, our technique constructs an approximation (and successive refinements, if necessary) of the input policy, and checks for errors. It terminates when an error has been found or the underlying bounded model checker has reached a predetermined bound.

3. We provide a detailed experimental comparison of MOHAWK against NuSMV [33], a well known model checking and bounded model checking tool, and RBAC-PAT [13, 46], a tool specifically designed for analyzing ARBAC policies. In comparison to the existing approaches, MOHAWK scales well with the size and complexity of the input policies.

   Our experimental evaluation uses a benchmark that includes a realistic case study for banking (Section 5.1). The case study has helped us understand the aspects of the ARBAC policy language that are likely to be used in creating real-world policies. In particular, we have discovered that the sources of complexity in ARBAC policies that we discuss in Section 4 can arise in realistic settings. Our benchmark is also publicly available along with the tool.

Organization: The remainder of our paper is organized as follows. In Section 2, we discuss access-control models and schemes. In Section 3, we describe the architecture of MOHAWK. In Section 4, we describe the sources of complexity from the standpoint of error finding and how MOHAWK deals with them. In Section 5, we present empirical results that demonstrate the efficacy of our approach. We discuss related work in Section 6 and conclude with Section 7.

2. PRELIMINARIES

In this section, we provide basic definitions and concepts relating to access-control policies, in particular the ARBAC framework. We also introduce the error-finding problem for access-control systems.

An access-control policy is a state-change system, $\langle \gamma, \psi \rangle$, where $\gamma \in \Gamma$ is the start or current state, and $\psi \in \Psi$ is a state-change rule. The pair $\langle \Gamma, \Psi \rangle$ is an access control model or framework.

The state, γ, specifies the resources to which a principal has a particular kind of access. For example, γ may specify that the principal Alice is allowed to read a particular file. Several different specifications have been proposed for the syntax for a state. Two well-known ones are the access matrix [15, 17] and Role-Based Access Control (RBAC) [10, 38]. In this paper, we focus on the latter to make our contributions concrete.

In RBAC, users are not assigned permissions directly, but via a role. Users are assigned to roles, as are permissions, and a user gains those permissions that are assigned to the same roles to which he is assigned. Consequently, given the set U of users, P of permissions and R of roles, a state γ in RBAC is a pair $\langle UA, PA \rangle$ where $UA \subseteq U \times R$ is the user-role assignment relation, and $PA \subseteq P \times R$ is the permission-role assignment relation.

RBAC also allows for roles to be related to one another in a partial order called a role hierarchy. However, as we point

	RBAC State
Roles	{BudgetCommitee, Finance, Acct, Audit, TechSupport, IT, Admin}
Users	{Alice, Bob}
UA	{⟨Bob, Acct⟩, ⟨Bob, Audit⟩, ⟨Alice, Admin⟩}
	State-Change Rule
can_assign	{⟨Admin, Finance, BudgetCommittee⟩, ⟨Admin, Acct ∧ ¬Audit, Finance⟩, ⟨Admin, TRUE, Acct⟩, ⟨Admin, TRUE, Audit⟩ ⟨Admin, TechSupport, IT⟩, ⟨Admin, TRUE, TechSupport⟩}
can_revoke	{⟨Admin, Acct⟩, ⟨Admin, Audit⟩, ⟨Admin, TechSupport⟩}

Figure 1: State and state-change rules for an ARBAC policy

out in Section 2.2 under "The role hierarchy," in the context of this paper, we can reduce the error-finding problems of interest to us to those for which the RBAC state has no role hierarchy.

Figure 1 contains a example of an RBAC state for a hypothetical company with 7 roles and 2 users, namely Alice and Bob. Alice is assigned to the Admin role. Bob is assigned to the Acct and Audit roles. For the sake of illustration we have only a limited number of roles in the example. We explain how to interpret the state-change rules in the next section.

2.1 ARBAC

The need for a state-change rule, ψ, arises from a tension between security and scalability in access control systems. Realistic access control systems may comprise tens of thousands of users and resources. Allowing only a few trusted administrators to handle changes to the state (e.g., remove read access from Alice) does not scale. A state-change rule allows for the *delegation* of some state changes to users that may not be fully trusted.

ARBAC [36] and administrative scope [9] are examples of such schemes for RBAC. To our knowledge, ARBAC is the first and most comprehensive state-change scheme to have been proposed for RBAC. This is one of the reasons that research on policy verification in RBAC [13,30,46], including this paper, focuses on ARBAC.

An ARBAC specification comprises three components, *URA*, *PRA*, and *RRA*. *URA* is the administrative component for the user-role assignment relation, *UA*, *PRA* is the administrative component for the permission-role assignment relation, *PA*, and *RRA* is the administrative component for the role hierarchy.

Of these, *URA* is of most practical interest from the standpoint of error finding. The reason is that in practice, user-role relationships are the most volatile [25]. Permission-role relationships change less frequently, and role-role relationships change rarely. Furthermore, as role-role relationships are particularly sensitive to the security of an organization, we can assume that only trusted administrators are allowed to make such changes.

PRA is syntactically identical to *URA* except that the rules apply to permissions and not users. Consequently, all our results in this paper for *URA* apply to *PRA* as well. We do not consider analysis problems that relate to changes in role-role relationships for the reasons we cited above.

In the remainder of this paper, when we refer to ARBAC, we mean the *URA* component that is used to manage user-role relationships.

URA. A *URA* specification comprises two relations, *can_assign* and *can_revoke*. The relation *can_assign* is used to specify under what conditions a user may be assigned to a role, and *can_revoke* is used to specify the roles from which users' memberships may be revoked. We call a member of *can_assign* or *can_revoke* a *rule*.

A rule in *can_assign* is of the form $\langle r_a, c, r_t \rangle$, where r_a is an administrative role, c is a precondition and r_t is the target role. An administrative role is a special kind of role associated with users that may administer (make changes to) the RBAC policy. The first component of a *can_assign* rule identifies the particular administrative role whose users may employ that rule as a state change.

A precondition is a propositional logic formula of roles in which the only operators are negations and conjunctions. Figure 1 contains the *can_assign* and *can_revoke* rules for our example RBAC state. An example of c is Acct ∧¬Audit in the *can_assign* rule that has Finance as the target role. For an administrator, Alice, to exercise the rule to assign a user *Bob* to Finance, Alice must be a member of Admin, *Bob* must be a member of Acct and must not be a member of Audit.

A *can_revoke* rule is of the form $\langle r_a, r_t \rangle$. The existence of such a rule indicates that users may be revoked from the role r_t by an administrator that is a member of r_a. For example, roles Acct, Audit, and TechSupport can be revoked from a user by the administrator Alice.

We point out that so long as r_a has at least one user, the rule can potentially fire as a state change. If r_a has no users, we remove the corresponding *can_assign* rule from the system as it has no effect on error finding. One of the consequences of this relates to what has been called the separate administration restriction. We discuss this in Section 2.2 below.

We have omitted some other details that are in the original specification for *URA* [36] because those details are inconsequential to the error-finding problem we address in this paper. For example, the original specification allows for the target role to be specified as a set or range of roles. We assume that it is a single role, r_t. A rule that has a set or range as its component for the target role can be rewritten as a rule for every role in that set or range. We know that roles in a range do not change, as we assume that changes to roles may be effected only by trusted administrators. Policy verification is not used for such changes.

2.2 The error-finding problem

The error-finding problem in the context of access-control policies arises because state changes may be effected by users that are not fully trusted, but an organization still wants to ensure that desirable security properties are met. The reason such problems can be challenging is that state-change rules are specified procedurally, but security properties of interest (e.g., Alice should never be able to read a particular file) are declarative [24].

A basic error-finding problem is safety analysis. In the context of RBAC and ARBAC, a basic safety question is: can a user u become a member of a role r? We call such a situation (in which the safety question is true), an *error*.

There are two reasons that the basic safety question such

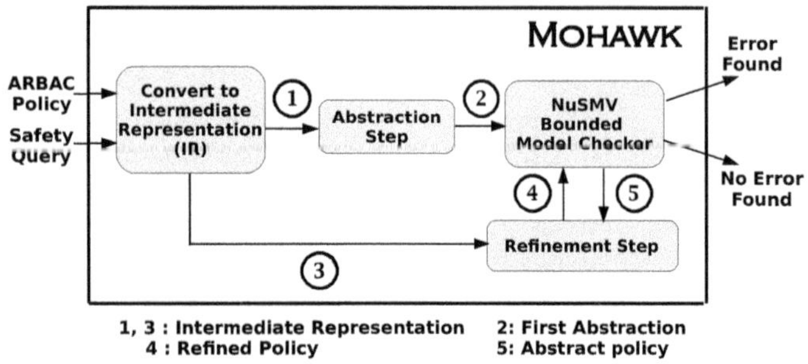

Figure 2: Mohawk Architecture

as the one from above has received considerable attention in the literature [21, 30, 39, 46]. One is that it is natural in its own right. The reason for asking such a question is that u should not be authorized to r. If the analysis reveals that he may be, by some sequence of state changes, then we know that there is a problem with the security policy. Another reason is that several other questions of interest, such as those related to separation of privilege, can be reduced to the basic safety question. This observation has been made before [21, 46].

An instance of an error-finding problem, in the context of this paper, specifies an ARBAC access control system, a user, and a role. It is of the form $\langle \gamma, \psi, u, r \rangle$. We ask whether u may become a member of r given the initial state $\gamma = \langle U, R, UA \rangle$, and state-change rule $\psi = \langle can\_assign, can\_revoke \rangle$.

The separate administration restriction. In the context of the error-finding problem, the separate administration restriction excludes administrative roles from the error-finding problem instance, i.e., administrative roles are not administered by the same rules as "regular" roles. We adopt the separate administration restriction in this paper. Some previous work [46] has considered subcases of when this restriction is lifted. We do not consider those subcases in this paper. We adopt the restriction because the original specification on ARBAC [36] adopts this restriction. Moreover, the separate administration restriction does not affect the complexity of the error-finding problem [40].

The role hierarchy. We assume that an RBAC state has no role hierarchy. The reason is that there is a straightforward, efficient reduction that has been presented in prior work from an error finding instance that has a role hierarchy to an error finding instance with no role hierarchy [39].

3. ARCHITECTURE OF MOHAWK

In this section, we describe MOHAWK's architecture (§3.1-§3.6), and illustrate our approach using an example (§3.7).

3.1 Abstraction Refinement in Mohawk

The general idea in an abstraction-refinement [6] technique is to first abstract (over or under approximate) a system represented typically as a logic formula, and check if a desired property holds in the abstraction, and iteratively refine as necessary. If the abstraction is an over approximation, i.e., the abstraction has more behaviors compared to its original, then the refinements restrict the abstraction's behavior on each iteration, so that it has fewer behaviors, until in the limit the abstraction equals the original. If the abstraction is an under approximation, i.e., the abstraction has fewer behaviors compared to its original, then the refinements relax the abstraction's behavior on each iteration, so that it has more behaviors, until in the limit the abstraction equals the original. Both techniques keep the errors one sided. In the case of over approximation, correctness of the abstraction corresponds with the original. In the case of under approximation, an error detected in the abstraction corresponds with the original.

MOHAWK uses an under approximation strategy [6]. Therefore, any error detected in an abstract policy exists in the original policy. Figure 2 illustrates the architecture of MOHAWK. MOHAWK accepts an ARBAC Policy $\langle U, R, UA,$ $can\_assign, can\_revoke \rangle$ and a safety query $\langle u, r \rangle$ as input. MOHAWK reports an error if it finds one. Otherwise, MOHAWK terminates and reports that it could not find any errors. In the following, we will refer to the role in the safety query as the query role. Briefly, MOHAWK works on the input as follows:

- **Input Transformation** (§3.2): MOHAWK transforms the policy and safety query into an intermediate representation (IR). The IR maintains a priority queue of roles based on how they are related to the query role, and uses this stratification to incrementally add roles, *can_assign*, and *can_revoke* rules in the refinement steps as necessary.

- **Abstraction Step** (§3.3): MOHAWK performs an initial abstraction step to produce an abstract policy.

- **Verification** (§3.4): In this step, MOHAWK invokes the NuSMV bounded model checker on the finite-state machine representation of the current abstract policy. If a counter example is produced by NuSMV, MOHAWK terminates and reports the error found. A counter example, in model-checking parlance, is a sequence of state transitions from the initial state to an error state of the input finite-state machine. For MOHAWK, the counter example reported corresponds to an error in the policy and is essentially a sequence of actions that enable the unauthorized user referred in the safety query to reach the query role.

- **Refinement Step** (§3.5): If no counter example is found in the previous step, MOHAWK refines the abstract policy. If no further refinements are possible, MOHAWK terminates and reports that it could not find any errors. MOHAWK may execute the verify-refine loop multiple times, until either MOHAWK identifies an error or no further refinements are possible.

Configurability of Abstraction-Refinement. MOHAWK's abstraction-refinement strategy is configurable. In abstraction-refinement techniques, there is an interplay between three factors, namely aggressiveness of the abstraction step, verification efficiency, and number of refinement steps. Aggressive abstraction-refinement makes the verification efficient at the cost of increasing the number of refinements. A less aggressive abstraction-refinement may reduce the number of refinements at the cost of making the verification harder. A key aspect of our approach is that, MOHAWK enables the user to control the aggressiveness of the abstraction and refinement steps. A configurable parameter k determines the number of queues of roles from the priority queues that are added to the abstract policy at each refinement step. The default value for k is one (The most aggressive setting for k).

3.2 Input Transformation

Figure 3 illustrates how a policy is specified in MOHAWK's input language. The "Roles", "Users", "UA", "CA", and "CR" keywords identify the lists of roles, users, user-role assignments, *can_assign* rules, and *can_revoke* rules respectively. The "ADMIN" key word identifies the list of admin users. In the example, Alice is the admin user and is assigned to Admin, which is the administrative role assumed in all the *can_assign* and *can_revoke* rules. The SPEC keyword identifies the safety query. In the example, the safety query is asking whether user Bob can be assigned to BudgetCommittee. In the intended policy, Bob cannot be assigned to BudgetCommittee. However, he can be assigned to the role in policy specified in Fig 3 because of the error we introduced in the *can_assign* rule. In Section 3.7, we show how MOHAWK identifies the error.

MOHAWK transforms the policy in the input into an intermediate representation, which enables efficient querying of the policy to facilitate the abstraction and refinement steps.

Related-by-Assignment. A role r_1 is said to be *Related-by-Assignment* to a role r_2, if $r_2 = r_1$ or r_2 appears in the precondition of at least one of the *can_assign* rules that have r_1 as their target role. *Related-by-Assignment* does not distinguish between positive and negative preconditions. The *Related-by-Assignment* relationship describes whether a user's membership to one role can affect the membership to another role. The *Related-by-Assignment* relationship between roles can be represented using a tree as shown in Figure 4, in which all nodes correspond to roles and a role r_2 appears as a child node of role r_1, if and only if the r_2 is *Related-by-Assignment* to r_1.

MOHAWK identifies all the roles *Related-by-Assignment* to the query role by performing a breadth-first search of the associated *can_assign* rules. The algorithm first assigns the highest priority to the query role and adds it to a work queue. While the work queue is not empty, the algorithm picks the next role in the work queue, and considers the *can_assign* rules that have the role being analyzed as their target role. All the roles in the preconditions in the *can_assign* rules are added to the work queue, and also added to the priority queue at the next lower priority compared to the role being analyzed. At the end of the analysis, we have a priority queue, in which all the roles *Related-by-Assignment* to the query role are inserted in the queues based on their priorities. Roles that directly affect the membership to the query role have the highest priority, while roles affecting the membership to roles that are *Related-by-Assignment* to the query role have a lesser priority.

3.3 Abstraction Step

In the initial abstraction step, MOHAWK constructs an abstract policy $\langle U', R', UA', can\_assign', can\_revoke' \rangle$, where

- U' contains the user in the safety query and admin users.
- R' contains the administrative roles, and roles from the first k queues in the priority queue.
- $UA' = \{(u, r) \mid (u, r) \in UA \land u \in U' \land r \in R'\}$
- *can_assign'* contains only *can_assign* rules in the input policy whose precondition roles and target roles are members of R'.
- *can_revoke'* contains only *can_revoke* rules from the input policy whose target roles are members of R'.

3.4 Verification

In the verification step, MOHAWK verifies the safety query in the abstract policy. On each verification step, MOHAWK translates the abstract policy to a finite-state-machine specification in the SMV language and the safety query to a LTL (Linear Temporal Logic) formula. If the model checker identifies a state in which the user is assigned to the role, it provides a counter example. The counter example corresponds to a sequence of assignment and revocation actions from initial authorization state that will result in the user being assigned to the role. On identifying a counter example, MOHAWK reports the error and terminates. Otherwise, MOHAWK refines the abstract policy in the refinement step.

In each step, the abstract policy contains a subset of the roles, UA, *can_assign*, and *can_revoke* rules in the complete policy. Therefore, the abstract policy permits only a subset of the administrative action sequences accepted in the full policy. Each action in the action-sequence identified by the counterexample corresponds to a *can_assign* or *can_revoke* rule that exists in both the abstract and original policies. Therefore, the counter example is true in the original policy also.

3.5 Refinement Step

An abstract policy verified in the previous step is refined as follows. (We use "$\leftarrow$" to represent instantiation.)

- $R' \leftarrow R' \cup R''$, where R'' is the set of roles from the next k queues from the priority queue.
- $UA' \leftarrow UA' \cup UA''$, where UA'' is the user's membership for the roles in R'', if there are any.
- $can\_assign' \leftarrow can\_assign' \cup can\_assign''$, where can_assign'' is the additional set of *can_assign* rules from the input policy whose preconditions and target roles are members of the updated R'.
- $can\_revoke' \leftarrow can\_revoke' \cup can\_revoke''$, where can_revoke'' is the additional set of *can_revoke* rules from the input policy whose target roles are members of R''.

If no additional refinements are possible, MOHAWK reports that no error was found.

3.6 On Completeness

Our abstraction-refinement technique is complete — we are no worse than conventional model-checking from the standpoint of completeness. If we do not find any errors at a particular refinement step, we can always continue to refine

```
Roles BudgetCommitee Finance Acct Audit
TechSupport IT Admin;

Users Alice Bob;

UA <Alice, Admin> <Bob, Acct> <Bob, Audit>;

CR <Admin, Acct> <Admin, Audit>
<Admin, TechSupport>;

CA <Admin, Finance, BudgetCommittee>
<Admin, Acct&Audit, Finance> <Admin, TRUE, Acct>
<Admin, TRUE, Audit> <Admin, TechSupport, IT>
<Admin, True, TechSupport>;

ADMIN Alice;

SPEC Bob BudgetCommittee;
```

Figure 3: An ARBAC policy in the Mohawk's input language

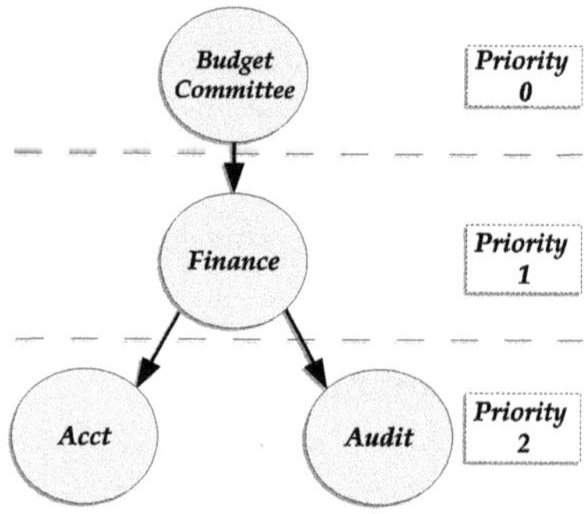

Figure 4: Related-by-assignment (RBA) relationship between roles with respect to BudgetCommittee.

Steps	Users	Roles	UA	*can_assign*	*can_revoke*	Result
Abstraction step	Alice, Bob	BudgetCommittee, Admin	⟨Alice, Admin⟩			No counterexample
Refinement 1	Alice, Bob	BudgetCommittee, Admin, Finance	⟨Alice, Admin⟩	⟨Admin, Finance, Budget-Committee, ⟩		No counterexample
Refinement 2	Alice, Bob	BudgetCommittee, Admin, Finance, Acct, Audit	⟨Alice, Admin⟩ ⟨Bob, Acct⟩ ⟨Bob, Audit⟩	⟨Admin, Finance, BudgetCommittee⟩ ⟨Admin, Acct∧Audit, Finance⟩ ⟨Admin, TRUE, Acct⟩ ⟨Admin, TRUE, Audit⟩	⟨Admin, Acct⟩ ⟨Admin, Audit⟩	**Counterexample found**

Table 1: Illustrating abstraction-refinement steps for the running example in Figure 3

till we check the entire policy. We can improve this approach further by incorporating techniques from the literature on estimating the *completeness threshold* for bounded model checking [7, 27]. Our main point here is that in our technique, we are optimistic about finding errors, and therefore, for a policy that, for example, has no errors, the abstraction-refinement steps that we undergo translate to pure overhead. However, in the case that errors do exist, it is likely that we will find them faster than conventional approaches. Our empirical results (see Section 5) bear this out.

3.7 Example

To illustrate MOHAWK's operations, we introduce an error in the policy of our running example in Fig 1. In the *can_assign* rule with target role Finance, we change c from Acct∧¬Audit to Acct∧Audit. The intent of the original policy is to assign the role Finance only to users who are in the Acct role and not in the Audit role. The error we introduced in the example by changing the *can_assign* rule will enable users who are in both Acct and Audit roles to be assigned to Finance. Figure 3 contains the erroneous policy in MOHAWK's input language.

Table 1 contains the abstraction-refinement steps for the example policy in Figure 3. Figure 4 contains the tree for the roles *Related-by-Assignment* with respect to the BudgetCommittee, which is the query role. In the priority queue, BudgetCommittee has priority 0, Finance has priority 1, and finally Acct and Audit have priority 2 (lower numbers indicate better priorities).

In the abstraction step, MOHAWK adds the users Alice and Bob, and roles BudgetCommittee and Admin. Bob is the user in the query, and Alice is the admin user. BudgetCommittee is the role from the queue with priority 0 and Admin is the admin role. The UA membership, (Alice, Admin), is added to the abstract policy. No *can_assign* or *can_revoke* rules are added because all of them require roles not added to the abstract policy. NuSMV does not identify a counter example for the abstract policy. Therefore, MOHAWK refines the policy.

In the first refinement step, MOHAWK adds Finance from the queue with priority 1. There are no changes to the users, UA, and *can_revoke*. The *can_assign* rule ⟨Admin, Finance, BudgetCommittee⟩ is added to the abstract policy. NuSMV still does not identify a counterexample. Therefore, MOHAWK further refines the abstract policy.

In the second refinement step, MOHAWK adds roles Audit and Acct, 2 UA memberships for Bob, 3 *can_assign* rules, and 2 *can_revoke* rules. Bob's membership to roles Acct and Audit are added to the abstract policy. The three additional *can_assign* rules added are ⟨Admin, Acct∧Audit, Finance⟩, ⟨Admin, TRUE, Audit⟩, and ⟨Admin, TRUE, Acct⟩. The additional *can_revoke* rules added are ⟨Admin, Acct ⟩ and ⟨Admin, Audit⟩. NuSMV identifies a counter example that has the following sequence of administrative actions:

1. Alice assigns Bob to Finance. This action is allowed because of the *can_assign* rule ⟨Admin, Acct∧Audit, Finance⟩.

2. Alice assigns Bob to BudgetCommittee. This action is allowed because of the *can_assign* rule ⟨Admin, Finance, BudgetCommittee⟩.

As a result of seeing this counter example, the administrator can fix the erroneous *can_assign* rule to enforce the correct policy.

As we have illustrated in the example, the abstract policy verified in each step is more constrained compared to the original policy. For example, the initial abstract policy does not allow any assignment and revocation actions. The subsequent two refinement steps add additional roles, *can_assign*, and *can_revoke* rules from the original policy. In effect, the abstraction step aggressively constrains the policy and the subsequent refinement steps relax the constraints to make the policy more precise compared to the earlier step, illustrating our under-approximation strategy.

3.8 Implementation

We implemented MOHAWK using Java. In addition to the abstraction-refinement approach, we implemented several supporting tools for MOHAWK. We have a tool for automatically converting a policy in the MOHAWK language to NuSMV specification. Also, we implemented a tool for creating complex ARBAC policies.

We also implemented two well-known static slicing techniques for ARBAC policies [21, 46]. The basic idea behind static slicing is to remove users, roles, *can_assign*, and *can_revoke* rules from the policies that are irrelevant to the safety question. There are two types of static slicing techniques, namely *forward pruning* [21] and *backward pruning* [21,46]. We implemented these techniques and analyzed the effect of static slicing on the ARBAC policies used in our experiments. We found that these techniques are not effective for realistic policies (Section 5.1).

4. SOURCES OF COMPLEXITY FOR ERROR FINDING

In this section, we describe the aspects that make error finding in the context of access control systems a difficult problem. We call these "sources of complexity." For each source of complexity, we give some intuition as to why it is a source of complexity. Previous work [21,39,46] on the verification problem alludes to some of these sources of complexity. Finally, we explain how MOHAWK's abstraction refinement strategy deals with these sources of complexity.

4.1 The Sources

Three aspects of access-control systems can bring complexity to the verification: (1) the syntax for the state, (2) the state-change rules, and, (3) the verification question of interest. In the context of (1), the size of the state is a source of complexity. In our case, this size is quantified by the number of roles in the RBAC component of the ARBAC policy. The rationale is that as the number of roles in the RBAC component increases, a verifier has to maintain a larger vector of user-role assignments, and also deal with more possible combinations of such assignments in considering state-changes.

The potential source (3) is not a source of complexity in our context. We study the basic question of safety. Given a state, checking whether the question is true or false is equivalent to an access-check. It has been observed in previous work [21] that more complex questions can be reduced to this rather basic notion of safety. Consequently, it appears that even more complex questions will not make the verification problem any more difficult.

The other sources of complexity are in the state-change rules. The component within the state-change rules that is relevant is the precondition. The specific aspects of preconditions that are complexity sources are (1) disjunctions — these are introduced by multiple *can_assign* rules with the same target role, (2) irrevocable roles — these are roles for which there is no *can_revoke* rule with any such role as the target, (3) mixed roles — these are roles that appear with and without negation in *can_assign* rules, and, (4) positive precondition roles — these are roles that appear without negation in *can_assign* rules.

Disjunctions. Given a safety instance, $\langle \gamma, \psi, u, r \rangle$ (see Section 2.2), we observe that determining whether the answer is true or not can be equivalent to determining the satisfiability of a boolean expression in Conjunctive Normal Form (CNF). This problem is known to be NP-complete.

Consider the following example. We have as target roles in *can_assign*, $r_1, \ldots, r_n$. The rule that corresponds to r_i in *can_assign* is $\langle r_a, c_i \wedge r_{i-1}, r_i \rangle$ where c_i is a disjunction of roles or their negations[1], and contains no roles from among $r_1, \ldots, r_n$. The only *can_assign* rule with r as the target role is $\langle r_a, r_n, r \rangle$, and u is assigned to r_0 in the start state.

In our example, the verification instance $\langle \gamma, \psi, u, r \rangle$ is true if and only if the boolean expression $c_1 \wedge \ldots \wedge c_n$ is satisfiable via the firing of *can_assign* and *can_revoke* rules. Indeed, this construction that we use as an example is similar to an NP-hardness reduction in previous work [21].

Irrevocable roles. A role $\widehat{r}$ is *irrevocable* if it is not a member of *can_revoke*. Once u is assigned to $\widehat{r}$, u's membership in $\widehat{r}$ cannot be revoked. Consider the case that an irrevocable role $\widehat{r}$ appears as a negated role in some *can_assign* rules. The challenge for a "forward-search" algorithm that decides the verification question $\langle u, r \rangle$ is that it is not obvious when u should be assigned to $\widehat{r}$.

In a path in the state-transition graph, if u is assigned to $\widehat{r}$ quite close to the start state, then it is possible that that action causes u to never be authorized to r on that path. Given a set of roles I, all of which appear negated in preconditions of *can_assign* rules and are irrevocable, such an algorithm must consider paths that correspond to every subset of I.

Stoller et al. [46] capture this requirement in what they call Stage 2 ("forward analysis") of their backward-search algorithm. The algorithm maintains a subset of I as an annotation in the state-reachability graph (or "plan," as they call it). They observe that their algorithm is doubly-exponential in the size of I.

Mixed roles. A mixed role is one that appears with negation and without in preconditions of *can_assign* rules[2]. Stoller et al. [46] show that the verification problem is fixed

[1]As we discuss in Section 2.1, disjunctions are disallowed in an individual *can_assign* rule. However, multiple rules with the same target role results in a disjunction of the preconditions of those rules. In our example, if $c_i = r_{i,1} \vee \ldots \vee r_{i,m}$, then we assume that we have the following *can_assign* rules with r_i as the target role: $\langle r_a, r_{i,1} \wedge r_{i-1}, r_i \rangle$, ..., $\langle r_a, r_{i,m} \wedge r_{i-1}, r_i \rangle$.

[2]We point out that a role does not appear with and without negation in the same *can_assign* rule. This is because conjunction and negation are the only operators in a rule (see Section 2.1), and therefore such a precondition is always false.

parameter tractable in the number of mixed roles. To see why the number of mixed roles is a source of complexity, consider the case that no role is mixed.

An algorithm can simply adopt the greedy approach of maximally assigning u to every role r_p that appears without negation, and revoking u from every role r_n that appears negated. Such an approach will not work for a mixed role. Given a mixed role r_m, it is possible that we may need to repeatedly assign u to it, and revoke u from it on a path to a state in which u is assigned to r.

A search algorithm must decide whether to revoke u from r_m in every state in which he is assigned to r_m, and whether to assign u to r_m in every state in which he is not assigned to r_m. In the worst case, every such combination must be tried for every mixed role.

Positive precondition roles. A positive precondition role is a role that appears without negation in a precondition. The number of positive precondition roles is a source of complexity. Sasturkar et al. [39] and Stoller et al. [46] observe that if we restrict each *can_assign* rule to only one positive precondition role, then the verification problem becomes fixed parameter tractable in the number of irrevocable roles.

An intuition behind this is that if there is at most one positive precondition role in every precondition of the *can_assign* rules, then the resultant CNF expression for which the model checker checks satisfiability comprises only of Horn clauses. We know that Horn Satisfiability is in **P**. If this restriction is lifted, then the corresponding satisfiability problem is NP-complete, as we discuss above under "Disjunctions."

We point out, however, that these are not unique to ARBAC. The access matrix scheme due to Harrison et al. [17], for example, has preconditions in its state-change rules as well. Similarly, in the context of RBAC, the work of Crampton and Loizou [9] on the scoped administration of RBAC, has what they call conditions on state-changes that are very similar to the preconditions of ARBAC.

4.2 Abstraction Refinement and the Sources of Complexity

An aspect from our approach that assuages the complexity is that we are goal-oriented in our abstraction-refinement algorithm (see Section 3). Recall that we create a priority queue of roles that are *Related-by-Assignment* to the query role, which is the role in the safety instance. This stratification of roles helps us eliminate roles that cannot affect the membership to the query role. A consequence of this is that a number paths from the start-state that do not lead to the error-state are removed.

Another aspect is that we optimistically look for short paths that lead from the start state to the error state, while not burdening the model checker with a lot of extraneous input. We first check whether we can reach the error state in zero transitions. In doing so, we ensure that the model checker is provided no state-change rules. We then check whether we can reach it in only a few transitions. In doing so, we provide the model checker with only those state-change rules that may be used for those few transitions. And so on.

Every source of complexity is associated with an intractable problem. For example, disjunctions are associated with satisfiability of boolean expressions in Conjunctive Normal Form (CNF). For a model-checker to check whether there is an error requires it to check whether a boolean expression in CNF that is embedded in the broader problem instance is satisfiable. The two aspects we discuss above result in fewer clauses in the corresponding boolean expression in the abstract policy and its refinements.

The numbers of irrevocable, mixed and positive precondition roles are fewer in the abstract policy and its refinements as well. Also, they pertain to fewer target roles. Consequently, the corresponding instances of intractable problems are smaller, and there are fewer possible paths for the model checker to explore than if such roles are strewn across rules for several target roles. Our empirical assessment that we discuss in the following section bears out these discussions.

5. RESULTS

Our experimental evaluation compares MOHAWK to current state-of-the-art verification tools for ARBAC policies, namely symbolic model checking, bounded model checking, and RBAC-PAT [46]. Note that although all the competing techniques were developed in the context of verification, they can also be used for the purposes of error finding. We chose NuSMV [33] as the reference implementation for both symbolic and bounded model checking. In the following, we use the terms MC and BMC to refer to NuSMV's symbolic model checker and bounded model checker respectively. Our evaluation focused on ascertaining the efficiency and the scalability of the tools in finding errors.

We measure the efficiency based on the absolute time taken to find an error. We measure the scalability with respect to the complexity sources (Section 4), namely number of roles, and four aspects of preconditions (number of disjunctions, number of irrevocable roles, number of mixed roles, and number of positive preconditions) in the input policies. Our case study (see Section 5.1) establishes that such features are required for creating realistic ARBAC policies. Our results can be summarized as follows:

Where Mohawk performs better: The mindset behind MOHAWK is that policies are likely to contain errors, and most of these errors can be found in only a few refinements. In other words, we are optimistic about finding errors. Consequently, we undergo the additional overhead of abstraction-refinement. For complex policies in which it is likely that there are several errors at various levels of refinement, it is likely that MOHAWK will outperform conventional approaches. MOHAWK is also likely to perform better on policies that contain several sources of complexity (see Section 4).

Where other tools may perform better: Other tools may perform better than MOHAWK in two particular cases that abstraction-refinement is unnecessary overhead. One is for the subcases for which the problem is in **P**. In this case, conventional model checking is likely to perform better than MOHAWK. Another is the case that there are only a few errors, and these errors require several refinement steps. It is not necessarily true that MOHAWK will perform worse in this case, as the fact that we use bounded model checking may in itself mitigate the effects of the overhead from abstraction-refinement. However, we acknowledge that it is possible that in such a case, abstraction-refinement adds overhead which may cause it to perform worse than other approaches.

In the following sections, we describe our case study,

		Num. of Roles, Rules	MC	BMC	RBAC-PAT		Mohawk
					Forward reachability	Backward reachability	
Case Study		612, 6142	M/O	31s	T/O	Err	2s
Test suite 1 *Poly-time verifiable*	1.	3, 15	0.097s	0.016s	0.625s	0.240s	0.382s
	2.	5, 25	0.050s	0.025s	0.695s	0.281s	0.431s
	3.	20, 100	M/O	0.103s	0.806s	Err	0.733s
	4.	40, 200	M/O	0.110s	0.780s	Err	0.379s
	5.	200, 1000	M/O	0.624s	1.471s	Err	0.477s
	6.	500, 2500	M/O	3.2s	2.177s	Err	0.531s
	7.	4000, 20000	M/O	414s	7.658s	Err	3.138s
	8.	20000, 80000	M/O	M/O	110s	Err	53s
	9.	30000, 120000	M/O	M/O	210s	Err	2m 14s
	10.	40000, 200000	M/O	M/O	6m 16s	Err	4m 32s
Test suite 2 *NP-Complete*	1.	3, 15	0.022s	0.021s	0.513s	0.241s	0.442s
	2.	5, 25	0.064s	0.026s	0.519s	0.252s	0.501s
	3.	20, 100	M/O	0.048s	0.512s	Err	0.436s
	4.	40, 200	M/O	0.122s	0.534s	Err	1.303s
	5.	200, 1000	M/O	0.472s	0.699s	Err	0.504s
	6.	500, 2500	M/O	1.819s	2.414s	Err	0.597s
	7.	4000, 20000	M/O	109s	311s	Err	2.753s
	8.	20000, 80000	M/O	M/O	T/O	Err	40s
	9.	30000, 130000	M/O	M/O	T/O	Err	1m 39s
	10.	40000, 200000	M/O	M/O	T/O	Err	4m 12s
Test suite 3 *PSPACE-Complete*	1.	3, 15	0.030s	0.102s	1.452s	0.665s	0.380s
	2.	5, 25	0.044s	0.033s	1.666s	0.881s	0.431s
	3.	20, 100	M/O	0.056s	1.364s	Err	0.381s
	4.	40, 200	M/O	0.169s	1.476s	Err	0.984s
	5.	200, 1000	M/O	0.972s	2.258s	Err	0.486s
	6.	500, 2500	M/O	2.422s	7.350s	Err	0.487s
	7.	4000, 20000	M/O	109s	511s	Err	2.478s
	8.	20000, 80000	M/O	M/O	T/O	Err	41s
	9.	30000, 130000	M/O	M/O	T/O	Err	2m 57s
	10.	40000, 200000	M/O	M/O	T/O	Err	6m 21s
Simple Policies	1.	12, 19	0.025s	0.022s	0.531s	0.238s	0.300s
	2.	20, 266	0.023s	0.026s	0.559s	0.247s	0.400s
	3.	32, 162	M/O	0.182s	1.556s	0.568s	0.830s

m	-	minutes	MC	-	NuSMV symbolic model checking	T/O	-	Time out after 60 mins
s	-	seconds	BMC	-	NuSMV bounded model checking	M/O	-	Memory out
ms	-	milliseconds	RBAC-PAT	-	Tool from Stoller et al. [13,46]	Err	-	Segmentation fault

Table 2: Evaluation of model-checking, bounded model-checking, RBAC-PAT, and Mohawk on various benchmarks.

benchmarks, experimental methodology and provide a summary of results.

5.1 Case Study

We conducted a case study for banking that has been vetted by a major financial institution. The case study involves several branches, and is realistic. We modeled several of the job functions at the branches, and the associated state-change rules. Our case-study has a number of similarities to an earlier case-study [41]. Our ARBAC policy has 612 roles and 6142 *can_assign* and *can_revoke* rules. Separation of privilege properties are of importance in banking [41]; commercial tools exist for checking this property for certain state-only schemes [1,2]. Hence, we focused on checking for errors that encode such properties. The particular separation of privilege property on which our case study is based expresses the constraint that in any branch, a user may be assigned to at most three of a set of five roles that are sensitive. The violation of this constraint can be checked by appropriately encoding a safety question. Our benchmarks (see Section 5.2) use similar safety questions.

We discussed this policy with the representatives of a leading bank, who agreed that enforcing separation of privilege is crucial for their operations and that our example is realistic [42]. Lack of such an enforcement can lead to *toxic pairs* of roles being assigned to the same user.

Our experience with the case study provides two insights about realistic policies. First, our case study affirms that the sources of complexity that we discuss in Section 4 occur in realistic policies. Second, realistic ARBAC policies are not amenable to static slicing techniques such as those proposed in prior work [21,46]. Static slicing techniques are effective only in cases where the role in question is dependent in particular ways only on a small set of roles, irrespective of the size of the policy (see Section 3.8). Such a dependency does not exist for the encoding of the separation of privilege property on which Table 2 is based, and for other properties we have investigated in our case-study.

We have tested our case study on all the error-finding tools for our safety question (see Table 2). MOHAWK identified an error in 2 seconds, BMC identified the same error in 31 seconds, and the other tools ran out of resources.

5.2 Benchmarks Used

We used two set of policies in our evaluation. Both are based on prior work [13,21,41,46]. The first set has not been used previously; we built it based on our case study, and the sources of complexity, given that they do indeed occur in practice. Our second set of policies has been used in the context of verification of ARBAC policies in prior work [13,46]. These policies are simpler than the policies in the first set.

Complex Policies (Set 1): We have created a test suite based on the case study, and the sources of complexity that we know occur in practice. As noted earlier, both from our case study and analysis we have concluded that the the number of roles (or size of the policy) and type of state change rules are sources of complexity in ARBAC policies. Depending on the type of state-change rules, the safety analysis problem for ARBAC is PSPACE-Complete, NP-Complete, or solvable in polynomial time [21]. Accordingly, we have created three sets of complex test suites with varying gradations of roles:

- **Test suite 1:** Policies with positive conjunctive *can_assign* rules and non-empty *can_revoke* rules. Error-finding problem is solvable in polynomial time for these policies.
- **Test suite 2:** Policies with mixed conjunctive *can_assign* rules and empty *can_revoke* rules. Error-finding problem is NP-Complete for these policies.
- **Test suite 3:** Policies with mixed conjunctive *can_assign* rules and non-empty *can_revoke* rules. The error-finding problem is PSPACE-Complete for these policies.

For each complex policy, we identified a user-role pair at random such that the role is reachable by an unauthorized user. Our results are for verifying this question. Recall that the basic safety question is determining whether a unauthorized user u can reach a role r. In our complex policies, a majority of the roles in the policy are related to the target role in the safety query. This is realistic, as it is similar to the policy in our case study.

Simple Policies (Set 2): This set comprises three ARBAC policies that have been used in previous work for the evaluation of RBAC-PAT [13,39,46]. The first policy is for a hypothetical hospital, and the second policy is for a hypothetical university. The third policy from [13] is a test case that has mixed preconditions. The first two policies were used in [46] for case studies. The third policy was used in [13], and a complete state-space exploration is reported to have taken 8.6 hours in RBAC-PAT. An important restriction in these policies is that they have at most one positive pre-condition per *can_assign* rule. As we explain in Section 5.4.2, answering the safety question for these policies was fairly easy for all the tools.

5.3 Experimental Methodology

All the experiments were conducted on a Macbook Pro laptop with an Intel Core 2 Duo 2.4 GHz processor and 4GB of RAM.

In all the experiments, the input to the error-finding tools consisted of an ARBAC policy and a safety question. We applied the static slicing techniques proposed in prior work [21,46] on all the policies prior to the experiments. The policies were encoded using the input language of the respective tools. MC and BMC use the SMV finite state machine language, while RBAC-PAT and MOHAWK have their own input language. We implemented a translation tool to convert policies in MOHAWK's input language to both SMV and RBAC-PAT input languages. We expected the tools to conclude that the role is reachable and provide the sequence of administrative actions that lead to the role assignment. In our evaluation, we had two users for each policy, namely the user in the safety question and the administrator. These are the only users required for answering the safety question. Moreover, static slicing techniques remove all users but the one that is relevant to the safety question.

5.4 Results Explained

We explain the results of our experimental evaluation below. Whenever we refer to MOHAWK below, we mean MOHAWK configured with aggressive abstraction-refinement, unless specified otherwise. For the policies in Table 2, on average we needed 2 refinements. The worst-case was for the policy from our case study, for which we needed 7 refinements.

5.4.1 Results on Complex Policies

The results of our evaluation on complex policies (Set 1) are contained in Table 2. Our results indicate that MOHAWK scales better than all the competing tools, irrespective of the complexity of the input policy. BMC scales better than MC, but still runs out of memory for large policies. RBAC-PAT's forward reachability, although slower compared to BMC, is effective for test suite 1, whose policies are verifiable in polynomial time. However, RBAC-PAT's forward reachability times out for large policies in test suites 2 and 3. The forward reachability algorithm in RBAC-PAT can be considered as a specialized model checking algorithm for ARBAC policies, and scales better than symbolic model checking. RBAC-PAT's backward reachability algorithm was faster compared RBAC-PAT's forward algorithm for a few small policies, but gave a segmentation fault for majority of the policies in all the test suites. It is unclear whether this is because of a bug in the implementation or if the tool ran out of memory. MOHAWK scales better compared to all the tools, and is orders of magnitude faster than competing tools for the larger and more complex policies.

MOHAWK (with aggressive abstraction-refinement) is slower compared to MC and BMC for small size policies. This is because these policies are so small that BMC can analyze them easily, but MOHAWK takes multiple iterations to arrive at the same answer. In other words, the policies are too simple, and the abstraction-refinement step creates unnecessary overhead. However, MOHAWK's abstraction-refinement step can be configured to be less aggressive for such policies. We ran MOHAWK with less aggressive abstraction-refinement for the smaller policies and got performance comparable to BMC.

MOHAWK is very efficient in finding errors in all the three test suites, although each of them belong to a different complexity class. This further underlines the effectiveness of the abstraction-refinement based technique in MOHAWK. Also, having a single technique that can perform well on large real-world policies that belong to different complexity classes is also useful from the point of view of maintaining and extending the tool. Furthermore, since our technique is not tied to specific model-checking algorithms, it can be used in conjunction with other algorithms such as RBAC-PAT's forward reachability.

5.4.2 Results on Simple Policies

The results of our evaluation on simple policies are summarized in Table 2. The first and second policies did not satisfy separate administration restriction, so we removed *can_assign* roles that have the administrative roles as target and used the modified policies in our evaluation.

BMC, RBAC-PAT, and MOHAWK were effective for all the three policies. The absolute differences in time taken to verify are not very significant because they are less than a second.

MOHAWK with aggressive abstraction-refinement is faster compared to RBAC-PAT's forward reachability, but slower compared to BMC and RBAC-PAT's backward reachability for these policies. However, the absolute slow down in each case is less than a second and is imperceptible to the user. MOHAWK's slowdown when compared to BMC is expected because of the small size of the policies. For the third test case, MC timed out. Both RBAC-PAT and MOHAWK with aggressive abstraction-refinement are slower compared to BMC, and MOHAWK is faster compared to RBAC-PAT's forward reachability algorithm and slightly slower compared to RBAC-PAT's backward reachability.

6. RELATED WORK

Counter-example guided abstraction refinement was originally developed in the context of model checking [6]. Since then the basic idea has been adapted in different ways in the context of bounded model-checking for hardware verification [27] and program analysis [4] to verify computer programs. The idea of abstraction refinement has also been adapted in the context of solvers for various theories such as modular and integer linear arithmetic [12]. To the best of our knowledge, MOHAWK is the first tool to adapt the paradigm of abstraction-refinement for finding errors in access-control policies.

We can classify verification problems in the context of access control broadly into two categories: state-only, and with state changes.

The work that falls in state-only considers only a given state, and verification of properties within that state. Examples of work that fall in this category include those of Jha et al. [22, 23], Hughes et al. [20], Hu et al. [18], Martin and Xie [31], Rao et al. [34], Kolovski [26], Zhao et al. [48], and Fisler et al. [11]. It is conceivable that our approach can be used in state-only contexts. Indeed, the work of Martin and Xie [31] considers testing of XACML policies by introducing what they call faults that are used to simulate common errors in authoring such policies. However, in this paper, we focus on access control systems that are characterized as state-change systems. Consequently, we focus on work that considers verification of such systems.

Plain model-checking approach has also been proposed for some state-change schemes [47]. As we have shown in Section 5, plain model checking does not scale adequately for verifying policies of very large sizes.

Work on safety analysis dates back to the mid-1970's; the work by Harrison et al. [17] is considered foundational work in access control. They were the first to provide a characterization of safety. They show also, that safety analysis for an access matrix scheme with state changes specified as commands in a particular syntax is undecidable. Since then, there has been considerable interest and work in safety, and more generally, security analysis in the context of various access control schemes.

Safety analysis in monotonic versions of the HRU scheme has been studied in [16]. Jones et al. [24] introduced the Take-Grant scheme, in which safety is decidable in linear time. Amman and Sandhu consider safety in the context of the Extended Schematic Protection Model (ESPM) [3] and the Typed Access Matrix model [37]. Budd [5] and Motwani et al. [32] studied grammatical protection systems. Soshi et al. [45] studied safety analysis in Dynamic-Typed Access Matrix model. These models all have subcases where safety is decidable. Solworth and Sloan [44] introduced discretionary access control model in which safety is decidable. This thread of research has proposed many new access control schemes, but has had limited impact on access control systems used in practice. This is potentially because the proposals were either too simplistic or too arcane to be useful. The focus of this paper is ARBAC, which was primarily proposed to meet the need of expressive access control schemes required for large-scale real-world deployments.

To our knowledge, Li and Tripunitara [29] were the first to consider security analysis in the context of ARBAC. Jha et al. [21] were the first to consider the use of model checking to for the verification problem of ARBAC. That work also identifies that the verification problem for ARBAC is PSPACE-complete. Subsequently, Stoller et al. [46] established that user-role reachability analysis is fixed parameter tractable with respect to number of mixed roles, irrevocable roles, positive preconditions, and goal size. Furthermore, they have proposed new model-checking algorithms for similar verification problems and implemented them in a tool called RBAC-PAT [13].

RBAC-PAT contains two algorithms for analyzing ARBAC policies, namely forward reachability and backward reachability. As we have shown in Section 5, forward reachability algorithm scales better compared to plain model checking, is effective for polynomial time verifiable policies, but does not scale adequately with complexity of the policies. We could not extensively evaluate the backward reachability algorithm because the implementation gave a segmentation fault for even moderately sized policies. In contrast, MOHAWK scales better and is efficient for identifying errors irrespective of the complexity of the policies. The key reason for MOHAWK's effectiveness is the abstraction-refinement approach that is goal oriented and optimally looks short paths that lead from the start path to the error state (Section 4.2).

Gofman et. al. [14] proposes incremental algorithms for analyzing the impact of changes to ARBAC policies by taking advantage of previous analysis results. Such incremental analysis is outside the scope of this paper.

7. CONCLUSION

We presented an abstraction-refinement based technique, and its implementation, the MOHAWK tool, for finding errors in ARBAC access-control policies. MOHAWK accepts an access-control policy and a safety question as input, and outputs whether or not an error is found. We extensively evaluated MOHAWK against current state-of-the-art tools for policy analysis. Our experiments show that in comparison with the current tools, MOHAWK scales very well with the complexity of policies and is also orders of magnitude faster. Analysis tools such as MOHAWK enable policy administrators to quickly analyze policies prior to deployment, thereby increasing the assurance of the system.

Acknowledgements

We thank Mikhail Gofman, Scott Stoller, C. R. Ramakrishnan, and Ping Yang for providing access to the RBAC-PAT tool and their experimental data.

8. REFERENCES

[1] Aveska. http://www.aveksa.com/solutions/access-control-automation.cfm.

[2] SailPoint. http://www.sailpoint.com/product/compliance-manager/policy-enforcement.php.

[3] P. Ammann and R. Sandhu. Safety analysis for the extended schematic protection model. *IEEE Symposium on Security and Privacy*, 1991.

[4] T. Ball and S. K. Rajamani. The SLAM project: debugging system software via static analysis. In *POPL '02: Proc. of the 29th ACM symposium on Principles of programming languages*, New York, NY, USA, 2002. ACM.

[5] T. A. Budd. Safety in grammatical protection systems. *Intl. Journal of Parallel Programming*, 12(6):413–431, 1983.

[6] E. Clarke, O. Grumberg, S. Jha, Y. Lu, and H. Veith. Counterexample-guided abstraction refinement for symbolic model checking. *J. ACM*, 50(5):752–794, 2003.

[7] E. Clarke, D. Kroening, J. Ouaknine, and O. Strichman. The completeness threshold for bounded model checking.

[8] E. M. Clarke, O. Grumberg, and D. A. Peled. *Model Checking*. The MIT Press, 1999.

[9] J. Crampton and G. Loizou. Administrative scope: A foundation for role-based administrative models. *ACM Trans. Inf. Syst. Secur.*, 6(2):201–231, 2003.

[10] D. F. Ferraiolo, D. R. Kuhn, and R. Chandramouli. *Role-Based Access Control*. Artech House, Inc., Norwood, MA, USA, 2003.

[11] K. Fisler, S. Krishnamurthi, L. A. Meyerovich, and M. C. Tschantz. Verification and change-impact analysis of access-control policies. In *ICSE '05: Proc. of the 27th Intl. conference on Software engineering*, 2005. ACM.

[12] V. Ganesh and D. L. Dill. A decision procedure for bitvectors and arrays. In *Computer Aided Verification,LNCS*, 2007.

[13] M. I. Gofman, R. Luo, A. C. Solomon, Y. Zhang, P. Yang, and S. D. Stoller. Rbac-pat: A policy analysis tool for role based access control. In *Proc. of the 15th Intl. Conference on Tools and Algorithms for the Construction and Analysis of Systems (TACAS)*, volume 5505, Springer-Verlag, 2009.

[14] M. I. Gofman, R. Luo, and P. Yang. User-role reachability analysis of evolving administrative role based access control. In *Proc. of the 15th European conference on Research in computer security*, Berlin, Heidelberg, 2010. Springer-Verlag.

[15] G. S. Graham and P. J. Denning. Protection — principles and practice. In *Proc. of the AFIPS Spring Joint Computer Conference*, volume 40, AFIPS Press, May 1972.

[16] M. A. Harrison and W. L. Ruzzo. Monotonic protection systems. *Foundations of Secure Computation*, 1978.

[17] M. A. Harrison, W. L. Ruzzo, and J. D. Ullman. On protection in operating systems. In *SOSP '75: Proc. of the fifth ACM symposium on Operating systems principles*, 1975. ACM.

[18] H. Hu and G. Ahn. Enabling verification and conformance testing for access control model. In *SACMAT '08: Proc. of the 13th ACM symposium on Access control models and technologies*, New York, NY, USA, 2008. ACM.

[19] V. C. Hu, D. R. Kuhn, and T. Xie. Property verification for generic access control models. In *EUC '08: Proc. of the 2008 IEEE/IFIP Intl. Conference on Embedded and Ubiquitous Computing*, 2008. IEEE Computer Society.

[20] G. Hughes and T. Bultan. Automated verification of access control policies using a sat solver. *Int. J. Softw. Tools Technol. Transf.*, 10(6):503–520, 2008.

[21] S. Jha, N. Li, M. Tripunitara, Q. Wang, and W. Winsborough. Towards formal verification of role-based access control policies. *IEEE Trans. Dependable Secur. Comput.*, 5(4):242–255, 2008.

[22] S. Jha and T. W. Reps. Model Checking SPKI/SDSI. *Journal of Computer Security*, 12(3–4):317–353, 2004.

[23] S. Jha, S. Schwoon, H. Wang, and T. Reps. Weighted Pushdown Systems and Trust-Management Systems. In *Proc. of TACAS*, New York, NY, USA, 2006. Springer-Verlag.

[24] A. K. Jones, R. J. Lipton, and L. Snyder. A linear time algorithm for deciding security. In *SFCS '76: Proc. of the 17th Annual Symposium on Foundations of Computer Science*, Washington, DC, USA, 1976. IEEE Computer Society.

[25] A. Kern. Advanced features for enterprise-wide role-based access control. In *ACSAC '02: Proc. of the 18th Annual Computer Security Applications Conference*, Washington, DC, USA, 2002. IEEE Computer Society.

[26] V. Kolovski, J. Hendler, and B. Parsia. Analyzing web access control policies. In *WWW '07: Proc. of the 16th Intl. conference on World Wide Web*, 2007. ACM.

[27] D. Kroening. Computing over-approximations with bounded model checking. *Electron. Notes Theor. Comput. Sci.*, 144:79–92, January 2006.

[28] N. Li, J. C. Mitchell, and W. H. Winsborough. Beyond proof-of-compliance: security analysis in trust management. *J. ACM*, 52(3):474–514, 2005.

[29] N. Li and M. V. Tripunitara. Security analysis in role-based access control. In *SACMAT '04: Proc. of the ninth ACM symposium on Access control models and technologies*, New York, NY, USA, 2004. ACM.

[30] N. Li and M. V. Tripunitara. Security analysis in role-based access control. *ACM Trans. Inf. Syst. Secur.*, 9(4):391–420, 2006.

[31] E. Martin and T. Xie. A fault model and mutation testing of access control policies. In *WWW '07: Proc. of the 16th Intl. conference on World Wide Web*, 2007. ACM.

[32] R. Motwani, R. Panigrahy, V. Saraswat, and S. Ventkatasubramanian. On the decidability of accessibility problems (extended abstract). In *STOC '00: Proc. of the thirty-second annual ACM symposium on Theory of computing*, New York, NY, USA, 2000. ACM.

[33] NuSMV. `http://nusmv.irst.itc.it/`.

[34] P. Rao, D. Lin, and E. Bertino. XACML function annotations. In *POLICY '07: Proc. of the Eighth IEEE Intl. Workshop on Policies for Distributed Systems and Networks*, Washington, DC, USA, 2007. IEEE Computer Society.

[35] J. H. Saltzer and M. D. Schroeder. The protection of information in computer systems. *Proc. of the IEEE*, 1975.

[36] R. Sandhu, V. Bhamidipati, and Q. Munawer. The arbac97 model for role-based administration of roles. *ACM Trans. Inf. Syst. Secur.*, 2(1):105–135, 1999.

[37] R. S. Sandhu. The typed access matrix model. In *Proc. IEEE Symposium on Research in Security and Privacy*, 1992.

[38] R. S. Sandhu, E. J. Coyne, H. L. Feinstein, and C. E. Youman. Role-based access control models. *IEEE Computer*, 29(2):38–47, 1996.

[39] A. Sasturkar, P. Yang, S. D. Stoller, and C. Ramakrishnan. Policy analysis for administrative role based access control. In *Proc. of the 19th Computer Security Foundations Workshop*. IEEE Computer Society Press, July 2006.

[40] A. Sasturkar, P. Yang, S. D. Stoller, and C. Ramakrishnan. Policy analysis for administrative role based access control. Technical report, Stony Brook University, 2006.

[41] A. Schaad, J. Moffett, and J. Jacob. The role-based access control system of a european bank: a case study and discussion. In *SACMAT '01: Proc. of the sixth ACM symposium on Access control models and technologies*, New York, NY, USA, 2001. ACM.

[42] Security Architect of a Leading Bank. Personal communication, 2010.

[43] K. Sohr, M. Drouineaud, G.-J. Ahn, and M. Gogolla. Analyzing and managing role-based access control policies. *IEEE Transactions on Knowledge and Data Engineering*, 20:924–939, 2008.

[44] J. A. Solworth and R. H. Sloan. A layered design of discretionary access controls with decidable safety properties. *IEEE Symposium on Security and Privacy*, 2004.

[45] M. Soshi. Safety analysis of the dynamic-typed access matrix model. In *Computer Security - ESORICS 2000*, LNCS, Springer Berlin / Heidelberg, 2000.

[46] S. D. Stoller, P. Yang, C. R. Ramakrishnan, and M. I. Gofman. Efficient policy analysis for administrative role based access control. In *CCS '07: Proc. of the 14th ACM conference on Computer and communications security*, 2007. ACM.

[47] N. Zhang, M. Ryan, and D. P. Guelev. Synthesising verified access control systems through model checking. *J. Comput. Secur.*, 16(1):1–61, 2008.

[48] C. Zhao, N. Heilili, S. Liu, and Z. Lin. Representation and reasoning on rbac: A description logic approach. In *ICTAC'05: Proc. of the 2nd Intl. Colloquium on Theoretical Aspects of Computing*, LNCS, Springer, 2005.

Trust-based Anonymous Communication: Adversary Models and Routing Algorithms

Aaron Johnson* Paul Syverson
U.S. Naval Research Laboratory
{aaron.m.johnson,paul.syverson}@nrl.navy.mil

Roger Dingledine Nick Mathewson
The Tor Project
{arma, nickm}@torproject.org

ABSTRACT

We introduce a novel model of routing security that incorporates the ordinarily overlooked variations in trust that users have for different parts of the network. We focus on anonymous communication, and in particular onion routing, although we expect the approach to apply more broadly.

This paper provides two main contributions. First, we present a novel model to consider the various security concerns for route selection in anonymity networks when users vary their trust over parts of the network. Second, to show the usefulness of our model, we present as an example a new algorithm to select paths in onion routing. We analyze its effectiveness against deanonymization and other information leaks, and particularly how it fares in our model versus existing algorithms, which do not consider trust. In contrast to those, we find that our trust-based routing strategy can protect anonymity against an adversary capable of attacking a significant fraction of the network.

Categories and Subject Descriptors

C.2.2 [**Networks**]: Network Protocols; C.2.0 [**Networks**]: General—*Security and protection*; C.4 [**Performance**]: Modeling techniques

General Terms

Security, Theory

Keywords

anonymous communication, onion routing, privacy, trust

1. INTRODUCTION

Existing anonymous communication theory and system design are generally based on the unrealistic assumption that both adversaries and vulnerability to their attacks are uniformly distributed throughout the communications infrastructure and that a larger network should better protect anonymity. But then if an adversary can control a significant fraction of the network, scaling the network to even tens or hundreds of thousands of nodes will not necessarily improve anonymity. This paper presents a model for routing traffic on an anonymity network where different users trust some parts of the network more than others, potentially allowing users to protect themselves even if large fractions of the network are compromised. We consider route selection for onion routing that makes use of that nonuniform trust and also protects despite an adversary's awareness of it.

While there have been many proposals for anonymous communication protocols [3, 7, 20, 40, 41], onion routing [26] is probably the most dominant. In particular, it enjoys a widely-deployed implementation in the Tor system [17, 49]. As of April 2011, the Tor network's roughly 2500 volunteer routers are used every day by several hundreds of thousands of users to carry about seventy terabytes of traffic [50]. Thus, though our model can apply to many protocols, we focus on onion routing for our examples to illustrate that the theory we introduce can be applied to real systems.

Onion routing, like most anonymous communication paradigms, derives its security from the (traditionally uniform) diffusion of trust throughout the system. In onion routing, users create a cryptographic circuit over a randomly chosen path and then use it to communicate bidirectionally with a destination. Onion routers are supposed to be run by distinct non-colluding entities, but enforcing non-collusion can be difficult. The routers of the Tor network, for example, are operated by volunteers whose identities and intentions are unverified. This choice has provided the network with the diversity and flexibility that has helped it grow to its current scale [16, 18]. But the number of routers that can be added by one entity is limited only by the number of IP addresses he can obtain.

This same general dependence on diffusion of trust applies to most anonymous communication schemes—both deployed anonymity networks, such as Mixmaster [35] and Mixminion [12], and those that have seen more theoretical consideration than actual use, such as the various treatments of Dining Cryptographers [2, 25, 27]. Most of the related research assumes that individual users can do little to learn which nodes are likely to be compromised. But onion routing was originally devised by the U.S. Naval Research Laboratory specifically to target an environment where large organizations or companies could use a network alongside ordinary citizens. What if the user is from an organization that *does* have the resources to investigate nodes, to operate

*This work was primarily done while at the Department of Computer Science at The University of Texas at Austin.

CCS'11, October 17–21, 2011, Chicago, Illinois, USA.
Copyright 2011 ACM 978-1-4503-0948-6/11/10 ...$10.00.

its own nodes, or to otherwise ensure the security of nodes against a particular adversary? Such an organization might run its own private network, in which it controls or vets all the nodes, and just use that. Even if such a private network hides which of its users is responsible for which connection, all traffic exiting it will be known to come from the organization running the network. Alternatively, the organization could run a subnet of the public network and preferentially use that subnet for its own traffic. This approach helps to resist first–last correlation (described below), but it exposes the organization to other attacks. Most significantly, to the extent that the organization is likelier than other users to use its own subnet, all the traffic carried on the subnet will be linked to the organization and therefore to some degree deanonymized. Even if the organization tries to keep its trust and use of its subnet a secret, usage patterns (as would happen if many users from the subnet make requests linkable to the organization) or inadvertent disclosures (as in unauthorized leaks [43]) could over time reveal its presence. We introduce a framework that can address such concerns.

We review related work in the next section. We set out our assumptions, describe our model for the network and adversaries, and provide corresponding definitions for trust and anonymity in Section 3. In Section 4, we use the model to design and analyze a novel path-selection algorithm for onion routing. We begin in Section 4.1 by considering the anonymity of a single connection. In particular, we use trust to obtain an algorithm that improves the posterior probability that an adversary assigns to a given user as the source of a connection given trust levels and the adversary's observations. We consider the value of this posterior for some typical usage scenarios, and compare it to the posterior probability under other path-selection algorithms. We also consider the effect of errors in assigning trust in these scenarios. Next, in Section 4.2, we examine the implications of making multiple connections over time and modify our path-selection algorithm to improve anonymity in this case.

Throughout the paper we try to keep our work applicable to real-world scenarios while remaining abstract enough to permit useful analysis. We hope our work here will provide a foundation for research in route selection so that ultimately users with large-resource, long-reach adversaries can have the assurances necessary to protect their communications.

2. RELATED WORK

The field of anonymous communication has grown vast. For recent general surveys, see Edman and Yener [22] or Danezis et al. [11]. Here we will focus on work related to our central topic, incorporating node trust into route selection. Two types of prior work are thus particularly relevant: First are papers that analyze the anonymity effects of restricted knowledge of the network by route selectors. Second are papers that also use trust in route selection. We also include a brief discussion of first–last correlation attacks.

The first work to consider general effects of route selection on a less than fully connected graph is Danezis's analysis of mix networks with restricted routes [9]. Route restriction was considered to ensure more traffic per link, but he also observed that if the network was an expander graph with N nodes, after $O(\log N)$ random hops a route will have nearly the same distribution on sources as in a fully connected graph.

Danezis and Clayton introduced "route fingerprinting" attacks that exploit the limited knowledge of the network that users must have for P2P anonymity designs to permit scaling [10]. To avoid such knowledge-based attacks, Tor requires that clients know about all the routers in the network. This choice obviously creates scaling problems, but because onion routing is not a P2P design, the number of clients is orders of magnitude larger than the number of routers. This hybrid approach has mitigated both scaling issues and some of the attacks that can arise from partial knowledge of the network. The current work is a generalization from the zero/one trust that is implied by knowledge or ignorance of network nodes [10] to a more fine-grained distinction of willingness to trust a node with one's traffic.

Using trust to make routing decisions in anonymity networks was first explicitly analyzed in [31]. (Prior suggestions of choosing so-called "entry guard" nodes based on trust did not describe how to make this choice or analyze use of trust [39].) Johnson and Syverson considered an adversary that would try to compromise a given fraction of the network's nodes. They used a notion of trust based on difficulty-of-compromise to examine the optimal strategy to resist the first–last correlation attack, depending on the resources of the adversary, the size of the network, and the distribution of trust on the nodes. They did not consider, as we do, that different users could have different distributions on trust or that different users could be concerned with attack by different adversaries. They also considered only how a user could resist correlation attacks given nonuniform trust in the network. They did not attempt a general analysis of other potential attacks in such a network or routing strategies to resist those attacks. Herein we consider additional attacks where the adversary makes inferences based on node selection rather than just trying to see the source and destination.

A very different notion of trust for anonymity networks concerns path formation that considers behavioral trust, such as performance reputation [15, 19]. Sassone et al. analyzed trust in this sense when an adversary compromises a fixed fraction of the network [42]. Users choose paths according to individual trust algorithms (independent of where the adversary exists). They analyze the probability that a user chooses an adversary node, and given that, the probability the adversary attaches to a user creating a path containing that node.

Onion routing's efficiency and bidirectionality make it fast and functional enough for popular online activities like web browsing and instant messaging, which in turn contributes to its success. But onion routing anonymity protocols are not the only ones that have been used for general public communication. In particular, systems based on passing discrete self-contained messages through "mixes" in a source-routed manner similar to onion routing [5, 6] have been used for public Internet communication via email. But even those that are designed to be practical or have been deployed and widely used [12, 28, 35] add much more latency and overhead compared with onion routing.

The added latency in mix systems is not just inefficiency. High-variance latency helps to protect against several types of attacks on anonymity that onion routing does not resist as well or at all, such as the first–last correlation attack [48] or various others [13, 23, 29, 30, 32, 33, 34, 36], although onion routing is more secure than mixing against some attacks [45, 46].

First–last correlation attacks require the adversary to match the timing pattern of messages coming from the user to the timing of messages going to the destination. This matching can either be done passively [1, 39] by simply using the timing pattern created by the user, or actively [51] by delaying messages to create timing watermarks. Extant defenses against first–last correlation are either ineffective in practice (padding) or impractical in effect (delaying and mixing) or, more typically, both. Simulation and experimentation have confirmed the obvious, that such attacks require trivial resources or analysis to be successful. If research does not uncover an effective and practical counter to first–last correlation, onion routing for low-latency use must simply accept it and strive to minimize its impact. For example, Tor contains no mixing or padding in its design [17].

3. MODEL

We describe a model to give semantics to the notion of trust in the context of anonymous communication. The model we present provides a foundation for using trust in designing and analyzing anonymity protocols, specialized to the particular setting of improving resistance to deanonymization and profiling for onion routing systems. It is part of a model intended to be general enough to reason about trust for various anonymity protocols, and for secure routing goals besides anonymity, such as route provenance. The more general model also describes other adversary goals beyond deanonymization and profiling, whether the anonymity protocols use onion routing or another approach. For example, an adversary may want to discover which of the various possible adversaries specific (classes of) users are trying to avoid, which could help indicate something about the likelihood that a given circuit belongs to a given user based on how well the circuit counters a given adversary. An adversary may also want to discover which network nodes are more trusted with respect to which adversaries. Among other things, this could indicate the resources deployed to protect a particular (class of) user's communication. Our focus in this paper is to provide a model and algorithms for onion routing that show how trust-aware route selection can greatly improve resistance to deanonymization and profiling. In particular, using trust can substantially improve security even when an adversary controls a significant portion of the network. The general model is more completely described in [47].

1. Let V be the set of nodes. And let $V = U \cup R \cup D$, where U is a set of users[1], R is a set of onion routers, and D is a set of destinations.
2. Let $E \subseteq \binom{V}{2}$ be the set of network links between nodes.
3. Let $\mathcal{A}$ be the set of adversaries.
4. Let $A_v \subseteq \mathcal{A}, v \in V$, be the adversaries with respect to which a node v wants privacy.
5. Let $C : 2^{\mathcal{A}\times(V\cup E)} \to [0,1]$ indicate the probability of a pattern of compromise among the nodes and links: for $c \in 2^{\mathcal{A}\times(V\cup E)}$, if $(a,x) \in c$, then adversary a has compromised x. C satisfies $\sum_{c\in 2^{\mathcal{A}\times(V\cup E)}} C(c) = 1$.
6. Let $C_v : 2^{\mathcal{A}\times(V\cup E)} \to [0,1], v \in V$, indicate the belief node v has in a pattern of compromise among nodes and links. The C_v satisfy $\sum_{c\in 2^{\mathcal{A}\times(V\cup E)}} C_v(c) = 1$.
7. Let $I_v \in \{0,1\}^*, v \in V$, be the inputs each node uses when running the protocol.

[1]Note that we say 'user' to refer to the human user and to the client software that creates connections on the user's behalf or sometimes to the computer on which that software runs. This overlap should not cause problems at the level at which we model systems. It should be clear from context which usage is intended if the distinction is important.

A protocol is run by the nodes over the network links in order to reach some collective state. For purposes of privacy, the relevant property of the protocol is the set of models that are consistent with the observations of an adversary during the protocol's execution. An adversary makes observations at the nodes and links he has compromised. A probabilistic protocol yields a distribution on the sets of possible models.

Investigating privacy in this model then becomes analyzing how likely the adversary is to be in a position to make good inferences about the model. Privacy may be quantified, for example, by the number of bits of node input learned for certain by the adversary. Or it could be that there are reasonable prior distributions that we can allow the adversary to put on the models, and privacy loss is measured by the mutual information between the observations and the models.

The model includes multiple adversaries. This is an important choice for modeling trust in anonymous communication, because a diverse set of users with varying goals and beliefs is necessary for the set to provide good anonymity. Part of that diversity occurs in the adversaries of a user. That means that we cannot require that each user relies on other network entities in the same way. Allowing users to use the network in different ways while still considering overall communication anonymity from their combined actions is a central issue for protocol design.

The adversaries themselves operate by controlling parts of the network. This models both that an adversary might provide some nodes and links to the network and that he might compromise some that are provided by others. We could restrict the adversary to controlling nodes alone, because an adversary that controls a link could be simulated for purposes of analysis by splitting any link and connecting the halves with a node controlled by the adversary. However, given that several attacks on anonymous communication protocols involve observing the network connections in particular [21, 37], it is useful to formally allow both types of compromise. Also, we allow different adversaries to compromise the same node at the same time.

Trust itself appears in our model in the distributions C_v. Trust in a node or link is given with respect to a set of adversaries $A \subseteq \mathcal{A}$. The trust of user u in, say, network link $e \in E$, with respect to A can be understood as a distribution over the ways 2^A in which the adversaries in A have compromised e. If, for example, the probability in C_u is high that some member of A has compromised e, then we can say that u has low trust in e. Ideally, from the user's perspective, the user's beliefs would be true, that is, C_u would equal C. Our model incorporates erroneous beliefs, though, because a user's beliefs affect her actions and may hurt anonymity when they differ from the truth.

Our analysis will assume a population $N \subseteq U$ of naïve users who think any router is as likely to be compromised as any other. It is within this population of users that we will hide the identity of a given user of the network. This approach is equivalent to assuming that the adversary can rule out all users other than u and the naïve users as being the source of a connection. Let $m = |R|$ be the number of routers. Let $n = |N|$ be the number of naïve users.

The naïve users share the same adversary, $A_n = \{a_N\}, n \in N$. Other users each have their own adversary, $A_u = \{a_u\}$. No router or destination has any adversary. The set of adversaries is $\mathcal{A} = a_N + \{a_u\}_{u \in U \setminus N}$.

The naïve users $n \in N$ hold the same beliefs about their adversary a_N. They believe each router is independently and equally likely to be compromised: $c^n_{a_N} = c_N$.

We assume user $u \in U$ believes that adversary $a \in \mathcal{A}$ compromises router $r \in R$ independently with probability $c^u_a(r)$. The *trust* of u in r with respect to a is then $\tau^u_a(r) = 1 - c^u_a(r)$. If clear from the context, we will drop the superscript u and the subscript a. The use of probabilities to represent trust reflects the uncertainty about the presence and power of an adversary when coordinating among many different parties over large networks. This uncertainty is best modeled directly, rather than giving the node too much power by assuming a known adversary or giving the adversary too much power by analyzing the worst case.

Furthermore, we assume that u believes with certainty either that a observes all links from u to the routers and destinations or that a observes none of them. That is, u believes with probability either one or zero that $\{u, v\}$ is compromised for all $v \in R \cup D$. Similarly, we assume that u believes with certainty either that a observes all links from a given destination $d \in D$ to R and U (if these conflict on a link in $U \times D$, the user believes that link is compromised). This models whether or not the user believes that he or his destination uses a hostile ISP. It will also be taken to include the case that the user visits a known hostile destination. If an adversary observes all traffic to and from a given user, we say that he observes the source links, and if he observes all traffic to and from a destination, we say that he observes the destination links. Our model can capture varying trust on the links as well as the routers, and incorporating this would better reflect reality; however, adding diverse link probabilities would complicate the analysis below. So, we restrict ourselves to analysis of varying router trust.

Finally, we assume that u does not believe a compromises users, destinations, or links between routers. As noted above, destination compromise is covered by an adversary observing the destination links. Similarly, the case of observed links between routers is subsumed by the adversary compromising either of the onion routers on that link.

Each user has as input a sequence of destinations $(d_1, d_2, \ldots)$ indicating connections over time. Routers and destinations have no inputs.

Anonymous-Communication Privacy.

We assume that users make connections according to a probabilistic process, and that the adversary uses it as a prior distribution to break privacy. Specifically, we assume that the source and destination of a given connection are independent of connections at other times. We also assume that the user and destination of a connection are independent. We acknowledge that this may not be true in practice—users communicate with different partners, application-layer protocols such as HTTP have temporal patterns of connection establishment, and so on. This assumption simplifies analysis, however, and isolates what the adversary can learn by observing the path.

We assume that the adversary's observations consist of a sequence of *active* links, that is, links carrying messages. We further assume that the adversary can determine (for example, via a correlation attack) when two observations correspond to the same connection.

We consider the privacy of the connections that each user makes (the user inputs) to be the most significant among the components of the model. We thus design our protocols to hide information about the connections, and analyze their privacy in most detail. We perform two types of privacy analysis on the connections. First, we consider the ability of the adversary to infer existence, source, and destination of a given connection, that is, to *deanonymize* the connection. Second, we consider the adversary's knowledge of all user connections over time, that is, his *profile* of each user's activity.

Deanonymization. This kind of analysis is useful when the privacy of a given connection is important, say, because it is particularly sensitive. For this analysis, we assume that the adversary has full knowledge of the model except for the user inputs. The analysis uses the posterior probability of deanonymizing the connection as a privacy metric. We want the probability that the adversary correctly names both the user and the destination of a given connection to be close to what it would be if he had not observed the network.

The correlation attack allows the adversary to infer the source and destination of a connection if he can observe both ends. Therefore, if the adversary can observe traffic from the user (either by compromising the entry router or by observing the user's connection to it) and can also observe traffic from the destination (either because he controls the destination or the last router on the path or observes the traffic between them) then the user has no anonymity. Otherwise, the adversary must use the parts of the connection that he can observe and determine the probability of each user being the source.

Profiling. This analysis is useful to understand the adversary's overall view of private inputs, which might be individually private but highly linked with one another. We use the entropy of user connections as a privacy metric in this case. Learning which connections are related helps the adversary to determine the set of destinations visited by some user. Such a profile, taken as a whole, may itself help identify the user if the adversary has background knowledge about the user's typical communication patterns. The adversary might also try to link connections that have identifying information in their traffic with connections that do not, thereby removing anonymity from those that do not and adding profiling information to both kinds of connections.

4. TRUST IN PATH SELECTION

The addition of trust gives users the ability to select routers that are not likely to be compromised by an adversary that they care about. Specifically, depending on various parameters, users of an onion-routing network who choose paths entirely out of highly trusted routers can sometimes minimize their risk of deanonymization via the correlation attack [31]. However, if other users are concerned about adversaries with a different trust distribution, using only highly trusted routers would lead to different users preferring different routers for their paths—and the choice of routers itself may identify the user. For example, an adversary that controls just the last router on a path observes the destination and the last two routers, and this information alone could deanonymize the user's connection.

By balancing between these effects, we can avoid deanonymization on a single connection. Users make multiple connections over time, however. If their paths change with every new connection, they run an increasing risk of selecting a path that has many compromised routers. An obvious way to avoid this problem is for each user to choose one fixed path to use for all of her connections.

While this strategy helps avoid deanonymization, choosing a single, static path allows an adversary to more easily link together connections from the same user. If the adversary observes the same set of routers in the same positions in two different circuits, he knows it is likely that they originate from the same user. Of particular concern is a malicious destination, because it always observes the *exit router*, that is, the last, static router. Combining static and random router choices allows us to balance avoiding deanonymization with avoiding profiling.

We analyze the impact of the above issues on path deanonymization and use the results of our analysis to motivate a path-selection algorithm. For the adversary types we analyze, the only nontrivial case will be when the adversary compromises destination links and some routers. Briefly stated, our algorithm for this case is to choose a static "downhill" path that picks each successive node from a pool that increases in size because the acceptable lower bound on node trust diminishes with each hop. Once the static path reaches the trust bottom, so that the pool includes all nodes, two dynamic hops are added to the end of the path. We do not claim that this is an optimal strategy. It does demonstrate how to use our model and analysis to easily do better than choosing nodes ignoring trust or using only the most trusted nodes. The details of how our analysis motivates the algorithm are set out below. Our analysis proceeds in two stages: first, we consider minimizing the chance of deanonymization of just a single connection, then second, we consider adapting to multiple connections to maintain good anonymity while also preventing profiling. We will be considering routing for a given user $u \in U$, and we will describe it with respect to the one adversary of u.

4.1 Path anonymity for a single connection

Suppose a user makes just one connection. She chooses a path for that connection based on her trust values for the routers. The adversary can learn about routers on that path by compromising them, compromising an adjacent router, or by observing source or destination links. He can link together routers as belonging to that circuit using the correlation attack. The adversary's ability to determine both source and destination of the circuit, and thereby deanonymize it, depends on these observations. We would like to choose paths to minimize the probability that he can do so.

The best way to select paths depends on the location and kind of adversary we are facing. There are four possibilities depending on whether the source links are compromised or not and whether the destination links are compromised or not. The cases that the source and destination links are either both unobserved or both observed are trivial. The user in these cases can do no better than directly connecting to the destination. If the adversary just observes source links, then we must try to hide the destination. If the adversary just observes destination links (or is the destination), then we must try to hide the user.

4.1.1 Source links observed

Suppose that the adversary observes the source links. Then the user is anonymous if and only if the adversary doesn't observe the destination. Therefore, we can maximize anonymity by choosing a one-hop path that maximizes $\tau(r_1)$, which is achieved by selecting a most-trusted router.

4.1.2 Destination links observed

Now suppose that the adversary observes the destination links. In this case, the adversary is able to learn about the final router, any router he has compromised, and any router adjacent to a compromised router. The adversary can determine that these routers are on the same path and what position they are in by using the correlation attack. Assuming that the adversary knows the user's trust values and the algorithm that the user uses to choose paths, then the adversary can use his observation to infer a distribution on the source of the circuit. We would like to minimize the probability that he assigns to the correct user.

We analyze this probability for a given user u with respect to the population of naïve users (that is, those users with no trust values or identical trust values).

Let P be a random ℓ-hop connection through the onion routing network, with P_i the ith router. Let S be the source (user) and Δ the destination. Let p be a connection made by user u. Let $A_R \subseteq R \cup D$ be the routers and destinations compromised by the adversary. Let the path positions observed by the adversary be $O = \{i : p_i \in A_R \vee p_{i-1} \in A_R \vee p_{i+1} \in A_R \vee (i = \ell \wedge \Delta \in A_R)\}$. Let q_1 be the probability of u making a connection consistent with the routers in p observed and not observed by A_R:

$$q_1 = \left(\frac{1}{n+1}\right) \prod_{i \in O} Pr[P_i = p_i | S = u] \cdot \prod_{i \notin O} \sum_{r \in R \setminus A_R} Pr[P_i = r | S = u].$$

Let q_2 be the probability that a naïve user other than u makes a connection consistent with A_R and p:

$$q_2 = \begin{cases} 0 & \text{if } p_1 \in A_R \\ \left(\frac{n}{n+1}\right) m^{-\ell} |R \setminus A_R|^{|\{i \notin O\}|} & \text{otherwise} \end{cases}$$

These expressions follow from the facts that each user is equally likely to be the source of a given connection and that naïve users choose routers uniformly at random.

Finally, let Y be the conditional probability that the source of a connection is u:

$$Y(A_R, p) = \frac{q_1}{q_1 + q_2}.$$

Y depends on the routers and destinations observed by the adversary and the probability distribution with which u selects a path. The routers in A depend on the trust values of the routers, and the destinations it observes are fixed. Y therefore is probabilistic with a distribution that depends on the path distribution of u and the trust values. The trust values are given, but we can choose the path distribution of u to optimize the distribution of Y.

There are several plausible criteria on the distribution of Y to use when optimizing the path distribution: the expectation $E[Y]$, a weighted expectation $E[f(Y)]$ for some weight function f, the probability $Pr[Y \geq \alpha]$ for some $\alpha \in (0, 1]$, and so on. Such criteria might lead to different optimal path distributions, because distributions of Y are not necessarily comparable (one may not stochastically dominate the other). We choose the expected value of Y as our criterion.

4.1.3 A Downhill Algorithm

Given the above framework, how can the users utilize trust to better protect their connections? As noted, more trust means lower chance of compromise, hence lower chance of observing the user, adjacent routers in the path, or the destination. On the other hand, a more trusted router is more likely to be associated with the user by someone who knows what adversary the user is trying to avoid. This suggests a routing algorithm in which the user chooses routers from sets with a decreasing minimum trust threshold (or, equivalently, increasing maximum risk of compromise). As these sets increase in size, they are more likely to contain a compromised router, but what that compromised router will see is also less identifying to the user.

Let ℓ be the length of the path. Let the acceptable level of risk in the ith hop be $\rho : [\ell] \rightarrow [0, 1]$ such that $\rho(i) < \rho(i + 1)$. The set of routers at the ith level is the "trust set" $T_i = \{r \in R : c(r) \leq \rho(i)\}$. The user chooses the ith hop independently and uniformly at random from T_i.

We can assume that the final trust set T_ℓ includes all of the routers R. The destination links are observed in this case, so we can't give the adversary any more observations by including all of R in a final trust set. And doing so may prevent the adversary from observing a trust set that is smaller than R and thus more associated with the user.

We want to set the parameters ℓ and $\rho(i)$ to minimize the expected posterior probability $E[Y]$. The straightforward algorithm for minimizing the expected value simply iterates over all possible path lengths and ways to set the trust thresholds at each path length. Let $\lambda \leq m$ be the maximum allowed path length. In practice, we only want to consider path lengths up to the point at which the latency becomes too high. The Tor network, for example, uses path lengths of 3. Let ν be the number of distinct trust values among the routers. The number of iterations is then $O(\lambda\nu^\lambda)$.

For each iteration, expected value is determined by calculating the posterior probability the adversary assigns to u for each possible set of compromised routers and each path:

$$E[Y] = \sum_{A_R \subseteq R} \prod_{a \in A_R} c(a) \prod_{a \notin A_R} (1 - c(a))$$
$$\sum_{p \in R^\ell} \prod_{i=1}^{\ell} Pr[P_i = p_i | S = u] Y(A_R + d, p).$$

Calculating the expectation from this expression involves summing over all 2^m possible adversary subsets, which takes far too long for any reasonably-sized anonymity network. However, in practice we do not expect the user to be able to make more than a handful of meaningful distinctions between routers on the basis of trust. If the number ν of distinct trust values is small, we can speed up the computation of the expectation by using the fact that our path distribution chooses all routers with the same trust value with equal probability.

4.1.4 Analyzing The Downhill Algorithm

We have calculated the optimal thresholds and the resulting expected posteriors for several plausible situations using a user population of $n = 1000$. The results appear in Table 1. They are given next to the anonymity of two other path algorithms for comparison: *i*) the user chooses each hop uniformly at random from the most-trusted nodes only and *ii*) the user chooses each hop uniformly at random from all routers. We also compare the results to a lower bound on $E[Y]$ of $c_{\min} = \min_r c(r)$. (The first node is compromised with probability at least $c_{\min}$, and $Y = 1$ in this case.) The situations we consider involve three different trust values, so we consider path lengths up to three. In Tables 1(b) and 1(c), the optimal thresholds skip one possible trust value and only use a two-hop path.

Table 1: Examples of optimal thresholds

(a) Small trusted and untrusted sets, for example when the user has information about a few good routers and a few bad routers, and has little information for the rest.

# Routers	5	1000	10
Prob. of compromise	0.01	0.1	0.9
Optimal thresholds	0.01	0.1	0.9

	Downhill	Trusted	Random	Lower bnd.
E[Y]	0.0274	0.2519	0.1088	0.01

(b) Small trusted, medium semi-trusted, large untrusted sets, for example when the adversary is strong, but the user and her friends run some routers.

# Routers	5	50	1000
Prob. of compromise	.001	0.05	0.5
Optimal thresholds	0.05	0.5	

	Downhill	Trusted	Random	Lower bnd.
E[Y]	0.0550	0.1751	0.4763	0.001

(c) Equally large trusted, semi-trusted, and untrusted sets, for example when the user assigns trust based on geographic regions.

# Routers	350	350	350
Prob. of compromise	0.1	0.5	0.9
Optimal thresholds	0.1	0.9	

	Downhill	Trusted	Random	Lower bnd.
E[Y]	0.1021	0.1027	0.5000	0.1

The table shows that using trust levels improves anonymity in each case against random route selection by factors of at least 4.0 and as much as 8.6. Similarly, we see improvements in each against the trusted-router strategy, from just a slight increase in the third situation when there are relatively many trusted routers to over a factor 3.1 improvement in the second situation when there are many untrusted routers. We can also see that in the first and third situations we achieve anonymity on the order of the best possible. Interestingly, we notice that in the first situation, using highly-trusted routers exclusively is worse than randomly choosing routers, but only because there are few highly-trusted routers. Using the downhill algorithm avoids that problem.

Figure 1 examines the effect of varying some of the trust values in the situation of Table 1(a). It shows the effect of

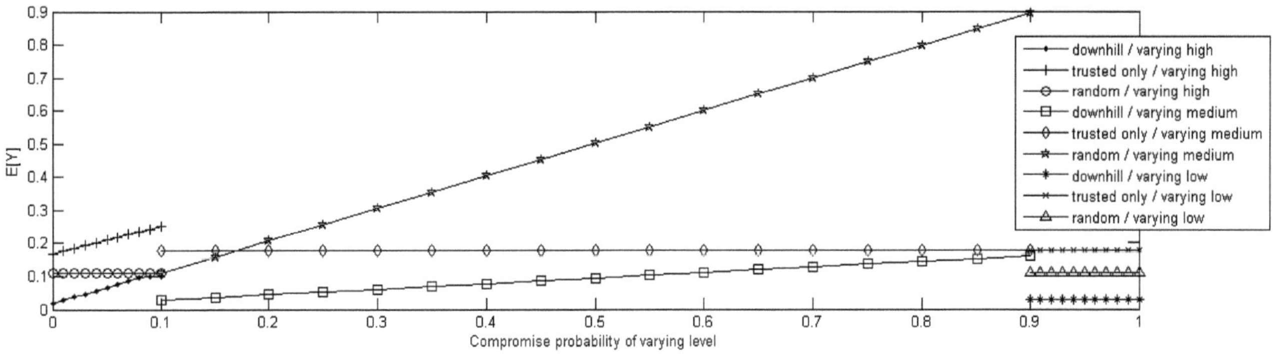

Figure 1: Anonymity when varying trust values of Table 1(a).

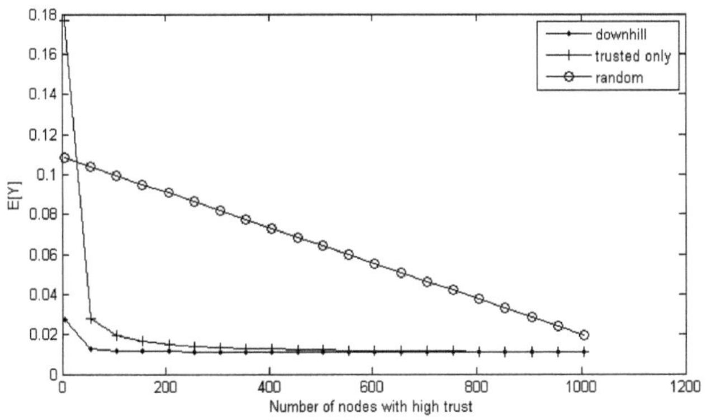

Figure 2: Anonymity when increasing number of high-trust nodes and decreasing number of medium-trust nodes in Table 1(a).

varying just high trust values, keeping the others at their original value, and the effects of the same process with the medium and low trust values. We can see that the change in the anonymity $E[Y]$ is roughly linear in the change in the trust values, and that the rate of the change increases as the trust change affects hops closer to the source. Furthermore, we see that choosing only trusted routers performs badly when the largest trust value isn't high, random selection performs badly when the average trust value isn't high, and the downhill-path algorithm always performs better than both and often much better.

Figure 2 examines the effect of trading off the number of high-trust and medium-trust nodes in the situation of Table 1(a). That is, it shows the variation in anonymity for that situation when there are x high-trust nodes and $1005 - x$ medium-trust nodes. The graph shows that using the downhill-trust or trusted-only algorithms quickly benefit from having larger numbers of high-trust nodes. This is because a selection of these is likely to be observed but not compromised. In contrast, random selection benefits roughly linearly in the number of routers shifted from medium to high trust.

Though these examples show very positive results for plausible scenarios, they are merely illustrative examples. There is no guarantee that they are representative of improvements when using trust values in deployed systems in actual use. But there is a more immediate concern. In the above calculations, we have assumed that the trust value assigned to a router by the user reflects the correct a priori probability of compromise of that router by the relevant adversary. What if the user was not correct in her assignment of trust?

4.1.5 *Correctness and Accuracy of Trust Assignments*

To assign trust values, the user must rely on some outside knowledge. This external information might include knowledge of the organizations or individuals who run routers—including both knowledge of their technical competence and the likelihood that those running a given router would intend to attack the user. Trust values might also be affected by computing platforms on which a router is running, geopolitical information about the router, knowledge about the hosting facility where a router might be housed or the service provider(s) for its access to the underlying communications network, and many other factors.

The process of assigning trust values is clearly uncertain, and we cannot expect the user to correctly assign values to all routers. Therefore, we consider the effect of errors in the believed trust values on the user's anonymity. First, we derive a bound on the effect that error in the trust value for a single router has on our anonymity metric, $E[Y]$. Second, we calculate the effect of a couple of types of errors in a specific scenario.

Let $r \in R$ be some router with an error of ϵ in its assumed trust value. Let $E_\epsilon[Y]$ be the expected posterior probability when the probability that r is compromised is $c(r) + \epsilon$. Let $S_i = T_i \setminus T_{i+1}$. Let k_1 be the first path position non-adjacent to the user for which r can be chosen, that is, for $r \in S_1$, let $k_1 = 2$, otherwise let k_1 be such that $r \in S_{k_1}$. Let k_2 be such that $r \in S_{k_2}$. Let μ_i be expected number of uncompromised routers in S_i given that r is uncompromised. Let $\mu_{\min} = \min_{1 \le i \le \ell} \mu_i$. Let P be a random path chosen by u according to the downhill algorithm. Let the probability that r is chosen i times in P be

$$\pi_r(i) = Pr[|\{j : P_j = r\}| = i] \tag{1}$$

$$\le \binom{\ell}{i} \prod_{j=k_1}^{k_1+i-1} 1/|T_j| \prod_{j=k_1+i}^{\ell} (1 - 1/|T_j|). \tag{2}$$

Let the ratio of the probability of u choosing a given router $s \in T_i$ at the ith step to the probability of a given naïve user doing the same be $\alpha_i = m/|T_i|$.

To express our bound succinctly, further let

$$a_i = \prod_{j=k_1-1}^{\min(k_1+3i-2,\ell)} \alpha_j,$$

$$b = \min(2\ell e^{-\mu_{\min}^{1/2}/4}, 1), \text{ and}$$

$$c_i = (1 + O(1/\mu_{\min}))^{\ell-i+1}(1 + O(\mu_{\min}^{-1/4}))^{\min(3i,\ell)}.$$

a_i bounds the relative increase in posterior probability gained from observing additional path positions. We use the Chernoff bound to obtain the bound b on the probability that, for all j, the number of uncompromised routers in S_j is within a factor $1 \pm \mu_{min}^{-1/4}$ of μ_j. c_i represents a bound on the relative posterior increase obtained from losing some unobserved positions and increasing the contribution of the retained unobserved positions. c_i is given explicitly in the proof, and its hidden constants are not large.

Then we can bound the effect of the error in r's trust value as follows:

THEOREM 1. *If $\mu_{\min} \geq 1$, then*

$$E_\epsilon[Y] - E[Y] \leq \epsilon\Bigg(Pr[P_1 = r] + (1 - Pr[P_1 = r])\cdot \left(b + (1-b)\sum_{i=0}^{\ell} \pi_r(i)(1 - 1/(c_i a_i))\right)\Bigg).$$

We omit the proof of the theorem for space.

We can see from Theorem 1 that the effect of the trust error is bounded by ϵ. Next, suppose that the expected number of uncompromised routers μ_i in each S_i is large. Suppose also that $r \notin T_1$. Then, the bound provided by the theorem approaches

$$\epsilon\left(\sum_{i=0}^{\ell} \pi_r(i)(1 - 1/a_i)\right).$$

This expression shows that the change in anonymity is determined by how often r is likely to be chosen in the path and how incriminating the observed positions are. Indeed, this expression goes to zero as the probability of choosing r in P goes to zero or as the values α_j of the observations go to one. These events happen when, for example, the smallest trust set containing r (i.e. T_{k_2}) grows, by Inequality 2 and the definition of the α_j.

We examine the concrete effect of trust errors by extending the scenario given in Table 1(a) to include errors. Figure 3 shows the anonymity when the user is incorrect about the trust level of a fraction of the nodes. Specifically, for a fraction x, x of the believed high-trust nodes have medium trust, $x/2$ of the believed medium-trust nodes have high trust, $x/2$ of the believed medium nodes have low trust, and x of the low-trust nodes have medium trust. The figure shows that using trust may actually be worse than choosing randomly if there are significant errors in the user's trust beliefs. In particular, as Theorem 1 describes, performance is particularly sensitive to errors in the most-trusted routers. Thus, even if the average trust values are lower than believed, as in Figure 3, the actual anonymity may be lower than believed if using trust.

Figure 4 also shows the effect of trust errors in the scenario of Table 1(a). The error it shows is an incorrect belief in the middle trust value. The anonymity is compared to that of the downhill algorithm using the correct trust values. We see that they are identical until the middle trust value reaches about .5. This is because the three-hop path is optimal in both cases until then, at which point it becomes optimal to use two hops. This illustrates that trust errors that leave the ordering of nodes by trust roughly the same may not change the optimality of the selected sequence of trust sets.

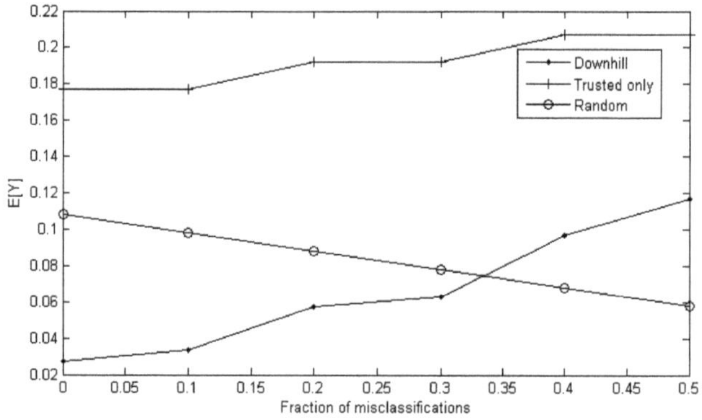

Figure 3: Anonymity when a fraction of nodes of Table 1(a) have incorrect trust values.

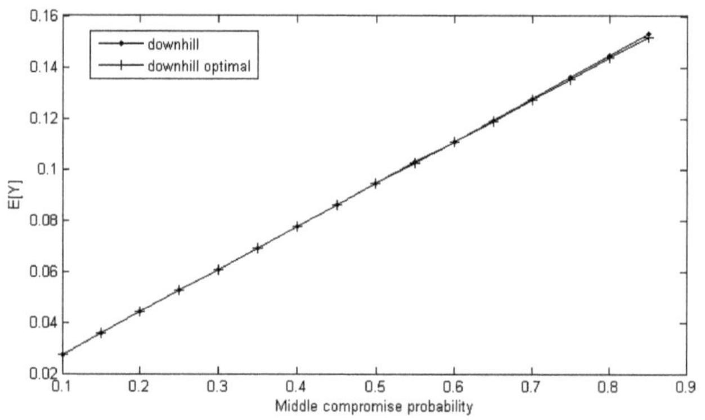

Figure 4: Anonymity from varying trust values of Table 1(a).

4.2 Path selection for multiple connections

The path-selection algorithm described is designed to protect the anonymity of one connection. However, users make multiple connections over time, and we want to maximize the probability that all of them have good anonymity.

If we were to simply use the given algorithm to choose a different path for every connection, users would be increasingly likely to have poor anonymity on at least one of their connections: each new connection would be another chance to select a compromised router. We want to maximize the probability that no connection has poor anonymity. This requirement would suggest that each user should maintain the same path across different connections—similar to the use of guard nodes in Tor suggested by Øverlier and Syverson [39].

However, doing so would make it easier for the adversary to link together different connections as coming from the same user. Suppose, for example, that the adversary observes the destination links and that users make repeated connections to the destination. The adversary would see multiple connections coming from the same router and can infer that they're more likely to come from the same user.

4.2.1 Path selection against different adversaries

If the adversary observes the source links, then he can already link connections together as belonging to the observed user. Therefore, in this case, we extend the path-selection algorithm from one connection to multiple connections by using the same path for all connections.

The difficult case is again when source links are unobserved, but the adversary observes the links of some of the destinations. For connections that are to unobserved destinations, the user should simply bypass the network entirely. For connections that are to observed destinations, we adapt the one-connection algorithm by using both static and dynamic components. First, as given in that algorithm, the user uses a decreasing sequence of trust thresholds to choose a path of length ℓ. At each hop, a router is chosen uniformly at random from all routers with trust value above the threshold at that hop. This path is *static*—it is chosen once at the start, and then the user uses it for all connections. Second, two routers are chosen uniformly at random from R and used as the $(\ell+1)^{st}$ and $(\ell+2)^{nd}$ hops. These hops are *dynamic*—a new random selection of these two hops is made for each new connection.

Combining static and dynamic hops in this way helps maintain anonymity over multiple connections while preventing them from being easily linked. The static portion of the path protects the source identity over all connections by preventing the source and her most-trusted routers from being observed even once. The last hop is dynamic so that the adversary observing destination links cannot use a static router to link together repeated connections from the same user. The $(\ell+1)^{st}$ hop is dynamic because the last hop is likely to be compromised on a fraction of connections equal to the fraction of routers that are compromised by the adversary. If this hop were static, the adversary could use it to link together destinations it observes from the last hop.

Of course, the $(\ell+1)^{st}$ router is also likely to be compromised on a fraction of the connections. When those connections are to destinations for which the links are observed, then they can be linked because of the static ℓ^{th} hop. However, multiple connections might not be only to such destinations. Due to uncertainty about the destination links or just for simplicity, users could use the downhill-trust algorithm to destinations with unobserved links. By using two dynamic routers as the final hops, linking unobserved destinations requires that both dynamic routers be compromised. Note that adding additional dynamic routers at the end provides no benefit, as the adversary can perform a correlation attack using only the first and last dynamic routers in order for the destinations to be observed and linked.

4.2.2 Analyzing path selection

In order to rigorously analyze the effectiveness of using static and dynamic routers together, we consider the problem of linking more precisely. The use of static components in the path means that if the adversary observes two different connections using the same static hops, they are more likely to belong to the same user.

Therefore, instead of looking only at his knowledge of a given connection, we must examine the adversary's overall view of which connections occurred. A user's private information consists of the sequence of connections that user makes over a given time period, where each connection consists of a user, a destination, and a start time. We examine user privacy over multiple connections by looking at the adversary's posterior distribution on the number of connections at the user's connection-start times and the sources and destinations of those connections. We use the entropy [14, 44] of this distribution as our metric of uncertainty. We will consider how this entropy is affected by adding dynamic routers at the end of the paths of some users.

Let $A_R \subseteq R$ be the routers compromised by the adversary. Let T be the set of start times of the connections for which u is the source. Let C^T be a random binary vector indicating the presence of a connection starting at the times in T. Let S^T be a random sequence of users indicating the sources for connections starting at times in T. Let D^T be a random sequence of destinations indicating the destinations for connections starting at times in T. Finally, let O_s indicate the adversary's observations when users only create and use the static part of the path, let O_{d_1} indicate the observations made by the adversary when users add one dynamic hop, and let O_{d_2} indicate the adversary's observations when users add a second dynamic hop after the first.

We are interested in how the entropy of the posterior distribution over connections given an adversary's observations changes when using dynamic hops. That is, we consider how $H(C^T, S^T, D^T|O_S)$, $H(C^T, S^T, D^T|O_{d_1})$, and $H(C^T, S^T, D^T|O_{d_2})$ compare. Using the chain rule of entropy [8] and the independence of S^T and D^T, we can express the entropy of the posterior as

$$H(C^T, S^T, D^T|O) = H(C^T|O) + H(S^T|C^T, O) + H(D^T|C^T, O), \quad (3)$$

where O is O_{d_1}, O_{d_2}, or O_s.

We first show that, assuming a user only makes connections over the anonymity network to destinations with observed links, then adding one dynamic hop to the static path can only increase the entropy over her connections.

THEOREM 2.

$$H(C^T, S^T, D^T|O_{d_1}) \geq H(C^T, S^T, D^T|O_s).$$

PROOF. The entropy $H(C^T|O = o)$ of the existence of connections at times in T does not change due to dynamic hops because the connections are always observed at the destination links.

The entropy $H(S^T|C^T, O = o)$ of connection sources can only change when a final static hop of a connection goes from being observed to unobserved. The final static router can become unobserved if the final static router is uncompromised and the penultimate static router is uncompromised. Then it becomes unobserved when the dynamic hop is uncompromised. To understand how the entropy can change, suppose the final static hop goes from being unobserved to being observed by removing the dynamic hop. Consider any value s^T of S^T and some set of observations o. s^T and o together imply a set of path selections for users in s^T. The conditional probability $Pr[S^T = s^T|O = o]$ is proportional to the probability that each user made the implied path selections. Removing a dynamic router from the end of a given connection can change this probability in two ways. First, the probability can decrease by a factor $1/m$, as the observation of the final static router implies that the source of the connection in s^T chose it in her path, and we can assume that the final static hop is chosen randomly from R. Second, it can send it to zero, if the source s^T assigned to the given connection is also assigned to another connection that is observed with a different final static router. Thus, the entropy can only decrease when the final static hop goes from being unobserved to being observed. This implies that the entropy can only increase when the final static hop switches from being observed to being unobserved.

The entropy $H(D^T|C^T, O = o)$ of connection destinations does not change, because all destinations of the user are assumed to be observed by the adversary.

Because no term of Equation 3 can decrease, the overall connection entropy $H(C^T, S^T, D^T|O = o)$ cannot decrease either. □

Next, we show that, again assuming a user only makes anonymous connections to observed destinations, using two dynamic hops has the same entropy as using one dynamic hop.

THEOREM 3.

$$H(C^T, S^T, D^T|O_{d_2}) = H(C^T, S^T, D^T|O_{d_1}).$$

PROOF. The proof of Theorem 2 shows that the first dynamic hop cannot change the entropy $H(C^T|O)$ of the connections or the entropy $H(D^T|C^T, O)$ of the destinations. Adding a second hop cannot change these for the same reason. In addition, the second hop cannot change the entropy $H(S^T|C^T, O)$ of the sources because it is only adjacent to the first dynamic hop, which is chosen at random by all users. Therefore, by Equation 3, adding a second hop cannot change the entropy $H(C^T, S^T, D^T|O_{d_1})$. □

Theorems 2 and 3 only show that adding dynamic hops doesn't decrease the connection entropy. This is not a particularly strong justification of their use. However, in general, this is the strongest claim we can make. Adding dynamic hops can increase the entropy by little or none if *i*) the adversary controls most of the network and thus most of the dynamic routers, *ii*) the adversary has compromised the user's initial, ultimate or penultimate static hops, or *iii*) each user has a unique pattern of observed hops not including the last hop.

5. CONCLUSION AND FUTURE WORK

The existing anonymous communication definitions and system models typically assume that all nodes in the network are the same, and that any part of the system is as likely to threaten security as any other. In this paper we have set out the first network and adversary model for anonymous communication that accounts for the diversity of trust that different users may have in elements of the network. The presented model is a specification for onion routing of a more general model we have developed to reason about various approaches to routing security [47]. We identified two important classes of privacy attacks in this model and presented an example of a routing algorithm motivated by resistance to them. Analysis of this algorithm in our model shows that it significantly improves the anonymity of onion routing, especially when an adversary can compromise a large fraction of the network.

An adversary that learns the trust placed in specific routers may learn something about the resources a user (or her organization) has applied to protect her communications. And, trust information must first be learned to be used in deanonymization as analyzed in Section 4.1. Given available space, we leave any discussion of how an adversary might learn trust values to future work. Similarly we do not discuss an adversary-learning adversary for either the usage scenario and algorithm we have described or for other cases. (For example, if Alice is a so-called "road warrior" travelling on behalf of her employer, and she wishes to log in from her hotel to her workstation back at her office, starting her circuits at highly trusted nodes would reveal something about who she is trying to hide from. Such a setting requires a complementary uphill-trust algorithm, although the complement is not simply a reverse of the downhill algorithm. There are other subtleties, such as the different need for dynamic hops.)

As in onion-routing networks, trust can play a role in mix networks too by helping to avoid compromised routers. But the adversary and communication assumptions are somewhat different, leading to different strategies. Our general model encompasses both of these types of anonymous communication as well as others; however, in this paper we limit discussion to onion-routing networks. We would like to investigate the impact of trust on other protocols to provide secure routes. The following are some of the other issues we intend to explore in future work: What impact might more user classes trying to avoid distinct nonuniform adversaries have on each other? How robust are our results when a fraction of users defect from the strategy that is optimal for a given non-naïve user, and what incentive mechanisms can induce them to cooperate? Note that users with flat trust distributions will choose ℓ=1 plus two dynamic hops—which is exactly the path-selection algorithm that Tor uses today [39]. The adversaries could employ other methods of attack, such as congestion attacks [23, 36], DoS attacks [4], changing the network topology, and manipulating the trust values. In addition to routers, we would like to investigate the effect of different trust values among links, to account for real-world Internet routing issues [21, 24]. We would like to investigate a *roving* adversary that tries to compromise different sets over time [38, 48]. The joint distribution of the events that adversaries compromise nodes could be arbitrary, instead of assuming independence of compromise between nodes. We could give the attacker a budget and assign costs to attempting compromise on a node. Users might have multiple adversaries. Every user could set a cost for every adversary of losing privacy to that adversary. Thus we could model the case where Alice doesn't want to be exposed by either Eve or Mallory, but would prefer one to the other.

Though just a simple example, we have shown that our new routing algorithm has significant security impact in plausible usage scenarios. Our model incorporates trust-based routing, a novel aspect of both anonymous communication in particular and secure communication in general. We hope that other researchers will see the potential of our approach and take up the above questions or be inspired to explore our model through questions of their own.

6. ACKNOWLEDGMENTS

The authors would like to thank Nick Hopper for much guidance in improving this paper. We would also like to thank George Danezis, Karsten Loesing, and the anonymous reviewers for helpful comments on drafts of this paper. This work supported by ONR, NSF, and DARPA.

7. REFERENCES

[1] K. Bauer, D. McCoy, D. Grunwald, T. Kohno, and D. Sicker. Low-resource routing attacks against Tor. In *Proceedings of the Workshop on Privacy in the Electronic Society (WPES 2007)*, Washington, DC, USA, October 2007.

[2] R. Beauxis and C. Palamidessi. Probabilistic and nondeterministic aspects of anonymity. *Theoretical Computer Science*, 410(41):4006–4025, 2009.

[3] A. Beimel and S. Dolev. Buses for anonymous message delivery. *Journal of Cryptology*, 16(1):25–39, 2003.

[4] N. Borisov, G. Danezis, P. Mittal, and P. Tabriz. Denial of service or denial of security? How attacks on reliability can compromise anonymity. In *Proceedings of the 14th ACM Conference on Computer and Communications Security (CCS)*, October 2007.

[5] J. Camenisch and A. Lysyanskaya. A formal treatment of onion routing. In V. Shoup, editor, *Advances in Cryptology – CRYPTO 2005: 25th Annual International Cryptology Conference*, pages 169–187. Springer-Verlag, LNCS 3621, August 2005.

[6] D. Chaum. Untraceable electronic mail, return addresses, and digital pseudonyms. *Communications of the ACM*, 4(2), 1981.

[7] D. Chaum. The dining cryptographers problem: Unconditional sender and recipient untraceability. *Journal of Cryptology: The Journal of the International Association for Cryptologic Research*, 1(1):65–75, 1988.

[8] T. M. Cover and J. A. Thomas. *Elements of information theory*. Wiley-Interscience, New York, NY, USA, 1991.

[9] G. Danezis. Mix-networks with restricted routes. In R. Dingledine, editor, *Privacy Enhancing Technologies: Third International Workshop, PET 2003*, pages 1–17. Springer-Verlag, LNCS 2760, 2003.

[10] G. Danezis and R. Clayton. Route fingerprinting in anonymous communications. In *Sixth IEEE International Conference on Peer-to-Peer Computing, P2P 2006*, pages 69–72. IEEE Computer Society Press, 2006.

[11] G. Danezis, C. Diaz, and P. Syverson. Anonymous communication. In B. Rosenberg, editor, *Handbook of Financial Cryptography*. CRC Press, 2010.

[12] G. Danezis, R. Dingledine, and N. Mathewson. Mixminion: Design of a Type III Anonymous Remailer Protocol. In *Proceedings of the 2003 IEEE Symposium on Security and Privacy*, pages 2–15, 2003.

[13] G. Danezis and A. Serjantov. Statistical disclosure or intersection attacks on anonymity systems. In *Proceedings of 6th Information Hiding Workshop (IH 2004)*, pages 293–308, 2004.

[14] C. Díaz, S. Seys, J. Claessens, and B. Preneel. Towards measuring anonymity. In R. Dingledine and P. Syverson, editors, *Privacy Enhancing Technologies, Second International Workshop, PET 2002, Revised Papers*, pages 54–68. Springer-Verlag, LNCS 2482, 2003.

[15] R. Dingledine, M. J. Freedman, D. Hopwood, and D. Molnar. A reputation system to increase MIX-net reliability. In I. S. Moskowitz, editor, *Information Hiding: 4th International Workshop, IH 2001*, pages 126–141, Pittsburgh, PA, USA, April 2001. Springer-Verlag, LNCS 2137.

[16] R. Dingledine and N. Mathewson. Anonymity loves company: Usability and the network effect. In R. Anderson, editor, *Fifth Workshop on the Economics of Information Security (WEIS 2006)*, June 2006.

[17] R. Dingledine, N. Mathewson, and P. Syverson. Tor: The second-generation onion router. In *Proceedings of the 13th USENIX Security Symposium*, pages 303–319. USENIX Association, August 2004.

[18] R. Dingledine, N. Mathewson, and P. Syverson. Deploying low-latency anonymity: Design challenges and social factors. *IEEE Security & Privacy*, 5(5):83–87, September/October 2007.

[19] R. Dingledine and P. Syverson. Reliable MIX cascade networks through reputation. In M. Blaze, editor, *Financial Cryptography, 6th International Conference, FC 2002*, pages 253–268. Springer-Verlag, LNCS 2357, 2003.

[20] S. Dolev and R. Ostrovsky. Xor-trees for efficient anonymous multicast and reception. *ACM Transactions on Information and System Security*, 3(2):63–84, 2000.

[21] M. Edman and P. Syverson. AS-awareness in Tor path selection. In S. Jha, A. D. Keromytis, and H. Chen, editors, *CCS'09: Proceedings of the 16th ACM Conference on Computer and Communications Security*, pages 380–389. ACM Press, 2009.

[22] M. Edman and B. Yener. On anonymity in an electronic society: A survey of anonymous communication systems. *ACM Computing Surveys*, 42(1), 2010.

[23] N. S. Evans, R. Dingledine, and C. Grothoff. A practical congestion attack on Tor using long paths. In *Proceedings of the 18th USENIX Security Symposium*, pages 33–50, Montreal, Canada, August 2009. USENIX Association.

[24] N. Feamster and R. Dingledine. Location diversity in anonymity networks. In *Proceedings of the Workshop on Privacy in the Electronic Society (WPES 2004)*, pages 66–76, 2004.

[25] S. Goel, M. Robson, M. Polte, and E. G. Sirer. Herbivore: A scalable and efficient protocol for anonymous communication. Technical Report 2003-1890, Cornell University, Ithaca, NY, February 2003.

[26] D. M. Goldschlag, M. G. Reed, and P. F. Syverson. Hiding routing information. In *Information Hiding: First International Workshop, Proceedings*, pages 137–150. Springer-Verlag, LNCS 1174, 1996.

[27] P. Golle and A. Juels. Dining cryptographers revisited. In *Advances in Cryptology – EUROCRYPT 2004*, pages 456–473, Interlaken, Switzerland, May 2004. Springer-Verlag, LNCS 3027.

[28] C. Gülcü and G. Tsudik. Mixing E-mail with Babel. In *Proceedings of the Network and Distributed Security Symposium (NDSS 1996)*, pages 2–16, 1996.

[29] A. Hintz. Fingerprinting websites using traffic analysis. In R. Dingledine and P. Syverson, editors, *Privacy Enhancing Technologies: Second International Workshop, PET 2002*, pages 171–178, San Francisco, CA, USA, April 2002. Springer-Verlag, LNCS 2482.

[30] N. Hopper, E. Y. Vasserman, and E. Chan-Tin. How much anonymity does network latency leak? *ACM Transactions on Information and System Security*, 13(2):13–28, 2010. February.

[31] A. Johnson and P. Syverson. More anonymous onion routing through trust. In *22nd IEEE Computer Security Foundations Symposium, CSF 2009*, pages 3–12, Port Jefferson, New York, July 2009. IEEE Computer Society.

[32] D. Kesdogan, D. Agrawal, and S. Penz. Limits of anonymity in open environments. In *Proceedings of Information Hiding Workshop (IH 2002)*, 2002.

[33] M. Liberatore and B. N. Levine. Inferring the source of encrypted HTTP connections. In R. N. Wright, S. De Capitani di Vimercati, and V. Shmatikov, editors, *CCS'06: Proceedings of the 13th ACM Conference on Computer and Communications Security*, pages 255–263. ACM Press, 2006.

[34] N. Mathewson and R. Dingledine. Practical traffic analysis: Extending and resisting statistical disclosure. In D. Martin and A. Serjantov, editors, *Privacy Enhancing Technologies, 4th International Workshop, PET 2004, Revised Selected Papers*, pages 17–34. Springer Verlag, LNCS 3424, 2005.

[35] U. Möller, L. Cottrell, P. Palfrader, and L. Sassaman. Mixmaster Protocol — Version 2. Draft, 2003.

[36] S. J. Murdoch and G. Danezis. Low-cost traffic analysis of Tor. In *Proceedings of the 2005 IEEE Symposium on Security and Privacy*, pages 183–195, 2005.

[37] S. J. Murdoch and P. Zieliński. Sampled traffic analysis by internet-exchange-level adversaries. In N. Borisov and P. Golle, editors, *Proceedings of the Seventh Workshop on Privacy Enhancing Technologies (PET 2007)*, Ottawa, Canada, June 2007. Springer.

[38] R. Ostrovsky and M. Yung. How to withstand mobile virus attacks. In *Proceedings of the Tenth ACM Symposium on Principles of Distributed Computing (PODC '91)*, pages 51–59. ACM Press, 1991.

[39] L. Øverlier and P. Syverson. Locating hidden servers. In *Proceedings of the 2006 IEEE Symposium on Security and Privacy*. IEEE CS, May 2006.

[40] C. Rackoff and D. R. Simon. Cryptographic defense against traffic analysis. In *Proceedings of ACM Symposium on Theory of Computing*, pages 672–681, 1993.

[41] M. Reiter and A. Rubin. Crowds: Anonymity for web transactions. *ACM Transactions on Information and System Security*, 1(1):66–92, 1998.

[42] V. Sassone, S. Hamadou, and M. Yang. Trust in anonymity networks. In P. Gastin and F. Laroussinie, editors, *CONCUR 2010 - Concurrency Theory: 21st International Conference*, pages 48–70. Springer-Verlag, LNCS 6269, 2010.

[43] B. Schneier. Secret German IP addresses leaked. Schneier on Security, `http://www.schneier.com/`, November 2008.

[44] A. Serjantov and G. Danezis. Towards an information theoretic metric for anonymity. In R. Dingledine and P. Syverson, editors, *Privacy Enhancing Technologies, Second International Workshop, PET 2002, Revised Papers*, pages 41–53. Springer-Verlag, LNCS 2482, 2003.

[45] P. Syverson. Why I'm not an entropist. In *Seventeenth International Workshop on Security Protocols*. Springer-Verlag, LNCS, 2009. Forthcoming.

[46] P. Syverson. Sleeping dogs lie in a bed of onions but wake when mixed. In *4th Hot Topics in Privacy Enhancing Technologies (HotPETs 2011)*, July 2011.

[47] P. Syverson, A. Johnson, R. Dingledine, and N. Mathewson. Trust-based anonymous communication: Adversary models and routing algorithms. Technical report, University of Texas at Austin, 2011.

[48] P. Syverson, G. Tsudik, M. Reed, and C. Landwehr. Towards an analysis of onion routing security. In H. Federrath, editor, *Designing Privacy Enhancing Technologies: International Workshop on Design Issues in Anonymity and Unobservability, Proceedings*, pages 96–114. Springer-Verlag, LNCS 2009, July 2001.

[49] The Tor project home page. `https://www.torproject.org/` .

[50] Tor metrics portal. https://metrics.torproject.org/, April 2011.

[51] Y. Zhu, X. Fu, B. Graham, R. Bettati, and W. Zhao. On flow correlation attacks and countermeasures in mix networks. In *Proceedings of Privacy Enhancing Technologies workshop (PET 2004)*, pages 207–225, 2004.

Cirripede: Circumvention Infrastructure using Router Redirection with Plausible Deniability

Amir Houmansadr† Giang T. K. Nguyen‡ Matthew Caesar‡ Nikita Borisov†
†Department of Electrical and Computer Engineering
‡Department of Computer Science
University of Illinois at Urbana-Champaign
{ahouman2,nguyen59,caesar,nikita}@illinois.edu

ABSTRACT

Many users face surveillance of their Internet communications and a significant fraction suffer from outright blocking of certain destinations. Anonymous communication systems allow users to conceal the destinations they communicate with, but do not hide the fact that the users are using them. The mere use of such systems may invite suspicion, or access to them may be blocked.

We therefore propose Cirripede, a system that can be used for *unobservable* communication with Internet destinations. Cirripede is designed to be deployed by ISPs; it intercepts connections from clients to innocent-looking destinations and redirects them to the true destination requested by the client. The communication is encoded in a way that is indistinguishable from normal communications to anyone without the master secret key, while public-key cryptography is used to eliminate the need for any secret information that must be shared with Cirripede users.

Cirripede is designed to work scalably with routers that handle large volumes of traffic while imposing minimal overhead on ISPs and not disrupting existing traffic. This allows Cirripede proxies to be strategically deployed at central locations, making access to Cirripede very difficult to block. We built a proof-of-concept implementation of Cirripede and performed a testbed evaluation of its performance properties.

Categories and Subject Descriptors

C.2.0 [**Computer-Communication Networks**]: General—*Security and protection*; E.3 [**Data**]: Data Encryption; K.4.1 [**Computers and Society**]: Privacy

General Terms

Algorithms, Design, Security

Keywords

Censorship-resistance, unobservability

1. INTRODUCTION

The Internet has become a serious threat to repressive regimes as it plays an increasingly powerful role in the free circulation of speech, information, and ideas. To counter this, countries that restrict political freedom and corporations that aim to silence whistleblowers limits open access to the Internet [61], thereby disrupting the free flow of information and ideas as well as preventing citizens and employees from sharing their own information with the world. To do this, repressive regimes leverage IP-address blocking, DNS hijacking, and TCP content filtering to block access to certain destinations or to prevent certain forms of content from being transmitted [3, 33]. To ensure compliance and to detect undercover political/social activists, repressive regimes also monitor usage by leveraging Deep Packet Inspection (DPI) and other technologies [33]. Consequences of non-compliance can be severe, ranging from identification and termination of employment to life-threatening prosecutions under repressive governments. Manipulating access to the Internet seems increasingly important in silencing corporate misconduct and for repressive governments to retain their power. Recent events in Tunisia, Libya, and the rest of the Middle East give strong indications that oppressive regimes can even be overthrown by the power of people mobilized to fight by organizing, communicating, and raising awareness through use of the Internet.

To help Internet users retain openness of communication, a number of systems have been developed, including *anti-censorship* and *anonymous communication* systems [2, 9, 13, 17, 30]. These systems, composed of computer and networking technologies, enable evasion of monitoring, blocking, and tracing of the information over the Internet. HTTP proxies [1, 9, 13] are the early circumvention tools that perform simple proxying of the HTTP requests in order to evade the IP-blocking and DNS hijacking techniques used by the early censors. The use of advanced content filtering by the censors [3, 15] led to the advent of more sophisticated circumvention tools such as Ultrasurf [2] and Psiphon [30]. These systems evade blocking techniques by avoiding firewalls and content-filtering systems. To evade monitoring, anonymous communication systems, such as Tor [17], were developed. These systems aim to hide the destinations a user visits from outside observers. Different designs have been proposed for anonymous communication, including the onion routing mechanisms [53] and the mix networks [12], each having different points of strengths and weaknesses.

While these systems are of great benefit, they share one common shortcoming: *they do not hide the fact that the user is using these technologies.* For example, a repressive regime in control of its nation's networks may not be able to detect which remote sites a Tor user is visiting, but it will be able to detect that the user is using Tor. This presents several problems. It calls attention to certain users of these services, which may bring about further investigation or detainment. In addition, if use of these services can be detected, access to them can also be blocked. For example, relays that run the Tor service have been blacklisted by several countries [4].

To address these issues, we need technologies that provide *unobservable* communication that circumvent monitoring and censorship technologies. As a first step in that direction, we describe *Cirripede*, a platform for unobservable communication with Internet destinations. From the perspective of a monitoring entity, a user of Cirripede appears to be making regular network connections, while the user is actually getting connected to destinations that are forbidden by that monitoring entity. To do this, Cirripede requires in-network support, through configuration changes and deployment of overlay nodes outside of the repressive regime's network. We envision these in-network changes may be offered as a service by some participating ISPs, or mandated/supported by non-repressive governments (or NGOs) to encourage the freedom of speech abroad.

In order to use Cirripede for the communication, a user needs to be registered in the system. This is performed by using covert channels inside the TCP headers of *legitimate traffic*. We design a cryptographic protocol that ensures that a client's registration messages can only be recognized by the Cirripede registration servers, whereas anyone else cannot distinguish them from regular traffic. The protocol uses public-key technology to eliminate the need of a (long-term) shared key between the Cirripede service and its clients.

The list of the registered clients is provided to border routers of participating ISPs, which *deflect* traffic from the clients to a Cirripede proxy. The proxy tunnels communication between the client and its true destination by replacing the encrypted payload of an HTTPS connection seemingly destined to a benign site. This provides a high-bandwidth channel that can be used to access a wide range of Internet services, including blocked websites and anonymous communication systems such as Tor. By strategically placing deflecting routers in the Internet core, it is possible to make the Cirripede service available to a large user population—we show that using *only two* tier-1 ASes can deliver Cirripede service to *all* Internet hosts. In this case, censors cannot block access to Cirripede without blocking a significant fraction of all Internet sites. Cirripede can operate on the existing router infrastructure using off-the-shelf networking tools, with low-cost commodity servers providing the registration and proxy services.

The rest of this paper is organized as follows; in Section 2, we define the problem targeted in this paper and describe the system model and assumptions. We describe the Cirripede design in Section 3. In Section 4, we address some technical and security issues of Cirripede in practice. Section 5 describes our prototype implementation on commodity hardware and opensource software. Section 6 describes a laboratory evaluation of our prototype implementation as well as studies Cirripede's usability under different deployment scenarios. In Section 7 we discuss the related work. Finally, the paper is concluded in Section 8.

2. PROBLEM STATEMENT AND THREAT MODEL

We consider the following problem: a client is being monitored by its host ISP, which we will call the warden. (Note that we use the term ISP loosely here; in the case of China, for example, the warden is comprised of all of the Chinese ISPs and monitors all traffic leaving China.) The client aims to communicate *unobservably* with a *covert destination*, without this communication being detected by the warden either directly or indirectly (by, e.g., observing that the client is using some sort of anonymous communication system). We assume that the warden can inspect the entirety of the traffic between the client and the outside world. Additionally, the warden can *block* traffic with certain destinations (including the covert destination), based on simple IP filtering and/or deep packet inspection. We assume, however, that the warden is only willing to perform *selective* blocking and is unwilling to block Internet access entirely, use a small "white list" of allowed sites, or block all HTTPS (port 443) traffic. As evidenced by the shutdown of Internet access in Egypt in January of 2011, there are some wardens who might take the above actions; we feel, however, that in the majority of cases, the wardens will be reluctant to take such drastic steps. (Indeed, the Internet shutdown in Egypt lasted only a week.) On the other hand, we assume that the warden *is* willing to block certain web sites and services (even popular ones) if it learns that they are being used to circumvent blocking.

Finally, we assume that the client is not privy to any secret information that is unavailable to the warden. In particular, we assume that the warden is aware of all the details of the system design, while the client relies on public information only. This is in contrast to previous proxy-based designs that assume, at a minimum, that the warden cannot learn the addresses of all proxies, yet must make the same proxy addresses available to a large population of users. In our case, the client only needs to obtain a public key of the system, which we assume is also available to the warden; we also assume that the warden can identify where the relevant proxies are located but is unable to prevent access to them without blocking a significant fraction of all Internet sites.

We assume that the warden does not actively tamper with the traffic sent by the client; we leave unobservability with respect to more active wardens to future work.

3. Cirripede ARCHITECTURE

The architecture of Cirripede is shown in Figure 1. The main components are:

- Client (C): the Internet user who aims to establish an unobservable connection with a covert destination (CD).
- Warden ISP: the network provider hosting client C.
- Covert destination (CD): a website, access to which is blocked by the warden ISP.
- Overt destination (OD): a website, access to which is allowed by the warden ISP. C communicates with this destination overtly to provide a carrier channel for covert communication with CD.
- Participating ISP: an ISP who participates in Cirripede by deflecting network traffic to Cirripede servers. This ISP must be on the (forward) network path from C to OD.

- Cirripede registration server (RS): a server that is part of the Cirripede infrastructure, used for registering clients who want to use the Cirripede service.
- Cirripede service proxy (SP): another server, also part of the Cirripede infrastructure, that connects with CD and proxies communications with it over the overt communication stream between C and OD.
- Deflecting router (DR): an Internet router, owned by a participating ISP, that deflects traffic from a registered client C to the service proxy SP.

We next provide an overview of the operation of Cirripede.

1. *Client registration:* A client C who wishes to use the Cirripede service first must register with Cirripede. Since its traffic is observed by the warden, C uses a covert channel in TCP headers to signal its intent to register and to establish a secret key, shared with Cirripede, to be used in later communication. The deflecting router DR mirrors part of all TCP traffic it sees to the registration server RS, which detects the covert registration message and instructs DR to redirect HTTPS traffic from C to the service proxy SP.
2. *Cover connection*: After registration, C makes a TCP connection with the overt destination OD, which is deflected by DR to SP.
3. *Covert communication*: C performs a TLS handshake with OD, which SP interposes upon. After the handshake, SP disconnects from OD and takes over the TLS connection, which is used to tunnel communication between C and CD.

We detail these steps in the following sections.

3.1 Client registration

The first step in using Cirripede is registration. The client must send a covert message to the registration server while avoiding detection by the warden ISP. We chose to use a covert channel embedded in TCP initial sequence numbers (ISNs) [41]. Each endpoint of a TCP connection selects a new initial sequence number for each connection, to prevent potential confusion between different TCP sessions that use the same ports [44]. These sequence numbers, however, should also be difficult to predict [6]. Modern operating systems, therefore, include a random component in the ISN generation that can be used to carry a covert message. Murdoch and Lewis [41] describe a covert channel that can embed 24 bits of covert information inside an ISN while faithfully mimicking the ISN generation algorithms of either Linux or OpenBSD. We adopt this channel for the purposes of our registration protocol. One particular advantage of using ISNs is that they are observed in the very first packet of the TCP session (the "SYN" packet); thus, to look for registrations sent over this channel, the registration server needs only examine a small fraction of the total packets seen by the deflection router. (See Section 7 for more details.) Each registration is valid for a registration time interval T to minimize the effect of failures, as described later.

3.1.1 Registration Protocol

The client uses the TCP ISN covert channel to announce its intention to use Cirripede. A simple approach would be to embed a special tag inside the ISN that will be recognized by the registration server. This, however, only obscures the behavior of the client from a warden who is completely unaware of Cirripede; if Cirripede became widely used, the warden could start looking for the embedded tag directly. To provide stronger protection from detection, we use a cryptographic registration protocol based on Diffie-Hellman key exchange [52].

The registration server creates a secret key k_{RS} and a Diffie-Hellman public key $K_{RS} = g^{k_{RS}}$, using some group $G = \langle g \rangle$ where the computational Diffie-Hellman assumption (CDH) is believed to hold. The client generates its own secret key k_C and public key $K_C = g^{k_C}$ and sends it to the registration server over the covert channel. This allows the client and the registration server to establish a shared key, $k_{C,RS} = g^{k_{RS}k_C}$, which is then used to generate a registration tag. In particular, the shared key is used to seed a cryptographically-strong pseudo-random number generator (PRNG), which is then used to produce an m-bit tag τ. Note that a secure PRNG will ensure that anyone not in possession of the secret key cannot distinguish it from random; we chose to use the AES-128 cipher in counter mode as the PRNG. Altogether, the client sends the following message over the covert channel:

$$K_C || \text{first } m \text{ bits of PRNG}(k_{C,RS})$$

To implement the Diffie-Hellman protocol, we chose to use Curve25519 [8], a state-of-the-art elliptic-curve Diffie-Hellman design. Curve25519 provides a high level of security and has a very fast implementation due to Bernstein[1]. It also uses a bit string encoding of group elements that makes it difficult for the warden to distinguish K_C from random to detect the use of Cirripede. The underlying group is an elliptic curve over F_p, where $p = 2^{255} - 19$, thus a uniformly random element of F_p, represented using 255 bits, will be distributed nearly identically to a uniformly random 255-bit string. Furthermore, although elliptic curve points are of the form $(x, y) \in F_p \times F_p$, for the purposes of Diffie-Hellman, it suffices to send the x coordinate only, as Bernstein's implementation does. This allows us to send K_C, along with a 33-bit tag τ, using a total of 36 bytes, carried over the ISN covert channel of 12 TCP connections.

The Curve25519 implementation in its recommended usage, however, produces only a fraction of all elements in F_p as public keys. First, the recommended domain for the secret key k_C uses only integers that are 0 mod 8, because active subgroup confinement attacks [34] can be used to determine k_C mod 8. Second, the recommended base point $g = 9$ in fact generates a subgroup of the elliptic curve of prime order p_1, whereas the curve itself has size $8p_1$. These choices can easily be adjusted in our scenario; learning k_C mod 8 is not helpful to an attacker, especially since k_C is only used once. Likewise, switching a generator of the full group allows an attacker to determine a few bits of information about k_C but does not invalidate the CDH assumption.

A more significant issue is that only approximately half of the elements of F_p form a valid x coordinate for the elliptic curve, and it is easy for the warden to check whether the client is sending a value that falls into this category over the ISN covert channel. If, over time, all of the ISNs from the client, decoded as elements of F_p, are valid x coordinates, the warden can be reasonably certain that the client is in fact using Cirripede. To address this, we follow the approach

[1] `http://cr.yp.to/ecdh.html`

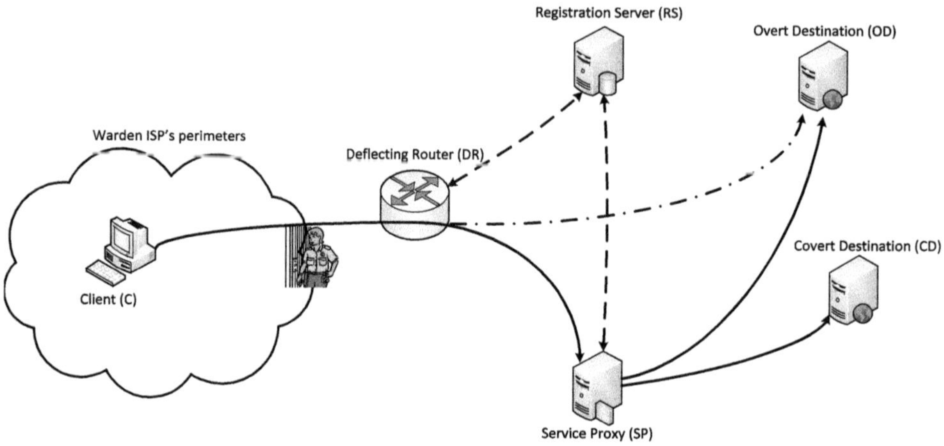

Figure 1: Cirripede architecture.

used in Telex [57] and use the *twist* of the elliptic curve. The x coordinates of points on the twist are precisely those points that are invalid x coordinates for the original curve. To avoid certain active attacks, Curve25519 was designed to have a twist group with order $4p_2$, where p_2 is a large prime, and thus the CDH is also believed to hold for the twist. The implementation can be made to use the twist group G' simply by choosing a generator g' of G'. The registration server has two public keys $K_{RS} = g^{k_{RS}}$ and $K'_{RS} = (g')^{k_{RS'}}$. The client randomly chooses to use the twist or the original curve, each with probability 1/2. The registration server can easily check whether K_C sent by the client belongs to the curve or the twist and use the corresponding secret key to complete the Diffie-Hellman protocol.

3.2 Traffic deflection

As mentioned in the previous subsection the *RS* needs to observe the contents of TCP SYN traffic, in order to perform the registration. To do this, the *DR*s must forward this information to the *RS*. Since the *DR* may be an existing router within the ISP network, to simplify deployment, we aim to minimize the required changes to *DR* hardware or vendor software. One way to do this is for the *DR* to simply forward all traffic to the *RS* in a similar manner to how scrubbing systems are deployed at some ISP networks (e.g., by using the ERSPAN primitive in Cisco IOS). Alternatively, the router can be configured to only forward TCP SYN traffic to the *RS* (e.g., by using the `match field tcp control bits eq 2 mask 0x3D` command in Cisco IOS). The *RS* in turn can write rules ("deflecting tables") into the *DR* to forward certain flows to the *SP*, in a similar fashion.

After a client C is registered, the registration server *RS* informs the deflecting routers to update their deflecting tables by adding an entry for C with the corresponding registration information. The registration information for a client includes the client's IP address and the registration expiration. At this point, any traffic from the client C being intercepted by any of the deflecting routers will be deflected to the service proxy *SP*.

3.3 Unobservable communication

Once the traffic from a registered client C is deflected by a deflecting router, the service proxy *SP* intercepts this traffic in order to start the unobservable communication with the client. The unobservable communication scheme is based on establishing covert communication using legitimate encrypted traffic, e.g., HTTPS traffic. Note that such unobservable communication can also be designed using the existing TCP/IP steganography techniques over a non-encrypted traffic; as mentioned in Section 7, that results in significantly lowering the capacity of the covert communication as compared to using HTTPS.

Figure 2 illustrates the sequence of the messages exchanged within the Cirripede system in order to establish an unobservable communication. Suppose that a client C has successfully been registered by Cirripede; thus, *SP* possesses the shared secret key $k_{C,RS}$. The client starts an HTTPS connection with an allowed overt destination *OD*. This traffic is deflected by a deflecting router *DR* toward the service proxy *SP*. Consequently, the following messages are exchanged in order to have the unobservable connection established:

1. Client C initiates an HTTPS connection with *OD*. This connection is deflected to and transparently proxied by the service proxy *SP* until C and *OD* complete their TLS handshake. (packets 1 to 4)
2. C sends a legitimate encrypted "application_data" TLS record (e.g., an HTTP GET request) to *OD* (this is to prevent connection termination due to a *false-connection* failure as discussed in Section 4.1). (packet 5)
3. *SP* terminates its TCP connection to *OD* on behalf of C. (packet 6)
4. *SP* uses the shared key $k_{C,RS}$ to derive a new shared TLS session key $k_{C,SP}$ (and initializes a new "cipher spec"[2]). Under the new cipher spec, *SP* sends an encrypted TLS record of a 64-byte message $M_1 = [M_0||r]$ to C to inform C of *SP*'s presence. M_0 is a fixed known 32-byte message and r is a 32-byte random number. (packet 7)
5. (C similarly derives $k_{C,SP}$ and initializes the new cipher spec.) C decrypts the TLS record received from *SP* and verifies that the cleartext contains the message M_0. At this time, C switches to using the new cipher spec for communication with *SP*.
6. C instructs *SP* to initiate a new connection to covert destination *CD*. (packet 8)
7. Finally, C communicates with *CD* through the existing

[2]`http://tools.ietf.org/html/rfc4346#section-7`

TLS connection, while appearing to the warden to be communicating with OD.

By having the CD be an entry point to an anonymous network like Tor, the client's traffic gets anonymized from Cirripede as well. This is discussed more in Section 4.3.

4. Cirripede IN PRACTICE

In this section we describe and address some of the technical and security issues of the Cirripede scheme. We start by listing two potential cases where Cirripede may not be able to join a new client, and our extensions to address them (Sections 4.1 and 4.2). We then describe some security properties of Cirripede (Section 4.3).

4.1 False connection failure

This is the case where an oblivious client $\hat{C}$, who is not trying to use Cirripede, is mistakenly registered by Cirripede's registration server. Because this may interfere with the client's normal Internet activity, Cirripede should minimize the rate of false-connection. As discussed in Section 3.1, the registration tag τ is 33-bit long. Thus, the false-connection rate is 2^{-33}, which is practically negligible for a given client. In the rare case of a false connection, the SP informs the RS to remove the mistakenly registered client $\hat{C}$ from the list of the registered clients, and the RS will consequently update the deflecting table of the DR routers by removing the entry corresponding to $\hat{C}$.

The following is another source that may cause a false-connection failure:

Clients with dynamic IPs: In many networks, IP addresses are assigned to the clients dynamically, e.g., using the DHCP protocol. In this case, it might happen that an oblivious client $\hat{C}$ gets assigned to an IP address that is currently registered with Cirripede.

Xie et al. [58] show that the inter-user duration of dynamic IP addresses, i.e., the time between two different clients using the same dynamic IP, depends on the type of the ISP and has a direct relation with the bandwidth provided by the ISP, but is typically on the order of several days. As an example, Comcast Cable has an inter-user duration of at least 10 days in more than 75% of the IP re-allocations. For the SBC DSL provider, this interval is about one day. As mentioned in Section 3.1, each client registration in Cirripede is valid for a registration time interval T. After the registration expires, the client needs to re-register with the Cirripede in order to use its service; this significantly reduces the rate of false-connection failures caused by dynamic IP re-assignments. In fact, the T value makes a tradeoff between the user's need for re-registration and the false-connections due to dynamic allocations of IP addresses.

4.2 Mis-connection failure

This is the case when a client C who has requested to be registered by Cirripede, by sending the registration request as mentioned before, has not been registered successfully. Since no confirmation message is sent to the requesting client during the client registration step, due to some technical constraints[3], there should be sufficient mechanisms by Cirripede in order to prevent possible connection failures. In particular, when a not-successfully registered client C tries to communicate with the service proxy SP by sending messages encrypted with $k_{C,SP}$, these messages directly reach OD, which cannot interpret them and will tear down the connection. In this case, the warden ISP can infer the client's anomalous behavior by observing frequent connection terminations for the client. To prevent the mis-connection failure, the first message that deviates from the TLS protocol—the "confirmation message"—is sent by SP. By having SP send the confirmation message, the client can reliably determine whether to continue communicating with OD or switch to communicating with SP.

[3]This requires deflecting routers to embed steganographic messages into the TCP headers.

4.3 Security analysis

Table 1 summarizes different security and privacy properties provided by Cirripede, as compared to other systems. A censorship circumvention tool or an anonymous network, e.g., Tor, do not provide unobservability from the warden ISP. Using Cirripede alone provides unobservability from the warden ISP, but it does not provide destination-anonymity from the Cirripede system itself: the service proxy knows the covert destination being targeted by a client. In some cases, a client does not trust the Cirripede service itself and requires destination-anonymity from the Cirripede as well. This can be easily provided by having the client use Cirripede to reach a traditional anonymous network like Tor, which is then used to reach the intended covert destination. In other words, in this case an entry point to the Tor network is requested for the CD destination. An alternative approach for providing destination-anonymity from Cirripede is to design a redundant structure for Cirripede; we leave this for future research.

The mentioned security and privacy promises of Cirripede are based on the assumption that Cirripede's private key is not compromised. Having the private key of Cirripede being compromised results in the exposure of Cirripede users as well as their covert destinations and contents of their covert communications, as is the case in other circumvention services, e.g., Tor.

As mentioned before, Cirripede relies on participating ISPs to deflect HTTPS traffic from registered clients to service proxies. In the following, we discuss the security and privacy promises of Cirripede considering different assumptions for the participating ISP.

Malicious participating ISPs: We consider a case where a participating ISP is malicious, i.e., tries to identify clients from its own network that use Cirripede. A participating ISP has access to the deflecting table, e.g., the list of registered clients, provided by Cirripede's registration server. However, as the communication of Cirripede is encrypted using a key shared between Cirripede and a client, a participating ISP will not be able to disclose either the covert destination address or the communicated content.

It may be possible to enforce two requirements to further reduce the consequences of having a malicious participating ISP; first, the participating ISPs are not selected from the countries under the control of the oppressive regimes. This reduces the chances of a malicious ISP to get access to the deflecting table of Cirripede. Second, for each newly registered client C the registration server RS only informs the DRs that belong to the participating ISPs other than C's host ISP. Hence, for a malicious ISP participating with Cirripede the maximum information disclosed will be only the identity of the registered clients that reside in other ISPs.

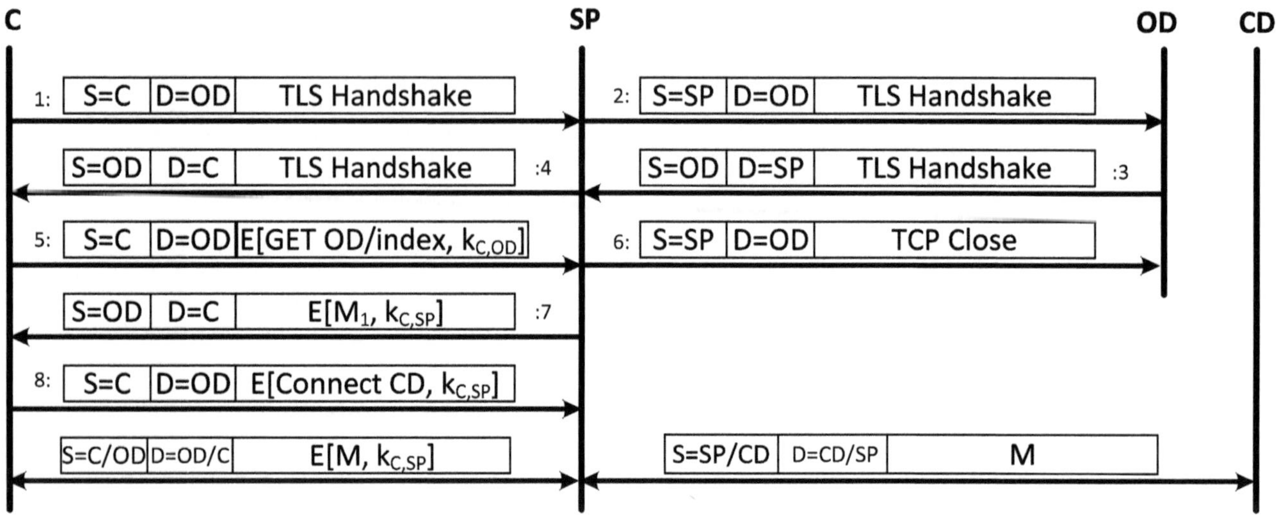

Figure 2: The connection sequence to perform the unobservable communication.

Table 1: Features provided by using different circumvention services.

Circumvention service being used	Source-Anonymity from destination	Destination-Anonymity from warden ISP	Destination-anonymity from circumvention service	Unobservability from warden ISP
None	No	No	N/A	No
Anonymous Network (Tor)	Yes	Yes	Yes	No
Cirripede only	Yes	Yes	No	Yes
Cirripede + Tor	Yes	Yes	Yes	Yes

Honest but curious participating ISPs: Similar to the case of a malicious participating ISP, an honest-but-curious ISP can only get information about the identity of registered clients that reside in other ISPs. However, no information about either of the covert destinations, nor the communication contents of the clients is disclosed to the participating ISPs.

5. PROTOTYPE IMPLEMENTATION

We have implemented a prototype of Cirripede on Linux.

5.1 Deflecting router

Without a real commercial router, we take advantage of the routing capabilities of Linux. The *DR* forwards copies of all TCP SYN packets to the *RS* by using the "TEE" target of `iptables`[4]. In order to deflect packets from registered sources to the *SP*, the *DR* uses policy-based routing. First, we create a new routing table `deflect`, which contains a single default route to the *SP*. (We assume the *SP* can be multiple hops away from the *DR*; thus, to ensure correct routing of deflected packets, which have *OD* as the destination IP address, the *DR* sends those packets to *SP* in an IP-in-IP tunnel.) Second, the *DR* uses the `ip rule` command to match the source IP addresses of registered clients and route them according to the `deflect` table.

[4]http://www.netfilter.org/projects/iptables/index.html

5.2 Registration server

The *RS* uses `libpcap`[5] to capture the TCP SYN packets forwarded to it by *DR*. From each captured packet, *RS* extracts the source IP address and the (24 LSB of the) ISN. The *RS* needs to accumulate 12 SYN packets from the client before it can attempt to validate the client as described in Section 3.1. (If the *RS* does not see a new SYN packet from a client after a *validation interval* of T_v seconds, then it removes the state for that client to reclaim memory.) If the client is validated, *RS* (1) notifies *SP* of the client IP address and the key $k_{C,RS}$, and (2) notifies *DR* to start deflecting the client's traffic.

5.3 Service proxy

At a high level, *SP* acts as a transparent proxy (i.e., client's packets have the *OD* for destination IP address), so the standard configurations necessary for transparent proxying apply. For the proxy software itself, we use `squid`[6] version 3.1.9, a popular HTTP proxy written in C++. We select `squid` only because it is mature and can act as a transparent proxy. We modify `squid` to receive notification packets from *RS* and maintain a mapping from registered client IP addresses to the corresponding $k_{C,RS}$ keys. For the TLS protocol, `squid` uses the OpenSSL 0.9.8q library[7].

Effectively, *SP* transparently intercepts and tunnels the client's TLS handshake with *OD*. When *SP* detects the

[5]http://www.tcpdump.org/
[6]http://www.squid-cache.org/
[7]http://www.openssl.org/

TLS handshake between the client and *OD* has completed, it "changes the CipherSpec" of the TLS connection with the client to use the stream cipher RC4 (though a real implementation should use the same cipher as agreed upon by the client and *OD*), and the "CipherSpec" (the cipher key and MAC secrets) is derived from $k_{C,RS}$. *SP* also clears the read and write TLS sequence numbers to 0. The *SP* then (optionally) closes its TCP connection with *OD* and immediately creates a new TCP connection to a local SOCKS proxy, for which we use 3proxy[8] version 0.6.1. (Alternatively, one could add the SOCKS protocol support into squid itself and not have to connect to a separate SOCKS proxy.) Afterwards, squid simply tunnels traffic between the client and the SOCKS proxy.

5.4 Client-side proxy

It is undesirable to require modifications to existing applications to use Cirripede. Thus we employ at the client host a local proxy, similar to the Tor proxy. This local proxy—henceforth referred to as *client proxy* or *CP*—exposes an apparent (see below) SOCKS interface. The *CP* is configured with the hostnames/IP addresses of two servers to whom packets from the client host will pass through a *DR*, though these two servers can be the same. The first one is used by the registration phase, and the second one is the *OD*. Upon starting, the *CP* will generate TCP traffic towards the *DR* to register itself with Cirripede. The generated TCP traffic needs to contain the special ISNs, so either kernel support or a userspace TCP stack is necessary. Our prototype *CP* simply generates SYN packets using raw sockets, without using a full application connection.

Then, applications at the client host can use *CP* as a regular SOCKS proxy. However, *CP* does not interpret the SOCKS requests. Instead, upon receiving the TCP connection of the request, it initiates an HTTPS connection to the *OD* and proceeds to complete the TLS handshake with *OD*. Then it "changes the CipherSpec" and clears the TLS sequence numbers similar to the *SP*, and then it expects the very next TLS record (of type "application_data") to contain the confirmation message. If that is the case, meaning *CP* is in fact connected to the *SP*, then *CP* proceeds to simply tunnel traffic between the application and *SP* over the TLS channel, without interpreting the SOCKS protocol. Otherwise, it rejects the SOCKS request.

6. EVALUATION

We evaluate the registration component and the throughput provided by Cirripede with experiments on the University of Utah's Emulab testbed [55]. Also, we use simulations to study the effect of *DR* deployment on the ability of clients to register with Cirripede.

6.1 Registration performance

6.1.1 Metrics

We are interested in the ability of the RS to handle real traffic load. The two main metrics are: (1) the fraction of registration signals that the RS can detect, and (2) the load on the RS (in particular, CPU and memory utilization).

[8]http://www.3proxy.ru/

6.1.2 Experiment setup and topology

For this experiment, we take an existing packet trace and embed registration signals into the existing packets, without introducing new packets. We use a one-hour trace [32] captured in March, 2011 at CAIDA's equinix-sanjose monitor, and filter it to keep only TCP SYN packets. We assume that all clients in the trace want to register; however, each client registers only once, at the earliest opportunity. Because we do not inject new packets, a client needs at least 12 SYN packets to register. Out of over 94 million SYN packets from over 6.4 million unique client IP addresses, we can embed only 1,069,318 complete registrations.

The experiment consists of two machines: the *DR* and the *RS*. Both are 2.4 GHz 64-bit Quad Core Xeon E5530 machines, with 12 GB of RAM, running Ubuntu 10.04 64-bit. The machines are connected via a 1 Gbps Ethernet link with zero latency. The *DR* simply uses tcpreplay[9] to replay the processed packet trace (which contains only TCP SYN packets) against the *RS*. The replay speed is about 41,000 packets/second, resulting in a replay duration of 2300 seconds, which puts more pressure on the *RS* than a live capture would have. The *RS* uses four threads, each handling a different set of clients, partitioned by the hash of the client IP address. The *validation interval* is one hour, effectively meaning the *RS* does not timeout any client during the experiment. The *RS* uses sar[10] to collect CPU and memory utilizations at two second intervals.

6.1.3 Results

The *RS* is able to receive 100% of packets that the *DR* successfully sends. It detects 1,038,689 registrations, which is a 97% success rate. We manually inspect a few of the missed registrations and find the cause to be out-of-order packets. Investigating further, we find via tcpdump that the network is at fault: the *DR* sends packets in the correct order, but they arrive at the *RS* re-ordered. In terms of the load on the *RS*, for the duration of the experiment, the average CPU utilization is 56% and the max 73%. The average memory utilization is 1.1 GB and the max 1.6 GB. The memory utilization increases through the experiment, but this is as expected because as noted above the *RS* does not timeout any client. From these results, we believe the registration component of Cirripede scales well.

6.2 Throughput performance

6.2.1 Metrics

For these experiments, we only measure the performance of downloading data from a web server (thus all clients are pre-registered with Cirripede before each experiment). The first metric we are interested in is the time to download the first byte. This is a measure of the perceived responsiveness of loading a website, especially for fetching small amounts of data such as a static web page. The second metric is the full page download time (though we only download a single file in our experiments, instead of a full web page containing multiple objects, possibly from different servers).

6.2.2 Experiment setup and topology

All hosts in the experiments, including the routers, are 2.4 GHz 64-bit Quad Core Xeon E5530 machines with 12 GB

[9]http://tcpreplay.synfin.net/

[10]http://sebastien.godard.pagesperso-orange.fr/

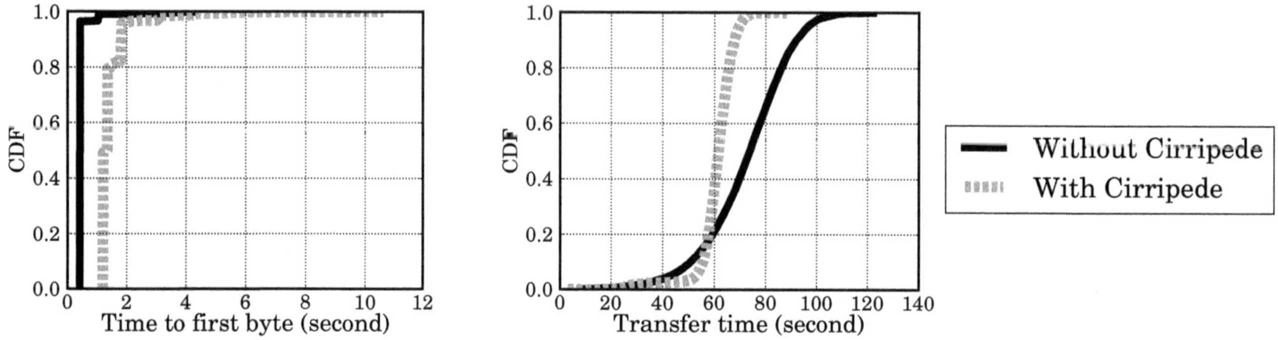

(a) (b)

Figure 3: CDF of the time to receive the first byte and the total time to download a 10 MB file, with and without using Cirripede, for 100 simultaneous clients, each downloading the file 100 times.

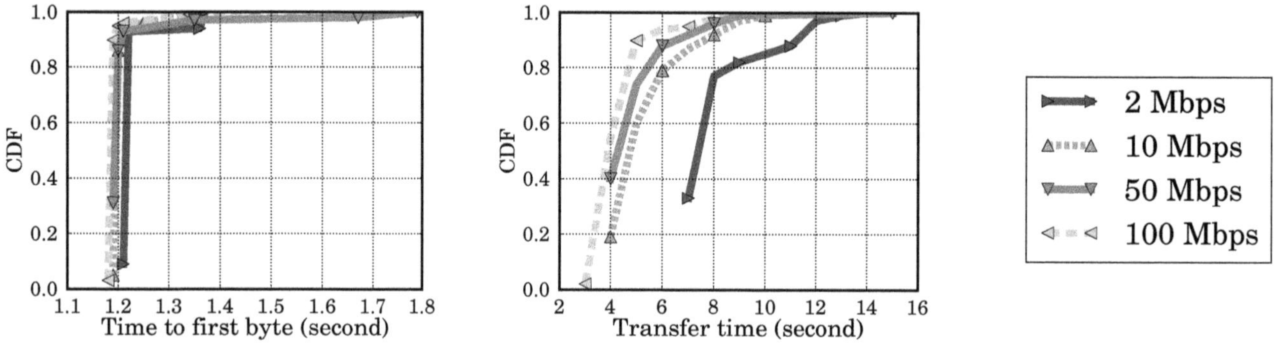

(a) (b)

Figure 4: CDF of the time to receive the first byte and the total time to download a 1 MB file for four simultaneous clients, each downloading the file 100 times using Cirripede.

of memory, running CentOS 5.5 64-bit. Unless otherwise specified, the links are 1 Gbps. Five servers run the Apache web server[11] version 2.2.3 with SSL support enabled. Five client hosts use `curl`[12] version 7.15.5 as the application to fetch files from the servers, using HTTP. Due to NIC limits, the clients are connected to the *DR* via two intermediate routers; however, in all experiments, the link bandwidths at the client hosts are the bottleneck. The *DR* is on the path between all client-server pairs. The *SP* is directly connected to the *DR*, and both the *SP* and *DR* have RTT of 150 ms to all clients and 50 ms to all servers. Thus, the effective RTT between all client-server pairs is 200 ms, approximating a client in Asia accessing a server in the US.

In the first set of experiments, all five client hosts have link bandwidths of 100 Mbps. On each client host, we launch 20 simultaneous "client" instances, each using `curl` to download a 10 MB file from a particular server 100 times over HTTP. Across all five client hosts, we have 100 "client" instances. We will compare results from using Cirripede and without using Cirripede.

In the second set of experiments, we use four client hosts, with different link bandwidths to the network: 2 Mbps, 10 Mbps, 50 Mbps, and 100 Mbps. Each client host runs only one client instance, using `curl` to download a 1 MB file from a server 100 times. All clients use the Cirripede service.

[11]http://www.apache.org/
[12]http://curl.haxx.se/

6.2.3 *Results*

For the first set of experiments, Figure 3(a) shows the results for the time to the first byte. We see that Cirripede adds a delay of no more than a few seconds, most of which is due to the two extra round-trips of the TLS handshake and the SOCKS request-response. Figure 3(b) compares the total download times. The main take-away point is that Cirripede provides comparable performance to the baseline of not using Cirripede. For this particular setup, Cirripede can also result in faster download time. This is because high latencies negatively affect TCP throughput. So, when we use the *SP*, the original TCP connection is split into two separate TCP connections, each with a lower RTT, so each of these two connections has a higher throughput than the original connection would have. Thus the effective end-to-end throughput is improved. (We performed separate experiments using a standard, non-Cirripede SOCKS proxy to confirm this behavior.)

Figure 4 shows the results of the second set of experiments. We can see in Figure 4(a) that as expected, higher bandwidths improve performance. However, because of the high RTTs between clients and servers, increasing the bandwidth yields diminishing returns for a standard TCP.

6.3 DR deployment simulation

In order to use Cirripede, a client needs to discover a path to a website that traverses a DR. To ensure this happens commonly, the provider of the Cirripede service needs to

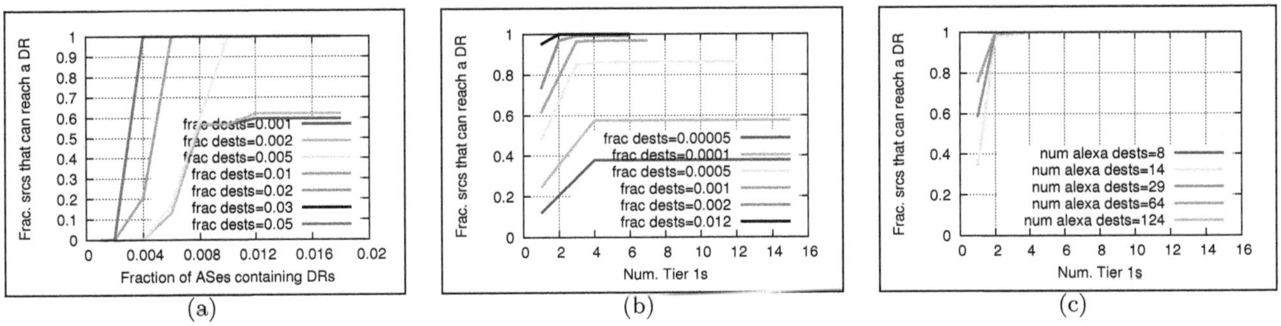

Figure 5: Fraction of sources that can utilize the system (i.e., that can discover a path that traverses a *DR*), when *DR*s are randomly placed (a) across all ASes (b) only tier-1 ASes, and (c) when the warden ISP attempts to block a randomly-selected fraction of most-popular web sites by Alexa Internet rank.

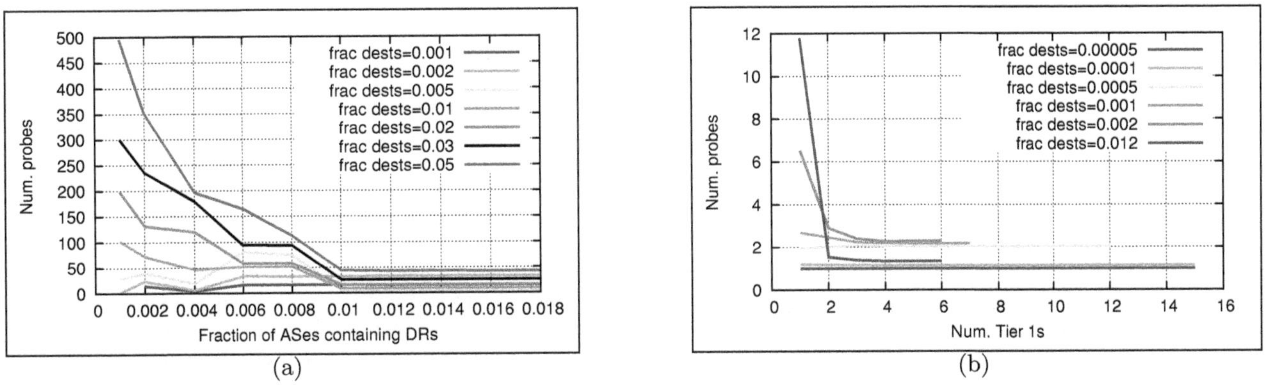

Figure 6: Average number of probes source needs to send before discovering a *DR*, when *DR*s are randomly placed (a) across all ASes (b) only tier-1 ASes.

make sure that sufficient *DR*s are deployed to "cover" most clients. However, for economic, business, and security considerations, the provider would like the number of *DR*s to be small, and deployed at trust-worthy ISPs or in locations under the provider's control.

To explore deployment considerations in practice, we performed a simulation study. We constructed a simple path-level simulator that reads in the Internet AS-level graph, allows us to place the system components of the Cirripede design at various ASes, and computes shortest policy-safe paths. We used the most recent CAIDA AS-level topology (sampled yearly, most recent sample on January 11, 2011). To compute shortest paths, we applied Gao-Rexford policies to the graph based on CAIDA's inferred AS-relationships. We performed two key experiments:

Fraction of clients that can utilize the network (Figure 5): First, we studied how many clients (source hosts) in the Internet would be able to join Cirripede, while varying the extensiveness of *DR* deployment. Figure 5a shows this result under the assumption that a random subset of ASes in the Internet act as *DR*s. We also vary the fraction of overt destinations the client is allowed to probe (in practice, the client may wish to limit the set of overt destinations probed, to reduce potential suspicion). We find that even if only 5% of overt destinations are allowed to be probed, then 0.4% of ASes deploying *DR*s is sufficient to enable all hosts in the Internet to join the Cirripede network. In practice, fewer ASes may suffice, if cooperation from ASes located near the repressive country/company are available. In addition, if *DR* functionality is located near the Internet core, fewer ASes suffice, as larger numbers of paths traverse these ASes. To study this, we evaluated performance under the assumption that only tier-1 ASes act as *DR*s, as shown in Figure 5b. Here we find that even if only one tier-1 AS deploys Cirripede, 97% of clients can use Cirripede, and this number increases to 100% if two tier-1 ASes participate. Since hosts that communicate often via Cirripede may appear suspicious to the warden ISP by contacting randomly-placed destinations, we repeated our study placing destinations according to the Alexa Internet Top Global Sites ranking (Figure 5c), and observed similar results (for example, if two tier-1 ISPs run Cirripede, and hosts are allowed to probe among the top-30 most popular sites, 100% of hosts are able to join Cirripede). Here, the client selects among the top-k most popular Alexa-ranked sites (each line in Figure 5c corresponds to a different value of k). Finally, Figure 5c shows the fraction of Alexa-ranked top web sites the warden ISP would have to block to prevent a host from joining Cirripede. We find that if hosts are allowed to probe the top 1000 Alexa-ranked sites, the warden would have to block more than 95% of these sites to be able to block hosts. We also note that if hosts are aware of which sites are blocked (e.g., if their join fails), they could simply continue to probe more sites.

Overhead required to join the network (Figure 6): To join the network, the client must discover a path to an overt destination that traverses a *DR*. However, the set of ASes containing *DR*s may wish to keep the fact that they are participating in Cirripede a secret. Hence, the client may have to "probe" multiple potential overt destinations before it can discover a path that traverses a *DR*. To speed joining, we would like the number of probes required to join the network to be low. Figure 6a shows the number of probes required under the assumption that a random subset of ASes in the Internet act as *DR*s. Here, we find that even if only 5% of overt destinations are allowed to be probed, the source only requires ten probes before discovering a path contained a *DR*. Under the assumption that *DR*s are only deployed at tier-1 ASes (Figure 6b), this value reduces to less than two. This happens because most Internet paths traverse tier-1 ASes, meaning the client usually finds a path through the selected tier-1 on the first probe.

7. RELATED WORK

7.1 Covert Channels

Covert channels provide a means for unobservable communication. These channels can be classified into covert timing channels and covert storage channels. Timing channels send information by embedding it inside the timing of a stream of packets [11, 49]. The use of timing channels can sometimes be detected using statistical tests by noticing the modifications they make to the ordinary distribution of packet timings [7, 10, 23]. To address this, newer channels use various models to generate timings with a target distribution [24, 29, 35, 48, 60]. However, it may nevertheless be possible to detect the use of such channels if the models do not capture all of the statistical properties of regular traffic; for example, Zander et al. [60] detect the use of covert channels that use i.i.d. traffic models [24, 48] by exploiting inter-packet timing correlations present in regular traffic.

Covert storage channels use some packet fields that are either unused or pseudo-random [25, 27, 41, 46]. Murdoch and Lewis [41] analyze a number of covert storage channels in TCP/IP; they show that a number of channels can be detected because the packet fields differ significantly from those generated by a regular TCP/IP stack. They also propose new covert channels that use TCP initial sequence numbers in a manner that is indistinguishable from either a Linux or an OpenBSD implementation. We use their channel in our registration protocol, see Section 3.1. Other research suggests the use of the IP header TTL field [59], IP addresses [26], TCP timestamp [25], and the order of the packets [22]. Lucena et al. identified a number of IPv6 header field that can be used for covert communication [36], and application-layer protocols, such as HTTP or DNS, can also be used for covert communications [5, 50].

The aforementioned channels typically have limited capacities: storage channels typically send a small number of bits per packet and timing channels likewise are subject to capacity bounds [42, 48]. Fortunately, the growing prevalence of end-to-end encryption creates a possibility for higher-bandwidth covert communication, since an observer not in possession of a secret key cannot learn the contents of an encrypted session. In particular, Cirripede captures HTTPS [45] connections to innocent-looking destinations and uses them for tunneling covert communication. Note that an observer may be able to detect differences in traffic patterns, such as packet sizes and timings, in tunneled traffic, so to ensure full unobservability, techniques to morph the traffic patterns should be used [47, 56]; we leave a full investigation of the application of these techniques to Cirripede to future work.

7.2 Blocking Circumvention

Censorship systems, such as the Great Firewall of China, use IP address blocking as their first line of defense [33]; a natural circumvention strategy is, therefore, to connect to forbidden destinations via proxies. This approach is used by the UltraSurf [2] and Psiphon [30] services; likewise, the Tor anonymous communication network [17] uses bridges that act as proxies for clients that cannot connection to Tor directly [16]. A key problem with this approach is how to distribute the IP addresses of proxies to users without their falling into the hands of the censors [20,38,39,51]; over time, it is expected that the censors can enumerate all proxy IP addresses [40], allowing them to block new users as well as identify past users in traces.

Infranet [19] attempts to disguise communication between the client and the circumvention proxy as a normal web browsing session: a client uses a covert channel based on the sequence of HTTP requests to communicate what true destination it wants to reach; the proxy then fetches the data and uses steganography to embed it inside images that it serves back to the client. However, as with other proxy approaches, it relies on the censor not knowing the proxy address. Burnett et al. propose Collage [19], which avoids this problem by using sites that share user-generated content, such as images on `flickr.com` for carrying forbidden content. Client requests are, likewise, sent via such images, improving unobservability, but significantly reducing the interactive performance of the client. A second problem is that a censor might discover which sites are used for such communication and block them entirely; for example, Burnett et al. consider sending user generated content via Twitter, which has already been blocked by several countries.

A key difference between Cirripede and the above proxy-based approaches is that, in our case, the proxy is embedded within the network itself, and blocking individual web sites is ineffective against Cirripede. Concurrently with our work, Wustrow et al. [57] and Karlin et al. [31] proposed circumvention systems—Telex and Decoy routing—that share this high-level strategy, though make slightly different design choices. Unlike Cirripede, Telex and Decoy routing do not use a registration protocol; instead, clients insert a signal directly into a TLS handshake. This strategy requires the service to monitor all port 443 traffic, including the payload, and reconstruct the underlying TCP sessions. In Cirripede, on the other hand, the registration server monitors only packet headers of TCP SYN packets, and the service proxy monitors only traffic from registered clients. This results in a significant reduction in traffic volumes: using two CAIDA traces gathered in March 2011 [32], we found that the volume (in IP datagram length in bytes) of SYN packets for all ports was only 4–7% that of port 443 traffic. On the other hand, adding signals to individual flows sidesteps issues around packet loss, dynamic IP addresses, and network address translation.

A second consequence of this strategy is that Telex and Decoy routing must hijack a TCP session already in place, whereas Cirripede (transparently) proxies the entire TCP session of registered users. Such hijacking is complicated by the possibility of asymmetric paths, which are common in the Internet [18], since only half of the connection might be seen by the server. Telex is designed to work only for symmetric communication paths, whereas Decoy routing handles this case by having the client use a covert channel to send information about the part of the connection unseen by the router. Hijacking must also be performed in real time, whereas the Cirripede registration process is more tolerant of processing delays at the service.

Telex uses a signaling protocol that, like Cirripede, uses Diffie-Hellman over an elliptic curve; it uses a different curve and has additional security features that protect against potential replay attacks by the warden. Decoy routing opts to use symmetric-key cryptography for signaling in order to achieve better scalability; it therefore requires each client to negotiate a shared key with the service using some out-of-band mechanism. Finally, Telex has some support for mimicking the TCP stack of the overt destination to avoid fingerprinting attacks [37] that could be used by the warden to detect the presence of a proxy. We leave a full analysis of the practical implications of the above design tradeoffs to future work.

7.3 Unobservable Communication

Vasserman et al. [54] create a membership concealing overlay network (MCON) for unobservable communication; they aim to make it difficult for either an insider or outsider adversary to learn the set of participating members. All communication in MCON takes place over links between individual members who trust each other. This is similar to previous "darknet" designs, such as WASTE [21], Turtle [43], and recent versions of Freenet [13, 14]; Vasserman et al. identify security flaws in those designs and propose improvements. To be effective, MCON requires a large number of participants to create a well-connected network, so that new clients can easily find points to join, whereas Cirripede requires a small number of servers, albeit well-placed in the network. The MCON evaluation further focuses on communication between members, rather than connection to external destinations. Another system for unobservable communication, NoneSuch [28], uses image steganography, similar to Collage. It uses the Usenet network for exchanging images and does not aim to address blocking by censors.

8. CONCLUSIONS

In this paper, we presented Cirripede, a system for unobservable communication with Internet destinations to circumvent monitoring and censoring technologies. Our design leverages in-network support to intercept client requests and redirect them to a covert destination, in a manner difficult to observe by adversaries who may control the client's access network. Through simulations on the Internet topology, we find that a small number of tier-1 ASes deploying our design can provide access to most end hosts in the Internet. Through an emulation-based study of an implementation of our design, we find that our design can process packets with low overheads.

Acknowledgments

We would like to thank Ian Goldberg, J. Alex Halderman, Josh Karlin, and Vern Paxson for helpful discussions about our design; we in particular are grateful for J. Alex Halderman for providing a detailed comparison of Telex and Cirripede. We also thank anonymous referees for their comments. This work was supported in part by NSF CNS 09-53655 and the Boeing Trusted Software Center at the Information Trust Institute, University of Illinois. Support for CAIDA's Internet Traces is provided by the National Science Foundation, the US Department of Homeland Security, and CAIDA Members.

9. REFERENCES

[1] DynaWeb. `http://www.dongtaiwang.com/home_en.php`.

[2] Ultrasurf. `http://www.ultrareach.com`.

[3] Defeat internet censorship: Overview of advanced technologies and products. White paper, Global Internet Freedom Consortium (GIFC), November 2007.

[4] Tor partially blocked in China, September 2007. `https://blog.torproject.org/blog/tor-partially-blocked-china`.

[5] M. Bauer. New covert channels in HTTP: adding unwitting Web browsers to anonymity sets. *Workshop On Privacy In The Electronic Society*, page 72, 2003.

[6] S. M. Bellovin. Security problems in the TCP/IP protocol suite. *ACM SIGCOMM Computer Communication Review*, 19(2):32–48, Apr. 1989.

[7] V. Berk, A. Giani, and G. Cybenko. Detection of covert channel encoding in network packet delays. Technical Report TR2005-536, Dartmouth College, Computer Science, Hanover, NH, Aug. 2005.

[8] D. Bernstein. Curve25519: New Diffie-Hellman Speed Records. In M. Yung, Y. Dodis, A. Kiayias, and T. Malkin, editors, *Public Key Cryptography - PKC 2006*, volume 3958 of *Lecture Notes in Computer Science*, pages 207–228. Springer Berlin / Heidelberg, 2006.

[9] J. Boyan. The anonymizer: Protecting user privacy on the web. *Computer-Mediated Communication Magazine*, 4(9), September 1997.

[10] Cabuk, Brodley, and Shields. IP covert timing channels: Design and detection. In *SIGSAC: 11th ACM Conference on Computer and Communications Security*. ACM SIGSAC, 2004.

[11] S. Cabuk. Network covert channels: Design, analysis, detection, and elimination, Jan. 2006.

[12] D. Chaum. Untraceable electronic mail, return addresses, and digital pseudonyms. *Communications of the ACM*, 4(2), February 1981.

[13] I. Clarke, O. Sandberg, B. Wiley, and T. W. Hong. Freenet: A distributed anonymous information storage and retrieval system. In *International Workshop on Design Issues in Anonymity and Unobservability*, pages 311–320, 2000.

[14] I. Clarke, O. Sandberg, B. Wiley, and T. W. Hong. Freenet: A distributed anonymous information storage and retrieval system. *International workshop on Designing privacy enhancing technologies: design issues in anonymity and unobservability*, page 46, 2001.

[15] R. Clayton, S. J. Murdoch, and R. N. M. Watson. Ignoring the great firewall of china. In G. Danezis and P. Golle, editors, *Privacy Enhancing Technologies*, volume 4258 of *Lecture Notes in Computer Science*, pages 20–35. Springer, 2006.

[16] R. Dingledine and N. Mathewson. Design of a blocking-resistant anonymity system. Technical report, The Tor Project.

[17] R. Dingledine, N. Mathewson, and P. Syverson. Tor: The Second-Generation Onion Router. In M. Blaze, editor, *Proceedings of the 13th USENIX Security Symposium*, pages 303–320, San Diego, CA, 2004. USENIX Association.

[18] M. Faloutsos, S. Krishnamurthy, and B. Huffaker. On routing asymmetry in the internet. In *GLOBECOM '05. IEEE Global Telecommunications Conference, 2005.*, 2005, 2005. IEEE.

[19] N. Feamster, M. Balazinska, G. Harfst, H. Balakrishnan, and D. Karger. Infranet: Circumventing web censorship and surveillance. In *Proceedings of the 11th USENIX Security Symposium (SECURITY-02)*, pages 247–262, Berkeley, CA, USA, Aug. 5–9 2002. USENIX Association.

[20] N. Feamster, M. Balazinska, W. Wang, H. Balakrishnan, and D. Karger. Thwarting Web Censorship with Untrusted Messenger Discovery. In *Privacy Enhancing Technologies 2003*, Dresden, Germany, March 2003.

[21] J. Frankel. http://waste.sourceforge.net.

[22] A. Galatenko, A. Grusho, A. Kniazev, and E. Timonina. Statistical covert channels through PROXY server. In V. Gorodetsky, I. V. Kotenko, and V. A. Skormin, editors, *MMM-ACNS*, volume 3685 of *Lecture Notes in Computer Science*, pages 424–429. Springer, 2005.

[23] S. Gianvecchio and H. Wang. Detecting covert timing channels: an entropy-based approach. In P. Ning, S. D. C. di Vimercati, and P. F. Syverson, editors, *ACM Conference on Computer and Communications Security*, pages 307–316. ACM, 2007.

[24] S. Gianvecchio, H. Wang, D. Wijesekera, and S. Jajodia. Model-based covert timing channels: Automated modeling and evasion. In *Recent Advances in Intrusion Detection*, pages 211–230. Springer, 2008.

[25] J. Giffin, R. Greenstadt, P. Litwack, and R. Tibbetts. Covert messaging through TCP timestamps. In *International Workshop on Privacy Enhancing Technologies (PET), LNCS*, pages 194–208, 2002.

[26] C. G. Girling. Covert channels in LAN's. *IEEE Transactions on Software Engineering*, SE-13(2):292–296, Feb. 1987.

[27] T. G. Handel and M. T. Sandford. Hiding data in the OSI network model. In *International Workshop on Information Hiding*, 1996.

[28] T. S. Heydt-Benjamin, A. Serjantov, and B. Defend. Nonesuch. In *Proceedings of the 5th ACM workshop on Privacy in electronic society - WPES '06*, page 1, New York, New York, USA, Oct. 2006. ACM Press.

[29] A. Houmansadr and N. Borisov. CoCo: coding-based covert timing channels for network flows. In *the 13-th Information Hiding Conference*. Springer, 2011.

[30] J. Jia and P. Smith. Psiphon: Analysis and estimation, 2004. `http://www.cdf.toronto.edu/~csc494h/reports/2004-fall/psiphon_ae.html`.

[31] J. Karlin, D. Ellard, A. W. Jackson, C. E. Jones, G. Lauer, D. P. Mankins, and W. T. Strayer. Decoy routing: Toward unblockable internet communication. In *USENIX Workshop on Free and Open Communications on the Internet*, Aug. 2011.

[32] kc claffy, D. Andersen, and P. Hick. The CAIDA anonymized 2011 internet traces - August 2011. `http://www.caida.org/data/passive/passive_2011_dataset.xml`.

[33] C. S. Leberknight, M. Chiang, H. V. Poor, and F. Wong. A taxonomy of Internet censorship and anti censorship, 2010. `http://www.princeton.edu/~chiangm/anticensorship.pdf`.

[34] C. Lim and P. Lee. A key recovery attack on discrete log-based schemes using a prime order subgroup. In B. S. Kaliski, editor, *Advances in Cryptology – CRYPTO '97*, volume 1294 of *Lecture Notes in Computer Science*, pages 249–263, Berlin, Heidelberg, 1997. Springer.

[35] Y. Liu, D. Ghosal, F. Armknecht, A.-R. Sadeghi, S. Schulz, and S. Katzenbeisser. Hide and seek in time - robust covert timing channels. In M. Backes and P. Ning, editors, *ESORICS*, volume 5789 of *Lecture Notes in Computer Science*, pages 120–135. Springer, 2009.

[36] N. B. Lucena, G. Lewandowski, and S. J. Chapin. Covert channels in ipv6. In G. Danezis and D. Martin, editors, *Privacy Enhancing Technologies*, volume 3856 of *Lecture Notes in Computer Science*, pages 147–166. Springer, 2005.

[37] G. F. Lyon. *Nmap Network Scanning.* Nmap project, 1999.

[38] M. Mahdian. Fighting Censorship with Algorithms. In P. Boldi and L. Gargano, editors, *Fun with Algorithms*, volume 6099 of *Lecture Notes in Computer Science*, pages 296–306. Springer Berlin / Heidelberg, 2010.

[39] D. McCoy, J. A. Morales, and K. Levchenko. Proximax: A Measurement Based System for Proxies Dissemination. In *Financial Cryptography and Data Security*, 2011.

[40] J. McLachlan and N. Hopper. On the risks of serving whenever you surf. *8th ACM workshop on Privacy in the electronic society*, page 31, 2009.

[41] S. J. Murdoch and S. Lewis. Embedding covert channels into TCP/IP. In M. Barni, J. Herrera-Joancomartí, S. Katzenbeisser, and F. Pérez-González, editors, *Information Hiding, 7th International Workshop, IH 2005, Barcelona, Spain, June 6-8, 2005, Revised Selected Papers*, volume 3727 of *Lecture Notes in Computer Science*, pages 247–261. Springer, 2005.

[42] J. A. OSullivan, P. Moulin, and J. M. Ettinger. Information theoretic analysis of steganography. In *IEEE Int. Symp. Information Theory*, page 297, 1998.

[43] B. Popescu, B. Crispo, and A. S. Tanenbaum. Safe and Private Data Sharing with {Turtle}: Friends Team-Up and Beat the System. In *12'th Cambridge International Workshop on Security Protocols*, Apr. 2004.

[44] J. Postel. Transmission control protocol. Technical Report RFC 793, DARPA, Sept. 1980.

[45] E. Rescorla. *HTTP Over TLS. RFC 2818.* May 2000.

[46] C. H. Rowland. Covert channels in the TCP/IP protocol suite. *First Monday*, 2(5), 1997.

[47] N. Schear. *Preventing Encrypted Traffic Analysis.* Ph.D., University of Illinois at Urbana-Champaign, 2011.

[48] S. H. Sellke, C.-C. Wang, S. Bagchi, and N. B. Shroff. Tcp/ip timing channels: Theory to implementation. In *INFOCOM*, pages 2204–2212. IEEE, 2009.

[49] G. Shah, A. Molina, and M. Blaze. Keyboards and covert channels. In *In Proceedings of the 2006 USENIX Security Symposium*, pages 59–75, 2006.

[50] M. Smeets and M. Koot. Research report: Covert channels. `http://gray-world.net/papers/rr_cc_univAmsterdam.pdf`, feb 2006.

[51] Y. Sovran, A. Libonati, and J. Li. Pass it on: social networks stymie censors. In *International Conference on Peer-to-peer Systems*, Feb. 2008.

[52] M. Steiner, G. Tsudik, and M. Waidner. Diffie-Hellman key distribution extended to groups. In C. Neuman, editor, *Proceedings of the 3rd ACM Conference on Computer and Communications Security*, pages 31–37, New Delhi, India, Mar. 1996. ACM Press.

[53] P. Syverson, G. Tsudik, M. Reed, and C. Landwehr. Towards an analysis of onion routing security. In H. Federrath, editor, *Proceedings of Designing Privacy Enhancing Technologies: Workshop on Design Issues in Anonymity and Unobservability*, pages 96–114. Springer-Verlag, LNCS 2009, July 2000.

[54] E. Y. Vasserman, R. Jansen, J. Tyra, N. Hopper, and Y. Kim. Membership-concealing overlay networks. In E. Al-Shaer, S. Jha, and A. D. Keromytis, editors, *Proceedings of the 2009 ACM Conference on Computer and Communications Security, CCS 2009, Chicago, Illinois, USA, November 9-13, 2009*, pages 390–399. ACM, 2009.

[55] B. White, J. Lepreau, L. Stoller, R. Ricci, S. Guruprasad, M. Newbold, M. Hibler, C. Barb, and A. Joglekar. An integrated experimental environment for distributed systems and networks. In *Proc. of the Fifth Symposium on Operating Systems Design and Implementation*, pages 255–270, Boston, MA, Dec. 2002. USENIX Association.

[56] C. V. Wright, S. E. Coull, and F. Monrose. Traffic Morphing: An Efficient Defense Against Statistical Traffic Analysis. In *NDSS*, 2009.

[57] E. Wustrow, S. Wolchok, I. Goldberg, and J. A. Halderman. Telex: Anticensorship in the network infrastructure. In *Proceedings of the 20th USENIX Security Symposium*, Aug. 2011.

[58] Y. Xie, F. Yu, K. Achan, E. Gillum, M. Goldszmidt, and T. Wobber. How dynamic are IP addresses? In J. Murai and K. Cho, editors, *Proceedings of the ACM SIGCOMM 2007 Conference on Applications, Technologies, Architectures, and Protocols for Computer Communications, Kyoto, Japan, August 27-31, 2007*, pages 301–312. ACM, 2007.

[59] S. Zander, G. J. Armitage, and P. Branch. An empirical evaluation of ip time to live covert channels. In *ICON*, pages 42–47. IEEE, 2007.

[60] S. Zander, G. J. Armitage, and P. Branch. Stealthier inter-packet timing covert channels. In J. Domingo-Pascual, P. Manzoni, S. Palazzo, A. Pont, and C. M. Scoglio, editors, *Networking (1)*, volume 6640 of *Lecture Notes in Computer Science*, pages 458–470. Springer, 2011.

[61] J. Zittrain and B. Edelman. Empirical Analysis of Internet Filtering in China. pages 70–77, 2003.

Forensic Investigation of the OneSwarm Anonymous Filesharing System

Swagatika Prusty Brian Neil Levine Marc Liberatore
Dept. of Computer Science, Univ. of Massachusetts Amherst
{swag, brian, liberato}@cs.umass.edu

ABSTRACT

OneSwarm is a system for anonymous p2p file sharing in use by thousands of peers. It aims to provide Onion Routing-like privacy and BitTorrent-like performance. We demonstrate several flaws in OneSwarm's design and implementation through three different attacks available to forensic investigators. First, we prove that the current design is vulnerable to a novel timing attack *that allows just two attackers attached to the same target to determine if it is the source of queried content. When attackers comprise 15% of OneSwarm peers, we expect over 90% of remaining peers will be attached to two attackers and therefore vulnerable. Thwarting the attack increases OneSwarm query response times, making them longer than the equivalent in Onion Routing. Second, we show that OneSwarm's vulnerability to traffic analysis by colluding attackers is much greater than was previously reported, and is much worse than Onion Routing. We show for this second attack that when investigators comprise 25% of peers, over 40% of the network can be investigated with 80% precision to find the sources of content. Our examination of the OneSwarm source code found differences with the technical paper that significantly reduce security. For the implementation in use by thousands of people, attackers that comprise 25% of the network can successfully use this second attack against 98% of remaining peers with 95% precision. Finally, we show that a novel application of a known TCP-based attack allows a single attacker to identify whether a neighbor is the source of data or a proxy for it. Users that turn off the default rate-limit setting are exposed. Each attack can be repeated as investigators leave and rejoin the network. All of our attacks are successful in a forensics context: Law enforcement can use them legally ahead of a warrant. Furthermore, private investigators, who have fewer restrictions on their behavior, can use them more easily in pursuit of evidence for such civil suits as copyright infringement.*

Categories and Subject Descriptors

C.2.4 [**Comp. Comm. Networks**]: Distributed Systems

General Terms

Security, Legal Aspects, Design

Keywords

Digital Forensics, Child Sexual Exploitation, P2P Networks

1. INTRODUCTION

OneSwarm [8, 9] is a peer-to-peer (p2p) system for anonymous file sharing that is actively used by thousands of peers and has been downloaded by hundreds of thousands of users. Like Gnutella, peers can query for content and download it from other users. The main design goal of OneSwarm is to resist monitoring and traffic analysis attacks that are easily performed on p2p file sharing networks such as Gnutella and BitTorrent [11]. In short, OneSwarm aims to provide Onion Routing-like privacy and BitTorrent-like performance. OneSwarm's architecture is based on a dense topology of peers to ensure availability of content, probabilistic forwarding of queries to neighbors to thwart traffic analysis, and application-level delays to thwart timing attacks.

OneSwarm provides privacy using a much different method than Onion Routing (OR), which is the architectural basis for Tor [6]. If a peer possesses queried content, it will not forward the query, and it will answer the query only after some delay; otherwise it forwards the query to each of its neighbors with probability p, again after some delay. Thus, as the original paper points out [8], colluding neighbors can determine the chance that a target possesses content when the query is not forwarded to them. For example, that analysis showed that with $p = 0.5$ and a population of 1,000 users, the chances are only 1% that 30 colluding attackers will succeed with 95% precision in determining that a specific, targeted peer is the source of a queried file. Users have downloaded and joined the system with these expectations.

The network is sure to receive the attention of many civil and government investigators. Our law enforcement partners were able to download images of the sexual abuse of prepubescent children through the OneSwarm system; our past work with law enforcement has demonstrated the same for Gnutella [11] and BitTorrent. We take the perspective of criminal forensic investigators that seek to meet standards of evidence for lawfully obtaining warrants for seizing and searching computers observed to be sharing child pornography. We note that, like all p2p networks, the vast majority of users are sharing copyrighted materials rather than child pornography, but as we explain below, investigations of copyright are easier than the criminal standard we hold to.

In this paper, we demonstrate several flaws in OneSwarm's design and implementation based on three different attacks that are available to investigators. First, we prove that OneSwarm is vulnerable to a novel timing attack that allows just two attackers attached to the same target to distinguish whether it is the source of queried content. When attackers comprise 15% of OneSwarm peers, we expect over 90% of remaining peers will be attached to two attackers and therefore vulnerable. The attack itself is simple: two attackers simultaneously query for the same content and they compare the *summed* response time. If the summed application delay is no greater than 600ms above the summed network roundtrip time to the target, then the neighbor target is the source. We derive the proper application-level delays that can deter this attack, but also show that the increased delays result in significantly higher path delays than are present in onion routing [20] architectures. Our attack does not distinguish whether a target is the source of a file or a trusted friend of the source, but as we discuss, both are crimes within our forensic goals.

Second, we show that OneSwarm's vulnerability to attackers that collude to compare probabilistically forwarded traffic is much greater than was previously reported. We use a corrected analysis that also considers the implications of content popularity and is based on a realistic legal model. As in papers that demonstrated flaws in the Vanish p2p system [7,25], we show that the steep growth in effectiveness of the attack as the population of attackers grows was not considered in the original analysis of OneSwarm. We show for this second attack that when investigators comprise just 25% of peers, over 40% of the network can be investigated with 80% precision to find sources of content that is not popular. The attack's success increases with content popularity.

Third, we analyze the OneSwarm source code and find that differences with the technical paper significantly reduce the security of the system. Specifically, the probability of forwarding is hard-coded to $p = 0.95$ instead of 0.5. For the implementation in use by thousands of people, attackers that comprise 25% of the network can successfully use this second attack against 98% of remaining peers with 95% precision due to this value of p. In comparison, should attackers comprise 25% of an Onion Routing network, at most 8% of the circuits are vulnerable in an analogous attack.

Finally, we demonstrate a novel application of a known TCP-based attack, which allows a single attacker to identify whether a neighbor is the source of data or a proxy for it. Using optimistic acknowledgements of data not yet received, an attacker can drive up a target's TCP send rate. If the target is a proxy rather than a source, it will run out of data to send before the true source can supply it. Hence, sources and proxies are distinguishable. Since this requires a single attacker, the entire network can be attacked with a trivial number of attackers — however, only users that turn off the default rate-limit setting are exposed. Onion Routing is not vulnerable to this attack, due to chained proxies. For this and the other two attacks, investigators can increase attack success by repeatedly leaving and re-joining the network to expose a new set of peers.

While our attacks are based on OneSwarm's design, our results are applicable to broad design principles for anonymous communication systems. For example, our TCP-based attack works on anonymous systems that don't use onion-based encrypted layers when streaming data, and several such open-source systems exist, including MUTE [16] and RShare [17]. We revalidate the common wisdom that there is a tradeoff between privacy and performance, and we quantify OneSwarm's anonymity so that it can be compared directly to Onion Routing. We also develop a different attacker model, one based on a conservative set of legal restrictions.

2. OVERVIEW OF ONESWARM

OneSwarm is a popular p2p system for anonymous file sharing. There are North American (`http://oneswarm.cs.washington.edu`), French (`https://forum.oneswarm-fr.net`), and Russian (`http://oneswarm.ru`) communities each with many thousands of users. Below, we include details of only the OneSwarm mechanisms that are relevant to our analysis. We examined the source code available from `http://www.cs.washington.edu/homes/isdal/OneSwarm-20110115.tar.bz2`, which is version 0.7. We note any relevant differences between the technical paper and source code.

OneSwarm is based on a dense topology of peers that discover each other through a community server. Neighboring peers can be *trusted* or *untrusted*. Trust is assigned by the user, and trusted peers see none of the delays or other mechanisms that OneSwarm introduces, as if they were standard BitTorrent peers. The content shared by trusted friends is displayed explicitly in the OneSwarm GUI.

Topology Construction. Each peer has 26 neighbors, and they can be added from out-of-band methods (such as email or social networking sites) as trusted or untrusted friends, or assigned as untrusted friends by the community server. The simplest method of investigation is to be randomly assigned to peers by the community server, and that is the case we focus on here. The source code assigns peers between 22 and 39 neighbors; as peers quit, community server can assign more peers to clients. When a target does have a trusted friend, all privacy controls are turned off, and therefore becoming a trusted friend is an appealing method of investigation; we don't investigate such an approach in this paper. But we do quantify the affect of trusted friends on our attacks, and we summarize the legal implications, which favor law enforcement, in Section 4.3.

Neighboring peers communicate via SSL over TCP. Key exchange is based on an underlying DHT; we elide the details. The public/private keypair used by each peer does not change and is stored on the local computer. The public keys of neighbors are also stored on the user's local computer. The user's keys and neighbors' keys are never deleted (until the application is uninstalled) and are useful corroborating evidence.

Searching for Content. OneSwarm is strongly linked to BitTorrent, and peers can search for content by flooding a query containing a text string or by a unique BitTorrent *infohash*, which is a standard method of uniquely identifying a torrent. When content is found, peers indicate they have a path to the content, without disclosing whether they are the source of the content or just a proxy to it. Pieces of the torrent are then swarmed from all remote peers that provide a path.

When a OneSwarm peer possesses queried content, it will return a *search reply* message after some delay but not forward the query any further. In the OneSwarm paper, the delay is selected uniformly at random from 150–300ms. The choice is consistent (random but deterministic) for the matching content (by info hash). Two neighbors that query a source for the same file will see the same delays. A peer that queries for two different files from the source will see different delays, but when a query is repeated it will see a consistent delay. In the source code, query replies are returned with a delay of 170–340ms. In the case of infohash searches, the delay is chosen on the basis of the infohash; for text searches, the delay is selected based on the content that matches the query. When intermediaries receive a search reply, they forward the message along the reverse path back to the original querier. The reply messages are forwarded by intermediaries with no delay in the source code, though the paper specifies that all OneSwarm protocol messages are delayed.

If the peer does not possess the queried content, it forwards the query to each of its neighbors with probability p; the choice to forward a specific query to a specific neighbor is random but deterministic. In the paper, forwarding of queries is delayed again by 150–300ms, a value chosen at random but again consistent for the specific query and the neighboring peer. In the software, query replies are forwarded without delay. In the paper, $p = 0.5$ is a suggested value, but it is stated that "privacy-conscious users are free to decrease their forwarding probability". However, the software follows a different design. p is set to a much higher value of 0.95 and there is not yet a user-visible method to change the value of p; users must edit and recompile the source. As we show, this setting greatly reduces the privacy of the system.

Once the querier receives a reply, the content is requested and relayed through the path of OneSwarm peers using the BitTorrent protocol. There are no direct downloads between peers unless they are neighbors, but peers cannot naively identify these direct connections.

OneSwarm messages have no time-to-live (TTL) fields, as they would allow attackers to determine if a neighbor is a source of a file by falsely setting the TTL of an outgoing query to 1. Without TTLs, queries might cause congestion collapse from unlimited traffic, and so OneSwarm uses another mechanism. As search replies are returned along the reverse path to the querier, *search cancel* messages are sent to any neighbor that received the original query. These cancel messages are sent without delay and are designed to catch up to and stop the propagating query.

Like BitTorrent, OneSwarm allows a form of parallel downloading (called *swarming*) that Onion Routing implementations, like Tor, do not support well. Our analysis of OneSwarm's privacy is so that users can evaluate if the performance benefits are worth the decline in security in comparison. The reason Onion Routing does not support swarming well is that a separate 3-proxy tunnel is needed to each peer offering part of a torrent.

Other details of OneSwarm's operation do not introduce vulnerabilities that we've discovered, and we do not describe them further here.

3. PROBLEM STATEMENT & MODEL

In this section, we provide a problem statement, attacker model, and our assumptions. Related work appears inline.

3.1 Problem Statement

OneSwarm was designed to thwart third parties from monitoring peers on its p2p network. For years, academic projects [3, 15] have measured p2p networks. Private companies such as DtecNet, Peer Media Technologies, and Media Defender have also monitored p2p networks to assist copyright holders in filing civil copyright infringement lawsuits.

For more than a decade [22], p2p networks have been an enormous venue for the distribution of child sexual abuse imagery, according to the US Dept. of Justice [21], past work by ourselves [11, 12], and others [5, 10]. Our work with law enforcement identified over 425,000 Gnutella users, as identified by application-level IDs, sharing known files of child pornography (CP) during 2010 [11]. Our focus is on US-based criminal investigations of OneSwarm peers for two reasons. First, criminal investigators are at a disadvantage compared to other civil investigators. The former are far more restricted by the legal process defined in the US for law enforcement. Accordingly, this process provides a lower bound on OneSwarm's vulnerabilities. Second, our law enforcement partners have verified there is CP shared on OneSwarm, and thus it is of interest to them.

Investigator Goals. The investigator is essentially an attacker, attempting to violate OneSwarm's privacy promises, though more limited in ability than is typically assumed [24]. Their goal is to *identify* a subset of all OneSwarm peers that are each sharing (or conspiring to share) one or more *files of interest*. The files are content that is known to be CP, and this represents a small fraction of files shared on the network. The overriding goal of the attacker is to gather evidence sufficient for a search warrant so that the physical location corresponding to a peer's IP address can be searched, and relevant physical evidence seized. Hence, we consider success only when evidence can be gathered that is sufficient at least for *probable cause*.

The OneSwarm threat model is designed to be resistant to the disclosure of user behavior to an attacker with control over a limited number of overlay nodes and that wishes to monitor millions of users. In contrast, our investigators want to quickly gather sufficient evidence for a subset of actors that are breaking the law, all while expending minimal resources. The investigator is not looking to catch everyone at once, but can repeat attacks over time.

Probable cause is a lower standard than the *beyond a reasonable doubt* standard needed for conviction. There is no quantitative standard for probable cause, and courts have defined it only qualitatively as a "fair probability" ; see *United States v. Sokolow*, 490 U.S. 1 (1989). Accordingly, we say a peer has been *identified* if the investigator's statistical confidence is above a level sufficient to serve as probable cause. While Isdal et al. analyze attacks requiring 95% precision, we believe that 80%, or perhaps even lower, is still a conservative quantification of this standard, though of course it depends on context. We evaluate different scenarios throughout this paper.

Evidence is *forensically valid* if gathered using techniques that are based on testable hypotheses, have a known error rate, are based on accepted scientific methods, and are peer reviewed; see *Daubert v. Merrell Dow Pharma.* 509 U.S. 579 (1993).

A basic tenet of criminal forensics is that investigators have limited resources. Like narcotics crimes, the number of persons arrested for CP possession is generally limited by investigator resources, not by the number of suspects. Each identified peer requires weeks of additional legal processing, and so maximizing the number identified is not necessary for success.

3.2 Model and Assumptions

The general approach adopted by law enforcement for investigating CP trafficking is based on a series of legal restrictions. We assume our attacker is in fact an investigator in the US and following these restrictions. The law places limits on how investigators can gather information prior to the receipt of a search warrant. The primary restriction is that investigators can only gather information in *plain view*. For p2p networks, any traffic is in plain view if either: *(i)* in the normal operation of the protocol the traffic can be observed by any peer on the normal path (for example, search queries that are broadcast to all peers, including the attacker); *(ii)* if the traffic is destined for the attacker (for example, a response to the attacker's search query). *U.S. v. Gabel*, 2010 WL 3927697 is a recent ruling that confirms this procedure's legality. We do not allow attackers in our model to analyze or compromise the contents of encrypted traffic. We do not allow attackers to seize or compromise peers through privilege escalation as that is outside the plain view standard.

Our attacker controls some fraction of all peers in the network. We detail three specific attacks on the anonymity of OneSwarm in the following sections, and describe the value of the evidence investigators discover from these attacks. Based on these attacks, an investigator can determine if a specific IP address is of interest. The first attack leverages timing information; the second leverages traffic information; the third leverages TCP information.

With a magistrate-ordered subpoena, the billing record of an IP address provides a specific geographic location. With the attack's evidence provided as part of a court-issued warrant, this location is searched, any computer systems and media are seized, and the media are examined for other evidence of the possession or distribution of CP. Such evidence includes CP burned to a DVD or other unassailable [2] evidence of intent to possess. Often the evidence gathered for the search warrant is not introduced at the criminal trial unless the search warrant is challenged; thus it is essential to investigations but must meet only the lower probable cause standard.

In comparison, a civil claim of copyright infringement need meet much lower standards. While a warrant cannot be issued by civil investigators, the billing records *and* computers at the location can be subpoenaed based on merely a *relevance* standard. Evidence is relevant if it "has a tendency to make any fact more probable or less probable than it would be without the evidence" [23]. As previous work has shown [14] this bar is very low, and the smallest success from our attacks would be sufficient for civil subpoena — precision of 95% confidence, as we can achieve, is for a civil subpoena extraordinarily high. Once at trial, only a *preponderance of evidence* standard must be met for a judgment to be awarded.

4. TIMING ATTACKS

In this section, we demonstrate that the current design of OneSwarm is subject to a novel timing attack. We also show that the deployed version of the system has this flaw. We then derive a configuration of OneSwarm delays that deters the attack; however, the new delays that OneSwarm enforces for responding to queries must be increased to 133%–400% of the delays imposed by Onion Routing. Further, the resultant search traffic on OneSwarm floods potentially thousands of nodes.

The basic design goal of OneSwarm is to prevent attackers from distinguishing between two cases for some targeted peer T and the source of some file (we use *file* and *content* synonymously):

- **Case A:** T **is** the source a particular file;
- **Case B:** T **is not** the source a particular file. Instead T is only a proxy on the path to some other peer it does not know, S, that is a source.

There is a major difference between the goals of the OneSwarm security model and the goals our forensic analysis. When the source of a file is a trusted friend, the OneSwarm design considers that as an example of Case B. In our analysis, we consider it as an example of Case A since the peer has explicit knowledge via the OneSwarm GUI of what its trusted friends are sharing on the network, and the peer is therefore a knowing source of the content as well; we return to this point in Section 4.3.

OneSwarm's design defeats a **Basic Timing Attack** where a single peer A issues a query to its neighbor T. The attacker compares the application-level response time to the network-based roundtrip time; if they are similar, then the attacker judges that T is the source.

To defeat the attack, when a peer *is* the source a requested file, it introduces an artificial delay of 150–300ms before answering queries, as described in Section 2. This response delay, r, is chosen randomly but deterministically for the specific file.

If a peer *does not* possess a queried file, it forwards the query on to its neighbors only after a delay, q, which is 150–300ms in the paper (but exactly 150ms in the current implementation). This added delay allows the original querier and intermediaries the chance to send a query *cancel message* that will catch up with the propagating query. Recall from Section 2 that the cancel messages are essential in preventing traffic explosions, since there are no TTL fields in OneSwarm messages.

OneSwarm peers do not keep a cache of previously answered queries. However, we discuss the effects of query and response caching on this attack later in the section and show that the attack is not substantively affected.

The attack makes use of two central variables:

- l is the one-way network layer delay between two peers. We assume such delays are symmetric and let $RTT = 2l$.
- δ is the application-level roundtrip delay in receiving OneSwarm search query responses from a source. Since OneSwarm enforces extra delays, this is not equal to the RTT.

4.1 The Twin Timing Attack

OneSwarm is vulnerable to a new attack using *simultaneous queries* from two attackers, which we dub the *twin timing attack*. The peers don't need synchronized clocks, but the two queries must be issued before the target changes from possessing the file to not possessing it, and before network-layer conditions change drastically. The complete attack appears in Algorithm 4.1 and refers to two attackers C_1 and C_2, both attached to a target peer T.

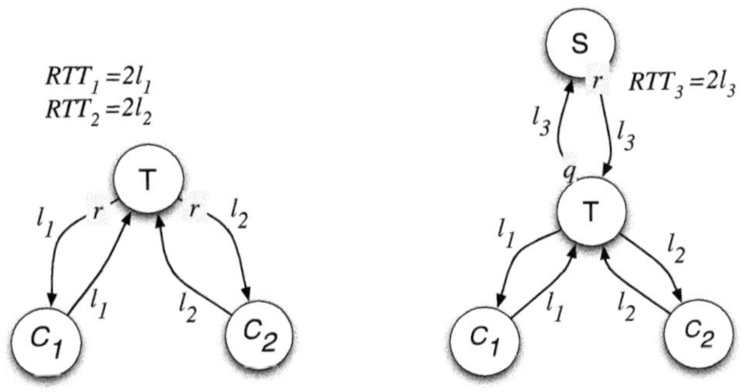

Figure 1: The attacker attempts to distinguish two scenarios. In Case A, peer T is the source of queried content. In Case B, peer S, one hop from T, is the source.

Algorithm 4.1: TWINTIMINGATTACK(T)

---

1. C_1 and C_2 each measure their respective network roundtrip time to T as RTT_1 and RTT_2, respectively.
2. C_1 and C_2 simultaneously query T for the same content.
3. Let δ_1 and δ_2 be the total delays after which C_1 and C_2 receive replies, respectively.
4. If $(\delta_1 + \delta_2) - (RTT_1 + RTT_2) < 600$ ms, then T is the source.

THEOREM 1: If T is the source of the queried content, then $(\delta_1 + \delta_2) - (RTT_1 + RTT_2) < 600$ ms; else T is not the source.

PROOF: This proof uses the delays defined in the OneSwarm paper; the case for the delays defined in the software is discussed subsequently. **Case A** is illustrated in Fig. 1(left) where

- T is the source of a file;
- l_1 is the network delay between C_1 and T;
- l_2 is the network delay between C_2 and T;
- r is the response delay at T for a query, whether by C_1 or C_2.

The total delay for each attacker is

$$\delta_1 = 2l_1 + r \quad (1)$$

$$\delta_2 = 2l_2 + r \quad (2)$$

Let sum_A equal the sum of δ_1 and δ_2 for Case A.

$$sum_A = 2l_1 + r + 2l_2 + r \quad (3)$$

Because r is chosen from 150–300ms, we can bound sum_A as

$$sum_A \leq 600 + 2l_1 + 2l_2 \quad (4)$$

Case B is illustrated in Fig. 1(right) and adds the following variables.

- T is not the source S;
- l_3 is the network delay between T and S;
- q is the delay at T before it forwards the query to S;

In this case, the total delays are

$$\delta_1 = 2l_1 + q + 2l_3 + r \quad (5)$$

$$\delta_2 = 2l_2 + q + 2l_3 + r \quad (6)$$

Let sum_B equal the sum of δ_1 and δ_2 for Case B.

$$sum_B = 2l_1 + 2q + 2l_2 + 2r + 4l_3 \quad (7)$$

Because all application-level delays are chosen from 150–300ms, we can bound sum_B as

$$sum_B \geq 600 + 2l_1 + 2l_2 + 4l_3 \quad (8)$$

Let RTT_1 and RTT_2 be the measure network roundtrip time to T from C_1 and C_2, respectively. When T is not the source (Case B), the difference of the summed network RTTs and the total response delay summed is *at least*

$$sum_B - (RTT_1 + RTT_2) \geq 600 + 4l_3 \quad (9)$$

When T is the source (Case A), the difference of the summed network RTTs and the total response delay summed is *at most*:

$$sum_A - (RTT_1 + RTT_2) \leq 600 \quad (10)$$

In short, the attack works because the minimum value of sum_B is always larger than maximum value of sum_A.

Therefore, if the difference between $2(l_1 + l_2)$ and $\delta_1 + \delta_2$ is less than 600 ms, T is the source or T is knowingly conspiring with the source as per Section 4.3. □

Caching query results. OneSwarm does not cache queries or query responses at peers. Doing so would thwart the attack as it would not be clear if a response was from a cached result or the original source. To defeat this defense, the timing would instead be on the request for the actual content. We assert that requests for content must also have delays as queries for content (forwarding and response) otherwise the Basic Timing Attack and variants would be possible. To defeat the twin timing attack on the requests for content, OneSwarm peers would have to cache actual content that was recently transferred, which is an enormous change to the OneSwarm's design. It would increase the resources required of peers dramatically.

4.2 Software Vulnerability to the Attack

In the OneSwarm software, r appears to be chosen between 170–340ms for text queries. If the node does not have the file, it will forward the query after a delay of $q = 150$ms but it appears that there are undocumented delays as well. An added detail is that if a query is for a specific infohash, the operation is slightly different. First, the source chooses a value for r between 170–340ms. Then, the querier learns the torrent's meta-information after this delay, it requests specific pieces, and the responses to each are delayed by 20–40ms by the source. We analyze only the text query process in this paper. When responses to a query are forwarded to an intermediate peer there is never a delay in forwarding. With these settings in the software, the proof remains valid. However, the multi-threaded nature of the software makes it impossible for us to be sure of its actual operation. In fact, in examining the software, we found unintended delays unknown to the developers themselves, which were fixed in later versions that we did not test. An added delay of about 100 ms is unintended in the code according to the developers. We rely on experimentation to empirically validate the attack on the software since its exact operation is unclear.

We implemented the attack on a set of four machines within our building on separate networks, taking the roles

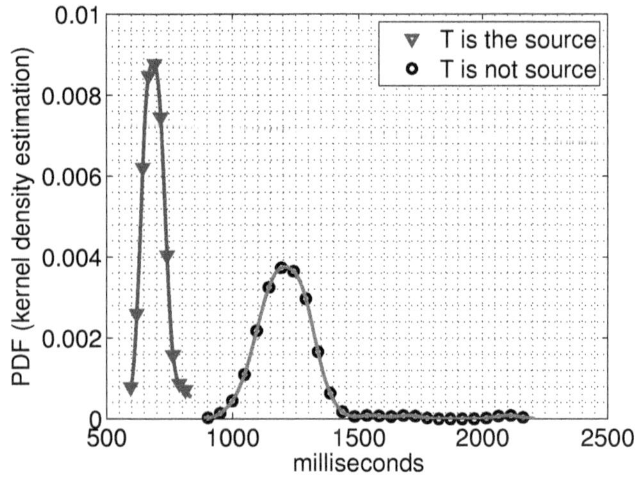

Figure 2: Results of the Twin Timing Attack implementation with 200 trials on a small network. The distribution of timing values is presented using a kernel density estimator. The two cases are from two distinctly different distributions.

shown in Figure 1. We did not attack any real users of OneSwarm because we did not have any ground truth for what they actually shared, so the experiments would have been impossible to evaluate. The attack fails when RTT variance is high and would be less successful across some Internet paths. However, if we had performed the attack on a node we controlled on the Internet, we would have not been able to isolate the aspects of OneSwarm's implementation that allow the attack. Moreover, we could not have asserted that the amount variance we observed would be typical of every path on the Internet. Stronger security is more often provided by a known design quality rather than relying on protean characteristics of Internet traffic that cannot be controlled or relied on, and we tested the former case here.

In our tests, each machine was running version 0.70 of OneSwarm; peers C_1 and C_2 were instrumented to display the relevant timing information, and network-level RTTs were determined by ICMP pings. We show the results of 200 trials of the attack in Figure 2 for 200 files, one trial per file. The results for each case is displayed using a kernel density estimator (KDE). The two cases, of possessing or proxying the file, are clearly and always differentiable as samples from distinct distributions. In our experiments, the maximum summed application-layer delay was 816 ms when T was not the source. The minimum application-layer delay when T was the source was 996 ms. The KDE representation of the distribution increases the maximum and minimum of each case, yet the distributions remain distinct. As we noted in the introduction, when attackers comprise 15% of OneSwarm network, we expect 90% of the remaining peers to be connected to two attackers and therefore vulnerable; see Eq. 20 in Section 5.

4.3 Trusted Neighbors

Trusted relationships are an important aspect of OneSwarm's design. When a neighbor is trusted, there are no delays for OneSwarm messaging. Accordingly, the Twin Timing Attack will not always distinguish between a target and its trusted friends as sources of a specific file, however, this is not a problem.

When peers act as a proxy for a trusted friend sharing child pornography, it is also a serious crime, and the attack's result is sufficient evidence of such criminal distribution. Filenames shared by trusted peers are shown in the target's GUI, and therefore a target of the Twin Timing Attack is distributing CP with knowing intent — the target can be charged with conspiracy to distribute; see 18 U.S.C. Sec. 2252A(b)(1). Furthermore, by setting a trusted relationship, the target gains a non-pecuniary benefit of better performance, which incurs a greater punishment; see US v. Schaefer, 472 F.3d 1219 sentencing memo, and USSG Sec. 2G2.2(b)(3)(B). Evidence found at the target could serve to support a search warrant of the trusted peer that is actually sourcing the child pornography, and so finding the proxy for a source of CP is a good strategy for investigators. In short, trusting a neighbor raises a significant criminal liability. While the system is designed to obscure whether a peer or its trusted neighbor is sharing a file, the distinction does not concern or thwart law enforcement investigations as in either case the target is breaking the law. The same conclusion can be drawn for civil investigations, where the bar of relevance is lower; see Section 3.2.

4.4 Deterring the Attack with Longer Delays

We now show that defeating the basic timing attack and the twin timing attack requires that the range of response delay r be larger than the forwarding delay q. However, the *search cancel* messages place a lower bound on the value of q. Under these constraints, finding content 1 hop away will require a delay of 4 times an expected Internet RTT. Finding content 3 hops away requires an additional delay of 12 times the expected RTT. While Onion Routing does not directly support search for content, its chain of 3 proxies (at a cost of 3 times the normal RTT) has much better performance when searching for torrents via Web sites, or when proxying the traffic of p2p systems that do support search.

First, we note that to defeat the Basic Timing Attack, OneSwarm enforces the following constraint for an expected RTT [8].

$$min(r) \geq RTT \tag{11}$$

With this minimum delay, a response from a target could appear to have come from a trusted peer, one hop away from the target. In the design, this value is chosen between 150–300ms to emulate the expected Internet delay of one to two hops.

THEOREM 2: To defeat the twin timing attack, the following constraint must hold

$$max(r) > min(q) - min(r) + RTT_3 \tag{12}$$

where RTT_3 is the roundtrip time between the Target and the Source as shown in Figure 1(right). We let $max(\cdot)$ and $min(\cdot)$ represent the maximum and minimum values of a given delay variable taken from uniform distributions.

PROOF: The twin timing attack is possible because of the difference between the summed total delay for Cases A and B. Based on logic similar to our proof of Theorem 1 (Eqs. 9 and 10), the attack is defeated if

$$min(sum_B) - max(sum_A) < 0 \tag{13}$$

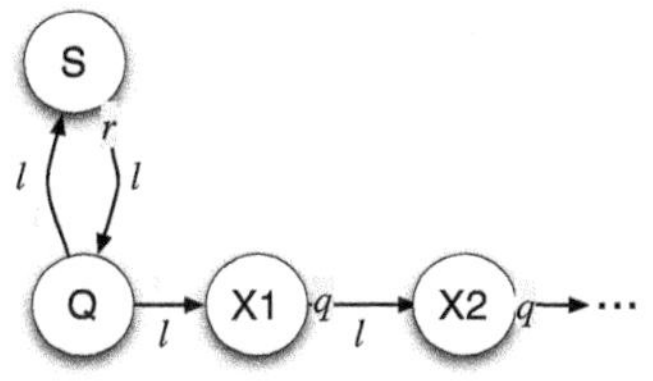

Figure 3: OneSwarm query and cancel message delays.

By first substituting Eqs. 3 and 7 (from the Proof of Theorem 1) into Eq. 13, it can be reduced to

$$min(2q + 2r + RTT_1 + RTT_2 + 2RTT_3) - max(2r - (RTT_1 + RTT_2)) \quad < 0 \qquad (14)$$

The target does not control the min or max values of the network-determined RTT, and thus must assume the worst case of $min(RTT) = max(RTT)$. Therefore, we have

$$min(q) + min(r) + RTT_3 - max(r) < 0$$

which is equivalent to Eq. 12. The Theorem holds, for example, when $q = 0$ and the range of r is greater than RTT_3. Since T can measure RTT_3 and it sets r, it can defeat the twin timing attack with correctly set delays. Moreover, it is not possible for the attacker to measure RTT_3. □

However, when $q = 0$, cancel messages will not work at all.

We now prove the constraints that are necessary for cancel messages to work correctly. Unlimited propagation of query messages would prevent OneSwarm from scaling to large topologies: all nodes would receive all query messages, which is untenable.

Cancel messages are illustrated in Fig. 3.

- Q is the querier of content;
- S is the source of the content;
- $X1$ will forward the query to its neighbors if not stopped by Q;
- q is the query delay randomly chosen by $X1$ before it forwards the query to the rest of the network.
- r is the response delay chosen at random by S for a query by Q.

Once Q receives a response from S, it will immediately forward a cancel message to $X1$. In this scenario, $X1$ is representative of T's 37 other neighbors; $X2$ is representative of $X1$'s neighbors, each having 38 neighbors, and so on.

THEOREM 3: For a querier's cancel messages to stop all instances of the query message within h hops of Q, then

$$max(r) < min(q)h - 2l. \qquad (15)$$

PROOF: We compare the latencies of the two messages as illustrated in the figure (dropping subscripts for link delays). For the cancel message to stop search queries within h hops, the following inequality must hold

$$max(r) + 2l + hl < h(min(q) + l) \qquad (16)$$

which directly reduces to Eq. 15. □

THEOREM 4: The constraints of the Basic Timing Attack, Twin Timing Attack, and search cancel messages imply that

$$min(q) > (6l)/(h - 1). \qquad (17)$$

PROOF: Starting from Eq. 12, we substitute $max(r)$ with the bound from Eq. 15. By then substituting $min(r)$ with the bound from Eq. 11, we have the inequality stated in Eq. 17. □

4.5 Performance Implications

Given that we have bounds on q and r that are required to defeat these attacks while ensuring cancel messages work, we can now determine the performance implications for OneSwarm. Specifically, we calculate the length of time to receive query responses from sources for these new delays. A large component delays in any implementation of Onion Routing come not from network latency, but rather from non-intentional application-layer queuing delays, and this is true in OneSwarm as well. Here, we perform a comparison of minimum delays imposed by the architecture of the systems that enables privacy, independent of traffic load or other external factors.

First, we determine for the existing OneSwarm implementation the number of hops queries can travel before being cancelled by a source one hop from a querier (as in Fig. 3. In the source code, $max(r) = 340$ms, $min(r) = 170$ms, and $q = 150$ms. Therefore, when $l \approx 75$ms, and from Eq. 15, we know that $h > (max(r) + 2l)/q = (340 + 150)/150 = 3.26$; therefore $h = 4$ since it can only take on an integer value. We can show that the earliest that messages can be stopped is $h > (min(r) + 2l)/q = (170 + 150)/150 = 2.13$; therefore, messages cannot be stopped before $h = 3$ hops from the querier. For smaller values of l, $2 \leq h \leq 3$, which we assume below as a conservative estimate.

Second, given this value, we can determine the number of peers that receive traffic for each query, even if answered by a direct neighbor. When $h = 2$, and $p = 0.95$ and with a full topology, each query will reach $(39 * 0.95)^2 = 1373$ peers. When $h = 3$ this value increases to 50,859 peers; the importance of limiting $h = 2$ is clear.

Third, given $h = 2$, we can now solve for values of q and r that protect OneSwarm users. From Eq. 17: $q > \frac{6l}{2-1} = 6l$; and from Eq. 11: $min(r) \geq 2l$; and from Eq. 12: $max(r) > 10l$.

Finally, these values allow us to compute, for a version of OneSwarm immune to timing attacks, the expected time t it takes to receive a response from a source x hops away is $E[t] = 8xl$. For x=1, $E(t) = 8l$; For x=3, $E(t) = 24l$.

In comparison, because Onion Routing always consists of a chain of 3 proxies, the delay in receiving data from a Torrent search engine is $E[t] = 6l$. Therefore, for any query, OneSwarm is always one RTT slower in terms of roundtrip delay; for many queries OneSwarm is about 4 times slower. The number of nodes that receive query traffic (in the thousands) is inefficient compared to contacting a single web server over an Onion Routing circuit.

5. COLLUSION ATTACK REVISITED

The *collusion attack* is a fundamental threat to OneSwarm peers as it based on only two aspects of the protocol's design: that queries are forwarded with probability p when the peer

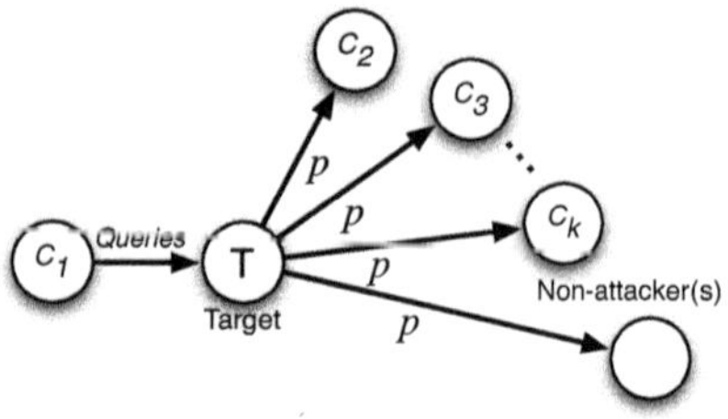

Figure 4: Setting for collusion attack. One attacker queries for content and the remaining attacker each have a probability p of receiving the query if T is not the source.

doesn't have requested content; and that each peer has up to 39 neighbors. If all other attacks we present in this paper are patched, the collusion attack remains. In this section, we demonstrate that Isdal et al. incorrectly calculate the chance of this attack in two ways. First, they overestimate the success of the attack by assuming attackers are chosen with replacement. Second, they underestimate the quick ramp up of the attack's success as the number of attackers grows. The collusion attack is significantly easier in OneSwarm than in OR. For example, we show the chances of success reach near 100% when attackers comprise 25% of the network, whereas success for OR would remain below 10%.

5.1 The Collusion Attack

As described in Section 2, if a peer receives a query and does not have the requested file, it forwards the query to only a subset of its neighbors. This subset is chosen based upon a forwarding probability p.[1] The decision to forward is decided independently for each piece of unique content and each neighbor and remains consistent.

The collusion attack is illustrated in Fig. 4. A set of k colluding attackers labeled $C_1, \ldots, C_k$ are directly connected to a target peer. When C_1 issues a query to target T that has the requested file, T does not forward the query on to its neighbors. Instead it sends back a reply after a randomly chosen delay. Therefore, if none of the other $k-1$ colluding attackers receive the query from T, there is a non-negligible probability that T may be sharing the file requested by C_1. This probability, which we call the attack's *precision*, is greater when k is larger. For law enforcement, higher precision better justifies having sufficient probable cause, as we discuss in Section 3.

Isdal et al. calculate that with $p = 0.5$, achieving 95% precision requires that at least $k = 6$ attackers (a querier and 5 colluders) to be directly connected to the target. The chance that a target that is not a source will forward the query to at least one of the $k-1$ colluders is [8]

$$1 - (1-p)^{k-1} \tag{18}$$

For example, we have $1-(1-0.5)^5 = 97\%$ (which is greater than 95%). Isdal et al. state the chances that 6 or more colluders are attached to a particular peer when $C = 30$ of the $N = 1000$ peers are attackers is "much less than 1%" and "given by the binomial CDF" [8]. While they don't state a formula, to use the binomial, we let A be a random variable

[1]Here $p = 1 - p_f$, where p_f is Isdal et al.'s notation for the probability of *not* forwarding a query.

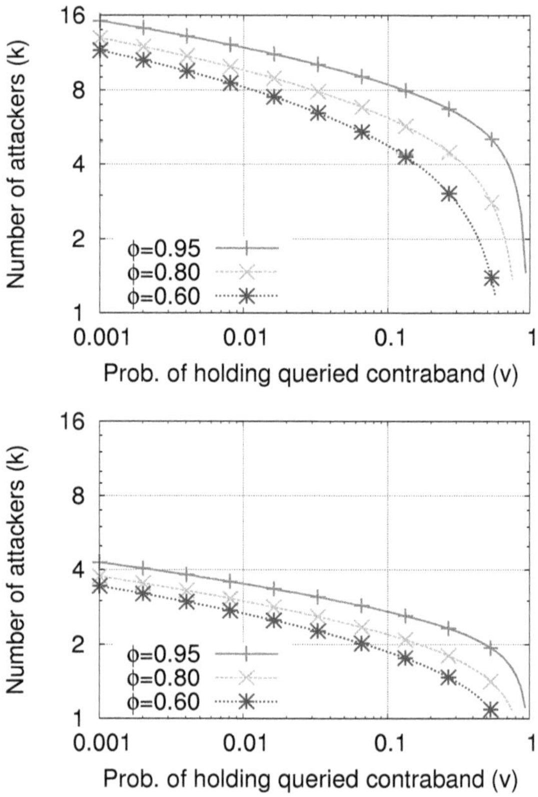

Figure 5: (top) For a fixed probability of forwarding $p = 0.5$ (the value suggested in the paper), the plot shows the required attackers k given the the popularity of content q from Eq. 23. Each line is a different precision require ϕ; (bottom) The same plot for fixed probability of forwarding $p = 0.95$ (the value hardcoded in software) again from Eq. 23. Both graphs use logscales.

that denotes the number of attackers assigned to a target. For N peers of which C are attackers, each with 26 neighbors, we have

$$P\{A \geq k\} = \sum_{i=k}^{26} \binom{26}{i} (\frac{C}{N})^i (1 - \frac{C}{N})^{26-i} \tag{19}$$

Unfortunately, the binomial is not entirely accurate, and the statement "much less than 1%" does not give a complete picture.

5.2 Re-Deriving the Attack

We re-derive the attack effectiveness with several changes. First, because community servers select neighbors for peers *without* replacement, the hypergeometric CDF is the correct model. Second, the paper states peers have 26 neighbors, but in the code, peers have at least 22 but up to 39 untrusted neighbors. We let U be the number of untrusted neighbors of a peer.

$$P\{A \geq k\} = \sum_{i=k}^{U} \frac{\binom{C}{i}\binom{N-C}{U-i}}{\binom{N}{U}} \tag{20}$$

Therefore, we have in the worst case that $U = 39$ for Eq. 20.

In the best case, $U = 0$. In reality, for each trusted neighbor, there is a probability that it is an undercover investigator, but it is not a scenario that we evaluate here.

The next step is to determine the value of k that defeats OneSwarm, and we do not use Eq. 18. Instead, we let X denote the event that the target T has content that was searched for, and let Y denote the event that none of the $k-1$ colluders were forwarded the search query issued by C_1. From Bayes' Theorem, we can define the precision of the collusion attack as

$$P(X|Y) = \frac{P(Y|X)P(X)}{P(Y|X)P(X) + P(Y|\bar{X})P(\bar{X})} \quad (21)$$

We know that $P(Y|X) = 1$ because given that T has the content, the $k-1$ colluders will not be forwarded the search query. In general, not every peer will have the files of interest that the attacker queries for; to model this situation simply, we let $P(X) = v$, where $0 \leq v \leq 1$ interpreted as the popularity of some file of interest being queried. We know that $P(Y|\bar{X}) = (1-p)^{k-1}$. Finally, we let $\phi = P(X|Y)$, and substituting we have

$$\phi = \frac{v}{v + (1-v)(1-p)^{k-1}} \quad (22)$$

Solving for k we get

$$k = 1 + \frac{\log\left(\left(\frac{v}{1-v}\right)\left(\frac{1-\phi}{\phi}\right)\right)}{\log(1-p)} \quad (23)$$

Fig. 5(top) plots Eq. 23 for $p = 0.5$ (the value suggested in the paper) showing the minimum k value required for different precision levels and v as an independent variable. Fig. 5(bottom) shows the same equation for $p = 0.95$ (the value hardcoded in software). Each plot shows three lines corresponding to precision values of 95%, 80%, and 60%. The first is the value used in Isdal et al., the second is conservative for probable cause, and the last is weak evidence for probable cause. (Note that the value of k is independent of U.)

For example, for $p = 0.5, v = 0.1$, and $\phi = 0.95$, then the attack requires $k = 8$ attackers (rather than 6); however, the more important point is that the value of k varies quite a bit with v. Roughly, as content is an order of magnitude more popular, k typically halves in size. Comparison of the two plots makes the obvious point that p also has a strong influence on k. Releasing the software with a higher value for p than documented in the paper reduced the required number of attackers by 60–75% in all cases. Finally, when $p = 0.95$, the plots demonstrate that values of $k \geq 4$ are definitely sufficient for probable cause for content that is sourced at only one in a thousand peers.

The *false positive rate* for the collusion attack is the probability that the target does not forward the query to any of the colluding attackers given that it is not the source of the file of interest:

$$FPR = (1-p)^{k-1} \quad (24)$$

This quantity is less than 0.0025 for $k \geq 3$ and $p = 0.95$. Thus investigators are at a very low risk of falsely suspecting any peer in OneSwarm as deployed. When $p = 0.5$ the false positive rate is less than 1.6% only when $k \geq 7$; note that for files less popular than $v \leq 0.06$, the same bound of $k \geq 7$ holds for precision values of 95% (see Fig. 5(top)) and so the requirement of a low FPR is not an significant issue for the investigator. Querying for multiple files of interest will affect the FPR, as we discuss in Section 5.3.

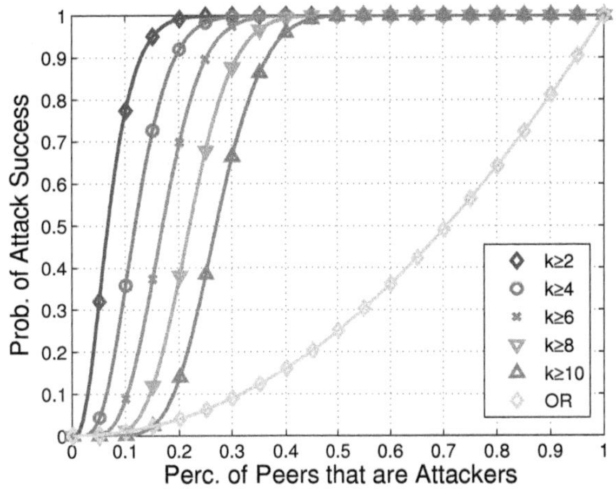

Figure 6: Plots of collusion attack success (Eq. 20 where $U = 39$) and first-and-last attack against OR (Eq. 25): The probability of success for the collusion attack on OneSwarm for a given required minimum value of k. The plot also shows the comparable attack success against OR (first and last peers on a circuit).

Comparison Against Onion Routing. Isdal et al. do not quantitatively compare OneSwarm directly against any other privacy mechanism. As a basic comparison we analyze the following simple OR attack. Peers hiding behind a OR circuit can be deanonymized if attackers are selected at random to be in the first and last positions. Selection of these nodes occurs without replacement. Once in these positions, attackers can use a well-known attack of sending a specific sequence of duplicate packets to determine if they are on the same path [20], essentially with a precision of 1 and FPR of 0. Therefore, the chances of a circuit being compromised in a OR network of N peers where C are attackers is

$$P\{A = 2\} = \left(\tfrac{C}{N}\right)\left(\tfrac{C-1}{N-1}\right). \quad (25)$$

Mechanisms such as *guard nodes* [26,27] can make this attack on OR more difficult. However, in general the simplicity of the model in Eq. 25 prevents us from comparing OneSwarm to Tor directly, instead of Onion Routing.

We use this passive attack because it's a tractable, conceptually simple presentation of the collusion attack on the OR architecture, allowing a straightforward comparison with OneSwarm's architecture. A more accurate model would consider the active attacks that are available against Tor, which are more effective than Eq. 25. This would require updating Bauer et al. [1] with the latest Tor path selection algorithm and measurements of Tor, to model weighted path selection. It wouldn't change our analysis of OneSwarm, and we expect it wouldn't change the relative comparison, barring a gross bias in the Tor route selection algorithm.

Fig. 6 compares effectiveness of these attacks against OneSwarm and OR. The plot is independent of a chosen value for p; to determine the required value of k, we first choose a value of p and consult Fig. 5(top or bottom). There are a number of implications to note. First, there is a non-linear, sharp increase in attacker success as they increase their proportion of the OneSwarm network. When the attack requires only that $k \geq 4$, the chances of success are 98% as attackers comprise 25% of peers in the network. Note that $k \geq 4$ is sufficient for even unpopular content when $p = 0.95$, which is the hard coded value in the released software. However, even if $p = 0.5$, requiring larger values of k, the effectiveness of the attack on OneSwarm grows far more quickly than the simple attack on OR.

All of the previous analysis assumes that the attackers join the network once. As such, they can only investigate peers to whom they've attached sufficient colluders. But attackers can repeatedly quit and rejoin the system with new identities, thereby investigating more and more peers over time. OneSwarm offers no Sybil attack protections.

Trusted Neighbors. Our attacks are worst case in that we assume the peer has 39 neighbors. To give a point of comparison, if the node has only $U = 20$ neighbors from the community server (and 19 trusted friends) then the investigator's job is harder. For example, the $k \geq 4$ line in Fig. 6 shifts roughly to almost where $k \geq 8$ is in the figure; these values can be compared more directly by re-plotting Eq. 20. Again, attackers can execute this attack as many times as necessary — churn in the OneSwarm population will force the community server to assign and re-assign new untrusted relationships.

5.3 Practical Considerations

The Multiple Comparison Problem. A naive version of the collusion attack would see investigators joining the network as described above. The investigator would then test each connected peer for possession of all known files of interest, and claim probable cause for each peer which was determined to have at least one file. This naive version is susceptible to the well-known *multiple comparison problem* of testing sets of hypothesis at once. We elide the analysis here, but we note the false positive rate quickly grows unusably high as the number of files tested per peer increases.

There are several ways to limit the effect of this problem, each of which centers around limiting the number of different files investigators check a peer for possession of. One such method is as follows. First, investigators survey the network for files of interest by searching for well-known keywords. In other p2p networks such as Gnutella and eDonkey2000, these files are typically named with explicit and descriptive names; our law enforcement partners confirm the same appears to be true of OneSwarm. The files are rank ordered by their apparent popularity in the system. Investigators then sweep through the network by performing the collusion attack for the top n files, where n is chosen to keep the FPR acceptably low. Only once these peers have been fully investigated, including offline searches and the subsequent legal process, do investigators repeat their survey to determine the next rank-ordered list to investigate.

Post-Warrant Confirmation. OneSwarm peers connect to one another using SSL bootstrapped by their RSA key pairs. A OneSwarm peer stores keys of neighbors and its own key on the local file system. Once a search warrant is executed and a machine seized, the investigator can tie that machine to specific network traffic based on the recovered key file. Even if the content has been deleted locally, the mechanism can confirm with cryptographic precision if this machine is the machine that transferred it. BitTorrent clients are subject to *forensic tagging* [12], in which investigators covertly ask remote machines to store nonces. These nonces can later be recovered to confirm that the correct machine was seized. However, OneSwarm makes this task redundant since all outgoing traffic is signed and the keys are stored persistently.

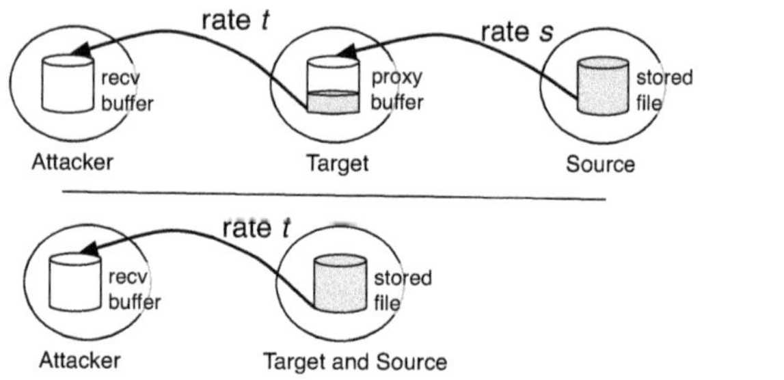

Figure 7: An attacker distinguishes two scenarios. In the first, the target is a proxy for the real source of a file. The goal is to increase the rate of transfer, t, from the target so that it is greater than the rate of transfer from the source, s. The buffer at the proxy should empty before the transfer is completed. In the second case, the target is the source, and therefore, for any value of t, the transfer should complete.

6. TCP-BASED ATTACKS

In this section, we demonstrate a novel adaptation of a known TCP-based attack [18] that can identify whether a OneSwarm peer is the source of data or a proxy. Peers that do not rate limit outgoing traffic are vulnerable. OneSwarm happens to turn on rate limiting by default to 80% of a test transfer to a central server, but nothing prevents eager users from turning off the rate limiting. A more robust defense without rate limiting is to probabilistically drop outgoing packets and audit incoming selective acks. In this section, we detail the attack and its limitations, show experimental results for a simplified implementation of the attack executed on a simple non-OneSwarm transfer, and we discuss defenses to the attack.

The attack leverages *optimistic acking* [18], where a receiver sends TCP acknowledgements for data before it is received, increasing throughput. Sherwood et al. [19] leverage the same mechanism to perform denial-of-service attacks against a server. Our contribution is in showing that the same mechanisms can be used to distinguish proxies from sources. The attack is not specific to OneSwarm; anonymous file-sharing protocol designers should be aware of the attack.

Fig. 7 illustrates our TCP attack scenario. An attacker requests a file from a target. The attacker induces a higher-bandwidth connection between itself and target than between the target and a potential source of data. If t can be made greater than any potential s and the target is not the source, it will stall out. The stall occurs because the target's application level buffers will run out before the actual source can fill them. Our tests show that it is possible to induce a sending rate that is higher than is typical even between nodes within the same building.

In our tests, we show that the attack can succeed in practice. In sum, OneSwarm is vulnerable (when rate-limiting is

Algorithm 6.1: DETECTPROXY(*maxExtra*, *rate*)

```
local p, ack, extra, lastReceived, maxReceived
while (download is not complete)
  do {
    p = RECEIVEPKT(timeoutValue)
    if timeout occurred
      then {
        ack = lastReceived
        extra = 0
        if too many timeouts
          then return ("proxy")
      }
      else {
        lastReceived = SEQNUM(p)
        if SEQNUM(p) > maxReceived
          then maxReceived = SEQNUM(p)
        extra += rate
        extra = MIN(extra, maxExtra)
        ack = maxReceived + extra
      }
    SENDACK(ack)
  }
return ("sender")
```

off) because it defends against only application-level timing and traffic attacks, and does not defend against an attacker breaking the underlying network abstraction.

Trusted Peers. When a peer has trusted peers (that are not undercover investigators), they reduce the chances that an investigator has an opportunity to execute the TCP attack, but do not affect the success of the attack itself. Vulnerable peers are those that have at least one untrusted relationship to an investigator; i.e., set $k = 1$ in Eq. 20.

6.1 Attack Details

We assume that targets of the attack follow TCP specifications properly, but we place no limit on the connection bandwidth between peers. The attacker does not follow TCP rules for receivers, by incorrectly acking packets that were lost and optimistically acking packets that have not yet been received. The receiver also always advertises a large TCP flow control window so as not to inhibit the sender.

The idealized attack algorithm is presented as pseudocode in Algorithm 6.1. The pseudocode assumes a TCP connection has been set up and a download requested via application-level messaging. The input to the algorithm is the rate at which the optimistic acking increases and the maximum value it can reach. Reasonable values can be found through heuristic hill-climbing.

Whenever a packet is received, the attacker sends an ack for the highest sequence number ever received from the sender, regardless of whether earlier bytes in the TCP flow were lost. Because acks are cumulative in TCP, the skipped over byte sequences are not a concern of the sender. Additionally, the receiver optimistically acks *extra* segments it has yet to receive but are likely on the way. The value of *extra* starts at 0 and the receiver increases it by *rate* bytes (and rounded to segment sizes) for each packet received, regardless of loss or duplication, until a given *maxExtra* value is reached.

The reason to grow this optimistic acking slowly is that the sender will silently drop acks for packets beyond what it has sent. If a sender receives overly optimistic acks, it will not close the connection, as TCP was designed to manage the occasional odd error. Accordingly, thoughtless optimistic acking by the attacker will have no effect, and the attacker must grow the window commensurately with the sender's values. As the window grows, heavy packet loss will occur, and the attack is partly blind in that sense.

If attacker grows the sender's window too aggressively, the RTT calculation at the sender can become mis-estimated as a very small duration, making a timeout exceedingly easy. When a timeout occurs, the sender will back off, cutting the rate drastically, and will resend old data, which is very bad for the attack. Therefore, if the receiver doesn't receive data by some timeout (250ms in our implementation), an ack packet is sent to the sender for the *latest* packet received, rather than the highest received. In our tests, this quickly re-initiates the data flow, and the attacker can return to acking the highest byte sent.

Pipelining. OneSwarm is BitTorrent based, and therefore requests for a file are piecewise. There are seven BitTorrent piece sizes in common use, and the most common are 256kB, 512kB, and 1MB. Our tests show that for the two smaller size, the sender barely gets out of slow start before the attack is complete. Inside of slow start, the congestion window is so small that the attack cannot achieve significant gains. However, pipelining of piece requests has been a feature since the protocol was introduced in 2003 to avoid reseting TCP's bandwidth algorithm and causing "disastrous" transfer rates [4]; this pipelining prevents the attack from stalling.

6.2 Attack Experimentation

We implemented the attack in about 700 lines of C++ to test its feasibility. The attack implementation and details of our measurement experiments (including packet header logs) are available from `http://traces.cs.umass.edu`. Our prototype implementation attacks the HTTP protocol rather than the BitTorrent protocol, as HTTP has fewer implementation details to manage. In principle, the same attack will work on pipelined BitTorrent requests. Further, our implementation does not implement the SSL handshake between peers that OneSwarm requires.

Methodology. We configured a network as shown in Fig. 7. We could not use PlanetLab for this experiment since it enforces a bandwidth cap, which is splits among all virtual hosts on each node [13]. The attacking machines were located at UMass, Wesleyan (CT), and UT Arlington (TX); the targets were a superset of the attacking machines and also included UCSB (CA); and the proxied sources at Central Michigan University, Harvey Mudd College (CA) and Mojohost, Inc. (FL). We chose these proxies to model relatively close (UCSB and HMC are both in CA) and distant (UCSB to Mojohost crosses the country) peers. We served the file directly through an httpd daemon from the targets, and we used netcat to act as an application-level proxy to the other sources. Our target file was a 10MB ISO image. We used wget as the well-behaved requester. We fixed the parameters of our attack implementation at relatively conservative values. We set the *maxExtra* value to 50 TCP segments for all connections, though in our experience this value should vary per bandwidth of the connection to the target. We report the bandwidth speedup of the attack, rather than seeking a *maxExtra* value that causes a timeout (as per Alg. 6.1). We ran measurement experiments across all paths (27 in total), varying type of retrieval (wget or tcp attack) and potential source (direct from UCSB, or proxied to either HMC or Mojohost). Each measurement was repeated five times.

Path			Target Possesses File		Target Proxies File	
Attacker	Target	Proxied Source	wget	attack (relative)	wget	attack (relative)
Wesleyan	UCSB	CMich	1.29 MB/s	*	686 KB/s	*
		HMC	1.25 MB/s	*	646 KB/s	*
		Mojohost	686 KB/s	*	714 KB/s	*
	UMass	CMich	3.66 MB/s	1.43	1.09 MB/s	*
		HMC	3.56 MB/s	1.96	1.04 MB/s	*
		Mojohost	3.57 MB/s	1.44	933 KB/s	*
	UTA	CMich	350 kB/s	1.90	311 KB/s	1.07
		HMC	385 KB/s	1.46	329 KB/s	1.05
		Mojohost	344 KB/s	1.26	304 KB/s	1.21
UMass	Wesleyan	CMich	281 KB/s	13.5	274 KB/s	4.42
		HMC	277 KB/s	13.6	292 KB/s	3.94
		Mojohost	270 KB/s	14.0	280 KB/s	3.74
	UCSB	CMich	446 KB/s	2.84	407 KB/s	1.75
		HMC	413 KB/s	3.13	475 KB/s	1.48
		Mojohost	402 KB/s	3.12	342 KB/s	2.06
	UTA	CMich	158 KB/s	10.4	168 KB/s	8.48
		HMC	183 KB/s	10.2	178 KB/s	7.95
		Mojohost	200 KB/s	8.76	209 KB/s	7.15
UTA	Wesleyan	CMich	94.7 KB/s	16.8	117 KB/s	11.3
		HMC	86.6 KB/s	19.2	115 KB/s	11.2
		Mojohost	93.7 KB/s	18.0	116 KB/s	12.2
	UCSB	CMich	1.61 MB/s	0.861	681 KB/s	0.976
		HMC	1.69 MB/s	0.793	659 KB/s	1.01
		Mojohost	1.41 MB/s	0.903	707 KB/s	0.920
	UMass	CMich	2.02 MB/s	0.750	1.25 MB/s	0.850
		HMC	3.58 MB/s	0.458	1.04 MB/s	1.02
		Mojohost	1.98 MB/s	0.678	1.03 MB/s	1.05

Table 1: Results of experiments that test our implementation of the TCP-based attack. Reading left-to-right, the first three columns denote a path, corresponding to the setup in Fig 7. The next pair of columns show, for the case where the target possesses the file, the mean throughput of the well-behaved downloader across five runs, and the relative mean throughput of the attack (for example, a value of 2.0 indicates the attack had twice the throughput of wget). The final pair of columns show the mean throughputs for the case where the target is proxying the file. The attack succeeds when the speedup for a possessed file is greater than the speedup of a proxied file (including timeouts). An asterisk indicates that all measurements timed out.

Results. Our results, shown in Table 1, show that the attack can differentiate between files served directly by the target, and files proxied by the target. Among all files made available by the target, those served at the highest rate are possessed by the target; those served at lower rates (or that result in timeouts) are proxied from a different source. The attack succeeds when the relative speedup of the attack (versus wget) is higher when the target is the source compared to when the target is the proxy; this is true in most cases even though *maxExtra* is fixed. While preliminary, these results indicate that the attack can succeed in practice, though we do not estimate error rates for this attack in general given these limited tests.

Limitations. We note that the attack depends upon the attacker being able to force the target to serve files faster than they can be retrieved from potential sources when proxied. This assumption does not always hold. The attacker could have poor connectivity to the target; this is easily detected in advance, and attackers can acquire high-bandwidth connections. Less avoidably, there could be rate limiting or traffic shaping in place, or the target, acting as a proxy, may have an extremely high bandwidth connection to the true source. In the latter case, the machines may be co-located, which is acceptable for a search warrant, or the owner of the machine may choose to cooperate with law enforcement in investigation of a crime. This type of cooperation is typical in practice, such as when investigations of non-anonymous systems lead to an innocent owner of an open Wi-Fi base station whose neighbor is using the connection illicitly.

Defenses. To detect this attack, nodes can purposefully drop outgoing packets from their TCP stream and determine if the remote peer requests the missing data or acknowledges receiving it. There is a patch[2] to an old version of the Linux kernel that addresses this vulnerability, but any such fix results in a non-standard TCP implementation and is unlikely to be deployed on a wide scale. To defend against the attack without detecting it, OneSwarm can force a bandwidth cap on peers that can't be turned off, which isn't done currently. Since OneSwarm is an open source project, investigators will know if and when such defenses are deployed.

7. CONCLUSIONS

OneSwarm is in use by thousands of peers and is of interest to criminal and civil investigators. We have detailed three attacks on the system that are available for use by investigators using only *plain view* data. We have quantified the

[2]See `https://www.kb.cert.org/vuls/id/102014`.

precision and error rates of two of these attacks so that they are applicable in legal context. Each attack can be repeated for increased success when investigators leave and re-join the network, exposing a different set of peers.

Our novel *timing attack* is successful with only two attackers as we show by proof and experimentation with the released software on a small network. We have described a defense and shown that it places delays on OneSwarm querying that is slower than the use of Onion Routing. We have re-analyzed the collusion attack, showing the vulnerability is much greater than was previously reported, and is much worse than OR's. Our revised model accounts for probabilistic forwarding, content popularity, precision, and details from OneSwarm's source code. We show for this second attack that when investigators comprise just 25% of peers, over 40% of the network can be investigated with 80% precision to find sources of content that is not popular. For the implementation in use by thousands of people, attackers that comprise 25% of the network can successfully use this second attack against 98% of remaining peers with 95% precision. Finally, we show that OneSwarm is vulnerable to a novel application of a known TCP-based attack, which allows a single attacker to identify whether a neighbor is the source of data or a proxy for it. An implementation of the attack succeeds given that the attacker's traffic is not shaped by third-party routers. Only users that turn off the default rate limit setting are exposed.

We provided the details of our attacks and results to the OneSwarm developers in May 2011. In August 2011, they reported that the following changes to OneSwarm have been made: the default value of p is set to 0.5, unintended forwarding latency has been decreased from about 100ms to less than 10ms, and the discrepancy between text search and hash search delays have been fixed.

Acknowledgements. This work was supported in part by NSF award CNS-1018615. We thank Cpl. Robert Erdely of the Pennsylvania State Police for verifying the presence of images of child sexual exploitation on OneSwarm. We thank Elizabeth Belding, Norman Danner, Danny Krizanc, Clay Shields, and Matthew Wright for providing resources for our TCP experiments. We thank Robert Walls and Brian Lynn for their insightful comments on the work.

8. REFERENCES

[1] K. Bauer, D. McCoy, D. Grunwald, T. Kohno, and D. Sicker. Low-Resource Routing Attacks Against Tor. In *Proc. ACM WPES*, pages 11–20, 2007.

[2] S. Brenner, B. Carrier, and J. Henninger. The Trojan Horse Defense in Cybercrime Cases. *Santa Clara Computer and High Technology Law Journal*, 21(1), 2004.

[3] J. Chu, K. Labonte, and B. N. Levine. Availability and Locality Measurements of Peer-to-Peer File Systems. In *Proc. ITCom: Scalability and Traffic Control in IP Networks II Conference*, volume SPIE 4868, pages 310–321, July 2002.

[4] B. Cohen. Incentives Build Robustness in BitTorrent. In *International Workshop on Peer-to-Peer Systems (IPTPS)*, Berkeley, CA, February 2003.

[5] L. Denoyer and M. Latapy. Measurement and Analysis of P2P Activity Against Paedophile. *Journée Données et Apprentissage Artificiel (DAPA)*, March 2009.

[6] R. Dingledine, N. Mathewson, and P. Syverson. Tor: The Second-Generation Onion Router. In *Proc. USENIX Security Symposium*, August 2004.

[7] R. Geambasu, T. Kohno, A. Levy, and H. M. Levy. Vanish: Increasing Data Privacy with Self-Destructing Data. In *Proc. USENIX Security Symposium*, 2009.

[8] T. Isdal, M. Piatek, A. Krishnamurthy, and T. Anderson. Privacy-preserving P2P data sharing with OneSwarm. In *Proc. ACM SIGCOMM*, pages 111–122, August 2010.

[9] T. Isdal, M. Piatek, A. Krishnamurthy, and T. Anderson. Privacy-preserving P2P data sharing with OneSwarm. Technical report, Dept. CS and Eng., Univ. of Washington, 2010. `http://oneswarm.cs.washington.edu/f2f_tr.pdf`.

[10] M. Latapy, C. Magnien, and R. Fournier. Quantifying paedophile activity in a large P2P system. In *IEEE Infocom Mini-Conference*. `http://antipaedo.lip6.fr`, April 2011.

[11] M. Liberatore, R. Erdely, T. Kerle, B. N. Levine, and C. Shields. Forensic Investigation of Peer-to-Peer File Sharing Networks. In *Proc. DFRWS Annual Digital Forensics Research Conference*, August 2010.

[12] M. Liberatore, B. N. Levine, and C. Shields. Strengthening Forensic Investigations of Child Pornography on P2P Networks. In *Proc. ACM Conference on Future Networking Technologies (CoNEXT)*, November 2010.

[13] L. Peterson, A. Bavier, M. E. Fiuczynski, and S. Muir. Experiences building PlanetLab. In *Proc. USENIX OSDI*, pages 351–366, 2006.

[14] M. Piatek, T. Kohno, and A. Krishnamurthy. Challenges and directions for monitoring P2P file sharing networks. In *Proc. USENIX Hot Topics in Security (HotSec)*, pages 12:1–12:7, July 2008.

[15] M. Ripeanu, I. Foster, and A. Iamnitchi. Mapping the Gnutella Network. *IEEE Internet Computing Journal*, 6(1):50–57, 2002.

[16] J. Rorher. MUTE. `http://mute-net.sourceforge.net`.

[17] RShare. `http://www.stealthnet.de/en\_index.php` and `http://www.planetpeer.de/wiki/index.php/RShare\_documentation\_\%28English\%29`.

[18] S. Savage, N. Cardwell, D. Wetherall, and T. Anderson. TCP congestion control with a misbehaving receiver. In *Proc. ACM SIGCOMM*, pages 71–78, October 1999.

[19] R. Sherwood, B. Bhattacharjee, and R. Braud. Misbehaving TCP receivers can cause Internet-wide congestion collapse. In *Proc. ACM CCS*, pages 383–392, Oct. 2005.

[20] P. Syverson, G. Tsudik, M. Reed, and C. Landwehr. Towards an Analysis of Onion Routing Security. In *Intl. Wkshp. on Designing Privacy Enhancing Technologies*, pages 96–114, July 2000.

[21] U.S. Dept. of Justice. National Strategy for Child Exploitation Prevention and Interdiction: A Report to Congress. `http://www.projectsafechildhood.gov/docs/natstrategyreport.pdf`, August 2010.

[22] U.S. General Accounting Office. File-Sharing Programs. Child Pornography Is Readily Accessible over Peer-to-Peer Networks. GAO-03-537T. Statement Before Congress; Linda D. Koontz, Information Management Issues, March 2003.

[23] U.S. Government. Federal Rules of Evidence. Rule 401. `http://www.law.cornell.edu/rules/fre/rules.htm`.

[24] R. J. Walls, B. N. Levine, M. Liberatore, and C. Shields. Effective Digital Forensics Research is Investigator-Centric. In *Proc. USENIX Workshop on Hot Topics in Security (HotSec)*, August 2011.

[25] S. Wolchok, O. Hofmann, N. Heninger, E. Felten, J. Halderman, C. Rossbach, B. Waters, and E. Witchel. Defeating Vanish with Low-Cost Sybil Attacks Against Large DHTs. In *Proc. ISOC Symposium Network and Distributed System Security (NDSS)*, February 2010.

[26] M. Wright, M. Adler, B. N. Levine, and C. Shields. An Analysis of the Degradation of Anonymous Protocols. In *Proc. ISOC Symposium Network and Distributed System Security (NDSS)*, pages 38–50, February 2002.

[27] M. Wright, M. Adler, B. N. Levine, and C. Shields. Defending Anonymous Communication Against Passive Logging Attacks. In *Proc. IEEE Symposium on Security & Privacy*, pages 28–41, May 2003.

Stealthy Traffic Analysis of Low-Latency Anonymous Communication Using Throughput Fingerprinting

Prateek Mittal, Ahmed Khurshid, Joshua Juen, Matthew Caesar, Nikita Borisov
University of Illinois at Urbana-Champaign
{mittal2, khurshi1, juen1, caesar, nikita}@illinois.edu

ABSTRACT

Anonymity systems such as Tor aim to enable users to communicate in a manner that is untraceable by adversaries that control a small number of machines. To provide efficient service to users, these anonymity systems make full use of forwarding capacity when sending traffic between intermediate relays. In this paper, we show that doing this leaks information about the set of Tor relays in a circuit (path). We present attacks that, with high confidence and based solely on throughput information, can (a) reduce the attacker's uncertainty about the bottleneck relay of any Tor circuit whose throughput can be observed, (b) exactly identify the guard relay(s) of a Tor user when circuit throughput can be observed over multiple connections, and (c) identify whether two concurrent TCP connections belong to the same Tor user, breaking unlinkability. Our attacks are stealthy, and cannot be readily detected by a user or by Tor relays. We validate our attacks using experiments over the live Tor network. We find that the attacker can substantially reduce the entropy of a bottleneck relay distribution of a Tor circuit whose throughput can be observed—the entropy gets reduced by a factor of 2 in the median case. Such information leaks from a single Tor circuit can be combined over multiple connections to exactly identify a user's guard relay(s). Finally, we are also able to link two connections from the same initiator with a crossover error rate of less than 1.5% in under 5 minutes. Our attacks are also more accurate and require fewer resources than previous attacks on Tor.

Categories and Subject Descriptors

C.2.0 [**Computer-Communication Networks**]: General—*Security and protection*

General Terms

Security, Measurement

Keywords

Anonymity, attacks, throughput

1. INTRODUCTION

With the advent of sophisticated monitoring technologies [2,3] coupled with coordination within governments and across businesses to exchange and mine information, communication on the Internet is increasingly becoming less private. At the same time, advancing use and pervasiveness of networks have increased the danger of misuse of that information, leading to potential invasions of user privacy, and fear of retribution against whistleblowers, unofficial leaks, and political activists. To counter this threat, *anonymous communication systems* such as Babel [22], Mixmaster [36], and Mixminion [14] improve anonymity by routing communication through an overlay network that masks identities of the endpoints. However, these systems work by introducing large and variable latencies between the endpoints, making them unsuitable for interactive applications. To fill this need, low-latency anonymous communication services like AN.ON [9], Onion Routing [47], Freedom [6], I2P [28] and Tor [16] were developed, which forward packets directly over low-delay circuits. Tor has achieved great success, servicing hundreds of thousands of users and carrying terabytes of traffic daily [48], and is currently being used as a crucial service by end users, government activists, journalists, as well as protecting business and military communications [49].

Low-latency anonymous communication networks are more vulnerable to a global passive adversary than other high-latency communication designs [12, 13, 36] because timing attacks can be used to link relayed copies of a communication stream [46]. Most users, however, are concerned about less powerful, *partial* adversaries who can observe (or even compromise) only a fraction of the network. A typical goal for low-latency systems is to ensure that an adversary who observes or controls a fraction f of the network can compromise the anonymity of f^2 of the flows. The hope is that making f large would require a high resource expenditure, especially as networks grow large (e.g., the Tor network had more than 2 000 active relays with an aggregate bandwidth of 4 Gbps as of May 2011[1]).

Further research has demonstrated that it is not, in fact, necessary to directly observe the network to learn where a flow is being forwarded. Instead, probes can be used to test a flow's presence at a particular location in the network by creating an observable interference pattern [11,19,38], or by

[1] `http://torstatus.blutmagie.de/`

otherwise correlating characteristics seen in the anonymous flow with a particular location [25]. In order to fully understand the risks of using a given anonymity network, it is necessary to understand what types of attacks of this class are possible and what resources are required for a certain probability of success. Such understanding will let users make informed security decisions; for example, a "low-resource" congestion attack on the Tor network originally proposed by Murdoch and Danezis in 2005 [38] is no longer considered practical for the current size of the network without new techniques to improve its scalability [19]. Users may also find comfort in the fact that the state-of-the-art attacks could be detected by Tor clients and relays, as they require the insertion of interference patterns or malicious content in flows.

In contrast, we examine a new collection of *stealthy* attacks on the Tor network that are based on detailed observations of the *throughput* of an anonymous flow. We called our attacks stealthy because, although they sometimes perform active *measurements*, they do so by acting as completely ordinary Tor clients, and therefore Tor users and relays cannot reliably detect that an attack is in progress. We observe that the throughput of a Tor flow can be used as a fingerprint of the bottleneck relay (i.e., the relay with minimal forwarding capacity in the flow path) used to forward it. By observing the dynamics of the throughput, it is also possible to identify when two flows share the same set (or subset) of relays. We note that in contrast to prior work, our attacks do not require the adversary to insert interference patterns or other malicious content in flows, and are thus not observable by a user/relay. We also perform a detailed study of how the throughput of the anonymous flow is influenced by scheduling, flow-control, and congestion-control algorithms at both the transport (i.e., TCP) and application (i.e., Tor) layer. We use the effects of these algorithms to design a passive attack that can show whether two flows share the same circuit and thus originate from the same user. To the best of our knowledge, this is the first study of flow throughput based attacks on Tor. Overall, our study demonstrates attacks that use threat models and resource requirements that differ significantly from attacks using other flow features. It also highlights the complexity of designing anonymous communication systems by demonstrating the impact that architectural and implementation decisions can have on the security of the system.

1.1 Overview of Attacks

Information leakage via circuit throughput: We show that it is possible to exploit heterogeneity of throughput of Tor relays to learn information about which relays used to forward a given stream. In particular, two circuits that share the same bottleneck relay will have highly correlated throughput. Thus, by forming one-hop probe circuits through all of the Tor relays, it is possible to gain some (probabilistic) information about the bottleneck relay of any Tor stream whose throughput can be observed. This observation also reveals some information about other relays forwarding the stream, since their observed one-hop throughput must be higher than the bottleneck. We performed our attacks on a subset of the live Tor network, and found that we were able to effectively reduce the entropy of the bottleneck relay distribution. Using this information, we were able to uncover the identities of the guard relay (the first relay in the path) over multiple connection attempts. We note that while learning a user's relays is not sufficient by itself to compromise the user identity in Tor, our attacks serve as a stepping stone for completely de-anonymizing the user; for example, several attacks in the literature rely on a user's guard relays being known to the adversary [11,24,25]. We also show that our attacks can also be applied to de-anonymize location hidden services that act as Tor relays.

Stream linkability attack: We show that throughput characteristics of two streams that are multiplexed over the same circuit have a unique characteristic: throughput of each stream repeatedly drops to zero during mutually exclusive periods of time, leading to a strong negative correlation. Thus if a client is communicating over Tor with two servers simultaneously, and if the servers collude, then they can reliably infer that they are communicating with the same client. Our experimental results indicate that after roughly 5 minutes of observations the attacker could reliably (with a crossover error rate of less than 1.5%) identify if the streams have been multiplexed over a common circuit. This is a significant improvement of the latency-based stream linking attack by Hopper et al. [24], which had a crossover error rate of 17% and required malicious content to be inserted into web pages.

We have validated all of our attacks using experiments over the live Tor network. Our source code and analysis scripts are available at our project webpage [1].

Roadmap. The rest of the paper is organized as follows. We present an overview of low-latency anonymity systems and discuss related attacks in Section 2. In Section 3 we show that there is a high degree of heterogeneity in observed circuit throughput in the Tor network, and that circuit throughput can be used to reduce the entropy of the corresponding Tor relays. We also present several *statistical disclosure attacks* based on information leakage from circuit throughput to uncover the identities of guard relays and relays that offer location-hidden services. We present our passive stream linkability attack in Section 4. Finally, we discuss the implications of our attacks in Section 5 and conclude in Section 6.

2. BACKGROUND AND RELATED WORK

We start by discussing work on designing low-latency anonymous communication systems. We then describe three key attacks on these systems: side channel attacks, latency attacks, and long-term attacks.

2.1 Tor Background

Tor [16] is a popular low-latency anonymous communication system. Deployed in 2003, Tor now serves hundreds of thousands of users and carries terabytes of traffic daily. As of May 2011, the network comprises more than 2 000 relays.[1] Users (clients) download a list of relays from central directory authorities and build anonymous paths (called *circuits*) using onion routing [46]. Tor clients build three-hop circuits for anonymous communication, where the three relays are respectively known as *guard*, *middle*, and *exit* relays. The guard relay is always chosen from a fixed set of three relays that is unique to each client, to prevent certain long term attacks on anonymous communication [50,51].In order to balance the load on the network, clients select Tor relays in proportion to their bandwidths (subject to certain constraints). A Tor client can multiplex individual TCP connections (called *streams*) over a single Tor circuit. The lifetime of a Tor circuit is generally set to 10 minutes. Finally, in addition to anonymous communication, Tor also provides support for *location-hidden services*; clients can connect to these services without knowing their network identity. We refer the interested reader to [16] for a more detailed description of Tor.

2.2 Tor Security

Traditional security analyses of Tor [16] assume that a user who controls (or observes) a fraction f of the network can compromise the anonymity of f^2 of all tunnels by end-to-end timing analysis (by observing the entry and exit point of a stream). Note that due to bandwidth-weighted relay selection, f is best thought of as the fraction of Tor bandwidth controlled or observed by an adversary. This simple model, however, abstracts away many important properties of the system that affect anonymity; recent research has shown that, when these properties are properly considered, the potential for anonymity compromise is significantly greater than predicted by the model. Some examples of such properties include the reliability of relays [10], the skew of the internal system clocks [37] and the topology of the underlying Internet paths used to forward traffic between relays [17, 20, 39]. A particular class of attacks uses side-channel information to determine whether an anonymous flow is forwarded by a particular Tor relay [7, 11, 19, 24, 38]; this effectively increases the fraction of the network that is observed (f) with a moderate resource expenditure. As our attacks fall into the same class, we next discuss these attacks in detail.

2.3 Circuit Clogging Attacks

Murdoch and Danezis [38] proposed an attack on the Tor network where an adversary aims to identify the Tor relays of a circuit by *modulating* the sending rate of traffic through a circuit, and studying the effect of the modulations on the *latency* characteristics (queueing delay) of individual Tor relays. A high correlation between the two indicates that the Tor relay is likely part of the original circuit. The attacks were tested in 2005, when the Tor network comprised only a handful of relays. Since 2005, the Tor network has grown in size by two orders of magnitude and Evans et al. [19] recently showed that the Murdoch–Danezis attack no longer works on the Tor network.

Evans et al. [19] proposed a variant of the Murdoch–Danezis attack where an adversary sets up a very long path through the Tor network, consisting of loops, such that the additional traffic introduced by an adversary gets amplified (in order to effectively congest a relay). There exist simple countermeasures to such an amplification attack, like imposing a bound on the maximum circuit length in Tor. Houmansadr and Borisov [26] also show that attempts to circumvent the bound by having the flow exit the Tor network and then re-enter it (by the means of forwarding proxies) can be mitigated using watermarking schemes. Note that without the ability to amplify traffic, significant resources are required in order to congest a relay.

Chakravarty et al. [11] proposed another variant of the Murdoch–Danezis attack in which an attacker modulates traffic rates of a circuit, and uses estimation tools to observe changes in forwarding capacity of Tor relays. In theory, their approach also allows the identification of Internet links used to carry an anonymous flow, with the potential to identify the identity of the Tor client. The attack, however, requires an extensive infrastructure of vantage points and maps of Internet topologies to be fully effective. Furthermore, the experimental evaluation of the attack showed only moderate success rates even under controlled settings; we expect this is because modulation of circuit rates does not have any impact on the forwarding capacity of nodes/links that are already operating at full capacity (such as some Tor relays).

Note that all of these attacks rely on coarse-grained effects of active modulation of circuit traffic. One mitigation for this attack approach is to reduce or eliminate the ability of two circuits to interfere with each other's performance by altering the packet scheduling algorithms used by Tor [33].

2.4 Latency Observations

Hopper et al. [24,25] studied information leaks in Tor that arise due to heterogeneous network latency. By measuring the round-trip times through a Tor circuit (using malicious JavaScript content inserted into web pages), it is possible to compute the likelihood of it following a particular path through the Tor network and eliminate some paths from consideration entirely. Additionally, it may be possible to learn information about the approximate geographic location of the client. Some of our attack scenarios are similar in spirit, but our attacks focus on throughput, rather than latency; in the stream linkability attack, we find that this results in significantly better accuracy.

A major limitation of circuit-clogging and latency attacks is that they are not stealthy; the traffic modulations and malicious content insertions can easily be detected by clients/Tor relays. In contrast, our attacks use finer-grained information about circuit throughput that can be obtained by a simple download through Tor, without actively modulating circuit traffic. Thus, our attacks are *stealthy* and cannot be detected by Tor relays and clients. Our techniques also enlarge the scope of possible threat models under which an attacker can perform traffic analysis. For example, prior attacks are only applicable to the scenarios where either the destination web server or the exit relay is compromised. In contrast, our attacks can be carried out by ISPs or other local traffic observers. Finally, the finer-grained information also allows us to achieve better accuracy while using fewer resources.

2.5 Long-Term Anonymity

If multiple communication rounds can be linked (e.g., if a user logs in frequently with a given pseudonym), the anonymity guarantees provided will degrade over time. For example, using the f^2 probability of circuit compromise, over a number of path reformulations, the chance that at least one tunnel will be observed at both the entry and exit approaches one [50, 51].This observation, along with attacks that can force reformulations to occur [4, 10, 40], motivates the use of guard relays in Tor, where each client uses a small fixed set of entry points into the network.

A similar degradation can be observed in mix-based systems, where observations of the set of active users [8, 43] or senders and recipients [30] at each communication round allows the use of *intersection attacks* to narrow down the set of potentially communicating parties. A statistical version of this attack (*statistical disclosure attack*) was proposed by Danezis [13]. Similarly, information learned by observing the

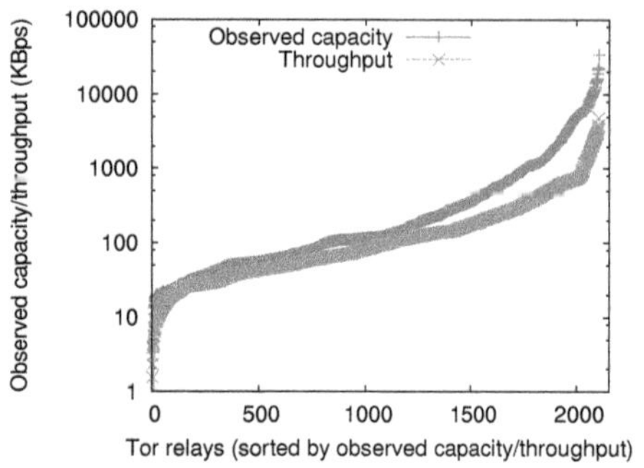

Figure 1: Observed capacity/throughput heterogeneity in the Tor network.

throughput of circuits can be used for a statistical disclosure attack, as we discuss in Section 3.

3. INFORMATION LEAKAGE VIA CIRCUIT THROUGHPUT

We next describe attacks on Tor that determine path information about a pair of circuits by correlating their observed throughput. We first motivate our approach by noting that the capacities of Tor relays are quite heterogeneous (Section 3.1). We then present an attack to determine if two circuits share a common sub-path (Section 3.2), and an attack to narrow in on which relays a given circuit traverses (Section 3.3). We combine these probabilistic observations over multiple circuit reformulations to de-anonymize guard relays (Section 3.4). Finally, we show the applicability of our attack on interactive traffic (Section 3.6).

3.1 Heterogeneity in the Tor Network

One fundamental observation used in our attacks is that the Tor network is composed of relays that have heterogeneous capacities. Figure 1 plots the advertised capacities of 2 104 Tor relays, collected from the Tor directory service. These capacity values are estimates based on the minimum of the maximum input or output bandwidth sustained over any ten second period at a particular Tor relay. This value is re-evaluated each day by every Tor relay and reported to the directory service. This information can be fetched using the *getinfo desc/all-recent* command. By analyzing these capacity values we can see that there is a significant degree of heterogeneity in the capacities of the Tor relays.

From Figure 1, we can see that around 38.6% of these Tor relays have capacity (plotted on a log scale) below 100 KBps. This increases the probability of the Tor network being the bottleneck for most of the flows passing through Tor and makes it vulnerable to our attacks.

In order to balance the load on the network, Tor clients select relays in proportion to their capacities. Let C_i denote the capacity of relay i. If there are X circuits being constructed in the network, then the expected number of circuits that choose any particular relay i is given by $X_i = 3 \cdot X \frac{C_i}{\Sigma_i C_i}$ (there is a factor of 3 because the Tor path consists of 3 relays). The capacity of relay i should be distributed evenly amongst circuits that traverse it, given by $\frac{C_i}{X_i} = \frac{\Sigma_i C_i}{3 \cdot X}$. Thus we can see that in an ideal scenario, the throughput received by all circuits should be homogeneous.[2]

Unfortunately, this is not the situation in the current Tor network. In spite of load balancing, there exists a large range of throughput that individual relays can sustain, as shown in Figure 1. To measure this, we individually probed the throughput of each available Tor relay using a 3-hop circuit with our own guard and exit relay. We used the stable version of Tor (Version 0.2.1.26, as of November 2010) to do the probing. We used two custom-built TCP client and server programs (details of these programs are presented in Section 3.2) to set up a flow through the relay being probed (using it as the middle relay). We ran both the client and the server programs at the same machine where the server sent data to the client as fast as possible (only limited by TCP's congestion control mechanism). We measured the throughput of the flow as observed by the client. Each relay was probed for 15 seconds, and we computed the average observed throughput over the last 10 seconds to avoid TCP's slow-start effect. As we probed each relay one by one, the entire experiment took about 18 hours to complete. Note that we chose a high capacity vantage point to perform this experiment so that it did not become the bottleneck. We were able to probe 2 104 out of 2 429 relays listed in the Tor network consensus on July 24, 2011. The remaining 325 relays did not respond to our circuit setup requests as they may have been offline when they were probed during our experiment.

There are three key factors that determine the throughput of a circuit: a) the capacity of the bottleneck relay, b) the number of active TCP flows between the bottleneck relay and the next hops and c) the number of other active circuits multiplexed over the TCP connection that carries the circuit in question[3]:

$$\text{throughput of circuit } i = \frac{\text{bottleneck relay bandwidth}}{\text{\# of TCP flows} \times \text{\# of circuits in } i\text{'s TCP flow}}$$

There are several reasons for the lack of perfect load balancing in the Tor network: a) the first hop relay is chosen from a fixed set of three guard relays, b) the last hop is chosen from the set of relays whose exit policy meets the client's requirements, c) the peak capacity advertised by a relay is capped to an arbitrary threshold, d) the clients are not privy to current levels of traffic in the network, and hence select relays in a fully decentralized fashion, and e) the clients cannot predict stream characteristics in advance when selecting circuits for anonymous communication. We note that most of these reasons are fundamental limitations for any secure low-latency anonymity system.

3.2 Circuit-Based Bandwidth Fingerprinting

In this section, we describe an attack that determines whether two circuits share a common sub-path by "fingerprinting" their communication. We do this by monitoring their throughput and using a simple statistical test to determine if their throughput is correlated. We consider three representative experimental scenarios:

[2]This is a slight simplification; some relays cannot be in the first or third position, and those that can are underweighted when selecting the middle relay.

[3]This formula makes the simplifying assumption that TCP results in fair sharing of bandwidth between flows. In reality, TCP is only RTT-fair [41]; this difference, however, has minimal impact on our analysis.

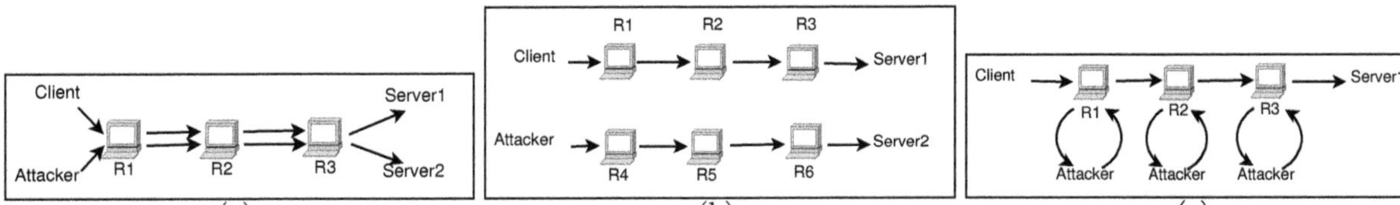

Figure 2: Experimental scenarios for circuit-based throughput fingerprinting: (a) *All-Common:* Two circuits sharing all three Tor relays have similar throughput characteristics. (b) *None-Common:* Two circuits without any common Tor relays do not have any similarity in their throughput characteristics. (c) *One-Common:* Two circuits with one or two common Tor relays will have similar throughput characteristics but only for the duration of time in which the common Tor relays are the bottleneck relays in the circuit.

All-Common (Figure 2(a)): If two Tor circuits have all relays in common, then the circuit throughput will be highly correlated. Since all three relays are common in both the circuits, any variation in the number of TCP flows or forwarding capacity at a relay will affect the throughput of both circuits in a similar fashion.

None-Common (Figure 2(b)): If two Tor circuits do not have any common relays, then the circuit throughput will not be correlated.

One-Common (Figure 2(c)): If two Tor circuits have at least one relay in common, but do not have all relays in common, then there are two cases. If the shared relay is the bottleneck in both the circuits (*One-Common-a*), then the circuit throughput will be highly correlated. If the shared relay is not the bottleneck in both the circuits (*One-Common-b*), then changes in its number of TCP flows or forwarding capacity will not affect the throughput of the two circuits, and thus their throughput will depend on their respective bottleneck relays.

We performed experiments on the live Tor network to verify these observations. We used two client nodes and two server nodes, located in four separate geographical regions. On the client machines, we ran the stable version of Tor as of November 2010 (Version 0.2.1.26). We used the default path selection in the Tor clients, but turned off the use of entry guards (by setting `UseEntryGuards=0`), so that our clients sample circuits from the space of all possible circuits. For our experiments with all three common relays, we disabled preemptive circuit setup on the Tor client at the attacker's machine (using `__DisablePredictedCircuits=1`). We used two custom-built TCP programs to work as the client and server in all of our experiments. The TCP client is a C program that connects with the TCP server, reads data sent by the server and computes the throughput of the flow periodically after a specific measurement interval. It uses the Tor SOCKS [31] interface to perform download via Tor. The TCP server is a multithreaded server written in C that waits for connection requests from clients and once connected sends random bytes to the client as fast as possible. The sending rate of the server is only limited by the TCP congestion control algorithm. For simplicity of presentation, our experiments in this section assume that a user is interested in bulk data transfer. Our attacks are also applicable to interactive traffic; we demonstrate this in Section 3.6.

For each experiment, we set up a stream at the honest client, recorded the circuit that the Tor client assigned to that stream, and built the same circuit at the attacker's client. We used an upper bound of 30 seconds as the synchronization delay, and after this delay, we set up a new stream at the attacker's client.

Results for *All-Common* (Figures 3(a) and 4(a)): We next present experimental results for the scenario where all three Tor relays are the same for both circuits. We performed 700 runs of this experiment, between November and December 2010. We found that the throughput values for the two circuits were highly correlated, measured using the Pearson product-moment correlation coefficient. Figure 3(a) illustrates an instance of this scenario, where correlation is depicted as a function of time. We also compute the 95% confidence interval for correlation using Fisher's Z transform [21]. We can see that after a time duration of 300 seconds, even the lower bound for the confidence interval is higher than 0.7. Figure 4(a) depicts the fraction of experiments where the correlation value is greater than a threshold as a function of time. In about 92% of the cases, the correlation was greater than a threshold value of 0.5 after a time duration of 300 seconds. Moreover, we can also see that correlation remains steady with time.

Results for *None-Common* (Figures 3(a) and 4(b)): Next, we consider the scenario where two circuits are completely disjoint. We performed 532 runs of this experiment in January 2011. In Figure 3(a), we can see that the correlation quickly approaches zero when the two circuits are comprised of disjoint relays. Figure 4(b) shows the full results for this scenario; we can see that in an overwhelming fraction of cases, the correlation quickly drops to zero—only 12 instances out of 532 had a correlation value greater than 0.5 for a time interval of 300 seconds (false positive percentage of only 2.2%). In our investigation of false positives, we found that many of the false positive instances occurred due to the geographic co-location of relays in the two circuits. For example, in four instances, the two circuits shared a relay that was part of the same subnet, like the **blutmagie** and **blutmagie4** relays. In one instance, the first 16 bits of the IPv4 address of two relays was the same (**ctor** and **cptnemo**, both located in Berlin), while in two other instances, IP geolocation databases indicate geographic closeness within tens of miles. However, geographic colocation could not explain the remaining five instances.

Results for *One-Common-a* (Figures 3(b) and 4(c)): Finally, we consider the scenario where two circuits have only a single common Tor relay. We build one-hop circuits through each of the relays in a client circuit. We performed 190 runs of this experiment for this scenario between November 2010 and February 2011. Figure 3(b) depicts the correlation as a function of time for two instances in this sce-

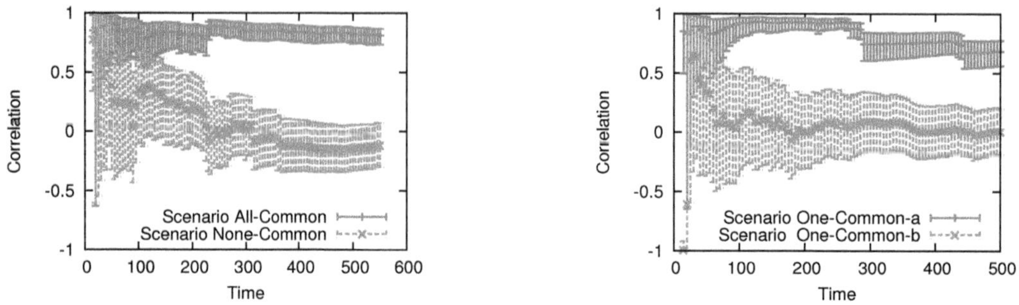

(a) (b)

Figure 3: (a) When the two circuits share all three relays (*All-Common*), the correlation is very high. When the circuits share no common relays (*None-Common*), the correlation is very low. (b) When the two circuits share a single relay, and that relay is the bottleneck on both paths (*One-Common-a*), then the correlation is high. If that relay is not the bottleneck on both paths (*One-Common-b*), then the correlation is low.

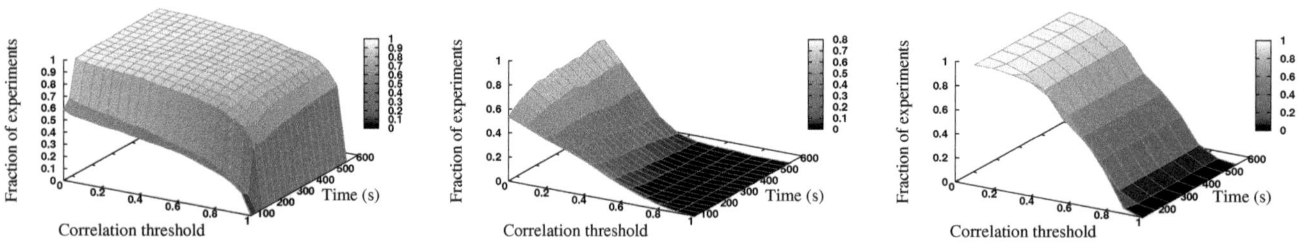

(a) c (b) c (c) c

Figure 4: Effect of correlation threshold on detection rate: (a) *All-Common*, (b) *None-Common*, (c) *One-Common-a*.

nario. In scenario *One-Common-a*, the common relay was the bottleneck relay for the full duration of 10 minutes, and we can see that the correlation value is similar to that of scenario *All-Common*. On the other hand, in scenario *One-Common-b*, the common relay was not the bottleneck relay, and we can see that the correlation is not statistically significant. When only a single relay is common between two circuits, we found that in many instances, correlation degrades over time, since the common relay may be a bottleneck only temporarily (not shown in Figure 3(b)). To address this issue, we modified the correlation analysis to consider *windows* (intervals) of time; for a particular size of the window, we compute the maximum correlation in the data over all time intervals greater than the window size (if the communication duration is smaller than the window size, we compute correlation as before). We probed all three relays for a client circuit in this experiment, but since only one of them may be the bottleneck at a time, we computed the maximum correlation amongst the three probes for different communication duration values. Figure 4(c) depicts the fraction of experiments that have correlation greater than a threshold value for different communication durations using a window size of 200 seconds. We can see that while correlation is not as high as the scenario where all three relays were common between two circuits, over 90% and 80% of the experiments still have correlation greater than 0.3 and 0.4 respectively after 300 seconds of communication. Next, we will use this observation to identify Tor relays.

Based on these experiments, we conclude that high correlation between circuit throughput indicates the presence of common Tor relay(s) in the two circuits. Note that the converse is not necessarily true.

3.3 Identifying Tor Relays

Threat model: Next, we present an attack where we try to identify one or more Tor relays being used by a particular flow. We call this flow the *target flow*. This flow can be any flow initiated by a Tor client over the Tor network to access a resource present at a particular server. We assume that the attacker can observe the throughput of the target flow. The attacker could have compromised the exit relay, the target web server, or the ISP forwarding the data; note that the attacker does not need to perform any modifications to the flow. The attacker tries to achieve its goal by probing different Tor relays; importantly, these probes can be launched from different vantage points than the target server. It builds one-hop circuits through these relays (Figure 5) and computes correlations between the throughput of the target flow and the *probe flows*. If the throughput of a probe flow is highly correlated with that of the target flow, then the server can assume that both the flows are actually traversing a common Tor relay. In this section, we show the success of the attacker at identifying Tor relays by running experiments over the live Tor network.

Experimental setup: In an ideal setting, the attacker will try to probe every relay in the Tor network and find

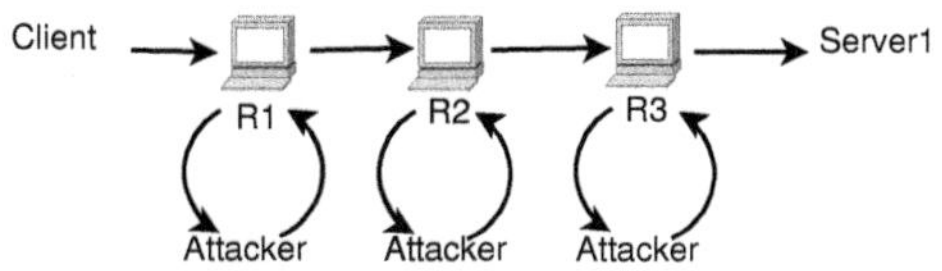

Figure 5: Identifying Tor relays attack: localizing which Tor relays are on a path by exploiting circuit throughput characteristics. Observe that the attack cost scales as $O(N)$.

the correlation between the probe flows and the target flow. However, in order to reduce the amount of resources required to perform this attack, we used a smaller set of 25 Tor relays for constructing circuits. To pick relays that are representative of the current Tor network, we selected relays with a probability proportional to their bandwidth using the Tor client. We performed our experiments during two different time period and used a different set of 25 relays in each period; we will refer to them as RELAY-SET-1 and RELAY-SET-2 (the list of Tor relays is available in the full version of this paper [34]).

Probe locations: We used 25 different Emulab [18] machines at the University of Utah to run the probe flows.[4] They were used to probe all the 25 Tor relays simultaneously. All of the probe flows originated from a single physical location, but we expect that their throughput was nevertheless shaped by the Tor overlay, rather than the access link: in a separate test, we were able to achieve 70 Mbps across the access link, far above the throughput of flows in the Tor network.

Single circuit experiments: In our first experiment, we set up a target flow between a client and a malicious server over a circuit that was constructed using a set of 25 Tor relays. We started all the probe flows simultaneously after the target flow ran for 50 seconds. Each probe flow lasted for 600 seconds, and we recorded the observed throughput every 0.1 seconds. Overall, we performed 40 measurements using RELAY-SET-1 in November 2010 and 150 measurements using RELAY-SET-2 in January-February 2011.

We use the entropy metric [15,44] (with a uniform prior) to quantify the attacker's uncertainty about the relays in a circuit (our computations are described in technical report [34]). Figure 6(a) depicts the CDF of the bottleneck relay entropy for varying window sizes using a correlation threshold of 0.4. We can see that while our attacks are not able to exactly identify the bottleneck relay, the bottleneck relay entropy is still drastically reduced. For example, using a window size of 300 seconds, the entropy in half of the cases is less than 2.5 bits (out of 4.6 bits). We found similar results for correlation thresholds 0.3 and 0.5.

In addition to being able to reduce the entropy of the bottleneck relay distribution, we can also learn some information about the target flow's non-bottleneck relays. Our attack observation is that if the mean throughput of a one-hop probe through a relay is less than the mean throughput of the target flow, then that relay is unlikely to be part of the target flow circuit. The expected drop in entropy for a given throughput is shown in Figure 6(b). We also plot the CDF of Tor circuit throughput for comparison. We can see that the circuits receiving a higher throughput have a lower entropy in the network. This is due to the presence of only a few high-throughput relays in the system; if high throughput is achieved, there are only a limited number of relays capable of providing this service. The average value of throughput observed in our experiment was 96 KBps thus yielding an expected instantaneous drop of about 18% in the total entropy at any given point in the experiment's run time.

We demonstrate the usefulness of this observation by eliminating relays with lower throughput than the target flow over a period of time. The results are plotted in Figure 6(c). By using this simple technique, we were able to reduce the entropy in our sample space by roughly 40% in the first ten seconds, and using a minute-long attack, we were able to reduce the entropy the bottleneck relay's sample space by roughly 45% as fluctuating probe bandwidth measurements allowed more relays to be eliminated from consideration.

3.4 Identifying Guard Relays

So far, we presented attacks that reduce the entropy of Tor relays in a single circuit. We now present attacks that can combine such probabilistic observations over multiple circuits, and identify a client's set of guard relays. Our observation is that the guard relays are more likely to be present in the anonymity set of bottleneck relays for a client's circuit, as compared to other relays (since the probability of the guard relays appearing in the client's circuit is much higher than other relays). Thus, over multiple circuit reformulations, the set of relays that appear in the anonymity set for a client's circuit with the highest frequencies are likely to be the guard relays.

Experimental setup: Here, in addition to restricting the client's Tor application in using relays from a selected set of 25 relays, we also restricted its choice of guard relay. With the help of the configuration options `EntryNodes`, `StrictEntryNodes`, `UseEntryGuards`, and `NumEntryGuards`, we configured the client's Tor application to always use a particular relay as the guard relay. The intuition behind this experiment is to analyze the vulnerability of using a fixed guard relay; i.e., we want to observe whether use of a fixed guard relay allows the attacker to combine probabilistic observations over multiple circuits and identify the guard relay. Similar to the experiments for identifying Tor relays, we used 25 different machines to do the probing where the target flow ran for 700 seconds and the probe flows ran for 600 seconds (within the lifetime of the target flow). We performed three experiments for this scenario, where we chose the guard relays to be `Fooligans`, `jalopy`, and `trusted`, respectively. We performed 50, 20, and 50 runs for the three experiments respectively, between November 2010 and February 2011. Note that we considered these three relays since we wanted to study the effectiveness of our attack against guard relays with very different capacities. `Fooligans`, `jalopy`, and `trusted` have a reported capacity of 82 KBps, 5.8 MBps, and 17.4 MBps, respectively (as of February 2011).

Results: Figure 7 show the number of times a particular relay was selected in the anonymity set for the bottleneck relay used by the target flow. We used a correlation threshold of 0.4, and set the window size to be 400. In Figure 7(a), we can see that the relay with the highest frequency of being in the anonymity set of bottleneck relays is `Fooligans`, which is indeed the guard relay for the client. In fact, in all three

[4]Note that we did not make use of Emulab's network emulation infrastructure and ran experiments on the production Tor network instead.

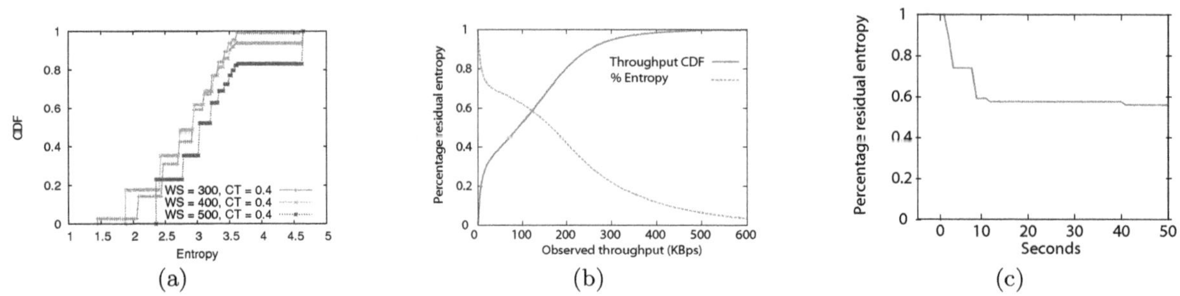

Figure 6: (a) Entropy of the anonymity set obtained through our de-anonymizing relay attack. (b) Entropy loss and CDF of observed throughput. (c) Decrease in entropy over six consecutive ten second intervals.

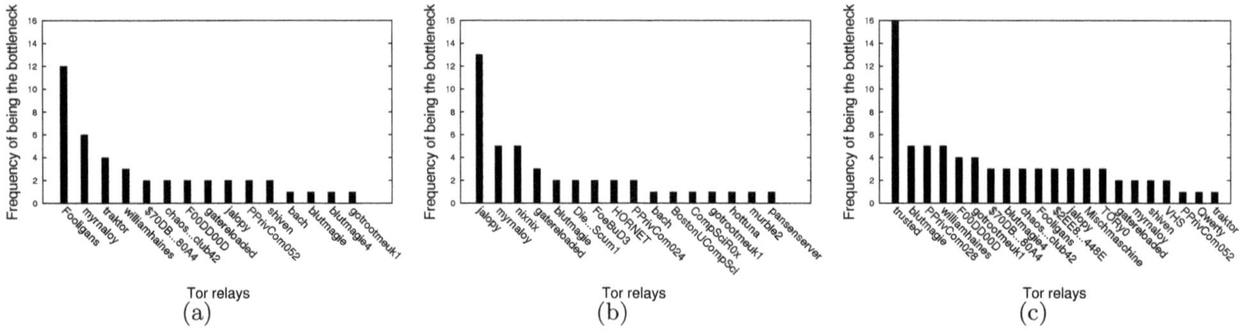

Figure 7: Number of times a particular relay was detected as a bottleneck, with guard relay (a) `Fooligans`, with observed capacity 82 KBps, (b) `jalopy`, with observed capacity 5.8 MBps, (c) `trusted`, with observed capacity 17.4 MBps, as of February 2011.

experiments, our attack was able to infer the identity of the guard relays, since they appeared in the anonymity set with the highest frequencies.

Observe that accounting for the fact that Tor clients use 3 guard relays by default (as compared to one in our experiments) would reduce the frequency of them being detected as a bottleneck relay by a factor of 3. However, note that our results are conservative since we selected relays from a limited pool of only 25 Tor relays. The current Tor network size is about 2 000 relays; application of this attack on the full Tor network would result in orders of magnitude reduction in the selection probability of relays which are not the guard relay, correspondingly reducing their frequency of being detected as a bottleneck relay. Thus in the full Tor network, even with 3 guard relays, we can expect the frequency of the guards being detected as the bottleneck relay to be much higher than a random relay in the network.

Finally, we note that our attack was able to identify the guard relay irrespective of its observed capacity. As the Tor network is heavily used by a large number of users, even high capacity relays become congested and cannot ensure enough throughput to all the flows. This causes them to affect flows' throughput in a way that can be detected through our one-hop relay identification attack. As the guard relay has a direct connection with the client, the severity of this attack is much higher than an attack that identifies the middle relays.

3.5 De-anonymizing Tor Relays Offering Location Hidden Service

In this section, we attempt to identify Tor relays that also offer location hidden services. The main purpose of a location hidden service is to remain anonymous while serving its clients. However, we show that when a Tor relay offers a location hidden service, it becomes susceptible to attacks. The observation that enables de-anonymization of location hidden servers is similar to our attack on guard relays, in that the location hidden service is likely to have the highest frequency of being part of the anonymity set of bottleneck relays for circuits connecting to that location hidden service. In order to assess the effectiveness of this attack, we set up our own Tor relay and advertised its existence to the Tor network. We also configured this machine to offer a location hidden service. We setup a target flow from a client machine to the location hidden service, and measured the flow throughput. While this target flow was active, we probed our Tor relay using a one-hop circuit as we did in Section 3.3. We ran this experiment 100 times and computed the correlation between the throughput of the target flow and the probe flows. Using a correlation threshold of 0.4, and window sizes of 300 and 400 seconds, we found that 15% and 9% of the target flows and the corresponding probe flows were highly correlated. Relating this observation with the observations from Section 3.3, we can conclude that our Tor relay will be placed in the anonymity set for bottleneck relays with a much higher probability than any other relay. Moreover, as there are usually 8 different relays/nodes including the server itself (the other seven relays comprise of three relays each for the client's circuit as well as the server's circuit, and a common meeting point for these circuits, called the *rendezvous* relay) in the path between the client and the server, each of them can become the bottleneck with 12.5% probability. Results from our experiment closely matches this value by identifying our Tor relay with roughly the same probability (9%-15%).

3.6 Applicability to Interactive Traffic

So far, we used bulk traffic in our experiments. We now investigate the accuracy of our attacks with interactive traffic (characterized by bursts of traffic followed by periods of inactivity). To evaluate our attacks, we first built a model for interactive traffic by collecting real packet level traces from a fast Tor guard relay at various times from April 24 through April 27. To preserve user privacy, we first used Mittal et al.'s [35] anonymizing framework to process the pcap traces; for each observed packet, the output of the framework was an anonymized client IP address, packet timestamp, and packet length. We performed the above data anonymization and minimization steps on the guard relay itself. The original pcap traces were deleted immediately afterwards[5]. Next, we analyzed the properties of the processed data. In total over the three days we observed 19 478 flows with 17 911 of these flows containing between one to ten packets. We surmise that these correspond to either preemptive circuits which were never actually used by Tor or failed circuit creation attempts. For the remaining flows, we break them up into ten-minute intervals and then calculate the fraction of 5 second sub-intervals where any traffic was observed. We next classify them into three categories based on the fraction of time they were observed sending data. We found 424 flows that transferred traffic for more than 90% of the time (non-interactive file downloads), 347 flows with between 50% and 90% utilization (interactive flows with moderate utilization), and 796 flows with less than 50% utilization (interactive flows with low utilization). We select only the flows comprising interactive traffic with moderate utilization, and use the distribution of their average burst sizes and gap times as a model for interactive traffic in our experiments. After computing the distribution of burst sizes and gap times, all intermediate data from previous steps was discarded to maintain the privacy of Tor users.

Next, we performed two experiments over the live Tor network, with 100 measurements each for the Scenarios All-Common and None-Common. In both experiments, we set up a bulk transfer flow (the attacker) and an interactive flow (the victim). For the interactive transfer, the TCP server was configured to send data to the victim in bursts where each burst was followed by a gap period. Both the burst size and the gap times were sampled from the observed distribution computed using real data. For both experiments, we computed the correlation in throughput of the attacker flow and the victim flow for those time intervals where the victim flow was active. We are interested in the fraction of measurements where the correlation was greater than a threshold. This metric corresponds to true positives for the Scenario All-Common, and false positives for the Scenario None-Common. The correlation threshold determines the trade off between the true positives and the false positives. Figure 8 depicts the ROC curve for our experiments. We found that for an estimated false positive rate of 0 (95% confidence interval is less than 3.5%), the true positive rate is

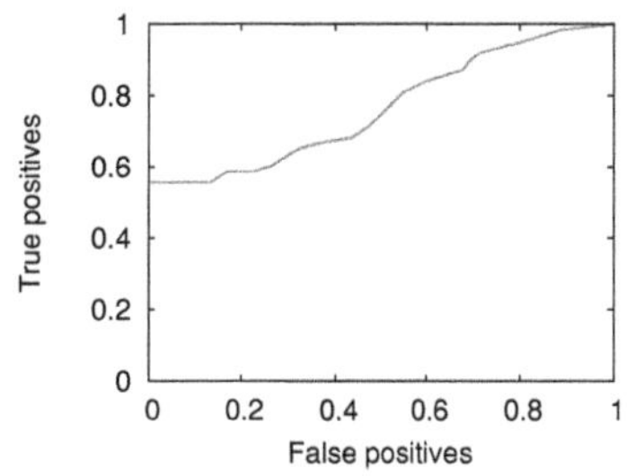

Figure 8: Attack on interactive traffic: ROC curve.

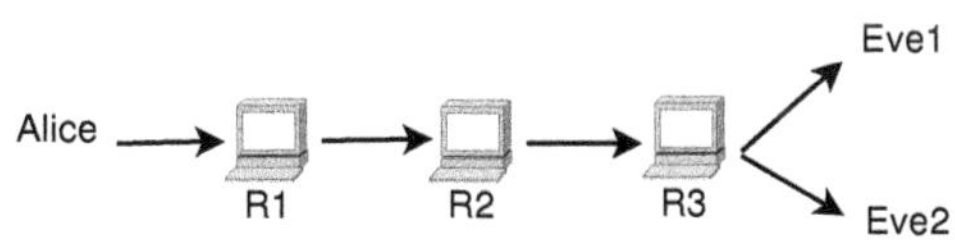

Figure 9: Stream fingerprinting attack: breaking unlinkability by exploiting stream throughput characteristics.

greater than 0.5. Our analysis demonstrates the applicability of our attacks on interactive traffic, though the accuracy in this case is lower than that of bulk traffic.

4. STREAM FINGERPRINTING

Circuits in Tor typically carry multiple *streams*, which correspond to individual TCP connections. By default, all streams created by a client within a 10 minute period are carried over the same circuit.[6] Tor uses a different scheduling mechanism to share bandwidth between streams than it does between circuits, providing an opportunity for new attacks that correlate streams. In particular, we will show that packet scheduling of streams that use the same circuit creates special characteristics that can easily be recognized by a completely passive attacker; this can be used to link the streams as belonging to the same user and thus compromise some of the unlinkability protections provided by Tor.[7]

4.1 Stream Throughput at Different Time Scales

Consider the scenario in Figure 9: Alice is communicating simultaneously with Eve1 and Eve2. Alice's Tor client multiplexes both streams over the same circuit, in this case consisting of Tor relays $R1$, $R2$, $R3$. Eve1 and Eve2 can see that both their connections are coming from the same exit node, and would like to learn if they are both communicating with the same person. We would expect that, since the streams share the same path through the network, they should exhibit similar throughput characteristics. Indeed, we find a very strong correlation between such streams; Figure 10(a) shows the results of one experiment, with a correlation of 0.93. However, as shown in Section 3, a high correlation is common among unrelated circuits that share the same bottleneck node, e.g., if $R3$ is the bottleneck for both streams.

However, there is a second effect that can be used to distinguish streams that share one or more common relays.

[5]In future work, we will enhance the anonymizing framework to perform the data minimization and anonymization steps in memory, in order to further minimize risk in case the guard relay is compromised during the data processing phase.

[6]This is governed by the `Max_Circuit_Dirtiness` parameter in Tor.

[7]It should be noted that exit relays can already perform such linking; our attacks, however, do not require the compromise of any relays in the Tor network.

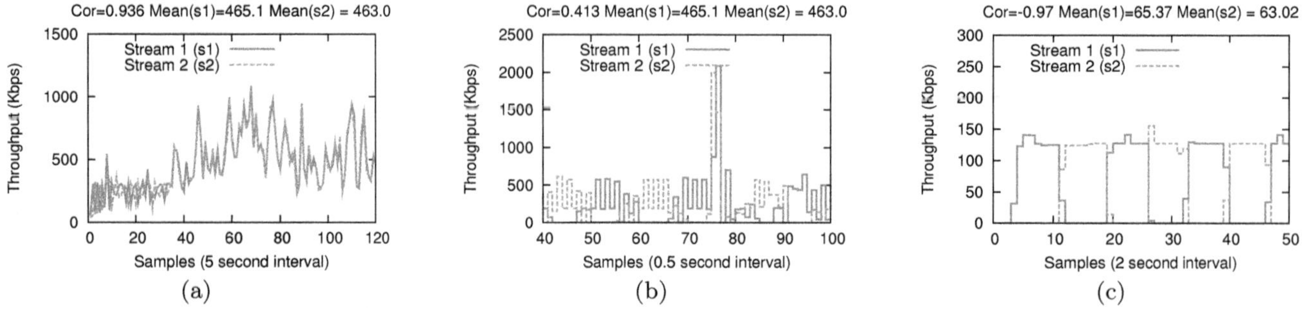

Figure 10: (a) Positive correlation between streams. (b) Batching effect when sampling every 0.5 seconds. (c) Batching effect when sampling every 2 seconds.

Tor implements stream-level throttling within circuits. This end-to-end flow control works as follows: each stream is initially allowed to send 500 of Tor's 512-byte cells (also called the *packaging window*). Upon successful reception of packets, the packaging window is incremented in blocks of 50 cells. Observe that if a stream is waiting for the packaging window to be incremented, then another stream that is being multiplexed on the same circuit can hog the circuit (*batching effect*) for a small time interval.

While the streams share the throughput fairly, flow- and congestion-control mechanisms in Tor result in batching behavior, where one stream may monopolize the circuit for some period of time, while the other streams lie idle. We can see this mutually exclusive use of the circuit by two streams when we sample the throughput at smaller time scales, as can be seen in Figures 10(b) and 10(c). We note that the length of the batches seems to be a multiple of 25 KB, corresponding to 50 of Tor's 512-byte cell, matching our intuition that 50-cell packaging window increments are responsible for the batching effect. This also means that the time scales necessary to observe this effect will vary depending on the throughput of the flow: in Figure 10(b), the mean throughput value is 450 Kbps and we observe the behavior sampling every 0.5 seconds, whereas in Figure 10(c), the mean throughput value is 66 Kbps, and we observe the behavior sampling every 2 seconds.

Based on these observations, we propose the following algorithm to infer whether the streams are coming from the same client:

1. We first check for strong correlation at macro-level time scales, as done in previous sections.
2. We define our micro-level time scale to be $\frac{25\text{ KB}}{\text{Throughput(KBps)}}$
3. We check for the batching effect at micro-level timescales. Namely, we compute the fraction of time when only one stream is active out of the total time that either stream is active, which shows the degree of "mutual exclusivity" between the two streams.

4.2 Results

To see how well the algorithm works, we performed an experiment in which a single client connects to two servers under our control, located in two different geographical locations, and simultaneously downloads data. Since the connections were made simultaneously, the two streams were multiplexed over the same Tor circuit. We performed a total of 225 runs between November 2010 and February 2011.

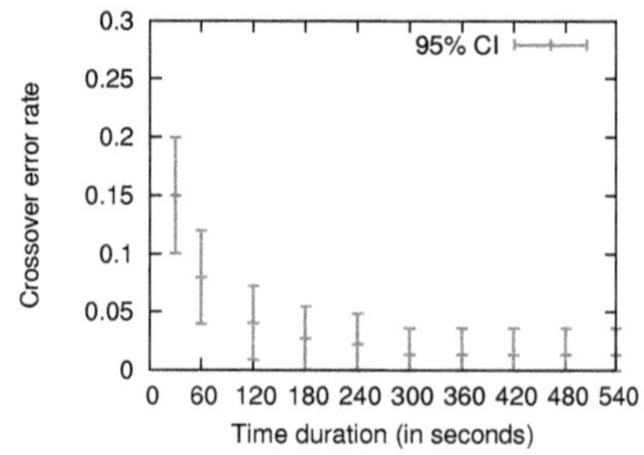

Figure 11: Stream linkability attack: crossover error rate as a function of time.

To check for false positives in our attack, we repeated the experiment with downloads by two different clients using separate circuits that have a common exit relay. We performed 225 iterations of this experiment in April 2011.

Recall that the tradeoff between false positives and false negatives is governed by the choice of the threshold values for correlation and mutual exclusiveness. As the threshold values are increased, the false positives decrease, but the false negatives increase. We plot the crossover error rate as a function of the communication duration in Figure 11. We can see that as the time duration is increased, the accuracy of our attack quickly improves. Even at a small duration of 120 seconds, our mean crossover error rate is less than 5%, which gets reduced to 1.3% beyond 300 seconds (with a 95% confidence interval of less than 4%).

Hopper et al. [24] analyzed a similar attack scenario, where latency information was used to determine if the same client is communicating with two servers. However, the crossover error rate in their attack was 17% even when the communication duration was 10 minutes. Note that throughput and latency provide orthogonal sources of information, and it may be interesting to combine our attacks with latency attacks to further improve accuracy. Finally, we also study the scenario where client Alice is communicating simultaneously on 3 streams, but only two of the destination endpoints are colluding. We found that the crossover error rate in this case was higher than the previous scenario, but still less than 8% when the communication duration is 300 seconds.

5. DISCUSSION

We discuss some issues and ramifications of our attacks:

Countermeasures: We now consider some possible ways to defend Tor users against our attacks. First, the circuit throughput fingerprinting attack relies on the existence of a shared bottleneck relay along the two paths. One countermeasure might be to use better load balancing within the Tor network. For example, preferring paths through higher capacity relays may make it more likely that the bottleneck is outside the Tor network. While it may be difficult to completely eliminate all bottlenecks within the Tor network, it may be possible to avoid making more sensitive relays as bottlenecks, for example by setting up paths such that guard relays are not the bottlenecks. In addition, multipath forwarding has been shown to give more even load balance in conventional networks [23]. Using multipath forwarding could reduce the number of bottlenecks by evenly distributing traffic over multiple paths, as well as "average out" short-term variations in throughput that arise from any single path. Also, since our attacks take some time to reliably associate the circuits, endpoints may periodically cycle through a small set of circuits, to reduce the amount of time they spend sharing a bottleneck with a malicious circuit. Another approach might be to change the effects that the bottleneck relay has on traffic. For example, relays may intentionally use an uneven rate allocation across flows, or inject spurious cross-traffic, to decouple throughput correlations in circuits they carry. Next, the stream linkability attack is based on Tor's intra-stream scheduling mechanism. To avoid this attack, Tor users may wish to perform heuristics at the client side to prevent circuit re-use for sensitive flows. In addition, better stream multiplexing algorithms [5] (e.g., algorithms that share bandwidth on a finer granularity) could eliminate the batching effects that we observed.

Alternative schemes to measure throughput: Our current attacks measure throughput by simply forwarding TCP traffic through the Tor relays. However, much work has been done in the networking community in the area of throughput probing, and it may be possible to leverage these techniques for improved performance. For example, instead of just monitoring flow throughput, techniques exist to monitor total *capacity* of the bottleneck link, by sending packets with precise timings [27, 29]. In situations where these techniques can be applied, correlation may be simplified, by revealing how much total capacity there is in nodes participating in the underlying channel. In addition, some of these techniques can measure throughput within short bursts of packets (e.g., packet pairs and packet trains [27, 29]), which may improve correlation for sessions of short duration.

Resource requirements: Our primary attacks are *stealthy* and do not require the attacker to congest Tor relays. Thus, the only cost incurred by an attacker is to create circuits to narrow the set of relays present in a circuit. To get a loose upper bound on the attacker's resource requirements, we note that the average throughput through a Tor relay from our study of 2,104 relays (Figure 1) is 226 KBps. Consider the very extreme case where the attacker simultaneously constructs one-hop circuits through each of the Tor relays in the entire network. The attacker would need to send 464.36 MBps (1632.51 GB per hour) of traffic. While this amount is higher than typical edge node bandwidth, the attacker may be able to acquire such bandwidth by using botnet hosts, or a hosted infrastructure such as Amazon EC2. Using EC2 pricing of $0.12 per GB, the attacker could send traffic for one hour with a cost of $196 (volume pricing for bandwidth in EC2 would reduce this cost for longer monitoring periods).

Impact of bulk traffic throttling: Recently, Tor implemented a mechanism that enables relay operators to throttle bulk traffic connections using a token bucket rate limiting system on traffic coming from non-relays. The rate limiting takes into account the burst rate and the long term throughput rate of a connection. The mechanism was first implemented in Tor-0.2.2.15-alpha, and thus did not impact our initial experiments conducted throughout November of 2010. However, as new versions of Tor were deployed throughout early 2011, we noticed that some of the attacker's probe circuits were getting throttled after roughly 300 seconds of high rate transfer down to a set limit of about 20 KBps. Note that the attacker can easily overcome the effects of throttling on its probe circuits by opening a new probe circuit when the current circuit begins to be throttled.

Ethics: Given that throughput information can leak information about clients, we conducted our study with some caution. In our experiments, we only attack the circuits created by our own experimental tool to avoid collecting information about non-participating clients. We also avoided launching large-scale attacks; we focus most of our experiments on only 25 Tor relays. All throughput data we collected was stored with strong encryption on machines behind a firewalled network. While analyzing traffic on a guard relay, we only recorded data pertaining to the distribution of burst sizes and gap times for the interactive traffic model (data-minimization). All other collected data (including outputs of various intermediate steps) was discarded to maintain the privacy of Tor users.

6. CONCLUDING REMARKS

To the best of our knowledge, our work comprises the first study of *throughput attacks* on anonymity systems. We presented attacks to identify Tor relays used by an existing connection, as well as techniques to identify the relationship between two streams, solely by monitoring their throughput. This calls into question, existing proposals to make observed bandwidth information public [32, 42, 45]. Our techniques are stealthy (cannot be detected by Tor users/relays) and low cost (do not require Tor relays to be congested). Moreover, our attacks use threat models and resource requirements that differ significantly from attacks using other flow features. Overall, our study highlights the complexity of designing anonymous communication systems.

Acknowledgments

We are grateful to Roger Dingledine for helpful discussions about Tor and for his guidance in shepherding our paper. We would like to thank Eugene Vasserman for suggesting the mechanism to probe Tor relays. This paper benefitted from discussions with George Danezis, Amir Houmansadr, Qiyan Wang, Giang Nyugen, Sonia Jahid and Xun Gong. Finally, we would like to thank the anonymous reviewers for their invaluable feedback on earlier drafts of this paper. This work was supported in part by NSF CNS 08-31488, 09-53655, 10-40391 and an International Fulbright S&T Fellowship.

7. REFERENCES

[1] http://netfiles.uiuc.edu/mittal2/www/throughput-fingerprinting.html.

[2] Cisco Systems, Inc., Cisco IOS Netflow. http://www.cisco.com/en/US/products/ps6601/products_ios_protocol_group_home.html.

[3] Symantec data loss prevention. http://www.symantec.com/business/products/family.jsp?familyid=data-loss-prevention.

[4] Abbott, T., Lai, K., Lieberman, M., and Price, E. Browser-based attacks on Tor. In *PETS* (2007).

[5] AlSabah, M., Bauer, K., Goldberg, I., Grunwald, D., McCoy, D., Savage, S., and Voelker, G. DefenestraTor: Throwing out windows in Tor. Tech. rep., University of Waterloo, 2011.

[6] Back, A., Goldberg, I., and Shostack, A. Freedom systems 2.1 security issues and analysis. White paper, Zero Knowledge Systems, Inc., May 2001.

[7] Back, A., Möller, U., and Stiglic, A. Traffic analysis attacks and trade-offs in anonymity providing systems. In *IH* (2001).

[8] Berthold, O., Federrath, H., and Köhntopp, M. Project "anonymity and unobservability in the Internet". In *10th Conf. on Computers, Freedom and Privacy* (2000).

[9] Berthold, O., Federrath, H., and Köpsell, S. Web MIXes: A system for anonymous and unobservable Internet access. In *Proceedings of Designing Privacy Enhancing Technologies: Workshop on Design Issues in Anonymity and Unobservability* (2000).

[10] Borisov, N., Danezis, G., Mittal, P., and Tabriz, P. Denial of service or denial of security? How attacks on reliability can compromise anonymity. In *CCS* (2007).

[11] Chakravarty, S., Stavrou, A., and Keromytis, A. D. Traffic analysis against low-latency anonymity networks using available bandwidth estimation. In *ESORICS* (2010).

[12] Chaum, D. Untraceable electronic mail, return addresses, and digital pseudonyms. *CACM 24*, 2 (1981).

[13] Danezis, G. Statistical disclosure attacks: Traffic confirmation in open environments. In *Proceedings of Security and Privacy in the Age of Uncertainty, (SEC2003)* (2003).

[14] Danezis, G., Dingledine, R., and Mathewson, N. Mixminion: Design of a Type III anonymous remailer protocol. In *IEEE S&P* (2003).

[15] Diaz, C., Seys, S., Claessens, J., and Preneel, B. Towards measuring anonymity. In *PETS* (2002).

[16] Dingledine, R., Mathewson, N., and Syverson, P. Tor: The second-generation onion router. In *USENIX Security* (2004).

[17] Edman, M., and Syverson, P. AS-awareness in Tor path selection. In *CCS* (2009).

[18] Emulab. EMULAB - Network Emulation Testbed Home. https://www.emulab.net/.

[19] Evans, N. S., Dingledine, R., and Grothoff, C. A practical congestion attack on Tor using long paths. In *USENIX Security* (2009).

[20] Feamster, N., and Dingledine, R. Location diversity in anonymity networks. In *WPES* (2004).

[21] Fisher, R. On the probable error of a coefficient of correlation deduced from a small sample. *Metron* (1921).

[22] Gulcu, C., and Tsudik, G. Mixing E-mail with Babel. In *NDSS* (1996).

[23] He, J., Suchara, M., Bresler, M., Rexford, J., and Chiang, M. Rethinking Internet traffic management: From multiple decompositions to a practical protocol. In *CoNext* (2007).

[24] Hopper, N., Vasserman, E. Y., and Chan-Tin, E. How much anonymity does network latency leak? In *CCS* (2007).

[25] Hopper, N., Vasserman, E. Y., and Chan-TIN, E. How much anonymity does network latency leak? *ACM Trans. Inf. Syst. Secur.* (2010).

[26] Houmansadr, A., and Borisov, N. SWIRL: A scalable watermark to detect correlated network flows. In *NDSS* (2011).

[27] Hu, N., Li, L., Mao, Z., Steenkiste, P., and Wang, J. A measurement study of Internet bottlenecks. *INFOCOM* (2005).

[28] I2P. I2P anonymous network. http://www.i2p2.de/index.html, 2003.

[29] Jacobson, V. Pathchar. http://www.caida.org/tools/utilities/others/pathchar/.

[30] Kesdogan, D., Agrawal, D., and Penz, S. Limits of anonymity in open environments. In *IH* (2002).

[31] Koblas, D., and Koblas, M. R. SOCKS. In *UNIX Security III Symposium* (1992).

[32] Loesing, K. Measuring the Tor network from public directory information. In *HotPets* (2009).

[33] McLachlan, J., and Hopper, N. Don't clog the queue! Circuit clogging and mitigation in P2P anonymity schemes. In *FC* (2008).

[34] Mittal, P., Khurshid, A., Juen, J., Caesar, M., and Borisov, N. Stealthy traffic analysis of low-latency anonymous communication using throughput-fingerprinting, 2011. Available at http://netfiles.uiuc.edu/mittal2/www/throughput-fingerprinting.pdf.

[35] Mittal, P., Paxson, V., Sommer, R., and Winterrowd, M. Securing mediated trace access using black-box permutation analysis. In *HotNets* (2009).

[36] Möller, U., Cottrell, L., Palfrader, P., and Sassaman, L. Mixmaster Protocol—Version 2. IETF Internet Draft, July 2003.

[37] Murdoch, S. J. Hot or not: Revealing hidden services by their clock skew. In *CCS* (2006).

[38] Murdoch, S. J., and Danezis, G. Low-cost traffic analysis of Tor. In *IEEE S&P* (2005).

[39] Murdoch, S. J., and Zieliński, P. Sampled traffic analysis by Internet-exchange-level adversaries. In *PETS* (2007).

[40] Overlier, L., and Syverson, P. Locating hidden servers. In *IEEE S&P* (2006).

[41] Padhye, J., Firoiu, V., Towsley, D., and Kurose, J. Modeling tcp throughput: a simple model and its empirical validation. *SIGCOMM Comput. Commun. Rev. 28* (October 1998), 303–314.

[42] Perry, M. Torflow: Tor network analysis. In *HotPets* (2009).

[43] Raymond, J.-F. Traffic analysis: Protocols, attacks, design issues, and open problems. In *Designing Privacy Enhancing Technologies* (2000).

[44] Serjantov, A., and Danezis, G. Towards an information theoretic metric for anonymity. In *PET* (2002).

[45] Snader, R., and Borisov, N. Eigenspeed: Secure peer-to-peer bandwidth evaluation. In *IPTPS* (2009).

[46] Syverson, P., Tsudik, G., Reed, M., and Landwehr, C. Towards an analysis of onion routing security. In *Designing Privacy Enhancing Technologies* (2000), pp. 96–114.

[47] Syverson, P. F., Goldschlag, D. M., and Reed, M. G. Anonymous connections and onion routing. *Security and Privacy, IEEE Symposium on 0* (1997).

[48] The Tor Project. Tor metrics portal. http://metrics.torproject.org/.

[49] The Tor Project. Who uses Tor. http://www.torproject.org/about/torusers.html.en. Accessed Februrary 2011.

[50] Wright, M., Adler, M., Levine, B. N., and Shields, C. An analysis of the degradation of anonymous protocols. In *NDSS* (2002).

[51] Wright, M., Adler, M., Levine, B. N., and Shields, C. Defending anonymous communication against passive logging attacks. In *IEEE S&P* (2003).

App Isolation: Get the Security of Multiple Browsers with Just One

Eric Y. Chen
Carnegie Mellon University
Mountain View, CA
eric.chen@sv.cmu.edu

Jason Bau
Stanford University
Stanford, CA
jbau@stanford.edu

Charles Reis
Google, Inc.
Seattle, WA
creis@google.com

Adam Barth
Google, Inc.
Mountain View, CA
abarth@google.com

Collin Jackson
Carnegie Mellon University
Mountain View, CA
collin.jackson@sv.cmu.edu

ABSTRACT

Many browser-based attacks can be prevented by using separate browsers for separate web sites. However, most users access the web with only one browser. We explain the security benefits that using multiple browsers provides in terms of two concepts: entry-point restriction and state isolation. We combine these concepts into a general *app isolation* mechanism that can provide the same security benefits in a single browser. While not appropriate for all types of web sites, many sites with high-value user data can opt in to app isolation to gain defenses against a wide variety of browser-based attacks. We implement app isolation in the Chromium browser and verify its security properties using finite-state model checking. We also measure the performance overhead of app isolation and conduct a large-scale study to evaluate its adoption complexity for various types of sites, demonstrating how the app isolation mechanisms are suitable for protecting a number of high-value Web applications, such as online banking.

Categories and Subject Descriptors

H.4.3 [**Information Systems Applications**]: Communications Applications—*Information browsers*; K.6.5 [**Management of Computing and Information Systems**]: Security and Protection

General Terms

Security, Design, Verification

Keywords

Web Browser Architecture, Isolation, Web Application Security, Security Modeling, Cross-Site Request Forgery, Cross-Site Scripting

1. INTRODUCTION

Security experts often advise users to use more than one browser: one for surfing the wild web and others for visiting "sensitive" web sites, such as online banking web sites [1, 2]. This advice raises a number of questions. Can using more than one browser actually improve security? If so, which properties are important? Can we realize these security benefits without resorting to the use of more than one browser?

In this paper, we seek to answer these questions by crystallizing two key security properties of using multiple browsers, which we refer to as *entry-point restriction* and *state isolation*. We find that these two properties are responsible for much of the security benefit of using multiple browsers, and we show how to achieve these security benefits in a single browser by letting web sites opt in to these behaviors.

Consider a user who diligently uses two browsers for security. This user designates one browser as "sensitive" and one as "non-sensitive". She uses the sensitive browser only for accessing her online bank (through known URLs and bookmarks) and refrains from visiting the general Web with the sensitive browser. Meanwhile, she uses only the non-sensitive browser for the rest of the Web and does not use it to visit high-value sites.

Using two browsers in this manner does have security benefits. For example, consider the case of reflected cross-site scripting (XSS). In a reflected XSS attack, the attacker crafts a malicious URL containing an attack string and navigates the user's browser to that URL, tricking the honest web site into echoing back the attack string in a dangerous context. The attack has more difficulty succeeding if the user runs more than one browser because the attack relies on *which* of the user's browsers the attacker navigates. If the attacker navigates the user's non-sensitive browser to a maliciously crafted URL on the user's bank, the attack will have no access to the user's banking-related state, which resides in another browser.

From this discussion, one might conclude that isolation of credentials and other state is the essential property that makes using two browsers more secure. However, another security property provided by using multiple browsers is equally important: entry-point restriction. To illustrate entry-point restriction by its absence, imagine if the attacker could arbitrarily coordinate navigation of the users' two browsers and open an arbitrary bank URL in the sensitive browser. Now, the attacker's maliciously crafted URL and attack string can be transplanted from the non-sensitive browser to the sensitive browser, leading to disaster.

In reality, it is extremely difficult for Web attackers to coordinate the navigation of two different browsers on the users' computer. This isolation between the two browsers provides the entry-point restriction property. Namely, sessions in the sensitive browser with an honest web site always begin with a fixed set of entry points (e.g., the site's home page or a set of bookmarks) and then proceed only to URLs chosen by the web site itself, not those chosen by a third party. Because the bank's entry points are restricted, the attacker is unable to inject the attack string into the user's session with the bank.

State isolation, in turn, augments the security provided by entry-point restriction when using two browsers. State isolation plays a critical role, for example, in preventing history sniffing [3, 4] and cache timing attacks [4, 5] because these attacks do not rely upon the attacker navigating the user's browser to a maliciously crafted URL. State isolation between browsers can even protect a user's high-value session data against exploits of browser vulnerabilities that give the attacker control of the rendering process [6, 7]. In concert, entry-point restriction and state isolation provide the lion's share of the security benefits of using two browsers.

In our example above, we use a single high-value site to illustrate the security benefit of isolation using *two* browsers, but the isolation benefits extend naturally to accessing multiple sites, each in their own browser. In this paper, we show that we can realize these security benefits within a single browser by allowing web sites to whitelist their entry points and request isolated storage. This is not a pinpoint defense against a specific attack but rather a general approach that has benefits in a number of attack scenarios.

The security benefits of our mechanism do come with a compatibility cost for certain types of web sites, as it places some limitations on deep links and third-party cookies. To avoid disrupting existing web sites, we advocate deploying our mechanism as an opt in feature. Furthermore, we hypothesize and experimentally verify the types of web sites that are suitable for our mechanism. Our experiments measured the number of entry points used by popular sites in a study of 10,551 browsers running Mozilla's Test Pilot platform [8]. Over 1 million links were included in our study. We discovered that many security sensitive sites such as online banking applications can easily deploy our mechanisms. However, highly social or content-driven applications such as Facebook and New York Times will have difficulties adopting our proposal.

To evaluate the security benefits of app isolation, we model our proposals in the Alloy language, leveraging previous work on modeling web security concepts in Alloy [9]. We enrich our existing Alloy model with new concepts, such as `EntryPoints` and `RenderingEngines`, to model the essential concepts in our proposal. Our analysis revealed two issues with our initial proposals: one related to HTTP redirects and one related to an unexpected interaction between entry-point restriction and state isolation. We repair these errors and validate that our improved proposals pass muster with Alloy.

We view our main contributions in this paper as follows.

- We crystallize the security benefits of using multiple browsers into two basic concepts.
- We provide a security mechanism that grants a single browser the security benefits of multiple browsers, compatible with certain types of existing sites.
- We validate the security of our mechanism using formal modeling, adjusting our design to patch uncovered vulnerabilities.
- We evaluate the compatibility of our mechanism using Mozilla's Test Pilot platform. We are the first to utilize this platform to conduct an academic study.

1.1 Organization.

The rest of this paper is organized as follows. Section 2 presents related app isolation work. Section 3 identifies the key security benefits of using multiple browsers. Section 4 discusses how browsers can identify apps that have opted in to our proposal. Section 5 and Section 6 describe our design in detail. Section 7 evaluates our proposal in terms of its security, complexity to adopt, and performance, and we conclude in Section 8.

2. BACKGROUND

In this section, we examine how the security properties of using multiple browsers have surfaced in related work and compare them to our proposal.

2.1 Isolation with multiple browsers

For users who choose to browse the web using multiple browsers, site-specific browsers (SSBs) can make the browsing experience simpler and more convenient. SSBs provide customized browsers that are each dedicated to accessing pages from a single web application. Examples of SSBs include Prism [10] and Fluid [11].

SSBs are simply special-purpose browsers and can provide the security benefits of using multiple general-purpose browsers. However, SSBs can become difficult to manage when users interact with and navigate between a large number of different web applications. We show that a single browser can realize the security benefits of SSBs without the management burden on the user. For example, our proposal allows users to seamlessly and securely follow a link from one app to another, even in a single browser tab.

2.2 Isolation within a single browser

The concept of finer-grained isolation inside a single browser has been explored by many researchers. However, prior work has not identified the essential factors needed for a single browser to achieve the same security benefits as using multiple browsers.

Recent browsers have begun employing sandbox technology that protects the local file system from attacks that exploit browser vulnerabilities. For example, Internet Explorer on Windows Vista introduced Protected Mode [12], which protects the local file system from being modified by a compromised rendering engine. The Google Chrome browser's sandbox additionally protects the local file system from being read by a compromised by a rendering engine [6]. Unfortunately, neither of these sandboxing technologies protect *web application* state, such as cookies and local storage data, from being accessed by a compromised rendering engine.

The OP browser [13] isolates plugins from state associated with other applications by enforcing restrictions on the cross-origin request API exposed to plugins. The Gazelle browser [14] goes a step further by restricting the cross-origin request API for the entire rendering engine. Under the Gazelle approach, a *web application*'s state is only visible to the rendering engine containing it. This prevents a malicious web entity from compromising its own rendering engine to gain access to the state of other web applications. However, because Gazelle denies rendering engines from requesting cross-origin resources unless their MIME type indicates a library format such as JavaScript or Cascading Style Sheets (CSS), it imposes a compatibility cost on many web sites [15].

One approach that can mitigate the compatibility costs of restricting the cross-origin request API is to allow an application to explicitly declare the URLs that compose it. One example of this approach is the Tahoma browser [16], which allows applications to specify a manifest file listing which URLs should be included in the same protection domain. Tahoma uses a separate state container for each application, so state associated with one application will be inaccessible in another. Although Tahoma realized the importance of isolating web application state, it did not incorporate the other benefit of using multiple browsers: restricting non-sensitive web sites from directing the user to a sensitive URL.

OMash [17] only attaches cookies to same-origin requests, effectively isolating state within a particular site. Each new entry into a site creates a new session. This approach mitigates reflected XSS, cross-site request forgery (CSRF), and click-jacking, since another site cannot hi-jack an existing session with a hyperlink or iframe. However, the drawback of OMash lies in its inability to maintain user state across multiple browsing sessions.

Content Security Policy [18] attempts to mitigate XSS by allowing web sites to only execute scripts from whitelisted external JavaScript files. SOMA [19] aims to alleviate XSS and CSRF by making the host of web content mutually approve the content request with the web content embedder. Unfortunately, both of these defenses are geared to counter individual attacks such as XSS and CSRF. They do not achieve the full security benefits as using multiple browsers, such as defenses against rendering engine exploits.

In contrast, our work aims to capture the same underlying properties of using separate browsers for sensitive web apps, gaining the security benefits in a single browser.

3. SECURELY ISOLATING WEB SITES

In this section, we investigate exactly which security benefits can be achieved by visiting sensitive web sites in a different web browser than non-sensitive web sites. We classify many common browser-based attacks and show that a large number of them can be mitigated through the use of multiple browsers. We then introduce two new mechanisms in a single browser that can be used to achieve these same benefits, for particular web sites that choose to opt in and accept the compatibility implications.

3.1 Benefits of Multiple Browsers

Suppose a user wishes to protect certain sensitive web sites from more dangerous ones by using two browsers, A and B. To achieve this, she must abide by the following rules:

1. Only type in passwords for sensitive web sites with Browser A. This rule ensures that user state for the sensitive web sites are stored only in Browser A.

2. Never type in URLs or click on bookmarks to non-sensitive web sites with Browser A, and never type into Browser A URLs received from non-sensitive web sites or other untrusted sources. This rule prevents Browser A from leaking any sensitive information to Browser B and prohibits Browser B from contaminating sensitive states in Browser A.

If the user strictly abides by the rules above, all sensitive state would reside in Browser A, isolated from non-sensitive web sites and unable to leak to Browser B. Furthermore, the integrity of Browser A is maintained because untrusted content in Browser B cannot infect Browser A, preventing attacks such as reflected XSS.

These rules prevent the "cross-origin" versions of the attacks listed in Table 1. We classify attacks as "cross-origin" if the attack is launched from a different origin than the victim origin, as opposed to "same-origin" attacks (such as one Facebook page trying to mount a CSRF attack on another Facebook page). Using a separate browser does not prevent the same-origin versions of these attacks, nor same-origin only attacks such as stored XSS, because the attacker resides in the same browser as the victim.

We provide a more thorough analysis of the cross-origin attacks from Table 1 below. We assume the attacker wishes to attack a victim web site to which the user has authenticated and can lure the user into visiting a malicious web site on a different origin. Furthermore, we assume that the user uses separate browsers according to the rules above.

- **Reflected XSS** – In a reflected XSS attack, the attacker lures the user into visiting a malicious URL inside the non-sensitive browser. This URL will allow the attacker's script to execute inside the victim's origin. However, because the user is authenticated to the victim site in the sensitive browser, the attacker's script will not have access to the user's session.

- **Session fixation** – In a session fixation attack, the attacker includes a known session ID inside a victim URL, then lures the user into visiting this URL and tricks her into logging in. Once the user is logged in, the attacker can freely impersonate the user with the shared session ID. However, because the user only types her password into the sensitive browser, the attack will fail.

- **Cross-origin resource import** – In a cross origin resource import attack, the attacker's page requests a sensitive resource from the victim's origin as a script or style sheet. If the user were authenticated to the victim site in the same browser, this request can leak confidential information to the attacker. However, the user is authenticated instead in the sensitive browser, thereby foiling the attack.

- **Click-jacking** – Click-jacking attacks overlay a transparent iframe from a victim page over a part of the attacker's page where the user is likely to click. This aims to trick the user into clicking somewhere on the

Cross-origin Attacks	Entry-point Restriction	State Isolation	Separate browser
Reflected XSS	✓		✓
Session Fixation	✓		✓
Cross-Origin Resource Import	✓	✓	✓
Click-jacking		✓	✓
CSRF	✓	✓	✓
Visited Link Sniffing		✓	✓
Cache Timing Attack		✓	✓
Rendering Engine Hi-jacking		✓	✓

Table 1: Cross-origin attacks mitigated by entry-point restriction, state isolation, and using separate browsers. Same-origin attacks, such as stored XSS, are not mitigated.

victim's page (e.g., the delete account button) without realizing it. Because the user is authenticated in the sensitive browser, clicking on the transparent victim iframe in the non-sensitive browser will cause no damage.

- **Cross-site request forgery** – In a traditional CSRF attack, the adversary makes subresource requests within a page she owns in an attempt to change the user's state on the victim's server. This attack succeeds because the user's credentials are attached to the attacker's subresource request. However, because the user authenticates only in the sensitive browser, the malicious request will not have a cookie attached, rendering it harmless.

- **Visited link sniffing** – The attacker's web site might attempt to sniff the user's browsing history by drawing visited links in a different color or style than unvisited ones, and then using JavaScript or CSS to discover which have been visited. Although a possible mitigation has been proposed and adopted by several major browsers [20], new attacks have been discovered that can detect browsing history despite the defense [21]. However, if the user uses separate browsers, these browsers have different history databases, so a web site in the non-sensitive browser is unable to discern the browsing history of the sensitive browser.

- **Cache timing attack** – Similar to visited link sniffing attacks, an attacker can measure the time to load a victim resource to determine if the user has visited it [4, 5]. Different browsers have different caches for their web resources, so web sites in the non-sensitive browser cannot detect cache hits or misses in the sensitive browser.

- **Rendering engine hi-jacking** – A powerful attacker might exploit a vulnerability in the browser's rendering engine to hi-jack its execution. For browsers with a single rendering engine instance (e.g., Firefox and Safari), this would let the attacker access all the user's state, such as the victim site's cookies and page contents. These attacks still apply to browsers with multiple rendering engine instances, if they rely on the rendering engine to enforce the Same-Origin Policy (e.g., Chrome and IE8). However, if the user logged in to the victim site with a different browser, the victim's cookies and sensitive pages will reside in an entirely different OS process. Assuming the exploited rendering engine is sandboxed, the attacker's exploit is unable to access this process.

3.2 Site Isolation in a Single Browser

As shown in the previous section, using a dedicated browser to visit certain sites mitigates a significant number of web attacks. This observation raises a question: which properties of browsing with a single browser make it vulnerable to these attacks? We believe the answer to this question can be summarized in three points:

1. Malicious sites are free to make requests to vulnerable parts of victim's site.

2. Malicious sites can make requests that have access to the victim's cookies and session data.

3. Malicious sites can exploit the rendering engine for direct access to in-memory state and to stored data from the victim site.

Our key observation is that these abilities are not fundamental flaws of browsing with a single browser but rather weaknesses of current browsers. We believe that for many types of web sites, it is possible to simulate the behavior of multiple browsers with a single browser by solving each of these weaknesses. These changes come with a compatibility cost, however, because benign third-party sites are also prevented from accessing the user's cookies. We evaluate the complexity that different types of sites face for adopting these changes in Section 7.2.

In the next three sections, we introduce mechanisms for removing these limitations in a single browser. First, we provide a means for web sites to opt in to this protection if they accept the compatibility implications. Second, we prevent untrusted third parties from making requests to vulnerable parts of these web sites. Third, we isolate the persistent and in-memory state of these sites from other sites. Because our approach works best with "app-like" web sites that contain sensitive user data and few cross-site interactions, we refer to this approach as *app isolation*.

4. IDENTIFYING ISOLATED WEB APPS

App isolation can provide a web site with the security benefits of running in a dedicated browser, but it comes at some compatibility cost. Isolating cookies and in-memory state not only prevents malicious web sites from compromising sensitive data, it can also hinder legitimate web sites from sharing information. For example, Facebook Connect[22] lets web sites access visitors' identifying information via Facebook, which would not work if Facebook was isolated in a separate browser. To remain compatible with web sites that desire this sharing, we employ an opt-in policy that lets web developers decide whether to isolate their site or web application from the rest of the browser.

We must choose the opt-in mechanism carefully to avoid introducing new security concerns, and we must consider the granularity at which the isolation should take effect. In this section, we first show the consequences of an inadequate opt-in mechanism using HTTP headers. Then, we describe a viable origin-wide approach with *host-meta*, and refine it to support sub-origin level web applications with manifest files.

Bootstrapping with HTTP headers.

As a straw man, we first consider identifying an isolated app using a custom HTTP header (e.g., X-App-Isolation: 1). If the browser receives this header on an HTTP response, the browser treats all future responses from the origin as belonging to the isolated app.

The primary disadvantage of this approach is that it does not verify that the given response has the privilege to speak for the entire origin. This lack of verification lets owners of portions of an origin (e.g., `foo.com/~username/`) opt the entire origin in to app isolation. A malicious sub-domain owner can use this mechanism to prevent desirable sharing on other parts of the origin, or he can misconfigure the app (e.g., listing a non-existent entry point) to perform a denial-of-service attack. Worse, bootstrapping with a custom HTTP response header might not enforce the policy for the initial request sent to the server, opening a window of vulnerability.

Bootstrapping with Host-meta.

To avoid attacks that grant the privileges of the entire origin to each resource, the browser can instead bootstrap app isolation using a file at a well-known location that can only be accessed by the legitimate owner of the origin. The *host-meta* mechanism is designed for exactly this reason [23]. With *host-meta*, the owner of the origin creates an XML file containing app isolation meta data located at `/.well-known/host-meta`. This meta data can include configuration information, such as a list of acceptable entry points. Because *host-meta* should be controllable only by the legitimate owner of the origin, an adversary controlling only a directory will not be able to influence the app isolation policy for the entire origin.

It is essential to retrieve *host-meta* information through a secure channel such as HTTPS. Otherwise, an active network attacker can replace the host-meta entries with bogus URLs, allowing the attacker to conduct denial-of-service or other misconfiguration attacks.

One downside of bootstrapping with *host-meta* is that is has poor performance because an additional round trip is required to fetch a resource if the host-meta file is not in the cache.

Bootstrapping with Manifest File.

The above proposals work at the granularity of an origin. However, it is also possible to isolate web apps at a finer granularity without violating the security concerns of "finer-grained origins" [24].

In the Chrome Web Store, web application developers package their applications using a manifest file [25]. This method of packaging web applications is becoming common; for example, Mozilla's Open Web Applications are also packaged using a such file [26]. The file includes a list of URL patterns that comprise the application, together with other meta data such as requested permissions. The manifest file provides extra context to the browser for how to treat the app, allowing it to enforce policies that might break ordinary web content. The Chrome Web Store also supports "verified apps [27]," in which the manifest file's author demonstrates that she has control over all origins included in the application's URL patterns.

We use additional syntax in the manifest to let applications in the Chrome Web Store opt in to app isolation. The URL patterns in the manifest might or might not span an entire origin, which would allow a site like Google Maps (e.g., `http://www.google.com/maps`) to opt into isolation features without affecting the rest of the origin. The Chrome Web Store already provides a mechanism for verifying that the manifest is provided by the web site author, which we leverage to prevent a malicious manifest file from bundling attacker URLs in the same app as a victim site.

The reason this does not run afoul of the typical security concerns of finer-grained origins is that our state isolation effectively separates the application's pages from the rest of the web, including non-application pages in the same origin. Origin contamination via scripts or cookies is blocked because an application page and a non-application page do not share the same renderer process or cookie store.

Both origin-level isolation using *host-meta* and application-level isolation using manifest files are viable opt in mechanisms. We leave it to browser vendors to decide on which method they deem appropriate. In the remainder of this paper, we refer to the unit of isolation as an *app*, whether designated as an origin or a collection of URLs in a manifest.

5. ENTRY-POINT RESTRICTION

Using multiple browsers securely requires the user to refrain from visiting a sensitive app at a URL that could be constructed by an attacker. Instead, the user always visits the app in the sensitive browser from a known starting point. Simulating this behavior with a single browser requires an intuitive way of visiting URLs of sensitive apps without compromising security. Our proposal for *Entry-point Restriction* provides a way to safely transition between sensitive and non-sensitive pages in a single browser, without altering the user's behavior.

In this section, we present the rules for entry-point restriction and discuss the challenges for selecting appropriate entry points. Table 1 lists attacks that are prevented by entry-point restriction.

5.1 Design

Under the entry-point restriction policy, we define an *entry point* to be a landing page of an app designated by the app's owner. Any app may choose to opt into entry-point restriction by providing at least one entry point.

Once an app opts into entry-point restriction, the browser may load a resource from the app if and only if at least one of the following statements holds true.

- The resource is requested by a page inside the app.
- The URL of the resource is a valid entry point for the app.

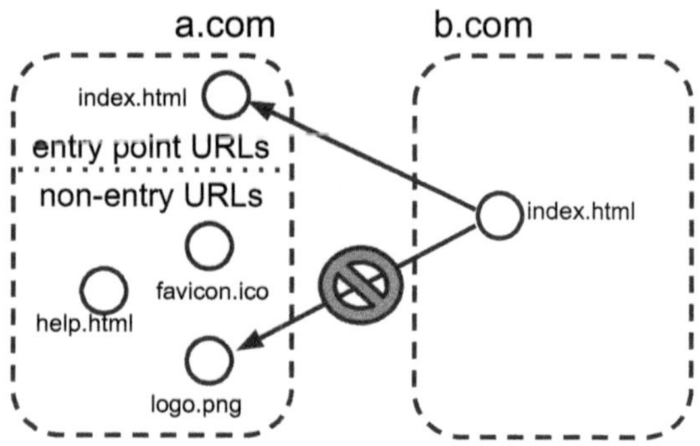

Figure 1: Entry-point Restriction

Figure 1 illustrates how entry-point restriction works in practice. Suppose `a.com` hosts its company logo at `a.com/logo.png`, and specifies an entry point at `a.com/index.html`. Meanwhile, `b.com/index.html` includes a hyperlink to `a.com/index.html` and embeds an image with the source attribute of `a.com/logo.png`. In this scenario, the user is able to follow the hyperlink because it points to a valid entry point. However, the logo will fail to load because it is a cross origin request to a non-entry-point URL.

Choosing entry points.

Entry points are whitelisted URLs or URL patterns that the app's owner trusts to load safely even when requested by an attacker's page. Therefore, it is crucial to choose these URLs with care. The goal is to select common landing pages that do not present opportunities for the attacker to exploit the user's credentials. We offer the following guidelines for selecting entry points.

- An entry point URL should cause no sensitive state changes, because an attacker may request it with the user's credentials.
- An entry point URL pattern should be as tightly constrained as possible, reducing the opportunity for attackers to place malicious code in the URL.
- An entry point URL should not return confidential information in a form that could be accessed on a cross-origin page, such as JSON.

In most cases, the default landing page for an app meets these guidelines. Many sites expect their users to arrive via multiple landing pages, creating a need to support multiple entry points. For example, an online banking site may have an English login page and a French login page. For additional flexibility, we also allow web sites to use wildcard characters in their entry point URLs (e.g., www.a.com/*/ where * represents any number of non-'/' characters). Allowing wildcards trades off some security benefits for compatibility because the number of wildcard characters and entry points is directly correlated with the size of the app's attack surface. However, this is still an improvement over having no such policy. We recommend that app owners restrict their policies as tightly as possible and use wildcards only when necessary.

It is important to note that not all web sites are well-suited for entry-point restriction. Some sites depend heavily on deep links to content, such as socially integrated sites like Facebook or content-oriented sites like New York Times. These sites will have a difficult time adopting the policy, because it is extremely difficult to identify all the URLs that legitimate sites may link to. We show in Section 7.2 that other types of sites, such as online banks, are amenable to these restrictions and can benefit from entry-point restriction.

Sub-resource restrictions.

By default, entry-point restriction must deny sub-resources at non-entry-point URLs from loading. This will prevent vulnerabilities such as reflected XSS and CSRF; however, it may also affect legitimate web pages. For example, loading a non-entry-point image will fail despite being typically a safe action.

Fortunately, this usability constraint can be alleviated. Entry-point restriction is only necessary because malicious requests will have the user's authentication tokens attached to them. Section 6 describes how State Isolation can be used to isolate these authentication tokens from sub-resource requests. When used in conjunction with state isolation, entry-point restriction can safely allow sub-resources at non-entry-point URLs.

5.2 Implementation

We implemented a proof-of-concept entry-point restriction mechanism in the Chromium browser. The entire system consists of less than 100 lines of C++ code. Our implementation enforces entry-point restriction inside Chromium's WebKit rendering engine. More specifically, we modified the *CanDisplay()* function of *SecurityOrigin*, which gets called before every web resource request. If the URL of a web resource violates the entry-point restriction policy, WebKit will not issue the network request.

Storing entry points.

Like most web resources, it is desirable for the browser to cache entry-point restriction information for performance. The exact caching method may differ depending on how apps opt into entry-point restriction.

If apps use host-meta to bootstrap app isolation, browsers could cache this information like conventional web resources. Users should be able to clear their app isolation information the same way they clear cookies or browsing histories. Most modern browsers offer users with private browsing features that allow them to browse without persistent storage [28]. To be compatible with these private browsing features, the host-meta information in such modes must be treated like cookies or browsing history, not being written to disk.

If apps instead use app manifests (such as the installed apps from the Chrome Web Store), the policies are stored in the browser's persistent app meta data. This essentially permits the browser to permanently cache the app isolation policies as long as the application is installed. To update the policy, developers can use the standard app update process.

6. STATE ISOLATION

The remaining security benefits of using multiple browsers shown in Table 1 result from isolating an app's state from other web sites. In traditional browsers, attackers can try to take advantage of persistent state, such as using an app's cookies in a CSRF attack. They can also try to directly access in-memory state by exploiting the browser's rendering engine and then inspecting memory.

We can simulate the state benefits of using a separate browser for an app with a single multi-process browser. This requires isolating both the in-memory and persistent state of the app from other web sites, using the process and storage architectures of the browser.

6.1 Design

Once the browser identifies the URLs comprising an isolated app (as discussed in Section 4), it can ensure instances of those pages are isolated in memory and on disk.

In-Memory State.

Any top-level page loaded from a URL in the app's manifest must be loaded in a renderer process dedicated to that app. Any sub-resource requests are then made from the same process as the parent page, even if they target URLs outside the app's manifest.

We treat sub-frames in the same manner as sub-resources. While this may open the app's process to attacks from a non-app iframe, the app does have some control over which iframes are present. Similarly, an app URL may be requested as an iframe or sub-resource outside the app process. The potential risk of this approach, that of framing attacks, is mitigated by persistent state isolation as described below, which ensures that such requests do not carry the user's credentials. This approach has the same security properties as loading the app in a separate browser.

Top-level pages from all other URLs are not loaded in the app's renderer process. Combined with an effective sandbox mechanism [6], this helps prevent an exploited non-app renderer process from accessing the in-memory state present in the app's process.

The browser kernel process can then take advantage of the process isolation between apps and other sites to enforce stricter controls on accessing credentials and other resources. HTTP Auth credentials, session cookies, and other in-memory state stored in the browser kernel is only revealed to the app's process.

Persistent State.

The browser kernel also creates a separate storage partition for all persistent state in the isolated app. Any requests from the app's renderer process use only this partition, and requests from other renderer processes do not have access to it. The partition includes all cookies, localStorage data, and other local state.

As a result, a user's session within an app process is not visible in other renderer processes, even if a URL from the app is loaded in an iframe outside the app process.

The storage partition can also isolate the browser history and cache for an app from that for other web sites. This can help protect against visited link and cache timing attacks, in which an attacker tries to infer a user's specific navigations within an app.

Combining with Entry-point Restriction.

When both entry-point restriction and state isolation are used together, the mechanisms complement each other and we can relax one of the restrictions for entry-point restriction. Specifically, a non-app page can be permitted to request non-entry-point URLs for sub-resources and iframes. This mimics the behavior when using a separate browser for the app, and it still protects the user because credentials are safely restricted to the app process.

6.2 Implementation

We implemented state isolation for apps in Chromium with roughly 1400 lines of code. For in-memory state isolation, Chromium already offers stricter process separation between installed web apps from the Chrome Web Store than most web sites. Pages from URLs in an app manifest are loaded in a dedicated app process. In the general case, Chromium avoids putting pages from different origins in the same process when possible, but cross-origin pages can share a process in many cases to avoid compatibility concerns [29].

However, we needed to strengthen Chromium's process isolation to more thoroughly prevent non-app pages from loading in the app's process. First, we needed to ensure that apps are not placed in general renderer processes if the browser's process limit is reached. Second, we needed to ensure navigations from an app URL to a non-app URL always exit the app's process.

For persistent state isolation, we changed Chromium to create a new URL context (a subset of the user's profile data) for each isolated app. The cookies, localStorage data, and other persistent information is stored on disk in a separate directory than the persistent data for general web sites. The browser process can ensure that this data is only provided to renderer processes associated with the app, and not to general renderer processes.

7. EVALUATION

In this section, we evaluate state isolation and entry-point restriction in three ways. First, we perform a formal analysis for the security properties of these mechanisms. Second, we experimentally assess the feasibility of various web sites adopting these mechanisms. Finally, we quantify their performance overhead relative to using one or multiple browsers.

7.1 Security

We used model-checking to evaluate the combined security characteristics of app isolation using both state isolation and entry-point restriction. Our approach consists of defining the security goals of app isolation, then modeling our implementation, its security goals, and attacker behavior in the web security framework described in [9] using Alloy [30, 31], a declarative modeling language based on first-order relational logic. We then analyze whether the expressed goals were met with the help of the Alloy analyzer software.

Security Goals.

The broad security goal of both our mechanisms are *isolation*. Isolation protects sensitive resources belonging to the app, such as non-entry URLs, scripts, and user credentials, against unauthorized use by web pages or scripts not belonging to the app. We distill two *isolation* goals which, if met, will provide the app with defenses against the attacks described in Section 3.1. (This property holds because the attacks either require an attacker to gain access to exploitable URLs within the app or use sensitive state from the app, or both.)

These goals are modeled by Alloy *assertions* (logical predicates whose consistency with the model may be checked) analogous to the following statements:

1. Browser contexts (pages or scripts) originating outside an app will not read or overwrite state issued within the app, such as credential cookies.

2. Browser contexts (pages or scripts) originating outside an app will not obtain a non-entry resource within the app.

Isolation Mechanisms.

We model entry-point restriction as an Alloy *fact* (a logic constraint which always holds), reproduced below. The *fact* states that the *browser* will not issue any cross-origin requests for a non-entry resource in an entry-restricting origin.

```
fact StrictEntryEnforcement {
  all sc:ScriptContext |
    sc.location=StrictEntryBrowser implies
      no areq:sc.transactions.req |
        areq.path=NON_ENTRY and
        isCrossOriginRequest[areq] and
        isRequestToStrictEntryOrigin[areq]
}}
```

To model state isolation, we refined the browser model of [9] by adding a set of `RenderingEngine`s associated with each `Browser`. Each `RenderingEngine` then runs a set of `ScriptContexts`, as shown in the Alloy *signatures* below:

```
sig Browser extends HTTPClient {
    engines: set RenderingEngine }

sig RenderingEngine {
   contexts: set ScriptContext,
   inBrowser : one Browser }
```

The actual state isolation is modeled by Alloy *facts*. The first fact states that each `cookie` in the model is tagged with the `RenderingEngine` of the `ScriptContext` in which it was first received. The next states that access to `cookies` are restricted to only `ScriptContexts` from an origin matching the domain setting of the `cookie` executing in a `RenderingEngine` matching the `cookie` tag.

Our app container model also includes a browser behavior relevant to app isolation, as described by Section 6.1: it associates a newly opened `ScriptContext` with the existing `RenderingEngine` of an app if the top-level URL of the new `ScriptContext` is within the app.

Finally, our modeling assumes that users will behave conservatively within an isolated app window, meaning attackers cannot get their `ScriptContexts` in the same `RenderingEngine` as an app when separate `RenderingEngines` exist.

Web and Rendering Engine Attacker.

We then modeled the abilities of the attacker. As described in [9], the abilities of web attackers include ownership of a web server by which they can introduce `ScriptContexts` under their control into the user's `browser`. Our modeled "rendering engine attackers" can additionally create scripts that compromise the `RenderingEngine` of the user's browser, giving them arbitrary control over other `ScriptContexts` on the same `RenderingEngine`, such as reading cookies, creating new `ScriptContexts`, sending requests, etc. However, our model assumes that storage isolation is enforced by an entity outside the rendering engines, like a browser kernel. Thus, the "rendering engine attacker" cannot compromise the storage isolation mechanism.

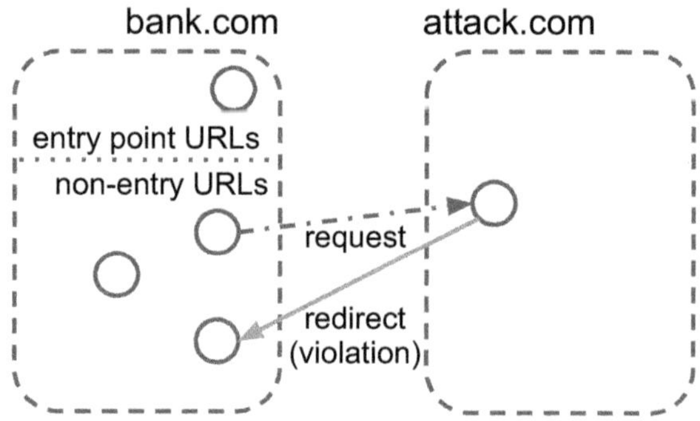

Figure 2: Entry-point restriction violation found by Alloy model.

Entry Restriction Results.

We first checked our implementation of entry restriction against the stated security goals and found that assertion 2 above was violated. We confirmed that this violation also existed in our implementation at that time and note (with some sheepishness) that the implementation bug resembles ones previously found by [9] in Referer validation defenses proposed by [32].

The violation, illustrated in Figure 2, occurs because of HTTP redirects. Suppose origin *bank.com* is a victim origin that uses entry-point restriction, and origin *attack.com* is a external origin that does **not** use entry-point restriction. A page created by *bank.com* is allowed by the browser to cause a request for a non-entry resource in *attack.com*, since *attack.com* does not use entry-point restriction. *attack.com* may then issue a redirect to the browser telling it to find the requested resource back at *bank.com*. The browser will then re-issue the request, now to *bank.com*, which will be granted by *bank.com* because the request was initiated by a context owned by *bank.com*. This violates the integrity goal because the external origin *attack.com* plays a role in redirecting the request back to *bank.com*, thus "requesting" the non-entry resource.

To fix this violation, we updated our implementation to keep track of all redirects experienced by a request and to refrain from sending a request for a non-entry resource to an entry-isolating domain if any external domains are recorded in the request's redirects. We verified that the model containing this fix now upholds the previously violated *integrity* assertion, up to the finite size we tried (up to 10 `NetworkEvents`, which are either requests or responses).

App Isolation Results.

We then used the model to check both app mechanisms (entry-point restriction and state isolation) and found that neither mechanism individually was able to uphold the security goals in the presence of the rendering engine attacker. For

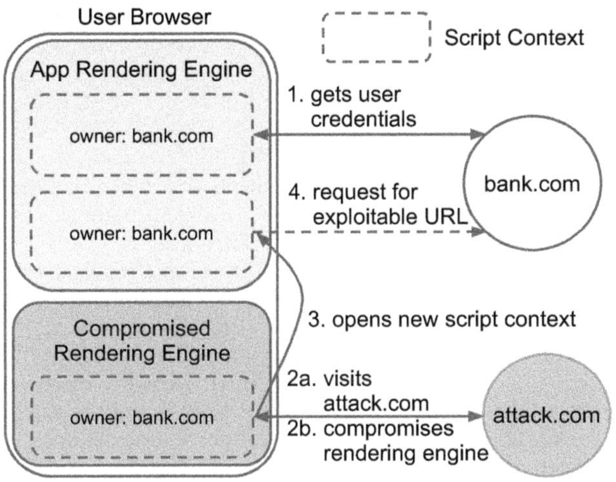

Figure 3: Isolation violation found by Alloy model. Request 4 to a non-entry URL, containing credentials issued within the app, is granted if entry-point restriction is absent or incorrect.

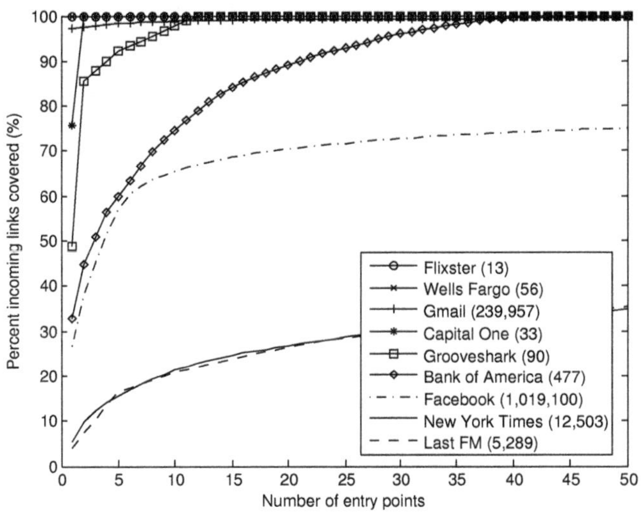

Figure 4: Entry points to popular sites observed by 10,551 Mozilla Test Pilot browsers. Numbers in parentheses indicate the total number of incoming links observed.

entry-point restriction without state isolation, there is only a single `RenderingEngine` for all `ScriptContexts`, letting the attacker trivially violate assertion 1 above by compromising the `RenderingEngine` and accessing cookies issued by the app. For state isolation without entry-point restriction, the Alloy analyzer found a violation of assertion 2 above that is very similar to the violation we found in the model with both mechanisms. We will therefore describe both results together in the next paragraphs.

When checking the model with both mechanisms, the Alloy analyzer found no violations to assertion 1 above but did find a violation for assertion 2. This violation occurs because our implementation at the time did not consider the app container as part of its notion of "same-origin" when applied to entry-point restriction. Figure 3 illustrates this violation, as well as the violation found for state isolation without entry-point restriction. The scenario is as follows:

Alice opens a session with *bank.com* as an app with a dedicated *app* renderer and receives credentials. Alice also visits *attack.com* with the browser's *ordinary* renderer, causing *attack.com* to send a script which compromises the *ordinary* renderer. The attacker creates a *bank.com* script context in the *ordinary* renderer. Then the attacker causes the *bank.com* script context to open a new window with top-level URL pointed at an exploitable non-entry URL within the *bank.com* app. This new window will open in the *app* renderer, because its initial URL is within the app, and its request for the non-entry URL will pass entry point checks, because the script context which caused the request is "same-origin" (owned by *bank.com*). Similarly, the request will also be sent if entry-point restriction is absent. This last request thus causes the attack to succeed.

The discovery of this vulnerability underscores two points regarding app containers. The first is that **both** entry-point restriction and state isolation mechanisms are necessary to stop a rendering engine attacker. The second is that the same-origin policy must be extended to include app containers. In effect, app containers divide a previously atomic origin into two new origins, one inside and one outside the container. As such, the entry-point restriction policy should have rejected the last request in our scenario, because its source was outside the app container and its target was inside. We implemented this updated notion of same-origin in our model and verified that both *assertions* were now upheld, up to the finite sizes we tried, again up to 10 `NetworkEvents`.

7.2 Complexity of Adoption

Entry-point restriction requires web sites to identify all URLs that they wish make public to other web sites. Highly socially integrated sites like Facebook or content-oriented sites like New York Times will have difficulty adopting entry-point restriction due to the inherent complexity in capturing all the possible entry points. On the other hand, we believe non-social web sites such as online banking applications will have an easier time identifying valid entry-points, making it practical to deploy entry-point restriction.

To gain additional insight into the effort required for different web sites to adopt entry-point restriction, we used the Mozilla Test Pilot platform [8]. Mozilla Test Pilot is a Firefox extension installed on more than 3 million active Firefox browsers. Our evaluation was performed on 10,551 of those browsers over a period of 3 days. In our study, we simulated entry-point restriction for 9 web sites shown in Figure 4. These sites consist of popular email and web applications, online banking pages of major financial institutions, news and social networks, and popular Chrome Web Store applications.

For each site, we gathered URL hashes of all *incoming links* to the site that appear on all pages that Test Pilot Browsers visited. Each incoming link represents either an actual HTML link or an embedded resource pointing to the site (e.g., `a.com/logo.png` would be an incoming link to `a.com`). Our results demonstrate several ideas. First, they verify our hypothesis that web sites that encourage the sharing of content will have a difficult time opting in to entry-point restriction (e.g., New York Times, Facebook, and Last.fm). Second, web sites with no intention of sharing content can opt in to entry-point restriction with relatively few entry points (e.g., Wells Fargo, Capital One and Flixster, a Chrome Web Store application). For certain sites such as Gmail and Bank of America, the compatibility with entry-point restriction is less clear. While 10 entry points can cover up to 95 percent of the incoming links, fully covering all incoming links appears to be a non-trivial task. For Gmail, we suspect this to be due to Gmail widgets, multiple login URLs (e.g., `mail.google.com/mail/u/0/`), and web mail portals from numerous organizations hosted by Gmail (e.g., `mail.google.com/a/west.cmu.edu/`). It is difficult to confirm this hypothesis from the data set, as we only collected hashes of the URLs to protect user privacy. For the online banking application for Bank of America, each entry point *path* is valid at a number of regional load-balancing *domains*, thus accounting for the large number of total entry point URLs.

Web applications that consist of multiple subdomains sometimes face an interesting challenge, if some subdomains are more amenable to app isolation than others. For example, a bank may have some of its login-guarded functionality on a **`online`** subdomain, while also having a separate **`creditcards`** subdomain with significant numbers of entry points. If pages on the **`creditcards`** subdomain can also recognize when a user is logged in, then it is difficult to isolate the two subdomains from each other. Such apps may either face difficulties adopting app isolation or be forced to specify less precise entry points.

To assist web site owners with identifying valid entry points and determining whether app isolation is suitable for their site, we propose a *report-only* mode similar to that of Content Security Policy [33]. Instead of enforcing a policy violation, report-only mode will send a violation report to the app's server. Report-only mode can thus be used to generate a suitable policy file that avoids false positives.

Web developers interested in adopting app isolation should consider the specific feature trade-offs they will be making. Their apps should have limited deep incoming links as entry points. They should not rely on authenticated resources from third parties, and they should not depend on their own authenticated resources being loaded on third party sites. Overall, we found that certain types of sites, including several online banks, do appear to be good candidates for adopting app isolation.

7.3 Performance

In this section, we evaluate the performance overhead of app isolation due to entry-point restriction and state isolation. While extra disk space is required for isolated caches, the overhead is generally far less than using multiple browsers.

7.3.1 Navigation Latency

In an entry-point restriction enabled browser, every web resource load for an app is preceded by an entry-point check. This check determines whether the URL of the web resource matches one of the known entry-points. Entry-point lookup can be made efficient using a hash table, imposing negligible cost on navigation latency. We measured the load times of the Alexa Top 100 Web sites with and without entry-point restriction enabled. For an artificially high list of 10000 entry points, the overhead incurred from hash table lookups was small enough to be lost in the noise (less than 0.1 ms per page load).

Besides entry-point lookup, policy files must also be fetched. The fetch of the policy file is done only once at app installation time, and thus we do not include it in the performance overhead.

7.3.2 Storage and Memory Overhead

To see the impact of state isolation, we measured the disk and memory space required for visiting 12 popular sites in their own tabs, similar to the sites used in Figure 4. Chromium stores a user's persistent state in a configurable profile directory, so we compared three conditions: all sites in a single Chromium profile, all in a single Chromium profile as isolated apps, and each in a separate Chromium profile. For sites that did not require HTTPS, we used pre-recorded network data to reduce variability. For Gmail, Bank of America, and Chase Bank, we logged into an account. We report the average of three trials.

Visiting all sites in a single profile required 19 MB of disk space. Using isolated apps required 86 MB, while multiple browsers required 117 MB. Each of these profiles includes a partial download of Chromium's Safe Browsing database (2.6 MB), which is a source of overhead for each additional browser profile.

We were surprised that isolated apps required over 4 times the space of a single profile. This is because Chromium aggressively allocates disk space for each cache. This behavior could be modified to be less aggressive for isolated apps. Users could also opt for an in-memory cache for isolated apps, which retains the security benefits and lowers the disk space required to 9.6 MB.

The total resident memory required for visiting all sites in separate tabs of a single profile was 729 MB.[1] We found that using isolated apps used a comparable 730 MB, while using a separate browser for each site used an aggregate of 1.83 GB memory.

These results show that by using isolated apps rather than multiple browsers, we can reduce the performance trade-off required for our security benefits.

8. CONCLUSION

We have shown that a single browser can achieve the security benefits of using multiple browsers, by implementing *entry-point restriction* and *state isolation* to isolate sensitive apps. These mechanisms might not be appropriate for every web site, but they can be effective for many high-value web sites, such as online banks. Using this approach, these high-value web sites can help protect themselves and their users from a broad spectrum of attacks with minimal effort.

9. REFERENCES

[1] R. Cook, "The Next Big Browser Exploit," *CSO Magazine*, p. 15, Feb 2008.

[2] E. Iverson, "Two Web Browsers can be More Secure than One." http://www.blueridgenetworks.com/securitynowblog/dual-web-browsers-can-avoid-information-disclosures

[3] D. Jang, R. Jhala, S. Lerner, and H. Shacham, "An empirical study of privacy-violating information flows in JavaScript web applications," in *Proceedings of the*

[1]Chromium over counts memory usage by not fully accounting for shared memory, but this is consistent across our three conditions.

17th ACM Conference on Computer and Communications Security. ACM, 2010, pp. 270–283.

[4] C. Jackson, A. Bortz, D. Boneh, and J. C. Mitchell, "Protecting browser state from web privacy attacks," in *Proceedings of the 15th International Conference on World Wide Web*, ser. WWW '06. New York, NY, USA: ACM, 2006, pp. 737–744. [Online]. Available: http://doi.acm.org/10.1145/1135777.1135884

[5] E. Felten and M. Schneider, "Timing attacks on web privacy," in *Proceedings of the 7th ACM Conference on Computer and Communications Security*. ACM, 2000, pp. 25–32.

[6] A. Barth, C. Jackson, and C. Reis, "The Security Architecture of the Chromium Browser," 2008 Technical Report.

[7] Mozilla Foundation Security Advisory 2009-29, "Arbitrary code execution using event listeners." http://www.mozilla.org/security/announce/2009/mfsa2009-29.html

[8] Mozilla, "Test Pilot," https://testpilot.mozillalabs.com/.

[9] D. Akhawe, A. Barth, P. E. Lam, J. Mitchell, and D. Song, "Towards a Formal Foundation of Web Security," *Computer Security Foundations Symposium, Proceedings of, IEEE*, vol. 0, pp. 290–304, 2010.

[10] Mozilla, "Prism," http://prism.mozillalabs.com/.

[11] T. Ditchendorf, "Fluid," http://fluidapp.com/.

[12] M. Silbey and P. Brundrett, "Understanding and working in Protected Mode Internet Explorer," 2006, http://msdn.microsoft.com/en-us/library/bb250462.aspx.

[13] C. Grier, S. Tang, and S. T. King, "Secure Web Browsing with the OP Web Browser," in *IEEE Symposium on Security and Privacy*, 2008, pp. 402–416.

[14] H. J. Wang, C. Grier, A. Moshchuk, S. T. King, P. Choudhury, and H. Venter, "The Multi-Principal OS Construction of the Gazelle Web Browser," in *USENIX Security Symposium*, 2009, pp. 417–432.

[15] L.-S. Huang, Z. Weinberg, C. Evans, and C. Jackson, "Protecting Browsers from Cross-Origin CSS Attacks," in *ACM Conference on Computer and Communications Security)*, 2010.

[16] R. S. Cox, S. D. Gribble, H. M. Levy, and J. G. Hansen, "A Safety-Oriented Platform for Web Applications," in *IEEE Symposium on Security and Privacy*, 2006, pp. 350–364.

[17] S. Crites, F. Hsu, and H. Chen, "OMash: enabling secure web mashups via object abstractions," in *ACM Conference on Computer and Communications Security*, 2008, pp. 99–108.

[18] S. Stamm, B. Sterne, and G. Markham, "Reining in the Web with Content Security Policy," in *International Conference on World Wide Web (WWW)*, 2010.

[19] T. Oda, G. Wurster, P. V. Oorschot, and A. Somayaji, "SOMA: Mutual Approval for Included Content in Web Pages," in *ACM Conference on Computer and Communications Security*, 2008.

[20] L. D. Baron. (2010) Preventing attacks on a user's history through CSS `:visited` selectors. http://dbaron.org/mozilla/visited-privacy

[21] Z. Weinberg, E. Y. Chen, P. Jayaraman, and C. Jackson, "I Still Know What You Visited Last Summer: Leaking browsing history via user interaction and side channel attacks," in *IEEE Symposium on Security and Privacy*, 2011.

[22] D. Morin, "Announcing Facebook Connect," 2008, https://developers.facebook.com/blog/post/108/.

[23] E. Hammer-Lahav, "Web Host Metadata," 2010, http://tools.ietf.org/html/draft-hammer-hostmeta-13.

[24] C. Jackson and A. Barth, "Beware of Finer-Grained Origins," in *Web 2.0 Security and Privacy*, 2008.

[25] Google, "Packaged Apps," http://code.google.com/chrome/extensions/apps.html.

[26] Mozilla, "Manifest File," https://developer.mozilla.org/en/OpenWebApps/The_Manifest.

[27] Google, "Verified Author," http://www.google.com/support/chrome_webstore/bin/answer.py?hl=en&answer=173657.

[28] G. Aggarwal, E. Bursztein, C. Jackson, and D. Boneh, "An Analysis of Private Browsing Modes in Modern Browsers," in *USENIX Security Symposium*, 2010, pp. 79–94.

[29] C. Reis and S. D. Gribble, "Isolating Web Programs in Modern Browser Architectures," in *ACM European Conference on Computer Systems (EuroSys)*, 2009.

[30] D. Jackson, "Alloy: a lightweight object modelling notation," *ACM Transactions on Software Engineering and Methodology (TOSEM)*, vol. 11, no. 2, pp. 256–290, 2002.

[31] ——, *Software Abstractions: Logic, Language, and Analysis*. The MIT Press, 2006.

[32] F. Kerschbaum, "Simple cross-site attack prevention," in *Security and Privacy in Communications Networks and the Workshops, 2007. SecureComm 2007. Third International Conference on*, Sept. 2007, pp. 464 –472.

[33] Mozilla, "CSP specification," 2011, https://wiki.mozilla.org/Security/CSP/Specification#Report-Only_mode.

Crouching Tiger – Hidden Payload: Security Risks of Scalable Vectors Graphics

Mario Heiderich
Chair for Network and Data Security
Ruhr-University Bochum, Germany
mario.heiderich@rub.de

Tilman Frosch
Chair for Network and Data Security
Ruhr-University Bochum, Germany
tilman.frosch@rub.de

Meiko Jensen
Chair for Network and Data Security
Ruhr-University Bochum, Germany
meiko.jensen@rub.de

Thorsten Holz
Chair for System Security
Ruhr-University Bochum, Germany
thorsten.holz@rub.de

ABSTRACT

Scalable Vector Graphics (SVG) images so far played a rather small role on the Internet, mainly due to the lack of proper browser support. Recently, things have changed: the W3C and WHATWG draft specifications for HTML5 require modern web browsers to support SVG images to be embedded in a multitude of ways. Now SVG images can be embedded through the classical method via specific tags such as `<embed>` or `<object>`, or in novel ways, such as with `<img>` tags, CSS or inline in *any* HTML5 document.

SVG files are generally considered to be plain images or animations, and security-wise, they are being treated as such (e.g., when an embedment of local or remote SVG images into websites or uploading these files into rich web applications takes place). Unfortunately, this procedure poses great risks for the web applications and the users utilizing them, as it has been proven that SVG files must be considered fully functional, one-file web applications potentially containing HTML, JavaScript, Flash, and other interactive code structures. We found that even more severe problems have resulted from the often improper handling of complex and maliciously prepared SVG files by the browsers.

In this paper, we introduce several novel attack techniques targeted at major websites, as well as modern browsers, email clients and other comparable tools. In particular, we illustrate that SVG images embedded via `<img>` tag and CSS can execute arbitrary JavaScript code. We examine and present how current filtering techniques are circumventable by using SVG files and subsequently propose an approach to mitigate these risks. The paper showcases our research into the usage of SVG images as attack tools, and determines its impact on state-of-the-art web browsers such as Firefox 4, Internet Explorer 9, and Opera 11.

Categories and Subject Descriptors

K.6.5 [**Security and Protection**]: Unauthorized access

General Terms

Security

Keywords

Scalable Vector Graphics; Web Security; Browser Security; Cross Site Scripting; Active Image Injections

1. INTRODUCTION

One of the factors behind the huge success of the World Wide Web is its ability and capacity for viewing image files within a web browser. Compared to the text-only formats, an image can convey considerably more information. A typical browser supports many different image file formats, such as JPEG, PNG and GIF files, whilst the vast majority of websites on the Web contain at least one graphic in either one form or another. Since image files are complex and need to be parsed and rendered before they can be displayed by a browser, it comes as no surprise that the images have security implications. To give an example, there were several cases in the past where the validation routine of image libraries contained security flaws leading to vulnerabilities [1, 2, 4]. For this reason, we need to consider the risk of images as the attack vectors.

One image format that has up till now received very limited scrutiny and little attention from the web development community is *Scalable Vector Graphics* (SVG [5]). This family of file formats comprises several specifications and specification drafts for composition and rendering of the vector based images and graphics. SVG is based on XML and was first published by the W3C in 1999. SVG images have not gained much traction from the web developers, as the support provided by major browsers was not consistent and only

Figure 1: A classic GhostScript/SVG example

a small subset of SVG features had been known to work reliably on a sufficiently large base of the web browsers. Browsers, like Firefox 1.5, already supported a decent subset of SVG features in November 2005, showcasing SVGs such as the famous *GhostScript Tiger* shown in Figure 1. This particular image is often used to illustrate the abilities of the vector based graphics to display complex structures. Other browsers, namely Internet Explorer, did not support SVG, unless a user installed an external plug-in.

All this has significantly changed with the recent appearance of HTML5: the W3C and WHATWG draft specifications for HTML5 *require* modern web browsers to support SVG images' embedment in a multitude of ways [25]. SVG images can now for example be engrafted in a given document either in the classical way via specific tags such as `<embed>` or `<object>` tags, or in the novel ways such as with `<img>` tags or inline in any HTML5 document. Internet Explorer 9 currently supports a large subset of SVG features as tests with the tech previews and available beta versions show. Furthermore, both Firefox and Webkit-based browsers, such as Chrome and Safari, as well as Opera, provide thorough SVG support.

Hitherto, SVG is mainly used in the context of screen and print design, as well as in the cartography and medical imagery, which all can be attributed to the lack of proper browser support [35]. This is however expected to change, owing to the SVG support being implemented in all modern web browsers, consequently lifting SVG files from being a niche format for W3C compliant and plug-in-equipped browsers only, to a widely used toolkit for enhancing images, diagrams and rich-text documents across the board. Depending on the rendering client's capabilities, an SVG file can contain interactive and animated elements. Processing events and raster images, embedding videos, and rich-text are also feasible. Contrary to popular belief, SVG files should thus not be considered to be plain images or animations, and it is necessary to treat them as fully functional, one-file web applications capable of potentially containing HTML, JavaScript, Flash and other interactive code structures.

In this paper, we elaborate on the security risks of improper SVG handling. We introduce several novel attack techniques of using SVG images to target modern, real life web applications (such as MediaWiki installations like Wikipedia, DeviantArt, and other high profile websites), as well as their unsuspecting users. Specifically, in Section 3 we present an *Active Image Injection* (AII) attack, in which arbitrary JavaScript code can be delivered via SVG files. Several other attacks such as SVG-based cross site scripting attacks or SVG chameleons (i.e., files that are interpreted differently depending on how they are opened) are also delivered. AII attacks are particularly important, since they are caused by faulty SVG implementations in modern browsers, thus affect all websites allowing users to embed external images – thereby our research significantly extends and partly falsifies the information available in the Browser Security Handbook, so far only covering risks connected to browser-deployed SVG in plugin containers. Furthermore, we discuss how current state-of-the-art filtering techniques are deceivable via using SVG files.

The basic idea behind all of our attacks is the fact that SVG files can accommodate active content, whereby browsers actually interpret this content due to its being standard-compliant. This idea is related to similar attacks that take advantage of code embedded in document formats [8,13,32] and we show that SVG images can be turned into an attack vector. In addition, we demonstrate the damaging potential of SVG files embedding arbitrary data formats and show how this property can be used to carry out attacks using Adobe Reader, Java Runtime Engine and Flash Player vulnerabilities. We discuss the impact of our attack on modern browsers such as Firefox 4, Internet Explorer 9, and Opera 11, showing that especially inline SVG grants new possibilities for bypassing website- and browser based XSS filters.

To mitigate the risks introduced by SVG-based attacks, we debate and evaluate several defense strategies. We showcase a filtering solution that is capable of removing potential malicious content from a given SVG file. Our approach does not break the functionality of the core features of fully interactive and descriptive SVG images. Instead, we extend an existing and widespread filtering software to support filtering of illegitimate and malicious content from SVG files, without damaging the benign file structure and contents. We have formerly implemented a prototype of the system and tested it with 105,509 SVG images obtained from Wikipedia. We found that we can filter 98.5% of the files without causing any difference in the visual appearance of the image, and for the remaining 1.5% we determined the visual deviation to be negligible in more than half of the cases.

In summary, we make the following contributions:

- We are the first ones to demonstrate the security risks tied to SVG files in the context of the World Wide Web and comparable client-server environments. Furthermore, we argue that SVG files must not be perceived as images, but rather full stack applications, provided the cases of them being rendered by a web browser or similar client software. This holds for SVG images rendered via `<embed>` and similar tags, as well as displayed as standalone file in modern web browsers.
- We show several innovative attack techniques illustrating the potential of maliciously crafted SVG files, which we call *Active Image Injection* (AII). We exhibit how SVG files can cause damage to major websites, and discuss the damage potential of SVG files embedding arbitrary data formats. The hereby discussed AII attacks affect a whole browser family, rendering *any* website leaving user submitted images vulnerable if the users visit it with the affected web browsers. Moreover, we show how inline SVG can be used to facilitate XSS filter bypasses on current web browsers.

- We introduce a defense solution to prevent SVG-based attacks by filtering potentially malicious content from a given SVG file. The large-scale evaluation results suggest that this approach can successfully defeat AII attacks on a practical level.

2. SVG BASICS AND SPECIFICS

This section provides a brief overview of the SVG file format and discusses the attack surface enabled by this image format, i.e., we illustrate the different ways available for an attacker to send arbitrary SVG files to a victim.

2.1 Overview and Benefits

The *Scalable Vector Graphics* (SVG) file format was introduced in 1999 when it was published by the W3C in an attempt to combine the best of both the specification drafts for *Precision Graphics Markup Language* (PGML) developed and published by Adobe, and the *Vector Markup Language* (VML) developed and published by Microsoft, Autodesk, Hewlett Packard, and others, all in 1998. SVG is a vector graphics format, i.e., it uses geometrical primitives such as points, lines and curves to describe an image, while it supports both static and dynamic content. The above mentioned static content and dynamic behavior are described in an XML-based format, which implies that SVG files are in fact text files.

The impact of SVG on the Internet can be described with the following characteristics:

- **Scalability**: SVG files are, as the name indicates, *scalable* based on their nature as vector graphics. This means that graphical output devices of any size can render SVG images without significant information loss or facing deficiencies in display quality. In times of websites' inhomogeneous output devices such as browsers, feed- and screen readers, smartphones and *Wireless Markup Language* (WML) compatible cellphones, this enables web developers to publish rich online documents without having to worry about the screen dimension of the device requesting the document.

- **Openness**: Unlike classical, raster-based image formats, SVG files are neither stored in a binary format nor is there a compression scheme rendering the actual content of the file unreadable for the human eye. SVG images can be enriched with meta-data and comments, so that a (handicapped) human as well as a program (e.g., a search engine or comparable parser) can effecively extract relevant information from the file in question. In this case accessibility is ensured by storing more descriptive information in a given file, compared to the rather limited possibilities of image comments provided by GIF and PNG files, or the embedded *Exchangeable Image File Format* (EXIF) data in RAW and JPEG images. Note that gzipped SVG files (also know as SVGZ) create an exception, for they do not use compression as means to reduce the file size.

- **Accessibility**: Related to the aforementioned openness, an SVG image can be enriched with sufficient meta-data and information to be *Web Accessibility Initiative* (WAI) compliant, i.e., visually impaired users can extract relevant information by having their tools parse and read the meta-data embedded in the SVG. Furthermore, screen-readers can (theoretically) parse SVG data and describe the shapes and visuals used by the image, allowing a broader range of users to benefit from its contents. In contrast, raster-based images are void of this kind of support.

The SVG family consists of several members and we use the following three file types as examples in later sections:

- **SVG Full 1.1**: SVG Full describes the full SVG feature set including 81 different SVG elements and tags. The specification is designed without a special focus on the devices parsing the SVG data.

- **SVG Basic 1.1**: SVG Basic is supposed to deliver a subset of the SVG Full specification to ease the implementation for developers of browsers for PDAs and handheld devices. SVG Basic only provides 70 of the 81 SVG elements specified in SVG Full 1.1. Contrary to SVG Tiny 1.2, the SVG Basic 1.1 features also include support for SVG fonts.

- **SVG Tiny 1.2**: SVG Tiny is specifically designed for smartphones and similar mobile devices with limited computing, rendering, and display capabilities. The subset of allowed SVG elements and tags has been reduced to 47 elements. SVG Tiny also ships several exclusive possibilities for event binding and external resource loading which we discuss in Section 3.

Additionally, the SVG specification provides interface descriptions for an *SVG Document Object Model* (DOM), which implies that SVG files also offer some dynamic capabilities. Users can create SVG files capable of providing event handling, effects, time-based changes and animations, as well as zoom effects and other helpful display enhancements. A large set of filters can be applied to the elements of SVG files to even more greatly increase the possibilities for image transformation and animation.

The ability to combine SVG with the *XML Linking Language* (XLink) features allows SVG files to link elements to other elements in the same image file, other image files or arbitrary objects referenced via *Uniform Request Identifiers* (URIs). Furthermore, these image files support the implementation of *International Color Consortium* (ICC) and *Standard Red-Green-Blue* (sRGB) color profiles, allowing the embedment of arbitrary content such as Flash, PDFs, Java and HTML via the `<foreignObject>` element.

2.2 HTML, SVG, and XML

Being historically an XML-based language, processing of SVG documents has been quite different from the way browsers process classic HTML websites. For instance, a slight violation of the XML syntax, such as missing closing tags or attribute value quotations, typically cause SVG processors to exit with an error. However, with the integration of SVG capabilities into modern browsers, this strict parsing approach got amalgamated with their more tolerant way of processing HTML, CSS, JavaScript and the like.

This mixture is causing browsers to process SVG through using two different processing modes: an HTML processor engine for CSS and JavaScript contents, and an additional SVG parser supporting XML-specific features like XML transformations (e.g. XSLT), XML Entity resolution, and tracking of XML Namespace bindings. Depending on the particular website's style of using SVG, the browser switches between the two processing modes on the go. For instance, encountering an inline `<svg>` tag within an HTML5 document causes the browser to switch from HTML mode to XML/SVG mode. Vice versa, if the browser encounters an HTML-specific tag (e.g. `<p>`) within an SVG mode context, it automatically closes all open SVG elements, switches to HTML mode, and renders the given tag.

As we show in the following sections, this approach is error-prone and may cause a lot of SVG-related vulnerabilities in most state-of-the-art browser engines.

2.3 Deployment Techniques

The capabilities, in terms of scripting and content inclusion of SVG files, strongly depend on how they are embedded in a website or loaded by the browser attempting to display them. In this section, we focus on five diverse manners of SVG files being deployed by a webserver or web application. In addition, we outline the attack surface we have discovered in connection to the five deployment techniques. The specific attack vectors we use are discussed in detail in Section 3, followed by Section 4 focusing on how to mitigate and defend against those attacks.

1. **SVG deployed via uploaded files**: A large number of tested web applications (e.g., MediaWiki and Wikipedia, OpenStreetMaps, DeviantArt, OpenClipArt, and several other free image hosting services) consider SVG files to be equivalent to raster images such as PNG, JPEG, and GIF files in terms of security implications. MediaWiki and Wikipedia claim to block the upload of SVG files containing script code, but we did manage to easily bypass this restriction. As we show in the next section, SVG files should be displayed and executed with a heavily limited set of features to prevent *universal XSS attacks*, since these files might contain scripts, embed arbitrary content and process events. In addition, we discovered alternative course of action for outmaneuvering the capability limitations of current browsers, which are used to protect sensitive DOM properties such as a website's cookies. Those are discussed in detail in Section 3.2

2. **SVG deployed via CSS backgrounds and *img* tags**: This way of deploying malicious SVG files can be considered as the most dangerous and effective attack, granted that the majority of the web applications judge `<img>` tags as part of user generated HTML to be harmless: `<img src="evil.svg">`
   Filter software, such as the HTMLPurifier [43], OWASP AntiSamy [16], and similar tools whitelist image tags and a large number of web applications allowing user generated HTML are prone to be sensitive to a novel class of attacks we term *active image injections*. Again, we underline that SVG files should be displayed and executed with a heavily limited set of features to prevent universal XSS attacks. In Section 3.2 and 3.5, we particularize on the attack vectors we discovered through using this presumably harmless way of deployment, and outline an innovative method of attacking browsers and high traffic web applications.

3. **SVG deployed via inline SVG**: The HTML5 specification draft suggests the web browsers to support websites providing *inline SVG*. This means a developer and an attacker are equally able to inject arbitrary SVG content right into the markup tree of a HTML document. The browser will then switch its parsing mode, use an intermediary layer to parse the (possibly non-well-formed) SVG content, clean it up, pass it on to the internal XML parser and layout engine, and then commence parsing and rendering the remaining optional HTML content. The last step likely includes even more inline SVG elements [17] that are capable of interacting with the already parsed content. In Section 3.4, we illustrate how this facilitates XSS filter bypasses of existing websites, filter libraries, and most importantly browsers and comparable user agents.

4. **SVG deployed as font file (*SVG Fonts*)**: The SVG standard specifies several possibilities to create font files completely consisting of SVG data [3]. Modern browsers allow their inclusion via CSS and the `@font` directive. In case when the browser supports SVG fonts, for every character with an SVG font assigned, the parser checks whether the character has a representation as an SVG path/glyph data and applies this to the view port if possible. SVG fonts provide a prominent range of features for detailed and complex font formatting, Unicode support, alternative glyphs, default behavior for missing glyphs, and more. We detected attack vectors allowing the deployment of arbitrary plug-in content via SVG fonts working on a variety of desktop and mobile user agents.

5. **SVG deployed via *iframe*, *embed*, or *object* tags**: The attack surface is comparably large to the one for the classic XSS and does not differ much from the regular `<iframe>` and `<script>` injections. It will thus not be discussed in more depth in this paper.

3. ATTACK VECTORS USING SVG FILES

Based on the prerequisites discussed in the previous section, we now introduce several different attacks based on SVG files and discuss their security impact.

3.1 Responsible Disclosure and Ethical Aspects

We describe several novel attacks related to SVG files and their security impact, ranging from universal XSS attacks to triggering vulnerabilities based on SVG images. Presenting such attacks is obviously an ethically sensitive area and one question that arises is if it is acceptable and justifiable to publish the attack details. In the following, we describe most attack vectors from a high-level point of view and do not present all implementation details. If a (legitimate) researcher is interested in test cases, we are happy to share them. Furthermore, we have contacted all major browser vendors and informed them about these problems. We are in contact with them and several reported problems have already been fixed. As a result, an attacker cannot easily take advantage of these identified attack vectors.

In addition, we introduce in Section 4 an approach to mitigate the attacks presented in this paper based on removing suspicious content from SVG files at the server side. We are in contact with the affected website's security teams, and discuss with them the possibility to deploy our countermeasure for these attacks. The WikiMedia team is interested in testing and deploying the tool we created and discuss in Section 4. Our mitigation approach can also be implemented as a local filter proxy to protect a web browser against malicious SVG images and we evaluate at the moment the effort required to implement this local mitigation approach.

3.2 Local JavaScript Execution and SVG Chameleons

One of the least sophisticated attack techniques (that is still rather likely to work in real-world scenarios) is tricking the victim into saving an SVG image from a website and opening it later on for repeated viewing pleasure. There are only a few ways for technically less affine users to tell a classic raster-based image (PNG/JPEG/GIF) apart from an SVG image. Once saved locally and double-clicked, the browser will open the file – since most users do not have a dedicated software installed that changes the application to handle the SVG MIME type. The SVG file is consequently opened from a *file* URI and in case it contains JavaScript, this code will be executed in the same context. Depending on the web browser the victim is using, the JavaScript can then attempt to read other files from the hard-disk or neighboring directories, and cause a data leakage incident. A thrifty adversary can cause the locally running JavaScript to load an applet from an arbitrary domain, thus even bypassing many of the security restrictions modern browsers apply for local script execution.

Similar attacks could be performed with *SVG Chameleons*, i.e., files containing both SVG and HTML content. Using in-line XML transformation (XSLT), we managed to craft an SVG file that acts like an image if embedded via `<img>`, CSS or similar ways, but unfolds to a full stack HTML file containing no SVG elements anymore as soon as opened directly [14]. This attack works with Gecko-based browsers, since it appears to be the only layout engine supporting in-line XSLT in SVG files. The attack would involve uploading an SVG Chameleon to a website such as Wikipedia, and trick the victim into right-clicking the image shown embedded and choosing to view the original. As soon as that happens, the XSLT will transform the SVG into an HTML file and execute embedded script code or worse [23].

Interestingly, some browsers such as Firefox do not allow cookie access in case the SVG file is being opened directly. This is especially important in cases where an attacker can upload SVG files to the same domain a targeted user is being logged into. The reason for that limitation is a different handling of the *SVGDOM* compared to the regular website's DOM. The SVGDOM does not know properties such as `document.cookie` or even `document.body`. We discovered ways to get around this limitation, though, by having the SVG create a `<foreignObject>` tag containing an Iframe loading the affected website. After the `onload` event of the Iframe, we injected JavaScript into its scope capable of extracting sensitive data such as the cookies and bypassing the more or less unconscious security restrictions.

3.3 Facilitating Cross Site Scripting Exploits

SVG images provide many possibilities for executing JavaScript in uncommon ways. Many of these are not known to typical web developers and thus are not covered by filter software protecting websites against XSS attacks. SVG Tiny, for example, allows to execute JavaScript by using a `handler` element with an `event` attribute, as shown in Listing 1. In case the event assigned to the handler element is specified as `load`, the text content of the handler element will be executed as JavaScript without any user interaction. Blacklist-based XSS filter systems are usually not aware of such ways of executing code, thus they are not capable of detecting this kind of attacks.

```
<svg xmlns="http://www.w3.org/2000/svg">
 <handler
  xmlns:ev="http://www.w3.org/2001/xml-
      events"
  ev:event="load">
     alert(1)
 </handler>
</svg>
```

Listing 1: Example for uncommon SVG-based JavaScript execution via <handler> tag

Another uncommon way of embedding malicious JavaScript in SVG files is shown in Listing 2. Using SVG's `<set>` tag, we dynamically equip an `<feImage>` tag with an `xlink:href` pointing to a `data:` URI. This kind of image element is meant to be used to apply overlay effects for SVG elements utilizing external resources. Shielded by the Base64 encoding, this URI contains another SVG image that itself contains malicious JavaScript – which is run immediately on loading the `<feImage>` tag.

```
<svg
 xmlns="http://www.w3.org/2000/svg"
 xmlns:xlink="http://www.w3.org/1999/xlink
     ">
 <feImage>
  <set
   attributeName="xlink:href"
   to="data:image/svg+xml;charset=utf-8;
   base64,PHN2ZyB4bWxucz0iaHR0cDovL3d3dy53
   My5vcmcvMjAwMC9zdmciPjxzY3JpcHQ%2BYWxl
   cnQoMSk8L3NjcmlwdD48L3N2Zz4NCg%3D%3D"/>
 </feImage>
</svg>
```

Listing 2: Example for uncommon SVG-based JavaScript execution via <set> tag

These and other ways of executing JavaScript from within an SVG file were used to bypass the filter used by the MediaWiki software, which is the most commonly used open source wiki software and, among many others, the platform used by Wikipedia. We established contact with the MediaWiki team and work together with them on mitigation and defense strategies against such attacks.

We also tried to load SVG images via a `Canvas` element in an HTML website and steal information by using the `canvas.toDataURL()` feature. This method is capable of freezing the optical state of a canvas element and transforming it into a dataURI for easy saving and later usage. This attack technique to steal data cross domains has been published by Lawrence in 2009 [30], but specifically aimed to steal pixel data cross domain for attacking CAPTCHA mechanisms and similar security instrumentations involving images. We attempted to use this attack technique in a novel context and steal whole website screenshots from SVG images being applied with a `<foreignObject>` tag and cross domain Iframes. Surprisingly, this did not work at all. All tested web browsers reacted with the expected behavior and threw security errors on attempting to execute the canvas.toDataURL() method when accessing the SVG with cross domain content.

3.4 Facilitating Filter Bypasses

One feature distinguishing the rendering behavior of HTML from XHTML and XML based websites and documents in browsers is the handling of entities in plain text tags. Plain text tags are HTML elements considered to contain plaintext information (such as <script> and <style> tags, as well as <noscript>, <noframes> and <nostyle> tags). While in HTML documents entities such as a will be treated as such, XHTML and XML documents will have the entity be treated like its canonical representation (e.g., the character a). In practice, this implies that within a XHTML/XML document the code <script>alert(1)</script> will execute the alert method, while an HTML document with the same content causes the script engine to throw an error.

Of course, this behavior applies for SVG files as well, since they are regular XML documents. Interesting in terms of web security, though, is the fact that the same applies for most web browsers to inline SVG. This implies that this behavior can be transported to regular HTML documents as soon as they contain an opening <svg> tag somewhere in the markup tree. While the aforementioned <script> tag example will not execute in an HTML document, the variation of <svg><script>=lert(1)<p> will do.

Note that the browser's parsers are also very tolerant about well-formedness of inline SVG, and neither require attribute delimiters nor balanced tags, nor even closing tags. The <p> element at the end of the example shown above indicates to the parser that the inline SVG just ended and an HTML section has started. Thus, the browser automatically closes both the <svg> and <script> tags, and thereby triggers the alert method to execute. This technique, combined with an injection, has been tested against the most common XSS filters and we managed to bypass most of them.

3.5 Active Image Injection

Several ways of abusing SVG files to execute JavaScript in situations where no script execution should happen at all have been fixed after we reported them back to browser vendors. Some vendors even completely restricted access to the DOM from an SVG context. This makes it very hard to execute same-domain JavaScript from within SVG files delivered via CSS, image tags, CSS fonts, or other ways in which browsers deliver images. Even if a web browser can be tricked into executing JavaScript via SVG deployment methods unintended for this, the script will run in the context of about:blank and cannot get access to the deploying website's DOM. This effectively disables XSS attacks, since they require their payload to execute on the targeted domain and not on a bogus fully qualified domain name (FQDN) such as about:blank.

A yet unsolved problem for several state-of-the-art web browsers is plugin content. The Opera browser, for instance, allows to use SVG files in order to deploy plugin content such as Flash, Java, and PDF files, depending on which plugins have been installed and registered on the user's system. This does not only hold for SVG files embedded via tags such as <embed>, <object>, or <iframe>, but also for <img> tags and CSS. This means that an attacker can execute arbitrary plugin code on a victim's machine *without* any user interaction by just having the victim browse a website containing an image tag. The image can be delivered from any arbitrary domain, thus most high-traffic websites and web applications allowing user generated image content are affected by this problem.

The Opera security team has been informed about this issue in summer 2010, but so far this vendor did not address the issue with a sufficient fix. This leaves applications such as Facebook, Google Mail, Yahoo! Mail, and many other websites prone to this kind of *Active Image Injection* attack – in case their users visit the page with Opera version 9 to 11. An example showcase has been set up to demonstrate the severity of the vulnerability, also trying to enforce an urgent fix from the Opera team [22].

Early versions of the Firefox 4 beta browser were prone to AII attacks as well, but these bugs have been spotted and fixed with Firefox 4 Beta 9, and did not surface in the final release version. Nevertheless, all browser vendors should monitor the security boundaries of SVG deployment closely, since small changes can cause vulnerabilities affecting a majority of web applications at once.

3.6 Browser Vulnerabilities

So far we covered attacks utilizing malicious SVG files to be instrumented in attacks against websites. We demonstrated how SVG files can be used to facilitate XSS attacks that bypass existing and well-configured filter mechanisms and security best practices, such as encoding user-generated data into HTML entities. SVG files can have other purposes for attackers, though, and be used to leverage attacks against the browser itself, or even against the underlying operating system. During our tests, it became evident that especially complex SVGs or SVG chameleons containing executable plugin code have the potential of easily crashing web browsers. We observed and reported several cases of memory corruption occurring in state-of-the-art browsers, which were caused by faulty or incomplete implementation of SVG features, or interference effects between the browser components delivering the SVG data and other components delivering embedded plugin code and Iframes.

One significant example showing the dangers of SVG files when used as attack tools against browsers is a specific bug in Opera version 11.50 24581. This version marked a turning point in the Opera browser history, since it was the first officially released version supporting inline SVG so far. We investigated an attack scenario where an attacker creates a website providing an SVG image as *favicon*. This SVG image deployed malicious content in form of a Flash file and a Java applet, as well as, an embedded PDF file. When opening the malicious website, the Opera browser attempted to load the *favicon* to decorate the loaded page's tab and address bar, as shown in Figure 2. Although this context should never execute plugin content or JavaScript at all, the browser started to play the Flash video we used for testing, and delivered the applet and PDF file – within the address bar as can be seen in Figure 2. The code was executed in the browser context, thus an exploit like this could easily haven been escalated from a proof of concept to a full attack, demonstrating how arbitrary vulnerabilities in browser plugins can be triggered via image files.

Furthermore, SVG-based attack vectors should be considered relevant for another category of software as well: mail clients such as Thunderbird and Opera Mail make use of the same (or only slightly modified) rendering and layout

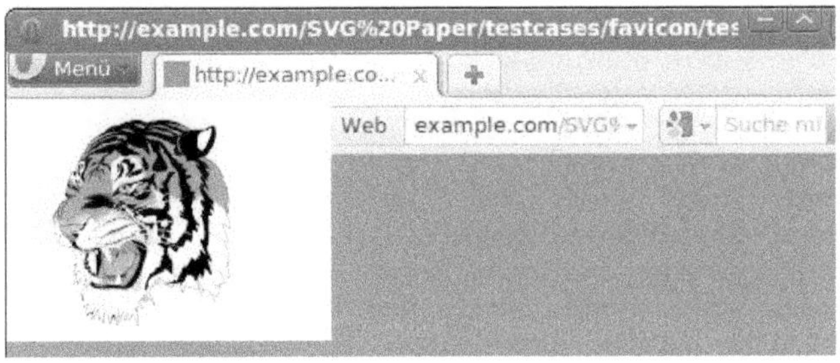

Figure 2: An SVG containing plugin content delivered via favicon

engines as their respective browser counterparts. We tested the latest versions of Opera Mail and Thunderbird 3.3, and discovered that both products allow usage of inline SVG inside HTML mails. One attack vector we crafted caused Thunderbird 3.3 alpha 3 to automatically store an SVG file in the temporary folder, open it, and execute JavaScript in the *file://* context. The only required user interaction is a click on an arbitrary part of the displayed mail body. Attacks like this can be used to place malicious software or to steal sensitive information from the */tmp* folder or other directories, depending on the location of the SVG file and the post-exploitation techniques used by the attacker.

4. MITIGATION TECHNIQUES

In the following section, we cover mitigation techniques to fend the attacks presented in the previous part. We start with a discussion of the common XML filtering and sanitization techniques, point out which problems occur when SVG is being used in modern web browsers, and list arguments as to why the classic and formerly approved approaches cannot be applied to SVGs used on the Internet. Based on these insights, we introduce and discuss *SVGPurifier*, a PHP-based, server-side SVG filter software we have developed to mitigate the identified attacks. What is more, we outline a set of recommendations for browser vendors addressing non-standard behavior that causes security problems with malicious SVG images and inline SVG parsing. Some of the listed issues have already been adopted by browser vendors during the preparatory phase of this paper completion.

4.1 XML Sanitization

The most common approach for verifying an XML document's validity is the use of *Document Type Definitions* (DTDs), *XML Schema*, or *RelaxNG* descriptions. All of these languages authorize a precise specification of which XML elements, attributes, and other tokens may be used within a specific XML document. For instance, the SVG Tiny specification provides a RelaxNG description of all XML elements and attributes that may be used in "Tiny"-compliant SVG documents. We have investigated these descriptions for practical usage in terms of removing malicious contents from SVG files. Unfortunately, we determined that their capabilities of restricting SVG contents are more focused on the XML documents' *structure* rather than restricting the content values of the SVG elements and attributes. Though both XML Schema and RelaxNG provision the means to restrict an SVG attribute value's data type to integer, string, URI, or other data types, we concluded this is insufficient for effectively filtering malicious SVG contents, such as those exemplified above.

For once, there is no feasible way to restrict the `xlink:href` attribute of `URI` data type to point to same-domain locations only, which would have been essential for resisting certain XSS attacks. The only viable way to perform such a verification while using XML Schema or RelaxNG capabilities comes down to setting the attribute's data type to a restricted string value that must conform to a given regular expression pattern. Expressing a value restriction as stated above would thus require a regular expression to be crafted for each type of restriction necessary for fending off the attacks. Although this might be (somehow and somewhat) feasible for same-domain URIs, it is easy to imagine this approach to fail for complete CSS declarations, Base64-encoded contents, and the like.

```
<!doctype html><svg><style>
&lt;img src=null onerror=alert(1)&gt;<p>
```

Listing 3: XML Entity Resolution leading to element injection

Another example that demonstrates the impossibility of XML Schema to remove suspicious content from a given file is shown in Listing 3. When processing this code fragment, Firefox 4 resolves the `<` entity automatically, resulting in the alert being triggered. The crux is that the XML entity introduces an additional HTML element "on the fly" during parsing. An XML Schema validator would seen a `<style>` element with odd contents, but nothing to be alerted about (note that the missing closing tags and attribute value quotations are added automatically by the parser engine.). However, the HTML renderer resolves the entities, hence introducing the additional `<img>` tag, and triggering the `onerror` event due to the missing `null` file.

To summarize, we established that common XML validator techniques, like XML Schema or RelaxNG validation are not capable of fending the specific SVG attack vectors described above. Especially in the case of inline SVG, where HTML, CSS, JavaScript, and SVG elements are mixed arbitrarily, the approach of XML Schema validation must be revoked as completely ineffective in practice.

4.2 SVG Purification

Due to the limitations discussed above, we require another way to prevent the attacks introduced in Section 3. The basic idea of our methodology is to *purify* SVG images, i.e., remove all suspicious content from a given file and preserve as much content as possible. As a result of this transformative process, the visual impact is minimized and the suspicious content is removed. Next, we discuss the overall design and present some implementation details.

The open source market provides a lot of tools claiming to possess the skills to filter user generated input for web applications in order to eliminate active markup and script code. Their main purpose is usually XSS mitigation and markup sanitation, as well as restructuring for validity and well-formedness' sake. For PHP-based web applications, several filtering solutions are available and those most commonly used include:

- *kses* [21], that has been incorporated into a highly customized version by the popular WordPress software.
- *htmlLawed* [37], which claims to be the fastest and most compact, yet complete solution.
- *HTMLPurifier* [43], which not only sanitizes data from possibly malicious code fragments, but also generates valid and well-formed XHTML output.

We analyzed all three XSS filters and have managed to bypass each of them, demonstrating that even the most sophisticated filtering software can never be able to fully protect against malicious markup. Some of the bypasses worked only for injections into SVG files, some even in a HTML/X-HTML context.

Despite these drawbacks of the server-side filtering approaches, we have decided to choose *HTMLPurifier* as the foundation for our SVG attack mitigation tool. One major reason for this determination was the fact that *HTMLPurifier* is very well maintained, receives frequent updates and security fixes. Another reason is the quality of filtering: we have only identified a few bypasses for this tool and every single one of them was fixed very quickly upon having contacted the developers. Still, most importantly, *HTMLPurifier's* internal API allows to filter arbitrary XML data and is not limited to HTML by design, unlike the other tested tools. This knowledge allowed us to create an *SVGPurifier* branch, a software that is using the *HTMLPurifier* API, but is not touching the core components. Our *SVGPurifier* has been supplied with a large array of data based on the SVG specifications defining which tags and attributes should be allowed in the user-generated SVG files. We explicitly *whitelist* tags and attributes, as well as the tag-attribute combinations and specific value ranges for attributes. Uncommon sources for cross-site scripting attacks, such as the `<set>` tag on older Webkit-based browsers, are limited by *SVGPurifier*.

The `<set>` tag can be used in SVG files, similarly to the timing driven equivalent `<animate>`, although the `attributeName` value can only consist of a limited amount of values. Specifically, we only allow those values which cannot be used to initiate or overwrite event handlers, change `xlink:href` values on the fly, or reposition elements and element groups on a website. Our tests showed that the `<set>` and `<animate>` tags can be used to assign `javascript:` and `data:` URIs to existing elements. This can either enable attacks by initiating malicious remote inclusions, or apply malicious URL schemes to the existing elements.

Attacks like the one just portrayed, as well as those shown in Listing 4, can be no longer carried out. Take account of the fact that the `<set>`/`<animate>` functionality is not removed completely, only the remote includes and the assignment of malicious URL handlers have been blocked. Furthermore, the resulys of our evaluation show that only two files out of more than 100,000 tested instances from the Wikipedia servers made use of the `<set>`/`<animate>` feature at all (see Section 5 for details).

```
<svg xmlns="http://www.w3.org/2000/svg">
  <set
    attributeName="onmouseover"
    to="alert(1)"/>
  <animate
    attributeName="onunload"
    to="alert(1)"/>
</svg>
```

Listing 4: Initiating JavaScript execution via set/animate elements

SVGPurifier completely forbids and removes `<script>` as well as `<foreignObject>` tags and event handler usage. Later versions of our purification approach might prove to add a supplementary scripting layer to allow basic JavaScript execution, but hinder scripts from reading, and overwriting sensitive data, or conduct other activities capable of leaking sensitive data or deploying malicious code [26]. As further elaborated on in Section 5, our tests showed that none of the analyzed and purified SVG used actual `<script>` tags. Surprisingly, a large percentage of the test files were making use of `<foreignObject>` tags. The reason behind it is that the software *Adobe Illustrator* uses this tag to hide proprietary meta-info in the SVG images generated by this tool [7]. Removing these tags does not affect the visual information provided by the SVG file.

Similar problems can be caused by maliciously crafted *SVG Cascading Stylesheets* (SVGCSS). SVG styles support more properties than classic CSS for (X)HTML documents and specifically extend the feature set with font formatting, typographic features, extended pointer event behavior, and the possibility to reference to other SVG elements containing definitions and visual effects. Arbitrary SVG elements can constitute reference to other SVG elements or even let external SVG files to borrow visual information or functionality including event handling. Those references can be defined via *FunctionIRI* or the fully qualified paths via protocol schemes such as data, HTTP and others. *SVGPurifier* guarantees that no external references can be loaded by elements allowing script execution. The `<use>` tag on modern Opera browser versions is conversely problematic. This tag can be utilized to include external resources executing JavaScript or providing links with potentially malicious URL handlers.

Currently, *SVGPurifier* scans style elements and attributes of the purified SVG for potentially malicious patterns and neutralizes them by overwriting certain parts of the payload. This includes replacing strings indicating the use of CSS expressions, Opera link and link target properties, as well as, data binding approaches with the placeholder `INVALID`. Listing 5 demonstrates an example for a purification result. Be assured that we do not forbid dangerous tags such as `<set>`, but analyze the attribute values and remove them in case an attack could be initiated by their contents.

```
// before
<svg xmlns="http://www.w3.org/2000/svg">
  <circle r="50" fill="red" cx="30" cy="30
      ">
    <set attributeName="onclick"
      to="javascript:alert(1)//">
    <set attributeName="fill" to="green">
  </circle>
</svg>

// after
<svg xmlns="http://www.w3.org/2000/svg">
<circle r="50" fill="red" cx="30" cy="30">
<set to="INVALID"></set><set attributeName
="fill" to="green"></set></circle></svg>
```

Listing 5: A malicious SVG before and after purification

Section 5 will further build upon the results of this purification process and furnish insight into how far this (for XML data unconventional) approach affects the visual information provided by the SVG test set.

SVGPurifier itself has undergone substantial testing from the security community during a public demonstration over a time-frame of several months [24]. The results helped us to refine the filtering mechanism and spot all the less obvious and difficult to find browser behaviors requiring dedicated fixes to deliver effective filtering and keep the security promise that the tool poses. During the testing phase we logged about 500 attempts targeted to break the filter functionality of the *SVGPurifier* and inject malicious content. Of those, about 15 were successful and resulted in the refinement of our algorithms. The *SVGPurifier* performance scales with the number of SVG tags and elements to sanitize, but can be considered uncritical since the main use case for the tool is on the server-side (e.g., each uploaded SVG image is transformed to remove suspicious content).

A server-side solution has the advantage that a website owner can performantly protect its users from attacks using SVGs and not requiring all users to upgrade their client-software. Our evaluation showed that the SVGPurifier was capable of removing malicious code in all of the discussed test cases. We examined possibilities to craft a purely client-side SVG filter combined with the possibility of limiting down DOM elements and their capabilities. Our initial research showed that this is feasible and considered as future work.

4.3 Unexpected Browser Behavior

We also found several cases of unusual and (depending on the execution context) often problematic browser behaviors that forced us to adapt *SVGPurifier* to address them:

- The Opera AII attacks mentioned in Section 3.5 have not been fixed by the vendor despite several bug reports from our side. This problem complicates the implementation of *SVGPurifier* since basically any external image resource loaded by an SVG file could contain suspicious plugin code and initiate an attack.

- Most browsers support the SVG `<use>` tag, but so far only Opera allows to include external SVG resources containing script code to execute, or links to show and point to possibly malicious URIs via URL handlers such as `javascript` and `data`. Most browsers tested permit utilizing the `<set>` as well as the `<animate>` tag to transform `xlink:href` attributes and set them with *JavaScript* and *data* URIs, too. This should be restricted by browsers for the sake of avoiding injection attacks via `<use>`, `<set>`, and `<animate>`. However, none of the over 100.000 SVG files we have tested during our evaluation actually used this feature.

- Plain text tags inside SVG images such as `<script>`, `<style>`, `<noscript>`, and similar tags allow to use HTML entities, giving them an equivalent syntactical meaning as their canonical forms. This was relevant for several of the XSS filter bypasses we described in Section 3.4. Especially the automated decoding of entities such as `<` and `>` could be used to bypass XSS filters and common protection mechanisms. Browsers therefore need to be more selective in determining which entities get automatically decoded and which do not. For example, Google Chrome went as far as to completely disable the automated decoding.

Some of these behaviors forced us to customize *SVGPurifier* and reduce the available feature set. Later versions of the tool might be less restrictive, assuming that the browser bugs get fixed and the market share of the affected browser versions shrinks to an insignificant level. Future versions of the tool will also be capable of handling external entities and place their proper value at the desired locations.

5. EVALUATION

We have implemented a prototype of *SVGPurifier*, consisting of 5,663 lines of PHP code. To evaluate the tool, we compiled a test set of SVG images obtained from Wikipedia. We chose this platform for several reasons: SVG images are widely used within Wikipedia, the content of the platform consists of the contributions from a large community, and among the contributors, the employment of a diverse set of tools to create the images can be observed. As a result, we have a heterogeneous test set that enables us to study the robustness and versatility of *SVGPurifier*.

To download the files, we used *wikix*, a tool that uses a snapshot of Wikipedia (exported as XML) to generate the URLs of the SVG files hosted at `upload.wikimedia.org`. The latest snapshot of the english Wikipedia at the time of writing has referenced a total of 112,646 SVG images. 105,509 were actually available for download at that time and we used those files for our evaluation.

5.1 Evaluation Setup

In order to minimize the impact of *SVGPurifier* on usability, the tool should not alter the visual appearance of an image since this would decrease the user experience. Our implementation only removes elements from an SVG file, thus (by construction) no new image element will appear in a purified image. However, the cleaning process might be too aggressive, i.e., cases where we remove elements that have a visual impact on the resulting image might occur. To evaluate this effect, we compare the original image with the purified one and determine if the file was altered during the process. Since the size of our test set is too large for a manual evaluation, we developed an approach to compare SVG files in an automated way.

Comparing two SVG images for similarity is difficult, resulting from the fact that there are countless ways of achieving the same visual appearance. Consequently, contrasting only the XML markup does not enable us to determine if a pair of images has the same visual appearance. Therefore, we decided to convert the SVG files to *Portable Network Graphics* (PNG) format and then perform the comparative step. PNG is a raster graphics format providing lossless data compression. Each pixel is defined in an 24 bit RGB colorspace with an optional 8 bit alpha channel (32 bit RGBA). Comparing two PNG files for similarity can thus be achieved by matching the value of each channel for each pair of pixels, which in turn results in a numerical value representing the absolute error a. A value of $a = 0$ indicates that no difference between the two images was found, while $a > 0$ denotes some discrepancy. Note that this evaluation measures the visual impact of our tool and approximates the deviation caused by the transformation process.

We tested the following four tools regarding their capability to convert SVG images to PNG format:

- Apache *batik* (`http://xml.apache.org/batik/`)
- *rSVG* (`http://librsvg.sourceforge.net/`)
- *GIMP* (`http://www.gimp.org/`)
- *Inkscape* (`http://inkscape.org/`)

Based on our test set, we have empirically found that the Apache *batik* toolkit was able to convert the largest number of files: only 23 of the 105,509 files could not be converted by the tool, prompting us to remove them from the test set. All files from the resulting evaluation set were converted to a PNG image with a fixed width, assuring the aspect ratio's preservation. As *batik* does not fully support declarative animations, we create static PNG images from the SVG files. In this manner, if an image was animated beforehand, we will only consider the visual state it is in before the animation begins. There are five different elements within a SVG file to accomplish animation: `<set>`, `<animate>`, `<animateMotion>`, `<animateColor>`, and `<animateTransform>`. A close analysis showed that only two SVG files in our test set actually contained one of these elements, which indicates that this feature is not (yet) widely used. We therefore consider comparison of static images exclusively to be only a minor limitation of our evaluation.

After converting images to PNGs, we compare the original and the purified image using the *ImageMagick* toolkit, which provides methods for a pixel-wise comparison of raster images, as well as, for gathering statistics on the amount of aberration. Furthermore, the tool is capable of creating *difference images* that visually indicate what regions of an image contain an error, which eventually enables us to manually examine cases in which actual changes occur. Other than determining the absolute number of pixels that differ between the two images, we calculate the normalized mean absolute error for each pair of images as metrics. We consider the normalized mean absolute error to be more relevant in our scenario than the root mean square error, as the former weights every aberration equally. Moreover, we log both the size of the original file, and that of the purified one, factually determining the compression ratio resulting from the purification process.

5.2 Evaluation Results

Based on the procedure outlined above, we analyzed all 105,486 files belonging to the evaluation set. For 98.5% of the samples, no visual difference exists in the appearance of the original versus the purified image (i.e., absolute error a is 0 and, therefore, all other error metrics are 0 as well). The 99th percentile of the normalized mean absolute error is 0.00000474877, where 0 represents no error at all and 1 indicates completely dissimilar images.

When investigating the error cases and the corresponding different images, we often found that although the image contained some kind of aberration that can be expressed numerically, a visual difference cannot be easily found by a human observer. Specifically, we manually analyzed 1,000 test cases in which the absolute error was larger than zero. We tried to determine in how many cases a human observer would notice an aberration. While this is not believed to be an approach that is valid overall (i.e., specific circumstances like medical applications require precise conversion), a visual impact in the context of a website exists only if a user can actually spot it.

During the manual inspection process, we spent about 10 seconds on each pair of the images to compare them (aided by the *difference image* to support the user). The results of this manual examination indicate that only 46.3% of the erroneous samples were perceived as different from their original. Since user experience may differ, we provide a website where we present all defective images complete with their original and the *difference images*, inviting others to freely inspect these cases [6].

Several side effects were observed during the purification process and the evaluation of this process' results. What was an additional positive side effect we found, was that due to the removal of elements not contributing to the visual appearance of the image, *SVGPurifier* actually compresses files with an average compression ratio of 2.6. Some files had a slightly larger file size after the purification process, which was caused by the transformation the tool has performed on broken files. In most cases, the increase in file size was based on the addition of missing closing tags by *SVGPurifier*.

1.59% of the files in our test set contained one or more instances of the `<foreignObject>` element. In the majority of the 1,686 cases, this element was used as what had appeared to be an artifact of *Adobe Illustrator* to store a base64-encoded representation of its proprietary AI file format within the SVG file. *SVGPurifier* deleted these elements and no visual impact resulted from this removal. However, the image size was reduced significantly.

6. RELATED WORK

Not surprisigly, being one of the most common problems in the area of web security, the Cross Site Scripting (XSS) problem has received a lot of attention during the last decade. [11,12,20,27–29,31,36,39,40,42]. On the offensive side, several different kinds of attacks were studied [12,28,31]. Approaches to prevent XSS attacks include information flow and taint tracking [20,36,39,40], and analysis on the client- or server-side [11,29,40]. John's dissertation elaborated on the attack and defense techniques in detail [27], while Phung et al. presented specific defense techniques against client side and JavaScript based attacks [38]. Nevertheless, none of these works dealt with the threat of malicious image files in the JavaScript execution context. In this paper, we introduce new innovative attacks that highlight the fact that in the era of HTML5, even a previously unsuspicious `<img>` tag may introduce security vulnerabilities due to the tight integration of SVG images into the modern browsers.

One exception is the work by Barth et al., who discussed attacks and mitigations around faulty and jaunty content sniffing [9]. Deprecated browsers such as Opera 9 and Internet Explorer 6 allowed to execute JavaScript by combining image tags with JavaScript URIs, but none of the tested modern browsers supports this kind of render behavior anymore, as this particular attack vector has been recently fixed. In contrast, the risks of Cross Site Scripting and related attacks against browsers induced by SVG images have not yet been investigated.

SVG as a subject itself surfaced rarely in the scientific security community. One notable exception is given by Damiani et al. [18], who dealt with access control requirements of parts of SVG files. Their assumption was that SVG files containing sensitive personal information should be rendered differently for different viewers, hence requiring some parts of an SVG document to be deleted (or kept encrypted). However, they did not manage to cope with the threat of misusing SVG files as attack vectors. In the same line of work, Mohammed et al. [33–35] investigated the use of SVG images in medical contexts, where certain security guarantees have to be granted for sensitive information contained in an SVG image. Again, their publication did not resolve the offensive use of SVG files.

One area of research closely related to the results presented in this paper deals with the problem of code embedded in document formats. For example, Backes et al. showed that maliciously prepared PostScript files can be used as an attacker vector [8], and Checkoway et al. discussed malicious TeX files that can, among other consequences, lead to an arbitrary code execution and data exfiltration based on TeX's Turing-complete macro language [13]. Even pure text files might contain shellcode as shown by Mason et al. [32]. We continue this line of scientific enquiry and present attacks related to SVG images.

An orthogonal area of research are alternative browser designs [10,15,19,41]. These browsers explore how the security of state-of-the-art browsers can be improved, for example by creating separate protection domains. The results presented in this paper need to be taken into account when designing more secure browser and especially the fact that `<img>` tags might lead to suspicious content have to be considered.

7. CONCLUSION

In this paper, we provide an overview of Scalable Vector Graphics (SVG) and their security impact on the World Wide Web as based on the new HTML5 specification drafts. We show that this image format (which exists for more than a decade), significantly changes the browser and web security landscape. We introduce several novel attacks against modern browsers and show that this phenomenon can have major impact on web applications that allow their users to post images. In particular, we illustrate that SVG images embedded via `<img>` tag and CSS can execute arbitrary JavaScript code and similar attacks. Subsequently, the discussed XSS filter bypasses, which work against several browsers, can have a similarly high impact on a targeted attack scenario.

To mitigate the attacks presented, we proposed *SVGPurifier* as a first practical solution available and capable of removing potentially malicious code from SVG files. We have empirically shown that the software is usable for real-world scenarios such as a purification of the SVG files stored by Wikipedia. We are in a discussion with the Wikipedia team, who might adopt *SVGPurifier* to their infrastructure. Furthermore, many of the identified attacks have already been fixed by major browser vendors.

8. REFERENCES

[1] National vulnerability database (NVD) (CVE-2007-1765). `http://web.nvd.nist.gov/view/vuln/detail?vulnId=CVE-2007-1765`, Mar. 2007.

[2] National vulnerability database (NVD) (CVE-2008-3702). `http://web.nvd.nist.gov/view/vuln/detail?vulnId=CVE-2008-3702`, Aug. 2008.

[3] Fonts – SVG 1.1 (Second Edition). `http://www.w3.org/TR/SVG/fonts.html`, June 2010.

[4] National vulnerability database (NVD) (CVE-2010-3113). `http://web.nvd.nist.gov/view/vuln/detail?vulnId=cve-2010-3113`, Aug. 2010.

[5] Scalable vector graphics (SVG) 1.1 (Second edition). `http://www.w3.org/TR/SVG11/`, June 2010.

[6] Svgpurifier: inaccurately converted images. `http://svgpurifier.nds.rub.de/`, May 2011.

[7] Adobe Systems Inc. Illustrator 10 XML Extensions Guide, Sept. 2001.

[8] M. Backes, M. Durmuth, and D. Unruh. Information Flow in the Peer-Reviewing Process. In *IEEE Symposium on Security and Privacy*, 2007.

[9] A. Barth, J. Caballero, and D. Song. Secure Content Sniffing for Web Browsers, or How to Stop Papers from Reviewing Themselves. In *IEEE Symposium on Security and Privacy*, 2009.

[10] A. Barth, C. Jackson, C. Reis, and Google Chrome Team. The Security Architecture of the Chromium Browser, 2008. `http://seclab.stanford.edu/websec/chromium/`.

[11] P. Bisht and V. N. Venkatakrishnan. XSS-GUARD: Precise Dynamic Prevention of Cross-Site Scripting Attacks. In *Conference on Detection of Intrusions and Malware & Vulnerability Assessment*, 2008.

[12] H. Bojinov, E. Bursztein, and D. Boneh. XCS: Cross Channel Scripting and its Impact on Web Applications. In *ACM Conference on Computer and Communications Security (CCS)*, 2009.

[13] S. Checkoway, H. Shacham, and E. Rescorla. Are Text-only Data Formats Safe? or, Use This LaTeX Class File to Pwn Your Computer. In *USENIX Workshop on Large-Scale Exploits and Emergent Threats (LEET)*, 2010.

[14] J. Clark. XSL transformations (XSLT). `http://www.w3.org/TR/xslt`, Nov. 1999.

[15] R. S. Cox, S. D. Gribble, H. M. Levy, and J. G. Hansen. A Safety-Oriented Platform for Web Applications. In *IEEE Symposium on Security and Privacy*, 2006.

[16] A. Dabirsiaghi. The OWASP AntiSamy project. `http://code.google.com/p/owaspantisamy/`, Apr. 2011.

[17] E. Dahlström. SVG and HTML. `http://dev.w3.org/SVG/proposals/svg-html/svg-html-proposal.html`, July 2008.

[18] E. Damiani, S. De Capitani di Vimercati, E. Fernandez-Medina, and P. Samarati. An access control system for SVG documents. *King's College, University of Cambridge, UK*, pages 29–31, 2002.

[19] C. Grier, S. Tang, and S. T. King. Secure Web Browsing with the OP Web Browser. In *IEEE Symposium on Security and Privacy*, 2008.

[20] M. V. Gundy and H. Chen. Noncespaces: Using Randomization to Enforce Information Flow Tracking and Thwart Cross-Site Scripting Attacks. In *Symposium on Network and Distributed System Security (NDSS)*, 2009.

[21] U. Harnhammar. kses - PHP HTML/XHTML filter. `http://sourceforge.net/projects/kses/`, Mar. 2010.

[22] M. Heiderich. Opera SVG AII testcase. http://heideri.ch/opera/, 2011.

[23] M. Heiderich. SVG chameleon via XSLT - HTML5 Security Cheatsheet. http://html5sec.org/#125, Mar. 2011.

[24] M. Heiderich and T. Frosch. SVGpurifier smoketest. http://heideri.ch/svgpurifier/SVGPurifier/, Apr. 2011.

[25] I. Hickson. HTML standard — the map element. http://whatwg.org/specs/web-apps/current-work/multipage/the-map-element.html#svg-0, Apr. 2011.

[26] L. Huang, Z. Weinberg, C. Evans, and C. Jackson. Protecting browsers from Cross-Origin CSS attacks. In *ACM Conference on Computer and Communications Security (CCS) 2010)*, 2010.

[27] M. Johns. *Code Injection Vulnerabilities in Web Applications - Exemplified at Cross-site Scripting.* PhD thesis, University of Passau, Passau, July 2009.

[28] C. Karlof, U. Shankar, J. D. Tygar, and D. Wagner. Dynamic Pharming Attacks and Locked Same-Origin Policies for Web Browsers. In *ACM Conference on Computer and Communications Security (CCS)*, 2007.

[29] E. Kirda, C. Kruegel, G. Vigna, and N. Jovanovic. Noxes: A Client-Side Solution for Mitigating Cross-Site Scripting Attacks. In *ACM Symposium On Applied Computing (SAC)*, 2006.

[30] E. Lawrence. Same origin policy part 1: No peeking. http://blogs.msdn.com/b/ieinternals/archive/2009/08/28/explaining-same-origin-policy-part-1-deny-read.aspx, Aug. 2009.

[31] M. Martin and M. S. Lam. Automatic Generation of XSS and SQL Injection Attacks with Goal-directed Model Checking. In *USENIX Security Symposium*, 2008.

[32] J. Mason, S. Small, F. Monrose, and G. MacManus. English Shellcode. In *ACM Conference on Computer and Communications Security (CCS)*, 2009.

[33] S. Mohammed, L. Chamarette, J. Fiaidhi, and S. Osborn. A Safe RSS Approach for Securely Sharing Mobile SVG Biomedical Images for Web 2.0. In *12th IEEE International Conference on Computational Science and Engineering*, 2009.

[34] S. Mohammed, J. Fiaidhi, H. Ghenniwa, and M. Hahn. Developing a Secure Web Service Architecture for SVG Image Delivery. *Journal of Computer Science*, 2(2):171–179, 2006.

[35] S. M. A. Mohammed and J. A. W. Fiadhi. Developing Secure Transcoding Intermediary for SVG Medical Images within Peer-to-Peer Ubiquitous Environment. In *CNSR '05 Proceedings of the 3rd Annual Communication Networks and Services Research Conference*, 2005.

[36] Y. Nadji, P. Saxena, and D. Song. Document Structure Integrity: A Robust Basis for Cross-site Scripting Defense. In *Symposium on Network and Distributed System Security (NDSS)*, 2009.

[37] S. Patnaik. htmLawed. http://www.bioinformatics.org/phplabware/internal_utilities/htmLawed/.

[38] P. H. Phung, D. Sands, and A. Chudnov. Lightweight Self-Protecting JavaScript. In *ACM Symposium on Information, Computer and Communications Security (ASIACCS)*, 2009.

[39] T. Pietraszek and C. V. Berghe. Defending Against Injection Attacks Through Context-Sensitive String Evaluation. In *Symposium on Recent Advances in Intrusion Detection (RAID)*, 2005.

[40] P. Vogt, F. Nentwich, N. Jovanovic, E. Kirda, C. Kruegel, and G. Vigna. Cross-Site Scripting Prevention with Dynamic Data Tainting and Static Analysis. In *Symposium on Network and Distributed System Security (NDSS)*, 2007.

[41] H. J. Wang, C. Grier, A. Moshchuk, S. T. King, P. Choudhury, and H. Venter. The Multi-Principal OS Construction of the Gazelle Web Browser. In *USENIX Security Symposium*, 2009.

[42] G. Wassermann and Z. Su. Static Detection of Cross-Site Scripting Vulnerabilities. In *International Conference on Software Engineering (ICSE)*, 2008.

[43] E. Z. Yang. HTML Purifier. http://htmlpurifier.org/, Mar. 2011.

Fear the EAR: Discovering and Mitigating Execution After Redirect Vulnerabilities

Adam Doupé, Bryce Boe, Christopher Kruegel, and Giovanni Vigna
University of California, Santa Barbara
{adoupe, bboe, chris, vigna}@cs.ucsb.edu

ABSTRACT

The complexity of modern web applications makes it difficult for developers to fully understand the security implications of their code. Attackers exploit the resulting security vulnerabilities to gain unauthorized access to the web application environment. Previous research into web application vulnerabilities has mostly focused on input validation flaws, such as cross-site scripting and SQL injection, while logic flaws have received comparably less attention.

In this paper, we present a comprehensive study of a relatively unknown logic flaw in web applications, which we call Execution After Redirect, or EAR. A web application developer can introduce an EAR by calling a redirect method under the assumption that execution will halt. A vulnerability occurs when server-side execution continues after the developer's intended halting point, which can lead to broken/insufficient access controls and information leakage. We start with an analysis of how susceptible applications written in nine web frameworks are to EAR vulnerabilities. We then discuss the results from the EAR challenge contained within the 2010 International Capture the Flag Competition. Finally, we present an open-source, white-box, static analysis tool to detect EARs in Ruby on Rails web applications. This tool found 3,944 EAR instances in 18,127 open-source applications. Finally, we describe an approach to prevent EARs in web frameworks.

Categories and Subject Descriptors

D.2.5 [**Testing and Debugging**]

General Terms

Security

Keywords

static analysis, web applications, execution after redirect

CCS'11, October 17–21, 2011, Chicago, Illinois, USA.

1. INTRODUCTION

An increasing number of services are being offered online. For example, banking, shopping, socializing, reading the news, and enjoying entertainment are all available on the web. The increasing amount of sensitive data stored by web applications has attracted the attention of cyber-criminals, who break into systems to steal valuable information such as passwords, credit card numbers, social security numbers, and bank account credentials.

Attackers use a variety of vulnerabilities to exploit web applications. In 2008, Albert Gonzalez was accused and later convicted of stealing 40 million credit and debit cards from major corporate retailers, by writing SQL injection attacks [20, 30]. Another common vulnerability, cross-site scripting (XSS), is the second highest-ranked entry on the OWASP top ten security risks for web applications, behind injection attacks like SQL injection [29]. Thus, SQL injection and XSS have received a large amount of attention by the security community. Other popular web application vulnerabilities include cross site request forgery (XSRF) [5], HTTP parameter pollution (HPP) [3, 12], HTTP response splitting [27], and clickjacking [2, 21].

In this paper, we present an in-depth study of a little-known real-world web application logic flaw; one we are calling Execution After Redirect (EAR). An EAR occurs because of a developer's misunderstanding of how the web application framework operates. In the normal workflow of a web application, a user sends a request to the web application. The web application receives this request, performs some server-side processing, and returns an HTTP response. Part of the HTTP response can be a notification that the client (a web browser) should look elsewhere for the requested resource. In this case, the web application sets the HTTP response code to `301`, `302`, `303`, or `307`, and adds a `Location` header [32]. These response codes instruct the browser to look for the resource originally requested at a new URL specified by the web application in the HTTP `Location` header [31]. This process is known as redirection[1]; the web application redirects the user to another resource.

Intuitively, one assumes that a redirect should end execution of the server side code; the reason is that the browser immediately sends a request for the new location as soon as the redirection response is received, and it does not process the rest of the web application's output. Some web frame-

[1]In this paper, we consider only HTTP server-side redirection. Other forms of redirection, executed on the client, exist such as JavaScript redirect or HTML meta refresh.

works, however, do not halt execution on a redirect. This can lead to EAR vulnerabilities.

Specifically, an EAR can be introduced when a web application developer writes code that issues an HTTP redirect under the assumption that the redirect will automatically halt execution of the web application. Depending on the framework, execution can continue after the call to the redirect function, potentially violating the security properties of the web application.

We define *halt-on-redirect* as a web framework behavior where server-side code execution halts on a redirect, thus preventing EARs. Unfortunately, some languages make halt-on-redirect difficult to implement, for instance, by not supporting a `goto`-type statement. Therefore, web frameworks differ in supporting halt-on-redirect behavior. This difference in redirect method semantics can increase the developer's confusion when developing applications in different frameworks.

In this paper, we present a comprehensive study of Execution After Redirect vulnerabilities: we provide an overview of EARs and classify EARs into different types. We also analyze nine web application frameworks' susceptibility to EARs, specifying their redirect semantics, as well as detailing what exactly makes them vulnerable to EARs. Moreover, we develop a novel static analysis algorithm to detect EARs, which we implemented in an open-source tool to analyze Ruby on Rails web applications. Finally, we discovered hundreds of vulnerabilities in open-source Ruby on Rails web applications, with a very low false positive rate.

In summary, this paper provides the following contributions:

- We categorize EARs and provide an analysis of nine frameworks' susceptibility to various types of EARs.
- We discuss the results from the EAR challenge contained within our 2010 International Capture the Flag Competition.
- We present an algorithm to statically detect EARs in Ruby on Rails applications.
- We run our white-box tool on 18,127 open-source Ruby on Rails applications, which found 3,944 EARs.

2. OVERVIEW OF EARS

An Execution After Redirect vulnerability is a logic flaw in web applications that results from a developer's misunderstanding of the semantics of redirection. Very often this misunderstanding is caused by the web framework used by the developer[2]. In particular, developers typically assume that the web application will halt after calling a function of the web framework that performs a redirect. Certain web frameworks, however, do not halt execution on a redirect, and instead, execute all the code that follows the redirect operation. The web browser perpetuates this misunderstanding, as it obediently performs the redirect, thus falsely indicating that the code is correct. As a result, when the developer tests the web application using the browser, the observed behavior seems in line with the intentions of the developer, and, consequently, the application is assumed to be correct.

[2] This misunderstanding was confirmed by a developer who responded to us when we notified him of an EAR in his code, who said, "I wasn't aware at all of this problem because I thought ruby on rails will always end any execution after a redirect." This example shows that developers do not always understand how their web framework handles redirects.

```
1  class TopicsController <
       ApplicationController
2   def update
3    @topic = Topic.find(params[:id])
4    if not current_user.is_admin?
5      redirect_to("/")
6    end
7    @topic.update_attributes(params[:topic])
8    flash[:notice] = "Topic updated!"
9   end
10 end
```

Listing 1: Example of an Execution After Redirect vulnerability in Ruby on Rails.

Note that an EAR is not a code injection vulnerability; an attacker cannot execute arbitrary code, only code already present after the redirect. An EAR is also different from XSS and SQL injection vulnerabilities; it is not an input validation flaw, but rather a mismatch between the developer's intentions and the actual implementation.

As an example, consider the EAR vulnerability in the Ruby on Rails code shown in Listing 1. The code appears to redirect the current user to "/" if she is not an administrator (Line 5), and, if she is an administrator, `@topic` will be updated with the parameters sent by the user in the `params` variable (Line 7). The code does not execute in this way, because Ruby on Rails does not support halt-on-redirect behavior. Thus, *any* user, not only the administrator, can update the topic, violating the intended authorization and compromising the security of the web application.

The simple way to fix Listing 1 is to add a `return` after the `redirect_to` call on Line 5. This will cause the `update` method to terminate after the redirect, thus, no additional code will be executed. Adding a return after all redirects is a good best practice, however, it is insufficient to prevent all EARs. Listing 2 depicts an example of an EAR that cannot be prevented by adding a return after a redirect. Here, the `redirect_to` on Line 4 is followed by a `return`, so there is no EAR in the `ensure_admin` method. However, `ensure_admin` is called by `delete` on Line 10, which calls `redirect_to` on Line 4. The `return` call on Line 5 will return the control flow back into the `delete` method, and execution will continue on Line 11. Thus, the `@user` object will still be deleted on Line 12, regardless of whether the `current_user` is an administrator or not, introducing an EAR. Unfortunately in some frameworks, the developer cannot simply use `exit` instead of return to halt execution after a redirect because the web application is expected to handle multiple requests. Therefore, calling `exit` would kill the web application and prevent further requests.

2.1 EAR History

Execution After Redirect vulnerabilities are not a new occurrence; we found 17 Common Vulnerabilities and Exposures (CVE) EAR vulnerabilities dating back to 2007. These CVE entries were difficult to find because EARs do not have a separate vulnerability type; the EAR CVE vul-

```
class UsersController <
    ApplicationController
  def ensure_admin
    if not current_user.is_admin?
      redirect_to("/")
      return
    end
  end

  def delete
    ensure_admin()
    @user = User.find(params[:id])
    @user.delete()
    flash[:notice] = "User Deleted"
  end
end
```

Listing 2: Example of a complex Execution After Redirect vulnerability in Ruby on Rails.

nerabilities we found[3] were spread across different Common Weakness Enumeration Specification (CWE) types: "Input Validation," "Authentication Issues," "Design Error," "Credentials Management," "Code Injection," and "Permissions, Privileges, and Access Control." These vulnerabilities types vary greatly, and this indicates that EARs are not well understood by the security community.

2.2 EARs as Logic Flaws

While logic flaws are typically thought of as being unique to a specific web application, we believe EARs are logic flaws, even though they are systemic to many web applications. Because an EAR is the result of the developer's misunderstanding of the web application framework, there is an error in her logic. The intuition is that the redirect is an indication of the developer's intent for ending server-side processing. A redirect can be thought of as a `goto` - the developer, in essence, wishes to tell the user to look somewhere else. However, it does not act as a `goto`, because the server-side control flow of the application is not terminated, even though that is how it appears from the perspective of the client.

There are almost no valid reasons to have code executed after a redirect method. The few exceptions are: performing cleanup actions, such as closing open files, and starting long-running processes, such as encoding a video file. In the former case, the cleanup code can be executed before a redirect, and in the latter case, long-running processes can be started asynchronously, alleviating the need to have code executed after a redirect.

Because there is no reason to execute code after a redirect, we can infer that the presence of code executed after a redirect is a logic flaw.

2.3 Types of EARs

Execution After Redirect logic flaws can be of two types: benign or vulnerable. A benign EAR is one in which no security properties of the application are violated, even though

[3]The interested reader is directed to the following EARs: CVE-2009-2168, CVE-2009-1936, CVE-2008-6966, CVE-2008-6965, CVE-2008-0350, CVE-2007-6652, CVE-2007-6550, CVE-2007-6414, CVE-2007-5578, CVE-2007-4932, CVE-2007-4240, CVE-2007-2988, CVE-2007-2776, CVE-2007-2775, CVE-2007-2713, CVE-2007-2372, and CVE-2007-2003.

```
$current_user = get_current_user();
if (!$current_user->is_admin())
{
   header("Location: /");
}
echo "Sensitive Information";
```

Listing 3: Example of an information leakage Execution After Redirect vulnerability in PHP. If the `current_user` is not an administrator, the PHP `header` function will be called, redirecting the user to "/". However, the sensitive information will still be returned in the output, thus leaking information. The fix is to call the `exit` function after the `header` call.

additional, unintended, code is executed after a redirect. For example, the code executed after the redirect could set a local variable to a static string, and the local variable is not used or stored. Although no security properties are violated, a benign EAR may indicate that a developer misunderstood the redirect semantics of the web framework, posing the risk that code will, in the future, be added after the redirect, elevating the EAR from benign to vulnerable.

A vulnerable EAR occurs when the code executed after the redirect violates the security properties of the web application. More specifically, in a vulnerable EAR the code executed after the redirect allows unauthorized modification to the state of the web application (typically the database), and/or causes leakage (reads and returns to the browser) of data to an unauthorized user. In the former case (e.g., see Listing 1), the integrity of the web application is compromised, while in the latter case, the confidentiality of the web application is violated (e.g., see Listing 3). Thus, every vulnerable EAR is an instance of broken/insufficient access controls, because the redirect call is an indication that the user who made the request is not allowed to access the requested resource.

EAR vulnerabilities can be silent. In a silent EAR, the execution of code does not produce any output. This lack of information makes silent EARs difficult to detect via a black-box approach, while information leakage EARs are easier to detect with black-box tools. Listings 1 and 2 are examples of silent EARs, and Listing 3 is an example of an information leakage EAR.

2.4 Framework Analysis

Web application frameworks vary on supporting halt-on-redirect behavior. Therefore, different frameworks provide protection against different kinds of EAR vulnerabilities. The differing semantics of redirects increases the confusion of developers. A developer we contacted said, "I didn't realize that [Ruby on Rails'] redirect_to was like PHP's header redirect and continued to run code." Thus, an understanding of the web framework's redirect semantics is essential to produce correct, EAR-free, code.

We analyzed nine of the most popular web frameworks to see how they differ with respect to their built-in redirect functions. The nine frameworks were chosen based on their StackOverflow activity, and include one framework for each of the Ruby, Groovy, and Python languages, three frameworks for the PHP language, one framework that can be applied to both C# and Visual Basic, and two frameworks for the Java language [7]. While the frameworks selected for analysis are not exhaustive, we believe they are diverse and popular enough to be representative of real-world usage.

To analyze the frameworks, we created nearly identical copies of a simple web service in each of the nine web frameworks. This web service provided access to four pages within the web application. The first was the root page, "/", which simply linked to the other three pages. The second was the redirect page, "/redirect", which was used to test proper redirect behavior. The third was the EAR page, "/ear", which called the framework's redirect function, appended a message to a log file regarding the request, and finally attempted to return a rendered response to the browser. The last page was the log page, "/log", which simply displayed the contents of the log file.

Using this design for the web application allowed us to check for integrity violations, represented by the appended log message, and confidentiality violations, represented by output sent after the HTTP redirect response when requesting the EAR page. We approached the implementation of this web application in each framework as many developers new to that framework would. That is, whenever possible, we followed the recommended tutorials and coding practices required to build a web application in the framework.

A brief background on the model-view-controller (MVC) software architecture is necessary to follow our analysis, as each framework analyzed fits the MVC pattern. The MVC architecture supports the separation of the persistent storage (model), the user interface (view), and the control flow (controller) [33]. More precisely, the models interact with the database, the views specify the output to return to the client, and the controllers are the glue that puts everything together. The controller must handle HTTP requests, fetch or update models, and finally return a view as an HTTP response. When following the MVC paradigm, a controller is responsible for issuing a redirect call.

The following sections describe our analysis of each framework's susceptibility to EAR vulnerabilities based on their redirect functions' use and documentation. We developed the test application in the latest stable version of each framework available at the time. The version numbers are listed adjacent to the framework name in the section headers.

2.4.1 Ruby on Rails 3.0.5

Ruby on Rails, commonly referred to as Rails, is a popular web application framework. Unfortunately, Rails is susceptible to EAR vulnerabilities. Rails provides the `redirect_to` function, which prepares the controller for sending the HTTP redirect. However, the redirect is not actually sent at this point, and code continues to execute following the call to `redirect_to`. In Rails, there is no mechanism to ensure that code halts following a redirect, thus if exit is called, a developer must return from the controller's entry function without executing additional code.

As previously mentioned in Section 2, the Ruby `exit` command cannot be used to halt the execution of a controller after a redirect. This is for two reasons: the first is that `redirect_to` does not immediately send output when it is called, thus if `exit` is called, the user will never see the redirect. The second reason is that Rails web applications are long-running processes that handle multiple incoming requests, unlike PHP, which typically spawns a new instance for each request. Therefore, calling `exit` to halt execution is not feasible, as it will terminate the Rails application, preventing it from handling further requests.

On a positive note, information leakage EARs are impossible in Rails web applications because a controller can either perform a redirect, or `render` a response (view) to the user. Any call to `render` after a redirect will result in Rails throwing a `DoubleRenderError`. This exception is thrown in all possible combinations: render after a redirect, render after a render, redirect after a render, and redirect after a redirect.

2.4.2 Grails 1.3.7

Grails is a framework written in Groovy, which was modeled after the Ruby on Rails framework. Thus, Grails behaves in a manner nearly identical to Rails with respect to redirects. Specifically, code will continue to execute following a call to the redirect function, and, therefore, the developer must take precautions to avoid creating an EAR vulnerability. Unfortunately, as of this writing, nowhere in the Grails documentation on redirects does it mention that code will continue to execute following a redirect [34].

Unlike Ruby on Rails, the behavior of Grails is somewhat less predictable when it comes to the order of view rendering and/or calls to redirect. To explain, we will say that to "render" means to output a view, and to "redirect" means to call the redirect function. As previously mentioned in Section 2.4.1, in Rails, only one render or one redirect may be called in a controller; a `DoubleRenderError` is thrown in the case of multiple calls. In Grails, however, the only redirect exception, `CannotRedirectException`, occurs when a redirect is called following another redirect. In cases where multiple calls to render are made, the final render is the only one that is sent to the browser. More importantly, in cases where both redirect and render are called, regardless of their order, the redirect is actually sent to the browser and the render call is simply ignored. Due to this behavior of Grails, it is not vulnerable to an information leakage EAR. However, like Rails, it is still vulnerable to silent EARs that violate the integrity of the application.

2.4.3 Django 1.2.5

Django is a Python web application framework that differs in its handling of redirects compared to the other frameworks (save for ASP.NET MVC). Rather than calling functions to render or perform the redirect, Django requires the developer to return an `HttpResponse` object from each controller. Django's documentation makes it clear that calling Django's `redirect` function merely returns a subclass of the `HttpResponse` object. Thus, there is no reason for the developer to expect the code to halt when calling `redirect`. The actual HTTP redirect is sent to the browser only if this object is also returned from the controller's entry point, thereby removing the possibility of further code execution [15]. Because the controller's entry point can only return a single `HttpResponse` object, the developer can rely completely on her browser for testing purposes. This behavior makes Django impervious to all EARs.

2.4.4 ASP.NET MVC 3.0

ASP.NET MVC is a web application framework developed by Microsoft that adds a Model-View-Controller paradigm on top of traditional ASP.NET, which includes the languages C# and Visual Basic [1]. ASP.NET MVC is similar to Django, in that all controllers must return an `ActionRe-`

sult object. In order to perform redirection, either a RedirectResult or RedirectToRouteResult object must be returned, which are both subclasses of ActionResult. Like Django, this behavior makes ASP.NET MVC impervious to all EARs.

2.4.5 Zend Framework 2.3

By default, the PHP based Zend Framework is not susceptible to EAR vulnerabilities because its redirect methods immediately result in the termination of server-side code. This default behavior is consistent in the two methods used to perform a redirect in the Zend Framework. The simplest method is by using the _redirect method of the controller, however, the recommended method is to use the Redirector helper object [36].

While the default behavior is not vulnerable to EARs, the Zend Framework supports disabling halt-on-redirect for both methods. The _redirect method will not halt when the keyword argument exit=False is provided as part of the call. Disabling halt-on-redirect when using the Redirector helper requires calling SetExit(False) on the Redirector helper object prior to making the redirect call. The latter method is particularly interesting because any code executed during the request has the ability to modify the behavior of redirects called using the Redirector helper. Fortunately, even when using the Redirector helper, the developer has the option of using a set of functions suffixed with "AndExit" that always halt-on-redirect.

When halt-on-redirect is disabled in Zend, it becomes vulnerable to integrity violation EARs. However, the default view rendering behavior no longer occurs. Thus, even when modifying the default behavior, information leakage EARs will never occur in the Zend Framework.

2.4.6 CakePHP 1.3.7

Similar to the Zend Framework, the CakePHP framework is also not susceptible to EAR vulnerabilities out of the box. By default, CakePHP's single redirect method immediately results in the termination of the PHP script. In a manner similar to the Zend Framework, this default behavior can be modified by setting the third argument of redirect to False, which in turn also disables the default mechanism for view rendering [11]. Thus CakePHP is vulnerable to EARs in exactly the same way as the Zend Framework.

2.4.7 CodeIgniter 2.0.0

Unlike the Zend Framework and CakePHP, CodeIgniter is a very lightweight PHP framework, and thus, it does not offer much out of the box. Nevertheless, the framework still provides a url helper class that contains a redirect method [16]. CodeIgniter's redirect method always exits after setting the redirect header; a behavior that cannot be changed. Therefore CodeIgniter is impervious to EARs when developers use only the provided redirect function. Unfortunately, the url helper class must be included manually. As a result, there is the risk that developers will not use the provided redirect function and instead introduce EARs by neglecting to call exit following a call to header("Location:<path>").

2.4.8 J2EE 1.4

Java 2 Platform, Enterprise Edition (J2EE) defines a servlet paradigm for the development of web applications and web application frameworks in Java. Thus, to perform a redirect in J2EE, or a J2EE-based framework, the developer calls HttpServletResponse.sendRedirect. This redirect function will clear out everything previously in the output buffer, set the Location header to the redirect location, set the response code to 302, and finally flushes the output buffer to the browser. However, sendRedirect does not halt execution of the servlet. Thus, only silent EARs are present in J2EE web applications, or any framework that is based on J2EE servlets.

2.4.9 Struts 2.2.3

Apache Struts is an MVC framework that is built on top of the servlet model provided by J2EE. Thus, Struts inherits all the potential vulnerabilities of the J2EE framework, specifically that silent EARs are possible but information leakage EARs are not possible. This is because to perform a redirect, the HttpServletResponse.sendRedirect method of J2EE must be called.

2.5 EAR Security Challenge

Each year since 2003, we have organized and hosted a security competition called the International Capture the Flag (iCTF). The competition pits dozens of teams from various universities across the world against each other in a test of their security prowess. While each iCTF has a primary objective, the competitions typically involve secondary security challenges tangential to the primary objective [14].

For the 2010 edition of the iCTF, we constructed a security challenge to observe the familiarity of the teams to Execution After Redirect vulnerabilities. The challenge involved a vulnerable EAR that violated both the confidentiality and the integrity of the web application. The confidentiality was violated when the web application's administrator view was leaked to unauthorized users following a redirect; the unauthorized users were "correctly" redirected to an error page. The information contained in the leaked view provided enough information to allow for an integrity violation had the database not purposefully been in a read-only state. More importantly, the initial data leak provided the means to leak further information, thus allowing teams to successfully solve the challenge [6].

The crux of the EAR challenge relied on the automatic redirecting of web browsers and other web clients, such as wget and curl. To our surprise, many of the teams relied only on the output produced by their web browser, and, therefore, failed to notice the leaked information. It is important to note that the teams in this competition are primarily made up of graduate and undergraduate level students from various universities; many would not be considered security professionals. Nevertheless, we assumed that the meticulous eye of a novice-to-intermediate level hacker attempting to break into a web service would be more likely to detect information leakage when compared to a web developer testing their application for "correct" page flow.

Of the 72 teams in the competition, 69 contacted the web server at least once. 44 of these 69 teams advanced past the first step, which required them to submit a file as per the web application's specifications. 34 of the 44 teams advanced past the second step, which required them to brute force a two-digit password. It was at this point that the EAR vulnerability was exposed to the teams, resulting in both a redirect to the unauthorized error page and the leak-

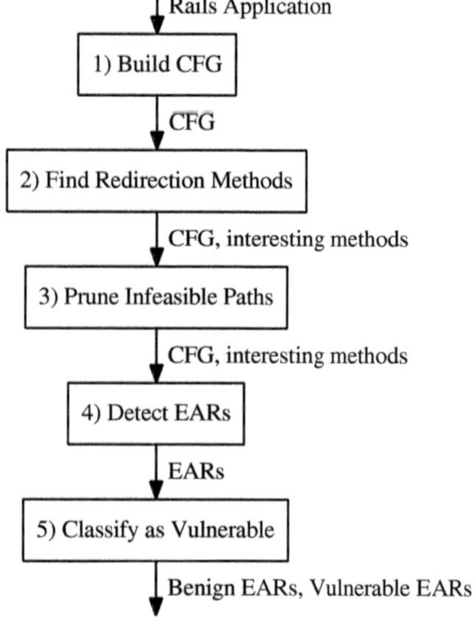

Figure 1: The logical flow of the white-box tool.

age of the administrator page as part of the HTTP redirect response. Of the 34 teams who made it this far, only 12 successfully discovered and exploited the vulnerability. The fact that only 12 out of 34 teams were successfully able to discover the information leaked to their browser in a hacking competition indicated that more research and exposure was necessary for EAR vulnerabilities.

3. EAR DETECTION

In this section, we discuss the design and implementation of our system to detect EAR vulnerabilities. This system uses static source code analysis to identify cases in which code might be executed after the call to a redirect function. We also introduce a heuristic to distinguish benign EARs from vulnerable EARs.

Our tool targets the Ruby language, specifically the Ruby on Rails web framework. We chose this framework for two reasons. First, Ruby on Rails is a very popular web framework, thus, there is a large number of open-source Ruby on Rails web applications available for inspection (e.g., on GitHub [19]). Second, due to the characteristics discussed in Section 2.4.1, all EARs present in Rails are silent. Thus, it is necessary to use a white-box tool to detect EARs in Ruby on Rails web applications. Again, it is important to note that redirects originate within the controllers[4], thus, our white-box tool operates specifically on controllers.

3.1 Detection Algorithm

The goal of our EAR detector is to find a path in the controller's Control Flow Graph (CFG) that contains both a call to a redirect method and code following that redirect method. An overview of our algorithm is given in Figure 1. The algorithm operates in five steps: (i) generate the CFG of the controller; (ii) find redirection methods; (iii) prune infeasible paths in the CFG to reduce false positives; (iv) detect EARs by finding a path in the CFG where code is executed after a redirect method is called; (v) use a heuristic to differentiate between benign and vulnerable EARs.

Step 1: Building the Control Flow Graph
We built our system on top of the Ruby parser presented by Furr et al. [18]. This parser first compiles Ruby into a subset of the Ruby language called Ruby Intermediate Language, or RIL. The purpose of RIL is to simplify Ruby code into an easier-to-analyze format. The simplification is performed by removing ambiguities in expressions, reducing Ruby's four different branches to one canonical representation, making method calls explicit, and adding explicit returns. At the end of the transformation, every statement in RIL is either a statement with one side effect or a branch. The parser generates the CFG of RIL.

Due to Ruby's dynamic nature, this CFG might be incomplete. In particular, strings containing Ruby code can be evaluated at run-time using the `eval` function, object methods can be dynamically called at run-time using the `send` function, and methods can be added to objects at runtime. We do not address EAR vulnerabilities associated with these language features. However, we have found that these features are rarely used in practice (see Section 3.2).

Step 2: Finding Redirection
To detect EARs, we must first find all program paths (from any program entry to any program exit point) in the CFG that call the Ruby on Rails method `redirect_to`. The reason is that we need to check these paths for the presence of code execution between the redirect call and the program exit point. Note that intra-procedural analysis is not enough to find all EARs. Consider the code in Listing 2. Simply looking in `ensure_admin` for code execution *after* the call to `redirect_to` and *before* the end of this method is not sufficient. Thus, we need to perform inter-procedural analysis to find all possible ways in which code execution can continue after a `redirect_to` call until the end of the program.

Our inter-procedural analysis proceeds as follows: we start by finding all methods that directly call `redirect_to`. These methods are added to a set called *interesting methods.* Then, for each method in the *interesting methods* set, we add to this set all methods that call it. This process is iterated until a fixpoint is reached, and no new interesting methods are found.

At this point, every element (method) in *interesting methods* can eventually lead to a `redirect_to` call. Whenever a call to an interesting method returns, its execution will continue after the call site in the caller. Thus, all paths from invocations of `redirect_to` until the end of the program are captured by the paths from all invocations (call sites) of interesting methods to the end of the methods that contain these calls. Now, to detect an EAR, we can simply look for code that is executed on a path from the call site of an interesting method until the end of the method that contains this call.

Step 3: Prune Infeasible Paths
Looking for all paths from the `redirect_to` method to the program exit point might lead to false positives due to infeasible paths. Consider the example in Listing 4. There

[4]Redirects can also occur in Rails' routing, before the request gets to the controller. However, EARs cannot occur in this context, because control flow never reaches a controller. Thus, we are not concerned with these redirects.

```
1  class UsersController <
       ApplicationController
2    def ensure_logged_in
3      if not current_user
4        redirect_to("/") and return false
5      end
6      @logged_in_users += 1
7      return true
8    end
9
10   def delete_all
11    if not ensure_logged_in()
12      return
13    User.delete(:all)
14   end
15 end
```

Listing 4: Example of potential false positive.

are no EARs in this code. The **redirect_to** on Line 4 will always return **true**, thus, **return false** (also on Line 4) will execute as well. Because of this, **ensure_logged_in** will always return **false** after performing a redirect. As a result, the call to **ensure_logged_in** on Line 11 will always return **false**, and the **return** on Line 12 will always occur.

The CFG for the code in Listing 4 is shown in Figure 2. With no additional processing, we would incorrectly report the path from **redirect_to** on Line 4 to the statement in Line 6. Moreover, we would also report an EAR because of the path from the redirect to the **User.delete** on Line 13. The first path is denoted as (1) in Figure 2, the second path as (2).

To prune infeasible paths in the CFG, we explore all paths that follow an interesting method. If *all* paths following an interesting method call return the same Boolean value, we propagate this Boolean constant to all the call sites of this method. Then, we recursively continue constant value propagation at all the call sites, pruning infeasible paths everywhere after the interesting method is called. We iteratively continue this process throughout the CFG; whenever we find a constant return value, we propagate this return value to all call sites.

Figure 2 shows the results of performing our pruning process on the CFG of Listing 4. Initially, all paths after the **redirect_to** in **ensure_logged_in** do not return the same Boolean, so we cannot conclude anything about the return value of **ensure_logged_in**. However, **redirect_to** always returns **true**. Therefore, we perform constant value propagation on the return value of **redirect_to**, which is used in a branch. As a consequence, we can prune all of the paths that result from the **false** branch. The edges of this path are labeled with (1) in Figure 2. Now, all paths from **redirect_to** return **false**, which means that **ensure_logged_in** will always return **false** after a redirect. We now perform constant value propagation at all the call sites of **ensure_logged_in**, removing all the paths labeled with (2). At this point, there is nothing more to be pruned, so we stop. It can be seen that there is no path from **redirect_to** to state-changing code (defined in the next step) along the solid lines.

Step 4: Detecting EARs

Once the CFG of the controller has been simplified and interesting method information has been extracted, we perform EAR detection. This is a fairly simple process; we traverse the CFG of every method to see if potentially problematic code can be executed after a call to an interesting method. We conservatively define such code as any statement that could possibly modify the program state, excluding statements that alter the control flow. This excludes **return** and branches, but includes assignment and method calls. As a special case, we also disregard all operations that set the **flash** or **session** array variable. These arrays are used in the former case to set a message to be displayed on the destination page, and in the latter case to store some information in the user's session. These calls are disregarded because they do no affect the state of the web application and are frequently called after redirection. We report as a potential EAR each method that executes potentially problematic code between the invocation of an interesting method and its return statements.

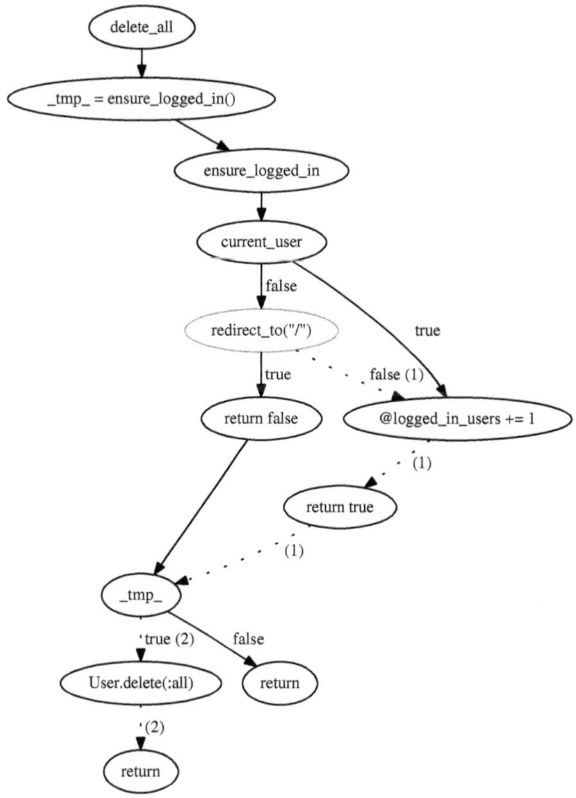

Figure 2: Control Flow Graph for the code shown in Listing 4. The dotted lines are paths removed from the CFG by Step 3 of the EAR detection algorithm.

Step 5: Distinguishing Between Benign and Vulnerable EARs

We also introduce a heuristic to identify vulnerable EARs. This heuristic looks for paths from an interesting method to a function that modifies the database. If one is found, the EAR is marked as vulnerable. We used the Rails documentation to determine the 16 functions that modify the database. Of course, this list can be easily extended. This process is not sound, because we perform no type analysis, and look only at the method names being called. Moreover, we do not analyze the models, only looking for this specific list. Despite these limitations, our results (Section 4.1) show

Type of EAR reported	Number reported
Benign	3,089
Vulnerable	855
Total	3,944
Total Projects	18,127
Any EAR	1,173
Only Benign	830
At least one vulnerable EAR	343

Table 1: Results of running the white-box detector against Ruby on Rails applications, 6.5% of which contained an EAR flaw. 2.9% of the projects had an EAR classified as vulnerable.

that this heuristic is still a good indicator of potentially vulnerable EARs that deserve the developer's attention.

3.2 Limitations

The white-box EAR detector is limited to analyzing Ruby on Rails applications, although the detection algorithm can be extended to any programming language and web framework. Detection is neither sound nor complete. False negatives can occur when a Rails application uses Ruby's dynamic features such as `eval` or `send` to execute a redirect. While such dynamic features are used extensively in the Ruby on Rails framework itself, they are rarely used by web applications written in Rails. Of the 3,457,512 method calls in controllers that we tested our tool on, there were 428 (0.012%) `eval` method calls and 2,426 (0.07%) `send` method calls, which shows how infrequently these are used in Rails web applications.

The white-box tool can report two types of false positives: false EARs, that is, the tool reports an EAR although no code can be executed after a redirect, or false vulnerable EARs, where the tool mistakes a benign EAR as vulnerable.

False EARs can occur for several reasons. One reason is that the path from the redirect function to the code execution that we found is infeasible. A typical example is when the redirect call and the code execution occur in opposite branches. The branch conditions for these are mutually exclusive, so there can never be a path from the redirect call to the code execution. Examples of this type of false positive are discussed in Section 4.1, and these could be mitigated by introducing better path sensitivity.

False vulnerable EARs are a problem caused by the heuristic that we use. The biggest issue is that we simply look for method calls that have the same name as method calls that update/change the database. However, we do not perform any type analysis to determine the *object* that the method is called on. Thus, methods such as `delete` on a hash table will trigger a false vulnerable EAR, since `delete` is also a method of the database object. Improved heuristics could be developed, for instance, that include the type of the object the method is being invoked on.

Despite these limitations, our experiments demonstrate that the tool works very well in practice. In addition, Ruby on Rails controllers are typically very small, as most application logic is present in the models. Thus, our tool works very well on these types of controllers. We provide[5] our tool to the community at large, so that others may use it to detect EARs in their code.

[5]`https://github.com/adamdoupe/find_ear_rails`

Classification after manual analysis	Number
True Vulnerable EARs	485
Benign EARs	325
No EARs (False Positives)	45

Table 2: Results of manually inspecting the 855 vulnerable EARs reported by our white-box tool. 40.1% were benign, and 5.3% were not EARs.

4. RESULTS

We used our EAR detection tool to find real-world EARs in open-source Ruby on Rails web applications. First, we downloaded 59,255 open-source projects from GitHub [19] that were designated as Ruby projects and that were not a fork of another project. We identified 18,127 of the downloaded Ruby projects that had an `app/controllers` folder, indicating a Ruby on Rails application.

Table 1 summarizes the results. In total, we found 3,944 EAR instances in 1,173 projects. 855 of these EARs, present in 343 projects, were classified as vulnerable by our system. This means that 6.5% of Rails applications we tested contained at least one EAR, and 29.3% of the applications containing EARs had an EAR classified as vulnerable.

Of the 1,173 projects that contained at least one EAR, we notified those project owners that had emails listed in their GitHub profile, for a total of 624. Of these project owners, 107 responded to our email. Half of the respondents, 49, confirmed the EARs we reported. 26 other respondents told us that the GitHub project was no longer being maintained or was a demo/toy. Three respondents pointed out false positives, which we confirmed, while 6 of the project owners said that there were not going to fix the EAR because there was no security compromise. The rest of the responses thanked us for the report but did not offer a confirmation of the reported EAR.

4.1 Detection Effectiveness

To determine the effectiveness of our tool, we manually inspected all 855 vulnerable EARs. The results are shown in Table 2. We manually verified that 485, or 59.9%, were true positives. Many of these were caused by ad-hoc authorization checks, where the developer simply introduced a redirect when the check failed. Some examples of security violations were allowing non-administrators access to administrator functionality, allowing modifications to items not belonging to the current user, and being able to sign up for a conference even though it was full.

Listing 5 shows an interesting example adapted from a real EAR where the redirect is followed by `and return` (Line 3), however, due to Ruby's semantics, this code contains an EAR. In Ruby, a `return` with no arguments returns `false`[6], thus, `redirect_to_login` will always return `false` (because of the "no argument" `return` call on Line 3). The result is that the `return` on Line 8 will never be executed, because `redirect_to_login` will always return `false`, and the short-circuit logic of `and` will cause Line 10 to be executed. This example shows that our tool discovers non-obvious EARs.

For vulnerable EARs, we consider two different types of false positives: false *vulnerable* EARs, which are benign

[6]Technically `nil`, but `nil` and `false` are equivalent for Boolean comparisons.

```
class BanksController <
    ApplicationController
  def redirect_to_login
    redirect_to("/login") and return
  end

  def create
    if not current_user.is_admin?
      redirect_to_login() and return
    end
    @bank = Bank.create(params[:bank])
  end
end
```

Listing 5: True positive Execution After Redirect vulnerability in Ruby on Rails.

EARs mistakenly reported as vulnerable, and false EARs (false positives).

As shown in Table 2, the white-box tool generated 45 false EARs, for a false positive rate of 5.3%. These false positives came from two main categories. About half of the false positives were due to impossible paths from the redirect methods to some code. An example of this is when a redirect method was called at the end of a branch that checked that the request was an HTTP GET, while the code executed after a redirect was in a branch that checked that the request was an HTTP POST. These two conditions are mutually exclusive, thus, this path is impossible. The other half of false positives were due to local variables that had the same name as a redirect method. The parsing library, RIL, mistakenly identified the local variable access as a method call to a redirect method. We are currently looking into fixing this issue in RIL, which will almost halve our false positive rate.

While our false EAR rate was only 5.5%, our vulnerable EAR detection heuristic had a higher false detection rate of 40.1%. The biggest culprit for false vulnerable EARs (72.9% of the instances) was due to no feasible path from the redirect to the method that changed the state of the database. For instance, the redirect method occurred in a branch that was taken only when a certain object was `nil`[7]. Later, the database method was called on this object. Thus, when the redirect happens, the object will be `nil`. Because of the presence of an EAR flaw, execution will continue and reach the database access method. However, since the object is `nil`, the database will not be affected. Because our heuristics cannot detect the fact that, after the redirect, the database function will always be called with a `nil` object, we report a vulnerability. The other common false vulnerable EAR were instances where the redirect method was called before code was executed, however, it was clear that the developer was fully aware of the redirect semantics and intended for the code to be executed.

We also checked that the false EAR rate did not differ significantly among the benign EARs by manually inspecting 200 random EARs reported as benign. We saw 13 false EARs in the manual inspection, for a false positive rate of 6.5%. Thus, the total false positive rate among the instances we manually inspected is 5.5%. We also did not see any vulnerable EARs among the benign EARs, thus, we did not see any false negative vulnerable EARs in our experiments.

[7] `nil` is Ruby's `null`

From our results, we can conclude that we detect EARs well. However, it is more difficult to distinguish between benign and vulnerable EARs. Classification could be improved by using a better heuristic to detect intended redirects. However, even though certain EARs might not be vulnerable at the moment, they are still programming errors that should be fixed. This is confirmed by the responses that we received from developers who were grateful for error reports even though they are not exploitable at the moment. Also, our tool reports one true vulnerability for every benign EAR mistakenly classified as vulnerable. This is well in line with the precision of previous static analysis tools [24,25,28].

4.2 Performance

To evaluate the performance of our tool, we measured the running time against the 18,127 Ruby on Rails applications. We ran our experiments on an Intel Core i7 with 12 gigabytes of RAM. Our algorithm scales linearly with the size of the CFG and is fast; no project took longer than 2.5 seconds even with the largest CFG size of 40,217 statements.

5. PREVENTION

The old adage "an ounce of prevention is worth a pound of cure" is true in software. Boehm showed that the later in an application's life-cycle bugs are caught, the more expensive they are to fix [8]. Thus, preventing certain types of bugs from even being introduced is attractive from both an economic standpoint, and a security perspective. Our recommendation to web frameworks, therefore, is to make Execution After Redirect vulnerabilities impossible to occur, by having every invocation of the redirect method halt execution, which we call halt-on-redirect behavior.

As we have shown in Section 2.4, some frameworks have already either adopted the approach of making EARs impossible, or their approach to generating HTTP responses makes EARs highly unlikely. For existing frameworks that wish to decrease the chance of EARs being introduced, such draconian measures may not be acceptable because they break backward-compatibility. Our suggestion in these cases is to make an application-wide setting to enable halt-on-redirect behavior, along with an argument to the redirect function to halt execution after the redirect. Of course, we suggest making halt-on-redirect the default behavior, however each framework will have to properly balance security and backward-compatibility.

To improve the security of Ruby on Rails, we are in discussions with the Rails development team about our proposed change. The difficulty with implementing halt-on-redirect behavior in Rails is that there are no `goto`s, and Rails applications run in a single-threaded context. This limits the two obvious forms of implementing halt-on-redirect: we cannot use a goto or language equivalent statement to jump from the end of the `redirect_to` method to the code after the controller is called. Moreover, we also cannot, at the end of the `redirect_to` method, send the HTTP response and cause the current thread to stop execution. PHP frameworks can use the `exit` function to implement halt-on-redirect behavior, because each request spawns a new PHP process.

Our proposed solution is to throw a new type of exception, `RedirectOccuredException`, at the end of the `redirect_to` body. In the Ruby on Rails framework core, where the controller is called, there is a catch block for this exception. While this will prevent almost all EARs, there is a possibility for code to be executed in an `ensure` block, Ruby's equivalent of a "finally" block. Code in this block will be executed regardless of a redirect. However, we believe this is semantically in line with the way the language should work: `ensure` blocks will always be executed, no matter what happens, and this is clear to the programmer via the language's semantics.

6. RELATED WORK

Specific instances of Execution After Redirect vulnerabilities have been previously identified. Hofstetter wrote a blog post alerting people to not forget to exit after a redirect when using the PHP framework CakePHP [22]. This discussion resulted in a bug being filed with the CakePHP team [9]. This bug was resolved by updating the CakePHP documentation to indicate the redirect method did not end execution [10].

Felmetsger et al. presented a white-box static analysis tool for J2EE servlets to automatically detect logic flaws in web applications. The tool, Waler, found Execution After Redirect vulnerabilities in a web application called Global Internship Management System (GIMS) [17]. However, neither Felmetsger nor Hofstetter identified EARs as a systemic flaw among web applications.

Wang et al. manually discovered logic flaws in the interaction of Cashier-as-a-Service (CaaS) APIs and the web applications that use them [35]. This is interesting because there is a three-way interaction between the users, the CaaS, and the web application. In our work, we consider one specific type of logic flaw across many applications.

Our white-box EAR detection tool uses the Ruby Intermediate Language (RIL) developed by Furr et al. [18]. RIL was used by An et al. to introduce static typing to Ruby on Rails [23]. They use the resulting system, DRails, on eleven Rails applications to statically discover type errors. DRails parses Rails applications by compiling them to equivalent Ruby code, making implicit Rails conventions explicit. This differs from our tool, which operates directly on the Rails application's control flow graph. Moreover, we are looking at a specific logic flaw, while DRails is looking for type errors.

Chaudhuri and Foster built a symbolic analysis engine on top of DRails, called Rubyx [13]. They are able to analyze the security properties of Rails applications using symbolic execution. Rubyx detected XSS, XSRF, session manipulation, and unauthorized access in the seven applications tested. Due to the symbolic execution and verifying of path conditions, false positives are reduced. However, Rubyx requires the developer to manually specify an analysis script that defines invariants on used objects, as well as the security requirements of the applications. Our tool, on the other hand, operates on raw, unmodified Rails applications, and does not require any developer input. This is due to the different focus; we are focusing on one specific type of flaw, while Rubyx is broader and can verify different types of security violations.

Our work is also related to numerous white-box tools that have previously been published. Huang et al. were one of the first to propose a static analysis tool for a server-side scripting language, specifically PHP. They implemented taint propagation to detect XSS, SQL injection, and general injection [24]. Livshits and Lam proposed a static analysis technique for Java web applications that used points-to analysis for improved precision [28]. Their tool detected 29 instances of SQL injection, XSS, HTTP response splitting, and command injection in nine open-source applications. Jovanovic et al. developed Pixy, an open-source static analysis tool to discover XSS attacks by performing flow-sensitive, inter-procedural, and context-sensitive data flow analysis on PHP web applications [26]. They later improved Pixy, adding precise alias analysis, to discover hundreds of XSS vulnerabilities in three PHP applications, half of which were false positives [25]. Balzarotti et al. used static and dynamic analysis to develop MiMoSa, a tool that performs inter-module data flow analysis to discover attacks that leverage several modules, such as stored XSS. They found 27 data flow violations in five PHP web applications [4].

All of these static analysis tools differ from our white box tool because we are not looking for unsanitized input vulnerabilities, but rather for unexpected execution that a developer did not intend. We also performed our analysis on a large corpus of real-world applications, and found a correspondingly large number of true vulnerable EARs.

7. CONCLUSIONS

We have described a new type of vulnerability, Execution After Redirect, and developed a novel static analysis tool to effectively find EARs. We showed that EARs are difficult to differentiate between benign and vulnerable. This difficulty is due to vulnerable EARs violating the specific logic of the web application. Better understanding of the application's logic should help differentiate vulnerable and benign EARs and it will be the focus of future work.

Acknowledgments

This work was also partially supported by the ONR under grant N000140911042 and by the National Science Foundation (NSF) under grants CNS-0820907, CNS-0905537, and CNS-0716095.

8. REFERENCES

[1] ASP.NET MVC. `http://www.asp.net/mvc`.

[2] Balduzzi, M., Egele, M., Kirda, E., Balzarotti, D., and Kruegel, C. A Solution for the Automated Detection of Clickjacking Attacks. In *Proceedings of the ACM Symposium on Information, Computer and Communications Security (AsiaCCS)* (Beijing, China, April 2010).

[3] Balduzzi, M., Gimenez, C., Balzarotti, D., and Kirda, E. Automated discovery of parameter pollution vulnerabilities in web applications. In *Proceedings of the 18th Network and Distributed System Security Symposium* (2011).

[4] Balzarotti, D., Cova, M., Felmetsger, V. V., and Vigna, G. Multi-module vulnerability analysis of web-based applications. In *Proceedings of the 14th ACM conference on Computer and communications security* (New York, NY, USA, 2007), CCS '07, ACM, pp. 25–35.

[5] Barth, A., Jackson, C., and Mitchell, J. C. Robust defenses for cross-site request forgery. In *Proceedings of the 15th ACM Conference on Computer and Communications Security (CCS 2008)* (2008).

[6] Boe, B. UCSB's International Capture The Flag Competition 2010 Challenge 6: Fear The EAR.

http://cs.ucsb.edu/~bboe/r/ictf10, December 2010.

[7] Boe, B. Using StackOverflow's API to Find the Top Web Frameworks. http://cs.ucsb.edu/~bboe/r/top-web-frameworks, February 2011.

[8] Boehm, B. W. *Software Engineering Economics*, 1st ed. Prentice Hall PTR, Upper Saddle River, NJ, USA, 1981.

[9] Include exit with a redirect call. http://replay.web.archive.org/20061011152124/https://trac.cakephp.org/ticket/1076, August 2006.

[10] docs should mention redirect does not "exit" a script. http://replay.web.archive.org/20061011180440/https://trac.cakephp.org/ticket/1358, August 2006.

[11] Cake Software Foundation, Inc. The CakePHP 1.3 Book. http://book.cakephp.org/view/982/redirect, 2011.

[12] Carettoni, L., and Di Paola, S. HTTP Parameter Pollution. OWASP AppSec Europe 2009, May 2009.

[13] Chaudhuri, A., and Foster, J. Symbolic security analysis of ruby-on-rails web applications. In *Proceedings of the 17th ACM Conference on Computer and Communications Security (CCS'10)* (2010), ACM, pp. 585–594.

[14] Childers, N., Boe, B., Cavallaro, L., Cavedon, L., Cova, M., Egele, M., and Vigna, G. Organizing large scale hacking competitions. In *Proceedings of the 7th international conference on Detection of intrusions and malware, and vulnerability assessment* (Berlin, Heidelberg, 2010), DIMVA'10, Springer-Verlag, pp. 132–152.

[15] Django Software Foundation. Django shortcut functions. http://docs.djangoproject.com/en/dev/topics/http/shortcuts/#django.shortcuts.redirect, 2011.

[16] EllisLab, Inc. CodeIgniter User Guide Version 2.0.2. http://codeigniter.com/user_guide/helpers/url_helper.html, 2011.

[17] Felmetsger, V., Cavedon, L., Kruegel, C., and Vigna, G. Toward Automated Detection of Logic Vulnerabilities in Web Applications. In *Proceedings of the USENIX Security Symposium* (Washington, DC, August 2010).

[18] Furr, M., hoon (David) An, J., Foster, J. S., and Hicks, M. The Ruby intermediate language. In *Proceedings of the ACM SIGPLAN Dynamic Languages Symposium (DLS)* (Oct. 2009).

[19] GitHub. http://github.com.

[20] Indictment in U.S. v. Albert Gonzalez. http://www.justice.gov/usao/ma/news/IDTheft/Gonzalez,%20Albert%20-%20Indictment%20080508.pdf, August 2008.

[21] Hansen, R. Clickjacking. http://ha.ckers.org/blog/20080915/clickjacking/, September 2008.

[22] Hofstetter, D. Don't forget to exit after a redirect. http://cakebaker.wordpress.com/2006/08/28/dont-forget-to-exit-after-a-redirect/, August 2006.

[23] hoon An, J., Chaudhuri, A., and Foster, J. Static typing for ruby on rails. In *Proceedings of the 24th IEEE/ACM Conference on Automated Software Engineering (ASE'09)* (2009), IEEE, pp. 590–594.

[24] Huang, Y.-W., Yu, F., Hang, C., Tsai, C.-H., Lee, D.-T., and Kuo, S.-Y. Securing web application code by static analysis and runtime protection. In *Proceedings of the 13th international conference on World Wide Web* (New York, NY, USA, 2004), WWW '04, ACM, pp. 40–52.

[25] Jovanovic, N., Kruegel, C., and Kirda, E. Pixy: A static analysis tool for detecting web application vulnerabilities (short paper). In *IN 2006 IEEE SYMPOSIUM ON SECURITY AND PRIVACY* (2006), pp. 258–263.

[26] Jovanovic, N., Kruegel, C., and Kirda, E. Precise alias analysis for static detection of web application vulnerabilities. In *Proceedings of the 2006 workshop on Programming languages and analysis for security* (New York, NY, USA, 2006), PLAS '06, ACM, pp. 27–36.

[27] Klein, A. Divide and conquer: HTTP response splitting, Web cache poisoning attacks, and related topics. http://www.packetstormsecurity.org/papers/general/whitepaper/httpresponse.pdf, 2004.

[28] Livshits, V. B., and Lam, M. S. Finding security vulnerabilities in java applications with static analysis. In *Proceedings of the 14th conference on USENIX Security Symposium - Volume 14* (Berkeley, CA, USA, 2005), USENIX Association, pp. 18–18.

[29] Open Web Application Security Project (OWASP). OWASP Top Ten Project. http://www.owasp.org/index.php/Top_10, 2010.

[30] Ortiz, C. Outcome of sentencing in U.S. v. Albert Gonzalez. http://www.justice.gov/usao/ma/news/IDTheft/09-CR-10382/GONZALEZ%20website%20info%205-11-10.pdf, March 2010.

[31] R. Fielding, J. Gettys, J. M. H. F. L. M. P. L. T. B.-L. RFC 2616: Hypertext Transfer Protocol – HTTP/1.1 Header Field Definitions. http://www.w3.org/Protocols/rfc2616/rfc2616-sec14.html#sec14.30, June 1999.

[32] R. Fielding, J. Gettys, J. M. H. F. L. M. P. L. T. B.-L. RFC 2616: Hypertext Transfer Protocol – HTTP/1.1 Status Code Definitions. http://www.w3.org/Protocols/rfc2616/rfc2616-sec10.html, June 1999.

[33] Reenskaug, T. Models - views - controllers. Tech. rep., Xerox Parc, 1979.

[34] SpringSource. Contollers - Redirects. http://www.grails.org/Controllers+-+Redirects, 2010.

[35] Wang, R., Chen, S., Wang, X., and Qadeer, S. How to shop for free online - security analysis of cashier-as-a-service based web stores. In *Proceedings of the 32nd IEEE Symposium on Security and Privacy* (Oakland, CA, May 2011), IEEE.

[36] Zend Technologies Ltd. Zend Framework: Documentation: Action Helpers - Zend Framework Manual. http://framework.zend.com/manual/en/zend.controller.actionhelpers.html#zend.controller.actionhelpers.redirector, 2011.

Automated Black-Box Detection of Side-Channel Vulnerabilities in Web Applications

Peter Chapman and David Evans
University of Virginia Computer Science
Charlottesville, Virginia, United States
http://www.cs.virginia.edu/sca

ABSTRACT

Web applications divide their state between the client and the server. The frequent and highly dynamic client-server communication that is characteristic of modern web applications leaves them vulnerable to side-channel leaks, even over encrypted connections. We describe a black-box tool for detecting and quantifying the severity of side-channel vulnerabilities by analyzing network traffic over repeated crawls of a web application. By viewing the adversary as a multi-dimensional classifier, we develop a methodology to more thoroughly measure the distinguishably of network traffic for a variety of classification metrics. We evaluate our detection system on several deployed web applications, accounting for proposed client and server-side defenses. Our results illustrate the limitations of entropy measurements used in previous work and show how our new metric based on the Fisher criterion can be used to more robustly reveal side-channels in web applications.

Categories and Subject Descriptors

D.4.6 [**Software**]: Security and Protection; K.6.5 [**Computing Milieux**]: Management of Computing and Information Systems

General Terms

Security, Measurement, Theory

1. INTRODUCTION

Communication between the client and server in a web application is necessary for meaningful and efficient operation, but without care, can leak substantial information through a variety of side-channels. Previous work has demonstrated the ability to profile transfer size distributions over encrypted connections in order to identify visited websites [6, 8, 30]. Today, such side-channel leaks are especially pervasive and difficult to mitigate due to modern web development techniques that require increased client-server communication [5]. The competitive marketplace encourages a dynamic and responsive browsing experience. Using AJAX and similar technologies, information is brought to the user on demand, limiting unnecessary traffic, decreasing latency, and increasing responsiveness. By design, this approach separates traffic into a series of small requests that are specific to the actions of the user [27].

Analyzing network activity generated by web applications can reveal a surprising amount of information. Most attacks examine the size distributions of transmitted data, since the most commonly used encryption mechanisms on the web make no effort to conceal the size of the payload. As a result, traffic patterns can be correlated with specific keypresses and mouse clicks. Fundamentally, these attacks leverage correlations between the network traffic and the collective state of the web application.

To assist developers who want to create web applications that are responsive but have limited side-channel leaks, we developed a system to automatically detect and quantify the side-channel leaks in a web application. Our system identifies side-channel vulnerabilities by extensively crawling a target application to find network traffic that is predictably associated with changes in the application state. We use a black-box approach for compatibility and accuracy. Driving an actual web browser enables the deployment of our tools on any website, regardless of back-end implementation or complexity. Further, by generating the same traffic as would be seen by an attacker we ensure that information leaks due to unpredictable elements such as plug-ins or third-party scripts are still detected.

Previous work has used the concept of an attacker's ambiguity set, measured either in reduction power [5, 22, 33] or conditional entropy [21, 33] to measure information leaks. Our results show that entropy-based metrics are very fragile and do not adequately measure the risk of information leaking for complex web applications under realistic conditions. As an alternative metric, we adopt the Fisher criterion [11] to measure the classifiability of web application network traffic, and by extension, information leakage.

Contributions and Overview. We consider two threat models for studying web application side-channel leaks: one where the attacker listens to encrypted wireless traffic and another where an attacker intercepts encrypted network traffic at the level of an Internet service provider (Section 3.2).

We present a black-box web application crawling system that logs network traffic while interacting with a website in the same manner as an actual user using a standard web browser, outputting a set of web application states and user actions with generated network traffic traces, conceptually represented as a finite-state machine (Section 3). We have developed a rich XML specification format to configure the crawler to interact effectively with many websites (Section 4.2).

Using the finite-state machine output of the web application exploration, we consider information leaks from the perspective of a multi-class classification problem (Section 5). In building our example nearest-centroid classifier, we enumerate three distance met-

CCS'11, October 17–21, 2011, Chicago, Illinois, USA.

rics that measure the similarity of two network traces. Using the same set of distance metrics, we measure the entropy of user actions in the web application in the same manner as prior work and show that the variation and noise in real web applications make the concept of an uncertainty set insufficient for describing information leaks (Section 5.2). This motivates an alternative measurement based on the Fisher criterion to quantify the classifiability and therefore information leakage of network traces in a web application based on the same set of distance metrics (Section 5.3).

We evaluate our crawling system and leak quantification techniques on several complex web applications. Compared to entropy-based metrics, we find the Fisher criterion is more resilient to outliers in trace data and provides a more useful measure of an applications vulnerability to side-channel classification (Section 6).

2. RELATED WORK

The study of side-channel vulnerabilities extends at least to the World War II [13]. Pervious work has considered side-channel vulnerabilities in a wide variety of domains, including cryptographic implementations [19], sound from dot matrix printers [1], and of course, web traffic [5, 6, 8, 30]. The most effective side-channel attacks on web applications have examined the size distributions of traffic [6, 8, 30]. The vulnerabilities stem from the individual transfer of objects in a web page, which vary significantly in size and quantity. Furthermore, due to the deployment of stream ciphers on the Internet [5], the sizes of objects are often visible in encrypted traffic. Tunneled connections [3, 21] and even encrypted wireless connections [3, 5] are vulnerable to these attacks.

The interactive traffic of modern web applications presents attackers with rich opportunities for side-channel attacks. Chen et al. demonstrated how an attacker could identify specific user actions within a web application based on intercepted encrypted traffic [5]. The leaks they found in search engines, a personal health information management system, a tax application, and a banking site required application-specific mitigation techniques for adequate and efficient protection. Search engine suggestions are a suitable example to demonstrate these attacks. As the user types a search query, the client sends the server the typed keys and the server returns a list of suggestions. An attacker can leverage the fact that the size of the suggestions sent after each keystroke vary depending on the typed letter to reconstruct search terms. Figure 1 shows how a single query is divided into a revealing series of network transfers. For a single letter, the attacker only needs to match the traffic to a set of 26 possibilities (letters A through Z). With the next letter, the attacker can use the reduced set of possibilities given by the first letter to drastically reduce the search space.

Side-Channel Vulnerability Detectors. Zhang et al. created Sidebuster [33], a tool that automates the detection of side-channel vulnerabilities in web applications built with the Google Web Toolkit (GWT) [16]. GWT developers write both the client and server code in Java and the framework generates the JavaScript code for the browser and automatically manages asynchronous communication. Every instance in the code where the client and server interact can be found through a straightforward static analysis. Sidebuster then quantifies the leaks using *rerun* testing, which initiates the statically discovered communication-inducing action using a simulated browser called HtmlUnit [4] and records the network traffic with Jpcap [14]. It measures the leaks by calculating the conditional entropy for each tested action. Sidebuster was tested on several demonstration applications and mock websites and shown to discover significant information leaks. We choose a black-box approach, in part, to create a leak discovery tool that is not limited to a particular implementation platform.

Black-box Web Application Exploration and Testing. Black-box exploration of traditional applications is often performed as part of test case generation [18, 23]. Many commercial automated black-box application security analysis tools are available (but none yet consider side-channel leaks) [2]. In the context of modern websites, black-box exploration is difficult since technologies such as AJAX break the traditional concept of a page. Crawljax was developed specifically to address the need to crawl the growing number of web sites employing AJAX elements [24, 25]. Our tool is built by extending Crawljax (see Section 4).

Side-Channel Leak Quantification. Current practice for quantifying the severity of web side-channels involves measuring the size of the attacker's uncertainty (or ambiguity) set in terms of reduction power [5, 22, 33] or bits of entropy [5, 8, 21, 33] as established in work measuring information flow in traditional software systems [26] and work specific to the web [20]. A primary goal is to quantify on average how well an attacker can determine the private state of the web application given a network trace. In that case it is also typical to simply measure the performance of a constructed classifier [6,22,30]. Section 5 discusses building a network trace classifier, measuring leaks in entropy bits, and our proposed method for quantifying leaks with the Fisher criterion.

Proposed Defenses. Prior work has developed a wide range of mitigation techniques for web side-channel leaks including random packet padding [5, 6, 8, 22], constant packet size [5, 6], and additional background traffic [6, 22]. The different defense strategies can be implemented in various points in the client-server interaction: in the application or server level of the host [5], through a local proxy [22], or in the web browser itself. The information available to the attacker affects the analysis and defenses of these leaks. While early work focused on intercepted HTTPS traffic [6], other work has considered other scenarios such as eavesdropping over a WPA/WPA2 connection [3, 5, 22]. Luo et al. developed HTTPOS, a client-side defense for the leaks [22]. HTTPOS is a local proxy that obfuscates network traffic by manipulating a wide range of HTTP, TCP, and IP protocol options and features such as adjusting the TCP window size, initiating TCP retransmissions, introducing timing delays, and even creating fake content requests. They target four threat models, two of which are shared with our work. In examining the applicability and effectiveness of packet padding defenses, Chen, et al. found that applications required specific and customized mitigation techniques, and proposed a devel-

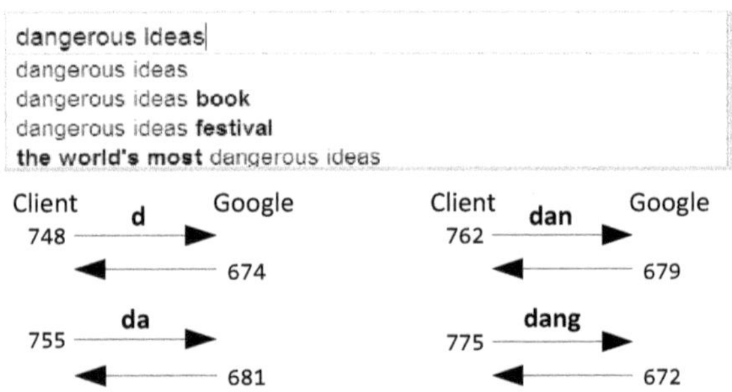

Figure 1: Search engines leak queries through the network traffic generated by auto-complete suggestions. The numbers indicate the number of bytes transferred.

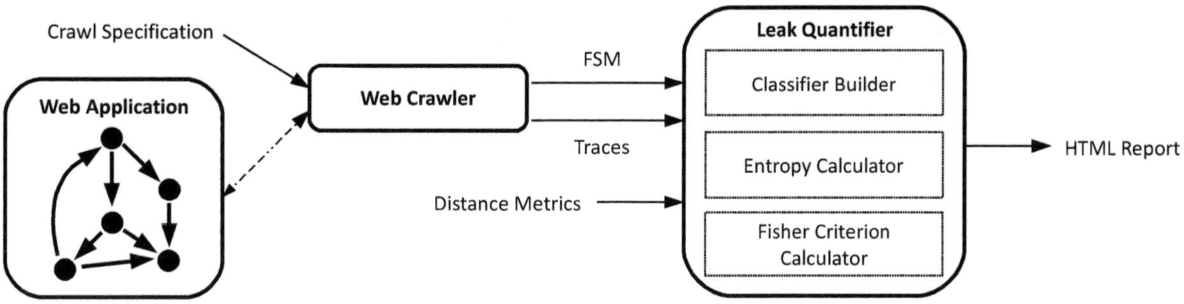

Figure 2: System Overview.

opment process for discovering, applying, and tuning defenses. We do not attempt to develop new defenses here, but rather to enhance understanding of side-channel leaks and to offer a side-channel leak quantification tool that can be used as a part of a mitigation process for typical web applications.

3. OVERVIEW

We built a completely dynamic, black-box side-channel vulnerability detection system. Figure 2 shows an overview of the system from the perspective of a developer. Using our system, a developer first creates an XML specification that assists the crawler in exploring the target website. The Web Crawler logs traffic while traversing the site (Section 4) and upon completion of a representative finite-state machine the Leak Quantifier analyzes the data to find relationships between user actions and network traffic (Section 5). A developer can use generated reports to pinpoint vulnerable areas of the site and devise effective and efficient mitigations. We do not attempt automatic mitigation here, although we believe the results produced by our tool could be used to automatically mitigate many leaks. Section 3.1 explains why we target a black-box solution; Section 3.2 clarifies the two threat models we consider.

3.1 Black-Box Analysis

Our approach does not assume any access to the server other than through standard web requests issued by a browser. There are many advantages to using a black-box, client-side only approach to perform the analysis. Generating actual user traffic makes experimental testing as close as possible to a real attack. Furthermore, a full browser such as Firefox can download and execute third-party scripts and plug-ins (e.g., Flash) which are crucial to realistic analysis since they could very easily be the the source of the leak. For example, an instructional Flash video could automatically play whenever the user of a tax site indicates they wish to obtain a certain tax credit. Although the remainder of the page may not result in distinguishable traffic, the streaming video could provide a clear indicator of the current state of the application.

Another advantage of a black-box approach is that our tool can be applied to any web application, regardless of its internal configuration. Section 6 reports on our experience applying our tool to several popular web applications. The primary limitation of the applicability of our system is that a standard Selenium installation cannot interact with items that are outside of the browser DOM (e.g., embedded Flash objects) or that do not fit well into the traditional web page model (e.g., HTML5 Canvas). Ongoing work is attempting to add stable Flash support to Selenium [12] which could be integrated into our testing framework.

3.2 Threat Model

We consider two threat models in this work: an attacker eavesdropping on encrypted wireless traffic and an attacker scanning through traffic directed through an ISP. For both cases, we assume an attacker targets a particular individual to learn as much information as possible from their encrypted web browsing. Most of our results may also apply to the scenario where a government agency, for example, is scanning a large amount of traffic from unknown individuals to find evidence of particular transactions, but we do not consider that scenario in this work.

WiFi Snooping. In the WiFi Snooping threat model, an attacker collects data over an encrypted wireless network. Example targets include high profile persons such as a politician or CEO, about whom sensitive information could be valuable to competitors or abused in devious ways. For example, one corporation could eavesdrop on its competitor's CEO's search queries to anticipate the competitors entry into a new market. Another possible attack would be a con-artist exploiting leaked sensitive information to customize a scam a particular victim. In our model, the WiFi snooper can see the size of network transfers and whether they are incoming our outgoing from the client but no other information about the data. We believe this model accurately reflects what an eavesdropper could learn since the access point (AP) announces its MAC address in the AP beacons and there are a variety of ways for the attacker to infer the target's MAC address.

ISP Sniffing. In our second threat model, the adversary taps directly into the traffic flowing through an ISP either with legal authority or by compromising network equipment. Such an attacker can observe the IP and TCP plain text packet headers in HTTPS communication including the source IP, destination IP, and the size of the encrypted payload.

4. CRAWLING WEB APPLICATIONS

The Crawler explores the target web application to build a finite-state machine (FSM) representation of the site. Each state in the FSM is a possible state of the DOM (Document Object Model) in the application saved as an HTML file. The transitions between states are the user actions that load new pages or trigger DOM changes, annotated with recorded network traffic over repeated trials. The FSM is the input into our leak quantifier which measures the degree to which paths through the state machine are consistent and identifiable.

Figure 3 shows the structure of the Crawler. We extend the Crawljax tool to manage the crawling process (Section 4.1). Selenium automates the Firefox actions needed to interact with the target web application. We use Jpcap to collect a network trace.

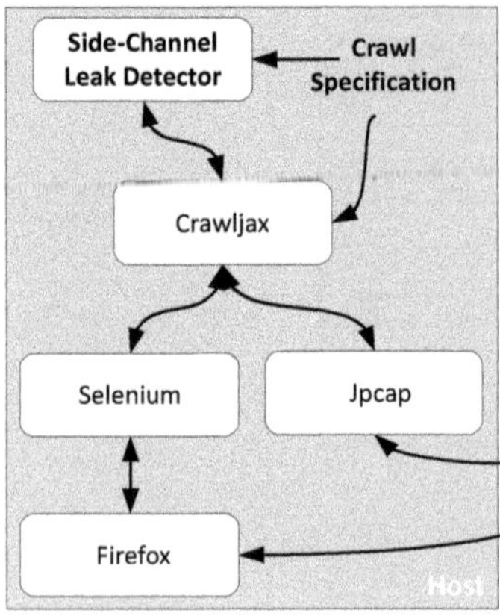

Figure 3: Crawling Web Applications.

```
<specification>
 <click>
  <tag>a</tag>
   <xpath>
    /HTML/BODY/DIV[2]/DIV[2]/A
   </xpath>
 </click>
 <waitFor>
   <id></id><value>footer</value><url>.</url>
 </waitFor>
 <matchOverride>
  <match>
   <pattern>
    <![CDATA[[\w\W]*(name="currentquestion")[\w\W]*?(<\/fieldset>)]]>
   </pattern>
   <replace></replace>
  </match>
 </matchOverride>
</specification>
```

Figure 4: Example Interaction Specification.

Since an exhaustive crawl is not possible for any interesting web application, we also extend Crawljax to allow developers to specify a directed crawl using a Crawl Specification, as described in Section 4.2. Since web services are often unreliable, it is necessary to repair the resulting FSMs, as described in Section 4.3.

4.1 Crawljax

Crawling modern web sites and services is challenging because of their highly dynamic nature and emphasis on client-side technologies that violate the traditional concept of a web page [25]. We build upon Crawljax [24], an open-source tool designed to check that sites are searchable, testable, and accessible. Crawljax attempts to construct a state machine of user interface states for web applications even in the presence of JavaScript and AJAX [25]. A web application state, with the default Crawljax settings, is a specific DOM configuration. If user actions such as clicks or keyboard actions result in changes to the DOM, Crawljax creates a new state and connects the two with a transition. To accomplish this, Crawljax drives an instance of the Selenium [15, 29] testing framework for black-box manipulation and state inference of the application. To support our goal of black-box detection of side-channel vulnerabilities of complex web applications, we made several changes to Crawljax, described next.

Logging Network Traffic. During execution Crawljax interacts with developer-specified elements and forms while monitoring the browser DOM to construct a corresponding state machine. We added network traffic logging to Crawljax. We used the existing plugin architecture built into Crawljax and the Jpcap Java library for network packet monitoring [14].For our experiments, we logged packet source, destination, length, and inter-packet timings. To improve robustness, our network plugins are also aware of basic TCP features such as sequence numbering and retransmission. Importantly, our tools do not use any knowledge unavailable to a potential adversary intercepting SSL-encrypted traffic. Experiments in the WiFi threat model ignore TCP features.

Caching. Unlike most previous experiments, the browser cache was left enabled to more accurately model typical web traffic. With Crawljax's depth-first search methodology, the cache is reset upon returning to the root of the website, which retains the functionality an attacker would face as the user goes through the site. Since Selenium does not currently include such functionality [28] we wrote a Firefox extension that communicates with our system.

4.2 Crawl Specification

Ideally, we would exhaustively visit every state of a web application. For any non-trivial application, state explosion makes such a goal infeasible. Hence, we developed a crawling specification that can be used to direct the navigation. A developer may provide three XML specifications to our system described in the following subsections: a required interaction specification that directs the crawl, an input specification for handling input fields, and a login specification for managing accounts. Regarding the developer burden of using our tool, writing the specification files is not harder than designing tests cases with the Selenium framework, a widely used tool for black-box web application testing. The primary task for the user of our system is to identify sections of the site that contain private interactions using the XPath notation and private content on the page with regular expressions and we advocate the use of of our tool as part of the development of privacy-sensitive applications.

Interaction Specification. At a minimum, a crawl specification must specify which elements on a site to click. This specification can specify click elements by tag, attribute, or an XPath [7]. Figure 4 shows an example of a interaction specification for the NHS Symptom Checker (see Section 6.3). It instructs the crawler to click on all anchor tags that satisfy the XPath expression, /HTML/BODY/DIV[2]/DIV[2]/A. This corresponds to the "next" button in the questionnaire. During exploration, the crawler will scan each page for elements satisfying the criteria, adding them to the depth-first search stack. The click element can be further refined with noClick elements that override the click specification.

A developer can use the waitFor element to specify a DOM element that indicates a web page has successfully loaded. This was added after we observed that occasionally a request will only be partially answered, causing only a portion of the page to load. When the described element appears in the DOM, Crawljax continues normally. If that particular request never completes fully, our system times out and retries the user action. The specification in Figure 4 tells the crawler to wait for the page footer to load.

By default, Crawljax defines two equivalent states as having a near identical Document Object Model representations (DOM). In reality, two instances of a web page may be semantically identical but have slightly differing DOMs. A developer can use matchOverride to enumerate a series of regular expression replacements to manipulate the DOM before the standard state comparison is performed. The example matchOveride in Figure 4 directs the crawler

```
<form>
  <beforeClickElement>
    <tag>input</tag>
    <xPath>
      <expression>
        /html/body/span/center/span/center/form[@id="gender"]
          /table/tbody/tr/td[2]/div/input
      </expression>
    </xPath>
  </beforeClickElement>
  <field>
    <id>female</id><value>false</value><value>true</value>
  </field>
  <field>
    <id>male</id><value>true</value><value>false</value>
  </field>
</form>
```

Figure 5: Example Input Specification.

to only examine the questions from the symptom checker for the state equivalence computation.

Input Specification. Many websites require user input for meaningful use. Due to the difficulties of inferring valid inputs, the developer must specify where and how to fill input fields in the application. The example input specification shown in Figure 5 was used to select the gender in NHS Symptom Checker. An input specification indicates how the fields will be populated with the beforeClickElement, which in this case would be the next button in the gender form. Additionally, the developer lists which field should be populated and all the possible inputs to try. The field tags in the example direct the crawler to first select the female option, follow that line of questions, and then return to select male. Specifications can also request performing a random subset of specified inputs. For example a developer may want to try random combinations of first and last names in order to get a larger sample. It may also be the case that progression in the application requires valid input (e.g., a Social Security Number), but the developer does not want network traffic to be tied to a specific input. Such functionality is implemented with the randomForm element.

Login Specification. Many real-world applications require existing user-accounts to function. Google Health requires login credentials to access the site. We extended Crawljax's basic support for form pages to allow the developer to list a series of accounts, from which one is chosen for a particular crawl. Using different accounts prevents logged traffic information from being over-fitted to a specific user. An example login specification for Google Health is shown in Figure 6. In this specification a URL is given to login at, the username and password along with where to input them, and what button to click to complete the login.

```
<preCrawl>
  <url><value>http://www.google.com/health</value></url>
  <input>
    <id>Email</id> <value>test@xkcd.com</value>
  </input>
  <input>
    <id>Passwd</id> <value>Tr0ub4dor&3</value>
  </input>
  <click><id>signIn</id></click>
</preCrawl>
```

Figure 6: Example Login Specification.

4.3 Crawl Repair

Since our crawling system triggers thousands of page loads when exploring externally operated complex web applications, errors often occur in the crawl. The most common failures were unfulfilled HTTP requests and generic application-level server-side errors. These failures result in incorrect network traces and even structurally different state machines, since application error pages or incomplete page loads prevent the crawler from finding new DOM elements with which to interact.

After a series of crawls the developer selects a trial as the ground-truth, presumably through manual analysis of the saved HTML states. We developed an accompanying tool to examine the suspect trials and repair the FSMs so that they are structurally equivalent. This involves removing states and transitions that do not exist in the selected trial and adding those as necessary. When adding new states to imperfect crawls we choose to disadvantage the attacker by assuming that no information was gained from that particular state transition in that trial. If desired, one could give the advantage to the attacker by replacing the missing data with the trace from the designated correct trial. In practice we found that within a trial the number of discovered errors is small; fewer than 1% of the number of total transitions need corrections.

5. LEAK QUANTIFICATION

Once the site exploration phase is complete, the leak quantifier analyzes the state machine of the web application to determine how vulnerable the network traffic is to reconstruction through the various side-channels. Each state transition contains a list of network transfers with information about the origin, destination, size, and time of the transfer as described in Section 4.1. To determine the similarity of two traces, we define a *distance metric*. Section 5.1 describes three different distance metrics we use based on different aspects of the network traces. Then, we consider two methods to quantify leaks in the web application: entropy (Section 5.2) and the Fisher criterion (Section 5.3).

Assumptions. A key assumption made throughout our leak quantification is that the adversary is able to track when state transitions begin and end. This is reasonable since the adversary can search for pauses in network traffic. For most web applications it is impractical to continually stream data between the client and the server due to the computational overhead and the bandwidth consumption, so traffic bursts reflect state transitions. For the WiFi threat model, we assume there is no other disruptive network traffic and that the attacker can distinguish whether packets are incoming to or outgoing from the victim, which is essentially a matter of identifying the MAC address of the target computer. Our last assumption is that the user starts at the root of the web application (e.g., the Google Health Dashboard or the NHS Symptom Checker welcome page) and makes forward progress through the application, not clicking back or randomly reloading pages. These assumptions favor the attacker, so potentially overestimate the amount of information available to an attacker in practice, although it seems likely that motivated attackers would be able to find ways to overcome violations of these assumptions.

Formalization. To formalize the problem as a multi-class classifier, we define x_i to be the set of examples belonging to class i, and x_i^j to be example j from the class. A *class* is the action or series of actions a user performed to reach a state in the web application. An example from a class is the set of network traces collected while those actions were performed. We assume the start and stop of page transitions are identifiable, so the function $t(x_i^j, k)$ yields the trace from example x_i^j for the kth transition. A network transfer is defined as the uninterrupted transmission of data (generally over TCP for our purposes) from one machine on the network to another. A trace is a list of network transfers of the form $src \rightarrow dst : bytes$ where src is the source, dst is the destination, and $bytes$ is the number of bytes of the transfered data as taken from the IP header. Given a transition v, $v[i]$ yields the ith transfer.

Impact of Threat Models. The threat models dictate the amount of information visible to the attacker. For the WiFi scenario, the attacker can only see the size of transfers and whether they were incoming or outgoing. Thus, all transfers are of the form $target \rightarrow accesspoint$ or $accesspoint \rightarrow target$. In the ISP threat model, the attacker has access to the plain text IP and TCP packet headers in in addition to the encrypted contents of the message. Since the ISP scenario allows the attacker to see the TCP packet headers, TCP protocol features such as ACKs and re-transmissions are easily identified. In anticipation of defenses designed to abuse these protocol features by sending fake ACKs or initiating unnecessary re-transmissions (as suggested by HTTPOS [22]), tests under the ISP threat model ignore both ACKs and re-transmissions. Unlike our other assumptions, this assumption favors the site operator by assuming the attacker's task is complicated by widespread deployment of these defenses, so underestimates the actual leakage in situations where these defenses are not used.

Baseline Classifier. To use as a baseline for testing the existence and exploitability of side-channel leaks, we construct a multi-class classifier, classifying network traces according to the action performed to generate them. Our classifier uses a nearest-centroid approach, assigning an unknown trace to the class of the nearest class centroid, where nearest is defined according to one of the distance metrics. Since the exact distribution of each class is unknown we estimate the centroid by attempting to create a trace that minimizes the Hamiltonian distance from the examples in the class. We validate the performance of the classifier by running K-fold cross-validation testing. The higher the success rate of the classifier, the more likely an attacker will be able to exploit a leak based on the properties measured in the metric. Ideally, a well protected system would not allow an attacker create a classifier that performs better than is possible with random guessing.

5.1 Distance Metrics

We use different distance metrics to test different environmental conditions and threat models to understand how conditions impact what vulnerabilities exist and the best methods to mitigate them.

Total-Source-Destination. The Total-Source-Destination (TSD) metric returns the summed difference of bytes transferred between each party. In a trace containing only a server and a client, it is the difference in the number of bytes transfered to the client, added to the difference in the number of bytes transfered to the server, as computed by Algorithm 1. The inputs are two transitions v and w, and the output measures the distance between the transitions. This metric is easily manipulated through basic packet padding which hides the actual lengths of the packets.

Size-Weighted-Edit-Distance. The Size-Weighted-Edit-Distance (SWED) adds robustness by tracking the control-flow of the transfered information. Unlike the Total-Source-Destination metric, the sequence of transfered data matters. Every transfer is treated as a symbol in a string of the sequence of transfers, $src \rightarrow dst$. The distance is the Levenshtein distance between the translated strings, but in order to give weight to the transfer sizes, the cost of each edit operation (insertion, deletion, and substitution) is the number

Algorithm 1 *TotalSourceDestination*(v, w)

distance = 0
for all $s \in Parties$ **do**
  for all $d \in Parties$ **do**
    $subdistance = 0$
    for all $i = 0 \rightarrow v.size$ **do**
      if $v[i].src = s \wedge v[i].dst = d$ **then**
        $subdistance = subdistance + v[i].bytes$
    for all $i = 0 \rightarrow w.size$ **do**
      if $w[i].src = s \wedge w[i].dst = d$ **then**
        $subdistance = subdistance - w[i].bytes$
    $distance = distance + abs(subdistance)$

of bytes being inserted or deleted. A minimum weight is set at a configuration value α, in order to lend sufficient weight to smaller transfers (TCP ACKs). If the source and destination are the same, the cost is simply the difference in transfer sizes.

Edit-Distance. Since the simple packet-padding defense dramatically affects the size distributions of transfers, we use the Edit-Distance (ED) metric to understand how well an attacker can do using only on the control flow of the network transfer. Like the previous metric, every transfer in the trace is a symbol in a string. The Edit-Distance is the Levenshtein distance between two strings where all edit operations have an equal cost. Since this metric is independent of the sizes of transfers, the Edit-Distance reveals how well an attacker can do against a perfect packet-padding strategy.

Random. The Random metric serves as a baseline in order to judge the distinguishability gained from the distance metrics beyond the assumption that the adversary can distinguish page breaks. In every metric, the nearest-centroid classifier will not consider classes that require a different number of transitions than the example in question. The Random assigns a random distance between 1 and 1000 regardless of the two examples being compared. Hence, the only useful classifiability gained from the Random metric is a result of the assumption that the adversary can identify when state transitions occur.

5.2 Entropy Measurements

Previous work measured the severity of leaks using bits of entropy [21,33] or reduction power [5,22,33]. Both measurements are a function of the size of the *uncertainty set* the attacker has for classifying a given network trace. In other words, given a network trace, how many classes can be eliminated as an impossibility for generating that trace. Logically, bits of uncertainty indicate the amount of ambiguity an attacker has in classifying a network trace. Using a concrete example, if a network trace is identical for four actions that trace is said to have $\log_2 4 = 2$ bits of entropy. Ideally we would measure the entropy for every possible network trace, looking at the number of classes that could possibly create each trace. To find the entropy of the system, we sum the entropy of each trace weighted by the probability of that trace occurring. In practice, however, it is infeasible to enumerate every possible trace so we use the corpus of those generated by our testing. To simplify our model we assume that each user action is equally probable. Together, the equation for calculating entropy is:

$$H(X) = \sum_{i=0}^{n} \frac{\log_2 p(\bar{x}_i)}{n}$$

where X is the tested system containing n classes, $\bar{x}_i$ is each centroid, and $p(\bar{x}_i)$ yields the size of the uncertainty set for the attacker.

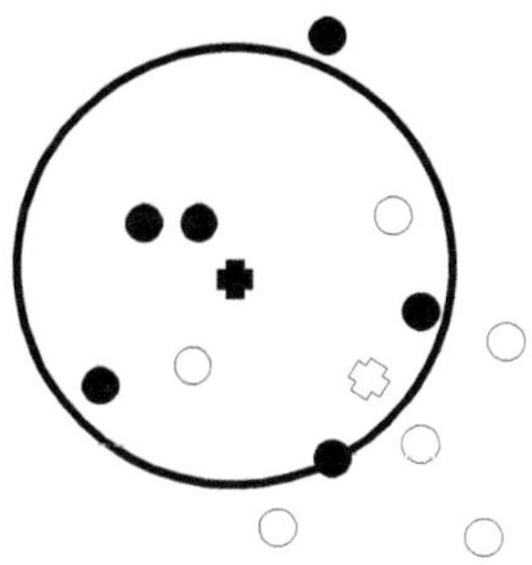

Figure 7: Entropy Distinguishability Threshold. Two classes are marked by different shadings with their respective centroids indicated by the + symbols. The 75% threshold for the dark class is the distance that contains 3/4 of the dark points. Since the centroid of the light class is within this threshold, we consider the classes indistinguishable at this threshold.

Note that if the uncertainty set is n for every trace, the resulting entropy is maximized at the desired $\log_2 n$. This is the conditional entropy metric used by Luo et al. [22].

The key difficulty in calculating entropy lies in determining the size of the uncertainty set for a given trace. In our analysis we take the estimated centroid for each class, then find the threshold distance from the centroid such that a certain percentage of the samples in the class are within that distance of the centroid. We use the threshold distance as the boundary for distinguishability. The number of centroids that fall within the threshold distance of the centroid yields $p(x_i)$ for this class. Figure 7 shows two classes considered indistinguishable given a threshold of of 75%.

The threshold for distinguishability in calculating entropy is often arbitrary. Depending on the choice, the resulting entropy value may not give a good measure of the attacker's likelihood of successfully exploiting a particular vulnerability (as demonstrated by our experimental results in Section 6). Additionally the boundary between distinguishable and indistinguishable classes is not necessarily strict and small changes can yield significant changes in entropy. It is desirable for our leak quantification to capture the relative distances of classes. Ignoring the relative distances can lead to misclassifying a system as invulnerable because each class appears indistinguishable but slight changes to the attacker strategy may yield an accurate classifier.

Ideally, defenses should generate network traces that are either exactly the same or entirely randomly distributed. If under the monitored properties the traces are either identical or entirely randomly distributed, the data is invulnerable to side-channel analysis. Our measurement should yield a meaningful value for this result. However, once the entropy measurement reaches its maximum value, each class is considered indistinguishable from every other class ignoring any notion of how distant or different classes are from one another. Two defenses that have maximum entropy values are not necessarily equally good considering a defense that barely establishes indistinguishability will be given the same value as a perfect defense. Our second metric is designed to overcome these limitations of the entropy measurement.

5.3 Fisher Criterion

Since we frame the goal of the attacker as a classifier, it is natural to borrow concepts from machine learning methods in constructing classifiers. We adopt the Fisher criterion as our measurement of classifiability [11]. The Fisher criterion was previously used by Guo et al. as the fitness function for a genetic programming algorithm to extract meaningful features for multi-class recognition problems [17], but we are not aware of any previous use in side-channel analysis.

The Fisher criterion is essentially the ratio of the between-class variance to the within-class variance of the data [31,32]. The higher the value, the more classifiable the data. The Fisher criterion is used as a tool in linear discriminant analysis to construct strong classifications. Since we are given the classifications (it is known which user actions created the network traces), we use the Fisher Criterion as a measurement of the severity of side-channel leaks. The Fisher criterion is calculated as:

$$F(X) = \frac{\sigma^2_{between}}{\sigma^2_{within}} = \frac{\sum_{i=0}^{n} m \cdot (\bar{x}_i - \bar{x})^2}{\sum_{i=0}^{n} \sum_{j=0}^{m} (x_i^j - \bar{x}_i)^2}$$

where n is the number of classes, m is the number of samples in each class, x_i^j denotes sample j in class i, $\bar{x}_i$ is the centroid of class i, and $\bar{x}$ is the total centroid. A Fisher criterion value greater than 1 has the physical meaning that the between-class variance is greater than the within-class variance. Although this may seem like a logical threshold for distinguishable classes, as has been previously claimed [31], our results do not support the existence of an absolute threshold.

The Fisher criterion is a better measurement of the classifiability of network traffic than previous entropy measures for two reasons: (1) it incorporates the distances between classes without the almost arbitrary distinction of distinguishable versus indistinguishable, increasing robustness against attack variations; (2) both the ideal and worst-case network trace distributions have associated values, 0 and ∞ respectively. The Fisher criterion approaches zero because either the within-class variance approaches infinity (the values within a class are random), or the between-class variance approaches 0 (all classes yield the same network traces). The Fisher criterion approaches infinity when the classes are well-separated and are well-defined, lending well to strong classifiability.

6. RESULTS

To evaluate the effectiveness of our black-box approach in side-channel leak quantification and the value of the Fisher criterion over conditional entropy, we tested our system on several existing web applications: search engines (Section 6.1), Google Health (Section 6.2), and the United Kingdom's National Health Service Symptom Checker (Section 6.3). Some of the search engines were tested and the Google Health application were also used in prior work [5]; the NHS Symptom Checker was chosen because it is a complex application that handles sensitive information.

For each application, we constructed crawl specification files as described in Section 4.2 and ran the crawlers on a variety of commodity hardware including desktops, laptops, and servers. The difficultly of writing these specifications varies as a function of website's complexity and adherence to standard web design practices such as using a RESTful [10] architecture and avoiding iframes. The average length of the constructed specifications is 4547 LOC ($\sigma = 7537$) according to CLOC [9]. A detailed breakdown of specification sizes can be found in Table 1. The Yahoo Search specification was the longest (17,589 LOC) as it includes an (automatically-generated) enumeration of three-letter combinations and the Bing specification was the shortest (45 LOC). Once the crawlers finish exploration of the web application, we quantified the leaks. The results of the leak quantification for each application are presented in the following subsections. During all tests, the browser cache was

Application	Interaction	Input	Login
Bing Suggestions	3	41	-
Google Search Suggestions	3	38	-
Google Instant	3	38	-
Yahoo Search	3	17589	-
Google Health	31	324	82
NHS Adult Male	37	286	-

Table 1: Specification Length. The 17589-line specification for Yahoo Search is automatically generated by enumerating all 3-letter combinations. The other specifications are manually generated. Only the Google Health specification includes a Login specification, since the other applications do not require user accounts.

left enabled, but reset upon returning to the root of the web application to ensure that the elements in the cache are only a function of the pages visited from the root.

We developed our tool and helper extensions for Firefox 3.6, although they could be adopted to any browser supported by Selenium. In fact, comprehensive site analysis may require using multiple browsers since uneven support of web standards may significantly vary the traffic signature from one browser to another. We have used our system on a variety of different systems running Windows XP, Windows 7, Ubuntu 9.10, and Ubuntu 10.04. Crawling a web application, just like performing any depth-first search, is trivially parallelized by assigning different instances to crawl different subtrees of the site. In addition to commodity desktops and laptops we tested our setup on a 64-machine cluster, demonstrating the ability for a developer to run very large crawls consisting of tens of thousands of pages in a matter of hours.

Section 6.4 uses our tools to analyze HTTPOS [22], a defense against side-channel attacks on the web. In Section 6.5, we test our results against a suite of general-purpose machine learning algorithms to confirm that our domain-specific methods are better than the best available general-purpose techniques.

6.1 Search Engine Suggestions

Chen et al. demonstrated how the Bing (http://bing.com), Google (http://encrypted.google.com), and Yahoo (http://search.yahoo.com) search engines leak queries through the network traffic generated by search suggestions [5]. Suggestion fields are particularly vulnerable to side-channel attacks because they update with every keystroke. Bing and Google search suggestions begin appearing after a single lowercase letter, so they were tested by scripting the typing of a single letter and measuring the accompanying network traffic. As demonstrated by Chen et al., the ability to distinguish a single letter allows the attacker to build up the entire query [5].

In September 2010, Google introduced Google Instant, which loads the search results as the user types a query. We evaluated Google Instant in the same manner as Bing and Google search suggestions. For Bing and Google search suggestions, classification performance is strong, reinforcing findings in prior work.

Yahoo's search suggestions do not begin appearing after three characters have been typed, increasing the state space for the first network transfer from 26 to $26^3 = 17,576$. We tested Yahoo Search to see how much delaying the suggestions mitigates the leak. The output of the classifier is a set of predicted classifications for a given example. The classification is considered correct if the actual example class is in the set.

Table 2 shows the results of our nearest-centroid classifier under the described metrics and proposed threat models for each search engine. Table 3 presents the entropy results. The distinguishability threshold greatly impacts the estimated bits of entropy in a query. For example, the classification accuracy using the Total-Source-Destination metric under the WiFi threat model is over 93% for Bing. The associated entropy calculation yields an average of 0.91 bits of uncertainty, meaning that on average the attacker's uncertainty set is $2^{0.91} = 1.88$. Considering the results of our classifier, 0.91 bits of entropy underestimates the classifiability of the data and a more appropriate 0.07 bits is only reached after ignoring the farthest 25% of sample points from the centroid. The inherent noise present in real world network traces shows the fragility of the entropy metric in the presence of classification outliers.

The calculated Fisher criterion values for the search suggestions in Table 4 give a more consistent view of the data while granting us new insights into the classifiability under the various metrics. Note that the Fisher criterion for the Edit-Distance metric is 0.00 for the search engine suggestions. This is logical considering the nature of search suggestion network traffic where almost every network trace is a short interaction between the client and the server consisting of a request, a response, and an acknowledgment. Under the Edit-Distance metric, each example trace is nearly identical and so reaches the goal Fisher criterion value of zero.

6.2 Google Health

We also tested our system on Google Health's (https://health.google.com) "Find a Doctor" feature. The "Find a Doctor" tool has been shown to leak the type of doctor a user searches and by extension a user's medical condition [5]. Since Google Health requires an account to function, we used the login functionality of our crawler described in Section 4.2. Using the application, the user inputs an area of medicine and a location. The crawler enumerates the areas of medicine in a drop-down menu to trigger searches for specialty doctors. The result of the search is a list of nearby doctors specializing in the requested medical field. As in Chen et al.'s work [5], we assume the adversary has a way to accurately determine the location (which is a reasonable assumption in cases where the adversary either knows the target's physical location or has access to the target's IP address).

The classifier performance (included in Table 4) is over 88% on the Google Health tool using the Total-Source-Destination metric, with similar results using Size-Weighted-Edit-Distance. The Edit-Distance metric yields little classification value, since like the search suggestions, the control-flows are largely similar. As seen in the other web applications, the entropy values (Table 3) decrease drastically as the threshold is decreased. However, we can observe that simply decreasing the threshold does not guarantee a repre-

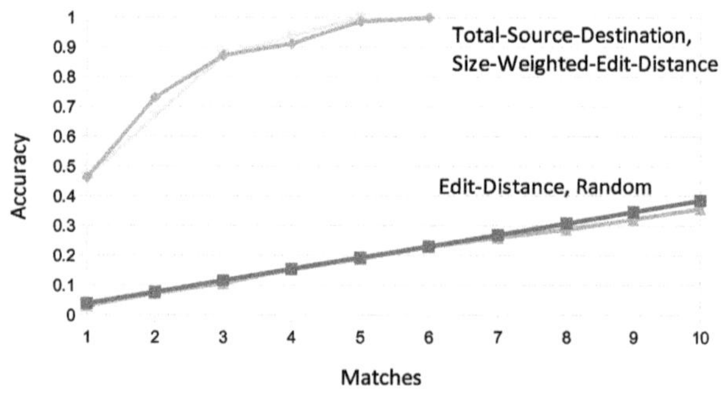

Figure 8: Performance of our Classifier. Our classifier performs well on Google Search suggestions when using the size-based metrics, but almost no better than random when sized is ignored.

Distance Metric		Bing		Google Search		Google Instant		Yahoo Search		Google Health		NHS	
Matches		1	10	1	10	1	10	1	10	1	10	1	10
Random		2.9	35.6	2.9	35.6	2.9	35.6	0.0	0.0	1.3	10.8	3.6	29.9
ISP	TSD	95.7	100.0	46.1	100.0	47.5	88.3	1.2	8.0	88.2	93.6	85.8	100.0
	SWED	96.3	100.0	46.1	100.0	7.3	52.6	1.1	7.9	81.8	91.9	31.0	89.7
	ED	3.7	37.0	3.8	39.5	7.7	56.0	0.0	0.0	2.0	11.1	5.8	38.3
WiFi	TSD	93.7	99.4	44.9	100.0	39.4	87.6	1.2	7.9	85.9	90.9	60.6	99.2
	SWED	94.7	98.8	44.9	100.0	29.6	83.0	1.2	7.9	81.8	89.6	46.9	97.7
	ED	3.7	37.0	3.8	38.5	31.5	86.7	0.0	0.1	2.7	19.9	46.1	98.1

Table 2: Nearest-Centroid Classifier Results. The value of *Matches* indicates the size of the set returned by the classifier. The results show the percentage of the time the correct classification is included time in the returned set of the given size. The metrics are Total-Source-Destination (TSD), Size-Weighted-Edit-Distance (SWED), and Edit-Distance (ED).

Distance Metric		Bing			Google Search			Google Instant		
Threshold		100%	75%	50%	100%	75%	50%	100%	75%	50%
Expected		4.70	4.70	4.70	4.70	4.70	4.70	4.70	4.70	4.70
ISP	TSD	0.42	0.07	0.07	0.42	0.07	0.07	4.70	1.97	1.09
	SWED	0.42	0.07	0.07	0.42	0.07	0.07	4.64	3.90	3.37
	ED	4.70	4.70	4.70	4.70	4.70	4.70	4.70	4.43	3.54
WiFi	TSD	0.91	0.07	0.07	2.95	2.40	0.44	4.70	2.02	1.02
	SWED	0.78	0.07	0.07	1.13	0.56	0.44	4.70	2.40	1.58
	ED	4.70	4.70	4.70	4.70	4.70	4.70	4.70	2.54	1.74
		Yahoo Search			Google Health			NHS		
Threshold		100%	75%	50%	100%	75%	50%	100%	75%	50%
Expected		14.01	14.01	14.01	6.63	6.63	6.63	8.87	8.87	8.87
ISP	TSD	7.86	6.80	5.05	0.58	0.05	0.01	5.13	2.83	1.92
	SWED	7.88	6.47	5.32	0.74	0.25	0.14	6.19	4.77	3.98
	ED	12.66	12.43	12.42	6.55	6.55	6.55	7.07	6.65	6.21
WiFi	TSD	7.91	6.62	5.04	0.71	0.05	0.01	4.76	2.70	1.83
	SWED	7.91	6.62	5.04	1.04	0.19	0.14	6.25	4.53	3.89
	ED	12.64	12.36	12.26	6.05	5.89	5.89	5.65	4.43	3.82

Table 3: Entropy Results (measured in bits of entropy).

Distance Metric		Bing	Google Search	Google Instant	Yahoo Search	Google Health	NHS
ISP	TSD	5.18	4.13	1.13	0.69	12.1	4.9
	SWED	0.17	41.7	0.34	0.59	18.0	3.3
	ED	0.00	0.00	0.22	0.56	0.0	1.8
WiFi	TSD	6.04	4.13	0.84	0.59	11.3	5.4
	SWED	1.26	41.7	0.76	0.58	10.8	3.2
	ED	0.00	0.00	0.79	0.51	3.0	5.0

Table 4: Fisher Criterion Results.

Application		Google Search							Google Instant						
Distance Metric		Accuracy (%)			Entropy (bits)			Fisher Criterion	Accuracy (%)			Entropy (bits)			Fisher Criterion
		1	3	10	100%	75%	50%		1	3	10	100%	75%	50%	
ISP	TSD	3.4	12.8	38.0	4.70	4.33	4.06	0.28	43.7	66.8	87.6	4.70	3.97	3.40	0.60
	SWED	3.8	11.1	38.0	4.70	4.43	3.52	0.43	8.2	20.4	51.4	4.16	3.61	3.55	0.55
	ED	3.4	9.4	35.5	4.70	4.58	3.51	0.14	8.7	19.0	55.0	4.70	4.55	3.81	0.47
WiFi	TSD	6.0	17.9	48.3	4.70	4.28	3.34	0.22	37.0	59.3	85.6	4.08	3.29	2.22	0.61
	SWED	3.8	11.1	35.0	4.67	4.46	3.91	0.23	27.2	47.6	82.2	4.38	3.70	2.67	0.57
	ED	6.8	11.1	35.5	4.70	4.52	3.93	0.37	26.2	49.8	81.5	4.16	3.61	3.55	0.69

Table 5: Leak Quantification Results for Google Search Suggestions and Google Instant while using HTTPOS.

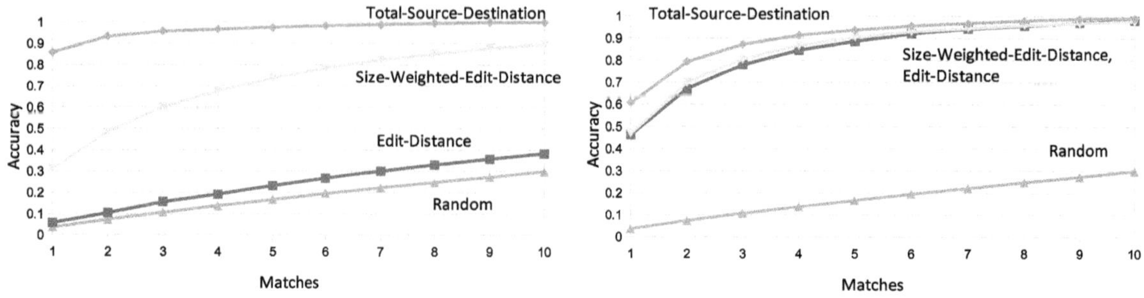

(a) ISP Threat Model (b) WiFi Threat Model

Figure 9: Classifier Performance on NHS Symptom Checker.

sentative result. For example, lowering the threshold to 50% with the Total-Source-Destination metric decreases the entropy to almost zero. Our classifier, on the other hand, is not able to classify roughly ten percent of the examples. Lowering the threshold in hopes of getting more accurate entropy values ignores actual sample points, even if they are outliers, and can result in underestimating the entropy. As expected from the classifier performance results, the Fisher criterion for the Edit-Distance under the ISP threat model is 0.00. Like the search suggestions, this is because the control flows are nearly identical for each query.

6.3 NHS Symptom Checker

To analyze our metrics on a more complex privacy-sensitive site, we also conducted an experiment using the Symptom Checker created by the United Kingdom's National Health Service (NHS). The NHS symptom checker asks a visitor a series of multiple-choice questions. The number of questions typically ranges from 10 to 30 before reaching a diagnosis, treatment advice, or a recommendation to seek medical attention. The answers to prior questions determine which questions are asked later as the system narrows down the possibilities. With the exception of three emergency questions determining whether an ambulance is needed urgently, the series of questions forms a tree. Using this property we were able to fully crawl every series of answers in the entire application.

We performed two sets of analysis for the NHS tool. The first is the subtree of the questionnaire for an adult male, the largest subtree after answering one's gender and age (468 states). We choose to do this in addition to the entire symptom checker for the subtree's interesting results and illustrate the power an attacker gains when starting with just two basic pieces of known context. The complete NHS symptom tracker has over 7300 paths through the questionnaire, each revealing different information about the user. Figure 9 summarizes the results.

To a much greater degree than the other web applications, the different threat models greatly affect classification performance. For example, using the Total-Source-Destination is significantly more effective in the ISP scenario than in the WiFi scenario. Loading full web pages, unlike the simple AJAX requests in the other applications, causes a significantly greater amount of noise due to TCP features such as ACKs and retransmissions. The inability to identify and filter out TCP features in the WiFi scenario greatly reduces classifiability for the Total-Source-Destination and Size-Weighted-Edit-Distance.

Edit-Distance Anomaly. Note that the Edit-Distance metric under the WiFi threat model performs better than under the ISP threat model. All metrics under in the ISP scenario ignore TCP features such as ACKs because they are easily manipulated either through padding the payload of ACK, by padding the transfers or by changing the TCP window size which indirectly manipulates the number of ACKs that will be sent. In the WiFi scenario, the attacker cannot filter out faked TCP ACKs, making classification more difficult. However, in our experiments TCP ACKs were legitimate and so when they are left in the trace they server as an indicator of the size of the transfer, and not random noise as would be expected in a strong defense system.

6.4 HTTPOS Defense

HTTPOS is a client-side defense against these attacks which substantially manipulates browser traffic to protect against analysis [22]. We deployed a prototype version of HTTPOS in the Firefox browser running our tests and measured its effectiveness. HTTPOS simply acts a SOCKS proxy and so we configured Firefox 3.6.17 to direct traffic through the HTTPOS system. We tested HTTPOS on Google search suggestions and Google Instant search, without a training phase and with all defenses enabled. The ability to easily apply and evaluate a previously published defense shows the flexibility of our system and the utility of the black-box approach for defense quantification and comparison.

The results of our initial tests are shown in Table 5. For search suggestions, HTTPOS is very effective. It significantly reduces the accuracy of our classifier across all metrics, resulting in performance only slightly better than random classification. However, in our experiments HTTPOS did not sufficiently mitigate the side-channel for Google Instant search. The accuracy using the TSD metric remained over 40%, which combined with successive letters in a search query, we still believe the tool to remain exploitable. This is due to the much greater variation in different flows found in a Google Instant search due to integration of images, embedded maps, and videos. Without a proper training phase HTTPOS is unaware of the degree of traffic manipulation necessary to suppress the leak. Also noteworthy is the increase in Fisher criterion values for the SWED and ED metrics under the ISP threat model. We were not able to identify the specific HTTPOS defense mechanism that causes this increase, but we advocate any new defense mechanisms be throughly tested for accidentally created side-channels. Taken together, these experiments validate the ability of HTTPOS to effectively manipulate network traffic to thwart side-channel attacks on simple flows, but for complex flows and pages a training phase is required. Such a restriction reduces the utility and real-world applicability of the defense, but the effectiveness of HTTPOS for the

Data Set	Best Classifier	Accuracy	Our Rate
Bing Suggestions	minimalist-boost	91.2	96.3
Google Search Suggestions	LogitBoost_weka_nominal	34.8	46.1
Google Instant	bonzaiboost-n200-d2	66.0	47.5
Google Health Find A Doctor	LogitBoost_weka_nominal	74.2	88.2
NHS Adult Male	FilteredClassifier_weka_nominal	78.1	85.8
HTTPOS on Google Search	bonzaiboost-n200-d2	7.1	6.8
HTTPOS on Google Instant	bonzaiboost-n200-d2	15.6	43.7

Table 6: MLComp Results. Running our datasets on generic, publicly available multi-class classifiers yields similar results to our nearest-centroid classifier. Each row of the table lists the best accuracy rate that any classifier had for that dataset as a percentage.

search suggestions shows that a generic client-side defense is still promising for many applications.

6.5 MLComp

MLComp (http://mlcomp.org) is a service for comparing machine learning algorithms on shared datasets. Users upload programs and data sets in a standard format, allowing others to test their algorithms against a variety of data sets, or choose good classification techniques for their datasets. We used MLComp to compare our classifiers with the best available generic classifiers on the site. Table 6 summarizes the accuracy of the best classifier for each dataset. As expected, the results generally show worse performance than our classifiers which are designed using domain-specific background knowledge, but in every case the best generic classifiers perform no less than 15% worse than ours. Larger datasets, such as Yahoo search, did not finish in the site's maximum computation time of 24-hours so are not included in this table.

7. CONCLUSION

Side-channel leaks of private data have been found in popular web applications. Without tools to precisely quantify the leaks, developers cannot eliminate side-channel leaks without also sacrificing the responsiveness expected of modern web applications. Our detection system infers a web application state machine only using network traffic and the browser DOM. Our dynamic, black-box approach allows us to experiment and identify side-channel vulnerabilities in real-world web applications without access to source code. The Fisher criterion metric we propose is able to estimate the severity of application leaks much more accurately than is possible with entropy-based metrics. We have demonstrated the applicability of our approach by performing side-channel vulnerability analysis on large systems. Mitigating side-channel leaks remains an elusive goal, but our results provide encouraging evidence the side-channel leaks can be found automatically in a robust way.

Availability

Our crawling framework and quantification tool is available under an open source license from http://www.cs.virginia.edu/sca.

Acknowledgments

The authors thank Shuo Chen and XiaoFeng Wang for introducing us to the interesting problem of web application side-channel leaks. We thank Daniel Xiapu Luo for generously providing us with an early version of HTTPOS. This material is based upon work partly supported by grants from the National Science Foundation and by the Air Force Office of Scientific Research under MURI award FA9550-09-1-0539.

8. REFERENCES

[1] Michael Backes, Markus Dürmuth, Sebastian Gerling, Manfred Pinkal, and Caroline Sporleder. Acoustic Side-Channel Attacks on Printers. In *19th USENIX Security Symposium*, 2010.

[2] Jason Bau, Elie Bursztein, Divij Gupta, and John Mitchell. State of the Art: Automated Black-Box Web Application Vulnerability Testing. In *31st IEEE Symposium on Security and Privacy*, 2010.

[3] George Dean Bissias, Marc Liberatore, David Jensen, and Brian Neil Levine. Privacy Vulnerabilities in Encrypted HTTP Streams. In *Privacy Enhancing Technologies Workshop*, 2005.

[4] Mike Bowler. HtmlUnit. http://htmlunit.sourceforge.net/.

[5] Shuo Chen, Rui Wang, XiaoFeng Wang, and Kehuan Zhang. Side-Channel Leaks in Web Applications: a Reality Today, a Challenge Tomorrow. In *31st IEEE Symposium on Security and Privacy*, 2010.

[6] Heyning Cheng and Ron Avnur. Traffic Analysis of SSL Encrypted Web Browsing. UC Berkeley CS 261 Final Report, http://www.cs.berkeley.edu/~daw/teaching/cs261-f98/projects/final-reports/ronathan-heyning.ps, 1998.

[7] James Clark and Steve DeRose. XML Path Language (XPath). http://www.w3.org/TR/xpath/, 1999.

[8] George Danezis. Traffic Analysis of the HTTP Protocol over TLS. http://research.microsoft.com/en-us/um/people/gdane/papers/TLSanon.pdf, 2009.

[9] Al Danial. CLOC: Count Lines of Code. http://cloc.sourceforge.net/, 2006–2011.

[10] Roy T. Fielding. *Architectural Styles and the Design of Network-Based Software Architectures*. PhD thesis, University of California, Irvine, 2000.

[11] Ronald A. Fisher. The Use of Multiple Measurements in Taxonomic Problems. *Annals of Eugenics*, 1936.

[12] Flash-Selenium Project. A Selenium Extension for Enabling Selenium to Test Flash Components, 2011.

[13] Jeffrey Friedman. TEMPEST: A Signal Problem. *Cryptologic Spectrum*, 2007.

[14] Keita Fujii. Jpcap. http://netresearch.ics.uci.edu/kfujii/jpcap/doc/.

[15] Grig Gheorghiu. A Look at Selenium. *Better Software*, 2005.

[16] Google. Google Web Toolkit. http://code.google.com/webtoolkit/.

[17] Hong Guo, Qing Zhang, and Asoke K. Nandi. Feature Generation Using Genetic Programming Based on Fisher Criterion. In *15th European Signal Processing Conference*, 2007.

[18] William G. J. Halfond and Alessandro Orso. Improving Test Case Generation for Web Applications using Automated

Interface Discovery. In 6th *Joint European Software Engineering Conference and ACM SIGSOFT Symposium on Foundations of Software Engineering*, 2007.

[19] Paul C. Kocher. Timing Attacks on Implementations of Diffie-Hellman, RSA, DSS, and Other Systems. In 16th *Annual Conference on Advances in Cryptology*, 1996.

[20] Mark Levene and George Loizou. Computing the Entropy of User Navigation in the Web. *International Journal of Information Technology and Decision Making*, 1999.

[21] Marc Liberatore and Brian Neil Levine. Inferring the Source of Encrypted HTTP Connections. In 13th *ACM Conference on Computer and Communications Security*, 2006.

[22] Xiapu Luo, Peng Zhou, Edmond W. W. Chan, Wenke Lee, Rocky K. C. Chang, and Roberto Perdiscio. HTTPOS: Sealing Information Leaks with Browser-side Obfuscation of Encrypted Flows. In *Network and Distributed System Security Symposium*, 2011.

[23] Atif M. Memon, Ishan Banerjee, and Adithya Nagarajan. GUI Ripping: Reverse Engineering of Graphical User Interfaces for Testing. In 10th *Working Conference on Reverse Engineering*, 2003.

[24] Ali Mesbah. Crawljax. http://crawljax.com/, 2008–2011.

[25] Ali Mesbah, Engin Bozdag, and Arie van Deursen. Crawling AJAX by Inferring User Interface State Changes. In *Eighth International Conference on Web Engineering*, 2008.

[26] Chunyan Mu and David Clark. Quantitative Analysis of Secure Information Flow via Probabilistic Semantics. In *International Conference on Availability, Reliability and Security*, 2009.

[27] Linda Dailey Paulson. Building Rich Web Applications with Ajax. *Computer*, October 2005.

[28] Selenium Issues. Clearing the Cache from Firefox Driver. http://code.google.com/p/selenium/issues/detail?id=548, 2010.

[29] Selenium Project. Selenium. http://seleniumhq.org/, 2004–2011.

[30] Qixiang Sun, Daniel R. Simon, Yi-Min Wang, Wilf Russell, Venkata N. Padmanabhan, and Lili Qiu. Statistical Identification of Encrypted Web Browsing Traffic. In *23rd IEEE Symposium on Security and Privacy*, 2002.

[31] Yong Xu and Guangming Lu. Analysis On Fisher Discriminant Criterion And Linear Separability Of Feature Space. In *International Conference on Computational Intelligence and Security*, 2006.

[32] Bing-Yi Zhang, Ya-Min Sun, Yu-Lan Bian, and Hong-Ke Zhang. Linear Discriminant Analysis in Network Traffic Modeling: Research Articles. *International Journal on Communication Systems*, February 2006.

[33] Kehuan Zhang, Zhou Li, Rui Wang, XiaoFeng Wang, and Shuo Chen. Sidebuster: Automated Detection and Quantification of Side-Channel Leaks in Web Application Development. In 17th *ACM Conference on Computer and Communications Security*, 2010.

Deobfuscation of Virtualization-Obfuscated Software

A Semantics-Based Approach

Kevin Coogan
Department of Computer Science
University of Arizona
P.O. Box 210077
Tucson, AZ 85721-0077
kpcoogan@cs.arizona.edu

Gen Lu
Department of Computer Science
University of Arizona
P.O. Box 210077
Tucson, AZ 85721-0077
genlu@cs.arizona.edu

Saumya Debray
Department of Computer Science
University of Arizona
P.O. Box 210077
Tucson, AZ 85721-0077
debray@cs.arizona.edu

ABSTRACT

When new malware are discovered, it is important for researchers to analyze and understand them as quickly as possible. This task has been made more difficult in recent years as researchers have seen an increasing use of virtualization-obfuscated malware code. These programs are difficult to comprehend and reverse engineer, since they are resistant to both static and dynamic analysis techniques. Current approaches to dealing with such code first reverse-engineer the byte code interpreter, then use this to work out the logic of the byte code program. This outside-in approach produces good results when the structure of the interpreter is known, but cannot be applied to all cases. This paper proposes a different approach to the problem that focuses on identifying instructions that affect the observable behavior of the obfuscated code. This inside-out approach requires fewer assumptions, and aims to complement existing techniques by broadening the domain of obfuscated programs eligible for automated analysis. Results from a prototype tool on real-world malicious code are encouraging.

Categories and Subject Descriptors

D.4.6 [**Operating Systems**]: Security and Protection—*Invasive Software*

General Terms

Security

Keywords

virtualization, deobfuscation, dynamic analysis

1. INTRODUCTION

Recent years have seen an increase in malware protected against analysis and reverse engineering using virtualization obfuscators such as VMProtect [16] and Code Virtualizer [11]. Such obfuscators embed the original program's logic within the byte code for a (custom) virtual machine (VM) interpreter. It is difficult to recover the logic of the original program because an examination of the executed code reveals only the structure and logic of the byte-code interpreter. Additionally, there may be an element of randomness introduced into the construction of the custom VM, so that successful reverse engineering of one instance of a virtualization-obfuscated program does not help us deal with a different program obfuscated using the same obfuscator. This makes the task of reverse engineering virtualization-obfuscated malware code a challenging one.

Existing techniques for reverse engineering of code protected by virtualization-obfuscation [6, 12, 13] first reverse engineer the VM interpreter; use this information to work out individual byte code instructions; and finally, recover the logic embedded in the byte code program. This outside-in approach is very effective when the structure of the interpreter meets certain requirements. However, when the interpreter uses techniques that do not fit these assumptions (e.g., direct-threading vs. byte-code interpretation), the deobfuscator may not work well. This approach may also not generalize easily to code that uses multiple layers of interpretation, since it may be difficult to distinguish between instruction fetches for various interpreters.

This paper presents a prototype tool that uses a different approach to dealing with virtualization-obfuscated programs. We note that for modern operating systems, programs interact with the system through a predefined interface, typically implemented as system calls. We also note that malicious code must use this interface if its behavior is to be meaningful or impactful in any way. We identify instructions that interact with the system, then use various analyses to determine which instructions affect this interaction, either directly or indirectly. The resulting set of instructions is an approximation of the original code, while the remaining instructions approximate the set of instructions that are semantically uninteresting and can be discarded.

The previous work mentioned above produces excellent results on those programs that match their assumptions. Because our approach does not attempt to recover the original instructions, but rather attempts to capture the relevant behavior of the code, it will not match those results for accuracy. However, our approach is more general, and can be applied to a wider range of obfuscation techniques. Thus, it should be seen as complementing existing approaches by providing information when others cannot.

The remainder of the paper is organized as follows: Section 2 describes the problem in detail and our approach to the analysis, Section 3.1 describes our methodology for evaluation of our results, Section 3.2 presents the results of our analysis, Section 5 discusses related works and Section 6 presents our conclusions.

2. DEOBFUSCATION

Static analysis of code that has been obfuscated using virtualization reveals only the structure of the virtual machine interpreter. Similarly, the dynamic trace of a virtualization obfuscated executable is a mix of virtual machine interpreter instructions and instructions performing the work of the original program. It is often difficult to see the boundaries between these two sets of instructions when looking at the trace. This task becomes even harder in the case that multiple interpreters are used, or when the interpreter dispatch routine performs multiple operations (e.g., decrypting the address of the next instruction).

Our approach is to try to identify instructions that are known to be part of the original code, and eliminating those that are not, while not assuming any information about the specific structure of the interpreter or its dispatch routines. In the remainder of this section, we present an outline of our overall approach, then discuss the parts of this approach that are original work in further detail.

2.1 Overall Approach

The analysis of an executable consists of the following steps:

1. Use a tracing tool such as qemu [3], OllyDbg, Ether [5], etc. to obtain a low level execution trace that provides, at each execution step, the address of the instruction executed, details about this instruction (byte sequence, mnemonic, operands, etc.), and the values of the machine registers.
2. Identify system calls and their arguments in this trace, using a database that gives information about arguments and return values of system calls.[1] In general, not all system calls may be of interest (e.g., those occurring in program start up or exit code may not be interesting), so we allow the user to optionally indicate which system calls to consider.
3. Use the available information to carry out analyses on the instruction trace. These analyses flag instructions that affect the values of arguments, as well as conditional control flow and the flow of control to system calls of interest. We refer to these instructions as *relevant instructions*.
4. Build a subtrace from those instructions that have been marked as relevant. This *relevant subtrace* approximates a dynamic trace of the original, unobfuscated code.

2.2 Value-based Dependence Analysis

To motivate our approach to deobfuscation, we begin by considering the semantic intuition behind any deobfuscation process. Obviously, when we simplify an obfuscated program, we cannot hope to recover the code for the original program for two reasons. First, in the case of malware we usually do not have access to the source code. Second, even where source code is available, the program may change during compilation, e.g., via compiler transformations such as in-lining or loop unrolling, so that the code for the final executable may be different from (though equivalent to) that of the original program. All we can require, then, is that the process of deobfuscation must be semantics-preserving: i.e., that the code resulting from deobfuscation be semantically equivalent to the original program.

In the context of malware analysis, a reasonable notion of semantic equivalence seems to be that of *observational equivalence*, where two programs are considered equivalent if they behave—i.e., interact with their execution environment—in the same way. Since a program's runtime interactions with the external environment are carried out through system calls, this means that two programs are observationally equivalent if they execute identical sequences of system calls (together with the argument vectors to these calls).

This notion of program equivalence suggests a simple approach to deobfuscation: identify all instructions that directly or indirectly affect the values of the arguments to system calls; these instructions are "semantically relevant." Any remaining instructions, which are by definition semantically irrelevant, may be discarded. The crucial question then becomes that of identifying instructions that affect the values of system call arguments: we discuss this issue in more detail in the remainder of this section.

The goal of dependence analysis is to work back from system call arguments to identify all instructions that directly or indirectly affect the values of those arguments. At first glance, this seems to be a straightforward application of dynamic program slicing [14], but this turns out to not be the case. The problem is that slicing algorithms follow all control and data dependencies in the code (an instruction I is *control-dependent* on an instruction J if the execution of J can affect whether or not control goes to I). Since the instructions that implement a byte-code operation are all control-dependent on the dispatch code in the interpreter, it follows that the code that evaluates system call arguments and makes the system calls will also be control dependent on the interpreter's dispatch code. The net result is that slicing algorithms end up including most or all of the interpreter code in the computed slice and so achieves little in the way of deobfuscation.

We use a different approach where we initially follow only data dependencies, then consider control transfers separately. We use a variation on the notion of *use-definition* (ud) chains [2]. Conventional ud-chains link instructions that use a variable (register, memory location) to the instruction(s) that define it. While ud-chains are usually considered in the context of static analysis of programs, it is straightforward to adapt them to dynamic execution traces. In this case, we must match each use of a variable with the instance of the instruction in the trace that defines it.

Because they do not follow control dependencies, ud-chains avoid the imprecision problem encountered with program slicing (control flow has to be identified separately in the deobfuscated code.) However, conventional ud-chains have precision problems of their own. Consider the following instruction sequence:

```
/*I1*/   mov eax, [ecx+edx]
/*I2*/   push eax
/*I3*/   call print
```

The argument to the print call is loaded from memory by instruction I_1, then pushed onto the stack by instruction I_2. A conventional ud-chain calculation would show that instruction I_1 uses ecx, edx, and the memory address pointed to by adding these values together. However, only the memory address is relevant to the *value* passed to the system call. This results in a loss of precision. What we should do, instead, is disregard the registers used for the address computation and trace back to find the (most recent) instruction that wrote to the memory location being accessed.

To deal with this issue, we define a notion of *value-based dependence*. The essential intuition here is that we focus on the flow of *values* rather than on details of the intermediate computations of

[1]Our current implementation uses DLL calls as a proxy for system calls, primarily because the Microsoft Windows API for DLLs is better documented and also more consistent across different versions of the Windows operating system. This generally causes the analysis to be sound but possibly conservative since not all DLL calls lead to system calls. It is straightforward to modify this to handle code that traps directly into the kernel without going through a DLL: it simply requires examining the argument values of instructions that trap into the operating system kernel, e.g., sysenter, to determine the syscall number and hence the system call itself.

the addresses of these values. This is done by redefining the set of locations used by an operand as follows:

use(*op*) =
  if *op* is a register r **then** $\{r\}$
  else if *op* specifies a memory address a **then** $\{a\}$
  else $\emptyset$;

We then identify the instructions that are *relevant* to the system calls executed by the program as follows. For each system call in the execution trace, we use ABI information to identify the arguments that are being passed; we initialize a set S to the locations holding these arguments. We then scan back in the trace, starting at the the system call, and process each instruction I as follows: if I defines a location $\ell \in$ S (which may be a register or a memory location) then I is marked as *relevant*, ℓ is removed from S, and the set of locations used by I according to our notion of value-based dependencies (see use() above) is added to S. This backward scan continues until S becomes empty or we reach the beginning of the trace. The effect of the value-based dependence analysis described above is that when an instruction I accesses a value from a memory location a, the dependence analysis works back to find the nearest previous instruction that wrote to location a but ignores the details of how the address a was computed by I.

Under certain conditions, the above algorithm may suffer from a lack of precision. The problem arises when the parameter in question is a pointer to a structure of some sort, and the function call is using an element of that structure. The trace-back based on the pointer itself only reveals the initialization of the structure. Without knowing the size of the structure, we will not recognize when elements of the structure are being set. To solve this problem, prior to performing our analysis, we must analyze the trace of the system calls to identify what values are used, and if those values are referenced using the pointer parameter.

For each system call, we create a set P, which holds all of the locations (register or memory locations) which might potentially be pointers, and a set M, which holds all of the memory locations that have been accessed through a pointer. Initially, P holds the stack locations of the parameters to the call, and M is empty since we have not encountered any uses yet. We scan forward through the trace of the system call and look at each instruction I. Typically, I will uses some number of locations (i.e., register and memory locations), which we will call ℓ_1 , ℓ_2 , ..., to define some location, which we will call ℓ_d. If I uses some location $\ell_i \in$ P to define ℓ_d, then ℓ_d may potentially also be a pointer and is added to P. Furthermore, if ℓ_i is known to access a memory location (e.g., eax in the instruction "move ebx, [eax]), then the value v stored at ℓ_i is also added to set M, since we know that it is a memory location accessed through a suspected pointer. Finally, if instruction I defines a location $\ell_d \in$ P, and I does not use any values from P, then we can assume that I is redefining ℓ_d as something other than a pointer that we are tracking, and we remove ℓ_d from P. The algorithm continues until P is empty, or until the end of the system call trace is reached. At this point, the set M contains a set of memory locations that we suspect are part of structures pointed to by one of the system call parameters. These locations are added to the set S above as part of the parameters passed to the call.

2.3 Relevant Conditional Control Flow

Value-based dependence analysis identifies the instructions that compute the values of system call arguments, but not the associated control flow instructions. The problem with identifying relevant control transfer instructions in virtualized code is that control transfers may be handled by the same dispatch code that handles other VM instructions. In the popular IA-32 (x86) architecture (the target of our analysis tool), conditional statements are typically implemented by setting the appropriate condition code flags in the designated eflags register, then executing a conditional branch statement, e.g., jnz that reads this register. The target of the branch statement is either the address given in the instruction or the address of the next instruction in the code, depending on the value stored in this eflags register. Hence, to recognize when conditional control flow is occurring, we can examine all control flow statements (e.g., jumps, conditional jumps, calls) to see how their target addresses are calculated. Any control flow instruction whose target address calculation is conditionally dependent on some previous value is an implementation of a conditional branch statement.

It is possible that conditional logic will not be implemented exactly as described above in virtualization-obfuscated code. For example, VMProtect eliminates the branch statements and moves the value of the flags register to other general purpose registers for manipulation. However, while theoretically possible, we are not aware of any obfuscation programs that implement conditional logic without the use of the value of the eflags register at some point in the code. Hence, we can examine target address calculations for any dependence on the value of the eflags register as an indication of conditional dependence. Even assuming that the flags register is used, there are still multiple ways to use this value to implement conditional logic. Thus, our approach must be general enough to handle any such implementation. We handle this problem through the use of an equational reasoning system that was developed in-house to handle x86 assembly code [4].

Our equational reasoning system translates each instruction in the dynamic trace into an equivalent set of equations. We note that in the dynamic trace, there may be multiple equations that define the same register or memory location. To maintain the original behavior of the trace, we number the variables as follows. A variable appearing on the left hand side of an equation (i.e., a variable that is being defined) is numbered according to the order that its instruction appears in the trace. A variable appearing on the right hand side of an equation (i.e., a variable that is being used) is numbered according to the instruction that defined it. These defining instructions are found by searching backwards through the trace to identify where the definition came from.

```
...
/*I10*/   mov ebx, 0x0
/*I11*/   pop eax
/*I12*/   add ebx, eax
/*I13*/   pop eax
/*I14*/   sub ebx, eax
```

(a)

...
ebx_{10} = 0x0
eax_{11} = ValueAt(M1000)
esp_{11} = esp_8 + 4
ebx_{12} = ebx_{10} + eax_{11}
$eflags_{12}$ = Flag(ebx_{10} + eax_{11})
eax_{13} = ValueAt(M1004)
esp_{13} = esp_{11} + 4
ebx_{14} = ebx_{12} - eax_{13}
$eflags_{14}$ = Flag(ebx_{12} - eax_{13})

(b)

Figure 1: Simple example of translating instructions into equivalent equations.

Consider the example in Figure 1. Figure 1(a) gives a snippet of x86 assembly code, and Figure 1(b) gives the equivalent equations generated by our system. We are assuming that the value of the stack pointer esp before instruction I_{10} executes is 1000. We use the notation "ValueAt(M1000)" to indicate the value stored at memory location 1000. Notice that the eax used in the equations for instruction I_{12} is not the same as the eax used in the equations for instruction I_{14}, as is indicated by our numbering scheme.

Also notice that we are explicitly handling the setting of the eflags register by generating its own equation. We introduce the "Flag" operation to indicate the calculation of the flag register value based on the expression passed as a parameter. So, for instruction I_{12}, ebx gets the result of adding ebx_{10} to eax_{11}, and the eflags register gets changed according the result of that same operation.

For our purposes here, we are primarily concerned with the calculation of the target addresses of control flow instructions. Specifically, as described, we need to determine if any component of the calculation of such a target address is dependent on the value of some flag calculation. With our equational reasoning system, we need to generate a simplified expression for the target address at the point it is used, then check that expression to see if it contains any calls to the "Flag" operation.

We must also account for the possibility of additional or trivial conditional logic added for the purpose of obfuscation. The obfuscation routine cannot change the behavior of the original program, but it can add branch statements that are always true or always false, to try to confuse analysis. For this reason, we can eliminate any conditional logic that reduces to a constant boolean value.

Next, we will examine several examples of increasing complexity to show how our system correctly identifies these conditional dependencies. First, we look at the simple example in Figure 2(a), where the normal branch instructions are used to implement conditional control flow. We know that the jnz instruction uses the value of the eflags register to decide whether or not to branch, so we add a new equation at the point of the jnz instruction to represent the value of the eflags register.

```
...
/*I10*/   cmp ebx, eax
/*I11*/   mov ebx, 0x0
/*I12*/   mov eax, 0x10
/*I13*/   jnz 10000
```

(a)

```
...
eflags10 = Flag(ebx7 cmp eax6)
ebx11 = 0x0
eax12 = 0x10
eflags13 = eflags10
```

(b)

Figure 2: Identifying control dependencies with branch instructions.

As seen in Figure 2(b), when we trace back to find the definition of the right hand side, we see that it is the value of eflags from instruction I_{10} that is being used. By substituting the definition of eflags_{10}, we see that the value of the flags register used by the conditional jump instrution is "Flag(ebx_7 cmp eax_6)."

Next, we consider a case where the standard branch instructions are not used. This case would be anticipated when analyzing virtualization-obfuscated code, since the dispatch routine typically handles all control flow. Consider the code snippet in Figure 3(a). We see that the indirect jump of instruction I_{16} is indexing into a table located at address 0x10000. The value of eax indexes into the table some number of 4-byte values. Instruction I_{10} sets eax equal to some index value to be used. Instructions I_{11} through I_{15} perform some comparison that sets the value of the flags register, then moves the flag value into the ebx register, and masks the value. The effect is as follows. If the result of the comparison turned on the "zero" flag, then the value of the ebx register after instruction I_{14} is one, otherwise, it is zero. The value in ebx is then added to the index value stored in eax such that the actual index value used in the jump depends on the result of the comparison in instruction I_{11}. In the context of virtualization-obfuscated code, the index value is the byte code of the next instruction, and the table contains the addresses of virtual instruction implementations.

```
...
/*I10*/   mov eax, index
/*I11*/   cmp ebx, ecx
/*I12*/   pushf
/*I13*/   pop ebx
/*I14*/   and ebx, 0x1
/*I15*/   add eax, ebx
/*I16*/   jump [eax*4 + 0x10000]
```

(a)

```
...
eax10 = index
eflags11 = Flag(ebx4 cmp ecx3)
esp12 = esp9 - 4
ValueAt(M1000)12 = eflags11
ebx13 = ValueAt(M1000)12
ebx14 = ebx13 & 0x1
eax15 = eax10 + ebx14
target16 = eax15 * 4 + 0x10000
```

(b)

Figure 3: Identifying control dependencies with no branch instructions.

To handle this case, we recognize the control flow statement is an indirect jump and depends on the target address calculation. We generate an equation for the target address calculation as seen in Figure 3(b), and simplify it as described before. The result is given in Figure 4, and shows that the target address depends on the result of the "Flag" operation. Thus, the indirect jump is acting as a conditional control flow statement.

$$\text{target}_{16} = \text{index} + (\text{Flag}(\text{ebx}_4 \text{ cmp ecx}_3)\ \&\ 0\text{x}1)$$

Figure 4: Result of target address simplification from Figure 3.

Finally, we examine a case inspired by the conditional control flow implementation that is used in VMProtect. We begin with the example in Figure 3, and add the use of indirection. In the code snippet of Figure 5(a), two index values are stored to adjacent locations in memory. The same trick is then used to conditionally load either the address of the first index or the address of the second index into the esi register. Finally, the value stored at the location in esi is loaded into the eax register, and the indirect jump calculates the address in the table to use.

For this example, let's assume that it was *index1* that was used in the calculation of the target address, and that the value of *address* was 5000. When we simplify our equation for target_{20}, we will substitute "ValueAt(esi_{18})" for "eax_{19}." By our assumption, we know that esi_{18} holds the value 5000, so we substitute the value at memory location 5000 which is *index1* from instruction I_{10}. Our simplified expression for the target is then "target_{20} = *index1* * 4 + 0x10000." From this result, it appears that this jump is not implementing conditional control flow. However, this is wrong. We know from our analysis of the code that the result of the compare instruction determines whether *index1* or *index2* is used to index into the table. The problem is that the conditional element has been hidden by a layer of indirection. When we calculate an expression for the target address, we are only using direct dependencies.

...
/*I_{10}*/ mov [*address*], *index1*
/*I_{11}*/ mov [*address + 4*], *index2*
/*I_{12}*/ mov esi, *address*
/*I_{13}*/ cmp ebx, ecx
/*I_{14}*/ pushf
/*I_{15}*/ pop ebx
/*I_{16}*/ and ebx, 0x1
/*I_{17}*/ mul ebx, 0x4
/*I_{18}*/ add esi, ebx
/*I_{19}*/ mov eax, [esi]
/*I_{20}*/ jump [eax*4 + 0x10000]

(a)

...
$\text{ValueAt}(address)_{10} = index1$
$\text{ValueAt}(address + 4)_{11} = index2$
$\text{esi}_{12} = address$
$\text{eflags}_{13} = \text{Flag}(\text{ebx}_4 \text{ cmp ecx}_3)$
$\text{esp}_{14} = \text{esp}_9 - 4$
$\text{ValueAt}(\text{M1000})_{14} = \text{eflags}_{13}$
$\text{ebx}_{15} = \text{ValueAt}(\text{M1000})_{14}$
$\text{esp}_{15} = \text{esp}_{14} + 4$
$\text{ebx}_{16} = \text{ebx}_{15} \& \text{0x1}$
$\text{ebx}_{17} = \text{ebx}_{16} * \text{0x4}$
$\text{esi}_{18} = \text{esi}_{12} + \text{ebx}_{17}$
$\text{eax}_{19} = \text{ValueAt}(\text{esi}_{18})$
$\text{target}_{20} = \text{eax}_{19} * 4 + \text{0x10000}$

(b)

Figure 5: Example of code using indirection to hide control dependencies.

To resolve this issue, we must account for any number of layers of indirection. We could analyze the code, as we did here, and recognizing that it was address 5000 that was used, and not 5004. However, this requires understanding how the code works at each step, and will quickly become more difficult as code complexity increases. Instead, we add new equations to our set that define where the calculation of memory addresses come from. We introduce a new variable for each memory access, named with the prefix "LOC" followed by the actual address that was accessed. Then a new equation is added that sets the value of that new variable according to how the calculation was done. Each variable is labeled with the order number as before to guarantee that they are unique. Figure 6 shows the addition of the memory location equation (marked *) for the memory access of instruction I_{19} in Figure 5. In practice, we would add similar equations for all memory accesses. These are omitted here for the sake of clarity.

...
$\text{ValueAt}(5000)_{10} = index1$
$\text{ValueAt}(5004)_{11} = index2$
$\text{esi}_{12} = 5000$
$\text{eflags}_{13} = \text{Flag}(\text{ebx}_4 \text{ cmp ecx}_3)$
$\text{esp}_{14} = \text{esp}_9 - 4$
$\text{ValueAt}(\text{M1000})_{14} = \text{eflags}_{13}$
$\text{ebx}_{15} = \text{ValueAt}(\text{M1000})_{14}$
$\text{esp}_{15} = \text{esp}_{14} + 4$
$\text{ebx}_{16} = \text{ebx}_{15} \& \text{0x1}$
$\text{ebx}_{17} = \text{ebx}_{16} * \text{0x4}$
$\text{esi}_{18} = \text{esi}_{12} + \text{ebx}_{17}$
(*) $\text{LOC\_5000}_{19} = \text{esi}_{18}$
$\text{eax}_{19} = \text{ValueAt}(\text{LOC\_5000}_{19})$
$\text{target}_{20} = \text{eax}_{19} * 4 + \text{0x10000}$

Figure 6: Equations augmented to handle indirection.

Now, for each memory access that is used to calculate the target address, we can start a new simplified expression for the address calculation. If this calculation shows some dependency on the "Flag" operation, then we know that the target address is indirectly conditionally dependent. Any memory access simplified expression that does not show any conditional dependence can be discarded because it is irrelevant. Returning to our example in Figure 5, we calculate all simplified expressions for memory access and get the results shown in Figure 7. Here we see the conditional dependence that we expect, and can mark the indirect jump of instruction I_{20} as implementing conditional control flow.

$\text{LOC\_5000}_{19} = \text{address} + ((\text{Flag}(\text{ebx}_4 \text{ cmp ecx}_3) \& \text{0x1}) * 4)$
$\text{target}_{20} = index1 * 4 + \text{0x10000}$

Figure 7: Result of target address simplification from Figure 5.

To handle multiple layers of indirection, we must account for all dependencies. We use an algorithm that propagates information forward as it scans over the equations in the trace. At each step, all control flow dependencies, direct and indirect, are collected as described above and associated with that equation. Later, if that equation is used in a target address calculation, the complete list of dependencies is known and can be scanned for conditional dependencies. The algorithm is presented in Figure 8.

Input: *List of Equations* : EqnList
Output: *List of simplified expressions* : SimpEqnList

```
Deps = ∅
SimpEqnList = ∅
for each equation in EqnList:
    if IsConditional(equation)
    then
        Deps = Deps ∪ equation
    endif
    MemAccesses = GetMemoryAccessesForEqn(equation)
    for each memAcc in MemAccesses:
        Deps = Deps ∪ memAcc→deps
    endfor
    ExprList = SimpEqnList ∪ equation
    for each term in equation:
        replacement = FindReplacement(EqnList, term)
        if replacement != ∅
        then
            ReplaceTerm(term, replacement)
            Deps = Deps ∪ replacement→deps
        endif
        equation→deps = Deps
    endfor
endfor
return SimpEqnList
```

Figure 8: Pseudocode of simplified expression and conditional dependency identification

2.4 Relevant Call-Return Control Flow

Functions are important mechanisms for code structuring, and are often the basic building blocks of a program during the design phase. Identifying functions during reverse-engineering and deobfuscation, then, would be a useful step towards program comprehension. In the case of unobfuscated, compiler generated code, this can often be a very straightforward task. For example, x86 compatible compilers such as gcc will typically use a standard preamble for functions that saves the base pointer, then points the base pointer to the top of the stack. Knowing this information, one can search through the code for these instructions and subsequently identify the beginning of many functions in the code. However, this technique is only a convention, and in the case where the code is to be purposefully obfuscated, it need not be followed. This section discusses the behavior of function calls and returns in various forms of obfuscation, their essential properties, and explains the technique we propose for identifying them.

```
1000        call 5000            1000        push 5000
...                              1004        ret
5000        pop eax              ...
5004        mov eax, [abc0]      5000        mov eax, [abc0]

            (a)                              (b)
```

Figure 9: examples of indirect jump

2.4.1 *Behavior of Function Calls and Returns*

In general, compiler generated, unobfuscated code uses the assembly instructions call and ret for function calls and returns, respectively. However, knowing how these instructions work allows one to use them for other purposes. For example, the call instruction pushes the address of the next instruction onto the stack, then jumps to its target address. The code in Figure 9(a) uses the call to jump to code at another location, then discards the return address, effectively implementing an indirect jump. A similar technique is often used in *position independent code* (PIC-code) by using a call instruction with a target address offset of 0. The effect is that the address of the next instruction is pushed onto the stack. As another example, the ret statement pops an address off the stack, then jumps to it. The code in Figure 9(b) pushes a hard-coded value onto the stack then executes a ret. The effect, as before, is equivalent to that of an indirect jump.

```
1000          call 5000 /* → f*/        1000          push 1008
1004   /*L*/ mov ebx, [eax]             1004          jmp 5000   /* → f*/
1008          inc ebx                   1008   /*L*/ mov ebx, [eax]
...                                     100C          inc ebx
5000   /*f*/ mov eax, [abc0]            ...
5004          ret   /* → L*/            5000   /*f*/ mov eax, [abc0]
                                        5004          ret   /* → L*/

        (a) no obfuscation                      (b) simple obfuscation

1000          push 1008                 1000          push 6000
1004          mov eax, 5000             1004   /*f*/ mov esx, [abc0]
1008          jmp [eax] /* → f*/        1008          ret   /* → L*/
100c   /*L*/ mov ebx, [eax]             ...
1010          inc ebx                   6000   /*L*/ mov ebx, [eax]
...                                     6004          inc ebx
5000   /*f*/ mov eax, [abc0]
5004          pop ebx
5008          jmp [ebx]   /* → L*/

    (c) another simple obfuscation              (d) extensive obfuscation
```

Figure 10: Examples of function call/return obfuscation

Similarly, we can use other instructions to simulate the behavior of a function call and return. Figure 10(a) presents an unobfuscated function call/return pair, as might typically be seen in compiler generated code. During execution, the call instruction at address 0x1000 pushes the address of the next instruction 0x1004 onto the runtime stack, then branches to the callee by copying the function address 0x5000 to the instruction pointer. The callee, when finished, pops the return address from the stack into the instruction pointer, resuming execution at the instruction immediately following the initial call. Figure 10(b) shows a semantically equivalent code snippet that uses simple obfuscation. The call instruction has been replaced by a push instruction that saves the return address to the stack, and a jmp instruction that copies the call target to the instruction pointer. Figure 10(c) gives a slightly more obfuscated version of the same code. Here, the target of the call and the return are both saved to a register first, then a jmp instruction moves the value in the machine register to the instruction pointer. These three examples suggest a possible necessary condition for call statements – that is, that they push the address of the textually following instruction onto the runtime stack, then copy the target of the call to the instruction pointer. Existing work [8] uses this assumption to identify function boundaries, and is capable of detecting the call/return pairs in Figures 10(a) - (c).

However, Figure 10(d) gives an example of a call/return pair that does not follow the above assumption. Here, the memory layout has been changed such that the call is executed by control "falling through" to the callee without explicit branching. The return address, which is initially pushed onto the stack, points to an instruction that is no longer adjacent in memory to the call instruction. This code would not be recognized as a call/return pair by existing techniques; however, from a dynamic point of view, it arguably has the identical behavior of the code in Figure 10(b). Furthermore, there is no technical reason that the return address has to be stored on the runtime stack. A program could easily maintain its own stack-like data structure apart from the system stack. In this case, read and write operations on the memory of this separate structure would substitute for push and pop operations in the traditional implementation. Finally, the value saved to memory does not even need to be the actual return address. Rather, it could be derived from the return address by some invertible transformation, and restored to original form at the last minute before the return. We have witnessed exactly these obfuscations in our work analyzing programs obfuscated by VMProtect and CodeVirtualizer.

2.4.2 *Identification Approach*

In order to correctly identify function call/return pairs in obfuscated code, we must first identify the essential properties of such pairs that do not rely on unnecessary conditions. Traditionally, a call is indicated by pushing the return address onto the runtime stack, and branching to the callee. The return is effected by retrieving this saved address and copying it to the instruction pointer. Our examples in Figure 10 demonstrate that many of these operations, such as saving the return address to the runtime stack, are not necessary but rather convenient conventions used by compilers that do not try to hide the functionality of code. When we try to identify what is common to all cases, it is much more general. We observe that a return address, in some form, must be saved by the caller before execution hits the target function. Furthermore, the return address must be retrieved by the callee, and used so that flow of control begins at this address after execution of the function. This suggests the following semantics:

Call: a code address is saved at the call site.
Return: the saved address is used for a control transfer at the return point.

Notice that calls and returns are defined as a pair of instructions, such that they cannot be identified individually. Based on this definition, the only tie between the call and return is the function's return address. We use this as a necessary condition for function call/return pairs. This approach handles all of the cases presented in Figure 10. However, we point out that our definition does have one, known shortcoming. In the case where a function pointer (i.e., address) is stored in memory, then used later to jump to that function, these instructions will be identified as a call/return pair. Our current results are virtually unaffected by this case, since the original source makes little or no use of function pointers, and the code is compiled on a commercial compiler. However, we are currently working to find a acceptable solution to the problem.

Next, we show why the above condition, while necessary, is not sufficient. Virtualized code presents an additional and significant challenge. First, because the interpreter makes use of the aforementioned techniques such as a simulated stack in place of the runtime stack. More importantly, because the same instruction used by the interpreter to implement byte-code dispatching can be used to implement function calls and returns. Figure 11 presents a fragment of a byte-code dispatching routine generated by VMProtect (instructions unrelated to dispatching logic are ignored). In this example, esi is used as the VM's instruction pointer by the interpreter. Instructions I_1 through I_4 load the encrypted byte-code from esi, decrypt it, then I_5 uses it as an index to locate the encrypted address of a byte-code handling subroutine in a dispatching table. Instruction I_6 decrypts the address, and eventually saves it at the top of the runtime stack. Finally, a ret instruction is used–similar to the example in Figure 10(b)–to jump to the byte-code handling subroutine.

```
/*I1*/   mov al, [esi]
/*I2*/   ror al, 0x4
/*I3*/   add al, 0x3e
/*I4*/   neg al
/*I5*/   mov edx, [eax*4+0x401e34]
/*I6*/   add edx, 0x5216a67c
/*I7*/   mov [esp+0x28], edx
/*I8*/   pushfd
/*I9*/   push dword [esp+0x30]
/*I10*/  ret 0x34
```

Figure 11: Examples of byte-code dispatching in code obfuscated using VMProtect

Typically, a similar set of dispatch instructions is used for each virtual instruction encountered by the interpreter. This code clearly meets the "save and use" of a target address definition that we present above. In this case, each iteration of the interpreter would be identified as a call/return pair, which is clearly not what we want. To eliminate these false positives, we add one additional step based on the concept of relevant instructions introduced earlier. The idea behind identifying instructions that contribute to the value of system calls is to separate the instructions of the virtual machine from the those of the original code. Thus, any call/return pair for which there are no relevant instructions in the call are semantically irrelevant, and can be ignored. We present the previous definition of calls and returns, along with the condition that there be at least one relevant instruction in the function call, as necessary and sufficient conditions for identifying call/return pairs.

While these conditions may be debatable, we argue that functions are not strictly necessary for the implementation of algorithms as computer code. Rather, they are abstractions that allow human programmers to more easily design and implement solutions. As such, it may be possible to generate assembly level code that meets our definition of a call/return pair, that was not intended by the programmer as an actual call to a function. Such cases are inevitable when analyzing the implementation of something that is, by definition, an abstraction. In these cases, we believe that any pairs that meet our definition are as good as intended call/return pairs.

With these conditions, identifying function call/return pairs becomes straightforward: identify all the address save/use pairs as candidates of function call/return pairs, then remove candidates that enclose no relevant instructions (as previously identified by value-based dependence analysis). The algorithm is shown in Figure 12.

2.5 Relevant Dynamic Trace

The final step is building the relevant subtrace. We use order numbers to combine the results of the previous steps in a meaningful way. The order number is a unique number for each instance of an instruction in the original dynamic trace that represents the order that instruction appears. Instructions labeled relevant because they contributed to the value of the system call parameters are added to the relevant subtrace in order. For call/return pairs, we add standard call and ret instructions at the appropriate locations, regardless of the obfuscated implementation. This works well because the original program is typically generated by a compiler using standard conventions. Similarly, for conditional control flow, we add a generic branch statement that will match with any standard branch statements.

```
Input: T : Trace
Output: P : List of identified call/return pairs
for u = sizeof(T) to 1 do:
    if instruction T[u] is indirect jump to address d
      AND T[u] is not marked as SAVE
      AND T[u] is not used as a DLL call
    then
      s = u;
      relevant_count = 0
      while s ≥ 1 do:
          if T[s] is relevant
          then
            relevant_count++;
          if T[s] initially saves d
          then
            mark T[s] as SAVE;
            mark T[u] as USE;
            if relevant_count > 0
            then
              /* call/return found */
              save (s, u) in P;
            break;
          else
            s--;
    else
      continue;
return P;
```

Figure 12: Pseudocode of function call/return identification algorithm

3. EXPERIMENTAL EVALUATION

3.1 Experimental Methodology

The evaluation of our approach to deobfuscation presents several significant problems that must be addressed. In essence, these problems point back to our previous discussion of program equivalence (see Section 2.2). We have argued that *observational equivalence* is a reasonable goal, but testing for such an equivalence can be difficult. It is necessary to identify the system calls, *and* the instructions that affect their parameters. To see why the system calls alone, or the calls and the values of their parameters are not enough, consider the following example. A program that takes 2 integers and outputs their sum will produce the same output as a program that takes two integers and outputs their product, if the inputs to both programs are 2 and 2. In its simplest form, the only system call required is the print statement.

Even if we take into account the relevant instructions, we need to account for them properly. Previous work by Sharif, *et al* [13] has built control flow graphs for the original program and the deobfuscated program to demonstrate similarity between the two. This approach becomes more difficult as the programs get larger and more complex. Furthermore, the idea is less applicable to our work than theirs. They use knowledge of the interpreter to identify where original instructions are stored in memory. In those cases where their code is applicable, they are able to recover most or all of the original instructions. Since we identify relevant instructions, control flow graphs of our results will not show the structure resulting from things like dead code, or branches not taken.

To further complicate this idea, there is no guarantee that the obfuscator will use the same instructions from the original program. We have seen how VMProtect and CodeVirtualizer rewrite call's as other semantically equivalent instructions. It is possible that obfuscators may rewrite other instructions. For example, the obfuscator may unroll some loops to hide part of the control flow graph, or it may rewrite a multiply operation as a loop of adds so that new control flow structure is found in the obfuscated code. Quantifying these differences likely will be impractical.

Unfortunately, we do not have a perfect solution to the problem, so we present an imperfect solution that we try to tune to what we know about the current state of virtualization-obfuscated code. Our approach is to treat the traces and relevant subtraces as sequences. We can then use known sequence matching algorithms to compare one trace to another. This approach is robust to the idea that we cannot recover the original code precisely. Matching will give us a score for our deobfuscation, regardless of how good our results are. These scores can be compared on a relative basis. While still imprecise, a score that is significantly higher than another should correspond to better matching.

This approach is also fairly flexible, and allows us to handle several of the issues presented by program equivalence. First of all, we know that the current virtualization programs that we examined rewrite library calls and some conditional branches using semantically equivalent instructions. It is a simple matter to replace library call implementations with a call statement at the appropriate place in the trace. Similarly, conditional branch implementations can be replaced with a generic jcc instruction that will match any conditional branch from the original code. Since the original code is compiled by a commercial compiler and will typically use a these standard instructions, this is a reasonable step, and provides good results. This approach also allows us to handle other instances of semantically equivalent instructions. For example, it is possible that an increment instruction could be rewritten as an add instruction. We can build equivalency classes into our matching algorithm as appropriate, so that an increment matches an instruction that adds one. In doing so, we are moving closer to the idea of comparing the behavior of two traces, and not their actual implementation. This idea is more robust and matches the intent behind program equivalence, since these cases truly are equivalent.

In addition to considering instruction operation equivalences, we must also consider how instruction operands are handled. This issue is especially relevant in the context of virtualization-obfuscated code. Due to the nature of the stack based approach used in the obfuscation programs we examined, it is possible, even likely, that the operands of the instructions will be different than in the original program. For example, in the sample files that we tested, VMProtect uses the esi register as the virtual machine instruction pointer. In CodeVirtualizer, the addresses of virtual instructions are always loaded into the al register. In both cases, the values to be operated on are stored on the virtual stack, and popped into machine registers when needed. There is no technical reason why the virtual machine would try to move these operands into the same registers that were used in the original code. To handle this, we cannot include the operands in the matching algorithm. Instead, we use only the opcode (add, call, etc.) to represent the instruction.

Next, we must consider to what we will match our results. We need to generate a trace of the original program on the same inputs. In order to present an unbiased representation of the original program, we must limit the amount of processing and analysis that is done to this trace. At the same time, we do not want to include instructions that may taint our results. As a result, we eliminate all instructions that result from library calls from both the original trace and the obfuscated trace. There are also a number of instructions that are part of the operating system initialization, and are included in every execution trace. We eliminate these instructions from both the original and obfuscated traces.

The matching algorithm itself is straightforward. Like our analysis, we use the knowledge of system calls as a guide. The traces are broken into segments, where a segment includes all instructions up to and including the next system call, or the end of the trace. In the case where the system calls between traces do not match exactly, we use the subset of calls that form a one-to-one correspondence between the two traces. Segments are then matched, and all segments are aggregated. A matching provides a score representing how many instructions from the original trace appear in either the obfuscated subtrace or our relevant subtrace.

As a final step, we wish to calculate how effective our analysis has been. To do this, we must take into account two competing factors. First, our analysis is trying to identify as many instructions from the original trace as possible. At the same time, we are trying to eliminate as many virtual machine instructions as we can. To this end, we present two numbers for each test. The first, which we call the *relevance score*, is the percentage of the instructions from the original trace that are included in the relevant subtrace. The second, which we call the *obfuscation score*, is the percentage of instructions added by the obfuscator that are correctly excluded from the relevant subtrace. It is easy to optimize either of these values individually, but achieving good (i.e., close to 100%) scores for both is difficult, and will provide a fair evaluation of our work.

Taking into account the above discussion and concerns, we present the following methodology for evaluating our analysis:

1. Original source code of a test program is compiled into an executable.
2. A dynamic trace is generated for the original executable on some input set.
3. An original subtrace is generated by including only instructions from the executable module.
4. The executable file is protected using an available virtualization-obfuscation technique.
5. A dynamic trace is generated for the obfuscated version of the executable.
6. We perform our analysis per Section 2 on the obfuscated subtrace, and generate a relevant subtrace.
7. The obfuscated subtrace is matched to the original subtrace, and scores are produced.
8. The relevant subtrace is matched to the original subtrace, and scores are produced.
9. The relevance score and obfuscation score are calculated.
10. The process is repeated for all combinations of virtualization-obfuscation techniques and input test files.

3.2 Experimental Results

To evaluate our analysis, we tested three toy programs simple enough that results could be checked by hand–an iterative factorial implementation, a matrix multiplaction program with double nested loops, and a recursive fibonacci implementation. We also tested two samples of malicious code–BullMoose and hunatcha–whose C source code was available from the VX Heavens web

Table 1: Results for programs obfuscated with VMProtect

Name	Original trace size	Obfuscated trace size	Relevant trace size	relevant matching	Rel. Score	Obf. Score
factorial	92	15365	222	54	58.7%	99.0%
matrx_mult	651	138798	597	345	53.0%	99.8%
fibonacci	151	16438	167	63	41.7%	99.4%
BullMoose	94	6900	376	36	38.3%	95.0%
hunatcha	2226	3327	1347	1347	60.5%	100.0%
md5	2257	77219	5347	1700	75.3%	95.1%

Table 2: Results for programs obfuscated with CodeVirtualizer

Name	Original trace size	Obfuscated trace size	Relevant trace size	relevant matching	Rel Score	Obf Score
factorial	92	172249	48720	56	60.9%	71.7%
matrx_mult	651	1571686	270143	454	69.7%	82.8%
fibonacci	151	223053	18560	102	67.5%	91.7%
BullMoose	94	120982	32817	67	71.3%	72.9%
hunatcha	2226	3881611	1066993	1524	68.5%	72.5%
md5	2257	5732714	2613431	2099	93.0%	54.4%

site [1]. Finally, we tested a simple benchmark utility that performs the md5 checksum. The results of our analysis on VMProtect obfuscated code are shown in Table 1 and the results of our analysis on CodeVirtualizer obfuscated code are shown in Table 2.

Table 1 shows that for most of our test programs, our analysis is able to identify better than half of the original programs instructions, while in all cases eliminating over 90% of the obfuscation introduced by VMProtect. Similarly, Table 2 shows even better results, identifying on average about 70% of original program instructions from CodeVirtualizer obfuscated code. However, our analysis fairs worse, eliminating about 75% of obfuscation instructions on average. Overall, these results are encouraging, since our approach only identifies those instructions that affect the behavior of the program. We anticipate that many of the "missed" instructions are performing functions like allocating memory or initializing data structures, and will not be caught by our analysis under any conditions. Hand analysis reveals that some of the missed instructions result from instruction implementations whose equivalences (see Section 3.1) were not anticipated. For example, some push and pop instructions were replaced with mov.

We note that, unlike the rest of our test programs, we were not able to achieve our results for the md5 benchmark program through totally automated means. The analysis of this program, even on the unprotected version, used excessive amounts of memory and crashed. The problem resulted from some of the return values of early calls to fopen and fread functions being used in later calculations. The resulting expressions were not able to be simplified easily by our equational reasoning system, which resulted in larger and larger expressions being generated late in the dynamic trace. We would also like to note, however, that our equational reasoning system allowed us to identify this problem easily, and also to select these function call return values for manual simplification. We were able to make these simplifications in about an hour, and feel that the results were still worth reporting.

We examined the results by hand, and found the reason for the lower obfuscation scores on CodeVirtualizer files as compared to VMProtect files. CodeVirtualizer uses an interesting technique that artificially creates a dependency between some original program instructions and the virtual machine interpreter instructions. We believe that this may result from the use of constant values that are stored in memory, and manipulated to add obfuscation. For example, instructions that require the constant 1, may instead use a reference to a variable that holds the value 1. Furthermore, if this variable is modified every time it is used (e.g., it is incremented then decremented just before use), this will create an artificial dependency between the use of the value, and all previous instances of manipulation. Of course, the obfuscator cannot change the function of the original program, so we believe these dependencies can be identified. We have had some success using code simplification techniques such as constant propagation and arithmetic simplification, but work on this issue continues.

The results in both tables also show the extraordinary increase in the number of executed instructions for both obfuscators. Our toy fibonacci program, for example, executes 151 instructions in the original trace. However, the VMProtect obfuscated version executes 16,438 instructions, and the CodeVirtualizer obfuscated version executes 223,053.

4. DEFEATING OUR ANALYSIS

The previous discussion begins to answer an obvious question: how would an attacker defeat our analysis? We must assume that once our analysis is known, malware authors will attempt to exploit its vulnerabilities. Our analysis is highly dependent on the output of our equational reasoning system, which attempts to build simplified equations for each instruction in the dynamic trace. In the case of the md5 analysis, we have seen how calls to fopen and fread could not be simplified away, leading to longer and longer expressions later in the trace of both the unprotected and protected versions of the test file. We have similar results when analyzing the CodeVirtualizer protected versions of code, which stores important values in encrypted form in memory, then decrypts these values before use. The decryption routine is difficult to simplify, and if properly chosen, could similarly cause runtime and memory usage issues in the equational reasoning system. Hence, any such algorithm, embedded in the code, that cannot be simplified away has the potential to cripple our analysis by making the problem impractical.

We have also seen how CodeVirtualizer builds artificial dependencies between the virtual machine code and the original program code. Since our analysis is based on the idea of separating these two sets of instructions, successfully building such dependencies has the effect of thwarting the analysis. If done properly, it may be possible to build such dependencies between most, or all, instructions in the trace, thus driving our obfuscation scores toward 0%. Because the obfuscation cannot change the function of the original program, we speculate that such dependencies can, in theory, be identified and handled. However, to date, we have not explored this idea in depth, and leave such analysis for future work.

5. RELATED WORK

The deobfuscation of code obfuscated using virtualization obfuscators has been discussed by Rolles [12], Sharif *et al.* [13], and Falliere [6]. These works follow the outside-in approach outlined in Section 1. Lau discusses the use of dynamic binary translation to deal with virtualization obfuscators [9].

There has been some work, in the programming language community, on using a technique called *partial evaluation* [7] for code specialization, in particular for specializing away interpretive code. However, the literature assumes that the program analysis and transformation are static, which suggests that its application to highly obfuscated malware binaries may not be straightforward.

The notion of obfuscation through virtualization has some similarities with the idea of *control flow flattening* [17]. Udupa *et al.* discuss techniques for deobfuscating code that has been subjected to this transformation [15]. These techniques are static, and therefore very different from the ideas presented here.

There is a rich body of work on various sorts of dependence analysis in the program analysis literature. The notion of ud-chains for relating uses and definitions of variables during static program analysis is well-established [2]. There is an extensive body of literature on program slicing [14], but as discussed earlier this technique seems too imprecise for our needs.

6. CONCLUSIONS

Virtualization-obfuscated programs are difficult to reverse engineer because examining the machine instructions of the program, either statically or dynamically, does little to shed light on the program's logic, which is hidden in the interpreted byte-code. Prior approaches to reverse-engineering virtualization-obfuscated programs typically work by first reverse engineering the byte-code interpreter, and then working back from this to work out the logic embedded in the byte code. This paper describes a different approach that focuses on identifying the flow of values to system call instructions. This new approach can be applied to a larger number of obfuscated binaries because it makes fewer assumptions about the nature of the virtual machine interpreter, and still produces good results on test files including two malware executables and one benchmark utility. On average, we identify 50% to 75% of instructions from the original program, while eliminating approximately 75% to 90% of instructions added by the obfuscator.

The system works by gradually adding instructions that are calculated to be of importance, and adding these to a relevant subtrace that represents the behavior of the original, unobfuscated program. Instructions that contribute to the values of system call arguments are included, as are call/return pairs, and conditional control flow statements. We note that our analysis only identifies conditional control flow statements of the original program that appear in the dynamic trace, and, thus, misses code paths that are not executed. In principle, it should be possible to extend multi-path analysis techniques (see, e.g., [10]) to the conditionals so identified. In practice, our intuition is that this will likely be challenging because virtualization-based obfuscation will mean that identifying path constraints (as in Moser et al's work) will not be straightforward. The issue is beyond the scope of this work, but would be interesting and relevant for future work.

Acknowledgements

This work was supported in part by the National Science Foundation via grant no. CNS-1016058, as well as by a GAANN fellowship from the Department of Education award no. P200A070545.

7. REFERENCES

[1] VX Heavens, 2011. `http://vx.netlux.org/`.

[2] A. V. Aho, R. Sethi, and J. D. Ullman. *Compilers – Principles, Techniques, and Tools*. Addison-Wesley, Reading, Mass., 1985.

[3] F. Bellard. QEMU, a fast and portable dynamic translator. In *USENIX Annual Technical Conference, FREENIX Track*, pages 41–46. USENIX, 2005.

[4] K. Coogan and S. Debray. Equational reasoning on x86 assembly code. *Source Code Analysis and Manipulation, IEEE International Workshop on*, 2011.

[5] A. Dinaburg, P. Royal, M. I. Sharif, and W. Lee. Ether: malware analysis via hardware virtualization extensions. In *Proceedings of the 2008 ACM Conference on Computer and Communications Security, CCS 2008, Alexandria, Virginia, USA, October 27-31, 2008*, pages 51–62, 2008.

[6] N. Falliere. Inside the jaws of Trojan.Clampi. Technical report, Symantec Corp., Nov. 2009.

[7] N. D. Jones, C. K. Gomard, and P. Sestoft. *Partial Evaluation and Automatic Program Generation*. Prentice Hall, 1993.

[8] A. Lakhotia, E. U. Kumar, and M. Venable. A method for detecting obfuscated calls in malicious binaries. *IEEE Transactions on Software Engineering*, 31(11):955–968, 2005.

[9] B. Lau. Dealing with virtualization packer. In *Second CARO Workshop on Packers, Decryptors, and Obfuscators*, May 2008.

[10] A. Moser, C. Kruegel, and E. Kirda. Exploring multiple execution paths for malware analysis. In *SP '07: Proceedings of the 2007 IEEE Symposium on Security and Privacy*, pages 231–245, 2007.

[11] Oreans Technologies. Code virtualizer: Total obfuscation against reverse engineering, Dec. 2008. `http://www.oreans.com/codevirtualizer.php`.

[12] R. Rolles. Unpacking virtualization obfuscators. In *Proc. 3rd USENIX Workshop on Offensive Technologies (WOOT '09)*, Aug. 2009.

[13] M. Sharif, A. Lanzi, J. Giffin, and W. Lee. Automatic reverse engineering of malware emulators. In *Proc. 2009 IEEE Symposium on Security and Privacy*, May 2009.

[14] F. Tip. A survey of program slicing techniques. *Journal of Programming Languages*, 3:121–189, 1995.

[15] S. K. Udupa, S. K. Debray, and M. Madou. Deobfuscation: Reverse engineering obfuscated code. In *Proc. 12th IEEE Working Conference on Reverse Engineering*, pages 45–54, Nov. 2005.

[16] VMProtect Software. Vmprotect software protection, 2008. `http://vmpsoft.com/`.

[17] C. Wang, J. Davidson, J. Hill, and J. Knight. Protection of software-based survivability mechanisms. In *Proc. International Conference of Dependable Systems and Networks*, July 2001.

The Power of Procrastination: Detection and Mitigation of Execution-Stalling Malicious Code

Clemens Kolbitsch
Vienna University of Technology
Vienna, Austria
ck@iseclab.org

Engin Kirda
Northeastern University
Boston, MA, USA
ek@ccs.neu.edu

Christopher Kruegel
UC Santa Barbara
Santa Barbara, CA, USA
chris@cs.ucsb.edu

Abstract

Malware continues to remain one of the most important security problems on the Internet today. Whenever an anti-malware solution becomes popular, malware authors typically react promptly and modify their programs to evade defense mechanisms. For example, recently, malware authors have increasingly started to create malicious code that can evade dynamic analysis.

One recent form of evasion against dynamic analysis systems is *stalling code*. Stalling code is typically executed before any malicious behavior. The attacker's aim is to delay the execution of the malicious activity long enough so that an automated dynamic analysis system fails to extract the interesting malicious behavior. This paper presents the first approach to detect and mitigate malicious stalling code, and to ensure forward progress within the amount of time allocated for the analysis of a sample. Experimental results show that our system, called HASTEN, works well in practice, and that it is able to detect additional malicious behavior in real-world malware samples.

Categories and Subject Descriptors

D.4.6 [**Operating Systems**]: Security and Protection

General Terms

Security

Keywords

Malware Analysis, Evasion, Emulation

1. INTRODUCTION

Malicious software (malware) is the driving force behind many security problems on the web. For example, a large fraction of the world's email spam is sent by botnets [16], Trojan programs steal account credentials for online banking sites [27], and malware programs participate in click fraud campaigns and distributed denial of service attacks [15].

Malware research is an arms race. As new anti-malware solutions are introduced, attackers are updating their malicious code to evade analysis and detection. For example, when signature-based anti-virus scanners became widely adopted, attackers started to use code obfuscation and encryption to thwart detection. As a consequence, researchers and security vendors shifted to techniques that focus on the runtime (dynamic) behavior of malware.

An important enabler for behavior-based malware detection are dynamic analysis systems (such as ANUBIS [2], CW-SANDBOX [3], NORMAN SANDBOX [4], and TEMU [25]). These systems execute a captured malware program in a controlled environment and record its actions (such as system calls, API calls, and network traffic). Based on the collected information, one can decide on the malicious nature of a program, prioritize manual analysis efforts [8], and automatically derive models that capture malware behaviors [14, 19]. Such models can then be deployed to protect end-users' machines.

As dynamic analysis systems have become more popular, malware authors have responded by devising techniques to ensure that their programs do not reveal any malicious activity when executed in such an automated analysis environment. Clearly, when malware does not show any unwanted activity during analysis, no detection models can be extracted. For anti-malware researchers, these evasion attempts pose a significant problem in practice.

A common approach to thwart dynamic analysis is to identify the environment in which samples are executed. To this end, a malware program uses checks (so-called red pills) to determine whether it is being executed in a virtual machine [13, 24] or a system emulator such as Qemu [20, 22, 23]. Whenever a malware program is able to detect that it is running inside such an environment, it can simply exit.

Reacting to the evasive checks (red pills), researchers have proposed more transparent analysis environments [11, 12]. Another approach has focused on the detection of differences between the execution of a program in a virtual platform and on real hardware [6, 17]. When such a discrepancy is identified, the checks responsible for the difference can be removed. Finally, systems that perform multi-path exploration [9, 21] or that identify "malicious triggers" [10] can detect and bypass checks that guard malicious activity.

In the next step of the arms race, malware authors have begun to introduce *stalling code* into their malicious programs. This stalling code is executed before any malicious behavior – regardless of the execution environment. The purpose of such evasive code is to delay the execution of malicious activity long enough so that automated analysis systems give up on a sample, incorrectly assuming that the program is non-functional, or does not execute any action of interest. It is important to observe that the problem of stalling code affects *all* analysis systems, even those that are fully transparent. Moreover, stalling code does not have to perform any checks.

Thus, systems that aim to detect malware triggers or that explore multiple execution paths do not reveal any additional behaviors.

With stalling code, attackers exploit two common properties of automated malware analysis systems: First, the time that a system can spend to execute a single sample is limited. Typically, an automated malware analysis system will terminate the analysis of a sample after several minutes. This is because the system has to make a trade-off between the information that can be obtained from a single sample, and the total number of samples that can be analyzed every day. Second, malware authors can craft their code so that the execution takes much longer inside the analysis environment than on an actual victim host. Thus, even though a sample might stall and not execute any malicious activity in an analysis environment for a long time (many minutes), the delay perceived on the victim host is only a few seconds. This is important because malware authors consider delays on a victim's machine as risky. The reason is that the malicious process is more likely to be detected or terminated by anti-virus software, an attentive user, or a system reboot.

In this paper, we present the first approach to detect and evade malicious stalling code, and to ensure forward progress within the amount of time allocated for the analysis of a sample. To this end, we introduce techniques to detect when a malware sample is not making sufficient progress during analysis. When such a situation is encountered, our system automatically examines the sample to identify the code regions that are likely responsible for stalling the execution. For these code regions (and these regions only), costly logging is disabled. When this is not sufficient, we force the execution to take a path that skips (exits) the previously-identified stalling code.

We implemented our approach in HASTEN, an extension for ANUBIS, our dynamic analysis system. Our experimental evaluation shows that HASTEN is effective in practice and can reveal additional behavior in real-world malware.

This paper makes the following contributions:

- We present the first approach to detect and deal with malicious stalling code in real-world malware, and to ensure forward progress within the amount of time allocated for the analysis of a malware sample.

- We propose HASTEN, a dynamic analysis system extension to detect and *passively* mitigate the impact of stalling code. To this end, we identify stalling code regions and execute them with reduced logging.

- We introduce an *active* extension to HASTEN that forces the execution of the malware to take a path that skips the previously-identified stalling code. This helps in cases where reduced logging is not sufficient.

2. PROBLEM DESCRIPTION

In this section, we discuss the problem of stalling code in more detail, and we show a real-world code example that implements such a mechanism.

2.1 Definition

We define a *stalling code region* as a sequence of instructions that fulfills two properties: First, the sequence of instructions runs considerably slower inside the analysis environment than on a real (native) host. In this context, "considerably slower" means that the slowdown is large compared to the average slowdown that the sandbox incurs for normal, benign programs. Examples of slow operations are system call invocations (because of additional logging overhead) and machine instructions that are particularly costly to emulate (e.g., floating point operations or MMX code).

```
unsigned count, t;

void helper() {
 t = GetTickCount();
 t++;
 t++;
 t = GetTickCount();
}
void delay() {
 count=0x1;
 do {
  helper();
  count++;
 } while
  (count!=0xe4e1c1);
}
```

Figure 1: Stalling code in W32.DelfInj

The second property of stalling code is that its entire execution must take a non-negligible amount of time. Here, non-negligible has to be put into relation with the total time allocated for the automated analysis of a program. For example, for a dynamic analysis system, this could be in the order of a few minutes. Thus, we expect the stalling code to run for at least several seconds. Otherwise, the analysis results would not be significantly affected. That is, when an instruction sequence finishes within a few milliseconds instead of microseconds, we do not consider this as stalling code.

Clearly, an attacker could create stalling code that stalls execution on the real host in the same way it does in the analysis environment. For example, the attacker could use sleep calls, or create high amounts of activity to delay execution. However, in practice, execution delays using sleep-like functions can be easily skipped, and delaying execution (for example, by raising the volume of activity) increases chances of being detected and terminated on a victim host.

Intuitively, our definitions imply that stalling code contains "slow" operations (to satisfy the first property), and that these operations are repeated many times (to satisfy the second property). As a result, attackers typically implement stalling code as loops that contain slow operations (and we will sometimes refer to stalling code as *stalling loops* in this paper).

2.2 Example of Stalling Code

Figure 1 shows a stalling loop implemented by real-world malware. This code was taken from a sample that was first submitted to the Anubis analysis system in February 2010. As the sample was only available in binary format, we reverse engineered the malware program and manually produced equivalent C code. Since the executable did not contain symbol information, we introduced names for variables and functions to make the code more readable. To determine the malware family that this sample belongs to, we submitted it to the popular VirusTotal service. VirusTotal uses around 40 anti-virus (AV) tools to scan each uploaded sample. All 40 AV scanners considered the file to be malicious, and most tools labeled our sample as *Trojan Win32.DelfInj*.

As can be seen in Figure 1, the code contains a number of unnecessary calculations involving the return value of the Windows `GetTickCount` function. According to documentation provided by Microsoft [5], `GetTickCount` "retrieves the number of milliseconds that have elapsed since the system was started, up to 49.7 days." It is typically used to measure the time that elapses between two events. In this scenario, however, the repeated invocations are not useful. In fact, the value of the variable `tick` is simply overwritten by subsequent calls to `GetTickCount`. Moreover, this loop is executed 15 million times. This strongly supports the intuition that the purpose of this code is to stall execution.

When the code shown in Figure 1 is run natively on a real processor, the loop executes and terminates in a matter of milliseconds.

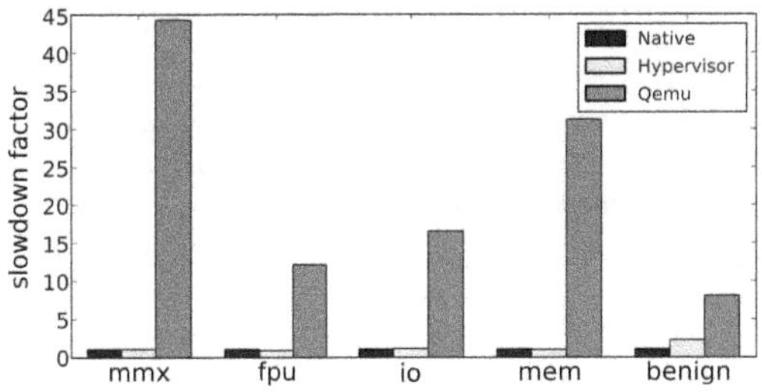

Figure 2: Slowdown for native, hypervisor-based, and emulated (Qemu) execution (native = baseline).

Interestingly, on the Qemu system emulator, the execution time is not significantly higher. This is because of the way in which the `GetTickCount` function is implemented on Windows. Instead of invoking an expensive system call to retrieve the number of milliseconds elapsed since system start-up, this value can be read directly from a kernel memory page that is mapped (read-only) into the address space of all user programs (the counter is updated periodically by the operating system).

Analyzing the stalling code inside ANUBIS, our Qemu-based dynamic analysis environment, yields a completely different result. In ANUBIS, `GetTickCount` is monitored and, thus, the system invokes a pair of log functions for each call to `GetTickCount` (one before the call, and one after returning). These log functions extract and write detailed information about the monitored function call. For the stalling code in Figure 1, this means that the logging functions of our analysis system are called 60 million times. Our estimates show that this would take about ten hours, which means that the attacker can successfully evade the analysis.

Note that excluding `GetTickCount` from the list of monitored functions would provide a solution in this specific example. However, the general problem that we address in this paper would still remain. We discovered various other samples in the wild that invoke different functions that are frequently monitored (such as `WriteFile`), and we cannot generally ignore them all. Furthermore, attackers can implement stalling code without targeting the overhead introduced by the monitoring system and instead make use of instructions that are particularly slow to emulate. Figure 2 shows four examples of programs that make heavy use of FPU, MMX, IO, and memory operations, each experiencing a significant slowdown (up to a factor of 45). In comparison, for benign applications average overheads stay below a factor of 10.

3. SYSTEM OVERVIEW

In this section, we present a high-level overview of HASTEN. The goal of our system is to detect stalling loops and to mitigate their effect on the analysis results produced by a sandbox (such as ANUBIS). In particular, our system must ensure that the analysis makes sufficient progress during the allocated analysis timeframe so that we can expose as much malicious activity as possible. To this end, HASTEN can operate in three modes: monitoring, passive, and active mode.

Monitoring mode. When the analysis of a malware sample is launched, HASTEN operates in monitoring mode. In this mode, the system performs lightweight observation of all threads of the process under analysis. The goal is to measure the *progress* of each thread, and to identify instances in which the execution might have entered a stalling region.

Passive mode. When the monitoring mode detects insufficient progress, this is typically due to slow operations that are executed many times. Thus, as a first step, HASTEN attempts to identify the code region that is repeatedly executed. To this end, our system starts to dynamically record information about the addresses of instructions (code blocks) that are executed. Using these addresses, we build a (partial) control flow graph (CFG) of the non-progressing thread. This CFG is then searched for loops.

Intuitively, the code that is identified by this process represents the stalling loop(s). For example, in the code snippet in Figure 1, our tool would identify the *do-while* loop in the `delay` function (Line 11-15). The stalling code region would also include the `helper` function (L. 3-8), since it is invoked inside the body of the loop (L. 12). Note that our system uses inter-procedural control flow analysis for loop detection. This allows us to handle cases in which a loop is not part of a single function, but the result of recursive function calls.

Once the stalling loop is identified, HASTEN adapts its analysis for this code region. More precisely, we first whitelist the code that is part of the stalling region. Note that this whitelist covers *only* those instructions (basic blocks) that have been executed previously by the malware. Thus, parts of a stalling loop that have not been executed before are not whitelisted. In the next step, the system limits (or turns off) detailed malware introspection for the whitelisted code regions. This approach significantly reduces (or removes) the overhead that is introduced by the analysis environment.

The passive mode is called "passive" because we do not interfere with the malware execution; we only modify the analysis environment to accelerate stalling loops.

Active mode. When HASTEN operates in active mode, it actively interferes with the execution of the binary. In particular, the tool attempts to force a stalling loop to exit (or, more precisely, to follow a code path that exits the whitelisted region that the previous analysis has identified; this might force execution into parts of a stalling loop that have not yet been executed). To this end, our system uses the previously-constructed CFG and identifies all nodes associated with conditional jumps that are *(i)* part of the stalling loop and that *(ii)* have one successor node that is not part of the whitelisted code region. That is, we identify all nodes through which there exists a path that exits the stalling code. At the next loop iteration, when such a conditional jump is encountered, HASTEN flips the check that this instruction implements (e.g., a *less-than* would be converted into a *greater-or-equal*). Hence, the thread is forced to continue execution along a path outside the stalling region.

Altering the flow of execution of a program (such as prematurely preempting a loop or following an "unexplored" path within the loop) can leave this program in an inconsistent state. Referring back to our example in Figure 1, one can see that the variable `count` will not have the expected value (`0xe4e1c1`) when HASTEN forces the loop to exit. This might be irrelevant, but at the same time, there is a possibility that it could also lead to program crashes. Malware authors could leverage these inconsistencies to expose the analysis system. For example, consider an attacker that calls `check`, shown in Figure 3, after the `delay` function (from Figure 1). If our system would preempt the loop, this comparison

```
// H4X0r: make sure delay loop was not interrupted
void check() {
 if (count!=0xe4e1c1) exit();
}
```

Figure 3: Malware code to check that the delay loop has not been interrupted.

would succeed, and the malware would terminate without revealing any additional malicious behavior.

To overcome this problem, our approach is as follows: Before we exit a whitelisted code region, we first analyze this region for all variables (memory locations) that the code writes as part of a computation (logic and arithmetic instructions). These memory locations are then marked with a special label (tainted), indicating that their true value is *unknown*. Whenever a machine instruction uses a tainted value as source operand, the destination is tainted as well. For this, we leverage the fact that we have implemented our prototype solution on an emulator-based analysis platform that already supports data flow (taint) tracking.

Whenever a tainted variable is used in a comparison operation or in an indirect memory access (using this variable as part of the address computation), HASTEN temporarily halts the execution of the malware process. It then extracts a backward slice that ends at the comparison instruction and that, when executed, will compute the correct value for this variable. To obtain this slice, we leverage a tool that we previously developed [18]. Once the slice is extracted, it is executed on a native machine. As a result, this computation does not incur any overhead compared to the execution on a real victim host.

4. MONITORING MODE

The goal of the monitoring mode is to determine whether a malware process has entered a stalling code region. To this end, HASTEN monitors the *progress* of a program under analysis. More precisely, the system monitors, for each thread, the frequencies, types, and return codes of all (native) system calls that this thread invokes.

System calls are the mechanism through which a process interacts with its environment and the operating system. Also, to perform security-critical tasks (such as spawning new processes, modifying files, or contacting network services), a program *must* invoke at least one system call. Thus, we believe that it is reasonable to monitor the progress of a running program by inspecting the system calls that it invokes. Moreover, all system calls use the same convention to report errors. That is, there are well-specified values that indicate a successful, or erroneous, invocation. This makes it easy to determine whether a system call has been successful or not (which is useful knowledge when reasoning about the progress of a process). Finally, almost all analysis systems already support the monitoring of system calls, and typically, this data can be collected efficiently.

Detecting progress. To measure the progress of a process, HASTEN periodically evaluates the system calls that each of its threads invokes. More precisely, after a thread has been scheduled for a time interval of length t, the system employs five simple detectors to evaluate the system calls that have been observed during that last period. Whenever one or more of these detectors reports insufficient progress, the system is switched into passive mode (explained in more detail in the following Section 5).

When choosing a concrete value for the time interval t, we need to balance two ends: Large values are more resistant against short sequences of unusual, repeated behavior; small values allow faster detection of abnormal activity. For our experiments, we have chosen a value of $t = 5$ seconds. This allows us to evaluate the progress multiple times during an analysis run (which is typically a few minutes) and yielded good results in our experiments. Our five detectors are discussed in the paragraphs below:

Detector for too few successful system calls: We expect to see a reasonably large number of successful system calls that reflect the normal interactions of a process with its environment and the OS. Thus, when our system does not observe any system calls (or too few of them), this is an indication of insufficient progress. This detector simply computes the total number of *successful* system calls S_s within the time interval t. An alarm is raised when this number is lower than a threshold $S_s < S_{min,s}$.

Detector for too many successful system calls: Interestingly, there is also the possibility that a malware process invokes too many system calls, even though no progress is made. Usually, the number of system calls a program executes is limited by the necessary data processing in between two calls, or delays introduced while waiting for IO completion. With some stalling loops, however, malware authors try to exploit the logging overhead of the analysis system and rapidly issue many calls. For this, one would typically select system calls that finish very quickly (e.g., NTCREATESEMAPHORE, as it does not need to wait for IO completion). This detector recognizes such attempts. An alarm is raised when the number of successful system calls exceeds a certain threshold $S_s > S_{max,s}$.

Detector for too many failed system calls: Of course, it is also possible to overload a sandbox with many invalid system calls (i.e., system calls with incorrect parameters). Invalid calls are quickly caught by the kernel, which checks the validity of the parameters (e.g., pointers should not be `NULL`) early on. Hence, they execute very fast on a victim host. Unfortunately, they still incur the full logging overhead on the analysis platform. Thus, this detector raises an alarm when the number of failed system calls exceeds a certain threshold $S_f > S_{max,f}$.

Detector for too many identical system calls: The previous two detectors identify cases in which stalling code attempts to overload the sandbox with excessive numbers of system calls. A more cautious attacker could attempt to hide stalling code by issuing fewer system calls (that stay under our thresholds) and inject additional computations between the call sites. However, even in this case, it is likely that we will observe the same (small) set of calls repeated many times (executed in a loop). This is different from normal program execution, where a program invokes more diverse system calls. The detector for identical system calls recognizes cases where most system calls seen within interval t belong to a small set. To this end, we compute the entropy S_e of the set of system calls during t. An alarm is raised when the entropy is below a threshold $S_e < S_{min,e}$.

Detector for too diverse system calls: To thwart the previous detector, a malware author could choose to execute a series of *randomly* chosen system calls to artificially increase the entropy. Although the stealth implementation of such an approach seems difficult (considering the detector for too many failed system calls), we add an additional detector that raises an alarm when the entropy exceeds a threshold that is atypical for normal program executions: $S_e > S_{max,e}$.

In our experiments, we found that the previously-described detectors are successful in identifying stalling code in real-world malware. However, if necessary, it is easy to develop additional heuristics and integrate them into our system.

Parameter computation. The choice of concrete parameter values used by the five detectors ($S_{min,s}$, $S_{max,s}$, $S_{max,f}$, $S_{min,e}$, and $S_{max,e}$) determines how often the system is switched into passive mode. When the thresholds are set too low, HASTEN might enter passive mode more often than necessary. When the thresholds are too high, the system might mistake stalling code for sufficient progress and, as a result, miss interesting activity. Because the cost of unnecessarily switching into passive mode is only a small performance hit, we prefer low thresholds that result in sensitive detectors.

To compute the necessary thresholds, we compiled a training set of 5,000 malware samples submitted to ANUBIS. We only selected samples that performed obvious malware activity (they produced network traffic, spawned additional processes, or opened a UI window). We assume that these samples do not contain stalling code because the analysis successfully exposed malicious behaviors. All samples from the training set were executed in HASTEN, counting the numbers of successful and failed system calls during each time period t, and computing their entropy. Then, the thresholds were set so that the numbers derived for the training samples do not trigger any detector. For more details about the parameter computation, the reader is referred to Appendix A.

5. PASSIVE MODE

When the previous monitoring phase detects that a thread makes insufficient progress, the system switches into passive mode (for this thread). When in passive mode, the system performs two steps.

In the first step, the system attempts to find code blocks that are repeatedly executed (as part of loops or through recursive function calls). To this end, the system starts to build a dynamic control flow graph (CFG) that covers the code that the thread is executing. This CFG is then searched for cycles, and all blocks that are part of a cycle are marked as (potential) stalling code. In the second step, HASTEN reduces (or disables) logging for all blocks that the previous step has marked as stalling code.

5.1 Identifying Stalling Code

Constructing the dynamic control flow graph. To build a dynamic, inter-procedural control flow graph, we need to keep track of which instructions the program executes. For this, we leverage the execution infrastructure of ANUBIS, which is based upon the system emulator Qemu. More precisely, whenever HASTEN is switched into passive mode, the system starts to instrument the first instruction of each translation block (which is roughly the Qemu-equivalent to a basic block) as well as all `call` and `ret` instructions. The first instruction of a basic block simply appends the value of the current instruction pointer `%eip` to a queue. This allows us to efficiently determine the sequence in which a thread has executed its basic blocks. The `call` and `ret` instructions additionally store the current value of the stack pointer. This makes it easier to handle non-standard function calls (when the callee does not return to the calling function).

The queue holding `%eip` information is processed periodically (during scheduling or when switching to kernel code). At this point, the sequence of values $(eip_1, eip_2, ..., eip_n)$ in the queue is used to construct the CFG: Each distinct eip_i value represents a different basic block, and hence, a different node in the control flow graph. Thus, for each $eip_i \; \forall i : 1 \leq i \leq n$, we check whether there exists already a corresponding node in the CFG. If not, it is added. Then, for each pair $(eip_i, eip_{i+1}) \; \forall i : 1 \leq i < n$, we insert an edge from the node associated with eip_i to the node associated with eip_{i+1} (if this edge does not exist). Finally, the queue is flushed, and the last element eip_n (which has not been processed so far) is inserted as the next head of the queue.

Every time the system processes the queue with the `%eip` values, there is potentially more information available that can be used to obtain a more complete picture of the program's CFG. However, we expect that there are diminishing returns. That is, after some time, all code blocks that are part of the stalling code region have been seen, and no new nodes are added to the CFG when the queue is processed. At this point, the CFG can be analyzed for stalling code regions. Note, we also trigger this analysis after a timeout T_r (currently set to 8 seconds). This handles cases where the stalling code contains a loop with many different paths so that a few more nodes are discovered and added every time.

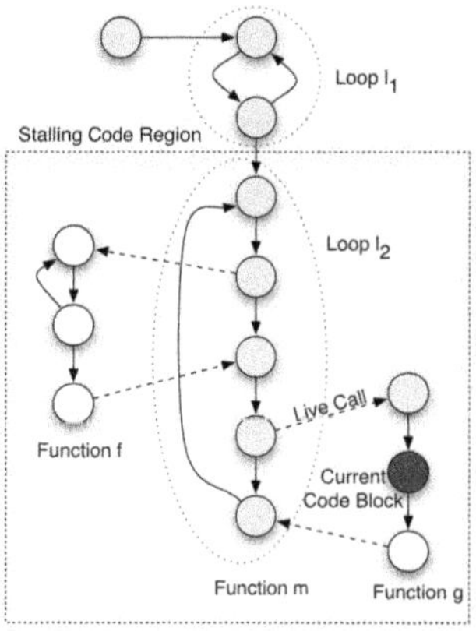

Figure 4: Example CFG for functions m, f, and g.

Finding live loops. To find stalling code, we analyze the CFG for loops. To this end, we use the algorithm proposed by Sreedhar et al. [26]. At this point, we have identified a number of loops in the dynamic control flow graph of the malware program. Some of these loops might be nested, but in most cases, we will find non-overlapping loops that belong to different functions. The question now is: Which of these loops (and which code blocks) should we consider to be part of the execution stalling region?

To answer this question, we first identify all code blocks that are *live* at the current point during the execution. Intuitively, live code blocks represent the code of all functions the program has started to execute, but have not returned yet. More precisely, we define live code blocks as follows:

> *Definition:* A code block b is live when there is a path in the inter-procedural CFG from the node that corresponds to block b to the node c that corresponds to the *current code block.* Moreover, this path can traverse only intra-procedural edges and *live call edges.*

The current code block is the code block that holds the currently-executing instruction (i.e., the code block that the instruction pointer `%eip` currently points to). A live call edge is an edge that has been introduced into the graph by a function call that has not returned yet. Consider a function f that invokes function g. This introduces an edge into the CFG from a node in f to a node in g. Initially, this edge is live, because the program executes instructions in g. When g returns, g is no longer live and its frame is removed from the stack. As a result, the call edge between f and g is no longer live. Of course, the edge in the CFG still remains.

Consider an example where a main function m first invokes f and then, after f has returned, a second function g. Figure 4 shows a CFG for this example. Let us further assume that the current code block is in function g (node in black). It can be seen that only the call edge between m and g is live. The live blocks for this program are represented as gray nodes. Note that the live blocks cover the loops in m and the first nodes in g.

To determine live call edges, we use a stack to track call and return instructions that the malware program executes. As mentioned previously, the stack pointer information associated with `call` and `return` instructions helps us to handle cases in which functions perform non-standard returns.

Finding stalling loops. Once we have determined all live code blocks, the next step is to identify *active loops*. Intuitively, an active loop is a loop that is still in progress; that is, it has not finished yet. We are only interested in active loops as potential stalling loops, since we assume that the stalling code is still running when we perform our analysis.

A necessary precondition for an active loop is that it contains code blocks that are live. However, this is not sufficient: Consider, again, the example in Figure 4. One can see that function m contains two sequential (non-nested) loops; l_1 followed by l_2. The current code block is in g, which is called from a node in l_2. This indicates that l_1 has finished. Thus, even though l_1 is live, it is not active. In our example, only l_2 is active.

To determine active loops, we first identify all live loops. This is straightforward: A live loop is a loop in the CFG with at least one node that corresponds to a live block (actually, because there is a path from all nodes inside a loop to all other nodes in that loop, either all nodes in a loop will be live, or none). Then, we mark as active all live loops where either *(i)* the current code block is part of the loop, or *(ii)*, a node with an outgoing, live call edge is part of the loop.

Note that all active loops within the same function (instance) are nested. To see this, consider all active loops within one function. They must contain either the node associated with the current code block or the node associated with the live call edge. In the case of recursive function calls, we need to distinguish between different instances of the same function, but for each instance, there can be at most one live call node.

Any active loop (or a combination thereof) is potentially responsible for stalling the execution. Thus, we can use different heuristics to pick the one(s) that is (are) most likely stalling. For example, we could pick the innermost active loop. This assumes that the execution is stalled inside the loop that is currently executing, and the code region for which logging is reduced is as small as possible (which is desirable). However, if the inner loop is only a part of a larger stalling loop, accelerating only this region is not sufficient. As an alternative, it is also possible to simply take the outermost loop. In this case, it is very likely that the stalling code is covered in its entirety. On the downside, reduced logging will be enabled for a larger portion of the malicious code. Thus, in our system, we pick the innermost, active loop as the stalling loop. This ensures the most accurate analysis results. In the following subsection, we discuss how we handle the situation when this innermost loop does not cover the entire stalling code region.

5.2 Reducing Analysis Overhead

Once the system has selected the active loop that is likely causing the execution to stall, we have to find the entire code that is part of the stalling code. Of course, the code blocks that are part of the selected, active loop are part of the stalling code, but this is not everything. We also need to add to the stalling region all code blocks that are reachable from any block in the loop body, even when these blocks are not live at the point in time. This is necessary because the stalling region must cover the entire code that is executed as part of the loop; including other functions that can be invoked by the loop, not only those parts that are currently live. However, it is important to remember that the stalling code region can only contain basic blocks that the program has executed previously (others are not part of our CFG).

To find the stalling code region, we find all code blocks b in the CFG so that there is a path from any active loop block to b. This is very similar to the analysis that finds live code blocks, but with the main difference that a path can pass through any call edge (and not only live call edges). All code blocks b that are found by this analysis are added to the stalling region. In the example shown in Figure 4, this means that the stalling code also includes code blocks in function f (since they are reachable from l_2 in m).

Once we have found all blocks that are part of the stalling code, we reduce the amount of analysis that is performed while this code is executing. More precisely, we temporarily disable logging of all functions that are not critical for the proper operation of the analysis system or that we consider highly security-critical. Examples for functions that are continued to be analyzed even in these situations are related to loading of libraries or spawning of new processes. Of course, this is done only for the selected thread and limited to the identified stalling code.

Whenever the execution exits the stalling region, we switch back to monitoring mode. To this end, we whitelist all blocks that are part of the stalling loop. Whenever execution encounters a non-whitelisted code block, the system is reverted back to monitoring mode, and the full analysis is re-enabled.

In case a stalling region contains multiple, nested loops, we first whitelist the innermost loop. When we later observe that this is not sufficient, the whitelisted region is successively extended to cover also the enclosing, parent loops. The details of the process are described in Appendix B.

6. ACTIVE MODE

In passive mode, HASTEN attempts to accelerate the execution of stalling loops by reducing the overhead associated with logging security-relevant functions. Unfortunately, this might not be sufficient to obtain progress. In particular, malware authors can write stalling code that exploits machine instructions that are very slow to emulate (such as floating point or MMX instructions). To address such types of stalling code, we introduce HASTEN's active mode. In active mode, the system forces the termination of the whitelisted stalling code. The purpose of this is to continue to explore the program execution further.

6.1 Modifying the Flow of Execution

When entering active mode, we first have to identify suitable nodes in the CFG that have an outgoing edge that exits the stalling loop. To this end, HASTEN searches all whitelisted code blocks that are part of the stalling region for those that end in a conditional branch. Then, the system checks whether any of these conditional branch instructions has a successor node that is *not* part of the stalling region. These instructions are marked as exit points. If the system fails to find at least one suitable exit point, HASTEN stops analysis and flags the analysis report for subsequent human analysis. Finally, we resume the execution of the malware.

Whenever the process subsequently attempts to execute an exit point instruction, HASTEN examines the operands of the branch operation and determines the path that the execution is about to take. When this path exits the stalling region, the process is allowed to continue. Otherwise, our system will dynamically invert the branch (for example, a *greater-than* operation is changed into *less-or-equal*). This means that HASTEN will take the first exit point that the execution encounters after switching into active mode. See Section 8 for a discussion of the implications of this approach. Once execution leaves the whitelisted code region, HASTEN re-enables full monitoring.

6.2 Handling Inconsistent Variables

When HASTEN changes the control flow and, thus, the execution of a process, the state of this process might become inconsistent. This is a problem when the program later tries to access or use variables that are modified by the stalling code (but that hold incorrect values). For example, the program could compute a magic value inside a stalling loop that is checked afterwards; a simple mechanism to detect whether an analysis system has skipped the stalling code.

To handle the problem of *inconsistent variables* (which are variables that hold potentially incorrect values), we use taint analysis to track memory locations that might hold incorrect values (as well as the variables that are derived from these memory locations). When the program later uses a potentially inconsistent variable, we extract a slice that efficiently computes the correct value.

In a first step, we need to determine all memory locations that can potentially be written by the stalling code. We can then assign a taint label to these variables that marks them as inconsistent. Our underlying analysis platform already supports the tracking of taint labels. That is, whenever a computation (or data transfer operation) involves at least one tainted source operand, the destination is tainted as well. As a result, at any later point in time, the system can determine whether the value of a memory location was derived from an inconsistent variable.

To approximate all locations that can be written by the stalling code, we use the following technique: While the program is executing in passive mode, we label the destinations of all arithmetic and logic operations. Given that the stalling code is executed many times, we assume that we see all write targets at least once.

Whenever a labeled (tainted) value is used as an operand in a control flow operation (a conditional or indirect branch), an indirect memory access, or an argument in a system call, HASTEN needs to step in. This is because using an incorrect value as input to these *fragile operations* might yield visibly incorrect program behavior (such as program crashes, invalid outputs, etc.). This is different from "normal" instructions, which HASTEN handles in a lazy fashion by simply propagating taint labels.

Efficiently computing inconsistent variables. Whenever HASTEN encounters a fragile instruction that uses a tainted operand, we need to efficiently compute its correct, expected value. To this end, we extract a backward slice from the malware program that contains exactly the instructions necessary to compute the inconsistent value.

To extract the slice, we leverage our previous work on INSPECTOR [18], a tool to extract stand-alone programs (gadgets) from malware programs. More precisely, the goal of INSPECTOR is to extract, from a given malware binary, a slice that computes the argument values of interesting (security-relevant) system calls. This is very similar to our problem, where we are interested in a slice that computes the value of an inconsistent variable.

To perform its task, INSPECTOR employs binary backward slicing. This process exploits the fact that detailed runtime information can be gathered from the dynamic execution of malware (such as the targets of indirect memory accesses and control flow instructions). This allows the extraction of complex slices that span multiple functions and involve elaborate memory access patterns. For space reasons, we have to refer the reader to our previous paper [18] for a detailed discussion of INSPECTOR.

Once our system has extracted a slice, it can be executed as a stand-alone program by the *slice player* that comes with INSPECTOR. Note that the slice player performs no instrumentation, and it can execute the code directly on a native host. Thus, the slices execute the stalling code very fast, basically as fast as on the victim's machine. For stalling code that exploits the overhead introduced by slow emulation, this can speed up execution by several orders of magnitude. Once the slice has computed the required value, it replaces the current (incorrect) value of the tainted variable, and HASTEN continues the execution of the malware process.

7. EVALUATION

In this section, we evaluate HASTEN's ability to mitigate stalling code in malware binaries. We show that detecting signs of low progress works on samples found in the wild, and we test the effectiveness of HASTEN's different modes.

7.1 Malware Data Set

To evaluate our system, we randomly selected 29,102 samples from the files that were submitted to ANUBIS between August 2010 and February 2011. When picking malware programs for our data set, we did not include any invalid Windows PE files or files that failed to load in the analysis environment (e.g., due to unresolved library dependencies). Moreover, we did not select any sample that terminated within the time allocated for the original analysis run (in our case, 240 seconds). The reason is that these samples have already revealed their entire malicious activity during the allocated analysis timeframe. Our data set represents a diverse mix of malware currently active on the Internet.

We also retrieved the analysis report generated for each of the samples. We refer to these reports as the *base run*, and we use the observed behavior as one part to evaluate whether HASTEN is successful in revealing additional behavior.

7.2 Measuring Behavior

The goal of HASTEN is to reveal additional behaviors in malware samples that contain stalling loops. To be able to measure this in an automated fashion, it would be tempting to simply re-run each sample in our system and compare the observed behavior to this sample's base run. However, this would not be fair. The reason is that the behavior exhibited by a sample can significantly depend on the date/time of analysis and the availability of remote resources.

Thus, for a fair evaluation of HASTEN, we re-ran each of the samples twice: First, we performed a *redundancy run* with identical settings compared to the base run; in parallel, we conducted a *test run* using HASTEN. In this way, we attempted to minimize external influences on the behavior of a sample by eliminating the time between *test* and *redundancy runs* for each binary.

Whenever a test run reveals added behavior compared to the redundancy run, we also compare the redundancy run to the (initial) base run. If these two runs differ considerably, it is possible that the detected, added behavior is independent of HASTEN. To assess the added behavior produced by HASTEN, we use three different metrics: *Optimistic improvement (OI)* considers any added behavior seen during the test run (over the redundancy run) as an improvement due to HASTEN. *Average improvement (AI)* takes into account randomness in malware executions. To this end, we do not attribute any added behavior to HASTEN when the test run produces less added behavior than the corresponding redundancy run over the base run. *Pessimistic improvement (PI)* counts added behavior in the test run as new only when redundancy and base runs do not differ.

Added behavior. To determine added behavior when comparing two analysis runs, we only take into account *persistent features* of the corresponding behavioral profiles: A persistent feature is an activity performed by the malware that is visible from the outside of the analysis sandbox or that introduces permanent changes to the system. Examples for such features are communicating over network sockets, writing to files in the file system, or opening graphical windows. Table 3 (Appendix C) lists all combinations of resources and actions that we considered persistent features in this paper. In our setting, focusing on persistent features is reasonable, since they are indicative of the typical behavior used to classify and detect malware.

7.3 Evaluation Results

We analyzed each of the 29,102 samples in our test set twice; once without HASTEN (redundancy run), and once with our system enabled (test run). HASTEN has a negligible impact on analysis performance in monitoring mode and only introduces small overheads in the other modes. We considered extending the analysis time for the test runs to compensate for this difference. However, this difference is difficult to predict precisely. Thus, we conservatively used the same timeout (240 seconds) for all evaluation runs.

Monitoring mode results. 9,826 (33.8%) of the analyzed malware programs exhibited insufficient progress at some point during the analysis. That is, at least one of the heuristics triggered. In 98.3% of these cases, observing too few successful system calls was the predominant cause for switching into passive mode. An excessive number of successful and failed system calls were observed in 1.5% and 0.3% of the cases, respectively. Throughout our experiments, the heuristics for identical or suspiciously diverse calls never triggered. This does not come as a surprise, however, as we introduced these to increase the burden to bypass our system. With attackers becoming aware our system, we expect these detectors to become more important.

For the 9,826 low progress samples, HASTEN switched into passive, and, if necessary, also into active mode. The remaining 19,276 programs showed good progress. While this number appears large at first glance, it makes sense. We do not expect that a majority of malware samples in the wild already contains stalling code against sandboxes.

Passive mode results. Whenever HASTEN switches into passive mode, the system starts to record the control flow of the thread that stalls and tries to extract live loops. For the 9,826 samples that exhibited stalling behavior, the tool was able to do so in 6,237 (63.5%) cases.

We manually inspected some of the remaining 3,589 cases to determine why no loop was identified, despite low progress. We found that many samples were in a "mostly waiting" state; that is, the threads were sleeping, occasionally interrupted by the OS that invoked a callback function. In other cases, we found that "stalling loops" were of short duration, and threads made progress before HASTEN could complete the analysis of the loop. We attribute these cases to the conservative thresholds that we selected for the detectors in monitoring mode. That is, the malware processes show signs of low progress but it is not due to malicious stalling. Thus, we cannot expect that HASTEN can extract added behavior. Note that the negative impact of switching into passive mode is minimal (only a small performance loss).

We further investigated the 6,237 samples for which HASTEN discovered insufficient progress *and* extracted a live loop. In 3,770 cases, the system only switched into passive mode. In the remaining 2,467 test runs, the system activated the passive and, subsequently, the active mode. Table 1 details our findings of new, added behavior observed during the test runs, using the average improvement metrics (for a detailed overview of added behaviors using the optimistic and pessimistic metrics, refer to Table 4 in Appendix D). The table also shows the number of malware labels assigned to different sets of malware samples by a popular anti-virus product. We used only the family portion of the malware labels for this analysis (that is, `W32.Allaple.A` becomes `allaple`). Of course, we are aware of the limitations of labels assigned by anti-virus products. We just provide these numbers to underline the heterogeneity of our malware data set.

The left side of Table 1 shows that the passive mode allowed HASTEN to observe new behaviors in 1,003 runs (26.6% of all passive-only runs). With 25.2% and 14.9%, file and registry modifications are the most prevalent behavior detected by HASTEN, respectively. Furthermore, 11.8% of samples in this class participated in new networking behavior, which can lead to the exposure of new command and control servers or drop zones on the Internet.

HASTEN detected added behavior in 1,447 more cases. However, due to the conservative nature of our evaluation, and since the redundancy run also produced additional features, we cannot conclusively attribute this to our approach.

For the remaining 1,320 analysis runs, we did not observe new behavior, but neither did the system advance into active mode. Typically, this means that HASTEN did not manage to build a whitelist in time that covers the entire stalling code. More precisely, while building the CFG, some paths inside the stalling code were initially not observed, or a deeply nested stalling loop is executed. As a result, HASTEN repeatedly hits non-whitelisted code, which switches the system back into monitoring mode. After monitoring progress for another time slot, passive mode is re-enabled, and a more complete whitelist is generated. However, the analysis timeout is encountered before this iterative process can complete. A longer timeout or more aggressive whitelisting could be used to address such situations.

Active mode results. For certain samples, HASTEN did not observe progress despite reduced logging. Thus, the system proceeds to actively interrupt stalling code to force forward progress. In our evaluation set, HASTEN modified the control flow of $2,467$ samples, revealing new behavior in 549 analysis runs (22.3%). The right-hand side of Table 1 shows details about the added behaviors.

While new behavior in passive mode always means additional, relevant activity, we need to be more careful in active mode: Since we actively change the flow of execution, we could follow infeasible paths that lead to errors (shown in the last row of Table 1). We handle inconsistent variables as discussed in the previous section, but the program might still show undesired behavior (such as premature program exits or exceptions). The reason is that the program could be forced down an error path that does not reference any tainted variable modified in the loop, but simply performs some clean-up activities and then raises an exception. A prominent example are the checks that are introduced by Microsoft's compiler to guard the return addresses on the stack against overflow corruption. As a result, when HASTEN encounters as exit point the conditional branch that checks for stack corruption and forces execution down this path, the program terminates with an exception (see the next Section 8 for a discussion on how this can be addressed). Of course, we discard all added behaviors that are due to exceptions (such as the start of the debugger).

Overall, HASTEN detected the use of inconsistent variables during 780 analysis runs in active mode. In 778 cases, INSPECTOR needed to be invoked once, for two runs, two invocations were necessary.

Discussion. Table 1 demonstrates that HASTEN was able to reveal interesting added behavior for 1,552 (1,003 + 549) samples, using the average improvement metrics. This number increases to 3,275 when considering the optimistic measure for additional behavior (as shown in Table 4). This behavior relates to significant activity, such as file system accesses or network traffic. Our numbers show that HASTEN successfully found additional behavior in 24.5% (or 52.5%, when using the optimistic metrics) of the 6,237 samples that contain some kind of loop that delays progress in a sandbox. The failure to expose additional behavior for the remaining samples has several reasons: Most often, some necessary resource (e.g., a command and control server) was no longer available, thus, the malware stopped its execution. In other cases, HASTEN switched

Table 1: Additional behavior observed in Hasten (using *average improvement*).

Description	Passive			Active		
	# samples	%	# AV families	# samples	%	# AV families
Runs total	**3,770**	–	319	**2,467**	–	231
Added behavior (any activity)	**1,003**	**26.6%**	119	**549**	**22.3%**	105
- Added file activity	949	25.2%	113	359	14.6%	79
- Added network activity	444	11.8%	52	108	4.4%	31
- Added GUI activity	24	0.6%	15	260	10.5%	51
- Added process activity	499	13.2%	55	90	3.6%	41
- Added registry activity	561	14.9%	82	184	7.5%	52
Ignored (possibly random) activity	**1,447**	**38.4%**	128	**276**	**11.2%**	72
No new behavior	**1,320**	**35.0%**	225	**1,642**	**66.5%**	174
- Exception cases	0	0.0%	0	277	11.2%	63

into passive mode towards the end of the analysis timeframe, and a timeout was encountered before additional behaviors could be exposed. Finally, in some cases, HASTEN selected an error path that lead to premature program termination.

We also wanted to understand in more detail the nature of the stalling code introduced by malware authors. To this end, we focused our attention on the 1,552 samples that revealed added behavior. While it is difficult to determine with certainty that a particular piece of code has been deliberately inserted by a malware author to prevent dynamic analysis, we checked for the presence of many repeated calls to API functions that serve no apparent purpose. In particular, during manual analysis of a few samples, we observed repeated calls to `GetTickCount` and `GetCommandLine`. We then checked the prevalence of these calls in the execution traces of the 1,552 samples. We found that more than a third of the samples (543) invoked one of these two functions more than 5,000 times inside a loop.

Even when considering the entire data set of 29,102 malware programs, a surprisingly large number of samples contains stalling code. This demonstrates that execution stalling is not a purely theoretical problem. Instead, a non-trivial fraction of malware in the wild already includes such evasive techniques. Thus, it is crucial that sandboxes are improved to handle this threat.

8. DISCUSSION AND LIMITATIONS

As mentioned previously, the fight against malicious code is an arms race, and malware authors always strive to improve their programs to resist new analysis and detection approaches. In this section, we discuss the robustness of our approach and possible, future improvements to further harden our techniques.

Malware authors can target each of the three modes of HASTEN: First, the stalling loop could be crafted so that it delays the execution of malicious activity in the sandbox without triggering any of the detectors in **monitoring mode**. To this end, a malware process would have to issue successful system calls with a frequency and diversity similar to non-stalling programs. To counter such mimicry attacks, we can add additional detectors that measure progress in different ways. For example, we could count, for each time interval, the number of distinct basic blocks that a program executes or the number of new (never before executed) basic blocks that Qemu, our system emulator, has to translate. For stalling code, we expect both values to be low. Moreover, we could opportunistically (and randomly) switch to passive mode every once in a while, even when no detector has raised an alert.

Likewise, it is possible that long-lasting operations (e.g., the decryption of large files) trigger one of our heuristics. Internally, we refer to this as *accidental stalling* code, since the malware author does not do this deliberately. This is similar to opportunistically switching to passive mode and introduces only a minor performance hit.

Passive mode is more difficult to exploit for the attacker. While we reduce the amount of information that is logged, we are careful to preserve all security-relevant information. To this end, we only whitelist code regions (basic blocks) that have previously been executed by the malware. For example, consider a malware author who puts a piece of malicious code into the body of a stalling loop and guards this code with a conditional branch. When the passive mode recognizes the stalling loop, it will only whitelist the part of the loop that has been executed before. The malicious code region, on the other hand, will be excluded from reduced logging. Moreover, certain security-critical system calls are always recorded.

The **active mode** seems most vulnerable to attacks since it modifies the normal flow of program execution, and, thus, could leave the program in an inconsistent state or force it along an impossible path. HASTEN addresses the problem of inconsistent program state by tracking the variables (memory locations) that stalling code modifies. Moreover, through taint analysis, all variables derived from these memory locations are tracked as well. Whenever the malware process attempts to check or use a potentially inconsistent variable, its execution is suspended. Then, the system generates a slice that will efficiently compute the variable's correct value, and this value is provided to the program before it is allowed to continue. Of course, a malware author can force our system to extract and execute slices. However, as described in more detail in [18], the slices that INSPECTOR generates are small, stand-alone executables (gadgets) that can be executed directly on a native host. Moreover, slice generation is fast. Thus, the stalling code will be run almost as fast as on a native (victim) machine.

An important limitation is our current, simple technique to determine all variables (memory locations) that stalling code can write to. Since this technique uses only dynamic information, it might miss certain locations. One way to address this problem is to incorporate static analysis to identify and taint such variables. This analysis can be conservative, as "over-tainting" can only result in unnecessary calls to INSPECTOR but will not cause incorrect program executions. Furthermore, it is possible that INSPECTOR cannot extract a proper slice to compute a needed value. This is less of a concern, as our previous work has shown that the tool is able to extract meaningful slices from real-world malware programs that span multiple functions and that contain non-trivial memory accesses. Also, INSPECTOR will report the failure to extract a slice, allowing further manual inspection.

An attacker could also try to force HASTEN to skip a stalling loop that contains malicious code (and thus, fail to observe malicious activity). This is difficult for the attacker because *all* conditional branches that exit any whitelisted stalling code region are possible exit points. In particular, when there is previously non-executed, malicious code inside a stalling loop, the branch that guards this malicious code is considered as a possible exit point (in addition to the loop exit). Recall that we only whitelist code that was previously executed; this implies that we will not whitelist the entire body of a stalling loop when there are paths through this loop that were not executed before.

In our current prototype, we force the program execution out of a stalling region through the first exit point that is encountered. This has two drawbacks. First, we might skip malicious code inside the loop (when the wrong exit point is chosen). Second, it is possible that HASTEN picks an incorrect (infeasible) loop exit path that later results in a program exception (as mentioned in the previous section, an example are error paths). To tackle these problems, we can leverage the fact that our system has full control over the analysis environment. More precisely, we can create a snapshot of the CPU and the memory before any active modification to the program's control flow. This way, HASTEN can later revert to previous snapshots and explore multiple exit paths in a more systematic fashion. This is similar in spirit to a multi-path exploration of the binary [21].

9. RELATED WORK

The idea of detecting and evading dynamic malware analyzers is not new. In the past, malware authors have introduced checks, so-called red pills, to detect execution inside a virtualized environment [13, 24]. Other work has proposed techniques to detect execution in system emulators, such as Qemu [20, 22, 23]. Yet other research [1, 7] has discussed practical fingerprinting techniques to recognize public, dynamic malware analyzers (e.g., ANUBIS [2], CWSANDBOX [3], JOEBOX, etc.). Fingerprinting a malware analysis system is particularly easy when the system provides a public interface that accepts submissions from anywhere.

To mitigate the problem of checks that detect malware analyzers, researchers have proposed transparent analysis environments [11, 12]. These systems leverage novel virtualization features of modern processors to implement a minimalistic hypervisor. This makes it more difficult to reveal the presence of the analysis platform.

Others have focused on the detection of differences between the execution of a program in a virtual or emulated platform, and on real hardware [6, 17]. The basic intuition is that any difference between the executions in two different environments (using deterministic replay) must be due to checks in a sample. If one can determine that a sample is trying to evade analysis, the evasive check can either be removed, or the sample can be marked for manual inspection.

Finally, checks that detect the analysis environment can also be bypassed by systems that perform multi-path exploration [9, 21, 28]. The idea is to first identify conditional branches that depend on some input read from the program's environment (file system, registry, network, ...). Once such a branch (check) is found, both alternative execution branches can be explored. When the system explores the branch that is different from the the current program execution, care must be taken to keep the program state consistent. In a related approach [10], the authors try to identify behaviors that are triggered by timer events.

The crucial difference between previous research and this work is that previous techniques focused on the detection and mitigation of evasive checks. Such checks are inserted by malware authors to identify dynamic analysis environments and, subsequently, change the behavior of their programs. In this paper, we present the first solution to the growing problem of dynamically analyzing malware samples that include stalling code. Stalling code does not use any checks, and it does not alter the flow of execution of the malware program in a dynamic analysis environment. As a result, transparent platforms or systems that detect and remove evasive checks are ineffective.

10. CONCLUSIONS

As new malware analysis solutions are introduced, attackers react by adapting their malicious code to evade detection and analysis. One recent form of evasion code for dynamic analysis systems is stalling code. In this paper, we present the first approach to detect and mitigate malicious stalling code, and to ensure forward progress within the amount of time allocated for the analysis of a sample. Our results show that HASTEN works well in practice, and is able to reveal additional behaviors in real-world malware samples that contain stalling code.

11. ACKNOWLEDGEMENTS

The research leading to these results has received funding from the European Union Seventh Framework Programme under grant agreement n. 257007 (SysSec), the Austrian Research Promotion Agency (FFG) under grant 820854 (TRUDIE), the NSF under grant CNS-1116777, the ONR under grant N000140911042, and the National Science Foundation (NSF) under grants CNS-0845559 and CNS-0905537. We also acknowledge Secure Business Austria for their support.

This publication reflects the views only of the authors, and the funding agencies cannot be held responsible for any use which may be made of the information contained therein.

12. REFERENCES

[1] Forum Posting - Detection of Sandboxes. http://www.opensc.ws/snippets/3558-detect-5-different-sandboxes.html, 2009.

[2] http://anubis.iseclab.org, 2010.

[3] http://www.cwsandbox.org, 2010.

[4] http://www.norman.com/enterprise/all_products/malware_analyzer/norman_sandbox_analyzer/en, 2010.

[5] http://msdn.microsoft.com/en-us/library/ms724408%28VS.85%29.aspx, 2010.

[6] BALZAROTTI, D., COVA, M., KARLBERGER, C., KRUEGEL, C., KIRDA, E., AND VIGNA, G. Efficient Detection of Split Personalities in Malware. In *Network and Distributed System Security Symposium (NDSS)* (2010).

[7] BAYER, U., HABIBI, I., BALZAROTTI, D., KIRDA, E., AND KRUEGEL, C. A View on Current Malware Behaviors. In *Workshop on Large-Scale Exploits and Emergent Threats (LEET)* (2009).

[8] BAYER, U., MILANI COMPARETTI, P., HLAUSCHEK, C., KRUEGEL, C., AND KIRDA, E. Scalable, Behavior-Based Malware Clustering. In *Network and Distributed System Security Symposium* (2009).

[9] BRUMLEY, D., HARTWIG, C., LIANG, Z., NEWSOME, J., SONG, D., AND YIN, H. Towards automatically identifying trigger-based behavior in malware using symbolic execution and binary analysis. Tech. Rep. CMU-CS-07-105, Carnegie Mellon University, 2007.

[10] CRANDALL, J., WASSERMANN, G., DE OLIVEIRA, D., SU, Z., WU, F., AND CHONG, F. Temporal Search: Detecting Hidden Malware Timebombs with Virtual Machines. In *Conference on Architectural Support for Programming Languages and Operating Systems (ASPLOS)* (2006).

[11] DINABURG, A., ROYAL, P., SHARIF, M., AND LEE, W. Ether: Malware Analysis via Hardware Virtualization Extensions. In *ACM Conference on Computer and Communications Security* (2008).

[12] FATTORI, A., PALEARI, R., MARTIGNONI, L., AND MONGA, M. Dynamic and Transparent Analysis of Commodity Production Systems. In *International Conference on Automated Software Engineering (ASE)* (2010).

[13] FERRIE, P. Attacks on Virtual Machines. In *Proceedings of the Association of Anti-Virus Asia Researchers Conference* (2007).

[14] FREDRIKSON, M., JHA, S., CHRISTODORESCU, M., SAILER, R., AND YAN, X. Synthesizing Near-Optimal Malware Specifications from Suspicious Behaviors. In *IEEE Symposium on Security and Privacy* (2010).

[15] FREILING, F., HOLZ, T., AND WICHERSKI, G. Botnet Tracking: Exploring a Root-Cause Methodology to Prevent Distributed Denial-of-Service Attacks. In *European Symposium On Research In Computer Security (ESORICS)* (2005).

[16] JOHN, J., MOSHCHUK, A., GRIBBLE, S., AND KRISHNAMURTHY, A. Studying Spamming Botnets Using Botlab. In *Usenix Symposium on Networked Systems Design and Implementation (NSDI)* (2009).

[17] KANG, M., YIN, H., HANNA, S., MCCAMANT, S., AND SONG, D. Emulating Emulation-Resistant Malware. In *Workshop on Virtual Machine Security (VMSec)* (2010).

[18] KOLBITSCH, C., HOLZ, T., KRUEGEL, C., AND KIRDA, E. Inspector Gadget: Automated Extraction of Proprietary Gadgets from Malware Binaries. In *IEEE Symposium on Security and Privacy* (2010).

[19] KOLBITSCH, C., MILANI COMPARETTI, P., KRUEGEL, C., KIRDA, E., ZHOU, X., AND WANG, X. Effective and Efficient Malware Detection at the End Host. In *Usenix Security Symposium* (2009).

[20] MARTIGNONI, L., PALEARI, R., ROGLIA, G. F., AND BRUSCHI, D. Testing CPU Emulators. In *International Symposium on Software Testing and Analysis (ISSTA)* (2009).

[21] MOSER, A., KRUEGEL, C., AND KIRDA, E. Exploring Multiple Execution Paths for Malware Analysis. In *IEEE Symposium on Security and Privacy* (2007).

[22] PALEARI, R., MARTIGNONI, L., ROGLIA, G. F., AND BRUSCHI, D. A Fistful of Red-Pills: How to Automatically Generate Procedures to Detect CPU Emulators. In *usenix-woot* (2009).

[23] RAFFETSEDER, T., KRUEGEL, C., AND KIRDA, E. Detecting System Emulators. In *Proceedings of the Information Security Conference* (2007).

[24] RUTKOWSKA, J. Red Pill... or how to detect VMM using (almost) one CPU instruction. `http://www.invisiblethings.org/papers/redpill.html`, 2004.

[25] SONG, D., BRUMLEY, D., YIN, H., CABALLERO, J., JAGER, I., KANG, M. G., LIANG, Z., NEWSOME, J., POOSANKAM, P., AND SAXENA, P. BitBlaze: A new approach to computer security via binary analysis. In *Conference on Information Systems Security (Invited Paper)* (2008).

[26] SREEDHAR, V. C., GAO, G. R., AND FONG LEE, Y. Identifying loops using DJ graphs, 1995.

[27] STONE-GROSS, B., COVA, M., CAVALLARO, L., GILBERT, B., SZYDLOWSKI, M., KEMMERER, R., KRUEGEL, C., AND VIGNA, G. Your Botnet is My Botnet: Analysis of a Botnet Takeover. In *ACM Conference on Computer and Communications Security (CCS)* (2009).

[28] WILHELM, J., AND CHIUEH, T.-C. A Forced Sampled Execution Approach to Kernel Rootkit Identification. In *Recent Advances in Intrusion Detection*. 2007.

APPENDIX

A. MONITORING MODE: PARAMETERS

Figures 5a and 5b show information about the number of successful and failed system calls, respectively, that we observed for the 5K malware samples in our training set (see Section 4). More precisely, the figures show, for a particular number n of system calls (depicted on the x-axis), the (absolute) number of time slots during which we have seen n system calls (depicted on the y-axis). For example, when analyzing the samples, we have recorded 150 successful system call invocations for roughly 1,000 intervals (see Figure 5a). Likewise, Figure 5c shows that the number of times (y-axis) a certain entropy value (x-axis) was encountered. Table 2 shows the thresholds that we derived from the training runs for HASTEN's detectors.

Table 2: Threshold values used in monitoring mode (for slot time duration $t = 5$ seconds).

Type	Name	Threshold (min)	Threshold (max)
Successful	$S_{min/max,s}$	3	600
Failed	$S_{max,f}$	–	900
Entropy	$S_{min/max,e}$	0.17	20.0

B. HANDLING NESTED STALLING LOOPS

When HASTEN operates in passive mode, its goal is to find and whitelist code that stalls execution. To this end, the system checks the program's dynamic CFG for loops. When a number of active, nested loops are found, HASTEN whitelists the innermost one (as discussed in Section 5.2). This is a problem when the innermost, active loop is only a part of the entire stalling code (we have encountered cases in real-world malware where a stalling loop is itself executed many times by an outer loop). In this case, the system reverts back to monitoring mode as soon as the innermost loop is finished. Unfortunately, the entire execution still does not make progress, and the outer loop will simply execute the inner loop again. Of course, the monitoring phase will detect insufficient progress, and the system will be switched into passive mode. However, our analysis will find the same active loops again. At this point, whitelisting the inner loop only would be the wrong solution. This would result in an execution where the system would constantly switch between monitoring and passive mode. To address this problem, the system keeps track of all loops that have been previously whitelisted. When we find that an active loop has been previously whitelisted, but no progress has been made, the system extends the whitelist to include the next enclosing loop. That is, nested loops are incrementally added to the whitelist, starting from the inner-most one, proceeding outwards.

C. PERSISTENT BEHAVIORAL FEATURES

Table 3: Persistent behavioral features.

Resource	Action
file	create, delete, write, open-truncate rename, set-information
network	*any*
registry	keys: create, delete, save, restore; set-value, set-information
process	create, terminate, set-information
driver	load, unload
GUI	open window

D. DETAILED FINDINGS

As mentioned in Section 7.2, we can use different approaches for measuring additional behavior. Table 4 shows additional behaviors detected by HASTEN as measured by the optimistic and pessimistic and metrics.

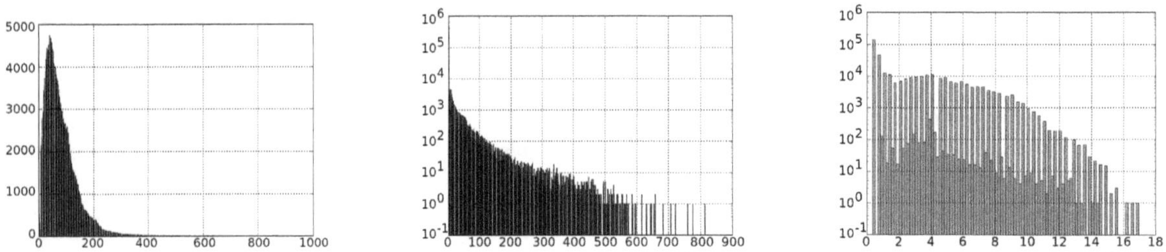

(a) Successful system calls S_s. (b) Failed system calls S_f. (c) System call entropy S_e.

Figure 5: Evaluating the progress of active samples by bucketing number of observed system calls (x-axis) and counting observed number of time-slots for each bucket (y-axis).

Table 4: Additional behavior observed in Hasten.

Description	Passive			Active		
	# samples	%	# AV families	# samples	%	# AV families
Runs total	3,770	–	319	2,467	–	231
	Optimistic Improvement					
Added behavior (any activity)	2,450	65.0%	188	825	33.5%	139
- Added file activity	1,873	49.7%	169	519	21.0%	100
- Added network activity	906	24.0%	73	128	5.2%	39
- Added GUI activity	28	0.7%	16	367	14.9%	69
- Added process activity	895	23.7%	79	127	5.1%	48
- Added registry activity	795	21.1%	107	224	9.1%	62
No new behavior	1,320	35.0%	225	1,642	66.5%	174
- Exception cases	0	0.0%	0	277	11.2%	63
	Pessimistic Improvement					
Added behavior (any activity)	416	11.0%	86	500	20.3%	94
- Added file activity	390	10.3%	80	314	12.7%	69
- Added network activity	257	6.8%	41	95	3.9%	29
- Added GUI activity	20	0.5%	12	249	10.1%	49
- Added process activity	177	4.7%	42	70	2.8%	34
- Added registry activity	331	8.8%	60	165	6.7%	46
Ignored (possibly random) activity	2,034	54.0%	156	325	13.2%	84
No new behavior	1,320	35.0%	225	1,642	66.5%	174
- Exception cases	0	0.0%	0	277	11.2%	63

MIDeA: A Multi-Parallel Intrusion Detection Architecture

Giorgos Vasiliadis
FORTH-ICS, Greece
gvasil@ics.forth.gr

Michalis Polychronakis
Columbia University, USA
mikepo@cs.columbia.edu

Sotiris Ioannidis
FORTH-ICS, Greece
sotiris@ics.forth.gr

ABSTRACT

Network intrusion detection systems are faced with the challenge of identifying diverse attacks, in extremely high speed networks. For this reason, they must operate at multi-Gigabit speeds, while performing highly-complex per-packet and per-flow data processing. In this paper, we present a multi-parallel intrusion detection architecture tailored for high speed networks. To cope with the increased processing throughput requirements, our system parallelizes network traffic processing and analysis at three levels, using multi-queue NICs, multiple CPUs, and multiple GPUs. The proposed design avoids locking, optimizes data transfers between the different processing units, and speeds up data processing by mapping different operations to the processing units where they are best suited. Our experimental evaluation shows that our prototype implementation based on commodity off-the-shelf equipment can reach processing speeds of up to 5.2 Gbit/s with zero packet loss when analyzing traffic in a real network, whereas the pattern matching engine alone reaches speeds of up to 70 Gbit/s, which is an almost four times improvement over prior solutions that use specialized hardware.

Categories and Subject Descriptors

C.2.0 [**General**]: Security and Protection

General Terms

Design, Performance, Security

Keywords

Intrusion Detection, Pattern Matching, Acceleration, GPU, NIDS

1. INTRODUCTION

Network intrusion detection systems (NIDS) are commonly classified into *anomaly-based* and *signature-based* systems. Anomaly-based systems are used to detect unknown attacks, but usually generate false positives [8,42]. In contrast, signature-based systems are typically more precise, but cannot detect attacks for which they do not have a signature, and therefore, they require continuous updating [33,36]. Due to their low false-positive rate and their higher performance, signature-based detection approaches are the basis for the majority of the existing NIDSs. Unfortunately, as the speed of network links increases, keeping up with the inspection of all traffic becomes quite challenging.

A number of approaches have been proposed to address the problem of matching stateful signatures in high-speed networks, both *hardware* and *software* based. Hardware-based implementations offer a scalable method of inspecting packets in high-speed environments [6,9,10,24,26,27,29,45]. These systems usually consist of special-purpose hardware, such as FPGAs, CAMs, and ASICs, that is used to process network packets in parallel. Although the use of specialized hardware achieves high processing rates, most implementations require custom programming, and are usually tied to the underlying device. As a consequence, they are very difficult to extend and reprogram. Additionally, most of these approaches focus on the raw inspection of the network packets alone, without implementing crucial functionalities of modern NIDSs, such as protocol analysis and application-level parsing.

In contrast, software implementations based on commodity processors are low-cost and easily programmable. The advent of multicore processors has lead researchers to employ them for high-speed traffic processing. Previous approaches have focused extensively on multi-core general-purpose processors [19, 20, 37, 39, 47], in which the NIDSs operations are decomposed to different processing elements. Graphics processors have also been used to boost computationally intensive tasks, like string searching [18, 41, 48] and regular expression matching [49].

The majority of these approaches take advantage of parallelism only at a single level, either through traffic splitting [21, 47], flow-level parallelization [19, 20, 39], or content inspection [18, 41, 48, 49]. In practice, however, the performance of modern NIDSs depends on several operations, including packet capture and decoding, TCP stream reassembly, and application-level protocol analysis. A scalable architecture *must* exploit parallelism for each operation individually, otherwise Amdahl's Law will fundamentally limit the performance that the hardware can provide [34].

In this paper, we present MIDeA, a new model for network intrusion detection systems, which combines commodity, general-purpose hardware components in a single-node design, tailored for high-performance network traffic analysis. Our system takes advantage of the parallelism offered by modern network interface cards, multiple CPUs, and multiple GPUs, to improve scalability and runtime performance. By mapping each operation to the appropriate device, we implemented a NIDS with no serialized components—no component needs to be synchronized and wait for another component to finish its execution, or contend for a shared resource. This design allows for significant performance gains. On a single box, MIDeA performs stateful packet analysis and inspection at 5.2 Gbit/s, while the raw processing throughput of the computationally-intensive pattern matching operations exceeds 70 Gbit/s when offloaded to the GPUs.

In summary, the main contributions of this work are:

- We introduce a novel multi-parallel architecture for high-performance processing and stateful analysis of network traffic. Our architecture is based on inexpensive, off-the-shelf, general-purpose hardware, and combines multi-queue NICs, multi-core CPUs, and multiple GPUs.

- We present our prototype implementation based on Snort [36], the most widely used open-source NIDS, demonstrating that the proposed model is practical and can be adopted by existing systems.

- We present the design and implementation of a number of system-level optimizations that improve end-to-end performance. We demonstrate that our implementation scales well with the number of processing units.

- We experimentally evaluate our prototype implementation under various configurations, and show that commodity hardware can be used effectively to drastically improve the performance of traffic processing applications. Our evaluation on 10 Gbit/s links demonstrates a significant increase in processing throughput compared to existing approaches.

The rest of the paper is organized as follows. Section 2 presents the design objectives and challenges of our proposed architecture. In Section 3, we describe the architecture of our parallel network intrusion detection system in detail. Section 4 presents optimizations implemented to overcome bottlenecks and reduce specific overheads. In Section 5, we thoroughly evaluate our architecture using different benchmarks and workloads. In Section 6, we discuss the limitations of our system and directions for future work. Finally, we discuss related work in Section 7 and conclude in Section 8.

2. DESIGN OBJECTIVES

We begin by discussing the design principles and practical challenges of mapping the different functional components of a signature-based network intrusion detection system to a multi-parallel system architecture.

Inter-flow Parallelism. Our aim is to design a NIDS architecture that scales with the number of available processing units, enabling it to operate at line-rates without packet loss. The primary role of a NIDS is to passively capture the network packets through the network interface (NIC), process them, and report any suspicious events. Therefore, the main tasks of the NIDS can be summarized as: (i) packet capturing, usually at multi-Gigabit rates, and (ii) packet processing, including TCP stream reassembly, application-level protocol parsing, and pattern matching.

In current hardware NIDS platforms [1,44], packet processing operates at line-rates, handling a single input port; therefore, the platform must inspect input traffic at several Gigabit per second. Existing software-based NIDS, in contrast, typically follow a multi-core approach and split the traffic at the flow-level to N slices, where N is the number of processing nodes available to the system [39,47]. Flow-based partitioning achieves an almost even processing load at all processing nodes, without requiring any intra-node communication for processing operations that are limited in scope to a single flow. Traffic is distributed using either an external traffic splitter—which is quite a costly solution—or a software-based load-balancing scheme, where a simple hash function is applied on each captured packet, based on which it is assigned to the appropriate node for processing.

Unfortunately, having many different cores receiving traffic from the same network interface or a shared packet queue, increases contention to the shared resource, which incurs additional delay in packet capturing [19,20]. This observation leads us to our first design principle: *traffic has to be separated at the network flow level using existing, commodity solutions, without incurring any serialization on the processing path.* In Section 3, we show how our system takes advantage of recent load-balancing technologies such as Receive-Side Scaling (RSS) [3], which allows different cores to receive portions of the monitored traffic directly. This inherently leads us to a multi-core architecture, in which each core runs a separate instance of the inspection engine, processing only a subset of the network flows.

Intra-flow Parallelism. Distributing the monitored traffic to different CPU cores offers significant performance benefits. Recent studies [20,39] have shown a close-to-linear speedup in the number of cores. However, the CPU is still saturated by the large number of diverse and computationally heavy operations it needs to perform: network flow tracking, TCP stream reassembly, protocol parsing, string searching, regular expression matching, and so on. The problem then is how to further parallelize content inspection on each core, enabling a further increase in the overall traffic processing throughput, *without* incurring any packet loss.

This leads us to our second design principle: *per-flow traffic processing should be parallelized beyond simple per-flow load balancing across different CPU cores.* To enable such "intra-flow" parallelism, network packets from the same flow have to be processed in parallel, while also maintaining flow-state dependencies. In Section 3.2.2, we discuss how our system can take advantage of multiple graphics processors to inspect high-volume traffic concurrently with the CPU cores. Intra-flow parallelism is achieved by buffering incoming packets and transferring them to the graphics card in large batches. Although this buffering scheme adds some latency to the processing path, it pays off in terms of the processing throughput that can be sustained.

By parallelizing both packet pre-processing and content inspection across multiple CPUs and GPUs, the proposed multi-parallel NIDS architecture can operate at line rate in multi-Gigabit networks using solely commodity components. Our parallelization scheme also leads to an architecture that is incrementally extensible in terms of hardware resources. We demonstrate that the overall processing throughput of the system can be increased simply by adding more processing elements.

Resulting Trade-off. A potential issue of our design is the data transfer operations that must take place between the memory address spaces of each device. Specifically, network packets are transferred from the NIC to the main memory of the host, and from there to the device memory of the GPU. However, the extra data transfers between the CPU and the GPU over the PCIe bus can be worth the computational gain offered by the GPU. To further mitigate this data transfer overhead, we have implemented a pipelining scheme that allows CPU and GPU execution to overlap, and consequently hides the added latencies. Although the raw computational power of the GPU offers enough performance benefits even when considering all data transferring overheads, the pipelining scheme that we introduce offers an additional level of parallelism to the overall execution path. In Section 4, we discuss in detail how these optimizations have been implemented in our system.

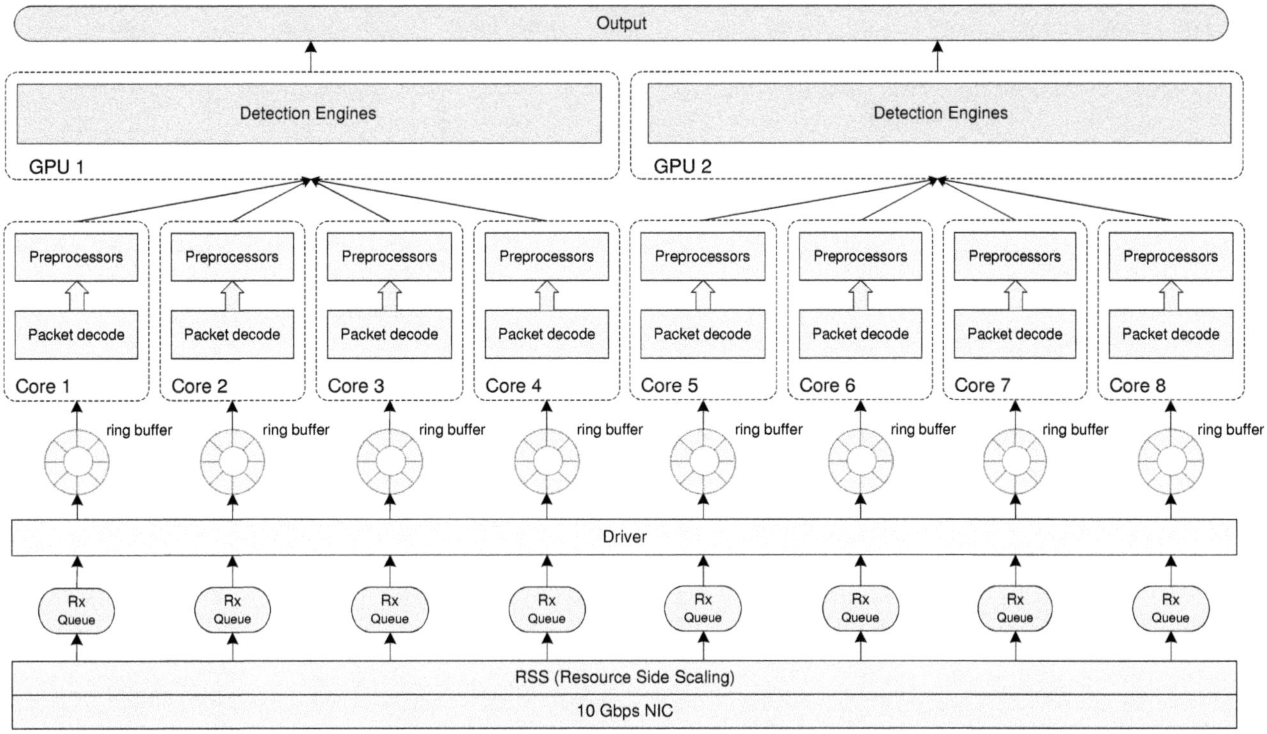

Figure 1: MIDeA architecture.

3. ARCHITECTURE

In this section, we describe the overall design of our multi-parallel network intrusion detection architecture. The key factors for achieving good performance are: (i) load balancing between processing units, and (ii) linear performance scalability with the addition of more processing units. Additionally, for high-performance packet capturing we consider the use of only inexpensive commodity NICs.

As shown in Figure 1, the NIDS application is mapped to the different processing units using both *task* and *data* parallelism across the incoming network flows. In particular, the network interface distributes the captured packets to the CPU-cores, ensuring flow-pinning and equal workload across the cores. Each CPU-core reassembles and normalizes the captured traffic before offloading it to the GPU for pattern matching. Any matching results are logged by the corresponding CPU-core using the specified logging mechanism, such as a file or database.

This design has a number of benefits: First, it does not require any synchronization or lock mechanisms since different cores process different data in isolation. Second, having several smaller data structures (such as the TCP reassembly tables) instead of sharing a few large ones, not only reduces the number of table look-ups required to find a matching element, but also reduces the size of the working set in each cache, increasing overall cache efficiency.

3.1 Packet Capturing

Our system uses 10GbE NICs, which are currently the state-of-the-art general-purpose network interfaces. Capturing packets at these rates is non-trivial and requires the coordinated effort of the network controller and the multi-core CPUs.

3.1.1 Multiqueue NICs

To avoid contention when multiple cores access the same 10GbE port, modern network cards can partition incoming traffic into several Rx-queues [28]. This allows each CPU core to access its own hardware queue independently, while the NIC controller is responsible for classifying incoming network packets and distributing them to the appropriate queue. The Rx-queues are not shared between the CPU cores, eliminating the need of synchronization. Each Rx-queue is dedicated to a specific user-level process that is mapped to a different core, as shown in Figure 1. Each user-level process fetches packets from a single queue and forwards them to the next processing module. The controller can set up a number of Rx-queues equal to the number of available CPU cores (the Intel 82599EB Ethernet controller [2] that we used in our implementation supports up to 128 Rx-queues).

To avoid costly packet copies and context switches between user and kernel space, we use the `PF_RING` network socket [11]. The most efficient way to integrate a `PF_RING` socket with a multi-queue NIC is to dedicate a separate ring buffer for each available Rx-queue [15]. Network packets of each Rx-queue are stored into a separate ring buffer and are pulled by the user-level process through DMA, without going through the kernel's network stack.

We also take into consideration the interrupt handling of each queue. In Linux, interrupts are handled automatically by the kernel through the `irqbalance` daemon. This daemon is responsible for evenly distributing interrupts from each Rx-queue to CPU cores, in a round-robin fashion. Unfortunately, this is not the optimal solution for multi-core systems, because distributing the handling of interrupts from a single Rx-queue to multiple cores results in cache invalidation and performance degradation [25]. This means that `irqbalance` does not guarantee that the interrupt of the next packet of the same flow will be handled by the same core. Therefore, we bind the interrupt handling of each Rx-queue to a specific CPU core by setting the corresponding `/proc/irq/X/smp_affinity` entry (where `X` is the IRQ number of each Rx-queue, which can be obtained from `/proc/interrupts`).

3.1.2 Load Balancing

A major implication when partitioning the incoming traffic to multiple instances is to guarantee that all packets of a specific flow will be processed by the same user-level process. It is also important to distribute the load equally to the different processing cores. Modern NICs [3] support *hash-based* (or *flow-based*), and *address-based* classification schemes. In hash-based schemes, such as Receive-Side Scaling (RSS), a hash function is applied to the protocol headers of the incoming packets in order to assign them to one of the Rx-queues. In address-based schemes, such as Virtual Machine Device Queues (VMDQ), each Rx-queue is assigned a different Ethernet address, to provide an abstraction of a dedicated interface to guest virtual machines.

For our purposes, we choose the hash-based method. The hash function, computed on the typical 5-tuple <ip_src, ip_dst, port_src, port_dst, protocol> achieves good distribution among the different queues. The RSS specification [28] allows the explicit parameterization of the tuple fields that will be used to compute the hash. Unfortunately, current RSS-enabled network interfaces (such as the Intel 82599EB that we used) use a fixed hashing type, which only ensures that the packets of the uni-directional streams of a connection will result to the same hash value. This means that the client-to-server stream of the flow will may end up to one Rx-queue, and the server-to-client stream to a different one.

In order to insure that packets of both directions end up into the same ring buffer, a symmetric hashing is further applied on the 5-tuple fields of each packet header. Eventually, all packets of the same flow will always be placed in the same ring buffer, and will be processed by the same user-level process. In addition, we bind the process that reads from each ring buffer to the same core using the CPU affinity of the Linux scheduler (see `sched_setaffinity(2)`), in order to increase cache locality. We assume that the monitored traffic consists of many different concurrent flows (at least as many as the available CPU cores), hence all processes are fed with data. This is not an issue even in small networks, since even a single host usually has tens of concurrent active connections.

3.2 Processing Engine

Incoming traffic is forwarded to the processing engines for analysis. Each processing engine is implemented as a single process and is mapped to a certain CPU core to avoid costs due to process scheduling. The basic functionality of each processing engine is to retrieve the network packets from its assigned hardware queue, decode them and apply higher-level protocol analysis, and finally transfer them to the GPU for content inspection.

3.2.1 Preprocessing

Preprocessing modules are built on top of the decoding subsystem and preprocessor engines of Snort 2.9. The purpose of the decoder is to parse the packet headers according to lower-layer protocols (Ethernet, IP, TCP, and so on). After packets have been decoded, they are sent through a preprocessing stage that includes *flow reassembly* and *protocol analysis*.

TCP packets are reassembled into TCP streams to build the entire application dialog before they are forwarded to the pattern matching engine. Packets that belong to the same direction of a TCP flow, are merged into a single packet by concatenating their payloads according to the TCP protocol. Inspecting the concatenation of several network packets, instead of each network packet separately, enables the handling of overlapping data and other TCP anomalies. This allows the detection engine to match patterns that span multiple packets. Content normalization is also applied for higher-level protocols, such as HTTP and DCE/RPC, to remove potential ambiguities and neutralize evasion tricks.

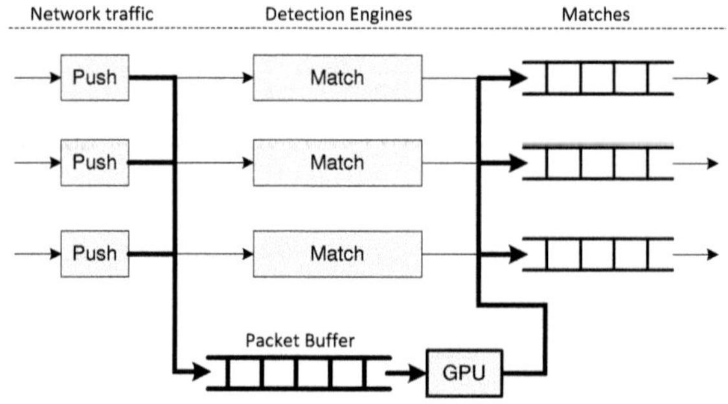

Figure 2: Batching different flows to a single buffer.

Once flow reassembly and normalization is complete, the data is forwarded to the detection engine, which performs signature matching on the incoming traffic. In existing NIDS like Snort [36], the detection signatures are organized in *port groups*, based on the source and destination port numbers of each rule. Additionally, a separate detection engine instance is used to search for the string patterns of a particular rule group. To achieve *intra-flow* parallelization, MIDeA takes advantage of the data-parallel capabilities of modern graphics processors.

Incoming traffic is transferred to the memory space of the GPU in batches. As we discuss in Section 5.2, small transfers results to significant PCIe throughput degradation, hence we batch lots of data together to reduce the PCIe transaction overhead. Also, instead of allocating a different buffer for each port group, we simply mark each packet so that it will be processed by the appropriate detection engine in the searching phase. Consequently, only one buffer is needed per process, instead of one for each port group, as shown in Figure 2. This results to significantly lower memory consumption and reduces response latency for port groups with low traffic. Whenever the buffer gets full, all packets are transferred to the GPU in one operation.

The buffer that is used to collect the network packets is allocated as a special type of memory, called page-locked or "pinned down" memory. Page-locked memory is a physical memory area that does not map to the virtual address space, and thus cannot be swapped out to secondary storage. The use of this memory area results to higher data transfer throughput between the host and the GPU device, because the GPU driver knows the location of the data in RAM and does not have to locate it—neither swap it from disk, nor copy it to a non-pageable buffer—before transferring it to the GPU. Data transfers between page-locked memory and the GPU are performed through DMA, without occupying the CPU.

3.2.2 Parallel Multi-Pattern Engine

A major design criterion for matching large data streams against many different patterns, is the choice of an efficient pattern matching algorithm. The majority of network intrusion detection systems use a flavor of the Aho-Corasick algorithm [5] for string searching, which uses a transition function to match input data. The transition function gives the next state $T[state, ch]$ for a given $state$ and a character ch. A pattern is matched when starting from the *start state* and moving from state to state, the algorithm reaches a *final state*. The memory and performance requirements of Aho-Corasick depend on the way the transition function is represented. In the full representation, each transition is represented with 256 elements, one for each 8-bit character. Each element contains the

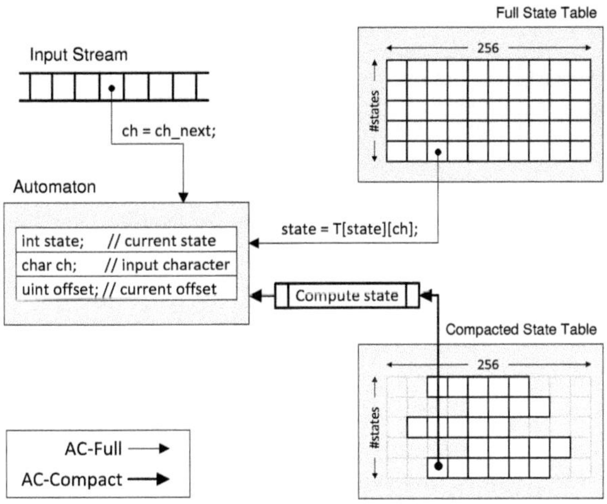

Figure 3: State tables of AC-Full vs. AC-Compact.

next state to move to, hence given an input character, the next state can be found in $O(1)$ steps. This gives a linear complexity over the input data, independently on the number of patterns, which is very efficient in terms of performance.

In the full state representation, hereinafter *AC-Full*, every possible input byte leads to *at most* one new state, which ensures high performance. Unfortunately, a full state representation requires large amounts of memory, even for small signature sets. When compiling the whole rule set of Snort, the size of the compiled state table can reach up to several hundreds Megabytes of memory. On most modern graphics cards, available memory is not a constraint any more, since they are usually equipped with ample amounts of memory—a GeForce GTX480 comes with 1.5GB of memory at a reasonable price. Unfortunately, in the CUDA runtime system [32], on which MIDeA is based, each CPU thread is executed in its own CUDA context. In other words, a different memory space has to be allocated in the GPU for each process, since they cannot share memory on the GPU device. As we discuss in Section 5.2, when using the AC-Full algorithm, only the detection engines of a single Snort instance can fit in the memory space of the GPU. That means that only one Snort instance can fully utilize the GPU at a time.

To overcome the memory sharing limitation of CUDA and maintain scalability, it is important to keep the memory requirements low. Instead of creating a full state table, we use a *compacted state table* structure for representing the compiled patterns [31]. The compacted state table is represented in a banded-row format, where only the elements from the first non-zero value to the last non-zero value of the table are actually stored. The number of the stored elements is known as the *bandwidth* of the sparse table. In our new implementation, *AC-Compact*, the next state is not directly accessible while matching input bytes, but it has to be computed, as shown in Figure 3. This computation adds a small overhead at the searching phase, which is amortized by the significantly lower memory consumption.

Moreover, it is common that many patterns are case-insensitive, or share the same final state in the transition table. Instead of inserting every different combination of lowercase and capital letters for the pattern, we simply insert only one combination (i.e., all characters are converted to lowercase), and mark that pattern in the pattern list as case-insensitive. In case the pattern is matched in a packet, an extra case-insensitive search should be made at the index where the pattern was found. If two patterns share the same final list (i.e.,

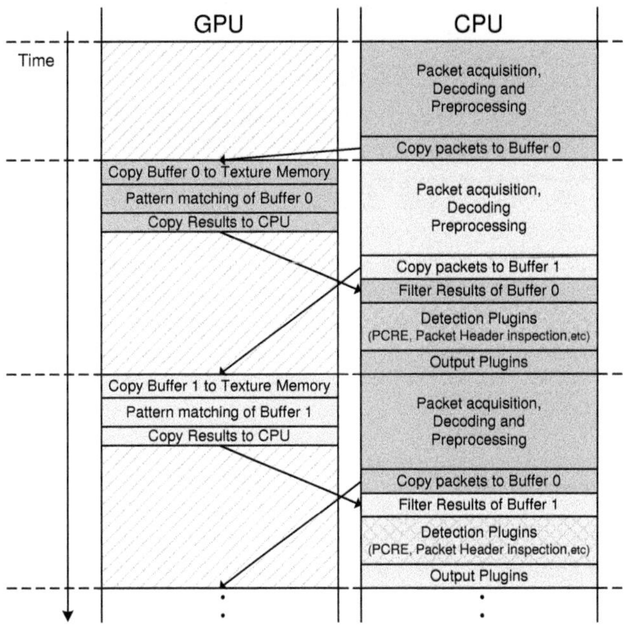

Figure 4: Execution flow of a single CPU process.

the match list contains more than one pointers to patterns), the patterns contained in the list have to be verified for finding the actual match.

Each packet is processed by a different GPU thread. Packets are stored into an array, which dimensions are equal to the number of the packets that are processed at once and the Maximum Transmission Unit (MTU). Packets that exceed MTU (which is 1500 bytes in Ethernet) are splitted down into several smaller ones, and are copied in consecutive rows in the array. To detect attacks that span multiple rows, each thread continues its search to the following portions of the packet (if any) iteratively, until a *final* or *fail state* is reached.

3.2.3 Multi-GPU Support

A key feature of MIDeA is its support for pattern matching using several GPUs at a data-parallel level. Modern motherboards, such as the one we used in our evaluation, support multiple GPUs on the PCI Express bus. MIDeA utilizes the different GPUs by dividing the incoming flows equally and performing the signature matching in parallel across all devices.

By default, MIDeA utilizes as many GPUs as it can find in the system; however, this can be controlled by defining the number of GPUs it should try to use in the configuration file. In the CUDA runtime system, on which MIDeA is based, each CPU process is bound to one device. To make multi-GPU computation possible, several host processes must then be created, with at least one process per device. A static GPU assignment is used for each process. Each process receives a uniform amount of flows, due to the load balancing scheme described in Section 3.1.2, and thus flows are equally distributed to the different GPUs.

4. PERFORMANCE OPTIMIZATIONS

Having described our architecture, we now go into a couple of optimizations that improve: (i) memory accesses on the GPU, and (ii) CPU and GPU execution through pipelining.

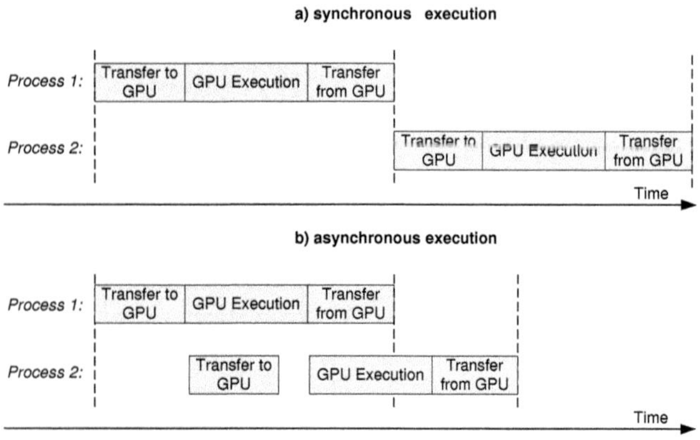

Figure 5: Data transfers and GPU execution of different processes can overlap.

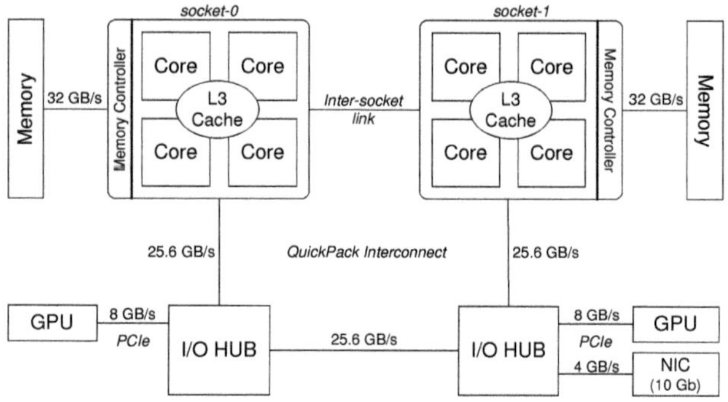

Figure 6: Hardware setup.

Optimizing GPU Memory Accesses. One important optimization for the GPU pattern matching algorithm is related to the way the input data are loaded from the device memory. Since pattern matching is performed byte-wise, each input symbol is represented with 8 bits. However, the minimum size for every device memory transaction is 32 bytes. Thus, by reading the input stream one byte at a time, the overall memory throughput may be reduced by a factor of up to 32.

We have found that memory is better utilized when multiple bytes are fetched at a time, instead of just one. To that end, we redesigned the input reading process so that each thread accesses data using the `int4` built-in data type (`int4` is a vector type, consisting of 4 integer variables). Data is stored into a 128-bit register, and is accessed a byte at a time. `Int4` is the largest data-type that can be used to read data from the *texture memory* of the device, utilizing up to 50% of the total GPU memory bandwidth.

Pipelined Execution. Our core idea for hiding the pattern matching computation time on the GPU is double buffering. Our architecture improves the achieved parallelism by pipelining the execution of CPU cores and the GPUs. For each process, when the first buffer becomes full, it is copied to a texture bounded array that can be later read by the GPU through the kernel invocation. While the GPU is performing pattern matching on the flows of the first buffer, the CPU processes newly arrived packets, as shown in Figure 4.

Moreover, on recent CUDA-enabled devices, it is possible to overlap kernel execution on the device with data transfers between the host and the device, even for different processes. The dedicated DMA engine of NVIDIA GPUs[1] allows the concurrent execution of a CUDA kernel along with data transfers over the PCIe bus. For example, while one process transfers the data to the GPU, another process can execute the pattern matching operations. This allows better GPU utilization, as depicted in Figure 5. As we discuss in Section 5.2.1, the performance improvement due to overlapping execution in the GPU is up to 330%.

5. EXPERIMENTAL EVALUATION

We evaluated the performance of our system under a variety of workloads. We first describe the experimental testbed (Section 5.1), and then analyze the performance of MIDeA under different scenarios using micro-benchmarks (Section 5.2), as well as high-level end-to-end performance measurements (Section 5.3).

[1]For devices with Compute Capability 1.1 or greater.

5.1 Experimental Setup

Hardware Setup. The overall architecture of our test system is shown in Figure 6. Our base system has two processor sockets, each with one Intel Xeon E5520 Quad-core CPU at 2.27GHz and 8192KB of L3-cache. Each socket has an integrated memory controller, connected to memory via a memory bus; this offers parallelism in memory accesses and, therefore, to higher aggregate and per-CPU bandwidth, as previous studies have shown [13]. The sockets are connected to each other and to the I/O hub via dedicated high-speed point-to-point links. The I/O hub is connected to the GPUs and the NIC via a set of PCIe buses: two PCIe 2.0 ×16 slots, which we populated with two GeForce GTX480 graphics cards, and one PCIe 2.0 ×8 slot holding one Intel 82599EB 10GbE NIC. To cover the needs for PCIe lanes, we acquired a motherboard with a dual I/O hub and a total of 72 lanes. Each NVIDIA GeForce GTX 480 is equipped with 480 cores, organized in 15 multiprocessors, and 1.5GB of GDDR5 memory.

Software. Our prototype runs on Linux 2.6.32 with the `ioatdma` and `dca` modules loaded. The `ioatdma` driver is required for supporting QuickPath Interconnect architecture of recent Intel processors. DCA (Direct Cache Access) is a NIC technology that directly places incoming packets into the cache of the CPU core for immediate access by the application. In all of our experiments we used the default rule set of Snort 2.8.6, which consists of 8,192 rules, comprising about 193,000 substrings for string searching. All default preprocessors, including `frag3`, `stream5`, `rpc_decode`, `ftp_telnet`, `smtp`, `dns`, and `http_inspect`, were enabled.

Traffic Generation. We used two servers for traffic generation to overcome the poor performance of the Linux kernel's network stack when sending small packets. The traffic generation servers and MIDeA are connected through a 10GbE switch. The test traffic, consisting of both generated synthetic traffic as well as real traffic traces, is sent using `tcpreplay` [4].

5.2 Micro-Benchmarks

We begin our evaluation by measuring the computational throughput of MIDeA using a varying number of CPU processes and GPU devices. Each process runs on a different CPU core, therefore we can utilize all cores by creating eight processes.

For the input data stream we used synthetic network traces of varying length with random payload. The data stream was carefully created to exercise most code branches, as well as different parameters of our implementation. To simulate the multi-queue capabilities of the NIC, we loaded the network packets of the trace file into separate queues (one for each core) using a simplified version of the Toeplitz hash function, which is used for RSS in modern NICs [28]. This is the "ideal NIC" case, where no overhead is

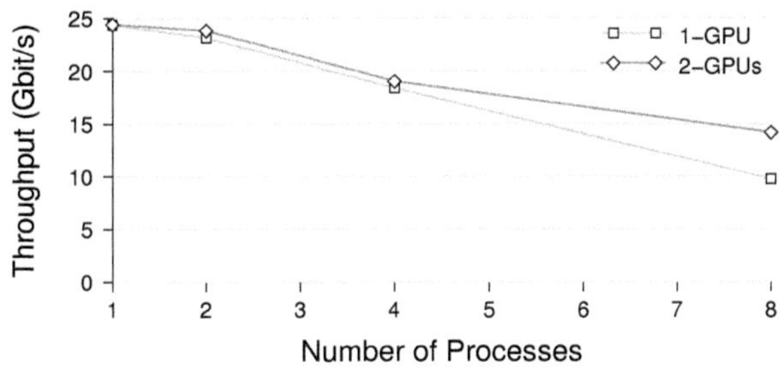

Figure 7: Per-process transfer rate between CPU and GPU.

Buffer Size	1KB	4KB	64KB	256KB	1MB	16MB
Host to Device	2.04	7.1	34.4	42.1	44.6	45.7
Device to Host	2.03	6.7	21.1	23.8	24.6	24.9

Table 1: Data transfer rate between host and device (Gbit/s).

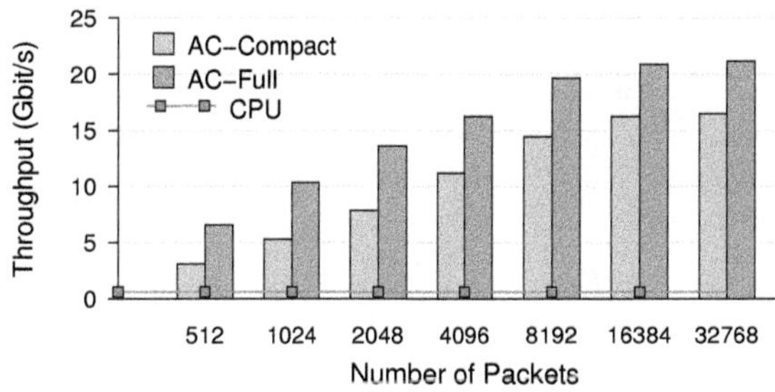

Figure 8: GPU throughput for AC-Full and AC-Compact.

#Rules	#Patterns	#States	AC-Full	AC-Compact
8,192	193,167	1,703,023	890.46 MB	24.18 MB

Table 2: Memory requirements of AC-Full and AC-Compact for the default Snort rule set.

added due to the transferring of the packets from the network interface to the host's main memory. All network packets are stored in memory, thus no blocks were transferred from disk when reading packets. We have verified the absence of I/O latencies using the `iostat(1)` tool.

5.2.1 GPU Performance

Data Transfer. Flows are transferred to each GPU device over the shared PCIe ×16 bus. PCIe uses point-to-point serial links, allowing more than one pair of devices to communicate with each other at the same time.

Table 1 shows the transfer rate of one process for moving data to a single GPU device, and vice versa, for different buffer sizes. We observe that with a large buffer, the rate of data transfer to the device is over 45 Gbit/s, while the transfer rate from the device to the host decreases to about 25 Gbit/s. This asymmetry in the data transfer throughput is probably related to the chosen hardware setup (i.e., the interconnection between the motherboard and the graphics cards), and has been also observed by other researchers [17]. We speculate that future motherboards will alleviate this asymmetry.

Figure 7 shows the transfer rate for a varying numbers of processes. The transfer costs include the copy of the network packets to the memory space of the GPU, and the copy of the results from the GPU to the host's memory. We can see that as the number of processes increases, the per-process throughput sustained by the PCIe bus slightly decreases. That is expected, since many processes contend for the same device through the same bus link. However, the aggregate throughput achieved by all processes increases, resulting to better PCIe bus utilization. As shown in Figure 7, for eight processes, the bidirectional PCIe throughput when using a single GPU reaches 9.7 Gbit/s per process, which in aggregate corresponds to 77.8 Gbit/s for all eight processes.[2] Adding one more GPU device results to a much higher throughput of 14.1 Gbit/s per process (113.3 Gbit/s in aggregate for all eight processes), since each GPU device is interconnected through dedicated PCIe lanes.

Computational Throughput. Having examined the data transfer costs, we now measure the GPU performance of the AC-Compact and AC-Full algorithms, described in Section 3.2.2.

Figure 8 shows the sustained throughput for pattern matching on a single GTX480. We fix the packet length to 1500 bytes and vary the number of packets that are processed at once from 512 to 32,768. Our AC-Full and AC-Compact implementations achieve a peak performance of 21.1 Gbit/s and 16.4 Gbit/s, respectively, including the data transferring costs to and from the device. The CPU achieves a performance of 0.6 Gbit/s for the AC-Full implementation, and thus a single GPU instance corresponds to 36.2 and 28.1 CPU cores for the AC-Full and AC-Compact implementations, respectively.

As expected, AC-Full outperforms AC-Compact in all cases. The added overhead of the extra computation that AC-Compact performs in every transition decreases its performance about 30%. The main advantage of AC-Compact is that it has significantly lower memory consumption than AC-Full. Table 2 shows the corresponding memory requirements for storing the detection engines of a single Snort instance. AC-Compact utilizes up to 36 times less memory, which makes it a better fit for a multi-CPU environment, due to CUDA's limitation of allocating a separate memory context for each host thread. Using AC-Compact, a single GTX480 card can store the detection engines of about 50 Snort instances ($50 \times 24.18MB \approx 1.2GB$). The remaining memory is used for storing the contents of network packets. If AC-Full is used, only one instance can fit in device memory. In all subsequent experiments we use the AC-Compact algorithm.

Utilization. We investigate the performance of the AC-Compact algorithm further, by varying the number of CPU processes that feed the GPU devices with data.

Figure 9(a) shows the aggregate data processing throughout of the GPU(s) for an increasing number of CPU processes. Figure 9(b) plots the same data normalized by the number of processes. It is clear that multiple processes offer an improvement even when utilizing only one GPU device. Currently, GPUs support multitasking through the use of "timesliced" context switching: each program receives a time slice of the GPU resources and cannot be suspended. When many processes use the same GPU device, data transfers and GPU execution may overlap, offering better GPU utilization. GPU executions have short run times, ranging from 100–300ns per packet, and hence, the GPU device can be effectively timesliced among the CPU processes.

We observe that with two spawned processes, the overhead of the AC-Compact implementation increases, since the 25 Gbit/s throughput achieved is greater than the 21.1 Gbit/s achieved by the AC-Full algorithm, as shown in Figure 8. Increasing to eight processes, a single GPU reaches a maximum of 48 Gbit/s throughput. The PCIe

[2]The capacity of PCIe ×16 v2.0 is 64 Gbit/s *for each* direction. In practice though, the theoretical maximum data rate diverges due to the 8b/10b encoding at the physical layer.

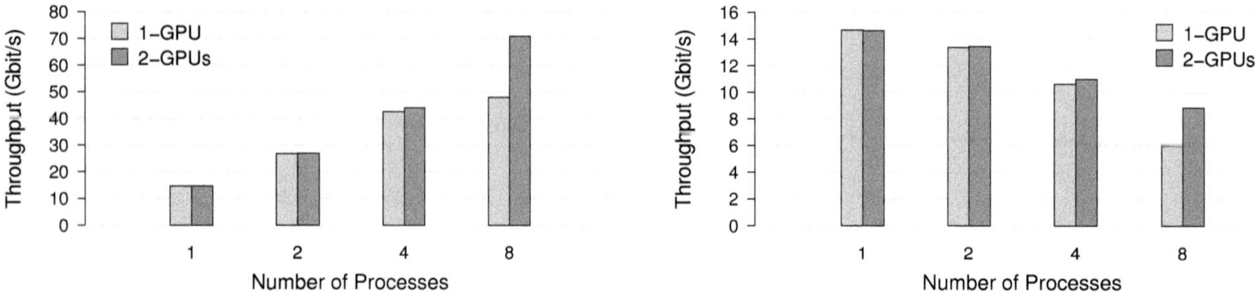

(a) Aggregate (b) Per-process

Figure 9: GPU throughput with an increasing number of CPU-processes up to the number of cores.

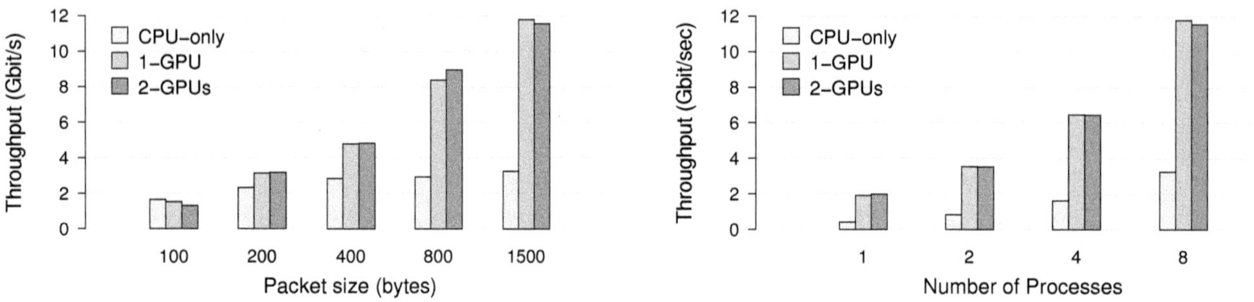

(a) Different packet sizes. (b) Different numbers of CPU processes.

Figure 10: Overall sustained throughput for different workloads and configurations.

bus saturation, which was shown in Figure 7, is the main reason for this upper bound. However, since the PCIe bus is a point-to-point link, adding one more GPU device to the system increases the aggregate GPU throughput to over 70 Gbit/s.

5.2.2 *Overall Performance*

Throughput. In our next experiment, we measured the overall processing throughput achieved by our multi-parallel implementation. Figure 10(a) shows the sustained throughput for different packet sizes. We observe that for very small packet sizes, the GPU-assisted design exhibits a slightly worse performance compared to the multi-core approach alone. The main reason for this is that the buffering overheads for very small packets are greater than the corresponding pattern matching costs, as shown in more detail in the following experiment. Therefore, it is better in terms of performance to match very small packets on the CPU, rather than transferring them to the GPU.

As a consequence, we adopted a simple opportunistic offloading scheme, in which pattern matching of very small packets is performed on the CPU instead of the GPU. Thus, only packets that exceed a minimum size threshold are copied to the buffer that is transferred to the GPU for pattern matching. The packets contain already the TCP reassembled stream of a given direction, hence no state needs to be shared between the CPU and the GPU. The minimum threshold can be inferred off line, using a simple profiling measurement, or automatically at runtime. For simplicity we currently use the former method, although we plan to implement an automated solution in the future.

Figure 10(b) shows the sustained throughput for a different number of CPU processes, using 1500-byte packets. We observe that as the number of processes increases, the sustained throughput also increases linearly. When pattern matching is offloaded on the GPU, the throughput of the legacy multi-core implementation is increased 3.5–4.5 times, depending on the number of processes. The maximum throughput achieved by our base system reaches about 11.7 Gbit/s when utilizing all resources—eight CPU cores and two GPUs.

Finally, we observe that switching from one to two GPUs does not offer significant improvements to the overall performance. This can be explained by the fact that GPU communication and computation costs are completely hidden by the overlapped CPU computation, as discussed in the following experiment.

Timing breakdown. We proceed and examine in greater detail the overall performance achieved by profiling each device separately. In Figures 11(a)–11(d) we plot the individual execution times for various packet lengths. We show the times of each device with different bars, since execution is performed in parallel. CPU and GPU execution is pipelined, hence the CPU can continue unaffected while GPU execution is in progress. Each bar represents the execution time of the two GPU devices, while the thin line on each bar represents the corresponding time when utilizing one GPU. We observe that even when a single GPU is used, the cost for the data transfers and the pattern matching on the GPU is completely hidden by the overlapped CPU workload, for all packet sizes.

The extra cost for packet buffering before transferring them to the GPU depends highly on the packet size. Small packets incur higher cost per-byte, due to the start-up overhead of the `memcpy(3)` function. 100-byte packets or smaller induce a prohibitively large overhead, in comparison with the pattern matching cost. We tried to optimize the copies using a byte-by-byte procedure instead of calling the `memcpy(3)`, however the overhead was still higher. Thereupon, we avoid the small-packets penalty by opportunistically offloading pattern matching computation on the GPU depending on the packet length.

Finally, we notice that GPU execution times for small packets

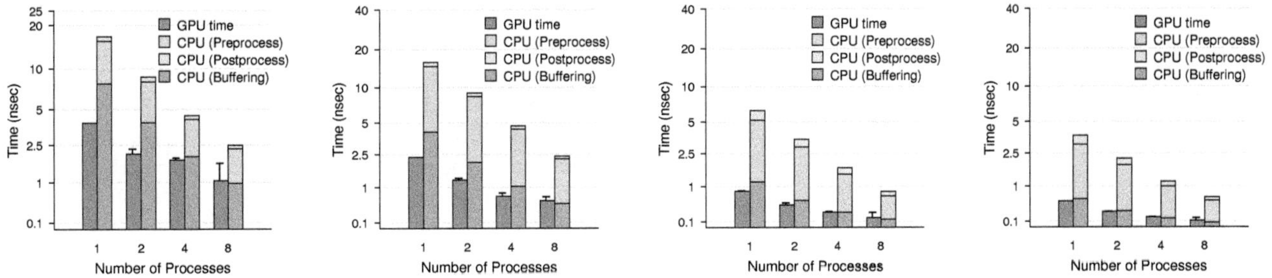

(a) 100-byte packets (b) 200-byte packets (c) 800-byte packets (d) 1500-byte packets

Figure 11: Breakdown of per-byte processing overhead for different packet sizes.

also increase. The main reason for this is that the dimensions of the buffer that is used for transferring the packets to the GPU are fixed, hence it is populated sparsely for small packets.

5.3 Overall Traffic Processing Throughput

In this section, we measure the end-to-end performance of our prototype implementation under realistic conditions.

5.3.1 Synthetic Traffic

Figure 12(a) shows the packet loss ratio for different packet sizes, when replaying traffic at varying rates. We plot values up to the maximum achieved replay rate, hence the smaller the packet size, the lower the replay rate reached. For example, for 200-byte packets, we managed to replay traffic at maximum rate of 1.86 Gbit/s, while for 1500-byte packets we achieved a rate of 7.67 Gbit/s.

Given these traffic replay rates, our prototype system begins to drop packets at 7.22 Gbit/s for 1500-byte packets, which is a 253% improvement over the traditional multi-core implementation. When processing smaller packets, the performance falls to 1.5 Gbit/s, which is slightly higher than the traditional multi-core implementation, although the drop rate is about 6.6 times lower.

Comparing the achieved throughput with the "ideal NIC" case in Figure 10(a), we observe that the NIC adds a variable overhead that depends on the size of the captured packets. It is clear that small packets add more latency to the capturing process than larger ones. For the traditional multi-core approach, we observe an extra overhead of 55% for 200-byte packets, that falls to 18% for 800-byte packets, and 13% for 1500-byte packets. Similarly, the extra overhead for the GPU-accelerated implementation is 110% for 200-byte packets, about 87% for 800-byte packets, and 52% for 1500-byte packets. We observe that the NIC overhead is larger in the GPU-accelerated implementation, and we speculate that this is an issue related to congestion in the PCIe controller.

5.3.2 Real Traffic

In our final experiment, we evaluate MIDeA in a scenario using real traffic. We used a trace of real network traffic (referred to as `UNI`), captured at the gateway of a large university campus with several thousands of users. Specifically, the trace spans 74 minutes, and includes all packets and their payloads, totalling 46 GB. Table 3 summarizes the most important properties of the trace.

To replay the captured trace at high-speed, it has to reside in the main memory of the host to avoid disk accesses. Unfortunately, the main memory of our two traffic generator machines is only 4GB, hence it is impossible to load the whole trace in memory. To overcome this issue, we split the trace to several 2GB parts. While one part is replayed, the other part is loaded into main memory. Since reading from disk is much slower, each part is replayed several times, up until the next part is fully loaded into memory. Using the above pre-fetching scheme, we successfully managed to replay the captured trace with speeds of up to 5.7 Gbit/s.

Packets	73,162,723
Packet size (min/max/avg)	60/1,514/ 679.57
IP Fragments	88,411
TCP sessions	185,642
UDP sessions	174,442
Triggered Snort Alerts	183,050

Table 3: `UNI` trace properties.

Model	Qty	Unit price
NIC: Intel 82599EB	1	$687
CPU: Intel Xeon E5520	2	$336
GPU: NVIDIA GTX480	2	$340

Table 4: Cost of MIDeA components (as of April 2011).

Figure 12(b) shows the dropped packets when increasing the traffic rate. We also annotate the throughput achieved when reading the network packets directly from main memory instead of the NIC. The traditional multi-core implementation starts to drop packets at 1.1 Gbit/s, while the ideal throughput is near 1.4 Gbit/s. When GPU acceleration is enabled, we did not observe any packet loss for speeds of *up to 5.2 Gbit/s*. For comparison, the ideal throughput is 7.8 Gbit/s.

6. DISCUSSION

So far in this paper we went over a detailed description of the design aspects, trade-offs, and performance issues of our proposed architecture. Even though we focused on the parallelization of an intrusion detection system, we strongly believe that the proposed model can benefit a variety of other network monitoring applications, such as traffic classification, content-aware firewalls, spam filtering, and other network traffic analysis systems. With this in mind, we could easily augment a router with multi-parallel network processing capabilities, expanding its functionality without affecting its normal packet routing operations [13].

Price/Performance. For our hardware setup, we have selected relatively low-end devices: two Intel Xeon E5520 processors, two NVIDIA GeForce GTX 480 graphics cards, and an Intel 82599EB 10GbE NIC. Table 4 shows the approximate cost of each component, as of April 2011. The total cost of our base system is about $2739, achieving a throughput per dollar cost of 1.8 Mbps/$.

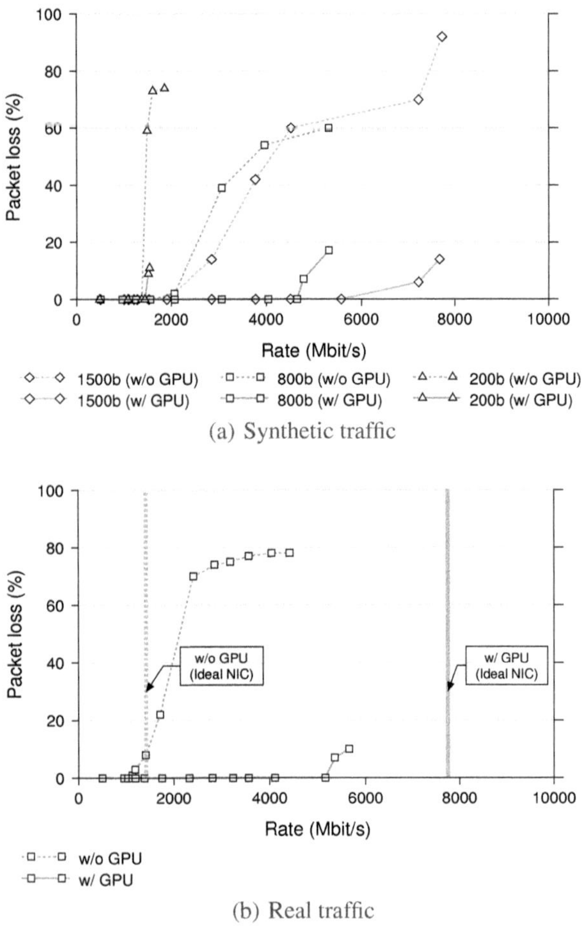

Figure 12: Observed packet loss for (a) synthetic and (b) real traffic, as a function of the traffic rate. MIDeA can handle real traffic speeds of up to 5.2 Gbit/s without dropping any packets.

Limitations and Future Work. In favor of programming simplicity, we chose to use processes instead of threads for parallelizing the CPU part of MIDeA. We believe that a multi-threaded implementation would further increase the complexity of the design without a significant increase in the overall throughput.

In our flow-based partitioning scheme, we avoid any communication between the cores. Traditional Snort-style signature matching does not require any communication for analysis outside the scope of a single flow. In case a network analysis system needs this functionality, e.g., for detecting DDoS attacks or malware propagation, a lightweight communication scheme needs to be integrated for coordinating the different cores [47].

The buffering of network packets, described in section 3.2.1, introduces an extra copy operation. This is mandatory for our design, considering that most packets have to be processed before matching them against signatures, and that transferring a single packet each time significantly reduces the PCIe throughput.

Finally, each process allocates a different memory space on the GPU, due to the restriction of the CUDA driver for preventing sharing of GPU memory between different processes. Although the same policy applies to threads, we believe that future releases of the CUDA driver will support device memory sharing. In that case, we could easily migrate to the faster AC-Full algorithm. We also believe that a shared GPU memory space would exhibit higher locality and increase the computational throughput.

7. RELATED WORK

Prior work has focused extensively on the use of specialized hardware to augment NIDSs capabilities. The majority of these approaches focus on improving deep packet inspection (DPI), which is the most computationally-intensive NIDS operation, using specialized hardware, such as FPGAs, ASICs, and TCAMs [9, 12, 27, 30, 45, 52]. Recently, Meiners et al. [27] proposed a custom regular expression matching approach based on TCAMs, which achieves a throughput of up to 18.6 Gbit/s; our corresponding pattern matching implementation alone reaches a 70 Gbit/s throughput, which is almost a four-times improvement, using commodity off-the-shelf equipment. Other approaches employ a pre-filtering mechanism based on FPGAs to reduce the amount of traffic sent to a software NIDS/NIPS for inspection [16,43]. Unfortunately, most implementations are tied to a specific architecture, and thus, are particularly difficult to extend and program. Any changes in the rule set require recompilation, regeneration of the automaton, resynthesis, replacement, and routing of the circuits, which is a time-consuming and difficult procedure.

Much work has also focused on improving the performance of detection mechanisms, such as string matching and regular expression matching [7, 22, 23, 40, 46, 51]. These works are orthogonal to ours, and can be integrated to our system to improve memory utilization and performance.

In another line of work, cluster-based approaches have been proposed for keeping-up with the increasing link speeds. Instead of having a single server to process all incoming traffic, a cluster of servers is used instead. The major issue then is how to partition the incoming traffic to the back-end servers, while supporting stateful processing. Kruegel et al. [21] propose a stateful slicing mechanism that divides the overall network traffic into subsets of manageable size, which are then processed by different sensors. Foschini et al. [14] extend that work with a parallel matching algorithm that allows communication between the sensors through a dedicated control plane. SPANIDS [38] uses a specialized FPGA-based switch, that takes into account flow information and the load of each server when redirecting network packets. Xinidis et al. [50] present an active splitter architecture that provides early filtering to reduce the load of the back-end sensors.

Other approaches attempt to improve the performance of NIDS using commodity hardware. Paxson et al. [35] and Valentin et al. [47] implemented a NIDS cluster that scales through the use of parallel nodes. Their system, based on Bro [33], demonstrates the ability to scale beyond the capacity of a single NIDS instance using commodity hardware, with the exception of the special purpose front-end hardware that was used to distribute traffic evenly across the back-end nodes. In Supra-linear Packet Processing [19], a single thread is responsible for packet gathering and dispatching, while many other threads are processing incoming flows in parallel. Thus, each processing thread handles a specific flow in isolation. Unfortunately, a lot of time is spent on context switches between threads, most likely due to high levels of locking contention to the shared packet queue.

To eliminate the excessive contention rates due to packet queue access in the packet processing architectures, flow-pinning is commonly used (i.e., all packets of a flow are "pinned" to be processed by a specific thread) [20]. This approach requires slightly more data storage to keep the incoming packets to separate queues. However, it allows most of the threads to work independently, which is a key characteristic of a good multi-threaded algorithm. Schuff et al. [39] evaluate different per-flow and intra-flow parallelization approaches. Although their results do not propose a clear winner, it seems that pure flow-concurrent parallelism performs better in almost all cases.

Recently, graphics processors have been used to boost computationally intensive tasks in intrusion detection systems. Gnort [48, 49] was the first attempt that sufficiently utilized the graphics processor for string searching and regular expression matching. Unfortunately, its single-threaded architecture restricts its scalability in the advent of multi-core CPUs. Many other approaches followed the above scheme [18, 41], without significant differences in the architecture and the performance benefits.

8. CONCLUSION

In this work, we designed and built a multi-parallel intrusion detection architecture, as a scalable solution for the processing and stateful analysis of network traffic. Our system achieves high performance, with a processing throughput that exceeds 5 Gbit/s for real traffic, and raw pattern matching speeds of 70 Gbit/s, using commodity off-the-shelf hardware, in a single box.

MIDeA has three levels of parallelization, at the NIC, the CPU, and the GPU levels. It consists of a multi-queue NIC, which distributes the incoming traffic across a set of multi-core CPUs for packet processing and analysis. Each CPU core is processing the traffic of only a subset of network flows. Having split the traffic to different cores, MIDeA further offloads the costly content inspection operations to a set of GPUs. By parallelizing both packet processing and content inspection across multiple CPU cores and graphics processors, MIDeA offers a scalable approach for building a multi-parallel NIDS, which can operate at speeds of several Gbit/s, while at the same time it has en extremely low price point.

9. ACKNOWLEDGMENTS

The authors would like to thank Evangelos Markatos for his invaluable comments and suggestions during the preparation of this paper. This work was supported in part by the Marie Curie Actions – Reintegration Grants project PASS, by the FP7-PEOPLE-2009-IOF project MALCODE and the FP7 project SysSec, funded by the European Commission under Grant Agreements No. 254116 and No. 257007, and by the project i-Code, funded by the Prevention, Preparedness and Consequence Management of Terrorism and other Security-related Risks Programme of the European Commission – Directorate-General for Home Affairs under Grant Agreement No. JLS/2009/CIPS/AG/C2-050. This publication reflects the views only of the authors, and the Commission cannot be held responsible for any use which may be made of the information contained herein.

10. REFERENCES

[1] Endace Security Manager. http://www.endace.com/endace-security-manager2.html.

[2] Intel 82599EB 10 Gigabit Ethernet Controller. http://ark.intel.com/Product.aspx?id=32207.

[3] Receive side scaling on Intel Network Adapters. http://www.intel.com/support/network/adapter/pro100/sb/cs-027574.htm.

[4] Tcpreplay. http://tcpreplay.synfin.net/.

[5] A. V. Aho and M. J. Corasick. Efficient String Matching: an Aid to Bibliographic Search. *Communications of the ACM*, 18(6):333–340, June 1975.

[6] Z. K. Baker and V. K. Prasanna. Time and Area Efficient Pattern Matching on FPGAs. In *Proceedings of the 12th ACM/SIGDA International Symposium on Field Programmable Gate Arrays (FPGA)*, 2004.

[7] M. Becchi and P. Crowley. A Hybrid Finite Automaton for Practical Deep Packet Inspection. In *Proceedings of the ACM International Conference on emerging Networking Experiments and Technologies Conference (CoNEXT)*, 2007.

[8] V. Chandola, A. Banerjee, and V. Kumar. Anomaly Detection: A Survey. *ACM Computing Surveys*, 41:15:1–15:58, July 2009.

[9] C. R. Clark, W. Lee, D. E. Schimmel, D. Contis, M. Koné, and A. Thomas. A Hardware Platform for Network Intrusion Detection and Prevention. In P. Crowley, M. A. Franklin, H. Hadimioglu, and P. Z. Onufryk, editors, *Proceedings of the 3rd Workshop on Network Processors and Applications (NP3)*, 2005.

[10] C. R. Clark and D. E. Schimmel. Efficient Reconfigurable Logic Circuits for Matching Complex Network Intrusion Detection Patterns. In *Proceedings of the International Conference on Field Programmable Logic and Applications (FPL)*, 2003.

[11] L. Deri. Improving Passive Packet Capture: Beyond Device Polling. In *Proceedings of 4th International System Administration and Network Engineering Conference (SANE)*, 2004.

[12] S. Dharmapurikar, P. Krishnamurthy, T. S. Sproull, and J. W. Lockwood. Deep Packet Inspection Using Parallel Bloom Filters. *IEEE Micro*, 24(1), 2004.

[13] M. Dobrescu, N. Egi, K. Argyraki, B.-G. Chun, K. Fall, G. Iannaccone, A. Knies, M. Manesh, and S. Ratnasamy. RouteBricks: Exploiting Parallelism to Scale Software Routers. In *Proceedings of the 22nd ACM SIGOPS Symposium on Operating Systems Principles (SOSP)*, 2009.

[14] L. Foschini, A. V. Thapliyal, L. Cavallaro, C. Kruegel, and G. Vigna. A Parallel Architecture for Stateful, High-Speed Intrusion Detection. In *Proceedings of the 4th International Conference on Information Systems Security (ICISS)*, 2008.

[15] F. Fusco and L. Deri. High Speed Network Traffic Analysis with Commodity Multi-core Systems. In *Proceedings of the 10th Internet Measurement Conference (IMC)*, 2010.

[16] J. M. Gonzalez, V. Paxson, and N. Weaver. Shunting: A Hardware/Software Architecture for Flexible, High-Performance Network Intrusion Prevention. In *Proceedings of the 14th ACM Conference on Computer and Communications Security (CCS)*, 2007.

[17] S. Han, K. Jang, K. Park, and S. Moon. PacketShader: A GPU-accelerated Software Router. In *Proceedings of the ACM SIGCOMM 2010 Conference on Applications, Technologies, Architectures, and Protocols for Computer Communications (SIGCOMM)*, August 2010.

[18] N.-F. Huang, H.-W. Hung, S.-H. Lai, Y.-M. Chu, and W.-Y. Tsai. A GPU-Based Multiple-Pattern Matching Algorithm for Network Intrusion Detection Systems. In *Proceedings of the 22nd International Conference on Advanced Information Networking and Applications - Workshops (AINAW)*, 2008.

[19] Intel Corporation. Supra-linear Packet Processing Performance with Intel Multi-core Processors, 2006.

[20] Intel Corporation. Removing System Bottlenecks in Multi-threaded Applications, 2008.

[21] C. Kruegel, F. Valeur, G. Vigna, and R. Kemmerer. Stateful Intrusion Detection for High-Speed Networks. In *Proceedings of the 23rd IEEE Symposium on Security and Privacy (S&P)*, May 2002.

[22] S. Kumar, B. Chandrasekaran, J. Turner, and G. Varghese. Curing Regular Expressions Matching Algorithms from Insomnia, Amnesia, and Acalculia. In *Proceedings of the 3rd ACM/IEEE Symposium on Architecture for Networking and Communications Systems (ANCS)*, 2007.

[23] S. Kumar, S. Dharmapurikar, F. Yu, P. Crowley, and J. Turner. Algorithms to Accelerate Multiple Regular Expressions Matching for Deep Packet Inspection. In *Proceedings of the ACM SIGCOMM 2006 Conference on Applications, Technologies, Architectures, and Protocols for Computer Communications (SIGCOMM)*, 2006.

[24] J. Lee, S. H. Hwang, N. Park, S.-W. Lee, S. Jun, and Y. S. Kim. A High Performance NIDS Using FPGA-based Regular Expression Matching. In *Proceedings of the 22nd ACM Symposium on Applied computing (SAC)*, 2007.

[25] B. H. Leitao. Tuning 10Gb Network Cards on Linux. In *Proceedings of the 2009 Linux Symposium*, July 2009.

[26] R.-T. Liu, N.-F. Huang, C.-H. Chen, and C.-N. Kao. A Fast String-matching Algorithm for Network Processor-based Intrusion Detection System. *ACM Transactions on Embedded Computing Systems*, 3(3):614–633, 2004.

[27] C. R. Meiners, J. Patel, E. Norige, E. Torng, and A. X. Liu. Fast Regular Expression Matching Using Small TCAMs for Network Intrusion Detection and Prevention Systems. In *Proceedings of the 19th USENIX Security Symposium*, 2010.

[28] Microsoft Corporation. Scalable Networking: Eliminating the Receive Processing Bottleneck - Introducing RSS, 2005.

[29] A. Mitra, W. Najjar, and L. Bhuyan. Compiling PCRE to FPGA for accelerating SNORT IDS. In *Proceedings of the 3rd ACM/IEEE Symposium on Architecture for Networking and Communications Systems (ANCS)*, 2007.

[30] J. Moscola, J. Lockwood, R. Loui, and M. Pachos. Implementation of a Content-Scanning Module for an Internet Firewall. In *Proceedings of 11th IEEE Symposium on Field-Programmable Custom Computing Machines (FCCM)*, 2003.

[31] M. Norton. Optimizing Pattern Matching for Intrusion Detection, July 2004.

[32] NVIDIA. NVIDIA CUDA Programming Guide.

[33] V. Paxson. Bro: A System for Detecting Network Intruders in Real-time. In *Proceedings of the 7th Conference on USENIX Security Symposium*, 1998.

[34] V. Paxson, K. Asanović, S. Dharmapurikar, J. Lockwood, R. Pang, R. Sommer, and N. Weaver. Rethinking Hardware Support for Network Analysis and Intrusion Prevention. In *Proceedings of the 1st USENIX Workshop on Hot Topics in Security (HotSec)*, 2006.

[35] V. Paxson, R. Sommer, and N. Weaver. An Architecture for Exploiting Multi-core Processors to Parallelize Network Intrusion Prevention. In *Proceedings of the 30th IEEE Sarnoff Symposium*, May 2007.

[36] M. Roesch. Snort: Lightweight Intrusion Detection for Networks. In *Proceedings of the 1999 USENIX Large Installation System Administration Conference (LISA)*, 1999.

[37] D. P. Scarpazza, O. Villa, and F. Petrini. Exact Multi-pattern String Matching on the Cell/B.E. Processor. In *Proceedings of the 5th Conference on Computing Frontiers (CF)*, 2008.

[38] L. Schaelicke, K. Wheeler, and C. Freeland. SPANIDS: A Scalable Network Intrusion Detection Loadbalancer. In *Proceedings of the 2nd Conference on Computing Frontiers (CF)*, 2005.

[39] D. L. Schuff, Y. R. Choe, and V. S. Pai. Conservative vs. Optimistic Parallelization of Stateful Network Intrusion Detection. In *Proceedings of the 12th ACM SIGPLAN Symposium on Principles and Practice of Parallel Programming (PPoPP)*, 2007.

[40] R. Smith, C. Estan, and S. Jha. XFA: Faster Signature Matching with Extended Automata. In *Proceedings of the 29th IEEE Symposium on Security and Privacy (S&P)*, 2008.

[41] R. Smith, N. Goyal, J. Ormont, K. Sankaralingam, and C. Estan. Evaluating GPUs for Network Packet Signature Matching. In *Proceedings of the International Symposium on Performance Analysis of Systems and Software (ISPASS)*, 2009.

[42] R. Sommer and V. Paxson. Outside the Closed World: On Using Machine Learning for Network Intrusion Detection. In *Proceeding of the 31st IEEE Symposium on Security and Privacy (S&P)*, 2010.

[43] H. Song, T. Sproull, M. Attig, and J. Lockwood. Snort Offloader: A Reconfigurable Hardware NIDS Filter. In *Proceedings of the 15th International Conference on Field Programmable Logic and Applications (FPL)*, 2005.

[44] Sourcefire. Sourcefire 3D System. `http://www.sourcefire.com/security-technologies/cyber-security-products/3d-system`.

[45] I. Sourdis and D. Pnevmatikatos. Pre-Decoded CAMs for Efficient and High-Speed NIDS Pattern Matching. In *Proceedings of the 12th Annual IEEE Symposium on Field Programmable Custom Computing Machines (FCCM)*, 2004.

[46] N. Tuck, T. Sherwood, B. Calder, and G. Varghese. Deterministic Memory-efficient String Matching Algorithms for Intrusion Detection. In *Proceedings of the 23rd IEEE International Conference on Computer Communications Conference (INFOCOM)*, 2004.

[47] M. Vallentin, R. Sommer, J. Lee, C. Leres, V. Paxson, and B. Tierney. The NIDS Cluster: Scalable, Stateful Network Intrusion Detection on Commodity Hardware. In *Proceedings of the 10th International Symposium on Recent Advances in Intrusion Detection (RAID)*, 2007.

[48] G. Vasiliadis, S. Antonatos, M. Polychronakis, E. P. Markatos, and S. Ioannidis. Gnort: High Performance Network Intrusion Detection Using Graphics Processors. In *Proceedings of the 11th International Symposium on Recent Advances in Intrusion Detection (RAID)*, 2008.

[49] G. Vasiliadis, M. Polychronakis, S. Antonatos, E. P. Markatos, and S. Ioannidis. Regular Expression Matching on Graphics Hardware for Intrusion Detection. In *Proceedings of the 12th International Symposium on Recent Advances in Intrusion Detection (RAID)*, 2009.

[50] K. Xinidis, I. Charitakis, S. Antonatos, K. G. Anagnostakis, and E. P. Markatos. An Active Splitter Architecture for Intrusion Detection and Prevention. *IEEE Transactions on Dependable and Secure Computing*, 3:31–44, January 2006.

[51] F. Yu, Z. Chen, Y. Diao, T. V. Lakshman, and R. H. Katz. Fast and Memory-efficient Regular Expression Matching for Deep Packet Inspection. In *Proceedings of the 2nd ACM/IEEE symposium on Architecture for Networking and Communications Systems (ANCS)*, 2006.

[52] F. Yu, R. H. Katz, and T. V. Lakshman. Gigabit Rate Packet Pattern-Matching Using TCAM. In *Proceedings of the 12th IEEE International Conference on Network Protocols (ICNP)*, October 2004.

BitShred: Feature Hashing Malware for Scalable Triage and Semantic Analysis

Jiyong Jang
Carnegie Mellon University
Pittsburgh, PA, USA
jiyongj@cmu.edu

David Brumley
Carnegie Mellon University
Pittsburgh, PA, USA
dbrumley@cmu.edu

Shobha Venkataraman
AT&T Labs – Research
Florham Park, NJ, USA
shvenk@research.att.com

Abstract

The sheer volume of new malware found each day is growing at an exponential pace. This growth has created a need for automatic malware triage techniques that determine what malware is similar, what malware is unique, and why. In this paper, we present BitShred, a system for large-scale malware similarity analysis and clustering, and for automatically uncovering semantic inter- and intra-family relationships within clusters. The key idea behind BitShred is using feature hashing to dramatically reduce the high-dimensional feature spaces that are common in malware analysis. Feature hashing also allows us to mine correlated features between malware families and samples using co-clustering techniques. Our evaluation shows that BitShred speeds up typical malware triage tasks by up to 2,365x and uses up to 82x less memory on a single CPU, all with comparable accuracy to previous approaches. We also develop a parallelized version of BitShred, and demonstrate scalability within the Hadoop framework.

Categories and Subject Descriptors

D.4.6 [**Operating Systems**]: Security and Protection—*Invasive software*

General Terms

Design, Performance, Security

Keywords

Malware Triage, Feature Hashing, Co-clustering, Hadoop

1. INTRODUCTION

The volume of new malware, fueled by easy-to-use malware morphing engines, is growing at an exponential pace [8]. In 2009 security vendors received upwards of 8,000 unique by hash malware samples per day [8], with the projected total to reach over 1,000,000 per day within the next 7 years. The sheer volume of malware means we need automatic methods for large-scale malware triage techniques and systems.

At a high level, triage has two steps. First, per-sample malware analysis is run on each sample to extract a set of features. Second, malware are compared in a pairwise fashion to determine similarity, e.g., in our work, like others, using the Jaccard distance. Once we determine what malware are similar, and what are the important semantic similarities and differences to known malware cases, triage can make informed decisions. For example, triage may perform further in-depth analysis on one representative malware sample per family that would be cost-prohibitive to do on the entire data set.

In this paper, we present BitShred, a system for large-scale malware similarity analysis and clustering, and for automatically uncovering semantic inter- and intra-family relationships within clusters. The main feature of BitShred is it is agnostic to the particular per-malware analysis routine, even when the extracted feature set has a very large feature space. Malware authors and defenders are caught in a cyclic battle where defenders invent ever-more advanced and accurate per-malware analyses for feature extraction, which are then defeated by new malware obfuscation algorithms. The cyclic battle brings the need for malware triage techniques that allow us to plug-in the latest or most appropriate analysis for feature extraction. We empirically show BitShred meets the desired requirement by demonstrating BitShred on two previously proposed per-sample analysis: dynamic behavior analysis from Bayer *et al.* [13] where the feature space is 2^{17}, and static code reuse detection as proposed in [9, 25, 38] where the feature space is 2^{128}.

The main issues for handling large volumes of malware are (a) efficiently representing malware features (so we can fit more in main memory without paging), and (b) comparing feature sets between malware, and (c) determining which features are correlated for malware groups. To give a sense of scale, currently over 8000 new malware per day are observed, requiring about 31 million comparisons to find families using hierarchical clustering. If we perform n-item analysis when $n = 16$ bytes, an exact representation of the features would require 2^{128} (2^{95} *gigabytes*) per sample. We could not perform all 31 million comparisons on previous data structures in 24 hours on a single CPU.

The central idea in BitShred is to use feature hashing [36, 37, 39]. Feature hashing allows for dramatic dimensionality reduction, so the hashed representation takes less room in memory, and is also L1/L2 cache efficient. The catch is that feature hashing introduces collisions in the reduced feature space. For example, we use a hash function that compresses the 2^{128} feature space down to 2^{18}, there will be an enormous number of collisions in the feature space. The surprising thing is that with feature hashing, we need just a single hash function for the dimensionality reduction of the feature space. Requiring only single hash function as well as dimensionality reduction have immediate performance implications. This result is backed by theory and experimentation that shows pairwise comparison, thus algorithms built on top like hierarchical clustering, will be close to exact.

Feature hashing allows us to also simultaneously mine correlated features between malware families and samples using co-clustering techniques. Clustering alone acts like a blackbox, telling us only that malware are grouped because they are similar. Co-clustering goes one step further and tells us why malware are similar by simultaneously clustering features. For example, co-clustering allows us to group two malware and to say the features that explain why they are similar (e.g., a significant amount of shared code) and why they are different (e.g., contacting different command and control hosts).

Contributions. Our main contribution is a system for performing the triage tasks described above that scales to data sets orders of magnitude larger than existing approaches. We present a theoretical analysis showing that feature hashing with the Jaccard offers near optimal results, and build a real system called BitShred that is independent of the particular per-malware analysis engine and works even for high-dimensional feature sets. We extensively evaluate BitShred's scalability, speed and accuracy using two different per-sample analysis: code similarity and dynamic behaviors. Our performance evaluation shows that BitShred can cluster over 116,000 malware per day on a single node, and over 1.9 million per day on a Hadoop cluster where we develop an optimal schedule that minimizes communication overhead and provides uniform node work. We also propose novel techniques based upon co-clustering adapted to BitShred for identifying similar or distinguishing semantic features in malware families.

2. THE CORE IDEA, FEATURE HASHING, AND THE RELATION TO PREVIOUS APPROACHES

We focus on any analysis that outputs a set of features that are Boolean, or can be encoded as Boolean variables. For example, in code reuse detection the features are whether a code fragment is present or not. Real-value features can be encoded by bucketizing them, where a Boolean feature is true if the feature falls within a particular bucket. This allows us to plug in many types of analysis.

2.1 Feature Hashing & Malware Similarity

We compute malware similarity using the Jaccard similarity metric. The Jaccard calculates the percentage of common features, with the idea that the larger the sharing is, the more alike the malware are, and is used extensively in previous work [13, 32]. More formally, given two feature sets g_a and g_b for malware s_a and s_b respectively, the Jaccard similarity (i.e., index) is:

$$J(g_a, g_b) = \frac{|g_a \cap g_b|}{|g_a \cup g_b|} \quad (1)$$

In order to motivate feature hashing, consider first using a standard implementation of Jaccard, e.g., as found in SimMetrics [5]. The advantage of this approach is the size of the feature data structure is linear in the number of features a malware sample actually presents, e.g., if our feature space is of size 2^{128} but a particular malware only has 2^{30} features, the data structure is still only 2^{30} in size. Unfortunately, set operations are not amenable to feature extraction using co-clustering, and the set union and intersection operations themselves are a bottleneck. In our experiments, we could only cluster about 2,388 malware/day using this approach (§ 5, labeled as exact Jaccard).

We take an approach of encoding features as a bitvector. The Jaccard becomes fast CPU-friendly logic operations:

$$J_{bv}(f_a, f_b) = \frac{S(f_a \wedge f_b)}{S(f_a \vee f_b)} \quad (2)$$

where f_i is the bitvector representation of the feature set for malware s_i and $S(\cdot)$ counts the number of set bits.

Feature hashing [36, 37, 39] is a specific way of encoding features as a bitvector. Most existing implementations of bitvector Jaccard, e.g., the one found in python, assume the feature space is completely encoded using index variables where feature 1 corresponds to bit 1, feature 2 to bit 2, feature 3 to bit 3, and so on. This scheme is impractical when the feature space is large, e.g., as in our case where such an encoding would result in a per-malware data structure that is gigabytes in size.

A more efficient encoding is to use Bloom filters, which we initially tried. A Bloom filter is a probabilistic data structure used to efficiently encode sets and perform set membership tests. Let $h_1, h_2, h_3, ..., h_k$ be a set of hash functions of type $D \rightarrow R$ and $|D| \gg |R|$, i.e., each hash is a compression function. A Bloom filter calculates $h_i(x) = d$ and sets the d'th bit in the m-length bitvector for all hash functions h_i and each feature value x. To test if an element x' is in the feature set, you check that the $h_i(x')$ bit is set for all i. If any are not set, then x' is not in the set. Bloom filters have false positives due to hash collisions, but never have a false negative. The false positive rate is reduced, all things being equal, by adding more hash functions.

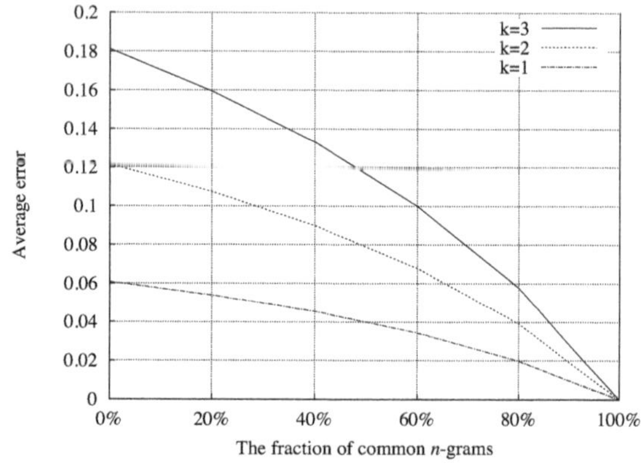

Figure 1: Error with various k where m=8,192

Bloom filters did not work well. The catch in our problem setting is we want to approximate the Jaccard, not perform set membership tests. We had naively estimated the error rate to be the expected Bloom filter collisions in the numerator divided by the expected number of Bloom filter collisions in the denominator, which is mathematically unsound: dividing two expected values will not provide the proper expectation of the Jaccard expression.

Feature hashing is similar to Bloom filters where we compute $h(x) = d$ and set the d'th bit, except that only a single hash function is used. We call the hashed version of features the *malware fingerprint*. Theorem 1 (§ 3.1) shows that the malware fingerprints provide a near-optimal approximation of the true Jaccard index. To the best of our knowledge, no previous work (e.g., [15]) has performed similar analysis. Indeed, the proof shows that increasing the number of hash functions increases error, which is why Bloom filters don't work well. This corresponds well to feature hashing, where only one hash function is used. Further, requiring only one hash has obvious performance improvement implications.

We also showed through simulations on random sets of n-grams, the use of single hash function minimized the difference between the Jaccard in Equation 1 and the bitvector Jaccard in Equation 2. In particular, we created two sets that contain 1000 n-grams each, with varying number of overlapping n-grams, and measured how much the bitvector Jaccard differs from the Jaccard. Figure 1 shows the average error as the fraction of common n-grams and the number of hash functions k vary (the standard deviation is very small and therefore, not shown). We note that the error increases as k increases, with minimum error achieved at $k = 1$, which is different from the usual Bloom filter set membership tests.

The theoretical and empirical analysis motivates feature hashing in BitShred. The main quality metric for our approach is how well our approach approximates a full set representation vs performance improvements. We show through numerous experiments that our approach has extremely high accuracy with up to 2,365 times speedup on a single CPU.

2.2 Co-clustering in BitShred

A BitShred fingerprint is a m-length bitvector where the intuition is a bit i is 1 if the particular malware sample has a feature g_i, and 0

$$\mathbf{M} = \begin{vmatrix} 0 & 1 & 1 & 0 & 1 \\ 1 & 0 & 0 & 1 & 0 \\ 0 & 1 & 1 & 0 & 1 \\ 1 & 0 & 0 & 1 & 0 \\ 1 & 0 & 0 & 1 & 0 \end{vmatrix} \Rightarrow \left|\begin{array}{ccc|cc} 1 & 1 & 1 & 0 & 0 \\ 1 & 1 & 1 & 0 & 0 \\ \hline 0 & 0 & 0 & 1 & 1 \\ 0 & 0 & 0 & 1 & 1 \\ 0 & 0 & 0 & 1 & 1 \end{array}\right| = \mathbf{M}'$$

Figure 2: $\mathbf{M}$ is co-clustered to identify the checkerboard sub-matrix $\mathbf{M}'$ of highly correlated malware/feature pairs.

otherwise. Given n malware samples, the m-sized list of BitShred fingerprints can be viewed as a matrix $\mathbf{M}$ of size $n \times m$ where each row is a malware fingerprint, and each column is a particular feature. This intuition leads us to the idea of using co-clustering (aka bi-clustering) to auto-correlate both features and malware simultaneously. Within the matrix, co-clustering does this by creating sub-matrices among columns (features) and rows (malware) where each sub-matrix is a highly correlated malware/feature pair.

Co-clustering allows us to discover substantial, non-trivial structural relationships between malware samples, many of which will not be discovered with simpler approaches. For example, consider how the following simple approaches for mining features between two malware families would be limited:

- Identify all common features between families. In BitShred, this is accomplished by taking the bitwise-and ($\wedge$) of the malware fingerprints. However, we would miss identifying code that is present in 99% of family 1 and 99% of family 2.
- Identify all distinctive features in a list of malware. In our setting, this is accomplished with bitwise xor ($\oplus$) of the fingerprints. This would have limited value for the same reasons as above.
- A third approach might be to cluster features either *before* or *after* the malware fingerprints have been clustered. Note, however, this approach would also result in misleading information, e.g., clustering features *after* the clustering malware fingerprints would not reveal structural similarity across fingerprints in different families, and clustering features *before* the malware fingerprints may result in poor malware clusters if there are many feature clusters that are common to multiple groups of malware fingerprint clusters.

We introduce some terminology to make co-clustering precise. A matrix is *homogeneous* if the entries of the matrix are similar, e.g., they are mostly 0 or mostly 1, and define the *homogeneity* of a matrix to be the (larger) fraction of entries that have the same value. Define a *row-cluster* to be a subset of the rows M (i.e., malware samples) that are grouped together, and a *column-cluster* to be a subset of the columns (i.e., the features) that are grouped together. The goal of co-clustering is to create a pair of row and column labeling vectors:

$$\mathbf{r} \in \{1, 2, ..., k\}^n \quad \text{and} \quad \mathbf{c} \in \{1, 2, ..., \ell\}^m$$

The sub-matrices created are homogeneous, rectangular regions. The number of rectangular regions is either given as input to the algorithm, or determined by the algorithm with a penalty function that trades off between the number of rectangles and the homogeneity achieved by these rectangles [1].

For example, Figure 2 shows a list of 5 malware BitShred fingerprints where there are 5 possible features. The result is the 5×5 matrix M. Co-clustering automatically identifies the clustering to produce sub-matrices, as shown by the checkerboard M'. The sub-matrices are homogeneous, indicating highly-correlated feature/-malware pairs. In this case the labeling vectors are $\mathbf{r} = (12122)^T$ and $\mathbf{c} = (21121)^T$. These vectors say that row 1 in $\mathbf{M}$ mapped to row cluster 1 (above the horizontal bar) in $\mathbf{M'}$, row 2 mapped to row cluster 2 (below the horizontal bar), etc., and similar for the column vectors for features. We can reach two clustering conclusions. First, the row clusters indicate malware s_1 and s_3 are in one family, and s_2, s_4, and s_5 are in another family. The column clusters say the distinguishing features between the two families are features 2, 3, and 5.

[1]The goal is to make the minimum number of rectangles which achieve the maximum homogeneity. For this reason, co-clustering algorithms ensure that homogeneity of the rectangles is penalized by the number of rectangles if they need to automatically determine k and ℓ.

2.3 Related Approaches

Feature Hashing and Locality Sensitive Hashing. Our main goal is to increase scalability in malware comparison, as well as enable data mining on co-occurring features. We are not alone. Bayer *et al.* [13] has made significant strides in this area by using locality sensitive hashing (LSH) [10]. The main idea in LSH is to define a hash function h such that $h(s_1) = h(s_2)$ if the two malware s_1 and s_2 are similar. The hash is run over all malware samples, and only those with unique hash values are compared. LSH is complementary to feature hashing, because it reduces the number of items while feature hashing reduces the number of features. While complementary, our evaluation shows that using feature hashing alone outperforms LSH alone by a factor of 2-to-1. Previous work has shown this bears on theoretical analysis as well [36]. While in our evaluation we focus on the effects of each algorithm independently, both feature hashing and locality-sensitive hashing could be combined in a real system.

Feature Hashing and graph analysis comparison. Others have proposed malware similarity methods that do not use boolean features. For example, the Zynamics BinDiff tool [7] and Hu *et al.* [21] use a similarity metric based upon isomorphisms between control flow and function call graphs. While we can compute call graph similarity based upon features, e.g., how many basic blocks are in common, our approach cannot readily be adapted to actually computing the isomorphism. Hu *et al.* argue that although graph-based isomorphism is expensive, it is less susceptible to being fooled by polymorphism. In Hu *et al.* 's implementation they return the 5 nearest neighbors, and achieve an 80% success rate in having 1 of the 5 within the same family on a data set of 102,391 samples. The query time was between 0.015s to 872s, with an average of 21s using 100MB of memory. We did not have access to their data set; results for the same size of our data set for finding nearest neighbor using the Jaccard are reported in § 5.1.

Classification vs. Clustering. Classification uses *labeled* samples to learn a rule for assigning labels to new samples. Feature hashing was previously used to build an efficient spam classifier [11], which is trained with labeled (i.e., spam/not-spam) emails and then determines whether an incoming email is spam or not. On the contrary, clustering groups *unlabeled* samples based on given similarity metrics. In our setting, (unlabeled) malware are grouped based upon similar features – static code or dynamic behaviors. To the best of our knowledge, ours is the first study to introduce clustering techniques combining feature hashing with the Jaccard and to present a theoretical proof of correctness.

2.4 Security and Rest of Paper

Security. Feature hashing, like LSH, uses a hash function which must be kept secret. If the hash function is known, then an attacker may be able to "fool" the algorithm into an atypical number of collisions, thus potentially reducing the overall accuracy. This problem is mitigated by using a keyed hash function as is usual, e.g., picking a secret key k and computing $h(k||s_a||k)$ for item s_a. For simplicity, in the rest of this paper we refer to the hash as simply h

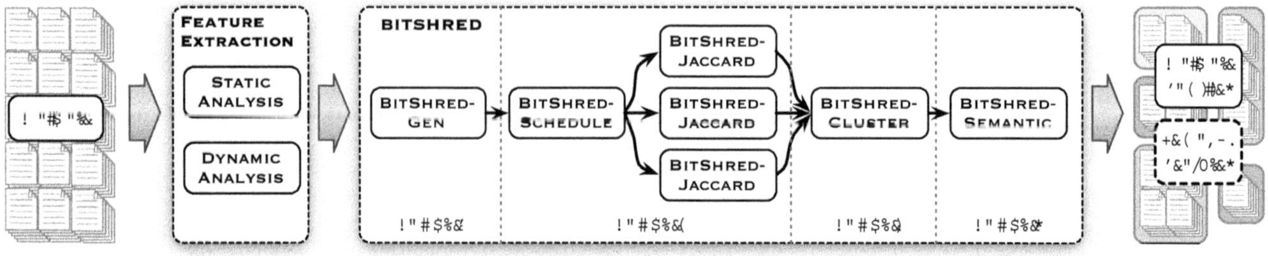

Figure 3: BitShred Overview

instead of a keyed variant, with the expectation it is used as a keyed function for security.

In the rest of this paper we describe BitShred, our system for malware triage and semantic feature identification on very large malware data sets based on the above ideas. We focus on the performance of our hash feature approach vs. previously proposed methods such as straight set-based analysis, winnowing, and locality sensitive hashing. The main conclusion is that BitShred provides the same accuracy but better performance. Better performance means we scale to much larger malware volumes, as well as deal with current volumes much more quickly. We also show that BitShred can be parallelized, which allows us to take advantage of infrastructures like supercomputers and Hadoop as performance requirements exceed that which can be provided by a single CPU.

Finally, we show BitShred in the context of an end-to-end system for malware triage. In our data set BitShred has above 90% accuracy at automatically identifying malware families and semantic features. While malware authors can always add more obfuscation and make analysis harder, thus decreasing accuracy of any system, the core concepts in BitShred can "plug-in" any malware analysis that outputs Boolean or (binary-encoded) integer-valued values, and speed it up while retaining similar accuracy to the exact Jaccard.

3. BITSHRED OVERVIEW

At a high level, BitShred takes in a set of malware, runs per-malware analysis, and then performs inter-malware comparison, correlation, and feature analysis, as shown in Figure 3. BitShred's job is to speed up subsequent correlation after using existing techniques to perform per-sample feature extraction. In our implementation, we experiment with using n-grams as proposed in [9, 25, 38] because the feature space is extremely large, and dynamic behavior analysis from Bayer *et al.* [13] because it has been shown effective.

Throughout the rest of this paper we use s_i to denote malware sample i, G to denote the set of all features, and g_i to denote the subset of all features G present in s_i.

We use full hierarchical clustering as a representative computationally expensive triage task. Hierarchical clustering has a lower bound of $s(s-1)/2$ comparisons for s malware to cluster [19]. Other problems, such as incremental clustering and finding nearest neighbor, are algorithmically less expensive. For example, incremental clustering, comparing incoming newly reported s' malware against s malware in a database, requires $s' \times s$ comparisons where $s' \ll s$. The nearest neighbor to a malware s_i can be performed by comparing it to all other samples, which is linear in s.

3.1 Single Node BitShred

In this section we describe the core components of BitShred: BITSHRED-GEN, BITSHRED-JACCARD, BITSHRED-CLUSTER and BITSHRED-SEMANTIC. In § 3.2, we show how the algorithm can be parallelized, e.g., to run on top of Hadoop or multi-core systems.

• **BITSHRED-GEN:** $G \rightarrow F$.

BITSHRED-GEN is an algorithm from the extracted feature set $g_i \in G$ to fingerprints $f_i \in F$ for each malware sample s_i. A BitShred fingerprint f_i is a bit-vector of length m, initially set to 0. BITSHRED-GEN performs feature hashing to represent feature sets g_i in fingerprints f_i. More formally, for a particular feature set we define a hash function $h : \chi \rightarrow \{0,1\}^m$ where the domain χ is the domain of possible features and m is the length of the bitvector. We use djb2 [14] and reduce the result modulo m. (Data reduction techniques such as locality-sensitive hashing [13] and Winnowing [34] can be used to pare down the data set for which we call BITSHRED-GEN and perform subsequent steps.)

• **BITSHRED-JACCARD:** $F \times F \rightarrow \mathbb{R}$.

BITSHRED-JACCARD computes the similarity $d \in [0,1]$ between fingerprints f_a and f_b using the bitvector Jaccard from Equation 2. A similarity value of 1 means the two samples are identical, while a similarity of 0 means the two samples share nothing in common (in our setting, this means they share no features in G).

Formally, Theorem 1 states that BITSHRED-JACCARD well-approximates the Jaccard index.

Theorem 1. Let g_a, g_b denote two sets of size N with c common elements, and f_a, f_b denote their respective fingerprints with bit-vectors of length m and k hash functions. Let Y denote $\frac{S(f_a \wedge f_b)}{S(f_a \vee f_b)}$. Then, for $m \gg N$, $\epsilon, \epsilon_2 \in (0,1)$,

$$Pr[Y \leq \frac{c(1+\epsilon_2)}{2N-c-m\epsilon}] \geq 1 - e^{-mq\epsilon_2^2/3} - 2e^{-2\epsilon^2 m^2/Nk}$$

and

$$Pr[Y \geq \frac{c(1-\epsilon_2)}{(2N-c)+m\epsilon}] \geq 1 - e^{-mq\epsilon_2^2/2} - 2e^{-2\epsilon^2 m^2/Nk}$$

for $q = 1 - 2\left(1-\frac{1}{m}\right)^{kN} + \left(1-\frac{1}{m}\right)^{k(2N-c)}$.

We defer a full proof to the Appendix. Note that because the goal of feature hashing is different from Bloom filters, our guarantees are not in terms of the false positive rate for standard Bloom filters, but instead are of how well our feature hashing data structure lets us approximate the Jaccard index.

• **BITSHRED-CLUSTER:** $(F \times F \times \mathbb{R}$ **list**$) \times \mathbb{R} \rightarrow C$.

BITSHRED-CLUSTER takes the list containing the similarity between each pair of malware samples, a threshold t, and outputs a clustering C for the malware. BITSHRED-CLUSTER groups two malware if their similarity d is greater than or equal to t: $d \geq t$. The threshold t is set by the desired precision tradeoff based upon past experience. While a smaller t divides malware into a few general families, a larger t discovers specific variants of a family. See § 5 for our experiments for different values of t.

BitShred currently uses an agglomerative hierarchical clustering algorithm to produce clusters in that the number of clusters is typically not known in advance. Initially each malware sample s_i is assigned to its own cluster c_i. The closest pair is selected and merged into a cluster. We iterate the merging process until there is no pair whose similarity exceeds the input threshold t. When there are multiple samples in a cluster, we define the similarity between cluster c_A and cluster c_B as the maximum similarity between all possible pairs (i.e., single-linkage), i.e., BITSHRED-JACCARD(c_A, c_B) $=$

(a) A typical matrix before co-clustering

(b) 8 different kinds of Trojan

(c) 3 different kinds of Adware

Figure 4: Semantic feature information. Grey dots represent 1 in the binary matrix, i.e., the presence of a feature.

$\max\{\text{BITSHRED-JACCARD}(f_i, f_j) | f_i \in c_A, f_j \in c_B\}$. We chose a single-linkage approach as it is efficient and accurate in practice.

• **BITSHRED-SEMANTIC:** $C \times F \to G'$.

Based on the BITSHRED-CLUSTER results, BITSHRED-SEMANTIC performs co-clustering on subset of fingerprints to cluster features as well as malware samples. Co-clustering yields correlated features-malware subgroups G' which shows the common or distinct features among malware samples, as discussed in § 2.2.

We have adapted the cross-associations algorithm [16], redesigned for the Map-Reduce framework [30], to BitShred fingerprints. The basic steps are row iterations and column iterations. A row iteration fixes a current column group and iterates over each row, updating r to find the "best" grouping. In our algorithm, we seek to swap each row to a row group that would maximize homogeneity of the resulting rectangles. The column iteration is similar, where rows are fixed. The algorithm performs a local optimal search (finding a globally optimal co-clustering is NP-hard [30]).

Unlike typical co-clustering problems, co-clustering in BitShred needs to operate on hashed features, i.e., recall that our fingerprints are not the features themselves, but hashes of these features. However, because our feature hashing is designed to approximately preserve structural similarities and differences between malware samples, we can apply co-clustering on our hashed features (just as if they were regular features) and still extract the structural relationships between the malware samples, and with the increased computational efficiency that comes from feature hashing.

Figure 4a shows a matrix before co-clustering where each row is a malware fingerprint and each column is a particular feature. Figure 4b and Figure 4c graphically depict the results of co-clustering on 8 different kinds of Trojan and 3 different kinds of Adware, respectively. Co-clustering reveals the semantic feature information, i.e., the checkerboard patterns which describe distinguishing or common features across the malware families. We discuss both inter- and intra-family feature extraction in detail in § 5.3.

3.2 Distributed BitShred

3.2.1 BITSHRED-SCHEDULE

There are two things we parallelize in BitShred: fingerprint generation in Phase 1, and the $s(s-1)/2$ fingerprint comparisons in Phase 2 during clustering. Parallelizing fingerprint generation is straight-forward: given s malware samples and r resources, we assign s/r malware to each node and run BITSHRED-GEN on each assigned sample.

Parallelizing BITSHRED-JACCARD in a resource and communication-efficient manner requires more thought. There are $s(s-1)/2$ comparisons, and every comparison takes the same fixed time, so if every node does $s(s-1)/2r$ comparisons all nodes do equal work. Unlike BITSHRED-JACCARD, comparisons between variable length of two sets take time (computation) depending on the length, thus distributing uniform node work is not simple.

To accomplish this we first observe that while the first malware needs to be compared against all other malware (i.e., $s-1$ fingerprint comparisons), each of the remaining malware require fewer than $s-1$ comparisons each. In particular, malware i requires only $s-i$ comparisons, and malware $s-i$ requires $s-(s-i)$ comparisons. The main insight is to pair the comparisons for malware i with $s-i$, so that the total comparisons for each pair is $s-i+s-(s-i) = s$. If we pair together the comparisons for malware i with $s-i$, the total comparisons for each pair is $s-i+s-(s-i) = s$. Thus, for each node to do uniform work, BITSHRED-SCHEDULE ensures that the $s-i$ comparisons for malware i are scheduled on the same node as the $s-(s-i)$ comparisons for malware $s-i$. BITSHRED-SCHEDULE then simply divides up the pairs among the r nodes.

Although there may be other protocols for distributing computations, we note that this approach is simple, and optimal in the sense that there all nodes do equal work and there is no inter-node communication during the s^2 Jaccard calculations.

3.2.2 *BitShred on Hadoop*

Our distributed implementation uses the Hadoop implementation of MapReduce [1, 17]. MapReduce is distributed computing technique for taking advantage of a large computer nodes to carry out large data analysis tasks. In MapReduce, functions are defined with respect to ⟨key,value⟩ pairs. MapReduce takes a list of ⟨key,value⟩ pairs, and returns a list of values. MapReduce is implemented by defining two functions:

1. MAP: $\langle K_i, V_i \rangle \to \langle K_o, V_o \rangle$ list. In the MAP step the master Hadoop node takes the input pair of type $\langle K_i, V_i \rangle$ and partitions into a list of independent chunks of work. Each chunk of work is then distributed to a node, which may in turn apply MAP to further delegate or partition the set of work to complete. The process of mapping forms a multi-level tree structure where leaf nodes are individual units of work, each of which can be completed in parallel. When a unit of work is completed by a node, the output $\langle K_o, V_o \rangle$ is passed to REDUCE.
2. REDUCE: $\langle K_o, V_o \rangle$ list $\to V_f$ list. In the REDUCE step the list of answers from the partitioned work units are combined and assembled to a list of answers of type V_f.

We also take advantage of the Hadoop distributed file system (HDFS) to share common data among nodes.

In phase 1, distributed BitShred produces fingerprints using the Hadoop by defining the following MapReduce functions:

1. MAP: $\langle K_i, s_i \rangle$ list $\rightarrow$ $\langle K_i, f_i \rangle$ list. Each MAP task is assigned the subset of malware samples s_i and creates fingerprints f_i to be stored on HDFS. Fingerprint files are named as K_i representing the index to the corresponding malware samples.
2. REDUCE. In this step, no REDUCE step is needed.

In phase 2, distributed BitShred runs BITSHRED-JACCARD across all Hadoop nodes by defining the following functions:

1. MAP: $\langle K_i, f_i \rangle$ list $\rightarrow$ $\langle \mathbb{R}, (s_a, s_b) \rangle$ list MAP tasks read fingerprint data files created during phase 1 and runs BITSHRED-JACCARD on each fingerprint pair, outputting the similarity $d \in \mathbb{R}$.
2. REDUCE: $\langle \mathbb{R}, (s_a, s_b) \rangle$ list $\rightarrow$ sorted $\langle \mathbb{R}, (s_a, s_b) \rangle$ list REDUCE gathers the list of the similarity values for each pair and returns a sorted list of pairs based upon similarity.

This phase returns a sorted list of malware pairs by similarity using standard Hadoop sorting. The sorted list is essential for the agglomerative single linkage clustering. In particular, malware s_i's family is defined as the set of malware whose distance is less than θ, thus all malware in the sorted list with similarity $> \theta$ are in the cluster.

4. IMPLEMENTATION

We have implemented single-node BitShred in 2000 lines of C code. Since BitShred is agnostic to the particular per-malware analysis methods, we only need individualized routines for extracting raw input features, before converting into fingerprints. In case of static code analysis, BitShred divides executable code section identified by `GNU BFD` library into n-grams and hashes each n-gram to create fingerprints. For dynamic behavior analysis, BitShred simply parses input behavior profile logs and hashes every behavior profile to generate fingerprints. We use `berkeley DB` to store and manage fingerprints database. After building the database, BitShred retrieves fingerprints from the database to calculate the Jaccard similarity between fingerprints. After applying an agglomerative hierarchical clustering algorithm, malware families are formed. We use graphviz and Cluto [24] for visualizing the clustering and family trees generated as shown in Figure 10, 11.

Distributed BitShred is implemented in 500 lines of Java code. We implemented a parser for extracting section information from Portable Executable header information because there is no `BFD` library for Java. In our implementation, we perform a further optimization that groups several fingerprints into a single HDFS disk block in order to optimize I/O. In the Hadoop infrastructure we use, the HDFS block size is 64MB. We optimize for this block size by dividing the input malware set so each node works on 2,048 malware samples at a time because 64MB = 32KB $\times$ 2048. That is, each MAP task is given 2,048 samples ($s_i, s_{i+1}, \cdots s_{i+2047}$) and generates a single file containing all fingerprints. We can similarly optimize for other block sizes and different bit-vector lengths, e.g, 64KB bit vectors result in batching 1,024 malware samples per node.

Distributed co-clustering is implemented in 1200 lines of Java code. We implemented a python-wrapper to iterate row and column operations to find an optimal co-clustering.

5. EVALUATION

We have evaluated BitShred for speed and accuracy using two types of per-sample analysis for features. First, we use a static code reuse detection approach where features are code fragments, and two malware are considered similar if they share common code fragments. Second, we use a dynamic analysis feature set where features are displayed behaviors, and two malware are considered similar if they have exhibit similar behaviors. Note that similarity is a set comparison, so order does not matter (e.g., re-ordering basic blocks is unlikely to affect the results). We stress that we are not advocating a particular approach such as static or dynamic analysis, but instead demonstrating how BitShred could be used once an analysis was selected.

Equipment. All single-node experiments were performed on a Linux 2.6.32-23 machine (Intel Core2 6600 / 4GB memory) using only a single core. The distributed experiments were performed on a Hadoop using 64 worker nodes, each with 8 cores, 16 GB DRAM, 4 1TB disks and 10GbE connectivity between nodes [2]. 53 nodes had a 2.83GhZ E5440 processor, and 11 had a 3GhZ E5450 processor. Each node is configured to allow up to 6 map tasks and up to 4 reduce tasks at one time.

Malware Dataset. We performed our experiments on a malware data set collected from a variety of open repositories such as Malware Analysis System (aka CWSandbox) [3], Offsensive Computing [4], and from our Universities infrastructure-wide security infrastructure inbetween 2009-2010. Our total data set consists of 655,360 unique samples by MD5 hash.

5.1 BitShred with Code Reuse as Features

Setup. Our static experiments are based upon reports that malware authors reuse code as they invent new malware samples [9, 25, 38]. Since malware is traditionally a binary-level analysis, not a source analysis, our implementation uses n-grams to represent binary code fragments. Malware similarity is determined by the percentage of n-grams shared.

We chose n-grams based analysis because it is one previously proposed approach that demonstrates a high dimensionality feature space. We set $n = 16$, so there are 2^{128} possible n-gram features. We chose 16 based upon experiments that show it would cover at least a few instructions (not shown for space reasons). We can use other features such as basic blocks, etc. as well by first building the appropriate feature and then defining a hash function on it; all possible extensions of the per-sample analysis is out of scope for this work. Surprisingly, even this simple analysis had over 90% accuracy when the malware is unpacked using off-the-shelf unpackers. Pragmatically, n-gram analysis also has the advantage of not requiring disassembling, building a control flow graph, etc., all of which are known hard problems on malware.

Single Node Performance. Table 1 shows BitShred's performance using a single node in terms of speed, memory consumed, and the resulting error rate. We limited our experiment to clustering 1,000 malware samples (which requires 499,500 pairwise comparisons) in order to keep the exact Jaccard time reasonable. The "exact Jaccard" row shows the overall performance when computing the set operations as shown in Equation 1 using the SimMetrics library [5]. Clustering using exact Jaccard took more than 4 hours, and required 644.13MB of memory. This works out to about 33 malware comparisons/sec and 2,388 malware clustered per day.

We performed two performance measurements with BitShred: one with 32KB fingerprints and one with 64KB fingerprints. With 64KB fingerprints, BitShred ran about 317 times faster than exact Jaccard. With 32KB fingerprints, BitShred runs about 2 times faster compared to 64KB fingerprints, and about 631 times faster than exact Jaccard.

Since BitShred uses feature hashing, hash collisions may impact the accuracy of the Jaccard distance computations. The overall error rate in the distance computations is a function of the fingerprint length, the size of the feature space, and the percentage of code that is similar. The statement in Theorem 1 formally expresses this tradeoff. We also made two empirical measurements. First, we computed the average error on all pairs, which worked out to be about 2% with 64KB fingerprints and 4% with 32KB fingerprints.

	Size of fingerprints	Time to compare every pair	Average error on all pairs	Average error on similar (>0.5) pairs	Malware comparisons per second	Malware clustered per day
EXACT JACCARD	644.13MB	4h 12m 16s	-	-	33	2,388
BS64K	62.50MB	48s	0.0199	0.0017	10,472	42,538
BS32K	31.25MB	24s	0.0403	0.0050	20,812	59,970
WINNOW (W4)	66.97MB	41m 5s	0.0019	0.0109	203	5,918
WINNOW (W12)	30.16MB	20m 35s	0.0081	0.0128	404	8,360
BS32K (W4)	31.25MB	24s	0.0159	0.0009	20,812	59,970
BS32K (W12)	31.25MB	24s	0.0062	0.0039	20,812	59,970
BS8K (W4)	7.81MB	6s	0.0649	0.0086	78,047	116,131
BS8K (W12)	7.81MB	6s	0.0247	0.0016	78,047	116,131

Table 1: BitShred (BS) vs. Jaccard vs. Winnowing. We show BitShred with several different fingerprint sizes.

The error goes up as the fingerprint size shrinks because there is a higher chance of collisions. We also computed the average error on pairs with a similarity of at least 50%, and found the error to be less than 1% of the true Jaccard. Note that the second metric (i.e., average error on pairs with higher similarity), is the more important metric – these are the numbers with the most impact on the accuracy, as these are the numbers that will primarily decide which family a malware sample belongs to. Thus, BitShred is a very close approximation indeed.

BitShred vs. Winnowing. In this paper so far we have considered techniques that provide an exact ranking between all pairs of malware. Nonetheless, malware practitioners are constantly facing hard choices on how much time to spend given finite computing resources, thus may want faster but approximate over theoretically correct but slower clustering. LSH is one type of data reduction technique that improves performance. Here we discuss another called *Winnowing*.

Winnowing, the algorithm used by the MOSS plagiarism detection tool, is a fuzzing hashing technique that selects a subset of features from a sample for analysis [34]. Let w be a window measured in some way, e.g., w statements, w consecutive n-grams, w behaviors, etc. Winnowing guarantees at least one shared unit in any window of length at least $w + n - 1$ will be included in the feature set [34]. In our evaluation we measure Winnowing because a) MOSS is well-known, and b) it corresponds to similarity detection based upon code as proposed in previous work [9, 25, 38], thus is directly related to our approach, and c) it is guaranteed to be within 33% of an upper bound on performance algorithms for similarity detection [34]. We compared in two settings: BitShred vs. Winnowing as in previous work, and BitShred extended to include Winnowing. Table 1 also shows these results for window sizes 4 (denoted as W4) and 12 (denoted as W12).

BitShred beats straight Winnowing. We reimplemented Winnowing as detailed in [34] using a 32-bit hash function as the original implementation is not public. For the purpose of performance comparison, we computed the similarity using SimMetrics library. BitShred is anywhere from 26-102 times faster, while requiring less memory. Winnowing does have a slightly better error rate, though none of the error rates is very high. A more interesting case is to consider pre-processing the feature set with Winnowing and then applying BitShred. With Winnowing applied, we can reduce the BitShred fingerprint size down to 8KB, allowing all 1,000 samples to be clustered in 6 seconds.

Figure 5 relates all experiments with respect to the total number of malware clustered per day. Recall there are about 8,000 new malware found per day. BitShred deals easily with current volumes, and has room to spare for future growth. Figure 5 also shows on the right-hand y-axis one reason BitShred is faster. Recall we mentioned exact Jaccard computations are slow in part because they use set operations. These, in turn, are not efficient on real architectures. BitShred's bitvector fingerprints, on the other hand, are L1/L2 cache friendly.

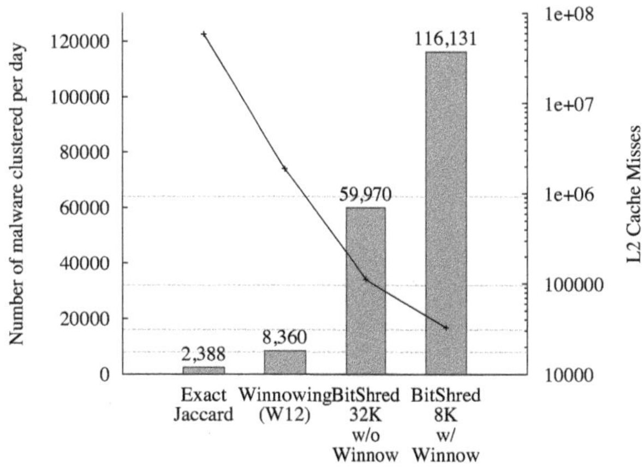

Figure 5: Overall malware clustered-per-day capabilities. We also report relative L1/L2 cache misses.

Distributed BitShred. We have implemented the Hadoop version of BitShred, and performed several experiments to measure overall scalability and throughput. We use up to 655,360 samples in this experiment. Note all samples were unpacked as the goal of this experiment is to measure overall performance and not accuracy.

Figure 6 shows the BITSHRED-GEN fingerprint generation time. In this experiment, we utilized 80 map tasks for small datasets (20,480 $\sim$ 81,920) and 320 map tasks for large datasets (163,840 $\sim$ 655,360). The total time to create fingerprints for all samples was 5m 45s with BS8K (W12) and 4m 40s with BS32K (W1). The graph also shows a linear trend in the fingerprint generation time, e.g., halving the total number of samples to 327,680 samples approximately halves the generation time to about 2m 54s and 2m 25s, respectively. BITSHRED-GEN performance slightly dropped at 163,840 samples because the startup and shutdown overhead of each map dominates the benefit of utilizing more maps.

Figure 7 shows the amount of time for computing the pairwise distance for the same sample set. We utilized 200 map tasks for small datasets and 320 map tasks for large datasets. Given the values in the graph, we can work out the number of comparisons per second. For example, 163,840 samples requires approximately 1.3×10^{10} comparisons, and takes 10m 15s with BS8K (W12), which works out to 21,823,888 comparisons/sec. 327,680 samples requires about 5.4×10^{10} comparisons, and takes 40m 55s with BS8K (W12), which works out to a similar 21,868,402 comparisons/sec.

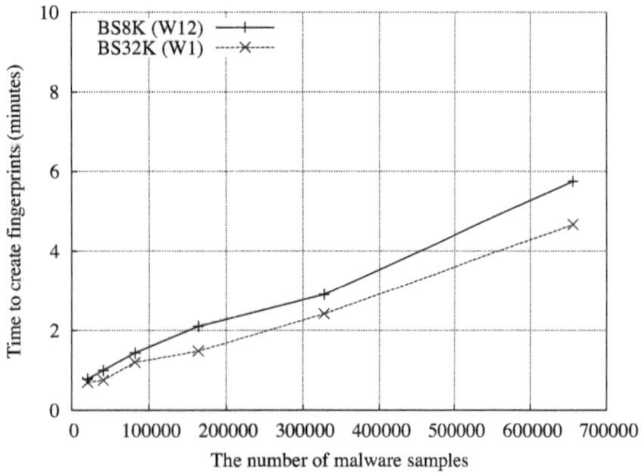

Figure 6: Performance of Distributed BITSHRED-GEN

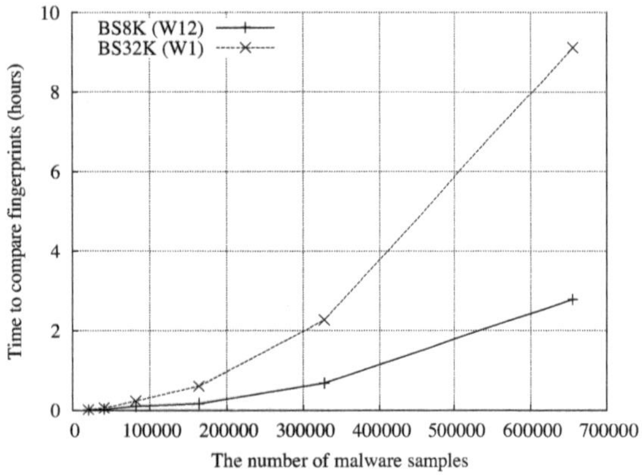

Figure 7: Performance of Distributed BITSHRED-JACCARD

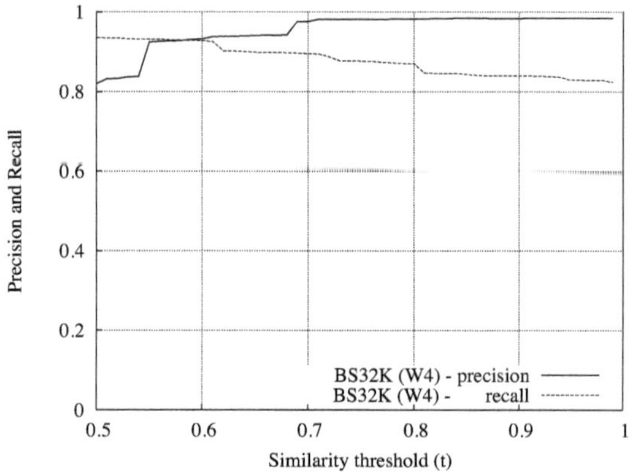

Figure 8: Precision and Recall (3,935 samples)

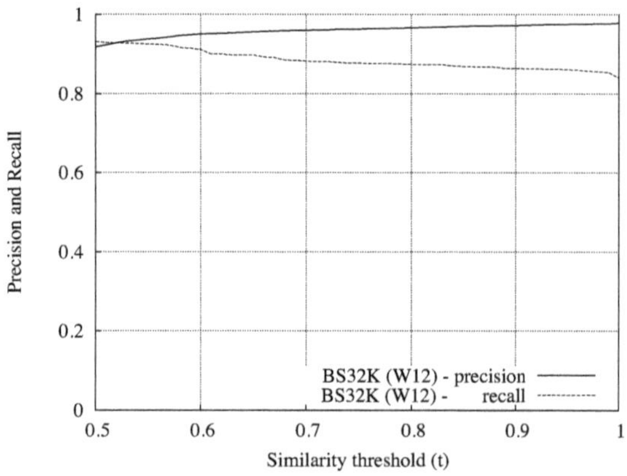

Figure 9: Precision and Recall (131,072 samples)

Overall, the distributed version achieved a pairwise comparison throughput of about 1.9×10^{12} per day. This works out to *full* hierarchical clustering over 1.9 million malware per day. In the case of *incremental* clustering, this works out to comparing over 190,000 malware per day against 10 million known malware that are already in a database.

Triage Tasks. Three common triage tasks are to automatically identify malware families via clustering [13], to identify the nearest neighbors to a particular malware sample [21], and to visualize malware by creating phylogenetic trees [23]. In this experiment we explore using BitShred with n-grams as the extracted features. While we stress that we are not advocating n-gram analysis, we also note it is interesting to see what the actual quality would be in such a system. We repeat these analysis in § 5.2 using dynamic behavior features.

• *Clustering.* We refer to how close a particular clustering is to the "correct" clustering with respect to labeled data set as the *quality* of a clustering. Overall quality will heavily depend upon the feature extraction tool (e.g., static or dynamic), the particular data set (e.g., because malware analysis often relies upon undecidable questions), and the quality of the reference data set.

To create a reference clustering data set, we used 30∼40 different anti-virus labels provided by VirusTotal [6]. First, we chose samples that were detected as malware by at least 20 anti-virus programs to get more reliable labels. We normalized and tokenized all the labels; then, we assigned the family name based upon only the tokens occurring at the majority of the detecting anti-virus programs. As a result, we had 3,935 samples.

The overall clustering quality is measured with respect to two metrics: precision and recall. Precision measures how well malware in separate families are put in different clusters, and recall measures how well malware within the same family are put into the same cluster. Formally, precision and recall are defined as:

$$\text{Precision} = \frac{1}{s}\sum_{i=1}^{c} \max(|C_i \cap R_1|, ..., |C_i \cap R_r|)$$

$$\text{Recall} = \frac{1}{s}\sum_{i=1}^{r} \max(|C_1 \cap R_i|, ..., |C_n \cap R_i|)$$

We clustered the reference data set 3,935 samples based upon n-grams. Figure 8 shows the overall quality of BitShred with Winnowing (BS32K (W4)). Surprisingly, simple n-gram analysis did quite well. When $t = 0.6$, BS32K (W4) clustering produced 200 clusters with a precision of 0.932 and a recall of 0.928 in 8 minutes.

For a larger-scale experiment, we unpacked 131,072 malware samples using off-the-shelf unpackers. We then clustered the malware and compared the identified families to a reference clustering using ClamAV labels [2]. Figure 9 shows the overall results with BitShred with Winnowing (BS32K (W12)). When $t = 0.57$, BS32K (W12) clustering produced 7,073 clusters with a precision of 0.942 and a recall of 0.922. It took about 27m with 256 map tasks.

• *Nearest Neighbor.* Hu *et al.* describe finding the nearest k-neighbors to a given sample as a common triage task [21] (§2.3). We have implemented similar functionality in BitShred by comparing the given malware to all other malware. We performed experiments finding the 5 nearest neighbors to randomly chosen malware samples on the 102,391 malware data set. We achieved the same 94.2% precision and 92.2% recall as above. The average time to find the neighbors was 6.8s (w/ BS8K) and 27s (w/ BS32K), using 25MB memory, with variance always under 1s.

• *Visualization.* We also have implemented several ways to visualize clustering within BitShred. First, we can create boxed malware

[2] Considerable amount of manual work is required to prepare a reference data set. For this reason, we simply used ClamAV as a reference for 131,072 samples.

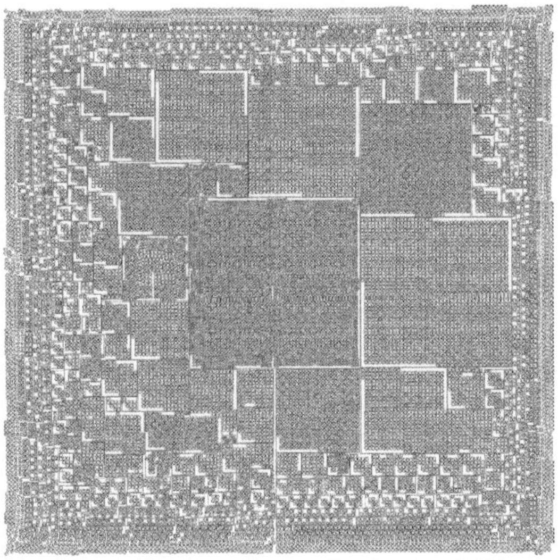

Figure 10: Clustering graph when $t = 0.57$

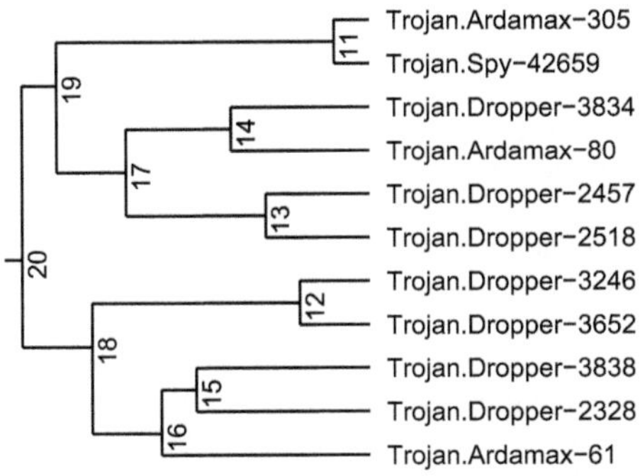

Figure 11: Lineage tree for a single malware family

graphs where each square represents a malware family, with circles representing individual samples. Figure 10 shows a clustering of 20,000 malware samples when $t = 0.57$ [3]. In the figure we can see larger families with many malware in the center, with the size of the family decreasing as we move to the edges. At the very edge are malware samples that cluster with no family.

Another way to visualize the results using BitShred is to create phylogenetic family trees based upon similarity [23]. The more alike two malware samples are, the closer they are on the tree. Figure 11 depicts an example tree created from our data set, labeled with ClamAV nodes. It is interesting to note ClamAV labels the malware as coming from three families: Spy, Dropper, and Ardamax. We manually confirmed that indeed all three were extremely similar and should be considered of the same family, e.g., Trojan.Ardamax-305 and Trojan.Spy-42659 are in different ClamAV families, but only differ in 1 byte.

5.2 BitShred with Dynamic Behaviors as Features

Static analysis may be fooled by advanced obfuscation techniques, which has led researchers to propose a variety of dynamic behavior-based malware analysis approaches, e.g., [12, 13, 28, 29, 33, 35]. One popular variant of this approach is to load the malware into a clean virtual machine. The VM is started, and observed behaviors such as system calls, conditional checks, etc. are recorded as features.

Bayer *et al.* provided us with their implementation of clustering, and the 2658 behavior profiles they used to measure accuracy from

[3]We pick 20,000 samples because larger numbers created graphs that hung our, and potentially the reviewers', PDF reader.

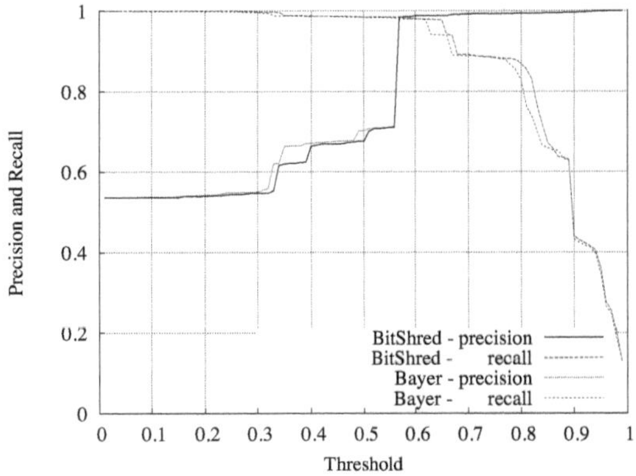

Figure 12: Clustering quality based upon behavior profiles

# of profiles	Clustering	Elapsed Time	Required Memory (max)
2,658	BAYER-EXACT	16s	86MB
	BITSHRED-EXACT	4s	12MB
75,692	BAYER-LSH	2h 25m 44s	4.3GB
	BITSHRED-SETBITS	24m 35s	89MB
	BITSHRED-EXACT	1h 2m 51s	89MB

Table 2: Scalability of Systems

their paper [13]. In this data set, each behavior profile is a list of feature index numbers. The total number of features was 172260. In our experiments, we used only a 1KB fingerprint size since the number of features was relatively small.

As shown in Table 2, an exact clustering took 16s and 86MB of memory using the code from Bayer *et al.* BitShred took 4s (4x as fast) and used 12MB of memory (7x less memory). The average error was 2% using the 1KB fingerprint. Figure 12 depicts the exact clustering vs BitShred as a function of precision and recall. Both had the same precision of .99 and recall of .98 when $t = .61$. Overall, BitShred is faster and uses less memory, while not sacrificing accuracy for dynamic analysis feature sets.

Although Bayer *et al.* made the 2658 profiles they used for accuracy, they did not provide all 75,692 profiles they used when measuring performance. In order to measure performance on this size of data, we synthetically generated 73,034 variants using the 2658 as a basis. We then ran the code from Bayer *et al.* on 75,692 profiles using the same parameters as described in [13]: $k = 10$, $l = 90$, and $t = 0.7$. BAYER-LSH took 2h 25m 44s using 4.3GB of memory and performed 236,132,556 distance computations. BITSHRED-SETBITS [4] took 24m 35s (5.9x as fast) using 89MB of memory (49x less memory) and computed similarity of 1,021,322,219 pairs when $t = 0.7$. (Note that BITSHRED-SETBITS performed 4.3x more distance computations.) Even BITSHRED-EXACT at 1h 2m 51s outperformed (2.3x as fast) BAYER-LSH.

5.3 Semantic Feature Information

Finally, we used the co-clustering phase in BitShred to identify semantic distinguishing features among malware families. We performed a variety of experiments and found that, overall, co-clustering automatically identified both inter-family and intra-family semantic features. Typical features identified included distinguishing register keys set and internet hosts contacted.

Co-clustering of Behavior-Based Profiles. We performed a full co-clustering on the entire dynamic analysis data set from § 5.2.

[4]We sorted the samples based upon the number of set bits in fingerprints. Then each sample only needed to be compared to the samples whose number of set bits are within the input threshold.

(a) A typical matrix before co-clustering.

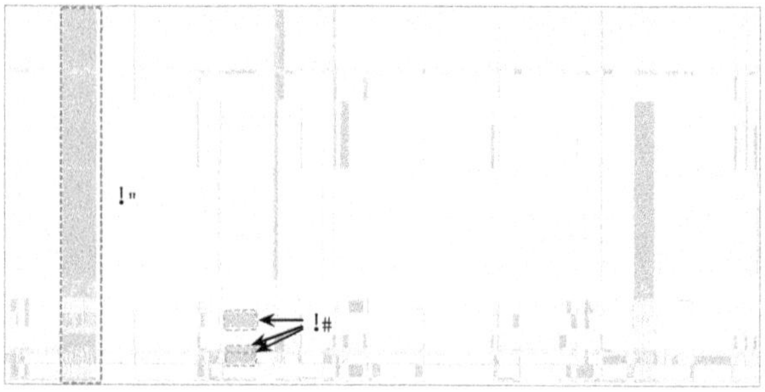

(b) Inter-family analysis based on dynamic behavior profile

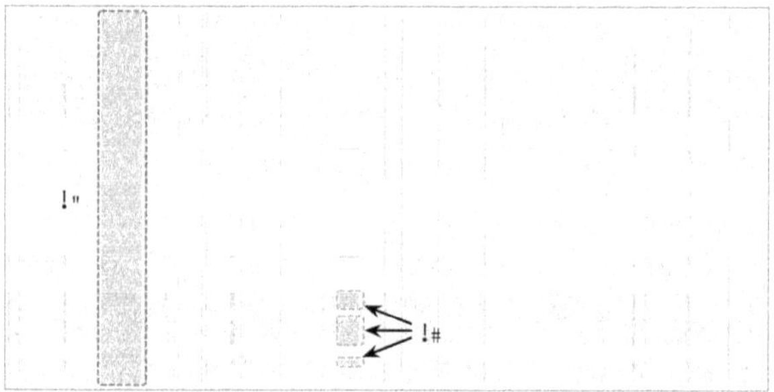

(c) Intra-family analysis based on dynamic behavior profile

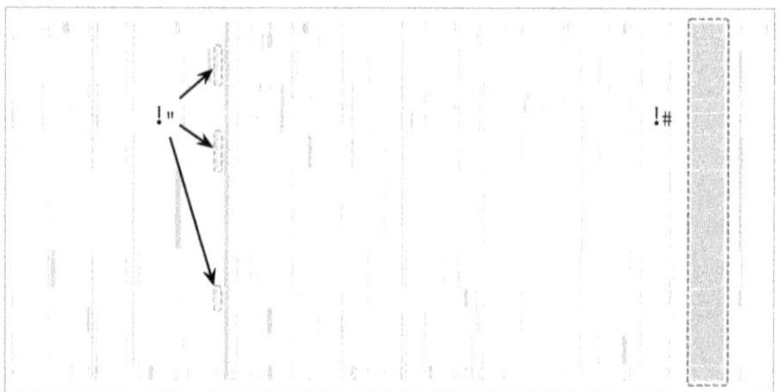

(d) Intra-family analysis based on static code analysis

(e) Inter-family analysis based on static code analysis

Figure 13: Feature extraction by co-clustering. Grey dots represent 1 in the binary matrix, i.e., the presence of a feature.

Figure 13a depicts the malware/feature matrix before co-clustering. We then co-clustered, which took 15 minutes.

Figure 13b shows the complete results. The checkerboard pattern corresponds to the sub-matrices identified as being homogeneous, i.e., corresponding malware/feature pairs that are highly correlated. For example, the large dark sub-matrix labeled g_8 corresponds to the fact that most malware had the same memory-mapped files including WS2HELP.dll, icmp.dll, and ws2_32.dll. The sub-matrix g_9 shows a commonality between two families, but no others. The commonality corresponds to opening the file \Device\KsecDD.

Figure 13c focuses on only the 717 samples in the Allaple malware family. One semantic feature, labeled g_3, is that almost all samples use the same memory-mapped files such as winrnr.dll, WS2HELP.dll, icmp.dll, and ws2_32.dll. More importantly, we also found that many family members were distinguished by the register entry they create (e.g., HKLM\SOFTWARE\CLASSES\-CLSID\{7BDAB28A-B77E-2A87-868A-C8DD2D3C52D3} in one sample) and the IP address they connect to, e.g., one sample connected to 24.249.139.x while another connected to 24.249.150.y (shown as g_4).

Co-clustering of n-gram features. We also experimented with co-clustering using the n-gram features. Figure 13d shows intra-family co-clustering for the Trojan.OnlineGames malware family. The features labeled g_2 correspond to all code from the code entry to a particular point that overlap. The feature set g_1 corresponds to new functionality in a few variants that makes tcp connections to a new host not found in previous variants.

We also performed inter-family analysis. In this set of experiments we envision that an analyst uses co-clustering to mine differences and similarities between malware family members or between malware families. We picked the Trojan.Dropper, Trojan.Spy, Trojan.OnlineGames, and Adware.Downloader families, which have 1280 total members. The total time taken by co-clustering was 10 minutes (about 2s per sample), with about 1 minute for each column and row iteration. We used 10 maps for each row iteration and 64 maps for column iteration.

Figure 13e shows the resulting co-clustering. Trojan.Dropper and Trojan.Spy were grouped together by co-clustering. This is accurate: we manually confirmed that the samples we have from those families are not well-distinguished. The submatrix labeled g_5 is one distinguishing feature corresponding to Adware.Downloader connecting to a particular host on the internet. The submatrix labeled g_6 corresponds to data section fragments shared between the Trojan family, but not present in Adware. The submatrix labeled g_7 corresponds to shared code for comparing memory locations. This code is shared between Adware.Downloader and Trojan.OnlineGames, but not Trojan.Spy/Trojan.Downloader.

6. RELATED WORK

We are not the first to propose the need for large-scale malware analysis and triage, e.g., [13, 21, 31] have similar goals. As discussed in § 2.3, the main difference in our work is scalability and co-clustering to automatically identify semantic features. Our work builds on per-sample analysis and feature extraction, which is an extremely active area of research including unpacking research [18, 20, 27, 33, 35], and even entire conferences like DIMVA.

While we focus on analyzing malware binaries, Perdisci *et al.* [32] have explored clustering based upon network behavior features. Their similarity metric is based upon the weighted combination of Euclidean distance, Levenshtein distance, and Jaccard distance. While BitShred could compute Hamming distance and Jaccard distance, we leave adapting the analysis, implementation, and experimentation for other distance metrics as future work.

Li *et al.* [26] argue it is difficult to get ground truth for clustering accuracy. In our setting the main metric is how close the feature-hashed version of clustering comes to the quality of an exact Jaccard clustering, which is different than looking for ground truth. Nonetheless, we do report overall clustering accuracy, where all the caveats from [26] apply.

7. CONCLUSION

In this paper we have presented *BitShred*, a system for large-scale malware triage and similarity detection. The key idea behind BitShred is using feature hashing to reduce the high-dimensional feature space in malware analysis, which is supported by theoretical and empirical analysis. Our approach makes inter-malware comparisons in typical large-scale triage tasks such as clustering and finding nearest neighbors up to 2,365x faster than existing methods while using less memory. As a result, BitShred scales to current and future malware volumes where previous approaches do not. We have also developed a distributed version of BitShred where $2x$ the hardware gives $2x$ the performance. In our tests, we show we can scale to up to clustering over 1.9 million malware per day. Finally, we have developed novel techniques based upon co-clustering to extract semantic features between malware samples and families. The extracted features provide insight into the fundamental differences and similarities between and within malware data sets.

Acknowledgment

This research was supported in part by sub-award PO4100074797 from Lockheed Martin Corporation originating from DARPA Contract FA9750-10-C-0170 for BAA 10-36. We would like to thank Malware Analysis System (aka CWSandbox) and Offensive Computing for providing malware data sets. We also would like to thank VirusTotal for providing the private API to access their resources.

References

[1] Apache hadoop. http://hadoop.apache.org/.

[2] CMU Cloud Computer Cluster. http://www2.pdl.cmu.edu/~twiki/cgi-bin/view/OpenCloud/ClusterOverview.

[3] Malware Analysis System. http://mwanalysis.org/.

[4] Offensive Computing. http://www.offensivecomputing.net/.

[5] SimMetrics. http://sourceforge.net/projects/simmetrics/.

[6] VirusTotal. http://www.virustotal.com/.

[7] zynamics bindiff. http://www.zynamics.com/bindiff.html.

[8] Symantec internet security threat report. http://www.symantec.com/business/theme.jsp?themeid=threatreport, April 2010.

[9] T. Abou-Assaleh, N. Cercone, V. Keselj, and R. Sweidan. N-gram-based detection of new malicious code. In *COMPSAC '04: Proceedings of the 28th Annual International Computer Software and Applications Conference - Workshops and Fast Abstracts*, 2004.

[10] A. Andoni and P. Indyk. Near-optimal hashing algorithms for approximate nearest neighbor in high dimensions. *Communications of the ACM*, 51(1):177–122, 2008.

[11] J. Attenberg, K. Weinberger, A. Dasgupta, A. Smola, and M. Zinkevich. Collaborative email-spam filtering with the hashing-trick. In *Proceedings of the Sixth Conference on Email and Anti-Spam*, 2009.

[12] M. Bailey, J. Oberheide, J. Andersen, F. J. Z. Morley Mao, and J. Nazario. Automated classification and analysis of internet malware. In *Proceedings of the Symposium on Recent Advances in Intrusion Detection*, September 2007.

[13] U. Bayer, P. M. Comparetti, C. Hlauschek, C. Kruegel, and E. Kirda. Scalable, behavior-based malware clustering. In *Proceedings of the Network and Distributed System Security Symposium*, 2009.

[14] D. Bernstein. http://www.cse.yorku.ca/~oz/hash.html.

[15] A. Broder and M. Mitzenmacher. Network applications of bloom filters: A survey. *Internet Mathematics*, 1(4):485–509, 2005.

[16] D. Chakrabarti, S. Papadimitriou, D. Modha, and C. Faloutsous. Fully automatic cross associations. In *Proceedings of ACM SIGKDD*, August 2004.

[17] J. Dean and S. Ghemawat. MapReduce: Simplified data processing on large clusters. In *Proceedings of the USENIX Symposium on Operating System Design and Implementation*, 2004.

[18] A. Dinaburg, P. Royal, M. Sharif, and W. Lee. Ether: malware analysis via hardware virtualization extensions. In *ACM CCS*, 2008.

[19] D. Eppstein. Fast hierarchical clustering and other applications of dynamic closest pairs. In *Proceedings of ACM Symposium on Discrete Algorithms (SODA)*, 1998.

[20] F. Guo, P. Ferrie, and T.-C. Chiueh. A study of the packer problem and its solutions. In *Proceedings of the International Symposium on Recent Advances in Intrusion Detection*, pages 98–115, 2008.

[21] X. Hu, T. cker Chiueh, and K. G. Shin. Large-scale malware indexing using function call graphs. In *Proceedings of the ACM Conference on Computer and Communications Security*, 2009.

[22] N. Jain, M. Dahlin, and R. Tewari. Using bloom filters to refine web search results. In *Proceedings of Eighth International Workshop on the Web and Databases (WebDB 2005)*, June 2005.

[23] M. Karim, A. Walenstein, A. Lakhotia, and L. Parida. Malware phylogeny generation using permutations of code. *Journal in Computer Virology*, 1(1):13–23, November 2005.

[24] G. Karypis. CLUTO: a clustering toolkit, release 2.1.1. Technical report, University of Minnesota, 2003.

[25] J. Z. Kolter and M. A. Maloof. Learning to detect and classify malicious executables in the wild. *Journal of Machine Learning Research*, 7:2721–2744, Dec. 2006.

[26] P. Li, L. Lu, D. Gao, and M. Reiter. On challenges in evaluating malware clustering. In *Proceedings of the International Symposium on Recent Advances in Intrusion Detection*, 2010.

[27] L. Martignoni, M. Christodorescu, and S. Jha. OmniUnpack: Fast, generic, and safe unpacking of malware. In *In Proceedings of the Annual Computer Security Applications Conference*, 2007.

[28] A. Moser, C. Kruegel, and E. Kirda. Exploring multiple execution paths for malware analysis. In *Proceedings of the IEEE Symposium on Security and Privacy*, 2007.

[29] A. Moser, C. Kruegel, and E. Kirda. Limits of static analysis for malware detection. In *Proceedings of the Annual Computer Security Applications Conference*, 2007.

[30] S. Papadimitrou and J. Sun. Disco: Distributed co-clustering with map-reduce. In *Proceedings of ICDM*, 2008.

[31] R. Perdisci, A. Lanzi, and W. Lee. Classification of packed executables for accurate computer virus detection. *Pattern Recogn. Lett.*, 29(14):1941–1946, 2008.

[32] R. Perdisci, W. Lee, and N. Feamster. Behavioral clustering of HTTP-based malware and signature generation using malicious network traces. In *Proceedings of NSDI*, 2010.

[33] P. Royal, M. Halpin, D. Dagon, R. Edmonds, and W. Lee. PolyUnpack: Automating the hidden-code extraction of unpack-executing malware. In *Proceedings of Computer Security Applications Conference*, December 2006.

[34] S. Schleimer, D. Wilkerson, and A. Aiken. Winnowing: Local algorithms for document fingerprinting. In *Proceedings of the ACM SIGMOD/PODS Conference*, 2003.

[35] M. Sharif, A. Lanzi, J. Giffin, and W. Lee. Automatic reverse engineering of malware emulators. In *Proceedings of the IEEE Symposium on Security and Privacy*, 2009.

[36] Q. Shi, J. Petterson, G. Dror, J. Langford, A. Smola, and S. Vishwanathan. Hash kernels for structured data. *Journal of Machine Learning Research*, 2009.

[37] Q. Shi, J. Petterson, G. Dror, J. Langford, A. Smole, A. Strehl, and V. Vishwanathan. Hash kernels. In *Proceedings of the 12th International Conference on Artificial Intelligence and Statistics (AISTATS)*, 2009.

[38] A. Walenstein and A. Lakhotia. The software similarity problem in malware analysis. In *Duplication, Redundancy, and Similarity in Software*, 2007.

[39] K. Weinberger, A. Dasgupta, J. Langford, A. Smola, and J. Attenberg. Feature hashing for large-scale multitask learning. In *Proceedings of ICML*, 2009.

APPENDIX

A. PROOF OF THEOREM 1

Our analysis shows that with high probability, the Jaccard index $\frac{|g_i \cap g_j|}{|g_i \cup g_j|}$ is well approximated by the $\frac{S(f_i \wedge f_j)}{S(f_i \vee f_j)}$, where f_i and f_j are the fingerprints of g_i and g_j. Throughout this analysis, we let c denote the number of shared elements between sets g_i and g_j; note that the Jaccard index $\frac{|g_i \cap g_j|}{|g_i \cup g_j|}$ is then $\frac{c}{2N-c}$. The focus of our analysis is to show that the ratio $\frac{S(f_i \wedge f_j)}{S(f_i \vee f_j)}$ is close to $\frac{c}{2N-c}$ with high probability (unlike other analyses [22] that restrict their focus to computing the expected value of $S(f_i \wedge f_j)$). We make the usual assumption that the hash functions used are k-wise independent.

We first consider the union $g_i \cup g_j$. We note that the bitvector obtained by computing the bitwise-or of the two fingerprints f_i and f_j is equivalent to the bitvector that would be obtained by directly inserting all the elements in $g_i \cup g_j$, if the same k hash functions are used on a bitvector of the same size.

Let the random variable U denote the number of bits set to 1 in $f_i \vee f_j$. Note that the set $g_i \cup g_j$ contains $2N - c$ elements. If these elements are inserted into a bitvector of size m with k hash functions, the probability q_u that a bit is set to 1 is: $1 - (1 - \frac{1}{m})^{k(2N-c)}$. We can use this to compute the expected value of U:

$$E[U] = mq_u = m\left(1 - \left(1 - \frac{1}{m}\right)^{k(2N-c)}\right) \quad (3)$$

As U is tightly concentrated around its expectation [15], we get:

$$Pr[|U - E[U]| \geq \epsilon m] \leq 2e^{-2\epsilon^2 m^2/(2N-c)k} \leq 2e^{-2\epsilon^2 m^2/Nk}.$$

Next, we consider the intersection $g_i \cap g_j$. Let the random variable I denote the number of bits set to 1 in $f_i \wedge f_j$. A bit z is set in $f_i \wedge f_j$ in one of two ways: (1) it may be set by some element in $g_i \cap g_j$, or (2) it may be set by some element in $g_i - (g_i \cap g_j)$ and by some element $g_j - (g_i \cap g_j)$. Let I_z denote the indicator variable for bit z in $f_i \wedge f_j$. Then,

$$\begin{aligned} Pr[I_z = 1] \;=\; & \left(1 - \left(1 - \frac{1}{m}\right)^{kc}\right) + \\ & \left(1 - \frac{1}{m}\right)^{kc}\left(1 - \left(1 - \frac{1}{m}\right)^{k(|g_i|-c)}\right) \\ & \cdot \left(1 - \left(1 - \frac{1}{m}\right)^{k(|g_j|-c)}\right) \end{aligned}$$

which may be simplified as:

$$1 - \left(1 - \frac{1}{m}\right)^{kN} - \left(1 - \frac{1}{m}\right)^{kN} + \left(1 - \frac{1}{m}\right)^{k(2N-c)}.$$

With linearity of expectation, we can compute $E[I]$ as $\sum_z Pr[I_z = 1]$, which reduces to:

$$E[I] = m\left(1 - 2\left(1 - \frac{1}{m}\right)^{kN} + \left(1 - \frac{1}{m}\right)^{k(2N-c)}\right). \quad (4)$$

Note that the random variables $I_1, I_2 \ldots I_m$ are negatively dependent, and so we can apply Chernoff-Hoeffding bounds to compute the probability that I deviates significantly from $E[I]$: e.g., $Pr[I \geq E[I](1+\epsilon_2) \leq e^{-mq\epsilon_2^2/3}$, where $q = 1 - (1 - \frac{1}{m})^{kN} - (1 - \frac{1}{m})^{kN} + (1 - \frac{1}{m})^{k(2N-c)}$.

We now turn to the ratio $\frac{S(f_i \wedge f_j)}{S(f_i \vee f_j)}$; let the random variable Y denote this ratio. We have just shown that U and I are both likely to remain close to their expected values, and we can use this to compute upper and lower bounds on Y – since U and I lie within an additive or multiplicative factor of their expectations with probability at least $1 - 2e^{-mq\epsilon_2^2/3}$ and $1 - 2e^{-2\epsilon^2 m^2/Nk}$ respectively, we can derive upper and lower bounds on Y that hold with probability at least $1 - 2e^{-mq\epsilon_2^2/3} - 2e^{-2\epsilon^2 m^2/Nk}$.

To do this, we first simplify the quantities $E[U]$ and $E[I]$. Assuming that $m \gg 2kN$, we can approximate $E[U]$ and $E[I]$ by discarding the higher-order terms in each of binomials in 3 and 4:

$$\begin{aligned} E[U] &\geq m\left(1 - \left(1 - \frac{k(2N-c)}{m}\right)\right) \\ &= mk\left(\frac{2N-c}{m}\right) = k(2N-c). \end{aligned}$$

Likewise, we can approximate $E[I]$ as:

$$\begin{aligned} E[I] &\leq m\left(1 - 2\left(1 - \frac{kN}{m}\right) + \left(1 - \frac{k(2N-c)}{m}\right)\right) \\ &= mk\left(\frac{c}{m}\right) = ck. \end{aligned}$$

Using these approximations for $E[I]$ & $E[U]$, we see that $Y \leq \frac{c(1+\epsilon_2)}{2N-c-m\epsilon}$, with probability at least $1 - e^{-mq\epsilon_2^2/3} - 2e^{-2\epsilon^2 m^2/Nk}$. We can compute a similar lower bound for Y, i.e., $Y \geq \frac{c(1-\epsilon_2)}{(2N-c)+m\epsilon}$, with probability at least $1 - e^{-mq\epsilon_2^2/2} - 2e^{-2\epsilon^2 m^2/Nk}$. Thus, this shows that with high probability, the ratio $\frac{S(f_i \wedge f_j)}{S(f_i \vee f_j)}$ is close to the Jaccard index $\frac{c}{2N-c}$, for appropriately chosen values of m and k. We have thus proven our Theorem 1.

Lastly, we give an example to illustrate our bounds in our application scenario. Suppose we set $\epsilon m \geq 5$, $m \approx 1000N$, $k = 6$. Then, our analysis shows us that with probability at least 95%, $Y \in \left(\frac{c(1-\frac{1}{\sqrt{2c}})}{2N-c+5}, \frac{c(1+\frac{4}{\sqrt{c}})}{2N-c-5}\right)$, i.e., that ratio of the bits set to the union is very close to the Jaccard index.

B. EXTENSION

Containment. BITSHRED-JACCARD measures the proportional similarity between features. However, we may want to also measure when one feature set is contained within another, e.g., whether one malware is completely contained in another code. For example, suppose malware A is the composition of two malware samples B and C, and suppose $|B| \gg |C|$. Then the similarity between A and C will be proportionally very low. An alternative similarity metric for this case can be given as:

$$\text{BITSHRED-JACCARD}_c(f_a, f_b) = \frac{S(f_a \wedge f_b)}{S(f_b)},$$

when f_i is the fingerprint for malware s_i and $|s_a| \gg |s_b|$.

Trace Equivalence Decision: Negative Tests and Non-determinism*

Vincent Cheval
LSV, ENS Cachan & CNRS
cheval@lsv.ens-cachan.fr

Hubert Comon-Lundh
LSV, ENS Cachan & CNRS
comon@lsv.ens-cachan.fr

Stéphanie Delaune
LSV, ENS Cachan & CNRS
delaune@lsv.ens-cachan.fr

ABSTRACT

We consider security properties of cryptographic protocols that can be modeled using the notion of trace equivalence. The notion of equivalence is crucial when specifying privacy-type properties, like anonymity, vote-privacy, and unlinkability.

In this paper, we give a calculus that is close to the applied pi calculus and that allows one to capture most existing protocols that rely on classical cryptographic primitives. First, we propose a symbolic semantics for our calculus relying on constraint systems to represent infinite sets of possible traces, and we reduce the decidability of trace equivalence to deciding a notion of symbolic equivalence between sets of constraint systems. Second, we develop an algorithm allowing us to decide whether two sets of constraint systems are in symbolic equivalence or not. Altogether, this yields the first decidability result of trace equivalence for a general class of processes that may involve else branches and/or private channels (for a bounded number of sessions).

Categories and Subject Descriptors

D.2.4 [**Program Verification**]: Formal Methods

General Terms

Security, Verification

1. INTRODUCTION

Security protocols are widely used today to secure transaction that rely on public channels like the Internet. It is therefore essential to obtain as much confidence as possible in their correctness. Starting in the 80s, many works have been devoted to the use of formal methods to analyse the security of these protocols (*e.g.* [17, 24]). In the case of a bounded number of sessions, secrecy preservation is co-NP-complete [21, 24], and for an unbounded number of sessions, several decidable classes have been identified (*e.g.* [17, 23]). Many tools have also been developed to automatically verify cryptographic protocols (*e.g.* AVISPA [6], ProVerif [9]).

Until recently, most efforts and successes only concerned trace properties, *i.e.* security properties that can be checked on each individual sequence of messages corresponding to an execution of the protocol. Secrecy and authentication are typical examples of trace properties. There are however several security properties, which cannot be defined as trace properties and require a notion of *behavioural equivalence.* We focus here on the notion of *trace equivalence* which is well-suited for the analysis of security protocols. Intuitively, two processes P and Q are trace equivalent, denoted $P \approx_t Q$, if any experiment performed by an attacker on both processes lead to the emission of two sequences of messages that are indistinguishable, *i.e.* the attacker can not observe any difference between these two sequences. The notion of trace equivalence is weaker than the notion of *observational equivalence* that has been the subject recently of several works [10, 15, 25]. Trace equivalence is probably more adequate to the formalization of privacy-type properties. Originally, observational equivalence is a bisimulation-based equivalence notion that has been introduced as a proof technique for trace equivalence [4]. In the present paper, we are interested in automating the proofs of trace equivalence.

Related work. A line of works consists in designing stronger notions of equivalences that imply observational equivalence (and thus trace equivalence). This approach has for instance been used in [7, 8, 25], relying on constraint solving techniques. ProVerif implements an algorithm, based on Horn clauses and dedicated resolution strategies, which is able to establish the observational equivalence between two processes written in the applied pi calculus [10]. However, all these methods check a stronger equivalence than observational equivalence and fail on some simple toy examples. Unfortunately, this is exactly the kind of situations we encountered in several case studies, *e.g.* the private authentication protocol [3], and e-passport protocols [5]. If we restrict our attention to *simple processes* with trivial else branches, then the strong notion of equivalence between two positive constraint systems used in [7] (or [25, 11]), is sufficient to decide trace equivalence. Another procedure for deciding trace equivalence has also been proposed in [18].

Another line of works [20, 12] is based on an extension of the small attack property of [24]: they show that, if two processes are not equivalent, then there must exist a small witness of non-equivalence. A decision of equivalence can be derived by checking every possible small witness. Again this result does not apply to protocols with non-trivial else branches.

In summary, there is no known result that is suitable to protocols such as the private authentication protocol [3], or the e-passport protocol described in [5]: these protocols require a conditional

*This work has been partly supported by the ANR projects AVOTÉ and PROSE, by the grant DIGITEO API from Région Île-de-France, and by the INRIA project SecSI.

(with a non-trivial else branch) to be modeled in accurate way. Moreover, the notion of equivalence used by ProVerif or the notion of diff-equivalence used in [8] are too strong to conclude on these case studies. For instance ProVerif yields a false negative in these examples, because the two (equivalent) processes do not have the same control structure.

Our contributions. Our main contribution consists in dropping the requirements on the conditionals and on the determinacy in previous algorithms that decide trace equivalence: we provide a new algorithm, that decides the trace equivalence of (possibly non-determinate, possibly with non-trivial else branches) processes, without replication and that use standard primitives, namely signature, hash function, pairing, symmetric and asymmetric encryptions.

We show that the trace equivalence of two processes without replication can be reduced to a notion of symbolic equivalence between sets of initial constraint systems, which we show next how to decide. In our class, we can model in particular conditionals (with non-trivial else branches), private channels, and non-deterministic choice. The private authentication protocol [3] and the various versions of the e-passport protocol [5] fall into our class.

This work is built upon a procedure that has been first described in [11]. However, non trivial conditionals and non-determinism force two main generalizations: we need to consider *sets of constraints* instead of individual constraints and we need also to consider *negative atomic constraints*, for instance disequalities. This yields difficult technical problems, which we will describe, as well as their solutions.

2. MODEL

This section introduces our process calculus, by giving its syntax and its semantics. This calculus is close to the original applied pi calculus [2] but we consider a fixed set of cryptographic primitives, namely signatures, pairing, hash function, symmetric and asymmetric encryptions. Participants in a protocol are modeled as processes, and the communication between them is modeled by means of message passing.

2.1 Syntax

To describe processes, one starts with an infinite set of *names* $\mathcal{N} = \{a, b, \ldots, sk, k, n, m, \ldots\}$ (which are used to model atomic data), an infinite set of *(first-order) variables* $\mathcal{X}^1 = \{x, y, \ldots\}$, and a set $\mathcal{F}$ of *function symbols* which is split into the set $\mathcal{F}_c$ of *constructors* and the set $\mathcal{F}_d$ of *destructors*. More specifically, we consider:

$$\mathcal{F}_c = \{\mathsf{senc}/2,\ \mathsf{aenc}/2,\ \mathsf{pub}/1,\ \mathsf{sign}/2,\ \mathsf{vk}/1,\ \langle\rangle/2,\ \mathsf{h}/1\}$$
$$\mathcal{F}_d = \{\mathsf{sdec}/2,\ \mathsf{adec}/2,\ \mathsf{check}/2,\ \mathsf{proj}_1/1,\ \mathsf{proj}_2/1\}.$$

This signature contains function symbols to model signature, pairing, hash function, symmetric and asymmetric encryptions.

Terms are defined as names, variables, and function symbols applied to other terms. Let $\mathsf{F} \subseteq \mathcal{F}$, $\mathsf{N} \subseteq \mathcal{N}$ and $\mathsf{V} \subseteq \mathcal{X}^1$, the set of terms built from N and V by applying function symbols in F is denoted by $\mathcal{T}(\mathsf{F}, \mathsf{N} \cup \mathsf{V})$. We write $vars^1(u)$ for the set of (first-order) variables occurring in a term u. The term u is said to be a *ground* term if $vars^1(u) = \emptyset$. We denote by $st(u)$ the set of subterms of u. The *constructor terms*, resp. *ground constructor terms*, are those in $\mathcal{T}(\mathcal{F}_c, \mathcal{N} \cup \mathcal{X}^1)$, resp. in $\mathcal{T}(\mathcal{F}_c, \mathcal{N})$. A ground constructor term is also called a *message*.

We model the properties of our cryptographic primitives by means of a term rewriting system. For instance, the first rule models the fact that the decryption of a ciphertext will return the associated plaintext when the right key is used to perform the decryption.

$$\begin{array}{rcl} \mathsf{sdec}(\mathsf{senc}(x,y),y) & \to & x \\ \mathsf{adec}(\mathsf{aenc}(x,\mathsf{pub}(y)),y) & \to & x \\ \mathsf{check}(\mathsf{sign}(x,y),\mathsf{vk}(y)) & \to & x \end{array} \qquad \begin{array}{rcl} \mathsf{proj}_1(\langle x,y\rangle) & \to & x \\ \mathsf{proj}_2(\langle x,y\rangle) & \to & y \end{array}$$

This term rewriting system is convergent. We denote by $t\downarrow$ the normal form of t. Moreover, to represent messages, we will only consider valid terms. A term u is *valid*, denoted $\mathsf{valid}(u)$, if $v\downarrow$ is a constructor term for any $v \in st(u)$.

We now consider a set $\mathcal{X}^2 = \{X, Y, \ldots\}$ of *second-order variables* and we write $vars^2(\cdot)$ the function that returns the set of second-order variables occurring in its argument. A *recipe* is a term built on $\mathcal{F}_c, \mathcal{F}_d$, a set of *parameters* $\mathcal{AX} = \{ax_1, \ldots, ax_n, \ldots\}$, that can be seen as pointers to the hypotheses (or known messages), and variables in $\mathcal{X}^2$. As in the applied pi calculus, all the function symbols are public, *i.e.* available to the attacker. Moreover, names are excluded from recipes: names that are known to the attacker must be given explicitly as hypotheses. We denote by Π the set of recipes, *i.e.* $\Pi = \mathcal{T}(\mathcal{F}, \mathcal{AX} \cup \mathcal{X}^2)$. A *ground recipe* ζ is a recipe that does not contain variables ($vars^2(\zeta) = \emptyset$) but only parameters. We denote by $param(\zeta)$ the set of parameters that occur in ζ. Intuitively, a ground *recipe* records the attacker's computation. It is used as a witness of how some deduction has been performed.

It is well-known that replication leads to undecidability [19] thus, we consider processes without replication. The grammar of our *plain processes* is as follows:

$$\begin{array}{l} P, Q, R := 0 \\ \quad P \mid Q \\ \quad P + Q \\ \quad \mathsf{new}\, x.P \\ \quad \mathtt{if}\ M_1 = M_2\ \mathtt{then}\ P\ \mathtt{else}\ Q \\ \quad \mathsf{in}(M, x).P \\ \quad \mathsf{out}(M, N).P \end{array}$$

where M_1, M_2, M, N are terms, and x is a variable. We denote by $fv(P)$ the free variables of P. This notion is extended as expected to multiset of processes.

At a particular point in time, while engaging in one or more sessions of one or more protocols, an attacker may know a sequence of messages $u_1, \ldots, u_n$. As in the applied pi calculus, such a sequence of messages is organized into a (concrete) frame $\phi = \{ax_1 \rhd u_1, \ldots, ax_n \rhd u_n\}$ where $u_1, \ldots, u_n$ are ground constructor terms. Its domain $dom(\phi)$ is the set $\{ax_1, \ldots, ax_n\}$ whereas its size $|\phi|$ is the integer n. A frame ϕ defines a substitution $\{ax \mapsto u \mid ax \in dom(\phi), ax \rhd u \in \phi\}$.

DEFINITION 1. *A* (concrete) process *is a pair* $(\mathcal{P}; \phi)$ *where:*

- ϕ *is a* (concrete) frame*; and*
- $\mathcal{P}$ *is a multiset of* plain processes *(defined above) such that* $fv(\mathcal{P}) = \emptyset$.

Additionally, we require processes to be variable distinct, i.e. *any variable is at most bound once.*

EXAMPLE 1. *We consider a protocol given in [3] designed for transmitting a secret without revealing its identity to other participants. In this protocol, A is willing to engage in communication with B and wants to reveal its identity to B. However, A does not want to compromise its privacy by revealing its identity or the identity of B more broadly. The protocol works as follows:*

$$\begin{array}{rcl} A \to B & : & \mathsf{aenc}(\langle N_a, \mathsf{pub}(A)\rangle, \mathsf{pub}(B)) \\ B \to A & : & \mathsf{aenc}(\langle N_a, \langle N_b, \mathsf{pub}(B)\rangle\rangle, \mathsf{pub}(A)) \end{array}$$

$$(\{\mathsf{in}(u,x).P\} \uplus \mathcal{P};\phi) \xrightarrow{\mathsf{in}(\xi,\zeta)} (\{P\{x \to t\}\} \uplus \mathcal{P};\phi) \quad \text{(IN)}$$
$$\text{if } \zeta,\xi \in \mathcal{T}(\mathcal{F}, dom(\phi)),\ \zeta\phi\downarrow = t,\ \xi\phi\downarrow = u\downarrow,\ \mathsf{valid}(t), \text{ and } \mathsf{valid}(u)$$

$$(\{\mathsf{out}(u,t).Q\} \uplus \mathcal{P};\phi) \xrightarrow{\mathsf{out}(\xi,ax_{|\phi|+1})} (\{Q\} \uplus \mathcal{P};\phi \cup \{ax_{|\phi|+1} \rhd t\downarrow\}) \quad \text{(OUT)}$$
$$\text{if } \xi \in \mathcal{T}(\mathcal{F}, dom(\phi)),\ \xi\phi\downarrow = u\downarrow,\ \mathsf{valid}(t), \text{ and } \mathsf{valid}(u)$$

Figure 1: Semantics

First A sends to B a nonce N_a and its public key encrypted with the public key of B. If the message is of the expected form then B sends to A the nonce N_a, a freshly generated nonce N_b and its public key, all of this being encrypted with the public key of A. Otherwise, B sends out a "decoy" message: $\mathsf{aenc}(N_b, \mathsf{pub}(B))$. This message should basically look like B's other message from the point of view of an outsider. This is important since the protocol is supposed to protect the identity of the participants.

A session of role B played by agent b with a can be modeled by the plain process $B(b,a)$ where $N = \mathsf{adec}(y, skb)$. Note that B is not given the value ska but is directly given the value $\mathsf{pub}(ska)$, that is the public key corresponding to A's private key.

$$\begin{aligned}
&B(b,a) \stackrel{\mathsf{def}}{=} \\
&\quad \mathsf{new}\ n_b.\mathsf{in}(c,y). \\
&\quad \mathsf{if}\ \mathsf{proj}_2(N) = \mathsf{pub}(ska)\ \mathsf{then} \\
&\quad \mathsf{out}(c, \mathsf{aenc}(\langle \mathsf{proj}_1(N), \langle n_b, \mathsf{pub}(skb)\rangle\rangle, \mathsf{pub}(ska))).0 \\
&\quad \mathsf{else}\ \mathsf{out}(c, \mathsf{senc}(nb, \mathsf{pub}(skb))).0
\end{aligned}$$

Intuitively, this protocol preserves anonymity if an attacker cannot distinguish whether b is willing to talk to a (represented by the process $B(b,a)$) or willing to talk to a' (represented by the process $B(b,a')$), provided a, a' and b are honest participants. For illustration purposes, we also consider the process $B'(b,a)$ obtained from $B(b,a)$ by replacing $\mathsf{else}\ \mathsf{out}(c, \mathsf{senc}(nb, \mathsf{pub}(skb))).0$ *by* $\mathsf{else}\ 0$. *We will see that the "decoy" message plays a crucial role to ensure privacy.*

A (concrete) process representing a session in which b plays B with a is $(\mathcal{P}_0;\phi_0)$ where $\mathcal{P}_0 = B(b,a)$, and

$$\begin{aligned}
\phi_0 = \{&ax_1 \rhd c,\ ax_2 \rhd a,\ ax_3 \rhd a',\ ax_4 \rhd b, \\
&ax_5 \rhd \mathsf{pub}(ska),\ ax_6 \rhd pub(ska'),\ ax_7 \rhd \mathsf{pub}(skb)\}
\end{aligned}$$

The purpose of ϕ_0 is to disclose the names of the agents and their public keys in order to make them available to the attacker.

2.2 Semantics

The operational semantics of processes is defined by the relation $\xrightarrow{\alpha}$ for which some rules are described in Figure 1. Of course, we have also some rules to deal with conditionals, internal communications, and choice operators. This relation transforms a concrete process into a concrete process. Note that the output of a term t is made "by reference" using the next parameter $ax_{|\phi|+1}$. Moreover, we check the validity of the terms that have to be evaluated during the execution. Note also that, since we authorize arbitrary terms for channels, we have to check whether the channel is known by the attacker or not.

EXAMPLE 2. *Continuing Example 1, we have that:*

$$\begin{aligned}
(\mathcal{P}_0;\phi_0) &\stackrel{\mathsf{def}}{=} (\{B(b,a)\};\phi_0) \\
&\xrightarrow{\tau} \xrightarrow{\mathsf{in}(ax_1, \mathsf{aenc}(\langle ax_1, ax_5\rangle, ax_7))} (\{P_1\};\phi_0) \\
&\xrightarrow{\mathsf{out}(ax_1, ax_8)} (\{0\};\phi_0 \cup \{ax_8 \rhd u\})
\end{aligned}$$

where $u = \mathsf{aenc}(\langle c, \langle n_b, \mathsf{pub}(skb)\rangle\rangle, \mathsf{pub}(ska))$ and for some plain process P_1.

Considering the same sequence of reductions starting from the process $(\{B(b,a')\};\phi_0)$ yields the process:

$$(\{0\};\ \phi_0 \cup \{ax_8 \rhd \mathsf{aenc}(n_b, \mathsf{pub}(skb))\}).$$

Indeed, in such a situation, the equality test will be false and the "decoy" message will be sent.

Intuitively, two processes are *equivalent* if they cannot be distinguished by any active attacker. Equivalences can be used to formalize many interesting security properties, in particular privacy-type properties, such as those studied in [16]. However, proofs are difficult because of the universal quantification over all contexts. For this reason, we consider here trace equivalence that intuitively captures the same notion. First, we introduce a notion of intruder's knowledge that has been extensively studied (see *e.g.* [1]).

DEFINITION 2. *Two concrete frames ϕ and ϕ' are statically equivalent, written $\phi \sim \phi'$, when $dom(\phi) = dom(\phi')$ and when:*

- *for any ground recipe ζ such that $param(\zeta) \subseteq dom(\phi)$, we have that $\mathsf{valid}(\zeta\phi)$ if, and only if, $\mathsf{valid}(\zeta\phi')$;*
- *for any ground recipes ζ,ζ' such that $param(\{\zeta,\zeta'\}) \subseteq dom(\phi)$, and $\mathsf{valid}(\zeta\phi)$, $\mathsf{valid}(\zeta\phi')$, we have that $\zeta\phi\downarrow = \zeta'\phi\downarrow$ if, and only if, $\zeta\phi'\downarrow = \zeta'\phi'\downarrow$.*

EXAMPLE 3. *Consider the two concrete frames introduced in Example 2:*

- $\phi_1 = \phi_0 \cup \{ax_8 \rhd \mathsf{aenc}(\langle c, \langle n_b, \mathsf{pub}(skb)\rangle\rangle, \mathsf{pub}(ska))\}$;
- $\phi_1' = \phi_0 \cup \{ax_8 \rhd \mathsf{aenc}(n_b, \mathsf{pub}(skb))\}$.

Actually, they are in static equivalence. This is a non-trivial equivalence. Intuitively, there is no test that allows one to distinguish these two frames since the decryption key skb is not available and the message stored in ax_8 can not be reconstructed (n_b is not available to the attacker).

Let $\mathcal{A}$ be the alphabet of actions for our semantics. For every $w \in \mathcal{A}^*$ the relation $\xrightarrow{w}$ on concrete processes is defined in the usual way. For $s \in (\mathcal{A} \smallsetminus \{\tau\})^*$, the relation $\stackrel{s}{\Rightarrow}$ on concrete processes is defined by: $(\mathcal{P}_A;\phi_A) \stackrel{s}{\Rightarrow} (\mathcal{P}_B;\phi_B)$ if, and only if there exists $w \in \mathcal{A}^*$ such that $(\mathcal{P}_A;\phi_A) \xrightarrow{w} (\mathcal{P}_B;\phi_B)$ and s is obtained by erasing all occurrences of τ.

Let $A = (\mathcal{P}_1;\phi_1)$ be an intermediate process. We define the following set:

$$\mathsf{trace}(A) = \{(s,\phi_2) \mid (\mathcal{P}_1;\phi_1) \stackrel{s}{\Rightarrow} (\mathcal{P}_2;\phi_2) \text{ for some } (\mathcal{P}_2;\phi_2)\}.$$

DEFINITION 3 (TRACE EQUIVALENCE $\approx_t$). *Let A and B be two concrete processes. The processes A and B are* trace equivalent, *denoted by $A \approx_t B$, if for every $(s,\phi) \in \mathsf{trace}(A)$ there exists $(s',\phi') \in \mathsf{trace}(B)$ such that $s = s'$ and $\phi \sim \phi'$ (and conversely).*

EXAMPLE 4. *Continuing Example 1, we have that:*

$$(\{B(b,a)\};\phi_0) \approx_t (\{B(b,a')\};\phi_0).$$

Again, this is a non-trivial equivalence that illustrates the anonymity property. However, as noticed in [14], the "decoy" message plays an important role. Indeed, considering now the process $B'(b,a)$, we have that:

$$(\{B'(b,a)\};\phi_0) \not\approx_t (\{B'(b,a')\};\phi_0).$$

This can be easily shown by considering the sequence of actions $s = \mathsf{in}(ax_1, \mathsf{aenc}(\langle ax_1, ax_5\rangle, ax_7)) \cdot \mathsf{out}(ax_1, ax_8)$. We have that $(s,\phi_1) \in \mathsf{trace}((\{B'(b,a)\};\phi_0))$ (as in Example 2). However, this sequence s does not exist for $(\{B'(b,a')\};\phi_0)$.

Now, we are able to state our main result:

THEOREM 1. *Let A and B be two concrete processes. The problem whether A and B are trace equivalent is decidable.*

3. SYMBOLIC SEMANTICS

In this section, we propose a symbolic semantics for our calculus following *e.g.* [8]. By treating inputs symbolically, our symbolic semantics avoids potentially infinite branching of execution trees due to inputs from the environment. Correctness is maintained by associating with each process a set of constraints on terms. We then define symbolic trace equivalence which is shown to be sound and complete with respect to concrete trace equivalence.

3.1 Initial constraint systems

An (initial) constraint system represents the possible executions of a protocol once an interleaving has been fixed.

DEFINITION 4. *An* initial constraint system *is either $\perp$ or a tuple $(\Phi; D; E)$ where:*

1. *Φ is a sequence of the form $\{ax_1 \rhd v_1, \ldots, ax_m \rhd v_m\}$ where $v_1, \ldots, v_m$ are terms;*
2. *D is a sequence of* deducibility constraints *$X_1, i_1 \overset{?}{\vdash} u_1 \wedge \ldots \wedge X_n, i_n \overset{?}{\vdash} u_n$ where*
   - *$X_1, \ldots, X_n$ are distinct second-order variables, $u_1, \ldots, u_n$ are terms, and $0 \leq i_1 \leq \ldots \leq i_n \leq m$;*
   - *for every $0 \leq k \leq m$, $vars^1(v_k) \subseteq \bigcup_{i_j < k}\{u_j\}$.*
3. *E is a conjunction of equations and disequations between terms such that $vars^1(E) \subseteq \{u_1, \ldots, u_n\}$.*

Note that each variable x occurs first in a deducibility constraint whose right member is exactly x. We also assume that the variables that occur in E have been introduced in a deducibility constraint. This allows us to ensure that once the ground recipes associated to the second order variables are fixed, then the values of the first-order variables are uniquely determined.

Note also that all the variables that occur in such a system are free. The variables X_i represent the recipes that might be used to deduce the right-hand side of the deducibility constraint. The indices indicate the *support* of the variable, *i.e.* which initial segment of the frame can be used. Note that Φ is not a concrete frame: the terms $v_1, \ldots, v_m$ are not necessarily ground and may contain some destructors.

DEFINITION 5. *A* solution *of an initial constraint system $\mathcal{C} = (\Phi; D; E)$ consists of a substitution σ mapping $vars^1(\mathcal{C})$ to ground constructor terms and a substitution θ mapping $vars^2(\mathcal{C})$ to ground recipes such that:*

- *for every $ax_i \rhd v_i$ in Φ, we have that $\mathsf{valid}(v_i\sigma)$;*
- *for every $X_i, j \overset{?}{\vdash} u_i$ in D, $param(X_i\theta) \subseteq \{ax_1, \ldots, ax_j\}$, $\mathsf{valid}(u_i\sigma)$, and $X_i\theta(\Phi\sigma)\downarrow = u_i\sigma\downarrow$;*
- *for every equation $u \overset{?}{=} v$ in E, $\mathsf{valid}(u\sigma)$, $\mathsf{valid}(v\sigma)$, and $u\sigma\downarrow = v\sigma\downarrow$;*
- *for every disequation $u \overset{?}{\neq} v$ in E, $\neg\mathsf{valid}(u\sigma)$, or $\neg\mathsf{valid}(v\sigma)$, or $u\sigma\downarrow \neq v\sigma\downarrow$.*

We denote by $\mathsf{Sol}_{\mathsf{init}}(\mathcal{C})$ the set of solutions of $\mathcal{C}$. By convention, we have that $\mathsf{Sol}_{\mathsf{init}}(\perp) = \emptyset$.

Let $\mathcal{C}$ be an initial constraint system and θ be a substitution such that $(\sigma,\theta) \in \mathsf{Sol}_{\mathsf{init}}(\mathcal{C})$ for some σ. Note that once θ is fixed, the associated substitution σ is uniquely defined.

EXAMPLE 5. *Let $\mathcal{C}_1 = (\Phi_1; D_1; E_1)$ where:*

- *$\Phi_1 = \phi_0 \cup \{ax_8 \rhd v_8\}$ where v_8 is equal to* $\mathsf{aenc}(\langle \mathsf{proj}_1(\mathsf{adec}(y, skb)), \langle n_b, \mathsf{pub}(skb)\rangle\rangle, \mathsf{pub}(ska))$
- *$D_1 = \{X, 7 \overset{?}{\vdash} c;\ Y, 7 \overset{?}{\vdash} y;\ Z, 7 \overset{?}{\vdash} c\}$; and*
- *$E_1 = \{\mathsf{proj}_2(\mathsf{adec}(y, skb)) \overset{?}{=} \mathsf{pub}(ska)\}$*

$\mathcal{C}_1$ is an initial constraint system. We can check that $(\sigma,\theta) \in \mathsf{Sol}_{\mathsf{init}}(\mathcal{C}_1)$ where:

- *$\theta = \{X \mapsto ax_1, Y \mapsto \mathsf{aenc}(\langle ax_1, ax_5\rangle, ax_7), Z \mapsto ax_1\}$;*
- *$\sigma = \{y \mapsto \mathsf{aenc}(\langle c, \mathsf{pub}(ska)\rangle, \mathsf{pub}(skb))\}$.*

The *structure* of an initial constraint system $\mathcal{C} = (\Phi; D; E)$ is given by $\{(X,i) \mid X, i \overset{?}{\vdash} u \in D \text{ for some } u\}$, and $dom(\Phi)$. We are now able to define our notion of *symbolic equivalence* between sets of initial constraint systems. This notion will be useful later on to define our notion of *symbolic trace equivalence* (see Section 3.2). The remaining of this paper is entirely devoted to the problem of deciding this notion of symbolic equivalence.

DEFINITION 6. *Let Σ and Σ' be two sets of initial constraint systems having the same structure. We have that $\Sigma \approx_{\mathsf{init}} \Sigma'$ if for all $\mathcal{C} \in \Sigma$, for all $(\sigma,\theta) \in \mathsf{Sol}_{\mathsf{init}}(\mathcal{C})$, there exists $\mathcal{C}' \in \Sigma'$ and a substitution σ' such that $(\sigma',\theta) \in \mathsf{Sol}_{\mathsf{init}}(\mathcal{C}')$ and $\Phi\sigma\downarrow \sim \Phi'\sigma'\downarrow$ where $\mathcal{C} = (\Phi; D; E)$, and $\mathcal{C}' = (\Phi'; D'; E')$ (and conversely).*

3.2 Symbolic calculus

From a concrete process $(\mathcal{P};\phi)$ we compute the set of initial constraint systems capturing its possible executions, starting from the symbolic process $(\mathcal{P};\phi;\emptyset;\emptyset)$.

DEFINITION 7. *A* symbolic process *is a tuple $(\mathcal{P}; \Phi; D; E)$:*

- *$\mathcal{C} = (\Phi; D; E)$ is an initial constraint system; and*
- *$\mathcal{P}$ is a multiset of plain processes with $fv(\mathcal{P}) \subseteq vars^1(\mathcal{C})$.*

The semantics of symbolic processes is defined by the relation $\xrightarrow{\alpha_s}_s$ for which some rules are described in Figure 2. This relation transforms a symbolic process into a symbolic process. The aim of this symbolic semantics is to avoid the infinite branching due to the inputs of the environment. This is achieved by keeping variables rather than input terms. The constraint system gives a finite representation of the value that these variables are allowed to take. As in our concrete semantics, we define $\xrightarrow{w}_s$ and $\overset{s}{\Rightarrow}_s$.

$$(\{\mathsf{in}(u,x).P\} \uplus \mathcal{P}; \Phi; D; E) \xrightarrow{\mathsf{in}(X,Y)}_s (\{P\} \uplus \mathcal{P}; \Phi; D'; E) \quad (\text{IN}_s)$$

where $D' = D \wedge X, |\Phi| \overset{?}{\vdash} u \wedge Y, |\Phi| \overset{?}{\vdash} x$ and Y, X are fresh variables

$$(\{\mathsf{out}(u,t).P\} \uplus \mathcal{P}; \Phi; D; E) \xrightarrow{\mathsf{out}(X, ax_{|\Phi|+1})}_s (\{P\} \uplus \mathcal{P}; \Phi \cup \{ax_{|\Phi|+1} \rhd t\}; D'; E) \quad (\text{OUT}_s)$$

with $D' = D \wedge X, |\Phi| \overset{?}{\vdash} u$ and X is a fresh variable

Figure 2: Symbolic semantics

DEFINITION 8. *Let $A = (\mathcal{P}_A; \phi_A)$ and $B = (\mathcal{P}_B; \phi_B)$ be two concrete processes. They are in* symbolic trace equivalence *if for every sequence tr_s of symbolic actions, we have:*

$$\{(\Phi'_A; D'_A; E'_A) \mid (\mathcal{P}_A; \phi_A; \emptyset; \emptyset) \overset{\mathsf{tr}_s}{\Rightarrow}_s (\mathcal{P}'_A; \Phi'_A; D'_A; E'_A)\}$$
$$\approx_{\mathsf{init}}$$
$$\{(\Phi'_B; D'_B; E'_B) \mid (\mathcal{P}_B; \phi_B; \emptyset; \emptyset) \overset{\mathsf{tr}_s}{\Rightarrow}_s (\mathcal{P}'_B; \Phi'_B; D'_B; E'_B)\}$$

We can show that symbolic trace equivalence exactly captures trace equivalence.

THEOREM 2. *Let $A = (\mathcal{P}_A; \phi_A)$ and $B = (\mathcal{P}_B; \phi_B)$ be two concrete processes. They are in trace equivalence if, and only if, they are in symbolic trace equivalence.*

Now, since the symbolic transition system is finite, we only have to show that symbolic trace equivalence is decidable. However, for processes with non-trivial branchings, the sets of constraints in Definition 8 are not reduced to singletons: we have to consider sets (disjunctions) of contraints.

EXAMPLE 6. *Actually, the system $\mathcal{C}_1$ (see Example 5) is one of the constraint systems obtained by applying our symbolic rules on $(\mathcal{P}_0; \phi_0; \emptyset; \emptyset)$ and considering $\mathsf{tr}_s = \mathsf{in}(X,Y) \cdot \mathsf{out}(Z, ax_8)$. The other one (for the same sequence tr_s) is $\mathcal{C}_2 = (\Phi_2; D_2; E_2)$ where $D_2 = D_1$,*

- *$\Phi_2 = \phi_0 \cup \{ax_8 \rhd \mathsf{aenc}(n_b, \mathsf{pub}(skb))\}$, and*
- *$E_2 = \{\mathsf{proj}_2(\mathsf{adec}(y, skb)) \overset{?}{\neq} \mathsf{pub}(ska)\}$.*

For the same sequence tr_s, similar constraint systems, denoted $\mathcal{C}'_1$ and $\mathcal{C}'_2$, can be derived for the process $(\{B(b,a')\}; \phi_0)$. The occurrences of ska will be replaced by ska'.

To establish symbolic trace equivalence between the processes $(\{B(b,a)\}; \phi_0)$ and $(\{B(b,a')\}; \phi_0)$, we will need in particular to check that $\{\mathcal{C}_1, \mathcal{C}_2\} \approx_{\mathsf{init}} \{\mathcal{C}'_1, \mathcal{C}'_2\}$.

4. FRAMEWORK

Our procedure for deciding symbolic equivalence between sets of constraint systems requires a slightly different setting from the one introduced in Section 3. Therefore, we adapt and generalize several notions and definitions. In particular, our algorithm (see Section 5) considers constructor terms only. In this section, we show how to get rid of destructor symbols and of some recipes, and we prove that our new notion of symbolic equivalence coincides with the one introduced in Section 3 on sets of initial constraint systems.

4.1 Frames

The purpose of a frame is to record the sequence of messages (or terms in a symbolic execution) that have been sent by the participants of the protocol. We extend this notion to record some additional information on attacker's deductions. Typically the element $\mathsf{sdec}(X, \zeta), i \rhd u$ records that, using a decryption with the recipe ζ, on top of a recipe X, allows one to get u (at stage i). After recording this information in the frame, we may forbid the attacker to use a decryption on top of X, forcing him to use this "direct access" from the frame.

DEFINITION 9 (FRAME). *A (ground)* frame *Φ is a sequence $\Phi = \zeta_1, i_1 \rhd u_1, \ldots, \zeta_n, i_n \rhd u_n$ where:*

- *$\zeta_1, \ldots, \zeta_n$ are (ground) recipes;*
- *$i_1, \ldots, i_n$ are integers; and*
- *$u_1, \ldots, u_n$ are (ground) constructor terms.*

The domain *of the frame Φ is $dom(\Phi) = \mathcal{AX} \cap \{\zeta_1, \ldots, \zeta_n\}$. It must be equal to $\{ax_1, \ldots, ax_m\}$ for some m that is called the* size *of Φ. Such a frame Φ defines a substitution on $dom(\Phi)$.*

In order to restrict the set of recipes we have to work with, we define the following set Π_r:

$$\Pi_r = \left\{ \xi \in \Pi \;\middle|\; \begin{array}{l} \mathsf{g}(\xi_1, \ldots, \xi_n) \in st(\xi) \text{ for some } \mathsf{g} \in \mathcal{F}_d \\ \quad \Rightarrow \mathsf{Top}(\xi_1) \notin \mathcal{F}_c \end{array} \right\}$$

where $\mathsf{Top}(u)$ denotes the root symbol of u.

For instance, $\mathsf{sdec}(\mathsf{senc}(ax_1, ax_1), ax_2)$ is *not* in Π_r. When checking static equivalence (resp. symbolic equivalence) between frames (constraint systems) that only contain constructor terms, we can restrict ourselves to consider only recipes that are in Π_r. Thus, in the remainder, we will only consider recipes in Π_r.

4.2 Constraint systems

We slightly generalize the constraint systems introduced in Section 3. Let us explain how and why. According to Section 3, we need to decide symbolic equivalence of sets (disjunctions) of constraint systems, *e.g.* $\{\mathcal{C}_1, \mathcal{C}_2\} \overset{?}{\approx} \{\mathcal{C}'_1, \mathcal{C}'_2\}$. We cannot split these sets and consider instead sets of pairs, because the solutions of, say, $\mathcal{C}_1$ might be covered by both $\mathcal{C}'_1$ and $\mathcal{C}'_2$ and, conversely, some solutions of $\mathcal{C}'_1$ might correspond to solutions of $\mathcal{C}_2$. Now, if we wish to apply a transformation rule, to one of the component, say $\mathcal{C}_1$, our choice must be consistent with the transformation performed on the other components $\mathcal{C}_2, \mathcal{C}'_1, \mathcal{C}'_2$. For instance if we guess that a key is deducible in $\mathcal{C}_1$ using a recipe ξ, we must consistently use ξ in the constraints $\mathcal{C}'_1, \mathcal{C}'_2$, and in turn in $\mathcal{C}_2$. In summary, we need to make this choice for the whole pair of sets. Now, if the key is assumed to be non-deducible in $\mathcal{C}_1$, this must also be recorded in the other components. In short, we need to split the solutions into disjoint sets *for every component*. This yields negative constraints, typically a constraint that states that a key is not deducible.

In summary, we extend the constraints, adding some negative information.

DEFINITION 10 (CONSTRAINT SYSTEM). *It is either $\perp$ or a tuple $(\Phi; D; E; E_\Pi; ND)$ where:*

1. Φ *is a frame, whose size is some* m;

2. D *is a sequence* $X_1, i_1 \overset{?}{\vdash} u_1; \ldots; X_n, i_n \overset{?}{\vdash} u_n$ *where*

   - $X_1, \ldots, X_n$ *are distinct second order variables,* $u_1, \ldots, u_n$ *are constructor terms, and we have that* $0 \leq i_1 \leq \ldots \leq i_n \leq m$.
   - *for every* $\xi, i \rhd u$ *in* Φ, $vars^1(u) \subseteq \bigcup_{i_j < i} vars^1(u_j)$;

3. $E = \bigwedge_k u_k \overset{?}{=} v_k \wedge \bigwedge_i \forall \tilde{x}_i \cdot [\bigvee_j u_{i,j} \overset{?}{\neq} v_{i,j}]$ *where the terms* $u_k, v_k, u_{i,j}$ *and* $v_{i,j}$ *are constructor terms.*

4. $E_r = \bigwedge_i \zeta_i \overset{?}{=} \zeta'_i \wedge \bigwedge_j \xi_j \overset{?}{\neq} \xi'_j \wedge \bigwedge_k \mathsf{Top}(\beta_k) \overset{?}{\neq} \mathsf{f}_k$ *where* $\zeta_i, \zeta'_i, \xi_j, \xi'_j, \beta_k$ *are recipes in* Π_r *and* f_k *are constructor symbols.*

5. $ND = \bigwedge_i \forall \tilde{x}_i.[u_i \overset{?}{\neq} v_i \vee \bigvee_j k_{i,j} \overset{?}{\not\vdash} w_{i,j}]$ *where* $u_i, v_i, w_{i,j}$ *are constructor terms and* $0 \leq k_{i,j} \leq m$.

In Section 2, we define $vars^1(\mathcal{C})$ as the set of all first order variables that occur in $\mathcal{C}$. With this extended definition of a constraint system, the set $vars^1(\mathcal{C})$ will denote the free variables that occur in $\mathcal{C}$, *i.e.* those that do not occur explicitly under a forall quantification.

In order to define the notion of solution for such a constraint system, we have first to give the semantics of the formulas ND and E. The formulas ND and E are logic formulas built upon elementary formulas using classical connectives. The semantics for the elementary formulas are given below and is extended as expected to general formulas. Let θ be a substitution mapping $vars^2(\mathcal{C})$ to ground recipes, and σ be a substitution mapping $vars^1(\mathcal{C})$ to ground constructor terms. We have that:

- $\sigma \models (i \overset{?}{\not\vdash} u)$ iff $\xi\Phi\sigma\!\downarrow \neq u\sigma\!\downarrow$ for any ground recipe $\xi \in \Pi_r$ with $param(\xi) \subseteq \{ax_1, \ldots, ax_i\}$;
- $\sigma \models u \overset{?}{\neq} v$, iff $u\sigma \neq v\sigma$;
- $\theta \models \xi_1 \overset{?}{=} \xi_2$ (resp. $\theta \models \xi_1 \overset{?}{\neq} \xi_2$) iff $\xi_1\theta = \xi_2\theta$ (resp. $\xi_1\theta \neq \xi_2\theta$);
- $\theta \models \mathsf{Top}(\xi) \overset{?}{\neq} \mathsf{f}$ iff $\mathsf{Top}(\xi\theta) \neq \mathsf{f}$.

DEFINITION 11. *A* solution *of* $\mathcal{C} = (\Phi; D; E; E_r; ND)$ *consists of a substitution* σ *mapping* $vars^1(\mathcal{C})$ *to ground constructor terms and a substitution* θ *mapping* $vars^2(\mathcal{C})$ *to ground recipes in* Π_r*, such that:*

1. *for every* $X_i, j \overset{?}{\vdash} u_i$ *in* D*, we have that* $X_i\theta(\Phi\sigma)\!\downarrow = u_i\sigma\!\downarrow$ *and* $param(X_i\theta) \subseteq \{ax_1, \ldots, ax_j\}$;
2. $\sigma \models ND \wedge E$ *and* $\theta \models E_r$.

We denote by $\mathsf{Sol}(\mathcal{C})$ *the set of solutions of* $\mathcal{C}$. *By convention,* $\mathsf{Sol}(\bot) = \emptyset$.

The *structure* of a system $\mathcal{C} = (\Phi; D; E; E_r; ND)$ is given by E_r, $\{(X, i) \mid X, i \overset{?}{\vdash} u \in D\}$, and $\{(\xi, i) \mid \xi, i \rhd u \in \Phi\}$. Two constraint systems $\mathcal{C}$ and $\mathcal{C}'$ have the *same structure* if their underlying structure are equal.

For this generalized notion of constraint systems, we can define the notion of symbolic equivalence accordingly.

DEFINITION 12. *Let* Σ *and* Σ' *be two sets of constraint systems having the same structure. We have that* $\Sigma \approx_s \Sigma'$ *if for all* $\mathcal{C} \in \Sigma$*, for all* $(\sigma, \theta) \in \mathsf{Sol}(\mathcal{C})$*, there exists* $\mathcal{C}' \in \Sigma'$ *and a substitution* σ' *such that* $(\sigma', \theta) \in \mathsf{Sol}(\mathcal{C}')$ *and* $\Phi\sigma\!\downarrow \sim \Phi'\sigma'\!\downarrow$ *where* $\mathcal{C} = (\Phi; D; E; E_r; ND)$*, and* $\mathcal{C}' = (\Phi'; D'; E'; E'_r; ND')$ *(and conversely).*

Note also that given an initial constraint system $\mathcal{C}_0 = (\Phi_0; D_0; E_0)$ that may contain some destructors, we can transform it into an "equivalent" constraint system $\mathcal{C} = (\Phi; D; E; E_r; ND)$ (without destructors) in the sense that:

- for every $(\sigma_0, \theta) \in \mathsf{Sol}_{\mathsf{init}}(\mathcal{C}_0)$ with recipes in Π_r, there exists $(\sigma, \theta) \in \mathsf{Sol}(\mathcal{C})$ such that $\Phi_0\sigma_0\!\downarrow = \Phi\sigma\!\downarrow$; and
- for every $(\sigma, \theta) \in \mathsf{Sol}(\mathcal{C})$, there exists $(\sigma_0, \theta) \in \mathsf{Sol}_{\mathsf{init}}(\mathcal{C}_0)$ such that $\Phi\sigma\!\downarrow = \Phi_0\sigma_0\!\downarrow$.

Roughly, the transformation consists in guessing the possible reductions, in the spirit of [13]. We write $\mathbf{Tr}(\mathcal{C}_0)$ to denote the result of applying the transformation to $\mathcal{C}_0$.

EXAMPLE 7. *Going back to the initial constraint system* $\mathcal{C}_1$ *(resp.* $\mathcal{C}_2$*) described in Example 5 (resp. Example 6), the constraint system* $\mathbf{Tr}(\mathcal{C}_1)$ *is obtained from* $\mathcal{C}_1$ *by applying the substitution* $\{y \mapsto \mathsf{aenc}(\langle y', \mathsf{pub}(ska)\rangle, pub(skb))\}$ *(and normalizing the result) whereas* $\mathbf{Tr}(\mathcal{C}_2)$ *is obtained from* $\mathcal{C}_2$ *by replacing its disequation with* $\forall y' \cdot y \overset{?}{\neq} \mathsf{aenc}(\langle y', \mathsf{pub}(ska)\rangle, \mathsf{pub}(skb))$. *Note that in both cases, we get rid of all the destructors.*

PROPOSITION 1. *Let* $\Sigma = \{\mathcal{C}_1, \ldots, \mathcal{C}_k\}$, $\Sigma' = \{\mathcal{C}'_1, \ldots, \mathcal{C}'_\ell\}$ *be two finite sets of initial constraint systems. We have that:*

$$\Sigma \approx_{\mathsf{init}} \Sigma' \quad \Leftrightarrow \quad \{\mathbf{Tr}(\mathcal{C}_i) \mid \mathcal{C}_i \in \Sigma\} \approx_s \{\mathbf{Tr}(\mathcal{C}'_i) \mid \mathcal{C}'_i \in \Sigma'\}$$

5. ALGORITHM

The main result of this section is a decision procedure for symbolic equivalence between sets of constraint systems obtained by applying our transformation $\mathbf{Tr}()$ on sets of initial constraint systems.

THEOREM 3. *Given two sets* Σ, Σ' *of initial constraint systems, it is decidable whether* $\{\mathbf{Tr}(\mathcal{C}) \mid \mathcal{C} \in \Sigma\} \approx_s \{\mathbf{Tr}(\mathcal{C}') \mid \mathcal{C}' \in \Sigma'\}$.

Our decision algorithm works by rewriting pairs of sets of constraint systems, until a trivial failure or a trivial success is found. These rules are branching: they rewrite a pair of sets of constraint systems into two pairs of sets of constraint systems. Transforming the pairs of constraints therefore builds a binary tree. Termination requires to follow a particular strategy that is explained in Section 5.3. The transformation rules are *sound*: if all leaves are success leaves, then the original pair of sets of constraint systems is equivalent. They are finally *complete*: if the two original sets of constraint systems are equivalent then all the leaves are success leaves.

5.1 Transformation rules

The transformation rules are displayed in Figure 3 for a single constraint system (we only write the components of the constraint systems that are modified during an application of an instance of a rule). Since we intend to decide symbolic equivalence between two sets of constraint systems, we will then explain how to apply these transformation rules in such a setting (see Section 5.2).

The CONS rule simply guesses whether the top symbol of the recipe is a constructor f. Either it is, and then we can split the

Transformation rules for satisfiability:

$$\underline{\textsc{Cons}(X,\mathsf{f})} : X, i \overset{?}{\vdash} t; E; E_r \quad \longrightarrow \quad X_1, i \overset{?}{\vdash} x_1; \cdots; X_n, i \overset{?}{\vdash} x_n; E \wedge t \overset{?}{=} \mathsf{f}(x_1,\ldots,x_n); E_r \wedge X \overset{?}{=} \mathsf{f}(X_1,\ldots,X_n)$$

$$\qquad\qquad\qquad\qquad \longrightarrow \quad X, i \overset{?}{\vdash} t\ ;\ E;\ E_r \wedge \mathsf{Top}(X) \neq \mathsf{f}$$

where $x_1,\ldots,x_n, X_1,\ldots X_n$ are fresh variables.

$$\underline{\textsc{Axiom}(X,\xi)} : \ X, i \overset{?}{\vdash} u;\ E;\ E_r \quad \longrightarrow \quad E \wedge u \overset{?}{=} v;\ E_r \wedge X \overset{?}{=} \xi$$

$$\qquad\qquad\qquad\qquad \longrightarrow \quad X, i \overset{?}{\vdash} u;\ E;\ E_r \wedge X \overset{?}{\neq} \xi$$

If $(\xi, j \rhd v) \in \Phi$ and $i \geq j$.

$$\underline{\textsc{Dest}(\xi, l \to r, i)} : E; ND \quad \longrightarrow \quad \mathsf{g}(\xi, X_2,\ldots,X_n), i \rhd w; X_2, i \overset{?}{\vdash} u_2; \ldots; X_n, i \overset{?}{\vdash} u_n; E_p \wedge v \overset{?}{=} u_1; ND$$

$$\qquad\qquad\qquad\qquad \longrightarrow \quad E;\ ND \wedge \forall \tilde{x} \cdot [v \neq u_1 \vee i \overset{?}{\nvdash} u_2 \vee \ldots \vee i \overset{?}{\nvdash} u_n]$$

If $(\xi, j \rhd v) \in \Phi$ with $j \leq i$. $X_2,\ldots,X_n$ are fresh variables, and $\tilde{x}$ are the variables that occur in $\mathsf{g}(u_1,\ldots,u_n) \to w$ a fresh renaming of the rewriting rule $l \to r$.

Additional transformation rules for static equivalence:

$$\underline{\textsc{Eq-left-left}(\xi_1,\xi_2)} : E \quad \longrightarrow \quad E \wedge u_1 \overset{?}{=} u_2 \qquad\qquad \longrightarrow \quad E \wedge u_1 \overset{?}{\neq} u_2$$

If $(\xi_1, i_1 \rhd u_1),\ (\xi_2 \rhd u_2) \in \Phi$ for some u_1, u_2, i_1, i_2.

$$\underline{\textsc{Eq-left-right}(\xi_1, X_2)} : E \quad \longrightarrow \quad E \wedge u_1 \overset{?}{=} u_2 \qquad\qquad \longrightarrow \quad E \wedge u_1 \overset{?}{\neq} u_2$$

If $(\xi_1, i_1 \rhd u_1) \in \Phi$ and $(X_2, i_2 \overset{?}{\vdash} u_2) \in D$ for some u_1, u_2, i_1, i_2 such that $i_2 < i_1$.

$$\underline{\textsc{Eq-right-right}(X,\xi)} : X, i \overset{?}{\vdash} u;\ E;\ E_r \quad \longrightarrow \quad E \wedge u \overset{?}{=} v;\ E_r \wedge X \overset{?}{=} \xi$$

$$\qquad\qquad\qquad\qquad \longrightarrow \quad X, i \overset{?}{\vdash} u;\ E \wedge u \overset{?}{\neq} v;\ E_r$$

where $\xi \in \mathcal{T}(\mathcal{F}_c, dom(\alpha))$ and $v = \xi\alpha$ with $\alpha = \{Y \mapsto u \mid (Y, j \overset{?}{\vdash} u) \in D \wedge j \leq i\}$.

$$\underline{\textsc{Ded-st}(\xi,\mathsf{f})} : E; ND \quad \longrightarrow \quad X_1, m \overset{?}{\vdash} x_1;\ \cdots;\ X_n, m \overset{?}{\vdash} x_n;\ E \wedge u \overset{?}{=} \mathsf{f}(x_1,\ldots,x_n);\ ND$$

$$\qquad\qquad\qquad\qquad \longrightarrow \quad E;\ ND \wedge \forall \tilde{x} \cdot [u \neq \mathsf{f}(x_1,\ldots,x_n) \vee m \overset{?}{\nvdash} x_1 \vee \ldots \vee m \overset{?}{\nvdash} x_n]$$

If $(\xi, i \rhd u) \in \Phi$. The sequences $\tilde{x} \overset{\mathsf{def}}{=} x_1,\ldots,x_n$, and $X_1,\ldots,X_n$ are sequences of fresh variables and m denotes the size of Φ.

All rules assume that the equations have a mgu that is eagerly applied to the resulting constraint, that the disequations have been simplified. Moreover, if there exists a constraint $X, i \overset{?}{\vdash} u$ with $u \notin \mathcal{X}^1$ and on which the rule Cons *and* Axiom *cannot be applied on it, and the rule* Dest *can not be applied anymore, then we replace $\mathcal{C}$ with $\bot$.*

Figure 3: Transformation rules

deducibility constraint, or it is not and we add a disequation on recipes forbidding this. The rule AXIOM also guesses whether a trivial recipe (a left member of the frame, typically an axiom ax_i) can be applied. If so, the constraint can simply be removed. Otherwise, we also add a disequation on recipes forbidding it. The DEST rule is more tricky. If v is a term of the frame, that can be unified with a non variable subterm of a left side of a rewrite rule (for instance v is a ciphertext), we guess whether the rule can be applied to v. This corresponds to the equation $u_1 \stackrel{?}{=} v$, that yields an instance of w, the right member of the rewrite rule, provided that the rest of the left member is also deducible: in case of symmetric encryption, we get a constraint $X_2, j \stackrel{?}{\vdash} u_2$. The various equality rules guess equalities between right-hand sides of deducibility constraints and/or members of the frame. Finally, the last transformation rule is the only rule that is needed to get in addition a static equivalence decision algorithm, as in [1]. Thanks to this rule, if a subterm of the frame is deducible, then there will be a branch in which it is deduced.

The idea behind these rules is to transform a system into simpler ones. Typically, as it is done in [11], we want to consider systems in which right-hand sides of deducibility constraints are distinct variables (assuming that the mgu corresponding to the equations has been applied on the constraints). However, in presence of disequations, putting the systems in such a form does not guarantee anymore that the two resulting systems will be in symbolic equivalence. Let us illustrate this using a simple example.

EXAMPLE 8. *Consider the constraint systems*

- $\mathcal{C} = (ax_1, 1 \rhd a;\ X, 1 \stackrel{?}{\vdash} x;\ \emptyset;\ \emptyset;\ \emptyset)$, *and*
- $\mathcal{C}' = (ax_1, 1 \rhd a;\ X, 1 \stackrel{?}{\vdash} x;\ x \stackrel{?}{\neq} \langle a, a\rangle;\ \emptyset;\ \emptyset)$.

Although these two systems have the expected form, they are not *in symbolic equivalence (consider for instance the recipe $\langle ax_1, ax_1\rangle$).*

Once the system is put in this kind of "pre-solved form", the basic idea will be to continue to apply our transformation rules to "match" the disequations of each constraint system. For this, we want to transform the disequations in which some names or universally quantified variable occur until obtaining disequations that only contain free variables and public function symbols. This will guarantee that there exists a recipe associated to this term and this gives us the way to match it in another constraint system. Once the system is transformed into such a new kind of "solved form", we can now easily conclude. Indeed, since we also take care of static equivalence on the resulting frames, disequations that correspond to public disequality tests are easily transferable from one constraint system to another without any additional checks.

EXAMPLE 9. *Continuing Example 8 and assuming that the pairing operator is the only constructor symbol, we will go on, applying* CONS. *Let $\Phi_0 = \{ax_1, 1 \rhd a\}$, $D = \{X_1, 1 \stackrel{?}{\vdash} x_1; X_2, 1 \stackrel{?}{\vdash} x_2\}$, and $E_r = \{X \stackrel{?}{=} \langle X_1, X_2\rangle\}$. One of the resulting pair will be the pair $(\mathcal{C}_1, \mathcal{C}'_1)$ where:*

- $\mathcal{C}_1 = (\Phi_0; D; x \stackrel{?}{=} \langle x_1, x_2\rangle; E_r; \emptyset)$;
- $\mathcal{C}'_1 = (\Phi_0; D; x \stackrel{?}{=} \langle x_1, x_2\rangle \wedge [x_1 \stackrel{?}{\neq} a \vee x_2 \stackrel{?}{\neq} a]; E_r; \emptyset)$;

Now, by applying the AXIOM *rule twice, one of the resulting pair will be the pair $(\mathcal{C}_2; \mathcal{C}'_2)$ where:*

- $\mathcal{C}_2 = (\Phi_0; \emptyset; x \stackrel{?}{=} \langle a, a\rangle; X = \langle ax_1, ax_1\rangle; \emptyset)$; *and*
- $\mathcal{C}'_2 = \bot$ *since the disequations will be trivially not satisfied.*

These two constraint systems are not in symbolic equivalence.

Now, to ensure that we will reach such a solved form in which all the disequations are matched, the rule EQ-RIGHT-RIGHT plays an important role.

EXAMPLE 10. *Consider the two constraint systems:*

- $\mathcal{C} = (\Phi_0; D_0; x \stackrel{?}{\neq} \mathsf{h}(y) \wedge x \stackrel{?}{\neq} y; \emptyset; \emptyset)$;
- $\mathcal{C}' = (\Phi_0; D_0; \emptyset; \emptyset; \emptyset)$

where $\Phi_0 = \{ax_1, 1 \rhd a\}$ and $D_0 = \{X, 1 \stackrel{?}{\vdash} x;\ Y, 1 \stackrel{?}{\vdash} y\}$.

We could apply CONS *replacing x with $\mathsf{h}(x')$ to simplify the disequation $x \stackrel{?}{\neq} \mathsf{h}(y)$ into $x' \stackrel{?}{\neq} y$. However, this operation will transform the other disequation, namely $x \stackrel{?}{\neq} y$, into $\mathsf{h}(x') \stackrel{?}{\neq} y$. Consequently, one of the resulting pair would be made up of two systems on which the* CONS *rule is again applicable. Instead of this, since the disequation $x \stackrel{?}{\neq} \mathsf{h}(y)$ does not contain any name, it can be matched to the other system, so we apply* EQ-RIGHT-RIGHT. *This leads us to the pairs $(\bot, \mathcal{C}'_1)$ and $(\mathcal{C}; \mathcal{C}'_2)$ where:*

- $\mathcal{C}'_1 = (\Phi_0; \{Y, 1 \stackrel{?}{\vdash} y\}; x \stackrel{?}{=} \mathsf{h}(y); X \stackrel{?}{=} \mathsf{h}(Y); \emptyset)$; *and*
- $\mathcal{C}'_2 = (\Phi_0; D_0; x \stackrel{?}{\neq} \mathsf{h}(y); \emptyset; \emptyset)$.

From the pair $(\bot, \mathcal{C}'_1)$ we will conclude that symbolic equivalence does not hold. Regarding the pair $(\mathcal{C}; \mathcal{C}'_2)$, we can go on and reach a solved form by applying EQ-RIGHT-RIGHT *obtaining again two pairs of constraint systems. The first one will be of the form $(\bot; \mathcal{C}'_3)$ and the second one will contain two systems in which all the disequations are matched.*

5.2 How to apply the rules

We explain here how the transformation rules can be used on a pair of sets of constraint systems, assuming that all the constraint systems have the same structure. Actually, the basic idea is to apply the same transformation rule (with the same parameters) on each constraint system. Note that, the parameters of a transformation rule only depend on the structure of the underlying constraint system. Thanks to this, the simultaneous application of a transformation rule can be defined in a natural way. It consists of applying the same instance of the transformation rule on each constraint system that occurs in the two sets. So an application of a rule on a pair (Σ, Σ') of sets of constraint systems will result in two pairs (Σ_1, Σ'_1) and (Σ_2, Σ'_2)

Let (Σ, Σ') be a pair of sets of constraint systems having the same structure. Let $\Sigma = \{\mathcal{C}_1, \ldots, \mathcal{C}_k\}$, $\Sigma' = \{\mathcal{C}'_1, \ldots, \mathcal{C}'_\ell\}$, and R be an instance of a transformation rule. An application of R on the pair (Σ, Σ') yields two pairs (Σ_1, Σ'_1) and (Σ_2, Σ'_2) such that:

- $\Sigma_i = \{\mathcal{C}_{i,1}, \ldots, \mathcal{C}_{i,k}\}$ for $i = 1, 2$; and
- $\Sigma'_i = \{\mathcal{C}'_{i,1}, \ldots, \mathcal{C}'_{i,\ell}\}$ for $i = 1, 2$.

where $(\mathcal{C}_{1,j}, \mathcal{C}_{2,j})$ (resp. $(\mathcal{C}'_{1,,j'}, \mathcal{C}'_{2,j'})$) is the pair of constraint systems obtained by applying R on $\mathcal{C}_j$ (resp. $\mathcal{C}'_{j'}$).

Actually, deciding symbolic equivalence between two sets raises two main issues:

- matching an existing solution from one set to the other;
- and deciding whether the two resulting frames are statically equivalence or not.

When checking static equivalence, we have to check that the same equalities hold in both resulting frames. So, in order to develop a simple test on leaves, it is important to gather the two resulting sets of constraint systems when the rule is used to check static equivalence on the resulting frames. This leads us to consider matrices of constraint systems and two kinds of applications for our rules: *internal* and *external*. An external application will apply a rule on the whole matrix while an internal application will apply a rule on one particular line (the same in both matrices) replacing this line with two new lines.

EXAMPLE 11. *Consider the following example where there is no deducibility constraint. The idea is to simply check whether static equivalence holds between sets of frames. Let* $\Phi_1 = \{ax_1, 1 \rhd k, ax_2, 2 \rhd a\}$ *and* $\Phi_2 = \{ax_1, 1 \rhd k, ax_2 \rhd \mathsf{senc}(a, k)\}$*. We consider the systems* $C_i = (\Phi_i; \emptyset; \emptyset; \emptyset; \emptyset)$ *for* $i = 1, 2$*. Now, we want to check whether* $\{C_1, C_2\} \approx_s \{C_2\}$*. Actually, symbolic equivalence does not hold since* $\Phi_1 \not\sim \Phi_2$*. However, applying* DEST*, the only rule that can be applied, will result in the pairs:*

$$(\{\bot, C_2'\}, \{C_2'\}) \qquad (\{C_1'', C_2''\}, \{C_2''\})$$

where C_1'' *(resp.* C_2''*) are obtained from* C_1 *(resp.* C_2*) by adding the non-deducibility constraints:*

- $\forall x, y \cdot [a \stackrel{?}{\neq} \mathsf{senc}(x, y) \vee \stackrel{?}{\nvdash} y]$ *in* C_1''*;*
- $\forall x, y \cdot [\mathsf{senc}(a, k) \stackrel{?}{\neq} \mathsf{senc}(x, y) \vee \stackrel{?}{\nvdash} y]$ *in* C_2''*.*

Note that no transformation rule is applicable on this pair. It is easy to see that symbolic equivalence holds for the first pair. Actually, symbolic equivalence also holds on the second pair taking into account the non-deducibility constraints. However, we do not want to solve these non-deducibility constraints. Instead, we apply DEST *internally, obtaining one leaf of the form:*

$$\begin{pmatrix} \bot & C_2' \\ C_1'' & C_2'' \end{pmatrix}, \begin{pmatrix} C_2' \\ C_2'' \end{pmatrix}$$

Then, on the leaves, we check that for each column of one matrix, there exist a column in the other matrix on which the constaint systems have the same status, i.e. $\bot$ *or not. Here, this test will trivially fail on our unique leaf allowing us to conclude that the two original sets* $\{C_1, C_2\}$ *and* $\{C_2\}$ *are* not *in symbolic equivalence.*

5.3 Strategy

Applying blindly the transformation rules does not always terminate (see [11] for an example). As in [11], to avoid non-terminating behaviors, we fix one of the constraint system, reduce it until reaching a "pre-solved form" (distinct variables in the right-hand sides of the deducibility constraints), and then move to the next system. Solving the second system does preserve the property on the first one. In this way we can reach constraint systems in "pre-solved" form.

This is not however sufficient: because of the disequations, it might be not so easy to decide the equivalence of such sets (or matrices) of constraint systems (see Example 8). Therefore, we further apply some transformation rules, that allow to simplify the disequalities. For this second phase, we only need the rules CONS, AXIOM, EQ-RIGHT-RIGHT. CONS is restricted to the situations in which there is a disequation $x \neq u$ and either u is not a name and contains a name, or else u is not a variable and contains a universally quantified variable. There is still one difficulty, because, as before, we may get a non terminating behavior.

EXAMPLE 12. *We consider a constraint system in "pre-solved" form such that:*

$$E = [x_1 \stackrel{?}{\neq} y \vee x_2 \stackrel{?}{\neq} a] \wedge y \stackrel{?}{\neq} \langle\langle x_1, x_2\rangle, b\rangle.$$

For sake of simplicity, we do not described Φ *and* D*. We simply assume that the frame contains the terms* a *and* b*. First, we apply* AXIOM *on* x_2 *(with* a*), on one branch we will obtain* $x_1 \stackrel{?}{\neq} y \wedge y \stackrel{?}{\neq} \langle\langle x_1, a\rangle, b\rangle$*. Then, applying* CONS *twice, we obtain* $x_1 \stackrel{?}{\neq} \langle\langle y_1, y_2\rangle, y_3\rangle \wedge [y_1 \stackrel{?}{\neq} x_1 \vee y_2 \stackrel{?}{\neq} a \vee y_3 \stackrel{?}{\neq} b]$*. Lastly, applying* AXIOM *on* y_3 *(with* b*), we obtain*

$$x_1 \stackrel{?}{\neq} \langle\langle y_1, y_2\rangle, b\rangle \wedge [y_1 \stackrel{?}{\neq} x_1 \vee y_2 \stackrel{?}{\neq} a]$$

getting back to the original set of disequations.

We therefore use the following strategy:

$$((\text{CONS} + \text{EQ-RIGHT-RIGHT})!; \text{AXIOM}!)!$$

where the exclamation mark means "as long as possible". This allows us in particular to avoid the non-terminating behavior described in Example 12. Now, we claim that irreducible constraints contain only disequations $x \neq u$ where u does not contain names or universally quantified variables and that the transformations are terminating.

The termination argument is as follows: EQ-RIGHT-RIGHT allows to "externalize" the disjunctions, splitting disjunctive constraints, each of which will appear in different matrices. Then, CONS will allow to decrease the heights of names and universally quantified variables. Finally, these measures may increase with AXIOM, but then the replacement substitutes a variable with support i with terms that only contain variables, whose support is strictly smaller than i. Furthermore, all these rules will keep the deducibility constraints in pre-solved form.

5.4 Correctness

The transformation rules yield a finite tree labeled with pairs of matrices of constraint systems. As briefly explained in Example 11, our test on the leaves consists of checking that for each column in one matrix, there exists a column in the other matrix such that each constraint system has the same status. We say that $\mathsf{LeafTest}(M, M') = \mathsf{true}$ when this syntaxic test holds on the leaf (M, M'). Otherwise, we say that $\mathsf{LeafTest}(M, M') = \mathsf{false}$.

PROPOSITION 2. *Let* (Σ_0, Σ_0') *be a pair of sets of constraint systems obtained by applying our transformation* $\mathbf{Tr}()$ *on sets of initial constraint systems, and consider a binary tree obtained by following the strategy described in Section 5.3.*

- soundness: *If all leaves of a tree are labeled with* (M, M') *such that* $\mathsf{LeafTest}(M, M') = \mathsf{true}$*, then* $\Sigma_0 \approx_s \Sigma_0'$*.*
- completeness: *If* $\Sigma_0 \approx_s \Sigma_0'$*, then all leaves of a tree are labeled with* (M, M') *with* $\mathsf{LeafTest}(M, M') = \mathsf{true}$*.*

The idea of the proof is to first analyse the structure of the leaves and then to show that our notion of equivalence is preserved through application of our transformation rules: for any transformation rule, if the two pairs of sets of constraint systems labeling the sons of a node are respectively in symbolic equivalence, then the same property holds for the father.

6. CONCLUSION

An Ocaml implementation of an early version of the procedure described in this paper has already been completed. This procedure extends [13] to set of constraints, including disequalities. Actually, checking symbolic equivalence between sets of constraint systems is quite efficient. However, the interleaving step, that is required for moving from symbolic equivalence to trace equivalence, is performed in a naive way and it appears that this step is expensive from the computation point of view. We tested this implementation on the private authentication protocol and the two versions of the e-passport protocol. Our implementation concludes within a few minutes for the private authentication protocol and the flawed version of the e-passport protocol (considering 2 sessions only). We also tried our implementation on the fixed version of the e-passport and it took more time (around 2 days).

In order to get an efficient procedure, it is necessary to come with some optimisations to reduce the search space and the number of interleavings. This problem is not specific to trace equivalence and has already been studied in the context of trace properties (*e.g.* [22]). However, discarding some "symbolic" interleavings appears to be challenging for equivalence-based properties. Finally, we would like to extend the method to other cryptographic primitives, typically blind signatures and zero-knowledge proofs.

7. REFERENCES

[1] M. Abadi and V. Cortier. Deciding knowledge in security protocols under equational theories. *Theoretical Computer Science*, 387(1-2):2–32, 2006.

[2] M. Abadi and C. Fournet. Mobile values, new names, and secure communication. In *Proc. 28th Symposium on Principles of Programming Languages (POPL'01)*, pages 104–115. ACM Press, 2001.

[3] M. Abadi and C. Fournet. Private authentication. *Theoretical Computer Science*, 322(3):427–476, 2004.

[4] M. Abadi and A. Gordon. A calculus for cryptographic protocols: The spi calculus. In *Proc. 4th Conference on Computer and Communications Security (CCS'97)*, pages 36–47. ACM Press, 1997.

[5] M. Arapinis, T. Chothia, E. Ritter, and M. Ryan. Analysing unlinkability and anonymity using the applied pi calculus. In *Proc. of 23rd IEEE Computer Security Foundations Symposium (CSF'10)*, pages 107–121. IEEE Computer Society Press, 2010.

[6] A. Armando et al. The AVISPA Tool for the automated validation of internet security protocols and applications. In *Proc. 17th Int. Conference on Computer Aided Verification (CAV'05)*, volume 3576 of *LNCS*, pages 281–285. Springer, 2005.

[7] M. Baudet. Deciding security of protocols against off-line guessing attacks. In *Proc. 12th Conference on Computer and Communications Security (CCS'05)*, pages 16–25. ACM Press, 2005.

[8] M. Baudet. *Sécurité des protocoles cryptographiques : aspects logiques et calculatoires*. Phd thesis, École Normale Supérieure de Cachan, France, 2007.

[9] B. Blanchet. An Efficient Cryptographic Protocol Verifier Based on Prolog Rules. In *Proc. 14th Computer Security Foundations Workshop (CSFW'01)*, pages 82–96. IEEE Comp. Soc. Press, 2001.

[10] B. Blanchet, M. Abadi, and C. Fournet. Automated verification of selected equivalences for security protocols. *Journal of Logic and Algebraic Programming*, 75(1):3–51, 2008.

[11] V. Cheval, H. Comon-Lundh, and S. Delaune. Automating security analysis: symbolic equivalence of constraint systems. In *Proc. 5th International Joint Conference on Automated Reasoning (IJCAR'10)*, volume 6173 of *LNAI*, pages 412–426. Springer-Verlag, 2010.

[12] Y. Chevalier and M. Rusinowitch. Decidability of symbolic equivalence of derivations. *Journal of Automated Reasoning*, 2011. To appear.

[13] H. Comon-Lundh and S. Delaune. The finite variant property: How to get rid of some algebraic properties. In *Proc. 16th International Conference on Rewriting Techniques and Applications (RTA'05)*, LNCS, pages 294–307. Springer, 2005.

[14] V. Cortier and S. Delaune. A method for proving observational equivalence. In *Proc. 22nd Computer Security Foundations Symposium (CSF'09)*, pages 266–276. IEEE Comp. Soc. Press, 2009.

[15] S. Delaune, S. Kremer, and M. D. Ryan. Symbolic bisimulation for the applied pi-calculus. In *Proc. 27th Conference on Foundations of Software Technology and Theoretical Computer Science (FSTTCS'07)*, pages 133–145, 2007.

[16] S. Delaune, S. Kremer, and M. D. Ryan. Verifying privacy-type properties of electronic voting protocols. *Journal of Computer Security*, 17(4):435–487, July 2009.

[17] D. Dolev and A. C. Yao. On the security of public key protocols. In *Proc. 22nd Symposium on Foundations of Computer Science (FCS'81)*, pages 350–357. IEEE Computer Society Press, 1981.

[18] L. Durante, R. Sisto, and A. Valenzano. Automatic testing equivalence verification of spi calculus specifications. *ACM Transactions on Software Engineering and Methodology*, 12(2):222–284, 2003.

[19] N. Durgin, P. Lincoln, J. Mitchell, and A. Scedrov. Undecidability of bounded security protocols. In *Workshop on Formal Methods and Security Protocols*, 1999.

[20] H. Hüttel. Deciding framed bisimulation. In *Proc. 4th Int. Workshop on Verification of Infinite State Systems (INFINITY'02)*, pages 1–20, 2002.

[21] J. Millen and V. Shmatikov. Constraint solving for bounded-process cryptographic protocol analysis. In *Proc. 8th ACM Conference on Computer and Communications Security (CCS'01)*. ACM Press, 2001.

[22] S. Mödersheim, L. Viganò, and D. A. Basin. Constraint differentiation: Search-space reduction for the constraint-based analysis of security protocols. *Journal of Computer Security*, 18(4):575–618, 2010.

[23] R. Ramanujam and S. Suresh. Tagging makes secrecy decidable for unbounded nonces as well. In *Proc. 23rd Conference on Foundations of Software Technology and Theoretical Computer Science (FSTTCS'03)*, 2003.

[24] M. Rusinowitch and M. Turuani. Protocol insecurity with finite number of sessions is NP-complete. In *Proc. 14th Computer Security Foundations Workshop (CSFW'01)*, pages 174–190. IEEE Comp. Soc. Press, 2001.

[25] A. Tiu and J. E. Dawson. Automating open bisimulation checking for the spi calculus. In *Proc. 23rd IEEE Computer Security Foundations Symposium (CSF'10)*, pages 307–321. IEEE Computer Society Press, 2010.

Extracting and Verifying Cryptographic Models from C Protocol Code by Symbolic Execution

Mihhail Aizatulin
The Open University

Andrew D. Gordon
Microsoft Research

Jan Jürjens
TU Dortmund & Fraunhofer ISST

ABSTRACT

Consider the problem of verifying security properties of a cryptographic protocol coded in C. We propose an automatic solution that needs neither a pre-existing protocol description nor manual annotation of source code. First, symbolically execute the C program to obtain symbolic descriptions for the network messages sent by the protocol. Second, apply algebraic rewriting to obtain a process calculus description. Third, run an existing protocol analyser (ProVerif) to prove security properties or find attacks. We formalise our algorithm and appeal to existing results for ProVerif to establish computational soundness under suitable circumstances. We analyse only a single execution path, so our results are limited to protocols with no significant branching. The results in this paper provide the first computationally sound verification of weak secrecy and authentication for (single execution paths of) C code.

Categories and Subject Descriptors

C.2.2 [**Computer-Communication Networks**]: Network Protocols—*Protocol verification*; D.2.4 [**Software Engineering**]: Software/Program Verification

General Terms

Security, Verification

1. INTRODUCTION

Recent years have seen great progress in formal verification of cryptographic protocols, as illustrated by powerful tools like ProVerif [8], CryptoVerif [7] or AVISPA [4]. There remains, however, a large gap between what we verify (formal descriptions of protocols, say, in the pi calculus) and what we rely on (protocol implementations, often in low-level languages like C). The need to start the verification from C code has been recognised before and implemented in tools like CSur [20] and ASPIER [13], but the methods proposed there are still rather limited. Consider, for example, the small piece of C code in fig. 1 that checks whether a message received from the network matches a message authentication code. Intuitively, if the key is honestly chosen and kept secret from the attacker then with overwhelming probability the event will be triggered only if another honest participant (with access to the key) generated the message. Unfortunately, previous approaches cannot prove this property: the analysis of CSur is too coarse to deal with authentication properties like this and ASPIER cannot directly deal with code manipulating memory through pointers. Furthermore the previous works do not offer a definition of security directly for C code, i.e. they do not formally state what it means for a C program to satisfy a security property, which makes it difficult to evaluate their overall soundness. The goal of our work is to improve upon this situation by giving a formal definition of security straight for C code and proposing a method that can verify secrecy and authentication for typical memory-manipulating implementations like the one in fig. 1 in a fully automatic and scalable manner, without relying on a pre-existing protocol specification.

```
void * key; size_t keylen;
readenv("k", &key, &keylen);
size_t len;
read(&len, sizeof(len));
if(len > 1000) exit();
void * buf = malloc(len + 2 * MAC_LEN);
read(buf, len);
mac(buf, len, key, keylen, buf + len);
read(buf + len + MAC_LEN, MAC_LEN);
if(memcmp(buf + len,
          buf + len + MAC_LEN,
          MAC_LEN) == 0)
  event("accept", buf, len);
```

in(x_1); **in**(x_2); **if** $x_2 = mac(k, x_1)$ **then event** $accept(x_1)$

Figure 1: An example C fragment together with the extracted model.

Our method proceeds by extracting a high-level model from the C code that can then be verified using existing tools (we use ProVerif in our work). Currently we restrict our analysis to code in which all network outputs happen on a single execution path, but otherwise we do not require use of any specific programming style, with the aim of applying our methods to legacy implementations. In particular, we do not assume memory safety, but instead explicitly verify it during model extraction. The method still assumes that the cryptographic primitives such as encryption or hashing

CCS'11, October 17–21, 2011, Chicago, Illinois, USA.

are implemented correctly—verification of these is difficult even when done manually [3].

The two main contributions of our work are:

- formal definition of security properties for source code;
- an algorithm that computes a high-level model of the protocol implemented by a C program.

We implement and evaluate the algorithm as well as give a proof of its soundness with respect to our security definition. Our definition of security for source code is given by linking the semantics of a programming language, expressed as a transition system, to a computational security definition in the spirit of [10, 19, 30]. We allow an arbitrary number of sessions. We restrict our definition to trace properties (such as weak secrecy or authentication), but do not consider observational equivalence (for strong secrecy, say).

Due to the complexity of the C language we give the formal semantics for a simple assembler-like language into which C code can be easily compiled, as in other symbolic execution approaches such as [14]. The soundness of this step can be obtained by using well-known methods, as outlined in the technical report [2].

Our model-extraction algorithm produces a model in an intermediate language without memory access or destructive updates, while still preserving our security definition. The algorithm is based on symbolic execution [21] of the C program, using symbolic expressions to over-approximate the sets of values that may be stored in memory during concrete execution. The main difference from existing symbolic execution algorithms (such as [12] or [18]) is that our variables represent bitstrings of potentially unknown length, whereas in previous algorithms a single variable corresponds to a single byte.

We show how the extracted models can be further simplified into the form understood by ProVerif. We apply the computational soundness result from [5] to obtain conditions where the symbolic security definition checked by ProVerif corresponds to our computational security definition. Combined with the security-preserving property of the model extraction algorithm this provides a computationally sound verification of weak secrecy and authentication for C.

Outline of our Method. The verification proceeds in several steps, as outlined in fig. 2. The method takes as input:

- the C implementations of the protocol participants, containing calls to a special function `event` as in fig. 1,
- an environment process (in the modelling language) which spawns the participants, distributes keys, etc.,
- symbolic models of cryptographic functions used by the implementation,
- a property that event traces in the execution are supposed to satisfy with overwhelming probability.

We start by compiling the program down to a simple stack-based instruction language (CVM) using CIL [25] to parse and simplify the C input. The syntax and semantics of CVM are presented in section 2. Due to space constraints the translation from C to CVM is in the technical report [2].

In the next step we symbolically execute CVM programs to eliminate memory accesses and destructive updates, thus obtaining an equivalent program in an intermediate model language (IML)—a version of the applied pi calculus extended with bitstring manipulation primitives. For each allocated memory area the symbolic execution stores an expression describing how the contents of the memory area have been computed. For instance a certain memory area might be associated with an expression $hmac(01\|x, k)$, where x is known to originate from the network, k is known to be an environment variable, and $\|$ denotes concatenation. The symbolic execution does not enter the functions that implement the cryptographic primitives, it uses the provided symbolic models instead. These models thus form the trusted base of the verification. An example of the symbolic execution output is shown at the bottom of fig. 1. We define the syntax and semantics of IML in section 3 and describe the symbolic execution in section 5.

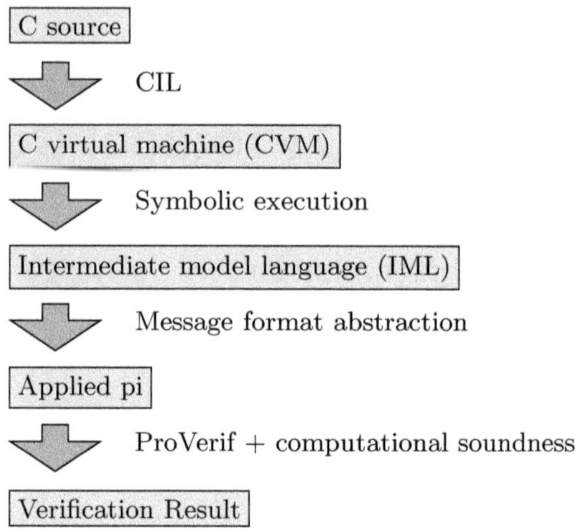

Figure 2: An outline of the method

Our definition of security for source code is given in section 4. The definition is generic in that it does not assume a particular programming language. We simply require that the semantics of a language is given as a set of transitions of a certain form, and define a computational execution of the resulting transition system in the presence of an attacker and the corresponding notion of security. This allows one to apply the same security definition to protocols expressed both in the low-level implementation language and in the high-level model-description language, and to formulate a correspondence between the two.

Given that the transition systems generated by different languages are required to be of the same form, we can mix them in the same execution. This allows us to use CVM to specify a single executing participant, but at the same time use IML to describe an environment process that spawns multiple participants and allows them to interact. In particular, CVM need not be concerned with concurrency, thus making symbolic execution easier. Given an environment process P_E with n holes, we write $P_E[P_1, \ldots, P_n]$ for a process where the ith hole is filled with P_i, which can be either a CVM or an IML process. The soundness result for symbolic execution (theorem 1) states that if $P_1, \ldots, P_n$ are CVM processes and $\tilde{P}_1, \ldots, \tilde{P}_n$ are IML models resulting from their symbolic execution then for any environment process P_E the security of $P_E[\tilde{P}_1, \ldots, \tilde{P}_n]$ with respect to a trace property ρ relates to the security of $P_E[P_1, \ldots, P_n]$ with respect to ρ.

To verify the security of an IML process, we replace its bitstring-manipulating expressions by applications of constructor and destructor functions, thus obtaining a process in the applied pi-calculus (the version proposed in [9] and augmented with events). We can then apply a computational soundness result, such as the one from [5], to specify conditions under which such a substitution is computationally sound: if the resulting pi calculus process is secure in a symbolic model (as can be checked by ProVerif) then it is asymptotically secure in our computational model (the probability of a successful attack is negligible [5]). The correctness of translation from IML to pi is captured by theorem 2 and the computational soundness for resulting pi processes is captured by theorem 3. The verification of IML (and these two theorems in particular) is described in section 6.

Theoretical and Practical Evaluation. Theorems 1 to 3 establish the correctness of our approach. In a nutshell, their significance is as follows: given implementations $P_1, \dots, P_n$ of protocol participants in CVM, which are automatically obtained from the corresponding C code, and an IML process P_E that describes an execution environment, if $P_1, \dots, P_n$ are successfully symbolically executed with resulting models $\tilde{P}_1, \dots, \tilde{P}_n$, the IML process $P_E[\tilde{P}_1, \dots, \tilde{P}_n]$ is successfully translated to a pi process P_π, and ProVerif successfully verifies P_π against a trace property ρ then $P_1, \dots, P_n$ form a secure protocol implementation with respect to the environment P_E and property ρ. We did not aim for completeness; our implementation work has been driven by examples and in our theory we have aimed to show soundness of our implementation.

We are aiming to apply our method to large legacy code bases like OpenSSL. As a step towards this goal we evaluated it on a range of protocol implementations, including recent code for smart electricity meters [27]. We were able to find bugs in preexisting implementations or to verify them without having to modify the code. Section 7 provides details.

The current restriction of analysis to a single execution path may seem prohibitive at first sight. In fact, a great majority of protocols (such as those in the extensive SPORE repository [26]) follow a fixed narration of messages between participants, where any deviation from the expected message leads to termination. For such protocols, our method allows us to capture and analyse the fixed narration directly from the C code. In the future we plan to extend the analysis to more sophisticated control flow by generalising our symbolic execution to an abstract interpretation [15].

Related Work. We mention particularly relevant works, a broader survey can be found in [2]. One of the first attempts at cryptographic verification of C code is contained in [20], where a C program is used to generate a set of Horn clauses that are then solved using a theorem prover. The method is implemented in the tool CSur. We improve upon CSur in two ways in particular.

First, we have an explicit attacker model with a standard computational attacker. The attacker in CSur is essentially symbolic—it is allowed to apply cryptographic operations, but cannot perform any arithmetic computations.

Second, we handle authentication properties in addition to secrecy properties. Adding authentication to CSur would be non-trivial, due to a rather coarse over-approximation of C code. For instance, the order of instructions in CSur is ignored, and writing a single byte into an array with unknown length is treated the same as overwriting the whole array. Authentication, however, crucially depends on the order of events in the execution trace as well as making sure that the authenticity of a whole message is preserved and not only of a single byte of it.

ASPIER [13] uses model checking to verify implementations of cryptographic protocols. The model checking operates on a protocol description language, which is rather more abstract than C; for instance, it does not contain pointers and cannot express variable message lengths. The translation from C to the protocol language is not described in the paper. Our method applies directly to C code with pointers, so that we expect it to provide much greater automation.

Corin and Manzano [14] report an extension of the KLEE test-generation tool [12] that allows KLEE to be applied to cryptographic protocol implementations (but not to extract models, as in our work). They do not extend the class of properties that KLEE is able to test for; in particular, testing for trace properties is not yet supported. Similarly to our work, KLEE is based on symbolic execution; the main difference is that [14] treats every byte in a memory buffer separately and thus only supports buffers of fixed length.

An advantage of the aforementioned tools (CSur, ASPIER, and KLEE) is that they do not share our limitation to single execution paths.

An online technical report includes more details and proofs of all results stated in this paper [2]. The implementation can be found at `http://github.com/tari3x/csec-tools`.

2. C VIRTUAL MACHINE (CVM)

This section describes our low-level source language CVM (C Virtual Machine). The language is simple enough to formalise, while at the same time the operations of CVM are closely aligned with the operations performed by C programs, so that it is easy to translate from C to CVM.

The model of execution of CVM is a stack-based machine with random memory access. All operations with values are performed on the stack, and values can be loaded from memory and stored back to memory. The language contains primitive operations that are necessary for implementing security protocols: reading values from the network or the execution environment, choosing random values, writing values to the network and signalling events. The only kind of conditional that CVM supports is a testing operation that checks a boolean condition and aborts execution immediately if it is not satisfied.

The fact that CVM permits no looping or recursion in the program allows us to inline all function calls, so that we do not need to add a call operation to the language itself. For simplicity of presentation we omit some aspects of the C language that are not essential for describing the approach, such as global variable initialisation and structures. We also restrict program variables to all be of the same size: for the rest of the paper we choose a fixed but arbitrary $N \in \mathbb{N}$ and assume $\texttt{sizeof}(v) = N$ for all program variables v. Our implementation does not have these restrictions and deals with the full C language.

Let $BS = \{0,1\}^*$ be the set of finite bitstrings with the empty bitstring denoted by ε. For a bitstring b let $|b|$ be the length of b in bits. Let *Var* be a countably infinite set of variables. We write $f \colon X \rightharpoonup Y$ to denote a partial function and let $\mathrm{dom}(f) \subseteq X$ be the set of x for which $f(x)$ is defined. We write $f(x) = \bot$ when f is not defined on x and use the notation $f\{x \mapsto a\}$ to update functions. A *partial algorithm* is an algorithm that implements a partial function.

Let **Ops** be a finite set of operation symbols such that

$b \in BS$, $v \in Var$, $op \in$ **Ops**		
$src ::=$ `read` | `rnd`		input source
$dest ::=$ `write` | `event`		output destination
$instr ::=$		instruction
	`Const` b	constant value
	`Ref` v	pointer to variable
	`Malloc`	pointer to fresh memory
	`Load`	load from memory
	`In` v src	input
	`Env` v	environment variable
	`Apply` op	operation
	`Out` $dest$	output
	`Test`	test a condition
	`Store`	write to memory
$P \in CVM ::= \{instr;\}^*$		program

Figure 3: The syntax of CVM.

each $op \in$ **Ops** has an associated arity $\mathrm{ar}(op)$ and an efficient partial algorithm $A_{op}\colon BS^{\mathrm{ar}(op)} \rightharpoonup BS$. The set **Ops** is meant to contain both the primitive operations of the language (such as the arithmetic or comparison operators of C) and the cryptographic primitives that are used by the implementation. The security definitions of this paper (given later) assume an arbitrary security parameter. Since real-life cryptographic protocols are typically designed and implemented for a fixed value of the security parameter, for the rest of the paper we let $k_0 \in \mathbb{N}$ be the security parameter with respect to which the operations in **Ops** are chosen.

The syntax of CVM is shown in fig. 3. To define the semantics of CVM we choose two functions that relate bitstrings to integer values, $\mathrm{val}\colon BS \to \mathbb{N}$ and $\mathrm{bs}\colon \mathbb{N} \to BS$ and require that for $n < 2^N$ the value $\mathrm{bs}(n)$ is a bitstring of length N such that $\mathrm{val}(\mathrm{bs}(n)) = n$. We allow bs to have arbitrary behaviour for larger numbers. The functions val and bs encapsulate architecture-specific details of integer representation such as the endianness. Even though these functions capture an unsigned interpretation of bitstrings, we only use them when accessing memory cells and otherwise place no restriction on how the bitstrings are interpreted by the program operations. For instance, the set **Ops** can contain both a signed and an unsigned arithmetic and comparison operators. Bitstring representations of integer constants shall be written as $i1$, $i20$, etc, for instance, $i10 = \mathrm{bs}(10)$.

We let $Addr = \{1, \ldots, 2^N - 1\}$ be the set of valid memory addresses. The reason we exclude 0 is to allow the length of the memory to be represented in N bits. The semantic configurations of CVM are of the form $(\mathcal{A}^c, \mathcal{M}^c, \mathcal{S}^c, P)$, where

- $\mathcal{M}^c\colon Addr \rightharpoonup \{0,1\}$ is a partial function that represents concrete memory and is undefined for uninitialised cells,
- $\mathcal{A}^c \subseteq Addr$ is the set of allocated memory addresses,
- $\mathcal{S}^c$ is a list of bitstrings representing the execution stack,
- $P \in CVM$ is the executing program.

Semantic transitions are of the form $(\eta, s) \xrightarrow{l} (\eta', s')$, where s and s' are semantic configurations, η and η' are environments (mappings from variables to bitstrings) and l is a protocol action such as reading or writing values from the attacker or a random number generator, or raising events. We give an informal overview of the semantics of CVM; the details are in the technical report [2]. Before the program is executed, each referenced variable v is allocated an address $\mathrm{addr}(v)$ in $\mathcal{M}^c$ such that all allocations are non-overlapping. If the program contains too many variables to fit in memory, the execution does not proceed. Next, the instructions in the program are executed one by one as described below. For $a, b \in \mathbb{N}$ we define $\{a\}_b = \{a, \ldots, a + b - 1\}$.

- `Const` b places b on the stack.
- `Ref` v places $\mathrm{bs}(\mathrm{addr}(v))$ on the stack.
- `Malloc` takes a value s from the stack, reads a value p from the attacker, and if the range $\{\mathrm{val}(p)\}_{\mathrm{val}(s)}$ does not contain allocated cells, it becomes allocated and the value p is placed on the stack. Thus the attacker gets to choose the beginning of the allocated memory area.
- `Load` takes values l and p from the stack. In case $\{\mathrm{val}(p)\}_{\mathrm{val}(l)}$ is a completely initialised range in memory, the contents of that range are placed on the stack. In case some of the bits are not initialised, the value for those bits is read from the attacker.
- `In` v `read` or `In` v `rnd` takes a value l from the stack. `In` v `read` reads a value of length $\mathrm{val}(l)$ from the attacker and `In` v `rnd` requests a random value of length $\mathrm{val}(l)$. The resulting value b is then placed on the stack. The environment η is extended by the binding $v \mapsto b$.
- `Env` v places $\eta(v)$ and $\mathrm{bs}(|\eta(v)|)$ on the stack.
- `Apply` op with $\mathrm{ar}(op) = n$ applies A_{op} to n values on the stack, replacing them by the result.
- `Out write` sends the top of the stack to the attacker and `Out event` raises an event with the top of the stack as payload. Events with multiple arguments can be represented using a suitable bitstring pairing operation. Both commands remove the top of the stack.
- `Test` takes the top of the stack and checks whether it is $i1$. If yes, the execution proceeds, otherwise it stops.
- `Store` takes values p and b from the stack and writes b into memory at position starting with $\mathrm{val}(p)$.

3. INTERMEDIATE MODEL LANGUAGE

This section presents the intermediate model language (IML) that we use both to express the models extracted from CVM programs and to describe the environment in which the protocol participants execute. IML borrows most of its structure from the pi calculus [1, 9]. In addition it has access both to the set **Ops** of operations used by CVM programs and to primitive operations on bitstrings: concatenation, substring extraction, and computing lengths of bitstrings. Unlike CVM, IML does not access memory or perform destructive updates.

The syntax of IML is presented in fig. 4. In contrast to the standard pi calculus we do not include channel names, but implicitly use a single public channel instead. This corresponds to our security model in which all communication happens through the attacker. The nonce sampling operation $(\nu x[e])$ takes an expression as a parameter that specifies the length of the nonce to be sampled—this is necessary in the computational setting in order to obtain a probability distribution. We introduce a special abbreviation for programs that choose randomness of length equal to the secu-

$b \in BS$, $x \in Var$, $op \in \mathbf{Ops}$

$e \in IExp ::=$		expression
	b	concrete bitstring
	x	variable
	$op(e_1, \ldots, e_n)$	computation
	$e_1 \| e_2$	concatenation
	$e\{e_o, e_l\}$	substring extraction
	$\mathrm{len}(e)$	length
$P, Q \in IML ::=$		process
	0	nil
	$!P$	replication
	$P \vert Q$	parallel composition
	$(\nu x[e]);\ P$	randomness
	$\mathbf{in}(x);\ P$	input
	$\mathbf{out}(e);\ P$	output
	$\mathbf{event}(e);\ P$	event
	$\mathbf{if}\ e\ \mathbf{then}\ P\ [\mathbf{else}\ Q]$	conditional
	$\mathbf{let}\ x = e\ \mathbf{in}\ P\ [\mathbf{else}\ Q]$	evaluation

Figure 4: The syntax of IML.

$$\begin{aligned}
&[\![b]\!] = b, \text{ for } b \in BS,\\
&[\![x]\!] = \bot, \text{ for } x \in Var,\\
&[\![op(e_1, \ldots, e_n)]\!] = A_{op}([\![e_1]\!], \ldots, [\![e_n]\!]),\\
&[\![e_1 \| e_2]\!] = [\![e_1]\!] \| [\![e_2]\!],\\
&[\![e\{e_o, e_l\}]\!] = \mathrm{sub}([\![e]\!], \mathrm{val}([\![e_o]\!]), \mathrm{val}([\![e_l]\!])),\\
&[\![\mathrm{len}(e)]\!] = \mathrm{bs}(|[\![e]\!]|).
\end{aligned}$$

Figure 5: The evaluation of IML expressions, whereby $\bot$ propagates.

rity parameter k_0 introduced in section 2: let $(\tilde{\nu} x);\ P$ stand for $(\nu \tilde{x}[k_0])$; $\mathbf{let}\ x = nonce(\tilde{x})\ \mathbf{in}\ P$, where $nonce \in \mathbf{Ops}$. Using *nonce* allows us to have tagged nonces, which will be necessary to link to the pi calculus semantics from [5].

For a bitstring b let $b[i]$ be the ith bit of b counting from 0. The concatenation of two bitstrings b_1 and b_2 is written as $b_1 \| b_2$.

Just as for CVM, the semantics of IML is parameterised by functions bs and val. The semantics of expressions is given by the partial function $[\![\cdot]\!]\colon IExp \rightharpoonup BS$ described in fig. 5. The partial function sub: $BS \times \mathbb{N} \times \mathbb{N} \rightharpoonup BS$ extracts a substring of a given bitstring such that $\mathrm{sub}(b, o, l)$ is the substring of b starting at offset o of length l:

$$\mathrm{sub}(b, o, l) = \begin{cases} b[o] \ldots b[o + l - 1] & \text{if } o + l \le |b|, \\ \bot & \text{otherwise.} \end{cases}$$

For a *valuation* $\eta\colon Var \rightharpoonup BS$ we denote with $[\![e]\!]_\eta$ the result of substituting all variables v in e by $\eta(v)$ (if defined) and then applying $[\![\cdot]\!]$.

The technical report [2] describes the detailed semantics of IML.

4. SECURITY OF PROTOCOLS

To define security for protocols implemented by CVM and IML programs we need to specify what a protocol is and give a mapping from programs to protocols. The notion of a protocol is formally captured by a *protocol transition system (PTS)*, which describes how processes evolve and interact with the attacker. A PTS is a set of transitions of the form $(\eta, s) \xrightarrow{l} \{(\eta_1, s_1), \ldots, (\eta_n, s_n)\}$, where η and η_i are environments (modelled as valuations), s and s_i are semantic configurations of the underlying programming language, and l is an action label. Actions can include reading values from the attacker, generating random values, sending values to the attacker, or raising events. We call a pair (η, s) an *executing process*. Multiple processes on the right hand side capture replication. Full details are in [2].

The semantics of CVM and IML are given in terms of the PTS that are implemented by programs. For a CVM program P we denote with $[\![P]\!]_C$ the PTS that is implemented by P. Similarly, for an IML process P the corresponding PTS is denoted by $[\![P]\!]_I$.

Given a PTS T and a probabilistic machine E (an attacker) we can execute T in the presence of E. The state of the executing protocol is essentially a multiset of executing processes. The attacker repeatedly chooses a process from the multiset which is then allowed to perform an action according to T. The result of the execution is a sequence of raised events. For a resource bound $t \in \mathbb{N}$ we denote with $\mathrm{Events}(T, E, t)$ the sequence of events raised during the first t steps of the execution. We shall be interested in the probability that this sequence of events belongs to a certain "safe" set. This is formally captured by the following definition:

Definition 1 (Protocol security) We define a *trace property* as a prefix-closed set of event sequences with efficiently decidable membership. For a PTS T, an attacker E, a trace property ρ and a resource bound $t \in \mathbb{N}$ let $\mathrm{insec}(T, E, \rho, t)$ be the probability $\Pr[\mathrm{Events}(T, E, t) \notin \rho]$. □

Since the semantics of CVM and IML are in the same formalism, we may combine the sets of semantic rules and obtain semantics $[\![\cdot]\!]_{CI}$ for mixed programs, where a CVM program can be a subprocess of a larger IML process. We add an additional syntactic form $[]_i$ (a hole) with $i \in \mathbb{N}$ and no reductions to IML. For an IML process P_E with n holes and CVM or IML processes $P_1, \ldots, P_n$ we write $P_E[P_1, \ldots, P_n]$ to denote process P_E where each hole $[]_i$ is replaced by P_i.

Being able to embed a CVM program within an IML process is useful for modelling. As an example, let P_1 be the CVM program resulting from the translation of the C code in fig. 1 and let P_2 be a description of another participant of the protocol, in either CVM or IML. Then we might be interested in the security of the following process:

$$P_E[P_1, P_2] = !((\tilde{\nu} k);\ ((!P_1)|(!P_2))),$$

where k is the free variable of P_1 (used as the key). A trace property ρ of interest might be, for instance, "Each event of the form $accept(x)$ is preceded by an event of the form $request(x)$", where *request* is an event possibly raised in P_2. The next section shows how we can relate the security of $P_E[P_1, P_2]$ to the security of $P_E[\tilde{P}_1, P_2]$, where IML process $\tilde{P}_1$ is a model of the CVM process P_1, extracted by symbolic execution.

5. CVM TO IML: SYMBOLIC EXECUTION

We describe how to automatically extract an IML model from a CVM program while preserving security properties. The key idea is to execute a CVM program in a symbolic semantics, where, instead of concrete bitstrings, memory locations contain IML expressions representing the set of all possible concrete values at a given execution point.

$v \in Var,\ i \in \mathbb{N}$

$pb \in PBase ::=$		pointer base
	stack v	stack pointer to variable v
	heap i	heap pointer with id i
$e \in SExp ::=$		symbolic expression
	$\mathrm{ptr}(pb, e)$	pointer
	$\ldots$	same as *IExp* in fig. 4

Figure 6: Symbolic expressions.

$$\begin{aligned}
&\mathrm{apply}(+_b, \mathrm{ptr}(pb, e_o), e) = \mathrm{ptr}(pb, e_o +_b e),\\
&\quad \text{for } e \in IExp,\\
&\mathrm{apply}(-_b, \mathrm{ptr}(pb, e_o), \mathrm{ptr}(pb, e_o')) = e_o -_b e_o',\\
&\mathrm{apply}(op, e_1, \ldots, e_n) = op(e_1, \ldots, e_n),\\
&\quad \text{for } e_1, \ldots, e_n \in IExp,\\
&\mathrm{apply}(\ldots) = \bot, \text{ otherwise.}
\end{aligned}$$

Figure 7: Operations on symbolic expressions.

To track the values used as pointers during CVM execution, we extend IML expressions with an additional construct, resulting in the class of *symbolic expressions* shown in fig. 6. An expression of the form $\mathrm{ptr}(pb, e_o)$ represents a pointer into the memory location identified by the *pointer base* pb with an offset e_o relative to the beginning of the location. We require that $e_o \in IExp$, so that pointer offsets do not contain pointers themselves. Pointer bases are of two kinds: a base of the form stack v represents a pointer to the program variable v and a base of the form heap i represents the result of a `Malloc`.

Symbolic execution makes certain assumptions about the arithmetic operations that are available in **Ops**. We assume that programs use operators for bitwise addition and subtraction (with overflow) that we shall write as $+_b$ and $-_b$. We also make use of addition and subtraction without overflow—the addition operator (written as $+_\mathbb{N}$) is expected to make the result wide enough to prevent truncation or overflow (say, $1 +_\mathbb{N} 1 = 10$) and the negation operator (written as $-_\mathbb{N}$) returns $\bot$ instead of a negative result. We assume that **Ops** contains comparison operators $=$, $\leq$, and $<$ such that $A_=(a, b)$ returns $i1$ if $\mathrm{val}(a) = \mathrm{val}(b)$ and $i0$ otherwise, similarly for the other operators. This way $\leq$ and $<$ capture unsigned comparisons on bitstring values. We assume **Ops** contains logical connectives $\neg$ and $\vee$ that interpret $i0$ as false value and $i1$ as true value. These operators may or may not be the ones used by the program itself.

To evaluate symbolic expressions concretely, we need concrete values for pointer bases as well as concrete values for variables. Given an *extended valuation* $\eta\colon Var \cup PBase \rightharpoonup BS$, we extend the function $[\![\cdot]\!]_\eta$ from fig. 5 by the rule:

$$[\![\mathrm{ptr}(pb, e_o)]\!]_\eta = \eta(pb) +_b [\![e_o]\!]_\eta.$$

When applying arithmetic operations to pointers, we need to make sure that the operation is applied to the pointer offset and the base is kept intact. Also we can only apply $-_b$ to pointers with (syntactically) equal bases. This behaviour is encoded by the function apply, shown in fig. 7.

As well as tracking the expressions stored in memory, we also track logical facts discovered during symbolic execution. To record these facts, we use symbolic expressions themselves, interpreted as logical formulas with $=$, $\leq$, and $<$ as relations and $\neg$ and $\vee$ as connectives. We allow quantifiers in formulas, with straightforward interpretation. Given a set Σ of formulas and a formula ϕ we write $\Sigma \vdash \phi$ iff for each Σ-consistent valuation η (that is, a valuation such that $[\![\psi]\!]_\eta = i1$ for all $\psi \in \Sigma$) we also have $[\![\phi]\!]_\eta = i1$.

To check the entailment relation, our implementation relies on the SMT solver *Yices* [17], by replacing unsupported operations, such as string concatenation or substring extraction, with uninterpreted functions. This works well for our purpose—the conditions that we need to check during the symbolic execution are purely arithmetic and are supported by Yices' theory.

The function getLen returns for each symbolic expression an expression representing its length:

$$\begin{aligned}
&\mathrm{getLen}(\mathrm{ptr}(\ldots)) = \mathrm{bs}(N),\\
&\mathrm{getLen}(\mathrm{len}(\ldots)) = \mathrm{bs}(N),\\
&\mathrm{getLen}(b) = \mathrm{bs}(|b|), \text{ for } b \in BS,\\
&\mathrm{getLen}(x) = \mathrm{len}(x), \text{ for } x \in Var,\\
&\mathrm{getLen}(op(e_1, \ldots, e_n)) = \mathrm{len}(op(e_1, \ldots, e_n)),\\
&\mathrm{getLen}(e_1 \| e_2) = \mathrm{getLen}(e_1) +_\mathbb{N} \mathrm{getLen}(e_2),\\
&\mathrm{getLen}(e\{e_o, e_l\}) = e_l.
\end{aligned}$$

We assume that the knowledge about the return lengths of operation applications is encoded in a fact set Σ_{op}. As an example, Σ_{op} might contain the facts:

$$\begin{aligned}
&\forall x, y, a\colon \mathrm{len}(x) = a \wedge \mathrm{len}(y) = a \Rightarrow \mathrm{len}(x +_b y) = a,\\
&\forall x\colon \mathrm{len}(sha1(x)) = i20.
\end{aligned}$$

We assume that Σ_{op} is consistent: $\emptyset \vdash \phi$ for all $\phi \in \Sigma_{op}$.

The transformations prescribed by the symbolic semantic rules would quickly lead to very large expressions. Thus the symbolic execution is parametrised by a simplification function simplify that is allowed to make use of the collected fact set Σ. We demand that the simplification function is sound in the following sense: for each fact set Σ, expression e and a Σ-consistent valuation η we have

$$[\![e]\!]_\eta \neq \bot \implies [\![\mathrm{simplify}_\Sigma(e)]\!]_\eta = [\![e]\!]_\eta.$$

The simplifications employed in our algorithm are described in the technical report [2].

The algorithm for symbolic execution is determined by the set of semantic rules presented in fig. 8. The initial semantic configuration has the form (`Init`, P) with the executing program $P \in CVM$. The other semantic configurations have the form (Σ, $\mathcal{A}^s$, $\mathcal{M}^s$, $\mathcal{S}^s$, P), where

- $\Sigma \subseteq SExp$ is a set of formulas (the path condition),
- $\mathcal{A}^s\colon PBase \rightharpoonup SExp$ is the symbolic allocation table that for each memory location stores its allocated size,
- $\mathcal{M}^s\colon PBase \rightharpoonup SExp$ is the symbolic memory. We require that $\mathrm{dom}(\mathcal{M}^s) = \mathrm{dom}(\mathcal{A}^s)$,
- $\mathcal{S}^s$ is a list of symbolic expressions representing the execution stack,
- $P \in CVM$ is the executing program.

The crucial rules are (S-Load) and (S-Store) that reflect the effect of storing and loading memory values on the symbolic level. The rule (S-Load) is quite simple—it tries to deduce from Σ that the extraction is performed from a defined memory range given by $\mathcal{M}^s$ (which is, in general, smaller than the allocated memory range given by $\mathcal{A}^s$), after which it represents the result of the extraction using an IML range

$$\frac{}{(\texttt{Init},\ P) \rightarrow (\Sigma_{op},\ \{\text{stack } v \mapsto \text{bs}(N) \mid v \in \text{var}(P)\},\ \{\text{stack } v \mapsto \varepsilon \mid v \in \text{var}(P)\},\ [],\ P)} \quad \text{(S-Init)}$$

$$\frac{}{(\Sigma,\ \mathcal{A}^s,\ \mathcal{M}^s,\ \mathcal{S}^s,\ \texttt{Const}\ b;\ P) \rightarrow (\Sigma,\ \mathcal{A}^s,\ \mathcal{M}^s,\ b :: \mathcal{S}^s,\ P)} \quad \text{(S-Const)}$$

$$\frac{}{(\Sigma,\ \mathcal{A}^s,\ \mathcal{M}^s,\ \mathcal{S}^s,\ \texttt{Ref}\ v;\ P) \rightarrow (\Sigma,\ \mathcal{A}^s,\ \mathcal{M}^s,\ \text{ptr}(\text{stack } v,\ i0) :: \mathcal{S}^s,\ P)} \quad \text{(S-Ref)}$$

$$\frac{e_l \in \mathit{IExp} \quad i \in \mathbb{N} \text{ minimal s.t. } pb = \text{heap } i \notin \text{dom}(\mathcal{M}^s)}{(\Sigma,\ \mathcal{A}^s,\ \mathcal{M}^s,\ e_l :: \mathcal{S}^s,\ \texttt{Malloc};\ P) \rightarrow (\Sigma,\ \mathcal{A}^s\{pb \mapsto e_l\},\ \mathcal{M}^s\{pb \mapsto \varepsilon\},\ \text{ptr}(pb, i0) :: \mathcal{S}^s,\ P)} \quad \text{(S-Malloc)}$$

$$\frac{pb \in \text{dom}(\mathcal{M}^s) \quad e = \text{simplify}_\Sigma(\mathcal{M}^s(pb)\{e_o, e_l\}) \quad \Sigma \vdash (e_o +_\mathbb{N} e_l \leq \text{getLen}(\mathcal{M}^s(pb)))}{(\Sigma,\ \mathcal{A}^s,\ \mathcal{M}^s,\ e_l :: \text{ptr}(pb, e_o) :: \mathcal{S}^s,\ \texttt{Load};\ P) \rightarrow (\Sigma,\ \mathcal{A}^s,\ \mathcal{M}^s,\ e :: \mathcal{S}^s,\ P)} \quad \text{(S-Load)}$$

$$\frac{e_l \in \mathit{IExp} \quad l = (\text{if } src = \texttt{read} \text{ then } \mathbf{in}(v);\ \text{else } (\nu v[e_l]);)}{(\Sigma,\ \mathcal{A}^s,\ \mathcal{M}^s,\ e_l :: \mathcal{S}^s,\ \texttt{In}\ v\ src;\ P) \xrightarrow{l} (\Sigma \cup \{\text{len}(v) = e_l\},\ \mathcal{A}^s,\ \mathcal{M}^s,\ v :: \mathcal{S}^s,\ P)} \quad \text{(S-In)}$$

$$\frac{}{(\Sigma,\ \mathcal{A}^s,\ \mathcal{M}^s,\ \mathcal{S}^s,\ \texttt{Env}\ v;\ P) \rightarrow (\Sigma,\ \mathcal{A}^s,\ \mathcal{M}^s,\ \text{len}(v) :: v :: \mathcal{S}^s,\ P)} \quad \text{(S-Env)}$$

$$\frac{e = \text{apply}(op, e_1, \ldots, e_n) \neq \bot}{(\Sigma,\ \mathcal{A}^s,\ \mathcal{M}^s,\ e_1 :: \ldots :: e_n :: \mathcal{S}^s,\ \texttt{Apply}\ op;\ P) \rightarrow (\Sigma,\ \mathcal{A}^s,\ \mathcal{M}^s,\ \text{len}(e) :: e :: \mathcal{S}^s,\ P)} \quad \text{(S-Apply)}$$

$$\frac{e \in \mathit{IExp} \quad l = (\text{if } dest = \texttt{write} \text{ then } \mathbf{out}(e);\ \text{else } \mathbf{event}(e);)}{(\Sigma,\ \mathcal{A}^s,\ \mathcal{M}^s,\ e :: \mathcal{S}^s,\ \texttt{Out}\ dest;\ P) \xrightarrow{l} (\Sigma,\ \mathcal{A}^s,\ \mathcal{M}^s,\ \mathcal{S}^s,\ P)} \quad \text{(S-Out)}$$

$$\frac{e \in \mathit{IExp}}{(\Sigma,\ \mathcal{A}^s,\ \mathcal{M}^s,\ e :: \mathcal{S}^s,\ \texttt{Test};\ P) \xrightarrow{\text{if } e \text{ then}} (\Sigma \cup \{e\},\ \mathcal{A}^s,\ \mathcal{M}^s,\ \mathcal{S}^s,\ P)} \quad \text{(S-Test)}$$

$$\frac{\begin{array}{c} e_h = \mathcal{M}^s(pb) \neq \bot \quad e_s = \mathcal{A}^s(pb) \neq \bot \quad e_{lh} = \text{getLen}(e_h) \quad e_l = \text{getLen}(e) \\ \text{either } \Sigma \vdash (e_o +_\mathbb{N} e_l < e_{lh}) \text{ and } e'_h = \text{simplify}_\Sigma(e_h\{i0, e_o\} \| e \| e_h\{e_o +_\mathbb{N} e_l, e_{lh} -_\mathbb{N} (e_o +_\mathbb{N} e_l)\}) \\ \text{or } \Sigma \vdash (e_o +_\mathbb{N} e_l \geq e_{lh}) \wedge (e_o \leq e_{lh}) \wedge (e_o +_\mathbb{N} e_l \leq e_s) \text{ and } e'_h = \text{simplify}_\Sigma(e_h\{i0, e_o\} \| e) \end{array}}{(\Sigma,\ \mathcal{A}^s,\ \mathcal{M}^s,\ \text{ptr}(pb, e_o) :: e :: \mathcal{S}^s,\ \texttt{Store};\ P) \rightarrow (\Sigma,\ \mathcal{A}^s,\ \mathcal{M}^s\{pb \mapsto e'_h\},\ \mathcal{S}^s,\ P)} \quad \text{(S-Store)}$$

Figure 8: The symbolic execution of CVM.

expression. The rule (S-Store) distinguishes between two cases depending on how the expression e to be stored is aligned with the expression e_h that is already present in memory. If e needs to be stored completely within the bounds of e_h then we replace the contents of the memory location by $e_h\{\ldots\}\|e\|e_h\{\ldots\}$ where the first and the second range expression represent the pieces of e_h that are not covered by e. In case e needs to be stored past the end of e_h, the new expression is of the form $e_h\{\ldots\}\|e$. The rule still requires that the beginning of e is positioned before the end of e_h, and hence it is impossible to write in the middle of an uninitialised memory location. This is for simplicity of presentation—the rule used in our implementation does not have this limitation (it creates an explicit "undefined" expression in these cases).

Since all semantic rules are deterministic there is only one symbolic execution trace. The sequence of transition labels produces an IML process that simulates the behaviour of the original CVM program. Formally, for a CVM program P, let L be the symbolic execution trace starting from the state $(\texttt{Init}, P)$. If L ends in a state with an empty program, let $\lambda_1, \ldots, \lambda_n$ be the sequence of labels of L and set $[\![P]\!]_S = \lambda_1 \ldots \lambda_n 0 \in \mathit{IML}$, otherwise set $[\![P]\!]_S = \bot$.

We shall say that a polynomial is *fixed* iff it is independent of the arbitrary values assumed in this paper, such as N or the properties of the set **Ops**. Our main result relates the security of P to the security of $[\![P]\!]_S$.

Theorem 1 (Symbolic Execution is Sound) *There exists a fixed polynomial p such that if $P_1, \ldots, P_n$ are CVM processes and $\tilde{P}_i := [\![P_i]\!]_S \neq \bot$ for all i then for any IML process P_E, attacker E, trace property ρ, and resource bound $t \in \mathbb{N}$:*

$$\begin{aligned} &\text{insec}([\![P_E[P_1, \ldots, P_n]]\!]_{CI}, E, \rho, t) \\ &\quad \leq \text{insec}([\![P_E[\tilde{P}_1, \ldots, \tilde{P}_n]]\!]_I, E, \rho, p(t)). \end{aligned} \quad \square$$

The condition that p is fixed is important—otherwise p could be large enough to give the attacker the time to enumerate all the 2^{2^N-1} memory configurations. For practical use the actual shape of p can be recovered from the proof of the theorem given in the technical report [2]. In particular, the proof shows that the execution time of the IML process is polynomial with respect to the execution time of the original C program.

Fig. 9 illustrates our method by showing how the symbolic execution proceeds for our example in fig. 1. For each line of the C program we show updates to the symbolic memory, the set of new facts, and the generated IML code if any. In our example `MAC_LEN` is assumed to be 20 and N is equal to `sizeof(size_t)`. The variables l, x_1, and x_2 are arbitrary fresh variables chosen during the translation from C to CVM. Below we mention details for some particularly interesting steps (numbers correspond to line numbers in fig. 9).

1. The call to `readenv` redirects to a proxy function that generates CVM instructions for retrieving the environment variable k and storing it in memory.

Line no.	C line	symbolic memory updates	new facts	generated IML line
1.	`readenv("k", &key, &keylen);`	stack $key \Rightarrow$ ptr(heap 1, $i0$) heap $1 \Rightarrow k$ stack $keylen \Rightarrow$ len(k)		
2.	`read(&len, sizeof(len));`	stack $len \Rightarrow l$	$\mathrm{len}(l) = iN$	$\mathbf{in}(l)$
3.	`if(len > 1000) exit();`		$\neg(l > i1000)$	
4.	`void * buf = malloc(len + 2 * MAC_LEN);`	stack $buf \Rightarrow$ ptr(heap 2, $i0$) heap $2 \Rightarrow \varepsilon$		
5.	`read(buf, len);`	heap $2 \Rightarrow x_1$	$\mathrm{len}(x_1) = l$	$\mathbf{in}(x_1)$
6.	`mac(buf, len, key, keylen, buf + len);`	heap $2 \Rightarrow x_1 \| mac(k, x_1)$		
7.	`read(buf + len + MAC_LEN, MAC_LEN);`	heap $2 \Rightarrow x_1 \| mac(k, x_1) \| x_2$	$\mathrm{len}(x_2) = i20$	$\mathbf{in}(x_2)$
8.	`if(memcmp(...) == 0)`			$\mathbf{if}\ mac(k, x_1) = x_2\ \mathbf{then}$
9.	`event("accept", buf, len);`			$\mathbf{event}\ accept(x_1)$

Figure 9: Symbolic execution of the example in fig. 1.

4. A new empty memory location is created and the pointer to it is stored in `buf`. We make an entry in the allocation table $\mathcal{A}^s$ with the length of the new memory location $(l +_b i2 * i20)$.
5. We check that the stored value fits within the allocated memory area, that is, $l \le l +_b i2 * i20$. This is in general not true due to possibility of integer overflow, but in this case succeeds due to the condition $\neg(l > i1000)$ recorded before (assuming that the maximum integer value $2^N - 1$ is much larger than 1000). Similar checks are performed for all subsequent writes to memory.
7. The memory update is performed through an intermediate pointer value of the form ptr(heap 2, $l +_b i20$). The set of collected facts is enough to deduce that this pointer points exactly at the end of $x_1 \| mac(k, x_1)$.
8. The proxy function for `memcmp` extracts values $e_1 = e\{l, i20\}$ and $e_2 = e\{l +_b i20, i20\}$, where e is the contents of memory at heap 2, and puts $cmp(e_1, e_2)$ on the stack. With the facts collected so far e_1 simplifies to $mac(k, x_1)$ and e_2 simplifies to x_2. With some special comprehension for the meaning of cmp we generate IML **if** $e_1 = e_2$ **then**.

6. VERIFICATION OF IML

The symbolic model extracted in fig. 9 does not contain any bitstring operations, so it can readily be given to ProVerif for verification. In general this is not the case and some further simplifications are required. In a nutshell, the simplifications are based on the observation that the bitstring expressions (concatenation and substring extraction) are meant to represent pairing and projection operations, so we can replace them by new symbolic operations that behave as pairing constructs in ProVerif. We then check that the expressions indeed satisfy the algebraic properties expected of such operations.

We outline the main results regarding the translation to ProVerif. The technical report [2] contains the details. The pi calculus used by ProVerif can be described as a subset of IML from which the bitstring operations have been removed. Unlike CVM and IML, the semantics of pi is given with respect to an arbitrary security parameter: we write $[\![P]\!]_\pi^k$ for the semantics of a pi process P with respect to the parameter $k \in \mathbb{N}$. In contrast, we consider IML as executing with respect to a fixed security parameter $k_0 \in \mathbb{N}$. For an IML process P we specify conditions under which it is translatable to a pi process $\tilde{P}$.

Theorem 2 (Soundness of the translation) *There exists a fixed polynomial p such that for any $P \in$ IML translatable to a pi process $\tilde{P}$, any attacker E, trace property ρ, and resource bound $t \in \mathbb{N}$:*

$$\mathrm{insec}([\![P]\!]_I, E, \rho, t) \le \mathrm{insec}([\![\tilde{P}]\!]_\pi^{k_0}, E, \rho, p(t)). \qquad \square$$

Backes et al. [5] provide an example of a set of operations $\mathbf{Ops}^S$ and a set of *soundness conditions* restricting their implementations that are sufficient for establishing computational soundness. The set $\mathbf{Ops}^S$ contains a public key encryption operation that is required to be IND-CCA2 secure. The soundness result is established for the class of the so-called *key-safe* processes that always use fresh randomness for encryption and key generation, only use honestly generated decryption keys and never send decryption keys.

Theorem 3 (Computational soundness) *Let P be a pi process using only operations in $\mathbf{Ops}^S$ such that the soundness conditions are satisfied. If P is key-safe and symbolically secure with respect to a trace property ρ (as checked by ProVerif) then for every polynomial p and attacker E the following function is negligible in k:* $\mathrm{insec}([\![P]\!]_\pi^k, E, \rho, p(k))$. $\square$

Overall, theorems 1 to 3 can be interpreted as follows: let $P_1, \ldots, P_n$ be implementations of protocol participants in CVM and let P_E be an IML process that describes an execution environment. Assume that $P_1, \ldots, P_n$ are successfully symbolically executed with resulting models $\tilde{P}_1, \ldots, \tilde{P}_n$, the IML process $P_E[\tilde{P}_1, \ldots, \tilde{P}_n]$ is successfully translated to a pi process P_π, and ProVerif successfully verifies P_π against a trace property ρ. Then we know by theorem 3 that P_π is a pi protocol model that is (asymptotically) secure with respect to ρ. By theorems 1 and 2 we know that $P_1, \ldots, P_n$ form a secure implementation of the protocol described by P_π for the security parameter k_0.

7. IMPLEMENTATION & EXPERIMENTS

We have implemented our approach and successfully tested it on several examples. Our implementation performs the conversion from C to CVM at runtime—the C program is instrumented using CIL so that it outputs its own CVM representation when run. This allows us to identify and compile the main path of the protocol easily. Apart from information about the path taken we do not use any runtime information and we plan to make the analysis fully static in future. The idea of instrumenting a program to emit a low-level set of instructions for symbolic execution at runtime as well as some initial implementation code were borrowed from the CREST symbolic execution tool [11].

Currently we omit certain memory safety checks and assume that there are no integer overflows. This allows us

	C LOC	IML LOC	outcome	result type	time
simple mac	~ 250	12	verified	symbolic	4s
RPC	~ 600	35	verified	symbolic	5s
NSL	~ 450	40	verified	computat.	5s
CSur	~ 600	20	flaw: fig. 11	—	5s
minexplib	~ 1000	51	flaw: fig. 12	—	15s

Figure 10: Summary of analysed implementations.

```
read(conn_fd, temp, 128);
// BN_hex2bn expects zero-terminated string
temp[128] = 0;
BN_hex2bn(&cipher_2, temp);
// decrypt and parse cipher_2
// to obtain message fields
```

Figure 11: A flaw in the CSur example: input may be too short.

to use the more efficient theory of mathematical integers in Yices, but we are planning to move to exact bitvector treatment in future.

The implementation comprises about 4600 lines of OCaml code. The symbolic proxies for over 80 of the cryptographic functions in the OpenSSL library comprise further 2000 lines of C code.

Fig. 10 shows a list of protocol implementations on which we tested our method. Some of the verified programs did not satisfy the conditions of computational soundness (mostly because they use cryptographic primitives other than public key encryption and signatures supported by the result that we rely on [5]), so we list the verification type as "symbolic", referring to Dolev and Yao's standard "symbolic" (or formal) model of cryptography [16]. In all three cases marked "verified" in fig. 10, we successfully verified the IML process using the ProVerif verifier for this formal model. In the NSL case, we can appeal to the computational soundness result to obtain a result in the computational model. In all cases we provide a guarantee that the C program correctly implements a much simpler IML process (theorem 1).

The "simple mac" is an implementation of a protocol similar to the example in fig. 1. RPC is an implementation of the remote procedure call protocol in [6] that authenticates a server response to a client using a message authentication code. It was written by a colleague without being intended for verification using our method, but we were still able to verify it without any further modifications to the code.

The NSL example is an implementation of the Needham-Schroeder-Lowe protocol written by us to obtain a fully computationally sound verification result. Masking the second participant's identity check triggers Lowe's attack [24] as expected. The technical report [2] shows the source code and the extracted models.

The CSur example is the code analysed in a predecessor paper on C verification [20]. It is an implementation of a protocol similar to Needham-Schroeder-Lowe. During our verification attempt we discovered a flaw, shown in fig. 11: the received message in buffer `temp` is being converted to a `BIGNUM` structure `cipher_2` without checking that enough bytes were received. Later a `BIGNUM` structure derived from `cipher_2` is converted to a bitstring without checking that the length of the bitstring is sufficient to fill the message buffer. In both cases the code does not make sure that the information in memory actually comes from the network, which makes it impossible to prove authentication properties. The CSur example has been verified in [20], but only for secrecy, and secrecy is not affected by the flaw we discovered. The code reinterprets network messages as C structures (an unsafe practise due to architecture dependence), which is not yet supported by our analysis and so we were not able to verify a fixed version of it.

```
unsigned char session_key[256 / 8];
...
// Use the 4 first bytes as a pad
// to encrypt the reading
encrypted_reading =
  ((unsigned int) *session_key) ^ *reading;
```

Figure 12: A flaw in the minexplib code: only one byte of the pad is used.

The minexplib example is an implementation of a privacy-friendly protocol for smart electricity meters [27] developed at Microsoft Research. The model that we obtained uncovered a flaw shown in fig. 12: incorrect use of pointer dereferencing results in three bytes of each four-byte reading being sent unencrypted. We found two further flaws: one could lead to contents of uninitialised memory being sent on the network, the other resulted in 0 being sent (and accepted) in place of the actual number of readings. All flaws have been acknowledged and fixed. An F# implementation of the protocol has been previously verified [28], which highlights the fact that C implementations can be tricky and can easily introduce new bugs, even for correctly specified and proven protocols. The protocol uses low-level cryptographic operations such as XOR and modular exponentiation. Under certain restrictions these primitives can be modelled in ProVerif [22, 23], but in general it is impossible obtain a computational soundness result for XOR [29]. Thus we could not use ProVerif to verify the metering protocol, but we are investigating the use of CryptoVerif for this purpose.

8. CONCLUSION

We presented methods and tools for the automated verification of cryptographic security properties of protocol implementations in C. More specifically, we provided a computationally sound verification of weak secrecy and authentication for (single execution paths of) C code. Despite the limitation of analysing single execution paths, the method often suffices to prove security of authentication protocols, many of which are non-branching. We plan to extend the analysis to more sophisticated control flow.

In future, we aim to provide better feedback in case verification fails. In our case this is rather easy to do as symbolic execution proceeds line by line. If a condition check fails for a certain symbolic expression, it is straightforward to print out a computation tree for the expression together with source code locations in which every node of the tree was computed.

Acknowledgements. Discussions with Bruno Blanchet, François Dupressoir, Bashar Nuseibeh, and Dominique Unruh were useful. We also thank George Danezis, François Dupressoir, and Jean Goubault-Larrecq for giving us access to the code of minexplib, RPC, and CSur, respectively. Bruno Blanchet, Ricardo Corin and François Dupressoir commented on a draft.

9. REFERENCES

[1] M. Abadi and C. Fournet. Mobile values, new names, and secure communication. In *ACM POPL*, pages 104–115, 2001.

[2] M. Aizatulin, A. D. Gordon, and J. Jürjens. Extracting and verifying cryptographic models from C protocol code by symbolic execution (long version). Available at `http://arxiv.org/abs/1107.1017`, 2011.

[3] J. B. Almeida, M. Barbosa, J. S. Pinto, and B. Vieira. Deductive verification of cryptographic software. In *NASA Formal Methods Symposium 2009*, 2009.

[4] A. Armando, D. A. Basin, Y. Boichut, Y. Chevalier, L. Compagna, J. Cuéllar, P. H. Drielsma, P.-C. Héam, O. Kouchnarenko, J. Mantovani, S. Mödersheim, D. von Oheimb, M. Rusinowitch, J. Santiago, M. Turuani, L. Viganò, and L. Vigneron. The AVISPA tool for the automated validation of internet security protocols and applications. In *CAV*, volume 3576 of *Lecture Notes in Computer Science*, pages 281–285. Springer, 2005.

[5] M. Backes, D. Hofheinz, and D. Unruh. CoSP: A general framework for computational soundness proofs. In *ACM CCS 2009*, pages 66–78, November 2009. Preprint on IACR ePrint 2009/080.

[6] J. Bengtson, K. Bhargavan, C. Fournet, A. D. Gordon, and S. Maffeis. Refinement types for secure implementations. In *CSF '08: Proceedings of the 2008 21st IEEE Computer Security Foundations Symposium*, pages 17–32. IEEE Computer Society, 2008.

[7] B. Blanchet. A computationally sound mechanized prover for security protocols. In *IEEE Symposium on Security and Privacy*, pages 140–154. IEEE Computer Society, 2006.

[8] B. Blanchet. Automatic verification of correspondences for security protocols. *Journal of Computer Security*, 17(4):363–434, 2009.

[9] B. Blanchet, M. Abadi, and C. Fournet. Automated verification of selected equivalences for security protocols. *Journal of Logic and Algebraic Programming*, 75(1):3–51, Feb.–Mar. 2008.

[10] M. Blum and S. Micali. How to generate cryptographically strong sequences of pseudo-random bits. *SIAM J. Comput.*, 13(4):850–864, 1984.

[11] J. Burnim and K. Sen. Heuristics for scalable dynamic test generation. In *ASE '08: Proceedings of the 2008 23rd IEEE/ACM International Conference on Automated Software Engineering*, pages 443–446. IEEE Computer Society, 2008.

[12] C. Cadar, D. Dunbar, and D. Engler. KLEE: Unassisted and automatic generation of high-coverage tests for complex systems programs. In *USENIX Symposium on Operating Systems Design and Implementation (OSDI 2008)*, San Diego, CA, Dec. 2008.

[13] S. Chaki and A. Datta. ASPIER: An automated framework for verifying security protocol implementations. In *Computer Security Foundations Workshop*, pages 172–185, 2009.

[14] R. Corin and F. A. Manzano. Efficient symbolic execution for analysing cryptographic protocol implementations. In *International Symposium on Engineering Secure Software and Systems (ESSOS'11)*, LNCS. Springer, 2011.

[15] P. Cousot and R. Cousot. Abstract interpretation: a unified lattice model for static analysis of programs by construction or approximation of fixpoints. In *Conference Record of the Fourth Annual ACM SIGPLAN-SIGACT Symposium on Principles of Programming Languages*, pages 238–252, Los Angeles, California, 1977. ACM Press, New York, NY.

[16] D. Dolev and A. Yao. On the Security of Public-Key Protocols. *IEEE Transactions on Information Theory*, 29(2):198–208, 1983.

[17] B. Dutertre and L. D. Moura. The Yices SMT Solver. Technical report, 2006.

[18] P. Godefroid, M. Y. Levin, and D. A. Molnar. Automated whitebox fuzz testing. In *Proceedings of the Network and Distributed System Security Symposium, NDSS 2008*. The Internet Society, 2008.

[19] S. Goldwasser and S. Micali. Probabilistic encryption. *Journal of Computer and System Sciences*, 28:270–299, 1984.

[20] J. Goubault-Larrecq and F. Parrennes. Cryptographic protocol analysis on real C code. In *Proceedings of the 6th International Conference on Verification, Model Checking and Abstract Interpretation (VMCAI'05)*, volume 3385 of *Lecture Notes in Computer Science*, pages 363–379. Springer, 2005.

[21] J. C. King. Symbolic execution and program testing. *Commun. ACM*, 19(7):385–394, 1976.

[22] R. Küsters and T. Truderung. Using ProVerif to Analyze Protocols with Diffie-Hellman Exponentiation. In *Proceedings of the 22nd IEEE Computer Security Foundations Symposium (CSF 2009)*, pages 157–171. IEEE Computer Society, 2009.

[23] R. Küsters and T. Truderung. Reducing protocol analysis with XOR to the XOR-free case in the horn theory based approach. *Journal of Automated Reasoning*, 46(3):325–352, 2011.

[24] G. Lowe. An attack on the Needham-Schroeder public-key authentication protocol. *Inf. Process. Lett.*, 56:131–133, November 1995.

[25] G. C. Necula, S. McPeak, S. P. Rahul, and W. Weimer. CIL: Intermediate Language and Tools for Analysis and Transformation of C Programs. In *Proceedings of the 11th International Conference on Compiler Construction*, CC '02, pages 213–228, London, UK, 2002. Springer-Verlag.

[26] Project EVA. Security protocols open repository, 2007. `http://www.lsv.ens-cachan.fr/spore/`.

[27] A. Rial and G. Danezis. Privacy-friendly smart metering. Technical Report MSR-TR-2010-150, 2010.

[28] N. Swamy, J. Chen, C. Fournet, K. Bharagavan, and J. Yang. Security programming with refinement types and mobile proofs. Technical Report MSR-TR-2010-149, 2010.

[29] D. Unruh. The impossibility of computationally sound XOR, July 2010. Preprint on IACR ePrint 2010/389.

[30] A. C. Yao. Theory and application of trapdoor functions. In *SFCS '82: Proceedings of the 23rd Annual Symposium on Foundations of Computer Science*, pages 80–91. IEEE Computer Society, 1982.

Modular Code-Based Cryptographic Verification

Cédric Fournet
Microsoft Research
fournet@microsoft.com

Markulf Kohlweiss
Microsoft Research
markulf@microsoft.com

Pierre-Yves Strub
MSR-INRIA Joint Centre
pierre-yves@strub.nu

ABSTRACT

Type systems are effective tools for verifying the security of cryptographic programs. They provide automation, modularity and scalability, and have been applied to large security protocols. However, they traditionally rely on abstract assumptions on the underlying cryptographic primitives, expressed in symbolic models. Cryptographers usually reason on security assumptions using lower level, computational models that precisely account for the complexity and success probability of attacks. These models are more realistic, but they are harder to formalize and automate.

We present the first modular automated program verification method based on standard cryptographic assumptions. We show how to verify ideal functionalities and protocols written in ML by typing them against new cryptographic interfaces using F7, a refinement type checker coupled with an SMT-solver. We develop a probabilistic core calculus for F7 and formalize its type safety in Coq.

We build typed module and interfaces for MACs, signatures, and encryptions, and establish their authenticity and secrecy properties. We relate their ideal functionalities and concrete implementations, using game-based program transformations behind typed interfaces. We illustrate our method on a series of protocol implementations.

Categories and Subject Descriptors

K.6.m [**Security and Protection**]: Security; F.3.1 [**Specifying and Verifying and Reasoning about Programs**]: Specification techniques.

General Terms

Security, Verification, Languages.

Keywords

Cryptography, refinement types, security protocols.

1. TYPECHECKING CRYPTOGRAPHY

One long-standing challenge for reliably building secure software is to integrate cryptographic expertise with general-purpose program verification.

Several research tools provide automated security analysis of code that uses cryptography; they can deal with sample protocol implementations written in C [32, 23, 28] or in ML [17, 16, 18, 19]. These tools can verify complex properties and reveal logical flaws in protocol designs and implementations. On the other hand, they rely on strong, symbolic assumptions on the underlying cryptographic primitives, treated as black boxes, as initially proposed by Dolev and Yao [27]. They formally restrict the power of the attacker, and are often at odds with weaker guarantees considered by the cryptographers who actually design and implement these primitives. In symbolic models, for instance, each primitive constructs syntactically-distinct symbolic terms, each subject to distinct rewrite rules, which makes it difficult to reflect attacks where the same bitstring may be successfully decrypted *and* parsed using different keys and message formats. Similarly, brute-force attacks on concrete bitstrings used as keys or passwords, or side-channel attacks on binary formats are difficult to reflect symbolically.

Formal Computational Cryptography The semantics of computational models are more complex, as they must account for adversaries with bounded computational capabilities and for small probabilities of failure, even with correct primitives and protocols. More fundamentally, computational models reason about *partial specifications* of cryptographic primitives. Instead of giving, for instance, rewrite rules that completely define their behavior, cryptographers provide minimal positive *functional guarantees*: what the protocol requires to run as intended, e.g. decryption of a correctly encrypted plaintext with the correct key will succeed; and minimal negative *security assumptions*: what a computationally-bounded adversary cannot achieve, except with a negligible probability, e.g. distinguish between encryptions of two different plaintexts. Thus, computational proofs must apply parametrically, for any concrete primitives that meet those functional and security hypotheses.

Direct vs Indirect Approaches The relation between symbolic and computational models for cryptography has been an active subject of research for the last ten years [see e.g. 39, 3, 5]. Despite impressive results, computational soundness holds only for a fraction of the primitives and patterns supported by symbolic verification tools; it also restricts their usage (for instance demanding tags to disambiguate parsing) and requires non-standard assumptions [e.g. type-*n* security, 3]. Thus, to tackle the details of existing protocol designs and implementations, with their own choice of cryptographic primitives and properties, one usually cannot first verify them symbolically then apply a generic computational soundness theorem. As advocated by Halevi [33], Datta et al. [25], Blanchet [20], Barthe et al. [9, 10], we follow a more direct approach: we design and adapt automated verification techniques for computational cryptography, rather than hypothetical symbolic abstractions.

Typing Cryptographic Primitives Types naturally capture partial cryptographic specifications. In the context of communications security, protocol code can be typechecked against abstract interfaces for their primitives, then linked to any implementation that meets this interface, with guaranteed security for the resulting executable. For example, Laud [40, 41] adapt type systems for symbolic security and establish their computational soundness with relatively minor changes to the typing rules.

Symbolic Typechecking with F7 (Review) Bengtson et al. [15] develop a general-purpose refinement type system and a prototype typechecker (F7) for verifying the code of protocols and applications written in F#, a dialect of ML for the .NET platform. Bhargavan et al. [19] extend their method by designing symbolic libraries for a wide range of cryptographic primitives and patterns and evaluating the performance of typechecking versus global verification by ProVerif, a leading protocol verifier [2]. Their approach relies on dual implementations for cryptography: a *concrete implementation* links to systems libraries and is used for running the protocol; another *symbolic implementation* defines cryptography in terms of programming-language abstractions such as seals [42] and algebraic data types. Formally, security holds only within the symbolic model. Following Dolev and Yao [27], concrete security also depends on a careful assessment of the presumed capabilities of adversaries versus those enabled by the symbolic libraries.

Cryptographic Verification with F7 In this paper, we introduce a modular method for programming and verifying cryptographic systems. Using F# and F7, we build computationally sound libraries for sample functionalities, and we use them to program and verify sample protocols. Our method is as follows: for each cryptographic functionality,

- we write a new refinement-typed *ideal interface* that captures its security guarantees;
- we program and typecheck an *ideal implementation* for this functionality, thereby verifying its security;
- we show how to substitute concrete cryptographic implementations for the ideal one, while preserving its security for all well-typed programs that use the functionality, under standard assumptions coded as games in ML.

We then automatically verify programs and protocols that use these functionalities by typechecking against their ideal interfaces. Although these interfaces differ from those used for symbolic verification, the F7 verification framework still applies; we can in particular re-typecheck existing code against our new interfaces, and thus verify their security in the computational model without modifying their specification. Our contributions are as follows:

(1) We adopt the "code-based game-playing" approach advocated by Bellare and Rogaway [13] for writing precise cryptographic proofs: we reason on cryptography using ML programs (rather than Turing machines) and conduct our security proofs by programming, typechecking, and reasoning on ML code (§2 to §6).

(2) We develop a probabilistic variant of RCF, the core typed calculus for F7. We have formalized our calculus and most of its metatheory in Coq [46], including all the key typing lemmas such as type safety and parametricity (§2).

(3) We program typed ideal functionalities for MACs and signatures, and establish their soundness for authenticity, assuming CMA security (§3).

(4) We define a notion of perfect secrecy and show how to automatically verify it by typing using parametricity (§4).

(5) We program parametrically typed ideal functionalities for CPA and CCA2 secure encryption, and establish that they are indistinguishable from concrete encryption (§5).

(6) We evaluate our method on cryptographic constructions, such as hybrid encryption and encrypt-then-MAC, and security protocols, including large implementations previously verified using symbolic models. To our knowledge, these are the largest protocols verified in the standard model (§6).

Our approach is modular, since the existence of ideal interfaces and implementations can be established separately for each cryptographic functionality, and since their composition preserves security. (Symbolic verification lacks this form of modularity, as it relies on a single definition of symbolic terms.) Our ideal implementations correspond to ideal functionalities in the universal composability model [22]; as required, concrete and ideal implementations are indistinguishable for all well-typed environments. Similarly, our use of refinement typed interfaces for ideal functionalities may be seen as a form of conditional simulatability [6].

The code fragments and interfaces listed in this paper are part of typed, executable programs. The source files, the formal Coq development, and a companion paper with additional details and proofs are available online.

Related Work We discuss only closely related work on cryptographic type systems, computational soundness for symbolic cryptography, and verification tools for computational cryptography. As regards perfect secrecy, our definitions and proof techniques rely on parametricity, a classic approach for symbolic security [see e.g. 42, 1, 21].

We adapt an existing type system and its implementation, but do not attempt to design a new one for reasoning about probability distributions or polynomial-time complexity. Many type systems have been developed specifically for computational cryptography, notably in the context of information flow security [e.g. 40, 41]. Beyond type systems, other verification techniques also rely on logical properties of protocols, using domain-specific axioms [29, 26].

CertiCrypt [9] and EasyCrypt [10] provide a framework and a tool to derive Coq proofs for cryptographic constructions. CryptoVerif [20] can verify the security of protocols under asymptotic assumptions, both expressed in a domain-specific pi calculus. It searches for a sequence of games, until it reaches a 'final game' such that the target security properties can be checked. Bhargavan et al. [16] build a model extractor from ML to CryptoVerif, and apply it to verify the cryptographic core of their TLS implementation. Their tools rely on global program transformations that do not scale well to large programs. Our approach is scalable and modular, but does require type annotations.

Our work can be seen as a typed variant of simulation-based security [22, 5, 37]. Using types to express constraints on environments, we achieve fine-grained modularity, giving for example an ideal functionality for CPA encryption.

Backes et al. [8] establish the asymptotic soundness of symbolic trace properties in RCF, the core calculus of F7, by translation to CoSP [7]. They do not rely on types; instead, they relate the seal-based symbolic cryptography of Bengtson et al. [15] to an algebraic Dolev-Yao model, then apply a general computational-soundness theorem. Our method seems more direct and compositional, and also applies to observational equivalences, such as indistinguishability.

2. COMPUTATIONAL RCF

We define a variant of RCF, with mutable references and probabilistic sampling, but without non-determinism: we need sampling to model cryptographic algorithms and probabilistic adversaries; we exclude non-determinism because it would yield too much power to computationally bounded adversaries, essentially giving them access to an NP oracle. Instead, as usual with concrete cryptography, we let the adversary schedule the computation. The resulting calculus has the same expressive power and complexity as probabilistic Turing machines, while retaining the high-level programming syntax and tools of ML. We stay as close as possible to the calculus of Bengtson et al. [15]. We adapt their type system and use F7, their typechecker, for all our experiments.

Core Syntax We give below our syntax for RCF, a formal core of F# with support for sampling and references. This syntax is a simplification of the concrete ML syntax supported by F# and F7; the technical report provides encodings and syntactic sugar showing how to support the ML code presented in the next sections.

Syntax of Values and Expressions

a,b,c	label
x,y,z	variable
ϕ	first-order logic formulas
$h ::=$	value constructor
inl	left constructor of sum type
inr	right constructor of sum type
fold	constructor of recursive type
$M,N ::=$	value
x	variable
$()$	unit
fun $x \to A$	function (scope of x is A)
(M,N)	pair
$h\,M$	construction
$\mathbf{read}_a$	reference reader
$\mathbf{write}_a$	reference writer
$A,B ::=$	expression
M	value
$M\,N$	application
let $x = A$ **in** B	let (scope of x is B)
let $(x,y) = M$ **in** A	pair split (scope of x, y is A)
match M **with**	constructor match
$h\,x \to A$ **else** B	(scope of x is A)
assume ϕ	assumption of formula ϕ
assert ϕ	assertion of formula ϕ
sample	fair coin toss
ref M	reference creation
true $\triangleq$ *inl* $()$ **false** $\triangleq$ *inr* $()$	

The syntax includes standard functional constructors, values, and expressions. It also has two expressions for specification purposes: **assume** and **assert** both take a formula ϕ as parameter. Informally, **assume** ϕ records ϕ as a new hypothesis, whereas **assert** ϕ records ϕ as a proof obligation, which should logically follow from the hypotheses recorded so far. Operationally, these expressions do not affect the rest of the computation. The formulas ϕ range over first-order logic with predicates on F# values; we omit their standard syntax.

Our first addition to RCF is the expression **sample**, which reduces to either **true** or **false** with probability $\frac{1}{2}$. This expression models a perfect source of random bits.

Instead of communications and concurrency, our calculus features references à la ML, via the presence of references creators, readers and writers. We use these imperative references for programming schedulers, communications, and stateful oracles. Formally, references are pairs of functions that read and write on a memory location. Each evaluation of **ref** allocates a fresh label a, and returns a pair $(\mathbf{read}_a, \mathbf{write}_a)$ for resp. reading and writing at location a. Following the syntax of ML, we write $!M$ and $M{:=}N$ for reference reading and writing, defined as

$$\begin{aligned} get\ c &\triangleq \mathbf{let}\ (x_1,x_2) = c\ \mathbf{in}\ x_1\ () \\ set\ c\ v &\triangleq \mathbf{let}\ (x_1,x_2) = c\ \mathbf{in}\ x_2\ v \end{aligned}$$

Conversely, our calculus does not include primitive comparison on arbitrary values ($M = N$), present in RCF. This restriction matters for modelling secrecy in §4, where we need to exclude comparisons on values with abstract types. (Comparisons on constructed values such as Booleans, pairs, and bitstrings are still enabled using **match**, so this restriction does not affect the expressive power of protocols and adversaries that exchange only first-order values.)

Probabilistic semantics We define a probabilistic reduction semantics. We write $[X,L,A] \to_p [X',L',B]$ when expression A reduces in one step to B, from store X to store X', under logical assumptions (i.e. sequence of formulas) L to L', with probability p ($0 < p \leq 1$); this relation is defined in the full paper. Stores are finite maps from labels to values and keep track of references creations and assignments in the usual way. We write $[X,L,A] \to_p^n [X',L',B]$ when $[X,L,A] \to_{p_1} \cdots \to_{p_n} [X',L',B]$ in n steps and p is the product $p_1 \cdots p_n$, and write $[X,L,A] \to_p^* [X',L',B]$ when $[X,L,A] \to_p^n [X',L',B]$ for some $n \geq 0$. Our reduction rules coincide with those of RCF, except for the presence of probability indices, the rules for references and assumption logging:

$$\begin{aligned} [X,L,\mathbf{ref}\ M] &\to_1 [X \uplus \{a \mapsto M\}, L, (\mathbf{read}_a, \mathbf{write}_a)] \\ [X \uplus \{a \mapsto M\}, L, \mathbf{read}_a\ ()] &\to_1 [X \uplus \{a \mapsto M\}, L, M] \\ [X \uplus \{a \mapsto M\}, L, \mathbf{write}_a\ N] &\to_1 [X \uplus \{a \mapsto N\}, L, ()] \\ [X,L,\mathbf{assume}\ \phi] &\to_1 [X, L \cup \{\phi\}, ()] \end{aligned}$$

the sampling rules $\mathbf{sample} \to_{\frac{1}{2}} \mathbf{true}$, $\mathbf{sample} \to_{\frac{1}{2}} \mathbf{false}$ and the stuttering rule on values $[X,L,M] \to_1 [X,L,M]$ which guarantees that every closed configuration performs a reduction step with total probability 1. For example, **let** x_0 = **sample in** ... **let** x_{n-1} = **sample in** $(x_0, \ldots, x_{n-1})$ reduces in $2n$ steps to each binary n-word with probability $\frac{1}{2^n}$ and may model a uniform random bitstring generator.

Runtime Safety A close expression A is *safe* if and only if, in all evaluations of A, all assertions succeed, that is, each time an **assert** is evaluated, its formula logically follows from the previously assumed formulas. More generally, we define a probabilistic notion of safety. Let P be a predicate over monotonic trace properties. The probability that $P(A)$ holds in $n \geq 0$ steps is defined as $q_n \triangleq \sum_{A \to_{p_1} \mathbf{A}_1 \ldots \to_{p_n} \mathbf{A}_n | P} (p_1 \ldots p_n)$ where the sum ranges over distinct configurations $\mathbf{A}_1, \ldots, \mathbf{A}_n$ up to relabeling. ($\mathbf{A}_i$ represent configurations with main expression A_i, and an expression A is treated as the configuration with an empty store and an empty log.) The series $(q_n)_{n \geq 0}$ is positive, increasing, and bounded by 1, so it has a limit $q \in [0,1] = \lim_{n \to \infty} q_n$. We let $\Pr[A \Downarrow M]$ be q when M is a closed value and P is "$\mathbf{A}_n$ has expression M". We similarly define the probability that A *terminates*, letting P be "$\mathbf{A}_n$'s expression is a value", and that A *fails*, letting P be "some $\mathbf{A}_i$ is a failing assert" (i.e. $\mathbf{A}_i = [X_i, L_i, E[\mathbf{assert}\ \ \phi]]$ for some evaluation context E and formula ϕ that does not follow from L_i). Hence, A is safe if and only if it fails with probability 0.

Type Safety We type expressions using dependent types, with the syntax below. The main addition to F# types are *refinement types*: an expression has type $x{:}T\{\phi\}$ when its values M (if any) have type T and, moreover, are such that formula $\phi\{M/x\}$ follows from prior assumptions. Dependent functions and dependent pairs bind a value variable x in the formulas within the types of the function result and the second element of the pair, respectively.

The main typing judgment is of the form $I \vdash A : T$, stating that expression A has type T in environment I. Following Bhargavan

Syntax of Types

$T,U,V ::=$	type	
	α	type variable
	unit	unit type
	$x{:}T \to U$	dependent function type (scope of x is U)
	$x{:}T * U$	dependent pair type (scope of x is U)
	$T + U$	disjoint sum type
	$\mu\alpha.T$	recursive type (scope of α is T)
	$x{:}T\{\phi\}$	refinement type (scope of x is ϕ)
bool $\triangleq$ unit + unit	**ref** $T \triangleq (() \to T) * (T \to ())$	

et al. [19], we do not rely on kinding (formally, we do not have the subtyping rule (Public Tainted)) and we use an auxiliary typing judgment $I \vdash B \rightsquigarrow I'$ stating that B is a module that is well-typed in environment I and that exports the typed interface I'. Formally, if we have $I \vdash B \rightsquigarrow I'$ and $I' \vdash A : T$, then also $I \vdash B \cdot A : T$ where $B \cdot A$ represents the composition of the F# modules B and A. We refer to the full paper for auxiliary definitions and the RCF typing rules.

We obtain a safety theorem for probabilistic RCF:

THEOREM 1 (SAFETY). If $\varnothing \vdash A : T$ then A is safe.

Concretely, to establish $I \vdash B \rightsquigarrow I'$, the F7 typechecker takes as input a series of interface definition files (with .fs7 suffixes) instead of typed environments I and I' plus an F# implementation file (with an .fs suffix) instead of the expression B. After typechecking with F7, all formulas can be erased to yield ordinary F# interfaces and implementations.

Security By Typing We use safety to model the security of protocols and their implementations, as follows. The protocol and its libraries are written as F# modules (say C_{PR}), using **assume** and **assert** to specify their security properties, whereas the adversary is their main programs (say A). The capabilities of the adversary are specified as a typed adversary interface I_{PR}: we let A range over arbitrary programs well-typed against this interface ($I_{\mathsf{PR}} \vdash A : T$) that do not use **assume** and **assert**.

Since the **assume** and **assert** specify what is actually verified by typing, one must carefully review them before interpreting formal safety as a meaningful security property. In this paper, we suppose in particular that, for all runs of our systems, the assumptions recorded in the global log are logically consistent, in the sense that we cannot derive false from them. Bhargavan et al. [19] rely on a similar logical-consistency hypothesis and provide simple syntactic conditions on assumed formulas to guarantee consistency. In comparison, our code uses only basic assumptions (e.g. to record runtime events) and their consistency is straightforward.

For protocols, we write the adversary interface I_{PR} so that all its functions operate on plain, unrefined types such as concrete bytes. Thus, our condition $I_{\mathsf{PR}} \vdash A : T$ expresses that the adversary can interact with the protocol only by calling these functions, using any concrete bytes that it can compute, and its formal typability does not exclude any such attack. For instance, I_{PR} may export functions to control the network, generate keys, and trigger runs of the protocol with various parameters, but keep some of the protocol keys private. Thus, by quantifying over all probabilistic runs of all resulting systems $C_{\mathsf{PR}} \cdot A$, we account for the potential behavior of C_{PR} when controlled by any active network attackers. To automatically verify the protocol, we let F7 check that it is a well-typed implementation of the interface I_{PR}, that is, $\varnothing \vdash C_{\mathsf{PR}} \rightsquigarrow I_{\mathsf{PR}}$. Then, by composing the two typing hypotheses on C_{PR} and A, we have $\varnothing \vdash C_{\mathsf{PR}} \cdot A : T$, and by Theorem 1, we conclude that $C_{\mathsf{PR}} \cdot A$ is safe for all active network attackers.

For cryptographic functionalities, the main focus in this paper, we write more precise typed interfaces, using refinement types to express (and typecheck) obligations that protocol designers need to comply with when using these functionalities. Our typed cryptographic interfaces enable us to treat protocols and adversaries as a single program when reasoning on cryptographic libraries. These interfaces may not directly correspond to a class of untyped adversaries. As illustrated for the RPC protocol at the end of §3, they complement more traditional bytes-only adversary interface: given a system composed of cryptographic libraries and protocol code, one can automatically verify by typing that the system exports this particular adversary interface. (See also the full paper for an extended discussion of adversary typability.)

Computational Complexity We finally define notions of termination and complexity. *Asymptotic security* is expressed for algorithms, protocols, and adversaries parameterized by a global *security parameter* $\eta \geq 0$, intuitively the length of the cryptographic materials in use. In this paper, we treat η as a symbolic integer constant in expressions and we often keep its instantiation implicit, writing for instance A instead of $(A_\eta)_{\eta \geq 0}$ for the series of expressions obtained by instantiating η with $0, 1, \ldots$.

- A series of probabilities $(q_\eta)_{\eta \geq 0}$ is *negligible* when, for any polynomial p, we have $\lim_{\eta \to \infty}(q_\eta * p(\eta)) = 0$; it is *overwhelming* when $1 - q_\eta$ is negligible.
- A closed expression A is asymptotically safe when its series of probabilities of failing is negligible.
- Closed expressions A^0 and A^1 are asymptotically indistinguishable, written $A^0 \approx_\varepsilon A^1$, when $|\Pr[A^0 \Downarrow M] - \Pr[A^1 \Downarrow M]|$ is negligible for all closed values M.
- A closed expression A has probabilistic polynomial-time complexity, or is p.p.t. for short, when there exists a polynomial p such that, for all $\eta \geq 0$, A_η terminates with probability 1 in at most $p(\eta)$ steps.

We extend our notions of polynomial-time complexity to typed, modular systems with first-order interfaces, that is, interfaces declaring values of base type and n-ary functions on such values. (In our F# programs, we treat curried functions as n-ary functions.)

(1) A closed first-order functional value is p.p.t. when its runtime is bounded by a polynomial in the size of its parameters. In the definition below, we let B range over modules that just bind such values—this ensures that B does not perform any computation on its own, or use any shared state.

(2) An open expression A such that $I \vdash A : T$ is p.p.t. when, for every $\vdash B \rightsquigarrow I$, the expression $B \cdot A$ is p.p.t.

(3) A module F such that $I \vdash F \rightsquigarrow I_F$ is p.p.t. when, for every p.p.t. expression A such that $I_F \vdash A$, the open expression $F \cdot A$ is p.p.t.

The third step is needed to support stateful modules, such as ideal functionalities that allocate a constant-size entry in a log each time they are called. For a given p.p.t. expression A, the size of the log is polynomial, which usually suffices to show that F is polynomial.

For functions on bitstrings, our definitions coincide with those used for Turing machines. Our definition for modules is similar to inexhaustible Turing machines [37] and reactive polynomial-time [34]. We leave as future work a more general treatment of complexity for higher-order modules; see for instance Kapron and Cook [35] for second-order functions, or Danielsson [24] for type-based verification of complexity.

3. AUTHENTICITY USING MACS

Message authentication codes (MACs) provide integrity protection based on keyed cryptographic hashes. We consider the properties of an F# module that implements this functionality. We begin with its plain F# programming interface:

```
type key              val GEN: unit → key
type text = bytes     val MAC: key → text → mac
type mac = bytes      val VERIFY: key → text → mac → bool
val macsize: int      val LEAK: key → bytes
val keysize: int
```

The interface declares types for keys, texts, and MACs. The type for keys is abstract, whereas those for texts and MACs are just type aliases for 'bytes', the type of concrete byte arrays, used for clarity in other declarations. The interface also declares symbolic constants for the sizes (in bytes) of MACs and keys, and four functions: to generate a fresh key; to produce a MAC given a key and a text; to verify whether a MAC is valid given a key and a text; and to serialize a key into bytes. This function is named *LEAK* since it will be used to model key compromise. (The full paper also discusses a converse function *COERCE* to turn bytes into keys.)

Concrete implementation (*C*) We give below a sample implementation of that interface based on the .NET cryptographic libraries, which we use for running our protocols.

```
open System.Security.Cryptography
let keysize = 16 (* 128 bits *)
let macsize = 20 (* 160 bits *)
type key = bytes
let GEN () = randomBytes keysize
let MAC k (t:text) = (new HMACSHA1(k)).ComputeHash t
let VERIFY k t sv = (MAC k t = sv)
let LEAK (k:key) = k
```

(For brevity, we often omit repeated declarations in code excerpts, such as **type** *text* = bytes; the complete source files are available online.) This F# code sets sizes for keys and MACs, uses concrete random bytes as keys, and just performs system calls to standard algorithms [36]. As with all practically deployed symmetric primitives, there is no formal security guarantee and the choice of algorithms is expected to evolve over time.

Ideal Interface (*I*) To capture the intended properties of MACs, we rely on another, refined *ideal interface* for the same module, written *I*, as follows:

```
type mac = b:bytes{Length(b) = macsize}
predicate val Msg: key * text → bool
val GEN: unit → key
val MAC: k:key → t:text{Msg(k,t)} → mac
val VERIFY: k:key → t:text → m:mac → v:bool{v=true ⇒ Msg(k,t)}
val LEAK: k:key{!t. Msg(k,t)} → b:bytes {Length(b) = keysize}
```

This refined interface is designed for protocol verification and is similar to those used for typing symbolic cryptography [19]. It declares the type of keys as abstract, thus preventing accidental key leakage in data sent on a public network or passed to *MAC*.

To support authentication properties, the interface introduces a logical predicate on keys and texts, *Msg(k,t)*, to indicate that *t* is an authentic message MACed with key *k*. This predicate occurs in the types of *MAC* and *VERIFY*, as a pre-condition for MACing and as a post-condition of successful MAC verification. The interpretation of *Msg(k,t)* is protocol-dependent: as illustrated at the end of this section, each protocol defines *Msg* according to the properties it wishes to authenticate using MACs, possibly giving a different interpretations to each key. In order to be safe for any logical definition of *Msg*, calls to *VERIFY* may succeed at most for texts previously passed as arguments to *MAC* with matching keys (until the key is leaked), thereby excluding the possibility of forging a MAC for any other text.

The pre-condition of *LEAK* accounts for dynamic key compromise: the protocol may call *LEAK* to access the actual key bytes, while other parts of the protocol still rely on the post-condition of *VERIFY*. To preserve safety, the precondition *!t, Msg(k,t)* demands that, before leaking the key, *Msg(k,t)* holds for all texts. (In F7 syntax, *!t* is logical universal quantification on *t*.) The function *LEAK* can be used to model the potential corruption of principals by leaking their keys to the adversary; see Bhargavan et al. [18, 19] and §6 for protocols verified by typing despite partial key compromise. (The function *COERCE* would have a similar pre-condition, so that any key supplied by the adversary is treated as compromised. Independently, the adversary may include its own copy of the concrete implementation *C*, and thus use any bytes as keys.)

In contrast with symbolic models, our texts and MACs are just concrete byte arrays. Taking advantage of refinements, the interface also enforces the consistency of sizes for MACs and key bytes. (In F7, *Length* is a logical library function.) Thus, for instance, typechecking would catch parsing errors leading to a call to *VERIFY* with a truncated MAC, as its argument would not match the refined type *mac*.

Intuitively, the ideal interface is too good to be true: a simple information-theoretic argument shows that any implementation such that (1) MACs are shorter than texts and (2) *MAC* and *VERIFY* communicate only through MACs must be unsafe. In particular, we do *not* have $\vdash C \rightsquigarrow I$. Next, we show how we can establish its weaker, asymptotic safety under cryptographic assumptions.

Security (*CMA*) Common assumptions on MACs are functional correctness and security. The correctness assumption, as well as other expected functional properties of our concrete implementation, are expressed using another *refined concrete interface* that declares

```
type mac = b:bytes{Length(b) = macsize}
predicate val GENerated: key → bool
predicate val MACed: key * text * mac → bool
val GEN: unit → k:key {GENerated(k)}
val MAC: k:key → t:text → m:mac {MACed(k,t,m)}
val VERIFY: k:key → t:text → m:mac →
  v:bool{ GENerated(k) ∧ MACed(k,t,m) ⇒ v = true }
val LEAK: k:key → b:bytes{Length(b) = keysize}
assume !k,t,m0,m1.
  GENerated(k) ∧ MACed(k,t,m0) ∧ MACed(k,t,m1) ⇒ m0 = m1
```

In this interface, written I^C in the following, two auxiliary predicates *GENerated* and *MACed* keep track of the results returned by *GEN* and *MAC*; the final assumption states that *MAC* is a deterministic function. These properties are easily met by any implementation that just recomputes the MAC for verification, as our concrete implementation does: to typecheck against I^C, it suffices to add events at the end of *GEN* and *MAC* to record their result.

The security assumption is expressed as a game. We adopt a standard notion, *resistance against existential Chosen Message forgery Attacks* (CMA), introduced by Goldwasser et al. [31] for signatures; we follow the presentation of Bellare et al. [14]. In this game, an adversary attempts to forge a valid MAC; to this end, it can adaptively call two *oracles* for computing and verifying MACs on a single, hidden key; the adversary wins if it can produce a text and a MAC such that verification succeeds but the text has not been passed to the MAC oracle. We set up this game using an F# module, written *CMA* and defined as follows:

```
let k = GEN()
let log = ref []
let mac t = log := t::!log; MAC k t
let verify t m =
  let v = VERIFY k t m in assert(not v || List.mem t !log); v
```

This code generates a key, implements the two oracles as functions using that key, and maintains a log of all texts passed as arguments to the *mac* function. We intend to run this code with an adversary given access to *mac* and *verify*, but not *k* or *log*. The verification oracle also tests whether any verified pair wins the game:

the **assert** claims that this does not happen: either v is false, or t is in the log. (In the asserted formula, || is logical disjunction.)

DEFINITION 1. *C is CMA-secure when, for all p.p.t. expressions A with no* **assume** *or* **assert** *such that mac: text → mac, verify: text → mac → bool* $\vdash$ *A: unit, the expression* $C \cdot CMA \cdot A$ *is asymptotically safe.*

We establish asymptotic safety for programs well-typed against the *ideal* interface of a CMA-secure MAC.

THEOREM 2 (ASYMPTOTIC SAFETY FOR MAC). Let C be p.p.t. CMA-secure and such that $\vdash C \rightsquigarrow I^C$. Let A be p.p.t. such that $I \vdash A : unit$. The expression $C \cdot A$ is asymptotically safe.

As illustrated at the end of this section, Theorem 2 usefully applies to expressions A composed of a fixed protocol and any adversaries typed against its protocol interface.

To prove Theorem 2, our main tool is an intermediate, well-typed functionality, written F and defined below, such that $C \cdot F$ implements the ideal interface I. We call $C \cdot F$ an ideal MAC implementation. Our next theorem states that the concrete and ideal implementations are indistinguishable; it can be used in compositional proofs relying on F. For example, §6 in the full paper uses it to show that encrypt-then-MAC implements authenticated encryption. (In terms of universal composability, C emulates F, with C as a simulator.)

THEOREM 3 (IDEAL FUNCTIONALITY FOR MAC). Let C be p.p.t. CMA-secure such that $\vdash C \rightsquigarrow I^C$. Let A be p.p.t. such that $I \vdash A$. We have $C \cdot A \approx_\varepsilon C \cdot F \cdot A$.

Ideal Functionality (F) Our ideal functionality re-defines the type for keys, now represented as integer indexes, and re-defines the functions *GEN*, *MAC*, *VERIFY*, and *LEAK* using those provided by any implementation of the refined concrete interface I^C. It maintains a global, private association table *ks* that maps each key index to some internal state, consisting of a concrete MAC key (*kv*), a list of previously-MACed texts (*log*), and a Boolean flag (*leaked*) indicating whether the key has been leaked or not. In the code below, qualified names such as **Mac**.*GEN* refer to entries from the concrete interface I^C, while names such as *GEN* refer to their re-definition. Our ideal functionality F is:

```
let ks = ref [] (* state for all keys generated so far *)
let GEN () =
  let k = list_length !ks
  let kv = Mac.GEN() in
  ks := (k,(kv,empty_log k,false_flag k))::!ks; k
let MAC k t =
  let (kv,log,leaked) = assoc k !ks in
  log := t:: !log; Mac.MAC kv t
let VERIFY k t m =
  let (kv,log,leaked) = assoc k !ks in
  Mac.VERIFY kv t m && (mem k t !log || !leaked)
let LEAK k =
  let (kv,log,leaked) = assoc k !ks in
  leaked := true; Mac.LEAK kv
```

where the functions *list_length*, *assoc*, and *mem* are the standard ML functions *List.length*, *List.assoc*, and *List.mem* with more precise refinement types, and where the functions *empty_log* and *false_flag* allocate mutable references that initially contain an empty list and **false**, respectively.

GEN allocates a key with index k (the number of keys allocated so far), generates a concrete key, and records its initial state, with an empty log and a flag set to **false**. When called with a key, the three other functions first perform a table lookup to retrieve its state (*kv,log,leaked*). *MAC* computes the MAC using the concrete key *kv* and adds the MACed text to the log. *VERIFY* performs the concrete MAC verification, then it corrects its result from **true** to **false** when (i) the concrete verification succeeds; but (ii) the text has not been MACed, as recorded in *log*; and (iii) the key has not been leaked, as recorded by *leaked*. *LEAK* returns the concrete key bytes, and sets the *leaked* flag to **true**.

The module $C \cdot F$ obtained by composing the concrete MAC implementation with F is a well-typed implementation of the ideal interface, as F corrects any unsafe verification of C, but it is unrealistic, as F relies on global shared state.

LEMMA 1 (TYPING). $I^C \vdash F \rightsquigarrow I$.

This lemma is proved by letting F7 typecheck F. Intuitively, it holds because the result of the verification function is always consistent with the log and the flag, whose refinement types record enough facts *Msg(k,t)* to establish the post-condition of *VERIFY*.

We provide a brief outline of the proof for Theorems 3 and Theorem 2, but refer to the full paper for the details. Classically, we rely on an "up to bad" lemma of [13], stating that $C \cdot F$ and C have exactly the same behaviour until F corrects a verification; when this happens, a related adversary wins against CMA. We use two main reductions, to account for dynamic key leakage, then for the use of multiple keys in F. To complete the proof of Theorem 2, we use Lemma 1 and the typing hypotheses of C and A to conclude from Theorem 1 that $C \cdot F \cdot A$ is perfectly safe.

Sample Protocol: An Authenticated RPC To illustrate the use of our MAC library for verification, we include the code of a sample protocol for remote procedure calls (RPC) adapted from Bhargavan et al. [19]. In the protocol, a client and a server exchange requests s and responses t coded as strings. To authenticate and correlate these strings, they use MACs computed from a shared key k:

```
let k = GEN()
let client s =
  assume (Request(s));
  send (concat (utf8 s) (MAC k (request s)));
  recv (fun msg →
    let (v,m') = split macsize msg in let t = iutf8 v in
    if VERIFY k (response s t) m' then assert(Response(s,t));())
let server () =
  recv (fun msg →
    let (v,m) = split macsize msg in let s = iutf8 v in
    if VERIFY k (request s) m then
     (assert (Request(s));
      let t = "22" in assume (Response(s,t));
      send (concat (utf8 t) (MAC k (response s t)))))
```

We omit the formatting functions, *request* and *response*, that compute the bytes actually MACed as tagged concatenations of their arguments. For simplicity we only consider the single key setting. Fournet et al. [30] show how to verify a variant of the protocol with multiple keys shared between pairs of principals using our MAC functionality; the details are available online.

Security is modelled as safety when running with an active adversary that calls the functions *client* and *server* (to trigger parallel sessions) and controls the network. To this end, these two functions include matching **assume** and **assert** for each message sent and accepted by the protocol, respectively. With this specification, type-safety entails two correspondence properties between these events, of the form "whenever the server accepts a request s, the client must have sent that request before" and similarly for responses. The protocol uses a single key, so its security depends on MACing unambiguous texts (formatted by *request* and *response*).

Let *Net* range over modules implementing the network and the scheduler, informally controlled by the adversary, with the following interface for the protocol:

$$I_{Net} \triangleq send\text{: bytes} \rightarrow \text{unit}, recv\text{: (bytes} \rightarrow \text{unit)} \rightarrow \text{unit}$$

In addition, *Net* may export an arbitrary interface I'_{NET} for the adversary. Let C_{RPC} be the sample protocol code above, after inlining its other (trusted) library functions, with the following interface for the adversary: $I_{\mathsf{RPC}} \triangleq$ *client*: string $\rightarrow$ unit, *server*: unit $\rightarrow$ unit

We arrive at the following computational safety theorem:

THEOREM 4 (RPC SAFETY). Let C be a CMA-secure p.p.t. module with $\vdash C \rightsquigarrow I^C$. Let *Net* be a module with $\vdash Net \rightsquigarrow I_{\mathsf{NET}}$, $\vdash Net \rightsquigarrow I'_{\mathsf{NET}}$, and $Net \cdot C_{\mathsf{RPC}}$ is p.p.t. Let A be a p.p.t. expression with $I'_{\mathsf{NET}}, I_{\mathsf{RPC}} \vdash A : unit$.

The expression $C \cdot Net \cdot C_{\mathsf{RPC}} \cdot A$ is asymptotically safe.

(Technically, we state our p.p.t. assumption on *Net* composed with C_{RPC} because *Net* has a second-order interface.) For each concrete definition of *Net*, we obtain a computational safety theorem against adversaries A with access to the network and the protocol, guaranteeing that the two correspondence properties discussed above hold with overwhelming probability.

The proof of Theorem 4 roughly consists of letting F7 typecheck $I_{\mathsf{NET}}, I \vdash C_{\mathsf{RPC}} \rightsquigarrow I_{\mathsf{RPC}}$. As a sanity check, we outline a broken (non-typable) variant $C^{\bullet}_{\mathsf{RPC}}$ and a sample adversary A that breaks response authentication (with probability 1). Suppose that the formatting functions *request* and *response* simply concatenate their arguments—without tagging. Any valid MAC for a request will also be accepted as a valid MAC for the empty response to that request. The adversary A below meets the conditions of Theorem 4, and tries this simple reflection attack by triggering a request, intercepting it, and sending back a fake response with the same MAC:

```
client "hello";
let msg = recv'() in
let (v,mac) = split macsize msg in
send' (concat (utf8 "") mac)
```

where *send'* and *recv'* are part of the attacker interface I'_{NET}. The expression $C \cdot Net \cdot C^{\bullet}_{\mathsf{RPC}} \cdot A$ reduces to a configuration of the form $[X, \{Request(\texttt{"hello"})\}, E[\textbf{assert}(Response(\texttt{"hello"},\texttt{""}))]]$, with a failing assertion as the the client accepts the fake response. As can be expected, the protocol $C^{\bullet}_{\mathsf{RPC}}$ does not typecheck, since the precondition for calling *MAC* would have to imply *Response*(s,"").

Bhargavan et al. [19] verify similar code by typing against symbolic cryptographic interfaces. Although we now rely on computational assumptions, our protocol code still typechecks essentially for the same reasons. In comparison with their symbolic theorem, ours is also simpler—we do not need to give our adversary access to the cryptographic library, since the adversary may include its own implementation of MAC algorithms.

Experimentally, we also test that our protocol code runs correctly, at least when compiled with a *Net* library and an adversary that implements a reliable network and a simple test. The rest of the code is available online, including a sample (harmless) adversary that correctly schedules clients and servers for testing, and another adversary that tries the attack described above.

Public-Key Signatures We have also applied our verification method to public-key signature schemes, under similar assumptions, using RSA as sample implementation. The main differences are that we have distinct types for public and private keys, and that we give the protocol (and the adversary) unconditional access to the bytes of public keys. See the full paper for the resulting ideal functionality.

4. PERFECT SECRECY BY TYPING

In this section and the next, we focus on a simple notion of perfect secrecy and on *indistinguishability*, its cryptographic counterpart. We let $\approx$ represent probabilistic equivalence between closed terminating expressions: two expressions are equivalent when they return values with identical probabilities. Our notion of secrecy concerns values given an abstract type, written α in this section. With encryptions, α will be the type of plaintexts. Intuitively, protocols given values of type α cannot directly operate on them [44]; we use this parametricity property to establish equivalences between implementations of α. (Roy et al. [45] similarly restrict protocols, using a notion of secretive traces for protecting nonces.)

DEFINITION 2. *For a fixed type variable α, let* secret types *be of the form $T_\alpha ::= \alpha \mid T \rightarrow T_\alpha$ where T ranges over base types. Let* secret interfaces *be of the form $I_\alpha = \alpha, x_1 : T_{\alpha,1}, \ldots, x_n : T_{\alpha,n}$ for some $n \geq 0$. Let P_α range over modules that define* **let** $x_i = v_i$ *for some pure total values v_i for $i = 1..n$, such that $\vdash P_\alpha \rightsquigarrow I_\alpha$.*

THEOREM 5 (SECRECY BY TYPING). Let A such that $I_\alpha \vdash A : bool$. For all P^0_α and P^1_α, we have $P^0_\alpha \cdot A \approx P^1_\alpha \cdot A$.

The proof relies on a variant of the subject reduction lemma, which we verified in COQ. Experimentally, we use F7 to automatically check the typing condition of Theorem 5.

For example, consider a protocol C that operates on a secret string s (formally a free variable of C) using operations defined in library P (including a definition of s), and an adversary A that tries to gain information on s by interacting with the protocol using interface I_C. We are thus interested in systems of the form $P \cdot C \cdot A$ with $\vdash P \cdot C \rightsquigarrow I_C$ and $I_C \vdash A : bool$. To prove that $P \cdot C$ does not leak any information on s, it suffices to verify that P defines only pure values, to write a secret interface of the form $I_\alpha = \alpha, s : \alpha, \ldots$ for P, and to typecheck that $\vdash P \rightsquigarrow I_\alpha$ and $I_\alpha \vdash C \rightsquigarrow I_C$. Theorem 5 then applies to $C \cdot A$ and any two variants P^0_α and P^1_α of P that differ only in their definition of s, and thus the probability $\Pr[P \cdot C \cdot A \Downarrow b]$ does not depend on the value of s.

A Module for Plaintexts In preparation to encryption in §5, we introduce a sample module for plaintexts, written P, with two interfaces: a *secret interface* I_{PLAIN} with abstract type α=*plain*; and another, *concrete interface* I^C_{PLAIN} that reveals the representation of *plain*. We begin with the latter:

```
val plainsize: int
type repr = b:bytes {Length(b) = plainsize}
type plain = repr
val plain: repr → plain
val respond: plain → plain
```

The constant *plainsize* and the type *repr* define a fixed-length, concrete representation of *plain* values. (We need to bound the length of plaintexts, as otherwise encryption would necessarily leak some information about plaintexts.)

We let I_{PLAIN} be I^C_{PLAIN} with the abstract type declaration **type** *plain* substituted for the type alias **type** *plain* = *repr*. The interface I_{PLAIN} is secret, and such that $\vdash P \rightsquigarrow I^C_{\mathsf{PLAIN}}$ implies $\vdash P \rightsquigarrow I_{\mathsf{PLAIN}}$. (It does not strictly match Definition 2 because of the integer constant *plainsize*; however Theorem 5 applies after inlining *plainsize* in P.) In both interfaces, the functions *plain* and *respond* stand for any code that operates concretely on secrets, for instance *respond* may compute responses to secret requests in an RPC protocol; this code may be hoisted to P in order to apply Theorem 5. The function *plain* (implemented as the identity function) maps representations to plaintexts; it is useful, for instance, to let the adversary provide chosen values for plaintexts. Conversely, a function *repr* from plaintexts to concrete representations, necessary for instance to marshal plaintexts before their concrete encryption, would break secrecy. As explained in the next section, however, the secret interface I_{PLAIN} still enables ideal encryption.

5. SECRECY USING ENCRYPTION

We consider the secrecy guarantees provided by encryption, We begin with public-key encryption, then briefly discuss symmetric encryption. As for MACs in §3, we have a basic F# interface and a more precise concrete F7 interface (written I^C_{ENC}) that expresses functional correctness and enforces consistent bytes lengths for encryption. We let C_{ENC} range over p.p.t. implementations of I^C_{ENC}. The full paper gives these interfaces and a sample implementation based on RSA-OAEP.

Our ideal interface for public-key encryption (I_{ENC}), parameterized by the plaintext type of I_{PLAIN}, is as follows:

```
predicate val PKey: bytes → bool
type pkey = pk:bytes{Length(pk)=pksize ∧ PKey(pk)}
type cipher = b:bytes {Length(b)=ciphersize}
type skey
val GEN: unit → pkey * skey
val ENC: pkey → plain → cipher
val DEC: skey → cipher → plain
```

The interface sets sizes for public keys and ciphertexts, and declares three algorithms: *GEN* generates keys, *ENC* encrypts using the public key, and *DEC* decrypts using the secret key. Secret keys *skey* are abstract and, in contrast with §3, the interface does not support their dynamic compromise, as this would lead to a well-known commitment problem [see e.g. 4]. Public keys *pkey* are concrete, fixed-length bytes; these keys may be passed to the adversary, who can then encrypt using its own implementation of *ENC*, or to other parties, who can authenticate them then encrypt their secrets. The refinement *PKey(pk)* tracks the public keys generated by *GEN* and prevents the use of untrusted keys.

Security of Encryption (CCA2) We use a standard notion of security, named indistinguishability under chosen-ciphertext attacks (CCA2) [43]. We follow the presentation of Bellare and Rogaway [12], allowing the adversary to perform multiple oracle encryptions. We formalize this notion as a game in F#, using two modules CCA^b for $b = 0, 1$ obtained from the code below by replacing *select* x_0 x_1 with x_0 and x_1, respectively.

```
let pk, sk = GEN ()
let log = empty_log pk
let enc x0 x1=
  let x = select x0 x1 in
  let v = ENC pk x in
  log := cons pk (v,x) !log; v
let dec v =
  match assoc pk v !log with
  | Some(x) → zero
  | None → DEC sk v
```

These modules generate a keypair then define oracles for encryption and decryption: the adversary is given access to *enc*, *dec* and *pk*, but not to the private decryption key *sk*. This is enforced by the interface

$$I_{cca} \triangleq pk{:}\ pkey,\ enc{:}\ plain \rightarrow cipher,\ dec{:}\ cipher \rightarrow plain$$

using the types of I^C_{PLAIN} and I^C_{ENC}. The oracle-encryption function *enc*, also known as a left-or-right oracle, encrypts either x_0 or x_1, depending on *b*; it also logs the pair (v,x) where v is the resulting ciphertext. The oracle-decryption function *dec* first checks whether its argument v is the result of an oracle encryption, and then returns a constant (*zero*), otherwise it performs the decryption. In the end, the adversary wins if it can guess *b*.

DEFINITION 3. *C_{ENC} is CCA2 secure when, for all p.p.t. modules P with $\vdash P \rightsquigarrow I^C_{\mathsf{PLAIN}}$ and A with $I^C_{\mathsf{PLAIN}}, I_{cca} \vdash A : bool$, we have $P \cdot C_{\mathsf{ENC}} \cdot CCA^0 \cdot A \approx_\varepsilon P \cdot C_{\mathsf{ENC}} \cdot CCA^1 \cdot A$.*

A first encryption theorem yields secrecy by typing for protocols whose plaintexts can be given a secret interface.

THEOREM 6 (ASYMPTOTIC SECRECY). *Let C_{ENC} be a p.p.t. CCA2-secure module with $I^C_{\mathsf{PLAIN}} \vdash C_{\mathsf{ENC}} \rightsquigarrow I^C_{\mathsf{ENC}}$. Let A be a p.p.t. expression with $I_{\mathsf{PLAIN}}, I_{\mathsf{ENC}} \vdash A : bool$.*

For any two pure p.p.t. implementations P^b of I_{PLAIN}, we have $P^0 \cdot C_{\mathsf{ENC}} \cdot A \approx_\varepsilon P^1 \cdot C_{\mathsf{ENC}} \cdot A$.

A second, more general theorem states the soundness of a well-typed ideal functionality for encryption F_{ENC}, defined below.

THEOREM 7 (IDEAL FUNCTIONALITY). *Let C_{ENC} be a p.p.t. CCA2-secure module with $I^C_{\mathsf{PLAIN}} \vdash C_{\mathsf{ENC}} \rightsquigarrow I^C_{\mathsf{ENC}}$, P a p.p.t. module with $\vdash P \rightsquigarrow I^C_{\mathsf{PLAIN}}$, and A a p.p.t. expression with $I^C_{\mathsf{PLAIN}}, I_{\mathsf{ENC}} \vdash A$. We have $P \cdot C_{\mathsf{ENC}} \cdot A \approx_\varepsilon P \cdot C_{\mathsf{ENC}} \cdot F_{\mathsf{ENC}} \cdot A$.*

In contrast with Theorem 6, Theorem 7 does not require that *A* be well-typed using secret plaintexts; instead, it says that, irrespective of I^C_{PLAIN}'s implementation, the use of encryption does not leak additional information about plaintexts. As illustrated in the rest of the paper, Theorem 7 is convenient for composing cryptographic modules, for instance with plaintexts carrying cryptographic materials such as short term keys.

Ideal Functionality (F_{ENC}) We let F_{ENC} be the module:

```
let ks = ref [] (* state for all keypairs generated so far *)
let zero = zeroCreate plainsize
let GEN () =
  let pk, sk = PKEnc.GEN ()
  ks := (pk,(sk, empty_log pk))::!ks; (pk,SK(pk))
let ENC pk x =
  let (sk,log) = assoc pk !ks in
  let c = PKEnc.ENC pk zero in log := cons pk (c,x) !log; c
let DEC (SK(pk)) c =
  let (sk,log) = assoc pk !ks in
  match assocc pk c !log with
  | Some(x) → x | None → plain (PKEnc.DEC sk c)
```

Our ideal functionality (for abstract plaintexts) calls a concrete public-key encryption module **PKEnc** (for plaintexts of type *repr*). It stores all concrete secret keys in a private association table *ks* indexed by public keys, together with a *log* of all ciphertext-plaintexts pairs for this key. It implements the type of secret keys as *SK* **of** *pkey*, also used to index the table. The refinement *PKey(pk)* of I_{ENC} ensures that all table lookups in *ks* succeed. To ideally encrypt *x*, F_{ENC} concretely encrypts *zero* (some constant *plainsize* bytes), and adds (c,x) to the log of the public key. To ideally decrypt *c*, F_{ENC} first searches for some (c,x) in the log; otherwise it concretely decrypts *c* and uses the function *plain* to turn the resulting *repr* into an abstract *plain*. Thus, F_{ENC} treats plaintexts parametrically, and can be typed using the secret interface I_{PLAIN}: we have $I_{\mathsf{PLAIN}}, I^C_{\mathsf{ENC}} \vdash F_{\mathsf{ENC}} \rightsquigarrow I_{\mathsf{ENC}}$ and this enables us to prove Theorem 6 from Theorems 5 and 7.

CPA Encryption and Authenticated Encryption We outline variants of our ideal interface for two other notions of security: resistance to chosen plaintext attacks (CPA) and authenticated encryption. We refer to the full paper and the code for the corresponding security definitions and variants of Theorems 6 and 7. We focus on symmetric encryptions, for simplicity and because authenticated encryption does not have a direct public-key analogue. (See also Küsters and Tuengerthal [38] for ideal functionalities for symmetric encryption with support for corruption.)

CPA Secure Encryption is an assumption weaker than CCA2, obtained by removing the decryption oracle, and meant to be used with authenticated ciphertexts.

Accordingly, our ideal CPA interface I^{cpa}_{SENC} declares

predicate val *ENCrypted*: *key* $*$ *plain* $*$ *cipher* $\rightarrow$ bool
val *ENC*: *k:key* $\rightarrow$ *p:plain* $\rightarrow$ *c:cipher* {*ENCrypted(k,p,c)*}
val *DEC*: *k:key* $\rightarrow$ *c:cipher* {$\exists$*p. ENCrypted(k,p,c)*} $\rightarrow$ *p:plain*

where the predicate *ENCrypted(k,p,c)* in the refinements ensures that a well-typed program never attempts to decrypt a ciphertext not produced by *ENC*. The interface also includes a logical assumption, stating that a ciphertext is the correct encryption of at most one plaintext for a given key.

Authenticated Encryption is a stronger notion that provides both secrecy and authenticity. Accordingly, our ideal interface I^{ae}_{SENC} declares

predicate val *Msg*: *key* $*$ *plain* $\rightarrow$ bool
val *ENC*: *k:key* $\rightarrow$ *p:plain* {*Msg(k,p)*} $\rightarrow$ *c:cipher*
val *DEC*: *k:key* $\rightarrow$ *c:cipher* $\rightarrow$ (*p:plain* {*Msg(k,p)*}) *option*

where the predicate *Msg* plays the same role as in §3. The precondition on *DEC* has disappeared, and *DEC* now returns an option: either some authentic plaintext, or *None* to report decryption error.

Sample Construction Hybrid encryption [12] supports public-key encryption for large plaintexts by encrypting them under a fresh symmetric key itself encrypted under the public key. To illustrate our method, we program hybrid encryption given a pair of public-key and symmetric-key encryptions and we show that, if both these encryptions are CPA, then hybrid encryption is also CPA. Our code defines:

```
let ENC pk t =
  let k = SEnc.GEN() in concat (PKEnc.ENC pk k) (SEnc.ENC k t)
let DEC sk c =
  let c0,c1 = split SEnc.ciphersize c in SEnc.DEC(PKEnc.DEC sk c0) c1
```

The code (C_{Hyb}) uses two encryption modules named **SEnc** and **PKEnc** (written C_{SENC} and C_{ENC} below), each parameterized by its own plaintext module (P and P_k): large, fixed-sized bytes for symmetric encryption and the resulting hybrid encryption, and symmetric keys for public-key encryption. Using F7, we verify that C_{Hyb} implements an interface ($I^{cpa,\mathsf{hyb}}_{\mathsf{ENC}}$, listed below) that includes a public key ideal interface for CPA and defines its *ENCrypted* predicate as a logical specification of hybrid encryption:

```
definition !pk,p,c. ENCrypted(pk,p,c) ⇔
  ∃c0,c1,k. (c = c0|c1 ∧ Length(k)=SEnc.keysize
  ∧ PKEnc.ENCrypted(pk,k,c0) ∧ Length(c0)=PKEnc.ciphersize
  ∧ SEnc.ENCrypted(k,p,c1) ∧ Length(c1)=SEnc.ciphersize)
val GEN: unit → pk:pkey * sk:skey {pk=PK(sk)}
val ENC: pk:pkey → p:plain → c:cipher {ENCrypted(pk,p,c)}
val DEC: sk:skey → c:cipher {∃p. ENCrypted(PK(sk),p,c)} →
  p:plain{ENCrypted(PK(sk),p,c)}
```

We outline a proof of our two encryption theorems for hybrid encryption. To prove the ideal-functionality theorem, we apply ideal-functionality theorems first to public-key encryption, then to symmetric-key encryption. Let P and A be the plaintext module and main expression (as in Theorem 7). Let P_k define symmetric keys as public-key encryptions plaintexts. Starting with our concrete implementation $C \triangleq C_{\mathsf{SENC}} \cdot P_k \cdot C_{\mathsf{ENC}} \cdot C_{\mathsf{Hyb}}$, we have

$$\begin{aligned} P \cdot C \cdot A &\approx_\varepsilon P \cdot C_{\mathsf{SENC}} \cdot P_k \cdot C_{\mathsf{ENC}} \cdot F_{\mathsf{ENC}} \cdot C_{\mathsf{Hyb}} \cdot A \\ &\approx_\varepsilon P \cdot C_{\mathsf{SENC}} \cdot F_{\mathsf{SENC}} \cdot P_k \cdot C_{\mathsf{ENC}} \cdot F_{\mathsf{ENC}} \cdot C_{\mathsf{Hyb}} \cdot A. \end{aligned}$$

To apply the ideal public-key and symmetric-key theorems, we let F7 verify their two typing hypotheses:

$$I^{C,\mathsf{ENC}}_{\mathsf{PLAIN}}, I_{\mathsf{ENC}} \vdash P \cdot C_{\mathsf{SENC}} \cdot C_{\mathsf{Hyb}} \rightsquigarrow I^{cpa,\mathsf{hyb}}_{\mathsf{ENC}}$$
$$I^{C,\mathsf{SENC}}_{\mathsf{PLAIN}}, I_{\mathsf{SENC}} \vdash P_k \cdot C_{\mathsf{ENC}} \cdot F_{\mathsf{ENC}} \cdot C_{\mathsf{Hyb}} \rightsquigarrow I^{cpa,\mathsf{hyb}}_{\mathsf{ENC}}.$$

and we conclude with ideal functionality $F \triangleq C_{\mathsf{SENC}} \cdot F_{\mathsf{SENC}} \cdot P_k \cdot C_{\mathsf{ENC}} \cdot F_{\mathsf{ENC}} \cdot C_{\mathsf{Hyb}}$. To prove the asymptotic secrecy theorem (with hypotheses similar to those of Theorem 6), we use our new ideal-functionality theorem twice and Theorem 5:

$$P_0 \cdot C \cdot A \approx_\varepsilon P_0 \cdot F \cdot A \overset{\text{Thm 5}}{\approx_\varepsilon} P_1 \cdot F \cdot A \approx_\varepsilon P_1 \cdot C \cdot A$$

To apply Theorem 5, we let F7 verify $I_{\mathsf{PLAIN}} \vdash F \rightsquigarrow I^{cpa,\mathsf{hyb}}_{\mathsf{ENC}}$.

The full paper also describes a broken, non-typable variant of hybrid encryption that "forgets" to encrypt its symmetric keys, a sample protocol that encrypts a secret, and a sample passive adversary that breaks asymptotic secrecy using its own concrete implementation of the decryption algorithm.

6. APPLICATIONS

We show how to compose the typed interfaces and functionalities given in §3 and §5 to verify larger programs.

Multiple Instances of Cryptographic Libraries Formally, a single protocol can use several copies of the same functionality, with distinct copies of their ideal interface and distinct abstract types to protect their keys. Asymptotic security then follows from repeatedly applying our authenticity and secrecy theorems. This enables us, for instance, to verify protocols that use both MACs and signatures, or protocols that encrypt values with different concrete types. The full paper illustrates this approach, showing for instance how to encrypt the keys of another functionality, and how to verify variants of our RPC protocol with authenticated encryption.

Sample Construction: Encrypt-then-MAC We realize authenticated encryption [11] using Encrypt-then-MAC. Given a CMA-secure MAC C_{MAC} and a CPA-secure encryption C_{SENC}, we build a module C_{EtM} such that $C \triangleq C_{\mathsf{SENC}} \cdot C_{\mathsf{MAC}} \cdot C_{\mathsf{EtM}}$ implements authenticated encryption, with ideal functionality $F \triangleq C_{\mathsf{SENC}} \cdot F^{cpa}_{\mathsf{SENC}} \cdot C_{\mathsf{MAC}} \cdot F_{\mathsf{MAC}} \cdot C_{\mathsf{EtM}}$. Using the theorems of §3 and §5, we show that, for any plaintext module P such that $\vdash P \rightsquigarrow I^{C}_{\mathsf{PLAIN}}$ and every p.p.t. A such that $I^{C}_{\mathsf{PLAIN}}, I^{ae}_{\mathsf{SENC}} \vdash A$, we have $P \cdot C \cdot A \approx_\varepsilon P \cdot F \cdot A$.

We also use F7 to verify that F implements the ideal authenticated encryption interface of §5, that is, $I_{\mathsf{PLAIN}} \vdash F \rightsquigarrow I^{ae}_{\mathsf{SENC}}$.

Sample Implementation: Secure Multiparty Sessions We outline the application of our method to larger existing protocols, and consider the cryptographic implementations of secure multiparty sessions of Bhargavan et al. [18], excluding their fixed key distribution sub-protocol.

Multiparty sessions are global, structured communication protocols. Sessions are specified using a declarative language that indicates who can send which messages, when, and what those messages can contain. From this high-level specification, one can infer generalized correspondence properties, named *session integrity*, that account for parallel runs of sessions and the compromise of some of their principals, and then generate custom cryptographic protocols that realize all these properties. To this end, Bhargavan et al. developed a verifying protocol compiler that generates both the protocol code (in F#) and detailed type annotations (in F7) embedding the multiparty session logic and the refinements for each of the MAC keys of the protocol—essentially a large definition of the predicate *Msg* presented in §3. The compiled code is independently verified by F7. Some of their sample protocols involve up to six roles and hundreds of different cryptographic messages formats, handled by more than 5 000 lines of ML protocol code and 4 000 lines of F7 declarations.

Nonetheless, the refined interface for MACs used for typechecking their protocols is almost identical to the ideal interface I_{MAC} of §3, thanks to its support for dynamic key generation and key compromise. Thus, we directly benefit from their symbolic verification effort: for each protocol implementation that they generate and typecheck against their cryptographic library interfaces, Theorem 2 applies and, assuming that their MAC algorithm is CMA-secure, the generated protocol is also asymptotically safe, and their notion of session integrity holds with overwhelming probability.

7. CONCLUSIONS AND FUTURE WORK

We have shown how to express and verify the computational security of sample cryptographic functionalities (once and for all) using ideal refinement-typed interfaces.

(1) The cryptographic proofs of these functionalities are independent and relatively simple; they mostly rely on programming and typechecking.

(2) The security proofs for protocols using these cryptographic functionalities entirely rely on automated typechecking, much as in prior work on symbolic verification.

(3) Their verified security properties are directly expressed as (asymptotic variants of) safety and perfect secrecy on the protocol code.

This yields an effective, modular method for specifying and verifying protocol code under standard assumptions.

Although we conducted our experiments using F# and F7, we would like to carry over our approach to protocols coded in lower-level languages such as C and C++. Refinement types are a convenient way to implement point (2) above, but any general-purpose static verification tool that can prove that a program conforms with our ideal interfaces will do.

Acknowledgments Many thanks to Martín Abadi, Aslan Askarov, Karthik Bhargavan, Avik Chaudhuri, Andy Gordon, Gurvan le Guernic, James Margetson, Tamara Rezk, Nikhil Swamy, Dimitrios Vytiniotis and the anonymous reviewers for their help.

References

[1] M. Abadi. Secrecy by typing in security protocols. *JACM*, 46(5), 1999.

[2] M. Abadi and B. Blanchet. Analyzing security protocols with secrecy types and logic programs. *JACM*, 52(1), 2005.

[3] M. Abadi and P. Rogaway. Reconciling two views of cryptography (the computational soundness of formal encryption). *J. Crypt.*, 15(2), 2002.

[4] M. Backes, B. Pfitzmann, and M. Waidner. Symmetric authentication in a simulatable Dolev-Yao-style cryptographic library. *Int. J. Inf. Sec.*, 4(3), 2005.

[5] M. Backes, B. Pfitzmann, and M. Waidner. The reactive simulatability (RSIM) framework for asynchronous systems. *Inf. Comput.*, 205(12), 2007.

[6] M. Backes, M. Dürmuth, D. Hofheinz, and R. Küsters. Conditional reactive simulatability. *Int. J. Inf. Sec.*, 7(2), 2008.

[7] M. Backes, D. Hofheiz, and D. Unruh. CoSP: A general framework for computational soundness proofs. In *ACM CCS 09*, 2009.

[8] M. Backes, M. Maffei, and D. Unruh. Computational sound verification of source code. In *ACM CCS 09*, 2010.

[9] G. Barthe, B. Grégoire, S. Heraud, and S. Z. Béguelin. Formal certification of ElGamal encryption. In *FAST 2008*, 2008.

[10] G. Barthe, B. Gregoire, S. Heraud, and S. Zanella Béguelin. Computer-aided security proofs for the working cryptographer. In *CRYPTO 2011*, 2011.

[11] M. Bellare and C. Namprempre. Authenticated encryption: Relations among notions and analysis of the generic composition paradigm. *J. Crypt.*, 21, 2008.

[12] M. Bellare and P. Rogaway. Introduction to modern cryptography. In *UCSD CSE 207 Course Notes*, 2005.

[13] M. Bellare and P. Rogaway. The security of triple encryption and a framework for code-based game-playing proofs. In *EUROCRYPT 2006*, 2006.

[14] M. Bellare, R. Canetti, and H. Krawczyk. Keying hash functions for message authentication. In *CRYPTO'96*, 1996.

[15] J. Bengtson, K. Bhargavan, C. Fournet, A. D. Gordon, and S. Maffeis. Refinement types for secure implementations. Technical Report MSR–TR–2008–118–SP1, Microsoft Research, 2008.

[16] K. Bhargavan, C. Fournet, R. Corin, and E. Zalinescu. Cryptographically verified implementations for TLS. In *ACM CCS 09*, 2008.

[17] K. Bhargavan, C. Fournet, A. D. Gordon, and N. Swamy. Verified implementations of the Information Card federated identity-management protocol. In *ASIACCS'08*, 2008.

[18] K. Bhargavan, R. Corin, P.-M. Dénielou, C. Fournet, and J. Leifer. Cryptographic protocol synthesis and verification for multiparty sessions. In *CSF 2009*, 2009.

[19] K. Bhargavan, C. Fournet, and A. D. Gordon. Modular verification of security protocol code by typing. In *POPL 2010*, 2010.

[20] B. Blanchet. A computationally sound mechanized prover for security protocols. In *IEEE Symposium on Security and Privacy*, 2006.

[21] B. Blanchet, M. Abadi, and C. Fournet. Automated verification of selected equivalences for security protocols. *JLAP*, 75(1), 2008.

[22] R. Canetti. Universally composable security: A new paradigm for cryptographic protocols. In *FOCS*, 2001.

[23] S. Chaki and A. Datta. ASPIER: An automated framework for verifying security protocol implementations. In *CSF 2009*, 2009.

[24] N. A. Danielsson. Lightweight semiformal time complexity analysis for purely functional data structures. In *POPL 2008*, 2008.

[25] A. Datta, A. Derek, J. C. Mitchell, V. Shmatikov, and M. Turuani. Probabilistic polynomial-time semantics for a protocol security logic. In *ICALP 2005*, 2005.

[26] A. Datta, A. Derek, J. C. Mitchell, and A. Roy. Protocol composition logic (PCL). *Electr. Notes Theor. Comput. Sci.*, 172, 2007.

[27] D. Dolev and A. Yao. On the security of public key protocols. *IEEE Transactions on Information Theory*, IT–29(2), 1983.

[28] F. Dupressoir, A. D. Gordon, J. Jürjens, and D. A. Naumann. Guiding a general-purpose C verifier to prove cryptographic protocols. In *CSF 2011*, 2011.

[29] N. A. Durgin, J. C. Mitchell, and D. Pavlovic. A compositional logic for proving security properties of protocols. *JCS*, 11(4), 2003.

[30] C. Fournet, K. Bhargavan, and A. Gordon. Cryptographic verification of protocol implementations by typechecking. In *FOSAD*, 2011.

[31] S. Goldwasser, S. Micali, and R. Rivest. A digital signature scheme secure against adaptive chosen-message attack. *SICOMP*, 17(2), 1988.

[32] J. Goubault-Larrecq and F. Parrennes. Cryptographic protocol analysis on real C code. In *VMCAI'05*, 2005.

[33] S. Halevi. A plausible approach to computer-aided cryptographic proofs. Cryptology ePrint Archive, Report 2005/181, 2005.

[34] D. Hofheinz, D. Unruh, and J. Müller-Quade. Polynomial runtime and composability. Cryptology ePrint Archive 2009-023, 2009.

[35] B. M. Kapron and S. A. Cook. A new characterization of type 2 feasibility. *SICOMP*, 25, 1996.

[36] H. Krawczyk, M. Bellare, and R. Canetti. HMAC: Keyed-hashing for message authentication, 1997. RFC 2104.

[37] R. Küsters. Simulation-based security with inexhaustible interactive Turing machines. In *CSFW 2006*, 2006.

[38] R. Küsters and M. Tuengerthal. Universally composable symmetric encryption. In *CSF*, 2009.

[39] P. Laud. Semantics and program analysis of computationally secure information flow. In *ESOP 2001*, volume 2028, Apr. 2001.

[40] P. Laud. Secrecy types for a simulatable cryptographic library. In *ACM CCS 09*, 2005.

[41] P. Laud. On the computational soundness of cryptographically-masked flows. In *POPL 2008*, 2008.

[42] J. H. Morris, Jr. Protection in programming languages. *CACM*, 16(1), 1973.

[43] C. Rackoff and D. R. Simon. Non-interactive zero-knowledge proof of knowledge and chosen ciphertext attack. In *CRYPTO'91*, 1991.

[44] J. C. Reynolds. Types, abstraction and parametric polymorphism. In *IFIP Congress*, 1983.

[45] A. Roy, A. Datta, A. Derek, and J. C. Mitchell. Inductive trace properties for computational security. *JCS*, 18(6), 2010.

[46] The Coq Development Team. *The Coq Proof Assistant Reference Manual – Version V8.3*, 2011.

Information-Flow Types for Homomorphic Encryptions

Cédric Fournet
Microsoft Research
fournet@microsoft.com

Jérémy Planul
MSR–INRIA Joint Centre
jeremy.planul@inria.fr

Tamara Rezk
INRIA Sophia Antipolis-Méditerranée
Tamara.Rezk@inria.fr

ABSTRACT

We develop a flexible information-flow type system for a range of encryption primitives, precisely reflecting their diverse functional and security features. Our rules enable encryption, blinding, homomorphic computation, and decryption, with selective key re-use for different types of payloads.

We show that, under standard cryptographic assumptions, any well-typed probabilistic program using encryptions is secure (that is, computationally non-interferent) against active adversaries, both for confidentiality and integrity. We illustrate our approach using ElGamal and Paillier encryption.

We present two applications of cryptographic verification by typing: (1) private search on data streams; and (2) the bootstrapping part of Gentry's fully homomorphic encryption. We provide a prototype typechecker for our system.

Categories and Subject Descriptors

K.6.m [**Security and Protection**]: Security; D.2.0 [**Software Engineering**]: Protection Mechanisms; F.3.1 [**Specifying and Verifying and Reasoning about Programs**]: Specification techniques.

General Terms

Security, Verification, Design, Languages.

Keywords

Secure information flow, cryptography, confidentiality, integrity, non-interference, type systems.

1. INTRODUCTION

Information flow security is a well-established, high-level framework for reasoning about confidentiality and integrity, with a clear separation between security specifications and mechanisms. At a lower level, encryption provides essential mechanisms for confidentiality, with a wide range of algorithms reflecting different trade-offs between security, functionality, and efficiency. Thus, the secure usage of adequate algorithms for a particular system is far from trivial.

Even with plain encryption, the confidentiality and integrity of keys, plaintexts, and ciphertexts are interdependent: encryption with untrusted keys is clearly dangerous, and plaintexts should never be more secret than their decryption keys. Integrity also matters: attackers may swap ciphertexts, and thus cause the declassification of the wrong data after their successful decryption. Conversely, to protect against chosen-ciphertext attacks, it may be necessary to authenticate ciphertexts, even when plaintexts are untrusted.

Modern encryption schemes offer useful additional features, such as the ability to blind ciphertexts, thereby hiding dependencies between encrypted inputs and outputs, and more generally to compute homomorphically on encrypted data, for instance by multiplying ciphertexts instead of adding their plaintexts. These features are naturally explained in terms of information flows; they enable computations at a lower level of confidentiality—homomorphic operations can be delegated to an "honest but curious" principal—but they also exclude CCA2 security and require some care in the presence of active adversaries.

In this paper, we develop an information-flow type system for cryptography, with precise typing rules to reflect the diverse functional and security features of encryption schemes. Our goal is to understand them better, and to guide protocol designers and programmers. We rely on standard cryptographic assumptions, expressed as probabilistic polynomial-time indistinguishability games —this level of detail is necessary to reliably capture the information flows of the underlying algorithms. Thus, our adversaries are probabilistic polynomial-time programs, with limited read and write access to data, that attempt to gain information about higher-confidentiality data, or to influence higher-integrity data, by interacting with our programs. Our main theorem states that well typed probabilistic polynomial programs using any combination of encryptions, blinding, homomorphic functions, and decryptions are such that our adversaries succeed only with a negligible probability. Depending on the relative security levels of keys, plaintexts, and ciphertexts, we propose different typing rules. Our rules are sound with regards to standard cryptographic assumptions such as CPA or CCA2; they enable the selective re-use of keys for protecting different types of payloads, as well as blinding and homomorphic properties.

Secure Distributed Computations Our work is part of a research project on the synthesis and verification of distributed cryptographic implementations of programs from a description of their information flow security requirements. Fournet et al. [10] present such a security compiler that automatically generates code for encryption and authentication. As illustrated in our programming examples, an important motivation for a new type system is to justify its efficient use of cryptography. For instance, we strive to re-use the same keys for protecting different types of data at different levels of security, so that we can reduce the overall cost of cryptographic protection. More generally, we would like to automatically generate well-typed code for performing blind computations, such as those supported by the systems of Henecka et al. [14] and Katz and Malka [15].

Formally, our work is based on the type system of Fournet and Rezk [9], who introduce the notion of *computational non-interference* against active adversaries to express information flow security in probabilistic polynomial-time cryptographic systems and present a basic type system for encryption and authentication mechanisms. In comparison, their typing rules are much more restrictive, and only support CCA2 public-key encryptions with a single payload type.

Applications We illustrate our approach using programming examples based on classic encryption schemes with homomorphic properties [8, 22]. We also develop two challenging applications of our approach. Both applications rely on a security lattice with intermediate levels, reflecting the structure of their homomorphic operations, and enabling us to prove confidentiality properties, both for honest-but-curious servers and for compromised servers controlled by an active attacker.

- We program and typecheck a practical protocol for private search on data streams proposed by Ostrovsky and Skeith III [21], based on a Paillier encryption of the search query. This illustrates that our types protect against both explicit and implicit information flows; for instance we crucially need to apply some blinding operations to hide information about secret loop indexes.
- We program and typecheck the bootstrapping part of Gentry's fully homomorphic encryption [11]. Starting from the properties of the bootstrappable algorithms given by Gentry–being CPA and homomorphic for its own decryption and for some basic operations—we obtain an homomorphic encryption scheme for an arbitrary function. This illustrates three important features of our type system: the ability to encrypt decryption keys (which is also important for typing key establishment protocols); the use of CPA encryption despite some chosen-ciphertext attacks; and an interesting instance of homomorphism where the homomorphic function is itself a decryption.

This paper exclusively treats public-key encryptions. We believe that their symmetric-key counterparts can be treated similarly. We also refer to Fournet and Rezk [9] for cryptographic types for authentication primitives, such as public-key signatures. This paper omits many details and all proofs. The full paper, programming examples, and a prototype typechecker for our system are available online at `msr-inria.inria.fr/projects/sec/cflow`.

2. PROGRAMS, TYPES, AND POLICIES

We use an imperative probabilistic WHILE language with security policies. A probabilistic semantics is necessary for modeling encryption security [13]. Shared memory is sufficient to model a wide range of interactions between programs and adversaries; for instance public untrusted variables model an open network.

Language The grammar for expressions and commands is

$$\begin{array}{lcl} e & ::= & x \mid op(e_1,\ldots,e_n) \\ P & ::= & x := e \mid x_1,\ldots,x_m := f(e_1,\ldots,e_n) \mid \\ & & P; P \mid \text{if } e \text{ then } P \text{ else } P \mid \text{while } e \text{ do } P \mid \text{skip} \end{array}$$

ASSIGNS
$$\frac{[\![e]\!](\mu) = v}{\langle x := e, \mu\rangle \rightsquigarrow_1 \langle \surd, \mu\{x \mapsto v\}\rangle}$$

SEQS
$$\frac{\langle P,\mu\rangle \rightsquigarrow_p \langle P_1,\mu_1\rangle \qquad P_1 \neq \surd}{\langle P;P',\mu\rangle \rightsquigarrow_p \langle P_1;P',\mu_1\rangle}$$

SEQT
$$\frac{\langle P,\mu\rangle \rightsquigarrow_p \langle \surd,\mu_1\rangle}{\langle P;P',\mu\rangle \rightsquigarrow_p \langle P',\mu_1\rangle}$$

SKIPS
$$\langle \text{skip},\mu\rangle \rightsquigarrow_1 \langle \surd,\mu\rangle$$

STABLE
$$\langle \surd,\mu\rangle \rightsquigarrow_1 \langle \surd,\mu\rangle$$

CONDTRUE
$$\frac{[\![e]\!](\mu) \neq 0}{\langle \text{if } e \text{ then } P \text{ else } P',\mu\rangle \rightsquigarrow_1 \langle P,\mu\rangle}$$

CONDFALSE
$$\frac{[\![e]\!](\mu) = 0}{\langle \text{if } e \text{ then } P \text{ else } P',\mu\rangle \rightsquigarrow_1 \langle P',\mu\rangle}$$

WHILETRUE
$$\frac{[\![e]\!](\mu) \neq 0}{\langle \text{while } e \text{ do } P,\mu\rangle \rightsquigarrow_1 \langle P; \text{while } e \text{ do } P,\mu\rangle}$$

WHILEFALSE
$$\frac{[\![e]\!](\mu) = 0}{\langle \text{while } e \text{ do } P,\mu\rangle \rightsquigarrow_1 \langle \surd,\mu\rangle}$$

FUN
$$\frac{p = [\![f]\!](\mu(y_1),\ldots,\mu(y_n))(\vec{v}) \qquad p > 0}{\langle \vec{x} := f(y_1,\ldots,y_n),\mu\rangle \rightsquigarrow_p \langle \surd,\mu\{\vec{x}\mapsto\vec{v}\}\rangle}$$

Figure 1: Probabilistic operational semantics

where op and f range over polynomial n-ary deterministic and probabilistic functions respectively, with arity $n \geq 0$.

Expressions e consist of variables and operations on data represented as bitstrings. We write op for nullary operations $op()$. We assume given standard functions for boolean and arithmetic constants $(0, 1, \ldots)$ and operators $(||, +, \ldots)$. We let $=_0$ be comparison on booleans, true when both its arguments are either 0 or non-0. We also have standard functions for pairs and functional arrays: we use $\langle e_0, e_1\rangle$ and $(e)_i$ for constructing and projecting pairs, and use $e[e_i]$ and update(x, e, e_i) for reading and updating arrays.

Commands P consist of variable assignments, using deterministic expressions and probabilistic functions (such as encryptions or key generations) composed into sequences, conditionals, and loops. We use syntactic sugar for arrays, writing $x[e_i] := e$ instead of $x :=$ update(x, e, e_i), and for loops, writing for $x := e$ to e' do P instead of $x := e$; while $x \leq e'$ do $\{P; x := x + 1\}$.

Semantics Configurations (s) range over pairs of a command and a memory, written $\langle P, \mu\rangle$, plus inert configurations, written $\langle \surd, \mu\rangle$, that represent termination with final memory μ.

Probabilistic reductions between distributions of configurations are based on a probabilistic transition relation $\rightsquigarrow_p$ defined in Figure 1. We lift these reduction steps to configuration distributions (d), and write $d \rightsquigarrow d'$ when, for all configurations s', we have $d'(s') = \sum_{s \rightsquigarrow_p s'} p \times d(s)$. We denote by $\rho_\infty(\langle P, \mu\rangle)$ the final distribution of memories after running program P with initial memory μ. We write $\Pr[\langle P, \mu\rangle; \varphi]$ for the probability that P terminates with a final memory that meets condition φ.

Confidentiality and Integrity We annotate variables, types, and commands with security labels. These labels specify the programmer's security intent, but they do not affect the behavior of programs. The security labels form a lattice $(\mathcal{L}, \leq)$ obtained as the product of two lattices, for confidentiality $(\mathcal{L}_C, \leq_C)$ and for integrity $(\mathcal{L}_I, \leq_I)$. We write $\bot_\mathcal{L}$ and $\top_\mathcal{L}$ for the smallest and largest elements of $\mathcal{L}$, and $\sqcup$ and $\sqcap$ for the least upper bound and greatest lower bound of two labels, respectively. We write $\bot_C$, $\bot_I$, $\top_C$, and $\top_I$ for the smallest and largest elements of $\mathcal{L}_C$ and $\mathcal{L}_I$, respectively.

For a given label $\ell = (\ell_C, \ell_I)$ of $\mathcal{L}$, the confidentiality label ℓ_C specifies a read level for variables, while the integrity label ℓ_I specifies a write level; the meaning of $\ell \leq \ell'$ is that ℓ' is at least as confidential (can be read by fewer entities) and at most as trusted (can be written by more entities) than ℓ [20]. We let $C(\ell) = \ell_C$ and $I(\ell) = \ell_I$ be the projections that yield the confidentiality and integrity parts of a label. We overload $\leq_C$ and $\leq_I$, writing $\ell \leq_C \ell'$ for $C(\ell) \leq_C C(\ell')$ and $\ell \leq_I \ell'$ for $I(\ell) \leq_I I(\ell')$. Hence, the partial order on $\mathcal{L}$ is defined as $\ell \leq \ell'$ iff $\ell \leq_C \ell'$ and $\ell \leq_I \ell'$. In examples, we often use a four-point lattice defined by $LH < HH < HL$ and $LH < LL < HL$, where for instance LH stands for low confidentiality and high integrity.

Types for Information-Flow Security We use the following grammar for security types:

$$\begin{array}{lll} \tau ::= t(\ell) \mid \tau * \tau \mid \mathsf{Array}\,\tau & & \text{Security types} \\ t ::= \mathsf{Data} & & \text{Payload Data types} \\ \quad \mid \mathsf{Enc}\,\tau\, K q \mid \mathsf{Ke}\,\mathsf{E}\, K \mid \mathsf{Kd}\,\mathsf{E}\, K & & \text{Encryption Data types} \end{array}$$

where $\ell \in \mathcal{L}$ is a security label, E is a set of security types, K is a key label, and q is an encryption index, as explained below. We have pairs at the level of the security types to keep track of tuples of values with different labels, e.g. for encrypting tuples.

Let L be the projection from security types to labels defined by $L(\tau * \tau') = L(\tau) \sqcap L(\tau')$, $L(\mathsf{Array}\,(\tau)) = L(\tau)$, and $L(t(\ell)) = \ell$. We overload $\leq$ for subtyping on security types (e.g. $t(\ell) \leq t(\ell')$ if $\ell \leq \ell'$) and as a relation between security types and labels (e.g. $t(\ell) \leq \ell$). We overload $\sqcup$ from labels to types (e.g. $t(\ell') \sqcup \ell \doteq t(\ell' \sqcup \ell)$). Memory policies are functions Γ from variables to security types. For a given policy Γ, we overload $\leq$ as a relation between variables, security types, and labels (e.g. $x \leq \ell$ if $\Gamma(x) \leq \ell$).

We explain our datatypes for encryptions, but defer their typing rules to the next sections. $\mathsf{Enc}\,\tau\, K$ represents an encryption of a plaintext with security type τ; $\mathsf{Ke}\,\mathsf{E}\,K$ and $\mathsf{Kd}\,\mathsf{E}\,K$ represent encryption and decryption keys, respectively, with a set E that indicates the range of security types τ for the plaintexts that may be encrypted and decrypted with these keys. This set enables us to type code that uses the same key for encrypting values of different types, which is important for efficiency.

The key labels K are used to keep track of keys, grouped by their key-generation commands. In a given program, there should be only one keypair generation for a given label. These labels are attached to the types of the generated keypairs, and propagated to the types of any derived cryptographic materials. They are used to match the usage of key pairs and to prevent key cycles.

The encryption indexes q are used to distinguish between different datatypes for encryptions, for instance when they range over different groups before and after some homomorphic operations. In all other cases, we use a single, implicit index $q = 0$.

Active adversaries For a given $\alpha \in \mathcal{L}$, we let α-adversaries range over commands A that read variables in a set $V_\alpha^C = \{x \mid x \leq_C \alpha\}$ and write variables outside a set $V_\alpha^I = \{x \mid x \leq_I \alpha\}$, that is, $rv(A) \subseteq V_\alpha^C$ and $wv(A) \cap V_\alpha^I = \emptyset$. We consider programs obtained by composing commands with diverse levels of trust, including any α-adversaries as well as fixed, trusted commands. To this end, we write $P[\_]$ for a command context (with a grammar obtained from that of P by adding a hole $\_$) and $P[P']$ for the command obtained by replacing each occurrence of $\_$ with P'.

$$\textsc{Var}\ \ \vdash x : \Gamma(x) \qquad \textsc{Op}\ \ \frac{op : \tau_1 \ldots \tau_n \to \tau \quad \vdash e_i : \tau_i \text{ for } i = 1..n}{\vdash op(e_1, \ldots, e_n) : \tau} \qquad \textsc{SubE}\ \ \frac{\vdash e : \tau \quad \tau \leq \tau'}{\vdash e : \tau'}$$

$$\textsc{Assign}\ \ \frac{\vdash e : \Gamma(x)}{\vdash x := e : L(x)} \qquad \textsc{ProbFun}\ \ \frac{\vdash e : \mathsf{Data}\,(\ell) \text{ for } e \in \vec{e} \quad \mathsf{Data}\,(\ell) \leq \Gamma(x) \text{ for } x \in \vec{x}}{\vdash \vec{x} := f(\vec{e}) : \ell}$$

$$\textsc{Seq}\ \ \frac{\vdash P : \ell \qquad \vdash P' : \ell}{\vdash P; P' : \ell} \qquad \textsc{Cond}\ \ \frac{\vdash e : \mathsf{Data}\,(\ell) \quad \vdash P : \ell \quad \vdash P' : \ell}{\vdash \mathsf{if}\ e\ \mathsf{then}\ P\ \mathsf{else}\ P' : \ell}$$

$$\textsc{While}\ \ \frac{\vdash e : \mathsf{Data}\,(\ell) \qquad \vdash P : \ell}{\vdash \mathsf{while}\ e\ \mathsf{do}\ P : \ell} \qquad \textsc{SubC}\ \ \frac{\vdash P : \ell \qquad \ell' \leq \ell}{\vdash P : \ell'} \qquad \textsc{Skip}\ \ \vdash \mathsf{skip} : \top^\mathcal{L}$$

$$\textsc{Hole}\ \ \vdash \_ : (C(\alpha), \top_I)$$

Figure 2: Non-cryptographic typing rules with policy Γ.

Figure 2 defines a type system that prevents information flows in command contexts that do not rely on cryptography: two runs of the command obtained by inserting α-adversaries, starting with initial memories that coincide on all variables in V_α^C (resp. outside V_α^I), yield final memory distributions that also coincide on those variables. The typing rules are standard, except for Rule Hole, which safely accounts for any α-adversary, and Rule ProbFun, which is a probabilistic version of Op. In Rule Op, the first hypothesis gives the type signature of *op*:

$$\begin{array}{rl} op & : \mathsf{Data}\,(\ell) * \cdots * \mathsf{Data}\,(\ell) \to \mathsf{Data}\,(\ell) \\ \langle\rangle & : \tau_0, \tau_1 \to (\tau_0 * \tau_1) \\ ()_i & : (\tau_0 * \tau_1) \to \tau_i \\ [] & : \mathsf{Array}\,(\tau) \\ \text{cell} & : \mathsf{Array}\,(\tau), \mathsf{Data}\,(L(\tau)) \to \tau \\ \text{update} & : \mathsf{Array}\,(\tau), \tau, \mathsf{Data}\,(L(\tau)) \to \mathsf{Array}\,(\tau) \\ + & : \mathsf{Array}\,(\tau), \tau \to \mathsf{Array}\,(\tau) \\ \text{size} & : \mathsf{Array}\,(\tau) \to \mathsf{Data}\,(L(\tau)) \end{array}$$

We assume that all primitive operations run in polynomial time in the size of their arguments, and that all primitive probabilistic functions yield distributions that are polynomial-time samplable. As we use cryptographic primitives, we assume that they take an additional parameter included in the initial memory whose length matches a security parameter η. We overload $\Pr[\langle P, \mu\rangle; \varphi]$ to denote a probability function parameterized by η. This function is deemed negligible when, for all $c > 0$, there exists η_c such that, for all $\eta \geq \eta_c$, we have $\Pr[\langle P, \mu\rangle; \varphi] \leq \eta^{-c}$.

3. TYPING ENCRYPTIONS

We consider cryptographic algorithms for asymmetric (public key) encryption. We model them in our language as probabilistic functions $\mathcal{G}_e$, $\mathcal{E}$, and $\mathcal{D}$ that meet both functional and security properties, given below.

Definition 1 (Encryption scheme). *Let pubkeys, seckeys, plaintexts, and ciphertexts be sets of polynomially-bounded bitstrings indexed by η. An asymmetric encryption scheme is a triple of algorithms $(\mathcal{G}_e, \mathcal{E}, \mathcal{D})$ such that*

1. $\mathcal{G}_e$, *used for* key generation, *ranges over pubkeys $\times$ seckeys;*

2. $\mathcal{E}$, *used for* encryption, *ranges over ciphertexts;*

3. $\mathcal{D}$, *used for* decryption, *ranges over plaintexts;*

4. *for all* $k_e, k_d := \mathcal{G}_e()$, *if* $y := \mathcal{E}(m, k_e)$ *with* $m \in$ *plaintexts, then* $\mathcal{D}(y, k_d) = m$.

Next, we recast the usual game-based definition of resistance against chosen plaintext attacks in our setting.

DEFINITION 2 (CPA SECURITY). *The scheme* $(\mathcal{G}_e, \mathcal{E}, \mathcal{D})$ *provides indistinguishability against adaptive chosen-plaintexts attacks when, for the commands*

$$E \doteq \mathsf{if}\ b = 0\ \mathsf{then}\ m := \mathcal{E}(x_0, k_e)\ \mathsf{else}\ m := \mathcal{E}(x_1, k_e)$$
$$\mathsf{CPA} \doteq b := \{0, 1\}; k_e, k_d := \mathcal{G}_e(); A[E]$$

and for any polynomials command context A *such that* $b, k_d \notin rv(A)$ *and* $b, k_d, k_e, \eta \notin wv(A)$, *the advantage of the adversary defined as* $|\Pr[\mathsf{CPA}; b =_0 g] - \frac{1}{2}|$ *is negligible.*

The definition involves an indistinguishability game where the adversary command A attempts to guess (and write in variable g) whether the oracle encrypts x_0 or x_1. This notion of security does not involve the decryption algorithm. In particular, it does not cover chosen-ciphertext attacks.

Typing CPA encryptions Figure 3 gives cryptographic rules for typing the algorithms of a CPA encryption scheme.

In Rule GENE for key generation, the first hypothesis requires that the encryption scheme (implicitly parameterized by the key label K) be at least CPA secure. The next two hypotheses give matching encryption-key and decryption-key types to variables k_e and k_d, with the same key label K and the same range of plaintexts E. The constraint $\tau \leq_C \ell_d$ for every type $\tau \in \mathsf{E}$ states that the decryption key k_d is at least as confidential as every plaintext, thereby preventing confidentiality leaks by key compromise. (The constraint appears in GENE rather than DECRYPT, to ensure that all copies of the decryption key are sufficiently confidential.)

In Rule ENCRYPT, the first three hypotheses bind types to the ciphertext y, plaintext e, and key k_e involved in the encryption; these types are related by $\tau \in \mathsf{E}$ and K. The type of y carries two security labels: ℓ_y, the level of the encryption, and $L(\tau)$ within $\mathsf{Enc}\ \tau\ K$, the level of the encrypted plaintext. The label ℓ_y in the typing of k_e records an ordinary flow from k_e to y: by subtyping, we must have $L(k_e) \leq \ell_y$. Conversely, there is no constraint on the flow from e to y, so our typing rule may be sound only with cryptographic assumptions: for confidentiality, this flow reflects that encryption is a form of declassification: e can be more confidential than y. In that case, that is $\tau \not\leq_C y$, we say that K *declassifies* $C(\tau)$. For integrity, this flow reflects that encryption is also a form of endorsement: intuitively, y is only a carrier for e, not in itself an observable outcome of the program; its integrity indicates that y is the result of a correct encryption, even when e itself is not trusted. Finally, the disjunction is a robustness condition on the encryption key, requiring that its integrity be sufficient to protect the confidentiality of the plaintext. The first disjunct excludes that an α-adversary may affect the encryption key (for instance overwriting it with a key she knows). The second disjunct states that the confidentiality protection provided by the key is nil, since an α-adversary may directly read the plaintext. Hence, in case E contains plaintexts with different levels of secrecy, a key with relatively low integrity may still be used to encrypt a plaintext with relatively low confidentiality.

In Rule DECRYPT, the first three hypotheses on the left bind types to the variables x, y, and k_d involved in the decryption; these types are related by τ and K. The label $L(x)$ flows from y to x, as in a normal assignment. The label ℓ_d and the hypothesis $\ell_d \leq_I x$ record integrity flows from k_d to x, as in a normal assignment. Conversely, there is no constraint on the confidentiality flow from k_d to the plaintext x, so our typing rule may be sound only with cryptographic assumptions. Informally, this reflects that the decrypted plaintext yield no information on the decryption key itself, thereby enabling decryptions of plaintexts with different confidentiality levels. When $\ell_d \not\leq_C x$, we say that K *declassifies* $C(\ell_d)$.

The disjunction deals with the integrity of the ciphertext y and the decryption key k_d, with three cases: either

- both ciphertext and decryption key have high integrity; or
- the plaintext is at least as confidential as the key; or
- cryptographic protection is nil, since an α-adversary may read the decryption key then decrypt the plaintext.

The first case intuitively reflects our CPA security assumptions: it requires that the integrity of the ciphertext and the decryption key suffices to guarantee a correct decryption.

When $y \not\leq_I \alpha$ and $\ell_d \not\leq_C \alpha$, the second case covers some chosen-ciphertext attacks, which may come as a surprise: in that case, we say that K *depends on* $C(x)$ and we rely on an additional safety condition (see also Example 3 and 4). When $\ell_d \not\leq_I \alpha$ and $\ell_d \not\leq_C \alpha$, the second case also cover compromise of the decryption key, which may then flow to the decrypted value, as discussed in Example 2.

Examples We provide a series of examples that illustrate the relative information-flow security properties of encryptions. In the examples, unless specified otherwise, we assume that α is *LH* and k_e, k_d is a secure keypair, that is, we set $L(k_e) = LH$ and $L(k_d) = HH$ and assume that $(\mathcal{G}_e, \mathcal{E}, \mathcal{D})$ is CPA. We also write for instance x_{LH} for a variable such that $L(x_{LH}) = LH$. We first encrypt a pair of mixed integrity into a ciphertext of high integrity:

EXAMPLE 1 (HIGHER-INTEGRITY ENCRYPTIONS). *Consider the command context*

$$k_e, k_d := \mathcal{G}_e(); x := \langle x_{HH}, x_{HL}\rangle; y_{LH} := \mathcal{E}(x, k_e); \_;$$
$$x' := \mathcal{D}(y_{LH}, k_d); x'_{HH} := (x')_0; x'_{HL} := (x')_1$$

Let $\Gamma(x) = \Gamma(x') = \mathsf{Data}\,(HH) * \mathsf{Data}\,(HL)$. *This command typechecks; it is safe, inasmuch as the adversary can influence the values of* x_{HL}, x'_{HL} *and of the ciphertext* y_{LH}, *but not the final value of* x'_{HH}.

Encrypting with a low-integrity key clearly leads to confidentiality leaks, as the adversary may overwrite the key with its own key before the encryption. Decrypting with a low-integrity decryption key may also be problematic, especially when the plaintext is not secret, as illustrated below:

EXAMPLE 2 (LOW-INTEGRITY KEYS). *Consider the command context*

$$k_e, k_d := \mathcal{G}_e(); k'_d := k_d; y_{LH} := \mathcal{E}(1, k_e); \_;$$
$$\mathsf{if}\ x_{HH}\ \mathsf{then}\ k''_d := k_d\ \mathsf{else}\ k''_d := k'_d; x_{LL} := \mathcal{D}(y_{LH}, k''_d)$$

We let k'_d *and* k''_d *be low-integrity copies of the decryption key, that is* $L(k'_d) = L(k''_d) = HL$. *The command is not typable, and is actually unsafe, since we may fill the hole with the command* $k'_d := 0$; *thus,* k''_d *to contain the correct key if and only if* $x_{HH} \neq 0$, *and the adversary can finally compare* x_{LL} *with* 1, *the correct decryption, and infer the confidential value* x_{HH}.

$$\frac{\begin{array}{l}\text{GENE}\\ (\mathcal{G}_e,\mathcal{E},\mathcal{D}) \text{ is CPA}\\ \Gamma(k_e)=\mathsf{Ke\,E}\,K(\ell_e)\\ \Gamma(k_d)=\mathsf{Kd\,E}\,K(\ell_d)\\ \forall\tau\in\mathsf{E},\tau\leq_C\ell_d\end{array}}{\vdash k_e,k_d:=\mathcal{G}_e()\,:\,\ell_e\sqcap\ell_d}
\qquad
\frac{\begin{array}{l}\text{ENCRYPT}\\ \Gamma(y)=\mathsf{Enc}\,\tau K(\ell_y)\\ \vdash e:\tau\qquad\tau\in\mathsf{E}\\ \vdash k_e:\mathsf{Ke\,E}\,K(\ell_y)\\ k_e\leq_I\alpha\ \textbf{or}\ \tau\leq_C\alpha\end{array}}{\vdash y:=\mathcal{E}(e,k_e)\,:\,\ell_y}
\qquad
\frac{\begin{array}{l}\text{DECRYPT}\\ \tau\leq\Gamma(x)\qquad\tau\in\mathsf{E}\\ \vdash y:\mathsf{Enc}\,\tau K(L(x))\\ \vdash k_d:\mathsf{Kd\,E}\,K(\ell_d)\qquad\ell_d\leq_I x\\ (y\leq_I\alpha\ \textbf{and}\ \ell_d\leq_I\alpha)\ \textbf{or}\ \ell_d\leq_C x\ \textbf{or}\ \ell_d\leq_C\alpha\end{array}}{\vdash x:=\mathcal{D}(y,k_d)\,:\,L(x)}$$

Figure 3: Typing rules for CPA encryption with policy Γ.

Similarly, since we rely on CPA (for chosen plaintext) and not CCA (for chosen ciphertext), decrypting a low-integrity ciphertext may also be problematic, as illustrated below:

EXAMPLE 3 (CHOSEN-CIPHERTEXT ATTACKS). *When decrypted, low-integrity ciphertexts may leak information about their decryption keys. For a given CPA encryption scheme $(\mathcal{G}_e,\mathcal{E},\mathcal{D})$, we derive a new scheme $(\mathcal{G}'_e,\mathcal{E}',\mathcal{D}')$ as follows:*

$$\mathcal{G}'_e() \doteq \mathcal{G}_e() \qquad \mathcal{E}'(x,k_e) \doteq 1|\mathcal{E}(x,k_e)$$
$$\mathcal{D}'(y,k_d) \doteq b|y' := y; \mathsf{if}\ b=0\ \mathsf{then}\ k_d\ \mathsf{else}\ \mathcal{D}(y',k_d)$$

(where $b|y' := y$ abbreviates decomposing y into b and y'). In the new scheme, decryption leaks its key when called on an ill-formed ciphertext (prefixed with a 0 instead of a 1).

Although this scheme is CPA, decryption of a low-integrity ciphertext may cause a confidentiality flow from k_d to the decrypted plaintext, letting the adversary decrypt any other value encrypted under k_e.

CPA versus chosen ciphertext attacks As illustrated in Sections 7 and 8, our typing rules for CPA allow the decryption of low-integrity ciphertexts when the plaintext is secret, as long as the resulting plaintext never flows to any cryptographic declassification.

We define a notion of key dependencies, used to express the absence of key cycles in Section 6, and we give a counter-example showing an implicit information flow for one such cycle.

DEFINITION 3 (KEY DEPENDENCIES). *For given policy, adversary, and typed command context P, K* depends on *K' when*

1. *K occurs in the set E' of plaintext types for K'; or*
2. *K depends on c, $c \leq_C c'$, and K' declassifies c'.*

EXAMPLE 4. *For a given CPA encryption scheme $(\mathcal{G}_e,\mathcal{E},\mathcal{D})$, we define a modified scheme $(\mathcal{G}_e,\mathcal{E}',\mathcal{D}')$ as follows:*

$$\mathcal{E}'(x,k_e) \doteq r := random\_plaintext();$$
$$\mathsf{if}\ \mathcal{D}(\mathcal{E}(r,k_e),x)=r\ \mathsf{then}\ 0|x\ \mathsf{else}\ 1|\mathcal{E}(x,k_e)$$
$$\mathcal{D}'(b|y',k_d) \doteq \mathsf{if}\ b=0\ \mathsf{then}\ k_d\ \mathsf{else}\ \mathcal{D}(y',k_d)$$

In the modified scheme, the encryption of a decryption key with the corresponding encryption key leaks the decryption key. This scheme is still CPA since an adversary would have to guess the decryption key for a successful attack. However, this scheme leaks k_d when the decryption of a compromised plaintext appears in an encryption:

$$k_e,k_d := \mathcal{G}_e(); y_{LL} := \mathcal{E}(0,k_e); \_;$$
$$x_{HL} := \mathcal{D}(y_{LL},k_d); y'_{LL} := \mathcal{E}(x_{HL},k_e);$$

This command has a key-dependency cycle, but it is otherwise typable, and it is unsafe: we may fill the hole with a command injecting an ill-formed ciphertext; thus $y'_{LL} = x_{HL} = k_d$ and the adversary can obtain the private key by reading y'_{LL}.

Typing CCA2 encryptions We recall the definition of CCA2, obtained from CPA by adding a decryption oracle:

DEFINITION 4 (CCA2 SECURITY). *The scheme $(\mathcal{G}_e,\mathcal{E},\mathcal{D})$ provides indistinguishability against adaptive chosen-plaintext and chosen-ciphertext attacks when, for the commands*

$$E \doteq \mathsf{if}\ b=0\ \mathsf{then}\ m := \mathcal{E}(x_0,k_e)\ \mathsf{else}\ m := \mathcal{E}(x_1,k_e);$$
$$log := log + m$$
$$D \doteq \mathsf{if}\ m \in log\ \mathsf{then}\ x := 0\ \mathsf{else}\ x := \mathcal{D}(m,k_d)$$
$$CCA \doteq b := \{0,1\}; log := \mathsf{nil}; k_e,k_d := \mathcal{G}_e(); A[E,D]$$

and for any polynomial command context A such that $b,k_d \notin rv(A)$ and $b,k_d,k_e,\eta,log \notin wv(A)$, the advantage of the adversary $|\Pr[CCA; b =_0 g] - \frac{1}{2}|$ is negligible.

If the scheme is CCA2 secure, we may use an additional rule for typing decryptions, given below.

$$\frac{\begin{array}{ll}\text{DECRYPT CCA2} & \\ \tau\leq\Gamma(x)\quad\tau\in\mathsf{E} & (\mathcal{G}_e,\mathcal{E},\mathcal{D}) \text{ is CCA2}\\ \vdash y:\mathsf{Enc}\,\tau K(L(x)) & \\ \vdash k_d:\mathsf{Kd\,E}\,K(\ell_d)\qquad\ell_d\leq_I x & \ell_d\leq_I\alpha\ \textbf{or}\ \ell_d\leq_C\alpha\\ \forall\tau'\in\mathsf{E},\tau'\leq\tau\sqcup(\bot,\top) & \end{array}}{\vdash x:=\mathcal{D}(y,k_d)\,:\,L(x)}$$

Except for the CCA2 cryptographic assumption, the rule differs from rule DECRYPT only on the last line of hypotheses, so DECRYPT CCA2 effectively adds a fourth case for decryptions of low-integrity ciphertexts. In this new case, the adversary may be able to mix encryptions for values of type τ with those of values of any other type $\tau' \in \mathsf{E}$, so we must statically exclude some of the resulting flows between plaintexts: τ and τ' must have the same datatypes at the same levels of confidentiality.

EXAMPLE 5 (CIPHERTEXT REWRITING). *Consider a command context using the same keypair for payloads at levels HH and LL:*

$$k_e,k_d := \mathcal{G}_e();$$
$$y_{LL} := \mathcal{E}(x_{LL},k_e); y'_{LL} := \mathcal{E}(x_{HH},k_e); \_; x'_{LL} := \mathcal{D}(y_{LL},k_d)$$

The command is not typable, and is unsafe: indeed, we may fill the hole with an adversary command $y_{LL} := y'_{LL}$, thereby causing the program to leak a copy of the secret x_{HH} into x'_{LL}.

4. BLINDING SCHEMES: SECURITY AND TYPING

Blinding schemes, also known as reencryption schemes, have been introduced by Blaze et al. [3] and can be seen as special cases of homomorphic encryption schemes. To precisely keep track of their information flows, we separate encryption into two stages, each with its own primitive and typing rule:

- Pre-encryption $\mathcal{P}()$ inputs a plaintext and outputs its representation as a ciphertext, but does not in itself provides confidentiality; it can be deterministic; it is typed as an ordinary operation and does not involve declassification.
- Blinding $\mathcal{B}()$ operates on ciphertexts; it hides the correlation between its input and its output, by randomly sampling another ciphertext that decrypts to the same plaintext; it is typed with a declassification, similarly to rule ENCRYPT.

As shown below, some standard encryption schemes can easily be decomposed into pre-encryption and blinding. This enables us for instance to blind a ciphertext without knowing its plaintext, and to perform multiple operations on ciphertexts before blinding. For conciseness, we may still write $\mathcal{E}$ instead of $\mathcal{P};\mathcal{B}$ when the two operations are executed together. We define the functional properties of blinding encryption schemes:

DEFINITION 5 (BLINDING SCHEME). *A blinding encryption scheme is a tuple $(\mathcal{G}_e, \mathcal{P}, \mathcal{B}, \mathcal{D})$ such that $(\mathcal{G}_e, \mathcal{P}; \mathcal{B}, \mathcal{D})$ is an encryption scheme and $\mathcal{B}$ is a probabilistic function such that, for all $k_e, k_d := \mathcal{G}_e()$, if v encrypts m, then $\mathcal{D}(v, k_d) = m$, where 'encrypts' is defined by*

1. *v encrypts m when $v := \mathcal{B}(\mathcal{P}(m, k_e))$ with $m \in$ plaintexts;*
2. *v' encrypts m when $v' := \mathcal{B}(v, k_e)$ and v encrypts m.*

Blinding hides whether an encrypted value is a copy of an other, as shown in the following example.

EXAMPLE 6. *Consider a service that, depending on a secret, either forwards or overwrites an encrypted message. We distinguish a third confidentiality level S such that $L \leq_C S \leq_C H$.*

$$k_e, k_d := \mathcal{G}_e(); y_{LH} := \mathcal{E}(m_{HH}, k_e);$$
$$\text{if } s_{SH} \text{ then } y_{SH} := \mathcal{P}(m_{SH}, k_e) \text{ else } y_{SH} := y_{LH};$$
$$y'_{LH} := \mathcal{B}(y_{SH}, k_e)$$

The resulting ciphertext y_{SH} is itself secret, as an adversary may otherwise compare it with y_{LH} and infer the value of s_{HH}. After blinding, however, y'_{LH} still protects the same message but can be safely treated as public, as an adversary reading y_{LH} and y'_{LH} learns nothing about m_{HH} or s_{SH}.

CPA for Blinding A blinding scheme $(\mathcal{G}_e, \mathcal{P}, \mathcal{B}, \mathcal{D})$ is secure enough to be used with our typing rules when $(\mathcal{G}_e, \mathcal{B}, \mathcal{D})$ is CPA. We have shown this property for the blinding schemes based on El-Gamal [8] $(\mathcal{G}_e^{\mathsf{E}}, \mathcal{P}^{\mathsf{E}}, \mathcal{B}^{\mathsf{E}}, \mathcal{D}^{\mathsf{E}})$, and Paillier [22] $(\mathcal{G}_e^{\mathsf{P}}, \mathcal{P}^{\mathsf{P}}, \mathcal{B}^{\mathsf{P}}, \mathcal{D}^{\mathsf{P}})$.

THEOREM 1. *$(\mathcal{G}_e^{\mathsf{E}}, \mathcal{B}^{\mathsf{E}}, \mathcal{D}^{\mathsf{E}})$ and $(\mathcal{G}_e^{\mathsf{P}}, \mathcal{B}^{\mathsf{P}}, \mathcal{D}^{\mathsf{P}})$ are CPA.*

Typing rules for Pre-Encryption and Blinding The typing rules for pre-encryption and blinding appear in Figure 4.

Rule PRE-ENCRYPT is similar to ENCRYPT, but constrains the confidentiality flow from e to y, which forbids any declassification by typing.

The first three hypotheses of the Rule BLIND bind types to the variables k_e, z, and y. These types are related by $\tau, \tau' \in \mathsf{E}$ and K, which are also typing assumptions for encryptions with key k_e. The label ℓ_y in the typing of k_e records the flow from k_e to y (by subtyping, we must have $k_e \leq \ell_y$). The label $L(\tau)$ in the typing of z records the flow from z to the encrypted value in y. The hypothesis $\tau \leq \tau'$ ensure the correctness of the flow from the encrypted value in z to the encrypted value in y. Similarly to ENCRYPT, there is no constraint on the flow from z to y, so our typing rule may be sound only with cryptographic assumptions. When $z \not\leq_C y$, we say that *K declassifies $C(z)$*.

5. HOMOMORPHIC ENCRYPTIONS

We now consider encryption schemes with homomorphic properties: some functions on plaintexts can instead be computed on their ciphertexts, so that the command that performs the computation may run at a lower level of confidentiality. These schemes enable private remote evaluation: supposing that f_K is a function that homomorphically compute a function f, a client may delegate its evaluation to a server as follows:

1. the client encrypts the secret plaintext x into z_1;
2. the server applies f_K to the encrypted value (possibly encrypting its own secret inputs);
3. the client decrypts the result.

Programmatically, to implement $x' := f(x)$, we use a sequence of three commands sharing the variables z and z' and the encryption key k_e:

$$z := \mathcal{E}(x, k_e); z' := f_K(z, k_e); x' := \mathcal{D}(z', k_d)$$

For simplicity, we do not consider probabilistic homomorphic functions, or homomorphic functions that take non-ciphertext arguments.

DEFINITION 6 (HOMOMORPHIC ENCRYPTION SCHEME). *An homomorphic encryption scheme is a tuple $(\mathcal{G}_e, \mathcal{P}, \mathcal{B}, \mathcal{D}, \mathcal{F})$ such that $(\mathcal{G}_e, \mathcal{P}, \mathcal{B}, \mathcal{D})$ is a blinding encryption scheme and $\mathcal{F}$ is a partial map on polynomial deterministic functions such that for all $k_e, k_d := \mathcal{G}_e()$, if v encrypts$_q$ m, then $\mathcal{D}(v, k_d) = m$, where 'encrypts' is defined by*

1. *v encrypts$_0$ m when $v := \mathcal{B}(\mathcal{P}(m, k_e))$ with $m \in$ plaintexts;*
2. *v' encrypts$_q$ m when $v' := \mathcal{B}(v, k_e)$ and v encrypts$_q$ m.*
3. *v encrypts$_{q'}$ $f(m_1, \ldots, m_n)$ when $f \mapsto f_K : q \rightarrow q' \in \mathcal{F}$, $v := f_K(v_1, \ldots, v_n)$, and each v_i encrypts$_q$ m_i for $i \in 1..n$.*

Homomorphic properties are usually incompatible with CCA2 security. Also, practical encryption schemes usually support a few fixed functions f, and often put limits on the number of consecutive applications of f_K. (This is the purpose of indexes in our model.) Intuitively, these homomorphic application are not perfect; they also produce noise, which may eventually leads to incorrect decryptions. For example, [4] provides a scheme with an unlimited number of additions but only one homomorphic multiplication. In our model, this translate to: $\mathcal{F} = \{+ \mapsto +_K : 0 \rightarrow 0; * \mapsto *_K : 0 \rightarrow 1; + \mapsto +_K : 1 \rightarrow 1\}$.

Figure 4 includes our additional rule for homomorphic computation, HOM-FUN. This rule is parametric on the homomorphic encryption scheme, and relies on a typing assumption on the corresponding 'virtual' computation on plaintexts, using a security policy extended with fresh plaintext variables: $\Gamma, x : \tau \sqcup \ell_y, \vec{x} : \vec{\tau} \sqcup \ell_y \vdash x := f(\vec{x}) : L(\tau) \sqcup \ell_y$.

The first hypotheses bind types to the variables k_e, y, and $\vec{z}$ involved in the homomorphic operation; these types are related by $\vec{\tau}, \tau \in \mathsf{E}$ and K, which describe the typing assumptions for encryptions with key k_e. They also ensure that the function f is homomorphically implementable in this encryption scheme with the corresponding indexes. The last hypothesis ensure that f would be typable if applied on the decrypted ciphertext. The label ℓ_y in the typing of k_e, y, and $\vec{z}$ records the flow from k_e and $\vec{z}$ to y.

Our typing rule ensures that if an homomorphic function types, its equivalent non-homomorphic version would also type, as illustrated in Example 7.

$$\frac{\begin{array}{l}\text{PRE-ENCRYPT}\\ \Gamma(y) = \mathsf{Enc}\,\tau K q(\ell_y)\\ \vdash e : \tau \quad\quad \tau \leq_C y\\ \vdash k_e : \mathsf{Ke}\,\mathsf{E}\,K(\ell_y)\\ \tau \in \mathsf{E}\end{array}}{\vdash y := \mathcal{P}(e, k_e) \;:\ell_y}$$

$$\frac{\begin{array}{l}\text{BLIND}\\ (\mathcal{G}_e, \mathcal{B}, \mathcal{D}) \text{ is CPA}\\ \Gamma(y) = \mathsf{Enc}\,\tau\, Kq(\ell_y) \quad\quad \tau' \leq \tau\\ \vdash z : \mathsf{Enc}\,\tau'\, Kq(L(\tau))\\ \vdash k_e : \mathsf{Ke}\,\mathsf{E}\,K(\ell_y) \quad\quad \tau, \tau' \in \mathsf{E}\\ k_e \leq_I \alpha \textbf{ or } \tau \leq_C \alpha\end{array}}{\vdash y := \mathcal{B}(z, k_e) \;:\ell_y}$$

$$\frac{\begin{array}{l}\text{HOM-FUN}\\ \mathcal{F}_K(f) = f_K : \vec{q} \rightarrow q'\\ \Gamma(y) = \mathsf{Enc}\,\tau\, Kq'(\ell_y)\\ \vdash z_i : \mathsf{Enc}\,\tau_i\, Kq_i(\ell_y) \quad\quad \text{for } z_i \in \vec{z}\\ \vdash k_e : \mathsf{Ke}\,\mathsf{E}\,K(\ell_y) \quad\quad \vec{\tau}, \tau \in \mathsf{E}\\ \Gamma, x : \tau \sqcup \ell_y, \vec{x} : \vec{\tau} \sqcup \ell_y \vdash x := f(\vec{x}) : L(\tau) \sqcup \ell_y\end{array}}{\vdash y := f_K(\vec{z}, k_e) \;:\ell_y}$$

Figure 4: Additional typing rules for pre-encryption, blinding, and encryption homomorphisms with policy Γ.

Examples The examples below use Paillier encryption, which enables us to add plaintexts by multiplying their ciphertexts. Thus, we use $f = +$ and $f_K = *$, and for $\mathcal{F}(+) = * : 0 \mapsto 0$ we obtain a single instance of rule HOM-FUN:

$$\frac{\begin{array}{l}\text{HOM-PAILLIER}\\ \Gamma(y) = \mathsf{Enc}\,(\mathsf{Data}\,(\ell))\, K\,(\ell_y)\\ \vdash z_i : \mathsf{Enc}\,(\mathsf{Data}\,(\ell_i))\, K\,(\ell_y) \text{ for } i = 0, 1\\ \vdash k_e : \mathsf{Ke}\,\mathsf{E}\,K(\ell_y) \quad\quad \mathsf{Data}\,(\ell), \mathsf{Data}\,(\ell_0), \mathsf{Data}\,(\ell_1) \in \mathsf{E}\\ \ell_0 \sqcup \ell_1 \sqcup \ell_y \leq \ell \sqcup \ell_y\end{array}}{\vdash y := z_0 * z_1 \;:\ell_y}$$

EXAMPLE 7. *To illustrate our typing rule, we compare two programs that perform the same addition, on plaintexts (on the left) and homomorphically (on the right):*

$$\begin{array}{llll} P \doteq & k_e, k_d := \mathcal{G}_e(); & P' \doteq & k_e, k_d := \mathcal{G}_e();\\ & z_1 := \mathcal{E}(x_1, k_e); & & z_1 := \mathcal{E}(x_1, k_e);\\ & x'_1 := \mathcal{D}(z_1, k_d) & & \\ & x := x'_1 + x'_1; & & y := z_1 * z_1;\\ & y := \mathcal{E}(x, k_e); & & \\ & r := \mathcal{D}(y, k_d); & & r := \mathcal{D}(y, k_d); \end{array}$$

Suppose that we type P with a policy Γ, then, relying on the plaintext-typing assumption in rule HOM-FUN, *we can also type P' with the same policy.*

EXAMPLE 8. *We show how to homomorphically multiply an encrypted value by a small integer factor.*

$$\begin{array}{l} k_e, k_d := \mathcal{G}_e(); y_{LH} := \mathcal{E}(x_{HH}, k_e); z_{SH} := \mathcal{E}(0, k_e);\\ \mathsf{for}\ i_{SH} := 1 \ \mathsf{to}\ n_{SH}\ \mathsf{do}\ z_{SH} := z_{SH} * y_{LH};\\ z_{LH} := \mathcal{B}(z_{SH}, k_e); \_; x_{HH} := \mathcal{D}(z_{LH}, k_d) \end{array}$$

By typing, we have that an honest-but-curious adversary ($\alpha = SH$) does not learn x_{HH}, and that a network adversary ($\alpha = LH$) learns neither x_{HH} nor n_{SH}. The latter guarantee crucially relies on blinding the result at the end of the loop, since otherwise the adversary may also iterate multiplications of y_{LH} and compare them to the result to guess n_{SH}.

Another classic example of homomorphic scheme is the ElGamal encryption, which enables us to multiply plaintexts by multiplying their ciphertexts; we omit similar, typable programming examples.

6. COMPUTATIONAL SOUNDNESS

We define security properties for probabilistic command contexts as computational variants of noninterference, expressed as games [9].

DEFINITION 7 (COMPUTATIONAL NON-INTERFERENCE). *Let Γ be a policy, α an adversary level, and P a command context.*

P is computationally non-interferent against α-adversaries when, for both $V = V^C_\alpha$ and $V = V^I_\alpha$, and for all polynomial commands J, B_0, B_1, T containing no cryptographic variables, such that $wv(B_b) \cap V = \emptyset$ and $rv(T) \subseteq V$, $\vec{A}$ α-adversaries such that $P[\vec{A}]$ is a polynomial command, $g \notin v(J, B_0, B_1, P, \vec{A})$, and some variable $b \notin v(J, B_0, B_1, P, \vec{A}, T)$ in the command

$$CNI \doteq b := \{0, 1\}; J; \mathsf{if}\ b = 0\ \mathsf{then}\ B_0\ \mathsf{else}\ B_1; P[\vec{A}]$$

if we have $\Pr[CNI; \bigwedge_{x \in rv(T)} x \neq \bot] = 1$, then the advantage $|\Pr[CNI; T; b =_0 g] - \frac{1}{2}|$ is negligible.

In the game, the command $J; \mathsf{if}\ b = 0\ \mathsf{then}\ B_0\ \mathsf{else}\ B_1$ probabilistically initializes the memory, depending on b. Definition 7, then runs the command context applied to adversaries $P[\vec{A}]$. Finally, T attempts to guess the value of b and set g accordingly. T cannot read cryptographic variables, which are not an observable outcome of the program. The condition $\bigwedge_{x \in rv(T)} x \neq \bot$ rules out commands T that may read uninitialized memory. Hence, the property states that the two memory distributions for $b = 0$ and $b = 1$ after running *CNI* cannot be separated by an adversary that reads V.

Besides the cryptographic assumptions, we state additional safety conditions for soundness.

DEFINITION 8. *Let $\alpha \in \mathcal{L}$ be security label. A command context P is safe against α-adversaries when $\Gamma \vdash P$ and*

1. *Each key label is used in at most one key generation.*
2. *Each key variable read in P is first initialized by P.*
3. *There is no dependency cycle between key labels.*

We rely on these conditions to apply cryptographic games in the proof of type soundness, for instance to guarantee the integrity of decrypted values. They can be enforced by static analysis, for instance by collecting all relevant static occurrences of variables and forbidding encryption-key generation within loops.

Condition 1 prevents decryption-key mismatches. Condition 2 recalls our assumption on uninitialized variables for keys. Condition 3 prevents leaks with low integrity ciphertext when using CPA.

We also assume that each static key label is associated to a fixed scheme for encryption that meets Definitions 1, 5, or 6 and we impose constraints on the length of ciphertexts in order to prevent information leakage via the length of encrypted messages (see appendix for a formal definition).

Relying on these conditions, we obtain our main security theorem: well-typed programs are computationally non-interferent.

THEOREM 2. *Let $\alpha \in \mathcal{L}$ be a security label. Let Γ be a policy. Let P be a polynomial-time command context, safe against α-adversaries. P satisfies computational non-interference against α-adversaries.*

The proof relies on a series of typability-preserving program transformations that match the structure of the games used in the cryptographic security assumptions (Definition 2). These transformations replace, one static key label at a time, couples of encryptions and decryption algorithms by an ideal implementation that maintains a global table for all values encrypted so far and encrypts 0s instead of the actual plaintexts.

7. PRIVATE SEARCH ON DATA STREAMS

We illustrate the use of Paillier encryption on a simplified version of a practical protocol developed by Ostrovsky and Skeith III [21] for privately searching for keywords in data streams (without the Bloom filter). The protocol has two roles: an agency P and a service S. Assume that the service issues, or processes, confidential documents such as mail orders or airline tickets, and that the agency wishes to retrieve any such document whose content matches some keywords on a secret black list. The two roles communicate using a public network. The black list is too sensitive to be given to the service. Conversely, the service may be processing a large number of documents, possibly at many different sites, and may be unwilling to pass all those documents to the agency.

We formally assume that the agency is more trusted than the service. We suppose that the documents are arrays of words, and that all words (including the keywords on the black list) appear in a public, trusted dictionary. We model the public network using variables shared between P and S. We rely on the additive property of Paillier encryption, detailed in Section 5. We code the protocol using three commands, explained below.

Initially, the agency generates a keypair and encodes the list of keywords as an array ($mask$) of encryptions indexed by the public dictionary that contains, for each word, either an encryption of 1 if the word appears in the black list or an encryption of 0 otherwise. The agency can distribute this array to the service without revealing the black list.

$$\begin{aligned} P_0 \doteq\ & k_e, k_d := \mathcal{G}_e(); \\ & \quad \text{for } i := 0 \text{ to } size(words) - 1 \text{ do} \\ & \quad \text{if } words[i] \in keywords \text{ then } wb := 1 \text{ else } wb := 0; \\ & \quad mask[i] := \mathcal{E}(wb, k_e) \end{aligned}$$

Then, for each document d, the service homomorphically computes the number of matching keywords, as the sum of the 0 and 1s encrypted in $mask$ for all indexes of the words ($d[j]$) present in the document, by multiplying those encryptions in e. Moreover, the service homomorphically multiplies e and the value of the document d (seen as a large integer) in z—the loop computes e^d, and may be efficiently replaced with a fast exponentiation. In particular, if they were no matches, z is just an encryption of 0. Finally, the serviceblinds both e and z before sending them to the agency—this step is necessary to declassify these encryptions without leaking information on the document.

$$\begin{aligned} S \doteq\ & e := 1; \\ & \text{for } j := 0 \text{ to } size(d) - 1 \text{ do} \\ & \quad e := e * mask[words^{-1}(d[j])]; \\ & e' := \mathcal{B}(e, k_e); z := 1; \\ & \text{for } j := 0 \text{ to } d - 1 \text{ do } z := z * e; \\ & z' := \mathcal{B}(z, k_e) \end{aligned}$$

Last, for each pair e' and z', the agency decrypts the value containing the number of matches (in n) and, if n is different from 0, retrieves the value of the document by decrypting the product and dividing by n.

$$\begin{aligned} P \doteq\ & n := \mathcal{D}(e', k_d); \\ & \text{if } n > 0 \text{ then} \\ & \quad nd := \mathcal{D}(z', k_d); log := log + (nd/n) \end{aligned}$$

Adding an outer loop for the documents processed by the service, the whole protocol is modelled as the command

$$\begin{aligned} Q \doteq\ & P_0; \\ & \text{for } l := 0 \text{ to } nb\_docs \text{ do} \\ & \quad d := docs[l]; S; P; \_ \end{aligned}$$

As discussed by Ostrovsky and Skeith III, this algorithm is reasonably efficient for the service, as it requires just a multiplication and a table lookup for each word in each document. Relying on Bloom filters, the authors of the protocol and Danezis and Diaz [6] develop more advanced variants, requiring less bandwidth and guaranteeing additional privacy properties for the service, but the overall structure of the protocol remains unchanged.

We now specify the security of the protocol as a policy Γ that maps the variable of Q to labels. We distinguish three levels of integrity: H for the agency, S for the service, and L for untrusted data, with $H <_I S <_I L$. k_e and $keywords$ have high integrity (H); all other variables have service integrity (S).

We also distinguish four levels of confidentiality: H and P for the agency, S for the service, and L for public data. With $L <_C P <_C H$ and $L <_C S <_C H$.

- $words$, $mask$, e', z', i, nb_docs, k_e are public (at level L);
- $docs$, d, e, z, j, l are readable by the service (S) and the agency;
- $keywords$, kd, bw are readable only by the agency (P);
- log, n, nd are also readable by the agency, but they depend on low-integrity decryptions, and thus should not flow to any further encryption with key k_e (H).

We prove the security properties of the protocol as instances of computational non-interference, established by typing our code with different choices of adversary level α.

THEOREM 3. *$\Gamma \vdash Q$ when α ranges over SH, SS, and LS, hence Q is computationally non interferent against these adversaries.*

The case $\alpha = SH$ corresponds to a powerful adversary that entirely controls the service but still learns nothing about the blacklist: it cannot distinguish between any two runs of the protocol with different values of $keywords$. If the service is honest but curious ($\alpha = SS$), the protocol also completes with the correct result. If the adversary controls only the network ($\alpha = LS$), it learns nothing either about the documents contents (*docs*).

8. BOOTSTRAPPING HOMOMORPHIC ENCRYPTIONS

Gentry [11] proposes a first fully homomorphic encryption (FHE) scheme, that is, a scheme that supports arbitrary computations on encrypted data, thereby solving a long-standing cryptographic problem [13]. Others, e.g. Smart and Vercauteren [23], develop more efficient constructions towards practical schemes.

These constructions are based on *bootstrappable encryption schemes*, equipped with homomorphic functions for the scheme's own decryption function as well as some more basic functions; these basic operations may represent e.g. logical gates. (Designing a bootstrappable encryption scheme is in itself very challenging, as it severely constrains the decryption algorithm, but is not our concern here.)

The bootstrap relies on a series of keys. Whenever the noise accumulated as the result of homomorphic evaluation needs to be canceled, the intermediate result (encrypted under the current key) is encrypted using the next encryption key, then homomorphically decrypted using an encryption of the current decryption key under the next encryption key. This bootstrapping yields an homomorphic scheme for any function as long as the computation can progress using other homomorphic functions between encryptions and decryptions to the next key. (Following Gentry's terminology, the resulting scheme is a *leveled* FHE: the key length still depends on the max size of the circuit for evaluating f; some additional key-cycle assumption is required to get a fixed-length key.)

Next, we assume the properties of the base algorithms given by Gentry—being CPA and homomorphic for its own decryption plus basic operations f_i that suffice to evaluate some arbitrary function f. We then show that these properties suffice to program and verify by typing the bootstrapping part of Gentry's construction, leading to homomorphic encryption for this arbitrary function f. Typing of Gentry's bootstrapping relies on typing rules for CPA with multiple keys and types of encrypted values, and on instances of rule HOM-FUN with $f = \mathcal{D}$.

We assume given a bootstrappable scheme using a set of homomorphic functions for decrypting and for computing: $\mathcal{F} = \{\mathcal{D} \mapsto \mathcal{D}_K : 0 \to 1; f^i \mapsto f^i_K : 1 \to 2 \text{ for } i = 1..n\}$.

We are now ready to program the bootstrapping for f. Both parties agree on the function to compute, f, and its decomposition into successive computation steps $(f_i)_{i=1..n}$ such that $f = f_1; \ldots; f_n$. This may be realized by producing a circuit to evaluate f and then letting the f_i be the successive gates of the circuit. For simplicity, we assume that each f_i operates on all the bits of the encrypted values; Gentry instead uses a tuple of functions $f_i^{j=1..w}$ for each step, each f_i^j computing one bit of the encrypted values. This more detailed bootstrapping can be typed similarly.

For the plaintexts, we write x_0 for the input, $x_1, \ldots x_{n-1}$ for the intermediate results, and x_n for the final result, so the high-level computation is just $x_i := f_i(x_{i-1})$ for $i = 1..n$.

The client generates all keypairs; encrypts the input using the first encryption key; encrypts each decryption key using the next encryption key; calls the server; and decrypts the result using the final key:

$$\begin{array}{lll} P_c \doteq ke_i, kd_i := \mathcal{G}_e(); & & \text{for } i = 1..n \\ \quad skd_i & := \mathcal{E}(kd_i, ke_{i+1}); & \text{for } i = 1..n-1 \\ \quad y_0 & := \mathcal{E}(x_0, ke_1); & \\ \quad \_; & & \text{calling the server} \\ \quad x_n & := \mathcal{D}(z_n, sk_n) & \end{array}$$

The message consists of the content of the shared variables y_0, ke_1, skd_1, ..., ke_{n-1}, skd_{n-1}, ke_n. The server performs the homomorphic computation for each f_i, interleaved with the re-keying.

$$\begin{array}{l} P_s \doteq \big(z_i := f^i_{K_i}(y_{i-1}, ke_i); \\ \quad t_i := \mathcal{E}(z_i, ke_{i+1}); \\ \quad y_i := \mathcal{D}_{K_{i+1}}(t_i, skd_i, ke_{i+1}); \big)_{\text{for } i=1..n-1} \\ \quad z_n := f^n_{K_n}(y_{n-1}, ke_n); \_ \end{array}$$

We specify the security of the protocol as a policy Γ that maps the variable of P_c and P_s to labels. We distinguish three levels of integrity: H for the agency, S for the service, and L for untrusted data, with $H <_I S <_I L$. ke_i and kd_i have high integrity (H) for $i = 1..n$; all other variables have service integrity (S).

Since our scheme is only CPA, we need $n+1$ levels of confidentiality to separate the results of low integrity decryptions: $H_0..H_n$ for the agency and L for public data, such that $L <_C H_0 <_C \cdots <_C H_n$.

- $ke_i, skd_i, z_i, t_i, y_i$ are public for $i = 1..n$ (at level L);
- x_0 is readable only by the agency (H_0);
- kd_i is readable only by the agency for $i = 1..n$ (H_i);
- x_n is also readable by the agency, but moreover it depends on low-integrity decryptions, and thus should not flow to any further encryption with any of the key ke_i for $i = 1..n$ (H_n).

Let $\tau_i = \mathsf{Data}\,(H_i S)$. We type our variables as follows, for $i = 1..n-1$.

$$\begin{array}{ll} \Gamma(ke_i) & = \mathsf{Ke}\,\mathsf{E}_i\,K_i(LH) \\ \Gamma(kd_i) & = \mathsf{Kd}\,\mathsf{E}_i\,K_i(H_iH) \\ \Gamma(x_0) & = \tau_0 \\ \Gamma(skd_i) & = \mathsf{Enc}\,(\mathsf{Kd}\,\mathsf{E}_i\,K_i(H_{i-1}S))K_{i+1}0(LS) \\ \Gamma(y_0) & = \mathsf{Enc}\,\tau_0\,K_1 0(LS) \\ \Gamma(z_i) & = \mathsf{Enc}\,\tau_{i-1}\,K_i 2(LS) \\ \Gamma(t_i) & = \mathsf{Enc}\,(\mathsf{Enc}\,\tau_{i-1}\,K_i 2(LS))\,K_{i+1}0(LS) \\ \Gamma(y_i) & = \mathsf{Enc}\,\tau_i\,K_{i+1}1(LS) \\ \Gamma(z_n) & = \mathsf{Enc}\,\tau_{n-1}\,K_n 2(LS) \\ \Gamma(x_n) & = \tau_n \end{array}$$

with the encrypted sets below, for $i = 2..n$:

$$\begin{array}{l} \mathsf{E}_1 = \{\tau_0\} \\ \mathsf{E}_i = \{\tau_{i-1}, \mathsf{Kd}\,\mathsf{E}_{i-1}\,K_{i-1}(H_{i-2}S), \mathsf{Enc}\,\tau_{i-1}\,K_{i-1}(HS)\} \end{array}$$

We verify that the commands above are typable with the resulting policy Γ:

THEOREM 4. *$\Gamma \vdash P_c[P_s]$ when α ranges over LS and LH, hence $P_c[P_s]$ is computationally non-interferent against these adversaries.*

The theorem yields strong indistinguishability guarantees. The case $\alpha = LS$ corresponds to an "honest but curious" adversary, who can observe all server operations on ciphertexts (that is, read all intermediate values) but still learn nothing about the plaintexts. The case $\alpha = LH$ corresponds to an active adversary in full control of the service, who can disrupt its operations, and still learns nothing about the plaintexts. To clarify these confidentiality guarantees, we verify by typing that our construction is in particular CPA. We let $\mathcal{S}$ abbreviate the scheme $(\mathcal{G}^h_e, \mathcal{E}^h, \mathcal{D}^h, \{f \mapsto f_K : 0 \to 1\})$ defined as follows:

$$\begin{array}{rl} ke, kd := \mathcal{G}^h_e() \doteq & \big(ke_i, kd_i \ := \ \mathcal{G}_e();\big)_{\text{for } i=1..n} \\ & \big(skd_i \ := \ \mathcal{E}(kd_i, ke_{i+1});\big)_{\text{for } i=1..n-1} \\ & ke \ := \ (ke_1, ..., ke_n, skd_1, skd_{n-1}); \\ & kd \ := \ (kd_1, kd_n) \\ y := \mathcal{E}^h(e, ke) \doteq & y \ := \ \mathcal{E}(e, (ke)_1); \\ y := f^h_K(z, ke) \doteq & y_0 \ := \ z; \\ & \big(z_i \ := \ f^i_{K_i}(y_{i-1}, (ke)_i); \\ & \ t_i \ := \ \mathcal{E}(z_i, (ke)_{i+1}); \\ & \ y_i \ := \ \mathcal{D}_{K_{i+1}}(t_i, (ke)_{i+n}, (ke)_{i+1});\big)_{\text{for } i=1..n-1} \\ & y \ := \ f^n_{K_n}(y_{n-1}, (ke)_n) \\ x := \mathcal{D}^h(y, kd) \doteq & \mathsf{if}\ is\_enc(y, (kd)_1) \\ & \mathsf{then}\ x := \mathcal{D}(y, (kd)_1) \\ & \mathsf{else}\ x := \mathcal{D}(y, (kd)_2) \end{array}$$

THEOREM 5. *$\mathcal{S}$ is a CPA homomorphic encryption scheme.*

9. RELATED WORK

Information flow policies and types Non-interference was introduced by Goguen and Meseguer [12]. Laud [17] introduces computational non-interference in a model with passive adversaries (CNIP). Laud and Vene [19] propose a type system (relying on CPA) to verify CNIP in a language with symmetric encryption but where decrypted values cannot be treated as keys. Fournet and Rezk [9] generalize CNIP to the active case, with adversaries that may interfere with the normal execution of programs, and also covers integrity properties. We present a type system (relying on CCA2) that enables typing of key establishment protocols. In a similar line of work, Smith and Alpízar [24] present a type system (relying on CCA2) with encryption and decryption but no explicit keys. Askarov et al. [1] propose a type system for cryptographically masked flows. Their system also handles key reuse for plaintexts at different levels, via subtyping, but their adversary model is weaker than ours, and excludes in particular chosen-ciphertext attacks. Laud [18] investigates conditions such that cryptographically masked flow imply secrecy and proposes a simpler computationally-sound execution model for passive adversaries.

Homomorphic encryptions The first CPA homomorphic encryption scheme is due to Goldwasser and Micali [13]. Additive homomorphic encryption schemes proved to be CPA include Benaloh [2] and Paillier [22]. ElGamal [8] is a CPA multiplicative homomorphic encryption scheme. Other schemes [4, 11] allow both addition and multiplication.

Protocol analysis featuring homomorphic encryptions Delaune et al. [7] and Lafourcade [16] analyse protocols featuring homomorphic encryptions using equational theories (see Cortier et al. [5]) to model homomorphisms.

Acknowledgments We thank Martín Abadi, Anupam Datta, Markulf Kohlweiss, Nikhil Swamy, and the anonymous reviewers for their comments.

References

[1] A. Askarov, D. Hedin, and A. Sabelfeld. Cryptographically-masked flows. In *Proceedings of the 13th International Static Analysis Symposium*, LNCS, 2006. Springer-Verlag.

[2] J. C. Benaloh. Secret sharing homomorphisms: Keeping shares of a secret sharing. In A. M. Odlyzko, editor, *CRYPTO*, volume 263 of *LNCS*, pages 251–260. Springer, 1986.

[3] M. Blaze, G. Bleumer, and M. Strauss. Divertible protocols and atomic proxy cryptography. In *EUROCRYPT*, pages 127–144, 1998.

[4] D. Boneh, E.-J. Goh, and K. Nissim. Evaluating 2-DNF formulas on ciphertexts. In *Theory of Cryptography (TCC)*, number 3378 in LNCS, pages 325–341. Springer, Feb. 2005.

[5] V. Cortier, S. Delaune, and P. Lafourcade. A survey of algebraic properties used in cryptographic protocols. *Journal of Computer Security*, 14(1):1–43, 2006.

[6] G. Danezis and C. Diaz. Space-efficient private search with applications to rateless codes. In *Financial cryptography and data security: 11th international conference, FC 2007, and 1st International Workshop on Usable Security, USEC 2007*, 2007.

[7] S. Delaune, P. Lafourcade, D. Lugiez, and R. Treinen. Symbolic protocol analysis in presence of a homomorphism operator and exclusive or. In M. Bugliesi, B. Preneel, V. Sassone, and I. Wegener, editors, *ICALP (2)*, volume 4052 of *LNCS*, pages 132–143. Springer, 2006.

[8] T. ElGamal. A public key cryptosystem and a signature scheme based on discrete logarithms. In *CRYPTO*, pages 10–18, 1984.

[9] C. Fournet and T. Rezk. Cryptographically sound implementations for typed information-flow security. In *35th Annual ACM SIGPLAN-SIGACT Symposium on Principles of Programming Languages (POPL'08)*, pages 323–335, Jan. 2008.

[10] C. Fournet, G. le Guernic, and T. Rezk. A security-preserving compiler for distributed programs: From information-flow policies to cryptographic mechanisms. In *ACM Conference on Computer and Communications Security*, pages 432–441, Nov. 2009.

[11] C. Gentry. Fully homomorphic encryption using ideal lattices. In *ACM symposium on Theory of computing (STOC)*, pages 169–178, 2009.

[12] J. A. Goguen and J. Meseguer. Security policies and security models. In *IEEE Symposium on Security and Privacy*, pages 11–20, 1982.

[13] S. Goldwasser and S. Micali. Probabilistic encryption & how to play mental poker keeping secret all partial information. In *ACM symposium on Theory of computing (STOC)*, pages 365–377, 1982.

[14] W. Henecka, S. Kögl, A.-R. Sadeghi, T. Schneider, and I. Wehrenberg. TASTY: tool for automating secure two-party computations. In *17th ACM Conference on Computer and Communications Security*, pages 451–462, Oct. 2010.

[15] J. Katz and L. Malka. Secure text processing with applications to private DNA matching. In *17th ACM Conference on Computer and Communications Security*, pages 485–492, Oct. 2010.

[16] P. Lafourcade. *Vérification des protocoles cryptographiques en présence de théories équationnelles.* Thèse de doctorat, Laboratoire Spécification et Vérification, ENS Cachan, France, Sept. 2006.

[17] P. Laud. Semantics and program analysis of computationally secure information flow. In *10th European Symposium on Programming (ESOP)*, volume 2028 of *LNCS*. Springer, Apr. 2001.

[18] P. Laud. On the computational soundness of cryptographically-masked flows. In *35th Annual ACM SIGPLAN-SIGACT Symposium on Principles of Programming Languages (POPL'08)*, pages 337–348, Jan. 2008.

[19] P. Laud and V. Vene. A type system for computationally secure information flow. In *Fundamentals of Computation Theory*, LNCS, pages 365–377. Springer, 2005.

[20] A. C. Myers, A. Sabelfeld, and S. Zdancewic. Enforcing robust declassification and qualified robustness. *Journal of Computer Security*, 14(2):157–196, 2006.

[21] R. Ostrovsky and W. E. Skeith III. Private searching on streaming data. In V. Shoup, editor, *Advances in Cryptology–CRYPTO 2005*, volume 3621 of *LNCS*, pages 223–240, 2005.

[22] P. Paillier. Public-key cryptosystems based on composite degree residuosity classes. In *EUROCRYPT*, pages 223–238, 1999.

[23] N. Smart and F. Vercauteren. Fully homomorphic encryption with relatively small key and ciphertext sizes. *Public Key Cryptography–PKC 2010*, pages 420–443, 2010.

[24] G. Smith and R. Alpízar. Secure information flow with random assignment and encryption. In *FMSE '06: fourth ACM workshop on Formal methods in security*, pages 33–44, 2006.

Cryptographic Primitives for Building Secure and Privacy Respecting Protocols

Keynote – 2010 ACM SIGSAC Outstanding Innovation Award

Jan Camenisch
IBM Research – Zurich
jca@zurich.ibm.com

ABSTRACT

Using the Internet and other electronic media for our daily tasks has become common. Thereby a lot of sensitive information is exchanged, processed, and stored at many different places. Once released, controlling the dispersal of this information is virtually impossible. Worse, the press reports daily on incidents where sensitive information has been lost, stolen, or misused - often involving large and reputable organizations. Privacy-enhancing technologies can help to minimize the amount of information that needs to be revealed in transactions, on the one hand, and to limit the dispersal, on the other hand. Many of these technologies build on common cryptographic primitives that allow for data to be authenticated and encrypted in such a way that it is possible to efficiently prove possession and/or properties of data revealing the data or side-information about it. Proving such statements is of course possible for any signature and encryption scheme. However, if the result is to be practical, special cryptographic primitives and proof protocols are needed.

In this talk we will first consider a few example scenarios and motivate the need for such cryptograph building block before we then present and discuss these. We start with efficient discrete logarithms based proof protocols often referred to as generalized Schnorr proofs. They allow one to prove knowledge of different discrete logarithms (exponents) and relations among them. Now, to be able to prove possession of a (valid) signature and a message with generalized Schnorr proofs, it is necessary that the signature and the message signed are exponents and that no hash-function is used in the signature verification. Similarly, for encryption schemes, the plain text needs to be an exponent. We will present and discuss a number of such signature and encryption schemes.

To show the power of these building blocks, we will consider a couple of example protocols such as anonymous access control and anonymous polling. We then conclude with a discussion on security definition and proofs. We hope that the presented building blocks will enable many new privacy-preserving protocols and and applications in the future.

Categories and Subject Descriptors

D.4.6 [**Operating Systems**]: Security and Protection—*access controls, authentication, cryptographic controls*; E.3 [**Data**]: Data Encryption—*Public key cryptosystems*

General Terms

Security

Keywords

Cryptographic Protocols, Privacy.

Acknowledgments

This talk covers work with a large number of co-authors I have had the pleasure to work with. Thank you all so much! Particular thanks go to Endre Bangerter, Patrik Bichsel, Christian Cachin, Maria Dubovitskaya, Thomas Gross, Susan Hohenberger, Markulf Kohlweiss, Anna Lysyanskaya, Joy Müller, Gregory Neven, Franz-Stefan Preiss, Abhi Shelat, Victor Shoup, Dieter Sommer, Markus Stadler.

Also, I was fortunate to have worked with the people involved in the PRIME and PrimeLife projects and my colleagues of the different incarnations of security group at IBM Research – Zurich. I have enjoyed countless fruitful discussions with them and many have become close friends.

Biography

Jan Camenisch received a Diploma in Electrical Engineering in 1993 and a Ph.D. in Computer Science in 1998 both from ETH Zurich. From 1998 until 1999 he has been Research Assistant Professor in Computer Science at the University of Aarhus, Denmark. Since 1999 he is Research Staff Member and project leader at IBM Research – Zurich. He was also the technical leader of the EU-funded projects PRIME (prime-project.eu) and PrimeLife (primelife.eu) which both contributed towards making on-line privacy a reality.

His research interests include public key cryptography; cryptographic protocols, in particular those supporting privacy and anonymity; practical secure distributed computation; and privacy-enhancing technologies.

CCS'11, October 17–21, 2011, Chicago, Illinois, USA.
ACM 978-1-4503-0948-6/11/10.

Process Out-Grafting: An Efficient "Out-of-VM" Approach for Fine-Grained Process Execution Monitoring

Deepa Srinivasan
NC State University
dsriniv@ncsu.edu

Zhi Wang
NC State University
zhi_wang@ncsu.edu

Xuxian Jiang
NC State University
jiang@cs.ncsu.edu

Dongyan Xu
Purdue University
dxu@cs.purdue.edu

ABSTRACT

Recent rapid malware growth has exposed the limitations of traditional *in-host* malware-defense systems and motivated the development of secure virtualization-based *out-of-VM* solutions. By running vulnerable systems as virtual machines (VMs) and moving security software from inside the VMs to outside, the out-of-VM solutions securely isolate the anti-malware software from the vulnerable system. However, the presence of semantic gap also leads to the compatibility problem in not supporting existing defense software. In this paper, we present *process out-grafting*, an architectural approach to address both isolation and compatibility challenges in out-of-VM approaches for fine-grained process-level execution monitoring. Specifically, by relocating a suspect process from inside a VM to run side-by-side with the out-of-VM security tool, our technique effectively removes the semantic gap and supports existing user-mode process monitoring tools without any modification. Moreover, by forwarding the system calls back to the VM, we can smoothly continue the execution of the out-grafted process without weakening the isolation of the monitoring tool. We have developed a KVM-based prototype and used it to natively support a number of existing tools without any modification. The evaluation results including measurement with benchmark programs show it is effective and practical with a small performance overhead.

Categories and Subject Descriptors

D.4.6 [**Operating Systems**]: Security and Protection - Invasive Software

General Terms

Security

Keywords

Virtualization, Process Monitoring, Semantic Gap

CCS'11, October 17–21, 2011, Chicago, Illinois, USA.

1. INTRODUCTION

Computer malware (e.g., viruses and trojans), in its seemingly infinite evolution of functionality and forms, is one of the largest threat that end users and enterprises are combating daily. A recent report from McAfee [3] shows a rapidly exploding malware growth with new record numbers "accomplished" in the last year. Specifically, as highlighted in the report, "McAfee Labs identified more than 20 million new pieces of malware in 2010," which translates into nearly 55,000 new malware samples discovered every day! Moreover, "of the almost 55 million pieces of malware McAfee Labs has identified and protected against, 36 percent of it was written in 2010!" This alarming trend reveals the disturbing fact that existing malware defenses fail to effectively contain the threat and keep up with the malware growth.

Especially, if we examine traditional anti-malware tools, they are typically deployed within vulnerable systems and could be the first targets once malware infect a computer system. In other words, though these traditional *in-host* tools are valuable in monitoring system behavior or detecting malicious activities (with their native access inside the systems), they are fundamentally limited in their isolation capability to prevent themselves from being infected in the first place. To address that, researchers propose *out-of-VM* approaches [8, 15, 20, 21, 30, 31, 37], which change the malware defense landscape by leveraging recent advances of virtualization to run vulnerable systems as VMs and then moving anti-malware tools from inside the systems to outside. By enlisting help from the underlying virtualization layer (or hypervisor), out-of-VM approaches can effectively overcome the isolation challenge that encumbers traditional in-host approaches. However, by separating anti-malware software from the untrusted systems, they also naturally encounter the well-known semantic gap challenge: these anti-malware software or tools – as out-of-VM entities – need to monitor or semantically infer various in-VM activities.

In the past several years, researchers have actively examined this semantic-gap challenge and implemented a number of introspection-based systems [12, 21] to mitigate it. For example, VMwatcher [21] proposes a guest view casting technique to apply the knowledge of inner guest OS kernel, especially the semantic definition of key kernel data structure and functionality, to bridge the semantic gap. Virtuoso [12] aims to automate the process of extracting introspection-relevant OS kernel information (by monitoring the execution of an in-guest helper program) for the construction of introspection-aware security tools. Though these systems make steady progresses in bridging the semantic gap, the gap still inevitably leads to a compatibility problem. In particular, none of these introspection-based systems is compatible with existing anti-malware software (including various system/process monitoring tools) that were designed to run within a host. Due to the lack of compatibility, significant effort and advanced mechanisms [12, 21] are still needed to re-engineer these tools and adapt them for different guest OSs. This is especially concerning when fine-grained monitoring of individual processes requires intercepting a wide variety of events (e.g. user-library function calls or system calls) and interpreting them meaningfully (e.g. to determine their arguments). Worse, these introspection-based solutions are sensitive to guest OS versions or variants and to some extent fragile to any change or patch to the guest OS. As a result, this compatibility problem severely limits the effectiveness and the adoption of these out-of-VM approaches.

In this paper, we present *process out-grafting*, an architectural approach that addresses both isolation and compatibility challenges for out-of-VM, fine-grained user-mode process execution monitoring. Similar to prior out-of-VM approaches, out-grafting still confines vulnerable systems as VMs and deploys security tools outside the VMs. However, instead of analyzing the entire VM on all running processes, out-grafting focuses on each individual process for fine-grained execution monitoring. More importantly, our approach is designed to naturally support existing user-mode process monitoring tools (e.g., *strace*, *ltrace*, and *gdb*) outside of monitored VMs on an internal suspect process, without the need of modifying these tools or making them introspection-aware (as required in prior out-of-VM approaches). For simplicity, we use the terms "production VM" and "security VM" respectively to represent the vulnerable VM that contains a suspect process and the analysis VM that hosts the security tool to monitor the suspect process.

To enable process out-grafting, we have developed two key techniques. Specifically, the first technique, *on-demand grafting*, relocates the suspect process on demand from the production VM to security VM (that contains the process monitoring tool as well as its supporting environment). By doing so, grafting effectively brings the suspect process to the monitor for fine-grained monitoring, which leads to at least two important benefits: (1) By co-locating the suspect process to run side-by-side with our monitor, the semantic gap caused by the VM isolation is effectively removed. In fact, from the monitor's perspective, it runs together with the suspect process inside the same system and based on its design can naturally monitor the suspect process without any modification. (2) In addition, the monitor can directly intercept or analyze the process execution even at the granularity of user-level function calls, without requiring hypervisor intervention, which has significant performance gains from existing introspection-based approaches.

To still effectively confine the (relocated) suspect process, our second technique enforces a mode-sensitive split execution of the process, thus the name *split execution*. Specifically, only the user-mode instructions of the suspect process, which is our main focus for fine-grained monitoring, will be allowed to execute in the security VM; all kernel-mode execution that requires the use of OS kernel system services is forwarded back to the production VM. By doing so, we can not only maintain a smooth continued execution of the suspect process after relocation, but ensure its isolation from our monitoring tools. Particularly, from the suspect process' perspective, it is still logically running inside the production VM. In the meantime, as the suspect process physically runs inside the security VM, the monitoring overhead will not be inflicted to the production VM, thus effectively localizing monitoring impact within the security VM.

We have implemented a proof-of-concept prototype on KVM/ Linux (version kvm-2.6.36.1) and tested it to out-graft various processes from different VMs running either Fedora 10 or Ubuntu 9.04. We have evaluated it with a number of different scenarios, including the use of traditional process monitoring tools, i.e., *strace*/*ltrace*/*gdb*, to monitor an out-grafted process from another VM. Note that these fine-grained process monitoring tools cannot be natively supported if the semantic gap is not effectively removed. Moreover, we also show that advanced (hardware-assisted) monitoring tools [26] can be deployed in the security VM to monitor a process in the production VM, while they may be inconvenient or even impossible to run inside the production VM. The performance evaluation with a number of standard benchmark programs shows that our prototype implementation incurs a small performance overhead and the monitoring overhead is largely confined within the security VM, not the production VM.

The rest of the paper is organized as follows: we first present the system design in Section 2. We then describe the implementation and evaluation in Sections 3 and 4, respectively. We discuss possible limitations and explore future improvements in Section 5. Finally, we describe related work in Section 6 and conclude the paper in Section 7.

2. SYSTEM DESIGN

2.1 Goals and Assumptions

Process out-grafting is a virtualization-based approach that advances current out-of-VM approaches for fine-grained process-level execution monitoring. It is introduced to effectively support existing user-mode process-level monitoring tools while removing the inherent semantic gap in out-of-VM approaches. To achieve that, we have three main design goals.

- *Isolation* Process out-grafting should strictly isolate process monitoring tools from the untrusted process. In other words, the untrusted process will be architecturally confined without unnecessarily exposing monitoring tools. This essentially achieves the same isolation guarantee as existing out-of-VM approaches.
- *Compatibility* Our solution should naturally support existing fine-grained process monitoring tools (e.g., *strace* /*ltrace*/*gdb*) without modification. Accordingly, all required semantic information by these tools need to be made available in the security VM.
- *Efficiency* Process out-grafting needs to efficiently support existing process monitoring tools without much additional performance overhead caused by isolation. Due to its process-level granularity, we also need to localize the monitoring overhead to the monitored process, without unnecessarily impacting the production VM as a whole.

In this work, we assume no trust from the suspect process being monitored. An attacker may also introduce malicious software (either user-mode or kernel-mode) to compromise the production VM. However, we assume the presence of a

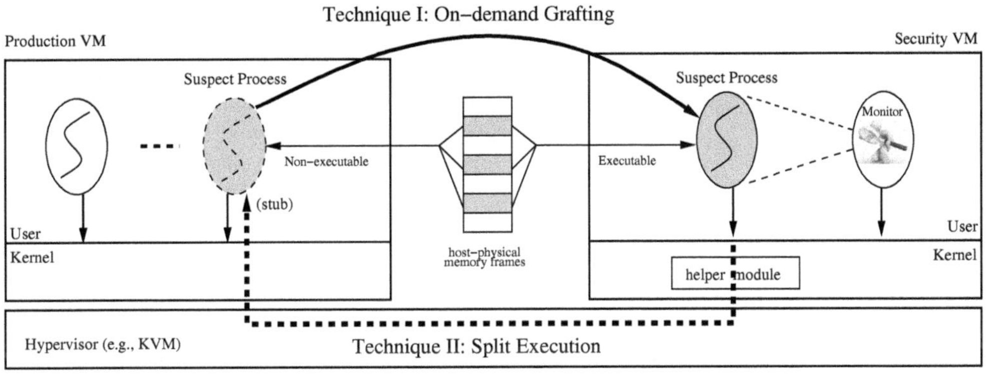

Figure 1: An Overview of Process Out-Grafting

trusted hypervisor [25, 40], which properly enforces the isolation between running VMs. By focusing on fine-grained user-mode process-level monitoring, our system does not address OS kernel monitoring. But a compromised OS kernel should not affect our design goals. Also, we do not attempt to hide the fact that an out-grafted process or malware is being actively monitored. But we do guarantee that the monitoring process itself cannot be disabled by the monitored process.

Figure 1 shows the overview of our system with two key techniques: *on-demand grafting* and *split execution*. Before presenting each technique in detail, we define some terminology used throughout the paper. Our system is designed to work with hardware virtualization extensions available in commodity CPUs, including support for efficient memory virtualization. Leveraging the underlying hardware support, a CPU can enter either host or guest mode. The hypervisor code runs directly in host mode while the VM runs in guest mode. In a virtualized system, there are three different kinds of memory addresses: A *guest-virtual* address is the virtual address observed by a running process inside the guest; a *guest-physical* address is the physical addresses seen by the guest when it runs in the guest mode; a *host-physical* address is the actual machine address seen by the CPU hardware. While executing in guest-mode, a VM never sees the host-physical addresses directly.

We point out that when memory virtualization support is enabled, the CPU utilizes an additional level of page tables managed by the hypervisor to translate from guest-physical to host-physical addresses (i.e., the Nested Page Table (NPT) [7] in AMD CPUs or the Extended Page Table (EPT) [18] in Intel CPUs). Since our current prototype uses an Intel processor, we simply use the term EPT to represent both. With that, the guest OS is free to manage its own guest-physical page frame allocation, with no intervention from the hypervisor. The hypervisor controls only the EPT to allocate host-physical memory, as needed for the guest. While the CPU EPT support significantly improves performance for the running VM [6, 7, 18], such support also poses challenges in our design and some of them will be highlighted below as we describe our system.

2.2 On-demand Grafting

Our first key technique is developed to re-locate a suspect process running in a production VM to a security VM for close inspection. Specifically, it enables efficient, native inspection from existing process-level monitoring tools by avoiding unnecessary hypervisor intervention and eliminating the inherent semantic gap from VM isolation. Relocating a suspect process can be initiated as determined by an administration policy, say a process can be brought under scrutiny either periodically, at random time intervals or using certain event triggers. The monitoring duration can be arbitrary, including the entire lifetime of a process. Regardless of the out-grafting policy, in this paper, we mainly focus on the mechanisms for the out-grafting support.

In order to out-graft a running process, we will need to first accurately locate it (e.g. using the base address of its page table directory). Once it is located, the hypervisor can then redirect or transfer its execution from the production VM into the security VM. In the following, we examine when, what, and how to transfer the suspect process execution across the two VMs.

2.2.1 When to Out-graft

To determine the appropriate moment for process execution transfer, we need to ensure it is safe to do so, i.e., the transfer will not corrupt the execution of the out-grafted process and the OS kernel. Particularly, once a process is selected for out-grafting, the hypervisor first pauses the production VM, which is akin to a *VM Exit* event and causes the VM's virtual CPU (VCPU) state to be stored in hypervisor-accessible memory. At this particular time, the to-be-grafted process may be running in either user- or kernel-mode. (If it is not actively running, it is then waiting in the kernel-mode to be selected or dispatched for execution.) If the VCPU state indicates the VCPU is executing the process in user mode, we can immediately start out-grafting the process.

On the other hand, if the VCPU was running in privileged mode (in the context of either the suspect process or another process), we should not start the out-grafting process to avoid leading to any inconsistency. For example, the suspect process may have made a system call to write a large memory buffer to a disk file. If its execution is transferred at this point to another VM, we may somehow immediately resume execution (in the security VM) at the next user-mode instruction following the system call. As we are only transferring the user-mode execution, this will implicitly assume the production VM kernel has already completed servicing the system call, which may not be the case. Therefore, we choose to wait till the process is selected to execute and eventually returns to user-mode. One way the hypervisor could detect this is by monitoring context switches that occur inside the VM. However, in systems that support EPT, the hypervisor is no longer notified of in-VM context switches. Instead, based on the process' page tables, we mark the

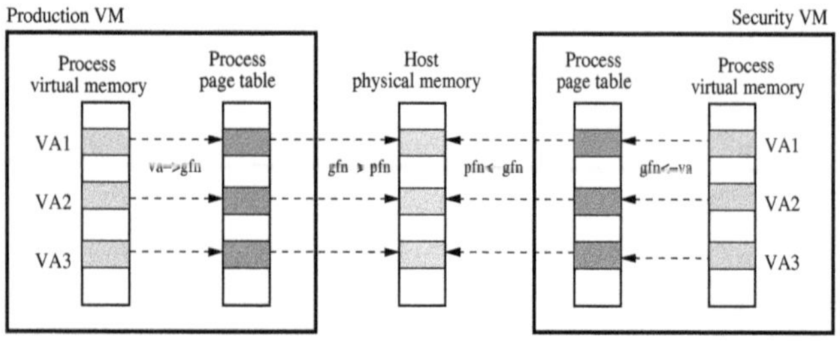

Figure 2: Out-grafted Process Memory Mapping in Production and Security VMs (*va*: virtual address; *gfn*: guest frame number; *pfn*: physical frame number)

corresponding user-level host-physical pages non-executable (NX) in the EPT. When the kernel returns control of the process back to user-mode, it will immediately cause a trap to the hypervisor and thus kick off our out-grafting process.

2.2.2 What to Out-graft

After determining the right moment, we then identify the relevant state that is needed to continue the process execution in the security VM. As our focus is primarily on its user-mode execution, we need to transfer execution states that the user-mode code can directly access (i.e. its code and data). It turns out that we only need to transfer two sets of states associated with the process: the execution context (e.g., register content) and its memory page frames. The hypervisor already identifies the process' register values from the VCPU state (stored in the hypervisor-accessible memory). To identify its memory page frames, we simply walk through the guest OS-maintained page tables (located from the guest *CR3*) to identify the guest-physical page frames for the user-mode memory of the process. For each such page, we then further identify the corresponding host-physical page frame from the EPT. At the same time, we mark NX bit on each user-mode page frame in EPT that belongs to the process. (Although this seems to duplicate the setting from Section 2.2.1, this is required in case the guest OS may allocate new pages right before we start to out-graft.) After that, if the user-level code is executed, inadvertently or maliciously, when the process has been out-grafted for monitoring, the hypervisor will be notified. Note that we mark the NX bit in the EPT, which is protected from the (untrusted) production VM.

We point out that the transferred resources or state do not include those OS kernel-specific states, which the process may access only via system calls (e.g. open file descriptors and active TCP network connections). This is important from at least three different aspects. First, the OS kernel-specific states are the main root cause behind the semantic gap challenge. Without the need of interpreting them, we can effectively remove the gap. Second, keeping these specific states within the production VM is also necessary to ensure smooth continued execution of the out-grafted process in the security VM – as the system call will be redirected back to the production VM. It also allows for later process restoration. Third, it reduces the state volume that needs to be transferred and thus alleviates the out-grafting overhead.

2.2.3 How to Out-graft

Once we identify those states (e.g., the execution state and related memory pages), we then accordingly instantiate them in the security VM. There are two main steps. First, we lock down the guest page table of the out-grafted process in the production VM. Specifically, we mark the page frames that contain the process' page table entries as read-only in the EPT so that any intended or unintended changes to them (e.g. allocating a new page or swapping out an existing page) will be trapped by the hypervisor. This is needed to keep in-sync with the out-grafted process in the security VM. These hardware-related settings are the only interposition we need from the hypervisor, which are completely transparent to, and independent of the monitoring tools (in the security VM). The lock-down of page tables is due to the previously described lack of hypervisor intervention over in-guest page tables. In our system, these settings are temporary and only last for the duration of our monitoring.

Second, we then populate the transferred states in the security VM. For simplicity, we collectively refer to those states as S_{rd}. For this, we prepare a helper kernel module (LKM) running inside the security VM. The hypervisor issues an upcall to the helper module to instantiate S_{rd}. In that case, the helper module retrieves S_{rd} and creates a process context within the security VM for the out-grafted process to execute. At this point, the memory content of the process needs to be transferred from the production VM to the security VM. In a non-EPT supported system, the hypervisor could simply duplicate the page table between the production and security VMs. In the presence of EPT however, we aim to avoid large memory transfers by enabling the memory transfer as follows: The helper module allocates the guest-physical page frames for those virtual addresses that were present in S_{rd} and sends this information to the hypervisor; The hypervisor then simply maps each such page to the host-physical page frame for the corresponding virtual address in the production VM. In other words, this mechanism ensures that a user-level virtual address A of the out-grafted process in the security VM and the user-level virtual address A of the process in the production VM are ultimately mapped to the same host-physical page (as illustrated in Figure 2). After that, the helper also ensures that any system call from the out-grafted process will not be serviced in the security VM. Instead, they will be forwarded back to the production VM and handled by our second key technique (Section 2.3).

When a process is out-grafted for monitoring, its state in the production VM is not destroyed. As mentioned earlier, the production VM still maintains the related kernel state, which not only serves the forwarded system calls but also greatly facilitates the later restoration of the process from the security VM back to the production VM. Meanwhile, because of the separate maintenance of the process page tables inside both VMs, we need to ensure they are kept in-sync. In particular, the production VM may make legitimate changes (e.g. swapping out a page). To reflect these changes back in the security VM, our previous read-only marking on related page tables can timely intercept any changes and then communicate the changes back to the security VM.

With the populated states in a new process inside the security VM, existing process-level monitoring tools such as *strace*, *ltrace*, and *gdb* can naturally access its state or monitor its execution. For example, when the out-grafted process executes system call instructions in the security VM (although they are not actually serviced by the security VM kernel), these can be examined in a semantically-rich manner (i.e., interpreting the arguments) without any modification to existing tools. Specifically, different from prior out-of-VM approaches, the monitor in our case no longer needs to walk through external page tables to identify the physical addresses for examination. In other words, they can be transparently supported! Finally, in order to support tools that may need to access disk files used by the monitored process, we make the file system that is used by the production VM available in the security VM. We mount this file system as read-only and non-executable. Note that the file system is accessed only by the monitor to access any semantic information. The requests by the out-grafted process to access files are not handled in the security VM, but in the production VM through forwarded system calls.

2.3 Mode-sensitive Split Execution

After selecting and out-grafting a process to the security VM, our second key technique ensures that it can smoothly continue its execution in the security VM, even though the out-grafted process may consider itself still running inside the same production VM. Also, we ensure that the untrusted process cannot tamper with the security VM, including the security VM's kernel and the runtime environment (libraries, log files etc.). We achieve this by splitting the monitored process' execution between the two VMs: all user-mode instructions execute in the security VM while the rest execute in the production VM. In the following, we describe related issues in realizing this mechanism and our solutions.

2.3.1 System Call Redirection

To continue the out-grafted process execution and isolate it from the security VM, there is a need for it to access the kernel-specific resources or states maintained in the production VM. For instance, if the process already opened a file for writing data, after the relocation to the security VM, it must be able to continue writing to it. As the process needs to make system calls to access them, we therefore intercept and forward any system call from the out-grafted process back to the production VM.

To achieve that, there exist two different approaches. The first one is to simply ask hypervisor to intervene and forward the system call (by crafting an interrupt and preparing the appropriate execution context). However, it will unfortunately impact the entire production VM execution. The second one is to have a small piece of stub in place of the out-grafted process. The stub is mainly designed to receive forwarded system calls from the security VM, invoke the same in the production VM, and then return the results back to the security VM. We take the second approach in our design as it can effectively localize the effect within the out-grafted process itself and avoid heavy hypervisor intervention for every forwarded system call.

The placement of the stub code deserves additional consideration. Since the guest page tables are not managed by the hypervisor, it cannot simply allocate a separate guest-physical page for the stub code. As our solution, we choose to temporarily "steal" an existing code page in the process, by saving the original content aside and overlaying it with the stub's code. Recall (from Section 2.2) that the host-physical memory frames corresponding to the process address space are mapped in both VMs. To steal a code page, the corresponding host-physical page frame is replaced with another one that contains the stub code. To protect it from

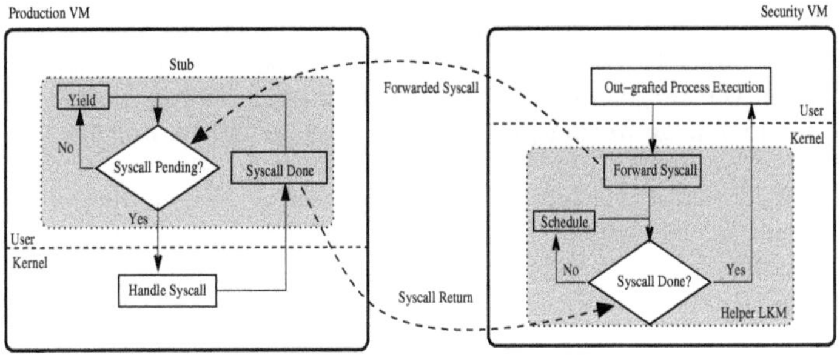

Figure 3: The Interplay Between the Stub (in Production VM) and the Helper LKM (in Security VM)

being tampered by the production VM, we mark it non-writable in the production VM's EPT for the duration of out-grafting.

The stub's main function is to proxy the forwarded system call from the security VM and replay it in the production VM. In order to facilitate direct communication without requiring hypervisor intervention, during the out-grafting phase, we set up a small shared communication buffer accessible to the stub and the helper module in the security VM. Also, note that if a system call argument is a pointer to some content in the process address space, our design ensures that there is no need to copy this data between the production and security VM. Since the process' memory is mapped in both VMs, the production VM kernel can simply access this as it would for any regular process. This eliminates unnecessary memory copy overhead.

An interesting dilemma arises if the stub code needs to use the stack. Specifically, the process' stack is part of its data pages and these pages are mapped faithfully in both VMs. Any user-space instructions in the out-grafted process will use this memory region as the stack. Further, these memory regions may also contain the arguments to be passed down to the production VM kernel for system calls. Hence, the stub code cannot use the original stack pointer as its stack frame, or it will collide with the user-mode execution in the security VM. In our design, we simply avoid using the stack in the stub code execution.

The interplay between the stub code and our helper module is shown in Figure 3. The stub code is self-contained and will directly invoke system calls without relying on any additional library calls. Its size has been kept to the minimum since we are overlaying over existing code memory for this. Also, the stub can handle signals from the production VM kernel and communicate them to the security VM helper module. Specifically, when the production VM invokes a previously registered signal handler, it will cause an exit to the hypervisor, which will be eventually relayed to the helper module to deliver the same signal to the out-grafted process for handling.

2.3.2 Page Fault Forwarding

In addition to forwarding system calls, we also need to forward the related page faults for the out-grafted process. More specifically, at the time when a process' execution is being redirected to the security VM, some of its pages may not be present (e.g., due to demand paging). Hence, when the process is executing in the security VM, if it accesses a non-present page, it will be trapped. Since the security VM has no knowledge of how to correctly allocate and populate a new page (e.g., in case of a file-mapped page), we forward page faults to the production VM. This also ensures that when the production VM kernel attempts to access a new memory page during process execution, it will be immediately available.

To forward related page faults, out helper module in the security VM registers itself to receive notification from the security VM kernel for any page fault (or protection fault) related to the out-grafted process. When it receives such a notification, it places the virtual address that causes the page fault and a flag to indicate a read-fault (including instruction fetches) or a write-fault, in the communication buffer and notifies the stub in the production VM. To service a page fault, the stub will attempt to either read in a byte from the address or write a byte to the address. This will cause the same page fault in the production VM. After completing this read or write, the stub sends a notification back to our helper module. The stub's write to the memory will be immediately overwritten with the correct value by the out-grafted processes when it re-executes a faulting instruction, thus ensuring correct process execution. Unlike a system call return value, the stub cannot return the guest-physical page allocated for the new address in the production VM. Instead, since we have write-protected the process page tables, when the production VM makes a change to it (i.e. to set the page table entries for the new page), this is intercepted by the hypervisor and our helper module will be notified. After that, it then allows the page fault handling routines in the security VM to continue processing. As previously described, instead of duplicating a memory page, we simply tell the hypervisor to map the same host-physical memory page corresponding to new page in the production VM.

Later on, if we decide not to continue monitoring the out-grafted process, we can place it back in the production VM. In this case, since we have already maintained synchronized page tables between the two VMs, we only need to restore the execution context states back in the production VM. For those memory pages overlaid for the stub use, they need to be properly restored as well. Specifically, if we find the VCPU was executing stub code, which is located in the user mode, we can simply change the VCPU state contents to restore the execution context. Otherwise, we need to detect when the user-mode execution resumes by marking the stub's code page as NX and then restore the VCPU values. In the security VM, any state for the out-grafted process is then simply destroyed (i.e. guest-physical page frames allocated to it are freed and helper module requests the hypervisor to release the mappings in the security VM EPT).

3. IMPLEMENTATION

We have implemented a process out-grafting prototype by extending the open-source KVM [2] hypervisor (version 2.6.36.1). All modifications required to support out-grafting are contained within the KVM module and no changes are required to the host OS. Our implementation increases KVM's 36.5K SLOC (x86 support only) by only 1309 SLOC, since most functionality required for out-grafting (e.g. manipulating a VM's architectural state) is already present in the stock KVM. Our prototyping machine runs Ubuntu 10.04 (Linux kernel 2.6.28) with an Intel Core i7 CPU and hardware virtualization support (including EPT). Though our prototype is developed on KVM, we believe it can be similarly implemented on other hypervisors such as Xen and VMware ESX. Our current prototype supports both 32-bit Fedora 10 and Ubuntu 9.04 as guests (either as the production VM or the security VM). In the rest of this section, we present details about our KVM-based prototype with Intel VT support.

3.1 On-demand Grafting

KVM is implemented as a loadable kernel module (LKM), which once loaded extends the host into a hypervisor. Each KVM-powered guest VM runs as a process on the host OS, which can execute privileged instructions directly on the CPU (in the so-called guest mode based on hardware virtualization support). The VM's virtual devices are emulated by a user-level program called QEMU [4] that has a well-defined *ioctl*-based interface to interact with the KVM module. In our prototype, we extend the interface to define the out-grafting command *graft_process*. This command accepts a valid page table base address (or guest *cr3*) to directly locate the process that needs to be out-grafted. The guest *cr3* could be retrieved either by converting from the process ID or process name via VM introspection, or directly reading from the guest kernel with a loadable kernel module.

Once the *graft_process* command is issued, the KVM module pauses the VM execution, which automatically saves the VM execution context information in the VM control structure (VMCS [19]). KVM provides a number of functions that wrap CPU-specific instructions to read and write to different fields in this VMCS structure. From this structure, we retrieve the current value of the VM's *cr3* register and compare with the argument to the *graft_process*. If they match and the current VCPU is running in user-mode, we then read the VCPU's register values (eax, ebx, esp etc.) and store them in memory. Otherwise, we take a walk through the process page table from the given base address to locate all the user-mode guest-physical page frames (*gfn*) used by the to-be-grafted process. Using the *gfn_to_pfn()* function in KVM, we obtain the host-physical page frames (*pfn*) and set the NX bit in the VM's EPT. As a result, when the VCPU returns back to execute any user-mode instruction in this process, an *EPT violation* occurs and the control is transferred to KVM. At this point, KVM can read the register values from VMCS and save a copy.

After retrieving its execution context (i.e., those register values), we then examine the page table (from the given base address) to determine which virtual addresses in the suspect process have pages allocated or present. That is, it determines the *gfn* for each virtual address and then invokes *gfn_to_pfn()* to determine the corresponding *pfn* in the production VM's EPT. KVM stores this information in a local buffer. It then makes an upcall in the form of a virtual IRQ to the security VM (using the *inject_irq()* function).

In the security VM, we have implemented a helper module which is registered to handle this (virtual) IRQ. The helper module then instantiates a process context for the out-grafted process so that it can continue the execution. Specifically, it first allocates a memory buffer and makes a hypercall to KVM with the address of this memory buffer, so that KVM can copy the state S_{rd} to it. Since spawning a new process is a complex task, our helper module creates a simple "dummy" process in the security VM, which executes in an infinite sleep loop. Upon the IRQ request from KVM, it proceeds to replace the dummy process with the out-grafted process state. Specifically, our helper module retrieves register values from S_{rd} and instantiates them in the dummy process (using the *pt_regs* structure) After that, we simply destroy any pages (i.e., via *do_unmap()*) allocated to the dummy process and then allocate "new" pages for virtual addresses, as indicated in S_{rd}. Note that we do not actually allocate new host-physical memory pages to accommodate these transferred memory pages. Instead, KVM simply maps (*__direct_map()*) those host-physical memory frames that are used by the out-grafted process to the dummy process in the security VM. After the mapping, the out-grafted process is ready to execute its user-mode instructions in the security VM. An execution monitor (such as *strace*) in this security VM can now intercept the process-related events it is interested in.

3.2 Mode-sensitive Split Execution

After relocating the suspect process to the security VM, any system call made from it will be intercepted by our helper module and forwarded back to the production VM. Specifically, our helper module wraps the exposed system call interface in the security VM to the out-grafted process. For each intercepted system call, we collect the corresponding system call number and its argument values in a data structure (*sc_info*) and save it in the shared communication buffer so the stub code in production VM will pick it up to invoke the actual system call. (As noted in Section 2.3.1, memory contents for pointer arguments are not copied since the user-level memory is present in both VMs).

More specifically, the stub code is created when the process is being out-grafted from the production VM to the security VM. Its main purpose is to proxy the forwarded system calls from the security VM to the production VM. As mentioned in Section 2.3.1, we need to "steal" an existing code page to host the stub code. We have written the stub code in a few lines of assembly with an overall size of 167 bytes. The stub code itself does not make any use of a stack while executing (Section 2.3.1). Similarly, with the help of KVM, we set up a shared communication buffer between the stub code and our helper module. When a system call is to be forwarded to the production VM, our helper module copies the *sc_info* data structure described above to this buffer. It then sets a flag (in the same buffer) to indicate to the stub that a new system call is to be serviced and waits in a loop for this flag to be cleared by the stub. To avoid blocking the entire security VM during this time, it yields from inside the loop.

The stub code checks the flag and then retrieves the *sc_info* values and copies them to the registers in the production VM. It then invokes the requested system call so that the production kernel can service the request. Once the request is complete, the stub places the return value in the buffer and modifies the flag indicating service completion. After that, our helper module in the security VM can now return the same value to the out-grafted process. In addition to forwarding system calls from the out-grafted process, we also need to forward related page faults to the production VM. Naturally, we leverage the above communication channel between the stub code and our helper module. Specifically, when a page fault occurs in the out-grafted process (while running in the security VM), the security VM's page fault handler invokes a callback defined in our helper module, which then forwards the page fault information to the stub. Based on the fault information, the stub either reads or writes a dummy value in the faulting address in the production VM to trigger a page fault of the same nature in the production VM. When the page fault handler in the production VM attempts to update the page tables with a new page table entry (pointing to a new page frame we denote by *gfn_p*), this causes an "EPT violation" and control is transferred to KVM. KVM examines the root cause and saves a copy of the *gfn_p->pfn* mapping while fixing the violation and resuming the production VM. The helper module notifies KVM with the new guest-physical frame it allocated in the security VM (*gfn_s*). KVM then maps *gfn_s* to *pfn* and ensures the same memory content is available in both VMs. After that, the out-grafted process can continue its execution with the new memory page.

3.3 Process Restoration

In our prototype, process out-grafting is initiated through a QEMU command *graft_process*. As mentioned earlier, other mechanisms can also be added to trigger the out-grafting process. An example is an event-based trigger that runs inside the production VM (Section 4).

In our current prototype, we also implemented another QEMU command *restore_process*, which can be invoked to notify KVM (via an *ioctl* interface) to restore the out-grafted process back to the production VM. Similar to the out-grafting procedure, when KVM receives the *restore_process* command, it injects an IRQ to the security VM, which will be received by the helper module. If the module is currently waiting on a forwarded system call's completion, the restoration operation cannot be immediately carried out. Instead, it will wait for the completion of the system call. After that, it fetches register values stored in the process' *pt_regs* data structure and sends this down to KVM with a hypercall. KVM then restores this register state back in the production VM. Due to the similarity with the earlier out-grafting steps, we omit the details here. The key difference however is that, instead of copying values *from* the VCPU fields, we copy values *to* it. For the page tables, as they are kept in-sync between the two VMs, no further actions will be needed. For those process contexts and guest memory pages allocated to the out-grafted process in the security VM, we simply discard them. At this point, the process can seamlessly resume its execution in the production VM.

4. EVALUATION

In this section, we first perform a security analysis on the isolation property from our approach. Then, we present case studies with a number of execution monitoring tools. Finally, we report the performance overhead with several standard benchmarks.

4.1 Security Analysis

Monitor isolation and effectiveness To allow for fine-grained out-of-VM process monitoring, one key goal is to ensure that the process monitoring tool and its supporting environment cannot be tampered with or disabled by the out-grafted process. In the following, we examine possible attacks and show how our system can effectively defend against them. Specifically, one main way that a suspect process can tamper with another process (or the monitor in our case) is through system calls. However, such attack will not work since our system strictly forwards all system calls from the suspect process back to the production VM. Moreover, the controlled interaction is only allowed from the monitoring process to the suspect process, *not* the other way around. From another perspective, the suspect process may choose to attack the (production VM) OS kernel when it services system calls (for e.g. exploiting a buffer overflow by sending in an invalid argument). Such attack will only impact the production VM and its own execution.

According to our threat model (Section 2), we stress that our system does not attempt to guarantee stealthy monitoring as out-grafted monitoring could be detected by sophisticated malware. But we do enable reliable monitoring in protecting our system from being tampered with by the suspect process. In addition, a strong administrative policy might reduce the time window for such out-grafting detection. For example, out-grafting can be initiated randomly (at any instance in a process' lifetime) and can span arbitrary durations. In such cases, malware would be forced to continuously check for out-grafting which can be costly and expose its presence. Note that the out-grafted process is ultimately serviced by the untrusted production VM, and as such, we cannot guarantee that it accurately services the out-grafted process' system calls, but any inappropriate handling of system calls will not violate the isolation provided by our approach.

Protection of helper components The out-grafting operation itself is initiated and controlled by the hypervisor and cannot be disabled by a malicious production VM kernel. However, there are two helper components in the production VM to support out-grafting: the stub code and shared communication buffer, which may be open to attack. We point out that since the stub code's host-physical page is marked as read-only in the EPT, any malicious attempts to write to it will be trapped by the hypervisor. The stub code's guest virtual-to-physical mapping cannot be altered by the production VM since the page tables of the process are write-protected by the hypervisor. The untrusted kernel in the production VM is responsible for scheduling the stub process as well as saving and restoring its execution context according to the scheduling policy. If it tampers with the execution context states (such as the instruction pointer), then the stub code itself will not execute correctly, which cascadingly affects the execution of the suspect process itself. As mentioned earlier, if the production VM does not properly serve the forwarded system calls or attempts to alter the system call arguments or return incorrect results, such behavior may result in incorrect execution for the out-grafted process, but will not affect the isolation or the integrity of our monitoring process.

4.2 Case Studies

Next, we describe experiments with a number of execution monitoring tools, including the most common ones: *strace*, *ltrace*, *gdb*, as well as an OmniUnpack[26]-based tool (to detect malware unpacking behavior). The common tools are used to demonstrate the effectiveness of our approach in removing the semantic-gap, while the OmniUnpack tool requires special hardware support for the monitoring in the security VM and such support may not be enabled or provided in production VM. As a test process for out-grafting, we chose the *thttpd* web server that uses both disk and network resources and has a performance benchmark tool readily available to automatically exercise it.

4.2.1 Tracing System Calls

In our first experiment, we demonstrate semantically-rich system call tracing. This type of monitoring has been widely applied to detect malicious behavior [13] such as accesses to sensitive resources or dangerous system calls. For this, we install the standard Linux *strace* tool in the security VM. *strace* makes use of the underlying OS facilities to monitor system calls invoked by another running process, which in our case logically runs in another VM. For each intercepted system call, it retrieves and parses the arguments. The results will allow us to know what file was opened by a process, what data is read from it etc.

In prior "out-of-VM" systems, the code to determine system call number and interpret each of its arguments has to be completely re-written. In fact, one of our earlier systems, i.e., VMscope [20], took one of the co-authors more than one month to correctly intercept and parse the arguments of around 300 system calls supported in recent Linux kernels. This task is expected to become even more complicated especially for closed-source OSs.

To better understand the effectiveness, we perform a comparative study. Specifically, we first run *strace* inside the production VM to monitor invoked system calls from *thttp* when it handles an incoming HTTP request. After that, we out-graft *thttp* and run *strace* in the security VM for out-of-VM monitoring when it handles another incoming HTTP request. Our results are shown in Figure 4. From the figure, we can verify that both *strace* runs lead to the same system call patterns in the handling of incoming HTTP requests by accurately capturing system calls invoked by the same *thttpd* process and interpreting each related argument.

4.2.2 Tracing User-level Library Calls

In our second experiment, we show the capability of reusing existing tools for user-level library call tracing. User-level library call tracing is a fine-grained monitoring technique that allows for understanding which library functions are being used by a running process and what are their arguments. It has advantages over system call tracing in collecting semantically-rich information at a higher abstraction level.

As one can envision, the number of library functions available to a program and the type and definition of each argument for such functions can be very large. This can make it complex, expensive, or even impossible to examine such events in a semantically-rich manner using prior "out-of-VM" approaches. Fortunately, in our approach, we can simply re-use an existing tool *ltrace* to intercept and interpret user-level library calls of a running process in one VM from another different VM. In our experiment, we found that *ltrace* extracts process symbol information from the process' binary image on disk. As we mounted the production VM's filesystem read-only in the security VM, *ltrace* works naturally with no changes needed. Our results show that *ltrace* indeed accurately captures and interprets the user-level library calls invoked by the out-grafted *thttpd* process. In a similar setting, we replace *ltrace* with *gdb*, which essentially allows for debugging an in-VM process from outside the VM!

4.2.3 Detecting Malware Unpacking Behavior

Most recent malware apply obfuscation techniques to evade existing malware detection tools. Code packing is one of the popular obfuscation techniques [17]. To detect packed code,

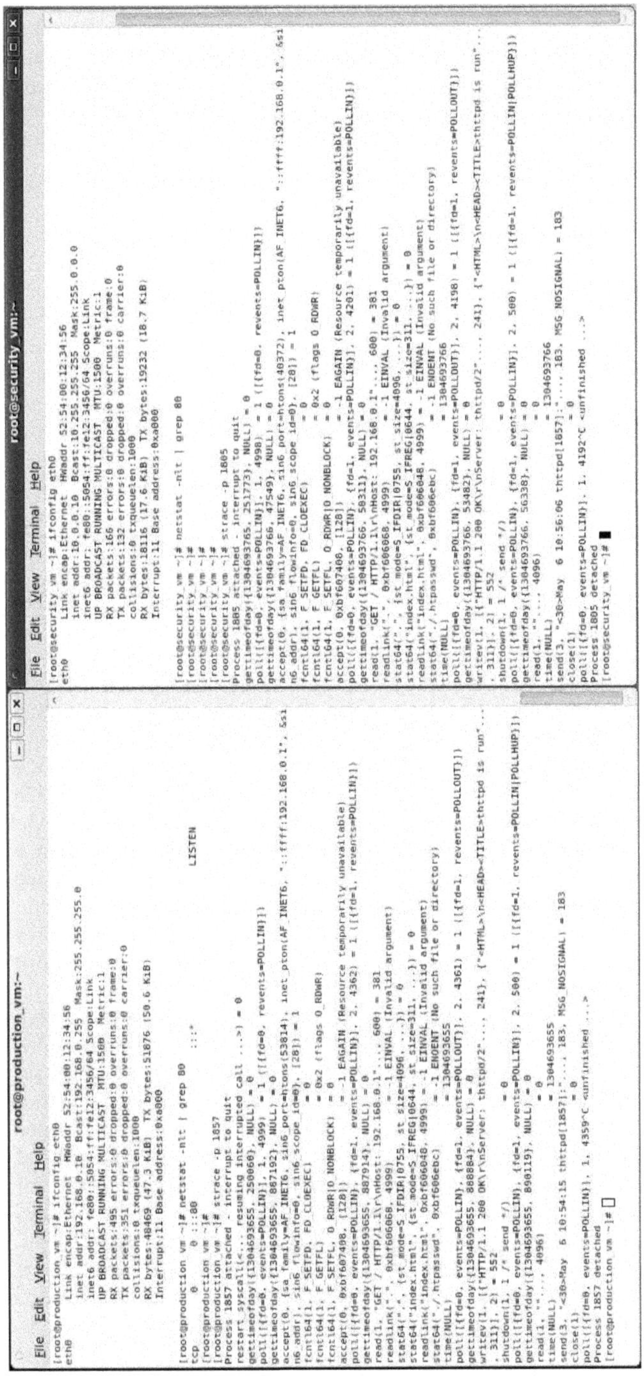

Figure 4: Comparison of strace results of the thttpd server when running inside the VM (on the bottom) and out-grafted to another VM (on the top)

efficient behavioral monitoring techniques such as OmniUnpack [26] have been developed to perform real-time monitoring of a process' behavior by tracking the pages it writes to and then executes from. When the process invokes a "dangerous" system call, OmniUnpack looks up its page list to determine whether any previously written page has been executed from. If so, this indicates packing behavior, at which point a signature-based anti-virus tool can be invoked to check the process' memory for known malware. Since OmniUnpack was developed only for Windows and also is not open source, we wrote a Linux tool that faithfully implements OmniUnpack's algorithm. We stress that if OmniUnpack was previously available for Linux, this porting step would not be necessary. In our Linux porting, we do not need to bridge the semantic gap or be aware of any prior introspection techniques. Instead, we just envision a Linux tool that will be used *in-host*. This experience also demonstrates the benefits from our approach.

In our test, we use the freely available UPX packer [5] to pack the Kaiten bot binary [1]. In this experiment, we also utilize a security-sensitive event trigger that initiates out-grafting when a suspect process invokes the *sys_execve* system call. The trigger is placed such that just before the system call returns to user-mode (to execute the first instruction of the new code), KVM is invoked to out-graft the process' execution to the security VM. Inside the security VM, we run the OmniUnpack tool to keep track of page accesses by the process. Since the system calls invoked by the process are also available for monitoring, OmniUnpack successfully detects the packing behavior.

We highlight several interesting aspects this experiment demonstrates. In the past, packer detection has required a trade-off between tool isolation and performance overhead. Specifically, in-host tools [26, 33], including OmniUnpack can efficiently detect packing behavior, but they are vulnerable to attack. "Out-of-VM" techniques [11] ensure packer detection is isolated, but introduce very high overhead, largely limiting its usability for offline malware analysis, not online monitoring. Using process out-grafting, we are able to effectively move an in-host tool "out-of-VM" without introducing significant overhead while still providing the needed isolation. Another interesting aspect is due to the fact that OmniUnpack requires the NX bit in the guest-page tables. For 32-bit Linux, this bit is available only if PAE support is enabled. In our experiments, we enabled PAE only in the security VM, whereas in the production VM page tables, the NX bit is still not available. Thus, if the monitoring tool requires additional features or support from the underlying OS, even if this support is not present in the production VM, we can take advantage of it in the security VM. Also, we point out that the process out-grafting happens at the very beginning of its execution. When a process begins execution, most of its code pages are not yet mapped in by the OS. As such, this experiment also thoroughly tests the page fault forwarding mechanisms in our system (Section 2.3).

4.3 Performance

To evaluate the performance overhead of our system, we measure two different aspects: the slowdown experienced by the production VM when a process is out-grafted for monitoring as well as the slowdown to the out-grafted process itself. The platform we use is a Dell T1500 system containing an Intel Core i7 processor with 4 cores, running at 2.6 GHz, and 4 GB RAM. The host OS is 32-bit Ubuntu 10.04 (Linux kernel 2.6.32) and the guests run 32-bit Fedora 10 (Linux kernel 2.6.27). Both VMs are configured with 1 virtual CPU each. The production VM is configured with 2047 MB memory and the security VM is configured with 1 GB memory. Table 1 lists the detailed configuration. In all experiments, the two VMs are pinned to run on separate CPU cores in the host (using the Linux *taskset* command).

Production VM overhead First, we measure the slowdown experienced by the VM (i.e. other normal pro-

Table 1: Software Packages in Our Evaluation

Name	Version	Configuration
Host OS	Ubuntu 10.04	Linux-2.6.32
Guest OS	Fedora 10	Linux-2.6.27
SPEC CPU 2006	1.0.1	integer suite
Apache	2.2.10	ab -c 3 -t 60
thttpd	2.25b	ab -c 1 -t 60

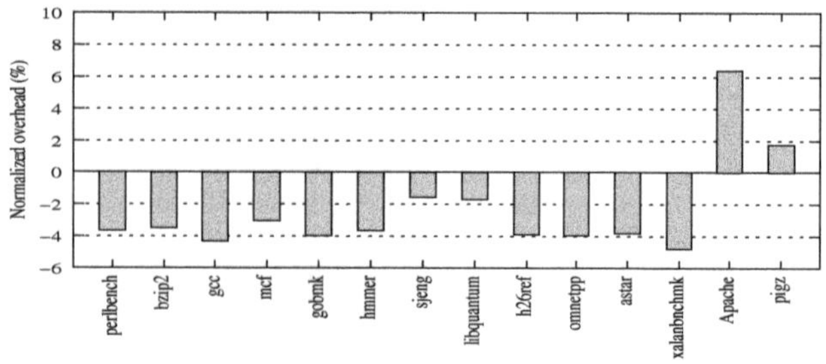

Figure 5: Production VM Slowdown with a Contending Process Out-grafted

cesses running in it) when we out-graft an unrelated process for monitoring. Specifically, we choose a standard CPU benchmark program, i.e., SPEC CPU 2006, and run it twice (1) either with another CPU-intensive process that spins in an infinite loop inside the same VM (2) or with the CPU-intensive process out-grafted to another VM. Our results show benchmarks experience speedups after out-grafting the CPU-intensive process. This is expected as a contending process has been moved to execute in a different VM for monitoring, which is running on a different core. This also confirms the monitoring overhead has been localized inside the security VM, not the production VM. Next, we measure the impact to *Apache* and *pigz* (or parallel *gzip*) when they run together either with *thttp* out-grafted or not. In our experiments, *Apache* and *thttpd* listen on different TCP ports, but their network traffic is handled by the same production VM kernel. Our results are shown in Figure 5. It is interesting to note that when *thttpd* is out-grafted, it is scheduled more often (since both *Apache* and *pigz* dominate it when they run in the same VM). However, the redirected system calls from *thttpd* will not get serviced until the stub is scheduled for execution in the production VM, thus its impact to the dominant processes is still low. Finally, we also measured the time it takes to identify the state for out-grafting during which time the production VM is paused. While this would vary depending on the memory size of a process, we observed an average time of $\sim 250\mu s$ in our current experiments. Opportunities still exist to further reduce it (e.g., with lazy updates – Section 5).

Out-grafted process slowdown Second, we measure the slowdown an out-grafted process may experience due to the fact that it is running in a different VM. For this, we first measure slowdown in two out-grafted processes: (1) The first one is a simple file copy command that transfers a *tar* file (421MB) from one directory to another in the production VM, which will result in lots of file-accessing system calls being forwarded. (2) The second is *thttpd*, for which we generate traffic using the *ab* benchmark program. In each set of experiments above, we have rebooted both VMs and physical machine after each run to avoid any caching interference. The average slowdown experienced by them is 35.42% and 7.38%, respectively. Moreover, we run a micro-benchmark program to measure the system call delay experienced by *sys_getpid()*. Our result shows that the average time of invoking *sys_getpid()* is $\sim 11\mu s$. As *sys_getpid()* simply obtains the process ID (after it has been forwarded), its slowdown is approximately equivalent to the system call forwarding latency.

5. DISCUSSION

While our prototype demonstrates promising effectiveness and practicality, it still has several limitations that can be improved. For example, our current prototype only supports out-grafting of a single process. A natural extension will be the support of multiple processes for simultaneous out-grafting. Note it is cumbersome and inefficient to iterate the out-grafting operation for each individual process. From another perspective, simultaneous out-grafting of multiple processes can also lead to the unique scenario where multiple security VMs can be engaged in monitoring different groups of out-grafted processes or different aspects of behavior.

Also, our current way of handling *sys_execve()* can be improved. Specifically, as this system call will completely change the memory layout of the out-grafted process, our current prototype simply chooses to first restore the process back to the production VM and then out-graft again the process immediately after this system call is completed by the production VM. Though this approach can leverage the functionalities we already implemented for *graft_process* and *restore_process*, an integrated solution is still desired. Moreover, our current prototype proactively maps all the (user-mode) memory pages at the very beginning when a process is out-grafted. A better solution will be to only map the currently executing code page to the security VM. For the rest of the pages, they can be lazily mapped when they are being actually accessed. This could further improve our system performance.

One caveat we experienced in our prototype development is related to shared pages. Specifically, most commodity OSs map the same physical pages for common shared library code among different processes. In our system, this means that a single host-physical page can contain code that is used across multiple processes in the production VM. Recall that our system directly maps this host-physical page to the out-grafted process in the security VM. If the monitoring tool modifies such code page (say to install certain code hooks), this could alter other process' behavior in the production VM. Fortunately, this can be resolved in a straightforward manner by co-operating the helper module and KVM to mark all executable code pages for the out-grafted process as read-only in the EPT. By applying the classic copy-on-write technique, if the monitor process (*not* the out-grafted process) attempts to write to this page, a separate copy of the page can be created.

Finally, with the wide adoption of virtualization in data centers, we also envision that different security VMs can be dispatched to each physical machine to inspect running guest VMs and their internal processes (for fine-grained execution monitoring). This is largely feasible as the semantic gap has been effectively bridged to support existing monitoring tools. On the other hand, with our current focus on examining individual suspect process for malicious behavior, we believe other interesting applications and opportunities (e.g., performance monitoring and intelligent parallel job scheduling) remain, which we plan to explore in the future.

6. RELATED WORK

Virtualization has been widely proposed to address various computer system problems, including enhancing the effectiveness and robustness of host-based monitoring tools. Specifically, it has been applied in offline malware analysis [9, 11], honeypot-based malware capture [20], intrusion analysis [23, 24] and malware detection [15, 21]. Among the most notable, Livewire [15] pioneered the concept of placing a monitor "out-of-VM" and applying VM introspection techniques to understand in-VM activities. A number of recent systems address the inherent semantic gap challenge to improve VM introspection for various purposes [8, 10, 21, 30, 31, 37]. For instance, one recent work Virtuoso [12] aims to effectively automate the process of building introspection-based security tools. Another system [10] proposes injecting stealthy agents into a monitored VM to solve the semantic gap problem and enhance out-of-VM tools. Similar to most of these efforts, our approach places security tools out-of-VM. However, our approach mainly differs from them in the way to address the semantic gap challenge. In particular, while prior approaches are sensitive to particular guest kernel versions or patches, our approach *brings* the suspect process to the security tool and allows for native support of existing tools. In other words, by effectively removing the semantic gap, our approach enables *re-use* of existing user-mode process monitoring tools. Further, our approach localizes the impact on the out-grafted process and avoids perturbing the monitored VM as a whole.

From another perspective, one recent system SIM [34] utilizes hardware features to place an "in-VM" monitor in a hypervisor-protected address space. While it is not physically running out-of-VM, SIM still suffers from the semantic-gap and cannot natively support existing monitoring tools. In other words, though the in-VM presence leads to unique performance benefits, there is a need to adapt existing tools to take advantage of the SIM support. Also, the main goal of SIM is to protect "kernel hook"-based monitors. Another recent system Gateway [38] leverages virtualization to detect kernel malware by monitoring kernel APIs invoked by device drivers. In contrast, our focus is for fine-grained process-level execution monitoring (e.g. *ltrace*) that typically requires user-mode interception. Process implanting [22] is another "in-VM" approach, where an "undercover agent" process is dynamically implanted in a target VM for surveillance and repair operations. Contrary to process out-grafting, process implanting relies on the integrity of the target VM's kernel and requires special modification to the program executed by the implanted process.

Process out-grafting requires redirecting the process execution across two different VMs, which bears certain similarities to well-known process migration mechanisms [28, 29, 35, 36]. However, one key difference is that process migration techniques typically move the entire execution states, including kernel-maintained resources while our approach only (temporarily) redirects the user-level execution of a process for secure monitoring. Moreover, most process migration techniques are typically applied for generic purposes such as fault-tolerance and load-balancing [28, 35] and do not consider the isolation challenge for secure monitoring.

We also notice that the idea of system call forwarding has been previously applied in systems to protect a critical application from an untrusted kernel [39]. In this case, a programmer can divide system calls into two sets so that each set will be serviced by either a trusted or untrusted kernel, respectively. In contrast, throughout the out-grafting duration, our system has one single kernel to serve all system calls for the out-grafted process. Moreover, due to the relocated user-level execution, we need to perform mode-sensitive split execution, which leads to an extra but unique need of forwarding page faults. System call forwarding between VMs has also been used [27] to improve the fidelity of runtime environment for better malware behavior monitoring, albeit without isolation guarantees. In contrast, we aim to address compatibility of existing process monitoring tools while ensuring their strong isolation in the context of VM introspection. Further, we dynamically create the memory mapping for the out-grafted process between the production VM and security VM. Also, our on-demand grafting allows for dynamically grafting the execution first and then *restoring* the execution back.

More generally, sandboxing and isolation techniques [14, 16, 32] have been widely researched and applied as effective mechanisms to confine an untrusted process' access to sensitive resources in the host system. Our work is related to them by essentially leveraging the VM isolation provided by the underlying virtualization layer. However, with an out-of-VM approach, process out-grafting can be applied on-demand, which provides certain flexibility in monitoring runtime behavior of suspect processes. Also, our approach is unorthodox when compared with traditional sandboxing and isolation techniques due to its split execution, i.e., the user-mode and kernel-mode execution of an out-grafted process run in two different VMs.

7. CONCLUSION

We have presented the design, implementation and evaluation of process out-grafting, an architectural approach to address isolation and compatibility challenges in out-of-VM approaches for fine-grained process-level execution monitoring. In particular, by effectively relocating a suspect process from a production VM to the security VM for close inspection, process out-grafting effectively removes the semantic gap for native support of existing process monitoring tools. Moreover, by forwarding the system calls from the out-grafted process back to the production VM, it can smoothly continue its execution while still being strictly isolated from the monitoring tool. The evaluation results with a number of performance benchmarks show its effectiveness and practicality.

Acknowledgements The authors would like to thank the anonymous reviewers for their insightful comments that helped improve the presentation of this paper. This work was supported in part by the US Air Force Office of Scientific Research (AFOSR) under Contract FA9550-10-1-0099 and the US National Science Foundation (NSF) under Grants 0852131, 0855297, 0855036, 0910767, and 0952640. Any opinions, findings, and conclusions or recommendations expressed in this material are those of the authors and do not necessarily reflect the views of the AFOSR and the NSF.

8. REFERENCES

[1] Kaiten. `http://packetstormsecurity.org/irc/kaiten.c`. [last accessed: May 2011].

[2] Kernel Virtual Machine. `http://www.linux-kvm.org`. [last accessed: May 2011].

[3] McAfee Threats Report: Fourth Quarter 2010. `http://www.mcafee.com/us/resources/reports/rp-quarterly-threat-q4-2010.pdf`. [last accessed: May 2011].

[4] QEMU. `http://www.qemu.org`. [last accessed: May 2011].

[5] UPX: The Ultimate Packer for eXecutables. `http://upx.sourceforge.net`. [last accessed: May 2011].

[6] Adams, K., and Agesen, O. A Comparison of Software and Hardware Techniques for x86 Virtualization. In *Proceedings of the 12th International Conference on Architectural Support for Programming Languages and Operating Systems* (2006).

[7] AMD. AMD-V Nested Paging. *AMD White Paper* (2008).

[8] Azab, A. M., Ning, P., Sezer, E. C., and Zhang, X. HIMA: A Hypervisor-Based Integrity Measurement Agent. In *Proceedings of the 25th Annual Computer Security Applications Conference* (2009).

[9] Bayer, U., Kruegel, C., and Kirda, E. TTAnalyze: A Tool for Analyzing Malware. In *Proceedings of the 15th Annual Conference of the European Institute for Computer Antivirus Research* (2006).

[10] cker Chiueh, T., Conover, M., Lu, M., and Montague, B. Stealthy Deployment and Execution of In-Guest Kernel Agents. In *BlackHat 2009*.

[11] Dinaburg, A., Royal, P., Sharif, M., and Lee, W. Ether: Malware Analysis via Hardware Virtualization Extensions. In *Proceedings of the 15th ACM Conference on Computer and Communications Security* (2008).

[12] Dolan-Gavitt, B., Leek, T., Zhivich, M., Giffin, J., and Lee, W. Virtuoso: Narrowing the Semantic Gap in Virtual Machine Introspection. In *Proceedings of the 32nd IEEE Symposium on Security and Privacy* (2011).

[13] Forrest, S., Hofmeyr, S., and Somayaji, A. The Evolution of System-Call Monitoring. In *Proceedings of the 24th Annual Computer Security Applications Conference* (2008).

[14] Garfinkel, T., Pfaff, B., and Rosenblum, M. Ostia: A Delegating Architecture for Secure System Call Interposition. In *Proceedings of the 11th Annual Network and Distributed System Security Symposium* (2004).

[15] Garfinkel, T., and Rosenblum, M. A Virtual Machine Introspection Based Architecture for Intrusion Detection. In *Proceedings of the 10th Annual Network and Distributed Systems Security Symposium* (2003).

[16] Goldberg, I., Wagner, D., Thomas, R., and Brewer, E. A. A Secure Environment for Untrusted Helper Applications: Confining the Wily Hacker. In *Proceedings of the 6th USENIX Security Symposium* (1996).

[17] Guo, F., Ferrie, P., and Chiueh, T.-c. A Study of the Packer Problem and Its Solutions. In *Proceedings of the 11th International Symposium on Recent Advances in Intrusion Detection.* (2008).

[18] Intel. Intel Virtualization Technology: Hardware Support for Efficient Processor Virtualization. *Intel(R) Technology Journal 10*, 3 (2006).

[19] Intel. *Intel 64 and IA-32 Architectures Software Developerś Manual Volume 3: System Programming Guide, Part 1 and Part 2*, (2010).

[20] Jiang, X., and Wang, X. "Out-of-the-Box" Monitoring of VM-Based High-Interaction Honeypots. In *Proceedings of the 10th International Symposium on Recent Advances in Intrusion Detection* (2007).

[21] Jiang, X., Wang, X., and Xu, D. Stealthy Malware Detection through VMM-based "Out-of-the-Box" Semantic View Reconstruction. In *Proceedings of the 14th ACM Conference on Computer and Communications Security* (2007).

[22] Gu, Z., Deng, Z., Xu, D., and Jiang, X. Process Implanting: A New Active Introspection Framework for Virtualization. In *Proceedings of the 30th IEEE Symposium on Reliable Distributed Systems* (2011).

[23] Joshi, A., King, S. T., Dunlap, G. W., and Chen, P. M. Detecting Past and Present Intrusions through Vulnerability-specific Predicates. In *Proceedings of the 20th ACM Symposium on Operating Systems Principles* (2005).

[24] King, S. T., and Chen, P. M. Backtracking Intrusions. In *Proceedings of the 19th ACM Symposium on Operating Systems Principles* (2003).

[25] Klein, G., Elphinstone, K., Heiser, G., Andronick, J., Cock, D., Derrin, P., Elkaduwe, D., Engelhardt, K., Kolanski, R., Norrish, M., Sewell, T., Tuch, H., and Winwood, S. seL4: Formal Verification of an OS Kernel. In *Proceedings of the 22nd Symposium on Operating Systems Principles* (2009).

[26] Martignoni, L., Christodorescu, M., and Jha, S. OmniUnpack: Fast, Generic, and Safe Unpacking of Malware. In *Proceedings of the 23rd Annual Computer Security Applications Conference* (2007).

[27] Martignoni, L., Paleari, R., and Bruschi, D. A Framework for Behavior-Based Malware Analysis in the Cloud. In *Proceedings of the 5th International Conference on Information Systems Security* (2009).

[28] Nuttall, M. A Brief Survey of Systems Providing Process or Object Migration Facilities. *ACM SIGOPS Operating Systems Review 28* (1994).

[29] Osman, S., Subhraveti, D., Su, G., and Nieh, J. The Design and Implementation of Zap: a System for Migrating Computing Environments. *ACM SIGOPS Operating Systems Review 36* (2002).

[30] Payne, B., de Carbone, M., and Lee, W. Secure and Flexible Monitoring of Virtual Machines. In *Proceedings of the 23rd Annual Computer Security Applications Conference* (2007).

[31] Payne, B. D., Carbone, M., Sharif, M., and Lee, W. Lares: An Architecture for Secure Active Monitoring Using Virtualization. In *Proceedings of the 29th IEEE Symposium on Security and Privacy* (2008).

[32] Provos, N. Improving Host Security with System Call Policies. In *Proceedings of the 12th USENIX Security Symposium* (2003).

[33] Royal, P., Halpin, M., Dagon, D., Edmonds, R., and Lee, W. PolyUnpack: Automating the Hidden-Code Extraction of Unpack-Executing Malware. In *Proceedings of the 22nd Annual Computer Security Applications Conference* (2006).

[34] Sharif, M. I., Lee, W., Cui, W., and Lanzi, A. Secure In-VM Monitoring Using Hardware Virtualization. In *Proceedings of the 16th ACM Conference on Computer and Communications Security* (2009).

[35] Smith, J. M. A survey of process migration mechanisms. *ACM SIGOPS Operating Systems Review 22* (1988).

[36] Smith, J. M. The Design and Implementation of Berkeley Lab's Linux Checkpoint/Restart. *Berkeley Lab Technical Report* (2002).

[37] Srivastava, A., and Giffin, J. Tamper-Resistant, Application-Aware Blocking of Malicious Network Connections. In *Proceedings of the 11th International Symposium on Recent Advances in Intrusion Detection* (2008).

[38] Srivastava, A., and Giffin, J. Efficient Monitoring of Untrusted Kernel-mode Execution. In *Proceedings of the 18th Annual Network and Distributed Systems Security Symposium* (2011).

[39] Ta-Min, R., Litty, L., and Lie, D. Splitting Interfaces: Making Trust between Applications and Operating Systems Configurable. In *Proceedings of the 7th Symposium on Operating Systems Design and Implementation* (2006).

[40] Wang, Z., and Jiang, X. HyperSafe: A Lightweight Approach to Provide Lifetime Hypervisor Control-Flow Integrity. *Proceedings of the 31st IEEE Symposium on Security and Privacy* (2010).

SICE: A Hardware-Level Strongly Isolated Computing Environment for x86 Multi-core Platforms*

Ahmed M. Azab
North Carolina State University
amazab@ncsu.edu

Peng Ning
North Carolina State University
pning@ncsu.edu

Xiaolan Zhang
IBM T.J. Watson Research Center
cxzhang@us.ibm.com

ABSTRACT

SICE is a novel framework to provide hardware-level isolation and protection for sensitive workloads running on x86 platforms in compute clouds. Unlike existing isolation techniques, SICE does not rely on any software component in the host environment (i.e., an OS or a hypervisor). Instead, the security of the isolated environments is guaranteed by a trusted computing base that only includes the hardware, the BIOS, and the System Management Mode (SMM). SICE provides fast context switching to and from an isolated environment, allowing isolated workloads to time-share the physical platform with untrusted workloads. Moreover, SICE supports a large range (up to 4GB) of isolated memory. Finally, the most unique feature of SICE is the use of multi-core processors to allow the isolated environments to run concurrently and yet securely beside the untrusted host.

We have implemented a SICE prototype using an AMD x86 hardware platform. Our experiments show that SICE performs fast context switching (67 μs) to and from the isolated environment and that it imposes a reasonable overhead (3% on all but one benchmark) on the operation of an isolated Linux virtual machine. Our prototype demonstrates that, subject to a careful security review of the BIOS software and the SMM hardware implementation, current hardware architecture already provides abstractions that can support building strong isolation mechanisms using a very small SMM software foundation of about 300 lines of code.

Categories and Subject Descriptors

D.4.6 [**Operating Systems**]: Security and Protection

*We would like to thank our shepherds Úlfar Erlingsson and Leendert van Doorn for helping us improve the quality of the paper, and Adrian Perrig and Jonathan McCune for their helpful discussion. This work is supported by U.S. National Science Foundation (NSF) under grant 0910767, the U.S. Army Research Office (ARO) under grant W911NF-08-1-0105 managed by NCSU Secure Open Systems Initiative (SOSI)), and an IBM Open Collaboration Faculty Award.

General Terms

Design, Security

Keywords

Isolation, Trusted Computing, Virtualization Security

1. INTRODUCTION

In the last few years, a significant portion of the IT industry has moved toward cloud computing. However, cloud computing services, particularly those relying on hardware sharing, have been the source of major security concerns.

Firstly, the owner of a workload that runs inside the cloud needs to trust the cloud service provider. This trust is imposed by the commodity x86 hardware architecture that gives full memory access to the highest privileged software, which is typically an OS or a hypervisor. Secondly, recent attacks [16, 32] and vulnerability reports [23, 24] show that hypervisors are subject to security exploits and can be compromised. These attacks form a major threat to users who intend to run their workloads beside other potentially malicious ones inside the cloud.

Thus, a need emerges for a solution that provides strong isolation to workloads running in the cloud, yet still allowing hardware sharing to reduce the operating costs. To provide strong isolation, we need to minimize the code base that is granted full access to the memory of running workloads. Thus, we can minimize the exposure to security vulnerabilities that can evade the isolation provided to these workloads. Moreover, this code base should be provided with enhanced security protection and the ability to attest to its integrity.

To achieve this objective, we introduce a prototype system that provides a strongly isolated execution environment, which relies on a trusted computing base (TCB) composed of the hardware, the BIOS, and the System Management Mode (SMM).

Our prototype represents a test system that aims to explore the capability of current hardware platforms in providing more secure isolated environments. We demonstrate that current hardware architecture already provides abstractions that can support strong isolation. Moreover, we show that building strong isolation mechanisms on top of those abstractions requires a very small software foundation of about 300 lines of code (LOC), which tremendously reduces the TCB size compared with previous techniques.

Since the SMM was neither designed nor implemented with high-assurance security mechanisms in mind, detailed security reviews by both CPU and platform vendors would be necessary to verify that current SMM implementations are properly done to support such strong isolation guarantees provided by our prototype in practice.

1.1 Previous Attempts

There have been a few recent attempts to tackle the problem of isolating sensitive workloads while eliminating the host OS or hypervisor from the TCB of these workloads. These attempts can be divided into two main categories: (1) microhypervisor-based approaches, and (2) hardware-based approaches.

Microhypervisor-based Approaches: These approaches rely on a thin, privileged software layer (i.e., a thin hypervisor) to provide the required isolation for sensitive workloads. Among the notable research efforts in this direction are NOVA [27] and Trustvisor [19].

NOVA proposes to replace current hypervisors with a microhypervisor that is around 9 KLOC in size. Despite having a small TCB compared to commodity hypervisors, NOVA is still responsible for several management tasks (e.g., address space management, interrupt and exception handling, and communication between the running workloads). Thus, its TCB is still relatively complicated.

Trustvisor minimizes the code base of the microhypervisor even further (about 2 KLOC for its core functions), so that it can be used for isolation purposes only. However, Trustvisor is only designed to handle workloads with a small code base and only supports systems with a single processor core. This makes it unsuitable for typical compute clouds.

An effort closely related to these microhypervisor-based approaches is seL4 [15]. seL4 proposes a technique to formally verify a microkernel, which is around 8.7 KLOC, to avoid security vulnerabilities. Although this microkernel can be used for isolation purposes, the formal verification process imposes several restrictions on the microkernel functionality. Thus, it cannot be extended to fully support all the functionalities required from micorhypervisors yet.

Hardware-based Approaches: These approaches rely on hardware security extensions to provide isolation for sensitive workloads. The main advantage of these approaches is the enhanced protection for the isolated workloads (compared with software based techniques).

One notable research effort in this direction is Flicker [20], which is a system that uses the late launch capability to run a secure verifiable workload. However, the late launch capability, provided by both Intel [11] and AMD [1], incurs significant overhead (in the magnitude of hundreds of milliseconds) on every context switch to the isolated environment. Hence, it cannot provide a practical solution for cloud computing environments.

Another effort, NoHype [14], also relies on hardware isolation through assigning dedicated processor cores to each running workload. However, NoHype still relies on a thin software layer to achieve the required protection and manage the hardware resources (e.g., page tables). Moreover, it requires architectural changes to processors and hardware peripherals, which are slow to realize.

It should be noted that all of the above techniques are research prototypes that make several simplifying assumptions about their target platforms. These assumptions may hinder the applicability or even weaken the security guarantees provided by these techniques. For instance, the formal verification introduced by seL4 does not include the firmware or the SMM code, which could negate all seL4 guarantees. Thus, a practical deployment of any of these research prototypes, including the prototype we present in this paper, requires a comprehensive consideration of the target platform that includes the full hardware and firmware specifications.

1.2 Introducing SICE

In this paper, we present SICE, which stands for Strongly Isolated Computing Environment, a framework that provides a hardware-level isolated execution environment for x86 hardware platforms. SICE's main objective is to minimize the TCB required to create an isolated execution environment on commodity x86 platforms. This isolated environment can be used to host a security sensitive workload.

SICE achieves this objective by relying on a TCB that is only composed of the hardware, the BIOS, and the SMM. The TCB, which is fundamentally different from previous research, gives SICE principal advantages over both microhypervisors and hardware-based isolation techniques. We summarize these advantages below.

Smaller Attack Surface: SICE utilizes the hardware protection provided by commodity x86 processors for the SMM and the memory that hosts its code, which is called System Management RAM (SMRAM). There are two fundamental differences between the SMM and microhypervisors.

First, the SMM can only be triggered by a single interface, which is to invoke a System Management Interrupt (SMI). In SICE, the SMI handler is required to execute one of only four functions upon receiving an SMI, which are to create, enter, exit and terminate an isolated environment. Implementing these functions requires the system to run *briefly* in the SMM. Moreover, the SMI handler is not required to handle any other interrupts because all interrupts are disabled upon entering the SMM mode. The SMI handler is also *not* responsible for managing the communication between running workloads. On the other hand, microhypervisors reside at the system's highest privileged level. Thus, they have to handle all system events (e.g., hypercalls, interrupts and exceptions). They are also required to manage the communication channels (e.g, shared memory pages) between different workloads.

Second, SICE uses the SMRAM to provide the needed memory isolation. After the SMRAM is initialized by the BIOS, it can be locked so that no software can access its contents except for the SMM code. The SMM code can manage the SMRAM through modifying only two registers, which has a huge impact on decreasing the size of the TCB. In contrast, microhypervisors that rely on hardware virtualization have to manage a different set of page tables for every isolated environment to provide memory protection.

To sum up, SICE's SMM code base is better protected and less complicated than any microhypervisor. Moreover, this code does not provide any functionality other than the required isolation, which results in a very small code base. For instance, our prototype SMI handler consists of around 300 LOC (excluding cryptographic libraries). This is around an order of magnitude less than current microhypervisors (e.g., Trustvisor and NOVA). As discussed in [15], this is a significant difference when it comes to verification cost. For instance, using the industry rules-of-thumb of $10K per LOC for common criteria certification as a guideline for the cost of code verification, the cost for verifying 500LOC is $5M versus $100M for 10 KLOC.

Compatibility with Existing Software Systems: Unlike isolation techniques that monopolize the highest privileged execution level of the target platform (e.g., Trustvisor), SICE does not exclude running legacy workloads (e.g., a hypervisor with multiple VMs) on the same physical platform. In other words, a platform using SICE can offer isolated environments, and at the same time accommodate legacy virtualization software.

Feasible Hardware-based Isolation: SICE uses existing hardware features to provide the required isolation. We have successfully implemented a SICE prototype using a commodity AMD processor. Thus, it does not require fundamental changes to current hardware architecture.

Moreover, our performance evaluation shows that SICE performs a secure context switching with an isolated environment that is four orders of magnitude faster than systems that rely on the late launch capability (e.g., Flicker [20]). It also uses multi-core processors to allow isolated workloads to run in parallel to a legacy hypervisor or OS. Thus, SICE avoids the two main drawbacks of using late launch, which are the high performance overhead, and the dedication of all system resources to only one isolated workload.

1.3 SICE Overview

SICE introduces novel techniques that allow the isolated workloads to run in parallel with a host OS or hypervisor. For convenience, we refer to the OS or hypervisor along with all the software running on it as the *legacy host*, a strongly isolated computing environment, which supports an isolated workload, as an *isolated environment*, and the code that manages the isolation between these environments as the *SMI handler*, or simply SICE.

The SMI handler, which represents the TCB of the isolated environments, resides inside the SMRAM. It is the only part of our framework that executes in the SMM. The SMI handler is responsible for two main tasks: 1) maintaining the memory isolation of the isolated environments, 2) securely initializing the isolated environments and attesting to their integrity. In SICE, these tasks require the SMI handler to run for a very short time.

An isolated environment is composed of two components: an isolated workload and a security manager. The isolated workload is a user-provided system that runs in the isolated environment. It can be any software, ranging from a single program (e.g., a program that manages secret keys) to a complete VM (e.g., a VM that runs a web server).

The security manager is a thin software layer that has limited functionalities such as handling exceptions and managing page tables. It is mainly responsible for confining the isolated workload. Due to the commodity hardware limitation on SMRAM size, SICE's unique hardware-level isolation is not used to protect the legacy host from the isolated environments. Thus, SICE uses the security manager to prevent the isolated workload from accessing the memory of the legacy host. A separate copy of the security manager is generated by SICE for every isolated workload running on the system. Both the security manager and the isolated workload run after the system returns from the SMM.

Though SICE requires the legacy host to trust the security managers, it does not weaken the hardware-level isolation provided to the isolated workloads. SICE uses SMM to protect isolated environments from the legacy host. Even if a malicious workload (in one isolated environment) compromises its own security manager and consequently the legacy host, it will not be able to compromise any other isolated environment running on the same platform.

SICE's protection of the legacy host may appear to be equivalent to those provided by microhypervisor-based approaches such as NOVA. Indeed, the security manager, which is a thin privileged software layer, is similar to a microhypervisor in terms of its required tasks and code size. However, SICE also provides hardware-level, stronger protection for the isolated environments, which are not available in microhypervisor-based approaches.

SICE provides two operating modes: *time-sharing mode* and *multi-core mode*. In both modes, the SICE philosophy is based on using the isolated environments to run security sensitive workloads, while the legacy host is used for running less sensitive workloads and managing hardware peripherals. In a typical execution scenario, a communication channel is used so that the legacy host provides hardware services (e.g., networking) to the isolated environments. The communication channel can be established using a shared memory outside of the memory range protected by SICE. Communication channels are not controlled or managed by the SMI handler. Thus, the code responsible for managing the communication is not a part of the TCB.

In the time-sharing mode, time multiplexing is used to share the hardware platform between the isolated environments and the legacy host. During the environment switching, SICE guarantees a fresh start of the processor, complete memory isolation between these environments, and a timely switching that does not largely impact the performance.

In the multi-core mode, SICE assigns one or more processor cores to each isolated environment, while the other cores are used to run the legacy host. SICE guarantees isolation of both the processor cores and the memory dedicated to each of the concurrently running environments.

In both modes, SICE attests to the integrity of each isolated environment to remote users, while avoids revealing sensitive information about the workload to the legacy host.

The current SICE design relies on hardware features provided by AMD processors. Some of these features are not currently supported by Intel processors, particularly the ability to resize the SMRAM at runtime and defining a separate SMRAM for each processor core. Proposing alternative techniques to implement SICE on Intel platforms will require further research. We discuss these issues in Appendix A.

We implement a prototype of SICE on an IBM LS22 blade server that uses AMD processors. We use our SICE prototype to run a complete Linux VM in the isolated environment. Our experimental evaluation shows that the time required to enter and exit an isolated environment using SICE is around 67 μs. We conduct experiments to evaluate the performance of the isolated VM. In the multi-core mode, SICE incurs a low (under 3%) overhead on VM operations that do not require frequent communication with the legacy host. The time-sharing mode shows a higher overhead (around 10%) due to the time for the context switching. A test dedicated to measure the performance of network emulation shows a higher overhead. However, this overhead is expected to decrease using an optimized implementation of network emulation for isolated VMs.

1.4 Summary of Contributions

We make several technical contributions in this paper:

- We provide a complete and feasible solution to share

hardware resources with an isolated execution environment that does not rely on any host software. Instead, it relies on a TCB that is around an order of magnitude smaller than the state-of-the-art systems.

- We provide a novel technique that allows concurrent execution of the isolated environments with the untrusted host environment.
- We provide attestation to the integrity of the isolated workloads without revealing sensitive information about the workloads to untrusted host software.
- We implement a prototype of SICE on an AMD platform. We use this prototype to evaluate the performance overhead introduced by SICE.

The rest of this paper is organized as follows. Section 2 provides background information on SMM. Section 3 discusses our assumptions and threat model. Section 4 presents SICE in detail. Section 5 presents our prototype implementation. Section 6 presents our experimental evaluation. Section 7 presents related work, and Section 8 concludes this paper with some future research directions. Finally, The Appendix discusses SICE's portability to Intel platforms.

2. BACKGROUND

In this section, we briefly give some background information on the System Management Mode (SMM).

Commodity x86 architecture supports the SMM as one of its operating modes. The processor enters the SMM when receiving an SMI. Upon an SMI, the processor saves its state to a dedicated state save map and switches to the SMM. To return from the SMM, the special instruction `RSM` restores the saved processor state and resumes normal execution.

SMM code is stored in a designated memory called SMRAM. To provide protection of the SMM code and data, both AMD and Intel provide the capability of locking the SMRAM. When the SMRAM is locked, all accesses to it, except from within the SMM, are prevented. All interrupts, including non-maskable ones, are disabled upon entering the SMM. Thus, no other code running on the system can interfere with the SMI handler.

Current hardware can support up to 4 GB of SMRAM. There are two types of SMRAM: the `ASeg`, which is located at a fixed low address, and the `TSeg` which is located at a variable base and has a variable size. SICE uses `TSeg` due to the flexibility it offers. Defining the SMRAM location and range differs slightly between AMD and Intel architectures. In the following, we take a closer look at AMD architecture, on which this paper focuses.

The AMD architecture defines the `TSeg` memory range using two Model Specific Registers (MSRs) that are local to each processor core. The first is `SMM_Addr`, which specifies the SMRAM base address, while the second is `SMM_Mask`, which specifies its range. Since MSRs are local to each processor core, all cores have to set their MSRs to provide complete protection of the SMRAM.

The `SMMLOCK` bit in the `HWCR` MSR can be set to prevent changing the `TSeg` range. Moreover, the AMD architecture uses a password mechanism to protect the modification of the `SMMLOCK` bit. When the SMRAM is unlocked, writes to the `SMM_KEY` MSR set the 64-bit password. When the SMRAM is locked, writing the correct password to the same MSR clears the `SMMLOCK` bit.

3. THREAT MODEL AND ASSUMPTIONS

Threat Model: SICE aims at defending against all malicious activities by software running in the legacy host that are targeted at compromising the isolation offered to the isolated environment (e.g., malicious activity that result from exploiting a vulnerability in the hypervisor). Specifically, SICE protects the isolated environment from all types of unauthorized memory accesses or any modification to its execution environment. The protection starts from the moment the isolated environment is initialized by SICE. Upon initialization, the initial image of the isolated workload, which is loaded by the legacy host, is measured so that SICE can further attest to its integrity.

We consider the following attacks out of the scope of this paper: Attacks aimed at the availability of SICE (e.g., denying its network access), and those that directly exploit vulnerabilities of the isolated environment through legitimate communication channels. Such attacks are not specific to the isolation mechanism, and should be addressed by other techniques such as keep-alive messages and patching the vulnerabilities. Moreover, SICE is not responsible for securing the hardware services provided by the host. Thus, the isolated workload should use other techniques to achieve this objective (e.g., encrypting its network traffic).

Side-channel attacks are also out of the scope of this paper. Adopting SICE prevents cache side-channels because the hardware automatically clears the cache upon entering and exiting from the SMM. However, these attacks in general are not unique to our approach and require further research.

Assumptions: We assume that our platform is physically secure (e.g., locked in a server room) so that an adversary cannot launch any hardware attack. Moreover, we assume that the target platform is equipped with trusted computing hardware, including the Core Root of Trust Measurement (CRTM) and Trusted Platform Module (TPM) [29]. This allows the attestation to the integrity of key software components (e.g., the SMI handler).

We assume that the SMM is properly isolated from other software running on the system and the hardware provides the SMRAM with proper isolation from all unauthorized memory accesses (e.g., cache poisoning, Direct Memory Access (DMA)). Recent incidents showed that attackers were able to subvert the SMRAM using cache poisoning [6, 33]. Fortunately, such attacks cannot be mounted on AMD platforms due to its SMRAM cache protection and can be easily defeated on Intel platforms using proper setting of the System Management Range Register (SMRR) [13].

4. SICE DESIGN

In this section, we present the design of SICE. The objective is to enable hardware-level strongly isolated computing environments that run in parallel with the legacy host on the same hardware platform.

Implementation requirements: To implement SICE, the SMI handler needs to be modified to include SICE's code. Recently, most hardware vendors use the BIOS to lock the SMRAM to prevent potential SMM misuse. Thus, SICE requires hardware vendors to allow adding its code to the SMI handler before locking the SMRAM.

The legacy host (e.g., the hypervisor) is required to add an interface that invokes an SMI to trigger SICE. Hardware management functions provided by the legacy host (e.g.,

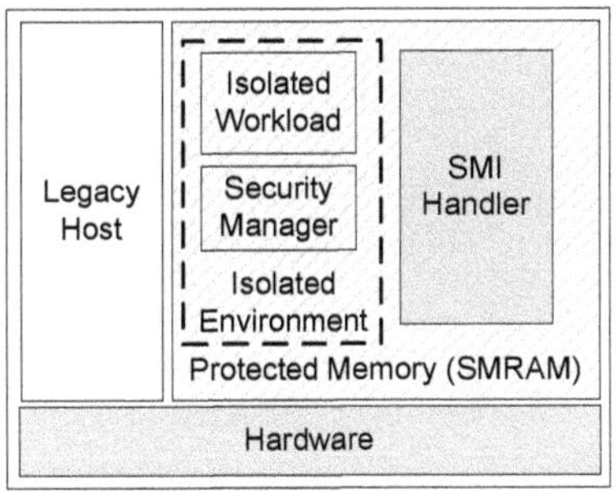

Figure 1: SICE Architecture

hardware device drivers) should be modified to use this interface to provide its services to the isolated environment. Note that the legacy host may refuse to invoke an isolated environment or deny it some services, thus threatening its availability. However, these attacks are easily detectable by SICE and its remote users (e.g., from the lack of response of the isolated workload), and can then be thwarted by replacing the faulty legacy host.

SICE Architecture: Figure 1 shows the architecture of SICE. It consists of three components: The SMI handler, the security manager, and the isolated workload. The security manager and the isolated workload constitute the isolated environment. SICE enables the isolated environment and the legacy host to share the physical platform's resources.

The security manager is a thin software layer that confines the isolated workload. It has limited functionalities such as handling exceptions and managing page tables. The initial image of the security manager should be loaded to the SMRAM, along with the SMI handler, upon the system initialization. Thus, we assume trust in both the SMI handler and the security manager based on the system's trusted boot, which can be attested to later using the TPM.

The isolated workload is a user-provided system that runs in the isolated environment. It can be any software, ranging from a single program to a complete VM. The only restrictions on this software are that it does not use more than 4GB of memory (due to SMRAM constraints) and that it does not manipulate hardware peripherals directly.

When the isolated environment is not actively running, its code and data are securely stored in the SMRAM (as shown in Figure 1). However, the SMM is a limited execution mode that is not suitable for running the isolated environment. For instance, code execution inside the SMM is slower than the protected mode [2]. Moreover, some hardware functionalities (e.g., starting a hardware assisted VM) are not supported in the SMM. Thus, SICE only uses the SMM to prepare and enter the isolated environment. SICE uses novel techniques to move the security manager and the isolated workload out of the SMRAM after the isolated environment is initialized.

In the following, we discuss SICE in a *time-sharing mode*, where the legacy host and the isolated environment time share the physical platform. We then present the *multi-core mode*, where the legacy host and the isolated environment run in parallel using multi-core processors.

4.1 Time-sharing Mode

In the time-sharing mode, SICE provides two important features: (1) fast context switch between the legacy host and the isolated environment (in the magnitude of few tens of microseconds), and (2) large protected memory range for the isolated workload (up to 4GB). The fast context switch allows the isolated workload to receive its input data and send its output to and from the legacy host without posing significant overhead on the system performance. The large protected memory range enables the isolated environment to securely keep its state across the context switches.

4.1.1 Initializing the Isolated Environment

Both the security manager and the SMI handler are initialized when the physical platform is booted. When an isolated workload is ready to be started, the legacy host first loads the initial image of this workload to a specific memory range. Then, it triggers SICE using an SMI. The SMI handler then measures the initial image of the isolated workload and copies it to the protected SMRAM. Details on measuring and attesting to the isolated environment are discussed in Section 4.3.

4.1.2 Entering the Isolated Environment

Figure 2 shows the process of entering the isolated environment. Whenever the legacy host requires the isolated workload to run, it triggers another SMI. The SMI then switches the processor's execution environment to the SMM and the execution jumps to the SMI handler. The SMI handler then prepares the isolated environment by changing the saved processor state so that the security manager, instead of the legacy host, runs after the processor returns from the SMM. The SMI handler also stores the processor state of the legacy host so that it can resume execution after the isolated environment finishes its execution.

In the time-sharing mode, SICE gives the isolated environment full control of the physical platform as soon as it runs. Thus, it changes the processor state (e.g., interrupt descriptors, system call handlers) so that only the security manager will have control after the SMI handler returns.

Unfortunately, the SMM cannot change most of the critical processor states (e.g., the interrupt descriptor table (IDT) register and the CR3 register). To overcome this challenge, the SMI handler relocates the code pointed to by the current processor state through modifying the page tables. Since the CR3 register is not writable, the SMI handler modifies the first level page table pointed to by the CR3 so that it directly points to the security manager. It also flushes the Translation Lookaside Buffer (TLB) to avoid potential race conditions with the cached page tables.

Before the SMI handler returns, we need to ensure that both the security manager and the isolated workload are accessible to the processor after it returns from the SMM. As shown in Figure 1, both the security manager and and the isolated workload are stored in the SMRAM before the isolated environment is entered. These two components need to be moved out of the SMRAM so that they can run after the processor returns from the SMM.

A straightforward solution is to copy the security manager and the isolated workload out of the SMRAM to an unprotected memory. However, this will introduce an unacceptable performance overhead.

To address this problem, we use the ability of AMD processors to resize the SMRAM during the system runtime. This feature, discussed in Section 2, relies on a password-protected mechanism to clear the SMM lock so that the `SMM_Addr` and the `SMM_Mask` registers can be updated.

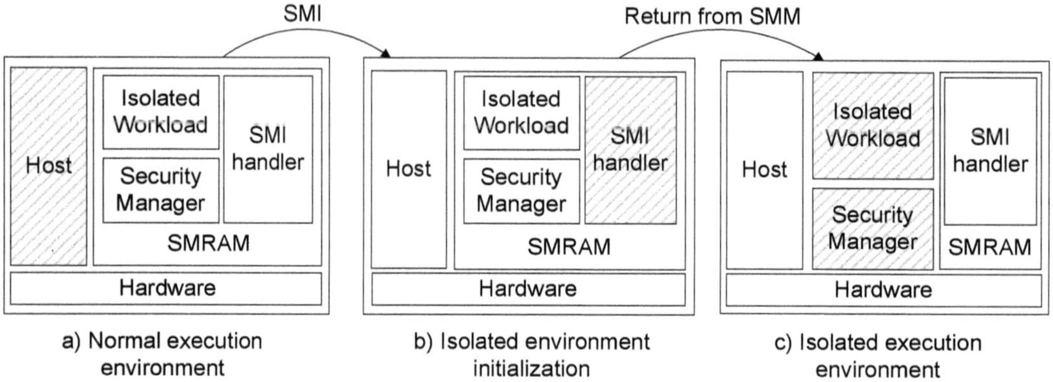

Figure 2: Entering SICE from the legacy host (actively running components are shaded): a) An SMI triggers SICE operations. b) The SMI handler prepares the isolated environment and the new SMRAM layout. c) After entering the isolated environment, the security manager prevents the isolated workload from accessing the legacy host memory.

Upon the initialization of the system, SICE generates a 64-bit random number, sets it as the password for locking/unlocking the SMRAM, and stores it inside the SMRAM. Before entering the isolated environment, the SMI handler uses this password to unlock the SMRAM and modify its protection range (by modifying the `SMM_Addr` and the `SMM_Mask` registers) to exclude both the security manager and the isolated workload. Thus, they can be accessed by the processor after the SMI handler returns.

As shown in Figure 2, the SMRAM protection remains for the SMI handler while the isolated workload runs. This guarantees that the SMI handler (including the SMRAM password) can never be accessed by any other software running on the system, including the isolated workload.

A subtle issue needs to be clarified. To guarantee full control over the system, the isolated environment should run in the highest privileged level after the SMI returns. However, this requires the legacy host to trigger the SMI from within the highest privileged level. In other words, the SMI cannot be triggered by a guest VM. Otherwise, the isolated environment will return to the context of a guest VM controlled by the legacy host.

To verify that the SMI is triggered by the highest privileged level, SICE requires the legacy host to disable virtualization by clearing the `SVME` bit in the `EFER` register before triggering the SMI. The SMI handler verifies that this bit is clear. Otherwise, it will not enter the isolated environment and keep the SMRAM protection for its memory.

4.1.3 Managing the Isolated Workload

Since the isolated workload is provided by the user, it is not trusted by SICE. Hence, it should not be allowed to tamper with the hardware configuration or access memory regions that belong to the security manager or legacy host.

Unfortunately, commodity hardware architecture cannot assign more than 4GB of memory to the SMRAM. Thus, using the SMRAM to protect the legacy host memory from the isolated workload will not be a feasible solution due to its restriction on the memory capacity of the legacy host.

To address this challenge, the security manager plays the role of a hypervisor and runs the isolated workload in the context of a guest VM. Therefore, the isolated workload's execution environment is restricted so that it cannot execute privileged instructions. Moreover, the security manager crafts the page tables of the isolated workload so that it can access a limited specific range of physical memory. Thus, the isolated workload cannot access any memory range that belongs to either the security manager or the legacy host.

4.1.4 Exiting the Isolated Environment

To allow the legacy host and the isolated environment to efficiently share the hardware resources, SICE provides a technique to securely and properly exit the isolated environment and return the execution back to the legacy host.

To return back to the legacy host, the isolated environment triggers an SMI. The SMI handler then: (1) Clears all general purpose registers, (2) flushes all cache levels, (3) uses the SMM password to change the SMRAM range so that it covers both the security manager and the isolated workload, and (4) restores all changes done to the legacy host page tables before the isolated environment was initialized.

The first two steps ensures that no sensitive data is leaked to the legacy host. The third step ensures the protection of the isolated environment's memory. Finally, the last step ensures that the legacy host resumes its operations correctly.

4.1.5 Terminating the Isolated Workload

When the isolated workload finishes execution, it needs to be securely terminated so that no confidential information are leaked to the legacy host. Thus, isolated workload termination requests must be forwarded to the SMI handler, which securely erases the memory belonging to the isolated workload and then removes it from the protected SMRAM.

4.2 Multi-core Mode

The SICE multi-core mode enables the legacy host and the isolated environments to run in parallel on different processor cores to better utilize the hardware resources.

Before presenting our solution, we first give some background information on multi-core processors. As shown in Figure 3, multi-core processors are equipped with one or more processing nodes. Each node has its own memory control hub (north bridge) and one or more processor cores. North bridge configuration registers can be accessed by any core on any node. On the other hand, each processor core has its own general-purpose registers, MSRs, APIC, and two

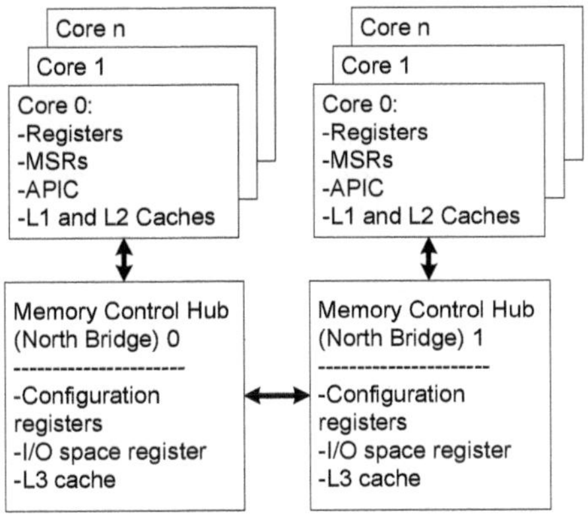

Figure 3: General multi-core processors architecture

levels of cache. These components can only be accessed by their designated core. Among these core-dependent components are the `SMM_Addr` and `SMM_Mask` MSRs that define the SMRAM memory range. Thus, each processor core can have its own protected SMRAM memory range that is independent from the SMRAM memory range defined on other processor cores that share the same node. SICE utilizes this architecture to provide the necessary protection for the isolated environment in the multi-core mode.

For simplicity, we assume a platform with two cores in our discussion: the *host core* that runs the legacy host, and the *isolated core* that runs the isolated environment. However, the same techniques can be used to assign more than one core to either the legacy host or the isolated environment. In general, two processor cores that belong to different execution environments can be either co-located on the same processing node or located among different nodes.

In the multi-core mode, SICE initializes the isolated environment in the same way as the time-sharing mode (i.e., by triggering an SMI in the legacy host). The SMI switches the execution environment of all processor cores that exist on the target platform to the SMM. The SMI handler performs a different task on each processor core. On the isolated core, the SMI handler prepares the isolated environment and returns to the security manager using the techniques described in Section 4.1.2. Meanwhile, on the host core, the SMI handler returns directly to the legacy host so that it can resume its operations at the same time.

Since both the legacy host and the isolated environment run in parallel on different processor cores, no context switching between these environments is needed.

To ensure the isolation between the legacy host and the isolated environments, SICE prevents the legacy host from affecting the execution of the isolated environment, and the isolated workload (excluding the security manager, which needs to be trusted by the legacy host) from affecting the execution of the legacy host. In particular, we need to prevent the interference through explicit inter-core communication as well as those through modifying each other's memory.

4.2.1 Handling Inter-core Communication

Communication between processor cores, which is done through Inter-Processor Interrupts (IPIs), can modify the execution environment on the recipient code by changing the execution path. This can pose a risk on the integrity of the isolated environment. Therefore, all IPIs should either be blocked or securely handled by the recipient core.

There are two types of IPIs: (1) Maskable IPIs that can be blocked by the recipient core's Advanced Programmable Interrupt Controller (APIC), and (2) non-maskable IPIs (e.g., NMI, SMI, startup, and INIT) that cannot be blocked.

Upon initializing the isolated environment, the SMI handler disables all maskable interrupts on the isolated core so that the host core cannot interfere with the isolated core. The security manager, which runs as a thin hypervisor on the isolated core, keeps these interrupts disabled.

On the other hand, non-maskable interrupts cannot be blocked. Moreover, a specific non-maskable interrupt, the startup interrupt, resets the processor core to start execution at a low physical memory address. Intuitively, this address can be modified by the host core to alter the course of execution on the isolated core.

To overcome this problem, SICE relies on the Global Interrupt Flag (GIF) introduced by AMD. When the GIF is clear, all interrupts, including non-maskable ones, are ignored or held pending. The security manager thus clears the GIF of the isolated core when the isolated environment is entered, and sets it only after the isolated environment completes its execution and all memory protection measures are taken.

The security manager then runs the isolated workload in the guest VM mode. Upon entering the VM mode, both global interrupts and maskable interrupts are re-enabled. Hence, the isolated workload can receive all interrupts including both IPIs and local processor interrupts. However, the received interrupts will cause a VM exit and jump to the security manager rather than modifying the execution environment.

Global interrupts are automatically disabled again before exiting the VM mode and jumping to the security manager. The security manager identifies the reason that causes the VM exit. If it is an interrupt that aims to modify the execution environment (e.g., INIT interrupt), then it indicates a malicious activity from the host core and all memory protection measures are taken. However, if the VM exit is caused by a local interrupt or an IPI, the interrupt is forwarded back to the isolated workload. This architecture allows the isolated workload to use IPIs as method of signaling, which is required to build a communication channel with the legacy host. This channel can be used to provide hardware services offered by the legacy host to the isolated workload.

On the other hand, SICE relies on hardware virtualization to prevent the isolated workload from perturbing the legacy host. The isolated workload, which runs in a guest VM, is not allowed to directly access the APIC to send any interrupts that can perturb the execution of the host core.

4.2.2 Memory Isolation

To prevent the legacy host from accessing the isolated environment's memory, SICE relies on a novel protection called the *memory double-view technique*, shown in Figure 4. This technique relies on the fact that AMD processor's SMRAM is defined based on the *core-dependent* MSRs. Thus, different cores can view the SMRAM differently depending on the values of their own `SMM_Addr` and `SMM_Mask` registers.

As shown in Figure 4, each processor core has its own view of the physical memory. From the host core's perspective, the isolated environment uses a physical memory that lies in the SMRAM memory range. Hence, the legacy host cannot

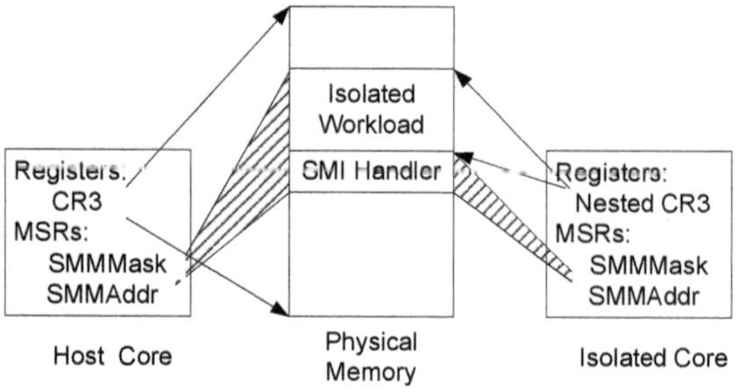

Figure 4: Double view of memory from different processor cores. From the host core's view, the isolated environment is part of the SMRAM. From the isolated workload's view, the SMI handler is protected by the SMRAM and the legacy host is protected by the security manager via hardware assisted paging.

access such memory due to the SMRAM protection. From the isolated core's perspective, the isolated environment lies within a normal memory region that is not part of the SMRAM. Hence, the isolated environment can run normally on the isolated core.

SICE also prevents the isolated workload from accessing the legacy host memory. The security manager, which plays the role of a hypervisor, restricts the isolated workload to its assigned physical memory. Nevertheless, a shared memory, which does not fall in the host core's SMRAM, is mapped to allow communication between the two environments.

4.3 Attestation and Secure Communication

Cloud computing users are required to trust the environment that runs their workloads. In SICE, attesting the integrity of the isolated environment is complicated by the fact that the legacy host has full access to all hardware peripherals and communication channels. In this section we provide a three-step solution to address this challenge.

Attesting to Integrity of SICE: SICE requires the platform to use standard trusted boot [28]. After a typical trusted boot, the TPM securely stores the measurement of the boot process, which includes the SMI handler, the code image of the security manager and the code that loads them and locks the SMRAM. The measurement is stored in TPM special registers that cannot be erased by malicious software.

The TPM can further use its private Attestation Identity Key (AIK) to attest to the integrity of this measurement to remote users. Unlike other system software that is continuously interacting with potential attackers, the SMI handler cannot be modified by any code running on the system and the trust in it can be maintained.

Attesting to Integrity of Isolated Workload: In turn, the SMI handler attests to the integrity of the isolated workload. It measures the isolated workload before it is first invoked and stores the measurement in the secure SMRAM.

To enable the attestation, we adopt an approach we previously used is HyperSentry [2]. Specifically, SICE generates a public/private key pair during system boot. The private key is securely stored in the SMRAM, and the public key is securely stored inside the TPM.

To attest to the integrity of the isolated workload, the SMI handler signs the measurement of the initial workload image using its private key. The remote user accepts the measurement output only if the private key matches the public key stored in, and attested to by, the TPM.

Secure Communication with the Isolated Environment: SICE allows the establishment of a secure communication channel between the isolated workload and its remote owner using standard cryptographic techniques. To enable the remote owner to authenticate the isolated workload, SICE provides a public/private key pair for the isolated workload. The public key is sent to the user as a part of the workload attestation evidence signed by the SMI handler. The private key is directly provided to the isolated workload. Thus, it is never exposed to potentially malicious code running inside the legacy host. On the other hand, the isolated workload should include the public key of its remote owner as a part of its initial image.

With both the security manager and the remote owner being able to validate each other's public keys, we can easily modify, for example, SSL for secure communication without leaking information to the (untrusted) legacy host.

4.4 Security Analysis

Now we discuss the security of the isolated environment, including its confidentiality, integrity, availability, and TCB. We also discuss the security implication of using the SMM.

4.4.1 The Security of the Isolated Environment

Confidentiality: To protect the confidentiality of the isolated environment, SICE prevents potential attackers from accessing its memory. SICE uses the SMRAM to achieve this objective. The hardware protects the SMRAM from access requests made by both the CPU and direct memory access (DMA) capable devices.

In the time-sharing mode, SICE modifies the SMRAM memory range according to the running environment. Whenever the legacy host is running, SICE extends the SMRAM to include the memory of the isolated environment. Thus, this memory is protected from all memory requests.

When the isolated environment is triggered, SICE takes two security measures to guarantee its confidentiality. First, SICE assures that the isolated environment fully controls physical platform. Hence, the legacy host is not active to threaten the isolated environment, given that modern processors do not use cached memory upon entering the SMM to avoid cache poisoning attacks [1, 13]. Second, SICE uses hardware DMA exclusion (e.g., AMD's DMA exclusion vector (DEV) [1] and Intel's VT-d [12]) to prevent DMA capable devices, which could be maliciously programmed, from accessing the protected memory.

In the multi-core mode, SICE's memory double-view technique provides the needed protection. According to architecture manuals, memory access requests made from a processor core are checked against its own SMRAM before being routed. Hence, the host core will not be able to access the protected memory that falls within its own SMRAM range. The same is true for requests to update or retrieve cache entries. Hence, cache poisoning is not possible.

In the multi-core mode, SICE cannot rely on hardware DMA exclusion because its control registers exist in the memory control hub, which is accessible by all processor cores. Thus, SICE relies on the SMRAM protection to prevent DMA access to the isolated environment's memory. Typically, the memory control hub does not allow DMA access to the SMRAM. However, the AMD hardware architecture manual does not precisely define which processor core's SMRAM range is used to prevent DMA access, particularly when different SMRAM ranges are defined on different cores. Thus, implementing SICE on a specific platform requires verifying which SMRAM range is protected from DMA. The specific processor core(s) that defines this range is the same one that should be used as the untrusted host core. As shown in figure 4, the host core's SMRAM memory range includes the whole memory range used by the running, one or more, isolated environments.

A final threat to the confidentiality of the isolated environment is brute force attacks against the SMM password. For each processor core, SICE generates a 64-bit random value to be used as the SMM password. Thus, it is computationally infeasible to break this password. The random password generation can be done using the TPM.

Integrity: In the time-sharing mode, the legacy host cannot threaten the integrity of the isolated environment because they do not run concurrently. In the multi-core mode, the host core cannot access the registers, MSRs and APIC of the isolated core. However, the host core can still modify system-wide configurations that rely on shared resources (e.g., the memory control hub and the IO control hub). Next, we prove that such configurations can only perturb the isolated environment, for example, by rebooting the system, without threatening its confidentiality or integrity.

According to the Advanced Configuration and Power Interface (ACPI) specification [10], processor cores keep their state as long as the processor runs in the S0 or S1 power modes. Thus, the isolated core will keep running the isolated environment as long as either S0 or S1 state is maintained. On the other hand, all other ACPI states will cause the processor core to lose its state and resume execution from the non-volatile memory (i.e., the BIOS). Since the BIOS belongs to the trusted computing base, changing the ACPI state will be detected by SICE. In all cases, the ACPI implementation of the target platform needs to be carefully reviewed to securely implement SICE.

As presented in Section 4.2, attacks that use IPI between processor cores are thwarted using APIC setting and the GIF of the processor core that runs the isolated environment.

Availability: SICE does not provide protection against attacks that target the availability of the isolated environment. Example attacks include perturbing the isolated environment through system reboots or denying it network access. However, this type of attacks is easily detectable by SICE and its remote users (e.g., from the lack of response of the isolated environment), and can be easily thwarted by removing the malicious code from the legacy host.

The TCB of SICE: SICE aims to minimize and enhance the protection of the TCB of the isolated environment so as to maximize its security.

The TCB of the isolated environment consists of the hardware, the BIOS, and the SMM. Using the SMM gives SICE two main advantages over microhypervisor-based isolation. First, SICE TCB enjoys the hardware protection provided for the SMRAM. Second, the SMM's attack surface is much smaller than that of microhypervisors. Thus, The TCB of the isolated environment is better protected and less complicated than that of microhypervisors. Section 1.2 compares the TCB of SICE with that of microhypervisors in detail.

Trusting the BIOS is required to start the trust chain based on the static root of trust management (SRTM) technique. However, recent incidents [17] show that the SRTM can be compromised. Nevertheless, SICE can adopt the Dynamic root of trust management (DRTM) to start the trust chain, which consequently eliminates the BIOS from the TCB. SICE can use the DRTM to invoke a trusted code that securely initializes the SMRAM, given that it will not be locked by the BIOS. A similar technique was used by Trustvisor [19] to initialize its TCB.

SICE requires the legacy host to trust the security manager(s). However, this does not make the security guarantee provided to the legacy host weaker than microhypervisor-based approaches such as NOVA, which assume trust in a thin hypervisor with typical duties. Indeed, SICE and the microhypervisor-based approaches provide similar security guarantees for the legacy host, while SICE additionally also provides a stronger protection for the isolated environments, as discussed in Section 1.3.

4.4.2 SMM Security

Despite being an integral part of the TCB of SICE, the SMM was not designed to provide security services. It was originally designed to create a shadow environment to run hardware management tasks. In the following, we discuss some of the important issues that need to be considered before deploying SICE, or any other system that relies on the SMM, in a production environment.

Legacy SMM Tasks: Intuitively, the TCB of SICE includes any code that exists in the SMRAM. To keep the TCB minimal, legacy system management tasks need to be eliminated from the SMM. This does not mean that SICE needs to completely eliminate them from the system. Instead, SICE can simply forward specific SMIs to (possibly relocated) legacy SMM code after taking the required memory protection measures.

Previous SMM Attacks: As mentioned in Section 3, there have been attempts to subvert the SMRAM using cache poisoning [6,33]. Although these attacks can be easily prevented by using proper hardware configuration, it shows that hardware vendors should undergo a rigorous review of the SMM security to avoid any further security problems.

It is worth mentioning that the implication of SMM attacks is beyond the systems that rely on the SMM for security. It is shown in [7] that a subverted SMM can be used to host a stealthy rootkit that undermines the security of any system. In general, trusting the underlying hardware, including the SMM, is imposed on all software systems.

Hardware Vendors Cooperation: As mentioned in Section 4, implementing SICE requires hardware vendors to allow adding its code to the SMI handler before locking the SMRAM. In fact, we advocate that SICE should be entirely implemented by hardware vendors. In this case, the system BIOS will be responsible for initializing SICE upon booting the system. This guarantees that SICE will always be compatible with the specification of the underlying hardware.

5. SICE PROTOTYPE: AN ISOLATED VM

In this section, we present a SICE prototype implemented on an IBM LS22 blade server, which is equipped with two 2.7GHz AMD Opteron 10h family quad-core processors. We use an Ubuntu 9.10 Linux as the OS. In our prototype, we replace the original SMI handler with SICE's SMI handler. Implementing the core functions of SICE's SMI handler,

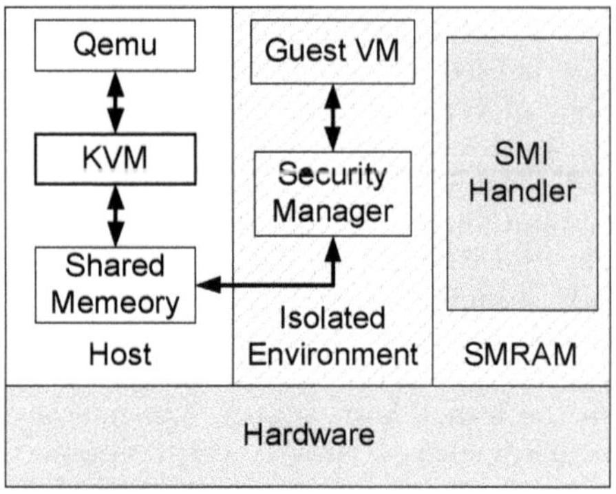

Figure 5: SICE Prototype

which are to prepare and enter the isolated environment, requires around 300 LOC (excluding cryptographic libraries)

As mentioned in Section 1.3, the isolated environment can support running any software, ranging from a single program to a complete VM. To run a single program inside SICE, it needs to be instrumented so that it directly runs on top of the security manager. The required instrumentation is similar to that required by previous research on running isolated security sensitive code (e.g., Flicker [20], Trustvisor [19]).

In our prototype, we use SICE to run a Linux VM, rather than running an instrumented single program. This is to demonstrate the flexibility provided to the isolated environment. Running a whole VM requires the ability to support a diverse set of applications, frequent context switching, and a large range of protected memory.

Figure 5 shows our SICE prototype. The security manager plays the role of the hypervisor in the isolated environment. It uses hardware assisted virtualization to manage and run the VM as the isolated workload. All hardware management functions are delegated to the legacy host, specifically, a modified version of Qemu/KVM [18] running in the legacy host. Qemu is a program that emulates hardware peripherals. KVM is a kernel module that manages other VM operations like scheduling and memory management.

We modified KVM so that it uses a shared memory to send the required VM configurations to the security manager. The same shared memory is used by the security manager to pass the information required to request hardware services from the legacy host. This architecture is mainly chosen to simplify the implementation efforts. In our prototype, the security manager is composed of around 2.1 KLOC, which is comparable to the size of current microhypervisors.

Our implementation provides both network interface and serial port emulation using Qemu. Networking is necessary to allow the VM to communicate with remote users, while the serial port is used as a console for debugging.

Our prototype does not support graphic display emulation, which is not necessary for cloud computing applications. Moreover, we do not support disk drive emulation because our experiments do not need a permanent storage.

Supporting a disk drive emulation is straightforward based on the technique used to implement the network interface emulation. However, the main question is how to secure the disk access from a compromised legacy host. The answer is dependent on the isolated workload rather than the isolation mechanism. For instance, security sensitive applications can either use full disk encryption (similar to Bitlocker [8]), or selectively encrypt secret files only (e.g., a file that contains user passwords). Other applications only need to keep secret data in memory without a permanent storage (e.g., web servers that process online purchases without storing customer credit card numbers).

In the following, we present more details about our prototype implementation.

5.1 Preparing and Initializing the VM

As discussed in Section 4.1.1, the legacy host provides SICE with the initial VM image, composed of the VM kernel and the initial ram disk. The SMI handler copies this image to the SMRAM. KVM also places the required VM configuration parameters (e.g., RAM size) in the shared memory then triggers an SMI to initialize the isolated workload. As mentioned in Section 4.3, the SMI handler measures the initial VM image to attest to its integrity to the remote owner of this VM. The integrity evidence should be extended to include the VM configuration parameters passed by KVM. Some of these parameters (e.g., the VM execution entry point, initial register values) are critical to its integrity.

The security manager prepares the VM page tables and its virtual machine control block (VMCB), based on the provided configuration parameters. The page tables are crafted using AMD's nested page tables (NPT) [1], which adds another layer to the virtual-to-physical memory translation.

5.2 Handling VM Exits

Certain events force the VM to exit its operations (e.g., external interrupts, page faults). These events need to be handled by the hypervisor.

We forward most of the VM exit events to KVM in the legacy host. Nevertheless, the security manager handles some specific VM exits that do not require much computation to avoid unnecessary context switching. Among these VM exit events are control register accesses and requests to execute privileged instructions like `CPUID` or `INVD`.

Other VM exists (e.g., writing to an IO port, accessing an IO memory) are directly forwarded to the legacy host. To preserve the VM confidentiality, the security manager should only send information that is necessary for handling the VM exits (e.g., VM exit reason and error code). This information is sent to the KVM in the legacy host through an established communication channel between the isolated environment and the legacy host.

5.3 Communication with the Legacy Host

Establishing a communication channel with the legacy host is not managed by the SMI handler. Instead, it is directly managed by the security manager and the legacy host. As discussed in Section 4, a shared memory that is outside the SMRAM protection is used to establish the communication between the legacy host and the isolated workload.

Signaling is required between the two environments to send notifications that data is placed into the shared memory. In the time-sharing mode, we use the context switching as the method of signaling. In the multi-core mode, IPIs between the host and the isolated cores are used for signaling, as discussed in Section 4.2.1.

5.4 Using Hardware Peripherals

In our prototype, hardware peripherals in the isolated workload are emulated using Qemu in the legacy host. There are three main methods to control a hardware peripheral:

IO ports, IO memory, and Direct Memory Access (DMA). When the VM accesses an IO port or an IO memory, a VM exit occurs and the control is transferred to the host to emulate the hardware access.

DMA requests work differently because DMA is supposed to directly read or write physical memory. In legacy VMs, Qemu is granted full access to the VM physical memory to emulate DMA accesses. However, since Qemu is located in the legacy host, SICE prevents it from directly accessing the memory of the isolated environment. Thus, our prototype modifies Qemu to send a request to the security manager with the address, size, and type (read or write) of the emulated DMA. The security manager in turn copies the required memory between the VM memory and the shared memory. To preserve the confidentiality of the isolated workload, the security manager only allows Qemu to retrieve or modify VM memory areas assigned to DMA operations.

In our prototype, the security manager handles DMA access to simplify our implementation. Nevertheless, this operations should be directly handled by the isolated VM by allowing it to directly access a part of the shared memory, which will reduce the tasks required from the security manager, and consequently reduce its code size.

5.5 Attestation

As mentioned in Section 4.3, the SMI handler should be a part of a trusted boot process. However, the LS22 servers, used for our implementation prototype, are not equipped with a TPM. Due to the lack of a TPM, the attestation process is not included in our prototype. Nevertheless, it is worth mentioning that static attestation using the TPM, signature key generation and signing are all known techniques that have been implemented previously.

It is worth mentioning here that implementing these cryptographic operations may increase the size of the code base of SICE. For instance, a typical SHA1 library is around 120 LOC. Other cryptographic functions (e.g., generating an RSA signature) can be done using the TPM.

6. EXPERIMENTAL EVALUATION

We perform a set of experiments to evaluate the performance of SICE. There are two anticipated sources of performance overhead associated with SICE. The first is the direct overhead resulting from entering/exiting the isolated environment. The second is the indirect overhead that results from the cache and TLB flushing required for SICE operations. On the other hand, running the isolated environment outside the SMM avoids any execution slow-down and is not anticipated to cause any performance overhead, compared to running the same workload without SICE.

In the rest of this section, we present a measurement of the anticipated overhead. First, we measure the execution time needed for a full context switching to and from the isolated environment. Second, we use the SICE prototype (See Section 5) to compare the performance of the isolated guest VM with the same VM running without SICE isolation.

6.1 SICE Execution Time

We measure the execution time needed to perform each of the four major steps of entering and exiting the isolated environment. The measured steps include: (1) triggering the SMI, (2) preparing the isolated environment by the SMI handler, (3) entering the isolated environment, and (4) returning to the legacy host. These measures are obtained from the average of 100 runs.

To precisely measure the end-to-end execution time of each step, we use the `RDTSC` instruction to read the processor's Time Stamp Counter (TSC). We then convert cycles to microseconds based on the TSC speed (2.7GHz in our experimental platform).

Table 1: SICE execution time

Operation	Time (in μs)	Std. Dev.
Triggering an SMI	6.8	0.074
Preparing the isolated env.	20.7	0.155
Entering the isolated env.	9.3	0.233
Exiting the isolated env.	30.1	0.644
Total (≈)	67	

Table 1 shows the experimental results for the time-sharing mode. Triggering an SMI and switching the processor context from the legacy host to the SMI handler needs an average of 6.8 μs. The SMI is invoked by the local APIC of the processor core by sending an IPI to all cores on the system.

The next step, which is to prepare the isolated environment, needs an average of 20.7 μs. The latency of this step is relatively high given that this step only requires changing a few entries in the page tables, modifying the interrupt vector table descriptor, and verifying the values of several registers and MSRs. We anticipate that this relatively high latency is caused by a slower processing speed in the SMM. A similar observation was made in [2].

The next step is entering the isolated environment. In this step, we execute the "return from SMM" instruction (`RSM`) to jump to the security manager. The time needed for this step is 9.3 μs, which is relatively high. We anticipate this latency is due to the change of the processor execution environment, particularly the page tables, which leads to invalidating all cache and TLB entries.

Finally, the time needed to return from the isolated environment to the legacy host is 30.1 μs, which is similar to executing all the previous steps in the reverse order (i.e., from the isolated environment to the legacy host). In total, the end-to-end time required to enter and exit the isolated environment is 67 μs.

In the time-sharing mode, the end-to-end execution time overhead obtained in this experiment occurs on every context switch between the isolated environment and the legacy host. A context switch is required every time the isolated environment needs a service from the legacy host. In contrast, it is a one-time overhead in the multi-core mode.

6.2 Isolated Environment Performance

Our next experiment is to evaluate the overall performance overhead on the isolated workload. We run this experiment using the same system configuration of our prototype system, discussed in Section 5. In our experiments, we assign a 256 MB to the VM. Our VM runs Linux kernel v2.6.28. and a ram disk that is equipped with BusyBox v1.10.2 [4]. (BusyBox is a program that combines common utilities into a single executable.)

To evaluate the performance of the guest VM, we assemble a set of tests and run each test on the same guest VM in three different environments: (1) unmodified Qemu/KVM using one processor core, (2) SICE time-sharing environment using a single processor core, and (3) SICE multi-core environment using two processor cores, used as the host core and the isolated core. In the multi-core test, we do not run any program other than Qemu/KVM on the host core, so that we can get a precise measurement of the performance overhead.

To measure the performance overhead, we use Qemu to emulate a serial port for the guest VM. We then configure the guest VM to use this serial console to accept shell command. Our performance measurement is the execution time needed for the guest VM to complete each of these tests. The execution time is calculated by using the **RDTSC** instruction in the legacy host. The time measurement is taken just before sending the last letter of the shell command (the carriage return) and right after the first response is received (echoing the carriage return).

To calculate the performance overhead of each test, we first measure T_K, the time needed to run the test using unmodified Qemu/KVM. Afterward, we measure T_S, the time needed to run the same experiment using SICE. The performance overhead is then calculated using the equation $(T_S - T_K)/T_K \times 100\%$.

We selected our test cases in three categories: The first is user level programs to test the user level operations of guest VMs running with SICE. The second is a group of tests that test the throughput of the guest VM kernel. The third tests the performance of the emulated network interface.

In the first category, we run three tests. The first measures the latency of copying a 2.1 MB file. Our prototype system does not support hard drive emulation. Thus the file is copied inside the virtual file system that represents the initial ram disk. Our main objective of this test is to estimate the impact of SICE on the guest VM memory operations, because it is basically a copy between two locations in memory rather than an actual disk access. The next two tests in the same category use the programs **gzip** and **gunzip** to compress and decompress the same file. These tests aim to test the impact of SICE on the guest VM's user level computations. The final results of these tests are obtained as an average of 100 runs.

In the second category, we measure the guest VM kernel responses to three main operations: **fork**, **getpid** and **insmod**. **fork** and **getpid** are tested using a custom program that directly calls these system calls 10,000 times and measures the average response time. For the **insmod** test case, we use the **insmod** program to insert a 16.4 KB loadable kernel module in the guest kernel. This test is repeated 10 times, and all test runs show very little variance.

In the last category, we run a single test that uses **wget** to retrieve a 156.6 KB file from an Apache server running in the legacy host. The test is repeated 10 times.

Figure 6 shows the results of our experiments. In the multi-core mode, all tests, except for **wget**, showed a slight performance overhead under 3%. We expect that the slight performance overhead is due to the time required to copy information to and from the shared memory between the legacy host and the security manager.

The **wget** test shows a 17% performance overhead. However, a significant portion of this overhead is due to the *non-optimized* implementation of the Qemu network emulator for SICE. When a packet is ready to be sent through the network, the VM sends an IO command to the network adapter to inform it that a packet is ready. In normal operations,

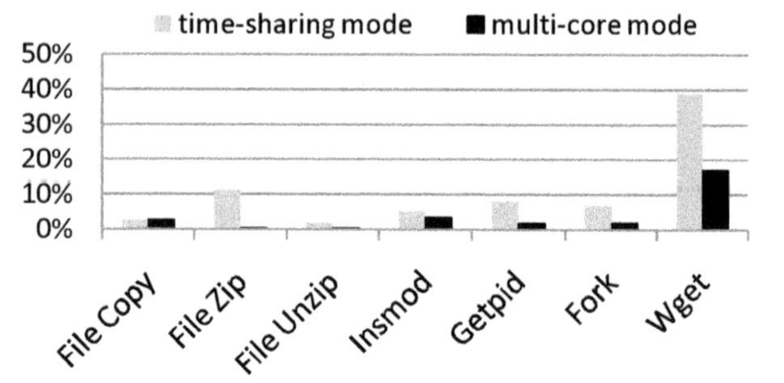

Figure 6: Performance overhead of an isolated VM compared with original Qemu/KVM

Qemu first receives this IO command, and then directly accesses the VM physical memory to emulate the DMA read of the packet. In our prototype, Qemu does not have direct access to the physical memory of the guest VM. Thus, we modified Qemu to send DMA requests to the security manager, which copies the packet from the protected guest VM memory to the shared memory so that Qemu can process it correctly. Similarly, an extra step is necessary when the VM receives a packet.

Hence, our prototype requires an extra communication step between Qemu in the legacy host and the security manager for every network packet. Intuitively, this extra communication step requires an extra context switch from the legacy host to the isolated environment in the time-sharing mode or an extra inter-process communication between the host core and the isolated core in the multi-core mode.

This extra communication step is the cause of the high overhead in the **wget** test. To support this claim, we measured the number of exits to and from the isolated environment during this test. In normal operations, there was an average of 1,249 guest VM exits that required hardware emulation by KVM and/or Qemu. In SICE's time-sharing mode, there was an average of 1,877 context switches between the isolated environment and the legacy host. There was a similar number of messages passed between the host core and the isolated core in the multi-core mode. This 50% increase in the communication time between the two environments explains the high overhead in this test.

To avoid this overhead, the VM device driver can be modified so that it uses the shared memory for the network adapter's DMA operations. Thus, the Qemu emulated driver would be able to directly read the passed packets without sending an extra request to the security manager.

The time-sharing mode showed a higher performance overhead, which is expectable due to the 67 μs needed to switch between the host and the isolated guest VM. The tests that show higher overhead, such as **gzip** and **wget**, are those that require a higher number of switching between the host and the isolated environment.

It is also noticeable that the time-sharing mode showed a higher overhead (around 40%) in the **wget** test. Receiving the target file in the normal VM operations needs 0.532 seconds compared to 0.739 seconds in the time-sharing mode. As mentioned above, this test requires 1,877 context switches from the isolated environment to the legacy host. Given that each context switch requires an average of 67 μs, the context switch overhead in this test was 0.126 seconds. This test clearly shows that the time-sharing mode is not suitable for operations that are IO intensive. It will be rather useful to run programs that require an enhanced isolation and a smaller IO footprint (e.g., a program that processes secret key operations).

7. RELATED WORK

Several researchers (e.g, [3, 5, 9, 22, 34]) attempted to use hypervisors to enable strong isolation between workloads running in a cloud computing environment. Nevertheless, recent attacks [16,32] and vulnerability reports [23,24] show that hypervisors are subject to security exploitation.

There have been several attempts (e.g., [2,30,31]) to verify the runtime integrity of hypervisors. These techniques still require cloud computing users to trust the host environment, which has a relatively large TCB and continuously interacts with mutually distrusted workloads.

As discussed in Section 1, the recent attempts that aim at eliminating the hypervisor from the TCB can be divided into microhypervisor-based and hardware-based approaches.

Hardware-based approaches: The introduction discussed how systems that rely on the late launch capability (e.g., Flicker [20], BIND [25]) fall short from our objectives. Moreover, Intel proposed a hardware service called Processor Measured Application Protection Service (P-MAPS) [21] to offer runtime memory isolation. However, there is insufficient detail about its ability to provide multi-core isolation. IBM also introduced interesting security features in its Cell Broadband Engine (Cell BE) architecture [26], which provides multi-core isolation. However, these features are unique to this specific architecture. SICE achieves the same level of isolation on the x86 architecture, which is used in the vast majority of general purpose computing platforms.

Microhypervisor-based approaches: We discussed two notable microhypervisors, NOVA [27] and Trustvisor [19], as well as seL4 [15] in the introduction. In particular, seL4 is a promising approach that uses formal verification to introduce a vulnerability-free microkernel, though it cannot be extended to commodity hypervisors due to its restrictions (e.g., it should run with interrupts mostly disabled). It would be interesting to study how we can apply formal verification to guarantee the integrity of SICE's security manager.

8. CONCLUSION

In this paper, we presented SICE, a research prototype that aims to explore the capability of current hardware platforms in providing more secure isolated environments. We demonstrated that current hardware architecture already provides abstractions such as SMM that can support strong isolation. We showed that building strong isolation mechanisms on top of the SMM abstraction requires a very small TCB of about 300 LOC, which tremendously reduces the TCB size compared with previous techniques. Nevertheless, practical deployment of SICE would require CPU and hardware platform vendors to undergo detailed security reviews of the BIOS software and the SMM implementation.

SICE provides a set of unique capabilities to the isolated environment, including (1) fast context switch to and from the legacy host, (2) protected concurrent execution with the legacy host, and (3) attestation to its integrity. Moreover, its ability to run isolated workloads concurrently with a legacy host provides a cost-effective solution to security sensitive workloads without using dedicated hardware platforms.

Our future research will focus on extending SICE to work on Intel platforms. In addition, we will explore how to apply formal verification methods on SICE's security manager.

9. REFERENCES

[1] Advanced Micro Devices. Amd64 architecture programmer's manual: Volume 2: System programming, September 2007.

[2] A. M. Azab, P. Ning, Z. Wang, X. Jiang, X. Zhang, and N. C. Skalsky. HyperSentry: enabling stealthy in-context measurement of hypervisor integrity. In *Proceedings of the 17th ACM conference on Computer and communications security (CCS '10)*, pages 38–49, 2010.

[3] S. Berger, R. Cáceres, D. Pendarakis, R. Sailer, E. Valdez, R. Perez, W. Schildhauer, and D. Srinivasan. TVDc: managing security in the trusted virtual datacenter. *SIGOPS Oper. Syst. Rev.*, 42(1):40–47, 2008.

[4] BusyBox. `http://www.busybox.net/`.

[5] X. Chen, T. Garfinkel, E. C. Lewis, P Subrahmanyam, C. A. Waldspurger, D. Boneh, J. Dwoskin, and D.R.K Ports. Overshadow: a virtualization-based approach to retrofitting protection in commodity operating systems. In *Proceedings of the 13th international conference on Architectural support for programming languages and operating systems (ASPLOS'13)*, pages 2–13, 2008.

[6] L. Duflot. Getting into the SMRAM: SMM reloaded. In *Proceedings of the 10th CanSecWest conference*, 2009.

[7] S. Embleton, S. Sparks, and C. Zou. SMM rootkits: a new breed of OS independent malware. In *Proceedings of the 4th international conference on Security and privacy in communication networks*, pages 1–12, August 2008.

[8] Niels Ferguson. Aes-cbc + elephant diffuser: A disk encryption algorithm for windows vista. Microsoft Corporation Technical Report, 2006.

[9] T. Garfinkel, B. Pfaff, J. Chow, M. Rosenblum, and D. Boneh. Terra: a virtual machine-based platform for trusted computing. In *Proceedings of the 19th ACM symposium on Operating systems principles (SOSP '03)*, pages 193–206, 2003.

[10] Hewlett-Packard, Intel, Microsoft, Phoenix, and Toshiba. Advanced configuration and power interface specification. revision 3.0b, October 2006.

[11] Intel Corporation. Trusted eXecution Technology preliminary architecture specification and enabling considerations. Document number 31516803, 2006.

[12] Intel Corporation. Intel virtualization technology for directed I/O. Document number 31516803, 2007.

[13] Intel Corporation. Software developer's manual vol. 3: System programming guide, June 2009.

[14] E. Keller, J. Szefer, J. Rexford, and R. B. Lee. Nohype: virtualized cloud infrastructure without the virtualization. In *Proceedings of the 37th annual international symposium on Computer architecture (ISCA '10)*, pages 350–361, 2010.

[15] G. Klein, K. Elphinstone, G. Heiser, J. Andronick, D. Cock, P. Derrin, D. Elkaduwe, K. Engelhardt, R. Kolanski, M. Norrish, T. Sewell, H. Tuch, and S. Winwood. sel4: formal verification of an OS kernel.

In *Proceedings of the ACM SIGOPS 22nd symposium on Operating systems principles (SOSP '09)*, pages 207–220, 2009.
[16] K. Kortchinsky. Hacking 3D (and breaking out of VMWare). In *Black Hat conference*, 2009.
[17] Dartmouth PKI Lab. TPM reset attack. `http://www.cs.dartmouth.edu/~pkilab/sparks/`. Accessed in August 2011.
[18] Kernel Based Virtual Machine. `http://www.linux-kvm.org/`.
[19] J. McCune, Y. Li, N. Qu, A. Datta, V. Gligor, and A. Perrig. Efficient TCB reduction and attestation. In *the 31st IEEE Symposium on Security and Privacy*, May 2010.
[20] J. McCune, B. Parno, A. Perrig, M. Reiter, and H. Isozaki. Flicker: an execution infrastructure for TCB minimization. In *Proceedings of the ACM European Conference on Computer Systems (EuroSys)*, March/April 2008.
[21] R. Sahita, U. Warrier, and P. Dewan. Dynamic software application protection. Intel Corporation, April 2009.
[22] R. Sailer, T. Jaeger, E. Valdez, R. Caceres, R. Perez, S. Berger, J. Griffin, and L. van Doorn. Building a MAC-based security architecture for the xen opensource hypervisor. In *Proceedings of the 21st Annual Computer Security Applications Conference (ACSAC)*, pages 276–285, 2005.
[23] Secunia. Vulnerability report: Vmware esx server 3.x. `http://secunia.com/advisories/product/10757/`. Accessed in August 2011.
[24] Secunia. Xen multiple vulnerability report. `http://secunia.com/advisories/44502/`. Accessed in August 2011.
[25] E. Shi, A. Perrig, and L. van Doorn. BIND: A fine-grained attestation service for secure distributed systems. In *Proceedings of the 2005 IEEE Symposium on Security and Privacy*, May 2005.
[26] K. Shimizu, H. P. Hofstee, and J. S. Liberty. Cell broadband engine processor vault security architecture. *IBM J. Res. Dev.*, pages 521–528, September 2007.
[27] U. Steinberg and B. Kauer. NOVA: a microhypervisor-based secure virtualization architecture. In *Proceedings of the 5th European conference on Computer systems (EuroSys'10)*, pages 209–222. ACM, 2010.
[28] Trusted Computing Group. `https://www.trustedcomputinggroup.org/`.
[29] Trusted Computing Group. TPM specifications version 1.2. `https://www.trustedcomputinggroup.org/downloads/specifications/tpm/tpm`, July 2005.
[30] J. Wang, A. Stavrou, and A. K. Ghosh. HyperCheck: A hardware-assisted integrity monitor. In *Proceedings of the 13th International Symposium on Recent Advances in Intrusion Detection (RAID'10)*, September 2010.
[31] Z. Wang and X. Jiang. HyperSafe: A lightweight approach to provide lifetime hypervisor control-flow integrity. In *Proceedings of the 31st IEEE Symposium on Security and Privacy*, May 2010.
[32] R. Wojtczuk and J. Rutkowska. Xen 0wning trilogy. In *Black Hat conference*, 2008.
[33] R. Wojtczuk and J. Rutkowska. Attacking SMM memory via Intel CPU cache poisoning. Invisible Things Lab, 2009.
[34] J. Yang and K. G. Shin. Using hypervisor to provide data secrecy for user applications on a per-page basis. In *Proceedings of the fourth ACM SIGPLAN/SIGOPS international conference on Virtual execution environments (VEE'08)*, pages 71–80, 2008.

APPENDIX

A. PORTABILITY TO INTEL PLATFORMS

In this section, we discuss the portability of SICE to Intel platforms. Although SMM is supported by both AMD and Intel, SICE uses some hardware features that are only provided by AMD. In the following, we discuss these features and propose alternative techniques for Intel platforms. Implementing SICE on Intel platforms using these techniques needs further research, particularly to achieve both the security and performance required from this system.

SMRAM Size and Location Modification: After the SMRAM is locked, Intel platforms do not allow runtime change of its size and location. This restriction has a direct impact on our techniques, which rely on changing the SMRAM size at run time to enable fast context switching to the isolated environment. However, some other Intel features can be used for SICE. For instance, new Intel hardware is equipped with special instructions to do a high throughput cryptographic operations using the Advanced Encryption Standard (AES). In the time-sharing mode, this feature can be used to encrypt and authenticate the memory of the isolated workload while the legacy host is running, and decrypt and verify the same memory in the isolated environment. Thus, the SMRAM can only be used as a permanent storage of encryption keys. Further research is needed to evaluate the feasibility and performance of this approach.

Memory Double-view: Intel platforms define the `TSeg` SMRAM in its memory controller hub, which is shared among multiple cores. Unless the implementation is modified to move the SMRAM definition to a core specific location, our memory double-view technique will not be able to isolate individual Intel processor cores.

Nevertheless, current Intel implementation can apply this technique on processor nodes as they do not share the same memory control hub, allowing a more coarse grained isolation of the resources on physical platforms.

Multi-core Protection: Intel does not provide a capability that can disable all system interrupts. As mentioned in Section 4.2, we rely on this capability to prevent the host core from using the startup IPI to modify the execution environment of the isolated core. However, the startup IPI can only set the instruction pointer to an address in the lowest 1MB of the physical memory. This address range can be easily modified to point to a non-writable memory chip.

AmazonIA: When Elasticity Snaps Back

Sven Bugiel*, Stefan Nürnberger*, Thomas Pöppelmann†, Ahmad-Reza Sadeghi*†, Thomas Schneider*

*System Security Lab / CASED, Technische Universität Darmstadt, Germany

†Fraunhofer SIT, Darmstadt, Germany

ABSTRACT

Cloud Computing is an emerging technology promising new business opportunities and easy deployment of web services.

Much has been written about the risks and benefits of cloud computing in the last years. The literature on clouds often points out security and privacy challenges as the main obstacles, and proposes solutions and guidelines to avoid them. However, most of these works deal with either malicious cloud providers or customers, but ignore the severe threats caused by unaware users.

In this paper we consider security and privacy aspects of *real-life* cloud deployments, independently from malicious cloud providers or customers. We focus on the popular Amazon Elastic Compute Cloud (EC2) and give a detailed and systematic analysis of various crucial vulnerabilities in publicly available and widely used Amazon Machine Images (AMIs) and show how to eliminate them.

Our Amazon Image Attacks (AmazonIA) deploy an automated tool that uses only publicly available interfaces and makes *no* assumptions on the underlying cloud infrastructure. We were able to extract highly sensitive information (including passwords, keys, and credentials) from a variety of publicly available AMIs. The extracted information allows to (i) start (botnet) instances worth thousands of dollars per day, (ii) provide backdoors into the running machines, (iii) launch impersonation attacks, or (iv) access the source code of the entire web service. Our attacks can be used to completely compromise several real web services offered by companies (including IT-security companies), e.g., for website statistics/user tracking, two-factor authentication, or price comparison. Further, we show mechanisms to identify the AMI of certain running instances.

Following the maxim "security and privacy by design" we show how our automated tools together with changes to the user interface can be used to mitigate our attacks.

Categories and Subject Descriptors

K.6.5 [**MANAGEMENT OF COMPUTING AND INFORMATION SYSTEMS**]: Security and Protection

General Terms

Security

Keywords

Cloud Computing, Privacy, Awareness, Attacks, App Store, Virtual Machine Images, Secure Shell

1. INTRODUCTION

Cloud computing offers fine-grained IT resources, including storage, networking, and computing platforms, on an on-demand and pay-per-use basis. The high usability of today's cloud computing platforms makes this rapidly emerging paradigm very attractive for customers who want to instantly and easily provide web-services that are highly available and scalable to the current demands [36].

In the most flexible service model of cloud computing, *Infrastructure-as-a-Service* (IaaS), customers can build entire *virtual infrastructures* by renting resources like storage, network, and computing platforms in form of virtual machines with administrative access to the whole operating system. Images of these virtual machines can easily be shared to be run by other users, similar to an app store for the cloud.

Albeit the various advantages of cloud computing, serious concerns about security and privacy hinder many users from "going into the cloud". Most solutions to preserve security and privacy in the cloud proposed so far consider potentially faulty/malicious cloud providers or technical savvy/rogue customers. However, the much more serious and ubiquitous threat of unaware users who unintentionally harm their own or others' security or privacy is often overseen.

The main goal of this paper is the investigation and evaluation of security and privacy threats caused by the unawareness of users in the cloud. Although the methods and techniques described in this paper are applicable to arbitrary IaaS providers, we focus on one of the major cloud providers, Amazon's Elastic Compute Cloud (EC2) [5] and adapt our terminology accordingly. In the following, we describe the players involved in the (Amazon) Cloud App Store and the resulting security challenges.

The Cloud App Store. As shown in Fig. 1, the Cloud App Store involves a Provider and typically two kinds of users, Publisher and Consumer. The *Provider*, Amazon in our case, operates the IaaS cloud infrastructure, authenticates users and bills them for the resources they consumed.

The *Publisher* creates and publicly offers cloud apps, called *Amazon Machine Images* (AMIs). For this, he selects an existing AMI (AMI-1 in Fig. 1), instantiates it ($\text{Instance-1}_{\text{AMI-1}}$), logs into the running instance to configure it, and finally publishes a snapshot as a new AMI (AMI-2).

The *Consumer* selects this AMI from a list of available AMIs, instantiates it ($\text{Instance-2}_{\text{AMI-2}}$), and uses it for her purposes. Optionally, a Publisher can declare an AMI as *paid AMI* to earn money from Consumers invoking it.

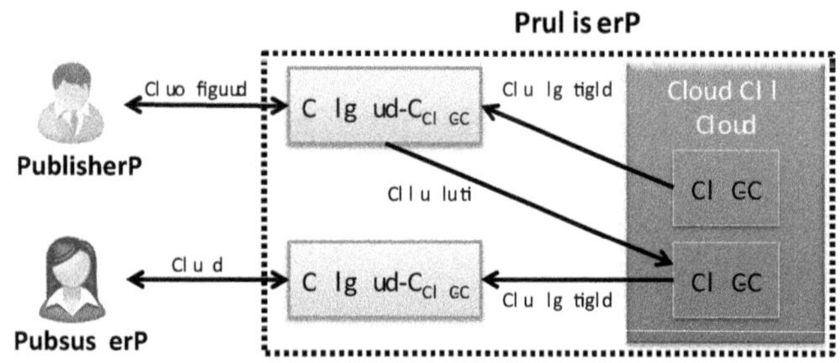

Figure 1: Basic System Model of Cloud App Store

The Cloud App Store poses security challenges for both, Consumers and Publishers (see also [48, 17]).

Security of Consumer. The Consumer must trust the Publisher not to include any malware into the AMI. Such a malicious AMI could contain a Trojan horse that spies on or modifies the Consumer's data, or a backdoor for malicious remote login. Even though full protection against such malicious AMIs is almost impossible, filters, virus scanners, and rootkit detectors could provide at least some level of protection [48].[1]

Security of Publisher. The Publisher on the other hand might accidentally publish AMIs that contain highly sensitive information. Examples include keys, credentials, passwords, command history/log files, or source code.

Although Amazon's user guide recommends to ensure that all confidential information is removed before publishing an AMI [12, Sharing AMIs Safely], many users seem to be unaware of the crucial consequences of ignoring these recommendations, do not have the appropriate tools at hand, or simply forgot private data in their AMIs.

The Gap between Theory and Practice. The Provider could filter AMIs for Trojans, backdoors, or confidential information to reduce the chance of malicious or sensitive data within AMIs. This was proposed in [48], but although the automated filtering system presented in that paper seems to be used already within the IBM SmartCloud [32], the explicit filtering rules are not available to the public.

In contrast, Amazon currently does not provide automated scanning of public AMIs as they are not responsible/liable for what users do with their own data. Though Amazon quickly reacts on incidents reported to their security hotline and informs affected customers, e.g., those running an AMI in which a backdoor was found [15].[2]

In this paper we show that these previously reported incidents are only the tip of the iceberg and many of the publicly available AMIs have severe security vulnerabilities leaking highly sensitive data.

Our Contribution and Outline.

After summarizing related work in §2 and giving background information on the Amazon Web Services (AWS) in §3 we present the following contributions.

Extraction of Sensitive Information from Public AMIs (cf. §4). Through an extensive analysis we were able to extract highly sensitive information from several publicly available EC2 AMIs. To make the analysis cost and time effective we developed an automated tool that uses different search strategies and exploits technology specific aspects of the Amazon cloud. The costs for running our attack were less than \$20 while the information we extracted from the AMIs would allow an attacker to cause financial damage of several \$10,000 per day and could severely harm the reputation of several companies that operate services in the cloud. After testing overall 1225 AMIs we got hold of the source code repositories, administrator passwords and other types of credentials of various web service providers.

SSH Vulnerabilities in AMIs (cf. §5). We discovered several vulnerabilities in AMIs that are introduced by incorrect usage and configuration of SSH. About one third of the tested 1100 public AMIs in Europe and the US-East region contain an SSH backdoor, i.e., a (forgotten) public key that allows remote login for the Publisher. We identified multiple instances that use the same SSH host key which allows an external attacker to correlate these instances running the same or a similar AMI, identify candidates for corresponding public AMIs, and mount several attacks, e.g., host impersonation.

Countermeasures (cf. §6). We provide several mechanisms to protect against our attacks on public AMIs. Besides organizational measures we propose to use our tools to enhance the security of the interfaces for publishing AMIs and also extensions to the interface of the Cloud App Store.

2. RELATED WORK

In this section we briefly revisit previous work on the security challenges of publicly sharing Virtual Machine (VM) images (AMIs in our terminology) on which we build our practical attacks. Afterwards we review the main related work on general cloud security, security aspects specific to the Amazon cloud, and methods for searching private data.

VM Image Analysis.

As summarized in §1, security and privacy risks for the Consumer and Publisher when sharing VM images have been identified in [48]. Shared VM images may contain either malware that was intentionally or unintentionally included by the Publisher. To protect against these threats, the authors propose filtering of VM images by the Provider which has been implemented in the Mirage image manage-

[1]In principle, this is similar to mobile app stores where downloaded apps must be trusted as well. Recently, Google's mobile app store withdrew 25 Android apps that were infected with malware [13]. As such attacks also harm the reputation of the mobile app store provider, some providers already review new apps submitted to the store to ensure that they perform as expected [9, 31].

[2]"For security reasons, we (Amazon) recommend that any instance based on a publicly available AMI that is distributed with an included SSH public key should be considered compromised and immediately terminated." [14]

ment system [38]. The IBM SmartCloud [32] deploys a system that is presumably based on (a mechanism like) Mirage for automated patching [52] and periodical malware scans [41] of public VM images.

We show that the risks pointed out in [48] ubiquitously occur in Amazon's Cloud App Store and have more severe consequences than previously thought. As our results show, Amazon does not apply any centralized filtering as proposed in [48], and considers this as the responsibility of cloud users. As countermeasure against these threats we propose tools and extensions to the user interface of the Cloud App Store that allow even technically less skilled users to protect their published AMIs from containing sensitive data.

General Cloud Security Challenges.

The risks and threats for cloud computing as analyzed in [23, 26, 21, 45] concern mainly the vulnerabilities inherent to cloud infrastructures, e.g., protection of the outsourced data and computations against eavesdropping and illegitimate modifications; new threats induced by sharing physical resources with other users' VMs (*multi-tenancy*); non-availability of the users' outsourced data and cloud-based services; or vendor lock-in to a single provider.

The security threats induced specifically by the usage model and capabilities of VMs, e.g., massive scalability and VM snapshots, i.e., copies of the current state of a VM, were discussed in [29, 40, 24]. These threats include, e.g., the rollback of a VM to an already compromised state, the conflict between traditional security management systems and the VMs' flexibility, or the loss of entropy upon state rollback affecting the freshness needed for cryptographic mechanisms and protocols.

Recent guidances and best practices aim at mitigating these threats and securing cloud computing [35, 22]. However, we show that many Publishers and Consumers do not adhere to these recommendations.

Amazon Specific Cloud Security Challenges.

The documentation of the Amazon Web Services (AWS) [8] contains several relevant security guidelines. Moreover, the Elastic Compute Cloud (EC2) [5], an integral part of AWS, has recently been subject to scientific and industrial security research as summarized next.

AWS Security Recommendations. An overview of the security processes in the AWS cloud infrastructure is given in [47]. Further, Amazon provides security guidelines and best practices on how to use AWS [19], including advises and references [43] on how customers can secure their AWS credentials in EC2 instances with respect to the risk of unintentionally embedding them in public AMIs. However, the proposed solutions require technical knowledge of the AWS mechanisms which conflicts with the high usability of the Cloud App Store. Thus, Cloud App Store users are either unaware of the security risks/guidelines or are only capable of using the store but not of implementing the security guidelines. This assumption is underlined by the high number and severity of our findings.

VM correlation. The possibility to gain insight into the EC2 network topology, and how to exploit this knowledge for placing a malicious VM A purposefully on the same physical host as a specific foreign VM B, and finally to eavesdrop on VM B via side-channels, was demonstrated in [39]. Our SSH correlation attack (cf. §5) provides additional information about running VMs that can be used to enhance their approach.

Malicious VMs. The attacks presented in [17] exploit design flaws of the EC2 Cloud App Store such as phishing by publishing a malicious AMI that appears high in the list of available AMIs. Our countermeasures proposed in §6 can be used to mitigate these attacks.

Private Data Search.

Several methods and sources exist to search for unintentionally leaked private data in public resources. Examples include recovery of sensitive data from second-hand harddrives [28], or "Google hacking" [16, 46] which allows to query the Google search engine to find private information in its indices, e.g., private keys, hashed passwords, or private information about a person.

3. BACKGROUND ON AWS

In this section we recall the main aspects of the Amazon Web Services (AWS) [8]: the Amazon Elastic Compute Cloud (EC2) [5] in §3.1 and authentication to AWS in §3.2. For detailed information we refer to Amazon's documentation on AWS [18]. Readers already familiar with AWS can skip this section.

3.1 Amazon's Elastic Compute Cloud (EC2)

In 2006, Amazon introduced the Elastic Compute Cloud (EC2) [5] as part of the Amazon Web Services (AWS). It allows users to run Virtual Machines (VMs) on-demand on the infrastructure provided by AWS. The VMs behave similar to a physical server and contain a full-blown operating system (currently supported are various Linux distributions, FreeBSD, OpenSolaris, and Windows). Running VMs are called *instances* and isolation between instances is enforced by the XEN hypervisor [19]. Fig. 2 illustrates the instantiation of VMs from Amazon Machine Images (AMIs) via the AWS Cloud App Store. When a Consumer starts a VM, she has to specify 1) an AMI from which the instance is derived (AMI-ID), 2) a type defining the resources available to the instance (Type), and 3) the geographical region in which the VM is deployed (Region) as described next.

Region and Type.

The Region defines one out of five EC2 data centers (two in the US, one in Europe, and two in Asia). To guarantee failsafe operation, each data center of a region is currently split into two or more independent *availability zones*.

The Type specifies how many resources are allocated for the instance (CPU, RAM, temporary disk space, speed of the network connection) and determines the costs ranging from $0.02 to $2.10 per instance operation hour. Besides costs for running instances, the user is also monthly charged for I/O usage and consumed network bandwidth.

Amazon Machine Images (AMIs).

Amazon introduced the concept of pre-built VM image templates, called Amazon Machine Images (AMIs) for rapid deployment of instances. An AMI contains a whole operating system together with applications and data. When an instance is started, a copy of the selected AMI is booted and control over the instance is handed over to the user. AMIs are managed in the *Cloud App Store* and are either provided

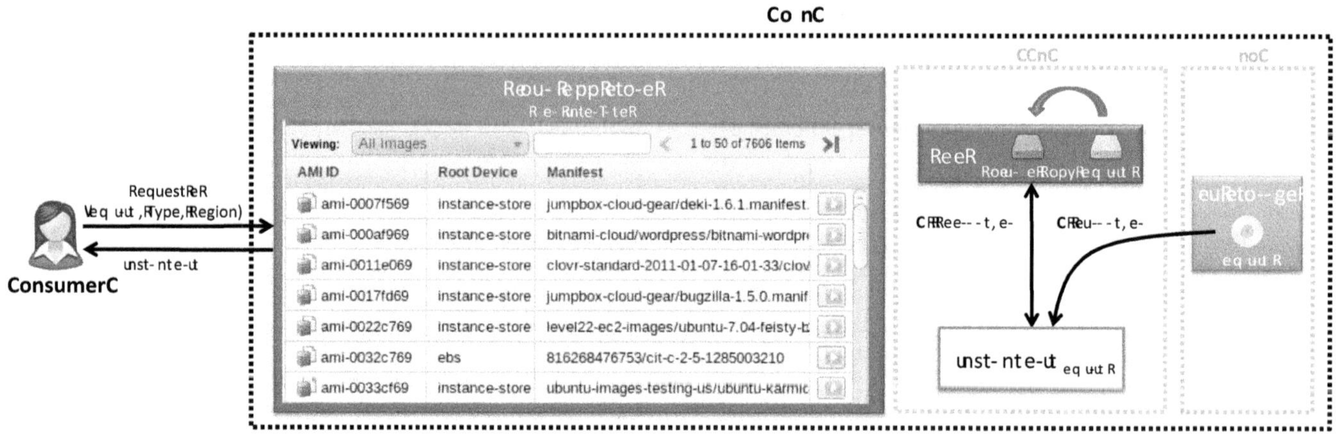

Figure 2: VM instantiation in Amazon AWS. The Consumer chooses the image (AMI-ID), resources (Type), and availability zone (Region) for her VM on the Web Interface of the AWS Cloud App Store. Depending on the type of the AMI, the VM is instantiated (Instance-ID$_{\text{AMI-ID}}$) either as (A) EBS-backed or (B) S3-backed.

directly by Amazon or by third party publishers. Users can take these public AMIs to create their own AMIs which are either kept for themselves (private AMIs), made accessible to a group of users (shared AMIs), or made publicly available for every user of EC2 (public AMIs) as shown in Fig. 1. AMIs are further distinguished by the storage type they are based on – either S3 or EBS – as described next.

S3-backed AMIs. S3-backed AMIs are stored on the highly available Simple Storage Service (S3) [7]. As shown in Fig. 2, S3-backed AMIs are instantiated by first copying the image onto the hard drive of a physical EC2 node which then boots the image. A new S3-backed AMI can be created from within a running S3-backed instance by a process called *bundling*, which stores the current state of the instance's file system on S3 and registers this state with the Cloud App Store as new AMI. The data in an S3-backed instance is only persistent for the life of the instance and lost upon instance termination or failure. This resembles the usage model of a live CD.

EBS-backed AMIs. EBS-backed AMIs reside on the Elastic Block Storage (EBS) [4]. EBS offers persistent, attachable block devices, called *volumes*, which can hold an arbitrary file system. When a user instantiates an EBS-backed AMI, a *bitwise* copy of the image is created on EBS and the VM is started from this new image as shown in Fig. 2. Storing the instance's data persistently on an EBS volume enables the user to stop the execution of an EBS-backed VM. He then has only ongoing costs for the storage occupied by the block device. New EBS-backed AMIs are created by storing a bitwise copy of the current state of a volume, called *snapshot*, on EBS and registering this snapshot with the Cloud App Store as new AMI. EBS volumes cannot only be used to hold bootable AMIs, but are also a general way to store persistent data. They can be attached on-the-fly to running instances (comparable to a USB flash drive in the cloud).

Networking.

All instances are executed in an environment which provides logging, monitoring, and security capabilities such as a simple firewall for inbound traffic (cf. [20]). On startup, the instance is assigned an external IPv4 address for Internet connectivity and an internal address for communication with other EC2 instances. The user is only charged for data traffic with the Internet over the external address.

3.2 Authentication in AWS

AWS uses different authentication mechanisms to provide authenticated access to the AWS account and to running instances as described next.

Authentication to the AWS Account. During the initial account creation and verification, an AWS Customer associates her email address with an AWS account, selects a password, and provides credit card and personal information for the monthly billing. After successful verification by Amazon she obtains a password to log into a web management system where she can inspect log files and the current account activity, change personal information, and manage instances. In this web management system, the Customer can register credentials for an Application Programming Interface (API) to control the life cycle of an instance by means of tools provided by 3rd parties or Amazon [34]. We refer to those credentials as *API keys*.[3] The API keys can be used for example to start or terminate instances, create EBS volumes, or to register public images. Moreover, API keys are required within an S3-backed instance during the bundling of the same instances in order to access the S3 storage. However, API keys do not provide direct access to personal or credit card information.

Authentication to Instances. After an instance has been started, the control needs to be securely transferred to the Customer by providing her with a secure and authenticated login channel. For this, Linux/Unix-based instances commonly use Secure Shell (SSH) [51]. Here, a customer generates an SSH key pair $(\mathsf{pk}, \mathsf{sk})$ and registers the public key pk with AWS. Upon instantiation of an AMI, this key is automatically made available to and imported by the SSH server running in the newly created instance and can be used for secure logins of the user who holds the corresponding secret key sk.

[3]Technically, API keys provide authorized access to a SOAP, Query, or REST-based web service.

4. AMI PRIVACY ANALYSIS

By systematically examining only little more than 10% of all public Linux-based AMIs we were able to extract a lot of private information. The results of our analysis are summarized in §4.1. To automate the analysis we implemented a tool as described in §4.2. We calculate the costs for analyzing all AMIs in §4.3 and discuss the reasons for and implications of our analysis in §4.4.

4.1 Our Findings

We analyzed a total of 1225 AMIs in the European and US-East region of the Amazon EC2 cloud. In our privacy analysis of these AMIs we discovered AWS API keys, private keys and credentials, and private data, including source code. For each of these categories we describe the possible threats and our findings next. A summary of our findings in EBS-backed AMIs is given in Tab. 1.

Finding	US-East-1		EU-West-1	
Analyzed AMIs	550	(100%)	550	(100%)
AWS API Keys	12	(2%)	2	(0.35%)
SVN Credentials	4	(0.7%)	3	(0.55%)
SSH/SSL User Keys	14	(2.5%)	5	(0.9%)
SSH Host Keys	205	(37%)	122	(22%)
SSH Backdoor	253	(46%)	93	(16%)

Table 1: Summary of the Findings of our Privacy Analysis of Public EBS-backed AMIs (April 2011)

4.1.1 AWS API keys

Our most significant findings are API keys (cf. §3.2) which could be used to abuse the AWS account of the AMI Publisher. Those keys had been used by the Publisher of the examined AMIs to query the AWS API, in most cases for authorization before publishing and registering the running instance as new AMI.

Threats. The presence of AWS API keys in public AMIs is a very serious threat to the owners of those keys. It allows the adversary to destroy the victim's virtual infrastructure or to create his own infrastructure at the expense of the victim [23]. For example, an attacker could discover multiple API keys in the public images of other customers. He then creates a public image of his own, which is configured to mount a DDoS attack against a chosen target. Using the discovered API keys he is able to instantiate several instances of his DDoS-image and run the attack at the expenses of the API keys' holders. This is in particular a problem as it is currently not possible to set a maximum limit of costs to prevent excessive usage in case of an accident (e.g., misconfiguration) or security breach [1]. With one AWS API key an attacker can cause costs of more than $3000 per day for running instances and additional charges for traffic and storage (cf. calculation in §A). Moreover, before the introduction of improved key management with the *Identity and Access Management (IAM)* [10] service in September 2010, customers had to use a single API key to control all their AWS services like EC2, the S3 storage or the SimpleDB database [42] engine. It seems that many EC2 customers have not migrated to this new service yet, e.g., because of unawareness or of being technically overwhelmed, and thus a discovered API key can be used to extract private information also from AWS services beyond EC2.

Findings. We retrieved 20 AWS API keys from S3 and EBS-backed AMIs in the US-East and European region.

4.1.2 Private Keys and Credentials

Private keys and login credentials are quite frequently stored or cached on a computer's hard drive. For instance, they are used to login to other hosts via SSH or to provide secure communication channels using SSL certificates.

Threats. Although most private keys are encrypted with a password when stored on disk, this data can be recovered [50]. Thus, these unintentionally published keys and credentials can compromise the security of the Publisher's IT infrastructure. For instance, an attacker can use private keys of SSH user authentication to log in to other hosts the key is authorized for. These hosts may be located within the virtual infrastructure of the Publisher in the cloud or even in the conventional IT infrastructure of the Publisher. Leaked private keys of valid SSL certificates that are used on commercial websites/services would allow an attacker to carry out man-in-the-middle attacks on those sites or implement ideal phishing attacks.

Findings. We discovered 16 unencrypted private keys for SSH user authentication, 3 unencrypted private keys of valid SSL certificates, and various other private keys. Most of the SSH keys we found were associated with an account with administrative privileges.

4.1.3 Private Data

Most AMIs contain information about their Publisher, resulting from the configuration and usage of the instance from which the AMI was created. This information can be obtained by analyzing, e.g., log, cache, or configuration files.

Threats. Private data can be used to profile Publishers, e.g., to identify their name, email address, other hosts they connected to, browser history, or their affiliation. The value of private information found by a random attacker is hard to estimate. However, leakage of private information might harm the reputation of a person or company, cause financial harm, or even entail legal consequences.

Findings. In one particular AMI we found a picture of the owner of the AMI, holding a badge stating his name and employing company. In other cases we were able to find out the name of the AMI publisher by using information in the bash history and the name of the SSH key used for login. However, we cannot give concrete numbers as privacy violations are hard to categorize.

4.1.4 Source Code

The Amazon cloud is well suited for software development and testing of new software products and especially start-up companies make use of it.

Threats. Obtaining and analyzing source code of new proprietary applications or websites allows an attacker to steal unpublished ideas and concepts. Moreover, it gives him enough insight to mount further attacks on these products (or their users) and even the ability to insert malicious code if he gains access to the source code repository.

Findings. We obtained credentials for 7 different private source code repositories. Most of these repositories were operated by businesses and the repository's copy stored in the AMI contained highly valuable intellectual property and hard coded passwords for administrative access.

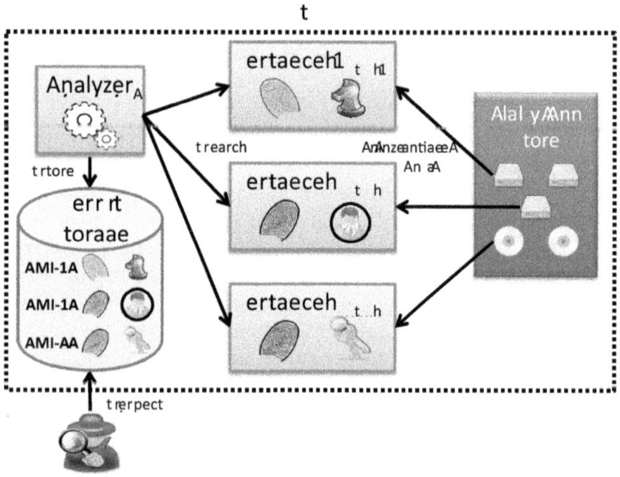

Figure 3: Approach for Analysis of AMIs

4.2 Tool for AMI Privacy Analysis

Next, we explain our tool for privacy analysis of AMIs and give details on its technical background and our strategy for cost- and time-efficient attacks. We have implemented our tool in the Python programming language and made use of the Boto library [34] in order to access the AWS API. We concentrated our analysis on Linux based AMIs, which form the majority of the provided AMIs (see [11] for detailed statistics), and thus designed our tools specifically for the Linux directory structure and key formats.

Fig. 3 depicts our approach of iteratively inspecting public AMIs for private information. It consists of (1) the instantiation of target AMIs, (2) the search for fingerprints, private information, or keys, and (3) the storing of the results in a data store. The last step (4) is a semi-automated inspection and analysis of all findings.

We describe how our tool accesses the data inside the AMIs (§4.2.1) and extracts private content from it (§4.2.2).

4.2.1 AMI Access

In order to analyze an AMI we mount its volume directly into the file system of our Analyzer instance (cf. Fig. 3). By running it in the cloud, we avoid expensive network traffic (e.g., downloading the image) and are able to profit from the scalability of cloud computing. Further by mounting target AMIs as volumes or via the SSH File System (SSHFS) [44] we minimize assumptions on the environment our analysis tools runs in (e.g., software dependencies). We describe the two methodologies in more detail next.

SSHFS. The SSHFS allows to mount remote volumes into the local file system by means of the SSH protocol. As SSH is the standard tool to perform system administration on EC2 Linux based instances and thus is supported by most AMIs, this approach is widely applicable. Although this method does not make any restrictions on where the Analyzer is run (e.g., it could be executed on a local host), deploying it on a dedicated EC2 instance reduces the network overhead significantly. Moreover, Amazon does not charge for cloud-internal data traffic.

EBS-Mount. Analyzing EBS-backed images is substantially faster than using SSHFS as EBS volumes provide raw

Pattern	Explanation (Common Usage)
*.pem	Specifies a file containing a private key, public key or a certificate
*.priv	File extension for *priv*ate keys
*.pub	Used to store *pub*lic keys
*.crt	*Cert*ificates
id_rsa	Default file name of private SSH keys
*.gpg | *.pgp	Files related to use with the encryption and signing application GPG/PGP
*.jks	Acronym for Java key-store [37]
secret | *key* | *private*	Potentially interesting files
.bash_history	User's history of executed commands
.svn/ | .git/ | .hg/	Common source code repositories

Table 2: Example of Search Patterns (* denotes the wildcard character and | alternatives)

disk access. As described in §3.1, EBS-backed images are stored on and booted from EBS volumes. Therefore, our analyzer tool first starts a public EBS-backed AMI to instantiate it on a new EBS volume. By dissolving the mapping between this instance and the new volume its file system is stored on, the tool obtains the EBS volume that contains the AMI to be tested. This EBS volume is then mounted by the Analyzer instance. This method allows also to analyze EBS-backed AMIs that are explicitly configured without SSH access (e.g., to protect the source code of an appliance).

4.2.2 Extraction of Private AMI Content

Once an AMI is mounted into the file system of the Analyzer instance, the Analyzer searches for keys and private information in the AMI and stores its findings locally for later evaluation. Some of the patterns for file or directory names that our tool is searching for are listed in Tab. 2. These patterns include common names for key files/stores, shell history files, and source code repository directories.

The primary targets of the automated search are high-value findings, i.e., private keys and credentials, usually to be discovered in the home directories of users, the home directory of the superuser (root), and common locations for (custom) programs and configuration files.

If a search result indicates the presence of further, not automatically discovered private data, e.g., a source code repository directory was found or the shell history is non-empty, we manually investigate the corresponding AMI for further findings such as source code or private information.

Forensic Analysis of EBS Volumes. As described in §3.1, EBS-backed AMI instances are created as a *bitwise* copy of the original AMI volume they are derived from and hence provide access to raw blocks on the newly created volume. This enables our analyzer to apply forensic methods [28, 27] in order to recover and scrutinize deleted files which may contain private information.

4.3 Costs for AMI Privacy Analysis

Our analysis tool described in §4.2 currently takes approximately 10 minutes to start and completely analyze an AMI. However, as Amazon charges for each started instance hour [3], the costs for starting an AMI are one instance hour. For EBS-backed AMIs the smallest available type is the "Micro" instance for \$0.03/h. The costs for S3-backed AMIs depend on the AMI's architecture: a 32-bit S3-backed AMI can be started as "Small" instance for \$0.10/h while 64-bit AMIs only support the "Large" instance type for \$0.40/h. A medium scale analysis can even be done "for free" as Amazon offers free services to new customers in the first year (currently 750 "Micro" instance hours per month plus some storage and traffic volume).

Costs of Our Analysis. During our analysis, we examined 1225 AMIs (100 S3-backed 32-bit AMIs, 25 S3-backed 64-bit AMIs and 1100 EBS-backed AMIs). As we have split our analysis into two months, the costs for starting the EBS-backed AMIs were covered by the free offer and for the S3-backed AMIs we paid in total \$20.

Costs for Analyzing All Public AMIs. Scanning *all* free and Linux based 9864 public AMIs that are currently available[4] (cf. Fig. 4) would cost approximately \$1550: Starting all AMIs would cost around 3058 "Micro" instance hours, 4449 "Small" instance hours, and 2357 "Large" instance hours to start all AMIs. As the Analyzer component of our tool takes on average 10 minutes per AMI this adds $\frac{9864*10}{60} =$ 1644 "Micro" instance hours. We note that such an exhaustive search can be highly parallelized and therefore carried out very fast, e.g., in less than one day with 70 analyzing instances, without increasing the costs.

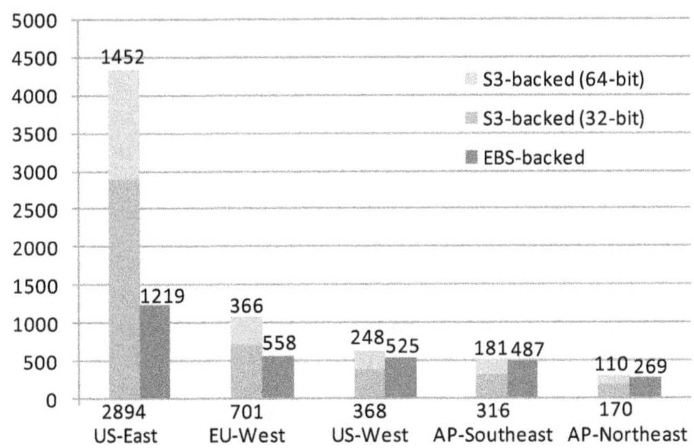

Figure 4: Linux Based Public AMIs per Region

Attack Optimization. One could even reduce the costs for the attack to almost zero by first scanning public AMIs that are likely to contain AWS API keys and then using these keys to start further analyzer instances at the expense of these initial victims. Candidates for the initial attacks are AMIs from inexperienced or unaware users, i.e., those who published only few AMIs or give suspicious names to their AMIs such as "backup" or "test".

4.4 Discussion

We discuss the reasons for and implications of our successful extraction of private information from public AMIs.

Reasons for Forgotten AWS API Keys.

We discovered AWS API keys in both S3- and EBS-backed AMIs. Our inspection of S3-backed AMIs revealed that those keys were unintentionally included during the bundling process when the AMI was created. Since S3-backed instances require an API key within the instance for bundling, the success rate to find API keys within this kind of AMIs is high. Our inspection of EBS-backed AMIs showed, that the Publishers used their API keys within their instances in order to access further AWS services such as S3 or EBS storage, and that the Publishers simply forgot to delete the key before publishing.

EBS Specific Problems.

In general our analysis shows that EBS-backed images contain more private information than S3-backed AMIs. We attribute this to the fact that data in EBS-backed instances is persistent (cf. §3.1). In fact, EBS-backed AMIs are much more dangerous than S3-backed AMIs for various reasons:

Loss of intellectual property. Publishers who want to protect their intellectual property by limiting access to the actual VM should not distribute it as an EBS-backed AMI. Indeed, in our analysis we found appliances which were configured explicitly without SSH access but could easily be inspected by mounting them as EBS volumes (cf. §4.2.1).

Forensic attacks. EBS backed AMIs or EBS volumes that once contained *any* valuable information, should not be made public. By applying forensic methods [27, 28] on a raw EBS volume we were able to reconstruct and inspect several deleted files, containing private information.

Snapshots. Snapshots are non-bootable EBS volumes with the purpose to ease sharing of (large volumes) of data. Snapshots can be created as new volume and filled with data, but they can also be created from instances. Thus, they also bare the risk of unintentionally publishing (forensically retrievable) private information. For instance, a first analysis of various snapshots revealed a private picture of the Publisher.

5. CLOUD SPECIFIC SSH THREATS

In this section we discuss vulnerabilities of the Secure Shell (SSH) protocol [30], which result from the cloud's dynamic nature and the usage model of AMIs. In particular, we evaluate SSH-based backdoors of instances (§5.1) and present new attacks due to the SSH-based identification of the AMI from which an instance is derived (§5.2).

SSH provides confidentiality and integrity, supports asymmetric key pairs for user authentication ($\mathsf{sk}_u, \mathsf{pk}_u$) and for host authentication (sk_h,pk_h). The SSH protocol is well-established and is the primary method for remote administration of Linux based instances in EC2 (cf. §3.2). For details on authentication in SSH we refer to §B.

5.1 AMIs with SSH Backdoor

Recently, Amazon informed several of its customers that a public AMI contained an SSH user authentication key pk_u and thus a backdoor allowing the publisher of the AMI who holds the corresponding sk_u to log into instances derived from that particular AMI [15]. Amazon strongly advises customers to terminate such instances and regards them as compromised [14]. However, this problem is not an isolated incident and, as we will show in this section, many of the publicly available AMIs contain SSH backdoors.

Threats. An SSH user authentication key deployed in a public AMI poses a severe threat to the AMI Consumer's privacy, as the key owner is able to log in to the affected Consumer's instances. A potentially malicious Publisher

[4]Note that the number of public AMIs changes frequently.

is thus able to deliberately eavesdrop or modify the Consumer's data and services in the instance.

Findings. Our analysis revealed that 30% of the 1100 analyzed EBS-backed AMIs in the European and US-East region at the time of the analysis contained pk_u and thus a backdoor for the AMI Publisher (detailed numbers are given in Tab. 1). By examining the affected AMIs we discovered that the backdoor problem is not limited to AMIs created by individuals, but also affects appliances of well-known open-source projects and even of companies that offer IT-security products. Moreover, our investigation yields that an overwhelming number of AMIs allows SSH login and that most users have administrative privileges[5].

5.1.1 Approach

Our approach to identify AMIs with a SSH backdoor is based on our analysis tool presented in §4.2. For this, we analyzed the *.ssh/authorized_keys* file. It is located in the users' home directories and contains the public keys pk_{u_i} of users that are allowed to log in.

5.1.2 Discussion

Reasons for Forgotten Public Keys. The reasons why such a huge number of AMIs contain backdoors for the Publisher are similar to those for unintended inclusion of private information as discussed in §4. However, the Publisher has no strong incentives to remove his public key before publishing an AMI, as the only negative consequence of not doing this is that he can be traced among AMIs.

Countermeasures against SSH Backdoors. In case a Consumer decides that she wants to run a particular AMI (e.g., because of the unique features offered by this AMI), she should check the *authorized_keys* file in every home directory and delete all public keys pk_u (except for her own). In addition to that she should examine the configuration of the SSH server in case other authentication methods (like insecure password authentication) are enabled or other locations for authorized keys are specified. Another countermeasure is to use the Amazon provided inbound firewall to generally restrict the IP range from which users are allowed to login via SSH. It also supports features for the implementation of a multi-tier infrastructure with a central gateway that validates access attempts to other instances [20].

5.2 AMI Identification via SSH

Some public AMIs contain an SSH host key pair $(\mathsf{sk}_h, \mathsf{pk}_h)$ which is generally used to prove the identity of the remote host to the client during login (cf. §B for details). Usually, a host key pair is generated from fresh entropy when installing SSH or the operating system. However, in cloud apps, where instances of an AMI are only a copy of the hard drive's state of an already configured machine, the SSH host key pair is not regenerated. Hence, all instances of an AMI are using the same SSH host key pair.

The severity of this vulnerability can be amplified by combining it with the technique for extracting information from public AMIs described in §4.2. The attacker can examine several (or all) public AMIs and extract the SSH host key pairs $(\mathsf{sk}_h, \mathsf{pk}_h)$ from it. Afterwards, he can use the host key fingerprint $\mathsf{f}(\mathsf{pk}_h)$ of an instance to look up the corresponding public AMI and the secret key sk_h.

[5]Many Linux distributions for EC2 allow the default user to execute commands as superuser via "sudo".

Attack	Prerequisites
Correlation of System Config.	-
Whitebox Attacks	public AMI identified
Impersonation Attacks	public AMI identified
Man-in-the-Middle Attacks	public AMI identified
Co-Location Attacks	public AMI identified
Phishing Attacks	owner of public AMI

Table 3: Attacks based on identical SSH host keys.

We describe the consequences of our attacks in §5.2.1, our findings in §5.2.2, our approach in §5.2.3, and the underlying causes in §5.2.4.

5.2.1 Threats

The possibility to identify instances that are using the same SSH host key or potentially even identifying the corresponding public AMI from which these instances are derived allows a variety of attacks as summarized in Tab. 3 and described in the following.

Correlation of System Configurations. Even if the attacker only detects instances with an identical fingerprint $\mathsf{f}(\mathsf{pk}_h)$, but does not manage to identify the corresponding AMI (e.g., because it is not public), he knows that these instances are likely to be instances of the same AMI (or a derived AMI). This enables him to discover test systems or forgotten servers which are not as secure as the productive system.

If the attacker identifies the corresponding public AMI he has more options:

Whitebox Attacks. The attacker can examine the contents of the AMI for potential vulnerabilities and misconfigurations like usage of default passwords or insecure services to launch attacks on the victim instance.

If the attacker extracts the host key pair $(\mathsf{sk}_h, \mathsf{pk}_h)$ from the AMI and has control over the network between the Consumer and the Provider (e.g., [25]) he can launch impersonation and man-in-the-middle attacks on SSH:

Impersonation Attacks. The attacker can redirect the SSH connection attempt of the Consumer to an instance under his control. In this case, verification of the host key fingerprint $\mathsf{f}(\mathsf{pk}_h)$ does not protect the Consumer as the attacker is able to equip his fake instance with the host key pair obtained from the public AMI. The Consumer may get suspicious that the impersonating instance is only similar to the expected environment, but there is a chance that the Consumer reveals private information or credentials before recognizing this, e.g., passwords upon login to other services. The attack especially works when automated scripts are used, e.g., a script that automatically uploads a backup copy onto an instance in the cloud. By impersonating this instance the attacker can obtain such a backup copy.

Man-in-the-Middle Attacks. If SSH is configured for password-based user authentication, an attacker can use sk_h to play as man-in-the-middle and eavesdrop or modify the communication between the Consumer and the VM.

Co-Location Attacks. The AMI type narrows down the possible instance type as 32-bit AMIs do not support the more powerful instance types because they cannot make use of the offered resources. This information can be exploited by an attacker to narrow down the search space in co-location attacks [39].

Phishing Attacks. If the attacker himself is the Publisher of the executed malicious AMI he can deniably identify victims of his own VM phishing attacks. The malicious AMI might contain intentionally embedded vulnerabilities [17, 48] or SSH backdoors (cf. §5.1).

5.2.2 Findings

Our analysis shows that approximately 29% of the 1100 analyzed AMIs (in US-East and EU-West) are misconfigured such that their derived instances do not recreate the SSH host key pair $(\mathsf{sk}_h, \mathsf{pk}_h)$ on first boot (cf. Tab. 1). We discovered that 62 distinct SSH host keys in the EC2 Tokyo region were used by more than one instance. We identified the public AMI of 11 of those host keys, which were contained in 278 instances running in this region.

Our experiment also revealed that $\frac{604}{2533} \approx 23\%$ of the instances in the Tokyo region with SSH access are using a non-unique host key pair $(\mathsf{sk}_h, \mathsf{pk}_h)$. However, we were not able to map all duplicate SSH host keys to public AMIs and believe that these misconfigured instances are derived from private AMIs owned by one user or a small group and are thus potential production or test systems with similar vulnerabilities (cf. *Correlation of System Configurations* described above).

5.2.3 Approach

Our approach for finding public AMIs using not freshly generated SSH host keys is illustrated in Fig. 5. Based on our analysis tool for public AMIs (cf. §4.2), we first extracted the SSH public key fingerprints $\mathsf{f}(\mathsf{pk}_h)$ of all AMIs in the Tokyo region and used this to obtain a mapping from 615 fingerprints to their corresponding AMI ID. Further, by making SSH connection attempts to all IP addresses in the Tokyo region's IP range (175.41.192.0/18), we gathered all mappings from IP addresses to host key fingerprints for the region. By matching the SSH fingerprints in both results, we found a mapping between the IP addresses of running instances to their corresponding AMI ID. Moreover, the diversity of SSH fingerprints in the region's IP range gave us the statistic about duplicated SSH host keys as explained in §5.2.2.

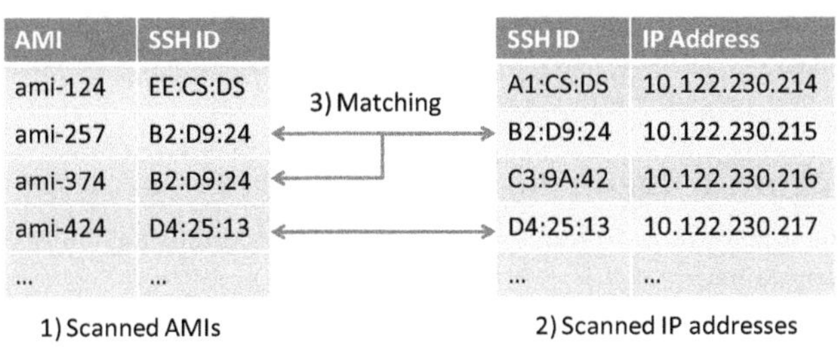

Figure 5: Matching Between AMIs and Instances

5.2.4 Discussion

In summary, our findings in §5.2.3 show that AMIs which do not recreate their SSH host key occur frequently.

The main reason for SSH host keys being included in public AMIs is presumably the same as for private information (cf. §4.4) and SSH user authentication keys (cf. §5.1.2) and, thus, countermeasures are similar. We therefore extend this discussion to the whole process of secure authentication and administration in the cloud, as it is negatively affected by the flexibility and usage model of computing clouds.

Alternatively, an attacker could use other publicly available information than the SSH host key to identify the AMI of an instance, e.g., the software version and configuration of a web-server running in the instance. However, the SSH host key is a much more distinguishing characteristic than the software configuration. Nevertheless, this is supplementary information to identify the AMI of an instance if more than one candidate image exists (e.g., *ami-257* and *ami-374* in Fig. 5).

Static vs. Dynamic Environments.

So far, the SSH protocol has been used mostly in and is designed for relatively static networks. Hence, manual verification of the host keys is only necessary in case of relatively infrequent changes to the underlying infrastructure (e.g., change of the server's IP address or hostname, or newly generated host key). In contrast, the cloud provides a highly dynamic environment with much shorter life time of instances and dynamically assigned IP addresses. Additionally, the use of preconfigured VMs instead of installation from scratch opens new vulnerabilities as shown in §5.2.

Trust on First Use.

This leads to the general challenge of secure authentication to started EC2 instances which is not sufficiently addressed in the current implementation of EC2 and even worse for AMIs with non-unique host keys. As described in §3 and shown in Fig. 2, the Consumer issues a request to start a public AMI and is returned the Instance-ID which can be used to look up the IP address of the instance (over the AWS API or Web Interface). When she connects to the IP address of this newly created instance, she has no prior knowledge on the contents of the AMI and its host key ("Trust-on-first-use", cf. [49]). The only option is to use an out-of-band method, provided by Amazon, to obtain the console output of the started instance to which the SSH server writes the host key fingerprint $\mathsf{f}(\mathsf{pk}_h)$ after the host key pair has been freshly created. However, as it takes a few minutes until the output of the console becomes available to the user, we assume that most users do not make use of this technique when establishing the first connection to a newly started instance. The situation is even worse when the instance's SSH server does not create a fresh host key pair where the user has no means to verify that he really connects to the machine he started.

This problem is aggravated when the instance is stopped and restarted with a newly assigned external IP address. In this case, the console output does not contain the host key fingerprint as no new host key was generated, and the user is forced to store the correct fingerprint upon the very first connect in order to be able to securely authenticate his instance after reboot or change of the external IP address.

6. COUNTERMEASURES

Finally, we present and discuss several countermeasures that create awareness, reduce the impact of lost credentials, or assist users in realizing that they accidentally published sensitive information. Some general countermeasures have been proposed and discussed in [48], however, we believe that the high popularity and deep integration of Amazon specific services, e.g., S3 and EBS, into the EC2 Cloud App Store prevents adoption of these countermeasures as it would require fundamental changes to the architecture. We therefore present mechanism that specifically address the environment provided by Amazon and its limitations.

Organizational Measures.

Most problems that led to our attacks could have been prevented by the Publishers themselves. Especially as most public AMIs do not provide any additional value to other consumers, e.g., due to lacking functionality and documentation, they should not have been made public in the first place. Therefore, the first and most effective step should be to provide better information to users on the risks they are facing when publishing an AMI and to create problem awareness. In addition to that, despite the novelty of cloud computing and AMI publishing, companies and individuals should develop and follow guidelines, best practices, and processes for releasing their AMIs to the public. In this case AMIs do not differ from documents, software, or mediums containing confidential information (e.g., discharging of old hard drives §2). Another effective way to reduce the impact of an accidentally lost AWS API key is the recently introduced AWS Identity and Access Management (IAM) [10]. It allows managing of multiple security credentials for an AWS account with a different set of permissions which could be used to limit the damage an attacker can cause (cf. §A).

Tool Assistance for the Publisher.

Additionally, Publishers can be protected by enhancing Amazon's toolchain.

S3-backed AMIs. As discussed in §4.4 some Publishers of S3-backed AMIs have exposed their AWS API key used for authorizing the bundling operation [2]. We propose to extend the bundling command in a way that a warning is issued in case the AWS API key is included into the new bundle (cf. Fig. 6 for an example) or information about the key is stored in the command line history. Moreover, the extension can provide a *safe bundling* option to warn Publishers about data which is potentially private (e.g., by applying search patterns similar to those in Tab. 2).

```
$ ec2-bundle-vol -k /root/sk-HKZYCLO.pem
WARNING: The key sk-HKZYCLO.pem used to
    authorize the bundling operation will be
    included in the image file. Publishing the
    AMI may leak it to the public!
Do you want to proceed (y/n): n
```

Figure 6: Improved Bundling Tool

EBS-backed AMIs. Protection for EBS-backed AMIs has to be implemented differently than for S3-backed AMIs. EBS-backed AMIs can be almost instantly generated out of running instances and made public entirely over the web interface. As the underlying storage engine just instructs the storage layer to create a bitwise copy of a volume, we have to apply different countermeasures. Here, Amazon could extend their interface to inform the user on potential risks of private data being included and also offer tools to deal with them. This can be realized by a service (e.g., a public AMI) that is given an EBS volume as input, creates a report on potential privacy problems, and outputs a low-level sanitized volume to prevent forensic analysis.

Regular Scanning.

As described in [33], Providers have to find a trade-off between the benefits of providing security measures and the costs for implementing and operating them. However, we believe that it is possible for a provider like AWS to regularly scan the provided AMIs (cf. cost analysis in §4.3) while still ensuring that the Provider does not take any liability on undiscovered problems. As hackers are likely to re-implement the techniques described in our paper (especially given the high damage that can be caused), public cloud service providers should take immediate action.

For this, Amazon and other providers could adopt our tools, eventually increase their efficiency by integrating them into their infrastructure, and scan the Cloud App Store regularly, or when a new AMI is published. Although the scanning may result in more time and effort for manually verification of the results and informing affected customers of a discovered vulnerability, this approach would underline a proactive approach to security problems.

Improving the Cloud App Store.

As we have described in §5 a great deal of AMIs, deployed by a large number of consumers, does not satisfy even lowest quality standards (e.g., contains an SSH backdoor). This situation can be improved by combing an automated rating system that checks AMIs for predefined properties together with a reputation system that allows users to evaluate the usefulness and quality of an AMI. Such features are commonly available in today's mobile app stores as well as for online auction and shopping platforms to rate vendors and products, but still missing in Amazon's Cloud App Store and its web console. Moreover, the AWS web console should be extended to provide more information on particular AMIs like the date of publishing or more detailed descriptions about the AMI's purpose and its publisher. A process for submitting AMIs and extended documentation already exists, but this information [6] is not available in the web console. Additionally, well known and trusted AMI Publishers could be rewarded with a special status visible to the consumer (star/gold Publisher). Before earning such a status, a Publisher would have to earn good reviews or pass an analysis of their AMIs by Amazon.

Acknowledgements

The authors would like to thank Michael Waidner for helpful discussions.

We would also like to thank the AWS security team for their quick, professional response after we have notified them about our findings and their immediate reaction to protect their customers.

The research leading to this paper was in part funded by the European Union's Seventh Framework Programme (FP7/2007-2013) under grant agreement n°257243 (TClouds project: `http://www.tclouds-project.eu`).

7. REFERENCES

[1] All Together Now: Amazon, we need those caps on billing. http://forums.aws.amazon.com/thread.jspa?threadID=50075#jive-message-217130.

[2] Amazon EC2: ec2-bundle-vol. http://docs.amazonwebservices.com/AmazonEC2/dg/2006-10-01/CLTRG-ami-bundle-vol.html.

[3] Amazon EC2 Pricing. http://aws.amazon.com/ec2/pricing.

[4] Amazon Elastic Block Store (EBS). http://aws.amazon.com/ebs/.

[5] Amazon Elastic Compute Cloud (Amazon EC2). http://aws.amazon.com/ec2/.

[6] Amazon Machine Images (AMIs) . http://aws.amazon.com/amis.

[7] Amazon Simple Storage Service (S3). http://aws.amazon.com/s3/.

[8] Amazon Web Services. http://aws.amazon.com.

[9] Apple App Store Review Guidelines. http://developer.apple.com/appstore/guidelines.html.

[10] AWS Identity and Access Management (IAM) Documentation. http://aws.amazon.com/documentation/iam/.

[11] The Cloud Market. EC2 Statistics. http://thecloudmarket.com/stats.

[12] Amazon Elastic Compute Cloud User Guide, 2011. http://awsdocs.s3.amazonaws.com/EC2/latest/ec2-ug.pdf.

[13] An Update on Android Market Security, March 3 2011. http://googlemobile.blogspot.com/2011/03/update-on-android-market-security.html.

[14] AWS Developer Forums: Email from Amazon EC2 about my AMI being compromised, April 8 2011. https://forums.aws.amazon.com/thread.jspa?messageID=235613.

[15] Compromised EC2 image includes root access SSH key, 2011. http://pastebin.com/q1VH4rmF.

[16] A. Abdelhalim and I. Traore. The impact of google hacking on identity and application fraud. In *Pacific Rim Conference on Communications, Computers and Signal Processing*, pages 240 –244. IEEE, 2007.

[17] N. Arvantis, M. Slaviero, and H. Meer. Clobbering the Cloud!, 2009. http://www.sensepost.com/labs/conferences/clobbering_the_cloud.

[18] Amazon Web Services Documentation. http://aws.amazon.com/documentation.

[19] Amazon Web Services: Overview of Security Processes, August 2010. http://awsmedia.s3.amazonaws.com/pdf/AWS_Security_Whitepaper.pdf.

[20] S. Bleikertz, M. Schunter, C. W. Probst, D. Pendarakis, and K. Eriksson. Security audits of multi-tier virtual infrastructures in public infrastructure clouds. In *ACM Cloud Computing Security Workshop (CCSW'10)*, pages 93–102. ACM, 2010.

[21] Y. Chen, V. Paxson, and R. H. Katz. What's new about cloud computing security? Technical Report UCB/EECS-2010-5, Jan 2010.

[22] Cloud Security Alliance (CSA). Security guidance for critical areas of focus in cloud computing v2.1, December 2009. https://cloudsecurityalliance.org/csaguide.pdf.

[23] Cloud Security Alliance (CSA). Top threats to cloud computing, March 2010. cloudsecurityalliance.org/topthreats/csathreats.v1.0.pdf.

[24] Ionut Constandache, Aydan Yumerefendi, and Jeff Chase. Secure control of portable images in a virtual computing utility. In *ACM workshop on Virtual machine security*, VMSec '08, pages 1–8. ACM, 2008.

[25] Danny Dolev and Andrew C. Yao. On the security of public key protocols. Technical report, 1981.

[26] European Network and Information Security Agency (ENISA). Cloud computing security risk assessment, May 2009. http://www.enisa.europa.eu/act/rm/files/deliverables/cloud-computing-risk-assessment/.

[27] S.L. Garfinkel. Automating disk forensic processing with SleuthKit, XML and Python. In *Workshop on Systematic Approaches to Digital Forensic Engineering*, pages 73–84. IEEE, 2009.

[28] S.L. Garfinkel and A. Shelat. Remembrance of data passed: a study of disk sanitization practices. *IEEE Security and Privacy*, 1(1):17 – 27, January 2003.

[29] T. Garfinkel and M. Rosenblum. When virtual is harder than real: security challenges in virtual machine based computing environments. In *Workshop on Hot Topics in Operating Systems (HotOS'05)*, page 20. USENIX, 2005.

[30] B. Hatch. SSH Host Key Protection, Oct 2004. http://www.symantec.com/connect/articles/ssh-host-key-protection.

[31] C. Heath. *Symbian OS Platform Security*. John Wiley & Sons, 2006.

[32] IBM Cooperation. IBM SmartCloud. http://www-935.ibm.com/services/us/igs/cloud-development/#tab:details-security.

[33] D. Molnar and S. Schechter. Self hosting vs. cloud hosting: Accounting for the security impact of hosting in the cloud. In *Workshop on the Economics of Information Security (WEIS 2010)*, June 2010.

[34] J. Murty. *Programming Amazon Web Services: S3, EC2, SQS, FPS, and SimpleDB*. O'Reilly Media, 2008.

[35] NIST. Guidelines on security and privacy in public cloud computing. 2011. Special Publication 800-144.

[36] NIST. The NIST Definition of Cloud Computing (Draft). 2011. Special Publication 800-145 (Draft).

[37] O. Pirttikoski and Y. Kortesniemi. Local Key and Certificate Storage in JDK 1.3. *Proceedings of the NordSec2000, Reykjavk, Iceland*, 2000.

[38] D. Reimer, A. Thomas, G. Ammons, T. Mummert, B. Alpern, and V. Bala. Opening black boxes: using semantic information to combat virtual machine image sprawl. In *SIGPLAN/SIGOPS international conference on Virtual execution environments (VEE'08)*, pages 111–120. ACM, 2008.

[39] T. Ristenpart, E. Tromer, H. Shacham, and S. Savage. Hey, you, get off of my cloud: exploring information leakage in third-party compute clouds. In *ACM conference on Computer and communications security (CCS'09)*, pages 199–212. ACM, 2009.

[40] T. Ristenpart and S. Yilek. Randomness goes bad:

Virtual machine reset vulnerabilities and hedging deployed cryptography. In *Network and Distributed Security Symposium (NDSS'10)*. ACM, 2010.
[41] M. Satyanarayanan, W. Richter, G. Ammons, J. Harkes, and A. Goode. The case for content search of vm clouds. In *Computer Software and Applications Conference Workshops (COMPSACW'10)*, pages 382 –387. IEEE, 2010.
[42] Amazon SimpleDB. `http://aws.amazon.com/simpledb`.
[43] S. Swidler. How to Keep Your AWS Credentials on an EC2 Instance Securely, August 2009. `http://shlomoswidler.com/2009/08/how-to-keep-your-aws-credentials-on-ec2.html`.
[44] M. Szeredi. SSH filesystem. `http://fuse.sourceforge.net/sshfs.html`.
[45] H. Takabi, J. B.D. Joshi, and G.-J. Ahn. Security and privacy challenges in cloud computing environments. *IEEE Security and Privacy*, 8:24–31, 2010.
[46] E.I. Tatlı. Google Reveals Cryptographic Secrets. In *Kryptowochenende 2006 – Workshop über Kryptographie. Universität Mannheim*, page 33, 2006.
[47] J. Varia. Architecting for the cloud: Best practices, January 2011. `http://media.amazonwebservices.com/AWS_Cloud_Best_Practices.pdf`.
[48] J. Wei, X. Zhang, G. Ammons, V. Bala, and P. Ning. Managing security of virtual machine images in a cloud environment. In *ACM Cloud Computing Security Workshop (CCSW'09)*, pages 91–96. ACM, 2009.
[49] Dan Wendlandt, David G. Andersen, and Adrian Perrig. Perspectives: Improving SSH-style host authentication with multi-path probing. In *USENIX 2008 Annual Technical Conference*, pages 321–334, Berkeley, CA, USA, 2008. USENIX Association.
[50] J. Yan, A. Blackwell, R. Anderson, and A. Grant. Password memorability and security: empirical results. *IEEE Security and Privacy*, 2(5):25 –31, 2004.
[51] T. Ylonen and C. Lonvick. The Secure Shell (SSH) Protocol Architecture. RFC 4251 (Proposed Standard), January 2006.
[52] W. Zhou, P. Ning, X. Zhang, G. Ammons, R. Wang, and V. Bala. Always up-to-date: scalable offline patching of vm images in a compute cloud. In *Annual Computer Security Applications Conference (ACSAC'10)*, pages 377–386. ACM, 2010.

APPENDIX

A. VALUE OF CAPTURED AWS API KEYS

We roughly estimate the potential financial damage that can be caused with a captured AWS API key. As the pricing is highly dynamic and depends on various factors we give a general overview only which may change over time.

It is not possible to set an upper limit on the money AWS will charge for service usage. There exist only limitations on the amount of resources a user can request at a time. These limits can be increased by contacting Amazon. A standard account is allowed to start 20 on-demand EC2 instances and to request 100 instances on the spot market. On the spot market, unused resources of EC2 are sold for a varying price, depending on the current demand. Given these limitations, an attacker can request 20 on-demand instances of the most expensive "Quadruple Extra Large" type ($2.10/h) and 100 "Quadruple Extra Large" type instances on the spot market (we assume $0.84/h). This leads to costs of $126/h or $3024/day. Note that this calculation is pessimistic as it does not include additional costs for network bandwidth, storage or I/O access. All in all, capturing an AWS API key allows an attacker to misuse simultaneously around 8000 GB memory and 3000 EC2 Compute Units (ECU), where one ECU is equivalent to the CPU capacity of a 1.0-1.2 GHz 2007 Opteron or 2007 Xeon processor.

B. SSH AUTHENTICATION

As described in §3.2, SSH [30] is the primary method for remote administration in EC2. The SSH protocol supports user authentication based on passwords or asymmetric key pairs and has built in protection against man-in-the-middle attacks as described next.

In the cloud environment mainly the asymmetric key based method is used. It is supported by the EC2 infrastructure as well as most public AMIs, and is considered to be more secure than password based authentication. As mentioned in §3.2, the AMI user's public key pk_u is imported by a newly created instance (called host in SSH context) from EC2 and the user then authenticates herself by proving possession of the associated secret key sk_u. In addition to that, SSH also supports a check of the host's identity to prevent an attacker from impersonating a remote host or launching a man-in-the-middle attack. This is realized with an unique and unforgeable asymmetric key pair $(\mathsf{sk}_h, \mathsf{pk}_h)$, called host key which is stored on the remote host. When a user connects to a host he has to verify that the fingerprint, i.e., a hash, $\mathsf{f}(\mathsf{pk}_h)$ of the host key belongs to the machine he wants to connect to (cf. Fig. 7). As no Certificate Authority is involved, it is the responsibility of the user to ensure the authenticity of the fingerprint when connecting to a new or unknown host, e.g., over an outbound channel. After the key has been accepted, the SSH client application caches the mapping between the key and the host's IP address or hostname.

```
john:~$ ssh ec2-user@47.127.0.233
The authenticity of host '47.127.0.233 (47.127.0.233)'
    can't be established.
RSA key fingerprint is
    f3:5a:f4:a2:f3:d1:e5:52:2c:e3:87:ff:07:13:01:11.
Are you sure you want to continue connecting (yes/no)?
```

Figure 7: SSH First Connection

Eliminating the Hypervisor Attack Surface for a More Secure Cloud

Jakub Szefer, Eric Keller, Ruby B. Lee and Jennifer Rexford
Princeton University
Princeton, NJ, USA
{szefer, ekeller, rblee, jrex}@princeton.edu

ABSTRACT

Cloud computing is quickly becoming the platform of choice for many web services. Virtualization is the key underlying technology enabling cloud providers to host services for a large number of customers. Unfortunately, virtualization software is large, complex, and has a considerable attack surface. As such, it is prone to bugs and vulnerabilities that a malicious virtual machine (VM) can exploit to attack or obstruct other VMs — a major concern for organizations wishing to move "to the cloud." In contrast to previous work on hardening or minimizing the virtualization software, we eliminate the hypervisor attack surface by enabling the guest VMs to run natively on the underlying hardware while maintaining the ability to run multiple VMs concurrently. Our NoHype system embodies four key ideas: (i) pre-allocation of processor cores and memory resources, (ii) use of virtualized I/O devices, (iii) minor modifications to the guest OS to perform all system discovery during bootup, and (iv) avoiding indirection by bringing the guest virtual machine in more direct contact with the underlying hardware. Hence, no hypervisor is needed to allocate resources dynamically, emulate I/O devices, support system discovery after bootup, or map interrupts and other identifiers. NoHype capitalizes on the unique use model in cloud computing, where customers specify resource requirements ahead of time and providers offer a suite of guest OS kernels. Our system supports multiple tenants and capabilities commonly found in hosted cloud infrastructures. Our prototype utilizes Xen 4.0 to prepare the environment for guest VMs, and a slightly modified version of Linux 2.6 for the guest OS. Our evaluation with both SPEC and Apache benchmarks shows a roughly 1% performance gain when running applications on NoHype compared to running them on top of Xen 4.0. Our security analysis shows that, while there are some minor limitations with current commodity hardware, NoHype is a significant advance in the security of cloud computing.

Categories and Subject Descriptors

C.0 [**General**]: System Architectures; D.4.6 [**Software Engineering**]: Operating Systems—*Security and Protection*

General Terms

Security

Keywords

Secure Cloud Computing, Hypervisor Security, Attack Vectors, Virtualization, Multicore, Hardware Security

1. INTRODUCTION

Cloud computing is transforming the way people use computers. Cloud computing is also transforming how networked services are run. The provider of a service (the cloud customer) is able to dynamically provision infrastructure to meet the current demand by leasing resources from a hosting company (the cloud infrastructure provider). The cloud infrastructure provider can leverage economies of scale to provide dynamic, on-demand infrastructure at a favorable cost. The provider does this by utilizing virtualization where virtual machines from multiple customers share the same physical server. This multi-tenancy, where mutually distrusting customers lease resources from the same provider, underscores the need for a secure virtualization solution.

Because of its central role, the virtualization software is a prime target for attacks. Unfortunately, the virtualization layer is quite complex and forms a very large trusted computing base (e.g. Xen has ~200K lines of code in the hypervisor itself ~600K in the emulator, and over 1M in the host OS). The large code base is not suitable for formal verification – the best formal verification techniques available today are only able to handle around 10K lines of code [18]. Further, bug reports such as those listed in NIST's National Vulnerability Database [6] show the difficulty of shipping bug-free hypervisor code. A malicious VM can exploit these bugs to attack the virtualization software. Exploiting such an attack vector would give the attacker the ability to obstruct or access other virtual machines and therefore breach confidentiality, integrity, and availability of the other virtual machines' code or data.

Such vulnerabilities make many companies hesitant about moving to the cloud [14]. If not for the security threat of attacks on a vulnerable virtualization layer, computing in the cloud has the potential to be *more* secure than in private facilities. This is due to the very nature of the large and critical data centers run by the cloud infrastructure providers. The level of physical security (cameras, personnel, etc.) found in these data centers is often cost prohibitive for individual customers.

Previous approaches to securing the virtualization software have limitations when applied to cloud computing. Approaches that minimize the hypervisor, e.g., [32], are not suitable for cloud computing infrastructures because they greatly reduce functionality. Approaches that introduce a new processor architecture, e.g., [10], cannot be deployed today. Approaches that add extra software to verify the integrity of the hypervisor, e.g., [9], add overhead, leave a small window open between the attack and the reactive defense, and do not protect against attacks that exploit bugs in the hypervisor for purposes other than injecting code or modifying the control flow (e.g., bugs which cause the hypervisor to crash).

In this paper we present our NoHype system that takes the novel approach of *eliminating* the hypervisor attack surface altogether. We remove the need for virtual machines to constantly interact with the hypervisor during their lifetime (e.g., by short-circuiting the system discovery and avoiding indirection). With NoHype, we (i) retain the ability to run and manage virtual machines in the same manner as is done today in cloud computing infrastructures, (ii) achieve this with today's commodity hardware, and (iii) prevent attacks from happening in the first place.

We previously proposed the high-level idea of NoHype in a position paper [16]. The previous work discussed how pre-allocation and virtualized I/O devices could be used to remove the hypervisor and motivated why this idea works in the setting of hosted cloud infrastructures. In this paper, we present the complete design, implementation, and evaluation of a working NoHype system on today's commodity hardware. This new work adds a significant level of depth through a complete prototype design and implementation, as well as new performance and security analysis which identifies and evaluates potential side-channels. In particular, we make the following new contributions:

- **An architecture which eliminates the hypervisor attack surface.** As we previously proposed [16], the architecture pre-allocates memory and processor cores (so a hypervisor does not have to do this dynamically) and uses only virtualized I/O devices (so a hypervisor does not have to emulate devices). New to this paper, the architecture also avoids the indirection of mapping physical interrupts and identifiers to the virtual ones (so a hypervisor does not have to be involved in any communication channels). Each of these is enabled by the unique use case of the cloud computing model.
- **A design which can be realized on today's commodity hardware.** We take advantage of modern hardware features to enforce the resource allocations as well as the common practice for cloud infrastructure providers to provide a set of kernel images. With this, we allow the guest operating systems to boot up as normal. This process is supported by a temporary hypervisor, which enables a slightly modified guest operating system to discover the environment at boot up and save this information about the system for later use.
- **A prototype implementation and system evaluation.** We built a NoHype prototype using an Intel Nehalem quad-core processor. We utilized Xen 4.0 to prepare the environment for the guest virtual machines, and a slightly modified version of Linux 2.6 for the guest operating system. Our performance evaluation through the use of SPEC 2006 [15] and Apache [1] benchmarks show roughly 1% faster run times. We also present a security analysis which shows that NoHype makes an improvement in the security of virtualization technology for hosted and shared cloud infrastructures.

The remainder of the paper is organized as follows. In Section 2 we discuss background information about virtualization. In Section 3 we discuss our threat model. In Section 4 we discuss the NoHype system architecture, while in Section 5 we discuss details of our prototype implementation. The security analysis is presented in Section 6. Finally, related works are discussed in Section 7 and we conclude in Section 8 including a discussion about future work where we discuss live virtual machine migration.

2. VIRTUALIZATION VULNERABILITIES

The purpose of a hypervisor is to present to the guest VM a view that appears as though the operating system and applications inside the VM are running directly on some given hardware. The hypervisor achieves this by emulating the underlying hardware and arbitrating access to it. Realizing this functionality requires a large and complex body of software. It also requires a significant and frequent interaction between the guest VMs and the hypervisor. This interaction is the basis of the security threat which a malicious VM can utilize to attack the hypervisor and exploit bugs in the hypervisor or supporting virtualization software to attack another VM.

2.1 Roles of Virtualization Software

Figure 1 shows the hypervisor, host OS, and emulator (e.g., QEMU) which form the virtualization layer. The dotted line outlines the components which are the trusted computing base in today's virtualization solutions. Highlighted in the figure are also the points of interaction and components which are involved in these interactions.

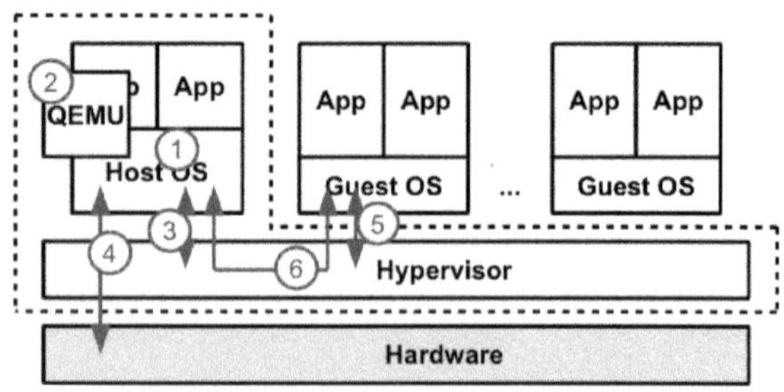

Figure 1: Roles of hypervisor.

An important and large part of the virtualization layer, in addition to the hypervisor, is the host OS (①) and the emulator (②). The host OS (Dom0 in Xen's terminology) has special management privileges and a system administrator uses the host OS to manage VMs on the system, e.g., launching and shutting down VMs. This causes the host OS to interact with the hypervisor via hypercalls (③). The

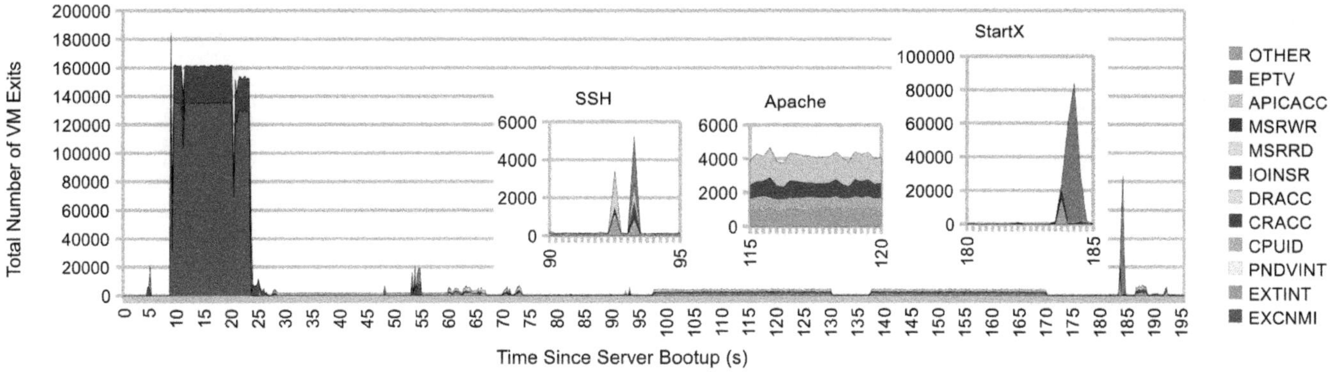

Figure 2: VM exits in stock Xen 4.0 during server bootup and runtime of a guest VM.

host OS may also include drivers for the physical devices which are used by the system (④). An emulator which emulates system devices that guest VMs interact with is also commonly run within the host OS. All together, this functionality requires over a million lines of code.

We now dicuss the roles of the hypervisor in emulating and managing the main resources in today's computer systems.

Processor cores: The first responsibility of any virtualization solution is the ability to arbitrate access to the processor cores as well as sometimes emulate their functionality. The hypervisor needs to cope with the dynamic addition and removal of VMs as they get started and stopped, as well as the ability to schedule multiple VMs on the same system. In addition to scheduling the VMs, the virtualization layer also uses the scheduler to periodically, every clock tick, run some of its own functionality – for example the hypervisor needs to check whether to deliver timer interrupts to the VM in this clock tick. The virtualization layer may also emulate the underlying processor as the presented processor cores may differ in capabilities from the actual cores.

Memory: The hypervisor is also in charge of managing the host physical memory of the system. Each VM is assigned some guest physical memory that the guest OS can manage and assign as virtual memory to the applications. Here, the virtualization layer can take a number of different approaches to managing the allocation of host physical memory among the various VMs. One popular use of virtualization is server consolidation which relies on the virtualization layer to dynamically manage the allocation of physical memory to the different VMs in the system.

I/O devices: Another important functionality of the virtualization layer is dealing with I/O devices such as a network interface card (NIC). Today's virtualization solutions commonly create virtual devices that they assign to the guest VMs. The virtualization layer needs to manage these virtual devices and emulate their behavior. There is also the option of dedicating physical devices to the VMs. In this situation, the virtualization layer only needs to assign and reclaim the devices. It does not need to emulate their behavior. In both cases, however, the emulator is needed to emulate the PCI (Peripheral Component Interconnect) bus. The guest OS interacts with the PCI bus during bootup to discover and configure the available devices.

Interrupts and Timers: The virtualization layer must also emulate the interrupt subsystem and timers for the guest VMs. For interrupts, the main parts of the underlying hardware interrupt subsystem emulated by the hypervisor include the I/O APIC[1] (which routes interrupts from devices to processor cores) and local APICs (which are attached to each core as an interface to the interrupt subsystem for sending and receiving interrupt messages to and form other local APICs or the I/O APIC). These APICs are emulated so the guest OS can use them to configure and manage interrupts inside the VM, while physical APICs are controlled by the hypervisor for the management of the physical platform. For timers, since the hypervisor utilizes the physical timer devices to get periodic clock ticks itself, it has to emulate the timer device for each guest VM. Today, VMs can be scheduled on different cores and as such, the interrupts and timers must first go through the hypervisor which will deliver the interrupts to the VM by utilizing its knowledge of the VM's current location.

2.2 Attack Surface

The virtualization layer is heavily involved throughout the lifetime of the guest VM. Each interaction between the VM and the hypervisor is then a potential attack vector that could be exploited by the guest. The guest OS interacts directly with the hypervisor (⑤) and indirectly with the host OS and the emulator (⑥) through VM exits (and hypercalls if paravirtualization is used). A VM exit is an event which occurs when the VM's code is interrupted and the hypervisor code begins to execute to handle some event (e.g., emulate memory access, deliver a virtual timer interrupt, etc.). A hypercall is similar to a system call and is used by guest VMs to request explicit service from the hypervisor. Hypercalls are not considered further as we are not using paravirtualization. VM exits are quite frequent even when the guest OS inside the VM is not doing any work; in an idle VM running on top of Xen 4.0, the VM exits occur ~600 times per second.

On a 64-bit Intel x86 architecture with virtualization extensions, there are 56 reasons for VM exits, and this forms the large attack surface which is the basis of the security threat. The reasons VM for exits are described in Table 1. Each VM exit causes the hypervisor code to run so the hypervisor can intervene when the guest OS performs some operation that caused the associated exit. This allows the hypervisor to maintain the abstraction of the system which it presents to the guest OSes, for example it can return different CPUID values than the values actually reported by the hardware.

In order to emphasize how often the large and complex

[1]APIC is the advanced programmable interrupt controller.

virtualization layer is needed, we examine the execution of an actual (non-paravirtualized) VM with the Xen hypervisor. Figure 2 shows a timeline of a Linux based VM pinned to a core and with a directly assigned NIC, booting up and running some programs on top of the Xen 4.0 hypervisor with no other VMs present. The most frequent reasons for exits are highlighted in the figure while others are grouped in the "other" category. The stacked area graph shows the number of VM exits during each 250ms interval.

First, the guest OS boots up, which is the first 75 seconds in the graph. A staggering 9,730,000 exits are performed as the system is starting up. This is an average of about 130,000 exits per second. The majority of the exits are the EPTV and EXCNMI VM exits, but exits such as CPUID are also present. These exits are due to interaction with hardware that is being emulated (EPTV and EXCNMI) or are part of system discovery done by the guest OS (CPUID).

Next, at around 90 seconds we show an SSH login event which causes a spike in VM exits (EXTINT and APICACC). Even with the directly assigned NIC, the hypervisor is involved in the redirection of the interrupts to the correct core and the EXTINT exit signals when an interrupt has come. The APICACC exits are due to the guest interacting with the local APIC (Advanced Programmable Interrupt Controller) which is used to acknowledge receipt of an interrupt, for example.

Then, at around 115 seconds we show execution of the Apache web server with a modest request rate. This causes many exits: EXTINT, CPUID, CRACC, APICACC. We found that libc and other libraries make multiple uses of CPUID each time a process is started and in Apache there are new processes started to handle each connection.

Finally, at around 180 seconds we show starting VNC (a graphical desktop sharing software) and running `startx` to start the X Window System. We can see the EPTV exits which are due to emulation of VGA once the graphical window system is started.

To summarize, different situations lead to different uses of VM exits and invocation of underlying hypervisor support. Each VM exit could be treated as a communication channel where a VM implicitly or explicitly sends information to the hypervisor so the hypervisor can handle the event. Each VM exit is then a potential attack vector as it is a window that the VM can use to attack the hypervisor (e.g., by exploiting a bug in how the hypervisor handles certain events). With NoHype, we eliminate these attack vectors.

3. THREAT MODEL

With NoHype, we aim to protect against attacks on the hypervisor by the guest VMs. A malicious VM could cause a VM exit to occur in such a manner as to inject malicious code or trigger a bug in the hypervisor. Injecting code or triggering a bug could potentially be used to violate confidentiality or integrity of other VMs or even crash or slow down the hypervisor, causing a denial-of-service attack violating availability. We eliminate the need for interaction between VMs and hypervisor, thus preventing such attacks.

To that end, we assume the cloud infrastructure provider is not malicious, and sufficient physical security controls are being employed to prevent hardware attacks (e.g., probing on the memory buses of physical servers) through surveillance cameras and restricted access to the physical facilities. We are not concerned with the security of the guest OSes,

Table 1: Selected reasons for VM exits [3].

VM Exit	Reason
EPTV	An attempt to access memory with a guest-physical address was disallowed by the configuration of the EPT paging structures.
APICACC	Guest software attempted to access memory at a physical address on the APIC-access page.
MSRWR	Guest software attempted to write machine specific register, MSR.
MSRRD	Guest software attempted to read machine specific register, MSR.
IOINSR	Guest software attempted to execute an I/O instruction.
DRACC	Guest software attempted to move data to or from a debug register
CRACC	Guest software attempted to access CR0, CR3, CR4, or CR8 x86 control registers.
CPUID	Guest software attempted to execute CPUID instruction.
PNDVINT	Pending virtual interrupt.
EXTINT	An external interrupt arrived.
EXCNMI	Exception or non-maskable interrupt, NMI.

but do require that a cloud provider makes available a set of slightly modified guest OS kernels which are needed to boot a VM. The responsibility of protecting software which runs *inside* the VMs is placed upon the customer. Also, in this work the security and correctness of the cloud management software is not covered. The cloud management software presents the interface that cloud customers use to request, manage and terminate virtual machines. It runs on dedicated servers and interacts with the NoHype servers. For the purpose of this paper, we assume it is secure, but will revisit this as potential future work.

4. NOHYPE SYSTEM ARCHITECTURE

In this section we present the NoHype system architecture which capitalizes on the unique use model of hosted and shared cloud infrastructures in order to eliminate the hypervisor attack surface. Rather than defending once these attack vectors have been utilized to attack the hypervisor, we take the new approach of removing the attack surface. In doing so, we have a goal of preserving the semantics of today's virtualization technology – namely that we can start VMs with configurable parameters, stop VMs, and run multiple VMs on the same physical server. Additionally, the NoHype architecture is designed to be realizable on today's commodity hardware. In subsequent sections we discuss the key ideas of the NoHype architecture which are:

- pre-allocating memory and cores,
- using only virtualized I/O devices,
- short-circuiting the system discovery process, and
- avoiding indirection.

4.1 Pre-allocating Memory and Cores

One of the main functions of the hypervisor is dynamically managing the memory and processor cores' resources toward the goal of overall system optimization. By dynamically managing the resources, VMs can be promised more resources than are actually physically available. This oversubscription is heavily used in enterprises as a way to consolidate servers. In a hosted cloud computing model, however, oversubscription is at odds with the expectations of the customer. The customer requests, and pays for, a certain set of resources. That is what the customer expects to receive and not the unpredictable performance and extra side channels often associated with oversubscription. Rather than relying on customers underutilizing their VMs, the cloud infrastructure provider could instead simply capitalize on the rapidly increasing number of cores and memory in servers to host more VMs per physical server (even without oversubscription). With NoHype we pre-allocate the processor cores and memory so that a hypervisor is not needed to manage these resources dynamically – this is possible in hosted cloud computing since the customer specifies the exact resources needed before the VM is created.

Today, the hypervisor dynamically manages the processor cores through the scheduling functionality. Since the number of cores is specified by the customer before the VM is created, in NoHype we dedicate that number of cores to the specific VM. This is not to be confused with pinning a VM (also called setting the processor core affinity of a VM), which is a parameter to the hypervisor scheduling function to configure the restrictions of which cores a given VM is allowed to run on. Additionally, today when the cores are not dedicated to a single VM and when the core which the VM is scheduled on can change, the hypervisor must emulate the local APIC by providing a timer and handling IPIs, which are functionalities that the guest OS would expect from a local APIC. Since with NoHype, a core is dedicated to a given VM, we no longer need to emulate this functionality and can allow a guest to use the local APIC directly. While this gives the guest OS direct control over the hardware local APIC and opens a new possibility for a guest VM to send a malicious interprocessor interrupt (IPI) to other VMs, we show in our security analysis in Section 6.2 that this can be handled with a slight modification to the way the guest VM handles IPIs.

Similar to pre-allocating processor cores, in NoHype we also pre-allocate the memory. In order to remove the virtualization layer, we can again capitalize on the use model where customers of the cloud infrastructure provider specify the amount of memory for their VMs. This means we can pre-allocate resources rather than having a hypervisor dynamically manage them. A key to isolating each virtual machine is making sure that each VM can access its own guest physical memory and not be allowed to access the physical memory of other VMs. Without an active hypervisor we must utilize the hardware to enforce the memory isolation by capitalizing on the hardware paging mechanisms available in modern processors.

4.2 Using only Virtualized I/O Devices

I/O devices are another important component that is addressed in the NoHype architecture. With NoHype, we dedicate I/O devices to the guest VM so we do not need virtualization software to emulate these devices. Of course, dedicating a physical I/O device to each VM does not scale. With NoHype, the devices themselves are virtualized. However, a VM running 'in the cloud' has no need for peripheral devices such as a mouse, VGA, or printer. It only requires network connection (NIC), storage, and potentially a graphics card (which is increasingly used for high-performance general-purpose calculations). So, only a limited number of devices with virtualization support is needed. Today, NICs with virtualization support are already popular and storage and graphics devices will be soon. Moreover, networked storage can be utilized in lieu of a virtualized (local) storage device – making the unavailability of virtualized storage devices only a minor limitation.

NoHype capitalizes on modern processors for both direct assignment of devices as well as virtualization extensions in modern commodity devices. VMs control the devices through memory-mapped I/O. The memory-management hardware of modern commodity processors can be configured so that the VM can only access the memory of the device that is associated with it (and the device can also only access the memory of its associated VM). Further, virtualization extensions are available in modern commodity devices. For example, SR-IOV[2] [7] enabled device announces itself as multiple devices on the PCI bus. The functionality of these devices is separated into board-wide functions (known as physical functions) which are controllable only by the host OS , and functions which are specific to the individual virtual devices (known as virtual functions) that can be assigned to different guest VMs.

4.3 Short-Circuiting the System Discovery

To run on a variety of platforms, most operating systems automatically *discover* the configuration of the underlying system. This is done by the guest OS kernel during its initial loading. To minimize changes to the guest OS, the NoHype architecture allows the guest OS to perform its normal bootup procedure, but slightly modifies it to cache system configuration data for later use. This is supported by a temporary hypervisor to overcome current limitations of commodity hardware. For example, to determine which devices are available, the guest OS will perform a series of reads to the PCI configuration space in order to determine what devices are present. This PCI configuration space, along with "system discovering" instructions such as CPUID, are not virtualized by today's hardware.

This modified guest OS kernel is provided by the cloud infrastructure provider – a practice that is common today to make it easier for customers to start using the cloud provider's infrastructure. This becomes a requirement in the NoHype architecture to ensure that no customer code executes while any underlying virtualization software is present – since the customer code may attempt to attack this temporary hypervisor. Additionally, as minimal changes are required to ensure all system information is discovered only during guest OS initialization, the cloud provider can make these minimal changes for the benefit of all of its customers. Importantly, this does not restrict what applications and guest OS kernel modules the customer can run, so restricting the customer's choice to a fixed set of guest OS kernels is not a significant problem.

Once the initial guest OS kernel bootup sequence is complete and the underlying system configuration has been learned by the guest OS, the temporary hypervisor is disabled. At this point the guest VM execution switches from code under the control of the cloud infrastructure provider to the customer's code which can run any applications and load any guest OS kernel modules desired.

In addition to supporting the device discovery and system information instructions, the guest OS will utilize one

[2]SR-IOV is the Single-Root I/O Virtualization specification.

additional device during its initialization. In particular, a high precision timer, such as the high-precision event timer (HPET), is needed temporarily during the boot process of the Linux kernel. First, it is used as an external reference to determine the clock frequency of the processor. The local APIC timer is configured to generate an interrupt in a certain number of clock cycles (rather than certain time). Therefore, it is important to know the exact frequency of the processor clock so the local APIC can be used as an accurate timer[3]. Second, this high precision timer is used to emulate the CMOS-based real-time clock – that is, the battery backed clock which tells the date and time. Again, the temporary hypervisor can emulate this functionality to let the guest discover the processor core's frequency and get the time of day. After this, the clock is not needed anymore[4].

Finally, since we allow this system discovery only during bootup, the OS must be sure to gather all of the information that may be needed over the lifetime of the VM. We capitalize on the fact that we are providing the guest OS kernel by making minor modifications so that the information is gathered during guest OS bootup and cached by the OS. This removes the need for instructions like the CPUID to run during the lifetime of the OS to determine hardware configuration, and therefore the need for a hypervisor response.

4.4 Avoiding Indirection

Today, because hypervisors present an abstracted view of a machine that is not a one-to-one mapping of virtual to real hardware, they must perform indirections that map the virtual view to real hardware. Since we are bringing the guest virtual machine in more direct contact with the underlying hardware, we avoid these indirections, and therefore, remove the need for a hypervisor to perform them.

One such indirection is involved in the communication between cores. Hypervisors present each VM with the illusion of running on a dedicated system. As such, the hypervisor presents each VM with processor IDs that start at 0. Today, the physical cores in the processor can be shared by more than one VM and the core that a VM is running on can be changed by the hypervisor's scheduler. Because of this, the hypervisor needs a map between the view presented to the VM and the current configuration in order to support communication between the VM's virtual cores. When dedicating cores to VMs, as is the case with NoHype, the guest VM can access the real processor ID and avoid the need for indirection.

Indirection is also used in delivering interrupts to the correct VM. For the same reason that the processor core ID requires indirection (VMs can share cores and can move between cores), the hypervisor has to handle the interrupts and route them to the correct VM. When dedicating cores to VMs, we remove the need for the re-routing as interrupts go directly to the target VM.

5. PROTOTYPE DESIGN

In this section we present the prototype of our NoHype system. Rather than write from scratch all of the necessary software to setup and boot a guest virtual machine, we instead utilize existing virtualization technology which must also provide this functionality. We base our prototype off of Xen 4.0, Linux 2.6.35.4 as the guest OS, and an Intel XEON W5580 processor. For the virtualized network card we used one with the Intel 82576 Ethernet controller. We utilized networked storage instead of a virtualized disk, since there are no commercially available drives which support SR-IOV at this time. In particular we used iPXE[5] for a network boot to fetch the guest OS kernel along with iSCSI [27] for the guest VM's storage.

In order to understand the details of what changes were required to the various software components, it is useful to understand what is happening during the various phases of execution. Shown in Figure 3 is a time line of a guest VM's life time – from creation to shutdown. The following subsections will detail each phase and discuss the changes we made to Xen or Linux to support that phase. We will wrap up the section by presenting an evaluation of the raw performance improvements seen with our prototype.

5.1 VM Creation

Independent of the interface that is presented to the customer for managing virtual machines, eventually, a request from the customer will result in a request sent by the cloud management software to the system software running on a specific server to create a virtual machine. This request will specify all of the configuration details, such as the amount of memory, the number of cores, and what (virtual) devices to assign to the VM.

During this phase all of the resources are pre-allocated and the virtualized I/O devices are assigned. Here, Xen already provides all of the required functionality. The management software runs in Dom0, Xen's privileged VM, and we restricted it to execute only on core 0, as shown in Figure 3(a). The VM initialization code then configures the hardware mechanisms which will enforce memory allocation – in particular, the extended page tables (EPT) in the Intel processors. With NoHype, we require that these tables be preset so that there is no need for a hypervisor which manages memory translation dynamically. Xen's VM initialization code already has such pre-setting of EPT entries for this purpose. The VM initialization code also includes the physical function driver for the NIC which sets up the registers in the device not accessible to guest VMs – e.g., the MAC address, multicast addresses, and VLAN IDs.

For pre-allocating processor cores, Xen's VM initialization code has the ability to pin a VM to a set of cores. It does this by setting the processor core affinity of the VM which causes the scheduler function to re-schedule the VM on the selected core and add it to the list of VMs for which it can choose between for that core. Note that while pinning sets which cores a given VM can run on, it does not restrict the pinning of multiple VMs to the same core. For NoHype, the management software needs to keep track of which cores are already assigned and only pin VMs to unused cores.

Finally, Xen's VM initialization code allocates the virtualized NIC(s) via the PCI pass through mechanism supported in Xen. That is, it sets EPT entries to enable the device's memory range to be mapped to the VMs memory space. It also utilizes the VT-d [4] extensions in the Intel architecture to allow the device to DMA directly into the VM's memory.

[3]In newer processors the local APIC runs at a fixed frequency regardless of the processor core's idle states [2] so it can be used to keep track of processor ticks.

[4]The network time protocol can be used to ensure the clock stays accurate.

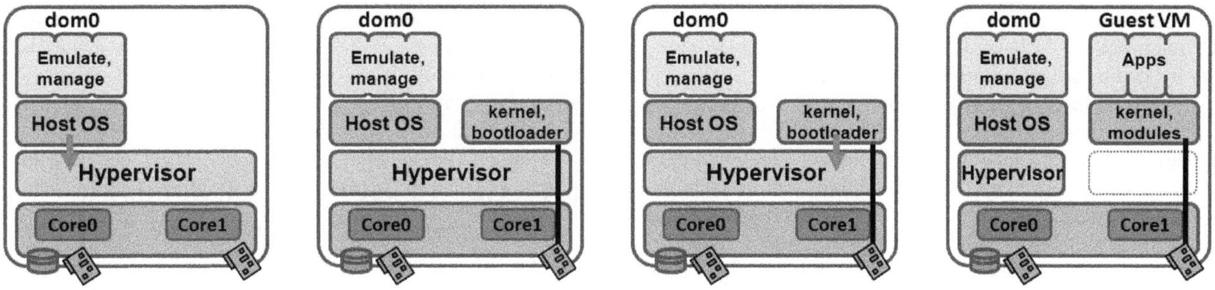

(a) Creation. (b)Bootup. (c) Disengagement (d) Execution/Shutdown.

Figure 3: The four stages of a VM's lifetime in a NoHype system.

5.2 Guest VM bootup

Once the VM is created, its boot process is kicked off, as seen in Figure 3(b). We piggyback on Xen's inclusion of a bootloader called "hvmloader" (hvm stands for hardware virtual machine, which indicates the processor has certain virtualization capabilities). The hvmloader is the first software that executes inside the guest VM. It has network boot capabilities through the inclusion of iPXE[5] which enables it to fetch, in our case, the guest OS kernel and initial RAM disk[5]. Once the guest OS kernel is loaded and ready to boot, the hvmloader sets the guest OS kernel parameters to pass information to the guest OS and jumps to the kernel.

During the operating system bootup, the guest OS kernel will perform a great deal of system discovery – in particular, device discovery as well as discovering the processor capabilities. We discuss each of these in further detail below. Recall that during this phase, a temporary hypervisor is present to support the system discovery.

5.2.1 Discovering Devices

In order to determine what devices are present, in particular PCI devices, the guest operating system queries a known range of memory addresses. If the response to the read of a particular memory address returns a well-known constant value, that means there is no device present at that address. Otherwise the device would return a device identifier. In Xen based VMs, reads to these addresses trap to the hypervisor. Xen then passes the request to QEMU running in Dom0 which handles it. In QEMU today, there is an assumption of a minimal set of devices being present (such as VGA). We modified QEMU to return "no device" for all but a network card.

Upon discovering the device, the guest OS then sets up the interrupts for that device by choosing vectors and setting up internal tables that associate the vectors with interrupt handler functions. When the guest OS configures the I/O APIC with this information, the request traps to the hypervisor which virtualizes the I/O APIC in software. Since the guest's view of available vectors does not match what is actually available, Xen chooses a vector which is free, and stores a mapping between the actual vector and what the guest expects. This means that Xen would typically handle the interrupt, perform a mapping, and then inject an interrupt with the mapped vector. However, since we will eventually be disengaging the hypervisor, we modified both Xen and the guest Linux kernel to make the vector chosen by each to be configurable. Linux is made configurable so that it chooses a vector which is actually available and so that it does not choose the same vector as another VM. Xen is made configurable so that the management software can ensure that the Xen vector assignment function will also choose this vector. Once the interrupts are set up, the guest OS sets up the device itself through the virtual function driver's initialization routine. In the particular NIC we used for our prototype, part of this initialization utilizes a mailbox mechanism on the NIC for interacting with the physical function driver in the host OS to perform a reset and retrieve the MAC address. After the virtual function driver is initialized, interaction with the physical function driver is not needed.

5.2.2 Discovering Processor Capabilities

In addition to needing to know which devices are available, the guest OS needs to know details about the processor itself – in particular, (i) the clock frequency, (ii) the core identifier, and (iii) information about the processor's features.

The frequency that the processor runs at must be calculated from a reference clock. For this, we provide a high precision event timer (HPET) device to the guest VM. Since this device is not virtualized in hardware, we only have a software virtualized HPET providing the guest VM with periodic interrupts during bootup when the operating system will need it. Once the operating system knows the clock frequency of the core, it can use the per-core local timer as its timer event source rather than the HPET.

The core identifier is used so that when the software running on one core wants to send an interprocessor interrupt (IPI) to another core, it knows what to set as the destination. In Xen, this identifier is assigned by Xen and any IPIs involve a mapping within the hypervisor to the actual identifier. In order to unwind this indirection, we modified Xen to pass the actual identifier of the core, which in Intel processors is the local advanced programmable interrupt controller (APIC) ID. This identifier can be obtained by the guest operating system in three ways, each of which we modified. First, it can be obtained in the *APIC ID* register within the local APIC itself. Second, it can be obtained through the CPUID instruction by setting the EAX register to '1'. Finally, it can be obtained with the Advanced Configuration and Power Interface (ACPI) table, which is written by the bootloader (hvmloader for Xen) as a way to pass information to the operating system.

Finally, information about the processor's features such

[5]The release version of Xen includes gPXE. iPXE is a more actively developed branch and one for which we added a driver for the Intel 82576 Ethernet controller.

as cache size and model number, are obtained through the CPUID instruction. This is an instruction that applications can use in order to do some processor-specific optimizations. However, in a virtual environment the capabilities of the processor are different than the actual capabilities, and therefore when the instruction is encountered, the processor causes an exit to the hypervisor which emulates the instruction. We modified the Linux kernel to perform this instruction during boot-up with each of the small number of possible input values, storing the result for each. We then make this information available as a system call. Any application that calls the CPUID instruction directly will have to be modified so they do not cause a VM exit. While this may sound like a major hurdle, in reality, it is not. We did not encounter any such applications, but instead encountered the use of the CPUID instruction in a small number of standard libraries such as libc which calls CPUID whenever a process is created. We modified libc to use the system call instead of the instruction. While these are not part of the guest OS kernel (and therefore not provided by the cloud provider), they can be made available for customers to easily patch their libraries and do not require a recompilation of the application. Further, for any application which does make use of CPUID and cannot be recompiled or modified, simple static binary translation can be used to translate the CPUID instruction into code which performs the system call and puts the results in the expected registers.

5.3 Hypervisor Disengagement

At the end of the boot process, we must disengage the hypervisor from any involvement in the execution of the guest VM. We achieve this through a guest OS kernel module which is loaded and unloaded within the init script of the initial RAM disk (initrd). As shown in Figure 3(c), this module simply makes a hypercall with an unused hypercall number (Dom0 communicates with the hypervisor through hypercalls). The handler for this particular hypercall will perform the hypervisor disengagement for that core and send an IPI to the other cores allocated to the VM to signal to them that they need to perform the core-specific disengagement functionality.

There are three main functions of this process. First, it must take steps to remove the VM from several lists (such as timers which are providing timer interrupts to the guest) as well as remove the set of cores from the online processor cores mask (so Xen does not attempt to send any IPIs to it). Second, the disengagement function must configure the hardware such that the guest has full control over the individual core. This includes settings within the virtual machine control structure (VMCS)[6] (e.g., setting the virtualize APIC access bit to 0) as well as mappings in the extended page tables (e.g., adding the local APIC's memory range so that it does not cause an EPT violation). Finally, we must initialize the local APIC registers with values that match what the guest operating system wrote. Before this disengagement, Xen makes use of the local APIC itself and presents a virtualized view to the guest (e.g., Xen uses a one-shot timer as its own timer source but presents a periodic timer to our Linux kernel). The disengagement function sets the registers in the actual local APIC with the values that are stored in the virtualized local APIC.

[6]The VMCS is used to manage transitions between the guest virtual machine and the hypervisor.

Once the hypervisor disengagement process completes, execution returns to the guest VM where the disengagement-initiator module is unloaded and the iSCSI drive(s) for the customer is mounted. Execution control is then transferred (for the first time) to the user's code.

5.4 Guest Execution and Shutdown

At this point, execution is under the complete control of the guest, as shown in Figure 3(d). It can run applications and load OS kernel modules. We have configured the system such that anything the virtual machine may need to do, it will be able to do. We consider any other actions to be illegal (and potentially malicious). Many actions, such as accessing memory outside of the allocated memory range, will cause an exit from the VM. Since we consider them illegal, they will result in the termination of this VM. Other actions, such as sending messages to the physical function driver via the mailbox functionality on a device, can be ignored.

Because of this restriction, we needed to modify the guest Linux kernel slightly – these modifications do not affect an application or kernel module's interaction with Linux. That is not to say we must trust the guest OS for the security of the entire system, simply that in order for the guest VM to run without causing a VM exit, Linux is configured to not access devices that it is not using. In particular, Linux assumes the presence of a VGA console and writes to the fixed I/O port whether there is a VGA console or not. We modified this assumption and instead made the use of a VGA console configurable. Additionally, Linux makes the assumption that if an HPET device is available for determining the clock frequency, it should be added to the list of clock sources. Each of the clocks in this list are periodically queried for its cycle count. As we have a time stamp counter (TSC) also available, the HPET is not needed. We added a configuration in Linux to specify whether the HPET device is to be added to the list of clock sources or not.

However, one limitation of completely removing the availability of an HPET device is that we are now relying on the local APIC timer. In processors before the current generation, this local APIC timer would stop when the core goes into a deep idle state. Recent processors with the Always Running APIC Timer (ARAT) feature are not subject to this limitation. Unfortunately, we built our prototype on a processor without this feature. To overcome this, rather than buying a new processor, we simply faked that we have it by (i) specifying that the processor has the ARAT capability in the response to the CPUID instruction, and (ii) using the Linux parameter, *max_cstate*, to tell Linux to not enter a deep idle state (clearly not ideal, but acceptable for a prototype).

Our timeline ends when the guest VM shuts down. A guest VM can initiate the shutdown sequence itself from within the VM. This will eventually result in an exit from the VM, at which point the VM is terminated. However, we cannot rely on customers to cleanly shutdown when their time is up. Instead, we need to be able to force the shutdown of a VM. We realize this by configuring the VMCS to specify that the VM should exit when the core receives a non-maskable interrupt (NMI). In this way, the hypervisor, restricted to running core 0 at this point, can send an NMI, forcing a VM exit, giving the VM exit handler the ability to shutdown the VM.

5.5 Raw Performance Evaluation

Our prototype was built as a demonstration that we can actually realize NoHype on today's commodity hardware. In addition to the security benefits, which we analyze in Section 6, removing a layer of software leads to performance improvements, since with NoHype, there will no longer be the number of VM exits as seen in Figure 2.

We experimented with both the SPEC benchmarks which analyze the performance of the system under different workloads as well as a VM running Apache to capture a common workload seen in cloud infrastructures today. In each case we ran the experiment with both NoHype and stock Xen with a hardware virtual machine guest. With the NoHype system, we utilized our modified Linux kernel, whereas in the Xen system we utilized the unmodified 2.6.35.4 Linux kernel. Each VM was configured with two cores, 4GB of memory, and two network cards that were passed through (one an Internet facing NIC, and one for communicating with the iSCSI server). There was no device emulation and no other VMs were running on the system which might interfere with performance.

Shown in Figure 4 are the results of our experiments. We saw an approximately 1% performance improvement across the board. The lone exception to this was the gcc benchmark, which saw better performance with Xen than with NoHype. We need to further investigate the cause of this, but believe it to be related to our modifications to the guest kernel. Also note that much of the major performance bottlenecks associated with virtualization are alleviated with the VT-d (to directly assign devices) and EPT (to allow VMs to manage page tables) technologies and therefore already used in Xen. Our performance improvement comes from removal of the VM exits and is on top of performance gained from using VT-d and EPT hardware.

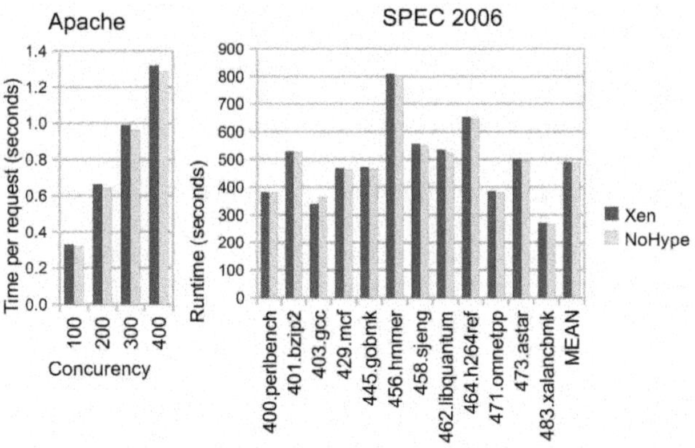

Figure 4: Raw performance of NoHype vs. Xen.

6. SECURITY ANALYSIS

In this section we present a security analysis of our NoHype architecture and its realization on today's commodity hardware. Our conclusion is that NoHype makes an important improvement in the security of virtualization technology for hosted and shared cloud infrastructures, even with the limitations due to today's commodity hardware.

6.1 Remaining Hypervisor Attack Surface

A NoHype system still requires system management software (performing some of today's hypervisor's duties) to be running on each server. While defending the interaction between the cloud manager and the system manager is our future work, here we have concentrated on the surface between the guest VM and the hypervisor which is much larger and more frequently used.

To initialize the guest VM, we use a temporary hypervisor and a slightly modified guest OS for performing system discovery tasks. The initial guest OS kernel is supplied and loaded by the cloud infrastructure provider, thus the customer has no control over the OS kernel which interacts with the temporary hypervisor. The temporary hypervisor is disabled (i.e., the VM is disengaged) before switching to the customer's code. By the time the customer's code runs, it does not require any services of the hypervisor (the system discovery data is cached and the devices, memory and cores are assigned). Any VM exit will trigger our kill VM routine as previously described, thus denying a malicious customer the opportunity to use a VM exit as an attack vector.

The ability of the guest VM to do something illegal, cause a VM exit, and trigger system management software to take action is itself a possible attack vector. The code handling this condition is in the trusted computing base (TCB) of a NoHype system, however, it is quite simple. After the VM is disengaged we set a flag in memory indicating that any VM exit should cause the VM to be terminated. The code base found in the temporary hypervisor and privileged system manger is never triggered by the guest VM after disengagement. Similarly, it cannot be triggered by any other running VM, as an exit from that VM will only trigger the kill VM routine.

6.2 VM to VM Attack Surface

After disengaging a VM, we give it full access to interprocessor interrupts (IPIs). One limitation of today's hardware is that there is no hardware mask which can be set to prevent a core from sending an IPI to another core. This introduces a new but limited ability for VM to VM communication. Now the VM has the ability to send an IPI to any other core without that core being able mask it or even know who sent it. The system management software which is pinned to one of the cores may also be a target of such an attack.

A preliminary pragmatic solution is presented here. Since the IPI does not contain any data and is only used as a trigger, the guest OS can defend against this attack by slightly modifying the way it handles IPIs. For each type of IPI, a shared region in memory can hold a flag that can be set by the sending core and then checked and cleared by the receiving core. Given that no VM can access memory of another VM, an attacker will not have the ability to set any of these flags. Therefore, the receiver of the IPI can simply ignore the IPI if the flag is not set.

While this ability for guest VMs to send IPIs poses very little security risk, it has the potential to enable an attacker to launch a denial of service attack by constantly sending IPIs to a given core. Fortunately, the extent to which they can possibly degrade performance is extremely limited. We set up an experiment by configuring an attacker VM with up to 8 cores, each sending IPIs at their maximum rate, and a victim with 2 cores. The results, shown in Figure 5, show that the performance degradation is limited to about 1%. Note that while we experimented with 8 cores, using 4 attacker cores was sufficient to saturate the rate at which IPIs can be sent in our test system. We used the Apache bench-

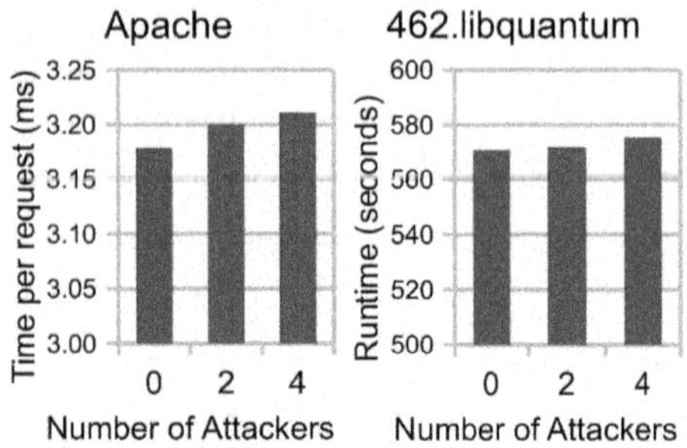

Figure 5: Effect of IPI attack on benchmarks.

mark and a compute intensive benchmark (462.libquantum) from the SPEC 2006 suite. Because the bus used to deliver IPIs is the same bus used for interrupts (the APIC bus), the performance of Apache was affected slightly more because it is a more interrupt driven application. The 462.libquantum benchmark is compute intensive and captures the overhead of simply having to process each interrupt.

6.3 Isolation between VMs

With NoHype, we rely on hardware mechanisms to provide isolation of access to shared resources. Most important are the confidentiality and integrity of each VM's memory. We utilize Xen's code which pre-sets the entries in the extended page tables (EPT) to assign physical pages to a particular VM. Any access to memory by a VM will cause the processor hardware to perform a translation using the EPT. When accessing memory outside of the given VM's allowed pages, a violation will occur and the VM will exit to the hypervisor context (which after disengagement is our kill VM routine). Because of this, the confidentiality and integrity are tied to the correctness of the hardware EPT implementation, which we believe will have undergone significant testing and verification. While all modern hypervisors also use the EPT mechanism, they may update the mapping when they provide additional capabilities such as transparent page sharing among VMs [8]. Consequently, isolation today depends not only on the hardware's correctness but also on the complex hypervisor software.

Also of importance is the performance isolation between VMs in the face of resource sharing. Without a hypervisor, as in NoHype, hardware is relied on to provide the isolation. The main shared resources of concern are the network card (and associated bandwidth) as well as the memory bus. The network card has queues with flow control mechanisms that provide a fair allocation of resources. The memory controller and bus, on the other hand, do not in today's processors [28].

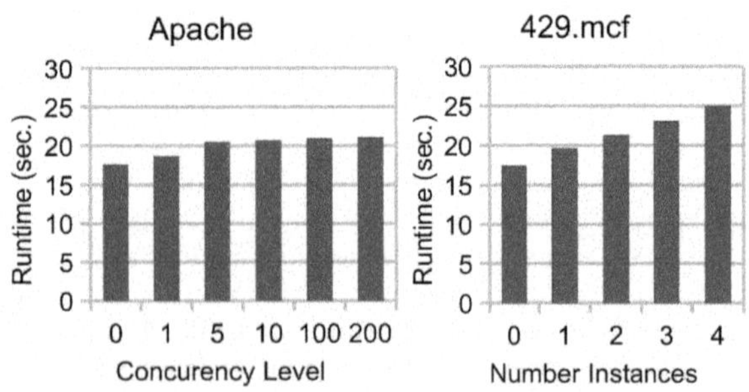

Figure 6: Quantification of the memory side-channel.

To quantify the quality of memory isolation, we ran one VM with a varying workload and examined the performance of a second VM with a fixed workload. In particular, the fixed workload VM had the memory intensive 429.mcf benchmark from SPEC 2006 suite running. In the varying workload VM we experimented with both Apache, under varying number of concurrent requests, as well as varying the number of instances of the 429.mcf benchmark. The results are shown in Figure 6. This experiment can be viewed either in terms of (i) an attacker attempting to affect the performance of a victim, or (ii) an attacker attempting to learn information about the victim (i.e., utilize it as a side channel to answer questions such as "how loaded is my competitor"). In either case, there is some interference between each workload, but we believe the interference is not significant enough to completely deny service or to learn sensitive information such as cryptographic keys [17].

6.4 VMs Mapping Physical Infrastructures

Work by Ristenpart, et al., [30] has raised the concern of infrastructure mapping attacks. With NoHype, the guest VMs have a more direct interaction with the hardware and could abuse that to try to map an infrastructure. One example may be a malicious VM reading the APIC ID numbers to identify the underlying physical cores and use that information to help narrow down where in the provider's infrastructure the VM is located. This may be mitigated by randomizing APIC IDs of the cores (which can be done at system boot time). Even if a malicious VM is able to determine that it is co-located with a victim VM, our approach of eliminating the attack surface denies it the opportunity to attack the hypervisor and by extension the victim VM.

7. RELATED WORK

The related work can be categorized in four main areas: minimizing the hypervisor, proposing a new processor architecture, hardening the hypervisor, or giving VMs more direct access to hardware.

Minimizing the hypervisor: Work on minimizing hypervisors aims to reduce the amount of code within the hypervisor, which should translate to fewer bugs and vulnerabilities. One example is SecVisor [32], a hypervisor which supports a single guest VM and protects that VM from rootkits. Another example is TrustVisor [26] which is a special-purpose hypervisor for protecting code and data integrity of selected portions of the application. Previous minimal hypervisors are not practical for deployment in the hosted cloud computing model where multiple VMs from multiple customers run on the same server. With NoHype, we show how to remove attack vectors (in effect also reducing the hypervisor) while still being able to support the hosted cloud computing model.

New processor architectures: In another approach, researchers propose building new processor architectures which explicitly offer new hardware functionality for improving security. Much work has been done on new hardware mechanisms for protecting applications and trusted software modules [24, 34, 21, 12], including Bastion [10] which uses a full hypervisor. Unfortunately, such approaches do require new microprocessors and cannot be deployed today, unlike our solution. Additionally, the use model for cloud computing has some similarities with that of mainframes. The architectures targeting these systems, such as the IBM System z [29], have support for creating logical domains which enforce partitioning of resources such as CPU and memory in hardware. In contrast, NoHype focuses on commodity x86 servers used by cloud infrastructure providers.

Hardening the hypervisor: Much of hypervisor-related work has centered around hardening of the hypervisor, such as [23, 31, 33]. Especially interesting is HyperSafe [35] which aims to protect a hypervisor against control-flow hijacking attacks. They use a non-bypassable memory lockdown technique (only a special routine in the hypervisor can write to memory) coupled with a restricted pointer indexing technique (all function calls in the hypervisor are transformed to jumps from a special table). While making it more difficult to subvert the hypervisor, these additions add about a 5% performance overhead and any bugs in the hypervisor could still be exploited through one of the attack vectors. Recently, HyperSentry [9] used the SMM (system management mode) to bypass the hypervisor for integrity measurement purposes. Unfortunately, the integrity measurements only reveal traces of an attack after it has already happened and are limited to protecting against attacks which persistently modify the hypervisor executable. While the authors report being able to invoke the measurement every 8 seconds in HyperSentry, this still leaves a window for attackers. Furthermore, their approach results in a 2.4% overhead if HyperSentry protections are invoked every 8 seconds. In contrast, NoHype prevents the attacks from happening in the first place, and does this with about a 1% performance improvement.

Direct access to hardware: NoHype shares much with exokernels such as ExOS [13] and Nemesis [22] which essentially reduce an operating system to providing only arbitration to shared resources and give applications more direct access to hardware. We capitalize on modern hardware advances to push it even further where the thin software layer from the exokernels is realized in hardware and full commodity operating systems can be run, rather than requiring applications to be redesigned for the exokernel environment. There have also been proposals that enable a single operating system to run without a virtualization layer but can insert a virtualization layer when needed – e.g., to run a second VM during planned maintenance [25] or to utilize migration for consolidation [19]. NoHype, on the other hand, can run multiple VMs simultaneously, each with direct access to its allocated hardware.

8. CONCLUSIONS AND FUTURE WORK

Today, the hypervisor is the all-powerful system software layer which controls the resources of a physical system and manages how they interact with the guest VMs. Because of its central role, the hypervisor, and other parts of the virtualization software, is a potent target for attacks, especially in shared infrastructures which allow multiple parties to run virtual machines. In this paper, we presented the complete design, implementation and evaluation of a working NoHype system on today's commodity hardware which removes the attack surface of the hypervisor and thus eliminates the vector by which VMs can exploit vulnerabilities. We do this by eliminating the VM's need for a hypervisor through (i) pre-allocation of processor cores and memory resources, (ii) using only virtualized I/O devices, (iii) supporting the system discovery process with a temporary hypervisor and a slightly modified guest OS, and (iv) avoiding any indirection that would necessitate having a hypervisor. This allows us to remove the interaction between the guest VMs and hypervisor and eliminate the attack surface which a malicious VM could use to compromise the virtualization layer, and then in turn attack or obstruct other VMs. In addition, our evaluation with benchmarks showed about 1% faster run times.

While NoHype significantly advances the security of shared cloud infrastructures, today's commodity hardware imposes some limitations; as future work, we will examine minimal hardware changes to further tighten the security of a NoHype system. Also, we will add support for live VM migration, particularly for the scenario where the initiator of the migration (the cloud provider) differs from the owner of the VM (the cloud customer). The disruption this process causes to the customer's VM depends on the workload of the VM [11], yet the provider does not know the workload or whether it is a particularly bad time to disrupt the guest VM. We believe the correct model for migration is for the provider to notify the customer ahead of time, allowing the customer to prepare for the transient disruption (e.g., by shedding load or redirecting new requests) and participate in the migration itself (e.g., through support for OS migration [20] in the guest). Finally, we plan to explore ways for the customer to run virtualization software of its own to enable nested virtualization, which may also aid in supporting live migration.

9. ACKNOWLEDGMENTS

This work was supported in part by National Science Foundation grants: EEC-0540832 and CCF-0917134. Eric Keller was supported through an Intel Ph.D. Fellowship. We also benefited from equipment donation from Intel.

We would like to thank Tim Deegan from Citrix, Andrew Warfield from University of British Columbia, and Don Banks from Cisco, for discussions and feedback on our NoHype design. Additionally, we would like to thank our shepherd, Herbert Bos, and the anonymous CCS reviewers for their comments and suggestions.

10. REFERENCES

[1] ab - Apache HTTP server benchmarking tool. `http://httpd.apache.org/docs/2.0/programs/ab.html`.

[2] Intel 64 and IA-32 Architectures Software Developer's Manual Volume 2A: Instruction Set Reference, A-M, page 274. `http://www.intel.com/products/processor/manuals/`.

[3] Intel 64 and IA-32 Architectures Software Developer's Manual Volume 3B: System Programming Guide, Part 2. `http://www.intel.com/products/processor/manuals/`.

[4] Intel Corporation: Intel Virtualization Technology for Directed I/O. `http://download.intel.com/technology/itj/2006/v10i3/v10-i3-art02.pdf`.

[5] iPXE: Open Source Boot Firmware. `http://ipxe.org/`.

[6] National Vulnerability Database, CVE and CCE Statistics Query Page. `http://web.nvd.nist.gov/view/vuln/statistics`.

[7] PCI SIG: PCI-SIG Single Root I/O Virtualization. `http://www.pcisig.com/specifications/iov/single_root/`.

[8] Understanding Memory Resource Management in VMware ESX Server. VMWare White Paper. 2009. www.vmware.com/files/pdf/perf-vsphere-memory_management.pdf.

[9] A. M. Azab, P. Ning, Z. Wang, X. Jiang, X. Zhang, and N. C. Skalsky. HyperSentry: Enabling stealthy in-context measurement of hypervisor integrity. In *ACM Conference on Computer and Communications Security (CCS)*, pages 38–49, October 2010.

[10] D. Champagne and R. B. Lee. Scalable architectural support for trusted software. In *IEEE International Symposium on High Performance Computer Architecture (HPCA)*, pages 1–12, Jan. 2010.

[11] C. Clark, K. Fraser, S. Hand, J. G. Hansen, E. Jul, C. Limpach, I. Pratt, and A. Warfield. Live migration of virtual machines. In *2nd Symposium on Networked Systems Design and Implementation (NSDI)*, 2005.

[12] J. Dwoskin and R. B. Lee. Hardware-rooted trust for secure key management and transient trust. In *ACM Conference on Computer and Communications Security (CCS)*, Oct. 2007.

[13] D. R. Engler, M. F. Kaashoek, and J. O'Toole. Exokernel: An operating system architecture for application-level resource management. In *Symposium on Operating Systems Principles (SOSP)*, December 1995.

[14] F. Gens. IT cloud services user survey, pt.2: Top benefits & challenges, Oct. 2008. http://blogs.idc.com/ie/?p=210.

[15] J. L. Henning. SPEC CPU2006 benchmark descriptions. *SIGARCH Comput. Archit. News*, 34:1–17, September 2006.

[16] E. Keller, J. Szefer, J. Rexford, and R. B. Lee. NoHype: Virtualized cloud infrastructure without the virtualization. In *International Symposium on Computer Architecture (ISCA)*, June 2010.

[17] J. Kelsey, B. Schneier, D. Wagner, and C. Hall. Side channel cryptanalysis of product ciphers. In J.-J. Quisquater, Y. Deswarte, C. Meadows, and D. Gollmann, editors, *Computer Security: ESORICS 98*, volume 1485 of *Lecture Notes in Computer Science*, pages 97–110. 1998.

[18] G. Klein, K. Elphinstone, G. Heiser, J. Andronick, D. Cock, P. Derrin, D. Elkaduwe, K. Engelhardt, R. Kolanski, M. Norrish, T. Sewell, H. Tuch, and S. Winwood. seL4: Formal verification of an OS kernel. In *Symposium on Operating Systems Principles (SOSP)*, pages 207–220, October 2009.

[19] T. Kooburat and M. Swift. The best of both worlds with on-demand virtualization. In *Workshop on Hot Topics in Operating Systems (HotOS)*, May 2011.

[20] M. A. Kozuch, M. Kaminsky, and M. P. Ryan. Migration without virtualization. In *Workshop on Hot Topics in Operating Systems (HotOS)*, May 2009.

[21] R. B. Lee, P. C. S. Kwan, J. P. McGregor, J. Dwoskin, and Z. Wang. Architecture for protecting critical secrets in microprocessors. In *International Symposium on Computer Architecture (ISCA)*, June 2005.

[22] I. Leslie, D. McAuley, R. Black, T. Roscoe, P. Barham, D. Evers, R. Fairbairns, and E. Hyden. The design and implementation of an operating system to support distributed multimedia applications. *IEEE Journal on Selected Areas in Communication*, 14(7), Sept. 1996.

[23] C. Li, A. Raghunathan, and N. K. Jha. Secure virtual machine execution under an untrusted management OS. In *Proceedings of the Conference on Cloud Computing (CLOUD)*, July 2010.

[24] D. Lie, C. Thekkath, M. Mitchell, P. Lincoln, D. Boneh, J. Mitchell, and M. Horowitz. Architectural support for copy and tamper resistant software. In *Architectural Support for Programming Languages and Operating Systems (ASPLOS)*, November 2000.

[25] D. E. Lowell, Y. Saito, and E. J. Samberg. Devirtualizable virtual machines enabling general, single-node, online maintenance. In *Architectural Support for Programming Languages and Operating Systems (ASPLOS)*, October 2004.

[26] J. M. McCune, Y. Li, N. Qu, Z. Zhou, A. Datta, V. Gligor, and A. Perrig. TrustVisor: Efficient TCB reduction and attestation. In *IEEE Symposium on Security and Privacy*, pages 143–158, May 2010.

[27] K. Z. Meth and J. Satran. Design of the iSCSI protocol. In *IEEE Symposium on Mass Storage Systems*, April 2003.

[28] T. Moscibroda and O. Mutlu. Memory performance attacks: Denial of memory service in multi-core systems. In *Proceedings of USENIX Security Symposium*, August 2007.

[29] L. Parziale, E. L. Alves, E. M. Dow, K. Egeler, J. J. Herne, C. Jordan, E. P. Naveen, M. S. Pattabhiraman, and K. Smith. Introduction to the new mainframe: z/VM basics, Nov. 2007. http://www.redbooks.ibm.com/redbooks/pdfs/sg247316.pdf.

[30] T. Ristenpart, E. Tromer, H. Shacham, and S. Savage. Hey, you, get off of my cloud: Exploring information leakage in third-party compute clouds. In *ACM Conference on Computer and Communications Security (CCS)*, November 2009.

[31] R. Sailer, E. Valdez, T. Jaeger, R. Perez, L. V. Doorn, J. L. Griffin, S. Berger, R. Sailer, E. Valdez, T. Jaeger, R. Perez, L. Doorn, J. Linwood, and G. S. Berger. sHype: Secure hypervisor approach to trusted virtualized systems. Technical Report RC23511, IBM Research, 2005.

[32] A. Seshadri, M. Luk, N. Qu, and A. Perrig. SecVisor: A tiny hypervisor to provide lifetime kernel code integrity for commodity OSes. *SIGOPS Oper. Syst. Rev.*, 41(6):335–350, December 2007.

[33] U. Steinberg and B. Kauer. NOVA: A microhypervisor-based secure virtualization architecture. In *European Conference on Computer Systems*, April 2010.

[34] G. E. Suh, C. W. O'Donnell, I. Sachdev, and S. Devadas. Design and implementation of the AEGIS single-chip secure processor using physical random functions. In *International Symposium on Computer Architecture (ISCA)*, June 2005.

[35] Z. Wang and X. Jiang. HyperSafe: A lightweight approach to provide lifetime hypervisor control-flow integrity. In *IEEE Symposium on Security and Privacy*, pages 380–395, May 2010.

How to Break XML Encryption*

Tibor Jager
Horst Görtz Institute for IT Security
Chair for Network- and Data Security
Ruhr-University Bochum
tibor.jager@rub.de

Juraj Somorovsky
Horst Görtz Institute for IT Security
Chair for Network- and Data Security
Ruhr-University Bochum
juraj.somorovsky@rub.de

ABSTRACT

XML Encryption was standardized by W3C in 2002, and is implemented in XML frameworks of major commercial and open-source organizations like Apache, redhat, IBM, and Microsoft. It is employed in a large number of major web-based applications, ranging from business communications, e-commerce, and financial services over healthcare applications to governmental and military infrastructures.

In this work we describe a practical attack on XML Encryption, which allows to decrypt a ciphertext by sending related ciphertexts to a Web Service and evaluating the server response. We show that an adversary can decrypt a ciphertext by performing only 14 requests per plaintext byte on average. This poses a serious and truly practical security threat on all currently used implementations of XML Encryption.

In a sense the attack can be seen as a generalization of padding oracle attacks (Vaudenay, Eurocrypt 2002). It exploits a subtle correlation between the block cipher mode of operation, the character encoding of encrypted text, and the response behaviour of a Web Service if an XML message cannot be parsed correctly.

Categories and Subject Descriptors

E.3 [**Data Encryption**]: Code breaking

General Terms

Security

1. INTRODUCTION

The W3C XML Encryption specification [6] today marks the de-facto standard for data encryption in complex distributed applications. The use of XML as core data syntax, e.g. for major business, e-commerce, financial, healthcare, governmental and military applications, has resulted in broad adoption of XML Encryption to protect confidential data—especially, but not exclusively, in the context of Web Services. On the technical level, the XML Encryption specification precisely describes the process and syntax to be used when applying a cryptographic algorithm for data encryption to arbitrary XML-structured data. Moreover, it also describes how to process this syntax in order to decrypt the encrypted contents at the data recipient's side. XML Encryption does not describe a new cryptographic algorithm itself, but merely allows a set of standard block ciphers, namely AES and Triple-DES (3DES), to be used at will. In order to be able to encrypt messages which are longer than the input size of the block cipher, the *cipher-block chaining* (CBC) mode of operation is used.

In this paper, we present an attack technique that enables an adversary to decrypt arbitrary data that have been encrypted according to the XML Encryption specification. Based on a cryptographic weakness of the CBC mode, we are able to perform a chosen-ciphertext attack which recovers the entire plaintext from a given ciphertext. The only prerequisite for this attack consists in availability of an "oracle" telling us whether a given ciphertext contains a "correctly formed" plaintext. "Correctly formed" means here that the plaintext contains a valid encoding (e.g. in UTF-8 or ASCII) of a message. In practice, this oracle may be provided for instance by a Web Service that returns suitable error messages, or that provides some other side-channel allowing us to distinguish correct from invalid ciphertexts, like a different timing of data processing, for instance.

To prove the practical relevance of our attack, we apply it examplarily to a realistic Web Service based on the Apache Axis2 [18] XML framework. Axis2 is one of the most popular frameworks to support the building of Web Services client and server applications. We show that a moderately optimized implementation of the attack is able to decrypt 160 bytes of encrypted data within 10 seconds by issuing 2,137 queries to the Web Service. The complexity of the attack grows only linearly with the ciphertext size, thus recovering a larger plaintext of 1,600 bytes takes about 100 seconds and 23,000 queries.

Despite the fact that the details of the attack, and thus our results in context of the Axis2 framework, are of course rather application-specific, we want to stress that the attack itself is generic, and can be adapted to other scenarios like alternate XML frameworks and possibly even other systems

*This work has been supported by the European Commission through the ICT programme under contract ICT-2007-216676 ECRYPT II and the Sec2 project of the German Federal Ministry of Education and Research (BMBF, FKZ: 01BY1030).

CCS'11 October 17–21, 2011, Chicago, Illinois, USA.

beyond XML Encryption as well. For instance, we have verified that the attack works against redhat JBoss [9] as well without any modifications.

In general chosen-ciphertext attacks can be avoided by ensuring the integrity of the ciphertext. One would therefore expect our attack can easily be thwarted by using XML Signature [7] to ensure integrity (note that XML Signature specifies not only classical public-key signatures, but also "secret-key signatures", i.e., message authentication codes). However, for several reasons this is not true, since we can show how to perform our attack *even if* either public-key or secret-key XML Signatures over the ciphertext are used. We achieve this either by applying classical Signature Wrapping [10] techniques, or by using a new attack technique that we call *Encryption Wrapping*. Thus, fixing current implementations or developing secure new implementations without changing the XML Encryption standard seems non-trivial. We illustrate this in more detail in the countermeasures section below.

RESPONSIBLE DISCLOSURE. The attack described in this paper was announced to the W3C XML Encryption Working Group and to several providers and users of implementations of XML Encryption in February 2011. This includes The Apache Software Foundation (Apache Axis2), redhat Linux (JBoss), IBM, Microsoft, and a governmental CERT. All have acknowledged the validity of our attack. The CERT has disclosed our attack to governmental CERTs of other countries. Furthermore, redhat has immediately forwarded a short announcement to the `vendor-sec` mailing list.

We are providing advice to developers that are working on fixes. As already mentioned, this is difficult without changing the standard itself (see Section 6 for details).

RELATED WORK AND OUR CONTRIBUTION. It is well-known that the CBC encryption mode is malleable unless additional methods for ensuring integrity are applied. This was exploited by Vaudenay [19], who showed that it is possible to decrypt a ciphertext which is encrypted in CBC mode by issuing a small number of queries to a so-called *padding oracle*. Subsequent work refines the idea of Vaudenay [19], for instance to other padding schemes and modes of operations [1, 14], random or secret initialization vectors [20], attacks on real-world systems like IPSec [3, 4] and ASP.NET, JSF CAPTCHA, the Ruby on Rails framework, and an OWASP security system [15, 5]. Duong and Rizzo [15, 5] also make the observation that a padding oracle does not only allow to decrypt ciphertexts, but also to obtain valid *encryptions* of arbitrary plaintexts. It is even possible to describe padding schemes which are secure against padding oracle attacks [1, 13], a corresponding formal security model was given by Paterson and Watson [13].

By their nature, padding oracle attacks work only for certain padding schemes. In particular, the above attacks are *not* applicable to XML Encryption, since the standard specifies a different padding scheme.

In contrast, we use the *encoding* of data as a side-channel that allows to attack encryption schemes using a weak mode of operation, which allows to exploit the in most cases inevitable fact that an adversary is able to observe whether a decrypted plaintext is processed by an application after decryption, or discarded since the encoding could not be recognized. Note that this works independent of the padding scheme, and thus potentially also in scenarios where padding oracle attacks are not applicable. Mitchell [11] has already outlined such a generalization of padding oracle attacks, but without giving any specific example.

Our attack on XML Encryption is highly efficient, as it needs only 14 queries per byte on average to break XML Encryptions. For comparison, the related attack of Rizzo and Duong [15] issues 128 oracle queries per byte on average in order to break CAPTCHA.

2. PRELIMINARIES

Throughout the paper we write $\{0,1\}^\ell$ to denote the set of all bit strings of length ℓ. For $a, b \in \{0,1\}^\ell$, we write $|a|$ to denote the length of a (i.e., $|a| = \ell$), $a \oplus b$ to denote the bitwise XOR of a and b, and $a||b$ to denote concatenation of a and b. We write $\{0,1\}^*$ shorthand for $\{0,1\}^* = \bigcup_{i=0}^{\infty}\{0,1\}^i$.

2.1 Block Ciphers

The XML Encryption standard specifies AES and Triple-DES (3DES) as block ciphers. Since our attack does not exploit specific properties of these algorithms, but works with any cipher in a similar way, we will consider an abstract block cipher in the following.

To this end, we define a *block cipher* as a pair of algorithms $(\mathsf{Enc}, \mathsf{Dec})$. The encryption algorithm $c = \mathsf{Enc}(k, m)$ takes as input a key $k \in \{0,1\}^\ell$ and an ν-byte plaintext $m \in \{0,1\}^n$, where $n = 8 \cdot \nu$,[1] and returns a ciphertext $c \in \{0,1\}^n$. The decryption algorithm $m = \mathsf{Dec}(k, c)$ takes a key k and a ciphertext c, and returns $m \in \{0,1\}^n$. For instance, if AES is used then we have $n = 128$ and thus $\nu = 16$.

2.2 Padding Scheme

Suppose we want to encrypt an XML message $m \in \{0,1\}^*$ of arbitrary bit-length $|m|$. Since XML data is represented by UTF-8 characters, we may always assume that $|m|$ is an integer multiple of 8. However, $|m|$ does not need necessarily be an integer multiple of the block size n of the block. Thus a padding algorithm π with inversion algorithm π^{-1} must be applied to the message, to obtain a padded message $m' = \pi(m)$ whose bit-length $|m'|$ is an integer multiple of n.

The XML Encryption standard specifies the usage of the following padding scheme π:

1. Calculate the smallest non-zero number *plen* of bytes that must be suffixed to the plain text to bring it up to a multiple of the block size n.

2. Append $plen - 1$ arbitrary pad bytes to m.

3. Set the last byte equal to *plen*.

For instance, the example given in [6] considers a three-byte message $m =$ `0x616263` and a block cipher with $n = 64$, so that $\nu = 8$. In this case, we have

$$\pi(m) = m' = \texttt{0x616263??????????05},$$

where ?? is an arbitrary byte value.

To remove the padding, one simply reads the last byte of m' and removes the required number of bytes to obtain m.

[1]Throughout the paper we assume that the block size n is always an integer multiple of 8.

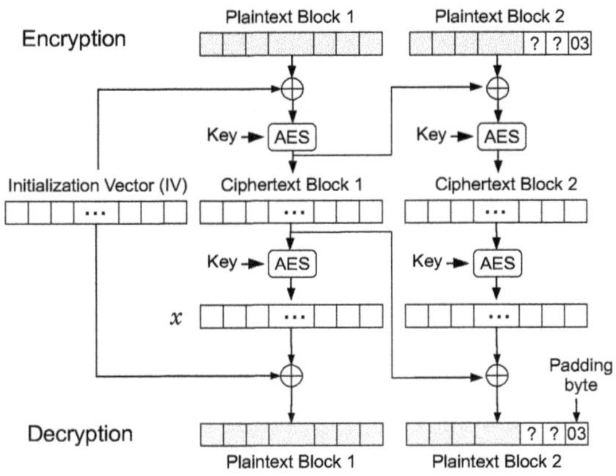

Figure 1: Illustration of the CBC mode of operation with the padding scheme from Section 2.2.

2.3 Cipher-Block Chaining

Cipher-block chaining (CBC) is the most popular block-cipher mode of operation in practice, and the only mode specified in the XML Encryption standard. It processes a message m', whose length is an integer multiple dn of the block size of $(\mathsf{Enc}, \mathsf{Dec})$, as follows.

- An *initialization vector* $iv \in \{0,1\}^n$ is chosen at random. The first ciphertext block is computed as

$$x := m_1' \oplus iv, \qquad C^{(1)} := \mathsf{Enc}(k, x). \qquad (1)$$

- The subsequent ciphertext blocks $C^{(2)}, \ldots, C^{(d)}$ are computed as

$$x := m_i' \oplus C^{(i-1)}, \qquad C^{(i)} := \mathsf{Enc}(k, x) \qquad (2)$$

  for $i = 2, \ldots, d$.

- The resulting ciphertext is $C = (iv, C^{(1)}, \ldots, C^{(d)})$.

See Figure 1 for an illustration of this scheme. The decryption procedure reverses this process in the obvious way.

In the sequel we will write $C = \mathsf{Enc}_{\mathsf{cbc}}(k, \pi(m))$ to denote encryption and $\pi(m) = \mathsf{Dec}_{\mathsf{cbc}}(k, C)$ to denote decryption in CBC mode.

3. BASIC IDEA OF THE ATTACK

In this section, we describe the basic idea behind our attack, and give a toy example which illustrates how to apply this idea in a simplified scenario. In Section 4 we will show how to adapt this idea to the "real world".

3.1 CBC-Mode is Malleable

One ingredient to our attack described below is that ciphertexts encrypted in CBC mode can be modified by an adversary such that the resulting ciphertext is related to the original ciphertext in a certain way. This works for *any* block cipher.

Suppose a ciphertext $C = (IV, C^{(1)}, \ldots, C^{(d)})$ encrypting a message $m = (m^{(1)}, \ldots, m^{(d)})$ in CBC mode is given. Then a related ciphertext can be constructed as follows. Let $IV' := IV \oplus msk$ for some $msk \in \{0,1\}^n$. Then the ciphertext

$$(IV', C^{(1)})$$

is a valid encryption of the message $m^{(1)} \oplus msk$. This can be seen by inspecting Equations (1). Similarly, Equations (2) show that the ciphertext

$$(C^{(i-1)} \oplus msk, C^{(i)})$$

is a valid encryption of the message $m^{(i)} \oplus msk$ for all $i \in \{2, \ldots, d\}$. Here we use that the decryption algorithm interprets $C^{i-1} \oplus msk$ as an initialization vector, if the ciphertext starts with this value.

In our attack described below, we choose different values for msk and send the resulting ciphertext to the XML server. The response (i.e., the type of error message or application response) of the server allows us to learn the plaintext contained in a given ciphertext.

3.2 A Toy Example

In this section we describe a simple attack on ciphertexts encrypted in CBC mode, which allows to recover the plaintext message, if a certain *oracle* (to be described below) is given. The actual attack on XML Encryption from Section 4 is based on the same idea, but in addition handles some technical obstacles that arise when the theoretical concept is adopted to the "real world".

In the following let us assume that a plaintext consists only of 8-bit characters (e.g. ASCII), and that no padding scheme is used (i.e., the length of the encrypted data is always an integer multiple of the block-length of the cipher). Let us partition the set of all characters into two sets $\mathcal{A}$ and $\mathcal{B}$. We say that $\mathcal{A}$ contains "Type-A" characters, and $\mathcal{B}$ contains "Type-B" characters. In this toy example we assume that $\mathcal{A} = \{w\}$ contains only a *single* character w. For instance, $w = \texttt{0x00}$ may be the `NULL` character.

DEFINITION 1. *We say that a ciphertext C is* well-formed *w.r.t. key k, if the plaintext $m = \mathsf{Dec}_{\mathsf{cbc}}(k, C)$ contains* only *Type-B characters.*

Let us assume that we are given a (not necessarily well-formed) ciphertext

$$C = (IV, C^{(1)}) = \mathsf{Enc}_{\mathsf{cbc}}(k, m)$$

consisting of an initialization vector IV and a single encrypted block $C^{(1)}$, which encrypts a message m. Furthermore, suppose that we may query an oracle $\mathcal{O}$. The oracle takes as input CBC-encrypted ciphertexts $C = (IV, C^{(1)})$. It computes the decryption $\mathsf{Dec}_{\mathsf{cbc}}(k, C)$ and replies as follows.

- $\mathcal{O}(C) = 1$, if the plaintext $m = \mathsf{Dec}_{\mathsf{cbc}}(k, C)$ contains *only* Type-B characters.
- $\mathcal{O}(C) = 0$, otherwise.

We will show how to use this oracle to recover the message m contained in $C = (IV, C^{(1)})$ byte-by-byte. To this end, we proceed in three steps.

1. Use the oracle to compute an initialization vector IV' such that $C' = (IV', C^{(1)})$ is well-formed.
2. Use the oracle to recover the CBC decryption intermediate value $x = \mathsf{Dec}(k, C^{(1)})$.
3. Recover the message m by computing $m = IV \oplus x$.

It is easy to compute an initialization vector IV' such that the ciphertext $C' = (IV', C^{(1)})$ is well-formed. To this end, we can first query the oracle whether $\mathcal{O}((IV, C^{(1)})) = 1$. In this case we can set $IV' := IV$. Otherwise we set IV' to a random bit string. The probability Π that this yields a well-formed ciphertext depends on the number ν of bytes per block. For the current definition of $\mathcal{A}$, the probability is equal to

$$\Pi(\nu) = (1 - 1/256)^{\nu}.$$

Thus, when using AES we have $\Pi(16) = (1 - 1/256)^{16} \approx 0.94$, while using 3DES we have $\Pi(8) \approx 0.97$. Thus, we can expect that we find a suitable IV' after a few trials. We query the oracle to test whether we are successful.

Now we have a well-formed ciphertext $(IV', C^{(1)})$. Next we show how to recover an arbitrary byte x_j of the CBC decryption intermediate value $x = \mathsf{Dec}(k, C^{(1)})$. To this end, let us write $IV' = (IV'_1, \ldots, IV'_\nu)$ and $IV'' = (IV''_1, \ldots, IV''_\nu)$ to denote the individual bytes of IV' and IV''. Next we modify the initialization vector IV' by XOR-ing a byte-mask msk to the j-th byte of IV', until a mask msk is found such that

$$\mathsf{Dec_{cbc}}(k, (IV'', C^{(1)})) = IV'' \oplus \mathsf{Dec}(k, C^{(1)}) = IV'' \oplus x$$

contains a character from $\mathcal{A} = \{w\}$. Since we have only modified the j-th byte of IV', we can conclude that

$$w = IV''_j \oplus x_j.$$

Thus we can recover x_j by computing $x_j = w \oplus IV''_j$. Since this procedure works for all j, we can thus determine x byte-wise.

Algorithm 1 Recovering x_j.

Input: A single-block ciphertext $C' = (IV', c^{(1)})$ and an index $j \in \{1, \ldots, \nu\}$.
Output: The j-th byte x_j of $x = \mathsf{Dec}(k, C^{(1)})$.
$msk := \mathtt{0x00}$
repeat
  $msk := msk + 1$
  $IV'' := IV' \oplus 0^{8(j-1)}||msk||0^{n-8j}$
until $\mathcal{O}((IV'', C^{(1)})) = 1$
return $x_j := w \oplus IV''_j$

Finally, if we are given $x = \mathsf{Dec}(k, C^{(1)})$, then we can recover the message m contained in the original ciphertext $(IV, C^{(1)})$ by computing $m = IV \oplus x$. The process of recovering x_1 is illustrated in Figure 2.

4. ATTACKING XML ENCRYPTION

In this section we show how to apply the attack described above on a real world Web Service framework. We have chosen Apache Axis2 [18], since it is one of the major frameworks. We start with some basics on how encryption in XML documents works, and how Axis2 handles incoming XML-based messages. These messages are formatted according to the SOAP standard [8], the details of this format are not relevant here and thus omitted. Then we describe how we can use such an Axis2-based Web Service endpoint as an oracle $\mathcal{O}_{\mathsf{Axis}}$ for our attack. Finally, we describe algorithms that execute the attack using this oracle by first preparing a given multi-block ciphertext (by e.g. adjusting the padding) and

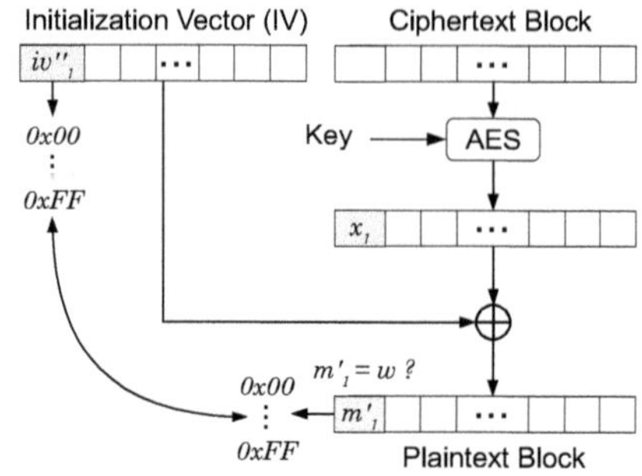

Figure 2: Using the malleability of CBC and the oracle $\mathcal{O}$ to recover x_1.

```
<EncryptedData
      Type='http://www.w3.org/2001/04/xmlenc#Element'
      xmlns='http://www.w3.org/2001/04/xmlenc#'>
   <EncryptionMethod
         Algorithm='http://www.w3.org...#aes256-cbc'>
   </EncryptionMethod>
   <KeyInfo xmlns='http://www.w3.org/2000/09/xmldsig#'>
      <KeyName>John Smith</KeyName>
   </KeyInfo>
   <CipherData>
      <CipherValue>A23B45C56...</CipherValue>
   </CipherData>
</EncryptedData>
```

Figure 3: Example of an XML Encryption metadata block

then recovering the plaintext byte-wise from such a prepared ciphertext.

4.1 XML and XML Encryption

XML. The *eXtensible Markup Language* [2], or XML for short, is a syntax for serializing tree-shaped data structures. An essential characteristic of the XML syntax is that the use of the '<' and '>' characters is allowed only for the declaration of XML element nodes. Hence, if a text node happens to contain any of these characters prior to XML serialization, it must be escaped to a different set of characters (here: `<` and `>`). In the same way, the ampersand (`&`) is escaped to `&`. These properties of XML are relevant to the attack description.

XML ENCRYPTION. Along with specifying XML, the W3C fostered the standardization of means to apply cryptographic primitives like digital signatures and encryption to arbitrary XML data. The resulting specifications were the *W3C XML Signature* recommendation [7] and the *W3C XML Encryption* recommendation [6].

We focus on the XML Encryption specification, of which a syntax example is given in Figure 3. As can be seen, the XML Encryption specification describes the encryption metadata, such as encryption key identifiers, algorithms, encryption schemes, etc. The most important part, however, is the `<CipherValue>` element, which contains the ciphertext of the original data.

When receiving an encrypted message, it is processed as follows. At first, it is necessary to search the whole XML document for `<EncryptedData>` elements. For each of these, the metadata elements containing key information must be parsed, processed, and used to gain the proper cryptographic key required for decryption. The mechanism for this task is out of scope for this paper, it can be assumed that the processing application has means to determine and gather the correct key based on the information from the `<KeyInfo>` element. Next, the content of the `<CipherValue>` is extracted and decoded in order to gather the ciphertext. Then, the decryption itself can be performed, using the algorithm specified in `<EncryptionMethod>`. Finally—and this is a crucial step for the attack described below—the decrypted contents are parsed and put back to the XML document tree. If an error occurs during the decryption or subsequent parsing process, this error is propagated to the XML processor, which typically raises an exception for the application to handle.

Since XML Encryption can be applied to arbitrary subtrees of an XML document tree, there are different types of encryption modes depending on the nature of the encrypted contents. *Encrypted Element* implies that a single XML element including all of its descendant nodes has been encrypted. *Encrypted Content* states that the ciphertext may contain arbitrary node types, e.g. multiple subsequent XML elements, comments, processing instructions etc. *Encrypted Text Content* is a special case of *encrypted content*, and implies that the ciphertext is completely made of text contents.

Though the `Type` attribute of the `<EncryptedData>` element gives a hint on which of these three cases applies, the common XML decryption frameworks in general do not treat them differently. Decryption, parsing, and processing works identical for all these cases.

4.2 Character Encondings

The XML Encryption standard prescribes that characters and symbols are encoded according to the UTF-8 code, which specifies a bit-representation of characters from various alphabets (latin, greek, cyrillic, hebrew, arabic, and countless more) plus many special symbols (e.g. from mathematics or music). The most important subset of UTF-8 characters consists of latin characters, arabic numerals, and some special symbols like `line feed` and `carriage return`. It is important to know that for these characters UTF-8 is identical to ASCII.

The ASCII code represents characters as single bytes, and allows to encode $2^7 = 128$ different characters, as depicted in Figure 4. Note that the encoding uses only 7 out of 8 bits, the most-significant bit is always equal to 0 for all ASCII characters.

Figure 4 lists also a classification of ASCII characters into "Type-A" and "Type-B" characters, which is not relevant yet, but will be useful to explain our attack.

4.3 The Axis2 Web Services Framework

In recent years many Web Services frameworks emerged [17, 16, 9]. One of the most popular open source Web Services Framework is Apache Axis2 [18]. The Rampart module of Axis2 contains an implementation of the WS-Security [12] standard, which allows to apply XML Encryption and XML Signature in SOAP messages.

To use a module in the Axis2 framework, the module must be engaged to the Axis2's message *flow*. A flow is a collection of modules, where each module takes the incoming SOAP message context, processes it, and passes it to the next module. When the SOAP message comes to the end of the flow, it is forwarded to a Message Receiver. The Message Receiver invokes the function implemented in the Service class and passes the result to the output flow.

The Axis2 flow consists typically of three modules, namely Transport, Security, and Dispatch. The Security module processes the security elements. In particular, encrypted elements are first *decrypted* and then *parsed* by an XML parser in order to update the SOAP message context. The decrypted and validated content is then passed on to the Dispatch module. Each module in the flow and the Message Receiver can stop the SOAP message processing if an error occurs. In this case the processing is terminated and an appropriate SOAP fault is returned.

We distinguish between two types of server responses. We say that a `security fault` is returned, if the server replies with a `WSDoAllReceiver: security processing failed` message. If an application-specific error or no error message is returned, then we say that the server replies with an `application response`.

4.4 Axis2 Security Faults

To construct our Axis2-based oracle $\mathcal{O}_{\mathsf{Axis}}$, we evaluate the SOAP faults returned by the security handler of an Axis2 server. This handler returns a `security fault` fault whenever a problem during the processing of security elements in a message occurs. This fault can have several reasons, which can be divided into two categories:

Decryption error. This results from incorrect padding.

> Recall that the last byte of a padded plaintext must include a valid padding number in the range from `0x01` (indicating only the last byte is padded) to `0x10` (indicating the whole last block is a padding block).

Parsing error. This error may have two reasons.

> Either the plaintext contains an "invalid" character. Invalid charactes are all ASCII characters from `0x00` to `0x1F`, except for `0x09` (`horizontal tab`), `0x0A` (`line feed`), and `0x0D` (`carriage return`).
>
> The other reason is that the syntax of the decrypted XML part is not valid. The latter means that the special escape character `0x26` (`&`) is not followed by a valid entity reference, or the bracket `0x3C` (`<`) is not properly closed.

Since in both cases the *same* error message is returned, we cannot distinguish between them.

4.5 An Axis-based Oracle

We classify the set of ASCII characters in two categories, which we call "Type-A" and "Type-B" characters. This classification is depicted in Figure 4. We denote with $\mathcal{A}$ the set of all Type-A characters, and with $\mathcal{B}$ the set of all Type-B characters. Observe that $\mathcal{A}$ contains primarily "invalid" characters, plus the reserved XML characters "&" and "<".

Based on this classification, we can construct an oracle $\mathcal{O}_{\mathsf{Axis}}$, which is similar to the oracle $\mathcal{O}$ from Section 3.2, as follows. $\mathcal{O}_{\mathsf{Axis}}$ takes as input a CBC-encrypted ciphertext $C = (IV, C^{(1)})$, which consists of an initialization vector IV and a single ciphertext block $C^{(1)} \in \{0,1\}^n$. It embeds the ciphertext C into a SOAP message, sends this document to the Axis2 server, and replies as follows.

Dec.	Hex	Char.	Type	Dec.	Hex	Char.	Type	Dec.	Hex	Char.	Type	Dec.	Hex	Char.	Type
	Block 0				Block 2				Block 4				Block 6		
0	00	NUL	A	32	20	SPC	B	64	40	@	B	96	60	`	B
1	01	SOH	A	33	21	!	B	65	41	A	B	97	61	a	B
2	02	STX	A	34	22	"	B	66	42	B	B	98	62	b	B
3	03	ETX	A	35	23	#	B	67	43	C	B	99	63	c	B
4	04	EOT	A	36	24	$	B	68	44	D	B	100	64	d	B
5	05	ENQ	A	37	25	%	B	69	45	E	B	101	65	e	B
6	06	ACK	A	38	26	&	**A**	70	46	F	B	102	66	f	B
7	07	BEL	A	39	27	'	B	71	47	G	B	103	67	g	B
8	08	BS	A	40	28	(	B	72	48	H	B	104	68	h	B
9	09	HT	**B**	41	29	)	B	73	49	I	B	105	69	i	B
10	0A	LF	**B**	42	2A	*	B	74	4A	J	B	106	6A	j	B
11	0B	VT	A	43	2B	+	B	75	4B	K	B	107	6B	k	B
12	0C	FF	A	44	2C	,	B	76	4C	L	B	108	6C	l	B
13	0D	CR	**B**	45	2D	-	B	77	4D	M	B	109	6D	m	B
14	0E	SO	A	46	2E	.	B	78	4E	N	B	110	6E	n	B
15	0F	SI	A	47	2F	/	B	79	4F	O	B	111	6F	o	B
	Block 1				Block 3				Block 5				Block 7		
16	10	DLE	A	48	30	0	B	80	50	P	B	112	70	p	B
17	11	DC1	A	49	31	1	B	81	51	Q	B	113	71	q	B
18	12	DC2	A	50	32	2	B	82	52	R	B	114	72	r	B
19	13	DC3	A	51	33	3	B	83	53	S	B	115	73	s	B
20	14	DC4	A	52	34	4	B	84	54	T	B	116	74	t	B
21	15	NAK	A	53	35	5	B	85	55	U	B	117	75	u	B
22	16	SYN	A	54	36	6	B	86	56	V	B	118	76	v	B
23	17	ETB	A	55	37	7	B	87	57	W	B	119	77	w	B
24	18	CAN	A	56	38	8	B	88	58	X	B	120	78	x	B
25	19	EM	A	57	39	9	B	89	59	Y	B	121	79	y	B
26	1A	SUB	A	58	3A	:	B	90	5A	Z	B	122	7A	z	B
27	1B	ESC	A	59	3B	;	B	91	5B	[	B	123	7B	{	B
28	1C	FS	A	60	3C	<	**A**	92	5C	\	B	124	7C	|	B
29	1D	GS	A	61	3D	=	B	93	5D	]	B	125	7D	}	B
30	1E	RS	A	62	3E	>	B	94	5E	^	B	126	7E	~	B
31	1F	US	A	63	3F	?	B	95	5F	_	B	127	7F	DEL	B

Figure 4: ASCII Character Encoding Table and Classification of Characters.

- $\mathcal{O}_{\mathsf{Axis}}(C) = 1$, if the Axis2 server returns a `security fault`.
- $\mathcal{O}_{\mathsf{Axis}}(C) = 0$, otherwise.

As described in Section 4.3, the Axis2 server will return no `security fault`, if

- the decryption $\pi(m) = IV \oplus \mathsf{Dec}(k, C^{(1)})$ yields a message with *valid padding*, and
- the plaintext $m = \pi^{-1}(\mathsf{Dec}_{\mathsf{cbc}}(k, C))$ has a valid XML structure. That is,
  - if m contains an XML tag `<a>` for some string `a`, then it must also contain the corresponding closing tag `</a>`,
  - if m contains the `&` ampersand character, then it must be a valid entity reference, like `>` for instance,
  - m does not contain any characters from `0x00` to `0x1F`, except for `0x09` or `0x0A` or `0x0D`.

Otherwise a `security fault` is returned. This allows us to use $\mathcal{O}_{\mathsf{Axis}}$ in a way similar to the oracle $\mathcal{O}$ from Section 3.2.

4.6 Using $\mathcal{O}_{\mathsf{Axis}}$ to recover plaintexts

In this section we describe an algorithm that uses the $\mathcal{O}_{\mathsf{Axis}}$ oracle to decrypt a given ciphertext $C = (IV, C^{(1)}, \ldots, C^{(d)})$. Note that C may consist of multiple blocks (i.e., $d \geq 1$). Due to the rather complex structure of the set $\mathcal{A}$ and some optimizations to reduce the number of oracle queries, this procedure is rather complex. For better readability, we present only simplified algorithms, which illustrate the basic attack idea better. However, we have implemented the optimized algorithms. We will furthermore make the (in practice reasonable) assumption that the plaintexts contains only ASCII characters, but no characters from the extended character set of UTF-8. The attack can however be extended to arbitrary UTF-8 characters.

First we need a new definition of well-formedness.

Definition 2. *We say that a single-block ciphertext* $C = (IV, C^{(1)})$ *is* well-formed *w.r.t. key* k, *if*

$$m = (m_1, \ldots, m_\nu) = \mathsf{Dec}_{\mathsf{cbc}}(k, C)$$

has a single byte padding (i.e. $m_\nu =$ `0x01`*) and consists only of Type-B characters (i.e.* $m_j \in \mathcal{B}$ *for all* $j \in \{1, \ldots, \nu-1\}$*).*

The algorithm is a composition of two sub-procedures, which we call FindIV and $\mathsf{FindXbyte}$.

- The FindIV procedure prepares the ciphertext for our attack. It takes as input a multi-block ciphertext $C = (IV, C^{(1)}, \ldots, C^{(d)})$ and an index $i \in \{1, \ldots, d\}$, and returns an initialization vector iv such that the ciphertext $c = (iv, C^{(i)})$ is well-formed.
- The $\mathsf{FindXbyte}$ procedure takes as input an index $j \in \{1, \ldots, \nu\}$ and a well-formed (w.r.t. the target key) single-block ciphertext $c = (iv, c^{(1)})$ such that $c^{(1)} = C^{(i)}$ (as provided by the FindIV procedure). It returns the j-th byte x_j of the CBC decryption intermediate value

$$x = (x_1, \ldots, x_\nu) = \mathsf{Dec}(k, C^{(i)}).$$

Using these procedures, Algorithm 2 recovers the plaintext m contained in C. The algorithm loops through all d ciphertext blocks of C, each time performing essentially three steps.

1. First, it calls the FindIV procedure, which computes an initialization vector iv such that $c = (iv, C^{(i)})$ is a well-formed ciphertext (Line 2).

2. Then it runs the FindXbyte procedure ν times to recover all ν decryption intermediate values
$$x^{(i)} = (x_1^{(i)}, \ldots, x_\nu^{(i)}) = \mathsf{Dec}(k, C^{(i)})$$
(Lines 3 to 5).

3. Knowledge of $x^{(i)} = \mathsf{Dec}(k, C^{(i)})$ allows us to recover the i-th plaintext block as
$$\begin{aligned} m^{(i)} &= \mathsf{Dec}(k, C^{(i)}) \oplus C^{(i-1)} \\ &= x^{(i)} \oplus C^{(i-1)} \end{aligned}$$
(Lines 6 and 7).

Algorithm 2 Using $\mathcal{O}_{\mathsf{Axis}}$ to recover plaintexts.

Input: $C = (C^{(0)} = IV, C^{(1)}, \ldots, C^{(d)})$
Output: $m = (m^{(1)}, \ldots, m^{(d)})$
1: **for** $i = 1$ **to** d **do**
2: $\quad iv := \mathsf{FindIV}(C, i)$
3: $\quad$ **for** $j = 1$ **to** ν **do**
4: $\quad\quad x_j^{(i)} := \mathsf{FindXbyte}(C^{(i)}, iv, j)$
5: $\quad$ **end for**
6: $\quad x^{(i)} := (x_1^{(i)}, \ldots, x_\nu^{(i)})$
7: $\quad m^{(i)} := x^{(i)} \oplus C^{(i-1)}$
8: **end for**
9: **return** $(m^{(1)}, \ldots, m^{(d)})$

Note that the above algorithm makes exactly d calls to the FindIV procedure and $d \cdot \nu$ calls to the FindXbyte procedure.

4.6.1 *Procedure* FindIV

In this section we describe the FindIV procedure. This procedure takes as input a ciphertext $C = (C^{(0)}, C^{(1)}, \ldots, C^{(d)})$ and an index i, and returns an initialization vector iv such that $(iv, C^{(i)})$ is a well-formed ciphertext.

For simplicity we explain the algorithm for the case where a block cipher with block size $\nu = 16$ bytes is used. This corresponds to the case where AES is used in the XML Encryption standard. With a few minor changes the procedure can be adapted to ciphertexts of arbitrary block length. Moreover, we suppose the input ciphertext has the following properties:

- The plaintext of $C' = (C^{(i-1)}, C^{(i)})$ does not contain any "Type-A" character, except for (possibly) the "<" character.

- Each encrypted block contains only incomplete XML elements (i.e. there exists no start tag followed by an element content and an end tag).

If the input ciphertext meets these ciphertext properties, then there are two more issues our FindIV procedure must solve. First, it has to remove all occurrences of the "<" character. Thus we obtain an *encrypted text content* ciphertext consisting only of characters from $\mathcal{B}$. Second, it sets the last byte of the newly created iv so that the padding byte becomes equal to `0x01`. Thus, we obtain a valid padded ciphertext with a single padding byte. These are exactly the prerequisites for our FindXbyte procedure.

We start the description of our FindIV procedure with an observation on the padding byte. The padding byte can be modified by changing the last byte of $C^{(i-1)}$. When we iterate over all the 256 possible values for the last byte $C_\nu^{(i-1)}$ of $C^{(i-1)}$, then we implicitly modify the last byte of the (padded) plaintext contained in $(C^{(i-1)}, C^{(i)})$. Note that in the case $\nu = 16$ there are at most 16 valid padding bytes, namely all values from `0x01` (one padding byte) to `0x10` (all 16 bytes are padding).

First observe that, since we know that the first bit of any ASCII character and any valid padding byte is always equal to 0, we can copy the first bit from the last byte of the original initialization vector $C^{(i-1)}$. Our algorithm iterates only over the remaining at most 128 possible values of the last byte of $C^{(i-1)}$.

Observe now that, if the plaintext of $(IV, C^{(i)})$ contains only characters from $\mathcal{B}$ (no "<" character), then $\mathcal{O}_{\mathsf{Axis}}$ returns exactly $\nu = 16$ responses such that $\mathcal{O}_{\mathsf{Axis}}(C) = 0$. Otherwise, the number of $\mathcal{O}_{\mathsf{Axis}}(C) = 0$ responses *depends on the position* of the first "<" character in the block. For example, if we get only one $\mathcal{O}_{\mathsf{Axis}}(C) = 0$ response, then this means that only one padding byte, namely `0x10` is valid. This implies that the first byte of the plaintext is equal to the "<" character. Similarly, if we get three $\mathcal{O}_{\mathsf{Axis}}(C) = 0$ responses it means that the paddings `0x10`, `0x0F`, and `0x0E` are valid and the "<" character stands on the third position.

For the purpose of getting the number of valid padding bytes we introduce the procedure in Algorithm 3, which collects all the valid padding masks.

Algorithm 3 GetValidPaddingMasks

Input: $IV, C^{(i)}$
Output: A set of valid padding masks $Pset$
$Pset := \emptyset$
for $j := 0x00$ **to** $0x7F$ **do**
$\quad IV' := IV \oplus (0^{n-8} || j)$
$\quad$ **if** $\mathcal{O}_{\mathsf{Axis}}(IV', C^{(i)}) = 0$ **then**
$\quad\quad Pset := Pset \cup IV'_\nu$
$\quad$ **end if**
end for
return $Pset$

Algorithm 3 computes a set of valid padding masks $Pset$. If $Pset$ contains $\nu = 16$ elements, then this tells us that the block does not include any "<" character. Otherwise, we learn that the "<" character stands on the position $pos := |Pset|$. We can simply change the "<" character by flipping the last bit of the IV_{pos}. We repeat the **`GetValidPaddingMasks`** procedure and the bit flipping until $|Pset| = \nu$.

After extraction of all the "<" characters, we set the last byte of iv to cause the padding `0x01`. To this end, we introduce another procedure, called **`GetIvWithPaddingMask01`**. This procedure gets as input IV and $Pset$ of $\nu = 16$ valid padding masks $msk0x01 \ldots msk0x10$. Since the padding mask $msk0x10$ differs from other paddings in the 4-th bit, we can distinguish it from other padding masks. Therefore, we can simply set the iv to:

$$iv := IV \oplus (0^{n-8} || (msk0x10 \oplus 0x11))$$

The complete procedure is depicted in Algorithm 4.

Algorithm 4 FindIV

Input: A ciphertext $C = (C^{(i-1)}, C^{(i)})$
Output: iv

```
IV := C^(i-1)
repeat
    Pset := GetValidPaddingMasks(IV, C^(i))
    pos := |Pset|
    IV_pos := IV_pos ⊕ 0x01
until |Pset| = ν
iv := GetIvWithPaddingMask01(PSet, IV)
return iv
```

EXTENSION OF FindIV FOR ARBITRARY XML DATA. In the description of the FindIV procedure we had to make some restrictions on the encrypted plaintext. It is possible to overcome these restrictions using very similar techniques. We omit the details due to space limitations.

4.6.2 *Procedure* FindXbyte

In this section we describe a procedure FindXbyte which takes as input a single-block ciphertext $C^{(i)}$, an initialization vector iv such that $c = (iv, C^{(i)})$ is well-formed, and an index $j \in \{1, \ldots, \nu\}$ (as provided by FindIV). The procedure returns the j-th byte of $x^{(i)} = \mathsf{Dec}(k, C^{(i)})$. Note that we have

$$\mathsf{Dec}(k, C^{(i)}) \oplus iv = \mathsf{Dec}_{\mathsf{cbc}}(k, (iv, C^{(i)})).$$

If $j = \nu$, i.e., the procedure is asked to return the ν-th byte of $x^{(i)}$, then the algorithm can compute $x_\nu^{(i)}$ without even querying the oracle. Recall that we know that the last plaintext-byte contained in c is the single-byte padding 0x01. Thus we have

$$\begin{aligned}(??, \ldots, ??, \texttt{0x01}) &= \mathsf{Dec}_{\mathsf{cbc}}(k, (iv, C^{(i)})) \\ &= x^{(i)} \oplus iv.\end{aligned}$$

This enables us to recover $x_\nu^{(i)}$ as $x_\nu^{(i)} = \texttt{0x01} \oplus iv_\nu$.

If $j \in \{1, \ldots, \nu - 1\}$, then we need to use the $\mathcal{O}_{\mathsf{Axis}}$ oracle to recover $x_j^{(i)}$. We do this by modifying the initialization iv and evaluating the response behaviour of the oracle. Let us write $iv = (iv_1, \ldots, iv_\nu)$ to denote individual bytes of iv, and $(iv_{j,1}, \ldots, iv_{j,8})$ to denote individual bits of byte iv_j. Similarly, we write $x_j^{(i)} = (x_{j,1}^{(i)}, \ldots, x_{j,8}^{(i)})$ to denote individual bits of byte $x_j^{(i)}$.

Determining the first bit $x_{j,1}^{(i)}$ is easy, since the first bit $m_{1,j}^{(i)}$ of an ASCII-encoded character $m_j^{(i)}$ is always equal to 0. Since we have

$$x^{(i)} = iv^{(i)} \oplus m^{(i)},$$

which implies that $x_{j,1}^{(i)} = iv_{j,1}^{(i)}$ for all $i \in \{1, \ldots, d\}$ and $j \in \{1, \ldots, \nu\}$.

To describe our algorithm to determine the remaining bits, let us divide the ASCII table into blocks, as depicted in Figure 4. The first four bits of an ASCII character determine to which block it belongs. For instance, 0x5A is a character from Block 5, 0x35 is from Block 3, and so on. This leads us to the following observations on the distribution of Type-A characters.

- Only Blocks 0 to 3 contain Type-A characters.
- There is only one block which *does not* contain any Type-B character, namely Block 1.
- Blocks 2 and 3 contain *exactly one* Type-A character, namely 0x26 in Block 1 and 0x3C in Block 2.
- The last four bits of 0x26 and 0x3C are *not equal.*

We use these observations as follows. In order to determine $x_{j,2}^{(i)}, x_{j,3}^{(i)}, x_{j,4}^{(i)}$, we first run Algorithm 5 to compute a set $Aset$ of bit masks. This algorithm initializes set $Aset$ to the empty set (Line 1). Then, by looping through all possible masks $msk \in \{\texttt{0x00}, \texttt{0x10}, \texttt{0x20}, \ldots, \texttt{0x70}\}$, the algorithm modifies the bits of the initialization vector which correspond to the bits $x_{j,2}^{(i)}, x_{j,3}^{(i)}, x_{j,4}^{(i)}$ (Line 4). The algorithm queries $\mathcal{O}_{\mathsf{Axis}}$ to test whether

$$\tilde{m}_j^{(i)} = x_j^{(i)} \oplus (iv_j \oplus msk)$$

is a Type-A character (Line 5). If true, the algorithm stores the corresponding mask msk in $Aset$ (Line 6).

Algorithm 5 Computing the set $Aset$.

Input: $c = (iv, C^{(i)})$, $j \in \{1, \ldots, \nu\}$
Output: Set $Aset \subseteq \{0, \ldots, 7\}$

```
1: Aset := ∅
2: for R = 0 to 7 do
3:     msk := 0xR0
4:     iv' := iv ⊕ 0^(8(j-1)) || msk || 0^(n-8j)
5:     if O_Axis((iv', C^(i))) = 1 then
6:         Aset := Aset ∪ {msk}
7:     end if
8: end for
9: return Aset
```

We can now observe that the set $Aset$ returned by Algorithm 5 contains always either one or two or three elements. To see this, recall that the last four bits of $m_j^{(i)}$ are never modified. Therefore we have

- $|Aset| = 1$ if and only if the *last* four bits of $m_j^{(i)}$ are equal to 0x?9, or 0x?A, or 0x?D (see the Type-B characters in Block 0).
- $|Aset| = 3$ if and only if the *last* four bits of $m_j^{(i)}$ are equal to 0x?6 or 0x?C (see the Type-A characters in Block 2 and Block 3).
- $|Aset| = 2$ otherwise.

If $|Aset| = 1$ and $Aset = \{msk\}$, then we learn that $m_j^{(i)} \oplus msk \in \{\texttt{0x19}, \texttt{0x1A}, \texttt{0x1D}\}$. Now observe that there is exactly one mask $msk' \in \{\texttt{0x25}, \texttt{0x26}, \texttt{0x21}\}$ such that $m_j^{(i)} \oplus msk \oplus msk' = \texttt{0x3C}$ is a Type-A character. Again we can use the oracle to determine msk'. This gives us an equation

$$x_j^{(i)} \oplus (iv_j \oplus msk) \oplus msk' = \texttt{0x3C}$$

Plaintext size (bytes)	Server requests			Time (seconds)
	FindIV	FindXbyte	Total	
16	32	130	162	0.975
160	449	1688	2137	9.6
1,600	7,453	16,356	23,809	98
16,000	81,155	161,433	242,588	1,039

Figure 5: Summary of Experimental Analysis

where only $x_j^{(i)}$ is unknown. Thus we can recover byte $x_j^{(i)}$. Note that in the case $|Aset| = 1$ we need at most two oracle queries to determine msk'.

If $|Aset| = 2$ or $|Aset| = 3$, then a procedure which applies the same principle as the above, but is slightly more complex, allows us to recover $x_j^{(i)}$, by issuing at most 23 oracle queries in total.

4.7 Attack Variations

A priori knowledge about the plaintext could improve the attack significantly. For instance, knowing the XML Schema which defines the structure of the XML document, one could skip decryption of blocks that contain the known plaintext, like XML element tags, and focus on the blocks that contain unknown contents. In the same line, if the attacker knows *a priori* that an encrypted text is, for instance, a credit card number, he can rule out any potential plaintext character that is not a digit.

Furthermore, it is obvious that knowledge of the $x^{(i)}$ bytes also allows an attacker to encrypt arbitrary messages. To this end, the attacker proceeds "from right to the left", i.e., starting with the last ciphertext block (see also [15]).

5. EXPERIMENTAL ANALYSIS

In order to investigate the feasibility and performance of our approach we developed a proof-of-concept implementation of the algorithms decribed in the previous section. We have implemented slightly optimized variants of the presented algorithms.

We measured the time and the number of server requests sent for different ciphertext sizes. Our implementation uses Java 6 and for the SOAP message handling, using a single thread. As a Web Services server, we used the recent Apache Axis2 Version 1.5.3 with Apache Rampart 1.5 module. Both application and Axis2 server were running on a single machine. For completeness, the machine was equipped with Linux Ubuntu 10.10 and Intel Core2 Duo P9700 processor (2 cores with 2.80 GHz).

SETTING. We implemented a simple Java class and deployed it on the Apache Axis2 server to create a Web Service endpoint. We secured the generated Web Services endpoint with the default XML Encryption setting so that the Axis2 server accepted only the SOAP messages with encrypted SOAP body. We used the AES block cipher with 128-bit key (but everything works the same way with 256-bit key).

We generated messages of various length and structure. The shortest messages consisted of 10 characters, thus fitted in a single AES block, and no '<' characters. Larger SOAP messages contained two '<' characters in each cipher block. The symmetric key was encrypted with the public key of the Axis2 server and put into the header of the SOAP message.

RESULTS. The results of our analysis with messages of size 1, 10, 100, and 1000 blocks are depicted in Figure 5. The first two columns in the table describe the plaintext length. The third column shows the number of requests sent by FindIV and FindXbyte. The overall time for the attack execution is listed in the last column.

ANALYSIS. Our results show the practicality of our attack. A single encrypted block can be decrypted with only 162 requests in less than one second. Moreover, it is also feasible to decrypt larger ciphertexts, decrypting 16,000 bytes takes only 17 minutes.

As we executed the tests on a single machine, the timing results are only approximate. For instance, one has to consider the delay by transporting the SOAP message over the network to the server and back. On the other hand, usage of a more powerful server would speed up the message processing.

In any case the experimental results show that the attack is applicable in practical real world scenarios, not only for very short messages but also for larger plaintexts.

6. COUNTERMEASURES

6.1 XML Signature on Ciphertext

The XML Signature standard [7] describes a method to digitally sign all request messages for ensuring their integrity, either using a public-key digital signature scheme or a secret-key message authentication code. A candidate countermeasure would be to apply XML Signatures in order to ensure the integrity of messages, and thus to thwart our attack. However, in the following we illustrate that unfortunately it is not that trivial in practice.

XML SIGNATURE WRAPPING. It is well-known that many Web Services implementations are vulnerable to *XML Signature Element Wrapping* attacks [10]. These attacks allow to modify a ciphertext without breaking the security of the digital signature scheme or message authentication code.

XML ENCRYPTION WRAPPING. Beyond the classical XML Signature Wrapping attacks, we furthermore developed a novel class of attacks that allow to mount our attack even if signature wrapping attacks are not applicable. We call these attacks *XML Encryption wrapping*. To illustrate the idea, consider a standard scenario where the SOAP body contains data encrypted with a symmetric key. This symmetric key is encrypted with the server's public key and put into the SOAP header. Along with the encrypted key the SOAP header includes a reference list, which tells the server which elements must be decrypted using the symmetric key. The whole SOAP body including the encrypted data is signed. We observed that it is possible to copy the encrypted data to the SOAP header and insert a new element to the encrypted data reference list. This forces the server to process both EncryptedData elements, and thus allows to bypass the XML Signature validation to perform the attack.

ANALYSIS. We have evaluated Apache Axis2 and JBossWS regarding their resistance against XML Signature Wrapping and Encryption Wrapping attacks. Our experiments showed that all Rampart configuration examples and all JBoss standard examples are vulnerable, and conjecture therefore that the majority of all practical applications is vulnerable to this attack.

6.2 Unified Error Messages

The possibly most obvious countermeasure to our attack consists in unifying the SOAP fault messages sent in response to invalid SOAP request messages so that an attacker can not distinguish between a decryption error and an application level error. However, this approach has some serious drawbacks.

At first, meaningful error messages are generally considered as "good programming practice". In fact, they are necessary for developers that have to implement client-side applications for encryption-enabled Web Services.

Secondly, even with unified SOAP fault messages, there are additional side-channels that can be exploited for determining what type of error a certain request message triggered. For instance, measuring the time consumed until a (unified) SOAP fault message arrives may already indicate the level in the application stack at which the error occurred.

Finally, we stress that this countermeasure is not effective when XML Encryption wrapping attacks as described above are applicable, since copying the encrypted data to a deeper level in the SOAP header would exclude them from XML Schema validation and business logic processing. Thus, the server responds with a SOAP fault *if and only if* the encrypted data in the SOAP header are incorrect.

6.3 Changing the Mode of Operation

One possibility to avoid our attack is to use a *symmetric* cryptographic primitive that does not only provide confidentiality, but also integrity. This can for instance be achieved by replacing the CBC mode of operation with a mode that provides message integrity. Adequate choices have for instance been standardized in ISO/IEC 19772:2009. We consider this solution as very recommendable for future versions of the XML Encryption standard. Unfortunately, this may bring deployment and backwards compatibility issues.

7. ACKNOWLEDGEMENTS

We would like to thank Meiko Jensen, Jörg Schwenk, Thorsten Holz, Sebastian Schinzel, and Stefan Wigchers for their contributions, and the anonymous reviewers for helpful remarks.

8. REFERENCES

[1] Black, J., and Urtubia, H. Side-channel attacks on symmetric encryption schemes: The case for authenticated encryption. In *USENIX Security Symposium* (2002), D. Boneh, Ed., USENIX, pp. 327–338.

[2] Bray, T., Paoli, J., Sperberg-McQueen, C. M., Maler, E., and Yergeau, F. Extensible Markup Language (XML) 1.0 (Fifth Edition). *W3C Recommendation* (2008).

[3] Degabriele, J. P., and Paterson, K. G. Attacking the IPsec standards in encryption-only configurations. In *IEEE Symposium on Security and Privacy* (2007), IEEE Computer Society, pp. 335–349.

[4] Degabriele, J. P., and Paterson, K. G. On the (in)security of IPsec in MAC-then-encrypt configurations. In *ACM Conference on Computer and Communications Security* (2010), E. Al-Shaer, A. D. Keromytis, and V. Shmatikov, Eds., ACM, pp. 493–504.

[5] Duong, T., and Rizzo, J. Cryptography in the web: The case of cryptographic design flaws in ASP.NET. In *IEEE Symposium on Security and Privacy* (2011).

[6] Eastlake, D., Reagle, J., Imamura, T., Dillaway, B., and Simon, E. XML Encryption Syntax and Processing. *W3C Recommendation* (2002).

[7] Eastlake, D., Reagle, J., Solo, D., Hirsch, F., and Roessler, T. XML Signature Syntax and Processing (Second Edition). *W3C Recommendation* (2008).

[8] Gudgin, M., Hadley, M., Mendelsohn, N., Moreau, J.-J., and Nielsen, H. F. SOAP Version 1.2 Part 1: Messaging Framework. *W3C Recommendation* (2003).

[9] JBoss Community. JBoss WS (Web Services Framework for JBoss AS).

[10] McIntosh, M., and Austel, P. XML signature element wrapping attacks and countermeasures. In *SWS '05: Proceedings of the 2005 workshop on Secure web services* (New York, NY, USA, 2005), ACM Press, pp. 20–27.

[11] Mitchell, C. J. Error oracle attacks on cbc mode: Is there a future for cbc mode encryption? In *ISC* (2005), pp. 244–258.

[12] Nadalin, A., Kaler, C., Monzillo, R., and Hallam-Baker, P. Web Services Security: SOAP Message Security 1.1 (WS-Security 2004). *OASIS Standard* (2006).

[13] Paterson, K. G., and Watson, G. J. Immunising CBC mode against padding oracle attacks: A formal security treatment. In *SCN* (2008), R. Ostrovsky, R. D. Prisco, and I. Visconti, Eds., vol. 5229 of *Lecture Notes in Computer Science*, Springer, pp. 340–357.

[14] Paterson, K. G., and Yau, A. Padding oracle attacks on the ISO CBC mode encryption standard. In *Topics in Cryptology – CT-RSA 2004* (Feb. 2004), T. Okamoto, Ed., vol. 2964 of *Lecture Notes in Computer Science*, Springer, pp. 305–323.

[15] Rizzo, J., and Duong, T. Practical padding oracle attacks. In *Proceedings of the 4th USENIX conference on Offensive technologies* (Berkeley, CA, USA, 2010), WOOT'10, USENIX Association, pp. 1–8.

[16] Robert A. van Engelen. The gSOAP Toolkit for SOAP Web Services and XML-Based Applications.

[17] Thai, T., and Lam, H. *.NET Framework Essentials*. 2001.

[18] The Apache Software Foundation. Apache Axis2.

[19] Vaudenay, S. Security flaws induced by CBC padding - applications to SSL, IPSEC, WTLS ... In *Advances in Cryptology – EUROCRYPT 2002* (Apr. / May 2002), L. R. Knudsen, Ed., vol. 2332 of *Lecture Notes in Computer Science*, Springer, pp. 534–546.

[20] Yau, A. K. L., Paterson, K. G., and Mitchell, C. J. Padding oracle attacks on CBC-mode encryption with secret and random IVs. In *Fast Software Encryption – FSE 2005* (Feb. 2005), H. Gilbert and H. Handschuh, Eds., vol. 3557 of *Lecture Notes in Computer Science*, Springer, pp. 299–319.

Ciphers That Securely Encipher Their Own Keys

Mihir Bellare*
UCSD

David Cash†
IBM Research

Sriram Keelveedhi‡
UCSD

ABSTRACT

In response to needs of disk encryption standardization bodies, we provide the first tweakable ciphers that are proven to securely encipher their own keys. We provide both a narrowblock design **StE** and a wideblock design **EtE**. Our proofs assume only standard PRP-CCA security of the underlying tweakable ciphers.

Keywords: Disk encryption, Ciphers, Key-dependent messages.

Categories and Subject Descriptors

E.3 [**Data**]: DATA ENCRYPTION

General Terms

Algorithms, Security, Theory

1. INTRODUCTION

In email archives of discussions of candidate enciphering schemes for disk encryption, conducted by the Security in Storage Working Group (IEEE P1619), one sees the intriguing comment "I have not received any meaningful response to the issue of grandma storing her keys on an encrypted drive. The WG must have considered it the first time it came up." The issue is whether it is safe to encipher the enciphering key itself. The group eventually came to the conclusion that key-enciphering security is important and desirable, for reasons that go beyond grandma. The presence of key-enciphering attacks on one candidate (LRW) then influenced rejecting it in favor of others on which attacks were not found.

Meanwhile, the group did value security proofs. EME [15], a wideblock cipher, is proven to achieve PRP-CCA security. (Disk encryption must be length preserving, so we are talking about ciphers, not randomized modes like CBC.) A variant EME2 [12] was standardized on the strength of these proofs, a host of efficiency properties, and the *presumed* security of enciphering the key.

If (as seems the consensus in this domain) key enciphering security is a requirement, and (as also seems the consensus) proofs are also important, a discrepancy becomes obvious, namely that, while there is a proof of PRP-CCA security, there is no proof of key enciphering security, confidence in the latter resting only on the absence of discovered attacks.

The question this raises is, can we fill the gap? We want efficient tweakable ciphers, both narrowblock (data is n bits long where n is the blocklength of the underlying blockcipher) and wideblock (data is mn bits long for $m \geq 2$). They should be not only proven PRP-CCA secure but also proven to securely encipher data that contains their own keys. (In the narrowblock case this means the message might equal the key, while in the wideblock case it means any block of the message might equal the key.) We do not want to use random oracles (ROs) but rather want to prove all this assuming only what was assumed for EME, namely the standard PRP-CCA security of the underlying blockcipher.

Is this possible? Proving security of encryption of key-dependent messages is notoriously hard. Standard reduction techniques fail completely. The first solutions [6] used ROs. Sophisticated, non-RO solutions based on novel techniques have emerged [7, 1, 8, 2] but they are far from practical.

In this paper we show nonetheless how to achieve the stated objective. We first provide **StE**, a simple and efficient transform that, applied to any tweakable PRP-CCA blockcipher, results in a tweakable narrowblock cipher that is not only proven PRP-CCA but also proven to securely encipher its own key, assuming only PRP-CCA security of the starting tweakable blockcipher. We then use **StE** as the basis for **EtE**, a transform that, applied to any tweakable PRP-CCA wideblock cipher, results in another tweakable wideblock cipher that, again, is not only proven PRP-CCA but also proven to securely encipher data containing its own key in any block, assuming only PRP-CCA security of the starting wideblock tweakable cipher and of the tweakable blockcipher underlying **StE**.

Motivated also by the above mentioned issues for disk encryption, Halevi and Krawczyk [13] had initiated the study

*Suppored in part by NSF grants CCF 0915675 and CNS 0904380.

†Part of this work was done while the author was at UCSD, supported by NSF grant CCS 0915675, and at Ruhr-Universität Bochum, supported by Eike Kiltz's Sofja Kovalevskaja Award from the Alexander von Humboldt Foundation.

‡Suppored in part by NSF grants CCF 0915675 and CNS 0904380.

of PRFs and PRPs secure for key dependent messages (KDMs). They were able to provide (1) standard model KDM secure PRFs, which are not invertible and thus cannot do disk encryption (2) KDM secure PRPs, but in the ideal cipher model. Ours are the *first* constructions of KDM secure PRPs with a proof of security in the standard (as opposed to random oracle or ideal cipher) model.

We instantiated **EtE** with AES as the base blockcipher, tweaked via XEX [18], and with EME as the base wideblock cipher. We implemented this with the AES-NI instruction set. We found that **EtE** is only 15% slower than plain EME.

BACKGROUND. Security for key-dependent data was first considered for (randomized) IND-CPA encryption [6], so that solutions (which were provided in the RO model by [6]) are necessarily length increasing. For disk encryption, the encryption function must be length preserving. The desired primitive is a tweakable cipher [16] $E\colon \{0,1\}^n \times \mathcal{T} \times \{0,1\}^{mn} \to \{0,1\}^{mn}$ that deterministically maps an n-bit key K, a tweak $T \in \mathcal{T}$ and an m-block plaintext M to an m-block ciphertext $E(K,T,M)$. (So n is both the keylength and the blocklength.) It must be invertible, meaning $E(K,T,\cdot)\colon \{0,1\}^{mn} \to \{0,1\}^{mn}$ is, for every K,T, a permutation whose inverse we denote by $E^{-1}(K,T,\cdot)$. This is a (tweakable) blockcipher, or a narrowblock design, if $m=1$, and a wideblock design if $m>1$. Both are of interest to the Security in Storage Working Group, the first under P1619 and the second under P1619.2. In disk encryption the tweak could be the sector number (wideblock) or the block index (narrowblock) and its use significantly increases security.

The standard security notion for a (tweakable) cipher is to be PRP-CCA secure [16]. (This is sometimes called strong PRP security following the terminology of [17].) We extend this to key dependent messages (KDM), defining what it means for E to be Φ-PRP-CCA secure where Φ is a class of functions that map n-bit keys to mn-bit inputs, following [6, 13]. The game picks a random challenge bit b, a random key K and a random permutation $\pi(T,\cdot)\colon \{0,1\}^{mn} \to \{0,1\}^{mn}$ for each T. It gives the adversary the standard oracles $\text{FN}, \text{FN}^{-1}$ from the PRP-CCA game and a new oracle KDFN. Oracle FN, on input T,M, returns $E(K,T,M)$ if $b=1$ and $\pi(T,M)$ otherwise; oracle FN^{-1}, on input T,C, returns $E^{-1}(K,T,C)$ if $b=1$ and $\pi^{-1}(T,C)$ otherwise; oracle KDFN, on input ϕ,T, where ϕ is required to be in Φ, returns $E(K,T,\phi(K))$ if $b=1$ and $\pi(T,\phi(K))$ otherwise. To ensure non-triviality, the adversary is required to be legitimate, meaning does not query $\text{FN}^{-1}(T,C)$ for a C previously received as a response to a $\text{KDFN}(T,\cdot)$ query. The adversary advantage is $2\Pr[b=b']-1$ where b' is its output bit. Φ-PRP-CCA security obviously implies PRP-CCA security for all Φ, and coincides with it when $\Phi=\emptyset$.

What we mean by "encrypting the key" depends on whether the design is narrowblock or wideblock. In the narrowblock case, we are concerned with the obvious, namely that the message equals the key, captured formally by letting Φ consist of the identity function id. For wideblock designs, we seek security when *any block* of the message equals the key. (This reflects P1619.2 requirements.) We clarify that the key may occur in multiple blocks but may not overlap between blocks. Thus if $M = M[1]\ldots M[m]$ is the message then $M[i]$ may equal the key K for any i but we do not allow K to start somewhere in one block and end somewhere in the next block. In Section 4 we specify a Φ, that we denote $\mathcal{ID}_m$, that captures this formally.

The Security in Storage Working Group advocates security for encrypting the key because users or the system may store the key on the disk but also because, if it would create a vulnerability, an attacker could attempt to manipulate the system so that it transfers the key from memory to the disk. Overall, they considered it important enough to reject candidates without the property.

Attacks of Halevi and Krawczyk [13] show that, unlike for randomized encryption [6], there is no cipher that is Φ-PRP-CCA secure for the class Φ of all functions. To achieve security, we must restrict the class somehow. The restriction we make, namely to consider encrypting the key, results in a class capturing practical attacks for which we will show security to be achievable.

Motivated by the concerns and needs of the Security in Storage Working Group that we have explained, Halevi and Krawczyk [13] introduced the notions of KDM secure PRFs and PRPs and asked whether there exist Φ-PRFs or Φ-PRPs for non-trivial Φ. (Meaning, Φ contains some interesting non-constant function such as the identity.) They were able to give a standard model construct in the PRF case, but it was not invertible and thus could not be used for disk encryption. They also gave a PRP but the proof is in the ideal cipher model. Left open by their work is to provide a Φ-PRP for non-trivial Φ in the standard model. We resolve this, providing not only constructs, but efficient ones, with proofs not only in the standard model but assuming only standard PRP security of the underlying blockcipher, for non-trivial Φ of practical interest, with tweaks, and for both the narrow and wide block settings.

APPROACH. First we address the narrowblock case, providing a transform **StE** that turns a given PRP-CCA tweakable blockcipher into a {id}-PRP-CCA tweakable blockcipher, meaning the constructed cipher not only preserves the PRP-CCA security of the base one but, assuming only PRP-CCA security of the latter, is proven to securely encrypt its key. **StE** is of interest in its own right as the first (tweakable) blockcipher that can provably encipher its own key under standard and minimal assumptions.

We would have liked to show that instantiating the base blockcipher of E of EME [15] with $F = \textbf{StE}[E]$ results in a wideblock cipher that can provably encipher its own key, but this does not work. Instead, we show how to add a pre-processing step to EME, or any other PRP-CCA secure wideblock cipher, to get another wideblock cipher that now, when instantiated with F as the underlying blockcipher, is $\mathcal{ID}_m$-PRP-CCA secure, meaning not only PRP-CCA secure but able to securely encipher messages that contain the key in any block. Let us now look at these two contributions more closely.

NARROWBLOCK DESIGN. Our starting point is a suggestion of [7] to securely encrypt keys with a *randomized* encryption scheme by exchanging the key with another point. To make this work for deterministic encryption we swap with a "hidden" point, the latter determined by encryption under the key of a constant. A crucial idea is to use tweaks, defining the hidden point via a tweak not used for anything else.

We take as given a tweakable blockcipher $E\colon \{0,1\}^n \times \mathcal{T} \times \{0,1\}^n \to \{0,1\}^n$ assumed to have normal, meaning PRP-CCA, security, but not necessarily able to securely encrypt its key. We pick an arbitrary tweak $\gamma \in \mathcal{T}$ for E and also an arbitrary point $\alpha \in \{0,1\}^n$. Both α and γ are public and known to the adversary. Our **StE** (Swap-then-Encipher) transform now turns E into another tweakable blockcipher $F\colon \{0,1\}^n \times \mathcal{T} \setminus \{\gamma\} \times \{0,1\}^n \to \{0,1\}^n$ whose tweakspace $\mathcal{T}\setminus\{\gamma\}$ is that of E with γ removed, meaning γ is not allowed as a tweak for F. We define F via

$\underline{F(K,T,M)}$
$H \leftarrow E(K,\gamma,\alpha)$
If $M = K$ then $Y \leftarrow E(K,T,H)$
Else If $M = H$ then $Y \leftarrow E(K,T,K)$
Else $Y \leftarrow E(K,T,M)$
Return Y

In Section 3 we show that F is invertible, as required to be a cipher. A curious aspect of the design is that at the third line we actually encrypt the key K with the original blockcipher E. Given that the latter may not necessarily be able to securely encrypt its key, why would this work? The answer is that we only do this if $M = H$ and we ensure the latter is very unlikely. Thus H is our "hidden" point.

Making sure H is hidden takes some care. It is not so merely because its computation depends on K, for the adversary will have an oracle that (at least in the real game) allow it to compute F under K for any tweak of the adversary's choice and this might be used to extract information about H. The crucial point is that γ, the tweak used in computing H, was removed from the tweak space of F so the adversary cannot use it.

The proof that F indeed securely encrypts its key is done by reduction to the assumed PRP-CCA security of E and is delicate due to the cyclic nature of the construction.

It is crucial for disk encryption that F is invertible. It is to ensure this that we need the swap that effectively exchanges the roles of K and H.

At first glance it would appear that **StE** doubles the cost since it requires two invocations of E, one to get H and the other to get Y. This, however, is also true of XEX-AES [18]: presented as a fast tweakable blockcipher, XEX actually requires two invocations of the underlying blockcipher. In both cases, however, the answer is the same, namely that the ciphers will be used in a mode where the extra blockcipher computation is done once and its cost is thus amortized out so that the effective cost of the cipher is one blockcipher call. Specifically if F, like XEX-AES, is used as the base blockcipher in a wideblock design to encipher a sector consisting of m blocks (eg. $m = 32$), we can compute H just once across the m encipherings so **StE** effectively involves just a single blockcipher invocation.

The IEEE 1619 standard for narrowblock encryption is based on XEX-AES [18]. **StE** is easily applied here, yielding an alternative narrowblock candidate that is as efficient as the current one when the cost of computing H is amortized out, but also has provable security for enciphering the key.

WIDEBLOCK DESIGN. EME [15] is a wideblock tweakable cipher that is proven PRP-CCA secure assuming only PRP-CCA security of the underlying blockcipher. It makes two passes through the data and runs at 2 blockcipher invocations per message block. One of its attractions, and its advantage over the earlier CMC [14], is that it is parallelizable. No attack is known when one encrypts messages containing the key in any block, but nor is there any proof that such an attack is absent.

We wish to enhance designs like EME so that PRP-CCA security is preserved but provable key-enciphering security is also added, without assuming any more of the underlying blockcipher than PRP-CCA security. Our **EtE** transform does just this. It makes an ECB pass through the data using $F = \mathbf{StE}[E]$ under one tweak and then applies any wideblock PRP-CCA cipher (EME would be one possibility) using F with another tweak. We prove that the resulting cipher is $\mathcal{ID}_m$-PRP-CCA secure assuming only that tweakable blockcipher E is PRP-CCA secure. Thus **EtE** provides a generic way to upgrade any PRP-CCA wideblock cipher to also be able to securely encipher messages containing the key in any block, at the cost of one extra blockcipher operation per block. The design preserves parallelizability, so that when instantiated with a parallelizable wideblock cipher like EME, the resulting cipher is also parallelizable.

INSTANTIATION AND IMPLEMENTATION. Getting the best out of **EtE** requires good choices for the underlying components and some optimizations. We use AES as the base blockcipher and XEX [18] to tweak it. We use EME as the wideblock cipher. Let J denote the resulting wideblock cipher as produced by **EtE**. We implemented J, as well as plain EME for comparison, on an Intel Xeon W3690 processor at 3.47 GHz with support for AES-NI running Linux version 2.6 with code compiled using `gcc -O3 -ftree-vectorize -msse2 -ffast-math` to enable vector instructions and perform other general optimizations. The base code was from Brian Gladman's EME2 implementation [10], which we modified to run as EME and use the hardware AES instructions. Our experiments show that J is only 15% slower than EME.

Recall that EME uses about two blockcipher calls per message block. Since J would thus use three blockcipher calls per message block, one might naively expect a 50% slowdown. However, EME computes various offsets that are added to the blockcipher inputs and outputs, and these computations are quite costly, so our simple ECB pass is less expensive compared to EME than one might imagine. We remark that AES-NI is now widely available in Intel and AMD processors on modern machines, and disk controllers might potentially have hardware AES support as well, so using AES-NI as a starting point is realistic.

A CCS 2011 reviewer asked us to also implement in eBASH. As of the time of writing this CCS abstract, we have not completed such an implementation.

2. PRELIMINARIES

NOTATION. By $\mathsf{Maps}(D,R)$ we denote the set of all functions $f\colon D \to R$. We denote by id the identity function. Some of our definitions and proofs are expressed via code-based games [5]. Recall that such a game — see Figure 1 for an example — consists of an INITIALIZE procedure, procedures to respond to adversary oracle queries, and a FINALIZE procedure. A game G is executed with an adversary A as follows. First, INITIALIZE executes. Then A executes, its oracle queries being answered by the corresponding procedures of G. When A terminates, its output becomes the input to FINALIZE, and the output of the latter is the output of the game. We denote by "G^A" the event that this game output takes value true. Boolean flags are assumed initialized to false. The running time of an adversary by convention is the worst case time for the execution of the adversary with the game defining its security, so that the time of the called game procedures is included.

TWEAKABLE BLOCKCIPHERS. A *tweakable blockcipher* [16] is a map E: $\{0,1\}^k \times \mathcal{T} \times \{0,1\}^m \to \{0,1\}^m$ that takes input a k-bit key K, a *tweak* T drawn from the tweakspace $\mathcal{T}$ and a m-bit message M to return an m-bit output $E(K,T,M)$. The map $E(K,T,\cdot)$: $\{0,1\}^m \to \{0,1\}^m$ that on input $M \in \{0,1\}^m$ returns $E(K,T,M)$ is required to be a permutation and its inverse is denoted $E^{-1}(K,T,\cdot)$.

The standard notion of security for a tweakable blockcipher is to be a tweakable pseudorandom permutation [16]. This can be considered under either chosen-plaintext attack (usually called PRP security) or chosen-ciphertext attack (usually called strong PRP security) [16, 17], but we will use the terms PRP-CPA and PRP-CCA as more indicative of the models and more consistent with notation for other primitives. We will be working with PRP-CCA. To define it consider games Real_E and Rand_E of Figure 1. In Rand, we are denoting by $\mathsf{TwPm}(\mathcal{T},\{0,1\}^m)$ the set of all π: $\mathcal{T} \times \{0,1\}^m \to \{0,1\}^m$ such that $\pi(T,\cdot)$ is a permutation on $\{0,1\}^m$ for each $T \in \mathcal{T}$. In this case, $\pi^{-1}(T,\cdot)$: $\{0,1\}^m \to \{0,1\}^m$ is the inverse of $\pi(T,\cdot)$. We define the prp-cca advantage of A as

$$\mathbf{Adv}_E^{\text{prp-cca}}(A) = \Pr[\mathrm{Real}_E^A] - \Pr[\mathrm{Rand}_E^A].$$

KDM PRP-CCA SECURITY. We extend PRP-CCA to allow for the encryption of key-dependent messages via games $\mathrm{Real}_{E,\Phi}$ and $\mathrm{Rand}_{E,\Phi}$ of Figure 1. Oracle KDFN takes input a tweak T and a function $\phi \in \mathsf{Maps}(\{0,1\}^k, \{0,1\}^m)$ and derives M as $\phi(K)$. If $\Phi \subseteq \mathsf{Maps}(\{0,1\}^k, \{0,1\}^m)$ we say that adversary A is Φ-restricted if the argument ϕ in its KDFN queries is always from Φ. We define the Φ-kdm-prp-cca advantage of such an A to be

$$\mathbf{Adv}_{E,\Phi}^{\text{prp-cca}}(A) = \Pr[\mathrm{Real}_{E,\Phi}^A] - \Pr[\mathrm{Rand}_{E,\Phi}^A].$$

We continue, thus, to denote the notion via prp-cca, the key-dependent messages indicated by the extra subscript Φ in the advantage function.

Consider the following strategy for A. It makes KDFN query T, id to get back a ciphertext C and then queries $\mathrm{FN}^{-1}(T,C)$. The response will be $M = \mathrm{id}(K) = K$, and now A has the key and can easily win. (That is, get a high advantage, for example by returning 1 if $E(K,T,M') = \mathrm{FN}(T,M')$ for some T and some $M' \neq M$, and 0 otherwise.) To preclude this, we require that A is *legitimate*, meaning that, for all T,ϕ, it never makes a $\mathrm{FN}^{-1}(T,C)$ query for C previously received in response to a $\mathrm{KDFN}(T,\phi)$ query. The analogy is the definition of IND-CCA secure encryption where the adversary is not allowed to query to the decryption oracle a ciphertext it previously received as a challenge. The (necessary) assumption that adversaries are legitimate is made throughout and is implicit in all our results. We remark that we do not need to prohibit A from query $\mathrm{FN}^{-1}(T,C)$ for C previously returned in response to query $\mathrm{FN}(T,M)$, because A already knows the message M it would get as response. So no restriction is present in the plain prp-cca notion. But when key-dependent messages are introduced, we must require legitimacy.

KDM-secure IND-CPA encryption was defined by [6]. Subsequently, KDM security of tweakable blockciphers was defined by Halevi and Krawczyk [13]. Because blockciphers, unlike encryption schemes, are deterministic, KDM security is not achievable when arbitrary functions ϕ are allowed in KDFN queries. This is analogous to what happens with related-key attacks (RKAs) and thus, as with the formalization of RKA security from [4], Halevi and Krawczyk [13] parameterize the advantage and definition of KDM security for tweakable blockciphers by a class Φ of functions. Our narrow-block design **StE** will achieve security when $\Phi = \{\mathrm{id}\}$, corresponding to encrypting the key. Our extended cipher **GStE** will achieve security for a broader class Φ and our wideblock design for Φ corresponding to any block of the message equaling the key.

Halevi and Krawczyk [13] do not explicitly state the legitimacy condition. They also allow the possibility of decryption of key-dependent ciphertexts, via an extra oracle. We have not considered this capability because, while plaintexts may be key dependent, we did not see why ciphertexts would be key dependent. Our schemes do not aim to achieve security in the presence of decryption of key-dependent ciphertexts.

3. NARROWBLOCK CIPHER

In this section we show how to construct a narrowblock tweakable blockcipher that can securely encipher its own key.

CONSTRUCTION. Let E: $\{0,1\}^n \times \mathcal{T} \times \{0,1\}^n \to \{0,1\}^n$ be a tweakable blockcipher whose key length and message length are the same value n. (For example, $n = 128$ for XEX-AES [18].) We fix an arbitrary tweak $\gamma \in \mathcal{T}$ as well as an arbitrary message $\alpha \in \{0,1\}^n$. Both γ and α are public parameters of the system known to the adversary. Our Swap-then-Encipher transform $\mathbf{StE}_{\gamma,\alpha}$ associates to E another tweakable blockcipher $F = \mathbf{StE}_{\gamma,\alpha}[E]$: $\{0,1\}^n \times \mathcal{T} \setminus \{\gamma\} \times \{0,1\}^n \to \{0,1\}^n$ whose tweak space $\mathcal{T} \setminus \{\gamma\}$ is that of E with the point γ removed. The function F is defined as follows:

$\underline{F(K,T,M)}$
$H \leftarrow E(K,\gamma,\alpha)$
If $M = K$ then $Y \leftarrow E(K,T,H)$
Else If $M = H$ then $Y \leftarrow E(K,T,K)$
Else $Y \leftarrow E(K,T,M)$
Return Y

Before considering security, We establish that F is invertible as required to be a tweakable blockcipher. Indeed, the inverse F^{-1} is given by

$\underline{F^{-1}(K,T,C)}$
$Y \leftarrow D(K,T,C)$
$H \leftarrow E(K,\gamma,\alpha)$
If $Y = K$ then $M \leftarrow H$
Else If $Y = H$ then $M \leftarrow K$
Return M

EFFICIENCY. In the form it is described above, evaluating F requires two calls to the underlying cipher E. But in practice we are enciphering a message consisting of multiple blocks. In this case the value $E(K,\gamma,\alpha)$ can be computed just once and then cached, which means each evaluation of $F(K,T,M)$ requires one call to E with the same key and tweak value. Similarly, $E(K,\gamma,\alpha)$ can also be cached for inversion. Thus, the amortized cost of $\mathbf{StE}_{\gamma,\alpha}$ is the same as that of E. We remark that the situation here is analogous to that of XEX [18]. XEX too needs two applications of the underlying blockcipher, but one can usually be amortized out. **StE** is no worse.

proc INITIALIZE // $\mathrm{Real}_E, \mathrm{Real}_{E,\Phi}$	proc INITIALIZE // $\mathrm{Rand}_E, \mathrm{Rand}_{E,\Phi}$
$K \leftarrow\!\!\$ \{0,1\}^k$	$K \leftarrow\!\!\$ \{0,1\}^k$; $\pi \leftarrow\!\!\$ \mathsf{TwPm}(\mathcal{T}, \{0,1\}^m)$
proc $\mathrm{FN}(T, M)$ // $\mathrm{Real}_E, \mathrm{Real}_{E,\Phi}$	proc $\mathrm{FN}(T, M)$ // $\mathrm{Rand}_E, \mathrm{Rand}_{E,\Phi}$
Return $E(K, T, M)$	Return $\pi(T, M)$
proc $\mathrm{KDFN}(T, \phi)$ // $\mathrm{Real}_{E,\Phi}$	proc $\mathrm{KDFN}(T, \phi)$ // $\mathrm{Rand}_{E,\Phi}$
$M \leftarrow \phi(K)$	$M \leftarrow \phi(K)$
Return $E(K, T, M)$	Return $\pi(T, M)$
proc $\mathrm{FN}^{-1}(T, C)$ // $\mathrm{Real}_E, \mathrm{Real}_{E,\Phi}$	proc $\mathrm{FN}^{-1}(T, C)$ // $\mathrm{Rand}_E, \mathrm{Rand}_{E,\Phi}$
Return $E^{-1}(K, T, C)$	Return $\pi^{-1}(T, C)$
proc $\mathrm{FINALIZE}(b')$ // $\mathrm{Real}_E, \mathrm{Real}_{E,\Phi}$	proc $\mathrm{FINALIZE}(b')$ // $\mathrm{Real}_E, \mathrm{Real}_{E,\Phi}$
Return $(b' = 1)$	Return $(b' = 1)$

Figure 1: Games $\mathrm{Real}_E, \mathrm{Rand}_E$ to define PRP-CCA security, and games $\mathrm{Real}_{E,\Phi}, \mathrm{Rand}_{E,\Phi}$ to define KDM PRP-CCA security of tweakable blockcipher E: $\{0,1\}^k \times \mathcal{T} \times \{0,1\}^m \to \{0,1\}^m$.

SECURITY. The following theorem says that $F = \mathbf{StE}_{\gamma,\alpha}[E]$ is a PRP-CCA that can securely encipher its own key, or more formally, that it is {id}-kdm-prp-cca secure, assuming only that E meets the standard PRP-CCA notion of security.

THEOREM 3.1. *Let E: $\{0,1\}^n \times \mathcal{T} \times \{0,1\}^n \to \{0,1\}^n$ be a tweakable blockcipher. Let $\gamma \in \mathcal{T}$ and $\alpha \in \{0,1\}^n$. Let $F = \mathbf{StE}_{\gamma,\alpha}[E]$: $\{0,1\}^n \times \mathcal{T} \setminus \{\gamma\} \times \{0,1\}^n \to \{0,1\}^n$ be the tweakable blockcipher associated to E via the $\mathbf{StE}_{\gamma,\alpha}$ transform as defined above. Let $\Phi = \{\mathrm{id}\}$ consist of the identity function. Let A be an adversary making at most Q oracle queries. Then there is an adversary B such that*

$$\mathbf{Adv}^{\text{prp-cca}}_{F,\Phi}(A) < 2 \cdot \mathbf{Adv}^{\text{prp-cca}}_{E}(B) + \frac{3Q}{2^n - 1} .$$

Moreover, the running time of B is about equal to the running time of A.

The intuition is that, during the $\mathrm{Real}_{F,\{\mathrm{id}\}}$ and $\mathrm{Rand}_{F,\{\mathrm{id}\}}$ games, an adversary is unlikely to trigger the test in lines 02 and 03 in the computation of F, except by submitting $\phi = \mathrm{id}$ to its oracle. Once this established, we can give a reduction to the prp-cca security of E. For the first part, we show that K and H are hard to guess using the prp-cca security of E. If the adversary guesses K, then we can show how to break the prp-cca security of E, a contradiction. We can show the same if the adversary guesses H. This is where we use the fact that the tweak γ is never allowed elsewhere, effectively making H look random. The proof implements this approach and deals with other complications.

PROOF. We begin with the games in Figure 2. Recall that here $\Phi = \{\mathrm{id}\}$, so it is assumed that $\phi = \mathrm{id}$ in any KDFN query. Game G_0 includes the boxed code and hence is the same as Real^A_F, and thus we have

$$\begin{aligned}\mathbf{Adv}^{\text{prp-cca}}_{F,\Phi}(A) &= \Pr[\mathrm{G}_0^A] - \Pr[\mathrm{G}_2^A] \\ &= \Pr[\mathrm{G}_1^A] - \Pr[\mathrm{G}_2^A] + \Pr[\mathrm{G}_0^A] - \Pr[\mathrm{G}_1^A] \\ &\leq \Pr[\mathrm{G}_1^A] - \Pr[\mathrm{G}_2^A] + \Pr[\mathrm{BAD}(\mathrm{G}_1^A)] .\end{aligned}$$

The inequality is by the Fundamental Lemma of Game Playing [5] since $\mathrm{G}_0, \mathrm{G}_1$ are identical until bad. We design adversary B_1 so that

$$\Pr[\mathrm{G}_1^A] - \Pr[\mathrm{G}_2^A] \leq \mathbf{Adv}^{\text{prp-cca}}_{E}(B_1) . \qquad (1)$$

The simulation is straightforward since G_1 does not include the boxed code. B_1 has oracles $\mathrm{FN}, \mathrm{FN}^{-1}$. It starts by letting $H \leftarrow \mathrm{FN}(\gamma, \alpha)$. It then runs A. When A makes a query (T, M) to its FN oracle, B_1 queries its own FN oracle with (T, M) and forwards the response to A. Similarly when A makes a query (T, C) to its FN^{-1} oracle, B_1 queries its own FN^{-1} oracle with (T, C) and forwards the response to A. When A queries its KDFN oracle with T, id, adversary B_1 responds with $\mathrm{FN}(T, H)$. When A halts with output b', so does B_1. We clearly have

$$\Pr[\mathrm{Real}^{B_1}_E] = \Pr[\mathrm{G}_1^A] .$$

Since the tweak γ is not used in any queries of A, the point H in G_2 is random and can be viewed as playing the role of K in game Rand_E. Thus we also have

$$\Pr[\mathrm{Rand}^{B_1}_E] = \Pr[\mathrm{G}_2^A] .$$

Thus we have Equation (1).

It remains to upper bound $\Pr[\mathrm{BAD}(\mathrm{G}_1^A)]$. Fix a point $\alpha' \in \{0,1\}^n \setminus \{\alpha\}$ and consider games $\mathrm{G}_3, \mathrm{G}_4$ of Figure 2. Game G_3 replaces the $M = K$ test from G_1 with the test $E(M, \gamma, \alpha') = H'$. The purpose is to avoid referring explicitly to K, thereby opening the way for a reduction to the assumed prp-cca security of E. This new test, however, will certainly return true if $M = K$ and hence

$$\begin{aligned}\Pr[\mathrm{BAD}(\mathrm{G}_1^A)] &\leq \Pr[\mathrm{G}_3^A] \\ &= \Pr[\mathrm{G}_3^A] - \Pr[\mathrm{G}_4^A] + \Pr[\mathrm{G}_4^A] .\end{aligned}$$

We stress that in G_4, where we move to the random world by replacing $E(K, \cdot, \cdot)$ by $\pi(\cdot, \cdot)$, the test still uses E, invoking the blockcipher here explicitly on inputs M, γ, α'. (The test does not use π.) We design adversary B_2 so that

$$\Pr[\mathrm{G}_3^A] - \Pr[\mathrm{G}_4^A] \leq \mathbf{Adv}^{\text{prp-cca}}_{E}(B_2) . \qquad (2)$$

The simulation is again straightforward now that K is not referred to explicitly in either game. B_2 has oracles $\mathrm{FN}, \mathrm{FN}^{-1}$. It starts by letting $H \leftarrow \mathrm{FN}(\gamma, \alpha)$ and $H' \leftarrow \mathrm{FN}(\gamma, \alpha')$ and

proc INITIALIZE // G_0, G_1
$K \leftarrow_{\$} \{0,1\}^n$; $H \leftarrow E(K, \gamma, \alpha)$

proc FN(T, M) // $\boxed{G_0}$, G_1
$X \leftarrow M$
If $M = K$ then bad $\leftarrow$ true ; $\boxed{X \leftarrow H}$
Else If $M = H$ then bad $\leftarrow$ true ; $\boxed{X \leftarrow K}$
Return $E(K, T, X)$

proc KDFN(T, ϕ) // G_0, G_1
Return $E(K, T, H)$

proc FN$^{-1}(T, C)$ // $\boxed{G_0}$, G_1
$X \leftarrow E^{-1}(K, T, C)$; $M \leftarrow X$
If $X = K$ then bad $\leftarrow$ true ; $\boxed{M \leftarrow H}$
Else If $X = H$ then bad $\leftarrow$ true ; $\boxed{M \leftarrow K}$
Return M

proc FINALIZE(b') // G_0, G_1, G_2
Return $(b' = 1)$

proc FINALIZE(b') // G_3, G_4
Return $(\mathsf{bad}_1 \vee \mathsf{bad}_2)$

proc INITIALIZE // G_2
$\pi \leftarrow_{\$} \mathsf{TwPm}(\mathcal{T}, \{0,1\}^n)$
$H \leftarrow \pi(\gamma, \alpha)$

proc FN(T, M) // G_2
Return $\pi(T, M)$

proc KDFN(T, ϕ) // G_2
Return $\pi(T, H)$

proc FN$^{-1}(T, C)$ // G_2
Return $\pi^{-1}(T, C)$

proc INITIALIZE // G_3
$K \leftarrow_{\$} \{0,1\}^n$
$H \leftarrow E(K, \gamma, \alpha)$
$H' \leftarrow E(K, \gamma, \alpha')$

proc INITIALIZE // G_4
$\pi \leftarrow_{\$} \mathsf{TwPm}(\mathcal{T}, \{0,1\}^n)$
$H \leftarrow \pi(\gamma, \alpha)$
$H' \leftarrow \pi(\gamma, \alpha')$

proc FN(T, M) // G_3
If $E(M, \gamma, \alpha') = H'$ then $\mathsf{bad}_1 \leftarrow$ true
Else If $M = H$ then $\mathsf{bad}_2 \leftarrow$ true
Return $E(K, T, M)$

proc KDFN(T, ϕ) // G_3
Return $E(K, T, H)$

proc FN$^{-1}(T, C)$ // G_3
$M \leftarrow E^{-1}(K, T, C)$
If $E(M, \gamma, \alpha') = H'$ then $\mathsf{bad}_1 \leftarrow$ true
Else If $M = H$ then $\mathsf{bad}_2 \leftarrow$ true
Return M

proc FN(T, M) // G_4
If $E(M, \gamma, \alpha') = H'$ then $\mathsf{bad}_1 \leftarrow$ true
Else If $M = H$ then $\mathsf{bad}_2 \leftarrow$ true
Return $\pi(T, M)$

proc KDFN(T, ϕ) // G_4
Return $\pi(T, H)$

proc FN$^{-1}(T, C)$ // G_4
$M \leftarrow \pi^{-1}(T, C)$
If $E(M, \gamma, \alpha') = H'$ then $\mathsf{bad}_1 \leftarrow$ true
Else If $M = H$ then $\mathsf{bad}_2 \leftarrow$ true
Return M

Figure 2: Games used in the proof of Theorem 3.1.

initializing boolean variables $\mathsf{bad}_1, \mathsf{bad}_2$ to false. It then runs A. When A makes a query (T, M) to its FN oracle, B_2 does the following:

If $E(M, \gamma, \alpha') = H'$ then $\mathsf{bad}_1 \leftarrow$ true
Else If $M = H$ then $\mathsf{bad}_2 \leftarrow$ true
Return FN(T, M) to A

Similarly when A makes a query (T, C) to its FN^{-1} oracle, B_2 does the following:

$M \leftarrow$ FN$^{-1}(T, C)$
If $E(M, \gamma, \alpha') = H'$ then $\mathsf{bad}_1 \leftarrow$ true
Else If $M = H$ then $\mathsf{bad}_2 \leftarrow$ true
Return M to A

When A queries its KDFN oracle with T, id, adversary B responds with FN(T, H). When A halts with output b', adversary B halts with output 1 if $(\mathsf{bad}_1 \vee \mathsf{bad}_2)$ has value true and 0 otherwise. We have

$$\Pr[\mathrm{Real}_E^{B_2}] = \Pr[\mathrm{G}_3^A] \text{ and } \Pr[\mathrm{Rand}_E^{B_2}] = \Pr[\mathrm{G}_4^A]$$

which implies Equation (2).

Let B be the adversary that picks c at random from $\{1, 2\}$ and runs B_c. Then at this point we have

$$\mathbf{Adv}_{F,\Phi}^{\text{prp-cca}}(A) \le 2 \cdot \mathbf{Adv}_E^{\text{prp-cca}}(B) + \Pr[\mathrm{G}_4^A]$$

and proceed to upper bound the last term above, considering separately the probability of setting bad_1 and that of setting bad_2. Since γ is not in the tweak space of F, game G_5 of Figure 3 picks π from $\mathsf{TwPm}(\mathcal{T} \setminus \{\gamma\}, \{0,1\}^n)$ rather than $\mathsf{TwPm}(\mathcal{T}, \{0,1\}^n)$, and picks H, H' as random, distinct points. The game can move the setting of bad_1 and the choice of H' to FINALIZE without impacting what is returned to the adversary. At the end of the execution, the set S can have size at most Q so

$$\Pr[\mathrm{G}_4^A \text{ sets } \mathsf{bad}_1] = \Pr[\mathrm{G}_5^A] \le \frac{Q}{2^n - 1} .$$

Bounding the probability that bad_2 is set in G_4 is more difficult because information about H does reach the adversary via the KDFN query. Our intent is to move to a game where H is not referred to in replying to adversary oracle queries. We begin with game G_6 of Figure 3 which samples π lazily. The arrays $\pi[\cdot,\cdot]$ and $\pi^{-1}[\cdot,\cdot]$ are assumed initially everywhere undefined, and get filled in as the game progresses. A test "If $\pi[T, M]$" returns true if $\pi[T, M]$ is defined, and false otherwise, and similarly for "If $\pi^{-1}[T, C]$". The game begins by picking a random Y_T for each T that is intended to stand for $\pi[T, H]$ but not assigned to the latter so as to avoid using H. Instead, whenever $\pi[T, H]$ or $\pi^{-1}[T, Y_T]$ are called for, the game sets bad and corrects via the boxed code, which is included in G_6. A variant of the Fundamental Lemma of Game Playing from [5] says that identical until bad games have the same probability of setting bad and hence

$$\Pr[\mathrm{G}_4^A \text{ sets } \mathsf{bad}_2] = \Pr[\mathrm{G}_6^A] = \Pr[\mathrm{G}_7^A] .$$

But game G_7, which excludes the boxed code, does not refer to H in replying to adversary oracle queries, and hence

$$\Pr[\mathrm{G}_7^A] = \Pr[\mathrm{G}_8^A] .$$

Since A is legitimate, a FN$^{-1}(T, C)$ query with $C = Y_T$ must occur before it receives Y_T from KDFN and hence is made with no knowledge of Y_T. Thus the probability that a query of A sets bad is at most 2^{-n}. (We remark that this is the place we use the assumption that A is legitimate, without which bad could be set with probability one.) On the other hand the set S has size at most Q at the end of the execution

$\underline{\text{proc Initialize}}$ // G_5
$\pi \leftarrow_\$ \mathsf{TwPm}(\mathcal{T} \setminus \{\gamma\}, \{0,1\}^n)$
$H \leftarrow_\$ \{0,1\}^n$; $S \leftarrow \emptyset$

$\underline{\text{proc Fn}(T, M)}$ // G_5
$S \leftarrow S \cup \{E(M, \gamma, \alpha')\}$
Return $\pi(T, M)$

$\underline{\text{proc KDFn}(T, \phi)}$ // G_5
Return $\pi(T, H)$

$\underline{\text{proc Fn}^{-1}(T, C)}$ // G_5
$M \leftarrow \pi^{-1}(T, C)$
$S \leftarrow S \cup \{E(M, \gamma, \alpha')\}$
Return M

$\underline{\text{proc Finalize}(b')}$ // G_5
$H' \leftarrow_\$ \{0,1\}^n \setminus \{H\}$
Return $(H' \in S)$

$\underline{\text{proc Initialize}}$ // G_6, G_7
For all $T \in \mathcal{T} \setminus \{\gamma\}$ do
  $Y_T \leftarrow_\$ \{0,1\}^n$; $R(T) \leftarrow \{Y_T\}$
$H \leftarrow_\$ \{0,1\}^n$

$\underline{\text{proc Fn}(T, M)}$ // $\boxed{G_6}$, G_7
If $\pi[T, M]$ then return $\pi[T, M]$
$C \leftarrow_\$ \{0,1\}^n \setminus R(T)$
If $M = H$ then $\mathsf{bad} \leftarrow \mathsf{true}$; $\boxed{C \leftarrow Y_T}$
$D(T) \leftarrow D(T) \cup \{M\}$; $R(T) \leftarrow R(T) \cup \{C\}$
$\pi[T, M] \leftarrow C$; $\pi^{-1}[T, C] \leftarrow M$
Return $\pi[T, M]$

$\underline{\text{proc KDFn}(T, \phi)}$ // G_6, G_7
Return Y_T

$\underline{\text{proc Fn}^{-1}(T, C)}$ // $\boxed{G_6}$, G_7
If $\pi^{-1}[T, C]$ then return $\pi^{-1}[T, C]$
$M \leftarrow_\$ \{0,1\}^n \setminus D(T)$
If $C = Y_T$ then $\mathsf{bad} \leftarrow \mathsf{true}$; $\boxed{M \leftarrow H}$
Else If $M = H$ then
  $\mathsf{bad} \leftarrow \mathsf{true}$
  $\boxed{M \leftarrow_\$ \{0,1\}^n \setminus (D(T) \cup \{H\})}$
$D(T) \leftarrow D(T) \cup \{M\}$; $R(T) \leftarrow R(T) \cup \{C\}$
$\pi[T, M] \leftarrow C$; $\pi^{-1}[T, C] \leftarrow M$
Return M

$\underline{\text{proc Finalize}(b')}$ // G_6, G_7
Return bad

$\underline{\text{proc Initialize}}$ // G_8
For all $T \in \mathcal{T} \setminus \{\gamma\}$ do
  $Y_T \leftarrow_\$ \{0,1\}^n$; $R(T) \leftarrow \{Y_T\}$
$S \leftarrow \emptyset$

$\underline{\text{proc Fn}(T, M)}$ // G_8
If $\pi[T, M]$ then return $\pi[T, M]$
$C \leftarrow_\$ \{0,1\}^n \setminus R(T)$
$S \leftarrow S \cup \{M\}$
$D(T) \leftarrow D(T) \cup \{M\}$
$R(T) \leftarrow R(T) \cup \{C\}$
$\pi[T, M] \leftarrow C$; $\pi^{-1}[T, C] \leftarrow M$
Return $\pi[T, M]$

$\underline{\text{proc KDFn}(T, \phi)}$ // G_8
Return Y_T

$\underline{\text{proc Fn}^{-1}(T, C)}$ // G_8
If $\pi^{-1}[T, C]$ then return $\pi^{-1}[T, C]$
$M \leftarrow_\$ \{0,1\}^n \setminus D(T)$
If $C = Y_T$ then $\mathsf{bad} \leftarrow \mathsf{true}$
Else $S \leftarrow S \cup \{M\}$
$D(T) \leftarrow D(T) \cup \{M\}$
$R(T) \leftarrow R(T) \cup \{C\}$
$\pi[T, M] \leftarrow C$; $\pi^{-1}[T, C] \leftarrow M$
Return M

$\underline{\text{proc Finalize}(b')}$ // G_8
$H \leftarrow_\$ \{0,1\}^n$
Return $(H \in S) \vee \mathsf{bad}$

Figure 3: More games used in the proof of Theorem 3.1.

of A with the game. So $\Pr[G_8^A] \le 2Q \cdot 2^{-n}$. Putting this together with the above concludes the proof. □

The IEEE 1619 standard for narrowblock encryption is based on XEX-AES [18]. **StE** is an alternative narrowblock candidate that is essentially as efficient as the current one but also has provable security for enciphering the key.

4. WIDEBLOCK CIPHER

We provide a simple and general way to enhance a given PRP-CCA wideblock cipher to be able to encrypt messages that might, in any block, contain the key. Our construction simply puts an ECB layer in front of the given cipher and then uses **StE** as the base tweakable blockcipher for both the ECB pass and the application of the wideblock cipher. This works for any given wideblock cipher that is a mode of operation of a blockcipher, meaning it uses the key only to key an underlying blockcipher, as is the case with EME and other standard designs. **StE** is used with one tweak for the ECB pass and then, by fixing a different tweak, yields a blockcipher to instantiate the wideblock mode of operation.

We begin, below, by defining what it means for a wideblock design to be a mode of operation and what it means to assume it is PRP-CCA secure. Then we provide our construction and prove it secure.

Modes. A wideblock mode of operation $\mathbf{WB} = (\mathsf{WB}, \mathsf{WB}^{-1})$ is a pair of oracle algorithms. Given oracle access to a permutation g: $\{0,1\}^n \to \{0,1\}^n$, algorithm WB takes input a tweak $T \in \mathcal{T}$ and an m-block message $X \in \{0,1\}^{mn}$ to return an m-block ciphertext denoted $\mathsf{WB}(T, X : g)$. Given oracle access to g^{-1}, algorithm WB^{-1} takes input a tweak $T \in \mathcal{T}$ and an m-block ciphertext $Y \in \{0,1\}^{mn}$ to return an m-block message denoted $\mathsf{WB}^{-1}(T, Y : g^{-1})$. It is required that $\mathsf{WB}^{-1}(T, \mathsf{WB}(T, X : g) : g^{-1}) = X$ for all choices of the inputs and oracles. Here $\mathcal{T}, n, m$ are the tweak space, blocklength and number of blocks associated to **WB**.

If N: $\{0,1\}^n \times \{0,1\}^n \to \{0,1\}^n$ is a blockcipher then **WB** associates to it a tweakable blockcipher $W = \mathbf{WB}[N]$ where W: $\{0,1\}^n \times \mathcal{T} \times \{0,1\}^{mn} \to \{0,1\}^{mn}$ is defined by $W(K, T, X) = \mathsf{WB}(T, X : E(K, \cdot))$ and $W^{-1}(K, T, Y) = \mathsf{WB}^{-1}(T, Y : E^{-1}(K, \cdot))$. EME is an example of a wideblock mode of operation that, in this way, transforms a given blockcipher into a wideblock tweakable cipher.

Let $\mathbf{WB} = (\mathsf{WB}, \mathsf{WB}^{-1})$ be a wideblock mode of operation. Consider the games of Figure 4 and let

$$\mathbf{Adv}^{\text{prp-cca}}_{\mathbf{WB}}(B) = \Pr[\mathrm{RO}^B_{\mathbf{WB}}] - \Pr[\mathrm{Rand}^B_{mn}] \,.$$

Game $\mathrm{RO}_{\mathbf{WB}}$ instantiates the oracles of WB and WB^{-1} with a random narrow block permutation and its inverse, respectively, while game Rand_{mn} responds to oracle queries via a random wideblock permutation. Now let

$$\mathbf{Adv}^{\text{prp-cca}}_{\mathbf{WB}}(Q, n, m, t) = \max_B \mathbf{Adv}^{\text{prp-cca}}_{\mathbf{WB}}(B)$$

where the maximum is over all adversaries B making at most Q oracle queries with the tweak argument in each query having length at most nt. Proving security of a mode of operation ubiquitously proceeds by upper bounding this advantage as a function of Q, n, m, t. This is a purely information

proc INITIALIZE // $\mathrm{RO}_{\mathbf{WB}}$ $\pi \leftarrow\!\!\$\ \mathsf{Pm}(\{0,1\}^m)$ proc $\mathrm{FN}(T, M)$ // $\mathrm{RO}_{\mathbf{WB}}$ Return $\mathsf{WB}(T, M:\pi)$ proc $\mathrm{FN}^{-1}(T, C)$ // $\mathrm{RO}_{\mathbf{WB}}$ Return $\mathsf{WB}^{-1}(T, C:\pi^{-1})$ proc FINALIZE(b') // $\mathrm{RO}_{\mathbf{WB}}$ Return $(b' = 1)$	proc INITIALIZE // Rand_{mn} $\pi \leftarrow\!\!\$\ \mathsf{TwPm}(\mathcal{T}, \{0,1\}^{mn})$ proc $\mathrm{FN}(T, M)$ // Rand_{mn} Return $\pi(T, M)$ proc $\mathrm{FN}^{-1}(T, C)$ // Rand_{mn} Return $\pi^{-1}(T, C)$ proc FINALIZE(b') // Rand_{mn} Return $(b' = 1)$	proc INITIALIZE // J $\pi \leftarrow\!\!\$\ \mathsf{TwPm}(\mathcal{T}, \{0,1\}^n)$ $K \leftarrow\!\!\$\ \{0,1\}^n$ proc $\mathrm{FN}(T, M)$ // J Return $\pi(T, M)$ proc $\mathrm{KDFN}(T, \mathrm{id}_M)$ // J For $i = 1, \ldots, m$ do If $M[i] = \bot$ then $M[i] \leftarrow K$ Return $\pi(T, M)$ proc $\mathrm{FN}^{-1}(T, C)$ // J Return $\pi^{-1}(T, C)$ proc FINALIZE(b') // J Return $(b' = 1)$

Figure 4: On the left are games $\mathrm{RO}_{\mathbf{WB}}, \mathrm{Rand}_{mn}$ to define security of wideblock mode of operation $\mathbf{WB} = (\mathsf{WB}, \mathsf{WB}^{-1})$. On the right is the final game J for the proof of Theorem 4.1.

theoretic setting, and absolute bounds are provided. For example, for EME, it is shown in [15] that this advantage is at most $7(Qt + qn + 1)^2/2^n$. (EME requires $m \leq n$, assumed in this bound.) PRP-CCA security of $\mathbf{WB}[N]$ follows from the assumption that N is a PRP-CCA secure blockcipher by a standard reduction argument.

CONSTRUCTION. Let ECB denote the oracle algorithm that given oracle access to a permutation g: $\{0,1\}^n \to \{0,1\}^n$, and given input $M = M[1] \ldots M[m] \in \{0,1\}^{mn}$, returns the m-bit string $C = \mathsf{ECB}(M:g)$ defined by $C[i] = g(M[i])$ for $1 \leq i \leq m$. Let $\mathbf{WB} = (\mathsf{WB}, \mathsf{WB}^{-1})$ be a wideblock mode of operation with tweakspace $\mathcal{T}$, blocklength n and number of blocks m. Let F: $\{0,1\}^n \times \{\gamma_1, \gamma_2\} \times \{0,1\}^n \to \{0,1\}^n$ be a tweakable blockcipher with a tweakspace of size two. (Of course, any tweakable blockcipher with an even larger tweakspace will do. Just drop all but two possible tweaks.) Our **EtE** (ECB-then-encipher) transform associates to **WB** and F a tweakable wideblock cipher $J = \mathbf{EtE}[\mathbf{WB}, F]$ where J: $\{0,1\}^n \times \mathcal{T} \times \{0,1\}^{mn} \to \{0,1\}^{mn}$ is defined as follows:

$J(K, T, M)$
01 $X \leftarrow \mathsf{ECB}(M : F(K, \gamma_1, \cdot))$
02 $Y \leftarrow \mathsf{WB}(T, X : F(K, \gamma_2, \cdot))$
03 Return Y

The inverse is defined by

$J^{-1}(K, T, Y)$
01 $X \leftarrow \mathsf{WB}^{-1}(T, Y : F^{-1}(K, \gamma_2, \cdot))$
02 $M \leftarrow \mathsf{ECB}(X : F^{-1}(K, \gamma_1, \cdot))$
03 Return X

We take advantage here of the fact that $\mathsf{ECB}(\cdot : g^{-1})$ is the inverse of $\mathsf{ECB}(\cdot : g)$.

When instantiated with EME in the role of **WB** this uses three blockcipher invocations per block, but retains the parallelizability of EME. F would be obtained by applying **StE** to some tweakable blockcipher with a tweakspace of size three.

THE CLASS $\mathcal{ID}_m$. We formally define the class Φ capturing occurrence of the key in any block of the message. Associate to any m-vector M over $\{0,1\}^n \cup \{\bot\}$ the function id_M: $\{0,1\}^n \to \{0,1\}^{mn}$ that on input a key $K \in \{0,1\}^n$ returns the message $M' = M'[1] \ldots M'[m]$ defined by $M'[i] = M[i]$ if $M[i] \neq \bot$ and $M'[i] = K$ if $M[i] = \bot$ for all $1 \leq i \leq m$. Then $\mathcal{ID}_m$ is the class of all id_M as M ranges over all m-vectors over $\{0,1\}^n \cup \{\bot\}$. This is the class Φ we will consider.

SECURITY. Assume **WB** is PRP-CCA secure and assume F is $\{\mathrm{id}\}$-PRP-CCA secure, meaning can safely encrypt its own key. We claim that J is $\mathcal{ID}_m$-PRP-CCA secure, meaning can safely encrypt messages that contain the key in any block.

THEOREM 4.1. *Let $\mathbf{WB} = (\mathsf{WB}, \mathsf{WB}^{-1})$ be a wideblock mode of operation with tweakspace $\mathcal{T}$, blocklength n and number of blocks m. Let F: $\{0,1\}^n \times \{\gamma_1, \gamma_2\} \times \{0,1\}^n \to \{0,1\}^n$ be a tweakable blockcipher. Let $J = \mathbf{EtE}[\mathbf{WB}, F]$ be the wideblock tweakable cipher associated to **WB** and F via the **EtE** transform as defined above. Let $\Phi = \mathcal{ID}_m$. Let A be an adversary making at most Q oracle queries with the tweak argument in each query having length at most nt. Then there is an adversary B such that*

$$\mathbf{Adv}^{\text{prp-cca}}_{J,\Phi}(A) \leq$$

$$2 \cdot \mathbf{Adv}^{\text{prp-cca}}_{F,\{\mathrm{id}\}}(B) + 2\delta(\mathbf{WB}) + \frac{2Q^2(m^2+2)}{2^{n+2}},$$

where $\delta(\mathbf{WB}) = \mathbf{Adv}^{\text{prp-cca}}_{\mathbf{WB}}(Q, n, m, t)$. Moreover, the running time of B is about equal to the running time of A.

The proof would seem at first to be a quite straightforward simulation in which KDFN queries of A can be answered via KDFN queries of B. The subtle issue is that B needs to be legitimate and this means it cannot answer all FN^{-1} queries of A. Ensuring B is legitimate makes the proof more involved.

PROOF. We begin with the games in Figure 5. We have

$$\begin{aligned} \Pr[\mathrm{Real}^A_{J,\mathcal{ID}_m}] &= \Pr[\mathrm{G}_0^A] \\ &= \Pr[\mathrm{G}_0^A] - \Pr[\mathrm{G}_1^A] + \Pr[\mathrm{G}_1^A] \\ &\leq \Pr[\mathrm{G}_1^A] + \Pr[\mathrm{BAD}(\mathrm{G}_1^A)], \end{aligned} \quad (3)$$

```
proc INITIALIZE // G0, G1
K ←$ {0,1}^n ; S ← ∅

proc FN(T, M) // G0, G1
X ← ECB(M : F(K, γ1, ·))
Y ← WB(T, X : F(K, γ2, ·))
Return Y

proc KDFN(T, id_M) // G0, G1
For i = 1, ..., m do
    If M[i] = ⊥ then M[i] ← K
X ← ECB(M : F(K, γ1, ·))
S ← S ∪ { X[i] : 1 ≤ i ≤ m }
Y ← WB(T, X : F(K, γ2, ·))
Return Y

proc FN^{-1}(T, C) // [G0], G1
X ← WB^{-1}(T, C : F^{-1}(K, γ2, ·))
S' ← { X[i] : 1 ≤ i ≤ m }
M ← ⊥
If S ∩ S' ≠ ∅ then bad ← true
    [M ← ECB(X : F^{-1}(K, γ1, ·))]
Else M ← ECB(X : F^{-1}(K, γ1, ·))
Return M

proc FINALIZE(b') // G0, G1
Return (b' = 1)
```

```
proc INITIALIZE // H
π ←$ TwPm({γ1, γ2}, {0,1}^n)
K ←$ {0,1}^n ; S ← ∅

proc FN(T, M) // H
X ← ECB(M : π(γ1, ·))
Y ← WB(T, X : π(γ2, ·))
Return Y

proc KDFN(T, id_M) // H
For i = 1, ..., m do
    If M[i] = ⊥ then M[i] ← K
X ← ECB(M : π(γ1, ·))
S ← S ∪ { X[i] : 1 ≤ i ≤ m }
Y ← WB(T, X : π(γ2, ·))
Return Y

proc FN^{-1}(T, C) // H
X ← WB^{-1}(T, C : π^{-1}(γ2, ·))
S' ← { X[i] : 1 ≤ i ≤ m }
M ← ⊥
If S ∩ S' ≠ ∅ then bad ← true
Else M ← ECB(X : π^{-1}(γ1, ·))
Return M

proc FINALIZE(b') // H
Return (b' = 1)
```

```
proc INITIALIZE // I0, I1
π1 ←$ TwPm({γ1}, {0,1}^n)
π2 ←$ TwPm(𝒯, {0,1}^n)
K ←$ {0,1}^n ; S ← ∅

proc FN(T, M) // I0, I1
X ← ECB(M : π1(γ1, ·))
Y ← π2(T, X)
Return Y

proc KDFN(T, id_M) // I0, I1
For i = 1, ..., m do
    If M[i] = ⊥ then M[i] ← K
X ← ECB(M : π1(γ1, ·))
S ← S ∪ { X[i] : 1 ≤ i ≤ m }
Y ← π2(T, X)
Return Y

proc FN^{-1}(T, C) // [I0], I1
X ← π2^{-1}(T, C)
S' ← { X[i] : 1 ≤ i ≤ m }
M ← ⊥
If S ∩ S' ≠ ∅ then bad ← true
    [M ← ECB(X : π1^{-1}(γ1, ·))]
Else M ← ECB(X : π1^{-1}(γ1, ·))
Return M

proc FINALIZE(b') // I0, I1
Return (b' = 1)
```

Figure 5: Games used in the proof of Theorem 4.1.

the inequality by the Fundamental Lemma of Game Playing [5]. We will design (legitimate!) B_1, B_2 so that

$$\Pr[G_1^A] - \Pr[H^A] \leq \mathbf{Adv}^{\text{prp-cca}}_{F,\{\text{id}\}}(B_1) \quad (4)$$

$$\Pr[\text{BAD}(G_1^A)] - \Pr[\text{BAD}(H^A)] \leq \mathbf{Adv}^{\text{prp-cca}}_{F,\{\text{id}\}}(B_2) \,. \quad (5)$$

Due to space restrictions, the descriptions of B_1, B_2 are omitted and can be found in the full version of this paper [3].

Let B pick $i \in \{1,2\}$ at random and run B_i, and let $\delta(F) = \mathbf{Adv}^{\text{prp-cca}}_{F,\{\text{id}\}}(B)$. Then from Equations (3), (4), (5) we have

$$\Pr[G_0^A] \leq 2\delta(F) + \Pr[H^A] + \Pr[\text{BAD}(H^A)] \,. \quad (6)$$

We will design B_3, B_4 so that

$$\Pr[H^A] - \Pr[I_1^A] \leq \mathbf{Adv}^{\text{prp-cca}}_{\mathbf{WB}}(B_3) \quad (7)$$

$$\Pr[\text{BAD}(H^A)] - \Pr[\text{BAD}(I_1^A)] \leq \mathbf{Adv}^{\text{prp-cca}}_{\mathbf{WB}}(B_4) \,. \quad (8)$$

Due to the space restrictions, the descriptions of B_3, B_4 are omitted and can be found in [3].

Recall that $\delta(\mathbf{WB}) = \mathbf{Adv}^{\text{prp-cca}}_{\mathbf{WB}}(Q, n, m, t)$. Then from Equations (6), (7), (8) we have

$$\Pr[G_0^A] - \Pr[I_1^A] \leq 2\delta(F) + 2\delta(\mathbf{WB}) + \Pr[\text{BAD}(I_1^A)] \,. \quad (9)$$

Consider game J of Figure 4. Composing a random permutation with any independently chosen permutation yields a random permutation, regardless of the distribution of the second permutation, so

$$\begin{aligned}
\mathbf{Adv}^{\text{prp-cca}}_{J,\mathcal{ID}_m}(A) &= \Pr[\text{Real}^A_{J,\mathcal{ID}_m}] - \Pr[\text{Rand}^A_{J,\mathcal{ID}_m}] \\
&= \Pr[G_0^A] - \Pr[J^A] \\
&= \Pr[G_0^A] - \Pr[I_0^A] \\
&= (\Pr[G_0^A] - \Pr[I_1^A]) + (\Pr[I_1^A] - \Pr[I_0^A]) \\
&\leq (\Pr[G_0^A] - \Pr[I_1^A]) + \Pr[\text{BAD}(I_1^A)] \,.
\end{aligned}$$

Putting this together with Equation (9) we have

$$\mathbf{Adv}^{\text{prp-cca}}_{J,\mathcal{ID}_m}(A) \leq 2\delta(F) + 2\delta(\mathbf{WB}) + 2 \cdot \Pr[\text{BAD}(I_1^A)] \,. \quad (10)$$

To complete the proof we show in [3] that $\Pr[\text{BAD}(I_1^A)] \leq Q^2(m^2+2) \cdot 2^{-n-2}$. □

5. IMPLEMENTATION

We describe a fast AES-based instantiation of **EtE**. As a starting point, we need an AES-based tweakable blockcipher. LRW [16] and XEX [15] are possible choices. Both of them require two calls to the base AES blockcipher, but with XEX, one of the calls can be can be made just once and the value cached as the cipher is used to encipher many message blocks. We thus choose XEX. Applying **StE** to XEX yields a tweakable blockcipher F. Now we need to pick a wideblock cipher to play the role of **WB**. We pick EME which uses about two blockcipher calls per message block together with overhead for offset computations. Let J be the wideblock tweakable cipher produced by applying **EtE**

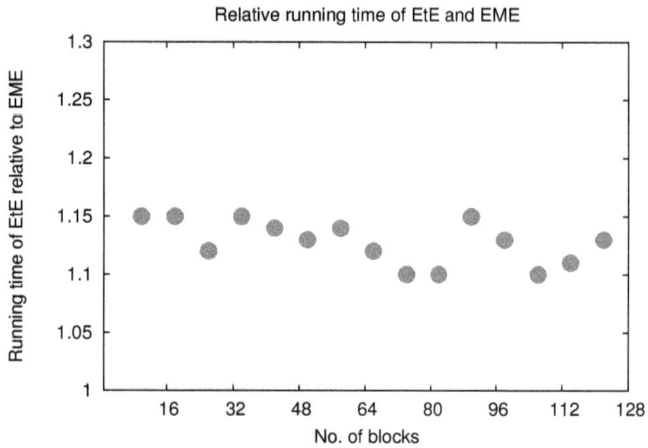

Figure 6: Running time of J on a scale where the running time of EME has been normalized to 1.

to **WB** and F. We have optimized J and then implemented it and compared its speed to that of EME.

XEX. XEX over a blockcipher E: $\{0,1\}^n \times \{0,1\}^n \to \{0,1\}^n$ has tweakspace $\{0,1\}^n \times \mathbb{I}$, where $\mathbb{I}$ is the set of integers $[1,\ldots,2^n-2]$. Arithmetic operations in XEX are done in the field $\mathrm{GF}(2^n)$, with elements of $\mathrm{GF}(2^n)$ viewed interchangeably as n-bit strings, integers in $[0,2^n-1]$ and as formal polynomials of degree $n-1$ with binary coefficients. Addition is bitwise XOR and multiplication of two points is performed by multiplying them as formal polynomials modulo the irreducible polynomial $p_{128}(x) = x^{127} + x^7 + x^2 + x + 1$. XEX is defined by $\tilde{E}_K^{(N,i)}(M) = E_K(M \oplus \Delta) \oplus \Delta$ where $\Delta = 2^i\mathsf{N}$ and $\mathsf{N} = E_K(N)$. For our purposes, we require a much smaller tweak space of two elements. We pick $t_0 = (0^n, 1)$ and $t_1 = (10^{n-1}, 1)$. Now, Δ can assume only two values (Δ_0, Δ_1) which can be precomputed and cached between successive calls, avoiding running E for the second time to calculate N. The XOR operations still remain, but they are parallelizable, using vector instructions [9].

EXPERIMENTS. We compare the speeds of **EtE** and EME on a processor that has the AES-NI support for executing AES in hardware [11]. Given that **EtE** is intended for use in disk encryption at the sector level, which happens in hardware, the use of AES-NI is realistic.

Our results show that encrypting with **EtE** is slower than EME by a modest 15% or less. We ran the tests described below on a Intel Xeon W3690 processor at 3.47 GHz with support for AES-NI running Linux version 2.6 with code compiled using gcc -O3 -ftree-vectorize -msse2 -ffast-math to enable vector instructions and perform other general optimizations. The base code was from Brian Gladman's EME2 implementation [10], which we modified to run as EME and use the hardware AES instructions.

6. REFERENCES

[1] B. Applebaum, D. Cash, C. Peikert, and A. Sahai. Fast cryptographic primitives and circular-secure encryption based on hard learning problems. In S. Halevi, editor, *CRYPTO 2009*, volume 5677 of *LNCS*, pages 595–618. Springer, Aug. 2009.

[2] B. Barak, I. Haitner, D. Hofheinz, and Y. Ishai. Bounded key-dependent message security. In H. Gilbert, editor, *EUROCRYPT 2010*, volume 6110 of *LNCS*, pages 423–444. Springer, May 2010.

[3] M. Bellare, D. Cash, and S. Keelveedhi. Ciphers that securely encipher their own keys. Cryptology ePrint Archive, 2011. http://eprint.iacr.org/.

[4] M. Bellare and T. Kohno. A theoretical treatment of related-key attacks: RKA-PRPs, RKA-PRFs, and applications. In E. Biham, editor, *EUROCRYPT 2003*, volume 2656 of *LNCS*, pages 491–506. Springer, May 2003.

[5] M. Bellare and P. Rogaway. The security of triple encryption and a framework for code-based game-playing proofs. In S. Vaudenay, editor, *EUROCRYPT 2006*, volume 4004 of *LNCS*, pages 409–426. Springer, May / June 2006.

[6] J. Black, P. Rogaway, and T. Shrimpton. Encryption-scheme security in the presence of key-dependent messages. In K. Nyberg and H. M. Heys, editors, *SAC 2002*, volume 2595 of *LNCS*, pages 62–75. Springer, Aug. 2003.

[7] D. Boneh, S. Halevi, M. Hamburg, and R. Ostrovsky. Circular-secure encryption from decision diffie-hellman. In D. Wagner, editor, *CRYPTO 2008*, volume 5157 of *LNCS*, pages 108–125. Springer, Aug. 2008.

[8] Z. Brakerski, S. Goldwasser, and Y. T. Kalai. Black-box circular-secure encryption beyond affine functions. In Y. Ishai, editor, *TCC 2011*, volume 6597 of *LNCS*, pages 201–218. Springer, Mar. 2011.

[9] N. Firasta, M. Buxton, P. Jinbo, K. Nasri, and S. Kuo. Intel AVX: New frontiers in performance improvements and energy efficiency. *Intel Software Network*, 2009.

[10] B. Gladman. Brian gladman's aes implementation. http://gladman.plushost.co.uk/oldsite/AES/index.php.

[11] S. Gueron. Advanced encryption standard (AES) instructions set. Intel, http://softwarecommunity.intel.com/articles/eng/3788.htm, 2010.

[12] S. Halevi. EME*: Extending EME to handle arbitrary-length messages with associated data. In A. Canteaut and K. Viswanathan, editors, *INDOCRYPT 2004*, volume 3348 of *LNCS*, pages 315–327. Springer, Dec. 2004.

[13] S. Halevi and H. Krawczyk. Security under key-dependent inputs. In P. Ning, S. D. C. di Vimercati, and P. F. Syverson, editors, *ACM CCS 07*, pages 466–475. ACM Press, Oct. 2007.

[14] S. Halevi and P. Rogaway. A tweakable enciphering mode. In D. Boneh, editor, *CRYPTO 2003*, volume 2729 of *LNCS*, pages 482–499. Springer, Aug. 2003.

[15] S. Halevi and P. Rogaway. A parallelizable enciphering mode. In T. Okamoto, editor, *CT-RSA 2004*, volume 2964 of *LNCS*, pages 292–304. Springer, Feb. 2004.

[16] M. Liskov, R. L. Rivest, and D. Wagner. Tweakable block ciphers. In M. Yung, editor, *CRYPTO 2002*, volume 2442 of *LNCS*, pages 31–46. Springer, Aug. 2002.

[17] M. Luby and C. Rackoff. How to construct pseudorandom permutations from pseudorandom functions. *SIAM Journal on Computing*, 17(2), 1988.

[18] P. Rogaway. Efficient instantiations of tweakable blockciphers and refinements to modes OCB and PMAC. In P. J. Lee, editor, *ASIACRYPT 2004*, volume 3329 of *LNCS*, pages 16–31. Springer, Dec. 2004.

Password-Protected Secret Sharing

Ali Bagherzandi
Dept. of Computer Science
University of California, Irvine
zandi@ics.uci.edu

Stanisław Jarecki
Dept. of Computer Science
University of California, Irvine
stasio@ics.uci.edu

Nitesh Saxena
Computer and Information Sciences
University of Alabama, Birmingham
saxena@cis.uab.edu

Yanbin Lu
Dept. of Computer Science
University of California, Irvine
yanbinl@ics.uci.edu

ABSTRACT

We revisit the problem of protecting user's private data against adversarial compromise of user's device(s) which store this data. We formalize the solution we propose as *Password-Protected Secret-Sharing* (PPSS), which allows a user to secret-share her data among n trustees in such a way that (1) the user can retrieve the shared secret upon entering a correct password into a reconstruction protocol, which succeeds as long as at least $t+1$ uncorrupted trustees are accessible, and (2) the shared data remains secret even if the adversary which corrupts t trustees, with the level of protection expected of password-authentication, i.e. the probability that the adversary learns anything useful about the secret is at most $q/|D|$ where q is the number of reconstruction protocol the adversary manages to trigger and $|D|$ is the size of the password dictionary.

We propose an efficient PPSS protocol in the PKI model, secure under the DDH assumption, using non-interactive zero-knowledge proofs with efficient instantiations in the Random Oracle Model. Our protocol is practical, with fewer than 16 exponentiations per trustee and $8t+17$ exponentiations per user, with $O(1)$ bandwidth between the user and each trustee, and only three message flows, implying a single round of interaction in the on-line phase. As a side benefit our PPSS protocol yields a new Threshold Password Authenticated Key Exchange (T-PAKE) protocol in the PKI model with significantly lower message, communication, and server computation complexities than existing T-PAKE's.

Categories and Subject Descriptors

D.4.6 [**Security and Protection**]: Cryptographic Controls; D.4.6 [**Security and Protection**]: Authentication

General Terms

Security, Algorithms

Keywords

Secret Sharing, Intrusion Tolerance, Password Authentication

1. INTRODUCTION

A user of computing technology, let's call her Alice, needs to store her valuable private data, e.g. texts, images, passwords, or keys, on her computer or any other electronic device. Alice's device, however, can fall prey to viruses or any other type of malware which could expose her data. Moreover, Alice's device could get lost or stolen and thus fall under control of someone whom Alice does not trust. On the other hand, Alice might want to have access to her private data on more than one device, and she would like her data protected from loss due to device failures.

Consider the general problem of protecting Alice's secret data, let's call it s, in the event of the compromise or failure of the device(s) on which s could be stored. Storing an encryption of s using a key derived from Alice's password is vulnerable to an off-line password dictionary attack once the device is corrupted, and it is also not robust to device failure. Without specialized hardware, Alice could instead outsource s to some trusted remote server, and authenticate to this server whenever she needs to retrieve s. Note that Alice cannot store any authentication token on her device, or otherwise the adversary who corrupts the device can still recover s by using this token to authenticate to the server. If we want a software-only solution, Alice could only use a human-memorable password for authentication to the server. Still, she would be placing all her trust in a single server.

Password-Protected Secret Sharing. To eliminate the bottleneck of a single trusted server we could secret-share s among a set of n trustees so that only a compromise of more than some threshold of trustees would disable the system or leak s. However, secret sharing by itself is not enough because Alice still needs some way to authenticate to these trustees to trigger the secret reconstruction protocol, and since she can only use human-memorable passwords, a black-box combination of password authentication and secret-sharing leaves us with two bad choices: Alice can use n independently chosen passwords, one for each trustee, which is impractical, or she can use the same password with all trustees, but this would eliminate all the benefits of secret-sharing, because a single corrupt trustee could recover this password via an off-line dictionary attack and use it to recover s by authenticating to the other trustees. This motivates the question of how to distribute Alice's data among n trustees so that: (1) Alice can retrieve her data by triggering a reconstruction protocol using only her password, and the reconstruction is guaranteed as long as at least $t+1$ honest trustees are available; and (2) Alice's data remains secret even when t trustees are corrupted, and the level of this protection is as expected of password-authenticated protocol, i.e. if Alice chooses her password uniformly in set D then the probability that adversary learns anything about Alice's data after triggering q instances of the reconstruction protocol is at most $q/|D|$ plus some negligible quantity. We call a protocol that satisfies these two properties a (t, n) *Password-Protected Secret Sharing (PPSS)*.

Two Implementation Settings. There are two basic implementation settings for a PPSS scheme. In the *roaming user setting* implicitly assumed above, Alice's device does not have any private storage, and the n trustees are implemented by n separate physical entities. This setting is highly robust, because the adversary can destroy Alice's data only by corrupting $n-t$ trustees, and it is easy to extend to multiple user devices, since a user device needs no private information. As for security, the loss of Alice's device(s) gives no information to the adversary, and Alice's data is secure even if the adversary corrupts t out of n trustees. However, Alice's data is vulnerable to on-line dictionary attacks against the trustees, and the adversary corrupting $t+1$ trustees recovers both Alice's data and her password, possibly after an off-line dictionary attack.

In a *private storage setting*, Alice can trade robustness for increased security by initializing an $(n, 2n-t)$ PPSS scheme, distributing n shares among the n trustees, and storing the remaining $n-t$ shares locally on her device. During reconstruction this device will use its shares to play the part of $n-t$ virtual trustees. The resulting system is less robust because Alice's data is lost after corruption of either $n-t$ trustees *or* of Alice's device. However, the system is more secure because an adversary learns Alice's data only after corrupting both $t+1$ trustees *and* Alice's device. Moreover, a network attacker can no longer stage an on-line dictionary attack, because the $n-t$ virtual trustees implemented by Alice's device do not need to respond to network requests.

Applications. A PPSS scheme can be implemented by a dedicated service provider as service to individual users, or it can be administered by users themselves, exploiting their real-world trust relationships, e.g. from on-line social networks such as *Facebook*. For example, using the PPSS scheme in a private storage setting Alice can improve the security of her data compared compared to local storage, at the price of risking data loss if $n-t$ out of n of her trustees become unavailable. The role of the trustees can also be played by different devices belonging to Alice herself. For example, Alice can use PPSS to off-load sensitive data from her mobile phone so that the adversary can gain control of this data only by stealing the phone together with t out of n of her additional devices, e.g. her home computer, her work computer, or even her Bluetooth-connected watch. Various types of trustees could be mixed, so the pool of Alice's own n devices can extend to computers of Alice's Facebook friends and to dedicated service providers. Moreover, each logical trustee can be assigned a different weight by playing the role of $k>1$ virtual trustees. In the PPSS protocol we propose this would increase trustee's computational cost only by replacing one exponentiation with one multi-exponentiation on k bases.

A PPSS scheme can be used to protect any sensitive data, including user's cryptographic keys, e.g. for decryption, signing, authentication, etc. One variant of such application is a *password management*, where Alice's data protected by a PPSS scheme are her passwords to various on-line services. Apart of convenience of having to remember only one "master password", used by the PPSS to recover all the other passwords, such scheme can improve security of password authentication because it allows Alice to use independent random keys instead of all her passwords except the master password. Currently several entities offer such password management service, e.g. LastPass [17] and Mozilla Weave Sync [20], but these are centralized solutions.

Scheme	MSJ06 [19]	RG06 [7]	Ours
Client Computation	$O(1)$	$O(1)$	$O(n)$
Server Computation	$O(n)$	$O(n^2)$	$O(1)$
Total Bandwidth	$O(n^2)$	$O(n^3)$	$O(n)$
Client/Server Messages	7	≥ 12	3

Figure 1: Previous TPAKE's versus our PPSS/TPAKE.

Related Work. The idea of password-authenticated recovery of secret-shared data was to the best of our knowledge proposed by Ford and Kaliski [11]. As pointed out by a subsequent paper by Jablon [14], the Ford-Kaliski protocol implicitly assumes a *public key infrastructure* (PKI) model, while the improvement given by [14] removed the need for trusted public keys, but both protocol handles only the $t = n$ case of secret-sharing, and neither paper clearly specified the security properties of such scheme nor did they formally argue the security of the protocols they proposed.

The notion of PPSS is closely related to Threshold Password Authenticated Key Exchange (T-PAKE) defined by MacKenzie et al. [19], who followed up on the work of [11, 14], in particular by defining a more general primitive than password-authenticated recovery of secret-shared data, namely a password-authenticated key exchange between a client and n servers. Indeed, any T-PAKE scheme can be used to implement a PPSS scheme at negligible extra cost: The client authenticates to the n trustees with a T-PAKE instance, and the trustees use the keys established by this instance to encrypt and authenticate their shares of Alice's secret. As we show in this paper, in the PKI model the implication works also in the opposite direction, i.e. a PPSS implies a T-PAKE with little extra costs: Alice picks a public key encryption key pair and shares the decryption key using a PPSS scheme. A T-PAKE protocol consists of a PPSS reconstruction followed by each server encrypting a fresh session key under Alice's public key. Alice decrypts these keys using the decryption key recovered in the PPSS instance. For server-to-client authentication each server signs its encrypted session key. In spite of this equivalence between PPSS and T-PAKE in the PKI model, it is productive to formally introduce PPSS as a separate notion, firstly because it is a natural functionality, a protocol that reconstructs a (long) secret if and only if supplied with a correct (short) password, but also because it is simpler than T-PAKE, since only the client has any output, and this output can be dependent across protocol sessions.

Specifically, MacKenzie et al. [19] showed a T-PAKE protocol in the PKI model secure under the Decisional Diffie-Hellman (DDH) assumption in the Random Oracle Model (ROM), while Di Raimondo and Gennaro [7] showed a T-PAKE without relying on ROM and trusted public keys, based on the PAKE of Katz-Ostrovsky-Yung [16]. The drawback of both T-PAKE's is several rounds of server-to-server communication, which is feasible if the servers communicate over a LAN network, as could be the case in fault-tolerant distribution of an authentication server which motivated the T-PAKE's of [19, 7], but the PPSS applications that motivate our work are user-centric and can involve highly heterogeneous trustees, in which case it would be preferable that each trustee communicates only with the user device. In such user-centric communication model, the T-PAKE of [19] requires exchange of 9 messages between the user and each trustee, with $O(n)$ bandwidth, and the costs of T-PAKE of [7] are even higher (see Table 1 below). For the special case of 2 servers these results were improved upon by Brainard et al. [3] in the PKI model, and by Katz et al. [15] in the model without trusted public keys, but even these

2-server T-PAKE's require, respectively, 7 and 5 messages in the user-centric communication model, assuming ROM.

MacKenzie and Reiter's "Capture-Resilient Device" protocols [18] considered essentially the same goals as a PPSS scheme cast in the private storage setting, but in a less general setting where the trust threshold is fixed at $t = 1$, i.e. where a single trustee, in addition to the client's device, is needed to reconstruct user's data. Their schemes considered not only password-protected storage of user's data, but also password-protected computation of RSA signatures and ElGamal decryption. Note that any T-PAKE protocol, including one implied by a PPSS scheme, can be used to implement such password-protected computation given a non-interactive threshold protocol for the respective computation. The servers simply encrypt the messages of the threshold function-computation protocol under the session keys generated by a T-PAKE instance. Thus the 2-party password-protected signature/decryption computation of [18] can be generalized to any (t, n) threshold using our PPSS and non-interactive threshold RSA signature of [24] and non-interactive threshold ElGamal decryption of [6]. (We note, however, that the protocols of [18] for the $t = 1$ case use only 2 messages, while those built using our PPSS scheme would take 3 messages.) Xu and Sandhu [26] consider the same notion of password-authenticated threshold signature computation called TPAKE-TSig, except that they consider it in the roaming user setting. Since their construction is exactly the composition of a T-PAKE and a threshold signature sketched above, their TPAKE-Sig protocol can only be as fast as a T-PAKE.

PPSS is remotely related to the "key-insulated" and "intrusion-resilient" cryptosystems introduced in [9, 8], which also concern protecting user's data against device corruption via secret-sharing user's private key among semi-trusted entities. However, they consider only embedded entities like smartcards or co-processors, to whom the user does not need to authenticate remotely.

Our Contributions. We present a practical PPSS scheme in the PKI model, where the client trusts some public key(s), provably secure under the DDH assumption, assuming non-interactive zero-knowledge proofs which can be efficiently instantiated in ROM. Our scheme requires fewer than 16 exponentiations per trustee and $8t + 17$ exponentiations per user, with $O(1)$ bandwidth between the user and each trustee, and only three message flows, implying a single round of interaction if trustees' first messages are precomputed. We also show that a PPSS implies a T-PAKE with very little computation and communication overhead, and no additional communication rounds. Thus our scheme implies a T-PAKE with fewer communication rounds, less bandwidth, and less server computation than existing T-PAKE's of [19, 7]. The exact cost comparison in the user-mediated communication model is shown in Table 1. For the special case of $n = 2$, our scheme has lower message complexity and server computation costs than even the 2-party T-PAKE's of Brainard et al. [3] and Katz et al. [15]. However, in the private storage setting and threshold t set at 1, our scheme is beaten by those of [18].

2. PPSS DEFINITION

A Password-Protected Secret Sharing (PPSS) scheme is a protocol involving $n + 1$ parties, a user U, and n servers $\mathsf{P}_1, ..., \mathsf{P}_n$. A PPSS scheme for secret space S and dictionary D is a tuple $(\mathsf{Init}, \mathsf{User}, \mathsf{Server})$, where $\mathsf{Init}(p, s)$ is an initialization algorithm which on inputs a secret $s \in S$ and password $p \in D$ generates $\mathsf{st} = (\mathsf{st}_0, \mathsf{st}_1, ..., \mathsf{st}_n)$ where st_0 are public parameters and st_i is the private state of server P_i; $\mathsf{User}(\tilde{p}, \mathsf{st}_0)$ is an interactive algorithm followed by U on its password $\tilde{p}$ (presumably equal to p) and parameters st_0; and $\mathsf{Server}(\mathsf{st}_i)$ is an interactive algorithm followed by P_i on input st_i. The Server algorithm has no local output, while the User algorithm has a local output which is either some bitstring s' or a special rejection symbol $\perp$. We require a PPSS protocol to be complete in the sense that if $\mathsf{PPSS}(p, \mathsf{st})$ is a random variable defined as the local output of algorithm $\mathsf{User}(p, \mathsf{st}_0)$ after an interaction with oracles $\mathsf{Server}(\mathsf{st}_1)$, ..., $\mathsf{Server}(\mathsf{st}_n)$ then $\mathsf{PPSS}(p, \mathsf{Init}(p, s)) = s$ for any $(s, p) \in S \times D$. To model concurrent execution of several PPSS protocol instances we denote by $\mathsf{User}^\diamond(p, \mathsf{st}_0)$ an oracle which allows the caller to interact with any number of $\mathsf{User}(p, \mathsf{st}_0)$ instances. Importantly, the caller sees only protocol messages output by each User instance it interacts with, and not the local output of any of these instances, although this view is crucially amended in the *strong security* notion below. Similarly, for any set B we denote by $\mathsf{Server}^\diamond(\mathsf{st}_{\overline{\mathsf{B}}})$ an oracle which allows the caller to interact with any number of $\mathsf{Server}(\mathsf{st}_i)$ instances for any i in $\overline{\mathsf{B}} \triangleq \{1, ..., n\} \setminus \mathsf{B}$. We say that probabilistic algorithm $\mathcal{A}$ interacts with at most q_U user sessions if in any of its executions $\mathcal{A}$ initializes at most q_U instances of $\mathsf{User}(p, \mathsf{st}_0)$ algorithm when interacting with oracle $\mathsf{User}^\diamond(p, \mathsf{st}_0)$, and we say that $\mathcal{A}$ interacts with at most q_S server sessions if in any execution of $\mathcal{A}$ we have $\sum_{i \in \overline{\mathsf{B}}} q_i \leq q_S$ where q_i is the number of $\mathsf{Server}(st_i)$ instances $\mathcal{A}$ initializes when interacting with oracle $\mathsf{Server}^\diamond(\mathsf{st}_{\overline{\mathsf{B}}})$.

We define security of a PPSS scheme in terms of advantage in distinguishing between PPSS instances initialized with two different secrets, where the adversary sees the public parameters st_0, the private states $\mathsf{st}_\mathsf{B} \triangleq \{\mathsf{st}_i\}_{i \in \mathsf{B}}$ of corrupted servers $\{P_i\}_{i \in \mathsf{B}}$, and has concurrent oracle access to instances of the user and server algorithms executing on inputs defined by the initialization procedure. Note that this defines a PPSS scheme in the PKI model, because the user algorithm is assumed to execute only on the st_0 parameters generated by $\mathsf{Init}(p, s)$, and this st_0 could be certified under a trusted public key instead of being stored locally. We call an (t, n)-threshold PPSS scheme secure if this advantage is bounded by $\frac{1}{|D|}$, the probability of guessing the password, times $\lfloor \frac{q_S}{t - t' + 1} \rfloor$ where $t' \leq t$ is the number of servers an adversary corrupts, plus at most a negligible amount. The last factor corresponds to the probability of success of an on-line dictionary attack in a threshold setting: An adversary who learns the shares of $t' \leq t$ servers can test any password $\tilde{p}$ in D by executing $\mathsf{User}(\tilde{p}, st_0)$ and interacting with any subset of $t - t' + 1$ uncorrupted servers. To the best of our knowledge all previous works on T-PAKE's bound attackers' success by $\frac{q_S}{|D|}$, which is higher than the above bound, except if the adversary corrupts the maximum threshold of servers, $t' = t$. In particular, if each server locally bounds the number of sessions it performs with the same user to k, such definition bounds the number of passwords which a network attacker can test to $n * k$ passwords, instead of the optimal number of $\lfloor \frac{n * k}{t+1} \rfloor$ passwords.

Formally, we call a PPSS scheme on dictionary D and secret space S is $(n, t, T, q_U, q_S, \epsilon)$*-secure* if for any $s_0, s_1 \in S$, any set B s.t. $t' \triangleq |\mathsf{B}|$ satisfies $t' \leq t$, and any algorithm $\mathcal{A}$ with running time T, we have

$$|p_0 - p_1| \leq \left\lfloor \frac{q_S}{t - t' + 1} \right\rfloor * \frac{1}{|D|} + \epsilon$$

where p_b is the probability that $\mathcal{A}(s_0, s_1, \mathsf{st}_0, \mathsf{st}_\mathsf{B})$ outputs 1 on access to q_U sessions with oracle $\mathsf{User}^\diamond(p, \mathsf{st}_0)$ and q_S sessions with oracle $\mathsf{Server}^\diamond(\mathsf{st}_{\overline{\mathsf{B}}})$, for st output by $\mathsf{Init}(p, s_b)$ on p chosen at random in D, with probability taken over all random processes.

To make a PPSS scheme easier to use as a building block, e.g. in a construction of a T-PAKE protocol in Section 4, the above security definition needs to be strengthened by allowing the adversary to learn whether honest user sessions output some reconstructed secret or reject. Intuitively, whenever any application employs a PPSS scheme to reconstruct a secret, it uses this reconstructed secret in some higher-level protocol, e.g. in the case of a T-PAKE to authenticate a key exchange, thus allowing a network adversary to learn whether the PPSS subprotocol accepted or rejected, as in the latter case the protocol built on top of PPSS will visibly diverge from its usual course. Formally, a PPSS scheme on dictionary D and secret space S is $(n, t, T, q_U, q_S, \epsilon)$-*strongly secure* if it satisfies the $(n, t, T, q_U, q_S, \epsilon)$-security definition above with the user oracle $\mathsf{User}^\diamond$ modified so that for every $\mathsf{User}(p, \mathsf{st_O})$ instance the adversary learns a bit which indicates whether this instance accepts, i.e. outputs some $s' \neq \perp$, or rejects, i.e. outputs $\perp$.

A practical PPSS scheme should satisfy two further properties, namely *robustness* and *soundness*. Robustness requires that a user communicating with n servers recovers the shared secret as long as at least $t+1$ of these servers follow the protocol. Soundness requires that even n corrupt servers cannot cause a user using the prescribed public parameters $\mathsf{st_O}$ to recover a secret which is different from the one which was initially shared. We differentiate between *weak soundness*, where this is required only for a user entering the correct password, and *strong soundness*, where this is required for any password the user enters, including incorrect ones. Formally a PPSS scheme on dictionary D and secret space S is (T, ϵ)-*robust* if for any $(s, p) \in S \times D$, any B s.t. $n - |\mathsf{B}| \geq t+1$, and any algorithm $\mathcal{A}$ with running time T, the probability that $s' \neq s$ where st is output by $\mathsf{Init}(p, s)$ and s' is output by $\mathsf{User}(p, \mathsf{st_O})$ interacting with $\mathcal{A}(s, p, \mathsf{st_B})$ and $\mathsf{Server}^\diamond(\mathsf{st}_{\bar{\mathsf{B}}})$, is bounded by ϵ. To formally define soundness we say that a PPSS scheme on dictionary D and secret space S is (T, ϵ)-*sound* if for any $(s, p, \tilde{p}) \in S \times D \times D$ and any algorithm $\mathcal{A}$ with running time T, the probability that $s' \notin \{s, \perp\}$ where st is output by $\mathsf{Init}(p, s)$ and s' is output by $\mathsf{User}(\tilde{p}, \mathsf{st_O})$ interacting with $\mathcal{A}(s, p, \tilde{p}, \mathsf{st})$, is bounded by ϵ. We define *weak soundness* in the same way but restricting $\tilde{p}$ to $\tilde{p} = p$.

3. PPSS PROTOCOL SECURE UNDER DDH

We describe the protocol for password protected secret sharing. We start by introducing the basic idea of our scheme, which can use any threshold homomorphic encryption. We then explain how to reduce the round complexity of this basic protocol using special properties of ElGamal. The resulting protocol involves only three message flows between the user and each server (and one round of interaction in an on-line phase), each message involving constant number of group elements. For exposition's sake, we first show this protocol secure only against honest-but-curious players, assuming secure channels (PPSS_1 in Figure 2), and then proceed to explain how we can address active threats and achieve security against malicious adversaries (PPSS_2 in Figure 3).

Basic PPSS Protocol. Our protocol can use any homomorphic encryption with a threshold decryption protocol, but for the sake of subsequent modifications we describe it instantiated with ElGamal. Let g be a generator of group G of prime order q. Take dictionary $D = \mathbb{Z}_q$ and message space $S = G$. Note that any other dictionary can be hashed into $\mathbb{Z}_q$ using a collision-resistant hash, and as we discuss later message space G can be easily extended to a standard message space of fixed-length bitstrings. For $(p, s) \in \mathbb{Z}_q \times G$, procedure $\mathsf{Init}(p, s)$ picks an ElGamal key-pair $(x, y = g^x)$, secret-shares x among servers using a (t, n) secret sharing [23] (i.e. $\mathsf{st}_j = x_j = f(j)$ where f is a random t-degree polynomial over $\mathbb{Z}_q$ s.t. $f(0) = x$), and outputs public parameter $\mathsf{st_O}$ which consists of public key y, a "shifted" ElGamal encryption of password p, $(c_p, d_p) = (g^{r_p}, y^{r_p} g^p)$, and a textbook ElGamal encryption of secret s, $(c_s, d_s) = (g^{r_s}, y^{r_s} s)$, for random r_p, r_s in $\mathbb{Z}_q$. The PPSS protocol between the user U on input $\tilde{p}$ and the servers $\{\mathsf{P}_j\}_{j=1}^n$ on inputs st_j proceeds as follows:

1. U sends an encryption of $\tilde{p}$, $(c_{\tilde{p}}, d_{\tilde{p}}) = (g^{r_{\tilde{p}}}, y^{r_{\tilde{p}}} g^{\tilde{p}})$, to each Server_j. Note that for a legitimate user, $\tilde{p} = p$.
2. P_j's randomize $(c_\delta, d_\delta) = (c_p / c_{\tilde{p}}, , d_p / d_{\tilde{p}})$ by each P_j returning $(c_{\beta_j}, d_{\beta_j}) = ((c_\delta)^{t_j}, (d_\delta)^{t_j})$ for $t_j \xleftarrow{r} \mathbb{Z}_q$.
3. U sends $(c_\beta, d_\beta) = (\prod_{i=1}^n c_{\beta_i}, \prod_{1=1}^n d_{\beta_i})$ to each P_j. Note that (c_β, d_β) is an ElGamal encryption of g^β where $\beta = \sum_{i=1}^n \beta_i = \delta_p \cdot \sum_{i=1}^n t_i$ and $\delta_p = p - \tilde{p}$.
4. P_j's threshold-decrypt $(c_\alpha, d_\alpha) = (c_s \cdot c_\beta, d_s \cdot d_\beta)$ [6], i.e. each P_j returns $z_j = (c_\alpha)^{x_j}$ and U interpolates any $t+1$ of these z_j's to $z = (c_\alpha)^x$ and outputs $\alpha = d_\alpha \cdot (z)^{-1}$.

Note that $\alpha = s \cdot g^{\sum_i \beta_i} = s \cdot g^{(p - \tilde{p}) \sum_i t_i}$. Hence, $\alpha = s$ if $\tilde{p} = p$; but α is random in G if $\tilde{p} \neq p$ and $\sum_i t_i$ is random in $\mathbb{Z}_q$.

This basic PPSS protocol is secure in the honest-but-curious setting under the DDH assumption on G. Moreover we have to assume secure channels between U and each P_j because $\alpha = s$ can be decrypted from the values (c_β, d_β) and z_j exchanged in the last two messages of this protocol. However, in the presence of malicious parties, and without secure channels, a whole range of issues needs to be addressed: For example, since the protocol relies on the homomorphic property of ElGamal encryption, a malicious user can recover s by setting $(c_{\tilde{p}}, d_{\tilde{p}})$ as a randomization of (c_p, d_p), thus ensuring that $\tilde{p} = p$ without the knowledge of p. In another example, a single malicious server can cancel out all other servers' contributions $(c_{\beta_j}, d_{\beta_j})$ to (c_β, d_β) so that the sum $\sum_i t_i$ hits some adversarially chosen value t. (The malicious server sets its $(c_{\beta_j}, d_{\beta_j})$ as an encryption of g^t divided by the product of all other $(c_{\beta_j}, d_{\beta_j})$'s.) This way the "ciphertext randomization" step (2) above fails its purpose of providing a random mask for s in the case $\tilde{p} \neq p$, and the value $\alpha = s \cdot g^{t(\tilde{p} - p)}$ which the user outputs allows the adversary to recover s in an off-line dictionary attack.

On-Line Non-Interactive PPSS Protocol. Before addressing the active threats, we observe that relying on specific properties of ElGamal Encryption, we can shave off one communication round in the above protocol, by combining the distributed ciphertext randomization step ($i.e.$ step 2) and the threshold decryption step ($i.e.$ step 4), given some precomputation from the Servers. The resulting protocol (Figure 2 below) involves only three communication flows, with the *on-line* phase, i.e. between User contributing its password $\tilde{p}$ and recovering the secret s, taking only two communication flows (hence the term *non-interactive on-line*).

Note that values z and d_β which the user needs to decrypt s in the basic PPSS protocol above are formed as $z = (c_\alpha)^x = (c_s \cdot c_\beta)^x = (g^{r_s + \delta_r \sum_i t_i})^x = y^{r_s} y^{\delta_r \sum_i t_i}$, where $\delta_r \triangleq r_p - r_{\tilde{p}}$, and $d_\beta = \prod_i d_{\beta_i} = y^{\delta_r \sum_i t_i} g^{\delta_p \sum_i t_i}$, where $\delta_p \triangleq p - \tilde{p}$. The decryption works because if $\delta_p = 0$ then $d_\beta = y^{\delta_r \sum_i t_i}$ and $s = d_s \cdot d_\beta \cdot (z)^{-1}$. At first it would seem that the randomization process which creates (c_β, d_β) in steps (2-3) must precede the threshold-decryption step (4), where z is distributively computed as $(c_\alpha)^x = (c_s \cdot c_\beta)^x$. To see how to combine these two steps, first observe that if the protocol is executed not by all n servers but by a subset V of $t+1$ servers, in particular if $(c_\beta, d_\beta) = (\prod_{i \in V} c_{\beta_i}, \prod_{i \in V} d_{\beta_i})$, and if each P_j in V computes

$$z_j = d_{\beta_j} \cdot (c_s \cdot c_\beta)^{-\lambda_j x_j} \quad (1)$$

where λ_j is a coefficient s.t. $x = \sum_{j \in V} \lambda_j x_j$, then U can still recover s as $s = d_s \cdot \prod_{j \in V} z_j = d_s \cdot d_\beta \cdot (c_s \cdot c_\beta)^{-x}$. Note that P_j can

$\underline{\mathsf{Init}(p,s)}$ (on public parameters g, q, n, t)

$x \xleftarrow{r} \mathbb{Z}_q, y \leftarrow g^x, \{x_i\}_{i=1}^n \xleftarrow{(n,t)} \mathsf{SS}(x), h \xleftarrow{r} G, (r_p, r_s) \xleftarrow{r} (\mathbb{Z}_q)^2, (c_p, d_p) \leftarrow (g^{r_p}, y^{r_p} h^p), (c_s, d_s) \leftarrow (g^{r_s}, y^{r_s} s)$

$\mathsf{st}_0 \leftarrow (g, y, h, (c_p, d_p), (c_s, d_s)), \{\mathsf{st}_i \leftarrow x_i\}_{i=1}^n$

$\underline{\mathsf{User}(\mathsf{st}_0, \tilde{p}) \rightleftharpoons (\mathsf{Server}_1(\mathsf{st}_0, \mathsf{st}_1), \cdots, \mathsf{Server}_n(\mathsf{st}_0, \mathsf{st}_n))}$

S1 (Server_j) : Pick $t_j \xleftarrow{r} \mathbb{Z}_q$. Compute $(a_j, b_j) \leftarrow (g^{t_j}, (c_p)^{t_j})$. Send (a_j, b_j) to User.

U1 (User) : Pick a set V of $t+1$ servers. Pick $r_{\tilde{p}} \xleftarrow{r} \mathbb{Z}_q$. Compute $\{e_j \leftarrow (a_j)^{r_{\tilde{p}}}\}_{j \in V}$ and $(c_{\tilde{p}}, d_{\tilde{p}}) \leftarrow (g^{r_{\tilde{p}}}, y^{r_{\tilde{p}}} h^{\tilde{p}})$. Compute $c_\beta \leftarrow \prod_{j \in V} (b_j / e_j)$. For all $j \in V$, send $(V, c_\beta, (c_{\tilde{p}}, d_{\tilde{p}}))$ to Server_j.

S2 (Server_j) : Compute $\lambda_j \leftarrow \frac{\prod_{i \in V/\{j\}}(-i)}{\prod_{i \in V/\{j\}}(j-i)} \bmod q$, $w_j \leftarrow (c_s \cdot c_\beta)^{\lambda_j \cdot x_j}$, $d_{\beta,j} \leftarrow (d_p / d_{\tilde{p}})^{t_j}$, and $z_j \leftarrow d_{\beta,j} / w_j$. Send z_j to User.

U2 (User) : Output $s \leftarrow d_s \cdot \prod_{j \in V} z_j$.

Figure 2: PPSS_1: Password-Protected Secret-Sharing secure against Honest-but-Curious Adversaries assuming Secure Channels

compute $d_{\beta_j} = (d_p / d_{\tilde{p}})^{t_j}$ using $d_{\tilde{p}}$ sent produced by U, but since $c_\beta = g^{\delta_r \sum_{j \in V} t_j}$ involves randomization factors $\{t_j\}_{j \in V}$ from all servers in V, computing c_β seems to require the three communication rounds of steps (1-3) above. However, it can be done in two rounds instead if each P_j first sends to U a pair of "randomization commitment" values, $(a_j, b_j) = (g^{t_j}, (c_p)^{t_j}) = (g^{t_j}, g^{r_p t_j})$, which allows U to return to all P_j's the c_β value computed as:

$$c_\beta = \prod_{j \in V} (b_j \cdot (a_j)^{-r_{\tilde{p}}}) \qquad (2)$$

This re-organization leads us to the PPSS_1 protocol shown in Figure 2: Each P_j computes its $(g^{t_j}, (c_p)^{t_j})$ randomization commitment in step **S1**. In step **U1** U chooses a set V of $t+1$ servers and sends to each server in V the c_β value computed as in equation 2 together with an encryption of $\tilde{p}$ (technically only sending the $d_{\tilde{p}}$ part of this ciphertext is necessary). In step **S2** each server computes its response z_j as in equation 1, and U in step **U2** decrypts s as $s = d_s \cdot \prod_{j \in V} z_j$. The PPSS_1 protocol in Figure 2 diverges in just one aspect from the above sketch: Namely, the base used in the shifted ElGamal encryption of the password is changed from g to a different random base h. This change is crucial to prevent an off-line dictionary attack that otherwise would be possible since in PPSS_1, unlike the basic PPSS protocol above, the user learns $a = \prod a_i = g^{\sum_i t_i}$. This value, together with user's output $\alpha = s \cdot g^{(p-\tilde{p}) \sum_i t_i}$ computed for an arbitrary $\tilde{p}$, allows an off-line dictionary attack, where each candidate password p' can be tested by checking if $s' = \alpha \cdot (a)^{\tilde{p}-p'}$ looks like a valid plaintext. On the other hand, if the shifted ElGamal encryption encrypts h^p instead of g^p then $\alpha = s \cdot h^{(p-\tilde{p}) \sum_i t_i}$ is a one-time pad encryption of s because under the DDH assumption $h^{\sum_i t_i}$ is a pseudorandom value, and hence so is $h^{\delta_p \sum_i t_i}$ for any $\delta_p \triangleq (p - \tilde{p})$, even given $a_i = g^{\sum_i t_i}$, if $\sum_i t_i$ is random in $\mathbb{Z}_q$.

Security against Malicious Adversaries. Somewhat surprisingly, combining the randomization step with threshold decryption step helps achieve security against malicious adversaries -albeit with additional modifications discussed below. The reason why this collapse of two computation steps makes security argument (and the necessary modifications to the protocol) easier, is that now the contribution of each P_j to threshold-decryption of $\alpha = s \cdot h^{\delta_p \sum_i t_i}$, technically value $w_j = (c_\alpha)^{\lambda_j x_j} = (c_s \cdot c_\beta)^{\lambda_j x_j}$ computed in step **S2**, is output "masked" with P_j's contribution to the "randomization" of the encryption $(c_p / c_{\tilde{p}}, d_p / d_{\tilde{p}})$ of $\delta_p = p - \tilde{p}$, i.e. with the value $d_{\beta,j} = (d_p / d_{\tilde{p}})^{t_j} = y^{\delta_r t_j} h^{\delta_p t_j}$. Intuitively, if $\delta_p \neq 0$, then variable $h^{\delta_p t_j}$ in $d_{\beta,j}$ acts like a pseudorandom mask (assuming DDH) even given values $(a_j, b_j) = (g^{t_j}, g^{r_p t_j})$. This allows us to argue that servers' responses z_j are indistinguishable from random group elements values on sessions where $\delta_p \neq 0$, and thus we are left only with the information released in sessions where $\tilde{p} = p$, i.e. where the adversary guesses the correct password.

It might seem that there is nothing to argue for sessions on which $\tilde{p} = p$, but this is not the case: In a standard password-authenticated protocol (PAKE), the attackers indeed win if they guess the password on any session. However, we have n servers, and an adversary who corrupts $t' \leq t$ of them needs to use the correct password on $t - t' + 1$ sessions with distinct uncorrupted servers in order to break the scheme. Thus the messages output by the first $t - t'$ sessions where adversary uses the correct password must still look indistinguishable from sessions with wrong passwords. Our scheme achieves this property for the following reasons. Firstly we are helped by the properties of Shamir secret-sharing of the decryption key x: If the only sessions on which the servers threshold decryption shares $w_j = (c_\alpha)^{\lambda_j x_j}$ are not masked with pseudorandom values are those where $\tilde{p} = p$ then, by the properties of Shamir secret sharing, the first $t - t'$ such shares produced by the uncorrupted servers, even given the t' shares x_j of corrupted servers, are still statistically independent of the decryption key x. Consequently, as long as $\tilde{p} = p$ on sessions with no more than $t - t'$ uncorrupted servers, adversary's interaction with the scheme effectively never uses the real decryption key x. Therefore in particular, until that point we can look at tuple (g, y, g^{t_j}, y^{t_j}) for each uncorrupted P_j as a DDH tuple, in which case even if $\delta_p = 0$, the value $d_{\beta,j} = y^{\delta_r t_j} h^{\delta_p t_j} = y^{\delta_r t_j} = y^{(r_p - r_{\tilde{p}}) t_j}$ still acts like a pseudorandom one-time pad masking the partial decryption w_j, even given $(a_j, b_j) = (g^{t_j}, g^{r_p t_j})$, provided that $r_{\tilde{p}} \neq r_p$ (which is easy to prevent, see below). Here we list the remaining differences between the resulting protocol, PPSS_2 in Figure 3, and PPSS_1 in Figure 2:

(1) A syntactic change is that in Figure 3 we use Server_j to denote the j-th *session* of the Server algorithm, i.e. $j \in \{1, ..., q_S\}$, and we use ID_j to denote the ID of the Server who executes this session, i.e. $ID_j \in \{1, ..., n\}$. This notation makes it clearer how the protocol executes in the concurrent setting, where each server runs many sessions of the Server algorithm.

(2) Another minor change is that the user pre-computes the λ_j coefficient for each server session in V. This is to keep the size of user's message constant. (The user could also compute $Q_j = (c_s \cdot c_\beta)^{\lambda_j}$ in step **S1** and send it instead of (λ_j, c_β), then Server_j would compute $w_j \leftarrow (Q_j)^{x_{ID_j}}$ and both parties would use Q_j in the proof π_{3j}. This change would have no effect on security and it would shift one exponentiation from the server to the user.)

(3) In PPSS_1 the server's responses z_i are sent back in cleartext,

$\underline{\mathsf{Init}(p,s)}$ (on public parameters g, q, n, t)

$x \xleftarrow{r} \mathbb{Z}_q$, $y \leftarrow g^x$, $\{x_i\}_{i=1}^n \xleftarrow{(n,t)} \mathsf{SS}(x)$, $(h, \hat{g}, \hat{h}, \hat{y}, \bar{g}) \xleftarrow{r} (G)^4$, $(r_p, r_s) \xleftarrow{r} (\mathbb{Z}_q)^2$, $(c_p, d_p) \leftarrow (g^{r_p}, y^{r_p} h^p)$, $(c_s, d_s) \leftarrow (g^{r_s}, y^{r_s} s)$
$\{r_i \leftarrow \mathbb{Z}_q; y_i \leftarrow g^{x_i} h^{r_i}\}_{i=1}^n$, $\mathsf{st}_0 \leftarrow (g, h, y, \{y_i\}_{i=1}^n, \hat{g}, \hat{h}, \hat{y}, \bar{g}, (c_p, d_p), (c_s, d_s))$, $\{\mathsf{st}_i \leftarrow (x_i, r_i)\}_{i=1}^n$

$\underline{\mathsf{User}(\mathsf{st}_0, \tilde{p}) \rightleftharpoons \{\mathsf{Server}_j(\mathsf{st}_0, \mathsf{st}_{ID_j})\}_{j=1}^n}$ (ID_j denotes Server ID of j-th Server session, $ID_j \in \{1, ..., n\}$.)

S1 (Server_j) : Pick $t_j \xleftarrow{r} \mathbb{Z}_q$. Compute $(a_j, b_j, \bar{a}_j) \leftarrow (g^{t_j}, (c_p)^{t_j}, (\bar{g})^{t_j})$, and $\pi_{1j} \leftarrow \mathcal{P}[\mathcal{L}_{S1}^{\mathsf{st}_0}]((a_j, b_j, \bar{a}_j), t_j)$.
Send $(ID_j, a_j, b_j, \bar{a}_j, \pi_{1j})$ to User.

U1 (User) : Pick set V of $t+1$ sessions $\{\mathsf{Server}_j\}_{j \in V}$ run by distinct servers s.t. $\{\mathcal{V}[\mathcal{L}_S^{\mathsf{st}_0}]((a_j, b_j, \bar{a}_j), \pi_{1j}) = 1\}_{j \in V}$.
Pick $r_{\tilde{p}} \xleftarrow{r} \mathbb{Z}_q$.

Compute: $\{e_j \leftarrow (a_j)^{r_{\tilde{p}}}\}_{j \in V}$, $c_\beta \leftarrow \prod_{j \in V}(b_j/e_j)$, $(c_{\tilde{p}}, d_{\tilde{p}}, \hat{c}_{\tilde{p}}, \hat{d}_{\tilde{p}}) \leftarrow (g^{r_{\tilde{p}}}, y^{r_{\tilde{p}}} h^{\tilde{p}}, (\hat{g})^{r_{\tilde{p}}}, (\hat{y})^{r_{\tilde{p}}} (\hat{h})^{\tilde{p}})$
$\{\lambda_j \leftarrow \frac{\prod_{i \in V/\{j\}}(-ID_i)}{\prod_{i \in V/\{j\}}(ID_j - ID_i)} \bmod q$, $\pi_{2j} \leftarrow \mathcal{P}[\mathcal{L}_U^{\mathsf{st}_0}]((a_j, e_j, c_{\tilde{p}}, d_{\tilde{p}}, \hat{c}_{\tilde{p}}, \hat{d}_{\tilde{p}}), (r_{\tilde{p}}, \tilde{p}))\}_{j \in V}$

Send $(\lambda_j, c_\beta, e_j, (c_{\tilde{p}}, d_{\tilde{p}}), (\hat{c}_{\tilde{p}}, \hat{d}_{\tilde{p}}), \pi_{2j})$ to Server_j.

S2 (Server_j) : Stop if $\mathcal{V}[\mathcal{L}_U^{\mathsf{st}_0}]((a_j, e_j, c_{\tilde{p}}, d_{\tilde{p}}, \hat{c}_{\tilde{p}}, \hat{d}_{\tilde{p}}), \pi_{2j}) = 0$. Pick $r_{z_j} \leftarrow \mathbb{Z}_q$.

Compute: $w_j \leftarrow (c_s \cdot c_\beta)^{\lambda_j \cdot x_{ID_j}}$, $d_{\beta,j} \leftarrow (d_p/d_{\tilde{p}})^{t_j}$, $z_j \leftarrow d_{\beta,j}/w_j$, $(c_{z_j}, d_{z_j}) \leftarrow (g^{r_{z_j}}, (c_{\tilde{p}})^{r_{z_j}} \cdot z_j)$
$\pi_{3j} \leftarrow \mathcal{P}[\mathcal{L}_{S2}^{\mathsf{st}_0, ID_j}]((c_{z_j}, d_{z_j}, c_{\tilde{p}}, a_j, d_p/d_{\tilde{p}}, (c_s \cdot c_\beta)^{\lambda_j}), (r_{z_j}, t_j, x_{ID_j}, r_{ID_j}))$

Send $((c_{z_j}, d_{z_j}), \pi_{3j})$ to User.

U2 (User) : Stop if $\exists_{j \in V}$, s.t. $\mathcal{V}[\mathcal{L}_{S2}^{\mathsf{st}_0, ID_j}]((c_{z_j}, d_{z_j}, c_{\tilde{p}}, a_j, d_p/d_{\tilde{p}}, (c_s \cdot c_\beta)^{\lambda_j}), \pi_{3j}) = 0$.
Output $s \leftarrow d_s \cdot (\prod_{j \in V} d_{z_j})/(\prod_{j \in V} c_{z_j})^{r_{\tilde{p}}}$.

Figure 3: PPSS_2: Password-Protected Secret-Sharing Protocol Secure against Malicious Adversaries

hence the protocol is insecure even with a passive eavesdropper on the channels between the user and the servers. To counter such eavesdropping attack, each server encrypts its response z_j in step **S2** using ElGamal encryption with user's value $c_{\tilde{p}} = g^{r_{\tilde{p}}}$ sent in step **U1** serving as an ElGamal public key, and the user will use $r_{\tilde{p}}$ to decrypt these ciphertexts in step **U2**. Even though $c_{\tilde{p}}$ is used as first part of user's ElGamal ciphertext $(c_{\tilde{p}}, d_{\tilde{p}})$ encrypting $\tilde{p}$, it turns out that we can re-use it for encrypting information from servers to the user. As for preventing more sophisticated man-in-the-middle attacks, both the user's and the servers' messages are accompanied by simulation-sound zero-knowledge proofs of well-formedness, and one consequence of these proofs is that they make it difficult for the man-in-the-middle adversary to re-use the messages from the honest parties.

(4) To enable efficient simulation of the honest parties in the protocol (and thus show that an attacker learns no useful information in an interaction with these parties), we could amend each protocol message with a proof of knowledge of the randomness used to create it (e.g. t_j in server's message **S1** or $r_{\tilde{p}}$ in user's message **U1**), but this would require concurrently extractable zero-knowledge proofs of knowledge, and even the most efficient such proofs, e.g. [10], would make the protocol significantly more expensive. However, the simulator turns out to need to compute only values which include adversarial players' randomness in the exponent, i.e. values of the form z^w where w is the randomness of the adversarially controlled party, and z is some group element known to the simulator. Therefore we can avoid the need for proofs of knowledge with a technique used before e.g. by Gennaro and Shoup [25]: If the simulator needs a value of the form z^w in computing a (simulated) response to some message, we extend that message by a value of the form $(g')^w$ where g' is an additional random group element in the parameter string, and include a zero-knowledge (and simulation-sound) proof that the message is formed using consistent randomness w. The simulator will then compute z^w by embedding z into g'. Such proofs, as opposed to concurrent proofs of knowledge, are inexpensive, and they can be made non-interactive in the Random Oracle Model. This is why we extend server's message **S1** with value $\bar{a}_j = (\bar{g})^{t_j}$, and user's message **U1** with value $\hat{c}_{\tilde{p}} = (\hat{g})^{r_{\tilde{p}}}$. (This is also why the secondary encryption of $\tilde{p}$ we discuss in the next item uses a new base $\hat{h}$ instead of h.)

(5) It seems difficult to simulate this protocol efficiently unless the simulator can test whether the user's ciphertext encrypts the correct password, e.g. because the simulator can replace the servers' responses by random values, as argued above, only if the user encrypts an incorrect password. However, since the adversary's view includes an encryption of the correct password, the DDH reduction which shows that this encryption is semantically secure cannot know the corresponding decryption key, and thus cannot perform such test. We overcome this quandary using the twin encryption paradigm used in the design of CCA-secure encryption or CMA-secure signatures starting with [21, 13]. Namely, we extend the user's message by a "secondary" encryption of $\tilde{p}$, under an independent ElGamal public key $\hat{y}$. For technical reasons it turns out that this encryption can re-use the same randomness $r_{\tilde{p}}$ used in the "primary" ciphertext $(c_{\tilde{p}}, d_{\tilde{p}})$, and so it suffices to extend the **U1** message by just one value $\hat{d}_{\tilde{p}} = (\hat{y})^{r_{\tilde{p}}} (\hat{h})^{\tilde{p}}$. The simulator can now test whether $(c_{\tilde{p}}, d_{\tilde{p}})$ encrypts $\tilde{p} = p$ by decrypting $(\hat{c}_{\tilde{p}}, \hat{d}_{\tilde{p}})$ – since by the soundness of the user's proof these two ciphertexts encrypt the same plaintext – using a trapdoor key $\hat{x} = DL(\hat{g}, \hat{y})$ which is independent of $x = DL(g, y)$. In this way the simulator can test for password correctness even as it embeds a DDH challenge into the primary key y and the public ciphertexts (c_p, d_p) and (c_s, d_s).

(6) For verifiability of Server_j's computation of the (encrypted) response z_j in step **S2**, we amend the public parameters with the set of Pedersen commitments $\{y_i = g^{x_i} h^{r_i}\}_{i=1}^n$ to the server's shares $\{x_i\}_{i=1}^n$ of the decryption key. Note that the Server_j sessions where the adversary guesses the correct password effectively implement an exponentiation oracle $z_z = F_j(m) = m^{x_{ID_j}}$, e.g. setting $c_\beta = m^{1/\lambda_j}/c_s$. Therefore the adversary who happens

to guess the password can adaptively choose t servers to query in this way (assume for simplicity that no servers are corrupted). This presents a problem which arises in adaptively secure threshold cryptosystems, e.g. [5]. Namely, if the simulator had to commit itself to n uncorrupted shares using a simpler perfectly binding commitment scheme, $y_i = g^{x_i}$, then it could consistently respond to such queries only by guessing at the beginning of the interaction the set of t servers which the adversary later chooses to query in this way. (Note that the simulator has to answer such queries correctly, as the adversary could test if $F_j(g^a) = (y_{ID_j})^a$.) This is why we use Pedersen commitments instead.

Non-Interactive Simulation-Sound Zero-Knowledge Proofs. To assure that protocol messages are well-formed we use simulation-sound non-interactive zero-knowledge (SS-NIZK) proofs [22], a slightly weaker notion than non-malleable NIZK's. Our protocols could also use interactive version of such proofs, which can be realized with comparable efficiency without Random Oracles – see e.g. [12], but using non-interactive proofs enables best round complexity and keeps a protocol write-up simple. Since these are standard notions, we recall only briefly that a NIZK proof system for language $\mathcal{L}$ is a triple of algorithms, prover $\mathcal{P}$ which produces a proof π on input a statement instance x and witness w, verifier $\mathcal{V}$ which accepts or rejects on input (x, π), and a simulator $\mathcal{S}$ which outputs a (simulated) proof on just the input x, using some trapdoors embedded in public parameters (or intercepting honest players' interaction with a hash function in ROM). We will use an exact security version of the SS-NIZK notion, calling such proof system $(T_S, q_P, \epsilon_{ZK}, \epsilon_{SS})$ *simulation-sound zero-knowledge* (SSZK) if there is a simulator algorithm $\mathcal{S}$ running in time T_S which answers up to q_P prover queries with simulated proofs on adaptively chosen statements of adversary's choice (which can include false statements) s.t. (1) the statistical difference between the view of an interaction with $\mathcal{S}$ and an interaction with the real prover is at most ϵ_{ZK}, and (2) the probability that any adversary interacting with $\mathcal{S}$ outputs a correct proof on a new false statement, i.e. a different from those for which it receives a simulated proof from $\mathcal{S}$, is at most ϵ_{SS}. We need such proofs for three languages corresponding to the three protocol messages, all parameterized by public parameters $\mathsf{st}_0 = (g, h, y, \{y_i\}_{i=1}^n, \hat{g}, \hat{h}, \hat{y}, \bar{g}, (c_p, d_p), (c_s, d_s))$:

$$\mathcal{L}_{S1}^{\mathsf{st}_0} = \{(a, b, \bar{a}) \in (G)^3 \mid \exists\, t \in \mathbb{Z}_q \text{ s.t. } (a, b, \bar{a}) = (g^t, (c_p)^t, (\bar{g})^t)\}$$

$$\mathcal{L}_{U}^{\mathsf{st}_0} = \{(a, e, c_{\tilde{p}}, d_{\tilde{p}}, \hat{c}_{\tilde{p}}, \hat{d}_{\tilde{p}}) \in (G)^6 \mid \exists\, (r_{\tilde{p}}, \tilde{p}) \in (\mathbb{Z}_q)^2 \text{ s.t. } (e, c_{\tilde{p}}, d_{\tilde{p}}, \hat{c}_{\tilde{p}}, \hat{d}_{\tilde{p}}) = (a^{r_{\tilde{p}}}, g^{r_{\tilde{p}}}, y^{r_{\tilde{p}}} h^{\tilde{p}}, (\hat{g})^{r_{\tilde{p}}}, (\hat{y})^{r_{\tilde{p}}} (\hat{h})^{\tilde{p}})\}$$

$$\mathcal{L}_{S2}^{\mathsf{st}_0, i} = \{(c_z, d_z, c_{\tilde{p}}, a, \Delta, P) \in (G)^6 \mid \exists\, (r_z, t, x, r) \in (\mathbb{Z}_q)^3 \text{ s.t. } (y_i, a, c_z, d_z) = (g^x h^r, g^t, g^{r_z}, (c_{\tilde{p}})^{r_z} \Delta^t P^{-x})\}$$

These languages involve equality relations on representations of some group elements in bases defined by other group elements. Well-known simulation-sound NIZKs for such relations in ROM are generalizations of Schnorr's proof of discrete logarithm knowledge and Chaum's proof of discrete logarithm equality, using the Fiat-Shamir heuristic, see e.g. [4]. The prover and the verifier in these proofs perform as many (multi)-exponentiations as are used to define the corresponding language, e.g. three for $\mathcal{L}_{S1}^{\mathsf{st}_0}$, five for $\mathcal{L}_{U}^{\mathsf{st}_0}$, and four for $\mathcal{L}_{S2}^{\mathsf{st}_0, i}$. (The verifier's computation can be reduced further using the techniques of batch verification of discrete-log based signatures, e.g. [2].) These proof systems achieve simulation sound zero knowledge with error bounds $\epsilon_{ZK} = (q_P \cdot q_H)/q$ and $\epsilon_{SS} = q_H/q$, where q_H is the upper bound on adversary's hash function queries, with the simulators whose running time is the same as that of the corresponding provers.

Efficiency, Standard Message Spaces, Soundness, Robustness. *Efficiency:* For efficiency estimates we assume that the SS-NIZK proofs are implemented in ROM, with proof verification implemented using multi-exponentiation and randomization of each verification equation, as in signature batch-verification of [2]. (This increases the soundness errors of these proofs by negligible amounts.) We count multi-exponentiations involving up to 5 bases as single "multiexp" operations, e.g. we estimate the verification costs of proofs $\pi_{1j}, \pi_{2j}, \pi_{3j}$ as 2, 4, and 3 multiexp's, respectively. To reduce user's costs we also arrange the $t+1$ proofs π_{2j} into a single proof showing consistency of $(c_{\tilde{p}}, d_{\tilde{p}}, \hat{c}_{\tilde{p}}, \hat{d}_{\tilde{p}})$ ciphertexts and $t+1$ proofs of consistency of each (a_j, e_j) pair with $c_{\tilde{p}}$. Under these assumptions the protocol costs $8t+17$ multiexp's for the user and 16 for each server. Using precomputation we can reduce the on-line cost to $7t+8$ multiexp's for the user and 6 for each server.

Message Space: Protocol PPSS_2 works on a non-standard message space, i.e. s must be an element of group G, but this can be easily changed to standard message spaces: Let l be a keylength of semantically secure symmetric encryption, and let G be a DDH group of order q where $|q| = 3l$. The public parameters string st_0 is amended by a random key k of a universal hash function H_k mapping elements of G onto l-bit bitstrings s.t. $H_k(x)$ is statistically indistinguishable from random 160-bit string if x is random in G. A modified PPSS protocol on password p and secret m, which is now any bitstring, runs the PPSS_2 protocol of Figure 3 on a random element s in G, and attaches to the public parameters st_0 the hash key k and a symmetric encryption of m under key $H_k(s)$. In the recovery protocol the user hashes the recovered value s to decrypt the shared secret m. Note that we can encrypt directly under $H(s)$ with a subgroup of size $|q| = \max(l, 160)$ assuming either a "Hashed Diffie-Hellman" assumption [1] or just DDH but modeling H as a random oracle.

Soundness: The PPSS protocol of Figure 3 satisfies only weak soundness, i.e. even malicious servers cannot make the user who runs on the correct password recover any other secret except of that which was initially shared. This follows from soundness of the SS-NIZK proof systems used in servers' messages, since these proofs effectively force the servers to perform the prescribed protocol. One easy way to extend this to strong soundness is to include a public key *pk* of an existentially unforgeable signature scheme in st_0, use the corresponding signature key to sign secret s, and run the PPSS algorithm as modified above on a concatenation of s with this signature. The protocol then proceeds as above except that at the end the user parses the recovered secret as $s|\sigma$ and outputs s only if σ is a valid signature on s under the key *pk* in st_0.

Robustness: Note that the PPSS protocol of Figure 3 does not satisfy robustness, because the user outputs $\perp$ if some server sessions in set V fail to send back correct responses in step **S2**. However, robustness can be achieved by modifying the PPSS_2 protocol as follows: If some sessions in V fail in step **S2**, the user marks the servers executing them as "dishonest" and restarts the protocol using a fresh set of $t+1$ server sessions, executed by servers which have not been marked. In the presence of $r \leq n - (t+1)$ active faults, this can take up to r rounds of interaction before all server sessions the user chooses are with non-faulty servers, which guarantees recovery of s. In practice such active attacks should be extremely rare because the attack reveals the servers corrupted by the adversary, in which case the user should eliminate, or clean-up, the attacked server(s) and re-initialize the protocol. Hence the adversary would achieve only a momentary slowdown of the secret-reconstruction protocol at a price of expulsion from the servers it has managed to corrupt. Random network errors are of greater concern, but in practice the user should ping each server before including its session in set V in step **U1**. Note that the user could compute its **U1** messages for n instead of $t+1$ distinct servers and only then settle on the set V, and the server's response **S2** involves only three multi-exponentiations computed on-line, namely d_{z_j}, verification of π_{2j}, and the fourth element of π_{3j}, which involves a flexible base. Thus at the price of increasing **U1**'s cost by a factor of $\frac{n}{t+1}$ we can reduce the computational cost contributing to the delay between the user's ping of the servers in step **U1** and receiving their responses, to three on-line multiexp's needed in step **S2**.

THEOREM 1. *Let G be a group of prime order q where the DDH problem is $(T_{ddh}, \epsilon_{ddh})$-hard, let $t_{\exp}$ be the time of full (multi)-exponentiation in G, let $\Pi[\mathcal{L}_U^{\mathsf{st}_0}]$, $\Pi[\mathcal{L}_{S1}^{\mathsf{st}_0}]$, and $\Pi[\mathcal{L}_{S2}^{\mathsf{st}_0,i}]$ be $(T_S, q_P, \epsilon_{ZK}, \epsilon_{SS})$-SSZK proof systems. Protocol* PPSS_2 *is a $(n, t, T, q_U, q_S, \epsilon)$ strongly secure* PPSS *scheme on message space G and dictionary $D \subseteq \mathbb{Z}_q$, as long as $\max(q_U, n \cdot q_S) \leq q_P$ and*

$$T \leq T_{ddh} - 3T_S - (10 + n + (8t+12)q_U + 10nq_S) \cdot t_e$$
$$\epsilon \leq 6\epsilon_{ZK} + (5q_U + 3nq_S + 4)(\epsilon_{ddh} + \epsilon_{SS})$$

PROOF. Let $\mathcal{A}$ be an algorithm followed by an adversary attacking the PPSS_2 scheme, running in time T, accessing at most q_U user and q_S server sessions, and corrupting servers $\{\mathsf{P}_i\}_{i \in \mathsf{B}}$ for some set B s.t. $|\mathsf{B}| = t' \leq t$. Figure 4 describes a series of games, $\mathsf{G}_0, \ldots, \mathsf{G}_8$, all initialized on secret s, where G_0 models the interaction of $\mathcal{A}$ with the PPSS_2 scheme, with slight modifications explained below, while games $\mathsf{G}_1, \ldots, \mathsf{G}_8$ are modifications of G_0 used in the security argument below. We first explain how the game G_0 models the interaction of $\mathcal{A}$ with the PPSS_2 scheme. The $\mathsf{Init}^\diamond$ procedure treats threshold (t, n) and the set of corrupted players B as parameters. Note that adversary $\mathcal{A}$ can engage in at most q_S sessions but it is up to $\mathcal{A}$ to decide which servers will be involved in these sessions. We handle this in the security game by creating q_S distinct sessions for each server, thus $n \cdot q_S$ total sessions, even though a q_S-limited adversary will utilize only q_S of them. We denote the identity of the server executing the j-th session, where $j = 1, .., n \cdot q_S$, as ID_j, which can be set w.l.o.g. as $ID_j = (j \bmod n) + 1$. Procedure $\mathsf{Init}^\diamond$ on input s picks $p \xleftarrow{r} D$ and follows the real initialization procedure $\mathsf{Init}(p, s)$ in generating the vector of initial states $\mathbf{st}$, including the parameters st_0 and the states st_i for each server P_i. $\mathsf{Init}^\diamond$ also executes the first step **S1** for all server sessions, and hands off to $\mathcal{A}$ the parameters st_0, the shares of corrupted servers $\mathsf{st}_B = \{x_i\}_{i \in B}$, and the first message on all nq_S sessions $\{\mathsf{Server}_j\}_{j=1}^{nq_S}$. Then $\mathcal{A}$ can make q_U queries to the $\mathsf{User}^\diamond$ oracle, which models execution of step **U1** of procedure $\mathsf{User}(\mathsf{st}_0, p)$, and q_S queries to the execution of step **S2** of the j-th sesssion of the Server procedure. Note that the inputs $\mathcal{A}$ provides to these oracles must syntactically conform to, respectively, a set of **S1** messages from some $t+1$ servers for the $\mathsf{User}^\diamond$ oracle, and user **U1** message in the case of the $\mathsf{Server}_j^\diamond$ oracle, but the adversary can choose these values at wish, in particular they do not have to equal to the corresponding variables produced by the oracles simulating the honest players.

Proof Roadmap. We will use the following notation: By $\mathsf{F}_{i,s}$ we denote event F defined in Figure 4 happening in the interaction between $\mathcal{A}$ and game G_i initialized on secret s, writing F_i if s is not even present in that game. By $p_i(s)$ we denote $\Pr[1 \leftarrow (\mathcal{A} \rightleftharpoons \mathsf{G}_i(s))]$. Since G_0 differs from the real interaction, we denote the corresponding probability in the real interaction as $\bar{p}_0(s)$. The intuition for the security proof is that the event F roughly corresponds to an adversary sending an encryption of the correct password on at least $t - t' + 1$ sessions run by distinct servers, in which case $\mathcal{A}$ could indeed learn s. The goal of the security argument is to show that for q_S, q_U, T satisfying the bounds in the theorem claim, and any s, s', it holds that

$$|\bar{p}_0(s) - \bar{p}_0(s')| \leq \lfloor \frac{q_S}{t - t' + 1} \rfloor * \frac{1}{|D|} + \epsilon' \quad (3)$$

where $\epsilon' = 6\epsilon_{ZK} + (5q_U + 3nq_S + 4)(\epsilon_{ddh} + \epsilon_{SS})$ This would follow if we showed that $|\bar{p}_0(s_1) - \bar{p}_0(s_0)| \leq \Pr[\mathsf{F}_8] + \epsilon'$ and $\Pr[\mathsf{F}_8] \leq \lfloor \frac{q_S}{t-t'+1} \rfloor * \frac{1}{|D|}$, and below we show this by showing indistinguishability of adversarial views each consecutive games, with the last game, G_8, releasing no information about either p or s, implying the above probability bound on F_8.

Let $p_i^{\neg\mathsf{F}}(s)$ denotes the joint probability $\Pr[1 \leftarrow (\mathcal{A} \rightleftharpoons \mathsf{G}_i(s)) \wedge \neg\mathsf{F}_{i,s}]$; let t_e be a time of a single (multi)-exponentiation in G; let the DDH problem be $(T_{ddh}, \epsilon_{ddh})$-hard in group G; and let proof systems $\Pi[\mathcal{L}_U^{\mathsf{st}_0}]$, $\Pi[\mathcal{L}_{S1}^{\mathsf{st}_0}]$ and $\Pi[\mathcal{L}_{S1}^{\mathsf{st}_0}]$ be $(T_S, q_P, \epsilon_{ZK}, \epsilon_{SS})$ simulation-sound zero-knowledge. Denote $T_{red} = (10+n+(8t+12)q_U + 10nq_S) \cdot t_e$: This is the maximum computational cost, in addition to simulating the ZK proofs, encountered by any of our reductions below. Assume that the bounds on q_U, q_S, T are satisfied as in the theorem claim, namely $\max(q_U, n \cdot q_S) \leq q_P$ and $T + (T_{red} + 3T_S) \leq T_{ddh}$. We will show the following four facts, for any s, s', for $\epsilon_{0,3} = 3\epsilon_{ZK} + (2q_U + nq_S)(\epsilon_{ddh} + \epsilon_{SS})$, $\epsilon_{4,5} = \epsilon_{ddh}$, and $\epsilon_{4,8} = (q_U + nq_S + 2)(\epsilon_{ddh} + \epsilon_{SS})$.

CLAIM 1. $|\bar{p}_0(s) - p_3(s)| \leq \epsilon_{0,3}$

CLAIM 2. $|p_3(s) - p_3(s')| \leq |p_4^{\neg\mathsf{F}}(s) - p_4^{\neg\mathsf{F}}(s')| + \max(\Pr[\mathsf{F}_{4,s}], \Pr[\mathsf{F}_{4,s'}])$

CLAIM 3. $\Pr[\mathsf{F}_{4,s}] \leq \lfloor \frac{q_S}{t-t'+1} \rfloor * \frac{1}{|D|} + \epsilon_{4,8}$

CLAIM 4. $|p_4^{\neg\mathsf{F}}(s) - p_4^{\neg\mathsf{F}}(s')| \leq 2\epsilon_{4,5}$

Summing these up we obtain that $|\bar{p}_0(s) - \bar{p}_0(s')| \leq 2(\epsilon_{0,3} + \epsilon_{4,5}) + \epsilon_{4,8} + \lfloor \frac{q_S}{t-t'+1} \rfloor * \frac{1}{|D|}$, which implies inequality 3, because $2(\epsilon_{0,3} + \epsilon_{4,5}) + \epsilon_{4,8} \leq \epsilon'$. Now, claim 1 follows from claims 5-7 below, because $\epsilon_{0,3}$ is the sum of the upper bounds on the distances $|p_{i-1}(s) - p_i(s)|$ for $i = 1, 2, 3$ in claims 5-7 below, and $|\bar{p}_0(s) - p_0(s)|$, which is bounded by $3\epsilon_{ZK}$. Claim 2 follows from claim 8 below: Note that $|p_3(s) - p_3(s')| = |(p_3^{\neg\mathsf{F}}(s) + p_3^{\mathsf{F}}(s)) - (p_3^{\neg\mathsf{F}}(s') + p_3^{\mathsf{F}}(s'))|$ is upper bounded by $|p_3^{\neg\mathsf{F}}(s) - p_3^{\neg\mathsf{F}}(s')| + \max(\Pr[\mathsf{F}_{3,s}], \Pr[\mathsf{F}_{3,s'}])$; and moreover by claim 8, it follows that $p_3^{\neg\mathsf{F}}(s) = p_4^{\neg\mathsf{F}}(s)$ and $\Pr[\mathsf{F}_{3,s}] = \Pr[\mathsf{F}_{4,s}]$ for all s. Claim 3 follows from claims 9-12 below, because (1) $\epsilon_{4,8}$ is the sum of the upper bounds on the distances $|\Pr[\mathsf{F}_{i-1,s}] - \Pr[\mathsf{F}_{i,s}]|$ shown for $i = 5, 6, 7, 8$ in claims 9-12, and (2) $\Pr[\mathsf{F}_{8,s}] \leq \lfloor \frac{q_S}{t-t'+1} \rfloor * \frac{1}{|D|}$ because G_8 releases no information about p. Claim 4 follows from claim 9 below because game G_5 is independent of secret s, and therefore for every s, s' we have that $p_5^{\neg\mathsf{F}}(s) = p_5^{\neg\mathsf{F}}(s')$.

CLAIM 5. *Games G_0 and G_1 are indistinguishable under DDH. Concretely, $|p_0(s) - p_1(s)| \leq q_U(\epsilon_{ddh} + \epsilon_{SS})$.*

PROOF. To show that G_0 and G_1 are indistinguishable, we make a hybrid argument over q_U user sessions. We define a series of intermediary games G_0^i, between G_0 and G_1, where G_0^i follows G_1 in the $\mathsf{User}^\diamond$ oracle calls on the first i user sessions, *i.e.* it picks $\hat{d}_{\bar{p}} \xleftarrow{r} G$, and then follows G_0 on the remaining sessions. Clearly, $\mathsf{G}_0^0 \equiv \mathsf{G}_0$ and $\mathsf{G}_0^{q_U} \equiv \mathsf{G}_1$. Let $p_0^i = \Pr[1 \leftarrow (\mathcal{A} \rightleftharpoons \mathsf{G}_0^i)]$. For each $i > 0$ we construct reduction $\mathcal{R}_{0,1}^i$ which on input a DDH challenge $(A, B, C) = (g^a, g^b, g^c)$ follows G_0 during $\mathsf{Init}^\diamond$ except

$\mathsf{Init}^{\diamond}$(on input s)

$x \xleftarrow{r} \mathbb{Z}_q, y \leftarrow g^x, \{x_i\}_{i=1}^n \xleftarrow{(n,t)} \mathsf{SS}(x)$	$y \xleftarrow{r} G, \{x_i\}_{i=1}^n \xleftarrow{(n,t)} \mathsf{SS}(0)$	G_4
$(h, \hat{g}, \hat{h}, \bar{g}) \xleftarrow{r} (G)^3$		
$\hat{y} \xleftarrow{r} G$	$\hat{x} \xleftarrow{r} \mathbb{Z}_q, \hat{y} \leftarrow (\hat{g})^{\hat{x}}$	G_3
$r_s \xleftarrow{r} \mathbb{Z}_q, (c_s, d_s) \leftarrow (g^{r_s}, y^{r_s} s)$	$(c_s, d_s) \xleftarrow{r} (G)^2$	G_5
$p \leftarrow D, r_p \xleftarrow{r} \mathbb{Z}_q, (c_p, d_p) \leftarrow (g^{r_p}, y^{r_p} h^p)$	$(c_p, d_p) \xleftarrow{r} (G)^2$	G_8

$\mathsf{idSet} \leftarrow \{\}, \mathsf{CpSet} \leftarrow \{\}, \mathsf{F} \leftarrow \mathsf{false}$

$\{\, t_j \xleftarrow{r} \mathbb{Z}_q, (a_j, b_j, \bar{a}_j) \leftarrow (g^{t_j}, (c_p)^{t_j}, \bar{g}^{t_j}), \pi_{1j} \leftarrow \mathcal{S}[\mathcal{L}_{S1}^{\mathsf{st_0}}](a_j, b_j, \bar{a}_j) \,\}_{j=1}^{n \cdot q_S}$

$\{\, r_i \xleftarrow{r} \mathbb{Z}_q,\ \mathsf{st}_i \leftarrow (x_i, r_i),\ y_i \leftarrow g^{x_i} h^{r_i} \,\}_{i=1}^n$

$\mathsf{st_0} \leftarrow (g, h, y, \{y_i\}_{i=1}^n, \hat{g}, \hat{h}, \hat{y}, \bar{g}, (c_p, d_p), (c_s, d_s)),\ \mathsf{Ret}(\mathsf{st_0}, \{\mathsf{st}_i\}_{i \in \mathsf{B}}, \{a_j, b_j, \bar{a}_j, \pi_{1j}\}_{j=1}^{n \cdot q_S})$

$\mathsf{User}^{\diamond}(\{ID_j, a_j, b_j, \bar{a}_j, \pi_{1j}\}_{j=1}^{t+1})$

If $(\exists_{j \in \{1,..,t+1\}}$ st $\mathcal{V}[\mathcal{L}_{S1}^{\mathsf{st_0}}]((a_j, b_j, \bar{a}_j), \pi_{1j}) = 0)$ then ABORT this session.

$r_{\tilde{p}} \xleftarrow{r} \mathbb{Z}_q, (c_{\tilde{p}}, \hat{c}_{\tilde{p}}) \leftarrow (g^{r_{\tilde{p}}}, (\hat{g})^{r_{\tilde{p}}}), \mathsf{CpSet} \leftarrow \mathsf{CpSet} \cup \{c_{\tilde{p}}\}, \{e_j \leftarrow (a_j)^{r_{\tilde{p}}}\}_{j=1}^{t+1}$

$d_{\tilde{p}} \leftarrow y^{r_{\tilde{p}}} h^p$	$d_{\tilde{p}} \xleftarrow{r} G$	G_7
$\hat{d}_{\tilde{p}} \leftarrow \hat{y}^{r_{\tilde{p}}} (\hat{h})^p$	$\hat{d}_{\tilde{p}} \xleftarrow{r} G$	G_1

$\{\pi_{2j} \leftarrow \mathcal{S}[\mathcal{L}_U^{\mathsf{st_0}}](a_j, e_j, c_{\tilde{p}}, d_{\tilde{p}}, \hat{c}_{\tilde{p}}, \hat{d}_{\tilde{p}})\}_{j=1}^{t+1},\ \mathsf{Ret}(\{e_j\}_{j=1}^{t+1}, (c_{\tilde{p}}, d_{\tilde{p}}), (\hat{c}_{\tilde{p}}, \hat{d}_{\tilde{p}}), \{\pi_{2j}\}_{j=1}^{t+1})$

$\mathsf{Server}_j^{\diamond}(\lambda_j, c_\beta, e_j, c_{\tilde{p}}, d_{\tilde{p}}, \hat{c}_{\tilde{p}}, \hat{d}_{\tilde{p}}, \pi_{2j})$

If $(\mathcal{V}[\mathcal{L}_U^{\mathsf{st_0}}]((a_j, e_j, c_{\tilde{p}}, d_{\tilde{p}}, \hat{c}_{\tilde{p}}, \hat{d}_{\tilde{p}}), \pi_{2j}) = 0)$ then ABORT this session.

If $(\hat{d}_{\tilde{p}}/(\hat{c}_{\tilde{p}})^{\hat{x}} = (\hat{h})^p)$ then $\mathsf{idSet} \leftarrow \mathsf{idSet} \cup \{ID_j\}$; If $|\mathsf{idSet}| > t - t'$ then set $\mathsf{F} \leftarrow \mathsf{true}$; $w_j \leftarrow (c_s \cdot c_\beta)^{\lambda_j \cdot x_{ID_j}}$

$d_{\beta,j} \leftarrow (d_p/d_{\tilde{p}})^{t_j}$	If $(\hat{d}_{\tilde{p}}/(\hat{c}_{\tilde{p}})^{\hat{x}} = (\hat{h})^p)$ then $d_{\beta,j} \leftarrow (d_p/d_{\tilde{p}})^{t_j}$ else $d_{\beta,j} \xleftarrow{r} G$	G_3	$d_{\beta,j} \xleftarrow{r} G$	G_6

$z_j \leftarrow d_{\beta,j} \cdot (w_j)^{-1}$	If $(c_{\tilde{p}} \in \mathsf{CpSet})$ then $z_j \xleftarrow{r} G$ else $z_j \leftarrow d_{\beta,j} \cdot (w_j)^{-1}$	G_2

$r_{z_j} \xleftarrow{r} \mathbb{Z}_q, (c_{z_j}, d_{z_j}) \leftarrow (g^{r_{z_j}}, (c_{\tilde{p}})^{r_{z_j}} \cdot z_j),\ \pi_{3j} \leftarrow \mathcal{S}[\mathcal{L}_{S2}^{\mathsf{st_0}, ID_j}](c_{z_j}, d_{z_j}, c_{\tilde{p}}, a_j, d_p/d_{\tilde{p}}, (c_s \cdot c_\beta)^{\lambda_j}),\ \mathsf{Ret}((c_{z_j}, d_{z_j}), \pi_{3j})$

Figure 4: Games G_0,G_1,...,G_8 used in the security proof of the PPSS protocol

In Figure 4, all games follow the code in boxes that span the width of the figure. However, if a line has two boxes, an unmarked one on the left and one marked "G_i" for some i on the right, then game G_j follows the box on the left for $j < i$ and the box on the right for $j \geq i$. In other words, the boxes on the right mark the differences from G_0 introduced in some game, which are then adhered to in each subsequent game. A special case is the second row of boxes in the code of oracle $\mathsf{Server}_j^{\diamond}$, which contain three boxes: Games $\mathsf{G}_0 - \mathsf{G}_2$ follow the unmarked left-most box, games $\mathsf{G}_3 - \mathsf{G}_5$ follow the middle box marked "G_3", and games $\mathsf{G}_6 - \mathsf{G}_8$ follow the right-most marked "G_6".

Game G_0 portrayed in Figure 4 differs from $\mathcal{A}$'s view of the real protocol in three ways: (1) Figure 4 does not include the interaction corresponding to step **U2** of the $\mathsf{User}^{\diamond}$ oracle. Recall that in the strong security notion the adversary receives a bit indicating whether the User protocol instance accepts or rejects its protocol session. However, in PPSS_2 this bit is determined by whether this User instance receives $t+1$ messages corresponding to server's steps **S1** and **S2** accompanied by proofs $\{\pi_{1j}, \pi_{3j}\}_{j=1}^{t+1}$ which pass the corresponding verification, hence this bit is publicly computable from the adversary's actions; (2) The $\mathsf{User}^{\diamond}$ oracle simulating step **U1** of the User algorithm does not return values λ_j and c_β, but these values are publicly computable from the inputs $\{ID_j, b_j\}_{j=1}^{t+1}$ sent by $\mathcal{A}$ to this User session and from its outputs $\{e_j\}_{j=1}^{t+1}$; (3) In G_0 all oracles output simulated proofs, while in the real interactions these proofs are output by respective prover algorithms on corresponding witnesses.

that it computes $\hat{g} \leftarrow g^{r_0}$ and $\bar{g} \leftarrow A^{r_1}$ for $r_0, r_1 \xleftarrow{r} \mathbb{Z}_q$ and embeds $\hat{y} \leftarrow B$. Then $\mathcal{R}_{0,1}^i$ follows G_0 in all Server$^\diamond$ calls, but for User sessions it follows G_1 on all sessions prior to the i-th session, and G_0 on all sessions from $i+1$ on, but on the i-th session it sets $\{e_j \leftarrow (a_j)^{1/(r_0 r_1)}\}_{j=1}^t$, $c_{\tilde{p}} \leftarrow A^{1/r_0}$, $d_{\tilde{p}} \leftarrow A^{x/r_0}h^p$, $\hat{c}_{\tilde{p}} \leftarrow A$, and $\hat{d}_{\tilde{p}} \leftarrow C^{1/r_0}(\hat{h})^p$. If (A, B, C) is a DDH tuple (g^a, g^b, g^{ab}) then $\mathcal{R}_{0,1}^i(A, B, C) \equiv \mathsf{G}_0^{i-1}$ because for the i-th session the user's output is computed as in G_0, with $r_{\tilde{p}} = a/r_0$ and $\hat{x} = DL(\hat{g}, \hat{y}) = b/r_0$. However if (A, B, C) is a random tuple then $\hat{d}_{\tilde{p}}$ is a random group element, as in G_1, and so $\mathcal{R}_{0,1}^i(A, B, C) \equiv \mathsf{G}_0^i$. It follows that $|p_0^i - p_0^{i+1}| \leq \epsilon_{ddh} + \epsilon_{SS}$, since we have to add the probability ϵ_{SS} that all proofs $\pi_{1,j}$ verify while some $(a_j, \bar{a}_j)$ sent to the i-th user session is not of the form $(g^{t_j}, (\bar{g})^{t_j})$ for some t_j. □

CLAIM 6. *Games G_1 and G_2 are indistinguishable under DDH. Concretely, $|p_1(s) - p_2(s)| \leq q_U(\epsilon_{ddh} + \epsilon_{SS})$.*

PROOF. We use a hybrid argument over q_U user sessions. For each $i \in [0, q_U]$, we define an intermediate game G_1^i which follows G_2 except that in Server$^\diamond$ oracle responses G_1^i decides whether z_j should be real or random based on whether $c_{\tilde{p}} \in \mathsf{CpSet}[1, i]$, the set of $c_{\tilde{p}}$'s output by the first i User$^\diamond$ oracle sessions. Note that $\mathsf{G}_1^0 \equiv \mathsf{G}_1$ and $\mathsf{G}_1^{q_U} \equiv \mathsf{G}_2$. Let $p_1^i = \Pr[1 \leftarrow (\mathcal{A} \rightleftharpoons \mathsf{G}_1^i)]$. For each $i \in [1, q_U]$ we show reduction $R_{1,2}^i$ which reduces breaking DDH to distinguishing between G_1^{i-1} and G_1^i. Let the DDH challenge be $(A, B, C) = (g^a, g^b, g^c)$. The reduction follows the Init$^\diamond$ procedure as in game G_1 except that it picks $r_0, r_1, \hat{x} \xleftarrow{r} \mathbb{Z}_q$ and sets $\hat{g} \leftarrow g^{r_0}$, $\bar{g} \leftarrow A^{r_1}$, and $\hat{y} \leftarrow (\hat{g})^{\hat{x}}$. For the user sessions, the reduction follows the code of G_1 except for i-th session, where it embeds $c_{\tilde{p}} \leftarrow A$ and computes $\hat{c}_{\tilde{p}} \leftarrow (c_{\tilde{p}})^{r_0}$, $d_{\tilde{p}} \leftarrow (c_{\tilde{p}})^x \cdot h^p$, $\hat{d}_{\tilde{p}} \leftarrow (\hat{c}_{\tilde{p}})^{\hat{x}} \cdot (\hat{h})^p$, and $e_j \leftarrow (\bar{a}_j)^{1/r_1}$ for all j. For the server sessions, the reduction $\mathcal{R}_{1,2}^i$ follows the code for G_1^{i-1} except for the sessions where $c_{\tilde{p}}$ is passed as input; where it computes $(c_{z_j}, d_{z_j}) \leftarrow (B^{r_{z_j}}, C^{r_{z_j}} \cdot z_j)$ where $z_j = d_{\beta,j}/w_j$. Thus reduction $R_{1,2}^i$ hits G_1^{i-1} on a DDH tuple and it hits G_1^i on a random tuple. The reduction relies on the correctness of server's messages sent to user's i-th session; but since the event that these are incorrect while servers' proofs verify is bounded by ϵ_{SS}, this yields $|p_1^i - p_1^{i+1}| \leq \epsilon_{ddh} + \epsilon_{SS}$, and the claim follows. □

CLAIM 7. *Games G_2 and G_3 are indistinguishable under DDH. Concretely, $|p_2(s) - p_3(s)| \leq (n \cdot q_S)(\epsilon_{ddh} + \epsilon_{SS})$.*

PROOF. We use a hybrid argument over nq_S server sessions to argue that G_2 and G_3 are indistinguishable. For each $i \in [0, nq_S]$, we define an intermediate game G_2^i which follows G_3 on calls to Server$_j^\diamond$ for $j \leq i$ and follows G_2 on calls to Server$_j^\diamond$ for $j > i$. Note that $\mathsf{G}_2^0 \equiv \mathsf{G}_2$ and $\mathsf{G}_2^{nq_S} \equiv \mathsf{G}_3$. Let $p_2^i = \Pr[1 \leftarrow (\mathcal{A} \rightleftharpoons \mathsf{G}_2^i)]$. For each $i \in [1, nq_S]$ we show reduction $R_{2,3}^i$ which reduces breaking DDH assumption to distinguishing between G_2^{i-1} and G_2^i. Let the DDH challenge be $(A, B, C) = (g^a, g^b, g^c)$. The reduction follows the Init$^\diamond$ procedure as in game G_3 except that it sets $(h, \hat{h}, \bar{g}) \leftarrow (B, C^{r_0}, g^{r_1})$ where $r_0, r_1 \xleftarrow{r} \mathbb{Z}_q$. Also, $\mathcal{R}_{2,3}^i$ computes $(a_j, b_j, \bar{a}_j)$ for all $j \in [nq_S]$ as in the protocol, except for $j = i$ where it sets $(a_i, b_i, \bar{a}_i) \leftarrow (A, A^{r_p}, A^{r_1})$. The reduction responds to Server$^\diamond$ queries for sessions $j < i$ as in G_3, for sessions $j > i$ as in G_2, while on the i-th session it computes $d_{\beta,i} \leftarrow (b_i/e_i)^x \cdot C^p \cdot (\hat{d}_{\tilde{p}}/(\hat{c}_{\tilde{p}})^{\hat{x}})^{-1/r_0}$. If (A, B, C) is a DDH tuple, and the oracle inputs are formed correctly, i.e. proof π_{2i} holds on the correct statement $(a_i, e_i, c_{\tilde{p}}, d_{\tilde{p}}, \hat{c}_{\tilde{p}}, \hat{d}_{\tilde{p}})$, then $d_{\beta,i} = y^{(r_p - r_{\tilde{p}})t_i} h^{(p-\tilde{p})t_i}$ as in G_2^{i-1}, where $t_i = a$, because in that case $C = h^{t_i}$. Otherwise, if (A, B, C) is a random tuple, then $d_{\beta,j}$ is random as in G_2^i. Since the views are correct except for probability ϵ_{SS}, we get that $|p_2^i - p_2^{i-1}| \leq \epsilon_{ddh} + \epsilon_{SS}$, and the claim follows. □

CLAIM 8. *For any s, $p_3^{\neg \mathsf{F}}(s) = p_4^{\neg \mathsf{F}}(s)$ and $\Pr[\mathsf{F}_{3,s}] = \Pr[\mathsf{F}_{4,s}]$.*

PROOF. We argue that under condition that event F does not happen the adversarial views in games G_3 and G_4 are identical. This immediately implies that (1) $\Pr[\mathsf{F}_{3,s}] = \Pr[\mathsf{F}_{4,s}]$, and (2) that the conditional probabilities $\Pr[1 \leftarrow (\mathcal{A} \rightleftharpoons \mathsf{G}_3(s)) \mid \neg \mathsf{F}_{3,s}]$ and $\Pr[1 \leftarrow (\mathcal{A} \rightleftharpoons \mathsf{G}_4(s)) \mid \neg \mathsf{F}_{4,s}]$ are the same, and hence the claim follows, because $p_i^{\neg \mathsf{F}}(s) = \Pr[1 \leftarrow (\mathcal{A} \rightleftharpoons \mathsf{G}_i(s)) \mid \neg \mathsf{F}_{i,s}] * \Pr[\mathsf{F}_{i,s}]$ To argue this, note that the only difference between G_3 and G_4 is that in G_3, x_i's are (n, t)-secret-sharing of a random value whereas in G_4 x_i's are (n, t)-secret-sharing of zero. Therefore unless adversary knows $t+1$ shares of x_i's, the view of the adversary in G_3 is identical to its view in G_4. Now, adversary gets to know $t' < t$ shares of x simply by corrupting t' servers. However server queries could possibly leak information about x_i's as in w_j value. But in any server query, if adversary does not use the legitimate password, w_j is masked with a random value in both G_3 and G_4; otherwise if adversary uses the legitimate password, unless event F happens, the number of distinct servers which adversary contacts is bounded by $t - t'$. Thus, unless event F happens, the maximum number of x_i shares that is effectively used in either game is bounded by t. □

CLAIM 9. *Games G_4 and G_5 are indistinguishable under DDH, i.e. $|p_4^{\neg \mathsf{F}}(s) - p_5^{\neg \mathsf{F}}(s)| \leq \epsilon_{ddh}$ and $|\Pr[\mathsf{F}_{4,s}] - \Pr[\mathsf{F}_{5,s}]| \leq \epsilon_{ddh}$.*

PROOF. The proof goes via an easy reduction from DDH which embeds the DDH challenge (A, B, C) by setting $(y, c_s, d_s) \leftarrow (A, B, C \cdot s)$. Note that neither game G_4 nor G_5 needs to know values x and r_s corresponding to (y, c_s, d_s). □

CLAIM 10. *Games G_5 and G_6 are indistinguishable under DDH, i.e. $|p_5(s) - p_6(s)| \leq (n \cdot q_S)(\epsilon_{ddh} + \epsilon_{SS})$ and $|\Pr[\mathsf{F}_{5,s}] - \Pr[\mathsf{F}_{6,s}]| \leq (n \cdot q_S)(\epsilon_{ddh} + \epsilon_{SS})$.*

PROOF. As in the proof of Claim 7, we use a hybrid argument over nq_S server sessions. For $i \in [0, nq_S]$ we define game G_5^i which follows G_6 on Server$_j^\diamond$ calls for $j \leq i$ and G_5 on Server$_j^\diamond$ calls for $j > i$. Note that $\mathsf{G}_5^0 \equiv \mathsf{G}_5$ and $\mathsf{G}_5^{nq_S} \equiv \mathsf{G}_6$. Let $p_5^i = \Pr[1 \leftarrow (\mathcal{A} \rightleftharpoons \mathsf{G}_5^i)]$ and let F_5^i denote event F in G_5^i. For each $i \in [1, nq_S]$ we show a DDH reduction $R_{2,3}^i$ which on input a tuple $(A, B, C) = (g^a, g^b, g^c)$ follows the Init$^\diamond$ procedure as in game G_5 except that it sets $(y, h, \hat{g}, \hat{h}, barg) \leftarrow (B, g^{r_0}, C^{r_3}, A^{r_1}, g^{r_2})$ where $r_0, r_1, r_2, r_3 \xleftarrow{r} \mathbb{Z}_q$. $\mathcal{R}_{2,3}^i$ computes all $(a_j, b_j, \bar{a}_j)$ as in the protocol except for $j = i$ where it sets $(a_i, b_i, \bar{a}_i) \leftarrow (A, A^{r_p}, A^{r_2})$. The reduction responds to Server$^\diamond$ queries for sessions $j < i$ as in G_6, for sessions $j > i$ as in G_5, while on the i-th session it computes $d_{\beta,i} \leftarrow C^{r_p} \cdot A^{p \cdot r_0} \cdot (\hat{d}_{\tilde{p}}/(\hat{c}_{\tilde{p}})^{\hat{x}})^{-r_0/r_1} \cdot (\hat{c}_{\tilde{p}})^{-1/r_3}$ If (A, B, C) is a DDH tuple, and proof π_{2i} holds on the correct statement $(a_i, e_i, c_{\tilde{p}}, d_{\tilde{p}}, \hat{c}_{\tilde{p}}, \hat{d}_{\tilde{p}})$, then $d_{\beta,i} = g^{x(r_p - r_{\tilde{p}})t_i} h^{(p-\tilde{p})t_i}$ as in G_5^{i-1}, where $t_i = a$ and $x = b$, because in that case $C = g^{x \cdot t_i}$. Otherwise $d_{\beta,j}$ is random, as in G_5^i. Since the views are correct except for probability ϵ_{SS}, we get both $|p_5^i - p_5^{i-1}| \leq \epsilon_{ddh} + \epsilon_{SS}$ and $|\Pr[\mathsf{F}_5^i] - \Pr[\mathsf{F}_5^{i-1}| \leq \epsilon_{ddh} + \epsilon_{SS}$, and the claim follows. □

CLAIM 11. *Games G_6 and G_7 are indistinguishable under DDH, i.e. $|\Pr[\mathsf{F}_{6,s}] - \Pr[\mathsf{F}_{7,s}]| \leq q_U(\epsilon_{ddh} + \epsilon_{SS})$.*

PROOF. The proof goes via a hybrid reduction from DDH over the User$^\diamond$ oracle sessions, for $i = 1, .., q_U$, and it is very similar to the reduction in the proof of Claim 5. The reduction picks $(\hat{g}, \bar{g}) \leftarrow (g^{r_0}, g^{r_1})$ for random r_0, r_1 and $\hat{y} = (\hat{g})^{\hat{x}}$ for random $\hat{x}$, and embeds the DDH challenge (A, B, C) by setting $y \leftarrow B$, and then in the i-th User$^\diamond$ session it assigns $c_{\tilde{p}} \leftarrow A$, $d_{\tilde{p}} \leftarrow C \cdot h^p$, $\hat{c}_{\tilde{p}} \leftarrow A^{r_0}$, $\hat{d}_{\tilde{p}} \leftarrow (\hat{c}_{\tilde{p}})^{\hat{x}}(\hat{h})^p$, and sets each e_j as $e_j \leftarrow (\bar{a}_j)^{1/r_0}$. □

$\mathsf{Init}(p)$ (on public parameters κ, n, t)

$(\mathsf{pk}, \mathsf{sk}) \leftarrow \mathsf{EKg}$, $\{(\mathsf{ssk}_i, \mathsf{vk}_i) \leftarrow \mathsf{SKg}\}_{i=1}^n$,
$(\tilde{\mathsf{st}}_0, \tilde{\mathsf{st}}_0, ..., \tilde{\mathsf{st}}_n) \leftarrow \mathsf{PPSS.Init}(p, \mathsf{sk})$
$\mathsf{st}_0 \leftarrow (\tilde{\mathsf{st}}_0, \mathsf{pk}, \{\mathsf{vk}_i\}_{i=0}^n)$, $\{\mathsf{st}_i \leftarrow (\tilde{\mathsf{st}}_i, \mathsf{ssk}_i)\}_{i=1}^n$

$\mathsf{Client}(\mathsf{st}_0, \tilde{p}, uId) \rightleftharpoons (\mathsf{Server}(\mathsf{st}_0, \mathsf{st}_1), \cdots, \mathsf{Server}(\mathsf{st}_0, \mathsf{st}_n))$

C1 (Client) Pick $sId \xleftarrow{r} \{0,1\}^\kappa$;
Send (uId, sId) to each Server;
Run $\mathsf{PPSS.User}(\tilde{st}_0, \tilde{p})$ with the Servers.

S1 (Server_j) Run $\mathsf{PPSS.Server}_j(\tilde{\mathsf{st}}_0, \tilde{\mathsf{st}}_j)$ with the Client;
On abort, assign $k_j \leftarrow \perp$ on session sId and stop.
Otherwise pick $k_j \xleftarrow{r} \{0,1\}^\kappa$;
Compute $\sigma_j \leftarrow \mathsf{Sign}(\mathsf{ssk}_{Id_j}, (uId, sId, k_j))$
Compute $e_j \leftarrow \mathsf{Enc}(\mathsf{pk}, (k_j, \sigma_j))$;
Send e_j to Client.

C2 (Client) Let $\hat{sk}$ be the output of the PPSS instance.
If $\hat{sk} = \perp$ then set $k_j \leftarrow \perp$ for all j and stop.
Let $(\hat{k}_j, \hat{\sigma}_j) \leftarrow \mathsf{Dec}(\hat{\mathsf{sk}}, e_j)$ for all Server_j;
For each j, if $\mathsf{Vrfy}(\mathsf{vk}_{Id_j}, \hat{\sigma}_j, (uId, sId, \hat{k}_j)) = 1$
then set $k_j \leftarrow \hat{k}_j$ on session sId with Server_j;
o/w set $k_j \leftarrow \perp$ on this session.

Figure 5: TPAKE from PPSS

CLAIM 12. *Games* G_7 *and* G_8 *are indistinguishable under DDH, e.g.* $|\Pr[\mathsf{F}_{7,s}] - \Pr[\mathsf{F}_{8,s}]| \leq \epsilon_{ddh}$.

PROOF. The proof goes via an easy reduction from DDH which embeds the DDH challenge (A, B, C) by setting $(y, c_p, d_p) \leftarrow (A, B, C \cdot h^p)$. Note that neither game G_7 nor G_8 needs to know values x and r_p corresponding to (y, c_p, d_p). □

4. EFFICIENT T-PAKE FROM PPSS

A password protected secret sharing (PPSS) scheme can be used as a black box to achieve a threshold password authenticated key exchange (T-PAKE) protocol (in the public key model) at very little additional cost. In particular, the round complexity of the resulting T-PAKE is the same as the PPSS because all the T-PAKE messages can be piggybacked onto the PPSS protocol flows. Figure 5 shows a secure T-PAKE protocol assuming that $\mathcal{E} = (\mathsf{EKg}, \mathsf{Enc}, \mathsf{Dec})$ is a chosen ciphertext attack secure public key encryption, $\mathcal{S} = (\mathsf{SKg}, \mathsf{Sign}, \mathsf{Vrfy})$ is a signature scheme which is existentially unforgeable under chosen message attack, and PPSS is a strongly secure password protected secret sharing protocol. For lack of space we omit the formal proof that this construction satisfies T-PAKE security, but, very briefly, the signatures and CCA encryption scheme ensure that the network adversary cannot re-route messages from a session in which honest players are involved, or modify them in any way, and hence in particular all User sessions are independent of each other. Then by the security of the PPSS scheme, except for $\lfloor q_S/(t-t'+1) \rfloor \cdot (1/|D|)$ probability, the view of the PPSS protocol initialized with the real decryption key sk is indistinguishable from a view where sk is replaced by an independent key, in which case CCA security of encryption ensures that $\mathcal{A}$ gets no information about any unrevealed session keys even given a capability to reveal any other session keys (handled by decryption queries in a reduction to CCA encryption security).

5. REFERENCES

[1] M. Abdalla, M. Bellare, and P. Rogaway. The oracle diffie-hellman assumptions and an analysis of DHIES. In D. Naccache, editor, *CT-RSA*, volume 2020 of *Lecture Notes in Computer Science*, pages 143–158. Springer, 2001.

[2] M. Bellare, J. A. Garay, and T. Rabin. Fast batch verification for modular exponentiation and digital signatures. In *EUROCRYPT*, pages 236–255, 1998.

[3] J. Brainard, A. Juels, B. Kaliski, and M. Szydlo. Nightingale: A new two-server approach for authentication with short secrets. In *12th USENIX Security Symp*, pages 201–213. IEEE Comp. Soc. 2003.

[4] J. Camenisch and M. Michels. Proving in Zero-Knowledge that a Number Is the Product of Two Safe Primes. In *EUROCRYPT'99*, volume 1592 of *LNCS*, pages 107–122, 1999.

[5] R. Canetti, R. Gennaro, S. Jarecki, H. Krawczyk, and T. Rabin. Adaptive security for threshold cryptosystems. In *CRYPTO'99*, volume 1666 of *LNCS*, pages 98–115, 1999.

[6] Y. Desmedt and Y. Frankel. Threshold Cryptosystems. In *CRYPTO '89*, volume 435 of *LNCS*, pages 307–315, 1990.

[7] M. Di Raimondo and R. Gennaro. Provably secure threshold password-authenticated key exchange. *J. Comput. Syst. Sci.*, 72(6):978–1001, 2006.

[8] Y. Dodis, M. K. Franklin, J. Katz, A. Miyaji, and M. Yung. Intrusion-resilient public-key encryption. In *CT-RSA*, pages 19–32, 2003.

[9] Y. Dodis, J. Katz, S. Xu, and M. Yung. Key-insulated public key cryptosystems. In L. R. Knudsen, editor, *EUROCRYPT*, volume 2332 of *Lecture Notes in Computer Science*, pages 65–82. Springer, 2002.

[10] M. Fischlin. Communication-efficient non-interactive proofs of knowledge with online extractors. In *Crypto'05*, 2005.

[11] W. Ford and B. S. K. Jr. Server-assisted generation of a strong secret from a password. In *WETICE*, pages 176–180, 2000.

[12] J. A. Garay, P. D. MacKenzie, and K. Yang. Strengthening zero-knowledge protocols using signatures. In E. Biham, editor, *EUROCRYPT*, volume 2656 of *Lecture Notes in Computer Science*, pages 177–194. Springer, 2003.

[13] S. Goldwasser, S. Micali, and R. L. Rivest. A "paradoxical" solution to the signature problem. In *IEEE Annual Symposium of Foundations of Computer Science (FOCS'84)*, pages 441–448, 1984.

[14] D. Jablon. Password authentication using multiple servers. In *CT-RSA'01: RSA Cryptographers' Track*, pages 344–360. Springer-Verlag, 2001.

[15] J. Katz, P. Mackenzie, G. Taban, and V. Gligor. Two-server password-only authenticated key exchange. In *Proc. Applied Cryptography and Network Security ACNSÄĂŹ05*, 2005.

[16] J. Katz, R. Ostrovsky, and M. Yung. Efficient password-authenticated key exchange using human-memorable passwords. In *Advances in Cryptology - EUROCRYPT 2001, International Conference on the Theory and Application of Cryptographic Techniques*, 2001.

[17] LastPass. Lastpass password manager, 2009. Available at `https://lastpass.com`.

[18] P. D. MacKenzie and M. K. Reiter. Networked cryptographic devices resilient to capture. *Int. J. Inf. Sec.*, 2(1):1–20, 2003.

[19] P. D. MacKenzie, T. Shrimpton, and M. Jakobsson. Threshold password-authenticated key exchange. *J. Cryptology*, 19(1):27–66, 2006.

[20] Mozilla Labs. Weave sync, 2009. Available at `http://labs.mozilla.com/projects/weave`.

[21] M. Naor and M. Yung. Public-key cryptosystems provably secure against chosen ciph. attacks. In *STOC*, pages 427–437. ACM, 1990.

[22] A. Sahai. Non-malleable non-interactive zero knowledge and adaptive chosen-ciphertext security. In *FOCS*, pages 543–553, 1999.

[23] A. Shamir. How to Share a Secret. *Commun. ACM*, 22(11):612–613, Nov. 1979.

[24] V. Shoup. Practical Threshold Signatures. In *EUROCRYPT'00*, volume 1807 of *LNCS*, pages 207–220, 2000.

[25] V. Shoup and R. Gennaro. Securing threshold cryptosystems against chosen ciphertext attack. *J. Cryptology*, 15(2):75–96, 2002.

[26] S. Xu and R. S. Sandhu. Two efficient and provably secure schemes for server-assisted threshold signatures. In *CT-RSA*, 2003.

Practical Delegation of Computation using Multiple Servers

Ran Canetti*
Tel Aviv University & Boston University
canetti@tau.ac.il

Ben Riva*
Tel Aviv University
benriva@tau.ac.il

Guy N. Rothblum†
Microsoft Research, Silicon Valley Campus
rothblum@alum.mit.edu

ABSTRACT

The current move to Cloud Computing raises the need for verifiable delegation of computations, where a weak client delegates his computation to a powerful server, while maintaining the ability to verify that the result is correct. Although there are prior solutions to this problem, none of them is yet both general and practical for real-world use.

We demonstrate a relatively efficient and general solution where the client delegates the computation to *several* servers, and is guaranteed to determine the correct answer as long as even a *single* server is honest. We show:

- A protocol for any efficiently computable function, with logarithmically many rounds, based on any collision-resistant hash family. The protocol is set in terms of Turing Machines but can be adapted to other computation models.
- An adaptation of the protocol for the X86 computation model and a prototype implementation, called Quin, for Windows executables. We describe the architecture of Quin and experiment with several parameters on live clouds. We show that the protocol is practical, can work with nowadays clouds, and is efficient both for the servers and for the client.

Categories and Subject Descriptors

K.6.5 [**Management of Computing and Information Systems**]: Security and Protection

General Terms

Algorithms, Experimentation, Security

*Research supported by the Check Point Institute for Information Security.

†Most of this work was done while the author was at the Department of Computer Science at Princeton University and Supported by NSF Grant CCF-0832797 and by a Computing Innovation Fellowship.

Keywords

Verifiable Computation, Cloud Computing

1. INTRODUCTION

These days, the IT world is moving towards the *pay-per-use* paradigm (aka Cloud Computing). Companies of all sizes reduce their computing assets and shift to a use of computing resources in the clouds. This shift is predicted to increase in the near future and become a significant portion of the IT market. One consequence of this shift is that the IT world outside the clouds is moving to a use of weaker and smaller computer devices, like Virtualized Thin Desktops, Tablet PCs and Smartphones. Whenever stronger resources are needed, those devices will use the cloud.

Since cloud services are often given by an outside entity with different interests than those of the client, this model carries within it many security problems. One problem, however, stands out as an inherent and very basic one: How can the client verify the correctness of the cloud's computation? This question is not easily answered by the existing tools of security and cryptography.

There are many possible reasons for a cloud to answer incorrectly. For instance, a cloud would like to improve its revenue by investing less resources while charging for more. Or, a cloud might benefit somehow from certain outputs of the computation, thus it can try to maximize specific results. Or, a disgruntled employee of the cloud provider could modify the executed program. Consequently, the client must be able to verify the correctness of that result. To be effective, we would like the verification process to use considerably *less* resources than those required to actually perform the computation from scratch.

This problem has been considered extensively in the theoretical computer science community, most notably by using Probabilistically Checkable Proofs (e.g., [15, 20]). (See Section 1.2.) However, although those solutions are very efficient in terms of asymptotic complexity, they are currently impractical.

A natural idea, pursued in this work, is to take the basic concept behind cloud computing, the pay-per-use paradigm, and extend it also for *integrity*. If a client wants to get better assurance of the integrity of his cloud computations, he can pay a little more to get such assurance. And if he already pays a little more, why should it be to the same cloud? He can split his payment among several clouds as they are all accessible on the net anyhow.

One simple way of achieving this goal could be to use a number of clouds, and then have the client execute the program by himself in case of inconsistency. However, what about the case where it is impossible or impractical for the client to execute the program even in case of inconsistency?

For this case, the following idea has been proposed: Instead of executing his program on one specific cloud provider, the client picks N different cloud providers. Next, the client asks each of those cloud providers to execute his program and return the output. Now, the client takes the plurality value of those answers to be the correct answer. As long as there is a majority of honest cloud providers (even if the client does not know which ones), the client gets the correct answer. Indeed, this approach is used in Grid Computing, e.g., BOINC [1].

The main downside of this approach is, of course, the need for an honest majority of clouds. In particular, this method requires at least three clouds to be viable. Can one do better? In particular, can we get practical efficiency improvements over the single cloud case, with access to only *two* clouds, only one of which is honest and for a client that *cannot* compute the function by himself?

We provide a positive answer to this question. Specifically, we are interested in the following model: The client asks for the result of the function $f(x)$ from two (or more) cloud servers. In case they make contradictory claims about $f(x)$, the client engages in a protocol with each of the servers, at the end of which the client can efficiently determine the true claim as long as there is at least *one* honest server. As for efficiency, we require that the computational requirements from an honest server are not much more than those required to compute the function in the first place, and that the client's running time is much smaller than the time required to compute the function. We call this model Refereed Delegation of Computation (RDoC) since the client acts like a referee.

Our model is closely related to the *Refereed Games (RG)* model of Feige and Kilian [10] where they focus on two unbounded competing servers and polynomial time referee/client. However, we are faced with the additional challenges of building protocols with efficient honest servers, with a super-efficient client and for any number of servers. In fact, our model can be also considered as *refereed games with multiple efficient servers* and super-efficient clients.

We remark that although our main motivation is a solution for the setting of cloud computing, our results are also useful for other client-server applications. E.g., Grid computing, or when using several processors for redundancy in realtime systems. (Indeed in the latter case there is a need to determine the identities of the faulty processors.)

1.1 Our Contributions

For the description here we restrict attention to the case when there are exactly two servers, one honest and one malicious (but the client does not know which is honest). We later show how to extend our protocol for more than two servers. We show an efficient and *full-information* RDoC protocol for any efficiently computable function, with logarithmically many rounds, based on any collision-resistant hash function family. Here, by full information we mean that the servers can see the full internal state of the client and the communication between the client and the servers is public. The honest servers' work grows only *quasi-linearly* with the complexity of the computation. This protocol is highly generic and can work with any reasonable computation model.

Previously, Feige and Kilian [10] gave a *private information* but unconditionally sound protocol with similar parameters. It also follows from their results that it is unlikely that an information-theoretically sound full-information protocol with similar performance can be obtained (in particular, this is impossible unless all of $\mathcal{P}$ can be computed in poly-logarithmic space).

Our protocol, which builds directly on the protocol of Feige and Kilian, is qualitatively more practical than known techniques for delegating computation in the single-server setting. In particular, all known protocols rely either on arithmetization and PCP techniques [20, 12], or provide only amortized performance advantages and rely on fully homomorphic encryption [11, 9]. Neither approach is currently viable in practice. Moreover, all known protocols work with the (arguably less practical) circuit representation of the computation.

At high level, in this protocol the client searches (using binary search) for inconsistencies between the intermediate states of the two servers' computations. On finding an inconsistency, the client can detect the cheater by performing only a *single step* of the delegated computation. The collision-resistant hash functions are used to allow the servers to "commit" to the (large) intermediate internal states of the computation using small commitments.

In addition, in contrast with prior protocols, our protocol is full-information (or *public coins*). This means that, in a setting where messages between clients and servers are digitally signed, the protocol guarantees that as soon as a server cheats, the client detects the cheating and obtains a publicly verifiable proof of this fact. This is a strong guarantee: we view the servers as *rational* self-interested parties (say cloud computing service providers). An honest server can convince even third parties that all of the cheating servers are cheaters. Assuming that pointing out cheaters is rewarded and cheating is penalized, playing honestly becomes (always) a dominant strategy for rational servers.

We stress that in case all servers agree upon the result, there are no overheads for the servers, nor for the client. The overhead kicks in only in case the servers do not agree. In this case, the overhead is only poly-logarithmic in the size of the computation.

Quin. We adapt the protocol for the X86 computation model. A simplistic adaptation would be to simply run a Turing Machine simulator for X86; but this would result in highly inefficient code. Instead, we adapt the protocol to the X86 computation model: Instead of Turing Machine transitions we have assembly instructions, and instead of working tapes we have the machine's stack and heap memories. This highly improves the practicality of the protocol, and shows its flexibility.

We present a prototype implementation of this adaptation for the Windows environment. Our implementation, which we call Quin, works directly with X86 assembly instructions. However, we do not require the programmer to write his code in assembly. The programmer can write his code in C language and later on build the program to run with our framework. This is an important feature since it makes the implementation almost transparent for the application programmer. Moreover, with small modifications to our prototype, it allows future support for other languages that compile to X86 assembly.

Since our protocol requires the ability to execute a program for a given number of steps, stop its execution and store its state to a file, and later on, be able to resume execution from a stored state, we use a binary instrumentation framework, Intel's PIN [17], to add assembly instructions for counting the number of executed instructions and comparing it to a given threshold. Then, we combine several low-level techniques that work directly with the process memory in order to efficiently dump/restore a state to/from a file.

Another requirement of our protocol is that the client should be able to simulate one step of the computation by himself, given only a small part of some stored state. While for Turing Machines this seems easy, for high-level languages it can be complicated (e.g., in Java, a single step can be a heavy computation that depends on many variables). However, focusing only on X86 instructions that are more "simple" and depend on a small number of variables (or memory), we can meet this requirement by using an X86 emulator that we feed with the required registers and memory data. We extend the Python X86 emulator PyEmu [3] to support emulation of instructions given only a remote access to the process memory (since we do not want to transfer the entire memory to the client).

Last, our protocol assumes that each execution of the delegated program is fully deterministic (i.e. for a fixed input, the Turing Machine's tableau must be the same for each execution of the machine on this input), and therefore, the delegated program has to use only deterministic system calls. However, useful library calls like `malloc()` are not deterministic and depend on the state of the operating system. We overcome this problem by implementing deterministic versions of `malloc()` and `free()` that use pre-allocated memory that is allocated in a nearly deterministic address. We suggest how to extend the idea of function stubs for other system/library calls.

We experiment with this prototype on live clouds and show that the overhead is almost *reasonable* for real-world applications. For some parameters we get a slowdown factor of "only" 8, compared to the original application. Furthermore, the result implies that a large portion of the overhead is due to implementation issues. Thus, a product-level implementation of the protocol could achieve much smaller overheads. See Section 4.4 for further details regarding the overheads.

1.2 Related Work

Prior work has studied the question of proving the correctness of general computations. (Most previous works focused on interactive proofs between a verifier and a prover. However, the problems are closely related: Given an interactive protocol for proving the correctness of a computation of f, one can easily get verifiable delegation of computation by asking the server for $y = f(x)$ and a proof that y is the correct result.) Babai *et al.* [7] consider this question in a setting where the prover is a non-adaptive oracle. Kilian [15] and Micali [20] build on their techniques and show efficient computationally sound protocols, whose security is based on cryptographic assumptions and where soundness holds only against computationally bounded cheating provers. Micali gets a non-interactive computationally sound proof based on the existence of a Random Oracle whereas Kilian gets a four-message interactive computationally sound proof assuming the existence of collision resistance hash family. Goldwasser *et. al.* [12] present an information theoretically sound interactive proof protocol for verifiable computation for any language in $\mathcal{L}$-uniform $\mathcal{NC}$.

We note that, with the exception of [12], the above works are based on Probabilistic Checkable Proofs (PCP) [6]. Although constructions of PCP are very efficient by means of asymptotic complexity, they are far from being practical.

Gennaro *et al.* [11], Chung *et. al.* [9] and Applebaum *et al.* [5] consider a model with a pre-processing stage. Based on the existence of a fully homomorphic encryption, they construct computationally sound protocols, where in an offline pre-processing stage the verifier runs in time proportional to the size of the computation. Afterwards, in a one-round online stage, the verifier (using the result of the pre-processing stage) runs in time proportional to the size of its inputs and the computation results. In these works, as long as the verifier does not encounter cheating provers, the same pre-processing information can be used in multiple rounds, yielding improved amortized complexity.

We remark that in all the above works, the verifier has to know all the inputs, including any randomness that the server uses for the computation (our protocol also shares this requirement).

A related proof model with several provers is the model of Multi-Prover Interactive Proofs, suggested by Ben-Or *et al.* [8]. In this model, even if *all* of the provers cheat, the verifier will detect that they are cheating. However, soundness is guaranteed assuming that malicious provers *cannot* communicate or coordinate their strategies during the protocol. This is in contrast to the refereed games of Feige and Kilian [10] and to our model, where soundness is guaranteed as long as one server is honest, even if all malicious servers communicate *during* the protocol. In addition, the client learns who are the cheating provers.

As for more applied prior work, there are works that in some sense restrict the computation type (e.g. [21] for computations that have short intermediate states, or, [13] for functions with easy to sample domains) and there are several works that use *trusted hardware* that allow almost any type of computation (e.g. [22, 18]). In the latter one, the client trusts some small tamper-resistant hardware (e.g. a tamper-proof coprocessor) that the server has, and using this hardware the server can prove the correctness of its computation. We note that using tamper-resistant hardware is conceptually similar to trusting another weak third-party (in this case, the hardware manufacturer). Nonetheless, this direction is very promising by means of practicality and generality.

There are works that consider verification of peers in distributed computations (e.g., [14] for verifying peers that are state machines) but usually these works assume the different players (i.e. the servers in our model) communicate among themselves or through a trusted server. In the model of cloud computing, we prefer that all communication will be held only between the client and the servers. That way, the servers do not know whom they are "playing" against (or even against how many) and the client does not have to trust any third party servers.

Our construction is not based on probabilistically checkable proofs or Fully Homomorphic Encryption, which are not practical yet, nor does it rely on trusted hardware. Furthermore, it does not require the *arguably* complex transformation of a Turing Machine program to a boolean circuit.

1.3 Organization

In Section 2 we define the model of Refereed Delegation of Computation (RDoC) and show how to extend RDoC with two servers to N servers. In Section 3.3 we present in detail our RDoC protocol. In Section 4 we describe the difficulties of implementing the protocol, our design choices, the adaptation of the protocol for X86 CPU and the architecture of Quin. In Section 4.4 we show experimental results of Quin on live clouds and in Section 4.5 we outline several future improvements.

2. REFEREED DELEGATION OF COMPUTATION

A refereed delegation of computation for a function f is a protocol between a client (or a referee) R and N servers $P_1, P_2, \dots, P_N$. All parties may use local randomness. The client and the servers receive an input x. The servers claim different results for the computation of $f(x)$ and the client should be able to determine the correct answer with high probability. We assume that at least one of the servers is honest.

DEFINITION 1 (REFEREED DELEGATION OF COMPUTATION). *Let $(P_1, P_2, \dots, P_N, R)$ be an ε-RDoC with N servers for a function f if the following holds:*

- *For any input x and for all $i \in \{1, \dots, N\}$, if server P_i is honest then for any $P_1^*, \dots, P_{i-1}^*, P_{i+1}^*, \dots, P_N^*$ the output of R is $f(x)$ w.p. at least $1 - \varepsilon$.*
- *The complexity of the client is at most quasi-linear in $|x|$ and the complexity of the (honest) servers is polynomial in the complexity of evaluating f.*

If soundness holds only for polynomially bounded (in $|x|$) servers then we say that it is a *computationally sound RDoC*. Furthermore, if the client starts by sending all its local random choices to *all* servers, and if all the communication between the client and the servers is public, we call it a *full-information* RDoC.

For completeness of the description, we briefly review the model of Refereed Games [10]. A refereed game (RG) for a language L is a protocol between a referee R and two competing *unbounded* servers P_1 and P_2. All three parties may use local randomness. The referee and the servers receive $x \in \{0,1\}^*$. Without loss of generality we can assume P_1 claims that $x \in L$ and P_2 claims that $x \notin L$, and the referee should be able to determine the correct answer with probability at least 2/3.

From Two Servers to N Servers. In the next sections we only discuss the case where there are two servers. Here we show how, given any RDoC with two servers and negligible error probability, one can construct a RDoC with N servers and negligible error probability, where we only need to assume that at least *one* of them is honest.

The idea is to execute the RDoC with two servers between each pair of servers. By the soundness of the RDoC with two servers, with high probability there exists an honest server P_i that convinces the client in *all* of his "games". The client outputs the claimed result of P_i.

This solution can be executed in parallel for all pairs, and therefore keeps the number of rounds the same. However, it requires $\frac{N\cdot(N-1)}{2}$ different executions of the protocol.

3. PROTOCOL FOR TURING MACHINES

3.1 Preliminaries: Merkle Hash Tree

Merkle Hash Tree (MHT) [19] is a common primitive that allows one to hash a long string of n characters in a where the hash can later be used to reveal any part of the string and supply a short proof of consistency. Given a collision-resistant hash function H and a string str of length n, the tree has n leaf nodes where leaf node i has the value of $H(str[i])$. The next level has the values of $H(H(str[i]) \circ H(str[i+1]))$ for $i = 1, 3, \ldots n-1$, and so on for the other levels. The highest level, the root, is the hash for the full string str. The proof of consistency for character i is the hash values along the path from the root to $H(str[i])$ and their siblings.

Given a Merkle Hash Tree of string str, denote by $MH_{root}(str)$ the value of the root, by $MH_{proof}(str, i)$ the proof of consistency for i-th character, and by VerifyMHProof$(root, i, str_i, p)$ the verification function that given a claimed $p = MH_{proof}(str, i)$ outputs True if p is a valid proof of consistency, and False otherwise. Note that the size of $MH_{root}(str)$ depends on the output length of the hash function and the size of $MH_{proof}(str, i)$ is logarithmic in the length of str.

Denote by $str_{[i]=x}$ the string that equals to str except for the i-th character that is x. We observe the following property of Merkle Hash Trees: Given a proof of consistency p for the i-th character of str, anyone can efficiently (i.e. in logarithmic time in the length of str) compute $MH_{root}(str_{[i]=x})$. This can be done by computing the hash of x and then iteratively computing the hashes along the path from i to the root.

3.2 Reduced Turing Machine Configuration

Given a Turing Machine configuration $(state, head, tape)$, let the *reduced-configuration* of $(state, head, tape)$ be the tuple

$$(\ state, head, tape[head], MH_{root}(tape)\ ).$$

For simplicity of the description, we denote by k the maximal length of the tape during the execution of the Turing Machine. Note that the size of the reduced-configuration is logarithmic in k, and therefore for computation of size T, it is at most logarithmic in T.

Given two reduced Turing Machine configurations $rc_1 = (s_1, h_1, v_1, r_1)$ and $rc_2 = (s_2, h_2, v_2, r_2)$ that are claimed to be consecutive, and a proof of consistency of the first configuration $p_1 = MH_{proof}(t, h_1)$ where t is the tape of configuration rc_1, one can efficiently verify this claim by checking the following:

1. Verify that VerifyMHProof(r_1, h_1, v_1, p_1) is True.
2. Simulate a single step of the Turing Machine on s_1, h_1, v_1 and get the next state s', new head position h' and the written character v'
3. Verify that $s' == s_2$ and $h' == h_2$.
4. Using p_1 and v', compute $r' = MH_{root}(t_{[h_1]=v'})$. (This can be done without knowing t using the previous observation.)
5. Verify that $r' == r_2$.

If one of the above checks fail, then the claim is false.

Denote by VerifyReducedStep(rc_1, rc_2, p_1) the function that given two reduced configurations rc_1, rc_2 and proof of consistency p_1 outputs False if any of the above checks fails, and True otherwise.

3.3 The Protocol

We base our protocol on the work of Feige and Kilian [10] where they present a refereed game with polynomial number of rounds and private communication channels (therefore not full information) for any *EXPTIME* language. Their protocol uses *arithmetization* for consistency checks and then takes advantage of the *locality* property of a single Turing Machine step (each Turing Machine transition uses only $O(1)$ *local* information: the current state, the current head position and the current character). In their protocol for languages in *EXPTIME*, the referee is polynomial in the length of the input x.

Their construction can be directly scaled-down for languages in P, yielding a protocol where the servers are polynomial in the input size and the referee is quasi-linear. Correctness remains unconditional. However, the protocol requires private communication channels between the referee and the two servers.

We modify their scaled-down protocol (for $\mathcal{P}$ languages) by replacing the use of arithmetization with Merkle Hash Trees. Although it gives only computational soundness, it greatly simplifies the protocol and gives us a negligible error probability for even one execution of the protocol. Since the main overhead of the protocol would be retrieving different states of the execution, this property is highly important. Our protocol is full-information and in particular does not require private communication channels. In a setting where messages between the players are digitally signed, the client can obtain a publicly verifiable proof that a server is cheating. (Note that in case of private channels/private-information, and specifically in the protocol of [10], colluding referee and server can forge together a transcript that incriminates an honest server of cheating. In the full-information model it is not possible.)

Given a Collision-Resistant Hash Function, our protocol is the following. The client requests each server to execute the Turing Machine that computes $f(x)$. In case they answer the same, by the assumption that one of them is honest, the answer is the correct one. Else, the client continues to a *binary-search* phase. The client asks the servers to send him the number of steps it takes to compute $f(x)$), takes the smaller answer as the current *bad row* variable, n_b, and sets to 1 the current *good row* variable, n_g. The client also asks for the maximal length of their stored configurations and takes the bigger answer to be k. Now, the client asks for the reduced configuration of the $(n_b - n_g)/2 + n_g$ configuration. If one of the answers is not a valid reduced configuration, the client outputs the value of $f(x)$ of the other server (this is the honest server). If answers match, he sets $n_g = (n_b - n_g)/2 + n_g$, otherwise, he sets $n_b = (n_b - n_g)/2 + n_g$. The client continues the binary search in that way till he gets $n_g + 1 = n_b$. Note that the servers do not have to remember *all* the configurations, instead, they can remember only two configurations, one for the last n_g and one for the last $(n_b - n_g)/2 + n_g$. Then, when asked for the next configuration, the server can continue the TM execution from one of those configurations. Overall, in worst case scenario, the servers execution time is not much more than executing the program twice.

Now, the client asks Server 1 for the consistency proof for configuration n_g, i.e. $p = MH_{proof}(t_{n_g}, h_{n_g})$. Denote by rc_{n_g} and rc_{n_b} the reduced configuration that Server 1 sent to the client. If VerifyReducedStep(rc_{n_g}, rc_{n_b}, p) is True, the client outputs the value of $f(x)$ of Server 1. Otherwise, he outputs the value of $f(x)$ of Server 2.

Overall we have:

THEOREM 1. *Assume the hash function in use is collision resistant. Then the above protocol is a computationally sound, full-information, RDoC with two servers and with negligible soundness ε for any function computable in polynomial time. For functions that can be computed by TMs taking $T(n)$ steps and $S(n)$ space on input x with $|x| = n$, the protocol takes $\log T(n) + 3$ rounds, the client runs in time $O(n + \kappa \log T(n) + \kappa \log S(n))$ and the servers run in time $O(T(n) + \kappa S(n) \log T(n))$, where κ is a security parameter.*

Note that in case both servers are honest, there is no overheads.

PROOF (SKETCH). By the specification of the protocol, if Server 1 is honest then it always successfully convinces the client (no matter what a malicious Server 2 does).

A malicious Server 1 can deceive the client to output a false value only if it can generate a fake consistency proof p that has the same root of the Merkle Hash Tree as in the correct reduced configuration n_g. Let π be the above protocol, and let π' be the above protocol with the following change: in the last step the client asks for the consistency proof from *both* servers and outputs the value of the server that was honest (i.e., its consistency proof was consistent with its reduced configurations n_g and n_b) or the output of Server 1 if they were both "honest" (i.e., both proofs were valid). Let ϵ be the probability that Server 1 cheats in π and let ϵ' be the probability Server 1 cheats in π'. Since a malicious Server 1 from protocol π can also cheat in protocol π' then $\epsilon \leq \epsilon'$. Now, assuming Server 1 in π' is malicious, then the client in protocol π' receives two different consistency proofs with the same root, thus, he gets a collision in some node along the path to index h_{n_g}. By the security of the collision resistant hash function, this can only happen with a negligible probability. Therefore, ϵ is negligible. □

3.4 Extensions

Reducing the number of rounds. In some scenarios, the number of rounds might still be the bottle-neck of the protocol. We can reduce the number of rounds by permitting larger messages and longer running time of the servers.

For any constant number t we can reduce the number of rounds to $\log_{t+1} T(n)$ (but slightly increase the communication size, by a factor of t) using the following idea. Instead of asking the servers for only one reduced configuration in each round, the client asks for t reduced configurations. Specifically, the client asks for the t steps that are equally spread between n_g and n_b. I.e., given $n_g = 100, n_b = 200, t = 4$, the client asks for $120, 140, 160$ and 180. Similar to the protocol from Section 3.3, the client updates n_g and n_b according to the servers' answers and continues to the next iteration of the binary (or $(t+1)$-ary) search.

More than two servers. In addition to the general method for extending the protocol to N servers from Section 2, we can extend this specific protocol also in the following way. The client executes a *Playoff* between all servers. In the first round, the client executes the protocol from Section 3.3 with all servers (he can do that because the protocol uses only public communication), where he marks a row as a good row only if all answers for this row match. At the end of the binary search, the client checks if the reduced configurations are consecutive for each one of the servers. After the execution of this protocol, at least one malicious server will be caught lying and will be declared as a cheater. The client continues to the next round with the other servers, again, executes the protocol to find at least one cheater and then excludes him (or them) from the next rounds. The protocol ends when all the remaining servers agree on the output.

Since the client excludes at least one malicious server in each round of the playoff, the number of rounds is bounded by the number of malicious servers.

Supporting large datasets. In order to support computations which use large datasets (e.g. Databases), we can use the Merkle Hash Trees again. We assume the client knows the root of the MHT of the data (either because he delegated the data in the past, or by keeping track of changes of the root). We modify the protocol from Section 3.3 to work with another tape that includes the dataset and we add to the reduced configuration also the root of the MHT of this tape, the current head position and the MHT proof for its current character. The rest of the protocol is the same. Note that the client has to know the root of the MHT at the beginning of the computation in order to be able to verify the initial configuration.

Reducing the server's overhead. In the worst case, the execution time of the servers in the protocol from Section 3.3 is not much more than executing the program twice. The server "pays" one execution time only for counting the number of instructions and then half execution time for getting to the middle configuration.

If we allow the servers to store more configurations then we can reduce the computation time for getting the middle configuration. Instead of just counting the number of instructions, the server also stores intermediate configurations. Let i be the current step of the execution. During the count of instructions, the server remembers the last three configurations for steps $i_3 = 2^{\lfloor \log(i) \rfloor}, i_1 = i_3/2$ and $i_2 = (i_3 - i_1)/2 + i_1$. Note that these values are changed only when $i = 2 * i_3$, and by storing also configuration $i_3 + i_1$, the server can compute them efficiently on-the-fly. In other words, the server always remembers at most four configurations and updates them during the counting (without rewinding the computation). Now, when requested for the middle configuration, the server takes the nearest stored configuration (either for i_1 or i_2) and continues the execution from that configuration. Overall, it reduces the computation of the middle configuration from half to one sixth in the worst case (resulting in overhead of $1\frac{4}{6}$ instead of 2). Repeating this method can reduce this overhead even more but with the price of larger storage.

4. QUIN: ADAPTATION AND IMPLEMENTATION OF THE PROTOCOL FOR X86

We show how to adapt the protocol from Section 3.3 for X86 CPU, and we present a prototype implementation that enables delegation of X86 executables for the Windows environment. Note that Windows is a closed-source OS, and our implementation does not require any changes to the OS. Everything runs in User-Mode. See [4] for the source code of the prototype.

4.1 The Difficulties and Design Choices

Although the protocol in Section 3.3 seems easy to describe with Turing Machines, its adaptation for real-world use is quite delicate. An implementation of it must have the following key properties:

- **Determinism:** The protocol highly depends on the determinism of the execution, therefore, the framework should be able to execute the program in a completely deterministic way, independently of the OS.

- **Stop, store and continue execution:** The protocol requires the ability to execute a program for a given number of steps, stop its execution and store its current state to a file. Later, we need to be able to continue the program execution from any previously stored state.

  At first, it seems obvious we can use a debugger. However, this is not the common functionality most debuggers provide. We require the ability to continue from *any* previously stored state, whereas a normal debugger stops on a pre-determined state and can continue execution only from that state.

- **Simulate an instruction:** In order to implement the last step of the protocol (VerifyReducedStep()), the client should be able to simulate any instruction given the instruction's operands.

When we were looking for candidate high-level languages we had two key observations:

- Since our client has to simulate one instruction by itself, we prefer to work with a language that has simple instructions. By simple we mean that any single instruction takes a small and bounded amount of time to compute, as opposed to, for example, a single line of Java code which can theoretically hide a very heavy computation. Ideally, we would like to work with something that is similar to RISC assembly or Java Bytecode.

- Interpreted languages like Java and Python have complex interpreters that have their own internal states, which are usually not deterministic. E.g., their native code cache or their internal memory management processes like the Garbage Collector. Therefore, storing a state of an interpreted-language program requires subtle changes of its interpreter to somehow make it more deterministic.

In addition, there are many non deterministic events that depend on the operating system, e.g., many OS interfaces return handles to some of the OS internal structures like a pointer to an opened file. Since most operating system calls are also non-deterministic, we require that the program will not make any non-deterministic operating system or standard library calls. We remark that this restriction can be bypassed by writing *function stubs* that preserve that determinism of the program. Currently, we implemented such stubs only for the essential `malloc()` and `free()` functions. See Section 4.5 for further discussion. Similarly, multi-threading could ruin the determinism, so we require that our delegated program use only one thread.

4.2 Adaptation of the Protocol for X86

We decided to implement the prototype directly with X86 assembly, for stand-alone programs. We believe that using X86 assembly is both cleaner to use and general for further development (e.g., using C++ programs instead of only C).

Instead of the Turing Machine's transitions table, the computation is described by assembly instructions. Each step of the protocol is now an execution of a single X86 instruction. When the client needs to compute a single step by himself, he should be able to execute a single X86 instruction given the needed registers and memory. We remark that some X86 instructions are non-deterministic by definition (e.g. CPUID, RDTSC) and we assume the program does not use them (this can be restricted during build).

The equivalent of a Turing Machine state is the current values of all the CPU registers (e.g., `eax`, `ebx`, etc). We initialize those registers before the execution of the program.

Last, we replace the Turing Machine working tapes with the process' stack and heap memories. We assume these memories are initialized to zero, which is the equivalent of an empty tape. Under reasonable assumptions on the cloud operating system we can work with fixed base-addresses for those memories and therefore get fully deterministic memory operations (i.e., even pointers to the memory will have deterministic addresses for each execution of the program).

The reduced-configuration equivalence in this model would be the values of all CPU registers (the equivalent to the Turing Machine's state and head position) and two hash values. Those hash values are the root values of the Merkle Hash Trees of the current stack and heap memories.

The proof of correctness of the resulting protocol is similar to the proof of protocol from Section 3.3.

4.3 System Architecture

The client has a source code in C of a program `prog.exe` that he wishes to delegate. The programmer does not have to write his program in some new or restricted language, he can write his program in the same way he writes any C program. For simplicity of the description here we assume that the input to the program is part of the program itself (hard-coded) and that the result of the program is an integer. Specifically, we assume there is a function with the prototype `int client_program()`. Those restrictions can be easily eliminated (e.g., by using a pre-allocated buffers for input/output before/after the program execution).

Given the source code, the client builds the program using a supplied makefile. This makefile basically links the program with a wrapper code, sets the code base-address to be static and statically links all libraries. We set the code base-address to be static so the operating system's loader will load the program to the same memory address for all executions. Similarly, since shared libraries can be loaded to any memory address, we statically link all libraries so they will be (again) loaded to specific memory addresses.

The wrapper code corresponds to the Turing Machine initialization. It initializes to zero all the general use registers and the required stack memory, it allocates a large amount of memory to be used as the program heap and calls `client_program()`. Also, the makefile links a code for `malloc()` and `free()` that uses the pre-allocated memory instead of the regular heap. Here we use the fact that Windows allocates large memory segments (e.g. 2 GB) in almost deterministic addresses. See Figure 1 for a pseudo-code of the wrapper function.

After the client builds his program with the supplied makefile, he sends the executable to each of the servers. Now, the protocol itself starts.

```
int main(){
    int i;
    int result;
    void *heap;
    char *stack;
    /* Init stack memory          */
    /* STACK_SIZE is usually 2^20 */
    _asm{
        mov stack, esp
    }
    for(i=0;i<STACK_SIZE;i++){
        *(stack-i) = 0;
    }
    /* Init heap memory           */
    /* HEAP_SIZE is usually 2^30  */
    heap = calloc(HEAP_SIZE);
    /* Init all registers         */
    _asm{
        mov eax,0
        mov ebx,0
        ...
        /* Setting esp to be the
           start of a memory page  */
        mov eax, esp
        and eax, 0xfff
        sub esp, eax
    }
    /* Execute original program    */
    _asm{
        call client_program()
        mov result, eax
    }
}
```

Figure 1: Quin wrapper function.

The prototype consists of three main tools: `QuinExecuter`, `QuinClient` and `QuinServer`. The client runs the `QuinClient` on his machine and the servers run `QuinServer` and `QuinExecuter` on their machines. `QuinExecuter` is a tool for executing a program for a given number of instructions. It can store the program state or continue execution from a previously stored state. `QuinClient` and `QuinServer` are python implementations of the protocol itself.

The Merkle Hash Tree is computed with granularity of a 4Kbyte (a page-size), i.e., the lowest level of the tree are hashes of 4Kbyte segments. (This is why our wrapper function moves the `esp` register to the beginning of a page.)

4.3.1 *QuinExecuter*

For executing a program for a given number of instructions, we need a way to count in real-time the number of executed instructions. There are several ways to do that:

- Use the CPU internal instructions counters: this is a very efficient method, but requires to change the OS in order to differentiate between our instructions and other OS instructions.

- Extend the compiler: instead of emitting the programmer's code as is, add to it few assembly instructions that increment a counter before each original assembly instruction.

  The downside is that we have to do it for every high level language compiler although the protocol itself works with the assembly instructions.

- Use OS debug API: execute the program *step-by-step*. Since it is *out-of-process* debugging, it is very inefficient.

- Static instrumentation: given an executable, transform it to a new executable with the other needed instructions (i.e., that increment a counter).

- Dynamic instrumentation: similar to static instrumentation, but done in run-time.

Our method of choice is to use a dynamic instrumentation tool, specifically Intel's PIN [17]. Although dynamic instrumentation has potential for substantial overheads over static instrumentation, PIN has many benefits for our use. PIN is very efficient (compared to other dynamic instrumentation frameworks), very convenient for rapid development, well supported by Intel, and most importantly, works the same in Windows and Linux environments. PIN runs the program inside a Virtual Machine and uses Just-In-Time (JIT) compilation of the instrumented code. The PIN developer writes a piece of code that is called a *PIN-tool*, which is a description of where to instrument and what code to put there. In order to run the PIN-tool, only four binary files are needed (`.exe` and `.dll` files), and no setup is required. The PIN-tool itself is another `.dll` binary.

`QuinExecuter` is basically a PIN-tool. The naive way to get our goal is that `QuinExecuter` adds instrumented code for counting steps and checking whether we reached the needed number of steps. This would be the main overhead of our implementation, as for each executed instruction of the original executable we add code that increments a 64 bit counter and checks whether this counter reached some threshold. This means that *for each* assembly instruction of the original program we add around 10-15 new assembly instructions. Our implementation actually uses a simple heuristic to reduce this overhead. Instead of adding the code for each instruction, we add the code only once for each *basic-block* (a sequence of code with only one entry point and one exit point). For each basic block we increment the counter according to the basic block's number of instructions. Since we want to be correct with a granularity of a single instruction, when we get close enough to our threshold (say, 500 instructions below the threshold), we re-instrument the code and add our code before each instruction (as in the naive way). We note that since we are interested in precise granularity for all types of computations, this heuristic seems to have the best tradeoff between efficiency and accuracy.

After it reaches the needed number of steps, it dumps the current state of the memories (we separate the stack and the heap for efficiency) and all the registers values to a file. When requested, it can do the opposite, start a new process, restore a state from a given file and continue the execution of the process from this state. The way it does those operations is by reading and writing directly the stack and the heap whenever needed.

In order to handle memory, we use the following two methods:

- **For stack memory:** In order to get full determinism, all memory should be initialized before use. Since the operating system do not initialize the stack by itself, our wrapper function does it before the call to `client_program()`. We use the maximal stack size that is defined during the program linkage.

- **For heap memory:** As already noted, we implemented our own `malloc()` and `free()`. Those functions uses a pre-allocated memory, and stores its state in a pre-defined memory areas, so when needed to dump or restore a state, our PIN-tool can work directly with those internal structures.

  For the protocol itself, we define the maximal size of the heap memory to be constant (e.g., 2^{30} bytes). As this memory is pre-allocated, we set this memory to zero before the execution of `client_program()`.

`QuinExecuter` is implemented in C and Assembly, and uses several low-level techniques in order to get efficient instrumented code.

We note that since we assume the client has the source-code of the delegated program, we could have chosen to change the build process in order to create a different executable that can directly give us the above functionalities. However, our future goal is to replace the use of our makefile (that adds the wrapper function) with another binary instrumentation, in a way that our PIN-tool could work directly with any stand-alone executable (e.g. commodity software). This PIN-tool will find `main()` and wrap it with our wrapper function using instrumentation. In addition, it will locate `malloc()` and `free()` and replace them with our implementation of those functions.

4.3.2 *QuinServer*

`QuinServer` is a pure Python program that takes an executable as input and implements the server side of the protocol. It is a state-machine. It waits for the client's connection and then waits for his commands. The first command the server receives is **RUN**, and, as a response, the server executes `QuinExecuter` with the input executable and returns its result to the client, including the returning value of `client_program()`, the number of steps of the execution and several other low-level information on the execution itself. Then, if the client decides to proceed to the binary search stage (in case of inconsistency between the servers' answers), the server receives the command **GetReducedState** i. As a response, the server now sends the values of all CPU registers and two hash values. Those hash values are the root values of the Merkle Hash Trees of the current stack and the current heap. This command is received for all the binary search requested configurations.

After the client finishes the binary search stage, it simulates one instruction based on the registers that the servers sent for the n_g step. In case the simulated instruction requires to use some memory, either from the stack or the heap, the client sends the command **GetMemory** i**, address**. Then, the server sends the memory value of the requested address, augmented with a Merkle Hash Tree proof that this value is consistent with the root values it sent before (for step i).

4.3.3 *QuinClient*

`QuinClient` is a python program that implements the client part of the protocol. It connects to the servers, sends the command **RUN** to all of them and compares their answers. In case of consistency, it can output the correct result of `client_program()` and quit. In case of inconsistency, it executes the binary search and finds the step where the servers disagree (by using the **GetReducedState** i command). Then, it simulates the instruction for step n_g using an open-source X86 emulator called PyEmu [3]. In order to support the use of PyEmu in our prototype, we implemented a new object that encapsulates the verifiable memory accesses using the **GetMemory** i command. When PyEmu needs some memory page, `QuinClient` asks one of the servers for it. The server sends that page along with Merkle Hash Tree proof for this page. Then, `QuinClient` verifies that proof and feeds PyEmu with the received page. Last, `QuinClient` uses the emulation result (the written memory data and the values of the registers) to compute the correct reduced configuration for step n_b, compares it to the servers' answers and declares the correct output. We remark that PyEmu does not support the full X86 instruction set, but it does support the instructions most compilers generate. (Also, it is easy to add other instructions if needed.) Quin inherits this limitation.

4.4 Evaluation

We conducted several experiments with our Quin prototype in order to test the practicality of our protocol. We separated the evaluation of the protocol and the evaluation of our main tool, `QuinExecuter`, in order to better understand where the bottle-necks are. We believe there are many possible directions for improving `QuinExecuter` and therefore we want to get the exact weight of its performance compared to the protocol's overall performance.

Since our goal is to check practicality of the protocol in real-world scenarios, we experimented with live cloud providers, Amazon EC2 and Rackspace Cloud, which are currently among the largest cloud providers. For our experiments we used the following setup: 1) Laptop installed with Windows Vista, Intel 2.2 GHz CPU, 1 GB of RAM. 2) EC2 virtual machines installed with Windows 2008 32bit, 5 EC2 compute units, 1.7 GB RAM and 160 GB storage. All are located in Amazon's Virginia region. 3) Rackspace virtual machines installed with Windows 2008 32bit, 2 GB RAM, 80 GB storage and default CPU. All are located in Rackspace's Chicago datacenter. The average round-trip time between the laptop and the clouds was 380ms (for packets of size 10K bytes).

As for the delegated program, we used a simple but very useful program, `Determinant.exe`, that computes the determinant of a given matrix. Although there are algorithms for computing determinant that run in time $O(n^3)$ (for $n * n$ matrix), we used the naive algorithm that runs in time $O(n!)$, and uses $O(n^3)$ space.

4.4.1 *QuinExecuter Performance*

In order to isolate the overhead of the `QuinExecuter` itself, we ran the following experiments:

1. Execution of the delegated program, `Det_quin.exe`, which is `Determinant.exe` wrapped with our wrapper function. The overhead of our wrapper function itself is negligible.

2. Execution of PIN with `Det_quin.exe`, without any instrumentation (i.e., `pin -- Det_quin.exe`). Since PIN is a dynamic instrumentation tool that uses dynamic translation (JIT), this gives us an estimation of the overhead of this translation (the PIN VM).

3. Execution of PIN with `Det_quin.exe`, with our PIN-tool (i.e., `pin -t quin.dll -- Det_quin.exe`). This is an execution of `Det_quin.exe` when we only count the number of executed instructions (by adding instrumentation code).

4. Execution of PIN with `Det_quin.exe`, with our PIN-tool, for N steps (i.e., `pin -t quin.dll -- Det_quin.exe -n N`). This is an execution of `Det_quin.exe` for N steps when we count the number of executed instructions and compare it to N. N is the total number of steps of the execution of `Det_quin.exe`. This is the heaviest instrumentation we use in the protocol since it adds code both for counting the number of executed instructions and for the comparison to N.

We ran the above experiments on an Amazon EC2 virtual machine and on a Rackspace Cloud virtual machine. The left side of Table 1 shows the results for those experiments. Each experiment was executed three times. The numbers in the table represent the average running times in seconds on Amazon EC2 and Rackspace Cloud, respectively, separated by slashes.

Matrix Size	Exp. 1	Exp. 2	Exp. 3	Exp. 4	Quin Total	Overhead Factor
10	2/1	3/3	7/7	15/15	381	190
11	21/19	23/21	69/67	156/143	694	33
12	252/230	256/242	829/803	1899/1720	2243	8

Table 1: Evaluation results of PIN-tool experiments and Quin performance

We can observe (from experiment 2) that PIN itself introduces an overhead of at least 1-2 seconds. This overhead is very influencing for the protocol since Quin executes PIN for each round of the binary search and for many short executions, so we get that for x rounds of the binary search we already have an overhead of at least x seconds, and in most cases this overhead is much larger.

Furthermore, we can see that adding even few instrumentation instructions increases the running time by large factors.

Those performance results are important, since it gives us a good estimation of the protocol performance. The protocol starts with executing `Det_quin.exe` and counting the number of steps, and then, continues to an execution of the heavier instrumentation for overall time that is proportional to the running time of the program once. So, in theory (without considering network latency, servers' overheads, etc) we expect that the protocol performance would be something that is proportional to the sum of the fourth and the fifth columns. (Note that these sums are bigger by factors of $10 - 20$ than the plain execution.)

4.4.2 *Performance of the Protocol*

We executed several experiments of the full protocol. For each experiment we ran the protocol several times with one cheating cloud that cheats on one out of three randomly chosen states. Those states were chosen to be close to the end of the computation (around 80%−85% of the total number of steps). We added to `QuinServer` a code that, when asked, tries to cheat on all configurations from some given step. Note that we focus on the efficiency of the clouds since the client's running time is very small (he just sends short TCP messages to each cloud, and receives short answers that are several hundreds of bytes for each round and around 5Kbyte for the last round).

After evaluating the performance of `QuinServer` and noticing that its execution is very expensive, we decided to modify the underlying protocol as following: If $(n_b - n_g)$ is greater than some threshold (e.g., 50M), instead of asking for configuration $(n_b - n_g)/2 + n_g$ the client asks for configuration $(n_b - n_g)/4 + n_g$. The rest of the protocol is the same. This change is essentially a tradeoff between the number of rounds (that is increased) and the number of executed instructions on the cloud (that is decreased proportionally to the distance of the last n_g configuration from the last configuration).

We used one virtual machine on each cloud provider (as our two clouds) and the laptop as our client. In the right side of Table 1 we show the average running times of the protocol for the program `Determinant.exe`. The numbers represent the total Quin running times as recorded by the client (where only few seconds, combined, are from the client work or from communication latency). We remark that there are major performance differences, both between Amazon EC2 and Rackspace Cloud and between different times of the day. The overhead factors are over the running times of `Det_quin.exe` from experiment 1.

We can observe that the overhead of the protocol is reduced when the original computation time grows. This suggests that the overhead of the protocol itself is lower, and there are many implementation overheads. E.g., the PIN VM overhead that adds at least 1-2 seconds for each round and the PIN-tool large overheads we saw in the previous section. We believe that a product-level implementation those parts can get much smaller overheads, presumably a factor of 10-20 times slower on average for all computations.

Recall that the protocol from Section 3 has no overhead for the servers in case both of them are honest. Therefore, since most of the time both servers are honest, a more efficient solution would be that the client starts by simply asking both servers for their answers, and only in case of inconsistent answers he proceeds to the full execution of Quin. This gives a solution with no overhead in case both servers are honest.

4.5 Restrictions and Further Improvements

Adding function stubs. Since the program has to be fully deterministic, it can not call any non-deterministic external libraries or OS APIs. This restriction can be overcome (to some extent) by adding function stubs that hide the OS non-deterministic factors. E.g., `fopen()` returns a pointer `FILE*` that points to some non deterministic address. One could implement the functions `ex_fopen()` and `ex_fread()` that instead of working with `FILE*`, they work with some file identifiers that are generated deterministically. Those functions use an internal table to translate that identifier to a matching `FILE*` pointer and call the required `fopen()` or `fread()`. Last, `QuinExecuter` should treat calls to `ex_fopen()` or `ex_fread()` as single instructions. Note that this workaround can work only for functions that are non-deterministic because of the OS implementation, and it can not work with functions that are non-deterministic by definition (e.g., functions that return current time or a packet from the network).

Different Operating Systems. Currently Quin runs only on Windows because we make use of some of the Windows Loader low-level properties. Since PIN supports Windows and Linux, under minor changes to our PIN-tool, `QuinExecuter` can be used also in Linux. As the delegated program is a plain stand-alone C program that can be executed on any OS, and since `QuinClient` and `QuinServer` are OS independent, an interesting improvement would be to generalize `QuinExecuter` to be OS independent.

Support any X86 executable. Our current prototype requires building the delegated executable with our supplied makefile. We stress that it is a design decision since our future goal is to replace the use of our makefile (that adds the wrapper function) with another binary instrumentation, in a way that our PIN-tool could work directly with any stand-alone executable (e.g. commodity software).

Static Instrumentation instead of Dynamic Instrumentation. The functionalities we need from PIN can be achieved by static instrumentation, which is much more efficient for cases of *instrument once, run many times*. We saw in our evaluation that `QuinExecuter` adds the largest overhead of the implementation, therefore, any performance improvement of it will dramatically improve the performance of the overall protocol.

There are several static instrumentation frameworks for Linux environments (e.g., DynInst [2], PEBIL [16]), but we did not find a convenient framework that works also for Windows executables.

Using several computers in each cloud. Since the main bottleneck of our implementation is the executions of `QuinExecuter`, we can use the following trick to reduce the overheads. Instead of running `QuinExecuter` separately for each query, the cloud can use several computers (or other CPU cores) and execute different executions of `QuinExecuter` in parallel. E.g., when queried for configuration i, the cloud executes `QuinExecuter` for i steps on one machine, but also `QuinExecuter` for $i+(n_b-i)/2$ steps on a second machine. Then, if the next query is for step $i+(n_b-i)/2$, the cloud could answer with the result sooner than in the sequential protocol.

Also, using parallel executions of `QuinExecuter`, we can efficiently reduce the number of rounds to $\log_{t+1} T + 3$ as described in Section 3.4.

Implementation for Interpreted Languages. As discussed before, interpreted languages such as Java and Python have complex interpreters that usually maintain an internal state that depends on many factors other then the program itself (e.g., garbage collector's tables). However, those interpreters already do many operations that we can use (e.g., most interpreters do just-in-time compilation, or have stubs for system calls). Therefore, if we could modify them to be more deterministic, we might gain a very efficient solution. During our work we have investigated several interpreters and we believe that the above can be done.

Another environment that is potentially relevant for our protocol is the *Platform as a Service* (e.g., Google App Engine), which usually provides kind of a stand-alone computation delegation service for one process and a restricted set of "system calls". Implementation of our protocol for interpreted languages may be very appealing for such services.

5. REFERENCES

[1] BOINC, Validation and replication. `http://boinc.berkeley.edu/trac/wiki/ValidationSummary`.

[2] DynInst, an application program interface for runtime code generation. `http://www.dyninst.org`.

[3] PyEmu, a python IA-32 emulator. `http://code.google.com/p/pyemu`.

[4] Quin's source code. `http://www.cs.tau.ac.il/~benriva/quin`.

[5] B. Applebaum, Y. Ishai, and E. Kushilevitz. From secrecy to soundness: efficient verification via secure computation. In *Proceedings of the 37th international colloquium conference on Automata, languages and programming*, pages 152–163. Springer-Verlag, 2010.

[6] S. Arora and S. Safra. Probabilistic checking of proofs: a new characterization of NP. *J. ACM*, 45:70–122, January 1998.

[7] L. Babai, L. Fortnow, L. A. Levin, and M. Szegedy. Checking computations in polylogarithmic time. In *Proceedings of the twenty-third annual ACM symposium on Theory of computing*, pages 21–32. ACM, 1991.

[8] M. Ben-Or, S. Goldwasser, J. Kilian, and A. Wigderson. Multi-prover interactive proofs: how to remove intractability assumptions. In *Proceedings of the twentieth annual ACM symposium on Theory of computing*, pages 113–131. ACM, 1988.

[9] K. M. Chung, Y. Kalai, and S. Vadhan. Improved delegation of computation using fully homomorphic encryption. In *Proceedings of the 30th annual conference on Advances in cryptology*, pages 483–501. Springer-Verlag, 2010.

[10] U. Feige and J. Kilian. Making games short (extended abstract). In *Proceedings of the twenty-ninth annual ACM symposium on Theory of computing*, pages 506–516. ACM, 1997.

[11] R. Gennaro, C. Gentry, and B. Parno. Non-interactive verifiable computing: outsourcing computation to untrusted workers. In *Proceedings of the 30th annual conference on Advances in cryptology*, pages 465–482. Springer-Verlag, 2010.

[12] S. Goldwasser, Y. T. Kalai, and G. N. Rothblum. Delegating computation: interactive proofs for muggles. In *Proceedings of the 40th annual ACM symposium on Theory of computing*, pages 113–122. ACM, 2008.

[13] P. Golle and I. Mironov. Uncheatable distributed computations. In *Proceedings of the 2001 Conference on Topics in Cryptology: The Cryptographer's Track at RSA*, pages 425–440. Springer, 2001.

[14] A. Haeberlen, P. Kuznetsov, and P. Druschel. PeerReview: Practical accountability for distributed systems. In *Proceedings of the 21st ACM Symposium on Operating Systems Principles*, pages 175–188. ACM, 2007.

[15] J. Kilian. A note on efficient zero-knowledge proofs and arguments (extended abstract). In *Proceedings of the twenty-fourth annual ACM symposium on Theory of computing*, pages 723–732. ACM, 1992.

[16] M. Laurenzano, M. M. Tikir, L. Carrington, and A. Snavely. PEBIL: Efficient static binary instrumentation for linux. In *ISPASS*, pages 175–183, 2010.

[17] C. K. Luk, R. Cohn, R. Muth, H. Patil, A. Klauser, G. Lowney, S. Wallace, V. J. Reddi, and K. Hazelwood. Pin: building customized program analysis tools with dynamic instrumentation. In *Proceedings of the 2005 ACM SIGPLAN conference on Programming language design and implementation*, pages 190–200. ACM, 2005.

[18] J. M. McCune, B. J. Parno, A. Perrig, M. K. Reiter, and H. Isozaki. Flicker: an execution infrastructure for tcb minimization. In *Proceedings of the 3rd ACM SIGOPS/EuroSys European Conference on Computer Systems 2008*, pages 315–328. ACM, 2008.

[19] R. C. Merkle. A digital signature based on a conventional encryption function. In *A Conference on the Theory and Applications of Cryptographic Techniques on Advances in Cryptology*, pages 369–378. Springer-Verlag, 1988.

[20] S. Micali. Computationally sound proofs. *SIAM J. Comput.*, 30:1253–1298, October 2000.

[21] F. Monrose, P. Wycko, and A. D. Rubin. Distributed execution with remote audit. In *Proceedings of the 1999 ISOC Network and Distributed System Security Symposium*, pages 103–113. The Internet Society, 1999.

[22] E. Shi, A. Perrig, and L. V. Doorn. Bind: A fine-grained attestation service for secure distributed systems. In *Proceedings of the 2005 IEEE Symposium on Security and Privacy*, pages 154–168. IEEE Computer Society, 2005.

Fashion Crimes: Trending-Term Exploitation on the Web

Tyler Moore
Wellesley College*
tmoore@cs.wellesley.edu

Nektarios Leontiadis
Carnegie Mellon University
leontiadis@cmu.edu

Nicolas Christin
Carnegie Mellon University
nicolasc@cmu.edu

ABSTRACT

Online service providers are engaged in constant conflict with miscreants who try to siphon a portion of legitimate traffic to make illicit profits. We study the abuse of "trending" search terms, in which miscreants place links to malware-distributing or ad-filled web sites in web search and Twitter results, by collecting and analyzing measurements over nine months from multiple sources. We devise heuristics to identify ad-filled sites, report on the prevalence of malware and ad-filled sites in trending-term search results, and measure the success in blocking such content. We uncover collusion across offending domains using network analysis, and use regression analysis to conclude that both malware and ad-filled sites thrive on less popular, and less profitable trending terms. We build an economic model informed by our measurements and conclude that ad-filled sites and malware distribution may be economic substitutes. Finally, because our measurement interval spans February 2011, when Google announced changes to its ranking algorithm to root out low-quality sites, we can assess the impact of search-engine intervention on the profits miscreants can achieve.

Categories and Subject Descriptors

K.4.1 [**Public Policy Issues**]: Abuse and crime involving computers

General Terms

Measurement, Security, Economics

Keywords

Online crime, search engines, malware, advertisements

1. INTRODUCTION

News travels fast. Blogs and other websites pick up a news story only about 2.5 hours on average after it has been reported by traditional media [21]. This leads to an almost continuous supply of new "trending" topics, which are then amplified across the Internet, before fading away relatively quickly.

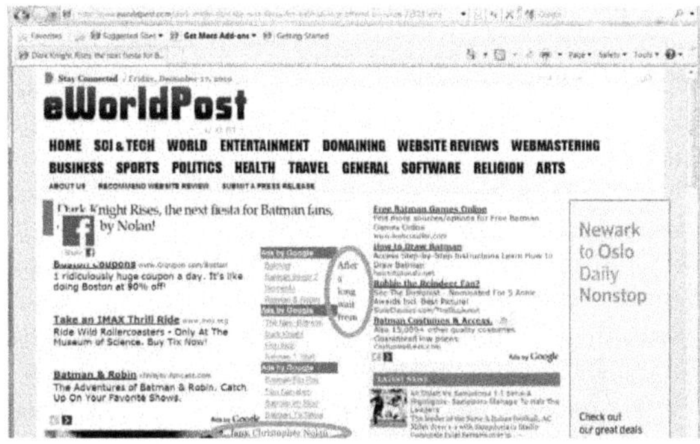

Figure 1: Ad-filled website appearing in the results for trending terms (only 8 words from the article, circled, appear on screen).

However narrow, these first moments after a story breaks present a window of opportunity for attackers to infiltrate web and social network search results in response. The motivation for doing so is primarily financial. Websites that rank high in response to a search for a trending term are likely to receive considerable amounts of traffic, regardless of their quality. Web traffic can in turn be monetized in a number of ways, as shown in related work [6, 10, 17, 20]. In short, manipulation of web or social network search engine results can be a profitable enterprise for its perpetrators.

In particular, the sole goal of many sites designed in response to trending terms is to produce revenue through the advertisements that they display in their pages, without providing any original content or services. Figure 1 presents a screenshot for `eworldpost.com`, which has appeared in response to 549 trending terms between July 2010 and March 2011. The actual article (circled) is hard to find, when compared to the amount of screen real estate dedicated to ads. Such sites are often referred to as "Made for AdSense" (MFA) after the name of the Google advertising platform they are often targeting. Whether such activity is deemed to be criminal or merely a nuisance remains an open question, and largely depends on the tactics used to prop the sites up in the search-engine rankings. Some other sites devised to respond to trending terms have more overtly sinister motives. For instance, a number of malicious sites serve malware in hopes of infecting visitors' machines [30], or peddle fake anti-virus software [2, 8, 36].

Both MFA and malware-hosting sites are enough of a scourge to trigger response from search engine operators. Google modified its search algorithm in February 2011 in part to combat MFA sites [35], and has long been offering the Google Safe Browsing API to block malware-distribution sites. Trending-term exploita-

*This work was primarily done while T. Moore was at Harvard University.

CCS'11, October 17–21, 2011, Chicago, Illinois, USA.

tion makes both MFA and malware sites even more dynamic than they used to be, thereby complicating the defenders' task.

This paper provides the first large-scale measurement and analysis of trending-term exploitation on the web. Based on a collection of over 60 million search results and tweets gathered over nine months, we characterize how trending terms are used to perform web search-engine manipulation and social-network spam. An important feature of our work is that we bring an outsider's perspective. Instead of relying on proprietary data tied to a specific search engine, we use comparative measurements of publicly observable data across different web search engines (Google, Yahoo!/Bing) and social network (Twitter) posts.

Our specific contributions are as follows. We (1) provide a methodology to automate classification of websites as MFA, (2) show salient differences between tactics used by MFA site operators and malware peddlers, (3) construct an economic model to characterize the trade-offs between advertising and malware as monetization vectors, quantifying the potential profit to the perpetrators, and (4) examine the impact of possible intervention strategies.

The rest of this paper is organized as follows. We introduce our measurement and classification methodology in Section 2. We analyze the measurements collected in Section 3 to characterize trending-term exploitation on the web. Notably, we uncover collusion across offending domains using network analysis, and we use regression analysis to conclude that both malware and MFA sites thrive on less popular and profitable trending terms. We then use these findings to build an economic model of attacker revenue in Section 4, and examine the effect of search-engine intervention in Section 5. We compare our study with related work in Section 6, before drawing brief conclusions in Section 7.

2. METHODOLOGY

We start by describing our methodology for data collection and website classification. At a high level, we need to issue a number of queries on various search engines for current trending terms, follow the links obtained in response to these queries, and classify the websites we eventually reach as malicious or benign. Within the collection of malicious sites so obtained, we have to further distinguish between malware-hosting sites and ad-laden sites. Moreover, we need to compare the results obtained with those collected from "ordinary," rather than trending, terms.

The data collection hinges on a number of design choices that we discuss and motivate here. Specifically, we must determine how to build the corpus of trending terms to use in queries ("*trending set*"); identify a set of control queries ("*control set*") against which we can compare responses to queries based on trending terms; decide on how frequently, and for how long, we issue each set of queries; and find mechanisms to classify sites as benign, malware-distributing, and MFA.

2.1 Building query corpora

Building a corpus of trending terms is not in itself a challenging exercise. Google, through Google Hot Trends [15], provides a list of twenty current "hot searches," which we determined, through pilot experiments, to be updated hourly. Likewise, Twitter avails a list of ten trending topics [37] and Yahoo! gives a "buzz log" [38] containing the 20 most popular searches over the past 24 hours.

These different lists sometimes have very little overlap. For instance, combining the 20 Yahoo! Buzz logs, 20 Google Hot Trends, and 10 Twitter Trending Topics, it is not uncommon to find more than 40 distinct trending terms over short time intervals. This would seem to make the case for aggregating all sources to build our query corpus. However, all search APIs limit the rate at which queries can be issued. We thus face a trade-off between the time granularity of our measurements and the size of our query corpus.

Trending set. Fortunately, we can capture most of the interesting patterns we seek to characterize by solely focusing on Google Hot Trends. Indeed, a recent measurement study conducted by John et al. [17] shows that over 95% of the terms used in search engine manipulation belong to the Google Hot Trends. However, because Twitter abuse may not necessarily follow the typical search engine manipulation patterns, we use both Google Hot Trends and the Twitter current trending topics in our Twitter measurements.

Hot trends, by definition, are constantly changing. We update our trending term corpus every hour by simply adding the current Google Hot Trends to it. Determining when a term has "cooled" and should be removed from the query corpus is slightly less straightforward. We could simply remove terms from our query corpus as soon as they disappear from the list of Google Hot Trends. However, unless all miscreants stop poisoning search results with a given term as soon as this term has "cooled," we would likely miss a number of attempts to manipulate search engine results. Furthermore, Hot Trends are selected based upon their rate of growth in query popularity. Terms that have fallen out of the list in most cases still enjoy a sustained period of popularity before falling.

We ran a pilot experiment collecting Google and Twitter search results on 20 hot terms for up to four days. As Figure 2(a) shows, 95% of all unique Google search results and 81% of Twitter results are collected within three days. Thus, we settled on searching for trending terms while they remain in the rankings, plus up to three days after they drop out of the rankings.

Control set. It is necessary to compare results from the trending set to a control set of consistently popular search terms, to identify which phenomena are unique to the trending nature of the terms as opposed to their overall popularity. We build a control list of the most popular search terms in 2010 according to Google Insights for Search [13]. Google lists the top 20 most popular search terms for 27 categories. These reduce to 495 unique search terms, which we use as a control set.

2.2 Data collection

For each term in our trending and control sets, we run automated searches on Google and Yahoo! between July 24, 2010 and April 24, 2011. We investigate MFA results throughout that period, and study the timeliness of malware identification between January 26 and April 24, 2011. We study Twitter results gathered between March 10 and April 18, 2011.

We use the Google Web Search API [1] to pull the top 32 search results for each term from the Google search engine, and the Yahoo! BOSS API to fetch its top 100 Yahoo! results for each term. Since the summer of 2010 Yahoo! and Bing search results are identical [23]. Consequently, while in the paper we refer to Yahoo! results, they should also be interpreted as those appearing on Bing. Likewise, we use the Twitter Atom API to retrieve the top 16 tweets for each term in Google's Hot Trends list and Twitter's Current Trends list. We resolve and record URLs linked from tweets, as well as the authors of these tweets linking to other sites.

Because all these APIs limit the number of queries that can be run, we had to limit the frequency with which we ran the search queries. To better understand the trade-offs between search frequency and comprehensiveness of coverage, we selected 20 terms from a single trending list and ran searches using the Google API every 10 minutes for one week. We then compared the results we could obtain using the high-frequency sampling to what we found when sampling less often. The results are presented in Figures 2(b) and 2(c). Sampling once every 20 minutes, rather than every 10

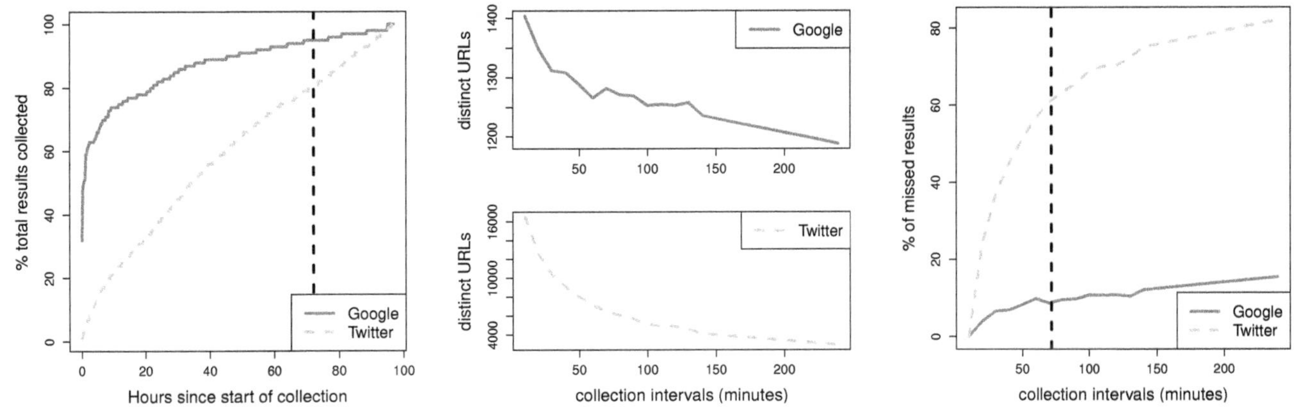

(a) New search results as a function of time in Twitter and Google. More than 80% of Google results appear within 3 days, while Twitter continuously produces new results.

(b) Number of distinct URLs collected using different collection intervals. The measurement lasted for two weeks using a fixed set of terms that was trending at the beginning of the experiment.

(c) Number of distinct URLs that we failed to collect using different collection intervals. The measurement lasted for two weeks using a fixed set of terms that was trending at the beginning of the experiment

Figure 2: Calibration tests weigh trade-offs between comprehensiveness and efficiency for collecting trending-term results.

minutes, caused 4% of the Google search results to be missed. Slower intervals caused more sites to be missed, but only slightly: 85% of the search results found when reissuing the query every 10 minutes could also be retrieved by sampling only once every 4 hours. So, even for trending topics, searching for the hot terms once every four hours provides adequate coverage of Google results. For consistency, we used the same interval on Twitter despite the higher miss rate. Twitter indeed continues producing new results over a longer time interval, primarily due to the "Retweet" function which allows users to simply repost existing contents.

2.3 Website classification

We next discuss how we classified websites as benign, malware-distributing, or ad-filled. We define a website as a set of pages hosted on the same second-level DNS domain. That is, `this.example.com` and `that.example.com` belong to the same website.[1] While we realize that different websites may be hosted on the same second-level domains, they are ultimately operated or endorsed by the same entity – the owner of the domain. Hence, in a slight abuse of terminology we will equivalently use "website" and "domain" in the rest of this discussion.

Malware-distributing sites. We pass all search results to Google's Safe Browsing API, which indicates whether a URL is currently infected with malware by checking it against a blacklist. Because the search results deal with timely topics, we are only interested in finding which URLs are infected near the time when the trending topic is reported. However, there may be delays in the blacklist updates, so we keep checking the results against the blacklist for 14 days after the term is no longer hot.

When a URL appears in the results and is only later added to the blacklist, we assume that the URL was already malicious but not yet detected as such. It is, of course, also possible that the reason the URL was not in the blacklist is that the site had not yet been infected. In the case of trending terms, however, a site appearing in results indicates a likely compromise, since the attacker's modus operandi is to populate compromised web servers with content that reflects trending results [17].

[1] So do `this.example.co.uk` and `that.example.co.uk`, as `co.uk` is considered a top-level domain; as are a few others (e.g., `ac.jp`) for which we maintain an exhaustive list.

The possibility of later compromise further justifies our decision to stop checking the search results against the blacklist after two weeks have passed. While it is certainly possible that some malware takes more than two weeks to be detected, the potential for prematurely flagging a site as compromised also grows with time. Indeed, in a study of spam on Twitter [10], the majority of tweets flagged by the Google Safe Browsing API as malicious were not added to the blacklist until around a month had passed. We suspect that many of the domains marked as malicious were in fact only compromised much later. Consequently, our decision to only flag malware detected within two weeks is a conservative one that minimize false positives while slightly increasing false negatives.

Dealing with long-delayed reports of malware poses an additional issue for terms from the control set, because these search results are more stable over time. Sometimes a URL appears in the results of a term for years. If that website becomes infected, then it would clearly be incorrect to claim that the website was infected but undetected the entire time. In fact, most malware appearing in the results for the control set are for websites that have only recently "pushed" their way into the top search results after having been infected. For these sites, delays in detection do represent harm.

We thus exclude from our analysis of malware in the control set URLs that appeared in the results between December 20-31, 2010, when we began collecting results for the control set. To eliminate the potential for edge effects, our analysis of malware does not begin until January 26, 2011. As in the trending set, we also only flag results as malware when they are detected within 14 days.

Finally, we note that sometimes malware is undetected by the SafeBrowsing API on the top-level URL, but that URLs loaded externally by the website are blocked. Consequently, our analysis provides an upper bound on malware success.

MFA sites. Automated identification of MFA sites is a daunting task. There are no clear rules for absolutely positive identification, and even human inspection suggests a certain degree of subjectivity in the classification. We discuss here a set of heuristics we use in determining whether a site is MFA or not.

While 182 741 different domains appeared in the top 32 Google and Yahoo! search results for trending terms over 9 months, only 6 558 (3.6%) appeared in the search results for at least 20 different trending terms. Because the goal of MFA sites is to appear high in the search results for as many terms as possible, we investigate further which of these 6 558 websites are in fact legitimate sources of information, and which are low-quality, ad-laden sites. To that effect we selected a statistically significant (95% confidence interval) random sample of 363 websites for manual inspection. From this sample, we identified five broad categories of websites indicative of MFA sites. All MFA sites appear to include a mechanism for automatically updating the topics they cover; differences emerge in how the resulting content is presented.

1. Sites which reuse snippets created by search engines and provide direct links to external sites with original content (e.g., `http://newsblogged.com/tornado-news-latest-real-time`).

2. Sites in blog-style format, containing a short paragraph of content that is likely copied from other sources and only slightly tweaked – usually by a machine algorithm, rather than a human editor (e.g, `http://toptodaynews.com/water-for-elephants-review`).

3. Sites that automatically update to new products for sale pointing to stores through paid advertisements (for instance, `http://tgiblackfriday.com/Online-Deals/-261-up-Europe-On-Sale-Each-Way-R-T-required--deal`).

4. Sites aggregating content by loading external websites into a frame so that they keep the user on the website along with their own overlaid ads (e.g., `http://baltimore-county-news.newslib.com/`).

5. Sites containing shoddily, but seemingly manually written content based on popular topics informed by trending terms (e.g., `http://snarkfood.com/mel-gibsons-mistress-says-hes-not-racist/310962/`).

Based on manual inspection of our random sample of 363 sites, we decided to classify websites in any of the first four categories as MFA, while rejecting sites in the fifth category. (Including those would have driven up the false positive rate to unacceptable levels.) This results in 44 of the 363 websites being tagged as MFA.

Subsequently, we used a supervised machine-learning algorithm (Bayesian Network [29] constructed using the K2 algorithm [7]) to automatically categorize the remaining 6 195 candidate websites.

The set of measures used to describe each page is a combination of structural and behavioral characteristics: (1) the number of internal links, i.e. links to the same domain as the web page under examination; (2) the number of external links, i.e. links directed to external domains; and (3) the existence of advertisements in the web page. We calculate these three quantities for each of the 6 558 domains by parsing the front page of the domain and a set of five additional web pages within the same domain, randomly chosen among the direct links existing in the front page.

We experimented with many more features in the classifier (e.g,, time since the website was registered, private WHOIS registration, number of trending terms where a website appears in the search results, presence of JavaScript, etc). As manual inspection confirmed, this did not improve classification accuracy beyond the three features described in the paper. MFA sites exhibit large numbers of external links but few internal links, because unlike external links to ads, internal links do not (directly) generate revenue.

We determine whether a website has advertisements by looking for known advertising domains in the collected HTML. Because these domains often appear in JavaScript, we use regular expressions to search throughout the page. We use manually-collected lists of known advertising domains used by Google and Yahoo!, complemented by the "Easy List" maintained by AdBlock Plus [3] (Jan. 12, 2011).

We used a subset of the 363 sample domains as a training set for the machine learning algorithm. We did not use the entire set because it is overcrowded with non-MFA domains (87% non-MFA vs. 13% MFA), which would lead to over-training the model towards non-MFA websites. By using fewer non-MFA websites in the training set (80% vs. 20%), we kept our model biased towards non-MFA websites, thereby maintaining the assumption of innocence while remaining able to identify obvious MFA instances.

We assessed the quality of our predictive model by performing 10 rounds of cross-validation [19], yielding a 87.3% rate of successful classifications. In the end, the algorithm classified 838 websites (0.46% of all collected domains) that appear in the trending set results as MFAs. The relatively small number of positive identifications allows for manual inspection to root out false positives. We find that 120 of the websites (consistent with the predicted 87.3% success rate) are likely false positives. We remove these websites from consideration when conducting the subsequent quantitative analysis of MFA behavior.

	Terms			Results			URLs			Domains		
	Total	Inf.	%	Total	Inf.	%	Total	Inf.	%	Total	Inf.	%
Malware												
Web Search												
Trending set	6 946	1 232	18	9.8M	7 889	.08	607K	1 905	.30	109K	495	.50
Control set	495	123	25	16.8M	7 332	.04	231K	302	.13	86K	123	.14
Twitter												
Trending set	1 950	46	2.4	466K	137	.03	355K	101	.03	43K	13	.03
Control set	495	53	11	1M	139	.01	825K	129	.02	98K	101	.02
Twitter trnd.	1 176	20	1.7	180K	24	.01	139K	21	.02	26K	9	.03
MFA sites												
Web Search												
Trending set	19 792	15 181	76.7	32.3M	954K	3.0	1.35M	83 920	6.2	183K	629	.34
Twitter												
Trending set	1 950	1 833	94	466K	32 152	6.9	355K	32 130	9.0	43K	141	.3
Twitter trnd.	1 176	1 012	86	179K	12 145	6.6	139K	12 144	8.7	26K	42	.2

Table 1: Total incidence of malware and MFA in web search and Twitter results.

3. MEASURING TRENDING-TERM ABUSE

3.1 Incidence of abuse

We now discuss the prevalence of malware and MFA in the trending search results. There are many plausible ways to summarize tens of millions of search results for tens of thousands of trending terms gathered over several months. We consider four categories: terms affected, search results, URLs and domains.

Table 1 presents totals for each of these categories. For web search, we observed malware in the search results of 1 232 of the 6 946 terms in the trending set. Running queries six times a day over three months yielded 9.8 million search results. Only 7 889 of these results were infected with malware – 0.08% of the total. These results corresponded to 607 156 unique URLs, only 1 905 of which were infected with malware. Finally, 495 of the 108 815 domains were infected.

How does this compare to popular search terms? As a percentage, more control terms were infected with malware, but that is due to their persistent popularity. Around the same number of search results were infected, but the control set included nearly twice as many overall results (because there were around 300 trending terms "hot" at any one time compared to the 495 terms always checked in the control set). 1 905 URLs were infected in the trending set, compared to only 302 in the control set.

The prevalence of malware on Twitter is markedly lower: only 2.4% of terms in the trending set were found to have malware, compared to 18% for search, and only 101 URLs on 13 distinct domains were found infected. While the number of infections observed is very small (0.03%), it is consistent with the proportion of malicious URLs observed by Grier et al. [10] on a significantly larger dataset

	Terms		Results	Domains		URLs	
	#	%	#	#	%	#	%
Trending terms – web search (point in time)							
detected	12.8	4.4	14.8	13.8	0.089	8.7	0.146
top 10	2.9	1.0	3.2	3.1	0.020	2.4	0.040
undetected	6.2	2.1	7.6	6.7	0.0	3.718	0.061
top 10	1.2	0.4	1.5	1.4	0.009	0.9	0.015
Control terms – web search (point in time)							
detected	9.5	1.9	14.1	11.5	0.043	8.9	0.067
top 10	3.1	0.6	3.9	3.7	0.014	3.1	0.023
undetected	1.0	0.2	1.0	1.0	0.0	0.856	0.006
top 10	0.1	0.0	0.1	0.1	0.000	0.1	0.001

Table 2: Prevalence of malware in trending and control terms, presented as the average prevalence of malware at every point in time when searches are issued.

of 25 million unique URLs. The control and Twitter-trending sets also reveal similarly low levels of infection.

Grier et al. observed a much higher proportion of "spammy" behavior on Twitter. Likewise, we observe substantial promotion of MFA websites on Twitter: 94% of trending terms contained tweets with MFA domains. While most terms are targeted, only a small number of domains are promoted – 141 in the trending set and 42 in the Twitter-trending set. Web search is also targeted substantially by MFA sites. 77% of terms in the trending set included one or more of the 629 MFA domains in at least one result.

From the figures in Table 1 alone, it would appear that malware on trending terms is largely under control, while MFA sites are relatively rampant. However, aggregating figures across a large period of time can obscure the potential harm of malware distributed via trending terms. Table 2 presents the malware infection rate at a single *point in time*: counting the number of terms and search results that are infected with malware for each of the trending terms within a 3-day window of rising. For example, on average, 12.8 trending terms are infected with malware that has already been flagged by the Safe Browsing API, which corresponds to 4.4% of recently hot terms at any given moment. A further 6.2 trending terms are infected but not yet detected by the blacklist. On average, 1.2 terms include a top 10 result that distributes malware and has not yet been detected by the Safe Browsing API. Viewed in this manner, the threat from web-based malware appears more worrisome.

But is the threat worse for trending terms? 9.5 control terms include detected malware at a given point in time, with one term infected but not yet detected. Hence, popular terms are still targeted for malware, but less frequently than trending terms and with less success. Finally, the false negative rate for the trending set is much higher than for the control set: 34% (7.6 results undetected compared to 14.8 detected) vs. 7% (1 undetected result compared to 14.1 detected).

3.2 Network characteristics

We next turn to characterizing how sites preying on trending terms are connected to each other. To prop up their rankings in Google, one would expect a group of sites operated by a same entity to link to each other – essentially building a "link farm [11]." Thus, we conjecture that looking at the network structure of both MFA and malware-serving sites may yield some insight on both the actors behind these attacks, and the way campaigns are orchestrated.

MFA domains. We build a directed graph G_{MFA} where each node corresponds to one of the 629 domains we identified as MFA sites, and each of the 3 221 (directed) edges corresponds to an HTML link between two domains. We construct the graph by fetching 1 000 backlinks for each of the sites from Yahoo! Site Explorer [39]. Extracting the strongly connected components from G_{MFA} yields family of sites that link to each other. We find 407 distinct strongly connected components, most (392) only contain singletons. More interestingly, 193 sites (30.7% of all MFA sites) form a strongly connected component. These nodes have on average a degree (in- and out-links) of 12.83, and an average path length between two nodes of 3.92, indicating a quite tightly connected network. It thus appears that a significant portion of all MFA domains may be operated by the same entity – or at the very least, by a unique group of affiliates all linking to each other. Further inspecting where these sites are hosted indicates that 130 of the 193 sites belong to one of only seven distinct Autonomous Systems (AS); here, sites within a same AS are usually hosted by the same provider, which confirms the presence of a fairly large, collusive, MFA operation.

Campaign ID	# Domains	Duration	Distinct ASes
949	590	>1 year	>200
5100	36	>8 months	1
5101	25	>8 months	1
5041	11	4 days	2
5053	10	2 days	1
4979	9	11 days	2
4988	9	8 days	2

Table 3: Malware campaigns observed.

Malware-serving sites. Examining the network characteristics of malware-distributing sites serves a slightly different purpose. Here, sites connected to each other are unlikely to be operated by the same entity, but are likely to have been *compromised* by the same group or as part of the same campaign. This is consistent with the behavior observed by John et al. [17], who found that miscreants add links between malicious websites to elevate PageRank. As with MFA sites, we build a directed graph G_{mal} where each node corresponds to one of the 6 133 domains we identified as malware-serving based on a longer collection of trending terms gathered from April 6, 2010 to April 27, 2011. Each (directed) edge corresponds to an HTML link between two malware-serving domains. G_{mal} contains 6 133 nodes and 18 864 edges, and 5 125 distinct strongly connected components, only 216 of which contain more than one node. Table 3 lists the largest strongly connected components ("campaigns") in G_{mal}. For each of the nodes in these campaigns, we look up the time at which they were first listed as infected. By comparing the first and last nodes to be infected within a given campaign, we can infer the campaign's duration. We also look up the number of distinct ASes in each campaign.

We observe divergent campaign behaviors, each characterized by markedly different attacker tactics. The largest campaign (949) is still ongoing at the time of this writing: nodes are compromised at a relatively constant rate, and are hosted on various ASes. This indicates a long-term, sustained effort. This campaign affects at least 9.6% of all the malware-infested sites we observed. Campaigns 5100 and 5101 are likely part of the same effort: all nodes share the same set of servers, and seem compromised by the same exploit. Interestingly, this campaign went unabated for at least 8 months (until Dec. 2010). Finally, the other four notable campaigns we observed target small sets of servers, that are compromised almost simultaneously, and all immediately link to each other.

Our definition of a campaign is extremely conservative: we are only looking for strongly connected components in the graph we have built. It is thus likely that many of the singletons we ob-

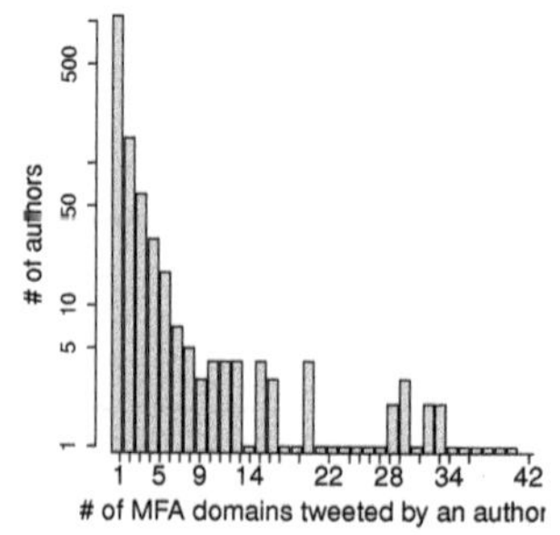

(a) Number of Twitter authors posting unique URLs containing MFA domains. Most authors post up to 14 distinct domains.

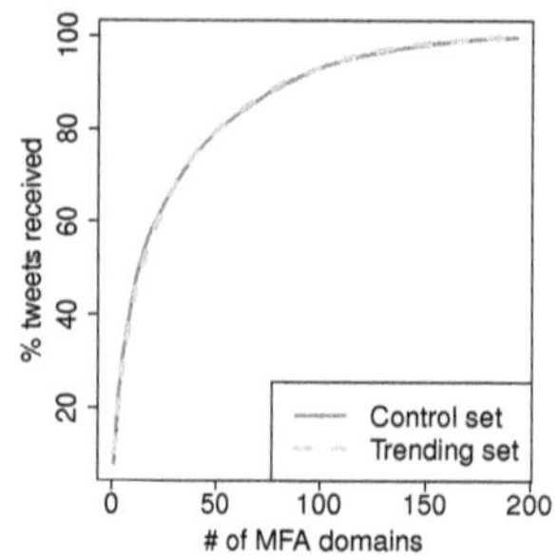

(b) CDF of tweets associated with MFA domains. The x-axis shows the number of domains associated with a portion of the tweets.

Figure 3: Trending-term exploitation on Twitter.

served are in fact part of larger campaigns. Further detection of such campaigns would require more complex clustering analysis. For instance, one could try to use the feature set of the classification algorithm as a coordinate system, and cluster nodes with nearby coordinates. However, it is unclear that this specific coordinate system would provide definitive evidence of collusion.

3.3 MFA in Twitter

We turn our attention now to the use of MFA links in Twitter posts. We are interested in measuring the amount of unique MFA-related URLs each malicious user posts, and the popularity of the MFA websites among them.

Figure 3(a) shows that 95% of the authors who post MFA URLs link to 5 domains or less – this amounts to about 20 000 posts. However, the remaining 5% is responsible for about 55 000 posts, and links to 870 domains. The control set gives similar numbers.

In other words, a small number of authors are responsible for wide promotional campaigns of MFA websites. The vast majority of authors post a small number of MFA links, and it is unclear whether they are actually malicious or not.

Similarly, the number of MFA domains that receive the majority of related tweets is small as Figure 3(b) shows. 50% of the MFA infected tweets direct users to 14 MFA domains, with the remaining 50% distributed across 180 MFA domains.

3.4 Search-term characteristics

We now examine how characteristics of the trending terms themselves influence the prevalence of malware and MFA sites in their search results. We focus on the importance of the term's category, popularity in searches, and expected advertising revenue.

Measuring term category, popularity and ad prices. We combine results from several Google tools in order to learn more about the characteristics of each of the trending terms. First, we classify the trending terms into categories using Google Insights for Search, which assigns arbitrary search terms to the most likely category, out of the same 27 categories used for constructing the control sample described in Section 2.1 above.

Second, Google offers a free service called Traffic Estimator that estimates for any phrase the number of global monthly searches averaged over the past year [14]. For trending terms, averaging over the course of a year significantly underestimates the search traffic when a term is peaking in popularity. Fortunately, Google also offers a measure of the relative popularity of terms through Google Trends [15], provided at the granularity of one week. The relative measure is normalized against the average number of searches for

Category name	%	CPC	Malware % terms	MFA % terms	MFA % top 10	coef.
Arts & Humanities	2.7	$0.44	20.1	40.6	6.8	
Automotive	1.3	$0.67	16.0	29.2	5.2	−0.0062
Beauty & Personal Care	0.8	$0.76	19.6	32.5	6.9	
Business	0.4	$0.87	7.4	32.9	6.9	
Computers & Electronics	2.4	$0.61	14.5	31.7	5.9	
Entertainment	30.6	$0.34	18.6	41.0	6.4	−0.0043
Finance & Insurance	1.4	$1.26	20.2	30.4	5.6	
Food & Drink	2.9	$0.43	17.1	49.5	7.9	+0.0105
Games	2.3	$0.32	13.4	30.0	5.6	−0.0073
Health	2.5	$0.85	14.1	27.6	5.9	−0.0046
Home & Garden	0.5	$0.76	7.1	29.7	7.2	
Industries	1.6	$0.50	26.1	38.6	6.6	−0.0072
Internet	0.7	$0.49	7.7	43.7	6.0	
Lifestyles	4.5	$0.33	25.4	45.8	6.5	
Local	11.0	$0.51	21.8	39.2	6.9	−0.0027
News & Current Events	3.6	$0.39	19.7	45.0	7.0	
Photo & Video	0.2	$0.59	0.0	21.9	6.4	
Real Estate	0.2	$1.02	6.2	34.2	6.5	
Recreation	1.0	$0.43	13.7	43.5	6.5	
Reference	1.4	$0.43	14.5	55.4	8.7	+0.0203
Science	1.4	$0.40	16.0	44.9	9.1	+0.0095
Shopping	3.2	$0.56	11.6	43.7	8.8	+0.0106
Social Networks	0.5	$0.19	27.8	59.1	6.4	
Society	5.1	$0.62	15.2	33.7	5.6	−0.0085
Sports	15.4	$0.38	20.7	44.9	6.9	−0.0044
Telecommunications	0.8	$0.91	10.9	36.4	4.6	
Travel	1.7	$0.88	10.1	29.3	6.4	
Average (category)	**3.7**	**$0.59**	**18.4**	**38.3**	**6.6**	

Table 4: Malware and MFA incidence broken down by trending term category.

the past year, precisely the figure returned by the Traffic Estimator. We obtain the *peak-popularity estimate* Pop(s) for a term s by multiplying the relative estimate for the week when the term peaked by the absolute long-run popularity estimate.

The Google Traffic Estimator also indicates the advertising value of trending terms, by providing estimates of the anticipated cost per click (CPC) for keywords. We collect the CPC for all trending and control terms. Many trending terms are only briefly popular and return the minimum CPC estimate of US$0.05. We use the CPC to approximate the relative revenue that might be obtained for search results on each term. The CPC is a natural proxy for the prospective advertising value of user traffic because websites that show ads are likely to present ads similar to the referring term.

Empirical analysis. Table 4 breaks down the relative prevalence of trending terms, and their abuse, by category. Over half of the terms fall into three categories – Entertainment, Sports and Local. These categories feature topics that change frequently and briefly rise from prior obscurity. 18% of trending terms include malware in their results, while 38% feature MFA websites in at least 1% of the top 10 results.

We observe some variation in malware and MFA incidence across categories. However, perhaps the most striking result from examining the table is that all categories are targeted, irrespective of the category's propensity to "trendiness." Miscreants do not seem to be specializing yet by focusing on particular keyword categories.

If we instead look at popularity and ad prices, substantial differences emerge. Figure 4 shows how the incidence of malware and MFA varies according to the peak popularity and ad price of the trending term. The left-most graph shows how malware varies according to the term's peak popularity. The least popular terms (less than 1 000 searches per day at their peak) attract the most malware in their top results. 38% of such terms include malware, while 9%

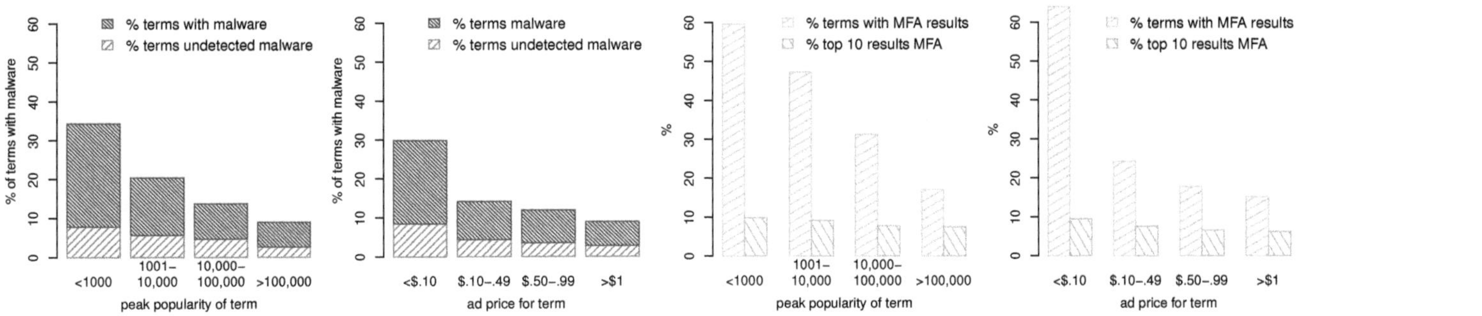

Figure 4: Exploring how popularity and ad price of trending terms affects the prevalence of malware (left) and ad-laden sites (right).

of these terms include malware that is not initially detected. As terms increase in peak popularity, fewer are afflicted by malware: only 6.2% of terms with peak popularity greater than 100 000 daily searches include malware in their results, and only 2% of terms include malware that is not immediately detected. A similar pattern follows for malware incidence according to the term's ad price. 30% of terms with ad prices under 10 cents per click had malware in their results, compared to 8.8% of terms with ad prices greater than $1 per click.

A greater fraction of terms overall include MFA websites in their results than malware (37% vs. 19%). Consequently, all proportions are larger in the two graphs on the right side of Figure 4. 60% of terms with peak popularity of less than 1 000 daily searches include MFA sites in their results. This proportion drops steadily until only 17.4% of terms attracting over 100 000 daily visits include MFA in the top 10 search results. A similar reduction can be seen for varying ad prices in the right-most figure. The two right figures show the percentage of all terms that have MFA, followed by the percentage of top 10 results that are MFA, for only those terms that have MFA terms present. Here we can see that the percentages remain relatively steady irrespective of term popularity and price. For unpopular terms, 10% of their results point to MFA, dropping modestly to 8% for the most popular terms. The drop is more significant for ad prices – from 10% to 6%. Consequently, while the success in appearing in results diminishes with popularity and rising ad prices, when a term does have MFA, a similar proportion of its results are polluted.

Of course, ad prices and term popularity are correlated – more popular search terms tend to attract higher ad prices, and vice versa. Consequently, we use linear regression to disentangle the effect both have on the prevalence of abuse.

Because the dependent variable is binary in the case of malware (either the term has malware present or does not), we use a logit model for the regression of the following form:

$$\text{logit}(p_{\text{HasMalware}}) = \beta + \text{AdPrice}x_1 + \log_2(\text{Popularity})x_2$$

We also ran a logit regression with the term's categories, but none of the category values were statistically significant. Thus, we have settled on this simpler model. The results of the regression reveal that a term's ad price and search popularity are both negatively correlated with the presence of malware in a term's search results, and the relationship is statistically significant:

	coef.	odds	Std. Err.	Significance
AdPrice	-0.509	.601	0.091	$p < 0.001$
$\log_2$(Popularity)	-0.117	0.889	0.012	$p < 0.001$

These coefficients mean that a $1 increase in the ad price corresponds to a 40% decrease in the odds of having malware in the term's results. Likewise, when the popularity of a term doubles, the odds of having malware in the term's results decreases by 11%.

We also devised a linear regression using the fraction of a term's top 10 results classified as MFA as the dependent variable:

$$\text{FracTop10MFA} = \beta + \text{AdPrice}x_1 + \log_2(\text{Popularity})x_2 + \text{Category}x_3 \,.$$

The Category variable is encoded as a 27-part categorical variable using deviation coding. Deviation coding is used to measure each categories' deviation from the overall mean value, rather than deviations across categories.

For this regression, the term's ad price and search popularity are both statistically significant and negatively correlated with the fraction of a trending term's top 10 results classified as MFA:

	coef.	Std. Err.	Significance
AdPrice	-0.0091	0.091	$p < 0.001$
$\log_2$(Popularity)	-0.004	0.012	$p < 0.001$
Coefficients for category variables in Tab. 4, R^2: 0.1373			

A $1 increase in the ad price corresponds to a 0.9% decrease in the MFA rate, while a doubling in the popularity of a search term matches a 0.4 percentage point decrease. This may not seem much, but recall that, on average, 6.6% of a term's top 10 results link to MFA sites. A 0.9% decrease in MFA prevalence represents a 13.2% decrease from the average rate.

Each of the coefficients listed in the right-most column in Table 4 are statistically significant (all have p values less than 0.001, except Local, Health, and Automotive, where $p < 0.05$). For instance, Food & Drink terms correspond to a 1 percentage point increase in the rate of MFA domains in their top 10 results, while Reference terms suffer a 2% higher MFA rate.

Implications of analysis. The results just presented demonstrate that, for both malware and MFA sites, miscreants are struggling to successfully target the more lucrative terms. An optimistic interpretation is that defenders manage to relegate the abuse to the more obscure terms that have less overall impact. A more pessimistic interpretation is that miscreants are having success in the tail of hot terms, which are more difficult to eradicate.

It is not very surprising that malware tends to be located in the results of terms that demand lower ad prices, given that higher ad prices do not benefit malware distribution. However, it is quite unexpected that the prevalence of MFA terms is negatively correlated with a term's ad price, since those promoting MFA sites would much prefer to appear in the search results of more expensive terms. One reason why malware and MFA appears less frequently on pages with higher ad prices could be that there is stronger legitimate competition in these results than for results fetching lower ad prices.

	# Visitors		
	Total	Period	Monthly Rate
MFA	39 274 200	275 days	4 284 458
Malware (trending set)			
detected	454 198	88 days	154 840
Bing, Yahoo!	189 511	88 days	64 606
undetected	143 662	88 days	48 975
Malware (control set)			
detected	12 825 332	88 days	4 372 272
Bing, Yahoo!	6 352 378	88 days	2 165 583
undetected	83615	88 days	28505

Table 5: Estimated number of visits to MFA and malware sites for trending terms.

Furthermore, there is a potential incentive conflict for search engines to eradicate ad-laden sites, when many of the pages run advertisements for the ad platforms maintained by the search engines. It is therefore encouraging that the evidence suggests that search engines do a better job at expelling MFA sites from the results of terms that attract higher ad prices.

Finally, the data helps to answer an important question: are malware and ad abuse websites competitors, or do they serve different parts of the market? The evidence suggests that, in terms of being a technique to monetize search traffic, malware and MFA behave more like substitutes, rather than complements. Both approaches thrive on the same types of terms, low-volume terms where ads are less attractive. Consequently, a purely profit-motivated attacker not fearful of arrest might choose between the two approaches, depending on which method generates more revenue.

4. ECONOMICS OF TRENDING-TERM EXPLOITATION

We next examine the revenues possible for both malware and ads, by first characterizing the volumes of population affected, before deriving actual expected revenues.

4.1 Exposed population

We first estimate the number of visits malware and MFA sites attract from trending-term searches. The cumulative number of visits over an interval t to a website w for a search term s is given by

$$V(w,s,t) = C(\text{Rank}(w,s)) \cdot \text{Pop}(s) \cdot \frac{4}{30 \times 24} \times t\,,$$

where Pop(s) is the monthly peak popularity of the term, as defined in Section 3.4. Rank(w, s) is the position in search results website w occupies in response to a query for s, and $C(r)$ defines a click probability function for search rank $1 \leq r \leq 10$ following the empirical distribution observed by Joachims et al. [16]. They found that 43% of users clicked on the first result, 17% on the second result, and 98.9% of users only clicked on results in the first page. We ignore results in ranks above 10 (i.e., $C(r) = 0$ for $r > 10$).

Pop(s) is measured at a monthly rate, so we normalize the visits to the four-hour interval between each search. We also weigh Google and Yahoo! search results differently. Google has reportedly an 64.4% market share in search, while Yahoo! and Bing have a combined market share of 30% [12]. Since our estimates are based on what Google observes, we anticipate that Yahoo! and Bing attract $\frac{30\%}{64.4\%} = 46.5\%$ of the searches that Google does.

The results are given in Table 5. MFA sites attract 39 million visits over nine months, or 4.3 million visits per month. For the

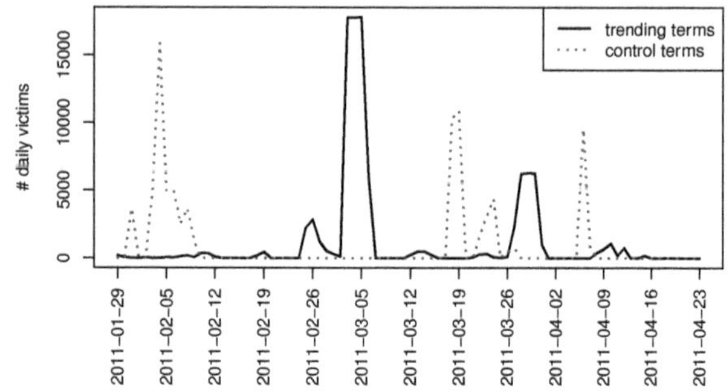

Figure 5: Number of estimated daily victims for malware appearing in trending and control terms.

malware results, we compare the estimated visits for both control and trending terms. While more users see malware in the results of control terms than trending terms (about 4.4 million versus about 200 000 per month over three months), over 99% of the visits from control terms are blocked by the Safe Browsing API. By contrast, 24% of the visits triggered from the results of trending terms are not blocked by the Safe Browsing API. In aggregate, trending terms expose around 49 000 victims per month to undetected malware, compared to about 28 000 for control terms.

The table also lists the number of Bing and Yahoo! users that encounter malware detected by Google's SafeBrowsing API. We cannot say for certain whether or not these users will be exposed to malware. If they attempt to visit the malicious site using the Chrome or Firefox browser then they would be protected, since Google's SafeBrowsing API is integrated into those browsers. Internet Explorer users would be protected only if the sites appear in IE's internal blacklist. Unfortunately, we could not verify this since the blacklist is not made publicly accessible.

The sums presented in the table mask several peculiarities of the data. First, for malware, the number of visitors exposed is highly variable. Figure 5 plots the number of daily victims over time. Most days the number of victims exposed is very small, often zero. Because terms in the control set are always very popular, successful attacks cause large spikes, but tend to be rare. On the other hand, trending terms exhibit frequent spikes, but many of the spikes are small. This is because many trending terms are in fact not very popular, even at their peak. A big spike, as happened around March 5, results from the conjunction of three factors: (1) the attacker must get their result towards the top of the search results; (2) the result cannot be immediately spotted and flagged; and (3) the trending term has to be popular enough to draw in many victims. Consequently, there is a downside to the constantly replenishing pool of trending terms for the attacker – they are often not popular enough for the attacker to do much damage. This is further exacerbated by the finding from the last section – more popular terms are less likely to be manipulated. At the same time, the figure demonstrates that even the odd success can reel in many victims.

Figure 6 plots the cumulative distribution of user visits compared to the affected domains. The graph indicates high concentration – most of the traffic is drawn to a small number of domains. The concentration of visitors is particularly extreme for malware, which makes sense given the spikes observed in Figure 5. The concentration in MFA sites shows that a few websites profit handsomely from trending terms, and that many more are less successful. This is consistent with our earlier finding that there are only a few large connected clusters of MFA sites linking to each other. One conse-

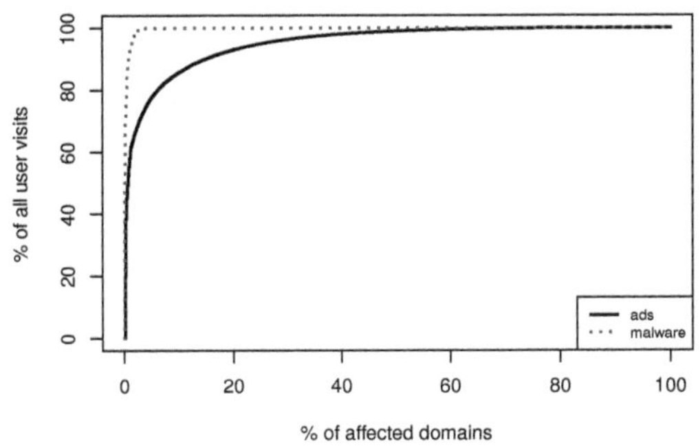

Figure 6: CDF of visits for domains used to transmit malware or ads in the search results of trending terms.

quence of this concentration is that we can approximate the revenue to the biggest players simply by considering aggregate figures.

4.2 Revenue analysis

We next compare revenues miscreants generate from MFA sites and from malware-hosting sites.

MFA revenue. Essentially, the aggregate revenue for MFA websites is a sum of the revenues generated by all MFA sites w obtained in response to all the search terms s considered. Each website generates a revenue equal to the number of website visitors times the advertising revenue that can be obtained from these visitors:

$$R_{\mathrm{MFA}}(t) = \sum_{w \in \mathrm{MFA}(s)} \sum_{s} V(w,s,t) \cdot (p_{\mathrm{PPC}} \cdot p_{\mathrm{clk}} \cdot r_{\mathrm{PPC}} + p_{\mathrm{banner}} \cdot r_{\mathrm{banner}} + p_{\mathrm{aff}} \cdot p'_{\mathrm{clk}} \cdot r_{\mathrm{aff}}) .$$

There are three broad classes of online advertising in use on MFA domains – pay-per-click (PPC) (e.g., Google AdSense), banners (e.g., Yahoo! Right Media) and affiliate marketing (e.g., Commission Junction). Banner advertisements are paid r_{banner} by the visit, PPC only pays r_{PPC} when the user clicks on an ad (which happens with probability p_{clk}), and affiliate marketing pays r_{aff} whenever a visitor clicks the ad and then buys something (which happens with probability p'_{clk}). By inspecting our corpus of MFA sites, we discover that 83% include PPC ads, 66% use banner ads, and 16% include affiliate ads. 50% of sites use two types of advertising, and 7% use all three. We include each type of advertisement in the revenue calculation with probability $p_{\mathrm{ad\ type}}$, and we assign the probability according to the percentage of MFA site visits that include each class of ad. For the MFA websites we have identified, $p_{\mathrm{PPC}} = 0.94$, $p_{\mathrm{banner}} = 0.53$, and $p_{\mathrm{aff}} = 0.33$.

To calculate the earning potential of each ad type, we piece together rough measures gathered from outside sources. Estimating the "click-through rate" (CTR) p_{clk} is difficult, as click-through rates vary greatly, and ad platforms such as Google keep very tight-lipped on average click-through rates. One Google employee reported that an average CTR is "in the neighborhood of 2%" [32]. We anticipate that the CTR for MFA sites is substantially higher than 2%, since sites have multiple ads aggressively displayed and little original content. Nonetheless, we assign $p_{\mathrm{clk}} = 0.02$.

To measure per-click ad revenue r_{PPC}, we turn to the CPC estimates Google provides for advertising keywords. We expect that more persistent search terms are likely to appear as keywords for ads, even on websites about trending terms. Hence, we assume that advertising revenue for trending terms matches the CPC for most popular keywords in the corresponding category. We assign the expected advertising revenue to the mean of ad prices for the 20 most popular search terms weighted by the amount each category is represented in the results from the trending set (see Table 4, column 1). This yields $r_{\mathrm{PPC}} = \$0.97$.

Calculating banner advertising revenue is a bit easier, since no clicks are required to earn money. Public estimates of average revenue are hard to come by, but the ad network Adify issued a press release stating that its median cost per 1 000 impressions in Q2 2010 was $5.29 [4], so we assign $r_{\mathrm{banner}} = \$0.00529$.

For affiliate marketing, we assume assume that $p'_{\mathrm{clk}} = p_{\mathrm{clk}} = 0.02$, the same as for PPC ads. To estimate the revenue r_{aff} that can be earned, we turn to Commission Junction (CJ), one of the largest affiliate marketing networks that matches over 2 500 advertisers with affiliates. CJ provides an estimate of expected earnings from advertisers per 100 clicks; we collected this estimate for all advertisers on Commission Junction in December 2009, and found it to be $26.49. Consequently, we estimate that $r_{\mathrm{aff}} = \$0.265$.

Putting it all together, we estimate the monthly revenue to MFA sites to be:

$$\begin{aligned} R_{\mathrm{MFA}}(1\text{ month}) =& 4\,284\,458 \times (0.94 \times 0.02 \times \$0.97 \\ &+ 0.53 \times \$0.00529 + 0.33 \times 0.02 \times \$0.265) \\ =& \$97\,637 . \end{aligned}$$

So, MFA sites gross roughly $100,000 per month from trending-term exploitation. There are, however, costs that are not factored into the above derivation, which makes it an upper bound. For instance, Google generally imposes a 32% fee on advertising revenues [24]. Furthermore, servers have to be hosted and maintained. As an example, most sites in the largest cluster in Section 3.2 are hosted by the same service provider, which charges $140/server/month. That cluster contains 193 nodes hosted on 155 unique servers, which, ignoring economies of scale, would come up to $21 700/month in maintenance. Nevertheless, it is worth noting that these costs can be amortized over other businesses – it is unlikely that such servers are only set up for the purpose of trending-term exploitation.

Malware revenue. Attackers have experimented with several different business models to monetize drive-by-downloads, from adware to credential-stealing trojans [31]. However, researchers have observed that attackers exploiting trending terms have tended to rely on fake antivirus software [2, 8, 36]. We therefore define the revenue due to malware in trending results as:

$$R_{\mathrm{mal}}(t) = \sum_{w \in \mathrm{mal(s)}} \sum_{s} V(w,s,t) \cdot p_{\mathrm{exp}} \cdot p_{\mathrm{pay}} * r_{\mathrm{AV}} ,$$

where we multiply the number of visits times the likelihood of exposure, the probability of a victim paying for the software, and the amount paid. For these figures, we turn to the analysis of Stone-Gross et al. [36], who acquired a copy of back-end databases detailing the revenues and expenses of three large fake antivirus programs, each of which were advertised by compromising trending search results. They found that 2.16% of all users exposed to fake antivirus ultimately paid for a "license," at an average cost of $58. We can use these figures directly in our model for the revenues due to malware, setting $p_{\mathrm{pay}} = 0.0216$ and $r_{\mathrm{AV}} = \$58$.

Unlike most drive-by-downloads, fake antivirus software does not need to exploit a vulnerability in the client visiting the infected search result in order for a user to be exposed. Instead, the server will use a server-side warning designed to appear as though it is on the client's machine, and then prompt a user to install software [2]. Because of this, every user that visits a link distributing fake AV is exposed, and so we assign $p_{\mathrm{exp}} = 1$. These parameters yield a

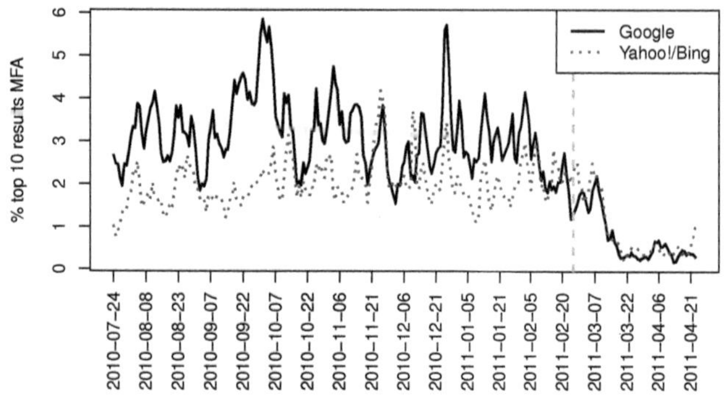

Figure 7: MFA prevalence in the top 10 search results fell after Google announced changes to its ranking algorithm on February 24, 2011, designed to counter "low-quality" results.

monthly revenue from malware of:

$$R_{\mathrm{mal}}(1 \text{ month}) = 48\,975 \times 1 \times 0.0216 \times 58 \approx \$61\,356\,.$$

Thus, malware sites (e.g., fake anti-virus sites) generate roughly $60,000/month just from trending-term exploitation.

Here too, there are costs associated with deploying these sites, but server maintenance is a lot cheaper than in the case of MFA sites, given that most machines hosting malware have been compromised rather than purchased. Bots go for less than a dollar [5, and references therein], while a compromised server (presumably with high quality network access) goes at most for $25 according to Franklin et al. [9]. Note that we do not adjust the returns on malware for the risk of being caught because the likelihood of being arrested for cyber-criminal activity is currently negligible in many jurisdictions where cyber-criminals operate.

One conclusion of this analysis is that malware and MFA hosting have quite different revenue models, but yield surprisingly similar amounts of money to their perpetrators. This lends further support to the hypothesis that they could be treated as substitutes.

5. SEARCH-ENGINE INTERVENTION

On February 24, 2011, following a series of high-profile reports of manipulation of its search engine (e.g., [33, 34]), Google announced changes to its search ranking algorithm designed to eradicate "low-quality" results [35]. Google defined low-quality sites as those which are "low-value add for users, copy content from other websites or sites that are just not very useful." The MFA sites examined in this paper certainly appear to match that definition. Because we were already collecting search results on the trending set, we can measure the effectiveness of the intervention in eradicating abuse targeting trending terms.

Figure 7 plots over time the average percentage of top 10 search results marked as MFA for terms in the trending set. From July to February, 3.1% of Google's top 10 results (solid line) for trending terms pointed to MFA sites, compared to 2.0% for Yahoo!'s top 10 results (dotted line). The vertical dashed line marks February 24, 2011, the day of Google's announcement. The proportion of MFA sites quickly fell, stabilizing a month later at a rate of 0.47% for Google. Curiously, Yahoo!'s share of top 10 MFA results also fell, to an average of 0.56%.

Landing in the top results tells only part of the story. The underlying popularity of the trending terms is also important. We compute the estimated site visits to MFA sites, which is more directly tied to revenue. Table 6 compares the number of visits referred to

	Monthly MFA visits		
	Pre-intervention	Post-intervention	% change
Google search	3 364 402	1 788 480	-47%
Google ads	2 989 821	1 763 709	-41%
Other ads	374 556	24 770	-93%
Yahoo!/Bing search	1 302 314	1 448 058	+11%
Google ads	1 204 928	1 424 323	+18%
Other ads	95 363	23 734	-75%
Total	**4 666 716**	**3 236 538**	**-31%**

Table 6: Estimated number of visits to MFA and malware sites for trending terms.

by Google and Yahoo! search results before and after the intervention. Between July 24, 2010 and February 24, 2011, MFA sites attracted 4.67 million monthly visits on average. Between March 10 and April 24, 2011, the monthly rate fell 31% to 3.2 million.

However, the changes differed greatly across search engines. Referrals from Google search results fell by 47%, while on Yahoo! and Bing the visits increased by 11%. The table also distinguishes between whether the MFA site uses Google ads or another provider. 81% of MFA sites show Google ads, which is not surprising given Google's dominance in pay-per-click advertising. It is an open question whether Google might treat MFA sites hosting its own ads differently than sites with other ads. Striking them from the search results reduces Google's own advertising revenue. However, it is in Google's interest to provide high-quality search results, the amount of foregone revenue is small, and is likely to be partly replaced by other search results. Our figures support the latter rationale. Sites with Google ads fell by 1.2 million visits, or 41%. Visits to sites not using AdSense fell by 91%, but, in absolute terms, the reduction was smaller than for sites with Google ads. By contrast, Yahoo! results with Google ads rose by 18%.

Using the pre- and post-intervention MFA visit rates into the revenue equations developed in Section 4.2, the average monthly take for MFA sites has fallen from $106 000 to $74 000. If this reduction holds over time, what are the implications for miscreants? First, they may decide to devote more effort to manipulating Yahoo! and Bing, despite their lower market penetration, since the MFA revenues are growing more equitable in absolute terms. Second, malware becomes more attractive as an alternative source of revenue, so one unintended consequence of the intervention to improve search quality could be to foster more overtly criminal activities harming consumers. Third, revenue models based on advertising require volume, and external efforts that reduce traffic levels can cause significant pain to the miscreant. By contrast, malware offers substantially more expected revenue per visitor, and is therefore likely to be much more difficult to eradicate.

Given the striking change in MFA prevalence following Google's intervention, it is worth checking whether this intervention alters the significance of the empirical conclusions reached in Section 3.4. We included a dummy variable into the MFA regression reflecting whether Google's intervention had yet occurred, and found that this inclusion does not alter the significance of the dependent variables presented in Section 3.4.

6. RELATED WORK

Our work inscribes itself in the body of literature on understanding the underground online economy. Some of the early econometric work in that domain revolves around quantities bartered in underground forums [9], and on email spam campaigns [18, 22]. Grier et al. [10] extend this literature to Twitter spam. Along the same lines, Moore and Clayton have published a series of papers characterizing phishing campaigns [25, 26, 27].

More recently, a number of papers have also started to investigate web-based scams. Christin et al. [6] study a specific web-based social engineering scam ("one click fraud"). Provos et al. describe in details how so called "drive-by-downloads" are used to automatically install malware [30, 31]. Cova et al. [8] and Stone-Gross et al. [36] focus on fake anti-virus malware, and provide estimates of the amount of money they generate. Stone-Gross et al. calculate, through recovery of the miscreants' transactions logs, that anti-virus campaigns gross between $3.8 and $48.4 million a year. Affiliates funneling traffic to miscreants get between $50,000 and $1.8 million in over two months. These totals are markedly higher than what we obtain, but they consider all possible sources of malware (botnets, search engine manipulation, drive-by-downloads) whereas we only look at the much smaller subset of search engine manipulation based on trending term exploitation.

A few recent works consider search engine manipulation. Leontiadis et al. [20] investigate search engine manipulation to promote potentially illicit online drugs. John et al. [17] present a case study of recent search engine manipulation campaigns, confirming that trending-term exploitation is an attack vector of choice. They then devise countermeasures to thwart search engine manipulation.

Our approach differs from the related work in that we focus on a specific phenomenon – trending-term exploitation – by investigating how it is carried out (e.g., search-engine manipulation, Twitter spam), as well as its purpose: malware distribution and monetization through advertisements. Our analysis thus sheds light on a specific technique used by miscreants that search-engine operators are battling to fend off.

7. CONCLUSION

We have undertaken a large-scale investigation into the abuse of "trending" terms, focusing on the two primary methods of monetization: malware and ads. We have found that the the dynamic nature of the trends creates a narrow opportunity that is being effectively exploited on web search engines and social-media platforms. We have presented statistical evidence that the less popular and less financially lucrative terms are exploited most effectively, and that the spoils of abuse are highly concentrated among a few players. We have developed an empirically grounded model of the earnings potential of both malware and ads, finding that each attracts aggregate revenues on the order of $100 000 per month. Finally, we have found that Google's intervention to combat low-quality sites has likely reduced revenues from trend exploitation by more than 30%.

There is a connection in our economic modeling to the battle over how to profit from typosquatting [28]. In both cases, Internet "bottom feeders" seek to siphon off a fraction of legitimate traffic at large scale. Several years ago, typosquatting was used in phishing attacks and to distribute malware. Today, however, typosquatting is almost exclusively monetized through pay-per-click and affiliate marketing ads [28], attracting hundreds of millions of dollars in advertising revenue to domain squatters via ad platforms.

The open question is whether a significant crackdown on, say, fake antivirus sales, will simply shift the economics in favor of low-quality advertising. However, while ad platforms might tolerate placing ads on typosquatted websites, advertising that lowers the quality of search results directly threatens the ad platform's core business of web search. Consequently, we are more optimistic that search engines might be willing to crack down on all abuses of trending terms, as we have found in our initial data analysis.

8. ACKNOWLEDGMENTS

We thank our anonymous reviewers for helpful feedback on this paper. This research was partially supported by CyLab at Carnegie Mellon under grant DAAD19-02-1-0389 from the Army Research Office, and by the National Science Foundation under ITR award CCF-0424422 (TRUST).

9. REFERENCES

[1] Google Web Search API. `https://code.google.com/apis/websearch/`.

[2] M. Abu Rajab, L. Ballard, P. Mavrommatis, N. Provos, and X. Zhao. The nocebo effect on the web: an analysis of fake anti-virus distribution. In *Proc. USENIX LEET'10*, San Jose, CA, April 2010.

[3] AdBlock. Adblock easy list. `https://easylist-downloads.adblockplus.org/easylist.txt`.

[4] Adify. Adify vertical gauge shows steady growth in seven of eleven critical verticals. `http://www.smartbrief.com/news/aaaa/industryMW-detail.jsp?id=732F69A7-9192-4E05-A261-52C068021634`. Last accessed May 5, 2011.

[5] N. Christin, S. Egelman, T. Vidas, and J. Grossklags. It's all about the Benjamins: Incentivizing users to ignore security advice. In *Proc. Financial Crypto.'11*, St. Lucia, Feb. 2011.

[6] N. Christin, S. Yanagihara, and K. Kamataki. Dissecting one click frauds. In *Proc. ACM CCS'10*, pages 15–26, Chicago, IL, Oct. 2010.

[7] G. Cooper and E. Herskovits. A Bayesian method for the induction of probabilistic networks from data. *Machine Learning*, 9(4):309–347, 1992.

[8] M. Cova, C. Leita, O. Thonnard, A. Keromytis, and M. Dacier. An analysis of rogue AV campaigns. In *Proc. RAID 2010*, Ottawa, ON, Canada, September 2010.

[9] J. Franklin, V. Paxson, A. Perrig, and S. Savage. An inquiry into the nature and causes of the wealth of internet miscreants. In *Proc. ACM CCS'07*, pages 375–388, Alexandria, VA, October 2007.

[10] C. Grier, K. Thomas, V. Paxson, and M. Zhang. @spam: The underground in 140 characters or less. In *Proc. ACM CCS'10*, pages 27–37, Chicago, IL, October 2010.

[11] Z. Gyöngyi and H. Garcia-Mollina. Link spam alliances. In *Proc. VLDB'05*, pages 517–528, Trondheim, Norway, Aug. 2005.

[12] Experian Hitwise. Experian hitwise reports bing-powered share of searches reaches 30 percent in march 2011, April 2011. `http://www.hitwise.com/us/press-center/press-releases/experian-hitwise-reports-bing-powered-share-of-s/`.

[13] Google Inc. Google insights for search. `http://www.google.com/insights/search/`.

[14] Google Inc. Google traffic estimator. `https://adwords.google.com/select/TrafficEstimatorSandbox`.

[15] Google Inc. Google trends. `http://www.google.com/trends/`.

[16] T. Joachims, L. Granka, B. Pang, H. Hembrooke, and G. Gay. Accurately interpreting clickthrough data as implicit feedback. In *Proc. ACM SIGIR'05*, pages 154–161, Salvador, Brazil, Aug. 2005.

[17] J. John, F. Yu, Y. Xie, M. Abadi, and A. Krishnamurthy. deSEO: Combating search-result poisoning. In *Proc. USENIX Security'11*, San Francisco, CA, August 2011.

[18] C. Kanich, C. Kreibich, K. Levchenko, B. Enright, G. Voelker, V. Paxson, and S. Savage. Spamalytics: An empirical analysis of spam marketing conversion. In *Proc. ACM CCS'08*, pages 3–14, Alexandria, VA, Oct. 2008.

[19] R. Kohavi. A study of cross-validation and bootstrap for accuracy estimation and model selection. In *Proc. IJCAI'95*, pages 1137–1145, Montreal, QC, Canada, Aug. 1995.

[20] N. Leontiadis, T. Moore, and N. Christin. Measuring and analyzing search-redirection attacks in the illicit online prescription drug trade. In *Proc. USENIX Security'11*, San Francisco, CA, August 2011.

[21] J. Leskovec, L. Backstrom, and R. Kleinberg. Meme-tracking and the dynamics of the news cycle. In *Proc. ACM KDD'09*, Paris, France, June 2009.

[22] K. Levchenko, N. Chachra, B. Enright, M. Felegyhazi, C. Grier, T. Halvorson, C. Kanich, C. Kreibich, H. Liu, D. McCoy, A. Pitsillidis, N. Weaver, V. Paxson, G. Voelker, and S. Savage. Click trajectories: End-to-end analysis of the spam value chain. In *Proc. IEEE Symp. Security & Privacy*, pages 431–446, Oakland, CA, May 2011.

[23] Microsoft. Microsoft, yahoo! change search landscape. `http://www.microsoft.com/presspass/press/2009/jul09/07-29release.mspx`.

[24] N. Mohan. The AdSense revenue share, May 2010. `http://adsense.blogspot.com/2010/05/adsense-revenue-share.html`.

[25] T. Moore and R. Clayton. Examining the impact of website take-down on phishing. In *Proc. APWG eCrime'07*, Pittsburgh, PA, October 2007.

[26] T. Moore and R. Clayton. Evil searching: Compromise and recompromise of internet hosts for phishing. In *Proc. Financial Crypto'09*, pages 256–272, Barbados, Feb. 2009.

[27] T. Moore, R. Clayton, and H. Stern. Temporal correlations between spam and phishing websites. In *Proc. USENIX LEET'09*, Boston, MA, April 2009.

[28] T. Moore and B. Edelman. Measuring the perpetrators and funders of typosquatting. In *Proc. Financial Crypto.'10*, pages 175–191, Tenerife, Spain, Jan. 2010.

[29] J. Pearl. Bayesian Networks: A Model of Self-Activated Memory for Evidential Reasoning. In *Proc. 7th Conf. of the Cognitive Science Society*, pages 329–334, Irvine, CA, Aug. 1985.

[30] N. Provos, P. Mavrommatis, M. Abu Rajab, and F. Monrose. All your iFrames point to us. In *Proc. USENIX Security'08*, San Jose, CA, August 2008.

[31] N. Provos, D. McNamee, P. Mavrommatis, K. Wang, and N. Modadugu. The ghost in the browser: Analysis of web-based malware. In *Proc. USENIX HotBots'07*, Cambridge, MA, April 2007.

[32] B. Schwarz. Google adwords click through rates: 2% is average but double digits is great, January 2010. `http://www.seroundtable.com/archives/021514.html`. Last accessed May 3, 2011.

[33] D. Segal. A bully finds a pulpit on the web. *New York Times*, November 2010. Article appeared in print on November 28, 2010, on page BU1 of the New York edition. Available online at `http://www.nytimes.com/2010/11/28/business/28borker.html`.

[34] D. Segal. The dirty little secrets of search. *New York Times*, February 2011. Article appeared in print on February 13, 2011, on page BU1 of the New York edition. Available online at `http://www.nytimes.com/2011/02/13/business/13search.html`.

[35] A. Singha. Finding more high-quality sites in search, February 2011. `http://googleblog.blogspot.com/2011/02/finding-more-high-quality-sites-in.html`.

[36] B. Stone-Gross, R. Abman, R. Kemmerer, C. Kruegel, D. Steigerwald, and G. Vigna. The underground economy of fake antivirus software. In *Proc. (online) WEIS 2011*, Fairfax, VA, June 2011.

[37] Twitter. Twitter developers trends resources. `http://dev.twitter.com/doc/get/trends/`.

[38] Yahoo! Inc. Yahoo buzzlog. `http://buzzlog.yahoo.com/overall/`.

[39] Yahoo! Inc. Yahoo site explorer. `http://siteexplorer.search.yahoo.com/`.

SURF: Detecting and Measuring Search Poisoning

Long Lu
College of Computing
Georgia Inst. of Technology
long@cc.gatech.edu

Roberto Perdisci
Dept. of Computer Science
University of Georgia
perdisci@cs.uga.edu

Wenke Lee
College of Computing
Georgia Inst. of Technology
wenke@cc.gatech.edu

ABSTRACT

Search engine optimization (SEO) techniques are often abused to promote websites among search results. This is a practice known as *blackhat SEO*. In this paper we tackle a newly emerging and especially aggressive class of blackhat SEO, namely *search poisoning*. Unlike other blackhat SEO techniques, which typically attempt to promote a website's ranking only under a limited set of search keywords relevant to the website's content, search poisoning techniques disregard any term relevance constraint and are employed to poison popular search keywords with the sole purpose of diverting large numbers of users to short-lived traffic-hungry websites for malicious purposes.

To accurately detect search poisoning cases, we designed a novel detection system called SURF. SURF runs as a browser component to extract a number of robust (i.e., difficult to evade) detection features from *search-then-visit* browsing sessions, and is able to accurately classify malicious search user redirections resulted from user clicking on poisoned search results. Our evaluation on real-world search poisoning instances shows that SURF can achieve a detection rate of 99.1% at a false positive rate of 0.9%. Furthermore, we applied SURF to analyze a large dataset of search-related browsing sessions collected over a period of seven months starting in September 2010. Through this long-term measurement study we were able to reveal new trends and interesting patterns related to a great variety of poisoning cases, thus contributing to a better understanding of the prevalence and gravity of the search poisoning problem.

Categories and Subject Descriptors

H.3.3 [**INFORMATION STORAGE AND RETRIEVAL**]: Information Search and Retrieval—*Relevance feedback*

General Terms

Security

Keywords

Search engine poisoning, Malicious search engine redirection, Detection, Measurement

CCS'11, October 17–21, 2011, Chicago, Illinois, USA.

1. INTRODUCTION

Search engines, capable of digging out the most relevant from oceans of information, have become web surfers' first choice when seeking information on the web. In fact, for most websites more than 70% of their visitors reach their pages through search engines [6]. Therefore, website owners always strive to attract more visits by optimizing their exposure in relevant search results. To fulfill this need, web developers use a number of search engine optimization (SEO) techniques, which can improve the visibility of a website to the search crawlers, highlight its relevance under certain search terms, and promote its raking in the search results.

Legitimate uses of SEO techniques are accepted and even encouraged by search engines [1]. However, dishonest web developers may choose to abuse these techniques in various ways to gain (or cheat) a favorable ranking in the search results, a practice known as *blackhat SEO*. In this case, search crawlers are presented with deceptive views of a website, which consist of specially crafted webpages with inflated relevance to a set of target search terms. Attempts to counter blackhat SEO have been proposed mainly in the information retrieval community [18, 24], but with very limited success against the recent surge of blackhat SEO adopters [11]. In the meantime, blackhat SEO has not captured sufficient attention from the security community, perhaps because such techniques have been historically employed by non-harmful websites, including some high profile ones [10], that execute overly aggressive marketing strategies to win search users from their competitors.

This paper tackles a newly emerging class of blackhat SEO techniques developed by Internet miscreants to lure search users into visiting malicious websites [7]. We refer to this new class of blackhat SEO as *search poisoning*. Unlike other blackhat SEO techniques, which typically attempt to promote a website's ranking only under a limited set of search keywords relevant to the website's content, search poisoning techniques disregard any term relevance constraint. In practice, search poisoning techniques target any search term that can maximize the number of incoming search users (e.g., popular keywords). This is in contrast with SEO or other blackhat SEO techniques adopted by regular websites, because if search poisoning were to be used to promote a regular website, users landing on the website via completely unrelated search terms may get annoyed and the website's reputation may be irreparably damaged. Therefore, we posit that search poisoning cannot be used for legitimate purposes and is only useful to short-lived traffic-hungry websites that aim to attract search users for malicious purposes.

We approach the search poisoning problem from a new angle, compared to previous work on blackhat SEO. We focus on detecting *malicious search user redirections*, an essential component of search poisoning that we discovered during our study (Section 2.2). To detect malicious search user redirections, we designed a novel detection system named **SURF** (Search User Redirection Finder), which runs as a browser component and is able to accurately detect poisoned search results. In this paper, we restrict our definition of "malicious search user redirections" to be any redirection that starts from a search landing page (i.e., the immediate page a search result points to) promoted by search poisoning and ends at an unwanted or malicious terminal page (i.e., the final destination of the redirection). We show that these malicious redirections can be characterized by a number of distinctive features that are collectively difficult to circumvent. SURF is designed to capture this very type of malicious redirections, and in turn to detect search poisoning instances. Other malicious redirections on landing pages not involving search poisoning are out of the scope of this work.

To detect search poisoning instances, SURF analyzes data collected during a *search-then-visit* browsing session and outputs a classification result, namely whether or not the monitored browsing session includes malicious search user redirections caused by a poisoned search result. As shown in Figure 1, the monitored browsing session starts from the search result page, passes by the landing page and possibly some intermediate pages, and stops at the terminal page to which the search user is eventually redirected. During this course, SURF collects the following information: (i) browser events to track page (and frame) loads and redirections; (ii) network information to model the redirection chain; and (iii) search result information to measure the poisoning likelihood of the landing page. From this information, SURF extracts a number of statistical features, which are then fed to a classifier trained to identify instances of search poisoning. Given the adversarial nature of classifying search poisoning instances, we selected our feature set with particular emphasis on individual feature *robustness* while retaining collective feature *generality*. To identify a suitable set of features, we performed a manual analysis of a dataset $\mathcal{S}_{study}$ containing 1,084 real-world search poisoning cases (see Section 2.2). We then experimented with 15 candidate features on a separate dataset $\mathcal{S}_{eval}$ containing 2,344 independently labeled samples of browsing sessions, 1,160 of which where related to search poisoning and there remaining 1,184 were not. Through feature selection, we refined the initial feature set down to 9 features based on which we evaluated SURF's classifier, which achieved an average true positive rate of 99.1% at a false positive rate of 0.9%.

To further demonstrate the effectiveness of SURF, we developed a prototype system and deployed it to classify daily popular search results obtained from both Google and Bing over a period of seven months (from September 2010 to April 2011). This large scale evaluation allowed us to conduct extensive measurements of real-world search poisoning cases, through which we observed that, on average, about 50% of popular searches contain poisoned results. During this measurement study we also observed a surge in both the volume of search poisoning instances and the variety of malicious content reached through poisoned search results.

In summary, this paper makes the following contributions:

- We clearly define search poisoning and distinguish it from other abuses of SEO techniques. We report an in-depth study to motivate and inspire countermeasures against this increasing threat.

- We design and evaluate SURF, a system that is able to detect search poisoning with a 99.1% true positive rate at a 0.9% false positive rate.

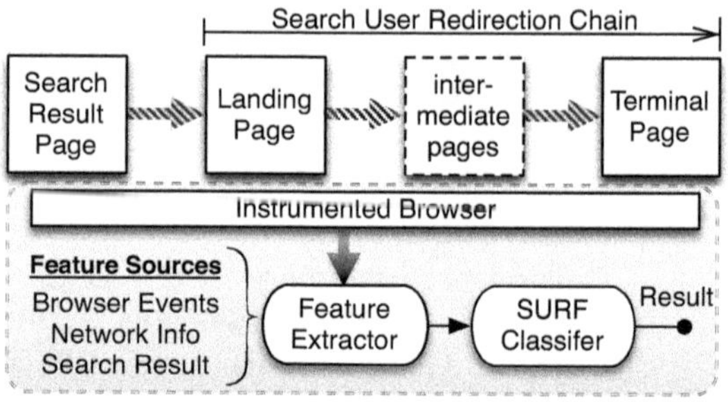

Figure 1: SURF Architecture

- Using a SURF prototype, we conducted a seven-month measurement study on poisoned popular search results, which highlights the severity of search poisoning and provides insight into its fast growing trends.

2. BACKGROUND AND PROBLEM STUDY

In this Section, we provide a brief overview of the fundamentals of search engines and the reason why search results are subject to manipulation. We then present a study of search poisoning based on real world data, and discuss the observations that inspired our detection approach.

2.1 Search Engine and Blackhat SEO

Search engines typically employ crawlers to discover newly created or updated webpages. Each crawled page is then indexed based on keywords retrieved from its content. Upon a search query, webpages are ranked based on their relevance to the search terms and presented to the user.

This gives the abusers the following advantages. First, search engines implicitly trust the authenticity of the content on the indexed webpages, even though the content is under complete control of the website owners. Second, a web server can easily distinguish between search crawlers and human visitors. It is this *implicit trust* and *distinguishability* that give rise to blackhat SEO, whereby a web server fulfills webpage requests from crawlers with specially crafted content having inflated relevance to a selected set of keywords, referred to as the *target keywords*. In addition, these crafted pages often contain large numbers of cross-reference hyperlinks to webpages that belong to the same blackhat SEO campaign. These hyperlinks have the effect of increasing the incoming link count for the promoted webpages, thus boosting the ranking in the search results.

Despite the fact that they involve some level of dishonesty, blackhat SEO techniques are sometimes used by legitimate businesses. In this paper, we distinguish between two types of blackhat SEO, namely *search inflating* and *search poisoning*. Search inflating aims to boost a website ranking through search keywords closely related to the promoted website, therefore only attracting users who search for topics related to the promoted website. On the other hand, search poisoning aims to boost a website's ranking though popular search keywords, regardless of whether these keywords are actually related to the promoted website's content or not. Unlike search inflating, which may be adopted by some legitimate websites, search poisoning only fits the need of visitor-hungry websites that simply want to increase the number of visitors for malicious purposes (e.g., for malware propagation purposes).

Most previous works on blackhat SEO detection apply lexical and structural analysis on page content [18, 22], or graph-based analysis on hyper-links [24]. However, very limited success has been achieved in practice [9], as the battle soon turned into an arms race. Having full control over webpage visibility and the freedom of adopting new evasion techniques gives adversaries significant upper hands, and makes it fundamentally difficult to design robust detection schemes based on lexical and structural analysis. To mitigate these problems, our approach aims to detect search poisoning instances using a set of features that are collectively difficult to evade because they are intrinsic to how search poisoning works, as we discuss in Section 3.2.1.

2.2 Search Poisoning Study

Search poisoning instances luring visitors to malware websites were first reported in 2007 [7]. However, until recently search poisoning has not been sufficiently studied, and has been only sporadically mentioned within the anti-malware community (mostly due to *fake AV* websites [20]).

To gain a more in-depth understanding of the search poisoning problem, we manually analyzed a dataset $\mathcal{S}_{study}$ containing 1,084 real-world search poisoning cases collected in September 2010. This preliminary study aimed to discover a set of robust features that can be leveraged for detection purposes, and to inspire our overall detection approach.

To collect the dataset $\mathcal{S}_{study}$ we proceeded as follows. We deployed an army of instrumented browsers, which on a daily basis automatically query Google and Bing with keywords that have been popular for the past 7 days. For each query, the browsers visited the top 100 URLs in the search results[1]. All network data and browsing events occurred during each browsing session were recorded as a browsing trace. This data collection process resulted in a very large dataset $\mathcal{D}$ containing over half a million browsing traces. $\mathcal{S}_{study}$ was derived from $\mathcal{D}$ using a simple heuristic to select traces that lead to malicious [3] or non-reputable webpages [4] with content irrelevant to the search keywords. This coarse-grained filtering yielded 1,084 highly likely search poisoning cases consisting of 596 unique landing URLs. It is worth noting that this dataset is not meant to be inclusive of all poisoning traces in $\mathcal{D}$, which is impossible to achieve without first developing a reliable detection system. However, our filtering heuristic produced a $\mathcal{S}_{study}$ dataset that exhibits satisfactory accuracy and sufficient diversity, as confirmed by our manual analysis. Therefore, $\mathcal{S}_{study}$ represents a reasonable base for our preliminary study of search poisoning.

Below we itemize our observations and lessons learned from our manual analysis, which inspired the choice of the statistical features used by SURF.

O1: Ubiquitous use of cross-site redirections

We found that over 98% traces in $\mathcal{S}_{study}$ contain one or more redirections that cross website boundaries. The remaining 2% of browsing traces that do not contain such redirections are mostly due to incompletely rendered webpages, or modal dialogs that require non-trivial user interactions to proceed. On the other hand, less than 6% of the entire traces in $(\mathcal{D} - \mathcal{S}_{study})$ involve cross-site redirections. This ubiquitous use of cross-site redirections can be intuitively explained by the high risk and low effectiveness of exposing the malicious terminal website directly to search engines for rank promotion (thus a separated landing website is needed). For example, search engines have various security detectors in place to filter known malicious webpages and downgrade ranks of suspicious ones. Therefore, directly promoting malicious webpages can be a vain attempt and risks to jeopardize the entire search poisoning campaign. In fact, as our study went deeper, more evidence emerged supporting the need for malicious search user redirection in search poisoning.

[1]excluding URLs already flagged as malicious by search engines.

O2: Search poisoning as a service

From all traces in S_{study} we extracted their chain of redirections, which are then used to compose a redirection graph, in which the nodes represent encountered domains and the directed edges represent redirections from one domain to another. Large numbers of inter-connected chains form subgraphs that represent different search poisoning campaigns. Two representative subgraphs are shown in Figure 2, as examples to illustrate our findings. Successful campaigns are able to employ many landing domains and target different search keywords to maximize the incoming search users. Figure 2 (top) shows a campaign that successfully poisoned over 28 "trendy" search keywords and injected at least 46 URLs into top search results. Furthermore, the variety of terminal domains supported by a single campaign suggests that specialized search poisoning services are available to all kinds of malicious websites for purchase. The graph also indicates a two-tier affiliate marketing model followed by this campaign. Some landing pages redirected search users to centralized "super affiliate" domains (circled in the graph), which then dynamically dispatch the lured users to different terminal domains. As a result, more intermediate webpages appeared in the redirection chains.

O3: Sophisticated poisoning and evasion tricks

Cloaking techniques [12] are commonly used in search poisoning (by 97% landing pages in S_{study}). Search crawlers are presented with specially crafted content with fake relevance. The malicious redirection process only starts when visited by search users that queried the target (poisoned) keywords, while blocking other visitors as an attempt to prevent security detectors reaching the malicious content or domains. By forging the browser's `User-Agent` strings, we managed to obtain the search crawler views of 26 landing pages in our S_{study} dataset that did not verify the crawler's source IP address. These views were carefully composed to mimic normal webpages (e.g., blogs or news sites), with highly relevant content (possibly scraped from elsewhere) organized in a smooth way. We noticed that this well-crafted content may easily fool human readers, and is therefore very likely to evade content-based blackhat SEO detectors. In addition, we discovered a handful of image-rich landing pages that likely targeted at multimedia searches.

Another way in which search poisoning try to evade detection is by hosting the landing pages on compromised websites. These websites typically have been indexed by search engines for quite some time and accumulated a non-trivial domain history or reputation. This can help search poisoning to bypass some security checks performed by search engines and to facilitate rank promotion. In our study dataset S_{study} we found that about 70% of the redirections start from domains with a fair reputation score in [4] and only 2% originate from blacklisted domains in [3].

O4: Persistence under transient appearances

To achieve a persistent poisoning effect, search poisoners have to accommodate for the volatility of popular search keywords. The bottom graph in Figure 2 shows a campaign that made multiple appearances on different popular search results across the entire study period: old landing domains had been active only for a limited time (a few days) before a new batch came in with a new set of poisoned search keywords. Rapidly rotating landing domains not only enable a wide coverage on trendy search topics, but also hinder detection efforts due to their transient appearance. Terminal domains behave in a similar way. An important difference is the fact that terminal domains tend to be disposable and have short registration periods (likely using domain tasting services), which further impedes blacklist-based detection.

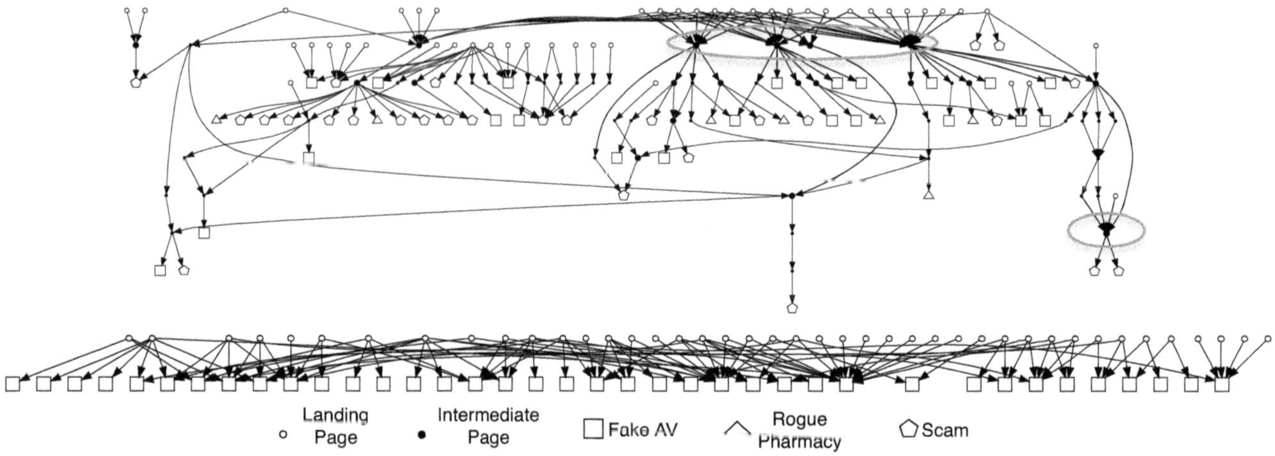

Figure 2: Redirection graphs of two search poisoning campaigns

O5: Various malicious applications

While previous reports always associate search poisoning with malware distribution websites [8, 14], search poisoning is used in a variety of other malicious applications. Figure 2 shows at least three types of malicious websites that use search poisoning to promote different types of cyber crimes, such as distributing fake AV software, hosting of rogue pharmacy sites, and other types of scams. Other types of uses (not reported in Figure 2) were also observed in S_{study}, such as sites that host drive-by download exploits, are part of click fraud schemes, or host phishing pages. Therefore, we argue that security solutions specific to individual types of malicious websites fail to thoroughly address the general search poisoning problem.

Lessons learned: Detecting search poisoning is a daunting task. Solely relying on identifying suspicious features associated with the landing pages (e.g., deceptive relevance, suspicious linkage structures, etc.) is immediately subject to evasion, given the attackers' freedom to craft the page content. At the same time, detecting malicious terminal pages is hindered by their diversity and conditional accessibility of the actual malicious content (in particular, malicious sites can detect crawlers and security scanners). However, our observations convey a positive message to the defenders: the malicious search user redirections are intrinsic to search poisoning cases and exhibit distinguishable behaviors that are difficult to avoid completely for search poisoning to be successful, as we further discuss in Section 3.2.1. SURF's design was inspired by these findings.

3. SURF DESIGN AND EVALUATION

Based on the lessons learned from our search poisoning study (Section 2.2), we set three primary design goals for our detection system:

- *Generality*: Search poisoning techniques are employed by attackers to promote a variety of malicious contents, and are not limited to luring users to visiting malware distribution pages. Therefore, SURF aims to detect generic search poisoning instances, regardless of the malicious content the attackers intend to promote.
- *Robustness*: While it is arguably impossible to completely prevent an arms race between defenders and attackers, we aim to identify features typical of search poisoning cases that are difficult to evade. In practice, we restrict SURF to using a set of *robust* features, which cannot be evaded by adversaries without incurring a significant cost (e.g., because of the need to completely change their attack strategy, or move to a different attack infrastructure).
- *Wide deployability*: Unlike most previous work on blackhat SEO detection, which is constrained by the dependency on search engine private data and only deployable at the search engine side, our approach aims to provide a solution that can be deployed at end-user's browsers (as a plugin), at automated security crawlers, and inside search engines. End-users can be protected from malicious terminal webpages hidden behind poisoned search results. At the same time, search engines or security vendors can deploy SURF in a "browsers farm" to accurately detect whether a search keyword is poisoned and harvest the malicious terminal page.

3.1 SURF System Overview

To meet the goals listed above, we designed SURF as a browser component. An overview of SURF is shown in Figure 1. In practice, SURF sits in a browser and observes search-related browsing sessions. Whenever a user submits a query to a search engine and receives the result page, SURF starts its monitoring on page loads and redirections, from the search result page, to the landing page (on user's click), and to the terminal page the user is eventually brought to (after going through several intermediate pages in some cases). During this course, SURF extracts a number of statistical features from a range of sources, such as browser events, network information regarding the domain names and IP addresses involved in the redirection chain, and the search results themselves (see Section 3.2 for details). The resulting feature vector is then sent to the *SURF Classifier*, which is trained to distinguish between normal redirections and *malicious search user redirections*. In practice, the *SURF Classifier* is a supervised statistical classifier trained using a labeled dataset containing examples of redirection chains resulted from clicking on either legitimate or a variety of poisoned search results. It is worth noting that our definition of "malicious search user redirections" in this paper is restricted to redirections following poisoned search results. Detecting other types of malicious redirection is out of the scope of this work. While the vast majority of redirections used by the search poisoning cases we encountered during our study (Section 2.2) only change the URLs of webpages' top frames, SURF also covers the malicious redirections that occur within dynamic subframes (e.g., an `iframe`).

3.2 Detection Features

Inspired by the study presented in Section 2.2, and keeping in mind the design goals outlined at the beginning of Section 3, we

Aspects	Features	Source*	Evasion Possibility
Redirection Composition	Total redirection hops	B	Low
	Cross-site redirection hops	B,N	Low
	Redirection consistency	B	Low
Chained Webpages	Landing to terminal distance	B,N	Low
	Page load/render errors	B,N	Low
	IP-to-name ratio	B	Medium
Poisoning Resistance	Keyword poison resistance	S	Low
	Search rank	S	Low
	Good rank confidence	S	Low

* B=browser events/data; N=network info; S=search result

Table 1: Feature selection

identified a set of nine statistical features that capture the characteristics of generic search poisoning instances, and that are difficult for the attacker to evade without incurring a significant cost (e.g., the attacker would need to move to a new search poisoning strategy and infrastructure). The features extracted by SURF are divided in three groups as summarized in Table 1 and detailed below.

Redirection composition: This group of three features aims at capturing discrepancies between the legitimate and malicious search user redirections. The `total redirection hops` records the number of redirections that transport the visitor from the landing page to a terminal page, whereas the `cross-site redirection hops` counts how many of these redirections cross website boundaries. In SURF, a cross-site redirection is a redirection that brings from a domain d_1 to a domain d_2, where the *second-level* domains[2] of d_1 and d_2 differ (e.g., `www.cnn.com` and `blogs.cnn.com` share the same second-level domain, while `www.cnn.com` and `www.bbc.com` do not). As noted in Section 2.2, the vast majority of poisoned search results rely on cross-site redirections to transport search users to the malicious terminal pages hosted on covert domains. On the other hand, legitimate search user redirections rarely send incoming visitors away to another websites, simply because of the common incentive of keeping as many visitors as possible within their own domain. The `redirection consistency` feature captures whether a redirection is only visible to targeted search users. In legitimate search user redirections, users who arrive to the landing page through a search engine or though a direct link (e.g., by typing the same URL on the browser's address bar, or clicking the hyperlink on a "non-search" website) will be redirected to the same terminal page displaying relevant content. This is in contrast with search poisoning cases, in which typically only users that reach the landing page through a search will be redirected to the malicious content, while other visitors will be presented with non-malicious content in an attempt to evade some detection systems or manual analysis (see Section 2.2). To measure redirection consistency, SURF can first command the browser to directly visit the landing page (thus effectively stripping the `Referrer` field in the HTTP request, for example), and then allows the user's click on the search result link to go through so that the two obtained sets of redirection events can be compared for consistency. When used at the search engine-level (e.g., in a "browsers farm"), SURF could perform this comparison on redirections obtained by visiting the landing page from different IP addresses to bypass some of the cloaking techniques discussed in Section 2.2 whereby the malicious content is not provided to IP addresses visiting the same landing page twice in a row. It is worth noting that such cloaking technique would not affect SURF's protection when deployed at end user's browsers. If the attacker refuses to offer the malicious content at the second visit (i.e., when SURF allows the user's click on a search result to go through), the user will not be exposed to the malicious content in the first place.

Chained webpages: This group of features measures three properties of the webpages involved in search user redirections. The `landing to terminal distance` feature measures the (approximate) geographical and topological distances between the landing page and the terminal page. In practice, to measure this distance we leverage information about the geo-location of the IPs where the two pages reside, the autonomous systems (AS) the IPs belong to, and the websites' domain names. The intuition is that malicious search user redirections always "travel" a long distance. The reason is that in search poisoning cases the landing page is usually hosted on a (likely compromised) website that belongs to a separate (usually legitimate) organization, while the terminal page is often hosted on a "bullet-proof" server provided by a different (usually not legitimate or boarder-line) organization often located in a different country.

The `page load/render errors` flags pages in the redirection chain that failed to load or render properly, due to exceptions or network errors. The intuition is that compromised pages are sometimes blacklisted or remediated, and the redirection chain to the malicious terminal page may end prematurely. The `IP-to-name ratio` feature represents the number of the redirection URLs that use an IP address (e.g., `http://192.168.0.1/index.php`) divided by the number of redirection URLs that instead use a domain name (e.g., `http://example.com/index.php`). This is motivated by the fact that a large number of search poisoning cases encountered in our study involve URLs that use IPs that are dynamically assigned to unnamed hosts, in an effort to bypass URL blacklists commonly available in major browsers.

Poisoning resistance: This group of features measure properties of the search keywords and their corresponding search results. The `keyword poison resistance` quantifies the difficulty of poisoning search results under a given keyword. We measure this feature using publicly available information. The basic idea is straightforward: given a certain search keyword, the competitiveness of promoting a link higher in the result rankings is reflected by how prominent the top ranked webpages are under that keyword. We use Google's PageRank [19] to measure the prominence of a website. The `keyword poison resistance` of a keyword k is defined as the average PageRank value of the top 10 ranked websites obtained from the search results under k. In practice, the higher the value of this feature, the more prominent websites competing for the top rank positions, and thus the more difficult for an attacker to poison the keyword and force a link to a rogue landing page to appear higher in the ranking.

From our study dataset S_{study} (see Section 2.2), we noticed that the distribution of poisoned keywords across different search poisoning cases is skewed towards keywords with low `keyword poison resistance`. This result was somewhat expected, because keywords that are popular and yet easier to poison than others tend to attract the attackers' attention. Another feature we consider is the `search rank` of a landing page. The higher the rank of a landing page, the lower the probability that the result has been poisoned. This follows directly from our previous argument that top ranked pages are often prominent websites, making it difficult for search poisoners to promote their sites ahead of these prominent sites. The `rank confidence` feature is computed by dividing the `keyword poison resistance` by the rank of a partic-

[2] The second-level domain of a domain name `d.c.b.a` is typically defined as `b.a`, where `a` is called the *top-level* domain. We leverage Mozilla's public domain suffix list to take effective top-level domains such as `co.uk` into account.

ular search result. The higher the `rank confidence`, the less likely that the result is poisoned.

3.2.1 *Qualitative Robustness Analysis*

Here we present a qualitative analysis of the robustness of SURF's statistical features against evasion attempts. A quantitative robustness analysis is discussed in Section 3.4.

Redirection composition: This group of features tries to capture the "search poisoning as a service" phenomenon discussed in Section 2.2. In practice, attackers often compromise several legitimate websites to host rogue landing pages, which use deceptive content to promote their ranks and at the same time redirect lured search users to the malicious terminal webpages. While in principle an attacker can attempt to evade this group of features, this would force the attacker to move to a completely different malicious network infrastructure in which all malicious redirections and terminal malicious pages are hosted on the same second-level domain, for example. In addition to incurring the significant cost of changing the malicious network infrastructure, this could also increase the risk of being detected by the compromised website's administrators, thus exposing search poisoning instances to a more prompt remediation, and end up sacrificing the established rogue landing pages which typically take considerable amount of time and efforts to mature.

Chained webpages: This group of features measure properties of the webpages involved in search user redirections. The `IP-to-name ratio`, while useful for classification in most practical cases, is not very difficult to evade because it only requires the attacker to register more domain names. However, we would like to emphasize that carrying an evasion attack on this feature will not significantly impact SURF's accuracy, as shown in the quantitative analysis in Section 3.4. The remaining two features are harder to evade. The `landing to terminal distance` feature depends on the attacker's network infrastructure, and therefore the same arguments we made for the *redirection composition* features hold in this case. The `page load/render errors` may depend, for example, on pages (and domains) along the redirection chain that have been blacklisted or remediated. Therefore, this feature is not under the attacker's direct control and is difficult to evade.

Poisoning resistance: Since these three features are derived from the search result pages themselves with the help of public PageRank data, which is determined by the search engine algorithms and out of attackers' control. Therefore these features are difficult to evade.

3.3 Prototype Implementation

SURF only requires a limited amount of data to be collected during *search-then-visit* browsing sessions, and can be easily incorporated into a browser as a plugin. To demonstrate the effectiveness of our detection approach, we implemented SURF on top of an instrumented version of Internet Explorer 8. This instrumented browser leverages `mshtml.dll` for HTML parsing and rendering, and is able to listen for event notifications (e.g., used to identify subframe redirections) and peek into browsing data (e.g., HTML code and user visible content) at different rendering stages. In addition, SURF is capable of emulating simple user interactions during visiting sessions that require certain user input to proceed (e.g., clicking on a message dialogue box, activating a mouse-over action, etc.).

To perform our evaluation of SURF, we used several instrumented browser instances and instructed them to retrieve lists of popular (or "trendy") search keywords, query each keyword on both Google and Bing, and visit the top 100 search results for each query. Our evaluation data collection started in September 2010. We deployed our browser on 20 virtual machines which would run daily to query search keywords that had reached popularity within the past seven days. In addition, our instrumented browser was enhanced with BLADE [16], which we used to protect the VMs from *drive-by download* malware infections and to log attempted exploits. The obtained browsing information for each browsing session was then saved for offline analysis. While we performed our evaluation offline for convenience reasons, mainly to be able to run cross-validation experiments on large datasets, once the statistical classifier has been trained SURF can detect search poisoning instance *online* (see Figure 1).

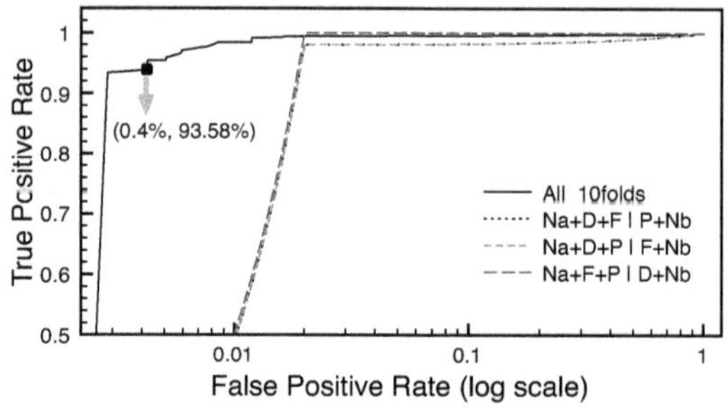

Figure 3: Threshold Curves (ROC)

3.4 Evaluation Results

Evaluation Dataset: To the best of our knowledge, there exist no public labeled dataset of search results and their related user redirection events related to search poisoning cases. Therefore, we chose to semi-manually label part of our dataset. In particular, we labeled browsing sessions collected during October 2010. In the following, we refer to obtain dataset as $\mathcal{S}_{eval}$. It is worth noting that $\mathcal{S}_{eval}$ differs from the $\mathcal{S}_{study}$ dataset that we used for the search poisoning study in Section 2.2 ($\mathcal{S}_{study}$ was collected one month earlier). This is to make sure that SURF does not "overfit" $\mathcal{S}_{study}$ because $\mathcal{S}_{study}$ inspired the choice of SURF's statistical features, and to avoid over-estimating SURF's accuracy. For the same reasons, none of the statistical features measured by SURF were used to guide our labeling. We simply semi-manually labeled the data using a separate set of heuristics based on the relation between the search terms and a (visual) analysis of the terminal page content rendered by the browser.

In practice, we labeled search poisoning cases related to three types of malicious activities: search result for popular search keywords that lead to irrelevant terminal pages serving (1) *drive-by download* malware, (2) *fake AV* software, or (3) hosting *rogue pharmacy* sites. We labeled all these cases as *poisoned* (or positive). At the same time, we labeled a search result as *non-poisoned* (or negative) only when all URLs appeared in redirection chain have a fair reputations (e.g., according to [4]) and none of them are flagged as malicious by website scanning or blacklisting services (e.g, using [3]). Overall, $\mathcal{S}_{eval}$ consists of 1,184 negative samples and 1,160 positive ones, with 585 fake AV, 414 drive-by download, and 161 rogue pharmacy cases.

To evaluate SURF and confirm it follows the design goals outlined at the beginning of Section 3, we conducted three different experiments. The first experiment aims to estimate SURF's accuracy, while the second attempts to show that SURF is able to detect generic search poisoning cases, and is not limited to one specific type of malicious content. The third experiment aims to show what features are the most important for classification, and how SURF may respond to evasion attempts on these features. Throughout all our experiments, we used Weka's `J48` decision tree classifier [13], which is an implementation of the well known C4.5 algorithm [5]. This choice is motivated by the fact that decision trees are efficient (both during the training and testing phases) compared to other statistical classifiers, and the resulting trained classifier can be easily interpreted.

Overall accuracy: To estimate SURF's detection rate and false positives, we performed a 10-fold cross validated of SURF's classifier on the $\mathcal{S}_{eval}$ dataset, achieving an average true positive rate of 99.1% at a 0.9% false positive rate. The ROC curve in Figure 3 shows a very slow decrease of the detection rate as the false positive rate is pushed down from 0.9% to 0.28%. Therefore SURF can satisfy a relatively wide range of usage scenarios with different levels of tolerance to false positives, while still maintaining a reasonably high true positive rate. In our SURF prototype we set the detection threshold to limit the false positive rate to 0.4% (marked point in Figure 3). We also analyzed the decision tree produced by the trained `J48` classifier and found that misclassifications were mainly caused by those rare cases in which poisoned search results achieved a top rank under a very competitive keyword, or cases in which a legitimate landing page redirects visitors to a very "distant" terminal page (see Section 3.2) and detours sampled visitors through third-party traffic analysis services.

Generality test: To confirm that SURF is able to detect generic search poisoning cases, regardless of the specific malicious content that they promote, we performed the following experiment. We prepared three datasets, $\mathcal{D}$, $\mathcal{F}$, and $\mathcal{P}$, containing labeled search poisoning example from the drive-by malware downloads, fake AV, and rogue pharmacy cases from $\mathcal{S}_{eval}$, respectively. In addition, we prepared two separate datasets, $\mathcal{N}_a$ and $\mathcal{N}_b$, containing randomly selected negative examples (i.e., legitimate search redirection cases). We then performed a 3-fold cross validation by using $\mathcal{D} \cup \mathcal{F} \cup \mathcal{N}_a$ for training, and testing on $\mathcal{P} \cup \mathcal{N}_b$ for the first fold, training on $\mathcal{D} \cup \mathcal{P} \cup \mathcal{N}_a$ and testing on $\mathcal{F} \cup \mathcal{N}_b$ for the second fold, and training on $\mathcal{F} \cup \mathcal{P} \cup \mathcal{N}_a$ and testing on $\mathcal{D} \cup \mathcal{N}_b$ for the third one. Figure 3 shows the three separate ROC curves (one per fold). Averaging the results of the 3-fold validation, we obtained a detection rate of 98% at a false positive rate of 1.8%. It is worth noting that while this result does not appear to be as good as the result obtained for the overall 10-fold cross validation experiment, our 3-fold evaluation presents SURF with much harder cases in which no examples of search poisoning instances of the same category used for testing are present in the training set. However, the high detection rate and relatively limited false positives demonstrate that the features used by SURF can indeed capture generic search poisoning properties, independent of the specific type of malicious content delivered by the terminal page.

Feature Robustness: This experiment attempts to quantify SURF's resistance to evasion effects on the statistical features. To perform the experiments, we ran SURF's classifier on 100 randomly chosen positive samples. We artificially modified the values of the features describing these 100 samples to simulate different evasion scenarios, and evaluated how the classifier's accuracy changed as a consequence. We first artificially set the `IP-to-name ratio` to zero, which is the most common value of the feature in negative samples. The `IP-to-name ratio` feature is the only one among SURF's features that is not difficult to evade. After altering this feature, only 1 out of 100 samples was misclassified, which suggests that the attacker cannot gain much by attempting to evade it. Despite the fact that other features are hard to evade (see Section 3.2.1), we nonetheless wanted to investigate the effect of altering the most discriminant features, i.e., the features that appeared close to the root of the decision tree. The `redirection consistency` and `landing to terminal distance` turned out to be the top two most discriminant features. Replacing their values with values drawn from negative samples caused 80 out of 100 samples to be misclassified. However, it is worth noting that evading these two features would require the attacker to change her malicious network infrastructure, thus incurring a significant cost, as discussed in Section 3.2.1.

4. DISCUSSION

At a first glance, our evaluation may seem unconvincing because we used a dataset labeled by ourselves. However, to the best of our knowledge, no public labeled dataset exists that contains browsing session data related to a variety of search poisoning instances. As discussed in Section 3.4, our semi-manual labeling process is based on a set of heuristics that do not overlap with any of the detection features measured by SURF. This allowed us to perform an unbiased evaluation. While we acknowledge that our semi-manual labeling can only help us collect partial "ground truth", it is extremely difficult, if not impossible, to obtain complete ground truth without a deterministic search poisoning detection system. In absence of such perfect search poisoning detector, our labeling method represents our best effort to produce a representative (even though not complete) ground truth that includes a variety of search poisoning instances leading to different types of malicious content.

During our feature selection process, we discarded a few candidate features that may help the classification accuracy but are not robust. For example, we chose not to include features based on measuring the relevance of the content of terminal pages to the search keywords because the content of the terminal pages is under complete control of the attacker, making these types of features easy to evade. Also, we did not include features related to the structure of the URLs involved in malicious search user redirections. These features usually require historical knowledge of the "normal" structure of the URLs for each particular website. While these type of features may be included in a search engine-side deployment of SURF, client-side deployments would not be able to collect and leverage this kind of information, and therefore we decided not to add them to our prototype implementation. Furthermore, an attacker has a non-negligible flexibility when choosing the structure of the redirection URLs, and therefore it is not clear how robust these features would be. We also considered some features based on domain or IP reputation scores. Though capable of reducing the false positive rate, these features were excluded from our selection because of their heavy dependence on external security services, and because we wanted to evaluate the detection accuracy of SURF based solely on the strengths of our own features. In practice, SURF implementations may opt to incorporate reputation-based features to improve classification accuracy.

When deployed at the search engine side (e.g., using a "browser farm"), SURF can be used to analyze suspicious search results and accurately detect poisoning cases. This can provide search engines with valuable information that goes beyond specific poisoning instances. For instance, the landing pages involved in search poisoning are often organized in a "botnet mode", so that the keywords to be poisoned can be periodically fetched from a command-and-control server. Therefore, detecting search poisoning cases can reveal information about compromised websites and botnet organizations. In addition, newly detected malicious terminal webpages may serve as labeled samples for malicious webpage detectors that require periodic re-training.

At the same time, SURF can be deployed at each single client to detect (and block) poisoned search results. A possible deployment scenario could include large numbers of client-side SURF installations that collaboratively detect search poisoning case and share information about the underlying malicious network infrastructures

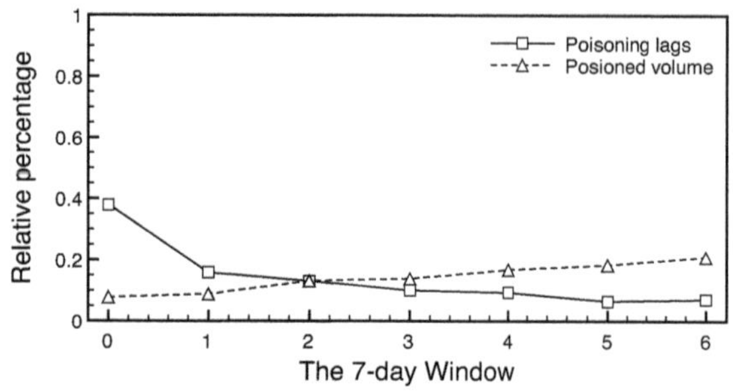

Figure 4: Micro measurement statistics

(e.g., domain names, IP address, etc.) through a cloud service, thus potentially improving SURF's detection accuracy.

5. EMPIRICAL MEASUREMENTS

To gain a deeper insight into the search poisoning problem, we performed a long-term (7 months, 212 days) measurement study. As discussed in Section 2, we manually analyzed data in the first month. We used SURF to analyze browsing data we collected in the next 6 months. During this period we instructed SURF to analyze over 12 millions search results from both Google and Bing collected by querying the top 40 "trendy" keywords [2]. In practice, once a search keyword appeared in the top 40 list on a given day, we used SURF to query the search engines for this keyword for the following 7 days. Overall, during our measurement study SURF automatically queried the search engines with 8,480 keywords. This long-term data collection process enabled us to study in-the-wild search poisoning instances from two different angles, a "micro measurement" study based on a 7-day window that focuses on how search poisoning evolves with respect to frequently changing keyword popularity, and a "macro measurement" study that looks at poisoning trends over the entire 7-month period.

5.1 Micro Measurements

Due to frequent changes in the trendy search keywords [2], we expected that some time (e.g., a few days) would be required for the attackers to poison the search terms and make their landing pages of choice appear in the related top search results. Surprisingly, our measurements on the micro developments of detected search poisoning cases suggest otherwise: adversaries are extremely responsive and have built effective approaches to promote rogue landing pages under the targeted trendy search keywords in a short time.

Among the 3,869 keywords for which we detected related poisoned search results, 38% of them had *poisoning lag* (i.e., the time it takes for the first poisoned result to be detected) of one day or less. This percentage decreases as the lag increases, and only 7% of the keywords had a poisoning lag of 7 days, as shown in Figure 4. This results suggest that the adversaries are capable of keeping up with search users' interests, and that the majority of their poisoning attempts succeed within the first 3 days.

We also found that the average life time of a rogue landing page involved in search poisoning is only 1.7 days. This indicates that adversaries favor a fast-switching strategy to reduce the exposure window, thus reducing the possibility of the rogue pages being detected and conserving the compromised landing sites for reuse in future poisoning attacks. However, the appearance of these rogue landing pages in the search results lasts for more than 3 days on average, until the page ranking is demoted due to the new information retrieved by the search crawlers. At the same time, the relative volume of detected rogue landing pages for a given poisoned keyword keeps increasing throughout the 7-day observation window, as shown by the *poisoned volume* increase in Figure 4 (the poisoned volume is relative to the total number of detected poisoned results during the 7-day period). We believe this fast paced operation proposes significant challenges for blacklisting and other traditional security solutions, making them inadequate to solve the search poisoning problem. In fact, well-known malicious webpage scanners (e.g., [3]) have failed to detect 78.9% of malicious terminal pages involved in the search poisoning cases detected by SURF (we scanned all the terminal pages using [3] on the same day when SURF detected the related search poisoning instance).

Our measurements show that the visiting traffic reaching a particular malicious terminal page is always contributed by multiple landing pages that appear in poisoned search results related to different search keywords. In particular, we found that during a 7-day period, for each given malicious terminal page, their visitors were supplied in average by 2.9 poisoned search keywords and 2.2 different rogue landing sites per keyword. We speculate this is a reflection of a growth in the "search poisoning as a service" phenomenon discussed in Section 2.2.

5.2 Macro Measurements

After examining the development of poisoned search results in the first 7 days period, we now zoom out our measurement window to consider the entire 7-month data collection period. Through these long-term measurements we aim to discover search poisoning's evolving trends and characteristics that are observable only throughout a long period of time. To highlight specific patterns and long-term trends, we divide the 7-month observation period in 31 epochs, where each epoch is equal to one week. Then, for each week we compute a number of statistics (discussed below), and plot how these statistics vary with respect to time.

During most epochs, we found that more than 50% of the search keywords that became popular on that epoch got poisoned. For this particular measurement, a search keyword is considered to be poisoned if at least one out of the top 100 search results for that keyword is related to a search poisoning instance. Figure 5 (left) plots the percentage of poisoned keywords for each week, broken down into different degrees of success in terms of search ranking. We can see that during some of the epochs, almost 60% of the trendy search keywords resulted in rogue landing pages that ranked within the top 50 search results. Furthermore, in some cases adversaries managed to promote their rogue landing pages up to the top 10 search results. These particularly successful attacks were related to about 15% of all poisoned keywords on average. These findings are alarming because they suggest that a large number of search users can easily be affected by search poisoning.

Figure 5 (right) shows two curves. One represents the number of rogue landing sites (counted as the number of distinct related domain names) that were involved in search poisoning cases, and the other the number of distinct (*landing domain*, *keyword*) pairs. The two peeks (marked by A and B in the figure) that appeared around Christmas time and the Super Bowl are not a coincidence. Our analysis shows that important predictable events can help adversaries to further increase their poisoning success rate, given the sufficiently large preparing time (enabled by the predictability of the events) and the interest of large number of search users in the events being exploited. At the same time, less predictable breaking news that receive broad attention for a not too short amount of time (e.g., a few days) are also an easy target for search poisoning. An example of this is the earthquake and tsunami that recently hit Japan (marked by C in Figure 5). Furthermore, as the targeted keywords (upper curve) fluctuated between attempts to leverage different events, the number of detected landing domains (lower curve) remained somewhat more stable, suggesting that search poisoning

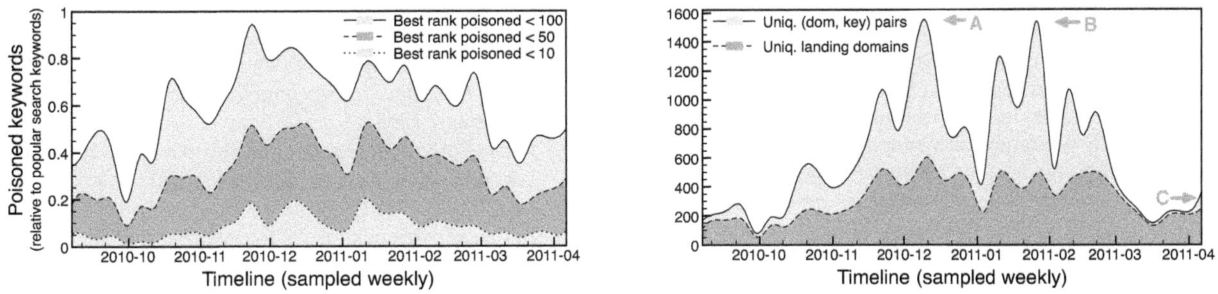

Figure 5: Poisoned keywords percentage (left) and landing domains engaging search poisoning (right)

operators have a solid footing in the search engines' indexes, and are ready to launch new attacks whenever the opportunity comes.

On average, users who fall victim of search poisoning are redirected at least twice, including one cross-domain redirection, before reaching the malicious terminal page. About 29% of these redirections were due to HTTP 30x responses. Not surprisingly, the majority of the remaining 70% were mostly due to client-side scripts (likely an attempt to evade security crawlers that do not support script execution). About 78% of the landing page URLs explicitly contained the targeted search keywords to boost the page relevance perceived by search crawlers. About 98% of the intermediate URLs include ID-like parameters to track unique visitors, identify search poisoning affiliates, or prevent repeated visits. In 94% of the cases, the terminal page URLs used domain names registered for less than a year, with many of these domain chosen to purposely deceive victim users and promote specific scams. Among the detected search poisoning cases, the most frequently used top-level domains (TLDs) for landing pages are `.com`, `.org`, `.net`, and `.info`, with a TLD distribution similar to regular websites. On the other hand, domains related to terminal pages were mostly registered under TLDs such as `.cc`, `.com`, `.in`, and `.net`, some of which are known to be malware friendly.

To have a sense of the variety of malicious content promoted by search poisoning, we surveyed 350 randomly chosen terminal pages. These 350 terminal pages were evenly distributed across our 7-months measurement period. The results are shown in Figure 6. We manually categorized the terminal pages based on data saved at the time when the page was visited by SURF, including screen shots of each rendered page. As expected, fake AVs are the most prevalent adopters of search poisoning during the entire 7-month period. However, we noticed that their pervasiveness started fading as other types of malicious terminal pages increased. Drive-by malware downloads and other browser exploitation techniques did not appear to be commonly leveraging search poisoning. On the other hand, various types of social engineering-based malicious pages are dominant players. The figure shows a clear surge of rogue search engine pages, which present the users with links seemingly relevant to the search keyword but aim to profit from user clicks.

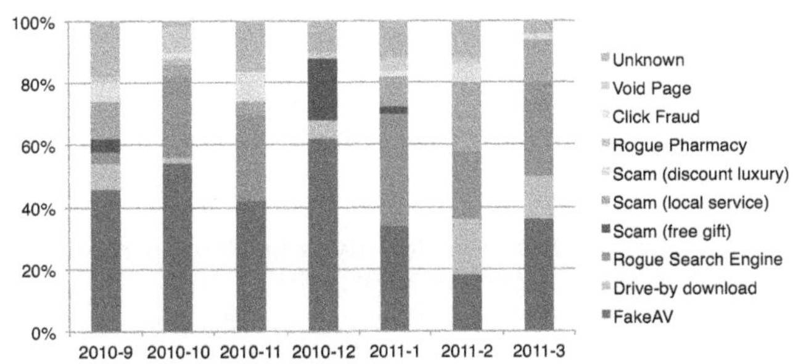

Figure 6: Terminal page variety survey

Scam pages (e.g., watch replicas, etc.) represent another significant fraction of the surveyed terminal pages. Regardless of their individual tactics, scam pages in general bait traps with free or unrealistically cheap goods to attract users and steal private information (e.g., credit card numbers, passwords, etc.). We also encountered a number of malicious terminal pages related to click fraud and rogue pharmacies. The terminal pages categorized as "void" typically contain clues of of certain types of maliciousness (e.g., based on their domain name patterns) but were inaccessible when visited due to unsuccessful DNS resolution, or webpage errors. SURF's ability to detect even these "void" malicious terminal pages supports our initial goal of building a detection system that is agnostic to the specific content of malicious pages promoted through search poisoning.

6. RELATED WORK

In this section, we identify and discuss two lines of work related to our detection system.

Blackhat SEO countermeasures: Blackhat SEO, which involves abusing search engine optimization techniques to achieve undeserved rankings, is not a new problem and has been studied for year, especially in the information retrieval community. Most proposed detection methods work at the search engine level and attempt to identify deceptive information introduced by the adversaries into the search index to influence the rankings of their websites. Various detection features explored by these methods mainly focus on two aspects of indexed webpages: intra-page characteristics [18,22,25] and inter-page linkages [24]. However, for adversaries with full control over their injected search landing pages, such features are not difficult to evade, sometimes even without requiring changes to their operation routines. In fact, this traditional way of countering blackhat SEO has failed to stop its rising trend [11]. SURF addresses search poisoning, a new class of blackhat SEO, building on the lessons learned from previous work and approaching the detection from a new angle using a set of feature that is more robust to evasion (see Section 3.2.1).

deSEO [15] is a very recent work done in parallel with SURF. It detects URLs from the search index that contain signatures derived from known search poisoning landing pages and exhibit patterns not previously seen by the search engine on the same domain. Since there is no need to crawl each URL, this approach scales much better than SURF when facing a huge volume of search results. However, deSEO is limited by the coverage of the URL signatures, and may only find a subset of what SURF detects. For example, about 12% landing page URLs detected by SURF in Section 5.2 do not contain trendy search keywords, and thus may be missed by deSEO. Moreover, SURF does not rely on any information internal to search engines and can be deployed at the client side, enabling single browsers to detect poisoned search results as well as malicious webpages behind them before the content is presented to the user.

Malicious webpage detection: SURF, when implemented as an automated detection agent, can be viewed as a dynamic crawler used to scan search results looking for poisoned ones. From this perspective, SURF is similar to many proposed systems that crawl the Internet for various kinds of malicious webpages [17,23]. Such systems always employ an army of browsing agents running in a controlled environment to visit suspicious URLs in batch and detect signs of specific types of malicious activities. SURF can be easily integrated into these systems and can enable the detection of search poisoning cases along with the related compromised landing page and malicious terminal pages. On the other hand, solely relying on malicious page detectors for finding poisoned search results may achieve limited success, because of the variety of terminal pages, many of which use social engineering attacks that are difficult to detect.

Applying machine learning techniques to data collected during a crawling session is also a common approach to detecting malicious webpages. A recent work [21] is able to detect URLs that lead to spam pages. Our work is different because SURF is not limited to detecting spam pages, and can instead detect generic search poisoning cases.

7. CONCLUSION

Search poisoning is an abuse of SEO techniques by which miscreants target any search term that can maximize the number of incoming search users to their malicious websites. We observed through an empirical study that a key characteristic of search poisoning is the ubiquitous use of cross-site redirections. We designed and implemented SURF, a novel detection system that runs as a browser component and is able to detect malicious search user redirections resulted from user clicking on poisoned search results. SURF extracts a number of detection features from *search-then-visit* browsing sessions. These features are robust and the resulting classifier is hard to evade because they capture the key properties of search poisoning (derived from our empirical study and analysis). Our evaluation showed that SURF can achieve a detection rate of 99.1% at a false positive rate of 0.9% on a dataset that contains real-world search poisoning instances. Using SURF, we also performed a long-term measurement study on search poisoning on the Internet over a period of seven months. Our study revealed new trends and interesting patterns related to a great variety of poisoning cases, and underscored the prevalence and gravity of the search poisoning problem.

8. ACKNOLEDGEMENT

The authors would like to thank the anonymous reviewers for helpful comments on earlier versions of the paper. This material is based upon work supported in part by the National Science Foundation under grant no. 0831300, the Department of Homeland Security under contract no. FA8750-08-2-0141, the Office of Naval Research under grants no. N000140710907 and no. N000140911042. Any opinions, findings, and conclusions or recommendations expressed in this material are those of the authors and do not necessarily reflect the views of the National Science Foundation, the Department of Homeland Security, or the Office of Naval Research.

9. REFERENCES

[1] Google search engine optimization. http://www.google.com/webmasters/.

[2] Google trends. http://www.google.com/trends.

[3] URLVoid: Scan a website with multiple scanning engines. http://www.urlvoid.com/.

[4] WOT: Web of trust. http://www.mywot.com/wiki/API.

[5] *C4.5: Programs for Machine Learning*. Morgan Kaufmann Publishers, 1993.

[6] Google drives 70 percent of traffic to most web sites. http://searchengineoptimism.com/Google_refers_70_percent.html, July 2006.

[7] Malware poisoning results for innocent searches. http://www.eweek.com/c/a/Security/Malware-Poisoning-Results-for-Innocent-Searches, November 2007.

[8] Barracuda labs 2010 mid-year security report. Technical report, Barracuda Networks Inc., 2010.

[9] Search engine optimization 'poisoning' way up this year. http://www.networkworld.com/news/2010/110910-seo-poisoning-increases.html, November 2010.

[10] The dirty little secrets of search. http://www.nytimes.com/2011/02/13/business/13search.html, February 2011.

[11] Google: Search engine spam on the rise. http://www.pcworld.com/article/217370/google_search, January 2011.

[12] Z. Gyöngyi and H. Garcia-Molina. Web spam taxonomy. Technical report, Stanford University, 2005.

[13] M. Hall, E. Frank, G. Holmes, B. Pfahringer, P. Reutemann, and I. H. Witten. The weka data mining software: an update. *SIGKDD Explor. Newsl.*, 11(1):10–18, 2009.

[14] F. Howard and O. Komili. Poisoned search results: How hackers have automated search engine poisoning attacks to distribute malware. Technical report, SophosLab, 2010.

[15] J. John, F. Yu, Y. Xie, M. Abadi, and A. Krishnamurthy. deSEO: Combating search-result poisoning. In *Proceedings of the 20th USENIX Security*, 2011.

[16] L. Lu, V. Yegneswaran, P. Porras, and W. Lee. Blade: an attack-agnostic approach for preventing drive-by malware infections. In *Proceedings of the 17th ACM CCS*, 2010.

[17] E. Moshchuk, T. Bragin, S. D. Gribble, and H. M. Levy. A crawler-based study of spyware on the web. In *Proceedings of the NDSS*, 2006.

[18] A. Ntoulas and M. Manasse. Detecting spam web pages through content analysis. In *In Proceedings of the 15th WWW*, 2006.

[19] L. Page, S. Brin, R. Motwani, and T. Winograd. The pagerank citation ranking: Bringing order to the web. Technical Report 1999-66, Stanford InfoLab, 1999.

[20] M. A. Rajab, L. Ballard, P. Mavrommatis, N. Provos, and X. Zhao. The nocebo effect on the web: an analysis of fake anti-virus distribution. In *Proceedings of the 3rd USENIX LEET*, 2010.

[21] K. Thomas, C. Grier, J. Ma, V. Paxson, and D. Song. Design and evaluation of a real-time url spam filtering service. In *In Proceedings of the IEEE S&P*, 2011.

[22] T. Urvoy, E. Chauveau, P. Filoche, and T. Lavergne. Tracking web spam with html style similarities. *ACM Trans. Web*, 2:3:1–3:28, March 2008.

[23] Y.-M. Wang, D. Beck, X. Jiang, and R. Roussev. Automated web patrol with strider honeymonkeys: Finding web sites that exploit browser vulnerabilities. In *Proceedings of the NDSS*, 2006.

[24] B. Wu and B. D. Davison. Identifying link farm spam pages. In *Proceedings of the 14th WWW*, 2005.

[25] B. Wu and B. D. Davison. Detecting semantic cloaking on the web. In *Proceedings of the 15th WWW*, 2006.

Cloak and Dagger: Dynamics of Web Search Cloaking

David Y. Wang, Stefan Savage, and Geoffrey M. Voelker
Deptartment of Computer Science and Engineering
University of California, San Diego

ABSTRACT

Cloaking is a common "bait-and-switch" technique used to hide the true nature of a Web site by delivering blatantly different semantic content to different user segments. It is often used in search engine optimization (SEO) to obtain user traffic illegitimately for scams. In this paper, we measure and characterize the prevalence of cloaking on different search engines, how this behavior changes for targeted versus untargeted advertising and ultimately the response to site cloaking by search engine providers. Using a custom crawler, called *Dagger*, we track both popular search terms (e.g., as identified by Google, Alexa and Twitter) and targeted keywords (focused on pharmaceutical products) for over five months, identifying when distinct results were provided to crawlers and browsers. We further track the lifetime of cloaked search results as well as the sites they point to, demonstrating that cloakers can expect to maintain their pages in search results for several days on popular search engines and maintain the pages themselves for longer still.

Categories and Subject Descriptors

H.3.5 [**Information Storage and Retrieval**]: Online Information Services—*Web-based services*

General Terms

Measurement, Security

Keywords

Cloaking, Search Engine Optimization, Web spam

1. INTRODUCTION

The growth of e-commerce in the late 20th century in turn created value around the attention of individual Internet users — described crassly by Caldwell as "The Great Eyeball Race" [3]. Since then, virtually every medium of Internet interaction has been monetized via some form of advertising, including e-mail, Web sites, social networks and on-line games, but perhaps none as successfully as *search*. Today, the top Internet search engines are a primary means for connecting customers and sellers in a broad range of markets, either via "organic" search results or sponsored search placements—together comprising a $14B marketing sector [16].

Not surprisingly, the underlying value opportunities have created strong incentives to influence search results—a field called "search engine optimization" or SEO. Some of these techniques are benign and even encouraged by search engine operators (e.g., simplifying page content, optimizing load times, etc.) while others are designed specifically to manipulate page ranking algorithms without regard to customer interests (e.g., link farms, keyword stuffing, blog spamming, etc.) Thus, a cat and mouse game has emerged between search engine operators and scammers where search operators try to identify and root out pages deemed to use "black hat" optimization techniques or that host harmful content (e.g., phishing pages, malware sites, etc.) while scammers seek to elude such detection and create new pages faster than they can be removed.

In this conflict, one of the most potent tools is *cloaking*, a "bait-and-switch" technique used to hide the true nature of a Web site by delivering blatantly different content to different user segments. Typically a cloaker will serve "benign" content to search engine crawlers and scam content to normal visitors who are referred via a particular search request. By structuring the benign version of this content to correspond with popular search terms—a practice known as keyword stuffing—Web spammers aggressively acquire unwitting user traffic to their scam pages. Similarly, cloaking may be used to prevent compromised Web servers hosting such scam pages from being identified (i.e., by providing normal content to visitors who are not referred via the targeted search terms). In response to such activity, search engine providers attempt to detect cloaking activity and delist search results that point to such pages.

In this paper, we study the dynamics of this cloaking phenomenon and the response it engenders. We describe a system called *Dagger*, designed to harvest search result data and identify cloaking in near real-time. Using this infrastructure for over five months we make three primary contributions. First, we provide a contemporary picture of cloaking activity as seen through three popular search engines (Google, Bing and Yahoo) and document differences in how each is targeted. Second, we characterize the differences in cloaking behavior between sites found using undifferentiated "trending" keywords and those that appear in response to queries for targeted keywords (in particular for pharmaceutical products). Finally, we characterize the *dynamic behavior* of cloaking activity including the lifetime of cloaked pages and the responsiveness of search engines in removing results that point to such sites.

The remainder of this paper is structured as follows. Section 2 provides a technical background on cloaking and the related work we build upon, followed by a description of Dagger's design and implementation in Section 3. Section 4 describes our results, followed in Section 5 by a discussion of our overall findings.

CCS'11, October 17–21, 2011, Chicago, Illinois, USA.

2. BACKGROUND

The term "cloaking", as applied to search engines, has an uncertain history, but dates to at least 1999 when it entered the vernacular of the emerging search engine optimization (SEO) market.[1] The growing role of search engines in directing Web traffic created strong incentives to reverse engineer search ranking algorithms and use this knowledge to "optimize" the content of pages being promoted and thus increase their rank in search result listings. However, since the most effective way to influence search rankings frequently required content vastly different from the page being promoted, this encouraged SEO firms to serve different sets of page content to search engine crawlers than to normal users; hence, cloaking.

In the remainder of this section we provide a concrete example of how cloaking is used in practice, we explain the different techniques used for visitor differentiation, and summarize the previous work that has informed our study.

2.1 An Example

As an example of cloaking, entering the query "bethenney frankel twitter" on Google on May 3, 2011 returned a set of search results with links related to Bethenney Frankel. (The appendix includes screenshots of this example, with Figure 11a showing a screenshot of the search results.) For the eighth result, the bold face content snippet returned by Google indeed indicates that the linked page includes the terms "bethenney frankel twitter" (in addition to other seemingly unrelated terms, a common indicator of keyword stuffing). Further, Google preview shows a snapshot of the page that the Google crawler sees. In this case it appears the link indeed leads to content with text and images related to "bethenney frankel". Upon clicking on this link on a Windows machine, however, we are sent through a redirect chain and eventually arrive at a landing page (Figure 11b). This page is an example of the fraudulent anti-virus scams that have become increasingly popular [5, 15] and shares little with "bethenney frankel twitter" (and indeed, both the previous snippet and any hints of the previewed snapshot do not appear). Finally, if we revisit the search result link but disguise our identity to appear as a search crawler (in this case by modifying the **`User-Agent`** string in our HTTP request header) we get redirected using a 302 HTTP code to the benign root page of the site (Figure 11c), presumably to avoid possible suspicion. This case represents a classic example of IP cloaking. The site is detecting Google IP addresses, as evidenced by the snippet and preview, and providing an SEO-ed page with text and images related to "bethenney frankel twitter" that it deceives Google into indexing. The core idea here is clear. The scammer is crafting content to reflect the transient popularity of particular terms (in this case due to Bethenney Frankel's sale of her cocktail line) and serving this content to search engine crawlers to capitalize on subsequent user queries, but then directs any user traffic to completely unrelated content intended to defraud them.

2.2 Types of Cloaking

For cloaking to work, the scammer must be able to distinguish between user segments based on some identifier visible to a Web server. The choice of identifier used is what distinguishes between cloaking techniques, which include *Repeat Cloaking*, *User Agent Cloaking*, *Referrer Cloaking* (sometimes also called "Click-through Cloaking"), and *IP Cloaking*.

[1]For example, in a September 2000 article in *Search Engine Watch*, Danny Sullivan comments that "every major performance-based SEO firm I know of does [use cloaking]" [19].

In the case of *Repeat Cloaking*, the Web site stores state on either the client side (using a cookie) or the server side (e.g., tracking client IPs). This mechanism allows the site to determine whether the visitor has previously visited the site, and to use this knowledge in selecting which version of the page to return. Thus first-time visitors are given a glimpse of a scam, in the hopes of making a sale, but subsequent visits are presented with a benign page stymieing reporting and crawlers (who routinely revisit pages).

In contrast, *User Agent Cloaking* uses the **`User-Agent`** field from the HTTP request header to classify HTTP clients as user browsers or search engine crawlers. User agent cloaking can be used for benign content presentation purposes (e.g., to provide unique content to Safari on an iPad vs. Firefox on Windows), but is routinely exploited by scammers to identify crawlers via the well-known **`User-Agent`** strings they advertise (e.g., Googlebot).

Referrer Cloaking takes the idea of examining HTTP headers even further by using the **`Referer`** field to determine which URL visitors clicked through to reach their site. Thus, scammers commonly only deliver a scam page to users that visit their site by first clicking through the search engine that has been targeted (e.g., by verifying that the **`Referer`** field is **`http://www.google.com`**). This technique has also been used, in combination with repeat cloaking and chains of Web site redirections, to create one-time-use URLs advertised in e-mail spam (to stymie security researchers). However, we restrict our focus to search engine cloaking in this paper.

Finally, one of the simplest mechanisms in use today is *IP Cloaking*, in which a scammer uses the IP address of the requester in determining the identity of the visitor. With an accurate mapping between IP addresses and organizations, a scammer can then easily distinguish all search engine requests and serve them benign content in a manner that is difficult to side-step. Indeed, the only clear way for search engine operators to mechanistically detect such cloaking is through acquiring fresh IP resources—but the signal of "delisting" seems to provide a clear path for efficiently mapping such address space even if it is initially unknown [1]. Although challenging to detect in principle since it would nominally require crawling from a Google IP address, in practice a crawler like Dagger can still detect the use of IP cloaking because cloakers still need to expose different versions of a page to different visitors (Section 3.3). As a result, we believe Dagger can detect all forms of cloaking commonly used in the Web today.

2.3 Previous work

The earliest study of cloaking we are aware of is due to Wu and Davidson [24]. They first developed the now standard technique of crawling pages multiple times (using both user and crawler identifiers) and comparing the returned content. Using this approach, they refer to situations in which the content differs as "syntactic cloaking", whereas the subset of these differences that are deemed to be driven by fraudulent intent (using some other classifier [25]) are termed "semantic cloaking".

Chellapilla and Chickering used a similar detection framework to compare syntactic cloaking on the most popular and monetizable search terms [4]. In this study, monetizability corresponds to the amount of revenue generated from users clicking on sponsored ads returned with search results for a search term. Using logs from a search provider, they found that monetized search terms had a higher prevalence of cloaking (10%) than just popular terms (6%) across the top 5000 search terms. While we do not have access to logs of search provider revenue, we also demonstrate significant differences in cloaking prevalence as a function of how search terms are selected.

Up to this point, all studies had focused exclusively on user agent cloaking. In 2006, Wang et al. extended this analysis to include referrer cloaking (called click-through cloaking by them), where pages only return cloaked content if accessed via the URL returned in search results [21]. Targeting a handful of suspicious IP address ranges, they found widespread referrer cloaking among the domains hosted there. In a related, much more extensive study, Wang et al. used this analysis in a focused study of redirection spam, a technique by which "doorway" Web pages redirect traffic to pages controlled by spammers [22]. Finally, Niu et al. performed a similar analysis incorporating referrer cloaking but focused exclusively on forum spamming [14].

These prior studies have used a range of different inputs in deciding whether multiple crawls of the same page are sufficiently different that cloaking has occurred. These include differences in the word distribution in the content of the two pages [4, 24], differences in the links in the page [24], differences in HTML tags [12] or differences in the chain of domain names in the redirection chain [21, 22]. A nice summary of these techniques as well as the different algorithms used to compare them is found in [12]. Our approach represents a combination of these techniques and some new ones, driven by a desire to support crawling and detection in near-real time (Section 3).

Finally, the use of cloaking is predominately driven by so-called "black hat" search engine optimization (SEO) in which the perpetrators seek to attract traffic by using various methods to acquire higher ranking in search engine results. Two contemporaneous studies touch on different aspects of this behavior that are echoed in our own work. John et al. examine one very large scale "link farm" attack used to create high rankings for "trending" search terms and thus attract large amounts of undifferentiated traffic [8]. While this particular attack did not use cloaking per se (except implicitly in the use of JavaScript redirection) we encounter similar structures driving the popularity of cloaked sites in our measurements. Leontiadis et al. perform a broad study of SEO-advertised pharmaceutical sites (driven by focused searches on drug-related terms) and note that cloaking is commonly used by compromised sites and, in part, serves the purpose of "hiding" the existence of such sites from normal visitors [10]. We explore both kinds of search traffic streams in our analysis (driven by trending and focused search terms) and find significant differences between them.

In general, most studies of cloaking have focused on a single snapshot in time. Moreover, the prevalence of cloaking reported in all such studies is difficult to compare due to variations in detection approach, differences in how search terms are selected and changes in scammer behavior during different time periods. Thus, one of our primary contributions is in extending these previous efforts to examine the dynamics of cloaking over time, uncovering the fine-grained variability in cloaking, the lifetime of cloaked search results (bounding the response time of search engines to cloaked results) and the duration of the pages they point to. Ultimately, these *dynamics* in the ranking of cloaked sites drive the underlying economics of their attack.

3. METHODOLOGY

Dagger consists of five functional components: collecting search terms, fetching search results from search engines, crawling the pages linked from the search results, analyzing the pages crawled, and repeating measurements over time. In this section, we describe the design and implementation of each functional component, focusing on the goals and potential limitations.

3.1 Collecting Search Terms

The first challenge in data collection is building a meaningful test set for measuring cloaking. Since our goal is to understand the dynamics of scammers utilizing cloaking in search results, we want to target our data collection to the search terms that scammers also target rather than a random subset of the overall search space. In particular, we target two different kinds of cloaked search terms: those reflecting popular terms intended to gather high volumes of undifferentiated traffic, and terms reflecting highly targeted traffic where the cloaked content matches the cloaked search terms.

For our first set of search terms, as with previous work we seed our data collection with popular *trending* search terms. We also enhance this set by adding additional sources from social networks and the SEO community. Specifically, we collect popular search terms from Google Hot Searches, Alexa, and Twitter, which are publicly available and provide real-time updates to search trends at the granularity of an hour.[2] We extract the top 20 popular search trends via Google Hot Searches and Alexa, which reflect search engine and client-based data collection methods, respectively, while the 10 most popular search terms from Twitter adds insight from social networking trends. These sources generally compliment each other and extend our coverage of terms. We found that terms from Google Hot Searches only overlapped 3–8% with trending terms from both Twitter and Alexa. Note that, for trending terms, the page being cloaked is entirely unrelated to the search terms used to SEO the page. A user may search for a celebrity news item and encounter a search result that is a cloaked page selling fake anti-virus.

For our second set of search terms, we use a set of terms catering to a specific domain: pharmaceuticals. We gathered a generic set of pharmaceutical terms common to many spam-advertised online pharmacy sites, together with best-selling product terms from the most popular site [11]. Unlike trending search terms, the content of the cloaked pages actually matches the search terms. A user may search for "viagra" and encounter a cloaked page that leads to an online pharmacy site selling Viagra.

We construct another source of search terms using keyword suggestions from Google Suggest. Google Suggest is a search term autocomplete service that not only speeds up user input, but also allows users to explore similar long-tail queries. For example, when users enter "viagra 50mg", they are prompted with suggestions such as "viagra 50mg cost" and "viagra 50mg canada". Specifically, we submit search terms from Google Hot Searches and the online pharmacy site to Google Suggest and use the result to create dynamic feeds of search terms for trending and pharmaceutical searches, respectively. While investigating SEO community forums, we found various software packages and services using popular search term services as seeds for extending the terms they target using suggestion services. Combined with a suggestion service, each search term forms the basis of a cluster of related search terms from lists of suggestions [23]. The main attraction of a suggestion service is that it targets further down the tail of the search term distribution, resulting in less competition for the suggestion and a potentially more advantageous search result position. Moreover, long-tail queries typically retain the same semantic meaning as the original search term seed. Furthermore, recent studies have shown superior conversion rates of long-tail queries [20].

3.2 Querying Search Results

Dagger then submits the terms, every four hours for trending

[2]We originally considered using an even broader range of search term sources, in particular Yahoo Buzz, Ask IQ, AOL Hot Searches, eBay Pulse, Amazon Most Popular Tags, Flickr Popular Tags, and WordPress Hot Topics. Since we detected no more than a few cloaked results in multiple attempts over time, we concluded that scammers are not targeting these search terms and no longer considered those sources.

queries and every day for pharmaceutical queries, to the three most actively used search engines in the US: Google, Yahoo, and Bing. With results from multiple search engines, we can compare the prevalence of cloaking across engines and examine their response to cloaking. From the search results we extract the URLs for crawling as well as additional metadata such as the search result position and search result snippet.

At each measurement point, we start with the base set of search terms and use them to collect the top three search term suggestions from Google Suggest.[3] For trending searches, Google Hot Searches and Alexa each supply 80 search terms every four-hour period, while Twitter supplies 40. Together with the 240 additional suggestions based on Google Hot Searches, our search term workload is 440 terms. Note that while overlap does occur within each four-hour period and even between periods, this overlap is simply an artifact of the search term sources and represents popularity as intended. For example, a term that spans multiple sources or multiple periods reflects the popularity of the term. For pharmaceutical queries, we always use a set of 230 terms composed of the original 74 manually-collected terms and 156 from Google Suggest.

Next, we submit the search terms and suggestions to the search engines and extract the top 100 search results and accompanying metadata. We assume that 100 search results, representing 10 search result pages, covers the maximum number of results the vast majority of users will encounter for a given query [17]. Using these results Dagger constructs an index of URLs and metadata, which serves as the foundation for the search space that it will crawl and analyze. At this point, we use a whitelist to remove entries in the index based on regular expressions that match URLs from "known good" domains, such as `http://www.google.com`. This step reduces the number of false positives during data processing. In addition, whenever we update this list, we re-process previous results to futher reduce the number of false positives. Afterwards, we group similar entries together. For example, two entries that share the same URL, source, and search term are combined into a single entry with the same information, except with a count of two instead of one to signify the quantity. As a result, for each search engine, instead of crawling 44,000 URLs for trending search results (440 search terms $\times$ 100 search results), on average Dagger crawls roughly 15,000 unique URLs in each measurement period.

3.3 Crawling Search Results

For each search engine, we crawl the URLs from the search results and process the fetched pages to detect cloaking in parallel to minimize any possible time of day effects.

Web crawler. The crawler incorporates a multithreaded Java Web crawler using the `HttpClient 3.x` package from Apache. While this package does not handle JavaScript redirects or other forms of client-side scripting, it does provide many useful features, such as handling HTTP 3xx redirects, enabling HTTP header modification, timeouts, and error handling with retries. As a result, the crawler can robustly fetch pages using various identities.

Multiple crawls. For each URL we crawl the site three times, although only the first two are required for analysis. We begin disguised as a normal search user visiting the site, clicking through the search result using Internet Explorer on Windows. Then we visit the site disguised as the Googlebot Web crawler. These crawls download the views of the page content typically returned to users and crawlers, respectively. Finally, we visit the site for a third time as a user who does not click through the search result to download the view of the page to the site owner. As with previous approaches, we disguise ourselves by setting the `User-Agent` and the `Referer` fields in the HTTP request header. This approach ensures that we can detect any combination of user-agent cloaking and referrer cloaking. Moreover, our third crawl allows us to detect pure user-agent cloaking without any checks on the referrer. We found that roughly 35% of cloaked search results for a single measurement perform pure user-agent cloaking. For the most part, these sites are not malicious but many are involved in black-hat SEO operations. In contrast, pages that employ both user-agent and referrer cloaking are nearly always malicious (Section 4.5).

[3]We only use three suggestions to reduce the overall load on the system while still maintaining accuracy, as we found no significant difference in our results when using five or even ten suggestions.

IP cloaking. Past studies on cloaking have not dealt with IP address cloaking, and the methodology we use is no different. However, because the emphasis of our study is in detecting the situation where cloaking is used as an SEO technique in scams, we do not expect to encounter problems caused by IP cloaking. In our scenario, the cloaker must return the scam page to the user to potentially monetize the visit. And the cloaker must return the SEO-ed page to the search crawler to both index and rank well. Even if the cloaker could detect that we are not a real crawler, they have few choices for the page to return to our imitation crawler. If they return the scam page, they are potentially leaving themselves open to security crawlers or the site owner. If they return the SEO-ed page, then there is no point in identifying the real crawler. And if they return a benign page, such as the root of the site, then Dagger will still detect the cloaking because the user visit received the scam page, which is noticeably different from the crawler visit. In other words, although Dagger may not obtain the version of the page that the Google crawler sees, Dagger is still able to detect that the page is being cloaked (see Appendix A for an illustrated example).

To confirm this hypothesis, we took a sample of 20K cloaked URLs returned from querying trending search terms. We then crawled those URLs using the above methodology (three crawls, each with different `User-Agent` and `Referer` fields). In addition, we performed a fourth crawl using Google Translate, which visits a URL using a Google IP address and will fool reverse DNS lookups into believing the visit is originating from Google's IP address space. From this one experiment, we found more than half of current cloaked search results do in fact employ IP cloaking via reverse DNS lookups, yet in every case they were detected by Dagger because of the scenario described above.

3.4 Detecting Cloaking

We process the crawled data using multiple iterative passes where we apply various transformations and analyses to compile the information needed to detect cloaking. Each pass uses a comparison-based approach: we apply the same transformations onto the views of the same URL, as seen from the user and the crawler, and directly compare the result of the transformation using a scoring function to quantify the delta between the two views. In the end, we perform thresholding on the result to detect pages that are actively cloaking and annotate them for later analysis.

While some of the comparison-based mechanisms we use to detect cloaking are inspired from previous work, a key constraint is our real-time requirement for repeatedly searching and crawling to uncover the time dynamics of cloaking. As a result, we cannot use a single snapshot of data, and we avoided intensive offline training for machine learning classifiers [4, 12, 24, 25]. We also avoided running client-side scripts, which would add potentially unbounded latency to our data collection process. Consequently, we do not directly measure all forms of redirection, although we do capture the same end result: a difference in the semantic content of the same URL [21, 22]. Since we continuously remeasure over time, manual inspection is not scalable outside of a couple of snapshots [14]. Moreover, even an insightful mechanism that compares the structure of two views using HTML tags, to limit the effects of dynamic content [12], must be applied cautiously as doing so requires significant processing overhead.

The algorithm begins by removing any entries where either the user or crawler page encountered an error during crawling (a non-200 HTTP status code, connection error, TCP error, etc.); on average, 4% of crawled URLs fall into this category.

At this point, the remaining entries represent the candidate set of pages that the algorithm will analyze for detecting cloaking. To start, the detection algorithm filters out nearly identical pages using text shingling [2], which hashes substrings in each page to construct signatures of the content. The fraction of signatures in the two views is an excellent measure of similarity as we find nearly 90% of crawled URLs are near duplicates between the multiple crawls as a user and as a crawler. From experimentation, we found that a difference of 10% or less in sets of signatures signifies nearly identical content. We remove such pages from the candidate set.

From this reduced set, we make another pass that measures the similarity between the snippet of the search result and the user view of the page. The snippet is an excerpt from the page content obtained by search engines, composed from sections of the page relevant to the original query, that search engines display to the user as part of the search result. In effect, the snippet represents ground truth about the content seen by the crawler. Often users examine the snippet to help determine whether to follow the link in the search result. Therefore, we argue that the user has an implicit expectation that the page content should resemble the snippet in content.

We evaluate snippet inclusion by first removing noise (character case, punctuation, HTML tags, gratuitous whitespace, etc.) from both the snippet and the body of the user view. Then, we search for each substring from the snippet in the content of the user view page, which can be identified by the character sequence '...' (provided in the snippet to identify non-contiguous text in the crawled page). We then compute a score of the ratio of the number of words from unmatched substrings divided by the total number of words from all substrings. The substring match identifies similar content, while the use of the number of words in the substring quantifies this result. An upper bound score of 1.0 means that no part of the snippet matched, and hence the user view differs from the page content originally seen by the search engine; a lower bound score of 0.0 means that the entire snippet matched, and hence the user view fulfills the expectation of the user. We use a threshold of 0.33, meaning that we filter out entries from the candidate set whose user view does not differ by more than two-thirds from the snippet. We chose this threshold due to the abundance of snippets seen with three distinct substrings, and 0.33 signifies that the majority of the content differs between the snippet and user view. In practice, this step filters 56% of the remaining candidate URLs.

At this point, we know (1) that the views are different in terms of unstructured text, and (2) that the user view does not resemble the snippet content. The possibility still exists, however, that the page is not cloaked. The page could have sufficiently frequent updates (or may rotate between content choices) that the snippet mismatch is misleading. Therefore, as a final test we examine the page structures of the views via their DOMs as in [12]. The key insight for the effectiveness of this approach comes from the fact that, while page content may change frequently, as in blogs, it is far less likely for the page structure to change dramatically.

We compare the page structure by first removing any content that is not part of a whitelist of HTML structural tags, while also attempting to fix any errors, such as missing closing tags, along the way. We compute another score as the sum of an overall comparison and a hierarchical comparison. In the overall comparison, we calculate the ratio of unmatched tags from the entire page divided by the total number of tags. In the hierarchical comparison, we calculate the ratio of the sum of the unmatched tags from each level of the DOM hierarchy divided by the total number of tags. We use these two metrics to allow the possibility of a slight hierarchy change, while leaving the content fairly similar. An upper bound score of 2.0 means that the DOMs failed to match any tags, whereas a lower bound score of 0.0 means that both the tags and hierarchy matched. We use a threshold of 0.66 in this step, which means that cloaking only occurs when the combination of tags and hierarchy differ by a third between the structure of the user and crawler views. We chose this threshold from experimentation that showed the large majority of cloaked pages scored over 1.0. Once we detect an entry as actively cloaking, we annotate the entry in the index for later processing.

When using any detection algorithm, we must consider the rate of false positives and false negatives as a sign of accuracy and success. Because it is infeasible to manually inspect all results, we provide estimates based on sampling and manual inspection. For Google search results, we found 9.1% (29 of 317) of cloaked pages were false positives, meaning that we labeled the search result as cloaking, but it is benign; for Yahoo, we found 12% (9 of 75) of cloaked pages were false positives. It it worth noting that although we labeled benign content as cloaking, they are technically delivering different data to users and crawlers. If we consider false positives to mean that we labeled the search result as cloaking when it is not, then there are no false positives in either case. In terms of false negatives, when manually browsing collections of search results Dagger detected cloaked redirection pages for the majority of the time. The one case where we fail is when the site employs advanced browser detection to prevent us from fetching the browser view, but we have only encountered this case a handful of times.

3.5 Temporal Remeasurement

The basic measurement component captures data related to cloaking at one point in time. However, because we want to study temporal questions such as the lifetime of cloaked pages in search results, Dagger implements a temporal component to fetch search results from search engines and crawl and process URLs at later points in time. In the experiments in this paper, Dagger remeasures every four hours up to 24 hours, and then every day for up to seven days after the original measurement.

The temporal component performs the same basic data collection and processing steps as discussed in the previous components. To measure the rate at which search engines respond to cloaking, we fetch results using the original search term set and construct a new index from the results that will capture any churn in search results since the original measurement. Then we analyze the churn by searching for any entry with a URL that matches the set of cloaked pages originally identified and labeled. Note that there still exists the possibility that for every cloaked page removed from the new index, another cloaked page, which originally was not a part of the index, could have taken its place. Therefore, this process does not measure how clean the search results are at a given time, just whether the original cloaked pages still appear in the search results.

To measure the duration pages are cloaked, the temporal component selects the cloaked URLs from the original index. It then performs the measurement process again, visiting the pages as both a user and a crawler, and applying the detection algorithm to the results. There still exists the possibility that pages perform cloaking at random times rather than continuously, which we might not de-

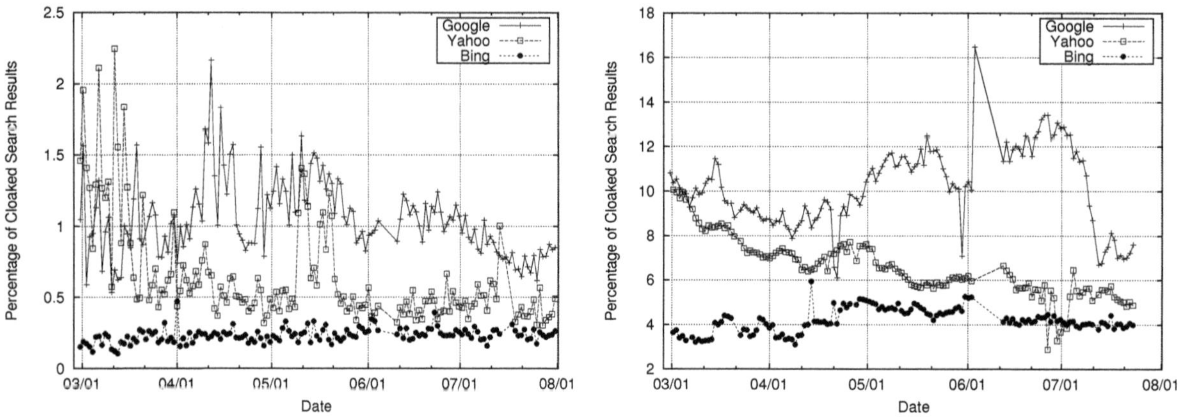

(a) Trends

(b) Pharmacy

Figure 1: Prevalence of cloaked search results in Google, Yahoo, and Bing over time for trending and pharmaceutical searches.

tect. However, we consider these situations unlikely as spammers need sufficient volume to turn a profit and hence cloaking continuously will result in far greater traffic than cloaking at random.

4. RESULTS

This section presents our findings from using Dagger to study cloaking in trending and pharmaceutical search results in Google, Yahoo, and Bing. We use Dagger to collect search results every four hours for two months, from March 1, 2011 through August 1, 2011, crawling over 47 million search results. We examine the prevalence of cloaking in search results over time, how cloaking correlates to the various search terms we use, how search engines respond to cloaking, and how quickly cloaked pages are taken down. We also broadly characterize the content of cloaked pages, the DNS domains with cloaked pages, and how well cloaked pages perform from an SEO perspective. Where informative, we note how trending and pharmaceutical cloaking characteristics contrast, and also comment on the results of cloaking that we observe compared with results from previous studies.

4.1 Cloaking Over Time

Figure 1a shows the prevalence of cloaking over time for trending search results returned from each search engine. We show the percentage of the cloaked search results averaged across all searches made each day. Recall from Section 3.3 that we crawl the top 100 search results every four hours for 183 unique trending search terms (on average) collected from Google Hot Searches, Google Suggest, Twitter, and Alexa, resulting on average in 13,947 unique URLs to crawl after de-duping and whitelisting. Although we crawl every four hours, we report the prevalence of cloaking at the granularity of a day for clarity (we did not see any interesting time-of-day effects in the results). For example, when cloaking in Google search results peaked at 2.2% on April 12, 2011, we found 2,094 out of 95,974 cloaked search results that day.

Initially, through May 4th, we see the same trend for the prevalence of cloaked search results among search engines: Google and Yahoo have nearly the same amount of cloaked results (on average 1.11% on Google and 0.84% on Yahoo), whereas Bing has 3–4$\times$ fewer (just 0.25%). One explanation is that Bing is much better at detecting and thwarting cloaking, but we find evidence that cloakers simply do not appear to target Bing nearly as heavily as Google and Yahoo. For instance, cloaked results often point to link farms, a form of SEO involving collections of interlinked pages used to boost page rank for sets of search terms. For large-scale link farms that we have tracked over time, we consistently find them in Google and Yahoo results, but not in Bing results.

Similarly, Figure 1b shows the prevalence of cloaking over time when searching for pharmaceutical terms. We crawl the top 100 search results daily for 230 unique pharmaceutical search terms collected from a popular spam-advertised affiliate program, further extended with Google Suggest, resuling in 13,646 unique URLs to crawl after de-duping and whitelisting. (Note that the gap in results in the first week of June corresponds to a period when our crawler was offline.) Across all days, we see the same relative ranking of search engines in terms of cloaking prevalence, but with overall larger quantities of cloaked results for the same respective time ranges: on average 9.4% of results were cloaked on Google, 7.7% results on Yahoo, and 4.0% on Bing.

The difference in quantities of cloaked results for trending and pharmaceutical terms reflects the differences between these two types of searches. In trending searches the terms constantly change, with popularity being the one constant. This dynamic allows cloakers to target many more search terms and a broad demographic of potential victims—anyone by definition searching using a popular search term—at the cost of limited time to perform the SEO needed to rank cloaked pages highly in the search results. In contrast, pharmaceutical search terms are static and represent product searches in a very specific domain. Cloakers as a result have much more time to perform SEO to raise the rank of their cloaked pages, resulting in more cloaked pages in the top results. Note, though, that these targeted search terms limit the range of potential victims to just users searching in this narrow product domain. Section 4.7 further explores the effects of SEO on cloaked results.

Looking at trends over time, cloakers were initially slightly more successful on Yahoo than Google for trending search terms, for instance. However, from April 1 through May 4th, we found a clear shift in the prevalence of cloaked search results between search engines with an increase in Google (1.2% on average) and a decrease in Yahoo (0.57%). We suspect this is due to cloakers further concentrating their efforts at Google (e.g., we uncovered new link farms performing reverse DNS cloaking for the Google IP range). In addition, we saw substantial fluctuation in cloaking from day to day. We attribute the variation to the adversarial relationship between cloakers and search engines. Cloakers perform blackhat SEO to artifically boost the rankings of their cloaked pages. Search engines refine their defensive techniques to detect cloaking either directly (analyzing pages) or indirectly (updating the ranking algorithm). We interpret our measurements at these time scales as

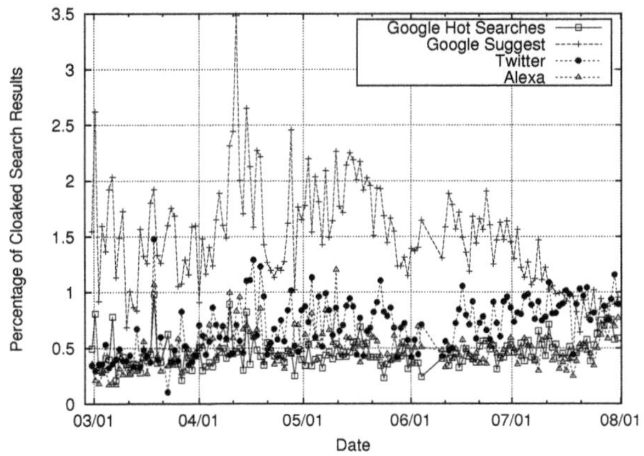

(a) Google

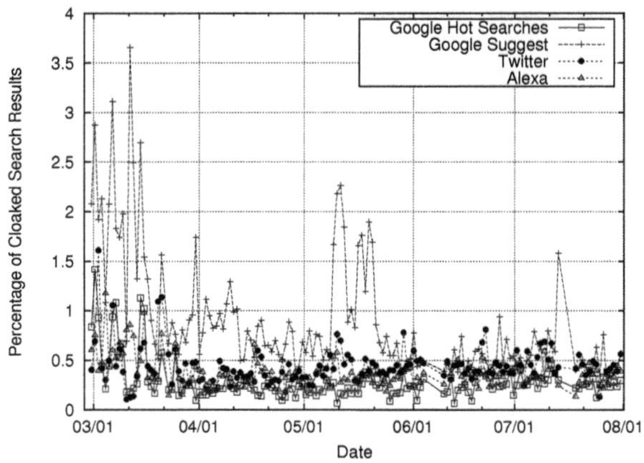

(b) Yahoo

Figure 2: Prevalence of cloaked search results over time associated with each source of trending search terms.

Search Term	% Cloaked Pages
viagra 50mg canada	61.2%
viagra 25mg online	48.5%
viagra 50mg online	41.8%
cialis 100mg	40.4%
generic cialis 100mg	37.7%
cialis 100mg pills	37.4%
cialis 100mg dosage	36.4%
cialis 10mg price	36.2%
viagra 100mg prices	34.3%
viagra 100mg price walmart	32.7%

Table 1: Top 10 pharmaceutical search terms with the highest percentage of cloaked search results, sorted in decreasing order.

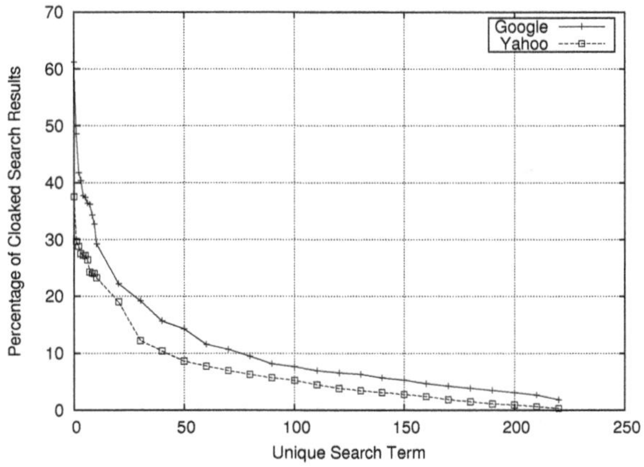

Figure 3: Distribution of percentage of cloaked search results for pharmaceutical search terms, sorted in decreasing order.

simply observing the struggle between the two sides. Finally, we note that the absolute amount of cloaking we find is less than some previous studies, but such comparisons are difficult to interpet since cloaking results fundamentally depend upon the search terms used.

4.2 Sources of Search Terms

Cloakers trying to broadly attract as many visitors as possible target trending popular searches. Since we used a variety of sources for search terms, we can look at how the prevalence of cloaking correlates with search term selection.

Figures 2a and 2b show the average prevalence of cloaking for each source on search results returned from Google and Yahoo, respectively, for trending searches; we do not present results from Bing due to the overall lack of cloaking. Similar to Figure 1, each point shows the percentage of cloaked links in the top 100 search results. Here, though, each point shows the average percentage of cloaked results for a particular source, which normalizes the results independent of the number of search terms we crawled from each source. (Because different sources provided different numbers of search terms, the percentages do not sum to the overall percentages in Figure 1.)

From the graphs, we see that, through May 4th, using search terms from Google Suggest, seeded initially from Google Hot Searches, uncovers the most cloaking. For Google search results, averaged across the days, Google Suggest returns 3.5× as many cloaked search results as Google Hot Searches alone, 2.6× as Twitter, and 3.1× as Alexa. Similarly, even when using Yahoo, Google Suggest returns 3.1× as many cloaked search results as Google Hot Searches alone, 2.6× as Twitter, and 2.7× as Alexa. As discussed in Section 3.1, cloakers targeting popular search terms face stiff SEO competition from others (both legitimate and illegitimate) also targeting those same terms. By augmenting popular search terms with suggestions, cloakers are able to target the same semantic topic as popular search terms. Yet, because the suggestion is essentially an autocomplete, it possesses the long-tail search benefits of reduced competition while remaining semantically relevant.

The above results demonstrate that the prevalence of cloaking in search results is highly influenced by the search terms. As another perspective, for each measurement period that crawls the search terms at a given point in time, we can count the number of cloaked results returned for each search term. Averaging across all measurement periods, 23% and 14% of the search terms accounted for 80% of the cloaked results from Google and Yahoo, respectively. For reference, Table 1 lists the results for the top 10 search terms on Google and Figure 3 shows the distribution of the percentage of cloaked search results for pharmaceutical search terms. The query "viagra 50mg canada" is the pharmaceutical term with the largest percentage of cloaked search results on Google with 61%. Yet, the median query "tramadol 50mg" contains only 7% of cloaked search results. Note that the percentages sum to much more than 100% since different search terms can return links to the same cloaked

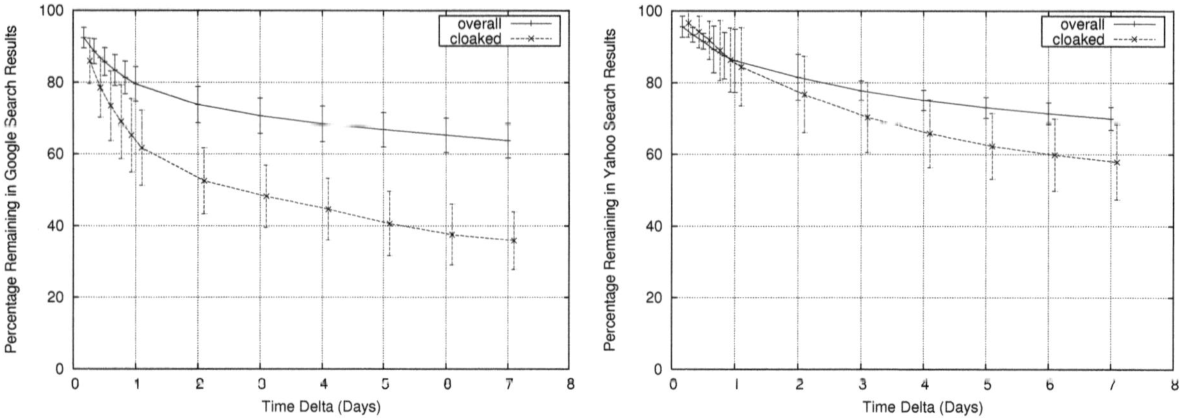

(a) Google (b) Yahoo

Figure 4: Churn in the top 100 cloaked search results and overall search results for trending search terms.

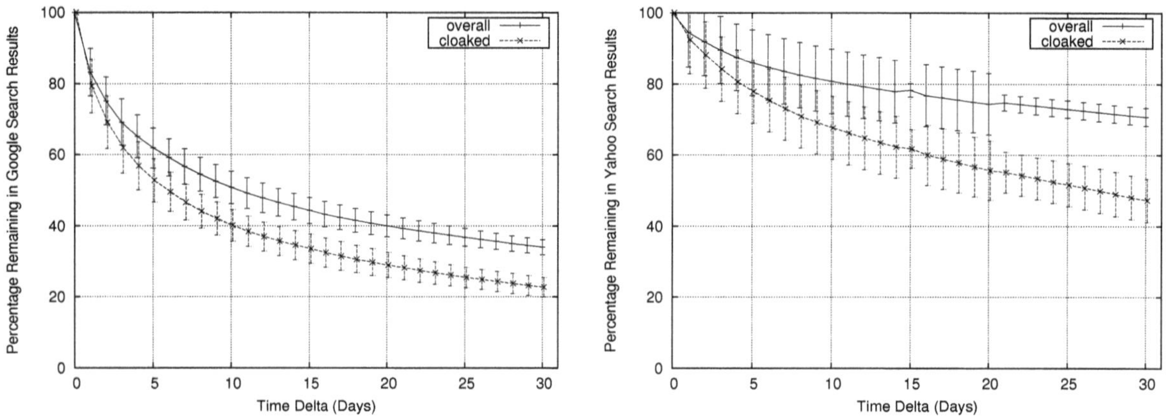

(a) Google (b) Yahoo

Figure 5: Churn in the top 100 cloaked search results and overall search results for pharmaceutical search terms.

pages. As an example in Figure 3, the sixth point shows the average percentage of cloaked search results, across all measurements, for the search term with the sixth highest percentage of cloaked search results. We plot the first 10 points with the most significant percentage of cloaked search results, then plot every 10th search term, for clarity. From these results we see high variance in the percentage of cloaked search results.

4.3 Search Engine Response

Next we examine how long cloaked pages remain in search results after they first appear. For a variety of reasons, search engines try to identify and thwart cloaking. Although we have little insight into the techniques used by search engines to identify cloaking,[4] we can still observe the external effects of such techniques in practice.

We consider cloaked search results to have been effectively "cleaned" by search engines when the cloaked search result no longer appears in the top 100 results. Of course, this indicator may not be directly due to the page having been cloaked. The search engine ranking algorithms could have adjusted the positions of cloaked pages over time due to other factors, e.g., the SEO techniques used by cloakers may turn out to be useful only in the short term. Either way, in this case we consider the cloaked pages as no longer being effective at meeting the goals of the cloakers.

[4]Google has a patent in the area [13], but we have not seen evidence of such a client-assisted approach used in practice.

To measure the lifetime of cloaked search results, we perform repeated search queries for every search term over time (Section 3.5). We then examine each new set of search results to look for the cloaked results we originally detected. The later search results will contain any updates, including removals and suppressions, that search engines have made since the time of the initial measurement. To establish a baseline we also measure the lifetime of all our original search results, cloaked or not. This baseline allows us to differentiate any churn that occurs naturally with those attributable to "cleaning". We perform these repeated searches on each term every four hours up to 24 hours and then every day up to seven days.

Figures 4a and 4b show the lifetime of cloaked and overall search results for Google and Yahoo for trending searches. Each point shows the average percentage of search results that remain in the top 100 for the same search terms over time. The error bars denote the standard devation across all searches, and we plot the points for "cloaked" slightly off-center to better distinguish error bars on different curves. The results, for both search engines, show that cloaked search results rapidly begin to fall out of the top 100 within the first day, with a more gradual drop thereafter. In contrast, search results in general have similar trends, but decline more gradually. For Google, nearly 40% of cloaked search results have a lifetime of a day or less, and over the next six days only an additional 25% drop from the top 100 results. In contrast, for the baseline only 20% of overall search results have a lifetime of a day of less, and

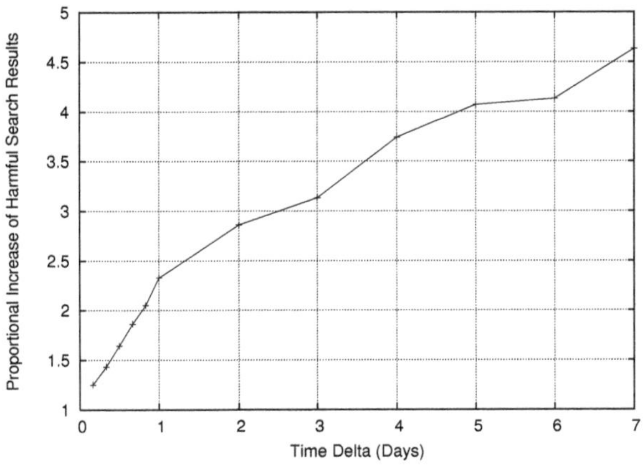

Figure 6: Increase in harmful trending search results over time on Google as labeled by Google Safe Browsing.

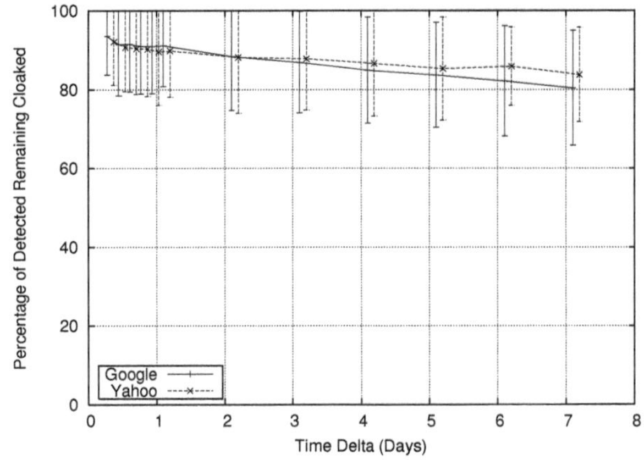

Figure 7: Duration pages are cloaked.

an additional 15% are cleaned after the next six days. Yahoo exhibits a similar trend, although with less rapid churn and with a smaller separation between cloaked and the baseline (perhaps reflecting differences in how the two search engines deal with cloaking). Overall, though, while cloaked pages do regularly appear in search results, many are removed or suppressed by the search engines within hours to a day.

Figures 5a and 5b show similar results for pharmaceutical searches. Note that the maximum time delta is 30 days because, unlike trending terms, the pharmacy search terms do not change throughout the duration of our experiment and we have a larger window of observation. While we still see similar trends, where cloaked search results drop more rapidly than the churn rate and Google churns more than Yahoo, the response for both Google and Yahoo is slower for pharmaceutical terms than for trending terms. For example, whereas 45% and 25% of cloaked trending search results were "cleaned" for Google and Yahoo, respectively, within two days, only 30% and 10% of cloaked pharmacy search results were "cleaned" for Google and Yahoo, respectively.

As another perspective on "cleaning", Google Safe Browsing [7] is a mechanism for shielding users by labeling search results that lead to phishing and malware pages as "harmful". These harmful search results sometimes employ cloaking, which Google Safe Browsing is able to detect and bypass. This insight suggests that the rate that Google is able to discover and label "harmful" search results correlates with the rate at which they can detect cloaking. We can measure this Safe Browsing detection by repeatedly querying for the same terms as described in Section 3.5 and counting the number of "harmful" search results.

As observed in Section 4.2, the prevalence of cloaking is volatile and depends heavily on the specific search terms. The prevalence of detected harmful pages is similarly volatile; although 37% of the results on average on Google are marked as harmful for the terms we search for, there is substantial variance across terms. Therefore, we normalize the change over time in the number of harmful search results labeled by Google Safe Browsing relative to the first measurement. Figure 6 shows the average normalized change in the number of harmful labels over time, across all queries on trending search terms. The number of harmful labels increases rapidly for the first day, with nearly 2.5× more labels than the original measurement, and then increases steadily over the remaining six days, where there are nearly 5× more labels than the original query. This behavior mirrors the results on cleaning above.

4.4 Cloaking Duration

Cloakers will often subvert existing pages as an SEO technique to capitalize on the already established good reputation of those pages with search engines. We have seen that the search engines respond relatively quickly to having cloaked pages in search results. Next we examine how long until cloaked pages are no longer cloaked, either because cloakers decided to stop cloaking or because a subverted cloaked page was discovered and fixed by the original owner.

To measure the duration that pages are cloaked, we repeatedly crawl every cloaked page that we find over time, independent of whether the page continues to appear in the top 100 search results. We then apply the cloaking detection algorithm on the page (Section 3.4), and record when it is no longer cloaked. As in Section 4.3, we crawl each page every four hours up to 24 hours and then every day up to seven days.

Figure 7 shows the time durations that pages are cloaked in results returned by Google and Yahoo. Each point shows the percentage of all cloaked pages for each measurement period that remain cloaked over time, and the error bars show the standard deviations across measurement periods. We see that cloaked pages have similar durations for both search engines: cloakers manage their pages similarly independent of the search engine. Further, pages are cloaked for long durations: over 80% remain cloaked past seven days. This result is not very surprising given that cloakers have little incentive to stop cloaking a page. Cloakers will want to maximize the time that they might benefit from having a page cloaked by attracting customers to scam sites, or victims to malware sites. Further, it is difficult for them to recycle a cloaked page to reuse at a later time. Being blacklisted by Google Safe Browsing, for instance, requires manual intervention to regain a positive reputation. And for those cloaked pages that were subverted, by definition it is difficult for the original page owners to detect that their page has been subverted. Only if the original page owners access their page as a search result link will they realize that their page has been subverted; accessing it any other way will return the original contents that they expect.

4.5 Cloaked Content

Since the main goal of cloaking as an SEO technique is to obtain user traffic, it is natural to wonder where the traffic is heading. By looking at the kind of content delivered to the user from cloaked search results, not only does it suggest why cloaking is necessary

Category	% Cloaked Pages
Traffic Sale	81.5%
Error	7.3%
Legitimate	3.5%
Software	2.2%
SEO-ed Business	2.0%
PPC	1.3%
Fake-AV	1.2%
CPALead	0.6%
Insurance	0.3%
Link farm	0.1%

Table 2: Breakdown of cloaked content for manually-inspected cloaked search results from Google for trending search terms. Note that "Traffic Sale" pages are the start of redirection chains that typically lead to Fake-AV, CPALead, and PPC landing pages.

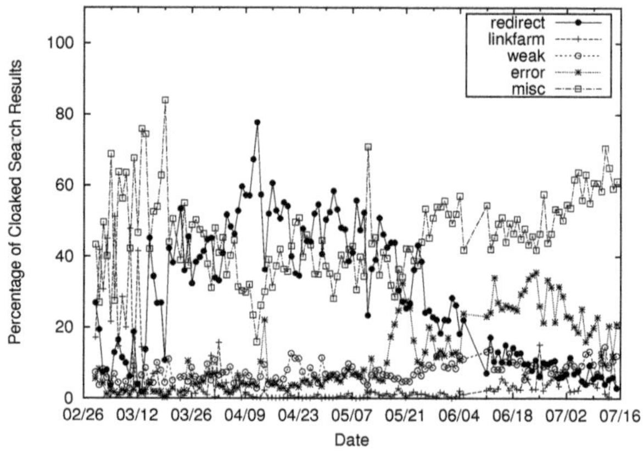

Figure 8: Proportional distribution of cloaked search results in Google over time for trending searches.

for hiding such content, but it also reveals the motives cloakers have in attracting users.

We have no fully automated means for identifying the content behind cloaked search results. Instead, we cluster cloaked search results with the exact same DOM structure of the pages as seen by the user when clicking on a search result. We perform the clustering on all cloaked search results from Google across all measurement points for trending searches. To form a representative set of cloaked pages for each cluster, we select a handful of search results from various measurement times (weekday, weekend, dayime, morning, etc.) and with various URL characteristics. We then manually label pages in this representative set to classify the content of the pages being cloaked.

We manually label the content of each cluster into one of ten categories: traffic sales, pay-per-click (PPC), software, insurance, Fake-AV, CPALead,[5] link farm, SEO-ed business, error, and legitimate. Traffic sales are cloaked search results with the sole purpose of redirecting users through a chain of advertising networks, mainly using JavaScript, before arriving at a final landing page. Although we are unable to follow them systematically, from manually examining thousands of traffic sales, we observed these search results directing users primarily to Fake-AV, CPALead, and PPC pages. Occasionally cloaked search results do not funnel users through a redirection chain, which is how we are able to classify the PPC, software, insurance, Fake-AV, and CPALead sets. The link farm set contain benign pages that provide many backlinks to boost the rankings of beneficiary pages. The SEO-ed business refers to businesses that employ black-hat SEO techniques, such as utilizing free hosting to spam a large set of search results for a single term. The errors are pages that have client side requirements we were unable to meet, i.e., having an Adobe Flash plugin. Finally, the legitimate set refers to pages that display no malicious behavior but were labeled as cloaking due to delivering differing content, as is the case when sites require users to login before accessing the content.

Table 2 shows the breakdown of cloaked search results after manually inspecting the top 62 clusters, out of 7671 total, which were sorted in decreasing order of cluster size. These 62 clusters account for 61% of all cloaked search results found in Google for trending searches across all measurement points. From this, we see that about half of the time a cloaked search result leads to some form of abuse. Further, over 49% of the time, cloaked search results sell user traffic through advertising networks, which will eventually lead to Fake-AV, CPALeads, or PPC.

Interestingly, the DOM structure of the largest cluster, which alone acounted for 34% of cloaked search results, was a single JavaScript snippet that performs redirection as part of traffic sales. Other large clusters that accounted for 1–3% of cloaked search results also consist primarily of JavaScript that performs redirection as part of traffic sales.

Despite the fact that the clusters we have examined account for 61% of all cloaked search results, there still exists 39% that have not been categorized and likely do not share the same distribution. While incrementally clustering, we noted that the top clusters grew larger and larger as more and more data was added. This suggests the presence of long-term SEO campaigns, as represented by the top clusters, that constantly change the search terms they are targeting and the hosts they are using. Therefore, since the uncategorized search results fall within the long tail, they are unlikely to be actively involved in direct traffic sales. Instead, we speculate that they fall in the link farm or legitimate sets given that those groups have the most difficult time in forming large clusters because they are not being SEO-ed as heavily across search terms.

The kinds of pages being cloaked is also dynamic over time. Figure 8 shows the classification of cloaked page content for search results from Google using trending terms, from March 1, 2011 through July 15, 2011. We classify the HTML of cloaked pages, using the file size and substrings as features, into one of the following categories: Linkfarm, Redirect, Error, Weak, or Misc. The Linkfarm category represents content returned to our "Googlebot" crawler that contains many outbound links hidden using CSS properties. The Redirect category represents content returned to a user that is smaller than 4 KB and contains JavaScript code for redirection, or an HTML meta refresh. The Error category represents user content that is smaller than 4 KB and contains a blank page or typical error messages. The Weak category contains user content below 4 KB in file size not already classified; similarly, the Misc category contains user content larger than 4 KB not already classified. As an example, on March 7th approximately 7% of the cloaked content detected were linkfarms, 53% were redirects, 6% were errors, 3% were weak and 31% were misc.

Looking at the trends over time reveals the dynamic nature of the content being hidden by cloaking. In particular, we saw a surge in redirects from March 15th to June 5th. During this period, the average distribution of redirects per day increased from 11.4% to

[5]Cost-per-action pages that ask a user to take some action, such as filling out a form, that will generate advertising revenue.

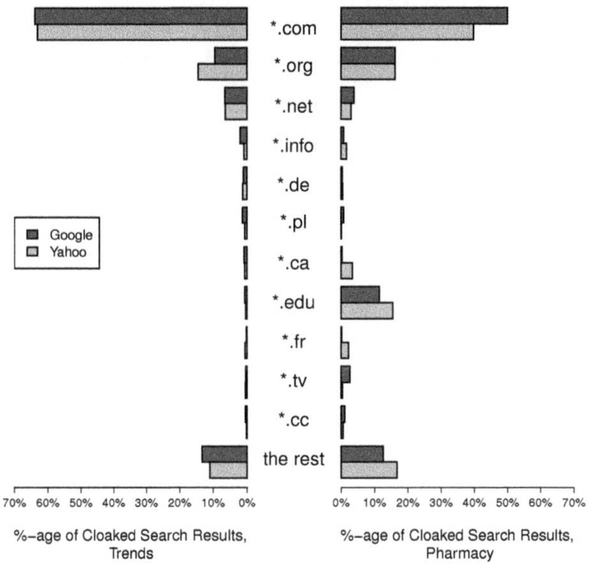

Figure 9: Histogram of the most frequently occuring TLDs among cloaked search results.

41.3% and later dropped off to 8.7%. Interestingly, as redirects begin to fall off, we see a corresponding increase in errors. During the high period of redirects, errors represented 8.0% of the average distribution, but afterwards represented 24.3%. One explanation of this correlation is that the infrastructure supporting redirects begins to collapse at this point. Anecdotally, this behavior matches the general time frame of the undermining of key Fake-AV affiliate programs [9], frequently observed at the end of the redirect chains.

4.6 Domain Infrastructure

Analyzing the underlying intent of cloaked pages confirmed again that cloakers are attempting to attract traffic by illegitimately occupying top search result positions for trending and pharmacy search terms and their suggestions. The implication is that the key resource that spammers must possess, to effectively utilize cloaking in their scams, is access to Web sites and their domains. Ideally, these sites should be established sites already indexed in search engines. Otherwise, solely using traditional SEO tactics, such as link farming, will have limited success in obtaining high search result positions. Recent reports confirm that many pages have been targeted and infected by well known exploits to their software platforms, and subsequently used to cloak hidden content from search engines [18].

In this section, we examine the top level domains (TLDs) of cloaked search results. Figure 9 shows histograms of the most frequently occuring TLDs among all cloaked search results, for both Google and Yahoo. We see that the majority of cloaked search results are in `.com`. Interestingly, cloaked search results from pharmaceutical queries utilize domains in `.edu` and `.org` much more frequently, where together they represent 27.6% of all cloaked search results seen in Google and 31.7% in Yahoo. For comparison, `.edu` and `.org` together represent just 10% in Google and 14.8% in Yahoo for trending searches. Cloakers spamming pharmaceutical search terms are using the "reputation" of pages in these domains to boost their ranking in search results similar to the recent accusations against `overstock.com` [6].

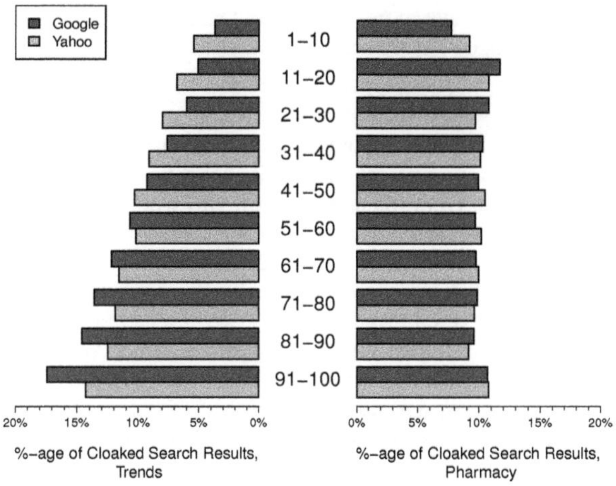

Figure 10: Distribution of cloaked search result positions.

4.7 SEO

Finally, we explore cloaking from an SEO perspective by quantifying how successful cloaking is in high-level spam campaigns. Since a major motivation for cloaking is to attract user traffic, we can extrapolate SEO performance based on the search result positions the cloaked pages occupy. For example, a campaign that is able to occupy search result positions between 1–20 is presumably much more successful than one that is only able to occupy search result positions between 41–60.

To visualize this information, we calculate the percentage of cloaked search results found between ranges of search result positions for each measurement. Then we take the average across all measurements. Again, we only focus on Google and Yahoo due to the lack of cloaked search results in Bing. For clarity, we bin the histogram by grouping every ten positions together, the default number of search results per page.

Figure 10 shows the resulting histograms for trending search terms and pharmaceutical terms, side by side. For trending searches we see a skewed distribution where cloaked search results mainly hold the bottom positions; for both Google and Yahoo, positions further away from the top contain more cloaking. Compared to the positions 1–10 on the first page of results, the number of cloaked search results are 2.1× more likley to hold a search result positon between 31–40 in Google, and 4.7× more likely to be in position 91–100; results for Yahoo are similar. In some ways, this distribution indicates that cloaking is not very effective for trending search terms. It does not lead to a higher concentration in the most desirable search result positions (top 20), likely due to the limited amount of time available to SEO. Although cloakers will have fewer opportunities for their scams as a result, presumably it still remains profitable for cloakers to continue the practice.

Interestingly, we see a very different trend in pharmaceutical searches where there is an even distribution across positions. The number of cloaked pages are just as likely to rank in the first group of search results (positions 1–10) as any other group within the top 100. Wu and Davison [24] had similar findings from 2005. One possible explanation is that the differences again reflect the differences in the nature of cloaked search terms. Cloaking the trending terms by definition target popular terms that are very dynamic, with limited time and heavy competition for performing SEO on those search terms. Cloaking pharmacy terms, however, is a highly focused task on a static set of terms, providing much longer time frames for performing SEO on cloaked pages for those terms. As a result, cloakers have more time to SEO pages that subsequently span the full range of search result positions.

5. CONCLUSION

Cloaking has become a standard tool in the scammer's toolbox and one that adds significant complexity for differentiating legitimate Web content from fraudulent pages. Our work has examined the current state of search engine cloaking as used to support Web spam, identified new techniques for identifying it (via the search engine snippets that identify keyword-related content found at the time of crawling) and, most importantly, we have explored the dynamics of cloaked search results and sites over time. We demonstrate that the majority of cloaked search results remain high in rankings for 12 hours and that the pages themselves can persist far longer. Thus, cloaking is likely to be an effective mechanism so long as the overhead of site placement via SEO techniques is less than the revenue obtained from 12 hours of traffic for popular keywords. We believe it is likely that this holds, and search engine providers will need to further reduce the lifetime of cloaked results to demonetize the underlying scam activity.

Acknowledgments

We thank Damon McCoy for insightful comments and discussion of this work, and we also thank the anonymous reviewers for their valuable feedback. This work was supported in part by National Science Foundation grants NSF-0433668 and NSF-0831138, by the Office of Naval Research MURI grant N000140911081, and by generous research, operational and/or in-kind support from Google, Microsoft, Yahoo, Cisco, HP and the UCSD Center for Networked Systems (CNS).

6. REFERENCES

[1] John Bethencourt, Jason Franklin, and Mary Vernon. Mapping Internet Sensors with Probe Response Attacks. In *Proceedings of the 14th USENIX Security Symposium*, Baltimore, MD, July 2005.

[2] Andrei Z. Broder. On the Resemblance and Containment of Documents. In *Proceedings of the Compression and Complexity of Sequences (SEQUENCES'97)*, pages 21–29, June 1997.

[3] Lee G. Caldwell. *The Fast Track to Profit*. Pearson Education, 2002.

[4] Kumar Chellapilla and David Maxwell Chickering. Improving Cloaking Detection Using Search Query Popularity and Monetizability. In *Proceedings of the SIGIR Workshop on Adversarial Information Retrieval on the Web (AIRWeb)*, August 2006.

[5] Marco Cova, Corrado Leita, Olivier Thonnard, Angelos Keromytis, and Marc Dacier. An Analysis of Rogue AV Campaigns. In *Proceedings of the 13th International Symposium on Recent Advances in Intrusion Detection (RAID)*, September 2010.

[6] Amir Efrati. Google Penalizes Overstock for Search Tactics. `http://online.wsj.com/article/SB10001424052748704520504576162753779521700.html`, February 24, 2011.

[7] Google Safe Browsing API. `http://code.google.com/apis/safebrowsing/`.

[8] John P. John, Fang Yu, Yinglian Xie, Arvind Krishnamurthy, and Martin Abadi. deSEO: Combating Search-Result Poisoning. In *Proceedings of the 20th USENIX Security Symposium*, August 2011.

[9] Brian Krebs. Huge Decline in Fake AV Following Credit Card Processing Shakeup. `http://krebsonsecurity.com/2011/08/huge-decline-in-fake-av-following-credit-card-processing-shakeup/`, August 2011.

[10] Nektarios Leontiadis, Tyler Moore, and Nicolas Christin. Measuring and Analyzing Search-Redirection Attacks in the Illicit Online Prescription Drug Trade. In *Proceedings of the 20th USENIX Security Symposium*, August 2011.

[11] Kirill Levchenko, Neha Chachra, Brandon Enright, Márk Félegyházi, Chris Grier, Tristan Halvorson, Chris Kanich, Christian Kreibich, He Liu, Damon McCoy, Andreas Pitsillidis, Nicholas Weaver, Vern Paxson, Geoffrey M. Voelker, and Stefan Savage. Click Trajectories: End-to-End Analysis of the Spam Value Chain. In *Proceedings of the IEEE Symposium and Security and Privacy*, Oakland, CA, May 2011.

[12] Jun-Lin Lin. Detection of cloaked web spam by using tag-based methods. *Expert Systems with Applications*, 36(4):7493–7499, 2009.

[13] Marc A. Najork. System and method for identifying cloaked web servers, United States Patent number 6,910,077. Issued June 21, 2005.

[14] Yuan Niu, Yi-Min Wang, Hao Chen, Ming Ma, and Francis Hsu. A Quantitative Study of Forum Spamming Using Contextbased Analysis. In *Proceedings of 15th Network and Distributed System Security (NDSS) Symposium*, February 2007.

[15] Moheeb Abu Rajab, Lucas Ballard, Panayiotis Mavrommatis, Niels Provos, and Xin Zhao. The Nocebo Effect on the Web: An Analysis of Fake Anti-Virus Distribution. In *Proceedings of the 3rd USENIX Workshop on Large-Scale Exploits and Emergent Threats (LEET'10)*, April 2010.

[16] Search Engine Marketing Professional Organization (SEMPO). State of Search Engine Marketing Report Says Industry to Grow from $14.6 Billion in 2009 to $16.6 Billion in 2010. `http://www.sempo.org/news/03-25-10`, March 2010.

[17] Craig Silverstein, Monika Henzinger, Hannes Marais, and Michael Moricz. Analysis of a Very Large Web Search Engine Query Log. *ACM SIGIR Forum*, 33(1):6–12, 1999.

[18] Julien Sobrier. Tricks to easily detect malware and scams in search results. `http://research.zscaler.com/2010/06/tricks-to-easily-detect-malware-and.html`, June 3, 2010.

[19] Danny Sullivan. Search Engine Optimization Firm Sold For $95 Million. `http://searchenginewatch.com/2163001`, September 2000. Search Engine Watch.

[20] Jason Tabeling. Keyword Phrase Value: Click-Throughs vs. Conversions. `http://searchenginewatch.com/3641985`, March 8, 2011.

[21] Yi-Min Wang and Ming Ma. Detecting Stealth Web Pages That Use Click-Through Cloaking. Technical Report MSR-TR-2006-178, Microsoft Research, December 2006.

[22] Yi-Min Wang, Ming Ma, Yuan Niu, and Hao Chen. Spam Double-Funnel: Connecting Web Spammers with Advertisers. In *Proceedings of the 16th International World Wide Web Conference (WWW'07)*, pages 291–300, May 2007.

[23] Wordtracker. Five Reasons Why Wordtracker Blows Other

Keywords Tools Away. `http://www.wordtracker.com/find-the-best-keywords.html`.

[24] Baoning Wu and Brian D. Davison. Cloaking and Redirection: A Preliminary Study. In *Proceedings of the SIGIR Workshop on Adversarial Information Retrieval on the Web (AIRWeb)*, May 2005.

[25] Baoning Wu and Brian D. Davison. Detecting Semantic Cloaking on the Web. In *Proceedings of the 15th International World Wide Web Conference*, pages 819–828, May 2006.

APPENDIX

A. CLOAKING ILLUSTRATION

Figure 11 uses browser screenshots to illustrate the effects of cloaking when searching on Google on May 3, 2011 with the terms "bethenney frankel twitter", a topic popular in user queries at that time. The top screenshot shows the first search results page with the eighth result highlighted with content snippets and a preview of the linked page; this view of the page corresponds to the cloaked content returned to the Google crawler when it visited this page. These search results are also examples of what Dagger obtains when querying Google with search terms (Section 3.2).

The middle screenshot shows the page obtained by clicking on the link using Internet Explorer on Windows. Specifically, it corresponds to visiting the page with the **User-Agent** field set to:

```
Mozilla/5.0 (compatible; MSIE 8.0; Windows NT 5.2;
Trident/4.0; Media Center PC 4.0; SLCC1; .NET CLR
3.0.04320)
```

and the **Referer** field indicating that the click comes from a search result for the terms "bethenney frankel twitter". This page visit corresponds to when Dagger crawls the URL as a search "user" (Section 3.3), displaying an advertisement for Fake-AV.

The bottom screenshot shows the page obtained by crawling the link while mimicking the Google crawler. Specifically, it corresponds to visiting the page with the **User-Agent** field set to:

```
Mozilla/5.0 (compatible; Googlebot/2.1;
+http://www.google.com/bot.html)
```

and corresponds to when Dagger visits the URL as a search "crawler". Note that this page also uses IP cloaking: the content returned to Dagger, which does not visit it with a Google IP address, is different from the content returned to the real Google search crawler (as reflected in the snippet and preview in the top screenshot). Nevertheless, because the cloaked page does return different content to search users and the Dagger crawler, Dagger can still detect that the page is cloaked.

(a) Google Search Results Page

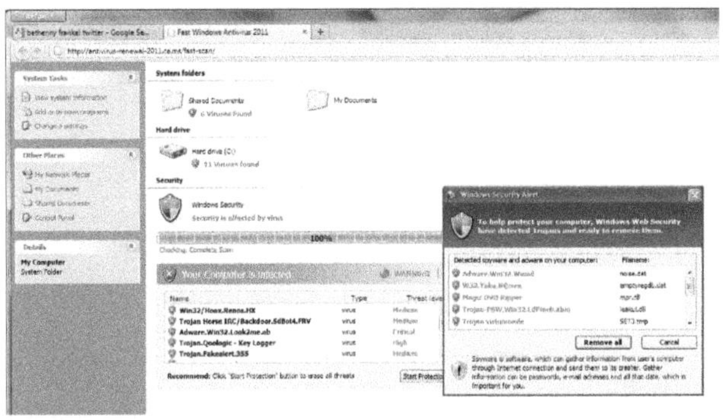

(b) User from Windows

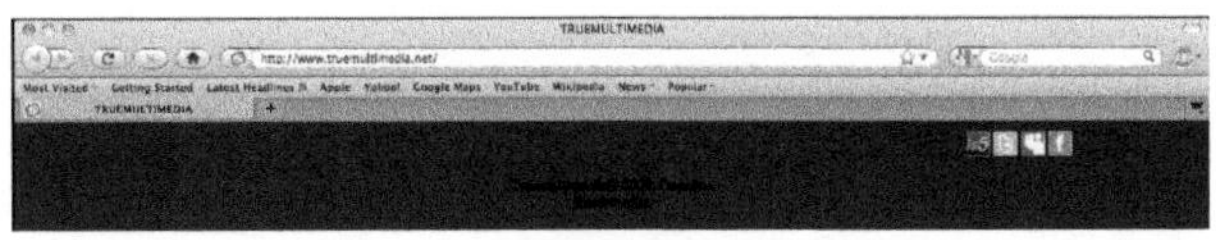

(c) Crawler

Figure 11: Example of cloaking in practice: (a) the first search results page for the query "bethenney frankel twitter", including the Google preview; (b) the page obtained by clicking on the highlighted link from a Windows machine (with **Referer** indicating a search result); and (c) the same page visited but with the **User-Agent** field in the HTTP request header set to mimic that of the Google search crawler.

Proofs of Ownership in Remote Storage Systems * †

Shai Halevi
IBM T. J. Watson Research Center
shaih@alum.mit.edu

Danny Harnik
IBM Haifa Research Labs
dannyh@il.ibm.com

Benny Pinkas
Bar Ilan University
benny@pinkas.net

Alexandra Shulman-Peleg
IBM Haifa Research Labs
shulmana@il.ibm.com

ABSTRACT

Cloud storage systems are becoming increasingly popular. A promising technology that keeps their cost down is *deduplication*, which stores only a single copy of repeating data. *Client-side deduplication* attempts to identify deduplication opportunities already at the client and save the bandwidth of uploading copies of existing les to the server.

In this work we identify attacks that exploit client-side deduplication, allowing an attacker to gain access to arbitrary-size les of other users based on a very small hash signatures of these les. More speci cally, an attacker who knows the hash signature of a le can convince the storage service that it owns that le, hence the server lets the attacker download the entire le. (In parallel to our work, a subset of these attacks were recently introduced in the wild with respect to the Dropbox le synchronization service.)

To overcome such attacks, we introduce the notion of proofs-of-ownership (PoWs), which lets a client e ciently prove to a server that that the client holds a le, rather than just some short information about it. We formalize the concept of proof-of-ownership, under rigorous security de nitions, and rigorous e ciency requirements of Petabyte scale storage systems. We then present solutions based on Merkle trees and speci c encodings, and analyze their security. We implemented one variant of the scheme. Our performance measurements indicate that the scheme incurs only a small overhead compared to naive client-side deduplication.

*The work of Benny Pinkas was supported by the SFEROT project funded by the European Research Council (ERC). The work of Danny Harnik and Alexandra Shulman-Peleg has received funding from the European Community's Seventh Framework Programme (FP7/2007-2013) under grant agreement n 257019.

†A full version of this paper appears in [13].

CCS'11, October 17–21, 2011, Chicago, Illinois, USA.

Categories and Subject Descriptors

H.3.5 [**Information Systems**]: Information storage and retrieval *On-line information services*

General Terms

Security

Keywords

Cloud storage, Deduplication, Merkle trees, Proofs of ownership.

1. INTRODUCTION

The rapid adoption of Cloud services is accompanied by increasing volumes of data stored at remote servers, so techniques for saving disk space and network bandwidth are needed. A central up and coming concept in this context is *deduplication*, where the server stores only a single copy of each le, regardless of how many clients asked to store that le. All clients that store the le merely use links to the single copy of the le stored at the server. Moreover, if the server already has a copy of the le, then clients do not even need to upload it again to the server, thus saving bandwidth as well as storage (this is termed client-side deduplication). Reportedly, business applications can achieve deduplication ratios from 1:10 to as much as 1:500, resulting in disk and bandwidth savings of more 90% [8]. Deduplication can be applied at the le level or at the block level, and this paper focuses on le-level deduplication. (Block-level deduplication is discussed briey in Section 6.)

In a typical storage system with deduplication, a client rst sends to the server only a hash of the le and the server checks if that hash value already exists in its database. If the hash is not in the database then the server asks for the entire le. Otherwise, since the le already exists at the server (potentially uploaded by someone else), it tells the client that there is no need to send the le itself. Either way the server marks the client as an owner of that le, and from that point on there is no di erence between the client and the original party who has uploaded the le. The client can therefore ask to restore the le, regardless of whether he was asked to upload the le or not.

Harnik et al. observed recently that client-side deduplication introduces new security problems [14]. For example, a server telling a client that it need not send the le reveals that some other client has the exact same le, which could be a sensitive information. The ndings in [14] apply to popular le storage services such as MozyHome and Dropbox, among others.

A New Attack The starting point of this work is a much more direct threat to storage systems that use client-side deduplication across multiple users. Specifically, by accepting the hash value as a proxy for the entire file, the server allows anyone who gets the hash value to get the entire file. Consider for example the following case: Bob is a researcher who routinely publishes hashes of his lab reports, as a time-stamp for the results of his research. Bob is also careful to daily backup his hard disk to an online file storage service. Alice is interested in learning the results of Bob's research. She signs up to the same storage service, asks to backup a file, and when asked to present its hash value she presents the value that was published by Bob as a time-stamp for his file. The service forgoes the upload, and just makes note that Alice and Bob uploaded the same file. Later on, Alice asks to recover that file and the service complies, sending her a copy of Bob's lab report.

The problem illustrated above stems from the fact that by learning just a small piece of information about the file, namely its hash value, an attacker is able to get the entire file from the server. This extra piece of information is not really meant to be secret, and in fact it must be computable from the file via a deterministic public algorithm which is shared by all clients.

A simplistic fix for this attack is to hash some context information together with the file, e.g., "`deduplication at cloud service XYZ`" and a system-wide random salt value (i.e., a single random value used for all files). This makes it highly unlikely for different applications to use the same hashing mechanism, thus preventing the specific attack from above. However, this solution still does not address the root cause of the attack: There is still a very short piece of information that represents the file, and an attacker that learns it can get access to the entire file. Although we plugged one avenue of leakage, there could be others.

Potential Attacks. Below we list some plausible attacks, supporting our main point that representing a large file by a small piece of not really secret information is a bad idea.

Usage of a common hash function This is essentially the attack described in the previous example, where the deduplication system uses a standard hash function. (It was recently reported that Dropbox uses SHA256 [1].) In that case it is plausible that an attacker can obtain hash values of files owned by other users (e.g., if these hash values are used elsewhere or the user publishes a signature on the file).

Using the storage service as an unintended CDN In this scenario, Alice the attacker uploads a copy of a (potentially huge, and possibly copyright infringing) file to the storage server and publishes the hash of that file (e.g., on her web page). Now anyone wishing to obtain the file can attempt to upload it to the storage service, present the hash value to the service and be identified as owning that file, and then ask to restore the file from the storage service. Hence Alice essentially uses the storage service as a *content distribution network* (CDN). This behavior may run afoul with the business model of that storage server, which is likely to be designed to support many uploads but very few restore operations. This behavior might also support piracy and copyright infringing behavior.

Server break-in Consider an attacker that is able to temporarily compromise a server machine, getting access to its internal cache, which includes the hash values for all the recently accessed files. Having obtained this (relatively small) piece of information, the attacker is now able to download all these files, which may include confidential files of others. The attacker can even publish these hash values, thus enabling anyone in the world to get these files.

Note that it is unlikely that the attacker can use a short compromise event to actually download all the large files, but the server cache may be many orders of magnitude smaller. Further, even if the server learns about the attack early on, there is not much that it can do about it. The only effective remedy that it has is to turn off client side deduplication for the affected files, essentially forever.

Malicious client software A similar attack is also possible on the client side. For example, Alice can install malicious software on the machine of Bob the victim. The malicious software can use a very low-bandwidth covert channel to send to Alice the hash of interesting file, and enable Alice to get the file from the server. (In fact, in [14] it was shown how to use the deduplication service itself as a low bandwidth covert channel. The attack described here can amplify this covert channel and enable the leakage of much more data.)

As opposed to the malicious software stealing Bob's access password to the storage server, the hash-based attack works no matter how well Bob protects his credentials (e.g., even if Bob uses an external device or some TPM-based scheme to authenticate to the server). Further, the usage of a stolen password can be identified by Bob checking his account login audit files. A hash based attack cannot be easily tracked since the attacker pose as legitimate users who happen to upload the same files as Bob.

The attack can be amplified even further in the following way. The examination of Dorredorf and Pinkas [7] revealed that the client software of several file storage services, including Dropbox, stores local unencrypted manifest files, written in SQLite format. These files include an entry for each file stored by the service, which includes the hash value of the file. A malicious software can leak to Alice the hash value of this file itself. Alice can use this value to recover the manifest file, and then use the hash values stored in the manifest file to recover all files stored by Bob. The implication is that a leakage of a short hash value, which is either 20 or 32 byte long (depending on the service), leaks all of Bob's files, in a way which is essentially undetectable.

Implementations of the attack. We stress that the attacks that we describe are not just theoretical. Independently of our work, the attack was very recently discovered by Wladimir van der Laan, who started an open-source project called Dropship that uses the Dropbox storage servers as a CDN. The Dropship project was withdrawn after Dropbox had asked in a really civil way that its creator take down the source code, since they felt that it is a violation of the TOS (Terms of Service) [1, 19].[1] This attack against Dropbox, as well as a similar attack that was implemented against another major file storage service, was also discovered and implemented by Dorrendorf and Pinkas [7]. (The

[1]It is interesting to note that even though the Dropbox service allows its users to share files by storing them on their public folder, Dropbox has actively tried to shutdown the Dropship service. This might be due to the fact that normal file sharing through the public folder is bandwidth limited, and since Dropship is better suited for sharing copyright infringing content.

name of the second service is withheld since the relevant company has not yet been noti ed.). Another recent and independent implementation of the attack on Dropbox was described by Mulazzani et al. [17].

Effect on open APIs for remote storage Given the attacks above it is clear that using only a small hash as a proxy for a large le is a security vulnerability. This issue must be addressed before creating open APIs for remote-storage that support client-side deduplication. We thus view a solution to this problem as an enabler for the creation of advanced open storage APIs.

1.1 Proofs of Ownership (PoWs)

To solve the problem of using a small hash value as a proxy for the entire le, we want to design a solution where a client proves to the server that it indeed has the le. We call a proof mechanism that prevents such leakage ampli cation a *proof of ownership* (PoW). We note that this is somewhat similar to proofs of retrievability (PORs) [15, 18] and proofs of data possession (PDPs) [3] with a role reversal (the client is the prover rather than the server). However, this role reversal is signi cant, and in particular the advanced POR and PDP protocols in the literature are inapplicable in our setting, see more discussion in Section 1.3.

We next discuss some important requirements that constrain our solutions:

Public hash function. To support cross-user deduplication, all clients must use the same procedure for identifying duplicate les. Hence this procedure must be **public**, which means that a determined attacker can learn it.

Bandwidth constraints. The protocol run between the server and client must be **bandwidth efficient**. Speci cally, it must consume a lot less bandwidth than the size of the le (otherwise the client could just upload the le itself).

Server constraints. The server typically has to handle a huge number of les. (For example, Mozy reports storing more than 25 Petabytes of data.) The les themselves are stored on a secondary storage with a large access time, and the server can store only a small amount of data per le in fast storage (such as RAM). Moreover, the server cannot a ord to retrieve the le or parts of it from secondary storage upon every upload request. The solution must therefore allow the server to store only an extremely **short information per file**, that will enable it to check claims from clients that they have that le.

Client constraints. The client should be able to e ciently prove to the server that it knows the le in question. This could be hard, e.g., if the le is very large and does not t in local memory. We therefore seek a solution where the client can compute the proof by making a **single pass** over the le (and using a reasonable amount of memory).

On the other hand, during the computation of the proof there should be **no very-short state** from which the proof can be computed. Otherwise the very-short state itself can serve as a proxy for the large le, and the system will remain vulnerable to some of the atacks above.

1.1.1 Our security definition

For security we want to ensure that as long as the le has a lot of min-entropy (from the attacker's perspective), the attacker has only a small chance of convincing the server. We stress that in many cases, an attacker may have some **partial information** about the le, e.g., it may know the format of the le, its language, or the contents of large portions in the le. Hence we require security even when the entropy of le (from the attacker's perspective) is much smaller than the le length, as long as there are still a lot of uncertainty left in the le.[2]

De ning what it means for the le to have a lot of min-entropy from the attacker's perspective turns out to be somewhat subtle. The formal de nition roughly follows the CDN /malicious-software attack scenarios. Speci cally, we consider an attacker that does not know all of the le, but has accomplices who have the le. The accomplices can interact with the storage server, and can help the attacker in arbitrary ways, subject to only two constraints. One constraint is that the total number of bits that the accomplices send to the attacker is much smaller than the initial min-entropy of the le (hence the le still has a lot of min-entropy even after all that communication). The other constraint is that the accomplices can only help the attacker during an o -line phase before the proof protocol begins, since otherwise the attacker could just relay messages back and forth between the server and an accomplice who has the le. (The no-man-in-the-middle restriction seems justi ed in many of the attack scenarios.) This formulation can be viewed as an instance of the bounded retrieval model [6, 9].

1.2 Our Solutions

In this work we consider a few di erent formal formulations of the intuitive requirement above and associated protocols that realize them. The rst solution is the most stringent in terms of security, but lacks in e ciency (mainly of computation time and memory requirements). The next solutions two solutions each improve on these aspects at the cost of relaxations on the security guarantees.

A general solution Our most stringent security requirement says that as long as the min-entropy in the original le *minus the number of bits sent to the adversary by the accomplices* is more than the security parameter, the adversary should not be able to convince the server that it has the le (except with insigni cant probability). This notion can be achieved by adopting the Merkle-tree-based proof-of-retrievability protocol. Namely, we rst encode the le using an erasure code, such that it is possible to recover the whole le from any (say) 90% of the encoded bits. We then build a Merkle tree over the encoded le, and have the server ask for a super-logarithmic number of leaves, chosen at random.

From the properties of the erasure code, if the adversary is missing any of the le then there are at least 10% of the leaves that it does not know. Moreover, if the le has high min-entropy from the adversary's perspective then it cannot even guess the value of these 10% leaves with any noticeable chance for success. Hence, it will be caught with overwhelming probability.[3] This solution is described in Section 3.

A more efficient solution using universal hashing The above solution is not as e cient for the client as we would like. First, computing the erasure code requires random

[2] Note that the security also holds for computational notions of entropy, e.g., if the adversary holds an encryption of the file.

[3] Without erasure codes, an adversary could have very high success probability on large files with small entropy, since the small entropy might mean that the adversary knows most of the file. The codes ensures that even a single unknown block of a large file will be extended to many unknown blocks in the encoded file.

access to bits of the le, hence for large les that do not t in RAM it entails too many disk accesses. Also, the server must ask for a number of leaves which is super-logarithmic in the security parameter, which means that the communication complexity of the proof protocol is $\omega(k \log k \log n)$ for an n-leaf tree and security parameter k.

We therefore seek more e cient protocols, even at the price of settling for a somewhat weaker form of security. Speci cally, we relax our security requirement by having an upper-threshold T such that if the attacker gets T bits from its accomplices then it is allowed to convince the prover (even if T is much smaller than the entropy of the le). This allows us to have a mechanism in which the client only needs $O(T)$ bits of internal memory in order to process the le, even if the le itself is much larger, and the communication in the protocol depends (polylogarithmically) on T and not on the size of the le. In realistic scenarios, we may get adequate security by setting T to be a rather large value (but not huge), e.g., 64 MByte. With this relaxation, a good solution would be to use universal hashing to hash the potentially large le into a *reduction buffer* of size at most 64MByte, and then implement the Merkle-tree protocol on the hashed values. This solution is described in Section 4.

A streaming scheme and implementation The more e cient solution can be implemented with reasonable memory, but universal hashing with such large output size is very expensive to compute. We, thus, optimize for a more practical solution for which we can still o er meaningful security analysis, albeit under some restrictions. We may argue that in realistic settings the input distribution (from the attacker's perspective) is not arbitrary, but rather is taken from a speci c class of distributions. Speci cally, these distributions capture cases in which there are parts of the le that the attacker may know and other parts that are essentially random. We formulate this condition (which is a generalization of block- xing distributions), and describe a protocol that can be proved secure for this class of input distributions. Roughly speaking, for these common input distributions we can replace the universal hashing with a procedure that generates a good erasure code over the reduction bu er.

We stress that it is impossible to verify experimentally the assumption about the input distribution, since it is an assumption about the view of an attacker. Still it seems a reasonable assumption to make in many settings (e.g., even les in a known format contain some le speci c information that is essentially random, see examples in Section 2.2.1). We also stress that we do not know of any e ciently computable input distributions under which there is an attack on our streaming scheme. It is interesting to either prove that no such distributions exist (maybe in the random-oracle model) or to exhibit one.

We implemented this streaming scheme and measured its expected e ect on performance of the system (see details of the implementation and test results in Section 5.3). For large les (over 2GByte) the overhead of our protocol above reading the le and computing its SHA256, is less than 50%, and this gure drops as the le grows. The overhead for smaller les is larger, yet it is still very bene cially to run the protocol when considering the saved data transfer times. When considering an average 5Mbps network, the protocol takes no more than 4% of the time it would have taken to transfer the le via the network (and less than 1% for large les). Even with a fast 100Mbps network, client-side deduplication with our protocol beats sending the entire le to the server already for les as small as 125KByte.

1.3 Related Work

As we mentioned above, proofs-of-ownership are closely related to proofs of retrievability (POR) [15, 18, 20] and proofs of data possession (PDP) [3]. The two main di erences are that (a) proofs of retrievability/data-possession often use a pre-processing step that cannot be used in proofs of ownership, and (b) our security notion is weaker than that of proofs of retrievability. We now elaborate:

No pre-processing step. In PORs/PDPs the input le is pre-processed by the client by embedding some secrets in it, which makes it possible for the server to later prove that it has the le by replying to the client queries with answers that are consistent with these secrets. In our setting, a new client comes with the only original le itself, we cannot embed secrets in it for the purpose of proofs. This rules out solutions based on MACs or signatures, for example the schemes from [3, 15, 18, 4].

Weaker security guarantee. Our de nition is not in the style of proofs-of-knowledge [11], in that we do not require extractions. Instead, we assume that the le is chosen from a distribution and talk about the success probability of the attacker given that distribution. In this sense, our de nition is somewhat reminiscent of the Storage-enforcing Commitment of Golle et al. [12]. It is obvious that our security notion is implied by the stronger extraction property. It is also not hard to show an example of a protocol which is secure according to our notion but does not have an e cient extractor.[4]

Another well studied, related problem is that of verifying the integrity of memory contents in computing platforms and ensuring that no memory corruption a ects the performed computations [10]. Many of these schemes utilize Merkle trees [16] for memory and data authentication.

2. PRELIMINARIES

We brie y survey the tools that we use and state our security de nition. Denote by $[n]$ the set $\{1, 2, \ldots, n\}$.

Error correction codes An $[n, k, d]$ is an encoding function $E : \{0,1\}^k \rightarrow \{0,1\}^n$, that has the property that for any two di erent values $x, y \in \{0,1\}^k$, the Hamming distance between $E(x)$ and $E(y)$ is at least d. The smallest distance between any two codewords is called the minimum-distance of the code. A code with minimum-distance d can recover from any $d-1$ erasures.

Pairwise independent hashing A family H of functions from $\{0,1\}^k$ to $\{0,1\}^n$ is pairwise independent (aka 2-universal) if for every two di erent values $x, y \in \{0,1\}^k$ and every two strings $a, b \in \{0,1\}^n$, when choosing at random $h \in_R H$ the probability that h maps x to a and y to b is exactly 2^{-2n}.

Collision resistant hashing A collision-resistant hash function has shorter output than input, and yet it is hard to nd

[4]For example, applying the solution of Section 3 to a one-way permutation of the file rather than to the file itself. One can extract the permuted file but cannot extract the file itself (still this adheres to the requirement of PoWs, since to answer correctly many bits have to be leaked).

e ciently two inputs that maps to the same output. Formally, a family of functions $\mathcal{H}$ is collision resistant if no e cient algorithm can nd, on input a random $h \in \mathcal{H}$, two di erent inputs $x \neq y$ such that $h(x) = h(y)$ (except with insigni cant probability). In practice we use a single function that accepts arbitrary-size input and has a xed-size output (e.g., SHA256 with 256 bits of output).

2.1 Merkle Trees

A Merkle tree provides a succinct commitment to a large bu er, such that it is later possible to open and verify individual blocks of the bu er without giving the entire bu er. To construct a Merkle tree we split the input bu er into blocks, then group the blocks in pairs and use a collision-resistant hash function to hash each pair. The hash values are then again grouped in pairs and each pair is further hashed, and this process is repeated until only a single hash value remains. This results in a binary tree with the leaves corresponding to the blocks of the input bu er and the root corresponding to the last remaining hash value. In order to commit to a bu er, one sends the root of the Merkle tree on this bu er. In order to open a commitment to a speci c block, the committer sends the hash value of this block, and all of the hashes needed to construct the path between the leaf and root of the merkle tree. Basically this consists of all of the hash values of siblings along the path from leaf to root (a total of h hash values on a 2^h sized bu er). The collision-resistance of the hash ensures that an e cient committer can only open to the original value.

All our solutions use the following basic proof protocol, between a veri er that has the root value of a Merkle tree on a bu er (and the number of leaves in the tree), and a prover who claims to know the underlying bu er. The veri er simply chooses u random choices of leaf indexes (u depends on the security parameter) and ask the prover for the value of the corresponding leaves. The prover replies with these leaves and with a sibling path for each one of them, and the veri er accepts if all these sibling paths are valid.

Our security proofs rely on a well-known Merkle-tree lemma, which says that every prover that passes the Merkle-tree protocol with high enough probability can be converted into an extractor that extracts most of the leaves of the tree. Details appear in the full version of this paper [13].

2.2 Proofs of Ownership

Proof-of-ownership is a protocol in two parts between two players on a joint input F (which is the input le). First the veri er summarizes to itself the input le F and generates a (shorter) veri cation information v. Later, the prover and veri er engage in an interactive protocol in which the prover has F and the veri er only has v, at the end of which the veri er either accepts or rejects. Hence a proof-of-ownership is speci ed by a summary function $S(\cdot)$ (which could be randomized and takes the input le F and a security parameter), and an interactive two-party protocol $(P \leftrightarrow V)$.

Validity. The scheme $\mathcal{P} = (S, \ )$ is valid if (a) S and are e cient, and (b) for every input le $F \in \{0,1\}^n$ and every value of the security parameter n, it holds that $(P(F, 1^n) \leftrightarrow V(S(F, 1^n))) \Rightarrow$ accept with all but a negligible probability (in n).

Efficiency. The main e ciency parameters of a proof-of-ownership are (a) the size of the summary information $v = S(F, 1^n)$, (b) the communication complexity of the protocol , and (c) the computation complexity of computing the function S and of the two parties in (all with respect to the le size $|F|$ and the security parameter n). We seek solutions where the dependence on the security parameter is linear, the computation complexity of S and P is linear in $|F|$ and the rest is at most (poly) logarithmic in $|F|$.

Another e ciency parameter that can be important is the space complexity of S, P when viewed as one-pass algorithms that access the input le in a streaming fashion. (This is signi cant since for large les we would like to read them sequentially from disk only once, and we do not have enough memory to store them all.)

2.2.1 *Security of Proofs-of-Ownership*

Our goal is to ensure that the le does not have a small representation that when leaked to an attacker allows the attacker to obtain the le from the server. Ideally, we would like the smallest representation of the le to be as long as the amount of entropy in the le itself. There are three regimes of parameters to keep in mind here:

Low-entropy files. These could be either small les, or large les that are mostly known. For example, consider two MS-Word documents describing two employees in a company. These les may be very large but di er on very few elds. Hence from the point of view of employee A, the le of employee B has very small entropy.

Medium-entropy files. These are les that have quite a lot of uncertainty, but still much less than their actual size. For example, consider an attacker that has a new movie with an invisible digital watermarking, and wants to get the non-watermarked movie from the storage server. Here the movie itself could be many megabytes long, and the only thing that the attacker does not know is the exact embedding of the watermarks which could be just a few kilobytes.

High-entropy files. These are large les that are mostly unknown to the attacker. For example, one can think of attackers that try to use the storage server as a content-distribution network (CDN): One client uploads the le to a server and sends a second client just a short message that allows the second client to get the le from the server.

To capture security our attack scenario postulates an arbitrary distribution $\mathcal{D}$ from which the input le F is chosen. The le is then given to the storage server who runs the summary function to get $v = S(F)$. Next there is a learning phase in which the adversary can set-up client accomplices and have them receive the le F and run the proof protocol with the server. The accomplices can interact freely with the adversary during the same learning phase.

Then the game moves to a proof phase , in which the adversary engages in the proof protocol with the server but cannot interact with the accomplices.[5]

Our rst (and strongest) security de nition (addressed in Section 3) roughly says that as long as the min-entropy in the original distribution is su ciently larger than the number of bits sent to the adversary by the accomplices, the adversary should not be able to convince the server that it has the le.

[5]We can even iterate between "learning phases" and "proof phases", as long as the accomplices cannot talk to the adversary concurrently with any run of the proof protocol.

Definition 1. *Fix parameters* $s \in \mathbb{N}, \varepsilon \in [0,1]$. *A scheme* $\mathcal{P} = (S, \ )$ *is a* strong proof of ownership with slackness s and soundness error ε *if for any* $t \in \mathbb{N}$ *and any input distribution* $\mathcal{D}$ *with* t *bits of min entropy, and any adversary as above that receives less than* $t - s$ *bits from the accomplices during the game, the adversary has probability of convincing the storage server that it has the file that is at most negligible in* s *more than* ε.

Our second de nition (addressed in Section 4) relaxes the restriction that the proof fails unless the accomplices send all the entropy of the le to the adversary. Instead, we have a leakage threshold T (set by the designers of the system) such that we allow the attacker to convince the server if it receives T or more bits from the accomplices, regardless of the entropy of the original le. This does not e ect much the low- or medium-entropy cases, but it weakens the defense in the high-entropy case. For example, if we set the threshold at 64Mbyte then the server can still be used as a CDN, except that the short message that clients must send to each other in order to use it will be 64Mbyte long.[6]

Definition 2. *Fix parameters* $s, T \in \mathbb{N}, \varepsilon \in [0,1]$. *A scheme* $\mathcal{P} = (S, \ )$ *is a* proof of ownership with leakage threshold T, slackness s, and soundness error ε, *if for any* $t \in \mathbb{N}$, *any input distribution* $\mathcal{D}$ *with* t *bits of min entropy, and any adversary as above that receives less than* $\min(T, t - s)$ *bits from the accomplices during the game, the verifier rejects the proof with all but negligibly more than* ε *probability.*

Our last de nition (addressed in Section 5) further relaxes the security requirement, in that we do not insist on protecting every input distribution, but just distributions taken from some class (which we believe captures all the input distributions that appear in practice).

Definition 3. *Fix parameters* $s, T \in \mathbb{N}, \varepsilon \in [0,1]$ *and a class* $\mathcal{CD}$ *of distributions. A scheme* $\mathcal{P} = (S, \ )$ *is a* proof of ownership with respect to $\mathcal{CD}$ with leakage threshold T, slackness s, and soundness error ε, *if for any* $t \in \mathbb{N}$, *any input distribution* $\mathcal{D} \in \mathcal{CD}$ *with* t *bits of min entropy, and any adversary as above that receives less than* $\min(T, t - s)$ *bits from the accomplices, the adversary has at most negligibly more than* ε *probability of convincing the storage server that it has the file.*

Note that our de nitions and solutions also generalize to a computational analog of entropy, i.e. the distribution is computationally indistinguishable from one with the relevant entropy. [7]

3. A MERKLE-TREE-BASED SOLUTION

Our rst solution is also a proof of retrievability protocol: in a nutshell it works by encoding the le using an erasure code, and then building a Merkle-tree over the encoded le. Speci cally, let $E : \{0,1\}^M \to \{0,1\}^{M'}$ be an erasure code, resilient to erasure of upto α fraction of the bits (for some constant $\alpha > 0$). Namely, from any $(1-\alpha)M'$ bits of $E(F)$ it is possible in principle to completely recover the original $F \in \{0,1\}^n$. For this application *it is not important that the recovery procedure be efficient*, in fact any code $E(\cdot)$ with minimum distance greater than $\alpha M'$ will do.

In addition, let H be a collision resistant hash function with output length of n bits (e.g., SHA256 with $n = 256$), and we denote by $MT_{H,b}(X)$ the binary Merkle tree over bu er X using b-bit leaves and the hash function H.

The Basic Construction[8] We use parameters $b = 256$ (the Merkle-tree leaf size), ε (the desired soundness bound), and α (the erasure recovery capability of the code). We use the collision-resistant hash function $H(\cdot)$ and the α-erasure-code $E(\cdot)$. On M-bit input le $F \in \{0,1\}^M$, the veri er computes the encoding $X = E(F)$ and then the Merkle tree $MT_{H,b}(X)$ and keeps only the root of the tree (and the number of leaves) as veri cation information. During the proof protocol, the veri ed chooses at random u leaf indexes, $\ell_1, \ldots, \ell_u$, where u is the smallest integer such that $(1-\alpha)^u < \varepsilon$. The veri er asks the prover for the sibling-paths of all the leaves, and accepts if all are valid with respect to $MT_{H,b}(X)$.

Theorem 1. *The basic construction is a proof-of-ownership protocol as per Definition 1 with soundness* $(1-\alpha)^u$.

4. PROTOCOLS WITH SMALL SPACE

The problem with using the generic solution from the previous section is that good erasure codes for very large les are expensive to compute. In particular, it seems that computing a good erasure code require random access to the le, which means that for les larger than the available memory this computation entails many accesses to the disk.

We get around this problem by introducing a security/space tradeo : Namely we allow the designer of the system to specify a memory-bound L such that (a) the client only needs roughly L bits of memory during the computation even for a very large les, but (b) leaking more than $O(L)$ bits may allow the adversary to cheat in the proof (even if the le has much higher entropy).

The idea is that instead of encoding the le with an erasure code, we hash it down to L bits using a hash function with public randomness, and then do the Merkle tree protocol over the hashed value. What makes this solution nontrivial is the fact that the adversary can choose the leakage functions depending on the public randomness, for example the adversary can ask to see $L/2$ bits of the hash value.

Using Pairwise Independent Hashing One solution that works is to use an arbitrary pairwise-universal hash family H that maps M bit les to (say) L bits. In is instructive to think of the setting $M \gg L \gg s$, and about input distribution $\mathcal{D}$ with $k = L + 2s$ bits of min-entropy. Note that with high probability over choice of $h \in H$ it is likely that $h(F)$ has high min-entropy, but this is not enough for us. For example, an adversary can try to nd a large set of blocks in the bu er $h(F)$ such that the projection of $h(F)$ onto these blocks has small min entropy. Then the adversary can ask for leakage only on these blocks, and hope that all the queries during the Merkle-tree hash will fall in this large set of blocks.

To show that this line of attack does not work we need to prove that when h is chosen at random from a pairwise

[6]See Section 6 for a way to add protection against CDN attacks also to our more efficient protocols from Sections 4 and 5.

[7]The reason is that since the verifier in a proof-of-ownership can be efficiently simulated, then an efficient strategy that fools the proof on a pseudo-entropy distribution, can be used to distinguish between the pseudo-entropy and real entropy distributions.

[8]Details and proof appear in the full version [13].

independent family, then with high probability *every* large subset of the blocks of $h(F)$ has high min-entropy. See full version [13] for details. Using this property we show that the small-space protocol based on universal hashing meets our intermediate security notion of De nition 2.

THEOREM 2. *The above protocol using pairwise-independent hash function to an L-bit buffer and Merkle-tree with basic block size b is a proof-of-ownership as per Definition 2, with leakage threshold* $T = L(\frac{1}{3} - \frac{1}{2b})$.

5. A STREAMING PROTOCOL

Although it is possible in principle to implement pairwise-independent hashing of M bits into an L-bit bu er in a one-pass fashion using only roughly L bits of memory (e.g., if we use linear hashing), such implementation would be prohibitively expensive for large M, L. In this section we present a variant of the space-e cient protocol that can be implemented much more e ciently, and for which we can still argue security in realistic settings. We pay for the e ciency by only being able to prove security for a more restrictive set of input distributions, and only under a (reasonable) assumption about the linear code that we obtain.

We present our scheme as a series of modi cations to the general universal hashing scheme using linear hashing. In the basic universal hashing scheme the le is viewed as a bit vector and multiplied by a random Boolean matrix. Namely, each bit in the le is XORed to a random subset of locations in the bu er (approximately to half of the locations). The main modi cations that we make are as follows:

Blocks vs. bits: Viewing the le as a bit vector is very taxing performance wise, as we need to process the bits individually. Instead we operate on blocks of B bits at a time (for example, $B = 512$ bits to match the block size of SHA256). For a le of M bits we denote the number of blocks by $m = \lceil M/B \rceil$, and the L-bit bu er holds $\ell = \lceil L/B \rceil$ blocks. All operations in the nal solutions will be XOR operations on blocks of bits, allowing for high performance.

Theoretically, this choice could severely hurt the properties of our encoding (since now the rst bits of the blocks never interact with the second bits of the blocks, etc.) But practically we can justify this choice under the assumption that real life uncertainty about le contents comes at the granularity of blocks, rather than uncertainty of single bits. Roughly, the attacker may have some parts of the le that it knows and others that it does not, and these parts are not individual bits but rather they are larger blocks. We thus prove the security of our scheme with respect to a input distributions that come in blocks, and argue that this should still provide adequate security in practical settings. See Section 5.1 for a precise description of the input distributions that we consider.

Sparse reduction and mixing phases: Even when working with full blocks, adding every input block to a large number of random locations requires an order of $m\ell$ operations, which is still too expensive. (Even for not-so-long les of size $\approx \ell$ blocks requires work that is quadratic in the bu er length, $O(\ell^2)$.) Instead we aim for a solution that takes as close to $m + \ell$ operations as we can get. Our encoding solution consists of two phases:

First we have a *reduction phase* in which the m-blocks le's content is reduced into the *reduction buffer* of ℓ blocks. In this stage each block from the le is XORed to a *constant* number of random locations in the bu er (where the constant is as small as 4 in our implementation). The small constant is signi cant for performance, but it means that we have poor di usion. For example starting from a le with only a single unknown block we end up with a bu er with only four unknown blocks.

To overcome this, we run a *mixing phase* on the bu er (this stage works on the bu er alone, not the original le). In this phase, we make several passes over the bu er, each time XORing every block into four other random locations in the bu er. This phase resembles the reduction phase but takes as input current blocks from the bu er rather than input blocks from the original le. Intuitively, this unbalanced Feistel structure should give us good di usion if we run enough passes, since each unknown block will eventually contaminate all the blocks in the bu er. (We evaluated the required number of passes experimentally, and observed that 4-5 passes are enough to get very good di usion.)

Cyclic shifts on blocks: Simply XORing full blocks onto the bu er causes an unknown block to cancel itself if it is XORed an even number of times. Hence in general we expect each unknown block to inuence only 50% of the blocks in the bu er, even after many passes. To get better di usion (without paying in performance) we apply a very simple cyclic shift to the block before XORing it. Speci cally, with $B = 512$-bit blocks, we XOR each block into four location, with shifts of 0,128,256 and 384 positions, respectively. (These shift values were chosen to give good performance on machines with word-size up to 128 bits.) With this twist each unknown block will inuence roughly 15 /16 of the blocks in the output bu er as opposed to only 1/2.

Using self contained pseudorandomness: As described so far, the transformation can be viewed as a xed linear mapping from an m-block le to an ℓ-block bu er. However, the description of this mapping is quite large: for each block position in the le/bu er we need to specify four indexes in the bu er where this block should be XORed. Note that the server and all clients have to agree on this mapping, so we cannot just let each of them choose it at random as they go along. Possible relief can be obtained by choosing this randomness once and for all and hard-wiring it in the code or to generate it pseudo-randomly from a short seed.

In our implementation we use a speedup that allows us to get the mapping for free : Observe that the client must anyway hash the input le, so that the server could compare the hash value and decide if that le already exists in the database. Hashing the le (say with SHA256) require applying the underlying SHA256 compression function to each block of the input le, thus computing a 256-bit chaining value that is used when hashing the next block. In our implementation these intermediate IV values double also as the speci cation of our mapping. Namely, we derive from each intermediate chaining value the four indexes that tell us where in the output bu er to XOR the current block. Under the *random oracle* model (where SHA256 is assumed to approximate a random function), this gives us the random mapping that we need (and we store these indexes and use them again during the mixing phase). This trick greatly improves performance, since the mapping can now be computed from the le using quantities that we have anyway.

Note that we are using a di erent set of pseudorandom

choices for di erent les, which heuristically could help security, but we are using it here as a performance optimization trick rather than a security enhancement mechanism.

5.1 Security of the Streaming Scheme

As we said above, for this implementation we can only prove security for a restrictive class of input distributions. This class is a (slight generalization of) *block-fixing distribution*: Essentially, from the attacker's perspective there are blocks in the input le that are completely random, and others that are fully known. We generalize block- xing distributions somewhat by allowing the random blocks to be chosen from a low-rank linear space, this captures for example the case where the same random block appears in the le several times. We argue that these generalized block- xing distributions are a reasonably good approximation to input distributions that can be found in practice, in that a real-world attacker may know some parts of a le (e.g., xed formatting), and may even know that some unknown parts must be equal to each other (e.g., the same information appears multiple times), but typically cannot know much more complicated information about the le.

A good way of thinking about this generalized bit- xing sources is that a length-M input le with k-bits of (min)-entropy is obtained by choosing a k-bit random vector $\vec{w} \in \{0,1\}^k$ and computing the le itself as $\vec{f} \leftarrow \vec{w} \cdot A + \vec{b}$ where $A \in \{0,1\}^{k \times M}$ and $\vec{b} \in \{0,1\}^M$ are chosen by the adversary (and A has full rank). This is generalized to B-bit blocks if each bit in w is replaced by a random B bit block but the operation of A remains the same (except applied to full blocks rather than bits).

Our hashing function can therefore be thought of as taking the adversarially encoded $\vec{f} = \vec{w} \cdot A + \vec{b}$ and re-encoding it as $\vec{r} \leftarrow h(\vec{f})$. If h itself is linear, $h(\vec{f}) = \vec{f} \cdot C$ (with $C \in \{0,1\}^{M \times L}$), then we can view the hashed image as a (coset of a) linear code, $E(\vec{w}) = \vec{w} \cdot AC + (\vec{b}C)$. We show below that the resulting scheme will be secure as long as the linear code generated by the matrix AC has large minimum distance.

THEOREM 3. *Consider a PoW scheme as described with the following parameters: ℓ is the number of blocks in the buffer, t is the number of challenges on Merkle-tree leaves, and C is the matrix representing the reduce and mix transformation from m blocks to ℓ blocks. If the matrix C in the scheme is chosen so that* for every *full-rank $k \times m$ matrix A it holds with high probability (over C) that the code generated by the rows of AC has minimum distance at least some d, then the scheme is a secure proof-of-ownership with soundness $(\frac{L-d+1}{L})^t$ with respect to generalized block-fixing distributions with min-entropy k.*

The proof of Theorem 3 is given in the full version [13]. For the security of our protocol we argue that when choosing a matrix C as a product of a random sparse reduction matrix R and many Feistel mixing steps M_i, we get a good code with high probability (for every full rank A). For example, if the code has minimum distance $\geq \ell/3$ then we get soundness of $(2/3)^t$. Unfortunately, it seems very hard to analyze the error-correction properties of such a construction, so we can only argue security under the unproven assumption that we get a good code. (In fact we can get by with a slightly weaker condition: Instead of requiring that the code AC does not have low-weight words, it is enough to assume that an e cient adversary cannot nd a low-weight word in this code.)

5.2 Implementation

Below we describe the actual implementation and parameters of our scheme.

Input: An M-bit file, broken into $m = \frac{M}{512}$ blocks.

Initialize buffer. A buffer is allocated with ℓ blocks of 512 bits, where $\ell = \min\{2^{20}, 2^{\lceil \log_2 m \rceil}\}$. (Note that 2^{20} blocks is 64MByte.)

Also allocate an IV buffer of m 256-bit IVs, set $IV[0]$ = SHA256-IV. We view each $IV[i]$ as both a 256-bit value and as an array of 4 indexes into Buffer.

Reduction phase. For each block $i \in [m]$:

1. Compute $IV[i] = \text{SHA256}(IV[i-1]; File[i])$

2. For $j = 0$ to 3:

3. $Block$ = Cyclic Shift of $File[i]$ by $j * 128$ bits.

4. XOR $Block$ into location $IV[i][j]$ in Buffer

Mixing phase. Repeat 5 times:

1. For each block $i \in [\ell]$, For $j = 0$ to 3:

2. $Block$ = Cyclic Shift of Buffer$[i]$ by $j * 128$ bits.

3. If $i \neq IV[i][j]$ then XOR $Block$ into location $IV[i][j]$ in Bu er

Figure 1: Outline of the implemented construction.

Block size: We use 512-bit blocks, which is also the block size of SHA256.

Buffer size: For smaller les uses a bu er roughly the size of the le.[9] For large les we limit the bu er to size 64MByte. This seems su cient for most applications (leaking 64MByte is quite a bit), and at the same time ts comfortably in main memory of contemporary machines.

Usage of Hash IVs: Hash IVs are computed in the reduction phase and then the same IVs are used again in the mixing phase. Each IV contains 256 bits and we typically use 80 (or less) of these bits as indexes for 4 locations in the bu er (there are at most 2^{20} blocks in the reduction bu er). If the bu er is longer than the input le then we use more bits from the IVs as indexes.

Number of iterations: The number of required iterations was tested empirically and shown in Figure 2. We see a convergence to a ecting 15/16 of the blocks within $4-5$ iterations. For the smaller bu er sizes, the mixing is slightly faster, and if a larger number of blocks is initially unknown, then the mixing may be as fast as 3 iterations. We set the number of iterations to 5 to accommodate for the largest bu er size (64MByte) and as low as one unknown block.

Number of challenge leaves: We set the number of challenge leaves in the Merkle tree to 20. Under the assumption that the code gives distance of $0.1L$ this will translate to a soundness error on the order of 2^{-66} if no leakage from accomplices is allowed, and to an error on the order of 2^{-20} if leakage of up to $0.4L$ is allowed. Note that the error does not have to be negligibly small, since the service can block

[9] The buffer size (in blocks) is rounded up to the next power of 2, to get a full binary Merkle tree over the buffer.

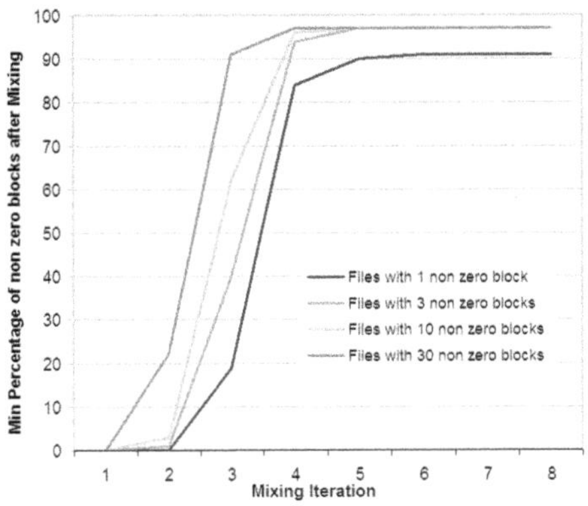

Figure 2: **Mixing iterations. The number of mixing passes needed to get full diffusion, when the input file has different numbers of unknown blocks.**

de-duplication attempts for a le once it has failed a PoW more than, say, 3 times.

5.3 Performance Evaluation

We implemented the PoW protocol[10] and below we evaluate its performance considering the following aspects:

Client time (C_{time}). This includes the time for reading the le from disk, computing its SHA256, performing the reduction and mixing phases, and computing the Merkle-tree over the resulting bu er. Our measurements show that the reduction phase adds less than 28% time over the insecure solution of just computing the SHA256 value of the le. The mixing and Merkle-tree times are relatively signi cant for small les (about 3 fold slowdown compared to the SHA256 computation), but once the le grows beyond 64MByte these times remain constant (844 and 1158ms respectively) since they are only applied to the 64MByte bu er. [11]

For les larger than 2GByte the overhead of our scheme (vs. only computing SHA256) is less than 50%. When further increasing the le size this overhead continues to decrease and the time to compute SHA256 becomes more dominant. These results are depicted in Figure 3.

Server time (S_{time}). This is the time spent by the server checking the Merkle tree authentication signatures. We observed that the overhead of these tests is very low, validating 20 sibling paths takes approximately 0.6 ms.

Network time (N_{time}). This is the estimated time required to transfer the protocol data. The overall size of the message transmitted by the protocol for 20 challenges is less than 20K. Thus, the network transmission time for a 5Mbps network is less than 0.1ms and is negligible.

Time savings by using deduplication. Figures 4 and 5 show the time-saving for the client by using deduplication (including the PoW overhead) compared to a policy of always sending the entire le to the server. We considered two network settings, one with an average speed for a fast network (5Mbps) [2] and the other being an extremely fast network (100Mbps). We observed that for the 5Mbps network, the PoW scheme always consumes less time than transmitting the le over the network (even for les of about 15KBytes). For the 100Mbps network deduplication (including the PoW) is faster than transmitting the le for sizes larger than 64KBytes. Furthermore, the bene t from using the PoW increases with the le size, e.g., for les larger than 1GByte the time consumed by PoW comprises of less than 1% and 20% of the upload time (for 5Mbps and 100Mbps respectively).

Overall, by using PoWs one can get the bene ts of client-side deduplication without sacri cing security. The bene ts become higher as les grow and for better deduplication ratio, as well as for slower networks.

[10]The measurements are done on random files in range 16KByte - 16GByte, Intel Xeon X5570 CPU, 2.93GHz. The protocol is implemented in C++ and uses SHA256 function of the Crypto++ [5].

[11]Note that the mixing and Merkle-tree computations can be performed after the client has sent the SHA256 value to the server and is waiting for the server to check if the file is already in the database and can be de-duplicated. Hence, in practice this time may be swallowed by the network latency.

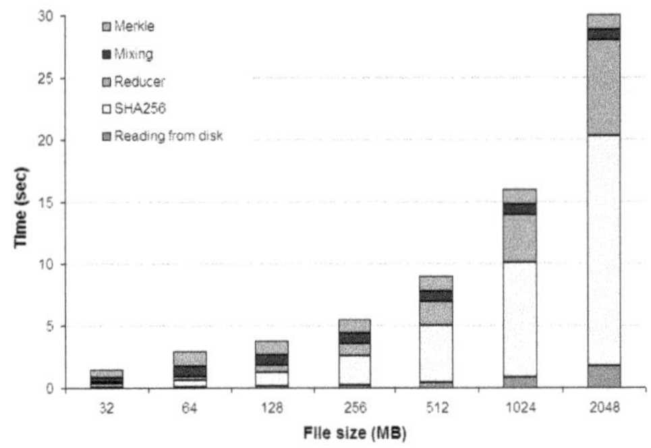

Figure 3: **Performance of PoW phases. The running times of the different stages of the PoW algorithm compared to the time to read the file from the disk or calculate its SHA256.**

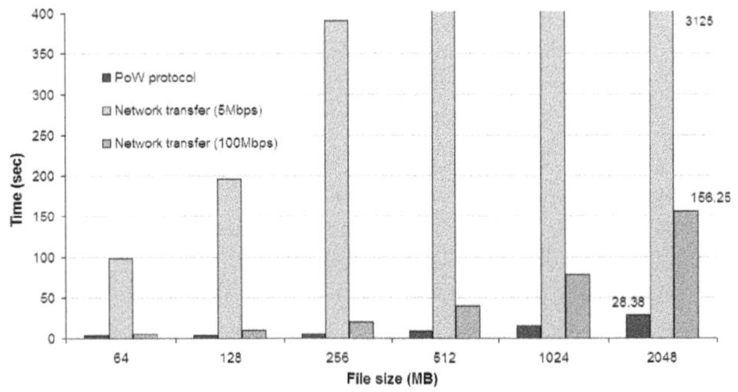

Figure 4: **PoW overall performance. Comparison of the overall time consumed by the PoW scheme to the time to send the file over the networks with 5Mbps and 100Mbps upload speed. The overall running times of the PoW scheme are calculated as $T = C_{time} + S_{time} + N_{time}$.**

6. ADDITIONAL COMMENTS AND CONCLUSIONS

In this work we put forward the notion of proof-of-ownership, by which a client can prove to a server that it has a copy of a le without actually sending it. This allows to counter attacks on le-deduplication systems where the attacker obtains a short summary of the le and uses it to fool the server into thinking that the attacker owns the entire le. We gave three de nitions for security in this setting and

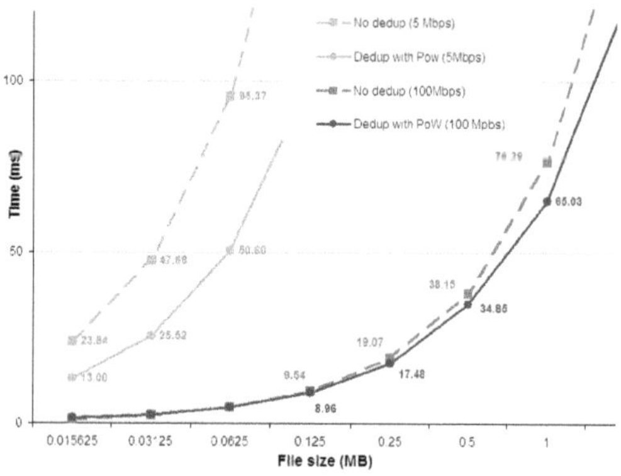

Figure 5: **Benefits of deduplication with PoW Comparisons between systems that perform deduplication with PoW to those that always transmit the data over the 5Mbps and 100Mbps networks respectively. We consider a relatively conservative workload in which only 50% of the data is deduplicated and we pay the overhead of the reduction phase of the PoW scheme for remaining 50% of the files.**

three matching protocols, the last of which is very practical. Our streaming protocol allows the designer of the scheme to set a threshold for how short a summary can a le have (e.g., 64MBytes in our implementation). This seem suitable for the attack scenarios of common hash functions, malicious software, or accidental leakage.

For CDN attacks the protection of our protocol is not as strong as one could hope for, but a very simple x can augment this streaming system also against CDN-type attacks: simply use two Merkle trees, one over the le itself and the other over the encoded bu er (and the server can keep only the hash of the two roots). Roughly speaking, the bu er-Merkle-tree addresses the low-entropy and medium-entropy cases while the le-Merkle-tree addresses the high-entropy case. This composed solution can run using small space with running time about twice higher that in Section 5.3. Note that this solution does not cover all ranges of the parameters. E.g., for a 16GByte le with 128MByte of entropy, an attacker can use only 64MByte of leakage and has a chance to convince the server. However, this parameter setting does not seem to appear much in typical applications.

We remark that the new attacks that we consider and our solutions to them are more relevant for le-level deduplication than for block-level deduplication. (Indeed, if an attacker can learn a hash value for each 8KByte block of the le, then it can probably learn also the blocks themselves and does not need to fool the storage server.) Note, however, that the attack remains relevant (and our solution useful) when a service uses both le- and block-level deduplication, as is likely to be the case in practical systems.

Acknowledgment: We thank Dalit Naor for her support throughout this work.

7. REFERENCES

[1] Dropship - dropbox api utilities. `https://github.com/driverdan/dropship`, April 2011.

[2] Akamai. *The State of the Internet*, 3rd Quarter 2010. www.akamai.com/stateoftheinternet.

[3] G. Ateniese, R. Burns, R. Curtmola, J. Herring, L. Kissner, Z. Peterson, and D. Song. Provable data possession at untrusted stores. In *ACM CCS '07*, pages 598 609. ACM, 2007.

[4] K. Bowers, A. Juels, and A. Opera. Hail: a high-availability and integrity layer for cloud storage. In *ACM CCS '09*, pages 187 198. ACM, 2009.

[5] W. Dai. *Crypto++ Library, 5.6.1, Jan, 2011.* http://www.cryptopp.com/.

[6] G. DiCrescenzo, R. J. Lipton, and S. Wal sh. Perfectly Secure Password Protocols in the Bounded Retrieval Model. In *TCC'06*, pages 225 244, 2006.

[7] L. Dorrendorf and B. Pinkas. Deduplication volnurabilities in major storage services. Under preparation, 2011.

[8] M. Dutch and L. Freeman. *Understanding data de-duplication ratios.* SNIA, February 2009. http://www.snia.org/.

[9] S. Dziembowski. Intrusion-Resilience Via the Bounded-Storage Model. In *TCC'06*, pages 207 224, 2006.

[10] R. Elbaz, D. Champagne, C. Gebotys, R. B. Lee, N. Potlapally, and L. Torres. Hardware mechanisms for memory authentication: A survey of existing techniques and engines. *ToCS IV, LNCS*, pages 1 22, March 2009.

[11] S. Goldwasser, S. Micali, and C. Racko . The Knowledge Complexity of Interactive Proof Systems. *SIAM J. Comput.*, 18(1):186 208, 1989.

[12] P. Golle, S. Jarecki, and I. Mironov. Cryptographic primitives enforcing communication and storage complexity. In *"Financial Cryptography '02"*, volume 2357 of *LNCS*, pages 120 135. Springer, 2003.

[13] S. Halevi, D. Harnik, B. Pinkas, and A. Shulman-Peleg. Proofs of ownership in remote storage systems. Cryptology ePrint Archive, Report 2011/207, 2011. `http://eprint.iacr.org/`.

[14] D. Harnik, B. Pinkas, and A. Shulman-Peleg. Side channels in cloud services, the case of deduplication in cloud storage. *IEEE Security and Privacy Magazine, special issue of Cloud Security*, 2010.

[15] A. Juels and B. S. Kaliski, Jr. Pors: proofs of retrievability for large les. In *ACM CCS '07*, pages 584 597. ACM, 2007.

[16] R. C. Merkle. A certi ed digital signature. In *Proceedings on Advances in cryptology*, CRYPTO '89, pages 218 238, New York, NY, USA, 1989. Springer-Verlag New York, Inc.

[17] M. Mulazzani, S. Schrittwieser, M. Leithner, M. Huber, and E. Weippl. Dark clouds on the horizon: Using cloud storage as attack vector and online slack space. In *USENIX Security*, 8 2011.

[18] H. Shacham and B. Waters. Compact proofs of retrievability. In *ASIACRYPT '08*, pages 90 107. Springer-Verlag, 2008.

[19] K. Thomas. Dropbox: A le sharer's dream tool? *PC World*, April 2011. `http://www.pcworld.com/businesscenter/article/226280/`.

[20] Q. Wang, C. Wang, J. Li, K. Ren, and W. Lou. Enabling public veri ability and data dynamics for storage security in cloud computing. In *ESORICS'09*, pages 355 370. Springer-Verlag, 2009.

How to Tell if Your Cloud Files Are Vulnerable to Drive Crashes

Kevin D. Bowers
RSA Laboratories
Cambridge, MA, USA
kbowers@rsa.com

Marten van Dijk
RSA Laboratories
Cambridge, MA, USA
marten.vandijk@rsa.com

Ari Juels
RSA Laboratories
Cambridge, MA, USA
ajuels@rsa.com

Alina Oprea
RSA Laboratories
Cambridge, MA, USA
aoprea@rsa.com

Ronald L. Rivest
MIT CSAIL
Cambridge, MA, USA
rivest@mit.edu

ABSTRACT

This paper presents a new challenge—verifying that a remote server is storing a file in a fault-tolerant manner, i.e., such that it can survive hard-drive failures. We describe an approach called the *Remote Assessment of Fault Tolerance* (RAFT). The key technique in a RAFT is to measure the *time taken* for a server to respond to a read request for a collection of file blocks. The larger the number of hard drives across which a file is distributed, the faster the read-request response. Erasure codes also play an important role in our solution. We describe a theoretical framework for RAFTs and offer experimental evidence that RAFTs can work in practice in several settings of interest.

Categories and Subject Descriptors

E.3 [**Data**]: [Data Encryption]

General Terms

Security

Keywords

Cloud storage systems, auditing, fault tolerance, erasure codes

1. INTRODUCTION

Cloud storage offers clients a unified view of a file as a single, integral object. This abstraction is appealingly simple. In reality, though, cloud providers generally store files/objects with redundancy or error correction to protect against data loss. Amazon, for example, claims that its S3 service stores three replicas of each object[1]. Additionally, cloud providers often spread files across multiple storage devices. Such distribution provides resilience against hardware failures, e.g., drive crashes (and can also lower latency across disparate geographies).

[1]Amazon has also recently introduced reduced redundancy storage that promises less fault tolerance at lower cost

CCS'11, October 17–21, 2011, Chicago, Illinois, USA.

The single-copy file abstraction in cloud storage, however, conceals file-layout information from clients. It therefore deprives them of insight into the true degree of fault-tolerance their files enjoy. Even when cloud providers specify a storage policy (e.g., even given Amazon's claim of triplicate storage), clients have no technical means of *verifying* that their files aren't vulnerable, for instance, to drive crashes. In light of clients' increasingly critical reliance on cloud storage for file retention, and the massive cloud-storage failures that have come to light, e.g., [8], it is our belief that remote testing of fault tolerance is a vital complement to contractual assurances and service-level specifications.

In this paper we develop a protocol for remote testing of fault-tolerance for stored files. We call our approach the *Remote Assessment of Fault Tolerance* (RAFT). A RAFT enables a client to obtain proof that a given file F is distributed across physical storage devices to achieve a certain desired level of fault tolerance. We refer to storage units as *drives* for concreteness. For protocol parameter t, our techniques enable a cloud provider to prove to a client that the file F can be reconstructed from surviving data given failure of any set of t drives. For example, if Amazon were to prove that it stores a file F fully in triplicate, i.e., one copy on three distinct drives, this would imply that F is resilient to $t = 2$ drive crashes.

At first glance, proving that file data is stored redundantly, and thus proving fault-tolerance, might seem an impossible task. It is straightforward for storage service $\mathcal{S}$ to prove knowledge of a file F, and hence that it has stored at least one copy. $\mathcal{S}$ can just transmit F. But how can $\mathcal{S}$ prove, for instance, that it has *three distinct copies* of F? Transmitting F three times clearly doesn't do the trick! Even proving storage of three copies doesn't prove fault-tolerance: the three copies could all be stored on the same disk!

To show that F isn't vulnerable to drive crashes, it is necessary to show that it is spread across multiple drives. Our approach, the Remote Assessment of Fault Tolerance, proves the use of multiple drives by exploiting drives' performance constraints—in particular bounds on the *time* required for drives to perform challenge tasks. A RAFT is structured as a timed challenge-response protocol. A short story gives the intuition. Here, the aim is to ensure that a pizza order can tolerate $t = 1$ oven failures.

> A fraternity ("Eeta Pizza Pi") regularly orders pizza from a local pizza shop, "Cheapskate Pizza." Recently Cheapskate failed to deliver pizzas for the big pregame party, claiming that their only pizza oven had suffered

> a catastrophic failure. They are currently replacing it with two new BakesALot ovens, for increased capacity and reliability in case one should fail.
>
> Aim O'Bese, president of Eeta Pizza Pi, wants to verify that Cheapskate has indeed installed redundant pizza ovens, without having to visit the Cheapskate premises himself. He devises the following clever approach. Knowing that each BakesALot oven can bake two pizzas every ten minutes, he places an order for two dozen pizzas, for delivery to the fraternity as soon as possible. Such a large order should take an hour of oven time in the two ovens, while a single oven would take two hours. The order includes various unusual combinations of ingredients, such as pineapple, anchovies, and garlic, to prevent Cheapskate from delivering warmed up pre-made pizzas.
>
> Cheapskate is a fifteen minute drive from the fraternity. When Cheapskate delivers the two dozen pizzas in an hour and twenty minutes, Aim decides, while consuming the last slice of pineapple/anchovy/garlic pizza, that Cheapskate must be telling the truth. He gives them the fraternity's next pregame party order.

Our RAFT for drive fault-tolerance testing follows the approach illustrated in this story. The client challenges the server to retrieve a set of random file blocks from file F. By responding quickly enough, $\mathcal{S}$ proves that it has distributed F across a certain, minimum number of drives. Suppose, for example, that $\mathcal{S}$ is challenged to pull 100 random blocks from F, and that this task takes one second on a single drive. If $\mathcal{S}$ can respond in only half a second[2], it is clear that it has distributed F across at least two drives.

Again, the goal of a RAFT is for $\mathcal{S}$ to prove to a client that F is recoverable in the face of at least t drive failures for some t. Thus $\mathcal{S}$ must actually do more than prove that F is distributed across a certain number of drives. It must *also* prove that F has been stored with a certain amount of *redundancy* and that the distribution of F across drives is *well balanced*. To ensure these two additional properties, the client and server agree upon a particular mapping of file blocks to drives. An underlying erasure code provides redundancy. By randomly challenging the server to show that blocks of F are laid out on drives in the agreed-upon mapping, the client can then verify resilience to t drive failures.

The real-world behavior of hard drives presents a protocol-design challenge: The response time of a drive can vary considerably from read to read. Our protocols rely in particular on timing measurements of disk seeks, the operation of locating randomly accessed blocks on a drive. Seek times exhibit high variance, with multiple factors at play (including disk prefetching algorithms, disk internal buffer sizes, physical layout of accessed blocks, etc.). To smooth out this variance we craft our RAFTs to sample *multiple* randomly selected file blocks per drive. Clients not only check the correctness of the server's responses, but also measure response times and accept a proof only if the server replies within a certain time interval.

We propose and experimentally validate on a local system a RAFT that can, for example, distinguish between a three-drive system with fault tolerance $t = 1$ and a two-drive system with no fault tolerance for files of size at least 100MB. Additionally, we explore the feasibility of the RAFT protocol on the Mozy cloud backup system and confirm that Mozy is resilient to at least one drive failure. We conclude that RAFT protocols are most applicable to test fault tolerance for large files in an archival or backup setting in which files are infrequently accessed and thus there is limited drive contention.

Our RAFT protocol presented in this paper is designed for traditional storage architectures that employ disk-level replication of files and use hard disk drives (HDDs) as the storage medium. While these architectures are still prevalent today, there are many settings in which our current protocol design is not directly applicable. For instance, the characteristics of HDD's sequential and random access do not hold for SSD drives or RAM memory, which could potentially be used for performance-sensitive workloads in systems employing multi-tier storage (e.g., [1,28]). Systems with data layout done at the block level (as opposed to file-level layout) are also not amenable to our current design, as in that setting timing information in our challenge-response protocol does not directly translate into fault tolerance. Examples of architectures with block-level data layout are chunk-based file systems [14,17], and systems with block-level de-duplication [7]. Other features such as spinning disks down for power savings, or replicating data across different geographical locations complicate the design of a RAFT-like protocol. Nevertheless, we believe that our techniques can be adapted to some of these emerging architectures and we plan to evaluate this further in future work.

RAFTs aim primarily to protect against "economically rational" service providers/adversaries, which we define formally below. Our adversarial model is thus a mild one. We envision scenarios in which a service provider agrees to furnish a certain degree of fault tolerance, but cuts corners. To reduce operating costs, the provider might maintain equipment poorly, resulting in unremediated data loss, enforce less file redundancy than promised, or use fewer drives than needed to achieve the promised level of fault tolerance. (The provider might even use too few drives accidentally, as virtualization of devices causes unintended consolidation of physical drives.) An economically rational service provider, though, *only* provides substandard fault tolerance when doing so reduces costs. The provider does not otherwise, i.e., maliciously, introduce drive-failure vulnerabilities. We explain later, in fact, why protection against malicious providers is technically infeasible.

1.1 Related work

Proofs of Data Possession (PDPs) [2] and Proofs of Retrievability (PORs) [9,10,21,31] are challenge-response protocols that verify the integrity and completeness of a remotely stored F. They share with our work the idea of combining error-coding with random sampling to achieve a low-bandwidth proof of storage of a file F. This technique was first advanced in a theoretical framework in [27]. Both [23] and [4] remotely verify fault tolerance at a logical level by using multiple independent cloud storage providers. A RAFT includes the extra dimension of verifying physical layout of F and tolerance to a number of drive failures at a single provider.

Cryptographic challenge-response protocols prove knowledge of a secret—or, in the case of PDPs and PORs, knowledge of a file. The idea of timing a response to measure remote physical resources arises in cryptographic *puzzle* constructions [11]. For instance, a challenge-response protocol based on a moderately hard computational problems can measure the computational resources of clients submitting service requests and mitigate denial-of-service attacks by proportionately scaling service fulfilment [20]. Our protocols here measure not computational resources, but the storage

[2] Of course, $\mathcal{S}$ can violate our assumed bounds on drive performance by employing unexpectedly high-grade storage devices, e.g., flash storage instead of rotational disks. As we explain below, though, our techniques aim to protect against economically rational adversaries $\mathcal{S}$. Such an $\mathcal{S}$ might create substandard fault tolerance to cut costs, but would not employ more expensive hardware just to circumvent our protocols. (More expensive drives often mean higher reliability anyway.)

resources devoted to a file. (Less directly related is physical distance bounding, introduced in a cryptographic setting in [6]. There, packet time-of-flight gives an upper bound on distance.)

We focus on non-Byzantine, i.e., non-malicious, adversarial models. We presume that malicious behavior in cloud storage providers is rare. As we explain, such behavior is largely irremediable anyway. Instead, we focus on an adversarial model ("cheap-and-lazy") that captures the behavior of a basic, cost-cutting or sloppy storage provider. We also consider an economically rational model for the provider. Most study of economically rational players in cryptography is in the multiplayer setting, but economical rationality is also implicit in some protocols for storage integrity. For example, [2,15] verify that a provider has dedicated a certain amount of storage to a file F, but don't strongly assure file integrity. We formalize the concept of self-interested storage providers in our work here.

A RAFT falls under the broad heading of cloud security assurance. There have been many proposals to verify the security characteristics and configuration of cloud systems by means of trusted hardware, e.g., [13]. Our RAFT approach advantageously avoids the complexity of trusted hardware. Drives typically don't carry trusted hardware in any case, and higher layers of a storage subsystem can't provide the physical-layer assurances we aim at here.

1.2 Organization

Section 2 gives an overview of key ideas and techniques in our RAFT scheme. We present formal adversarial and system models in Section 3. In Section 4, we introduce a basic RAFT in a simple system model. Drawing on experiments, we refine this system model in Section 5, resulting in a more sophisticated RAFT which we validate against the Mozy cloud backup service in Section 6. In Section 7, we formalize an economically rational adversarial model and sketch matching RAFT constructions. We conclude in Section 8 with discussion of future directions.

2. OVERVIEW: BUILDING A RAFT

We now discuss in further detail the practical technical challenges in building a RAFT for hard drives, and the techniques we use to address them. We view the file F as a sequence of m blocks of fixed size (e.g., 64KB).

File redundancy / erasure coding. To tolerate drive failures, the file F must be stored with redundancy. A RAFT thus includes an initial step that expands F into an n-block erasure-coded representation G. If the goal is to place file blocks evenly across c drives to tolerate the failure of any t drives, then we need $n = mc/(c-t)$. Our adversarial model, though, also allows the server to drop a portion of blocks or place some blocks on the wrong drives. We show how to parameterize our erasure coding at a still higher rate, i.e., choose a larger n, to handle these possibilities.

Challenge structure. (*"What order should Eeta Pizza Pie place to challenge Cheapskate?"*) We focus on a "layout specified" RAFT, one in which the client and server agree upon an exact placement of the blocks of G on c drives, i.e., a mapping of each block to a given drive. The client, then, challenges the server with a query Q that selects exactly one block per drive in the agreed-upon layout. An honest server can respond by pulling exactly one block per drive (in one "step"). A cheating server, e.g., one that uses fewer than c drives, will need at least one drive to service *two* block requests to fulfill Q, resulting in a slowdown.

Network latency. (*"What if Cheapskate's delivery truck runs into traffic congestion?"*) The network latency, i.e., roundtrip packet-travel time, between the client and server, can vary due to changing network congestion conditions. The client cannot tell how much a response delay is due to network conditions and how much might be due to cheating by the server. Based on the study by Lumezanu et al [24] and our own small-scale experiments, we set an upper bound threshold on the variability in latency between a challenging client and a storage service. We consider that time to be "free time" for the adversary, time in which the adversary can cheat, prefetching blocks from disk or perform any other action that increases his success probability in the challenge-response protocol. We design our protocol to be resilient to a bounded amount of "free time" given to the adversary.

Drive read-time variance. (*"What if the BakesALot ovens bake at inconsistent rates?"*) The read-response time for a drive varies across reads. We perform experiments, though, showing that for a carefully calibrated file-block size, the response time follows a probability distribution that is stable across time and physical file positioning on disk. (We show how to exploit the fact that a drive's "seek time" distribution is stable, even though its read bandwidth isn't.) We also show how to smooth out read-time variance by constructing RAFT queries Q that consist of *multiple* blocks per drive.

Queries with multiple blocks per drive. (*"How can Eeta Pizza Pie place multiple, unpredictable orders without phoning Cheapskate multiple times?"*) A naïve way to construct a challenge Q consisting of multiple blocks per drive (say, q) is simply for the client to specify cq random blocks in Q. The problem with this approach is that the server can then schedule the set of cq block accesses on its drives to reduce total access time (e.g., exploiting drive efficiencies on sequential-order reads). Alternatively, the client could issue challenges in q steps, waiting to receive a response before issuing a next, unpredictable challenge. But this would require c rounds of interaction.

We instead introduce an approach that we call *lock-step* challenge generation. The key idea is for the client to specify query Q in an initial step consisting of c random challenge blocks (one per drive). For each subsequent step, the set of c challenge blocks depends on the *content* of the file blocks accessed in the last step. The server can proceed to the next step only after fully completing the last one. Our lock-step technique is a kind of repeated application of a Fiat-Shamir-like heuristic [12] for generating q independent, unpredictable sets of challenges non-interactively. (File blocks serve as a kind of "commitment.") The server's response to Q is the aggregate (hash) of all of the cq file blocks it accesses.

3. FORMAL DEFINITIONS

A Remote Assessment of Fault Tolerance $\mathcal{RAFT}(t)$ aims to enable a service provider to prove to a client that it has stored file F with tolerance against t drive failures. In our model, the file is first encoded by adding some redundancy. This can be done by either the client or the server. The encoded file is then stored by the server using some number of drives. Periodically, the client issues challenges to the server, consisting of a subset of file block indices. If the server replies correctly and promptly to challenges (i.e., the answer is consistent with the original file F, and the timing of the response is within an acceptable interval), the client is convinced that the server stores the file with tolerance against t drive failures. The client can also reconstruct the file at any time from the encoding stored by the server, assuming at most t drive failures.

3.1 System definition

To define our system more formally, we start by introducing some notation. A file block is an element in $B = GF[2^{\ell}]$. For convenience we also treat ℓ as a security parameter. We let f_i denote the ith block of a file F for $i \in \{1, \ldots, |F|\}$.

The RAFT system comprises these functions:

- $\mathsf{Keygen}(1^\ell) \xrightarrow{R} \kappa$: A key-generation function that outputs key κ. We denote a keyless system by $\kappa = \phi$.

- $\mathsf{Encode}(\kappa, F = \{f_i\}_{i=1}^m, t, c) \rightarrow G = \{g_i\}_{i=1}^n$: An encoding function applied to an m-block file $F = \{f_i\}_{i=1}^m$; it takes as additional input fault tolerance t and a number of c logical disks. It outputs encoded file $G = \{g_i\}_{i=1}^n$, where $n \geq m$. The function Encode may be keyed, e.g., encrypting blocks under κ, in which case encoding is done by the client, or unkeyed, e.g., applying an erasure code or keyless cryptographic operation to F, which may be done by either the client or server.

- $\mathsf{Map}(n, t, c) \rightarrow \{C_j\}_{j=1}^c$: A function computed by both the client and server that takes the encoded file size n, fault tolerance t and a number c of logical disks and outputs a logical mapping of file blocks to c disks or $\perp$. To implement Map the client and server can agree on a mapping which each can compute, or the server may specify a mapping that the client verifies as being tolerant to t drive failures. (A more general definition might also include $G = \{g_i\}_{i=1}^n$ as input. Here we only consider mappings that respect erasure-coding structure.) The output consists of sets $C_j \subseteq \{1, 2, \ldots, n\}$ denoting the block indices stored on drive j, for $j \in \{1, \ldots, c\}$. If the output is not $\perp$, then the placement is tolerant to t drive failures.

- $\mathsf{Challenge}(n, G, t, c) \rightarrow Q$: A (stateful and probabilistic) function computed by the client that takes as input the encoded file size n, encoded file G, fault tolerance t, and the number of logical drives c and generates a challenge Q consisting of a set of block indices in G and a random nonce ν. The aim of the challenge is to verify disk-failure tolerance at least t.

- $\mathsf{Response}(Q) \rightarrow (R, T)$: An algorithm that computes a server's response R to challenge Q, using the encoded file blocks stored on the server disks. The timing of the response T is measured by the client as the time required to receive the response from the server after sending a challenge.

- $\mathsf{Verify}(G, Q, R, T) \rightarrow b \in \{0, 1\}$: A verification function for a server's response (R, T) to a challenge Q, where 1 denotes "accept," i.e., the client has successfully verified correct storage by the server. Conversely 0 denotes "reject." Input G is optional in some systems.

- $\mathsf{Reconstruct}(\kappa, r, \{g_i^*\}_{i=1}^r) \rightarrow F^* = \{f_i^*\}_{i=1}^m$: A reconstruction function that takes a set of r encoded file blocks and either reconstructs an m-block file or outputs failure symbol $\perp$. We assume that the block indices in the encoded file are also given to the Reconstruct algorithm, but we omit them here for simplicity of notation. The function is keyed if Encode is keyed, and unkeyed otherwise.

Except in the case of Keygen, which is always probabilistic, functions may be probabilistic or deterministic. We define $\mathcal{RAFT}(t) = \{\mathsf{Keygen}, \mathsf{Encode}, \mathsf{Map}, \mathsf{Challenge}, \mathsf{Response}, \mathsf{Verify}, \mathsf{Reconstruct}\}$.

3.2 Client model

In some instances of our protocols called *keyed protocols*, the client needs to store secret keys used for encoding and reconstructing the file. *Unkeyed protocols* do not make use of secret keys for file encoding, but instead use public transforms.

If the Map function outputs a logical layout $\{C_j\}_{j=1}^c \neq \perp$, then we call the model *layout-specified*. We denote a *layout-free* model one in which the Map function outputs $\perp$, i.e., the client does not know a logical placement of the file on c disks. In this paper, we only consider layout-specified protocols, although layout-free protocols are an interesting point in the RAFT design space.

For simplicity in designing the Verify protocol, we assume that the client keeps a copy of F locally. Our protocols can be extended easily via standard block-authentication techniques, e.g., [25], to a model in which the file is maintained only by the provider and the client deletes the local copy after outsourcing the file.

3.3 Drive and network models

The response time T of the server to a challenge Q as measured by the client has two components: (1) Drive read-request delays and (2) Network latency. We model these two protocol-timing components as follows.

Modeling drives.

We model a server's storage resources for F as a collection of d independent hard drives. Each drive stores a collection of file blocks. The drives are stateful: The timing of a read-request response depends on the query history for the drive, reflecting block-retrieval delays. For example, a drive's response time is lower for sequentially indexed queries than for randomly indexed ones, which induce seek-time delays [30]. We do not consider other forms of storage here, e.g., solid-state drives[3].

We assume that all the drives belong to the same class, (e.g. enterprise class drives), but may differ in significant ways, including seek time, latency, and even manufacturer. We will present disk access time distributions for several enterprise class drive models. We also assume that when retrieving disk blocks for responding to client queries in the protocol, there is no other workload running concurrently on the drive, i.e. the drive has been "reserved" for the RAFT[4]. Alternatively, in many cases, drive contention can be overcome by issuing more queries. We will demonstrate the feasibility of both approaches through experimental results.

Modeling network latency.

We adapt our protocols to handle variations in network latency between the client and cloud provider. Based on the results presented in [24] and our own small-scale experiments, we set an upper bound threshold on the variability in observed latency between the vast majority of host pairs. We design our protocol so that the difference in timing to reply successfully to a challenge between an

[3]At the time of this writing, SSDs are still considerably more expensive than rotational drives and have much lower capacities. A typical rotational drive can be bought for roughly \$0.07/GB in capacities up to 3 TBs, while most SSDs cost more than \$2.00/GB are are only a few hundred GBs in size. For an economically rational adversary, the current cost difference makes SSDs impractical.

[4]Multiple concurrent workloads could skew disk-access times in unexpected ways. This was actually seen in our own experiments when the OS contended with our tests for access to a disk, causing spikes in recorded read times.In a multi-tenant environment, users are accustomed to delayed responses, so reserving a drive for 500 ms. to perform a RAFT test should not be an issue.

adversarial and an honest server is at least the maximum observed variability in network latency.

3.4 Adversarial model

We now describe our adversarial model, i.e., the range of behaviors of $\mathcal{S}$. In our model, the m-block file F is chosen uniformly at random. This reflects our assumption that file blocks are already compressed by the client, for storage and transmission efficiency, and also because our RAFT constructions benefit from random-looking file blocks. Encode is applied to F, yielding an encoded file G of size n, which is stored with $\mathcal{S}$.

Both the client and server compute the logical placement $\{C_j\}_{j=1}^{c}$ by applying the Map function. The server then distributes the blocks of G across d real disks. The number of actual disks d used by $\mathcal{S}$ might be different than the number of agreed-upon drives c. The actual file placement $\{\mathcal{D}_j\}_{j=1}^{d}$ performed by the server might also deviate arbitrarily from the placement specified by the Map function. (As we discuss later, sophisticated adversaries might even store something other than unmodified blocks of G.)

At the beginning of a protocol execution, we assume that no blocks of G are stored in the high-speed (non-disk) memory of $\mathcal{S}$. Therefore, to respond to a challenge Q, $\mathcal{S}$ must query its disks to retrieve file blocks. The variable T denotes the time required for the client, after transmitting its challenge, to receive a response R from $\mathcal{S}$. Time T includes both network latency and drive access time (as well as any delay introduced by $\mathcal{S}$ cheating).

The goal of the client is to establish whether the file placement implemented by the server is resilient to at least t drive failures.

Our adversarial model is validated by the design and implementation of the Mozy online backup system, which we will discuss further in Section 6.2. We expect Mozy to be representative of many cloud storage infrastructures.

Cheap-and-lazy server model.

For simplicity and realism, we focus first on a restricted adversary $\mathcal{S}$ that we call *cheap-and-lazy*. The objective of a cheap-and-lazy adversary is to reduce its resource costs; in that sense it is "cheap." It is "lazy" in the sense that it does not modify file contents. The adversary instead cuts corners by storing less redundant data on a smaller number of disks or mapping file blocks unevenly across disks, i.e., it may ignore the output of Map. A cheap-and-lazy adversary captures the behavior of a typical cost-cutting or negligent storage service provider.

To be precise, we specify a cheap-and-lazy server $\mathcal{S}$ by the following assumptions on the blocks of file F:

- **Block obliviousness:** The behavior of $\mathcal{S}$ i.e., its choice of internal file-block placement $(d, \{\mathcal{D}_j\}_{j=1}^{d})$ is independent of the content of blocks in G. Intuitively, this means that $\mathcal{S}$ doesn't inspect block contents when placing encoded file blocks on drives.

- **Block atomicity:** The server handles file blocks as atomic data elements, i.e., it doesn't partition blocks across multiple storage devices.

A cheap-and-lazy server may be viewed as selecting a mapping from n encoded file blocks to positions on d drives without knowledge of G. Some of the encoded file blocks might not be stored to drives at all (corresponding to dropping of file blocks), and some might be duplicated onto multiple drives. $\mathcal{S}$ then applies this mapping to the n blocks of G.

General adversarial model.

It is also useful to consider a general adversarial model, cast in an experimental framework. We define the security of our system $\mathcal{RAFT}(t)$ according to the experiment from Figure 1. We let $\mathcal{O}(\kappa) = \{\mathsf{Encode}(\kappa,\cdot,\cdot,\cdot), \mathsf{Map}(\cdot,\cdot,\cdot), \mathsf{Challenge}(\cdot,\cdot,\cdot,\cdot), \mathsf{Verify}(\cdot,\cdot,\cdot,\cdot), \mathsf{Reconstruct}(\kappa,\cdot,\cdot)\}$ denote a set of RAFT-function oracles (some keyed) accessible to $\mathcal{S}$.

Experiment $\mathsf{Exp}_{\mathcal{S}}^{\mathcal{RAFT}(t)}(m,\ell,t)$:
  $\kappa \leftarrow \mathsf{Keygen}(1^{\ell})$;
  $F = \{f_i\}_{i=1}^{m} \leftarrow_R B^m$;
  $G = \{g_i\}_{i=1}^{n} \leftarrow \mathsf{Encode}(\kappa, F, t, c)$;
  $(d, \{\mathcal{D}_j\}_{j=1}^{d}) \leftarrow \mathcal{S}^{\mathcal{O}(\kappa)}(n, G, t, c,$ "store file");
  $Q \leftarrow \mathsf{Challenge}(n, G, t, c)$;
  $(R, T) \leftarrow \mathcal{S}^{\{\mathcal{D}_j\}_{j=1}^{d}}(Q,$ "compute response");
  if $\mathsf{Acc}_{\mathcal{S}}$ and $\mathsf{NotFT}_{\mathcal{S}}$
    then output 1,
  else output 0

Figure 1: Security experiment

We denote by $\mathsf{Acc}_{\mathcal{S}}$ the event that $\mathsf{Verify}(G, Q, R, T) = 1$ in a given run of $\mathsf{Exp}_{\mathcal{S}}^{\mathcal{RAFT}(t)}(m,\ell,t)$, i.e., that the client / verifier accepts the response of $\mathcal{S}$. We denote by $\mathsf{NotFT}_{\mathcal{S}}$ the event that there exists $\{\mathcal{D}_{i_j}\}_{j=1}^{d-t} \subseteq \{\mathcal{D}_j\}_{j=1}^{d}$ s.t. $\mathsf{Reconstruct}(\kappa, |\{\mathcal{D}_{i_j}\}_{j=1}^{d-t}|, \{\mathcal{D}_{i_j}\}_{j=1}^{d-t}) \neq F$, i.e, the allocation of blocks selected by $\mathcal{S}$ in the experimental run is not t-fault tolerant.

We define $\mathsf{Adv}_{\mathcal{S}}^{\mathcal{RAFT}(t)}(m,\ell,t) = \Pr[\mathsf{Exp}_{\mathcal{S}}^{\mathcal{RAFT}(t)}(m,\ell,t) = 1] = \Pr[\mathsf{Acc}_{\mathcal{S}} \text{ and } \mathsf{NotFT}_{\mathcal{S}}]$. We define the *completeness* of $\mathcal{RAFT}(t)$ as $\mathsf{Comp}^{\mathcal{RAFT}(t)}(m,\ell,t) = \Pr[\mathsf{Acc}_{\mathcal{S}} \text{ and } \neg\mathsf{NotFT}_{\mathcal{S}}]$ over executions of honest $\mathcal{S}$ (a server that always respects the protocol specification) in $\mathsf{Exp}_{\mathcal{S}}^{\mathcal{RAFT}(t)}(m,\ell,t)$.

Our general definition here is, in fact, a little too general for practical purposes. As we now explain, there is no good RAFT for a fully malicious $\mathcal{S}$. That is why we restrict our attention to cheap-and-lazy $\mathcal{S}$, and later, in Section 7, briefly consider a "rational" $\mathcal{S}$.

Why we exclude malicious servers.

A *malicious* or fully Byzantine server $\mathcal{S}$ is one that may expend arbitrarily large resources and manipulate and store G in an arbitrary manner. Its goal is to achieve $\leq t-1$ fault tolerance for F while convincing the client with high probability that F enjoys full t fault tolerance.

We do not consider malicious servers because there is no efficient protocol to detect them. A malicious server can convert any t-fault-tolerant file placement into a 0-fault-tolerant file placement very simply. The server randomly selects an encryption key λ, and encrypts every stored file block under λ. $\mathcal{S}$ then adds a new drive and stores λ on it. To reply to a challenge, $\mathcal{S}$ retrieves λ and decrypts any file blocks in its response. If the drive containing λ fails, of course, the file F will be lost. There is no efficient protocol that distinguishes between a file stored encrypted with the key held on a single drive, and a file stored as specified, as they result in nearly equivalent block read times.[5]

3.5 Problem Instances

A RAFT *problem instance* comprises a client model, an adversarial model, and drive and network models. In what follows, we

[5]The need to pull λ from the additional drive may slightly skew the response time of $\mathcal{S}$ when first challenged by the client. This skew is modest in realistic settings. And once read, λ is available for any additional challenges.

propose RAFT designs in an incremental manner, starting with a very simple problem instance—a cheap-and-lazy adversarial model and simplistic drive and network models. After experimentally exploring more realistic network and drive models, we propose a more complex RAFT. We then consider a more powerful ("rational") adversary and further refinements to our RAFT scheme.

4. THE BASIC RAFT PROTOCOL

In this section, we construct a simple RAFT system resilient against the cheap-and-lazy adversary. We consider very simple disk and network models. While the protocol presented in this section is mostly of theoretical interest, it offers a conceptual framework for later, more sophisticated RAFTs.

We consider the following problem instance:

Client model: Unkeyed and layout-specified.

Adversarial model: The server is cheap-and-lazy.

Drive model: Time to read a block of fixed length ℓ from disk is constant and denoted by τ_ℓ.

Network model: The latency between client and server (denoted L) is constant in time and network bandwidth is unlimited.

4.1 Scheme Description

Our RAFT construction encodes the entire m-block file F with an erasure code that tolerates a certain fraction of block losses. The server then spreads the encoded file blocks evenly over c drives and specifies a layout. To determine that the server respects this layout, the client requests c blocks of the file in a challenge, one from each drive. The server should be able to access the blocks in parallel from c drives, and respond to a query in time close to $\tau_\ell + \mathsf{L}$.

If the server answers most queries correctly and promptly, then blocks are spread out on disks almost evenly. A rigorous formalization of this idea leads to a bound on the fraction of file blocks that are stored on any t server drives. If the parameters of the erasure code are chosen to tolerate that amount of data loss, then the scheme is resilient against t drive failures.

To give a formal definition of the construction, we use a maximum distance separable (MDS), i.e., optimal erasure code with encoding and decoding algorithms ($\mathsf{ECEnc}, \mathsf{ECDec}$) and expansion rate $1+\alpha$. ECEnc encodes m-block messages into n-block codewords, with $n = m(1+\alpha)$. ECDec can recover the original message given any αm erasures in the codeword.

The scheme is the following:

- $\mathsf{Keygen}(1^\ell)$ outputs ϕ.
- $\mathsf{Encode}(\kappa, F = \{f_i\}_{i=1}^m, t, c)$ outputs $G = \{g_i\}_{i=1}^n$ with n a multiple of c and $G = \mathsf{ECEnc}(F)$.
- $\mathsf{Map}(n, t, c)$ outputs a balanced placement $\{C_j\}_{j=1}^c$, with $|C_j| = n/c$. In addition $\cup_{j=1}^c C_j = \{1, \ldots, n\}$, so consequently $C_i \cap C_j = \phi, \forall i \neq j$.
- $\mathsf{Challenge}(n, G, t, c)$ outputs $Q = \{i_1, \ldots, i_c\}$ consisting of c block indices, each i_j chosen uniformly at random from C_j, for $j \in \{1, \ldots, c\}$. (Here, we omit nonce ν.)
- $\mathsf{Response}(Q)$ outputs the response R consisting of the c file blocks specified by Q, and the timing T measured by the client.
- $\mathsf{Verify}(G, Q, R, T)$ performs two checks. First, it checks *correctness* of blocks returned in R using the file stored locally by the client[6]. Second, the client also checks the *promptness* of the reply. If the server replies within an interval $\tau_\ell + \mathsf{L}$, the client outputs 1.
- $\mathsf{Reconstruct}(\kappa, r, \{g_i^*\}_{i=1}^r)$ outputs the decoding of the file blocks retained by $\mathcal{S}$ (after a possible drive failure) under the erasure code: $\mathsf{ECDec}(\{g_i^*\}_{i=1}^r)$ for $r \geq m$, and $\perp$ if $r < m$.

The security analysis of the protocol is deferred to the full version of the paper [5]. Here we summarize the main result.

THEOREM 1. *For fixed system parameters c, t and α such that $\alpha \geq t/(c-t)$ and for constant network latency and constant block read time, the protocol satisfies the following properties for a cheap-and-lazy server $\mathcal{S}$:*
1. The protocol is complete: $\mathsf{Comp}^{\mathcal{RAFT}(t)}(m, \ell, t) = 1$.
2. If $\mathcal{S}$ uses $d < c$ drives, $\mathsf{Adv}_{\mathcal{S}}^{\mathcal{RAFT}(t)}(m, \ell, t) = 0$.
3. If $\mathcal{S}$ uses $d \geq c$ drives, $\mathsf{Adv}_{\mathcal{S}}^{\mathcal{RAFT}(t)}(m, \ell, t) \leq 1 - B(c, t, \alpha)$ *where* $B(c, t, \alpha) = \frac{\alpha(c-t)-t}{(1+\alpha)(c-t)}$.

Multiple-step protocols.

We can make use of standard probability amplification techniques to further reduce the advantage of a server. For example, we can run multiple steps of the protocol. A step for the client involves sending a c-block challenge, and receiving and verifying the server response. We need to ensure that queried blocks are different in all steps, so that the server cannot reuse the result of a previous step in successfully answering a query.

We define two queries Q and Q' to be *non-overlapping* if $Q \cap Q' = \emptyset$. To ensure that queries are non-overlapping, the client running an instance of a multiple-step protocol maintains state and issues only queries with block indices not used in previous query steps. We can easily extend the proof of Theorem 1 (3) to show that a q-step protocol with non-overlapping queries satisfies $\mathsf{Adv}_{\mathcal{S}}^{\mathcal{RAFT}(t)}(m, \ell, t) \leq (1 - B(c, t, \alpha))^q$ for a server $\mathcal{S}$ using $d \geq c$ drives.

5. NETWORK AND DRIVE TIMING MODEL

In the simple model of Section 4, we assume constant network latency between the client and server and a constant block-read time. Consequently, for a given query Q, the response time of the server (whether honest or adversarial) is deterministic. In practice, though, network latencies and block read times are variable. In this section, we present experiments and protocol-design techniques that can be used to adapt our simple RAFT protocol to more practical settings.

5.1 Network model

We present some experimental data on network latency between hosts in different geographical locations based on the Lumezanu et al. study [24], and quantify the amount of variance it exhibits over time. We discuss how our RAFT protocol can be made robust against variability in network latency. We also show how to reduce the communication complexity of our protocol—thereby eliminating network-timing variance due to fluctuations in network bandwidth.

[6]Recall we assume a copy of the file is kept by the client to simplify verification, though this is not necessary.

Network latency model.

Lumezanu et al. [24] present a study that measures the network latency between 1715 pairs of hosts at various time intervals within a two month period. Their goal is to study the occurrence and characteristics of triangle inequality violations in the Internet. In one of their experiments, they measure the variability of network latency among pairs of hosts over time. Their findings indicate that for about 88% of host pairs in their trace, the standard deviation of network latency is less than 100ms. Another metric of variability is the inter-quartile range of the latency distribution (defined as the difference between 75th and 25th percentiles). They show that less than 10% of the host pairs have inter-quartile higher than 40ms, suggesting that the variance in network latency is caused by outliers farther away from the mean, rather than values closer to the mean.

For our purposes, we are interested in estimating the maximum difference between round-trip times observed at various times between the same pair of hosts. While the study does not give us directly an estimate for this metric, we can approximate the 99th percentile of the difference, for instance, by three standard deviations, i.e., 300ms (which for the normal distribution cover 99.7% of the distribution).

To validate this choice of parameters, we perform our own small-scale experiments. We pinged two hosts (one in Santa Clara, CA, USA and one in Shanghai, China) from our Boston, MA, USA location during a one week interval in March 2010. We observed that the ping time distribution is heavy tailed with spikes correlated in time, most likely due to temporary network congestion.

The ping times to Santa Clara ranged from 86 ms to 463 ms, with 90th, 99th and 99.9th percentiles at 88ms, 95ms and 102ms, respectively. Ping times to Shanghai exhibit more variability across the larger geographical distance and range between 262 ms and 724 ms. While daily spikes in latency raise the average slightly, 90% of readings are still less than 278 ms. These spikes materially lengthen the tail of the distribution, however, as the 99% (433 ms) and 99.9% (530 ms) thresholds are no longer grouped near the 90% mark, but are instead much more spread out. To summarize, the 99th percentile of the difference in network latency is 9 ms for Santa Clara and 171 ms for Shanghai. The 99.9th percentile results in 16ms for Santa Clara, and 268ms for Shanghai. We believe therefore that a choice of three standard deviations (300ms) is a reasonable maximum variability in network latency we can set in our RAFT experiments.

In our RAFT protocol, we consider a response valid if it arrives within the maximum characterized network latency. We then adopt the bounding assumption that the difference between minimum and maximum network latency is "free time" for an adversarial server. That is, during a period of low latency, the adversary might simulate high latency, using the delay to cheat by prefetching file blocks from disk into cache. This strategy would help the server respond to subsequent protocol queries faster, and help conceal poor file-block placement. If the amount of data which can be read during this "free time" is small compared to the size of the file, the effect is insignificant. We quantify this precisely in the full version of the paper [5].

Limited network bandwidth.

In the basic protocol from Section 4, challenged blocks are returned to the client as part of the server's response. To minimize the bandwidth used in the protocol, the server can simply apply a cryptographically strong hash to its response blocks together with a nonce supplied by the client, and return the resulting digest. The client can still verify the response, by recomputing the hash value locally and comparing it with the response received from the server.

5.2 Drive model

We now look to build a model for the timing characteristics of magnetic hard drives. While block read times exhibit high variability due to both physical factors and prefetching mechanisms, we show that for a judicious choice of block size (64KB on a typical drive), read times adhere to a stable probability distribution. This observation yields a practical drive model for RAFT.

Drive characteristics.

Magnetic hard drives are complex mechanical devices consisting of multiple platters rotating on a central spindle at speeds of up to 15,000 RPM for high-end drives today. The data is written and read from each platter with the help of a disk head sensing magnetic flux variation on the platter's surface. Each platter stores data in a series of concentric circles, called tracks, divided further into a set of fixed-size (512 byte) sectors. Outer tracks store more sectors than inner tracks, and have higher associated data transfer rates.

To read or write to a particular disk sector, the drive must first perform a *seek*, meaning that it positions the head on the right track and sector within the track. Disk manufacturers report average seek times on the order of 2 ms to 15 ms in today's drives. Actual seek times, however, are highly dependent on patterns of disk head movement. For instance, to read file blocks laid out in sequence on disk, only one seek is required: That for the sector associated with the first block; subsequent reads involve minimal head movement. In constrast, random block accesses incur a highly variable seek time, a fact we exploit for our RAFT construction.

After the head is positioned over the desired sector, the data is read from the platter. The data transfer rate (or throughput) depends on several factors, but is on the order of 300MB per second for high-end drives. The disk controller maintains an internal cache and implements complex caching and prefetching policies. As drive manufacturers give no clear specifications of these policies, it is difficult to build general data access models for drives [30].

The numbers we present in this paper are derived from experiments performed on a number of enterprise class SAS drives, all connected to a single machine running Red Hat Enterprise Linux WS v5.3 x86_64. We experimented with drives from Fujitsu, Hitachi, HP[7], and Seagate. Complete specifications for each drive can be found in Table 1.

Modeling disk-access time.

Our basic RAFT protocol is designed for blocks of fixed-size, and assumes that block read time is constant. In reality, though block read times are highly variable, and depend on both physical file layout and drive-read history. Two complications are particularly salient: (1) Throughput is highly dependent on the absolute physical position of file blocks on disk; in fact, outer tracks exhibit up to 30% higher transfer rates than inner tracks [29] and (2) The transfer rate for a series of file blocks depends upon their relative position; reading of sequentially positioned file blocks requires no seek, and is hence much faster than for scattered blocks.

We are able, however, to eliminate both of these sources of read-time variation from our RAFT protocol. The key idea is to *render seek time the dominant factor* in a block access time. We accomplish this in two ways: (1) We read *small* blocks, so that seek time

[7]Upon further inspection, the HP drive is actually manufactured by Seagate. Nearly all drives available today are in fact made by one of three manufacturers.

Manufacturer	Model	Capacity	Buffer Size	Avg. Seek / Full Stroke Seek	Latency	Throughput
Hitachi	HUS153014VLS300	147 GB	16 MB	3.4 ms./ 6.5 ms.	2.0 ms.	72 - 123 MB/sec
Seagate	ST3146356SS	146 GB	16 MB	3.4 ms./6.43 ms.	2.0 ms.	112 - 171 MB/sec
Fujitsu	MBA3073RC	73.5 GB	16 MB	3.4 ms./8.0 ms.	2.0 ms.	188 MB/sec
HP	ST3300657SS	300 GB	16 MB	3.4 ms./6.6 ms.	2.0 ms.	122 - 204 MB/sec

Table 1: Drive specifications

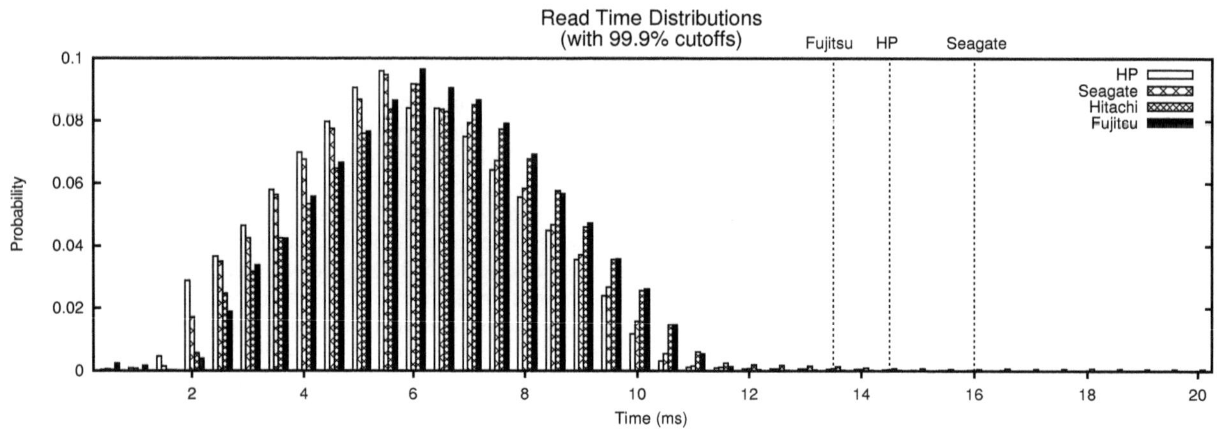

Figure 2: Read time distribution for 64KB blocks

dominates read time and (2) We access a *random* pattern of file blocks, to force the drive to perform a seek of comparable difficulty for each block.

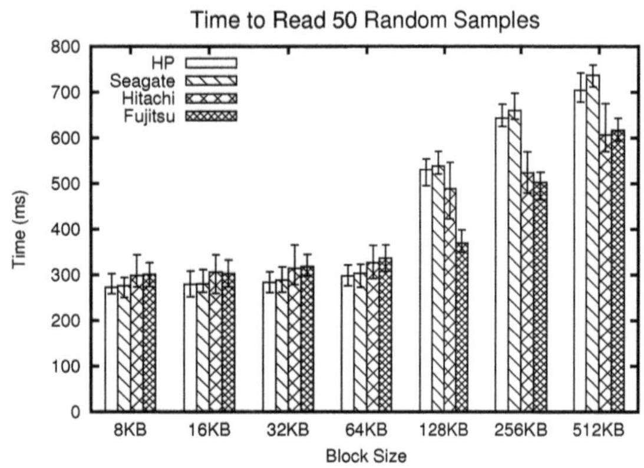

Figure 3: Read time for 50 random blocks

As Figure 3 shows, the time to sample a fixed number of random blocks from a 2GB file is roughly constant for blocks up to 64KB, regardless of drive manufacturer. We suspect that this behavior is due to prefetching at both the OS and hard drive level. Riedel et al. also observe in their study [29] that the OS issues requests to disks for blocks of logical size 64KB, and there is no noticeable difference in the time to read blocks up to 64KB.

For our purposes, therefore, a remote server can read 64KB random blocks at about the same speed as 8K blocks. If we were to sample blocks smaller than 64KB in our RAFT protocol, we would give an advantage to the server, in that it could prefetch some additional file blocks essentially for free. For this reason, we choose to use 64KB blocks in our practical protocol instantiation.

Figure 2 depicts the read time distributions for a random 64KB block chosen from a 2GB file. To generate this distribution, 250 random samples were taken from a 2GB file. The read time for each request was recorded. This was repeated 400 times, for a total of 100,000 samples, clearing the system memory and drive buffer between each test. The operating system resides on the Hitachi drive, and occasionally contends for drive access. This causes outliers in the tests (runs which exceed 125% of average and contain several sequential reads an order of magnitude larger than average), which were removed. Additional tests were performed on this drive to ensure the correctness of the results. By comparison, the variability between runs on all other drives was less than 10%, further supporting the OS-contention theory.

While the seek time average for a single block is around 6 ms, the distribution exhibits a long tail, with values as large as 132 ms. (We truncate the graph at 20 ms for legibility.) This long tail does not make up a large fraction of the data, as indicated by the 99.9% cutoffs in figure 2, for most of the drives. The 99.9% cutoff for the Hitachi drive is not pictured as it doesn't occur until 38 ms. Again, we expect contention from the OS to be to blame for this larger fraction of slow reads on that drive.

Read times for blocks of this size are dominated by seek time and not affected by physical placement on disk. We confirmed this experimentally by sampling from many files at different locations on disk. Average read times between files at different locations differed by less than 10%. The average seek time for 64KB blocks does, however, depend on the size of the file from which samples are being taken, as shown in Figure 4.

We observe that the average block read time increases with the file size, due to more head movement. While this relationship is fairly linear above a certain point (close to 40MB files), small files exhibit significantly reduced average block read times, likely due to the disk buffer. Once the file is small enough to fit in the disk buffer, the drive will respond from its cache without performing the

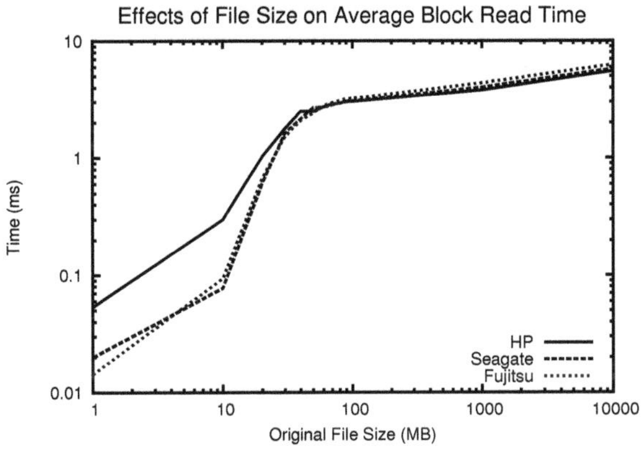

Figure 4: Effects of file size on average block retrieval time

physical seek, returning data much more quickly. This indicates that RAFTs will not work for files smaller than the combined disk buffer sizes of the drives being used to store the file, an hypothesis we confirm in our experimental evaluation.

In the next section, we modify our basic protocol to smooth out seek-time variance. The idea is to sample (seek) many randomly chosen file blocks in succession.

6. PRACTICAL RAFT PROTOCOL

In this section, we propose a practical variant of the basic RAFT protocol from Section 4. As discussed, the main challenge in practical settings is the high variability in drive seek time. The key idea in our practical RAFT here is to smooth out the block access-time variability by requiring the server to access multiple blocks per drive to respond to a challenge.

In particular, we structure queries here in multiple *steps*, where a step consists of a set of file blocks arranged such that an (honest) server must fetch one block from each drive. We propose in this section what we call a *lock-step protocol* for disk-block scheduling. This lock-step protocol is a non-interactive, multiple-step variant of the basic RAFT protocol from Section 4. We show experimentally that for large enough files, the client can, with high probability, distinguish between a correct server and an adversarial one.

6.1 The lock-step protocol

A naïve approach to implementing a multiple-step protocol with q steps would be for the client to generate q (non-overlapping) challenges, each consisting of c block indices, and send all qc distinct block indices to the server. The problem with this approach is that it immediately reveals complete information to the server about all queries. By analogy with job-shop scheduling [26], the server can then map blocks to drives to shave down its response time. In particular, it can take advantage of drive efficiencies on reads ordered by increasing logical block address [32]. Our lock-step technique reveals query structure incrementally, and thus avoids giving the server an advantage in read scheduling. Another possible approach to creating a multi-step query would be for the client to specify steps interactively, i.e., specify the blocks in step $i+1$ when the server has responded to step i. That would create high round complexity, though. The benefit of our lock-step approach is that it generates steps unpredictably, but non-interactively.

The lock-step approach works as follows. The client sends an initial one-step challenge consisting of c blocks, as in the basic RAFT protocol. As mentioned above, to generate subsequent steps non-interactively, we use a Fiat-Shamir-like heuristic [12] for signature schemes: The block indices challenged in the next step depend on all the block contents retrieved in the current step (a "commitment"). To ensure that block indices retrieved in next step are unpredictable to the server, we compute them by applying a cryptographically strong hash function to all block contents retrieved in the current step. The server only sends back to the client the final result of the protocol (computed as a cryptographic hash of all challenged blocks) once the q steps of the protocol are completed.

The lock-step protocol algorithms Keygen, Encode, Map, and Reconstruct are similar to our basic RAFT. Let h be a cryptographically secure hash function with fixed output (e.g., from the SHA-2 family). Assume for simplicity that the logical placement generated by Map in the basic RAFT protocol is $C_j = \{jn/c, jn/c+1, \ldots, jn/c+n/c-1\}$. We use c suitable hash functions that output indices in C_j: $h_j \in \{0,1\}^* \rightarrow C_j$. (In practice, we might take $h_j(x) = h(\tilde{j}||x) \mod C_j$, where $\tilde{j}$ is a fixed-length index encoding.)

The Challenge, Response, and Verify algorithms of the lock-step protocol with q steps are the following:

- In Challenge(n, G, t, c), the client sends an initial challenge $Q = (i_1^1, \ldots, i_c^1)$ with each i_j^1 selected randomly from C_j, for $j \in \{1, \ldots, c\}$, along with random nonce $\nu \in_U \{0,1\}^l$.

- Algorithm Response(Q) consists of the following steps:

1. $\mathcal{S}$ reads file blocks $f_{i_1^1}, \ldots, f_{i_c^1}$ specified in Q.

2. In each step $r = 2, \ldots, q$, $\mathcal{S}$ computes $i_j^r \leftarrow h_j(i_1^{r-1}||\ldots||i_c^{r-1}||f_{i_1^{r-1}}||\ldots||f_{i_c^{r-1}}||h(\nu, j))$. If any of the block indices i_j^r have been challenged in previous steps, $\mathcal{S}$ increments i_j^r by one (in a circular fashion in C_j) until it finds a block index that has not yet been retrieved. $\mathcal{S}$ schedules blocks $f_{i_j^r}$ for retrieval, for all $j \in \{1, \ldots, c\}$.

3. $\mathcal{S}$ sends response $R = h(f_{i_1^1}||\ldots||f_{i_c^1}||\ldots||f_{i_1^q}||\ldots||f_{i_c^q}||\nu)$ to the client, who measures the time T from the moment when challenge Q was sent.

- In Verify(G, Q, R, T), the client checks first correctness of R by recomputing the hash of all challenged blocks, and comparing the result with R. The client also checks the timing of the reply T, and accepts the response to be prompt if it falls within some specified time interval (experimental choice of time intervals within which a response is valid is dependent on drive class and is discussed in Section 6.2 below).

Security of lock-step protocol. We omit a formal analysis. Briefly, derivation of challenge values from (assumed random) block content ensures the unpredictability of challenge elements across steps in Q. $\mathcal{S}$ computes the final challenge result as a cryptographic hash of all qc file blocks retrieved in all steps. The collision-resistance of h implies that if this digest is correct, then intermediate results for all query steps are correct with overwhelming probability.

6.2 Experiments for the lock-step protocol

In this section, we perform experiments to determine the number of steps needed in the lock-step protocol to distinguish an honest server using c drives from an adversarial server employing $d < c$ drives. As discussed in Section 3.3, we evaluate both servers that "reserve" drives for RAFT testing, as well as services operating under contention.

6.2.1 *Reserved drive model*

We begin by looking at the "reserved" drive model, which we can test locally. The first question we attempted to answer with our tests is if we are able to distinguish an honest server from an adversarial

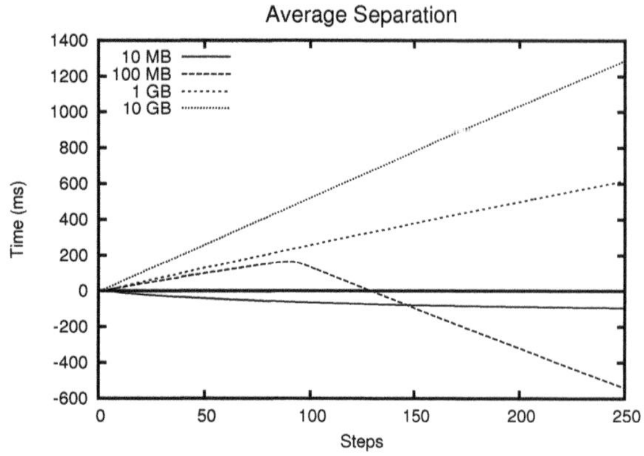

Figure 5: Average difference between adversarial and honest response times in a challenge

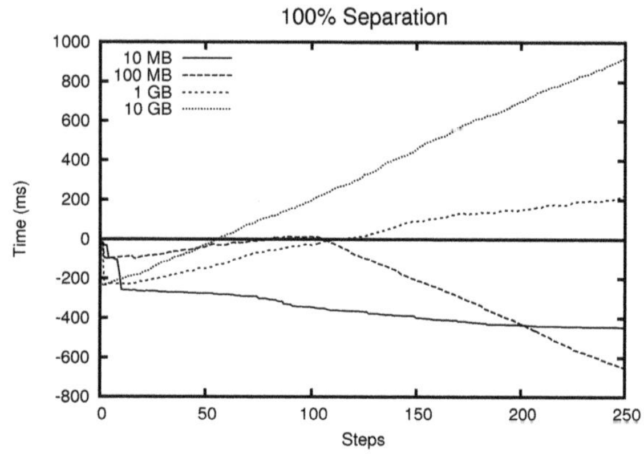

Figure 6: Complete separation of adversarial and honest response times in a challenge

one employing fewer drives based only on disk access time. Is there a range where this can be done, and how many steps in the lock-step protocol must we enforce to achieve clear separation? Intuitively, the necessity for an adversarial server employing $d \leq c-1$ drives to read at least two blocks from a single drive in each step forces the adversary to increase its response time when the number of steps performed in the lock-step protocol increases.

Detailed experiments for $c = 3$ drives.

In practice, files are not typically distributed over a large number of drives (since this would make meta-data management difficult). Here, we focus on the practical case of $c = 3$. The file sizes presented are those of the original file before encoding and splitting across drives. Files are encoded to survive one drive failure in the honest server case and are evenly spread over the available drives. The adversarial server must store the same total amount of information in order to respond to challenges, but does so using one fewer drive than the honest server. The adversarial server spreads the encoded file evenly across two drives and must perform a double read from one of the drives in each step of the lock-step protocol.

For each file size, we performed 200 runs of the protocol for both the honest and adversarial servers. The honest server stores data on the HP, Seagate, and Fujitsu drives, while the adversary uses only the HP and Seagate drives. We show in Figure 5 the average observed difference between the adversarial and honest servers' time to reply to a challenge as a function of the number of steps in the protocol. In Figure 6, we show the 100% separation between the honest and adversarial servers defined as the difference between the minimum adversarial response time and the maximum honest response time in a challenge. Where the time in the graph is negative, an adversary using two drives could potentially convince the client that he is using three drives as promised.

One way for the adversary to cheat is to ignore the protocol entirely and instead read the whole file sequentially into memory and then respond to challenges. In the 10 MB file case this becomes the optimal strategy almost immediately, and thus both the average and complete separation graphs are entirely negative. For the 100 MB file this strategy becomes dominant around 100 steps. At this point, reading the file sequentially becomes faster than performing 100 random seeks. The turning point for the larger files is much higher and thus not visible in these graphs. Since an adversary can choose how to respond to the challenges, and may in fact read the file into memory to answer queries, a RAFT will only be effective for relatively large files.

We plot in Figures 7-10 the actual read-time histograms for both honest and adversarial servers for the shown number of steps in the lock-step protocol. Using 10 steps for the 10 MB file achieves no separation between honest and adversarial servers, due to the fact that the file fits completely in the disk buffer (running for more steps would only benefit the adversary). For a 100MB file, there is a small separation (of 14ms) between the adversarial and honest servers at 100 steps.[8] On the other hand, an honest server can respond to a 175 step challenge on a 1 GB file in roughly one second, a task which takes an adversary almost 400 ms more, and with 250 steps over a 10 GB file we can achieve nearly a second of separation between honest and adversarial servers. As discussed in Section 5.1, this degree of separation is sufficient to counteract the variability in network latency encountered in wide area networks. As such, a RAFT protocol is likely to work for files larger than 100MB when the latency between the client and cloud provider experiences little variability, and for files larger than 1GB when there is highly variable latency between the client and cloud provider.

Simulated experiments for $c > 3$ drives.

We have been comparing in all our experiments so far an honest server using $c = 3$ drives to an adversary using $d = 2$ drives. We now perform some simulations to test the effect of the number of drives the file is distributed across on the protocol's effectivness. Figure 11 shows, for different separation thresholds (given in milliseconds), the number of steps required in order to achieve 95% separation between the honest server's read times and an adversary's read times for a number of drives c ranging from 3 to 11. The honest server stores a 1 GB file, encoded for resilience to one drive failure, evenly across the available number of drives, while the adversarial server stores the same file on only $c - 1$ drives, using a balanced allocation across its drives optimized given the adversary's knowledge of Map.

The graph shows that the number of steps that need to be performed for a particular separation threshold increases linearly with the number of drives c used by the honest server. In addition, the number of steps for a fixed number of drives also increases with larger separation intervals. To distinguish between an honest server using 5 drives and an adversarial one with 4 drives at a 95% sepa-

[8]Running more than 100 steps for a 100 MB file would not benefit us here as the adversary would simply switch to a strategy of reading the entire file into memory and then answering the challenge from memory.

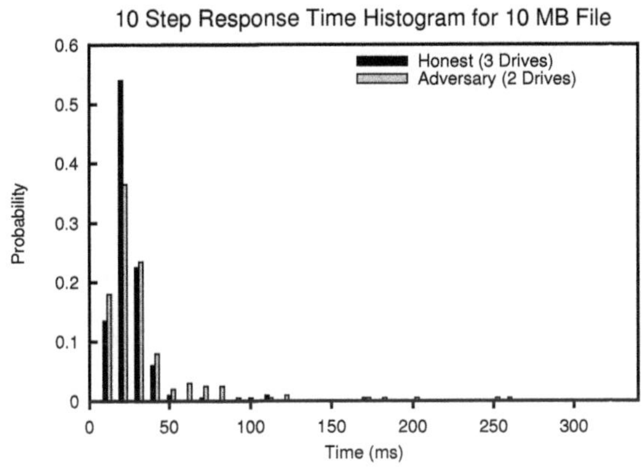

Figure 7: Read-time histogram at 10 steps for a 10 MB file

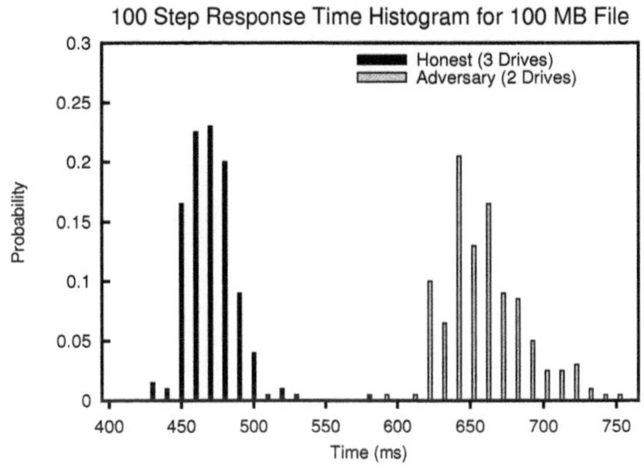

Figure 8: Read-time histogram at 100 steps for a 100 MB file

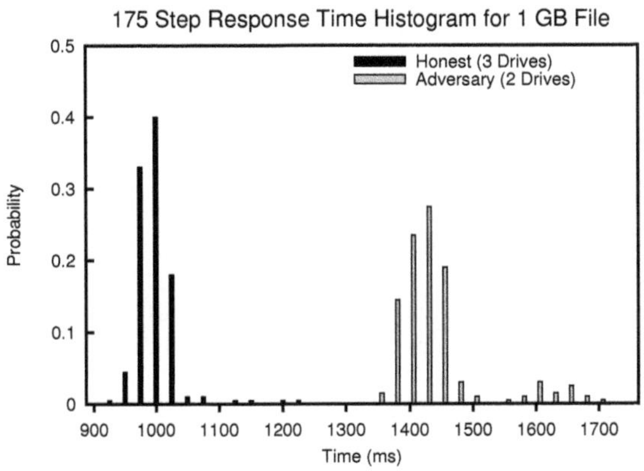

Figure 9: Read-time histogram at 175 steps for a 1 GB file

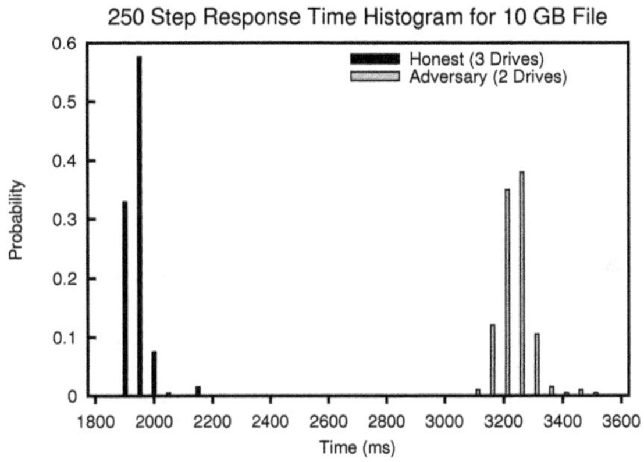

Figure 10: Read-time histogram at 250 steps for a 10 GB file

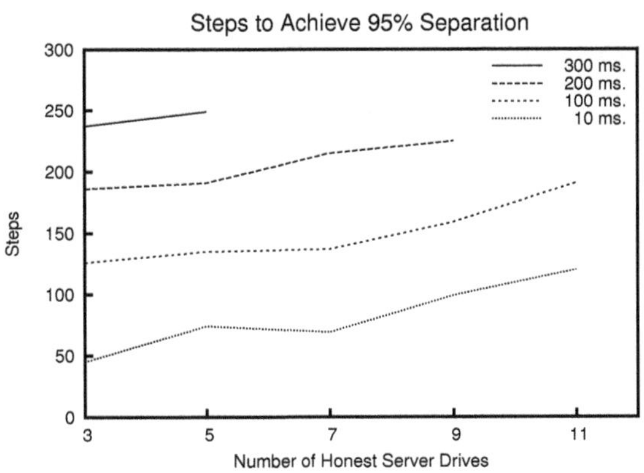

Figure 11: Effect of drives and steps on separation

ration threshold of 100ms, the lock-step protocol needs to use less than 150 steps. On the other hand, for a 300ms separation threshold, the number of steps increases to nearly 250.

More powerful adversaries.

In the experiments presented thus far we have considered an "expected" adversary, one that uses $d = c - 1$ drives, but allocates file blocks on disks evenly. Such an adversary still needs to perform a double read on at least one drive in each step of the protocol. For this adversary, we have naturally assumed that the block that is a double read in each step is stored equally likely on each of the $c - 1$ drives. As such, our expected adversary has limited ability to select the drive performing a double read.

One could imagine a more powerful adversary that has some control over which drive performs a double read. As block read times are variable, the adversary would ideally like to perform the double read on the drive that completes the first block read fastest (in order to minimize its total response time). We implement such a powerful adversary by storing a full copy of the encoded file on each of the $d = c - 1$ drives available. In each step of the protocol, the adversary issues one challenge to each drive, and then the fourth challenged block to the drive that completes first.

We performed some experiments with a 2GB file. We implemented the honest server using all four of our test drives and issuing a random read to each in each step of the protocol. We then removed the OS drive (Hitachi) from the set, and implemented both the expected and the powerful adversaries with the remaining (fastest) three drives. We show in Figure 12 the average time to respond to a challenge for an honest server using $c = 4$ drives, as well as for the expected and powerful adversaries using $d = 3$ drives (the time shown includes the threading overhead needed to issue blocking read requests to multiple drives simultaneously, as well as the time to read challenged blocks from disk).

The results demonstrate that even if a powerful adversarial server is willing to store triple the necessary amount of data, it is still distinguishable from an honest server with a better than 95% probability using only a 100-step protocol. Moreover, the number of false

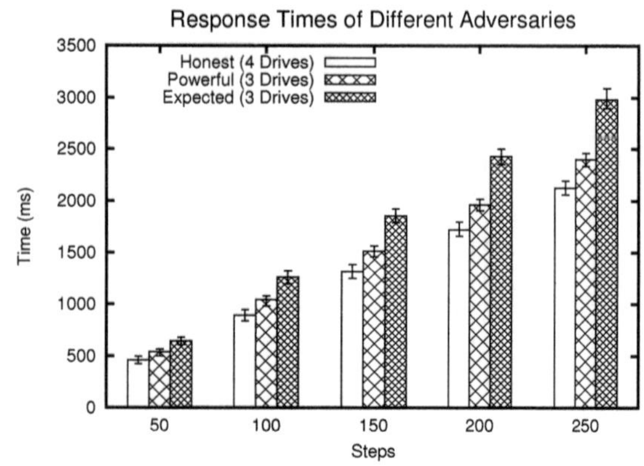

Figure 12: Time to complete lock-step protocol

negatives can be further reduced by increasing the number of steps in the protocol to achieve any desired threshold.

6.2.2 *Contention model*

We now turn to look at implementing RAFT in the face of contention from other users. For that, we performed tests on Mozy, a live cloud backup service. As confirmed by a system architect [19], Mozy does not use multi-tiered storage: Everything is stored in a single tier of rotational drives. Drives are not spun down and files are striped across multiple drives. An internal server addresses these drives independently and performs erasure encoding/decoding across the blocks composing file stripes. Given Mozy's use of a single tier of storage, independently addressable devices, and internal points of file-block aggregation and processing, we believe that integration of RAFT into Mozy and other similar cloud storage systems is practical and architecturally straightforward.

To demonstrate the feasibility of such integration, we performed a simple experiment. This experiment shows that even with no modification or optimization for RAFT, and in the face of contention from other users, it is possible to achieve a very basic RAFT-style demonstration that files span multiple drives.

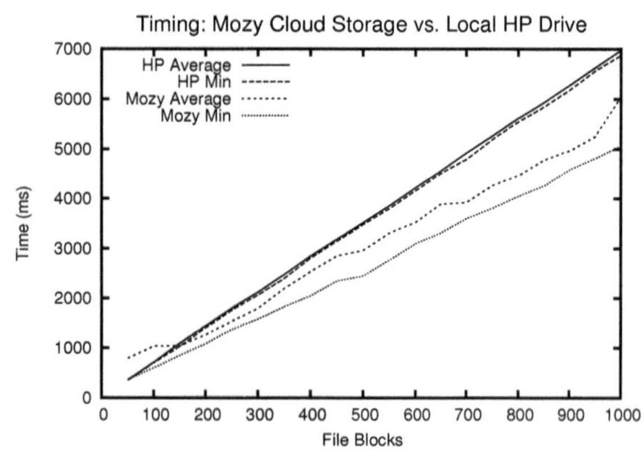

Figure 13: Comparing block retrieval on Mozy and a local drive

In this experiment, we had a remote client upload a large (64GB) file into Mozy. The client then issued several requests for randomly located bytes in the file.[9] The client measured the time required for Mozy to return the requested blocks. The time seen by the client also includes roughly 100 ms. of round-trip network latency (measured by pinging the Mozy servers). For comparison, we ran the same tests locally on the HP drive and report the results in Figure 13. Once the number of requested blocks is greater than 150, Mozy is able to retrieve the blocks and transmit them over the network faster than our local drive can pull them from disk. For example, 500 requested blocks were returned from Mozy in 2.449 seconds. By comparison, the same task took 3.451 seconds on the HP drive. Mozy consistently retrieved the blocks 15% faster (and occasionally up to 30% faster) than would be consistent with the use of a single, high-performance drive. Even with *no modification* to Mozy, we are already able to demonstrate with a RAFT like protocol that Mozy distributes files across at least two drives.

Of course, with an integrated RAFT system in Mozy, we would expect to achieve a stronger (i.e., higher) lower bound on the number of drives in the system, along with a proof of resilience to drive crashes. RAFT's suitability for Mozy promises broader deployment opportunities in cloud infrastructure.

7. RATIONAL SERVERS

The cheap-and-lazy server model reflects the behavior of an ordinary substandard storage provider. As already noted, an efficient RAFT is not feasible for a fully malicious provider. As we now explain, though, RAFTs can support an adversarial server model that is stronger than cheap-and-lazy, but not fully Byzantine. We call such a server *rational*. We show some RAFT constructions for rational servers that are efficient, though not as practical as those for cheap-and-lazy servers.

A rational server $\mathcal{S}$ aims to constrain within some bound the drive and storage resources it devotes to file F. Refer again to Experiment $\mathsf{Exp}_{\mathcal{S}}^{\mathcal{RAFT}(t)}(m, \ell, t)$ in Figure 1. Let $\rho(d, \{\mathcal{D}_j\}_{j=1}^d)$ be a *cost function* on a file placement $(d, \{\mathcal{D}_j\}_{j=1}^d)$ generated by $\mathcal{S}$ in this experiment. This cost function ρ may take into account d, the total number of allocated drives, and $|\mathcal{D}_j|$, the amount of storage on drive j. Let R denote an upper bound on ρ. We say that $\mathcal{S}$ is (ρ, R)-constrained if it satisfies $\rho(d, \{\mathcal{D}_j\}_{j=1}^d) \leq R$ for all block placements it generates. Roughly speaking, within constraint R, a rational server $\mathcal{S}$ seeks to maximize $\Pr[\mathsf{Acc}_{\mathcal{S}}]$. Subject to maximized $\Pr[\mathsf{Acc}_{\mathcal{S}}]$, $\mathcal{S}$ then seeks to maximize the fault-tolerance of F. Formally, we give the following definition:

DEFINITION 1. *Let p be the maximum probability $\Pr[\mathsf{Acc}_{\mathcal{S}}]$ that a (ρ, R)-constrained server $\mathcal{S}$ can possibly achieve. A (ρ, R)-constrained server $\mathcal{S}$ is* rational *if it minimizes $\Pr[\mathsf{NotFT}_{\mathcal{S}}]$ among all (ρ, R)-constrained servers $\mathcal{S}'$ with $\Pr[\mathsf{Acc}_{\mathcal{S}'}] = p$.*

A rational adversary can perform arbitrary computations over file blocks. It is more powerful than a cheap-and-lazy adversary. In fact, a rational adversary can successfully cheat against our RAFT scheme above. The following, simple example illustrates how a rational $\mathcal{S}$ can exploit erasure-code *compression*, achieving $t = 0$, i.e., no fault-tolerance, but successfully answering all challenges.

EXAMPLE 1. *Suppose that $\mathcal{S}$ aims to reduce its storage costs, i.e., minimize $\rho(d, \{\mathcal{D}_j\}_{j=1}^d) = \sum_j |\mathcal{D}_j|$. Consider a $\mathcal{RAFT}(t)$ with (systematic) encoding G, i.e., with $\{g_1, \ldots, g_m\} = \{f_1, \ldots, f_m\} = F$ and parity blocks $g_{m+1}, \ldots, g_n$. $\mathcal{S}$ can store $\{f_j\}_{j=1}^m$ individually across m disks $\{\mathcal{D}_j\}_{j=1}^m$ and* discard all parity blocks.

[9]We use bytes to ensure the requested block is on a single drive since we don't know the granularity with which Mozy stripes files.

To reply to a RAFT challenge, $\mathcal{S}$ retrieves every block of F (one per disk) and recomputes parity blocks on the fly as needed.

7.1 Incompressible erasure codes

This example illustrates why, to achieve security against rational adversaries, we introduce the concept of *incompressible* erasure codes. Intuitively, an incompressible file encoding / codeword G is such that it is infeasible for a server to compute a compact representation G'. I.e., $\mathcal{S}$ cannot feasibly compute G' such that $|G'| < |G|$ and $\mathcal{S}$ can compute any block $g_i \in G$ from G'. Viewed another way, an incompressible erasure code is one that lacks structure, e.g., linearity, that $\mathcal{S}$ can exploit to save space.[10]

Suppose that $\mathcal{S}$ is trying to create a compressed representation G' of G. Let $u = |G'| < n = |G|$ denote the length of G'. Given a bounded number of drives, a server $\mathcal{S}$ that has stored G' can, in any given timestep, access only a bounded number of file blocks / symbols of G'. We capture this resource bound by defining $r < n$ as the maximum number of symbols in G' that $\mathcal{S}$ can access to recompute any symbol / block g_i of G.

Formally, let $IEC = (\mathsf{ECEnc} : SK \times B^m \rightarrow B^n, \mathsf{ECDec} : PK \times B^n \rightarrow B^m)$ be an (n, m)-erasure code over B. Let $(sk, pk) \in (SK, PK) \leftarrow \mathsf{Keygen}(1^\ell)$ be an associated key-generation algorithm with security parameter ℓ. Let $A = (A_1, A_2^{(r)})$ be a memoryless adversary with running time polynomially bounded in ℓ. Here r denotes the maximum number of symbols / blocks that A_2 can access over G'.

Experiment $\mathsf{Exp}_A^{IEC}(m, n, \ell; u, r)$:
  $(sk, pk) \leftarrow \mathsf{Keygen}(1^\ell)$;
  $F = \{f_i\}_{i=1}^m \stackrel{R}{\leftarrow} B^m$;
  $G = \{g_i\}_{i=1}^n \leftarrow \mathsf{ECEnc}(sk, F)$;
  $G' \in B^u \leftarrow A_1(pk, G)$;
  $i \stackrel{R}{\leftarrow} Z_n$;
  $g \leftarrow A_2^{(r)}(pk, G')$;
  if $g = g_i$
    then output 1,
  else output 0

Figure 14: IEC Security Experiment

Referring to Figure 14, we have the following definition:

DEFINITION 2. *Let* $\mathsf{Adv}_A^{IEC}(m, n, \ell, u, r) = \Pr[\mathsf{Exp}_A^{IEC}(m, n, \ell; u, r) = 1] - u/n$. *We say that IEC is a* (u, r)-*incompressible code (for* $u < n$, $r < n$*) if there exists no* A *such that* $\mathsf{Adv}_A^{IEC}(m, n, \ell; u, r)$ *is non-negligible.*

In the full version of the paper [5], we prove the following theorem (as a corollary of a result on arbitrary (u, d)-incompressible IECs). It shows that given an IEC and a slightly modified query structure, a variant of our basic scheme, $\mathcal{RAFT}'(t)$, is secure against rational adversaries:

THEOREM 2. *For a* $\mathcal{RAFT}(t)$ *using a* $(n-1, d)$-*incompressible IEC, a* (ρ, R)-*constrained rational adversary* $\mathcal{S}$ *with* d *drives has advantage at most* $\mathsf{Adv}_{\mathcal{S}}^{\mathcal{RAFT}(t)}(m, \ell, t) \leq 1 - B(c, t, \alpha)$, *where* $B(c, t, \alpha)$ *is defined as in Theorem 1.*

We propose two constructions for incompressible erasure codes, with various tradeoffs among security, computational efficiency, and key-management requirements:

[10]Incompressibility is loosely the inverse of local decodability [22].

Keyed RAFTs Adopting the approach of [16, 21], it is possible to encrypt the parity blocks of G (for a systematic IEC) or all of G to conceal the IEC's structure from A. (In a RAFT, the client would compute Encode, encrypting blocks individually under a symmetric key κ—in practice using, e.g., a tweakable cipher mode [18].) Under standard indistinguishability assumptions between encrypted and random blocks, this transformation implies (u, r)-incompressibility for any valid $u, r < n$. While efficient, this approach has a drawback: Fault recovery requires use of κ, i.e., client involvement.

Digital signature with message recoverability A digital signature $\sigma = \Sigma_{sk}[m]$ with message recoverability on a message m has the property that if σ verifies correctly, then m can be extracted from σ. (See, e.g., [3] for PSS-R, a popular choice based on RSA.) We conjecture that an IEC such that $g_i' = \Sigma_{sk}[g_i]$ for a message-recoverable digital signature scheme implies (u, r)-incompressibility for any valid $u, r < n$. (Formal proof of reduction to signature unforgeability is an open problem.)

This RAFT construction requires use of private key sk to compute encoding G or to reconstruct G after a data loss. Importantly, though, it doesn't require use of sk to construct F itself after a data loss. In other words, encoding is keyed, but *decoding* is keyless.

The construction is somewhat subtle. A scheme that *appends* signatures that lack message recovery does not yield an incompressible code: A can throw away parity blocks and recompute them as needed provided that it retains all signatures. Similarly, applying signatures only to parity blocks doesn't work: A can throw away message blocks and recompute them on the fly.[11]

8. CONCLUSION

We have shown how to bring a degree of transparency to the abstraction layer of cloud systems in order to reliably detect drive-failure vulnerabilities in stored files. Through theory and experimentation, we provided strong evidence that our Remote Assessment of Fault Tolerance (RAFT) works in realistic settings. With careful parametrization, a RAFT can handle the real-world challenges of network and drive operation latency for large files (at least 100MB) stored on traditional storage architectures.

We believe that RAFT has a clear deployment path in systems such as Mozy, where a cloud server can request data in parallel from multiple drives and aggregate it before communicating with the client. Such infrastructure is likely common for providers offering fault-tolerant cloud storage. As we have shown, some level of data dispersion can already be evidenced in Mozy even without server-side modification. It remains an open problem to build a full end-to-end RAFT protocol integrated into an existing cloud infrastructure and demonstrate its feasibility in practice.

With their unusual combination of coding theory, cryptography, and hardware profiling, we feel that RAFTs offer an intriguing new slant on system assurance. RAFT design also prompts interesting new research questions, such as the modeling of adversaries in cloud storage systems, the construction of provable and efficient incompressible erasure codes, and so forth.

[11]Message-recoverable signatures are longer than their associated messages. An open problem is whether, for random F, there is some good message-recoverable signature scheme over blocks of G that has no message expansion. Signatures would be existentially forgeable, but checkable against the client copy of F.

Acknowledgments

We wish to extend our thanks to Burt Kaliski for his comments on an early draft of this paper, and to Erik Riedel for clearing up questions about hard drive operation. We also thank Tom Ristenpart for shepherding the paper and to the anonymous reviewers for their helpful comments.

9. REFERENCES

[1] D. G. Andersen, J. Franklin, M. Kaminsky, A. Phanishayee, L. Tan, and V. Vasudevan. FAWN: A fast array of wimpy nodes. In *Proc. ACM SOSP*, 2009.

[2] G. Ateniese, R. Burns, R. Curtmola, J. Herring, L. Kissner, Z. Peterson, and D. Song. Provable data possession at untrusted stores. In *Proc. ACM CCS*, pages 598–609, 2007.

[3] M. Bellare and P. Rogaway. The exact security of digital signatures: How to sign with RSA and Rabin. In U. Maurer, editor, *Proc. EUROCRYPT '96*, volume 1070 of *LNCS*, pages 399–416. Springer-Verlag, 1989.

[4] K. Bowers, A. Juels, and A. Oprea. HAIL: A high-availability and integrity layer for cloud storage. In *Proc. ACM CCS '09*, pages 187–198, 2009.

[5] K. D. Bowers, M. van Dijk, A. Juels, A Oprea, and R. Rivest. How to tell if your cloud files are vulnerable to drive crashes, 2010. IACR ePrint manuscript 2010/214.

[6] S. Brands and D. Chaum. Distance-bounding protocols (extended abstract). In *Proc. EUROCRYPT '93*, pages 344–359. Springer, 1993. LNCS vol. 765.

[7] A. Clements, I. Ahmad, M. Vilayannur, and J. Li. Decentralized deduplication in san cluster file systems. In *Proc. USENIX Annula Technical Conference*, 2009.

[8] J. Cox. T-Mobile, Microsoft tell Sidekick users we 'continue to do all we can' to restore data. *Network World*, October 13, 2009.

[9] R. Curtmola, O. Khan, R. Burns, and G. Ateniese. MR.PDP: Multiple-replica provable data possession. In *Proc. 28th IEEE ICDCS*, 2008.

[10] Y. Dodis, S. Vadhan, and D. Wichs. Proofs of retrievability via hardness amplification. In *Proc. TCC*, 2009.

[11] C. Dwork and M. Naor. Pricing via processing or combatting junk mail. In E.F. Brickell, editor, *Proc. CRYPTO '92*, pages 139–147. Springer, 1992. LNCS vol. 740.

[12] A. Fiat and A. Shamir. How to prove yourself: Practical solutions to identification and signature problems. In *Proc. CRYPTO'86*, volume 263 of *LNCS*, pages 186–194. Springer, 1986.

[13] T. Garfinkel, B. Pfaff, J. Chow, M. Rosenblum, and D. Boneh. Terra: a virtual machine-based platform for trusted computing. In *Proc. ACM SOSP*, pages 193–206, 2003.

[14] S. Ghemawat, H. Gobioff, and S.T. Leung. The Google file system. In *Proc. ACM SOSP*, pages 29–43, 2003.

[15] P. Golle, S. Jarecki, and I. Mironov. Cryptographic primitives enforcing communication and storage complexity. In *Proc. Financial Cryptography*, pages 120–135. Springer, 2002. LNCS vol. 2357.

[16] P. Gopalan, R. J. Lipton, and Y. Z. Ding. Error correction against computationally bounded adversaries, October 2004. Manuscript.

[17] The Hadoop distributed file system. `http://hadoop.apache.org/hdfs`.

[18] S. Halevi and P. Rogaway. A tweakable enciphering mode. In D. Boneh, editor, *Proc. CRYPTO'03*, volume 2729 of *LNCS*, pages 482–499. Springer, 2003.

[19] Mozy CTO J. Herlocker. Personal Communication, 2011.

[20] A. Juels and J. Brainard. Client puzzles: A cryptographic countermeasure against connection depletion attacks. In *Proc. ISOC NDSS*, pages 151–165, 1999.

[21] A. Juels and B. Kaliski. PORs–proofs of retrievability for large files. In *Proc. ACM CCS 2007*, pages 584–597, 2007.

[22] J. Katz and L. Trevisan. On the efficiency of local decoding procedures for error-correcting codes. In *Proc. STOC*, pages 80–86, 2000.

[23] R. Kotla, L. Alvisi, and M. Dahlin. Safestore: a durable and practical storage system. In *Proc. USENIX'07*, pages 10:1–10:14, Berkeley, CA, USA, 2007. USENIX Association.

[24] C. Lumezanu, R. Baden, N. Spring, and B. Bhattacharjee. Triangle inequality variations in the internet. In *Proc. ACM IMC*, 2009.

[25] R. Merkle. A certified digital signature. In *Proc. Crypto 1989*, volume 435 of *LNCS*, pages 218–238. Springer-Verlag, 1989.

[26] J.F. Muth and G.L. Thompson. *Industrial scheduling*. Prentice-Hall, 1963.

[27] M. Naor and G. N. Rothblum. The complexity of online memory checking. In *Proc. 46th IEEE FOCS*, pages 573–584, 2005.

[28] J. Ousterhout, P. Agrawal, D. Erickson, C. Kozyrakis, J. Leverich, D. Mazières, S. Mitra, A. Narayanan, G. Parulkar, M. Rosenblum, S. M. Rumble, E. Stratmann, and R. Stutsman. The case for RAMClouds: Scalable high-performance storage entirely in dram. *SIGOPS Operating Systems Review*, 43(4):92–105, 2009.

[29] E. Riedel, C. Van Ingen, and J. Gray. A performance study of sequential I/O on Windows NT 4.0. Technical Report MSR-TR-97-34, Microsoft Research, September 1997.

[30] C. Ruemmler and J. Wilkes. An introduction to disk drive modeling. *IEEE Computer*, 27(3):17–29, 1994.

[31] H. Shacham and B. Waters. Compact proofs of retrievability. In *Proc. Asiacrypt 2008*, volume 5350 of *LNCS*, pages 90–107. Springer-Verlag, 2008.

[32] B. L. Worthington, G. R. Ganger, and Y. N. Patt. Scheduling algorithms for modern disk drives. In *Proc. ACM Sigmetrics*, pages 241–251, 1994.

Sedic: Privacy-Aware Data Intensive Computing on Hybrid Clouds

Kehuan Zhang, Xiaoyong Zhou,
Yangyi Chen and XiaoFeng Wang
School of Informatics and Computing
Indiana University, Bloomington, IN, USA
{kehzhang, zhou, yangchen, xw7}@indiana.edu

Yaoping Ruan
IBM T.J. Watson Research Center
Hawthorne, NY, USA
yaoping.ruan@us.ibm.com

ABSTRACT

The emergence of cost-effective cloud services offers organizations great opportunity to reduce their cost and increase productivity. This development, however, is hampered by privacy concerns: a significant amount of organizational computing workload at least partially involves sensitive data and therefore cannot be directly outsourced to the public cloud. The scale of these computing tasks also renders existing secure outsourcing techniques less applicable. A natural solution is to split a task, keeping the computation on the private data within an organization's private cloud while moving the rest to the public commercial cloud. However, this *hybrid cloud computing* is not supported by today's data-intensive computing frameworks, *MapReduce* in particular, which forces the users to manually split their computing tasks. In this paper, we present a suite of new techniques that make such privacy-aware data-intensive computing possible. Our system, called *Sedic*, leverages the special features of MapReduce to automatically partition a computing job according to the security levels of the data it works on, and arrange the computation across a hybrid cloud. Specifically, we modified MapReduce's distributed file system to strategically replicate data, moving sanitized data blocks to the public cloud. Over this data placement, map tasks are carefully scheduled to outsource as much workload to the public cloud as possible, given sensitive data always stay on the private cloud. To minimize inter-cloud communication, our approach also automatically analyzes and transforms the reduction structure of a submitted job to aggregate the map outcomes within the public cloud before sending the result back to the private cloud for the final reduction. This also allows the users to interact with our system in the same way they work with MapReduce, and directly run their legacy code in our framework. We implemented Sedic on Hadoop and evaluated it using both real and synthesized computing jobs on a large-scale cloud test-bed. The study shows that our techniques effectively protect sensitive user data, offload a large amount of computation to the public cloud and also fully preserve the scalability of MapReduce.

Categories and Subject Descriptors

K.6.5 [**Security and Protection**]: Unauthorized access

General Terms

Security

Keywords

Cloud security, MapReduce, data privacy, computation split, automatic program analysis

CCS'11, October 17–21, 2011, Chicago, Illinois, USA.

1. INTRODUCTION

With the rapid growth of information within organizations, ranging from hundreds of gigabytes of satellite images to terabytes of commercial transaction data, the demands for processing such data are on the rise. Meeting such demands requires an enormous amount of low-cost computing resources, which can only be supplied by today's commercial cloud-computing systems: as an example, Amazon Elastic Compute Cloud (EC2) can easily handle terabytes of data at a price as low as 0.015 dollar per hour. This newfound capability, however, cannot be fully exploited without addressing the privacy risks it brings in: on one hand, organizational data contains sensitive information (e.g., financial data, health records, etc.) and therefore cannot be shared with the cloud provider without proper protection; on the other hand, today's commercial clouds do not offer high security assurance, a concern that has been significantly aggravated by the recent incidents of Amazon outages [13] and the Sony PlayStation network data breach [10], and tend to avoid any liability [36]. As a result, attempts to outsource the computations involving sensitive data are often discouraged.

A natural solution to this problem is cryptographic techniques for secure computation outsourcing, which has been studied for a decade [38, 17, 19, 16]. However, existing approaches are still not up to the challenge posed by data-intensive computing. For example, homomorphic encryption [30, 46, 49] was found to be prohibitively expensive for a large-scale computation [25]. As another example, the secret-sharing techniques underlying most outsourcing proposals can lead to intensive data exchanges between the share holders on different clouds during a computation involving an enormous amount of data, and are therefore hard to scale.

Secure hybrid-cloud computing. Oftentimes, a data-intensive computation involves both public and sensitive data. For example, a simple `grep` across an organizational file system encounters advertising slogans as well as lines of commercial secrets. Also, many data analysis tasks, such as intrusion detection [8], targeted advertising [14], etc., need to make use of the information from public sources, sanitized network traces and social-network data [9] for example, as well as information within an organization. If the computation on the public data can be separated from that on the sensitive data, the former can be comfortably delegated to the public commercial clouds and the latter, whose scale can be much smaller than the original task, will become much easier to handle within the organization. Such a split of computation is an effective first step to securely outsource computations and can be naturally incorporated into today's cloud infrastructure, in which a public cloud typically receives the computation "overflow" from an organization's internal system when it is running out of its computing resources. This way of computing, involving both the private cloud within an organization and the public commercial cloud, is called *hybrid cloud computing* [29]. The hybrid cloud has already been adopted by most organizational cloud users and is still undergoing a rapid development, with new techniques mushroomed to enable a smoother inter-cloud coordination (e.g. [18]). It also presents a new opportunity that makes practical, secure outsourcing of computation tasks possible.

However, today's cloud-based computing frameworks, such as *MapReduce* [22], are not ready for secure hybrid-cloud computing: they are designed to work on a single cloud and not aware of the presence of the data with different security levels, which forces cloud users to manually split and re-arrange each computation job across the public/private clouds. This lack of a framework-level support also hampers the reuse of existing data-processing code, and therefore significantly increases the cloud users' programming burden. Given the fact that privacy concerns have already become the major hurdle for a broader adoption of the cloud-computing paradigm [37], it is in urgent need to develop practical techniques to facilitate secure data-intensive computing over hybrid clouds.

Our work. To answer this urgent call, a new, generic secure computing framework needs to be built to support automatic splitting of a data-intensive computing job and scheduling of it across the public and private clouds in such a way that data privacy is preserved and computational and communication overheads are minimized. Also desired here is accommodation of legacy data-processing code, which is expected to run directly within the framework without the user's manual interventions. In this paper, we present a suite of new techniques that make this happen. Our system, called *Sedic*, includes a privacy-aware execution framework that automatically partitions a computing job according to the security levels of the data it involves, and distributes the computation between the public and private clouds. Sedic is based on MapReduce, which includes a "map" step and a "reduce" step: the map step divides input data into lists of key-value pairs and assigns them to a group of concurrently-running *mappers*; the reduce step receives the outputs of these mappers, which are intermediate key-value pairs, and runs a *reducer* to transform them into the final outputs. This way of computation is characterized by its simple structure, particularly the map operations that are performed independently and concurrently on different data records. This feature is leveraged by our execution framework to automatically decompose a computation on a mixture of public and sensitive data, which is actually difficult in general. More specifically, Sedic transparently processes individual data blocks, sanitizes those carrying sensitive information along the line set by the smallest data unit ("*record*") a map operation works on, and replicates these sanitized copies to the public cloud. Over those data blocks, map tasks are assigned to work solely on the public or sensitive data within the blocks. These tasks are carefully scheduled and executed to ensure the correctness of the computing outcomes and the minimum impacts on performance. In this way, the workload of map operations is distributed to the public/private clouds according to their available computing resources and the portion of sensitive data in the original dataset.

A significant technical challenge here is that reduction usually can not be done on private nodes and public nodes separately and only private nodes are suitable for such a task in order to preserve privacy. This implies that the intermediate outputs of computing nodes on the public cloud need to be sent back to the private cloud for reduction, which could bring in a significant communication overhead. To reduce such inter-cloud data transfer as well as move part of the reduce computation to the public cloud, we developed a new technique that automatically analyzes and transforms reducers to make them suitable for running on the hybrid cloud. Our approach extracts a *combiner* from the original reducer for preprocessing the intermediate key-value pairs produced by the public cloud, so as to compress the volume of the data to be delivered to the private cloud. This was achieved, again, by leveraging the special features of MapReduce: its reducer needs to perform a *folding* operation on a list, which can be automatically identified and extracted by a program analyzer embedded in Sedic. If the operation turns out to be associative or even commutative, as happens in the vast majority of cases[1] , the combiner can be built upon it and deployed to the public cloud to process the map outcomes. In our research, we implemented Sedic on *Hadoop* [28] and evaluated it over *FutureGrid* [40], a large-scale, cross-the-country cloud testbed. Our experimental results show that the techniques effectively protected confidential user data and minimized the workload of the private cloud at a small overall cost.

Contributions. The contributions of the paper are summarized as follows:

• *A new and user-transparent secure data-intensive computing framework.* We have developed the first hybrid-cloud based secure data-intensive computing framework. Our framework ensures that sensitive user data will not be exposed to the public cloud without the user's consent, while still letting the public cloud shoulder most of the computing workload when possible. Also important is the transparency our design offers, which enables cloud users to work on the framework in exactly the same way they use the original MapReduce. As a result, legacy MapReduce jobs can be directly executed within the framework. An additional benefit that comes with this transparency is the flexibility of our computing framework: not only can it outsource all non-sensitive map tasks, but our approach can also automatically move them back to the organization perimeter when necessary (e.g., when the public cloud suffers an outage). It is important to note that these properties are achieved when the scalability of MapReduce is fully preserved. This is by no means trivial given the complexity of this execution framework, which involves carefully-designed algorithms for achieving high performance, such as the replication strategies of its distributed file system, task assignment and scheduling and others.

• *Automatic reducer analysis and transformation.* We have built a new program analysis tool that automatically evaluates and transforms the reduction structure of a computing job to optimize it for hybrid-cloud computing. The tool breaks down a reducer into components that can work on the public and private clouds respectively, which not only moves part of the reduce computation away from the private cloud but also helps control the amount of the intermediate outcomes to be delivered back to the private cloud which could cause significant delay and bandwidth charges on today's cloud model. Since inter-cloud data transfers are known to be a bottleneck in cloud computing, the new techniques offer a critical support that makes secure hybrid-cloud computing practical.

• *Implementation and evaluation.* We have implemented our design and evaluated it over a large-scale cloud testbed, using both real and synthesized MapReduce jobs. Our experimental study demonstrates that the new techniques we propose are both effective and practical.

Sedic is designed to protect data privacy during map-reduce operations, when the data involved contains both public and private records. This protection is achieved by ensuring that the sensitive information within the input data, intermediate outputs and final results will never be exposed to untrusted nodes during the computation. Another important concern in data-intensive computing is integrity, i.e., whether the public cloud honestly performs a computing task and deliveries the right results back to the private cloud. We chose to address the confidentiality issue first, as it has

[1] As a prominent example, 10 out of all 11 examples coming with Hadoop distribution contain commutative and associative folding loops.

already impeded the extensive use of the computing resources offered by the public cloud [4]. By comparison, many cloud users today live with the risk that their computing jobs may not be done correctly on the public cloud. As a prominent example, the National Institutes of Health still prohibits outsourcing of the computation involving human DNA data to the commercial cloud, though the same tasks on non-human genomes has already been delegated to Amazon EC2 [35].

Roadmap. The rest of the paper is organized as follows. Section 2 outlines the high-level design of Sedic and also explicates our objectives and adversary model. Section 3 and 4 describes the details of our secure execution framework and code transformation tool, including our implementation of these techniques. Section 5 reports our experimental study that evaluates the performance of Sedic. Section 6 surveys related prior research. Section 7 discusses the limitation of our current design and possible future research, and Section 8 concludes the paper.

Table 1: Steps for a Privacy-Aware MapReduce

Users	• Label sensitive data, which can be done through a data-tagging tool (Section 3.1). • Submit to Sedic labeled data and a MapReduce job.
Sedic	• Analyze and transform the reduction structure of the job (Section 4). • Partition and replicate the data according to security labels (Section 3.1). • Create and schedule mappers across the public/private clouds (Section 3.2). • Combine the results on the public cloud and complete the reduction on the private cloud (Section 3.3).

2. OVERVIEW

In this section, we first explain the properties expected from Sedic and then present its high-level design and the adversary model used in our research.

2.1 Background and Design Objectives

MapReduce. MapReduce is a software framework for supporting data-intensive computing, such as web searching [22], document format conversion [43], genome sequence analysis [42, 34] and others. The computation within this framework first divides the input data into lists of key-value pairs and assigns them to a group of concurrently-running problem solvers, i.e., the mappers. Each mapper is iteratively invoked by the node that performs the computation (called *tasktracker* in Hadoop terminology) to convert an input pair into one or more intermediate key-value pairs. These pairs are fed into the reducers to transfer the pairs with the same key into a list of output pairs. Although conceptually simple, this computing framework includes a set of complicated mechanisms to ensure the scalability and fault tolerance during a computation, through replicating data and scheduling the map-reduce operations dynamically to nodes capable of undertaking the workloads. It also supports a user-defined combiner structure that allows the nodes running mappers to reduce the amount of the data that needs to be delivered to the reducers, thereby limiting bandwidth consumption. MapReduce has many open-source implementations, among which the most popular one is *Hadoop* [28]. Hadoop includes a distributed file system (HDFS) that offers reliable and high-performance storage services for MapReduce applications, and a runtime framework that manages MapReduce jobs through job submission control, task scheduling and fault tolerance. Another prominent implementation is Twister [27], which supports iterative MapReduce computations. With its distributed computing nature, MapReduce has been one of the most adopted application running on cloud.

Objectives. The original MapReduce framework does not support the operation over the hybrid cloud to process the data with different security levels. We developed Sedic to enhance MapReduce to make it suitable for performing a privacy-aware data intensive computing. More specifically, our system has been designed to achieve the following objectives:

• *High privacy assurance.* Only the public data, as indicated by the user, can be handed over to the public commercial cloud.

• *Moving workload to the public cloud when possible.* When the private cloud is about to run out of its computing resources, we need to move as much computation to the public cloud as possible, given the privacy of user data is preserved.

• *Scalability.* The system should preserve the scalability of the MapReduce framework. The overhead incurred by privacy protection should be kept low.

• *Limited inter-cloud data transfer.* Inter-cloud data transfer is traditionally deemed as a very expensive operation. The bandwidth offered by today's Internet cannot sustain intensive data exchanges during the computation involving a large amount of data.

• *Ease to use.* The system should be transparent to the users, keeping the MapReduce interfaces they are familiar with, and also support a convenient migration of legacy *jobs* (i.e, MapReduce programs) to the new execution framework. These jobs can either run without any modifications, or be converted to optimize their performance through automatic program transformation.

As discussed before, the MapReduce framework is highly complicated, employing various mechanisms to improve its performance. Therefore, it is challenging to build privacy protection into the framework to meet the above requirements without undermining its scalability. Here, we present a design that makes this happen, as illustrated in Figure 1. We also prototyped the design over Hadoop. The architecture and individual components of our system are surveyed in Section 2.2 and elaborated in Section 3 and 4.

2.2 Design

The design of Sedic is meant to be generic, supporting execution of not only the MapReduce job designed for it but also legacy jobs without altering the way the user interacts with the original MapReduce platform. It includes an execution framework and auxiliary tools. The framework performs privacy-aware map-reduce operations on the data with different security labels (either *sensitive* or *public*). The auxiliary tools are used to help cloud users label their data and transform the code of their MapReduce jobs for better performance. What is expected here is that one only needs to indicate which part of the data is sensitive, and the execution framework then takes over to automatically partition the data, create and schedule map tasks on the data according to its security labels over the public/private clouds, and strategically arrange the reduce tasks to minimize inter-cloud communication. The steps for performing such a privacy-aware MapReduce are summarized in Table 1.

Specifically, before submitting a MapReduce job to the execution framework, the user can run our data-tagging tool to locate sensitive data, for example, the content involving special strings like credit-card numbers, within her dataset, and mark such data items as "sensitive". The labeled data is then uploaded to the private cloud, which is connected to the public cloud through a virtual private network[2]. The distributed file system (DFS) of this hybrid cloud breaks the data into blocks according to their security labels and places them across the clouds strategically: the blocks containing public or sensitive data only are replicated to the public or private cloud respectively, while the others are propagated through two types of replicas, the original ones stored on the private cloud and the sanitized ones, which are cleaned of sensitive information, disseminated to the public cloud (Section 3.1). Over these data blocks, the private cloud creates map tasks, which are assigned to the nodes that host the data (Section 3.2). Such data replication and task assignment strategies, together our improvement on the execution mechanism of cloud nodes, ensure that the map tasks are computed correctly and efficiently. The results output by the nodes are delivered to the reducer to complete the computation (Section 3.3).

The reduce operation typically happens on the private cloud, as it inputs both public and sensitive data. This requires that all the mapping outcomes produced by the public cloud be transferred to the private cloud. To avoid the huge communication overhead incurred thereby and further move the computation to the public cloud, Sedic employs an automatic program analysis tool to evaluate and transform the reduction structure of a MapReduce job (Section 4). Specifically, when the user uploads her job, the tool is invoked to identify the loop within the reducer for folding the input key-value list. Once such an operation is found to be associative and commutative, which is often true for real MapReduce jobs, the loop is extracted to build a combiner and the rest of the reduce code is exported as a new reducer. The combiner is then deployed to the public cloud to pre-process mapping outcomes, which helps bring down the workload of the private cloud and reduce the volume of the data that needs to be sent to the new reducer.

2.3 Adversary Model

We consider an adversary who intends to acquire sensitive user information and has a full control of the public cloud. On the other hand, we assume that the private cloud is trustworthy: specifically, the adversary has no access to the nodes on the cloud and its underlying network, and therefore cannot launch such attacks as eavesdropping. Under this adversary model, Sedic is designed to ensure the confidentiality of a computation, though the powerful adversary can still compromise its integrity, i.e., rendering the outcomes of the computation incorrect. As discussed before, our focus on confidentiality is based on the observation that today's cloud users seem to be more willing to live with the risk of getting unreliable computing results than the threat to their private data. Finally, we assume that the absence of some records in the data blocks processed by the public cloud does not leak out information. Note that this is all that the adversary can see from a public node: Sedic ensures that the sensitive information in input/intermediate/output data never gets out of the privacy cloud.

3. THE EXECUTION FRAMEWORK

In this section, we elaborate our design of the privacy-aware execution framework within Sedic, as illustrated in Figure 1, and its implementation over Hadoop.

3.1 Data Labeling and Replication

Sensitive data labeling. As discussed before, to perform a privacy-aware MapReduce on her data, all a user needs to do is marking out the data she deems to be sensitive, and then submits the data and her computing job to Sedic, just as she would do when interacting with the original MapReduce platform. Data labeling can be done manually when only a very small amount of contiguous sensitive content is involved, or through a data-tagging tool that comes with Sedic. In our research, we implemented such a tool as a simple string scanner that searches a given dataset for the keywords or other text patterns that describe sensitive user information like social security numbers, credit-card numbers and others. Once the target is found, a security label is created to record the location of the information: the one built into our prototype is a tuple (⟨`filename, offset, length`⟩). Also, in the case that a dataset contains multiple files, individual files can be automatically labeled according to their access privileges within file systems. For example, all except those accessible to the public should be marked as sensitive data. All the labels for a dataset are included in a meta-data file, which is submitted, together with the dataset, to Hadoop Distributed File System (HDFS).

Data uploading. To compute over a dataset, a Hadoop user first needs to upload it to HDFS, which further places and replicates the data to the nodes across a cloud. Specifically, HDFS has two types of nodes: *namenode* that maintains the meta information of the whole file system, particularly the *inode* for each file that documents its attributes (file name, modification time, etc), and *datanode* that keeps the actual data. The data stored on the datanode is organized as *blocks*, each containing 64 MB by default. The locations of the blocks that belong to the same file are recorded by the `BlockInfo` array within the file's inode. To upload a file, the user first uses her Hadoop client to contact a namenode, which creates an inode for the file, locates an available block within HDFS and sends its whereabout back to the client. According to the information, the client communicates with the datanode hosting that block to transfer its data. If the size of the file exceeds 64 MB, the client continues to request blocks from the namenode, until all the data has been uploaded. This process also includes data replication, which we discuss later.

To protect private user data from the public cloud, which is not trusted, we modified the Hadoop client and HDFS to ensure that a file with some sensitive content are uploaded through the namenode on the private cloud. Specifically, the client first contacts such a node to build an inode for the file, which includes the security labels associated with the file. To this end, we extended Hadoop's `INodeFile` class by adding a new private field, `secureMeta`, which is an array for accommodating locations of sensitive data. The content of `secureMeta` is built upon the security labels: for each label, the namenode puts in the array the location of the data record that carries the sensitive content indicated by the label. According to such meta-data, whenever the client asks for storage to upload the data involving sensitive records, the namenode first allocates to it a data block from a private datanode, i.e., the one on the private cloud. The positions of these records are also given to the datanode as the meta-data of the block to protect the records from being disclosed during the follow-up replication process.

Data replication. The data uploading process always comes with replication, which HDFS uses for the purposes of performance enhancement and fault tolerance. For each block of user data a Hadoop client requests space for, a namenode tries to replicate it to multiple data blocks on different datanodes. The number of replicas, called *replication factor*, can be specified in a Hadoop configuration file and is set to 3 by default. The replication process starts from the first datanode receiving data from the client. One by one, the data is streamed to the next datanode selected by the namenode from the prior one. This operation can also be triggered by a periodic checking performed by HDFS: once a block is found to be under-replicated, the namenode allocates space and directs datanodes to make copies of it.

The replication mechanism used in Sedic improves over that of

[2] This can be done, for example, through Amazon Virtual Private Cloud [3] when the EC2 is used as the public cloud.

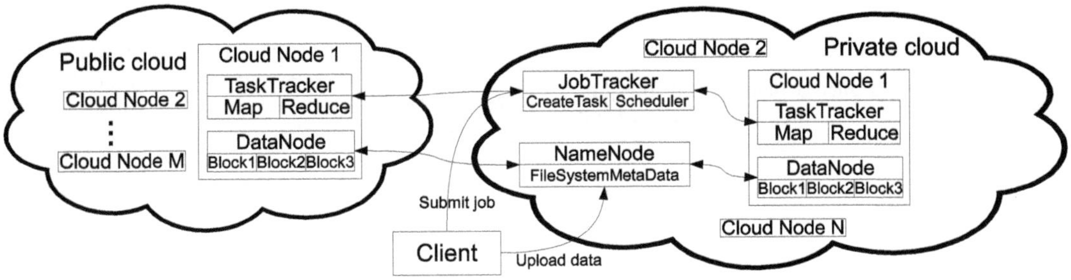

Figure 1: A Framework for Privacy-Aware MapReduce

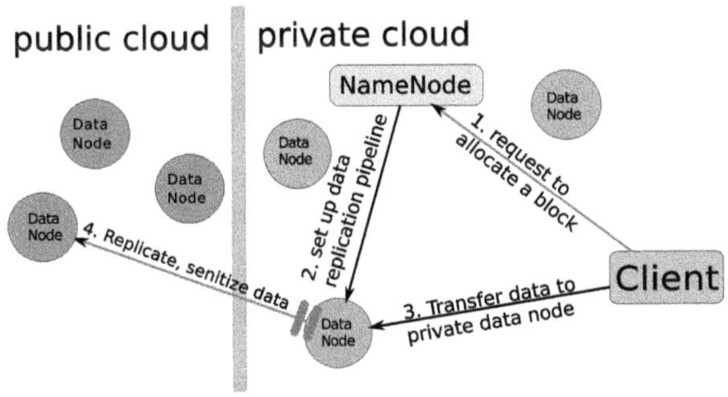

Figure 2: Data Replicate

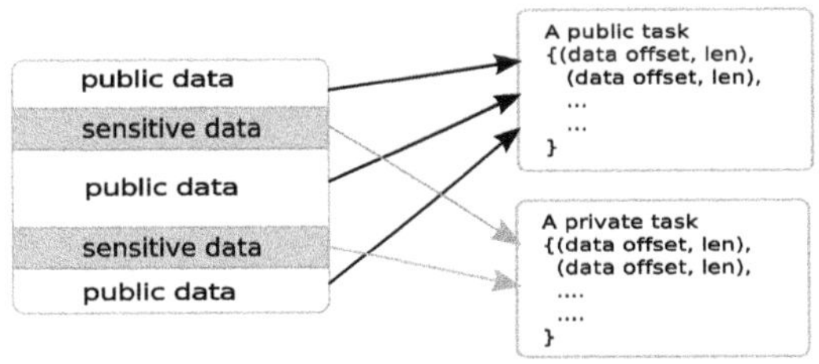

Figure 3: Task Management

Hadoop, making it suitable for operating on sensitive data in a hybrid cloud environment. Our approach ensures that the blocks with all sensitive data are only replicated to private datanodes. On the other hand, those with public data only are first sent to the public cloud, which causes the their follow-up replications more likely to happen there, due to the data locality strategy taken by Hadoop [28]. For the blocks with both public and sensitive data, the namenode first uses private datanodes to replicate them and then propagates their public data to the public nodes. This arrangement makes it possible to outsource the computation on the public data to the public cloud, while keeping the operations on the private data within the private cloud.

When replicating a data block, a private datanode copies not only the block but also its meta-data to the next node, if the recipient is also within the private cloud. Otherwise, the sender first zeros out all the sensitive records on the data block, according to the meta-data, before propagating it to a public datanode. The public node also receives the meta-data, which indicates the locations of the blank records within the block that should not be operated on. As a result of this replication, the blocks with both public and sensitive records get two types of replicas, the original versions and the sanitized ones. Figure 2 illustrates the replication process. Note that oftentimes, such an inter-cloud data transfer only happens when a new file is being uploaded, which places replicas on the public cloud. After that, the cloud user can run different jobs over this data placement. Actually, many users today already have their public data stored on the commercial cloud.

3.2 Map Task Management

Task creation and submission. After uploading data to HDFS, the client needs to submit a computing job, which includes the Java code for the mapper, reducer, other optional functions such as combiner and job configuration parameters, particularly the paths for the input and output files of the job. The node on the cloud that receives such a job is called *job submission node*. This node contains a *jobtracker* that works with the client to break the job into tasks before assigning them to the *tasktrackers* on a set of datanodes to run. More specifically, the client provides the jobtracker with a description of the map tasks over the data blocks of a file it submitted. Such a description is a list of `FileSplit` objects, with each of them associated with a map task. A `FileSplit` object carries two parameters, the offset for the start of a contiguous region within the file, a 64-MB block typically, and its length. A map task will process all the records within that block, from the beginning to the end.

To create the map tasks over the blocks with different security levels, we modified `InputSplit` to add in a security tag `sensitive`. This tag is set to sensitive when the block associated with a task carries all private content, and to public when it contains no secret at all. For the block with both types of data, a Sedic client generates two map tasks, one sensitive and one public. The offsets of these tasks point to where public or sensitive data begins and their length parameters describe the sizes of the contiguous content with the same security label within a block. To handle the block with several interleaved segments with disparate security levels, we changed `FileSplit` to specify multiple offset-length pairs. The idea is to use one map task to handle all public data of the block and the other to process the sensitive one. This treatment ensures the correctness of the keys produced by these two tasks, which often depend on the locations of individual records, as well as that of the values, since each of such segments carries integer number of records, the smallest data unit a mapper works on, as described before. The task creation is shown in Figure 3.

Task scheduling. Scheduling those map tasks to cloud nodes is done by the Hadoop jobtracker. Upon receiving a list of task descriptions, the jobtracker first creates `TaskInProgress` objects for the tasks on the list, and then assembles these objects into a `JobInProgress` queue. Whenever a "heartbeat" signal comes, indicating that a tasktracker of a node is ready to run a new task, the jobtracker looks up the queue and locates the most appropriate task for that node, the one whose data block is stored on the node, for example. This task scheduling process becomes privacy-sensitive in Sedic: we revised the jobtracker, which sits on the private cloud, to tag the `TaskInProgress` objects according to the `sensitive` fields within the `InputSplit` objects, and schedule the tasks based on their tags. Simply put, a sensitive task is always scheduled to a private datanode, which often hosts the related data block, while a public task is more likely to be handed over to a public datanode to outsource the map computation.

Task execution. A tasktracker assigned a map task by the jobtracker executes the task over the data block stored on its local host or downloaded from other nodes. In Hadoop, this proceeds as follows. The mapper reads a record from the block through a `RecordReader` object, which makes a socket connection to `DataXceiverServer`, a service maintained by the datanode that hosts the block. Each time a record is processed, the mapper gets the next one by calling the method `nextKeyValue` through the connection. This happens even when the block is co-located with the tasktracker on the same node.

A problem of this data-access mechanism is that it only reads contiguous data: whenever the read stops (e.g., due to the need of moving the read pointer to skip some data), HDFS discontinues the current connection. Given a data block often contains disconnected segments of public or sensitive data, a mapper has to call `seek` to adjust the read pointer after finishing its work on one segment, which interrupts connections. As a result, new connections need to be made continuously, which incurs a huge overhead. For example, establishing a connection takes `DataXceiverServer` (on the sender side) several hundred milliseconds to create a new `BlockSender` object for delivering data to `RecordReader` (on the receiver side).

Our solution to this problem is to read all the data segments the mapper needs within one block through a single connection. To this end, we modified `RecordReader` and `DataXceiverServer` to pass the offset-length pairs to `BlockSender`, which was also enhanced to perform both read and seek operations on a block file according to these pairs. This ensures that a connection will be torn down only after all required data is given to the mapper.

3.3 Reduction Planning

The scheduling of the reduce task poses yet another technical challenge. The reducer receives the outputs from the mappers running on sensitive data, and therefore cannot be directly executed on the public cloud. A straightforward solution here is to move all the map outcomes produced by the public cloud back to the private cloud. This, however, can incur a huge amount of inter-cloud communication, which we intend to avoid. For example, finding the TCP ports connected by each host requires a large number of port information to be transferred back to private cloud for reduce operations. Alternatively, we can carefully plan the scheduling of map tasks to ensure that the total amount of the map output to be generated by the public cloud does not exceed an upper limit set by the user according to the bandwidth she is willing to use and the delay she can tolerate. More specifically, the user is supposed to specify to Sedic the amount of output data produced by mapping one record and a threshold that represents the maximum amount of data to be sent from the public cloud to the private cloud. When scheduling a map task to a node on the public cloud, the jobtracker estimates the output volume the task will produce according to the size of the data it works on. Once the aggregated volume of the outsourced tasks is found to exceed the threshold, we stop moving computation to the public cloud. The problem of this simple treatment is that it constrains the amount of computation that can be undertaken by the public cloud.

More desired here is to let the public cloud perform part of the reduce operation, which not only cuts down the volume of the data that needs to be sent back, but also moves part of the computation away from the private cloud. What we can leverage are the properties of reducers: they all contain a fold loop that works on a list and in the vast majority of cases, such an operation is associative and commutative. Examples include counting the number of occurrences of a keyword in a large database and comparing the edit distances of different alignments to find the smallest one. For these reducers, Sedic extracts their loops to build combiners, which process the data on the public cloud and deliver their outcomes to the private cloud to complete the computation. Sedic provides an automatic program analysis tool that evaluates the source code of a reducer to determine its features and perform code transformation when necessary, which is elaborated in Section 4.

4. AUTOMATIC REDUCER ANALYSIS AND TRANSFORMATION

In this section, we present a suite of new techniques that optimize the reduction structure of a MapReduce job for secure and efficient computing of the job over a hybrid cloud. These techniques perform an automatic analysis and transformation on a reducer's Java source code, as soon as the job is submitted to the jobtracker, which enables the Sedic framework to schedule the reduce tasks in a way that minimizes the inter-cloud communication as well as the workload of the private cloud. Their design and implementation are elaborated below.

4.1 Automatic Analysis

The idea. The MapReduce computing framework has its origin in functional programming [23]. The reduce operation actually comes from *fold*, a high order function that aggregates elements on a list. Although the reducer of real-world job can be more complicated than fold, which is rather straightforward, it typically contains a fold component, in the form of a loop, to combine the values of the same keys from an input list. If the fold is associative, we can run it on the public cloud to partially process map outcomes. For example, given an associative fold $f([a_1, a_2, a_3, a_4, a_5, a_6]) = f([f([a_1, a_2]), f([a_3, a_4]), f([a_5, a_6])])$, we can outsource $f([a_1, a_2])$ and $f([a_5, a_6])$ to the pubic cloud if only a_3 and a_4 are sensitive. This move also helps reduce the communication overhead caused by sending the map outputs back to the private cloud, since the fold component partially combines these outputs. We can do even better when the fold is also commutative, which allows us to compute $f([a_1, a_2, a_5, a_6])$ on the public node in the above example. Actually, real-world reducers are often associative and commutative. In the cases they are not, their fold components typically have these properties. Figure 4 presents an example: although a reducer that calculates the mean of its input values is clearly not associative, its fold loop, which does the sum, is.

Before a fold operation can be outsourced, it needs to be analyzed to find out whether these desired properties are there. To see how to do this, let us first take a close look at the operation. Consider a list $[a_1, \cdots, a_n]$. A fold on the list can be described as $f([a_1, \cdots, a_n]) = g([g([\cdots g([g([a_1, a_0]), a_2]) \cdots]), a_n])$, where g is a function that works only on a two-element list and a_0 the initial value. Essentially, g describes the operation performed on a list member and an intermediate aggregation outcome at every iteration of the fold loop. If the operation is associative and commutative, so will be the whole fold loop. In other words, all we need to study here is what happens in a single iteration. In the rest of the section, we describe our analysis techniques, which first check the loop dependence of the fold and then evaluate the operation between a list member and the intermediate value in an iteration. We also prototyped our approach using Soot [11], a Java optimization framework.

Reducer analysis. The first step to analyzing a reducer is to locate its fold component. As discussed before, fold is typically performed through a loop in Java or other imperative programming languages. Actually, the loop is mandated by the reduce interface

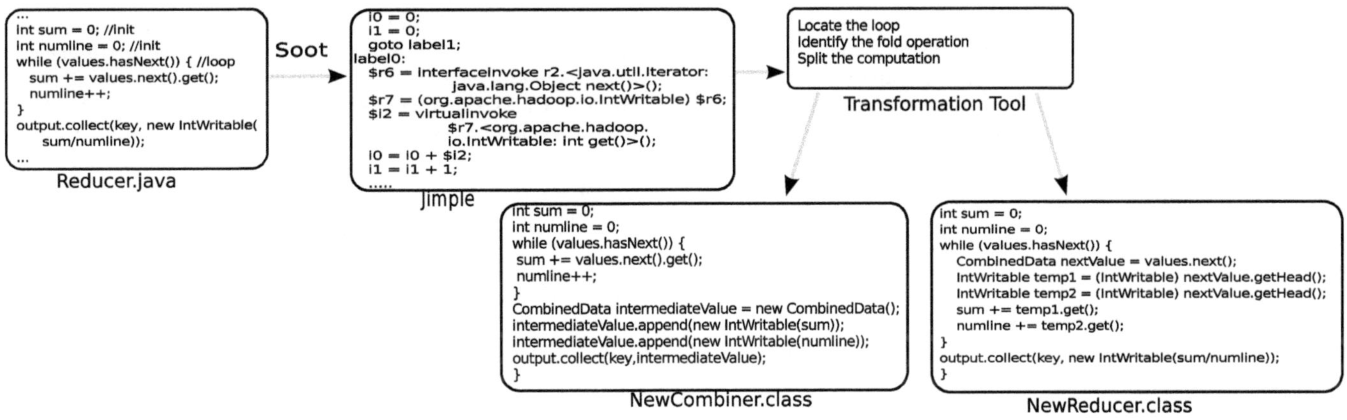

Figure 4: Reduce Structure

provided by Hadoop, which keeps the input values in an iterator. Our approach utilizes Soot to convert the Java source code of a reducer to *Jimple* intermediate representation and then runs the API `LoopFinder()` to identify this fold loop, which is characterized by its operations on these input values. All the follow-up analysis mainly happens to that loop. Specifically, we first perform a loop dependence analysis to check whether there exists any variable that is first defined within one iteration and later used in another iteration. If there is no such a variable, we conclude that the loop dependence does not exist and the loop can be used to build a combiner (Section 4.2), as it is both associative and commutative. This happens in the cases such as filtering, which drops the values above or below a certain threshold, `Grep`, `Sort`, etc.

If the dependence relations are found, our approach moves on to perform a liveness analysis on their causal variables. Specifically, the analysis utilizes a Soot API `SimpleLiveLocals` to find out those still alive posterior to the loop and put them in a set D. These variables not only carry the dependence but also produce the outcomes of the fold operation, and therefore are the keys for understanding the fold's properties. The follow-up analysis backtracks the define-use chain of each variable $v \in D$ within an iteration, starting from the first use of v outside the loop. The objective here is to discover all the variables and operations that define v across all execution paths in the iteration. This evaluation ends when it hits the input key-value list or moves out from the scope the iteration.

For each execution path discovered, our approach checks all the operators that define the loop-dependent variables. The fold becomes associative and commutative if these properties hold across all the paths. This can only be verified empirically, as the problem in general is undecidable. However, all we really need here is just a *sufficient* condition that covers the operations a real-world reducer performs, which are typically simple. Specifically, a form of the computation analyzed in our research is as follow: for each execution path i in an iteration with a path condition P_i, the reducer calculates an aggregation $v \longleftarrow v \bigotimes \delta_i$, where δ_i, which is a function, and P_i do not contain any loop-dependent variables, and $\bigotimes$ is an operator. Essentially, this computation aggregates all δ_i for each input key-value pair using $\bigotimes$. It is clearly associative and commutative if $\bigotimes$ has all these properties. Such a type of aggregation, though simple, actually generalizes the fold operations performed by the vast majority of real-world MapReduce jobs. A prominent example is sum that adds the values of the same key together. Other examples include finding the optimal alignment between two strings, where the edit distance is minimal (operator here is min), and calculating different statistics according to the values of the inputs, which are loop independent.

```
...
int sum = 0;
int i;
for (IntWritable val : values) {
        i = val.get();
        if(i > 10)
                sum += i;
}
result.set(sum);
context.write(key, result);
...
```

Figure 5: Code analysis example

Such an aggregation can be identified from the define-use chain of the variable v. Our approach evaluates all the statements on the chain to ensure that v is the only loop-dependent variables used, and the operation on the variable only happens between it and the program elements independent of other iterations, and always through the same, associative and commutative operator. We also check all the branch conditions encountered, which need to be loop independent. For the example in Figure 5, our analyzer backtracks the statements that work on the live variable `sum`, which cause the loop dependence. All such statements meet the above conditions, particularly, the addition operator is associative and commutative. Therefore, we conclude that the fold loop has all the desired properties and can be used to build a combiner. In our research, we implemented this automatic analysis in the prototype.

4.2 Code Transformation

Once the fold loop is found to be associative and commutative, Sedic uses it to build a combiner, which is deployed to both the public cloud and the private cloud to preprocess map outputs. The results of this operation are fed to a new reducer on a private node to complete the computation. In this section, we describe our code transformation technique that supports this data processing.

Our approach. Like the code analyzer, our transformation tool was also implemented as a Soot `jtp` pass [11]. It works on the Jimple representation of the Hadoop job the user uploads and saves the new code to a newly-created combiner class `CombinedData` before resubmitting the modified job to the cloud. Specifically, the tool separates the fold loop from the rest part of the reducer. As illustrated in Figure 4, the loop sits right between variable declarations/initializations and the posterior loop operations that ultimately export the outcomes of the computation to `outputCollect` of a Hadoop job. Using the information provided by the code analyzer, our tool locates the fold loop and its related variable declarations on Soot's structural representation of Jimple code, and copies these nodes to the new combiner class. The new program structure is then converted directly into Java class files by Soot. Note that when the whole reducer includes just an associative and commutative loop and standard output functions (e.g., `Context.write`), our tool simply adds `SetReducer` to the original job to make the reducer also the combiner with proper initial value adjustment.

Although conceptually simple, this code transformation does bring in a few interesting technical issues. First, the handling of the variables in the reducer needs to be well thought-out. Remember that the combiner generated thereby is supposed to be run on both the public and private clouds. If we simply copy to it the variables and their initializations from the original reducer, we could end up with aggregating the initial values of these variables multiple times, which leads to an incorrect outcome. To see how this could happen, let us look at the example in Figure 4. In the fold loop that does the sum, if we keep the initial value of the aggregation variable `i0 = 5` in the combiner, this value will be added twice to its partial sums produced on both the public cloud and the private cloud, and added again by the new reducer, making the final result larger than what it is supposed to be by 10. Our solution is to set the initial value of the fold operation to an identity element of the fold operator $\otimes$ to avoid this double-counting. For example, when the operator is an addition, we can set the value to 0; when it is a multiplication, we initialize it as 1. The original initial values are only aggregated by the new reducer. Second, although the new reducer and combiner share large amount of code with the original reducer, a naive copy of Jimple `Stmt` from original reducer will not work because the `ValueBox`es in each Jimple `Stmt` refers to variables in original reducer. Besides copying the `Local` chain and `Trap` chain, we also patch the values in each `ValueBox` so it refers to variables in the new `Local` chain. Finally, we also need to add an interface between the new combiner and the new reducer. Specifically, our tool sets all the live variables of the fold loop as the output of the combiner and put them into a data structure called `CombinedData`, which is essentially a list of output objects. We further modify the loop within the new reducer, which extracts elements from the lists provided by the combiners on both clouds and aggregates these elements using the operator $\otimes$. We also need to remove the computation of δ from the reducer to avoid duplicate computation of δ.

An example. For the example in Figure 4, the reducer calculates the mean of input values. Our code analyzer identifies the fold loop on the structural representation of the code, moves it, together with all related variables, to the new combiner class and further modifies the reducer structure. Such code is finally converted into Java class files. For the ease of understanding, we also present the Java source code of the combiner and reducer here, though the output of our tool is actually Java bytecode.

5. EVALUATION

In this section, we report the evaluation study of our privacy-aware MapReduce framework. Our objective is to understand whether these techniques are capable of significantly reducing the workload of the private cloud, scaling to a large amount of data and also maintaining an acceptable level of overall overheads, particularly a limited inter-cloud communication cost. To this end, we evaluated the performance of realistic, large-scale Hadoop jobs using our prototype, over a large-scale cloud test-bed. The details of the study are elaborated here.

5.1 Experimental Setting

Here, we describe the setting of our experimental study, including the MapReduce jobs and the data we used to evaluate our prototype, and our hybrid cloud-computing environment.

Computing jobs and data. In our study, we ran five Hadoop jobs over our prototype to evaluate its effectiveness and performance, which include a data analysis for target marketing, two intrusion detection analyses and two jobs for preparing spam detection. The target-marketing analysis was designed to understand the public's responses to different brand names. More specifically, we utilized Hadoop's `Grep` implementation to evaluate one day Twitter data we captured on April 16th, 2010, in an attempt to find out the comment words (e.g., "wonderful", "worst", etc.) associated with different product brand names. We randomly select some user and mark their tweets as sensitive date, just as if they set their privacy preferences to share data only with their friends. The two examples for intrusion detection systems (IDS) were all based on the DARPA Intrusion Detection Evaluation dataset [5]. The dataset includes the sniffing data from external networks, which was marked as public in our study, as well as that from the internal network, which was considered to be sensitive. Our analyses on the data involved finding all the ports connected by each IP address and determining the amount of traffic generated by individual hosts. The last two jobs prepared a Naive Bayesian classifier for detecting email spam: one of them counted the occurrences of a set of words on a spam keyword list and the other counted the total number of words in a large dataset. We utilized the published Enron email dataset [6] as the private data and a SPAM archive [12] as the public data. These jobs and their related datasets are described by Table 2 and 3. We also performed an additional experiment to understand the performance of Sedic on the dataset with various proportions of sensitive records, using a job that computed the average lengths of packet payloads over the IDS dataset. The code of the job came from Hadoop sample code [28].

Table 2: Descriptions of Hadoop Jobs

Job	Data set	Descriptions
Port Scan Detection	IDS data set	Find the TCP ports connected by each host
Traffic Statistics	IDS data set	Count the total amount of the traffic generated by each host (for detecting denial of service attacks)
Email Word Count	Spam data set	Count the total number of words in the spam dataset (for calculating Bayes probability)
Spam Keyword Count	Spam date set	Count the occurrences of each keyword on a given spam keyword list file(for calculating Bayes probability)
Grep	Twitter	Search for word patterns according to predefined regular expressions within the dataset, e.g., brand names and comment words such as awesome, wonderful, worst etc.

The hybrid cloud. We built our hybrid cloud on FutureGrid [7], an NSF-supported, across-the-country cloud test-bed [40]. The public cloud included 3 nodes located at the University of Chicago. Each machine has 8-core 2.93 GHz Intel Xeon, 24 GB memory, 862 GB local disk and Linux 2.6.18. The private cloud involved 3 nodes at Indiana University, each with 8 to 24 cores of Intel Xeon CPUs, 32G or 48GB memory, 1.6TB disk and also Linux 2.6.18. These two clouds were connected by a 40 MBps link.

5.2 Experimental Results

In our experiment, we evaluated both the effectiveness of our code transformation tool and the performance of our execution framework, which includes computational and communication overheads.

Code transformation. Like the typical reduction performed in a

Table 3: Descriptions of Datasets

Name	Sensitive Data	Public Data	Size of Sensitive Data	Size of Public Data	Percentage of Sensitive Content
IDS data set	The tcpdump files for inside	The tcpdump files for outside	17GB	15GB	54%
Spam data set	The Enron Email Dataset	SPAM archive download from http://untroubled.org/spam/	1.3GB	0.8GB	62%
Twitter data set	Tweets from randomly chosen users who are assumed to prefer to protect their tweets	Tweets from other users	123MB	491MB	20%

MapReduce job, all the reducers encountered in our experimental study were pretty simple. Actually, most jobs simply summed up the values produced by mappers according to the keys. Our analysis tool easily identified the fold loops within them and determined that they were all commutative and associative. These reducers were also set as combiners so that they could combine the data at the public and private clouds respectively, and then reduce the outputs on the private node. The exceptions include the tasks for collecting all the ports associated with individual IP addresses and for determining the average lengths of packet payloads. The fold loop of the former did not have a loop dependency and therefore was directly used as a combiner. The latter calculated the mean of all its inputs, which was analyzed and transformed as described in Section 4.2.

Performance. We ran the job that computes average payload lengths on the IDS dataset to analyze the performance of our execution platform in the presence of different public/sensitive data mixtures. Specifically, we considered the situation that sensitive data was uniformly distributed to every data block, since it represents the worst-case scenario with the most negative impact on the performance of our system. Under this scenario, we gradually raised the proportion of sensitive information, from 10% to 50%, to evaluate the amount of the computation being outsourced to the public cloud. The workload here was measured by the total task execution time, which was summed over the execution time of individual tasks (map and reduce) processed by private nodes. Such workload was compared with that of running the whole job within the private cloud, which we call *baseline*, to estimate the ratio of the computation being outsourced to the public cloud. We got all the runtime statistics from Hadoop log files, which has the detailed information about each task, including the starting time, running on which TaskTracker and finishing time. The outcomes of this study are illustrated by Figure 6. The workload the private cloud shouldered increases from about 69.68 seconds (an outsource ratio about 76%), when 10% of the dataset was sensitive, to about 168.88 seconds (about 40% of outsource ratio), when 40% of the data was private, compared with that caused by running the whole job on the private nodes. The workload dropped a bit when the ratio of the sensitive data went to 50%, probably due to the randomness in execution. Remember that the map task undertaken by the private cloud only processes the sensitive records within each block (Section 3.2). However, there apparently were noticeable overheads associated with initializing the task and seeking for these records within a block, which brought down the performance.

The performance of other jobs are described in Table 4. What we can see here is that all of them successfully moved a large portion of computation to the public cloud, in accordance with the ratio of the private information within the individual datasets they worked on. This even happened to the job that processed the Twitter dataset, whose distribution of sensitive data was more even compared with the other two datasets. In some cases, the outsource ratios are even higher than the proportion of the public data within the dataset (Word Count). We believe that this was caused by the randomness in the job execution. The overall job execution time was also low

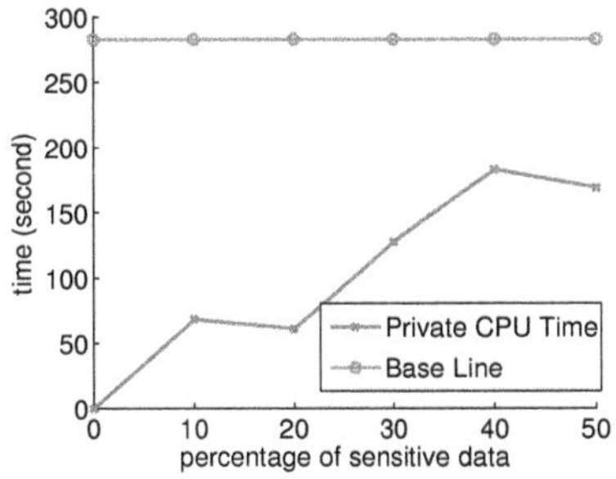

Figure 6: Performance vs. Sensitive Data Ratio

for our prototype: as an example, for port scan detection, it took about 3 minutes to complete the whole job (on 6 nodes, 3 private and 3 public), even below the baseline, which used about 6 minutes (on 3 private nodes). This is actually quite reasonable, given the fact that our hybrid-cloud computing leveraged the resources from the public cloud.

Communication overheads. Our experiments also show that the new reduction structure automatically generated by Sedic did contribute to the effective control of inter-cloud data transfers, one of the major hurdles to the extensive use of cloud computing. Specifically, we compared the bandwidth consumption of the original Hadoop jobs with that incurred after their reducers were transformed. The results are presented in Table 4. As we can see here, in the presence of code transformation, the flood of the traffic stream between the public and the private clouds was reduced to trickles: for example, in the case of port scan detection, over 1.5 GB data was reduced to merely 8.2 MB using the automatically generated combiner on the public cloud. This saving in bandwidth consumption can significantly improve the performance of hybrid-cloud computation, given the fact that inter-cloud bandwidth is typically low. For example, the link between Amazon EC2 and Amazon S3 is around 50MBps [1] and the connections EC2 receives from the outside are often less than 10MBps [2]. The experimental results offer strong evidence that our code analysis and transformation techniques indeed work.

6. RELATED WORK

Security protection in cloud computing. Most system security research on the cloud focuses on data-storage security [47] and virtualization security [33]. Little effort has been made to facilitate security and privacy protections during the computation specific to this new computing platform (despite the rich literature on more generic secure-computing techniques). One exception is Airavat [41], a system that ensures mandatory access control and differential privacy [26] when MapReduce operations are performed on sensitive data. Different from Airavat, which trusts the cloud platform it is running upon, our work aims at protecting sensitive data from the public cloud, which will be achieved by a security mechanism designed for the hybrid-cloud platform.

Table 4: Performance

ID	Job	Task Execution Time of the Whole Job (Baseline, in seconds)	Total Task Execution Time in Private Cloud(in seconds)	Outsource Ratio	Public Data Ratio	Inter-cloud Communication w/o Transformation (in Bytes)	Inter-cloud Communication w. Transformation (in Bytes)
1	Port scan detection	1909.79	928.86	51%	46%	1512075005	8215706
2	Traffic statistics	1723.87	890.25	48%	46%	672975164	582889
3	Word count	148.48	66.12	55%	38%	422691678	294
4	Spam Keyword Count	155.70	99.03	36%	38%	68598926	13173
5	Grep	17.85	5.24	71%	80%	2158	156

Secure computation outsourcing. Secure computation outsourcing has been studied for more than a decade. Early research is mainly on delegating cryptographic operations (e.g., modular exponentiations) to a set of untrusted helpers [38, 31]. More recent studies include the techniques for secure computing of edit distances and string alignments [19, 16, 32, 20, 44], which are too heavyweight for data-intensive computations. Effort has also been made to securely outsource the computations such as linear algebra operations [15] and machine-learning tasks [25]. For example, Peer-for-Privacy decomposes a category of data mining algorithms into vector addition steps and distributes them to multiple nodes on a cloud, which can be securely evaluated through a special secret sharing scheme [25]. All these approaches, however, incur a large amount of communication during the computation. Also, secret-sharing based approaches may bring in new policy challenges: once the data has been shared to multiple parties, an organization completely loses the control of it, since these parties can work together to restore the data; it is still unclear whether the organization needs to sign an agreement with each of them, which these parties may want to avoid for liability concerns [36], and if so, what the agreement will look like. This concern is also applied to the approaches that decompose a computation problem [44] into small sub-problems and allocates them to multiple problem solvers, under the assumption that these parties will not collude.

Computation split. The idea of splitting a computation among multiple parties for security purposes has been explored under different scenarios. For example, Swift [21] uses a secure information-flow analysis [39] to partition a web application into client and server components. Other examples include distributing a genomic computation to two or more parties [44, 48]. However, none of these techniques are designed for data-intensive computations, the focus of our research.

7. DISCUSSION

Sedic is designed to work on the data whose sensitive records are known to its owner and can therefore be marked out. This is true in most real-life situations: for example, documents in organizations' file systems oftentimes are already labeled by their access privileges. On the other hand, there are situations when the owner herself has no idea about which part of the data is sensitive. A prominent example here is *mapping of human DNA sequences*, which is also known as *read mapping* [45]. The task is to align a short human DNA sequence to a long reference genome, so as to identify the genetic location of the sequence. The challenge here is that before the alignment, we have no idea where the sequence belongs, no to mention whether it carries sensitive information. In this case, we have to come up with a specific solution to such a problem, by carefully considering its special features.

Our approach is built upon Hadoop, which does not support iterative MapReduce [23]. To execute a task that needs to perform multiple rounds of map-reduce operations, we have to break it down into multiple Hadoop jobs. Also, Sedic requires an additional step to label the output of one job so that its follow-up job can be split between the public and the private clouds. In the future research, we plan to move our design to Twister [27] to support iterative MapReduce, which is important to a set of data mining analyses [24]. We could also embed a lightweight information-flow tracking and declassification mechanisms into the execution framework to enable automatic labeling of a job's sensitive outputs.

The design of Sedic can also be improved. For example, our experimental study found that the data block involving public or sensitive data alone can be more efficiently processed than those containing both types of information. A straightforward solution seems to be simply re-organizing the data, clustering sensitive records from different blocks into new blocks. This approach, however, could cause the outcomes of the computation to be incorrect, as the keys generated by mappers are often related to the positions of the blocks in the datasets. To solve this problem, we need to attach such position information to individual records being clustered. The question is, whether the extra workload to process such information can lead to a significant performance degradation. This will be investigated in the future research.

Our current code analysis and transformation tool can only handle the type of the reducers as described in Section 4.1. This approach seems to be good enough, as the vast majority of the reducers in real-world jobs are rather simple. However, it is still important to understand whether there are strong demands for more complicated reduction operations, which may not be associative. If such demands are indeed there, the analysis and transformation techniques certainly need to be improved to accommodate the new applications. This issue, again, is on our research agenda.

8. CONCLUSION

Commercial cloud services, such as the Amazon EC2, enable their customers to process a large amount of data at a low cost. This benefit, however, comes with privacy risks: the computing tasks of organizations often involves sensitive data and therefore cannot be directly delegated to the public cloud without proper protection. Such protection cannot be expected from traditional secure outsourcing techniques, which often cannot handle the large amount of data such computation involves. A more practical solution is to split the computation so as to move the workload unrelated to sensitive data to the commercial cloud, while keeping the rest within an organization's private cloud. This hybrid computing paradigm needs to be supported by a new privacy-aware computation framework. To this end, we present Sedic, the first secure data-intensive computing system, in this paper. Our approach leverages the special features of MapReduce to schedule individual map tasks over a carefully planned data placement, in a way that the tasks within the private cloud only work on sensitive data and those on the public cloud only processes public data. As a result, all the workload that does not involve private information can be offloaded to the low-cost commercial cloud. To avoid an intensive data exchange between clouds, Sedic also automatically analyzes the reducer of a legacy MapReduce job to extract a combiner for aggregating the map outcomes on the public cloud. We implemented our techniques on Hadoop and evaluated our prototype on FutureGrid, a large-scale cloud test-bed. Our study shows that without jeopardizing user privacy, Sedic effectively outsourced a large amount of computing workload to the public cloud, fully preserved the scalability of MapReduce and also conveniently accommodated legacy computing jobs.

Acknowledgements

We thank Kumar Bhaskaran, Milton H. Hernandez and Xiaolan (Catherine) Zhang for their valuable comments and advices, and Vijay Naik for his knowledge about hybrid cloud. We also thank anonymous reviewers for their insightful comments. Kehuan Zhang was also supported in part by the NSF CNS-0716292, CNS-1017782 and the IBM internship program.

9. REFERENCES

[1] Network performance within amazon ec2 and to amazon s3. http://blog.rightscale.com/2007/10/28/network-performance-within-amazon-ec2-and-to-amazon-s3/, 2008.

[2] Testing amazon web services bandwidth. http://jonathanmaim.com/2008/05/testing-amazon-web-services-bandwidth.html, 2008.

[3] Amazon virtual private cloud. http://aws.amazon.com/vpc/, 2011.

[4] Awareness, trust and security to shape government cloud adoption. http://www.lockheedmartin.com/data/assets/isgs/documents/CloudComputingWhitePaper.pdf, 2011.

[5] Darpa intrusion detection data set. http://www.ll.mit.edu/mission/communications/ist/corpora/ideval/data/index.html, 2011.

[6] Enron email dataset. http://www.cs.cmu.edu/~enron/, 2011.

[7] Future grid portal. https://portal.futuregrid.org/, 2011.

[8] An introduction to distributed intrusion detection systems. http://www.symantec.com/connect/articles/introduction/distributed/intrusion/detection/systems, 2011.

[9] Social media data helping to target extend demand gen campaigns. http://www.demandgenreport.com/archives/feature-articles/594-social-media.html, 2011.

[10] Sony: Hacker stole playstation users' personal info. http://edition.cnn.com/2011/TECH/gaming.gadgets/04/26/playstation.network.hack/index.html, 2011.

[11] Soot: a java optimization framework. http://www.sable.mcgill.ca/soot/, 2011.

[12] Spam archieve. http://untroubled.org/spam/, 2011.

[13] Summary of the amazon ec2 and amazon rds service disruption in the us east region. http://aws.amazon.com/message/65648/, 2011.

[14] Target marketing. http://en.wikipedia.org/wiki/Target_market, 2011.

[15] M. J. Atallah and K. B. Frikken. Securely outsourcing linear algebra computations. In *Proceedings of the 5th ACM Symposium on Information, Computer and Communications Security*, ASIACCS '10, pages 48–59, New York, NY, USA, 2010. ACM.

[16] M. J. Atallah, F. Kerschbaum, and W. Du. Secure and private sequence comparisons. In *Proceedings of the 2003 ACM workshop on Privacy in the electronic society*, WPES '03, pages 39–44, New York, NY, USA, 2003. ACM.

[17] M. J. Atallah and J. Li. Secure outsourcing of sequence comparisons. *Int. J. Inf. Secur.*, 4:277–287, October 2005.

[18] D. Bernstein, E. Ludvigson, K. Sankar, S. Diamond, and M. Morrow. Blueprint for the intercloud - protocols and formats for cloud computing interoperability. *Internet and Web Applications and Services, International Conference on*, 0:328–336, 2009.

[19] M. Blanton and M. Aliasgari. Secure outsourcing of dna searching via finite automata. In S. Foresti and S. Jajodia, editors, *DBSec*, volume 6166 of *Lecture Notes in Computer Science*, pages 49–64. Springer, 2010.

[20] F. Bruekers, S. Katzenbeisser, K. Kursawe, and P. Tuyls. Privacy-preserving matching of dna profiles. Technical Report Report 2008/203, ACR Cryptology ePrint Archive, 2008.

[21] S. Chong, J. Liu, A. C. Myers, X. Qi, K. Vikram, L. Zheng, and X. Zheng. Secure web applications via automatic partitioning. *SIGOPS Oper. Syst. Rev.*, 41:31–44, October 2007.

[22] J. Dean and S. Ghemawat. Mapreduce: simplified data processing on large clusters. *Commun. ACM*, 51:107–113, January 2008.

[23] J. Dean and S. Ghemawat. Mapreduce: simplified data processing on large clusters. *Commun. ACM*, 51:107–113, January 2008.

[24] A. P. Dempster, N. M. Laird, and D. B. Rubin. Maximum likelihood from incomplete data via the em algorithm. *JOURNAL OF THE ROYAL STATISTICAL SOCIETY, SERIES B*, 39(1):1–38, 1977.

[25] Y. Duan, N. Youdao, J. Canny, and J. Zhan. P4p: Practical large-scale privacy-preserving distributed computation robust against malicious users abstract. In *Proceedings of the 19th USENIX Security Symposium*, Washington, DC, August 2010.

[26] C. Dwork. Differential privacy. In *in ICALP*, pages 1–12. Springer, 2006.

[27] J. Ekanayake, H. Li, B. Zhang, T. Gunarathne, S.-H. Bae, J. Qiu, and G. Fox. Twister: A runtime for iterative mapreduce. Technical report, Indiana University, Bloomington, IN, 2010.

[28] T. A. S. Foundation. Apache Hadoop Project. http://hadoop.apache.org/, 2010.

[29] B. Furht. Cloud computing fundamentals. In B. Furht and A. Escalante, editors, *Handbook of Cloud Computing*, pages 3–19. Springer US, 2010.

[30] C. Gentry. Fully homomorphic encryption using ideal lattices. In *Proceedings of the 41st annual ACM symposium on Theory of computing*, STOC '09, pages 169–178, New York, NY, USA, 2009. ACM.

[31] S. Hohenberger and A. Lysyanskaya. How to securely outsource cryptographic computations. In J. Kilian, editor, *Theory of Cryptography*, volume 3378 of *Lecture Notes in Computer Science*, pages 264–282. Springer Berlin / Heidelberg, 2005.

[32] S. Jha, L. Kruger, and V. Shmatikov. Towards practical privacy for genomic computation. In *2008 IEEE Symposium on Security and Privacy*, 2008.

[33] A. V. Konstantinou, T. Eilam, M. Kalantar, A. A. Totok, W. Arnold, and E. Snible. An architecture for virtual solution composition and deployment in infrastructure clouds. In *Proceedings of the 3rd international workshop on Virtualization technologies in distributed computing*, VTDC '09, pages 9–18, New York, NY, USA, 2009. ACM.

[34] B. Langmead, M. Schatz, J. Lin, M. Pop, and S. Salzberg. Searching for SNPs with cloud computing. *Genome Biology*, 10(11):R134+, November 2009.

[35] A. W. S. LLC. Amazon Elastic Compute Cloud (Amazon EC2). http://aws.amazon.com/ec2/, 2010.

[36] A. W. S. LLC. Amazon Web Services Customer Agreement. http://aws.amazon.com/agreement/, 2010.

[37] M. C. I. Lockheed Martin, LM Cyber Security Alliance. Awareness, trust and security to shape government cloud adoption. http://www.lockheedmartin.com/data/assets/isgs/documents/CloudComputingWhitePaper.pdf, April 2010.

[38] T. Matsumoto, K. Kato, and H. Imai. Speeding up secret computations with insecure auxiliary devices. In *Proceedings of the 8th Annual International Cryptology Conference on Advances in Cryptology*, pages 497–506, London, UK, 1990. Springer-Verlag.

[39] A. C. Myers and B. Liskov. Protecting privacy using the decentralized label model. *ACM Trans. Softw. Eng. Methodol.*, 9(4):410–442, 2000.

[40] NSF. Award abstract #091081 - futuregrid: An experimental, high-performance grid test-bed, 2009.

[41] I. Roy, S. T. V. Setty, A. Kilzer, V. Shmatikov, and E. Witchel. Airavat: Security and privacy for mapreduce. In *NSDI*, pages 297–312. USENIX Association, 2010.

[42] M. C. Schatz. CloudBurst: highly sensitive read mapping with MapReduce. *Bioinformatics*, 25(11):1363–1369, 2009.

[43] A. W. Services. Aws case study: Washington post. http://aws.amazon.com/solutions/case-studies/washington-post/, December As of 2010.

[44] D. Szajda, M. Pohl, J. Owen, and B. G. Lawson. Toward a practical data privacy scheme for a distributed implementation of the smith-waterman genome sequence comparison algorithm. In *NDSS*. The Internet Society, 2006.

[45] C. Trapnell and S. L. Salzberg. How to map billions of short reads onto genomes. *Nature biotechnology*, 27(5):455–457, May 2009.

[46] M. van Dijk, C. Gentry, S. Halevi, and V. Vaikuntanathan. Fully homomorphic encryption over the integers. In H. Gilbert, editor, *Advances in Cryptology - EUROCRYPT 2010*, volume 6110 of *Lecture Notes in Computer Science*, pages 24–43. Springer Berlin / Heidelberg, 2010.

[47] C. Wang, Q. Wang, K. Ren, and W. Lou. Privacy-preserving public auditing for data storage security in cloud computing. In *Proceedings of the 29th conference on Information communications*, INFOCOM'10, pages 525–533, Piscataway, NJ, USA, 2010. IEEE Press.

[48] R. Wang, X. Wang, Z. Li, H. Tang, M. K. Reiter, and Z. Dong. Privacy-preserving genomic computation through program specialization. In *CCS '09: Proceedings of the 16th ACM conference on Computer and communications security*, pages 338–347, New York, NY, USA, 2009. ACM.

[49] Z. Yang, S. Zhong, and R. N. Wright. Privacy-preserving classification of customer data without loss of accuracy. In *In SIAM SDM*, pages 21–23, 2005.

iSpy: Automatic Reconstruction of Typed Input from Compromising Reflections

Rahul Raguram, Andrew M. White, Dibyendusekhar Goswami,
Fabian Monrose and Jan-Michael Frahm
Department of Computer Science, University of North Carolina at Chapel Hill
Chapel Hill, North Carolina
{rraguram,amw,dgoswami,fabian,jmf}@cs.unc.edu

ABSTRACT

We investigate the implications of the ubiquity of personal mobile devices and reveal new techniques for compromising the privacy of users typing on virtual keyboards. Specifically, we show that so-called compromising reflections (in, for example, a victim's sunglasses) of a device's screen are sufficient to enable *automated* reconstruction, from video, of text typed on a virtual keyboard. Despite our deliberate use of low cost commodity video cameras, we are able to compensate for variables such as arbitrary camera and device positioning and motion through the application of advanced computer vision and machine learning techniques. Using footage captured in realistic environments (e.g., on a bus), we show that we are able to reconstruct fluent translations of recorded data in almost all of the test cases, correcting users' typing mistakes at the same time. We believe these results highlight the importance of adjusting privacy expectations in response to emerging technologies.

Categories and Subject Descriptors: K.4.1 [Computers and Society]: Privacy

General Terms: Human Factors, Security

Keywords: Compromising Emanations; Mobile Devices

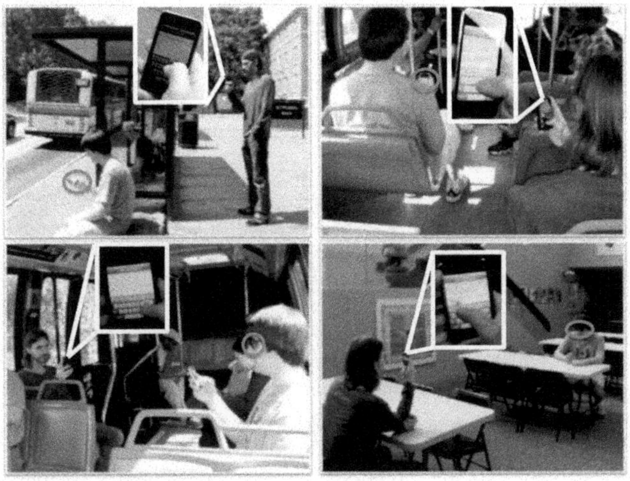

Figure 1: Some example threat scenarios that we investigated. Video was recorded in both indoor and outdoor environments, using various consumer video cameras. top: shoulder surfing, bottom: reflection surfing, bottom right: key *pop-out* event.

1. INTRODUCTION

The ability to obtain information without the owner's knowledge or consent is one which has been sought after throughout human history, and which has been used to great effect in arenas as diverse as war, politics, business and personal relationships. Accordingly, methods and techniques for compromising – and protecting – communications and data storage have been studied extensively. However, the ubiquity of powerful personal computing devices has changed how we communicate and store information, providing new possibilities for the surreptitious observation of private messages and data. In particular, mobile phones have become omnipresent in today's society, and are used on a daily basis by millions of us to send text messages and emails, check bank balances, search the internet, and even make purchases. And while some of us may be concerned with – and take steps to prevent – shoulder-surfing and direct observation of the text we input into these devices (see Figure 1), how many of us spare a second glance for the person facing us across the aisle on our morning bus ride?

In this work, we show that automated reconstruction of text typed on a mobile device's virtual keyboard is possible via *compromising reflections*, e.g., those of the phone in the user's sunglasses. Such *compromising reflections* have been exploited in the past for reconstructing text displayed on a screen [2, 3], but these approaches require expensive, high-powered telescopic lenses. Our approach operates on video recorded by inexpensive commodity cameras, such as those found in modern smartphones. The low resolution of these cameras makes visual analysis difficult, even for humans, and severly limits the possibility of directly identifying on-screen text. What makes this threat practical, however, is that most modern touchscreen smartphones make use of a *virtual keyboard*, where users tap keys on-screen. In the absence of tactile feedback, visual confirmation is typically provided to the user via a key *pop-out* effect, as illustrated on the bottom right of Figure 1. Note that although the on-screen text is essentially unreadable, the pop-out event provides a strong

CCS'11, October 17–21, 2011, Chicago, Illinois, USA.

visual cue to help identify the letter that was tapped. The approach we take in this paper exploits this effect in order to recover the text typed by the user.

Recent work has also explored the feasibility of reconstructing text typed on a full-sized physical keyboard based on video from compromised web-cams [4]. In that scenario, both the camera and keyboard are stable and in known positions relative to each other. In our case, both the phone and the camera are free to move and can be positioned arbitrarily with respect to each other, adding considerable difficulty to any automated visual analysis. To further complicate matters, the user's fingers often occlude portions of the visual keyboard. We apply a variety of state-of-the-art techniques to overcome these and other challenges.

As we show later, the approach we take offers much promise in two real-world threat models, namely: (1) *direct surveillance*, wherein we assume the adversary is able to direct the camera towards the screen of the mobile device (e.g., over the victim's shoulder) and capture visual cues from the virtual keyboard, and (2) *indirect surveillance*, wherein the adversary takes advantage of indirect views of the virtual keyboard obtained, for example, via "compromising reflections" of the phone in the victim's sunglasses.

In both cases, we assume only inexpensive, commodity video cameras, without any telescopic lenses or additional high-end equipment. In addition, we make no limiting assumptions about the capture setup, the motion of the phone, or the typing style of the user. Thus, the only input we assume is a video sequence, either direct or indirect, of a user typing on a virtual keyboard. We then use a number of computer vision techniques to process the recorded video, identifying, for each frame, potential keys that were pressed. This visual detection, coupled with a language model, enables us to achieve surprisingly accurate sentence retrieval results, even under challenging real-world scenarios.

Our ability to reconstruct text typed on virtual keyboards from compromising reflections underscores the need to continually reevaluate our preconceptions of privacy – or the lack thereof – in modern society. Even cryptography and secure devices are of little use when, across the aisle, someone who appears to be reading email on their phone is in fact surreptitiously recording every character we type.

2. RELATED WORK

By now, it is well understood that electronic, electro-optical and electromechanical devices give off some form of unintentional electromagnetic signals that can inadvertently leak sensitive information. The risks from these so-called "*compromising emanations*" were noted over half a century ago, and led to the introduction of emission-security tests standards to control leakage from digital electronics, particularly when pertaining to classified information [23]. Although the nature of these emissions has changed with evolving technology, side-channel attacks continue to surface [11, 16, 17, 21, 28, 31].

More recently, both visual emanations (e.g., from reflections on curved surfaces of close-by objects such as tea pots) and acoustic emanations (e.g., from key presses on a keyboard or from the sounds made by dot-matrix printers) [1, 32] have been used to undermine the confidentiality of information displayed or entered into commodity devices. More closely related is the work of Backes et al. [2, 3] on "*compromising reflections*" that presents eavesdropping techniques for exploiting optical emanations using telescopic equipment. There, the authors show that an adversary is able to successfully spy from distances as far as 30 meters away, and in certain cases, can even read large text reflected in the eyeball of the victim. In this work, we focus on a related, but different, problem: namely, exploring the feasibility of automatic generation of transcripts from low-resolution, indirect footage captured using inexpensive, and ubiquitous, consumer electronics.

Also germane to this paper is the work of Balzarotti et al. [4] that explores the idea of automatically reproducing text from surveillance video – albeit from a camera mounted directly above a terminal – that captures a user's typing as she inputs data at the keyboard. Similar to Balzarotti et al., we apply the noisy channel model to help recover sequences of words from streams of frames (with guessed labels); both works also employ an n-gram language model. However, the error model employed by Balzarotti et al. only accounts for the deletion of identified characters and the substitution of one character for another. In contrast, our model allows for insertions, deletions, and substitutions, with substitutions weighted according to the distance between the two characters on the keyboard. Moreover, unlike Balzarotti et al., our frame parsing model handles spacing, allowing for the insertion and removal of spaces. An additional challenge in our setting is the need to overcome significant instability in the captured footage, as well as operate at a far lower resolution.

A more distantly related problem is that of extracting captions in broadcast news in order to provide search metadata for digital archives. In these works, the low resolution of characters within the video makes the problem of segmenting characters quite challenging, so much so that video OCR typically does not perform well without significant text enhancement [13]. As we show later, the problem is exacerbated in our context, where we operate on even lower resolutions and must simultaneously deal with instability in the video (e.g., due to both camera and phone motion).

3. OUR APPROACH

Our approach consists of a number of stages, each a difficult problem requiring the application of advanced computer vision and machine learning techniques. At a high level, the approach we take is to first detect and track the phone across the frames of a video sequence. As we do so, stable and distinctive feature points are extracted from the phone area in each frame, and subsequently used to compute stabilizing image transformations. These transformations help eliminate the effects of camera and phone motion. The stabilized video frames are also aligned to a reference image of the phone (obtained, for instance, from the user manual of the device of interest). In this aligned state, pop-out events for each key are then localized to specific known regions of the keyboard, and we train classifiers to recognize when a particular key has been pressed. The result is that for each frame, we output a set of possible key pop-out events. To account for missed and spurious detections, we subsequently use a language model to impose additional constraints, thus refining the output of the computer vision modules. Finally, we evaluate the effectiveness of our approach using established metrics, designed to correlate well with human judgements, for scoring machine translations. Next, we discuss each component of the overall design (given in Figure 2) in turn.

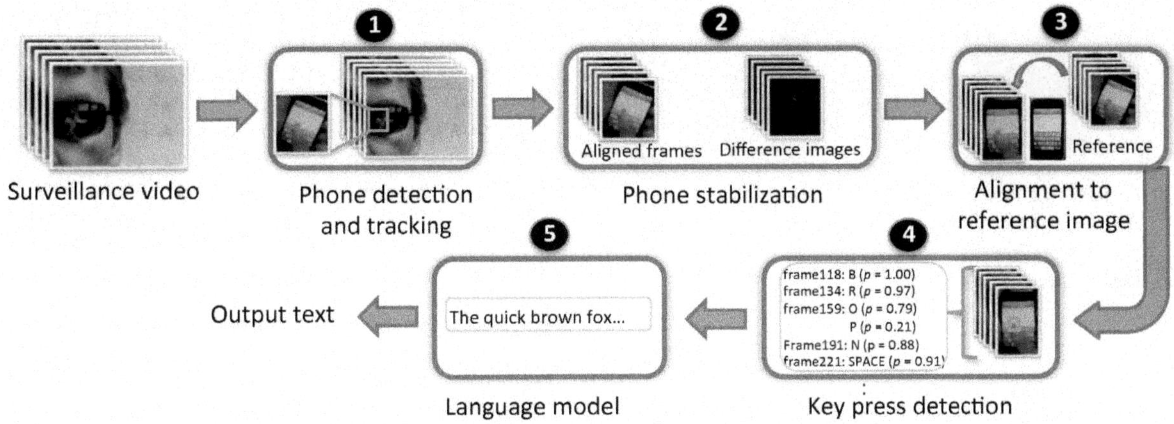

Figure 2: Overview of our approach for typed input reconstruction from video.

3.1 Phone detection and tracking (Stage ❶)

Given a surveillance video, one of the most basic challenges we face is in determining the location of the phone in the video. It is often the case that the phone occupies only a small spatial region of the image, with the remaining portion being unrelated background clutter (e.g., the phone in Figure 3 only occupies 1.8% of the total image area). Indeed, the visual features on the background are invariably "distracting" for subsequent stages of our approach, since they vastly outnumber the visual features on the phone itself. Determining the location of the phone in the video thus enables us to focus specifically on the object of interest, eliminating all irrelevant background information. Hence, our goal in this stage is to compute (for every frame) an approximate spatial region, or bounding box, that contains the phone.

The domains of *object detection* and *object tracking* have received widespread attention in computer vision, due to the ubiquitous nature of these problems [8, 15, 27, 29, 30]. In certain applications, such as frontal-view face detection, modern techniques are capable of providing very accurate results; indeed, most consumer point-and-shoot cameras today come equipped with built-in face detection technology. The approach we take in this paper involves the formulation of the tracking problem as one of binary classification [9, 15, 27]. The intuition is to train binary classifiers to distinguish the appearance of the object being tracked from that of the background. This training is either performed *offline* (using a dedicated training phase prior to running the tracking algorithm), or *online* (where the appearance of the object is learned *during* the tracking process). In the former case, tracking is typically very fast, since the classifiers have been pre-trained beforehand. The latter, while slower, is capable of adapting on-the-fly to changes in appearance of the object. In our setting, the appearance of the object being tracked can vary considerably, based on the model of the phone, the relative orientation between the surveillance cameras and the user, the ambient lighting conditions, occlusions, etc. Hence, to handle this appearance variability, we elect to perform online training, learning the appearance of the phone during the tracking process.

We base our phone tracker on the techniques proposed in [8, 27], which describe an online AdaBoost [7] feature selection algorithm for tracking. At a high level, *boosting* is a classification scheme that works by combining a number of so-called *weak learners* into a more accurate *ensemble* classifier. A weak learner may be thought of as a "rule of thumb" that only has to perform slightly better than chance – for example, in a binary classification problem, the error rate must be less than 50%. These can be as simple as a threshold on a feature value. The intuition is that a combination of these "weak" rules will often be much more accurate than any individual rule. Given a set of training images, where each image is labeled as positive (containing the phone) or negative (not containing the phone), we obtain a training set $\chi^L = \{\langle \mathbf{x}_1, y_1\rangle, ..., \langle \mathbf{x}_{|\chi^L|}, y_{|\chi^L|}\rangle\}$, where $\mathbf{x}_i$ is an m-dimensional feature representing the ith training image, and $y_i \in \{+1, -1\}$ is the corresponding label. As suggested by Grabner et al. [8], we use three different types of image features, concatenated to form the vectors $\mathbf{x}_i$: Haar-like features [30], orientation histograms [20] and local binary patterns [24].

Initially, each training example is given a uniform weight $p(\mathbf{x}_i) = 1/|\chi^L|$. During the first round of training, we select a weak learner that has the lowest weighted classification error, given χ^L and $p(\mathbf{x})$, and add that learner to our ensemble. Following this, the weights $p(\mathbf{x}_i)$ of the misclassified training examples are increased, while the weights of the correctly classified samples are decreased. At each subsequent training iteration, we select a weak learner h_i that does well on the training examples that were hard for the previous weak learners. The final ensemble classifier is then computed as a linear combination of the selected weak learners, with the weight of each learner being proportional to its accuracy.

While the above discussion describes an offline version of boosting, the online variant assumes that one training example is available (for instance, by drawing an approximate bounding box in the first video frame). This image region becomes the positive training sample, and negative examples are extracted from the surrounding background regions. Given this data, multiple training iterations of the online boosting algorithm are performed as above. In the next frame, the ensemble classifier is evaluated at a number of possible image locations (e.g., in a search window surrounding the object's position in the first frame), with each location being assigned a confidence value. The target window is then shifted to the new location of the maxima,

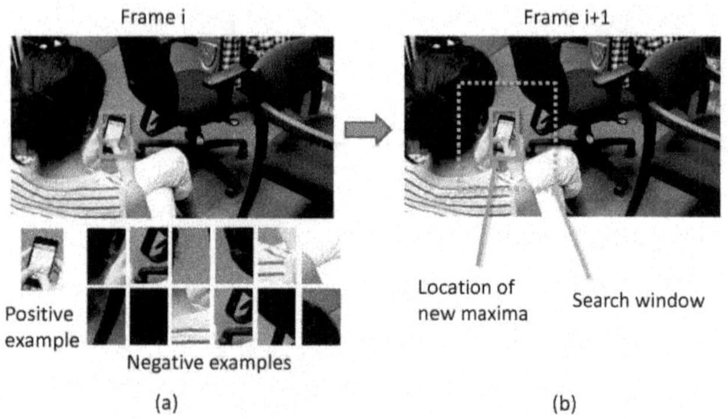

Figure 3: Phone tracking: (a) User-selected bounding box highlighting our positive example for training. (b) In the next frame, the classifier is evaluated within a search window, and the position of the maximum response defines the phone's new location.

and the classifier is updated using new positive and negative training examples so as to become discriminative to variable object/background appearance. The operation of the tracker is illustrated in Figure 3. Note that this is the *only* stage of our overall approach that requires user input – the user simply needs to draw a single rectangular bounding box around the phone area in the first video frame. All subsequent stages of the algorithm are fully automatic. The output of this module is the phone's location in each frame, allowing all further processing steps to focus on the phone.

3.2 Phone stabilization (Stage ❷)

The phone tracking stage provides, for every frame of video, the coordinates of a bounding box that contains the phone. Given these subimages, the next step is to compensate for the effects of phone and camera motion. As discussed earlier, we do not impose any constraints on the motion of either the camera or the user. While this enables us to operate in a wide range of real-world threat scenarios, it also results in a tremendous degree of variability in the appearance of the phone within each detected subwindow. Explicitly compensating for this motion would allow us to effectively reduce one dimension of variability, resulting in a more "stable" set of image frames to work with.

Before presenting the details of our stabilization algorithm, we introduce the notion of a *homography* [10]. In computer vision parlance, a homography is a 2D projective transformation that relates two images of the same planar surface. In our setting, the phone represents a (mostly) rigid, planar object, and we capture multiple images of this plane from potentially different viewpoints. The images that we capture – specifically, the portions of the image that contain the phone – are related to each other via a 2D homography transformation. Note that in the case of reflections, the image of the phone can be distorted due to the curvature of the sunglasses. We do not explicitly model this in the current system, but rather assume that the sunglasses are approximately locally planar. Since the phone occupies only a small area of the sunglasses, this approximation proves to be sufficient in practice.

The 2D homography transformation has a number of important practical applications, one of which is image stabilization. Given two views of a rigid planar object, along with the homography $\mathbf{H}$ between them, the homography can be used to *warp* one of the images in order to align it with the other. In other words, if we were given access to $\mathbf{H}$ with respect to the phone, then we could align the phone in neighboring frames of a video sequence, thereby removing the effects of phone and camera motion. In short, the basic idea is to compute pairwise homographies between phones in video frames, chaining them together to align all phones in the frames to a common reference frame. The problem now reduces to that of automatically determining the transformation $\mathbf{H}$, given two neighboring video frames I_t and I_{t+1}. This is a well studied problem in computer vision, and several algorithms have been proposed to automatically estimate this transformation.

The approach we take involves two key steps. In our **feature extraction and matching** step, we extract stable, repeatable and distinctive *feature points* in the two images, with the intuition being that we would like to identify matching points in the captured images that correspond to the same 3D point on the phone. For this we use the Scale Invariant Feature Transform, or SIFT [22]. Each SIFT feature consists of a 2D image location, scale, orientation vector, and a 128-dimensional *feature descriptor* which represents a histogram of gradient orientations centered around the extracted feature. The main point is that a pair of features in two images that correspond to the same point in 3D space will have similar SIFT descriptors. The SIFT representation is powerful in practice, and its popularity stems from their ability to tolerate a wide range of scale and illumination changes, as well some degree of viewpoint variation. For this task, we use a fast in-house GPU implementation of SIFT extraction and matching[1], capable of processing more than 12 frames per second on a standard graphics card.

For our **robust homography estimation** step, we compute the homography $\mathbf{H}$ from N "true" feature matches between the two images using the normalized Direct Linear Transformation (DLT) algorithm [10]. One limitation here, however, is that doing so requires a minimum of $N = 4$ feature matches between the two images. Additionally, the DLT algorithm is sensitive to outliers, or mismatched features. To combat this problem, we turn to the field of *robust statistics* [12], where the problem of estimating quantities from data that has been corrupted by noise and outliers has been well studied. Perhaps the most popular of these *robust estimators* is Random Sample Consensus (RANSAC). The popularity of RANSAC, particularly in computer vision – where noisy and outlying image measurements are practically unavoidable – is primarily due to its ability to tolerate a high level of data contamination. In our approach, we apply a fast, real-time variant of RANSAC, called ARRSAC (Adaptive Real-Time Random Sample Consensus) [26], which simultaneously estimates the 2D homography, as well as returning the set of "true" feature correspondences. The resulting homography can then be used to align the phone images together, thus nullifying the effects of scene and camera motion.

The two steps outlined above are illustrated in Figure 4. Figures 4(a)-(c) denote the process of SIFT feature extraction, matching, and robust homography estimation, respectively. Notice that the incorrect feature matches present

[1]Available online: `http://cs.unc.edu/~ccwu/siftgpu`

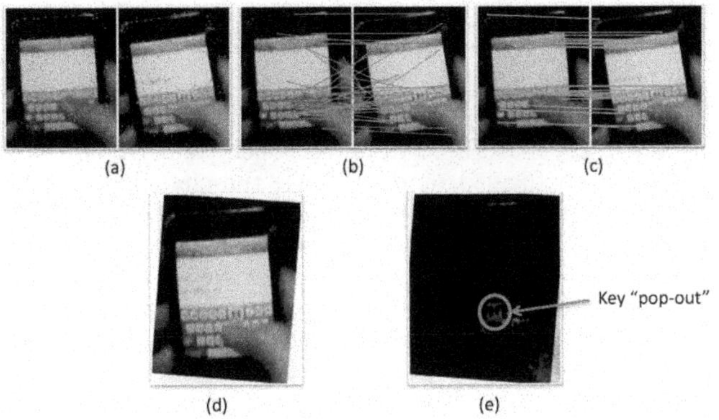

Figure 4: Automatic phone stabilization of two video frames.

in Figure 4(b) are "cleaned up" by ARRSAC, which selects the set of true correspondences (shown in Figure 4(c)) out of the potential correspondences (Figure 4(b)). These true correspondences are then used to estimate the homography between the two frames. Figure 4(d) shows the two frames aligned with respect to each other, and Figure 4(e) represents the pixel-wise difference between the images after alignment. In the difference image, dark pixels represent areas of low image difference, and lighter pixels represent areas of high difference. Two points are pertinent: first, since the difference image consists mainly of dark pixels, this is an indication that the homography-based alignment has accurately aligned the images to each other; and second, observe that the key pop-out event becomes apparent in the difference image. We will leverage these observations later.

3.3 Alignment to reference image (Stage ❸)

In the previous section, we showed how one could compensate for the effects of scene and camera motion by aligning the video frames using a robust homography estimation procedure. However, while this results in a stabilized video, one other aspect of appearance variation that remains unaccounted for is the relative positioning between the surveillance camera and the user. Note that we do not assume that the camera has a clean, frontal view of the screen of the device; rather, the surveillance camera can be oriented arbitrarily with respect to the user. Given that our ultimate goal is the detection of pressed keys, we now reduce the difficulty of our problem further by aligning the stabilized video to a *reference phone image*. This image can be obtained easily, in a number of ways: for example, by taking a single frontal-view photograph of the phone or using a photo from a reference manual. Alternatively, it would also be possible to automatically infer the keyboard layout by using character frequency analysis.

Given a reference image, the process of aligning the stabilized video to this reference image can be carried out in much the same way as before; that is, by detecting features in the reference image and the video frames, matching them, and computing a robust homography estimate which can then be used to warp all the video frames to the reference. In principle, we actually need to align only a *single* video frame to the reference image, since the frames of the video sequence have already been aligned to each other by pairwise homographies. More specifically, let $\mathbf{H}_{j+1,j}$ be the homography

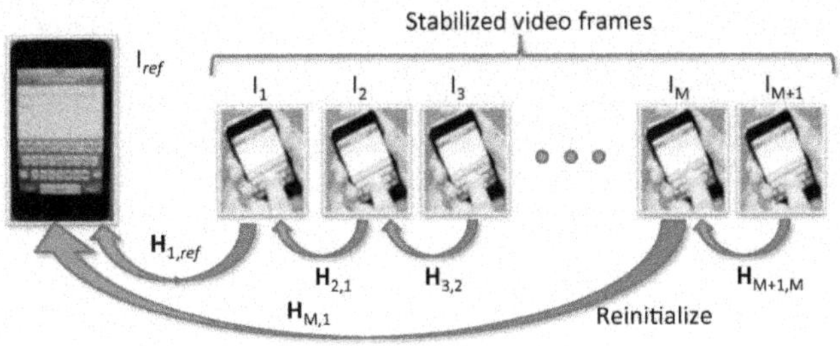

Figure 5: Iterative procedure to align video frames to the reference image (I_{ref}). To prevent long-term drift, the frames are periodically reinitialized with respect to the reference image.

that transforms video frame I_{j+1} to frame I_j. Assuming that I_1 denotes the first video frame, the transformation between frame I_{j+1} and frame I_1 can be computed by chaining together all previous pairwise transformations:

$$\mathbf{H}_{j+1,1} = \prod_{k=1}^{j} \mathbf{H}_{k+1,k}. \tag{1}$$

In theory, given a single transformation $\mathbf{H}_{1,ref}$, that aligns frame I_1 to the reference image I_{ref}, then by extension, one can align the entire video to the reference image. However, one important issue arises in practice: error propagation. Since the transformations are chained together, even a small error in the estimation of homography $\mathbf{H}_{j+1,j}$ propagates to all subsequent transformations. For a reasonably long video sequence, this invariably leads to "drift", where the alignment progressively deteriorates as more frames are aligned to the reference image.

To combat this effect, we instead perform a more careful alignment process, depicted in Figure 5. We begin by aligning frame I_1 to the reference image I_{ref}, via a robust homography $\mathbf{H}_{1,ref}$, estimated using the techniques introduced in Section 3.2. We then align subsequent frames of video by chaining together pairwise homography transformations – the difference being that every M frames ($M = 50$ in our experiments), we re-initialize our transformation with respect to the reference image by recomputing the video-to-reference image homography. We use the newly estimated homography as the base transformation for the next window of M frames.[2] This process of inter-frame homography estimation is much more accurate, as well as far more efficient, than performing alignment to the reference image. The reason is that the change in appearance of the phone between two successive video frames is often very small, while the change in appearance between the phone image in a random video frame (captured under arbitrary pose and lighting conditions) and the reference image is much larger.

3.4 Key press detection (Stage ❹)

Thus far, we have focused primarily on accounting for sources of appearance variability: phone and camera motion and the spatial relationships between the user and the

[2]In particular, we perform a non-linear minimization of the estimation error [10] with respect to the reference image. This is a common trick often used in practice to prevent drift, and also helps prevent catastrophic failure in the event of failed alignments.

surveillance system. The net effect of the operations performed thus far is to convert an arbitrary, free-form video sequence into one that has been aligned to a stable, *known* reference frame. There is a significant advantage to doing so: by aligning the video to a known coordinate frame, we know precisely which regions to inspect in order to find key pop-out events. More specifically, once the video frames have been aligned to the reference image, we can isolate the key pop-out event of each key on the virtual keypad to a *specific spatial location* (derived, for example, by overlaying 2D boxes on the reference image).

Although we have greatly simplified the problem, we are still faced with challenges. For one, because we are operating at a fairly low resolution, coupled with the fact that the appearance of the keys is often "blurred out," one can not readily apply OCR techniques to recover the characters in the isolated frames. Moreover, in several cases the pop-out events are occluded. As an experiment, we applied a popular open source OCR engine (`tesseract-ocr`) [3] to stabilized frames from Stage ❸. The results were an abysmal failure – no characters were correctly recognized.

Another complication is that the 2D boxes constituting the keypad grid are overlapping – in other words, the key pop-out events for neighbouring keys have a non-negligible area of overlap. To address this, we do not make any final decisions at this stage; rather, for each frame, we inspect each key location independently and assign a score to each key, which may be interpreted as the probability of the key having been pressed in that frame. These scores, along with their key labels, are then used in the final stage.

Training a key press classifier. The basic idea we use to identify key press events is to exploit the fact that we have a known, regular grid, and train a binary classifier for each key on the keypad. The classifier for each key focuses on a specific bounding box on the reference keypad, and aims to distinguish between a key pop-out event and the "background". We again make use of AdaBoost classifiers, introduced in Section 3.1, to perform this classification. In addition, since we have explicitly compensated for multiple sources of appearance variation, we can, at this stage, use an offline training procedure in order to have a classifier that is capable of rapid classification when processing each frame of video. Since we are operating on small image patches, and some illumination variation remains, we use dense SIFT descriptors as the features for each patch (i.e., a SIFT descriptor is extracted for each pixel in the patch, and concatenated to form a feature vector).

For each key on the keypad, we train a binary classifier, by providing positive and negative examples of key pop-out events. This data is obtained by running a representative collection of training videos through Stages ❶-❸, subsequently labeling each aligned frame with the key pressed for the frame. For example, to detect the tapping of the letter 'C', we extract a positive training patch from the 2D box corresponding to that letter, and negative patches for all other letters, at their respective locations. Each classifier is then trained offline using the acquired samples.

On detecting keyboard layout mode: While the above discussion focuses primarily on the alphabet keys, the same principles apply for special characters and numbers. On a smartphone, there is usually a special key that allows one to toggle between alphabet and numeric/special character mode. There are a couple of strategies one could adopt to detect keyboard toggle: (*a*) train a classifier that inspects the entire keyboard area to detect when the keyboard layout has been toggled, and then use the classifiers for the appropriate keys in each layout or (*b*) at each key pop-out location, run the classifiers for all keys that could potentially pop out at that location, and select the classifier that yields the highest score. In this work, we chose to pursue the latter option, and have used that approach to successfully detect numbers interspersed with alphabet characters.

Testing the classifier. Given a test video, and a pool of trained key press classifiers, we run the test video through Stages ❶-❸. Then, for every frame of video, each classifier inspects its respective image patch and outputs a classification score (the probability of that key having been pressed in the frame). We reject detections that score less than 0.5. Note that each classifier is run independently, and so there could potentially be multiple keys that pass this threshold. For each frame, we store all potential key labels and scores. Once a key pops-out on the keypad, it typically stays in this state for a fixed amount of time (e.g., about 0.25s on the `iPhone`); this fact can be used to parse the detected sequence of keys in order to identify tentative character breaks.

The observant reader would have noticed by now that we have yet to discuss the issue of the "space" bar. On many popular smartphones we examined (e.g., the `iPhone` and `NexusOne`), there is no pop-out event for the space bar. However, it is still possible to obtain a reasonable estimate of the locations of the spaces in typed text, by performing some straightforward post-hoc analysis. Given a sequence of identified key press events, we determine the median time interval t between successive key presses. If we now reinspect our key press detections, we can label the frames lying between two widely separated[4] key presses as potential space events. Additionally, the visual classifier we use to determine the space key event inspects a larger region of the keyboard, with the intuition being that when users press the space, a large portion of the keyboard is visible. This is by no means foolproof: a few spaces may be missed, and false spaces may be inserted when the user pauses between keystrokes. However, coupled with an image-based classifier, this analysis can still provide useful information.

3.5 Parsing and Language Modeling (Stage ❺)

Once we have identified key labels for each frame in a video, along with potential character breaks and spaces, the issue of identifying typed words still remains. We can view this task in terms of the *noisy channel* problem, often encountered in speech recognition: given a sequence of observations (labeled frames), find the most likely sequence of intended words. This process is often referred to as *maximum-likelihood decoding* [14].

The noisy channel problem is often formulated in a Bayesian framework. Let $P(w|o)$ represent the probability of a word sequence w given an observation sequence o. Then the decoding problem is that of finding $\hat{w} = \text{argmax}_w P(w|o)$. Us-

[3]See `http://code.google.com/p/tesseract-ocr/`

[4]A threshold of $1.5t$ appears to be effective in practice.

ing Bayes' rule, this can be reformulated as

$$\hat{w} = \underset{w}{\text{argmax}} \frac{P(o|w)P(w)}{P(o)} = \underset{w}{\text{argmax}}\, P(o|w)P(w)$$

where $P(o|w)$ represents the probability of observing a sequence o given that the sequence w was intended. The prior $P(w)$ represents the probability of observing word sequence w in the language of interest. The denominator can be safely omitted as it does not depend on w.

To solve the noisy channel decoding problem, speech recognition systems have long employed *cascades* of component models, where each model represents one conceptual stage in the task of transcribing speech. For instance, one such cascade might consist of three models: 1) an *acoustic model* which transforms an acoustic signal into component sounds, 2) a *pronunciation model* which converts sequences of sounds to individual words, and 3) a *language model*, which governs the combination of words into phrases and sentences. In this case, $P(w)$ represents the language model. The likelihood $P(o|w)$ can be further decomposed into sub-models, such as the acoustic and pronunciation models, representing intermediate stages. Commonly, these sub-models are assumed to be independent.

We draw on a large body of work on speech recognition cascades that has proven to be very useful in our context. However, in traditional speech recognition systems, the interaction between components often cannot be modeled explicitly, i.e., each step is performed independently. Pereira and Riley [25] proposed an elegant solution to this problem, representing each model and submodel as a *weighted finite-state transducer (WFST)*, thereby allowing for decoding to range over the entire cascade simulataneously. While a full treatment of weighted finite-state transducers is beyond the scope of this paper, we remind the reader that a finite-state transducer is a finite-state machine with both an input and an output tape and thus represents a mapping between sequences from two alphabets; applying weights to each arc then allows for scoring each path through the transducer. A finite-state *acceptor* can be viewed as the special case where the input and output tapes are identical. Multiple finite-state automata can be combined in various ways: for example, a speech recognition cascade can be represented as the *composition* of individual transducers for each stage. The resulting cascade can then be composed with an acceptor representing an input sequence, which transforms the decoding problem into that of finding the shortest path through the resulting weighted finite-state transducer.

In what follows, we apply weighted finite-state transducers to solve the noisy channel decoding problem in a manner similar to that of speech recognition cascades. That is, we utilize a language model and define a number of component models which, when combined, provide a probabilistic mapping from frame label sequences to word sequence. More specifically, we first apply a frame parsing model, $\mathcal{F}$, which maps sequences of frame labels to character strings. We then apply an edit distance model, $\mathcal{E}$, which maps each character string to a (weighted) set of similar character strings and helps account for errors made by the typist, the recognition algorithm, and the frame parser. Next, a dictionary model $\mathcal{D}$ is applied, discarding those paths resulting in invalid words. Finally, the language model $\mathcal{L}$ is applied, accounting for unlikely words and sequences of words in English.

Each component model is represented as a weighted finite-state machine, and the application of each is performed by composition. The resulting cascade WFST is then composed with the input sequence, represented as acceptor $\mathcal{I}$, resulting in a weighted transducer which maps from the input sequence to word sequences. We then search this transducer for the shortest path, which corresponds to the most likely sequence of words given the input sequence. We use the OpenFST library[5] to construct, combine, optimize and search our model cascade.

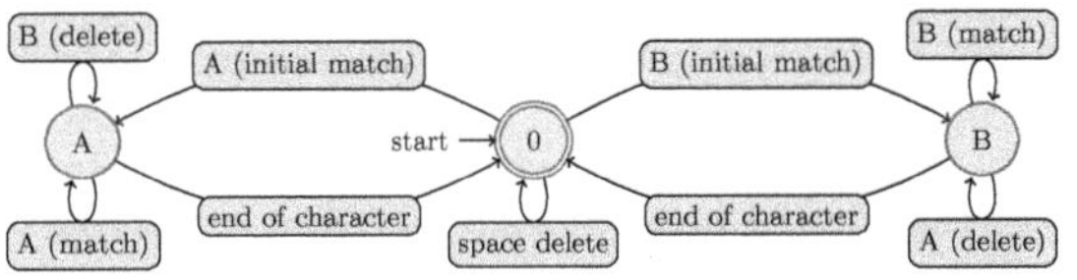

Figure 6: Simplified frame parsing WFST, with only two characters, that maps a sequence of labeled frames to characters.

The frame parsing WFST (Figure 6) allows for character break and space insertion as well as frame, break, and space deletion and is parametrized by weights on each of these actions. Each path starts at the zero state, representing the beginning of the frame label sequence. Upon encountering a frame labeled with a character, a transition is made to a character-dependent state (A or B, in this example) and that character is output. Subsequent frames with the same label are ignored freely, while those with a different character label are dropped with a penalty. In a typical path, once a character break appears in the frame stream, the transition back to the start state is made, from which the string can end or a new character can begin. Thus an input stream 'AA|BB' would be output as 'A|B' in a typical path. Other paths are possible, however, which insert or drop characters breaks and spaces with certain penalties; the same input would also generate, amongst other outputs, 'A' and 'A|A|B', albeit with a lower probability.

Our edit distance is based on the distance between keys on the keyboard and is intended to correct any misclassifications by the recognition algorithm. It can also automatically correct typing mistakes. The distance between two characters is straightforward. If both keys are in the same row, then the distance is the number of keys between them. If the keys are not in the same row, we calculate the distance as though they were in the same row (with rows aligned on the left-hand edge) and apply a multiplicative penalty for each row the two keys are apart. This distance is then normalized to be between zero and one; we take the additive inverse to obtain a probability estimate, which is weighted with a parameter. Similarly, the insertion and deletion costs are represented as probabilities and weighted with parameters, which allow for tuning the effects of the edit distance on the overall cascade. For efficiency, we limit the number of contiguous edits to two.

A simplified view of the edit distance WFST appears in Figure 7. For the edit distance WFST, the most likely path is a loop in the start state, in which case the output string is identical to the input string. However, an edit (substitution, insertion, or deletion) can be made, with a penalty, at any position in a word, resulting in a path which transitions to state 1; a second edit can then be made, transitioning to state 2. From either of these states, a match – or the end of

[5]`www.openfst.org`

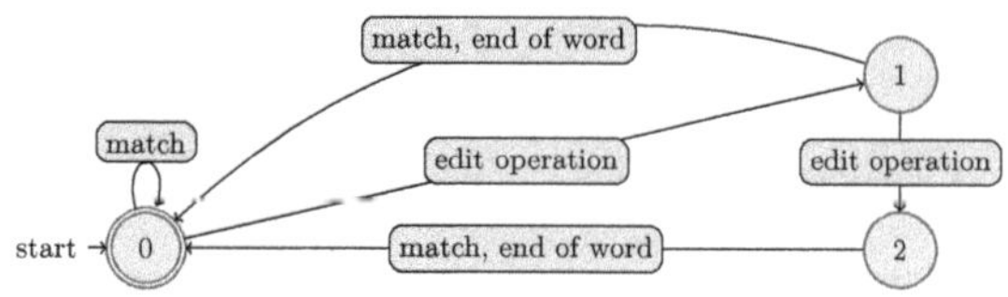

Figure 7: Simplified edit distance WFST mapping sequences of characters to similar sequences.

a word – is required to return to the zero state, which limits to 2 the number of edits which can be made in a row.

The dictionary used is based on the medium-sized word list from the Spell Checker Oriented Word Lists (SCOWL)[6], from which we removed roman numerals and the more obscure abbreviations and proper nouns. Finally, the language model used is a unigram model, i.e., simple word frequencies, trained on the well-known Brown corpus [6].

4. EVALUATION

Recall that our primary goal is to explore the feasibility of exploiting compromising reflections using low cost consumer devices, and to impose very few conditions on the capture environment. Towards this end, we experimented with capture devices ranging from a mid-range consumer grade device (a Canon VIXIA HG21 Camcorder, retailing for about $1000) to low cost, hand-held devices (Kodak PlayTouch and Sanyo VPC-CG20, costing $90 and $140, respectively). The Kodak PlayTouch camera, for instance, has a form factor very similar to a smartphone, thus allowing for unobtrusive capture in real-world settings.

Our capture settings ranged from cameras mounted near the ceiling of an indoor office environment to hand-held capture performed outdoors. For example, we recorded video footage at a bus stop as well as on a moving bus. In the indoor setup, the distance between the user and the camera was approximately 14 feet, while the outdoor capture was done at distances ranging from 4-7 feet (for instance, looking over a person's shoulder while sitting on a bus). At these distances, the pixel dimensions of the phone in the captured video ranged from about 49x75 to 114x149 (*widthxheight*). In addition to low resolution, these datasets present numerous other challenges: unstable video, motion blur, reflections from other objects, etc. See `http://cs.unc.edu/~rraguram/ispy` for some examples.

In total, we collected 18 videos (containing 39 sentences) from ten different users typing on the **iPhone**. Our experimental setup covered a number of practical use-cases designed to elicit a variety of typing styles (and speeds), and includes scenarios where subjects (a) typed short passages of text from *The Art of War* and David Kahn's *The Codebreakers* (b) simply typed whatever came to mind and (c) typed responses to text messages (e.g., '*What time shall we meet?*') sent to the phone. In each case, subjects were instructed to use the phone as they normally would. All subjects routinely use smartphones.

4.1 Evaluating Output Quality

We now turn our attention to how we measure the quality of our reconstructions. The problem we face here is similar to that found in both the automated speech recognition and machine translation (MT) communities, which has addressed many of the challenges associated with scoring the output of such systems. While humans are the target audience for MT systems (and therefore remain the ultimate arbiters of output quality), evaluations using human judges pose several obstacles. For one, evaluations using *experts* can be prohibitively expensive; conversely, hiring non-experts leads to issues with reliability and inconsistency. More pragmatically, progressive development necessitates frequent changes, evaluating the effectiveness of which requires rapid prototyping and testing.

Automated evaluation, on the other hand, allows system designers to quickly test new ideas while providing a consistent basis for comparing multiple approaches. Ideally, such automated evaluations would produce results similar to those of human experts, who typically assess the *adequacy*, or how well the appropriate meaning is conveyed, and *fluency* of a translation on a sentence-by-sentence basis. Similarly, state-of-the-art automated MT evaluation techniques score a *hypothesis* (i.e., the machine translation) by comparing it with one or more *reference* (i.e., expert) translations. The performance of these automated evaluation techniques is judged according to how well the assigned scores correlate with those assigned by experts.

Scoring our inferences. Before proceeding further, we note that automated MT evaluation remains an area of active research, with entire conferences dedicated to the topic. Nevertheless, one widely adopted metric for producing scores at the segment level is the Metric for Evaluation of Translation with Explicit ORdering [19]. METEOR accounts for position-independent matching of words (i.e., to model adequacy) and differences in word order (i.e., to model fluency). More specifically, the METEOR metric is the combination of a weighted f-score and a *fragmentation penalty*. The f-score is defined as the harmonic mean of unigram *precision* p and *recall* r. In this context, precision is the ratio of the number of (non-unique) words which occur in both the reference and the hypothesis to the total number of (non-unique) words in the hypothesis. Recall is the ratio of the number of words present in both hypothesis and reference translation to the number of words in the reference.

Denkowski and Lavie [5] have extensively explored the space of tunable parameters, and have identified different sets of values that correlate well with human evaluations on different tasks; we use the Human-Targeted Edit Rate parameter set with synonym matching disabled. As a guideline for METEOR scores, Lavie [18] suggests that scores of 0.5 and higher indicate *understandable* hypotheses, while scores of 0.7 and higher indicate *good* or *fluent* hypotheses.

4.2 Results

A boxplot of the METEOR scores for our reconstructions of the sentences typed in our collected videos is provided in Figure 8(a). Notice that in both the direct and indirect cases, more than 35% (8/23 and 6/16, respectively) of our hypotheses achieve *perfect* scores, and none score below the 0.5 threshold representing "understandable" translations. We provide a few examples of our hypothesized transcripts in Table 1, where we also list the input as actually typed by the user and the reference text used for scoring.

[6] `wordlist.sourceforge.net`

		Sentence	Scenario	Score
1	Typed:	to be prepared beforehand for any contingency is the greatest of virtues	Sunglasses	
	Reference:	to be prepared beforehand for any contingency is the greatest of virtues	Canon	0.92
	Hypothesis:	to be prepared beforehand for any contingency _ the greatest of virtues	66x104	
2	Typed:	i freaked out by the *possibilitu* of someone else *reafing* this	Direct, on-bus	
	Reference:	i freaked out by the possibility of someone else reading this	Kodak	0.65
	Hypothesis:	i *created* out by the possibility of *committee* else reading *the*	114x149	
3	Typed:	i can levitate birds	Sunglasses	
	Reference:	i can levitate birds	Sanyo	0.54
	Hypothesis:	i can *hesitate* birds	92x107	

Table 1: Example hypotheses from our reconstruction process. Under 'Scenario' is given the details of the capture scenario for each hypothesis, including camera type and phone image resolution. Note that Sentence 2 was captured on a bus.

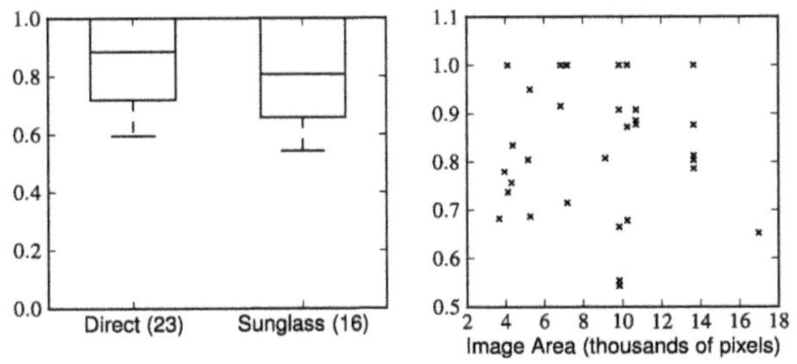

(a) METEOR scores (with number of sentences).

(b) Plot of input area size against METEOR scores.

System-Level Analysis. It is also instructive to consider evaluations at the level of entire corpora of documents, i.e., the system level. System-level analysis offers a different perspective and, in particular, smooths the dependency of the scoring on the length of the sentence. For instance, even a single mistake in a short sentence can lead to a relatively low METEOR score, as in Table 1 (Sentence 3). System-level analysis does not depend as strongly on the length of invididual sentences and can therefore alleviate this issue to some extent. The formulae are the same as at the sentence-level, but instead, (*i*) the system-level precision is calculated as the ratio of the sum of the counts of matched words over all sentences to the total number of words over all hypothesis sentences, and (*ii*) the fragmentation penalty is calculated based on the total number of contiguous subsequences and unigram matches over all sentences.

To better judge how well the system-level scores generalize, we also provide confidence intervals based on *bootstrap resampling*, a common statistical technique for estimating the distribution of a quantity, which consists of sampling (with replacement) from the set used to derive a statistic and calculating a *bootstrap statistic* based on the new sample. This process is repeated many times, resulting in an empirical distribution over the statistic of interest. For direct surveillance, we achieve a system-level METEOR score of 0.89, with a bootstrapped 95% confidence interval of $[0.84, 0.93]$. In the indirect surveillance case, we achieve a lower, yet still respectable, system score of 0.77, with a bootstrapped 95% confidence interval of $[0.70, 0.86]$.

Impact of Input Resolution. To gain a deeper understanding of the influence of the various input resolutions (of the phone's screen) on our ability to reconstruct the typed text, we plot the area (in pixels) of each input, against the ultimate METEOR score (Figure 8(b)). The figure shows no correlation, as evidenced by a correlation coefficient (Pearsons's r-value) of 0.07.

Isolated Word-Unit Matching. Lastly, there are a number of scenarios where an attacker might not wish to apply the dictionary matching and language modeling stages: for instance, when the text of interest is a secure password. Unfortunately, METEOR is not well-suited to evaluating accuracy in this scenario since we are interested in the ability to reconstruct isolated *word units*, i.e., sequences of contiguous non-space characters, rather than phrases. For this reason, we give instead precision and recall scores, based on the number of word units which match between what was actually typed and our reconstructed text. The results are for the same sets of sentences as in the evaluation above, but *without* the application of edit distance, dictionary, or language models. In this analysis, we achieve precision and recall, respectively, of 0.75 and 0.78 for direct surveillance and 0.64 and 0.65 for indirect surveillance – in all cases, the accuracy is high enough to recover more than half of any typed passwords. In addition, our single-character precision and recall scores are 94% and 98%, respectively, in the direct case, and 92% and 97% in the indirect case – certainly accurate enough for password guessing, particularly given that we have a reasonable prior distribution over characters to drive password space exploration.

5. SUMMARY & LIMITATIONS

We explore the feasibility of automatically reconstructing typed input in low resolution video, of, e.g., compromising reflections, captured in realistic scenarios. While our results are certainly disconcerting, it is prudent to note that there are some important issues that remain open. Low pixel resolution of the phone image is one of the key problems we encountered. It can be caused by a variety of factors, including camera aperture, wide angle lenses, motion blur, and large standoff distance. All of these make the phone's appearance so blurry that no reliable features can be extracted, and so our phone stabilization (Stage ❷) and alignment (Stage ❸) methods fail in certain cases. We believe this could be addressed by using more sophisticated (and expensive) capture techniques, as in [3], which addresses the allied problem of *capturing* clear images from reflections.

Finally, there are potential defenses against the attacks proposed in this work. One, in the indirect case, is the application of an anti-reflective coating, such as is common on modern eyeglasses, on the reflection surface. Reducing the brightness of the screen would also have a detrimental effect on any reconstruction. Finally, one might disable the visual key press confirmation mechanism which we leverage in this work. Obviously, our approach is not applicable to situations where there is no visual key press confirmation. Hence, devices that lack this effect – for instance, tablets, or devices that use Swype – are not vulnerable to our attack. How to effectively handle these kinds of devices is an interesting direction to explore. Incorporating temporal information through optical flow could potentially extend our approach to cover these types of input. Lastly, as suggested by Backes et al. [3], one could use secondary reflections in the environment when direct line-of-sight to the target is infeasible.

Nevertheless, the fact that we can achieve such high accuracy underscores the practicality of our attack, and aptly demonstrates the threats posed by emerging technologies.

6. ACKNOWLEDGMENTS

We thank the anonymous reviewers for their insightful comments. We also thank Pierre Georgel for helpful suggestions in improving this work and Enrique Dunn, Jared Heinly, Alex Keng, Megha Pandey, Anusha Sethuraman, Rohit Shah, Vishal Verma, and Enliang Zheng for assisting in our data collection efforts. This work is supported in part by NSF grant CNS-0852649.

References

[1] D. Asonov and R. Agrawal. Keyboard acoustic emanations. In *Proceedings of IEEE Symposium on Security and Privacy*, 2004.

[2] M. Backes, M. Dürmuth, and D. Unruh. Compromising reflections-or-how to read LCD monitors around the corner. In *Proceedings of the IEEE Symposium on Security and Privacy*, 2008.

[3] M. Backes, T. Chen, M. Duermuth, H. Lensch, and M. Welk. Tempest in a teapot: Compromising reflections revisited. In *Proceedings of the IEEE Symposium on Security and Privacy*, 2009.

[4] D. Balzarotti, M. Cova, and G. Vigna. ClearShot: Eavesdropping on keyboard input from video. In *Proceedings of the IEEE Symposium on Security and Privacy*, 2008.

[5] M. Denkowski and A. Lavie. Choosing the right evaluation for machine translation: an examination of annotator and automatic metric performance on human judgment tasks. In *Proceedings of the AMTA*, 2010.

[6] W. N. Francis and H. Kucera. Brown corpus manual. Technical report, Dept. of Linguistics, Brown University, 1979.

[7] Y. Freund and R. E. Schapire. A decision-theoretic generalization of on-line learning and an application to boosting. In *Proceedings of the* 2nd *European Conf. on Computational Learning Theory*, pages 23–37, 1995.

[8] H. Grabner, M. Grabner, and H. Bischof. Real-time tracking via on-line boosting. In *British Machine Vision Conference*, volume 1, pages 47–56, 2006.

[9] H. Grabner, C. Leistner, and H. Bischof. Semi-supervised on-line boosting for robust tracking. *European Conf. on Computer Vision*, pages 234–247, 2008.

[10] R. I. Hartley and A. Zisserman. *Multiple View Geometry in Computer Vision.* Cambridge University Press, 2000.

[11] H. J. Highland. Electromagnetic radiation revisited. *Computer Security*, 5:85–93, June 1986.

[12] P. J. Huber. *Robust Statistics.* John Wiley & Sons, 1981.

[13] K. Jung, K. I. Kim, and A. K. Jain. Text information extraction in images and video: a survey. *Pattern Recognition*, 37(5):977 – 997, 2004.

[14] D. Jurafsky and J. H. Martin. *Speech and Language Processing: An Introduction to Natural Language Processing, Computational Linguistics, and Speech Recognition.* Prentice Hall, 2008.

[15] Z. Kalal, K. Mikolajczyk, and J. Matas. Forward-backward error: Automatic detection of tracking failures. *Int. Conference on Pattern Recognition*, 2010.

[16] M. Kuhn. Electromagnetic eavesdropping risks of flat-panel displays. In *Privacy Enhancing Technologies*, 2004.

[17] M. G. Kuhn. Optical time-domain eavesdropping risks of CRT displays. In *Proceedings of the IEEE Symposium on Security and Privacy*, 2002.

[18] A. Lavie. Evaluating the output of machine translation systems. AMTA Tutorial, 2010.

[19] A. Lavie and M. J. Denkowski. The METEOR metric for automatic evaluation of machine translation. *Machine Translation*, 23:105–115, September 2009.

[20] K. Levi and Y. Weiss. Learning object detection from a small number of examples: the importance of good features. In *Computer Vision and Pattern Recognition*, 2004.

[21] J. Loughry and D. A. Umphress. Information leakage from optical emanations. *ACM TISSEC*, 5, August 2002.

[22] D. Lowe. Distinctive image features from scale-invariant keypoints. *Int. Journal of Computer Vision*, 60(2), 2004.

[23] NSA. TEMPEST: A signal problem. *Cryptologic Spectrum*, 2(3), 1972.

[24] T. Ojala, M. Pietikäinen, and T. Mäenpää. Multiresolution gray-scale and rotation invariant texture classification with local binary patterns. *IEEE Trans. Pattern Anal. Machine Intelligence*, 24:971–987, July 2002.

[25] F. C. N. Pereira and M. Riley. Speech recognition by composition of weighted finite automata. *The Computing Research Repository*, cmp-lg/9603001, 1996.

[26] R. Raguram, J.-M. Frahm, and M. Pollefeys. A comparative analysis of RANSAC techniques leading to adaptive real-time random sample consensus. In *European Conference on Computer Vision*, pages II: 500–513, 2008.

[27] S. Stalder, H. Grabner, and L. V. Gool. Beyond semi-supervised tracking: Tracking should be as simple as detection, but not simpler than recognition. *Workshop on On-line Learning for Computer Vision*, pages 1409–1416, Sept. 2009.

[28] W. van Eck. Electromagnetic radiation from video display units: an eavesdropping risk? *Computer Security*, 4: 269–286, December 1985.

[29] P. A. Viola and M. J. Jones. Rapid object detection using a boosted cascade of simple features. In *Computer Vision and Pattern Recognition*, 2001.

[30] P. A. Viola and M. J. Jones. Robust real-time face detection. *Int. Journal of Computer Vision*, 57(2), 2004.

[31] M. Vuagnoux and S. Pasini. Compromising electromagnetic emanations of wired and wireless keyboards. In *Proceedings of the* 18th *USENIX Security Symposium*, 2009.

[32] L. Zhuang, F. Zhou, and J. D. Tygar. Keyboard acoustic emanations revisited. *ACM TISSEC*, 13, November 2009.

Televisions, Video Privacy, and Powerline Electromagnetic Interference

Miro Enev
University of Washington
miro@cs.washington.edu

Sidhant Gupta
University of Washington
sidhant@cs.washington.edu

Tadayoshi Kohno
University of Washington
yoshi@cs.washington.edu

Shwetak N. Patel
University of Washington
shwetak@cs.washington.edu

ABSTRACT

We conduct an extensive study of information leakage over the powerline infrastructure from eight televisions (TVs) spanning multiple makes, models, and underlying technologies. In addition to being of scientific interest, our findings contribute to the overall debate of whether or not measurements of residential powerlines reveal significant information about the activities within a home. We find that the power supplies of modern TVs produce discernible electromagnetic interference (EMI) signatures that are indicative of the video content being displayed. We measure the stability of these signatures over time and across multiple instances of the same TV model, as well as the robustness of these signatures in the presence of other noisy electronic devices connected to the same powerline.

Categories and Subject Descriptors

K.6.5 [**Management of Computing and Information Systems**]: Security and Protection—*Unauthorized access*; I.5.4 [**Pattern Recognition**]: Applications—*Signal Processing*; I.5.1 [**Pattern Recognition**]: Models—*Neural Nets*

General Terms

Security, Experimentation

Keywords

Information leakage, powerline security, electromagnetic interference

1. INTRODUCTION

It is known that consumer electronic devices can leak *some* information over powerlines, such as whether a particular device is on or off [10, 23], or even information about specific keystrokes on a keyboard [3, 28]. However, this knowledge is limited. In many cases, when faced with a given technology and asked whether it leaks private information over the powerline, our only possible answer is either a "maybe" or a "probably." The device probably leaks information about whether it is on or off. It might also leak more fine-grained information, but exactly what information we do not know. Moreover, even if we can make an educated guess that a device might leak some particular form of information, we do not know how stable that information leakage channel is over time or over multiple instances of the same technology, nor how robust that information leakage is against interference from other devices connected to the same powerline.

In tandem with the above observations, we find that numerous technologies are being developed that will measure information from residential powerlines. For example, utility (power) companies are seeking to deploy smart meters that measure fine-grained power usage for billing and demand-prediction [27], and ubiquitous computing (ubicomp) systems similarly measure the powerline for activity recognition purposes [10, 11, 23]. Future versions of these technologies may measure even more information. Returning to the above-mentioned information leakage knowledge gap, there is enough information today for privacy advocates to argue that these powerline measurement should be treated as private [20], thus motivating proposed policy changes, recommendations to industry, and research on privacy-preserving mechanisms for powerline measurements (e.g., [24]). Those opposed to these recommendations argue that the privacy concerns are overinflated. Unfortunately, the existence of the knowledge gap means that both sides of the debate are proceeding with incomplete knowledge and hence positions based in part on conjecture. Thus, in addition to being of scientific interest, new research is needed to inform this debate.

While it is infeasible to completely close this knowledge gap and study *all* electronic devices and root out *all* powerline information leakage channels, it is feasible — even if daunting — to rigorously and extensively study individual artifacts or classes of artifacts. For this study, we choose to focus extensively on one of the most ubiquitous classes of consumer electronic devices: modern televisions (TVs). We choose TVs, rather than toasters or ovens, because TVs have complex internal states — functions of the screen content being displayed — and thus present the *potential* for rich information leakage.

Separately, our choice of TVs was driven by the legal status of TVs and video viewing habits. Specifically, the U.S. Video Protection Privacy Act of 1998 states that an

Television Name	Technology	Date of Fabrication	Price (USD)
Panasonic-42-A	Plasma	Sept 2010	$1099
Panasonic-42-B	Plasma	Sept 2010	$1099
Samsung-58-A	Plasma	Sept 2010	$2599
Samsung-58-B	Plasma	Sept 2010	$2599
Samsung-32	LCD	Oct 2007	$896
Sharp-42	LCD	Sept 2008	$1399
Sharp-32-A	LCD	Dec 2009	$499
Sharp-32-B	LCD	Dec 2009	$499

Table 1: A summary of the tested TVs showing make, technology, date of manufacture, and price for each device.

individual's video viewing records must be kept confidential. Any research finding to the contrary — that a measurements of a home's powerline could reveal private information about someone's video viewing habits — could thus have significant legal ramifications.

For breadth and depth, we obtained a collection of eight TVs spanning three manufacturers (Panasonic, Samsung, and Sharp),[1] two technologies (LCD and Plasma), and three sizes (32", 42", and 58"); see Table 1. We repeatedly played video sequences on each of these TVs while recording the electromagnetic interference (EMI) that these TVs produced as measured on the powerlines; we obtained these measurements using a separate single sensor attached to the same powerline, though explicitly *not* between the TV and the powerline itself. Our sensor's access to the powerline thus matches the access afforded to any other consumer electronic plugged in somewhere within a home. We analyzed the EMI in the frequency domain. We obtained initial measurements in a clean laboratory setting, and then collected further measurements in unrestricted home environments with diverse collections of other noisy electronics attached to the same powerline.

We find that all but the Sharp 32″ TVs produce a significant amount of stable, robust information leakage over the powerline via EMI. As an example, for the Panasonic 42″ TVs in a laboratory setting, we find that we can correctly match a random 15 minute EMI trace from a movie to a database of EMI signatures totaling 1200 movie minutes 96% of the time (the remaining 4% were below our matching threshold, not incorrectly matched); the hit rate drops to 92% in noisy home environments. More broadly, we sought to develop an infrastructure capable of exploring answers to the following five questions:

- Do TVs of different makes, models, and technologies produce repeatable EMI, when given repeated screen content?
- Does different screen content produce differentiable EMI from a given TV?
- Is EMI consistent across multiple instances of TVs from the same model family?
- Can we determine if someone is watching a particular video by matching an EMI sample to a database of EMI signatures?
- Can we match EMI recorded in a lab setting to EMI extracted in homes, especially when those homes might have a diverse array of other consumer electronics connected to the same powerline?

In general, we find that we are able to answer all these questions affirmatively, though with some caveats and clarifications, e.g., clarifications on what it means for an EMI trace to be "repeatable" or "consistent" and weaker results with the Sharp 32″ TVs. Although explicitly not our primary goal, we also sought to conduct a preliminary investigation into the following question:

- Can we learn to predict what EMI a TV would produce given *only* screen content, i.e., without previous EMI traces for that TV model when displaying the content in question?

To summarize, our primary contribution is an extensive study of powerline EMI information leakage from a diverse collection of modern TVs, as well as the discovery that significant, stable, and robust information is, in fact, leaked from these devices. Fortunately, from a privacy perspective, we also observe that today's utility companies are *not* collecting the granularity of information necessary for repeating our analyses, and the ubicomp technologies from the research community that could collect this type of information are not yet widely deployed. Nevertheless, these technologies are surprisingly near-term, e.g., smart meters exist today that report samples at 1 Hz but collect measurements at 3 kHz [7] (our approach in contrast samples at 500 kHz and uses measurements at 2 Hz) and we anticipate higher sampling rates in the near future.

Although these emerging technologies enable important applications, we stress here that the policies enacted today could help inform future utility and ubicomp deployments, and hence we argue that it is important to understand these findings today, before new technologies in or attached to the home begin to collect and store fine-grained powerline measurements at a large scale.

2. TECHNICAL FOUNDATIONS

Modern consumer electronics utilize switched mode power supplies (SMPS), which are increasingly employed due to their higher efficiency and smaller form factor. Energy Star even mandates the use of this kind of power supply for most consumer electronic devices. We anticipate that the prevalence of SMPS will only increase as hardware manufacturers face continued pressure from political and market forces demanding higher levels of efficiency and miniaturization. The materials described here are either known or easily inferred from past work and an understanding of how electrical devices operate, e.g., [10].

SMPS as EMI Sources. Despite the advantages SMPS provide, one side effect of SMPS's operation is that they inadvertently produce electromagnetic interference (EMI). The EMI is a consequence of the voltage conversion method that SMPS employ and it's characteristics are proportional to the rate at which the conversion in the power supply takes place. This rate, also known as the switching frequency, is dynamically adjusted to meet the power requirements of the appliance driven by the SMPS. In sum, the changing power demands of an electronic device cause dynamic adjustments to the SMPS's switching frequency which in turn modulates

[1]We do not have any reason to believe that our results are specific to these manufacturers.

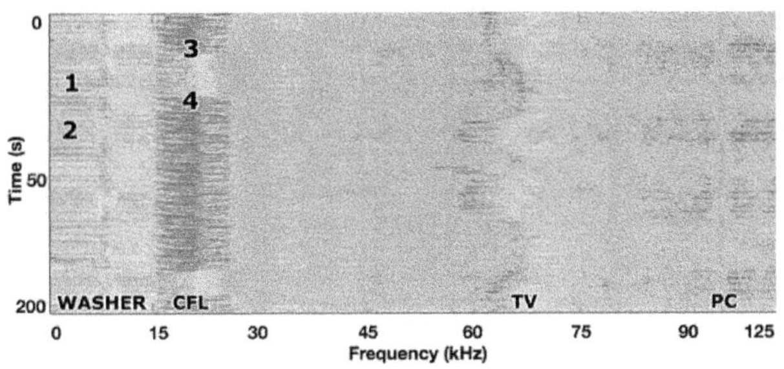

Figure 1: Frequency spectrogram showing various electrical appliances in the home. Washer cycle on (1) and off (2). CFL lamp turning off briefly (3) and then on (4). Note that the TV's (Sharp 42" LCD) EMI shifts in frequency, which happens as screen content changes.

the EMI signal. To prevent high levels of inadvertent EMI from adversely influencing the operation of neighboring devices, the Federal Communications Commission (FCC) in the U.S. limits the amount of interference that a device can emit to -40dBm for the frequency range of 1–500 kHz (47CFR part 15/18 Consumer Emission Limits); however the regulation threshold is weak from an information leakage perspective since EMI measurements can be accurately done using inexpensive hardware (the circuit we describe is sensitive to -100 dBm).

Noise Propagation. The EMI generated by SMPS devices is coupled onto the powerline and propagates throughout the electric infrastructure (i.e., a home) while retaining its signal qualities. In our tests we were able to capture robust signals several hundred feet away from the EMI source. We leverage this property and demonstrate that a single sensor anywhere along a home's powerline (including outdoor outlets) can observe the conducted EMI signals from numerous connected SMPS-based devices.

Signal Characteristics. The raw signals we gather with our powerline interface (PLI) (detailed in Section 5) are not particularly meaningful unless analyzed in the frequency domain. To transform the signal from a sequence of data points in time to a set of energies at various frequencies, we digitize the analog readings and compute a Fast Fourier Transform (described in detail later in the paper). The goal of these engineering operations is to allow us to analyze EMI fluctuations as changes in power over frequency space (visualized in Figure 1).

Figure 1 presents a waterfall plot of the EMI observed in a typical home; note the rich information landscape which unfolds when the frequencies of EMI signals (horizontal axis) are plotted against time (vertical axis). In this snapshot we observe that several devices are in continuous operation (PC, television, and washer) while others are turning on and off (compact fluorescent lamp (CFL)).

There are several interesting features in this data, which provide a good reference point for discussing the general EMI signal characteristics that we observed across our many experiments. In particular:

- Each SMPS device produces some conducted EMI, and the presence or absence of this signal is a direct consequence of the power state of the device.
- The EMI signature of each device is centered around the switching frequency of its power supply; different devices often occupy distinct frequency ranges allowing for their noise signals to coexist with minimal interference. However signal overlap is possible, and increasingly likely if many active devices share the same powerline.
- Changes in EMI can manifest in frequency shifts, energy density changes, or both. These properties are visible in Figure 1 as the TV exhibits frequency shift EMI, while the washer signal produces density changes.

Note that EMI signals vary as a function of the operation of the device, e.g., washer EMI increases in energy density when the barrel is rotated during the spin cycle, and TV EMI is modulated in frequency as the screen content changes. We explore this phenomenon more deeply in our investigations below.

3. RELATED WORK

Our work builds on and complements past work in the activity recognition, energy monitoring, and information leakage.

Activity Recognition & Energy Monitoring. Detecting electrical device activity and power consumption in the home has historically been done in the distributed sensing model wherein each device being tracked is instrumented with a dedicated sensor. This one-sensor-per-device model is limiting because, as the name suggests, every monitored device requires separate sensor installation and maintenance. However, research dating from the 1980s in single-point sensing of electrical events has focused on the design of new in-line metering techniques for monitoring whole-house appliance usage [11]. This early work used a current sensor installed in-line with a home's power meter to monitor voltage and current waveforms from the incoming power to the home. The methods used in these original studies combined measurements of (1) step changes in power, (2) the active and reactive power of the home, and (3) time of day statistics. These data sources were combined to detect and classify individual appliance usage.

Recent advances in infrastructure-mediated sensing (IMS) from the ubicomp literature have provided an alternative approach for detection of events on the home's utility infrastructure [6, 9, 10, 22, 23]. These methods focus on leveraging incidental signals such as the EMI from electrical appliances and water pressure changes from plumbing fixtures for inferring appliance usage and thus in-home activity from a single-point. We were inspired by this line of work and have based our sensor architecture on the design of a power line interface introduced in [10] to capture EMI present on a home's powerline. The primary focus of the existing research on electrical sensing has been on detecting and differentiating between appliances, whether by measurements of overall power consumption [11] or via the presence/absence of characteristic signals in the EMI when analyzed in the frequency domain [10].

To surface privacy concerns, Molina-Markham et al. recently highlighted that monitoring the home's aggregate power consumption can reveal private information about a homeowner's activity [21]. This work used methods from prior work in the energy monitoring and ubiquitous computing communities. Specifically, these authors use power usage patterns of the on/off states of electrical device to show that privacy inferences are possible using seemingly innocuous data (e.g., power activity every few hours during the night may indicate regular feedings of a newborn).

Unlike prior work, which analyzes the state and identity of appliances, we use a different method to track a continuously varying signal. If we compare the EMI acquisition sensor to a microphone, an appropriate analogy would be that previous work has been able to detect the presence of speech and potentially who is speaking while our contribution enables us to understand *what* is being said. Concurrent to our own work, Clark et al. study powerline information leakage when a PC visits a Web page [5]. They evaluated their approach with eight websites and a single PC; their measurements instrument the connected outlet, whereas our measurements can take place anywhere on the powerline.

Security & Information Leakage. In the security literature, evidence suggests that the government has long known that ancillary EM emissions from CRT monitors leak private information about what those devices might be displaying [8, 12, 16]. Early work on studying electromagnetic leakage from CRTs has since been extended to flat-panel displays [17] and wired and wireless keyboards [3, 28].

There are important commonalities between all these works, e.g., they all seek to extract as much information as possible from the observed EMI noise. There are, however, also important differences. We focus on modern LCD and Plasma systems manufactured between 2007 and 2010. More fundamentally, we find that there are inherent differences in the types of signals we analyze. For example, both [3] and [28] leverage EMI resulting from a keyboard's digital transmission of bits corresponding to key presses. Past works on CRTs/LCDs similarly looked at analog/digital transmissions within the TVs [8, 12, 16, 17], however there is an *additional* level of indirection in the EMI information leakage that we exploit in this paper. Specifically, although the TV's video content is transmitted digitally within the TV, we do not knowingly extract any information about that digital content. Rather, we extract information from EMI emitted from the TV's power supply as it drives the video display, which consumes varying power.

The security community has also explored numerous other classes of information leakage, including: the time to perform various tasks (e.g., [13]), optical emanations (e.g., [19] for network appliances and [15] for CRTs), acoustic emanations (e.g., for printers [4], CPUs [26], and keyboards [1]), and reflections (e.g., [2]). There is also security research focused on the modern television showing that it is possible to infer what someone is watching over an encrypted wireless video stream from the size of the transmitted packets [25]; that approach exploits information leakage through variable bitrate encoding schemes, which was pioneered in [29]. Related to power consumption, but far afield from our own work, is the broad area of power analysis and differential power analysis for cryptographic processors [14].

4. CONTEXT AND THREAT MODEL

This work focuses on understanding and assessing how information might leak from a highly popular consumer electronic device: the TV. In this section we characterize the threat models under which our results are the most applicable. We stress, however, that (in our opinion) the results in this paper are of scientific interest independent of any particular threat model or policy question.

We consider three key axes for our threat model: the type of attacker, the adversarial goals, and the adversarial resources. We consider each in turn.

Attacker Type. We consider two key types of attackers:

- **Intentional Attacker.** An entity seeking to violate the privacy of an individual; may attach an adversarial monitoring device to the victim's powerline.
- **Unintentional "Attacker."** A party that attaches a monitoring device to a powerline for *legitimate* purposes (e.g., a smart meter or a ubicomp device). The word "attacker" is in quotes because the party in question is not malicious. Rather, the attached device will record measurements from the powerline for *non-malicious* purposes. The device may store those measurements locally or transmit (a function of) those measurements to an external server for processing and/or storage.

An intentional attacker could, for example, plug a sensor into an exterior outlet on a neighbor's home and thereby monitor EMI on the neighbor's powerline. We observe, however, that if the attacker could enter the neighbor's home, then the attacker might also explore even more devious attacks, such as hiding a webcam in a sensitive location. Thus, the most likely intentional attacker is one that does not have direct physical access to the monitored space (the interior of a home, apartment, or dorm room) but that does have direct physical access to the powerline (e.g., via an external outlet). The device could also be disguised as a different device, such as a harmless power adaptor or DVD player.

A more pressing concern is likely the unintentional "attacker." Consider, for example, this scenario recounted in a recent joint filing before the State of California by the Center for Democracy & Technology and the Electronic Frontier Foundation [20]:

> Government agents issued a subpoena to the suspect's utility to obtain energy usage records and then used a utility-prepared "guide for estimating appropriate power usage relative to square footage, type of heating and accessories, and the number of people who occupy the residence" to show that the suspect's power usage was "excessive" and thus "consistent with" a marijuana-growing operation.

As smart meters and ubicomp devices begin to collect increasingly fine-grained measurements from the home powerline for legitimate purposes (e.g., demand prediction, activity recognition, green energy recommendations), it is important to understand how those measurements could be misappropriated in the future.

Adversarial Goals. We consider two adversarial goals:

- **Target Video Identification.** An adversary might seek to determine whether the victim is watching a *target video.*
- **Target Channel Identification.** An adversary might seek to infer what TV channel the victim is watching.

In both cases the adversary might either be an intentional attacker or someone analyzing the data collected by an unintentional "attacker." For target video identification, the adversary may seek to determine whether the victim is viewing a video from a "watch list" of sensitive titles, e.g., politically sensitive videos, religious videos, terrorist training videos. For target channel identification, we observe that the channel a person watches may reveal private information, e.g., political views, religion, known languages. The severity of these adversarial goals may be a function of the environment in which the victim lives. Within the U.S., we recall that an individual's video viewing records is considered highly sensitive pursuant to the Video Protection Privacy Act.

Our choice of these adversarial goals is driven by scale. For target channel identification, the attacker may know that a victim is watching one of a handful (a dozen or possibly a hundred) channels. Determining which channel a person is watching out of a small finite set of possible channels is far more feasible than determining which video a person is watching from the set of all possible videos. For target video identification, the goal is still significantly more feasible than determining which video a person is watching from the set of all possible videos — rather, the adversary must only be able to detect the viewing of specific videos.

Although we did not explore the following, we conjecture that our approach could also be used to estimate whether an individual is watching a pirated movie, *if* that pirated movie has some (possibly slight) deviation from the authorized copy of that movie. For example, if a pirated movie begins with a characteristic opening sequence — e.g., the opening animation inserted by the pirating organization, or an opening sequence that announces that the video is for the exclusive use by members of the Academy of Motion Picture Arts and Sciences — then that opening sequence might reveal itself in the leaked EMI. We explicitly did not investigate the identification of pirated content. But, as evidence of plausibility, over the course of our experiments we did develop the capability to visually distinguish between the splash screens for different studios (e.g., MGM, Twentieth Century Fox, etc.). The lack of these splash screens or the FBI warning screen on a DVD could also be an indicator.

Adversarial Resources. Finally, in addition to assuming that the attacker has the ability to obtain sufficient quality measurements from the victim's powerline, we assume that the attacker knows the type of TV that the victim is using. Although not the focus of this paper, we consider extensions in Section 10 where this is not necessary. Although outside the scope of this paper, we also conjecture that a second level classifier could be designed to infer the model of TV based on the operational characteristics of the SMPS, which is also discussed in prior work [10]. Finally, we assume that the attacker has access to the videos that he or she seeks to identify (e.g., DVDs for the target videos or feeds from all the channels that the victim might be watching).

5. SYSTEM DESCRIPTION

We now turn our attention to describing the data acquisition and post-processing components we used for our experiments. See Figure 2.

EMI Capture Hardware and Signal Processing. Our system consists of three main components. First, we connect a custom power line interface (PLI) module to any available electrical outlet in the recording environment to gather the conducted EMI signal. Second, we use a high-speed data acquisition module to digitize the incoming analog signals from the PLI. Lastly, we use a data collection and analysis PC

Figure 2: Components of our EMI capture hardware: Power Line Interface (P) for filtering 60 Hz signal voltage sensing, high speed digitizer (U) for analog to digital conversion of signals and an isolation transformer (I) for filtering EMI from other devices in our laboratory environment. The Sharp 42" LCD TV and the data logging PC are also visible. We also connect a spectrum analyzer (S) for debugging purposes and for visualizing the real-time EMI signal as a waterfall plot.

running our software to condition and process the incoming signals from the digitizer.

Harvesting EMI. The power line interface (PLI) that we designed to capture EMI was modeled on the circuit described in [10] with slight modifications to increase sensitivity at a broader frequency range. Our PLI module is essentially a high pass filter, composed of 3 resistors and 2 capacitors arranged as depicted in the schematic in Figure 3. This circuit design yields a RC high-pass filter which has two important properties. First, as in [10] it removes the 60 Hz frequency which is the rate at which alternating current (AC) is supplied in the U.S.; if this filter is not included, the 60 Hz signal would overwhelm our capture system yielding unusable data (and also potentially damaging any connected low voltage hardware). Second, the filter has a flat frequency response between 6 and 30,000 kHz which allows us to capture any conducted EMI in this expansive frequency band.

Post Processing and Automation. To transform the EMI data into the frequency domain, we fed the analog signal from the PLI into a USRP (Universal Software Radio Peripheral), which acts as a high-speed digitizer. We set the sampling rate of the USRP to 500 kHz, which allows us to effectively analyze the spectrum from 0 to 250 kHz (under the Nyquist Theorem). We found no interesting television signals beyond 250 kHz.

The digitized data from the USRP is then streamed in real time over a USB 2.0 connection to a PC running customized GNU Radio software. The PC processes the incoming data and computes a Blackman-Harris windowed (size half of FFT

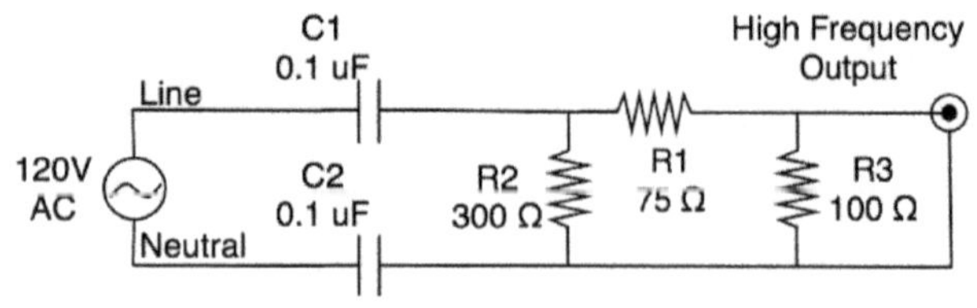

Figure 3: Schematic of the Power Line Interface, modified from [10] for broader sensitivity.

length) Fast Fourier Transform (FFT) 122 times a second to produce a vector of 2048 points which are spread uniformly over the spectral range (from 0 to 250 kHz). Next we compute the squared magnitude of each FFT vector and store the result on disk for post-processing. Our experimental infrastructure is highly automated; it can automatically stream video content to TVs while simultaneously logging EMI signals.

Lab vs Home Setup. Over the course of our experimental analysis we collected EMI data from lab and home settings. During lab recordings, we connected the TV being tested and our PLI sensor to the output of an isolation transformer (model Tripp Lite IS500HG). The isolation transformer reduces electrical noise and EMI present on the power line and presents a cleaner AC power at it's output [2]. Generally, isolation transformers are used to protect against electric shock, or to suppress electrical noise in sensitive devices such as high-end audio systems.

Conversely, in home recordings, we did not use the isolation transformer but rather connected the PLI directly to any available electrical outlet. This meant that we were no longer guaranteed a clean electrical background, and our target EMI could now be affected by the noise produced by any of the devices on the powerline.

6. SELECTION OF TVS AND MOVIES

To evaluate the level of EMI based information leakage in modern TVs, we procured a set of eight TVs that differ along a number of axes including: manufacturer (Panasonic, Samsung, Sharp), display technology (LCD or Plasma), size (32″, 42″, 58″), and date of manufacturing (2007–2010).

Table 1 summarizes our hardware selection. We opted for an equal distribution of LCDs and Plasmas — the two dominant technologies currently on the market. Furthermore we deliberately selected three pairs of duplicate TV models to enable analysis of EMI signature similarity across identical hardware. This table also introduces a naming scheme which we use in the remainder of the paper. Under this convention, television names include manufacturer, size, and model-pair information. For example the name Samsung-32 indicates that the Samsung TV is 32″ and that we have only one model instance; similarly, Panasonic-42-A is a 42″ Panasonic TV which is the first of a pair (as indicated by the "A").

Next we needed to choose what video signals to send to the TVs while recording EMI. For experimental feasibility, we opted to create a 20 movie database. To make our movie selection systematic, we chose four top-rated films within each of five distinct genres (ratings were extracted from the Internet movie database, `imdb.com`). Since these movies had variable running times, we limited our analysis to the first 60 minutes of each DVD video stream. Table 2 lists the movies that constitute our library. Looking ahead, our results suggest that our methodology is applicable far beyond a collection of 20 target movies. Nevertheless, we note that past work on video information leakage also studied a similarly-sized collection of movies (26 movies), though in a very different context (information leakage from streaming encrypted video data) [25]. Returning to the threat model in Section 4, we also argue that distinguishing between 20 movies approximates the adversarial goal of target channel identification. In our experiments we also embed random portions of these 20 movies into streaming TV signals and assess our ability to detect the embedded videos, thereby approximating the adversarial goal of target video identification.

Genre	Movie
Action	(1) Lord of the Rings: Return of the King, (2) Star Wars V: Empire Strikes Back, (3) The Bourne Ultimatum, (4) The Matrix
Animation	(5) Wall-E, (6) Shrek 2, (7) The Lion King, (8) Aladdin
Comedy	(9) Office Space, (10) Meet the Parents, (11) The Hangover, (12) Wedding Crashers
Documentary	(13) Planet Earth: Fresh Waters, (14) Food Inc., (15) An Inconvenient Truth, (16) Top Gear (Season 4;Episode 7)
Drama	(17) The Shawshank Redemption, (18) American Beauty, (19) Titanic, (20) Requiem for a Dream

Table 2: List of twenty movies that we included in our dataset selected such that they span various genres.

7. DATA COLLECTION PROCEDURE

We performed recordings on each of our 8 TVs in a lab environment where we could carefully regulate the electrical conditions. This data accounted for 13 days of EMI traces, and provided the foundation of most of our analysis. Next, we selected a single TV (Panasonic-42-B) and deployed our system to three home locations to gather data in electrically uncontrolled settings. Lastly, we recorded EMI from 20 hours of broadcast programming, which was the basis of the experiment described in Section 9.5.

Lab Recording. During lab recordings, we plugged a given TV and our voltage sensor into an isolation transformer to remove interference from other electrical devices in the building. We then streamed our database of 20 movies twice[3] while logging EMI in the 6 to 250 kHz range.

Home Recording. To evaluate EMI based information leakage under a more naturalistic setting, we also performed data collection in three homes with distinct sizes, neighborhoods, ages (1906, 2003, 2009), and styles (apartment, suburban house, multi-family home) on a subset of our movie database (12 movies, 15 minutes each). Table 3 shows the

[2]We recognize that a 'Line Impedance Stabilization Network' LISN device would have provided a more optimally stable and repeatable signal; however, we expect a LISN to only improve the already high matching accuracies achieved with our acquisition hardware.

[3]Two runs of our movie library were recorded on each TV to investigate the repeatability of EMI signatures.

ID	Style/ Year Built	Size/Floors
H1	Single family Home/2003	3000 sq. ft/ 2 flrs
H2	Apartment/2009	657 sq. ft/ 1 flr
H3	Multi-family Home/1906	800 sq. ft/ 3 flrs(*)

Table 3: A summary of the homes showing the style, size and number of floors. (*) 800 sq. ft refers to only one apartment in a converted multi-family home.

specifications for these residences. During the home data collection, we did not prevent occupants from actuating electrical devices and we also did not use the isolation transformer. Also, we plugged in our sensor in a arbitrarily chosen electrical outlet that was available. Thus, we captured not only the EMI from the TV but also any number of active electrical devices operating in the home under natural conditions (e.g., lamps, kitchen appliances, computers, other televisions). Many times during our home data collection EMI from other devices overlapped with the EMI from the TV under investigation. In addition, Home#2 used power line communication (PLC) during recordings, however we did not observe significant signal interference since home PLC signals are typically narrow-band in our recording range.

8. SIGNAL CONDITIONING

Automated Signal Identification. To facilitate analysis we needed to devise a method for extracting meaningful signals from the FFT data captured using our hardware. Recalling the properties of EMI we described in Section 2, we see that there are two critical questions which must be answered in order to track the signature of a particular device: (1) in what range of the frequency spectrum does the EMI signal reside, and (2) in what way does the EMI signal fluctuate with changes in device state.

Although it is often possible to answer both of these questions by visual inspection of a spectrum analyzer during device operation, we sought to develop a systematic search procedure which played a 5 minute custom software-generated video while performing a range sweep to find EMI changes that are strongly correlated in time with the controlled signal. The search method was designed to determine the EMI frequency range, fluctuation type (frequency or energy density), and to ultimately produce a 1-dimensional time series representation (EMI trace) normalized to the 0:1 domain.

The search algorithm requires FFT samples extracted from EMI over the 0 to 250 kHz frequency range collected during controlled video signal playback (36600 total FFT samples). Given this input our procedure analyzes subsets (windows) of the frequency spectrum and correlates their EMI trace (computed as both energy density and frequency shift) to the trace of brightness changes in the software-generated video [4]. At the end of the sweep, the optimal 1-dimensional EMI trace is returned which produced maximal correlations to the control signal (the search is performed across all frequency windows and signal types). The functions we applied are shown below in pseudo-code using the array syntax *initial-value:final-value* common to the MATLAB programming language. Smoothing is done using a 4th order Butterworth filter with a cutoff frequency of 10 kHz; decimation is done using eighth-order lowpass Chebyshev Type I filter with

[4]Our experiments led us to conclude that artificially generated color gradients work well as control signals.

Television Name	Freq. Range	Signal Type
Panasonic-42-A/B	1 to 60 kHz	Energy Density
Samsung-58-A/B	45 to 55 kHz	Frequency Shift
Samsung-32	10 to 50 kHz	Energy Density
Sharp-42	60 to 90 kHz	Frequency Shift
Sharp-32-A/B	35 to 40 kHz	Energy Density

Table 4: Frequency regions and EMI signal types for our 8 TVs.

a cutoff frequency of $0.8 * (Fs/2)/r$ where $r = 20$ is the decimation factor; standard normalization is performed to shift the domain to 0:1.

Using the EMI search procedure, we were able to characterize the EMI signatures for all of the TVs in the lab setting (Table 4). In addition, the search method proved invaluable when we analyzed EMI from home recordings as different residences had unique levels of dynamic background noise which overlapped with tracking ranges we found in lab; our methods were always able to find frequency regions minimally influenced by the other powerline noise and thus enabled us to recover the TV EMI signal (due to harmonics).

EMI search procedure:

```
var EMI := fft(range := 0 : 250kHz, time := 1 : 36600);
  var target := brightnessGradient(controlVideo);
    begin
      for r := 1 to 250 step 2 do
        for len := 10 to 60 step 10 do
          if r + len > 250 then continue fi;
          rEnd := r + len;
          [freqEMI, densEMI] := extractEMI(r, rEnd);
          fCorr(r, len) := xcorr(freqEMI, target);
          dCorr(r, len) := xcorr(densEMI, target);
        od
      od
      [optRange, sigType] := max_{r,len}(fCorr, dCorr)
      proc extractEMI(start, end) ≡
        type1 := sum(EMI(start : end, 1 : 36600);
        type2 := maxIndex(EMI(start : end, 1 : 36600);
        densEMI := normalize(decimate(smooth(type1)))
        freqEMI := normalize(decimate(smooth(type2)))
      .
    end
```

9. ANALYSIS AND RESULTS

We began by experimentally establishing that individual televisions produce repeatable EMI traces when the same video content is shown multiple times. Building on this result, we show that the EMI signals produced by multiple TVs of the same model are highly correlated given identical video inputs. We then use our collection of 20 movies to study the ability of an attacker to match the EMI collected from one movie with a database of previously collected EMI measurements from all 20 movies. Together, these results suggest that an attacker can use TV EMI to accomplish the target channel identification goal from Section 4 with high confidence. Next, we study the feasibility of our approach in three home environments, where additional signals sources are active on the power line. The data from homes also allows us to reason about the possibility of matching EMI traces gathered in an electrically clean setting to those collected

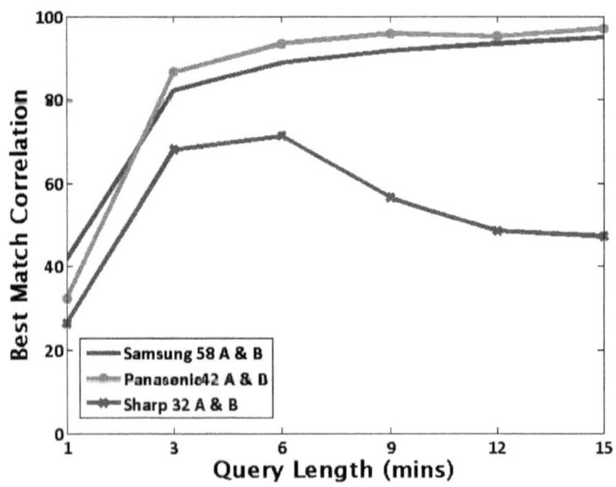

Figure 4: Cross Correlation results at various query lengths.

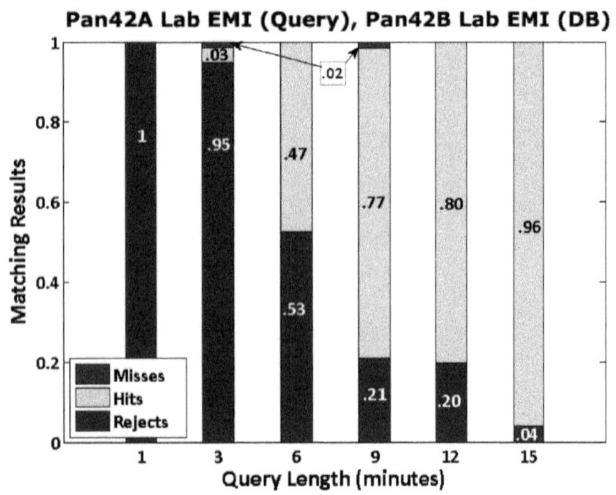

Figure 5: Matching results for Pan-42-A vs Pan-42-B for varying query lengths.

from noisy environments (i.e., matches are possible between lab and home EMI). Finally, we showcase the robustness of our methods by accurately identifying segments of EMI from our movie database that have been embedded within a stream of foreign EMI (20 hours of local television broadcasting), thus providing strong evidence that an attacker can also use TV EMI to accomplish the target video identification goal from Section 4 with high confidence.

9.1 Signal Repeatability in Lab

Individual TVs. The first question we sought to answer was whether repeated video content played on a target TV would produce consistent EMI. To test this, we computed the cross-correlation of a movie's EMI trace between multiple recording sessions. The left column of Table 5 contains the cross-correlation statistics when this computation was applied to every movie in our database and repeated for each TV, using only the first 15 minutes of each trace. These levels of high cross-correlation suggest that for most televisions multiple runs of identical video content produced consistently similar EMI. The exceptions, which we consider in more

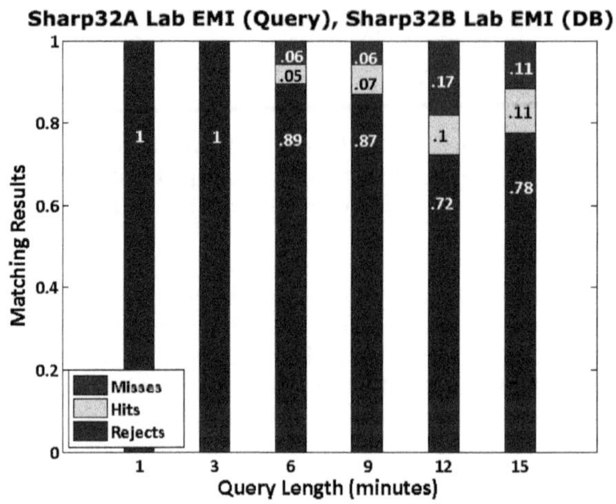

Figure 6: Matching results for Sharp-32-A vs Sharp-32-B for varying query lengths.

depth later, are the Sharp 32″ TVs. Conversely, dissimilar video content tended to produce highly uncorrelated EMI traces. The latter conclusion was drawn from the results of our followup experiment which analyzed the potential for similarity between EMI traces from different video streams. More specifically, we recorded the highest levels of cross-correlation possible while matching a movie against all other films in the database (itself excluded); our measurements are reported in the right column of Table 5.

Model Families. While the above findings indicate significant information leakage within a TV, it's not clear whether this leakage poses a significant threat to privacy. The question arises: can an attacker infer information from the EMI of a TV that he or she is not able to physically access? We explore that question here by assessing how similar the EMI is between two TVs of the same model. We performed this test by replicating the methods above, but instead of comparing EMI signals from multiple recording sessions on a single TV we analyzed the correlations between EMI signals between single sessions of EMI recorded on TVs within the same model family (i.e., Panasonic-42-A vs Panasonic-42-B, Samsung-58-A vs Samsung-58-B, and Sharp-32-A vs Sharp-32-B). As before, we computed the EMI similarity of identical content (Table 6, left column) as well as distinct content (each movie against all others, Table 6, right column).

Discussion. The experiments suggested that, with few exceptions, EMI from identical video signals are highly repeatable while distinct video sources yield independent EMI signals. These results were shown to hold within individual TVs as well as across pairs of TVs within a model family. In both cases, the Sharp 32″ TVs produced outlier data points, reflecting a significant decrease in EMI consistency relative to the averages of other TVs. We attribute this to the fact that these devices had the least dynamic EMI (minimally modulated by screen content changes) within the televisions we tested. We tested the power consumption of the Sharp 32″ TVs and found that their power draw changed by only 1W (175W to 176W) when playing a software generated custom video, whereas the Sharp 42″ TV exhibited a 24W (190W to 214W) change using the same video signal. Thus we attribute the small dynamic shifts in EMI of the Sharp 32″ to

TV	Cross Correlation Same Content (%)		Cross Correlation Different Content (%)	
	Average	Standard Deviation	Average	Standard Deviation
Panasonic-42-A	98.18	±2.77	60.36	±12.83
Panasonic-42-B	98.99	±0.98	59.51	±12.97
Samsung-58-A	97.47	±1.97	53.29	±10.22
Samsung-58-B	96.71	±2.73	53.37	±9.70
Samsung-32	98.26	±5.21	65.56	±16
Sharp-42	97.30	±8.26	63.45	±12.84
Sharp-32-A	60.03	±8.12	56.41	±5.10
Sharp-32-B	60.91	±8.39	56.39	±5.79

Table 5: Analysis of EMI signal similarity given identical and different video content within a TV - averaged over the 15 minute intro segment of all movies.

TV	Best Cross Correlation Same Content (%)		Best Cross Correlation Different Content (%)	
	Average	Standard Deviation	Average	Standard Deviation
Panasonic-42-A and B	96.82	±4.67	59.93	±12.85
Samsung-58-A and B	94.96	±9.23	59.30	±10.09
Sharp-32-A and B	77.21	±18.84	53.31	±12.96

Table 6: Analysis of EMI signal similarity given identical and different video content between TV pairs (averaged over all movies). For this we used randomly selected 15 minute streams from each 60 minute movie

the power consumption characteristics of the circuitry. There is also a possibility that this particular model incorporates a fixed frequency power supply.

9.2 Signal Matching and Query Length

Our initial experiments suggested that extracted EMI signals are consistent within TVs as well as between identical models using cross correlations computed over 15 minute segments of content. We next evaluated how varying the length of EMI traces impacts signal repeatability and differentiability.

We designed a search procedure that would take as input a full EMI trace of a movie and extract 10 query segments (of variable lengths) from multiple (randomly chosen) starting indexes along the 60 minute stream. Each query segment would then be matched against the EMI signals of the entire movie database (using sliding-window cross correlation), and the highest correlated match would be returned. This technique is also referred to as matched filtering in signal processing communities. We applied this procedure to find matching signals between TVs of the same model; query data would be extracted from the EMI library of the first TV in the pair, and the database signals would come from the other (e.g., query = EMI from Panasonic-42-A, database = EMI from Panasonic-42-B).

We performed a series of runs using query lengths ranging between 1 and 15 minutes (1, 3, 6, 9, 12 and 15 mins) and in each instance computed the cross correlation between the query and its best match (averaged across 10 samples for each query length). The matching results for the three TV model pairs are show in Figure 4. Even short length queries tend to find highly correlated matches in the database. In particular, for TVs with repeatable EMI signals, once the query length reaches 6 minutes the correlation reaches 93.7%.

Interestingly, for the Sharp-32-A and B TVs, longer queries led to degraded performance. We attribute this to the weak EMI signatures of these TVs (as previously mentioned) which are susceptible to noise whenever the EMI signal is not being modulated along its entire dynamic range. However, the Sharp-42 performed very well with just short queries.

9.3 Reducing False Matches

Usually the best correlated match to a query (returned by our search procedure) was taken from the trace of the same movie in the database; however this was not always the case and we address this issue in the current section. To develop a method that would reduce false matches, we modified our matching algorithm to withhold query responses unless the top correlation match was a "clear winner" and was separated from the next best candidate by a margin of 5%. We experimented with multiple settings of this threshold parameter (including setting its value to be proportional to the number of samples in the query) but found that the 5% level provided a good trade-off between numbers of false positives and rejected samples given the query lengths and dataset size we tested (we provide a lengthier discussion of the threshold value choice in the Appendix B).

Given this modified search procedure, each query could be classified into one of three bins:

- **Miss:** the search engine is confident in the match (accept) but there is a mismatch between the search engine's best guess and the query origin. (Failure.)
- **Hit:** the search engine is confident in the match (accept) and the match was the movie from which the query itself was extracted. (Success.)
- **Reject**: the best match was a not a "clear winner," and the matching algorithm chooses not to respond. (Neither success nor failure.)

In Figure 5 and Figure 6 we respectively show the distribution of queries into these bins as a function of query length for the TVs which were the best (Panasonic 42″) and worst performers (Sharp 32″) on the test for signal repeatability within a model family.

We note that the Sharp 32″ A vs B data causes a very high rejection rate due to the consistent lack of a "clear winner,"

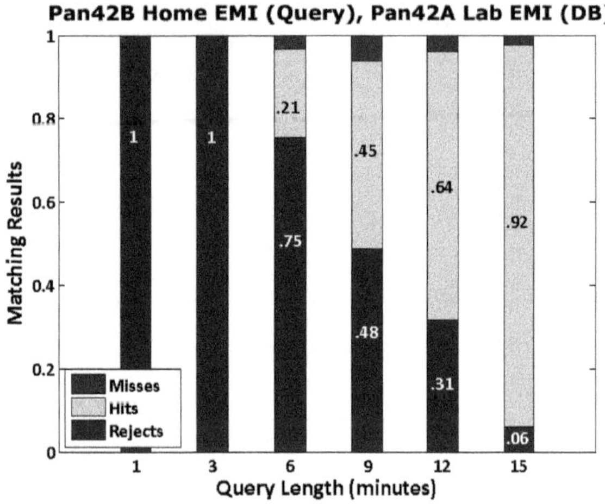

Figure 7: Distribution of queries into rejected, hit and miss for lab vs home data for Panasonic-42.

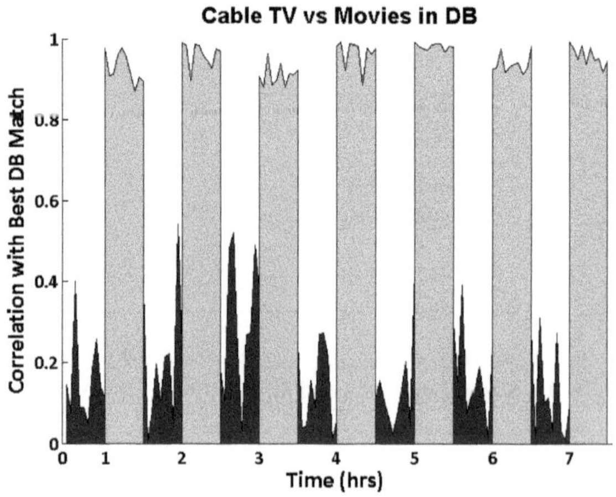

Figure 8: Cross correlation for target (green) movies embedded in broadcast content (blue).

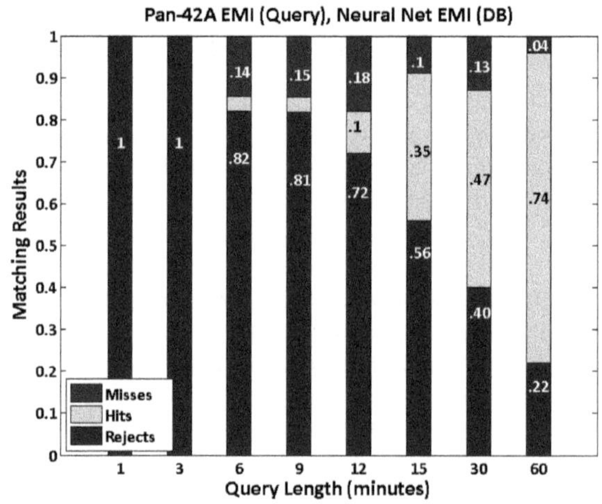

Figure 9: Matching results for Panasonic-42-A EMI queries against neural network database.

in addition further strengthening the hypothesis that the Sharp 32″ A & B are very sensitive to noise. Conversely the Panasonic 42″ A vs B data quickly reaches a high hit rate (and low rejection rate). In all cases the miss rate was low. This method is therefore less influenced by noise; queries that result in a match (non-reject) have a high probability of being correct.

9.4 Home Results

Having found evidence of significant information leakage within a lab setting, we next turned to evaluating our approach in a more natural environment. We wanted to deploy a TV in multiple homes and see if we could match queries from home EMI to lab EMI datasets. In choosing which television to utilize for our residential recordings, we initially restricted the candidate pool to TVs for which we had duplicate models (Panasonic-42-A&B, Samsung-58-A&B, and Sharp-32-A&B). We rejected the Sharp 32″ TVs based on their weak EMI signatures. Given the choice between the Panasonic 42″ TVs and Samsung 58″ TVs, we selected the smaller TVs because they were significantly easier to transport.

We set up our system (Panasonic-42-B, PLI, and logging equipment) in three different homes (see Table 3, along with Appendix C) and in each context recorded a smaller version of our database (3 hours total — first 15 minutes of the first 12 movies). Next we matched queries extracted from home EMI (Panasonic-42-B) against the EMI signature database collected in the lab (Panasonic-42-A) using the search system which had the capacity to reject searches that did not produce "clear winners" (as described previously). The results of this analysis are shown in Figure 7.The hit rate for 15 minute queries drops from 96% in the lab environment with no misses to 92% in the home environment with a 2% miss rate.

9.5 Searching for Target Content

The above results show that our small collection of 20 movies yield distinguishable EMI when displayed on modern TVs; this emulates the target channel identification adversarial goal in Section 4. We now turn to experimentally emulating a target video identification attack scenario (recall again Section 4). Under this scenario, a person might be watching arbitrary TV content, and the attacker wishes to determine whether that content corresponds to some target (e.g., censored, banned, sensitive) content. To explore this adversarial goal, we recorded 20 hours of EMI while the TV was tuned to over-the-air HD television broadcast.

Figure 8 shows the results of running our matching framework on EMI from one hour long chunks of over the air broadcast interleaved with one hour movies (the targets) from our database. Given a query length of 6 or more minutes the over the air cable data never returned a match because matches could not pass the confidence threshold. Conversely, the content embedded from our "sensitive" database had a rejection rate of 3.3% and a hit rate of 95.06%. This demonstrates that target videos were clearly detectable when intermingled with non-target videos.

10. EXTENSION: MODELS OF EMI

The results in the previous sections motivated us to ask the following question: can we reverse engineer the method by which a TV produces EMI as a function of its video input? Such a tool could be used to build a database of EMI models to predict noise signatures without needing physical access to target devices (after the training phase). It would also be plausible to learn to recreate EMI from a home TV without ever seeing a TV of that type, provided that there are samples of data from periods during which the TV displays known content (e.g., if the user is watching one of five news channels in the morning, the system could build a model for the TV to try and detect whether the user is watching some specific show later).

We investigate the plausibility of learning a model to recreate the EMI of one TV (Panasonic-42-A) by framing the problem as an instance of supervised learning, where the goal is to approximate how the various hardware components of the device (taken together as a black box) modulate the SMPS and produce EMI from video input. To tackle this problem we chose to use recurrent neural networks (RNN) because the EMI we are seeking to replicate is a continuous time signal which exhibits non-stationarity (i.e., the current state of the EMI depends on the past several samples) hence ruling out the possibility of using popular stationary methods for supervised learning (i.e., Support Vector Machines). A further motivation to use RNNs comes from their ability to accommodate for non-linear interactions between the input and output which we could not rule out from the processes that shape electromagnetic interference.

Features from Video Frames. The input to our model, is a sequence of video frames arriving at a rate of 30FPS (NTSC) with typical DVD resolution of 720 x 480 pixels. In its raw form the input dimensionality at each sample is extremely high (3 x 720 x 480 per frame) and prohibitively large for model training. Thus, we opted to compress each video frame into a 11 element vector which extracts selected features (meant to capture key statistics for each frame) from the visual content and greatly reduce the complexity of the learning problem. The features we compute from each frame are listed below:

- **Brightness:** cumulative sum of averaged RGB intensities (based on pixel values).
- **Flux:** change in brightness between consecutive frames.
- **Edge Intensity:** pixelsum of a Canny Edge filter.
- **FFT:** slope of the best fit line to an FFT.
- **Color:** mean and standard deviations for gaussians fitted to R, G, and B color histograms (6 params).
- **Bitrate:** kbits/second computed using FFMPEG.

These features were post processed in a fashion very similar to the signal conditioning of the EMI. In particular, we performed normalization (0 to 1 scale), smoothing (Butterworth filter with 10kHz cutoff frequency) and decimation (10 samples per second).

Network Structure. RNNs are a class of neural networks in which intermediate layers (i.e., those separating input and output) have connections to neighboring layers as well as (re)connections to themselves; these properties lead to self feedback (memory) which enable dynamic temporal behavior [20]. At time t the network input layer consisted of a video frame represented as a 11 element feature vector. The input layer was connected to the first of 3 hidden layers (connected in succession, each composed of 11 neurons to match the dimensionality of the input) and the final hidden layer was connected to a scalar output layer representing the normalized time series EMI at time t.[5]

Training. The training phase began with randomly initialized network parameters which were tuned using backpropagation through time (BPTT) via the Levenberg-Marquardt gradient method. The criterion for performance was how well the network output matched test EMI (measured as mean squared normalized error). Each training session concluded when the optimization converged or after 50 epochs (whichever came first).

Results. We used our neural network to generate a database of *synthetic EMI* (i.e., given *only* video data) and performed matching searches using *real* TV EMI traces as queries. Prior to defining our training and target sets, we systematically removed the five movies with the globally lowest self similarity measures across all TVs (Wedding Crashers, The Hangover, Meet the Parents, Office Space, Top Gear). This eliminates noise artifacts during training *and* approximates the goal of only plausibly detecting target videos with high self similarity.

The remaining 15 movies were divided into random sets of 10 training movies and 5 target movies, and for each training/target combination we evaluated matching performance using our thresholding method (Section 9.3) which rejected queries unless there was a .05 gap in the cross-correlation of the best candidate match and the runner up. For each combination of training and target movie sets we computed matching using a database of neural network EMI (generated for the 5 target movies) and queried using real TV EMI (from 10 test movies — the 5 target movies with generated EMI via the neural network and the 5 movies originally excluded due to low self similarity). The average cross correlation of the neural network output and the ground truth EMI of the Panasonic-42-A for the 5 target movies was .88 (for a query length of 60 minutes). Figure 9 shows the results of submitting real EMI for the 5 target movies into our query matching system (the hit rate at 60 minutes is .74, lower than .88, because of the .05 threshold gap). Figure 10 visually shows the alignment between the generated EMI for a target movie and real EMI for that movie. The matching database correctly rejected EMI from the five movies originally excluded because of low self similarity with average probability 96.8 (averaged across query lengths longer than 15 minutes).

Using brightness as an isolated input to train a network generates signals that are .73 correlated with real EMI for the target movies (other features produce an average of .17 correlation). In future work it would be worthwhile to use hypothesis driven regression models to strengthen our understanding of generative EMI sources, however such analysis will require careful experimentation with secondary sources of EMI signal modulation (e.g., display processing circuitry) â as suggested by our results and confirmed by [18].

It is important to stress that the above analysis should only be viewed as evidence of plausibility — the primary focus of our work is on the experimental analysis of real EMI as discussed in the previous sections. Our results here do, however, suggest that it is feasible to use supervised methods to train generative models of EMI.

[5]Though we cannot claim that this network structure is globally optimal for our problem, it offered high performance and low overfitting after experimenting with a large set of multi-layered neuron arrangements.

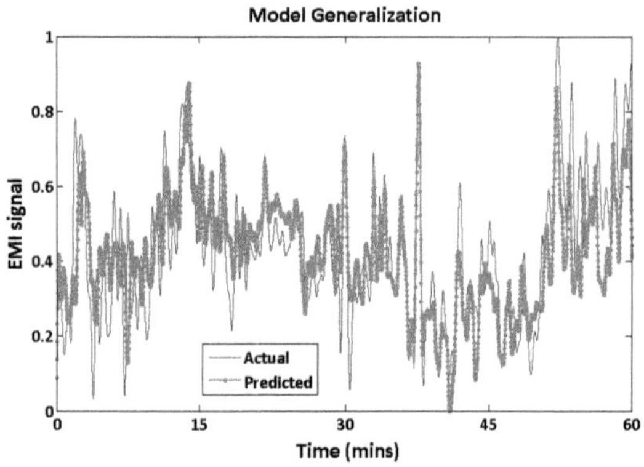

Figure 10: Neural network predictions (driven via visual features) vs. actual EMI of a 60 minute movie not included in the training set (Bourne Ultimatum).

11. DISCUSSION

Applicability to Other Devices. To better understand the scope of information leakage exposed via conducted EMI from SMPS, we executed a survey of other common home electronics: a personal computer, a laptop, a laser printer, a DVD player, a game console, and a washing machine. Our aim was to assess whether these SMPS-based appliances similarly produce noise signatures as a function of their device operation. Recall that past work on conducted EMI information leakage, such as works focused on keyboards [3, 28], observed EMI that was a direct function of electrical signals — bits — already communicated within the device in question; SMPS were not designed to carry digital signals, yet we observed that many appliances do yield EMI signal fluctuations that are correlated with the various functions supported by the device in question.

We found that the laser printer generated increased electromagnetic interference while warming up and during the printing process that engages the motors. In the case of the personal computer and laptop, we observed increases in EMI amplitude while running a collection of intensive CPU/memory/disk benchmarks. The DVD player's (with internal FM Radio) EMI was affected by volume changes, and the game console produced different EMI signals depending on whether it was in the main menu or in the process of rendering a game. The washer produced EMI bursts whenever the barrel rotated during the wash cycle.

Defenses and Challenges. There are several potential countermeasures for minimizing information leakage through EMI. One simple defense mechanism is to connect SMPS based devices to a powerline isolator similar to the one used in our laboratory experiments. The internal transformer provides enough isolation such that the high frequency noise does not pass back over the powerline (assuming the isolator itself has not been compromised). This capability is found in some newer line conditioners and in some instances of uninterruptible power supplies (UPSs).

A potential whole home solution, which does not require installing a device behind every electronic appliance, would be to inject random high-energy broadband noise over the powerline. In addition to traditional challenges with randomness, a key pragmatic challenge with this approach is that it must conform to FCC regulations. In addition, this would cause problems with legitimate powerline-based communication systems like broadband over powerline and X10(r) home automated systems. A more practical approach could be to identify potential devices that may be leaking information by observing the power line and only blocking certain frequency bands using an active noise rejection system or informing the home owner where to install line isolators.

It might be tempting to fall back on an out-of-band solution and ask for new regulation on how SMPS power supplies are built. In addition the political challenges with such a solution, this approach is also faced with the following tension: it may be impossible to fully defend against such information disclosure while still being in compliance with Energy STAR. Said another way, existing regulation within the U.S. may make it difficult or infeasible to implement defenses since the costs of privacy (increased consumption and decreased efficiency) are in direct conflict with recent legislation. This creates a fundamental challenge: to develop systems that are both highly energy efficient and private.

Through this contribution we assess the key features of SMPS information leakage over the powerline, and provide a knowledge base to aid in future efforts for mitigating the tension between device functionality and privacy.

12. CONCLUSIONS

We conducted an extensive study of powerline information leakage from eight modern TVs spanning two technologies (LCD, Plasma), three sizes (32″, 42″, 58″), and three manufacturers (Panasonic, Samsung, Sharp). We find that these TVs generally produce stable, robust EMI signals on the powerline that correlate with the video being displayed. We discuss two adversarial goals that do not require an adversary to pre-train on the set of *all possible* movies, but rather train on a *small set* of video content/movies (e.g., to infer whether a person is watching a target, sensitive video or whether a person is watching a target, sensitive channel), and we describe two different classes of adversaries (intentional adversaries that might attach malicious hardware to a home's powerline and unintentional adversaries — e.g., ubicomp devices — that might unwittingly collect and storing privacy-compromising measurements from the home's powerline). Next, we experimentally evaluate our approach with 20 movies in both a clean laboratory setting and electrically noisy home environments with other active devices connected to the powerline. Subsequently, we describe extensions to our core work that allow an attacker to infer information from a home's TV's EMI without ever requiring access to that TV or another TV of the same model (by dynamically learning a model of the TV's EMI signatures as a function of known video content). Lastly, we close with a discussion of some defenses, as well as fundamental challenges to fully defending against this threat (e.g., complete defenses may be in violation of Energy STAR).

Acknowledgements

We thank Lee Tien for his insights, feedback, and encouragement, and we thank a Shane Clark, Alexei Czeskis, Tamara Denning, Daniel Halperin, Eric Larson, and Franziska Roesner for valuable comments on earlier drafts of this paper. This work was supported in part by NSF Award CNS-0846065 and an Alfred P. Sloan Research Fellowship.

References

[1] Dmitri Asonov and Rakesh Agrawal. Keyboard acoustic emanations. In *IEEE Symposium on Security and Privacy*, 2004.

[2] M. Backes, M. Dürmuth, , and D. Unruh. Compromising reflections – or – how to read lcd monitors around the corner. In *IEEE Symposium on Security and Privacy*, 2008.

[3] Andrea Barisani and Daniele Bianco. Sniffing keystrokes with lasers/voltmeters: Side channel attacks using optical sampling of mechanical energy and power line leakage. In *Black Hat Technical Security Conference: USA*, 2009.

[4] R. Briol. Emanations: How to keep your data confidential. In *Symposium on Electromagnetic Security for Information Protection*, 1991.

[5] Shane S. Clark, Jacob Sorber, Kevin Fu, and Erik Learned-Miller. Current Events: Compromising Web Privacy by Tapping the Electrical Outlet. Technical Report UM-CS-2011-030, Department of Computer Science, University of Massachusetts Amherst, Amherst, MA, July 2011.

[6] G. Cohn, S. Gupta, J. Froehlich, E. Larson, and S. Patel. GasSense: Appliance-level, single-point sensing of gas activity in the home. In *International Conference on Pervasive Computing*, 2010.

[7] Analog Devices. Analog devices power measure ic for smart meters. Analog.com, `http://www.analog.com/en/analog-to-digital-converters/energy-measurement/products/index.html`, 2010.

[8] V.W. Eck. Electromagnetic radiation from video display units: An eavesdropping risk? *Computers and Security*, 4:269–286, 1985.

[9] J. Froehlich, E. Larson, T. Campbell, C. Haggerty, J. Fogarty, and S.N. Patel. HydroSense: Infrastructure-mediated single-point sensing of whole-home water activity. In *International Conference on Ubiquitous Computing*, 2009.

[10] S. Gupta, S.N. Patel, and M.S. Reynolds. ElectriSense: Single-point sensing using EMI for electrical event detection and classification in the home. In *International Conference on Ubiquitous Computing*, 2010.

[11] G. Hart. Advances in nonintrusive appliance load monitoring. In *EPRI Information and Automation Conference*, 1991.

[12] History of Tempest. Cryptome, `http://cryptome.org/tempest-old.htm`, 2000.

[13] P.C. Kocher. Timing attacks on implementations of Diffie-Hellman, RSA, DSS, and other systems. In *Advances in Cryptology*, 1996.

[14] P.C. Kocher, J. Jaffe, and B. Jun. Differential power analysis. In *Advances in Cryptology*, 1999.

[15] M.G. Kuhn. Optical time-domain eavesdropping risks of CRT displays. In *IEEE Symposium on Security and Privacy*, 2002.

[16] M.G. Kuhn. Compromising emanations: Eavesdropping risks of computer displays. University of Cambridge Technical Report UCAM-CL-TR-577, 2003.

[17] M.G. Kuhn. Electromagnetic eavesdropping risks of flat-panel displays. In *Workshop on Privacy Enhancing Technologies*, 2004.

[18] M.G. Kuhn. Compromising emanations of lcd tv sets. In *IEEE International Symposium on Electromagnetic Compatibility - Aug 11-19 (to appear)*, 2011.

[19] J. Loughry and D. A. Umphress. Information leakage from optical emanations. *ACM Transactions on Information and System Security*, 5:262–289, August 2002.

[20] Jennifer Lynch and Lee Tien. Joint comments of the Center for Democracy & Technology and the Electronic Frontier Foundation on proposed policies and findings pertaining to the smart grid. Comments to the the Public Utilities Commission of the State of California, `http://www.eff.org/files/CDTEFFJointComment030910.pdf`, 2010.

[21] Molina-Markham, P. Shenoy, K. Fu, E. Cecchet, and D. Irwin. Private memoirs of a smart meter. In *ACM Workshop on Embedded Sensing Systems for Energy-Efficiency in Building*, 2010.

[22] S.N. Patel, M.S. Reynolds, and G.D. Abowd. Detecting human movement by differential air pressure sensing in HVAC system ductwork: An exploration in infrastructure mediated sensing. In *International Conference on Pervasive Computing*, 2008.

[23] S.N. Patel, T. Robertson, J.A. Kientz, M.S. Reynolds, and G.D. Abowd. At the flick of a switch: Detecting and classifying unique electrical events on the residential power line. In *International Conference on Ubiquitous Computing*, 2007.

[24] Alfredo Rial and George Danezis. Privacy-preserving smart metering. Microsoft Research Technical Report MSR-TR-2010-150, 2010.

[25] T.S. Saponas, J. Lester, C. Hartung, S. Agarwal, and T. Kohno. Devices that tell on you: Privacy trends in consumer ubiquitous computing. In *USENIX Security Symposium*, 2007.

[26] M. R. Spiegel. *Theory and Problems of Probability and Statistics*, chapter 14 (Correlation Theory). McGraw-Hill, 1992.

[27] The benefits of smart meters. California Public Utilities Commision, `http://www.cpuc.ca.gov/PUC/energy/Demand+Response/benefits.htm`, 2010.

[28] M. Vuoagnoux and S. Pasini. Compromising electromagnetic emanations of wired and wireless keyboards. In *USENIX Security Symposium*, 2009.

[29] C. V. Wright, L. Ballard, F. Monrose, and G. M. Masson. Language identification of encrypted VoIP traffic: Alejandra y Roberto or Alice and Bob? In *USENIX Security Symposium*, 2007.

APPENDIX

A. TWO EMI TYPES

EMI signal fluctuations can be manifested as frequency shifts or variations in energy density. The following figure shows examples of these two types of EMI signals.

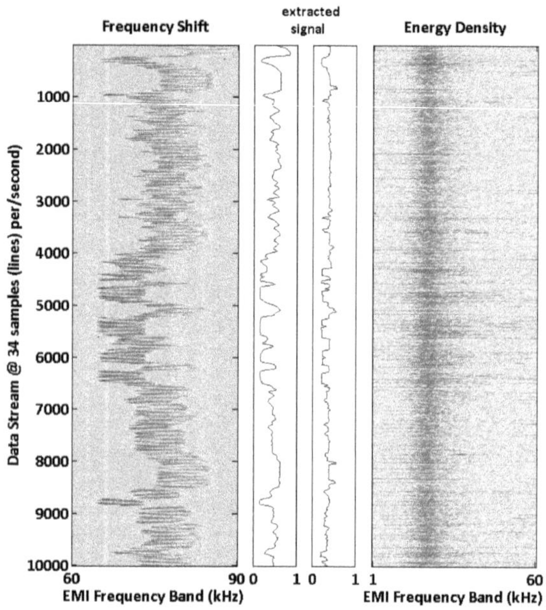

The Sharp-42 TV is shown on the left; changes in screen content cause a shift in the center frequency of the EMI. The white strip on left shows the signal obtained by tracking the EMI on left. The Panasonic-42-A TV is shown on the right; changes on screen manifest as change in the Energy density of the EMI. Tracking total energy over time yields the signal shown in white strip on the right.

B. REDUCING FALSE MATCHES USING A CONFIDENCE THRESHOLD

The following figure shows average hit rates (solid lines) and reject rates (dashed lines) as a function of threshold setting for confidence gap between the top match and the runner-up for 6 minute queries. The blue lines represent the average hit and reject rates for the 6 TVs (excluding the Sharp 32" A&B); and the red lines depict the average hit and reject rates for the Sharp 32" A&B. Note that the Sharp TVs produce significantly higher reject rates because they produce signals that are not good at discriminating between movies.

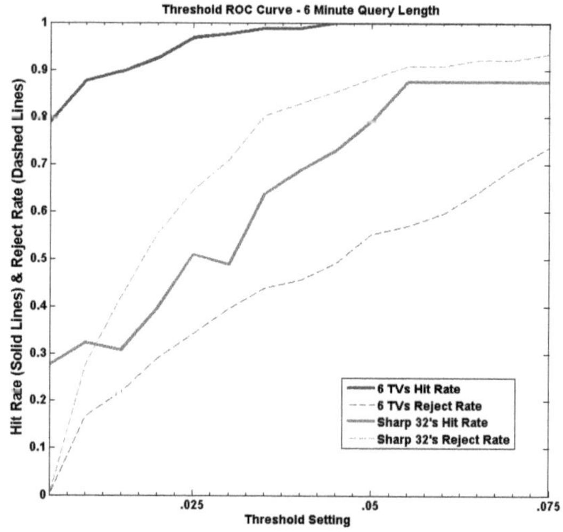

To clarify this figure, note that hit rate is *not* 1 minus the reject rate. Rather, the accept rate (not shown) is 1 minus the reject rate. The hit rate is the number of correct matches divided by the number of queries not rejected. The reject rate gets higher as we require a larger gap between the winner and the runner up. The accept rate (not shown) will simultaneously decrease. However, the hit rate (shown) does increase with larger threshold values. For our experiments we select a threshold of .05, which yields a hit rate.

C. HOME EMI

The following figure shows EMI recorded from Home 3. Note that multiple devices were in operation at any given time, and despite signal overlaps our EMI extraction algorithm was able to successfully track the TV noise signature.

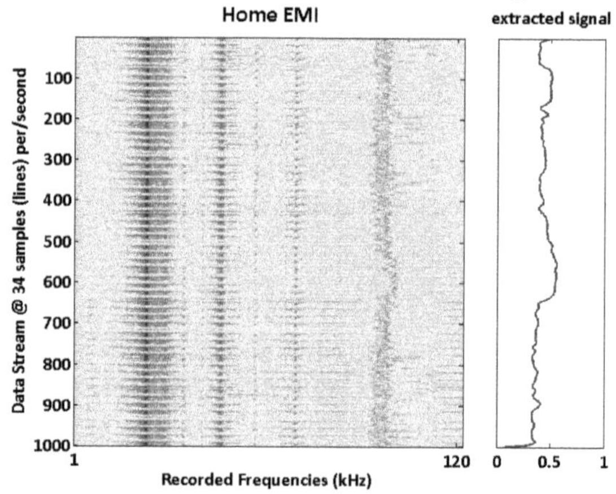

(sp)iPhone: Decoding Vibrations From Nearby Keyboards Using Mobile Phone Accelerometers

Philip Marquardt*
MIT Lincoln Laboratory
244 Wood Street, Lexington, MA USA
philip.marquardt@ll.mit.edu

Arunabh Verma, Henry Carter and Patrick Traynor
Georgia Institute of Technology
{arunabh.verma@, carterh@, traynor@cc.}gatech.edu

ABSTRACT

Mobile phones are increasingly equipped with a range of highly responsive sensors. From cameras and GPS receivers to three-axis accelerometers, applications running on these devices are able to experience rich interactions with their environment. Unfortunately, some applications may be able to use such sensors to monitor their surroundings in unintended ways. In this paper, we demonstrate that an application with access to accelerometer readings on a modern mobile phone can use such information to recover text entered on a nearby keyboard. Note that unlike previous emanation recovery papers, the accelerometers on such devices sample at near the Nyquist rate, making previous techniques unworkable. Our application instead detects and decodes keystrokes by measuring the relative physical position and distance between each vibration. We then match abstracted words against candidate dictionaries and record word recovery rates as high as 80%. In so doing, we demonstrate the potential to recover significant information from the vicinity of a mobile device without gaining access to resources generally considered to be the most likely sources of leakage (e.g., microphone, camera).

Categories and Subject Descriptors

K.6.5 [**Management of Computing and Information Systems**]: Security and Protection—*invasive software*

General Terms

Security

Keywords

mobile phones, information leakage, accelerometer

1. INTRODUCTION

Mobile phones are becoming increasingly powerful devices. In addition to being able to run applications ranging from email clients to web browsers, a progressively sophisticated set of sensors are enabling these devices to more actively interface with the world around them. From gestures captured by accelerometers for games to augmented reality applications displaying metadata tags on video from the camera in real-time, mobile phones are becoming adept at capturing and harnessing rich features and data from their surroundings.

Unfortunately, the array of sensors in these devices can also be used in unintended ways. As many have suggested, malware could potentially gain access to a mobile phone's camera to take photos or video of the owner and their surroundings [16, 37]. In cases where the camera may not be pointed at an interesting target, a malicious application could instead attempt to activate the device's microphone and record ambient sounds or syphon GPS data to track the target's location [17, 13, 23, 21]. Recognizing the potential for the leakage of sensitive information, many modern mobile phone operating systems provide mechanisms by which access to such sensors is protected by explicit permission from the user. For instance, the manifest files included with every Android application provide an unambiguous list of all of permissions an application may ever request at installation time. Should an application not request access to these resources[1] or the user deny the application such rights, the application will not be able to potentially abuse these resources. However, access to all of the sensors contained in these devices are not so tightly controlled.

In this paper, we demonstrate that unfettered access to the accelerometers available on many mobile phones can allow for significant unintended leakage of information from a user's environment. We show that a malicious application with access to the accelerometer feed can record and reconstruct the keypresses made on a nearby keyboard based solely on the observed vibrations. We develop profiles for pairs of keypress events using a neural network, which creates an abstract representation of the relationship between consecutive events. We then recover the typed content by translating from our intermediary form to English words using a number of different dictionaries. Such tasks are not a trivial application of standard techniques, especially when compared to previous efforts in this space. Specifically, we must overcome much lower sensor sampling rates than has been experienced in the related acoustic and electromagnetic-based eavesdropping attacks, which makes deciphering individual keypresses extremely difficult.

Through this, we make the following contributions in this paper:

- **Recover keystrokes with far less precise monitoring equipment:** We note that while a number of related efforts analyze

*Work conducted while at Georgia Institute of Technology

[1]Specifically, the manifest file would need to contain `RECORD_AUDIO`, `CAMERA` and `ACCESS_FINE_LOCATION` [2].

CCS'11, October 17–21, 2011, Chicago, Illinois, USA.

keyboard emanations, our techniques overcome a noteworthy disadvantage. Most critically, the sampling rates of the devices used to recover acoustic and electromagnetic emanations are six (2.5 GHz) [40] and two (44.1 kHz) [3] orders of magnitude *greater* than that of the accelerometers running in a modern mobile phone (100 Hz).

- **Develop an infrastructure for characterizing keypress vibrations:** We capture, analyze and develop profiles of pairs of keypress events on a nearby keyboard based on the vibrations created when they are pressed. Our inputs are then processed using a neural network to create an intermediary representation of the relative position and distance between keypress pairs, which is combined with candidate dictionaries to successfully recover words at rates as high as 80%.

- **Provide effective mitigation techniques:** In spite of a rich resource management options, we demonstrate that mobile phones lack sufficient policies to prevent such attacks. We offer suggestions to dramatically reduce the effectiveness of these kinds of attacks without appreciably affecting other applications requiring legitimate access to the accelerometers.

Note that for all its apparent obstacles, our approach has a significant advantage over previous work. Attacks designed to compromise keystrokes using electromagnetic and acoustic emanations have thus far required that an adversary gain undetected physical access to the space occupied by their target. Our approach eliminates this requirement by allowing our malicious application to run on a device most users are likely to already be carrying with them.

The remainder of this paper is organized as follows: Section 2 discusses important related work and provides context for our contributions; Section 3 describes our attack and threat model in detail; Section 4 attempts to apply previously used methods and demonstrates why they do not work in this setting; Section 5 describes our model and experimental setup in detail; Section 6 offers experimental results; Section 7 discusses a number of related issues and mitigation strategies; Section 8 provides concluding remarks.

2. RELATED WORK

The emanations of electrical and mechanical devices have long been known to expose information about their users' activities. As early as the 1940s, scientists working on the TEMPEST project demonstrated the ability to capture the electromagnetic signals generated by the Bell 131-B2 teletype terminal, which was used to encrypt communications by the US military [29]. These techniques were improved and used during the Vietnam War to detect Viet Cong trucks at distances of up to ten miles [28]. More recently, researchers applied similar techniques to CRT [39] and LCD [27] monitors and demonstrated the ability to recover their contents both at great distance and through significant obstacles (e.g., brick walls). Similar attacks on electromagnetic emanations have since been demonstrated against Smart Cards [31], CMOS chips [1], serial port cables [34] and keyboards [40]. While such an attack vector was certainly within the capabilities of sophisticated adversaries, its use by the general public has thus far been fairly limited.

Optical emanations and reflections also offer a potential source of information. Kuhn [26] demonstrated that temporal variations of the diffuse reflections of CRT monitors could be processed to reveal the contents displayed on the screen. Backus et al. [7] were able to capture the content from any monitor based on mirroring by nearby objects with high reflectiveness, including soda bottles, tea pots and eye glasses. This work was later extended to capture reflections directly from a target's eye [5]. While these attacks are effective at distances of up to 30 meters, they are difficult to execute without a constant and unobstructed line of sight, which may potentially expose the presence of the adversary.

Figure 1: Our experimental placement of a mobile phone running a malicious application attempting to recover text entered using the nearby keyboard.

The acoustic emanations made by a range of devices are more easily captured by less capable adversaries. For instance, using a simple consumer-grade microphone, the contents of printouts made by a dot-matrix printer can be recognized with high accuracy [11, 6]. Recognizing this, the research community has spent significant effort recreating key presses on computer keyboards through such auditory channels. Specifically, previous work has shown the ability to recover greater than 80% of keyboard presses given substantial training [3], without training [42] and based on acoustic dictionaries [10]. While such approaches are certainly more within the reach of the adversary, they are extremely difficult to scale to large deployments as they require that a microphone is physically located near all potential targets at all times.

The vibrations caused by physical activities can also be exploited to surreptitiously leak information. For instance, laser vibration systems focused on flat surfaces such as windows can recover both voiced conversations and typing [8]. As such systems are becoming more readily available to the public [22], their use becomes more practical. However, like the above acoustic case, the scalability of their deployment makes large-scale attacks using such equipment difficult. Through the use of compromised mobile phones, our work focuses on taking advantage of such side channels while making such attacks significantly more scalable.

3. ATTACK DESCRIPTION AND THREAT MODEL

Many previous emanation papers have been successful because they were able to deploy sensitive equipment near their intended target. From microphones to an antenna, previous attacks require an adversary to violate the physical security of the area near their target. This observation does not make such attacks impossible, but certainly increases both difficulty and likelihood of detection. Our attack instead attempts to recover emanations with a device that the target themselves will bring near the keyboard.

Mobile phones perfectly match this description. These devices contain a range of sensors (e.g., camera, microphone, GPS) through which a malicious program could potentially eavesdrop upon a target [32, 38]. Such attacks have long been expected and can easily be prevented by denying access to such resources [24, 9]. Access to information generated by accelerometers, however, is not protected in any current mobile phone operating system. Accordingly, we investigate whether or not this sensor can record nearby phenomenon with sufficient accuracy to recover sensitive information.

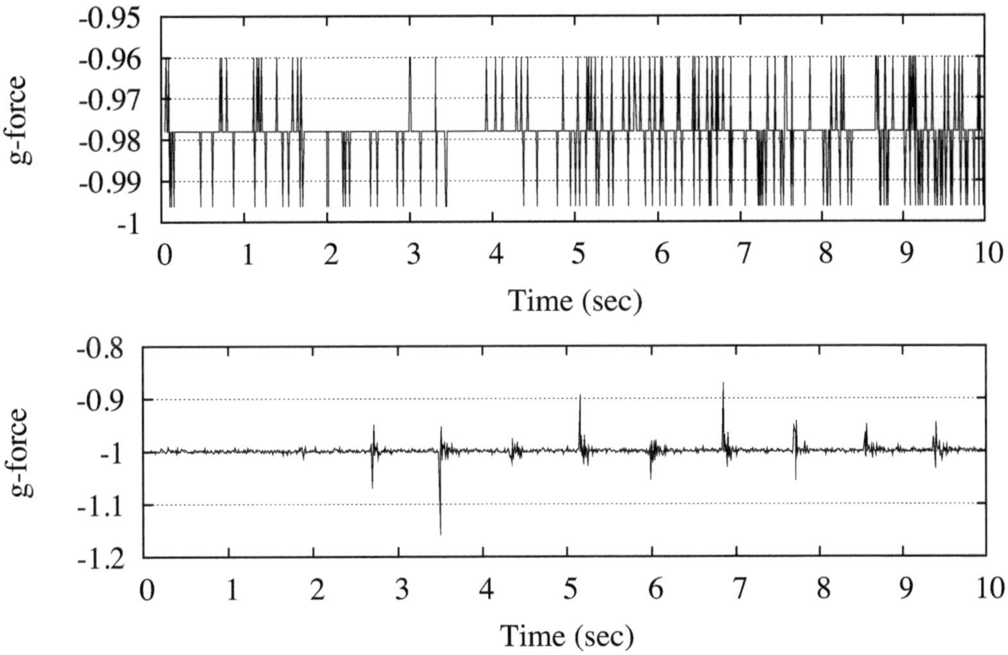

Figure 2: A comparison of accelerometer readings from an iPhone 3GS (top) and an iPhone 4 (bottom) during the spaced and repeated pressing of a single key. Note that keypress events are easily recognizable on the iPhone4, whereas they are indistinguishable on the iPhone 3GS.

Our attack is based on a simple observation. Specifically, many users place their mobile devices on their desk when they are working so that their are easily accessible. Figure 1 shows our experimental setup. An adversary attempting to recover sensitive information entered by a user on a desktop computer would operate as follows: the adversary would install a malicious application on the mobile phone belonging to their target. This step could be by gaining physical access to the device or through social engineering (e.g., suggesting an innocuous and seemingly useful application to a colleague, spam, etc). Secondly, the application will record accelerometer data. This operation need not occur constantly, but could instead occur by explicit wake up (e.g., text message trigger) or by periodic sampling for activity. Finally, the malicious application has some means of exfiltrating the observed data. This channel could via a direct connection to the Internet or potentially indirectly through another application. We do not assume access to any additional resources.

4. APPLICATION OF PREVIOUS TECHNIQUES

A number of papers have recently been published on the decoding of keyboard emanations. Two questions naturally arise. First, given that the accelerometers found in current mobile phones sample at rates that are orders of magnitude smaller than previous acoustic and electromagnetic attacks, *can keypresses even be detected by these sensors?* Secondly, if such events can be observed, *can previously developed methodology (i.e., identifying individual keys using neural networks) be blindly applied to identify keystrokes?*

We answer the first question by comparing the capabilities of two different phones - the iPhone 3GS and the iPhone 4. Figure 2 shows the raw amplitude readings from the z-axis accelerometers on these devices when placed two inches from the left side of a QWERTY-style keyboard. Most noticeably, generic keypress events are unidentifiable on the iPhone 3GS. The relatively noisy output generated by the accelerometers on the iPhone 3GS provide very few differentiable features over which classification could occur. The presence of a better accelerometer and a gyroscope on the iPhone 4 provides significantly improved separation of keypresses and shows 9 distinct events. This observation leads us to assert that accelerometer-based eavesdropping could potentially be implemented on some phones.

Having satisfactorily determined that keypress events are observable using the accelerometers included on a currently available mobile phone, we attempt to determine whether such events are measurably different enough to allow for classification. Asonov et al. [3] showed accuracies of 79% by processing acoustic emanations using microphone signals digitized with a standard PC sound card with 44.1 kHz sampling rate. In their experiments, audio samples were captured and feature vectors were created using FFT values for each sample. These feature vectors were used to train a neural network for classification.

Our initial experiments aimed to recreate the methods used in the acoustic work. We gathered samples using an iPhone 4 on a wooden surface located 2 inches from a wireless Apple Bluetooth keyboard. Each alphabetic key was sampled 150 times by gathering x, y, z values from the raw accelerometer output. Due to the constraints on the accelerometer hardware, our sample rates were limited to 100 Hz, 441 times less than Asonov et al. The raw output was then processed through several algorithms for creating feature vectors, including mean, min, max, FFT, MFCC and other time window values. We trained and tested a neural network using a 70%/30% data split. As expected, our overall accuracies (25.89%) were significantly lower than Asonov et al. (78.85%). Specifically, only 3 letters out performed the acoustic results, 'a', 'e', and 'o'. However, overall the accuracies of our initial results

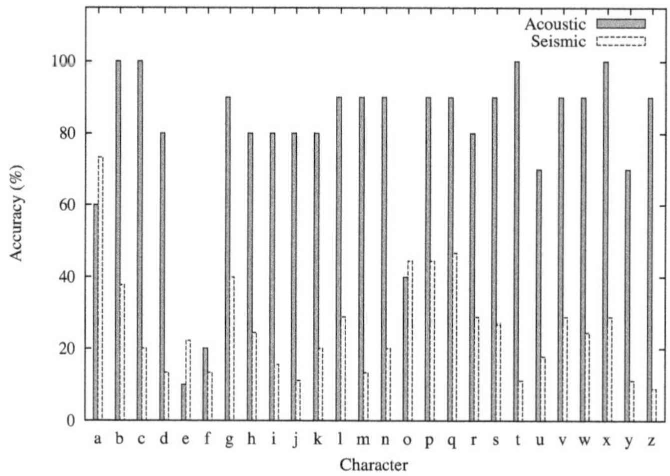

Figure 3: Comparison of the per-letter accuracies for acoustic (theirs) and seismic (ours) emanations using the methodology by Asonov et al. [3]. Note that our proposed use of accelerometer provides significantly less accurate results (25.89% vs 78.85%) based on this approach. Accordingly, a different approach is necessary.

were well below the results gathered in the acoustic experiments. Figure 3 shows comparative results for each alphabetic key.

These initial results tell us that while keypress events are detectable, the direct application of previous techniques does not provide an effective means of recovering text entered on a nearby keyboard. We therefore investigate an approach more suited to our limited sampling abilities.

5. MODELING KEYPRESS EVENTS

In this section, we present our model for identifying keypress events. We then discuss our experimental setup and processing architecture.

5.1 Keypress Event Modeling

Because of the extremely low sampling rates available to accelerometers and our previously demonstrated difficulty in recognizing individual keys, we instead attempt to characterize pairs of keypresses and their relation to each other. Let P_i, P_j equal sequential keypress events. We characterize the relation between two successive events, $rel(P_i, P_j)$ using the following two features:

- **Horizontal Orientation:** The location $loc(P_i)$ of each keypress event relative to a 'central-line' dividing the keyboard into *left* and *right* partitions.

- **Distance Between Consecutive Keypresses:** For a threshold distance in keys α, we define the distance $dist(P_i, P_j)$ of consecutive keypress events as being either *near* or *far*, where $near < \alpha$ and $far \geq \alpha$.

We define consecutive keypress events as $rel(P_i, P_j) = loc(P_i) || loc(P_j) || dist(P_i, P_j)$, where || represents feature concatenation. A word is thus composed of a series of concatenated event-pairs, referred to as its 'word-profile'. As an example, assuming $\alpha = 3$ and a central-line marking all keys including and to the left of 't', 'g' and 'b' on a standard QWERTY keyboard as *left* and all keys including and to the right of 'y', 'h' and 'n' as *right*, the word "canoe" would be represented as:

LLN.LRF.RRF.RLF.

Note that for the five letter word "canoe", there are four pairs of consecutive keypresses: "ca", "an", "no", and "oe". Accordingly, all words of length n will be represented as abstract strings of length $n - 1$ in our system. These abstract words can then be processed for content using dictionaries as discussed below. We note that as there are only two one letter words in English (e.g., 'a' and 'I'), that we can identify such words as a special case in our architecture.

5.2 Framework Overview

To convert raw accelerometer data into dictionary words, our framework consists of a two phase process: the *learning* and *attack* phases. Figure 4 provides an overview of this process.

5.2.1 Learning Phase

Before we begin training our learner, our framework defines a preprocessing step needed to build the training data. This step consists of determining parameters for where the keyboard will be split for *left-right* and *near-far* labeling (α and central-line) . Once these parameters are defined, we build training data and word-profiles from different predefined English dictionaries for use during the learning and attack phases. To avoid over-fitting in the learners, the preprocessing step also ensures that the training data has an equal distribution of features.

After preprocessing, our framework trains the model through data collection, feature extraction, word labeling, and supervised learning processes.

Data Collection: When a key is pressed, the iPhone's accelerometer senses the surface vibrations and gives outputs values of the instantaneous acceleration on the x, y, and z axes. Our 'Data-Collector' application running on the iPhone records these acceleration values at a variable sampling rate (100Hz on average) along

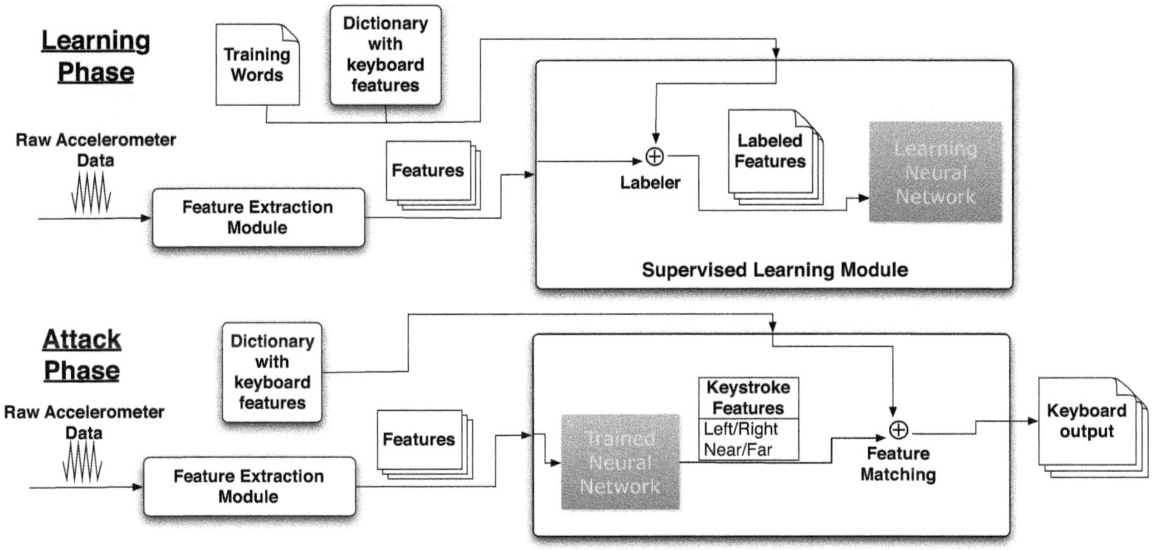

Figure 4: The Data Processing Architecture. This diagram provides a high level overview of the architecture used for training the neural network and for analyzing keyboard input during an attack.

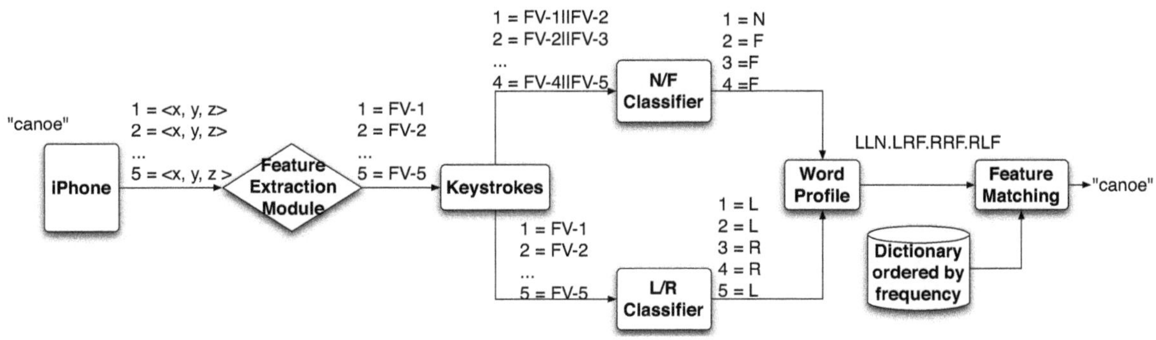

Figure 5: An example of identifying a single word "canoe". As the victim types, raw x, y, and z values are captured and converted to feature vectors. These feature vectors are analyzed by two classifiers, creating a word profile that is used to select the best possible match from a dictionary of words.

with the key that was pressed. At the start of the learning phase, we type all the letters in the English alphabet (a through z) 150 times each (with no fixed ordering or timing) on the target keyboard. The 'Data-Collector' application continuously records the seismic emanations produced by these key-presses resulting in the raw-acceleration dump for learning phase D_L of 3900 distinct keypress events corresponding to all the alphabets (150 times).

Feature Extraction: The raw acceleration values collected are then processed to extract relevant features to be used to train the model. Due to the iPhone accelerometer's low sampling rate, we were unable to obtain satisfactory classifier performance by only using features gathered in previous emanations work [3]. Therefore, we use a combination of time-domain, frequency-domain and cepstral features to construct our 'feature-vector'. Asonov et al. [3] determined a key-press is approximately 100 ms long guiding us to use the same time window for our feature extraction calculations. From the raw acceleration (x, y, z) values stored in D_L, we calculate time-domain features including root mean square (rms), skewness, variance, and kurtosis and combine those with spectral and cepstral features such as fast Fourier transform (FFT) and mel-frequency cepstrum coefficients (MFCCs) respectively. The final feature-vector corresponding to the x, y, z accelerations of a key-press (P_i) is denoted as: $FV(P_i) =<$ mean, kurtosis, variance, min, max, energy, rms, mfccs, ffts $>$. At the end of this step, we have a set (SF) containing 150 feature-vectors (FVs) corresponding to each English letter. i.e., $SF = \{FV(P_i) \mid \forall P_i \in D_L\}$

Word Labeling: Once the feature vectors are extracted from the raw accelerometer data, the framework creates a training set by labeling individual key and key-pair samples based on the defined dictionary. To prevent over-training, a preprocessing step is performed which determines the number of samples to take per dictionary character by finding an even distribution of *left* (L) and *right* (R) and *near* (N) and *far* (F) labels.

Each word in the training dictionary is broken down into its constituent characters and character-pairs. As described earlier, a word of length n letters would be broken into n characters and $n-1$ character-pairs. For each character, we randomly select 100 feature vectors that correspond to that character from the Feature Extraction step and label each of these feature vectors as *left* (L) or *right* (R) based on the Word Labeling step. In a similar manner, for each character-pair we construct 100 composite feature vectors by concatenating 100 random feature vectors corresponding to the first character and 100 random feature vectors corresponding to the second character. Each of these composite feature vectors is labeled *near* (N) or *far* (F), again using the labels from the Word Labeling step. Once this process is completed for every character and character-pair in the dictionary, the labeled feature vectors can be used to train the neural networks in the last step.

Supervised Learning: The final step of the learning phase consists of training a model that will be used during the attack phase to classify each key and key-pair accordingly. We built two separate models by training a *left-right* neural network and a *near-far* neural network for classifying *left-right* and *near-far* feature-vectors respectively. Both neural networks where trained using 500 training cycles and a learning rate of 0.3.

5.2.2 *Attack Phase*

Our framework defines process for the attack phase much in the same way the learning phase was defined by attempting to recover words through data collection, feature extraction, key-press classification, and word matching.

Data Collection: When the 'Data-Collector' application becomes malicious, the same properties and procedures apply to the attack phase that existed in the learning phase with the exception of the ability to tag an accelerometer with the appropriate key-press. Under these circumstances we're provided with a raw-acceleration dump for attack phase D_A of all the key-presses entered by the victim minus the character pressed.

Feature Extraction: After the raw-acceleration data is collected by the malicious application, the attack phase then calculates the same features that were derived during the learning phase. The feature-vectors are then used to create two sets of data, one for classifying *left* vs. *right* and one for classifying *near* vs. *far*.

Key-press Classification: Once the data has been processed, our framework attempts to classify each vector. The model produced by the *left-right* neural network is used to predict the L/R label for each individual key-press while the model produced by the *near-far* neural network is use to predict the N/F label for each pair of key-presses. Each word is then labeled with its appropriate word profile using the predicted labels and sent to the word matcher.

Word Matching: The word matcher takes each predicted word profile of length $n - 1$ and assigns a score against each word in the dictionary with length n. Algorithm 1 defines the scoring algorithm. The scored dictionary words are then sorted and the top two scores are presented as candidate predictions for the given predicted profile.

Algorithm 1 Word matcher scoring

$curScore = 0$
for all $words$ in dic of $len(n)$ **do**
  for $i = 0$ to 2 **do**
    if $dic.word.profile[i] = prediction.profile[i]$ **then**
      if $dic.word.profile[i] = L$ or $dic.word.profile[i] = R$ **then**
        $curScore++$
      else if $dic.word.profile[i] = N$ or $dic.word.profile[i] = F$ **then**
        $curScore++$
      end if
    end if
  end for
end for
return $curScore$

5.3 Experimental Setup

In all of our experiments, we set the target desktop computer on a wooden desk. We then placed the iPhone used to collect keyboard vibrations beside the target computer's keyboard. To maintain consistency, we always placed the phone at a distance of two inches from the left hand side of the keyboard. *It is important to note that there is nothing inherently desirable about the orientation of the device used in our experiments.* The attack will work if the device is trained in any orientation. All raw accelerometer readings were collected by the phone, then uploaded to a remote server. This server ran the data processing and classification algorithms used to analyze the collected accelerometer readings.

The hardware and software components used to perform the experiments are described below:

1. Keyboard: We used Apple A1255 Wireless Bluetooth keyboard. Bluetooth was used so that we could send the typed characters to the data-collector application running on the iPhone while collecting accelerometer readings. We did this to automatically and accurately label the collected data during the Learning phase and to match the classifier's predicted word-profile to the actual word-profile in the Attack phase.

2. Phone and Accelerometer: We used the iPhone 4 (running firmware no. 03.10.01). The phone contains an ST-LIS331DLH accelerometer; operating with sensitivity of 1 mg/digit, g-range of $\pm 2g$ and Acceleration noise density of 218 $\frac{\mu g}{\sqrt{Hz}}$ [41]. The maximum accelerometer sampling rate achievable in our experiments was 100Hz.

3. Signal Processing: For calculating the FFT coefficients, we used MATLAB's Discrete Fourier transform function (FFT).The mel-frequency cepstral coefficients values were calculated using its Voicebox toolbox [12]. For MFCC calculations, we set the number of channels in the Mel Scale Filter Bank to 32 and use 3 MFCCs computed for the frame-duration of 0.025s and frame step of 0.01s.

4. RapidMiner / Machine learning: We used the RapidMiner (version 5.0.010) data mining application and libraries for training and testing our neural network models and developing our framework. This choice was motivated by RapidMiner's extensibility and integration in Java-based applications, the core of our framework.

6. EXPERIMENTAL RESULTS

To test the accuracy of our attack, we performed four experiments, varying the test sentences and the target dictionary used to match word profiles. In our first experiment, we demonstrate the accuracies that the L/R and N/F classifiers are capable of achieving by analyzing a single test sentence from the Harvard Sentences [30]. We chose this list of sentences because it is phonetically-balanced, i.e. it uses specific English phonemes with a uniform distribution. In our second experiment, we examine the system's potential for text recovery using a small dictionary of the first ten Harvard sentences and attempting to recover the same ten Harvard sentences as test data. In our third experiment, we calibrate our work against previous research in this space by re-creating the experiment used by Berger et al. [10] in order to gauge the relative accuracy of our approach against very large dictionaries. Finally, we simulate a real-world attack on a piece of written media selected from the USAToday [14]. We construct a dictionary based on the context of the target article using related news stories, then type the article as test data.

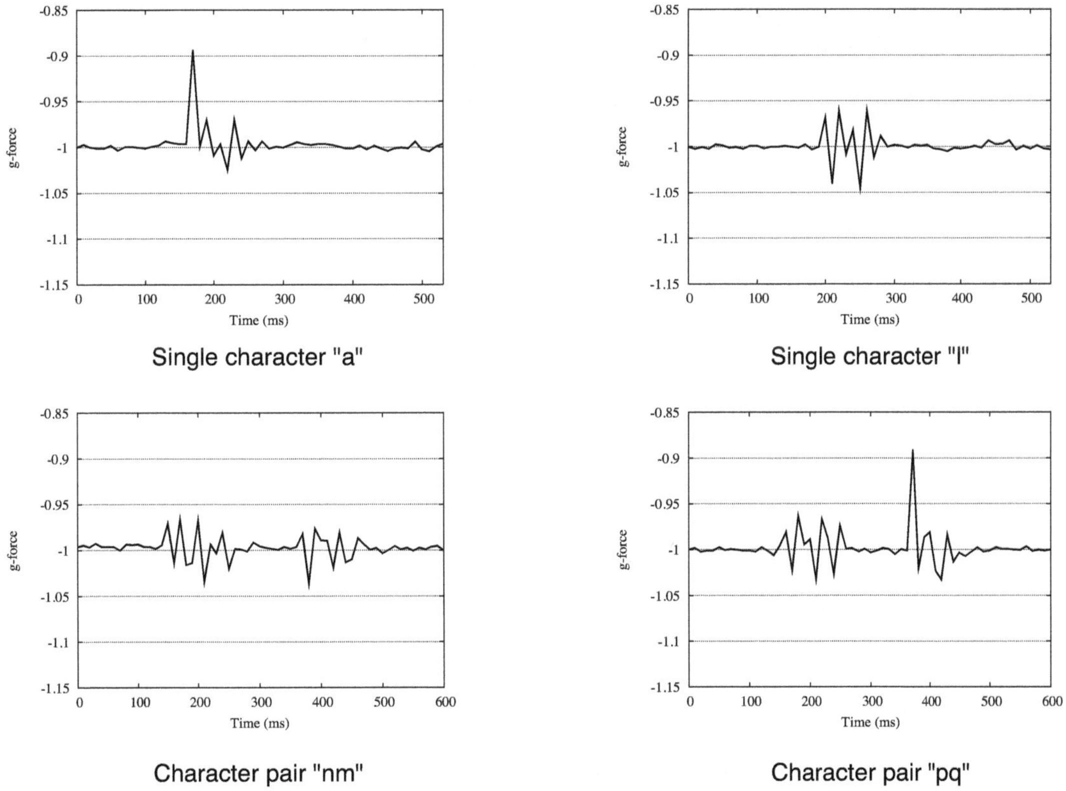

Figure 6: Examples of g-force measurements for L/R keypresses and N/F pairs. Note the distinct difference between left and right characters "a" and "l", as well as the varying level of contrast between near and far pairs "nm" and "pq". Also, left and right characters are even distinguishable across graphs, with "a" and "q" creating similar left side vibrations while "l", "n", "m", and "p" create similar right side vibrations.

6.1 Feature Accuracy

Our first analysis of these three experiments examined the base accuracy of both classifiers in correctly distinguishing letters as L/R and pairs as N/F. Figure 6 shows examples of the g-force measured by the accelerometer for two individual keypresses and two pairs. Even viewing with the naked eye, the difference between keypresses on the left end of the keyboard ("a") and the right end ("l") is significant. When visually examining concatenated pairs, the difference between two adjacent keypresses ("nm") is minimal when contrasted to the difference in two distant keypresses ("pq"). Our results demonstrate that for a majority of keypresses and keypress pairs, these differences are distinguishing enough to correctly identify the approximate location of a keypress on the keyboard. Moreover, these results reinforce the results shown in Figure 3. The keypresses of letters in close proximity, such as "nm", create very similar vibrations, making it incredibly difficult to identify the specific key pressed. Thus, our method of identifying a region rather than a specific key provides a more feasible means of differentiating between keypresses.

In our first experiment, the L/R classifier was able to correctly identify 91% of the individual keypresses as right or left, and 70% of the keypress pairs as near or far. As the size of our test data grew, these percentages declined. For the second experiment, our L/R accuracy was 84% and our N/F accuracy 65%. This drop in accuracy is to be expected with more keypresses, as the target will exhibit minor inconsistencies in striking the same key over time. Considering that many emails sent are no more than one or two sentences, these experiments represent a significant leakage of information.

6.2 Recovering Text

Our next analysis examined the percentage of text recovered by the matcher given the word profiles produced by the neural networks. When examining the preliminary results of our experiment, we noted that the overall percentages of words recovered noticeably dropped due to the frequency of two and three letter words in the analyzed text. Since these words are generally articles and conjunctions (e.g. an, the, and, or), they can be easily interpolated by examining the semantics of the recovered text. In our experiments, we opted to consider only "long" words of four letters or more in all final percentages of recovered words. In each figure, the "short" words will be denoted with asterisks.

In the first two experiments, the dictionary contained a small set of words containing the test data exactly. Our first experiment took vibrations from typing a single sentence and attempted to analyze the text. In Figure 7, we show the results of this experiment and compare the recovered sentence to the actual typed sentence. For each word profile, the matcher returned a list of possible results for that profile weighted by frequency of use. For the first Harvard sentence, 80% of the words were correctly identified as the first choice for their interpreted word profile. In the second experiment, we expanded the test data to the first ten Harvard sentences. For this larger analysis, 46% of the words were correctly identified as the first choice for their interpreted word profile. However, if we

```
          1st Choice Correct = 80%
          L/R Accuracy = 91.07%
          N/F Accuracy = 70.15%

     Typed Text: The birch canoe slid on the smooth planks
 Recovered Text: *** punch canoe slid ** *** smooth planks
```

Figure 7: Experiment 1. In this experiment, we attempted to interpret a single sentence, shown here. Our dictionary was composed of words from the first ten Harvard sentences. The first line shows the sentence as it was typed, and the second line shows the sentence as our program analyzed it. A string of asterisks represents a word of three letters or fewer, all of which were omitted.

```
          1st or 2nd Choice Correct = 72.92%
          L/R Accuracy =83.95%
          N/F Accuracy = 64.88%

     Typed Text: Glue the sheet to the dark blue background
 Recovered Text: Glue *** sheet ** *** well hogs background
                                         blue

     Typed Text: These days a chicken leg is a rare dish
 Recovered Text: These days * chicken *** ** * rare dish
```

Figure 8: Experiment 2. Again using the first ten Harvard sentences as a dictionary, we attempted to interpret all ten sentences and selected two to display here. We again show the text as it was typed and as our program analyzed it. If the correct word was weighted second by the matcher, it is listed below the first choice word, which is written in line. A string of asterisks represents a word of three letters or fewer, all of which were omitted from the analysis.

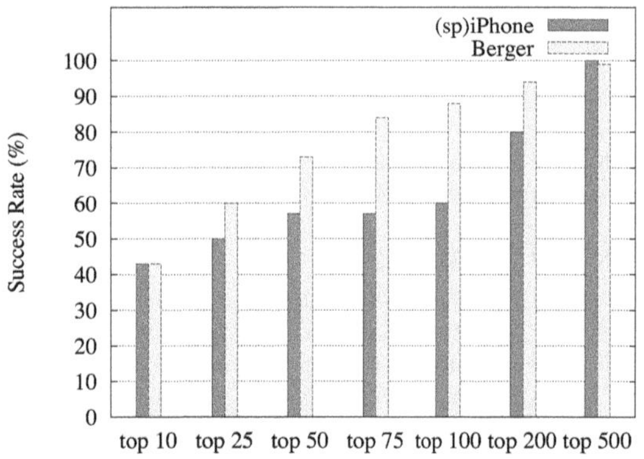

Figure 9: A comparison of accuracy of our ((sp)iPhone) and the acoustic dictionary techniques proposed by Berger et al [10]. Note that in spite of our dramatically reduce sampling rate, our results are roughly comparable for a very large dictionary (i.e., 57,000+ words).

also consider the words ranked second most likely by the matcher, this accuracy rises to 73%, as shown in Figure 8. By examining the semantics of a captured sentence, we can easily choose the correct choice between the top two choices for a word profile.

6.3 Comparison to Previous Work

In an attempt to calibrate this work against previous efforts in this space, we re-created the experiment from the work by Berger et al. [10]. This work cites a "corn-cob" dictionary of approximately 58,000 words and attempts to use the acoustic emanations of a keyboard to recover 27 test words ranging in length from 7-13 characters. In our experiment, we used a portion of the same dictionary, containing approximately 57,500 words (all the words with 4 or more characters). Rather than using the same 7-13 character word list, we selected 30 words from a randomly chosen USAToday article [14] (announcing a court ruling to keep then candidate Rahm Emanuel on the ballot for the February 2011 Chicago mayoral election), ranging in length from 4-9 characters. This test word set better demonstrates the practical accuracy of our technique by using a test sample from written media rather than an arbitrary selection of long words. The comparison is shown in Figure 9.

After running our list of test words through the data processing architecture, our techniques demonstrated comparable accuracies to that of Berger et al. [10]. Our technique placed the correct guess in the top 10 potential words selected for each test word 43% of the time, matching the work of Berger. When examining the number of correct terms in the top 50 potential words selected, our accuracy trailed somewhat at 56%, compared to 72% for the acoustic work. However, it is important to notice two distinct challenges faced by our technique. First, the frequency which we sample vibrations is two full orders of magnitude smaller than in the acoustic emanation work. With this extremely limited bandwidth, we are still able to match the acoustic accuracy in the top 10 potential words selected. Second, our word list uses words of 4-9 characters in length, as opposed to the 7-13 character words used in the previous work. The dictionary attacks used in both works allow longer words to be identified more easily since there are fewer potential matches in the dictionary of terms.

6.4 A More Realistic Attack

To demonstrate the feasibility of our technique in a real-world

```
1-5 Choice Correct = 80.00%
L/R Accuracy =78.58%
N/F Accuracy = 61.09%

Typed Text: The Illinois Supreme Court has ruled that Rahm Emanuel is eligible to

            run for mayor of Chicago and ordered him to stay on the ballot

Recovered Text:  ***  Illinois Supreme about *** ruled part wait Emanuel ** chicagos **
                                   among                    Rahm             eligible
                                   might
                                   night
                                   Court
            *** *** names ** Chicago  *** printed *** ** look ** *** ballot
                                          members
                                          grinned
                                          ordered
```

Figure 10: Experiment 4. Using news articles as a dictionary, we analyzed the typed contents of a USAToday article. Here we show an excerpt as it was typed and as our program analyzed it. If the correct word was weighted between second and fifth choice by the matcher, it is listed below the words that were weighted more heavily. A string of asterisks represents a word of three letters or fewer, all of which were omitted from the analysis.

attack, we examined the following scenario. Since an attacker may know the general context of a target's message, it is reasonable to construct a dictionary based upon terms that are likely to appear in the target's writing. So we constructed a dictionary using seven news articles related to Rahm Emanuel (from the New York Times [20, 18, 19] and USAToday [36, 15, 25, 35]) that were published during the week before the target text. This simulates eavesdropping on the reporter typing the USAToday piece. We again apply the methodology by Berger et al [10] to measure our results.

We again examined the same words of our test sample (from Experiment 3), this time using our 799 word context-aware dictionary. In 40% of the tests, our technique selected the correct word as first choice, and 53% fell in the first or second choice, as shown in Figure 10. The correct word fell in top 5 predictions for 80% of the tests. Based on these results, it is apparent that an attacker could easily recover a dangerous amount of text captured using our technique, simply by knowing some context for the target's writing.

7. DISCUSSION

7.1 Recognition versus Distance

Our experiments thus far have been conducted with the mobile phone located within two inches of the targeted keyboard. We believe that this is reasonable given the dimensions of most desks and the assumption that many users will wish to have their mobile phone with reach while working at their computer. However, our analysis would not be complete without an understanding of how increasing the distance between the mobile phone and its target impact recovery.

As expected, even small increases in distance dramatically reduce the effectiveness of this attack. Between absorption and attenuation of signal based on the Inverse Square Law, our accuracy drops rapidly at distance of one foot. Distinguishing keystrokes from noise at two feet is extremely difficult, effectively disrupting the attack. Beyond this range, our mechanism quickly approaches random guessing as the received signals are simply too small to meaningfully distinguish between. As we discuss in one of the following subsections, this simple observation functions as a powerful mitigation to these attacks.

Due to the low sensitivity of the accelerometer, the distance limitation is a difficult problem to overcome. Environmental factors, such as the surface characteristics of the desk (discussed further in the following section), add more complexity to this challenge. In the wrong conditions, even a small increase in distance could completely inhibit the attack, while good conditions could facilitate keystroke recognition from well over a distance of one foot. Because of variable environmental conditions, we can only guarantee proper functionality within one foot.

7.2 Challenges and Limitations

We examined three additional challenges that could be encountered with this application. Our first potential challenge relates to the orientation of the monitoring device. In all of our experiments, we positioned the mobile device vertically to the left of the keyboard, as shown in Figure 1. However, if this orientation were to change, the vibrations measured for the same keystrokes would be captured differently on the device's x and y axes. On first review, this would seem to cause errors in accuracy. The first strategy for compensating for a change in orientation would be to simply re-train the neural network to identify keystrokes coming from a device in the new orientation. However, according to the work of Zhuang et al. [42], the neural network *does not have to be re-trained* in this manner. Instead, the keystrokes could potentially be identified based on measuring their frequency. By using this technique to analyze vibrations captured by the mobile device in *any* orientation, we believe that we can produce similar results regardless of the orientation of the mobile device. We plan to explore this issue in future work.

The second potential challenge we considered was ambient vibrations. There is a plethora of possible scenarios where vibrations in the environment around the device could potentially garble the keystroke information being collected. Some of these vibrations could be subtle or consistent enough that our application would be able to distinguish keystroke information from the ambient noise. For example, if an office is adjacent to an air conditioning unit, a consistent vibration could potentially be detected and filtered out. However, other more obtrusive possibilities also exist. In skyscrapers, the movement of the building itself could be detected, causing periodic interference with keystroke detection. Users who bounce their knee or habitually tap on their desk would also send significant vibrations into the device, again causing a loss of pertinent data. This problem, although not common in most work environments, still merits further consideration with regards to the overall accuracy of this attack.

Typing speed is also likely to pose a problem to some recovery scenarios. Like previous studies [3], we limited the rate at which we typed so that easily distinguishable characters could be recorded and a proof of concept implementation of the attack created. However, some users that type very fast are likely to cause problems to the current Data-Collector. These problems arising from such behavior are not likely to be a result of keypresses overlapping - each keypress lasts roughly 100 ms and a user typing a key every 100 ms would be able to type approximately 120 words per minute (i.e., the extreme high range for professional typists [4]). Instead, the rapid movement of hands on the surfact is likely to cause addition noise, potentially making recognition more difficult. We intend to study this issue in greater depth in our future work.

The final challenge we considered was desk surface characteristics. The capability of an accelerometer to detect vibrations in a desk is directly dependent on the surface's ability to amplify or dampen these vibrations. In all of our experiments, we recorded keystrokes on the most common desk surface, wood. To begin to answer the question of the impact of surface characteristics on accuracy, we performed additional experiments on a ceramic tile surface. As would be expected from a rigid surface, keystroke vibrations on ceramic tile were not carried to the device at all, completely inhibiting the use of our application. The extent of this limitation to other surfaces, such as metal or plastic, merits some further consideration. However, we consider vibration-inhibiting surfaces such as tile to be minor special cases when evaluating the overall usefulness of our application.

7.3 Mitigation Strategies

The attack discussed in this paper demonstrates the need for careful thinking about how the array of sensors now available to mobile phones can be accessed. While access to the most obvious candidates for information leakage (e.g., camera, microphone, GPS) is increasingly being protected, we have shown that access to seemingly innocuous sensor data can result in the accurate recovery of potentially sensitive data. As a result, we now offer a number of short and long term mitigation strategies and mechanisms to address these problems.

The simplest mechanism is in preventing mobile phones from coming too close to keyboards. Some businesses and many government buildings already forbid their employees from carrying such devices on the premises. However, such an approach may be too restrictive for most corporate and home environments, especially given the common and legitimate use of mobile phones in these settings. Alternatively, a party concerned about such eavesdropping can place their mobile phone in a briefcase, backpack or handbag which they regularly carry. Finally, a user may simply place their mobile device on a separate surface. As our experiments have demonstrated, the accelerometers contained in mobile phones at the time of this writing are not nearly sensitive enough to detect and uniquely identify keypress generated vibrations.[2]

In the long term, mobile device operating systems should provide more finer-grained control to their resources. It is likely that attacks using other unregulated sensors in unintended ways will be possible on these platforms. Such access need not simply be Boolean in this particular case. Instead, we can limit the sampling rate to take advantage of the information theoretic lower bounds for avoiding aliasing based on the Nyquist-Shannon sampling theorem [33]. Specifically, an observed signal must be sampled at the Nyquist rate, at least two times the rate of the highest frequency, to prevent signals from becoming indistinguishable from each other. From our experiments, we determined that the highest observed frequency in our dataset was approximately 15 Hz. Accordingly, by providing all applications with less than 30 Hz resolution to accelerometer data by default, such attacks become theoretically impossible. This approach will be particularly successful for applications such as text editors which are likely to only use accelerometer data to rotate the contents of the screen based on the user turning their phone. However, the use of a decreased sampling rate may not be appropriate for applications such as games which may require more accurate measurements of movement (e.g., driving games in which the car is steered by rotating the phone). These applications should instead be given explicit access to a high-sampling permission, much as application manifests for Android can be written for fine and coarse-grained GPS access [2].

8. CONCLUSION

Mobile phones contain an array of powerful sensors. While access to many of the most obvious sources of information is generally restricted, the use of a number of a number of other seemingly innocuous sensors is not. In this paper, we demonstrate that unfettered access to accelerometer data allows a malicious application to recover and decode the vibrations caused by keypresses on a nearby keyboard. By characterizing consecutive pairs of keypress events, we demonstrate the ability to recover as much as 80% of typed content. We then provide a number of short and long term mitigation strategies. In so doing, we demonstrate that access to increasingly capable sensors by applications running on mobile phones must be more carefully regulated.

Acknowledgments

This work was supported in part by the US National Science Foundation (CNS-0916047, CAREER CNS-0952959). Any opinions, findings, conclusions or recommendations expressed in this publication are those of the authors and do not necessarily reflect the views of the National Science Foundation.

9. REFERENCES

[1] D. Agrawal, J. Rao, and P. Rohatgi. The EM side-channels. In *Proceedings of the Workshop on Cryptographic Hardware and Embedded Systems (CHES)*, 2002.

[2] Android Developers. Manifest.permission. `http://developer.android.com/reference/android/Manifest.permission.html`, 2010.

[3] D. Asonov and R. Agrawal. Keyboard Acoustic Emanations. In *Proceedings of the IEEE Symposium on Security and Privacy*, 2004.

[2]Assuming that the device is not placed on a highly amplifying surface.

[4] R. Ayres and K. Martinas. 120 WPM for Very Skilled Typist. *On the Reappraisal of Microeconomics: Economic Growth and Change in a Material World*, page 41, 2005.

[5] M. Backes, T. Chen, M. Durmuth, H. P. A. Lensch, and M. Welk. Tempest in a Teapot: Compromising Reflections Revisited. In *Proceedings of the IEEE Symposium on Security and Privacy (OAKLAND)*, 2009.

[6] M. Backes, M. Duermuth, S. Gerling, M. Pinkal, and C. Sporleder. Acoustic Side-Channel Attacks on Printers. In *Proceedings of the USENIX Security Symposium (SECURITY)*, 2010.

[7] M. Backes, M. Durmuth, and D. Unruh. Compromising Reflections – or – How to Read LCD Monitors Around the Corner. In *Proceedings of the IEEE Symposium on Security and Privacy (OAKLAND)*, 2008.

[8] A. Barisani and D. Bianco. Sniffing Keystrokes With Lasers and Voltmeters. In *Proceedings of Black Hat USA*, 2009.

[9] D. Barrera, H. Kayacik, P. van Oorschot, and A. Somayaji. A Methodology for Empirical Analysis of the Permission-Based Security Models and its Application to Android. In *Proceedings of the ACM Conference on Computer and Communications Security (CCS)*, 2010.

[10] Y. Berger, A. Wool, and A. Yeredor. Dictionary Attacks Using Keyboard Acoustic Emanations. In *Proceedings of the ACM Conference on Computer and Communications Security (CCS)*, 2006.

[11] R. Briol. Emanation: How to keep your data confidential. In *Symposium on Electromagnetic Security For Information Protection*, 1991.

[12] M. Brookes. Voicebox: Speech processing toolbox for matlab. `http://www.ee.ic.ac.uk/hp/staff/dmb/voicebox/voicebox.html`.

[13] L. Cai, S. Machiraju, and H. Chen. Defending Against Sensor-Sniffing Attacks on Mobile Phones. In *Proceedings of ACM SIGCOMM Workshop on Networking, Systems, Applications on Mobile Handhelds (MobiHeld)*, 2009.

[14] C. Camia. Rahm emanuel can run for chicago mayor. `http://content.usatoday.com/communities/onpolitics/post/2011/01/chicago-mayor-rahm-emanuel-/1`, January 2011.

[15] C. Camia. Rahm emanuel to fight to get onto chicago ballot. `http://content.usatoday.com/communities/onpolitics/post/2011/01/rahm-emanuel-chicago-mayor-court-ruling-/1`, January 2011.

[16] Z. Cheng. Mobile Malware: Threats and Prevention. `http://www.mcafee.com/us/local_content/white_papers/threat_center/wp__malware_r2_en.pdf`, 2007.

[17] D. Dagon, T. Martin, and T. Starner. Mobile Phones as Computing Devices: The Viruses are Coming! *IEEE Pervasive Computing*, 3(4):11–15, October - December 2004.

[18] M. Davey. Emanuel keeps campaigning, as he fights to get back on the ballot. `http://thecaucus.blogs.nytimes.com/2011/01/25/emanuel-keeps-campaigning-as-he-fights-to-get-back-on-the-ballot/?scp=8&sq=Rahm+Emanuel&st=nyt`, January 2011.

[19] M. Davey. Emanuel raises $10 million for chicago mayor's race. `http://query.nytimes.com/gst/fullpage.html?res=9B00E0DC1E3EF932A15752C0A9679D8B63&scp=10&sq=Rahm+Emanuel&st=nyt`, January 2011.

[20] M. Davey and J. Schwartz. Emanuel back on ballot; court will hear case. `https://www.nytimes.com/2011/01/26/us/politics/26rahm.html?scp=9&sq=Rahm+Emanuel&st=nyt`, January 2011.

[21] M. Egele, C. Kruegel, E. Kirda, and G. Vigna. PiOS: Detecting Privacy Leaks in iOS Applications. In *Proceedings of the ISOC Network and Distributed Systems Security (NDSS) Symposium*, 2011.

[22] Electromax International, Inc. Spy Surveillance: Laser Listening Systems. `http://www.electromax.com/laser.html`, 1998.

[23] W. Enck, P. Gilbert, B.-G. Chun, L. P. Cox, J. Jung, P. McDaniel, and A. N. Sheth. TaintDroid: An Information-Flow Tracking System for Realtime Privacy Monitoring on Smartphones. In *Proceedings of the USENIX Symposium on Operating Systems Design and Implementation (OSDI)*, 2010.

[24] W. Enck, M. Ongtang, and P. McDaniel. On Lightweight Mobile Phone Application Certification. In *Proceedings of the ACM Conference on Computer and Communications Security (CCS)*, 2009.

[25] J. Keen. Rahm emanuel's mayoral bid hits pothole. `http://www.usatoday.com/news/politics/2011-01-25-emanuel25_ST_N.htm`, January 2011.

[26] M. G. Kuhn. Optical time-domain eavesdropping risks of CRT displays. In *Proceedings of the IEEE Symposium on Security and Privacy (OAKLAND)*, 2002.

[27] M. G. Kuhn and R. J. Anderson. Soft Tempest: Hidden Data Transmission Using Electromagnetic Emanations. *Information Hiding*, Lecture Notes in Computer Science 1525:124–142, 1998.

[28] B. C. Nalty. The War Against Trucks Aerial Interdiction in Southern Laos 1968-1972. Office of Air Force History, Washington, DC, 2005.

[29] National Security Agency. TEMPEST. `http://www.nsa.gov/public_info/files/cryptologic_spectrum/tempest.pdf`, 2007.

[30] I. S. on Subjective Measurements. Ieee recommended practices for speech quality measurements. *IEEE Transactions on Audio and Electroacoustics*, 17:227–46, 1969.

[31] J.-J. Quisquater and D. Samyde. ElectroMagnetic Analysis (EMA): Measures and Counter-Measures for Smart Cards. In *Proceedings of the International Conference on Research in Smart Cards (E-SMART)*, 2001.

[32] R. Schlegel, K. Zhang, X. Zhou, M. Intwala, A. Kapadia, and X. Wang. Soundcomber: A Stealthy and Context-Aware Sound Trojan for Smartphones. In *Proceedings of the ISOC Network and Distributed Systems Security (NDSS) Symposium*, 2011.

[33] S. W. Smith. *The Scientist and Engineer's Guide to Digital Signal Processing*. Elsevier/Newnes Publishing, 2002.

[34] P. Smulders. The Threat of Information Theft by Reception of Electromagnetic Radiation from RS-232 Cables. *Computers and Security*, 9(1):53–58, 1990.

[35] D. Stanglin. Court puts rahm emanuel back on ballot, agrees to hear case. `http://content.usatoday.com/communities/ondeadline/post/2011/01/`

rahm-emanuel-back-on-the-ballot-pending-possible-court-hearing/1, January 2011.

[36] D. Stanglin. Rahm emanuel to fight ruling booting him from mayoral ballot. http://content.usatoday.com/communities/ondeadline/post/2011/01/court-says-rahm-emanuel-ineligible-to-run-for-chicago-mayor/1, January 2011.

[37] T. Thomas. Malware on the Move. http://mobile-security-software-review.toptenreviews.com/malware-on-the-move.html, 2008.

[38] P. Traynor, C. Amrutkar, V. Rao, T. Jaeger, P. McDaniel, and T. La Porta. From Mobile Phones to Responsible Devices. *Journal of Security and Communication Networks (SCN)*, To Appear 2011.

[39] W. Van Eck. Electromagnetic Radiation from Video Display Units: An Eavesdropping Risk? *Computers and Security*, 4:269–286, 1985.

[40] M. Vuagnoux and S. Pasini. Compromising Electromagnetic Emanations from Wired and Wireless Keyboards. In *Proceedings of the USENIX Security Symposium (SECURITY)*, 2009.

[41] www.st.com. Lis331dlh. http://www.st.com/stonline/products/literature/ds/15094.pdf, July 2009.

[42] L. Zhuang, F. Zhou, and J. D. Tygar. Keyboard Acoustic Emanations Revisited. In *Proceedings of the ACM Conference on Computer and Communications Security (CCS)*, 2005.

Predictive Mitigation of Timing Channels in Interactive Systems

Danfeng Zhang
zhangdf@cs.cornell.edu

Aslan Askarov
aslan@cs.cornell.edu

Andrew C. Myers
andru@cs.cornell.edu

Department of Computer Science
Cornell University
Ithaca, NY 14853

Abstract

Timing channels remain a difficult and important problem for information security. Recent work introduced predictive mitigation, a new way to mitigating leakage through timing channels; this mechanism works by predicting timing from past behavior, and then enforcing the predictions. This paper generalizes predictive mitigation to a larger and important class of systems: systems that receive input requests from multiple clients and deliver responses. The new insight is that timing predictions may be a function of any public information, rather than being a function simply of output events. Based on this insight, a more general mechanism and theory of predictive mitigation becomes possible. The result is that bounds on timing leakage can be tightened, achieving asymptotically logarithmic leakage under reasonable assumptions. By applying it to web applications, the generalized predictive mitigation mechanism is shown to be effective in practice.

Categories and Subject Descriptors

C.2.0 [**Computer-Communication Networks**]: General—*Security and protection*

General Terms

Security

Keywords

Timing channels, mitigation, interactive systems, information flow

1. Introduction

The time at which a computing system performs some observable action such as sending a network packet can in principle encode an unbounded amount of information about what is happening inside the system, creating a *timing channel* [1]. An adversary able to accurately measure this time may learn confidential information from this side channel (e.g., [2, 3, 4, 5]); an adversary able to influence this time may additionally use it as a covert channel to communicate confidential information (e.g., [6, 7, 8]).

CCS'11, October 17–21, 2011, Chicago, Illinois, USA.

Though the recent work cited above demonstrates the threat of timing channels, controlling them without compromising functionality is typically considered to be extremely challenging or even infeasible [9, 10, 11]. Recent work on timing channels has focused on quantitatively bounding what can be learned from timing channels rather than on blocking them entirely (e.g., [12, 13, 14]).

Recent work by Askarov et al. introduced a new mechanism called *predictive mitigation* for bounding information leakage via timing channels [14]. Unlike work focusing on preventing leakage of keys from cryptographic operations (such as [12, 13]), predictive mitigation applies to any computing system, making few assumptions about the nature of the computation being performed. However, as we argue, the original predictive mitigation mechanism is impractical for many real-world systems where timing channels are of concern—especially networked servers such as web applications. Therefore, this paper generalizes predictive mitigation to take advantage of more knowledge about the system whose timing channels are being mitigated, significantly improving the tradeoff between security and performance.

Contributions. The contributions of this work are both theoretical and practical. On the theoretical side, the theory of predictive mitigation is extended in several ways:

- **Inputs.** The model of the mitigated system is extended to account for inputs to the system, so output timing can be predicted from public (that is, nonconfidential) attributes of inputs such as request time.
- **Threads.** In [14], the system being mitigated is a black box. Here the system is modeled more concretely as containing multiple threads which communicate with the outside over different output channels. This more detailed modeling enables tighter leakage bounds.
- **Composition.** In general, a system employing predictive mitigation may be composed of several communicating components, each individually mitigated. The theory of composing predictive mitigation is developed.

This new theory of predictive mitigation has been put into practice as in an implementation of predictive mitigation for web applications. For example, we implement a standardized server-side wrapper that can mitigate timing leaks from any web application.

An important contribution of this paper is an empirical evaluation of how predictive mitigation performs when applied to real applications with different characteristics. We examine its impact on latency, throughput, and maximum timing leakage of wrapped web applications. The results from this implementation suggest that the generalized predictive mitigation mechanism appears to be practical and offers a significant improvement on the original predictive mitigation method.

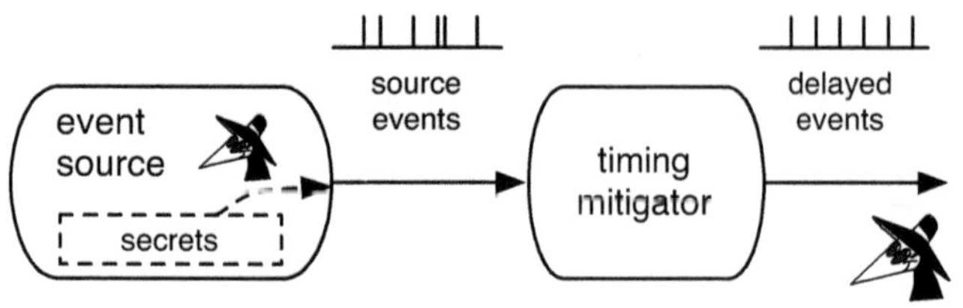

Figure 1: Predictive mitigation

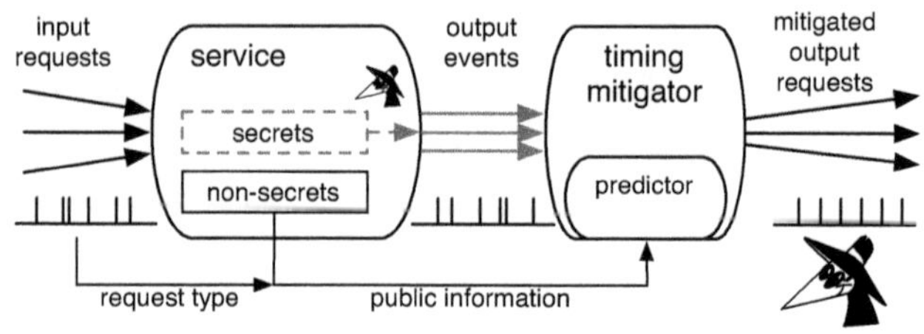

Figure 2: Predictive mitigation of an interactive system

The rest of the paper is structured as follows. Section 2 introduces the extended form of predictive mitigation in the context of the prior work. Section 3 presents different ways to construct predictive mitigators depending on the concurrency model and on what information is considered public. Section 4 analyzes information leakage under various mitigation schemes and assumptions about applications. Section 5 develops formal results on the composition of predictive mitigators. Experiments with applying predictive mitigation to real applications are presented in 6. Related work is discussed in Section 7; the paper concludes in Section 8.

2. Predictive mitigation

Timing channels can be divided into *internal* and *external* timing channels [15]. Predictive timing mitigation is a general method for limiting leakage through *external* channels: those in which the timing measurement is taken external to the system. Because measurement is external, methods that control internal timing channels by preventing effective timing measurement within the system (e.g., [16, 17, 18, 19]) cannot be applied.

Unlike timing mitigation methods that add random delays (e.g., [20, 16]), predictive mitigation bounds the amount of information that leaks through the timing channel, by delaying events according to a schedule that is predicted in advance.

2.1 Background

In the original predictive mitigation work, the system is modeled abstractly as an event source connected to a timing mitigator, as depicted in Figure 1. The timing of events produced by the event source is in general influenced by confidential information. Further, the adversary may be able to affect how confidential information influences timing, enabling timing to be used as a covert channel. For example, the adversary might install software onto the event source to modulate the timing of generated events [7].

Events from the event source are delayed by the timing mitigator to reduce the bandwidth of the timing channel. The adversary is assumed to be able to observe the timing of events leaving the mitigator,[1] but can affect the mitigator *only* via the input stream of source events. Generating fake events does not help; the adversary is assumed to be able to identify them.

At any point, the mitigator has a schedule describing when events are supposed to be released. The schedule is a sequence of predictions, each associated with a future point in time. As long as events arrive according to (or ahead of) the schedule, leakage must be low because the number of possible system behaviors observable by the adversary is small.

The event source might fail to behave according to the schedule, in which case the adversary may learn information. The mitigator responds to the misprediction by selecting a new schedule in a way that ensures that total leakage through the timing channel is bounded. The period during which the schedule correctly predicts behavior is called an epoch. Schedules are chosen in such a way that the number of epochs grows slowly with time.

For example, consider the following simple "fast doubling" mitigation scheme described by Askarov et al. [14]: initially, the mitigator has a schedule of predictions at evenly spaced intervals. If the event source fails to deliver events quickly enough, the resulting misprediction causes the mitigator to generate a new schedule in which the interval between predictions is doubled.

We can bound the amount of information that leaks through the adversary's observations through a combinatorial analysis of the number of possible distinct observations the adversary can make. An observation consists of a sequence of times at which events are released by the mitigator. Because events are released in accordance with schedules, the number of possible observations is limited; therefore, the information-theoretic entropy of the timing channel is bounded. This in turn bounds the capacity of the timing channel. In total time T, there can be no more than $\log(T+1)$ epochs,[2] each of which leaks no more than $\log(T+1)+1$ bits of information. Therefore, this simple scheme releases no more than $(1+\epsilon)\log^2 T$ bits of information, where ϵ is small for large T [14]. As this bound shows, it is possible to ensure leakage is asymptotically sublinear over time.

Note that this argument is all about the capacity of the timing channel, without any assumptions about how efficiently secrets are encoded into this channel. The bound applies even if the adversary is perfectly encoding secrets into event timing. But if the adversary does not have this level of control, the bound is likely to be quite conservative.

2.2 Generalizing predictive mitigation

The prior work on predictive mitigation assumes very little about the event source, which means that it can be applied to a wide range of systems. Predictive mitigation can address even difficult low-level timing channels such as those created by hardware contention at the level of the processor or the bus, as long as the mitigator is able to delay externally visible events to precisely the time predicted by the schedule.

However, the very generality of predictive mitigation can make the leakage bounds conservative, and performance of the system is then hurt because the mitigator excessively delays the release of events. By refining the system model, we can make more accurate predictions and also bound timing leakage more accurately. The result is a better tradeoff between security and performance.

Timing channels in network-based services are particularly of interest for timing channel mitigation. These services are interactive systems that accept input requests from a variety of clients and send back responses. Figure 2 illustrates how we extend predictive mitigation for such a system.

Here, the abstract event source used by the prior work is replaced

[1]The adversary may also be able to partly observe the *contents* of events leaving the mitigator, but this is a storage channel [1], the control of which is orthogonal to the goals of this work.

[2]All logarithms here use base 2.

by a more concrete interactive system that accepts input messages on multiple input channels and delivers output messages to corresponding output channels. Output messages are passed through the timing mitigator, as before, and released by the timing mitigator in accordance with the prediction for that message. If a message arrives early, the mitigator delays it until the predicted time. If it does not arrive in time—a misprediction has happened—the mitigation starts a new epoch and makes a new, more conservative prediction.

This scheme significantly generalizes the original predictive mitigation scheme. First, the time to produce each event is predicted separately, rather than requiring the mitigator to predict the entire schedule in advance—which is rather difficult for an interactive system. Second, the prediction may be computed using any public information in the system. This public information may be anything deemed public (the "non-secrets" in the diagram), possibly including some information about input requests. For example, the mitigator may use the time at which a given input request arrives to predict the time at which the corresponding output will be available for release. The model also permits the content of input requests to be partly public. Each request has an application-defined *request type* capturing what information about the request is public. If no information in the request is public, all requests have the same request type.

To see why this generalizes the original predictive mitigation scheme, consider what happens if the prior history of mitigator predictions is the *only* information considered public when predicting the time of output events. In this case, all predictions within an epoch can be generated at the start of the epoch, yielding a completely determined schedule for the epoch. By contrast, our generalized predictive mitigation can make use of information that was not known at the start of the epoch, such as input time. Therefore, predictions can be made dynamically within an epoch.

2.3 Leakage measures

Two ways to measure information leakage have recently been popular. The information-theoretic measure of *mutual information* has a long history of use; it is advocated, for example, by Denning [21], and has been used for the estimation of covert channel capacity, including timing channel capacity, in much prior work (e.g., [22, 23, 24]). Recently, *min-entropy leakage* has become a popular measure, motivated by the observation that two systems with the same leakage according to mutual information may have very different security properties [25].

Prior work on timing channel mitigation has used one or both of these measures. Fortunately, the style of analysis used here and in prior work on predictive mitigation is sufficiently conservative that it bounds both the mutual information and the min-entropy measures of leakage.

The information-theoretic (Shannon) entropy of a finite distribution X over its n possible values is written as $\mathcal{H}(X)$. It achieves its maximal value of $\log(n)$ bits when all n possible values have equal probability. Suppose that O is the distribution over n possible timing observations by the adversary, and S is the distribution over possible secrets that the adversary wants to learn. The mutual information between O and S, written $\mathcal{I}(O;S)$, is equal to $\mathcal{H}(O) - \mathcal{H}(O|S)$, where $\mathcal{H}(O|S)$ is the conditional entropy of O on S—how much entropy remains in O once S is fixed. In our context, the conditional entropy describes how effectively the adversary encodes the secrets S into the observations O. But since conditional entropy is always positive, the mutual information between O and S is at most $\mathcal{H}(O)$, or $\log(n)$.

Smith argues [25] that the min-entropy of a distribution is a better basis for assessing the vulnerability introduced by quantitative leakage because it describes the chance that an adversary is able to guess the value of the secret in one try. The min-entropy of a distribution is defined as $\mathcal{H}_\infty(O) = -\log V(O)$ where $V(O)$ is the worst-case *vulnerability* of O to being guessed: the maximum over the probabilities of all values in O. Let us write $P(o|s)$ for the probability of observation o given secrets s. Köpf and Smith [13] show that the min-entropy channel capacity from S to O is equal to $\log \sum_{o \in O} \max_{s \in S} P(o|s)$. This capacity is maximized when $P(o|s) = 1$ at all o, in which case it is equal to $\log(n)$. Therefore $\log(n)$ is a conservative bound on this measure of leakage as well.

3. Predictions for interactive systems

The system model described in Section 2.2 permits a great deal of flexibility in constructing predictions. We now begin to explore the possibilities.

Throughout the rest of the paper we assume that the mitigator has an internal state, denoted by $\mathbf{St}$. In the simplest schemes, the state only records the number of epochs N, that is, $\mathbf{St} = N$. But more complex internal state is possible, as discussed in Section 4.2.

3.1 Inputs, outputs, and idling

For simplicity, we assume that inputs to and outputs from the interactive system correspond one-to-one: each input has one output and vice versa. If inputs can cause multiple output events, this can be modeled by introducing a schedule for delivering the multiple outputs as a batch.

Many services generate output events only as a response to some external input. In the absence of inputs, such systems are idle and produce no output. If the predictor cannot take this into account when generating predictions, the failure to generate output produces gratuitous mispredictions. With generalized predictive mitigation, these mispredictions can be avoided.

For example, consider applying the original predictive mitigation scheme to a service that reliably generates results in 10ms. If the service is idle for an hour, the series of ensuing mispredictions will inflate the interval between predicted outputs to more than an hour, slowing the underlying service by more than five orders of magnitude. Clearly this is not acceptable.

Consider inputs arriving at times $inp_1, inp_2, \ldots inp_n, \ldots$, where each inp_i is the time of input i. We assume that the mitigator has some public state $\mathbf{St}$, and that this state always includes the index of the current mitigation epoch, denoted by N. Let the prediction for events for state $\mathbf{St}$ be described by a function $p(\mathbf{St})$, where p gives a bound on how long it is expected to take to compute an answer to a request in state $\mathbf{St}$.

Whenever the structure of the mitigator state is understood, we use more concrete notation. For example, in the simple mitigator we have $\mathbf{St} = N$, so we we write $p(N)$ for $p(\mathbf{St})$. Simple fast doubling has the prediction function $p(N) = 2^{N-1}$. For more complex predictors, p might depend on other (public) parameters as well. If $S_N(0)$ is the time of the start of the N-th epoch, subsequent event i in epoch N is predicted to occur at time $S_N(i)$:

$$S_N(i) = \max(inp_i, S_N(i-1)) + p(N)$$

The two terms in the above expression correspond to the predicted start of the computation for event i and the predicted amount of time it takes to compute the output, respectively. To predict the start of computation for event i, we take the later of two times: the time input i is available, and the time event $i-1$ is delivered.

3.2 Multiple input and output channels

Now let us consider mitigation on multiple channels, where requests on different channels may be handled in parallel.

There are at least two reasonable concurrency models. The first model assumes that every request type has an associated process and that processes handling requests of one type do not respond to requests of other types. The second model assumes a shared pool of worker processes that can handle requests of any type as they become available.

In either model, the mitigator is permitted to use some information about which channel an input request arrives on and about the content of the request. This information about the channel and the request is considered abstractly to be the request type of the request. There is a finite set of request types numbered $1, \ldots, R$. Requests coming at time inp with request type r are represented as a pair (inp, r). A *request history* is a sequence of requests $(inp_1, r_1) \ldots (inp_i, r_i) \ldots$, where inp_i is the time of request i, and r_i is the type of the request: $1 \le r_i \le R$.

The mitigator makes predictions separately for each request type; however, with multiple request types, an epoch is a period of time during which predictions are met for *all* request types. A misprediction for one request type causes an epoch transition for the mitigator, and may change predictions for every request type. We denote the prediction for computation when mitigator is in state $\mathbf{St}$ on request type r by a function $p(\mathbf{St}, r)$. When the state consists only of the number of epochs ($\mathbf{St} = N$), we simply write $p(N, r)$.

3.2.1 Individual processes per request type

In the case where each request type has its own individual process, the prediction for output event i is

$$S_N(i) = \max(inp_i, S_N(j)) + p(N, r_i)$$

where j is the index of the previous request of type r_i; that is, $j = \max\{j' \mid j' < i \wedge r_i = r_{j'}\}$. Hence $S_N(j)$ is the prediction of the previous request of type r_i. We define $S_N(j)$ to be zero when there are no previous requests of the same type.

Example. Consider a simple system with two request types A and B (for clarity we index request types with letters), and consider a mitigator with these prediction functions $p(N, r)$ for $N = 1$:

N	$p(N, A)$	$p(N, B)$
1	10	100

Assume the following input history: $(2, A)$, $(4, B)$, $(6, A)$, and $(30, B)$. That is, two inputs of type A arrive at times 2 and 6, and two of type B arrive at times 4 and 30.

The inputs $(2, A)$ and $(4, B)$ are the first requests of the corresponding types. The predictions for these requests are

$$S_1(1) = \max(2, 0) + 10 = 12$$
$$S_1(2) = \max(4, 0) + 100 = 104$$

For the next request of type A, the prediction is

$$S_1(3) = \max(6, 12) + 10 = 22$$

This prediction takes into account the amount of time it would take for the process for request type A to finish processing the last input and then to delay the message for $p(1, A)$. Similarly, the predicted output time for the fourth request $(30, B)$ is

$$S_1(4) = \max(30, 104) + 100 = 204$$

3.2.2 Shared worker pool

For a shared pool of worker processes, predictions must be derived more carefully. Suppose the system has at least n worker processes that handle input requests. To compute a prediction for input request i that arrives at time inp_i with type r_i, the mitigator needs to know two terms: when the handling of that request will start, and an estimate of how long it takes to complete the request. We assume that the completion estimate is given by $p(N, r)$ and focus instead on the first term. The main challenge is to predict when a worker will be available to process a request. For this we introduce a notion of *worker predictions*. Intuitively, worker predictions are a data structure internal to the mitigator that allows it to predict when different requests will be picked up by worker processes.

Concretely, worker predictions are n sets $W_1, \ldots, W_n$ in which every W_m contains pairs of the form (i, q). When $(i, q) \in W_m$, it means request i is predicted to be delivered at time q by worker m. Therefore, a given index i appears in at most one of the sets W_m. The function $\mathsf{avail}(W)$ predicts when a worker described by set W will be available, by choosing the time when the worker should deliver its last message.

$$\mathsf{avail}(W) \triangleq \begin{cases} \max\{q \mid (i, q) \in W\} & \text{if } W \neq \emptyset \\ 0 & \text{otherwise} \end{cases}$$

We describe next the algorithm for computing worker predictions.

Initialization. In the initial state of worker predictions, all sets W_m (for $1 \le m \le n$) are empty.

Prediction. Given an event i with input time inp_i and request type r_i, the prediction $S_N(i)$ is computed as follows:

1. The earliest available worker j is predicted to handle request i. Therefore, we find j such that $\mathsf{avail}(W_j) = \min_{1 \le m \le n}\{\mathsf{avail}(W_m)\}$
2. Since worker j is assumed to handle request i, we make the following prediction q for the i-th output:

$$q = \max(inp_i, \mathsf{avail}(W_j)) + p(N, r_i)$$

The prediction for S_N is $S_N(i) = q$.

3. Finally, worker predictions are updated with prediction (i, q):

$$W_j := W_j \cup \{(i, q)\}$$

Misprediction. When a misprediction occurs, the mitigator resets the state of worker predictions. Consider a misprediction at time τ_N, which defines the start time of epoch N. We reset the state of worker predictions as follows:

1. For every worker m, we find the earliest undelivered request i'; that is, request received before the misprediction but not delivered by the mitigator at τ_N :

$$i' = \min\{i \mid (i, q) \in W_m \wedge inp_i < \tau_N \le q\}$$

2. If such i' cannot be found, that is, the set in the previous equation is empty, we set W_m to $\emptyset$. Otherwise, we let $q' = \tau_N + p(N, r_{i'})$ and set $W_m = \{(i', q')\}$.
3. Note that the above step resets the state of each W_m in the worker predictions. Using these reinitialized states, we can compute predictions for the unhandled requests, i.e., all requests j with predicted time q such that $q \ge \tau_N$ according to the steps 1) and 2) described in *Prediction*.

An example using shared worker pool is presented in the Appendix.

4. Leakage analysis

As in [14], we can use a combinatorial analysis to bound how much information leaks via predictive mitigation in interactive systems. One difference is that we take into account the interactive nature of our model and derive bounds based on the number of input requests and the elapsed time. To conservatively estimate leakage we bound the number of possible timing variations that an adversary can observe, as a function of the running time T and the length of the input history M. Per Section 2.3, the leakage is at most the log of the number of possible observations.

We show that a leakage bound of $O(\log T \times \log M)$ can be attained, with a constant factor that depends on the choice of *penalty policy*. When there is a worst-case execution time for every request, a tighter bound of $O(\log M)$ can be derived.

4.1 Bounding the number of variations

To bound the number of possible timing variations, we need to know three values: (1) the number of timing variations within each epoch, (2) the number of variations introduced by the schedule selector, and (3) the number of epochs.

Let us consider the number of variations within each epoch. Because messages within a single epoch are delivered according to predictions, the only source of variations within an individual epoch is *whether* there is a misprediction, and if so, *when* the misprediction occurs. This can be specified by the *length* of the epoch. When the mitigator has received at most M messages, the length of any single epoch can be at most $M + 1$.

When the mitigator transitions from epoch n to epoch $n + 1$, it chooses the schedule for the next epoch. Since the predictor can rely on public information, the "schedule" is actually an algorithm parameterized by public inputs. However, this algorithm may be chosen based on non-public inputs, in which case the choice of schedule may convey additional information to the adversary. Following [14], we denote by Λ_N the number of possible schedules when transitioning between epochs n and $n + 1$. Its value depends on the details of the schedule selector. For simple mitigation schemes, where the choice of the next schedule does not depend on secrets, we have $\Lambda_N = 1$. For *adaptive* mitigation [14], where the choice of schedule depends on internal state such as the size of the mitigator's message buffer, Λ_N may be greater than one.

Consider a mitigator that at time T has received at most M requests and reached at most N epochs. The number of possible timing variations of such a mitigator is at most

$$(M+1)^N \cdot \Lambda_1 \dots \Lambda_N$$

Measured in bits, the corresponding bound on leakage is the logarithm of the number of variations:

$$N \cdot \log(M+1) + \sum_{i=1}^{N} \log \Lambda_i$$

Note that for the simple doubling scheme, because $\Lambda_i = 1$, we also have $\sum_{i=1}^{N} \log \Lambda_i = 0$.

We can enforce an arbitrary *enforcing bound* on leakage. Denote by $B(T, M)$ the amount of information permitted to be leaked by the mitigator. Enforcing bound $B(T, M)$ is satisfied if the mitigator ensures this inequality holds:

$$N \cdot \log(M+1) + \sum_{i=1}^{N} \log \Lambda_i \leq B(T, M)$$

This equation requires a relationship between the number of epochs, the elapsed time, and the number of received messages. The exact nature of this relationship is determined by *penalty policies*.

4.2 Penalty policies

Recall that the function $p(\mathbf{St}, r)$ predicts a bound on computation time for request type r in state $\mathbf{St}$. The intuition is that the more mispredictions have happened in the past (as recorded in $\mathbf{St}$), the larger is the value of $p(\mathbf{St}, r)$. The computation is *penalized* by delivering its response later.

Designing a penalty policy function opens up a space of possibilities. The question is how mispredictions on different request types are interconnected—for example, whether a particular request type should be penalized for mispredictions on other request types, and if so, then how much.

On one side of the spectrum, we can use a *global penalty policy* that penalizes *all* request types when a misprediction occurs. If all request types are penalized, it becomes harder to trigger mispredictions on any of them in future. Therefore, this policy provides a tight bound on N. Intuitively, an adversary gains no additional power to leak information by switching between request types. However, performance of all request types is hurt by mispredictions on any request type.

On the other end of the spectrum is a *local penalty policy* in which request types are not penalized by mispredictions on other types. This improves performance but offers weaker bounds on leakage. To see this, assume that the number of mispredictions a single request type can make is N. Since penalties are not shared between request types, with R types, as many as $R \times N$ mispredictions can occur. Timing leakage might be high if R is large; intuitively, the adversary can attack each request type independently.

Aiming for more control of the tradeoff between security and performance, we explore penalty policies that fill in the space between the global and local penalty policies. The key insight is that the request types with few mispredictions contribute little to total leakage, so they should share little penalty. This insight brings an l-level *grace period* policy. In a l-level grace period policy, request type r is only penalized by other types when the number mispredictions on r is greater than l.

For more complex penalty policies, leakage analysis becomes more challenging. In Section 4.4, we present an efficient and precise way of bounding N for some penalty policies.

4.3 Generalized penalty policies

Let us refine the state $\mathbf{St}$ to record the number of mispredictions for each request type. If m_r denotes the number of mispredictions on request type r, the mitigator state contains a vector of mispredictions counts $\vec{m} = m_1, \dots, m_R$. Initially all m_r are zero. When a misprediction happens on request type r, vector entry m_r is increased by one. In the following, we assume $\mathbf{St} = \vec{m}$, and write the penalty function as $p(\vec{m}, r)$.

Recall that during an epoch, predictions for all types are met. Given a vector of mispredictions $\vec{m}$, the number of epochs N is simply $N = 1 + \sum_{i=1}^{R} m_i$. Thus, the problem of bounding N is the same as bounding the sum $\sum_{i=1}^{R} m_i$.

For convenience, let us focus on a family of penalty functions p that are a composition of three functions:

$$p(\vec{m}, r) = q(r) \times (\phi \circ \mathrm{idx})(\vec{m}, r)$$

Here function $\phi(n)$ is a *baseline penalty* function, which given a penalty index n returns the prediction for n. The penalty index represents how severely this request type is penalized. It is computed by function $\mathrm{idx}(\vec{m}, r)$, which returns the value of the index in the current state $\vec{m}$ for request type r. Finally, $q(r)$ returns an initial penalty for request type r, and allows us to model different initial estimates of how long it takes to respond to the request of type r. For instance, if one knows that request type r_1 needs at least one second, and request type r_2 needs at least 100 seconds, then one can set $q(r_1) = 1, q(r_2) = 100$.

Examples. For penalty policies based on fast doubling, we set $\phi(n) = 2^n$, and $q(r) = q_0$ for all r with some initial quantum q_0. For the global penalty policy, idx can be set to $\mathrm{idx}(\vec{m}, r) = \sum_{i=1}^{R} m_i$. For the local penalty policy, idx is chosen as $\mathrm{idx}(\vec{m}, r) = m_r$. For an l-level grace period policy, we define idx to depend on the parameter l:

$$\text{idx}(\vec{m}, r) = \begin{cases} m_r & \text{if } m_r \leq l \\ \sum_{i=1}^{R} m_i & \text{otherwise} \end{cases}$$

4.4 Generalized leakage analysis

As discussed earlier, different penalty functions yield different bounds on N. While it is possible to analyze such bounds for specific penalty policies, in general it is hard to bound leakage for more complex penalty policies.

This section describes a precise method for deriving such bounds for several classes of penalty policies. We transform the problem of finding a bound on the number of epochs N into an optimization problem with R constraints, where R is the number of request types. These constraints can be nonlinear in general, but all considered classes of penalty functions can be solved in constant time.

We focus on penalty functions where $p(\vec{m}, r)$ is monotonic. Because monotonicity is natural for a "penalty", this requirement does not really constrain the generality of the analysis.

State validity. We write $\vec{0}$ for the initial state $\vec{0}$ in which no mispredictions have happened. At the core of our analysis are two notions: state reachability and state validity. Informally, a state $\vec{m}$ is reachable at time T if there is a sequence of mispredictions that, starting from $\vec{0}$, lead to $\vec{m}$ by time T. To bound the number of possible epochs N at time T, it is sufficient to explore the set of all reachable states, looking for $\vec{m}$ in which $1 + \sum_{i=1}^{R} m_i$ (and therefore N) is maximized.

Enumerating all reachable states may be infeasible. In particular, an exact enumeration requires detailed assumptions about the thread model presented in Section 3.2. Instead, we overapproximate the set of reachable states for efficient searching of the resulting larger space.

For this, we define the notion of state validity at time T. State validity at time T is similar to reachability at time T, except that we focus only on the predicted time to respond to a request, ignoring the time needed to execute earlier requests.

We first introduce the notion of a valid successor:

DEFINITION 1 (VALID SUCCESSOR). *A state $\vec{m}'$ is a* valid successor *of type j ($1 \leq j \leq R$) for state $\vec{m}$ when $m'_j = m_j + 1$ and $m'_i = m_i$ for $i \neq j$.*

For example, with three different request types ($R = 3$), the state $(0, 0, 1)$ is a valid successor of type 3 for state $\vec{0}$.

We can then define state validity:

DEFINITION 2 (STATE VALIDITY FOR TIME T). *For penalty function $p(\vec{m}, r)$, a state $\vec{m}$ is a* valid state for time T *if there exists a sequence of request types $j_1, \ldots j_{n-1}, j_n$, such that, if $m_0 = \vec{0}$, it holds that for all i, $1 \leq i \leq n$ we have*

- *$\vec{m}_i$ is valid successor of type j_i for state $\vec{m}_{i-1}$.*
- *$p(\vec{m}_{i-1}, r_{j_i}) \leq T$*
- *$\vec{m}_n = \vec{m}$*

The second condition approximates whether the state $\vec{m}_{i-1}$ can make one more transition: if execution time is predicted to exceed T, no more transitions are possible.

Example. Consider the simple case of one request type and time 6 with prediction function $p(\vec{m}, r) = 2^{m_r}$.

State $\vec{m} = (3)$ is a *valid* state for time 6. Consider the request type sequence $1, 1, 1$. We have $\vec{m}_0 = \vec{0}$. Since $\vec{m}_1$ is a valid successor of type 1 for state $\vec{m}_0$, we have $\vec{m}_1 = (1)$. Similarly, we have $\vec{m}_2 = (2)$ and $\vec{m}_3 = (3)$. It is easy to check that $p(\vec{m}_0) = 1 \leq 6$, $p(\vec{m}_1) = 2 \leq 6$ and $p(\vec{m}_2) = 4 \leq 6$. Since $\vec{m}_3 = \vec{m}$, $\vec{m}$ is valid by definition.

However, state $\vec{m}' = (4)$ is not *valid*. Otherwise, since there is only one request type in this example, j_n must be 1. Therefore, $\vec{m}_{n-1}$ must be (3) because $\vec{m}_n$ is a valid successor of type 1 for $\vec{m}_{n-1}$. However, $p(\vec{m}_{n-1}) = 8 > 6$. This contracts the definition of validity.

4.4.1 Transforming to an optimization problem

In this part, we show how to get the maximal $\sum_{i=1}^{R} m_i$ among all valid states when prediction function $p(\vec{m}, r)$ is monotonic. First, we show a useful lemma, proved in the appendix.

LEMMA 1. *Assume $p(\vec{m}, r)$ is monotonic. If $\vec{m}$ is a valid successor of some type j for $\vec{m}'$ such that $p(\vec{m}', j) \leq T$, then*

$$\vec{m} = (m_1, \ldots, m_R) \textit{ is valid for } T \iff$$
$$\vec{m}'' = (m_1, \ldots, m_{j-1}, 0, m_{j+1}, \ldots, m_R) \textit{ is valid for } T$$

Lemma 1 allows us to describe valid states by R constraints. To see this, first observe that because $\vec{m}$ is valid for T, there are some j_1 and $\vec{m}'$ such that $\vec{m}$ is a valid successor of $\vec{m}'$ of type j_1. By Definition 1, $p(\vec{m}', j_1) \leq T$. This is our first constraint on the space of valid states.

By Lemma 1, the validity of $\vec{m}$ for T implies the validity of $(m_1, ..., m_{j_1-1}, 0, \ldots, m_R)$ for T. Repeating the previous step, there is some $j_2 \neq j_1$ and $\vec{m}''$ where $(m_1, ..., m_{j_1-1}, 0, \ldots, m_R)$ is a valid successor of $\vec{m}''$ of type j_2; this gives us the second constraint, $p(\vec{m}'', j_2) \leq T$. Proceeding as above, we obtain R constraints such that $\vec{m}$ is valid iff all constraints are satisfied.

Based on the properties of p, our analysis proceeds as follows. We present two different classes of p in the order of difficulty of analyzing them, starting from the easiest.

Symmetric predictions. We first look at prediction policies in which all request types are penalized *symmetrically*:

1. for all i, j, such that $1 \leq i, j \leq R$ it holds that $p(m_1, \ldots, m_i, \ldots, m_j, \ldots m_R, i) = p(m_1, \ldots, m_j, \ldots, m_i, \ldots m_R, j)$.
2. for all i, j, k, such that $1 \leq i, j, k \leq R$, where $i \neq k$, and $j \neq k$ it holds that $p(m_1, \ldots, m_i, \ldots m_j, \ldots m_R, k) = p(m_1, \ldots, m_j, \ldots m_i, \ldots m_R, k)$.

These properties allow us to reorder the request types in R constraints that we have obtained earlier. For example, the first of the obtained constraints can be rewritten as $p((m_{j_1} - 1, \ldots, m_R), 1) \leq T$. Moreover, this allows us to rename the variables in the constraints without loss of generality:

$$\begin{cases} p((m_1 - 1, m_2, \ldots, m_R), 1) & \leq T \\ p((0, m_2 - 1, \ldots, m_R), 2) & \leq T \\ \ldots \\ p((0, 0, \ldots, m_R - 1), R) & \leq T \end{cases}$$

Thus, bounding N is equivalent to finding the maximum sum $\sum_{i=1}^{R} m_i$ satisfying all the conditions.

Examples. It is easy to verify that starting with same initial quantum, global, local, and l-level grace period policies penalize all request types symmetrically. We proceed with the analysis of these policies below.

1. Consider the global penalty function with fast doubling and the starting quantum $q_0 = 1$. The j-th constraint in the above system has the form

$$2^{(\sum_{i=j}^{R} m_i - 1)} \leq T$$

Here, $N = 1 + \sum_{i=1}^{R} m_i \leq \log T + 2$. This is very close to the bound $\log(T+1)+1$ given in [14].[3]

Using the leakage bound derived in Section 4.4, we obtain that for global penalty policy, when the mitigator runs for at most time T the leakage is bounded by function $B(T, M)$ where

$$B(T, M) = (\log T + 2) \cdot \log(M + 1)$$

2. Now consider the local penalty policy with the same penalty scheme and initial quantum. We have R constraints of the form:

$$2^{m_i - 1} \leq T, 1 \leq i \leq R$$

It is easy to derive $N \leq R \cdot (\log T + 1) + 1$.

Using this bound for N, we obtain that at running time time T, leakage is bounded by function $B(T, M, R)$ such that

$$B(T, M, R) = (R \cdot (\log T + 1) + 1) \cdot \log(M + 1)$$

3. We revisit the l-level grace period policy last. In this case, the j-th constraint can be split into two cases:

$$\begin{cases} m_j - 1 \leq \log T & \text{when } m_j - 1 \leq l \\ \sum_{i=j}^{R} m_i - 1 \leq \log T & \text{when } m_j - 1 > l \end{cases}$$

In general, l is ordinarily smaller than $\log T$, so N is maximized when $m_i = l + 1, 1 \leq i \leq R - 1$ and $m_R = \lfloor \log T \rfloor + 1$. Thus, $N \leq (R - 1) \cdot (l + 1) + \log T + 2$.

Using this bound for N we obtain that at running time T, leakage is bounded by function $B(T, M, R, l)$ such that

$$B(T, M, R, l) = \log(M + 1) \cdot ((R - 1) \cdot (l + 1) + \log T + 2)$$

Partially symmetric predictions. Request types starting with different initial quanta, such as the setup in Section 4.5, make the prediction function asymmetric.

Let $q_{min} = \min_{i=1}^{R} q(r)$, and replace $p(r)$ with q_{min} for all prediction functions. The upper bound N of these functions overapproximates that of asymmetric functions since any valid state using the latter functions must be valid for the former ones. Therefore, we can obtain R constraints, as for symmetric predictions.

Non-symmetric predictions. For other types of penalty functions, we can still try to partition request types into subsets such that in each subset, request types are penalized symmetrically. We then generate constraints for validity of subsets.

More formally, we say a vector of mispredictions $\vec{m}'$ is a *subvector* of $\vec{m}$ if and only if $m'_i = 0 \vee m'_i = m_i, 1 \leq i \leq R$. A set of vectors $\vec{m}^1, \ldots, \vec{m}^k$ is a *partition* of $\vec{m}$ if all vectors are subvectors of $\vec{m}$ and for all m_i, there is one and only one $\vec{m}^j$ such that $m^j_i = m_i$.

The following lemma shows that the condition that $\vec{m}$ is valid is stronger than the validity of all subvectors. Thus, the constraints on vectors in a partition overapproximates those on the validity of $\vec{m}$.

LEMMA 2. *When $p(\vec{m}, r)$ is monotonic, $\vec{m}$ is valid at time T $\Longrightarrow$ any subvector of $\vec{m}$ is valid at time T.*

Since there are R non-zero mispredictions among all vectors in the partition, this estimation still gives R constraints.

4.5 Security vs. performance

As discussed informally earlier, the global penalty policy enforces the best leakage bound but has bad performance; the local penalty policy has the best performance but more leakage. We explore this tradeoff between security and performance through simulations.

[3]Though [14] does not consider request types, the penalty policies considered there are effectively global penalty policies.

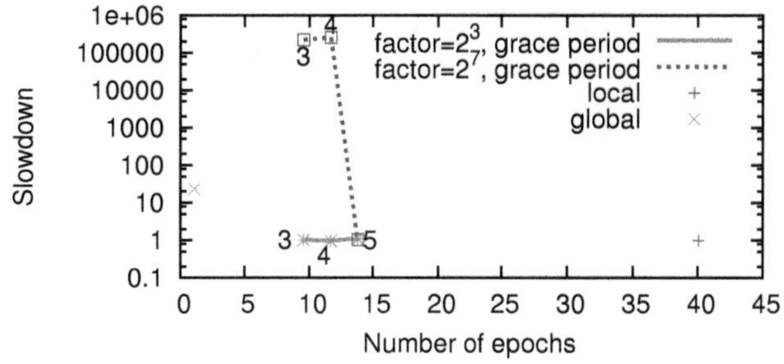

Figure 3: Performance vs. security

Simulation setup. We simulate a set of interactive system services characterized by various distributions over execution time. Initial penalty is set to be the mean of the execution time distribution. The fast doubling scheme is used, so the prediction function is

$$p(\vec{m}, r) = q(r) \times 2^{\text{idx}(\vec{m}, r)}$$

where $q(r)$ is the mean time of simulated type r. The form of $\text{idx}(\vec{m}, r)$ is defined by penalty policies.

To see the performance for requests with different variances in execution time, we simulate both *regular types* and *irregular types*. For regular types, the simulated execution time follows Poisson distribution with different means, since page view requests to a web page can be modeled as a Poisson process; for irregular types, execution time follows a perturbed normal distribution which avoids negative execution time.

Result. The results in Figure 3 demonstrate the impact of execution-time variation on performance. The x-axis in Figure 3 shows the bound on number of epochs N and the y-axis shows the slowdown for all simulated request types. All values shown are normalized so that the local policy has a slowdown of 1 and so that for the number of epochs, the global policy has value 1. The standard deviation is equal to the mean multiplied by a factor ranging from 2^3 to 2^7, generating around 3 to 7 mispredictions. The number on each line denotes the grace-period level.

The results confirm the intuition that the global penalty policy has the best security but bad performance, and the local policy has the best performance. However, the l-level grace period policies have considerably fewer epochs N, yet performance similar to that of the local policy when l is no less than m_{r_i} for most types.

When the variance of execution time increases, small grace-period level ($l = 3, 4$) can bring slowdown that is orders of magnitude higher than in the global case. The reason is that each irregular request type can trigger l mispredictions. Once misprediction of a request type is larger than l, $\text{idx}(\vec{m}, r)$ returns a large number. However using a larger grace-period level ($l = 5$) could restore performance at the cost of more leakage.

Penalty policies with other forms are possible to provide more options between the trade-off of security and performances. We leave a more comprehensive analysis of more penalty policies as future work.

4.6 Leakage with a worst-case execution time

In the analysis above, no assumption is made about execution time for each request type. The adversary can delay responses for an arbitrarily long time to covertly convey more information.

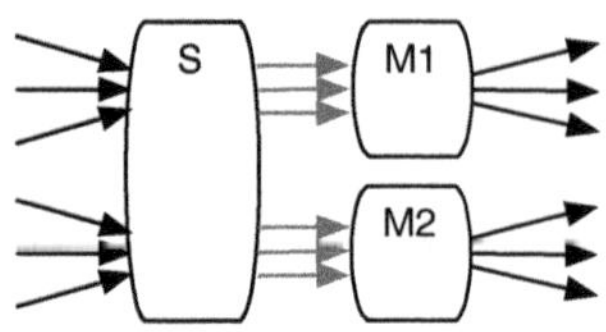

Figure 4: Parallel composition of mitigators

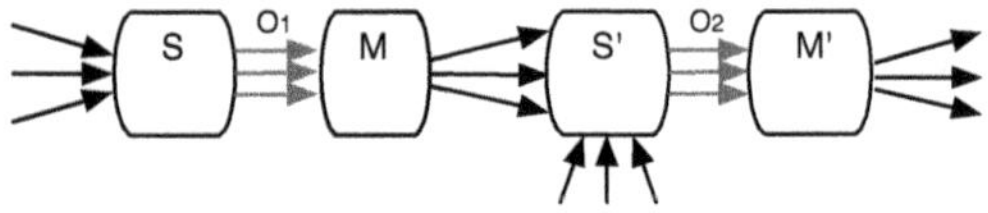

Figure 5: Sequential composition of mitigators

However, for some specific platforms, such as real-time systems and web applications with a timeout setting, we can assume a worst-case execution time T_w. Given this constraint, we can derive a tighter leakage bound.

The analysis works similarly to that in Section 4.3, but instead of using the conservative constraint $p(\vec{m}_{i-1}, r_{j_i}) \leq T$ as in Definition 2, worst-case execution time provides a tighter estimation:

$$p(\vec{m}_{i-1}, r_{j_i}) \leq T_w$$

Compared with bounding running time T, this condition more precisely approximates whether the state $\vec{m}_{i-1}$ can make one more misprediction to $\vec{m}_i$. The reason is that whenever $p(\vec{m}_{i-1}, r_{j_i}) > T_w$, the state $\vec{m}_{i-1}$ cannot have another misprediction because execution is bounded by T_w. Therefore, we can reuse the bound on the number of epochs in Section 4.3 by replacing T with T_w.

For example, total leakage with the assumption of worst-case execution time T_w for the global penalty policy is bounded by

$$B(T, M) = (\log T_w + 2) \cdot \log(M + 1)$$

This logarithmic bound is asymptotically the same as that achieved by the less general bucketing scheme proposed by Köpf et al. [12] for cryptographic timing channels.

For the l-grace-period penalty policy we can perform a similar analysis to derive a bound on leakage:

$$B(T, M, R, l) = \log(M + 1) \cdot ((R - 1) \cdot (l + 1) + \log T_w + 2)$$

5. Composing mitigators

If timing mitigation is used, we can expect large systems to be built by composing mitigated subsystems. Askarov et al. [14] show empirically that composing mitigators sequentially performs well, which makes sense because mitigated output has more predictable timing. However, the prior work did not analyze leakage.

We analyze composed mitigators by considering the leakage of two gadgets: two mitigators connected either in parallel or sequentially (Figures 4 and 5). More complex systems with mitigated subsystems can be analyzed by decomposing them into these gadgets.

Parallel composition. Figure 4 is an example of parallel composition of mitigators, in which requests received by the system are handled by two independent mitigators. The bound on the leakage of the parallel composition is no greater than the sum of the bounds of the independent mitigators. To see this, denote by P the total number of variations of the parallel composition, and denote by V_1 and V_2 the number of timing variations of the first and second mitigators, respectively. We know $P \leq V_1 \cdot V_2$; consequently, the total leakage of parallel composition $\log P$ is bounded by $\log V_1 + \log V_2$. The same argument generalizes to n mitigators in parallel.

Sequential composition. Suppose we have a security-critical component, such as an encryption function, and leakage from this component is controlled by a mitigator that guarantees a tight bound, say at most 10 bits of the encryption key. We can show that once mitigated, leakage of the encryption key can never exceed 10 bits, no matter how output of that component is used in the system. This is true for both Shannon-entropy and min-entropy definitions of leakage.

Consider sequential composition of two systems as depicted in Figure 5. Suppose that the secrets in the first system are S, and that the outputs of the first and the second mitigators are O_1 and O_2 respectively. We consider how much the output of each of the mitigators leaks about S.

As discussed in Section 2.3, the leakage of the first mitigator using mutual information is $\mathcal{I}(S; O_1)$ and the leakage of the second is $\mathcal{I}(S; O_2)$. Then we can show that the second mitigator leaks no more information about S_1 than the first does. We formalize this in the following lemma.

LEMMA 3. $\mathcal{I}(S; O_1) \geq \mathcal{I}(S; O_2)$

A similar result holds for min-entropy leakage.

LEMMA 4. $V(S|O_1) \geq V(S|O_2)$

Both of these lemmas are proved in the appendix.

Discussion. Parallel and sequential composition results enable deriving conservative bounds for networks of composed subsystems. The bounds derived may be quite conservative in the case where parallel mitigated systems have no secrets of their own to leak. If the graph of subsystems contains cycles, it cannot be decomposed into these two gadgets. We leave a more comprehensive analysis of mitigator composition to future work.

6. Experiments

To evaluate the performance and information leakage of generalized timing mitigation, we implemented mitigators for different applications. The widely used Apache Tomcat web container was modified to mitigate a local hosted application. We also developed a mitigating web proxy to estimate the overhead of mitigating real-world applications—a non-trivial homepage that results in 49 different requests and a HTTPS webmail service that requires stronger security.

We explored how to tune this general mechanism for different security and performance requirements. The results show that mitigation does slow down applications to some extent; we suggest the slowdown is acceptable for some applications.

6.1 Mitigator design and its limitations

We define the system boundary in the following way. Inputs enter the system at the point when Tomcat dispatches requests to the servlet or JSP code. Results returned from this code are considered outputs. Thus, all timing leakage arising during the processing of the servlet and the JSP files is mitigated.

This implementation of mitigation has limitations. Because of shared hardware and operating-system resources such as filesystem caches, memory caches, buses, and the network, the time required to deliver an application response may convey information about sensitive application data. Our current implementation strategy, chosen for ease of implementation, prevents fully addressing these timing channels where they affect timing outside the system boundary as defined.

To completely mitigate timing channels, mitigation should be integrated at the operating system and hardware levels. For example, the TCP/IP stack might be extended to support delaying packets until a mitigator-specified time. With such an extension, all timing channels, including low-level interactions via hardware caches and bus contention, would be fully mitigated. Although we leave the design of such a mechanism to future work, we see no reason why a more complete mitigation mechanism would significantly change the performance and security results reported here.

6.2 Mitigator implementation

We implemented the mitigator as a Java library containing 201 lines of Java code, excluding comments and the configuration file. This library provides two functions:

```
Mitigator startMitigation (String requestType);
void      endMitigation   (Mitigator miti);
```

The function `startMitigation` should be invoked when an input is available to the system, passing an application-specific request type identifier. The function `endMitigation` is used by the application when an output is ready, and the mitigator for the related input is required for this interface. Calling `endMitigation` blocks the current thread until the time predicted by the mitigator.

Instead of optimizing for specific applications, we heuristically choose the following parameters for all experiments: 1. *Initial penalty*: the initial penalty for all request types is 50 ms, a delay short enough to be unnoticeable to the user. 2. *Penalty policy*: we use the 5-level grace period policy since it provides good tradeoff between security and performance as shown in 4.5. 3. *Penalty function*: most requests are returned within 250 ms, and the distribution is quite even. We evenly divide the first 5 epochs to make predictions more precise: 50 ms, 100 ms, 150 ms, 200 ms, 250 ms, doubling progressively thereafter. 4. *Worst-case execution time* T_w: We assume worst-case execution time for requests T_w to be 300 seconds. This is consistent with Firefox browser version 3.6.12, which uses this value as a default timeout parameter.

6.3 Leakage revisited

Applying the experiment settings into the formula from Section 4.6 with R request types, the following leakage bound obtains:

$$\begin{aligned}&((R-1)\cdot(l+1)+(\log T_w+2))\cdot\log(M+1)\\=&((R-1)\cdot 6+(\log 300000+2))\cdot\log(M+1)\\\leq&(6\cdot R+15)\cdot\log(M+1)\end{aligned}$$

where M is the number of inputs using the simple doubling scheme.

Intuitively, introducing more request types helps make the prediction more precise for each request, because processing time varies for different kinds of requests. However, the leakage bound is proportional to the number of request types. So it is important to find the right tradeoff between latency and security.

6.4 Latency and throughput

To enable the mitigation of unmodified web applications, we modified the open source Java Servlet and JavaServer Pages container Tomcat 6.0.29 using the mitigation library.

Experiment setup. Mitigating Tomcat requires only three lines of Java code: one line generating a request type id from the HTTP request, one line to start the mitigation, and another line to end mitigation after the servlet is finished. We deployed a JSP wiki application, JSPWiki[4], in the mitigating Tomcat server to evaluate how mitigation affects both latency and throughput. Measurements

[4]http://www.jspwiki.org

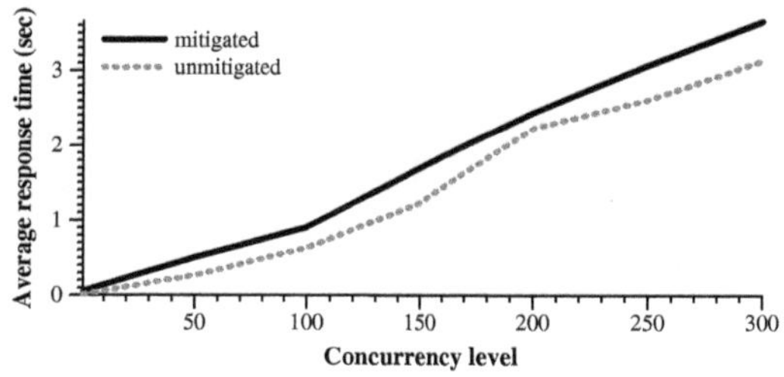

Figure 6: Wiki latency with and without mitigation

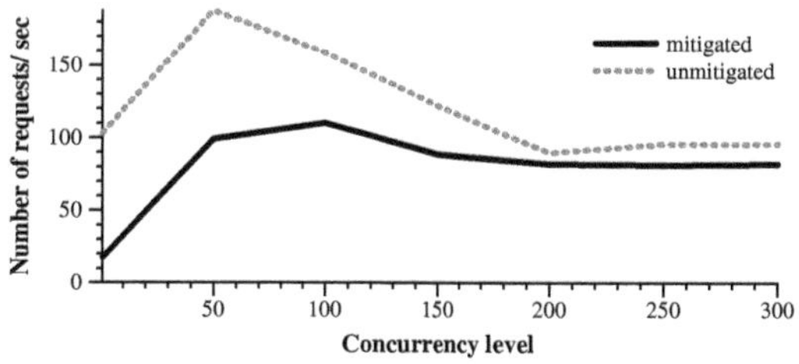

Figure 7: Wiki throughput with and without mitigation

were made using the Apache HTTP server benchmarking tool *ab*.[5] Since we focus on the latency and throughput overhead of requesting the main page of the wiki application, the URI is used as the request type identifier.

Results. We measured the latency and throughput of the main page of JSPWiki for both the mitigated and unmitigated versions. We used a range of different concurrency settings in *ab*, controlling the number of multiple requests to perform at a time. The size of the Tomcat thread pool is 200 threads in the current implementation. For each setting, we measured the throughput for 5 minutes. The results are shown in Figure 6 and Figure 7.

When the concurrency level is 1—the sequential case—the unmitigated Wiki application has a latency around 11ms. Since the initial penalty is selected to be 50ms in our experiments, the average mitigated latency rises to about 57ms: about 400% overhead. This is simply an artifact of the choice of initial penalty.

As we increase the number of concurrent requests, the unmitigated application exhibits more latency, because concurrent requests compete for limited resources. On the other hand, the mitigation system is predicting this delayed time, and we can see that these predictions introduce less overhead: at most 90% after the concurrency level of 50; an even smaller overhead is found for higher concurrency levels.

The throughput with concurrency level 1 is much reduced from the unmitigated case: only about 1/5 of the original throughput. However, when the concurrency level reaches 50, throughput increases significantly in both cases, and the mitigated version has 52.73% of the throughput of the unmitigated version. For higher levels of concurrency, the throughput of the two versions is similar.

6.5 Real-world applications with proxy

We evaluated the latency overhead of predictive mitigation on existing real-world web servers. To avoid the need to deploy predictive mitigation directly on production web servers, we introduce a mitigating proxy between the client browser and the target host. We modified an open source Java HTTP/HTTPS proxy, *Lit-*

[5]http://httpd.apache.org/docs/2.0/programs/ab.html

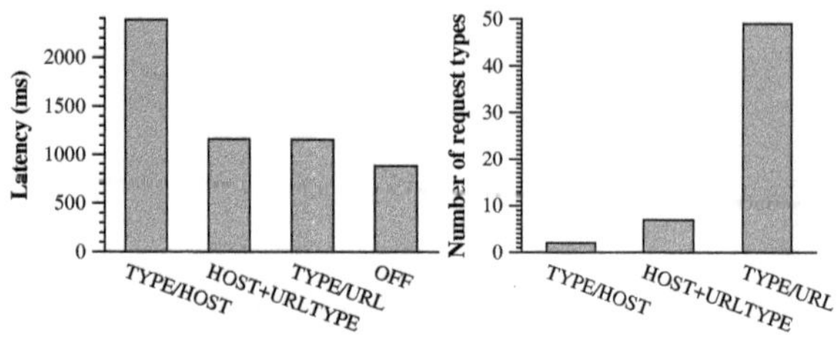

Figure 8: Latency for an HTTP web page

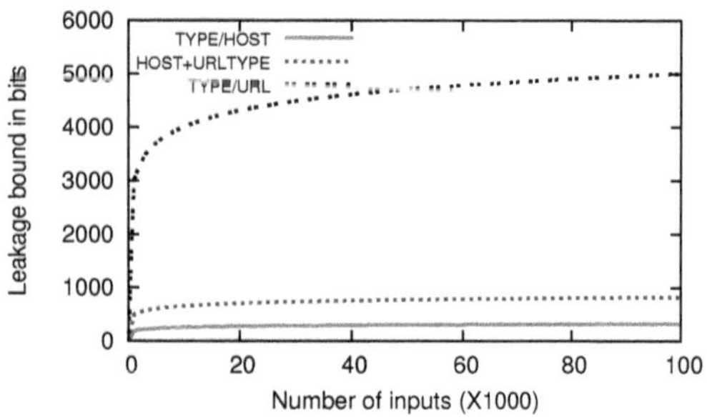

Figure 9: Leakage bound for an HTTP web page

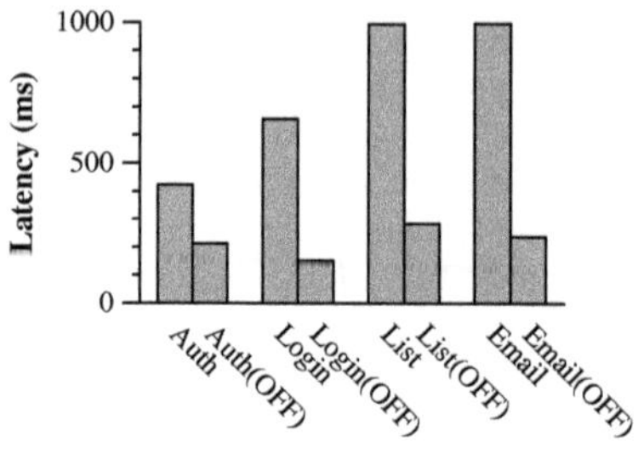

Figure 10: Latency overhead for HTTPS webmail service

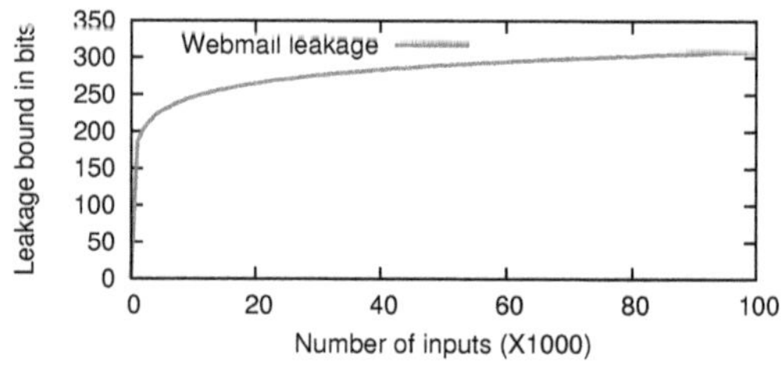

Figure 11: Leakage bound for HTTPS webmail service

tleProxy[6], to use the mitigation library, adding about 70 LOC. We used it to evaluate latency with two remote web servers: a HTTP web page and an HTTPS webmail service.

With mitigation again done entirely at user level, timing channels that arise outside the mitigation boundary cannot be mitigated. The mitigation boundary is defined as follows: the mitigating proxy treats requests from client browser as inputs, and forwards these requests to the host. The response from the host is regarded as an output in the black-box model.

The proxy mitigates both the response time of the server and the round-trip time between the proxy and server. Only the first part corresponds to real variation that would occur with a mitigating web server. To estimate this part of latency overhead, we put the proxy in a local network with the real host. Because we found measured little variation in this configuration, the results here should estimate latency for real-world applications reasonably accurately.

6.5.1 HTTP web page

Unlike the previous stress test that requests only one URL, we evaluated latency overhead using a non-trivial HTTP web page, a university home page that causes 49 different requests to the server. Multiple requests bring up the opportunity of tuning the tradeoff between security and performance. Various ways to choose request types were explored:

1. TYPE/HOST: all URLs residing on the same host are treated as one request type, that is, they are predicted the same way.
2. HOST+URLTYPE: requests on the same host are predicted differently based on the URL type of the request. We distinguish URL types based on the file types, such as JPEG files, CSS files and so on. Each of them corresponds to a different request type.
3. TYPE/URL: individual URLs are predicted differently.

Figure 8 shows the latency of loading the whole page and the number of request types with these options. The results show that latency in the most restrictive TYPE/HOST case almost triples that of the unmitigated case. HOST+URLTYPE and TYPE/URL options have similar latency results, with about 30% latency overhead.

[6]http://www.littleshoot.org/littleproxy/index.html

From the security point of view, the TYPE/HOST option only results in two request types: one host is in the organization, and the other one is `google-analytics.com`, used for the search component in the main page. HOST+URLTYPE introduces 6 more request types, while using the TYPE/URL option, there are as many as 49 request types. The information leakage bounds for different options are shown in Figure 9.

The HOST+URLTYPE choice provides a reasonable tradeoff: it has roughly a 30% latency overhead, yet information leakage is below 850 bits for 100,000 requests.

6.5.2 HTTPS webmail service

We also evaluate the latency with a webmail service based on Windows Exchange Server. After the user passes Kerberos-based authentication (Auth), he is redirected to the login page (Login) and may then see the list of emails (List) or read a message (Email).

Request type selection. This application accesses sensitive data, so we evaluate performance with the most restrictive scheme: one request type per host. There are actually two hosts: one host is used to serve only AuthPage.

Results. We measured the latency overhead of four representative pages for this service. Each page generates from 6 to 45 different requests. The results in Figure 10 show that the latency overhead ranges from 2 times to 4 times for these four pages; in the worst case, latency is still less than 1 second. Also, this overhead can be reduced with different request type selection options.

Figure 11 shows the leakage bound of this mitigated application. The leakage is limited to about 300 bits after 100,000 requests and grows slowly thereafter.

7. Related work

The most closely related work is that of Askarov et al. [14]. Comparisons to that work have been made throughout the paper; at a high level, the generalized predictive mitigation scheme makes possible the practical application of predictive mitigation to general services. The simple predictive mitigator defined by Askarov et al. is manifestly unsuitable to this task, as discussed in Section 3.1.

Köpf et al. [12, 13] introduced the mechanism of *bucketing* to mitigate timing side channels in cryptographic operations, achieving asymptotically logarithmic bounds on information leakage but with stronger assumptions than in this work. Their security analyses rely on the timing behavior of the system agreeing with a previously measured distribution of times; therefore they implicitly assume that the adversary does not control timing, and that there is a worst-case execution time. The bucketing approach does not achieve logarithmic bounds for general computation.

The NRL Pump [26] and its follow-ups, like Network Pump [27], are also network service handling that handle requests. The Pump work addresses timing channels arising from message acknowledgments (which correspond to but are less general than outputs in this work). Acknowledgment timing is stochastically modulated using a moving average of past activity, and leakage in one window does not affect later windows. Therefore the NRL/Network Pumps can enforce only a linear leakage bound.

Much other work has studied timing channels at the network level, exploring techniques such as adding random delays or periodic quantization of time (e.g., [24, 20]). For discussion of this prior work, see [14]. Work on language-based security has also addressed timing channels, especially for internal timing channels, and this also is covered in [14].

8. Conclusion

Predictive mitigation as introduced earlier offered the possibility of mitigating timing channels in general computations, but was impractical as a way to build real networked services. In this work, we have both generalized and refined the original model of predictive mitigation to apply to interactive systems. The experimental results from the implementation of this generalized prediction mitigation scheme suggest that it may be a practical way to mitigate timing channels in a variety of networked services.

Acknowledgments

We thank Owen Arden for useful discussions about this work, Jed Liu and the anonymous reviewers for helpful feedback about the paper.

This work was funded by a grant from the Office of Naval Research (ONR N000140910652), and by two grants from the NSF: 0424422 (the TRUST center), and 0964409.

9. References

[1] B. W. Lampson, "A note on the confinement problem," *Comm. of the ACM*, vol. 16, no. 10, pp. 613–615, Oct. 1973.

[2] P. Kocher, "Timing attacks on implementations of Diffie–Hellman, RSA, DSS, and other systems," in *Advances in Cryptology—CRYPTO'96*, Aug. 1996.

[3] D. Brumley and D. Boneh, "Remote timing attacks are practical," *Computer Networks*, Jan. 2005.

[4] D. Osvik, A. Shamir, and E. Tromer, "Cache attacks and countermeasures: the case of AES," *Topics in Cryptology–CT-RSA 2006*, Jan. 2006. [Online]. Available: http://www.springerlink.com/index/F52X1H55G1632L17.pdf

[5] A. Bortz and D. Boneh, "Exposing private information by timing web applications," in *Proc. 16th Int'l World-Wide Web Conf.*, May 2007.

[6] G. Shah, A. Molina, and M. Blaze, "Keyboards and covert channels," *Proc. 15th USENIX Security Symp.*, Aug. 2006.

[7] H. Meer and M. Slaviero, "It's all about the timing..." in *Proc. Black Hat USA*, 2007.

[8] Y. Liu, D. Ghosal, F. Armknecht, A. Sadeghi, and S. Schulz, "Hide and seek in time—robust covert timing channels," in *ESORICS*, 2009.

[9] R. G. Gallagher, "Basic limits on protocol information in data communication networks," *IEEE Transactions on Information Theory*, vol. 22, no. 4, Jul. 1976.

[10] M. Padlipsky, D. Snow, and P. Karger, "Limitations of end-to-end encryption in secure computer networks," Mitre Corp., Tech. Rep. ESD TR-78-158, 1978.

[11] I. S. Moskowitz and M. H. Kang, "Covert channels—here to stay?" in *COMPASS '94*, 1994.

[12] B. Köpf and M. Dürmuth, "A provably secure and efficient countermeasure against timing attacks," in *2009 IEEE Computer Security Foundations*, Jul. 2009.

[13] B. Köpf and G. Smith, "Vulnerability bounds and leakage resilience of blinded cryptography under timing attacks," in *2010 IEEE Computer Security Foundations*, Jul. 2010.

[14] A. Askarov, D. Zhang, and A. C. Myers, "Predictive black-box mitigation of timing channels," in *ACM Conf. on Computer and Communications Security (CCS)*, 2010, pp. 297–307.

[15] A. Sabelfeld and D. Sands, "Probabilistic noninterference for multi-threaded programs," in *Proc. 13th IEEE Computer Security Foundations Workshop*. IEEE Computer Society Press, Jul. 2000, pp. 200–214.

[16] W.-M. Hu, "Reducing timing channels with fuzzy time," in *IEEE Symposium on Security and Privacy*, 1991, pp. 8 – 20.

[17] J. Agat, "Transforming out timing leaks," in *Proc. 27th ACM Symp. on Principles of Programming Languages (POPL)*, Boston, MA, Jan. 2000, pp. 40–53.

[18] S. Zdancewic and A. C. Myers, "Observational determinism for concurrent program security," in *Proc. 16th IEEE Computer Security Foundations Workshop*, Pacific Grove, California, Jun. 2003, pp. 29–43.

[19] A. Russo, J. Hughes, D. Naumann, and A. Sabelfeld, "Closing internal timing channels by transformation," in *Proc. 11th Annual Asian Computing Science Conference (ASIAN)*, 2006.

[20] J. Giles and B. Hajek, "An information-theoretic and game-theoretic study of timing channels." *IEEE Transactions on Information Theory*, vol. 48, no. 9, pp. 2455–2477, 2002.

[21] D. E. Denning, *Cryptography and Data Security*. Reading, Massachusetts: Addison-Wesley, 1982.

[22] J. K. Millen, "Covert channel capacity," in *Proc. IEEE Symposium on Security and Privacy*, Oakland, CA, Apr. 1987.

[23] ——, "Finite-state noiseless covert channels," in *Proc. 2nd IEEE Computer Security Foundations Workshop*, Jun. 1989, pp. 11–14.

[24] I. S. Moskowitz and A. R. Miller, "The channel capacity of a certain noisy timing channel," *IEEE Trans. on Information Theory*, vol. 38, no. 4, pp. 1339–1344.

[25] G. Smith, "On the foundations of quantitative information flow," *Proc. 12th Intl' Conf. on Foundations of Software Science and Computation Structures*, pp. 388–402, 2010.

[26] M. H. Kang and I. S. Moskowitz, "A pump for rapid, reliable, secure communication," in *ACM Conf. on Computer and Communications Security (CCS)*, Nov. 1993, pp. 119–129.

[27] M. H. Kang, I. S. Moskowitz, and D. C. Lee, "A network pump," *IEEE Transactions on Software Engineering*, vol. 22, pp. 329–338, 1996.

[28] T. Cover and J. Thomas, *Elements of information theory.* Wiley, 2006.

APPENDIX

Example of shared worker pool

Reusing the settings from the example in Section 3.2.1, we have four inputs: $(2, A)$, $(4, B)$, $(6, A)$ and $(30, B)$, and prediction function $p(1, A) = 10$ and $p(1, B) = 100$. Suppose we have two shared workers.

As described above, the worker predictions are both initialized to be empty: $W_1 = \emptyset$ and $W_2 = \emptyset$. For the first input, both workers are available; that is, $\mathsf{avail}(W_1) = \mathsf{avail}(W_2) = 0$ since W_1 and W_2 are all empty sets now. We break the tie by selecting the worker with smaller index, worker 1, and then we set the prediction for input $(2, A)$ as

$$S_1(1) = \max(2, 0) + 10 = 12$$

Finally, the worker prediction of worker 1 is updated to $\{(1, 12)\}$.

For the second input, $\mathsf{avail}(W_1) = 12$ and $\mathsf{avail}(W_2) = 0$. Worker 2 is the earliest available worker. Similarly to the first input, the prediction for the second output is $S_1(2) = \max(4, 0) + 100 = 104$. The worker prediction of worker 2 is updated to $\{(2, 104)\}$.

Computation of the predicted worker becomes more interesting for the third input $(6, A)$. We have

$$\begin{aligned} \mathsf{avail}(W_1) &= \max\{q \mid (i, q) \in \{(1, 12)\}\} = 12 \\ \mathsf{avail}(W_2) &= \max\{q \mid (i, q) \in \{(2, 104)\}\} = 104 \end{aligned}$$

The mitigator picks the worker with earliest availability, worker 1. The third output is predicted at: $S_1(3) = \max(6, 12) + 10 = 22$, and the prediction for worker 1 is updated to $\{(1, 12), (3, 22)\}$.

For the last input $(30, B)$, the mitigator first computes the available times for both workers:

$$\begin{aligned} \mathsf{avail}(W_1) &= \max\{q \mid (i, q) \in \{(1, 12), (3, 22)\}\} = 22 \\ \mathsf{avail}(W_2) &= \max\{q \mid (i, q) \in \{(2, 104)\}\} = 104 \end{aligned}$$

Based on these values, the mitigator picks worker 1 as the predicted worker for the fourth input. The prediction for corresponding output is $S_1(4) = \max(30, 22) + 100 = 130$, and the prediction of worker 1 becomes $\{(1, 12), (3, 22), (4, 130)\}$.

Proof of Lemma 1

Proof. $\Longleftarrow$: since $\vec{m}''$ is valid, there is sequence of request types where all intermediate states satisfy the constraints. Further, we can construct a sequence of request types from $\vec{m}''$ to $\vec{m}$ by appending j to the previous sequence until $\vec{m}_i = \vec{m}$. Since $p(\vec{m}', j) \leq T$ and p is monotonic, all new states corresponding to this sequence still satisfy the constraints.

$\Longrightarrow$: by definition, there is a sequence of request types $r_1, \ldots, r_n$ such that all intermediate states satisfy constraints. Moreover, there must be a point i in this sequence such that $\forall l < i, r_l \neq j$ and $r_i = j$. Thus, the j-th element of $\vec{m}_{i-1}$ is 0.

Then, a new sequence of request types $p_1, \ldots, p_m$ exists such that $p_l = r_l, 0 \leq l \leq i-1$. For $l \geq i$, if $r_l = j$, skip this type. Otherwise, add the same type to sequence $\vec{p}$. By this construction, two properties of states occurring with $\vec{p}$ are that the j-th element is always 0, and that there is a corresponding state with sequence $\vec{r}$ such that they only differ in the j-th element. We denote the final states with request type sequence $\vec{r}$, $\vec{p}$ as $\vec{m}^r$ and $\vec{m}^p$ respectively. Since state $\vec{m}^r$ satisfies $p(\vec{m}^r, r_l) \leq T$, by monotonicity, corresponding state $\vec{m}^p$ also satisfies this condition. Since $m_n^r = \vec{m}''$, $\vec{m}''$ is valid at T.

□

Proof of Lemma 2

Proof. By definition, there is a sequence of request types $j_1, \ldots, j_n$ such that all conditions in Definition 2 are satisfied. For any subvector of $\vec{m}$, say $\vec{m}'$, we can take a projection of the sequence so that only the request types nonzero in the subvector are kept.

By monotonicity, it is easy to check that all conditions hold in the definition. Moreover, $\vec{m}_n = \vec{m}'$. So $\vec{m}'$ is valid by definition.

□

Proof of Lemmas 3 and 4

We can view the outputs O_1 and O_2 as discrete random variables. Since the second service and its mitigator do not share secret S, the conditional distribution of O_2 depends only on O_1 and is conditionally independent of S (in other words, random variables S, O_1, O_2 form a Markov chain). Denoting the probability mass function of a discrete random variable X as $P(X)$, the joint distribution of these three random variables has probability mass function $P(s, o_1, o_2) = P(s)P(o_1|s)P(o_2|o_1)$. The marginal distribution $P(o_2, s)$ is $\sum_{o_1 \in O_1} P(s, o_1, o_2)$, and for any o_1, we have $\sum_{o_2 \in O_2} P(o_2|o_1) = 1$.

Proof of Lemma 3.

Proof. The proof follows from the standard *data-processing inequality* [28] and the symmetry of mutual information:

$$\begin{aligned} \mathcal{I}(S; O_2) + \mathcal{I}(S; O_1|O_2) &= \mathcal{I}(S; O_1, O_2) \\ &= \mathcal{I}(S; O_1) + \mathcal{I}(S; O_2|O_1) \end{aligned}$$

Note that S and O_2 are conditionally independent given O_1, since the second mitigator produces outputs based on only the output of the first mitigator M, public inputs, and secrets other than S. Thus $\mathcal{I}(S; O_2|O_1) = 0$. Replacing this term with zero in the above equation, we get

$$\mathcal{I}(S; O_2) + \mathcal{I}(S; O_1|O_2) = \mathcal{I}(S; O_1)$$

Also, we know that $\mathcal{I}(S; O_1|O_2) \geq 0$, so we have

$$\mathcal{I}(S; O_1) \geq \mathcal{I}(S; O_2)$$

□

Proof of Lemma 4. As discussed in Section 2.3, min-entropy channel capacity is defined as the maximal value of $\log \frac{V(S|O)}{V(S)}$ among all distributions on S. So it suffices to show $V(S|O_1) = V(S|O_2)$ for any distribution on S.

$$\begin{aligned} V(S|O_2) &= \sum_{o_2 \in O_2} \max_{s \in S} P(s)P(o_2|s) \\ &= \sum_{o_2 \in O_2} \max_{s \in S} \sum_{o_1 \in O_1} P(s, o_1, o_2) \\ &= \sum_{o_2 \in O_2} \max_{s \in S} \sum_{o_1 \in O_1} P(s)P(o_1|s)P(o_2|o_1) \\ &\leq \sum_{o_2 \in O_2} \sum_{o_1 \in O_1} P(o_2|o_1) \max_{s \in S} P(s)P(o_1|s) \\ &= \sum_{o_1 \in O_1} \max_{s \in S}(P(s)P(o_1|s)) \sum_{o_2 \in O_2} P(o_2|o_1) \\ &= \sum_{o_1 \in O_1} \max_{s \in S} P(s)P(o_1|s) \\ &= V(S|O_1) \end{aligned}$$

WAPTEC: Whitebox Analysis of Web Applications for Parameter Tampering Exploit Construction

Prithvi Bisht
University of Illinois
Chicago, USA
pbisht@cs.uic.edu

Timothy Hinrichs
University of Chicago
Chicago, USA
tlh@uchicago.edu

Nazari Skrupsky
University of Illinois
Chicago, USA
nskroups@cs.uic.edu

V.N. Venkatakrishnan
University of Illinois
Chicago, USA
venkat@cs.uic.edu

Abstract

Parameter tampering attacks are dangerous to a web application whose server fails to replicate the validation of user-supplied data that is performed by the client. Malicious users who circumvent the client can capitalize on the missing server validation. In this paper, we describe WAPTEC, a tool that is designed to automatically identify parameter tampering vulnerabilities and generate exploits by construction to demonstrate those vulnerabilities. WAPTEC involves a new approach to whitebox analysis of the server's code. We tested WAPTEC on six open source applications and found previously unknown vulnerabilities in every single one of them.

Categories and Subject Descriptors

D.4.6 [**Security and Protection**]: Verification; K.4.4 [**Electronic Commerce**]: Security; K.6.5 [**Security and Protection**]: Unauthorized access

General Terms

Languages, Security, Verification

Keywords

Parameter Tampering, Exploit Construction, Program Analysis, Constraint Solving

1. INTRODUCTION

Interactive processing and validation of user input is increasingly becoming the de-facto standard for applications programmed for the Web. With the advent of client-side scripting, there has been a rapid transition in the last few years to process and validate user input in the browser itself, before it is actually submitted to the server. Some of the advantages of client-side processing is the elimination of delays associated with purely server-side data validation, and reduction of server-side loads.

Consider the example of a shopping cart application, where inputs such as the items in the shopping cart, submitted by a user are supplied as parameters to the server side. The server often makes certain assumptions about those parameters, e.g., the credit card expiration date is valid (not a past date). Most of those assumptions are being enforced by JavaScript on the client side, thereby avoiding extra round trips to the server caused by incorrect data entry. However, malicious clients often circumvent the client-side validation (e.g., craft HTTP requests by hand), and supply invalid data to the server. The correct way to program these applications is to ensure that the server performs the same (or stricter) validation checks that are performed at the client. If this is not the case with a server, then it is vulnerable to parameter tampering attacks.

Prior work [7] identifying such vulnerabilities in web applications used a blackbox approach that involved generating opportunities for potential tampering vulnerabilities. This blackbox approach, while being most suitable for testing web sites whose server side code isn't available, involves human labor in converting opportunities to actual exploits.

This paper improves the state-of-art by seeking a fully automated approach to identify the presence of such vulnerabilities in a web application, thus eliminating the need for a human in the loop. Since there is no human in the loop, our approach must identify such vulnerabilities without resulting in false alarms. Therefore, our approach must include mechanisms to *confirm* the existence of each potential vulnerability it identifies.

The basic problem of detecting parameter tampering vulnerabilities is to identify validation checks that are "missing" in a server. This can be done if we have a formal specification of the set of checks that must be performed by the server. Developing such specifications is often done through a manual process, and is a difficult task for legacy applications.

The key idea explored in this paper stems from the observation that in a web application, a client code already constitutes a description of the server's intentions regarding parameter validation checks. We can therefore, extract a specification directly from the client code. This specification can then be used to check the server side code for vulnerabilities.

Using the above observation, we develop a new formulation of this problem of automatically detecting parameter tampering vulnerabilities. In our formulation, a web application is said to be vulnerable when the server-side parameter validation is weaker than client-side validation. In other words, the server performs fewer checks than the client as to the well-formedness of the client supplied input. Such weaknesses point to security vulnerabilities on the server that can be exploited by malicious users. Whenever we find such a weakness, our approach automatically generates a concrete instance of the vulnerability in the form of an *exploit*.

Our approach tool that we call WAPTEC (Whitebox Analysis for Parameter Tampering Exploit Construction), performs web application vulnerability analysis by combining techniques from for-

Listing 1: client.js

```
1 function validateForm(){
2
3     var q = document.getElementById("quantity");
4     var n = document.getElementById("name");
5
6     if(q < 0 || n.length() > 10){
7       return false; // show error, don't submit
8     } else {
9       return true;  // submit form
10    }
11 }
```

Listing 2: server.php

```
$ca = $_POST['card'];
if($ca matches 'card-1'|'card-2')
    // generate HTML to show a
    //selected card in the form

$n = $_POST['name'];
if( strlen($n) > 10 )
    $n = substr ($n, 10);

if($_GET['op'] == "purchase"){

 $cost = $_POST['quantity'] * $price + $shipping;

 if(isset($_POST['discount']))
   $cost = $cost - $_POST['discount'] * $cost / 100;

 $q = "INSERT INTO orders ('name', 'address', 'card',
        'cost') ";
 $q .= " VALUES ('$n', '$_POST[address]', $ca, $cost)
        ;";

 mysql_query($q);
 if(mysql_error())
   $html .= " Please specify an address";
}
```

mal logic and constraint solving, symbolic evaluation and dynamic program analysis. Our approach implementation is targeted towards applications written using the LAMP (Linux, Apache, MYSQL, PHP) stack, one of the most widely used development and deployment platforms for web applications.

Due to the inherent multi-tiered nature of a LAMP application, the analysis that we need has to reason about the client side code that validates user supplied inputs, the server side transaction processing logic and (often) the database used for persistent storage. These tiers are implemented as different modules in different languages (HTML / JavaScript, PHP and SQL), and our core analysis needs to abstract the validation logic in each of these tiers and reason about them. While the Links [9, 10] programming language and several other frameworks [1, 8, 2] facilitate principled construction of multiple tiered applications, they are not applicable to reason across the three tiers of existing (legacy) LAMP applications.

To the best of our knowledge, this paper presents the first analysis that presents a uniform framework to reason about the three different tiers of an interactive LAMP application. Since our analysis spans the client, server and database, it is comprehensive and precise about its understanding of the validation performed on web application inputs, and identifies vulnerabilities "by construction". We discuss the design and implementation of this framework in this paper.

We evaluated six open source web applications using WAPTEC and were able to find 45 previously unknown vulnerabilities spanning every single one of these applications. These vulnerabilities have serious real world consequences including privilege escalation to an administrator account, overwriting files on the web server and denial of service. Furthermore, we show how our approach eliminates false positives and false negatives that are inherent in a black-box approach.

This paper is organized as follows: Section 2 presents a running example used in the rest of this paper. Section 3 provides a high-level overview of the basic ideas behind our approach. Section 4 describes the architecture of WAPTEC and its different components. Section 5 presents the implementation of WAPTEC. Section 6 presents an evaluation of our approach over several open source web applications. Section 7 presents related work. In Section 8 we conclude.

2. RUNNING EXAMPLE

Our main thesis is that it is possible to use the client of a web application as a specification of the server's intended behavior. The basis for this thesis stems from the following observations:

- Validation checks that are implemented at a client convey the "intention" of the server side of a web application.
- Server code on occasion does not replicate these intended checks often leading to security flaws.

The second point is worth further elaborating. The reason for the omission of security checks is multi-fold: first, not all web developers are aware of the security concerns about data received from a client cannot be trusted to respect these intended checks and therefore need to be replicated. Secondly, the client and the server often originate from two different codebases, the typical example is that a client is written in JavaScript and the server in one of the many platforms such as PHP, ASP or Java. When there are two codebases, improvements made to one (such as additional new validation checks and maintenance updates) do not always translate to changes to the other, leading to security violations. In this work, our aim is to detect such mismatches through automated code analysis.

We illustrate the general ideas in this work with the help of a running example. Consider a web application that provides a shopping checkout form with textfields `name`, `address`, item `quantity`, a dropdown menu displaying previously used credit cards to pick the `card` for the current purchase and a hidden field `op` that is set to "purchase". (These fields assume the usual meaning as in a typical shopping session). Listing 1 and 2 list the client side and server side code of this application, respectively.

The client side code in Listing 1 performs its validation checks at lines 6 through 7. The code checks if the `quantity` field is a positive integer, and if the supplied `name` is less than 10 characters, and submits input to the server if these conditions are met.

The server side code shown in Listing 2 computes the cost of purchase and inserts this into the `orders` database. To illustrate the basic parameter tampering attack, notice that the validation check for `quantity` is not replicated in the server. It is therefore possible that a malicious client can perform this attack by submitting a negative quantity field, reducing the cost computed to a low value.

In order to uncover this attack, the client JavaScript code in Listing 1 must be analyzed, leading to the inference that the constraint on the `quantity` field restricts it to a non-negative number. Similarly, the server PHP code in Listing 2 must be analyzed to infer

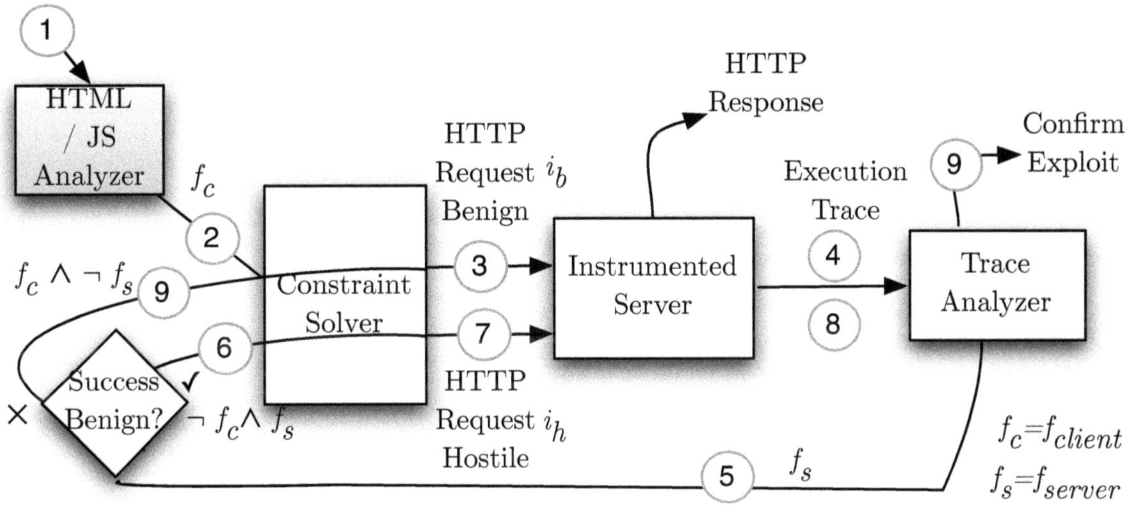

Figure 1: System Workflow

that it does not impose any constraints on this field. In addition, the following challenges need to be addressed as well.

Restrictive servers. While servers occasionally fail to replicate client checks, they are often designed to be more restrictive than clients in processing user input. In our example, note that the client restricts the length of the `name` field to 10 characters or less. On an input that does not meet this constraint (has 11 or more characters), the server chooses to "sanitize" this field by considering only the first 10 characters of the submitted value. A naive approach that doesn't satisfy the client restrictions and fails to consider the effect of sanitization in reaching a sensitive operation on the server will generate a false alarm. Our analysis is designed to factor such changes to input and avoids generating false alarms (§4.2).

Handling database operations. Any server side analysis should not only consider the effect of server side code, but also the effect of its database operations. For instance, database operations may further constrain data submitted by a client through integrity constraints. Failing to consider these constraints will also generate false alarms. For example, say the `address` field in database has an integrity constraint that ensures that it is not `null`. Failing to consider such constraints will generate false alarms. Our approach is designed to correctly handle the effect of such database constraints (§4.3).

Negative Parameter Tampering. Sometimes a server side file, such as `server.php` is written to handle multiple forms. In the above example, the server-side code additionally checks for parameter `discount`. While this code was intended for processing a totally different form that contains discounts for the user, it is not uncommon for LAMP applications to reuse the code that has some shared processing of content. An exploit that introduces this field `discount` can result in providing unlimited discounts to the total price. We call this *negative* tampering, as it is performed by an input field that is not present in the original form. By whitebox analysis of server side code, we are able to identify such vulnerabilities. We found a zero-day negative tampering attack on the open source application `dcpportal` that enables privilege escalation of an ordinary user to an administrator (§6).

3. APPROACH OVERVIEW

WAPTEC's basic approach to identifying parameter tampering exploits (inputs the client rejects but the server accepts) on a web application is a two-step process: (i) find server control paths that if taken result in the input being accepted, i.e., paths that lead to sensitive operations (such as the `INSERT` query in line 17 of our running example), and (ii) find inputs leading to each such control path that the client rejects (such as submitting a negative quantity to the server). In WAPTEC, step (i) is accomplished using a form of constraint-guided search that probes the server with inputs that the server ought to accept and then analyzes the code the server executed to determine if that control path led to a sensitive sink. We call any input the server ought to accept that results in execution of a sensitive operation a *benign input*. Step (ii) is also accomplished by probing the server with inputs and checking for a sensitive sink on the resulting control path, though this time the inputs are those the server ought to reject. Any input the server ought to reject that results in execution of a sensitive operation is a *hostile input*. Hostile inputs are *correct by construction* parameter tampering exploits.

Unlike many bug-finding program analysis efforts, WAPTEC leverages the existence of client-side code (a web form) for both steps. When searching for a benign input in step (i), WAPTEC only generates inputs that the web form accepts and would submit to the server; moreover, because the client code is relatively simple to analyze, WAPTEC extracts a logical representation of all such inputs (f_{client}) and utilizes constraint-solving technology to directly construct an input the client accepts (i.e., without fuzzing). While the server does not accept every input the client accepts, therefore requiring constraint-guided search, the client side code is a good enough approximation that WAPTEC often finds a benign input on the first try.

When searching for attacks on a given control path on the server in step (ii), WAPTEC again uses f_{client} to generate inputs, but in this case the inputs are designed to be hostile. The main thesis of WAPTEC's approach is that if the client code rejects an input, the server ought to reject it as well; thus, every input satisfying the negation of f_{client} is a potential hostile input (parameter tampering exploit), which constraint solvers can again construct directly. Furthermore, WAPTEC uses the logical representation of f_{client} to group all the potential exploits by the vulnerabilities they illustrate and generates one (or any number) of exploits per distinct vulnerability.

Below we describe WAPTEC's two step approach in more detail and refer to the steps shown in Figure 1.

3.1 Finding benign inputs

The purpose of a web form that validates user input is to reject inputs that the server will (or in practice *should*) reject. The converse is also often true: if the web form accepts an input the server will also accept it. We can therefore reasonably treat the constraints the web form checks as an approximate specification for the server's intended behavior. WAPTEC extracts the constraints enforced by the web form (which we call f_{client}) using program analysis, which is accomplished by the HTML / JavaScript Analyzer in step 2 of Figure 1. For our running example, the client formula is $quantity \geq 0 \wedge len(name) \leq 10 \wedge card \in \{card\text{-}1|card\text{-}2\} \wedge op = \text{"}purchase\text{"}$ where the first two constraints are contributed by JavaScript and the rest are derived from HTML.

To find a benign input, WAPTEC starts by using its Constraint Solver component to find any input that satisfies f_{client} and then submits that input to the server (step 3). To check whether or not the input reaches a sensitive sink (i.e., is benign), WAPTEC analyzes the code executed by the server using its Trace Analyzer component (step 4). If the server reaches a sensitive sink, the input is benign. However, sometimes the input fails to reach a sensitive sink because the server enforces more constraints than the client. These extra constraints can arise, for example, because the server has more information than the client (e.g., the list of existing usernames). In our running example, the input satisfying f_{client} might be $quantity = 3, name = \text{"}JohnDoe\text{"}, card = card\text{-}1, op = \text{"}purchase\text{"}$. The server rejects this input because it requires $address$ to have a non-null value (i.e., $address$ is a required value).

When an input that satisfies f_{client} fails to reach a sensitive sink, WAPTEC attempts to augment f_{client} with additional constraints, the intention being that any input satisfying the augmented f_{client} will lead to a sensitive sink. To compute this augmentation, WAPTEC examines the execution trace of the code the server executed on the failed input, and computes a logical formula representing that code trace (called f_{server}, computed in step 5, by the Trace Analyzer). The intuition is that f_{server} represents (the conjunction of) the conditions on the server's inputs that if true will always lead to the same control path. Since that control path fails to lead to a sensitive sink, every input leading to a sensitive sink must falsify one of the conditions on the path, i.e., it must satisfy the negation of f_{server}. Thus, the augmentation of f_{client} when no success sink is found is $f_{client} \wedge \neg f_{server}$ (step 9). In our example, the augmented f_{client} would be $quantity \geq 0 \wedge len(name) \leq 10 \wedge card \in \{card\text{-}1|card\text{-}2\} \wedge op = \text{"}purchase\text{"} \wedge required(address)$, where $required(x)$ means variable x is required to have a value.

This process then repeats, starting with the augmented f_{client}, finding an input that satisfies it, and iterating until WAPTEC finds a benign input. At a high level, this process generates a series of inputs, where each subsequent input has a better chance of being a benign input than all of the previous.

Once WAPTEC finds a benign input, it performs a depth-limited version of the procedure above to find additional, nearby control paths that lead to sensitive operations. To do that, WAPTEC analyzes the trace to extract f_{server}, which is a conjunction $C_1 \wedge \cdots \wedge C_n$. For each C_i, WAPTEC adds $\neg C_i$ to (the augmented) f_{client}, finds a satisfying input, and checks if that input leads to a sensitive operation. We call this process perturbation, since WAPTEC attempts to perturb the constraints leading to one sensitive sink to find additional sinks. Since each C_i can potentially produce a distinct control path leading to a sensitive sink, after this depth-limited search WAPTEC has between 1 and $n + 1$ control paths leading to sensitive operations. The perturbation process is motivated by the intuition that small changes to successful inputs may still drive execution successfully to sensitive sinks, which are often clustered together, and hence after finding a single sink, there is a high likelihood of finding additional sinks nearby. It is noteworthy that WAPTEC does not perturb a path that has no sensitive sinks because all the paths that it would reach by perturbation are already reachable by the augmentation of f_{client} by $\neg f_{server}$.

3.2 Finding hostile inputs

For each control path WAPTEC finds that leads to a sensitive sink, it attempts to generate inputs that the server ought not accept but that lead to that same sink. Generating inputs the server ought not accept is straightforward: find solutions to the negation of f_{client}, for if the client rejects a given input, we can be assured the server will reject it as well (or else the client fails to expose the server's full functionality to users). Generating inputs that cause the server to follow the same control path and therefore arrive at the same sensitive sink is likewise straightforward: find solutions to f_{server}. Thus, generating inputs that follow the same control path and therefore are accepted by the server but that the server should not accept amounts to finding a solution to $\neg f_{client} \wedge f_{server}$ (step 6). Conceptually, every such solution amounts to a parameter tampering exploit, but to ensure the input is in fact an exploit, we submit it to the server (step 7) and ensure it reaches a success sink (steps 8 and 9).

Furthermore, instead of generating one input for $\neg f_{client} \wedge f_{server}$, WAPTEC generates one input for each disjunct δ in the disjunctive normal form of $\neg f_{client}$ by finding a solution to $\delta \wedge f_{server}$. Each of those inputs satisfies a logically distinct set of constraints and hence is likely to represent a logically distinct vulnerability. Each $\delta \wedge f_{server}$ can be construed as a distinct server-side vulnerability witnessed by one of the exploits WAPTEC finds.

In our running example, the negation of f_{client} is $quantity < 0 \vee len(name) > 10 \vee op! = \text{"}purchase\text{"} \vee card \notin \{card\text{-}1|card\text{-}2\}$. There is a control path through the server where f_{server} includes $required(address) \wedge \neg len(name) > 10$. Thus, to construct an exploit, WAPTEC uses the Constraint Solver to find one solution to the formula $quantity < 0 \wedge required(address) \wedge \neg(len(name) > 10)$ and another solution to the formula $len(name) > 10 \wedge required(address) \wedge \neg(len(name) > 10)$. In the first case, the server executes an INSERT operation, and is deemed an exploit (hostile). This exploit illustrates the vulnerability where $quantity$ is given a negative value. The second formula is not satisfiable and therefore there is no exploit reported.

The pseudo-code for steps (i) and (ii) of our approach can be found in Algorithms 1 and 2, respectively.

3.3 Soundness

It is important to describe at a high level the mechanisms that we use for generating the client formula f_{client} and the server formula f_{server}, and their implications for the correctness of our approach.

The client formula f_{client} is generated by the HTML / JavaScript Analyzer (shown in Figure 1), and is based on our prior work [7]. The analyzer uses symbolic evaluation [20] to compute the client formula f_{client}. Since the formula is statically computed from the

Algorithm 1 WAPTEC (url)

```
f_client := clientAnalyzer(url)
Q := {true}
loop
    α := pop(Q)
    ν := solve(f_client ∧ α)
    (success, f_server) := server(url, ν)
    if success then
        genHostiles(url, f_client, f_server)
        for all C_i | f_server = C_1 ∧ ··· ∧ C_m do
            ν := solve(f_client ∧ α ∧ ¬C_i)
            (success, f_server) := server(url, ν)
            if success then genHostiles(url, f_client, f_server)
    else
        Q := Q ∪ {α ∧ ¬C_i | ¬f_server = ¬C_1 ∨ ··· ∨ ¬C_m}
        Q := simplify(Q)
        if empty(Q) then return
```

Algorithm 2 GENHOSTILES(url,f_{client},f_{server})

```
for all δ ∈ DNF(¬f_client) do
    ν := solve(δ ∧ f_server)
    success := server(url, ν)
    if success then print Exploit found: ν
```

source, the generated formula is in fact an approximation. Specifically, due to the nature of the approximations made in [7], f_{client} is an *under-approximation* of the constraints the client enforces, which means that every time an input is generated that satisfies f_{client}, it is indeed the case that this input will lead to a successful form submission from the client. Similarly, $\neg f_{client}$, represents an *over-approximation* of input instances that are rejected by the client (e.g., line 7 of client code listing 1 in our running example). Inputs satisfying $\neg f_{client}$ are therefore not necessarily rejected, but we can always execute those inputs in the actual client code to ensure they are rejected by the client.

In our approach, the server side behavior is obtained by dynamic analysis of server side code. This means that the server side formula f_{server} will be specifically tied to each run, and is generated from the program trace induced by the run. By its very nature, dynamic analysis only considers the operations done by code that is executed; hence, f_{server} precisely captures the server behavior for the run without any approximations.

Since f_{server} is precise, and WAPTEC can verify that any solution to $\neg f_{client} \wedge f_{server}$ is actually rejected by the client, all the exploits WAPTEC reports are concrete parameter tampering exploits. Our implementation seeks to find such exploits.

3.4 Discussion

Section 2 described several challenges that WAPTEC addresses. Here we explain how those challenges are met by the algorithms just discussed.

Multi-tier analysis. The algorithms above are written as though WAPTEC is faced with analyzing only a single program, but in reality there are three programs written in different languages that it must analyze: the web form, the server code, and the database. To reason about the combination of these three programs, WAPTEC analyzes each program individually and extracts the relevant semantics into logical formulas (more specifically the logic of strings). Once the important portions of the three programs are expressed in a common language, reasoning about the combination is much simpler and can be carried out as described in this section. Details on translating web forms into logic can be found in Section 4.1; details on translating server code (one trace at a time) into logic can be found in Section 4.2; details on translating database code into logic can be found in Section 4.3.

Negative parameter tampering. Discovering attacks that utilize variables not appearing in the client-side web form (i.e., negative parameter tampering attacks) is a natural side-effect of our basic algorithm. Such variables appear in the server-side code, and when the server processes any given input, f_{server} will therefore include those variables. In our running example, line 14 checks if the variable *discount* has a value. Therefore, every f_{server} generated from an input that fails to set *discount* will always include the constraint $\neg required(discount)$. When the input fails to reach a sensitive sink, f_{client} is augmented with $required(discount)$, and when the input succeeds in reaching a sensitive sink, the perturbation process includes $required(discount)$ as one perturbation. In both cases, subsequent attempts to find satisfying inputs require *discount* to be assigned a value.

Sanitization. Sometimes before validating user input, the server sanitizes those inputs. Sanitization violates the premise that if the client rejects an input so should the server. For example, instead of rejecting a *name* value that is longer than 10 characters, the server truncates *name* to 10 characters. WAPTEC can avoid triggering false positives for some sanitization cases because of the way it constructs f_{server} from a trace of the server's code (§4.2).

4. WAPTEC ARCHITECTURE

The previous section outlined high level challenges in designing a whitebox analysis tool to detect parameter tampering attacks. Specifically, we note that different components of a web application are written in different programming languages: client side code is written in HTML / JavaScript, server side code is written in server side programming languages such as PHP, JSP, etc., and finally, database schema is written in languages such as SQL. To compute formulas that represent restrictions imposed on inputs, we need to bridge the gap between different programming languages and express constraints imposed by them uniformly in terms of first-order logical formulas. Expressing constraints uniformly would then enable generation of benign and hostile inputs by solving formulas involving f_{client} and f_{server}.

This section discusses technical challenges faced in assimilating constraints from various components of a LAMP web application and algorithms that address them. f_{client} is computed from the client-side code and involves analysis of HTML / JavaScript code relevant to a web form (Section 4.1). f_{server} is computed from the server-side code and involves extracting constraints from PHP server-side code (Section 4.2) and SQL databases (Section 4.3).

4.1 Extracting constraints from client-side code

The client-side web form is typically expressed in HTML and JavaScript both of which encode restrictions on user inputs. We analyze HTML code of the web form to extract constraints implied by various form fields e.g., a drop down menu implies a range constraint on value of the user input. JavaScript validation code associated with the form is symbolically executed to extract conditions that, if satisfied, indicate successful input validation at the client. All restrictions imposed by HTML and JavaScript together then provide the client-side formula f_{client}. Generation of f_{client} is based on our prior work NoTAMPER[7] which provides a detailed treatment.

Listing 3: Trace generated for running example

```
1  $main_ca = $_POST['card'];                 //
2  if($main_ca matches 'card-1|card-2'){   //
3
4  }
5
6  $main_n = $_POST['name'];
7  if(! strlen($main_n) > 10 ) {
8  }
9
10 if($_GET['op'] == "purchase"){
11
12      $main_cost = $_POST['quantity'] * 100 + 10;    //
            where $price is 100
13
14      if(!isset($_POST['discount']){
15   }
16
17      $main_q = "INSERT INTO order ('name','address', '
            card', 'cost')";
18      $main_q = "INSERT INTO order ('name', 'address',
            'card', 'cost')" . "VALUES('" .  $main_n .
            "', '" .  $_POST['address'] . "'" .  $main_ca
             . "," . $main_cost .  ");";
19
20      mysql_query ($main_q);
21      $_wb_status = "SUCCESS";          // query
            execution denoted by SUCCESS status
22
23 }
```

4.2 Extracting constraints from server-side code

The formula f_{server} represents server side validation and sanitization of user inputs. To generate f_{server}, we first capture a trace comprising of statements that the server executed to process user inputs. For the running example (Listing 2), Listing 3 shows the generated trace for inputs `card='card-1'`, `name='alice'`, `address='wonderland'`, `op='purchase'` and `quantity=1`. Each line in the generated trace Listing 3 corresponds to the line in the running example Listing 2 that generated it.

To generate f_{server}, we need to identify statements in a trace that correspond to validation / sanitization done by the server side code. The server-side code may perform user input validation and sanitization in the following three ways: a) explicit validation of desired properties of user inputs in conditional statements and b) implicit validation / sanitization of user inputs through inbuilt functions in server-side code and c) implicit validation / sanitization of user inputs by database. In the running example (Listing 2), validation of the `card` parameter at line 2 illustrates explicit validation, truncation of the `name` parameter at line 8 illustrates explicit sanitization (as execution of line 8 ensures that value of the `name` parameter will contain 10 or less characters) and rejection of null value for the parameter `address` exemplifies database sanitization / validation. f_{server} is essentially computed by identifying and analyzing all the three types of validation / sanitization constructs present in a trace. We focus on the first two types of validation / sanitization constructs here and the database validation / sanitization is discussed in the next section (Section 4.3).

Extracting constraints due to explicit validation. Explicit validation of user inputs is captured by `IF` statements appearing in a trace e.g., four `IF` statements shown in the trace in Listing 3, capturing validation of parameters `card`, `name`, `op` and `discount`, respectively. To learn the constraint being checked by an `IF` statement, we analyze its condition argument. Each such condition argument is then repeatedly expanded until it only contains user inputs, concrete values and operators. For example, the `IF` statement on Line 2 (Listing 3) checks if $\texttt{\$main\_ca matches } '\texttt{card} - 1|\texttt{card} - 2'$. We expand `$main_ca` with `$_POST['card']` because of the assignment statement on Line 1. Intuitively, starting from the `IF` statement the above process walks backwards in the trace and replaces server-side variables appearing in conditions with values assigned to them until the condition is expressed in terms of inputs, concrete values and operators.

A challenge in precisely capturing explicit validation in `IF` statements stems from the presence of irrelevant statements. A naive approach that considers all `IF` conditions as relevant to a sink would report imprecise results. For example, consider the first `IF` statement in the trace (Listing 3). This `IF` statement checks the value of parameter `card` and sets the HTML form to show the selected entry. Although the trace contains check on `card`, it does not prevent the query computed at line 20 from using malicious values of `card`. Similarly, a form may contain several parameters but a server side sink may only use some of them. Therefore, our analysis must factor whether a tampered parameter is actually going to be used at a sensitive operation.

WAPTEC identifies conditionals relevant to a given sink by employing data- and control-dependency analysis: the data dependency analysis identifies conditionals that actually contributed data to a sink, and the control dependency analysis identifies conditionals that actually dictated control flow to a sink. For the running example, the query executed at line 20 is neither data nor control dependent on conditional statement at line 2 and hence this conditional is ignored while analyzing sink at line 20.

For the trace in Listing 3 the above process contributes the following constraints to the f_{server} formula:

$$len(name) \leq 10 \wedge op = \text{"}purchase\text{"} \wedge \neg isset(discount).$$

Extracting implicit constraints due to sanitization. The server-side sanitization of user inputs may inherently enforce constraints on user inputs. For example, at line 8 (Listing 2) server-side variable `$n` which contains value of the parameter `name`, is sanitized. In specific, by truncating the `name` parameter with `substr` function, the server-side code ensures that after this sanitization the contents of `$n` variable will have 10 or less characters i.e., it implicitly enforces the constraint $len\ (name)\ \leq\ 10$.

WAPTEC avoids analyzing paths that would result in generating false alarms due to such sanitization. To see, we revisit the basic process by which WAPTEC identifies paths to a success sink. Notice that we demand that this path is satisfied by an input that satisfies f_{client}. In the event the server chooses to apply sanitization of input to satisfy f_{client}, such a path will not be considered by WAPTEC for trace analysis, because a benign input will never traverse that path. For example, in Listing 2, the statement in Line 8 will never be executed by WAPTEC.

Nevertheless, an application may have incomplete or partial sanitization. To handle these cases, we capture such implicit constraints by analyzing the sink expression (e.g., SQL query), and demanding that f_{client} be held true by the sink expression. We express the sink expression purely in terms of user inputs and concrete values by following a process similar to expansion of `IF` conditions. The resulting SQL sink expressions are then parsed with a SQL parser thus identifying data arguments to SQL queries which contain user inputs (or a function of user inputs). Currently, the restrictions on the operators appearing in the sink expression are limited to the language (shown in Table 1) supported by the underlying solver (as described in §5.2).

4.3 Extracting constraints from database

Database query operations present interesting consequences for approaches that analyze server-side code. With respect to such operations, many security analysis approaches limit their reasoning to reachability, e.g., most tainting approaches aim to find if a tainted data item can reach a database query execution location. Without analyzing outcome of the query execution, such approaches will result in imprecision as database engine may either sanitize hostile inputs to comply with its schema or reject them. For blackbox approaches, database triggered sanitization may result in false alarms. Additionally, whitebox approaches that ignore these constraints may never generate a benign set of inputs that will be truly accepted at the sink. For our running example, without considering database constraint (NOT NULL) on the `address` field, it is not possible to generate acceptable benign inputs. Note that this also forbids discovery of legitimately exploitable parameters for such sinks, thus resulting in false negatives e.g., the `quantity` exploit cannot be constructed without providing a non-null address value.

We first note that the database schema is a sequence of SQL queries that creates different tables and views and expresses certain restrictions on data that can be inserted into each column of a table. Suppose we know that a user input u is being inserted into a column c of a table, then all constraints implied on c by the database schema, must be satisfied (if validation) or will be enforced when data is added to the database (if sanitization). However, finding the mapping between u (typically server-side variables) and c (column name in a database table) is challenging as it requires bridging the namespace differences between application code and database schema i.e., application code and database tables may refer to same data with different names. WAPTEC analyzes database schema and queries issued in traces to build a mapping between server-side variables and database columns which enables it to then express constraints imposed by database in terms of user inputs.

In the first step, this analysis parses the schema of an application's database. For each table creation statement we analyze the column definitions that typically specify constraints on values that can be stored e.g., `"NOT NULL"` clause enforces non-null values whereas `enum` specifies domain of accepted values. We handle `MySQL` formatted schemas and extract such conditions in the solver language.

In the second step, we generate a symbolic query for SQL sinks found in traces and parse them. This parsing enables us to map table column names to program variables. For example, on parsing a symbolic SQL query `"insert into T (uid, ... values( '$_GET[u]',..."`, we can associate column `uid` of table `T` to program variable `$_GET[u]`. Once this mapping is available, we generate constraints by replacing column names with program variables in constraints generated by the first step e.g., if `uid` column had a `NOT NULL` constraint, this analysis will yield a constraint `(NOT NULL u)`.

Discussion. The above discussion highlights the relationships between server variable names, client form field names and database field names as intended by typical web applications. These relations are important from the perspective of sanitization as well. We already discussed a precise way to handle the effect of sanitization that requires the client validation to hold at the sink expression, (and is therefore safe for such operation). However, such an approach needs to make an assumption that the database field corresponding to the sink expression represents a corresponding client form field (that is transformed to the sink expression with some form of sanitization). While the discussions in this section suggest that such an assumption is reasonable across a large class of web applications, and indeed holds in the applications that we analyzed, it is very easy to construe examples where it could break. For instance, consider a (contrived) web application which assigns a sink expression to a value that does not satisfy client validation, and the intention behind such an assignment may be beyond the inference of any automated mechanism. More generally, the above discussion raises the need for a *specification* that provides a mapping between client inputs and database fields. While such specifications were not needed for the applications we analyzed, the availability of such specifications will be able to broaden the applicability of our analysis.

5. IMPLEMENTATION

To generate f_{server}, we need a trace of statements executed by the server-side code. Section 5.1 provides the high-level details behind a program transformation that enables PHP applications to generate a trace and facilitate computation of f_{server}. Generating benign and hostile inputs entails solving logical formulas and Section 5.2 describes the implementation details of the solver.

5.1 Trace generation transformation

Computation of f_{server} entails reasoning about server-side processing of user inputs e.g., properties of user inputs checked by the server-side code. We capture the server-side processing of user inputs in traces which contain program statements executed by the server-side code to process user inputs. To generate such traces we perform source-to-source transformation of applications written in `PHP` language. The transformed applications are then deployed and generate traces apart from processing user inputs.

Alternate implementation. The other choice for capturing such traces is to instrument a `PHP` interpreter itself. Although, this approach requires less effort on a per application basis, it may require extensive changes to the `PHP` interpreter. Also, there are considerable analysis needs that led us to adopt a program rewriting route. First, we needed taint tracking to identify the flow of untrusted inputs. Second, we needed data and control flow analysis required to identify conditions only relevant to the sink. Third, to handle PHP5 object-oriented features, we need to unambiguously identify each object in order to avoid name collisions. While these can be done by hacking various internal parts of a PHP interpreter, such changes would generally not be portable across revisions to the interpreter. Our implementation does so in a much cleaner fashion while retaining portability across various PHP interpreters and is not broken by revisions to the interpreter.

Avoiding name collisions. Traces are straight-line `PHP` programs comprising only of assignments, calls to inbuilt functions and `IF-THEN` statements. A challenge in reporting variable names in traces is caused by the possibility of *name collisions*. As traces are straight-line programs, all functions (except `PHP` inbuilt) executed by the web application need to be in-lined. As this in-lining merges variables from several lexical scopes it could result in *name collisions* and could generate traces that misrepresent run of the web application e.g., name-collisions could result in traces that incorrectly capture use / reachability of an important variable. To avoid name collisions, program transformation attaches a unique prefix to each variable name being reported in the trace. To compute these prefixes, we use function / method signatures and for variables appearing in classes, a per object unique identifier is used additionally (as described below).

PHP object-oriented features. Object-oriented features are often used in `PHP` programs (2 of the 6 applications we evaluated were object-oriented and used inheritance). As multiple instantiations of a class yield objects with same methods, method signatures are same for all such objects. Thus prefixing signatures to

Class	Examples	Instances
Equality *	$=, \neq$	$x \neq y$
Numeric *	$+, *, -, /, <, >$	$x < 7$
Modal	$required$	$required(x)$
Regex *	$\in, \notin$	$x \in$ `[abc]*`
PHP	$trim, len, concat$	$len(x) < len(concat(y, z))$

Table 1: WAPTEC **constraint language**

variable names may still lead to name collisions in object-oriented programs. Further, a member variable can be accessed using multiple namespaces e.g., by using the *this* operator (inside methods) or by using names assigned to objects. Although, all such instances are accessing the same memory region, a naive renaming scheme may lose precision by failing to identify these accesses with a single variable name.

The main changes required to classes are for computing unique prefixes for variables. Here, the transformer adds an *id* member variable to the class definition to hold the unique identifier for each instance of the class. The constructor methods are augmented to initialize the *id* variable to a unique value. Further, inheritance is inherently handled in this scheme as the *id* member of inheriting class shadows the *id* member of base class. With the help of *id* variable, accesses to a member variable through an object ($\$o \rightarrow member_1$) or the `this` operator ($\$this \rightarrow member_1$) are uniformly transformed as $v\_\$id\_member_1$. This enables subsequent analysis to correctly identify accesses to a single memory location from disparate namespaces.

As f_{server} mainly concerns processing of user inputs, the transformer ensures that the generated traces only contain statements manipulating user inputs. We use standard taint tracking techniques to track user inputs and only include statements manipulating tainted arguments in traces. Special care was needed to initialize and propagate taint as PHP recursively defines some of the inbuilt arrays e.g., super global array GLOBALS contains itself as a member.

5.2 String solver

The string solver component analyzes logical formulae to construct inputs that are fed to the server; some of those inputs the system was designed to accept, while other inputs are intended to expose server-side vulnerabilities. The string solver component of WAPTEC was built on top of Kaluza [21], a state-of-the-art solver that finds variable assignments satisfying string and numeric constraints. The main challenge in building the string solver component was translating the WAPTEC constraint language into the language supported by Kaluza.

Constraint language. WAPTEC allows all boolean combinations of the atomic constraints shown in Table 1. The equality and numeric constraints are standard; regular expression constraints require a variable to belong to a given regular expression; PHP constraints include functions from PHP and JavaScript such as *trim* (found in e.g., the MyBloggie application) for removing whitespace from the ends of a string and *strpos* for computing the index at which one string appears inside another string. Kaluza roughly supports those categories of constraints marked with an asterisk, plus functions for computing the length of a string and concatenating two strings. Thus, translating WAPTEC's constraint language to Kaluza's language requires handling modals and PHP functions.

Static versus dynamic typing. Besides the difference in atomic constraints, there is a more fundamental difference between the constraint languages of Kaluza and WAPTEC. Kaluza requires every variable to have a single type and does not provide functions to cast from one type to another[1], whereas PHP allows variables to take on arbitrary values. This mismatch makes the translation difficult because a constraint such as $x \neq 0 \wedge x \neq$ "0" causes a type error in Kaluza but appears frequently in the semantics of PHP, e.g., when defining whether a variable evaluates to true or false.

Our approach approximates the semantics of PHP functions with a combination of type inference to detect type mismatches, type resolution to choose one type for mismatched arguments, static casting to convert problematic arguments to the chosen types, and type-based simplification to eliminate constraints that do not actually affect the satisfiability of the constraints but cause Kaluza to throw type errors.

Untranslatable constraints. Some of WAPTEC's constraints cannot faithfully be translated into Kaluza's constraint language. For example, PHP employs a number of built-in data structures not handled by Kaluza, and PHP functions often accept and return such data structures. For example, MyBloggie employs the *preg_replace* function, which is a regular-expression version of a string replacement operation. *preg_replace* can both accept and return arrays as arguments. Arrays are difficult to translate to Kaluza because they correspond to an unknown number of variables, and Kaluza expects a fixed number of variables in the constraints. Another example of a function we did not translate is found in DCP-Portal application: the *md5* function computes the MD5 hash of its argument.

For constraints that cannot be translated to Kaluza's language, WAPTEC simply drops those constraints, producing a constraint set that is weaker than it ought to be, potentially leading to unsoundness and incompleteness in the search for parameter tampering exploits. However, because WAPTEC always checks if the variable assignment produced by the solver satisfies the original constraints, unsound results are never reported.

Disjunction. As mentioned above, disjunction is employed heavily by WAPTEC, and while Kaluza handles disjunction natively, the search for parameter tampering exploits sometimes requires finding different solutions for different disjuncts in a set of constraints—functionality Kaluza does not support. Thus WAPTEC manages disjunctions itself, sometimes converting to disjunctive normal form (DNF)[2] explicitly.

6. EVALUATION

We evaluated the effectiveness of WAPTEC on a suite of 6 open source PHP applications that were chosen to reflect prevalent application domains in commonplace settings. Table 2 provides background information on these applications (lines of code, number of files, and functionality). The test suite was deployed on a Mac Mini (1.83 GHz Intel, 2.0 GB RAM) running the MAMP application suite, and WAPTEC was deployed on an Ubuntu workstation (2.45Ghz Quad Intel, 2.0GB RAM).

Experiments. We evaluated our approach by conducting two sets of experiments. In the first set of experiments, we ran WAPTEC to automatically analyze the chosen web forms and identify parameter tampering exploits that are correct by construction. In the second set of experiments, we ran NoTamper, a blackbox version of WAPTEC developed in our previous work [7], on the same web forms. We compared the results of the two experiments to quantify

[1]Type casting functions, while included in the documentation, were unavailable at the time of evaluation.

[2]In our experience, converting to DNF was usually inexpensive (despite its worst-case exponential behavior) because of the structural simplicity of the constraint sets.

Application	Size (KLOC)	Files	Use	Exploits
SnipeGallery	9.1k	54	Image Mgmt	2
SPHPBlog	26.5k	113	Blog	1
DcpPortal	144.7k	484	Content Mgmt	32
PHPNews	6.4k	21	News Mgmt	1
Landshop	15.4k	158	Real Estate	3
MyBloggie	9.4k	59	Blog	6

Table 2: Summary of WAPTEC **results**

the benefits of using whitebox analysis over blackbox analysis in the context of parameter tampering attacks.

Results summary. The outcome of the first set of experiments is summarized in Table 2. We evaluated one form in each application. WAPTEC *found a total of 45 exploits. We manually verified all of these exploits.* For each application shown in column 1, the last column shows reported exploits. As shown in this table, WAPTEC successfully generated one or more exploits for each application in the test suite underscoring a widespread lack of sufficient replication of the client-side validation in the corresponding server-side code. A detailed report of exploits found by WAPTEC can be found at *http://sisl.rites.uic.edu/waptec*. We discuss a few interesting exploits below and use them to motivate discussion in Section 6.2 that discusses improvements made by WAPTEC (whitebox) over our prior work NoTamper (blackbox).

6.1 Exploits

Privilege escalation. The `dcpportal` application allows guests to register for an account. The registration form solicits standard information, such as name, e-mail, username, password, etc. Upon normal registration, a user is provided with an account having basic privileges. When the form is submitted, the server-side form processing code validates the provided information and checks if a cookie `make_install_prn` is set. When this cookie is set to 1, the user is registered with administrative privileges. By setting this cookie, it is possible for an attacker to register an account with escalated privileges.

Discovery of the above vulnerability required WAPTEC to construct a negative parameter tampering exploit i.e., the client-side formula f_{client} for this form did not contain any restriction on the parameter `make_install_prn` however the server side formula f_{server} checked its value. The whitebox view of the server-side code enabled WAPTEC to set this additional parameter and escalate privileges of user being registered to an administrator.

After confirming the exploit, we analyzed the application to understand the root cause of this flaw. We found that the application used cookie `make_install_prn` during initial installation to allow creation of an administrator account. To patch this vulnerability, the application can use additional server-side state (e.g., sessions) to avoid depending on the cookie value alone or have a separate form for this purpose.

Duplicate users. The `dcpportal` application requires unique usernames comprising of at most 32 alphanumeric characters for new account registrations. The client-side allows only 32 alphanumeric characters, while the server-side enforces uniqueness by checking that the database does not contain a matching username before creating an account. Further, during insertion of new user details, the database enforces the length by truncating usernames to 32 characters.

During vulnerability analysis, WAPTEC recognized that the server fails to enforce the length constraint before checking for existing usernames. For this vulnerability, WAPTEC generated hostile inputs that exceeded 32 characters, which in this case caused the username existence check to always return false. This is because usernames stored in the database are truncated to 32 characters and checking for usernames of length > 32 will always return false. In addition to this, the server also fails to replicate the alphanumeric constraint on `username` and WAPTEC generated a hostile input that contained invalid characters. When confirming these exploits, we were able to refine them. Although true account duplication works only for long usernames, it is possible to create imposter accounts by appending url encoded whitespace to existing usernames.

Blog category hijacking. `mybloggie`, a blogging application, allows registered users to submit posts to the blog. When submitting a post, users are asked to choose a category for the current post from a drop-down list of existing categories. By submitting a value not in that list, an attacker can submit posts that will appear in a category that will be created in the future. This may negatively impact effectiveness / quality of the future category thus this attack can hijack a future blog category. WAPTEC computed formulas f_{server} and f_{client} for this form, revealed missing validation of submitted category value by the server-side code and was exploited by supplying an out of range value.

Additional exploits. Below we briefly describe one exploit from each of the other four applications we evaluated.

phpnews, a news management application, allows administrators to modify certain files through a form which contains name of the file as a hidden field. The server-side code fails to validate that the file name is not tampered and as a result attackers can update existing files, create arbitrary files and / or corrupt files of other applications deployed on the same web server.

snipegallery, a photo album application, allows users to arrange albums hierarchically by selecting a parent category for each new album from a drop down list. By selecting a value not in that list, the new album becomes invisible; furthermore, additional analysis shows that a carefully constructed parent album value leads to a SQL injection attack.

landshop, a real estate application, includes a form with a hidden field not pertinent to that form. When the value of this field is set to the ID of an existing listing (which are displayed prominently on the site), that listing is deleted from the application whether the user is the owner or not.

sphpblog, a blogging application, allows users to choose a language for the blog from a drop down menu. By selecting a language value not in the drop down menu, an attacker can make the application unusable and thus conduct a denial-of-service attack.

6.2 Comparison of whitebox and blackbox results

The results of the comparison are summarized in Table 3. For each application, this table reports the number of confirmed exploits found by NoTamper (column 2) and WAPTEC (column 3). The next two columns report false positives reported by NoTamper, which were eliminated in WAPTEC, and false negatives reported by WAPTEC that NoTamper failed to find. In total, the blackbox approach resulted in 23 false positives, and 24 fewer confirmed exploits when compared to the whitebox approach. Further, for `dcpportal` and `mybloggie` applications WAPTEC found several exploitable sinks for each negated disjunct of f_{client} e.g., for `dcpportal` column 3 shows 16(32) - each hostile input generated by negating 16 f_{client} disjuncts was used in 2 distinct sinks and hence were exploitable (total 32 exploits). We wish to note that all

Application	Conf. exploits BlackB.	WhiteB.	False pos. BlackBox	False neg. BlackBox
SnipeGallery	2	2	1	0
SPHPBlog	1	1	0	0
DcpPortal	13	16(32)	9	19
PHPNews	1	1	0	0
Landshop	3	3	1	0
Mybloggie	1	5(6)	12	5
Total	21	45	23	24

Table 3: Comparing whitebox and blackbox analysis results

Application	Formula Complexity			Avg. trace size (KB)	Time (sec)
SnipeGallery	11	5	11	5	41
SPHPBlog	37	1	1	1	4
DcpPortal	187	2	48	135	10,042
PHPNews	1	1	1	1	12
Landshop	20	2	8	20	60
MyBloggie	37	5	4	738	2,082

Table 4: Additional WAPTEC **results**

these disjuncts would have contributed to one hostile each, at best, in NoTAMPER.

In the rest of this section we will refer to exploits described in Section 6.1 to highlight features of WAPTEC (whitebox) that enable it to produce better results than NoTAMPER (blackbox).

Multiple sink analysis. A single form input can be used by the server at multiple sensitive operations and can potentially cause problems at each such operation. The duplicate user exploit in `dcpportal` demonstrates a case where a single hostile input exploited multiple sinks. When WAPTEC negated the 32 alphanumeric character length constraint, it produced an invalid string that was used at two sinks. The string was first used in a sink that checked if a duplicate username exists in the database, and later it was inserted into the database at a second sink. WAPTEC detected that the malformed username was used at both sinks and reported an exploit for each. On the contrary, NoTAMPER reported a single vulnerability for a similar hostile input. This is because NoTAMPER is incapable of reasoning about multiple sinks and, therefore, suffers from false negatives.

Negative tampering. WAPTEC showcased that it can uncover negative tampering vulnerabilities by discovering the privilege escalation exploit in `dcpportal`. While exploring additional server-side form processing code, WAPTEC found a conditional that depended on value of a parameter `make_install_prn` which is not found in the client-side formula. To explore this branch, it satisfied the conditional by setting the cookie `make_install_prn` to 1. By analyzing data and control dependencies, it then determined that this branch modifies parameter values used in the sink, and therefore, reported the exploit. NoTAMPER is inadequate to discover such exploits because that requires analysis of server-side form processing logic to uncover hidden functionality, which is out of scope for a blackbox tool.

Sanitization. As mentioned in Section 4.2, WAPTEC fundamentally avoids paths that may sanitize inputs by computing benign inputs that satisfy f_{client} and hence are not needed to be sanitized. For cases where filter functions appear in conditional expressions, WAPTEC maps built-in functions to constraints implied by them. In contrast, NoTAMPER is unable to detect the presence of sanitization routines on the server-side beyond using simple heuristics to guess. To account for database constraints, WAPTEC adds them into f_{server} and checks for errors / warnings on database operations. Ignoring database constraints can lead to false positives e.g., during testing of the registration form for `dcpportal`, database constraints helped to avoid a false positive. In this example, the hostile input was produced by negating a range constraint on the `birthdate` parameter in f_{client}, and f_{server} did not contain the range constraint. The server's response returned a success page, so NoTAMPER recognized a vulnerability. However, the default action by the database converted the invalid date to '0000-00-00'. Another example was found while testing the `snipegallery` application. The hostile input was produced by negating a length constraint found in f_{client}, and f_{server} did not contain the replicated length constraint. However, database implicitly enforced the length check and this attack did not succeed. Without considering sanitization and database constraints, such false positives cannot be avoided.

Required variables. Another source of false positives for NoTAMPER is attributed to required variables that are enforced only at the server-side. In these cases, the client contains insufficient information to generate a truly benign input that satisfies the server's demand for certain variables. Any required variables in f_{server} can easily be identified in a whitebox approach through code analysis, but have to be heuristically determined in a blackbox approach. For example, NoTAMPER failed to catch the category hijacking exploit in the `mybloggie` application because of missed required variables. In this example, the server-side code required the client to set value of either `submit` or `preview` parameter. As NoTAMPER failed to set any of these values, the server generated a response page containing the same form for both benign and hostile inputs thus resulting in a false positive.

WAPTEC demonstrated that a whitebox approach produces improved results over the blackbox approach used by NoTAMPER. WAPTEC uncovered a greater number of exploits and eliminated false positives and false negatives by precisely reasoning about form inputs across the entire application (client and server). In contrast, NoTAMPER is limited to using constraints implied by the client-side code and employs heuristics to determine if the server-side code accepted / rejected inputs and thus inherently suffers from false positives and false negatives.

Although WAPTEC results are consistently better than NoTAMPER, both of these approaches have their own utility. As NoTAMPER does not rely on analyzing server-side code, it could be employed to analyze a wider range of applications and websites. However if the source code is available, a whitebox analysis based approach like WAPTEC could be employed to perform deeper code analysis to pinpoint more security problems. Further, by ensuring production of exploits by construction, the whitebox approach can reduce the human effort in confirming exploits that may be unavoidable in blackbox approaches.

6.3 Complexity and performance

For each evaluated application, Table 4 captures complexity of generated formulas (column 2 - client-side constraints, column 3 - server-side constraints, column 4 - database constraints), average size of generated traces (column 5 - kilo bytes) and average time taken to run the tool (column 6 - seconds).

Outliers. The most notable application we tested, `dcpportal`, included the largest formula complexities, the largest number of exploits, and the longest running time. The larger the formula complexity, the larger and more complex the form; hence, a longer running time is to be expected. The large number of exploits is partially attributed to large formula complexity because the potential number of exploit generation attempts is larger; however, the presence of a large number of confirmed exploits points to poor server-side validation of inputs.

Manual intervention. In a preliminary analysis of the chosen applications, we selected forms that contained interesting client side specifications and collected login credentials necessary to access them (in 5 applications). We also extracted form action parameters in cases where applications reused processing code between multiple forms (total of 4). These hints were necessary to facilitate automatic analysis and to restrict exploration of server-side code pertaining to other forms. Overall, it required typically less than 5 minutes to collect this data for each form.

7. RELATED WORK

The related work is organized along the dimensions of various contributions of WAPTEC.

Multi-tier reasoning of web applications. Web applications, those following LAMP model in specific, are inherently multi-tiered: client-side code written in HTML / JavaScript, server-side code written in PHP and database schema expressed in MySQL. To precisely construct parameter tampering exploits, WAPTEC reasons across these tiers and expresses them uniformly in the language of the solver. To the best of our knowledge, WAPTEC is the first work that offers a systematic multi-tiered analysis for legacy web applications. Most existing works on web application analysis do not reason across all tiers. Balzarotti et al. [5] offer a system that tries to reason across modules of a web application to find data and work flow attacks on web applications and in doing so offer limited support for finding URLs embedded in JavaScript and HTML code. Programming languages such as Links [9, 10] and frameworks such as [1, 8] offer principled construction of multi-tiered applications, however do not assist analysis of legacy web applications. In contrast, WAPTEC offers a much powerful analysis framework that combines concolic analysis of the HTML / JavaScript with static analysis of runtime traces for legacy web applications.

Specification inference. AutoISES [25] is an approach for C program bug detection that mines for common security-related patterns and identifies deviations from these as vulnerabilities. Engler [12] detects security bugs in C programs by mining temporal safety patterns and checking for inconsistencies. Srivastava [23] et al. exploit the difference between multiple implementations of the same application programming interface to detect security violations. Felmetsger et al. [13] monitor normal execution of a web application to infer a set of behavioral specification to find paths in program that will likely violate these specifications and hence may indicate missing checks. In contrast to these approaches, in our problem context, we are analyzing the two distinctive code bases of a single web application and have developed techniques to check consistencies between these two code bases.

Test input generation. A rich literature exists on automating the task of test input generation [21, 16, 19, 11, 14, 15, 22]. Saxena et al. Kudzu [21] combines the use of random test generation and symbolic execution for testing JavaScript applications with a goal to find code injection vulnerabilities in the client-side code that result from untrusted data provided as arguments to sensitive operations. Halfond et al. [16] employ symbolic execution and constraint solving to infer web application interfaces for improved testing and analysis of web applications. Kieżun et al. [19] use symbolic execution and a library of attack strings to find code injection attacks in web applications. Sen et al. [22] propose a technique that combines concrete and symbolic execution to avoid redundant test cases as well as false warnings. Authors of [15, 14] propose techniques to record an actual run of the program under test on either a well-formed input [15] or random inputs [14], symbolically evaluate the recorded trace, and gather constraints on inputs capturing how the program uses these. The collected constraints are then negated one by one and solved with a constraint solver, producing new inputs that exercise different control paths in the program. Although WAPTEC aims to find hostile inputs and in that sense is similar to these approaches, our formulation of the parameter tampering problem as one checking the consistency of the server and client codebases and development of web application specific methods such as perturbation that are specialized to this problem makes it distinctive.

Emmi et al. [11] concolically execute server-side code and analyze executed SQL queries to find missing database records to improve branch coverage in testing. WAPTEC tests legacy applications that typically contain relevant records in databases and extracts database constraints to improve precision of results. A key technical difference is that Emmi et al. decode WHERE clauses to reason about "missing records" in the current database and do not elaborate satisfying "database metadata" (typically database table schema) to generate such inputs. WAPTEC's database handling criteria is based on such schema analysis. In particular, it relies on the insight that database schema encodes constraints that must be satisfied by acceptable hostile and benign inputs.

Input validation. The lack of sufficient input validation is a major source of security vulnerabilities in web applications, including the type of vulnerabilities reported in this paper. As a result, there is a fairly well developed body of literature in server side techniques that attempt to curb the impact of untrusted data. Attacks such as SQL injection and Cross-site Scripting are well studied (e.g., [24] and many others) examples in which untrusted data can result in unauthorized actions in a web application. WAPTEC is similar to such studies in the sense that it can find vulnerabilities that could be exploited by SQL injection or Cross-site Scripting attacks. However, WAPTEC uses client-side code as a specification of the expected server-side behavior and hence is able to also find logic vulnerabilities that do not necessarily require code injection. Few recent works have focused on automatically discovering parameter pollution [3] and parameter tampering vulnerabilities [7]. Bethea et al. [6] discuss enforcement strategies for misbehaving clients in the context of online games. Jayaraman et al. [18] present an approach to enforce intended sequence of requests in web applications to prevent request integrity attacks.

Sanitization. Sanitization of inputs is an effective layer of defense for attacks that ride user inputs. Typically sanitization aims to re-write hostile inputs to render them benign. Unfortunately, there is no standard technique to sanitize user inputs which often results in vulnerable applications that inadequately sanitize inputs. Saner [4] attempts to identify and validate adequacy of sanitization routines in web applications. It models sanitization performed by web application as an automata and detects inadequacy by finding nonempty intersections with automata characterizing successful attacks. Recently, BEK [17] proposes a language for writing sanitizers that enables systematic reasoning about their correctness. To select a server-side control path to analyze, WAPTEC generates inputs that satisfy the client-side validation. In general, this leads to selection of paths in the server-side code that do not sanitize user inputs. For cases where sanitization is performed on all control paths, WAPTEC offers a limited reasoning of sanitization. In summary, all of the above research works provide the much needed starting points for sound reasoning about sanitization in web applications, an important area that needs further research.

8. CONCLUSION

In this paper, we presented WAPTEC, an approach and tool for automatically generating exploits for parameter tampering vulnerabilities. Our approach uses a combination of formal logic and constraint solving, symbolic evaluation and dynamic analysis. We presented an evaluation of six open source applications and our tool was able to find at least one exploit in every single application. Our paper illustrates that it is indeed possible to extract and use specifications of intended behavior from its own (client side) code. The numerous exploits found by our approach further illustrate that there does exist a gap between validation checks that must happen in a web application and those that actually happen.

Acknowledgements

This work was partially supported by National Science Foundation grants CNS-0845894, CNS-0917229 and CNS-1065537. Thanks are due to Kalpana Gondi for her helpful comments. Finally, we thank the anonymous referees for their feedback.

9. REFERENCES

[1] Google Web Toolkit. `http://www.google.com/webtoolkit/`.

[2] Ruby on Rails. `http://www.rubyonrails.org/`.

[3] BALDUZZI, M., GIMENEZ, C. T., BALZAROTTI, D., AND KIRDA, E. Automated Discovery of Parameter Pollution Vulnerabilities in Web Applications . In *18th Annual Network and Distributed System Security Symposium* (San Diego, CA, USA, 2011).

[4] BALZAROTTI, D., COVA, M., FELMETSGER, V., JOVANOVIC, N., KRUEGEL, C., KIRDA, E., AND VIGNA, G. Saner: Composing Static and Dynamic Analysis to Validate Sanitization in Web Applications. In *SP'08: Proceedings of the 29th IEEE Symposium on Security and Privacy* (Oakland, CA, USA, 2008).

[5] BALZAROTTI, D., COVA, M., FELMETSGER, V. V., AND VIGNA, G. Multi-Module Vulnerability Analysis of Web-based Applications. In *CCS'07: Proceedings of the 14th ACM Conference on Computer and Communications Security* (Alexandria, Virginia, USA, 2007).

[6] BETHEA, D., COCHRAN, R., AND REITER, M. Server-side Verification of Client Behavior in Online Games. In *NDSS'10: Proceedings of the 17th Annual Network and Distributed System Security Symposium* (San Diego, CA, USA, 2010).

[7] BISHT, P., HINRICHS, T., SKRUPSKY, N., BOBROWICZ, R., AND VENKATAKRISHNAN, V. NoTamper: Automatic Blackbox Detection of Parameter Tampering Opportunities in Web Applications. In *17th ACM Conference on Computer and Communications Security* (Chicago, Illinois, USA, 2010).

[8] CHONG, S., LIU, J., MYERS, A. C., QI, X., VIKRAM, K., ZHENG, L., AND ZHENG, X. Secure Web Application via Automatic Partitioning. *SIGOPS Oper. Syst. Rev. 41*, 6 (2007), 31–44.

[9] COOPER, E., LINDLEY, S., WADLER, P., AND YALLOP, J. Links: Web programming without tiers. In *FMCO* (2006).

[10] CORCORAN, B. J., SWAMY, N., AND HICKS, M. Cross-tier, label-based security enforcement for web applications. In *Proceedings of the ACM SIGMOD International Conference on Management of Data (SIGMOD)* (June 2009), pp. 269–282.

[11] EMMI, M., MAJUMDAR, R., AND SEN, K. Dynamic Test Input Generation for Database Applications. In *ISSTA'07: Proceedings of the 2007 International Symposium on Software Testing and Analysis* (London, UK, 2007).

[12] ENGLER, D., CHEN, D. Y., HALLEM, S., CHOU, A., AND CHELF, B. Bugs as Deviant Behavior: A General Approach to Inferring Errors in Systems Code. In *18th ACM Symposium on Operating Systems Principles* (Banff, Alberta, Canada, 2001).

[13] FELMETSGER, V., CAVEDON, L., KRUEGEL, C., AND VIGNA, G. Toward Automated Detection of Logic Vulnerabilities in Web Applications. In *19th USENIX Security Symposium* (Washington, DC, USA, 2010).

[14] GODEFROID, P., KLARLUND, N., AND SEN, K. DART: Directed Automated Random Testing. *SIGPLAN Not. 40*, 6 (2005), 213–223.

[15] GODEFROID, P., LEVIN, M. Y., AND MOLNAR, D. A. Automated Whitebox Fuzz Testing. In *NDSS'08: Proceedings of the 15th Annual Network and Distributed System Security Symposium* (San Diego, CA, USA, 2008).

[16] HALFOND, W., ANAND, S., AND ORSO, A. Precise Interface Identification to Improve Testing and Analysis of Web Applications. In *ISSTA'09: Proceedings of the ACM SIGSOFT International Symposium on Software Testing and Analysis* (Chicago, IL, USA, 2009).

[17] HOOIMEIJER, P., LIVHSITS, B., MOLNAR, D., SAXENA, P., AND VEANES, M. Fast and Precise Sanitizer Analysis with BEK. In *20th USENIX Security Symposium* (San Francisco, CA, USA, 2011).

[18] JAYARAMAN, K., LEWANDOWSKI, G., TALAGA, P. G., AND CHAPIN, S. J. Enforcing Request Integrity in Web Applications. In *DBSec'10: Proceedings of the 24th Annual IFIP WG 11.3 Working Conference on Data and Applications Security and Privacy* (Rome, Italy, 2010).

[19] KIEŻUN, A., J. GUO, P., JAYARAMAN, K., AND D. ERNST, M. Automatic Creation of SQL Injection and Cross-site Scripting Attacks. In *ICSE'09: Proceedings of the 31st International Conference on Software Engineering* (Washington, DC, USA, 2009).

[20] KING, J. C. Symbolic execution and program testing. *Commun. ACM 19*, 7 (1976).

[21] SAXENA, P., AKHAWE, D., HANNA, S., MAO, F., MCCAMANT, S., AND SONG, D. A Symbolic Execution Framework for JavaScript. In *31st IEEE Symposium on Security and Privacy* (Oakland, CA, USA, 2010).

[22] SEN, K., MARINOV, D., AND AGHA, G. CUTE: A Concolic Unit Testing Engine for C. In *10th European Software Engineering Conference*.

[23] SRIVASTAVA, V., BOND, M. D., MCKINLEY, K. S., AND SHMATIKOV, V. A Security Policy Oracle: Detecting Security Holes using Multiple API Implementations. In *ACM Conference on Programming Language Design and Implementation* (San Jose, CA, USA, 2011).

[24] SU, Z., AND WASSERMANN, G. The Essence of Command Injection Attacks in Web Applications. In *33rd symposium on Principles of programming languages* (Charleston, SC, USA, 2006).

[25] TAN, L., ZHANG, X., MA, X., XIONG, W., AND ZHOU, Y. AutoISES: Automatically Inferring Security Specifications and Detecting Violations. In *17th USENIX Security Symposium* (San Jose, CA, USA, 2008).

Context-Sensitive Auto-Sanitization in Web Templating Languages Using Type Qualifiers

Mike Samuel
Google Inc.
Mountain View, CA, USA
mikesamuel@gmail.com

Prateek Saxena
Computer Science Division
UC Berkeley
Berkeley, CA, USA
prateeks@cs.berkeley.edu

Dawn Song
Computer Science Division
UC Berkeley
Berkeley, CA, USA
dawnsong@cs.berkeley.edu

ABSTRACT

Scripting vulnerabilities, such as cross-site scripting (XSS), plague web applications today. Most research on defense techniques has focused on securing existing legacy applications written in general-purpose languages, such as Java and PHP. However, recent and emerging applications have widely adopted web templating frameworks that have received little attention in research. Web templating frameworks offer an ideal opportunity to ensure safety against scripting attacks by secure construction, but most of today's frameworks fall short of achieving this goal.

We propose a novel and principled type-qualifier based mechanism that can be bolted onto existing web templating frameworks. Our solution permits rich expressiveness in the templating language while achieving backwards compatibility, performance and formal security through a context-sensitive auto-sanitization (CSAS) engine. To demonstrate its practicality, we implement our mechanism in Google Closure Templates, a commercially used open-source templating framework that is used in GMail, Google Docs and other applications. Our approach is fast, precise and retrofits to existing commercially deployed template code without requiring any changes or annotations.

Categories and Subject Descriptors: D.4.6 Operating Systems: Security and Protection; D.1.2 Programming Techniques: Automatic Programming

General Terms: Languages, Security

Keywords: Cross-site Scripting, Type Systems

1. INTRODUCTION

Scripting vulnerabilities, such as cross-site scripting [36] and cross-channel scripting [6], are pervasive in web applications [1, 7, 8, 10, 41], embedded systems [6, 17] and on smartphone platforms [9]. A central reason for this wide-spread prevalence is the ad-hoc nature of output generation from web applications today. Web applications emit code intermixed with data in an unstructured way. *Web application output* is essentially text strings which can be emitted from the server-side code (in Java or PHP) or from client-side code in JavaScript. When a portion of the application output controlled by the attacker is parsed by the browser as a script, a scripting attack results.

The predominant first-line of defense against scripting vulnerabilities is *sanitization*—the process of applying encoding or filtering primitives, called *sanitization primitives* or *sanitizers*, to render dangerous constructs in untrusted inputs inert [1, 38, 49, 50]. However, the practice of manually applying sanitizers is notoriously prone to errors [1, 27, 33, 41–43].

Web Templating Frameworks. To streamline the output generation from application code, numerous web templating frameworks have recently emerged and are gaining wide-spread adoption [11–14, 20, 25, 34, 40, 44, 45, 48, 53, 54]. Web templating frameworks allow developers to specify their application's output generation logic in code units or modules called *templates*. Templates take *untrusted inputs* which may be controlled by the attacker and emit web application outputs, such as HTML or CSS code, as strings. String outputs from templates are composed of static or constant strings written by developers, which are explicitly trusted, and untrusted inputs which must be sanitized. These templates can be compiled into a *target language*, such as JavaScript or Java/PHP, as code functions that take untrusted data as template arguments and emit the application's output as strings. Templates are written in a different language, called a *templating language*, the semantics of which are much simpler as compared to that of the target language. Notably, complex constructs such as JavaScript's `eval` and `document.write` are not included in the templating language. Code external to templates is responsible for invoking compiled templates to obtain the string outputs and evaluating/rendering them in the browser.

Vision. Ideally, we would like to create web applications that are secure by construction. In fact, web templating frameworks offer an ideal opportunity to relieve the developers from the burden of manual sanitization by *auto-sanitizing*—inserting sanitization primitives automatically during the compilation of templates to server-side or client-side code. Despite this ideal opportunity, research so far has not broached the topic of building auto-sanitization defenses in today's commercial templating frameworks.

Challenges. In this work, we first identify the following practical challenges in building reliable and usable auto-sanitization in today's web templating frameworks:

- *Context-sensitivity.* XSS sanitization primitives vary

significantly based on the *context* in which the data sanitized is being rendered. For instance, applying the default HTML escaping sanitizer is recommended for untrusted values placed inside HTML tag content context [38]; however, for URL attribute context (such as `src` or `href`) this sanitizer is insufficient because the `javascript` URI protocol (possibly masked) can be used to inject malicious code [21]. We say, therefore, that each sanitization primitive *matches* a context in which it provides safety. Many developers fail to consistently apply the sanitizers matching the context, as highlighted in a recent study performed on a large commercial application well-audited for security [43].

- *Complexity of language constructs.* Templating languages today permit a variety of complex constructs: support for string data-type operations, control flow constructs (`if-else`, loops) and `calls` to splice the output of one template into another. Untrusted input variables may, in such languages, be used in one context along one execution path and a different context along another path. With such rich language features, determining the context for each use of untrusted input variables becomes a path-sensitive, global data-flow analysis task. Automatically applying correct sanitization on all paths in templating code becomes challenging.
- *Backwards compatibility with existing code.* Developers may have already applied sanitizers in existing template code at arbitrary places; an auto-sanitization mechanism should not undo existing sanitization unless it is unsafe. For practical adoption, auto-sanitization techniques should only supplement missing sanitizers or fix incorrectly applied ones, without placing unnecessary restrictions on where to sanitize data.
- *Performance Overhead.* Auto-sanitized templates should have a minimal performance overhead. Previous techniques propose parsing template outputs with a high-fidelity HTML parser at runtime to determine the context [5]. However, the overhead of this mechanism may be high and undesirable for many practical applications.

Context-sensitive Auto-sanitization Problem. We observe that a set of contexts in which applications commonly embed untrusted data is known [50]. And, we assume that for each such context, a matching sanitizer is externally provided. Extensive recent effort has focused on developing a library of safe or correctly-implemented sanitization primitives [22, 23, 29, 30, 38, 41]. We propose to develop an automatic system that, given a template and a library of sanitizers, automatically sanitizes each untrusted input with a sanitizer that matches the context in which it is rendered. By auto-sanitizing templates in this context-sensitive way, in addition to enforcing the security properties we outline in Section 2.2, templating systems can ensure that scripting attacks never result from using template outputs in intended contexts.

Our Approach & Contributions. In this paper, we address the outlined challenges with a principled approach:

- *Type Qualifier Based Approach.* We propose a type-based approach to automatically ensure context sensitive sanitization in templates. We introduce *context type qualifiers*, a kind of type qualifier that represents the *context* in which untrusted data can be safely embedded. Based on these qualifiers, which refine the base type system of the templating language, we define a new type system. Type safety in our type system guarantees that well-typed templates have all untrusted inputs context-sensitively sanitized.
- *Type Inference during Compilation.* To transform existing developer-written templates into well-typed templates, we develop a Context-Sensitive Auto-Sanitization (CSAS) engine which runs during the compilation stage of a web templating framework. The CSAS engine performs two high-level operations. First, it performs a static type inference to infer context type qualifiers for all variables in templates. Second, based on the inferred context types, the CSAS engine automatically inserts sanitization routines into the generated server-side or client-side code. To the best of our knowledge, our approach is the first principled approach using type qualifiers and type inference for context-sensitive auto-sanitization in templates.
- *Real-world Deployability.* To show that our design is practical, we implement our type system in Google Closure Templates, a commercially used open-source templating framework that is used in large applications such as GMail and Google Docs. Our implementation shows that our approach requires less than 4000 lines of code to be built into an existing commercial web framework. Further, we show that retrofitting our type system to existing templates used in commercial applications requires no changes or annotations to existing code.
- *Improved Security.* Our approach eliminates the critical drawbacks of existing approaches to auto-sanitization in today's templating frameworks. Though all the major web frameworks today support customizable sanitization primitives, a majority of them today do not automatically apply them in templates, leaving this error-prone exercise to developers. Most others automatically sanitize all untrusted variables with the same sanitizer in a *context-insensitive* manner, a fundamentally unsafe design that provides a false sense of security [50]. Google AutoEscape, the only context-sensitive abstraction we are aware of, does not handle the richness of language features we address. We refer readers to Section 7 for a detailed comparison.
- *Fast, Precise and Mostly Static Approach.* We evaluate our type inference system on 1035 existing real-world Closure templates. Our approach offers practical performance overhead of 3 – 9.6% on CPU intensive benchmarks. In contrast, the alternative runtime parsing approach incurs 78% - 510% overhead on the same benchmarks. Our approach performs all parsing and context type inference statically and so achieves significantly better performance. Our approach does not sacrifice any precision in context-determination as compared to the runtime parsing approach— it defers context-sensitive sanitization to runtime for a small fraction of output operations in which pure static typing is too imprecise. Hence, our type system is *mostly static*, yet precise.

2. PROBLEM DEFINITION

The task of auto-sanitization is challenging because state-

Base Types	$\alpha ::=$	$\beta \mid \eta \mid \beta_1 \rightarrow \beta_2 \rightarrow \ldots \beta_k \rightarrow$ unit
	$\beta ::=$	bool | int | string | unit
Commands	$S ::=$	**print** $(e : \beta)$
		$\mid (v : \beta) := (e : \beta)$
		| **callTemplate** $f\ (e_1, \ldots, e_k)$
		$\mid c_1\ ;\ S_1$
		| **if**(e : *bool*) **then** S_1 **else** S_2 **fi**
		| **while**(e : *bool*) S_1
		| **return**;
Expressions	$e ::=$	$(e_1 : \texttt{int}) \oplus (e_2 : \texttt{int})$
		$\mid (e_1 : \texttt{bool}) \odot (e_2 : \texttt{bool})$
		$\mid (e_1 : \texttt{string}) \cdot (e_2 : \texttt{string})$
		| **const** $(i : \beta)$
		$\mid v : \beta$
		| **San** $(f, e : \beta)$
	$v ::=$	*Identifier*

Figure 1: The syntax of a simple templating language. $\oplus$ represents the standard integer and bitvector arithmetic operators, $\odot$ represents the standard boolean operations and $\cdot$ is string concatenation. The *San* expression syntactically refers to applying a sanitizer.

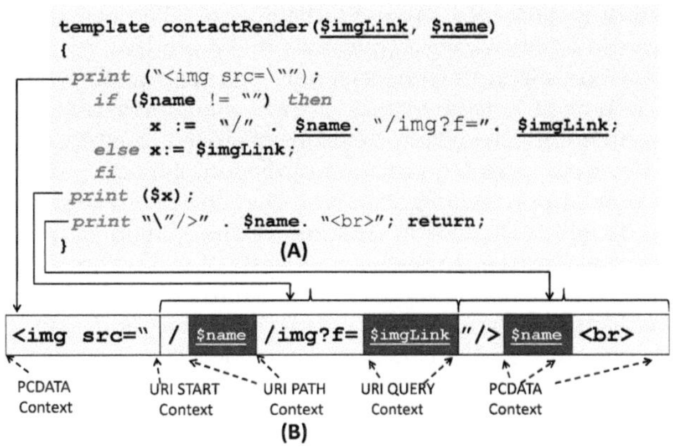

Figure 2: (A) shows a template used as running example. (B) shows the output buffer after the running example has executed the path including the true branch of the `if` statement.

of-the-art templating frameworks don't restrict templates to be straight-line code. In fact, most templating frameworks today permit control-flow constructs and string data operations to allow application logic to conditionally alter the template output at runtime. To illustrate the issues, we describe a simple templating language that captures the essence of the output-generating logic of web applications. We motivate our approach by showing the various challenges that arise in a running example written in our templating language.

2.1 A Simple Templating Language

Our simple templating language is expressive enough to model Google Closure Templates and several other frameworks. We use this templating language to formalize and describe our type-based approach in later sections. It is worth noting that the simple templating language we present here is only an illustrative example—our type-based approach is more general and can be applied to other templating languages as well.

The syntax for the language is presented in Figure 1. The templating language has two kinds of data types in its base type system: the primitive (`string, bool, int`) types and a special type (denoted as η) for *output buffers*, which are objects to which templates write their outputs. Figure 2(A) shows a running example in our templating language. For simplicity, we assume in our language that there is only a single, global output buffer to which all templates append their output, similar to the default model in PHP.

Command Semantics. The primary command in the language is the `print` command which appends the value of its only operand as a string to the output buffer. The running example has several `print` commands. Note that the syntax ensures that the output buffer (η-typed object) can not be reassigned, or tampered with in the rest of the command syntax.

Templates are akin to functions: they can call or invoke other templates via the `callTemplate` command. This command allows a template to invoke another template during its execution, thereby splicing the callee's outputs into its own. Parameter passing follows standard pass-by-value semantics.

The templating language allows control-flow commands such as `for` and `if-then-else` to allow dynamic construction of template outputs. It supports the usual boolean and integer operations as well as string concatenation. We exclude more complex string manipulation operations like string substitution and interpolation functions from the simple language; with simple extensions, their semantics can be modeled as string concatenations [41].

Restricting Command Semantics. The semantics of the templating language is much simpler than that of a general-purpose language that templates may be compiled to. Notably, for instance, the templating language does not have any dynamic evaluation commands such as JavaScript's `eval` or `document.write`. Therefore, final code evaluation in DOM evaluation constructs or serialization to the HTTP response stream is performed by external application code. For instance, Figure 3 below shows a JavaScript application code written outside the templating language which invokes the function compiled from the running example template. It renders the returned result string dynamically using a `document.write`. Therefore, the template code analysis does not need to model the complex semantics of `document.write` [1].

```
<script>
var o = new soy.StringBuilder();
contactRender({O: o, imglink: $_GET('extlink'),
               name: [$_GET('name')] }));
document.write(o);
</script>
```

Figure 3: Psuedo-code of how external application code, such as client-side Javascript, can invoke the compiled templates.

2.2 Problem Definition & Security Properties

In this paper, we focus on the following problem: given a templating language such as the one in Section 2.1, and a set of correct sanitization routines for different contexts, the goal is to automatically apply the correct sanitization primitives during compilation to all uses of untrusted inputs in constructing template outputs, while satisfying the following properties.

[1]The semantics of `document.write` varies based on whether the `document` object is open or closed.

Property NOS: No Over-Sanitization. The templating language allows string expressions to be emitted at `print` operations. String expressions may be constructed by concatenation of constant/static strings and untrusted input variables; only the latter should be sanitized or else we risk breaking the intended structure of the template output. For instance in our running example, the auto-sanitization engine should *not* place a sanitizer at the statement `print ($x)`, because the expression `x` consists of a constant string as well as untrusted input value. Sanitizing at this print statement may strip out the / or ? characters rendering the link unusable and breaking the intended structure of the page.

Property CSAN: Context-Sensitive Sanitization. Each untrusted input variable should be sanitized with a sanitizer matching the context in which it is rendered in. However, this is challenging because untrusted inputs may be used in two different contexts along two different paths. In our running example, the `$imgLink` variable is used both in a URI context as well as a HTTP parameter context, both of which have different sanitization requirements. Similary, untrusted inputs can be rendered in two different contexts even along the same path, as seen for the variable `$name` in Figure 2 (B). We term such use of inputs in multiple contexts as a *static context ambuiguity*, which arise because of path-sensitive nature of the template output construction logic and because of multiple uses of template variables. Section 4 describes further scenarios where context ambiguity may arise.

Property CR: Context Restriction. Template developers should be forbidden from mistakenly using untrusted values in contexts other than ones for which matching sanitizers are available. Certain contexts are known to be hard to sanitize, such as in an unqouted JavaScript string literal placed directly in a JavaScript eval [21], and thus should be forbidden.

Determining Final Output Start/End Context. For each template, we infer the contexts in which the template's output can be safely rendered. However, since the final output is used external to the template code, providing a guarantee that external code uses the output in an intended context is beyond the scope of our problem. For example, it is unsafe for external code to render the output of the running example in a JavaScript `eval`, but such properties must be externally checked.

2.3 Motivation for Our Approach

If a templating langauge has no control-flow or `callTemplate` constructs and no constructs to create string expressions, all templates would be straight-line code with `prints` of constant strings or untrusted variables. Auto-sanitizating such templates is a straight-forward 3-step process— (a) parse the template statically using a high-fidelity parser (like HTMLPurify [23]), (b) determine the context at each `print` of untrusted inputs and (c) apply the matching sanitizer to it. Unfortunately, real templating languages are often richer like our templating language and more sophisticated techniques are needed.

One possible extension of the approach for straight-line code is to defer the step of parsing and determing contexts to runtime execution [5]. We call this approach a *context-sensitive runtime parsing* (or CSRP) approach, where a parser parses all output from the compiled template, determines the context of each `print` of untrusted input and sanitizes it at runtime. This approach has additional performance overhead due to cost of parsing all application output at runtime, as previously shown [5] and as we evaluate in Section 6. If string operations are supported in the language, the performance penalty may be exacerbated because of the need for tracking untrusted values during execution.

Instead, we propose a new "mostly static" approach which off-loads expensive parsing steps to a static type analysis phase. Contexts for most uses of untrusted data can be statically determined and their sanitizers can be selected during compile-time; only a small fraction need the more expensive CSRP-like sanitizer selection in our approach—hence our approach is "mostly static".

Assumptions. Our type-based approach relies on a set of assumptions which we summarise below:

1. *Canonical Parser.* To reliably determine the contexts in which untrusted inputs are rendered, constant/static strings in templates must parse according to a canonical grammar which reliably parses in the same way across major browsers. This restriction is necessary to ensure that our context determination is consistent with its actual parsing in the client's browser, which is challenging because browser parsing behaviors vary in idiosyncratic ways. In our approach, templates not complying with our canonical grammar do not typecheck as per our type rules defined in section 4. Google AutoEscape based frameworks such as GWT and CTemplate already tackle the practical issue of developing such a canonical grammar [11, 13, 20]; our engine leverages this existing code base.
2. *Sanitizer Correctness.* As mentioned previously, we assume that a set of contexts in which applications commonly render untrusted inputs is known and their matching sanitizers are externally available. Creating sanitizers that work across major browser versions is an orthogonal challenge being actively researched [22, 23].
3. *End-to-End Security.* As explained earlier, if the external code renders the template outputs in an unintended context or tampers with the template's output before emitting it to the browser, the end-to-end security is not guaranteed. Ensuring correctness of external code that uses template outputs is beyond the scope of the problem we focus here—lint tools, static analysis and code conformance testing can help enforce this discipline externally.

3. OUR APPROACH

In our type-based approach, we enforce the aforementioned security properties by attaching or qualifying variables and expressions in templates with a new kind of qualifier which we call the *context type qualifier.* Type qualifiers are a formal mechanism to extend the basic type safety of langauge to enforce additional properties [16]. Context type qualifiers play different roles for the various expressions they qualify. For an untrusted input variable, the context type qualifier captures the contexts in which the variable can be safely rendered. An untrusted input becomes safe for rendering in a certain context only after it is sanitized by a sanitizer matching that context. Unsanitized inputs have the `UNSAFE` qualifier attached, and are not safe to be a part

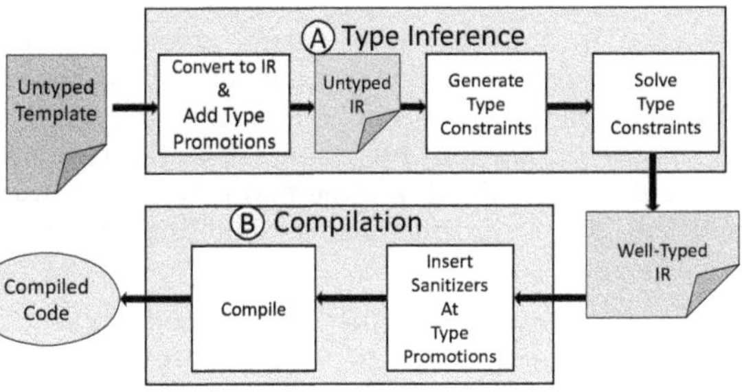

Figure 4: Overview of our CSAS engine.

Types	τ ::=	$\mathcal{Q}_1\ \beta \mid \mathcal{Q}_2\ \eta$	
Base Types	α ::=	$\beta \mid \eta \mid \beta_1 \to \beta_2 \to \ldots$ unit	
	β ::=	bool | int | string | unit	
Type Qualifiers	$\mathcal{Q}$ ::=	$\mathcal{Q}_1 \mid \mathcal{Q}_2 \mid \vec{\mathcal{Q}_1} \to [\mathcal{Q}_2 \to \mathcal{Q}_2]$	
	$\mathcal{Q}_1$ ::=	UNSAFE	
		| $\mathtt{STATIC}_{c_1 \hookrightarrow c_2}$	$c_1, c_2 \in \mathcal{C}$
		| $\mathtt{DYN}_{SC}$	$SC \in 2^{\mathcal{C} \times \mathcal{C}}$
	$\mathcal{Q}_2$ ::=	$\mathtt{CTXSTAT}_c$	$c \in \mathcal{C}$
		| $\mathtt{CTXDYN}_S$	$S \in 2^{\mathcal{C}}$
Contexts	$\mathcal{C}$ ::=	PCDATA | RCDATA | ...	

Figure 5: The final types τ are obtained by augmenting base types of the language α with type qualifiers $\mathcal{Q}$

of any expression that is used in a `print` statement. For constant/static string expressions, context type qualifiers capture the result of parsing the expression, that is, the start context in which the expression will validly parse and the context that will result after parsing the expression. When the template code constructs an output string expression by concatenating a constant string and an untrusted input, a type rule over context qualifiers of the two strings ensures that the untrusted input is only rendered in contexts for which it is sanitized.

This rule only enforces the `CSAN` property in the concatenation operation. Several additional rules are needed to enforce all the outlined security properties to cover all operations in our templating language. We describe the full type system with formal type rules over context type qualifiers in section 4. The type safety of the type system implies that the security properties outlined in Section 2.2 are enforced.

CSAS Engine. The input to our auto-sanitization engine is an existing template which may be completely devoid of sanitizers. We call these templates *untyped* or vanilla templates. The task of our auto-sanitization engine is two-fold: (a) to convert untyped or vanilla templates into an internal representation (or IR) complying with our type rules (called the well-typed IR), and (b) to compile the well-typed IR to the target language code with sanitization. We develop a CSAS engine in the compiler of a templating framework to handle these tasks. Figure 4 shows the CSAS architecture. It has two high-level steps: (A) Type Qualifier Inference, and (B) Compilation of CSAS templates.

The qualifier inference step transforms the vanilla template into a well-typed IR and automatically infers the type qualifiers for all program expressions in the IR. The inferred type qualifiers exactly determine where and which sanitizers are required for untrusted inputs. The well-typed IR must conform to the type rules that we define in Section 4. The step (B) compiles the well-typed IR and inserts sanitization primitives and additional instrumentation in the final compiled code. The detailed design of the CSAS engine is presented in Section 5.

4. THE CONTEXT TYPE SYSTEM

In this section, we formally describe our type qualifier mechanism that refines the base type system of the language defined in Section 2.1. We define the associated type rules to which well-typed IR code must conform after the type inference step.

4.1 Key Design Points

The CSAS engine must track the parsing context induced by the application's output at each program point. Each string expression, when parsed by the browser, causes the browser to transition from one context to another. We term this transition induced on the browser by parsing strings as a *context transition*, denoted by the notation $c_1 \hookrightarrow c_2$.

Notion of Context Type Qualifiers. Qualifiers play different roles for different kinds of expressions.

For constant/static strings, the context type qualifier captures the context transition it induces when parsed by our canonical grammar. For example, the constant string `<a href="` is qualified with a $\mathtt{STATIC}_{\mathtt{PCDATA} \hookrightarrow \mathtt{URI\_START}}$ context type qualifier indicating that it parses validly as per our canonical grammar (HTML 5), causing the browser to transition from `PCDATA` context (start of tag) to the `URI_START` context. Unsanitized input variables are by default qualified `UNSAFE`. The type system qualifies them with a $\mathtt{STATIC}_{c \hookrightarrow c'}$ context qualifier, where c and c' are contexts, only after the variable is sanitized with a sanitizer matching the context c. The sanitizer ensures that the untrusted input safely renders in context c—we define this correctness property of the sanitizer more precisely in Section 4.2. Variables qualified `UNSAFE` are not permitted to be used in string expressions that are emitted to the output buffer.

When data is emitted to the output buffer, the analysis engine must track which context the output buffer is in. The global output buffer (base type η) is also qualified with a different set of context type qualifiers, which indicate the context it is in at any given point in the program. For instance, the output buffer which is in a `URI_START` context, say just after `<a href="` is written to it, is annotated with a $\mathtt{CTXSTAT}_{\mathtt{URI\_START}}$ context qualifier. The context-sensitivity property is enforced by matching the context type qualifiers of the output buffer and the string expression being written at each `print` command. For example, when an untrusted variable is emitted to a $\mathtt{CTXSTAT}_c$ qualified buffer, it must have the $\mathtt{STATIC}_{c \hookrightarrow c'}$ qualifier attached, ensuring that it has been sanitized (or made safe) for rendering in context c.

We formally define the qualifiers in Figure 5. As explained, the type system defines two separate sets of type qualifiers: $\mathcal{Q}_1$ and $\mathcal{Q}_2$. Type qualifiers $\mathcal{Q}_2$ annotate the output buffer, which is an object of base type η, whereas the set $\mathcal{Q}_1$ exclusively qualifies other typed expressions. Type qualifiers of the form $\vec{\mathcal{Q}_1} \to [\mathcal{Q}_2 \to \mathcal{Q}_2]$ are inferred for each template function, which capture the expected qualifier types for the arguments and the template's effect on the output buffer, as explained in further detail in Section 4.2.

Handling Context ambiguity with Flow-Sensitivity. Untrusted inputs may be used in different contexts along different or even the same program paths. This leads to

```
template StatAmb($imgLink, $name)
{
    if ($name == "") then print ("<img src=\"");
    else print ("<div>"); fi
    print ($imgLink);
    if ($name == "") then print ("\" />");
    else print ("</div>"); fi; return;
}
```

Figure 6: An example of a template with static context ambiguity requiring a mixed static-dynamic approach.

context ambiguity, as explained in Section 2.2. A standard flow-insensitive type inference algorithm would infer that such an untrusted input has no single precise context qualifier because of its ambiguous usage in multiple different contexts. To handle such context ambiguity, we design our type system to be *flow-sensitive*— a flow-sensitive type system permits program variables to have varying type qualifiers at different program locations [16].

Mixed Static-Dynamic Typing. Flow-sensitive typing does address static ambiguity to a large extent, but not all of the cases we observe in practice. Consider a template such as the one in Figure 6. In one branch the program writes `<div>` and in the other it writes `<img src="` to the global output buffer. The context that output buffer is in at the join point is statically ambiguous, and consequently, statically selecting sanitizers on subsequent `print` statements in the template is not possible. Similar examples of static ambiguity have been shown to arise in large legacy applications [43].

Our approach avoids throwing type errors for such static ambiguous types by using the following approach: we further divide the type qualifiers into *statically-qualified* and *dynamically-qualified* sets. Qualifiers $\mathcal{Q}_2$ for the output buffer are either static qualifiers ($\mathtt{CTXSTAT}_C$) or dynamic ($\mathtt{CTXDYN}_S$). At a given program location, if the output buffer is unambiguously determined to be in a single context c, a static qualifier is attached to it. In contrast, when the embedding context of the buffer is statically ambiguous (or imprecise), as in the example of Figure 6, it is over-approximated by a set of contexts S and is qualified with the dynamic qualifer $\mathtt{CTXDYN}_S$. $\mathtt{CTXDYN}_S$ signifies that the buffer is in one of the contexts determined by the set S. Sanitizers can be statically selected for statically-qualified objects since their contexts are precisely known. For dynamically-qualified buffers, the context-sensitive runtime parsing (or CSRP) approach is employed—data written to such buffers is parsed and sanitized at runtime.

Qualifiers $\mathcal{Q}_1$ for other program expressions are similarly partitioned into static or dynamic sets—for instance, a string expression used in a `print` statement with a dynamically-qualified output buffer is also dynamically-qualified in our type system using the $\mathtt{DYN}_S$ qualifier. The set S is a static over-approximation of the set of context transitions that the string expression can induce. Sanitizer selection can be done statically for statically-qualified (such as $\mathtt{STATIC}_{c_1 \hookrightarrow c_2}$) expressions and these sanitizers can be placed during compilation. For dynamically-qualified expressions, however, since the context of the output buffer is known only at runtime, the sanitizer selection is performed by the CSRP approach. Specifically, the CSAS engine inserts additional instrumentation for dynamically-qualified string expressions to keep the untrusted substrings in the expression separate from constant substrings. At runtime, when such an expression is being used in a `print`, it is parsed at runtime as per the dynamically-determined start context and the necessary sanitization primitives are applied to the untrusted substrings. In our evaluation, less than 1% of the expressions were dynamically-qualified; a large majority of the cases do not incur the cost of runtime parsing, enabling our type system to be "mostly static".

Handling Context Ambiguity for Templates. Static context ambiguity may manifest for template start and end contexts as well. A template may be invoked in multiple starting contexts or may be expected to return in multiple ending contexts. In such cases, our CSAS engine resolves the ambiguity purely statically, by cloning templates. For templates that may start or end in more than one context, the CSAS engine generates multiple versions of the template during compilation, each specializing to handle a specific pair of start and end contexts.

Inferring Placement of Sanitizers. Our engine can insert sanitizers into code in which developers have manually applied some sanitizers (chosen from the sanitization library), without undoing existing sanitization if it is correct. Our type rules require additional sanitizers to only be inserted at `print` statements and at *type promotion* operations. Type promotion operations identify points where expressions need to be converted from `UNSAFE`-qualified types to statically- or dynamically-qualified types. These type promotion commands have the form $v := (Q)e$, where Q is a qualified type which are introduced by the CSAS engine when converting templates into the IR. Note that this design separates the type inference task from the type safety rules — type promotions may be added anywhere in the IR by the type qualifier inference algorithm, as long as the resulting IR conforms to the type rules after inference.

4.2 Static Type Rules

In this section, we define a set of type rules which impose static restrictions `S0` - `S4` to acheive the 3 properties (`CR`, `CSAN` and `NOV`) described in Section 2.2.

The type system is subdivided into two main kinds of typing judgements, one for typing language expressions (Figure 7) and one for typing language commands (Figure 8). In our type rules, Γ denotes the type environment that maps program variables, the output buffer (denoted by the symbol ρ) and template name symbols to qualifiers $\mathcal{Q}$.

In a flow-sensitive type system like ours, type qualifier for variables change from one program location to another. Therefore, typing judgements for the language commands (Figure 8) capture the effects of command execution on type environments and have the form $\Gamma \vdash c \Longrightarrow \Gamma'$. This judgement states that the command c is well-typed under the type environment Γ and its execution changes the type environment Γ to Γ'. The expression typing judgement $\Gamma \vdash e : Q$ is standard: it states that at the given program location, the expression e has a type qualifier Q under the environment Γ. All expressions that are neither statically-qualified nor dynamically-qualified, map to `UNSAFE` in Γ. The set of declared variables $\mathcal{V}$ and a map $\mathcal{LF}$ from statement labels to their enclosing functions are assumed to be pre-computed and available externally.

Defining Sanitizer Correctness. The soundness of our type system relies on the correctness of externally provided sanitizers. To define sanitizer correctness more precisely, we

$$\frac{v \in \mathcal{V} \qquad \{v \mapsto Q\} \in \Gamma}{\Gamma \vdash v : Q}\text{T-VAR} \qquad \frac{\alpha_i \neq \texttt{string} \qquad c \in \mathcal{C}}{\Gamma \vdash \mathbf{const}(i : \alpha_i) : \texttt{STATIC}_{c \hookrightarrow c}}\text{T-CONST} \qquad \frac{IsParseValid(s, c_1, c_2)}{\Gamma \vdash \mathbf{const}(s : \texttt{string}) : \texttt{STATIC}_{c_1 \hookrightarrow c_2}}\text{T-CONSTSTR}$$

$$\frac{\Gamma \vdash e_1 : \texttt{STATIC}_{c \hookrightarrow c} \qquad \Gamma \vdash e_2 : \texttt{STATIC}_{c \hookrightarrow c} \qquad c \in \mathcal{C}}{\Gamma \vdash (e_1 : \texttt{bool}) \odot (e_2 : \texttt{bool}) : \texttt{STATIC}_{c \hookrightarrow c}}\text{T-BOOL} \qquad \frac{\Gamma \vdash e_1 : \texttt{STATIC}_{c \hookrightarrow c} \qquad \Gamma \vdash e_2 : \texttt{STATIC}_{c \hookrightarrow c} \qquad c \in \mathcal{C}}{\Gamma \vdash (e_1 : \texttt{int}) \oplus (e_2 : \texttt{int}) : \texttt{STATIC}_{c \hookrightarrow c}}\text{T-INT}$$

$$\frac{\Gamma \vdash e_1 : \texttt{STATIC}_{c_1 \hookrightarrow c_2} \qquad \Gamma \vdash e_2 : \texttt{STATIC}_{c_2 \hookrightarrow c_3}}{\Gamma \vdash (e_1 : \texttt{string}) \cdot (e_2 : \texttt{string}) : \texttt{STATIC}_{c_1 \hookrightarrow c_3}}\text{T-STRCAT-STAT} \qquad \frac{\Gamma \vdash e : \texttt{UNSAFE} \quad SanMap(c_1 \hookrightarrow c_2, f) \qquad c_1, c_2 \in \mathcal{C}}{\Gamma \vdash \mathbf{San}(f, e) : \texttt{STATIC}_{c_1 \hookrightarrow c_2}}\text{T-SAN}$$

$$\frac{IsParseValid(s, c_1, c_2)}{\Gamma \vdash \mathbf{const}(s : \texttt{string}) : \texttt{DYN}_{\{c_1 \hookrightarrow c_2\}}}\text{T-CSTRDYN} \qquad \frac{\Gamma \vdash e_1 : \texttt{DYN}_{S_1} \qquad \Gamma \vdash e_2 : \texttt{DYN}_{S_2}}{\Gamma \vdash (e_1 : \texttt{string}) \cdot (e_2 : \texttt{string}) : \texttt{DYN}_{S_1 \bowtie S_2}}\text{T-STRCAT-DYN}$$

Figure 7: Type Rules for Expressions.

$$\frac{\Gamma \vdash e : Q \qquad v \in \mathcal{V}}{\Gamma \vdash v := e \Longrightarrow \Gamma[v \mapsto Q]}\text{T-ASSIGN} \qquad \frac{\Gamma \vdash e : Q \qquad Q \leq Q'}{\Gamma \vdash v_1 := (Q')e \Longrightarrow \Gamma[v_1 \mapsto Q']}\text{T-PROM} \qquad \frac{\Gamma_0 \vdash c_1 : \Gamma_1 \qquad \Gamma_1 \vdash S : \Gamma_2}{\Gamma_0 \vdash c_1; S \Longrightarrow \Gamma_2}\text{T-SEQ}$$

$$\frac{\Gamma \vdash e : \texttt{STATIC}_{c_1 \hookrightarrow c_2} \qquad \Gamma \vdash \rho : \texttt{CTXSTAT}_{c_1}}{\Gamma \vdash \mathbf{print}(e) \Longrightarrow \Gamma[\rho \mapsto \texttt{CTXSTAT}_{c_2}]}\text{T-PRINT-STATIC-1} \qquad \frac{\Gamma \vdash e : \texttt{DYN}_{S_1} \quad \Gamma \vdash \rho : \texttt{CTXDYN}_{S_2} \qquad |CDom(S_1, \mathcal{C}) \cap S_2| \neq 0}{\Gamma \vdash \mathbf{print}(e) \Longrightarrow \Gamma[\rho \mapsto \texttt{CTXDYN}_{CRange(S_1, S_2)}]}\text{T-PRINT-DYN-2}$$

$$\frac{Q_\rho = \texttt{CTXSTAT}_{c_\rho} \qquad Q_{\rho'} = \texttt{CTXSTAT}_{c_{\rho'}} \qquad \begin{matrix}\Gamma \vdash f : (Q_1, Q_2 \dots Q_k) \to [Q_\rho \to Q_{\rho'}] \\ c_\rho, c_{\rho'} \in \mathcal{C} \qquad \bigwedge_{i \in \{1 \dots k\}} (\Gamma \vdash e_i : Q_i)\end{matrix} \qquad \begin{matrix}\Gamma \vdash \rho : Q_\rho \\ \bigwedge_{i \in \{1 \dots k\}} ((Q_i \leq \texttt{STATIC}_{c_i \hookrightarrow c_{i'}}) \wedge (c_i \in \mathcal{C}) \wedge (c_{i'} \in \mathcal{C}))\end{matrix}}{\Gamma \vdash \mathbf{callTemplate}f(e_1, e_2, \dots, e_k) \Longrightarrow \Gamma[\rho \mapsto \texttt{CTXSTAT}_{c_{\rho'}}]}\text{T-CALL}$$

$$\frac{\begin{matrix}\Gamma \vdash \rho : \texttt{CTXSTAT}_c \qquad c \in \mathcal{C} \qquad \{\ell \mapsto f\} \in \mathcal{LF} \\ \Gamma \vdash f : (Q_1, Q_2 \dots Q_k) \to [Q_\rho \to Q_{\rho'}] \qquad Q_{\rho'} = \texttt{CTXSTAT}_c\end{matrix}}{\Gamma \vdash \ell : \mathbf{return;} \Longrightarrow \Gamma}\text{T-RET-STAT} \qquad \frac{\begin{matrix}\Gamma \vdash \rho : Q \\ c \in \mathcal{C} \qquad Q = \texttt{CTXDYN}_S \qquad |S| = 1 \qquad c \in S \qquad \{\ell \mapsto f\} \in \mathcal{LF} \\ \Gamma \vdash f : (Q_1, Q_2 \dots Q_k) \to [Q_\rho \to Q_{\rho'}] \qquad Q_{\rho'} = \texttt{CTXSTAT}_c\end{matrix}}{\Gamma \vdash \ell : \mathbf{return;} \Longrightarrow \Gamma[\rho \mapsto \texttt{CTXSTAT}_c]}\text{T-RET-DYN}$$

$$\frac{\Gamma_0 \vdash S_1 : \Gamma \qquad \Gamma_0 \vdash S_2 : \Gamma}{\Gamma_0 \vdash \mathbf{if}(e)\mathbf{then}S_1\mathbf{else}S_2 \Longrightarrow \Gamma}\text{T-IFELSE} \qquad \frac{\Gamma \vdash S \Longrightarrow \Gamma}{\Gamma \vdash \mathbf{while}(e)S \Longrightarrow \Gamma}\text{T-WHILE}$$

Figure 8: Type Rules for Commands. The output buffer (of base type η) is denoted by the symbol ρ.

reuse the notion of *valid syntactic forms*, formalized by Su et. al. [47]. A sanitizer f is *correct* for a context transition $c_s \hookrightarrow c_e$, if all strings sanitized with f are guaranteed to parse validly starting in context c_s yielding an end context c_e according to our canonical grammar, and if the sentential forms generated during such a parse are valid syntactic forms as per the application's intended security policy [47]. In other words, sanitized strings can span different contexts, but all the intermediate contexts induceded during parsing untrusted strings should be syntactically confined to non-terminals allowed by the application's policy. We assume that a relation $SanMap$, mapping each possible context-transition to a matching sanitizer, is available externally.

S0: No Implicit Type Casts. Our type system separates UNSAFE-qualified, statically-qualified and dynamic-qualified types. It does not permit implicit type conversions between them. Type qualifier conversions are *only* permitted through explicit type promotion operations, according to a *promotibility* relation $\leq$ defined in Figure 9.

$$\frac{}{q \leq q} \qquad \frac{c \in S \qquad S \in 2^{\mathcal{C}}}{\texttt{CTXSTAT}_c \leq \texttt{CTXDYN}_S} \qquad \frac{c_1, c_2 \in \mathcal{C}}{\texttt{UNSAFE} \leq \texttt{STATIC}_{c_1 \hookrightarrow c_2}} \qquad \frac{S \in 2^{\mathcal{C} \times \mathcal{C}}}{\texttt{UNSAFE} \leq \texttt{DYN}_S}$$

Figure 9: The promotibility relation $\leq$ between type qualifiers

Our promotibility relation is different from the standard subtyping relation ($\preceq$)—for example, the following subsumption rule applies in standard subtyping, but our promotibility relation does not adhere to it:

$$\frac{\Gamma \vdash e : Q_s \qquad Q_s \preceq Q_t}{\Gamma \vdash e : Q_t}\text{T-SUB}$$

The static type qualifier-based restrictions S1 and S3 defined below together satisfy the no over-sanitization (NOS) property. Similarly, S2 ensures the context restriction (CR) property. The S3 and S4 together satisfy the context-sensitivity (CSAN) property while maintaining strict separation between dynamically-qualified and statically-qualified expressions.

S1: No Sanitization for Constants. The rules T-CONST, T-CONSTSTR and T-CSTRDYN show that constant string values acquire the type qualifier without any sanitization. These values are program constants, so they are implicitly trusted.

S2: Canonical Parsing. The qualifier parameters (denoting the context-transitions) for trusted constant strings are inferred by parsing them according to the canonical grammar. We assume the availability of such a canonical grammar (assumption 1 in Section 2.3), embodied in a predicate $IsParseValid$ defined below.

DEFINITION 1. *$IsParseValid$ is a predicate of type* `string` $\times \mathcal{C} \times \mathcal{C} \to$ `bool`*, such that $IsParseValid(s, c_1, c_2)$ evaluates to true if and only if the data string s parses validly as per the assumed canonical grammar starting in context c_1 yielding a final context c_2.*

S3: Safe String Expression Creation. The rules for concatenation do not permit strings qualified as UNSAFE to be used in concatenations, forcing the type inference engine to type promote (and hence sanitize) operands *before* they can be used in concatenation opertions. The T-STRCAT-STAT rule ensures that only statically safe strings can be concatenated whereas the T-STRCAT-DYN rule constructs dynamically qualified strings. The latter rule conservatively over-approximates the result's dynamic set of context-transitions that could occur at runtime. For over-approximating sets, we define an inner-join $S_1 \bowtie S_2$ as the set of all context transitions $c_1 \hookrightarrow c_2$ such that $c_1 \hookrightarrow c_3 \in S_1$ and $c_3 \hookrightarrow c_2 \in S_2$.

S4: Context-Sensitive Output. The rules for print commands ensure that the emitted string expression can not be UNSAFE-qualified. Further, the type rule T-PRINT-STATIC-1 ensures that the context type qualifier of the emitted string matches the context of the output buffer, when both of them are statically-qualified.

Only dynamically-qualified strings can be emitted to dynamically qualified output buffers—a strict separation between dynamic and static type qualified expressions is maintained. The T-PRINT-DYN-2 type rule capture this case. This requires a runtime parsing, as described in section 4.3, to determine the precise context. The static type rules compute the resulting context for the output buffer by an over-approximate set, considering the context-transition sets of two dynamically-qualified input operands. To compute the resulting context set, we define 2 operations over a context-transition set S for a dynamically qualified type $\texttt{DYN}_S$:

$$CDom(S, E) = \{C_i | C_i \hookrightarrow C_e \in S, C_e \in E\}$$

$$CRange(S, B) = \{C_i | C_s \hookrightarrow C_i \in S, C_s \in B\}$$

Control flow Commands. Type rules T-IFELSE and T-WHILE for control flow operations are standard, ensuring that the type environment Γ resulting at join points is consistent. Whenever static context ambiguity arises at a join point, the types of the incoming values must be promoted to dynamically-qualified type to conform to the type rules. Our type inference step (as Section 5.1 explains) introduces these type promotions at join points in the untyped IR, so that after type inference completes, the well-typed IR adheres to the T-IFELSE and T-WHILE rules.

Calls and Returns. In our language, templates do not return values but take in parameters passed by value. In addition, templates have side-effects on the global output buffer. For a template f, Γ maps f by name to a type $(Q_1, Q_2, \ldots Q_k) \rightarrow [Q_\rho \rightarrow Q_{\rho'}]$, where $(Q_1, Q_2, \ldots Q_k)$ denotes the expected types of its arguments and $Q_\rho \rightarrow Q_{\rho'}$ denotes the side-effect of f on the global output buffer ρ. The T-CALL rule imposes several restrictions.

First, it enforces that each formal parameter either has a statically-qualified type or is promotible to one (by relation $\leq$). Second, it ensures that the types of actual parameters and the corresponding formal parameters match. Finally, it enforces that each (possibly cloned) template starts and ends in statically precise contexts, by ensuring that Q_ρ and $Q_{\rho'}$ are statically-qualified. The output buffer (ρ) can become dynamically qualified within a template's body, as shown in example of Figure 6, but the context of ρ should be precisely known at the return statement. In the example of Figure 6, the context of ρ is ambiguous at the join-point of the first if-else block. However, we point out that at the return statement the dynamically qualified set of contexts becomes a singleton, that is, the end context is precisely known. The T-RET-DYN rule applies in such cases and soundly converts the qualifier for ρ back to a statically-qualified type.

For templates that do not start and end in precise contexts, our CSAS engine creates multiple clones of the template, as explained in Section 5.1.3, to force conformance to the type rules.

4.3 Sanitization

Handling manually placed sanitizers. The T-SAN rule converts the type of the expression e in the sanitization expression $San(f, e)$ from UNSAFE to a statically-qualified type $\texttt{STATIC}_{c_1 \hookrightarrow c_2}$, only if f is a correct sanitizer for the context transition $c_1 \hookrightarrow c_2$ according to the externally specified $SanMap$ relation.

Auto-sanitization Only at Type Promotions. Other than T-SAN, the T-PROM type rule is the only way an UNSAFE-qualified string can become statically-qualified. The CSAS engine inserts statically selected sanitizers during compilation only at the type promotion command that promote UNSAFE-qualified to statically-qualified strings. For such a command $v := (\texttt{STATIC}_{c_1 \hookrightarrow c_2})e$, the CSAS engine's compilation step automatically inserts the sanitizer which matches the start context c_1 and will ensure that parsing v will safely end in context c_2 .

Type Promotion from UNSAFE to Dynamic. For dynamically qualified strings, the CSAS engine needs to perform runtime parsing and sanitization. To enable this for dynamically-qualified strings, our instrumentation uses an auxiliary data structure, which we call the CSRP-expression, which keeps constant substrings separate from the untrusted components. For conceptual simplicity, our CSRP-expression data structure is simply a string in which untrusted substrings are delimited by special characters $\llparenthesis\rrparenthesis$. These special delimiters are not part of the string alphabet of base templating language.

The T-PROM rule permits promotions from UNSAFE-qualified strings to dynamically-qualified expressions. The CSAS engine inserts instrumentation during compilation to insert the special characters $\llparenthesis\rrparenthesis$ around the untrusted data and to initialize this CSRP-expression with it. The concatenation operation over regular strings naturally extends to CSRP-expressions.

Runtime Parsing and Sanitization. At program points where the output buffer is dynamically-qualified, the CSAS engine adds instrumentation to track its *dynamic context* as a metadata field. The metadata field is updated at each `print`. When a CSRP-expression is written to the output buffer at runtime, the CSRP-expression is parsed starting in the dynamically-tracked context of the output buffer. This parsing procedure internally determines the start and end context of each untrusted substring delimited by $\llparenthesis\rrparenthesis$, and selects sanitizers for them context-sensitively.

We detail the operational semantics for the language and sketch the soundness proof for our type system in the appendix A.

5. CSAS ENGINE

We present the design and implementation of the CSAS engine in this section. The CSAS engine performs two main steps of inferring context type qualifiers and then compiling well-typed IR to JavaScript or server-side Java code with sanitization logic.

5.1 Type Qualifier Inference & Compilation

The goal of the type inference step is to convert untyped or vanilla templates to well-typed IR. In the the qualifier inference step, the CSAS engine first converts template code to an internal SSA representation (untyped IR). The qualifier inference sub-engine is also supposed to add additional type promotions for untrusted inputs, where sanitization primitives will eventually be placed. However, the qualifier inference sub-engine does not *apriori* know where all sanitizations will be needed. To solve this issue, it inserts a set of candidate type promotions, only some of which will be compiled into sanitizers. These candidate type promotions include *type qualifier variables*, i.e., variables whose values are context types and are to be determined by the type inference. They have the form $v' := (Q)e$ where Q is a type qualifier variable, and its exact value is a context type to be determined by the type qualifier inference sub-engine. Next, the type qualifier inference step solves for these qualifier variables by generating type constraints and solving them.

Once constraint solving succeeds, the concrete context type for each qualifier variable is known. These context types can be substituted into the candidate type promotions; the resulting IR is well-typed and is guaranteed to conform to our type rules. In the final compilation step, only some of the candidate type promotions are turned into sanitizer calls. Specifically, type promotions in well-typed IR that essentially cast from a qualified-type to itself, are redundant and don't require any sanitization, whereas those which cast `UNSAFE`-qualified variables into other qualified values are compiled into sanitizers as described in section 4.3.

5.1.1 Inserting Type Promotions with Qualifer Variables

Candidate type promotions are introduced at the following points while converting templates to the untyped IR:

- Each `print` (e) statement is turned into a `print` (v') statement in the IR by creating a fresh internal program variable v'. The CSAS engine also inserts a type promotion (and assignment) statement $v' := (Q)\ e$ preceeding the print statement, creating a qualifier variable Q.
- Each $v = \phi(v_1, v_2)$ statement is turned into equivalent type promotions $v := (Q_1)\ v_1$ and $v := (Q_2)\ v_2$ in the respective branches before the join point, by creating new qualifier variables Q_1 and Q_2 .
- Parameter marshalling from actual parameter "a" to formal parameter "v" is made explicit via a candidate promotion operation $v := (Q)\ a$, by creating new qualifier variable Q.
- A similar type promotion is inserted before the concatenation of a constant string expression with another string expression.

5.1.2 Constraint Solving for Qualifier Variables

The goal of this step is to infer context type qualifiers for qualifier variables. We analyze each template's IR starting with templates that are used by external code— we call these public templates. We generate a version of compiled code for each start and end context in which a template can be invoked, so we try to analyze each public template for each choice of a start and end context. Given a template T, start context c_s and end context c_e, the generic type inference procedure called $TempAnalyze(T, c_s, c_e)$ is described below.

$TempAnalyze(T, c_s, c_e)$ either succeeds having found a satisfying assignment of qualifier variables to context type qualifiers, or it fails if no such assignment is found. It operates over a call-graph of the templates in depth-first fashion starting with T, memoizing the start and end contexts for each template it analyzes in the process. When analyzing the body of a template in IR form, it associates a typemap $\mathcal{L}$ mapping local variables to type qualifiers at each program location. At the start of the inference for T, all local variables are qualified as `UNSAFE` in $\mathcal{L}$. The analysis proceeds from the entry to the exit of the template body statement by statement, updating the context qualifier of each program variable. The context of the output buffer is also updated with the analysis of each statement.

Type rules defined in Figure 8 can be viewed as inference rules as well: for each statement or command in the conclusion of a rule, the premises are type constraints to be satisfied. Similar constraints are implied by type rules for expressions. Our type inference generates and solves these type constraints during the statement by statement analysis using a custom constraint solving procedure.

Several of our type rules are non-deterministic. As an example, the rules `T-CONSTSTR` and `T-CSTRDYN` have identical premises and are non-deterministic because the language syntax alone is insufficient to separate statically and dynamically qualified types. Our constraint solving procedure resolves such non-determinism by backtracking to find a satisfying solution to the constraints. Our inference prefers the most precise (or static) qualifiers over less precise (dynamic) qualifiers as solutions for all qualifier variables during its backtracking-based constraint solving procedure. For instance, consider the non-determinism inherent in the premise involving $IsParseValid$ used in the `T-CONSTSTR` and `T-CSTRDYN` rules. $IsParseValid$ is a one-to-many relation and a constant string may parse validly in many start contexts. Our constraint solving procedure non-deterministically picks one such possible context transition initially, trying to satisfy all instances of the `T-CONSTSTR` rule before that of the `T-CSTRDYN` rule and refines its choice until it finds a context transition under which the static string parses validly. If no instance of the `T-CONSTSTR` rule matches, the engine tries to satisfy the `T-CSTRDYN` rule. Similar, backtracking is also needed when analyzing starting and ending contexts of templates when called via the `callTemplate` operation.

5.1.3 Resolving Context Ambiguity by Cloning

The static typing `T-CALL` rule for `callTemplate` has stringent pre-conditions: it permits a unique start and end context for each template. A templates can be invoked in multiple different start (or end) contexts—our inference handles such cases while keeping the consistency with the type rules by cloning templates. We memoize start and end contexts inferred for each template during the inference analysis. If during constraint generation and solving, we find that a template T is being invoked in start and end contexts different from the ones inferred for T previously during the inference, we create a clone T'. The cloned template has the same body but expects to begin and end in a different start and end context. Cloned templates are also compiled to separate functions and the calls are directed to the appropriate functions based on the start and end contexts.

6. IMPLEMENTATION & EVALUATION

We have implemented our CSAS engine design into a state-of-the-art, commercially used open-source templating framework called Google Closure Templates [45]. Closure Templates are used extensively in large web applications in-

Contexts
HTML PCDATA
HTML RCDATA
HTML TAGNAME
HTML ATTRIBNAME
QUOTED HTMLATTRIB
UNQUOTED HTMLATTRIB
JS STRING
JS REGEX
CSS ID, CLASS, PROPNAME, KEYWDVAL, QUANT
CSS STRING, CSS QUOTED URL, CSS UNQUOTED URL
URL START, URL QUERY, URL GENERAL

Figure 10: A set of contexts $\mathcal{C}$ used throughout the paper.

cluding Gmail, Google Docs and other Google properties. Our auto-sanitized Closure Templates can be compiled both into JavaScript as well as server-side Java code, enabling building reusable output generation elements.

Our implementation is in 3045 lines of Java code, excluding comments and blank lines, and it augments the existing compiler in the Closure Templates with our CSAS engine. All the contexts defined in Figure 10 of the appendix are supported in the implementation with 20 distinct sanitizers.

Subject Benchmarks. For real-world evaluation, we gathered all Closure templates accessible to us. Our benchmarks consist of 1035 distinct Closure templates from Google's commericially deployed applications. The templates were authored by developers prior to our CSAS engine implementation. Therefore, we believe that these examples represent unbiased samples of existing code written in templating languages.

The total amount of code in the templates (excluding file prologues and comments outside the templates) is 21,098 LOC. Our benchmarks make heavy use of control flow constructs such as `callTemplate` calls. Our benchmark's template call-graph is densely connected. It consists of 1035 nodes, 2997 call edges and 32 connected components of size ranging from 2 - 12 templates and one large component with 633 templates. Overall, these templates have a total of 1224 print statements which write untrusted data expressions. The total number of untrusted input variables in the code base is 600, ranging from $0-13$ for different templates. A small ratio of untrusted inputs to untrusted `print` shows that untrusted inputs are used in multiple output expressions, which are one of the main reasons for context ambiguity that motivate our flow-sensitive design.

Evaluation Goals. The goal of our evaluation is to measure how easily our principled type-based approach retrofits to an existing code base. In addition, we compare the security and performance of our "mostly static", context-sensitive approach to the following alternative approaches:

- *No Auto-Sanitization.* This is the predominant strategy in today's web frameworks.
- *Context-insensitive sanitization.* Most remaining web frameworks supplement each output `print` command with the same sanitizer.
- *Context-sensitive runtime parsing sanitization.* As explained earlier, previous systems have proposed determining the contexts by runtime parsing [5]. We compare the performance of our approach against this approach.

6.1 Compatibility & Precision

Our benchmark code was developed prior to our type system. We aim to evaluate the extent to which our approach can retrofit security to existing code templates. To perform this experiment, we disabled all sanitization checks in the benchmarks that may have been previously applied and enabled our auto-sanitization on all of the 1035 templates. We counted what fraction of the templates that were transformed to well-typed compiled code. Our analysis is implemented in Java and takes 1.3 seconds for all the 1035 benchmarks on a platform with 2 GB of RAM, an Intel 2.6 MHz dual-core processor running Linux 2.6.31.

Our static type inference approach avoids imprecision by cloning templates that are called in more than one context. In our analysis, 11 templates required cloning which resulted in increasing the output **print** statements (or sinks) from 1224 initially to 1348 after cloning.

Our main result is that all 1348 output sinks in the 1035 templates were auto-sanitized. No change or annotations to the vanilla templates were required. We test the outputs of the compiled templates by running them under multiple inputs. The output of the templates under our testing was unimpacted and remained completely compatible with that of the vanilla template code.

Our vanilla templates, being commercially deployed, have existing sanitizers manually applied by developers and are well-audited for security by Google. To confirm our compatibility and correctness, we compared the sanitizers applied by our CSAS engine to the those pre-applied in the vanilla versions of the benchmarked code manually by developers. Out of the 1348 print statements emitting untrusted expressions, the sanitization primitives on untrusted inputs exactly match the pre-applied sanitizers in all but 21 cases. In these 21 cases, our CSAS engine applies a more accurate (`escapeHtmlAttribute`) sanitizer versus the more restrictive sanitizer applied previously (`escapeHTML`) by the developer. Both sanitizers defeat scripting attacks; the pre-existing sanitizer was overly restrictive rendering certain characers inert that weren't dangerous for the context. This evaluation strengthens our confidence that our approach does not impact/alter the compatibility of the HTML output, and that our CSAS engine implementation applies sanitization correctly.

Our type qualifier inference on this benchmark statically-qualified expressions written to all but 9 out of the 1348 sinks. That is, for over 99% of the output sinks, our approach can statically determine a single, precise context.

In these 9 cases, the set of ambiguous contexts is small and a single sanitizer that sanitizes the untrusted input for all contexts in this set can be applied. In our present implementation, we have special-cased for such cases by applying a static sanitizer, which is safe but may be over-restrictive. We have recently implemented the CSRP scheme using an auxiliary data structure, as described in Section 4.3, in jQuery templates for JavaScript [28]; we expect porting this implementation to the Google Closure compiler to be a straightforward task in the future.

6.2 Security

To measure the security offered by our approach as compared to the context-insensitive sanitization approach, we count the number of sinks that would be auto-sanitized correctly in our 1035 templates. We assume that a context-insensitive sanitization would supplement the HTML-entity encoding sanitizer to all sinks, which is the approach adopted in popular frameworks such as Django [14]. Picking another sanitizer would only give worse results for the context-

	No Saniti- zation	Context-Insensitive	Context-Sensitive Runtime Parsing	Our Approach
Chrome 9.0	227	234 (3.0%)	406 (78.8%)	234 (3.0%)
FF 3.6	395	433 (9.6%)	2074 (425%)	433 (9.6%)
Safari 5.0	190	195 (2.5%)	550 (189%)	196 (3.1%)
Server:Java	431	431 (0.0%)	2972 (510%)	431 (0.0%)
# of Sinks Auto-Prot.	0/ 1348 (0%)	982 / 1348 (72%)	1348 / 1348 (100%)	1348 / 1348 (100%)

Figure 11: Comparing the security and runtime overhead (ms.) comparison between our approach and alternative existing approaches for server-side Java and client-side JavaScript code generated from our benchmarks. The last line shows the number of sinks auto-protected by each approach.

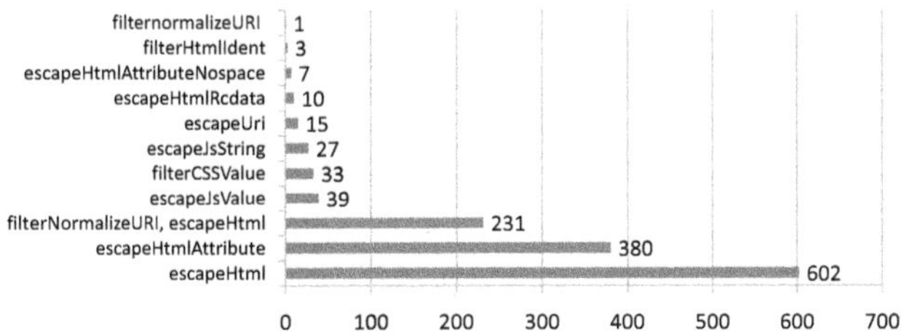

Figure 12: Distribution of inserted sanitizers: inferred contexts and hence the inserted sanitizer counts vary largely, therefore showing that context-insenstive sanitization is insufficient.

insensitive scheme— we show that the most widely inserted sanitizer in auto-sanitization on our benchmarks is also `escapeHtml`, the HTML-entity encoding sanitizer.

The last row in Figure 11 shows the number of sinks auto-protected by existing approaches. Context-insensitive sanitization protects 72% of the total output prints adequately; the auto-sanitization is insufficient for the remaining 28% output `print` opertions. Clearly, context-insensitive sanitization offers better protection than no sanitization strategy. On the other hand, context-sensitive sanitization has full protection whether the context-inference is performed dynamically or as in our static type inference approach. Figure 12 shows that the inferred sanitizers varied significantly based on context across the 1348 output points, showing the inadequacy of context-insensitive sanitization.

6.3 Performance

We measure and compare the runtime overhead incurred by our context-sensitive auto-sanitization to other approaches and present the results in Figure 11. Google Closure Templates can be compiled both to JavaScript as well as Java. We measure the runtime overhead for both cases. For compiled JavaScript functions, we record the time across 10 trial runs in 3 major web browsers. For compiled Java functions, we record the time across 10 trial runs under the same inputs.

The baseline "no auto-sanitization" approach overhead is obtained by compiling vanilla templates with no developer's manual sanitizers applied. For our approach, we enable our CSAS auto-sanitization implementation. To compare the overhead of context-insensitive auto-sanitization, we simply augment all output points with the `escapeHtml` sanitizer during compilation. A direct comparison to Google AutoEscape, the only context-sensitive sanitization approach in templating systems we know of, was not possible because it does not handle rich language features like if-else and loops which create context ambiguities and are pervasive in our benchmarks; a detailed explanation is provided in Section 7. To emulate the purely context-sensitive runtime parsing (CSRP) approach, we implemented this technique for our templating langauge. For Java, we directly used an off-the-shelf parser without modifications from the open-source Google AutoEscape implementation in GWT [15]. For JavaScript, since no similar parser was available, we created a parser implementation mirroring the Java-based parser. We believe our implementation was close to the GWT's public implementation for Java, since the overhead is in the same ballpark range.

Results. For JavaScript as the compilation target, the time taken for parsing and rendering the output of all the compiled template output (total 782.584 KB) in 3 major web browsers, averaged over 10 runs, is shown in Figure 11. The costs lie between 78% and $4.24x$ for the pure CSRP approach and our approach incurs between $3-9.6\%$ overhead over no sanitization. The primary reason for the difference between our approach and CSRP approach is that the latter requires a parsing of all constant string and context determination of untrusted data at runtime— a large saving in our static type inference approach. Our overhead in JavaScript is due to the application of the sanitizer, which is why our sanitization has nearly the same overhead as the context-insensitive sanitization approach.

For Java, the pure CSRP approach has a 510% overhead, whereas our approach and context-insensitive approach incur no statistically discernable overhead. In summary, our approach achieves the benefits of context-sensitive sanitization at the overhead comparable to a large fraction of other widely used frameworks.

We point out that Closure templates capture the HTML output logic with minimal subsidiary application logic — therefore our benchmarks are heavy in string concatenations and writes to output buffers. As a result, our benchmarks are highly CPU intensive and the runtime costs evaluated here may be amortized in full-blown applications by other latencies (computation of other logic, database accesses, network and file-system operations). For an estimate, XSS-GUARD reports an overhead up to 42% for the CSRP approach [5]. We believe our benchmarks are apt for precisely measuring performance costs of the HTML output logic alone. Further performance optimizations can be achieved for our approach as done in GWT by orthogonal optimizations like caching which mask disk load latencies.

7. RELATED WORK

Google AutoEscape, the only other context-sensitive sanitization approach in templating frameworks we are aware of, does not handle the rich language constructs we support— it does not handle conditionals constructs, loops or call operations [3]. It provides safety in straight-line template code for which straight-line parsing and context-determination suffice. To improve performace, it caches templates and the sanitization requirements for untrusted inputs. Templates can then be included in Java code [15] and C code [3]. As we outline in this paper, with rich constructs, path-sensitivity becomes a challenging issue and sanitization requirements for untrusted inputs vary from one execution path to the other. AutoEscape's caching optimization does not directly extend to code where sanitization requirements vary depending on executed paths. Our approach, instead, solves the challenges arising from complex language features representative of richer templating systems like Closure Templates.

Context-inference and subsequent context-sensitive placement for .NET legacy applications is proposed in our recent work [43]. The approach proposed therein, though sound, is a per-path analysis and relies on achieving path coverage by dynamic testing. In contrast, the type-based approach in this work achieves full coverage since it is based on static type inference. The performance improvements in our recent dynamic approach relies heavily on the intuition that on most execution paths, developers have manually applied context-sensitive sanitization correctly. The type-based approach in this work can apply sanitization correctly in code completely lacking previous developer-supplied sanitization. A potential drawback of our static approach is that theoretically it may reject benign templates since it reasons about all paths, even those which may be potentially infeasible. In our present evaluation we have not seen such cases.

Analysis techniques for finding scripting vulnerabilities has been widely researched [1, 2, 6, 18, 24, 27, 31–33, 37, 41, 42, 51, 52]. Defense architectures have targeted three broad categories: server-side techniques [5, 32, 43, 49, 52], purely browser-based techniques [4, 35] and client-server collaborative defenses [19, 26, 36, 46]. Unlike browser-based and client-server defenses, purely server-side approaches are applicable to the server code without requiring modifications to web browsers. Our techniques are an example of this fact.

Among server-side approaches, strong typing has been proposed as a XSS defense mechanism in the work by Robertson et. al [39]. Our approach significantly contrasts theirs in that it does not require any annotations or changes to the existing code, does not rely on strong typing primitives in the base language such as monads and is a mixed static-dynamic type system for existing web templating frameworks and for retrofitting to existing code.

8. CONCLUSIONS

We present a new auto-sanitization defense to secure web application code from scripting attacks (such as XSS) by construction. We introduce context type qualifiers, a key new abstraction, and develop a type system which is directly applicable to today's commercial templating languages. We have implemented the defense in Google Closure Templates, a state-of-the-art templating system that powers GMail and Google Docs. We find that our mostly static system has low performance overheads, is precise and requires no additional annotations or developer effort. We hope that our abstractions and techniques can be extended to other complex languages and frameworks in the future towards the goal of eliminating scripting attacks in emerging web applications.

9. ACKNOWLEDGEMENTS

We thank Avik Chaudhuri, David Wagner, Joel Weinberger, Devdatta Akhawe, Stephen McCamant, Adrian Mettler, Pongsin Poosankam and the anonymous reviewers for their insightful comments to improve this manuscript. This material is based upon work partially supported by the NSF under Grants No. 0311808, 0832943, 0448452, 0842694, 0627511, 0842695, 0831501, and 0424422, by the AFRL under Grant No. P010071555, by the ONR under MURI Grant No. N000140911081, and by the MURI program under AFOSR Grants No. FA9550-08-1- 0352 and FA9550-09-1-0539. The second author is also supported by the Symantec Research Labs Graduate Fellowship. The third author conducted part of the work as a visiting faculty at Google.

10. REFERENCES

[1] D. Balzarotti, M. Cova, V. Felmetsger, N. Jovanovic, E. Kirda, C. Kruegel, and G. Vigna. Saner: Composing Static and Dynamic Analysis to Validate Sanitization in Web Applications. In *Proceedings of the IEEE Symposium on Security and Privacy*, Oakland, CA, May 2008.

[2] S. Bandhakavi, S. T. King, P. Madhusudan, and M. Winslett. VEX: Vetting browser extensions for security vulnerabilities, 2010.

[3] Google autoescape implementation for ctemplate (c code). `http://google-ctemplate.googlecode.com/svn/trunk/doc/auto_escape.html`.

[4] D. Bates, A. Barth, and C. Jackson. Regular expressions considered harmful in client-side XSS filters. In *Proceedings of the 19th international conference on World wide web*, WWW '10, 2010.

[5] P. Bisht and V. N. Venkatakrishnan. XSS-GUARD: Precise dynamic prevention of cross-site scripting attacks. In *Detection of Intrusions and Malware, and Vulnerability Assessment*, 2008.

[6] H. Bojinov, E. Bursztein, and D. Boneh. XCS: Cross channel scripting and its impact on web applications. In *CCS*, 2009.

[7] Google Analytics XSS vulnerability. `http://spareclockcycles.org/2011/02/03/google-analytics-xss-vulnerability/`.

[8] Google XSS Flaw in Website Optimizer Scripts explained. `http://www.acunetix.com/blog/web-security-zone/articles/google-xss-website-optimizer-scripts/`.

[9] How I met your girlfriend, DEFCON'10. `ohack.us/xss/2010-defcon.ppt`.

[10] XSS Attack Identified and Patch-Twitter. `http://status.twitter.com/post/1161435117/xss-attacklinebreak-identified-and-patched`.

[11] ClearSilver: Template Filters. `http://www.clearsilver.net/docs/man_filters.hdf`.

[12] CodeIgniter/system/libraries/Security.php. `https://bitbucket.org/ellislab/codeigniter/src/8af0fb079f90/system/libraries/Security.php`.

[13] Ctemplate: Guide to Using Auto Escape. `http://google-ctemplate.googlecode.com/svn/trunk/doc/auto_escape.html`.

[14] django: Built-in template tags and filters. `http://docs.djangoproject.com/en/dev/ref/templates/builtins`.

[15] Google autoescape implementation for gwt (java code). `http://code.google.com/p/google-web-toolkit/source/browse/tools/lib/streamhtmlparser/streamhtmlparser-jsilver-r10/streamhtmlparser-jsilver-r10-1.5.jar`.

[16] J. S. Foster, T. Terauchi, and A. Aiken. Flow-sensitive type qualifiers. In *Proceedings of the ACM SIGPLAN 2002 Conference on Programming language design and implementation*, PLDI '02, 2002.

[17] B. Gourdin, C. Soman, H. Bojinov, and E. Bursztein. Towards secure embedded web interfaces. In *Proceedings of the Usenix Security Symposium*, 2011.

[18] A. Guha, S. Krishnamurthi, and T. Jim. Using static analysis for ajax intrusion detection. In *Proceedings of the 18th international conference on World wide web*, WWW '09.

[19] M. V. Gundy and H. Chen. Noncespaces: using randomization to enforce information flow tracking and thwart cross-site scripting attacks. *16th Annual Network & Distributed System Security Symposium*, 2009.

[20] Google Web Toolkit: Developer's Guide – SafeHtml. `http://code.google.com/webtoolkit/doc/latest/DevGuideSecuritySafeHtml.html`.

[21] R. Hansen. XSS cheat sheet. `http://ha.ckers.org/xss.html`.

[22] P. Hooimeijer, B. Livshits, D. Molnar, P. Saxena, and M. Veanes. Fast and precise sanitizer analysis with BEK. In *Proceedings of the Usenix Security Symposium*, 2011.

[23] HTML Purifier : Standards-Compliant HTML Filtering. http://htmlpurifier.org/.

[24] Y.-W. Huang, F. Yu, C. Hang, C.-H. Tsai, D.-T. Lee, and S.-Y. Kuo. Securing web application code by static analysis and runtime protection. In *Proceedings of the 13th international conference on World Wide Web*, WWW '04.

[25] JiftyManual. http://jifty.org/view/JiftyManual.

[26] T. Jim, N. Swamy, and M. Hicks. BEEP: Browser-enforced embedded policies. *16th International World World Web Conference*, 2007.

[27] N. Jovanovic, C. Krügel, and E. Kirda. Pixy: A static analysis tool for detecting web application vulnerabilities (short paper). In *IEEE Symposium on Security and Privacy*, 2006.

[28] Quasis demo - javascript shell 1.4. http://js-quasis-libraries-and-repl.googlecode.com/svn/trunk/index.html.

[29] A. Kieżun, V. Ganesh, P. J. Guo, P. Hooimeijer, and M. D. Ernst. HAMPI: A solver for string constraints. In *International Symposium on Software Testing and Analysis*, 2009.

[30] kses - PHP HTML/XHTML filter. http://sourceforge.net/projects/kses/.

[31] B. Livshits and M. S. Lam. Finding security errors in Java programs with static analysis. In *Proceedings of the Usenix Security Symposium*, 2005.

[32] B. Livshits, M. Martin, and M. S. Lam. SecuriFly: Runtime protection and recovery from Web application vulnerabilities. Technical report, Stanford University, Sept. 2006.

[33] M. Martin and M. S. Lam. Automatic generation of XSS and SQL injection attacks with goal-directed model checking. In *17th USENIX Security Symposium*, 2008.

[34] The Mason Book: Escaping Substitutions. http://www.masonbook.com/book/chapter-2.mhtml.

[35] L. Meyerovich and B. Livshits. ConScript: Specifying and enforcing fine-grained security policies for JavaScript in the browser. In *IEEE Symposium on Security and Privacy*, May 2010.

[36] Y. Nadji, P. Saxena, and D. Song. Document structure integrity: A robust basis for cross-site scripting defense. In *NDSS*, 2009.

[37] A. Nguyen-Tuong, S. Guarnieri, D. Greene, J. Shirley, and D. Evans. Automatically hardening web applications using precise tainting. *20th IFIP International Information Security Conference*, 2005.

[38] XSS Prevention Cheat Sheet. http://www.owasp.org/index.php/XSS_(Cross_Site_Scripting)_Prevention_Cheat_Sheet.

[39] W. Robertson and G. Vigna. Static Enforcement of Web Application Integrity Through Strong Typing. In *Proceedings of the USENIX Security Symposium*, Montreal, Canada, August 2009.

[40] Ruby on Rails Security Guide. http://guides.rubyonrails.org/security.html.

[41] P. Saxena, D. Akhawe, S. Hanna, F. Mao, S. McCamant, and D. Song. A symbolic execution framework for JavaScript. Technical Report UCB/EECS-2010-26, EECS Department, University of California, Berkeley, 2010.

[42] P. Saxena, S. Hanna, P. Poosankam, and D. Song. FLAX: Systematic discovery of client-side validation vulnerabilities in rich web applications. In *17th Annual Network & Distributed System Security Symposium, (NDSS)*, 2010.

[43] P. Saxena, D. Molnar, and B. Livshits. SCRIPTGARD: Automatic context-sensitive sanitization for large-scale legacy web applications. In *Proceedings of the ACM Computer and communications security(CCS)*, 2011.

[44] Smarty Template Engine: escape. http://www.smarty.net/manual/en/language.modifier.escape.php.

[45] Google Closure Templates. http://code.google.com/closure/templates/.

[46] S. Stamm. Content security policy, 2009.

[47] Z. Su and G. Wassermann. The essence of command injection attacks in web applications. 2006.

[48] Template::Manual::Filters. http://template-toolkit.org/docs/manual/Filters.html.

[49] Ter Louw, Mike and V.N. Venkatakrishnan. BluePrint: Robust Prevention of Cross-site Scripting Attacks for Existing Browsers. In *Proceedings of the IEEE Symposium on Security and Privacy*, 2009.

[50] J. Weinberger, P. Saxena, D. Akhawe, M. Finifter, R. Shin, and D. Song. A Systematic Analysis of XSS Sanitization in Web Application Frameworks. In *Proceedings of the European Symposium on Research in Computer Security*, 2011.

[51] Y. Xie and A. Aiken. Static detection of security vulnerabilities in scripting languages. In *Proceedings of the Usenix Security Symposium*, 2006.

[52] W. Xu, S. Bhatkar, and R. Sekar. Taint-enhanced policy enforcement: A practical approach to defeat a wide range of attacks. *USENIX Security Symposium*, 2006.

[53] Yii Framework: Security. http://www.yiiframework.com/doc/guide/1.1/en/topics.security.

[54] Zend Framework: Zend_Filter. http://framework.zend.com/manual/en/zend.filter.set.html.

APPENDIX

A. OPERATIONAL SEMANTICS

We have discussed the static type rules in Section 4. In this section, we describe the various runtime parsing checks that our CSAS engine inserts at various operations to achieve type safety. We do this by first presenting a big-step operational semantics for an abstract machine that evaluates our simple templating language. We sketch the proof for the soundness of our type system based on the operational semantics.

$$\frac{c \in \mathcal{C}}{M \vdash \mathbf{const}(n) \Downarrow \langle n, c \hookrightarrow c\rangle}\text{E-CINT} \qquad \frac{c \in \mathcal{C}}{M \vdash \mathbf{const}(b) \Downarrow \langle b, c \hookrightarrow c\rangle}\text{E-CBOOL}$$

$$\frac{IsParseValid(s, c_1, c_2)}{M \vdash \mathbf{const}(s) \Downarrow \langle s, c_1 \hookrightarrow c_2\rangle}\text{E-CONST} \qquad \frac{}{M \vdash \mathbf{const}(s) \Downarrow \lhd s \rhd}\text{E-STRING-DYN}$$

$$\frac{\begin{array}{c}M \vdash e_1 \Downarrow \langle b_1, c \hookrightarrow c\rangle \\ M \vdash e_2 \Downarrow \langle b_2, c \hookrightarrow c\rangle\end{array}}{M \vdash e_1 \odot e_2 \Downarrow \langle b_1 \odot b_2, c \hookrightarrow c\rangle}\text{E-BL} \qquad \frac{\begin{array}{c}M \vdash e_1 \Downarrow \langle n_1, c \hookrightarrow c\rangle \\ M \vdash e_2 \Downarrow \langle n_2, c \hookrightarrow c\rangle\end{array}}{M \vdash e_1 \oplus e_2 \Downarrow \langle n_1 \oplus n_2, c \hookrightarrow c\rangle}\text{E-INT}$$

$$\frac{M \vdash e_1 \Downarrow \langle s_1, c_1 \hookrightarrow c_2\rangle \qquad M \vdash e_2 \Downarrow \langle s_2, c_3 \hookrightarrow c_4\rangle \qquad c_2 = c_3}{M \vdash e_1 \cdot e_2 \Downarrow \langle s_1 \cdot s_2, c_1 \hookrightarrow c_4\rangle}\text{E-CAT-STAT}$$

$$\frac{M \vdash e_1 \Downarrow \lhd s_1 \rhd \qquad M \vdash e_2 \Downarrow \lhd s_2 \rhd}{M \vdash e_1 \cdot e_2 \Downarrow \lhd s_1 \cdot s_2 \rhd}\text{E-CAT-DYN}$$

$$\frac{M \vdash e \Downarrow s \qquad SanMap(c_1 \hookrightarrow c_2, f) \qquad s' = f(s) \qquad c_1, c_2 \in \mathcal{C}}{M \vdash \mathbf{San}(f, e) \Downarrow \langle s', c_1 \hookrightarrow c_2\rangle}\text{E-SAN}$$

$$\frac{M \vdash e \Downarrow s \qquad SanMap(c_1 \hookrightarrow c_2, f) \qquad \underline{s' = f(s)} \qquad c_1, c_2 \in \mathcal{C}}{M \vdash v := (\mathtt{STATIC}_{c_1 \hookrightarrow c_2})e \Downarrow M[v \mapsto \langle s', c_1 \hookrightarrow c_2\rangle]}\text{E-PROM-ST}$$

$$\frac{M \vdash e \Downarrow s}{M \vdash v := (\mathtt{DYN}_{\mathcal{S}})e \Downarrow M[v \mapsto \lhd (\!| s |\!) \rhd\rangle]}\text{E-PROM-DYN}$$

$$\frac{M \vdash e \Downarrow \langle s, c_1 \hookrightarrow c_2\rangle}{M \vdash v := (\mathtt{STATIC}_{c_1 \hookrightarrow c_2})e \Downarrow M}\text{E-CAST-1} \qquad \frac{M \vdash e \Downarrow \lhd s \rhd}{M \vdash v = (\mathtt{DYN}_{\mathcal{S}})e \Downarrow M}\text{E-CAST-2}$$

$$\frac{M \vdash e \Downarrow \langle s, c_1 \hookrightarrow c_2\rangle \qquad M \vdash \rho \Downarrow \| s', c \| \qquad c = c_1}{M \vdash print(e) \Downarrow M[\rho \mapsto \| s' \cdot s, c_2 \|]}\text{E-PRN-STAT}$$

$$\frac{M \vdash e \Downarrow \lhd s \rhd \qquad M \vdash \rho \Downarrow \| s', c \| \qquad \boxed{(s'', c_2) = CSRP(c, \lhd s \rhd)}}{M \vdash print(e) \Downarrow M[\rho \mapsto \| s' \cdot s'', c_2 \|]}\text{E-PRN-DYN}$$

$$\frac{M \vdash e \Downarrow true \qquad M \vdash S_1 \Downarrow M'}{M \vdash \mathbf{if}(e)\mathbf{then}S_1\mathbf{else}S_2 \Downarrow M'}\text{E-IF} \qquad \frac{M \vdash e \Downarrow false \qquad M \vdash S_2 \Downarrow M'}{M \vdash \mathbf{if}(e)\mathbf{then}S_1\mathbf{else}S_2 \Downarrow M'}\text{E-EL}$$

$$\frac{\begin{array}{c}M \vdash e \Downarrow true \\ M \vdash S; \mathbf{while}(e)S \Downarrow M'\end{array}}{M \vdash \mathbf{while}(e)S \Downarrow M'}\text{E-WHLTRUE} \qquad \frac{M \vdash e \Downarrow false}{M \vdash \mathbf{while}(e)S \Downarrow M}\text{E-WHLFALSE}$$

$$\frac{M \vdash e \Downarrow x}{M \vdash v := e \Downarrow M[v \mapsto x]}\text{E-ASSIGN} \qquad \frac{M \vdash c \Downarrow M' \qquad M' \vdash S \Downarrow M''}{M \vdash c; S \Downarrow M''}\text{E-SEQ}$$

Figure 13: Operational Semantics for the typed language. Sanitization routines inserted by the CSAS engine after inference are shown Underlined. Runtime parsing and other checks inserted are shown $\boxed{Boxed}$, which may produce runtime errors evaluating to `CFail`.

The evaluation rules are shown in Fig 13. Commands operate on a memory M mapping program variables to *values*. Each premise in an evaluation rule has the form $M \vdash e \Downarrow v$ which means that the expression e evaluates to a final value v under the state of the memory M. Command evaluation judgements have the form $M \vdash c \Downarrow M'$ which states that under the memory M evaluation of the command c results in a memory M'. We omit the rules for template calls and returns here which follow standard call-by-value semantics for brevity.

Values. The values produced during the evaluation of the language are mainly of two kinds: (a) V_β values for the data elements of base type β and (b) V_η for objects of base type η. Runtime errors are captured by a third, explicit `CFail` value. The syntax of values is described in Figure 14.

$$
\begin{array}{ll}
Value ::= & V_\beta | V_\eta | \texttt{CFail} \\
\\
V_\beta ::= & \langle Val, CTran \rangle | \lhd Expr \rhd | Val \\
Ctran ::= & \mathcal{C} \hookrightarrow \mathcal{C} \\
Val ::= & b | i | s \\
Expr ::= & Val | Expr \cdot Expr | (\!| Val |\!) \\
\\
V_\eta ::= & \| s, EmbCtx \| \\
EmbCtx ::= & \mathcal{C}
\end{array}
$$

Figure 14: Syntax of Values

The universe of **string**, **int** or **bool** base typed values is denoted by the letters s,i, and b letters respectively in the syntax above and the standard concatenation operation is denoted by "·". The V_β values are of three kinds:

1. Untrusted or unsanitized values are raw untrusted string, integer or boolean values.
2. Other values which are auto-sanitized statically or correspond to program constants are tuples of the form $\langle v, Ctran \rangle$ where $Ctran$ is a metadata field. The $Ctran$ metadata field indicates that the value v safely induces a context transition $Ctran$.
3. The remaining values are a special data-structure $\lhd Expr \rhd$, called the CSRP-expression, which is used for dynamically sanitized values. The data structure stores concatenation expressions, conceptually separating the untrusted peices from trusted peices. In our syntax, we separate untrusted substrings of string expressions by delimiting them with special delimiters, $(\!|$ and $|\!)$, which are assumed to be outside the string alphabet of the base language.

The global output buffer has a value of the form $\| s, EmbCtx \|$, where s is the string buffer consisting of the application's output. The $EmbCtx$ metadata field is the context as a result of parsing s according to our canonical grammar.

Type Safety. Note that the operational semantics ensure the 3 security properties outlined in section 2.2. The `CR` is explicit in the representation of output buffer values—parsing the output buffer at any point results in a permitted context defined in $\mathcal{C}$. Property `NOS` is similarly ensured in the `E-CONST` rule, which evaluate to values of the form $\langle v, Ctran \rangle$. Such values are never sanitized.

Property `CSAN` is immidiate for `E-PRN-STAT` evaluation rule which ensures that the output buffer's context matches the start context in the $Ctran$ field of the written string expression. For the evaluation rule `E-PRN-DYN`, the soundness relies on the procedure $CSRP$ shown boxed which takes a CSRP-expression and a start context to parse the expression in. This procedure parses the string expression embedded in the CSRP-expression, while sanitizing all and only the untrusted substrings delimited by $(\!| |\!)$ context-sensitively. If it succeeds it returns a tuple containing the sanitized string expression and the end context.

In order to formalize and sketch the proof of the soundness of our type system, we first define a relation $\mathcal{R}$ mapping types to the set of valid values they correspond to. At any given point in the program, if the type of a variable or object is Q under the typing environment Γ, then its value must correspond to the typing constraints. The relation $\mathcal{R}$ is defined as follows, assuming $\mathcal{U}$ is the universe of strings, integer and boolean values:

DEFINITION 2. ***(Relation*** $\mathcal{R}$***)***

$$
\begin{array}{ll}
\mathcal{R}(\mathit{UNSAFE}) & = \{v | v \in \mathcal{U}\} \\
\mathcal{R}(\mathit{STATIC}_{c1 \hookrightarrow c2}) & = \{\langle v, c1 \hookrightarrow c2 \rangle | v \in \mathcal{U}, IsParseValid(v, c_1, c_2)\} \\
\mathcal{R}(\mathit{DYN}_S) & = \{\lhd v \rhd | v \in \mathcal{U}\} \\
\mathcal{R}(\mathit{CTXSTAT}_c) & = \{\| s, c \| | c \in \mathcal{C}\} \\
\mathcal{R}(\mathit{CTXDYN}_S) & = \{\| s, c \| | c \in \mathcal{C}, c \in S\}
\end{array}
$$

At any program location, we define a notion of a well-typed memory M as follows:

DEFINITION 3. ***(Well-Typedness)*** *A memory is well-typed with respect to a typing environment* Γ*, denoted by* $M \models \Gamma$*, iff*

$$\forall x \in Dom(M), M[x] \in \mathcal{R}(\Gamma[x])$$

We define the two standard progress and preservation theorems that establish soundness our type system below. Progress states that if the memory if well-typed, then the abstract machine defined in the operational semantics does not get "stuck"— that is, there is at least one evaluation rules that can be applied to the well-typed terms. Preservation states that at any evaluation step if all the subterms (used in the premises) are well-typed then the deduced term is also well-typed.

The machine may get stuck for several reasons. It may be due to the runtime boxed checks failing. This is intended semantics of the language and such behavior is safe. The machine may also get stuck because no evaluaion rule may apply, or in other words, the memory state is such that the semantics do not define how to evaluate further. To distinguish these two cases, we define a value called `CFail`, which the boxed procedure $CSRP$ evaluates to when it fails. Other stuck states may result from reaching an inconsistent memory states for which no evaluation rule applies. We point out the abstract operational semantics we describe here are non-deterministic. Therefore, only when all non-deterministic evaluations of an instance of the procedure $CSRP$ fail, does the boxed check fail and the **print** statement evaluate to the `CFail` runtime error.

THEOREM 1. *(Progress and Preservation for Expressions). If* $\Gamma \vdash e : T$ *and* $M \models \Gamma$*, then either* $M \vdash e \Downarrow \texttt{CFail}$ *or* $M \vdash e \Downarrow v$ *and* $v \in \mathcal{R}(T)$*.*

PROOF. By induction on the derivation of $\Gamma \vdash e : T$. □

THEOREM 2. *(Progress and Preservation for Commands). If* $M \models \Gamma$ *and* $\Gamma \vdash c \Longrightarrow \Gamma'$*, then either* $M \vdash c \Downarrow \texttt{CFail}$ *or* $M \vdash c \Downarrow M'$ *where* $M' \models \Gamma'$*.*

PROOF. By induction on the derivation of $\Gamma \vdash c \Longrightarrow \Gamma'$. The definition of relation $\mathcal{R}$ serves as the standard inversion lemma. □

SCRIPTGARD: Automatic Context-Sensitive Sanitization for Large-Scale Legacy Web Applications

Prateek Saxena
UC Berkeley
Berkeley, CA
prateeks@cs.berkeley.edu

David Molnar
Microsoft Research
Redmond, WA
dmolnar@microsoft.com

Benjamin Livshits
Microsoft Research
Redmond, WA
livshits@microsoft.com

ABSTRACT

We empirically analyzed sanitizer use in a shipping web application with over 400,000 lines of code and over 23,244 methods, the largest empirical analysis of sanitizer use of which we are aware. Our analysis reveals two novel classes of errors: context-mismatched sanitization *and* inconsistent multiple sanitization. *Both of these arise* not *because sanitizers are incorrectly implemented, but rather because they are not placed in code correctly. Much of the work on cross-site scripting detection to date has focused on finding missing sanitizers in programs of average size. In large legacy applications, other sanitization issues leading to cross-site scripting emerge.*

To address these errors, we propose SCRIPTGARD, *a system for ASP.NET applications which can detect and repair the incorrect placement of sanitizers.* SCRIPTGARD *serves both as a testing aid to developers as well as a runtime mitigation technique. While mitigations for cross site scripting attacks have seen intense prior research, we consider both server and browser context, none of them achieve the same degree of precision, and many other mitigation techniques require major changes to server side code or to browsers. Our approach, in contrast, can be incrementally retrofitted to legacy systems with no changes to the source code and no browser changes. With our optimizations, when used for mitigation,* SCRIPTGARD *incurs virtually no statistically significant overhead.*

Categories and Subject Descriptors

D.4.6 [**Operating Systems**]: Security and Protection—*invasive software*;
D.1.2 [**Programming Techniques**]: Automatic Programming—*program transformation, program modification*

General Terms

Security, Languages, Vulnerabilities

CCS'11, October 17–27, 2011, Chicago, Illinois, USA.

Keywords

Cross-site scripting, Runtime analysis, Web applications

1. INTRODUCTION

Web applications are explosively popular, but they suffer from cross-site scripting (XSS) [4, 32] and cross-channel scripting (XCS) [5]. At the core of these attacks is injection of JavaScript code into a context not originally intended. These attacks lead to stolen credentials and actions performed on the user's behalf by an adversary. Ideally, we would create systems that resist attacks by construction. Recent projects such as BLUEPRINT have proposed primitives to encode HTML output in a safe way [20]. Unfortunately, these techniques are difficult to apply to legacy web applications because they make fundamental changes to the way an application creates HTML for consumption by the web browser. Mitigations are needed for XSS attacks against web applications that can be incrementally retrofitted to existing code.

Prior work: Much work in this space has focused on missing sanitizers and was performed on relatively small applications. The effort described in this paper goes well beyond that, specifically focusing on applications approaching half a million lines of code and above. We empirically analyze sanitization in a widely used Web application with over 400,000 lines of code, the largest application analysis of which we are aware. In this process, we discovered two novel classes of errors: *context-mismatched sanitization* errors and *inconsistent multiple sanitization* errors. These sanitization errors arise from subtle nesting of HTML contexts and sharing of dataflow paths in the application. Unlike previously reported errors, mismatched sanitization is not due to faulty or missing sanitizers; each individual sanitizer in our test application is *correct* to the best of our knowledge. The new categories of errors only became apparent because of the scale and complexity of the applications we target, however, we believe that they represent a new frontier of complexity, shared by other applications of a similar scale.

As a point of comparison, it is instructive to consider HTML templating systems such as Google GWT or CTemplates, which employs Google AutoEscape's auto-sanitization to remove the need for manual sanitization [10]. Such systems are much easier to sanitize as compared to large-scale *legacy* code that we focus on. For instance, developers are forced to separate untrusted variables from HTML structure explicitly in templates, unlike in legacy code. Their mechanisms does not need to handle the nesting of HTML contexts and sharing of dataflow paths, because they work with specific frameworks.

Consistent Sanitizer Placement: Context-mismatched sanitization errors arise because developers accidentally mismatch the choice of sanitizer with the web *browser context*, the browser's parsing state when processing the sanitized data. This happens when the browser's actual parsing state or context is different from what the developer expects, allowing unintended characters like single quotes in sanitized data. Moreover, we discover inconsistent multiple sanitization errors, in which the *combination* of sanitizers leads to problems. For example, we find that two sanitizers in our test application are not commutative: the order of application matters, only one order is safe, yet both orders appear in our empirical study.

We propose the problem of *consistent sanitizer placement*: apply a sequence of sanitizers, chosen from a pre-specified set, to an untrusted input such that it is safe for all the possible browser contexts in which it is rendered. Sanitization is also needed for cases where data must be encoded to avoid causing functionality errors in a specific context, such as encoding URLs in JavaScript. Prior work does not model the notion of browser contexts precisely, rendering it unable to detect these classes of errors. Depending on the configuration/policy of the application and the authority of the adversary who controls the sanitized data, these inconsistencies may or may not yield cross site scripting attacks, but these remain errors in sanitization practice.

ScriptGard: We develop ScriptGard, a system for detecting these sanitization errors, and repairing them by automatically choosing the appropriate sanitizer. Our system requires no changes to web browsers or to server side source code. Instead, we use binary rewriting of server code to embed a *browser model* that determines the appropriate browser parsing context when HTML is output by the web application. In contrast, projects such as Blueprint have proposed primitives to encode HTML output in a safe way [20], but at the cost of requiring large scale server code changes.

Unlike existing template-based HTML writing systems, such as ASP.NET's web and HTML controls, ScriptGard performs *context-sensitive* sanitization. ScriptGard allows developers to create custom nesting of HTML contexts, which we show in Section 6 is common in our test application, without sacrificing the consistency of the sanitization process. During analysis, ScriptGard employs *positive taint-tracking*, which contrasts with traditional taint-tracking because it is conservative (hence does not miss identifying sources of untrusted data) and can provide defense against cross channel-scripting attacks [5, 13]. For example, a recent vulnerability in Google Analytics was due to a non-traditional source of untrusted input, namely event logs [30], which our approach would detect.

We implement our analysis in ScriptGard, which uses binary rewriting techniques to instrument applications running on the ASP.NET platform. We stress, however, that the analyses we perform are general and could be ported to other platforms with sufficient engineering work. ScriptGard can be used either as a testing aid or as a runtime mitigation. As a testing aid, ScriptGard points out sanitizers that are not correct for the runtime parsing context. Our dynamic technique ensures that these reports are for specific, reproducible test cases that exhibit inconsistent sanitization.

As a runtime mitigation, we show how ScriptGard can leverage a *training phase* where it runs with full instrumentation on a target application to learn correct sanitizers for different program paths. Then in deployment, only a lighter path detection instrumentation is necessary. We adapt techniques from preferential path profiling [7]; with this optimization trick, ScriptGard incurs virtually no statistically significant overhead when auto-correcting inconsistently sanitized paths we tested.

1.1 Contributions

This paper makes the following contributions.

Testing for sanitizer placement errors: In Section 2, we identify two new classes of errors: *context-mismatched sanitization* and *inconsistent multiple sanitization*. We implement a novel analysis that combines automatic server-side instrumentation with a browser model to find inconsistent sanitization. We further refine this analysis with *positive taint tracking* to conservatively over-estimate potentially adversarial inputs, which has been applied to SQL injection in the past, but not to cross site scripting errors [13]. Because we use both server and browser modeling, we find potential sanitization flaws that would be missed with techniques that focus exclusively on the server [2, 17, 21].

Runtime auto-sanitization: We show how our analysis can determine the correct sanitization at runtime. While we show the cost to run the full ScriptGard instrumentation is a high multiple of the original run time, we propose a mechanism for using preferential path profiling techniques [7] to shift most of this cost to a pre-deployment *training phase*. With this optimization trick, deployed auto-correction incurs virtually negligible overhead. Our system changes only the server side runtime, requiring no changes to server code or to the browser.

Evaluation and empirical study: In Section 6 we evaluate both the testing approach as well as runtime auto-sanitization on an application with over 400,000 lines of code. We performed our security testing on a set of 53 large web pages derived from 7 sub-applications built on top of our test application. Each page contains 350–900 DOM nodes. Out of 25,209 total paths exercised, we found context-mismatched sanitization on 1,207 paths ScriptGard analyzed, 4.7% of the total paths analyzed. We also observed an additional 285 instances of inconsistent multiple sanitization errors. Our runtime mitigation technique safeguards against these inconsistent uses of sanitizers by automatically correcting them at runtime.

1.2 Paper Organization

The rest of this paper is organized as follows. Section 2 gives a description of the context-sensitive vulnerabilities ScriptGard is designed to prevent. Section 3 provides an overview of the ScriptGard architecture. Section 4 formalizes the vulnerabilities and provides a notion of correctness. Section 5 provides specific details of ScriptGard implementation. Section 6 gives an experimental evaluation of our techniques. Finally, Sections 7 and 8 describe related work and conclude.

2. SANITIZER CONSISTENCY

In this section, we systematically explain the two new class of sanitization errors we commonly observe in our empirical

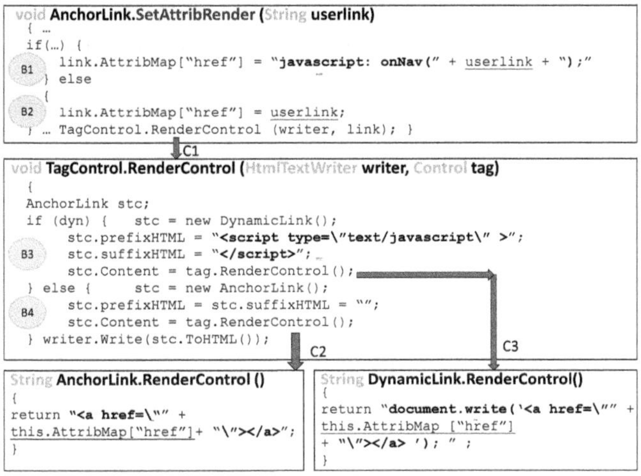

Figure 1: Running example: C# code fragment illustrating the problem of automatic sanitizer placement. Underlined values are derived from untrusted data and require sanitization; function calls are shown with thick black arrows C1-C3 and basic blocks B1-B4 are shown in gray circles.

analysis: *context-mismatched sanitization* and *inconsistent multiple sanitization*, both of which demonstrate that placement of sanitizers in legacy code is a significant challenge even if the sanitizers themselves are securely constructed.

It is well-known that script-injection attack vectors are highly *context*-dependent — a string such as `expression: alert(a)` is innocuous when placed inside a HTML tag context, but can result in JavaScript execution when embedded in a CSS attribute value context. In fact, the set of contexts in which untrusted data is commonly embedded by today's web applications is well-known. Sanitizers that secure data against XSS in each of these contexts are publicly available [10, 27]. We assume that contexts and their corresponding functionally correct sanitizers, shown in Figure 7, are standard and available.

2.1 Inconsistent Multiple Sanitization

Figure 1 shows a fragment of ASP.NET code written in C# which illustrates the difficulty of sanitizer placement. This running example is inspired by code from the large code base we empirically analyzed. Consider the function `DynamicLink.RenderControl` shown in the running example, which places an untrusted string inside a double-quoted `href` attribute which in turn is placed inside a JavaScript string. This code fragment places the untrusted string into two *nested contexts* — when the browser parses the untrusted string, it will first parse it in the JavaScript string literal and then subsequently parse it as a URI attribute.

In Figure 7 we show a sanitizer specification that maps functions to contexts. In particular, two sanitizer functions, `EcmaScriptStringEncode` and `HtmlAttribEncode`, are applied for the JavaScript string context and the HTML attribute context, respectively. However, developers must understand this order of parsing in the browser to apply them in the correct order. They must choose between the two ways of composing the two sanitizers shown in Figure 2.

It turns out that the first sequence of sanitizer composition is *inconsistent* with the nested embedding contexts, while the other order is safe or consistent. We observe that the standard recommended implementation for these sanitizers [27], even in widely deployed public web frameworks and libraries (Django, GWT, OWASP, .NET) do not commute. For instance, `EcmaScriptStringEncode` simply transforms all characters that can break out of JavaScript string literals (like the " character) to Unicode encoding (`\u0022` for "), and, `HtmlAttribEncode` HTML-entity encodes characters (`"` for "). This is the standard recommended behavior these sanitizers [27] with respect to respective contexts they secure.

```
document.write('<a href=" +
HtmlAttribEncode(EcmaScriptStringEncode(this.AttribMap["href"]))
+...
```

(a) Method 1

```
document.write('<a href=" +
EcmaScriptStringEncode(HtmlAttribEncode(this.AttribMap["href"]))
+...
```

(b) Method 2

Figure 2: Different sanitization approaches.

Example 1. The attack on the wrong composition is very simple. The key observation is that applying `EcmaScriptStringEncode` first encodes the attacker-supplied " character as a Unicode representation `\u0022`. This Unicode representation is not subsequently transformed by the second `HtmlAttribEncode` sanitization, because `\u0022` is a completely innocous string in the URI attribute value context.

However, when the web browser parses the transformed string first (in the JavaScript string literal context), it performs a Unicode decode of the dangerous character `\u0022` back to ". When the browser subsequently interprets this in the `href` URI attribute context the attacker's dangerous " prematurely closes the URI attribute value and can inject JavaScript event handlers like `onclick=...` to execute malicious code. This may also enable parameter pollution attacks in URLs [1]. It is easy to confirm that the other composition of correct sanitizers is definitely safe. ■

2.2 Context-Mismatched Sanitization

Even if sanitizers are designed to be commutative, developers may apply a sanitizer that does not match the context altogether; we call such an error as a *context-mismatched sanitization* inconsistency. Context-mismatched sanitization is not uncommon in real applications. To intuitively understand why, consider the sanitization requirements of the running example again.

Notice that the running example has 4 control-flow paths corresponding to execution through the basic-blocks (B1,B3), (B1,B4), (B2,B3) and (B2,B4) respectively. Each execution path places the untrusted `userlink` input string in 4 different contexts (see Figure 3). Determining the browser context is a path-sensitive property, and the developer may have to inspect the global control/data flow to understand in which contexts is a data variable used. This task can be error-prone because the code logic for web output may be spread across several classes, and the control-flow graph may not be explicit (especially in languages with inheritance). We show how two most prevalent sanitization strategies fail to work on this example.

Failure of output sanitization: Consider the case in which the application developer decides to delay all sani-

HTML output	Nesting of contexts
<script type="text/javascript"> document.write(' <a href="javascript: onNav(TOENCODE)";></a>); </script>	JavaScript String Literal, Html URI Attribute, JavaScript Number
<a href="javascript: onNav(TOENCODE);"></a>	Html URI Attribute, JavaScript Number
<a href="TOENCODE"></a>	Html URI Attribute
<script type="text/javascript"> document.write('<a href=" TOENCODE"> </a>'); </script>	JavaScript String Literal, Html URI Attribute

Figure 3: HTML outputs obtained by executing different paths in the running example. TOENCODE denotes the untrusted string in the output.

tization to the *output* sinks, i.e., to the `writer.Write` call in `TagControl.RenderControl`. There are two problems with doing so, which the developer is burdened to identify manually to get the sanitization right. First, the execution paths through basic-block B3 embed the untrusted data in a `<SCRIPT>` block context, where paths through basic-block B4 place it in a HTML tag context. As a result, *any* sanitizer picked cannot be consistent for both such paths. Second, even if the first concern did not exist, sanitizing the `stc.Content` variable at the output point is *not* correct. The `stc.Content` is composed of trusted substrings as well as untrusted data — if the entire string is sanitized, the sanitizer could change programmer-supplied constant strings in a way that breaks the intended structure of the output HTML. For example, if the basic-block B1 executes, the untrusted data would be embedded in a JavaScript number context(`javascript: OnNav()` explicitly by the programmer. If we applied `HtmlAttribEncode` to the `stc.Content` the `javascript:` would be eliminated breaking the application's intended behavior.

Failure of input sanitization: Moving sanitization checks to earlier points in the code, say at the input interfaces, is not a panacea either. The readers can verify that moving all sanitization to a code locations earlier in the dataflow graph continues to suffer from path-sensitivity issues. Sanitizing in basic-blocks B1 and B2 is not sufficient, because additional contexts are introduced when blocks B3 and B4 are executed. Sanitization locations midway in the dataflow chain, such the concatenation in function `AnchorLink.SetAttribRender`, are also problematic because depending on whether basic-block B1 executes or B2 executes, the `this.AttribMap["href"]` variable may have trusted content or not.

2.3 Why is Consistency Hard?

Expressive languages, such as those of the .NET platform, permit the use of string operations to construct HTML output as strings with trusted code intermixed with untrusted data. Plus, these rich programming languages allow developers to write complex dataflow and control flow logic. We summarize the following observations that exist in large legacy applications authored on such rich programming environments:

- **String outputs:** String outputs contain trusted constant code fragments mixed with untrusted data.
- **Nested contexts:** Untrusted data is often embedded in nested contexts.
- **Intersecting data-flow paths:** Data variables are used in conflicting or mismatched contexts along two or more intersecting data-flow paths.
- **Custom Output Controls:** Frameworks such as .NET encourage reusing output rendering code by providing built-in "controls", which are classes that render untrusted inputs in HTML codes. Large applications extensively define custom controls, perhaps because they find the built-in controls insufficient. The running example is typical of such real-world applications — it defines its own custom controls, `DynamicLink`, to render user-specified links via JavaScript.

In this paper, we empirically analyze the extent to which these inconsistency errors arise in practical real-world code. In security-conscious applications, such as the ones we study, security audits are routine and use of lint tools can enforce simple discipline. In particular, notice that running example code is careful to restrict the browser context in which data is allowed to be embedded. For instance, it rigorously appends quotes to each attribute value, as recommended by security guidelines [27].

We point out that state-of-the-art static analysis tools which scale to hundred-thousand LOC applications, presently are fairly limited. Most existing tools detect data-flow paths with sanitizers missing altogether. This class of errors is detected by several static or dynamic analysis tools (such as CAT.NET [22] or Fortify [9]). In this paper, we focus instead on the errors where sanitization is present but is inconsistent.

3. SCRIPTGARD APPROACH

ScriptGard employs a dynamic analysis approach to detecting and auto-correcting context-inconsistency errors in sanitization. At a high-level, the overall architecture for ScriptGard is shown in Figure 4. ScriptGard has two main components: (a) a training or analysis phase, and (b) a runtime auto-correction component. In the analysis step, ScriptGard traces the dynamic execution of the application on test inputs. By tracking the flow of trusted values, ScriptGard can identify all untrusted data embedded in the application's output. Given a trace of an application's execution, ScriptGard is capable of mapping the trace to a static program path. ScriptGard is able to determine the correct sequence of sanitizers that should be applied on this program path, by parsing the application's output.

The results of our analysis phase are cached in a *sanitization cache*, which records all execution paths that were seen to have context-inconsistency sanitization errors. This cache serves as a basis for runtime auto-correction of the application during deployed operation. Our intuition is that context-inconsistency arises in a relatively small fraction of the application's code paths. ScriptGard's architecture repairs the placement of sanitizers only on these execution paths by using a light-weight instrumentation. The auto-correction component deploys a low-overhead path-detection

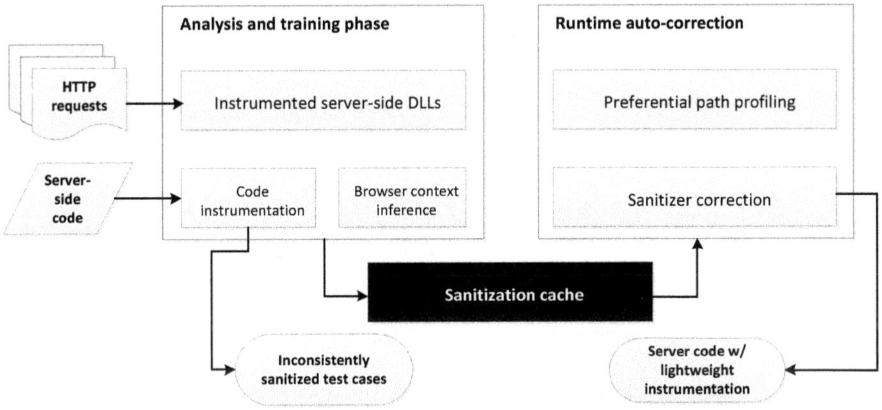

Figure 4: ScriptGard architecture.

technique that detects when these problematic paths are executed at runtime and applies the correct sanitization to untrusted values. The primary motivation for this architecture is to enable separation of expensive analysis to be performed prior to deployment, leaving only low-overhead components enabled at runtime. Another key feature of our auto-correction component is that it requires no updates or changes to the application code, thereby avoiding a long develop-review-patch development cycle.

Requirements: ScriptGard requires a map between browser contexts and sanitizer functions appropriate for those contexts. In practice this correspondence is specified by security architects or other experts and can be done once and for all.

Figure 7 shows the example sanitization specification for the running example as well as the applications we study. The sanitizer `SimpleHTMLFormatting` transforms the input such that its output can only contain certain permitted HTML tags such as `<b>`, `<a>` and so on, with the goal of preventing a browser from executing any JavaScript from the resulting string. In contrast, the sanitizer `EcmaScriptStringEncode` takes JavaScript literals and converts them to Unicode. Such conversion is necessary because the JavaScript parser converts Unicode to some other representation for string data. A similar function `UrlPathEncode` performs percent-encoding. This percent encoding is required because the URL parser will decode URLs on entry to the parser.

Reasoning about the localized correctness and completeness properties of the context-sanitizer mapping is an independent problem of interest; techniques for such correctness checking are an area of active research [2, 15, 17]. In this work, we assume the functional completeness and correctness for the specifications.

3.1 Training Phase

ScriptGard employs a dynamic analysis which treats each executed path as a sequence of *traces*. Each trace is conceptually a sequence of dataflow computation operations that end in a write to the HTTP stream or an *output sink*. As we highlighted in Section 2, we must consider traces because sanitizer placement is *path-sensitive*. ScriptGard's dynamic analysis checks if the sanitization applied on any untrusted trace is correct. For each untrusted trace observed during program execution, ScriptGard first determines a mapping for each program trace $\vec{t}$ to a sequence of sanitizer functions, $f_1, f_2, \ldots, f_k$, to apply, and second the portion of the output string that should be sanitized.

We call the first step *context inference*. The second step is achieved by a technique called *positive taint-tracking*. If the sequence of sanitizers applied on a trace does not match the inferred sequence, ScriptGard discovers a violating path and it adds the corrected sanitizer sequence for this path to the sanitization cache.

Positive Tainting: We have discussed untrusted execution traces in the abstract, but we have not talked about how ScriptGard determines which traces are untrusted and, therefore, need to be sanitized. Exhaustively identifying all the sources of untrusted data can be challenging [19]. Recent work has shown that failure to identify non-web related channels, such as data read from the file system, results in cross-channel scripting attacks [5].

Instead of risking an incomplete specification, which would miss potential vulnerabilities, ScriptGard takes a conservative approach to identifying untrusted data: it employs *positive tainting*, which is a modification of traditional (or negative tainting) used in several previous systems [12, 18, 26, 31, 35, 36]. Instead of tracking untrusted (negative) data as it propagates in the program, we track all safe data. Positive tainting is conservative because if input specifications are incomplete, unknown sources of data are treated as unsafe by default. We describe details of these two steps in Section 5.

3.2 Runtime Auto-Correction

From the training phase, ScriptGard builds a *sanitization cache*, which is a map between code paths and the correct sequence of sanitizers to apply for the browser context reached by that code path. Then at runtime, ScriptGard detects which path is actually executed by the program. If the path has been seen in the training phase, then ScriptGard can look up and apply the correct sanitizer sequence from the cache, obviating the need for the full taint flow instrumentation.

If the path has not been seen in the training phase, then the owner of the web site has a policy choice. One choice is

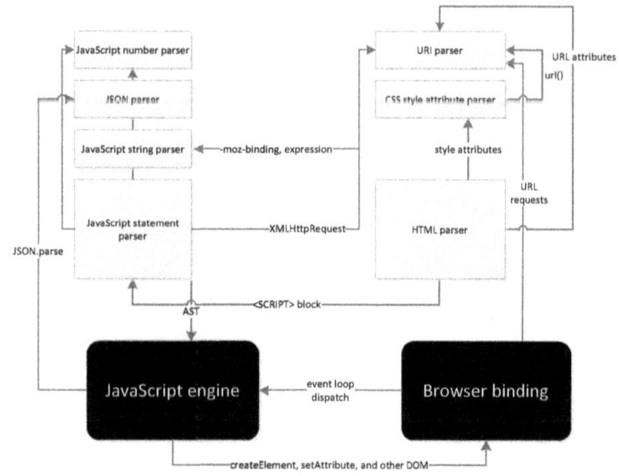

Figure 5: An abstract model of an HTML 5-compliant Web browser. Gray boxes represent various parsers for the browser sub-grammars. Black boxes are the major browser execution components.

to drop the request, then immediately re-execute the application with all SCRIPTGARD checks enabled. This is secure but adds signficant user latency. The other choice is to allow the request to complete, but then log the path taken for later analysis. This is not secure but preserves the performance of the application. We leave this choice up to the application administrator.

The common overhead for runtime in both policy choices comes from the cost to detect the path executed by the application. We leverage a technique called *preferential path profiling*, as first used in the Holmes statistical debugging project [7]. Preferential path profiling is a technique for adding lightweight instrumentation to a program to detect if the program executes one of a set of "preferred" paths known in advance of deployment. The technique uses an optimized way of labeling code blocks and updating state during execution to reduce overhead. We report overhead on our application in Section 5.

4. FORMALIZATION

In this section, we formalize our approach and the security properties we aim to achieve. We start with an abstract model of the browser. This allows us to define precisely what we mean by a *browser parsing context*. The notion of a context is closely tied to sanitizers that are used, as discussed previously in Section 2. For example, `HtmlAttributeEncode` will properly escape strings in the HTML attribute context, but it is inconsistent to use in other contexts. That in turn allows us to precisely characterize context-sanitizer mismatches. We then define what it means for a server-side program to prevent all such context-sanitizer mismatches. Finally, we show that our strategy in SCRIPTGARD in fact transforms programs into ones that ensure dynamically that no context-sanitizer mismatches are possible.

4.1 Browser Model: Definitions

We begin with a browser model as illustrated in Figure 5. For our purposes, we model a web browser as a parser consisting of sub-parsers for several languages. Of course, a real browser has a great deal of implementation issues and side effects to grapple with, but these are out scope of the problems we consider here.

More precisely, we treat the browser as a *collection* of parsers for different HTML standard-supported languages. Figure 5 shows the sub-grammars corresponding to the HTML language, JavaScript language, and the languages for web addresses and inline style attributes.

Because inconsistent application behavior may depend on context that are more fine-grained that regular HTML or JavaScript parsing, we can further divide each sub-grammar into partitions. For instance, the figure shows the JavaScript grammar further subdivided into the string literal sub-grammar, JSON sub-grammar, statement sub-grammar and the number sub-grammar. Formally, we model the browser as a composition of multiple sub-grammars.

Definition 1. *Let $G_1, G_2, ...G_n$ be n sub-grammars, where each context-free grammar $G_i = (V_i, \Sigma_i, S_i, P_i)$ is a quadruple consisting of a set of non-terminals V_i, terminals Σ_i , start symbol S_i and productions P_i.*

Let $\mathcal{T}$ be a set of grammar cross-grammar transition symbols *and the grammar transition productions $P_\mathcal{T}$, be a set of productions of the form $A \rightarrow T_i$ or $T_i \rightarrow B$, such that $A \in V_i$, $B \in V_j$ $(i \neq j)$ and $T_i \in \mathcal{T}$.*

We define a web browser as a grammar $\mathcal{G} = \{V, \Sigma, \mathcal{S}, P\}$, with non-terminals $V = V_1 \cup V_2 ... \cup V_n$, terminals $\Sigma = \cup\Sigma_i$, start symbol $\mathcal{S}$ and a set of productions $P = P_\mathcal{T} \cup P_1 \cup P_2 ... P_n$.

Conceptually, parsers for various languages are invoked in stages. After each sub-parser invocation, if a portion of the input HTML document is recognized to belong to another sub-language, that portion of the input is sent to the appropriate sub-language parser in the next stage. As a result, any portion of the input HTML document may be recognized by one or more sub-grammars. Transitions from one sub-grammar to another are restricted through productions involving special transition symbols defined above as $\mathcal{T}$, which is key for our formalization of context. In a real web browser, each transition from one sub-grammar to another may be accompanied by a one or more transduction steps of the recognized input.

Example 2. For instance, data recognized as a JavaScript string is subject to Unicode decoding before being passed to the AST. In addition, HTML 5-compliant browsers subject data recognized as a URI to percent-encoding of certain characters before it is sent to the URI parser [8].

This form of encoding can be modeled using additional rules in either of the sub-grammars. While restricting the browser formalism to a context-free grammar might elide some of the real-world complexities, we find this to be a convenient way for defining the notion of context, which appears to match the reality quite well. ■

Browser Parsing Contexts: We formally define the notion of a *browser parsing context* here, with reference to the grammar $\mathcal{G}$. Intuitively, a context reflects the state of the browser at a given point reading a particular piece of input HTML. Each step in the derivation, denoted by $\Rightarrow$ applies a production rule and yields a "sentential form", i.e., a sequence consisting of non-terminals and terminals. We model the parsing context as a sequence of transitions made by the parser between the sub-grammars in $\mathcal{G}$, only allowing the derivations that denote transition from one sub-grammar to another.

Definition 2. *Let derivation $D : \mathcal{S} \Rightarrow^* \gamma$ correspond to the sequence $(P_1, P_2, ...P_k)$ of production rule applications to derive a sentential form γ from the start symbol $\mathcal{S}$.*

A browser context $\mathcal{C}_\mathcal{D}$ induced by a derivation D is defined as a projection $(P_1, P_2, \ldots P_k) \rightarrow_\downarrow (P'_1, P'_2 \ldots P'_l)$, that preserves only the productions P'_i in the set of grammar transitions $P_\mathcal{T}$.

Our grammars are deterministic, so the notion of inducing a parsing context is well-defined. The browser enters a particular context as a result of processing a portion of the input.

Definition 3. *We say that an input I induces browser context $\mathcal{C}$, if*

- *$D : \mathcal{S}(I) \Rightarrow^* \gamma$ (on input I, $\mathcal{S}$ reduces to γ following derivation $\mathcal{D}$), and*
- *$\mathcal{D}$ induces context C.*

Sanitizers: A complex modern web application typically has a variety of both server- and client-side *sanitizers*. We make the simplifying assumption that sanitizers are *pure*, i.e. lacking side-effects. Our review of dozens of real-life sanitizers confirms this assumption. We model sanitizers as abstract functions on strings. Formally,

Definition 4. *A* sanitizer *is a function $f : string \mapsto string$.*

Definition 5. *A context-sanitizer map is*

$$\psi(\mathcal{C}) = \vec{f}$$

where $\mathcal{C}$ is a context and $\vec{f}$ is a sequence of sanitizers.

The goal of sanitization is typically to remove special characters that would lead to a sub-grammar transition. For example, we often do not want a transition from the HTML parsing context to the JavaScript parsing context, which would be enabled by inserting a `<SCRIPT>` block in the middle of otherwise non-offending HTML. Of course, this is but one of many ways that the parser can transition to a different context. Next, we define the *correctness* of a sequence of sanitizers. The intuition is that is after sanitization, the state of parsing is confined to a single context.

Definition 6. *Let input $\mathcal{I}$ consist of the* parsed *and* non-parsed *portion: $\mathcal{I} = [\mathcal{I}_P \circ \mathcal{I}_{NP}]$. Let input $\mathcal{I}_P$ induce browser context $\mathcal{C}$ such that $\psi(\mathcal{C}) = \vec{f}$. Then we say that the context-sanitizer map is* correct *if when $\vec{f}(\mathcal{I}_{NP})$ is reduced, the grammar never leaves context $\mathcal{C}$.*

In other words, applying the correct sequence of sanitizers "locks" a string in the current context. In particular, a string locked in the HTML context cannot cause the browser to transition to the JavaScript context, leading to a code injection.

4.2 Server-side Program: Definitions

So far, our discussion has focused on parsing HTML strings within the browser regardless of their source. Our goal is to produce HTML on the server that will always have consistent sanitization. Server-side programs take both untrusted and trusted inputs. Untrusted inputs are the well-known sources of injection possibilities such as HTML form fields, HTML headers, query strings, cookies, etc. Trusted inputs are often read from configuration files, trusted databases, etc. Note that the notion of what is trusted and what is not is often not clear-cut. Section 3.1 describes how ScriptGard addresses this problem. Next, we define what it means for a program to properly sanitize its inputs.

Definition 7. *A server-side program $\mathcal{P} : \mathcal{I} \rightarrow \mathcal{O}$ defines a relation from untrusted user inputs I to output string $\mathcal{O}$. The program interprocedural data flow graph is a graph $\langle \mathcal{N}, \mathcal{E} \rangle$ with designated sets of nodes*

$$\langle Src, Snk, San \rangle \subseteq \langle \mathcal{N} \times \mathcal{N} \times \mathcal{N} \rangle$$

where Src are the sources that introduce an untrusted inputs in $\mathcal{P}$, Snk are the sinks that write strings to the output HTTP stream, and San are the sanitizers used by the program.

Without loss of generality, we assume that sink nodes either write untrusted strings to the output stream or trusted strings, but never strings containing both. Sink operations with mixed content can be translated to an equivalent dataflow graph with only exclusively trusted or untrusted sink nodes using sink node splitting: the output of a mixed string $Snk(q_1 + q_2 + \cdots + r_1 + \ldots q_n)$ can be split into a sequence of exclusive sink writes $Snk(q_1)$, $Snk(q_2) \ldots, Snk(r), \ldots, Snk(q_n)$.

Definition 8. *An* untrusted execution trace *t of program $\mathcal{P}$ is a sequence of executed nodes*

$$\vec{t} = n_1, \ldots, n_k \in \mathcal{N}$$

such that $n_1 \in Src$, $n_k \in Snk$.

Definition 9. *Let t be an untrusted execution trace $\vec{t} = n_1 \ldots n_k$ and let $\vec{f} = f_1, \ldots, f_m$ be a sequence of sanitizers such that $f_1, \ldots, f_m$ is a subsequence of $n_2, \ldots, n_{k-1}$.*

For all inputs $\mathcal{I}$, let O be the total output string just before the execution of the sink node in $\vec{t}$. We say that trace $\vec{t}$ is properly sanitized *if $\mathcal{O}$ induces context $\mathcal{C}$ and $\psi(\mathcal{C}) = \vec{f}$.*

In other words, for all possible trace executions, we require that the proper set of sanitizers be applied on trace for the expected parsing context. Note that *trusted* traces are allowed to change the browser context. A common example of that is

```
output.WriteLine("<SCRIPT>");
output.WriteLine("alert('hi');");
output.WriteLine("</SCRIPT>");
```

where each string is a sink and the first and third lines correspond to browser state transitions.

Theorem 1. *If untrusted trace $\vec{t}$ is properly sanitized, assume the browser has read string $\mathcal{O}$ which induces context $\mathcal{C}$. Then reading the rest of the string output produced by $\vec{t}$ cannot induce any contexts $\mathcal{C}' \neq \mathcal{C}$.*

Proof: *Let input $\mathcal{I} = [\mathcal{I}_P \circ \mathcal{I}_{NP}]$. By Definition 9, for all input-output pairs $\mathcal{I}_P \rightarrow \mathcal{O}$, $\vec{t}$ contains sanitizers $\vec{f}$ correct for any context $\mathcal{C}$ inducible by $\mathcal{O}$. By Definition 6, we know that applying $\vec{f}$ to the remainder of the input $\mathcal{I}_{N\mathcal{P}}$ cannot leave context $\mathcal{C}$.*

For reasons of correctness, we wish to ensure that all untrusted execution traces are properly sanitized.

Definition 10. *A server-side program $\mathcal{P}$ is* properly sanitized *if for every untrusted execution trace $\vec{t}$ of $\mathcal{P}$, $\vec{t}$ is properly sanitized.*

As an obvious corollary, if the program is properly sanitized, then no untrusted input to the server program can force the browser to change its context.

5. IMPLEMENTATION DETAILS

We now describe our implementation in more detail, with reference to the ASP.NET framework. This section first describes positive taint tracking implemented in SCRIPTGARD in Section 5.1, and then context inference and auto-correcting runtime sanitization in Sections 5.2 and 5.3.

5.1 Positive Taint Tracking

We describe our full implementation for positive taint tracking for strings in the .NET platform. The .NET runtime supports two kinds of string objects: *mutable* and *immutable* objects. Immutable objects, instances of the `System.String` class, are called so because their value cannot be modified once it has been created [23]. Methods that appear to modify a `String` actually return a new `String` containing the modification. The .NET language also defines mutable strings with its `System.Text.StringBuilder` class, which allows in-place modification of string values; but all access to the characters in its value are mediated through methods of this class [24]. In essence, all strings in .NET are objects, whose values are accessed through public methods of the class — the language does support a primitive `string` type but the compiler converts `string` type to the `String` object and uses class methods whenever the value of a primitive `string` type is manipulated.

Using the encapsulation features offered by the language, we have implemented the taint status for each string object rather than keeping a bit for each character. The taint status of each string object maintains metadata that identifies if the string is untrusted and if so, the portion of the string that is untrusted. Our implementation maintains a weak hash table for each object, which keys on weak references to objects, so that our instrumentation does not interfere with the garbage collection of the original application objects and scales in size. Entries to freed objects are therefore automatically dropped. Taint propagation, capturing direct data dependencies between string objects, is implemented by using wrapper functions for all operations in string classes. Each wrapper function updates the taint status of string objects at runtime.

We use CCI Metadata [34], a robust static .NET binary rewriting infrastructure to instrument each call to the string object constructors with taint propagation methods. The .NET language is a stack-based language and CCI Metadata provides the ability to interpose on any code block and statically rewrite it. Using this basic facility, we have implemented a library that allows caller instrumentation of specified functions, which allows redirection of original method calls to static wrapper methods of a user-defined class. Redirection of virtual function calls is handled the same way as static calls with the exception that the wrapper function accepts the instance object (sometimes referred to as the `this` parameter) is received as the first argument to the wrapper function.

Soundness Considerations: We explain how our positive taint implementation is sound, i.e., does not miss identifying untrusted data, with exception identified in point 5 below. We show that this exception are rare in our test program.

1. The language encapsulation features provide the guarantee that all access to the string values are only permitted through the invocation of methods defined in the string classes.
2. All constant strings belong to the immutable string primitive type. Any modification to the primitive value by the program is compiled to a conversion to an object of the string class, which invokes the string class constructors. Thus, we can safely track all sources of taint by instrumenting these constructors.
3. The string classes `System.String` and `System.Text.StringBuilder` are both *sealed* classes; that is, they cannot be inherited by other classes. This eliminates the possibility that objects that we do not track could invoke methods on the string classes.
4. Conversion between the two string classes is possible. This involves the call to the `Object.ToString` generic method. Statically, we instrument all these calls, and use .NET's built-in reflection at runtime to identify if the dynamic instance of the object being converted to a string and perform the taint metadata update.
5. String class constructors which convert values from non-string types are treated as safe (or positively tainted) by default. This is because we do not currently track taint status for these types. In principle, this is a source of potential unsoundness in our implementation. For example, the following code will lead our tracking to treat untrusted data as trusted:

```
String untrusted = Request.RawUrl;
var x = untrusted.ToCharArray();
....
String outputstr = new String(x);
httpw.Write(outputstr);
```

   Fortunately, these constructors are rare in practice. Figure 11(a) shows the distribution of functions instrumented by SCRIPTGARD. The key finding is that potentially unsound constructions occur only in 42 out of 23,244 functions instrumented for our application. Our implementation ignores this source of false negatives presently; we can imagine verifying that these do not interfere with our needs using additional static analysis or implement more elaborate taint-tracking in the future.

Output: The result of SCRIPTGARD's analysis is three pieces of information. First, SCRIPTGARD marks the portion of the server's output which is not positively tainted. The untrusted texts are delimited using special markers consisting of characters that are outside the alphabet used by the application legitimately. Second, for each string written to the HTTP output stream, it records the sequence of propagators (such as string concatenation, format-string based substitution) applied on the output text fragment. In essence, this allows SCRIPTGARD to (a) separate strings that are used for constructing HTML output templates from other strings, and, (b) identify the propagator that places the untrusted data into an output template. Third, it records a path string identifying the control flow path leading to each HTML output sink operation.

In addition to the above information, SCRIPTGARD gathers the sequence of sanitizers applied to a given untrusted data. To do this, each sanitizer is instrumented similarly to surround the input data with additional special markup identifying that sanitizer's application to the input data. The knowledge of the untrusted data along with the nesting of sanitizers is thus encoded in the HTML output of the server. This output is then subject to the context inference step, which is described next.

5.2 Context Inference

For a given analyzed path the server outputs a HTML response encoding the information identifying sub-strings that are untrusted, as well as, the sequence of sanitizers applied. SCRIPTGARD employs a web browser to determine the contexts in which untrusted data is placed, in order to check if the sanitization sequence is consistent with the required sequence.

In our implementation, we use an HTML 5 compliant parser used in the C3 browser, that has been developed from scratch using code contracts to be as close to the current specification as possible. It has a fast JavaScript engine as well. The parser takes an HTML page as input. In the page, untrusted data is identified by special markup. The special markup is introduced at the server's output by our positive taint-tracking.

We augment the HTML parser to track the sequence of browser contexts in which data marked as untrusted appears. In our implementation for HTML, we treat each context to be (a) the state of the lexer (as defined in the HTML 5 draft specification), (b) the stack of open elements (as defined in the HTML 5 draft specification), and (c) specific information about the local state of the parse tree (such as the name of current tag or attribute being processed).

We apply techniques similar to string accenting for tracking untrusted data in other contexts [6]; DOM nodes that correspond to untrusted data are also marked. Similar context tracking is applied for the JavaScript parser. For the policy of our applications and the policies identified in previous work [20], we have found this level of tracking to be adequate.

Using context information, SCRIPTGARD decides the correct sequence of sanitizers to apply for a given untrusted execution trace. To determine the correct sanitizer sequence, SCRIPTGARD applies for each context in the trace, in the nesting order, the appropriate sanitizer from the input sanitization specification. The inferred chain of sanitizers is guaranteed to be correct for the trace, eliminating multiple sanitization errors that could have resulted from manual placement.

5.3 Runtime Sanitization Auto-Correction

During analysis or training, for each untrusted trace writing to sink operation S, SCRIPTGARD records the static program path by profiling. It also record the first propagator P in the dataflow computation, typically a string concatenation or format-string based string substitution, that places the untrusted data inside the trusted output string emitted at S. SCRIPTGARD instruments the deployed application with a low-overhead runtime path detector. During deployed operation, If the currently executing path is is in the sanitization cache, SCRIPTGARD sanitizes the untrusted substring(s) in the output string using the following technique.

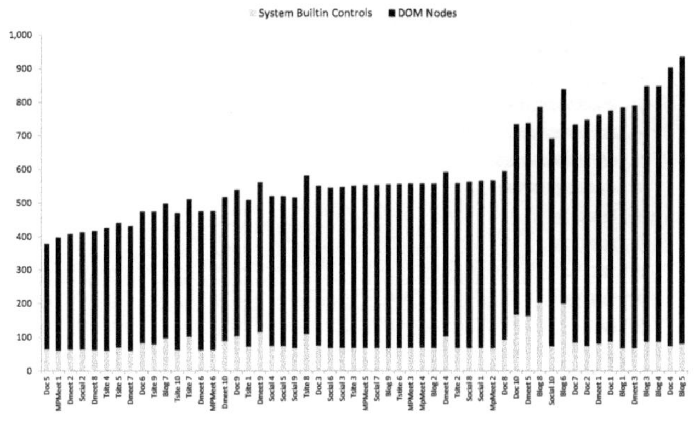

Figure 6: Distribution of DOM sizes, in nodes, across our training HTML pages.

HTML Sink Context	Correct sanitizer that suffices
HTML Tag Context	`HTMLEncode, SimpleTextFormatting`
Double Quoted Attribute	`HTMLAttribEncode`
Single Quoted Attribute	`HTMLAttribEncode`
URL Path attribute	`URLPathEncode`
URL Key-Value Pair	`URLKeyValueEncode`
In Script String	`EcmaScriptStringEncode`
CDATA	`HTMLEncode`
Style	`Alpha − numerics`

Figure 7: Sanitizer-to-context mapping for our test application.

Rewriting untrusted output: SCRIPTGARD maintains a *shadow copy* of the untrusted data. If the path is not in the sanitization cache, the actual value of the untrusted data is used at output sink. If the path is in the sanitization cache, the shadow copy is sanitized, then the results are output.

To do this, SCRIPTGARD instrumentation-based program transformation for maintaining shadow copies for each untrusted trace computation. Each untrusted trace computation is essentially a sequence of string propagator operations like string concatenation and format-string based substitution writing at a sink S. At string propagators using untrusted inputs, the added instrumentation creates a shadow copy of the untrusted data, and delimits it with special markup. At S, if the path executed is in the sanitization cache, the added instrumentation strips the actual value and markup out, applies the sanitization on the shadow copy, and writes it to the output stream. Finally, at S, if the path is not in the sanitization cache, the instrumentation strips the shadow value out and writes the actual value to the output stream leaving the application behavior unchanged for such paths.

6. EVALUATION

Our evaluation focuses on a large legacy application of over 400,000 lines of server-side C# code. We accessed 53

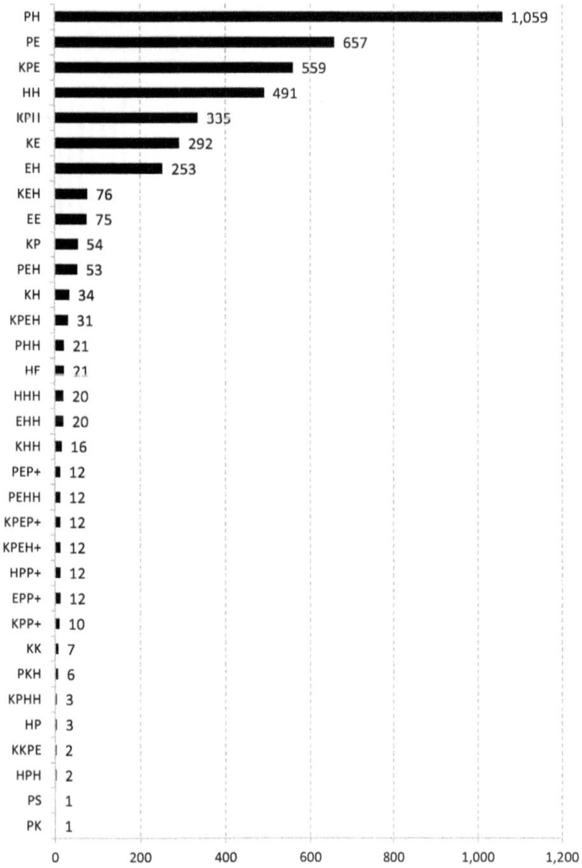

Figure 8: Histogram of sanitizer sequences consisting of 2 or more sanitizers empirically observed in analysis, characterizing sanitization practices resulting from manual sanitizer placement. E,H,U, K,P,S denote sanitizers `EcmaScriptStringLiteralEncode`, `HtmlEncode`, `HtmlAttribEncode`, `UrlKeyValueEncode`, `UrlPathEncode`,`SimpleHtmlEncode` respectively.

distinct web pages, which we subjected to ScriptGard analysis. Figure 6 shows the size of the various web pages in terms of the number of DOM nodes they generate from their initial HTML output (ignoring dynamic updates to the DOM via JavaScript, etc.). Page sizes range from 350 to 900 nodes. Our analysis statically instrumented 23,244 functions.

Our application uses custom objects that handle their own rendering. Figure 6 shows a majority of the DOM nodes in the applications' outputs are derived from custom objects. The language-based solution of ScriptGard, as opposed to .NET runtime library-specific solution, allows it to directly analyze these custom objects.

Figure 7 shows the mapping between contexts and sanitization functions for our application; which is a strict subset of mapping in previous work [20]. In particular, it permits only quoted attributes which have well-defined rules for sanitization [27]. Furthermore, it always sets the page encoding to UTF-8, eliminating the possibility of character-set encoding attacks [14]. We arrived at the result in Figure 7 after several interactions with the application's security engineers.

6.1 Analysis Results

Context-mismatched sanitization: Figure 9 shows that ScriptGard exercised 25,209 paths on which sanitization was applied. Of these, 1,558 paths (or 6.1%) were improperly sanitized. Of these improperly sanitized paths, 1,207 (4.7% of the total analyzed paths) contained data that could not be proven safe by our positive taint tracking infrastructure, so therefore are candidates for runtime automatic choice of sanitization. The remaining 1.4% of paths were sanitizing trusted strings improperly; ScriptGard does not consider these to be safe, therefore they do not need runtime correction.

We used Red Gate's .NET Reflector tool, combined with other decompilation tools, to further investigate the executions which ScriptGard reported as improperly sanitized. Our subsequent investigation reveals that errors result because it is difficult to manually analyze the calling context in which a particular potion of code may be invoked. In particular, the source and the sink may be separated by several intervening functions. Since ScriptGard instruments all string operations, we can count how far sources and sinks are removed from each other, as shown in 11(b). In Figure 10, we graph the distribution of these lengths for a randomly selected sample of untrusted paths. This shows that a significant fraction of the chains are long and over 200 of them exceed 5 steps.

Our data on the length of def-use chains is consistent with those reported in previous static analysis based work [18]. As explained in Section 2, the sharing of dataflow paths can result in further ambiguity in distinguishing context at the HTML output point in the server, as well as, in distinguishing trusted data from untrusted data. In our investigation we observed the following cases:

- A single sanitizer was applied in a context that did not match. Typically, the sanitizer applied was in a different function from the one that constructed the HTML template. This suggests that developers may not fully understand how the context — a global property — impacts the choice of sanitizer, which is a local property. This is not surprising, given the complexity of choices in Figure 7.
- A sanitizer was applied to trusted data (on 1.4% of the paths in our experiment) We still report these cases because they point to developer confusion. On further investigation, we determined this was because sinks corresponding to these executions were shared by several dataflow paths. Each such sink node could output potentially untrusted data on some executions, while outputting purely trusted data on others.
- More than one sanitizer was applied, but the applied sanitizers were not correct for the browser parsing context of the data[1].

Inconsistent Multiple Sanitization: We found 3,245 paths with more than one sanitizer. Of these, 285 (or 8%) of the paths with multiple sanitization were inconsistent with the context. The inconsistent paths fell into two categories: first, we found 273 instances with

[1]Errors where the combination was correct but the ordering was inconsistent with the nested context are reported separately as inconsistent multiple sanitization errors.

Web Page	Sanitized Paths	Inconsistently sanitized	
		Total	Highlight
Home	396	14	9
A1 P1	565	28	22
A1 P2	336	16	11
A1 P3	992	26	21
A1 P4	297	44	35
A1 P5	482	22	17
A1 P6	436	23	18
A1 P7	403	19	13
A1 P8	255	22	18
A1 P9	214	16	12
A1 P10	1,623	18	14
A2 P1	315	16	12
A2 P2	736	53	47
A2 P3	261	21	16
A2 P4	197	16	12
A2 P5	182	22	18
A2 P6	237	22	18
A2 P7	632	20	16
A2 P8	450	23	19
A2 P9	802	26	22
A3 P1	589	25	21
A3 P2	2,268	18	14
A3 P3	389	16	12
A3 P4	477	103	15
A3 P5	323	24	20
A3 P6	292	51	45
A3 P7	219	16	12
A3 P8	691	25	21
A3 P9	173	16	12
A4 P1	301	24	20
A4 P2	231	30	25
A4 P3	271	28	22
A4 P4	436	38	32
A4 P5	956	36	24
A4 P6	193	24	18
A4 P7	230	36	32
A4 P8	310	24	20
A4 P9	200	24	18
A4 P10	208	24	20
A4 P11	498	34	29
A4 P12	579	34	29
A4 P13	295	25	20
A4 P14	591	104	91
A5 P1	604	61	55
A5 P2	376	25	21
A5 P3	376	25	21
A5 P4	401	26	21
A5 P5	565	31	26
A5 P6	493	34	29
A5 P7	521	34	29
A5 P8	427	24	20
A5 P9	413	24	20
A5 P10	502	28	23
Total	25,209	1,558	1,207

Figure 9: Characterization of the fraction of the paths that were inconsistently sanitized. The right-most column indicates which fraction of those paths could not be proved safe and so were highlighted by our analysis. The difference between last and second last colmn is that some paths sanitize constant strings or provably trusted data.

the (**EcmaScriptStringLiteralEncode**)(**HtmlEncode**)+ pattern applied. As we saw in Section 2, these sanitizers do not commute, and this specific order is inconsistent. Second, we found 12 instances of the (**EcmaScriptStringLiteralEncode**)(**UrlPathEncode**)+ pattern. This pattern is inconsistent because it does not properly handle sanitization of URL parameters. If an adversary controls the data sanitized, it may be able to inject additional parameters.

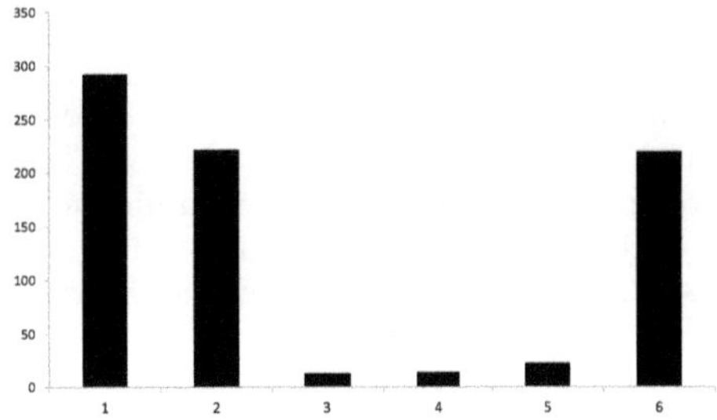

Figure 10: Distribution of lengths of paths that could not be proved safe. Each hop in the path is a string propagation function. The longer the chain, the more removed are taint sources from taint sinks.

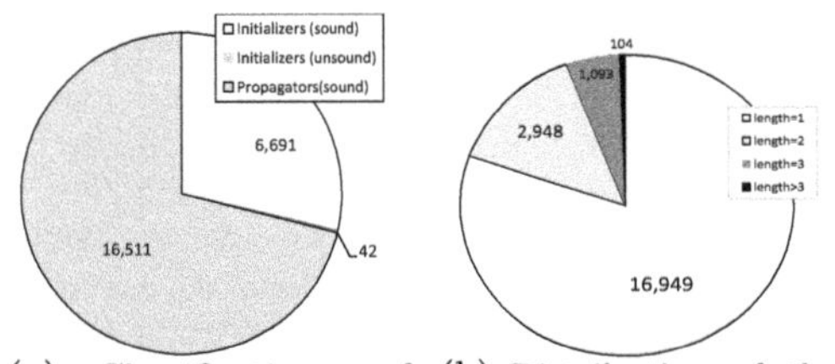

(a) Classification of functions used for ScriptGard instrumentation.

(b) Distribution of the lengths of applied sanitization chains, showing a sizable fraction of the paths have more than one sanitizer applied.

Figure 11: Characterizing ScriptGard instrumentation.

We found an additional 498 instances of multiple sanitization that were superfluous. That is, sanitizer A was applied before sanitizer B, rendering sanitizer B superfluous. While not a security bug, this multiple sanitization could break the intended functionality of the applications. For example, repeated use of **UrlKeyValueEncode** could lead to multiple percent encoding causing broken URLs. Repeated use of **HtmlEncode** could lead to multiple HTML entity-encoding causing incorrect rendering of output HTML.

We also observed that nesting of parsing contexts is common. For example a URL may be nested within an HTML attribute. Figure 11(b) shows the histogram of sanitizer sequence lengths observed. The inferred context for a majority of these sinks demanded the use of multiple sanitizers. Figure 8 shows the use of multiple sanitizers in the application is widespread, with sanitizer sequences such as **UrlPathEncode HtmlEncode** being most popular. In our application, these sanitizers are not commutative, i.e. they produce different outputs if composed in different orders, which means that paths with different orderings produce different behavior.

Because ScriptGard is a dynamic technique, all paths found can be reproduced with test cases exhibiting the context-inconsistent sanitization. We investigated a small fraction of these test cases in more depth. We found that while the sanitization is in fact inconsistent, injecting strings in these contexts did not lead to privilege escalation attacks. In part this is because our positive tainting is conservative: if we cannot prove a string is safe, we flag the path. In other cases, adversary's authority and the policy of the test application made it impossible to exploit the inconsistency.

6.2 Runtime Overhead

For our experiments, the server was a dual core Intel machine running at 3.16 GHz with 4 GB of RAM, 250 GB of 7200 RPM disk, running Windows Server 2008. Our client was a Core 2 Duo Intel machine running at 2.67 GHz with 8 GB of RAM, 160 GB of 7200 RPM disk, running 64-bit Windows 7. We connected the client and server directly using a network switch.

Full overhead: We started by measuring the overhead of the full SCRIPTGARD instrumentation, including positive taint flow and output parsing. Then we measured the overhead that would be incurred by the deployment phase of path preferential profiling techniques. While the full instrumentation incurs a huge overhead, the preferential profiling incurs negligible overhead.

We took nine URLs, each of which triggered complicated processing on the server to create the resulting web page. For each URL we first warmed the server cache by requesting the URL 13 times. We then measured the *time to first byte* of 13 additional queries to the server for the URL. Time to first byte is appropriate here because we are interested in the overhead added by SCRIPTGARD to server processing. Finally, we took the 75th percentile result, following web performance analysis practice used by colleagues at our institution responsible for a large public facing web site. Unfortunately, we found overheads of over 175.6x for the full analysis, for example a URL that took 0.53 seconds to load without instrumentation took 92.73 seconds to load with all checks.

PPP: Fortunately, we can shift much of this overhead to a pre-release phase by using preferential path profiling (PPP) techniques. As we described above, the optimizations in PPP include a smart way of numbering code blocks and a way to avoid updating global state when certain "preferred" paths are taken.

We used a wide-area network simulator running on the server to emulate conditions of a typical IEEE 802.11b link between the client and the server, to produce realistic network conditions for evaluating the total overhead. We then instrumented our application using preferential path profiling and performed training on a set of 19 URLs. To test the worst-case performance from PPP, we then chose 19 URLs completely different from those that were used during training. We then visited each URL 20 times and measured the time to first byte.

Figure 12 graphs the time to first byte for each of our test URLs, in milliseconds, after removing the first visit. To account for outliers, the time measurement represents the 75th percentile of the measurements over a series of 19 samples. Our graph shows error bars representing one standard deviation in each direction.

Figure 13 shows the median for each URL visited and the overhead for each of the 19 URLs. The average overhead for using preferential path profiling is actually negative, which we attibute to the overhead being too small to be statistically significant. We report overhead both for direct connection to the switch and for when the network simulator is in use configured to simulate an 802.11 connection. Our results show that while the runtime overhead of the full SCRIPTGARD analysis is prohibitive, the deployment overhead can be decreased greatly by shifting analysis to a training phase.

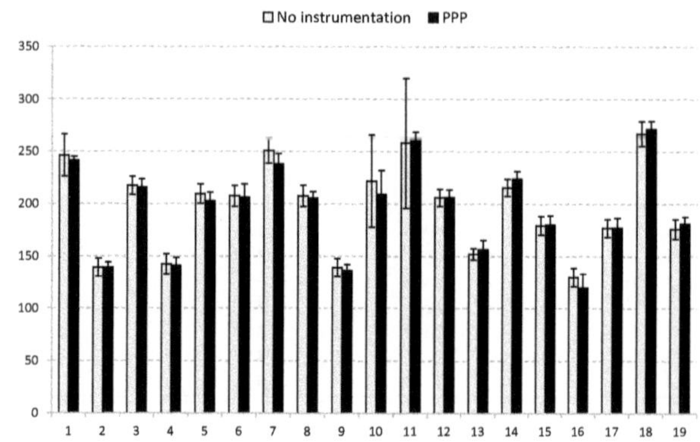

(a) Overhead over a switch.

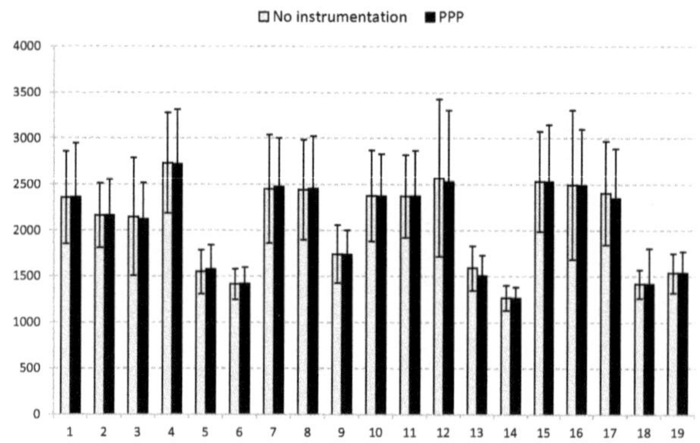

(b) Overhead over an 80211b connection.

Figure 12: Overhead of PPP on 19 URLs. Time is in milliseconds. Top of bar is the 75th percentile of 20 samples.

7. RELATED WORK

Many defense techniques for scripting attacks have been proposed, which we discuss next. SCRIPTGARD targets a new class of context-inconsistency errors.

Defense Techniques: Browser-based mitigations, such as Noncespaces, XSS Auditor, or DSI make changes to the web browsers that make it difficult for an adversary's script to run [3, 11, 25]. These approaches can be fast, but they require all users to upgrade their web browsers.

A server side mitigation, in contrast, focuses on changing the web application logic. BLUEPRINT describes mechanisms to ensure the safe construction of the intended HTML parse tree on the client using JavaScript in a browser-agnostic way [20]. However, issues in applying BLUEPRINT's mechanisms to various context still exist and developers may place them wrongly. Our work addresses this separate aspect of the problem, in a way that does not require any manual effort from developers.

XSS-GUARD [4] proposes techniques to learn allowed scripts from unintended scripts. The allowed scripts are then white-listed. Like SCRIPTGARD, it employs a web browser for its analysis, but the two approaches are fundamentally different. SCRIPTGARD's defense is based on automatic server-side sanitizer placement, rather than browser-based white-listing of scripting in server output. XSS-GUARD's techniques are intended for applications that allow rich HTML, where designing correct sanitizers becomes challenging. SCRIPTGARD target applications with fairly re-

Switch			80211b		
None	PPP	Overhead	None	PPP	Overhead
246.0	241.3	-1.93%	2,355.5	2,358.2	0.12%
139.3	139.3	0.00%	2,163.2	2,163.2	0.00%
217.3	215.5	-0.81%	2,146.5	2,121.2	-1.18%
142.5	141.0	-1.05%	2,731.8	2,719.0	-0.47%
209.5	202.5	-3.34%	1,548.7	1,574.4	1.66%
207.5	206.3	-0.60%	1,413.4	1,416.4	0.21%
250.5	238.0	-4.99%	2,451.7	2,476.5	1.01%
207.5	205.5	-0.96%	2,442.2	2,455.7	0.55%
139.3	136.3	-2.15%	1,742.2	1,739.9	-0.13%
221.8	209.0	-5.75%	2,376.2	2,370.7	-0.23%
258.0	260.3	0.87%	2,373.0	2,373.5	0.02%
206.0	206.3	0.12%	2,571.8	2,527.5	-1.72%
152.3	156.5	2.79%	1,588.9	1,505.9	-5.22%
215.8	224.0	3.82%	1,266.9	1,261.4	-0.43%
179.5	180.3	0.42%	2,533.5	2,530.8	-0.11%
130.0	119.8	-7.88%	2,493.5	2,489.2	-0.17%
177.0	177.3	0.14%	2,408.0	2,350.5	-2.39%
267.0	271.3	1.59%	1,416.1	1,413.1	-0.21%
176.3	181.0	2.70%	1,534.9	1,538.4	0.23%
Average		*-0.60%*	**Average**		*-0.13%*
Median		*-0.90%*	**Median**		*-0.45%*

Figure 13: PPP overhead statistics . Time is in milliseconds, 75th percentile reported from 20 samples.

strictive policies that have already addressed the sanitizer-correctness issue.

Google AutoEscape is a context-sensitive auto-sanitization mechanism for Google's GWT and CTemplates templating frameworks. As explained earlier, the templating languages it auto-sanitizes are much simpler and AutoEscape does not need to handle if-else or loop constructs which create path-senstivity a major issue. SCRIPTGARD's target is towards large-scale legacy applications, where sanitization placement logic is complex and already deployed, so rewriting all such logic is not practical.

SECURIFLY translates bug specifications written in a special program query to runtime instrumentation that detects these bugs [21]. Our approach reasons both about the browser context as well as the server state, allowing us to tackle sanitizer placement problems not detected by SECURIFLY.

Software security analysis of web applications: Software security focuses on using program analysis to find security critical bugs in applications. The WebSSARI project pioneered these approaches for web applications, and several static analysis tools have been propose [16, 35]. Runtime approaches, like ours, has the advantage of demonstrating clear, reproducible test cases over static analysis tools. Multiple runtime analysis systems for information flow tracking have been proposed, including Haldar *et al.* for Java [12] and Pietraszek *et al.* [28] and Nguyen-Tuong *et al.* for PHP [26]. Typically systems use *negative tainting* to specifically identify untrusted data in web applications applications [18, 19, 21, 36]. While negative taint is preferable for finding bugs, it is less desirable for mitigations because it requires specifying all sources of taint. Our design distinguishes itself from most previous work in that it tracks *positive taint*, which is conservative default fail-close approach, and side-steps identifying all sources of taint. The main exception is WASP [13], which does use positive taint, but which concerned SQL injection attacks, which do not exhibit the path sensitivity, use of multiple sanitizers, and need for a browser model to determine if data is a potential cross site scripting attack. WASP was also evaluated on much smaller applications (maximum 20,000 lines of code) than considered in this work.

Sanitizer correctness: Balzarotti *et al.* show that custom sanitizer routines are often incorrectly implemented [2].

Livshits *et al.* developed methods for determining which functions in a program play the role of sanitizer. Their MERLIN system is also capable of detecting missing sanitizers [19]. SCRIPTGARD's analysis is complementary to these works. Sanitizers may be present, and they may be functionally correct for contexts they are intended to be used in. Incorrect placement, however, can introduce errors.

The Cross-Site Scripting Cheat Sheet shows over two hundred examples of strings that exercise common corner cases of web sanitizers [29]. The BEK project proposes a systematic domain-specific languages for writing and checking sanitizers [15, 33].

8. CONCLUSIONS

We analyzed a set of 53 large web pages in a large-scale web application with over 400,000 lines of code. Each page contained 350–900 DOM nodes. We found 285 multiple-encoding issues, as well as 1,207 instances of inconsistent sanitizers, establishing the prevalence of our two new problem classes and the effectiveness of SCRIPTGARD as a testing aid. With preferential path profiling, when used for mitigation, SCRIPTGARD incurs virtually no statistically significant overhead on cached paths.

9. ACKNOWLEDGMENTS

We would like to give special thanks to Patrice Godefroid, who has been most instrumental in helping us define the problems. Kapil Vaswani made the ppp tool work with our application. We also thank Kapil Vaswani, David Wagner, Herman Venter, Joel Weinberger, Peli de Halleux, Nikolai Tillmann, Devdatta Akhawe, Adrian Mettler, Dawn Song, our anonymous reviewers, and other Microsoft colleagues. The first author performed this work while interning at Microsoft Research.

10. REFERENCES

[1] M. Balduzzi, C. Gimenez, D. Balzarotti, and E. Kirda. Automated discovery of parameter pollution vulnerabilities in web applications. In *Proceedings of the Network and Distributed System Security Symposium*, 2011.

[2] D. Balzarotti, M. Cova, V. Felmetsger, N. Jovanovic, E. Kirda, C. Kruegel, and G. Vigna. Saner: Composing Static and Dynamic Analysis to Validate Sanitization in Web Applications. In *Proceedings of the IEEE Symposium on Security and Privacy*, Oakland, CA, May 2008.

[3] D. Bates, A. Barth, and C. Jackson. Regular expressions considered harmful in client-side XSS filters. *International World Wide Web Conference*, 2010.

[4] P. Bisht and V. N. Venkatakrishnan. XSS-GUARD: precise dynamic prevention of cross-site scripting attacks. In *Detection of Intrusions and Malware, and Vulnerability Assessment*, 2008.

[5] H. Bojinov, E. Bursztein, and D. Boneh. XCS: Cross channel scripting and its impact on web applications. In *CCS*, 2009.

[6] S. Chen, D. Ross, and Y.-M. Wang. An analysis of browser domain-isolation bugs and a light-weight defense mechanism. In *Proceedings of the Conference on Computer and Communications Security*, October 2007.

[7] T. Chilimbi, B. Liblit, K. Mehra, A. V. Nori, , and K. Vaswani. Holmes: Effective statistical debugging via efficient path profiling. In *Proceedings of the International Conference on Software Engineering*, May 2009.

[8] D. Connolly and C. M. Sperberg-McQueen. Web addresses in HTML 5. `http://www.w3.org/html/wg/href/draft#ref-RFC3986`, 2009.

[9] Fortify, Inc. Fortify SCA. `http://www.fortifysoftware.com/products/sca/`, 2006.

[10] Google. Google auto escape. `http://google-ctemplate.googlecode.com/svn/trunk/doc/auto_escape.html`, 2011.

[11] M. V. Gundy and H. Chen. Noncespaces: using randomization to enforce information flow tracking and thwart cross-site scripting attacks. 2009.

[12] V. Haldar, D. Chandra, and M. Franz. Dynamic taint propagation for Java. In *Proceedings of the Annual Computer Security Applications Conference*, Dec. 2005.

[13] W. G. Halfond, A. Orso, and P. Manolios. WASP: Protecting web applications using positive tainting and syntax-aware evaluation. *IEEE Transactions on Software Engineering*, 34(1), 2008.

[14] Y. HASEGAWA. UTF-7 XSS cheat sheet. `http://openmya.hacker.jp/hasegawa/security/utf7cs.html`, 2005.

[15] P. Hooimeijer, B. Livhsits, D. Molnar, P. Saxena, and M. Veanes. Fast and precise sanitizer analysis with bek. In *Proceedings of the Usenix Security Symposium*, Aug. 2011.

[16] N. Jovanovic, C. Kruegel, and E. Kirda. Pixy: A static analysis tool for detecting Web application vulnerabilities (short paper). In *Proceedings of the IEEE Symposium on Security and Privacy*, 2006.

[17] A. Kieżun, V. Ganesh, P. J. Guo, P. Hooimeijer, and M. D. Ernst. HAMPI: A solver for string constraints. In *International Symposium on Software Testing and Analysis*, 2009.

[18] B. Livshits and M. S. Lam. Finding security errors in Java programs with static analysis. In *Proceedings of the Usenix Security Symposium*, 2005.

[19] B. Livshits, A. V. Nori, S. K. Rajamani, and A. Banerjee. Merlin: Specification inference for explicit information flow problems. In *Proceedings of the Conference on Programming Language Design and Implementation*, June 2009.

[20] M. T. Louw and V. N. Venkatakrishnan. Blueprint: Robust prevention of cross-site scripting attacks for existing browsers. In *Proceedings of the IEEE Symposium on Security and Privacy*, 2009.

[21] M. Martin, B. Livshits, and M. S. Lam. SecuriFly: runtime vulnerability protection for Web applications. Technical report, Stanford University, 2006.

[22] Microsoft Corporation. Microsoft code analysis tool .NET, 2009. `http://www.microsoft.com/downloads/en/details.aspx?FamilyId=0178e2ef-9da8-445e-9348-c93f24cc9f9d&displaylang=en`,.

[23] Microsoft Corporation. String class (system), 2010. `http://msdn.microsoft.com/en-us/library/system.string.aspx`.

[24] Microsoft Corporation. StringBuilder class, 2010. `http://msdn.microsoft.com/en-us/library/system.text.stringbuilder(v=VS.80).aspx`.

[25] Y. Nadji, P. Saxena, and D. Song. Document structure integrity: A robust basis for cross-site scripting defense. In *Proceedings of the Network and Distributed System Security Symposium*, 2009.

[26] A. Nguyen-Tuong, S. Guarnieri, D. Greene, J. Shirley, and D. Evans. Automatically hardening Web applications using precise tainting. In *Proceedings of the IFIP International Information Security Conference*, 2005.

[27] Open Web Application Security Project. The ten most critical Web application security vulnerabilities. `http://umn.dl.sourceforge.net/sourceforge/owasp/OWASPTopTen2004.pdf`, 2004.

[28] T. Pietraszek and C. V. Berghe. Defending against injection attacks through context-sensitive string evaluation. In *Proceedings of the Recent Advances in Intrusion Detection*, Sept. 2005.

[29] RSnake. XSS cheat sheet for filter evasion. `http://ha.ckers.org/xss.html`.

[30] B. Schmidt. google-analytics-xss-vulnerability, 2011. `http://spareclockcycles.org/2011/02/03/google-analytics-xss-vulnerability/`.

[31] E. J. Schwartz, T. Avgerinos, and D. Brumley. All you ever wanted to know about dynamic taint analysis and forward symbolic execution (but might have been afraid to ask). In *Proceedings of the IEEE Symposium on Security and Privacy*, 2010.

[32] Ter Louw, Mike and V.N. Venkatakrishnan. BluePrint: Robust Prevention of Cross-site Scripting Attacks for Existing Browsers. In *Proceedings of the IEEE Symposium on Security and Privacy*, 2009.

[33] M. Veanes, B. Livshits, and D. Molnar. Decision procedures for composition and equivalence of symbolic finite state transducers. Technical Report MSR-TR-2011-32, Microsoft Research, 2011.

[34] H. Venter. Common compiler infrastructure: Metadata API, 2010. `http://ccimetadata.codeplex.com/`.

[35] Y. Xie and A. Aiken. Static detection of security vulnerabilities in scripting languages. In *Proceedings of the Usenix Security Symposium*, 2006.

[36] W. Xu, S. Bhatkar, and R. Sekar. Taint-enhanced policy enforcement: A practical approach to defeat a wide range of attacks. In *Proceedings of the Usenix Security Symposium*, 2006.

Fortifying Web-Based Applications Automatically

Shuo Tang
University of Illinois
201 N Goodwin Ave
Urbana, IL 61801
stang6@illinois.edu

Nathan Dautenhahn
University of Illinois
201 N Goodwin Ave
Urbana, IL 61801
dautenh1@illinois.edu

Samuel T. King
University of Illinois
201 N Goodwin Ave
Urbana, IL 61801
kingst@illinois.edu

ABSTRACT

Browser designers create security mechanisms to help web developers protect web applications, but web developers are usually slow to use these features in web-based applications (web apps). In this paper we introduce ZAN[1], a browser-based system for applying new browser security mechanisms to legacy web apps automatically. Our key insight is that web apps often contain enough information, via web developer source-code patterns or key properties of web-app objects, to allow the browser to infer opportunities for applying new security mechanisms to existing web apps. We apply this new concept to protect authentication cookies, prevent web apps from being framed unwittingly, and perform JavaScript object deserialization safely. We evaluate ZAN on up to the 1000 most popular websites for each of the three cases. We find that ZAN can provide complimentary protection for the majority of potentially applicable websites automatically without requiring additional code from the web developers and with negligible incompatibility impact.

Categories and Subject Descriptors

K.6.5 [**Management of Computing and Information Systems**]: Security and Protection

General Terms

Security, Design

Keywords

Web security, client-side defense, cookies, frame busting, JSON

1. INTRODUCTION

The Web has become a popular platform for building web-based applications (web apps) and providing convenient and diverse services for users. One contributing factor in this rise in popularity is the features that browser developers add to browsers. Unfortunately, these new features have also created new avenues for attack. For example, web app developers can use frames (or `IFRAME`s) to compose web apps out of gadgets from different websites, but attackers can use frames to embed legitimate web apps inside of attack pages to trick users via "clickjacking" [17].

Browser developers have implemented security features to help web developers improve the security of web apps. Three examples of recent browser security features are `HttpOnly` cookies [2] that enable web developers to specify cookies that should be inaccessible from JavaScript, `X-Frame-Options` [21] to enable web developers to prevent their pages from being framed, and `JSON.parse()` [1] to enable web developers to deserialize JavaScript Object Notation (JSON) text safely without executing JavaScript code.

However, web developers have been slow to use these new browser security features [30, 26]. We surveyed the Alexa top 100 websites [6], and found that these security mechanisms are not used widely:

- There are at least 34 websites that do not set the `HttpOnly` attribute on their credential cookies.
- Only 11 websites use `X-Frame-Options` to prevent their main or login pages from being framed.
- Only 4 out of 16 websites that use JSON within five seconds after the page loads use `JSON.parse()` to deserialize JSON text.

In this paper we present ZAN – a browser-based system that fortifies web apps by applying new security mechanisms to existing web apps automatically. Our key insight is that the browser often has enough information to determine when new security features could be applied to existing web applications. This information can come from detecting common patterns in the code that web developers write or from identifying fundamental features of key web-app objects, like cookies. Our goal is to add simple mechanisms to narrow the attack surface or mitigate the damage of a web-based attack without requiring input from users or additional effort from web developers. We also aim to minimize incompatibilities induced by our system.

In general ZAN works by interposing on key states and events within the browser to detect candidates for applying stronger security mechanisms automatically. For example, ZAN inspects all cookies set by the web server to detect certain key words (e.g., "token" or "session") or randomness

[1] ZAN means awesome in Chinese.

(e.g., hashed values) commonly observed in authentication cookies used by web apps. When ZAN detects a combination of these conditions, it sets the HttpOnly attribute for these cookies to make them inaccessible from JavaScript, preventing authentication cookie theft via cross-site scripting (XSS) attacks.

Our contributions are:

- We design and implement ZAN, a browser-based system for applying new security features to existing web apps.
- We show that web apps often contain enough information to allow ZAN to infer opportunities for applying new security mechanisms to legacy web apps.
- We develop simple and effective algorithms for applying these principles to three browser security mechanisms: `HttpOnly` cookies (Section 4), `X-Frame-Options` (Section 5), and `JSON.parse()` (Section 6).
- We evaluate these algorithms in a real browser on popular websites to demonstrate ZAN's ability to prevent attacks without affecting compatibility or adding overhead to the system.

2. BACKGROUND

When the Web was first invented, it was a collection of static web pages. Now, the Web has evolved into a platform for deploying applications. With almost equivalent functionality as their desktop counterparts, web apps provide people applications such as email, banking, gaming, social networking and video streaming. Users invariably put private information into web apps, such as addresses, health records, social security numbers and credit card numbers, intensifying the need for more secure web apps.

In the contemporary Web, most security decisions are predicated on the origin of the web apps – this security model is called the same-origin policy (SOP). An origin of a web app is define as the `<protocol, domain name, port>` tuple of the uniform resource locator (URL) it originates from. Loosely speaking, The SOP acts as a non-interference policy for the Web and the SOP provides isolation for web pages and states originating from different origins. If the browser runs one web app from `victim.com` and another from `attack.com`, the browser isolates these two web apps from each other. For a more complete discussion of this policy, please see a recent paper by Singh, *et al.* [30].

Unfortunately, the SOP is not always effective at guarding the Web. Several attack scenarios operate without violating this policy, such as XSS and the frame-based attacks we discuss in Section 5. XSS is effectively a form of code injection attack, where an attacker injects malicious scripts into the victim web app and operates using the victim's origin and credentials. Potential damage an XSS could cause includes stealing the victim's credentials, gaining elevated access privileges to sensitive page content, and carrying out actions on behalf of the victim. In fact, XSS is the most prevalent vulnerability on modern computer systems, accounting for more vulnerabilities than all other vulnerabilities combined [32].

3. DESIGN

In this section, we discuss the threat model that ZAN considers, and the high-level design of ZAN.

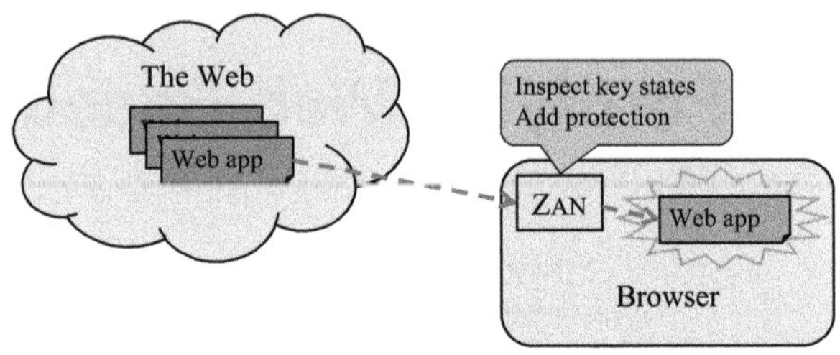

Figure 1: Deployment of Zan. Zan works by interposing on key states and events of web apps within the browser to detect candidates for adding or improving protection automatically.

3.1 Threat model

Our primary goal is to narrow the attack surface of web apps or to mitigate the damage of a successful attack. In our threat model, we assume that an attacker controls a malicious website and can serve sophisticated crafted web apps to the user, or that the attacker can escape sanitization processes to inject malicious scripts into legitimate web apps. We focus on non-memory based attacks and assume that the browser ZAN uses is faithful. Attacks that take control over a browser are still possible, such as a scenario involving buffer overflow. In these cases, it would require a better design and architecture of the browser system [14, 10, 41, 34] to improve the overall system security. It is also possible that the attacker could completely compromise a trusted website, rendering ZAN – a client-side system – ineffective. This is a separate aspect of web security that we do not address in this paper.

3.2 Design principles

As shown in Figure 1, ZAN works as a module in browsers by interposing on key states and events to infer opportunities to apply security mechanisms. In general, this approach is feasible because web apps often present enough information at the client side so that ZAN is able to use it to identify important objects or existing unreliable protection logic. For example, cookies that contain authentication tokens would likely be obfuscated and have special names. In other cases, the same JavaScript-based defense workarounds are often included, though might having variants, in multiple websites (e.g., frame busting code we will discuss in Section 5).

In designing and implementing ZAN's different mechanisms, we adhere to the following three principles:

1. *Use only information at the client side.* We already see slow adoption of new secure mechanisms in web app development. We hope a pure client-side solution could relieve the burden of web app developers.

2. *Make the mechanisms simple.* Browsers are already complex artifacts. New mechanisms should be simple and efficient in order to avoid introducing new vulnerabilities.

3. *Maintain compatibility of the web apps.* It is necessary not to break the Web. A protection mechanism that results in the loss of functionality is practically useless.

3.3 Methodology

ZAN relies on source-code patterns and key objects' characteristics to infer opportunities for applying new secure mechanisms to legacy web apps. For the mechanisms that ZAN includes, we first study a set of websites to capture characteristics of interest of their unknown underlying patterns.

In this paper, we use a consistent set of websites as the initial training data. We first pick the top 100 websites according to Alexa [6]. Because shopping and banking websites contain valuable data, we also include the top six websites in each category according to Alexa. Of course, if one of these is also in the top 100 websites, we skip it. We also use the top four web-mail sites. In the remainder of this paper, *top websites* are always used to refer to the 116 websites described in this subsection unless explicitly stated otherwise.

By analyzing the top websites, we are able to produce classifiers to identify candidates for applying new security mechanisms. To evaluate ZAN's efficiency and compatibility impact, we then extend our experiments to up to 1000 popular websites. At the same time, we could potentially tweak these classifiers for better protection and compatibility based on the new websites we test.

For the websites we study, some offer several services using a single domain and employ different security mechanisms among those services. To avoid ambiguity, we choose to analyze the main service, or the front page service when we refer to a website. For example, Google offers searching, calendar, documents, and many more within `google.com`, but we always refer to Google search when we talk about `google.com`.

4. CASE STUDY: COOKIE PROTECTION

The first security enhancement that ZAN enables is adding `HttpOnly` attributes to credential cookies automatically. We begin the discussion with cookie related issues as it is chronologically the first available feature among the three we cover in the paper. And `HttpOnly` is the earliest and most wildly used one among the three security mechanisms.

4.1 Cookies

A cookie, or an HTTP cookie, is a piece of text stored on a user's computer by his or her browser, typically consisting of one or more name-value pairs that the server and client pass back and forth. Cookies were invented by Lou Montulli at Netscape in 1994 to facilitate electronic commerce applications [20]. Initially developed as a method for implementing reliable virtual shopping carts, cookies were later pervasively used as the *de facto* way of authenticating users to web sites and storing the login information so that a web user does not have to keep entering their username and password each time he or she visits the same web site. Cookies can also be used to store identifiers so that web servers can track what the users have done during the visit.

In today's Web, part of cookie manipulation, like other computation, is pushed to the client side. For example, in Facebook's user sampling and tracking module, the session identifier is generated using JavaScript in the browser. A web app could also use `document.cookie` to set a cookie and then try to read it back to test if the browser has cookie support. As web apps continue to provide more versatile features, they also need a way to access local storage. Before HTML5 local storage [38] was introduced, web developers chose to use cookies for storing data in the client.

4.2 Attacks on cookies

Since cookies often contain time sensitive information, such as credentials, and are relatively easy to access using client-side scripts, cookie theft is a common result in Web-based attacks, such as XSS. For example, in a successful XSS attack, the attacker from `attack.com` could easily steal the victim's cookie using the following script:

```
var url
  = 'http://attack.com/stole.cgi?text='
  + escape(document.cookie);
var img = new Image();
img.src = url;
```

In the malicious script, the attacker uses `document.cookie` to retrieve the content of the list of cookies that the user has for the page, and embeds it into the query payload of a fake URL pointed to the attacker's web site. The attacker then creates a JavaScript image object on the fly and sets its source path to the fake URL. As a result, this list of cookies is sent to the `attack.com` server.

Cookies also pose a privacy threat [28] and enable the CSRF attack [42]. Mitigation methods are feasible but beyond the scope of this paper [9].

4.3 Alleviating cookie theft

An intuitive way to stop cookie theft in Web-based attacks is to address XSS. However, despite many efforts to prevent XSS, such as client-side approaches [25, 12], server-side approaches [35], or hybrid client-server approaches [23, 16], XSS remains the top vulnerability [4].

There are also other ways of alleviating cookie theft. One could use HTTP authentication instead of a cookie-based approach. As the authentication information is not available to JavaScript in the cookies, nothing could be revealed to an attacker with an XSS attack. Also, one could tie session cookies to the IP address that the user originates from and only permit that IP to use the cookies, rendering the stolen cookie useless in most situations. But it is possible that an attacker could spoof the IP address, or is behind the same Network Address Translation (NAT) firewall or web proxy, thus breaking down the protection.

A declarative method, `HttpOnly`, has also been proposed. First introduced in 2002 in Internet Explorer 2.0 [2], the `HttpOnly` cookie attribute has been implemented in all major browsers. If the optional `HttpOnly` flag is included in the HTTP response header for a cookie, the cookie cannot be accessed by client-side scripts. As a result, the browser would not reveal authentication cookies to the attacker in an XSS attack if they are properly tagged with `HttpOnly` flags.

Surprisingly, the `HttpOnly` attribute has not been thoroughly deployed in today's Web, even though it was invented almost 9 years ago. For the top websites, our survey shows that of the 93 websites that we are able to obtain accounts for and login to, 39 still have not incorporated `HttpOnly`.

4.4 Applying HttpOnly automatically

Fortunately, credential cookies often exhibit certain characteristics. We studied the 54 websites that use `HttpOnly` cookies. In some cases, cookies with `HttpOnly` are not necessarily used for authentication, but at least should not be

Phrase	Count
*sid$	122
auth	23
session	21
∧nid$	18
token	14
*sess$	11
other	174
Total	383

Table 1: Common phrases (case insensitive) used as the names of `HttpOnly` cookies in top websites, where * means any combination of characters, while ∧ and $ means the beginning and end of string respectively.

Property	HttpOnly		Non-HttpOnly	
	Aver.	Stdev.	Aver.	Stdev.
Entropy	4.00	1.60	2.83	1.82
Length	102	128	48	83

Table 2: Average and standard deviation of entropy and lengths of `HttpOnly` cookie values and non-`HttpOnly` ones in the top websites that use `HttpOnly`.

accessed by client-side scripts. Still, analysis on the whole set would give a close enough estimation of characteristics for the login cookies. The preliminary experiments show that they generally exhibit three key properties:

- They tend to have English phrases related to authentication in their names such as token, session, and so on.
- Their values exhibit greater randomness than non-`HttpOnly` cookies.
- They use relatively long strings for their values compared to the cookies without `HttpOnly`.

Table 1 shows the distribution of meaningful English phrases in the names of `HttpOnly` cookies. It shows that at least 54% of them use phrases related to authentication, indicating that we could use cookie name as one hint to decide if a cookie should be tagged as `HttpOnly`.

A well-known way to measure the randomness of a string is to calculate its entropy. There are many entropy models, and in ZAN we use the Shannon Entropy Equation defined as:

$$H(X) = -\sum_{x \in \mathcal{X}} p(x) \log_b p(x)$$

where $p(x)$ is the *probability mass function* of a character x appeared in the string X [29].

We show the average and standard deviation of our entropy calculations in Table 2. `HttpOnly` cookies have an average of 1.17 more bits of entropy than cookies without the `HttpOnly` attribute. Table 2 also shows that `HttpOnly` cookies on average have 54 more characters than non-`HttpOnly` ones. These are not coincidences. It is common that credential cookies are encrypted using hashing algorithms such as MD5 or SHA1. At the same time, web sites need to use long enough strings for session tokens in order to avoid collision among different users.

Using data provided in Table 2, we can use a standard *Gaussian distribution classifier* to decide if a cookie resembles a credential one. The classifier we use in ZAN is

$$\tau = \frac{\mu_h - \mu_{nh}}{\sigma_h + \sigma_{nh}} \sigma_{nh} + \mu_{nh}$$

where μ_h and σ_h are the mean and standard deviation for `HttpOnly` cookies respectively, while μ_{nh} and σ_{nh} are the mean and standard deviation for non-`HttpOnly` ones. τ defines the delineation between `HttpOnly` cookies and non-`HttpOnly` cookies, so we then can assume that a cookie with entropy greater than 3.45 bits or containing 70 or more characters is likely one that should be tagged with `HttpOnly`.

Based on the above information, we developed an algorithm that automatically detects credential cookies. The algorithm is defined as:

```
1 if (origin == JS || hasHttpOnlyAttr())
2       return;
3 for c in (the list of cookies)
4   if (c.name is common phrase)
5     if (entropy(c.value) > 3.45)
6       || len(c.value) > 70)
7       c.httponly = true;
8   else
9     if (entropy(c.value) > 3.45
10       && len(c.value) > 70)
11       c.httponly = true;
```

When a list of cookies is passed in with an HTTP request, we apply the algorithm to their name-value pairs. First, we only examine network cookies (lines 1 and 2). For cookies that are set by JavaScript, we skip the algorithm because they are by definition not `HttpOnly` cookies. Meanwhile, when `HttpOnly` is already present, we honor the web developer's decision and ignore the rest of the algorithm (lines 1 and 2).

Next for each cookie in the list, we check if it uses one of the common phrases presented in Table 1 as its name. For the one that uses a common phrase, we assume it is most likely a credential cookie and use a relatively loose classifier on the entropy and length of its value. We would tag cookie with `HttpOnly` as long as *either* its entropy or length falls into the range of a credential cookie. For the one that does not use common phrase, we use a relatively tight standard. Only when *both* its entropy and length meet the bar of credential cookie, we would apply `HttpOnly` on it.

The overall algorithm is conservative to some extent as we will show in the experiments later in this section. We choose to be conservative because setting `HttpOnly` on too many cookies would sometimes affect the compatibility and usability of web apps. If a cookie that is supposed to be used by JavaScript has been set with `HttpOnly`, the web app could function incorrectly. Meanwhile, missing a single credential cookie is not a serious problem as long as the attacker is not able to retrieve the complete set of authentication cookies.

4.5 Experiments

4.5.1 Implementation

ZAN is implemented on top of the open source version of the OP web browser, which is called OP2 [15]. The version of OP2 we choose uses the Qt framework 4.6 [3], and WebKit r54749 [5]. We opt to use OP2 as it provides a clear and

		Predicted	
		Positive	Negative
Actual	Positive	103	29
	Negative	4*	164

Figure 2: Confusion matrix [19] for Zan's cookie protection algorithm.

robust architecture for implementing the security features we describe in this paper. Nonetheless, ZAN does not rely on any special feature that is only available in OP2. And we believe that it is fairly straightforward engineering effort to implement ZAN in other browsers such as Internet Explorer, Firefox, Chrome, and so on.

For the cookie protection algorithm, we modify the cookie subsystem in OP2 to enable our algorithm. OP2 uses a clear message passing mechanism for cookie access and ZAN interposes the messages passed into the cookie subsystem. Each time the cookie subsystem receives a list of cookies from an HTTP response, ZAN applies the algorithm described previously to the cookies, and tags `HttpOnly` attribute appropriately. There is no need to modify the cookie read procedure, because the cookie subsystem then prevents `HttpOnly` cookies from being accessed by client-side script.

4.5.2 Coverage

Our algorithm is designed to prevent credential cookies from being stolen by XSS. While this protection could not eliminate all the aftermath of an XSS attack, it certainly minimizes the damage one can cause. Conceptually, we need to prove that our algorithm can identify at least one authentication cookie so that the attacker cannot use the stolen cookies to log in to the corresponding website.

To evaluate how effectively our algorithm detects credential cookies, in our current effort, we apply it to top 300 popular websites according to Alexa. Unlike the other two cases of this paper, it is infeasible to evaluate cookie protection automatically. Most websites employ mechanisms to prevent non-human users from obtaining accounts and/or logging in, such as using CAPTCHAs. Unless we could use a large group of users to test for us, it is hard to extend the experiments to a significantly larger scale. Even established research that aims to study the Web in large scale shies away from this problem. For example, Singh *et al.* did not log into the websites they surveyed [30].

Out of the 300 websites, 136 have authentication cookies but do not incorporate `HttpOnly` as shown in Figure 2. To simulate an attack we log in to each of the websites. Then, we delete all of the cookies that ZAN marks as `HttpOnly`. After erasing the `HttpOnly` cookies we attempt to continue our login session. If we cannot continue using the website as the logged-in user (e.g., being kicked back to login page), we consider this a successful defense because it implies that at least one of the cookies ZAN identified was needed for authentication at the website. Thus, if an attacker had stolen the cookies via JavaScript then the set of cookies they would have access to would not allow authenticated requests.

Out of the 136 websites, ZAN was able to apply `HttpOnly` to 110 automatically. There are 29 websites for which our algorithm could not detect credential cookies, mostly due to either low entropy or short value and irregular cookie names. For example, `Craigslist.com` had credential cookies using seemingly common *Login* name, but this name was infrequent in our data set, so we did not detect this cookie.

Of the 107 websites that ZAN did set `HttpOnly` cookies for, the algorithm identified authentication cookies correctly for 103 of them (i.e., ZAN ended the session after we deleted the `HttpOnly` cookies). It is very interesting that the four websites were able to continue the session despite the deletion of seemingly credential cookies. For example, we discarded a cookie that had name "PHPSESSIONID" from `imageshark.us`, but the user session persisted despite its removal.

4.5.3 Compatibility impact

In general, it is very rare, if any, for a well designed website to use client-side scripting to access authentication cookies. So the question is whether a non-credential cookie that is designed to be used in JavaScript has been incorrectly tagged with `HttpOnly` by ZAN.

However, without full knowledge of the usage of each cookie, it is infeasible to carry out a complete quantitative analysis. Instead, to have a close estimation, we opt to manually test the popular fuctions of these 136 websites in depth. To our best effort, we could not observe any noticeable breakdown of web pages. We understand that a client-side solution like ZAN needs to maintain compatibility very well and a thorough test is much required. However, we argue that the whole algorithm can be tweaked to be more aggressive or conservative to accommodate the majority of websites in practice.

5. CASE STUDY: FRAME-BASED ATTACK

In this section we discuss the state of the art in frame-based attacks and defense techniques. We also describe our algorithm for providing a more complete defense against frame-based attacks.

Back in the era of Netscape Navigator in early 1990s, the HTML `FRAME` element was introduced to allow web developers to delegate a portion of their document's visual display to another entity. These frames can then be navigated to independent documents, which can delegate their share of the screen further to sub-frames. The `FRAME` tag was inflexible and was replaced by the more versatile `IFRAME` tag, which was introduced by Internet Explorer in 1997.

`IFRAME`s enable modern browsers to display one web document inside another at an arbitrary position, creating a complex frame hierarchy. However, browsers present only the URL of the main, or top-level, frame to the users in the address bar. Consequently, it is infeasible for an average user to distinguish sub-frames from other parts of a page. This inconsistency, coupled with flexible display overlaying mechanisms available in browsers, creates the opportunities for frame-based attacks.

5.1 Frame-based attacks

Frame-based attacks were first reported in 2008 when Robert Hansen and Jeremiah Grossman introduced the term "clickjacking" [17]. In a clickjacking attack, the attacker chooses a clickable region on the target website that the user is currently authenticated on (e.g., a "like" button in a Facebook page). To perform the attack, a malicious website will load a page from the victim website inside an `IFRAME`, using Cascading Style Sheets (CSS) to make it transparent. At the same time, this transparent clickable element is placed on top of some visible, fake, but interesting clickable gadget (e.g., click to win a free iPad). As a result, the user would effectively "like" an attackers chosen page in Facebook instead of unrealistically winning a free iPad when he or she clicks it. Evidence shows that major websites such as Facebook and Twitter have already suffered from clickjacking attacks [11, 36]. There are also other variants of this same basic attack that use similar mechanisms to induce users to click on a page unwittingly.

As the Web evolves, the capability of frame-based attacks also improves. In recent research, Paul Stone demonstrated the next generation clickjacking by showing four new techniques [31]. In the new attack scenarios, the attacker could potentially use the drag-and-drop API in HTML5 and some social engineering to inject text into form fields of the victim's browser, which could be used to send fake emails from a user's account. An attacker could also extract content from the enclosed frame, which could be used to steal sensitive information such as passwords, or tokens that are used to authenticate a session and guard against cross-site request forgery (CSRF) [42] attacks. Stone also showed that it is possible to use this new technique to achieve login detection that is used to facilitate CSRF or other clickjacking attacks.

5.2 Preventing framing

Fortunately, while a number of different techniques have been discovered to carry out frame-based attacks, they can mostly be defended against.

Frame busting was the first technique that was suggested to counter clickjacking attacks [17]. Frame busting often refers to a snippet of JavaScript code included in a web app that intends to prevent this web app from being included in a sub-frame. A simple example of frame busting is shown here:

```
if (top.location != self.location)
  top.location = self.location;
```

Typically, frame busting includes a conditional statement to detect if the web app is embedded in a frame. If so, the next statement acts as the countermeasure to break out and load the web app in place of the web site that is framing it. Unfortunately, this JavaScript-based approach is not always effective, and there is a list of ways to defeat it as described by Rydstedt *et al.* [26]. For example, a malicious site may try to use the `onbeforeunload` Document Object Model (DOM) event to prevent a framed site from navigating to a different URL, or merely disable scripting in the framed web page.

Another option for preventing web apps from being framed is the `X-Frame-Options` introduced by Internet Explorer 8 [21], which now widely implemented in all modern browsers. `X-Frame-Options`, as a declarative method, provides a clear and robust approach to avoid unsolicited framing. `X-Frame-Options` can be used either in an HTTP response header of a web page or as an HTML "http-equiv" META tag in the web page itself. `X-Frame-Options` has two options: (1) *DENY* – the browser prevents the page from rendering if it will be contained within a frame; and (2) *SAMEORIGIN* – the browser blocks rendering only if the origin of the top-level browsing context is different than the origin of the content containing the `X-Frame-Options` directive. We also observe a third option – *ALLOW* – used by some `IFRAME`ed advertisements. We posit that it is used to

Defense	Front page	Login page
Frame busting	19	34
`X-Frame-Options`	7	14

Table 3: Frame busting and `X-Frame-Options` usage among top websites.

Type	Number
`top != self`	17
`parent.frames.length != 0`	2
`parent.frames.length > 0`	2
`top.location != self.location`	4
`window.self != window.top`	3
`top.location != location`	3
`window.top != window`	2
`top.location != window.location`	1

Table 4: Patterns used in conditional statements for detecting framing in frame busting code. This table shows the distribution of the frame detection code found in the 34 websites shown in Table 3. `self != top` is put in the same category of `top != self`. And `!=` is considered the same as `!==`. Whitespace is ignored.

advise the browser to allow the embedding in any case. Although more robust than frame busting, `X-Frame-Options` also has a potential pitfall. When `X-Frame-Options` is included in the HTTP header, a web proxy could strip it, leaving the page unprotected.

However, like the `HttpOnly` attribute, anti-framing mechanisms are not sufficiently incorporated in top websites. Some websites use frame busting code and a few have started to use the new `X-Frame-Options` feature (Table 3).

5.3 Robust anti-framing

As discussed above, both frame busting and `X-Frame-Options` have shortcomings and they are also poorly incorporated in top websites. To better counter frame-based attacks, we implement the following algorithm for each `IFRAME` in ZAN.

```
1 if(hasXFrameOptions())
2       return;
3 state = init;
4 for s in (all JS statements):
5   if(state == init && isFrameDetect(s))
6       state = nav;
7   if(state == nav && isTopFrameNav(s))
8       injectXFrameOption();
```

When `X-Frame-Options` is present in a web app, we honor whatever the web developer sets and ignore the rest of the algorithm (lines 1 and 2).

Next, the algorithm detects conditional statements that are predicated on detecting framed pages (line 5). Fortunately, frame detection code tends to exhibit some fairly simple patterns. For the 34 websites we found with frame busting code, the frame detection patterns we found are shown in Table 4. To find frame detection code, the `isFrameDetect()` function inspects JavaScript statements to check for one of the patterns listed in Table 4.

However, using frame detection code alone would induce false positives because these basic patterns are also used

Type
`top.location = loc`
`top.location.href = loc`
`top.location.replace(loc)`
`parent.location.href = loc`

Table 5: Frame busting navigation countermeasures used when framing is detected. This table shows the four navigation countermeasures we observed from websites that deploy frame busting code.

		Predicted	
		Positive	Negative
Actual	Positive	87	2
	Negative	0 (or 7*)	911 (or 904*)

Figure 3: Confusion matrix for Zan's frame busting code detection algorithm.

for functionality other than frame busting in web apps. To reduce false positives, we only inject **`X-Frame-Options`** if we also detect a countermeasure navigation statement (line 7). To find countermeasure navigation statements, our **`isTopFrameNav()`** function searches JavaScript statements for one of the patterns shown in Table 5. In these navigation countermeasures, loc could be any URL that the web author wants to use for replacing the top-level frame. The patterns we detect are less diverse than what we observe for frame detection. A recent study suggests that other countermeasures as well [26], but our evaluation indicates these four work well for top websites.

When ZAN detects frame detection code and countermeasure navigation statements, we apply **`X-Frame-Options`** with the SAMEORIGIN option to framed web apps (line 8), preventing them from being displayed as frames inside web pages that are from different origins.

This heuristic algorithm will not detect all frame busting code and it could detect frame busting code when there is none, but it is simple, efficient, and accurate for the websites that we examine (see experimental results later in this section for more details). The algorithm also has some flexibility built in. Browser developers could adjust the number of frame detection or frame navigation statements the algorithm searches for in order to trade-off more aggressive security against compatibility.

One alternative and more aggressive defense could be applying **`X-Frame-Options`** to any web pages that have username and password fields, thus protecting login sites from frame-based attacks. However, we did not evaluate this more aggressive defense in this paper.

5.4 Experiments

5.4.1 Implementation

For the frame-based attack defense, we modify the HTML parser used in WebKit. All HTML and JavaScript source code (even the external code) is processed first through the HTML parser. ZAN uses simple string pattern matching routines to detect the existence of frame busting code using the algorithm proposed earlier in this section, and then applies the same anti-framing method that the **`X-Frame-Options`** implementation uses in WebKit. Detecting login pages is quite a mature topic. Most modern browsers detect the password form field to enable automatic login. bWe instead use this method to apply **`X-Frame-Options`** to them.

5.4.2 Coverage

To test our frame defense we try to frame a website that ZAN injects **`X-Frame-Options`** into and we confirm that ZAN prevents framing. We verify that the five attack scenarios that are applicable to WebKit [26] can be mitigated in ZAN because ZAN does not rely on the correct execution of frame busting code.

Meanwhile, we also need to test whether our algorithm is able to cover all of the potential opportunities to apply stronger defenses. For our frame defense we visited the 89 websites out of top 1000 websites that have frame busting code, and ZAN correctly applied **`X-Frame-Options`** to 87 of them as shown in Figure 3. In fact, during the experiments, we found additional patterns of frame busting code and used them to improve our algorithm. As a result, if any of these websites is unwittingly framed, ZAN is able to stop its rendering. There are still two websites that ZAN cannot handle. One website (**`renren.com`**) uses an unorthodox way to detect framing, which is infeasible to be incorporated in ZAN's algorithm. The other copies its **`self.location`** to a variable and use the variable to compare to **`top.location`**. ZAN was not able to detect this case. Interestingly most of the websites in our test that do use **`X-Frame-Options`** also include frame busting code. Thus, had an HTTP proxy stripped the **`X-Frame-Options`** from the HTTP response header, ZAN would still protect the site.

One thing we want to point out is that ZAN's robust anti-framing mechanism is used to improve existing protection rather than adding new protection to random websites. It is infeasible for ZAN to decide whether a website can be used in **`IFRAME`**s legitimately without hints like frame busting code, although we do provide an aggressive option for protecting all login pages.

5.4.3 Compatibility impact

One potential issue that ZAN could cause is to stop rendering frames that do not actually have frame busing code. To test our frame defense we ran two experiments. First, we visited all of the top 1000 websites and measured ZAN's effects on any of the benign **`IFRAME`**s included in these sites. Then, we manually framed the 911 websites that did *not* have frame busting code and visited these framed sites to see if ZAN applied **`X-Frame-Options`** incorrectly and prevented their rendering.

ZAN did not affect the display of any benign **`IFRAME`**s in the top 1000 websites and 904 of the 911 manually framed websites that do not include frame busting code. ZAN incorrectly stopped the rendering of 7 web pages. The 7 websites actually include frame busting code, but use conditional statements to disable its execution in certain scenarios. For example, Wikipedia use an **`if`** statement to disable the frame busting logic in its main page (but not in the login page). Since we use string pattern matching instead of relying on complex control flow analysis in Zan, we are unable to eliminate this false positive. Nevertheless, in typical usage scenarios, these websites are not embedded in cross-orgin **`IFRAME`**s. So ZAN will not affect their normal functions.

During the experiments, we also found that statements

used in frame busting code were used for other purposes. However, the framing detection-like statements and navigation countermeasure statements are not close to each other in JavaScript code in these cases. As a result, we modify ZAN's algorithm to add a requirement for the distance between the two statements (i.e., the countermeasure statement should not be too far away following the framing detection statement) when trying to identify frame busting code, and successfully reduced false positive numbers.

6. CASE STUDY: SECURE JSON PARSING

Before the era of "Web 2.0", a full page re-load was required to update information on a webpage. The problem with this approach is that it is neither efficient or elegant. In terms of efficiency, the server was required to send a full version of the page to the client even for minimal content modifications, and in terms of elegance it forced visual resets of the screen requiring the client to wait while the refresh occurred. As such, websites needed a way to update information on the page less obtrusively, thus, Ajax was developed to enable asynchronous communication between the client and server. Ajax originally used the `XMLHttpRequest` object to transfer `XML` formatted data. Recently JSON has become an `XML` replacement in Ajax because it is simple and can be easily encoded into several popular programming languages.

6.1 JSON and exploiting JSON

JSON is a subset of the object literal notion of JavaScript. Originally specified by Douglas Crockford in RFC 4627, JSON is now supported in all major browsers as part of JavaScript. JSON can be used in client-side scripts to facilitate easy data exchange with servers. Below is an example of a simple JSON string:

```
{ "employee" : [
    {"name": "Alice", "sex": "female"},
    {"name": "Bob", "sex": "male"} ] }
```

In this example, the JSON string represents an object that contains a single member "employee", which contains an array containing two objects, each containing "name", and "sex" members.

JSON is often used together with XMLHttpRequests to enable the browser to exchange data asynchronously with the server. If an XMLHttpRrequest returns the above JSON string stored in a variable called `jsonText`, it can be converted into a JavaScript object using the JavaScript `eval()` function, which invokes the JavaScript compiler as shown in the following code snippet:

```
jsonObject = eval('(' + jsonText + ')')
```

Since JSON is a proper subset of JavaScript, the compiler will correctly parse the text and produce an object structure. For example, one can use `jsonObject.employee[0].name` to access the first employee's name. To avoid ambiguity in JavaScript's syntax, it is also recommended that the JSON text be wrapped in parentheses as shown in the statement above.

However, since `eval()` invokes the complete JavaScript compiler, it could execute any JavaScript program besides JSON, leading to potential security vulnerabilities. Typically in a web app, JSON is used over XMLHttpRequest, which is commonly restricted to only communicate with the origin that the web app comes from. Thus, the source is trusted. However, if the server does not provide correct JSON encoding, or it embeds user supplied content in JSON text without rigorous sanitization, it could deliver problematic JSON text to the client that could contain malicious scripts (e.g., CVE-2007-3227). The `eval()` function would then execute the script, resulting in an XSS attack. Assume in the above example, the name of an employee is provided by the user. If the user could enter a malicious script such as `", "arb": alert(document.cookie), "": "` instead of a real name,the resulting JSON text would become:

```
...
  {
      "name": "",
      "arb": alert(document.cookie),
      "": "",
      "sex": "female"
  },
...
```

When evaluated, the web page displays an alert showing the cookies for the active session. This threat has already been reported for real world websites such as in Google's personalized homepage and can be used for more serious script injection attacks [27].

6.2 Native JSON

To minimize script injection via JSON parsing, it is suggested that web developers use regular expressions to validate the data prior to invoking `eval()`. However, browser developers added a new function, `JSON.parse()`, as a safer and more robust alternative to `eval()` that parses JSON text without executing scripts.

`JSON.parse()`, which only recognizes JSON text, rejects all possible embedded malicious scripts. Additionally, `JSON.parse()` only parses JSON text that adheres to the JSON standard and will reject any malformed JSON text. Fortunately, browsers implement functions for converting JavaScript data structures into JSON text. These serialization and deserialization routines are well supported in most recent browsers as *Native JSON*. However, web developers have been slow to adopt this new security feature as well.

6.3 Automating native JSON adoption

To prevent script injection via JSON, ZAN inspects all strings passed into the JavaScript `eval()` function:

```
1 s = fixupEvalString(evalString);
2 if(s.startWith("({") && s.endWith("})"))
3     return zanParse(s);
4 if(s.startWith("([") && s.endWith("])"))
5     return zanParse(s);
6 ...
```

If the algorithm detects a string that looks like a JSON object, it will pass that string to the `JSON.parse()` function automatically. Our logic for detecting JSON objects checks the beginning and end of the eval string to find the "({" and "})" (line 2) or the "([" and "])" (line 4) strings respectively. These checks will find and thwart cases where developers use JSON objects but an attacker passes unsanitized JavaScript into the JSON object.

For the websites we examined, we found a few cases where web developers use JSON, but the JSON text was not formatted according to the strict JSON grammar. To ensure

		Predicted	
		Positive	Negative
Actual	Positive	76	3
	Negative	0	922

Figure 4: Confusion matrix for Zan's secure JSON parsing algorithm.

that these almost-valid JSON strings can pass our inspection we used a modified `JSON.parse()` parser for parsing JSON text with a slightly updated grammar to handle these cases (lines 3 and 5). Specifically, we allow single quotes in addition to double quotes and we accept name strings that omit enclosing quotes. Additionally, we have a function that fixes up eval strings to make our detection logic easier by remove some whitespace to ensure that the JSON brackets and braces make it to the beginning and the end of the eval string (line 1). With these modifications, the ZAN algorithm successfully parses all JSON objects we observed in our tests.

Although this algorithm is simple, efficient, and effective, there are a few cases where it could fail. A web developer could use a JSON object that deviates from the JSON standard, but is still detected by our algorithm as JSON, resulting in a failed parse. We found a few cases of this type of deviation, which resulted in our updated grammar, but other similar instances are possible. Another problematic scenario is when an attacker replaces JSON text altogether with malicious JavaScript, which we would pass to `eval()`, missing the attack.

6.4 Experiments

6.4.1 *Implementation*

For automatic `JSON.parse()` adoption, implementation is very straightforward. We modify the `eval()` implementation in the JavaScript engine of WebKit. By detecting and fixing JSON strings, we are able to pass them to the dedicated `JSON.parse()` function instead of using the general-purpose `eval()` function.

6.4.2 *Coverage*

To test our JSON parsing defense we manually craft three attacks that simulate the script injection vulnerabilities we describe earlier in this section. In all of our tests ZAN detected the JSON text and ran it through the `JSON.parse()` parser, which "correctly" failed to parse the text and return a null object as expected. Certainly, if an attacker is able to replace a JSON string completely with malicious JavaScript code, he or she can elude ZAN's protection. However, in this case, the attacker would have almost complete control of the web server. It is unrealistic to defend at the client side any more.

We also visited the top 1000 popular websites and found that 79 deserialize JSON text using `eval()`. ZAN was able to run JSON objects on 76 of these sites through the `JSON.parse()` parser correctly as shown in Figure 4. ZAN missed three websites because they did not wrap JSON strings in parentheses. We also observed that some websites mixed JSON text within legitimate JavaScript code that is passed to `eval()`. In these few cases, ZAN is not able to add protection. Generally, had an attacker injected a malicious playload into the JSON text, ZAN would be able to prevent its execution for any of the 76 websites.

6.4.3 *Compatibility impact*

There are two possible cases in which ZAN causes incompatibility: 1) incorrectly recognizing a benign JavaScript code snippet in `eval()` as JSON string; 2) producing a different object after fixing and parsing the JSON string. For our experiments, ZAN's automatic use of the `JSON.parse()` function did not affect any of the 1000 websites we visited. In other words, all eval strings were processed identically in ZAN when compared to processing them with `eval()`. However, we recognize that we did have to add to the grammar of our `JSON.parse()` parser in order to maintain this compatibility. It is possible that websites outside of our data set could induce false positives, but our evidence suggests that our techniques would be robust.

7. DISCUSSION

While ZAN shows promising results, it is not a perfect solution yet and should be complementary to server-side effort. In this section, we discuss the lessons we learned through designing and implementing ZAN, and also articulate some issues related to the approach of ZAN.

7.1 Use of heuristics

In this paper, we advocate a pure client-side defense as we observe that web app developers are slow to adopt new security mechanisms. While ZAN does not require extra work on the server side, it uses heuristics to recover implicit information at the client side.

Heuristics-based approaches in most cases cannot be 100 percent accurate. Two typical concerns are: 1) whether an approach adds or improves protection for all possible candidates; 2) whether it results in incompatible web apps.

While our experiments suggest that ZAN performs adequately well for top 1000 popular websites, it is possible that less popular websites with poor design could be problematic. For example, one could use clear-text authentication cookies or irregular JSON strings. Nevertheless, with larger scale real world experiments, the classifiers that ZAN uses could be changed to accommodate more websites. As long as ZAN maintains compatibility, it could be adopted by mainstream browsers to provide "free" extra protection. In fact, there are real world examples of heuristics-based client-side protection. For example, Internet Explorer 8 uses heuristics to implement its XSS filters [25].

7.2 Deployment

When introducing a new mechanism to the Web, especially solely at the client side, we have to think about how to deploy it and whether it will cause new problems.

We argue that ZAN can be incorporated into modern web browsers gradually. Browsers with and without ZAN capability will not present a fundamentally different interpretation of the same web app. ZAN does not rely on any events or states that can be multiplexed for different purposes. For example, credential cookies should only be used for authentication between browsers and servers. It is very rare, if any, for a well designed website to use client-side scripting to access authentication cookies. It is also possible that an attacker could inject frame busting-like code into a web app using XSS to confuse ZAN. However, ZAN would not stop rendering of the web app unless it is embedded in a cross-origin frame, which is uncommon.

At the same time, ZAN always obeys the web developers' decisions. For example, if a website already uses `HttpOnly` tags, ZAN will not modify the cookies for the website. If a website specifies `X-Frame-Options`, even if it is the ALLOW type, ZAN will skip its frame busting detection code for this website. Moreover, we can always allow web developers to disable ZAN using an extra HTTP header like disabling XSS filters [25] if needed.

It is reported that existing client-side defenses such as XSS filters in Internet Explorer have introduced new vulnerabilities into the browsers [24]. As browsers are already complex artifacts, adding complex defense mechanisms would be problematic. However, we argue that all the mechanisms we demonstrate are simple (less than 100 lines of code each), and do not change the structure or internal execution of a web page. Our secure JSON deserialization does change the JSON strings a little bit, but what ZAN tries to do is enforce better format according to standards. Nevertheless, it is infeasible to prove that there are no new vulnerabilities added. The only way we can do is to keep ZAN simple.

7.3 Performance overhead

We also need to make sure that ZAN does not incur noticeable performance overhead for web browsing. Microbenchmarks suggest that the cost of these three algorithms is less than 10 milliseconds even in worst cases. Additionally, computation of these algorithms can be overlapped with network latencies. In general, during the experiments, we did not observe any measurable amount of overhead.

8. ADDITIONAL RELATED WORK

In addition to the projects we discussed previously in this paper, there are a number of other related works. These related projects fit into one of three main categories: XSS defenses, clickjacking defenses, and cookie protection.

8.1 XSS defenses

XSS defenses are closely related to our `HttpOnly` cookie defense because one common use of XSS is to steal authentication cookies via injected JavaScript, which is something our defense is designed to prevent.

XSS Auditor [12] and IE8 [25] use heuristics to detect script-like entities embedded in URLs to prevent reflected XSS attacks. While Alhambra [33] uses heuristics to determine if a script should be executed or not in order to prevent XSS. A number of recent projects enable the programmer to use annotations to specify portions of the HTML document where the browser prevents scripts from running [18, 40, 13, 35, 39]. Similarly, two recent projects propose automated client/server hybrid systems [23, 16] that automatically mark portions of the HTML where scripts are not allowed to run. Finally, the Firefox NoScript extension [22] white-lists trusted script source locations. ZAN differs from these approaches because it focuses on identifying and isolating authentication cookies rather than determining what JavaScript code should be allowed to run.

8.2 Clickjacking defenses

Clickjacking defenses are related to our `X-Frame-Options` defense because it is enabled by attackers including framed pages and occluding the framed content to fool users.

ClearClick, which is part of NoScript [22], tries to prevent clickjacking by notifying the user anytime they interact with a framed element that has been occluded. This mechanism essentially infers the user's intent by reasoning about visual elements and any occlusion that the page might induce on embedded elements. ClickIDS [7] uses ClearClick as part of an automated testing tool that synthesizes clicks on pages and runs them with and without ClearClick enabled. By comparing the results of the two pages they can infer a possible clickjacking attack by detecting differences between the two. Our complementary `X-Frame-Options` defense differs from these techniques by instead inferring programmer intentions (i.e., frame busting code) and preventing the page from being framed rather inferring user intentions.

8.3 Cookie protection

One recent project that aims to protect cookies is the Doppelganger project [28]. It provides more flexible cookie policies by recording and replaying web sessions to detect if modifying a cookie would affect a web site. This information enables Doppelganger to make decisions about deleting cookies that would otherwise be stored by the browser.

Barnett also tried to use cookie name to identify authentication cookies and apply `HttpOnly` tags [8]. However, his approach requires server-side efforts and works only with Apache. Moreover, he did not take randomness and length of a cookie into account.

Recent work by Vogt *et al.* [37], proposes using dynamic taint tracking to prevent cookies from being sent to a remote site via JavaScript. In our work we strive to identify and isolate login cookies, whereas they assume that cookies are tainted and track the effects of these cookies as JavaScript code accesses them. One could imagine combining these two complementary techniques so that the taint tracking system only taints cookies that ZAN identifies as `HttpOnly` cookies.

9. CONCLUSIONS

In this paper we presented a browser-based approach for automatically adding new security features to existing web apps. ZAN accomplishes this by inspecting events and states in the browser to exploit opportunities for retrofitting legacy web apps with new security features. We presented three algorithms: `HttpOnly` cookie designation, which automatically restricts access to authentication cookies, `X-Frame-Options` specification, which denies the inclusion of web apps in `IFRAME`s, and `JSON.parse()`, which detects `eval()` calls on JSON text and parses them in safe routines. Each of these algorithms capitalizes on unique details about applications to provide automated security mechanisms.

One key aspect of our approach is that our algorithms are simple. As browsers are complex artifacts, it is necessary to maintain this feature for the development of practical systems. Despite their simplicity, our algorithms are effective at improving the security of several of the websites we evaluated. Furthermore, two of our algorithms, `HttpOnly` and `IFRAME` defense, are tunable and can be adjusted by browser developers to trade-off security against compatibility.

As web apps become increasingly popular, improving their security becomes paramount. Browser developers have been proactive in providing new security mechanisms, but web developers have either been too slow to adopt these new features or managed complex code bases that make it difficult to adapt legacy systems. ZAN is a system that can provide complimentary protection of legacy web apps where web developers fail to use the security mechanisms available to them in a timely fashion.

10. ACKNOWLEDGMENTS

We would like to thank Carl Gunter, Hank Levy, José Meseguer, and Pablo Montesinos who provided valuable feedback on this paper. We also would like to thank the anonymous reviewers for their thorough and helpful comments and feedback. This research was funded in part by NSF grants CNS 0834738 and CNS 0831212, grant N0014-09-1-0743 from the Office of Naval Research, and AFOSR MURI grant FA9550-09-01-0539.

11. REFERENCES

[1] JSON in JavaScript. `http://www.json.org/js.html`.

[2] Mitigating cross-site scripting with HTTP-only cookies. `http://msdn.microsoft.com/en-us/library/ms533046.aspx`.

[3] Qt - A Cross-platform application and UI. `http://qt.nokia.com/`.

[4] Symantec internet security threat report april 2010. `http://www.symantec.com/business/theme.jsp?themeid=threatreport`.

[5] The WebKit Open Source Project. `http://webkit.org/`.

[6] Alexa. Alexa top 500 global sites. `http://www.alexa.com/topsites`.

[7] M. Balduzzi, M. Egele, E. Kirda, D. Balzarotti, and C. Kruegel. A solution for the automated detection of clickjacking attacks. In *Proceedings of the 5th ACM Symposium on Information, Computer and Communications Security*, ASIACCS '10, pages 135–144, New York, NY, USA, 2010. ACM.

[8] R. Barnett. Helping protect cookies with httponly flag. `http://blog.modsecurity.org/2008/12/helping-protect-cookies-with-httponly-flag.html`, 2008.

[9] A. Barth, C. Jackson, and J. C. Mitchell. Robust defenses for cross-site request forgery. In *Proceedings of the 15th ACM Conference on Computer and Communications Security*, pages 75–88, 2008.

[10] A. Barth, C. Jackson, C. Reis, and The Google Chrome Team. The security architecture of the chromium browser, 2008. `http://crypto.stanford.edu/websec/chromium/chromium-security-architecture.pdf`.

[11] BBC. Facebook "clickjacking" spreads across site, June 2010. `http://www.bbc.co.uk/news/10224434`.

[12] Google Inc. Chromium. `http://www.chromium.org/chromium-os`.

[13] Google Inc. Google Caja. `http://code.google.com/p/google-caja/`.

[14] C. Grier, S. Tang, and S. T. King. Secure web browsing with the OP web browser. In *Proceedings of the 2008 IEEE Symposium on Security and Privacy*, pages 402–416, May 2008.

[15] C. Grier, S. Tang, and S. T. King. Designing and implementing the OP and OP2 web browsers. *ACM Trans. Web*, 5:11:1–11:35, May 2011.

[16] M. V. Gundy and H. Chen. Noncespaces: Using randomization to enforce information flow tracking and thwart cross-site scripting attacks. In *Proceedings of the Network and Distributed System Security Symposium*, February 2009.

[17] R. Hansen and J. Grossman. Clickjacking, September 2008. `http://www.sectheory.com/clickjacking.htm`.

[18] T. Jim, N. Swamy, and M. Hicks. Defeating script injection attacks with browser-enforced embedded policies. In *Proceedings of the 16th international conference on World Wide Web*, WWW '07, pages 601–610, New York, NY, USA, 2007. ACM.

[19] R. Kohavi and F. Provost. Glossary of terms. *Machine Learning*, 30(2):271–274, 1998.

[20] D. M. Kristol. Http cookies: Standards, privacy, and politics. *ACM Trans. Internet Technol.*, 1:151–198, November 2001.

[21] E. Lawrence. Combating clickjacking with X-Frame-Options, March 2010. `http://blogs.msdn.com/b/ieinternals/archive/2010/03/30/combating-clickjacking-with-x-frame-options.aspx`.

[22] G. Maone. NoScript - JavaScript/Java/Flash blocker for a safer Firefox experience!, 2008. `http://noscript.net/`.

[23] Y. Nadji, P. Saxen, and D. Song. Document structure integrity: A robust basis for cross-site scripting defense. In *Proceedings of the Network and Distributed System Security Symposium*, February 2009.

[24] E. V. Nava and D. Lindsay. Abusing internet explorer 8's xss filters. `http://p42.us/ie8xss/Abusing_IE8s_XSS_Filters.pdf`, 2010.

[25] D. Ross. IEBlog : IE8 Security Part IV: The XSS Filter, 2008. `http://blogs.msdn.com/ie/archive/2008/07/01/ie8-security-part-iv-the-xss-filter.aspx`.

[26] G. Rydstedt, E. Bursztein, D. Boneh, and C. Jackson. Busting frame busting: a study of clickjacking vulnerabilities at popular sites. In *in IEEE Oakland Web 2.0 Security and Privacy (W2SP 2010)*, 2010.

[27] P. Saxena, S. Hanna, P. Poosankam, and D. Song. FLAX: Systematic Discovery of Client-side Validation Vulnerabilities in Rich Web Applications. In *Proceedings of the 17th Network and Distributed System Security Symposium (NDSS)*, February 2010.

[28] U. Shankar and C. Karlof. Doppelganger: Better browser privacy without the bother. In *Proceedings of the 13th ACM Conference on Computer and Communications Security (CCS)*, pages 154–167, 2006.

[29] C. E. Shannon. A mathematical theory of communication. *The Bell System Technical Journal*, 27:379–423,623–656, July, October 1948.

[30] K. Singh, A. Moshchuk, H. J. Wang, and W. Lee. On the incoherencies in web browser access control policies. In *Proceedings of the IEEE Symposium on Security and Privacy*, May 2010.

[31] P. Stone. Next generation clickjacking, April 2010. `http://www.contextis.co.uk/resources/white-papers/clickjacking/Context-Clickjacking_white_paper.pdf`.

[32] Symantec Inc. Symantec global Internet security threat report: Trends for 2008, April 2009.

http://www.symantec.com/business/theme.jsp?themeid=threatreport.

[33] S. Tang, C. Grier, O. Aciicmez, and S. T. King. Alhambra: a system for creating, enforcing, and testing browser security policies. In *Proceedings of the 19th international conference on World wide web*, WWW '10, pages 941–950, New York, NY, USA, 2010. ACM.

[34] S. Tang, H. Mai, and S. T. King. Trust and protection in the illinois browser operating system. In *Proceedings of the 9th USENIX Conference on Operating Systems Design and Implementation*, OSDI'10, Berkeley, CA, USA, 2010. USENIX Association.

[35] M. Ter Louw and V. Venkatakrishnan. Blueprint: Robust prevention of cross-site scripting attacks for existing browsers. In *Proceedings IEEE Symposium on Security and Privacy*, pages 331–346, May 2009.

[36] Twitter. Clickjacking blocked, February 2009. http://blog.twitter.com/2009/02/clickjacking-blocked.html.

[37] P. Vogt, F. Nentwich, N. Jovanovic, E. Kirda, C. Kruegel, and G. Vigna. Cross-site scripting prevention with dynamic data tainting and static analysis. In *Proceedings of the Network and Distributed System Security Symposium (NDSS)*, February 2007.

[38] W3C. HTML 5. http://www.w3.org/TR/html5/.

[39] W3C. The iframe element. http://www.w3.org/TR/html5/the-iframe-element.html.

[40] H. J. Wang, X. Fan, J. Howell, and C. Jackson. Protection and communication abstractions for web browsers in MashupOS. In *Proceedings of the 21st ACM Symposium on Operating Systems Principles (SOSP)*, October 2007.

[41] H. J. Wang, C. Grier, A. Moshchuk, S. T. King, P. Choudhury, and H. Venter. The multi-principal OS construction of the Gazelle web browser. In *Proceedings of the 2009 USENIX Security Symposium*, August 2009.

[42] W. Zeller and E. W. Felten. Cross-site request forgeries: Exploitation and prevention. Technical report, Princeton University, October 2008. http://www.freedom-to-tinker.com/sites/default/files/csrf.pdf.

Android Permissions Demystified

Adrienne Porter Felt, Erika Chin, Steve Hanna, Dawn Song, David Wagner
University of California, Berkeley
{ apf, emc, sch, dawnsong, daw }@ cs.berkeley.edu

ABSTRACT

Android provides third-party applications with an extensive API that includes access to phone hardware, settings, and user data. Access to privacy- and security-relevant parts of the API is controlled with an install-time application permission system. We study Android applications to determine whether Android developers follow least privilege with their permission requests. We built Stowaway, a tool that detects overprivilege in compiled Android applications. Stowaway determines the set of API calls that an application uses and then maps those API calls to permissions. We used automated testing tools on the Android API in order to build the permission map that is necessary for detecting overprivilege. We apply Stowaway to a set of 940 applications and find that about one-third are overprivileged. We investigate the causes of overprivilege and find evidence that developers are trying to follow least privilege but sometimes fail due to insufficient API documentation.

Categories and Subject Descriptors

D.2.5 [**Software Engineering**]: Testing and Debugging; D.4.6 [**Operating Systems**]: Security and Protection

General Terms

Security

Keywords

Android, permissions, least privilege

1. INTRODUCTION

Android's unrestricted application market and open source have made it a popular platform for third-party applications. As of 2011, the Android Market includes more applications than the Apple App Store [10]. Android supports third-party development with an extensive API that provides applications with access to phone hardware (e.g., the camera), WiFi and cellular networks, user data, and phone settings.

Access to privacy- and security-relevant parts of Android's rich API is controlled by an install-time application permission system. Each application must declare upfront what permissions it requires, and the user is notified during installation about what permissions it will receive. If a user does not want to grant a permission to an application, he or she can cancel the installation process.

Install-time permissions can provide users with control over their privacy and reduce the impact of bugs and vulnerabilities in applications. However, an install-time permission system is ineffective if developers routinely request more permissions than they require. Overprivileged applications expose users to unnecessary permission warnings and increase the impact of a bug or vulnerability. We study Android applications to determine whether Android developers follow least privilege or overprivilege their applications.

We present a tool, Stowaway, that detects overprivilege in compiled Android applications. Stowaway is composed of two parts: a static analysis tool that determines what API calls an application makes, and a permission map that identifies what permissions are needed for each API call. Android's documentation does not provide sufficient permission information for such an analysis, so we empirically determined Android 2.2's access control policy. Using automated testing techniques, we achieved 85% coverage of the Android API. Our permission map provides insight into the Android permission system and enables us to identify overprivilege.

We apply Stowaway to 940 Android applications from the Android Market and find that about one-third of applications are overprivileged. The overprivileged applications generally request few extra privileges: more than half only contain one extra permission, and only 6% request more than four unnecessary permissions. We investigate causes of overprivilege and find that many developer errors stem from confusion about the permission system. Our results indicate that developers are trying to follow least privilege, which supports the potential effectiveness of install-time permission systems like Android's.

Android provides developer documentation, but its permission information is limited. The lack of reliable permission information may cause developer error. The documentation lists permission requirements for only 78 methods, whereas our testing reveals permission requirements for 1,259 methods (a sixteen-fold improvement over the documentation). Additionally, we identify 6 errors in the Android permission documentation. This imprecision leaves developers to supplement reference material with guesses and message boards. Developer confusion can lead to overprivileged applications, as the developer adds unnecessary permissions in an attempt to make the application work correctly.

Contributions. We provide the following contributions:

1. We developed Stowaway, a tool for detecting overprivilege in Android applications. We evaluate 940 applications from the Android Market with Stowaway and find that about one-third are overprivileged.
2. We identify and quantify patterns of developer error that lead to overprivilege.
3. Using automated testing techniques, we determine Android's access control policy. Our results represent a fifteen-fold improvement over the documentation.

Other existing tools [11, 12] and future program analyses could make use of our permission map to study permission usage in Android applications. Stowaway and the permission map data are available at `android-permissions.org`.

Organization. Section 2 provides an overview of Android and its permission system, Section 3 discusses our API testing methodology, and Section 4 describes our analysis of the Android API. Section 5 describes our static analysis tools for detecting overprivilege, and Section 6 discusses our application overprivilege analysis.

2. THE ANDROID PERMISSION SYSTEM

Android has an extensive API and permission system. We first provide a high-level overview of the Android application platform and permissions. We then present a detailed description of how Android permissions are enforced.

2.1 Android Background

Android smartphone users can install third-party applications through the Android Market [3] or Amazon Appstore [1]. The quality and trustworthiness of these third-party applications vary widely, so Android treats all applications as potentially buggy or malicious. Each application runs in a process with a low-privilege user ID, and applications can access only their own files by default. Applications are written in Java (possibly accompanied by native code), and each application runs in its own virtual machine.

Android controls access to system resources with install-time permissions. Android 2.2 defines 134 permissions, categorized into three threat levels:

1. *Normal* permissions protect access to API calls that could annoy but not harm the user. For example, `SET_WALLPAPER` controls the ability to change the user's background wallpaper.
2. *Dangerous* permissions control access to potentially harmful API calls, like those related to spending money or gathering private information. For example, Dangerous permissions are required to send text messages or read the list of contacts.
3. *Signature/System* permissions regulate access to the most dangerous privileges, such as the ability to control the backup process or delete application packages. These permissions are difficult to obtain: Signature permissions are granted only to applications that are signed with the device manufacturer's certificate, and SignatureOrSystem permissions are granted to applications that are signed or installed in a special system folder. These restrictions essentially limit Signature/System permissions to pre-installed applications, and requests for Signature/System permissions by other applications will be ignored.

Applications can define their own permissions for the purpose of self-protection, but we focus on Android-defined permissions that protect system resources. We do not consider developer-defined permissions at any stage of our analysis. Similarly, we do not consider Google-defined permissions that are included in Google applications like Google Reader but are not part of the operating system.

Permissions may be required when interacting with the system API, databases, and the message-passing system. The public API [2] describes 8,648 methods, some of which are protected by permissions. User data is stored in *Content Providers*, and permissions are required for operations on some system Content Providers. For example, applications must hold the `READ_CONTACTS` permission in order to execute READ queries on the Contacts Content Provider. Applications may also need permissions to receive *Intents* (i.e., messages) from the operating system. Intents notify applications of events, such as a change in network connectivity, and some Intents sent by the system are delivered only to applications with appropriate permissions. Furthermore, permissions are required to send Intents that mimic the contents of system Intents.

2.2 Permission Enforcement

We describe how the system API, Content Providers, and Intents are implemented and protected. To our knowledge, we are the first to describe the Android permission enforcement mechanisms in detail.

2.2.1 The API

API Structure. The Android API framework is composed of two parts: a library that resides in each application's virtual machine and an implementation of the API that runs in the system process(es). The API library runs with the same permissions as the application it accompanies, whereas the API implementation in the system process has no restrictions. The library provides syntactic sugar for interacting with the API implementation. API calls that read or change global phone state are proxied by the library to the API implementation in the system process.

API calls are handled in three steps (Figure 1). First, the application invokes the public API in the library. Second, the library invokes a private interface, also in the library. The private interface is an RPC stub. Third, the RPC stub initiates an RPC request with the system process that asks a system service to perform the desired operation. For example, if an application calls `ClipboardManager.getText()`, the call will be relayed to `IClipboard$Stub$Proxy`, which proxies the call to the system process's `ClipboardService`.

An application can use Java reflection [19] to access all of the API library's hidden and private classes, methods, and fields. Some private interfaces do not have any corresponding public API; however, applications can still invoke them using reflection. These non-public library methods are intended for use by Google applications or the framework itself, and developers are advised against using them because they may change or disappear between releases [17]. Nonetheless, some applications use them. Java code running in the system process is in a separate virtual machine and therefore immune to reflection.

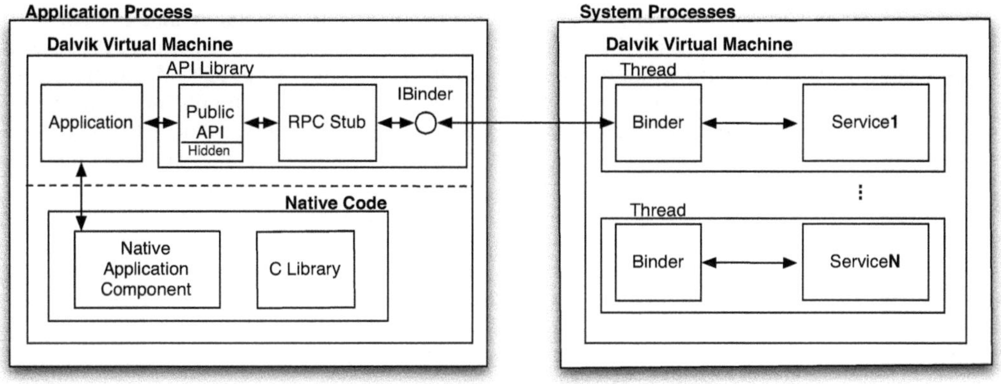

Figure 1: The architecture of the Android platform. Permission checks occur in the system process.

Permissions. To enforce permissions, various parts of the system invoke a permission validation mechanism to check whether a given application has a specified permission. The permission validation mechanism is implemented as part of the trusted system process, and invocations of the permission validation mechanism are spread throughout the API. There is no centralized policy for checking permissions when an API is called. Rather, mediation is contingent on the correct placement of permission validation calls.

Permission checks are placed in the API implementation in the system process. When necessary, the API implementation calls the permission validation mechanism to check that the invoking application has the necessary permissions. In some cases, the API library may also redundantly check these permissions, but such checks cannot be relied upon: applications can circumvent them by directly communicating with the system process via the RPC stubs. Permission checks therefore should not occur in the API library. Instead, the API implementation in the system process should invoke the permission validation mechanism.

A small number of permissions are enforced by Unix groups, rather than the Android permission validation mechanism. In particular, when an application is installed with the `INTERNET`, `WRITE_EXTERNAL_STORAGE`, or `BLUETOOTH` permissions, it is assigned to a Linux group that has access to the pertinent sockets and files. Thus, the Linux kernel enforces the access control policy for these permissions. The API library (which runs with the same rights as the application) can accordingly operate directly on these sockets and files, without needing to invoke the API implementation in the system process.

Native Code. Applications can include native code in addition to Java code, but native code is still beholden to the permission system. Attempts to open sockets or files are mediated by Linux permissions. Native code cannot communicate directly with the system API. Instead, the application must create Java wrapper methods to invoke the API on behalf of the native code. Android permissions are enforced as usual when the API calls are executed.

2.2.2 Content Providers

System Content Providers are installed as standalone applications, separate from the system process and API library. They are protected with both static and dynamic permission checks, using the same mechanisms that are available to applications to protect their own Content Providers.

Static declarations assign separate read and write permissions to a given Content Provider. By default, these permissions are applied to all resources stored by the Content Provider. Restrictions can also be applied at a finer granularity by associating permissions with a path (e.g., `content://a/b`). For example, a Content Provider that stores both public and private notes might want to set a default permission requirement for the whole Content Provider, but then allow unrestricted access to the public notes. Extra permission requirements can similarly be set for certain paths, making data under those paths accessible only if the calling application has the default permissions for the provider as well as the path-specific permissions.

Content Providers can also enforce permissions programmatically: the Content Provider code that handles a query can explicitly call the system's permission validation mechanism to require certain permissions. This gives the developer greater control over the granularity of the permission enforcement mechanism, allowing her to selectively require permissions for query values or database data.

2.2.3 Intents

Android's Intent system is used extensively for inter- and intra-application communication. To prevent applications from mimicking system Intents, Android restricts who may send certain Intents. All Intents are sent through the ActivityManagerService (a system service), which enforces this restriction. Two techniques are used to restrict the sending of system Intent. Some Intents can only be sent by applications with appropriate permissions. Other system Intents can only be sent by processes whose UID matches the system's. Intents in the latter category cannot be sent by applications, regardless of what permissions they hold, because these Intents must originate from the system process.

Applications may also need permissions to receive some system Intents. The OS uses the standard Android mechanism for restricting its Intent recipients. An application (in this case, the OS) may restrict who can receive an Intent by attaching a permission requirement to the Intent [13].

3. PERMISSION TESTING METHODOLOGY

Android's access control policy is not well documented, but the policy is necessary to determine whether applications are overprivileged. To address this shortcoming, we empirically determined the access control policy that Android enforces. We used testing to construct a permission map that identifies the permissions required for each method in the Android API. In particular, we modified Android 2.2's permission verification mechanism to log permission checks as they occur. We then generated unit test cases for API calls, Content Providers, and Intents. Executing these tests allowed us to observe the permissions required to interact with system APIs. A core challenge was to build unit tests that obtain call coverage of all platform resources.

3.1 The API

As described in §2.2.1, the Android API provides applications with a library that includes public, private, and hidden classes and methods. The set of private classes includes the RPC stubs for the system services.[1] All of these classes and methods are accessible to applications using Java reflection, so we must test them to identify permission checks. We conducted testing in three phases: feedback-directed testing; customizable test case generation; and manual verification.

3.1.1 Feedback-Directed Testing

For the first phase of testing, we used Randoop, an automated, feedback-directed, object-oriented test generator for Java [20, 22]. Randoop takes a list of classes as input and searches the space of possible sequences of methods from these classes. We modified Randoop to run as an Android application and to log every method it invokes. Our modifications to Android log every permission that is checked by the Android permission validation mechanism, which lets us deduce which API calls trigger permission checks.

Randoop searches the space of methods to find methods whose return values can be used as parameters for other methods. It maintains a pool of valid initial input sequences and parameters, initially seeded with primitive values (e.g., `int` and `String`). Randoop builds test sequences incrementally by randomly selecting a method from the test class's methods and selecting sequences from the input pool to populate the method's arguments. If the new sequence is unique, then it is executed. Sequences that complete successfully (i.e., without generating an exception) are added to the sequence pool. Randoop's goal is full coverage of the test space. Unlike comparable techniques [4,9,21], Randoop does not need a sample execution trace as input, making large-scale testing such as API fuzzing more manageable. Because Randoop uses Java reflection to generate the test methods from the supplied list of classes, it supports testing non-public methods. We modified Randoop to also test nested classes of the input classes.

Limitations. Randoop's feedback-guided space exploration is limited by the objects and input values it has access to. If Randoop cannot find an object of the correct type needed to invoke a method in the sequence pool, then it will never try to invoke the method. The Android API is too large to test all interdependent classes at once, so in practice many objects are not available in the sequence pool. We mitigated this problem by testing related classes together (for example, `Account` and `AccountManager`) and adding seed sequences that return common Android-specific data types. Unfortunately, this was insufficient to produce valid input parameters for many methods. Many singleton object instances can only be created through API calls with specific parameters; for example, a `WifiManager` instance can be obtained by calling `android.content.Context.getSystemService(String)` with the parameter `"wifi"`. We addressed this by augmenting the input pool with specific primitive constants and sequences. Additionally, some API calls expect memory addresses that store specific values for parameters, which we were unable to solve at scale.

Randoop also does not handle ordering requirements that are independent of input parameters. In some cases, Android expects methods to precede each other in a very specific order. Randoop only generates sequence chains for the purpose of creating arguments for methods; it is not able to generate sequences to satisfy dependencies that are not in the form of an input variable. Further aggravating this problem, many Android methods with underlying native code generate segmentation faults if called out of order, which terminates the Randoop testing process.

[1]The operating system also includes many internal methods that make permission checks. However, applications cannot invoke them because they are not currently exposed with RPC stubs. Since we are focused on the application-facing API, we do not test or discuss these permission checks.

3.1.2 Customizable Test Case Generation

Randoop's feedback-directed approach to testing failed to cover certain types of methods. When this happened, there was no way to manually edit its test sequences to control sequence order or establish method pre-conditions. To address these limitations and improve coverage, we built our own test generation tool. Our tool accepts a list of method signatures as input, and outputs at least one unit test for each method. It maintains a pool of default input parameters that can be passed to methods to be called. If multiple values are available for a parameter, then our tool creates multiple unit tests for that method. (Tests are created combinatorially when multiple parameters of the same method have multiple possible values.) It also generates tests using null values if it cannot find a suitable parameter. Because our tool separates test case generation from execution, a human tester can edit the test sequences produced by our tool. When tests fail, we manually adjust the order of method calls, introduce extra code to satisfy method pre-conditions, or add new parameters for the failing tests.

Our test generation tool requires more human effort than Randoop, but it is effective for quickly achieving coverage of methods that Randoop was unable to properly invoke. Overseeing and editing a set of generated test cases produced by our tool is still substantially less work than manually writing test cases. Our experience with large-scale API testing was that methods that are challenging to invoke by feedback-directed testing occur often enough to be problematic. When a human tester has the ability to edit failing sequences, these methods can be properly invoked.

3.1.3 Manual Verification

The first two phases of testing generate a map of the permission checks performed by each method in the API. However, these results contain three types of inconsistencies. First, the permission checks caused by asynchronous API calls are sometimes incorrectly associated with subsequent API calls. Second, a method's permission requirements can be argument-dependent, in which case we see intermittent or different permission checks for that method. Third, permission checks can be dependent on the order in which API calls are made. To identify and resolve these inconsistencies, we manually verified the correctness of the permission map generated by the first two phases of testing.

We used our customizable test generation tool to create tests to confirm the permission(s) associated with each API method in our permission map. We carefully experimented with the ordering and arguments of the test cases to ensure that we correctly matched permission checks to asynchronous API calls and identified the conditions of permission checks. When confirming permissions for potentially asynchronous or order-dependent API calls, we also created confirmation test cases for related methods in the pertinent class that were not initially associated with permission checks. We ran every test case both with and without their required permissions in order to identify API calls with multiple or substitutable permission requirements. If a test case throws a security exception without a permission but succeeds with a permission, then we know that the permission map for the method under test is correct.

Testing The Internet Permission. Applications can access the Internet through the Android API, but other packages such as `java.net` and `org.apache` also provide Internet access. In order to determine which methods require access to the Internet, we scoured the documentation and searched the Internet for any and all methods that suggest Internet access. Using this list, we wrote test cases to determine which of those methods require the `INTERNET` permission.

3.2 Content Providers

Our Content Provider test application executes **`query`**, **`insert`**, **`update`**, and **`delete`** operations on Content Provider URIs associated with the Android system and pre-installed appliactions. We collected a list of URIs from the **`android.provider`** package to determine the core set of Content Providers to test. We additionally collected Content Provider URIs that we discovered during other phases of testing. For each URI, we attempted to execute each type of database operation without any permissions. If a security exception was thrown, we recorded the required permission. We added and tested combinations of permissions to identify multiple or substitutable permission requirements. Each Content Provider was tested until security exceptions were no longer thrown for a given operation, indicating the minimum set of permissions required to complete that operation. In addition to testing, we also examined the system Content Providers' static permission declarations.

3.3 Intents

We built a pair of applications to send and receive Intents. The Android documentation does not provide a single, comprehensive list of the available system Intents, so we scraped the public API to find string constants that could be the contents of an Intent.[2] We sent and received Intents with these constants between our test applications. In order to test the permissions needed to receive system broadcast Intents, we triggered system broadcasts by sending and receiving text messages, sending and receiving phone calls, connecting and disconnecting WiFi, connecting and disconnecting Bluetooth devices, etc. For all of these tests, we recorded whether permission checks occurred and whether the Intents were delivered or received successfully.

[2]For those familiar with Android terminology, we searched for Intent *action* strings.

4. PERMISSION MAP RESULTS

Our testing of the Android application platform resulted in a permission map that correlates permission requirements with API calls, Content Providers, and Intents. In this section, we discuss our coverage of the API, compare our results to the official Android documentation, and present characteristics of the Android API and permission map.

4.1 Coverage

The Android API consists of 1,665 classes with a total of 16,732 public and private methods. We attained **85%** coverage of the Android API through two phases of testing. (We define a method as *covered* if we executed it without generating an exception; we do not measure branch coverage.) Randoop attained an initial method coverage of 60%, spread across all packages. We supplemented Randoop's coverage with our proprietary test generation tool, accomplishing close to 100% coverage of the methods that belong to classes with at least one permission check.

The uncovered portion of the API is due to native calls and the omission of second-phase tests for packages that did not yield permission checks in the first phase. First, native methods often crashed the application when incorrect parameters were supplied, making them difficult to test. Many native method parameters are integers that represent pointers to objects in native code, making it difficult to supply correct parameters. Approximately one-third of uncovered methods are native calls. Second, we decided to omit supplemental tests for packages that did not reveal permission checks during the Randoop testing phase. If Randoop did not trigger at least one permission check in a package, we did not add more tests to the classes in the package.

4.2 Comparison With Documentation

Clear and well-developed documentation promotes correct permission usage and safe programming practices. Errors and omissions in the documentation can lead to incorrect developer assumptions and overprivilege. Android's documentation of permissions is limited, which is likely due to their lack of a centralized access control policy. Our testing identified 1,259 API calls with permission checks. We compare this to the Android 2.2 documentation.

We crawled the Android 2.2 documentation and found that it specifies permission requirements for 78 methods. The documentation additionally lists permissions in several class descriptions, but it is not clear which methods of the classes require the stated permissions. Of the 78 permission-protected API calls in the documentation, our testing indicates that the documentation for 6 API calls is incorrect. It is unknown to us whether the documentation or implementation is wrong; if the documentation is correct, then these discrepancies may be security errors.

Three of the documentation errors list a different permission than was found through testing. In one place, the documentation claims an API call is protected by the Dangerous permission `MANAGE_ACCOUNTS`, when it actually can be accessed with the lower-privilege Normal permission `GET_ACCOUNTS`. Another error claims an API call requires the `ACCESS_COARSE_UPDATES` permission, which does not exist. As a result, 5 of the 900 applications that we study in §6.2 request this non-existent permission. A third error states that a method is protected with the `BLUETOOTH` permission, when the method is in fact protected with `BLUETOOTH_ADMIN`.

Permission	Usage
BLUETOOTH	85
B1UETOOTH_ADMIN	45
READ_CONTACTS	38
ACCESS_NETWORK_STATE	24
WAKE_LOCK	24
ACCESS_FINE_LOCATION	22
WRITE_SETTINGS	21
MODIFY_AUDIO_SETTINGS	21
ACCESS_COARSE_LOCATION	18
CHANGE_WIFI_STATE	16

Table 1: Android's 10 most checked permissions.

The other three documentation errors pertain to methods with multiple permission requirements. In one error, the documentation claims that a method requires one permission, but our testing shows that two are required. For the last two errors, the documentation states that two methods require one permission each; in practice, however, the two methods both accept two permissions (i.e., they are ORs).

4.3 Characterizing Permissions

Based on our permission map, we characterize how permission checks are distributed throughout the API.

4.3.1 API Calls

We examined the Android API to see how many methods and classes have permission checks. We present the number of permission checks, unused permissions, hierarchical permissions, permission granularity, and class characteristics.

Number of Permissions Checks. We identified 1,244 API calls with permission checks, which is 6.45% of all API methods (including hidden and private methods). Of those, 816 are methods of normal API classes, and 428 are methods of RPC stubs that are used to communicate with system services. We additionally identified 15 API calls with permission checks in a supplementary part of the API added by a manufacturer, for a total of 1,259 API calls with permission checks. Table 1 provides the rates of the most commonly-checked permissions for the normal API.

Signature/System Permissions. We found that 12% of the normal API calls are protected with Signature/System permissions, and 35% of the RPC stubs are protected with Signature/System permissions. This effectively limits the use of these API calls to pre-installed applications.

Unused Permissions. We found that some permissions are defined by the platform but never used within the API. For example, the BRICK permission is never used, despite being oft-cited as an example of a particularly dire permission [26]. The only use of the BRICK permission is in dead code that is incapable of causing harm to the device. Our testing found that 15 of the 134 Android-defined permissions are unused. For each case where a permission was never found during testing, we searched the source tree to verify that the permission is not used. After examining several devices, we discovered that one of the otherwise unused permissions is used by the custom classes that HTC and Samsung added to the API to support 4G on their phones.

Hierarchical Permissions. The names of many permissions imply that there are hierarchical relationships between them. Intuitively, we expect that more powerful permissions should be substitutable for lesser permissions relating to the same resource. However, we find no evidence of planned hierarchy. Our testing indicates that BLUETOOTH_ADMIN is not substitutable for BLUETOOTH, nor is WRITE_CONTACTS substitutable for READ_CONTACTS. Similarly, CHANGE_WIFI_STATE cannot be used in place of ACCESS_WIFI_STATE.

Only one pair of permissions has a hierarchical relationship: ACCESS_COARSE_LOCATION and ACCESS_FINE_LOCATION. Every method that accepts the COARSE permission also accepts FINE as a substitute. We found only one exception to this, which may be a bug: `TelephonyManager.listen()` accepts either ACCESS_COARSE_LOCATION or READ_PHONE_STATE, but it does not accept ACCESS_FINE_LOCATION.

Permission Granularity. If a single permission is applied to a diverse set of functionality, applications that request the permission for a subset of the functionality will have unnecessary access to the rest. Android aims to prevent this by splitting functionality into multiple permissions when possible, and their approach has been shown to benefit platform security [15]. As a case study, we examine the division of Bluetooth functionality, as the Bluetooth permissions are the most heavily checked permissions.

We find that the two Bluetooth permissions are applied to 6 large classes. They are divided between methods that change state (BLUETOOTH_ADMIN) and methods that get device information (BLUETOOTH). The `BluetoothAdapter` class is one of several that use the Bluetooth permissions, and it appropriately divides most of its permission assignments. However, it features some inconsistencies. One method only returns information but requires the BLUETOOTH_ADMIN permission, and another method changes state but requires both permissions. This type of inconsistency may lead to developer confusion about which permissions are required for which types of operations.

Class Characteristics. Figure 2 presents the percentage of methods that are protected per class. We initially expected that the distribution would be bimodal, with most classes protected entirely or not at all. Instead, however, we see a wide array of class protection rates. Of these classes, only 8 require permissions to instantiate an object, and 4 require permissions only for the object constructor.

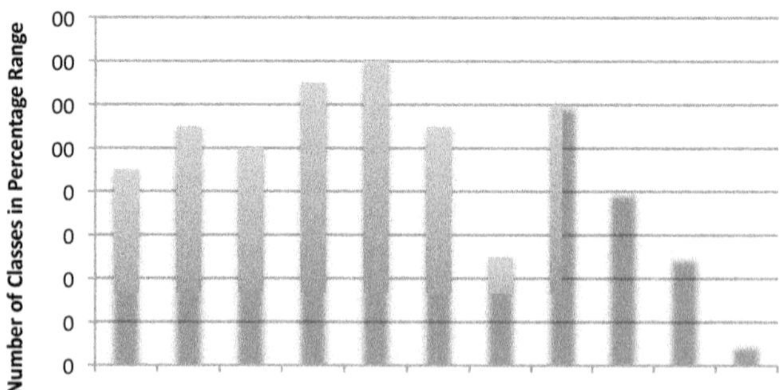

Figure 2: A histogram of the number of classes, sorted by the percentage of the classes' methods that require permissions. The numbers shown represent ranges, i.e., 10% represents [10 – 20%). We only consider classes with at least 1 permission check.

4.3.2 *Content Providers and Intents*

We examined Content Providers to determine whether they are protected by permissions. We investigated a total of 62 Content Providers. We found that there are 18 Content Providers that do not have permissions for any of the methods that we tested (insert, query, update, and delete). All of the Content Providers that lack permissions are associated with the `content://media` content URI.

We examined Intent communication and measured whether permissions are required for sending and receiving Intents. When sending broadcast Intents, 62 broadcasts are prohibited by non-system senders, 6 require permissions before sending the Intent, and 2 can be broadcast but not received by system receivers. Broadcast receivers must have permissions to receive 23 broadcast Intents, of which 14 are protected by a Bluetooth permission. When sending Intents to start Activities, 7 Intent messages require permissions. When starting Services, 2 Intents require permissions.

5. APPLICATION ANALYSIS TOOL

We built a static analysis tool, Stowaway, which analyzes an Android application and determines the maximum set of permissions it may require. Stowaway analyzes the application's use of API calls, Content Providers, and Intents and then uses the permission map built in §3 to determine what permissions those operations require.

Compiled applications for the Android platform include Dalvik executable (DEX) files that run on Android's Dalvik Virtual Machine. We disassemble application DEX files using the publicly available Dedexer tool [23]. Each stage of Stowaway takes the disassembled DEX as input.

5.1 API Calls

Stowaway first parses the disassembled DEX files and identifies all calls to standard API methods. Stowaway tracks application-defined classes that inherit methods from Android classes so we can differentiate between invocations of application-defined methods and Android-defined inherited methods. We use heuristics to handle Java reflection and two unusual permissions.

Reflection. Java reflection is a challenging problem [6, 18, 24]. In Java, methods can be reflectively invoked with `java.lang.reflect.Method.invoke()` or `java.lang.reflect.Constructor.newInstance()`. Stowaway tracks which Class objects and method names are propagated to the reflective invocation. It performs flow-sensitive, intra-procedural static analysis, augmented with inter-procedural analysis to a depth of 2 method calls. Within each method body, it tracks the value of each String, StringBuilder, Class, Method, Constructor, Field, and Object. We also track the state of static member variables of these types. We identify method calls that convert strings and objects to type Class, as well as method calls that convert Class objects to Methods, Constructors, and Fields.

We also apply Android-specific heuristics to resolving reflection by handling methods and fields that may affect reflective calls. We cannot model the behavior of the entire Android and Java APIs, but we identify special cases. First, `Context.getSystemService(String)` returns different types of objects depending on the argument. We maintain a mapping of arguments to the types of return objects. Second, some API classes contain private member variables that hold references to hidden interfaces. Applications can only access these member variables reflectively, which obscures their type information. We created a mapping between member variables and their types and propagate the type data accordingly. If an application subsequently accesses methods on a member variable after retrieving it, we can resolve the member variable's type.

Internet. Any application that includes a *WebView* must have the Internet permission. A WebView is a user interface component that allows an application to embed a web site into its UI. WebViews can be instantiated programmatically or declared in XML files. Stowaway identifies programmatic instantiations of WebViews. It also decompiles application XML files and parses them to detect WebView declarations.

External Storage. If an application wants to access files stored on the SD card, it must have the `WRITE_EXTERNAL_STORAGE` permission. This permission does not appear in our permission map because it (1) is enforced entirely using Linux permissions and (2) can be associated with any file operation or API call that accesses the SD card from within the library. We handle this permission by searching the application's string literals and XML files for strings that contain `sdcard`; if any are found, we assume `WRITE_EXTERNAL_STORAGE` is needed. Additionally, we assume this permission is needed if we see API calls that return paths to the SD card, such as `Environment.getExternalStorageDirectory()`.

5.2 Content Providers

Content Providers are accessed by performing a database operation on a URI. Stowaway collects all strings that could be used as Content Provider URIs and links those strings to the Content Providers' permission requirements. Content Provider URIs can be obtained in two ways:

1. A string or set of strings can be passed into a method that returns a URI. For example, the API call `android.net.Uri.parse("content://browser/bookmarks")` returns a URI for accessing the Browser bookmarks. To handle this case, Stowaway finds all string literals that begin with `content://`.
2. The API provides Content Provider helper classes that include public URI constants. For example, the value of `android.provider.Browser.BOOKMARKS_URI` is `content://browser/bookmarks`. Stowaway recognizes known URI constants, and we created a mapping from all known URI constants to their string values.

A limitation of our tool is that we cannot tell which database operations an application performs with a URI; there are many ways to perform an operation on a Content Provider, and users can set their own query strings. To account for this, we say that an application may require any permission associated with any operation on a given Content Provider URI. This provides an upper bound on the permissions that could be required in order to use a specific Content Provider.

5.3 Intents

We use ComDroid [8] to detect the sending and receiving of Intents that require permissions. ComDroid performs flow-sensitive, intra-procedural static analysis, augmented with limited inter-procedural analysis that follows method invocations to a depth of one method call. ComDroid tracks the state of Intents, registers, sinks (e.g., `sendBroadcast`), and application components. When an Intent object is instantiated, passed as a method parameter, or obtained as a return value, ComDroid tracks all changes to it from its source to its sink and outputs all information about the Intent and all components expecting to receive messages.

Stowaway takes ComDroid's output and, for each sent Intent, checks whether a permission is required to send that Intent. For each Intent that an application is registered to receive, Stowaway checks whether a permission is required to receive the Intent. Occasionally ComDroid is unable to identify the message or sink of an Intent. To mitigate these cases, Stowaway searches for protected Intents in the list of all string literals in the application.

6. APPLICATION ANALYSIS RESULTS

We applied Stowaway to 940 Android applications to identify the prevalence of overprivilege. Applications with unnecessary permissions violate the principle of least privilege. Overprivilege undermines the benefits of a per-application permission system: extra permissions unnecessarily condition users to casually accept dangerous permissions and needlessly exacerbate application vulnerabilities.

Stowaway calculates the maximum set of Android permissions that an application may need. We compare that set to the permissions actually requested by the application. If the application requests more permissions, then it is overprivileged. Our full set of applications consists of 964 Android 2.2 applications.[3] We set aside 24 randomly selected applications for tool testing and training, leaving 940 for analysis.

6.1 Manual Analysis

6.1.1 Methodology

We randomly selected 40 applications from the set of 940 and ran Stowaway on them. Stowaway identified 18 applications as overprivileged. We then manually analyzed each overprivilege warning to attribute it to either tool error (i.e., a false positive) or developer error. We looked for false positives due to three types of failures:

1. Stowaway misses an API, Content Provider, or Intent operation that needs a permission. For example, Stowaway misses an API call when it cannot resolve the target of a reflective call.
2. Stowaway correctly identifies the API, Content Provider, or Intent operation, but our permission map lacks an entry for that platform resource.
3. The application sends an Intent to some other application, and the recipient accepts Intents only from senders with a certain permission. Stowaway cannot detect this case because we cannot determine the permission requirements of other non-system applications.

We reviewed the 18 applications' bytecode, searching for any of these three types of error. If we found functionality that could plausibly pertain to a permission that Stowaway identified as unnecessary, we manually wrote additional test cases to confirm the accuracy of our permission map. We investigated the third type of error by checking whether the application sends Intents to pre-installed or well-known applications. When we determined that a warning was not a false positive, we attempted to identify why the developer had added the unnecessary permission.

We also analyzed overprivilege warnings by running the application in our modified version of Android (which records permission checks as they occur) and interacting with it. It was not possible to test all applications at runtime; for example, some applications rely on server-side resources that have moved or changed since we downloaded them. We were able to test 10 of the 18 application in this way. In each case, runtime testing confirmed the results of our code review.

6.1.2 False Positives

Stowaway identified 18 of the 40 applications (45%) as having 42 unnecessary permissions. Our manual review determined that 17 applications (42.5%) are overprivileged, with a total of 39 unnecessary permissions. This represents a **7%** false positive rate.

All three of the false warnings were caused by incompleteness in our permission map. Each was a special case that we failed to anticipate. Two of the three false positives were caused by applications using `Runtime.exec` to execute a permission-protected shell command. (For example, the `logcat` command performs a `READ_LOGS` permission check.) The third false positive was caused by an application that embeds a web site that uses HTML5 geolocation, which requires a location permission. We wrote test cases for these scenarios and updated our permission map.

Of the 40 applications in this set, 4 contain at least one reflective call that our static analysis tool cannot resolve or dismiss. 2 of them are overprivileged. This means that 50% of the applications with at least one unresolved reflective call are overprivileged, whereas other applications are overprivileged at a rate of 42%. However, a sample size of 4 is too small to draw conclusions. We investigated the unresolved reflective calls and do not believe they led to false positives.

6.2 Automated Analysis

We ran Stowaway on 900 Android applications. Overall, Stowaway identified 323 applications (35.8%) as having unnecessary permissions. Stowaway was unable to resolve some applications' reflective calls, which might lead to a higher false positive rate in those applications. Consequently, we discuss applications with unresolved reflective calls separately from other applications.

6.2.1 Applications With Fully Handled Reflection

Stowaway was able to handle all reflective calls for 795 of the 900 applications, meaning that it should have identified all API access for those applications. Stowaway produces overprivilege warnings for 32.7% of the 795 applications. Table 2 shows the 10 most common unnecessary permissions among these applications.

56% of overprivileged applications have 1 extra permission, and 94% have 4 or fewer extra permissions. Although one-third of applications are overprivileged, the low degree of per-application overprivilege indicates that developers are attempting to add correct permissions rather than arbitrarily requesting large numbers of unneeded permissions. This supports the potential effectiveness of install-time permission systems like Android's.

We believe that Stowaway should produce approximately the same false positive rate for these applications as it did for the set of 40 that we evaluated in §6.1. If we assume that the 7% false positive rate from our manual analysis applies to these results, then 30.4% of the 795 applications

[3] In October 2010, we downloaded the 100 most popular paid applications, the 764 most popular free applications, and 100 recently added free applications from the Android Market.

Permission	Usage
ACCESS_NETWORK_STATE	16%
READ_PHONE_STATE	13%
ACCESS_WIFI_STATE	8%
WRITE_EXTERNAL_STORAGE	7%
CALL_PHONE	6%
ACCESS_COARSE_LOCATION	6%
CAMERA	6%
WRITE_SETTINGS	5%
ACCESS_MOCK_LOCATION	5%
GET_TASKS	5%

Table 2: The 10 most common unnecessary permissions and the percentage of overprivileged applications that request them.

	Apps with Warnings	Total Apps	Rate
Reflection, failures	56	105	53%
Reflection, no failures	151	440	34%
No reflection	109	355	31%

Table 3: The rates at which Stowaway issues overprivilege warnings, by reflection status.

are truly overprivileged. Applications could also be *more* overprivileged in practice than indicated by our tool, due to unreachable code. Stowaway does not perform dead code elimination; dead code elimination for Android applications would need to take into account the unique Android lifecycle and application entry points. Additionally, our overapproximation of Content Provider operations (§5.2) might overlook some overprivilege. We did not quantify Stowaway's false negative rate, and we leave dead code elimination and improved Content Provider string tracking to future work.

6.2.2 The Challenges of Java Reflection

Reflection is commonly used in Android applications. Of the 900 applications, 545 (61%) use Java reflection to make API calls. We found that reflection is used for many purposes, such as to deserialize JSON and XML, invoke hidden or private API calls, and handle API classes whose names changed between versions. The prevalence of reflection indicates that it is important for an Android static analysis tool to handle Java reflection, even if the static analysis tool is not intended for obfuscated or malicious code.

Stowaway was able to fully resolve the targets of reflective calls in 59% of the applications that use reflection. We handled a further 117 applications with two techniques: eliminating failures where the target class of the reflective call was known to be defined within the application, and manually examining and handling failures in 21 highly popular libraries. This left us with 105 applications with reflective calls that Stowaway could not resolve or dismiss, which is 12% of the 900 applications.

Stowaway identifies 53.3% of the 105 applications as overprivileged. Table 3 compares this to the rate at which warnings are issued for applications without unhandled reflections. There are two possible explanations for the difference: Stowaway might have a higher false positive rate in applications with unresolved reflective calls, or applications that use Java reflection in complicated ways might have a higher rate of actual overprivilege due to a correlated trait.

We suspect that both factors play a role in the higher overprivilege warning rate in applications with unhandled reflective calls. Although our manual review (§6.1) did not find that reflective failures led to false positives, a subsequent review of additional applications identified several erroneous warnings that were caused by reflection. On the other hand, developer error may increase with the complexity associated with complicated reflective calls.

Improving the resolution of reflective calls in Android applications is an important open problem. Stowaway's reflection analysis fails when presented with the creation of method names based on non-static environment variables, direct generation of Dalvik bytecode, arrays with two pointers that reference the same location, or `Method` and `Class` objects that are stored in hash tables. Stowaway's primarily linear traversal of a method also experiences problems with non-linear control flow, such as `jumps`; we only handle simple `gotos` that appear at the ends of methods. We also observed several applications that iterate over a set of classes or methods, testing each element to decide which one to invoke reflectively. If multiple comparison values are tested and none are used within the block, Stowaway only tracks the last comparison value beyond the block; this value may be `null`. Future work may be able to solve some of these problems, possibly with the use of dynamic analysis.

6.3 Common Developer Errors

In some cases, we are able to determine why developers asked for unnecessary permissions. Here, we consider the prevalence of different types of developer error among the 40 applications from our manual review and the 795 fully handled applications from our automated analysis.

Permission Name. Developers sometimes request permissions with names that sound related to their applications' functionality, even if the permissions are not required. For example, one application from our manual review unnecessarily requests the MOUNT_UNMOUNT_FILESYSTEMS permission to receive the android.intent.action.MEDIA_MOUNTED Intent. As another example, the ACCESS_NETWORK_STATE and ACCESS_WIFI_STATE permissions have similar-sounding names, but they are required by different classes. Developers often request them in pairs, even if only one is necessary. Of the applications that unnecessarily request the network permission, 32% legitimately require the WiFi permission. Of the applications that unnecessarily request the WiFi permission, 71% legitimately need the network permission.

Deputies. An application can send an Intent to another *deputy* application, asking the deputy to perform an operation. If the deputy makes a permission-protected API call, then the deputy needs a permission. The sender of the Intent, however, does not. We noticed instances of applications requesting permissions for actions that they asked deputies to do. For example, one application asks the Android Market to install another application. The sender asks for INSTALL_PACKAGES, which it does not need because the Market application does the installation.

We find widespread evidence of this type of error. Of the applications that unnecessarily request the CAMERA permission, 81% send an Intent that opens the default Camera application to take a picture. 82% of the applications that unnecessarily request INTERNET send an Intent that opens a URL in the browser. Similarly, 44% of the applications that unnecessarily request CALL_PHONE send an Intent to the default Phone Dialer application.

Related Methods. As shown in Figure 2, most classes contain a mix of permission-protected and unprotected methods. We have observed applications that use unprotected methods but request permissions that are required for other methods in the same class. For example, `android.provider.Settings.Secure` is a convenience class in the API for accessing the Settings Content Provider. The class includes both setters and getters. The setters require the `WRITE_SETTINGS` permission, but the getters do not. Two of the applications that we manually reviewed use only the getters but request the `WRITE_SETTINGS` permission.

Copy and Paste. Popular message boards contain Android code snippets and advice about permission requirements. Sometimes this information is inaccurate, and developers who copy it will overprivilege their applications. For example, one of the applications that we manually reviewed registers to receive the `android.net.wifi.STATE_CHANGE` Intent and requests the `ACCESS_WIFI_STATE` permission. As of May 2011, the third-highest Google search result for that Intent contains the incorrect assertion that it requires that permission [25].

Deprecated Permissions. Permissions that are unnecessary in Android 2.2 could be necessary in older Android releases. Old or backwards-compatible applications therefore might have seemingly extra permissions. However, developers may also accidentally use these permissions because they have read out-of-date material. 8% of the overprivileged applications request either `ACCESS_GPS` or `ACCESS_LOCATION`, which were deprecated in 2008. Of those, all but one specify that their lowest supported API version is *higher* than the last version that included those permissions.

Testing Artifacts. A developer might add a permission during testing and then forget to remove it when the test code is removed. For example, `ACCESS_MOCK_LOCATION` is typically used only for testing but can be found in released applications. All of the applications in our data set that unnecessarily include the `ACCESS_MOCK_LOCATION` permission also include a real location permission.

Signature/System Permissions. We find that 9% of overprivileged applications request unneeded Signature or SignatureOrSystem permissions. Standard versions of Android will silently refuse to grant those permissions to applications that are not signed by the device manufacturer. The permissions were either requested in error, or the developers removed the related code after discovering it did not work on standard handsets.

We can attribute many instances of overprivilege to developer confusion over the permission system. Confusion over permission names, related methods, deputies, and deprecated permissions could be addressed with improved API documentation. To avoid overprivilege due to related methods, we recommend listing permission requirements on a per-method (rather than per-class) basis. Confusion over deputies could be reduced by clarifying the relationship between permissions and pre-installed system applications.

Despite the number of unnecessary permissions that we can attribute to error, it is possible that some developers request extra permissions intentionally. Developers are incentivized to ask for unnecessary permissions because applications will not receive automatic updates if the updated version of the application requests more permissions [15].

7. RELATED WORK

Android Permissions. Previous studies of Android applications have been limited in their understanding of permission usage. Our permission map can be used to greatly increase the scope of application analysis. Enck et al. apply Fortify's Java static analysis tool to decompiled applications; they study their API use [11]. However, they are limited to studying applications' use of a small number of permissions and API calls. In a recent study, Felt et al. manually classify a small set of Android applications as overprivileged or not, but they were limited by the Android documentation [15]. Kirin [12] reads application permission requirements during installation and checks them against a set of security rules. They rely solely on developer permission requests, rather than examining whether or how permissions are used by applications. Barrera et al. examine 1,100 Android applications' permission requirements and use self-organizing maps to visualize which permissions are used in applications with similar characteristics [5]. Their work also relies on the permissions requested by the applications.

Vidas et al. [27] provide a tool that performs an overprivilege analysis on application source code. Their tool could be improved by using our permission map; theirs is based on the limited Android documentation. Our static analysis tool also performs a more sophisticated application analysis. Unlike their Eclipse plugin, Stowaway attempts to handle reflective calls, Content Providers, and Intents.

In concurrent work, Gibler et al. [16] applied static analysis to the Android API to find permission checks. Their permission map includes internal methods within the system process that are not reachable across the RPC boundary, which we excluded because applications cannot access them. Unlike our dynamic approach, their static analysis might have false positives, will miss permission checks in native code, and will miss Android-specific control flow.

Java Testing. Randoop is not the only Java unit test generation tool. Tools like Eclat [21], Palulu [4] and JCrasher [9] work similarly but require an example execution as input. Given the size of the Android API, building such an example execution would be a challenge. Enhanced JUnit [14] generates tests by chaining constructors to some fixed depth. However, it does not use subtyping to provide instances and relies on bytecode as input. Korat [7] requires formal specifications of methods as input, which is infeasible for post-facto testing of the Android API.

Java Reflection. Handling Java reflection is necessary to develop sound and complete program analyses. However, resolving reflective calls is an area of open research. Livshits et al. created a static algorithm which approximates reflective targets by tracking string constants passed to reflections [18]. Their approach falls short when the reflective call depends on user input or environment variables. We use the same approach and suffer from the same limitations. They improve their results with developer annotations, which is not a feasible approach for our domain. A more advanced technique combines static analysis with information about the environment of the Java program in order to resolve reflections [24]. However, their results are sound only if the program is executed in an identical environment as the original evaluation. Even with their modifications, they are able to resolve only 74% of reflective calls in the Java 1.4 API. We do not claim to improve the state of the art in resolving Java reflection; instead, we focus on domain-specific heuristics for how reflection is used in Android applications. We are the first to discuss reflection in Android applications.

8. CONCLUSION

In this paper, we developed tools to detect overprivilege in Android applications. We applied automated testing techniques to Android 2.2 to determine the permissions required to invoke each API method. Our tool, Stowaway, generates the maximum set of permissions needed for an application and compares them to the set of permissions actually requested. Currently, Stowaway is unable to handle some complex reflective calls, and we identify Java reflection as an important open problem for Android static analysis tools.

We applied Stowaway to 940 Android applications and found that about one-third of them are overprivileged. Our results show that applications generally are overprivileged by only a few permissions, and many extra permissions can be attributed to developer confusion. This indicates that developers attempt to obtain least privilege for their applications but fall short due to API documentation errors and lack of developer understanding.

Acknowledgements

We thank Royce Cheng-Yue and Kathryn Lingel for their help testing the API and Content Providers. This work is partially supported by NSF grants CCF-0424422, 0311808, 0832943, 0448452, 0842694, a gift from Google, and the MURI program under AFOSR grant FA9550-08-1-0352. This material is also based upon work supported under a NSF Graduate Research Fellowship. Any opinions, findings, conclusions, or recommendations expressed here are those of the authors and do not necessarily reflect the views of the NSF.

9. REFERENCES

[1] Amazon Appstore for Android. `http://www.amazon.com/mobile-apps/b?ie=UTF8&node=2350149011`.

[2] Android Developers Reference. `http://developer.android.com/reference/`.

[3] Android Market. `http://www.android.com/market/`.

[4] Artzi, S., Ernst, M., Kiezun, A., Pacheco, C., and Perkins, J. Finding the needles in the haystack: Generating legal test inputs for object-oriented programs. In *Workshop on Model-Based Testing and Object-Oriented Systems* (2006).

[5] Barrera, D., Kayacik, H., van Oorschot, P., and Somayaji, A. A methodology for empirical analysis of permission-based security models and its application to android. In *Proc. of the ACM conference on Computer and Communications Security* (2010).

[6] Bodden, E., Sewe, A., Sinschek, J., and Mezini, M. Taming reflection: Static analysis in the presence of reflection and custom class loaders. Tech. Rep. TUD-CS-2010-0066, CASED, Mar. 2010.

[7] Boyapati, C., Khurshid, S., and Marinov, D. Korat: Automated testing based on Java predicates. In *Proc. of the 2002 ACM SIGSOFT International Symposium on Software Testing and Analysis* (2002).

[8] Chin, E., Felt, A. P., Greenwood, K., and Wagner, D. Analyzing Inter-Application Communication in Android. In *Proc. of the Annual International Conference on Mobile Systems, Applications, and Services* (2011).

[9] Csallner, C., and Smaragdakis, Y. JCrasher: an automatic robustness tester for Java. *Software: Practice and Experience 34*, 11 (2004).

[10] Distimo. The battle for the most content and the emerging tablet market. `http://www.distimo.com/blog/2011_04_the-battle-for-the-most-content-and-the-emerging-tablet-market`.

[11] Enck, W., Octeau, D., McDaniel, P., and Chaudhuri, S. A Study of Android Application Security. In *USENIX Security* (2011).

[12] Enck, W., Ongtang, M., and McDaniel, P. On lightweight mobile phone application certification. In *Proc. of the ACM conference on Computer and Communications Security* (2009).

[13] Enck, W., Ongtang, M., and McDaniel, P. Understanding Android security. *IEEE Security and Privacy 7*, 1 (2009).

[14] Enhanced JUnit. `http://www.silvermark.com/Product/java/enhancedjunit/index.html`.

[15] Felt, A. P., Greenwood, K., and Wagner, D. The Effectiveness of Application Permissions. In *Proc. of the USENIX Conference on Web Application Development* (2011).

[16] Gibler, C., Crussell, J., Erickson, J., and Chen, H. AndroidLeaks: Detecting Privacy Leaks in Android Applications. Tech. rep., UC Davis, 2011.

[17] Hackborn, D. Re: List of private / hidden / system APIs? `http://groups.google.com/group/android-developers/msg/a9248b18cba59f5a`.

[18] Livshits, B., Whaley, J., and Lam, M. S. Reflection Analysis for Java. In *Asian Symposium on Programming Languages and Systems* (2005).

[19] McCluskey, G. Using Java Reflection. `http://java.sun.com/developer/technicalArticles/ALT/Reflection/`, 1998.

[20] Pacheco, C., and Ernst, M. Randoop. `http://code.google.com/p/randoop/`.

[21] Pacheco, C., and Ernst, M. Eclat: Automatic generation and classification of test inputs. *European Conference on Object-Oriented Programming* (2005).

[22] Pacheco, C., Lahiri, S., Ernst, M., and Ball, T. Feedback-directed random test generation. In *Proc. of the International Conference on Software Engineering* (2007).

[23] Paller, G. Dedexer. `http://dedexer.sourceforge.net`.

[24] Sawin, J., and Rountev, A. Improving static resolution of dynamic class loading in java using dynamically gathered environment information. *Automated Software Eng. 16* (June 2009), 357–381.

[25] Stack Overflow. Broadcast Intent when network state has changend. `http://stackoverflow.com/questions/2676044/broadcast-intent-when-network-state-has-changend`.

[26] Vennon, T., and Stroop, D. Threat Analysis of the Android Market. Tech. rep., SMobile Systems, 2010.

[27] Vidas, T., Christin, N., and Cranor, L. Curbing Android Permission Creep. In *W2SP* (2011).

"These Aren't the Droids You're Looking For": Retrofitting Android to Protect Data from Imperious Applications

Peter Hornyack* pjh@cs.washington.edu
Seungyeop Han* syhan@cs.washington.edu
Jaeyeon Jung† jjung@microsoft.com
Stuart Schechter† stuart.schechter@microsoft.com
David Wetherall* djw@cs.washington.edu

University of Washington* Microsoft Research†

ABSTRACT

We examine two privacy controls for Android smartphones that empower users to run permission-hungry applications while protecting private data from being exfiltrated:

(1) covertly substituting shadow data in place of data that the user wants to keep private, and
(2) blocking network transmissions that contain data the user made available to the application for on-device use only.

We retrofit the Android operating system to implement these two controls for use with unmodified applications. A key challenge of imposing shadowing and exfiltration blocking on existing applications is that these controls could cause *side effects* that interfere with user-desired functionality. To measure the impact of side effects, we develop an automated testing methodology that records screenshots of application executions both with and without privacy controls, then automatically highlights the visual differences between the different executions. We evaluate our privacy controls on 50 applications from the Android Market, selected from those that were both popular and permission-hungry. We find that our privacy controls can successfully reduce the effective permissions of the application without causing side effects for 66% of the tested applications. The remaining 34% of applications implemented user-desired functionality that required violating the privacy requirements our controls were designed to enforce; there was an unavoidable choice between privacy and user-desired functionality.

Categories and Subject Descriptors

D.4.6 [**Operating Systems**]: Security and Protection; K.4.1 [**Computers and society**]: Public Policy Issues—*Privacy*

General Terms

Design, Security

1. INTRODUCTION

When a user prepares to install an application on the increasingly-popular Android platform, she will be presented with an ultimatum: either grant the application every permission demanded in its manifest or abandon the installation entirely. Even when a user agrees that an application should have access to sensitive data to provide functionality she desires, once the application has access to these data it may misappropriate them and exfiltrate them off the device. Despite the permission disclosures provided by the Android platform, the power of permission ultimatums and the inevitability that data will be misappropriated for exfiltration have created an application ecosystem in which privacy-invasive applications are commonplace [8]. U.S. federal prosecutors have even taken notice, initiating a criminal investigation into the misappropriation of users' data by mobile applications [3].

We have developed a system, called AppFence, that retrofits the Android operating system to impose privacy controls on existing (unmodified) Android applications. AppFence lets users withhold data from imperious applications that demand information that is unnecessary to perform their advertised functionality and, for data that are required for user-desired functions, block communications by the application that would exfiltrate these data off the device.

When an application demands access to sensitive data a user doesn't want it to have, AppFence substitutes innocuous *shadow data* in its place. For example, an application that demands a user's contacts may receive shadow data that contains no contact entries, contains only those genuine entries not considered sensitive by the user, or that contains shadow entries that are entirely fictional. Similarly, an application that demands the unique device ID (IMEI number), which is frequently used to profile users across applications, may instead receive the hash of the device ID salted with a device secret and the application name. This shadow data provides the illusion of a consistent device ID within the application, but is different from the ID given to other applications on the same device. Presenting a different device ID to each application thwarts the use of this ID for cross-application profiling. In other words, when an application demands the device ID for the purpose of linking the user to a cross-application profile, shadowing the device ID empowers users to reply that their device is "not the droid you're looking for."

Shadowing prevents the ingress of sensitive data into applications, breaking applications that truly require the correct data to provide functionality the user wants. For example, a user cannot examine or search her contacts if the application only has access to an empty shadow contact list. For data that *is* allowed to enter the application, we introduce a complementary data-egress control to prevent information from being misappropriated and sent off the device: *exfiltration blocking*. We extend the TaintDroid information-flow tracking system [8] to track data derived from information the user considers private, then block unwanted transmissions of these data. For each sensitive data type in the system, AppFence can be configured to block messages containing data of that particular type.

In this paper, we first measure how 110 popular permission-hungry applications use the private information that they have access to. We expose the prevalence of third-party analytics libraries packaged within the studied applications and reveal that these applications send sensitive data over encrypted channels (Section 2). This investigation of existing applications' behavior guided us to design two privacy controls, shadowing and exfiltration blocking, that protect against undesired uses of the user's sensitive data by applications (Section 3). We then study the potential side effects of these two privacy controls on the user experience of 50 applications. We develop a novel testing methodology for efficiently and reliably repeating experiments to investigate the user-discernable side effects that result when privacy controls are imposed on applications. The testing process records applications' screenshots and highlights the differences between executions so that they can be easily analyzed visually (Section 4). The evaluation that we performed using this methodology shows that, by combining shadowing and exfiltration blocking, it is possible to eliminate all side effects in the applications we studied except for those that represent a direct conflict between user-desired functionality and the privacy goal that our controls enforce—that private data must not leave the device (Section 5). We discuss future and related work in Sections 6 and 7, and we conclude in Section 8.

We make the following three contributions. First, we provide an extensive analysis of information exposure by Android applications in terms of types of information investigated, forms of exposure including encryption, and exposure patterns to advertising and analytics servers. Second, we present two privacy controls for reducing sensitive data exposure and show experimentally that the controls are promising: the privacy controls reduced the effective permissions of 66% of the 50 applications in our testbed without side effects. Last, we develop a novel testing methodology to detect side effects by combining automated GUI testing with visual highlighting of differences between application screenshots. This methodology allows us to characterize the side effects of the tested applications, revealing some common functionalities of Android applications that require the exposure of the user's sensitive data and are thus unavoidably in conflict with the goal of privacy controls.

2. PRIVACY RISKS ON ANDROID

To inform the design of our privacy controls, we performed several initial measurements and analyses of today's Android applications. As an application cannot misappropriate data it does not have access to, we first measured the prevalence with which applications request access to each type of potentially sensitive data. We then determined the prevalence with which applications exfiltrate data of each type and where they send the data to.

2.1 Application selection

We used three sets of applications for our initial measurements (described in this section) and in-depth experiments (described in Section 5). We began with a set of **1100** popular free Android applications, which we obtained by sampling the 50 most popular applications from each of 22 categories listed by the Android Market in November 2010. We examined this set of applications to identify a set of 11 permissions that applications must request to access sensitive data (Section 2.2). We also analyzed this set of applications to identify third-party packages that applications include for advertising and analytics (A&A) purposes (Section 2.4).

From the set of 1100 applications, we then selected a subsample of **110** applications for deeper analysis. For each type of permission used to access sensitive data, we included in the subsample at least 10 applications that used the permission, drawing first from those applications that contained a third-party A&A package and, if more applications were needed, next drawing from the set of applications without A&A packages but that still required Internet access.[1] We did not exclude any awkward or challenging applications when sampling the 110 applications. This subsample is intentionally biased in favor of *permission-hungry* applications: those that require the most permissions. This bias toward permission-hungry applications only increases the likelihood that our experiments in Section 5 will cause side effects when imposing privacy controls. In other words, this sampling overestimates side effects, leading to a conservative (high) estimate of the actual rate of side effects for the privacy controls in our experiments.

For our in-depth experiments in Section 5, which required scripting user inputs for each application to automate testing, we further subsampled the 110 applications; the labor-intensive nature of writing the test scripts limited us to automating 50 of the 110 applications. To select the **50** applications, we first excluded applications that did not transmit any type of sensitive data during our preliminary analyses; again, this increased the likelihood of identifying side effects in our experiments. We also excluded five applications that could not be tested using a single device with automated user behavior (for example, the `Bump` application requires two devices for its primary functionality). From the remaining pool of applications, we randomly selected 50 of them to be scripted; Appendix B lists the resulting set of applications.

2.2 Sources of sensitive information

By examining the applications in our 1100-application sample, we identified 11 permissions that could result in the disclosure of 12 types of sensitive information: `location`, `phone_state` (granting access to phone number & unique device ID information types as well as call state), `contacts`, user `account` information, `camera`, `microphone`, browser `history & bookmarks`, `logs`, `SMS messages`, `calendar`, and `subscribed_feeds`. We measured the prevalence with which applications demanded each permission by pars-

[1]Fewer than 10 applications requested access to the subscribed_feeds and calendar permissions.

Resource type	Applications
phone_state	374 (34.0%)
location	368 (33.5%)
contacts	105 (9.5%)
camera	84 (7.6%)
account	43 (3.9%)
logs	38 (3.5%)
microphone	32 (2.9%)
SMS messages	24 (2.2%)
history & bookmarks	19 (1.7%)
calendar	9 (0.8%)
subscribed_feeds	2 (0.2%)

Table 1: Of the 1100 popular Android applications we examined, those that required both access to a resource containing sensitive data and access to the Internet (through which data might be exfiltrated)

ing the applications' manifests using the publicly available Android `aapt` tool [13]. We find that 605 applications (55%) require access to at least one of these resources and access to the Internet, resulting in the potential for unwanted disclosure. We present these results broken down by resource type in Table 1.

2.3 Misappropriation

Prior work has revealed that some Android applications do exploit user data for purposes that may not be expected nor desired by users. Enck *et al.*, who developed the TaintDroid information-flow tracking system extended in our work, used this system to analyze 30 Android applications that required access to the Internet and either users' location, camera, or microphone [8]. They found that half of these applications shared users' locations with advertisement servers. The problem is not unique to Android. Egele *et al.* used static analysis to track information flow in popular iPhone applications and discovered that many contained code to send out the unique device ID [7]. Smith captured network traffic to observe iPhone applications transmitting device IDs [18]. The Wall Street Journal commissioned its own study of 50 iPhone applications and 50 Android applications, also using a network-observation approach [22, 23]. The article suspects that these unique IDs are so commonly transmitted because they can be used to profile users' behaviors across applications.

2.4 A profile of the profilers

Given the existing concerns over cross-application profiling of user behavior, we examined our sample of 1100 applications to identify third-party advertising and analytics (A&A) libraries that might build such profiles. We used the Android `apktool` [1] to disassemble and inspect application modules to identify the most commonly used libraries. We found eight A&A packages, listed in Table 2. AdMob was the most popular A&A package, employed by a third of our sample applications, followed by Google Ads. Google acquired AdMob in 2010; the combined application market share of AdMob and existing Google Ads and Analytics packages was 535 of our 1100 applications (49%). We also found that 591 applications (54%) have one or more A&A packages included in their code. Moreover, 361 of these applications (33%) demand access to the Internet and at least one of the resource types identified in Table 1, enabling the potential for disclosure of sensitive information to these third party servers.

	Applications	
	all	sensitive
A&A Module	1100	605
admob.android.ads	360 (33%)	225 (37%)
google.ads	242 (22%)	140 (23%)
flurry.android	110 (10%)	88 (15%)
google.android.apps.analytics	91 (8%)	66 (11%)
adwhirl	79 (7%)	67 (11%)
mobclix.android.sdk	58 (5%)	46 (8%)
millennialmedia.android	48 (4%)	47 (8%)
qwapi.adclient.android	39 (3%)	37 (6%)

Table 2: The prevalence of third-party advertising and analytics modules in our sample of 1100 Android applications, and a subset of 605 applications that demand access to at least one resource containing potentially sensitive information.

A&A destination	Any	IMEI	Loc
*.admob.com	57	0	11
*.doubleclick.net	36	0	0
data.flurry.com	27	2	15
*.googlesyndication.com	24	0	0
*.mydas.mobi	23	0	0
*.adwhirl.com	21	0	0
*.mobclix.com	17	10	6
*.google-analytics.com	17	0	0
tapad.jumptap.com	6	0	0
droidvertising.appspot.com	5	0	0
*.mojiva.com	4	0	0
ad.qwapi.com	2	0	0
*.greystripe.com	2	2	0
*.inmobi.com	1	0	1

Table 3: The number of applications (from our 110 application sample) that sent any communication to the A&A server, number that sent the unique device ID (IMEI), and number that sent the user's location.

2.5 Where sensitive information goes

Not all applications that request permission to access sensitive information will exfiltrate it. We ran an experiment to identify the prevalence with which applications transmit each type of sensitive information off the user's device and where they send it to. Performing this preliminary study required us to enhance TaintDroid, as it had previously only tracked five of the 12 data types examined in our study, and it did not track traffic sent through SSL. With our modifications, TaintDroid is able to detect sensitive data even when it has been obfuscated, encrypted using AES, or transmitted via SSL, although it is still limited in that it cannot track information leaked through control flow operations; we discuss this issue of leaks via implicit flows in Section 3.3. We also added instrumentation to record the identity of communicating parties and the traffic going to, and coming from, these parties.

To perform this analysis, we manually executed each of the applications in our 110-application subsample for about

Resource		Demanded	Sent to Anywhere		A&A	
phone_state	IMEI	83	31	37%	14	17%
	Phone#	83	5	6%	0	0%
location		73	45	62%	30	41%
contacts		29	7	24%	0	0%
camera		12	1	8%	0	0%
account		11	4	36%	0	0%
logs		10	0	0%	0	0%
microphone		10	1	10%	0	0%
SMS/MMS messages		10	0	0%	0	0%
history&bookmarks		10	0	0%	0	0%
calendar		8	0	0%	0	0%
subscribed_feeds		1	0	0%	0	0%

Table 4: The prevalence of permissions demanded by applications in the sample used for our initial information flow experiments. Note that the sum of the application counts is greater than 110 as many applications require access to multiple data types. For each data type, we tracked applications that demanded access to that data type and measured the fraction that transmitted messages tainted by that data type.

five minutes, exercising the application's main features and any features we thought might require the use or exfiltration of sensitive data (the same methodology is used in [22, 23]). We augmented the list of A&A domain names previously obtained through static analysis by observing traffic from these 110 applications and manually inspecting the sites they contacted to verify which third-parties were A&A servers. The resulting list of domain names of A&A servers can be found in Table 3.

For each sensitive resource, Table 4 shows the number of applications in our 110-application subsample that demanded access to it, and the fraction that we observed transmitting messages tainted by data from this resource out to the Internet. The only data types we see transmitted are device ID (IMEI), phone number, location, contacts, camera, account, and microphone. Some applications may send more information than we observed as we could not guarantee that all code paths were executed. In addition, the 110-application subsample contains a disproportionate number of permission-hungry applications as described in Section 2.1 and therefore this bias should be reflected when weighing the results reported in this section against the general population of Android applications. Table 3 shows the breakdown of A&A destinations that collected tainted data from applications. We observed that location was sent to `AdMob`, `Flurry`, `Mobclix`, and `Inmobi`, and device ID was sent to `Flurry`, `Mobclix`, and `Greystripe`.

Phone number. Five applications transmitted phone numbers. Two applications required users to register a phone number, so they filled in the device's phone number by default when the user completed the registration form (but the user could then modify the phone number if desired). The third application used the phone number to create a custom unique device identifier, so the phone number was not disclosed directly in the payload. However, two applications–Dilbert comic viewer and Mabilo ringtones downloader–sent the device's phone number with no discernable legitimate purpose!

Contacts. Seven applications transmitted contacts. Two did so to perform contact-specific searches, and three sent contacts as requested by the user. One, a reverse phone number lookup application (`Mr. Number`), sent contact entries to its own servers; it asks the user to opt in, but only after it has already sent the data to its servers. An instant messaging application (`KakaoTalk`) sent the phone numbers collected from the user's entire address book to its servers to automatically add other users of the application. The transmission took place without any notice and this feature is turned on by default. Additionally, six of the seven applications sent the device ID along with the contacts, making it easy for applications to link contacts with other information that is commonly collected as described below.

Device ID. 31 applications transmitted the device ID (IMEI). As reported by previous studies, the use of the device ID by applications is prevalent. 11 applications employed SSL secure connections when they transmitted the device ID to application servers. We find that these encrypted transmissions of the device ID sometimes accompany other sensitive data such as contacts and phone number. We find seven game applications that send the device ID over SSL along with a score to store high scores using a third-party company.

Location. 45 applications transmitted location data. Third-party servers are the most common destinations for location data; 30 applications shared location data with A&A servers. All but two of these 30 shared location data with A&A servers exclusively. Half (15) employ the `Flurry` analytics package, which uses a binary (non-human readable) data format when sending out location data to the Flurry server. Prior investigations that observed network traffic alone would not have detected the transmission of this information.

Camera & Microphone data. We observed that one application sent a photo and another application sent a voice memo. Both cases are triggered by explicit user requests.

Account. The account resource is used to store profile and authentication information for online accounts that the user has access to. Four applications transmitted data tainted by the `account` resource; all uses appear legitimate. One security application used account data to send email to the user's Gmail account. One multimedia application used account data to allow the user to register her Facebook account for creating personal profiles. One music sharing application used account data to authenticate the user with its server. One application used account data to access the Android Market for providing enhanced services.

2.6 Informing privacy controls

Our preliminary analysis can guide the selection of privacy control mechanisms for protecting sensitive data. One simple approach would be to block *all* access to the Internet by the application. While this obviously would impede user-desired functionality in some cases, we wondered if it might be sufficient in others. Having intercepted and observed all Internet communications to and from these applications, we show the fraction of each application's Internet traffic that is used for advertising and analytics (A&A) in Figure 1. Of the 97 applications in our 110 application sample that accessed A&A servers, 23 (24%) communicated exclusively with A&A

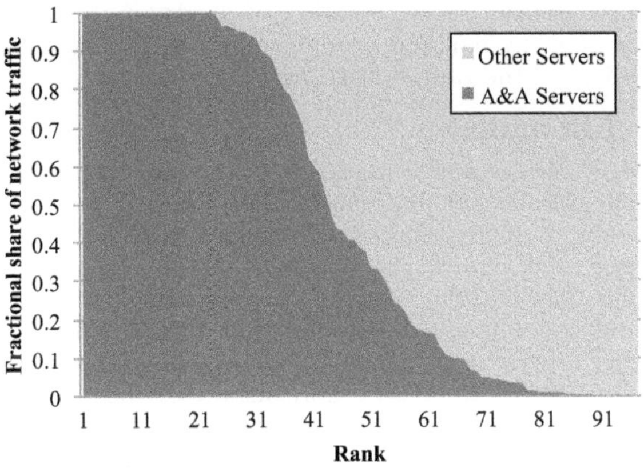

Figure 1: The fraction of network traffic (bytes inbound + bytes outbound) sent to A&A servers.

servers during our observations. While these could presumably provide the same functionality if one simply denied all access to the network, the rest would likely exhibit side effects.

Given the variation in the types of sensitive data, ways of using this data for user-desired features, and ways to misuse this data, it may simply not be possible to apply a single, one-size-fits-all policy that can protect data while minimizing side effects. Thus, we set out to explore a choice of privacy controls that could be customized to balance the needs of applications with the privacy requirements of their users.

3. PRIVACY CONTROLS

AppFence implements data *shadowing*, to prevent applications from accessing sensitive information that is not required to provide user-desired functionality, and *exfiltration blocking*, to block outgoing communications tainted by sensitive data. Either (or even both) of these controls may be applied to limit an application's misuse of a sensitive data type.

3.1 Data shadowing

Since today's applications do not suspect the use of shadowing, we opt for simple shadow data rather than developing more elaborate ruses to fool applications that might attempt to detect shadowing. However, our implementation can be easily extended to support more sophisticated shadow data than what is presented below if it becomes necessary to do so.

Android applications use the file system to access the camera, microphone, and logs. When applications try to open these resources, we provide the illusion of opening an empty file. Similarly, we shadowed browser metadata (history and bookmarks), SMS/MMS messages, subscribed feeds, contacts, accounts, and calendar entries by returning an empty set of data.

When applications request the device's location, we return the coordinates 37.421265, -122.084026.

When applications request the device's phone state, we construct phone state with a fixed phone number (1 650 623 4000) and an application-specific device ID. The shadow device ID (IMEI) is generated by hashing a three-tuple containing the device ID, application name, and a secret salt randomly generated for the device. The salt ensures that an application that is granted access to the device ID cannot be linked to an application that is granted access to the shadow ID. The result of the hash is a string containing 15 decimal digits—the proper format for a GSM IMEI number.

The Android phone state permission also grants access the software version number (IMEI/SV), SIM serial number, voice mail number, and subscriber ID (IMSI). We did not observe any applications use these data, and thus did not test any shadowing strategies for them.

Implementation

The Android architecture sandboxes each running application within a Dalvik virtual machine. Virtual machines are isolated from each other by running each in its own process. The Android operating system includes the Android core libraries, which are contained in each VM, as well as the Android framework, a set of centralized services and managers that reside outside of the VMs. Applications access the core libraries and framework through the Android API.

To impose privacy controls on unmodified applications, AppFence modifies the Android core libraries and Android framework. Figure 2 shows the components of the Android architecture that we modified for shadowing. The modified libraries and framework that guard access to sensitive data reside outside of the application sandbox imposed by the Dalvik virtual machine. We rely on the sandbox to prevent the application from tampering with these components. As native libraries are not sandboxed, AppFence prevents applications from loading their own native libraries (Android's core native libraries are still loaded on demand as applications require them). At the time of testing, the use of native libraries was exceptionally rare; not one application that we examined with AppFence (including all applications in our 110-application sample) required its own native libraries.

For simple resources such as the device ID, phone number, and location, we return shadow values directly from the managers in the Android framework code. More complex resources, such as the user's calendar and contact list, are accessed through Android's `content provider` framework [11]. Applications identify the resource they wish to access via a URI. For example, the calendar may be queried with the string `content://calendar`. For these content provider resources, we replace the cursor that would normally be returned by the content manager with a shadow database cursor. For our experiments we return an empty database cursor, though one could instead create a shadow database and return a cursor to it.

3.2 Exfiltration blocking

To block exfiltration of data, we intercept calls to the network stack to (1) associate domain names with open sockets and (2) detect when tainted data is written to a socket. When an output buffer contains tainted data, we drop the buffer and choose one of two actions: we may drop the offending message *covertly*, misleading the application by indicating that the buffer has been sent, or *overtly*, emulating the OS behavior an application would encounter if the buffer were dropped as a result of the device entering airplane mode (all wireless connections disabled).

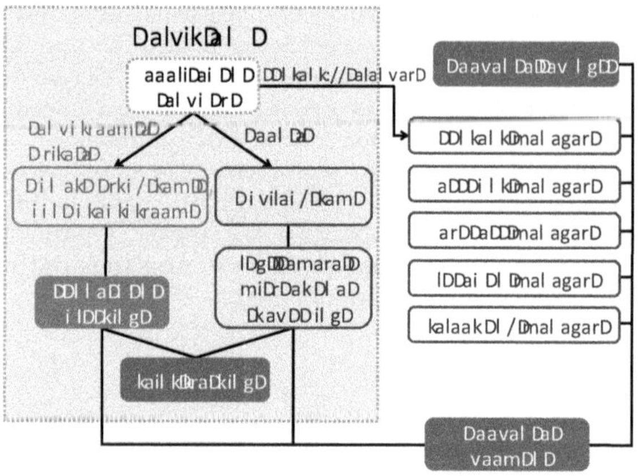

Figure 2: AppFence system architecture. The Dalvik VM sandboxes the application and contains the Android core libraries. Resource managers reside in the Android framework outside of the VMs. Existing resource manager and file system components are modified for shadowing, while exfiltration blocking introduces new components (solid boxes) for connection blocking and taint tracking. The AppFence daemon runs as a native library, and is controlled by the AppFence settings application.

Implementation

To monitor and block network traffic, we modify both the Java code and native code in the Android networking stack. Figure 2 shows key modules that we instrumented or created for exfiltration blocking.

When an application writes to a socket's output stream, the buffer is sent to the `sendStream()` method within the `OSNetworkSystem` core library. We modified `sendStream` so that if the buffer is tainted by data that should not be sent to its intended destination, we drop the buffer. When SSL sockets are used, we capture `write` calls to the `SSLOutputStream` class.

To emulate airplane mode, we first return error code `SOCKERR_TIMEOUT`, then block the next send with error code `SOCKERR_EPIPE`. If the application tries to open a new socket (via a `socket.connect()` call), we finally return a `SocketException` with error code `SOCKERR_ENETUNREACH`. Subsequent attempts to open sockets or send data will be allowed until we next encounter tainted data bound for a forbidden destination.

In order to facilitate user configuration and testing, we separate the policy specification mechanism into a service (daemon) that can be configured automatically or by users. Our privacy controls obtain their policies from this daemon. The privacy controls can be enabled globally or on a per-application basis.

AppFence relies on the open-source TaintDroid platform which, at the time of our testing, did not yet fully support just-in-time (JIT) compilation. We have thus initially implemented AppFence for Android version 2.1, which does not use JIT compilation. Android 2.1 represented 15% of the Android installations accessing the Android Market as of August 2011 [14]. We did not encounter any compatibility issues running applications on Android 2.1.

Our combined implementation of shadowing and exfiltration blocking required introducing or modifying roughly 5,000 lines of the Android platform code.

3.3 Limitations

One of the known limitations of our implementation is that the TaintDroid information flow tracking system, on which we built AppFence's exfiltration blocking feature, does not track information leaked through *control flow* operations. Applications intent on circumventing exfiltration blocking could move data using control flow operations. Tracking control flow may have reasonable overhead, especially if the code to do so is only activated when a tainted variable is loaded into the register space, but could raise the rate of false positives.

Still, actively circumventing AppFence would not be without consequences for software developers. Static analysis could be used to identify sections of code that appear to be designed to transfer data using control flow, exposing applications that actively attempt to subvert users' desired privacy policies. If application developers are found to be actively targeting and circumventing AppFence's exfiltration blocking controls, they may undermine their ability to employ the traditional excuse used to defend developers of privacy-invasive applications—that they operate openly with the implicit consent of a user base that is happy to reveal information.

An application that is aware of AppFence can detect the presence of exfiltration blocking. For example, an application could open two independent sockets, transmit tainted data over only one of those sockets and untainted data over the other socket, and have the server report back what it received. Similarly, shadow data may also not be convincing enough to fool an application. Applications that detect the presence of privacy controls could refuse to provide user-desired functionality until the controls are deactivated.

4. TEST METHODOLOGY

The primary cost of imposing privacy controls on applications is the introduction of side effects that negatively impact the user's experience. To enable the evaluation of our AppFence system, we developed a novel test methodology that allows us to automate the execution of applications and easily measure and characterize side effects introduced by the privacy controls. Our methodology overcomes the two main obstacles to systematic testing of the interaction between AppFence's privacy controls and applications: the ability to reproduce program executions (reproducibility), and the ability to detect side effects (detection). We describe how we use automated GUI testing and screenshot comparisons to tackle these issues in the next subsections.

We focus on *user-visible* side effects as the metric for evaluating AppFence because shadowing and exfiltration blocking have equivalent benefits when applied to the applications in our test bed; given that AppFence-unaware applications do not (at least to our knowledge) deliberately circumvent the information flow tracking used to block exfiltration, both privacy controls are equally effective on today's applications. We do not measure the performance impact of our privacy controls; the underlying information flow tracking provided by TaintDroid is fast enough to run applications in real-time with modest slowdown (worst case increase in CPU utilization of 14%), and beyond this we witnessed no discernable impact as applications with and without our privacy controls enabled ran side by side.

4.1 Automated application runs

Reproducibility is difficult because different runs of the same application may exercise different code paths. Furthermore, variations in user inputs, their timing, system state, and other factors may cause results to change. To minimize these variations, we built a test infrastructure that automates human usage patterns to remove variations in users' choices of actions and their timing. To this end we used the Android GUI testing system provided by the TEMA project [15, 20], which leverages the Android `monkey` event generator. The test system supports a scripting language in which user actions are expressed via high-level commands such as *TapObject*, *PressKey* and *SelectFromMenu*. Commands were sent from our PC running the GUI testing system to our Nexus One devices via a USB cable.

As described in Section 2.1, we selected 50 applications to be scripted for our experiments (these are listed in Appendix B). We scripted each application to perform its main tasks as we expected users to perform them. Our scripts are not guaranteed to cover all possible code paths, and so our results may not detect all uses of sensitive data by an application or all of the side effects of our privacy controls. The average time to execute each test script – excluding installation, uninstallation and cleanup – was 3.5 minutes, with an average of 24 script commands. We created a master test script that configures an Android device, enables the AppFence privacy controls for experimental configurations or disables them for the baseline configuration, and then tests all applications. For each application, the script installs and launches the application, executes the GUI test adapter to provide inputs, uninstalls the application, and then removes any changes to the device state caused by the application; we refer to these steps as an application *execution*.

4.2 Detecting changes in behavior

Detecting whether side effects impact *user*-desired functionality is a determination that eventually requires consultation of a user. However, placing a human in the loop can introduce bias and slow the process down, running counter to our goal of systematic, automated testing. To reduce the scalability constraints and bias caused by human evaluation, we leverage the insight that side effects are likely easy to detect and confirm if the visual outputs of the baseline and experimental executions can be compared side by side. We employed a feature of the GUI testing system to capture a screenshot from the Android device after every command in the test script. We first ran each test script with our baseline configuration—no resources were replaced with shadow resources and no attempts to exfiltrate data were blocked. We then ran each test script with our experimental configurations, in which either data shadowing or exfiltration blocking was activated. For each experimental execution, we automatically generated a web page with side-by-side screenshots from the baseline execution and the experimental execution, along with a visual `diff` of the two images. We found that these outputs could be scanned quickly and reliably, with little ambiguity as to whether a side effect had been captured in the image logs, as shown in Figure 3.

(a) Baseline execution (b) With exfiltration blocking (c) Visual diff between (a) and (b)

Figure 3: Detecting side effects using visual diff: The red shaded region in (c) highlights the advertising banner missing from (b).

We also monitored the tainted data exposure across test runs and found that it is not deterministic: it is possible for applications to transmit tainted data in some test runs but not others. We took steps to mitigate the underlying sources of variation during our testing. For example, we discovered that many applications request the most recent calculated location, without asking for the phone to access the GPS; they may do this to avoid the latency required to obtain updated location data, or to avoid the battery drain of activating the GPS unit. If a null location is returned, or if the last known location is stale (e.g. more than 60 minutes old), applications will often proceed without location data. To avoid inconsistencies during our testing, we modified the Android framework to always return a fixed default location, rather than null, when no last known location is available. To account for remaining variations in our testing, we examined the results of at least two test executions for every experimental configuration, and used additional executions and manual log inspection to resolve inconsistent application behavior.

5. EXPERIMENTS

This section shows the experimental results of testing AppFence's privacy controls on the 50 applications for which we generated test scripts (see Appendix B). We discuss the side effects resulting from the privacy controls and evaluate their impact on the user experience.

5.1 Experimental configurations

We executed applications over eight different experimental configurations. The control configuration, which did not have any privacy controls activated, represents how users run applications on Android today. In the *shadowing* configuration, sensitive data was replaced by shadow data, as described in Section 3.1. The remaining six configurations implemented some form of message blocking, three of which used overt blocking (simulating airplane mode) and three of which used covert blocking (pretending that blocked messages were actually sent). One pair of *exfiltration blocking* configurations (one covert, one overt) blocked messages tainted by sensitive data regardless of the server to which they were destined. Like data shadowing, these configurations are destination-agnostic. A pair of *destination-specific exfiltration blocking* configurations only blocked tainted messages if they were destined to known advertising & analytics

	Shadowing		Exfiltration blocking of *tainted* messages to... *all* destinations Covert	Overt	*only* A&A servers Covert	Overt	Blocking *all* messages to A&A servers Covert	Overt
None	28	(56%)	16 (32%)	16 (32%)	45 (90%)	45 (90%)	19 (38%)	18 (36%)
Ads absent	0	(0%)	11 (22%)	11 (22%)	4 (8%)	4 (8%)	29 (58%)	26 (52%)
Less functional	14	(28%)	10 (20%)	10 (20%)	0 (0%)	0 (0%)	0 (0%)	1 (2%)
Broken	8	(16%)	13 (26%)	13 (26%)	1 (2%)	1 (2%)	2 (4%)	5 (10%)

Table 5: The side effects of imposing privacy controls on all 12 categories of sensitive data for 50 test applications.

(A&A) servers. Finally, to examine the benefits of exfiltration blocking over more naïve approaches, a *destination blacklisting* pair blocked all traffic to known A&A servers, regardless of whether it was tainted by sensitive data or not. The list of known A&A servers can be found in Table 3.

We divided the possible side effects impacting the user experience into four categories based on severity: the privacy controls had no side effect (*none*); advertisements no longer appeared (*ads absent*); the application still performed its primary purpose but failed to perform a less-important secondary function, or was otherwise *less functional*; or the application no longer fulfilled its primary purpose or crashed (*broken*). We then classified each application into one of these categories, based on the most severe side effect we observed in the entire execution of the application under our test script.

The definition of less functional (as opposed to broken) is somewhat subjective, and will vary according to the individual user. When classifying applications, we carefully considered the primary purposes for which a user would run a particular application, and when judgment calls were necessary, we made them in favor of more severe impacts. A detailed explanation of when we considered each application to be less functional is presented in Appendix A. Because we are concerned with evaluating the potential negative impact of our privacy controls on the *user's* experience, we do not consider the absence of advertisements to be a side effect, nor do we study the impact on application developers or their advertising and analytics partners.

5.2 Coarse-grained controls

Our first experiment examines the side effects of imposing privacy controls on all 12 data types simultaneously. We begin with such a coarse-grained analysis because it allows us to identify the best applications for further examination; those that are not impacted by coarse-grained privacy controls will not require more detailed analysis. Our results are summarized in Table 5. Advertising & analytics (A&A) servers don't generally provide user-desired functionality, so it is not surprising that the naïve approach of blocking tainted messages sent to known A&A servers has fewer side effects than approaches that block messages to other servers as well. However, even blocking just tainted messages to known A&A servers can cause disruption to the user experience if applications fail to handle blocking gracefully. For example, after a connection to an A&A server failed, one application assumed that the network was unavailable and abandoned all network access. Blocking all messages sent to A&A servers, rather than just those messages tainted by sensitive data, caused slightly more applications to break. Closer inspection revealed that these applications send untainted communications to A&A servers upon launch, which may cause them to wait indefinitely for a response (covert mode) or receive a socket exception that is interpreted as network unavailability (overt mode). For all exfiltration blocking configurations, we found negligible differences in the occurrence of side effects caused by overt blocking versus covert blocking.

Alas, blocking only A&A servers only defends against behavioral advertising which, despite its popularity, is likely the least pernicious threat to sensitive data. More nefarious applications can circumvent such blacklist approaches, for example by proxying communications to A&A servers through their own (first party) servers. Preventing exfiltration of data through non-A&A servers requires one of our destination-agnostic approaches, i.e. using shadowing or using exfiltration blocking of tainted messages to all destinations. Table 5 shows that overall, shadowing causes fewer and less severe side effects than exfiltration blocking; a more detailed analysis is presented in the following section.

5.3 Fine-grained controls

We ran a second experiment to determine which resources were causing side effects when destination-agnostic privacy controls were applied. This required us to re-run our tests, applying privacy controls individually to each type of sensitive information. However, we only had to do so for those applications that were less functional or were broken when privacy controls had been applied to all types of information. For each resource (row) and privacy control (column) in Table 6, the corresponding entry shows the number of applications that experienced side effects as a result of imposing the privacy control on that resource.

Our results reflect that data types that are rarely directly presented to the user – device ID, location, and phone number – are best protected by shadowing. Shadowing did not break any applications that attempted to send the device ID or phone number to their servers. Six applications did become less functional when the device ID was shadowed—all were games that could still track their high scores, but not build cross-application high-score profiles. In contrast, eight applications that access the device ID broke when overt exfiltration blocking was imposed, and another seven were less functional. Many of these applications send data upon launch, then wait for a response before continuing, and thus break when exfiltration blocking is imposed. Others included the device ID in login information sent over an encrypted (SSL) socket, which we blocked. Because applications use the device ID in a way that is not directly visible to the user, shadowing the device ID can be less disruptive to the user experience than actively blocking the communication.

When controlling access to the user's location, shadowing also had slightly fewer side effects than exfiltration blocking.

	Breaks *or* less functional			Breaks (*only*)		
		Exfiltration blocking			Exfiltration blocking	
	Shadowing	Covert	Overt	Shadowing	Covert	Overt
device ID	6/43 (14%)	16/43 (37%)	15/43 (35%)	0/43 (0%)	9/43 (21%)	8/43 (19%)
location	10/36 (28%)	14/36 (39%)	14/36 (39%)	5/36 (14%)	8/36 (22%)	8/36 (22%)
contacts	4/14 (29%)	2/14 (14%)	2/14 (14%)	2/14 (14%)	1/14 (7%)	1/14 (7%)
history&bookmarks	1/3 (33%)	0/3 (0%)	0/3 (0%)	0/3 (0%)	0/3 (0%)	0/3 (0%)
phone number	0/43 (0%)	3/43 (7%)	3/43 (7%)	0/43 (0%)	3/43 (7%)	3/43 (7%)
SMS	1/2 (50%)	0/2 (0%)	0/2 (0%)	1/2 (50%)	0/2 (0%)	0/2 (0%)
calendar	1/4 (25%)	0/4 (0%)	0/4 (0%)	0/4 (0%)	0/4 (0%)	0/4 (0%)

Table 6: For each type of sensitive information, the fraction of applications that require this information that *either* break or are less functional as a result of imposing a destination-agnostic privacy control (first three data columns), followed by the subset of *only* those applications that break – rather than just become less functional – as a result of these controls (the last three data columns). *Data types not represented by rows in this table did not cause our privacy controls to induce side effects.*

Like the device ID, location coordinates are rarely presented to the user directly; rather, they are usually used to download information about a given location. Thus, exfiltration blocking will prevent any information from being retrieved, whereas shadowing will result in data being retrieved for the shadow location instead of the actual location. For some applications, data for the shadow location was not better than no data at all (as with exfiltration blocking), so these applications (14%) were classified as broken. However, the difference between the number of applications that were broken or less useful with location shadowing (28%) versus those broken or less useful with exfiltration blocking (39%) shows that some applications exfiltrated location data for purposes (such as analytics) that did not cause user-visible side effects when the location was shadowed. For these applications that use location data in a way that is not visible to the user, shadowing is a more appropriate privacy control than exfiltration blocking.

The results demonstrate that exfiltration blocking is best used for data that applications display to the user or allow the user to navigate. For example, whereas data shadowing causes four applications that use contacts to break or become less functional, only one of these applications is impacted by exfiltration blocking. Similar results are seen in Table 6 for bookmarks, SMS messages, and calendar entries.

Shadowing and exfiltration blocking are complementary, and when used together can produce fewer side effects than either can alone. While 28 of the 50 applications in our sample (56%) run side effect-free with just shadowing and merely 16 applications (32%) are side effect-free with exfiltration blocking, 33 (66%) could run side effect-free if the most appropriate privacy control (i.e. as determined by an oracle) could be applied to each application. Section 6.1 describes how we might determine appropriate privacy settings in the future.

The benefits of having two privacy controls to choose from are also apparent from Table 7, which presents another view of the data from our fine-grained analysis. This table characterizes the types of application functionality that were impacted by our privacy controls, and shows which data types led to side effects for shadowing, exfiltration blocking, or both. Many of the rows in this table show that for particular functionalities and data types, one control exhibits the side effect but the other does not, indicating that AppFence can avoid impacting this type of functionality if the appropriate privacy control is used.

Table 7 also offers further insight into the behavior of the tested applications. For example, returning to the previous discussion of applications that use location data in ways that are not visible to users, these applications are precisely those listed in the rows of the table for which exfiltration blocking of the location data type made applications broken or less functional while shadowing had no side effects.

Finally, Table 7 provides insight into the 34% of applications that exhibit side effects that were *unavoidable*: those side effects that occurred regardless of which privacy control was used. These are represented by the five rows in Table 7 in which both the shadowing and exfiltration blocking columns list that some side effect was present. In *every* instance, these side effects were the result of a direct conflict between the goal of imposing a privacy control (keeping information from leaving the device) and the functionality desired by the user. This functionality included sharing contacts with others (FindOthers), broadcasting the user's location to others (GeoBroadcast), performing a query containing the user's location on a remote server (GeoSearch), and building a cross-application profile of the user on a remote server (GameProfile). All of these are features that violate the privacy requirement by design, and represent a nearly-unavoidable[2] choice between the functionality desired and the privacy goal. For this minority of applications, the user cannot have her privacy and functionality too.

6. FUTURE WORK

This section discusses promising avenues to explore in order to further strengthen AppFence. In particular, we discuss how to address the problems of determining which privacy controls to apply to which applications and data types, and preventing applications from circumventing exfiltration blocking.

6.1 Determining privacy settings

While a user's privacy goals can be met by choosing the right privacy controls, the responsibility for making the correct choice must fall somewhere. To allow for more informed choices, we envision that AppFence could report application

[2]Outside of rearchitecting both client *and server* to support private-information retrieval protocols.

Impacted functionality	Sh	EB	Data type	Applications impacted
Launch:	*Application can't launch because required network transaction contains sensitive data*			
	-	⊗	Phone #	`dilbert`, `yearbook`
	-	⊗	Device ID	`dex`, `docstogo`, `kayak`, `moron`, `yearbook`
	-	⊗	Location	`dex`, `docstogo`, `moron`
Login:	*User can't login because login request contains sensitive data*			
	-	⊗	Device ID	`assistant`, `tunewiki`
Query:	*User can't receive response to a query because query contains sensitive data*			
	-	⊗	Device ID	`wnypages`, `yellowpages`
	-	⊗	Location	`manga`
	-	⊗	Phone #	`callerid`
	-	⊗	Contacts	`callerid`
	-	⊖	Device ID	`iheartradio`
GameProfile:	*Can't access cross-application high-score profile associated with device ID*			
	⊖	⊖	Device ID	`droidjump`, `mario`, `papertoss`, `simon`, `smiley_pops`, `trism`
	-	⊖	Location	`papertoss`
GeoSearch:	*Can't perform geographic search*			
	⊗	⊗	Location	`compass`, `dex`, `starbucks`, `wnypages`, `yellowpages`
	⊖	⊖	Location	`apartments`, `iheartradio`, `npr`, `yearbook`
GeoBroadcast:	*Can't broadcast geographic location to others*			
	⊖	⊖	Location	`heytell`
FindOthers:	*Can't learn which contacts are also using this application*			
	⊖	⊖	Contacts	`mocospace`
SelectRecipient:	*Can't select contacts with whom to call, message, or share*			
	⊗	-	Contacts	`callerid`, `heytell`
	⊖	-	Contacts	`quickmark`
DeviceData:	*Can't access bookmarks, SMS messages, calendar reminders, or other device data*			
	⊖	-	Bookmarks	`skyfire`
	⊗	-	SMS	`sqd`
	⊖	-	Calendar	`tvguide`

'-': no side effect, '⊖': application less functional, '⊗': primary application functionality breaks.

Table 7: The types of application functionality that were impacted by AppFence's privacy controls. The symbols in the shadowing (Sh) and exfiltration blocking (EB) columns indicate the severity of the side effects observed when privacy controls were applied to the given data types. Applications may be listed multiple times if they exhibited side effects for multiple functionalities or for different data types.

behaviors to a server and that users could report side effects. This data would reveal how applications use data and whether they will exhibit side effects if privacy controls are applied. Open problems to achieve this goal include finding ways to crowdsource the construction of application profiles while respecting users' privacy, detecting attempts by developers to compromise the integrity of this system to the advantage of their applications, and finding the right set of choices to present to users based on the data available.

6.2 Hampering evasion

As we discussed in Section 3.3, applications may be able to exploit limitations of AppFence's information flow tracking, which only monitors data flow operations, to circumvent exfiltration blocking.

Tracking information flow through control dependencies may broaden the set of data that is marked as tainted and result in false positives, which would in turn result in the unwarranted blocking of messages from an application. One promising option is to continue information flow tracking that is less likely to overtaint, and simultaneously use a more aggressive tracking that may overtaint. When AppFence detects a message that is tainted only by the more aggressive flow tracking it would allow the message. However, it would also report the event and the conditions that led up to it, to our servers for further analysis. We would then perform more comprehensive offline analysis (e.g. influence analysis [16]) to detect the cause of the difference between more and less aggressive tainting.

Alas, we cannot prevent applications from exploiting side channels (e.g. cache latency) to cleanse data of taint and circumvent exfiltration blocking. As shadowing prevents applications from ever accessing private data, it may always be the safest way to protect data from truly malicious applications. Data shadowing can be extended to offer finer-granularity controls such as shadowing location with a nearby but less private place, e.g. the city center. However, this kind of context-dependent control would require more configuration, warranting more research to make such controls practical and useful.

7. RELATED WORK

The use of shadow resources dates back at least as far as 1979, when the `chroot` operation was introduced to run

UNIX processes with a virtualized view of the file system hierarchy. Shadow password files allow system components that once accessed the real password files to get some of the information in that file without exposing the password hashes. Honeypots and Honeynets [17, 19, 21] have popularized the use of shadow resources to run malware while studying its behavior and limiting its potential to do damage. The prefix *honey* is frequently used for shadow resources created for the purpose of attracting an adversary and/or monitoring the adversary's behavior.

Felt and Evans propose a data shadowing scheme, called privacy-by-proxy [10]. Their mechanism is similar to our data shadowing as it provides a fake placeholder to third-party Facebook applications rather than the user's real information but the privacy-by-proxy is only effective to applications that access the user's information for the sole purpose of displaying the exact information back to the user. A recent paper by Beresford *et al.* also argues for replacing sensitive user data with "mock" (shadow) information. They apply data shadowing for a limited number of data types to 23 applications selected from those that were previously examined by Enck *et al.* using TaintDroid. However, they only tested to determine if shadowing could be applied to applications without causing them to crash–they did not measure user-discernable side effects [5]. Zhou *et al.* present a similar system that uses shadow data to provide a "privacy mode" for untrusted applications [27].

The Privacy Blocker application [2] performs static analysis of application binaries to identify and selectively replace requests for sensitive data with hard-coded shadow data. This binary-rewriting approach requires that each target application be rewritten and reinstalled, whereas AppFence performs data shadowing on unmodified applications at runtime. AppFence's dynamic approach also supports exfiltration blocking, which requires the hostname or IP address of the destination server that can only known for certain at runtime. However, this increased control over privacy comes at the price of deployability: AppFence requires modifications to the underlying operating system, whereas Privacy Blocker only requires the user to install an application.

There is also a wealth of prior work on the use of information-flow tracking to protect data confidentiality and integrity. Yin *et al.*'s Panorama uses dynamic information-flow tracking (DIFT) to perform offline analysis of data exfiltration by malware [26]. Chow *et al.*'s TaintBochs [6] uses DIFT to analyze the lifetime of security-critical data in memory, finding vulnerabilities when applications free memory containing encryption keys without first deleting them. Wang *et al.*'s PRECIP [25] tracks sensitive data (e.g., clipboard and user keystrokes) in Windows at the system-call level – tainting system objects – to prevent malicious processes from gaining access to them. However, it does not track taint propagation within applications and so the taint is lost when data is copied between objects. Perhaps most relevant is Vachharajani *et al.*'s RIFLE [24], which enforces security policies at runtime by translating programs into a custom instruction set architecture enhanced to track information flow.

Others have have worked to detect potential abuses of permissions and data by Android applications. Enck *et al.* [9] have developed a lightweight security checker, called Kirin, that analyzes manifest files to identify permissions that are dangerous when combined.

Android applications obtain user consent for all the permissions they will require at the time they are installed [12]. An alternative approach, to obtain consent for access to a resource at the time it is requested, is used for certain resources on Apple's iOS platform (e.g. location [4]). Requiring consent at time of access gives users more granular control over the time at which applications can access sensitive resources, and likely reduces the success rate of ultimatums. It does so at a cost of more frequent user interruptions. The Android team argues that the usability cost of time-of-access consents work "to the detriment of security" [12]. Regardless of when permissions are granted, neither the time-of-install nor the time-of-access consent model can prevent applications from misappropriating them.

8. CONCLUSION

AppFence offers two different approaches for protecting sensitive data from today's Android applications: shadowing sensitive data and blocking sensitive data from being exfiltrated off the device. We find that these privacy controls are complementary. For the 50 applications we studied, 34% of those have a direct conflict between the desired functionality and the privacy constraint our controls were designed to enforce—ensuring that sensitive data never leave the device. The testing methodology that we have developed for assessing side effects proves valuable for characterizing the types of application functionality that may be impacted by privacy controls. For the remaining applications, all side effects could be avoided with the right choice of either data shadowing or exfiltration blocking. How to help a user to make the right choice, however, remains a challenge to be addressed in future research.

Acknowledgments

We would like to thank Intel Labs for supporting this work, William Enck for sharing Android application binaries and Byung-Gon Chun, Peter Gilbert, Daniel Halperin, Patrick Gage Kelley, Robert Reeder, Anmol Sheth, the anonymous reviewers, and our shepherd, Ninghui Li for providing valuable feedback. This work was supported by National Science Foundation award CNS-0917341.

9. REFERENCES

[1] android-apktool: Tool for reengineering Android apk files. http://code.google.com/p/android-apktool/.

[2] Privacy Blocker. http://privacytools.xeudoxus.com/.

[3] S. T. Amir Efrati and D. Searcey. Mobile-app makers face U.S. privacy investigation. http://online.wsj.com/article/SB10001424052748703806304576242923804770968.html, Apr. 5, 2011.

[4] Apple Inc. iPhone and iPod touch: Understanding location services. http://support.apple.com/kb/HT1975, Oct. 22, 2010.

[5] A. R. Beresford, A. Rice, N. Skehin, and R. Sohan. MockDroid: Trading privacy for application functionality on smartphones. In *Proceedings of the 12th Workshop on Mobile Computing Systems and Applications (HotMobile)*, 2011.

[6] J. Chow, B. Pfaff, T. Garfinkel, K. Christopher, and M. Rosenblum. Understanding data lifetime via whole system simulation. In *USENIX Security Symposium*, 2004.

[7] M. Egele, C. Kruegel, E. Kirda, and G. Vigna. PiOS: Detecting privacy leaks in iOS applications. In *NDSS*, 2011.

[8] W. Enck, P. Gilbert, B.-G. Chun, L. P. Cox, J. Jung, P. McDaniel, and A. N. Sheth. TaintDroid: An information-flow tracking system for realtime privacy monitoring on smartphones. In *OSDI*, 2010.

[9] W. Enck, M. Ongtang, and P. McDaniel. On lightweight mobile phone application certification. In *CCS*, 2009.

[10] A. Felt and D. Evans. Privacy protection for social networking APIs. In *Proceedings of Web 2.0 Security And Privacy (W2SP)*, 2008.

[11] Google Inc. Android developers: Content providers. `http://developer.android.com/guide/topics/providers/content-providers.html`.

[12] Google Inc. Android developers: Security and permissions. `http://developer.android.com/guide/topics/security/security.html`.

[13] Google Inc. Android developers: Using aapt. `http://developer.android.com/guide/developing/tools/aapt.html`.

[14] Google Inc. Android developers: Platform versions. `http://developer.android.com/resources/dashboard/platform-versions.html`, Aug. 2011.

[15] A. Jääskeläinen. *Design, Implementation and Use of a Test Model Library for GUI Testing of Smartphone Applications.* Doctoral dissertation, Tampere University of Technology, Tampere, Finland, Jan. 2011.

[16] J. Newsome, S. McCamant, and D. Song. Measuring channel capacity to distinguish undue influence. In *Proceedings of the ACM SIGPLAN Fourth Workshop on Programming Languages and Analysis for Security*, June 15, 2009.

[17] N. Provos. A virtual honeypot framework. In *USENIX Security Symposium*, 2004.

[18] E. Smith. iPhone applications & privacy issues: An analysis of application transmission of iPhone unique device identifiers (UDIDs). In *Technical Report*, 2010.

[19] L. Spitzner. *Honeypots: Tracking Hackers.* Addison-Wesley, Boston, MA, Sept. 10, 2002.

[20] Tampere University of Technology. Introduction: Model-based testing and glossary. `http://tema.cs.tut.fi/intro.html`.

[21] The Honeynet Project. *Know Your Enemy: Revealing the Security Tools, Tactics, and Motives of the Blackhat Community.* Addison-Wesley, 2001.

[22] S. Thurm and Y. I. Kane. The Journal's cellphone testing methodology. The Wall Street Journal. Dec. 18, 2010. `http://online.wsj.com/article/SB10001424052748704034804576025951767626460.html`.

[23] S. Thurm and Y. I. Kane. Your apps are watching you. The Wall Street Journal. Dec. 18, 2010. `online.wsj.com/article/SB10001424052748704694004576020083703574602.html`.

[24] N. Vachharajani, M. J. Bridges, J. Chang, R. Rangan, G. Ottoni, J. A. Blome, G. A. Reis, M. Vachharajani, and D. I. August. RIFLE: An architectural framework for user-centric information-flow security. In *MICRO*, 2004.

[25] X. Wang, Z. Li, N. Li, and J. Y. Choi. PRECIP: Practical and retrofittable confidential information protection. In *NDSS*, Feb. 2008.

[26] H. Yin, D. Song, M. Egele, C. Kruegel, and E. Kirda. Panorama: capturing system-wide information flow for malware detection and analysis. In *CCS*, 2007.

[27] Y. Zhou, X. Zhang, X. Jiang, and V. Freeh. Taming information-stealing smartphone applications (on Android). In *International Conference on Trust and Trustworthy Computing (TRUST)*, 2011.

APPENDIX

A. WHEN APPLICATIONS ARE "LESS FUNCTIONAL"

When evaluating the impact of privacy controls on user experience, we consider certain side effects to render an application "less functional" when the application is able to perform its primary purpose but cannot perform some secondary function. In this appendix we explain the precise circumstances that led us to classify applications as less functional.

device ID (IMEI): We classified as less functional games that could not load a cross-application high-score profile because the profile is associated with the true device ID. Additionally, we classified the `iheartradio` application as less functional because its searches for nearby radio stations failed due to the inclusion of the device ID with the search request.

location: We included those applications where location proximity would have provided enhanced, but not core, functionality. For example, the `npr` radio application enhances its primary service by identifying the user's local stations, `yearbook` offers local chat in addition to its other chat options, and `heytell` allows users to optionally include their current location along with sent messages. We also included some applications that could no longer automatically capture the user's location, but offered users the option of manually entering their location (e.g. the `apartments` apartment-hunting application). Finally, the `papertoss` application became less functional when its high-score profile failed to load because it sends the user's location along with the request.

contacts: We included one chat application, `mocospace`, that could no longer add users' local contacts to the server-side chat contacts database. We also classified as less functional a barcode scanning application, `quickmark`, that offers the ability to send a bar code image to someone in the contacts book, but was not able to do so if contacts were protected by our privacy controls.

bookmarks: We included a browser, `skyfire`, that could still browse the web but was not be able to read or save bookmarks if they were protected.

calendar: We classified as less functional the `tvguide` application that cannot add reminders to the user's calendar if the calendar has been replaced by a shadow calendar.

B. APPLICATIONS SCRIPTED FOR AUTOMATED TESTING

#	application	package name
1	antivirus	com.antivirus
2	apartments	com.cellit.forrent
3	assistant	com.netgate
4	astrid	com.timsu.astrid
5	autorun	com.rs.autorun
6	avril	com.ringtone.avrillavigne
7	basketball	com.droidhen.basketball
8	bible	com.faithcomesbyhearing.android.bibleis
9	callerid	net.bsdtelecom.calleridfaker
10	christmas	com.maxdroid.christmas
11	chuck_norris	com.bakes.chucknorrisfacts
12	compass	com.a0soft.gphone.aCompass
13	dex	com.mportal.dexknows.ui
14	dilbert	com.tarsin.android.dilbert
15	docstogo	com.dataviz.docstogo
16	droidjump	com.electricsheep.edj
17	espn	com.espnsport
18	flightview	com.flightview.flightview_free
19	fmlife	fmlife.activities
20	heytell	com.heytell
21	howtotie	com.artelplus.howtotie
22	iheartradio	com.clearchannel.iheartradio.controller2
23	kayak	com.kayak.android
24	manga	com.ceen.mangaviewer
25	mario	de.joergjahnke.mario.android.free
26	minesweeper	artfulbits.aiMinesweeper
27	mocospace	com.jnj.mocospace.android
28	moron	com.distinctdev.tmtlite
29	mp3_ringtone	net.lucky.star.mrtm
30	musicbox	com.dreamstep.musicbox
31	npr	org.npr.android.news
32	papertoss	com.bfs.papertoss
33	princesses	com.socialin.android.puzzle.princess
34	quickmark	tw.com.quickmark
35	simon	com.neilneil.android.games.simonclassic
36	simpsons	us.sourcio.android.puzzle.simpson
37	skyfire	com.skyfire.browser
38	slotmachine	com.slot.slotmachine
39	smarttactoe	com.dynamix.mobile.SmartTacToe
40	smiley_pops	com.boolbalabs.smileypops
41	sqd	com.superdroid.sqd
42	starbucks	com.brennasoft.findastarbucks
43	taskos	com.taskos
44	trism	com.feasy.tris2.colorblocks
45	tunewiki	com.tunewiki.lyricplayer.android
46	tvguide	com.roundbox.android.tvguide.presentation.activity
47	videopoker	com.infimosoft.videopoker
48	wnypages	com.avantar.wny
49	yearbook	com.myyearbook.m
50	yellowpages	com.avantar.yp

Privacy and Accountability for Location-based Aggregate Statistics

Raluca Ada Popa
MIT
ralucap@mit.edu

Andrew J. Blumberg
University of Texas, Austin
blumberg@math.utexas.edu

Hari Balakrishnan
MIT
hari@mit.edu

Frank H. Li
MIT
frankli@mit.edu

ABSTRACT

A significant and growing class of location-based mobile applications aggregate position data from individual devices at a server and compute aggregate statistics over these position streams. Because these devices can be linked to the movement of individuals, there is significant danger that the aggregate computation will violate the *location privacy* of individuals. This paper develops and evaluates PrivStats, a system for computing aggregate statistics over location data that simultaneously achieves two properties: first, provable guarantees on location privacy even in the face of any side information about users known to the server, and second, privacy-preserving accountability (i.e., protection against abusive clients uploading large amounts of spurious data). PrivStats achieves these properties using a new protocol for uploading and aggregating data anonymously as well as an efficient zero-knowledge proof of knowledge protocol we developed from scratch for accountability. We implemented our system on Nexus One smartphones and commodity servers. Our experimental results demonstrate that PrivStats is a practical system: computing a common aggregate (e.g., count) over the data of $10,000$ clients takes less than 0.46 s at the server and the protocol has modest latency (0.6 s) to upload data from a Nexus phone. We also validated our protocols on real driver traces from the CarTel project.

Categories and subject descriptors: C.2.0 [Computer Communication Networks]: General–*Security and protection*
General terms: Security

1. INTRODUCTION

The emergence of location-based mobile services and the interest in using them in road transportation, participatory sensing [28, 21], and various social mobile crowdsourcing applications has led to a fertile area of research and commercial activity. At the core of many of these applications are mobile nodes (smartphones, in-car devices, etc.) equipped with GPS or other position sensors, which (periodically) upload time and location coordinates to a server. This information is then processed by the server to compute a variety of aggregate statistics.

As primary motivation, consider applications that process streams of GPS position and/or speed samples along vehicle trajectories, sourced from smartphones, to determine current traffic statistics such as average speed, average delay on a road segment, or congestion at an intersection. Several research projects (e.g., CarTel [21], Mobile Millennium [27]) and commercial products (e.g., TomTom [34]) provide such services. Another motivation is social mobile crowdsourcing, for example, estimating the number of people at a restaurant to determine availability by aggregating data from position samples provided by smartphones carried by participating users.

A significant concern about existing implementations of these services is the violation of user *location privacy*. Even though the service only needs to compute an aggregate (such as a mean, standard deviation, density of users, etc.), most implementations simply continuously record time-location pairs of all the clients and deliver them to the server, labeled by which client they belong to [21, 27, 22]. In such a system, the server can piece together all the locations and times belonging to a particular client and obtain the client's path, violating her location privacy.

Location privacy concerns are important to address because many users perceive them to be significant (and may refuse to use or even oppose a service) and because they may threaten *personal security*. Recently (as of the time of writing this paper), two users have sued Google [26] over location data that Android phones collect citing as one of the concerns "serious risk of privacy invasions, including stalking." The lawsuit attempts to prevent Google from selling phones with software that can track user location. Just a week before, two users sued Apple [25] for violating privacy laws by keeping a log of user locations without offering users a way to disable this tracking or delete the log. Users of TomTom, a satellite navigation system, have expressed concern over the fact that TomTom logs user paths and sells aggregate statistics (such as speeding hotspots) to the police, who in turn install speed cameras [34]. A study by Riley [35] shows even wider location privacy fears: a significant number of drivers in the San Francisco Bay Area will not install toll transponders in their cars because of privacy concerns. Moreover, online databases are routinely broken into or abused by insiders with access; if that happens, detailed records of user mobility may become known to criminals, who can then attempt security attacks, such as burglarizing homes when they know that their residents are away [40].

In this paper, we design, implement, and evaluate **PrivStats**, a practical system for computing aggregate statistics in the context of mobile, location-based applications that achieves both strong guar-

CCS'11, October 17–21, 2011, Chicago, Illinois, USA.

antees of location privacy and protection against cheating clients. PrivStats solves two major problems: it provides formal location privacy guarantees against *any side information* (SI) attacks, and it provides client *accountability without a trusted party*. Because of these contributions, in comparison to previous systems [16], CliqueCloak [14], [19], [24], [20], and Triplines [18], PrivStats provides the strongest formal privacy and correctness guarantees while making the weakest trust assumptions.

Side information refers to any out-of-bound information the server may have, which, when used together with the data the server gets in a system, can help the server compromise user location privacy. Some previous work ensures that clients upload data free of identifiers (they upload approximate time, location, and data sample), but even when all data is anonymized, a considerable amount of private location information can still leak due to side information. As a simple example, if the server knows that Alice is the only person living on a street, it can infer that Alice just left or arrived at her house when receiving some speed updates from that street. SI can come in many forms and has been shown to leak as much as full client paths in some cases: Krumm [24], as well as Gruteser and Hoh [17], show that one can infer driver paths from anonymized data and then link them to driver identities using side information such as knowledge of map, typical driving behavior patterns, timing between uploads, and a public web service with addresses and names. Despite SI's ability to leak considerable location privacy, previous systems for mobile systems aggregates either do not address the problem at all, or they only treat specific cases of it, such as areas of low density (see §10).

Our first contribution is to provide *an aggregate statistics protocol with strong location privacy guarantees, including protection against any general side information attack.* We formalize our guarantees by providing a definition of location privacy, termed *strict location privacy* or SLP (Def. 2), which specifies that the server learns nothing further about the location of clients in the face of arbitrary side information other than the desired aggregate result; then, in §5, we provide a protocol, also termed SLP, that provably achieves our definition.

While we manage to hide most sources of privacy leakage in our SLP protocol without any trust assumptions, hiding the number of tuples generated by clients information-theoretically can be reduced, under reasonable model assumptions, to a problem in distributed algorithms that can be shown to be impossible to solve. The reason is that it requires synchronization among a set of clients that do not know of each other. Our solution is to use a lightweight and restricted module, the *smoothing module* (SM), that helps clients synchronize with respect to the number of tuples upload and performs one decryption per aggregate. We distribute the SM on the clients (each "client SM" is responsible for handling a few aggregates) so as to ensure that at most a small fraction of SMs misbehave. We provide our strong SLP guarantees for all aggregates with honest SMs, while still ensuring a high level of protection for compromised SMs:

- A compromised SM cannot change aggregate results undetectably and cannot collude with clients to allow them to corrupt aggregates.
- Although a malicious SM opens the doors to potential SI leakage from the number of uploads and the values uploaded, a significant degree of privacy remains because client uploads are always anonymized, free of timing and origin information. Our SM is distributed *on the clients*, resulting in few compromised client SMs in practice.
- Our design of the SM (§5) facilitates distribution and ensuring its correctness: the SM has light load, ≈ 50 times less load than the server, performs two simple tasks summing up to only 62 lines of code (excluding libraries) which can be easily scrutinized for correctness, and only uses constant storage per aggregate.
- In contrast to our limited SM, trusted parties in previous work [18, 14, 20, 16] had the ability to fully compromise client paths and modify aggregate results when corrupted; at the same time, their use still did not provide general SI attack protection.

Since clients are anonymous, the problem of accountability becomes serious: malicious clients can significantly affect the correctness of the aggregate results. Hoh et al. [19] present a variety of attacks clients may use to change the aggregate result. For example, clients might try to divert traffic away from a road to reduce a particular driver's travel time or to keep low traffic in front of one's residence, or divert traffic toward a particular road-way to increase revenue at a particular store. A particular challenge is that accountability and privacy goals are in tension: if each client upload is anonymous, it seems that the client could upload as many times as she wishes. Indeed, most previous systems [16, 14, 24, 20] do not provide any protection for such client biasing attacks and the few that provide such verification ([18, 19]) place this task on heavily loaded trusted parties that when compromised can release full location paths with user identities and can corrupt aggregate results.

Our second contribution is *a privacy-preserving accountability protocol without any trusted parties* (§6). We provide a cryptographic protocol for ensuring that each client can upload at most a fixed quota of values for each aggregate. At the core of the protocol, is an efficient zero-knowledge proof of knowledge (ZKPoK) that we designed from scratch for this protocol. The zero-knowledge property is key in maintaining the anonymity of clients. Therefore, no trusted party is needed; in particular, the SM is not involved in this protocol.

Finally, our third contribution is an implementation of the overall system on Nexus One smartphones and commodity servers (§9). One of our main goals was to design a practical system, so we strived to keep our cryptographic protocols practical, including designing our ZKPoK from scratch. Computing a common aggregate (e.g. count) over the data of 10^4 clients takes less than 0.46 s at the server, the protocol has modest latency of about 0.6 s to upload data from a Nexus phone, and the throughput is linearly scalable in the number of processing cores. We believe these measurements indicate that PrivStats is practical. We also validated that our protocols introduce little or no error in statistics computation using real driver traces from the CarTel project [21].

2. MODEL

In this section, we discuss the model for PrivStats. Our setup captures a wide range of aggregate statistics problems for mobile systems.

2.1 Setting

In our model, we have many clients, a server, and a smoothing module (SM). *Clients* are mobile nodes equipped with smartphones: drivers in a vehicular network or peers in a social crowdsourcing application. The *server* is an entity interested in computing certain aggregate statistics over data from clients. The SM is a third party involved in the protocol that is distributed on clients.

We assume that clients communicate with the server and the SM using an anonymization network (e.g., Tor), a proxy forwarder, or other anonymizing protocol to ensure that privacy is not compromised by the underlying networking protocol. In this paper, we assume these systems succeed in hiding the origin of a packet from an adversary; it is out of our scope to ensure this. We assume that these systems also hide network travel time; otherwise clients must introduce an appropriate delay so that all communications have roughly the same round trip times.

Clients can choose which aggregates they want to participate in; they can opt-out if the result is deemed too revealing.

A *sample* is a client's contribution to an aggregate, such as average speed, delay on a road, or a bit indicating presence in a certain restaurant. Clients can generate samples periodically, as is the case in vehicular systems, or at certain location/times, as is the case for social mobile crowdsourcing systems. A *sample point* is a pair consisting of a location and a time interval where/when clients should generate a sample. We say that a client *passes through a sample point* if the client passes by the location and in the time interval of a sample point.

An aggregate to be computed consists of a sample point and the type of data clients should sample. The server may only be interested in computing certain aggregates. We assume that clients know the aggregates of interest (e.g., from a public database or a deterministic algorithm), that is, at which sample points they should upload and what kind of samples they should generate. We assume that each aggregate has an identifier id, with the mapping between identifiers and aggregates publicly known (e.g., a hash). Therefore, clients generate tuples of the form $\langle \mathsf{id}, \mathsf{sample} \rangle$, meaning that their sample for aggregate id is sample. We denote by *aggregate result* the result of the aggregation of all client samples for an aggregate. Each aggregate has an associated *sample interval* denoting an interval of acceptable values for the sample. For example, suppose that $\mathsf{id} = 2$ corresponds to an aggregate with sample point road segment S and time interval between T_1 = 4.00 pm to T_2 = 4.15 pm, and type of sample "average speed" (the sample interval could be 0 mph – 100 mph). A client passing through S, in the interval of time $[T_1, T_2]$ should take a sample of their average speed. The client generates the tuple: $\langle 2, 24 \text{ mph} \rangle$. Finally, the aggregate result over all clients could be 30 mph. (Note that the server may choose to compute the function in "real time" or at some later point in time.)

To preserve privacy, clients in PrivStats will transform these tuples (e.g., encrypt and add cryptographic tokens) and use a certain upload strategy to upload the transformed tuples to the server. Note that clients are not uploading their identity with the tuples, unlike in some existing systems [21, 12].

2.2 Threat Model

The server *cannot be trusted to protect the privacy of clients*: the server might attempt to recover the path of a given client and release this information to third parties without a client's consent or knowledge (e.g., for advertising), or hackers could break into the server and steal location data about particular users. These attacks can use any side information. However, the server is trusted to compute the aggregate statistics correctly: this is its goal.

Clients are also untrusted: they may attempt to bias the aggregate result (e.g., to convince a server that the road next to their house is crowded and no more traffic should come). There are two such potential threats: uploading a large number of samples or uploading samples with out-of-range samples, both of which could change an aggregate result significantly. However, each client is allowed to upload within a server-imposed quota and an acceptable interval of sample values; checking that the sample uploaded is precisely correct is out-of-scope. (See §9.2 for more details).

The smoothing module (SM) can misbehave by trying to change aggregate results or colluding with clients to help them bias statistics; PrivStats prevents such behavior. To guarantee full side information protection, the requirement on the SM is that it does not leak timing or decrypted samples.

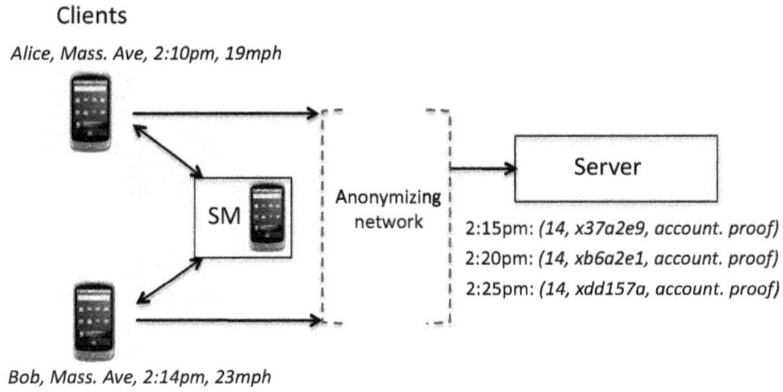

Figure 1: Architecture of PrivStats.

3. SIDE INFORMATION AND LOCATION PRIVACY

Side information can leak information about client paths even when the server receives tuples without identities. As already discussed, the number of tuples in areas of low density can leak privacy. Krumm [24] as well as Gruteser and Hoh [17] inferred driver paths and their identities using SI such as knowledge of map, driving patterns, upload timing, and a public web service. Driving patterns coupled with sample values can also leak private information. For example, if the server knows that client Bob is a habitual speeder, tracking uploads with high speed values will likely indicate his path. Other two interesting examples of SI are physical observation and information about someone else's path. For an example of the latter, assume that the server knows that Alice and Bob both went on street A and then it sees one upload from street B1 and one upload from B2, which follow directly from A. Knowing that Bob's house is on B1, it can infer that Alice went on B2. To quantify how much privacy is leaked, Shokri et al. [38] offer a framework for quantifying privacy leakage in various location privacy schemes that also takes into account side information.

We now provide a definition of location privacy that is resilient to arbitrary side information. SI can come in different forms and reveal varying degrees of information, making it challenging to provide theoretical guarantees. For example, one can never guarantee that the path of a client between point A and point B will remain unknown because the client may simply be observed physically at some location. Moreover, one cannot prevent the adversary from having SI: such SI can come from a variety of out-of-bound sources (public databases, physical observation, collusion with clients, personal knowledge of a driver's trends, etc.). Instead, the idea is that the protocol should not reveal any *additional* information about client paths beyond what the server already knows and the desired aggregate result. In short, the protocol should reveal nothing else other than the aggregate result.

Consider the following example. Alice, Bob, and some other clients volunteer to participate in an average speed computation on street S_1 for time interval 7 am to 9 am. Now suppose that the server has the following side information about the clients: on the days that Alice goes to work, she leaves home on street S_1 at 8:15 am; also, Bob is a speeder and tends to drive significantly faster than the average driver. If the protocol satisfies our definition, the server will learn the average speed, say 30 mph, and nothing else. In particular, the server will not learn how many people passed through the street or whether there was an upload at 8:15 am (and hence whether Alice went to work). Moreover, the server will not see the individual speed values uploaded so it cannot determine if there were some high speeds corresponding to Bob.

I. System setup (Runs once, when the system starts).

1: Server generates public and private keys for accountability by running *System setup* from §6.
2: Both Server and SM generate public and private keys for the aggregation protocols by running *System setup* from §5.

II. Client join (Runs once per client, when a client signs up to the system).

1: Client identifies herself and obtains public keys and capabilities to upload data for accountability (by running *Client join*, §6) from Server and public keys for aggregation (by running *Client join*, §5) from SM. Server also informs Client of the aggregates Server wants to compute, and Client decides to which aggregates she wants to contribute (i.e., generate tuples).

III. Client uploads for aggregate id (Runs when a client generates a tuple $\langle \mathsf{id}, \mathsf{sample} \rangle$)

1: Client runs SLP's *Upload* protocol (§5) by communicating with the SM for each $\langle \mathsf{id}, \mathsf{sample} \rangle$ and produces a set of transformed tuples $\mathcal{T}_1, \ldots, \mathcal{T}_k$ and a set of times, $t_1, \ldots, t_k$, when each should be uploaded to Server.
2: For each i, Client uploads $\mathcal{T}_i$ to Server at time t_i.
3: Client also proves to Server using the *Accountability upload* protocol, §6, that the upload is within the permissible quotas and acceptable sample interval.

IV. Server computes aggregate result id (Runs at the end of an aggregate's time interval).

1: Server puts together all the tuples for the same id and aggregates them by running *Aggregation* with SM, §5.

Figure 2: Overview of PrivStats.

For a security parameter k and an aggregate function F (which can also be a collection of aggregate functions), consider a protocol $\mathbb{P} = \mathbb{P}^F(k)$ for computing F. For example, the SLP protocol (§5) is such a protocol $\mathbb{P}$ where F can be any of the aggregates discussed in §7. Let R be a collection of raw tuples generated by users in some time period; that is, R is a set of tuples of the form $\langle \mathsf{id}, \mathsf{sample} \rangle$ together with the precise time, client network information, and client id when they are generated. R is therefore the private data containing the paths of all users and should be hidden from the server. We refer to R as a *raw-tuple configuration.* Let SI be some side information available at the server about R. Using $\mathbb{P}$, clients transform the tuples in R before uploading them to the server. (The sizes of R, F, and SI are assumed to be polynomial in k.)

The following definition characterizes the information available at the server when running protocol $\mathbb{P}$. Since we consider a real system, the server observes the timing and network origin of the packets it receives; a privacy definition should take these into account.

DEF. 1 (SERVER'S VIEW.). *The view of the server,* $\mathsf{View}_{\mathbb{P}}(R)$, *is all the tuples the server receives from clients or SM in* $\mathbb{P}$ *associated with time of receipt and any packet network information, when clients generate raw tuples* R *and run protocol* $\mathbb{P}$.

Let $\mathcal{D}$ be the domain for all raw-tuple configurations R. Let res be some aggregate result. Let $\mathcal{R}^F(\mathsf{res}) = \{R \in \mathcal{D} : F(R) = \mathsf{res}\}$ be all possible collections of raw tuples where the associated aggregate result is res.

Security game. We describe the SLP definition using a game between a challenger and an adversary. The adversary is a party that would get access to all the information the server gets. Consider a protocol $\mathbb{P}$, a security parameter k, a raw-tuple domain $\mathcal{D}$, and an adversary Adv.

1: The challenger sets up $\mathbb{P}$ by choosing any secret and public keys required by $\mathbb{P}$ with security parameter k and sends the public keys to Adv.
2: Adv chooses SI, res, and $R_0, R_1 \in \mathcal{R}^F(\mathsf{res})$ (to facilitate guessing based on SI) and sends R_0 and R_1 to the challenger.
3: Challenger runs $\mathbb{P}$ producing $\mathsf{View}^{\mathbb{P}}(R_0)$ and $\mathsf{View}^{\mathbb{P}}(R_1)$, and sends them to Adv. It chooses a fair random bit b and sends $\mathsf{View}^{\mathbb{P}}(R_b)$ to Adv. ($\mathsf{View}^{\mathbb{P}}$ usually contains probabilistic encryption so two encryptions of R_b will lead to different values.)
4: The adversary outputs its best guess for b^* and wins this game if $b = b^*$. Let $\mathsf{win}^{\mathbb{P}}(\mathsf{Adv}, k) := \Pr[b = b^*]$ be the probability that Adv wins this game.

DEF. 2 (STRICT LOCATION PRIVACY – SLP). *A protocol* $\mathbb{P}$ *has strict location privacy with respect to a raw-tuple domain,* $\mathcal{D}$, *if, for any polynomial-time adversary* Adv, $\mathsf{win}^{\mathbb{P}}(\mathsf{Adv}, k) \leq 1/2 +$ *negligible function of* k.

Intuitively, this definition says that, when the server examines the data it receives and any side information, all possible configurations of client paths having the same aggregate result are equally likely. Therefore, the server learns nothing new beyond the aggregate result.

Strict location privacy and differential privacy. The guarantee of strict location privacy is complementary to those of differential privacy [11], and these two approaches address different models. In SLP, the server is untrusted and all that it learns is the aggregate result. In a differential privacy setting, the *server is trusted and knows all private information of the clients*, clients issue queries to the database at the server, and clients only learn aggregate results that do not reveal individual tuples. Of course, allowing the server to know all clients' private path information is unacceptable in our setting. PrivStats' model takes the first and most important step for privacy: hiding the actual paths of the users from the server. Actual paths leak much more than common aggregate results in practice. A natural question is whether one can add differential privacy on top of PrivStats to reduce leakage from the aggregate result, while retaining the guarantees of PrivStats, which we discuss in §8.

4. OVERVIEW

PrivStats consists of running an aggregation protocol and an accountability protocol. The aggregation protocol (§5) achieves our strict location privacy (SLP) definition, Def. 2, and leaks virtually nothing about the clients other than the aggregate result. The accountability protocol (§6) enables the server to check three properties of each client's upload *without* learning anything about the identity of the client: the client did not exceed a server-imposed quota of uploads for each sample point, did not exceed a total quota of uploads over all sample points, and the sample uploaded is in an acceptable interval of values.

Figure 1 illustrates the interaction of the three components in our system on an example: computation of aggregate statistic with id 14, average speed. The figure shows Alice and Bob generating data when passing through the corresponding sample point and then contacting the SM to know how many tuples to upload. As we explain in §5, we can see that the data that reaches the server is anonymized, contains encrypted speeds, arrives at random times independent of the time of generation, and is accompanied by accountability proofs to prevent malicious uploads. Moreover, the number of tuples arriving is uncorrelated with the real number.

Figure 2 provides an overview of our protocols, with components elaborated in the upcoming sections.

5. AGGREGATION: THE SLP (STRICT LOCATION PRIVACY) PROTOCOL

A protocol with strict location privacy must hide all five leakage vectors (included in Def. 1): client identifier, network origin of packet, time of upload, sample value, and number of tuples generated for each aggregate (i.e., the number of clients passing by a sample point). The need to hide the first two is evident and we already discussed the last three vectors in §3.

Hiding the identifier and network origin. As discussed in §2, clients never upload their identities (which is possible due to our accountability protocol described in §6). We hide the network origin using an anonymizing network as discussed in §2.1.

Hiding the sample. Clients encrypt their samples using a (semantically secure) homomorphic encryption scheme. Various schemes can be used, depending on the aggregate to be computed; Paillier [30] is our running example and it already enables most common aggregates. Paillier has the property that $E(a) \cdot E(b) = E(a+b)$, where $E(a)$ denotes encryption of a under the public key, and the multiplication and addition are performed in appropriate groups. Using this setup, the server computes the desired aggregate on encrypted data; the only decrypted value the server sees is the final aggregate result (due to the SM, as described later in this section).

It is important for the encryption scheme to be *verifiable* to prevent the SM from corrupting the decrypted aggregate result. That is, given the public key PK and a ciphertext $E(a)$, when given a and some randomness r, the server can verify that $E(a)$ was indeed an encryption of a using r, and there is no b such that $E(a)$ could have been an encryption of b for some randomness. Also, the holder of the secret key should be able to compute r efficiently. Fortunately, Paillier has this property because it is a trapdoor permutation; computing r involves one exponentiation [30].

Hiding the number of tuples. The server needs to receive a number of tuples that is independent of the actual number of tuples generated. The idea is to arrange that the clients will *upload in total a constant number of tuples*, U_{id}, for each aggregate id. U_{id} is a publicly-known value, usually an upper bound on the number of clients generating tuples, and computed based on historical estimates of how many clients participate in the aggregate. §9 explains how to choose U_{id}.

The difficulty with uploading U_{id} in total is that clients do not know how many other clients pass through the same sample point, and any synchronization point may itself become a point of leakage for the number of clients.

Assuming that there are no trusted parties (i.e., everyone tries to learn the number of tuples generated), under a reasonable formalization of our specific practical setting, the problem of hiding the number of tuples can be reduced to a simple distributed algorithms problem which is shown to be impossible (as presented in a longer version of our paper at `http://nms.csail.mit.edu/projects/privacy/`). For this reason, we use a party called the *smoothing module* (SM) that clients use to synchronize and upload a constant number of tuples at each aggregate. The SM will also perform the final decryption of the aggregate result. The trust requirement on the SM is that it does not decrypt more than one value for the server per aggregate and it does not leak the actual number of tuples. Although the impossibility result provides evidence that some form of trust is needed for SLP, we do not claim that hiding the number of tuples would remain impossible if one weakened the privacy guarantees or altered the model. However, we think our trust assumption is reasonable, as we explain in §8: a malicious SM has limited effect on privacy (it does not see the timing, origin, and identifier of client tuples) and virtually no effect on aggregate results (it cannot decrypt an incorrect value or affect accountability). Moreover, the SM has light load, and can be distributed on clients ensuring that most aggregates have our full guarantees. For simplicity, we describe the SLP protocol with one SM and subsequently explain how to distribute it on clients.

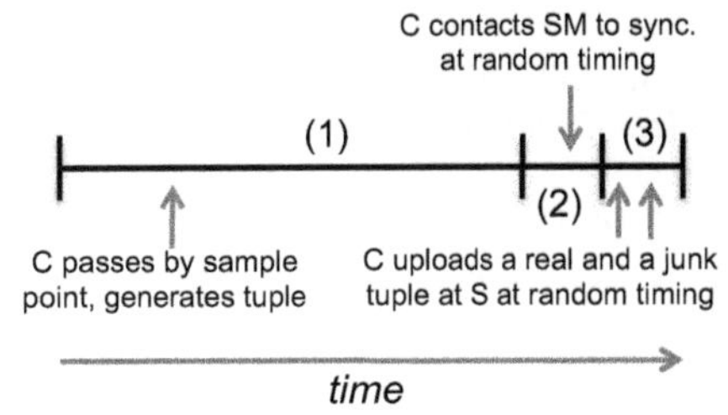

Figure 3: Staged randomized timing upload for a client C: (1) is the generation interval, (2) the synchronization interval, and (3) the upload interval.

Since the number of real tuples generated may be less than U_{id}, we will arrange to have clients occasionally upload *junk* tuples: tuples that are indistinguishable from legitimate tuples because the encryption scheme is probabilistic. Using the SM, clients can figure out how many junk tuples they should upload. The value of the junk tuples is a neutral value for the aggregate to be computed (e.g., zero for summations), as we explain in §7.

To summarize, the SM needs to perform only two simple tasks:

- Keep track of the number of tuples that have been uploaded so far (s_{id}) for an aggregate (without leaking this number to an adversary). Clients use this information to figure out how many more tuples they should upload at the server to reach a total of U_{id}.
- At the end of the time period for an aggregate id, decrypt the value of the aggregate result from the server.

Hiding timing. Clients upload tuples according to a staged randomized timing algorithm described in Figure 3; this protocol hides the tuple generation time from both the server and the SM. The generation interval corresponds to the interval of aggregation when clients generate tuples, and the synchronization and upload interval are added at the end of the generation interval, but are much shorter (they are not points only to ensure reasonable load per second at the SM and server).

We now put together all these components and specify the SLP protocol. Denote an aggregate by id and let quota be the number of samples a client can upload at id. Let $[t_{s0}, t_{s1}]$ be the sync. interval.

I. System setup: SM generates a Paillier secret and public key.
II. Client joins: Client obtains the public key from the SM.
III. Upload:

∘ GENERATION INTERVAL

1: Client generates a tuple ⟨id, sample⟩ and computes $\mathcal{T}_1 := \langle \text{id}, E[\text{sample}] \rangle$ using SM's public key.
2: Client selects a random time t_s in the sync. interval and does nothing until t_s.

∘ SYNCHRONIZATION INTERVAL

3: Client ↔ SM : At time t_s, Client requests s_{id}, the number of tuples other clients already engaged to upload for id from SM ($s_{\text{id}} = 0$ if Client is the first to ask s_{id} for id).
4: Client should upload $\Delta s := \min(\text{quota}, \lceil U_{\text{id}}(t_s - t_{s0})/(t_{s1} - t_{s0}) \rceil - s_{\text{id}})$ tuples. If $\Delta s \leq 0$, but $s_{\text{id}} < U_{\text{id}}$, assign $\Delta s := 1$. (In parallel, SM updates s_{id} to $s_{\text{id}} := \Delta s + s_{\text{id}}$ because it also knows quota and it assumes that Client will upload her share.)
5: Client picks Δs random times, $t_1, \ldots, t_{\Delta s}$, in the upload interval to use when uploading tuples.

∘ UPLOAD INTERVAL:

6: Client → Server : The client uploads Δs tuples at times $t_1, \ldots, t_{\Delta s}$. One of the tuples is the real tuple $\mathcal{T}_1$, the others, if any, are junk tuples.

IV. Aggregation:

1: At the end of the interval, Server computes the aggregate on encrypted samples by homomorphically adding all samples for id.
2: Server ↔ SM : Server asks SM to decrypt the aggregate result. SM must decrypt only one value per aggregate. Server verifies that SM returned the correct decrypted value as discussed.

The equation for Δs is designed so that for each time t in the synchronization interval, approximately a total of $U_{\text{id}}(t - t_{s0})/(t_{s1} - t_{s0})$ tuples have been scheduled by clients to be uploaded during the upload interval. Therefore, when t becomes t_{s1}, U_{id} tuples should have been scheduled for upload.

We assign $s_{\text{id}} := 1$ when Δs comes out negative or zero because as long as $s_{\text{id}} < U_{\text{id}}$, it is better to schedule clients for uploading in order to reach the value of U_{id} by the end of the time interval; this approach avoids too many junk tuples (which do not carry useful information) being uploaded later in the interval if insufficiently many clients show up then. Moreover, this ensures that, as long as U_{id} is an upper bound on the number of clients passing by, few clients will refrain from uploading in practice.

Choice of U_{id} and quota. A reasonable choice for quota is 3 and $U_{\text{id}} = \text{avg}_{\text{id}} + \text{std}_{\text{id}}$, where avg_{id} is an estimate of the average of clients passing through a sample point and std_{id} of the standard deviation; both these values can be deduced based on historical records or known trends of the sample point id. We justify and evaluate this choice of U_{id} and quota in §9.2.

Let $\mathcal{D}^*$ be the set of all raw-tuple configurations in which clients succeed in uploading U_{id} at sample point id. Raw-tuple configurations in practice should be a subset of this set for properly chosen U_{id} and quota.

THEOREM 1. *The SLP protocol achieves the strict location privacy definition from Def. 2 for $\mathcal{D}^*$.*

PROOF. Due to space constraints, we provide a high-level proof leaving a mathematical exposition for an extended version of this paper (`http://nms.csail.mit.edu/projects/privacy/`); nevertheless, the proof is easy enough to understand in such terms.

According to Def. 2, we need to argue that the information in the view of the server (besides the aggregate result and any SI the server already knows) when clients generate two different collections of raw tuples, R_0 and R_1, is indistinguishable. The information that reaches the server for id is a set of tuples consisting of three components: time of receipt, network origin, and encrypted sample. Due to our U_{id} scheme, the number of tuples arriving at the server in both cases is the same, U_{id}. Next, our staged upload protocol ensures that the timing of upload is uniformly at random distributed and the network origin is hidden. The encryption scheme of the samples is semantically secure so, by definition, any two samples encrypted with this scheme are indistinguishable to any polynomial adversary. Since all these three components are independent of each other, the total set of tuples for R_0 and R_1 are indistinguishable. □

Note that this theorem assumes that the clients, server, and SM run the SLP protocol correctly; specifically, the server performs all tasks in the protocol correctly, although it may try to infer private information from the data it receives. In §8, we discuss the protection PrivStats provides when these parties deviate from the SLP protocol in various ways.

Note that we provide the SLP guarantees as long as clients succeed in uploading U_{id} tuples (as captured in the definition of $\mathcal{D}^*$). In the special cases when an aggregate is usually popular (so it has high U_{id}), but suddenly falls in popularity (at least quota $= 3$ times less), clients may not be able to reach U_{id}. One potential solution is to have clients volunteer to "watch" over certain sample points they do not necessarily traverse, by uploading junk tuples within the same quota restrictions, if s_{id} is significantly lower than U_{id} towards the end of the synchronization interval.

Also note that the results of an aggregate statistics are available at the server only at the end of the generation, synchronization, and upload intervals. The last two intervals are short, but the first one is as long as the time interval for which the server wants to compute the aggregate. This approach inherently does not provide real-time statistics; however, it is possible to bring it closer to real-time statistics, if the server chooses the generation interval to be short, e.g., the server runs the aggregation for every 5 minutes of an hour of interest.

5.1 Distributing the Smoothing Module

So far, we referred to the smoothing module as one module for simplicity, but we recommend the SM be distributed on the clients: this distributes the already limited trust placed on the SM. Each client will be responsible for running the SM for one or a few aggregate statistics. We denote by a *client SM* the program running on a client performing the task of the SM for a subset of the sample points. Therefore, each physical client will be running the protocol for the client described above and the protocol for one client SM (these two roles being logically separated).

A set of K clients will handle each aggregate to ensure that the SLP protocol proceeds even if $K - 1$ clients become unavailable (e.g., fail, lose connectivity). Assuming system membership is public, anyone can compute which K clients are assigned to an aggregate id using consistent hashing [23]; this approach is a standard distributed systems technique with the property that, roughly, load is balanced among clients and clients are assigned to aggregates in a random way (see [23] for more details).

The design of the SM facilitates distribution to smartphones: the SM has light load (≈ 50 times less than the server), performs two simple tasks, and uses constant storage per aggregate (see §9).

We now discuss how the the two tasks of a client SM – aggregate result decryption and maintaining the total number of tuples – are accomplished in a distributed setting.

During system setup, one of the K clients chooses a secret and a public key and shares them with the other $K-1$ clients. The server can ask any SM to decrypt the aggregate result: since the server can verify the correctness of the decryption, the server can ask a different SM in case it establishes that the first one misbehaved. Client SMs should notify each other if the server asked for a decryption to prevent the server from asking different client SMs for different decryptions. Decryption is a light task for client devices because it happens only once per aggregate.

For a given aggregate, the aggregate result will be successfully decrypted if at least one of K client SMs is available. K should be chosen based on the probability that clients become unavailable, which depends on the application. Since it is enough for only one SM to function for correctness, in general we expect that a small number for K (e.g., $K = 4$ should suffice in practice).

For maintaining the total number of tuples, we designed our staged timing protocol (Fig. 3) in such a way that client SMs need only be available for the synchronization time interval. This interval is shorter than the generation interval. A client should ask each client SM corresponding to a sample point for the value of s_{id} in parallel. Since some client may not succeed in contacting all the client SMs, the client SMs should synchronize from time to time. To facilitate client SMs synchronization, each client should choose a random identifier for the request and provide it to each client SM so that SMs can track which requests they missed when they synchronize. (As an optimization, for very popular aggregates, one might consider not trying to hide the number of tuples because the leakage is less for such aggregates. For example, an aggregate can be conservatively considered popular if there are at least 1000 clients passing per hour.)

Our strict privacy guarantees will hold for an aggregate if none of the K client SMs for that aggregate are malicious. Since the fraction of malicious clients is small in practice, our strong privacy guarantees will be achieved for most of the aggregates.

6. ACCOUNTABILITY

Since each client uploads tuples anonymously, malicious clients might attempt to bias the aggregates by uploading multiple times. In this section, we discuss PrivStats's accountability protocol, which enforces three restrictions to protect against such attacks: a quota for each client's uploads for each sample point, a total upload quota per client, and a guarantee that each sample value must be within an acceptable interval. The protocol must also achieve the conflicting goal of protecting location privacy. The most challenging part is to ensure that each client uploads within quota at each sample point; the other two requirements are provided by previous work.

We note that the SM is not involved in any part of accountability; the server will perform the accountability checks by itself. This is one of the main contributions of PrivStats: with no reliance on a (even partially or distributed) trusted party, the server is able to enforce a quota on the number of uploads of each client without learning who performed any given upload.

The idea is to have each client upload a *cryptographic token* whose legitimacy the server can check and which does not reveal any information about the client; furthermore, a client cannot create more that her quota of legitimate tokens for a given aggregate. Thus, if a client exceeds her quota, she will have to re-use a token, and the server will note the duplication, discarding the tuple.

Notation and conventions. Let SK_s be the server's secret signing key and PK_s the corresponding public verification key. Consider an aggregate with identifier id. Let T_{id} be the token uploaded by a client for aggregate id. All the values in this protocol are computed in $\mathbb{Z}_n$, where $n = p_1p_2$, two safe prime numbers, even if we do not always mark this fact. We make standard cryptographic assumptions that have been used in the literature such as the strong-RSA assumption.

6.1 Protocol

For clarity, we explain the protocol for a quota of one tuple per aggregate id per client and then explain how to use the protocol for a larger quota.

The accountability protocol consists of an efficient *zero-knowledge proof of knowledge* protocol we designed from scratch for this problem. Proofs of knowledge [15], [3], [36] are proofs by which one can prove that she knows some value that satisfies a certain relation. For example, Schnorr [36] provided a simple and efficient algorithm for proving possession of a discrete log. The zero-knowledge [15] property provides the guarantee that no information about the value in question is leaked.

System setup. The server generates a public key (PK_s) and a private key (SK_s) for the signature scheme from [10].

Client joins. Client identifies herself to Server (using her real identity) and Server gives Client one capability (allowing her to upload one tuple per aggregate) as follows. Client picks a random number s and obtains a blind signature from Server on s denoted $\mathsf{sig}(s)$ (using the scheme in [10]). The pair $(s, \mathsf{sig}(s))$ is a capability. A capability enables a client to create exactly one correct token T_{id} for each aggregate id. The purpose of $\mathsf{sig}(s)$ is to attest that the capability of the client is correct. Without the certification provided by the blind signature, Client can create her own capabilities and upload more than she is allowed.

The client keeps s and $\mathsf{sig}(s)$ secret. Since the signature is blind, Server never sees s or $\mathsf{sig}(s)$. Otherwise, the server could link the identity of Client to $\mathsf{sig}(s)$; it could then test each token T_{id} received to see if it was produced using $\mathsf{sig}(s)$ and know for which tuples Client uploaded and hence her path. By running the signing protocol only once with Client, Server can ensure that it gives only one capability to Client.

Accountability upload

1. Client $\rightarrow$ Server : Client computes $T_{\mathsf{id}} = \mathsf{id}^s \mod n$ and uploads it together with a tuple. Client also uploads a zero-knowledge proof of knowledge (ZKPoK, below in Sec. 6.2) with which Client proves that she knows a value s such that $\mathsf{id}^s = T_{\mathsf{id}} \mod n$ and for which she has a signature from the server.
2. Server $\rightarrow$ Client : Server checks the proof and discards the tuple if the proof fails or if the value T_{id} has been uploaded before for id (signaling an overupload).

We prove the security of the scheme in Sec. 6.2 and the appendix. Intuitively, T_{id} does not leak s because of hardness of the discrete log problem. The client's proof is a zero-knowledge proof of knowledge (ZKPoK) so it does not leak s either. Since T_{id} is computed deterministically, more than one upload for the same id will result in the same value of T_{id}. The server can detect these over-uploads and throw them away. The client cannot produce a different T^*_{id} for the same id by using a different s^* because she cannot forge a signature of the server for s^*; without such signature, Client cannot convince Server that she has a signature for the exponent of id in T^*_{id}. Here we assumed that id is randomly distributed.

Quotas. To enforce a quota > 1, the server simply issues a quota of capabilities during registration. In addition, the server may want to tie quotas to aggregates. To do so, the server divides the aggregates into categories. For each category, the server runs system setup separately obtaining different SK_s and PK_s and then gives a different number of capabilities to clients for each category.

Quota on total uploads. We also have a simple cryptographic protocol to enforce a quota on how much a client can upload in total over all aggregates, not presented here due to space constraints; however, any existing e-cash scheme suffices here [8].

Ensuring reasonable values. As mentioned, in addition to quota enforcement, for each tuple uploaded, clients prove to the server that the samples encrypted are in an expected interval of values (e.g., for speed, the interval is $(0, 150)$) to prevent clients from uploading huge numbers that affect the aggregate result. Such proof is done using the efficient interval zero-knowledge proof of [5]; the server makes such interval publicly available for each aggregate. We discuss the degree to which fake tuples can affect the result in section 9.2.

6.2 A Zero-Knowledge Proof of Knowledge

We require a commitment scheme (such as the one in [31]): recall that a commitment scheme allows a client Alice to commit to a value x by computing a ciphertext ciph and giving it to another client Bob. Bob cannot learn x from ciph. Later, Alice can open the commitment by providing x and a decommitment key that are checked by Bob. Alice cannot open the commitment for $x' \neq x$ and pass Bob's verification check.

Public inputs: id, T_{id}, PK_s, g, h
Client's input: s, $\sigma = \mathsf{sig}(s)$.
Server's input: SK_s

CONSTRUCTION 1. ***Proof that*** Client ***knows*** s ***and*** σ ***such that*** $\mathsf{id}^s = T$ ***and*** σ ***is a signature by*** Server ***on*** s.

1. Client *computes a Pedersen commitment to* s*:* $\mathsf{com} = g^s h^r \mod n$*, where* r *is random.* Client *proves to* Server *that she knows a signature* $\mathsf{sig}(s)$ *from the server on the value committed in* com *using the protocol in [10].*
2. Client *proves that she knows* s *and* r *such that* $T_{\mathsf{id}} = \mathsf{id}^s$ *and* $\mathsf{com} = g^s h^r$ *as follows:*
   (a) Client *picks* k_1 *and* k_2 *at random in* $\mathbb{Z}_n$*. She computes* $T_1 = g^{k_1} \mod n$*,* $T_2 = h^{k_2} \mod n$ *and* $T_3 = \mathsf{id}^{k_1} \mod n$ *and gives them to the server.*
   (b) Server *picks* c *a prime number, at random and sends it to* Client.
   (c) Client *computes* $r_1 = k_1 + sc$*,* $r_2 = k_2 + rc$ *and sends them to* Server.
   (d) Server *checks if* $\mathsf{com}^c T_1 T_2 \stackrel{?}{\equiv} g^{r_1} h^{r_2} \mod n$ *and* $T_{\mathsf{id}}^c T_3 \stackrel{?}{\equiv} \mathsf{id}^{r_1} \mod n$*. If the check succeeds, it outputs "ACCEPT"; else, it outputs "REJECT".*

This proof can be made non-interactive using the Fiat-Shamir heuristic [13] or following the proofs in [5]; due to space limits, we do not present the protocol here. The idea is that the client computes c herself using a hash of the values she sends to the server in a way that is computationally infeasible for the client to cheat.

THEOREM 2. *Under the strong RSA-assumption, Construction 1 is a zero-knowledge proof of knowledge that the client knows* s *and* σ *such that* $\mathsf{id}^s = T_{\mathsf{id}} \mod n$ *and* σ *is a signature by the server on* s*.*

Due to space constraints, the proof is presented in a longer version of this paper at `http://nms.csail.mit.edu/projects/privacy/`.

6.3 Optimization

To avoid performing the accountability check for each tuple uploaded, the server can perform this check probabilistically; with a probability q, it checks each tuple for aggregate id. If the server notices an attempt to bias the aggregate (a proof failing or a duplicate token), it should then check all proofs for the aggregate from then on or, if it stored the old proofs it did not verify, it can check them all now to determine which to disregard from the computation. Note that the probability of detecting an attempt to violate the upload quote, Q, increases exponentially in the number of repeated uploads, n: $Q = 1 - (1 - q)^n$. For $q = 20\%$, after 10 repeated uploads, the chance of detection is already 90%. We recommend using $q = 20\%$, although this value should be adjusted based on the expected number of clients uploading for an aggregate.

6.4 Generality of Accountability

The accountability protocol is general and not tied to our setting. It can be used to enable a server to prevent clients from uploading more than a quota for each of a set of "subjects" while preserving their anonymity. For example, a class of applications are online reviews and ratings in which the server does not need to be able to link uploads from the same user; e.g., course evaluations. Students would like to preserve their anonymity, while the system needs to prevent them from uploading more than once for each class.

7. AGGREGATE STATISTICS SUPPORTED

SLP supports any aggregates for which efficient homomorphic encryption schemes and efficient verification or proof of decryption exist. Additive homomorphic encryption (e.g., Paillier [30]) already supports many aggregates used in practice, as we explain below. Note that if verification of decryption by the SM is not needed (e.g., in a distributed setting), a wider range of schemes are available. Also note that if the sample value is believed to not leak, arbitrary aggregates could be supported by simply not encrypting the sample.

Table 1 lists some representative functions of practical interest supported by PrivStats. Note the generality of sum and average of functions — F could include conditionals or arbitrary transformations based on the tuple. When computing the average of functions, some error is introduced due to the presence of junk tuples because each sample is weighted by the number of uploads. However, as we show in §9.2, the error is small (e.g., $< 3\%$ for average speed for CarTel).

Note in Table 1 that count is a special case and we can make some simplifications. We do not need the SM at all. The reason is that the result of the aggregate itself equals the number of tuples generated at the sample point, so there is not reason to hide this number any more. Also, since each sample of a client passing through the sample point is 1, there is no reason to hide this value, so we remove the sample encryptions. As such, there is no need for the SM any more. Instead of contacting the SM in the sync. interval (Fig. 3), clients directly upload to the server at the same random timing.

Additive homomorphic encryption does not support median, min, and max. For the median, one possible solution is to approximate it with the mean. One possible solution is to use order-preserving encryption [4]: for two values $a < b$, encryption of a will be smaller than encryption of b. This approach enables the server to directly compute median, min, and max. However, it has the drawback that the server learns the order on the values. An alternative that leaks less information is as follows: To compute the min, a client needs to upload an additional bit with their data. The bit is 1 if her sample is smaller than a certain threshold. The server can collect all values with the bit set and ask the SM to identify and decrypt the minimum. (Special purpose protocols for other statistics are similar.)

Table 1: Table of aggregate statistics supported by PrivStats with example applications and implementation.

Aggregation	Example Application	Implementation
Summation	No. of people carpooled through an intersection.	Each client uploads encryption of the number of people in the car. Junk tuples are encryptions of zero.
Addition of functions $\sum F(\text{tuple}_i)$	Count of people exceeding speed limit. This is a generalization of summation.	Each client applies F to her tuple and uploads encryption of the resulting value. Junk tuples are encryptions of zero.
Average	Average speed or delay.	See average of functions where $F(\text{tuple}) = \text{sample}$.
Standard Deviation	Standard deviation of delays.	Compute average of functions (see below) where $F(\text{tuple}) = \text{sample}^2$ and denote the result Avg_1. Separately compute $F(\text{tuple}) = \text{sample}$ and denote the result Avg_2. The server computes $\sqrt{\mathsf{Avg}_2 - (\mathsf{Avg}_1)^2}$. This procedure also reveals average to the server, but likely one would also want to compute average when computing std. deviation.
Average of functions $\sum_{i=1}^{N} F(\text{tuple}_i)/N$	Average no. of people in a certain speed range. Average speed and delay. This is a generalization of average.	If count (see below) is also computed for the sample point, compute $\sum_{i=1}^{N} F(\text{tuple}_i)$ as above instead, and then the server can divide by the count. Otherwise, compute summation of functions, where junk tuples equal real tuples. The server divides the result by the corresponding U_{id}.
Count	Traffic congestion: no. of drivers at an intersection.	The SM is not needed at all for count computation. Clients do not upload any sample value (uploading simply $\langle \text{id} \rangle$ is enough to indicate passing through the sample point). There are no junk tuples.

8. PRIVACY ANALYSIS

We saw that if the clients, smoothing module, and the server follow the SLP protocol, clients have strong location privacy guarantees. We now discuss the protection offered by PrivStats if the server, SM, or clients maliciously deviate from our strict location privacy protocol.

Malicious server. The server may attempt to ask the SM to decrypt the value of one sample as opposed to the aggregate result. However, this prevents the server from obtaining the aggregate result, since the SM will only decrypt once per aggregate id, and we assume that the server has incentives to compute the correct result. Nevertheless, to reduce such an attack, the SM could occasionally audit the server by asking the server to supply all samples it aggregated. The SM checks that there are roughly U_{id} samples provided and that their aggregation is indeed the supplied value.

The server may attempt to act as a client and ask the SM for s_{id} (because the upload is anonymous) to figure out the total number of tuples. Note that, if the aggregate is not underpopulated, if the server asks for s_{id} at time t, it will receive as answer approximately $U_{\text{id}}(t - t_{s0})/(t_{s1} - t_{s0})$, a value it knew even without asking the SM. This is one main reason why we used the "growing s_{id}" idea for the sync. interval (Fig. 3), as opposed to just having the SM count how many clients plan to upload and then informing each client of the total number at the end of the sync. interval, so that they can scale up their uploads to reach U_{id}. Therefore, to learn useful information, the server must ask the SM for s_{id} frequently to catch changes in s_{id} caused by other clients. However, when the server asks the SM for s_{id}, the helper increases s_{id} as well. Therefore, the SM will reach the U_{id} quota early in the sync. interval and not allow other clients to upload; hence, the server will not get an accurate aggregate result, which is against its interest.

Malicious SM. Since the server verifies the decryption, the SM cannot change the result. Even if the SM colludes with clients, the SM has no effect on the accountability protocol because it is entirely enforced by the server. If the SM misbehaves, the damage is limited because clients upload tuples without identifiers, network origin, and our staged timing protocol for upload hides the time when the tuples were generated even from the SM. A compromised SM does permit SI attacks based on sample value and number of tuples; however, if the SM is distributed, we expect the fraction of aggregates with a compromised SM to be small and hence our SLP guarantees to hold for most aggregates.

The SM may attempt a DoS attack on an aggregate by telling clients that U_{id} tuples have already been uploaded and only allowing one client with a desired value to upload. However, the server can easily detect such cheating when getting few uploads.

Malicious clients. Our accountability protocol prevents clients from uploading too much at an aggregate, too much over all aggregates, and out-of-range values. Therefore, clients cannot affect the correctness of an aggregate result in this manner. As mentioned in §2, we do not check if the precise value a client uploads is correct, but we show in §9.2 that incorrect value in the allowable range likely will not introduce a significant error in the aggregate result.

Colluding clients may attempt to learn the private path of a specific other client. However, since our SLP definition models a general adversary with access to server data, such clients will not learn anything beyond the aggregate result and the SI they already knew (which includes, for example, their own paths). A client may try a DoS attack by repeatedly contacting the SM so that the SM thinks U_{id} tuples have been uploaded. This attack can be prevented by having the SM also run the check for the total number of tuples a client can upload; U_{id} for a popular aggregate should be larger than the number of aggregates a client can contribute to in a day. For a more precise, but expensive check, the SM could run a check for the quota of tuples per aggregate, as the server does.

Aggregate result. In some cases, the aggregate result itself may reveal something about clients' paths. However, our goal was to enable the server to know this result accurately, while not leaking additional information. As mentioned, clients can choose not to participate in certain aggregates (see §2).

Differential privacy protocols [11] add noise into the aggregate result to avoid leaking individual tuples; however, most such protocols leak all the private paths to the server by the nature of the model. §3 explains how the SLP and differential privacy models are complementary. A natural question is whether one can add differential privacy on top of the PrivStats protocol, while retaining PrivStats' guarantees. At a high level, the SM, upon decrypting the result, may decide how much noise to add to the result to achieve differential privacy, also using the number of true uploads it knows (the number of times it was contacted during the sync. interval). The design of a concrete protocol for this problem is future work. Related to this question is the work of Shi et al. [37], who proposed a protocol combining data hiding from the server with differentially-private aggregate computation at the server; they consider the different

End-to-end metric	Result
Setup	0.16 s
Join, Nexus client	0.92 s
Join, laptop client	0.42 s
Upload without account., Nexus	0.29 s
Upload with account., Nexus	2.0 s
Upload with 20% account., Nexus	0.6 s
Upload without account., laptop	0.094 s
Upload with account., laptop	0.84 s
Aggregation (10^3 samples)	0.2 s
Aggregation (10^4 samples)	0.46 s
Aggregation (10^5 samples)	3.1 s

Table 2: End-to-end latency measurements.

setting of n parties streaming data to a server computing an overall summation. While this is an excellent attempt at providing both types of privacy guarantees together, their model is inappropriate for our setting: they assume that a trusted party can run a setup phase for each specific set of clients that will contribute to an aggregate ahead of time. Besides the lack of such a trusted party in our model, importantly, one does not know during system setup which specific clients will pass through each sample point in the future; even the number n of such clients is unknown.

9. IMPLEMENTATION AND EVALUATION

In this section, we demonstrate that PrivStats can run on top of commodity smartphones and hardware at reasonable costs. We implemented an end-to-end system; the clients are smartphones (Nexus One) or commodity laptops (for some social crowd-sourcing applications), the server is a commodity server, and the SM was evaluated on smartphones because it runs on clients. The system implements our protocols (Fig. 2) with SLP and enforcing a quota number of uploads at each aggregate per client for accountability.

We wrote the code in both C++ and Java. For our evaluation below, the server runs C++ for efficiency, while clients and SM run Java. Android smartphones run Java because Android does not fully support C++. (As of the time of the evaluation for this paper, Android NDK lacks support for basic libraries we require.) We implemented our cryptographic protocols using NTL for C++ and BigInteger for Java. Our implementation is $\approx$ 1300 lines of code for all three parties, not counting libraries; accountability forms 55% of the code. The core code of the SM is only 62 lines of code (not including libraries), making it easy to secure.

9.1 Performance Evaluation

In our experiments, we used Google Nexus One smartphones (1GHz Scorpion CPU running Android 2.2.2., 512 MB RAM), a commodity laptop (2.13 GHz Intel Pentium CPU 2-core, 3 GB RAM), a commodity server (2.53GHz Intel i5 CPU 2-core, 4 GB RAM), and a server with many cores for our scalability measurements: Intel Xeon CPU 16 cores, 1.60 GHz, 8 GB RAM. In what follows, we report results with accountability, without accountability (to show the overhead of the aggregation protocols), and with 20% of uploads using accountability as recommended in §6.3.

Table 2 shows end-to-end measurements for the four main operations in our system (Fig. 2); these include our operations and network times. We can see that the latency of setup and join are insignificant, especially since they only happen once for the service or once for each client, respectively.

The latency of upload, the most frequent operation, is measured from the time the client wants to generate an upload until the upload is acknowledged at the server, including interaction with the SM. The latency of upload is reasonable: 0.6 s and up to 2 s for Nexus.

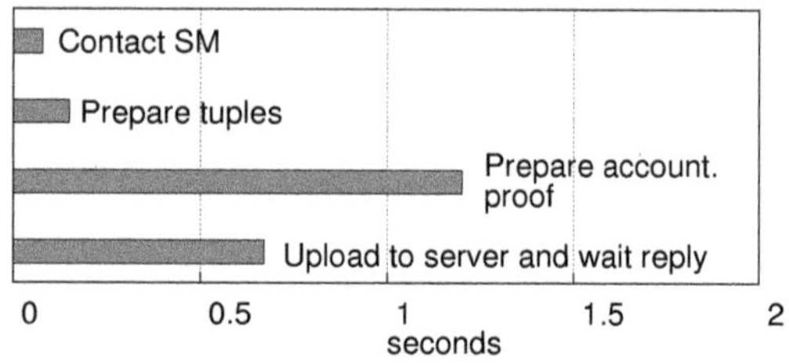

Figure 4: Breakdown of Nexus upload latency.

Server 0.29 s	Client laptop 0.46 s	Client Nexus 1.16 s

Table 3: Runtime of the accountability protocol.

Server metric	Measurement
Upload latency, with account.	0.3 s
Upload latency, no account.	0.02 s
Throughput with 0% account.	2400 uploads/core/min
Throughput with 20% account.	860 uploads/core/min
Throughput with 100% account.	170 uploads/core/min

Table 4: Server evaluation for uploads. Latency indicates the time it takes for the server to process an upload from the moment the request reaches the server until it is completed. Throughput indicates the number of uploads per minute the server can handle.

Since this occurs either in the background or after the client triggered the upload, the user does *not* need to wait for completion. Figure 4 shows the breakdown into the various operations of an upload. We can see that the accountability protocol (at client and server) takes most of the computation time (86%). The cost of accountability is summarized in Table 3.

For aggregation, we used the Paillier encryption scheme which takes 33 ms to encrypt, 16.5 ms to decrypt, and 0.03 ms for one homomorphic aggregation on the client laptop, and 135 ms to encrypt and 69 ms to decrypt on Nexus. The aggregation time includes server computation and interaction with the SM. The latency of this operation is small: 0.46 s for 10^4 tuples per aggregate, more tuples than in the common case. Moreover, the server can aggregate samples as it receives them, rather than waiting until the end.

In order to understand how much capacity one needs for an application, it is important to determine the throughput and latency at the server as well as if the throughput scales with the number of cores. We issued many simultaneous uploads to the server to measure these metrics, summarized in Table 4. We can see that the server only needs to perform 0.3 s of computation to verify a cryptographic proof and one commodity core can process 860 uploads per minute, a reasonable number. We parallelized the server using an adjustable number of threads: each thread processes a different set of aggregate identifiers. Moreover, no synchronization between these threads was needed because each aggregate is independent. We ran the experiment on a 16-core machine: Fig. 5 shows that the throughput indeed scales linearly in the number of requests.

We proceed to estimate the number of cores needed in an application. In a social crowd-sourcing application, suppose that a client uploads samples on the order of around 10 times a day when it visits a place of interest (e.g., restaurant). In this case, one commodity core can already serve about 120,000 clients.

In the vehicular case, clients upload more frequently. If n is the number of cars passing through a sample point, a server core working 24 h can thus support $\approx 24 \cdot 60 \cdot 860/n$ statistics in one day. For instance, California Department of Transportation statistics

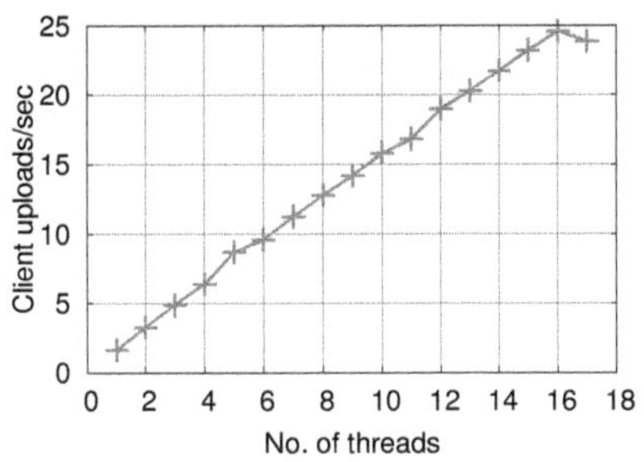

Figure 5: Throughput at the server versus number of parallel threads, showing linear scaling on a 16-core machine.

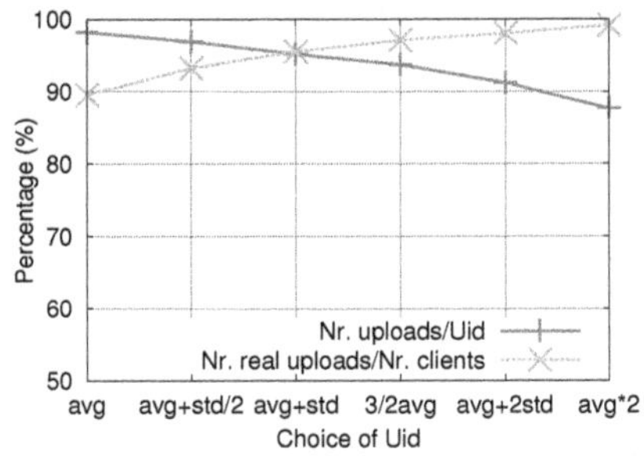

Figure 6: Total uploads at the server divided by U_{id}, and the number of clients that upload over total clients passing by a sample point.

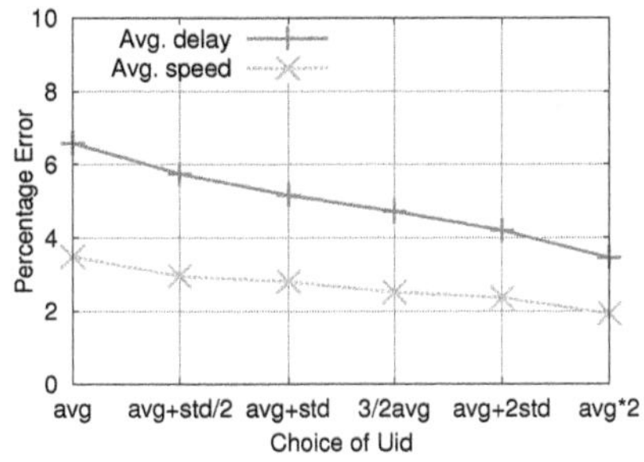

Figure 7: CarTel data showing the error in computing the average delay or speed for various choices of U_{id}.

[7] indicate that there are about $2,000$ cars on average passing in an hour through a highway lane. In this setting, one core supports about ≈ 620 different aggregates. Of course, the precise number depends on the application, but this estimation suggests our protocol is feasibly efficient.

We experimented with the SM as well; the throughput of s_{id} requests was mostly limited by how many http requests the smartphone can process. This is because the SM has very little work to do. The SM spends ≈ 140 ms for decryption and proof of decryption per aggregate (once per aggregate), and < 5ms per s_{id} request on a smartphone (once per client), while the server performs 300 ms worth of checks on a commodity server (once per client), resulting in more than 50 times more work than the SM especially when considering the different device capacities.

Bandwidth and storage usage are evaluated in a longer version of our paper to be found at `http://nms.csail.mit.edu/projects/privacy/`.

9.2 Accuracy and Effectiveness

In this section we evaluate the accuracy of our protocol and its robustness against malicious uploads. In the process, we justify recommended values for quota and U_{id}, the total number of tuples to be uploaded for aggregate id.

As mentioned in §5, we suggest quota $= 3$. Our reasoning is the following: On the one hand, we want the quota to be as small as possible to limit the error malicious clients can introduce into the aggregate. On the other hand, a quota of 1 or 2 would make it difficult for clients to upload U_{id} tuples in total: for aggregates with an unexpectedly low client turnout, participating clients need to upload more tuples in the place of missing clients to reach U_{id}.

We first analyze how much a single client can affect the aggregates by malicious uploads. Let N be the number of clients uploading for a certain aggregate, I the interval of accepted values, and μ the aggregate result when all clients are honest. For example, using the statistics in [7], N can be 2000 clients in an hour. For average speed computation, $I = (0, 100)$ mph and μ might be 60 mph, for instance. The highest change in the average that a client can induce is $\pm|I|\mathsf{quota}/N$ and the maximum fractional error is $\pm|I|\mathsf{quota}/N\mu$, where $|I|$ is the length of the interval I. We can see that if N is large (a popular area), the error introduced by a client is small. For our example, this is equal to ± 0.15 mph and 0.25% for quota $= 3$, both rather small.

Next, we evaluate the accuracy of our scheme both analytically and empirically against real traces. We obtained real traces from the CarTel project testbed, containing an average of ≈ 400 one-day paths of taxi drivers in the Boston/MA area for each month of year 2008 driving mainly through the Boston area, but extending to MA, NH, RI, and CT areas. In-car devices report segment id (a segment is a part of a road between two intersections), time, average speed on the segment and average delay on the segment. We considered that an aggregate is computed on each segment in every hour. We restricted our attention to aggregates with at least 50 drivers, which is most often the case in practice. We averaged all the results reported below over each month of the year and over all aggregates considered.

As discussed in §7, for "count" aggregates we do not need the SM and we have no U_{id}. For non-count aggregates, the choice of U_{id} imposes a mild tradeoff between accuracy of aggregate result and privacy. A low U_{id} may not allow some drivers to upload (because at most U_{id} tuples must reach the server), while a large U_{id} may be hard for clients to achieve in cases with an unexpectedly low client turnout because each client can at most upload quota tuples. If the server receives a lower number of tuples than U_{id}, the server learns some information about the clients because the number of tuples uploaded is no longer independent of the number of tuples generated. If the number of tuples uploaded tends to be close to U_{id} for most cases, then little information is leaked.

U_{id} should be chosen as a function of the historical number of uploads at an aggregate point, as follows. In Figure 6, we vary U_{id} by using combinations of avg – the average number of uploads at a sample point in all our trace over a year – and std – the corresponding standard deviation. In practice, avg and std can be obtained based on historical data or estimates of the traffic at a sample point. The decreasing line represents to what extent clients can upload U_{id} in total; as expected, this decreases as U_{id} increases. The increasing line shows the percentage of clients passing through the sample point that can upload at least one tuple. Fortunately, we can see that for most values of U_{id}, both metrics are high, typically greater than 90%. This means that our U_{id}-upload protocol is feasible to achieve in practice and does not significantly affect the accuracy of the aggregate.

Examining Fig. 6, $U_{\text{id}} = \mathsf{avg} + \mathsf{std}$ seems to be the best choice. We can gain some intuition as follows. Even if the turnout at a sample point is larger than avg by a standard deviation, most clients should still be able to upload. At the same time, U_{id} cannot be too much larger than avg for cases when there is a small turnout. We tried larger quotas of 4 and 5 and found that $U_{\text{id}} = \mathsf{avg} + (\mathsf{quota} - 1)/2 \cdot \mathsf{std}$ still represents the intersection of the lines in Fig. 6.

Finally, we examine the accuracy error introduced by our protocol for this choice of U_{id}. Count aggregates of course introduce no error. For summation-type aggregates (see §7), the increasing line in Fig. 6 provides this answer. If every value summed comes from the same distribution, the error is roughly 5% which we consider reasonable, especially since summation-type averages are less common.

For average-type aggregation (§7), the accuracy is very high: even if only a subset of the clients may be able to upload in certain cases, this subset is chosen at random from all clients passing through the sample point due to the random timing in the sync. interval (See §5 and Fig. 3). Assuming each client's value is taken from the same distribution, the expected average of tuples is equal to the real expected average; moreover, due to the law of large numbers, for popular aggregates (which therefore also have larger U_{id}), the observed average will become very close to the real one. For aggregates with as few as ≈ 100 uploads per aggregate (as is the case in Cartel), the errors were already small: Fig. 7 shows that the error in average delay is at most 5% and the error in average speed is 3%.

We do not claim that CarTel traffic patterns are representative, but one can use a similar analysis of historical data to deduce proper U_{id} for other cases. In fact, we expect our protocol to be even more effective in practice because the CarTel network is very small (≈ 30 drivers); in a system with more participants, both metrics in Fig. 6 will simultaneously be larger, many values of U_{id} will be suitable, and errors of averages smaller due to the law of large numbers.

10. RELATED WORK

Aggregate statistics for location privacy. Systems such as [16], CliqueCloak [14], [19], [24], [20], and Triplines [18], address the same problem as PrivStats. Their approaches are to use trusted parties to aggregate time-consecutive driver uploads for the same location, to avoid uploading in sensitive areas, to distort spatially and temporally locational services, or to "cloak" the data using spatial and temporal subsampling techniques.

One problem with these solutions is that they neither provide rigorous privacy guarantees nor protect against side information. As discussed in §3, even if a server only sees anonymized tuples, considerable private information can leak due to SI. For example, in [20, 18], a trusted party aggregates the upload of each driver on a piece of road with the uploads of other $k-1$ drivers close in time and location to provide k-anonymity. While one individual tuple has k-anonymity, when intersecting the sets of k-anonymity for a path, the driver may not be necessarily k-anonymous over her entire path among other drivers and their paths. And of course SI can cause further violations of k-anonymity.

Another difficulty with most of these solutions is their reliance on fully trusted intermediaries between drivers and server. For example, trusted parties in [16, 14, 18, 19] receive tuples with clients identifiers in plaintext and are supposed to remove them from the tuple. If these parties are compromised or collude with other trusted parties in the system, so are the paths of the drivers, as they have access to driver identifiers. In our work, if the SM gets compromised, the server will still only see anonymized tuples (see §8), and the use of the SM achieves stronger security.

Moreover, accountability has previously either been ignored (allowing drivers to bias significantly the aggregate result) [16, 14, 24, 20] or handled by having tuples contain driver identifiers [18, 19]. For instance, in [18, 19], users upload tuples containing their identities to a trusted party that checks if clients have uploaded too much, while another trusted party performs aggregation. If these trusted parties collude, driver paths with identities leak.

Other related work. We now discuss systems for protecting location privacy that target different but related problems.

VPriv [32] and PrETP [2] compute functions over a particular driver's path as opposed to computing statistics over the paths of *multiple* clients; for instance, they can compute the total toll that driver Alice has to pay based on how much she drove in a month. They associate the result of a function to a client's id, whereas PrivStats keeps clients anonymous and computes statistics over all clients. VPriv and PrETP also use the general zero-knowledge concept, but the actual cryptographic proofs and protocols are different from ours and inapplicable to our setting: in VPriv and PrETP, all the clients who provide data for a function must be online and perform work at the same time, which is impractical for aggregates with hundreds of clients. Moreover, these protocols do not support aggregates over data from different clients.

Furthermore, VPriv is vulnerable to side information because the server sees anonymized tuples with time and location information. VPriv acknowledges this problem, but does not solve it, leaving it for future work. PrETP also suffers from SI, but to a lesser extent than VPriv. Finally, VPriv and PrETP do not provide our type of accountability: clients can upload as many times as they desire. They have a random spot check scheme involving a trusted party that makes sure that clients upload at least once per location. Our accountability protocol uses no trusted parties, leaks no privacy, and most importantly performs different enforcements.

SEPIA [6] uses special-purpose secure-multiparty protocols to compute aggregate statistics over network traffic. However, the approach in SEPIA is not plausible in our usage scenario. Some trusted "input peers" provide network data, and a cluster of "privacy peers" performs all the computation on this data. The protocol relies on a majority of the privacy peers to not collude. In contrast to our system, these peers perform almost all computation, and if they collude, all client data is visible. Furthermore, input peers are trusted, so SEPIA does not provide any accountability checks against abusive clients. SEPIA also does not hide the number of tuples for each aggregate.

There has also been recent work by Narayanan et al. [29], Zhong et al. [41], and Puttaswamy and Zhao [33] on preserving location privacy in location-based social networking applications, an area also full of location privacy concerns. This work has a different goal than ours: it allows users to exchange location-based information with friends while protecting their privacy (against disclosure to both the server and to friends).

Shokri et al. [38] provide a framework for quantifying location privacy as a way of comparing various location privacy schemes. Given a certain adversarial goal and models of adversarial knowledge and of a location privacy scheme, the framework enables quantification of the performance of the adversary. The authors also argue that side information (which they call "prior knowledge") should be considered when analyzing privacy. However, this work has a different goal than PrivStats, does not provide a definition of privacy resilient to side information, and does not propose protocols for accountable and location private computation of aggregate statistics.

Work on e-cash [9] is related to our accountability protocol (§6): one might envision giving each client a number of e-coins to spend on every aggregate. This approach fits well in spam control applications [1, 39]. However, it is not practical in our setting: coins must be tied to a particular location, time interval, and sample type, which requires generating a prohibitively large number of coins. Other work [8] gives each user n coins for each time period. Again, we need the coins tied to sample points, so this is not feasible. Also, e-cash adds a lot of complexity (and thus slowdown) to identify double-spenders, which we do not require. Our accountability protocol is simple, specific to our setting, and fast.

Finally, we remark that our approach complements work on differential privacy [11], as we discussed in §8.

11. CONCLUSION

In this paper, we presented PrivStats, a system for computing aggregate statistics for mobile, location-based applications that achieves both strong guarantees of location privacy and protection against cheating clients. PrivStats solves two major problems not solved by previous work: it ensures that no further information leaks even in the face of arbitrary side information attacks, and it provides client accountability without a trusted party. We implemented PrivStats on commodity phones and servers, and demonstrated its practicality.

12. ACKNOWLEDGMENTS

We thank Nickolai Zeldovich, Mike Walfish, Arvind Narayanan, and the anonymous reviewers for useful comments and feedback. This work was supported in part by NSF grants 0931550 and 0716273.

13. REFERENCES

[1] M. Abadi, A. Birrell, M. Burrows, F. Dabek, and T. Wobber. Bankable postage for network services. In *ASIAN*, 2003.

[2] J. Balasch, A. Rial, C. Troncoso, B. Preneel, I. Verbauwhede, and C. Geuens. PrETP: Privacy-preserving electronic toll pricing. *Usenix Security*, 2010.

[3] M. Bellare and O. Goldreich. On defining proofs of knowledge. *CRYPTO*, 1992.

[4] A. Boldyreva, N. Chenette, Y. Lee, and A. O'Neill. Order-preserving symmetric encryption. In *EUROCRYPT*, 2009.

[5] F. Boudot. Efficient proofs that a committed number lies in an interval. *EUROCRYPT*, 2000.

[6] M. Burkhart, M. Strasser, D. Many, and X. Dimitropoulos. SEPIA: Privacy-preserving aggregation of multi-domain network events and statistics. *Usenix Security*, 2010.

[7] California Department of Transportation. Caltrans guide for the preparation of traffic impact studies.

[8] J. Camenisch, S. Hohenberger, M. Kohlweiss, A. Lysyanskaya, and M. Meyerovich. How to win the clonewars: Efficient periodic n-times anonymous authentication. In *CCS*, 2006.

[9] J. Camenisch, S. Hohenberger, and A. Lysyanskaya. Balancing accountability and privacy using e-cash. *Security and Cryptography for Networks*, 2006.

[10] J. Camenisch and A. Lysyanskaya. A Signature Scheme with Efficient Protocols. *Security and Cryptography for Networks*, 2002.

[11] C. Dwork. Differential privacy: A survey of results. In *TAMC 1-19*, 2008.

[12] E-ZPass. How it works. http://www.ezpass.com/index.html.

[13] A. Fiat and A. Shamir. How to prove yourself: Practical solutions to identification and signature problems. *CRYPTO*, 1986.

[14] B. Gedik and L. Liu. Location privacy in mobile systems: A personalized anonymization model. In *ICDCS*, 2005.

[15] S. Goldwasser, S. Micali, and C. Rackoff. The knowledge complexity of interactive proof-systems. *Symposium on the Theory of Computation*, 1985.

[16] M. Gruteser and D. Grunwald. Anonymous usage of location-based services through spatial and temporal cloaking. In *MobiSys*, 2003.

[17] M. Gruteser and B. Hoh. On the anonymity of periodic location samples. In *IEEE Pervasive Computing*, 2005.

[18] B. Hoh, M. Gruteser, R. Herring, J. Ban, D. Work, J.-C. Herrera, A. Bayen, M. Annavaram, and Q. Jacobson. Virtual trip lines for distributed privacy-preserving traffic monitoring. In *Mobisys*, 2008.

[19] B. Hoh, M. Gruteser, H. Xiong, and A. Alrabady. Enhancing security and privacy in traffic-monitoring systems. In *IEEE Pervasive Computing*, 2006.

[20] B. Hoh, M. Gruteser, H. Xiong, and A. Alrabady. Preserving privacy in GPS traces via uncertainty-aware path cloaking. In *CCS*, 2007.

[21] B. Hull, V. Bychkovsky, K. Chen, M. Goraczko, A. Miu, E. Shih, Y. Zhang, H. Balakrishnan, and S. Madden. CarTel: A Distributed Mobile Sensor Computing System. *Sensys*, 2006.

[22] N. Husted and S. Myers. Mobile location tracking in metro areas: Malnets and others. In *CCS*, 2010.

[23] D. Karger, E. Lehman, T. Leighton, M. Levine, D. Lewin, and R. Panigrahy. Consistent hashing and random trees: Distributed caching protocols for relieving hot spots on the World Wide Web. In *STOC*, 1997.

[24] J. Krumm. Inference attacks on location tracks. In *IEEE Pervasive Computing*, 2007.

[25] J. Lowensohn. Apple sued over location tracking in iOS. http://news.cnet.com/8301-27076_3-20057245-248.html, 2011. CNET News.

[26] E. Mills. Google sued over Android data location collection. http://news.cnet.com/8301-27080_3-20058493-245.html, 2011. CNET News.

[27] Mobile Millennium. http://traffic.berkeley.edu/.

[28] M. Mun, S. Reddy, K. Shilton, N. Yau, P. Boda, J. Burke, D. Estrin, M. Hansen, E. Howard, and R. West. PEIR, the personal environmental impact report, as a platform for participatory sensing systems research. In *MobiSys*, 2009.

[29] A. Narayanan, N. Thiagarajan, M. Lakhani, M. Hamburg, and D. Boneh. Location privacy via private proximity testing. *NDSS*, 2011.

[30] P. Paillier. Public-key cryptosystems based on composite degree residuosity classes. In *EUROCRYPT*, 1999.

[31] T. P. Pedersen. Non-interactive and information-theoretic secure verifiable secret sharing. *CRYPTO*, 1991.

[32] R. A. Popa, H. Balakrishnan, and A. J. Blumberg. VPriv: Protecting privacy in location-based vehicular services. *Usenix Security*, 2009.

[33] K. Puttaswamy and B. Zhao. Preserving privacy in location-based mobile social applications. *International Workshop on Mobile Computing and Applications*, 2010.

[34] R. Reid. TomTom admits to sending your routes and speed information to the police, 2011. CNET UK.

[35] P. Riley. The tolls of privacy: An underestimated roadblock for electronic toll collection usage. In *Third International Conference on Legal, Security, and Privacy Issues in IT*, 2008.

[36] C. P. Schnorr. Efficient identification and signatures for smart cards. *CRYPTO*, 1989.

[37] E. Shi, T.-H. H. Chan, E. Rieffel, R. Chow, and D. Song. Privacy-preserving aggregation of time-series data. In *NDSS*, 2011.

[38] R. Shokri, G. Theodorakopoulos, J.-Y. L. Boudec, and J.-P. Hubaux. Quantifying location privacy. In *IEEE Symposium on Security and Privacy*, 2011.

[39] M. Walfish, J. Zamfirescu, H. Balakrishnan, D. Karger, and S. Shenker. Distributed quota enforcement for spam control. In *NSDI*, 2006.

[40] WMUR. Police: Thieves robbed home based on Facebook, 2010. http://www.wmur.com/r/24943582/detail.html.

[41] G. Zhong, I. Goldberg, and U. Hengartner. Louis, Lester, and Pierre: Three protocols for location privacy. International Conference on Privacy-Enhancing Technologies, 2007.

Auctions in Do-Not-Track Compliant Internet Advertising

Alexey Reznichenko
MPI-SWS
areznich@mpi-sws.org

Saikat Guha
Microsoft Research India
saikat@microsoft.com

Paul Francis
MPI-SWS
francis@mpi-sws.org

ABSTRACT

Online tracking of users in support of behavioral advertising is widespread. Several researchers have proposed non-tracking online advertising systems that go well beyond the requirements of the Do-Not-Track initiative launched by the US Federal Trace Commission (FTC). The primary goal of these systems is to allow for behaviorally targeted advertising without revealing user behavior (clickstreams) or user profiles to the ad network. Although these designs purport to be practical solutions, none of them adequately consider the role of the ad auctions, which today are central to the operation of online advertising systems. This paper looks at the problem of running auctions that leverage user profiles for ad ranking while keeping the user profile private. We define the problem, broadly explore the solution space, and discuss the pros and cons of these solutions. We analyze the performance of our solutions using data from Microsoft Bing advertising auctions. We conclude that, while none of our auctions are ideal in all respects, they are adequate and practical solutions.

Categories and Subject Descriptors

K.4.1 [**Public Policy Issues**]: Privacy

General Terms

Design, Economics, Human Factors

Keywords

Auctions, Online Advertising, Privacy, Targeting

1. INTRODUCTION

Third-party tracking of users is widespread and increasing [17]. One of the primary purposes of user tracking is behavioral advertising. Although many companies that participate in tracking and behavioral profiling claim to not gather Personally Identifying Information (PII), it is often easy to link tracking information with PII [16]. Concern over tracking continues to grow, and has led for instance to the Do-Not-Track initiative launched by the Federal Trace Commission (FTC), and proposals for a do-not-track registry [23]. Do-not-track, however, requires a public that is largely unaware of tracking to opt-out. It also forces a trade-off between tracking and behavioral targeting: a compromise that industry is not prepared to make. Not surprisingly, do-not-track has not gained a lot of traction with the public, and ad networks are actively fighting it.

Several recent research projects take a different tack (Adnostic [24], Nurikabe [18], and Privad [13]). Rather than simply opting out of tracking, or pushing for data-protection after the fact, they propose alternative advertising technologies that allow for behavioral targeting without requiring tracking. These are meant to be practical alternatives that industry finds attractive. None of these systems, however, adequately explore how to operate the auctions that are critical to current advertising systems. Without this component, these systems leave unanswered what revenue the *broker* (i.e. an ad network like Google) can earn, thereby reducing the likelihood that a non-tracking[1] advertising system will be of commercial interest. In this paper, we look at the problem of running auctions that leverage a *user profile* for ad ranking while keeping the user profile private.

Although the non-tracking advertising systems cited above differ in significant ways, they all share several key design components. All systems propose a *software agent* that runs at the client and generates a user profile. All systems at least share the privacy goal that this profile not be revealed. All these designs propose that the broker transmit multiple ads to the client, not all of which match the user profile. For instance, the ads may all be within a given interest category. The client then locally selects from among these ads which best match the user profile, and display these to the user. The client reports the result of this selection anonymously, and without letting the broker link together different components of the user profile. The key privacy mechanisms are therefore anonymity and unlinkability.

What does this have to do with auctions? The most common pricing model for online advertising systems today is Pay Per Click (PPC): the advertiser does not pay the broker for showing an ad to a user, rather it pays only if the user clicks on an ad. The broker selects which ads to show through an auction whereby advertisers bid against each other. In a PPC system, the broker maximizes revenue by ranking the competing ads according to

CCS'11, October 17–21, 2011, Chicago, Illinois, USA.

[1]By non-tracking, we mean no third-party tracking.

the *Bid* × *ClickProbability* product, and transmitting the highest ranking ads to the client where they are displayed in rank order. Of course, the broker doesn't know the precise click probability for every ad. Rather, the broker tries to predict the click probability as best it can. This prediction is based on a number of inter-related factors such as the ad keywords, the landing page keywords, the user search terms or keywords associated with the web-page being browsed, stored user characteristics, and so on.

The user profile has a strong effect on click probability. To give a simple example, say a user searches for "running shoe". Whether the user is a man or a woman, or prefers brand-name products or discount products, plays an important role in which running shoe ad he or she is more likely to click on. In a do-not-track compliant advertising system, the broker does not know the user profile: if the auction takes place at the broker in the same way that it does today, then the user profile will not be factored into the result. Therefore the highest *Bid* × *ClickProbability* ads won't be selected, leading to less revenue than should otherwise be possible.

This paper characterizes the problem, and proposes three basic solutions, one of which is a variant of a method proposed in [12]. Following the lead of the initial work on non-tracking advertising, this paper takes a pragmatic approach to the problem. It looks for a good trade-off between strict privacy guarantees and practical business and deployment concerns. As such, this paper explores the pros and cons of the three approaches in terms of not just privacy (both user and advertiser), but also revenue, overhead, and vulnerability to attack. It uses around 2TB of auction traces from Microsoft Bing to guide and validate the design choices.

Altogether, this paper makes the following contributions: 1) It proposes two new non-tracking auction designs, and a third based on the previous work but substantially improved. 2) It analyzes the trade-offs between these three designs in terms of privacy properties, auction properties, and fraud resistance. 3) It analyzes the effect of bid churn and auction timing on revenue and ad ranking using a trace of Bing search advertising auctions, and uses this analysis to argue for the feasibility of the solutions.

2. BACKGROUND

This section describes how current online advertising systems such as Google and Microsoft work, and then describes an abstract alternative advertising model patterned after existing proposals for *non-tracking advertising*. In the process, we establish terminology and define the basic components.

2.1 Current 2nd Price Ad Systems

In current ad systems [7,11,20], *advertisers* submit *ads* to a *broker*. Associated with each ad is a *bid*, one or more *keywords*, and optionally some targeting information like demographics (location, age, gender) or interests. When a *client* computer does a search or receives a web page with *adboxes* (space to place an ad), the broker identifies the ads that match the search terms or keywords associated with the web page, and runs an auction. The auction ranks the selected ads in order of highest expected revenue (*Bid* × *ClickProbability*), and transmits some number of ads to the client. As already discussed, many factors are considered in estimating click probability. In this paper, we refer to all of these factors taken together as a *quality score* Q, where a higher value means higher expected click probability. Denoting bid as B, the ranking then is in order of the product $(B \times Q)$.

When a user clicks on an ad, the ad ID is transmitted to the broker. The broker computes Cost per Click (CPC), that is, the price that the advertiser must pay, using a *second-price auction* [8]. In this approach, the price paid is pegged to the bid of the ad that is ranked immediately below the clicked ad. To give a simple example, suppose that advertiser A is willing to pay as much as $5 for a click, and advertiser B is willing to pay $10. In a second-price auction, A could go ahead and bid $5 and B could bid $10. B would win, but would only pay incrementally more than A's (2nd-price) bid, say $5.01.

Second-price auctions allow bidders to bid the maximum that they are willing to pay, rather than frequently modify their bid in search of the value incrementally higher than the next lower bidder. Specifically, the CPC is computed as:

$$CPC = B_n \left(\frac{Q_n}{Q_c} \right)$$

where B_n and Q_n are the bid and quality score of the next lower ranked ad, and Q_c is the quality score of clicked ad. This CPC formula captures the minimum amount the advertiser would have had to bid to beat the next-ranked ad in a first-price auction. Note that it prevents the advertiser from paying more than it bid, even when the next-ranked in fact bid more.

2.2 Abstract Non-tracking Advertising

In this section, we describe an abstract non-tracking advertising system that captures key aspects of the three existing non-tracking advertising designs.

The principle components of the abstract non-tracking advertising system include those of today's tracking systems, the *broker*, the *client*, and the *advertiser*. A *user profile* is stored at the client (i.e. the user's computer, or a device trusted by the user: the distinction is not important for our purposes). Each ad is associated with targeting information. The user profile is defined as that information needed to determine how well an ad's targeting matches the user. To produce the user profile, the client monitors user behavior (i.e. the user's searching, browsing, purchases, and so on).

The privacy goals of the abstract non-tracking system are:

- Anonymity: the broker cannot associate any unit of learned information with any user PII (including network address), and
- Unlinkability: the broker cannot associate separate units of learned information with a single (anonymous) client. This prevents a broker from building up a user profile, and then associating it with a known user using externally gathered knowledge.

The broker is assumed to be honest-but-curious. We believe that this is close to reality (brokers like Google can generally be trusted to do what they claim they are doing). Nevertheless, we believe it is wise to avoid making it possible for brokers to obtain high-value information through hard-to-detect cheating, and our designs reflect this belief.

Figure 1 illustrates the basic architecture and message exchange of an abstract non-tracking advertising systems. The network layer address of all messages is anonymized, which we represent as an anonymizing proxy. Messages are encrypted to prevent viewing by the anonymizing proxy. The

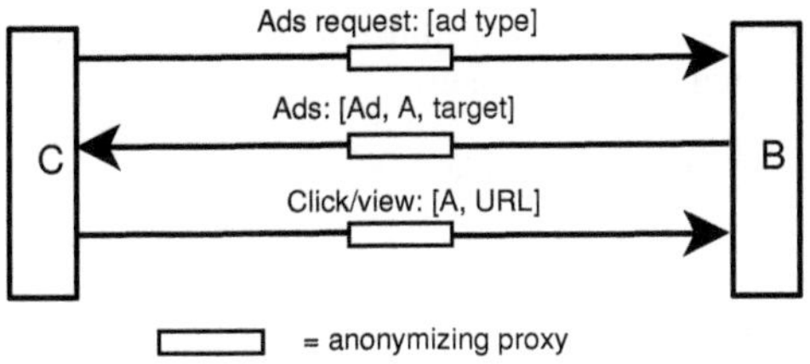

Figure 1: Abstract non-tracking advertising system. B is the broker, C is the client. Communications is through an anonymizing proxy. [x] denotes encryption of x.

client requests a set of ads of a given type (i.e. for a given product or service). The request must be generic enough that a substantial set of clients can have legitimately made the request (i.e. K-anonymity and L-diversity). A set of ads matching the type, each with identifier A and associated targeting information, are transmitted to the client and stored. When an adbox is presented to the client, for instance on a web page, the client selects among the stored ads those that best match the user profile, and puts them in the ad box for viewing by the user. The client reports the view and click of the ad A on a webpage with the given URL. There is nothing in the messages that allows the broker to link different messages as coming from the same user.

Our model has two necessary channels of communications between client and broker, ad delivery, and view and click reporting. Both channels present opportunities for the broker to learn information contained in user profiles, and current non-tracking advertising designs protect these channels. Any new information that must be conveyed for the purpose of the auction must also be protected.

3. AUCTION GOALS

The privacy goals for the auction component of a non-tracking advertising system are the same as described in Section 2: anonymity and unlinkability. This section describes the goals of the auction itself.

The primary goal of the auction in a non-tracking advertising system is to provide a second-price auction mechanism that achieves close-to-ideal ranking of ads (i.e., in order of $Bid \times ClickProbability$). For today's tracking advertising systems, leveraging the user profile is straightforward, since the broker itself accumulates and maintains this information. In a non-tracking system, the broker does not have user profile information, but does have other information that goes into the quality score Q. In other words, part of the information used to produce Q is in the broker, and part is in the client. Therefore, we define a *user score* U which directly reflects the effect of the user profile, when matched against an ad's targeting information, on click probability. We define a second quality score G, that reflects the remaining "global" information known to the broker.

Specifically, this results in an ideal ranking and CPC of:

$$Rank \Rightarrow B \times G \times U \quad (1)$$

$$CPC = B_n \left(\frac{G_n \times U_n}{G_c \times U_c} \right) \quad (2)$$

For example, U could be a positive real value greater or less than 1 that raises or lowers the click probability proportionally to its effect on the click probability defined by G. Section 7 briefly discusses how U may be computed.

In current tracking advertising systems, the click normally takes place almost immediately after the view, and so CPC is normally computed shortly after the ranking. As a result, the parameters that go into determining the ranking (B and Q) do not change much between ranking and CPC. In non-tracking advertising systems, as explained later, some time may pass between when B is set by the advertiser and when the ad is ranked, or between when an ad is ranked and when CPC is calculated. Therefore, we set the following goals with respect to ranking and CPC calculation:

- The B, G, and U used for CPC calculation are the same as the B, G, and U used for ranking. Note in particular that if they are not the same, then it is possible for instance for the CPC to be higher than the submitted bid of the clicked ad.
- The delay between ranking and CPC calculation is small enough that the churn in B, G, or U does not have a significant impact on rankings, CPC values, and broker revenue.

What exactly comprises user score U depends on the client profiler and can vary from system to system. We can, however, classify user information into three time frames. At the time frame of months or even years are user demographics like gender, location, language, age, salary, and so on. User interests can also last years (e.g. coin collecting), but more typically last weeks (a new car), days (a new pair of shoes), or minutes (a pizza). If we assume that matching ads to the content of a web page or search page increases click probability, then user score can change in seconds or less. For instance, a user might be interested in tennis and music, but the user score for tennis ads may increase while the user is looking at a tennis website, and vice versa for music ads.

We do not make any assumptions about the relative importance of B, G, or U. An ideal auction design however must allow for this flexibility.

Besides the basic goal of running an auction that leverages the user profile while prohibiting the broker from reconstructing it, there are a few additional related goals that are important:

- to maintain the privacy offered to the advertisers themselves. In particular, to prevent advertisers from learning each other's bids and budgets.
- to maintain the level of click-fraud defense in current tracking systems.
- to minimize the overhead of the auction.

As will become apparent in subsequent sections, our designs do not perfectly achieve all of these goals. Rather, our designs offer trade-offs between these goals.

Note finally that it is possible that the value of U may correlate with the probability that the user will buy the product or service being advertised assuming that the user has clicked. If this is the case, then the advertiser would want to express multiple bids as a function of U, since different U's would produce different revenues for the advertiser. We do not address this capability in this paper, but rather leave it for future work should it turn out to be important.

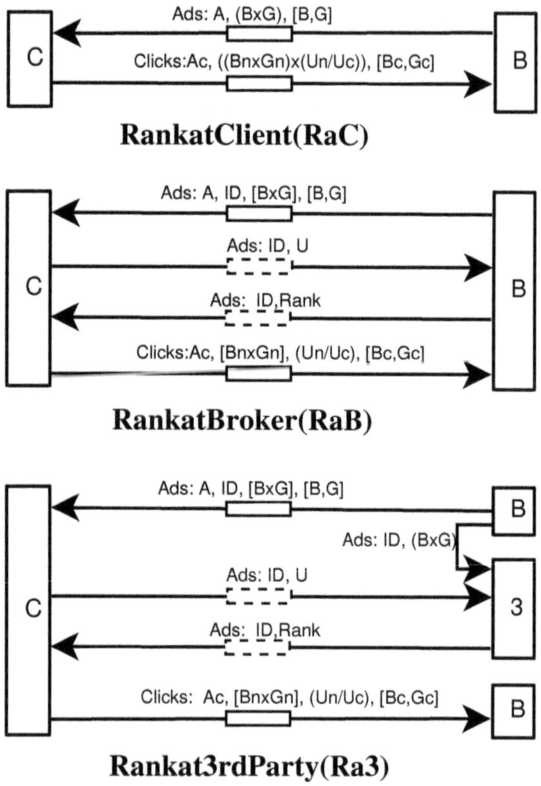

Figure 2: Three basic auction schemes. A is an ad ID unique to the ad, while ID is an Ad ID unique to the combination of ad and client. The subscripts 'c' and 'n' refer to the clicked ad and the next ranked ad respectively. [x] denotes encryption of x. Messages between client and broker pass through anonymizing proxies. Messages through solid-line proxies are encrypted. Messages though dotted-line proxies are in the clear.

4. DETAILED DESIGNS

To run the auction specified in Section 3, the system doing the ranking must have access to the bid B, the broker quality score G, and the user score U. This means that either 1) B and G are sent to the client, 2) U is sent to the broker, or 3) B, G, and U are all sent to a 3rd party (Figure 2). These basic approaches are explored in the following sections.

4.1 Rank-at-Client (RaC)

In this approach, the following information is transmitted with the ad to the client along with everything else required by the advertising system (e.g. targeting information, not shown):

A: The ad ID.

$(B \times G)$: A single value which is the product of $(B \times G)$.

$[B, G]$: The individual values B and G, encrypted with a symmetric key known only to the broker.

When a collection of ads arrive at the client, it ranks all ads using $(B \times G \times U)$. Note that in this case U is current, while $(B \times G)$ is more-or-less older. If the user clicks on an ad, then the client computes the following values and transmits them to the broker:

A_c: The ad ID of the clicked ad.

$((B_n \times G_n) \times (U_n/U_c))$: A single value which is the $(B_n \times G_n)$ product of the next-ranked ad times the ratio (U_n/U_c) of the user score of the next-ranked ad U_n and the user score of the clicked ad U_c.

$[B_c,G_c]$: The encrypted B and G for the clicked ad as received earlier from the broker.

Upon reception of this message, the broker decrypts $[B_c,G_c]$. It uses G_c and $((B_n \times G_n) \times (U_n/U_c))$ to compute the CPC as shown in Equation 2. The broker also compares the resulting CPC with the decrypted B_c. If $CPC > B_c$, then the broker knows that the client is engaged in click fraud, and the broker can ignore the message. If $CPC \leq B_c$, then the broker can accept the message, although this doesn't mean that the client is not engaged in click-fraud. Other mechanisms, such as statistical analysis, must be used to detect it as is done today.

Variation: It may not be necessary to transmit the encrypted values $[B_c,G_c]$. This is because B_c and G_c can be looked-up using the ad ID A_c. The danger here is that the looked-up values may be different from the B_c and G_c values used to rank the ads. How different depends on the level of churn in B and G values, which we found to be minimal in the Bing auction trace (Section 6). Therefore, it may well suffice to use looked-up values rather than values stored along with the ad at the client. Note that this variation applies to RaB and Ra3 as well.

4.2 Rank-at-Broker (RaB)

One concern with RaC is that the value (BxG) exposes information about the advertiser (see Section 5.1.3). This can be avoided if the ranking is done at the broker. The RaB scheme presented here is similar to the approach proposed by Privad in [12]. We present it here for completeness.

Along with the ad, the broker transmits the following to the client:

A: The ad ID.

ID: An identifier unique to this specific delivery of this ad (among all other deliveries). In other words, the same ad delivered to other clients would have a different values of ID.

$[B \times G]$: A single value which is the product of $(B \times G)$, encrypted with a symmetric key known only to the broker.

$[B, G]$: The values B and G, encrypted with a symmetric key known only to the broker.

The client computes a user score U for each ad (in the absense of knowledge of what web page the ad may be shown on). In order to obscure the user profile, the client assigns a random value for U for those ads for which the client has a very low user score (for instance because the demographic doesn't match that of the user).

Clients transmit the ID,U tuples to the broker via a proxy. These messages are not encrypted. The proxy also remembers which IDs were received from which clients.

For each received ID, the broker looks up the current values of B and G. It then uses B, G, and U to rank each received ad among a large number of recently received ads (say, those received over the last hour), and associates a rank number *Rank* to each ad. Closely ranked ads may have the same ranking number. The broker transmits the ID,*Rank* tuple back to the proxy.

The proxy looks up which client is associated with each ID, and forwards the message on to the client. The client disregards the ads related to the low user scores, and uses the remaining ranking for selecting ads to put in ad boxes.

When a user clicks on an ad, it transmits the following information to the broker:

A_c: The ad ID of the clicked ad.

$[B_n \times G_n]$: The encrypted $(B \times G)$ for the next-ranked ad received earlier.

(U_n/U_c): A single value which is the ratio of the user score of the next-ranked ad U_n and the user score of the clicked ad U_c.

$[B_c,G_c]$: The encrypted B and G for the clicked ad received earlier.

Upon reception of this message, the broker decrypts $[B_n \times G_n]$ and $[B_c,G_c]$. It uses G_c, $(B_n \times G_n)$, and (U_n/U_c)) to compute the CPC as shown in Equation 2. As with RaC, the broker also compares the resulting CPC with the decrypted B_c for click fraud.

The proxy prevents the broker from learning the identity of the client whose ads are being ranked. The per-client-per-ad unique ID prevents the proxy, which does know the client identity (network address), from learning which ad, and therefore what targeting information, is being referred to.

Even with the noise added to low user scores, we are concerned that the non-noise user scores can be interpreted at the broker as a kind of fingerprint over the set of ads (i.e., ads targeted to men should have uniformly higher scores for men, and lower scores for women). In this way, the broker could potentially tease out the profile of users.

4.3 Rank-at-3rd-Party (Ra3)

This approach is similar to RaB, but prevents the fingerprinting mentioned above. The main difference between Ra3 and RaB is that in Ra3, the broker additionally sends the unique ad IDs and $(B \times G)$ products to a 3rd party system which is trusted not to collude with the broker. This information must be delayed long enough that the 3rd party system cannot use a timing attack to correlate the values associated with a single user. This 3rd party also receives the user scores from the clients, and based on this information, ranks ads in the same way the broker does in the RaB approach. Since, unlike the broker, it does not know which ads were transmitted to the same client, it cannot fingerprint the clients.

4.4 Homomorphic Encryption Variant (RaC, RaB, and Ra3)

A variation on all three auction designs is to use homomorphic encryption (e.g., ElGamal [9]), which allows for multiplication operations on encrypted data. This may be used to defend against certain attacks by the broker as described in Sections 5.1.1 and 5.3.3. When a user clicks on an ad, the client encrypts (U_n/U_c) with the broker's public key. In the case of RaC, it also encrypts $(B_n \times G_n)$ with the broker's public key. In the case of RaB and Ra3, the broker provides the encrypted $[B_n \times G_n]$, but using its public key instead of a symmetric key. For all three schemes, the broker provides $[1/G_c]$, again encrypted with the broker's public key. Using homomorphic property of the encryption, the client is able to calculate:

$$[B_n \times G_n] \times \left[\frac{U_n}{U_c}\right] \times [1/G_c] = \left[B_n \left(\frac{G_n \times U_n}{G_c \times U_c}\right)\right]$$

and transmit the resulting value in the click report. Upon receiving a click report, broker decrypts the value to obtain the CPC. Although homomorphic encryption is relatively expensive, there is no need to do the operation in real-time. Rather, the client can do the operation when it has spare CPU cycles before transmitting, and the broker can likewise run the operations later on as batch processing.

5. AUCTION ANALYSIS

This section analyzes the three types of auctions in terms of privacy, auction quality, and attacks on the auction systems.

5.1 Privacy Properties

In this section, we look at the information that is conveyed for the sake of the auction between honest-but-curious players, and determine whether it constitutes a privacy threat. In Section 5.3 we relax this assumption.

5.1.1 *Broker analyzes* (U_n/U_c) *(RaB and Ra3)*

In order to exploit this value to gather more information about the user profile, the broker would have to first tease apart the values of U_n and U_c, then use the value combined with the ad targeting to reverse engineer the user profile, and then use the user profile knowledge to link together multiple reports. The first step may be made difficult by making (U_n/U_c) relatively coarse-grained, thus making it harder to uniquely factor out its components. The second step is made difficult simply by the sheer number of clients that are likely to have similar user scores. Thus, we conclude that exposure of (U_n/U_c) does not constitute a serious threat.

5.1.2 *Broker analyzes* $((B_n \times G_n) \times (U_n/U_c))$ *(RaC)*

This value is more difficult to reverse engineer than (U_n/U_c), and is therefore also not a threat.

5.1.3 *Client analyzes* $(B \times G)$ *(RaC)*

An advertiser can use this value to determine the broker quality score G assigned by the broker to its own ads. This can be done by the advertiser simply creating a client that receives its own ads, and using the known value of B to factor out G. Whether this is a problem needs to be decided by the broker, though we point out that today Google reveals a coarse-grained quality score to its advertising customers.

The product $(B \times G)$ to the client also reveals the overall ranking of an ad to anyone running a client, including the advertiser's competitors. From this, they can also roughly estimate the advertiser's bids. It is not clear that this is a problem, for two reasons. First, in today's advertising systems, an advertiser can see how its competitors rank relative to itself simply by observing how ads are displayed. RaC makes it easier and cheaper to obtain this ranking information, but does not fundamentally change an advertiser's ability to do so. Second, historically in traditional advertising (print, TV, radio), advertisers can monitor how much advertising their competitors do, and can generally know the cost of that advertising. While certainly all things being equal advertisers would like to keep this information secret, historically the inability to do so has not, for the most part, prevented companies from advertising.

If exposing the product $(B \times G)$ to the client is an acceptable privacy loss, then RaC should be the preferred auction method for its overall simplicity and lower overhead. If it is not acceptable, then RaB and Ra3, which both avoid exposing this information, may be preferred.

5.2 Auction Properties

In this section, we discuss the various shortcomings of each of the approaches with respect to the auction properties, especially ranking results and revenue.

5.2.1 System delays

There are several potential delays in the non-tracking advertising systems that can change both the rankings and the computed CPC. With RaC, there is a delay between when the ad was transmitted and adbox time when the ranking takes place. With RaB and Ra3, there is a delay between when the ranking occurs and adbox time when the ranking is actually used. In either case, the bid B or the broker quality score G used for ranking may no longer be correct, and an out-of-date ranking takes place.

During the design of the auction approaches, these delays were a major concern. As it turns out, at least for the auction data from Bing search advertising auctions (Section 6), the delays have only a minor impact on both broker revenue and advertiser costs, even when the delay is several hours or a day. Nevertheless, this may not be the case for other systems or future systems, and so it remains important that these delays are engineered to be minimal. This could be done, for instance, by having clients frequently request small numbers of new ads.

5.2.2 Client selection

A problem encountered by non-tracking advertising is that the broker does not know which clients are the best clients to send an ad to. For instance, suppose that some number of clients M have requests ads for watches. The broker does not know which clients may be interested in cheap watches, and which in expensive. The advertiser, however, might not have enough budget to pay for all the clicks that would result if all watch ads are sent to all interested users.

Lets assume that the broker knows the clicks per delivered-ad rate. From this, it can determine the number of clients N that should receive the ad without exhausting the advertisers budget. If it randomly chooses N clients among the interested clients, then it will not be sending all ads to the most interested clients.

One way to solve this problem is for the broker to go ahead and send the ad to all interested clients, but to also send a parameter giving the minimum user score that a client must have in order to show the ad. This way, only the best matching clients will show the ad. The broker may be able to establish the expected click per delivered-ad rate for various user scores, and therefore predict the setting of the user score based on the number of clients. If the broker predicts too high, then it can lower the minimum user score and send this to clients, thus causing more clients to show the ad.

5.2.3 Auction Scope

An important aspect of the auction is the scope of the auction, by which we mean the set of ads that compete in any given auction. As a general rule, the more ads that compete, the higher the CPC. This is simply because the more ads there are, the more probabilistically likely the next-ranked ad will have a $(B \times G \times U)$ closer to that of the clicked ad. On the other hand, the larger the auction scope, the less fair it is in the sense that very different types of ads must compete. A local pizza store may not wish to compete with Mercedes for ad boxes.

The auction scope for search or contextual systems like Bing and Google is the set of ads whose keywords match that of the search or web page. Today's ad exchanges, where advertisers bid in real time, typically for adboxes on premium publishers, have a potentially much broader scope because any advertiser can bid. The auction scope in a non-tracking advertising system is tunable. It may be all ads in a client, or all ads within an ad type (i.e. an interest). What's more, interests may be hierarchical (sports/tennis/clothing/shoes), and may be more general or more specific, thus allowing for substantial flexibility in auction scope.

5.3 Attacks

In this section, we relax our assumption of honest-but-curious players, and consider a number of malicious attacks and defenses.

5.3.1 Client click fraud

The client can commit a form of click fraud by lying about the value of $((B_n \times G_n) \times (U_n/U_c))$ (RaC) or (U_n/U_c) (RaB or Ra3). By inflating or deflating these values, the client can cause advertisers to pay more or less, and cause publishers to earn more or less. At a high level, this is very similar to normal forms of click fraud that occur today, and in this sense our auctions do not allow fundamentally new forms of click fraud. Privad describes how to defend against click-fraud even with anonymizing brokers [12]. The same method may be used here. The basic idea is that the proxy tags reports with a per-report unique identifier. If the broker suspects click fraud, it informs the proxy of the report ID of the suspicious report. If a given client is suspected more times than some threshold, its reports can be tagged by the proxy as coming from a suspected client. In some cases the broker may suspect click fraud simply because the 2nd price is impossibly high (i.e. higher than the 1st price bid). In most cases, however, the broker may suspect click fraud through statistical analysis of the reports for given advertisers or publishers.

5.3.2 Proxy fingerprints client user scores and resulting ranking (RaB and Ra3)

It is difficult but conceivable in RaB and Ra3 that the proxy could determine user profiles through observation of the client user scores and rankings. For instance, the proxy could establish a number of fake clients that pretend to have various profile attributes, and establish fingerprints of the resulting user scores and rankings. One way to do this might be to determine $(B \times G)$ given user scores and corresponding ad ranks, and use these values as the fingerprint. The proxy could then compare these fingerprints with the corresponding fingerprints of real clients. It could be that the signal-to-noise ratio is high enough to successfully pull off this attack. One way to prevent this would be to encrypt user scores and rankings. The user scores could be encrypted using the brokers (RaB) or 3rd-party's (Ra3) public key, and the rankings could be encrypted using symmetric keys created by the clients and conveyed securely to the broker or 3rd-party. These symmetric keys would be frequently modified to prevent the broker or 3rd-party from linking user scores with the same client, and possibly launching a similar fingerprint attack.

5.3.3 *Broker manipulates* $[B_n \times G_n]$ *(RaB, Ra3)*

A malicious broker could launch an attack on a non-tracking advertising system to identify clients by inserting unique IDs into the encrypted fields $[B, G]$ or $[B \times G]$. Once a client is identified in this way, unlinkability is lost, and the broker can build up client profiles. The broker can then potentially identify the client through external means. There is some cost to this approach, as the broker must "waste" ads to do the tracking[2]. The homomorphic encryption variant described in Section 4.4 defends against this attack. Because the client multiplies the received encrypted fields with other fields, the values generated by the broker are obscured.

5.4 Discussion

RaB, which was proposed in [12], is a weak system because it opens up a fingerprinting attack at the broker. Ra3 solves this problem, though at the expense of requiring yet another administratively distinct and non-colluding system. Nevertheless, we consider it to be better than RaB.

If exposing the $(B \times G)$ product to the client is not a problem for the broker and advertisers, then RaC is better than Ra3 because it is simpler, incurs less overhead and latency, and does not require the 3rd party. In addition, it has no issues here with respect to user score churn, because ranking takes place at ad view time. If exposing $(B \times G)$ is a problem, however, then Ra3 appears to be a reasonable approach.

6. EFFECT OF CHURN

Section 5.2 describes how various delays in all three auction systems may distort rankings and CPC computation. How detrimental this delay is depends on how much churn there is. Churn may affect rank, CPC value, and ultimately revenue. RaC is affected by churn in B and G, while RaB and Ra3 are additionally affected by churn in U. In this section, we use trace data from Microsoft's Bing advertising platform to study in depth the effect of auction delays on B and G from both the advertiser and broker perspective. We find that, while churn exists, it has only a negligible impact on broker revenue and advertiser costs.

6.1 What Causes Churn?

$B \times G$ for an ad changes when either B or G changes. B can change in one of three ways: first, the advertiser can manually update the bid; second, the ad network can automatically update the bid (as directed by the advertiser); third, a 3rd-party may update the bid on the advertiser's behalf. Each of these has different churn characteristics:

Advertiser: Manual updates, we believe, cause very little churn since they are reactive over a long feedback cycle. Advertisers receive updated campaign information (i.e. how many clicks, actual amount charged, budget left) at fairly coarse intervals (few times a day). This limits the number of informed changes to their campaigns.

Ad Network: The advertiser can invoke functionality provided by the ad network to optimize his bidding strategy. For example, the ad network may allow the advertiser to set a preferred rank (e.g. position 4), and the ad network automatically lowers or raises the bid to satisfy the request based on the market. Other examples may include automatically modifying bids to meet a target number of impressions per day (while still being charged only for clicks), or modifying bids based on time of day etc. Some of this functionality (e.g. modify bids based on time-of-day) can be implemented in the client and would therefore not result in any added churn. Other functionality (e.g. preferred rank) tends to be implemented today as a periodic update (once every few hours).

3rd Party: Search Engine Optimization (SEO) companies optimize their client's bidding strategy in real-time [6] e.g. based on trending terms, real-time click-through rates, etc. This could potentially result in high bid churn, however, due to the premium nature of these SEO services, only a small number of ads would be affected.

Aside from changes in B, G can also change. Recall G in our model is a function of what the broker knows: G is computed based on the ad (past CTR, landing page quality, etc.). G is largely a property of the ad itself, which we don't expect to change quickly or dramatically. In any event, our Bing auction trace unfortunately does not allow us to validate our assumption since it does not isolate user-derived components of G from other components.

6.2 How Does Churn Affect Auctions?

Today auctions take place at the time when an ad is displayed to the user; ranking and CPC calculations can immediately reflect any changes in B or G. Privacy preserving auctions described in Section 4 are limited in terms of how fast new B and G information can be incorporated. Since G does not rapidly change over time or can be engineered to remain relatively stable (e.g., using U to reflect short-term changes in click probability), the main source of churn is the changes in B. To understand the effects of churn in B values, we simulate auctions that use stale B information for ranking and CPC computation, and then compare the resulting ranking and CPC computation with auctions that use up-to-date B information.

6.3 Dataset

For our trace driven simulations, we sampled around 2TB of log data from Bing's auction engine spanning a 48 hour period starting September 1, 2010. The data covers over 150M auctions for over 18M unique ads shown to North American Bing search users across all search topics. The trace record for an auction lists all the ads that participated in it (whether the ad was ultimately shown or not), the bids corresponding to each ad, the corresponding quality scores,

[2]One might argue that the same attack can be launched simply be creating unique Ad IDs transmitted in the clear. However, this attack can at least be detected by third parties, for instance running honey-farms of clients.

and which if any of the ads were ultimately clicked by the user.

6.4 Methodology

We re-compute auction rankings and the CPC for each auction in our dataset using stale bid information; we vary staleness from 1 minute to 2 days.

Auction rankings are re-computed using bid and quality data from the trace. Since our trace does not show when the advertiser updated the bid, we infer the time based on multiple auctions that a given ad participates in. If the bid for the ad is the same for two consecutive auctions, we infer that the bid did not change during that interval. If the bid is different, we infer that the bid changed sometime between the two auctions; we use the mid-point as the time of change. To simulate an auction at time T with stale information from d minutes ago, we simply use the bids current as of time $T-d$ in our trace. The quality score in the trace is based on user features (e.g. search query), which correspond to U in private auctions; since the client always has the current value of U we use the same quality score for simulated auctions as in the trace.

CPCs are re-computed based on the re-computed auction rankings (using the second-price formula of Equation 2). In other words, for an adbox at time T in the trace, we compute the ranking based on bid values recorded at time $T - d$ and populate the adbox using resulting ranking. If the user clicked on an ad in this adbox, the bid of the next lower ranked ad B_n that we use in the CPC computation is the stale B_n taken at time $T - d$.

One limitation we face is that we cannot predict the change in user behavior when auction rankings change. Consider, for example, two ads A_1 and A_2 where in the trace they are ranked 1 and 2, while in the simulated stale auction they are ranked 2 and 1 respectively. If the user clicked A_2 in the trace, what might we expect the user to click in our simulation? One option is to model the user as clicking the same ad he clicked in the trace; thus in this case the user clicks A_2 in the simulation. Another option is to model the user as clicking the same position he did in the trace; in this case the user clicks position 2 (A_1 in the simulation). In reality, the user model is neither of these two extremes — it is well-known that both ad content and rank effect click-through rates (CTR) [10]. To account for this, we simulate 5 user models: 1) same position, 2) 75% same position and 25% same ad, 3) 50%-50%, 4) 25% same position and 75% same ad, and 5) same ad. Thus we establish an envelope of possible user behavior to get a sense of the upper- and lower-bounds of our simulation results. Note that always clicking on the same ad is a strictly conservative estimate. This is because an ad that was clicked in the trace but is not shown to the user in our simulation (due to being ranked too low) would not get clicked; at the same time, under the same-ad model, an ad that was not shown in the trace (due to being ranked too low) and was therefore not clicked would have no chance of getting clicked even if it were to be shown to the user in the simulation. This asymmetry biases the simulation towards fewer clicks (and therefore lower revenues). The only user model immune to this limitation is the same-position model.

A second limitation we face is that we cannot predict how advertisers would change their bidding strategy in response to auctions being based on stale information. Enterprising advertisers or SEOs, may for instance, attempt to predict what bid they might want to make 1hr hence, and enter it into the system well in advance. Advance bidding would reduce the effective staleness of information. For our purposes, we assume the bidding strategy does not change.

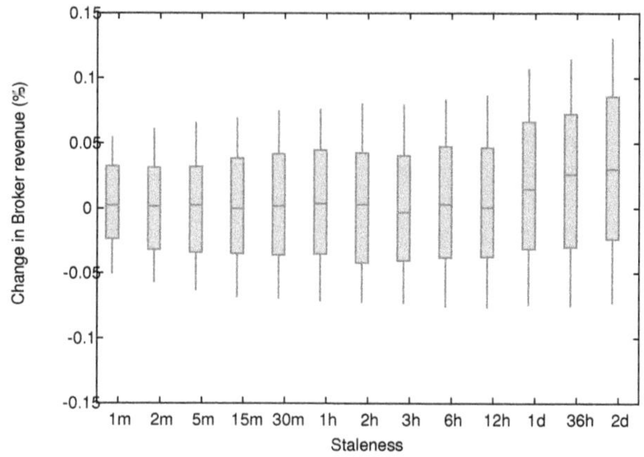

Figure 3: Change in broker revenue

6.5 Simulation Results

Overall our simulations show that there is no appreciable change in broker revenue for using stale bid information; even in the most conservative cases, the revenue is within ±0.1% of today. For advertisers, while stale bids affect their auction rankings, they do so in a balanced manner with cases of higher-than-today rank canceling out cases of lower-than-today rank resulting in zero net change.

Figure 3 plots the change in broker revenue compared to today as a function of the staleness of information used and the user model. The x-axis varies the stateless of bids from 1 minute to 2 days. The box-and-whisker plot varies the user model with the top whisker showing the outcome where the user clicks the same position, and the bottom whisker showing when the user clicks the same ad; the top edge of the box shows 75% same position and 25% same ad, and vice versa for the bottom edge of the box; the line in the middle shows the 50%-50% case.

The first observation we make from Figure 3 is that under a 50-50 user model, change in revenue is practically 0% even with bid information as stale as up to 12 hours. Under the 75-25 and 25-75 models, the change is almost always between ±0.05%, and only in the extreme cases 100-0 or 0-100 does it pass ±0.1%. More importantly, the change increases very gradually. This is good news since it means a private advertising system would not have a hard delay deadline beyond which there would be disproportionate change in revenue. Instead the system can strive to do the best it can, and reduce revenue change proportionally. The extremely gradual rate of change also means that system design trade-offs can be biased towards scalability and other engineering goals without much concern to revenue since it changes very little in the first place.

At first blush the effect of the "same-ad" user-model appears to be to reduce the revenue, but this is deceptive. As mentioned earlier, the more the user clicks on the same-ad (going from 0% to 100% from the top whisker to bottom), the more biased the simulation is towards fewer clicks and

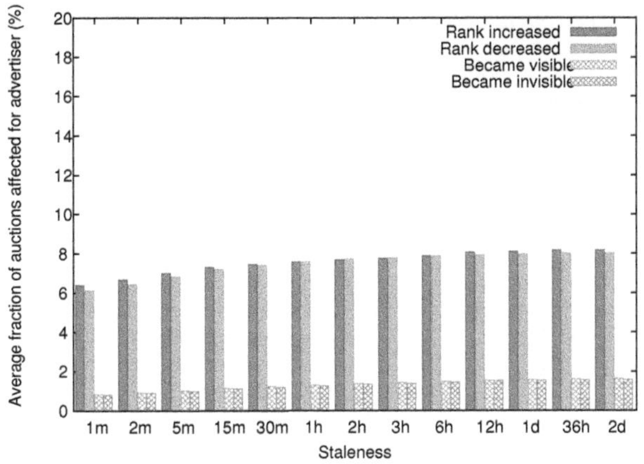

Figure 4: Fraction of auctions with modified rankings

therefore less revenue. Recall that only the top-whisker is unaffected by this simulation bias.

The second observation we make from Figure 3 is the slight upwards trend of the top-whisker signifying higher revenues as more stale information is used. This suggests a consistent trend of advertisers (as a whole) reducing their bids over time. We don't know the cause of this trend.

Next we turn to the advertiser perspective. We compute for each ad the fraction of auctions where the user-visible simulated ranking increased or decreased compared to the trace, and whether the ad became visible or invisible due to being ranked high-enough or too-low as compared to the trace. Figure 4 plots the average of these numbers across all ads as a function of the staleness of bid information used.

We first observe that both increased ranks and decreased ranks are roughly equal, and so average to nearly zero. The same is true for ads becoming visible or invisible. While this is consistent with the revenue change in Figure 3 averaging out to zero, we note that there are other ways the revenue could average out to zero while being unfair to advertisers. For instance, fewer increased ranks could have been compensated by more cases where the ad became visible thus still resulting in zero revenue change while being unfair to the advertiser; luckily, this is not the case.

We observe next that there is a very small impact of staleness on change in ranks; it begins with around 12% of auctions for 1 minute stale data, and quickly converges to around 16%. The reason this number is high is because of the cascade effect — if a single ad jumps from a low rank to a high rank, it causes all the ads in between to register a "change" in rank; thus a single change in bid can affect up to ten ads. The impact, however, is very little; the ad jumping from low to high might register a change of 10 ranks, however, the other 10 ads would register a change of only 1 rank each (not captured in the graph). Overall we found a median *net change* of 1 rank for every 820 auctions the ad participates in.

To summarize, based on extensive simulations across varying degrees of staleness and different user-models, there is little impact on broker revenue as compared to today, and little impact on advertiser fairness as compared to today.

7. COMPUTING USER SCORE

So far, we have assumed the existence of a user score U that, when multiplied with the quality score G produces the expected click probability at the client for a given ad. Because clicks are relatively rare, it may be difficult to estimate U at the client based purely on the click history of the client. Therefore, we require that the broker anonymously and unlinkably gathers detailed click statistics from clients in order to improve click probability estimates at individual clients. In what follows, we sketch out an approach.

There are a number of measurable attributes $X = \{x_1, x_2, ... x_L\}$ at the client that may help in prediction of click probability. For instance, the level of interest (high or low) in the ad's product or service, the quality of the match between the targeting and the user, the context of the webpage, as well as the user's historic CTR. The idea is that each client reports this information anonymously to the broker for each ad that it views and clicks. These reports contain: {Ad-ID, X, click}, where X is the values of the attributes, and 'click' indicates whether or not the ad was clicked. Given this information from many clients, the broker can determine the effect of the attributes on click probability, and convey this information to the client as a function f of the attributes such that $U = f(X)$, along with the ad. This allows the client to compute U by measuring the attributes and plugging them into the provided function. As mentioned, U in RaC can be computed at viewing time with the latest set of attributes without churn issues since that's when the ranking takes place. The function f for a new ad can be initially set to that of similar existing ads until enough data for the new ad is gathered. The details of this are left as future work.

One concern is that the set of attribute values X is unique for a given user. Several factors can mitigate this concern. First, the attributes may be fairly coarse-grained, thus broadening the set of users to which they apply. Second, some of the attributes may be hard to correlate using external knowledge, such as the user's CTR. Third, attributes like level of interest change from interest to interest, and even within an interest over time, and therefore are hard to link to the same user. Fourth, some attributes are not specific to the user, for instance webpage context. Finally, the only information beyond the attribute values that is leaked is the ad viewed. In particular, the user's click-stream is not exposed. We believe that it is reasonable to establish public policies that determine the nature of the attributes in such a way that meaningful privacy is preserved.

8. RELATED WORK

There is a substantial body of work on cryptographic protocols for privacy preserving auctions. Depending on the underlying security model these proposals can be classified into the following three categories. In the first category, there are protocols that rely on computation that is distributed among auctioneers who jointly determine the outcome of an auction using threshold multi-party computation (e.g., [14, 15, 22]). The second category of protocols introduces a semi-trusted third party, aka an "auction issuer" or "auction authority", in addition to the auctioneer, and uses asymmetric multi-party computation technique, such as Yao's garbled circuit (e.g., [1, 2, 5, 19, 21]). Finally, protocols in the third category allow bidders to cooperatively compute the auction outcome without relying on any trusted third party (e.g., [3,4]). The primary goal of all these proposals, and many others not cited, is to keep bids and selling price secret from the auctioneer and other auction participants. The problem that we address in this paper is different. This paper is primarily concerned with protecting the user, not the bidder (i.e. advertiser). Indeed the user does not exist in the prior work. In any event, the high computational and communication complexity imposed by aforementioned secure auction protocols make them impractical for our problem.

9. SUMMARY AND FUTURE DIRECTIONS

This paper addresses the challenge of designing an online advertising auction for a non-tracking advertising system that leverages the user profile information while keeping the user profile private. We broadly explore the design space, proposing three types of auctions, and analyzing their properties with respect to privacy, auction quality and vulnerability to attack. Overall, we find that two of the systems, Rank-at-Client (RaC) and Rank-at-3rd-Party (Ra3), are very acceptable designs. RaC is simpler and more efficient, but has the drawback that information about ad quality and bid is leaked. On the other hand, this is information that can today be determined by placing ads and monitoring the resulting ranking. Finally, noting that our auction designs suffer delays that cause out-of-date bid information to be used in rankings, we use Bing advertising system auction trace to determine the effect of these delays. We find the effect to be very minimal, and so conclude that our auction designs are viable.

As future work, we plan to implement the auction system to operate with a medium-scale deployment of Privad planned for next year (several 10's of thousands of users). Along with this, we plan to design and deploy mechanisms to compute U, and measure their effectiveness. We also plan to do a measurement study of ads served by Bing to determine to what extent advertisers can reverse-engineer each other's bids in today's systems. This will quantify how much advertiser privacy loss is incurred by the Rank-at-Client scheme. Each of the non-tracking advertising schemes so far proposed makes the tacit assumption that there is only a single broker, and a single profiler operating at each client. We are interested in exploring what happens if there are multiple brokers with competing profilers in each client. In particular, the profilers should be able to dynamically compete for ad boxes in real time, thus adding a new element to the auction that is not unlike the way ad exchanges operate today. What's more, these clients may also need to compete with existing tracking advertising systems in real-time auctions run by existing ad exchanges. We plan on designing and testing mechanisms that allow this.

10. REFERENCES

[1] M. Abe and K. Suzuki. M+ 1-st Price Auction Using Homomorphic Encryption. In *Proceedings of the 5th International Workshop on Practice and Theory in Public Key Cryptosystems*, pages 115–124. Springer-Verlag, 2002.

[2] O. Baudron and J. Stern. Non-interactive Private Auctions. In *Proceedings of the 5th International Conference on Financial Cryptography*, pages 364–378. Springer-Verlag, 2002.

[3] F. Brandt. Fully private auctions in a constant number of rounds. In *Proceedings of the 7th international conference on Financial cryptography*, pages 223–238. Springer-Verlag, 2003.

[4] F. Brandt and T. Sandholm. Efficient privacy-preserving protocols for multi-unit auctions. In *Proceedings of the 9th international conference on Financial cryptography and Data Security*, pages 298–312. Springer-Verlag, 2005.

[5] C. Cachin. Efficient private bidding and auctions with an oblivious third party. In *Proceedings of the 6th ACM conference on Computer and communications security*, pages 120–127. ACM, 1999.

[6] S. Clifford. Instant Ads Set the Pace on the Web. *The New York Times*, 2010. `http://tinyurl.com/yl8dt29`.

[7] DoubleClick. DART for Advertisers. `http://www.doubleclick.com/products/dfa/index.aspx`, 2009.

[8] B. Edelman, M. Benjamin, and M. Schwarz. Internet Advertising and the Generalized Second-Price Auction: Selling Billions of Dollars Worth of Keywords. *American Economic Review*, 97(1):242–259, Mar. 2007.

[9] T. ElGamal. A public key cryptosystem and a signature scheme based on discrete logarithms. *Information Theory, IEEE Transactions on*, 31(4):469–472, 2002.

[10] J. Feng, H. Bhargava, and D. Pennock. Implementing sponsored search in web search engines: Computational evaluation of alternative mechanisms. *INFORMS Journal on Computing*, 19(1):137, 2007.

[11] Google, Inc. AdWords: Advertise Your Business on Google. `http://adwords.google.com/`.

[12] S. Guha, B. Cheng, and P. Francis. Privad: Practical Privacy in Online Advertising. In *Proceedings of the 8th Symposium on Networked Systems Design and Implementation (NSDI)*, Boston, MA, Mar 2011.

[13] S. Guha, A. Reznichenko, K. Tang, H. Haddadi, and P. Francis. Serving Ads from localhost for Performance, Privacy, and Profit. In *Proceedings of HotNets '09*.

[14] H. Kikuchi. (M+ 1) st-Price Auction Protocol. In *Proceedings of the 5th International Conference on Financial Cryptography*, pages 351–363. Springer-Verlag, 2002.

[15] H. Kikuchi, S. Hotta, K. Abe, and S. Nakanishi. Distributed auction servers resolving winner and winning bid without revealing privacy of bids. In *Parallel and Distributed Systems: Workshops, Seventh International Conference on, 2000*, pages 307–312. IEEE, 2000.

[16] B. Krishnamurthy and C. Wills. On the Leakage of Personally Identifiable Information Via Online Social Networks. In *Proceedings of WOSN '09*.

[17] B. Krishnamurthy and C. Wills. Privacy diffusion on the web: A longitudinal perspective. In *Proceedings of the 18th International Conference on World Wide Web (WWW '09)*, Madrid, Spain, 2009.

[18] D. Levin, B. Bhattacharjee, J. R. Douceur, J. R. Lorch, J. Mickens, and T. Moscibroda. Nurikabe: Private yet Accountable Targeted Advertising. Under submission. Contact `johndo@microsoft.com` for copy, 2009.

[19] H. Lipmaa, N. Asokan, and V. Niemi. Secure Vickrey auctions without threshold trust. In *Proceedings of the 6th international conference on Financial cryptography*, pages 87–101. Springer-Verlag, 2002.

[20] Microsoft, Inc. Start advertising on Yahoo! Search and Bing. `https://adcenter.microsoft.com/`.

[21] M. Naor, B. Pinkas, and R. Sumner. Privacy preserving auctions and mechanism design. In *Proceedings of the 1st ACM conference on Electronic commerce*, pages 129–139. ACM, 1999.

[22] K. Sako. An Auction Protocol Which Hides Bids of Losers. In *Proceedings of the Third International Workshop on Practice and Theory in Public Key Cryptography*, pages 422–432. Springer-Verlag, 2000.

[23] Stanford. Do Not Track Universal Web Tracking Opt-Out. `donottrack.us`.

[24] V. Toubiana, A. Narayanan, D. Boneh, H. Nissenbaum, and S. Barocas. Adnostic: Privacy Preserving Targeted Advertising. In *Proceedings of NDSS '10*.

Practical PIR for Electronic Commerce*

Ryan Henry
Cheriton School of Computer Science
University of Waterloo
Waterloo ON Canada N2L 3G1
rhenry@cs.uwaterloo.ca

Femi Olumofin
Cheriton School of Computer Science
University of Waterloo
Waterloo ON Canada N2L 3G1
fgolumof@cs.uwaterloo.ca

Ian Goldberg
Cheriton School of Computer Science
University of Waterloo
Waterloo ON Canada N2L 3G1
iang@cs.uwaterloo.ca

ABSTRACT

We extend Goldberg's multi-server information-theoretic private information retrieval (PIR) with a suite of protocols for privacy-preserving e-commerce. Our first protocol adds support for single-payee tiered pricing, wherein users purchase database records without revealing the indices or prices of those records. Tiered pricing lets the seller set prices based on each user's status within the system; e.g., non-members may pay full price while members may receive a discounted rate. We then extend tiered pricing to support group-based access control lists with record-level granularity; this allows the servers to set access rights based on users' price tiers. Next, we show how to do some basic bookkeeping to implement a novel top-K replication strategy that enables the servers to construct bestsellers lists, which facilitate faster retrieval for these most popular records. Finally, we build on our bookkeeping functionality to support multiple payees, thus enabling several sellers to offer their digital goods through a common database while enabling the database servers to determine to what portion of revenues each seller is entitled. Our protocols maintain user anonymity in addition to query privacy; that is, queries do not leak information about the index or price of the record a user purchases, the price tier according to which the user pays, the user's remaining balance, or even whether the user has ever queried the database before. No other priced PIR or oblivious transfer protocol supports tiered pricing, access control lists, multiple payees, or top-K replication, whereas ours supports all of these features while preserving PIR's sublinear communication complexity. We have implemented our protocols as an add-on to Percy++, an open source implementation of Goldberg's PIR scheme. Measurements indicate that our protocols are practical for deployment in real-world e-commerce applications.

General Terms

Algorithms, Design, Security

Categories and Subject Descriptors

K.4.4 [**Computers and Society**]: Electronic Commerce—*security, payment schemes*; H.2.0 [**General**]: Security, integrity, and protection; H.2.4 [**Database Management**]: Systems—*distributed databases, query processing.*

*An extended version of this paper is available [36].

Keywords

Private information retrieval, PIR, e-commerce, access control, zero-knowledge proofs, privacy-enhancing technologies, PETs.

1. INTRODUCTION

Private information retrieval (PIR) provides a means of querying a database without the database being able to learn any information about the query [22]. In multi-server PIR, ℓ database servers each possess a replica of the database and a user submits his query to some size-k (or larger) subset of these servers in such a way that no server (or coalition of servers up to some threshold t) can learn the user's query. One can view the database X as consisting of n bits organized into r records, each of size $b = n/r$ bits. We follow the usual convention of specifying a PIR query by the index i of interest. Thus, in a PIR query, the user retrieves the record at index i without the servers learning any information about i. We note, however, that existing approaches allow one to build queries that are more expressive on top of this basic setup; for example, keyword-based lookups [21] or simple SQL queries [48]. Using these techniques in conjunction with the ideas in this paper is straightforward.

Existing multi-server PIR schemes offer information-theoretic privacy protection for the user's query, but they allow a dishonest user to obtain additional information, such as the record at index $j \neq i$, or the exclusive-or of some subset of records in the database [31]. However, for many real-world applications, protecting database privacy by preventing dishonest users from learning extra information about the database is advantageous. Examples abound in online sales of digital goods, such as a pay-per-download music store [1] where users must pay for each song they download, a pay-per-retrieval DNA database [17], a stock-information database [31], or a patent database [2]. In all of these practical situations, it is necessary to guarantee the seller of these digital goods that users learn exactly the database record of interest and nothing more. In some scenarios it may even be desirable to sell database records according to a *tiered pricing plan* whereby different users pay different prices for each record depending on, e.g., their membership status or geographic location.

Symmetric private information retrieval (SPIR) [31] adds an additional restriction to PIR that prevents the user from learning information about any records except for the one he requested, thus addressing the need for simultaneous user and database privacy; however, no existing SPIR scheme supports both (tiered) record-level pricing and access control lists. Some oblivious transfer (OT) schemes [1, 17–19] offer one or the other of these functions, but no scheme in the literature provides them both. Moreover, OT schemes generally have no requirement for sublinear communication complexity, which renders them useless for online sales of some types of digital goods, such as multimedia data, where the bandwidth requirement is high. Some schemes even require the user to download an encrypted copy of the *entire database* (e.g., [17–19]) and later purchase decryption keys for individual encrypted records. This allows one to amortize the cost of many transactions, but renders the scheme unsuitable for applications in which the contents of the database change frequently. Storing the database in an encrypted format also limits the usefulness of the database for other applications that need ready access to the cleartext data. Other OT-based schemes [1] require the database servers to store state information, such as the number of purchases made by a user, or his remaining balance, which might leak information about the user's queries or enable the server to link his purchases.

In this paper, we present a protocol that extends the open-source PIR scheme by Goldberg [33] to a priced symmetric private information retrieval (PSPIR) scheme offering tiered pricing with record-level granularity. Our initial PSPIR construction is a simple 'single payee' scheme wherein a single *content provider* (CP) sells digital goods through a distributed database and collects all proceeds from these sales. We then extend this simple scheme in three important ways. First, we introduce a slight modification to the protocol that enables the database servers to control access to individual records by implementing group-centric access control lists. Next, we propose a novel top-K replication strategy that makes it possible for the database servers to periodically identify and replicate the K most popular records to a smaller database — i.e., to construct a bestsellers list — thus facilitating more efficient retrieval for these most popular items. Finally, we show how to adapt the single-payee scheme to scenarios in which multiple (possibly competing) CPs sell their own digital goods through a common database and, using a distributed bookkeeping protocol, determine to what portion of the proceeds from these sales each seller is entitled. These enhancements provide a stronger and more realistic model of private information retrieval that enables e-commerce to coexist happily with strong privacy protection.

In our model, users belong to different pricing tiers and pay (perhaps different amounts) for each record; moreover, the database may require users to have explicit authorization to access some or all of the records in the database. In particular, tiered pricing logically groups users into different price tiers and allows the database to set the price and availability of each record with respect to each tier (a price tier is then roughly analogous with a *group* in the context of access control). Our approach enforces these constraints without revealing the user's price tier to the servers during a protocol run. Thus, when combined with an anonymous communications channel, our protocols maintain user anonymity in addition to query privacy; that is, the database servers do not learn any information about the identity nor the query of the user. More specifically, queries do not leak information about the index or price of the purchased record, the price tier according to which the user pays, the user's remaining balance, or even whether the user has ever queried the database before.

Outline.

We organize the remainder of this paper as follows: §2 introduces our system model, including our design goals and threat model, and an example use case for our scheme. §3 presents our notation and the basic building blocks we use in our protocols. Our main contribution follows in §4, where we describe each of our constructions in depth. In §5, we discuss our implementation and the results of some empirical performance evaluations we ran on it. We then proceed to differentiate our approach from related solutions in §6, and finally conclude the paper with a summary in §7.

2. SYSTEM MODEL

Our basic scenario consists of three parties: the *user* interested in purchasing digital goods, the *server* having a database containing potentially tens or hundreds of gigabytes of data that is divided into r records (or files), and the *bank*, an independent issuer of digital *wallets* (see below). We build our scheme from multi-server information-theoretic PIR; thus, the server is actually comprised of ℓ independent PIR servers that each hosts a complete replica of the database. Users submit their queries to any subset of at least $k > \ell/2$ servers of their choosing. We associate one or more price lists $\vec{p}_1, \ldots, \vec{p}_T$ with the database, where there are T tiers and each price list specifies a price for each of the r individual records. For simplicity, we represent price lists by length-r vectors of nonnegative integers (or $\perp$ to indicate that a record is unavailable in this price plan), although representations that are more efficient are typically possible and using one of these representations changes the protocols only superficially. Users' wallets are kept with any non-rerandomizable (one-show) anonymous credential scheme, such as that of Brands [10] or that of Au *et al.* [3]; the wallet encodes as attributes a *balance* and the index π of the price list according to which the owner of that wallet must pay, called that user's *price tier* or simply his *tier*. (For example, one price tier might apply to members while another price tier might apply to non-members; in general, any number of tiers may exist, although a large number of tiers might adversely affect system performance.) The tier π is encoded in the credential in a special way: each wallet encodes a collection of T attributes $x_1, \ldots, x_T$ such that $x_i = 1$ if $i = \pi$ and $x_i = 0$ otherwise. The bank initially issues each user with a wallet encoding the balance 0; users may charge their wallets at any time using, e.g., a prepaid credit card obtained via cash transaction from a grocery store. We make no assumptions regarding noncollusion between the bank and the database servers; indeed, it is not even required that the bank and database servers be different entities, although synchronization challenges may emerge in the case of a distributed bank. We do not discuss the full semantics of the bank, since this is not our focus in this paper and such details depend on the chosen credential system.

To query for the record at index β, the user must first prove that his wallet encodes sufficient funds to purchase that particular record according to his tier. To do so, the user must send his current wallet to each of at least k servers, which makes the task of detecting double spending particularly easy (via the pigeonhole principle) since the wallet is not rerandomizable and $k > \ell/2$. Along with his query response, the user receives a cryptographically signed *receipt* encoding the price paid for the query and the wallet used to make the payment. The user then uses this receipt to *refresh* his wallet with the bank; i.e., to obtain a new wallet (which is unlinkable to his old wallet) encoding his new remaining balance. This refreshing step does not reveal any information to the bank about the user's (old or new) balance, his tier, or the price encoded in the receipt.

Before discussing our constructions in further detail, we first present our high-level design goals and our threat model, as well as some motivation by way of a simple example use case that uses our full suite of protocols.

2.1 Design goals

We are interested in enhancing Goldberg's PIR protocol to yield a scheme with the following properties.

Utility.

In addition to PIR's standard functionality, we seek to provide the database servers with the following capabilities.

Tiered pricing: Users pay predetermined amounts for each retrieved record. The system assigns each user to a price tier and the prices they pay depend on both this tier and the particular records they purchase.

Access control: The database servers may set the availability of each record with respect to users of each price tier.

Replication: The database servers can dynamically learn which records are most popular without revealing information about individual users' query patterns. This allows popular records to be accessed at a lower computation and communication cost than their less popular counterparts.

Bookkeeping: A common database may sell records from multiple CPs while ensuring that each CP receives the correct share of profits based on sales of its own records.

Security and privacy.
Traditional databases can already offer all of the above functionality, and more. What makes our situation unique is that we wish to provide this functionality while offering strong privacy protection, both for users and for CPs.

Correctness: Users with sufficient funds and privileges can always retrieve a consistent copy of their desired record.

Query privacy: The database servers and bank learn no nontrivial information about the records accessed by a user.

User anonymity: The database servers and the bank learn only that 'some user with sufficient funds and privileges retrieved some record'; i.e., they learn no other information about a user's identity (including whether or not this user has previously queried the database), the price he pays for a record, or the past or present balance encoded in his wallet.

Database privacy: Dishonest users cannot learn any extra information about database records that they do not purchase.

Practicality.

Computational cost: Any increase in the computational cost of the underlying PIR scheme should be small and scale sublinearly in n and at most linearly in r.

Query size: The size of users' queries should increase by no more than a small multiplicative factor as compared to the underlying PIR scheme. Furthermore, the size of the query response should increase by no more than a small additive constant.

Round complexity: The protocols should add at most one additional round of interaction to the PIR protocol, per query.

2.2 Threat model

We consider a threat model in which users of the system are potentially malicious, while database servers and CPs (as well as the bank) are honest-but-curious (i.e., semi-honest); however, Goldberg's PIR scheme — and by extension, our own proposed scheme — is robust against some threshold of malicious database servers as well. Users of our system have obvious incentives for being malicious; for example, they may wish to learn about records that they cannot afford (or for which they simply do not want to pay), or to retrieve records for which they do not have authorization. Moreover, in e-commerce situations, unscrupulous competitors may try to subvert the bookkeeping and replication functionality by acting as users and submitting specially crafted, malformed queries. The system must provide the database servers with strong security guarantees against all such attacks.

Honest-but-curious database servers may collude among themselves (and the bank) to try to reveal the identity of a user, the price tier or balance encoded in his wallet, or the content of his queries. The system should be secure against attacks on user anonymity regardless of who may be colluding with whom, and should be secure against attacks on query privacy provided an honest majority exists among the database servers.[1] Malicious database servers may also try to compromise the integrity of the system by refusing to respond to user queries or by returning incorrect results in an effort to prevent a user from obtaining his desired record or a valid receipt. The system should be robust to some number of malicious database servers and should allow affected users to learn the identity of whichever servers misbehave. We do not consider the case of an actively malicious bank, but we do note that a fair exchange protocol such as the one proposed by Camenisch *et al.* [18] can also mitigate threats associated with a malicious bank.

We argue that our assumption of semi-honest database servers is realistic for many practical e-commerce scenarios, particularly in the multiple-payee variant of our protocol where the CPs themselves may host some or all of the database servers. In this setting, several distinct and possibly competing CPs cooperate to provide a value-added service to their customers (i.e., a privacy-preserving way to purchase their digital goods). On the one hand, the CPs have a vested interest in cooperating, since providing this service to their customers would otherwise be infeasible. On the other hand, competing CPs have an incentive not to divulge additional information about customer spending to one another, lest this information help the other CPs gain a competitive advantage over them.

2.3 A hypothetical use case

As a hypothetical use case to motivate our protocols, we consider an online seller of e-books akin to Amazon's Kindle Store. One can easily envision similar use cases for other online retailers (e.g., Google's Android Market); we consider an e-book store because the size of these increasingly popular digital goods makes them ideal candidates for distribution using PIR. In light of the Amazon's 2010 lawsuit against the state of North Carolina seeking to prevent the disclosure of customer purchase records [44], we also feel it is especially fitting to demonstrate how our platform could replace Amazon's current e-book sales model to provide a more privacy-friendly experience for customers, and to mitigate the risk of such egregious attacks on privacy in the future.

Suppose a number of independent publishers wish to team up to form a privacy-preserving alternative to the Kindle Store, wherein users can purchase electronic copies of these publishers' books without revealing their identities or facilitating the construction of privacy-invasive dossiers detailing their purchasing habits.[2]

Each publisher hosts a database server containing a replica of the entire e-book catalogue and users purchase e-books from this data-

[1] Of course, if sufficiently many database servers collude to reveal the content of a user's query, they may learn some information about that user's identity; for example, by noting if the user retrieves a record that is only available to certain tiers of users, or by making inferences based on external knowledge. We cannot protect against such attacks, so in these cases we aim only to minimize the information made available to the adversary.

[2] If the publishers desire an Amazon-style recommendation system, existing approaches to privacy-preserving targeted advertising [34, 38, 56] may apply; however, we leave further investigation of this idea for future work.

base using PSPIR. Periodically, (for example, weekly) the publishers cooperate to learn to what portion of the profits each is entitled. They also use this opportunity to determine the top-K best sellers, which they subsequently replicate to a smaller database to facilitate faster purchases of these books. Much like Amazon does with the Kindle Store [26], the publishers can sell the same e-book to users that are registered in different geographical locations for different prices, thus enabling them to recoup costs associated with, e.g., service fees incurred by offering customers free 3G service to purchase their books from a mobile device.

3. BUILDING BLOCKS

This section introduces our notation and the cryptographic primitives that we use in our construction.

For notational convenience, we use δ_{ij} to denote the well-known Kronecker delta function; that is, $\delta_{ij} = 1$ if $i = j$, and $\delta_{ij} = 0$ otherwise. We also define the complementary Kronecker delta function, $\bar{\delta}_{ij} = (1 - \delta_{ij})$. We use $\mathbb{Z}_m$ to denote the ring of integers modulo m (or the finite field of order m when m is prime); we will represent elements of $\mathbb{Z}_m$ by elements of $\{0, \ldots, m-1\}$. $\mathbb{Z}_m[x]$ denotes the ring of polynomials with coefficients in $\mathbb{Z}_m$, and $(\mathbb{Z}_m)^r$ the set of length-r vectors over $\mathbb{Z}_m$ (and similarly for $(\mathbb{Z}_m[x])^r$). We write $a \in_R \mathbb{Z}_m$ to mean that a is selected uniformly at random from $\{0, \ldots, m-1\}$. The notation $a \| b$ denotes concatenation (as strings) of values a and b. $\kappa \in \mathbb{N}$ is a parameter used to tune the soundness versus performance of certain zero-knowledge proofs.

Let $\mathbb{G}_1$, $\mathbb{G}_2$ and $\mathbb{G}_T$ be cyclic groups of prime order q (which we shall express multiplicatively). We assume throughout the existence of a bilinear pairing function $e : \mathbb{G}_1 \times \mathbb{G}_2 \to \mathbb{G}_T$; we also assume that $g, h \in \mathbb{G}_1$, $\hat{g} \in \mathbb{G}_2$ and $g_T, h_T \in \mathbb{G}_T$ are known generators of their respective groups, where $g_T = e(g, \hat{g})$ and $h_T = e(h, \hat{g})$. The crucial property of e is that of bilinearity: $e(g^a, \hat{g}^b) = e(g, \hat{g})^{ab}$ for all $a, b \in \mathbb{Z}_q$. If $\mathbb{G}_1 = \mathbb{G}_2$, the pairing is called *symmetric*; otherwise it is *asymmetric*. Elements of $\mathbb{G}_1$ in asymmetric pairings are shorter than in symmetric pairings. The pairing e we assume in this work is asymmetric.

3.1 Shamir secret sharing

We make extensive use of Shamir's polynomial secret sharing scheme [54] to share field elements among the servers. An element $a \in \mathbb{Z}_q$ is shared by choosing a polynomial $f_a(x) = a_t x^t + \cdots + a_1 x + a \in \mathbb{Z}_q[x]$ with each non-constant coefficient $a_i \in_R \mathbb{Z}_q$ and the constant term equal to the shared value; server j's share of a is then $f_a(j) \in \mathbb{Z}_q$. Any subset of at least $t+1$ servers can cooperate to reconstruct a using Lagrange interpolation [45, Ch. 12]; however, t or fewer colluding servers cannot deduce any nontrivial information about a. Such a scheme is called a $(t+1, \ell)$-threshold secret sharing scheme, since a threshold of at least $t+1$ out of ℓ servers must cooperate to recover the secret value. In general, any choice of $0 < t < \ell$ will suffice, however our top-K replication protocol requires that $t \le \lfloor (\ell - 1)/2 \rfloor$. We recommend $t = \lfloor (\ell - 1)/2 \rfloor$, which ensures that the protocols are secure whenever an honest majority exists among the servers. We write $[a]_q$ to denote a Shamir secret sharing of $a \in \mathbb{Z}_q$ among the ℓ servers; that is, $[a]_q = \langle f_a(1), \ldots, f_a(\ell) \rangle$ where the jth component of this vector is known only to server j.

Computing with Shamir secret shares.

Suppose $[a]_q$ and $[b]_q$ are two shared secrets and $c \in \mathbb{Z}_q$ is a public scalar. We write $[a]_q \oplus [b]_q$, $[a]_q \ominus [b]_q$ and $[a]_q \odot [b]_q$ to denote the component-wise sum, difference and product, respectively, of $[a]_q$ and $[b]_q$ (and similarly for $[a]_q \oplus c$, $[a]_q \ominus c$ and $[a]_q \odot c$). Observe that $[a]_q \oplus [b]_q = [a+b]_q$ and $[a]_q \ominus [b]_q = [a-b]_q$ (and similarly for $[a]_q \oplus c$ and $[a]_q \ominus c$), and that $c \odot [a]_q = [c \cdot a]_q$. Moreover, the product $[a]_q \odot [b]_q$ yields a $(2t+1, \ell)$-threshold sharing of $a \cdot b$; thus, when $t \le \lfloor (\ell - 1)/2 \rfloor$ as we require above, the servers can still interpolate to recover this product.

It is possible to construct algorithms for more complex operations using the above facts; e.g., distributed pseudorandom number generation [4], testing equality [25], or evaluating order predicates [46]. Indeed, we implicitly use these more complex operations for top-K replication, but do not discuss them in depth. The interested reader can consult Nishide and Ohta's paper [46] for further details on how to implement them.

3.2 Goldberg's PIR scheme

Goldberg's PIR scheme [33] is a multi-server information-theoretic scheme with good support for query robustness against colluding servers. It provides a t-private v-Byzantine-robust k-out-of-ℓ scheme for $0 < t < k \le \ell$ and $v < k - \lfloor \sqrt{kt} \rfloor$ protection. In other words, users submit their queries to at least k out of the ℓ servers, and the system can tolerate up to v servers being Byzantine (i.e., responding incorrectly) without inhibiting the ability of users to retrieve the correct record, and t servers colluding without compromising users' query privacy. The scheme also optionally supports τ-independence [30], a property that prevents the database servers from learning the contents of the database with information-theoretic protection against coalitions of up to τ servers.

The scheme structures the n-bit database X as an $r \times s$ matrix D over $\mathbb{Z}_q$, where r is the number of records, b is the size of each record (in bits), $w = \lfloor \lg q \rfloor$ is the word size, and $s = b/w$ is the number of words per record. For minimal communication, $b = \sqrt{wn}$. The user's query is a standard basis vector $\vec{1}_\beta \in (\mathbb{Z}_q)^r$, which has all elements 0 except for index β where it is 1. The scheme uses Shamir secret sharing to split $\vec{1}_\beta$ into k parts $\vec{\rho}_1, \ldots, \vec{\rho}_k$, which the user sends to the respective PIR servers.

A user queries for the record at index β by choosing a vector of r polynomials, $\vec{f} = \langle f_1, \ldots, f_r \rangle$, each of degree (at most) t, with uniformly random coefficients from $\mathbb{Z}_q$ for the non-constant terms. The constant term of f_i is $\delta_{i\beta}$. In addition, the user chooses k distinct server indices $I_1, \ldots, I_k$ and forms k vectors of $\mathbb{Z}_q$ elements by evaluating $\vec{f}$ component-wise at the k respective indices; that is $\vec{\rho}_j = \langle f_1(I_j), \ldots, f_r(I_j) \rangle$. The user forwards $\vec{\rho}_j$ to server I_j, while each server I_j computes an s-element vector $R_j = \vec{\rho}_j \cdot D$ and returns it back to the user. Finally, the user computes the record at index β from the R_j by using Lagrange interpolation (and also Guruswami-Sudan list decoding [35] if some servers are Byzantine or malicious).

3.3 Threshold BLS signatures

The BLS signature scheme [8] is a 'short' signature scheme that uses a pairing function for signature verification. The signer's private signing key is a random integer $x \in \mathbb{Z}_q$, and the corresponding public verification key is $(\hat{g}, \hat{g}^x)$ (recall that $\hat{g}$ is a generator of $\mathbb{G}_2$). Given the signing key x and a message m, the signature is computed via $\sigma = h^x$ where $h = \text{hash}(m)$ is a cryptographic hash of m; the verification equation is $e(\sigma, \hat{g}) \stackrel{?}{=} e(h, \hat{g}^x)$. We use the (k, ℓ)-threshold variant (and also the (k, k)-threshold variant) of BLS signatures; in both cases, the signing keys are evaluations of a polynomial of degree $k - 1$ and the master secret is the constant term of this polynomial. The user recombines signature shares via Lagrange interpolation in the exponent. Note that by publishing the individual 'verification key shares' of each signer, threshold BLS signatures provide some level of robustness against Byzantine signers since each signature share can also be verified independently by using the signer's public verification key share.

3.4 Polynomial commitments

Polynomial commitments [40] allow a prover to form constant-sized commitments to polynomials in such a way that a verifier can later use these commitments to confirm evaluations of the committed polynomials without revealing any additional information about them. We use the $\texttt{PolyCommit}_{\text{DL}}$ construction of Kate *et al.* [40], which provides unconditional hiding if the commitment is opened to at most $t-1$ evaluations (for a degree-t polynomial) and computational hiding under the discrete log (DL) assumption if the polynomial is opened at a tth point ($t+1$ or more openings is sufficient to interpolate and thus recover the committed polynomial), as well as their $\texttt{PolyCommit}_{\text{Ped}}$ construction, which offers unconditional hiding even when t evaluations are revealed. Their constructions are based on the polynomial remainder theorem: if f is a polynomial, then the remainder obtained by dividing $f(x)$ by $x-r$ equals $f(r)$; in other words, $x-r$ divides $f(x)-f(r)$. We describe how $\texttt{PolyCommit}_{\text{DL}}$ works, and refer the reader to [40] for details on the similar $\texttt{PolyCommit}_{\text{Ped}}$ construction. A commitment to the polynomial $f(x) = a_t x^t + \cdots + a_1 x + a_0$ in $\texttt{PolyCommit}_{\text{DL}}$ has the form $C_f = (g^{\alpha^t})^{a_t} \cdots (g^{\alpha})^{a_1} g^{a_0} = g^{f(\alpha)}$, where α is secret, $g \in \mathbb{G}_1$ is a generator, and all bases (as well as $\hat{g}$ and $\hat{g}^{\alpha}$) are part of the commitment scheme's public key. If $\texttt{PolyCommit}_{\text{Ped}}$ commitments are used, then the public key includes the additional values $h^{\alpha^t}, \ldots, h^{\alpha}, h$, where $h \in \mathbb{G}_1$ is a generator whose discrete logarithm with respect to g is unknown. To open an evaluation of f at $x = r$, the prover invokes $\texttt{CreateWitness}\,(f, r)$, which outputs a polynomial commitment w to the quotient obtained upon division of $f(x) - f(r)$ by $x - r$; the commitment w is called a *witness*. The verifier can confirm the claimed evaluation by checking if $\texttt{Ver}\,(C_f, r, f(r), w) = \left[e(C_f, \hat{g}) \stackrel{?}{=} e(w, \hat{g}^{\alpha}/\hat{g}^{r}) \cdot e(g, \hat{g})^{f(r)}\right]$ is $\texttt{true}$. Note that in [40], polynomial commitments are constructed over a symmetric pairing, whereas in this work we construct our polynomial commitments over an asymmetric pairing, since we wish to reuse this pairing for *short* threshold BLS signatures.

Much like traditional discrete logarithm commitments [27] and Pedersen commitments [52], polynomial commitments are additively homomorphic and scalar multiplication of committed values can be computed by exponentiating the commitment by the scalar. We exploit both of these facts extensively in our protocols.

3.5 Zero-knowledge proofs

Our protocols employ several standard zero-knowledge proofs (ZKPs) from the literature: proofs of knowledge of a committed value [53], range proofs [9] to prove that a committed value is non-negative, proofs of knowledge of a discrete log representation of a number [11], and proofs that a commitment opens to the product of the openings of two other commitments [20]. We refer the interested reader to the respective papers for more details on each of these proofs, or to [16] for a self-contained treatment of all of the aforementioned proofs. We also use some efficient batch proof techniques [6, 7] to achieve practicality in our protocols; the rest of this section describes these batch proofs.

3.5.1 *Proving equality of 1-out-of-r discrete logs.*

We combine the batch verification techniques of Bellare *et al.* [6, 7] with Cramer *et al.*'s [24] technique for proving the disjunction of two or more propositions to yield efficiently verifiable proofs of equality of 1-out-of-r discrete logarithms. That is, given bases g and h and two sets of inputs $g_1, g_2, \ldots, g_r$ and $h_1, h_2, \ldots, h_r$, to prove the predicate $\bigvee_{i=1}^{r} \left(\log_g(g_i) = \log_h(h_i)\right)$ without revealing which particular statements are true and which are false.

A detailed description of how to implement this proof is provided in Appendix A, and it is proved secure by Bellare *et al.* [7, Theorem 2.2].

3.5.2 *Proving that a vector of commitments opens to a standard basis vector.*

We introduce a new proof that allows one to efficiently prove that a vector of r commitments opens to an r-dimensional standard basis vector (i.e., a length-r vector containing a single 1 and the rest 0). Our proof uses a special case of the batch proof of equality of 1-out-of-r discrete logarithms from the previous section as a subroutine. In particular, we use the special case in which $g_1 = g_2 = \cdots = g_r$ and the h_i are all different, but $\log_{h^\gamma}(h_i) = a_i$ is known to the verifier, where γ is randomly chosen by the prover and unknown to the verifier. In our protocol, the prover actually wishes to prove to the verifier that the *vector of polynomials* committed to by a vector of polynomial commitments evaluate to a standard basis vector at $x = 0$. However, modifying our approach as described here to handle other types of commitments (e.g., Pedersen commitments) is straightforward and modifying it to handle different evaluation points is trivial.

Let $\vec{a} = \langle a_1, \ldots, a_r \rangle \in_R (\mathbb{Z}_{2^\kappa})^r$. The key observation behind our approach is as follows: if $\vec{v}$ is a standard basis vector, then $\vec{v} \cdot \vec{a} = a_i$ for some $1 \le i \le r$; conversely, if $\vec{v}$ is not a standard basis vector, then with high probability $\vec{v} \cdot \vec{a} \ne a_i$ for any $1 \le i \le r$.

A detailed description of how to implement this proof is provided in Appendix B, and it is proved secure in the extended version of this paper [36, Appendix A].

3.5.3 *Batch verification of evaluations of polynomial commitments at a common point.*

In [40], Kate *et al.* show how to open *a single polynomial commitment* to *a set of evaluations* at the same time with a single witness element, a technique they call *batch opening*. We flip this proof around and show how to verify the evaluations of *a set of polynomial commitments* at *a single point*, a technique we call *batch verification*. Batch verification can be either *cooperative* or *noncooperative*. The cooperative form of the protocol is interactive (though it can be made noninteractive using the Fiat-Shamir heuristic [28]), and uses only a single witness element, while the noncooperative form is noninteractive and uses one witness element per commitment. As the name implies, the noncooperative form of batch verification does not require the prover's cooperation; i.e., only the verifier changes. In particular, the verifier combines all of the witnesses (and commitments) into a single witness (and commitment) at verification time to significantly reduce verification time at the cost of a negligible decrease in soundness.

A detailed description of how to implement cooperative batch verification is provided in Appendix C, and it is proved secure in the extended version of this paper [36, Appendix B].

4. CONSTRUCTIONS

We now describe the full details of our constructions. We develop our scheme incrementally in three steps. First, we describe how to convert Goldberg's multi-server PIR into SPIR. We then describe the basic single-payee PSPIR construction and show how to extend it to support access control lists. Finally, we discuss our approach to bookkeeping and use this to add support for top-K replication and to construct multiple-payee PSPIR.

4.1 Symmetric PIR construction

The first step in our construction is to convert Goldberg's PIR scheme into SPIR; that is, we augment the scheme to enforce the additional property that no query will ever reveal information about more than a single record, under some mild computational assumptions. This property implies that no coalition of users can use knowledge obtained from one or more PIR queries to learn any information about a record that they did not purchase in one of those queries. We accomplish this with the aforementioned proof that a vector of commitments opens to a standard basis vector. In particular, the user (querying servers with indices $I_1, \ldots, I_k$ for the record at index β using his current wallet, `wallet`) does the following:

1. chooses $\vec{f} = \langle f_1, \ldots, f_r \rangle \in_R (\mathbb{Z}_q[x])^r$ such that $\deg(f_i) \leq t$ and $f_i(0) = \delta_{i\beta}$,
2. computes a vector $\vec{C}$ of component-wise $\texttt{PolyCommit}_{\mathrm{DL}}$ commitments to the polynomials in $\vec{f}$,
3. computes k vectors $\vec{\rho}_j = \langle f_1(I_j), \ldots, f_r(I_j) \rangle$ of evaluations of the polynomials in $\vec{f}$, and k witnesses w_j that attest to the fact that the r evaluations in $\vec{\rho}_j$ are correct using cooperative batch verification (made noninteractive via Fiat-Shamir), for $1 \leq j \leq k$,
4. computes the set S of commitment values from the proof that the polynomials committed to in $\vec{C}$ open to a standard basis vector at $x = 0$, and
5. sends $(\vec{C}, S, \texttt{wallet}, \vec{\rho}_j, w_j)$, to server I_j for $1 \leq j \leq k$.

Note that each server receives different vectors of evaluation points and witnesses, but the same wallet and sets of commitments. Upon receiving these values, each server I_j

6. ensures that it has not seen `wallet` in an earlier query,
7. verifies that the evaluations in $\vec{\rho}_j$ are correct using cooperative batch verification (with witness w_j),
8. computes a (k, ℓ)-threshold BLS signature share σ_j on the value $\vec{C} \| S \| \texttt{wallet}$, and
9. sends σ_j to the user.

After receiving signature shares from each server, the user

10. combines $\sigma_1, \ldots, \sigma_k$ into a signature σ on $\vec{C} \| S \| \texttt{wallet}$,
11. computes the challenge $c = \text{hash}(\sigma)$ and uses this challenge to compute the set V of responses to complete the aforementioned proof that the polynomials committed to in $\vec{C}$ open to a standard basis vector at $x = 0$, and
12. sends (σ, V) to server I_j for $1 \leq j \leq k$.

Upon receipt of this response, each server I_j

13. verifies that σ is a valid signature on $\vec{C} \| S \| \texttt{wallet}$, and
14. computes $c = \text{hash}(\sigma)$ and checks if the responses in V are valid responses for this challenge.

Recall that in Goldberg's PIR scheme, the user recovers the record by Lagrange interpolation at the point $x = 0$. It is apparent that the above proof convinces the database servers that the query only reveals information about a single record *when the responses are interpolated at the point* $x = 0$, but we must also consider a clever user that chooses the polynomials in his query non-randomly. In this case, the polynomials might be chosen such that interpolating at some other point $x = a$ reveals information about some other database record. This is unsurprising, since it is known that information-theoretic SPIR is impossible to achieve without some interaction between the servers, or a shared secret among them [31]. We thus introduce a shared secret key sk, known to all the servers but unknown to the users. (Note that the servers must already share a copy of the database, so requiring them to share an additional secret key is reasonable.) To prevent the above attack, server I_j

15. seeds a pseudorandom generator (PRG) with $F_{sk}(\vec{C})$, where F is a pseudorandom function family,
16. uses the PRG to generate a common pseudorandom nonce and appends it to the database as an ephemeral $(r+1)^{\text{th}}$ database record for this query,[3]
17. uses the PRG to generate $t - 1$ random $\mathbb{Z}_q$ elements from which it forms a common pseudorandom polynomial $g \in \mathbb{Z}_q[x]$ of degree (at most) t with $g(0) = 0$,
18. computes and appends $g(I_j)$ to $\vec{\rho}_j$, and
19. encodes the query response exactly as in Goldberg's original construction. Note that when encoding the response, the servers include the ephemeral $(r+1)^{\text{th}}$ record in the database, and also include their respective evaluations of the pseudorandom polynomial g in the query as if the user had submitted it as part of his original query.

This last set of steps effectively *rerandomizes* the user's query. The user decodes the responses to his rerandomized query in the usual way (see §3.2).

Note that this SPIR construction preserves the t-privacy and v-Byzantine-robustness properties of the underlying PIR protocol; however, our approach to rerandomizing user queries prevents us from inheriting the scheme's optional τ-independence property.

Theorem 1. *The above modifications convert Goldberg's multi-server information-theoretic PIR into multi-server SPIR. Query privacy is provided information theoretically against up to $t - 1$, and computationally against t (under the DL assumption), colluding servers; the database's privacy is protected computationally (under the t-SDH assumption [40]).*

The proof of this theorem is in the extended version of this paper [36, Appendix C].

4.2 Single-payee PSPIR

Next, we extend the above SPIR construction to single-payee PSPIR. To do this, we augment the protocol as follows. First, we have the user compute a commitment, called a *receipt*, that encodes the price of the requested record under the price tier encoded in his wallet. The user proves in zero-knowledge that the receipt is well-formed (i.e., that it encodes the correct price) and that the balance in his wallet is sufficient to purchase the record at that price; once convinced by this proof, the database servers issue a threshold BLS signature on the user's receipt and wallet. The user can later exchange his wallet and this signed receipt with the bank to retrieve a new wallet for use in a future transaction. We also discuss how a user can recharge the balance in his wallet, and then point out a simple trick that enables the servers to enforce access control lists with only a slight modification to the PSPIR protocol.

[3]It is important that no other values are used to seed the PRG, since the user might otherwise replay $\vec{C}$ to retrieve a different nonce and potentially leak some information about other database records.

Proving sufficient funds and computing the receipt.

To compute the receipt, the user and each database server independently compute a commitment to the price of the record encoded in the user's query for each price tier. This is done by taking advantage of the homomorphic properties of polynomial commitments: each party computes the T polynomial commitments $P_i = \prod_{j=1}^{r} C_j^{p_{ij}}$ for $1 \leq i \leq T$, where p_{ij} is the jth component of $\vec{p_i}$. (Recall that $\vec{p_i}$ is the tier i price list.) Note that P_i is a commitment to a polynomial $f_{P_i} = \vec{f} \cdot \vec{p_i}$ whose constant coefficient is equal to the price of record β in $\vec{p_i}$ (i.e., $f_{P_i}(0) = p_{\pi i}$). Next, the user

1. chooses $\gamma_0, \gamma_1 \in_R \mathbb{Z}_q$ and computes the $\texttt{PolyCommit}_{\text{Ped}}$ commitment $\mathcal{C}_P = P_\pi(h^\alpha)^{\gamma_1} h^{\gamma_0}$, where π is the price tier encoded in `wallet`,

2. computes a Pedersen commitment $\texttt{Receipt}_P = g_{\text{T}}^{p_{\pi\beta}} h_{\text{T}}^{\gamma_0}$ and the witness $w_P = g^{\phi(\alpha)} h^{\gamma_1}$ where $\phi(x)$ is the quotient upon division of $f_{P_\pi}(x) - f_{P_\pi}(0)$ by $x - 0$,

3. computes Π_P, a ZKP of knowledge of $(x_1, \ldots, x_T, b)$ and (γ_0, γ_1, p) such that $\mathcal{C}_P = P_1^{x_1} \cdots P_T^{x_T} (h^\alpha)^{\gamma_1} h^{\gamma_0}$ (recall that $x_i = \delta_{i\pi}$), $\texttt{Receipt}_P = g_{\text{T}}^{p} h_{\text{T}}^{\gamma_0}$, $b - p \geq 0$, and `wallet` encodes attributes $x_1, \ldots, x_T$ and balance b, and

4. sends the tuple $(\mathcal{C}_P, w_P, \texttt{Receipt}_P, \Pi_P)$ to server I_j for $1 \leq j \leq k$.

Upon receiving these values, each server I_j

5. verifies that the proof Π_P is correct,

6. checks if $e(\mathcal{C}_P, \hat{g}) \stackrel{?}{=} e(w_P, \hat{g}^\alpha) \cdot \texttt{Receipt}_P$,

7. computes a (k, ℓ)-threshold BLS signature share ς_j on the value $\texttt{wallet} \| \texttt{Receipt}_P$, and

8. sends ς_j to the user.

If any verification step above fails, then the servers abort immediately; otherwise, the servers proceeds to process the user's query as usual. The user recombines the signature shares ς_j, $1 \leq j \leq k$, to recover the signature ς on $\texttt{wallet} \| \texttt{Receipt}_P$.

Remark 1. To improve performance, our implementation of the above protocols (as described in [36, Appendix D]) diverges somewhat from the above descriptions. In particular, each of the ZKPs used in the SPIR construction are computed noninteractively using Fiat-Shamir, and the commitments and responses from this proof are transmitted to each server as early as possible, thus allowing the servers to begin verification before the user completes the proof. Then, instead of computing $\texttt{Receipt}_P$ noninteractively, each server issues a threshold BLS signature share on `wallet`, all common values from this proof, and all commitment values from the proof that $\texttt{Receipt}_P$ is valid; the user recombines these signature shares to produce a challenge value for this latter proof, then transmits the recombined signature and his responses to each server. This convinces the servers that they each saw the same wallet and query in the earlier SPIR proof.[4]

[4]The reason we describe the protocols as above is to make the SPIR construction secure *on its own*. In our implementation, the security of the SPIR relies on successful verification of the subsequent receipt proof (which is acceptable, since the servers do not respond to the query until they have verified both proofs).

Refreshing the wallet.

Before performing subsequent queries, the user must refresh his wallet with the bank. To do so, the user sends the tuple of values $(\varsigma, \texttt{Receipt}_P, \texttt{wallet})$ to the bank, who verifies that ς is a valid signature on $\texttt{wallet} \| \texttt{Receipt}_P$. If so, the user and the bank run the credential issuing protocol for the credential system (see §2) that represents the wallet. At the end of this protocol, the user has a new unlinkable (even to the bank) wallet `wallet'` encoding the same tier as `wallet` and a balance equal to the price committed to in $\texttt{Receipt}_P$ subtracted from the balance encoded in `wallet`. The user may similarly *recharge* his wallet with additional funds by first 'purchasing' a receipt that encodes a negative price using, for example, a prepaid credit card. Note that in this procedure, the bank does not learn the balance in the new or the old wallet, or the price encoded in the receipt; in fact, the bank cannot even distinguish between a user that is refreshing his wallet and one who is recharging it.

Supporting access control lists.

We now describe a simple modification to implement access control lists atop our PSPIR construction. The idea is to impose a maximum balance b_{max} on users' wallets, and then require all users to prove that their new balance does not exceed b_{max} each time they refresh or recharge their wallets with the bank. The bank will refuse to issue any wallet without such a proof, thus ensuring that no user's balance ever exceeds b_{max}. The remainder of the protocol remains unchanged, except that a price of $\perp$ in $\vec{p_\pi}$ is treated as a price of $b_{\text{max}} + 1$, which, by our restriction above, no user can afford. Thus, this simple modification effectively prevents users in price tier π from purchasing any record marked as $\perp$ in $\vec{p_\pi}$.

4.3 Bookkeeping

This section discusses our approach to bookkeeping. At a high level, our idea uses the additive and multiplicative homomorphic properties of Shamir secret shares to maintain and compute on shares of aggregate counts of the number of times each database record is retrieved (and at what price). In Goldberg's original PIR construction, the database servers do not maintain any state information — the only information they store is the actual database contents. We augment the database with two additional columns of state information; i.e., we require the database servers to store two w-bit words of state (Shamir secret shares) per database record, which are the length-r vectors of shares $\vec{\mathbf{c}_j} = \langle [c_1]_q, \ldots, [c_r]_q \rangle$ and $\vec{\mathbf{d}_j} = \langle [d_1]_q, \ldots, [d_r]_q \rangle$.

Our initial idea was for servers to maintain a running sum of all queries they witness between successive bookkeeping operations. Unfortunately, this naive solution requires all servers to be involved in all queries, since if server j aggregates a query but server j' does not, their shares will be inconsistent and interpolate to an unpredictable value that does not reflect the actual number of queries per record. However, requiring all servers to participate in all queries hurts availability since the failure of a single database server would render the system inoperable. (It also hurts efficiency by requiring additional bandwidth and computational power be devoted to each query.) Moreover, even if all servers aggregate all queries, this only enables them to track the number of times each record is retrieved, but not the prices paid for them. We solve the first problem by having the user reveal which subset Q of database servers are involved in each query, and then use this knowledge to convert the Shamir secret shares into additive shares; therefore, all servers must be online to compute on the shared bookkeeping data, but they do not need to be online during every query. To solve the second problem, we have the user (querying for record β under price tier π)

include the additional vector of shares $\vec{\varrho}_j$ of $(p_{\pi\beta} \cdot \vec{1}_\beta)$ along with his query.[5] The servers convert both vectors into additive shares and aggregate them into $\vec{\mathbf{c}_j}$ and $\vec{\mathbf{d}}_j$, which are then vectors of shares of the number of times each record was retrieved, and the total price paid for those retrievals, respectively.

After each bookkeeping operation, database server j reinitializes the auxiliary vectors $\vec{\mathbf{c}_j}$ and $\vec{\mathbf{d}}_j$ back to the length-r zero vector, chooses a new private signing key x_j for BLS signature generation, and publishes the corresponding verification key $(\hat{g}, \hat{g}^{x_j})$. By having each server choose its signing key independently, every subset Q of k servers has a unique public verification key pk_Q for (k, k)-threshold BLS signatures; this key is easily computable using Q via the expression $pk_Q = \prod_{I_j \in Q} (\hat{g}^{x_{I_j}})^{\lambda_{Q,j}} \bmod q$ where $\lambda_{Q,j} = \prod_{I_i \in Q - \{I_j\}} I_j \cdot (I_j - I_i)^{-1} \bmod q$. Users then reveal Q during each query, and the servers append an unambiguous string representation of Q to the message resulting in the signature σ. The servers accept the signature as valid if and only if verification succeeds using verification key pk_Q, where Q is the set of servers encoded in the message. Similarly, the servers encode Q into the signature ς on the user's receipt, and the user transmits Q along with the receipt to the bank.

This ensures that each server involved in a query sees a consistent set Q of other servers; however, a malicious user may still disrupt the bookkeeping process by neglecting to send the tuple (σ, V) to any nontrivial subset of Q on Step 12 of the SPIR protocol. The servers that do receive (σ, V) will aggregate the user's query into $\vec{\mathbf{c}_j}$ and $\vec{\mathbf{d}}_j$, while those that do not will not (thus resulting in inconsistent shares among the servers in Q). We therefore rely on the bank to facilitate atomicity to the query aggregation process. Instead of returning the regular query response $\vec{\rho}_j \cdot D$, the servers use the PRG (seeded with their shared secret and the user's wallet) to produce a common $\mathbb{Z}_q$ element for blinding, Γ, and return $\vec{\rho}_j \cdot D + \Gamma$. When the user sends $(\varsigma, Q, \texttt{wallet}, \texttt{Receipt}_P)$ to the bank, the bank 1) verifies that ς is a valid signature on $\texttt{wallet} \| \texttt{Receipt}_P \| Q$ using pk_Q, 2) computes and sends Γ to the user, and 3) notifies each server in Q that the transaction involving `wallet` is complete. At this point, all servers can safely update their aggregate shares.

Top-K replication.

Given the above modifications, supporting top-K replication is straightforward. When a query $(\vec{C}, S, \texttt{wallet}, \vec{\rho}_j, w_j, Q)$ arrives at server I_j, it temporarily stores $\vec{\rho}_j$. Upon notification of the query's success from the bank, server I_j accumulates the query by computing $\vec{\mathbf{c}_j} = \vec{\mathbf{c}_j} + \lambda_{Q,j} \cdot \vec{\rho}_j$.Computing the top-$K$ records from these shares is then a straightforward application of Burkhart and Dimitropoulos' [14] *privacy-preserving top-K* (PPTK) algorithm. The algorithm outputs the top-K largest shares in $\vec{\mathbf{c}_j}$ without revealing any additional information about the value of any share. After the top K are revealed, the servers replicate these to a smaller database and reinitialize $\vec{\mathbf{c}_j}$ to the length-r zero vector.

Multiple-payee PSPIR.

Supporting multiple payees in the tiered pricing model is slightly more involved than is supporting top-K replication. Due to space constraints, we only address the simpler case of a single-tiered pricing scheme, and then briefly outline how to extend this approach to a system with multiple price tiers (and access control lists). Full details of the more general construction are available in the extended version of this paper [36].

The single-tier case simplifies the construction in two important ways: first, the user need not send or prove statements about the additional vector of shares $\vec{\varrho}_j$ as above and, second, the servers only need to store a single additional column of auxiliary information. Consider the above PSPIR construction with a single price list $\vec{p} = \langle p_1, \ldots, p_r \rangle$ for all users, and a set of m CPs $\mathbf{CP} = \{\mathrm{CP}_1, \ldots, \mathrm{CP}_m\}$. For ease of presentation, we define $r_1 = 0$ and $r_{m+1} = r$, and assume that CP_i $(1 \leq i \leq m)$ owns the records at indices $r_i + 1$ through r_{i+1}. The amount payable to CP_i is then computed by summing the additive shares $\sum_{i=r_i+1}^{r_{i+1}} p_i \cdot [c_i]_q$.

With tiered pricing, the computation is conceptually similar but requires cooperation from the user. The user sends the vector of shares $\vec{\varrho}_j$ described above along with his query. The server chooses a random length-r vector of challenges $\vec{c} \in (\mathbb{Z}_q)^r$ (via Fiat-Shamir) and computes the T dot products $[e_i]_q = (\vec{\varrho}_j - \vec{p}_i \boxdot \vec{\rho}_j) \cdot \vec{c}$, where $\boxdot$ denotes component-wise multiplication of two vectors, for $1 \leq i \leq T$. If $\vec{\varrho}_j$ is well-formed, then $[e_i]_q = [0]_q$ for $i = \pi$; otherwise, $[e_i]_q \neq [0]_q$ for any $1 \leq i \leq T$ with overwhelming probability. The user then proves that $[e_i]_q = [0]_q$ for $i = \pi$ using a proof similar to the existing proof of correctness for the receipt. Once convinced, server j is convinced that $\vec{\varrho}_j$ is a vector of commitments to the correct price, and can safely aggregate $\vec{\varrho}_j$ into $\vec{\mathbf{d}}_j$.

Bookkeeping frequency.

Bookkeeping necessarily leaks some information about user queries. In the extreme case, where only a single user queries the database between bookkeeping operations, bookkeeping may completely reveal that user's query. At the other end of the spectrum, when every record is accessed hundreds or thousands of times between bookkeeping operations, the information leakage is minimal and likely not at all invasive to any user's privacy. However, prolonging the period between bookkeeping limits its usefulness in the case of top-K replication, and may be economically unacceptable in the case of multiple-payee PSPIR. Thus, a great deal of discretion is necessary on the part of the database servers in determining how often to run the bookkeeping protocols. For databases with consistently high usage, a simple bookkeeping schedule such as once per week or once per month may suffice, whereas those databases with lower usage may need to wait until the servers answer some threshold number of queries. In general, the bookkeeping policy is highly dependent both on the characteristics of the database and the business logic of its operators. We leave an in-depth investigation of this privacy-utility tradeoff as an important area for future work.

5. IMPLEMENTATION & EVALUATION

We implemented the protocols described in this paper using Ben Lynn's Pairing-Based Cryptography (PBC) [43] library with Aniket Kate's PBCWrapper [39] package for C++ Wrapper classes, Victor Shoup's NTL [55] with the GNU Multi-Precision Arithmetic Library [29] for multi-precision arithmetic, and OpenSSL [50] for hash functions (we use SHA-256). All experiments use a value of $\kappa = 40$ for the soundness parameter. Our PSPIR implementation is built atop Ian Goldberg's implementation of his PIR protocols, Percy++ [32]. For our evaluation, we implemented the protocol as a standalone add-on to Percy++, but we will later integrate it with the Percy++ library. We used the BigInteger-based version of Martin Burkhart's SEPIA library [13] and his PPTK [14] protocol for our top-K replication benchmarks. All measurements were taken in Ubuntu Linux 10.04.1 LTS running on a machine with Dual Intel

[5]Note that $\vec{\varrho}_j \neq p_{\pi\beta} \cdot \vec{\rho}_j \bmod q$, which would reveal the price $p_{\pi p}$ to the servers; rather, $\vec{\varrho}_j$ is an independently chosen vector of shares. Of course, $\vec{\varrho}_j - p_{\pi\beta} \cdot \vec{\rho}_j$ yields shares of the length-r zero vector, which is the property we exploit to let the user prove the well-formedness of $\vec{\varrho}_j$.

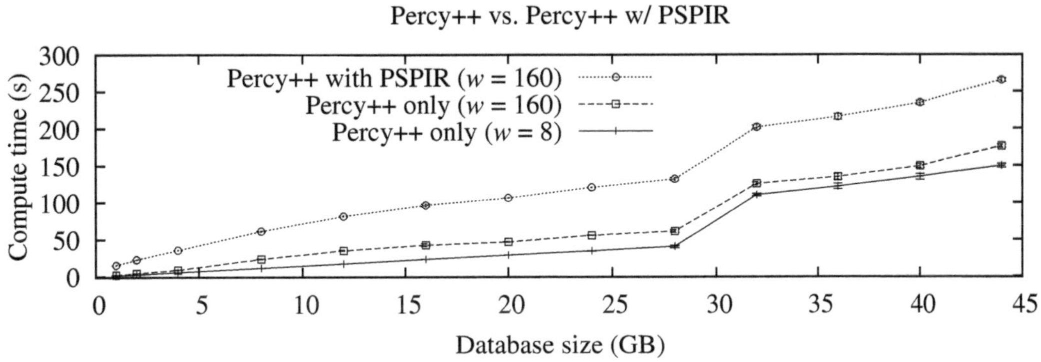

Figure 1: Query execution time for Percy++ with and without PSPIR ($k = 4$, $t = 2$). The percent compute time attributable to the PSPIR enhancements decreases monotonically from $\approx 86\%$ for a 1 GB database down to $\approx 33\%$ for a 44 GB database. Percy++ starts carrying the extra overhead of disk reads after a 28 GB database, which exceeds available RAM. The $w = 8$ plot shows the execution time for Percy++ using its performance-optimal parameter choices, whereas the $w = 160$ plot shows Percy++ with parameters needed to ensure the security of PSPIR. The Percy++ with PSPIR plot shows the combined cost of Percy++ with $w = 160$ and the PSPIR enhancements. Error bars are plotted for all data points, but are small and may therefore be difficult to see. For comparison, downloading a 44 GB database in OT-based schemes takes over 11 hours at 9 Mbps, which is the average Internet bandwidth in Canada and the US [49].

Xeon E5420 2.50 GHz CPUs and 32 GB memory. The value of q (the order of the pairing groups and the modulus for the polynomial operations) was 160 bits long.

5.1 Experiments

We measured the performance of the PSPIR and top-K replication protocols for various values of the PIR parameters n (the size of the database), b (the size of each record in the database), k (the number of servers participating in each query), and t (the number of servers that can collude without affecting query privacy).

Experiment 1. Our first experiment measures the computational overhead added to Percy++ by the PSPIR enhancements. We generated databases of sizes ranging from 1 GB to 44 GB containing random data and took measurements for both Percy++ and the Percy++ with PSPIR.

In Figure 1, we plot the results for parameters $k = 4$, $t = 2$, and $b = \sqrt{160n}$, which is the communication-optimal record size for this PIR scheme. We observe that PSPIR results in a moderate increase in compute times, with the percent compute time attributable to the PSPIR enhancements decreasing monotonically from about 86% for a 1 GB database down to just 33% for a 44 GB database. The upward bump just before 30 GB marks the point after which the database no longer fits in available memory. From that point on, every query bears more overhead from disk reads. In terms of communication overhead, PSPIR increases Percy++'s query size, which is itself just k times the size of the retrieved record, by a multiplicative factor of about 5. However, it increases each server's response by only 46 bytes, which corresponds to two $\mathbb{G}_1$ elements (BLS signature shares).

The PSPIR compute time scales linearly with k and $r = n/b$. In our implementation, the cost is independent of t except for a one-time preprocessing step at the client. (The size of the long-term polynomial commitment public key and Percy++'s client-side compute time are also linear in t. This latter cost consistently accounted for less than one percent of overall compute time in our experiments.) The bottleneck operation for the client is computing commitments, while for the server it is processing the actual PIR query. In both cases, the bottleneck operation increases with r. Top-K replication or bucketization [47] can enable one to trade some privacy to support larger values of r with little to no additional compute time or communication overhead.

Experiment 2. Our next experiment evaluates the impact of top-K replication; i.e., it studies the performance gains for the users when all queries for the K most popular records go to the smaller replicated database. In this experiment, we assume that all records are physically replicated to a second set of database servers, thus increasing the maximum database size for which both the top-K and non-top-K records fit in physical memory. Alternatively, the database servers could simply publish a list of indices for the top-K records and allow users to perform PIR on just this subset of the database; this would result in identical performance when the entire database fits in physical memory and somewhat lower performance otherwise. All trials of the top-K experiment used a query distribution that we generated at random using a bounded Pareto distribution that satisfies the 80/20 rule; i.e., about 80% of queries are for just 20% of the database records, with the number of queries per record bounded between 0 and 10,000. As such, we use $K = \lfloor r/5 \rfloor$. We chose an 80/20 distribution because such distributions are commonly observed in the wild, but we emphasize that the actual performance gains that a database can expect from top-K replication is highly dependent on the underlying query distribution. Figure 2 plots the mean query execution time for top-K and non-top-K queries, as well as the average (amortized) cost per query when 80% of queries are top-K queries and 20% are not. Note that the average query execution time is well below that of Percy++ without PSPIR functionality (cf. Figure 1).

We also measured the cost to the servers of actually computing the top-K using the SEPIA library. We found that using 160-bit secret shares results in poor performance compared to the benchmarks presented by Burkhart *et al.* [15]. Fortunately, in our case we can assert that all shared secrets are much smaller than $q/2$, which enables us to eliminate two-thirds of the computation in the bottleneck 'less than' computation. Furthermore, about 86% of the remaining computation time is spent generating random bit-wise secret shares modulo q. These random shares can be precomputed between top-K computations, resulting in a respectable 57 less-than operations per second in our tests. This still leads to significant computation times to isolate the top-K using Burkhart *et al.*'s PPTK algorithm [14] when the database size is large; thus, we fur-

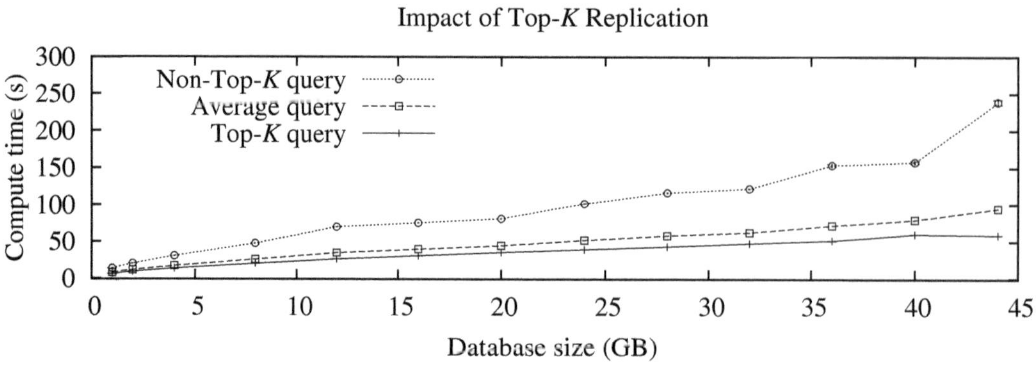

Figure 2: Query execution time for Percy++ with PSPIR and top-K replication ($k = 4$, $t = 2$, $K = \lfloor r/5 \rfloor$). Queries follow a bounded Pareto distribution that satisfies the 80/20 rule; thus, 80% of queries are for the top-K entries and 20% are for the remaining $r - K$ entries (labelled 'Non-Top-K' on the plot). The average query cost for the top-K replicated database ranges from just 51% that of an equivalent non-replicated database for a 1 GB database down to 36% for a 44 GB database. Error bars are plotted for all data points, but are small and may therefore be difficult to see.

ther optimize the algorithm by relaxing PPTK to a 'top-K-ish' algorithm. This reduces computation times quite significantly. For example, with a 1 GB database ($r = 7328$ records) and a bounded 80/20 Pareto distribution our modified PPTK takes an average of about 9700 comparisons (≈ 2.8 minutes) to find the top 19–21% of records, whereas standard PPTK takes about 14600 comparisons (≈ 4.2 minutes); for a 20 GB database ($r = 32768$ records) this figure is about 33500 comparisons (≈ 11.0 minutes) for our relaxed PPTK versus 137500 comparisons (≈ 40.2 minutes) for standard PPTK, and for a 44 GB database ($r = 48603$ records) it is about 48605 comparisons (≈ 14.2 minutes) for our relaxed PPTK versus 197500 comparisons (≈ 57.7 minutes) for standard PPTK. Moreover, a large fraction of trials with standard PPTK had no solution (i.e., no unique top-K) and the algorithm therefore returned only the top-K-ish anyhow. Note that we generated our test sets using a bounded 80/20 Pareto distribution and then used the CDF for this distribution as an 'initial guess' in the PPTK algorithm. In practice, such an accurate guess will typically not be available and the actual number of comparisons will be greater than our predictions. Nonetheless, we feel confident in concluding that even for large databases with imperfect knowledge of the underlying query distribution, the cost of computing the top-K will be quite reasonable.

6. RELATED WORK

The related bodies of work are symmetric private information retrieval (SPIR), oblivious transfer (OT), OT with access control (OTAC), and priced OT (POT).

OT schemes allow a database X consisting of two records and a user holding an index $i \in \{0, 1\}$ to run a protocol that results in the user learning the ith record and no information the $(1 - i)^{\text{th}}$ record, while the database learns nothing about i. Unlike PIR and SPIR, however, OT schemes have no sublinear communication requirements. Brassard *et al.* [12] considered the more general notion of 1-out-of-n OT, where the database holds n records and the user learns the record at index i, and learns nothing about the remaining $n - 1$ records [51]; the database still learns nothing about i.

SPIR schemes [31] address the honest-user assumption of PIR by additionally preserving database privacy so that dishonest users cannot learn any information about other database records beyond the record retrieved. All existing communication-efficient 1-out-of-n OT schemes are essentially single-server SPIR, whereas all existing communication-efficient distributed OT schemes [31] (i.e., two or more servers) of 1-out-of-n OT schemes are essentially multi-server SPIR. The first work on preserving database privacy against dishonest users in a multi-server PIR setting was by Gertner *et al.* [31]. They propose a single-round ℓ-server SPIR scheme with communication complexity $O(\log n \cdot n^{1/(2\ell-1)})$ for $\ell \geq 2$ and a $O(\log n)$-server scheme with communication complexity $O(\log^2 n \cdot \log\log n)$. Kushilevitz and Ostrovsky [42] briefly discuss how to convert their single-server PIR into SPIR using general zero-knowledge proof techniques, however they propose no concrete constructions. No existing SPIR scheme simultaneously provides support for both access control and tiered pricing.

Several OTAC schemes [17, 23, 57] were recently proposed. As with our approach, these schemes typically consist of three parties: user, database, and issuer. The issuer provides users needing access to the database with credentials encoding the access rights of users as an attribute set. The database encrypts its content under an access policy specific to each record and makes the encrypted contents available to users for download. A user with a valid credential can run the OTAC protocol with the database to obtain a decryption key for a particular record. After the protocol, the database learns that a user with a valid credential has obtained a key, but learns nothing about the user's credential or the decryption key issued. User's download the entire encrypted database and use the key obtained to decrypt the desired record. Zhang *et al.* [57] used attribute-based encryption to specify record-level access policies in disjunctive form without requiring duplication of database records. However, these schemes do not consider an economic model where users pay for each record and their high communication overhead makes them considerably more costly than SPIR.

POT schemes [1, 18] were originally introduced by Aiello *et al.* [1] to explore the difference between physical goods requiring close monitoring of inventory level and digital goods that are essentially of unlimited supply. In their model, users first deposit some money with the database and then proceed to buy multiple digital goods from the database, such that the total price of purchased goods does not exceed the user's deposit/balance. The database does not learn which digital goods the user has purchased. However, since the database tracks the users' accounts, all queries by a single user are linkable; thus, the approach lacks the anonymity properties that we seek. This enables the database server to deduce the number of digital goods a particular user has purchased, the average price of those purchases, and the user's spending pattern [18]. Furthermore, the scheme provides no way for users to recharge their balance, which means that when a user's balance becomes lower than the price of any record, the remaining balance is rendered useless. Camenisch *et al.* [18] address these problems by encoding users' wallets in an anonymous credential so that the database is no longer required to maintain user-specific state information; as a result, user purchases become unlinkable. They also lay out an extension that makes use of a trusted third party to facilitate a *fair purchase* protocol; i.e., an optimistic fair exchange protocol to prevent the database server from cheating by not sending the correct decryption key (or wallet) to the user.

All of the above priced and access-control-capable OT and SPIR schemes lack some ingredients necessary for deployment in a practical setting. The foremost missing ingredient is the right combination of functionalities for access control, tiered pricing, support for multiple payees, sublinear communication complexity, and availability of practical implementations. The SPIR schemes [31, 42] provide no pricing or access control functions. OT schemes (i.e., 1-out-of-n) have prohibitively expensive communication costs and require a static encrypted database, which potentially breaks other applications using the same database. In particular, existing OTAC schemes [17, 23, 57] do not provide pricing functions, while the POT schemes [1, 18], on the other hand, provide no access control functions. Note that one cannot simply adopt our approach of setting the price of a record higher than the maximum wallet balance, since all users in these schemes pay according to the same price list (and thus would automatically have the same access privileges). Moreover, no existing POT scheme supports multiple payees selling goods through a common database.

Much like our top-K replication strategy, a few research efforts have also focused on increasing the practicality of PIR by finding ways around PIR's linear computational requirements. Beimel *et al.* [5] propose preprocessing, which enables PIR servers to answer queries with only sublinear computation by precomputing and storing some extra information (the size of which is polynomial in the database size n). Ishai *et al.* [37] propose a different approach called batch coding that — while still requiring linear computation — enables the servers to process several PIR queries by the same user simultaneously, thus providing an amortized cost per query that is strictly smaller than n. Nearest to our own work, Olumofin and Goldberg [47] recently proposed an approach to indexing and partitioning large databases into highly diverse bucket portions that users can query independently. This approach makes querying such large databases with PIR practical, and simplifies the tradeoff between privacy and runtime; however, it does not include any way for the database servers to dynamically learn about and exploit the relative popularities of individual records to improve performance, as does the top-K approach taken in this work.

7. CONCLUSION

We have extended Goldberg's multi-server information-theoretic PIR with a suite of protocols for privacy-preserving e-commerce. Our protocols add support for tiered pricing with multiple payees, group-based access control lists with record-level granularity, and dynamic top-K replication, while preserving the sublinear communication complexity of PIR; no other scheme for priced retrieval using PIR or OT supports tiered pricing, multiple payees, access control, or dynamic replication. We have implemented the single-payee variant of our PSPIR protocol atop Percy++, an open-source implementation of Goldberg's PIR scheme, and evaluated its performance empirically. We also evaluated the cost and impact of top-K replication. Our measurements indicate that this combination of protocols results in performance that is acceptable for deployment in real-world e-commerce applications. Furthermore, the extensive functionality of our protocols, SPIR's sublinear communication costs, and the ability to operate on an unencrypted database, makes our approach more practical than competing OT-based approaches. For future work, we intend to optimize our implementation and add full support for multiple payees (which we do not expect to significantly alter the runtime), and to incorporate our protocols into Percy++.

Acknowledgements. We are extremely thankful to Martin Burkhart for his assistance with SEPIA. This research is supported by NSERC, OGS, mprime, and a Cheriton Graduate Scholarship.

REFERENCES

[1] W. Aiello, Y. Ishai, and O. Reingold. Priced Oblivious Transfer: How to Sell Digital Goods. In *Proceedings of EUROCRYPT 2001*, Innsbruck, Austria, May 2001.

[2] D. Asonov. *Querying Databases Privately: A New Approach To Private Information Retrieval*, volume 3128 of *LNCS*. Springer, 2004.

[3] M. H. Au, W. Susilo, and Y. Mu. Constant-Size Dynamic k-TAA. In *Proceedings of SCN 2006*, Maiori, Italy, September 2006.

[4] J. Bar-Ilan and D. Beaver. Non-Cryptographic Fault-Tolerant Computing in Constant Number of Rounds of Interaction. In *Proceedings of PODC 1989*, Edmonton, AB, August 1989.

[5] A. Beimel, Y. Ishai, and T. Malkin. Reducing the Servers' Computation in Private Information Retrieval: PIR with Preprocessing. In *Proceedings of CRYPTO 2000*, Santa Barbara, CA, August 2000.

[6] M. Bellare, J. A. Garay, and T. Rabin. Batch Verification with Applications to Cryptography and Checking. In *Proceedings of LATIN 1998*, Campinas, Brazil, April 1998.

[7] M. Bellare, J. A. Garay, and T. Rabin. Fast Batch Verification for Modular Exponentiation and Digital Signatures. In *Proceedings of EUROCRYPT 1998*, Espoo, Finland, May 1998.

[8] D. Boneh, B. Lynn, and H. Shacham. Short Signatures from the Weil Pairing. *Journal of Cryptology*, 17(4):297–319, January 2004.

[9] F. Boudot. Efficient Proofs that a Committed Number Lies in an Interval. In *Proceedings of EUROCRYPT 2000*, Bruges, Belgium, May 2000.

[10] S. Brands. Restrictive Blinding of Secret-Key Certificates. In *Proceedings of EUROCRYPT 1995*, Saint-Malo, France, May 1995.

[11] S. A. Brands. *Rethinking Public Key Infrastructures and Digital Certificates: Building in Privacy*. MIT Press, 2000.

[12] G. Brassard, C. Crépeau, and J.-M. Robert. All-or-Nothing Disclosure of Secrets. In *Proceedings of CRYPTO 1986*, Santa Barbara, CA, 1986.

[13] M. Burkhart. SEPIA: Security through Private Information Aggregation. Version 0.8.2.

[14] M. Burkhart and X. Dimitropoulos. Fast Privacy-Preserving Top-k Queries using Secret Sharing. In *Proceedings of ICCCN 2010*, Zurich, Switzerland, August 2010.

[15] M. Burkhart, M. Strasser, D. Many, and X. A. Dimitropoulos. SEPIA: Privacy-Preserving Aggregation of Multi-Domain Network Events and Statistics. In *Proceedings of USENIX Security 2010*, Washington, DC, August 2010.

[16] J. Camenisch. *Group Signature Schemes and Payment Systems Based on the Discrete Logarithm Problem*. PhD thesis, ETH Zurich, 1998. Reprint as vol. 2 of *ETH Series in Information Security and Cryptography*, Hartung-Gorre Verlag, Konstanz, 1998.

[17] J. Camenisch, M. Dubovitskaya, and G. Neven. Oblivious Transfer with Access Control. In *Proceedings of ACM CCS 2009*, Chicago, IL, November 2009.

[18] J. Camenisch, M. Dubovitskaya, and G. Neven. Unlinkable Priced Oblivious Transfer with Rechargeable Wallets. In *Proceedings of FC 2010*, Tenerife, Canary Islands, January 2010.

[19] J. Camenisch, M. Dubovitskaya, G. Neven, and G. M. Zaverucha. Oblivious Transfer with Hidden Access Control Lists. In *Proceedings of PKC 2011*, Taormina, Italy, March 2011.

[20] J. Camenisch and M. Michels. Proving in Zero-Knowledge that a Number Is the Product of Two Safe Primes. In *Proceedings of EUROCRYPT 1999*, Prague, Czech Republic, May 1999.

[21] B. Chor, N. Gilboa, and M. Naor. Private Information Retrieval by Keywords. Cryptology ePrint Archive, Report 1998/003, 1998. `http://eprint.iacr.org/`.

[22] B. Chor, O. Goldreich, E. Kushilevitz, and M. Sudan. Private Information Retrieval. In *Proceedings of FOCS 1995*, Milwaukee, WI, October 1995.

[23] S. E. Coull, M. Green, and S. Hohenberger. Controlling Access to an Oblivious Database Using Stateful Anonymous Credentials. In *Proceedings of PKC 2009*, Irvine, CA, March 2009.

[24] R. Cramer, I. Damgård, and B. Schoenmakers. Proofs of Partial Knowledge and Simplified Design of Witness Hiding Protocols. In *Proceedings of CRYPTO 1994*, Santa Barbara, CA, August 1994.

[25] I. Damgård, M. Fitzi, E. Kiltz, J. B. Nielsen, and T. Toft. Unconditionally Secure Constant-Rounds Multi-party Computation for Equality, Comparison, Bits and Exponentiation. In *Proceedings of TCC 2006*, New York, NY, March 2006.

[26] B. Doe. The Kindle in Australia, October 2009.

[27] P. Feldman. A Practical Scheme for Non-interactive Verifiable Secret Sharing. In *Proceedings of FOCS 1987*, Los Angeles, CA, October 1987.

[28] A. Fiat and A. Shamir. How to Prove Yourself: Practical Solutions to Identification and Signature Problems. In *Proceedings of CRYPTO 1986*, Santa Barbara, CA, 1986.

[29] Free Software Foundation. The GNU Multiple Precision (GMP) Arithmetic Library. Version 5.0.1.

[30] Y. Gertner, S. Goldwasser, and T. Malkin. A Random Server Model for Private Information Retrieval. In *Proceedings of RANDOM 1998*, Barcelona, Spain, October 1998.

[31] Y. Gertner, Y. Ishai, E. Kushilevitz, and T. Malkin. Protecting Data Privacy in Private Information Retrieval Schemes. In *Proceedings of STOC 1998*, Dallas, TX, May 1998.

[32] I. Goldberg. Percy++ / PIR in C++. Version 0.7.1.

[33] I. Goldberg. Improving the Robustness of Private Information Retrieval. In *Proceedings of IEEE S&P 2007*, Oakland, CA, May 2007.

[34] S. Guha, B. Cheng, and P. Francis. Privad: Practical Privacy in Online Advertising. In *Proceedings of NSDI 2011*, Boston, MA, March 2011.

[35] V. Guruswami and M. Sudan. Improved Decoding of Reed-Solomon and Algebraic-Geometric Codes. In *Proceedings of FOCS 1998*, Palo Alto, CA, November 1998.

[36] R. Henry, F. Olumofin, and I. Goldberg. Practical PIR for Electronic Commerce. Tech. Report CACR 2011-04, University of Waterloo, 2011.

[37] Y. Ishai, E. Kushilevitz, R. Ostrovsky, and A. Sahai. Batch Codes and Their Applications. In *Proceedings of STOC 2004*, Chicago, IL, June 2004.

[38] A. Juels. Targeted Advertising... And Privacy Too. In *CT-RSA*, San Francisco, CA, April 2001.

[39] A. Kate. PBCWrapper: C++ Wrapper Classes for the Pairing-Based Cryptography Library. Version 0.8.0.

[40] A. Kate, G. M. Zaverucha, and I. Goldberg. Constant-Size Commitments to Polynomials and Their Applications. In *Proceedings of ASIACRYPT 2010*, Singapore, December 2010.

[41] A. Kate, G. M. Zaverucha, and I. Goldberg. Polynomial Commitments. Tech. Report CACR 2010-10, University of Waterloo, 2010.

[42] E. Kushilevitz and R. Ostrovsky. Replication Is Not Needed: Single Database, Computationally-Private Information Retrieval. In *Proceedings of FOCS 1997*, Miami Beach, FL, October 1997.

[43] B. Lynn. PBC Library: The Pairing-Based Cryptography Library. Version 0.5.11.

[44] D. McCullagh. Amazon Fights Demand for Customer Records. In *CNET News*. April 2010. `http://news.cnet.com/8301-13578_3-20002870-38.html`.

[45] A. J. Menezes, P. C. van Oorschot, and S. A. Vanstone. *Handbook of Applied Cryptography*. CRC Press, 2001.

[46] T. Nishide and K. Ohta. Constant-Round Multiparty Computation for Interval Test, Equality Test, and Comparison. *IEICE Transactions*, 90-A(5):960–968, 2007.

[47] F. Olumofin and I. Goldberg. Preserving Access Privacy Over Large Databases. Tech. Report CACR 2010-33, University of Waterloo, 2010.

[48] F. G. Olumofin and I. Goldberg. Privacy-Preserving Queries over Relational Databases. In *Privacy Enhancing Technologies*, Berlin, Germany, July 2010.

[49] Ookla Net Metrics. Canada and US Source Data. `http://www.netindex.com/source-data/`.

[50] OpenSSL Project. OpenSSL: The Open Source toolkit for SSL/TLS. Version 1.0.0.

[51] R. Ostrovsky and W. E. Skeith III. A Survey of Single-Database Private Information Retrieval: Techniques and Applications. In *Proceedings of PKC 2007*, Beijing, China, April 2007.

[52] T. P. Pedersen. Non-Interactive and Information-Theoretic Secure Verifiable Secret Sharing. In *Proceedings of CRYPTO 1991*, Santa Barbara, CA, August 1991.

[53] C.-P. Schnorr. Efficient Identification and Signatures for Smart Cards. In *Proceedings of CRYPTO 1989*, Santa Barbara, CA, August 1989.

[54] A. Shamir. How to Share a Secret. *Communications of the ACM*, 22(11):612–613, November 1979.

[55] V. Shoup. NTL: A Library for doing Number Theory. Version 5.5.2.

[56] V. Toubiana, H. Nissenbaum, A. Narayanan, S. Barocas, and D. Boneh. Adnostic: Privacy Preserving Targeted Advertising. In *Proceedings of NDSS 2010*, San Diego, CA, February 2010.

[57] Y. Zhang, M. H. Au, D. S. Wong, Q. Huang, N. Mamoulis, D. W. Cheung, and S.-M. Yiu. Oblivious Transfer with Access Control : Realizing Disjunction without Duplication. In *Proceedings of Pairing 2010*, Yamanaka Hot Spring, Japan, December 2010.

APPENDIX

A. PROVING EQUALITY OF 1-OUT-OF-r DISCRETE LOGARITHMS

Let g and h be (known) generators of a group $\mathbb{G}$ (of order q) with $\log_g(h)$ unknown to the verifier, and let $g_1, g_2, \ldots, g_r$ and $h_1, h_2, \ldots, h_r$ be given. The proof works as follows:

Prover knows: $x = \log_g g_j = \log_h h_j$ and index j

Verifier learns: that $\log_g g_{j'} = \log_h h_{j'}$ for at least one j'

1. The prover chooses $\gamma_1, \ldots, \gamma_r \in_R \mathbb{Z}_q$ and $c'_1, \ldots, c'_r \in \mathbb{Z}_{2^\kappa}$, then computes and sends the commitments $\eta_i = g^{\gamma_i} g_i^{c'_i \bar{\delta}_{ij}}$ and $\zeta_i = h^{\gamma_i} h_i^{c'_i \bar{\delta}_{ij}}$ to the verifier, for $1 \le i \le r$.

2. The verifier chooses and sends $c \in_R \mathbb{Z}_{2^\kappa}$ to the prover.

3. The prover sets $c_i = c'_i$ and $v_i = \gamma_i$ for $i \in [1, r] - \{j\}$ and computes $c_j = c - \sum_{i=1}^{r} c'_i \bar{\delta}_{ij} \bmod 2^\kappa$ and $v_j = \gamma_j - c_j x \bmod q$, then sends the pair $(\vec{c}, \vec{v})$ to the verifier, where $\vec{c} = \langle c_1, \ldots, c_r \rangle$ and $\vec{v} = \langle v_1, \ldots, v_r \rangle$.

4. The verifier chooses $\vec{b} = \langle b_1, \ldots, b_r \rangle \in_R (\mathbb{Z}_{2^\kappa})^r$ and computes $v = \vec{v} \cdot \vec{b}$. The verifier accepts if and only if $\prod_{i=1}^{r} \eta_i^{b_i} \stackrel{?}{=}$

$g^{\upsilon}\left(\prod_{i=1}^{r} g_i^{b_i c_i}\right), \prod_{i=1}^{r} \zeta_i^{b_i} \stackrel{?}{=} h^{\upsilon}\left(\prod_{i=1}^{r} h_i^{b_i c_i}\right)$ and $c \stackrel{?}{\equiv} \sum_{i=1}^{r} c_i \bmod 2^{\kappa}$ all hold.

Note that the above batch verification equation is more efficient than checking each of the r verification equations independently, since both b_i and c_i are *short* exponents; moreover, in our own application (see §3.5.2), we take advantage of some properties of the special case we are proving to further reduce verification costs.

B. PROVING THAT A VECTOR OF COMMITMENTS OPENS TO A STANDARD BASIS VECTOR

Prover knows: a length-r vector of polynomials $\vec{f} \in (\mathbb{Z}_q[x])^r$
Verifier learns: a length-r vector $\vec{C}$ of component-wise commitments to polynomials in $\vec{f}$ and that $\vec{f}$ evaluates component-wise to a standard basis vector at $x = 0$

1. The prover computes and sends $\vec{C}$ to the verifier.
2. The verifier chooses a vector of challenges $\vec{a} \in_R (\mathbb{Z}_{2^\kappa})^r$ and sends it to the prover; meanwhile, the verifier computes $C_a = \prod_{i=1}^{r} C_i^{a_i}$, where C_i and a_i are the ith components of $\vec{C}$ and $\vec{a}$, respectively. Note that C_a is a commitment to the dot product $f_a = \vec{f} \cdot \vec{a}$.
3. The prover computes the dot product $f_a = \vec{f} \cdot \vec{a}$ and engages in a zero-knowledge proof of knowledge of the evaluation of f_a at $x = 0$ with the verifier, such as by using the technique described in [41, Appendix D].
4. Let $Y = g_{\mathrm{T}}^{\gamma \cdot y}$ be the (blinded) commitment to $y = f_a(0)$ from this last proof of knowledge. The prover sends $\nu = h^{\gamma}$ together with proof that γ is the same randomness used to blind Y, and engages in a batch proof of equality of 1-out-of-r discrete logarithms to prove $\bigvee_{i=1}^{r}\left(\log_{g_{\mathrm{T}}} Y = \log_h \nu^{a_i}\right)$.

Remark 2. Because we are dealing with the special case of the batch proof of equality of 1-out-of-r discrete logarithms in which $g_1 = g_2 = \cdots = g_r = Y$ and $\log_{\nu}(h_i) = a_i$ is known to the verifier, the following optimizations apply: instead of checking

$$\prod_{i=1}^{r} \eta_i^{d_i} \stackrel{?}{=} g^{\upsilon}\left(\prod_{i=1}^{r} g_i^{c_i d_i}\right) \text{ and }$$

$$\prod_{i=1}^{r} \zeta_i^{d_i} \stackrel{?}{=} h^{\upsilon}\left(\prod_{i=1}^{r} h_i^{c_i d_i}\right)$$

in the verification equation, the verifier computes $w_1 = \vec{c} \cdot \vec{d} \bmod q$ and $w_2 = \sum_{i=1}^{r} a_i c_i d_i \bmod q$ and checks if

$$\prod_{i=1}^{r} \eta_i^{d_i} \stackrel{?}{=} g^{\upsilon} Y^{w_1} \text{ and }$$

$$\prod_{i=1}^{r} \zeta_i^{d_i} \stackrel{?}{=} h^{\upsilon} \nu^{w_2}.$$

This reduces the cost of verification from 2 full length exponentiations and $6r$ 'short' exponentiations (i.e., exponentiations with κ-bit exponents) to 4 full length exponentiations and $2r$ short exponentiations.

C. VERIFYING EVALUATIONS OF POLYNOMIAL COMMITMENTS AT A COMMON POINT

Prover knows: a length-r vector of polynomials $\vec{f} \in (\mathbb{Z}_q[x])^r$
Verifier learns: a length-r vector $\vec{C}$ of component-wise commitments to polynomials in $\vec{f}$, a component-wise evaluation $\vec{\rho}$ of $\vec{f}$ at $x = x_0$, and the evaluation point x_0

1. The prover computes and sends $\vec{C}$ and $\vec{\rho}$ to the verifier.
2. The verifier chooses $\vec{a} = \langle a_1, \ldots, a_r \rangle \in_R (\mathbb{Z}_{2^\kappa})^r$ and sends it to the prover; meanwhile, the verifier computes the dot product $\rho_a = \vec{\rho} \cdot \vec{a}$ and the commitment $C_a = \prod_{i=1}^{r} C_i^{a_i}$.
3. The prover computes the dot product $f_a = \vec{f} \cdot \vec{a}$ and the witness $w_a = \texttt{CreateWitness}(f_a, x_0)$, then sends w_a to the verifier.
4. The verifier checks if $\texttt{Ver}(C_a, x_0, \rho_a, w_a) \stackrel{?}{=} \texttt{true}$.

The noninteractive form of batch verification works similarly, except the prover computes and sends a vector of witnesses to the verifier (one for each polynomial commitment), and *the verifier* combines the witnesses locally by computing $w_a = \prod_{i=1}^{r} w_i^{a_i}$; in particular, the vector $\vec{a}$ is local to the verifier and the prover never sees it.

Countering GATTACA: Efficient and Secure Testing of Fully-Sequenced Human Genomes

Pierre Baldi[†,‡] Roberta Baronio[†] Emiliano De Cristofaro[‡] Paolo Gasti[‡] Gene Tsudik[‡]

[†] Institute for Genomics and Bioinformatics [‡] Department of Computer Science
{pfbaldi,rbaronio,edecrist,pgasti,gts}@uci.edu
University of California, Irvine

ABSTRACT

Recent advances in DNA sequencing technologies have put ubiquitous availability of fully sequenced human genomes within reach. It is no longer hard to imagine the day when everyone will have the means to obtain and store one's own DNA sequence. Widespread and affordable availability of fully sequenced genomes immediately opens up important opportunities in a number of health-related fields. In particular, common genomic applications and tests performed *in vitro* today will soon be conducted computationally, using digitized genomes. New applications will be developed as genome-enabled medicine becomes increasingly preventive and personalized. However, this progress also prompts significant privacy challenges associated with potential loss, theft, or misuse of genomic data. In this paper, we begin to address genomic privacy by focusing on three important applications: *Paternity Tests*, *Personalized Medicine*, and *Genetic Compatibility Tests*. After carefully analyzing these applications and their privacy requirements, we propose a set of efficient techniques based on *private set operations*. This allows us to implement in *in silico* some operations that are currently performed via *in vitro* methods, in a secure fashion. Experimental results demonstrate that proposed techniques are both feasible and practical today.

Categories and Subject Descriptors: E.3 [Data Encryption]: Secure Multi-party Computation

General Terms: Security.

Keywords: Privacy, DNA, Cryptographic Protocols.

1. INTRODUCTION

Over the past four decades, DNA sequencing has been one of the major driving forces in life-sciences, producing full genome sequences of thousands of viruses and bacteria, and dozens of eukaryotic organisms, from yeast to man (e.g., [2, 30, 40, 76]). This trend is only being accentuated by modern High-Throughput Sequencing (HTS) technologies: the first diploid human genome sequences were recently produced [52, 74, 78] and a project to sequence 1,000 human genomes has been essentially completed [19, 43, 66]. Different HTS technologies are competing to sequence an individual human genome — composed of about 3 billion DNA nucleotides (or bases) — for less than $1,000 by 2012 [65], and even less than $100 five years later, reaching the point where human genome sequencing will be a commodity costing less than an X-ray or an MRI scan. Ubiquity of human and other genomes creates enormous opportunities and challenges. In particular, it promises to address one of the greatest societal challenges of our time: the unsustainable rise of health care costs, by ushering a new era of genome-enabled predictive, preventive, participatory, and personalized medicine ("P4" medicine). In time, genomes could become part of the *Electronic Medical Record* of every individual [38].

However, widespread availability of HTS technologies and genomic data exacerbates ethical, security, and privacy concerns [11]. A full genome sequence not only uniquely identifies each one of us; it also contains information about, for instance, our ethnic heritage, disease predispositions, and many other phenotypic traits [23, 64]. Traditional approaches to privacy, such as de-identification [54], become completely moot in the genomic era, since the genome itself is the ultimate identifier. To further compound the privacy problem, health information is increasingly shared electronically among insurance companies, health care providers and employers. This, coupled with the possibility of creating large centralized genome repositories, raises the specter of possible abuses.

Some federal laws have been passed to begin addressing privacy issues. The 2003 Health Insurance Portability and Accountability Act (HIPAA) provides a general framework for protecting and sharing Protected Health Information (PHI) [20, 49, 55]. In 2008, the Genetic Information Nondiscrimination Act (GINA) was adopted to prohibit discrimination on the basis of genetic information. with respect to health insurance and employment [73]. While providing general guidelines and a basic safety net, current legislation does not offer detailed technical information about safe and privacy-preserving ways for storing and querying genomes. In short, technical issues of security and privacy for HTS and genomic data remain both important and relatively poorly understood.

While privacy issues are not yet hampering progress in basic genomic research, it is not too early to start investigating them, particularly, in light of their complexity, potential impact on society, and current efforts to reform the health care system. It remains unclear where personal genomic information will be stored, who will have access to it, and how it will be queried and shared. To remain flexible, we can imagine a general framework comprised of two kinds of basic entities: (1) Data Centers where genomic data is stored, and (2) Agents/Agencies interested in querying this data. Granularity of Data Centers could vary. At one end of the spectrum, every individual could be her own Data Center and store the genome on a personal computer, cell phone, or some other device. At the other extreme, we could envision national or even international Data Centers storing millions (or even billions) of genomic sequences. Data Centers could also be envisioned at the granularity of family, school, pharmacy, laboratory, hospital, city, county or state. Likewise, many different types of Agents/Agencies are conceivable, ranging from individuals and personal physicians, to family members, pharmacies, hospitals, insurance companies, employers and government agencies (e.g., the FBI), or international organizations. Various Agents/Agencies might be allowed to query different aspects of genomic data and might be required to satisfy different query privacy requirements. In addition, one could imagine cases (e.g., criminal search or proprietary diagnostic technology) where both the genomic data and queries against it must remain private.

The main security and privacy challenge is how to support such queries with low storage costs and reasonably short query times, while satisfying privacy and security requirements associated with a given type of transaction. Unfortunately, current methods for privacy-preserving data querying do not scale to genomic data sizes. Several cryptographic techniques have been proposed that — though not addressing the case of fully-sequenced genomes — focus on private computation over genomic fragments. Specifically, they allow two or more parties to engage in protocols that reveal only the end-result of a given computation on their respective genomic data, without leaking any additional information. The main thrust of this paper is to adapt and deploy efficient cryptographic techniques to address specific genomic queries and applications, described below.

1.1 Applications

As mentioned above, availability of affordable full genome sequencing makes it increasingly possible to query and test genomic information not only *in vitro*, but also *in silico* using computational techniques. We consider three concrete examples of such tests and corresponding privacy-relevant scenarios.

Paternity Tests establish whether a male individual is the biological father of another individual, using genetic fingerprinting. Advances in biotechnology facilitated DNA paternity tests and stimulated the creation of hundreds of online companies offering testing via self-administered cheek swabs for as little as $79 (e.g., `http://www.gtldna.net`). However, this practice raises several security and privacy concerns: the testing company must be trusted with privacy and accuracy of test results, as well as with swabs that might yield full genome sequencing. We believe that, ideally, any two individuals, in possession of their genomes should be able to conduct a privacy-preserving paternity test with no involvement of any third parties. Only the outcome of the test ought to be learned by one or both parties and no other sensitive genomic information should be disclosed.

Personalized Medicine is recognized as a significant paradigm shift and a major trend in health care, moving us closer to a more precise, powerful, and holistic type of medicine [77]. With personalize medicine, treatment and medication type/dosage would be tailored to the precise genetic makeup of individual patient. For example, measurements of *erbB2* protein in breast, lung, or colorectal cancer patients are taken before selecting proper treatment. It has been showed that the trastuzumab monoclonal antibody is effective only in patients whose genetic receptor is over-expressed [63]. Furthermore, the FDA has recently recommended testing for the thiopurine S-methyltransferase (*tpmt*) gene, prior to prescribing for 6-mercaptopurine and azathioprine — two drugs used for treating childhood leukemia and autoimmune diseases. The *tpmt* gene codes for the TPMT enzyme that metabolizes thiopurine drugs: genetic polymorphisms affecting enzymatic activity are correlated with variations in sensitivity and toxicity response to such drugs. Patients suffering from this genetic disease (1 in 300) only need 6-10% of the standard dose of thiopurine drugs; if treated with the full dose, they risk severe bone marrow suppression and subsequent death [1]. Not surprisingly, experts predict that availability of full genome sequencing will further stimulate development of personalized medicine [29].

Genetic Tests are routinely used for several purposes, such as newborn screening, confirmational diagnostics, as well as pre-symptomatic testing, e.g., predicting Huntington's disease [34] and estimating risks of various types of cancer. We focus on genetic *compatibility* tests, whereby potential or existing partners wish to assess the possibility of transmitting to their children a genetic disease with Mendelian inheritance [56]. Modern genetic testing can accurately predict whether a couple is at risk of conceiving a child with an autosomal recessive disease. Consider, for instance, *Beta-Thalassemia minor*, that causes red cells to be smaller than average, due to a mutation in the *hbb* gene. It is called *minor* when the mutation occurs only in one allele. This *minor* form has no severe impact on a subject's quality of life. However, the *major* variant — that occurs when both alleles carry the mutation — is likely to result in premature death, usually, before age twenty. Therefore, if both partners silently carry the *minor* form, there is a 25% chance that their child could carry the major variety. Another example is the *Lynch Syndrome* (also known as Hereditary Nonpolyposis Colon Cancer), a genetic condition — most commonly inherited from a parent — associated with the high risk of colon cancer [45]. Parents with this syndrome have a 50% chance of passing it on to their children. Since the possibility of inheritance is maximized if both parents carry the mutations, testing for Lynch Syndrome is crucial.

Note on Non-human Genomes: Although this paper focuses on human genomes, some aforementioned scenarios apply to other organisms, e.g., crops and animals [3]. For instance, a paternity test may certify a purebred dog's bloodline or genetic tests may determine the quality of a racing horse. In fact, DNA "barcodes" identifiers are already embedded in genomes of genetically modified species. Conceivably, future veterinary treatments may also involve elements of personalized medicine for animals.

1.2 Roadmap

Motivated by the emerging affordability of full genome sequencing, we combine domain knowledge in biology, genomics, bioinformatics, security, privacy and applied cryptography in order to better understand the corresponding security and privacy challenges. In particular, we analyze specific requirements of three types of applications discussed above: Paternity Tests, Personalized Medicine and Genetic Tests. In the process, we carefully consider today's *in vitro* procedure for each application and analyze its security and privacy requirements in the digital domain. This type of approach allows us to gradually craft specialized protocols that incur appreciably lower overhead than state-of-the-art. However, as is well known, "lower overhead" does not necessarily imply practicality. Therefore, we demonstrate — via experiments on commodity hardware — that proposed protocols are indeed viable and practical *today*. Source code of our implementations is publicly available. We hope that it can help in developing privacy-aware operations on full genomes and allows individuals (in possession of their sequenced genomes) to run genetic tests with privacy.

Organization. We overview related work in the next section. Then, Sec. 3 introduces biological and cryptographic background used throughout the rest of the paper. The core of the paper is in Sec. 4

that includes step-by-step design of protocols for each aforementioned application. It also presents experimental results. Next, Sec. 5 provides security arguments for proposed protocols, followed by the summary and the discussion of future work in Sec. 6.

2. RELATED WORK

Motivated by the sensitivity of genomic information, the security research community has begun to develop mechanisms to enable secure computation on genomic data. A number of cryptographic protocols have been proposed for private searching, matching and evaluating similarity of strings, including DNA sequences. Also, prior work has considered specific (privacy-preserving) genomic operations. This section overviews relevant prior results and highlights their potential limitation.

Searching and Matching DNA

Troncoso-Pastoriza, et al. [71] proposed a privacy-preserving and error-resilient protocol for string searching. In it, one party (e.g., Alice), with her own DNA snippet, can verify the existence of a short template (e.g., a genetic test held by a service provider – Bob) within her snippet. This technique handles errors and maintains privacy of both the template and the snippet. Each query is represented as an automaton executed using a finite state machine (FSM) in an oblivious manner. Communication complexity is $O(n \cdot (|\Sigma| + |Q|))$, where n is snippet length, $|\Sigma|$ – alphabet size (i.e., 4 for DNA), and $|Q|$ – number of states. Computational complexity is $O(n \cdot |\Sigma| \cdot |Q|)$ and $O(n \cdot |Q|)$ cryptographic operations for Alice and Bob, respectively. However, the number of FSM states is always revealed to all parties. To obtain error-resilient and approximate DNA matching, [71] also shows how to construct an automaton that, given Alice's string x, accepts all strings with Levenshtein distance [51] at most d from x.

Blanton and Aliasgari [4] improve on [71], reducing Alice's work by a factor of $|\Sigma|$ and Bob's — by a factor of $\log(|Q|)$, incurring, however, a potentially increased communication complexity (if the security parameter is smaller than $\log(|Q|)$). This work also introduces a protocol for secure outsourcing of computation to an external service provider and a modified *multi-party* protocol.

A set of cryptographic protocols for secure pattern matching are presented in [27] and [36]. Given a binary string T of length n, held by Alice, and a binary pattern p of length m, held by Bob, pattern matching lets Bob learn all locations in T where p appears. Secure computation guarantees that nothing except m is learned by Alice, and nothing about T is revealed to Bob (besides n and locations where p appears). [27] proposes one such protocol, secure in the semi-honest setting, based on homomorphic encryption, with $O(m + n)$ communication and computation complexities. It includes another protocol, secure in the malicious setting, based on secure oblivious automata evaluation, with quadratic complexity and m rounds. Subsequently, [36] presented an improved protocol, with malicious security, using homomorphic encryption and incurring $O(m + n)$ complexity.

Another related result is the recent work in [47]. It realizes secure computation of the CODIS test [69] (run by the FBI for DNA identity testing), that could not be implemented using pattern matching or FSM. It achieves efficient secure computation of function $M(T, p, e, l) = 1$ iff $|l_{max}(T, p) - l| \leq \varepsilon$, where T is a DNA fragment, p a pattern, (ε, l) some additional information, and $l_{max}(T, p) \geq 0$ is the largest integer l' for which $p^{l'}$ appears as a substring in T. A general technique for secure text processing is introduced, combining garbled circuits and secure pattern matching. (The latter is reduced to private keyword search and solved using Oblivious Pseudorandom Functions (OPRF-s) [24, 35].) The resulting protocol can compute several functions (including CODIS) on sample T and pattern p, using the number of circuits linear in the number of occurrences of p. Complexity incurred by the underlying keyword search protocol is linear in $|T|$. However, common knowledge of some threshold on the number of occurrences needs to be assumed.

Similarity of DNA Sequences

Another set of cryptographic results focus on privately computing the *edit distance* of two strings α, β of size m and n, respectively.[1] Privacy-preserving computation of Smith-Waterman scores [67] has also been investigated and used for sequence alignment.

Jha, et al. [42] proposed techniques for secure edit distance using garbled circuits [79], and showed that the overhead is acceptable only for small strings (e.g., a 200-character strings require 2GB circuits). For longer strings, two optimized techniques were proposed; they exploit the structure of the dynamic programming problem (intrinsic to the specific circuit) and split the computation into smaller component circuits. However, a quadratic number of oblivious transfers is needed to evaluate garbled circuits, thus limiting scalability of this approach. For example, 500-character string instances take almost one hour to complete [42]. Optimized protocols also extend to privacy-preserving Smith-Waterman scores [67], a more sophisticated string comparison algorithm, where costs of delete/insert/replace operations, instead of being equal, are determined by special functions. Again, scalability is limited: experiments in [42] show that evaluation of Smith-Waterman for a 60-character string takes about 1,000 seconds.

Somewhat less related techniques include [44] that proposed a cryptographic framework for executing queries on genomic databases where privacy is attained by relying on two anonymizing and non-colluding parties. Danezis, et al. [14] used negative databases to test a single profile against a database of suspects, such that database contents cannot be efficiently enumerated.

Specialized Protocols

Wang, et al. [75] proposed techniques for computation on genomic data stored at a data provider, including: edit distance, Smith-Waterman and search for homologous genes. Program specialization is used to partition genomic data into "public" (most of the genome) and "sensitive" (a very small subset of the genome). Sensitive regions are replaced with symbols by data providers (DPs) before data consumers (DCs) have access to genomic information. DCs perform concrete execution on public data and symbolic execution on sensitive data, and may perform queries to DPs on sensitive nucleotides. However, only queries that do not let DCs reconstruct sensitive regions are allowed by DPs and generic two-party computation techniques are used during query execution. Portions of sensitive data are public information. We note that, due to the current limited knowledge of human genome, parts that are considered non-sensitive today may actually become sensitive later.

Finally, Bruekers, et al. [6] presented privacy-preserving techniques for a few DNA operations, such as: identity test, common ancestor and paternity test, based on STR (Short Tandem Repeat; see Sec. 3.1). Homomorphic encryption is used on alleles (fragments of DNA) to compute comparisons. Testing protocols tolerate a small number of errors, however, their complexity increases with the number of tolerated errors [4]. Also, [6] leaves as an open problem the scenario where an attacker (honestly) runs the protocol

[1] Edit distance is the minimum number of operations (delete, insert, or replace) needed to transform α into β.

but executes it on arbitrarily chosen inputs. In this setting, attackers, given STR's limited entropy, can "lie" about their STR profiles and run multiple dependent protocols thus reconstructing the other party's profile.

Using Current Techniques?

We aim to obtain secure and private computation on fully sequenced genomes, in scenarios where individuals possess their own genomic data. As discussed in Sec. 1, we focus on paternity testing, personalized medicine and genetic compatibility testing. Prior work has yielded a number of elegant (if not always efficient) cryptographic protocols for secure computation on DNA sequences. However, we identify some notable open problems:

1. ***Efficiency:*** Most current protocols are designed for DNA snippets (e.g., hundreds of thousands nucleotides) and it is unclear how to scale them to full genomes (i.e., three billion nucleotides).
2. ***Error Resilience:*** Most prior work attempts to achieve resilience to sequencing errors *in computation* (e.g., using approximate matching or distance with errors). Not surprisingly, this results in: (i) significant computation and communication overhead, and (ii) ruling out more efficient and simpler cryptographic tools, i.e., those geared for exact matching. (Whereas, our goal is error-resilience by design.) Also, as the cost of full genome sequencing drops, so do error rates. By increasing the number of sequencing runs, the probability of sequencing errors can be rapidly reduced.
3. ***Inter-String Distance:*** Analyzing the distance between sequenced strings works for the creation of phylogenetic trees, parental analysis, and homology studies. However, it does not suit applications, such as genetic diseases testing, that require much more complex comparisons.
4. ***Paternity Testing:*** To the best of our knowledge, the only available technique for privacy-preserving genetic paternity testing is [6]. However, it does not prevent a participant from manipulating its input to reconstruct the counterpart's profile. Also, as shown in Sec. 4.1, overhead can be significantly reduced using techniques that obtain error resilience by design.
5. ***Genetic Testing via Pattern Matching:*** The use of pattern matching over full genomes to test for genetic compatibility and/or personalized medicine is not straightforward. Suppose that a party wants to privately search for certain gene mutation, e.g., Beta-Thalassemia. The pattern representing this mutation might be very short — a few nucleotides — but needs to be searched in the full genome, as restricting the search to the specific gene would trivially expose the nature of the test. Therefore, naïve application of pattern matching would return all locations (presumably millions) where the pattern appears. This would be detrimental to both privacy and efficiency of the resulting solution. We could modify the pattern to include nucleotides expected to appear immediately before/after the mutation, such that, with high probability, this pattern would appear at most once. However, this needs to be done carefully, since: (i) nucleotides added to the pattern must appear in *all* human genomes, and (ii) the choice of pattern length should not expose the mutation being searched. Plus, extending the pattern would also increase computation and communication overhead.

3. PRELIMINARIES

This section provides some relevant biology and cryptography background information.

3.1 Biology Background

Genomes represent the entirety of an organism's hereditary information. They are encoded either in DNA or, for many types of viruses, in RNA. The genome includes both the genes and the non-coding sequences of the DNA/RNA. For humans and many other organisms, the genome is encoded in double stranded deoxyribonucleic acid (DNA) molecules, consisting of two long and complementary polymer chains of four simple units called nucleotides, represented by the letters A, C, G, and T. The human genome consists of approximately 3 billion letters.

Restriction Fragment Length Polymorphisms (RFLPs) refers to a difference between samples of homologous DNA molecules that come from differing locations of restriction enzyme sites, and to a related laboratory technique by which these segments can be illustrated. In RFLP analysis, a DNA sample is broken into pieces (digested) by restriction enzymes and the resulting restriction fragments are separated according to their lengths by gel electrophoresis. Thus, RFLP provides information about the length (but not the composition) of DNA subsequences occurring between known subsequences recognized by particular enzymes. Although it is being progressively superseded by inexpensive DNA sequencing technologies, RFLP analysis was the first DNA profiling technique inexpensive enough for widespread application. It is still widely used at present. RFLP probes are frequently used in genome mapping and in variation analysis, such genotyping, forensics, paternity tests and hereditary disease diagnostics. (For more details, see [61].)

Single Nucleotide Polymorphisms (SNPs) are the most common form of DNA variation occurring when a single nucleotide (A, C, G, or T) differs between members of the same species or paired chromosomes of an individual [68]. The average SNP frequency in the human genome is approximately 1 per 1,000 nucleotide pairs.[2] SNP variations are often associated with how individuals develop diseases and respond to pathogens, chemicals, drugs, vaccines, and other agents. Thus SNPs are key enablers in realizing *personalized medicine* [9]. Moreover, they are used in genetic disease and disorder testing, as well as to compare genome regions between cohorts in genome-wide association studies.

Short Tandem Repeats (STRs) occur when a pattern of two or more nucleotides are repeated and repeated sequences are directly adjacent to each other. The pattern can range in length from 2 to 50 nucleotides or so. Unrelated people likely have different numbers of repeat units in highly polymorphic regions, hence, STRs are often used to differentiate between individuals. STR *loci* (i.e., locations on a chromosome) are targeted with sequence-specific primers. Resulting DNA fragments are then separated and detected using electrophoresis. By identifying repeats of a specific sequence at specific locations in the genome, it is possible to create a genetic profile of an individual. There are currently over 10,000 published STR sequences in the human genome.

3.2 Cryptography Background

We now overview a set of cryptographic concepts and tools used in the rest of the paper. For ease of exposition, we omit basic notions and refer to [31, 46, 57] for details on various cryptographic primitives, such as hash functions, number-theoretic assumptions, as well as encryption and signature schemes.

Private Set Intersection (PSI) [25]: a protocol between Server

[2]NCBI maintains an interactive collection of SNPs, dbSNP, containing all known genetic variations of the human genome [59].

with input $\mathcal{S}=\{s_1,\ldots,s_w\}$, and Client with input $\mathcal{C}=\{c_1,\ldots,c_v\}$. At the end, Client learns $\mathcal{S}\cap\mathcal{C}$. PSI securely implements: $\mathcal{F}_{\mathsf{PSI}}$: $(\mathcal{S},\mathcal{C})\mapsto(\perp,\mathcal{S}\cap\mathcal{C})$.

Private Set Intersection Cardinality (PSI-CA) [25]: a protocol between Server with input $\mathcal{S}=\{s_1,\ldots,s_w\}$, and Client with input $\mathcal{C}=\{c_1,\ldots,c_v\}$. At the end, Client learns $|\mathcal{S}\cap\mathcal{C}|$. PSI-CA securely implements: $\mathcal{F}_{\mathsf{PSI\text{-}CA}}:(\mathcal{S},\mathcal{C})\mapsto(\perp,|\mathcal{S}\cap\mathcal{C}|)$.

Authorized Private Set Intersection (APSI) [16]: a protocol between Server with input $\mathcal{S}=\{s_1,\ldots,s_w\}$, and Client with input $\mathcal{C}=\{c_1,\ldots,c_v\}$ and $\mathcal{C}_\sigma=\{\sigma_1,\ldots,\sigma_v\}$. At the end, Client learns: $\mathsf{ASI}\stackrel{\text{def}}{=}\mathcal{S}\cap\{c_i \mid c_i\in\mathcal{C}\ \wedge\ \sigma_i \textit{ valid auth. on } c_i\}$. APSI securely implements: $\mathcal{F}_{\mathsf{APSI}}:(\mathcal{S},(\mathcal{C},\mathcal{C}_\sigma))\mapsto(\perp,\mathsf{ASI})$.

Adversarial Model. We use standard security models for secure two-party computation. One distinguishing factor is the adversarial model that is either semi-honest or malicious. (In the rest of this paper, the term *adversary* refers to insiders, i.e., protocol participants. Outside adversaries are not considered, since their actions can be mitigated via standard network security techniques.)

Following definitions in [31], protocols secure in the presence of *semi-honest adversaries* assume that parties faithfully follow all protocol specifications and do not misrepresent any information related to their inputs, e.g., size and content. However, during or after protocol execution, any party might (passively) attempt to infer additional information about the other party's input. This model is formalized by considering an ideal implementation where a trusted third party (TTP) receives the inputs of both parties and outputs the result of the defined function. Security in the presence of semi-honest adversaries requires that, in the real implementation of the protocol (without a TTP), each party does not learn more information than in the ideal implementation.

Security in the presence of *malicious parties* allows arbitrary deviations from the protocol. However, it does not prevent parties from refusing to participate in the protocol, modifying their inputs, or prematurely aborting the protocol. Security in the malicious model is achieved if the adversary (interacting in the real protocol, without the TTP) can learn no more information than it could in the ideal scenario. In other words, a secure protocol emulates (in its real execution) the ideal execution that includes a TTP. This notion is formulated by requiring the existence of adversaries in the ideal execution model that can simulate adversarial behavior in the real execution model.

Although security arguments in this paper are made with respect to semi-honest participants, extensions to malicious participant security (with the same computation and communication complexities) have already been developed for our cryptographic building blocks: PSI, PSI-CA and APSI. We consider these extensions to be out of the scope of this paper.

4. GENOME TESTING

We now explore efficient techniques for privacy-preserving testing on fully sequenced genomes. Unlike most prior work (reviewed in Sec. 2), we do not seek generic solutions for genomic computation. Instead, we focus on a few specific real-world applications and, for each, capitalize on domain knowledge to propose an efficient privacy-preserving approach.

Notation. We assume that each participant has a digital copy of her fully sequenced genome denoted by $\mathcal{G}=\{(b_1||1),\ldots,(b_n||n)\}$, where $b_i\in\{\text{A, G, C, T, –}\}$, n is the human genome length (i.e., $3\cdot10^9$), and "||" denotes concatenation. The "–" symbol is needed to handle DNA mutations corresponding to *deletion*, i.e., where a portion of a chromosome is missing [53]. It is also used when the sequencing process fails to determine a nucleotide. This data may be pre-processed in order to speed up execution of specific applications. For example, parties may pre-compute a cryptographic hash, $\mathrm{H}(\cdot)$, on each nucleotide, alongside its position in the genome, i.e., for each $(b_i||i)\in\mathcal{G}$, they compute $hb_i=\mathrm{H}(b_i||i)$.[3]

We use the notation $|str|$ to denote the length of string str, and $|A|$ to denote the cardinality of set A. Finally, we use $r\leftarrow R$ to indicate that r is chosen uniformly at random from set R.

Experimental Setup. The rest of this section includes some experimental results. Unless explicitly stated otherwise, all experiments were performed on a Linux Desktop, with an Intel Core i5-560M (running at 2.66 GHz). All tests were run on a single processor core and all code is written in C, using OpenSSL and GMP libraries. Cryptographic protocols use the SHA-1 hash function and 1024-bit moduli. Source code of our experiments is available at `http://sprout.ics.uci.edu/projects/privacy-dna`.

4.1 Genetic Paternity Test

A Genetic Paternity Test (GPT) allows two individuals with their respective genomes to determine whether there exists a biological parent-child relationship between them. A ***Privacy-Preserving Genetic Paternity Test*** (PPGPT) achieves the same result without revealing any information about the two genomes. In the following, we refer to the two participants as Client and Server. Only Client receives the outcome of the test.

Strawman Approach

Genomics studies have shown that about 99.5% of any two human genomes are identical. Humans carry two copies of each chromosome, inherited one from the mother and one from the father. Thus, genomes carried by two individuals tied by a parent-child relationship show an even higher degree of similarity. As a result, one immediate computational technique for GPT is to compare the candidate's genome with that of the child; the test returns a positive result if the percentage of matching nucleotides is above a given threshold τ, i.e., significantly higher than 99.5%.

First-Attempt Protocol. At first glance, protecting privacy is relatively easy: recent proposals for Private Set Intersection Cardinality (PSI-CA) protocols [17, 25, 48, 72] offer efficient and private two-party computation of the number of set elements shared by two parties. Thus, to perform PPGPT, two participants just need to run PSI-CA on input of their respective genomes.

We select the PSI-CA construction from [17] (shown in Fig. 1) since it offers the best communication and computation complexities. Also, we use PSI-CA rather than PSI since *semi-honest* participants only need to learn *how similar* their genomes are. Whereas, PSI would also reveal *where* the two genomes differ and/or where they have common features.

We emphasize that this approach provides very accurate results, and is not significantly affected by potential sequencing errors. In fact, given expected error ratio ε, one can simply modify threshold τ to accommodate errors. This is because ε is expected to be significantly smaller than the difference between τ and the percentage of nucleotides that any two individuals share.

Unfortunately, since the number of nucleotides in the human genome is extremely large (about $3\cdot10^9$), this technique, though optimal in terms of accuracy, is impractical using current commodity

[3] In case of *insertion* mutation in the genome, e.g., an 'A' is added between positions 35 and 36, genome pre-processing computes $\mathrm{H}(\text{A}||35||1)$. Similarly, if insertion involves multiple nucleotides. Since insertions are rare in human genomes, we do not consider them in this paper.

Client, on input $\mathcal{C} = \{c_1, \ldots, c_v\}$	[Common Input: $(p, q, g, \mathrm{H}, \mathrm{H}')$]	Server, on input $\mathcal{S} = \{s_1, \ldots, s_w\}$
		Offline $\{\hat{s}_1, \ldots, \hat{s}_w\} \leftarrow \Pi(\mathcal{S})$, with Π random permutation $R_s \leftarrow \mathbb{Z}_q,\ R'_s \leftarrow \mathbb{Z}_q, Y = g^{R_s}$ $\forall j\ 1 \le j \le w,\ ks_j = \mathrm{H}(\hat{s}_j)^{R'_s}$
Offline $R_c \leftarrow \mathbb{Z}_q,\ R'_c \leftarrow \mathbb{Z}_q, X = g^{R_c}$ $\forall i\ 1 \le i \le v,\ a_i = \mathrm{H}(c_i)^{R'_c}$	$X, \{a_1, \ldots, a_v\}$ $\longrightarrow$	**Online** $\forall i\ 1 \le i \le v,\ a'_i = (a_i)^{R'_s}$ $(a'_{\ell_1}, \ldots, a'_{\ell_v}) = \Pi(a'_1, \ldots, a'_v)$ $\forall j\ 1 \le j \le w,\ ts_j = \mathrm{H}'(X^{R_s} \cdot ks_j)$
Online $\forall i\ 1 \le i \le v,\ tc_{\ell_i} = \mathrm{H}'((Y^{R_c})(a'_{\ell_i})^{1/R'_c})$ **Out**: $\lvert\{ts_1, \ldots, ts_w\} \cap \{tc_{\ell_1}, \ldots, tc_{\ell_v}\}\rvert$	$Y, \{a'_{\ell_1}, \ldots, a'_{\ell_v}\}$ $\longleftarrow$ $\{ts_1, \ldots, ts_w\}$	

Figure 1: PSI-CA protocol from [17]. It executes on common input of two primes p and q (such that $q|p-1$), a generator g of a subgroup of size q and two hash functions, H and H$'$, modeled as random oracles. All computation is mod p.

hardware, as it requires both parties to perform online computation over the entire genome. Specifically, PSI-CA entails a number of (short) modular exponentiations linear in the input size. Table 1 estimates execution times and bandwidth incurred by this naïve approach. Since Client's online computation depends on that of the Server, a single test would consume approximately 10 days.

	Offline	Online	
	Time	Time	Size
Client	4.5 days	4.5 days	358 GB
Server	4.5 days	4.5 days	414 GB

Table 1: Computation and communication costs of the first straw-man PPGPT protocol.

Improved Protocol. Since about 99.5% of the human genome is the same, two parties would only need to compare the remaining 0.5%. Unfortunately, there is yet not enough statistical knowledge to pinpoint *where* exactly this 0.5% occurs. Nonetheless, experts claim that, in practice, comparing a properly chosen 1% of the genome yields an accuracy comparable to analyzing the entire genome [28]. Running times and bandwidth overhead required by this improved method are presented in Table 2.

	Offline	Online	
	Time	Time	Size
Client	67 mins	67 mins	3.57 GB
Server	67 mins	67 mins	4.14 GB

Table 2: Computation and communication costs of improved PPGPT protocol. Computation is performed over 1% of the human genome.

Efficient RFLP-based PPGPT

We now present a very efficient technique for Privacy-Preserving Genetic Paternity Testing (PPGPT). To construct it, we take advantage of domain knowledge in genomics and build upon effective *in vitro* techniques (RFLP or SNP) rather than generic computational techniques. First, we design a protocol that implements RFLP-based GPT. Next, we propose a cryptographic technique for secure computation of this protocol that realizes PPGPT. Finally, we show that the technique used for computing RFLP-based GPT can be easily adapted to perform SNP-based GPT.

As discussed in Sec. 3.1, RFLPs use specific restriction enzymes (e.g., HaeIII, PstI, and HinfI), to digest a genome into hundreds of smaller fragments. Following the deterministic and well-known process, enzymes cut the DNA at each occurrence of a given pattern (e.g., "CTGCAG" with PstI). Next, a subset of these fragments is selected using a small number of probes for well-known markers, which are located in known areas of the genome. In an RFLP-based paternity test, this process is applied to the DNA of the two tested individuals. If resulting fragments have comparable lengths, then the test returns a positive with certain confidence, based on the exact number of fragments of the same length.

There are a few slightly different ways to select the type and the number of markers, thus identifying exactly which fragments to compare. For the sake of reliability, one needs to use markers that are rare enough (i.e., occur in unrelated individuals with very low probability) while common enough to occur in at least one of the tested subjects. Currently, public databases and scientific literature offer thousands available probes for RFLP in human genomes [10, 62, 70]. However, to reduce the cost of in vitro tests, only a small subset of them is actually used [18]. Different laboratories consider various accuracy/cost trade-offs. Some compare as few as 9-15 DNA markers, returning a positive result whenever fewer than two fragments do not match [12], with an estimated 99.9% accuracy. Meanwhile, others use up to 25 markers and return a positive whenever fewer than two fragments do not match, thus providing significantly higher accuracy, i.e., about 99.999% [22, 50].

In the United States, these testing methodologies follow precise regulations issued by the American Association of Blood Banks (AABB) and are considered legally admissible as evidence in the court of law. Since our PPGPT technique closely mimics the *in vitro* procedure, it achieves the same level of accuracy. Nevertheless, as the cost of RFLP emulation on digitalized genomes is not significantly affected by the number of selected markers, we can anticipate increasing the number of markers to improve accuracy. We could perform tests with 50 markers and show that this only adds a small cost. However, selection of additional markers is out of the scope of this paper, as their introduction does not change the algorithm's functionality presented below.

RFLP-based Protocol. This protocol involves two individuals, on private input of their respective fully sequenced genomes. We distinguish between Client and Server, to denote the fact that only the former learns the test outcome. The protocol is run on common input of: a threshold τ, a set of enzymes $E = \{e_1, \ldots, e_j\}$, and a set of markers $M = \{mk_1, \ldots, mk_l\}$. Each participant also inputs its digitized genome.

1. First, participants emulate the digestion process of each enzyme $e_i \in E$ on their genome. Consider, for instance, the PstI enzyme: whenever the string `CTGCAG` occurs, the enzyme cuts the genome in two fragments, so that the first ends with `CTGCA` and the second starts with `G`. As a result, genomes are digested into a large number of fragments of variable length.
2. Next, participants probe the fragments using markers in M. During this process, each participant selects up to l fragments $\{frag_1, \ldots, frag_l\}$ (e.g., $l = 25$), corresponding to M. All remaining fragments are discarded. Public markers are chosen such that each appears in at most one sequence.
3. Client builds the set $F_C = \{(|frag_i^{(c)}|, mk_i)\}_{i=1}^{l}$. For each marker i not corresponding to any fragment, $frag_i^{(c)}$ is replaced with the empty string. Similarly, Server builds $F_S = \{(|frag_i^{(s)}|, mk_i)\}_{i=1}^{l}$
4. Client and Server run the PSI-CA protocol described in Fig. 1, on respective inputs: F_C and F_S. Client learns $pt = |F_C \cap F_S|$, i.e., how many of its and Server's fragments are of the same size.
5. Client learns the test result by comparing pt to threshold τ.

Why Compare Lengths? It might seem that comparing string *lengths* is unreliable since two same-length strings might encode completely different content, while our protocol would consider these strings as matching. In practice, however, this well-established technique yields false positives with ***extremely low probability***. Sequences are selected using markers, i.e., according to (part of) their content. Selection of markers, in turn, guarantees that they appear only in one specific position in the entire genome. Edges of each fragment are content-dependent as well, since enzymes digest them according to a specific pattern of nucleotides. Therefore, two unrelated sequences of the same length would not be compared and two same-length sequences containing the same marker should be indeed considered matching.

Furthermore, this approach boosts the resilience of PPGPT against sequencing errors. Only errors occurring in the pattern digested by enzymes (or in the markers) influence the result of the RFLP-based PPGPT. However, since patterns and markers are relatively short compared to the size of the genome, this happens with very low probability, since sampling errors are uniformly distributed. However, if we let participants compare hashes of fragments, rather than their length, even a moderate error rate would severely increase the probability of false negatives, since even a single sequencing error would affect the final outcome of the test. Moreover, the main purpose of the PPGPT presented in this paper is not to improve accuracy of the *in vitro* test currently used, but to efficiently and securely replicate it *in silico*.

PSI-CA or PSI? The use of PSI-CA, rather than PSI, is needed to minimize information learned by Client from protocol execution. With PSI, if the number of matches is sufficiently high (even if the test is negative), Client would learn the lengths of several Server's fragments: it could then use this information to perform a paternity test between the party previously playing the role of Server and any other individual (although with slightly lower reliability).

SNP-based Protocol. SNP-based tests are replacing RFLP-based tests due to their better performance [7]. While this technique is not yet considered legally admissible in court, it is expected to eventually supersede its RFLP-based counterpart. Our RFLP-based protocol can be extended to perform paternity testing using SNPs: instead of selecting fragments using enzymes and markers, the SNP-based test selects fragments using a set of known SNPs. Since the rest of the protocol is unchanged and the size of the set of SNPs is usually 52 elements [7], the new protocol performs almost identically to the RFLP-based PPGPT protocol with 50 fragments.

Performance Evaluation. We now measure performance of the RFLP-based protocol on the Intel Core i5-560M testbed. The (offline) time needed to emulate the enzyme digestion process on the full genome is 74 seconds. This computation is performed only once, thus, it does not affect the time required to perform the interactive protocol. Finally, in order to assess the practicality of the protocol on embedded devices, we also measured its performance on a modern smartphone — a Nokia N900 equipped with ARM Cortex A8 CPU running at 600 MHz. Table 3 summarizes the online cost of the RFLP-based protocol, measuring computation and communication overhead, using different numbers of markers, on both i5-560M and A8 processors.

	Offline (Time)		Online (Time/size)		
Entity (markers)	i5-560M	A8	i5-560M	A8	Size
Client (25)	3.4 ms	323 ms	3.4 ms	323 ms	3 KB
Server (25)	3.4 ms	323 ms	3.4 ms	323 ms	3.5 KB
Client (50)	6.7 ms	645 ms	6.7 ms	645 ms	6 KB
Server (50)	6.7 ms	645 ms	6.7 ms	645 ms	7 KB

Table 3: Computation and communication costs of RFLP-based PPGPT technique, testing 25 and 50 fragments.

For the sake of completeness, we compared our results to prior work on privacy-preserving paternity testing, presented in Figure 3 of [6]. Following a conservative approach, we instantiate: (i) the cheapest protocol variant, which tolerates no error, and (ii) the most efficient additively homomorphic cryptosystem among those suggested, i.e., modified ElGamal [21]. Also, we only count the number of modular exponentiations. Given that the paternity test is performed over n alleles (with n ranging from 13 to 67 for increasing accuracy) we estimate the following costs. In step (2) of the protocol, the party obtaining the test result computes $8n$ modified ElGamal encryptions, thus, incurring $24n$ (short) modular exponentiations. In the i5-560M testbed, this takes from 43ms to 224ms, depending on n. In step (3), the other party needs to obtain the encrypted sum using homomorphic properties: it does so by performing $30n$ exponentiations. This takes between 54 and 262ms on the i5-560M testbed. Even ignoring all other operations in [6] and without pre-computation, our most accurate test (using 50 markers) is about 5 times faster than the least accurate test in [6] (using 13 alleles).

4.2 Personalized Medicine

Personalized Medicine (PM) is increasingly used to provide patients with drugs designed for their specific genetic features. As discussed in Sec. 1, in the context of PM, drugs are associated with a unique genetic fingerprint. Their effectiveness is maximized in patients with a matching DNA [37]. To this end, genomes need to be compared against the fingerprint and a patient need to surrender her DNA to a physician or a pharmaceutical company.

One privacy-preserving approach is to let the patient independently run specialized software over her genome and identify a match (or lack thereof) with a given drug's fingerprint. This way, the patient would learn whether the drug is appropriate. However, pharmaceuticals may consider DNA fingerprints of their drugs to be trade secrets and thus might be unwilling to reveal them. At the same time, for every new drug, pharmaceuticals are required to obtain approval from appropriate government entities, e.g., the Food and Drug Administration (FDA) in case of the United States.

We now introduce a technique for ***Privacy-Preserving Personalized Medicine Testing*** (P^3MT), involving the following steps:

- Following positive clinical trials, a pharmaceutical company obtains FDA approval on a specific DNA fingerprint fp and receives a corresponding authorization, $auth$.
- The pharmaceutical and the patient engage in a protocol, where the former inputs $(fp, auth)$ and the latter inputs her genome.
- At the end of the protocol, the pharmaceutical learns whether the patient's genome matches fingerprint fp, provided that $auth$ is a valid authorization of fp.

Privacy requirements are that: (1) the company learns nothing about patient genome besides the part matching the (authorized) fingerprint, and (2) the patient learns nothing about fp or $auth$.

P^3MT Instantiation

We now present a specific P^3MT instantiation. It involves: (1) an authorization authority (e.g., the FDA) denoted as CA, (2) a pharmaceutical — Client, and (3) a patient — Server.

Our cryptographic building block is Authorized Private Set Intersection (APSI) [8, 15, 16], hence, our Client/Server/CA notation. We select one specific APSI construction in [15], illustrated in Fig. 2, since it currently offers lowest communication and computation complexity. (Moreover, it can be instantiated in the malicious model with only a small constant additional overhead.) For efficiency reasons, $R_{c:i}$'s and R_s are chosen uniformly at random from $W = [1..\lfloor\sqrt{N}/2\rfloor]$, rather than from $\mathbb{Z}_{N/2}$, as in the original version of the protocol. In fact, as proved in [32], the distribution of $g^x \bmod N$ with $x \leftarrow W$ is computationally indistinguishable from the distribution defined by g^x with $x \leftarrow [1..\phi(N)]$. This change does not affect protocol security arguments. Thus, we do not provide a new proof for APSI in this paper.

P^3MT involves two phases: *offline* and an *online*.

During the *offline* phase:

1. CA generates RSA public-private keypair $((N, e), d)$, publishes (N, e), and keeps d private.
2. Client prepares a fingerprint of drug $\mathcal{D}$: $fp(\mathcal{D}) = \{(b_j^* || j)\}$, where each b_j^* is expected at position j of a genome suitable for $\mathcal{D}$.
3. Client obtains from CA an authorization $auth(fp(\mathcal{D}))$, where $auth(fp(\mathcal{D})) = \{\sigma_j \mid \sigma_j = \mathrm{H}(b_j^* || j)^d \bmod N\}$.
4. Server runs the offline stage of the APSI protocol in Fig. 2, on input, $\mathcal{G} = \{(b_1 || 1), \ldots, (b_n || n)\}$, and publishes resulting $\{ts_1, \ldots, ts_n\}$.

During the *online* phase:

1. Client and Server run the online part of the APSI protocol in Fig. 2. Recall that Client's input is $(fp(\mathcal{D}), auth(fp(\mathcal{D})))$, and Server's is $\mathcal{G}$.
2. After the interaction, Client obtains $fp(\mathcal{D}) \cap \mathcal{G}$, and uses this information to determine whether Server is well-suited for drug $\mathcal{D}$.

We note that $auth$ is needed to limit the scope of the test on a patient DNA: the FDA can guarantee that: (i) fp only covers the appropriate set of required nucleotides, and (ii) pharmaceuticals cannot input arbitrary portions of a patient genome.

The proposed P^3MT protocol is resilient against (randomly distributed) sequencing errors. The size of the fingerprint input by Client in the protocol is negligible compared to the size of the entire genome. Thus, positions corresponding to Client input are affected by errors with extremely low probability.

Performance Evaluation. To estimate the efficiency of the P^3MT protocol, we consider two genetic tests commonly performed in the context of personalized medicine: the analysis of *hlu-B* and *tpmt* genes. Our choice is also motivated by the size of their fingerprints that, according to genomics experts, is representative of most personalized medicine tests.

First, we look at the *hla-B*5701* allelic variant, one G→T mutation associated with extreme sensitivity to abacavir, a drug used in HIV treatment [58]. In diploid organisms (such as humans), mutation may occur in either chromosome inherited from the parents. Thus, the related fingerprint contains 2 (*nucleotide, position*) pairs. We also consider the analysis of *tpmt* typically done before prescribing 6-mercaptopurine to leukemia patients. As shown in [80], two alleles are known to cause the *tpmt* disorder: (1) one presents a mutation G→C in position 238 of gene's c-DNA, (2) the other presents one mutation G→A in position 460 and one A→G in position 719.[4] Therefore, the resulting fingerprint contains these 6 (nucleotide, position) pairs.

In the underlying APSI protocol (Fig. 2), cryptographic operations on Server genome do not depend on Client input. Therefore, they can be computed offline, once for all possible tests. Moreover, we have designed the P^3MT protocol to be as generic as possible. Our protocol runs on the whole Server's genome — with linear complexity — in order to address future scenarios where genomics advances will cause better understanding of many more regions of human genomes. To reduce offline costs, we apply reference-based compression [5, 13] – a technique commonly used to efficiently represent genomic information. In particular, Server input consists of all differences between its genome and the reference sequence. We emphasize that this technique does not require any biological correctness of the reference genome that is only used for compression [39]. This allows us to reduce the size of Server input to about 1% of the entire genome.

Test	Party	Offline	Online	
		Time	Time	Size
*hla-b**5701	Client	–	0.82 ms	256 B
	Server	206 mins	0.82 ms	4.14 GB
tpmt	Client	–	2.46 ms	768 B
	Server	206 mins	2.46 ms	4.14 GB

Table 4: Computation and communication costs of P^3MT protocol for *hla-b* (2-nucleotide fingerprint) and *tpmt* (6-nucleotide fingerprint) tests.

Table 4 summarizes execution time and bandwidth costs of the P^3MT protocol used for testing *hla-B* and *tpmt*. These costs cannot be meaningfully compared to prior work, since, to the best of our knowledge, there is no other technique targeting privacy-preserving personalized medicine testing. Furthermore, as mentioned in Sec. 2, there are no current techniques that enforce fingerprint *authorization* by a trusted entity, such as the FDA. Also, prior work is essentially designed for operation on DNA snippets, and it is unclear how to efficiently adapt it to full genomes. Although a detailed experimental study is out of scope of this paper, we intend to include it as part of future work.

4.3 Privacy-Preserving Genetic Compatibility Testing

Genetic Compatibility Testing (GCT) can predict whether potential partners are at risk of conceiving a child with a recessive genetic disease. This occurs when both partners carry at least one

[4]For more details on *tpmt* and c-DNA, refer to [60] and [53], respectively.

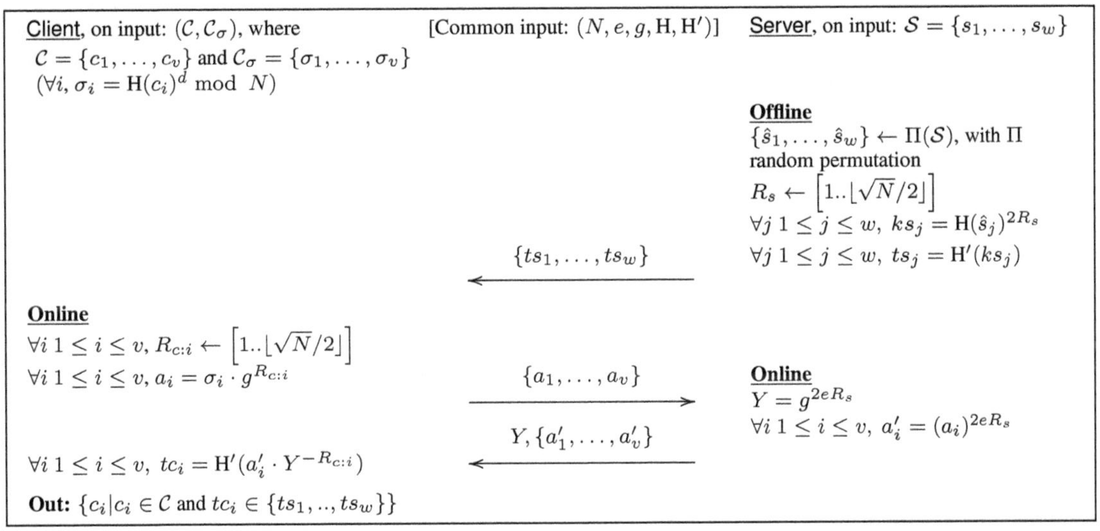

Figure 2: APSI Protocol from [15] (simplified for semi-honest security). The protocol is run on common input of RSA modulus $N = pq$ (with p and q safe primes), public exponent e, a random element g in $\mathbb{Z}_N^*$ and two hash functions, H and H$'$, modeled as random oracles. All computation is mod N.

gene affected by mutation, i.e., they are either asymptomatic carriers or actual disease sufferers. As in the Beta-Thalassemia example discussed in Sec. 1, asymptomatic carriers usually need to learn whether their potential partner is also a carrier of the same disease, since this would pose a serious risk to their potential off-spring.

To achieve genetic compatibility testing with privacy we introduce the concept of ***Privacy-Preserving Genetic Compatibility Testing*** (PPGCT) that allows participants to run GCT without disclosing to each other: (1) any other genomic information, and (2) which disease(s) they are carrying or being tested for.

Current biological knowledge of the human genome allows screening for a genetic disease associated with one SNP in a specific gene. In other words, most well-characterized genetic diseases are caused by a mutation in a single gene. However, we anticipate that, in the near future, researchers will develop tests for more complex diseases (e.g., diabetes or hypertension) involving multiple genes and multiple mutations. Therefore, we aim to design PPGCT techniques not limited to single-mutation diseases. Additional motivating examples for PPGCT include compatibility testing for sperm and organ donors.

The proposed PPGCT protocol involves two participants: Client and Server. Client runs on input of a fingerprint of a genetic disease $\hat{\mathcal{D}}$. Server runs on input of its fully-sequenced genome $\mathcal{G}$. At the end of the interaction, Client learns the output of the test, i.e., whether Server carries disease $\hat{\mathcal{D}}$.

Our cryptographic building block is Private Set Intersection (PSI) [15, 16, 25, 41]. We select the specific PSI construction in [41], shown in Fig. 3, since it achieves the best communication and computation complexity. It can also be instantiated in the malicious model with only a small constant additional overhead.

The PPGCT protocol involves the following steps:

1. Client builds a fingerprint corresponding to her genetic diseases $fp(\hat{\mathcal{D}}) = \{(b_j^*||j)\}$, where each b_j^* *is expected at position j of a genome with disease* $\hat{\mathcal{D}}$.
2. Client and Server run the PSI protocol in Fig. 3 on respective inputs: $fp(\hat{\mathcal{D}})$ and $\mathcal{G}$.
3. Client obtains $fp(\hat{\mathcal{D}}) \cap \mathcal{G}$, and uses this information to determine whether Server carries disease $\hat{\mathcal{D}}$.

The change from PSI-CA to PSI is motivated as follows. Depending on the disease being tested, a positive outcome occurs if the genome contains either: (1) the entire disease fingerprint, or (2) a given subset of nucleotides. In case of (1), the test result is positive only if: $fp(\hat{\mathcal{D}}) \subset \mathcal{G}$, i.e., $fp(\hat{\mathcal{D}}) \cap \mathcal{G} = fp(\hat{\mathcal{D}})$: if this happens, there is actually no difference between the output of PSI and that of PSI-CA. However, PSI-CA is preferred over PSI since, if the test is negative, less information about Server genome is revealed to Client. In case of (2), cardinality of set intersection is insufficient to assess the test result, since Client needs to learn which fingerprint nucleotides appear in Server's genome.

Similar to its P^{3}MT counterpart, the PPGCT protocol is resilient to uniformly distributed errors. In particular, since input size of Client is small, corresponding positions in Server genome are affected by errors with very low probability.

Open Problem: Unfortunately, a malicious Client could potentially *harvest* Server's genetic information (in addition to that needed for the compatibility test) by inflating its input. For instance, a healthy Client could learn whether or not Server carries a given genetic disease, unrelated to the compatibility testing.

Performance. As concrete examples, we use genetic compatibility tests for two genetic disorders: Roberts syndrome and Beta-Thalassemia. We chose them since they are fairly common and the size of their fingerprints is representative of that in most genetic compatibility tests.

Similar to P^{3}MT, we stress that cryptographic operations performed on Server genome, in the underlying PSI protocol, do not depend on Client input. Therefore, these operations can be pre-computed (just once) ahead of time.

First, we consider testing for Roberts syndrome. an autosomal genetic disorder, characterized by pre- and post-natal growth deficiency, limb malformations, and distinctive skull and facial abnormalities. As shown in [33], there are 26 single point mutations (in the *esco2* gene) causing this syndrome. Since humans are diploid organisms, we expect Roberts syndrome fingerprint to contain about 52 (nucleotide, location) pairs.

Next, we turn to Beta-Thalassemia. As pointed out in [26], more than 250 mutations in the *hbb* gene have been found to cause this disorder and most of them involve a change in a single nucleotide. Although reliable techniques to perform this test *in silico* are not yet available, it is reasonable to assume that the size of the Beta-Thalassemia fingerprint would include $2 \times 250 = 500$ (*nucleotide, location*) pairs.

Table 5 summarizes run time (computational) and bandwidth requirements for the PPGCT protocol for Roberts syndrome and Beta-Thalassemia, respectively. Following the same arguments as in P^{3}MT experiments, we let Server input the portion of its genome that differs from the reference genome, i.e., about 1%.

Test	Party	Offline Time	Online Time	Online Size
Roberts syndrome	Client	–	7.26 ms	62.5 KB
	Server	67 mins	7.26 ms	4.14 GB
Beta-Thalassemia	Client	–	70 ms	6.5 KB
	Server	67 mins	70 ms	4.14 GB

Table 5: Computation and communication costs of the PPGCT protocol for Beta-Thalassemia (500-nucleotide fingerprint) and Roberts syndrome (52-nucleotide fingerprint) tests.

Performance of the PPGCT protocol cannot be meaningfully compared to prior work. As discussed in Sec. 2, it is not trivial to adapt current secure pattern matching techniques to genetic compatibility testing on fully sequenced genomes. An experimental study (including the adaptation of such techniques) is left for future work.

5. SECURITY DISCUSSION

We now discuss security properties of protocols presented in this paper. In general, security of each protocol is based on that of the underlying building blocks. Therefore (and due to space limitations), we omit proof details and defer them to the extended version of this paper. Also, out cryptographic building blocks (PSI-CA, APSI, and PSI) can be generally used in a *black-box* manner. One can select any instantiation without affecting security of our protocols, as long as the chosen construction yields secure PSI/APSI/PSI-CA functionality. However, we pick specific instantiations to maximize protocol efficiency. As discussed earlier, we consider semi-honest adversaries (participants). Nevertheless, we are not restricted to this model, since our cryptographic building blocks are (provably) adaptable to the malicious participant model, incurring a small constant extra overhead.

PPGPT. We now show that RFLP-based PPGPT protocol (Sec. 4.1) is secure against semi-honest adversaries. We assume that PSI-CA performs secure computation of the $\mathcal{F}_{\text{PSI-CA}}$ functionality, in the presence of semi-honest participants. We select the construction in [17], that is secure under the One-More-DH assumption in the Random Oracle Model (ROM).
We divide the protocol in two phases. In the first, both Client and Server privately and independently perform the RFLP-related computation on their respective inputs. (This covers steps 1 to 3 of PPGPT). At the end of this phase, Client and Server construct sets F_C and F_S, respectively. Clearly, during this phase, neither participant learns anything about the other's input. During the second phase (steps 4-5), participants use F_C and F_S as their respective inputs to PSI-CA. Given the security of the latter, Client only learns $|F_S \cap F_C|$. PSI-CA protocols may reveal $|F_S|$ to Client and $|F_C|$ to Server. However, $|F_S| = |F_C| = l$, which is already known to both parties.

P^{3}MT. Similarly, security of the P^{3}MT protocol (in Sec. 4.2), against semi-honest Client and Server, stems from security of the underlying protocol — APSI. That is, if APSI performs secure computation of the $\mathcal{F}_{\text{APSI}}$ functionality in the presence of semi-honest participants, then P^{3}MT is also secure. This holds since a semi-honest participant with a non negligible advantage in distinguishing between real and simulated executions of P^{3}MT would have the same advantage in distinguishing between real and simulated executions of APSI. Although one can use APSI as a black box, for efficiency reasons, we prefer instantiations that allow precomputation on Server input. In our instantiation, we select the APSI construction in [15], proven secure under the RSA and DDH assumptions (in ROM).

PPGCT. Finally, security of the PPGCT protocol (Sec. 4.3) against semi-honest adversaries relies on that of the underlying PSI protocol, to which it is immediately reducible. (In other words, a semi-honest participant with a non-negligible advantage in distinguishing between real and simulated executions of PPGCT would have the same advantage in distinguishing between real and simulated executions of PSI.) Again, although one can use PSI as a black box, for efficiency reasons, we need PSI instantiations that allow pre-computation on Server input, such as OPRF-based constructs [15, 16, 35, 41]. We chose the PSI from [41], proven secure under the One-More-DH assumption (in ROM).

6. CONCLUSIONS AND FUTURE WORK

This paper identified and explored three popular privacy-sensitive genomic applications: (i) paternity tests, (ii) personalized medicine and (iii) genetic compatibility testing. Unlike most previous work, we focused on fully sequenced genomes. This scenario poses new challenges, both in terms of privacy and computational cost. For each application, we proposed an efficient construction, based on well-known cryptographic tools: Private Set Intersection (PSI), Private Set Intersection Cardinality (PSI-CA), and Authorized Private Set Intersection (APSI). Experiments show that these protocols incur online overhead sufficiently low to be practical today. In particular, our protocol for privacy-preserving paternity testing is significantly less expensive — in both computation and communication — than prior work. Furthermore, all protocols presented in this paper have been carefully constructed to mimic the state-of-the-art of (*in vitro*) biological tests currently performed in hospitals and laboratories.

Items for future work include, but are not limited to:

- Introducing privacy-preserving genetic paternity testing based on STR and/or SNP comparison.
- Exploring privacy-preserving techniques to realize genetic ancestry testing, i.e., to discover whether or not individuals are related up to a certain degree.[5]
- Extending the paternity test protocol to allow both participants to determine whether the other party introduced correct input according to some auxiliary authorization. (Note that APSI does not suffice since one of the parties might alter its input so that the test is negative).
- Investigation of additional privacy-sensitive applications for fully-sequenced genomes, such as certified forensic identification, where the subject of investigation must prove the authenticity of its input; privacy-preserving organ recipients compatibility, where a subject efficiently identifies a matching sample without revealing information about her genome.
- Extending our experiments to include adaptation of secure pattern matching and text processing to personalized medicine and genetic compatibility testing on full genomes.

Acknowledgements. We are grateful to Christophe Magnan for

[5] For an example of ancestry testing services, refer to `http://23andme.com`.

Client, on input $\mathcal{C} = \{c_1, \ldots, c_v\}$	[Common Input: $(p, q, g, \mathrm{H}, \mathrm{H}')$]	Server, on input $\mathcal{S} = \{s_1, \ldots, s_w\}$
		Offline
		$\{\hat{s}_1, \ldots, \hat{s}_w\} \leftarrow \Pi(\mathcal{S})$, with Π random permutation
		$R_s \leftarrow \mathbb{Z}_q$
	$\{ts_1, \ldots, ts_w\}$ $\longleftarrow$	$\forall j\ 1 \leq j \leq w,\ ts_j = \mathrm{H}'(\mathrm{H}(\hat{s}_j)^{R_s})$
Online		**Online**
$\forall i\ 1 \leq i \leq v, R_{c:i} \leftarrow \mathbb{Z}_q$		
$\forall i\ 1 \leq i \leq v,\ a_i = \mathrm{H}(c_i)^{R_{c:i}}$	$\{a_1, \ldots, a_v\}$ $\longrightarrow$	$\forall i\ 1 \leq i \leq v,\ a'_i = (a_i)^{R_s}$
$\forall i\ 1 \leq i \leq v,\ tc_i = \mathrm{H}'((a'_i)^{1/R_{c:i}})$	$\{a'_1, \ldots, a'_v\}$ $\longleftarrow$	
Out: $\{c_i \mid c_i \in \mathcal{C}$ and $tc_i \in \{ts_1, .., ts_w\}\}$		

Figure 3: PSI Protocol from [41] (simplified for semi-honest security). It runs on common input of two primes p and q (s.t. $q|p-1$), a generator g of a subgroup of size q and two hash functions, H and H$'$, modeled as random oracles. All computation is mod p.

useful hints about the testing environment and to anonymous ACM CCS'11 reviewers for helping us improve the paper. Work of Pierre Baldi is supported, in part, by grants: NIH LM010235 and NIH-NLM T15 LM07443.

References

[1] A. Abbott. Special section on human genetics: With your genes? Take one of these, three times a day. *Nature*, 425(6960), 2003.

[2] M. Adams et al. The Genome Sequence of Drosophila melanogaster. *Science*, 287(5461), 2000.

[3] J. Beckmann and M. Soller. Restriction fragment length polymorphisms and genetic improvement of agricultural species. *Euphytica*, 35(1), 1986.

[4] M. Blanton and M. Aliasgari. Secure outsourcing of dna searching via finite automata. In *DBSec*, 2010.

[5] M. Brandon, D. Wallace, and P. Baldi. Data structures and compression algorithms for genomic sequence data. *Bioinformatics*, 25(14), 2009.

[6] F. Bruekers, S. Katzenbeisser, K. Kursawe, and P. Tuyls. Privacy-Preserving Matching of DNA Profiles. `http://eprint.iacr.org/2008/203`, 2008.

[7] C. Børsting et al. Performance of the SNPforID 52 SNP-plex assay in paternity testing. *Forensic Science International: Genetics*, 2(4), 2008.

[8] J. Camenisch and G. Zaverucha. Private intersection of certified sets. In *FC*, 2009.

[9] B. Carlson. SNPs – A shortcut to personalized medicine. *Genetic Engineering & Biotechnology News*, 2008.

[10] Center for Applied Genomics, University of Toronto. Database of Genomic Variants. `http://projects.tcag.ca/variation`, 2011.

[11] F. Collins and V. McKusick. Implications of the Human Genome Project for medical science. *Jama*, 285(5), 2001.

[12] L. Cunningham. High-stakes Test. Daily Business Review, 2003.

[13] K. Daily et al. Data structures and compression algorithms for high-throughput sequencing technologies. *BMC bioinformatics*, 11(1), 2010.

[14] G. Danezis et al. Efficient negative databases from cryptographic hash functions. In *ISC*, 2007.

[15] E. De Cristofaro, J. Kim, and G. Tsudik. Linear-complexity private set intersection protocols secure in malicious model. In *Asiacrypt*, 2010.

[16] E. De Cristofaro and G. Tsudik. Practical Private Set Intersection Protocols with Linear Complexity. In *FC*, 2010.

[17] E. De Cristofaro and G. Tsudik. Fast and Private Computation of Set Intersection Cardinality. Cryptology ePrint Archive, 2011.

[18] N. Dracopoli, J. Haines, and B. Korf. *Current protocols in human genetics*. John Wiley & Sons, 1994.

[19] R. Durbin et al. A map of human genome variation from population-scale sequencing. *Nature*, 467(7319), 2010.

[20] M. Durham. How Research Will Adapt to HIPAA: A View from Within the Healthcare Delivery System. *Am. JL and Med.*, 28, 2002.

[21] T. ElGamal. A public key cryptosystem and a signature scheme based on discrete logarithms. *IEEE transactions on Information Theory*, 31(4), 1985.

[22] D. Endean. RFLP analysis for paternity testing: observations and caveats. In *International Symposium on Human Identification*, 1989.

[23] J. Fowler, J. Settle, and N. Christakis. Correlated genotypes in friendship networks. *Proceedings of the National Academy of Sciences*, 108(5), 2011.

[24] M. Freedman, Y. Ishai, B. Pinkas, and O. Reingold. Keyword search and oblivious pseudorandom functions. In *TCC*, 2005.

[25] M. Freedman, K. Nissim, and B. Pinkas. Efficient private matching and set intersection. In *Eurocrypt*, 2004.

[26] Genetics Home Reference. HBB Gene. `http://ghr.nlm.nih.gov/gene/HBB`.

[27] R. Gennaro, C. Hazay, and J. Sorensen. Text Search Protocols with Simulation Based Security. In *PKC*, 2010.

[28] R. Gibbs and A. Singleton. Application of genome-wide single nucleotide polymorphism typing: Simple association and beyond. *PLoS Genet*, 2(10), 10 2006.

[29] G. Ginsburg and H. Willard. Genomic and personalized medicine: foundations and applications. *Translational Research*, 154(6), 2009.

[30] A. Goffeau et al. Life with 6000 Genes. *Science*, 1996.

[31] O. Goldreich. *Foundations of cryptography: Basic applications*, chapter 7.2.2. Cambridge Univ Press, 2004.

[32] O. Goldreich, R. Israel, and V. Rosen. On the security of modular exponentiation with application to the construction of pseudorandom generators. *Journal of Cryptology*, 16, 2000.

[33] M. Gordillo et al. The molecular mechanism underlying Roberts syndrome involves loss of ESCO2 acetyltransferase activity. *Human molecular genetics*, 17(14), 2008.

[34] J. Gusella et al. A polymorphic DNA marker genetically linked to Huntington's disease. *Nature*, 306(5940), 1983.
[35] C. Hazay and Y. Lindell. Efficient protocols for set intersection and pattern matching with security against malicious and covert adversaries. In *TCC*, 2008.
[36] C. Hazay and T. Toft. Computationally secure pattern matching in the presence of malicious adversaries. *Asiacrypt*, 2010.
[37] J. Ho, Choi, et al. Replication study of SNP associations for colorectal cancer in Hong Kong Chinese. *British Journal of Cancer*, 2010.
[38] M. Hoffman. The genome-enabled electronic medical record. *Journal of Biomedical Informatics*, 40(1), 2007.
[39] M. Hsi-Yang Fritz, R. Leinonen, G. Cochrane, and E. Birney. Efficient storage of high throughput dna sequencing data using reference-based compression. *Genome Research*, 21(5), May 2011.
[40] International Human Genome Sequencing Consortium. Initial sequencing and analysis of the human genome. *Nature*, 409, 2001.
[41] S. Jarecki and X. Liu. Fast Secure Computation of Set Intersection. In *SCN*, 2010.
[42] S. Jha, L. Kruger, and V. Shmatikov. Towards practical privacy for genomic computation. In *S&P*, 2008.
[43] J. Kaiser. A plan to capture human diversity in 1000 genomes. *Science*, 319, 2008.
[44] M. Kantarcioglu, W. Jiang, Y. Liu, and B. Malin. A cryptographic approach to securely share and query genomic sequences. *Transactions on Information Technology in Biomedicine*, 12(5), 2008.
[45] F. Kastrinos et al. Risk of pancreatic cancer in families with Lynch syndrome. *JAMA: The Journal of the American Medical Association*, 302(16), 2009.
[46] J. Katz and Y. Lindell. *Introduction to modern cryptography*. Chapman & Hall/CRC, 2008.
[47] J. Katz and J. Malka. Secure text processing with applications to private dna matching. In *CCS*, 2010.
[48] L. Kissner and D. Song. Privacy-preserving set operations. In *Crypto*, 2005.
[49] J. Kulynych and D. Korn. The New HIPAA (Health Insurance Portability and Accountability Act of 1996) Medical Privacy Rule. *Circulation*, 108, 2003.
[50] E. Lander. DNA fingerprinting on trial. *Nature*, 339(6225), 1989.
[51] V. Levenshtein. Binary codes capable of correcting deletions, insertions, and reversals. In *Soviet Physics Doklady*, volume 10, 1966.
[52] S. Levy et al. The diploid genome sequence of an individual human. *PLoS biology*, 5(10), 2007.
[53] R. Lewis and A. Reynolds. *Human genetics: concepts and applications*. McGraw-Hill, 2003.
[54] B. Malin. An evaluation of the current state of genomic data privacy protection technology and a roadmap for the future. *Journal of the American Medical Informatics Association*, 12(1), 2005.
[55] A. McGuire and R. Gibbs. Currents in Contemporary Ethics: Meeting the Growing Demands of Genetic Research. *JL Med. & Ethics*, 34, 2006.
[56] V. McKusick and S. Antonarakis. *Mendelian inheritance in man: a catalog of human genes and genetic disorders*. John Hopkins University Press, 1994.
[57] A. Menezes, P. Van Oorschot, and S. Vanstone. *Handbook of applied cryptography*. CRC, 1997.
[58] S. Migueles et al. HLA B* 5701 is highly associated with restriction of virus replication in a subgroup of HIV-infected long term nonprogressors. *Proceedings of the National Academy of Sciences*, 97(6), 2000.
[59] National Center for Biotechnology Information (US). Single Nucleotide Polymorphism Database. `http://www.ncbi.nlm.nih.gov/projects/SNP/`.
[60] National Center for Biotechnology Information (US). TPMT thiopurine S-methyltransferase. `http://1.usa.gov/orAYkF`.
[61] National Center for Biotechnology Information (US). Restriction Fragment Length Polymorphism (RFLP). `http://1.usa.gov/pha5sw`, 2011.
[62] NCBI. Genome Mapping. `http://1.usa.gov/oWNiYo`, 2011.
[63] A. Prat and J. Baselga. The role of hormonal therapy in the management of hormonal-receptor-positive breast cancer with co-expression of her2. *Nature Clinical Practice Oncology*, 5(9), 2008.
[64] ScientificMatch.com. `http://scientificmatch.com`, 2011.
[65] R. F. Service. The race for the $1000 genome. *Science*, 311, 2006.
[66] N. Siva. 1000 Genomes project. *Nature biotechnology*, 26(3), 2008.
[67] T. Smith and M. Waterman. Identification of common molecular subsequences. *Journal of Molecular Biology*, 147, 1981.
[68] P. Stenson et al. The human gene mutation database: 2008 update. *Genome Medicine*, 1(1), 2009.
[69] The Federal Bureau of Investigation. Combined DNA Index System (CODIS). `http://www.fbi.gov/about-us/lab/codis`, 2011.
[70] T. Tokino et al. Isolation and mapping of 62 new RFLP markers on human chromosome 11. *American journal of human genetics*, 48(2), 1991.
[71] J. Troncoso-Pastoriza, S. Katzenbeisser, and M. Celik. Privacy preserving error resilient dna searching through oblivious automata. In *CCS*, 2007.
[72] J. Vaidya and C. Clifton. Secure set intersection cardinality with application to association rule mining. *Journal of Computer Security*, 13(4), 2005.
[73] M. Wadman. Genetics bill cruises through senate. *Nature*, 453, 2008.
[74] J. Wang et al. The diploid genome sequence of an Asian individual. *Nature*, 456(7218), 2008.
[75] R. Wang, X. Wang, Z. Li, H. Tang, M. Reiter, and Z. Dong. Privacy-preserving genomic computation through program specialization. In *CCS*, 2009.
[76] R. Waterston et al. Initial sequencing and comparative analysis of the mouse genome. *Nature*, 420(6915), 2002.
[77] A. Weston and L. Hood. Systems biology, proteomics, and the future of health care: toward predictive, preventative, and personalized medicine. *Journal of proteome research*, 3(2), 2004.
[78] D. Wheeler et al. The complete genome of an individual by massively parallel DNA sequencing. *Nature*, 452(7189), 2008.
[79] A. Yao. Protocols for secure computations. In *FOCS*, 1982.
[80] C. Yates et al. Molecular diagnosis of thiopurine S-methyltransferase deficiency: genetic basis for azathioprine and mercaptopurine intolerance. *Annals of internal medicine*, 126(8), 1997.

Automatically Optimizing Secure Computation

Florian Kerschbaum
SAP Research
Karlsruhe, Germany
florian.kerschbaum@sap.com

ABSTRACT

On the one hand, compilers for secure computation protocols, such as FairPlay or FairPlayMP, have significantly simplified the development of such protocols. On the other hand, optimized protocols with high performance for special problems demand manual development and security verification. The question considered in this paper is: Can we construct a compiler that produces optimized protocols? We present an optimization technique based on logic inference about what is known from input and output. Using the example of median computation we can show that our program analysis and rewriting technique translates a FairPlay program into an equivalent – in functionality and security – program that corresponds to the protocol by Aggarwal et al. Nevertheless our technique is general and can be applied to optimize a wide variety of secure computation protocols.

Categories and Subject Descriptors

D.3.4 [**Programming Languages**]: Processors—*Optimization*; D.4.6 [**Operating Systems**]: Security and Protection—*Cryptographic controls*

General Terms

Security, Programming Languages

Keywords

Secure Two-Party Computation, Programming, Optimization

1. INTRODUCTION

Secure (Multiparty) computation protocols [4, 7, 15, 31] allow a number of parties the computation of a function on joint input without disclosing anything except what can be inferred by one party's input and output. This offers an intriguing solution to many real-world problems where collaboration is prevented by the reluctance to disclose one's data. Privacy-preserving data mining [2, 21] is just one example of many.

Secure computation protocols are notoriously difficult to develop, since they require a high degree of domain expertise. Compilers, such as FairPlay [23] or FairPlayMP [6], have significantly simplified their development. They implement general techniques – the protocols of Yao [31] and Beaver et al. [4], respectively – in a cryptographic protocol layer and translate a program describing the ideal functionality into a circuit that is then interpreted by this layer. This reduces the development of the protocol to programming the ideal functionality.

Unfortunately, the compiler approach can be quite inefficient and is currently not amenable to large problem instances. Fortunately, a large body of work exists on optimized secure computation protocols for special problems. Besides the specification of the protocol itself, optimized protocols usually require a hand-crafted proof of security. These proofs are difficult and can be omitted in the compiler approach, since they are implicit in the cryptographic protocol layer.

Naturally, the question arises if a compiler could also produce optimized protocols. In programming languages the optimizing techniques of compilers have already overtaken the capabilities of even the most skilled assembler programmers. In this paper we present an optimization technique for a secure computation compiler. To the best of our knowledge this is the first such technique. Our optimizer takes as input a FairPlay program in the *Secure Function Definition Language* (SFDL). It outputs a Java program with several calls to FairPlay as a subroutine.

The basic idea is as follows: Everything that can be inferred from one's input and output is known. All known information can be revealed during the computation and does not have to be computed securely. Via logic inference we (under-) estimate the knowledge of each agent about a program's variables. Then we extract all operations on known data to the Java program of the local agent. This can significantly reduce the functionality that needs to be computed securely and the size of the circuit(s).

This paper contributes

- *logic inference rules* about an agent's knowledge in a SFDL program.
- a *program transformation* based on the result of the inference.
- an *evaluation* based on example applications of median and weighted average.

We present our optimization technique using a running example of median computation. In Section 2 we present this example in detail with program code for SFDL, optimized version as suggested by Aggarwal et al. [1] and performance comparison. Then, based on this example we show our inference rules and transformation technique in Section 3. We report our evaluation including the examples of oblivious transfer and weighted average in Section 4. Finally, we describe related work in Section 5 and conclude the paper in Section 6.

2. RUNNING EXAMPLE

As a running example in this paper we consider the joint computation of the median. We consider two parties – Alice and Bob – and each party has a set of n (distinct) integers. Alice and Bob want to jointly compute the median element of the union of their sets without disclosing anything else.

We implement the distributed algorithm by Aggarwal et al. [1]. Let each party's set be sorted in ascending order. The algorithm proceeds in several rounds. In each round each party chooses the median element of its set and then the parties compare these two elements. The party with the lower median disposes all elements below its median and the party with the higher median disposes all elements above its median. They begin a new round with these newly formed sets until each set has size 1 in which case they choose the lower one as the joint median.

We implemented this algorithm in SFDL of the FairPlay system [23]. This is not straightforward, since efficiently accessing the median of a variably sized array requires division which is not available in SFDL. This problem can be avoided by unrolling the loops and precomputing the division. In order not to complicate the exposition we choose $n = 2$. Furthermore, to simplify the analysis to be presented in this paper we replace arrays with structures of scalar variables. The resulting program is depicted in Listing 1.

Aggarwal et al. [1] not only present a distributed algorithm, but a distributed, secure protocol. The key insight of their protocol is that given the output of the joint median, the result of each comparison can be inferred. Then, in order to implement an efficient, secure algorithm it is only necessary to implement the comparisons using secure computation and all other operations can be implemented locally at the party's site. In Listing 1 the two relevant comparisons are depicted in lines 17 and 25.

The protocol by Aggarwal et al. can no longer be implemented as a single FairPlay program. Instead we implemented it using the L1 language and system for mixed-protocol secure computation [30]. The resulting program is depicted in Listing 2.

In L1 the same program is executed by both parties; except lines preceded by numbers are only executed by the parties with the respective identifiers. These identifiers are also returned by the call to the built-in function `id()`. The function call `comp32` in lines 9 and 17 invokes a secure computation of a comparison using the local input x, i.e. each party submits its variable x to a joint secure computation protocol.

The similarity between the two programs is not surprising, since they implement the same algorithm. Nevertheless, they compile into two very different protocols. While the FairPlay program implements Yao's protocol, the L1 program invokes secure computation only for the comparisons.

```
1  program Median {
2  type Elem        = Int<32>;
3  type AliceInput  = struct {Elem x,
4                             Elem y};
5  type AliceOutput = Elem;
6  type BobInput    = struct {Elem x,
7                             Elem y};
8  type BobOutput   = Elem;
9  type Input  = struct {AliceInput  alice,
10                       BobInput    bob};
11 type Output = struct {AliceOutput alice,
12                       BobOutput   bob};
13
14 function Output out (Input in) {
15    var Elem a, b;
16
17    if (in.alice.x <= in.bob.x) {
18       a = in.alice.y;
19       b = in.bob.x;
20    } else {
21       a = in.alice.x;
22       b = in.bob.y;
23    }
24
25    if (a <= b) {
26       out.alice = a;
27       out.bob   = a;
28    } else {
29       out.alice = b;
30       out.bob   = b;
31    }
32 }
33 }
```

Listing 1: Median Computation in FairPlay

```
1  include "utilYaoOTs.l1";
2  include "compareYao.l1";
3
4  int Median() {
5     int x = loadInt("input_x" + id());
6     int y = loadInt("input_y" + id());
7     int a;
8
9     if (comp32(x) == 1) {
10       1: a = y;
11       2: a = x
12    } else {
13       1: a = x;
14       2: a = y;
15    }
16
17    if (comp32(a) == 1) {
18       1: send(2, "a", a);
19       2: a = readInt("a");
20    } else {
21       1: a = readInt("a");
22       2: send(1, "a", a);
23    }
24
25    return a;
26 }
27
28 Median();
```

Listing 2: Median Computation in L1

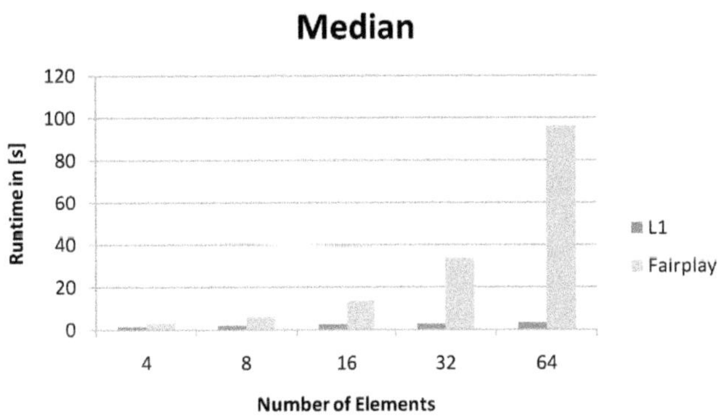

Figure 1: Secure Median

The result is a striking difference in performance. We ran experiments with both protocols for different joint set sizes $2n = 4, 8, 16, 32, 64$. The performance measurements are depicted in Figure 1. For only 64 elements in the joint set the L1 implementation already outperforms the FairPlay implementation by more than a factor of 30.

The research question of this paper is: Given the similarity between the two programs can we compile the FairPlay program into the protocol of the L1 program? Furthermore, can we design an optimization algorithm that is not only applicable to Aggarwal et al.'s median computation, but is generic?

3. TRANSFORMATION

3.1 Semi-Honest Security

We consider secure computation protocols secure in the semi-honest model [14]. Loosely speaking, an adversary in the semi-honest model adheres to the protocol, but may keep a record of the interaction and later try to infer additional information from it. A protocol secure in the semi-honest model, keeps everything about a party's input confidential that cannot be inferred from one's input and output.

Goldreich [14] defines security in the semi-honest model. The view $VIEW^{\Pi}(x, y)$ of a party during protocol Π on this party's input x and the other party's input y is its input x, the outcome of its coin tosses and the messages received during the execution of the protocol.

DEFINITION 1. *We say a protocol* Π *computing* $f(x, y)$ *is secure in the* semi-honest *model, if for each party there exist a polynomial-time simulator* S *given the party's input and output is computationally indistinguishable from the party's view* $VIEW^{\Pi}(x, y)$*:*

$$S(x, f(x, y)) \stackrel{c}{=} VIEW^{\Pi}(x, y)$$

FairPlay programs are secure in the semi-honest model by construction. L1 programs need to be proven secure manually, but can also implement more efficient protocols. Aggarwal et al.'s protocol is secure, if (correctly) implemented in L1.

Semi-honest security ensures confidentiality except what can be inferred from one's input and output. This inference is the basis of our optimization. We construct a program analysis technique for FairPlay programs that infers what is known from input and output. If our optimized protocol reveals this additional information – but nothing else –, then this does not violate semi-honest security, since it can be constructed by the simulator. We need to be very careful that our analysis is safe and always underestimates the possible inferences from input and output.

3.2 Algorithm

In our algorithm to transform a SFDL program we use labeling of variables. Each variable in the program is assigned any of two labels: $\{A\}$ or $\{B\}$. Labels are non-exclusive, i.e. a variable may be assigned none, one or two labels. The contents of a variable labeled $\{A\}$ is (always) known to Alice and the contents of a variable labeled $\{B\}$ is (always) known to Bob. A variable without labels is secret and can only be implemented using secure computation while a variable with both labels is public information and can be freely shared. The program text is known to both parties and so are all constants in the program. Our algorithm for optimizing a SFDL program proceeds as follows:

1. We convert the SFDL program into single-static assignment (SSA), 3-operand code form.
2. We use our inference algorithm to infer the labels of each variable.
3. We segment the program into different protocols. Each statement of which all variables are known to any party are executed locally by that party. Only statements with operands whose intersection of labels is empty will be executed using a secure computation as in FairPlay.

We give two examples of our segmentation of a program into protocols. Consider the addition expression in Listing 3. We have written the labels of the variables in subscript.

$a_{A} = b_{A} + c_{A\,B};$

Listing 3: Local Computation

This statement can be executed locally at Alice's site, since she knows all variables and the result a can be used as input in subsequent computations. Now, consider the comparison expression in Listing 4.

$a_{A\,B} = b_{A} < c_{B};$

Listing 4: Secure Computation

This statement must implemented as a secure computation. It is the program representation of Yao's millionaires' problem [31] where two parties compare private numbers.

3.3 Static Single Assignment

We convert the SFDL program into static single assignment (SSA) [9] form. In SSA each variable is assigned at most once and never changed afterwards. If a variable is changed in the original program, a new variable is introduced in SSA.

```
a = b ? c : d;
```

Listing 5: Conditional Assignment

```
program Median {

function Output out (Input in) {
    var Boolean a, d;
    var Elem    b, c;

    a = in.alice.x <= in.bob.x;
    b = a ? in.alice.y  : in.alice.x;
    c = a ? in.bob.x    : in.bob.y;

    d = b <= c;
    out.alice = d ? b : c;
    out.bob   = d ? b : c;
}
}
```

Listing 6: Single Static Assignment Form

We also unroll all loops – in SFDL loops have a constant number of iterations –, inline all functions – in SFDL there is no recursion –, and transform all if statements to conditional assignments. A conditional assignment has the form of Listing 5 where the variable a is assigned either the value of c or d depending on the truth value of the condition b.

Furthermore, we resolve complex expressions and transform all expressions into 3-operand code (except conditional assignments which have four operands). Each statement takes two operands (and an operator) as input and assigns the result (a new) operand as output.

The result of our SSA transform is depicted in Listing 6. We have omitted the type declarations for brevity as they are the same as in Listing 1. The challenge for our inference is now to determine that both Boolean variables, a and d, are (always) known to both, Alice and Bob, if they know their respective input and output.

3.4 Inference

Our inference algorithm (under-)estimates the knowledge about variables given one's input and output. In the notion of information flow, we try to determine whether there is an *inevitable* flow of information from the input to that variable or from that variable to the output. We differ from language-based information flow [29] which tries to detect and prevent *possible* information flows. One particular challenge in our inference is therefore that the flow of information may occur differently as possible flows depending on the state of program, but does occur inevitably in all possible states. We address this challenge by using a more powerful logic.

Furthermore, all (sensible) secure computations involve a declassification (release) of private information. Assuming that information flow is admissible, our inference algorithm indicates the earliest possible declassification operation in order to later increase the performance of the protocol. We present the details in Section 3.5.

3.4.1 Epistemic Modal Logic

We use epistemic modal logic (EML) [16] to reason about the knowledge of the protocol participants. Let p be a proposition which can be either true (p) or false ($\neg p$). We consider a single agent (either Alice or Bob) and use the modal operator K to denominate its knowledge. When we write

$$Kp$$

we mean that the agent knows p. EML only considers truthful knowledge, i.e.

$$Kp \Rightarrow p$$

Although the agent's knowledge is certain, the agent might consider different *possible worlds*. A possible world is an interpretation of propositions assigning them a truth value. One of the possible worlds is the real world, but the agent cannot differentiate between them. For example, let $\mathcal{W}_1$ and $\mathcal{W}_2$ be two different, possible worlds. A proposition p might be true in world $\mathcal{W}_1$, but false in world $\mathcal{W}_2$. We write

$$\mathcal{W}_1 \vDash p$$
$$\mathcal{W}_2 \vDash \neg p$$

As already mentioned we consider one agent at a time and using the possible worlds we can define the meaning of knowledge. Let there be n possible worlds $\mathcal{W}_1, \ldots, \mathcal{W}_n$. If and only if the proposition p is true in all possible worlds, then the agent knows p. We write

$$\mathcal{W}_j \vDash Kp \Leftrightarrow \forall(1 \le i \le n)\mathcal{W}_i \vDash p$$

This implements one of the simplest Kripke structures [20]. Introducing "logical and" for complex propositions ϕ and ψ we can summarize our simplified EML variant as

$$\begin{array}{ll} \mathcal{W} \vDash p & \text{if } p \text{ is assigned true in } \mathcal{W} \\ \mathcal{W} \vDash \neg\phi & \text{if } \mathcal{W} \nvDash \phi \\ \mathcal{W} \vDash \phi \wedge \psi & \text{if } \mathcal{W} \vDash \phi \text{ and } \mathcal{W} \vDash \psi \\ \mathcal{W} \vDash K\phi & \text{if for all } \mathcal{W}_i \vDash \phi \end{array}$$

3.4.2 Traces

In the remainder of this section we will consider wlog Alice as the agent. We create possible worlds by tracing the program. Each possible world contains one trace of the program. The trace is a set of propositions where each proposition is generated by a possible assignment in the program.

For integers we follow the assumption by Aggarwal et al. and assume that each input is unique. This assumption is not essential in our inference and can be easily lifted by adapting the algorithm to generate the traces. No further changes are necessary, but Aggarwal et al.'s protocol is then insecure and our running example no longer works. We therefore trace each integer variable in Alice's input as a unique identifier from the set $\{A1, \ldots, An\}$. We trace each integer variable in Bob's input as the identifier B. Boolean variables may be traced as either $true$ or $false$.

```
a = in.alice.x + in.bob.y
```

Listing 7: Integer Assignment

An assignment creates a new entry in the trace. An assigned integer variable is added to the trace with the intersection of the identifiers of its operands (with $\bot$ marking the empty set). In Listing 7 we add to the trace the proposition

$$\mathcal{W} \vDash a = \bot$$

```
a = in.alice.x < in.bob.y
```

Listing 8: Boolean Assignment

Each Boolean assignment with integer operands doubles the number of possible worlds. For each existing world $\mathcal{W}$

$$\mathcal{W} \models a = false$$
$$\mathcal{W} \models b = A1$$
$$\mathcal{W} \models c = B$$
$$\mathcal{W} \models d = false$$
$$\mathcal{W} \models out.alice = B$$

Figure 2: Trace

we create a new world $\mathcal{W}'$. In the example of Listing 8 we add to the trace of world $\mathcal{W}$ the proposition

$$\mathcal{W} \models a = true$$

In world $\mathcal{W}'$ we copy all of the previous trace (except, of course, the trace of a) of the world $\mathcal{W}$ and then add the proposition

$$\mathcal{W}' \models a = false$$

For Boolean assignments with Boolean operands we optimize this to a single proposition in all possible worlds by evaluating the expression.

Conditional assignments as in Listing 5 interpret the truth assignment of the condition. In worlds with the proposition $b = true$ we add a proposition for a with the trace of c and in worlds with the proposition $b = false$ we add a proposition for a with the trace of d.

In our example of the median computation (Listing 6) we get four possible worlds: one for each trace of a and d. We show one of the four traces in Figure 2.

Each variable is a proposition. The proposition is true in a possible world, if the contents of a variable is known to Alice in this world, i.e. under the assumption of a specific trace. If a variable a is known to Alice in all worlds, i.e. proposition a is true, then then the proposition Ka is true and we add the label $\{A\}$ to the variable.

It is important to note that we consider all possible traces. This may include invalid traces of unreachable code. Since we perform static analysis, we must either over- or underestimate the reachable code. By considering all unreachable code our analysis is safe. An additional, invalid trace can only reduce the set of labels of a variable, since even in the invalid trace the variable must be known to Alice in order to result in a label $\{A\}$ for the variable.

3.4.3 *Rules*

Initially only input and output are known to Alice (in all worlds). Further knowledge needs to be inferred via rules. We present these rules in this section.

Rules are logical deductions of propositions. Our rules are true in all worlds, although they might make a reference to a trace proposition. Let ϕ, ψ and χ be propositions. We write

$$\phi \wedge \psi \Rightarrow \chi$$

or

$$\frac{\phi \quad \psi}{\chi}$$

as a shortcut for

$$\neg((\phi \wedge \psi) \wedge \neg\chi)$$

We use the SSA form of the program and for each statement we add several rules. As we try to infer additional knowledge about program variables from input and output, we can distinguish two types of rules. Forward rules try to infer knowledge about the result of a statement from knowledge about its input. Backward rules try to infer knowledge about the input of a statement from knowledge about its result and maybe partial input. Forward and backward rules are true and applied concurrently during the logical inference. Only their combination enables us to make the necessary inferences. We have rules for expressions (3 operand code), conditional assignments, symbolic computation and previous knowledge.

Expressions.

```
a = b + c
d = e * f
```

Listing 9: Expression Assignment

The forward rule for expressions is simple. If both operands are known then, then the assigned variable is known. For the example in Listing 9 we write

$$\frac{b \quad c}{a} \qquad \frac{e \quad f}{d}$$

The backward rules for expressions are already more complex. Whether there is a backward rule depends on the operator. For addition (+) and subtraction (−) there are backward rules.

$$\frac{a \quad c}{b} \qquad \frac{a \quad b}{c}$$

But for multiplication ($*$) and (integer) division (/) there are none. This is for safety reasons. While in (modular) addition and subtraction it is always possible to compute the inverse, this is not always the case for multiplication and division. Consider multiplication by 0: the result is 0 independent of the value of the other operand.

Conditional Assignment.

The forward rule for conditional assignments is similar. Nevertheless we distinguish between the two possible worlds by making a reference to the trace proposition. Consider the example in Listing 5: we construct the following forward rules

$$\frac{b \quad b = true \quad c}{a} \qquad \frac{b \quad b = false \quad d}{a}$$

For conditional assignments there are two different backward rules. One for the assigned operand and one for the condition. The backward rules for the operands are as follows.

$$\frac{b = true \quad a}{c} \qquad \frac{b = false \quad a}{d}$$

We emphasize that these rules do not require knowledge of the condition. This is safe (as we will show at the example of oblivious transfer in Section 4.1), since the conclusion is only true in half of the possible worlds and therefore no further inference on labels is feasible.

The backward rule for the condition is our most complex rule. For its understanding we need to consider a specific world (trace). For example, consider the trace of Figure 2 and the conditional assignment in line 12 of the corresponding Listing 6. It is the final output assignment for Alice of the median computation.

Our intuition is the following: If the agent Alice knows the assigned variable (*out.alice*) and the trace of the variable ($out.alice = B$) only occurs in possible worlds with a specific condition ($d = false$), then the agent knows the condition. In other words: Alice can infer the condition from observing the known and unique output for that condition. This rule combines our tracing, backward rules and EML. We can express the uniqueness of the trace as Alice's knowledge

$$K(out.alice = B \Rightarrow d = false)$$

Recall that the modal operator K ranges over all possible worlds. The entire rule for the example is as follows

$$\frac{out.alice \quad out.alice = B \quad K(out.alice = B \Rightarrow d = false)}{d}$$

In the median example this means that Alice knows that in the last comparison her value was larger, because the output is a value of Bob. Recall that she can distinguish her and Bob's values, because all inputs are distinct.

Symbolic Computation.

In addition to the evaluation of statements we need to perform some symbolic computation. We can infer additional knowledge about the program's state by manipulating its symbols. Particularly, we introduce propositions for the lower-than relation into our inference.

Let a and b be two variables. Then the (true) proposition lt_a_b means that (in this possible world)

$$lt\_a\_b \Leftrightarrow a < b$$

```
c = z ? y : x;
a = b <= c;
d = e ? f : c;
```

Listing 10: Comparison Example

First, we need to tie the symbolic computation to the program. Consider the example in Listing 10. We deduce a proposition lt_c_b, if $a = false$ is in the trace and the variable a is known to the agent Alice.

$$\frac{a \quad a = false}{lt\_c\_b}$$

We also deduce knowledge about program variables from symbolic knowledge. We can omit the trace proposition, since our deduction of symbolic knowledge is always correct and safe.

$$\frac{lt\_c\_b}{a}$$

We need to take care of conditional assignments and track variable renaming. Variable tracking works, again, backward and forward. In the example of Listing 10 we write

$$\frac{e = false \quad lt\_c\_b}{lt\_d\_b} \qquad \frac{z = false \quad lt\_c\_b}{lt\_x\_b}$$

There are many such rules, one for each direction, condition truth value, front or back position of the variable in the proposition and integer variable that is not c.

Second, we implement mathematical axioms, such as negation and transitivity. Since all inputs are distinct, the lower-than relation can be inverted for negation.

$$\frac{\neg lt\_a\_b}{lt\_b\_a}$$

The lower-than relation is also transitive.

$$\frac{lt\_a\_b \quad lt\_b\_c}{lt\_a\_c}$$

Unfortunately, propositions in EML are simple, such that when using symbolic computation on n variables the number of rules increases to $O(n^3)$ with only transitivity already. Also, each conditional assignment introduces $O(n)$ variable renaming rules. We must therefore take care to restrict symbolic computation to the minimum set of variables necessary. We use symbolic computation only for variables appearing as operands in comparison statements.

Nevertheless, in our running example of median computation symbolic computation is necessary. The agent Alice needs to infer that in the world of the trace in Figure 2 the condition $in.alice.x > in.bob.x$ in the first comparison is true, since $in.alice.x > in.bob.y$ from the second comparison and $in.bob.y > in.bob.x$ in all of its inputs.

Assumptions.

Of course, we need to start out with the propositions that input and output are known.

$$K in.alice.x$$
$$K in.alice.y$$
$$K out.alice$$

But as seen in the previous example we need to also encode the assumptions about the input. Following the assumption of Aggarwal et al. we start out with the propositions

$$K lt\_in.alice.x\_in.alice.y$$
$$K lt\_in.bob.x\_in.bob.y$$

Note that these assumptions could also be encoded in the program. If the program would start with a sorting routine of the inputs, then the subsequent inference would remain. The sorting routines would also be marked as local by our optimization technique, since they operate on local input only. They would then be executed at the local site's before the secure computation. This shows another advantage of our technique[1].

3.4.4 Deduction

We can now enter all possible worlds (traces) and rules into a theorem prover. If it can deduce knowledge about the variables, we can assign the labels. Let ϕ be the propositions for all possible worlds and ψ all rules derived from the program. We then enter the following theorem for each variable, e.g. a

$$\phi \wedge \psi \Rightarrow Ka$$

If the theorem can be proven, we assign the label $\{A\}$ to the variable a. We create one such theorem for each variable. If the theorem cannot be proven, we do not assign a label.

We then repeat the process with Bob as the agent. The derivation algorithm for the rules and traces remains unchanged, but some propositions in the rules made in Section 3.4.3 "Assumptions" change, since now Bob's input and output are known instead of Alice's. Also, the propositions in the traces change, since Bob can distinguish its integer input variables, but not Alice's. We also create one theorem for each variable for Bob.

[1]We have omitted this option in order to stay truthful to the example of Aggarwal et al.

```
program Median {

function Output out (Input in) {
    var Boolean a A B, d A B;
    var Elem    b A, c B;

    a A B = in.alice.x A <= in.bob.x B;
    b A=a A B? in.alice.y A: in.alice.x A;
    c B=a A B? in.bob.x B  : in.bob.y   B;

    d A B = b A <= c B;
    out.alice  A = d A B ? b A: c B;
    out.bob    B = d A B ? b A: c B;
}
}
```

Listing 11: Assigned Labels

Finally, we assign the labels. The result of the median example is depicted in Listing 11. As we have pointed out in the beginning of the paper, the challenge is to infer the labels on the variables `a` and `d`. We show a complete deduction of Ka for Alice in Appendix A.

3.5 Segmentation

We can now segment the program of the median computation and perform selected computations at the local sites. The first statement in line 7 needs to be performed as a secure computation, since the intersection of labels is empty. Nevertheless, the result of the secure computation can be made available to both, Alice and Bob. This computation is an instance of Yao's millionaires' problem. Line 8 can be performed solely by Alice and line 9 solely by Bob. Line 11 is a secure computation again.

For lines 12 and 13 we need to implement a special routine. Although the intersection of labels is empty, Alice (or Bob) needs to learn the output of the computation. Therefore for output variables assigned in conditional statements, in case the operand is only known by the other party, we need to implement a send and receive message operation. Care must be taken and this routine only applies, if the condition variable is public and known to both, Alice and Bob, and not in our further example of oblivious transfer where the condition is only known to Alice and which must be implemented as a secure computation. The transmission operations are also implemented locally at Alice's and Bob's site, respectively.

If you compare this segmentation with the L1 program of Listing 2 the program transform is completely successful (except some syntactical constructs). We encode our segmented program as a Java program that calls FairPlay as a subroutine for its secure computation. We have transformed a (relatively) inefficient FairPlay program using program analysis into an efficient protocol similar to the hand-crafted one by Aggarwal et al.

4. FURTHER EXAMPLES

In this section we consider further examples in order to validate our optimization technique. First, we consider 1-out-of-2 oblivious transfer [11] and show that our inference is safe, i.e. the optimized protocol still implements secure oblivious transfer. Second, we use our optimization to reduce joint lot size computation [3] to weighted average computation.

```
program Median {
type Elem        = Int<32>;
type AliceInput  = Boolean;
type AliceOutput = Elem;
type BobInput    = struct {Elem x,
                           Elem y};
type Input  = struct {AliceInput  alice,
                      BobInput    bob};
type Output = struct {AliceOutput alice};

function Output out (Input in) {
out.alice = in.alice ? in.bob.x : in.bob.y;
}
}
```

Listing 12: Oblivious Transfer

4.1 Oblivious Transfer

Oblivious transfer (OT) can be implemented with the SFDL program shown in Listing 12. Of course, it is not best practice to implement OT using SFDL, since FairPlay uses an optimized OT protocol to implement Yao's protocol. It is much more efficient to use such an optimized protocol directly. We can nevertheless test if our optimization technique is safe.

OT is implemented as a single conditional assignment without intermediate variables. Therefore only traces and the rules for conditional assignments apply. There are four possible worlds – two for Alice and two for Bob – depending on the condition `in.alice`.

First, in Alice's case the backward rule for the operand applies. In one world she learns `in.bob.x` and in the other `in.bob.y`. Then also the forward rule applies, but she already knows `out.alice`. Alice cannot distinguish Bob's input, therefore the backward rule for the condition does not apply. Since Alice only learns either of Bob's inputs in a single world, she does not gain knowledge in all worlds and no new labels are created.

Second, in Bob's case no rule applies. Neither backward rule applies, since he does not know `out.alice`. The forward rule also does not apply, since he does not know the condition `in.alice`.

Therefore no optimization is possible using our inference algorithm. This is good news, since OT is an elementary cryptographic primitive and any "optimization" at the language layer would show that our inference algorithm is unsafe. We show next that a slight deviation in just one rule could already lead to such unsafe inferences.

Assume we would change the forward rule by omitting the proposition *in.alice* of the condition, as we have done in the backward rule, resulting in the rules below

$$\frac{in.alice = true \quad in.bob.x}{out.alice} \qquad \frac{in.alice = false \quad in.bob.y}{out.alice}$$

Then, Bob would learn `out.alice` in both worlds. Furthermore, the backward rule for the condition would apply and Bob would also learn `in.alice`. A complete breakdown of the safety of the optimization. It is therefore necessary to include the condition in the forward rule, but not the backward rule for the operand.

```
1  program Median {
2  type Elem         = Int<32>;
3  type AliceInput   = struct {Elem d,
4                              Elem fV,
5                              Elem hV,
6                              Elem c};
7  type AliceOutput = Elem;
8  type BobInput     = struct {Elem d,
9                              Elem fB,
10                             Elem hB};
11 type BobOutput    = Elem;
12 type Input   = struct {AliceInput   alice,
13                        BobInput     bob};
14 type Output  = struct {AliceOutput  alice,
15                        BobOutput    bob};
16
17 function Output out (Input in) {
18    var Elem a, b, c, d, e, f, g, h, i;
19
20    a = 2 * in.alice.d;
21    b = a * in.alice.fV;
22    c = in.alice.d / in.alice.c;
23    d = c * in.alice.hV;
24
25    e = 2 * in.bob.d;
26    f = e * in.bob.fB;
27
28    g = f + b;
29    h = in.bob.hB + d;
30    i = g / h;
31
32    out.alice = i ** 2;
33    out.bob   = i ** 2;
34 }
35 }
```

Listing 13: Joint Economic Lot Size

4.2 Weighted Average

We now consider an example from business administration. When placing an order buyer and vendor need to agree on an order quantity or lot size. Both, buyer and vendor, know the (yearly) demand d of the buyer as part of their contract, but they also have private information. The buyer has holding costs h_B per item and fixed ordering costs f_B per order. The vendor has holding costs h_V per item, fixed setup costs f_V per order and capacity c. They can jointly compute the optimal lot size q using Banerjee's formula [3] below

$$q = \sqrt{\frac{2d(f_B + f_V)}{h_B + \frac{d}{c}h_V}}$$

Since information such as costs and capacities is very sensitive, it is sensible to implement the computation securely. Buyer and vendor can do so using the (extended) SFDL program in Listing 13 where Alice is the vendor and Bob the buyer. We extend SFDL with multiplication (∗) and integer division (/) which are parsed, but not implemented in FairPlay. This has been fixed in FairPlayMP. Furthermore, we introduce the operator (∗∗) for integer roots which cannot be parsed by FairPlay. Therefore we need to execute the resulting protocols using the L1 system.

The program is entirely constructed from assignment expressions. Therefore only its forward and backward rules apply. Recall that constants are public and known to both, Alice and Bob.

As a result of our analysis intermediate variables `a`, `b`, `c`, `d` and `i` are known to Alice. Variables `e`, `f` and `i` are known to Bob. Therefore the first segment of the program (lines 20 - 23) can be executed locally at Alice's site and the second segment (lines 25 and 26) can be executed locally at Bob's site. Only the middle segment (lines 28 - 30) need to be executed as a secure computation. The final segments can be executed locally again, at either party's site.

Thus, we have optimized the protocol significantly. Instead of securely computing a square root – amongst other arithmetic operations –, we have reduced the problem to securely computing a weighted average. This significantly increases the efficiency of the protocol by locally computing several expensive operations and shows another successful application of our optimization technique. All our optimizations (including segmentation) were performed automatically.

We stress that we prepared the SFDL program, such that the optimizer yields the best result. We structured the arithmetic in order to form groups of operations that can be optimized into local computations. We nevertheless anticipate that this optimization can also be performed automatically in the future. Techniques, such as term rewriting, offer excellent capabilities for such transforms.

5. RELATED WORK

There are several systems for implementing secure computation. We classify them into systems specifying the ideal functionality and systems specifying the protocol description. Furthermore, we look at the examples used in our paper.

The positive effect on performance of performing as many computations as possible locally has been confirmed by [18]. [26] also tries to deduct local computations, but only considers the parties' input and not also their output as we do.

5.1 Ideal Functionality Specification

FairPlay [23] provides a generic system for secure two-party computation. The FairPlay system comprises a procedural language, called *Secure Function Definition Language* (SDFL), a compiler that translates SDFL programs into one-pass Boolean circuits that can be securely evaluated using the protocol suggested by [31]. Originally, i.e., as presented in [23], the FairPlay system supported only secure two-party computations written in SDFL 1. This system served as a basis for the development of the FairPlayMP system [6]. FairPlayMP supports the secure evaluation of multi-party computations written in SFDL 2. Some circuit optimization techniques for FairPlay are presented in [28].

There are other compilers [12, 32] which produce safe code for a program according to an information flow policy in a distributed environment. Nevertheless, they do not allow to specify any secure computation and offer no secure implementation for the resulting information flow.

Just FairPlay and FairPlayMP are instances of systems which only describe the ideal functionality of a secure computation, i.e. *what* is to be implemented by the protocol. The burden of finding the ideal protocol is with the compiler. To the best of our knowledge we present the first technique that automatically optimizes such a program.

5.2 Protocol Description Specification

Next to FairPlay and its specification of the ideal functionality, there are several secure computation implementations where the programmer can give the compiler hints on how to optimize. In the Secure Multiparty Computation Language (SMCL) [25] the programmer specifies the ideal functionality, but may specify also the visibility of variables as secret, private or public. This is similar to our (party-specific) labels, but we infer the labels automatically via program analysis and do not burden the programmer. The TASTY compiler and its TASTYL language [17] allow implementing mixed-protocol implementations using not only Yao's protocol, but also (additively) homomorphic encryption. The programmer can specify in TASTYL which protocol is to be used for which operation. This results in significantly more efficient, yet always provably secure protocols. The VIFF framework [10] extends the Python language using a library. It offers the programmer several primitives for secure computation, but the protocol description is up to the programmer. The Sharemind framework [8] offers an interpreter for an assembler-like language implementing secure protocols. The programmer has to specify the protocol description using the primitives. The L1 system [30] allows specifying protocol descriptions with many primitives including Yao's protocol and homomorphic encryption. It also offers a library for network communication.

All of these languages, compilers or frameworks are instances of systems where the programmer can – at least partially – specify *how* the protocol is implemented. This approach leads to significantly more efficient protocols, but puts an additional burden on the programmer. In this paper we have chosen a different approach. We use program analysis to infer the optimal protocol from the ideal functionality, but, of course, our techniques are also applicable in combination with other, programmer specified optimizations. To the best of our knowledge we are the first to present a fully automatic technique.

5.3 Examples

We use several optimized protocols as our examples. Our running example of the median computation by Aggarwal et al. [1] was one of the first instances of a (hand-)optimized secure computation protocol. Our optimization technique was able to even slightly exceed the manual optimization.

Oblivious transfer (OT) is a long known primitive in cryptography. 1-out-of-2 OT was introduced by Even et al. [11]. Our optimization was not able to improve its programming language specification. On the one hand, this is good, because our optimization is safe. After all, Kilian has shown that cryptography can be founded on OT [19]. On the other hand, it shows that our optimization technique cannot optimize the cryptographic implementation. This is not surprising, since it only consider the ideal functionality. There are several (cryptographically) optimized protocols for OT, e.g. [13, 22, 24].

Our last example is joint lot size computation as weighted average. This has been introduced in [27]. It shows the manifold applications of secure computation. Our optimization technique was able to match the manual optimization, if the program was accordingly structured.

6. CONCLUSIONS

We have presented the first technique to automatically optimize a secure computation program. Our program analysis infers what a party knows from input and output. This additional information is then used to perform several computations locally instead of as a secure protocol. We have shown using the running example of median computation that our optimization technique can match (and even exceed) those performed manually by the programmer. Using our implementation we were able to compile and execute an SFDL program as Aggarwal et al.'s protocol.

As the performers of an automated analysis related to Aggarwal et al.'s protocol we would like to make a few comments on this protocol. First, our analysis underpins that the protocol is *secure*. Our analysis is crafted carefully to be safe and resulted in a slightly more revealing protocol than the manually designed one. Second, our analysis shows that protocol is very slightly *inefficient*. Our analysis concludes – and it is very easy to verify manually – that the last comparison can also be implemented as a Yao's millionaire's protocol. Aggarwal et al. recommend to use a minimum computation that outputs the minimum element. This is very slightly less efficient, but avoids sending the output by one party. Our compiled protocol is therefore slightly more efficient.

For future work we see two open problems. First, our analysis works on protocols secure in the semi-honest model. We would like to extend this to protocols secure in the malicious model. One can adapt the compiler from the semi-honest to the malicious model by Goldreich [14], but this could be too inefficient. Second, our prototypical implementation uses the ModLeanTab theorem prover [5]. We can perform the compilation of the median example in roughly one minute, but the majority of the time is spent on proving the theorems. A more efficient algorithm that scales to large programs and maybe avoids theorem proving is desirable.

7. ACKNOWLEDGEMENTS

We are grateful to Axel Schröpfer for implementing the L1 examples and performing the experiments and to Achim Brucker and Marcel Jünemann for implementing SSA and the transformation.

8. REFERENCES

[1] G. Aggarwal, N. Mishra, and B. Pinkas. Secure computation of the k-th ranked element. In *EUROCRYPT'04: Advances in Cryptology*, 2004.

[2] R. Agrawal and R. Srikant. Privacy-preserving data mining. *ACM SIGMOD Record*, 29(2), 2000.

[3] A. Banerjee. A joint economic-lot-size model for buyer and supplier. *Decision Sciences*, 17, 1986.

[4] D. Beaver, S. Micali, and P. Rogaway. The round complexity of secure protocols. In *STOC'90: Proceedings of the 22nd ACM Symposium on Theory of Computing*, 1990.

[5] B. Beckert and R. Gore. In *CADE'98: Proceedings of the International Conference on Automated Deduction*, 1998.

[6] A. Ben-David, N. Nisan, and B. Pinkas. Fairplaymp: a system for secure multi-party computation. In *CCS'08: Proceedings of the 15th ACM Conference on Computer and Communications Security*, 2008.

[7] M. Ben-Or, S. Goldwasser, and A. Wigderson. Completeness theorems for non-cryptographic fault-tolerant distributed computation. In *STOC'88: Proceedings of the 20th ACM Symposium on Theory of Computing*, 1988.

[8] D. Bogdanov, S. Laur, and J. Willemson. Sharemind: a framework for fast privacy-preserving computations. In *ESORICS'08: Proceedings of the 13th European Symposium on Research in Computer Security*, 2008.

[9] R. Cytron, J. Ferrante, B. K. Rosen, M. N. Wegman, and F. K. Zadeck. Efficiently computing static single assignment form and the control dependence graph. *ACM Transactions Programming Languages and Systems*, 13(4), 1991.

[10] I. Damgård, M. Geisler, M. Krøigaard, and J. B. Nielsen. Asynchronous multiparty computation: theory and implementation. In *PKC'09: Proceedings of the 12th International Conference on Practice and Theory in Public Key Cryptography*, 2009.

[11] S. Even, O. Goldreich, and A. Lempel. A randomized protocol for signing contracts. *Communications of the ACM*, 28(8), 1985.

[12] C. Fournet, G. L. Guernic, and T. Rezk. A security-preserving compiler for distributed programs: from information-flow policies to cryptographic mechanisms. In *CCS'09: Proceedings of the 16th ACM Conference on Computer and Communications Security*, 2009.

[13] C. Gentry and Z. Ramzan. Single-database private information retrieval with constant communication rate. In *ICALP'05: Proceedings of the 32nd International Colloquium on Automata, Languages and Programming*, 2005.

[14] O. Goldreich. *Foundations of Cryptography*, volume 2. Cambridge University Press, 2004.

[15] O. Goldreich, S. Micali, and A. Wigderson. How to play any mental game. In *STOC'87: Proceedings of the 19th ACM Symposium on Theory of Computing*, 1987.

[16] J. Y. Halpern. Reasoning about knowledge: a survey. In D. M. Gabbay, C. J. Hogger, and J. A. Robinson, editors, *Handbook of Logic in Artificial Intelligence and Logic Programming*, volume 4. Oxford University Press, 1995.

[17] W. Henecka, S. Kögl, A.-R. Sadeghi, T. Schneider, and I. Wehrenberg. Tasty: tool for automating secure two-party computations. In *CCS'10: Proceedings of the 17th ACM Conference on Computer and Communications Security*, 2010.

[18] Y. Huang, D. Evans, J. Katz, and L. Malka. Faster secure two-party computation using garbled circuits. In *Proceedings of the 20th USENIX Security Symposium*, 2011.

[19] J. Kilian. Founding crytpography on oblivious transfer. In *STOC'88: Proceedings of the 20th ACM Symposium on Theory of Computing*, 1988.

[20] S. Kripke. A semantic analysis of modal logic i: normal modal propositional calculi. *Zeitschrift für Mathematische Logik und Grundlagen der Mathematik*, 9, 1963.

[21] Y. Lindell and B. Pinkas. Privacy-preserving data mining. In *CRYPTO'00: Advances in Cryptology*, 2000.

[22] H. Lipmaa. An oblivious transfer protocol with log-squared communication. In *ISC'05: Proceedings of the 8th International Conference on Information Security*, 2005.

[23] D. Malkhi, N. Nisan, B. Pinkas, and Y. Sella. Fairplay—a secure two-party computation system. In *Proceedings of the 13th USENIX Security Symposium*, 2004.

[24] M. Naor and B. Pinkas. Efficient oblivious transfer protocols. In *SODA'01: Proceedings of the 12th ACM-SIAM Symposium on Discrete Algorithms*, 2001.

[25] J. D. Nielsen and M. I. Schwartzbach. A domain-specific programming language for secure multiparty computation. In *PLAS'07: Proceedings of the ACM Workshop on Programming Languages and Analysis for Security*, 2007.

[26] A. Paus, A.-R. Sadeghi, and T. Schneider. Practical secure evaluation of semi-private functions. In *ACNS'09: Proceedings of the 7th International Conference on Applied Cryptography and Network Security*, 2009.

[27] R. Pibernik, Y. Zhang, F. Kerschbaum, and A. Schröpfer. Secure collaborative supply chain planning and inverse optimization - the jels model. *European Journal of Operational Research*, 208(1), 2011.

[28] B. Pinkas, T. Schneider, N. P. Smart, and S. C. Williams. Secure two-party computation is practical. In *ASIACRYPT'09: Advances in Cryptology*, 2009.

[29] A. Sabelfeld and A. C. Myers. Language-based information-flow security. *IEEE Journal on Selected Areas in Communications*, 21(1), 2003.

[30] A. Schröpfer, F. Kerschbaum, and G. Müller. L1 – an intermediate language for mixed-protocol secure computation. In *COMPSAC'11: Proceedings of the 35th IEEE Computer Software and Applications Conference*, 2011.

[31] A. C.-C. Yao. How to generate and exchange secrets. In *FOCS'86: Proceedings of the 27th IEEE Symposium on Foundations of Computer Science*, 1986.

[32] S. Zdancewic, L. Zheng, N. Nystrom, and A. C. Myers. Untrusted hosts and confidentiality: Secure program partitioning. In *SOSP'01: Proceedings of the 18th ACM Symposium on Operating System Principles*, 2001.

APPENDIX

A. MEDIAN EXAMPLE

Assumptions:

$$
\begin{array}{l}
K\mathit{in.alice.x} \\
K\mathit{in.alice.y} \\
K\mathit{out.alice} \\
K\mathit{lt\_in.alice.x\_in.alice.y} \\
K\mathit{lt\_in.bob.x\_in.bob.y}
\end{array}
$$

Trace of world $\mathcal{W}_1$:

$$
\begin{array}{l}
\mathcal{W}_1 \models a = \mathit{true} \\
\mathcal{W}_1 \models b = A2 \\
\mathcal{W}_1 \models c = B \\
\mathcal{W}_1 \models d = \mathit{true} \\
\mathcal{W}_1 \models \mathit{out.alice} = A2
\end{array}
$$

Inference in world $\mathcal{W}_1$:

$$
\dfrac{\dfrac{d = \mathit{true} \quad \mathit{out.alice}}{b} \quad b = A2 \quad K(b = A2 \Rightarrow a = \mathit{true})}{\mathcal{W}_1 \models a}
$$

Trace of world $\mathcal{W}_2$:

$$
\begin{array}{l}
\mathcal{W}_2 \models a = \mathit{false} \\
\mathcal{W}_2 \models b = A1 \\
\mathcal{W}_2 \models c = B \\
\mathcal{W}_2 \models d = \mathit{true} \\
\mathcal{W}_2 \models \mathit{out.alice} = A1
\end{array}
$$

Inference in world $\mathcal{W}_2$:

$$
\dfrac{\dfrac{d = \mathit{true} \quad \mathit{out.alice}}{b} \quad b = A1 \quad K(b = A1 \Rightarrow a = \mathit{false})}{\mathcal{W}_2 \models a}
$$

Trace of world $\mathcal{W}_3$:

$$
\begin{array}{l}
\mathcal{W}_3 \models a = \mathit{true} \\
\mathcal{W}_3 \models b = A2 \\
\mathcal{W}_3 \models c = B \\
\mathcal{W}_3 \models d = \mathit{false} \\
\mathcal{W}_3 \models \mathit{out.alice} = B
\end{array}
$$

Inference in world $\mathcal{W}_3$:

$$
\dfrac{\mathit{in.alice.x} \quad \dfrac{a = \mathit{true} \quad \dfrac{d = \mathit{false} \quad \mathit{out.alice}}{c}}{\mathit{in.bob.x}}}{\mathcal{W}_3 \models a}
$$

Trace of world $\mathcal{W}_4$:

$$
\begin{array}{l}
\mathcal{W}_4 \models a = \mathit{false} \\
\mathcal{W}_4 \models b = A1 \\
\mathcal{W}_4 \models c = B \\
\mathcal{W}_4 \models d = \mathit{false} \\
\mathcal{W}_4 \models \mathit{out.alice} = B
\end{array}
$$

Inference in world $\mathcal{W}_4$:

$$
\dfrac{\dfrac{\mathit{lt\_in.bob.x\_in.bob.y} \quad \dfrac{a = \mathit{false} \quad \dfrac{a = \mathit{false} \quad \dfrac{\dfrac{\mathit{out.alice} \quad \mathit{out.alice} = B \quad K(\mathit{out.alice} = B \Rightarrow d = \mathit{false})}{d} \quad d = \mathit{false}}{\mathit{lt\_c\_b}}}{\mathit{lt\_c\_in.alice.x}}}{\mathit{lt\_in.bob.y\_in.alice.x}}}{\mathit{lt\_in.bob.x\_in.alice.x}}}{\mathcal{W}_4 \models a}
$$

Global inference:

$$
\dfrac{\mathcal{W}_1 \models a \quad \mathcal{W}_2 \models a \quad \mathcal{W}_3 \models a \quad \mathcal{W}_4 \models a}{Ka}
$$

VMCrypt - Modular Software Architecture for Scalable Secure Computation

Lior Malka
Intel (work done while at UMD)
lior34@gmail.com

ABSTRACT

Garbled circuits play a key role in secure computation, but existing implementations do not scale and are not modular. In this paper we present VMCrypt, a library for secure computation. This library introduces novel algorithms that, regardless of the circuit being garbled or its size, have a very small memory requirement and use no disk storage. By providing an API (*Abstract Programming Interface*), VMCrypt can be integrated into existing projects and customized without any modifications to its source code. We measured the performance of VMCrypt on several circuits with hundreds of millions of gates. These are the largest *scalable* secure computations done to date.

Categories and Subject Descriptors

C.2.0 [**Computer-Communication Networks**]: General—*security and protection*

General Terms

Security, Performance, Algorithms

Keywords

Secure Computation, Software API, Scalable

1. INTRODUCTION

Secure computation enables parties to collaborate while keeping their information private. Specifically, a two-party protocol for secure computation allows a server (holding input x) and a client (holding input y) to compute $f(x\ y)$ such that either party learns nothing beyond the output of f.

Yao's Garbled Circuits Technique [31] is central to secure computation. The first phase in this approach is to create a representation of f as a boolean circuit C. Next, in the *garbling* phase, the server chooses secret keys (called *wire labels*) for each wire in C, encrypts a *a lookup table* for each gate, and sends all lookup tables (the *garbled circuit*) to the client. The server also sends wire labels corresponding to x. Wire labels corresponding to y require oblivious transfer (OT). Finally, in the *evaluation phase* the client uses the wire labels for x and y to decrypt the lookup tables until the output gates are decrypted and $f(x\ y)$ is revealed.

Yao's technique has been implemented in Fairplay [21] and TASTY [11], but these works focused on automation aspects of secure computation (more details in Section 1.3). This paper, however, is concerned with software engineering challenges.

The first challenge is scalability. Suppose, for example, that f computes the intersection of databases x and y. The circuit C representing $f(x\ y)$ could easily have billions of gates. Holding it memory would require terabytes of RAM. Wire labels or lookup tables would require a large hard drive. Read/write operations will paralyze the operating system. Recompilation (needed in Fairplay and TASTY) will take a significant amount of time, ruling out secure computation on the fly.

The second challenge is software modularity. Consider, for example, a scenario where garbled circuits are to be integrated into an application that already has a client and a server, and that, in addition, a specific method of encryption should be used for garbling. The source code of the garbled circuit software can be modified to accommodate this integration, but this would significantly increase development costs and is likely to introduce bugs into the source. Ideally, developers would be provided with an *abstract programming interface* (API) so that they can customize the software without modifying the source code. This includes customizing the client and the server, the OT protocol, garbling, encryption, and so on. Also, modules should be designed in such a way that developers can use them to build a protocol with any level of security (we have implemented the curious-but-honest protocol). Another objective would be to allow developers to replace parts of their circuits with improved implementations by other developers, making modular not only the software, but also the circuits themselves. Finally, developers must be able to test circuits for correctness automatically, without having to run the secure protocol.

1.1 Our Results

We present VMCrypt - a fully customizable Java library for secure computation. VMCrypt introduces novel algorithms that, regardless of the circuit being garbled or its size, have a very small memory footprint and use no disk storage. VMCrypt comes with a *Developers Manual* [19] and provides tools for debugging and validation.

To describe VMCrypt, we use the example of the database

CCS'11, October 17–21, 2011, Chicago, Illinois, USA.

search protocol, where the server has records $\langle x_i \; p_i \rangle$, and the client, who holds y, wants to learn all p_i for which $x_i = y$. We denote the circuit for this protocol by `DBSearch`.

Unlike Fairplay programs, VMCrypt circuits (called *components*) are simply Java classes. They are compiled once and for all and receive their parameters at run time, via the constructor. For example, `DBSearch` is instantiated at run time by executing `Component c = new DBSearch(` $_x$ $_p$ N`)`, where $_x$ and $_p$ denote the bit length of x and p, and N is the number of records in the database. In a realistic scenario where the number of records in the database changes daily, components allow us to start a VMCrypt protocol on the fly, whereas with Fairplay we need an expensive offline phase for recompilation (we compare with Fairplay because TASTY combines homomorphic encryption and garbled circuits. However, as we later show, the same applies to TASTY).

The second difference between VMCrypt and Fairplay relates to how circuit descriptions are maintained in memory. In earlier versions of VMCrypt, constructing a component (e.g., `new DBSearch(` $_x$ $_p$ N`)`) would have immediately created an instance of this object in memory. In the case of `DBSearch`, the size of the object is linear in $N(_x + _p)$. Thus, instantiating `DBSearch` is worse than holding the entire database in memory. This is clearly infeasible. Worse, it excludes secure computation from consumer devices such as laptops and cell phones. Fairplay suffers from the same issue.

VMCrypt solves this problem. Intuitively, it has an underlying virtual machine that loads and destructs hardware descriptions dynamically, during execution. This mechanism is transparent to the developer. It works for circuits of any size, and guarantees that the client and the server hold only a small part of the circuit in memory. See Section 3 for details.

To describe the third difference between VMCrypt and Fairplay, recall that in Yao's protocol the client evaluates the function after receiving the garbled circuit from the server. This requires storage (e.g., a hard drive) for wire labels or lookup tables, which, as our tests show, can reach gigabytes of data. Writing this much data to the hard-disk will paralyze the operating system and slow down execution.

VMCrypt eliminates the need for storage, which also improves running time. To achieve this, we introduce a new variant for Yao's protocol. Informally, our protocol divides the number n of input wires into segments of a constant size s (e.g., $s = 100$). In iteration i, the server issues the i-*th* segment of s wire labels to the client, following which it garbles the part of the circuit corresponding to this segment. The lookup tables are sent directly into the network. The client reads the lookup tables from the network and evaluates the i-th part of the circuit. This continues until the entire circuit is evaluated. To achieve this, we garble, evaluate, and execute OT at the same time (rather than sequentially). Interleaving OT in Yao's protocol is highly non trivial, especially because we execute OT in bulk, which is several orders of magnitude faster. Our new protocol is also attractive because it can be multi-threaded, which may further improve performance. More details, and a security proof, are given in Section 2.

We stress that all VMCrypt mechanisms (e.g., storing only part of the circuit in memory, or garbling the circuit in chunks) are completely transparent to developers. VMCrypt developers only need to describe the circuit (what we call *a component*) they want to securely compute and the input to the circuit.

1.2 Performance

Taking `DBSearch` again as an example, Fairplay compilation alone takes 50 seconds and 0 7 GB memory (23% of a 3 GB RAM) when the database size is 40 records. The Fairplay compiler crashes after 3 minutes when the number of records is increased to 55.

With VMCrypt, when the database size is 10 000, the entire protocol terminates after 19 seconds. Moreover, each party (and the Java virtual machine that executes it) uses only 0 15 GB memory (4 8% of 3 GB). Even if we increase the database size to 1 million (which increases the size of the circuit to 100 million gates), the parties still use the same amount of memory.

VMCrypt has gone through rigorous performance analysis. To show that it scales on circuits with a wide structure we tested it on the `DBSearch` circuit. To show that VMCrypt scales regardless of wiring patterns, we implemented the set intersection circuit, which has a highly connected structure. To show that VMCrypt scales on wide and deep circuits, we implemented the minimum circuit. To show VMCrypt modularity, all circuits have been developed and tested without modifying VMCrypt source code. To show that performance is truly linear, each circuit was tested on inputs of increasing length (as opposed to breaking the input into small pieces and modifying VMCrypt source code to evaluate several smaller circuits). To show scalability we evaluated circuits with hundreds of millions of gates. As our tests show, VMCrypt would scale on any circuit with any number of gates (e.g., billions). See Section 5.

1.3 Related Work

Secure computation has been used recently to implement systems for privacy-preserving face recognition, fingerprint matching, and DNA processing (c.f., [13, 7, 28, 24, 1, 8]). Other optimizations for garbled circuits, such as the free XOR technique [15] and others [17, 14, 27, 26, 6] has been proposed. Techniques for secure computation based on homomorphic encryption (c.f., [25, 5, 10, 30, 29]) have also been studied.

Fairplay [21, 2] demonstrated the feasibility of two-party secure computation based on garbled circuits. Automation and benchmarking of cryptographic protocols were studied in, e.g., [3, 4, 18, 23].

The comparison of VMCrypt to Fairplay applies also to TASTY [11]. TASTY combines the benefits of homomorphic encryption and garbled circuits. It uses a high level language, which requires recompilation and rules out executing secure protocols on the fly. TASTY does not provide an API (indeed, this was not a design requirement), and therefore integrating it into other applications requires modifying TASTY source code. TASTY would run out of memory on any large circuit. In fact, TASTY does not deal with large circuits, except for one example where memory consumption climbs as the circuit reaches 4 2 million gates, and crashes thereafter.

Prior to this work, we showed that faster execution times can be achieved by constructing circuits from Java classes [9]. The software from [9] was not designed to provide an API, and it does not include any of the innovations presented in this paper. Similarly, it does not scale and it requires the use of storage. Specifically, it crashes on large circuits and exhibits non-linear running time, problems which we avoided in [9] by manually instantiating many small circuits and rewriting the source code for each circuit.

2. OVERVIEW OF VMCRYPT

This section gives a high level overview of VMCrypt. Components are described in detail in the next section.

Once a component has been written, VMCrypt provides the developer with a test tool to validate that the component indeed computes the correct function. This tool, implemented in class `TestModule`, creates an instance of `StandardInput`, which holds the input bits. Similarly, it creates an instance of `StandardOutput`, and assigns the output bus of the component to point at it. After the component computes, its output is stored in the `StandardOutput` object. If the component implements interface `Testable`, then the test tool can automatically validate the component for correctness. The test tool iterates over all inputs to obtain a full functional coverage of the component. The advantage of our tool over Fairplay is that a component can be validated on all inputs, without having to run the secure protocol.

The preceding discussion gives the impression that the component is a passive description of a circuit, and that the test tool somehow processes this description. This impression is wrong. The entire work is done by the component, and the same applies to garbling and evaluation. We describe this process in more detail.

Each VMCrypt binary gate has a method `notify` that takes three arguments: *a port, an object*, and *a function.* In the case of the test module, the function is class `Calculate`, and the object, which represents an input, is a bit (0 or 1). The port, which is 0 or 1, tells the gate which input wire is receiving the object. Once both inputs arrive, the gate invokes the `compute` method of the function, passing these inputs as arguments. Next, the gate notifies its output wire with the output of this function. This process continues until the entire circuit is computed. The process of garbling and evaluating a circuit uses the same `notify` method, except that different functions and objects are passed as arguments.

VMCrypt presents a new variant for Yao's protocol, in which the circuit is garbled in chunks. We use a `Notifier` (see Figure 1), which has a very simple task: to obtain a segment (shown as a bracket) of pairs of wire labels, and for each pair in the segment, notify the component with this pair. More precisely, the notifier notifies the component with an object and a function that gates pass execution to once they have all their inputs ready. On the server side the function is `Garble` and the object is a `WireLabelPair`. On the client side the function is `Eval` and the object is `WireLabel`. Both functions implement abstract class `Function`.

Once the notification process begins, gates receive objects on all of their input wires and pass execution to the function. In the case of the garble function, gates receive wire label pairs, lookup tables are written into the network, and gates notify their output wires with a wire label pair. In the case of the evaluation function, gates receive wire labels, lookup tables are decrypted, and gates notify their output wires with wire labels. The notifiers repeat this, segment by segment, until the entire component is notified. Immediately after the server sends the last lookup table, the client computes the output. The component builds and destructs parts of its description during the notification process, which we describe in the next section.

Oblivious transfer is not executed before or after the garbling; it is interleaved in the garbling. What makes this possible is abstract class `WireLabelTransport`. VMCrypt provides a server side implementation for this class called `WLTPServer` (*wire label transport protocol, server side*) and a client side called `WLTPClient`. The role of the wire label transport protocol is to guarantee that when the notifier on the server side receives a segment of wire labels, the notifier on the client side already has them. This enables the server to stream lookup tables, knowing that the client will be able to decrypt them on the fly and discard them immediately. The obvious implication of this streaming is that no storage is necessary for either wire labels or lookup tables. This is a significant advantage because the garbled circuit can be very large. Moreover, time consuming read/write operations are eliminated, thus reducing running time. A

We briefly sketch the proof of security. The idea is identical to the classic proof [16]. The simulation begins when the simulator $\mathcal{S}$ sends the evaluator $\mathcal{E}$ a garbled circuit with a random output. Of course, the circuit is sent in chunks, and OT is interleaved in the garbling. After all OT operations are over, $\mathcal{S}$ learns the input of $\mathcal{E}$. It then queries the ideal functionality, learns the real output, and sends $\mathcal{E}$ a permutation that maps the random output to the real output. Since the ideal and the real views of $\mathcal{E}$ are computationally indistinguishable, the protocol is secure in the honest but curios setting.

In the rest of this section we describe the wire label transport protocol parameters, starting with the OT sub protocol. VMCrypt provides two OT implementations [22, 12], but of course any OT protocol can be passed as an argument. The second parameter is an implementation of interface `WireLabelGenerator`. The role of this interface is to provide wire label pairs for the wire label transport protocol. A standard implementation of this interface would simply return two random strings as a `WireLabelPair`, but VMCrypt implements the "free XOR" idea [15] and therefore our implementation of this interface produces a pair $\langle r \ r \oplus R \rangle$, where r is a freshly chosen random string, and R is a fixed random string. To use standard garbling, all that one needs to do is provide the standard implementation for `WireLabelGenerator`, with the corresponding implementations of `Function` for garbling and evaluation, and pass them as arguments to the respective classes.

The third parameter to the wire label transport protocol is a class that implements interface `CircuitInput`. For any i, this interface provides a method that answers whether wire i corresponds to a server input or not, and another method that returns the value on this wire (0 or 1). The wire label transport protocol uses the `CircuitInput` interface to find which input wire belongs to which party, and what is the value of this input. Implementations of `CircuitInput` play another important role: if a party has an input that is too large to hold in memory (e.g., a database), then `CircuitInput` can read it from its origin segment by segment, as opposed to loading it all at once in the beginning.

To avoid expensive OT per wire, we execute OT in bulk. However, recall that we interleave OT in the garbling, which means that we do not know in advance how many (and which) wire labels require OT. To overcome this, we implement what we call *an OT bucket.* Specifically, in the wire

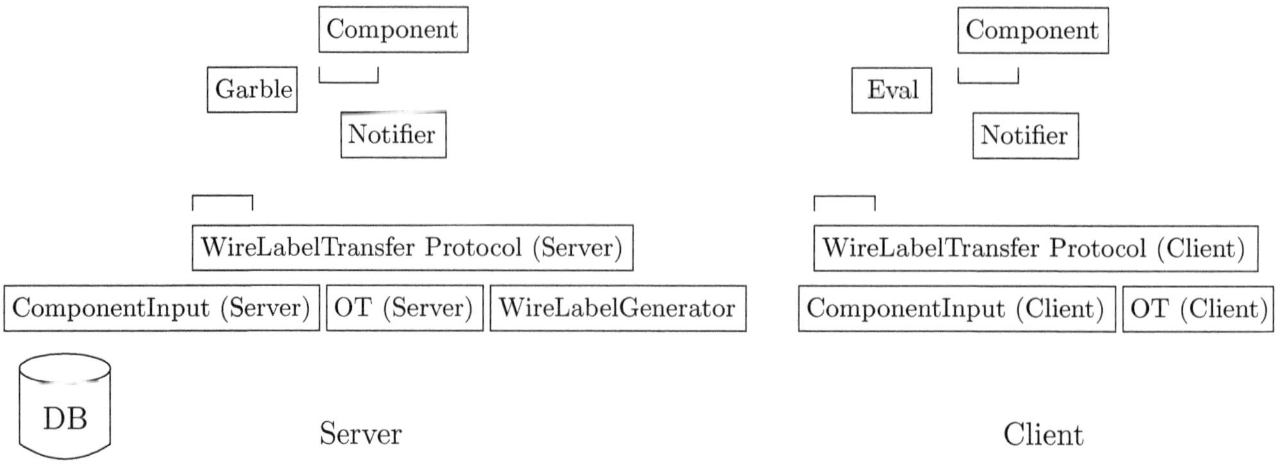

Figure 1: Overview of main VMCrypt modules

label transport protocol (server side) the OT bucket contains pairs of random strings $\langle r_{j\,0}\ r_{j\,1}\rangle$, as opposed to wire label pairs. On the client side it contains one string $r_{j\,b}$ per pair, where $b \in \{0\ 1\}$ is the client input at wire index j. Wire labels are transferred as follows. If $\langle W^{i\,0}\ W^{i\,1}\rangle$ is a wire label pair corresponding to a server input b, then $W^{i\,b}$ is sent to the client. Otherwise, $\langle W^{i\,0} \oplus r_0\ W^{i\,1} \oplus r_1\rangle$ is sent, where $\langle r_0\ r_1\rangle$ is the pair of masks at the top of the OT bucket. This works because the wire label transport protocol examines future segments to find what the client will need when future wires are reached. When the bucket is empty, the OT protocol is invoked to refill it.

Earlier in this section we described the test tool, which validates that a component indeed computes the function at hand. This may not be sufficient for debugging, because a developer may want to see how a signal passes through a circuit. The developer may also want to collect statistics, like network traffic, or number of gates. To support this, VMCrypt provides class `Monitor`, which is a tool for visualizing the execution of VMCrypt modules. The monitor allows developers to see what is happening inside components and protocols in real time. Modules report events by calling monitor method `report`. They pass the event itself and a string that includes values of relevant variables. The monitor displays the `ID` of the component with each report. The `ID` is a pair of integers `(depth,index)`. When sub components are built, they are assigned `depth` that is one higher than their enclosing component, and a unique `index` within this component. By providing the `ID`, VMCrypt helps developers identify which part of the component is reporting. Events are implemented in classes `ComponentEvent` and `ProtocolEvent`. They describe useful information such as when components build and destruct, or when protocols start and end. There are currently thirty one events in VMCrypt, and they can be extended of course. Events also provide runtime statistics, such as network traffic, execution times, and execution progress.

3. THE COMPONENT MODULE

The component module is the heart of VMCrypt. It has been redesigned four times from scratch to guarantee that performance does not depend on circuit topology. We start with the original design and explain how it evolved to the current version.

First version. The first version of the component module was inspired by the minimum function, which plays a central role in privacy-preserving systems [7, 28, 24, 1]. We defined two types of components: `Gate` and `Circuit`. We also provided wires to connect them. Our idea was that developers would be able to construct small circuits, and then use them as building blocks for larger circuits. For example, a bit multiplexer (Figure 2 a) would be built in a low-level manner, from gates and wires. A string multiplexer, on the other hand, would be built from the bit multiplexer. Next, a multiplexer and a comparator can be used to build a circuit for finding the minimum of two numbers (Figure 2 b), which is then used to build a circuit for finding the minimum of N numbers (Figure 2 c). This approach is similar to programming in $C++$ in the sense that developers have both the low-level power of C and the modularity provided by an object-oriented language. Another advantage of this approach is that developers can share components or replace them with better implementations.

To instantiate a circuit for finding the minimum of N numbers whose bit length is *arity*, VMCrypt developers use the following standard Java syntax: `Component c = new MIN(`N *arity*`)`. The problem is that, even for modest values $N = 1\ 000\ 000$ and $arity = 64$, the number of wires needed to connect the `BinaryMIN` circuits is $3 * arity * (N-1) = 194$ million wires (excluding wires and gates inside the `BinaryMIN`). Moreover, wires are implemented as lists (class `Vector` in Java) to allow fan out degree higher than 1. Thus, the memory needed to instantiate the `MIN` circuit is prohibitive. The code of this version was used in [8].

Second version. The objective of the second version was to provide components for wireless circuit design. We added a new component, called a `Switch`, that can route signals to its sub components without wires. The idea is simple: when the switch receives a signal and a wire index (called *a port*), it compares the in-degree of the first sub component with the port. If the port is smaller, then the sub component receives the signal. Otherwise, the in-degree is subtracted from the port, and the switch iterates on the next sub component (of course, like all other mechanisms,

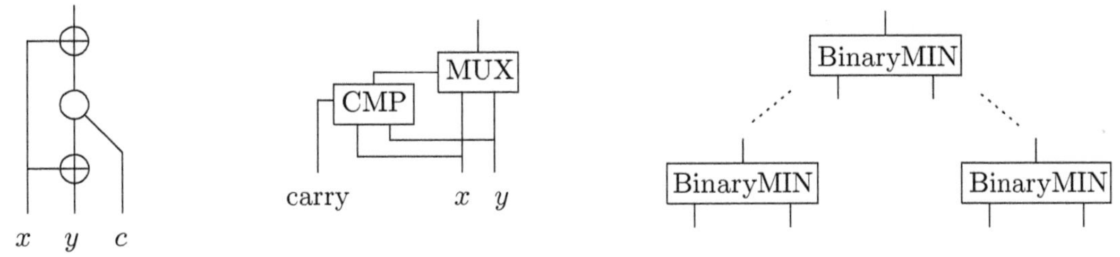

(a) BitMUX (b) BinaryMIN (c) MIN

Figure 2: Components of the MIN circuit due to [14, 28]

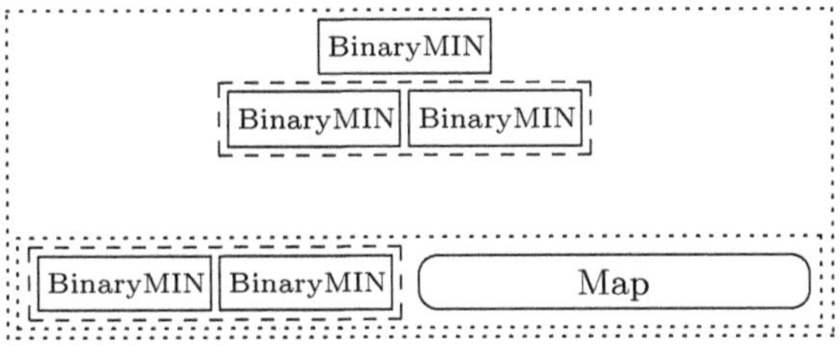

Figure 3: The `MIN` component.

this is automatically taken care of by the component and is transparent to the developer).

The switch brings up a difficult dilemma that is general to all the components. That is, should we equip a switch with output wires or not? Without output wires components will not be able to connect to each other. With them we create the same amount of wires that we wanted to eliminate in the first place. Our solution was to replace output wires of components other than gates with one pointer, and allow input wires only in circuits. Thus, gates will still be able to send signals to multiple components, but non-gate components will only be able to send signals to one component. In the rare case where this would be too restrictive, we provide a `Splitter`, which enables routing to multiple components. This dilemma represents a conflict between utility, usability, and efficiency, that predominated throughout the entire development process.

The other problem with the switch was that routing a signal requires linear time (as opposed to constant when using wires). This becomes quadratic per component, and increases the running time considerably. To solve this problem we introduced the `UniSwitch`. This component contains multiple copies of the same sub component. Thus, it can route a signal in constant time by dividing the value of the port by the in-degree of this sub component. The `UniSwitch` turned out to be very useful as it enables constructing components that mimic a **`for`** loop.

Let us use these components to build the `MIN` component without wires. As shown in Figure 3, this component has a `BinaryMIN` circuit at the root, and a `UniSwitch` containing `BinaryMIN` at each layer, except the base, which is a `Switch` containing two sub components: a `UniSwitch` and a component called a `Map`. The map requires almost no memory as it contains nothing inside. When it receives input on port i, it simply outputs it on port $m(j)$, where m is the function implemented by the map (the identity in this case). The map is used here to pass the signal one level up in case that the tree is not perfect. Notice that all the components reside inside a `Switch` whose input layer is the base layer.

Having built `MIN`, let us revisit the java statement `Component c =` **`new`** `MIN(`N *arity*`)`, which motivated all the new components in the second version. This statement no longer creates millions of wires. However, since all the `BinaryMIN` circuits are made of wires and gates, the `MIN` circuit still requires an unacceptable amount of memory.

Third version. The third version of the component module introduced the `Bus`. If VMCrypt has one most important module, the bus would be it. The bus has a very simple task: it counts the number of signals leaving the component. When this number reaches zero, the bus invokes the `destruct` method of the component. This removes the component from memory. All VMCrypt components have a bus, except for gates, which self destruct.

Clearly, there is no point in having a bus if the entire component resides in memory; the bus has a value only if components are built *after* their instantiation. Thus, all VMCrypt components (except gates) build when they receive their first signal, and destruct immediately when they output their last signal. We call this *the notification principle.* To see the power of this principle, notice that even when a component is built, its sub components will not be built until they receive input, and this of course applies recursively. Consequently, VMCrpyt components have a very lean memory footprint.

Let us see how much memory the `MIN` component (Figure 3) requires now. The first signal will build the base layer, which contains two components, but only the `UniSwitch` will build because the `Map` received no signal yet (assuming the signal comes from the left). Inside the `UniSwitch`, only the leftmost `BinaryMIN` circuit is built because the other ones received no inputs yet. Because the `BinaryMIN` is also built from sub components, only those that receive this signal will be built, and so on. Eventually, the signal will hit a gate, who will store it and wait for the other signal (assuming a binary gate). When this signal arrives, the gate computes, destructs, notifies its output wire, and the process continues. When the `BinaryMIN` fires its last output, it is destructed by its bus. In the case of a `UniSwitch`, even the reference to this object is removed from memory. Hence, the `UniSwitch` from the base layer becomes empty. Since each layer notifies the one above it, the `Switch`, which contains all these layers, requires $\log(N)$ references to components of type `UniSwitch` that are either empty or contain one `BinaryMIN`. Notice that this is not a flaw in VMCrypt; it is due to the underlying recursive algorithm we are using. To further improve the notification process we added a `Buffer` to components of type `Circuit`. The buffer will build the circuit and flush only after all signals have arrived. Overall, this reduces the amount of time components (both inside and outside the circuit) reside in memory as well as the number of these components.

The notification principle confronted us with the following problem. Consider the `MIN` circuit from Figure 2 c. The `BinaryMin` circuits (Figure 2 b) that make up this circuit take a carry bit (either 0 or 1) as input. Thus, the moment this value becomes available, all of them will be notified and hence built. The amount of memory required for this build is like having the entire `MIN` circuit in memory, which is clearly unacceptable. In our component for set intersection we faced the same problem. There, we have multiple copies of a sub component for set membership, and all of them are notified with the same set. The issue with our design is that ports have no control over when they receive notifications.

Fourth version. The fourth version introduces *pulling* and *pushing* ports. A component with a pulling port does not need to be connected to another component in order to receive its signals. Instead, it pulls them from a global *pulling-pushing table*, called `PTable`.

The most important aspect of pulling ports is that they can control when they want to be notified. For example, in the scenario mentioned above with the `MIN` circuit (Figure 2 c), the `BinaryMin` circuits will not build when the carry bit becomes available. Instead, they decide when to pull this value from the table. Of course, pulling is useless without pushing and therefore any output port can push a value into the table. In the `MIN` circuit scenario, for example, the carry bit will be initially pushed into the table, and components will pull it from the table.

The table presents several design challenges. Consider, for example, a component that has only pulling ports (we call it a *pulling component*). According to the notification principle, this component will never get notified and hence never built. The question is therefore who will notify this component and when. We decided that this will be specified by the enclosing component. That is, a component specifies pulling ports, pulling sub components, and a counter. The component increases its counter on each notification. If the counter equals to the in-degree of the component, then all pulling ports and pulling sub-components are notified. Thus, pulling can occur before, after, or while the component is receiving notifications. There is another issue. Recall that the role of the bus is to destruct a component once the component fired its last output. If some signals go to the `PTable` instead, the bus would not know about them and therefore never destruct the component. This problem has a recursive nature because components are nested. We solved this problem by allowing these *pushing signals* to continue to notify buses. Components, however, can ignore them.

We did not conceive situations where a port pulls a value that has not been pushed yet, but to allow this flexibility the table stores references to components making such requests and notifies them as soon as the value becomes available. We decided that only components (but no other object) will push values into the table. This preserves modularity because, by including pulling and pushing information in the component, developers can freely exchange components.

To see how a `PTable` works in practice, consider the VMCrypt component for set intersection from Figure 4. Intuitively, this component pushes the set $X = \{x_1 \quad x_{m\ 1}\}$ of the server into the table, and then each y_i from the client set $Y = \{y_1 \quad y_n\}$ is tested for membership in X by pulling X from the table. In detail, the component contains two sub components of type `UniSwitch`. The first `UniSwitch` pushes X into the table using m copies of the identity map (recall that only components can push. It turns out that `Map` is ideal for this purpose). The second `UniSwitch` contains n copies of a `Switch` for set membership. This `Switch` contains three sub components. The first is a map that pushes y_i into row m of the table. The second is a `UniSwitch` that contains m copies of the equality component `EQ` (of type `Circuit`). The j-th `EQ` circuit pulls to its leftmost ports the value stored in the table at row m (initially y_0) and to its rightmost ports the value stored in the table at row j (which is x_j). That is, it checks whether y_i and x_j are equal. Thus, the `UniSwitch` containing the `EQ` circuits outputs a sequence of m bits that are all 0 if and only if $y_i \in X$. Because this output is fed into an `OR` component (of type `Circuit`), the i-th `Switch` for set membership will output 1 if and only if $y_i \in X$.

How much memory did the `PTable` save? Suppose that we compute set intersection on databases of size $N = 1\ 000\ 000$ and that for efficiency we hash set elements into 20 byte strings (that is, $arity = 160$ bits). This requires $N(N * arity) + N * arity$ wires. The minimum memory cost for a wire is 8 bytes (a reference to the wire plus a reference in the wire itself). Thus, we would need a fantastic amount of 320 terabytes RAM.

Let us examine what happens in memory when the set intersection component computes. The component is first notified with the bits of x_0 and therefore only the `Map` exists fully in memory. There is nothing inside the map, but notice that now we also need to store information about which ports are pushing. Since all ports are pushing, this requires an array of size *arity*, which is the bit length of set elements. Once the map fires its last signal it is destructed by its bus and the `UniSwitch` in which this map resided becomes empty again. This repeats until $x_0 \quad x_{m\ 1}$ are pushed. Now the table contains the entire set X. This is not a flaw in VMCrypt; it is a consequence of the underlying algorithm we are using for set intersection. Next, we notify the component with the bits of y_0. As before, this causes the map to build and push y_0 into the table. After the map destructs, the `UniSwitch` containing the `EQ` circuit is built. Next, the first equality circuit builds, computes, destructs, and the `UniSwitch` containing it becomes empty again. The output of the `EQ` notifies the `OR` component. Since the `OR` was implemented as a circuit and circuits have a buffer, the output of `EQ` is stored in this buffer and the `OR` is not built yet. After the last `EQ` circuit produces its output, the `UniSwitch` containing the `EQ` destructs and the buffer of the `OR` is full. This causes the buffer to build the `OR` and flush all the signals into it. The `OR` computes, destructs, and sends its output to its enclosing component, the `Switch`. Since the out-degree of the `Switch` is also 1, it also destructs. Now we are at the same state as in the beginning because all the components inside the set intersection component are empty. This entire process repeats with $y_1 \quad y_{n\ 1}$, and finally the set intersection component destructs.

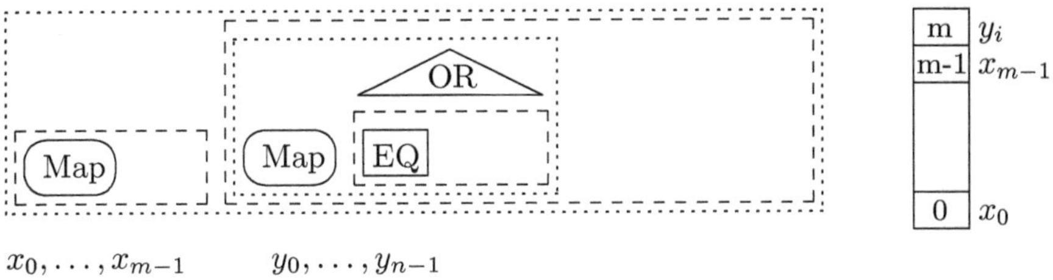

Figure 4: The set intersection component implemented in VMCrypt.

4. CREATING A NEW COMPONENT

This section describes how to create a VMCrypt component. For lack of space, we only provide an overview. See [20, 19] for details.

We start with an overview of the component hierarchy (Figure 5). The root of this hierarchy is `BaseComponent`. Objects of this class have an `ID`, which is a pair of integers `(depth,index)`. The only role of the `ID` is in validation. Class `Gate` is extended by two classes: `BinaryGate` for binary gates and `UniGate` for unary gates. All gates receive their type (e.g., XOR, OR, NOT) during instantiation, and their output wire (initially empty) is also created during instantiation. The classes `Map, UniSwitch, Switch` and `Circuit` are derived from `Component`. The main difference between a `Component` and `Gate` is that the former has a `Bus`, which also implies that it is built only when notified, whereas the later has an output wire and is built when instantiated.

Components are created in VMCrypt by writing a new Java class. Whether created from existing components or from scratch, developing new components is 100% modular - it requires no access to any source code. To create a new component, we need to choose a sub class of `Component` to extend, and the type of sub components. Notice that we can also add new building blocks to VMCrypt by deriving directly from `Component`, whereas in Fairplay the language is final and cannot be extended.

Class Map. A map is a component that maps an input from one port to another. A map only needs to implement abstract method `map`. For example, the identity map code is as follows:

```
class IDMap extends Map {
  IDMap(Bus bus, int inDegree) {
    super(bus, inDegree);
  }
  int map(int port) {
    return port;
  }
  public String name() {
    return "IDMap";
  }
}
```

The `name` method returns the name of the component and is used only for testing purposes. The `notify` method, which handles notifications from other components, is implemented in class `Map`. Notice that components like `Map` are not the only notifiable modules; a wire, a bus, and other modules also have a `notify` method.

Like all sub classes of `Component`, the constructor of `Map` passes three arguments to the constructor of `Component`: `inDegree, outDegree` and a `bus`. Those are data members of `Component`. In the case of `Map`, the value of `inDegree` is passed both as `inDegree` and `outDegree`, which is why our constructor for `IDMap` only takes `inDegree` as an argument.

Class Component. The most important data member of `Component` is the bus. We illustrate the role of the bus using the minimum component (Figure 3). The base layer of this component is a `Switch` with two sub components: a `UniSwitch` and an `IDMap`. Figure 6 shows this `Switch` with its two subcomponents (the `BinaryMIN` inside the `UniSwitch` are not shown). Each component has a `Bus` shown as a grey rectangle. As we mentioned above, all sub classes of `Component` must pass to the constructor of `Component` an instance of class `Bus`. This instance stores a reference (called `out`) to a notifiable object that will receive the output of the component. In the case of the minimum circuit, for example, we first instantiate the layer above the base layer (call it L), then we create a new bus that will point at it by writing `Bus bus = new Bus(`L`)`, and finally we invoke the constructor of the `Switch` with `bus` as argument. This bus is shown in Figure 6 at the top left corner of the `Switch`. In addition to directing the output, the bus is responsible for destructing a component once it has fired its last signal. For this, the bus maintains a counter. The only role of the `outDegree` variable is to set this counter. Consider now the sub components of the `Switch`. Their output is intended to L, yet their busses point at the bus of the `Switch`. Why? because the bus of the `Switch` must be able to count all the signals leaving the component. If some signals are missing, then it will never destruct the `Switch`.

Let us see how the bus works in practice. Suppose that the first signal the `Switch` from Figure 6 receives is on port 0. It will pass it to the `UniSwitch`, who will process it and fire a new signal on, say, port 0. If the `outDegree` of the `UniSwitch` is, say, 8, then the counter in the bus of the `UniSwitch` is now $8 - 1 = 7$. Similarly, if the `outDegree` of the `Switch` is, say, 16, then the bus of the `Switch` updates its counter to $16 - 1 = 15$. Of course, it also passes the signal from the `UniSwitch` out (to the layer above), on the same port it was received, which is 0. The type of bus that we use in the `UniSwitch` would not work in the `IDMap`. To see why, consider what happens when the `Switch` routes signals to the `IDMap`. Suppose that the `inDegree` of the `UniSwitch` is 16 and that the `Switch` receives a signal on port 16. Since 16 does not fall in the range $0 - 15$, the `Switch` will pass it to the `IDMap` on port $16 - 16 = 0$. Since the map is the identity function, the bus of the `IDMap` will pass this signal to the bus of the `Switch` on port 0, which will override outputs of the `UniSwitch`. Thus, when we instantiate the `IDMap`, we pass to it an `OffsetBus`, which offsets the port.

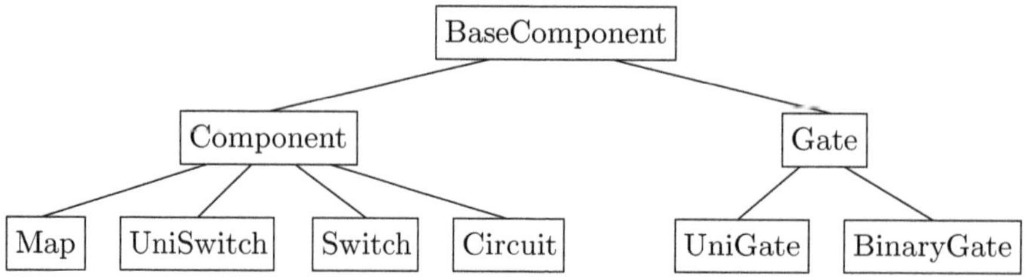

Figure 5: Class hierarchy of components.

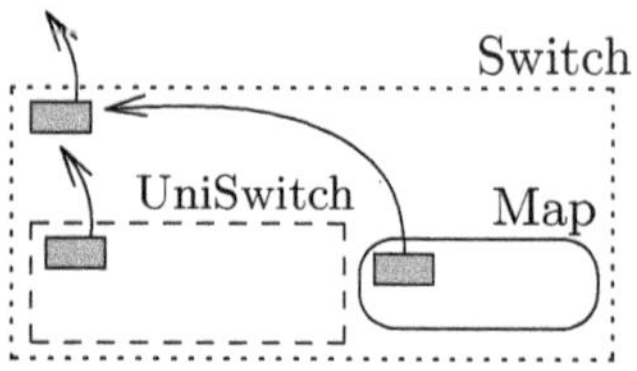

Figure 6: The role of the Bus.

In this scenario we want the output of the `IDMap` appearing immediately to the right of the output of the `UniSwitch`, and since the `outDegree` of the `UniSwitch` is 8, we instantiate this bus by writing `OffsetBus offsetBus = new OffsetBus(`*bus* `8)`, where *bus* is the bus of the `Switch`. Any output of the `IDMap` on port i will now be given to the bus of the `Switch` on port $8 + i$.

Unlilke `outDegree` and `Bus`, the role of `inDegree` depends on the component and the sub component. In a `Map`, the `inDegree` and `outDegree` are always the same, but `inDegree` is never used. Similarly, `Switch` and `UniSwitch` never use their own `inDegree`. However, the `Switch` uses the `inDegree` of its sub components for routing. This is why all classes derived from `BaseComponent` have an `inDegree()` method. The `UniSwitch` takes two parameters: `inputTab` and `outputTab`. When a signal is received on port i, it is given to the sub component at index $index = \lfloor i \ \texttt{inputTab} \rfloor$. If this sub component outputs a signal on port j, then the bus of the `UniSwitch` will output it on port $index*\texttt{outputTab}+j$. Class `Circuit` is the only component that uses its `inDegree`: when a circuit is built, it instantiates `inDegree` objects of class `Wire` and stores them in an array of size `inDegree`.

Circuits. Class `Circuit` is the only component with input wires. Like in a `Switch`, the sub components of `Circuit` can be of any type derived from `BaseComponent`. To create a circuit in VMCrypt, we need to implement two methods: one that instantiates sub components and another that connects them. As an example, we implement the bit multiplexer from Figure 2 a. The skeleton of our class is:

```
class BitMUX extends Circuit<BinaryGate> {
  BitMUX(Bus bus) {
    super(bus, 3,1);
  }
  public String name() {
    return "BitMUX";
  }
}
```

The numbers 3 and 1 are the `inDegree` and `outDegree` of the component, respectively. Class `Circuit` has an array called `components`. When a circuit receives its first input, its `define_sub_components()` method is called. In the case of the `BitMUX`, for example, this method will initiate `components` to be `XOR` and `AND` gates. Next, class `Circuit` will initialize its `inputWires` array to size `inDegree` (which is 3 in our case), create empty wires, and invoke method `connect_wires()` to connect wires to gates.

Once building blocks like `BitMUX` are built, higher level circuits can be built more easily. For example, our `MUX` on strings of length *arity* instantiates *arity* elements of `BitMUX` in `define_sub_components()`, and connects their input and output wires in `connect_wires()`.

Classes Switch and UniSwitch. Creating a component from classes `Switch` and `UniSwitch` is even simpler than class `Circuit`. In the case of `UniSwitch`, we only need to implement a method returning an instance of the sub component. In a `Switch`, on the other hand, each sub component can be from a different class, so like in `define_sub_components()`, we instantiate all the sub components, and connect them using a `Bus`, or a `Splitter` when necessary.

5. PERFORMANCE

We analyze VMCrypt performance on circuits which have been developed without modifying VMCrypt source code. Each circuit has different structural properties and was tested on inputs of increasing length to show that performance does not depend on size or structure. We are not aware of such rigorous analysis in prior work.

All tests were executed on a Thinkpad X301 laptop with 3 GB RAM and a 1 6 GHz Intel Core2 Duo processor running Ubuntu Linux. Two Java Virtual Machines (JVM) were run on this computer; one for each party. To guarantee that performance is measured in a standard setting, we did not configure the JVM (e.g., by increasing the size of the heap). Parties communicated through the loopback network interface. Running the parties side by side means that the same machine was stressed with twice the amount of work, for both TCP (packet handling, checksums, etc.) and Yao's protocol.

Encryption was implemented with SHA-1 modeled as a random oracle, which provides much better performance compared to number theoretic based pseudo-random generators (PRGs). Wire label length was 120 bits. We remark that our communication complexity is exactly four encryptions (one lookup table) per gate and one OT per wire. This is the absolute minimum. By maintaining party state, we avoid sending metadata (describing what is being sent), gate numbers, wire index, etc. Thus, any other protocol can only

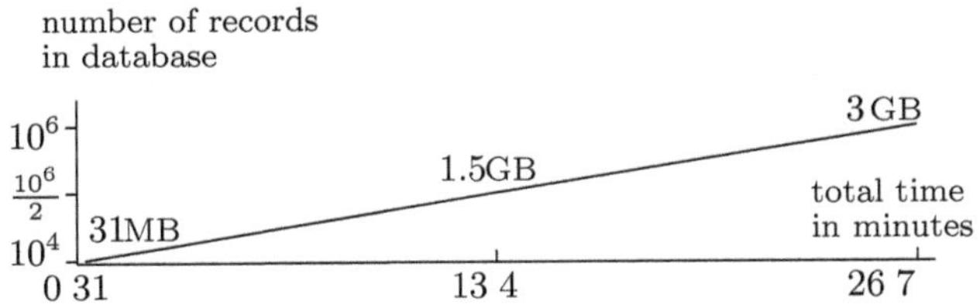

Figure 7: Running time of secure database search.

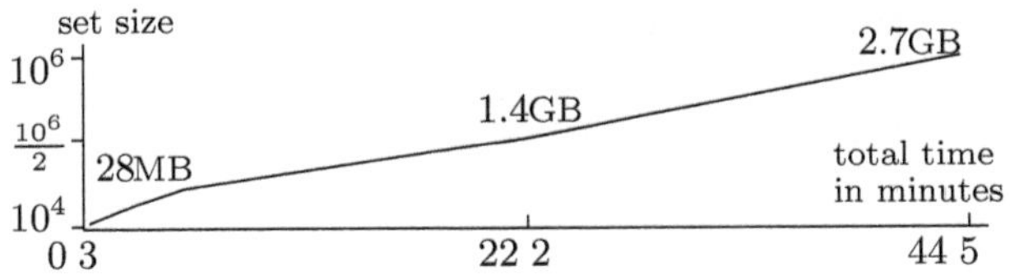

Figure 8: Running time of secure minimum.

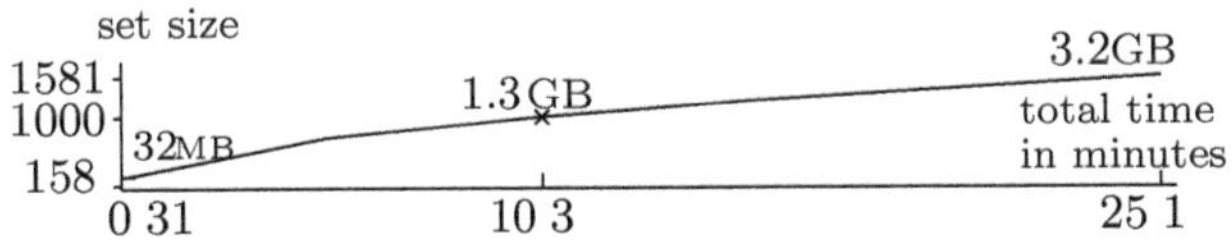

Figure 9: Running time of secure set intersection.

have equivalent or worse communication complexity. Formally, the communication complexity is exactly $4n*L+k*|x|$ bytes, where n is the number of non-XOR gates in the circuit, L is the byte length of a ciphertext (encryption), $|x|$ is the length of the input of the evaluator, and k is a small constant that depends on the OT communication complexity.

We start with the database search function. The input to this function is an array of records $\langle x_i\ p_i\rangle$ and a string y, where x_i and p_i are viewed as columns in a database table. The output is all p_i for which $x_i = y$. In VMCrypt it is implemented as component `DBSearch`. In Fairplay [21] it was implemented as *Keyed Database Search (KDS)*.

Since Fairplay circuit parameters are passed at compile time, the compiler must be run in each execution. Thus, we compared the performance of our full protocol with that of the Fairplay compiler [21] alone (ignoring the time and memory it takes to actually execute the Fairplay protocol). Since the time and memory complexity of the Fairplay compiler are not reported in the literature, we carried our own test on a table where the length of each of x_i p_i and y is 20 bits. When the table size is $N = 20$ records, the compiler runs for 10 seconds. When $N = 40$ the running time is 50 seconds. Obviously, this is not linear. When $N = 55$ the compiler runs for 3 minutes and then crashes with a Java `Out Of Memory` Error. In the case of $N = 40$, memory consumption climbs gradually to 23% of the RAM. When $N = 55$, it reaches 26%.

In VMCrypt, when $N = 10\ 000$ the running time of the secure database search protocol is 19 seconds. Figure 7 describes the running time (in minutes) and communication complexity for values of N up to 1 million. The component with 1 million records has 100 million gates and 60 million lookup tables (the number of non-XOR gates).

We discuss Figure 7 and other statistics. First and foremost, although the full hardware description of the circuit for database search is linear in N, the client and the server each used the same amount of memory, namely, 4 8% RAM. Secondly, the running time is linear in the database size. This was not the case with earlier versions of VMCrypt, and therefore should not be taken for granted (see discussion in Section 3). Thirdly, the very large amounts of data sent confirm that parallelizing Yao's protocol yields significant savings on disk read and writes. Finally, 84% of the running time was consumed by cryptographic operations and communication (this was measured by comparing with the running time of calculating the component). In other words, VMCrypt overhead was only 16% . Other implementations also have an overhead, but unfortunately such statistics are not provided in the literature.

Our next test was the minimum component, implemented in VMCrypt as class `MIN` (Figure 3). This component takes N integers (of length 20 bits each) and outputs their minimum. In our experiment, half of the integers belong to the client and half belong to the server. We remark that, in practice, parties will have shares of the integers, and the function would first add the shares and then find the minimum.

The running time (in minutes) and communication complexity of the protocol for secure minimum are given in Figure 8. These are linear in N because, as with the `DBSearch` component, the underlying (non-secure) algorithm runs in linear time. On average, parties used 5% of the memory (independently of N), and VMCrypt overhead was 10%. Notice that the running time is almost double that of the `DBSearch` component. This is because half of the inputs required oblivious transfer, and the number of lookup tables was almost double (the `MIN` component with 1 million inputs had 110 million gates and 90 million lookup tables).

Our last test was the set intersection component, implemented as class `SetIntersection` (Figure 4). This component takes two sets of size N and M, and outputs their intersection. We fixed the bit length of set elements to 20 bits. To simplify the presentation we chose $N = M$. The running time (in minutes) and communication complexity of the protocol for secure set intersection are given in Figure 9.

Notice that, unlike previous tests, the size of the set intersection component is quadratic in N due to the underlying (non-secure) algorithm it implements. For comparability with previous tests, we chose values of N ranging from 158 to 1581. Thus, when $N = 158$ we have $N^2 \cong 10^4$ and the component has 1 million gates and 0 5 million lookup tables. Similarly, when $N = 1581$ we have $N^2 \cong 10^6$ and the component has 100 million gates and 50 million lookup tables. On average, parties used 5% of the memory (independently of N), and VMCrypt overhead was 15%.

6. REFERENCES

[1] M. Barni, T. Bianchi, D. Catalano, M. D. Raimondo, R. D. Labati, and P. Faillia. Privacy-preserving fingercode authentication. In *MM&Sec'*, Roma, Italy, 2010. ACM.

[2] A. Ben-David, N. Nisan, and B. Pinkas. Fairplaymp: a system for secure multi-party computation. In *ACM Conference on Computer and Communications Security*, pages 257–266, 2008.

[3] D. Bogdanov, S. Laur, and J. Willemson. Sharemind: A framework for fast privacy-preserving computations. In *ESORICS*, pages 192–206, 2008.

[4] I. Damgård, M. Geisler, M. Krøigaard, and J. B. Nielsen. Asynchronous multiparty computation: Theory and implementation. In *Public Key Cryptography*, pages 160–179, 2009.

[5] I. Damgård and M. Jurik. A generalisation, a simplification and some applications of paillier's probabilistic public-key system. In *Public Key Cryptography*, pages 119–136, 2001.

[6] I. Damgård and C. Orlandi. Multiparty computation for dishonest majority: From passive to active security at low cost. In *CRYPTO*, pages 558–576, 2010.

[7] Z. Erkin, M. Franz, J. Guajardo, S. Katzenbeisser, I. Lagendijk, and T. Toft. Privacy-preserving face recognition. In *Privacy Enhancing Technologies*, pages 235–253, 2009.

[8] D. Evans, Y. Huang, J. Katz, and L. Malka. Efficient privacy-preserving biometric identification. In *Proceedings of the 17th conference Network and Distributed System Security Symposium, NDSS 2011.*

[9] D. Evans, Y. Huang, J. Katz, and L. Malka. Faster secure two-party computation using garbled circuits. To appear in the 20th USENIX Security Symposium.

[10] C. Gentry. Fully homomorphic encryption using ideal lattices. In *STOC*, pages 169–178, 2009.

[11] W. Henecka, S. Kögl, A.-R. Sadeghi, T. Schneider, and I. Wehrenberg. Tasty: Tool for automating secure two-party computations. In *ACM Conference on Computer and Communications Security*, 2010.

[12] Y. Ishai, J. Kilian, K. Nissim, and E. Petrank. Extending oblivious transfers efficiently. In *CRYPTO*, pages 145–161, 2003.

[13] S. Jha, L. Kruger, and V. Shmatikov. Towards practical privacy for genomic computation. In *IEEE Symposium on Security and Privacy*, pages 216–230, 2008.

[14] V. Kolesnikov, A.-R. Sadeghi, and T. Schneider. Improved garbled circuit building blocks and applications to auctions and computing minima. In *CANS*, pages 1–20, 2009.

[15] V. Kolesnikov and T. Schneider. Improved garbled circuit: Free XOR gates and applications. In *ICALP '08: Proceedings of the 35th international colloquium on Automata, Languages and Programming, Part II*, pages 486–498, Berlin, Heidelberg, 2008. Springer-Verlag.

[16] Y. Lindell and B. Pinkas. A proof of security of yao's protocol for two-party computation. *J. Cryptology*, 22(2):161–188, 2009.

[17] Y. Lindell, B. Pinkas, and N. P. Smart. Implementing two-party computation efficiently with security against malicious adversaries. In *SCN*, pages 2–20, 2008.

[18] P. D. MacKenzie, A. Oprea, and M. K. Reiter. Automatic generation of two-party computations. In *ACM Conference on Computer and Communications Security*, pages 210–219, 2003.

[19] L. Malka. VMCrypt 1.4 developers manual. *http://www.lior.ca/publications/VMCrypt_Manual_Rev1.0.pdf.*

[20] L. Malka. VMCrypt - modular software architecture for scalable secure computation. *EPrint report 2010/584*, 2010.

[21] D. Malkhi, N. Nisan, B. Pinkas, and Y. Sella. Fairplay—a secure two-party computation system. In *SSYM04: Proceedings of the 13th conference on USENIX Security Symposium*, pages 20–20, Berkeley, CA, USA, 2004. USENIX Association.

[22] M. Naor and B. Pinkas. Efficient oblivious transfer protocols. In *SODA*, pages 448–457, 2001.

[23] J. D. Nielsen and M. I. Schwartzbach. A domain-specific programming language for secure multiparty computation. In *PLAS*, pages 21–30, 2007.

[24] M. Osadchy, B. Pinkas, A. Jarrous, and B. Moskovich. Scifi - a system for secure face identification. In *IEEE Symposium on Security and Privacy*, pages 239–254, 2010.

[25] P. Paillier. Public-key cryptosystems based on composite degree residuosity classes. In *EUROCRYPT'99: Proceedings of the 17th international conference on Theory and application of cryptographic techniques*, pages 223–238, Berlin, Heidelberg, 1999. Springer-Verlag.

[26] A. Paus, A.-R. Sadeghi, and T. Schneider. Practical secure evaluation of semi-private functions. In *ACNS*, pages 89–106, 2009.

[27] B. Pinkas, T. Schneider, N. P. Smart, and S. C. Williams. Secure two-party computation is practical. In *ASIACRYPT*, pages 250–267, 2009.

[28] A.-R. Sadeghi, T. Schneider, and I. Wehrenberg. Efficient privacy-preserving face recognition. In *ICISC*, pages 229–244, 2009.

[29] N. P. Smart and F. Vercauteren. Fully homomorphic encryption with relatively small key and ciphertext sizes. In *Public Key Cryptography*, pages 420–443, 2010.

[30] M. van Dijk, C. Gentry, S. Halevi, and V. Vaikuntanathan. Fully homomorphic encryption over the integers. In *EUROCRYPT*, pages 24–43, 2010.

[31] A. C.-C. Yao. How to generate and exchange secrets (extended abstract). In *FOCS*, pages 162–167, 1986.

CCS'11 Print Proceedings Author Index

www.ingramcontent.com/pod-product-compliance
Ingram Content Group UK Ltd.
Pitfield, Milton Keynes, MK11 3LW, UK
UKHW051420290926
15471UKWH00009B/1701